THE
ALL ENGLAND
LAW REPORTS
1981

Volume 2

Editor
PETER HUTCHESSON LL M
Barrister, New Zealand

Assistant Editor
BROOK WATSON
of Lincoln's Inn, Barrister
and of the New South Wales Bar

Consulting Editor
WENDY SHOCKETT
of Gray's Inn, Barrister

London
BUTTERWORTHS

ENGLAND: Butterworth & Co (Publishers) Ltd
              London: 88 Kingsway, WC2B 6AB

AUSTRALIA: Butterworths Pty Ltd
              Sydney: 271–273 Lane Cove Road, North Ryde, NSW 2113
              Also at Melbourne, Brisbane, Adelaide and Perth

CANADA: Butterworth & Co (Canada) Ltd
              Toronto: 2265 Midland Avenue, Scarborough M1P 4S1

NEW ZEALAND: Butterworths of New Zealand Ltd
              Wellington: 33–35 Cumberland Place

SOUTH AFRICA: Butterworth & Co (South Africa) (Pty) Ltd
              Durban: 152–154 Gale Street

USA: Butterworth & Co (Publishers) Inc
              Boston: 10 Tower Office Park, Woburn, Mass 01801

Butterworth & Co (Publishers) Ltd

1981

ISBN 0 406 85141 7

Typeset by CCC, printed and bound in Great Britain by William Clowes (Beccles) Limited, Beccles and
London

House of Lords

The Lord High Chancellor: Lord Hailsham of St Marylebone

Lords of Appeal in Ordinary

Lord Wilberforce
Lord Diplock
Lord Edmund-Davies
Lord Fraser of Tullybelton
Lord Russell of Killowen

Lord Keith of Kinkel
Lord Scarman
Lord Roskill
Lord Bridge of Harwich

Court of Appeal

The Lord High Chancellor

The Lord Chief Justice of England: Lord Lane

The Master of the Rolls: Lord Denning

The President of the Family Division: Sir John Lewis Arnold

Lords Justices of Appeal

Sir John Frederick Eustace Stephenson
Sir Frederick Horace Lawton
Sir Roger Fray Greenwood Ormrod
Sir Sebag Shaw
Sir George Stanley Waller
Sir James Roualeyn Hovell-Thurlow-
  Cumming-Bruce
Sir Edward Walter Eveleigh
Sir Henry Vivian Brandon
Sir Sydney William Templeman

Sir John Francis Donaldson
Sir John Anson Brightman
Sir Desmond James Conrad Ackner
Sir Robin Horace Walford Dunn
Sir Peter Raymond Oliver
Sir Tasker Watkins VC
Sir Patrick McCarthy O'Connor
Sir William Hugh Griffiths
Sir Michael John Fox

Chancery Division

The Lord High Chancellor

The Vice-Chancellor: Sir Robert Edgar Megarry

Sir Peter Harry Batson Woodroffe Foster
Sir John Norman Keates Whitford
Sir Ernest Irvine Goulding
Sir Raymond Henry Walton
Sir Christopher John Slade
Sir Nicolas Christopher Henry Browne-
Wilkinson

Sir John Evelyn Vinelott
Sir George Brian Hugh Dillon
Sir Martin Charles Nourse
Sir Douglas William Falconer
Sir Jean-Pierre Frank Eugene Warner
Sir Peter Leslie Gibson
(appointed 27th April 1981)

Queen's Bench Division

The Lord Chief Justice of England

Sir Alan Abraham Mocatta
(retired 31st May 1981)
Sir John Thompson
Sir Helenus Patrick Joseph Milmo
Sir Joseph Donaldson Cantley
Sir Hugh Eames Park
Sir Stephen Chapman
(retired 17th April 1981)
Sir Bernard Caulfield
Sir Hilary Gwynne Talbot
Sir William Lloyd Mars-Jones
Sir Ralph Kilner Brown
Sir Phillip Wien
(died 11th June 1981)
Sir Peter Henry Rowley Bristow
Sir Hugh Harry Valentine Forbes
Sir Robert Hugh Mais
Sir Neil Lawson
Sir David Powell Croom-Johnson
Sir John Raymond Phillips
Sir Leslie Kenneth Edward Boreham
Sir John Douglas May
Sir Michael Robert Emanuel Kerr
Sir Alfred William Michael Davies
Sir John Dexter Stocker
Sir Kenneth George Illtyd Jones
Sir Haydn Tudor Evans
Sir Peter Richard Pain
Sir Kenneth Graham Jupp
Sir Robert Lionel Archibald Goff
Sir Stephen Brown

Sir Roger Jocelyn Parker
Sir Ralph Brian Gibson
Sir Walter Derek Thornley Hodgson
Sir James Peter Comyn
Sir Anthony John Leslie Lloyd
Sir Frederick Maurice Drake
Sir Brian Thomas Neill
Sir Roderick Philip Smith
(died 12th April 1981)
Sir Michael John Mustill
Sir Barry Cross Sheen
Sir David Bruce McNeill
Sir Harry Kenneth Woolf
Sir Thomas Patrick Russell
Sir Peter Edlin Webster
Sir Thomas Henry Bingham
Sir Iain Derek Laing Glidewell
Sir Henry Albert Skinner
Sir Peter Murray Taylor
Sir Murray Stuart-Smith
(appointed 27th April 1981)
Sir Christopher Stephen Thomas Jonathan
Thayer Staughton
(appointed 27th April 1981)
Sir Donald Henry Farquharson
(appointed 27th April 1981)
Sir Anthony James Denys McCowan
(appointed 2nd June 1981)
Sir Iain Charles Robert McCullough
(appointed 9th June 1981)

Family Division

The President of the Family Division

Sir John Brinsmead Latey
Sir Alfred Kenneth Hollings
Sir Charles Trevor Reeve
Sir Francis Brooks Purchas
Dame Rose Heilbron
Sir Brian Drex Bush
Sir Alfred John Balcombe
Sir John Kember Wood

Sir Ronald Gough Waterhouse
Sir John Gervase Kensington Sheldon
Sir Thomas Michael Eastham
Dame Margaret Myfanwy Wood Booth
Sir Christopher James Saunders French
Sir Anthony Leslie Julian Lincoln
Dame Ann Elizabeth Oldfield Butler-Sloss
Sir Anthony Bruce Ewbank

CITATION

These reports are cited thus:

[1981] 2 All ER

REFERENCES

These reports contain references to the following major works of legal reference described in the manner indicated below.

Halsbury's Laws of England

The reference 35 Halsbury's Laws (3rd Edn) 366, para 524, refers to paragraph 524 on page 366 of volume 35 of the third edition, and the reference 26 Halsbury's Laws (4th Edn) para 577 refers to paragraph 577 on page 296 of volume 26 of the fourth edition of Halsbury's Laws of England.

Halsbury's Statutes of England

The reference 5 Halsbury's Statutes (3rd Edn) 302 refers to page 302 of volume 5 of the third edition of Halsbury's Statutes of England.

The Digest

References are to the replacement volumes (including reissue volumes) of The Digest (formerly the English and Empire Digest), and to the continuation volumes of the replacement volumes.

The reference 44 Digest (Repl) 144, 1240, refers to case number 1240 on page 144 of Digest Replacement Volume 44.

The reference 28(1) Digest (Reissue) 167, 507, refers to case number 507 on page 167 of Digest Replacement Volume 28(1) Reissue.

The reference Digest (Cont Vol D) 571, 678b, refers to case number 678b on page 571 of Digest Continuation Volume D.

Halsbury's Statutory Instruments

The reference 12 Halsbury's Statutory Instruments (Third Reissue) 125 refers to page 125 of the third reissue of volume 12 of Halsbury's Statutory Instruments; references to subsequent reissues are similar.

CORRIGENDA

[1981] 2 All ER
p 267. **Finnigan v Sandiford.** Line *c* 2 should read '... for the purpose of effecting the arrest ...'
p 458. **Lonrho Ltd v Shell Petroleum Co Ltd.** Counsel for Shell should read *'Peter Curry QC, Brian Davenport QC* and *Gordon Langley'.*
p 555. **Westminster City Council v Haymarket Publishing Ltd.** Line *g* 2 should read '... would indemnify the defendants ...' Page 556, line *b* 5 should read '(2) On the true construction ...'

Cases reported in volume 2

National Panasonic (UK) Ltd v Commission of the European Communities

(Case 136/79)

COURT OF JUSTICE OF THE EUROPEAN COMMUNITIES

JUDGES KUTSCHER (PRESIDENT), O'KEEFFE, TOUFFAIT (PRESIDENTS OF CHAMBERS), MERTENS DE WILMARS, PESCATORE, LORD MACKENZIE STUART, BOSCO, KOOPMANS AND DUE

ADVOCATE-GENERAL J-P WARNER

18th MARCH, 30th APRIL, 26th JUNE 1980

European Economic Community – Restrictive trade practices – Investigation of undertakings – Investigation without previous notification – Powers of Commission – Whether undertaking may be investigated only after being asked for information – Whether investigation without previous notification interference with undertaking's right to privacy – EEC Treaty, art 85 – EEC Regulation No 17 of 6th February 1962, art 14 – European Convention for the Protection of Human Rights and Fundamental Freedoms 1950, art 8(2).

European Economic Community – Secondary legislation – Construction – Aids to interpretation – Whether statements made by Council members when adopting regulation may be looked at – Whether reference may be made to debates of European Parliament – Whether views of Commission staff may be referred to.

Acting under the authority of a decision adopted by the Commission of the European Communities under art 14[a] of EEC Regulation No 17 of 6th February 1962, and without any prior warning to the applicant, two inspectors of the Commission, accompanied by an official from the Office of Fair Trading, arrived at the applicant's sales office in Slough for the purpose of examining the applicant's books and records, making any necessary copies and demanding oral explanations of documents. The decision specified that the Commission had evidence leading it to believe that, in breach of art 85[b] of the EEC Treaty, the applicant was requiring from its trade customers a covenant not to export the applicant's products to the Federal Republic of Germany. A request by one of the applicant's directors that the inspectors await the arrival of the applicant's solicitor was refused. The inspectors then carried out the investigation and left on the same day taking with them copies of a number of documents and notes made during the investigation. The applicant applied to the Court of Justice of the European Communities seeking the annulment of the decision, the return of the copies of the documents, the

---

destruction of the notes taken and an undertaking that the Commission would make no
further use of the information that it had obtained during the course of the *a*
investigation. The applicant contended, inter alia, that the search was unlawful since on
its true construction art 14, like art 11^c, required the Commission to make a request to
an undertaking such as the applicant to provide the information required before issuing
an investigation decision. The applicant also contended that the search was unlawful
because it infringed the applicant's right to privacy, contrary to art 8^d of the European
Convention for the Protection of Human Rights and Fundamental Freedoms 1950.   *b*

Held – The application would be dismissed for the following reasons—
   (1) Although art 11 of Regulation No 17 expressly provided for a two-stage procedure
whereby an undertaking could be required to submit to an investigation only where the
Commission had previously asked those concerned for the necessary information, art 14
of that regulation contained no such restriction. The difference in the procedures was *c*
explained by the diversity of the needs met by the two provisions: whereas the procedure
contained in art 11 was to enable the Commission to collect information not already in
its possession and which in general it could not collect without the co-operation of the
undertaking concerned, the procedure contained in art 14 was in general designed to
enable the Commission to check information already in its possession by means of an
examination of the books and records of an undertaking (see p 12 *c* to *g* and *j* and p 15 *a* *d*
c, post).
   (2) Although the European Economic Community was bound to respect the
constitutional traditions of member states and the fundamental rights embodied in the
European Convention on Human Rights, art 8 of that convention, while upholding the
right to privacy, also permitted an interference with that right if it was 'in accordance
with law and [was] necessary in a democratic society in the interests of . . . the economic *e*
well-being of the country . . .' Since the aim of Regulation No 17 was to prevent
competition from being distorted to the detriment of the public interest, individual
undertakings and consumers and since the exercise of the powers given to the
Commission by that regulation contributed to the maintenance of the system of
competition intended by the EEC Treaty and which undertakings were absolutely
bound to comply with, it could not be said that Regulation No 17, by giving the *f*
Commission the power to carry out investigation without previous notification,
infringed any right of the applicants which was guaranteed by the European Convention
on Human Rights (see p 13 *c* to *g*, p 14 *c* and p 15 *a c*, post).
   Per the Advocate-General. Since what members of the Council of the European
Economic Community do when they adopt a regulation is to agree on the text and since
they do not necessarily all have the same views as to its meaning, it is not permissible as *g*
an aid to interpretation of a regulation to look at what individual members of the
Council said at the time, still less at the debates of the European Parliament or the views
of the staff of the Commission of the European Communities (see p 7 *d* to *g*, post);
Stauder v City of Ulm [1969] ECR 419 distinguished.

Notes   *h*
For investigation by the Commission of infringements of EEC rules on competition, see
Supplement to 39A Halsbury's Laws (3rd Edn) para 180.
   For the EEC Treaty, art 85, see 42A Halsbury's Statutes (3rd Edn) 1178.
   For EEC Regulation No 17 of 6th February 1962, arts 11, 14, see ibid 1195, 1196.

Cases cited   *j*
Acciaieria e Tubeficio di Brescia v High Authority of the European Coal and Steel Community
   Case 31/59 [1960] ECR 71, CJEC.

---

c   Article 11, so far as material, is set out at p 11 *f g*, post
d   Article 8 is set out at p 8 *c d*, post

a
Inland Revenue Comrs v Rossminster Ltd [1980] 1 All ER 80, [1980] AC 952, [1980] 2 WLR
1, HL; *rvsg* [1979] 3 All ER 385, QBD and CA, Digest (Cont Vol E) 316, 2153f.
Milac GmbH Gross- und Aussenhandel v Hauptzollamt Freiburg Case 28/76 [1976] ECR 1639,
CJEC.
Nold (J), Kohlen- und Baustoffgrosshandlung v EC Commission Case 4/73 [1974] ECR 491,
[1974] 2 CMLR 338, CJEC.
Stauder (Eric) v City of Ulm, Sozialamt Case 29/69 [1969] ECR 419, [1970] CMLR 112,
b
CJEC.
Transocean Marine Paint Association v EC Commission Case 17/74 [1974] ECR 1063, CJEC.

Application

By an application dated 23rd August 1979 National Panasonic (UK) Ltd applied to the
Court of Justice of the European Communities for, inter alia, (1) the annulment of the
decision of the Commission of the European Communities of 22nd June 1979 concerning
c an investigation to be made at the applicant's premises at Slough, Berkshire, pursuant to
art 14(3) of EEC Regulation No 17 of 6th February 1962, and (2) an order that the
Commission (a) return to the applicant all its documents copied by the Commission's
officials or destroy such copies, (b) destroy all notes made by the officials at the time of or
subsequent to the investigation and in relation thereto, and (c) undertake not to make
any further use of such documents, notes or information obtained during the course of
d the investigation. The language of the case was English. The facts are set out in the
opinion of the Advocate-General.

David Vaughan for the applicant.
John Temple Lang, of the Commission's Legal Service, for the Commission.

e 30th April.   **The Advocate-General (J-P Warner)** delivered the following opinion:
My Lords, this action is brought under art 173 of the EEC Treaty by an English
company, National Panasonic (UK) Ltd, to challenge a decision of the Commission dated
22nd June 1979 requiring it to submit to an investigation pursuant to art 14(3) of
Regulation No 17 of 6th February 1962.
       Article 14 of Regulation No 17 is, so far as material, in these terms:
f

'*Investigating powers of the Commission.*—1. In carrying out the duties assigned to it
... by provisions adopted under Article 87 of the Treaty, the Commission may
undertake all necessary investigations into undertakings... To this end the officials
authorised by the Commission are empowered: (*a*) to examine books and other
business records; (*b*) to take copies of or extracts from the books and business
g records; (*c*) to ask for oral explanations on the spot; (*d*) to enter any premises, land
and means of transport of undertakings.
       '2. The officials of the Commission authorised for the purpose of these
investigations shall exercise their powers upon production of an authorisation in
writing specifying the subject matter and purpose of the investigation and the
penalties provided for in Article 15(1)(*c*) in cases where production of the required
h books or other business records is incomplete. In good time before the investigation,
the Commission shall inform the competent authority of the Member State in
whose territory the same is to be made of the investigation and of the identity of the
authorised officials.
       '3. Undertakings ... shall submit to investigations ordered by decision of the
       Commission. The decision shall specify the subject matter and purpose of the
j investigation, appoint the date on which it is to begin and indicate the penalties
provided for in Article 15(1)(*c*) and Article 16(1)(*d*) and the right to have the decision
reviewed by the Court of Justice.
       '4. The Commission shall take decisions referred to in paragraph 3 after
consultation with the competent authority of the Member State in whose territory
the investigation is to be made.

'5. Officials of the competent authority of the Member State in whose territory the investigation is to be made may, at the request of such authority or of the Commission, assist the officials of the Commission in carrying out their duties. *a*

'6. Where an undertaking opposes an investigation ordered pursuant to this Article, the Member State concerned shall afford the necessary assistance to the officials authorised by the Commission to enable them to make their investigation. Member States shall, after consultation with the Commission, take the necessary measures to this end . . .'   *b*

National Panasonic (UK) Ltd, the applicant, is a wholly-owned subsidiary of a Japanese company, Matsushita Electric Trading Co Ltd which is itself a wholly-owned subsidiary of another Japanese company, Matsushita Electric Industrial Co Ltd. The applicant is the exclusive distributor in the United Kingdom, Ireland and Iceland of electrical and electronic goods, such as television sets, wireless sets, video cassette systems, high-fidelity *c* equipment and dictating machines, manufactured by the Matsushita group and sold under various trade marks and names, in particular 'National Panasonic' and 'Technics'. (I shall refer to those goods, compendiously, as 'Panasonic equipment'). Another wholly-owned subsidiary of the Matsushita group is National Panasonic Vertriebsgesellschaft mbH, a German company, which distributes Panasonic equipment in the Federal Republic.   *d*

On 11th January 1977 the German company notified to the Commission an agreement relating to the distribution of Panasonic equipment in Germany, with a request for negative clearance or exemption under art 85(3) of the treaty. The notification did not suggest that the agreement was supported by any export ban imposed in any other member state.

Certain evidence that reached the Commission gave rise, however, to a suspicion in its *e* mind that export bans were being imposed within the Community in respect of Panasonic equipment. In particular the Commission was led to suspect, rightly or wrongly, that the applicant was operating a ban on exports from the United Kingdom to Germany. Some particulars of that evidence were given to us by the Commission, but I need not, I think, go into it.

One of the grounds on which the validity of the decision of 22nd June 1979 is *f* challenged by the applicant is that it was inadequately reasoned. I must therefore read the main recitals in its preamble. After referring to art 85 of the treaty, to art 14(3) of Regulation No 17 and to the fact that the Commission had consulted 'the competent authority of the relevant Member State for the purpose of Art 14(4) of Regulation No 17' (ie the Director General of Fair Trading), the preamble continued:

'WHEREAS   *g*

'NATIONAL PANASONIC (UK) LTD is a subsidiary company of MATSUSHITA ELECTRIC INDUSTRIAL COMPANY of Japan and is the exclusive distributor of NATIONAL PANASONIC and TECHNICS consumer electronic products in the United Kingdom;

'A selective distribution agreement for NATIONAL PANASONIC and TECHNICS equipment in the Federal Republic of Germany was notified to the Commission on *h* 11 January 1977 by NATIONAL PANASONIC VERTRIEBSGESELLSCHAFT mbH together with a request for negative clearance or exemption under Article 85(3) of the EEC Treaty;

'The Commission has obtained documentary evidence and other information indicating that NATIONAL PANASONIC (UK) LTD has required trade customers not to re-export NATIONAL PANASONIC and TECHNICS products to other EEC Member States;

'The Commission therefore has grounds for believing that NATIONAL PANASONIC *j* (UK) LTD has participated and is still participating in agreements and concerted practices the object and effect of which is to insulate national markets within the EEC from the competitive effect of parallel imports from other Member States;

'If established, the foregoing would constitute a serious infringement of Article

85 of the EEC Treaty and would be relevant to the Commission's assessment
a   of the selective distribution agreement notified by NATIONAL PANASONIC
VERTRIEBSGESELLSCHAFT;
'In order for the Commission to ascertain all the relevant facts and circumstances
a decision must be adopted requiring NATIONAL PANASONIC (UK) LTD to submit to an
investigation and to produce the requisite business records.'

b   Lastly the preamble summarised the effect of arts 15(1)(c) and 16(1)(d) of Regulation
No 17, the full texts of which were annexed to the decision.
The operative part of the decision consisted of three articles.
By art 1 the applicant was required to submit to an investigation at its business
premises at Slough in Berkshire. It was to permit the Commission officials authorised to
carry out the investigation to enter its premises during normal office hours and was to
c   produce the business records required by them for examination and photocopying,
including certain categories of documents that were listed in the article. It was also to
give such explanations regarding the subject matter of the investigation as those officials
might require.
Article 2 provided that the investigation should be carried out at the business premises
of the applicant in Slough and should begin on or after 25th June 1979.
d   Article 3, after stating that the decision was addressed to the applicant, went on:

'It shall be notified by being handed over personally immediately before the
invesigation is to begin to a representative of the undertaking by the Commission's
officials authorised for the purposes of the investigation.
'Proceedings against this Decision may be instituted in the Court of Justice of the
European Communities in Luxembourg in accordance with Article 173 of the EEC
e   Treaty. As provided by Article 185 of the EEC Treaty, such proceedings shall not
have suspensory effect.'

The investigation took place on 27th June 1979. It was conducted by two Commission
officials, who were accompanied by an official from the Office of Fair Trading.
Consistently with art 3 of the decision, the applicant did not receive prior notice of the
f   investigation.
In their pleadings the parties give accounts of the investigation that differ in minor
respects. I do not think, however, that the differences are relevant to any of the issues in
the case.
The officials arrived at the applicant's premises at about 10 am. The decision was
served on Mr Aoki, the applicant's sales director, who signed a minute of its
g   notification. The nature and purpose of the investigation were explained to him and he
passed the information on by telephone to Mr Imura, the managing director. Mr Imura
sent Mr Maskrey, who was described as the applicant's 'legal and training manager', to
join the officials and Mr Aoki. The applicant's solicitor, Mr Robinson, was contacted at
his office in Norwich and arrangements were made for him to be brought by air and road
to Slough. A request (made either by Mr Aoki or by Mr Maskrey) that the investigation
h   be postponed until the arrival of Mr Robinson was refused by the inspectors who began
their work at about 10.45 am.
Mr Imura, Mr Aoki and other senior executives of the applicant left the premises at
lunch time because they had previously arranged to attend a trade exhibition in Cardiff.
Mr Robinson arrived at 1.30 pm. He was introduced to the officials and a copy of the
decision was given to him. He was informed of what the officials had so far done and he
j   stayed for the remainder of the investigation.
The investigation ended at about 5.30 pm. The Commission officials took with them
copies of a number of documents from the applicant's files, according to the Commission
26, consisting of 50 pages in all, according to the applicant a greater number. They did
not take, nor of course were they empowered to take, originals, which is one of the

features that distinguish this case from *Inland Revenue Comrs v Rossminster Ltd* [1980] 1
All ER 80, [1980] AC 952, to which some reference was made during the argument.

The applicant's case, as first put forward in its application, rested on four distinct
grounds: (1) that art 14 of Regulation No 17, on its correct interpretation, did not permit
the Commission to issue a decision requiring an undertaking to submit to an
investigation without first requesting it to do so by 'the informal procedure'; (2) that the
decision of the Commission was inadequately reasoned; (3) that in proceeding by way of
decision instead of by way of informal request the Commission had ·infringed the
principle of proportionality; and (4) that the Commission had infringed the applicant's
fundamental rights.

As the argument developed those grounds appeared to merge into each other, the
essence of the applicant's complaint being that it had had no warning of the investigation.

Nevertheless, the first question is whether art 14, correctly interpreted, provides, as the
applicant contends, for an obligatory two-stage procedure under which the Commission
must begin by informally requesting the undertaking concerned to submit to an
investigation on the basis only of an authorisation under para 2 of that article, and may
resort to a binding decision under para 3 only if that request is not complied with or is
incompletely complied with, or whether, as the Commission contends, the article confers
on it a discretion to carry out an investigation either on the basis of an authorisation
under para 2 only or on the basis of a decision under para 3, without its being bound to
use the former procedure before adopting the latter.

There is no doubt that the actual wording of art 14 is inapt to impose on the
Commission the obligation for which the applicant contends. Nor indeed did counsel
for the applicant seek to argue otherwise. His submission was that the court should leave
aside the wording of the article and look to its spirit and purpose. As to that the
Commission pointed out, rightly in my opinion, that the spirit and purpose of art 14
would be defeated if the Commission were always obliged to adopt a procedure that
would give the undertaking concerned an opportunity to hide or destroy relevant
documents. The Commission also relied on the judgment of this Court in *Acciaieria e
Tubeficio di Brescia v High Authority* [1960] ECR 71. That authority is not of course
directly in point since the court was there concerned with the interpretation of art 47 of
the ECSC Treaty, but there is a similarity between that article and art 14 of Regulation
No 17, and the judgment does at least show that the court will not readily imply into
such a provision a requirement that information should be sought before any
investigation is carried out. It is significant, I think, that the court there held (at 80) that
there was 'nothing in the letter, spirit or aim of the first paragraph of Article 47 to
prohibit information being obtained and a check being made at the same time'.

In support of the applicant's contention five arguments were put forward.

First, it was pointed out that art 11 of Regulation No 17, on requests by the
Commission for information, undoubtedly prescribes an obligatory two-stage procedure;
and reference was made to what I said about that in *Transocean Marine Paint Association
v Commission* [1974] ECR 1063 at 1089–1090. The same 'must' be true, it was submitted,
of art 14. In my opinion that is not so, because neither the wording nor the purpose of
the two articles is the same. As to the wording paras 2 to 4 of art 11 lay down a procedure
under which the Commission may send to an undertaking a request for information.
Then para 5 provides:

'Where an undertaking . . . does not supply the information requested within the
time limit fixed by the Commission, or supplies incomplete information, the
Commission shall by decision require the information to be supplied . . .'

Thus failure to obtain a satisfactory answer to a request for information is, under art 11,
expressly made a condition precedent to the adoption of a decision. There is no
corresponding language in art 14. Given the proximity of the two provisions, their
different language must, in my opinion, mean that they are intended to operate

differently. As to purpose, art 11 enables the Commission to seek, and if necessary to
a compel, the co-operation of the undertaking concerned in providing information, which
may or may not be contained in documents in the possession of the undertaking. Article
14 in contrast enables the Commission to take action to obtain evidence directly through
its own officials.

The applicant's second argument was also based on art 11. Pointing to the power in
art 14(1)(c) to 'ask for oral explanations on the spot', the applicant submitted that, unless
b its interpretation of art 14 were adopted, that article could be used by the Commission
to circumvent the two-stage procedure prescribed by art 11. In my opinion that is not
so, because, as was submitted by the Commission, the only explanations that can be
sought under art 14(1)(c) are explanations relating to the books and records under
examination or their contents.

Third, it was argued on behalf of the applicant that support for its interpretation of art
c 14 was to be found in a passage in the Report of the European Parliament's Internal
Market Committee on the proposal that ultimately became Regulation No 17, the
'Deringer Report' (European Parliament Document 57/1961), in a speech made to the
European Parliament on 19th October 1961, during the debate on that proposal, by Dr
Hans von der Groeben, the member of the Commission then responsible for competition
policy, and in an article written by Dr W Schlieder, the Commission's Director General
d for Competition, in Der Betriebs-Berater (1962, p 311). Those passages do, I think,
suggest that their authors regarded arts 11 and 14 (which were arts 9 and 11 respectively
in the proposal) as laying down similar procedures. That, however, cannot, in my view,
provide guidance as to the intentions of the Council when it enacted Regulation No 17.
As I ventured to point out in *Milac v HZA Freiburg* [1976] ECR 1639 at 1664, what the
members of the Council do when they adopt a regulation is to agree on a text. They do
e not necessarily all have the same views as to its meaning. That is to be sought, if
necessary, by judicial interpretation of the text. It cannot be sought by inquiry from
individual members of the Council. A fortiori can it not be sought by ascertaining the
views of particular members of the Parliament or of the Commission, let alone of
members of the Commission's staff, however eminent and however much they may
have been concerned in the preparation of the text. The authority relied on on behalf of
f the applicant for the contrary view was the judgment of this court in *Stauder v City of Ulm*
[1969] ECR 419. That case, however, was about a decision of the Commission adopted
under the management committee procedure. It was discovered that, whilst the French
and Italian texts of the decision accorded with what the management committee had
agreed on, the German and Dutch texts did not. Not surprisingly the Court held that the
French and Italian texts were to be preferred. That authority would only be in point here
g if the text of Regulation No 17 in one or more of the official languages of the Community
were found not to accord with the text agreed on by the Council. It does not support the
proposition for which it was relied on by the applicant. I ought to add that the
Commission drew our attention to a passage in a book written by Dr Deringer in which
he clearly expressed the view that art 14 did not impose an obligatory two-stage procedure
(see The Competition Law of the European Economic Community (1968, p 335)).
h Indeed the parties in their pleadings exhaustively reviewed the opinions of learned
writers on that question and it is manifest that, on balance, they favour the view
contended for by the Commission.

Fourth, the applicant relied on what it described as the practice of the Commission.
This led to a discussion of the manner in which the Commission had operated art 14 in
the past. I need not, I think, go into the details of it. It transpired that the Commission
j had resorted to decisions under art 14(3) without prior notice much more frequently
since the beginning of 1979 than previously. On behalf of the Commission it was
explained to us that that was because, as Community law became better known and
clearer in its content, undertakings were more and more tending to conceal their cartels,
particularly the more obviously unjustifiable ones. Be that as it may, it does not seem to

be that the nature of the powers conferred on the Commission by art 14 can depend on
the manner in which it has thought fit to exercise them in the past.

Lastly on this first question, the applicant referred to fundamental rights. Although
its argument here had of course a similarity to its argument in support of its fourth
ground of challenge to the validity of the Commission's decision, there was an essential
difference. Its argument here was that, in the absence of clear words relieving the
Commission from any obligation to give prior notice of an investigation, art 14 must be
interpreted in such a way as to encroach as little as possible on an undertaking's
fundamental rights, ie as requiring such prior notice. The fundamental rights relied on
by the applicant were the right to privacy, the right to be heard (with the concomitant
right to be told what was proposed), the right 'to prepare for the investigation', and the
right to appeal to this Court and seek a stay from it.

On the right to privacy the applicant relied on art 8 of the European Convention on
Human Rights (TS 71 (1953); Cmd 8969), which is in these terms:

'(1) Everyone has the right to respect for his private and family life, his home and
his correspondence.

'(2) There shall be no interference by a public authority with the exercise of this
right except such as is in accordance with the law and is necessary in a democratic
society in the interests of national security, public safety or the economic well-being
of the country, for the prevention of disorder or crime, for the protection of health
or morals, or for the protection of the rights and freedoms of others.'

The wording of that article might at first sight suggest that it applied only to an
individual and his home. This court, however, in the *Acciaieria di Brescia* case [1960]
ECR 71 at 90 clearly considered that the right to privacy extended to business premises,
whether those of an individual or of a company. That must indeed be so, for a public
authority cannot in a 'democratic society' be permitted to invade private property save
under a specific power conferred by law. The applicant did not deny that an invasion of
privacy might, in accordance with para (2) of art 8, be authorised by law in the interests
of 'the economic well-being of the country'. The burden of its submission was that the
person concerned should be given advance notice of such a proposed invasion. But there
is nothing in art 8 to that effect, nor was any authority cited on behalf of the applicant in
support of the proposition. Moreover, if the proposition were correct, most of the
powers of inspection and search conferred on national authorities, such as police, fiscal,
public health, and weights and measures authorities, quite apart from those concerned
with the enforcement of competition law, would be invalid.

What is somewhat unusual about art 14, if it means what to my mind it does, is that
the Commission is empowered to proceed without any sort of warrant from a judicial
authority. In general, though not always, the laws of member states require officers of
a public authority to have such a warrant before they may enter private premises.
Indeed the Deringer report suggested, citing the German constitution, that such a
requirement should be written into what are now arts 11 and 14 of Regulation No 17;
it pointed out that the right to have a decision of the Commission reviewed by this court
did not afford the same safeguard (see para 121 of that report). One may speculate as to
why that suggestion was not adopted, but one cannot in my opinion conclude, from the
fact that it was not, that art 14 is to be interpreted as conferring on an undertaking a right
to prior notice of an investigation.

As to the right to be heard I will say at once that I was unimpressed by an argument
put forward by the Commission which rested on art 19 of Regulation No 17. That article
lists certain categories of decisions that the Commission may not take without giving the
undertakings concerned an opportunity of being heard. It does not mention decisions
under art 14. A right to be heard may however exist although no legislation expressly
confers it; consider for instance the *Transocean Marine Paint Association* case [1974] ECR
1063. Nevertheless, the rule that a person whose rights are liable to be affected by an

administrative decision is entitled to be heard by the authority concerned is only a
a general rule. It is subject to exceptions. No-one has ever succeeded in categorising the
exceptions or in defining the circumstances in which they exist. Perhaps I may without
undue egotism refer to the discussion of that problem at the 8th Congress of the FIDE at
Copenhagen in 1978 (see the report of the proceedings at that congress, vol 3, pp 1–6 and
1–7, vol 1, pp 40–41). But one of the exceptions must be, in my opinion, where the
purpose of the decision would or might be defeated if the right were accorded. One
b comes back here, of course, to the Commission's point that the purpose of carrying out
an investigation without warning is to forestall the possible destruction or concealment
of relevant documents. Nor is it as if an undertaking affected by such an investigation
were left without a remedy. Its right to have the decision of the Commission reviewed
by the court is expressly preserved by art 14. True that remedy can only be invoked, if
the Commission is right, after the investigation has taken place, but that does not make
c it an ineffective remedy. The court may, as the Commission concedes, if it holds the
decision to have been unlawful, order the Commission to return to the undertaking any
copies of documents obtained as a result of the investigation and to refrain from using
any information so obtained.

As to the third fundamental right claimed on behalf of the applicant, the right 'to
prepare for the investigation', by taking legal advice, marshalling the documents
d considered by the undertaking to be relevant and not privileged from disclosure, and
ensuring that 'suitable senior executives and lawyers' can be present, I think it enough to
say that no authority whatever was cited on behalf of the applicant for the existence of
any such right.

The last 'fundamental right' claimed on behalf of the applicant was no more, really,
than a right to apply to this court for a stay of the investigation. That right was said to
e be conferred by art 185 of the treaty, which reads:

> 'Actions brought before the Court of Justice shall not have suspensory effect. The
> Court of Justice may, however, if it considers that circumstances so require, order
> that application of the contested act be suspended.'

Any right conferred by art 185 to apply to the court for an order suspending the
f application of a decision of the Commission under art 14 of Regulation No 17 can,
however, only be ancillary to the right to bring an action challenging the validity of that
decision under art 173 of the treaty. It is a right, therefore, that can be invoked only after
the decision has been adopted. So its existence cannot lead to the conclusion that the
Commission is bound under art 14 to adopt an informal procedure of the kind contended
for by the applicant as a preliminary to adopting the decision.

g   For those reasons I am of the opinion that art 14 is not to be interpreted in the manner
contended for by the applicant.

I can deal much more shortly with the second, third and fourth grounds on which the
applicant challenged the Commission's decision. Those grounds were of course relied on
on the footing that art 14 did not provide for a compulsory two-stage procedure.

The second was, your Lordships remember, that the decision was inadequately
h reasoned and the third was that it infringed the principle of proportionality. I take them
together because, as counsel for the applicant said at the hearing, they were linked. The
argument in support of them was, as I understood it, essentially this. Either the
Commission had reason to fear that the applicant might hide or destroy evidence, in
which case the Commission should have so stated in the preamble to its decision, so as to
justify its proceeding by way of immediate decision rather than by way of informal
j request first, or the Commission had no such fear, in which case the course it took was
disproportionate to the circumstances. I would reject that argument, if only because it
seems to me obvious that a recital that the Commission had reason to fear that an
undertaking might conceal or destroy evidence is not one that it can be required to
include in a decision addressed to that undertaking, or indeed to anyone.

As to the applicant's fourth ground, I think that I have said enough about fundamental rights to show that in my opinion no such rights of the applicant were infringed by the *a* Commission. It was not contended on behalf of the applicant that art 14 itself, if interpreted as not imposing a two-stage procedure, infringed anyone's fundamental rights. Nor do I think it could have been.

In the result I am of the opinion that this action should be dismissed with costs.

b

26th June. **THE COURT OF JUSTICE** delivered its judgment which, having summarised the facts, procedure and submissions of the parties, dealt with the law as follows:

1. By application of 24th August 1979, National Panasonic (UK) Ltd, a company incorporated in the United Kingdom (hereinafter referred to as 'National Panasonic'), *c* requests, under arts 173 and 174 of the EEC Treaty, the annulment of the Commission decision of 22nd June 1979 concerning an investigation to be made pursuant to art 14(3) of Regulation No 17 of 6th February 1962 of the Council. By the same application, the applicant requests in addition that the Commission should be ordered to return to National Panasonic all documents copied by the officials of the Commission during that investigation, to destroy the notes made at that time and to undertake not to make any *d* further use of such documents or notes or information.

2. The applicant is a company formed under English law and is a subsidiary of the Japanese Matsushita Electric Industrial Co and the exclusive distributor in the United Kingdom of National Panasonic and Technics electronic goods intended for sale to consumers. Another subsidiary of the Matsushita group is National Panasonic Vertriebsgesellschaft mbH, which is incorporated in the Federal Republic of Germany *e* and distributes National Panasonic products in that member state.

3. On 11th January 1977 National Panasonic Vertriebsgesellschaft mbH notified the Commission of an agreement relating to the distribution of National Panasonic products and requesting negative clearance or an exemption under art 85(3) of the treaty.

4. Although the notification did not indicate whether or not the agreement contained a prohibition on exports to another member state, information obtained by the *f* Commission showed that National Panasonic required its resellers not to re-export National Panasonic and Technics products to other member states.

5. On the basis of that information, the Commission considered that it was necessary to believe that the applicant had participated and was still participating in agreements and concerted practices contrary to art 85 of the EEC Treaty and therefore decided to carry out an investigation pursuant to Regulation No 17 of the Council and more *g* particularly to art 14(3) thereof. For that purpose on 22nd June 1979 it adopted the contested decision, art 3 of which provided, inter alia that it would be notified by being handed over personally immediately before the investigation was to begin to a representative of the undertaking by the Commission's officials authorised for the purposes of the investigation.

6. The investigation in question was carried out on 27th June 1979 by two officials *h* authorised by the Commission who, accompanied by an official of the Office of Fair Trading, which is the competent authority in the United Kingdom and which must be consulted under art 14(4) of Regulation No 17, arrived at National Panasonic's sales offices in Slough, Berkshire, and, after notifying their decision by handing it over personally to the directors of the company, in fact carried out the investigation without awaiting the arrival of the company's solicitor. They left the company's offices on the *j* same day with copies of several documents and notes made during the investigation.

7. The applicant contests the validity of that investigation, maintaining that the Commission decision ordering it is unlawful. It puts forward four submissions in support of its application, alleging that that decision is in breach of art 14 of Regulation

a No 17 and of fundamental rights, that it failed to state reasons properly or at all for the decision and that it violates the doctrine of proportionality.

(a) *The infringement of art 14 of Regulation No 17*

8. The applicant maintains first of all that the contested decision is unlawful because it does not comply with the spirit and letter of the provisions of art 14(3) of Regulation No 17 of the Council. To this end it maintains that on a proper construction those b provisions provide for a two-stage procedure which permits the Commission to adopt a decision requiring an undertaking to submit to an investigation only after attempting to carry out that investigation on the basis of a written authorisation to its own officials. This interpretation is confirmed, according to the applicant, by art 11 of the same regulation which is similar in structure and provides for a two-stage procedure and by art 13(1) which makes a distinction between an investigation carried out by the Commission c informally and that ordered by decision.

9. These arguments do not appear to be well founded. In order to enable the Commission to accomplish its task of ensuring that the rules of competition in the Common Market are complied with, the eighth recital of the preamble to Regulation No 17 provides that it—

d   'must ... be empowered, throughout the common market, to require such
      information to be supplied and to undertake such investigations as are necessary to
      bring to light any agreement, decision or concerted practice prohibited by Article
      85(1) or any abuse of a dominant position prohibited by Article 86.'

For this purpose, that regulation provides for separate procedures, which shows that the exercise of the powers given to the Commission with regard to information and e investigations is not subject to the same conditions.

10. Article 11(2), (3) and (5), which concern the Commission's power to request the information it considers necessary, provide as follows:

f   '2. When sending a request for information to an undertaking or association of
      undertakings, the Commission shall at the same time forward a copy of the request
      to the competent authority of the Member State in whose territory the seat of the
      undertaking or association of undertakings is situated.
      '3. In its request the Commission shall state the legal basis and the purpose of the
      request and also the penalties provided for in Article 15(1)(b) for supplying incorrect
      information.
      '5. Where an undertaking or association of undertakings does not supply the
g   information requested within the time limit fixed by the Commission, or supplies
      incomplete information, the Commission shall by decision require the information
      to be supplied. The decision shall specify what information is required, fix an
      appropriate time-limit within which it is to be supplied and indicate the penalties
      provided for in Article 15(1)(b) and Article 16(1)(c) and the right to have the decision
      reviewed by the Court of Justice.'

h It follows from those provisions that the article in question in fact stipulates, for the exercise of that power, a two-stage procedure, the second stage of which, involving the adoption by the Commission of a decision which specifies what information is required, may only be initiated if the first stage, in which a request for information is sent to the undertakings or associations of undertakings, has been carried out without success.

11. On the other hand, art 14 of the same regulation on the 'investigating' powers of j the Commission is different in structure. Article 14(2) and (3), which define the conditions for the exercise of those powers, provide as follows:

     '2. The officials of the Commission authorised for the purpose of these
     investigations shall exercise their powers upon production of an authorisation in

writing specifying the subject matter and purpose of the investigation and the
penalties provided for in Article 15(1)(c) in cases where production of the required *a*
books or other business records is incomplete. In good time before the investigation,
the Commission shall inform the competent authority of the Member State in
whose territory the same is to be made of the investigation and of the identity of the
authorised officials.

'3. Undertakings and associations of undertakings shall submit to investigations
ordered by a decision of the Commission. A decision shall specify the subject *b*
matter and purpose of the investigation, appoint the date on which it is to begin and
indicate the penalties provided for in Article 15(1)(c) and Article 16(1)(d) and the
right to have the decision reviewed by the Court of Justice.'

This provision does not of course prevent the Commission from carrying out an
investigation solely pursuant to a written authorisation given to its officials without *c*
adopting a decision, but in other respects it contains nothing to indicate that it may only
adopt a decision within the meaning of art 14(3) if it has previously attempted to carry
out an investigation by mere authorisation. Whereas art 11(5) expressly makes the
adoption of a Commission decision subject to the condition that the latter has previously
asked for the necessary information by means of a request addressed to those concerned
and specifies in art 11(3) the essentials which such a request must contain, art 14 makes *d*
the investigating procedure by means of a decision subject to no preliminary of this kind.

12. The applicant wrongly relies in support of its argument on the wording of art
13(1) of the same regulation which provides that, at the request of the Commission, the
national authorities must undertake the investigations which the Commission considers
to be necessary under art 14(1) or which it has ordered by decision pursuant to art
14(3). By making a distinction between the two investigatory procedures, that provision *e*
clearly shows by the use of the word 'or' that those two procedures do not necessarily
overlap but constitute two alternative checks the choice of which depends on the special
features of each case.

13. The difference in the rules on this subject contained in arts 11 and 14 is explained,
moreover, by the diversity of the needs met by those two provisions. Whereas the
information which the Commission considers it necessary to know may not as a general *f*
rule be collected without the co-operation of the undertakings and associations of
undertakings possessing this information, investigations, on the other hand, are not
necessarily subject to the same condition. In general they aim at checking, by measures
such as those listed in the second sub-paragraph of art 14(1) of Regulation No 17, the
actual existence and scope of information which the Commission already has and do not
therefore necessarily presuppose previous co-operation by undertakings or associations of *g*
undertakings in possession of the information necessary for the check.

14. The applicant maintains in another connection that if it were necessary to interpret
art 14 differently from art 11, that is as meaning that it permits the Commission to adopt
an investigation decision without previously carrying out an investigation such as that
provided for in art 14(2), the Commission might, by having recourse to the procedure
laid down in the same article for requests for information, escape the conditions laid *h*
down in art 11 and thus evade the guarantees given by the latter to the undertakings and
associations of undertakings concerned.

15. Such arguments do not however take into account the distinction made by the
regulation itself between the 'information' referred to in art 11 and the 'investigation'
referred to in art 14. The fact that the officials authorised by the Commission, in
carrying out an investigation, have the power to request during that investigation *j*
information on specific questions arising from the books and business records which
they examine is not sufficient to conclude that an investigation is identical to a procedure
intended only to obtain information within the meaning of art 11 of the regulation.

16. For all these reasons, it is necessary to dismiss the first submission as unfounded.

(b) *The infringement of fundamental rights*

a   17. The applicant then claims that by failing previously to communicate to it beforehand the decision ordering an investigation in question, the Commission has in this instance infringed fundamental rights of the applicant, in particular the right to receive advance notification of the intention to apply a decision regarding it, the right to be heard before a decision adversely affecting it is taken and the right to use the opportunity given to it under art 185 of the treaty to request a stay of execution of such

b   a decision. The applicant relies in particular on art 8 of the European Convention for the Protection of Human Rights and Fundamental Freedoms (TS 71 (1953); Cmd 8969) whereby 'Everyone has the right to respect for his private and family life, his home and family life, his home and his correspondence'. It considers that those guarantees must be provided mutatis mutandis also to legal persons.

        18. As the court stated in its judgment in *J Nold, Kohlen- und Baustoffgrosshandlung v EC*

c   *Commission* [1974] ECR 491 at 507, 'fundamental rights form an integral part of the general principles of law, the observance of which the [Court of Justice] ensures', in accordance with constitutional traditions common to the member states and with international treaties on which the member states have collaborated or of which they are signatories.

        19. In this respect it is necessary to point out that art 8(2) of the European Convention,

d   in so far as it applies to legal persons, whilst stating the principle that public authorities should not interfere with the exercise of the rights referred to in art 8(1), acknowledges that such interference is permissible to the extent to which it—

        'is in accordance with the law and is necessary in a democratic society in the interests of national security, public safety or the economic well-being of the

e   country, for the prevention of disorder or crime, for the protection of health or morals, or for the protection of the rights and freedom of others.'

        20. In this instance, as follows from the seventh and eighth recitals of the preamble to Regulation No 17, the aim of the powers given to the Commission by art 14 of that regulation is to enable it to carry out its duty under the EEC Treaty of ensuring that the

f   rules on competition are applied in the Common Market. The function of these rules is, as follows from the fourth recital of the preamble to the treaty, art 3(f) and arts 85 and 86, to prevent competition from being distorted to the detriment of the public interest, individual undertakings and consumers. The exercise of the powers given to the Commission by Regulation No 17 contributes to the maintenance of the system of competition intended by the treaty which undertakings are absolutely bound to comply

g   with. In these circumstances, it does not therefore appear that Regulation No 17, by giving the Commission the powers to carry out investigations without previous notification, infringes the right invoked by the applicant.

        21. Moreover, as regards more particularly the argument that the applicant was in this instance denied the right to be heard before a decision was taken regarding it, it is necessary to state that the exercise of such a right of defence is chiefly incorporated in

h   legal or administrative procedures for the termination of an infringement or for a declaration that an agreement, decision or concerted practice is incompatible with art 85, such as the procedures referred to by Regulation 99/63 of the Commission of 25th July 1963. On the other hand, the investigation procedure referred to in art 14 of Regulation No 17 does not aim at terminating an infringement or declaring that an agreement, decision or concerted practice is incompatible with art 85; its sole objective is to enable

j   the Commission to gather the necessary information to check the actual existence and scope of a given factual and legal situation. Only if the Commission considers that the data for the appraisal thereof collected in this way justify the initiation of a procedure under regulation 99/63 must the undertaking or association of undertakings concerned be heard before such a decision is taken, pursuant to art 19(1) of Regulation No 17 and to the provisions of Regulation 99/63. Precisely this substantive difference between the decisions taken at the end of such a procedure and decisions ordering an investigation explains the wording of art 19(1) which, in listing the decisions which the Commission cannot take before giving those concerned the opportunity of exercising their right of defence, does not mention that laid down in art 14(3) of the same regulation.

22. Finally, the argument that the absence of previous information deprived the applicant of the opportunity of exercising its right under art 185 of the treaty to request the court for a stay of execution of the decision in question is contradicted by the very provisions of art 185. That article presupposes in fact that a decision has been adopted and that it is effective, whereas the previous notification, which the applicant complains that the Commission did not send it, should have preceded the adoption of the contested decision and could not have been binding.

23. In view of these considerations, the second submission is not well founded.

(c) Absence of a statement of the reasons on which the decision was based

24. The applicant also maintains that the contested decision is irregular in that it failed to state or to state properly the reasons on which it was based, in particular because it in no way indicates the reasons why the Commission applied art 14(3) of Regulation No 17 in this instance without attempting first of all to carry out an informal investigation.

25. Article 14(3) of Regulation No 17 itself lays down the essential constituents of the statement of the reasons on which a decision ordering an investigation is based by providing that it—

'shall specify the subject matter and the purpose of the investigation, appoint the date on which it is to begin and indicate the penalties provided for in Article 15(1)(c) and Article 16(1)(d) and the right to have the decision reviewed by the Court of Justice.'

26. It is an established fact that the preamble to the contested decision states the purpose, which is to check facts which might show the existence of an export ban contrary to the treaty, and indicates the penalties laid down in arts 15(1)(c) and 16(1)(d) of Regulation No 17. It is also established that arts 1 and 2 of that decision state the subject matter of the investigation decided on and the place where and date on which that investigation will be carried out. Finally, the second paragraph of art 3 of the decision indicates the possibilities of instituting proceedings before the Court of Justice against such a decision in accordance with art 173 of the treaty.

27. In view of these factors, it follows that the contested decision fulfils the requirements laid down in Regulation No 17 as regards the statement of the reasons on which it is based and that it is necessary to dismiss this submission as unfounded.

(d) The violation of the principle of proportionality

28. The applicant points out in addition that the principle of proportionality, as established by the case law of the Court of Justice, implies that a decision ordering an investigation adopted without the preliminary procedure may only be justified if the situation is very grave and where there is the greatest urgency and the need for complete secrecy before the investigation is carried out. It points out, finally, that the contested decision violates such a principle by not indicating in the statement of the reasons on which it is based that any of those facts exists.

29. The Commission's choice between an investigation by straightforward authorisation and an investigation ordered by a decision does not depend on the facts relied on by the applicant but on the need for an appropriate inquiry, having regard to the special features of the case.

30. Considering that the contested decision was aimed solely at enabling the Commission to collect the necessary information to appraise whether there was any

a infringement of the treaty, it does not therefore appear that the Commission's action in this instance was disproportionate to the objective pursued and therefore violated the principle of proportionality.

31. For all these reasons, since this last submission cannot be accepted either, it is necessary to dismiss the application as unfounded.

Costs

b 32. Under art 69(2) of the Rules of Procedure, the unsuccessful party should be ordered to pay the costs.

33. Since the applicant has failed in its submissions, it must be ordered to pay the costs.

c On those grounds, the court hereby: (1) dismisses the application as unfounded; (2) orders the applicant to pay the costs.

Agents: *Lovell, White & King* (for the applicant); *Legal Service of the EC Commission.*

Andrew Durand Esq   Barrister.

d

Lambert v Roberts

QUEEN'S BENCH DIVISION
DONALDSON LJ AND KILNER BROWN J
e 11th, 19th DECEMBER 1980

Road traffic – Breath test – Driving a motor vehicle on a road – Requirement to take breath test – Requirement made on defendant's property after defendant protesting that constable a trespasser – Whether requirement to take breath test lawful – Whether constable's implied licence to go onto defendant's property revoked – Road Traffic Act 1972, s 8(1).

f

A uniformed police constable in a police car followed the defendant's car along a road because the defendant was exceeding the speed limit. When the defendant's car turned into the private driveway of the defendant's house the constable approached the defendant on foot in the driveway to tell him that he had been exceeding the speed limit. The constable smelt alcohol on the defendant's breath and, pursuant to s 8(1)[a] of *g* the Road Traffic Act 1972, required him to provide a specimen for a breath test. The defendant refused to comply with the request and stated that the constable was on private property. The constable said he would wait for ten minutes before taking a breath test. During the ten minutes the defendant and members of his family stated to the constable that he was on private property and was a trespasser. The defendant refused to take a breath test at the end of the ten minutes and again stated that the *h* constable was a trespasser. The constable, pursuant to s 8(3)[a] of the 1972 Act, arrested the defendant for failing to provide a breath test and took him to the police station where he again refused to take a breath test and also refused to provide a specimen of his blood or urine for testing. The defendant was charged, inter alia, with failing without reasonable excuse to provide a specimen for a breath test, contrary to s 8(3), and with failing to

j *a* Section 8, so far as material, provides:
'(1) A constable in uniform may require any person driving or attempting to drive a motor vehicle on a road . . . to provide a specimen of breath for a breath test there or nearby, if the constable has reasonable cause—(*a*) to suspect him of having alcohol in his body . . .
'(3) A person who, without reasonable excuse, fails to provide a specimen of breath for a breath test under subsection (1) . . . above shall be guilty of an offence . . .'

provide a blood or urine specimen, contrary to s 9(3) of the Act. The magistrates decided that the constable's implied permission or licence to enter the defendant's property had *a* been revoked by the statements of the defendant and his family that the constable was on private property and was a trespasser and accordingly the constable was not entitled to require the defendant to provide a specimen for a breath test under s 8(1), and the defendant's arrest and the subsequent request for a blood or urine specimen were unlawful. The magistrates accordingly dismissed the charges. The prosecutor appealed.

b

Held – The appeal would be dismissed for the following reasons—

(1) The magistrates were entitled to take the view that the statements of the defendant and his family had revoked the constable's implied licence to enter the defendant's property, even though the statements could be viewed merely as disputing the constable's right to require a breath test on the defendant's property and not as revoking his licence to enter (see p 19 *d e* and p 20 *f*, post).

c

(2) Since the constable's licence to enter the defendant's property had been revoked, he ceased to be acting in the execution of his duty while he remained on the property and was not entitled to require the defendant to take a breath test under s 8(1) of the 1972 Act. It followed that the request made on the defendant's property to take a breath test was unlawful, and that the defendant's arrest and the subsequent requirement to provide a blood or urine specimen were also unlawful (see p 19 *e f* and p 20 *e f*, post); *Davis v Lisle* *d* [1936] 2 All ER 213 and *Morris v Beardmore* [1980] 2 All ER 753 applied; dictum of Lord Diplock in *Morris v Beardmore* [1980] 2 All ER at 756 explained.

Notes

For the power to require a specimen of breath for a breath test and the power of arrest following refusal to provide a specimen, see Supplement to 33 Halsbury's Laws (3rd Edn) para 1061A.3–6.

e

For the Road Traffic Act 1972, ss 8, 9, see 42 Halsbury's Statutes (3rd Edn) 1651, 1655.

Cases referred to in judgments

Davis v Lisle [1936] 2 All ER 213, [1936] 2 KB 434, 105 LJKB 593, 155 LT 23, 100 JP 280, 34 LGR 253, 30 Cox CC 412, DC, 15 Digest (Reissue) 985, 8553.

Morris v Beardmore [1980] 2 All ER 753, [1980] 3 WLR 283, HL. *f*

R v Jones [1970] 1 All ER 209, [1970] 1 WLR 211, 134 JP 215, [1970] RTR 56, CA, Digest (Cont Vol C) 932, *322kl*.

Appeal

The prosecutor, George Patrick Lambert, appealed by case stated from a decision of the justices for the County of Bedford sitting at Biggleswade dismissing two charges brought *g* against the respondent, Clive James Roberts, that when driving a motor vehicle on a road he failed without reasonable excuse to provide a breath specimen when required to do so by a uniformed police constable, contrary to s 8(3) of the Road Traffic Act 1972, and, having been arrested under s 8(5) of the 1972 Act for refusing to provide a breath specimen, while at a police station failed without reasonable excuse to provide a specimen of blood or urine for a laboratory test when required to do so by a police constable, *h* contrary to s 9(3) of the 1972 Act. The facts as found by the justices, the justices' conclusions and the questions for the opinion of the court are set out in the judgment of Donaldson LJ.

Geoffrey Dallas Mercer for the prosecutor.
Mark Lowe for the respondent.

j

Cur adv vult

19th December. The following judgments were read.

DONALDSON LJ. On 13th August 1980 the respondent appeared before the justices for the County of Bedford sitting at Biggleswade to answer three motoring charges. The

first alleged that he had exceeded a speed limit. The second alleged that when driving a
a motor vehicle on a road, namely the A507, he failed without reasonable excuse to
provide a specimen of breath when required to do so by a uniformed police constable,
contrary to s 8(3) of the Road Traffic Act 1972. The third alleged that, having been
arrested under s 8 of the 1972 Act, while at a police station he failed without reasonable
excuse to provide a specimen of blood or urine for a laboratory test when required to do
so by a police constable, contrary to s 9(3) of the 1972 Act.
b   The two 'breathalyser' charges were dismissed by the justices and the prosecutor now
appeals by case stated. The facts as found by the justices were as follows:

'At 11.12 p.m. on Thursday 29 May 1980, Police Constable Tinkler was on duty
in uniform driving a marked Police car along the A507 road at Clifton in the
County of Bedfordshire, travelling from the direction of the Henlow roundabout
c   towards Shefford. He was accompanied by P.C. Shotbolt who was acting as
observer. For a distance of two tenths of a mile they followed and checked the speed
of a Ford Escort Motor Car, index number VBH 557N—the speed recorded on the
speedometer of the Patrol Car was a constant 60 miles per hour. Whilst travelling
along the A507 road the Escort car indicated a left turn and then turned left into
Hitchin Lane. The Police vehicle followed, and the Escort car then turned right
d   into a private driveway leading to the rear of number 12 Hitchin Lane. P.C. Tinkler
followed the car along the driveway on foot and saw the vehicle come to a stop and
he approached the driver, the sole occupant of the vehicle, the Respondent Mr
Roberts. The Officer then told the Respondent that he had checked the speed of his
car along the A507 road for two tenths of a mile at a constant speed of 60 miles an
hour, and informed him that that part of the road was restricted to a speed limit of
e   40 miles an hour, and he cautioned the Respondent who replied to the effect that he,
the Respondent was on private property and that they were trespassing. At that
point the Officer noticed that the Respondent's breath smelt strongly of intoxicating
liquor, and he told the Respondent that as he had just committed a moving traffic
offence, he required the Respondent to provide a specimen of breath for a breath
test. On being asked whether he was willing to provide such a breath specimen the
f   Respondent replied, "Yes". The Officer then asked him if it was more than twenty
minutes since he had last consumed an alcoholic drink and the Respondent replied,
"No, only about ten minutes". The Officer then informed him that he could wait
for another ten minutes before giving the breath test. The Respondent replied, "All
right, I want to make a telephone call to my Solicitor because I'm on private
property and I want to make sure that what you are doing is right". The Officer
g   then agreed to his making a telephone call provided that he could accompany the
Respondent, and he followed him into his house where the Respondent's wife was
present, and the Officer and the Respondent then went to the Respondent's mother's
house at 14 Hitchin Lane where the Respondent made a telephone call. Following
that telephone call the Officer and the Respondent went back to the Respondent's
home and waited in his kitchen until the ten minutes had elapsed. At the expiration
h   of that time the Officer informed the Respondent that the twenty minutes had now
elapsed since he had last consumed alcohol and he was required to provide a
specimen of breath for a breath test, and the Respondent replied that he was waiting
for a telephone call before doing anything. The Officer then offered him an
Alcotest R80 device and told him to inflate the bag and informed him of the
consequences of refusing or making no attempt to inflate it and asked the
j   Respondent if he understood, the Respondent replied, "Yes but I'm not going to
inflate it until I've had the 'phone call". The Officer offered the breath test device
again, the Respondent again refused and made reference to the fact that the Officer
was on private property and a trespasser, and the Officer told him that he was being
arrested for refusing to provide a specimen of breath for a breath test. At this point
the telephone bell rang in the house next door and the Respondent attempted to

brush past the two Officers in an attempt to answer it, and the Officers pursued him into the garden, arrested him, and handcuffed him.'   *a*

Perhaps I should interpolate at this point that the house next door was the respondent's mother's house, and it was possible to get from one to the other without going on to the public highway.

Resuming the facts as found by the justices:

'The events inside the house occurred in the presence of the Respondent's wife, *b* then in the presence of his mother, and later in the presence of an aunt who came on the scene from the Respondent's mother's house having received the second telephone call. At various times these three persons protested to the Police about their attempts to obtain a breath specimen when on private property. They also protested about the methods used in arresting the Respondent. Following his arrest, the Respondent was conveyed to Biggleswade Police Station where in due *c* course he was required to provide a specimen of breath and then of blood or of urine, and he was told of the consequences of a failure to provide a specimen. The Respondent indicated that he was unwilling to provide a specimen. P.C. Tinkler then asked him to listen carefully to a second request, and then made a formal request for a specimen of blood and explained again the consequences of a failure to provide such a specimen. The Respondent again refused to supply it. At 12.35 a.m. *d* on the following day he was formally charged with the three offences and cautioned, and to each charge the Respondent replied, "No", he was then bailed to appear at Biggleswade Magistrates' Court.'

The justices' conclusions are expressed in the following terms:

'We were of the opinion that by the time he was formally required to provide a *e* specimen of breath for a breath test, that is while he was still on the driveway to his house, the Respondent had stated that he was on private property, and that he subsequently refused to comply with the Police Officer's requirement because he believed that the Police had no right to administer a breath test in those circumstances, and that he wished to obtain advice over the telephone from his Solicitor before he would agree to take a test. By the time that requirement was *f* repeated some ten minutes later the Police Officers could have been in no doubt that they were on the Respondent's private property, that the Respondent was objecting strongly to providing the breath specimen in those circumstances, and they had been told by the Respondent on at least four occasions that they were on private property and were trespassers. They were also told this by the Respondent's wife and at a later stage by his mother. For these reasons we came to the conclusion that *g* we should apply the principles laid down in the case of *Morris v Beardmore* and hold that the Police Officer had acted unlawfully in requiring the Respondent to give a breath test and in effecting an arrest on that requirement being refused. It followed that having come to that conclusion, the further requirement made at Biggleswade Police Station that the Respondent should provide a specimen of blood or of urine for a laboratory test was unlawful, and we therefore acquitted the Respondent on *h* both charges.'

The questions for the opinion of this court which are posed by the case stated are as follows:

'i. Were we right to form the view on the facts found by us that the Police permission or licence to be on the Respondent's private property had been revoked *j* by the Respondent's initial statement that they were on private property and trespassing, reinforced during the ten minutes which followed by statements to the same effect made to the Officers, not only by the Respondent but also by his wife and his mother?

'ii. Were we right to apply the principles laid down in the case of *Morris a* v *Beardmore* to the facts found by us in this case, namely that a Police Constable in uniform, making a requirement under Section 8(1) of the Road Traffic Act 1972, who had had his licence or permission to be on private property withdrawn by the occupier, thereby lost his right, whilst remaining on the property as a trespasser, to require the Defendant to give a breath test, and thereupon his power of arrest in the event that his request be refused?'

b Although s 8(1) and (3) of the Road Traffic Act 1972 are in terms confined to breath tests of 'any person driving or attempting to drive a motor vehicle on a road or other public place', it is well settled law that a requirement to take a breath test can be made off the road so long as it is made in the course of a chain of action following sufficiently closely on an observed driving on the road (see *R v Jones* [1970] 1 All ER 209, [1970] 1 WLR 211). Accordingly, no problem arises out of the mere fact that the first requirement *c* to provide a specimen of breath was made when the respondent was off the road.

The problem with which this appeal is concerned arises out of the fact that this requirement was made at a time when the police officer was on the respondent's own driveway and, as the justices have found, after he had revoked his licence to be there.

The first question posed by the justices is whether they were right to form the view that this licence was revoked. There can be no doubt that in the absence of a locked gate *d* or some notice such as 'police keep out', police officers, like all other citizens, have an implied licence to enter on a driveway and to approach the door of a dwelling house if they have, or reasonably think that they have, legitimate business with the occupier. But it is a licence which is revocable without prior notice. In the present case the justices have found that the respondent's statement that the police officer was on private property and that the police officers were trespassing was such a notice. I am quite unable to say *e* that this was wrong, although an alternative view of the respondent's conduct, taken as a whole, is that he was simply disputing the right of the police officers to require a breath test on private property but was not effectively revoking their licence.

Once the licence was revoked, the police officers were under a duty to withdraw from the respondent's property with all reasonable speed and, if they did not do so, they were not thereafter acting in the execution of their duty (see *Davis v Lisle* [1936] 2 All ER 213, *f* [1936] 2 KB 434). They did not do so and the question is whether in the light of that failure they were still entitled to require the respondent to take a breath test.

This was considered by the House of Lords, in the context of s 8(2) and (5) of the Road Traffic Act 1972, in *Morris v Beardmore* [1980] 2 All ER 753, [1980] 3 WLR 283. The decision is recorded in the headnote in the All England Law Reports as follows:

g 'Because a constable's power under s 8(2) of the 1972 Act to require a person to provide a specimen of breath was a serious erosion of the citizen's common law rights, it was to be presumed that, in the absence of express provision to the contrary, Parliament did not intend any further encroachment on those rights by a constable acting unlawfully, whether in breach of the criminal law or the civil law. In order to be able validly to require a person to take a breath test a constable not only had to be in uniform but had to be acting in the execution of his duty, *h* which he was not if at the time of making the request he was a trespasser on the premises of the person to whom he had made the request; and evidence of an accused's failure to comply with a request in such circumstances was not admissible under the rule that all relevant evidence ought to be admitted at trial no matter how it was obtained but subject to judicial discretion to exclude it, because evidence of an accused's failure to comply with a requirement to provide a specimen of breath *j* was not evidence of an offence that the accused had already committed but direct evidence of the ingredients of the offence itself. Since it was not disputed that the police officers were trespassing at the time they required the appellant to provide a specimen for a breath test it followed that the appeal would be allowed.'

It was contended on behalf of the prosecutor that that decision is distinguishable because it related to s 8(2), requiring a breath test following an accident, and not to s 8(1), requiring a breath test on a road or other public place. This distinction is difficult to *a* maintain in principle, because the question of the rights of a trespassing police officer can only arise when the motorist has left the road or other public place and when it does arise the same issues are involved whether the requirement is based on s 8(1) or on s 8(2).

However, some superficial support for this submission is to be derived from the speech of Lord Diplock who said ([1980] 2 All ER 753 at 756, [1980] 3 WLR 283 at 287): 'Different considerations may apply where the requirement to undergo a breath test is *b* made under sub-s (1) [of s 8].' Lord Edmund-Davies does not appear to have made any such distinction. Lord Keith confined his consideration to s 8(2). Lord Scarman treated the two subsections as indistinguishable and there are no signs that Lord Roskill was minded to make any distinction.

What then is the explanation of Lord Diplock's caveat? I think that it may be attributable to a point spelt out by Lord Keith when he said ([1980] 2 All ER 753 at 762, *c* [1980] 3 WLR 283 at 295):

> 'It can be envisaged that circumstances may arise where the requirement to undergo a breath test is made by a police constable in a situation where he, and perhaps also the person of whom the requirement is made, are trespassers on the property, enclosed or unenclosed, of a third party. It is to be understood that the reasons for holding the requirement to have been invalid in the present case have no *d* necessary application to that situation.'

It is inherently more likely that both motorist and police officers will be trespassing on the property of a third party in a 'hot pursuit' case under s 8(1) than where s 8(2) applies. But in the present case the property was not that of a third party and, in my judgment, the decision in *Morris v Beardmore* obliges us to hold that the justices were *e* correct in concluding that the original request to take a breath test was not lawfully made. This being the case, the arrest and subsequent requirement to give a specimen of blood or urine at the police station were also unlawful and the respondent was entitled, as a matter of law, to be acquitted of both the breathalyser offences.

KILNER BROWN J. I agree.   *f*

Appeal allowed.

The court refused leave to appeal to the House of Lords but certified, under s 33(2) of the Criminal Appeal Act 1968, that the following point of law of general public importance was involved in the decision: whether a constable in uniform who is on private property and whose permission to *g* *remain thereon is subsequently withdrawn by the owner or occupier is empowered under s 8(1) and (3) of the Road Traffic Act 1972 to require that owner or occupier to provide a specimen of breath for a breath test and, in the event of refusal to provide such a specimen, to effect a lawful arrest of that person.*

2nd March 1981. The Appeal Committee of the House of Lords (Lord Diplock, Lord Keith of *h* *Kinkel and Lord Bridge of Harwich) dismissed a petition by the prosecutor for leave to appeal.*

Solicitors: *Morris, Bridgman*, Bedford (for the prosecutor); *Balderton, Warren & Co* (for the respondent).

Sepala Munasinghe Esq   Barrister. *j*

a

Joyce v Yeomans

COURT OF APPEAL, CIVIL DIVISION
WALLER, BRANDON LJJ AND SIR DAVID CAIRNS
4th, 5th, 8th, 9th DECEMBER 1980

b *Appeal – Evidence – Medical evidence – Conflicting medical evidence – Trial judge preferring medical evidence called by defendant to that called by plaintiff – Interference with judge's preference – Principles on which appellate court should act.*

Damages – Personal injury – Loss of future earnings – Child – Serious disablement – Injuries accelerating onset of epilepsy – Epilepsy affecting child's education – Epilepsy likely to lead to loss of future earnings – Correct basis of assessment of damages.

c

Interest – Damages – Personal injury – Loss of earning capacity – Damages awarded to cover risk that plaintiff might have to take less well paid employment or be without employment – Whether interest payable on award.

d Shortly before his tenth birthday, the plaintiff, a fairly bright boy, sustained severe injuries, including a head injury, when a car driven by the defendant ran into him. Not long afterwards he began having epileptic fits. He passed his eleven-plus examination and began attending a grammar school but the fits got worse, his behaviour at school deteriorated and he was not able to attend school regularly on account of the fits. His school work suffered and he was unable to pass any O levels. He brought an action against the defendant claiming damages for negligence. At the trial, two doctors, who were called as expert witnesses by the plaintiff, stated that in their opinion his head injury suffered in the accident was the cause of his epilepsy. A third doctor, called by the defence, stated that in his opinion the plaintiff had been a potential epileptic from birth and the head injury had merely accelerated the onset of the fits, which would in any event probably have started by the time he was 14. The judge accepted the medical *f* evidence submitted by the defence and awarded the plaintiff £7,500 damages, with interest, to cover both pain, suffering and loss of amenities and also the injury to his earning capacity. The plaintiff appealed, contending (i) that the judge's finding as to the cause of the epilepsy should be reversed because it was against the weight of the evidence and, so far as expert witnesses were concerned, the trial judge did not have any significant advantage over the Court of Appeal in forming a correct judgment between conflicting *g* views, and (ii) that the amount awarded was inadequate in that it allowed very little margin for the injury to the plaintiff's earning capacity, which should, in any event, have been calculated separately on a multiplier/multiplicand basis.

e

Held – (1) Although the demeanour of medical witnesses was not as important as that of other witnesses of fact, it was nonetheless material for the purpose of assessing the *h* value of their evidence, and an appellate court ought not lightly to interfere with the findings of a trial judge on such evidence since he had the advantage of seeing and hearing the witnesses. In the circumstances there was no reason to fault the finding of the trial judge (see p 24 *e* to p 25 *a*, p 26 *g* to p 27 *c* and *f* to p 28 *a*, post); *Watt (or Thomas) v Thomas* [1947] 1 All ER 582 applied; *Stojalowski v Imperial Smelting Corpn (NSC) Ltd* (1976) 121 Sol Jo 118 distinguished.

j   (2) The court was not bound in a case like the plaintiff's to calculate the loss of earning capacity on a mathematical basis by taking a multiplier/multiplicand and (per Waller LJ and Sir David Cairns) it would not be appropriate to apply that method in the circumstances because there were so many imponderables. Interest could not however be awarded on the damages for loss of earning capacity (see p 25 *g* and *j* to p 26 *a* and *e* to *g*, p 27 *c* to *f* and p 28 *d e*, post); *Clarke v Rotax Aircraft Equipment Ltd* [1975] 3 All ER 794 applied.

(3) The sum awarded by the judge did not adequately reflect the very real and substantial injury to the plaintiff's earning capacity by reason of the onset of the epilepsy *a* just as he was about to start at grammar school, and damages of £13,500, consisting of £6,000, with interest, for the pain, suffering and loss of amenities, and £7,500, without interest, for the loss of earning capacity would be substituted for the judge's award (see p 26 *a* to *g*, p 27 *f* and p 28 *b* to *e*, post).

Notes   *b*
For damages for future pecuniary loss in personal injuries cases, see 12 Halsbury's Laws (4th Edn) paras 1146, 1156, 1157, and for cases on the subject, see 51 Digest (Repl) 814–817, 3707–3725.

Cases referred to in judgments
Clarke v Rotax Aircraft Equipment Ltd [1975] 3 All ER 794, [1975] 1 WLR 1570, [1975] *c*
   ICR 440, CA, Digest (Cont Vol D) 692, 182ca.
Stojalowski v Imperial Smelting Corpn (NSC) Ltd (1976) 121 Sol Jo 118, CA.
Watt (or Thomas) v Thomas [1947] 1 All ER 582, [1947] AC 484, [1947] LJR 515, 176 LT
   498, HL, 51 Digest (Repl) 815, 3713.

Cases also cited   *d*
Moeliker v A Reyrolle and Co Ltd [1977] 1 All ER 9, [1977] 1 WLR 132, CA.
Pickett v British Rail Engineering Ltd [1979] 1 All ER 774, [1980] AC 136, HL.
Smith v Manchester Corpn (1974) 17 KIR 1, CA.

Appeal
This was an appeal by the plaintiff, Michael Joyce, an infant suing by his father and next *e* friend Michael Joyce, against the judgment of Thompson J, given on 5th July 1979, whereby he ordered that the defendant, Derek Yeomans, pay to the plaintiff the sum of £11,597·69, consisting of £7,500 general damages, £42·55 special damages and £4,055·14 agreed interest on the general and special damages. The facts are set out in the judgment of Waller LJ.

                                                                             f
R N Titheridge QC and *Maura Logan* for the plaintiff.
Richard Clegg QC and *Michael Brompton* for the defendant.

WALLER LJ. This is an appeal from a decision of Thompson J given on 5th July 1979 when he awarded £7,500 to the plaintiff. The plaintiff was a boy who was born in 1963 who had a serious accident in February 1973, when he was a few months short of his *g* tenth birthday. The accident happened when he was watching the snow in the evening, and a car skidded into a garden, causing him a head injury, some 6 inches in length, a rupture of the spleen, a fracture of the clavicle, and he was in hospital only a few weeks. He recovered well at that stage, but he did complain of some 'dizzy' spells. By October 1973 he was getting visual disturbance, hallucinations, and in February 1974 an EEG revealed a focal abnormality of a temporal lobe and temporal lobe epilepsy was *h* diagnosed. At that stage he was about to start at grammar school, and he did start at grammar school in September 1974 when he was 11 years of age. The attacks that he was having then were such that he was put on to phenobarbitone, and during the first three years that he was at grammar school his general performance and behaviour was poor to bad. During that period he had four or five grand mal attacks, and in 1975 there was another EEG which confirmed an earlier one, although later there were two others *j* which showed no abnormality.

   In February 1975 he was seen by Dr Evans. There was a claim against the defendant at this time, and Dr Evans was asked to examine the boy and make a report, and he did so in February 1975. His conclusion was that the plaintiff was suffering from epilepsy. He said in his report:

a
'It seems that since the accident Michael has developed attacks of minor epilepsy which arise, in all probability, from an epileptic focus in the posterior temple region of the brain. It is unlikely, in my opinion, that the epileptic focus was due to the head injury that occurred in the accident in question. In all probability the epileptic focus has been present since birth and the head injury in question had the effect of bringing out epileptic attacks which would, in any case, have developed in the next few years.'

b
Dr Evans thought that that would have been probably before the age of 14.

The contrary view was expressed in July 1975 by Dr Gordon who, having described the epileptic seizures, said this;

c
'As they have only occurred since the accident and as I was unable to obtain any history of a possible cause prior to the accident, I feel it must be presumed that the minor seizures have resulted from the head injury.'

There was then an exchange of reports, but neither doctor accepted the view of the other. At the trial, evidence was given by Dr Evans for the defendant and by Dr Neary and Dr McKinlay for the plaintiff. Dr Neary was called into the case at a late stage because what appears to have been the best qualified medical witness of the defendant, Dr
d Liversedge, had unfortunately died.

At the trial the judge accepted the evidence of Dr Evans. He said:

'Dr Evans is in the minority amongst the doctors whose opinions I have before me. Nonetheless, I accept his view as correct. What the accident did in the case of the plaintiff was, in my judgment, to bring on attacks of epilepsy earlier than, had
e there been no accident, they would have been likely to manifest themselves.'

Counsel for the plaintiff has submitted that the judge was wrong in preferring the evidence of Dr Evans. He submitted, in a very persuasive argument, that Dr Evans in the course of his evidence had said that in his experience one-third to one-half of his patients who had temporal lobe epilepsy did not give a history of any disturbance or
f occurrence at birth or before (that is to say, before the epilepsy started) and therefore, counsel for the plaintiff submitted, when considering this case, at the most, it was only an even chance that there was some previous predisposing factor and that accordingly there was insufficient evidence to upset what he submitted was the primary inference that the epilepsy was caused by the accident. He further submitted that in cross-examination Dr Evans agreed that it was one of the factors which he took into consideration which could have happened without a predisposing cause. He submitted
g that this was a case in which the judge's finding of fact could be interfered with.

As I have said, Dr Evans, who is a consultant neurologist and fellow of the Royal College of Physicians, expressed the view quoted above; he had told the defendant's solicitors to send his opinion to those representing the plaintiff because he thought they might agree it. They did not. The defendant then went to Dr Liversedge, another consultant neurologist and fellow of the Royal College of Physicians and he said in his
h report, expressing the view that this was probably a result of the accident:

'. . . it is extremely difficult to suport the view that his epilepsy was in any way constitutional and I would be inclined to agree with the opinion expressed by Dr. Gordon that these attacks are post-traumatic, particularly in view of the focal abnormality on the electroencephalograph. In short, therefore, I would disagree
j with Dr. Evans's conclusions. This is clearly a very important case and for this reason I think we must carry out one of the new E.M.I. Scans, which will be most helpful in establishing the presence or the absence of any focal change due to trauma.'

So an EMI scan was done and it was negative. Dr Liversedge said that that was

encouragement for the future but did not alter his opinion, but one cannot help having
the impression that Dr Liversedge thought that the EMI scan would be decisive in his   *a*
favour.

At the trial as I have already said, Dr Neary gave evidence instead of Dr Liversedge, and
Dr Evans also gave evidence. I think I should quote just one or two of Dr Evans's answers
because it is his evidence that is being attacked. Dealing with the EMI scan in answer to
the judge's question: 'You would expect it to be shown in the temporal region if there
had been brain damage caused by the accident?', he said, 'That is what I mean, yes'. And   *b*
so he was attaching some importance to that particular factor. He also said that he would
expect post-traumatic amnesia of more than 24 hours as being the kind of factor he was
looking for if it was to be attributed to the accident; and in this case the post-traumatic
amnesia was said to 12 to 24 hours.

He also said that he would have looked for a history of complications, such as a
depressed fracture or a blood clot or, he said, 'a history of epilepsy within 7 days of the   *c*
impact but none of those arose'. He thought that the symptoms of post-traumatic
epilepsy should have developed earlier than in fact they did. He said that about 50% of
patients developed this within 12 months, and he was apparently excluding such
symptoms as appeared within 11 months in this case.

He also relied on the head injury as not being the kind of head injury which he would
expect to cause temporal lobe epilepsy. He agreed, as I have already said, that each one   *d*
of those things might not have happened with epilepsy caused directly by the accident,
but he was relying on all of them.

Counsel for the plaintiff sought to rely on *Stojalowski v Imperial Smelting Corpn (NSC)
Ltd* (1976) 121 Sol Jo 118 where this court did reverse the view of a medical witness
which had been formed by the judge. The abbreviated report is accurate so far as it goes,
but a perusal of the transcript reveals a totally different situation from the present case in   *e*
that there were a number of factors in the case which were impossible to reconcile with
the evidence of the witness.

The demeanour of a medical expert giving evidence is probably not so important as
that of other witnesses of fact when the value of his evidence is being assessed, but in my
opinion the observations of Lord Thankerton in the well-known case of *Watt (or Thomas)
v Thomas* [1947] 1 All ER 582 at 587, [1947] AC 484 at 487–488, where he was   *f*
considering the position of an appellate court when dealing with a finding of fact by the
judge, should be borne in mind. He set out two principles which I will quote:

'I. Where a question of fact has been tried by a judge without a jury, and there
is no question of misdirection of himself by the judge, an appellate court which is
disposed to come to a different conclusion on the printed evidence should not do so
unless it is satisfied that any advantage enjoyed by the trial judge of having seen and   *g*
heard the witnesses, could not be sufficient to explain or justify the trial judge's
conclusion . . .

'III. The appellate court, either because the reasons given by the trial judge are
not satisfactory, or because it unmistakably so appears from the evidence, may be
satisfied that he has not taken proper advantage of his having seen and heard the
witnesses, and the matter will then become at large for the appellate court.'   *h*

In this case the judge had three medical witnesses of high qualifications. There was no
question of other credible witnesses giving evidence contradicting the facts on which the
experts gave their opinion. In this case there was no dispute about the basic facts, and on
those basic facts two different opinions were expressed. I do not know how the learned
judge made his decision, but the care with which Dr Evans examined the facts and the   *j*
opinions which he expressed about them were very much matters for the trial judge. I
can only say that reading the reports, the view of Dr Evans is more convincingly put
forward. Furthermore, it seems reasonably clear that Dr Liversedge expected the EMI
scan to confirm his view but it did not.

In his evidence Dr Evans explained in detail how he arrived at his opinion, and having

heard the argument of counsel for the plaintiff and having read all the evidence relevant
a to this issue, I see no reason to fault the finding of the judge. Dr Evans had obviously
given careful consideration to his view and to the contrary view, and there were ample
grounds on which he could so find. Accordingly, this ground of appeal fails.

The second ground of appeal by counsel for the plaintiff is against the amount of
damages awarded. The judge awarded £7,500 on a total award covering the head injury,
the loss of the spleen, the fractured clavicle and the accelerated onset of epilepsy. It also
b covered the injury to the plaintiff's earning capacity.

It was submitted on behalf of the plaintiff that the judge's figure was inadequate and
did not truly reflect the damage suffered by the plaintiff. On the basis of the evidence of
Dr Evans, the plaintiff was someone who would probably suffer from temporal lobe
epilepsy and in any event it would most likely occur in the plaintiff's teens, that is to say,
at 14 or 15. It might not happen at all but this was very unlikely. As a result of the
c accident the plaintiff had epilepsy starting at the age of 10 and the attacks were very
much worse and more frequent than they would otherwise have been. There were, as
I have already mentioned, four or five grand mal attacks which, the evidence was, would
have been unlikely had it not been for the accident.

The effect of the attacks on the plaintiff's education was serious. He missed a number
of days at each of his first three years at grammar school; 20% of the days in the first year,
d 16% of the days in the second year and 10% of the days in the third year. His behaviour
was not good. He was difficult and troublesome. He had done well in his eleven-plus
examination and might have done quite well at grammar school, but probably not up to
university standard.

The effect of the epilepsy was such that he could not pass any O levels. Dr Evans, in
his report, described it in this way: 'The emotional problems of settling into a Grammar
e School where the standards are high and the competition is greater' were factors that had
disturbed the plaintiff's behaviour. The aggravation of those problems by the loss of
time on account of fits and the fact that he was receiving phenobarbitone, which in itself
has the effect of causing behavioural disturbances in children, continued until the end of
1976. At the time of the hearing he had not had any fits for about six months and had
no behavioural disturbance whatsoever and was settling in well at his new job.

f   In evidence, in answer to the learned judge, Dr Evans said: 'A substantial part of his
failure in grammar school can be laid at the door of his epilepsy.' Then later he said that
was true to a considerable extent. The doctor explained that he thought that the falling
off between his primary school and the behaviour at his grammar school was largely
attributable to the epilepsy.

I agree with the judge that the assessment of damage is an exercise in guesswork. The
g judge assessed the damage at £7,500 but he did not divide that figure between pain and
suffering and loss of amenity on the one hand, and injury to earning capacity on the
other. He awarded, with the consent of counsel for the defendant in the court below,
interest on the whole figure.

Counsel for the plaintiff submitted that the figure of £7,500 was such that there was
very little margin for injury to earning capacity. The plaintiff's injuries consisted of the
h ruptured spleen (although it is said that its removal does not do any harm, nevertheless
the cases show that a figure in the region of £1,500 or £2,000 would not be excessive for
this alone), the fractured clavicle which would add a little, but not very much to that
figure, the onset of epilepsy which would probably have occurred one day but might not,
and which was worse in its effect than it would otherwise have been, and when all these
matters are taken into account the total figure must be getting near the £7,500 mark and
j therefore, leaving a very small margin for injury to earning capacity.

Counsel for the plaintiff has submitted that the injury to earning capacity should be
calculated on a multiplier/multiplicand basis and he suggested figures of very considerable
size. He submitted that the average weekly earnings should be a basis and arrived at a
weekly loss of, as I say, very considerable sums.

I agree with counsel for the defendant that the multiplier/multiplicand basis is

inappropriate in a case of this sort, although I do not accept his submission that the figure
could properly be contained in the balance of the figure which the judge had found. The *a*
plaintiff has, in my opinion, sustained a very real and substantial injury to his earning
capacity by the reason of the onset of epilepsy just as he was starting at grammar school;
his education has been seriously interfered with. Instead of being a boy with three, four
or even five O levels but not quite good enough to go to university, he has no O levels at
all. Instead of being a boy with a remote chance of never having epilepsy, he has had it
in a serious form and in any event sooner than he otherwise would.   *b*

In the doctor's view he was always, with that remote exception, going to be ineligible
for those jobs which bar an epileptic, the police which he favoured, jobs involving
moving machinery, and so on. On the other hand, he has lost the educational advantages
which might well have helped to minimise the limitations imposed on a known
epileptic. He may be able to do something to repair that loss by adult education, but that
is a possibility, not a probability.   *c*

In my opinion, the figure which should be awarded for this is, with great respect to the
judge, much greater than could be contained in the margin to which I referred earlier.
I would therefore consider separately the two figures.

In my judgment a fair figure for the pain and suffering, loss of amenity and the
general embarassment resulting from the earlier and more serious attacks of epilepsy,
and the loss of the spleen and the fractured clavicle which I have already mentioned, *d*
would be the sum of £6,000. The injury to his earning capacity resulting from the
serious educational loss is, as I have already said, a serious one and should include
something for being deprived of the remote chance of never having epilepsy at all.

I have already said that I do not accept the multiplier/multiplicand method of
calculation. There are so many imponderables. For example, how long will the plaintiff
live? What job will he in fact get? What sort of job would he have got if he had had the *e*
epilepsy later in his life? All of those are capable of a wide variety of answers.

I therefore would assess a figure which in my judgment would properly compensate
the plaintiff for all those matters, and the figure I would award would be one of £7,500
for this part of the damage.

Having regard to the decision of this court in *Clarke v Rotax Aircraft Equipment Ltd*
[1975] 3 All ER 794 at 798, [1975] 1 WLR 1570 at 1576 this figure for loss of earning *f*
capacity is in the same situation as damages for loss of future earnings, and does not carry
interest.

I would therefore allow this appeal and substitute for the figure of £7,500 with
interest which was accepted by the defendant in the court below, a figure of £6,000,
together with interest up to the date of judgment and a further £7,500 without interest.

g

BRANDON LJ. I agree that the appeal should be allowed and that damages should be
awarded in accordance with the judgment which Waller LJ has just given.

The appeal raises two questions of some general importance. The first question is the
extent to which it is legitimate for an appellate court to interfere with the findings of fact
of a trial judge based on the evidence of expert witnesses, in this case, medical expert
witnesses.   *h*

It has been suggested in argument, and there is some support for the suggestion
derived from *Stojalowski v Imperial Smelting Corpn (NSC) Ltd* (1978) 121 Sol Jo 118 to
which Waller LJ referred, that, where expert witnesses are concerned, the trial judge has
no significant advantage over an appellate court in forming a correct judgment between
conflicting views. I do not think that the authority referred to does, or was intended to,
go as far as that. In my judgment, even when dealing with expert witnesses, a trial judge *j*
has an advantage over an appellate court in assessing the value, the reliability and
impressiveness of the evidence given by experts called on either side.

There are various aspects of such evidence in respect of which the trial judge can get
the 'feeling' of a case in a way in which an appellate court, reading the transcript,

a cannot. Sometimes expert witnesses display signs of partisanship in a witness box or lack of objectivity. This may or may not be obvious from the transcript, yet it may be quite plain to the trial judge. Sometimes an expert witness may refuse to make what a more wise witness would make, namely, proper concessions to the viewpoint of the other side. Here again this may or may not be apparent to an appellate court but plain to the trial judge. I mention only two aspects of the matter, but there are others.

b I do not think that the authorities on the right of an appellate court to interfere with the findings of fact of a trial judge based on witnesses of simple fact are entirely applicable to cases where the finding is based on expert evidence, but I certainly would not go to the other extreme and say that the trial judge has no advantage over an appellate court because the witnesses are expert. I think he has certain advantages, not perhaps so great as those applicable where witnesses are witnesses of fact, but nevertheless significant advantages which an appellate court ought not to ignore.

c The second matter of general interest is whether and to what extent in a case of this kind the loss of future earning capacity should be calculated on some kind of mathematical basis, that is to say by taking a multiplier and multiplicand. Waller LJ has expressed the view that, on the facts of this particular case, any attempt to arrive at a figure for damages on a basis of a multiplier and a multiplicand would be inappropriate because of the very great number of imponderables which exist.

d I feel it right to express my view that, while a court is not bound to arrive at a multiplier and a multiplicand in a case of this kind in order to assess the damages, it would not be erring in law if it attempted to do so. The basis for finding a multiplicand is slender but judges are often faced with having to make findings of fact on evidence which is slender and much less convincing than would be desirable. Therefore it seems to me to be open to the court to approach the problem by putting a figure on the loss of e earning capacity on a weekly or annual basis and applying a multiplier to that figure.

I do however think that if that method is adopted, then the court should take a very careful look at the ultimate result in the round in order to see whether it seems a sensible figure in general terms or not.

In this case, having approached the matter perhaps from a slightly different angle from that of Waller LJ I nevertheless agree entirely with the figure of £7,500 at which he has f arrived by a more general approach.

SIR DAVID CAIRNS. I agree that this appeal should be allowed and that the judgment should be varied in the manner indicated by Waller LJ in his judgment.

On the issue whether the head injury resulting from the accident was the cause of epilepsy in a boy who up to the time of the accident had no tendency to epilepsy, or was g rather the agent activating a latent epilepsy which would probably have become active without any such injury within the next few years, I am of opinion that the judge was entitled to prefer the evidence of Dr Evans to that of other medical witnesses, and that no sufficient reason is shown why we should reverse his finding.

I do not consider that anything that was said in the judgment in the case of *Stojalowski v Imperial Smelting Corpn (NSC) Ltd* (1976) 121 Sol Jo 118 meant, or was intended to mean, h that the Court of Appeal is in every case in as good a position as the trial judge to assess the value of expert evidence given before him. It is clear from what Waller LJ has said in his judgment today, that that was not the intention of the court. If I had thought that it was so intended at the time when the judgments were delivered in the *Stojalowski* case, I should have expressed my dissent from it, though recognising that the other two members of the court had far greater experience than I had had in evaluating oral j evidence of doctors.

In *Stojalowski* the effect of a whole body of written and oral evidence was such as to convince the court that the evidence of a witness whom the judge had accepted as reliable was in fact untrue.

In the present case, the evidence seems to me to be very finely balanced. Dr Evans

expressed his opinion firmly and gave several reasons for it. I do not accept the
submission made in this court that his reasons were demolished in cross-examination. *a*
The transcript of the opposing evidence has not convinced me that the judge was wrong
in his finding on that matter, and in the circumstances I am of opinion that that finding
cannot be disturbed.

I am, however, satisfied that the judge must have underestimated the effect on the
plaintiff's prospects of the interference with his education by the occurrence of epilepsy
when it did occur. The effects, other than those which relate to earnings, of the injuries *b*
that he had, the initial pain and suffering, the probability that the epileptic fits were
more frequent and more severe than they would have been if the epilepsy had become
active later, the possibility that it would never have become active, the probable loss of
some pleasure in his employment as well as loss of earnings, must be regarded as
represented by most of the £7,500 award. I do not think that left to myself I would have
attributed as much as £6,000 to those other elements, but I do not feel strongly enough *c*
about that matter to dissent from that assessment.

If then only £1,500 out of the £7,500 is to be considered as representing loss of
earning capacity, I am satisfied that despite all the uncertainties of the case, that figure is
substantially too small.

I do not find it useful in this case to make any attempt to work out a multiplier and a
multiplicand. I regard it as essentially a case in which the best approach is that of going *d*
straight to estimating in the round what the figure should be and I agree that that figure
should be £7,500.

I further agree, following *Clarke v Rotax Aircraft Equipment Ltd* [1975] 3 All ER 794,
[1975] 1 WLR 1570 that the interest, while payable on the £6,000, is not payable on the
£7,500.

e

Appeal allowed. Judge's order varied. Leave to appeal to the House of Lords refused.

Solicitors: *Lickfolds, Wiley & Powles*, agents for *Taylor, Hindle & Rhodes*, Manchester (for
the plaintiff); *James Chapman & Co*, Manchester (for the defendant).

William Hoskins Esq   Barrister.

Jelley v Iliffe and others

COURT OF APPEAL, CIVIL DIVISION

STEPHENSON, CUMMING-BRUCE AND GRIFFITHS LJJ

27th, 28th NOVEMBER, 16th DECEMBER 1980

Family provision – Person who immediately before deceased's death was being maintained by deceased – Dependant – Substantial contribution by deceased towards applicant's needs otherwise than for full valuable consideration – Full valuable consideration – Maintenance of applicant immediately before death of deceased – Assumption of responsibility for maintenance – Widower living rent free in widow's house – Couple pooling resources to pay living expenses – Widower helping to care for house and garden and providing widow with companionship – Relationship lasting for eight years – Widower's application for reasonable provision out of widow's estate struck out as disclosing no reasonable cause of action – Whether applicant 'being maintained' by widow 'immediately before' her death – Whether applicant receiving a substantial contribution towards his needs otherwise than for full valuable consideration – Whether deceased assuming responsibility for applicant's maintenance – Inheritance (Provision for Family and Dependants) Act 1975, ss 1(1)(e) (3), 3(4).

In 1971 the applicant, a widower who had been living with his married daughter, went to live with the deceased, the widow of his brother-in-law, in the deceased's house which had been conveyed to her by her children (who had been entitled to it under their father's will) on the understanding that she would leave it to them on her death. The applicant and the deceased agreed to share the accommodation in the house and to pool their incomes, including their old age pensions, to meet their common living expenses. The applicant provided some furniture for the house, looked after the garden and did household jobs. and provided the deceased with companionship. She provided him with rent-free accommodation and cooked and washed for him. Their relationship continued for eight years until the deceased's death in 1979. By her will, made in 1972, the deceased left all her property including the house (which was valued at £16,000 and was the main part of her estate) to her children and made no provision for the applicant. The applicant applied under s 1(1)[a] of the Inheritance (Provision for Family and Dependants) Act 1975 for reasonable financial provision out of the deceased's estate on the gound that immediately before her death he was being maintained by her within s 1(1)(e) of that Act. On an application by the deceased's children, the registrar struck out the application on the ground that the evidence in support of it did not disclose a reasonable cause of action. On appeal by the applicant, the judge upheld the registrar's decision on the ground that the deceased's provision of rent-free accommodation for the applicant did not, in all the circumstances, amount to an assumption of responsibility for his maintenance for the purposes of s 1(1)(e). The applicant appealed seeking restoration of his application.

Held – (1) The concept of maintainance in s 1(1)(e) of the 1975 Act was similar to the concept of matrimonial maintenance (consisting mainly of financial provision for a spouse and the provision of accommodation) and s 1(1)(e) was to be considered in that light (see p 34 *f* to *h* and p 38 *c d*, post).

(2) By virtue of s 1(3) of the 1975 Act an applicant was 'being maintained' for the purposes of s 1(1)(e) only if the deceased, otherwise than for full valuable consideration (which was not limited to benefits provided under a contract), was making a substantial contribution in money or money's worth towards the applicant's reasonable needs immediately before his death, for the deeming provision of s 1(3) exhaustively defined

---

a   Section 1, so far as material, is set out at p 33 *b* to *e*, post

the meaning of 'being maintained' in s 1(1)(e), so that a state of affairs which did not come
within s 1(3) could not be described as 'being maintained' for the purposes of s 1(1)(e).   *a*
Moreover, 'immediately before the death of the deceased' in s 1(1)(e) did not refer to the
de facto situation at death but to the general arrangements for maintenance which had
existed during the deceased's lifetime (see p 34 *j* to p 35 *b* and p 38 *c* to *g*, post); *Re
Beaumont (deceased)* [1980] 1 All ER 266 applied.

(3) The bare fact that the applicant was being maintained by the deceased under an
arrangement subsisting at the deceased's death was sufficient to, and generally did, raise *b*
a presumption that the deceased had assumed responsibility for his maintenance within
s 3(4)[b] of the 1975 Act, and it was unnecessary to prove any other overt act demonstrating
the assumption of responsibility because (per Griffiths LJ) the words 'assumed . . .
responsibility for' in s 3(4) meant 'had undertaken' to provide maintenance. Moreover,
it was not necessary for an applicant to prove that the deceased had intended to maintain
him after his or her death, and it was sufficient if the deceased's conduct was such that the *c*
applicant had been made wholly or partially dependent on the deceased for his
maintenance during the deceased's lifetime, for the object of the 1975 Act in creating the
class of persons entitled to claim under s 1(1)(e) was to remedy the injustice of a person
being put by the deceased in a position of dependency and then deprived of financial
support after the deceased's death (see p 35 *e* to p 36 *b* and p 38 *c d* and *g* to p 39 *b e f*, post);
Re Beaumont (deceased) [1980] 1 All ER 266 not followed.   *d*

(4) In determining for the purposes of s 1(3) whether the deceased was making a
substantial contribution to the applicant's needs otherwise than for full valuable
consideration the court had to take a broad commonsense view of the relationship
between the parties and had to strike a balance between the benefits received by the
applicant from the deceased against those provided by the applicant to the deceased. If
there was doubt whether the balance tipped in favour of the deceased's contribution *e*
being the greater, the matter had to go to trial. If, however, the balance was bound to
come down in favour of the applicant's contribution being the greater, or if the
contributions were equal and there was, therefore, no dependency of the applicant on the
deceased because either the deceased depended on him or there was a mutual dependency,
the application should be struck out under the court's inherent jurisdiction as being
bound to fail, in order to save the costs of further proceedings which would probably *f*
have to come out of the estate (see p 36 *c* to *e g* and *j* to p 37 *a d g h* and p 38 *c d f* to *j*, post).

(5) The benefit of rent-free accommodation was a significant contribution to a person's
reasonable needs and in the case of an old age pensioner was a substantial contribution to
his reasonable needs. Moreover, where that benefit had been provided by the deceased
over a period of eight years that amounted to an assumption of responsibility for the
applicant's maintenance. Unless, therefore, the applicant's contributions to the deceased *g*
equalled or outweighed the benefit of the rent-free accommodation, he would qualify as
a dependant under s 1(1)(e). Since, on the applicant's affidavits, it was not clear beyond
doubt that his contributions had equalled or outweighed the benefit of rent-free
accommodation, there was an arguable case that he was being maintained by the deceased
within s 1(1)(e). It followed that his application ought not to have been struck out, and
that the matter should be allowed to proceed to trial. The appeal would therefore be *h*
allowed (see p 36 *h j*, p 37 *c* to *e* and *j* to p 38 *d* and p 39 *g* to p 40 *b*, post).

Notes

For persons for whom provision may be made out of the deceased's estate, and for
matters to which the court is to have regard, see 17 Halsbury's Laws (4th Edn) paras 1321,   *j*
1337.

For the Inheritance (Provision for Family and Dependants) Act 1975, ss 1, 3, see 45
Halsbury's Statutes (3rd Edn) 496, 501.

---

b   Section 3(4) is set out at p 33 *f g*, post

Cases referred to in judgments

a   *Beaumont (deceased), Re, Martin v Midland Bank Trust Co Ltd* [1980] 1 All ER 266, [1980] Ch 444, [1979] 3 WLR 818.

Coventry (deceased), Re [1979] 3 All ER 815, [1980] Ch 461, [1979] 3 WLR 802, CA, Digest (Cont Vol E) 224, 7680a.

Wilkinson (deceased), Re, Neales v Newell [1978] 1 All ER 221, [1978] Fam 22, [1977] 3 WLR 514, 24 Digest (Reissue) 697, 7510.

b

Appeal

By an originating summons dated 14th August 1979 the appellant, Thomas William Jelley, applied in the Coventry District Registry of the Family Division for an order, as a person who immediately before the death of Florence Lilian May Iliffe ('the deceased') was being maintained wholly or partly by her, that he was entitled to reasonable financial c   provision for his maintenance out of her estate on the ground that she had not made reasonable provision for his maintenance after her death. The respondents to the application were John Joseph Iliffe, Peter Shirley Iliffe and Betty Arnold, the deceased's children. On the application of the respondents Mr District Registrar Donaldson, on 13th June 1980, ordered that the originating summons be struck out on the ground that the evidence in support of it disclosed no cause of action. On 28th October 1980 Bush d   J sitting at Birmingham dismissed the appellant's appeal from the registrar's order. The appellant applied to the Court of Appeal for leave to appeal and on the hearing of the appeal for an order restoring the originating summons. The facts are set out in the judgment of Stephenson LJ.

Victor Joffe for the appellant.
e   *Cleveland M G Butterfield* for the respondents.

STEPHENSON LJ. Mr Jelley appeals against the dismissal of his application under the Inheritance (Provision for Family and Dependants) Act 1975 that reasonable financial provision for his maintenance be made out of the estate of Florence Lilian May Iliffe deceased.

f   He made his application on 19th August 1979. The respondents to this appeal, who are her three children, the first being the sole proving executor of, and one of the beneficiaries under, her will, met that application with an application to strike it out under the court's inherent jurisdiction on the ground that the evidence in support of it disclosed no reasonable cause of action in that when it came to be considered it would be bound to fail.

g   The appellant's application had been issued in the Family Division, Coventry District Registry (in accordance with RSC Ord 99, which permitted it to be taken out in the Chancery Division also), and on 13th June 1980 the district registrar ordered 'that the action to be struck out under Order 18 rule 19(1)(a)' (sic), and gave leave to appeal. On 28th October 1980 Bush J, sitting at Birmingham, dismissed the appellant's appeal and refused leave to appeal. We have given the appellant leave to appeal and have heard his h   appeal by which he asks us to restore his originating summons and let his application be heard on the merits.

    The district registrar reached his decision on the evidence of affidavits sworn by the appellant and his two daughters on the one hand, and the deceased's son (the first respondent) and one of her daughters (the third respondent) on the other. The judge had before him a further affidavit from the appellant, and also an affidavit from the j   proprietress of a seaside hotel, which may have been before the registrar. There was no oral evidence or cross-examination on the affidavits, but we were informed by counsel for the appellant that he had no further evidence to put before the court if the matter should go to trial. We have an agreed note of the judge's judgment, which he has not had an opportunity of approving. It contains a clear statement of the undisputed facts and of his reasons for dismissing the appeal.

The deceased was the widow of the appellant's brother-in-law, who died in 1970. The appellant's wife, who died in 1968, was her sister-in-law. In 1971 the appellant went to *a* live with the deceased in a house at 113 Southfield Road, Hinckley. Her husband had left the house to her for her life and after her death to their three children, but by a deed of arrangement in 1970 they conveyed the freehold to her. It was clearly understood by them (and they said by the appellant also, though he denied it) that the house should go to the children after her death. And so it did. By her will made on 22nd May 1972, of which the first respondent and the appellant were executors and trustees, she left all her *b* property, real and personal, to them on trust to divide her residuary estate between her three children in equal shares. At her death on 8th April 1979 the house, valued at £16,000, constituted by far the greatest part of her estate, which was valued when probate was granted to the first respondent at £17,303·86 net.

Ten days after Mrs Iliffe's death, solicitors wrote to the respondent's solicitors a letter before application, which was read by the judge. They wrote: *c*

'We act on behalf of Thomas William Jelley, the common law husband of Mrs. Iliffe. We understand from our client that Mrs. Iliffe died on the 8th April, 1979. We understand from our client that he lived with Mrs. Iliffe for eight years and has made substantial contributions to her maintenance and advancement. He has contributed both to the purchase of furniture at 113 Southfield Road and has carried *d* out certain improvements to the property at his own expense. In consequence we are of the opinion that the Will does not make any financial provisions for Mr. Jelley and accordingly we regard the situation as one where our client is entitled to make an application under the Inheritance (Provision for Family and Dependants) Act 1975. If such an application were to be made we are satisfied that the Courts would provide the provisions for our client to enable him to adequately maintain *e* himself. We understand that the deceased's estate consists of ready cash of somewhere in the region of £2,700 and the freehold property, 113 Southfield Road, Hinckley. Our client's only capital is some £1,800. We look forward to hearing from you with your client's proposals as to entering into a Deed of Family Arrangement to enable adequate provisions to be made to our client without the necessity of an application being made to the Court.' *f*

The appellant had suggested to the deceased that he should leave the house where he was living with a married daughter who was willing to keep him; but the deceased told him that she was lonely and frightened, he had known her nearly all her life and he thought he could help to look after her house and garden. So in March 1971 he moved in. In his first affidavit, at para 11 he swore: *g*

'I contributed to the home by providing my own furniture in the first instance and subsequently by providing many more articles of furniture and household use fitting carpets curtains tiles a bath and toilet and gates fencing water butt and greenhouse for the outside of the property out of my savings which in 1971 amounted to over £1,000·00.'

There was, as the judge said, 'some dispute' whether the appellant was merely a lodger *h* with the deceased or whether, as he said, they were really living as man and wife. There was the evidence of the hotel proprietress that they shared a double room on holiday together. He was about 64 and she three years younger when they started to live together. Whatever the sleeping arrangements in 1971 or later were, they agreed to share the accommodation at her house and thereafter they must be assumed to have lived as the appellant swore they did in para 2 of his first affidavit: *j*

'Immediately before her death and since the time we had commenced to live together the deceased was maintaining me and making a substantial contribution otherwise than for full valuable consideration in money or money's worth towards my reasonable needs in that she was providing me with accommodation at 113 a   Southfield Road and a home there and she and I had pooled our respective incomes and latterly our old age pensions, mine of £20·23 per week and hers of £20·10 per week towards our common living expenses. In addition we received £10·40 per week attendance allowance from 11th November 1978 for the period of the deceased's last illness.'

b   The judge read the relevant provisions of the 1975 Act, which are as follows. Section 1 reads:

'(1) Where after the commencement of this Act a person dies domiciled in England and Wales and is survived by any of the following persons—(a) the wife or husband of the deceased; (b) a former wife or former husband of the deceased who has not remarried; (c) a child of the deceased; (d) any person (not being a child of the deceased) who, in the case of any marriage to which the deceased was at any time a
c   party, was treated by the deceased as a child of the family in relation to that marriage; (e) [the relevant paragraph] any person (not being a person included in the foregoing paragraphs of this subsection) who immediately before the death of the deceased was being maintained, either wholly or partly, by the deceased; that person may apply to the court for an order under section 2 of this Act on the ground that the disposition of the deceased's estate effected by his will or the law relating to
d   intestacy, or the combination of his will and that law, is not such as to make reasonable financial provision for the applicant.
'(2) In this Act "reasonable financial provision" . . . (b) in the case of any other application made by virtue of subsection (1) above, means such financial provision as it would be reasonable in all the circumstances of the case for the applicant to receive for his maintenance.
e   '(3) For the purposes of subsection (1) (e) above, a person shall be treated as being maintained by the deceased, either wholly or partly, as the case may be, if the deceased, otherwise than for full valuable consideration, was making a substantial contribution in money or money's worth towards the reasonable needs of that person.'

f   Section 3(4) reads:

'Without prejudice to the generality of paragraph (g) of subsection (1) above, where an application for an order under section 2 of this Act is made by virtue of section 1 (1) (e) of this Act, the court shall, in addition to the matters specifically mentioned in paragraphs (a) to (f) of that subsection, have regard to the extent to which and the basis upon which the deceased assumed responsibility for the
g   maintenance of the applicant, and to the length of time for which the deceased discharged that responsibility.'

(Paragraph (g) of s 3(1) requires the court, on hearing an application, to take into account any other matter, including the conduct of the applicant or any other person, which in the circumstances of the case the court may consider relevant.)
h   The judge then said:

'We have two people living together as man and wife pooling their incomes and one of them happens to own the house in which they live. Does the provision of rent free accommodation amount to a substantial contribution to his mainte-nance? Was it intended by the deceased that that should be maintenance of Mr
j   Jelley in money's worth and intended by her to continue until his death? I do not think that it was intended by Mrs Florence Iliffe that it was to be and Mr Jelley was aware of this. I do not think for one minute that she assumed a responsibility in money or money's worth for Mr Jelley. They were living together and it just so happened that she owned the house in which they both lived. It was no more than that. Interesting to see how he first put it.'

The judge then referred to the first paragraph of the letter of 18th April 1979 and para
11 of the appellant's first affidavit, which I have read. He continued: *a*

'... in other words he is saying, "I was the one who has been maintaining the
other party to our agreement. I am the one who has been making substantial
contributions." The Act does not cater for reimbursement in those circumstances.
The provision of rent free accommodation is insignificant in relation to those acts.
One must find maintenance in money or money's worth and an assumption of such
responsibility by the deceased. In my view Mr Jelley comes nowhere near proving   *b*
the matters he must prove. I find as a fact that both of the requirements of this Act
are absent. The registrar was perfectly right and I take the view that this action
should be struck out and the appeal dismissed.'

In interpreting the Act and deciding whether the judge's reasoning and conclusions
are correct, we have in mind that he had the help of the decisions of Arnold J in *Re* *c*
Wilkinson [1978] 1 All ER 221, [1978] Fam 22 and of Sir Robert Megarry V-C in *Re
Beaumont (deceased)* [1980] 1 All ER 266, [1980] Ch 444. Also that he has not had a
chance to revise or correct the note of his judgment which I have just read.

The 1975 Act gave a statutory right to apply to the court for reasonable financial
provision out of deceaseds' estates not only to their families but to certain other
'dependants'. Not only spouses and children and other members of a deceased's family, *d*
who were dependent on him (or sometimes her) for support during his (or her) lifetime,
but have been denied it after the death of their supporter, can be awarded financial
provision by the court. A person might maintain or help to maintain others, of whom
a man's mistress is perhaps the most obvious example, and those in her position may
under the statute be able to obtain money from his estate.

Section 1(1)(e) defines one new class which qualifies for the right to apply for such *e*
provision. The question which, like the district registrar and Bush J, this court has to
decide is whether on the evidence, which must at this stage be accepted as true, the
appellant comes within the defined class and qualifies for that right. Whether there is
anything else in the statute, particularly in ss 1(3) and 3(4), which affects that definition
and that right is a question we have to consider. Whether the appellant will succeed in
his application is not a question we have to consider except (an important exception) in *f*
so far as it might be plain that his application would be bound to fail.

In answering the question whether the statute gives the appellant the right which the
registrar and judge have denied him we, like the statute, are concerned with dependency
for support of that kind well known to family law as maintenance. What may be called
matrimonial maintenance is mainly, if not exclusively, of two kinds, financial provision
or the provision of accommodation in a house. A man maintains his wife and children *g*
by providing them with somewhere to live or by paying contributions of money or by
both, and if he does that he maintains them, he assumes the responsibility of maintaining
them and he discharges that responsibility as long as he continues to do so. That it seems
to me is the background against which we have to consider the relevant provisions of the
Act extending the right to apply for financial provision to those who have been
maintained by a deceased person during his lifetime and immediately before his death, *h*
and to consider counsel's submissions on those provisions and their true interpretation.

I respectfully agree with Sir Robert Megarry V-C for the reasons that he gives in his
exposition of the statute in *Re Beaumont* [1980] 1 All ER 266 at 270–276, [1980] Ch 444
at 450–458, on all points but one. (1) The deeming provision in s 1(3) exhaustively or
exclusively defines what s 1(1)(e) means by 'being maintained', and does not include in
those words a state of affairs which is not within s 1(1)(e) and would extend its ambit. To *j*
qualify within s 1(1)(e) a claimant must satisfy s 1(3) as if before the words 'if the
deceased' the draftsman of s 1(3) had inserted the word 'only'. (2) In considering whether
a person is being maintained 'immediately before the death of the deceased' it is the
settled basis or general arrangement between the parties as regards maintenance during

the lifetime of the deceased which has to be looked at, not the actual, perhaps fluctuating,
a variation of it which exists immediately before his or her death. It is, I think, not
disputed that a relationship of dependence which has persisted for years will not be
defeated by its termination during a few weeks of mortal sickness. (3) Like Sir Robert
Megarry V-C I reject the contention that the parenthetical words in s 1(3), 'otherwise
than for full valuable consideration', apply only to full valuable consideration under a
contract and agree with him and with Arnold J that they apply whenever full valuable
b consideration is given, whether under contract or otherwise. Counsel supported the
appellant's argument against that interpretation by a reference to ss 10(2)(*b*) and 11 (2)(*c*),
where the same phrase is clearly used in the context of a disposition or contract for the
benefit of a donee. But even without referring to the Law Commission's Second Report
on Family Property: Family Provision on Death (Law Com No 61), on which the statute
was based, the narrower construction which has so far been rejected would exclude from
c its benefits those family arrangements which it seems designed to recognise as often
requiring a continuation of support after the death of the supporter.

Where, however, I feel bound to part company from Sir Robert Megarry V-C is in his
interpretation of assumption of responsibility for the maintenance of the supported
person. I do not question his opinion that the requirement of s 3(4) that the court should
'have regard to the extent to which and the basis upon which the deceased assumed
d responsibility for the maintenance of the applicant, and to the length of time for which
the deceased discharged that responsibility' implies or 'assumes' (in another sense) that at
the first stage, when the court is considering the applicant's right to apply under s 1(1)(*e*),
he must prove that the deceased did 'assume responsibility' for his maintenance. But I
cannot, with respect, agree with him, in spite of counsel's submission for the respondents
that I should, that the bare fact of maintenance raises no presumption that responsibility
e for it has been assumed. I am of opinion that it generally does. I would not disagree
with Sir Robert Megarry V-C when he says ([1980] 1 All ER 266 at 276, [1980] Ch 444
at 458):

'The word "assumes" . . . seems to me to indicate that there must be some act or
acts which demonstrate an undertaking of responsibility, or the taking of the
responsibility on oneself.'
f

And the Act, here and elsewhere, has drawn a distinction between assuming and
discharging responsibility. But how better or more clearly can one take on or discharge
responsibility for maintenance than by actually maintaining? A man may say he is
going to support another and not do it, promise to pay school fees but not pay; but if he
does pay them, has he not both assumed and discharged responsibility for them whether
g or not he covenants to pay them? Surely A shoulders the burden of supporting B by
supporting him. If B is A's mistress and he maintains her by providing her with
accommodation or money or both, has he not assumed or taken on responsibility for her
maintenance? If it be said, as counsel for the respondents submitted, that he has a moral
obligation which makes the assumption of responsibility easier to presume, is the
presumption nevertheless not to be made where provision of a share in a home and/or
h financial support is made out of the donor's generosity of heart to a poor relation or
friend? It may be that the presumption can be rebutted by circumstances including a
disclaimer of any intention to maintain. But here there is, in my judgment, a distinction
to be drawn between an intention to maintain during the lifetime of the giver who has
something to offer and an intention to provide continuing support after death. I cannot
help thinking that there is some confusion between the two, if not in Sir Robert Megarry
j V-C's judgment, at least in the judgment of Bush J and in the argument by which counsel
for the respondents has sought to support it. If it is necessary, or relevant, to prove an
intention on the part of the deceased to maintain a dependant qualified to apply under
s 1(1)(*e*), after the deceased's death, the only cases in which there will be the required
qualification will be those where the deceased's intention has been defeated by accident,

eg by his dying intestate leaving children or having made an invalid will in the
dependant's favour.

a

I do not read the Act as expressing so limited a legislative intention. Its object is surely
to remedy, wherever reasonably possible, the injustice of one, who has been put by a
deceased person in a position of dependency on him, being deprived of any financial
support, either by accident or by design of the deceased, after his death. To leave a
dependant, to whom no legal or moral obligation is owed, unprovided for after death
may not entitle the dependant to much or indeed any financial provision in all the
circumstances, but he is not disentitled from applying for such provision if he can prove
that the deceased by his conduct made him dependent on the deceased for maintenance,
whether intentionally or not.

b

Accordingly, I am of opinion that the court has to consider whether the deceased,
otherwise than for valuable consideration (and irrespective of the existence of any
contract), was in fact making a substantial contribution in money or money's worth
towards the reasonable needs of the appellant, on a settled basis or arrangement which
either was still in force immediately before the deceased's death or would have lasted
until her death but for the approach of death and the consequent inability of either party
to continue to carry out the arrangement. To discover whether the deceased was making
such a contribution the court has to balance what she was contributing against what he
was contributing, and if there is any doubt about the balance tipping in favour of hers
being the greater contribution, the matter must, in my opinion, go to trial. If, however,
the balance is bound to come down in favour of his being the greater contribution, or if
the contributions are clearly equal, there is no dependency of him on her, either because
she depended on him or there was mutual dependency between them, and his application
should be struck out now as bound to fail. Where what B does gives full valuable
consideration for the substantial contribution A makes, there is no dependency and B's
claim under the Act should be struck out.

c

d

e

The balancing of imponderables like companionship and other services, on which the
court has somehow to put a financial value, against contributions of money or
accommodation is a hard task, as Arnold J found in *Re Wilkinson* [1978] 1 All ER 221,
[1978] Fam 22, a case of two arthritic sisters, in which he found 'with considerable
uncertainty' that the services of the sister who was taken into the deceased sister's house
were just outweighed by what the deceased gave her in board and lodging enough to
entitle her to go on with her application. In *Re Beaumont*, which was on the facts much
closer to this case, Sir Robert Megarry V-C did not weigh the contributions of man and
mistress in a balancing operation because he held that there had been no assumption of
responsibility for maintenance of the man by what the deceased mistress had contributed
in accommodation and money. It is an operation which it may be said should be left to
the later stage of trial, but if it can be done at this stage and plainly results in the scales
ending level or the applicant's scale descending under the weight of his greater
contribution then the right course is to save the costs of further proceedings, which will
probably come out of the estate, may be charged to the legal aid fund, and are likely to
leave little or nothing for the applicant or the deceased's estate. Such litigation in respect
of small estates should be discouraged as far as justly possible, as this court recently
repeated in *Re Coventry* [1979] 3 All ER 815, [1980] Ch. 461.

f

g

h

Can this difficult operation be carried out at this stage and plainly produce that result?
I have no doubt that the provision of free accommodation in these times is a substantial
contribution to the needs of the accommodated and was a substantial contribution to the
appellant's reasonable needs. If in describing the deceased as one who 'happens to own
the house in which they live' the judge intended to treat that as an accidental and
therefore insignificant circumstance, I cannot agree with him. It might qualify the
appellant to pursue his claim because the pooling of their incomes and the remaining
contributions of aid and comfort which each gave to the other cancelled out. In my
judgment the statute, whether literally or purposively construed, requires the court to

j

take a broad commonsense view of the question whether the applicant for the statutory
a relief was a dependant of the deceased before death, and the ordinary man's answer to
what, on this approach, is the right question, 'Was this man dependent on this woman
during her lifetime for maintenance, or did he give as good as he got?' might be (without
regard to nice differences between the facts in this and other cases) that each was partly
dependent on the other and he gave her, in companionship (whether or not it amount
to consortium) and help in money and in furnishing her house and caring for her and her
b house and garden, as much as she gave him in companionship and rent-free
accommodation and money and looking after him by cooking and cleaning.

I do not therefore agree with the judge that the appellant was the one who had been
making substantial contributions, if by that he meant that the appellant was the only
one. Nor would I accept that the deceased's provision of rent free accommodation was
insignificant in relation to those acts of his. I find here, unlike the judge, maintenance
c in money and money's worth for a long time and an assumption of responsibility for
such maintenance by the deceased to a considerable extent and on a settled basis. But I
do not think her intention to continue such maintenance until *his* death (as the judge is
noted as saying), or his awareness (or ignorance) that such was not her intention, is
relevant to the question whether he qualifies for any financial provision after *her* death.
And I find also that the appellant was helping to maintain her by his contributions
d financially and otherwise and so giving *some* valuable consideration for her contribution
to their life together.

But how can we decide now whether the appellant was on balance being maintained
in the sense required by the statute and so is a defendant qualified to claim that the
deceased ought to have made some financial provision for him after her death? The
qualifying status of dependency is a question of fact which can only be decided against
e an applicant if there is no evidence on which it could be answered in his favour, and,
although we were told that the appellant is probably not in a position to call any further
evidence, I do not think we should rule out his application now and prevent the court to
which the discretion has been given from exercising it after hearing all the evidence.

The judge seems to have struck out the application because he did not find maintenance
in money or money's worth or an assumption of responsibility for such maintenance by
f the deceased. The finding of no maintenance may have been based mainly on a view of
assumption of responsibility which he shared with Sir Robert Megarry V-C but which I
consider mistaken. But it is, I think, clear from his reference to 'both of the requirements
of the Act' that it was based also on his opinion either that the deceased had not made a
substantial contribution to the applicant's maintenance or that he had given full valuable
consideration for the substantial contribution which she made.

g With that second reason after considerable hesitation I feel unable to agree. There
must be few cases indeed when the result of the balancing of contributions of deceased
and alleged dependant is so plain before trial that the court is entitled to strike out an
application under s 1(1)(e) of the 1975 Act. In many cases of mutual dependency there
must be real doubt whether an applicant will be able to prove dependency within
s 1(1)(e), and whether if he does the court will make any financial provision for him out
h of the deceased's estate. If there is such doubt the case is not one for the exercise of the
court's inherent jurisdiction to stop it without a full hearing, because the court cannot say
that it is bound to fail.

Here there are several indications that the appellant's case is likely to fail. He did a lot
for the deceased, perhaps enough to equal what she did for him, including the provision
of rent free accommodation, so he may not have been on balance dependent on her.
j Then the house was her children's until they conveyed it to her and she remained under
a moral obligation to leave it back to them on her death. He had a home with a daughter
to go to. He first applied to live on in the deceased's house after her death, later changed
his mind and applied for financial provision. These are all matters of conduct to which
the court would have to have regard under s 3(1)(g) in determining whether it should

give him any money and if so, how much. On the affidavit evidence it is hard to see how
a court could award him anything out of an estate as small as this, which the deceased *a*
wanted her children to enjoy after they had been so generous as to convert her life
interest in the house into absolute ownership. If the appellant has indeed no further
evidence to adduce at the hearing he would be well advised not to pursue his application,
particularly with the prospects of any property he may recover being charged to the legal
aid fund in payment of his costs.

I should like to save him and the deceased's estate all further expense by affirming the *b*
judge's order and dismissing the appeal. But I do not believe that the prospects of failure
are plain enough. It is only in plain cases that this drastic jurisdiction should be
exercised, even where a doubtful dependant seeks the statutory provision out of a small
estate. To invoke the jurisdiction in cases which are not plain is not to save costs but to
increase them. Even when the case is plain there will often be two sets of proceedings,
for an applicant will seldom be content to accept the decision of a master or registrar or *c*
to stop short of a judge, and there may sometimes be a second appeal, as in this case.

For these reasons I would allow the appeal and let the claim proceed.

Cumming-Bruce LJ is unable to be present today, but he authorises me to say that he
has read the judgment which I have just delivered and the judgment which Griffiths LJ
is about to deliver, and agrees with both those judgments.

d

GRIFFITHS LJ. I agree with the construction of s 1(1)(e) of the Inheritance (Provision
for Family and Defendants) Act 1975 expounded by Sir Robert Megarry V-C in *Re
Beaumont* [1980] 1 All ER 266, [1980] Ch 444. I adopt his reasoning and set out the
following conclusions.

Section 1(3) contains an exhaustive definition of the words 'being maintained' where *e*
they appear in s 1(1)(e).

The words 'immediately before the death of the deceased' in s 1(1)(e) cannot be
construed literally as applying to the de facto situation at death but refer to the general
arrangements for maintenance subsisting at the time of death. So that if for example the
deceased had been making regular payments to the support of an old friend the claim
would not be defeated if those payments ceased during a terminal illness because the *f*
deceased was too ill to make them.

Section 1(3) requires the court to balance the benefits received by the applicant from
the deceased against those provided by the applicant to the deceased. In striking the
balance the phrase 'for full valuable consideration' is not to be construed as being limited
to benefits provided under a contract. Only if the balance comes down heavily in favour
of the applicant will it be shown that the deceased was 'making a substantial contribution *g*
in money or money's worth towards the reasonable needs' of the applicant. In striking
this balance the court must use common sense and remember that the object of
Parliament in creating this extra class of persons who may claim benefit from an estate
was to provide relief for persons of whom it could truly be said that they were wholly or
partially dependent on the deceased. It cannot be an exact exercise of evaluating services
in pounds and pence. By way of example, if a man was living with a woman as his wife *h*
and providing the house and all the money for their living expenses she would clearly be
dependent on him, and it would not be right to deprive her of her claim by arguing that
she was in fact performing the services that a housekeeper would perform and it would
cost more to employ a housekeeper than was spent on her and indeed perhaps more than
the deceased had available to spend on her. Each case will have to be looked at carefully
on its own facts to see whether common sense leads to the conclusion that the applicant *j*
can fairly be regarded as a dependant.

The difficulty I have is to know what significance to attach to the words 'assumed
responsibility for the maintenance of the applicant' in s 3(4). Section 1(1)(e) appears to
me to be aimed at giving relief to persons where the relationship to the deceased is such

that it is highly unlikely that any formal arrangements will have been made between
a them. Obvious examples are the elderly but impoverished relative of friend who is
taken into the deceased's household and given free board and lodging and treated as a
member of the family. Or a man living with a woman out of wedlock but supporting
her as he would a wife. In such circumstances I would not as a general rule expect to find
any formal declaration of assumption of responsibility, but it cannot have been the
intention that such cases should fail for want of some such formality. I read 'assumed
b responsibility for' as being equivalent to 'has undertaken' and not adding much to the
fact of maintenance. In this approach I part company with Sir Robert Megarry V-C for
as I read his judgment he attaches more significance to the 'assumption of
responsibility'. He says ([1980] 1 All ER 266 at 276, [1980] Ch 444 at 458):

> 'The word "assumes", too, seems to me to indicate that there must be some act or
> acts which demonstrate an undertaking or responsibility, or the taking of the
> *c* responsibility on oneself. It may be that in some cases where there is neither a
> negation of responsibility nor a positive undertaking of it, it will be possible to infer
> from the circumstances attending the fact of maintenance that there has indeed
> been an undertaking of responsibility. But it is for the plaintiff to establish that
> there has been an assumption of responsibility, and not for the defendants to have
> to rebut any presumption of an assumption of responsibility which is to be drawn
> *d* from the bare fact of maintenance.'

It is of course possible to envisage situations in which a deceased was making regular
payments to some person's support while at the same time making it quite clear that the
recipient could not count on their continuing. But I regard such a situation as likely to
be the exception rather than the rule.
e In practice the evidence of the applicant will reveal the relationship with the deceased
and if it also shows an arrangement subsisting at the time of death under which the
deceased was making a substantial contribution in money or money's worth to the
reasonable needs of the applicant it will, as a general rule, be proper to draw the inference
that the deceased has undertaken to maintain the applicant and thus 'assumed
responsibility for the maintenance' within the meaning of s 3(4). It should not be
f necessary to search for any other overt act to demonstrate the 'assumption of
responsibility'. If such an overt act were necessary I suspect that most claims intended to
be covered by the 1975 Act would fail.
With these considerations in mind I turn to the facts of the present case. Ever since
they started to live together the deceased provided the appellant with free accommodation. I cannot in these days regard the benefit of free accommodation as insignificant; for
g a man living on an old age pension it is a substantial contribution in money's worth to
his reasonable needs. From the fact that the relationship had continued for eight years
I draw the inference that the deceased had undertaken to provide this free accommodation
for the appellant and she was maintaining him within the meaning of s 1(1)(e) unless it
can be said that the appellant was giving 'full valuable consideration' in return for his free
accommodation. He was not paying anything for it, but it is said that he was rendering
h services by looking after the garden and being a man about the house, doing various odd
jobs and some internal decoration.
On the other hand the deceased was, until her illness, doing the cooking and cleaning,
and I should have thought that on the face of it they were contributing about equally to
their common well-being in what they did for one another. It may well be that when
the claim is investigated and the witnesses cross-examined a different picture will emerge,
j but I feel quite unable to say that, on the face of the appellant's affidavits, the position was
so clear that it was right to strike out his claim as showing no cause of action. The fact
that the appellant was provided with free accommodation for eight years raises to my
mind an arguable case that he was being partly maintained by the deceased within the
meaning of s 1(1)(e).

I reach this conclusion with some reluctance because I appreciate how undesirable it is that small estates should be eaten up by the cost of litigation, as looks likely to happen *a* if this case now has to go back for a further hearing. But the beneficiaries under the deceased's will have brought it on themselves by moving to strike out the appellant's claim rather than meeting it and seeking to defeat it on the merits.

I agree that this appeal should be allowed.

Appeal allowed. Leave to appeal to the House of Lords refused.   *b*

Solicitors: *Donald Nelson & Co,* agents for *T P Keith Oakey & Co,* Hinckley (for the appellant); *Headleys,* Hinckley (for the respondents).

Patricia Hargrove Barrister.

c

Manson v Duke of Westminster and others

COURT OF APPEAL, CIVIL DIVISION   *d*
STEPHENSON, BRANDON LJJ AND SIR DAVID CAIRNS
3rd, 4th, 5th NOVEMBER, 12th DECEMBER 1980

Landlord and tenant – Leasehold enfranchisement – Tenancy at low rent – Letting value – Tenancy granted during period of rent restriction – Premium paid for grant of lease – Determination of 'letting value' – Landlords obtaining maximum rent permitted by statute but not *e* *obtaining maximum premium on open market – When premium decapitalised total value to landlord not exceeding two-thirds of letting value – Whether letting value restricted to rent or including annual value of maximum premium obtainable on open market – Leasehold Reform Act 1967, s 4(1) proviso.*

In 1945 in return for a premium payment of £500 the tenant's predecessor in title was *f* granted a lease of a house for a term of 40½ years at a rent of £100 per year. Under the Rent and Mortgage Interest Restrictions Act 1939 the rent under the lease was the maximum then permitted by law for the premises although there was at that time no limit on the premium a landlord could ask for a lease for 14 years or more. The tenant acquired the lease in 1973 and resided in the house from May 1973. In May 1978 he gave notice to the landlords under the Leasehold Reform Act 1967 that he wished to acquire the freehold on the basis that he had a long tenancy at a low rent and fell within *g* the appropriate rateable value. The landlords disputed his right to do so, on the ground that 'at the commencement of the tenancy the rent payable under the tenancy exceeded two-thirds of the letting value of the property (on the same terms)' and was thereby deemed by the proviso to s 4(1)[a] of the 1967 Act not to be a 'low rent' and that the tenancy was therefore excluded from the terms of the 1967 Act. The landlords *h* contended that the 'letting value of the property' was the rent they could have obtained on the open market in 1945 and that having regard to the statutory restrictions then in force the £100 per year that they had obtained was that rent. The tenant contended that 'the letting value of the property' referred to the total consideration, including not only the rent but also any premium, obtainable on the terms of the transaction, and that if £100 were to exceed two-thirds of the letting value the total letting value, including the *j* decapitalised value of any premium, had to be no more than £150. The landlords conceded that the lease could have been granted at a premium considerably greater than that which they had in fact obtained and which when decapitalised would have meant

---

a   Section 4(1), is set out at p 43 *a b,* post

a that the total letting value was greater than £150 if that value included the maximum premium payable on the open market. The county court judge held that for the purposes of the proviso to s 4(1) the letting value was to be ascertained by taking into account the premium that could reasonably have been obtained in the open market at the commencement of the tenancy and that the rent at that date was less than two-thirds of such a letting value of the premises. The judge accordingly ordered that the tenant was entitled to acquire the freehold. The landlords appealed.

b

Held – (1) On the true construction of the proviso to s 4(1) of the 1967 Act the 'letting value of the property' was the value in annual terms of the total amount, including any premium, paid by the tenant to the landlord, because—

(a) (per Stephenson LJ and Sir David Cairns) that was the natural meaning of the expression 'letting value' and it did not lead to such inconsistency, absurdity or
c inconvenience as to be contrary to Parliament's intention (see p 44 *d* and *g* to *j*, p 45 *j*, p 46 *h j*, p 48 *d* to *f* and p 50 *g h*, post); dictum of Lord Blackburn in *River Wear Comrs v Adamson* [1874–80] All ER Rep at 12 and *King v Earl Cadogan* [1915] 3 KB 485 applied;

(b) (per Brandon LJ) on the basis that the court was precluded by authority from holding that the 'letting value' was the annual rent obtainable in the open market irrespective of any statutory limit, a meaning of 'letting value' which included the
d decapitalised value of any lawfully obtainable premium was to be preferred to a meaning which excluded any premium, because it was contrary to common sense and reality to regard the rent under a tenancy as the sole benefit derived by the landlord when he may have derived a further and possibly very substantial benefit by way of a premium (see p 50 *c d g h*, post); *Gidlow-Jackson v Middlegate Properties Ltd* [1974] 1 All ER 830 criticised.

(2) Accordingly, the letting value of the house occupied by the tenant was at the
e commencement of the tenancy the annual rent then obtainable in the open market having regard to the statutory limit on rents imposed by the 1939 Act but with the addition of the decapitalised value of any premium lawfully obtainable. Since on that basis the rent at the commencement of the tenancy was less than two-thirds of the letting value inclusive of the maximum premium then obtainable, the judge had been right to order that the tenant was entitled to acquire the freehold. The appeal would accordingly
f be dismissed (see p 48 *f g* and p 50 *f g*, post).

Per Curiam. In the context of the proviso to s 4(1) the payment of a premium should be regarded as the consideration for which a lease is granted and not as part of 'the same terms' of the lease (see p 47 *b* to *d*, p 49 *b* to *d* and p 50 *g h*, post); *Hill v Booth* [1929] All ER Rep 84 applied.

g **Notes**
For when a tenancy of property is a tenancy at a low rent, see Supplement to 23 Halsbury's Laws (3rd Edn) para 1750.

For the Leasehold Reform Act 1967, ss 1, 4, see 18 Halsbury's Statutes (3rd Edn) 634, 640.

h **Cases referred to in judgments**
Gidlow-Jackson v Middlegate Properties Ltd [1974] 1 All ER 830, [1974] QB 361, [1974] 2 WLR 116, 27 P & CR 378, [1974] RVR 5, CA, Digest (Cont Vol D) 576, 1488a.
Hill v Booth [1930] 1 KB 381, [1929] All ER Rep 84, 99 LJKB 49, 142 LT 80, CA, 31(1) Digest (Reissue) 374, 2993.
Jones v Wrotham Park Settled Estates [1979] 1 All ER 286, [1980] AC 74, [1979] 2 WLR
j 132, sub nom *Wentworth Securities Ltd v Jones* 38 P & CR 77, [1979] RVR 315, HL, Digest (Cont Vol E) 359, 1497a.
King v Earl Cadogan [1915] 3 KB 485, CA.
Methuen-Campbell v Walters [1979] 1 All ER 606, [1979] QB 525, [1979] 2 WLR 113, 38 P & CR 693, CA, Digest (Cont Vol E) 358, 1491c.
R v Braddon and Speke (1684) 9 State Tr 1127.

Rawlence v Croydon Corpn [1952] 2 All ER 535, [1952] 2 QB 803, 116 JP 515, 50 LGR 576,
  CA, 26 Digest (Repl) 684, *18.*
River Wear Comrs v Adamson (1877) 2 App Cas 743, [1874–80] All ER Rep 1, 47 LJQB
  193, 37 LT 543, 42 JP 244, 3 Asp MLC 521, HL, 17 Digest (Reissue) 175, *544.*
Samrose Properties v Gibbard [1958] 1 All ER 502, [1958] 1 WLR 235, CA, 31(2) Digest
  (Reissue) 1033, *8189.*

Cases also cited
Davey, Re [1947] 1 All ER 90, CA.
Newman v Dorrington Developments Ltd [1975] 3 All ER 928, [1975] 1 WLR 1642.

Appeal
By a lease dated 12th July 1945 the then landlords, the Duke of Westminster and others,
in consideration of the sum of £500 paid for the grant of a lease demised the house and
premises at 42 Chester Row, London SW1 to one Walter William John Wright for a term
of 40½ years commencing on 29th September 1945 at a rent of £100 per annum. On
27th August 1945 Mr Wright assigned the lease to a Mrs Gabrielle Ormrod for £1,350.
On 8th January 1973 the tenant, Louis Joshua Manson, acquired the residue of the lease
for £18,500 and resided there from May 1973. On 12th May 1978 the tenant gave
notice under the Leasehold Reform Act 1967 to the landlords, the present trustees of the
Grosvenor Estates, being the fifth Duke of Westminster, the Hon Gerald Grosvenor, John
Nigel Courtenay James and Patrick Geoffrey Corbett, of his wish to acquire the freehold
of the premises. The landlords denied his claim. By an application dated 7th March
1979 the tenant applied to the West London County Court pursuant to s 20 of the 1967
Act for an order that he was entitled to the freehold of the premises. On 5th November
1979 his Honour Judge Corcoran made the order sought. The landlords appealed. The
facts are set out in the judgment of Stephenson LJ.

Edward Nugee QC and *Terence Etherton* for the landlords.
Kenneth J Farrow for the tenant.

Cur adv vult

12th December. The following judgments were read.

STEPHENSON LJ. This is an appeal by the landlords of a leasehold house, 42 Chester
Row, London SW1, against an order of his Honour Judge Corcoran made in the West
London County Court on 5th November 1979 declaring their tenant to be entitled to
acquire the freehold of the house pursuant to the Leasehold Reform Act 1967.
  Section 1(1)(*a*) of that Act conferred on a tenant of a leasehold house, occupying the
house as his residence, a right to acquire on fair terms the freehold or an extended lease
of the house and premises where—

  'his tenancy is a long tenancy at a low rent and the rateable value of the house and
  premises on the appropriate day is not (or was not) more ... if it is in Greater
  London, than £400 ...'

For tenancies created before 18th February 1966, s 118(1) of the Housing Act 1974 raised
that figure to £1,500 and altered the appropriate day from 23rd March 1965 to 1st April
1973. A 'long tenancy' means a tenancy granted for a term of years certain exceeding 21
years: see s 3(1) of the 1967 Act.
  The meaning of 'low rent' is given in s 4(1), on the proviso to which this appeal
turns. The subsection provides:

a   'For purposes of this Part of this Act a tenancy of any property is a tenancy at a low
rent at any time when rent is not payable under the tenancy in respect of the
property at a yearly rate equal to or more than two-thirds of the rateable value of the
property on the appropriate day or, if later, the first day of the term: Provided that
a tenancy granted between the end of August 1939 and the beginning of April 1963
otherwise than by way of building lease (whether or not it is, by virtue of section
3(3) above, to be treated for other purposes as forming a single tenancy with a
b   previous tenancy) shall not be regarded as a tenancy at a low rent if at the
commencement of the tenancy the rent payable under the tenancy exceeded two-
thirds of the letting value of the property (on the same terms).'

On 12th May 1978 the tenant gave notice of his claim under the 1967 Act and on 3rd
July 1978 the landlords gave notice in reply that they did not admit—

c   'your right on the grounds that the tenancy is not a tenancy at a low rent in that
at the commencement of the tenancy rent payable under the tenancy exceeded two-
thirds of the letting value of the property (Proviso to Section 4(1) of the Leasehold
Reform Act 1967).'

The tenant applied to the county court pursuant to s 20 of the 1967 Act on 7th March
d   1979 for an order determining that he was entitled to acquire the freehold. By their
answer the landlords put him to proof of the occupation of the house as his residence
which the Act requires and denied that the rent of £100 per year payable under the lease
was a low rent as defined by s 4 of the Act.

At the hearing the tenant admittedly satisfied every statutory requirement except
one. He was a tenant of this house pursuant to a lease dated 12th July 1945 granted for
e   a term of 40 years and one-half of another year from 29th September 1945 at a rent of
£100 per year, which he acquired by an assignment dated 8th January 1973 for a
premium of £18,500. He has occupied it as his residence since May 1973. Its rateable
value on 1st April 1973 was £1,076. His rent of £100 a year was payable at a yearly rate
much less than two-thirds of that rateable value. But his tenancy was granted between
the end of August 1939 and the beginning of April 1963 otherwise than by way of a
f   building lease. So the judge had to decide the question whether at the commencement
of the tenancy, in 1945, that rent payable under it 'exceeded two-thirds of the letting
value of the property (on the same terms)'. If it did exceed that proportion of that value,
the tenant was not entitled to acquire the freehold because the rent was too high. If it did
not, it was a low rent and he was entitled to acquire the freehold.

That was the only issue ultimately left for the judge to decide. It depended on the
g   meaning of the words 'the letting value' in their context. He accepted the tenant's
construction of the words and decided the issue in his favour. The landlords ask this
court to accept their construction of the words and decide in their favour that he is not
entitled to the declaration granted by the judge.

The landlords' case is that the 'letting value of the property (on the same terms)' means
simply the rent which the landlords could have obtained in the open market if they had
h   offered the property for letting on the terms of the lease. And that means in this case the
rent of £100 a year which is the maximum rent they could have lawfully obtained. The
tenant's case is that that value means the whole consideration for which the landlords
could have let the property in the open market, including a premium in addition to the
rent. And that means in this case a sum to be calculated by decapitalising the obtainable
premium which, when added to the £100 rent, would bring the obtainable consideration
j   above the minimum amount required to prevent the £100 exceeding two-thirds of that
consideration.

The rent of £100 a year was admitted to be the highest rent which the landlords could
exact in 1945. Tenancies of dwelling houses within the 1967 Act are not generally
tenancies controlled by the Rent Acts because the rent of the former must not equal or

exceed two-thirds of the rateable value whereas the rent of the latter must. But this house is subject to new control under the Rent and Mortgage Interest Restrictions Act 1939, £100 a year is the standard rent and there were no permitted increases entitling the landlords to recover more. It was also common ground that as the law stood in 1945 there was nothing to prevent the landlords charging and recovering a premium as the term of this lease was not less than 14 years. Furthermore the landlords did not challenge, and the judge accepted, the evidence of an experienced valuer and chartered surveyor called by the tenant that 7% was the correct percentage to apply to a premium in order to obtain its annual equivalent by decapitalisation and that to produce by this means the £50 a year necessary to keep the £100 a year rent down to two-thirds of the sum of those two amounts the minimum amount required as capital premium was £581. Finally it was conceded by the landlords that they could not call evidence to discharge the burden imposed on them by s 4(5) of proving that less than £581 could be lawfully exacted from a tenant in the open market on 29th September 1945.

So the tenant's right to acquire the freehold rests on the single question whether the court can take into account a premium in assessing 'the letting value of the property (on the same terms)'.

My first impression was that the court can and should take it into account as the judge did, because the natural and ordinary meaning of the words would not be limited to the rent but would include any other consideration, certainly any other consideration in cash, which the landlords would get for letting the house.

The expression is not defined in the 1967 Act. The industry of counsel has not found it in any other statute. The expression 'the lettable value of the premises' occurs in the Liabilities (War-Time Adjustment) Act 1944, s 6, where it was defined as—

'the rent at which in the opinion of the court the premises might reasonably be expected to let, or, as the case may be, might reasonably have been expected to let, under a tenancy for one year granted upon the same terms and conditions (so far as applicable) as those upon which the debtor is holding the premises.'

But 'the letting value' is not an expression of legal art, as Stamp LJ said in *Gidlow-Jackson v Middlegate Ltd* [1974] 1 All ER 830 at 840, [1974] QB 361 at 376; and, though he went on to use 'letting value' and 'lettable value' as apparently convertible terms, I derive no more help from the definition in the 1944 Act than from the absence of any definition in the 1967 Act. In that case this court held that the letting value of the property could not exceed the amount of rent at which the property could lawfully be let and the standard rent was the letting value. But there was no premium for the lease granted in that case and no possibility of lawfully exacting it and so no question whether a premium could be included in that value was raised or considered, let alone decided. Unhelped and unhampered by any statutory definition or judicial authority I would have thought a landlord who had been paid a good-sized premium by the tenant of his property would be astonished if he were told by an estate agent or his legal adviser, or by a judge, that the letting value of the property was confined to the rent. That value is what the property would be worth to him if he let it; and I agree with counsel for the tenant that, if the landlord had asked an estate agent what it would be worth to him if he let it, the estate agent would surely reply: 'You can get a rent of no more than £100 a year, but you can charge a premium if you are prepared to give up possession of it for 14 years.' The letting value of a property is its value to the landlord in annual or perhaps other periodic terms. Its value to him as a landlord is what he is paid for it by his tenant, and all that he is paid, and until I heard the cogent submissions of counsel for the landlords I wondered, reacting as did Sir George Jeffreys CJ, three centuries ago to an attempt to introduce hearsay evidence (*R v Braddon and Speke* (1684) 9 State Tr 1127 at 1189) 'to hear any man that wears a gown, to make a doubt of it'. But a doubt of it counsel certainly has made.

His submissions in the form in which he recorded them for our assistance are these.

1. The natural meaning of 'letting value' is rental or annual value and that is the meaning of those words in s 4(1) of the 1967 Act.

2. If the natural meaning of 'letting value' is the total consideration for which a property can be let, nevertheless for the purposes of s 4(1) the meaning of the phrase 'letting value' is restricted to rental or annual value.

3. The conclusion in 2 above is based on the following reasons. (1) Parliament cannot have intended that rent should be compared with something other than rental value, for that would be to compare like with unlike. It would also be unfair to the landlord, for whose very benefit the proviso to s 4(1) was inserted, because the proviso requires the actual rent to be compared with 'the letting value'. (2) In the only other statutory provision in which the phrase 'letting value' appears, namely s 15(2) of the 1967 Act, letting value means and can only mean the rental or annual value. (3) The 'building lease' exception in s 4(1)(d) of the 1967 Act is only explicable on the basis that a premium cannot be taken into account in ascertaining the 'letting value'. (4) The proviso to s 4(1) requires the rent to be compared with the letting value *on the same terms*. One of the terms of the letting is the payment of a premium, and that shows that 'letting value' in the section is something other than a premium. Further, to take into account the actual premium is inconsistent with the contention that 'letting value' means the best consideration that could have been obtained and not the actual consideration obtained. (5) If letting value meant total consideration, there would be great and possibly insuperable problems of valuation. It would mean reduction to an annual value of the best consideration that could have been obtained regardless of what was actually obtained, eg an infinite variety of combinations of premium and rent. It would also pose extraordinary problems of valuation where part of the consideration for the letting was or might have been the execution of works to the premises. Parliament cannot have intended these difficulties of valuation: see the simple treatment of premiums for income tax purposes. (We were referred to the Income and Corporation Taxes Act 1970, s 80.) (6) When Parliament enacted the 1967 Act, it must be taken to have been aware that premiums had formerly been chargeable and had in fact been charged in respect of Rent Act premises, and Parliament would have dealt specifically with premiums if it had intended premiums to be taken into account in ascertaining the letting value. (7) In the long history of rent restrictions and landlord and tenant legislation since 1914, the court has always drawn a sharp distinction between a genuine premium and a mere commuted rent. (We were referred to *Samrose Properties Ltd v Gibbard* [1958] 1 All ER 502, [1958] 1 WLR 225.) If Parliament had intended that in the 1967 Act a premium should be decapitalised for the purposes of s 4(1), it would have said so and provided how it should be done. Further, if it is proper to treat the premium as a commuted rent, then the commuted rent would exceed the standard rent under the Rent Act and would not be enforceable as rent. (8) The intention of Parliament, as disclosed by the White Paper, Leasehold Reform in England and Wales (Cmnd 2916 (1966)), referred to in the judgment of Lord Denning MR in *Gidlow-Jackson v Middlegate Properties Ltd* [1974] 1 All ER 830 at 835, [1974] QB 361 at 370, was to distinguish between long tenancies at a low rent and long tenancies at a high rent; this is also borne out by the long title to the 1967 Act. The tenancy in the present case is a tenancy at a rack rent because it reserved the best rent obtainable at the grant of the tenancy. (9) The 1967 Act is an expropriatory Act, and if there are genuine doubts as to the meaning of 'letting value' that phrase should be construed in favour of the landlord. Further the proviso to s 4(1) was inserted for the benefit of the landlord, and for that reason, if there is genuine doubt as to the meaning of 'letting value', the phrase should be construed in favour of the landlord. (We were referred to *Methuen-Campbell v Walters* [1979] 1 All ER 606 at 610, 615, 619, 620, [1979] QB 525 at 529, 536, 541, 542 and to *Jones v Wrotham Park Estates* [1979] 1 All ER 286 at 295, [1980] AC 74 at 113.)

Counsel's argument has not altered my first impression and I do not accept his first submission. His second submission I find formidable, in particular the first two reasons which he has submitted for restricting the natural meaning of the words.

(1) I agree that the value to be compared with the rent must be in one sense an annual or rental value. It is not expressed as 'the full net annual value of the house', the phrase *a* considered in *Rawlence v Croydon Corpn* [1952] 2 All ER 335, [1952] 2 QB 803; but the 'yearly rate' expressed in sub-s (1) must, I think, be implied in the proviso.

It is however, in my judgment, fallacious to conclude that the value to be compared cannot include a lump sum capable of being decapitalised, or 'rentalised' (to use counsel's alternative). A premium is the capital value of the difference between the actual rent and the best rent that might otherwise be obtained: see *King v Cadogan* [1915] 3 KB 485 at *b* 492. Decapitalisation is an exercise carried out whenever an annuity is bought or in reverse whenever judgment under Lord Campbell's Act (the Fatal Accidents Act 1846) is delivered. It is an exercise which these landlords carry out when they grant a lease for any term from 21 to 60 years at a standard rent: they require in addition to an undertaking to carry out tenant's repairs a 'cash payment (representing part of the annual value capitalised)'. It was agreed that the tenant would have signed an acceptance of an *c* offer of the 1945 lease in those terms (though the particular document had been destroyed); and the unchallenged evidence of the tenant's surveyor was that the annual equivalent of the premium was obtained by dividing it by the year's purchase figure in Parry's Valuation Tables for 40½ years at 7% (though the landlords used 6%) with a sinking fund of 2% (untaxed).

(2) The 1967 Act gives the tenant who qualifies for purchase of the freehold the *d* alternative right to acquire a 50 years' extension of his lease. Section 15(2) provides:

'The new tenancy shall provide that as from the original term date the rent payable for the house and premises shall be a rent ascertained or to be ascertained as follows:—(a) the rent shall be a ground rent in the sense that it shall represent the letting value of the site (without including anything for the value of buildings on *e* the site) for the uses to which the house and premises have been put since the commencement of the existing tenancy, other than uses which by the terms of the new tenancy are not permitted or are permitted only with the landlord's consent; (b) the letting value for this purpose shall be in the first instance the letting value at the date from which the rent based on it is to commence ... (c) the letting value at either of the times mentioned shall be determined not earlier than twelve months *f* before that time (the reasonable cost of obtaining a valuation for the purpose being borne by the tenant) ...'

It was rightly conceded by counsel for the tenant that the letting value there referred to is a hypothetical rent and nothing else. But that letting value is 'the letting value of the site', which would be the ground rent. No premium would be payable for the site *g* in the circumstances postulated in s 15, and what we have to interpret is 'the letting value of the property', where payment of a premium for the lease of the property would often be payable, even when the property and the lease were controlled by the Rent Acts. Premiums could lawfully be exacted from the tenants of such properties from 1920 to 1949 if the term was 14 years or more and from 1957 to 1967 (and 1969 onwards) if the term was 21 years or more; but no premium was lawful between 1949 and 1957 or *h* between 1967 and 1969: see the Rent Act 1920, s 8(3), the Landlord and Tenant (Rent Control) Act 1949, s 2, the Rent Act 1957, s 21, the Leasehold Reform Act 1967, s 39, and the Housing Act 1969, s 81. I am accordingly of the opinion that there is nothing in s 15(2) to restrict the meaning of the words used in the proviso to s 4(1), and to give 'the letting value of the property' in s 4 a wider meaning than the 'letting value of the site' in *j* s 15 would not involve a difference of definition.

I find less force in the rest of counsel's reasons.

(3) His argument on the building lease exception is that if a premium is to be decapitalised then the cost of building the house must be treated in the same way. If this were done the rent under the building lease would almost always be under two-thirds of

the rent plus the decapitalised value of the house so the exception is unnecessary.

a Counsel's answer for the tenant is that the value to be taken into account is not the cost to the tenant but the value to the landlord and that the value to him of the reversion will be far less than the cost of building the house (indeed with a 99-year lease it will be a very small sum) and there may well be cases where the rent would exceed two-thirds of the rent plus the decapitalised value of the reversion. Both arguments proceed on the basis that the hypothetical lease is a building lease. On that basis, which I think must be right,

b I find the answer for the tenant convincing.

(4) I understood counsel for the landlords to concede in his reply that the payment of a premium was not one of the 'terms' of the lease, but the consideration for the grant of the lease, as counsel for the tenant had argued in reliance on *Hill v Booth* [1930] 1 KB 381, [1929] All ER Rep 84. Though there are difficulties in either interpretation, I prefer the second thoughts of counsel for the landlord on this point. Since letting value is to be

c assessed on the basis of a hypothetical letting and since rent and premium are mutually dependent on each other, it seems right to consider a hypothetical premium as well as a hypothetical rent. If the premium is one of the 'terms' referred to in the parenthesis and if the hypothetical premium has to be the same as the actual premium, there will be hardly any tenancies granted in the years covered by the proviso in which the actual rent is less than two-thirds of the hypothetical rent.

d (5) The problems of valuation which the judge's interpretation of letting value would create are not, in my opinion, great enough to drive me to the landlords' interpretation and are certainly not insuperable. The combinations of rent plus premium actually obtained are nothing like infinite; and I would confine the total consideration to the total consideration in cash and exclude from the letting value of the property any other part of the consideration such as the execution of works of repair undertaken as a condition

e of the grant of the 1945 tenancy.

(6) and (7) The history of premiums charged for Rent Act premises and the presumption that Parliament had them in mind when enacting this proviso do not lead to the conclusion that by not mentioning them or providing for their decapitalisation Parliament intended to exclude them from the letting value of such premises. It would indeed be odd if Parliament had lost sight not only of such an important factor as

f premiums in causing low rents to be charged but of all the enactments dealing with such premiums to which I have already referred. After all, for every tenancy granted in the 24 years to which the proviso applies, a premium could lawfully be charged except for tenancies controlled by the Rent Acts which were granted in eight of those years. But if Parliament had premiums in mind it is difficult to suppose that it would not have regarded them as an obvious part of the letting value of Rent Act premises requiring

g specific exclusion rather than specific inclusion. To have disregarded them would have produced an anomaly arising from Parliament's alternating intention to allow them, on which counsel for the tenant relied. The tendency would be for rents to be nearer the permitted rent during those years when premiums were forbidden than at other times. So if one house with a permitted rent of £100 a year were let in 1948 on a 30-year lease at a rent of £20 a year with a premium of £2,000 and an exactly similar house with the

h same permitted rent were let in 1950 on a 30-year lease at a rent of £100 a year with no premium it might well be that if letting value is to be tested by rent alone the first tenant would be able to enfranchise and the second would not. I think there is some force in counsel's argument that this would be an unacceptable anomaly.

(8) and (9) It is plain that the 1967 Act is an expropriatory Act, that the proviso to s 4(1) was inserted for the benefit of landlords and, without recourse to the White Paper,

j that it expressed the intention of Parliament to distinguish between long tenancies at a low rent and long tenancies at a high rent (and, of course, to exclude short tenancies at any rent). The landlord is being required to submit to a compulsory purchase of his freehold property by a leaseholder who has a long tenancy at a low rent. The dividing line between low rents within the Act and high rents outside it is not fixed at any

boundary between ground rents and rack rents but by the figure of two-thirds of the
rateable value. But, as inflation operating on that figure between 1939 and 1963 would *a*
have 'enfranchised' leases at a rent which could not have been considered low at the
commencement of the tenancy, the proviso introduced the letting value instead of the
rateable value to prevent injustice which the landlords would have suffered without that
substitution.

I would, however, respectfully follow the judgments in this court and in the House of
Lords in the cases cited by counsel for the landlords and regard the expropriatory nature *b*
of the 1967 Act as of little weight in construing its provisions, and I would not regard the
standard rent of £100 a year, to which the Rent Acts restricted the rent of this house, as
a rack rent even in 1945. There is therefore nothing in those last reasons submitted by
counsel for the landlords that weighs against the construction of counsel for the tenant
which the judge accepted.

I return therefore to Lord Wensleydale's golden rule cited by Lord Blackburn in *River* *c*
Wear Comrs v Adamson (1877) 2 App Cas 743 at 764–765, [1874–80] All ER Rep 1 at 12:

> '. . . that we are to take the whole statute together, and construe it all together,
> giving the words their ordinary signification, unless when so applied they produce
> an inconsistency, or an absurdity or inconvenience so great as to convince the Court
> that the intention could not have been to use them in their ordinary signification,
> and to justify the Court in putting on them some other signification, which, though *d*
> less proper, is one which the Court thinks the words will bear.'

It may be that in inserting the proviso to s 4(1) and replacing the value to the tenant
(rateable value) by the value to the landlord (letting value) as the basis of distinction
between high and low rents Parliament gave inadequate consideration to that alternative
basis and to an important class of tenancies within which this tenancy and (we are told) *e*
a number of others granted by these landlords fall, and, like this court in *Gidlow-Jackson*
v Middlegate Properties Ltd, did not have premiums in mind. In doubt whether it did or
did not, the right course for the courts is to apply the golden rule. Its application leads
to no inconsistency or absurdity or inconvenience so great as to be contrary to
Parliament's intention. Not to apply it would have the absurd result of making a
property which could be let at £100 a year with a premium of £2,000 of equal letting *f*
value to another similar property which could be let at £100 a year with no premium.
Either construction may give rise to anomalies but to none greater than that. Balancing
them as best I can I conclude that the judge was right to come down in favour of what
I agree is the natural meaning of the proviso. I would accordingly dismiss the appeal.

BRANDON LJ. The question to be decided on this appeal is what meaning is to be *g*
given to the expression 'the letting value of the property (on the same terms)' appearing
at the end of the proviso to s 4(1) of the Leasehold Reform Act 1967.

The proviso was inserted for the benefit of landlords, in order to exclude from the
enfranchisement provisions of the 1967 Act houses the rents of which had been proper
market rents at the times when the relevant tenancies of them were granted but which, *h*
as a result of inflation between 1939 and 1963, had become less than two-thirds of the
rateable values of such houses on the appropriate day, namely (subject to later statutory
provisions) 23rd March 1965.

In the present case the relevant tenancy was granted on 12th July 1945 for a term of
40½ years commencing on 29th September 1945 at a rent of £100 a year on payment of
a premium of £500. The house was subject to new control under the Rent and Mortgage *j*
Interest Restrictions Act 1939, and £100 was the standard rent under the provisions of
that Act. The premium of £500 paid by the tenant was a lawful payment, since there
was at that time no statutory prohibition on the taking of a premium by a landlord on
the grant of a lease for 14 years or more.

In construing the expression 'the letting value of the property (on the same terms)' in
relation to these facts two potentially interlocking questions arise.

a

The first question is whether the words 'letting value of the property' mean (a) the
annual rent obtainable in the open market, irrespectively of any limit imposed in the
form of a standard rent or otherwise by the Rent Acts, or (b) the annual rent obtainable
in the open market having regard to such limit, without any addition for the decapitalised
value of any premium lawfully obtainable, or (c) the annual rent obtainable in the open
market having regard to such limit, but with an addition for the decapitalised value of

b

any premium lawfully obtainable.

The second question is whether the words in brackets 'on the same terms' include or
exclude the payment by the tenant of the premium of £500.

I think it convenient to answer the second question first. In my view the words in
brackets 'on the same terms', though capable of including the payment of the premium,
should, in the context in which they are found, be construed as not doing so. The

c

payment of the premium should rather be regarded as the consideration for which the
lease was granted: see *Hill v Booth* [1930] 1 KB 381, [1929] All ER Rep 84. I take that view
because the contrary view would, as it seems to me, result in relatively few tenants
satisfying the requirements of a tenancy at a low rent under the proviso to s 4(1).

Turning to the first question, I shall examine it first of all as an ordinary question of

d

statutory construction, without regard to any authority on it which may be binding on
me.

In my view meaning (a) above, namely the annual rent obtainable in the open market,
irrespectively of any limit imposed in the form of a standard rent or otherwise by the
Rent Acts, is the meaning which fits best with the purpose of the proviso to s 4(1). This
proviso was inserted, as I indicated earlier, for the benefit of landlords. Its purpose, as it

e

seems to me, was to substitute for a comparison of the annual rent payable under the
tenancy with a rateable value fixed perhaps many years after the commencement of the
tenancy, and therefore a value much increased by inflation, a comparison with a value
which would more nearly accord with that which would have been the rateable value of
the property at the commencement of the tenancy if an up-to-date revaluation of rateable
values had taken place at a reasonable time before or after such commencement.

f

Meaning (a) is the only one of the three possible meanings referred to above which is
capable of achieving this result, or something approximating to it. It follows that,
unhampered by any authority binding on me, I should be disposed to adopt meaning (a).

Section 4(5) of the 1967 Act puts on a landlord the burden of proving that a tenancy
coming within the proviso to s 4(1) is not a tenancy at a low rent. In the present case the
landlords called no evidence to show that, at the time of the commencement of the

g

tenancy on 29th September 1945, the annual rent obtainable for the house in the open
market on the same terms, irrespectively of any limit imposed by the Rent Acts, was less
than £150. It follows that, if meaning (a) were to be adopted, the tenant's claim would
succeed, although on a different basis from that relied on by the county court judge, who
adopted meaning (c) for the expression concerned.

While this would be my approach to the case if the matter were free of authority, it

h

seems that I am precluded from adopting meaning (a) by the earlier decision of this court
in *Gidlow-Jackson v Middlegate Properties Ltd* [1974] 1 All ER 830, [1974] QB 361. In that
case it was held that the 'letting value of the property' for the purposes of the proviso to
s 4(1) of the 1967 Act could not exceed the amount of rent lawfully exigible by the
landlords under the Rent Acts. The lease there concerned had been granted in 1952, at
which time it would have been unlawful for a landlord to require the payment of a
premium on a lease of whatever length. It follows that the court was not concerned

j

with, and did not have present to its mind, the complications arising from a premium
having been paid by the tenant on the grant of the lease concerned, or of the landlords,
though constrained by the Rent Acts with regard to the maximum amount of rent
exigible by them, being lawfully entitled to require the payment of a premium on the

grant of a long lease of the property. It was, accordingly, without regard to such complications that the court rejected meaning (a), and gave no consideration at all to the *a* choice between meanings (b) and (c).

I am not at all sure that, if the complications arising from a premium lawfully paid by a tenant and lawfully exigible by a landlord had been raised in *Gidlow-Jackson v Middlegate Properties Ltd*, the decision of the court to reject meaning (a) would have been the same. I recognise, however, that I am bound by that decision and am therefore precluded from adopting meaning (a) in the present case. It seems to me desirable nevertheless that the *b* decision in *Gidlow-Jackson v Middlegate Properties Ltd* should be reviewed by the House of Lords as soon as a suitable case for such review arises.

On the footing that this court is precluded from adopting meaning (a), I agree with the view of Stephenson LJ that meaning (c) should be preferred to meaning (b), as it was by the county court judge. I agree with that view mainly because it seems to me that it would be contrary to common sense, and to the realities of the matter, in assessing the *c* letting value of a rent-controlled house to regard the maximum rent exigible by the landlord under the Rent Acts as the sole benefit by him from the tenancy, and to disregard the further benefit (which may be very substantial) obtainable by him in the form of a premium lawfully exacted by him from the tenant in consideration of the grant of a long lease.

Although, with meaning (a) excluded as a possibility by authority, I prefer meaning *d* (c) to meaning (b), I think it right to point out that the adoption of meaning (c) produces some strangely anomalous results, because of the repeated changes during the material period in the law relating to the right of a landlord to require the payment of a premium on the grant of a lease.

The relevant period for the purposes of the proviso to s 4(1) of the 1967 Act is the end of August 1939 to the beginning of April 1963. During this period the situation with *e* regard to a landlord taking a premium on the grant of a lease was this: from 1939 to 1949 premiums were lawful in the case of leases for 14 years or more; from 1949 to 1957 premiums were unlawful in the case of any lease for however long; from 1957 to 1963 premiums were lawful again in the case of leases for 21 years or more.

It follows that, if meaning (c) is adopted, a tenant's chances of acquiring the freehold of a house let to him on a long lease were and are much better if his lease was granted *f* between 1939 and 1949 or between 1957 and 1963, when premiums were lawful, than if it was granted to him between 1949 and 1957, when premiums were unlawful.

For the reasons which I have given I should prefer, if not bound by authority, to support the decision of the county court judge on a basis different to that on which he relied. Bound by authority as I am, however, I agree with Stephenson LJ that the decision of the learned county court judge should be supported on the basis on which it *g* was given, and that the appeal should be dismissed accordingly.

SIR DAVID CAIRNS. I agree that this appeal should be dismissed for the reasons given by Stephenson LJ in his judgment.

I agree with Brandon LJ that the question whether *Gidlow-Jackson v Middlegate Properties Ltd* [1974] 1 All ER 830, [1974] QB 361 was rightly decided might well, on a *h* suitable occasion, be considered by the House of Lords, but I express no conclusion whether, if the decision of the Court of Appeal in that case were not binding on us, I should have held that the effect of the Rent Acts should, in the case of a rent-controlled house, be taken into account for the purposes of the proviso to s 4(1) of the Leasehold Reform Act 1967.

j

Appeal dismissed. Leave to appeal to the House of Lords granted.

Solicitors: *Mansons* (for the tenant); *Boodle, Hatfield & Co* (for the landlords).

Patricia Hargrove   Barrister.

Littlewood v Rolfe and another

QUEEN'S BENCH DIVISION
HIS HONOUR EDGAR FAY QC SITTING AS A DEPUTY JUDGE OF THE HIGH COURT
21st NOVEMBER, 1st DECEMBER 1980

Agricultural holding – Tenancy – Death of tenant – Eligibility of survivor of tenant for grant of new tenancy – Applicant not fully eligible for grant of new tenancy – Applicant entitled 'to be treated as eligible' if condition as to livelihood 'satisfied to a material extent' – Material extent – Widow applying for grant of tenancy of husband's holding – Widow and husband deriving joint livelihood partly from working on farm and partly from other work over period of 44½ months – Whether widow's principal source of livelihood derived 'to a material extent' from work on farm over period of five years – Agriculture (Miscellaneous Provisions) Act 1976, ss 18(2), 21(1)(b).

In October 1975 the husband was granted the tenancy of a farm, and he and his wife and their two children moved from London to live on the farm intending to make it their permanent home. Throughout the period of 44½ months from 1st October 1975 to 13th June 1979, when the husband died, the wife worked on the farm although not always full-time. From 1st October 1975 to 13th June 1977 she worked part-time on the farm and part-time as a nurse, the couple's joint livelihood being derived equally from the farm and her earnings as a nurse. From 13th June 1977 to the latter part of 1978 both the husband and the wife worked full-time on the farm and derived their joint livelihood from it. From 1978 until the husband's death the wife worked full-time on the farm and the husband worked partly on the farm and partly in other employment, and they derived their joint livelihood equally from the farm and the husband's other employment. On the husband's death the wife applied to an agricultural land tribunal for a direction under s 20(1)[a] of the Agriculture (Miscellaneous Provisions) Act 1976 that she was entitled to a tenancy of the farm. Although the wife satisfied the conditions for eligibility for a tenancy by succession specified in paras (a) and (c) of the definition of 'eligible person' in s 18(2)[b] of the 1976 Act, she did not satisfy the condition specified in para (b) of that definition that she had for a period of five years in the seven years preceding her husband's death derived her only or principal source of livelihood from her work on the farm. By s 21(1) and (3)[c] of that Act a person who, though not fully

---

a   Section 20(1) provides: 'Any eligible person may within the relevant period apply to the Tribunal for a direction entitling him to a tenancy of the holding.'

b   Section 18, so far as material, provides:
   '(1) Where after the passing of this Act the sole (or sole surviving) tenant of an agricultural holding dies and is survived by . . . (a) the wife . . . of the deceased . . . the following sections of this Part of this Act . . . shall apply . . .
   '(2) In the following provisions of this Part of this Act . . . "eligible person" means (. . . without prejudice to section 21 of this Act) a survivor of the deceased in whose case the following conditions are satisfied—(a) he falls within paragraphs (a) to (d) of subsection (1) above; (b) in the seven years ending with the date of death his only or principal source of livelihood throughout a continuous period of not less than five years, or two or more discontinuous periods together amounting to not less than five years, derived from his agricultural work on the holding or on an agricultural unit of which the holding forms part; and (c) he is not the occupier of a commercial unit of agricultural land within the meaning of Part II of the Agriculture Act 1967 or, if he is, occupies it as a licensee only . . .'

c   Section 21, so far as material, provides:
   '(1) This section applies to any survivor of the deceased who for some part of seven years ending with the date of death engaged (whether full-time or part-time) in agricultural work on the holding, being a person in whose case—(a) the conditions specified in paragraphs (a) and (c) of the definition of "eligible person" in section 18(2) of this Act are satisfied; and (b) the condition

(Continued on p 52)

satisfying that condition, 'satisfied [it] to a material extent' was nevertheless 'to be treated as an eligible person' if it appeared to the tribunal that in all the circumstances it was fair and reasonable for that person to apply for a tenancy. The wife accordingly applied for a determination by the tribunal under s 23(1) that she be treated as an eligible person notwithstanding her failure to fulfil the condition as to livelihood. The wife contended in regard to that condition that her only or principal source of livelihood had, to a material extent, been derived from her work on the farm for a period of five years preceding her husband's death. The tribunal held that the condition could only be satisfied 'to a material extent' if the applicant 'almost' fulfilled the condition, and held that the wife had not almost fulfilled it because during the relevant five-year period she had derived her only source of livelihood from the farm for only two years, and had derived her principal livelihood from the farm for only 44½ months which was less than 75% of the five-year period. The tribunal dismissed the wife's application. She appealed by way of case stated to the High Court.

Held – Having regard to the fact that an applicant wishing to be 'treated as an eligible person' had to show, under s 21(3) of the 1976 Act, that it was fair and reasonable in all the circumstances for him to be so treated, the expression 'to a material extent' in s 21(1)(b) was to be widely construed. Accordingly, a wife seeking a tenancy under the 1976 Act in succession to her husband satisfied 'to a material extent' the condition as to livelihood specified in para (b) of the definition of 'eligible person' in s 18(2) of that Act if in terms of value an important part of the joint livelihood of herself and her husband had been derived for a substantial period of time from their work on the husband's holding. The period of 44½ months during which an important part of the husband and wife's joint income had been derived from the farm was a substantial period and the wife accordingly satisfied the condition in para (b) to a material extent. The case would therefore be remitted to the tribunal for it to consider further whether in all the circumstances it would be fair and reasonable for the wife to apply for a direction entitling her to a tenancy of the farm (see p 58 d to p 59 a, post).

Dictum of Lord Russell in *Jackson v Hall* [1980] 1 All ER at 189 considered.

Notes
For succession on death of a tenant of an agricultural holding, see Supplement to 1 Halsbury's Law (4th Edn) para 1011A.1–3.

For the Agriculture (Miscellaneous Provisions) Act 1976, ss 18, 21, see 46 Halsbury's Statutes (3rd Edn) 31, 38.

Cases referred to in judgment
Clark v Bernard (March 1980, unreported), Agricultural Land Tribunal.
Colson v Midwood (June 1979, unreported), Agricultural Land Tribunal.
Dagg v Lovett (February 1979, unreported), Agricultural Land Tribunal.
Jackson v Hall [1980] 1 All ER 177, [1980] AC 854, [1980] 2 WLR 118, HL.
Judge v Umpleby (deceased) (July 1978, unreported), Agricultural Land Tribunal.

(Continued from p 51)
specified in paragraph (b) of that definition, though not fully satisfied, is satisfied to a material extent.

'(2) A person to whom this section applies may within the relevant period apply to the Tribunal for a determination that he is to be treated as an eligible person for the purposes of this Part of this Act.

'(3) If on an application under this section—(a) the Tribunal are satisfied that the applicant is a person to whom this section applies; and (b) it appears to the Tribunal that in all the circumstances it would be fair and reasonable for the applicant to be able to apply under section 20 of this Act for a direction entitling him to a tenancy of the holding, the Tribunal shall determine that he is to be treated as an eligible person for the purposes of this Part of this Act, but shall otherwise dismiss the application . . .'

Case stated

a On 13th September 1979 Mrs Edna Ada Littlewood applied to the Agricultural Land Tribunal for the East Midland Area for a declaration under s 20 of the Agriculture (Miscellaneous Provisions) Act 1976 that she was entitled to succeed to a tenancy of a holding known as land at Habblesthorpe, North Leverton and South Leverton, formerly held by her husband, and for a determination under s 21 of that Act that she was to be treated as an eligible person to apply for the tenancy. On 2nd April 1980 the tribunal

b determined that the applicant had failed to prove that she was an eligible person or was to be treated as such and dismissed her application. At the applicant's request the tribunal stated a case for the opinion of the High Court, the question for the court being whether an applicant could satisfy the requirement of para (*b*) of the definition of 'eligible person' in s 18(2) of the 1976 Act to 'a material extent', within s 21(1)(*b*) of the Act, if the period of the tenancy itself was less than 75% of the period of five years specified in para

c (*b*) and during the period of the tenancy the applicant had derived less than 75% of his livelihood from his work on the holding. By a notice of motion dated 15th August 1980 the applicant moved the court for determination of those questions of law. The landlords of the holding, Thomas Donald Rolfe and Rita Rolfe, were the respondents to the motion. The facts are set out in the judgment.

d *H Richards* for the applicant.
Christopher Priday for the respondents.

Cur adv vult

1st December. **HIS HONOUR EDGAR FAY QC** read the following judgment:
e This is an appeal by way of case stated from the Agricultural Land Tribunal for the East Midland Area. The applicant had applied to that tribunal for a declaration that she should be treated as an eligible person to apply to succeed to the tenancy of an agricultural holding formerly held by her husband, who had died on 13th June 1979.

The tribunal heard her application on 2nd April 1980 and dismissed it. The appeal requires this court to pronounce on the interpretation of a section of the Agriculture Acts
f which has caused controversy and has led to differing decisions by different tribunals.

The matter arises in this way. Section 20 of the Agriculture (Miscellaneous Provisions) Act 1976 confers on certain relatives of a deceased tenant of an agricultural holding the right to apply for a declaration entitling him to a tenancy of the holding. If the applicant is what the Act calls an 'eligible person' the tribunal have to decide whether he is, in their opinion, a suitable person to become a tenant of the holding. If they decide that he is,
g then, subject to certain qualifications irrelevant to this decision, they give a declaration entitling him to a tenancy. The applicant has thus to be both eligible and suitable.

Eligibility is defined in s 18 of the 1976 Act. It requires the satisfaction of three conditions. The first is relationship to the deceased; the list of relatives includes the widow. The third is that the applicant is not the occupant of a commercial unit of agricultural land; this is not in question here and it is agreed that the first and third
h conditions are satisfied. The second condition, in para (*b*) of the definition of 'eligible person' in s 18(2), is that—

> 'in the seven years ending with the date of death his only or principal source of livelihood throughout a continuous period of not less than five years, or two or more discontinuous periods together amounting to not less than five years, derived from his agricultural work on the holding or on an agricultural unit of which the
j holding forms part.'

This condition has two elements: one, that the applicant's only or principal source of livelihood has been derived from his work on the holding; the other, that this derivation of livelihood has enured for five years.

In the present case this condition is not satisfied. There is a shortfall in the period and there may be a difficulty over the principal source of livelihood point. But Parliament has provided for cases where the second condition is not fully satisfied; this is by s 21 of *a* the 1976 Act. Its somewhat convoluted provisions provide that on application under the section the tribunal have power to determine that the applicant is an eligible person. They must exercise this power in the applicant's favour if they are satisfied that he is a person to whom the section applies and also that in all the circumstances it would be fair and reasonable for the applicant to be able to apply under s 20 of the Act for a declaration entitling him to a tenancy of the holding. Subsection (1) of s 21 enacts that the applicant *b* is a person to whom the section applies if the first and third conditions of the definition of eligible person in s 18 are satisfied and if—

'(b) the condition specified in paragraph (b) of that definition, though not fully satisfied, is satisfied to a material extent.'

The result of all this verbiage is that one who fails to pass the second condition may, *c* nevertheless, be deemed to pass. But if he does a further hurdle is placed in the way, namely the need to show that it is fair and reasonable to make the order.

Now this deemed eligibility depends on whether the second condition is 'satisfied to a material extent' and what I have to determine in this case is what those deceptively simple words mean.

Let me now go back to the facts and the findings. Attached to the tribunal's stated case *d* is the tribunal's written decision and scheduled to that decision is the tribunal's written findings and reasons. In para 1 of this schedule the tribunal sets out its findings of fact in 11 numbered sub-paragraphs, as follows:

'i. the applicant is a woman aged forty. Michael Jack Littlewood ("the deceased") was her husband and died on 13 June 1979 aged 39;

'ii. Thomas Donald Rolfe and Rita Rolfe ("the landlords") granted the deceased a *e* tenancy of 5 fields at North Leverton with Habblesthorpe and South Leverton in the County of Nottingham ("the holding"). The holding was 26·774 acres and the tenancy commenced on 1 October 1975;

'iii. the deceased or the applicant [it should be 'the deceased *and* the applicant'] also owned a further almost 25 acres of land in the same area. That land was an agricultural unit of which the holding forms part. The holding and that agricultural *f* unit are collectively called "the farm";

'iv. the deceased and the applicant together with 2 children they then had moved to the area from London in the summer of 1975. The deceased then worked full time on the farm until the latter part of 1978 when he obtained employment as a nurse. The applicant had worked as a pupil nurse at the Royal Free Hospital in London training to become a state enrolled nurse;   *g*

'v. throughout the period between 1 October 1975 and 13 June 1979, some 44½ months, the applicant did agricultural work on the farm;

'vi. between 1 October 1975 and 13 June 1977, some 20½ months, the applicant was working either full time or part time at Worksop Victoria and Kilton Hospital ("the hospital");

'vii. between 1 October 1975 and 31 October 1976 the applicant worked full *h* time either as a pupil nurse or as a state enrolled nurse. She was earning between 1 October 1975 and 31 July 1976 at the gross annual rate of £1953, and for a very short period between 1 August 1976 and 20 August 1976 at the gross annual rate of £2,052, and between 20 August 1976 and 31 October 1976 at the gross annual rate of £2,184. The applicant ceased being a pupil nurse in May 1976. The Tribunal presume that was at the end of May, a period of 8 months since 1 October 1975;   *i*

'viii. between 1 November 1976 and 13 June 1977 the applicant worked part time (half the normal working hours) at the hospital earning at the gross annual rate of £1,092;

'ix. for exactly two years as it turned out the applicant worked on the farm without having earnings from any other employment;

'x. the deceased's drawings from the farm were as follows:

a
i.   year ended 31 March 1976   £1565·34
ii. year ended 31 March 1977   £1918·46
iii. year ended 31 March 1978   £2009·97
iv. year ended 31 July 1979   £1608·85

'xi. the applicant is a courageous and industrious woman, who much impressed the Tribunal as a witness. She had worked hard on the farm despite her other

b employment as a nurse, despite the birth of her third child, David, born on 24 September 1977, and despite the untimely and sudden death of her husband, the deceased.'

Pausing there, it is clear that the period during which the applicant derived her livelihood wholly or partly from the farm was 44½ months as against the 60 months required by the second condition of eligibility. Throughout that period she is found, as

c a fact, to have worked hard on the farm. She and her husband derived their livelihood partly from the farm and partly from nursing. The livelihood aspects may be divided into three periods: first, from 1st October 1975 to 13th June 1977, when the husband is working full-time on the farm and the wife is working part-time on the farm; second, from 13th June 1977 to what is called 'the latter part of 1978', when both were working full-time on the farm and, third, from the latter part of 1978 down to 13th June 1979,

d the date of the husband's death, when the wife was working full-time and the husband part-time on the farm. The joint livelihood of husband and wife was derived wholly from the farm during the second period. During the first period it would seem to have been derived almost equally from the farm and from the wife's nursing. We are not told what the husband earned when nursing for the last six or seven months of his life but the proportion derived from the two pursuits are likely to have been similar to the period

e when it was the wife who was nursing.

The case stated makes, in para 7, a further finding, namely that 'livelihood' might include other means of support such as the provision of food, clothing and shelter and that that other means of support was present only to a very small and limited extent. This I take to refer to the shelter of the farmhouse and to such foodstuffs as came off the farm.

f On those facts the tribunal decided by a majority that the applicant's principal source of livelihood did not come from her work on the farm during any period in which she worked full- or part-time as a nurse. They went on to consider, under s 21 of the 1976 Act, whether the second condition had been satisfied to a material extent and they said this, in para 6 of their findings:

g 'The decision of the Tribunal by a majority was: i. That the specified condition could be satisfied under s. 21(1)(b) of the Act only if the applicant almost fulfilled its requirements. The Tribunal was referred to the speech of Lord Russell in *Jackson v Hall* ([1980] 1 All ER 177 at 189, [1980] AC 854 at 893) where he said this about s. 21: "Section 21 in effect enables the tribunal to treat as an eligible person 'Any survivor of the deceased' who does not quite fulfil the earlier requirements for

h eligibility related to the activities of the applicant during the seven years preceding the death of the tenant."; ii. the test of satisfaction of the specified condition to a material extent under s. 21(1)(b) of the Act must be applied by considering: a. the length of the continuous period during which the applicant's principal source of livelihood derived from her agricultural work on the farm; b. the proportion of the applicant's livelihood derived from her agricultural work on the farm and derived,

j on the other hand, from her work elsewhere during any period when her principal source of livelihood was *not* derived from her agricultural work on the farm; iii. that even if the applicant's principal source of livelihood derived from agricultural work on the farm throughout the whole period from 1 October 1975 until 13 June 1979, nevertheless, as that period was less than 75% of the required period of 5 years the specified condition was not satisfied to a material extent; iv. that on the facts found the only period during which the applicant's principal source of livelihood derived from her agricultural work on the farm was the period of 2 years from 13 June 1977 *a* until 13 June 1979.'

The crucial part of this finding is the holding that 'satisfied to a material extent' means 'almost fulfilled'. If that is its meaning, their decision must clearly be right. But counsel for the applicant contends that a much wider meaning should be attached to the phrase. Both he and counsel for the respondents helpfully put before me certain decisions of other agricultural land tribunals touching on the interpretation. These are, of course, *b* not binding on me, but I find it helpful to see how other minds have approached this question.

Before I come to them, however, I would deal with the tribunal's reference to what Lord Russell said in *Jackson v Hall*. That was a case which went to appeal on the meaning of the third of the three conditions of eligibility together with the question of the date at which the applicant had to be eligible. It was in no way concerned with the *c* interpretation of s 21. Lord Russell, whose words on the subject are quoted in full in the passage I have read from the tribunal's findings, was referring to the section by way of what he described as a summary of the statutory provisions. Lord Fraser did the same where he summarised the second condition and added ([1980] 1 All ER 177 at 185, [1980] AC 854 at 888): '. . . though that condition may be relaxed by the tribunal under s 21(1)(b) if it has been not fully satisfied but satisfied to a material extent.' Lord Russell's *d* words can have no binding effect in these circumstances. The words themselves are not open to controversy if they bear a literal meaning. The tribunal has gone further and found in them an implied assertion that one who goes beyond a 'not quite' test is outwith the section. Lord Russell did not say that, although it may be that this was in his mind on first impression and without argument on the point.

Tribunals have, however, been wrestling with s 21 and hearing argument on it for *e* some time. I was referred to four decisions. In *Judge v Umpleby (deceased)* (July 1978, unreported) the Yorkshire/Lancashire Area Tribunal had this to say in para 22:

> 'It was accepted by Mr Maguire that the provision in s 21(1)(b) of the Act that this condition need only be satisfied to a material extent applied not only to the *period* during which the applicant's source of livelihood had derived from her work on the *f* holding, but also to the *extent* to which her livelihood had so derived. In other words, he accepted that it would be sufficient for the applicant to show that throughout the period in question, or some material part thereof, a material source of her livelihood had derived from her agricultural work on the holding, although it fell short of being her only or principal source of livelihood. In making this concession, Mr Maguire said that he did so in the light of s 21(6) of the Act. In the *g* view of the tribunal this concession was rightly and properly made, and represented a correct interpretation of the relevant law.'

In para 31:

> 'The tribunal did not consider it possible or realistic to make any precise *h* mathematical calculations of the extent to which any of these other benefits could be said to have been attributable to the applicant's work on the holding. Accordingly it was in our view impossible to say that we were satisfied that for at least five out of seven years ending with her father's death the applicant had derived her *principal* source of livelihood from her agricultural work in the holding. However, we were quite satisfied that for at least five of these years she had derived a *material* source of *j* livelihood from her agricultural work on the holding or (to put it in a slightly different way) had derived her livelihood from such work to a material extent. In other words, but for the rewards in cash and kind that she received for her agricultural work on the holding, she would have been materially worse off throughout this period.'

Next is *Dagg v Lovett* (February 1979, unreported) where the Northern Area Tribunal
a said in their decision:

> 'This section [that is s 21(2) of the 1976 Act] provides for applicants to be treated
> as eligible where they cannot show that they fully satisfy the requirements of [para
> (*b*) of the definition of 'eligible person' in s 18(2)] but can show that they satisfy these
> requirements to a material extent. What then is to be taken to be the interpretation
> of the word "material" in this context? Mr Price suggested that it was to be taken
> b to mean "more than minimal"; "there was," he said, "salt in seawater to a material
> extent in the ordinary meaning of the word." The tribunal did not take this view.
> It surely could not be the intention of the Act that applicants who clearly failed to
> pass the first hurdle should be admitted under this section. If it were, what would
> be the value of the test at [para (*b*)]? Its effect would be stultified. This tribunal take
> the view that the meaning to be given to the word "material" in this section is
> c "substantial in terms of time and important in terms of value".'

In *Colson v Midwood* (June 1979, unreported) the Eastern Area Tribunal adopted a
narrower construction. They said in their decision:

> '". . . the conditions . . . though not fully satisfied [are] satisfied to a material
> extent" (s 21(1)(*b*)). This provision is applicable both to cases where there is a failure
> d to satisfy [para (*b*) of the definition of 'eligible person' in s 18(2)] as to proportion of
> livelihood coming from agricultural work and to the period. There have been
> conflicting decisions but in our opinion s 21(6) makes the matter clear. As to what
> is a material extent, either as to amount or period, we do not think that this means
> that the source of livelihood must be shown to be only just below 51% or the period
> to be very nearly 60 months. But on the other hand we do not think it is enough
> e for an applicant to show merely that a "substantial" proportion of his (or her)
> livelihood has come from agricultural work or, as the case may be, that such has
> been the position for a substantial part of the full five-year period. If this had been
> all that was required the section could, and indeed surely would, have been quite
> differently and much more simply worded. Again hard and fast lines cannot be
> drawn but in our opinion though an applicant need not show that he (or she) has
> f come "within a hair's breadth" of full compliance it must be shown on the facts that
> there has not been a really large failure.'

Finally, in *Clark v Bernard* (March 1980, unreported) the South-Eastern Area Tribunal
said:

> 'The personal aspects of hardship that may ensue from the decision were not, in
> g the tribunal's view, relevant to this application and therefore attention was devoted
> to deciding whether the conditions specified in [para (*b*) of the definition of 'eligible
> person' in s 18(2)] of the Act were satisfied to a material extent. This was not easy.
> It was felt that it should not be done solely on the basis of any mathematical
> percentage or proportion. It was also felt that it would be unwise to do anything
> other than to consider the meaning of the word "material". That is the word in the
> h Act and if Parliament had wished to substitute some other word it would have done
> so. It is not proposed to enter into any lengthy discussion on what "material", in the
> context in which it is used, could otherwise mean. Certainly other meanings could
> be attempted. Definitions in the Oxford Dictionary include "of much consequence"
> and "important". If this is the right approach, it has to be considered, on the facts
> of this case, whether Mr Clark has brought himself, to the tribunal's satisfaction,
> j within the conditions of [para (*b*)], *to a material extent*.'

There has thus been a whole gamut of interpretation, from the strict 'only just failing'
view of the tribunal in the present case, to the wide interpretation accorded in *Dagg
v Lovett*. This underlines the difficulty of the task of interpretation, and, when I find
Viscount Dilhorne saying in *Jackson v Hall* [1980] 1 All ER 177 at 183, [1980] AC 854 at

885, 'My Lords, it is to be regretted that this lengthy and no doubt expensive litigation has been brought about by the inadequacy of the drafting of this Act', I feel disposed, *a* respectfully, to echo his sentiments.

'Satisfied to a material extent.' It is a strange phrase. 'Extent' presents no difficulty; nor does 'satisfied' in the context, although it is a misuse of the word to apply it to a condition which, ex hypothesi, is not satisfied. The crux of the question is the word 'material'. It is an adjective frequently used by lawyers: they speak of material facts, of material considerations. In this sense it means relevant to the matter in hand, but it can *b* hardly mean relevant here. It has another sense: of something substantial, more than minimal; that seems to have been the path followed by the Northern and Yorkshire/Lancashire tribunals.

Counsel for the respondents argues that because this litigation takes away a landlord's right to possession it ought to be narrowly construed. On the other hand the policy of Part II of the 1976 Act is clearly to create new rights in deserving persons with a view, I *c* would think, to preserving that family continuity which has long been a feature of English farming life. It can equally well be argued that a wide construction is needed to give effect to the policy of the Act.

I do not find either of these approaches compelling. I do, however, find some assistance in s 21(3)(b), the paragraph setting up the further hurdle to the successor tenant of whether the order is fair and reasonable. I think this points to a wide interpretation of *d* the words 'material extent'. If the 'not quite' view were right and the let-out consisted of what may be called 'the hard luck cases' (where the applicant has 59 months instead of 60, or 49% in livelihood instead of the 51% which would make it the principal source) then it is difficult to see how any tribunal could find that it was not fair and reasonable to make the order bearing in mind that the applicant still has the final hurdle of suitability to surmount. On the other hand, if jurisdiction is given over a wide spectrum *e* of facts by a beneficial interpretation of the word 'material', the tribunal will have a real task in deciding where lies fairness and reasonableness.

I therefore find that the tribunal erred in law in following the narrow interpretation. But I must go beyond this and endeavour to afford some guidance for those who have to solve these difficult problems. I agree wholeheartedly with the view that no mathematical formula can be laid down. Percentages of fulfilment, when worked out, *f* are a useful guide to put the facts of finance or of time in perspective and to help judge their weight, but I would think it wrong to try to impose a mathematical cut-off point to what is material. After considerable casting about I do not feel that I can do better by way of definition than to adopt what the Northern Area tribunal said, in *Dagg v Lovett*, namely that 'material' means 'substantial in terms of time and important in terms of value'. *g*

The case stated in the present appeal asks me to say whether an applicant can satisfy the requirement 'to a material extent' if the period of tenancy itself was less than 75% of the period of five years. It was in fact 44½ months against the 45 months which would be 75%. My answer to that question is Yes. I can envisage that 50% could well, in some circumstances, be satisfaction to an extent that was material in the sense of substantial. Here a young couple took on a farm, no doubt hoping to make their permanent home *h* there and bring their children up there. These are relevant facts when considering whether the period is deemed to be satisfied.

The tribunal pose a similar question as regards principal source of livelihood. I do not think one can approach the question of source of livelihood of husband and wife in two separate compartments. Husbands and wives usually pool their income. Here the husband and wife had two sources of income between them for part of the time and one *j* source only, namely the farm, for another part. The figures in this case show that an important part of the joint income at all times was the farm and I entertain no doubt that, applying the interpretation that I have to the word 'material', this applicant has brought herself within s 21 of the 1976 Act.

I accordingly remit the case to the tribunal with the direction that they find that the a applicant is a person to whom s 21 applies and with the further direction that they do now proceed to consider the question whether in all the circumstances it would be fair and reasonable for the applicant to be able to apply under s 20 of the 1976 Act for a direction entitling her to a tenancy of the holding.

Order accordingly.

b Solicitors: *Hancock & Willis*, agents for *Hodgkinson & Tallents*, Newark (for the applicant); *Collyer-Bristow*, agents for *Hayes, Son & Richmond*, Gainsborough (for the respondents).

K Mydeen Esq   Barrister.

c

Pedro v Diss

QUEEN'S BENCH DIVISION
LORD LANE CJ AND WEBSTER J
d 17th NOVEMBER, 9th DECEMBER 1980

Police – Assault on constable in execution of duty – Execution of duty – Metropolitan police constable stopping and searching suspect – Constable detaining suspect against his will but not arresting him – Suspect assaulting constable – Whether at time of assault constable acting unlawfully or in execution of his duty – Metropolitan Police Act 1839, s 66 – Police Act 1964,
e *s 51(1).*

A metropolitan police constable saw the appellant in the doorway of a private house and thought he was loitering there. As the constable approached the house, the appellant walked off round the corner. The constable went up to him, told him that he was a police officer and asked him what he was doing by the door. The appellant started to f walk off but the constable stopped him and asked him whether he lived in the house. The appellant refused to answer. The constable, suspecting that the appellant might have on him property stolen from the house or housebreaking implements, told him that he wanted to search him. The appellant resisted at first but then allowed himself to be searched. The constable found two keys on the appellant and asked him whether they were the keys to the house. The appellant did not reply and started to walk away. The g constable thereupon took hold of him by the arm and told him that he wanted him to return to the house with him. The appellant tried to pull away but the constable led him to the house, where he once more asked him whether he lived there. The appellant swore at the constable and then hit him. The constable caught hold of the appellant's clothing and the appellant hit him again before being arrested. Only then did he tell the h constable that his brother lived in the house. The appellant was subsequently charged with assaulting a police constable in the execution of his duty, contrary to s 51(1)[a] of the Police Act 1964, and convicted. He appealed contending that he could not be guilty of the offence because at the time of the assault the constable was acting unlawfully by holding him against his will without arresting him. The constable contended that he was acting lawfully in the execution of his duty at the time because s 66[b] of the Metropolitan Police Act 1839 gave him, as a metropolitan police constable, the power not j only to stop and search the appellant but also to detain him.

---

a   Section 51(1), so far as material, provides: 'Any person who assaults a constable in the execution of his duty . . . shall be guilty of an offence . . .'

b   Section 66 is set out at p 62 e to g, post

Held – A metropolitan police constable was obliged, when detaining a person under s 66 of the 1839 Act, to inform him that he was no longer a free man and to tell him the grounds on which he was being detained. On the evidence the constable had not done so and therefore could not rely on s 66 to justify the detention of the appellant. He was therefore not acting in the execution of his duty but unlawfully at the time of the assault. Accordingly the appeal would be allowed and the appellant's conviction quashed (see p 63 *d* to *j* and p 64 *d*, post).

Christie v Leachinsky [1947] 1 All ER 567, *Ludlow v Burgess* [1971] Crim LR 238 and *R v Inwood* [1973] 2 All ER 645 applied.

Per Curiam. Although a person who is being lawfully arrested or detained by a police officer may not rely on the justification of self-defence if he assaults the police officer in order to resist or escape arrest or detention, a person who is not being lawfully arrested or formally and lawfully detained may do so (see p 64 *b c*, post); *Kenlin v Gardiner* [1966] 3 All ER 931 approved.

Notes

For the meaning of arrest, see 11 Halsbury's Laws (4th Edn) paras 99–101, and for cases on arrest generally, see 14(1) Digest (Reissue) 189–194, *1343–1391*.

For powers of arrest by a constable, see 11 Halsbury's Laws (4th Edn) para 111, and for cases on the subject, see 14(1) Digest (Reissue) 203–206, *1477–1492*.

For assaulting a constable in the execution of his duty, see 11 Halsbury's Laws (4th Edn) para 962, and for cases on the subject, see 15 Digest (Reissue) 985–991, *8546–8590*.

For the Metropolitan Police Act 1839, s 66, see 25 Halsbury's Statutes (3rd Edn) 251.

For the Police Act 1964, s 51, see ibid 364.

Cases referred to in judgment

Christie v Leachinsky [1947] 1 All ER 567, [1947] AC 573, [1947] LJR 757, 176 LT 443, 111 JP 224, 45 LGR 201, HL, 14(1) Digest (Reissue) 206, *1491*.

Kenlin v Gardiner [1966] 3 All ER 931, [1967] 2 QB 510, [1967] 2 WLR 129, 131 JP 91, DC, 15 Digest (Reissue) 991, *8590*.

Ludlow v Burgess [1971] Crim LR 238, DC.

R v Inwood [1973] 2 All ER 645, [1973] 1 WLR 647, 137 JP 559, 57 Cr App R 529, CA, 14(1) Digest (Reissue) 190, *1353*.

Cases also cited

Atkinson v Walker [1976] RTR 118, DC.

Dallison v Caffery [1964] 2 All ER 610, [1965] 1 QB 148, CA.

Daniel v Morrison (1979) 70 Cr App R 142, DC.

Donnelly v Jackman [1970] 1 All ER 987, [1970] 1 WLR 562, DC.

Ghani v Jones [1969] 3 All ER 1700, [1970] 1 QB 693, CA.

Hadley v Perks (1866) LR 1 QB 444.

R v Brown (1976) 64 Cr App R 231, CA.

R v Grant [1980] RTR 280, CA.

R v Lemsatef [1977] 2 All ER 835, [1977] 1 WLR 812, CA.

R v Waterfield, R v Lynn [1963] 3 All ER 659, [1964] 1 QB 164, CCA.

Rice v Connolly [1966] 2 All ER 649, [1966] 2 QB 414, DC.

Willey v Peace [1950] 1 All ER 724, [1951] 1 KB 94, DC.

Case stated

This was an appeal by way of case stated by the justices of the East Central Petty Sessional Division of the Inner London Area in respect of their adjudication at the Highbury Corner Magistrates' Court on 28th September 1979 whereby they found the appellant, Ya Ya Pedro, guilty of assaulting the respondent, Pc Martin Diss, a constable of the

Metropolitan Police, in the execution of his duty contrary to s 51(1) of the Police Act
a 1964. The facts are set out in the judgment of the court.

James Wood and *Adrian Fulford* for the appellant.
Ann Goddard for the respondent.

Cur adv vult

b
9th December. **LORD LANE CJ** read the following judgment of the court: This is an
appeal by way of case stated by the justices of the East Central Petty Sessional Division of
the Inner London Area in respect of an adjudication at the Highbury Corner Magistrates'
Court on 28th September 1979.

On 2nd July 1979 an information was laid by the respondent, a police constable, that
c on 1st July 1979 the appellant had assaulted him in the execution of his duty, contrary
to s 51(1) of the Police Act 1964. The justices found that the appellant had assaulted the
respondent. They held that at the time when he was assaulted the respondent was acting
in the execution of his duty and they accordingly convicted the appellant who was later
fined £50 by different justices. The question for the opinion of this court was whether
on the facts found by the justices they were correct in holding that the respondent was
d acting in the execution of his duty at the time when he was assaulted. The facts found
can be quite shortly stated.

On Sunday, 1st July 1979, at about 12.45 am, the respondent was in plain clothes as a
passenger in a marked police vehicle with two other officers travelling south in Holloway
Road. As the officers passed the junction with Fairmead Road on their right, the
respondent saw by the first door on the right in Fairmead Road, which was the door to
e a private residence, three youths, one of whom was the appellant, who appeared to the
respondent to be loitering around the doorway. The police vehicle was turned round
and driven back towards Fairmead Road and as it approached this road the youths walked
into Holloway Road and along Holloway Road in a northerly direction. The police
officers got out of the vehicle and the respondent went up to the appellant, identifying
himself as a police officer, and said: 'What were you doing by that door?' The appellant
f began to walk away from the respondent who stepped in front of him and said: 'Do you
live there?' The appellant replied: 'I'm not talking to you man. Fuck off.' The
respondent was suspicious that the appellant might have on him property stolen from
the building or housebreaking implements and decided to search him. He said: 'I want
to search you.' The appellant replied: 'You are not touching me, cunt.' The respondent
searched the appellant who at first attempted to resist but then allowed the search. The
g respondent found on the appellant two Yale keys on a ring and said: 'Are these the keys
to the house?' The appellant again began to walk off and the respondent took hold of
him by the left arm and said: 'I want you to come back around the corner to the
house.' The appellant attempted to pull away but the respondent led him round to the
side of the house and said: 'Do you live here?' The appellant replied: 'Fucking cunt', and
then swung backwards with his left arm hitting the respondent in the chest with his
h elbow. As he did this the respondent caught hold of the appellant's clothing and the
appellant punched the respondent in the chest with his right hand and attempted to get
away. The appellant was then restrained with the assistance of the two other officers.
The appellant was arrested and cautioned and made no reply. It was later established that
the appellant's brother lived at the address.

The question asked by the justices which we have to decide, namely whether the
j respondent was acting in the execution of his duty at the time when he was assaulted, can
be answered conclusively by reference to a decision of this court in *Ludlow v Burgess*
[1971] Crim LR 238, unless that case can be distinguished. In that case three youths,
including the defendant, were charged with assaulting a constable in the execution of his
duty, contrary to s 51 of the Police Act 1964. The justices found that the constable was
kicked on the shin while he was boarding a bus by one of the youths. He had reason to

believe it was deliberate, but the defendant claimed it was an accident and expressed his
opinion in strong language. The constable, who did not have his warrant card with him, *a*
told him to stop using foul language and informed him that he was a police officer. As
the defendant started to walk away, the constable put his hand on his shoulder, not with
the intention of arresting the defendant, but to detain him for further conversation and
inquiries, so that the defendant struggled and kicked the constable. The two other
youths then assaulted the constable. The justices rejected a submission by the youths
that there was no case to answer and convicted them. The youths appealed. The *b*
Divisional Court, allowing their appeal, held that the detention of a man against his will
without arresting him was an unlawful act and a serious interference with a citizen's
liberty. Since it was an unlawful act it was not an act done in the execution of the
constable's duty.

The facts of this case are so strikingly similar to the facts in *Ludlow*'s case that the
decision in that case, unless it can be distinguished, would compel us to the conclusion *c*
that the respondent was not acting in the execution of his duty when, as the appellant
began to walk off for the second time, the respondent took hold of him by the left arm
and, as the appellant attempted to pull away, led him round to the side of the house.
That action on the part of the respondent carried out, as the justices found, before he
arrested the appellant was a detention by the appellant against his will without arresting
him of the same nature in similar circumstances as the detention in *Ludlow*'s case, so that *d*
when, thereafter and before he was arrested, the appellant assaulted the respondent, we
would be constrained by that decision to decide that the respondent was not acting in the
course of his duty, even if we were to be in some doubt about the matter which in fact
we are not. But the respondent seeks to distinguish the present case from that of *Ludlow*'s
case in reliance on the provisions of s 66 of the Metropolitan Police Act 1839. That
section provides: *e*

'Any person found committing any offence punishable either upon indictment
or as a misdemeanor upon summary conviction, by virtue of this Act, may be taken
into custody without a warrant by any constable, or may be apprehended by the
owner of the property on or with respect to which the offence shall be committed,
or by his servant or any person authorised by him, and may be detained until he can *f*
be delivered into the custody of a constable to be dealt with according to the law;
and every such constable may also stop, search and detain any vessel, boat, cart or
carriage in or upon which there shall be reason to suspect that anything stolen or
unlawfully obtained may be found, and also any person who may be reasonably
suspected of having or conveying in any manner anything stolen or unlawfully
obtained.'

g

Section 24 of the Metropolitan Police Courts Act 1839 contained the following
provisions:

'Every person who shall be brought before any of the said magistrates charged
with having in his possession or conveying in any manner anything which may be
reasonably suspected of being stolen or unlawfully obtained, and who shall not give
an account to the satisfaction of such magistrate how he came by the same, shall be *h*
deemed guilty of a misdemeanor, and shall be liable to a penalty of not more than
five pounds, or, in the discretion of the magistrate, may be imprisoned in any gaol
or house of correction within the metropolitan police district, with or without hard
labour, for any time not exceeding two calendar months.'

Section 55 of the Metropolitan Police Courts Act provided that that Act and the *j*
Metropolitan Police Act should be construed together as one Act, and there can be little
doubt, therefore, but that the purpose of the power of detention conferred by s 66 of the
Metropolitan Police Act 1839, in the context of s 24 of the Metropolitan Police Courts
Act 1839, was to enable a police constable in the metropolis, when he had stopped or

searched a person whom he reasonably suspected of having or conveying in any manner

a anything stolen or unlawfully obtained, to bring that person before a magistrate so that he could be charged under s 24 of the Metropolitan Police Courts Act. While s 24 was in force, therefore, it would probably have been unnecessary to decide whether the detention in question was synonymous with an arrest, or whether it included a detention which fell short of a formal arrest.

But s 24 of the Metropolitan Police Courts Act 1839 was repealed by the Criminal Law

b Act 1977. Section 66 of the 1839 Act now stands, for practical purposes, on its own and it may now in certain circumstances be necessary to decide what is meant by the word 'detain' in that section. This court has been asked to decide that question, and under what circumstances, after a person has been stopped and searched, the power to detain arises. For it is said on behalf of the respondent that from the moment when he stepped in front of the appellant until the moment of the assault and subsequent arrest he, the

c respondent, was acting in exercise of the powers conferred on him by s 66 and was, therefore, acting in the execution of his duty. The respondent was a police constable of the metropolis ('such constable' within the meaning of the section); as the justices found he suspected that the appellant might have on him stolen property and, by inference from the facts, that suspicion was reasonable; he stopped the appellant and searched him; and, so it was contended, when he took hold of the appellant's left arm he was detaining

d him within the meaning of s 66 in circumstances which gave him a power to do so. In our view, however, in the circumstances of this case it is not necessary for us to decide whether that last contention was correct because, in our judgment, the respondent is unable to rely on the detention as a detention under that section, whatever such a detention means or comprehends, for the following reason.

In *R v Inwood* [1973] 2 All ER 645, [1973] 1 WLR 647 the Court of Appeal held that

e a police constable carrying out an arrest was under an obligation to ensure that the arrested person understood that he was no longer a free man and that, where there was a dispute whether such a person was aware that he had been arrested, the question was one of fact for the jury; and in *Christie v Leachinsky* [1947] 1 All ER 567, [1947] AC 573 the House of Lords held that, apart from special circumstances, which in our view do not exist in the present case, an arrest without warrant can be justified only if it is an arrest

f on a charge made known to the person arrested.

In our view, whatever be the meaning of the word 'detention' in s 66 of the 1839 Act, the principle of those two decisions must apply just as much to a detention under that section as to an ordinary arrest. Thus a police constable, if he is to rely on the detention as a detention under that section, must in one way or another make it known to the person detained that he is no longer a free man and the grounds on which he is being

g detained. Here there is no finding that the respondent, at any stage before the arrest which occurred after the assault, made known to the appellant the fact that he was no longer a free man (although such a finding might possibly be inferred from the words, 'I want you to come back around the corner to the house' after he took hold of the appellant by the arm); and there is no finding, not even any suggestion arising by inference out of the findings, that the respondent made known to the appellant the

h grounds on which he was being detained. Quite apart from the findings, it seems virtually certain that he did no such thing, because we were told in argument that his powers of detention under s 66, whatever precisely they may be, first occurred to anyone connected with this case only after the hearing before the justices.

Accordingly, in our judgment, the respondent cannot rely on the detention in fact as a detention in law under s 66 of the 1839 Act, so that, for the reasons that we have already

j given and in accordance with the decision in *Ludlow's* case in our judgment he was not acting in the execution of his duty when the appellant assaulted him.

In these circumstances it is unnecessary for us to decide a number of the other issues raised in argument, for instance whether the stopping of the appellant before he was searched or the search itself on the facts found were lawful, either by virtue of the respondent's powers under s 66 or by virtue of any other powers. But there are two general observations which we should make.

Firstly, s 66 of the 1839 Act confers on police constables in the metropolis powers which extend, to a not insignificant degree, beyond their common law or other statutory powers. In our view, therefore, that section is to be strictly construed.

Secondly, compliance with the requirements of a lawful arrest in accordance with the decisions of *R v Inwood* [1973] 2 All ER 645, [1973] WLR 647 and *Christie v Leachinsky* [1947] 1 All ER 567, [1947] AC 573 and with the requirements of a lawful detention if in any respect it differs from a lawful arrest is not a mere formality. As this court decided in *Kenlin v Gardiner* [1966] 3 All ER 931, [1967] 2 QB 510, a person who is being lawfully arrested by a police officer or, it follows from our judgment, a person who is being lawfully detained, may not rely on the justification of self-defence if he assaults the police officer in order to resist or escape arrest or detention; but a person who is not being lawfully arrested, or formally and lawfully detained, may do so. This distinction, although a matter of law, is a distinction of which, we suspect, most people are aware. It is a matter of importance, therefore, to a person at the moment when he is first physically detained by a police officer, to know whether that physical detention is or is not regarded by that officer as a formal arrest or detention. That is one of the reasons why it is a matter of importance that the arresting or detaining officer should make known to the person in question the fact that, and the grounds on which, he is being arrested or detained.

In our judgment, therefore, this appeal should be allowed, the conviction must be quashed and the fine remitted.

Appeal allowed.

Solicitors: *Bindman & Partners* (for the appellant); *R E T Birch* (for the respondent).

N P Metcalfe Esq   Barrister.

a   # Regalian Securities Ltd v Ramsden

HOUSE OF LORDS

LORD WILBERFORCE, LORD SALMON, LORD RUSSELL OF KILLOWEN, LORD KEITH OF KINKEL AND
LORD ROSKILL

16th, 17th MARCH, 9th APRIL 1981

b   *Rent restriction – Long tenancy at low rent – Separate dwelling – Tenant purchasing remainder
of long lease – Premises consisting of penthouse comprising maisonette with self-contained flat
attached – Premises originally used as family home – Tenant subletting maisonette for latter part
of long lease – Sublease expiring day before expiry of long lease – Subtenant refusing to give up
occupation of maisonette on expiry of sublease – Tenant in occupation of flat on expiry of long
lease – Whether tenant entitled to Rent Act protection for whole of penthouse – Whether penthouse*
c   *let as one separate dwelling – Landlord and Tenant Act 1954, ss 1, 2(1), 22(3) – Rent Act 1977,
ss 1, 2(1)(a).*

On 29th September 1936 R took a long lease of a newly built penthouse (comprising a
maisonette with a self-contained flat attached) for himself, his family and his domestic
staff. The lease was due to expire on 29th September 1978. In 1973, when he no longer
d   required the maisonette, R assigned the lease of the whole penthouse to the appellant,
who was his son and who was living in the flat. The appellant in turn sublet the
maisonette to B, a family friend, for the remainder of the term of the headlease less one
day. In 1975 B assigned the sublease to C, who, without any legal right to do so,
continued to occupy the maisonette after 28th September 1978. When the headlease
expired on 29th September 1978 the head landlords wished to obtain possession of the
e   penthouse. However, the appellant claimed that on the expiry of the headlease he was,
by virtue of ss 2(1) and 22(3) of the Landlord and Tenant Act 1954[a], entitled under s 1 of
that Act to the protection of the Rent Act 1977 in respect of the whole of the penthouse
(even though he was only occupying the flat) because the penthouse was let to him as 'a
separate dwelling' within the meaning of s 22(3) and he was in residential occupation.
The landlords sought a declaration that s 1 of the 1954 Act did not apply to the tenancy
f   on the grounds that (1) on the term date (which was the material date) the penthouse was
not 'let as a separate dwelling' within s 22(3) because on that date it comprised a self-
contained maisonette and a self-contained flat each occupied and used as a separate
dwelling by C and the appellant respectively and (2) that, in any event, the appellant,
having sublet the maisonette, reserving only a nominal reversion, could not be said to be
occupying it as a residence on the term date. The appellant claimed that, if C had vacated
g   the maisonette when he should have done, he (the appellant) would have become
entitled to possession of the whole penthouse on the day before the expiry of the
headlease. The appellant further claimed that he intended to use the whole penthouse
as his residence in the future. The judge accepted that claim and dismissed the landlords'
application. On appeal, the Court of Appeal ([1980] 2 All ER 497) held that the appellant
was not entitled to protection under the 1977 Act in respect of the whole of the
h   penthouse on the ground that under s 22(3) of the 1954 Act the court was required to
consider the nature of the premises at the date of the expiry of the headlease and the
purpose for which they were then being used, and at that date the penthouse had been
divided into two separate dwellings which were being used by the appellant and C as
separate dwellings. The court further held that the appellant was entitled to the
protection of the 1977 Act in respect of the flat alone. The appellant appealed to the
j   House of Lords in respect of the Court of Appeal's refusal to grant him protection for the
whole of the penthouse and the landlords cross-appealed in respect of the grant of
protection for the flat on the ground that on a true construction of Part I of the 1954 Act

---

a   Sections 1, 2(1) and 22(3) are set out at p 71 *f g* and p 72 *b*, post

and the 1977 Act the appellant would not have been entitled by virtue of the 1977 Act to retain possession of part only of the premises comprised in the original tenancy.   *a*

Held – When determining for the purposes of s 2(1) of the 1954 Act whether a long tenancy at a low rent qualified for the protection of the 1977 Act, the requirement in s 22(3) of the 1954 Act that the court was to have regard to the 'nature of the property' and the 'purpose for which it . . . was used' applied only to the question arising under s 1[b] of the 1977 Act whether the premises were let as a separate dwelling at the end of the   *b* tenancy and not to the question arising under s 2(1)(a)[c] of the 1977 Act whether the tenant was occupying the dwelling as his residence. Since the nature of the penthouse had remained the same, there having been no structural alteration to the premises, and since the purpose for which it was let, namely residential use, had remained the same throughout the tenancy, the penthouse was deemed by s 22(3) of the 1954 Act to be let at the end of the tenancy on the same basis as at the beginning of the tenancy, namely as   *c* a separate dwelling. On the question whether the appellant was occupying the dwelling as his residence, the subletting of part of the penthouse did not deprive the appellant of the protection of the 1977 Act in respect of the whole of the penthouse, notwithstanding C's unlawful occupation of the maisonette on the expiry of the headlease, since, on the day the headlease expired, the only person entitled to lawful possession of the maisonette and therefore of the whole of the penthouse was the appellant, who intended to use it as   *d* his residence. The appellant's appeal would accordingly be allowed. It followed that the landlords' cross-appeal in respect of the grant of protection to the appellant for the flat failed, but in any event a tenant could become a statutory tenant under s 2(1)(a) of the 1977 Act of part only of the premises comprised in the original tenancy (see p 67 *d e*, p 68 *f* to p 69a, p 73 *d* to *h* and p 74 *a* to p 75 *a* and *h j*, post).

Herbert v Byrne [1964] 1 All ER 882 applied.   *e*
Haines v Herbert [1963] 3 All ER 715 approved.
Decision of the Court of Appeal [1980] 2 All ER 497 reversed in part.

Notes
For tenancies protected under Part I of the Landlord and Tenant Act 1954, see 23 Halsbury's Laws (3rd Edn) 841, para 1632, and for cases on the subject, see 31(2) Digest   *f* (Reissue) 1134, 8768–8770.

For the Landlord and Tenant Act 1954, ss 1, 2, 3, 22, see 18 Halsbury's Statutes (3rd Edn) 728, 730, 749.

Cases referred to in opinions
Crown Lodge (Surbiton) Investments Ltd v Nalecz [1967] 1 All ER 489, [1967] 1 WLR 647,   *g* CA, 31(2) Digest (Reissue) 1134, 8769.
Haines v Herbert [1963] 3 All ER 715, [1963] 1 WLR 1401, 31(2) Digest (Reissue) 1134, 8770.
Herbert v Byrne [1964] 1 All ER 882, [1964] 1 WLR 519, CA, 31(2) Digest (Reissue) 1134, 8768.
Horford Investments Ltd v Lambert [1974] 1 All ER 131, [1976] Ch 39, [1973] 3 WLR 872,   *h* 27 P & CR 88, CA, Digest (Cont Vol D) 593, 8058a.

Appeal
The appellant, Jack R Ramsden, appealed by leave of the House of Lords granted on 5th June 1980 against a decision of the Court of Appeal (Lord Denning MR, Bridge and Oliver LJJ) ([1980] 2 All ER 497) dated 1st April 1980 allowing an appeal by the   *j* respondents, Regalian Securities Ltd, the head landlords of premises known as Flats 83, 84 and 85 Vandon Court, Petty France, London SW1 ('the premises'), consisting of a maisonette and a flat, against the judgment of her Honour Judge Rowland given in the

---

b   Section 1 is set out at p 72 *c d*, post
c   Section 2(1), so far as material, is set out at p 72 *d e*, post

Westminster County Court on 24th September 1979 whereby she dismissed the
a respondents' application for a declaration under s 2(2) of the Landlord and Tenant Act
1954 that the tenancy of the premises created by a lease made on 1st October 1936
between Frank Lewis Griggs and Victor Ramsden and subsequently vested in the
appellant was not to be treated for the purposes of Part I of the 1954 Act as a tenancy to
which s 1 of that Act applied. The Court of Appeal allowed the appeal as to the
maisonette only but affirmed the judge's decision in respect of the flat. The respondents
b by a cross-notice appealed by leave of the House of Lords granted on 5th June 1980
against that part of the Court of Appeal's order which related to the flat. The facts are set
out in the opinion of Lord Roskill.

Patrick Garland QC and *Mark Blackett-Ord* for the appellant.
Robert Pryor and *Nicholas Dowding* for the respondents.

c   Their Lordships took time for consideration.

9th April. The following opinions were delivered.

LORD WILBERFORCE. My Lords, I have had the benefit of reading in advance the
speech prepared by my noble and learned friend Lord Roskill. I agree with it and would
d allow the appeal and dismiss the cross-appeal.

LORD SALMON. My Lords, I have had the advantage of reading in draft the speeches
prepared by my noble and learned friends Lord Russell and Lord Roskill. For the reasons
they have given I too would allow the appeal and dismiss the cross-appeal.

e **LORD RUSSELL OF KILLOWEN.** My Lords, in 1936 the father of the appellant
persuaded the builder of a block of flats in Petty France, SW1 to change in part the plans
so as to constitute a penthouse which he wished to lease as a residence for his family. This
having been done, a lease of the penthouse was granted to the father for a term expiring
on 29th September 1978, and for the next 37 years the father made it his family home.
The penthouse consisted of a maisonette on the eighth and ninth floors and an adjacent
f flat on the ninth floor intended primarily for staff of the household. The front door of
the flat was conveniently disposed beside a door leading into the maisonette. It is
common ground that notwithstanding the form of construction of the penthouse this
was a lease of one dwelling house.
In 1973 the father, being of a good age, wished to retire and to live in the country. In
March 1973 he assigned the lease of the penthouse to the appellant for a payment of
g £10,000. The appellant's employment was then largely out of London but he wished,
as the judge found, to preserve the family home (the penthouse) for his own family
home in the future. Shortly after the assignment, the appellant subleased the maisonette
to a friend, Mr de Bye, for the rest of the term less one day. The appellant lived from
time to time thereafter in the flat. In 1975 de Bye assigned the sublease of the maisonette
to one Carter. Under the sublease it was, of course, the duty of Carter to vacate the
h maisonette 24 hours before the term date of the lease and make it available for occupation
by the appellant. He did not in fact do so, asserting without justification in law that he
had a right to stay there. Carter could not be evicted by the appellant without a court
order, and remained in de facto occupation of the maisonette until after the lease term
date. In fact, the appellant made no attempt to secure Carter's eviction until after the
conclusion of the case (next mentioned) before the county court judge, when he
j established a right against the reversioners to remain after the lease term date as tenant
under Part I of the Landlord and Tenant Act 1954; any earlier attempt would have been
fruitless had the appellant failed against the reversioners.
Part I of the 1954 Act contains provisions whereby a tenant under a particular type of
tenancy is afforded the protection of the Rent Acts, and the tenancy is continued beyond
the term date of the tenancy, though with a number of provisions affecting the terms of
the continued tenancy. It was and is the contention of the appellant that his lease of the

penthouse fulfilled the requirements of the 1954 Act in this regard, and the judge so held. The Court of Appeal reversed the judge as to the maisonette, but (apparently *a* without objection by the present respondent reversioners) held that the appellant was entitled under the Act to a continuation of the lease so far as concerned the flat. The Appeal Committee of this House gave leave to the appellant to appeal to your Lordships, and to the respondents to cross-appeal as to the flat. It is convenient here to notice that it was accepted for the respondents that if the appeal were to succeed the cross-appeal must fail. There is provision (s 2(2)) for application to the court for decision of such *b* questions before the term date of the tenancy in question. On 3rd April 1978 the respondents applied for an order declaring that the tenancy of the penthouse is not to be treated for the purposes of Part I of the 1954 Act as a tenancy to which s 1 of the Act applies. That application was, on 24th September 1979, dismissed.

Section 1 of the Act is the section which if applicable confers on a tenant protection of the Rent Acts.
c
Section 2(1) requires the tenancy to be a long tenancy at a low rent. The lease of the penthouse was such. It also requires the tenancy to be one as respects which for the time being the 'qualifying condition' is fulfilled. The qualifying condition requires that the circumstances (as respects the property comprised in the tenancy, the use of the property and all other relevant matters) are such that on the coming to an end of the tenancy at that time the tenant would, if the tenancy had not been a long tenancy at a low rent, be *d* entitled by virtue of the Rent Acts to retain possession of the whole or part of the property comprised in the tenancy.

Section 22(3) of the Act is also to be noted. In effect it provides that in considering the 'nature of the property' at the time of the creation of the tenancy it is to be deemed to have been the same as its nature at the time in relation to which the question arises (here the term date); and secondly that the purpose for which the property was let under the *e* tenancy is deemed to have been the purpose for which the property is used at that time.

It appears to me that s 22(3) operates and operates only in relation to the first part of the qualifying condition under s 2(1), and that in the instant case there was no such operation. The nature of the property, the penthouse, remained the same: there had been no structural alteration; the purpose for which the penthouse was used was and remained the same, residential use.
f
I come back, then, to the question of the second branch of the qualifying condition. There is I apprehend ample authority for the proposition that a tenant entitled to the protection of the Rent Acts in respect of a dwelling house does not lose that protection if he sublets part of the dwelling comprised in the tenancy provided that he does not mean to abandon for the future all intention of ever occupying the sublet part as his residence. And this approach has been carried through into consideration of the 1954 *g* Act: see *Herbert v Byrne* [1964] 1 All ER 882, [1964] 1 WLR 519 which in my opinion was rightly decided. There was ample evidence on which the county court could find that the appellant intended to occupy the whole penthouse when it should become available, as in law it would have before the term date had Carter vacated the maisonette in accordance with his obligations under the sublease. Had Carter fulfilled his obligations, and had the appellant promptly moved in a bed, table and chair, the matter would not *h* have allowed doubt; and I cannot think that Carter's obduracy (based on an erroneous view of his legal rights) can affect the situation under the Act.

The Court of Appeal admitted evidence designed to show that the judge's findings of the intentions of the appellant were, or might have been, erroneous. The respondents sought in the alternative a new trial. In common with your Lordships I did not find the new evidence at all cogent, and declined to order a new trial.
j
Accordingly I would allow the appeal, dismiss the cross-appeal, and restore the order of the county court judge, the costs in the Court of Appeal and in this House to be paid by the respondents.

LORD KEITH OF KINKEL. My Lords, for the reasons given in the speech to be delivered by my noble and learned friend Lord Roskill, which I have had the advantage

of reading in draft and with which I agree, I too would allow the appeal and dismiss the
a cross-appeal.

LORD ROSKILL. My Lords, this appeal concerns a penthouse on the eighth and
ninth floors of Vandon Court, Petty France, Westminster, SW1. That penthouse
comprised a maisonette on the eighth and ninth floors, the flat numbers of which were
83 and 84, and a self-contained flat on the ninth floor, the flat number of which was
b 85. To avoid confusion, I shall call that self-contained flat on the ninth floor (85) 'the flat',
and numbers 83 and 84 on the eighth and ninth floors 'the maisonette'. When I refer to
'the penthouse' I shall use that phrase to describe the totality of these premises.
   The appellant claims the protection accorded to residential tenants by Part I of the
Landlord and Tenant Act 1954 in respect of the penthouse. The respondents (whom I
shall call 'the landlords') dispute that claim. They took advantage of the provisions of
c s 2(2) of the 1954 Act to start proceedings against the appellant on 3rd April 1978 in the
Westminster County Court for an order that the appellant's tenancy of the penthouse
was not to be treated as a tenancy to which Part I of the 1954 Act applied. For the reasons
given in a careful reserved judgment dated 24th September 1979, the learned county
court judge (her Honour Judge Rowland) dismissed the landlords' application. The
landlords appealed to the Court of Appeal (Lord Denning MR, Bridge and Oliver LJJ)
d ([1980] 2 All ER 497) which on 1st April 1980 allowed the landlords' appeal in relation
to the maisonette but affirmed the decision of the learned judge in relation to the flat.
The Court of Appeal refused the appellant leave to appeal to your Lordships' House. But
such leave was granted by an Appeal Committee on 5th June 1980, which also gave the
landlords leave to appeal against that part of the Court of Appeal's order which related to
the flat. Hence the landlords' cross-appeal with which I shall deal later.
e   The history of the penthouse and of the lease which became vested in the appellant is
fully set out in the learned judge's judgment. I can summarise the main facts as follows.
   1. Vandon Court was being built in 1936. Its owner was a Mr Griggs, who was a
friend of the appellant's father. He became interested in the construction, and in the
result, with Mr Grigg's agreement, he employed his own architect to redesign the top of
Vandon Court so as to create what ultimately became the penthouse. The penthouse was
f a single family home, the flat being intended for domestic staff. I need not trouble your
Lordships with the details of the accommodation. Suffice it to say that at no time
between 1936 and the end of 1978 were any structural alterations made to any part of the
penthouse.
   2. On 1st October 1936 Mr Griggs granted the appellant's father a lease of the
penthouse for 42 years from 29th September 1936 at the yearly rate of £300. It was
g common ground that from that day until 9th March 1973 (that is for some 37 years) the
penthouse was occupied by the appellant's father, and his family, as a single family home
or, to use the language used by Russell LJ in *Horford Investments Ltd v Lambert* [1974] 1 All
ER 131 at 135, [1976] Ch 39 at 46, as 'one unit of habitation'. In the language of the Rent
Acts, the penthouse was throughout that period of some 37 years let and used as 'a
separate dwelling'. The lease contained in cl 2(9) a covenant against user for trade,
h professional or business purposes.
   3. In 1973 the appellant's father, then 81 years of age, decided to live in the country.
On 9th March 1973 he assigned the residue of the term of years created by the 1936 lease
of the penthouse to the appellant for the sum of £10,000. But the appellant had no
immediate need of the penthouse. On 15th March 1973 he granted to a Mr de Bye (who
was a friend of the appellant's father) an underlease of the maisonette for a sum of £8,600
j and a yearly rental of £228. The term of that underlease was for the residue of the term
of the 1936 lease, less one day. But before and after the 1936 lease became vested in the
appellant he had used the flat for his own purposes, and he continued to do so after he
married in 1965, when he was in London on business, or for visits with his wife. The
details of his movements over this period will be found in the learned judge's
judgment. Since July 1978, that is, since the present proceedings were begun, the
appellant has been working mainly in London and since then has used the flat for some

two to three days each week. At about the same time as the appellant acquired the 1936 lease from his father, he spent some £5,500 modernising the flat.

4. On 25th March 1975 Mr de Bye assigned the residue of his underlease of the maisonette to a Mr Carter. The underlease contained no prohibition against assignment. The underlease thus expired by effluxion of time on 28th September 1978. The 1936 lease expired by effluxion of time on 29th September 1978. Mr Carter did not, however, leave the maisonette on 28th September 1978. Though he could not, of course, on or after that date, have been evicted from the maisonette without an order of the court, it was common ground that thenceforth he had no legal entitlement to possession of the maisonette. A possession order was ultimately obtained against him, and your Lordships were told that he finally left the maisonette in March 1980, having seemingly continued to occupy it for some eighteen months as a trespasser.

5. Though certain of the facts which I have summarised have been in dispute at the trial, the landlords expressly accepted before your Lordships' House that (i) until the assignment in March 1973 the appellant's father had occupied the penthouse as a separate dwelling, (ii) on the term date of the 1936 lease, that is to say 29th September 1978, the appellant was in occupation of the flat as a residence, (iii) after the term date of the underlease, that is 28th September 1978, Mr Carter had no contractual or statutory right to remain in possession of the maisonette save that he could not be lawfully evicted without a court order.

At the conclusion of her judgment, the learned judge made the following findings:

'I take the following view. I reject the contention on behalf of the applicant [that is, the landlords] that the subletting changed the character of the original single unit into two separate dwellings. There are no physical structural alterations. It is not a case of a home subsequently converted into separate flats. In my view the premises remain the same single unit as when built and let as such and used by one family for 37 years until 1973. I find the purpose of the respondent [that is, the present appellant] in purchasing the remainder of the lease of the penthouse was to keep the family home. He sublet the maisonette because he had no immediate use for more than the domestic flat. I find that he had and retained an intention to reoccupy the penthouse as a family home and that the terms of the sublease were designed to preserve the penthouse for such future occupation when required. The family furniture remained and still remains in the maisonette. His work commitments now require a family home in London. I find his original intention crystallised into an immediate intention before the relevant term date through the exigencies of his employment and his large family and domestic staff requirements. I am satisfied that he intends to occupy the whole penthouse as a family home in the near future and that it is a settled intention ... On the issue of occupation of the domestic flat I find that the respondent never abandoned his occupation of it. He always retained it, never let it and in 1973 spent £5,500 modernising it. He spent occasional nights there, sometimes with his wife. It was his only home for eight months in 1976. Since July 1978 with the transfer of his employment to London publishers he has occupied it several days each week. In my view whatever his past use of it, it was his London home at the relevant term date. I find that the respondent at the relevant term date had a settled intention to occupy the whole penthouse as a family home as soon as he could move his family there, was in regular personal residence of the domestic flat which I find constitutes a part of the penthouse and that he thus satisfies the requirements of the qualifying condition under the 1954 Act.'

In the Court of Appeal the landlords sought to challenge (among other matters) the learned judge's findings regarding 'the family furniture' having remained and still remaining in the maisonette. To this end it was sought to produce further evidence regarding the furniture. It was said that not only had the learned judge made a wrong finding of fact in this connection, as the new evidence was alleged to show, but that this alleged error vitiated her finding regarding the appellant's 'settled intention' regarding the penthouse. The landlords, by amendment of their notice of appeal to the Court of

Appeal, asked for a new trial because of this new evidence. But in view of their partial
_a_ success in that court that submission was understandably not pursued. The same request
was, however, made of your Lordships' House; indeed learned counsel for the landlords
made this his first submission at the outset of his address.

Lord Denning MR observed in his judgment in the Court of Appeal that it was not
altogether clear to whom the furniture belonged. He added ([1980] 2 All ER 497 at
500): 'At all events, no help can be gained from the furniture'. My Lords, I respectfully
_b_ agree with this view. Your Lordships were, however, invited to examine, and did
examine, the new evidence placed before the Court of Appeal. Much reliance was placed
on exhibit DJS 5 to an affidavit by a Mr Sheahan, a legal executive with the landlords'
solicitors. This exhibit is described in the affidavit as a 'draft letter' from Mr de Bye to the
appellant's then solicitors. How the landlords' solicitors acquired this document is not
explained, and I am quite unable to see how this document could possibly be admissible
_c_ evidence against the appellant. But whatever the arrangements were regarding the
furniture, this so-called new evidence leaves a very clear impression on my mind that
those arrangements were informal. Certainly I can see nothing which casts sufficient
doubt on the foundation of the learned judge's findings regarding the appellant's
intention, which is the important matter which would justify your Lordships taking the
extreme step, after proceedings which have now occupied the time of three tribunals, of
_d_ ordering a new trial. As I have already said, I respectfully agree with the observations
made by Lord Denning MR on this point. In my opinion, this appeal must be decided
on the basis of the learned judge's findings of fact which I have already stated. I would
therefore, without hesitation, refuse that application by the landlords.

Part I of the 1954 Act gave to certain residential tenants the protection of the Rent Acts
to which, apart from those statutory provisions, such tenants would not have been
_e_ entitled. The Rent Acts were defined in s 22(1) of the 1954 Act as meaning the Rent and
Mortgage Interest Restrictions Acts 1920 to 1939 and the Landlord and Tenant (Rent
Control) Act 1949. To secure Rent Act protection for such residential tenants the
following provisions were enacted in the 1954 Act. I should perhaps explain that I quote
these provisions as originally enacted and ignore any subsequent amendments and re-
amendments which are presently irrelevant:

_f_

'**1.** On the termination in accordance with the provisions of this Part of this Act
of a tenancy to which this section applies the tenant shall be entitled to the protection
of the Rent Acts subject to and in accordance with those provisions.

'**2.**—(1) The foregoing section applies to any long tenancy at a low rent, being a
tenancy as respects which for the time being the following condition (hereinafter
_g_ referred to as "the qualifying condition") is fulfilled, that is to say that the
circumstances (as respects the property comprised in the tenancy, the use of that
property, and all other relevant matters) are such that on the coming to an end of the
tenancy at that time the tenant would, if the tenancy had not been one at a low rent,
be entitled by virtue of the Rent Acts to retain possession of the whole or part of the
property comprised in the tenancy.

'(2) At any time before, but not more than twelve months before, the term date
_h_ application may be made to the court as respects any long tenancy at a low rent, not
being at the time of the application a tenancy as respects which the qualifying
condition is fulfilled, for an order declaring that the tenancy is not to be treated for
the purposes of this Part of this Act as a tenancy to which the foregoing section
applies; and where such an application is made—(_a_) the court, if satisfied that the
tenancy is not likely, immediately before the term date, to be a tenancy to which the
_j_ foregoing section applies, but not otherwise, shall make the order; (_b_) if the court
makes the order, then notwithstanding anything in subsection (1) of this section the
tenancy shall not thereafter be treated as a tenancy to which the foregoing section
applies . . .

'**3.**—(1) A tenancy which is current immediately before the term date and is then
a tenancy to which section one of this Act applies shall not come to an end on that
date except by being terminated under the provisions of this Part of this Act, and if

not then so terminated shall subject to those provisions continue until so terminated and shall, while continuing by virtue of this section, be deemed (notwithstanding *a* any change in circumstances) to be a tenancy to which section one of this Act applies ...

'**22** ... (3) In determining, for the purposes of any provision of this Part of this Act, whether the property comprised in a tenancy, or any part of that property, was let as a separate dwelling, the nature of the property or part at the time of the creation of the tenancy shall be deemed to have been the same as its nature at the *b* time in relation to which the question arises, and the purpose for which it was let under the tenancy shall be deemed to have been the same as the purpose for which it is or was used at the last-mentioned time.'

When the landlords began the instant proceedings, the relevant provisions regarding Rent Act protection were no longer to be found in the statutes originally referred to in s 22(1) of the 1954 Act, but in the Rent Act 1977. The most relevant provisions of the *c* 1977 Act are as follows:

'**1.** Subject to this Part of this Act, a tenancy under which a dwelling-house (which may be a house or part of a house) is let as a separate dwelling is a protected tenancy for the purposes of this Act. Any reference in this Act to a protected tenant shall be construed accordingly. *d*

'**2.**—(1) Subject to this Part of this Act—(a) after the termination of a protected tenancy of a dwelling-house the person who, immediately before that termination, was the protected tenant of the dwelling-house shall, if and so long as he occupies the dwelling-house as his residence, be the statutory tenant of it ...

'(3) In subsection (1)(a) above and in Part I of Schedule 1, the phrase "if and so long as he occupies the dwelling-house as his residence" shall be construed as it was *e* immediately before the commencement of this Act (that is to say, in accordance with section 3(2) of the Rent Act 1968).

'(4) A person who becomes a statutory tenant of a dwelling-house as mentioned in subsection (1)(a) above is, in this Act, referred to as a statutory tenant by virtue of his previous protected tenancy ...'

Schedule 23, para 16 reads thus: *f*

'In section 22(1) of the Landlord and Tenant Act 1954, in the definition of "the Rent Act", for "the Rent Act 1968" ... substitute ... "the Rent Act 1977" ...'

I should explain in connection with this last citation that the reference to the Rent Act 1968, which was deleted by para 16 of Sch 23, was inserted by Sch 15 to the Rent Act 1968, which had in this respect substituted a reference to that Act for the original *g* definition in s 22(1) of the 1954 Act. Thus, by 1978 when the instant proceedings were begun, the relevant protection accorded by the 1954 Act had to be determined by reference to the Rent Act 1977. But, as already stated, s 2(3) of the 1977 Act enjoined that the phrase in s 2(1)(a) 'if and so long as he occupies the dwelling-house as his residence' should be construed in accordance with s 3(2) of the Rent Act 1968. Reference back to that subsection shows that it provided that that same phrase— *h*

'shall be construed as requiring the fulfilment of the same, and only the same, qualifications (whether as to residence or otherwise) as had to be fulfilled before the commencement of this Act to entitle a tenant, within the meaning of the Increase of Rent and Mortgage Interest (Restrictions) Act 1920, to retain possession, by virtue of that Act and not by virtue of a tenancy, of a dwelling-house to which that Act *j* applied.'

Thus, one is taken right back to the Increase of Rent and Mortgage Interest (Restrictions) Act 1920. I think I need only refer to s 12(2) and s 15(1) of the 1920 Act. The purpose of this convoluted series of references back, both in the 1977 and in the 1968 Acts, and thence to the 1920 Act, must, I think, and indeed counsel for the appellant so submitted, have been to preserve, unchanged, that vast body of judge-made law on the

sufficiency or insufficiency of residence in this context. That body of case law will be
a found collected in Megarry on The Rent Acts (10th Edn, 1968, p 184ff).

It is against this complex statutory background that I turn to consider the application
of the facts found by the learned judge to the requirements of the 1954 Act which have
to be complied with before the protection accorded by that Act can be successfully
claimed by a tenant. The structure and intention of ss 1 and 2 of the 1954 Act seem
reasonably plain. The provisions are designed to give Rent Act protection to tenancies
b otherwise excluded from such protection, because they are long tenancies at low rents.
If they are long tenancies at low rents, then 'the qualifying condition' has to be satisfied
before protection is accorded. The qualifying condition is—

c   'that the circumstances (as respects the property comprised in the tenancy, the use
       of that property, and all other relevant matters) are such that on the coming to an
       end of the tenancy at that time the tenant would, if the tenancy had not been one
       at a low rent, be entitled by virtue of the Rent Act to retain possession of the whole
       or part of the property comprised in the tenancy.'

There is no question that the terms of the headlease satisfied the requirements of being
a long tenancy at a low rent. The crucial question is, therefore, whether on the term
d date, 29th September 1978, the appellant would as a tenant have been entitled to retain
possession of the whole or part of the property comprised in the tenancy.

The effect of s 2(1) of the 1954 Act has been fully considered in three decisions of the
Court of Appeal, *Haines v Herbert* [1963] 3 All ER 715, [1963] 1 WLR 1401, *Herbert v
Byrne* [1964] 1 All ER 882, [1964] 1 WLR 519 (the court consisted of Lord Denning MR,
Russell and Salmon LJJ) and *Crown Lodge (Surbiton) Investments Ltd v Nalecz* [1967] 1 All
e ER 489, [1967] 1 WLR 647. In each of the two last-mentioned cases Lord Denning MR
analysed the structure of this section, and on both occasions emphasised the importance
of looking at 'the whole house', and in *Herbert v Byrne* he italicised the word 'whole'. I
respectfully agree with him, and adopt his analysis. The court has to concern itself with
the position as between landlord and tenant, and not, at least at the outset of its inquiry,
look into the position between the tenant and any subtenants. The court must look at
f the totality of that which was the subject matter of the letting, s 22(3) enjoining it to treat
the factual situation at the term date regarding the nature of the property and the
purpose for which the property was let as that nature and purpose which had subsisted
at the beginning of the tenancy. In passing, I would observe that, as my noble and
learned friend Lord Russell pointed out during the hearing, s 22(3) plays little if any part
in the determination of this appeal since the nature of the property was the same in 1978
g as in 1936 (there had been no structural alteration whatever) and the purpose for which
that property was let was the same (namely residential). Moreover, as *Herbert v Byrne*
shows, the fact that there is a subletting of one or more parts of the property in question
does not of itself mean that the tenant has ceased to occupy the whole property as his
residence: see in particular the judgment of Lord Denning MR ([1964] 1 All ER 882 at
885, [1964] 1 WLR 519 at 525–526).
h
Counsel for the landlords founded much of his argument on the supposed irrelevancy
of the learned judge's finding as to the appellant's intention regarding the occupation of
the penthouse. Any relevant intention must, he argued, be capable of being put into
practical effect during the term of the tenancy, and what was found to have been the
appellant's intention on 29th September 1978 could never have been put into effect on
or before that date, since Mr Carter was then still in occupation of the maisonette albeit
j as a trespasser. It was only present intention that was relevant, and not intention as to the
future after the term date. The appellant as lessor to Mr Carter was responsible for that
which Mr Carter did or omitted to do, and he must bear the consequences of Mr Carter's
trespass which involved that there was no practical possibility of the appellant gaining
possession of the maisonette, and thus possession of the penthouse as distinct from his
existing possession of the flat, on the one crucial day, namely 29th September 1978.
Counsel for the landlords described that one day reversion as a conveyancing device to

prevent the conversion of an underlease into what, in the absence of such a single day, would be an assignment. Too much weight was not to be attached to its existence.

My Lords, the decisions of the Court of Appeal in both *Haines v Herbert* and *Herbert v Byrne* militate strongly against the landlords' submissions on the question of intention. In the former case the tenant had 'the intention of reconverting the whole messuage into one dwelling-house' (see [1963] 3 All ER 715 at 719, [1963] 1 WLR 1401 at 1407 per Harman LJ) but had not done so before the term date. That did not prevent there being a single occupation on the term date. In the latter, the tenant 'had formed the intention to make the new premises in the fullest sense his home, at least as soon as they were fully fit for occupation as such . . .' (see [1964] 1 All ER 882 at 887, [1964] 1 WLR 519 at 527 per Russell LJ). Salmon LJ emphasised the same point (see [1964] 1 All ER 882 at 888, [1964] 1 WLR 519 at 529).

But, my Lords, I do not think it would be possible to accept this part of the argument by the landlords without disapproving at least a part of the reasoning in *Haines v Herbert*, and in truth the decision in *Herbert v Byrne*. My Lords, even if I had any doubt as to the correctness of those decisions, and of the reasoning which led to them, which I emphatically do not, I would not willingly have suggested that your Lordships' House should overrule those decisions nearly twenty years after they were given. In the interval many cases must have been decided in county courts on the foundation there laid by the Court of Appeal, and it would be wrong now to disturb that secure foundation.

The Court of Appeal reached its decision in the present case by, in effect, treating the existence of the underlease of the maisonette to Mr Carter as determinative of the crucial issue whether the penthouse was, on the term date, let to the appellant as a separate dwelling. But, quite apart from the fact that the term date of the underlease was one day earlier than the term date of the lease to the appellant, the decisions to which I have referred, and in particular the decision in *Herbert v Byrne*, show that the existence of subletting, even of protected subletting, is in no way determinative of the issue. Counsel for the landlords did not shrink from inviting your Lordships' House to say that *Herbert v Byrne* was wrongly decided in this respect. In my view, if I may respectfully say so, *Herbert v Byrne* is in this respect, too, correctly decided, and for the reasons I have already given, I would not, even if I had thought otherwise, have been prepared to suggest that it should be overruled. Of course, if in a particular case, a landlord could show abandonment by the tenant of his right to possession (for example) by reason of one or more sublettings so that there was clearly no intention at any time thereafter to resume possession, the position might well be different. Where I respectfully differ from the Court of Appeal is that I think it failed sufficiently to distinguish between the landlords and the appellant as tenant under the 1936 lease on the one hand and the position between the appellant as lessor and Mr Carter as lessee under the underlease on the other. It directed attention to the latter rather than to the former, which as the cases show is what the 1954 Act enjoins the court to do. Indeed, I venture to think that the decision of the Court of Appeal in the present appeal is inconsistent with its previous decision in *Herbert v Byrne*, to which Lord Denning MR and Bridge LJ referred, but which was not discussed in detail in their judgments.

My Lords, I am clearly of the view that on the term date, one day after the expiry of the underlease, the penthouse was let to the appellant as a separate dwelling house because (1) there had initially been a single letting of the penthouse at a single rent for residential purposes, (2) the underlease had expired by effluxion of time on 28th September 1978, (3) Mr Carter's occupation on 29th September 1978 was unlawful, (4) the only person entitled to lawful possession, not only of the flat but also of the maisonette, and therefore of the penthouse, on 29th September 1978 was the appellant, (5) it was on that date, the term date, the appellant's settled intention to occupy the penthouse as a family house as soon as he could move there, (6) notwithstanding Mr Carter's unlawful occupation, the appellant was in possession of the penthouse on the term date with that settled intention.

It follows that I find myself in general agreement with the very clear judgment of the learned county court judge and I would allow the appeal and restore her decision, dismissing the landlords' application under the 1954 Act.

a Counsel for the landlords conceded that if the appellant's appeal should succeed, the landlords' cross-appeal must fail. I agree that this is so. Strictly, therefore, it is unnecessary therefore for your Lordships to express any view on the cross-appeal. But your Lordships may, nevertheless, think it right to do so in order to dispose of the argument skilfully advanced in its support, lest otherwise it reappears in some later case. The submission proceeded on the footing that, as the Court of Appeal held, there was not one separate dwelling house, the penthouse was not let as a separate dwelling

b house, the maisonette and the flat were each so separately let. But since the flat was only a part of what had been let in 1936, the Rent Act 1977 (which had become the relevant statute to write into ss 1 and 2 of the 1954 Act as I have already said) does not allow protection of a part of a tenancy. Only the whole tenancy can now be protected under the 1954 Act. This ingenious argument was, your Lordships were told, advanced in the Court of Appeal but not pressed, since it seemingly found little favour in that court. The

c landlords, content with victory in respect of the maisonette, did not seek to press their victory to the point of gaining possession of the flat as well. But your Lordships were also told that when the appellant obtained leave to appeal to your Lordships' House it was ordered that the landlords should be at liberty to cross-appeal if they so wished notwithstanding what had happened in the Court of Appeal. Your Lordships have not, therefore, had the advantage of the views of the Court of Appeal on the subject of the

d cross-appeal.

My Lords, the argument is admirably stated in the landlords' printed case, and I shall not repeat what is there fully set out. It depends for its validity on the fact that s 1 of the 1977 Act attaches protection to the tenancy under which the dwelling house is let as a separate dwelling, and not to the dwelling house itself, as in the earlier statutes. It seems that this change of language was first made in s 1 of the Rent Act 1965. It was continued

e in s 1 of the Rent Act 1968, a consolidating Act, and in effect repeated in s 1 of the Rent Act 1977, also a consolidating Act. My Lords, legislative accidents can happen, but it would be strange indeed if the effect of the changes made in 1965, and continued in 1968 and 1977, which were designed to increase the protection accorded to tenants by restoring to them the right to retain possession of certain premises (see the long title of the 1965 Act) were to have the inadvertent result when those provisions are written into the 1954

f Act of depriving persons admittedly up to 1965 entitled to protection in respect of part of the tenancy falling within the 1954 Act of that protection. Those who gained protection in 1965 can, if this argument be right, only have gained it at the expense of others who lost protection which had existed between 1954 and 1965.

The landlords' submissions involve that the relevant provisions of the 1977 Act must be treated as so inconsistent with those of the 1954 Act that the former must be regarded

g as impliedly repealing the latter. My Lords, I freely confess that I would only accept this argument if I saw no escape from it as a matter of construction, for I find it impossible to believe that the framers of the 1977 Act and its predecessors can possibly have intended this result.

My Lords, a close examination of the relevant provisions has led me to the conclusion that this argument is, in truth, ill-founded. Counsel for the appellant drew your

h Lordships' attention to s 2(3) of the 1977 Act and its predecessors. I have already traced the legislative history of this subsection through to its source, and I shall not repeat it again. I see no need to trace through the judicial history of the phrase which is also long and complex. Suffice it to say that under the law, as so preserved, a statutory tenant may be a statutory tenant of only a part of what he has hitherto been the contractual tenant. On that view the problem disappears. I would, therefore, dismiss the cross-appeal in

j addition to allowing the appeal.

Appeal allowed; cross-appeal dismissed. Order of her Honour Judge Rowland of 24th September 1979 restored.

Solicitors: *Watkins, Pulleyn & Ellison* (for the appellant); *Thornton, Lynne & Lawson* (for the respondents).

Mary Rose Plummer   Barrister.

Rank Film Distributors Ltd and others v Video Information Centre and others

HOUSE OF LORDS

LORD WILBERFORCE, LORD DIPLOCK, LORD FRASER OF TULLYBELTON, LORD RUSSELL OF KILLOWEN AND LORD ROSKILL

2nd, 3rd, 4th, 5th, 9th MARCH, 8th APRIL 1981

Practice – Inspection of property – Property subject matter of action or in respect of which question arising – Privilege against self-incrimination – Order requiring disclosure of information – Defendants pirating films and selling unauthorised video cassettes – Defendants ordered to disclose information regarding pirating and selling cassettes – Information likely to result in defendants being prosecuted for conspiracy to defraud – Whether defendants entitled to claim privilege against self-incrimination in respect of disclosure of information.

The appellants, who were film companies owning the copyright to films produced and made by them, believed that certain unauthorised persons were engaged in pirating copies of their films and recording and selling unauthorised video cassettes of them. The respondents were suspected of selling the cassettes. The appellants accordingly issued a writ against the suspected unauthorised persons seeking an injunction restraining them from infringing the appellants' copyright. The appellants also sought and were granted Anton Piller orders which, inter alia, required the respondents to disclose (i) the names and addresses of persons who supplied the cassettes and customers who bought them, (ii) all invoices, letters and other documents relating to the cassettes, and (iii) the whereabouts of all pirate cassettes and master copies known to the respondents. The respondents applied to the court to have the orders varied by expunging the requirements as to disclosure, on the grounds that by disclosing the information they might incriminate themselves and the orders therefore infringed the privilege against self-incrimination. The respondents contended that if they were compelled to disclose the information they would incriminate themselves by providing evidence on which they could be prosecuted and convicted of (i) contravention of s 21 of the Copyright Act 1956, (ii) contravention of s 18 of the Theft Act 1968 and (iii) conspiracy to defraud at common law. A person associated with the respondents in the pirating of the films was in the course of being prosecuted on charges of conspiracy to defraud. The judge dismissed the respondents' application but on appeal the Court of Appeal ([1980] 2 All ER 273) held that the orders requiring disclosure should be expunged because they were contrary to the principle of privilege against self-incrimination. The appellants appealed to the House of Lords seeking reinstatement of the orders. The appellants, while recognising the existence of privilege against self-incrimination by discovery, contended that the court ought to compel the respondents to disclose the information sought while imposing a restriction on the information being used in a criminal prosecution of the respondents.

Held – Since a charge against the respondents of conspiracy to defraud would not be a contrived, fanciful or remote possibility but an appropriate and exact description of what the respondents and the other persons involved had done, it was clear that disclosure by the respondents of the information sought would tend to expose them to such a charge, which would be a serious charge and would, if proved, attract heavy penalties. It followed that the claim of privilege against self-incrimination should be upheld. Moreover, there was no way in which the court could compel disclosure while at the same time protecting the respondents from the consequences of self-incrimination, since an express restriction imposed by the court on the use of any information disclosed would be binding only on the appellants and not on anyone else who brought a criminal

a prosecution and in any event would not bind a criminal court to exclude the information
as inadmissable evidence. The appeal would accordingly be dismissed (see p 80 *h* to p 81
b and *f* to *j*, p 82 *a* to *c g h*, p 84 *a b e* to *g* and p 86 *b* to *d*, post).

Riddick v Thames Board Mills Ltd [1977] 3 All ER 677 distinguished.

Per Curiam. In cases involving large scale and systematic infringements of copyright,
offences against s 21 of the 1956 Act are probably too trivial, having regard to the
maximum penalty of a £50 fine, to be taken into account when considering whether a
b claim for privilege against self-incrimination should succeed. Furthermore, the risk of
a successful prosecution under s 18 of the 1968 Act, which applies to theft of 'property',
is too remote to be considered because copyright is not 'property' for the purposes of s 18
(see p 80 *g h*, p 81 *h*, p 82 *g h*, p 83 *h* to p 84 *a* and p 86 *b* to *d*, post).

Per Lord Russell. Because the privilege against incrimination could largely deprive
the owner of a copyright of his just rights to the protection of his property, legislation
c similar to s 31 of the 1968 Act would be welcome; the aim of such legislation should be
to remove the privilege while at the same time preventing the use in criminal
proceedings of statements which would otherwise be privileged (see p 86 *c d*, post).

Decision of the Court of Appeal [1980] 2 All ER 273 affirmed.

d **Notes**

For privilege from production of documents exposing a party to penalties, see 13
Halsbury's Laws (4th Edn) para 92, and for cases on the subject, see 18 Digest (Reissue)
19, 149–152, 97–102, 1195–1246 and 22 Digest (Reissue) 433–437, 4310–4346.

For the Copyright Act 1956, s 21, see 7 Halsbury's Statutes (3rd Edn) 171.

For the Theft Act 1968, ss 18, 31, see 8 ibid 794, 802.

e

Cases referred to in opinions

Alterskye v Scott [1948] 1 All ER 469, 18 Digest (Reissue) 62, 426.

Anton Piller KG v Manufacturing Processes Ltd [1976] 1 All ER 779, [1976] Ch 55, [1976]
f 2 WLR 162, CA, Digest (Cont Vol E) 338, *1238b*.

Attorney-General v Conroy (1838) 2 Jo Ex Ir 791, 18 Digest (Reissue) 247, **1249*.

Chadwick v Chadwick (1852) 22 LJ Ch 329, 20 LTOS 272, 16 Jur 1060, 18 Digest (Reissue)
 151, *1230*.

Distillers Co (Biochemicals) Ltd v Times Newspapers Ltd [1975] 1 All ER 41, [1975] QB 613,
 [1974] 3 WLR 728, Digest (Cont Vol D) 277, *495a*.

EMI Ltd v Sarwar and Haidar [1977] FSR 146.
g *Jackson v Benson* (1826) 1 Y & J 32, 148 ER 574, 22 Digest (Reissue) 440, *4376*.

London (Mayor and citizens) v Levy (1803) 8 Ves 398, 32 ER 408.

Norwich Pharmacal Co v Customs and Excise Comrs [1973] 2 All ER 943, [1974] AC 133,
 [1973] 3 WLR 164, [1974] RPC 101, HL, 18 Digest (Reissue) 8, *23*.

R v Sang [1979] 2 All ER 1222, [1980] AC 402, [1979] 3 WLR 263, 143 JP 606, HL, Digest
h (Cont Vol E) 137, *3913a*.

Reynolds v Godlee (1858) 4 K & J 88, 32 LTOS 35, 70 ER 37, 18 Digest (Reissue) 88, *635*.

Riddick v Thames Board Mills Ltd [1977] 3 All ER 677, [1977] QB 881, [1977] 3 WLR 63,
 CA, Digest (Cont Vol E) 180, *495b*.

*Rio Tinto Zinc Corpn v Westinghouse Electric Corpn, RTZ Services Ltd v Westinghouse Electric
 Corpn* [1978] 1 All ER 434, [1978] AC 547, [1978] 2 WLR 81, HL: *rvsg sub nom Re*
j *Westinghouse Electric Corpn Uranium Contract Litigation MDL Docket No 235* [1977] 3 All
 ER 703, [1977] 3 WLR 430, CA, Digest (Cont Vol E) 222, *7114a*.

Scott v Scott [1913] AC 417, [1911–13] All ER Rep 1, 82 LJP 74, 109 LT 1, HL, 16 Digest
 (Reissue) 170, *1693*.

Triplex Safety Glass Co Ltd v Lancegaye Safety Glass (1934) Ltd [1939] 2 All ER 613, [1939]
 2 KB 395, 108 LJKB 762, 160 LT 595, CA, 18 Digest (Reissue) 245, *1933*.

Interlocutory appeal

The appellants, Rank Film Distributors Ltd, Universal City Studios Inc, Cinema *a*
International Corpn (UK), ITC Entertainment Ltd, ITC Film Distributors Ltd and EMI
Film Ltd, the plaintiffs in an action against the respondents, Video Information Centre
(a firm), Michael Anthony Lee, Susan Gomberg, Stylestone Ltd, Videochord Ltd and
Michael George Dawson, appealed against the decision of the Court of Appeal (Bridge
and Templeman LJJ, Lord Denning MR dissenting) ([1980] 2 All ER 273, [1980] 3 WLR
487) on 15th February 1980 allowing in part the respondents' appeal against the decision *b*
of Whitford J on 31st July 1979 to refuse to discharge or vary two orders made by Walton
J on 2nd and 5th July 1979. The orders made by Walton J, which were made on ex parte
applications, ordered, inter alia, (i) the second, third and sixth defendants to disclose the
names and addresses of persons, films or companies to whom they had supplied or
offered to supply to them or who were engaged in the production, distribution or sale of
illicit copies of films used or intended to be used in making illicit copies of films, (ii) the *c*
second, third and sixth defendants to disclose by affidavit all invoices, labels, books of
account, letters lists or other documents within their possession, power, custody and
control relating to illicit films supplied by or to the defendants, (iii) the second, third and
fourth defendants to permit representatives of the plaintiffs to enter four named premises
for the purpose of looking for, inspecting and photographing all illicit copy films, labels
or packaging, invoices, bills, letters, notes or other documents, equipment, films *d*
(including video cassettes and master tapes) and blank film stock, and removing into the
custody of the plaintiffs' solicitors all or any such items except equipment, (iv) all the
defendants, except the sixth defendant, and/or the person appearing to be in charge of
the four named premises to produce to the person serving the order all such films, labels,
packaging, invoices, bills, letters, other documents or film stock, and (v) all the defendants
to disclose to the person serving the order the whereabouts of all illicit copy films or *e*
masters for making copies known to the defendants. The facts are set out in the opinion
of Lord Wilberforce.

Donald Nicholls QC, Hugh Laddie and *Jeremy Davies* for the appellants.
Colin Ross-Munro QC and *Daniel Serota* for the first four respondents.
The fifth and sixth respondents did not appear.   *f*

Their Lordships took time for consideration.

8th April. The following opinions were delivered.

LORD WILBERFORCE. My Lords, this appeal relates to two interlocutory orders *g*
made by Walton J on 2nd and 5th July 1979. They are of a type which have come to be
known as Anton Piller orders, so called after a tortious infringer of copyright whose case
reached the Court of Appeal in 1976 (see *Anton Piller KG v Manufacturing Processes Ltd*
[1976] 1 All ER 779, [1976] Ch 55).
    They are designed to deal with situations created by infringements of patents, trade
marks and copyright, or more correctly with acts of piracy which have become a large *h*
and profitable business in recent years. They are intended to provide a quick and
efficient means of recovering infringing articles and of discovering the sources from
which these articles have been supplied and the persons to whom they are distributed
before those concerned have had time to destroy or conceal them. Their essence is
surprise. Because they operate drastically and because they are made, necessarily, ex
parte, i e before the persons affected have been heard, they are closely controlled by the *j*
court (see the judgment of Lord Denning MR in *Anton Piller KG v Manufacturing Processes
Ltd* [1976] 1 All ER 779 at 783, [1976] Ch 55 at 61). They are only granted on clear and
compelling evidence, and a number of safeguards in the interest of preserving essential
rights are introduced. They are an illustration of the adaptability of equitable remedies
to new situations.

In this case we are concerned with video tapes of films. The appellant plaintiffs
a represent the owners of the copyright in nearly every feature film in the English
language shown in this country, each representing a large investment, many of them
very valuable properties. The respondent defendants are persons alleged to be concerned
with the wholesale pirating of these films by distributing video tapes illegally made from
master tapes, themselves made from the original 35 mm films, copyright in which
belongs to the appellants. Those concerned in the present appeal are the first three
b respondents, effectively Mr Lee and Ms Gomberg, who own the Video Information
Centre. The sixth respondent, Mr Dawson, who owns or controls the fifth respondent
and between whom and Lee/Gomberg a business relationship appears to exist, had a
laboratory in Essex which was raided by the police in April 1979 and where 400 illicit
copy films were seized and a Rank reproducing machine was found. Mr Dawson is in
the course of being prosecuted on charges of alleged conspiracy to defraud. He did not
c take the present proceedings to the Court of Appeal and is not a party to the appeal to this
House. So far as Lee/Gomberg are concerned, it is enough to say that the evidence is
strong and clear that they have engaged in the distribution and sale of pirated copy video
tapes on a very large scale, to Kuwait and other places. It amply satisfied the requirements
laid down by the Chancery judges for the making of an Anton Piller order. The case is
one for an order to be made in such terms as will give the maximum legally possible
d protection to the appellants to whose business the respondents' activities represent a
major threat.

The main question before this House is whether Mr Lee and Ms Gomberg can avail
themselves of the privilege against self-incrimination in order to deprive the appellants
of an important part of the relief which they seek. It may seem to be a strange paradox
that the worse, ie the more criminal, their activities can be made to appear, the less
e effective is the civil remedy that can be granted, but that, prima facie, is what the
privilege achieves. The orders under appeal are elaborate. A summary of their effect is
sufficient. They included:

1. Injunctions from making or dealing with illicit copies of any of the appellants'
films; no question arises as to these.

2. An injunction restraining the respondents from warning third parties of the
f existence of these proceedings except for the purpose of obtaining legal advice; no
question.

3. An order relating to the identity of those concerned with the first and fifth
respondents; no question.

4. An order—

g
> 'that the Defendants Michael Anthony Lee and Susan Gomberg do each forthwith
> disclose to the person who shall serve this Order upon them the names and addresses
> of all persons firms or companies known to them (i) to whom or to which the
> Defendants or one or more of them have supplied or offered to supply illicit copy
> films or films used or intended to be used for making illicit copy films with the
> quantities and dates thereof (ii) who have supplied or offered to supply the
> Defendants or one or more of them with illicit copy films or films used or intended
h > to be used for making illicit copy films with the quantities and dates thereof and (iii)
> who are engaged in the production distribution offer for sale or sale of illicit copy
> films or films used or intended to be used for making illicit copy films.'

5. An order—

j
> 'that the Defendants Michael Anthony Lee and Susan Gomberg and each of them
> do within 4 days after service upon them of this Order make and serve upon the
> Plaintiffs' Solicitors an affidavit setting forth the information which they are
> required to give pursuant to the foregoing part of this Order and exhibiting thereto
> all invoices labels books of account letters lists or other documents within their
> respective possession power custody or control which relate to each and every illicit

copy film supplied or offered by or to the Defendants or one or more of them or to
any business relating thereto.'

6. An order that Mr Lee, Ms Gomberg . . . do forthwith permit two persons authorised
by the appellants to enter certain premises between specified hours for the purpose of
looking for and inspecting illicit copy films and defined categories of documents . . . for
the purpose of removing into the appellants' solicitors' custody all such films and
documents and to produce to the person serving the orders all the illicit copy films and
documents referred to above.

7. An order—

'that each of the Defendants do forthwith disclose to the person who shall serve
this order upon that Defendant the whereabouts of all illicit copy films or masters
for making the same known to that Defendant.'

Thus, for present purposes, the orders fall under three heads:
(1) Requiring the respondents to supply information.
(2) Requiring the respondents to allow access to premises for the purpose of looking
for illicit copy films and to allow their being removed to safe custody.
(3) Requiring the respondents to disclose and produce documents.

The orders under (2) were upheld by the Court of Appeal, and this part of the court's
decision was not seriously contested in this House. In any event I am satisfied that there
was jurisdiction to make these orders and that the privilege against self-incrimination has
no application to them. The privilege against self-incrimination is invoked as regards (1)
and (3). The essential question being whether the provision of the information or
production of the documents may tend to incriminate the respondents, it is necessary to
see what possible heads of criminal liability there may be. There are three.
(1) Section 21 of the Copyright Act 1956 creates summary offences under a number
of headings, some of which would have potential applicability to the respondents. For
a first offence there is a maximum fine of £50 however many infringing articles are
involved.
(2) Conspiracy to commit a breach of s 21 of the 1956 Act. By virtue of the Criminal
Law Act 1977 no greater punishment can be imposed for such a conspiracy then for the
substantive offence under s 21.
(3) Conspiracy to defraud, an offence at common law left unaffected by the 1977 Act.
As to (1) and (2), I think that a substantial argument could be raised that these should
not be taken account of in connection with a claim for privilege. The criminal offences
created by s 21 cover almost precisely the same ground as the bases for civil liability
under the Copyright Act 1956. I would be reluctant to hold that in civil proceedings for
infringement based on specified acts the defendants could claim privilege against
discovery on the ground that those same acts establish a possible liability for a petty
offence. In practice, as one would suppose, s 21 is very rarely invoked; only one case
came to our knowledge, namely of one prosecution in 1913 under the 1911 Act, and
potential liability under it might well be disregarded as totally insubstantial. The same
argument would apply as regards conspiracy to breach it.
However, it is only too clear (and I deliberately use the language of reluctance) that
supply of the information and production of the documents sought would tend to expose
the respondents to a charge of conspiracy to defraud. In the very nature of this activity,
a number of persons are certain to be involved in it, in printing the master tapes, copying
from the master tapes, seeking and accepting orders, and distributing the illicit copies.
A charge of conspiracy to defraud, so far from being as it sometimes is, a contrived
addition to other charges, is here an appropriate and exact description of what is being
done. So far from it being contrived, fanciful, or imagined, it is the charge on which Mr
Dawson, who appears on the existing evidence to be closely connected with Mr Lee and
Ms Gomberg, is to stand trial. It cannot be said that charges under this head would be

nothing but charges under s 21 of the 1956 Act under another name. An essential
a ingredient in them is dishonesty, which may exist in cases brought under s 21, but which
may not. The much heavier penalties also make it more likely that charges would be
brought of conspiracy to defraud. Unless some escape can be devised from this
conclusion, the privilege must inevitably attach.

Counsel for the appellants courageously attempted to suggest an escape route on the
following lines. The courts, he submitted, must in all cases try to reconcile protection of
b a defendant from possible self-incrimination with doing justice to a plaintiff. Whatever
may have been the position when the privilege was first worked out by the judges,
modern procedure is now more flexible, and makes it possible to do justice without
denying protection. It is all the more necessary to find a flexible approach, because so
many actions which formerly involved civil liability only are now, by modern trends in
legislation, made criminal offences. Thus many ordinary cases of 'passing off' are now
c offences under the Trade Descriptions Act 1968. If full scope is given to the privilege
against self-incrimination, potential plaintiffs, in this area of industrial property, will fail
to get a remedy in the civil courts. Counsel was at pains to make clear that he was not,
in these submissions, attempting to negate or undermine the privilege against self-
incrimination. This has been too long established in our law as a basic liberty of the
subject (in other countries it has constitutional status) to be denied. It has received
d modern recognition in the Civil Evidence Act 1968, s 14, and in this House.

It is certainly correct to say that existing law and practice to some extent prevent
matter disclosed on discovery in civil proceedings from being used to the prejudice of the
disclosing party. The protection is described with different words: the matter must not
be used for an 'improper' purpose (see *Alterskye v Scott* [1948] 1 All ER 469) or a 'collateral
object' (see Bray on Discovery (1885, p 238)) or, most strongly, 'otherwise than in the
e action in which they are disclosed' (see *Distillers Co (Biochemicals) Ltd v Times Newspapers
Ltd* [1975] 1 All ER 41 at 48, [1975] QB 613 at 621 per Talbot J).

In the most recent case (*Riddick v Thames Board Mills Ltd* [1977] 3 All ER 677 at 687,
[1977] QB 881 at 896) Lord Denning MR used the words 'for any ulterior or alien
purpose'. But it has never been held that these expressions, however wide, extend to
criminal proceedings; if they did there would be no need for the privilege. Counsel for
f the appellants was therefore obliged to suggest that, even granting this, the courts had
power positively to decide in a particular case, as the counterpart of the obligation to
disclose, that any matter which is compulsorily disclosed as the result of the court's
process should be inadmissible in evidence. But I cannot accept that a civil court has any
power to decide in a manner which would bind a criminal court that evidence of any
kind is admissible or inadmissible in that court. Certainly a criminal court always has a
g discretion to exclude evidence improperly obtained if to admit it would unfairly
prejudice a defendant. But to substitute for a privilege a dependence on the court's
discretion would substantially be to the defendant's detriment. That the civil court has
not the power to declare evidence inadmissible is strikingly shown by s 31 of the Theft
Act 1968 which contains an express provision by which a person is obliged to answer
questions put in proceedings for the recovery of property and to comply with orders
h made in such proceedings and which states that no statement or admission so made shall
be admissible in evidence against the person concerned in proceedings for an offence
under the Act. Infringement of copyright is not theft, so this section cannot be invoked.

The appellants' submission amounts to a request to the courts, by judicial decision, to
extend this statutory provision to civil proceedings generally, or at least to these
proceedings. But this, in my opinion, the courts cannot do. I should add that *Riddick's*
j case is no support for the proposition that answers or documents extracted in civil
proceedings are inadmissible in criminal proceedings: the remark of Lord Denning MR
in the Court of Appeal ([1980] 2 All ER 273 at 281, [1980] 3 WLR 487 at 507) is made
with reference to an argument for applying the Theft Act, s 31 by analogy (which I
cannot accept) and clearly does not represent Lord Denning MR's view as to *Riddick's* case
(see [1980] 2 All ER 273 at 279, [1980] 3 WLR 487 at 504).

There are some further points on this aspect of the case. First, I do not think that
adequate protection can be given by extracting from the plaintiffs, as a term of being   *a*
granted an Anton Piller order, an undertaking not to use the information obtained in
criminal proceedings. Even if such an undertaking were binding (see to the contrary
Triplex Safety Glass Co Ltd v Lancegaye Safety Glass (1934) *Ltd* [1939] 2 All ER 613, [1939]
2 KB 395) the protection is only partial, viz against prosecution by the plaintiff himself.
Moreover, whatever direct use may or may not be made of information given, or
material disclosed, under the compulsory process of the court, it must not be overlooked   *b*
that, quite apart from that, its provision or disclosure may set in train a process which
may lead to incrimination or may lead to the discovery of real evidence of an
incriminating character. In the present case, this cannot be discounted as unlikely; it is
not only a possible but probably the intended result. The party from whom disclosure
is asked is entitled, on established law, to be protected from these consequences. Second,
and this was very much an argument of last resort, counsel for the appellants suggested   *c*
that protection could be given by a hearing, wholly or in part, in camera. But such
procedure is totally alien, except in the most exceptional cases, to our procedure and I do
not think that so wide an extension of it as the submission involves ought to be
contemplated. Third, there are some procedural considerations. The appellants argued
that, even if, in principle, the privilege against self-incrimination is capable of attaching
in cases such as the present, that should not prevent the order for information and   *d*
production being made; the defendant should be left to raise the question of privilege,
if he wishes, and if necessary the court should rule on it. The difficulty is, however, that
the orders are intended to take effect immediately on the arrival of the plaintiff's
representatives (including, under existing practice, a solicitor) at the defendant's premises,
and if the defendant were to refuse to comply, even in reliance on the privilege, he
might, at least technically, be liable in contempt. I do not think that this problem is for   *e*
this House to resolve. Attention can merely be drawn to it, and in due course, no doubt,
forms of order will be worked out which will enable the orders to be as effective as
practicable while preserving the defendant's essential rights. All that this House can do
is to decide that the privilege against self-incrimination is capable of being invoked. I
would so decide.

Some other points were taken by the respondents as to the orders made in this case.   *f*
Some were said to be too widely expressed, in particular one which required each
defendant to disclose the whereabouts of all illicit copy films or masters (ie master copies)
for making the same known to that defendant. I can see that they may have force, but
the proper forum for them to be raised and debated is in the Chancery Division before
judges particularly experienced in the framing and controlling of interlocutory orders.
The record shows that they are fully sensitive to the need for keeping these orders within   *g*
due limits.

I would dismiss the present appeal.

LORD DIPLOCK. My Lords, I have had the advantage of reading in draft a copy of
the speech of my noble and learned friend Lord Wilberforce. For the reasons he has
given, I too would dismiss this appeal.   *h*

LORD FRASER OF TULLYBELTON. My Lords, recent technical developments
have made it possible for anyone who can get a cinema film into his possession for a few
hours to transpose it on to magnetic tape. Having made a master copy on magnetic tape
he can make hundreds of copies from it which can then be inserted in cassettes and sold
to the public. These cassettes can be played on a domestic television set provided it has   *j*
a suitable attachment, called a video cassette recorder (VCR), which can now be bought
for a few hundred pounds. Unauthorised copies are sold to the public at prices of £100
or £150 each and the owners of the copyright suffer serious loss as a result.

The appellants are, or represent, the owners of nearly every major English language
cinema film shown in public cinemas in the United Kingdom. The first four respondents

are alleged to be dealers in pirated copies of many of these films, and the fifth and sixth
a respondents are alleged to be makers of pirate copies. The appellants are naturally
concerned to protect their valuable copyright in these films. Ordinary actions against
dealers in illicit films are of little avail to the copyright owners because the dealers are
unlikely to be able to pay substantial damages and injunctions against them merely close
down one outlet for the films and do not prevent the manufacture of more unauthorised
copies which can then be sold through other outlets. The main concern of the appellants
b is, therefore, to trace the whereabouts of the master tapes in order to take action against
those who control them. For this purpose a form of order has been devised which is
generally referred to as an Anton Piller order, from the case of *Anton Piller KG v
Manufacturing Processes Ltd* [1976] 1 All ER 779, [1976] Ch 55. These orders are only
made when the plaintiff produces strong prima facie evidence of infringement of his
copyright. They are made on the ex parte application of the plaintiff, are served on the
c defendants without previous notice and order the defendants to make immediate
discovery of documents and to give immediate answers to interrogatories designed to
find out particularly the names and addresses of their suppliers. Orders of that general
nature, tending gradually to increase in stringency (see *EMI Ltd v Sarwar and Haidar*
[1977] FSR 146), have been found effective and have been made in several reported cases
in England as well as in New Zealand (apparently independently of the English
d development) and also in South Africa, Australia and elsewhere, apparently following the
English practice. Now for the first time the defendants have objected to making
discovery and to answering the interrogatories on the ground that by doing so they
might incriminate themselves. If the objection is well founded the usefulness of the
Anton Piller type of order will be much reduced if not practically destroyed.
     In the present case, two orders were made by Walton J on 2nd and 5th July 1979
e respectively. The order of 2nd July, which was directed to the first four respondents, was
a long, complicated document. The part of it to which the respondents object on the
ground that it might require them to incriminate themselves is the part which ordered
them to disclose to the person who served the order the names and addresses, so far as
known to them, of all customers to whom they had supplied illicit films and of all
persons who had supplied them or offered to supply them with illicit films. It also
f ordered them to permit the person who served the order to 'enter forthwith' their
premises for the purpose of looking for, inspecting and photographing documents
relating to illicit copy films, but the objection of self-incrimination is not made against
this part of the order. By 5th July, when the second order was made, the appellants had
apparently discovered the name of the sixth respondent, and by the order of that date
each of the six respondents was ordered to disclose to the person who served the order the
g whereabouts of all illicit films, or masters for making them, known to that respondent.
This order is said to infringe the privilege against self-incrimination.
     The respondents assert that, if they are compelled to disclose the information
mentioned in the parts of the orders to which they object, they will run a real risk of
providing evidence tending to show that they have been guilty of criminal offences.
Three offences are particularly suggested, namely (1) contravention of s 21 of the
h Copyright Act 1956, (2) the common law offence of conspiracy to defraud, and possibly
(3) an offence against s 18 of the Theft Act 1968. The risk of prosecution under the Theft
Act 1968 may, I think, be disregarded as remote, because that Act applies to theft of
'property' which is defined in a way that does not appear to include copyright, but only,
so far as this appeal is concerned, to the physical objects such as tapes and cassettes which
are of small value by themselves. The risk of prosecution under s 21 of the Copyright
j Act 1956 is theoretically greater because acts which are infringements of copyright,
including the making of unauthorised copies (s 13(5)) and knowingly importing or
selling infringing copies (s 16(2) and (3)(*a*)) are very likely also to be offences under s
21(1). But the offences created by s 21 are only ancillary remedies for breach of copyright,
as appears from the cross-heading to Part III of the Act, and they are treated as
comparatively trivial with a maximum penalty (as amended) of £50. It would, in my

opinion, be unreasonable to allow the possibility of incrimination of such offences to obstruct disclosure of information which would be of much more value to the owners of *a* the infringed copyright than any protection they might obtain from s 21.

But conspiracy to defraud is a different matter. It is a serious offence. The risk of those who deal in or manufacture illicit films being prosecuted for it is by no means remote or fanciful. Indeed the sixth respondent is now facing prosecution on that ground for the matters with which this appeal is concerned. Subject to a point, to be noticed hereafter, with regard to an offence of conspiracy, the possibility of prosecution on this ground does *b* therefore raise the question whether the defendant can rely on the privilege against being compelled to incriminate himself. The privilege itself is well established in English law. It is impliedly recognised by s 14(1) of the Civil Evidence Act 1968, and authority for its existence is to be found in *Triplex Safety Glass Co Ltd v Lancegaye Safety Glass (1934) Ltd* [1939] 2 All ER 613, [1939] 2 KB 395 and in *Rio Tinto Zinc Corpn v Westinghouse Electric Corpn* [1978] 1 All ER 434, [1978] AC 547. The appellants do not *c* dispute the existence of a privilege against compulsory self-incrimination by discovery or by answering interrogatories. But their counsel presented a powerful argument to the effect that the privilege ought not to be upheld in its simple form, to the serious prejudice of the appellants, when the object of the privilege could be attained in a way that would not prejudice the interests of parties such as the appellants. It could be attained, according to the argument, by compelling the discovery and answers, while *d* relying on a restriction, express or implied, against the use of information thereby disclosed in any prosecution of the party making the discovery.

At one stage, the argument seemed to depend on the possibility that the court which ordered the discovery might place an express restriction on the use of any information disclosed. In my opinion, any argument on that basis must be rejected. A restriction by the court making the order would, no doubt, be effective to bind the party who obtained *e* the order, but it can hardly be suggested that it would be effective to prevent a prosecutor in the public interest from using or an English criminal court (a fortiori a Scottish criminal court if a conspiracy were prosecuted in Scotland) from admitting the information in evidence at a trial. All evidence which is relevant is prima facie admissible in a criminal trial, although the trial judge has a discretion to exclude evidence which, though admissible, has been obtained by unfair means from the accused after commission *f* of the offence (see *R v Sang* [1979] 2 All ER 1222, [1980] AC 402). But it is obvious that a person who has to rely on an exercise of judicial discretion is in a less secure position than one who, by relying on the privilege, can avoid providing the information in the first place. We were referred to some old cases where the court had considered the restrictions on the use of documents which it ordered to be disclosed. In one case the court required an undertaking by the party in whose favour the order was made not to *g* use answers for the purpose of enforcing penalties (see *Jackson v Benson* (1826) 1 Y & J 32, 148 ER 574) and in another case Page Wood V-C said that the court had a right to say to the person who has obtained the production of documents, 'Those documents shall never be used *by you* except under the authority of the Court' (my emphasis) (see *Reynolds v Godlee* (1858) 4 K & J 88 at 92, 70 ER 37 at 39). Such qualified restrictions are clearly of much less value to the party making discovery than the privilege itself would have been. *h*

The main basis of the argument was an implied rule, said to be derived from *Riddick v Thames Board Mills Ltd* [1977] 3 All ER 677, [1977] QB 881, to the effect that evidence which has been disclosed under compulsion in a civil action cannot be used against a person who has disclosed it for the purposes of another civil action or of a criminal prosecution. It was argued that any incriminating information disclosed by a person making discovery or answering interrogatories would enjoy complete protection by *j* reason of that rule, because the information would have been given under compulsion, in respect that refusal to give it would be contempt of court. I would make one preliminary observation on that argument. It seems to me to go much too far. If it is well founded, it means that the established practice whereby judges warn witnesses that they need not answer questions addressed to them in oral examination in court, if the

answers might tend to incriminate them, is unnecessary, because refusal to answer
a would, in the absence of the warning, be contempt of court and any incriminating
evidence having been given under compulsion would not be admissible against them in
criminal proceedings. I approach a proposition leading to that result with some
scepticism. In any event, *Riddick* was concerned only with the question of the use to
which documents recovered on discovery could be put by the party who had obtained
discovery. Lord Denning MR stated the principle in a sentence thus ([1977] 3 All ER 677
b at 688, [1977] QB 881 at 896):

> 'A party who seeks discovery of documents gets it on condition that *he* will make
> use of them only for the purposes of that action and for no other purpose.' (My
> emphasis.)

That statement of principle would have to be extended to include cases such as *Norwich*
c *Pharmacal Co v Customs and Excise Comrs* [1973] 2 All ER 943, [1974] AC 133, where an
order was made for discovery of information for the purpose of its being used in another
action. The principle is, I think, that information is not to be used by the party who gets
discovery for purposes other than that for which production was ordered. But *Riddick*
had nothing to do with the use of information for prosecution in the public interest. On
the contrary, both Lord Denning MR and Stephenson LJ referred with approval to the
d observations of Talbot J in *Distillers Co (Biochemicals) Ltd v Times Newspapers Ltd* [1975] 1
All ER 41 at 48, [1975] QB 613 at 621 recognising that there might be a public interest
in favour of disclosure which would override the public interest in the administration of
justice which goes to preserve the confidentiality of documents disclosed on discovery
(see [1977] 3 All ER 677 at 688, 694, [1977] QB 881 at 896, 901). That is clearly correct.
If a defendant's answers to interrogatories tend to show that he has been guilty of a
e serious offence I cannot think that there would be anything improper in his opponent
reporting the matter to the criminal authorities with a view to prosecution, certainly if
he had first obtained leave from the court which ordered the interrogatories, and
probably without such leave. If that is right the object of the privilege against self-
incrimination would not be completely achieved by relying on any rule which can be
derived from *Riddick*.
f   Moreover, if the incriminating information given on discovery or in answer to
interrogatories were disclosed subsequently in open court in the civil action, it might be
heard and might then be used in a criminal prosecution against the defendant. In an
attempt to meet this difficulty counsel for the appellants submitted that the defendant's
interests could be protected by the courts sitting in camera whenever incriminating
information disclosed on discovery was to be referred to. Such procedure would raise
g considerable practical difficulties and it would also be objectionable on principle. There
are cases where in order that justice may be done the court has to sit in camera (see *Scott*
v Scott [1913] AC 417, [1911–13] All ER Rep 1), but it is important that such cases should
be limited to those where proceedings in private are absolutely necessary in the interests
of justice. If the procedure for which the appellants are contending would lead to more
frequent hearings in camera, as I think it would, then that is an additional argument
h against adopting it. Accordingly I reach the conclusion, with some regret, that the
respondents' objection based on the fear of self-incrimination is well founded and ought
to be upheld.
          An alternative and narrower contention was advanced by counsel for the appellants to
cover the event of his being unsuccessful on the main contention. This narrower
contention raises the point about a charge of conspiracy to which I have already referred.
j It was said that there is a special exception to the privilege against self-incrimination
where the incrimination relates to the offence of conspiracy, because of the wide range
of facts that might be included in that offence. There is some support for this argument
in observations by judges in cases to which we were referred (see *London (Mayor and*
citizens) v Levy (1803) 8 Ves J 398, 32 ER 408, *Attorney General v Conroy* (1838) 2 Jo Ex Ir
791 and *Chadwick v Chadwick* (1852) 22 LJ Ch 329), but in my opinion they do not

provide any clear principle on which an exception to the general rule against compulsory self-incrimination could be based. They do not appear to have been followed in recent years. Accordingly I would not accept the narrower submission on this point.

The order of 2nd July 1979 was criticised as being too wide, particularly in so far as it called on the respondents to disclose the names of all persons who are engaged in the production, distribution and sale of illicit films, and not merely those persons with whom the defendants have had business dealings. In my opinion that criticism was justified and the order ought to have been restricted in that way.

For these reasons I would dismiss the appeal.

LORD RUSSELL OF KILLOWEN. My Lords, for the reasons contained in the speeches of my noble and learned friends Lord Wilberforce and Lord Fraser I concur in the dismissal of this appeal. Inasmuch as the application of the privilege in question can go a long way in this and other analogous fields to deprive the owner of his just rights to the protection of his property I would welcome legislation somewhat on the lines of s 31 of the Theft Act 1968; the aim of such legislation should be to remove the privilege while at the same time preventing the use in criminal proceedings of statements which otherwise have been privileged.

LORD ROSKILL. My Lords, I have had the advantage of reading in draft the speeches of my noble and learned friends Lord Wilberforce and Lord Fraser. I agree with them and for the reasons they give I too would dismiss this appeal.

Appeal dismissed.

Solicitors: *Clifford-Turner* (for the appellants); *Cutner Bond* (for the first four respondents).

Mary Rose Plummer   Barrister.

Henry Moss of London Ltd and another v Customs and Excise Commissioners

COURT OF APPEAL, CIVIL DIVISION
LORD DENNING MR, SHAW AND TEMPLEMAN LJJ
2nd, 3rd DECEMBER 1980

Value added tax – Zero-rating – Exported goods – Proof of export – Conditions imposed by commissioners – Validity – Conditions stating that exported goods to be zero-rated only if specified method of proof complied with – Whether conditions unreasonable – Finance Act 1972, s 12(7) – Value Added Tax (General) Regulations 1975 (SI 1975 No 2204), reg 44(1) – Customs and Excise Notice 703, para 10(b)(c).

Regulations – Validity – Challenging – Appeal or judicial review – Proper method of challenge an application for judicial review – RSC Ord 53.

In the course of carrying on a substantial export trade, the taxpayers made wholesale sales over the counter to overseas trading customers who had no place of business in the United Kingdom. The taxpayers kept a record of such transactions at the time the sales took place, and, in accordance with para 30[a] of Customs and Excise Notice 703, each

---

a Paragraph 30, so far as material, provides: 'Suppliers should arrange for customers who buy goods and take delivery of them in the United Kingdom for ... export, under the arrangements described in [paragraph 10], to obtain proof of export and send it to them in order that the supply may be zero-rated . . .'

customer was given an export form and was instructed to have it stamped at the port of
a departure by the customs officer as proof of export and to return it to the taxpayer by
post. Most customers failed to return the forms. The Customs and Excise Commissioners
assessed the taxpayers to value added tax in respect of the supply of goods to those
customers. The taxpayers appealed to a value added tax tribunal against the assessments,
contending that the supplies fell to be zero-rated under s 12(7)[b] of the Finance Act 1972
and reg 44(1)[c] of the Value Added Tax (General) Regulations 1975, since the goods had
b in fact been exported, and, although the taxpayers had not complied with the
requirements of conditions (b) and (c) of para 10[d] of Notice 703 that the goods be
exported and proof of export obtained within one month of the supply and that the
proof be obtained as required by para 30 and retained for inspection by the commissioners,
the taxpayers had complied, so far as it lay within their power, with the conditions
imposed by the commissioners. The tribunal dismissed the appeal because the taxpayers
c had not complied with conditions (b) and (c), but the judge reversed that decision on the
ground that those conditions were unreasonable and therefore void, since the only
method of proof acceptable under them was virtually impossible for the taxpayers to
secure as it depended on action by customers who were outside their control. The
commissioners appealed to the Court of Appeal.

d **Held** – The appeal would be allowed for the following reasons—
   (1) Since the commissioners were not required by s 12(7) of the 1972 Act to make any
provision for the zero-rating of goods for export, since the object of the conditions
imposed by the commissioners was to ensure that any concession they might make with
respect to the zero-rating of such goods was not abused, since the conditions imposed
were practical and effective, and since (per Templeman LJ) it was not suggested that there
e was any other method whereby abuse could be prevented without intolerable delay,
uncertainty and expense, it could not be said that the conditions imposed by Notice 703
were unreasonable. Moreover, if a taxpayer felt that he was otherwise unlikely to
achieve the co-operation of a customer, he merely needed to require payment by the
customer of the whole or part of the appropriate value added tax as a deposit until the
proof of export was returned (see p 90 *j* to p 91 *h* and p 92 *a e* and *g*, post).
f   (2) On its true construction s 12(7) of the 1972 Act did not impose any limit on the
conditions that the commissioners could impose, provided they were bona fide directed
to defining the concession being granted and to ensuring that it was not abused (see p 90
h j and p 91 *d f* and *j* to p 92 *b* and *f g*, post).
   Per Curiam. The proper way to challenge the validity of regulations and administrative
directions made under the authority of a statute is by way of an application under RSC
g Ord 53 for judicial review (see p 90 *g*, p 91 *f g* and p 92 *a b*, post).

Notes
For the zero-rating of supplies of goods to overseas persons, see 12 Halsbury's Laws (4th
Edn) paras 919, 922.
   As from 17th November 1980 reg 44 of the Value Added Tax (General) Regulations
1975 has been replaced by reg 44 of the Value Added Tax (General) Regulations 1980, SI
h 1980 No 1536.

Case referred to in judgments
Associated Provincial Picture Houses Ltd v Wednesbury Corpn [1947] 2 All ER 680, [1948] 1
   KB 223, [1948] LJR 190, 177 LT 641, 112 JP 55, 45 LGR 635, CA, 45 Digest (Repl) 215,
   189.

j
Cases also cited
Customs and Excise Comrs v C & A Modes [1979] STC 433.

---

b   Section 12(7) is set out at p 88 *f g*, post
c   Regulation 44(1), so far as material, is set out at p 88 *h*, post
d   Paragraph 10, so far as material, is set out at p 89 *a* to *f*, post

Customs and Excise Comrs v Cure & Deeley Ltd [1961] 3 All ER 641, [1962] 1 QB 340.
Customs and Excise Comrs v J H Corbitt (Numismatists) Ltd [1979] STC 504, [1979] 3 WLR *a*
291, CA; *rvsd* [1980] 2 All ER 72, [1980] 2 WLR 653, [1980] STC 231, HL.

Appeal
The taxpayer companies, Henry Moss of London Ltd and The London Mob (Great
Portland Street) Ltd, appealed against the order of Forbes J ([1979] STC 657) setting aside
the decision of a value added tax tribunal sitting in London given on 19th October 1977, *b*
whereby in an appeal against an assessment by the Customs and Excise Commissioners
under s 40 of the Finance Act 1972 the tribunal had held that the supply of certain goods
to their overseas customers did not fall to be zero-rated under s 12(7) of that Act. The
facts are set out in the judgment of Lord Denning MR.

Simon D Brown for the commissioners.   *c*
Janek Matthews for the taxpayer companies.

LORD DENNING MR. This is another case about value added tax. We have before
us two business houses in London which deal in ladies' dresses and blouses. They are
wholesalers. They sell to overseas buyers. Some of their goods are sent direct to shippers
who export them to buyers abroad. But some of them are sold over the counter to *d*
buyers who say they come from overseas and want to take the goods with them. The
question is whether value added tax is payable on goods sold over the counter to overseas
buyers.
    When these ladies' dresses and blouses are sold over the counter in England, for use
here, they are subject to value added tax. They are positive-rated. But goods which are
exported or shipped overseas are exempt from value added tax. They are zero-rated. *e*
This is done by these provisions of the Finance Act 1972. Section 12(6) provides:

> 'A supply of goods is zero-rated by virtue of this subsection if the Commissioners
> are satisfied that the person supplying the goods—(a) has exported them . . .'

That subsection deals with a direct export from the trader here to an overseas
destination. It does not cover sales over the counter. These are dealt with by s 12(7), *f*
which provides:

> 'The Commissioners may by regulations make provision for the zero-rating of
> supplies of goods, or of such goods as may be specified in the regulations, in cases
> where the Commissioners are satisfied that the goods have been or are to be
> exported and such other conditions, if any, as may be specified in the regulations or
> the Commissioners may impose are fulfilled.'   *g*

Then the Value Added Tax (General) Regulations 1975, SI 1975 No 2204, reg 44(1) says:

> '. . . where the Commissioners are satisfied that goods have been supplied to a
> person not resident in the United Kingdom, a trader who has no place of business
> in the United Kingdom, or an overseas authority, and that the goods are to be
> exported, the supply, subject to such conditions as they may impose, shall be zero- *h*
> rated.'

Those provisions show that, although goods are supplied over the counter by the
wholesaler here, they can be zero-rated if the commissioners are satisfied that they are to
be exported overseas.

Paragraph 10 of the Customs and Excise Notice   *j*
    Under those provisions, conditions have been made by the commissioners in their
Customs and Excise Notice 703. Paragraph 10 says:

> 'Supplies of goods in the United Kingdom to overseas traders who have no place
> of business in the United Kingdom . . .'

a Stopping there, that is what happened in this case. Many people come here from the Middle East, Nigeria and so forth. They are the overseas traders. They have not got a place of business here. But they buy from these wholesalers. The paragraph goes on:

'Supplies of goods [to those people] may be zero-rated subject to the following conditions. (a) At the time when the goods are supplied, the supplier must keep a special record of the transaction, supported by evidence that the supply was to a trader having no place of business in the United Kingdom . . .'

b We have illustrations of that. These companies kept books. They set out the transactions in the following way:

'Item	Customer	Country	Invoice No
1 & 2	Seta Bulei	Turkey	011254 & 011446'

c Condition (b) says:

'The goods must be exported and proof of export obtained within one month of the time of supply.'

So, in order that the goods may be zero-rated, they must supply proof of export within a month. Condition (c) deals with the required proof:

d 'Proof of export must be obtained as required by paragraph 30 and retained for inspection by Customs and Excise.'

Before I turn to para 30, I will read condition (d):

'The goods must not be used between the time of supply and exportation, whether for their normal purpose or, for example, for display, exhibition or copying.'

e Then there follows this general provision:

'If any of these conditions are not complied with, or if the goods are not shown to the satisfaction of Customs and Excise to have been exported within the time allowed, the supplier must account for tax on the supply at the appropriate positive rate.'

f It is clear therefore that a wholesaler who supplies goods over the counter must comply with all those conditions; otherwise he is liable to pay value added tax. It is up to the wholesaler to see that the conditions are complied with.

g **Paragraph 30 of the Customs and Excise Notice**
I turn now to para 30 which is mentioned in condition (c). It is long and complicated. So I will summarise it. It lays down the requirements which the wholesaler must satisfy in order for the goods to qualify for zero-rating. The customs officers issue to the wholesalers a number of certificates in blank numbered Form C.273. When an overseas trader buys goods over the counter, and says they are for export, the wholesaler has to fill h in a certificate on Form C.273 in duplicate and hand it to the overseas trader together with the goods, together with a stamped addressed envelope for its return. The certificate is like an invoice. It gives full details of the goods and the prices, saying that they are for export. The overseas trader is told to take that certificate to the airport together with the goods, and present it to the customs officer at the airport. The customs officer will then stamp the certificate and retain the duplicate. He hands the stamped certificate to the j overseas trader, who is told to put it in the envelope and post it in the post box at the airport. When the wholesaler receives back the certificate duly stamped by the customs officer, it is accepted as proof of export such as to satisfy condition (c).
Now that system in para 30 is excellent, so long as the overseas trader does everything that he is told. But the plain fact is that the overseas traders do not do it. As it turns out, 99% of the overseas traders do not return the certificate at all to the wholesalers. They

just put the goods into their baggage and carry them off without troubling with the
certificate at all.

    It is this glaring failure which led the judge to find that the system invoked by para 30
was unreasonable and invalid. To this I will return later.

The course of events

    When the wholesalers made their returns of value added tax, they claimed that the
goods sold over the counter were zero-rated. But, as they could not produce the standard
certificate C.273, the customs authority charged them the full amount of value added
tax.

    The wholesalers then said to the customs authority, 'It is not our fault that the overseas
traders failed to return certificate C.273. We can prove that in some cases the goods were
in fact exported.' This plea was sympathetically received by the customs authorities.
Their officers examined the documents of the wholesalers and were satisfied that in some
cases the goods had in fact been exported. They allowed these to be zero-rated. The
wholesalers felt that many more ought to have been zero-rated. So they appealed to the
tribunal. The tribunal heard a lot of evidence. They held that there were several other
cases in which the goods had in fact been exported; but they felt that, in point of law,
they should not be zero-rated, because condition 10(c) had not been fulfilled. The
certificates C.273 had not been stamped or returned to the wholesalers. So the tribunal
rejected the appeal of the wholesalers.

The appeal

    From the decision of the tribunal, the wholesalers appealed to the High Court. Such
an appeal is permissible on a point of law under the Tribunals and Inquiries Act 1971 and
the Tribunals and Inquiries (Value Added Tax Tribunals) Order 1972, SI 1972 No 1210.
The appeal was heard by Forbes J. He held that the conditions made by the
Commissioners of Customs and Excise were unreasonable. He applied the familiar test
contained in *Associated Provincial Picture Houses Ltd v Wednesbury Corpn* [1947] 2 All ER
680, [1948] 1 KB 223. He held that they were so unreasonable that no reasonable
authority could have formulated them. So he held that condition 10(c) about the
certificates was bad. On that account he allowed the appeal, and said that all goods
should be zero-rated which the traders could prove had in fact been exported, even
though the conditions had not been fulfilled.

    Now there is an appeal to this court from that decision. At the outset I must mention
a point of procedure. Strictly speaking the point taken about the invalidity of the
conditions was not available on an appeal properly so called. It should have been made
by an application under RSC Ord 53 for judicial review. That is the proper way of
challenging the validity of regulations and conditions. But counsel for the Commissioners
of Customs and Excise invited us to deal with the case as if there had been an application
for judicial review. We gladly do so. Because it is important that the commissioners,
and everyone else, should know whether the conditions are valid or not.

    In considering the condition, I would first like to say this. You have to remember that
the ladies' dresses and blouses were sold to individuals over the counter in this country.
To an ordinary person, they would be positive-rated. It is only by way of exemption, if
they are proved to be for export, that they are zero-rated. Section 12(6) and (7) makes it
clear that it is for the commissioners to be 'satisfied' that they have been exported. It
seems to me that the commissioners were entitled to impose very strict conditions for
being satisfied. Unless there were strict conditions, value added tax could be evaded very
easily. A customer could go into a shop and say to the shopkeeper, 'I want these goods
for shipment overseas.' The shopkeeper could then say, 'Very well; you may have them
for shipment overseas. You have given me your word, and that is good enough.' The
customer might never send them overseas at all. In which case, the customer would
have the goods in his hands in this country without paying any value added tax on
them. So it was necessary for the commissioners to devise machinery to prevent people
from getting out of paying value added tax in that way.

It seems to me that the machinery is just about as good as could be devised, to stop
a evasion. All that the shopkeeper has to do is to say to the customer, 'You will not have
to pay value added tax on these goods as long as you go through the necessary machinery.
I will give you an invoice. When you arrive at the airport, hand it to the customs
officer. He will be satisfied that the goods are being shipped. He will give you a
certificate, which you must post to us. Here is a stamped addressed envelope for the
purpose.' So long as the customer is trustworthy, that should be satisfactory. If the
b shopkeeper is doubtful about his customer, he can say, 'I must ask you to pay a deposit
to cover the value added tax. I will be charged value added tax if you do not ship the
goods. If you do ship them, and post the certificate to me, I will return the deposit.'

It seems to me, in the very difficult circumstances of cases of this kind, to prevent the
wholesale evasion of paying value added tax, this is a sensible and reasonable provision
made by the customs authorities to deal with the matter. I do not think these conditions
c were in any way invalid.

This morning counsel for the taxpayer companies took a point which impressed me
for a time. He said that the statute says that the commissioners have to be 'satisfied' that
the goods were exported and such 'other conditions are fulfilled'. Those other conditions,
he said, must be something different from the satisfaction. The satisfaction is not to be
limited by any conditions. So long as evidence is adduced sufficiently to satisfy the
d commissioners, he submitted, that is good enough. If the commissioners were not
satisfied, the supplier can appeal to the tribunal under s 40(1)(c) of the 1972 Act.

Although that argument was attractively put, it seems to me erroneous. The
governing words are in s 12(7): 'The Commissioners may by regulations make provision
for the zero-rating of supplies of goods . . .' Those wide words cover the mode of proof
of satisfaction as well as other conditions.
e In my opinion, the regulations and conditions are perfectly valid. They have been
rightly applied in this case. The tribunal rejected any claim for zero-rating unless the
conditions were complied with. That was the right approach to this case. The
Commissioners of Customs and Excise did allow exemption in a few cases, by way of
concession, because they were satisfied that the goods had been exported. But the strict
law on the matter is that, unless the conditions are complied with, the goods are not zero-
f rated. They are positive-rated.

It seems to me that the tribunal came to a correct decision. So I would be in favour of
reversing the decision of Forbes J and restoring the decision of the tribunal.

SHAW LJ. I agree. The first argument of the taxpayer companies was that it is
unreasonable to require from a trader who seeks exoneration under s 12(7) of the Finance
g Act 1972 from the imposition of value added tax that he should provide a certificate,
since he has no control over his customer and cannot ensure that he will return the
certificate of shipment which is required by the conditions imposed by the
commissioners. It seems to me that amongst commercial people practical steps can be
taken at least to encourage the customer to return the certificate of shipment. He could
be asked to deposit with the trader a sum sufficiently large to persuade him to return the
h document when it has been duly stamped by the customs officer.

I see nothing unreasonable in the condition. That view is reinforced by the fact that
there is no statutory right to exoneration under s 12(7). It is a concession which is made;
and those who make the concession, namely the commissioners, are entitled to impose
whatever conditions are practical. They are not bound to make any concession at all.

As to the second point which counsel for the taxpayer companies argued very
j attractively, I cannot in the end accept that what the condition as to the provision of the
document requires is something which impinges on the question of the satisfaction of
the commissioners that the goods have been exported. It is a condition which stands by
itself. That the commissioners have to be satisfied that the goods have been exported or
are to be exported simply serves to define the area in which the concession is possible at
all. The conditions on which that concession is to be made are a totally different matter,

and they include the requirement in a practical and clear form of some indication that there has indeed been an export. That provision is amply justified in order to make the administration of the concession workable. a

I too would therefore allow the appeal and restore the decision of the tribunal.

TEMPLEMAN LJ. I agree. Two companies resist the payment of value added tax on goods which were exported. Section 12(7) of the Finance Act 1972 empowers, but does not direct, the Commissioners of Customs and Excise by regulations to make provision b for the zero-rating of supplies of goods specified in the regulations where the commissioners are satisfied that the goods have been or are to be exported, and such other conditions as may be specified in the regulations are fulfilled.

The commissioners did make regulations and they have imposed conditions. In the present case the conditions were not fulfilled. The conditions require, inter alia, the taxpayer to produce a certificate of shipment on the duplicate of Form C.273; and no c such certificate was produced.

Forbes J held that this condition was unreasonable because the taxpayer could not comply with the condition without the co-operation of the customer, and experience shows that the customer does not co-operate. The taxpayer could bring pressure to bear on the customer by requiring payment by the customer of the whole or part of the appropriate value added tax as a deposit until the certificate is produced. It is alleged that d such pressure would be ruinous to the export trade of the taxpayer. Whether this be true or not, and I know not, the taxpayer has a choice. He can trust the customer, and pay the tax if his trust is misplaced, or he can take steps to obtain security so as to ensure that the customer performs his part of the operation.

The object of the condition was to ensure that the concession, which the commissioners were not bound to make, but which they did make, and thought proper to make, under e s 12(7), was not abused. No one has suggested any method whereby abuse can be prevented without intolerable delay, uncertainty and expense, save for the method prescribed by the commissioners. That being so, I cannot accept that the condition is unreasonable.

Counsel for the taxpayer companies contended in the alternative that, on the true construction of s 12(7), the commissioners had no power to prescribe conditions which f define the exact method whereby the commissioners are to be satisfied that goods have been exported. In my judgment, s 12(7) does not impose any limit on the conditions which the commissioners may impose, provided that they are bona fide directed to defining the concession which they are granting, and to ensuring that the concession is not abused. In my judgment, the conditions which have been attacked are necessary conditions to prevent abuse of the concession which the commissioners are empowered g to make, and I should be very sorry to come to the conclusion that they are precluded by statute from doing what is necessary to secure that no abuse takes place.

I too would allow the appeal.

Appeal allowed. Leave to appeal to the House of Lords refused.

Solicitors: *Solicitor for the Customs and Excise; Max Bitel, Greene & Co* (for the taxpayer companies).

Sumra Green   Barrister.

a Inland Revenue Comrs v National Federation of Self-Employed and Small Businesses Ltd

HOUSE OF LORDS

LORD WILBERFORCE, LORD DIPLOCK, LORD FRASER OF TULLYBELTON, LORD SCARMAN AND LORD ROSKILL

b 10th, 11th, 12th, 16th MARCH, 9th APRIL 1981

Judicial review – Declaration – Locus standi – Sufficient interest – Revenue introducing special arrangement to prevent tax evasion by certain casual workers in future – Revenue agreeing not to assess and collect tax due from workers in respect of years prior to April 1977 – Taxpayers' association applying for judicial review in form of declaration that Revenue acting unlawfully in c *agreeing not to assess and collect tax due from workers – Whether applicants having 'sufficient interest' to apply for judicial review – RSC Ord 53, r 3(5).*

There was a long standing practice in Fleet Street for casual employees on national newspapers to receive their wages without deduction of tax and to supply fictitious names and addresses when drawing their pay in order to avoid tax. Their true identities d were known only to their unions which operated a closed shop and controlled all casual employment on the newspapers. In order to prevent the evasion of tax by the casual employees, the Revenue made a special arrangement with the employers, the employees and the unions whereby the employees were required to register with the Revenue and submit tax returns for the previous two years (1977–78 and 1978–79) in return for an undertaking by the Revenue that they would not investigate tax evaded prior to 1977. e The applicant, a federation of self-employed persons and small businessmen which claimed to represent a body of taxpayers, applied for judicial review under RSC Ord 53[a] seeking (i) a declaration that the Revenue had acted unlawfully in making the arrangement and (ii) an order of mandamus directing the Revenue to assess and collect tax on the newspaper employees as required by law. The Revenue opposed the application on the ground that the applicant did not have 'a sufficient interest in the f matter' relating to the application as required by Ord 53, r 3(5) for the court to grant it the necessary leave to apply for judicial review. The Divisional Court upheld that contention and refused the applicant leave. The applicant appealed to the Court of Appeal ([1980] 2 All ER 378) which held that, as a preliminary issue and on the assumption that the Revenue had acted unlawfully, the applicant was not a mere busybody but had a genuine grievance and therefore had a sufficient interest for the g purposes of r 3(5). The Revenue appealed, contending that the duties imposed on them by the tax legislation, including in particular the duty of confidentiality as between the Revenue and each individual taxpayer, precluded the possibility of any other taxpayer or group of taxpayers from having any 'sufficient interest' in the performance by the Revenue of their statutory duties.

h   **Held** – The appeal would be allowed for the following reasons—
        (1) The question whether for the purposes of RSC Ord 53, r 3(5) an applicant for judicial review had a 'sufficient interest in the matter to which the application relates' was not, except in simple cases where it was obvious that the applicant had no sufficient interest, a matter to be determined as a jurisdictional or preliminary issue in isolation on the applicant's ex parte application for leave to apply. Instead it was properly to be j   treated as a possible reason for the exercise of the court's discretion to refuse the application when the application itself had been heard and the evidence of both parties presented, since it was necessary to identify 'the matter' to which application related

---

a   Order 53, so far as material, is set out at p 116 b to e, post

before it was possible to decide whether the applicant had a sufficient interest in it (see
p 96 *h* to p 97 *a*, p 101 *b* to *e*, p 105 *g* to *j*, p 106 *e* to *g*, p 107 *d* and *f* to *j*, p 110 *d e*, p 113   *a*
g to *j*, p 115 *g h* and p 121 *f*, post).

(2) Whether an applicant for mandamus had a sufficient interest in the matter to
which the application related, for the purposes of Ord 53, r 3(5) depended on whether the
definition (statutory or otherwise) of the duty alleged to have been breached or not
performed expressly or impliedly gave the applicant the right to complain of the breach
or non-performance. Since the tax legislation, far from expressly or impliedly conferring   *b*
on a taxpayer the right to make proposals about another's tax or to inquire about such
tax, in fact indicated the reverse by reason of the total confidentiality of assessments and
negotiations between individuals and the Revenue, and since on the evidence the
Revenue in making the impugned arrangement were genuinely acting in the care and
management of taxes under the powers entrusted to them, the application made by the
applicant would be dismissed because the applicant did not have a sufficient interest for   *c*
the purposes of r 3(5), or (per Lord Diplock) because it had not been shown that the
Revenue had acted ultra vires or unlawfully in making the arrangement (see p 97 *h j*,
p 98 *j* to p 99 *c*, p 100 *f* to *j*, p 101 *j* to p 102 *b*, p 107 *c d*, p 108 *c d f* to *j*, p 111 *e f*, p 112
b c, p 114 *f* to *h*, p 119 *e* to *g*, p 120 a to *g* and p 121 *a* to *f*, post); *Arsenal Football Club Ltd
v Ende* [1977] 2 All ER 267 distinguished.

Per Lord Wilberforce. As a matter of general principle a taxpayer has no sufficient   *d*
interest in asking the court to investigate the tax affairs of another taxpayer or to
complain that the latter has been underassessed or overassessed; indeed there is a strong
public interest that he should not (see p 99 *a b*, post).

Decision of the Court of Appeal sub nom *R v Inland Revenue Comrs, ex parte National
Federation of Self-Employed and Small Businesses Ltd* [1980] 2 All ER 378 reversed on other
grounds.   *e*

Notes
For declaratory judgments, see 1 Halsbury's Laws (4th Edn) paras 185–187, and for cases
on the subject, see 30 Digest (Reissue) 189–194, 202–234.

Cases referred to in opinions
Allen v Gulf Oil Refining Co Ltd [1981] 1 All ER 353, [1981] 2 WLR 188, HL.
Arsenal Football Club Ltd v Ende [1977] 2 All ER 267, [1979] AC 1, [1977] 2 WLR 974, 141   *f*
     JP 314, 75 LGR 483, HL, Digest (Cont Vol E) 500, *1367a*.
Attorney General (on the relation of McWhirter) v Independent Broadcasting Authority [1973]
     1 All ER 689, [1973] QB 629, [1973] 2 WLR 344, CA, Digest (Cont Vol D) 269, *3785a*.
Burmah Oil Co Ltd v Bank of England (Attorney General intervening) [1979] 3 All ER 700,
     [1980] AC 1090, [1979] 3 WLR 722, HL, Digest (Cont Vol E) 184, *1277a*.
Congreve v Inland Revenue Comrs [1948] 1 All ER 948, 30 Tax Cas 163, [1948] LJR 1229,   *g*
     41 R & IT 319, HL, 28(1) Digest (Reissue) 443, *1590*.
Gouriet v Union of Post Office Workers [1977] 3 All ER 70, [1978] AC 435, [1977] 3 WLR
     300, 141 JP 552, HL, Digest (Cont Vol E) 168, *3776a*.
Income Tax Special Comrs v Linsleys (Established 1894) Ltd [1958] 1 All ER 343, [1958] AC
     569, [1958] 2 WLR 292, 37 Tax Cas 677, 51 R & IT 127, 37 ATC 26, [1958] TR 21, HL,
     28(1) Digest (Reissue) 416, *1515*.   *h*
Latilla v Inland Revenue Comrs [1943] 1 All ER 265, [1943] AC 377, 25 Tax Cas 107, 112
     LJKB 158, 168 LT 411, HL, 28(1) Digest (Reissue) 442, *1587*.
Napier, Ex parte (1852) 18 QB 692, 21 LJQB 332, 17 Jur 380, 19 LTOS 214, 118 ER 261,
     16 Digest (Reissue) 328, *3430*.
Padfield v Minister of Agriculture, Fisheries and Food [1968] 1 All ER 694, [1968] AC 997,
     [1968] 2 WLR, HL, 25 Digest (Reissue) 140, *1148*.   *j*
R v Askew (1768) 4 Burr 2186, 98 ER 139, 13 Digest (Reissue) 255, *2270*.
R v Barker (1762) 3 Burr 1265, 1 Wm Bl 352, 97 ER 823, 16 Digest (Reissue) 321, *3363*.
R v Cotham [1898] 1 QB 802, 67 LJQB 632, sub nom *R v Pilkington etc (Justices) and
     Wallace, ex parte Williams, R v Cotham etc (Justices) and Webb, ex parte Williams* 78 LT
     468, 62 JP 435, DC, 16 Digest (Reissue) 404, *4454*.

R v *Customs and Excise Comrs, ex parte Cooke and Stevenson* [1970] 1 All ER 1068, [1970]
 a   1 WLR 450, DC, 16 Digest (Reissue) 327, 3420.
R v *Greater London Council, ex parte Blackburn* [1976] 3 All ER 184, [1976] 1 WLR 550, 140
    JP 617, 74 LGR 464, CA, Digest (Cont Vol E) 587, *183a*.
R v *Guardians of Lewisham Union* [1897] 1 QB 498, 66 LJQB 403, 76 LT 324, 61 JP 151, DC,
    16 Digest (Reissue) 332, 3468.
R v *Hereford Corpn, ex parte Harrower* [1970] 3 All ER 460, [1978] 1 WLR 1424, 134 JP
 b   665, Digest (Cont Vol C) 646, *41a*.
R v *Income Tax Special Purposes Comrs, ex parte Cape Copper Mining Co Ltd* (1888) 21 QBD
    313, [1886–90] All ER Rep 1139, 2 Tax Cas 332, 57 LJQB 513, 59 LT 455, 53 JP 84,
    CA, 16 Digest (Reissue) 349, 3656.
R v *Lords Comrs of the Treasury* (1872) LR 7 QB 387, 41 LJQB 178, 26 LT 64, 36 JP 661,
    12 Cox CC 277, DC, 16 Digest (Reissue) 346, 3635.
 c R v *Northumberland Compensation Appeal Tribunal, ex parte Shaw* [1951] 1 All ER 268,
    [1951] 1 KB 711, 115 JP 79, 49 LGR 123, DC; *affd* [1952] 1 All ER 122, [1952] 1 KB
    388, 116 JP 54, 50 LGR 193, 2 P & CR 361, CA, 16 Digest (Reissue) 425, 4686.
R v *Russell, ex parte Beaverbrook Newspapers Ltd* [1968] 3 All ER 695, [1969] 1 QB 342,
    [1968] 3 WLR 999, 133 JP 27, DC, 14(1) Digest (Reissue) 222, 1603.
R v *Thames Magistrates' Court, ex parte Greenbaum* (1957) 55 LGR 129, CA, 26 Digest
 d   (Repl) 482, 1692.
Stott, Ex parte [1916] 1 KB 7, 85 LJKB 502, 114 LT 234, 80 JP 169, DC, 45 Digest (Repl)
    214, 179.
Vestey v Inland Revenue Comrs [1977] 3 All ER 1073, [1979] Ch 177, [1978] 2 WLR 136,
    [1977] STC 414; *varied* [1979] 3 All ER 976, [1980] AC 1148, [1980] STC 10, HL,
    Digest (Cont Vol E) 307, *1584a*.
 e *Vestey v Inland Revenue Comrs (No 2)* [1979] 2 All ER 225, [1979] Ch 198, [1978] 3 WLR
    693, [1978] STC 567; *varied* [1979] 3 All ER 976, [1980] AC 1148, [1980] STC 10, HL,
    Digest (Cont Vol E) 307, *1584a*.

Interlocutory appeal
 The Crown appealed against the decision of the Court of Appeal (Lord Denning MR and
 f Ackner LJ, Lawton LJ dissenting) ([1980] 2 All ER 378, [1980] QB 407, [1980] STC 261),
 allowing an appeal by the National Federation of Self-Employed and Small Businesses
 Ltd ('the federation') against the refusal by the Divisional Court of the Queen's Bench
 Division (Lord Widgery CJ and Griffiths J) ([1980] 2 All ER 378, [1980] STC 261) to grant
 leave to the federation to apply for judicial review in the following form: (i) a declaration
 that the Board of Inland Revenue acted unlawfully in granting to the casual workers in
 g Fleet Street an 'amnesty' in relation to their evasion of tax prior to 6th April 1977 and (ii)
 an order of mandamus directed to the Board to assess and collect income tax from the
 casual workers according to the law. The facts are set out in the opinion of Lord
 Wilberforce.

 The Lord Advocate (*Rt Hon Lord Mackay of Clashfern QC*), *Patrick Medd QC* and *Brian*
 h   *Davenport QC* for the Crown.
 R J Harvey QC and *Stephen Silman* for the federation.

 Their Lordships took time for consideration.

 9th April. The following opinions were delivered.
 j

 LORD WILBERFORCE. My Lords, the respondent federation, whose name
 sufficiently describes its nature, is asking for an order on the Commissioners of Inland
 Revenue to assess and collect arrears of income said to be due by a number of people
 compendiously described as 'Fleet Street casuals'. These are workers in the printing

industry who, under a practice sanctioned apparently by their unions and their employers, have for some years been engaged in a process of depriving the Inland *a* Revenue of tax due in respect of their casual earnings. This they appear to have done by filling in false or imaginary names on the call slips presented on collecting their pay. The sums involved were very considerable. The Inland Revenue, having become aware of this, made an arrangement, which I explain in more detail later, under which these workers are to register in respect of their casual employment, so that in the future tax can be collected in the normal way. Further, arrears of tax from 1977–78 are to be paid and *b* current investigations are to proceed, but investigations as to tax lost in earlier years are not to be made. This arrangement, described inaccurately as an 'amnesty', the federation wishes to attack. It asserts that the Revenue acted unlawfully in not pursuing the claim for the full amount of tax due. It claims that the Board exceeded its powers in granting the 'amnesty'; alternatively that, if it had power to grant it, reasons should be given and that those given cannot be sustained; that the Board took into account matters to which *c* it was not entitled to have regard; that the Board ought to act fairly as between taxpayers and has not done so; and that the Board is under a duty to see that income tax is duly assessed, charged and collected.

The proceedings have been brought by the procedure now called 'judicial review'. There are two claims: the first for a declaration that the Board of Inland Revenue 'acted unlawfully' in granting an amnesty to the casual workers; the second for an order of *d* mandamus to assess and collect income tax from the casual workers according to the law. These two claims rest, for present purposes, on the same basis, since a declaration is merely an alternative kind of relief which can only be given if, apart from convenience, the case would have been one for mandamus.

In RSC Ord 53, dating from 1977, which introduced the simplified remedies by way of judicial review it is laid down in r 3(5) that: *e*

'The Court shall not grant leave unless it considers that the applicant has a sufficient interest in the matter to which the application relates.'

The issue which comes before us is presented as one related solely to the question whether the federation has the 'sufficient interest' required.

In the Divisional Court, when the motion for judicial review came before it, the point *f* as to locus standi was treated as a preliminary point. 'Before we embark on the case itself,' said Lord Widgery CJ, 'we have to decide whether the federation has power to bring it at all' (see [1980] 2 All ER 378 at 382, [1980] STC 261 at 265). After hearing argument, the court decided that it had not. The matter went to the Court of Appeal ([1980] 2 All ER 378, [1980] QB 407, [1980] STC 261), and again argument was concentrated on the preliminary point, though it, and the judgments, did range over the *g* merits. The Court of Appeal by majority reversed the Divisional Court and made a declaration that 'the [federation] have a sufficient interest to apply for Judicial Review'. On final appeal to this House, the two sides concurred in stating that the only ground for decision was whether the federation has such sufficient interest.

I think that it is unfortunate that this course has been taken. There may be simple cases in which it can be seen at the earliest stage that the person applying for judicial *h* review has no interest at all, or no sufficient interest to support the application; then it would be quite correct at the threshold to refuse him leave to apply. The right to do so is an important safeguard against the courts being flooded and public bodies harassed by irresponsible applications. But in other cases this will not be so. In these it will be necessary to consider the powers or the duties in law of those against whom the relief is asked, the position of the applicant in relation to those powers or duties, and the breach *j* of those said to have been committed. In other words, the question of sufficient interest cannot, in such cases, be considered in the abstract, or as an isolated point: it must be taken together with the legal and factual context. The rule requires sufficient interest *in the matter to which the application relates*. This, in the present case, necessarily involves the

whole question of the duties of the Inland Revenue and the breaches or failure of those
duties of which the federation complains.

a

Before proceeding to consideration of these matters, something more needs to be said
about the threshold requirement of 'sufficient interest'. The courts in exercising the
power to grant prerogative writs, or since 1938 prerogative orders, have always reserved
the right to be satisfied that the applicant had some genuine locus standi to appear before
it. This they expressed in different ways. Sometimes it was said, usually in relation to
certiorari, that the applicant must be a person aggrieved, or have a particular grievance

b

(see *R v Thames Magistrates' Court, ex parte Greenbaum* (1957) 55 LGR 129); usually in
relation to mandamus, that he must have a specific legal right (see *R v Guardians of
Lewisham Union* [1897] 1 QB 498, *R v Russell* [1968] 3 All ER 695, [1969] 1 QB 342);
sometimes that he must have a sufficient interest (see *R v Cotham* [1898] 1 QB 802
(mandamus), *Ex parte Stott* [1916] 1 KB 7 (certiorari)). By 1977 when RSC Ord 53 was
introduced the courts, guided by Lord Parker CJ, in cases where mandamus was sought,

c

were moving away from the *Lewisham Union* test of specific legal right to one of sufficient
interest.

In *R v Russell* Lord Parker CJ had tentatively adhered to the test of legal specific right,
but in *R v Customs and Excise Comrs, ex parte Cooke and Stevenson* [1970] 1 All ER 1068,
[1970] 1 WLR 450 he had moved to sufficient interest. Shortly afterward the new rule

d

(RSC Ord 53, r 3) was drafted with these words.

RSC Ord 53 was, it is well known, introduced to simplify the procedure of applying
for the relief formerly given by prerogative writ or order, so the old technical rules no
longer apply. So far as the substantive law is concerned, this remained unchanged; the
Administration of Justice (Miscellaneous Provisions) Act 1938 preserved the jurisdiction
existing before the Act, and the same preservation is contemplated by legislation now

e

pending. The Order, furthermore, did not remove the requirement to show locus
standi. On the contrary, in r 3 it stated this in the form of a threshold requirement to be
found by the court. For all cases the test is expressed as one of sufficient interest in the
matter to which the application relates. As to this I would state two negative
propositions. First, it does not remove the whole, and vitally important, question of
locus standi into the realm of pure discretion. The matter is one for decision, a mixed

f

decision of fact and law, which the court must decide on legal principles. Second, the
fact that the same words are used to cover all the forms of remedy allowed by the rule
does not mean that the test is the same in all cases. When Lord Parker CJ said that in
cases of mandamus 'the test may well be stricter' (sc than in certiorari) (see *R v Russell*
[1968] 3 All ER 695 at 697, [1969] 1 QB 342 at 348 and in *R v Customs and Excise Comrs,
ex parte Cooke and Stevenson* [1970] 1 All ER 1068 at 1072, [1970] 1 WLR 450 at 455 'on

g

a very strict basis'), he was not stating a technical rule, which can now be discarded, but
a rule of common sense, reflecting the different character of the relief asked for. It would
seem obvious enough that the interest of a person seeking to compel an authority to carry
out a duty is different from that of a person complaining that a judicial or administrative
body has, to his detriment, exceeded its powers. Whether one calls for a stricter rule than
the other may be a linguistic point; they are certainly different and we should be unwise

h

in our enthusiasm for liberation from procedural fetters to discard reasoned authorities
which illustrate this. It is hardly necessary to add that recognition of the value of guiding
authorities does not mean that the process of judicial review must stand still.

In the present case we are in the area of mandamus, an alleged failure to perform a
duty. It was submitted by the Lord Advocate that in such cases we should be guided by
the definition of the duty, in this case statutory, and inquire whether expressly, or by

j

implication, this definition indicates, or the contrary, that the complaining applicant is
within the scope or ambit of the duty. I think that this is at least a good working rule
though perhaps not an exhaustive one.

The Commissioners of Inland Revenue are a statutory body. Their duties are,
relevantly, defined in the Inland Revenue Regulation Act 1890 and the Taxes

Management Act 1970. Section 1 of the 1890 Act authorises the appointment of commissioners 'for the collection and management of inland revenue' and confers on the *a* commissioners 'all necessary powers for carrying into execution every Act of Parliament relating to inland revenue'. By s 13 the commissioners must 'collect and cause to be collected every part of inland revenue and all money under their care and management and keep distinct accounts thereof'.

The 1970 Act provides (s 1) that 'Income tax ... shall be under the care and management of the Commissioners'. This Act contains the very wide powers of the *b* Board and of inspectors of taxes to make assessments on persons designated by Parliament as liable to pay income tax. With regard to casual employment, there is a procedure laid down by statutory instrument, the Income Tax (Employment) Regulations 1973, SI 1973 No 334, reg 50, by which inspectors of taxes may proceed by way of direct assessment or in accordance with any special arrangements which the Commissioners of Inland Revenue may make for the collection of the tax. As I shall show later it was a *c* 'special arrangement' that the commissioners set out to make in the present case.

From this summary analysis it is clear that the Commissioners of Inland Revenue are not immune from the process of judicial review. They are an administrative body with statutory duties, which the courts, in principle, can supervise. They have indeed done so: see *R v Income Tax Special Comrs* (1888) 21 QB 313, [1886–90] All ER Rep 1139 (mandamus) and cf *Income Tax Special Comrs v Linsleys (Established 1894) Ltd* [1958] 1 All *d* ER 343, [1958] AC 569, where it was not doubted that a mandamus could be issued if the facts had been right. It must follow from these cases and from principle that a taxpayer would not be excluded from seeking judicial review if he could show that the Revenue had either failed in their statutory duty toward him or had been guilty of some action which was an abuse of their powers or outside their powers altogether. Such a collateral attack, as contrasted with a direct appeal on law to the courts, would no doubt be rare, but *e* the possibility certainly exists.

The position of other taxpayers, other than the taxpayers whose assessment is in question, and their right to challenge the Revenue's assessment or non-assessment of that taxpayer, must be judged according to whether, consistently with the legislation, they can be considered as having sufficient interest to complain of what has been done or omitted. I proceed thereto to examine the Revenue's duties in that light. *f*

These duties are expressed in very general terms and it is necessary to take account also of the framework of the income tax legislation. This establishes that the commissioners must assess each individual taxpayer in relation to his circumstances. Such assessments and all information regarding taxpayers' affairs are strictly confidential. There is no list or record of assessments which can be inspected by other taxpayers. Nor is there any common fund of the produce of income tax in which income taxpayers as a whole can *g* be said to have any interest. The produce of income tax, together with that of other inland revenue taxes, is paid into the Consolidated Fund which is at the disposal of Parliament for any purposes that Parliament thinks fit.

The position of taxpayers is therefore very different from that of ratepayers. As explained in *Arsenal Football Club Ltd v Ende* [1977] 2 All ER 267, [1979] AC 1, the amount of rates assessed on ratepayers is ascertainable by the public through the valuation *h* list. The produce of rates goes into a common fund applicable for the benefit of the ratepayers. Thus any ratepayer has an interest, direct and sufficient, in the rates levied on other ratepayers; for this reason, his right as a 'person aggrieved' to challenge assessments on them has long been recognised and is so now in the General Rate Act 1967, s 69. This right was given effect to in *Ende's* case.

The structure of the legislation relating to income tax, on the other hand, makes clear *j* that no corresponding right is intended to be conferred on taxpayers. Not only is there no express or implied provision in the legislation on which such a right could be claimed, but to allow it would be subversive of the whole system, which involves that the commissioners' duties are to the Crown, and that matters relating to income tax are between the commissioners and the taxpayer concerned. No other person is given any

right to make proposals about the tax payable by any individual; he cannot even inquire
a as to such tax. The total confidentiality of assessments and of negotiations between
individuals and the Revenue is a vital element in the working of the system. As a matter
of general principle I would hold that one taxpayer has no sufficient interest in asking the
court to investigate the tax affairs of another taxpayer or to complain that the latter has
been underassessed or overassessed; indeed there is a strong public interest that he should
not. And this principle applies equally to groups of taxpayers: an aggregate of individuals
b each of whom has no interest cannot of itself have an interest.

That a case can never arise in which the acts or abstentions of the Revenue can be
brought before the court I am certainly not prepared to assert, nor that, in a case of
sufficient gravity, the court might not be able to hold that another taxpayer or other
taxpayers could challenge them. Whether this situation has been reached or not must
depend on an examination, on evidence, of what breach of duty or illegality is alleged.
c On this, and relating it to the position of the complainant, the court has to make its
decision. I find it necessary to state the circumstances in some detail.

The evidence consists of affidavits from Mr L F Payne, vice-president of the federation,
Sir William Pile, chairman of the Board of Inland Revenue, and Mr J A P Hoadley,
principal inspector of taxes, in charge of the Inland Revenue Special Offices. These
together present a picture of clarity. It is not often that a court on summary proceedings
d has so much and so relevant information.

Mr Payne's affidavit sets out very fairly the facts as known to him regarding the
employment of the 'casuals' and the Revenue's actions with regard to the income tax they
ought to have paid. He also gives a number of examples of what he claims to be the very
different attitude, viz one of strictness and even severity, taken by the Revenue as regards
persons represented by the federation. I think that these examples, while explaining the
e indignation of the federation and its members as regards the state of affairs in Fleet Street,
cannot be judged on their merits on the material we have. Even if there were not
another side to the taxpayers' presentation (and the Revenue suggest there may be) it is
not suggested that, and is impossible to see how, any success in these proceedings would
in any tangible way profit, or affect, the persons concerned or others like them.

On the other hand, as I suggested in *Ende's* case, a sense of fairness as between one
f taxpayer or group of taxpayers and another is an important objective, so that a sense of
unfairness may be the beginning of a recognisable grievance. I say the beginning,
because the income tax legislation contains a large number of anomalies which are
naturally not thought to be fair by those disadvantaged.

In this context Mr Payne also refers to the approach of the Revenue adopted in relation
to self-employed workers in the construction industry (commonly known as 'the lump'),
g who were found to be evading tax on a large scale. In this case the Revenue persuaded
Parliament to enact legislation of a stringent character. But I think that this has no
relevance for the present issue. Finally, Mr Payne agrees that the new arrangements
made by the Inland Revenue may be effective in securing that tax will be paid in the
future on casual earnings. But he complains of the 'amnesty' granted as regards arrears
before 1977.

h Sir William Pile gives a general description of the scope and nature of the duties of the
Inland Revenue with regard to the assessment and collection of taxes. He draws attention
to the large number of potential taxpayers (about 25 million) the huge sums involved,
and the limitations on the Board's manpower. His evidence is that it is impossible for the
Board to collect all the tax that is due, and that decisions have to be taken by way of 'care
and management' of the taxes to collect as much as is practicable, by cost-effective
j methods. He denies any discrimination as between self-employed and other taxpayers.
Such differences as exist are ascribable to difference of law and of fact. The cases cited by
Mr Payne are in his opinion contentious. As regard the 'casuals', the Board approved the
proposals made by Mr Hoadley and considered that it had good and sufficient justification
for doing so. This was clearly a 'management' decision.

Mr Hoadley explains the way in which the special offices came to investigate the problem of casual workers in Fleet Street and the difficulties of discovering the facts. There is, and I think Mr Payne agrees, no way in which the names and addresses of the *a* defaulting 'casuals' could be obtained, unless their unions were willing to reveal them. Estimating that about £1m of tax a year were being lost, he decided that action was needed to stop this loss for the future. After reflection he considered that the best way to do so was by way of a special arrangement. In order to make such an arrangement effective, the co-operation of the employers, the workers and the unions was essential. For this purpose he had lengthy discussions in the summer of 1978 with the employers *b* and the three unions involved, and as a result introduced a special arrangement in March 1979. This provided a method which would ensure that for the future tax would either be deducted at source or would be properly assessed. As regards the past, Mr Hoadley made it clear to the union representative that, if the arrangement were generally accepted, then if a casual worker registered with the inspector before 6th April 1979 and co-operated fully and promptly in settling his tax affairs (including the payment of any *c* outstanding tax) investigation into tax lost would not be carried out for years before 1977–78, ie before 6th April 1977. Investigations into incorrect returns would be unaffected. As I have indicated, to call this an 'amnesty' is liable to mislead.

Mr Hoadley expressed the conviction that an attempt to collect the whole amount due from hostile workers whose identity was unknown, for a period more than two years in the past, would have been unlikely to produce any substantial sums of money and would *d* have delayed or even frustrated the new arrangement. He denied that he made the arrangement under pressure from the unions; he made his own decision and told them of it.

In the Court of Appeal a good deal was made of the possibility of industrial action. But for this element, I think that Lord Denning MR would have come to the conclusion that the federation had no sufficient interest in the affairs of the 'casuals'. But he was *e* impressed with the possibility that the Revenue had taken their decision because of threats of industrial action, and consequent pressure by employers. After carefully examining the evidence, I reach the conclusion that it does not support the argument. It was dealt with quite frankly by Mr Hoadley. He knew, of course, that the newspaper industry is vulnerable to strikes. He said that the possibility of industrial action would not prevent him from seeking a settlement. But he would not get one without co- *f* operation from the casuals and the unions, and if the latter did not co-operate neither would the employers. I think that all this was part of the process of obtaining the arrangement and that it cannot be said that these very real considerations were outside what a person seeking, in the best interest of the Revenue, to obtain an agreement could properly take into account.

Finally, Mr Hoadley dealt very fully and adequately with all Mr Payne's other points. *g* His affidavit is very full and candid and I have only summarised the main points.

On the evidence as a whole, I fail to see how any court considering it as such and not confining its attention to an abstract question of locus standi could avoid reaching the conclusion that the Inland Revenue, through Mr Hoadley, were acting in this matter genuinely in the care and management of the taxes, under the powers entrusted to them. This has no resemblance to any kind of case where the court ought, at the instance *h* of a taxpayer, to intervene. To do so would involve permitting a taxpayer or a group of taxpayers to call in question the exercise of management powers and involve the court itself in a management exercise. Judicial review under any of its headings does not extend into this area. Finally, if as I think, the case against the Revenue does not, on the evidence, leave the ground, no court, in my opinion, would consider ordering discovery against the Revenue in the hope of eliciting some impropriety. Looking at the matter *j* as a whole, I am of opinion that the Divisional Court, while justified on the ex parte application in granting leave, ought, having regard to the nature of 'the matter' raised, to have held that the federation had shown no sufficient interest in that matter to justify its application for relief. I would therefore allow the appeal and order that the originating motion be dismissed.

LORD DIPLOCK. My Lords, this appeal provides the House with its first occasion to
a consider what changes, if any, to public law in England have been made by the new RSC
Ord 53, which came into effect on 11th January 1978 and provides for applications for
judicial review of the legality of action or inaction by persons or bodies exercising
governmental powers.

It is, in my view, very much to be regretted that a case of such importance to the
development of English public law under this new procedure should have come before
b this House in the form that it does as a result of what my noble and learned friend Lord
Wilberforce has described as the unfortunate course that was taken in the courts below
when, leave to apply for judicial review having been previously granted ex parte, the
application itself came on for hearing. This has had the result of deflecting the Divisional
Court and the Court of Appeal from giving consideration to the questions (1) what was
the public duty of the Board of Inland Revenue of which it was alleged to be in breach,
c and (2) what was the nature of the breaches that were relied on by the federation.
Because of this, the judgment of the Court of Appeal against which appeal to your
Lordships' House is brought takes the form of an interlocutory judgment declaring that
the federation 'have a sufficient interest to apply for Judicial Review herein'.

As Lord Wilberforce has pointed out, these two omitted questions need to be answered
in the instant case before it is possible to say whether the federation has 'a sufficient
d interest in the matter to which the application relates', since, until they are answered,
that matter cannot be identified. This is likely also to be the case in most applications for
judicial review that are not on the face of them frivolous or vexatious. Your Lordships
have accordingly heard full argument on both these questions.

As respects the statutory powers and duties of the Board of Inland Revenue, these are
described and dealt with in several of your Lordships' speeches. It would be wearisome
e if I were to repeat what already has been, and later will be, better said by others. All that
I need say here is that the Board are charged by statute with the care, management and
collection on behalf of the Crown of income tax, corporation tax and capital gains tax.
In the exercise of these functions the Board have a wide managerial discretion as to the
best means of obtaining for the national exchequer from the taxes committed to their
charge the highest net return that is practicable having regard to the staff available to
f them and the cost of collection. The Board and the inspectors and collectors who act
under their directions are under a statutory duty of confidentiality with respect to
information about individual taxpayers' affairs that has been obtained in the course of
their duties in making assessments and collecting the taxes; and this imposes a limitation
on their managerial discretion. I do not doubt, however, and I do not understand any of
your Lordships to doubt, that if it were established that the Board were proposing to
g exercise or to refrain from exercising their powers not for reasons of 'good management'
but for some extraneous or ulterior reason that action or inaction of the Board would be
ultra vires and would be a proper matter for judicial review if it were brought to the
attention of the court by an applicant with 'a sufficient interest' in having the Board
compelled to observe the law.

As respects what were alleged to be breaches of their statutory duty by the Board on
h which the federation relied, the evidence as to the way in which the Board and their
inspector in charge of the negotiations dealt with the problem of the Fleet Street casuals
and as to the reasons why they acted as they did, is set out in all necessary detail in Lord
Wilberforce's speech. All this evidence was before the Divisional Court and the Court of
Appeal had they chosen to look at it. It is enough for me to say that I agree with my
noble and learned friend that no court considering this evidence could avoid reaching the
j conclusion that the Board and their inspector were acting solely for 'good management'
reasons and in the lawful exercise of the discretion which the statutes confer on them.

For my part, I should prefer to allow the appeal and dismiss the federation's application
under Ord 53 not on the specific ground of no sufficient interest but on the more general
ground that it has not been shown that in the matter of which complaint was made, the
treatment of the tax liabilities of the Fleet Street casuals, the Board did anything that was

ultra vires or unlawful. They acted in the bona fide exercise of the wide managerial
discretion conferred on them by statute. Since judicial review is available only as a   *a*
remedy for conduct of a public officer or authority which is ultra vires or unlawful, but
not for acts done lawfully in the exercise of an administrative discretion which are
complained of only as being unfair or unwise, there is a sense in which it may be said that
the federation had not a sufficient interest in the matter to which its application related;
but this is not a helpful statement: it would be equally true of anyone, including the
Attorney General, who sought to complain.   *b*

It would be very much to be regretted if, in consequence of the unfortunate form in
which the instant appeal came before this House, anything that is said by your Lordships
today were to be understood as suggesting that the new Ord 53, r 3(5) has the effect of
reviving any of those technical rules of locus standi to obtain the various forms of
prerogative writs that were applied by the judges up to and during the first half of the
present century, but which have been so greatly liberalised by judicial decision over the *c*
last thirty years. It is for this reason that I venture to state how, in my view, Ord 53
would have applied to the federation's application if, instead of its locus standi being
considered in isolation, the proper course had been followed at the hearing of the
application in the Divisional Court.

My Lords, Ord 53 was made by the Rule Committee under the powers conferred on
them by s 99 of the Supreme Court of Judicature (Consolidation) Act 1925 and s 10 of the *d*
Administration of Justice (Miscellaneous Provisions) Act 1938. Rules of court made
under these sections are concerned with procedure and practice only; they cannot alter
substantive law, nor can they extend the jurisdiction of the High Court. But in the field
of public law where the court has a discretion whether or not to make an order
preventing conduct by a public officer or authority that has been shown to be ultra vires
or unlawful, the question of what qualifications an applicant must show before the court   *e*
will entertain his application for a particular kind of order against a particular class of
public officer or authority seems to me to be one of practice rather than of jurisdiction.
It has been consistently so treated by the courts over the past thirty years.

Before the new Ord 53 was substituted for its predecessor, the private citizen who
sought redress against a person or authority for acting unlawfully or ultra vires in the
purported exercise of statutory powers had to choose from a number of different   *f*
procedures that which was the most appropriate to furnish him the redress that he
sought. The major differences in procedure, including locus standi to apply for the relief
sought, were between the remedies by way of declaration or injunction obtainable by a
civil action brought to enforce public law and the remedies by way of the prerogative
orders of mandamus, prohibition or certiorari which lay in public law alone; but even
between the three public law remedies there were minor procedural differences, and the   *g*
locus standi to apply for them was not quite the same for each, although the divergencies
were in process of diminishing.

Your Lordships can take judicial notice of the fact that the main purpose of the new
Ord 53 was to sweep away these procedural differences including, in particular,
differences as to locus standi, to substitute for them a single simplified procedure for
obtaining all forms of relief, and to leave to the court a wide discretion as to what   *h*
interlocutory directions, including orders for discovery, were appropriate to the particular
case.

In the instant case, in the Divisional Court and the Court of Appeal alike, the argument
for the Board was put on the footing that notwithstanding this unification of procedure
for obtaining the various remedies available in public law, including those which had
been available in private law only, the new Ord 53 had left unchanged the basis on which *j*
an applicant was recognised as having locus standi to apply for each individual form of
relief sought. In the instant case these were a declaration and an order of mandamus.

As respects the claim for a declaration considerable reliance was placed on the recent
decision of this House in *Gouriet v Union of Post Office Workers* [1977] 3 All ER 70, [1978]
AC 435, which held that a private citizen, except as relator in an action brought by the

Attorney General, has no locus standi in private law as plaintiff in a civil action to obtain
a either an injunction to restrain another private citizen (in casu a trade union) from
committing a public wrong by breaking the criminal law or a declaration that his
conduct is unlawful unless the plaintiff can show that some legal or equitable right of his
own has been infringed or that he will sustain some special damage over and above that
suffered by the general public. This decision is, in my view, irrelevant to any question
that your Lordships have to decide today. The defendant trade union in deciding to
b instruct its members to take unlawful industrial action was not exercising any
governmental powers; it was acting as a private citizen and could only be sued as such in
a civil action under private law. It was not amenable to any remedy in public law. Lord
Wilberforce and I were at pains to draw this distinction.

In contrast to this, judicial review is a remedy that lies exclusively in public law. In
my view the language of r 1(2) and (3) of the new Ord 53 shows an intention that on an
c application for judicial review the court should have jurisdiction to grant a declaration
or an injunction as an alternative to making one of the prerogative orders, whenever in
its discretion it thinks that it is just and convenient to do so, and that this jurisdiction
should be exercisable in any case in which the applicant would previously have had locus
standi to apply for any of the prerogative orders. The matters specified in sub-paras (*a*)
and (*b*) of r 1(2) as matters to which the court must have regard make this plain. So if,
d before the new Ord 53 came into force, the court would have had jurisdiction to grant
to the applicant any of the prerogative orders it may now grant him a declaration or
injunction instead, notwithstanding that the applicant would have no locus standi to
claim the declaration or injunction under private law in a civil action against the
respondent to the application because he could not show that any legal right of his own
was threatened or infringed.

e So I turn first to consider what constituted locus standi to apply for one or other of the
prerogative orders immediately before the new Ord 53 came into force.

In the earlier cases a more restrictive rule for locus standi was applied to applications
for the writ of mandamus than for writs of prohibition or certiorari; and since mandamus
was the prerogative order sought by the federation in the instant case your Lordships
have been referred to many of them, reliance being placed in particular on the brief
f extempore judgment of Wright J delivered at the end of the last century in *R v Guardians
of Lewisham Union* [1897] 1 QB 498. He there said (at 500) that an applicant for a
mandamus 'must first of all shew that he has a legal specific right to ask for the
interference of the Court'. The law has not stood still since 1897. By 1977 this was no
longer correct, and I have no hesitation in saying that it is inconceivable that mandamus
would have been refused in the circumstances of that case if it had come before a
g Divisional Court at any time during the last twenty years.

The rules as to 'standing' for the purpose of applying for prerogative orders, like most
of English public law, are not to be found in any statute. They were made by judges; by
judges they can be changed, and so they have been over the years to meet the need to
preserve the integrity of the rule of law despite changes in the social structure, methods
of government and the extent to which the activities of private citizens are controlled by
h governmental authorities that have been taking place continuously, sometimes slowly,
sometimes swiftly, since the rules were originally propounded. Those changes have
been particularly rapid since the 1939–45 war. Any judicial statements on matters of
public law if made before 1950 are likely to be a misleading guide to what the law is
today.

In 1951 the decision of the Divisional Court in *R v Northumberland Compensation Appeal*
j *Tribunal* [1951] 1 All ER 268, [1951] 1 QB 711 resurrected error of law on the face of the
record as a ground for granting certiorari. Parliament by the Tribunals and Inquiries Act
1958 followed this up by requiring reasons to be given for many administrative decisions
that had previously been cloaked in silence; and the years that followed between then
and 1977 witnessed a dramatic liberalisation of access to the courts for the purpose of
obtaining prerogative orders against persons and authorities exercising governmental

powers. This involved a virtual abandonment of the former restrictive rules as to the
locus standi of persons seeking such orders. The process of liberalisation of access to the *a*
courts and the progressive discarding of technical limitations on locus standi is too well
known to call for detailed citation of the cases by which it may be demonstrated. They
are referred to and discussed in Professor H W R Wade's Administrative Law (4th Edn,
1977, pp 543–546 (prohibition and certiorari) and pp 610–612 (mandamus)). The
author points out there that, although lip service continued to be paid to a difference in
standing required to entitle an applicant to mandamus on the one hand and prohibition *b*
or certiorari on the other, in practice the courts found some way of treating the locus
standi for all three remedies as being the same. A striking example of this is to be found
in *R v Hereford Corpn, ex parte Harrower* [1970] 3 All ER 460, [1970] 1 WLR 1424, where
the applicants were treated as having locus standi in their capacity as ratepayers though
their real interest in the matter was as electrical contractors only. For my part I need only
refer to *R v Greater London Council, ex parte Blackburn* [1976] 3 All ER 184, [1976] 1 WLR *c*
550. In that case Mr Blackburn, who lived in London with his wife who was a ratepayer,
applied successfully for an order of prohibition against the council to stop them acting in
breach of their statutory duty to prevent the exhibition of pornographic films within
their administrative area. Mrs Blackburn was also a party to the application. Lord
Denning MR and Stephenson LJ were of opinion that both Mr and Mrs Blackburn had
locus standi to make the application: Mr Blackburn because he lived within the *d*
administrative area of the council and had children who might be harmed by seeing
pornographic films and Mrs Blackburn not only as a parent but also on the additional
ground that she was a ratepayer. Bridge LJ relied only on Mrs Blackburn's status as a
ratepayer, a class of persons to whom for historical reasons the Court of King's Bench
afforded generous access to control ultra vires activities of the public bodies to whose
expenses they contributed. But now that local government franchise is not limited to *e*
ratepayers, this distinction between the two applicants strikes me as carrying technicality
to the limits of absurdity having regard to the subject matter of the application in the
Blackburn case. I agree in substance with what Lord Denning MR there said, though in
language more eloquent than it would be my normal style to use ([1976] 3 All ER 184
at 192, [1976] 1 WLR 550 at 559):

> 'I regard it as a matter of high constitutional principle that if there is good ground *f*
> for supposing that a government department or a public authority is transgressing
> the law, or is about to transgress it, in a way which offends or injures thousands of
> Her Majesty's subjects, then any one of those offended or injured can draw it to the
> attention of the courts of law and seek to have the law enforced, and the courts *in
> their discretion* can grant whatever remedy is appropriate.' (My emphasis.)

The reference here is to flagrant and serious breaches of the law by persons and *g*
authorities exercising governmental functions which are continuing unchecked. To
revert to technical restrictions on locus standi to prevent this that were current thirty
years ago or more would be to reverse that progress towards a comprehensive system of
administrative law that I regard as having been the greatest achievement of the English
courts in my judicial lifetime.

The reliance by Bridge LJ in *R v Greater London Council, ex parte Blackburn* on Mrs *h*
Blackburn's status as a ratepayer to give her locus standi reflects a special relationship
between ratepayers and the rate-levying authority and between one ratepayer and
another, which is of ancient origin and antedates by centuries the first imposition of taxes
on income. This led the Board in the instant case to seek to rely on the decision of this
House in *Arsenal Football Club Ltd v Ende* [1977] 2 All ER 267, [1979] AC 1 as authority *j*
for a proposition of law that a taxpayer lacked a sufficient interest in what the Board did
in dealing with the tax affairs of other taxpayers to clothe the court with jurisdiction to
entertain his application for an order of mandamus, however flagrantly the Board, in
their dealing with those other taxpayers, had flouted the law. So, it was contended, no
question of discretion could arise. The *Arsenal Football Club* case had been decided before

the new Ord 53 had been made; but, in any event, it was not concerned with an
a application for a prerogative order: it turned on whether a ratepayer who complained
that the value for the hereditament of another ratepayer published in the valuation list
was too low was 'person aggrieved' by that low valuation within the meaning of s 69 of
the General Rate Act 1967, notwithstanding that, since the raising of the valuation of the
hereditament could have no effect on the amount of rates payable by the objecting
ratepayer, no financial interest of his own was affected. The question before this House
b was one of statutory construction only. It was held that the objecting ratepayer was a
'person aggrieved', not only in his capacity as a ratepayer in the same London borough as
that in which the hereditament that was the subject of his complaint was situated but
also as a ratepayer of another London borough within the precepting area of the GLC.
The case is thus illustrative of the liberal attitude of the courts in granting access to legal
remedies for those complaining of failure of public officers to perform their duties. He
c was held, however, not to be a person aggrieved in his capacity as a taxpayer despite the
fact that any shortfall in the rate yield due to the undervaluation of the hereditament
would be made up from central funds to which all taxpayers in Great Britain contribute.
A line, it was said, has to be drawn somewhere, and his interest as a taxpayer was too
remote to qualify him as a person aggrieved by a single entry in the valuation list for
rating purposes of a London borough.

d   My Lords, the expression 'person aggrieved' is of common occurrence in statutes and,
in its various statutory contexts, has been the subject of considerable judicial exegesis. In
the past, however, it had also sometimes been used by judges to describe those persons
who had locus standi to apply for the former prerogative writs or, since 1938, prerogative
orders. It was on this somewhat frail ground that it was argued that the distinction
drawn in the *Arsenal Football Club* case between Mr Ende's grievance as a ratepayer and his
e grievance as a taxpayer was relevant to the question whether the federation as
representing taxpayers was entitled to locus standi in the instant case. However this may
have been before the new Ord 53 was made, the draftsman of that order avoided using
the expression 'a person aggrieved', although it lay ready to his hand. He chose instead
to get away from any formula that might be thought to have acquired, through judicial
exposition, a particular meaning as a term of legal art. The expression that he used in
f r 3(5) had cropped up sporadically in judgments relating to prerogative writs and orders
and consisted of ordinary English words which, on the face of them, leave to the court
an unfettered discretion to decide what in its own good judgment it considers to be 'a
sufficient interest' on the part of an applicant in the particular circumstances of the case
before it. For my part I would not strain to give them any narrower meaning.

The procedure under the new Ord 53 involves two stages: (1) the application for leave
g to apply for judicial review, and (2) if leave is granted, the hearing of the application
itself. The former, or 'threshold', stage is regulated by r 3. The application for leave to
apply for judicial review is made initially ex parte, but may be adjourned for the persons
or bodies against whom relief is sought to be represented. This did not happen in the
instant case. Rule 3(5) specifically requires the court to consider at this stage whether 'it
considers that the applicant has a sufficient interest in the matter to which the application
h relates'. So this is a 'threshold' question in the sense that the court must direct its mind
to it and form a prima facie view about it on the material that is available at the first
stage. The prima facie view so formed, if favourable to the applicant, may alter on
further consideration in the light of further evidence that may be before the court at the
second stage the hearing of the application for judicial review itself.

The need for leave to start proceedings for remedies in public law is not new. It
j applied previously to applications for prerogative orders, though not to civil actions for
injunctions or declarations. Its purpose is to prevent the time of the court being wasted
by busybodies with misguided or trivial complaints of administrative error, and to
remove the uncertainty in which public officers and authorities might be left whether
they could safely proceed with administrative action while proceedings for judicial
review of it were actually pending even though misconceived.

My Lords, I understand that all your Lordships are agreed that, on the material that was before the Divisional Court on the ex parte application by the federation for leave to *a*
apply for judicial review of the so-called 'amnesty' extended to the Fleet Street casuals, the court was justified in exercising its discretion in favour of granting the leave sought. The only evidence that was before the court was the affidavit of Mr Payne, the contents of which have been summarised by my noble and learned friend Lord Wilberforce. It made out a prima facie case, albeit a somewhat flimsy one, that the Revenue had differentiated between three classes of defaulting taxpayers, (1) the Fleet Street casuals, all *b*
of whom were members of powerful trade unions, (2) owners of small businesses, who were not members of trade unions and on whose behalf the federation purported to be acting, and (3) perhaps more significantly, self-employed workers in the construction industry, popularly referred to as 'the lump', to whom powerful trade unions were bitterly opposed. In the absence of any other explanation, the leniency with which tax defaulters in the first class had been treated as contrasted with the severity with which *c*
those in the two latter classes were pursued gave rise, it was suggested by the federation, to reasonable suspicion that the Revenue had granted the amnesty not for any reasons of good management but simply in response to trade union pressure.

The complaint made by the federation was not preferential treatment of individual taxpayers but of all taxpayers falling within a particular class comprising 4,000 to 5,000 members whose unpaid taxes, recovery of which up to April 1977 was to be abandoned, *d*
were of the order of £1m a year. Consideration of the federation's complaint would not involve any departure from the Board's statutory duty to preserve the confidentiality of information obtained by their inspectors and collectors about individual taxpayers' affairs, since ex hypothesi the members of this class of taxpayers had made no returns and had not provided any information about their affairs.

My Lords, at the threshold stage, for the federation to make out a prima facie case of *e*
reasonable suspicion that the Board in showing a discriminatory leniency to a substantial class of taxpayers had done so for ulterior reasons extraneous to good management, and thereby deprived the national exchequer of considerable sums of money, constituted what was in my view reason enough for the Divisional Court to consider that the federation, or, for that matter, any taxpayer, had a sufficient interest to apply to have the question whether the Board were acting ultra vires reviewed by the court. The whole *f*
purpose of requiring that leave should first be obtained to make the application for judicial review would be defeated if the court were to go into the matter in any depth at that stage. If, on a quick perusal of the material then available, the court thinks that it discloses what might on further consideration turn out to be an arguable case in favour of granting to the applicant the relief claimed, it ought, in the exercise of a judicial discretion, to give him leave to apply for that relief. The discretion that the court is *g*
exercising at this stage is not the same as that which it is called on to exercise when all the evidence is in and the matter has been fully argued at the hearing of the application.

The analysis to which, on the invitation of the Lord Advocate for the Crown, the relevant legislation has been subjected by some of your Lordships, and particularly the requirement of confidentiality which would be broken if one taxpayer could complain that another taxpayer was being treated by the Revenue more favourably than himself, *h*
means that occasions will be very rare on which an individual taxpayer (or pressure group of taxpayers) will be able to show a sufficient interest to justify an application for judicial review of the way in which the Revenue have dealt with the tax affairs of any taxpayer other than the applicant himself.

Rare though they may be, however, if, in the instant case, what at the threshold stage was suspicion only had been proved at the hearing of the application for judicial review *j*
to have been true in fact (instead of being utterly destroyed), I would have held that this was a matter in which the federation had a sufficient interest in obtaining an appropriate order, whether by way of declaration or mandamus, to require performance by the Board of statutory duties which for reasons shown to be ultra vires they were failing to perform.

a It would, in my view, be a grave lacuna in our system of public law if a pressure group, like the federation, or even a single public spirited taxpayer, were prevented by outdated technical rules of locus standi from bringing the matter to the attention of the court to vindicate the rule of law and get the unlawful conduct stopped. The Attorney General, although he occasionally applies for prerogative orders against public authorities that do not form part of central government, in practice never does so against government departments. It is not, in my view, a sufficient answer to say that judicial review of the actions of officers or departments of central government is unnecessary because they are b accountable to Parliament for the way in which they carry out their functions. They are accountable to Parliament for what they do so far as regards efficiency and policy, and of that Parliament is the only judge; they are responsible to a court of justice for the lawfulness of what they do, and of that the court is the only judge.

I would allow this appeal on the ground on which, in my view, the Divisional Court c should have dismissed it when the application came to be heard, instead of singling out the lack of a sufficient interest on the part of the federation, viz that the federation completely failed to show any conduct by the Board that was ultra vires or unlawful.

LORD FRASER OF TULLYBELTON. My Lords, I agree with all my noble and d learned friends that this appeal should be allowed. I agree with the reasoning of Lord Wilberforce and Lord Roskill but I wish to explain my reasons in my own words.

The application by the federation in the appeal for judicial review under RSC Ord 53 was refused by the Divisional Court on the ground that the applicants did not have a 'sufficient interest' in the matter to which the application related, as required by r 3 of that order. The decision of the Divisional Court was reversed by the Court of Appeal, by e majority. Some of my noble and learned friends who heard the appeal consider that the appeal should be allowed and the application refused on the wider ground that it has no prospect of success on the merits. I agree that it does not, because the relief sought is a judicial review in the form of a declaration that the Revenue 'acted unlawfully' and an order of mandamus that they assess and collect income tax 'according to the law', but for the reasons explained by my noble and learned friend Lord Wilberforce it is clear that the f Revenue did not act unlawfully. So the application cannot succeed on its merits.

But the question whether the federation has a sufficient interest to make the application at all is a separate, and logically prior, question which has to be answered affirmatively before any question on the merits arises. Refusal of the application on its merits therefore implies that the prior question has been answered affirmatively. I recognise that in some cases, perhaps in many, it may be impracticable to decide whether g an applicant has a sufficient interest or not, without having evidence from both parties as to the matter to which the application relates, and that, in such cases, the court before whom the matter comes in the first instance cannot refuse leave to the applicant at the ex parte stage, under r 3(5). The court which grants leave at that stage will do so on the footing that it makes a provisional finding of sufficient interest, subject to revisal later on, and it is therefore not necessarily to be criticised merely because the final decision is h that the applicant did not have sufficient interest. But where, after seeing the evidence of both parties, the proper conclusion is that the applicant did not have a sufficient interest to make the application, the decision ought to be made on that ground. The present appeal is, in my view, such a case and I would therefore dismiss the appeal on that ground. When it is also shown, as in this case, that the application would fail on its merits, it is desirable for that to be stated by the court which first considers the matter in j order to avoid unnecessary appeals on the preliminary point.

The rules of court give no guidance as to what is a sufficient interest for this purpose. I respectfully accept from my noble and learned friends who are so much more familiar than I am with the history of the prerogative orders that little assistance as to the sufficiency of the interest can be derived from the older cases. But while the standard of sufficiency has been relaxed in recent years, the need to have an interest has remained and the fact that r 3 of Ord 53 requires a sufficient interest undoubtedly shows that not every applicant is entitled to judicial review as of right.

The new Ord 53, introduced in 1977, no doubt had the effect of removing technical and procedural differences between the prerogative orders, and of introducing a remedy by way of declaration or injunction in suitable cases, but I do not think it can have had the effect of throwing over all the older law and of leaving the grant of judicial review in the uncontrolled discretion of the court. On what principle, then, is the sufficiency of interest to be judged? All are agreed that a direct financial or legal interest is not now required, and that the requirement of a legal specific interest laid down in *R v Guardians of Lewisham Union* [1897] 1 QB 498 is no longer applicable. There is also general agreement that a mere busybody does not have a sufficient interest. The difficulty is, in between those extremes, to distinguish between the desire of the busybody to interfere in other people's affairs and the interest of the person affected by or having a reasonable concern with the matter to which the application relates. In the present case that matter is an alleged failure by the Revenue to perform the duty imposed on them by statute.

The correct approach in such a case is, in my opinion, to look at the statute under which the duty arises, and to see whether it gives any express or implied right to persons in the position of the applicant to complain of the alleged unlawful act or omission. On that approach it is easy to see that a ratepayer would have a sufficient interest to complain of unlawfulness by the authorities responsible for collecting the rates. Even if the General Rate Act 1967 had not expressly given him a right to propose alteration in the valuation list if he is aggrieved by any entry therein, he would have an interest in the accuracy of the list which is the basis for allocating the total burden of rates between himself and other ratepayers in the area. The list is public and is open for inspection by any person. The position of the taxpayer is entirely different. The figures on which other taxpayers have been assessed are not normally within his knowledge and the Commissioners of Inland Revenue and their officials are obliged to keep these matters strictly confidential: see the Inland Revenue Regulation Act 1890, ss 1(1) and 39 and the Taxes Management Act 1970, ss 1 and 6 and Sch 1. The distinction between a ratepayer and a taxpayer that was drawn in *Arsenal Football Club Ltd v Ende* [1977] 2 All ER 267, [1979] AC 1 for the purposes of defining a person aggrieved under the General Rate Act 1967 is also relevant to the present matter.

The federation is a body with some 50,000 members, but its counsel conceded, rightly in my opinion, that if it had a sufficient interest to obtain judicial review, then any individual taxpayer, or at least any payer of income tax, must also have such an interest. I can see no justification for treating payers of income tax as having any separate interest in the matter now complained of from that of persons who pay other taxes. All taxpayers contribute to the general fund of revenue and the sense of grievance which the federation claims to feel because of the difference between the Revenue's treatment of the Fleet Street casuals and their treatment of private traders might be felt just as strongly by any honest taxpayer who pays the full amount of taxes of any kind to which he is properly liable. But if the class of persons with a sufficient interest is to include all taxpayers it must include practically every individual in the country who has his own income, because there must be few individuals, however frugal their requirements, who do not pay some indirect taxes including value added tax. It would, I think, be extravagant to suggest that every taxpayer who believes that the Inland Revenue or the Commissioners of Customs and Excise are giving an unlawful preference to another taxpayer, and who feels aggrieved thereby, has a sufficient interest to obtain judicial review under Ord 53. It may be that, if he was relying on some exceptionally grave or widespread illegality, he could succeed in establishing a sufficient interest, but such cases would be very rare indeed and this is not one of them.

For these reasons I would allow the appeal on the ground that the federation has no sufficient interest in the matters complained of.

LORD SCARMAN. My Lords, the National Federation of Self-Employed and Small Businesses Ltd is an applicant for judicial review. The federation seeks a declaration and

an order of mandamus. It is asking the court to declare illegal a policy decision by the
a Revenue not to collect back tax from the casual printers of Fleet Street and to order the
Revenue to collect the tax. The decision was taken by the Revenue pursuant to a special
arrangement under which the Revenue agreed not to seek to collect the tax of past years
if the casuals would comply with arrangements facilitating the collection of tax for
future years. The details of the arrangement are fully set out in the affidavit evidence.
The federation alleges that the special arrangement ('amnesty' is what it understandably
b but inaccurately calls it) when contrasted with the Revenue's relentless pursuit of
federation members who are suspected of not paying their taxes is a breach of the
Revenue's duty to treat taxpayers fairly, that the duty is owed to the general body of
taxpayers and that the federation and its members have a genuine grievance which
entitled them to seek the assistance of the court. The Revenue deny the existence of any
such duty owed to the federation, its members or the general body of taxpayers, though
c they acknowledge the importance, as a matter of policy, of treating taxpayers fairly. The
Revenue deny, therefore, that the federation (or its members) has a sufficient interest in
the matter to entitle it to relief by way of judicial review. Put shortly, if there is no legal
duty, there can be no interest which a court can protect.

The application for judicial review was introduced by rules of court in 1977. The new
RSC Ord 53 is a procedural reform of great importance in the field of public law, but it
d does not, indeed cannot, either extend or diminish the substantive law. Its function is
limited to ensuring 'ubi jus ibi remedium'.

The new procedure is more flexible than that which it supersedes. An applicant for
relief will no longer be defeated merely because he has chosen to apply for the wrong
remedy. Not only has the court a complete discretion to select and grant the appropriate
remedy, but it now may grant remedies which were not previously available. Rule 1(2)
e enables the court to grant a declaration or injunction instead of, or in addition to, a
prerogative order where to do so would be just and convenient. This is a procedural
innovation of great consequence, but it neither extends nor diminishes the substantive
law. For the two remedies (borrowed from the private law) are put in harness with the
prerogative remedies. They may be granted only in circumstances in which one or other
of the prerogative orders can issue. I so interpret Ord 53, r 1(2) because to do otherwise
f would be to condemn the rule as ultra vires.

The appeal is said by both parties to turn on the meaning to be attributed to Ord 53,
r 3(5), which has been described as the heart of the Order. It is in these terms:

> 'The Court shall not grant leave unless it considers that the applicant has a
> sufficient interest in the matter to which the application relates.'

g There is, my Lords, no harm in so describing the issue, so long as it is remembered that
the right to apply for a prerogative order is a matter of law, not to be modified or
abridged by rule of court. The right has always been, and remains today, available only
at the discretion of the High Court which has to be exercised on the facts of the particular
case and according to principles developed by the judges. The case law, as it has
developed and continues to develop in the hands of the judges, determines the nature of
h the interest an applicant must show to obtain leave to apply. The rule, however, presents
no problems of construction. Its terms are wide enough to reflect the modern law
without distorting or abridging the discretion of the judges, and it draws attention to a
feature of the law, which has been overlooked in the present case. The sufficiency of the
applicant's interest has to be judged in relation to the subject matter of his application.
This relationship has always been of importance in the law. It is well illustrated by the
j history of the development of the prerogative writs, notably the difference of approach
to mandamus and certiorari, and it remains a factor of importance in the exercise of the
discretion today.

I therefore accept that one may properly describe the question for the House's decision
as being whether the federation has shown that it has a sufficient interest in the matter
to which its application relates to apply for a declaration and an order of mandamus
directed to requiring the Commissioners of Inland Revenue to fulfil their public duty.

The question is far from easy to answer, raising some complicated issues as to the rights of the private citizen to invoke the aid of the courts in compelling the performance of   a
public duty or in righting public wrongs, rights whose scope and effect derive not from RSC Ord 53 but from the common law developed by the judges.

The federation obtained leave ex parte to apply for judicial review. It then sought an order for discovery of documents from the master, but no order was made pending the hearing, inter partes, of a preliminary issue on the locus standi point. The Divisional Court decided the preliminary issue against the federation, basing itself on dicta to be   b
found in the speeches in *Arsenal Football Club Ltd v Ende* [1977] 2 All ER 267, [1979] AC 1. The Court of Appeal, by a majority, allowed the federation's appeal, holding, as Lord Denning MR put it, that the federation and its members 'are not mere busybodies' but 'have a genuine grievance' (see [1980] 2 All ER 378 at 392, [1980] QB 407 at 425, [1980] STC 261 at 276). Ackner LJ, after remarking that it had been *assumed* (by counsel's concession limited to the argument on the preliminary issue) that the Board acted   c
unlawfully, held that 'the body of taxpayers represented by the federation can reasonably assert a genuine grievance' (see [1980] 2 All ER 378 at 399, [1980] QB 407 at 433, [1980] STC 261 at 282).

As others of your Lordships have already commented, the decision to take locus standi as a preliminary issue was a mistake and has led to unfortunate results. The matter to which the application relates, namely the legality of the policy decision taken by the   d
Revenue to refrain from collecting tax from the Fleet Street casuals, was never considered by the Divisional Court and was dealt with by concession in the Court of Appeal. Yet there were available at both hearings very full affidavits from which the circumstances in which the policy decision, which is challenged, was taken, and the Revenue's explanation, clearly emerge.

In your Lordships' House the Lord Advocate, who now appears for the Commissioners   e
of Inland Revenue, has withdrawn the concession. He was right to do so. He has put at the forefront of his argument a reasoned analysis of the statutory duties of the Revenue, and has invited the House to hold that the statutory code neither recognises nor imposes on the Revenue a duty such as the federation alleges to the general body, or any group of taxpayers.

Before I consider this submission, it is necessary to deal with a subsidiary point taken   f
by the Lord Advocate. He submitted that, notwithstanding the language of Ord 53, r 1(2) the court has no jurisdiction to grant to a private citizen a declaration save in respect of a private right or wrong, and he relied on the House's decision in *Gouriet v Union of Post Office Workers* [1977] 3 All ER 70, [1978] AC 435. Declaration is, of course, a remedy developed by the judges in the field of private law. *Gouriet's* case is authority for the proposition that a citizen may not issue a writ claiming a declaration or other   g
relief against another for the redress of a public wrong unless he can persuade the Attorney General, on his 'relation', to bring the action. The case has nothing to do with the prerogative jurisdiction of the High Court; and it was decided before the introduction of the new Ord 53, at a time when a declaration could not be obtained by a private citizen unless he could show (as in a claim for injunction) that a private right of his was threatened or infringed. The new order has made the remedy available as an alternative,   h
or an addition, to a prerogative order. Its availability has, therefore, been extended, but only in the field of public law where a prerogative order may be granted. I have already given my reasons for the view that this extension is purely a matter of procedural law, and so within the rule-making powers of the Rule Committee. I therefore reject this submission of the Lord Advocate.

I pass now to the two critical issues. (1) The character of the duty on the Revenue and   j
the persons to whom it is owed. Is it legal, political or merely moral? (2) The nature of the interest which the applicant has to show. It is an integral part of the Lord Advocate's argument for the Crown that the existence of the duty is a significant factor in determining the sufficiency of an applicant's interest.

The duty

a   Mandamus is the most elusive of the prerogative writs and orders. The nature of the interest an applicant must show, the nature of the duty which it is available to enforce, and the persons or bodies to whom it may issue have varied from time to time in its development. It is, of course, a judicial remedy; it is equally clear that it is a remedy to compel performance of a public legal duty, that it does not go to the Crown itself and that it is available only if the applicant shows a sufficient interest. In his book Judicial Review

b   of Administrative Action (3rd Edn, 1973, App 1, p 515) the late Professor S A de Smith, discussing the historical origins of the prerogative writs, commented that 'Through the writ of mandamus the King's Bench compelled the carrying-out of ministerial duties incumbent upon both administrative and judicial bodies'. Lord Mansfield CJ clearly developed a very liberal view as to its availability. 'It ought to be used upon all occasions where the law has established no specific remedy, and where in justice and good

c   government there ought to be one': see *R v Barker* (1762) 3 Burr 1265 at 1267, 97 ER 823 at 824. But it does not lie to compel performance of a moral duty: see *Ex parte Napier* (1852) 18 QB 692, 118 ER 261. Nor may it be used to enforce a duty owed exclusively to the Crown: see *R v Lords Comrs of the Treasury* (1872) LR 7 QB 387. It has, however, been recognised by the judges as a remedy for certain forms of abuse of discretion, on the principle that the improper or capricious exercise of discretion is a failure to exercise the

d   discretion which the law has required to be exercised: see *R v Askew* (1768) 4 Burr 2186 at 2188–2169, 98 ER 139 at 141 per Lord Mansfield CJ, and, in modern times, *Padfield v Minister of Agriculture, Fisheries, and Food* [1968] 1 All ER 694, [1968] AC 997. The Lord Advocate accepted, as I understand his argument, this broad approach. But he strenuously submitted that the law imposed no such public legal duty as that for which the federation contends.

e   He submitted that one must examine what he appropriately described as 'the statutory code' to determine whether a duty owed to the applicant is expressly or impliedly recognised by the law. If this be an invitation to consider the relevant statutory provisions against a general background of legal principle developed by the judges, I accept it. For this is the common law approach to statute law.

First, then, 'the statutory code'. It is to be found in the Inland Revenue Regulation Act

f   1890 and the Taxes Management Act 1970. Commissioners are appointed 'for the collection and management of inland revenue': see s 1(1) of the Inland Revenue Regulation Act 1890. They 'shall collect and cause to be collected every part of inland revenue': see s 13(1). 'Inland revenue' means the revenue and taxes 'placed under the care and management of the Commissioners': see s 39. The Taxes Management Act 1970 places income tax under their care and management and for that purpose confers

g   on them and inspectors of tax very considerable discretion in the exercise of their powers. It also imposes on them the very significant duty of confidence in investigating, and dealing with, the affairs of the individual taxpayers. Indeed, the Lord Advocate relied on the existence of this duty as an indication that the statute imposed no duty owed to a taxpayer (or the general body of taxpayers) in respect of the collection of taxes due from another taxpayer, and he made particular reference to ss 1 and 6 of and Sch 1

h   to the Act. He rightly observed that in the daily discharge of their duties inspectors are constantly required to balance the duty to collect 'every part' of due tax against the duty of good management. This conflict of duties can be resolved only by good managerial decisions, some of which will inevitably mean that not all the tax known to be due will be collected.

On this analysis of the statutes the Lord Advocate submitted that the law neither

j   imposes nor recognises a duty owed to an individual taxpayer or a group of taxpayers to collect from other taxpayers all the tax due from them. He supported his submission by a reference to *R v Lords Comrs of the Treasury*; and he emphasised that Parliament and, since 1967, the Parliamentary Commissioner exist to redress the sort of grievance asserted by the federation in this case. His ultimate characterisation of the Revenue's failure in

this case, if it was a failure, was 'maladministration', not breach of any public duty owed
at law to the general body of taxpayers.

While I reject his conclusion, I accept much, but not all, of his submission. The
analysis of the statutory provisions is clearly correct. They establish a complex of duties
and discretionary powers imposed and conferred in the interest of good management on
those whose duty it is to collect the income tax. But I do not accept that the principle of
fairness in dealing with the affairs of taxpayers is a mere matter of desirable policy or
moral obligation. Not do I accept that the duty to collect 'every part of inland revenue'
is a duty owed exclusively to the Crown. Notwithstanding the *Treasury* case in 1872, I
am persuaded that the modern case law recognises a legal duty owed by the Revenue to
the general body of the taxpayers to treat taxpayers fairly, to use their discretionary
powers so that, subject to the requirements of good management, discrimination
between one group of taxpayers and another does not arise, to ensure that there are no
favourites and no sacrificial victims. The duty has to be considered as one of several
arising within the complex comprised in the care and management of a tax, every part
of which it is their duty, if they can, to collect.

Authority for this view is plentiful, albeit only persuasive in character. Viscount
Simon LC in *Latilla v Inland Revenue Comrs* [1943] 1 All ER 265 at 266, [1943] AC 377 at
381, 25 Tax Cas 107 at 117, discussing the evil of tax avoidance schemes, commented
that 'one result of such methods, if they succeed, is . . . to increase, *pro tanto*, the load of
tax on the shoulders of the great body of good citizens . . .' In the *Arsenal* case [1977] 2
All ER 267 at 272, [1979] AC 1 at 17 Lord Wilberforce commented, admittedly in the
context of rates but in terms which cannot rationally exclude a taxpayer, that 'To produce
a sense of justice is an important objective of taxation policy'. In *Vestey v Inland Revenue
Comrs* [1977] 3 All ER 1073 at 1098, [1979] Ch 177 at 197, [1977] STC 414 at 439
Walton J said that it is in 'the interest not only of all individual taxpayers . . . but also in
the interests of the Revenue . . . that the tax system should be fair', and in *Vestey v Inland
Revenue Comrs (No 2)* [1979] 2 All ER 225 at 234, [1979] Ch 198 at 204, [1978] STC 567
at 575 that—

> 'even if, contrary to my views, extra-statutory concessions are permissible and do
> form part of our tax code, nevertheless they do represent a published code, which
> applies indifferently to all those who fall, or who can bring themselves, within its
> scope.'

In the same case, when it reached the House, Lord Edmund-Davies, speaking of the
House's decision in *Congreve v Inland Revenue Comrs* [1948] 1 All ER 948, 30 Tax Cas 163,
said ([1979] 3 All ER 976 at 1003, [1980] AC 1148 at 1196, [1980] STC 10 at 37):

> 'But if it be permitted to stand, we have the deplorable situation that the Inland
> Revenue can *capriciously* select which of several beneficiaries they are going to
> tax . . .' (My emphasis.)

The duty of fairness as between one taxpayer and another is clearly recognised in these
(and other passages) in the modern case law. Is it a mere moral duty, a matter for policy
but not a rule of law? If it be so, I do not understand why distinguished judges allow
themselves to discuss the topic: they are concerned with law, not policy. And is it
acceptable for the courts to leave matters of right and wrong, which give rise to genuine
grievance and are justiciable in the sense that they may be decided and an effective
remedy provided by the courts, to the mercy of policy? Are we in the twilight world of
'maladministration' where only Parliament and the ombudsman may enter, or on the
commanding heights of the law? The courts have a role, long established, in the public
law. They are available to the citizen who has a genuine grievance if he can show that
it is one in respect of which prerogative relief is appropriate. I would not be a party to
the retreat of the courts from this field of public law merely because the duties imposed
on the Revenue are complex and call for management decisions in which discretion must
play a significant role.

a
If it be urged that the House took a different view in the *Arsenal Football Club* case, I would reply that the view there expressed, in so far as it concerned whether the Revenue owed a legal duty to the general body of taxpayers, was obiter. The case should, perhaps, be considered more in the context of an applicant's interest than in that of the nature of the duty placed on the public authority, for it turned on the meaning to be attributed to a person 'aggrieved' in s 69 of the General Rate Act 1967.

b
It is, however, not decisive of either issue, and, for the reasons given by Ackner LJ in the Court of Appeal, I would refuse to introduce into the public law the fine distinction, which the House in that case considered to exist, between the duty of a rating authority and the duty of a taxing authority. I am, therefore, of the opinion that a legal duty of fairness is owed by the Revenue to the general body of taxpayers. It is, however, subject to the duty of sound management of the tax which the statute places on the Revenue.

c
The interest
The sufficiency of the interest is, as I understand all your Lordships agree, a mixed question of law and fact. The legal element in the mixture is less than the matters of fact and degree, but it is important, as setting the limits within which, and the principles by which, the discretion is to be exercised. At one time heresy ruled the day. The decision of the Divisional Court in *R v Guardians of Lewisham Union* [1897] 1 QB 498 at 500 was

d
accepted as establishing that an applicant must establish 'a legal specific right to ask for the interference of the court' by order of mandamus: see per Wright J. I agree with Lord Denning MR in thinking this was a deplorable decision. It was at total variance with the view of Lord Mansfield CJ. Yet its influence has lingered on, and is evident even in the decision of the Divisional Court in this case. But the tide of the developing law has now swept beyond it, as the Court of Appeal's decision in *R v Greater London Council, ex parte*

e
Blackburn [1976] 3 All ER 184, [1976] 1 WLR 550 illustrates. In the present case the House can put down a marker buoy warning legal navigators of the danger of the decision. As Professor Wade pointed out (see Administrative Law (4th Edn, 1977, p 610)), if the *Lewisham* case were correct, mandamus would lose its public law character, being no more than a remedy for a private wrong.

f
My Lords, I will not weary the House with citation of many authorities. Suffice it to refer to the judgment of Lord Parker CJ in *R v Thames Magistrates' Court, ex parte Greenbaum* (1957) 55 LGR 129, a case of certiorari, and to the words of Lord Wilberforce in *Gouriet v Union of Post Office Workers* [1977] 3 All ER 70 at 84, [1978] AC 435 at 482, where he stated the modern position in relation to prerogative orders:

'These are often applied for by individuals and the courts have allowed them liberal access under a generous conception of locus standi.'

g
The one legal principle, which is implicit in the case law and accurately reflected in the rules of court, is that in determining the sufficiency of an applicant's interest it is necessary to consider the matter to which the application relates. It is wrong in law, as I understand the cases, for the court to attempt an assessment of the sufficiency of an applicant's interest without regard to the matter of his complaint. If he fails to show,

h
when he applies for leave, a prima facie case, or reasonable grounds for believing that there has been a failure of public duty, the court would be in error if it granted leave. The curb represented by the need for an applicant to show, when he seeks leave to apply, that he has such a case is an essential protection against abuse of legal process. It enables the court to prevent abuse by busybodies, cranks and other mischief makers. I do not see any further purpose served by the requirements for leave.

j
But, that being said, the discretion belongs to the court; and, as my noble and learned friend Lord Diplock has already made clear, it is the function of the judges to determine the way in which it is to be exercised. Accordingly I think that the Divisional Court was right to grant leave ex parte. Mr Payne's affidavit of 20th March 1979 revealed a prima facie case of failure by the Inland Revenue to discharge their duty to act fairly between taxpayer and taxpayer. But by the time the application reached the Divisional Court for

a hearing, inter partes, of the preliminary issue two very full affidavits had been filed by
the Revenue explaining the management reasons for the decision not to seek to collect *a*
the unpaid tax from the Fleet Street casuals. At this stage the matters of fact and degree
on which depends the exercise of the discretion whether to allow the application to
proceed or not became clear. It was now possible to form a view as to the existence or
otherwise of a case meriting examination by the court. And it was abundantly plain on
the evidence that the federation could show no such case. But the Court of Appeal,
misled into thinking that, at that stage and notwithstanding the evidence available, locus *b*
standi was to be dealt with as a preliminary issue, assumed illegality (where in my
judgment none was shown) and, on that assumption, held that the federation had
sufficient interest. Were the assumption justified, which on the evidence it was not, I
would agree with the reasoning of Lord Denning MR and Ackner LJ. I think the
majority of the Court of Appeal, in formulating a test of genuine grievance reasonably
asserted, was doing no more than giving effect to the general principle which Lord *c*
Mansfield CJ had stated in the early days on the remedy. Any more stringent test would,
as Professor Wade observes, open up 'a serious gap in the system of public law' (see
Administrative Law (4th Edn, 1977, p 612)).

Lastly, I wish to comment shortly on the duty of confidence owed by the Revenue to
every taxpayer and the right to discovery. The duty of confidence can coexist with the
duty of fairness owed to the general body of taxpayers. It is, however, of great importance *d*
when discovery is sought by an applicant, as happened in this case. On general principles,
discovery should not be ordered unless and until the court is satisfied that the evidence
reveals reasonable grounds for believing that there has been a breach of public duty, and
it should be limited strictly to documents relevant to the issue which emerges from the
affidavits. The Revenue in any event will have the right in respect of certain classes of
document to plead 'public interest immunity', of which in a proper case the court will be *e*
the arbiter: see Burmah Oil Co Ltd v Bank of England [1979] 3 All ER 700, [1980] AC
1090. In the present case, had the federation shown a sufficient interest, I doubt whether
any legitimate objection could have been taken to discovery of documents relevant to the
making of the special arrangement. Such documents would be unlikely to contain any
information about the affairs of any Fleet Street casual who had succeeded by various
devices in avoiding his identity being discovered by the searches of the Revenue. But, be *f*
that as it may, discovery can safely be left to the discretion of the court guided by the law
as I believe it to be.

The federation, having failed to show any grounds for believing that the Revenue have
failed to do their statutory duty, has not, in my view, shown an interest sufficient in law
to justify any further proceedings by the court on its application. Had it shown
reasonable grounds for believing that the failure to collect tax from the Fleet Street *g*
casuals was an abuse of the Revenue's managerial discretion or that there was a case to
that effect which merited investigation and examination by the court, I would have
agreed with the Court of Appeal that it had shown a sufficient interest for the grant of
leave to proceed further with its application. I would, therefore, allow the appeal.

LORD ROSKILL. My Lords, the appellants, the Commissioners of Inland Revenue, *h*
seek the reversal of an order dated 27th February 1980 made by the Court of Appeal
(Lord Denning MR and Ackner LJ, Lawton LJ dissenting) declaring that the respondent,
the National Federation of Self-Employed and Small Businesses Ltd, had a 'sufficient
interest' to apply for judicial review in these proceedings against the Revenue. In
making that declaration the Court of Appeal reversed an order of the Divisional Court
(Lord Widgery CJ and Griffiths J) dated 22nd November 1979 refusing an application for *j*
judicial review against the Revenue, on the ground that the federation had no such
'sufficient interest'.

My Lords, these proceedings were begun by the federation which, on 22nd March
1979, applied ex parte for leave to apply for an order for judicial review by way of
mandamus and a declaration against the Revenue. The ex parte application was made in

due form under RSC Ord 53. The original statement lodged in support of the application
a claimed, first, a declaration that the Revenue had exceeded their powers in granting what
was called an 'amnesty' to casual workers in Fleet Street and, second, an order of
mandamus directing the Revenue to assess and collect income tax from those casual
workers in Fleet Street 'according to law'. A subsequent amended statement substituted
for the original declaration sought a declaration that the Revenue acted unlawfully in
granting that 'amnesty'. On that ex parte application leave was granted. The hearing
b inter partes took place on 21st and 22nd November 1979, when, as I have already stated,
the federation's application was refused for want of 'sufficient interest'.

When the ex parte application was heard, the only evidence before the Divisonal Court
was an affidavit from a Mr Payne, a vice-president of the federation. But on the hearing
inter partes the Divisional Court also had long affidavits from Sir William Pile, then
chairman of the Board of Inland Revenue, and a Mr Hoadley, a principal inspector of
c taxes. Mr Hoadley had been personally responsible for the negotiations which led to the
so-called 'amnesty' of which the federation sought to complain. After these affidavits
had been sworn and before that hearing inter partes the federation had taken out a
summons for discovery against the Revenue. By agreement, this summons was treated
as a summons for the discovery of specific documents. On 5th November 1979 Master
Sir Jack Jacob QC dismissed that summons for the reasons given in a judgment of which
d your Lordships have a note. An appeal to the Divisional Court from that dismissal was
adjourned by agreement pending the final determination of these proceedings.

My Lords, when the matter came before the Divisional Court inter partes it was
apparently agreed that the question whether or not the federation had a 'sufficient
interest' to bring these proceedings at all should be dealt with as a preliminary point (see
the judgment of Lord Widgery CJ ([1980] 2 All ER 378, [1980] STC 261)). When the
e federation appealed to the Court of Appeal that preliminary point was the only issue
before that court as it had been before the Divisional Court. Moreover, in their printed
case, the Revenue averred that this was the only issue to be determined by your Lordships'
House, the Revenue contending that, as a matter of law, the federation had no 'sufficient
interest'.

My Lords, your Lordships' House has often protested about the taking of short cuts in
f legal proceedings, most recently in *Allen v Gulf Oil Refining Ltd* [1981] 1 All ER 353,
[1981] 2 WLR 188. The number of cases in which it is legitimate to take such short cuts
is small and in my opinion the present was not such a case. Indeed, many of the
difficulties which were canvassed at length in arguments before your Lordships' House
would have been avoided had this particular short cut not been taken. With profound
respect to the Divisional Court, this course was especially inappropriate where the grant
g or refusal of the remedy sought by way of judicial review is, in the ultimate analysis,
discretionary, and the exercise of that discretion and the determination of the sufficiency
or otherwise of the applicant's interest will depend not on one single factor (it is not
simply a point of law to be determined in the abstract or on assumed facts) but on the due
appraisal of many different factors revealed by the evidence produced by the parties, few
if any of which will be able to be wholly isolated from the others.

h My Lords, much time was spent in the courts below and in argument before your
Lordships' House with citation of well-known cases, some of now respectable antiquity
in which prerogative orders or formerly prerogative writs have been allowed to issue or
have been refused. With all respect to the authority of the judges by whom those cases
were decided, such decisions are today of little assistance for two reasons. First, in the last
thirty years, no doubt because of the growth of central local government intervention in
j the affairs of the ordinary citizen since the 1939–45 war, and the consequent increase in
the number of administrative bodies charged by Parliament with the performance of
public duties, the use of prerogative orders to check usurpation of power by such bodies
to the disadvantage of the ordinary citizen, or to insist on due performance by such
bodies of their statutory duties and to maintain due adherence to the laws enacted by
Parliament, has greatly increased. The former and stricter rules determining when such

orders, or formerly the prerogative writs, might or might not issue, have been greatly
relaxed. It is unnecessary in the present appeal to trace through a whole series of *a*
decisions which demonstrate that change in legal policy. The change is well known, as
are the decisions.

Second, since those cases were decided and following the change in legal policy to
which I have just referred, Ord 53 was introduced into the Rules of the Supreme Court
in 1977. For ease of reference I set out the most relevant parts of certain of the rules of
that Order: *b*

'**1.**—(1) An application for—(a) an order of mandamus, prohibition or certiorari
. . . shall be made by way of an application for judicial review in accordance with the
provisions of this Order.

'(2) An application for a declaration or an injunction (not being an injunction
mentioned in paragraph (1)(b)) may be made by way of an application for judicial
review, and on such an application the Court may grant the declaration or injunction *c*
claimed if it considers that, having regard to—(a) the nature of the matters in
respect of which relief may be granted by way of an order of mandamus, prohibition
or certiorari, (b) the nature of the persons and bodies against whom relief may be
granted by way of such an order, and (c) all the circumstances of the case, it would
be just and convenient for the declaration or injunction to be granted on an
application for judicial review.   *d*

'**2.** On an application for judicial review any relief mentioned in rule 1(2) or (2)
may be claimed as an alternative or in addition to any other relief so mentioned if
it arises out of or relates to or is connected with the same matter.

'**3.**—(1) No application for judicial review shall be made unless the leave of the
Court has been obtained in accordance with this rule.

'(2) An application for leave must be made ex parte to a Divisional Court of the *e*
Queen's Bench Division . . .

'(5) The Court shall not grant leave unless it considers that the applicant has a
sufficient interest in the matter to which the application relates . . .'

My Lords, I would make these comments on Ord 53 at this juncture. First, the
changes thereby effected, though seemingly changes in procedure and thus made as part *f*
of the Rules of the Supreme Court, were and were intended to be far reaching. They
were designed to stop the technical procedural arguments which had too often arisen and
thus marred the true administration of justice, whether a particular applicant had
pursued his claim for relief correctly, whether he should have sought mandamus rather
than certiorari, or certiorari rather than mandamus, whether an injunction or
prohibition, or prohibition rather than an injunction, or whether relief by way of *g*
declaration should have been sought rather than relief by way of prerogative order. All
these, and the like technical niceties, were to be things of the past. All relevant relief
could be claimed under the general head of 'judicial review', and the form of judicial
review sought or granted (if at all) was to be entirely flexible according to the needs of the
particular case. The claims for relief could be cumulative or alternative under r 2 as
might be most appropriate. Second, relief by way of declaration, or injunction, was *h*
made a form of judicial review to be granted in an appropriate case having regard to the
factors mentioned in r 1(2). Third, Ord 53 took effect on 11th January 1978, some six
months after the decision of your Lordships' House in *Gouriet v Union of Post Office
Workers* [1977] 3 All ER 70, [1978] AC 435, on 26th July 1977, an authority much relied
on by the learned Lord Advocate on behalf of the Revenue in support of his submissions
regarding the circumstances in which declarations might be granted. But *Gouriet's* case *j*
was a relator action and was not concerned with prerogative orders or judicial review,
and the relevant observations of your Lordships must be read in the light of that fact and
of the subsequent enactment of Ord 53.

My Lords, I venture to draw attention to the passage in the speech of Lord Wilberforce
in *Gouriet's* case [1977] 3 All ER 70 at 84, [1978] AC 435 at 482–483 where he stated that

the courts had granted individuals more liberal access in the case of application for
a prerogative writs and orders, and had adopted a more generous concept of locus standi
in those cases, for the individual was then seeking to enforce a public right, and to invite
the court to control by use of the prerogative power alleged abuse of authority or
jurisdiction.

Fourth, as already stated, the discretionary nature of the remedy of judicial review is
emphasised by the fact that r 3(1) denies the individual the right to apply for judicial
b review unless leave so to apply has first been obtained ex parte. Fifth, the court is
enjoined by r 3(5) not to grant leave unless the applicant has a 'sufficient interest' in the
matter to which the application relates, plain words of limitation on an applicant's right
to relief.

In my opinion it is now clear that the solution to the present appeal must lie in the
proper application of the principles now enshrined in Ord 53, in the light of modern
c judicial policy to which I have already referred, to the facts of the present case without
excessive regard to the fetters seemingly previously imposed by judicial decisions in
earlier times and long before that modern policy was evolved or Ord 53 was enacted.

My Lords, the all important phrase in r 3(5) is 'sufficient interest'. Learned counsel
were agreed that this phrase had not been used in any previous relevant enactment. My
Lords, careful review of the earlier authorities in which learned counsel for both parties
d engaged reveals that many different phrases have been used in different cases to describe
the required standing of a particular applicant for what is now described as judicial
review before the courts would entertain his application. He might be 'a party' to the
relevant proceedings. He might be 'a person aggrieved'. He might be 'a person with a
particular grievance'. He might be a 'stranger'. All those, and some other phrases, will
be found in the cases. None is exhaustive or indeed definitive and indeed in this field it
e would be, I think, impossible to find a phrase which was exhaustive or definitive of the
class of person entitled to apply for judicial review. No doubt it was for this reason that
the Rule Committee of the Supreme Court in 1977 selected the phrase 'sufficient interest'
as one which could sufficiently embrace all classes of those who might apply and yet
permit sufficient flexibility in any particular case to determine whether or not 'sufficient
interest' was in fact shown. So far as the researches of counsel went, the origin of this
f phrase appears to lie in an interlocutory observation made by the court in R v Cotham
[1898] 1 QB 802 at 804, and in its use by Avory J in his judgment in Ex parte Stott [1916]
1 KB 7 at 9.

Your Lordships' attention was drawn to a note to Ord 53 in the Supreme Court
Practice 1979 (vol 1, para 53/1-14/20-22, p 831), which your Lordships were told bore
the authority of Master Sir Jack Jacob QC. The learned editor stated that that which was
g a 'sufficient interest appears to be a mixed question of fact and law; a question of fact and
degree and the relationship between the applicant and the matter to which the
application relates, having regard to all the circumstances of the case'. With this
admirably concise statement, I respectfully agree.

The learned Lord Advocate founded his main submission for the Crown on s 1 of the
Inland Revenue Act 1890 which still remains on the statute book and ss 1 and 6 of and
h Sch 1 to the Taxes Management Act 1970. Those statutory provisions, he claimed,
defined the relevant duties of the Revenue. They established not only the Revenue's
duties, but also their strict obligation of confidentiality as between the Revenue and each
individual taxpayer, subject only to the exceptions for which the statutes made express
provision. The subject matter of the present application was the alleged liability of
others to pay income tax and averred a duty on the Revenue to assess and collect tax on
the Fleet Street casual workers identified as a class but not individually. But, the learned
j Lord Advocate submitted, the duties of the Revenue, as circumscribed by these statutes,
precluded the possibility of any other individual taxpayer, or the federation as a
representative group of other taxpayers, from having any 'sufficient interest' in the
performance by the Revenue of their statutory duties, vis-à-vis the Fleet Street casual
workers, so that there was no jurisdiction to grant the federation the relief which it

sought. The learned Lord Advocate sought to distinguish the rating cases, such as *Arsenal Football Club Ltd v Ende* [1977] 2 All ER 267, [1979] AC 1, on the ground that in *a* rating law there was a statutory duty to publish a valuation list containing specific valuations and correct any valuations in that list which might be shown to be wrong. Thus there was, under the rating legislation, a community of interest between ratepayers which did not exist as between taxpayers. Reliance was also placed on the fact that Mr Ende's attempt to prove his locus standi as a taxpayer as well as a ratepayer failed on the ground that the former interest was too remote. Nowhere in the two statutes to which *b* your Lordships were referred was there any express provision which recognised any interest by one taxpayer in the affairs of another taxpayer, or in the assessment and collection of tax on and from such other taxpayer. Unless there was a relevant duty cast by statute on the Revenue in which the federation could show a 'sufficient interest', there could be no jurisdiction to make an order for judicial review, there being no relevant relationship on the part of the federation to the subject matter of its application.   *c*

My Lords, at an early stage of his submissions, the learned Lord Advocate accepted that the question raised in the instant appeal involved the performance by the Revenue of a public duty. In my opinion that concession (if concession be the right word) was clearly properly made. But once it is made, I find it difficult to see how it can be said that there is no jurisdiction of the court to allow relief against the Revenue by way of a judicial review. The Revenue are, and must as a public body charged with the performance of *d* a public duty of crucial importance be, amenable to the general law and liable to possible correction if their statutory powers are exceeded, or their statutory duties are not lawfully discharged. But to say that, and to accept that there is jurisdiction to grant relief against the Revenue in a proper case, is a very different matter from saying that in the instant case relief should be granted to the federation as being possessed of that 'sufficient interest' which is a condition precedent to its obtaining the relief which it seeks.   *e*

Counsel for the federation contended that not only was there jurisdiction to grant the relief sought but that his client had a 'sufficient interest' to be granted that relief because once it was accepted that the Revenue were a statutory body charged with the performance of a public duty any member of the public had a right to come to the court and complain that that duty had not been performed in some relevant respect, and that this right of that member of the public did not depend on the precise nature of the *f* obligation cast by the statute on the Revenue. More narrowly, counsel for the federation argued that an individual taxpayer had as much interest in the performance by the Revenue of their statutory duty as the ratepayer in *Ende's* case and was not too remote from the Revenue in seeking to insist on performance of their duty in accordance with the law, a submission which found favour in the Court of Appeal with Ackner LJ. Ultimately counsel did not go so far as to assert that the Revenue's statutory duty *g* required them in every case to exact every penny which might be lawfully exigible from each individual taxpayer, but he asserted that there was already some evidence in the present case, and that after discovery against the Revenue there might well be further evidence, that in granting the so-called 'amnesty' and in agreeing to forgo collection of past arrears of tax from the Fleet Street casual workers, the Revenue had been moved by impermissible influences, such as fears of industrial action in Fleet Street, and thus had *h* failed to perform the statutory duties with which they were charged in accordance with the law. Hence, he argued that the relief sought should be granted. These casual workers, it was said, had defrauded the general body of taxpayers, and it was the right of the federation, as the representative of a substantial body of taxpayers who like others were adversely affected by these frauds by the casual workers not only escaping the normal consequences of such fraud but positively gaining as a result of the 'amnesty', to *j* complain and to seek strict enforcement of the Revenue's statutory duty to assess and collect the tax due from these casual workers.

My Lords, Lord Denning MR was willing to accept the wider of these propositions founded on what he had previously said in *Attorney General (on the relation of McWhirter) v Independant Broadcasting Authority* [1973] 1 All ER 689 at 696, [1973] QB 629 at 646 and

again in a revised form in *R v Greater London Council, ex parte Blackburn* [1976] 3 All ER
a 184 at 792, [1976] 1 WLR 550 at 559. He accepted that Lord Wilberforce had expressly
disapproved the former passage in his speech in *Gouriet's* case but claimed that that
disapproval was limited to relator actions such as *Gouriet's* case was. My Lords, with
profound respect I cannot agree. Though Lord Wilberforce's disapproval was, of course,
made in the context of a relator action, the view of Lord Denning MR, if applied to all
applications for judicial review, would extend the individual's right of application for
b that relief far beyond any acceptable limit, and would give a meaning so wide to a
'sufficient interest' in Ord 53, r 3(5) that they would in practice cease to be, as they were
clearly intended to be, words of limitation on that right of application.

More powerful support for the narrower submission of counsel for the federation is to
be found in the judgment of Ackner LJ. Ackner LJ found it impossible to distinguish
between the position of a ratepayer who was entitled to the relief sought, as for example
c in *Ende's* case, and a taxpayer who, it was said, was not entitled to the like relief. The test,
according to Ackner LJ, was whether the assertion of the grievance could be justified on
reasonable grounds.

Both Lord Denning MR and Ackner LJ proceeded on the basis that it should be
assumed (Lord Denning MR went so far as to say that it was a matter of concession) that
the Revenue had acted unlawfully because they had no dispensing power. My Lords,
d there was certainly some confusion in the Court of Appeal as to what was conceded or
what was to be assumed, a confusion not resolved before your Lordships' House. But
whatever may have been assumed or conceded, or thought to have been assumed or
conceded in the Court of Appeal, the learned Lord Advocate was not prepared to invite
the making of any assumption or to make any concession before your Lordships' House,
and I think he was right to adopt this attitude. For my part, I decline in a matter of this
e kind to make any assumption of any kind, let alone an assumption of illegality on the
part of the Revenue. This appeal must be determined on the totality of the evidence as
it was before the Divisional Court and the Court of Appeal. No question of any
dispensing power is involved. The Revenue were in no way arrogating to themselves a
right or inviting assumption of an arrogation to themselves of a right not to comply with
their statutory obligations under the statutes to which I have referred. On the contrary,
f their whole case was that they had made a sensible arrangement in the overall
performance of their statutory duties in connection with taxes management, an
arrangement made in the best interests of everyone directly involved and, indeed, of
persons indirectly involved, such as other taxpayers, for the agreement reached would be
likely to lead ultimately to a greater collection of revenue than if the agreement had not
been reached or 'amnesty' granted.

g My Lords, with profound respect to both courts below I do not think that either
approached this application for judicial review on a correct basis in point of law. In my
opinion the Divisional Court was wrong for the reasons I have given for refusing relief
for it dealt with the relevant issue as a matter of jurisdiction and not as one of overall
discretion. I also think that the majority of the Court of Appeal was wrong in granting
the relief claimed either on the wider ground Lord Denning MR preferred or on the
h narrower ground which appealed to Ackner LJ.

My Lords, I hope I yield to no one in stressing the importance that relief by way of
judicial review should be freely available in whatever form may be appropriate in a
particular case, and it is today especially important not to cut down by judicial decision
the scope of Ord 53 in creating modern procedure for applications for judicial review.
I emphasise in particular that relief by way of declaration is expressly made a form of
j judicial review additional to or alternative to relief by way of prerogative order or
injunction. The court has a general discretion which, if any, relief shall be granted, and
many of the old decisions restricting the circumstances in which declarations may be
granted to establish legal rights seem to me to be no longer in point. On the other hand,
it is equally important that the courts do not by use or misuse of the weapon of judicial
review cross that clear boundary between what is administration, whether it be good or

bad administration, and what is an unlawful performance of the statutory duty by a body
charged with the performance of that duty. If the body against which an order of a
judicial review is sought is for some reason not amenable to such an order, then clearly
there is no jurisdiction to allow the order to go. But once that body is admitted to be, as
the Revenue are admitted to be, a statutory body charged with the performance of a
public duty, then it is clear that there is jurisdiction to grant an order of judicial review
in a proper case; and to the extent that the learned Lord Advocate contended otherwise
I reject his argument. But the arguments that he advanced on jurisdiction which I have b
rejected become highly relevant when the question of 'sufficient interest' arises. The
first question must be to inquire what is the relevant duty of the statutory body against
which the order is sought, of the performance or non-performance of which complaint
is sought to be made. For that I turn to the sections of the statutes on which the learned
Lord Advocate relied. The Revenue are responsible for the overall management of the
relevant part of the taxation system of this country, and for the assessment and collection c
of taxes from those who are, by law, liable to pay them. Such assessment and collection
is a confidential matter between the Revenue and each individual taxpayer. Such
confidence is allowed to be broken only in those exceptional circumstances for which the
statute makes express provision.

The next matter is to consider the complaint made and the relief sought. It is clear
that the federation is seeking to intervene in the affairs of individual taxpayers, the Fleet d
Street casual workers, and to require the Revenue to assess and collect tax from them
which the Revenue have clearly agreed not to do. Theoretically, but one trusts only
theoretically, it is possible to envisage a case when because of some grossly improper
pressure or motive the Revenue have failed to perform their statutory duty as respects a
particular taxpayer or class of taxpayer. In such a case, which emphatically is not the
present, judicial review might be available to other taxpayers. But it would require to be e
a most extreme case for I am clearly of the view, having regard to the nature of the
Revenue's statutory duty and the degree of confidentiality enjoined by statute which
attaches to their performance, that in general it is not open to individual taxpayers or to
a group of taxpayers to seek to interfere between the Revenue and other taxpayers,
whether those other taxpayers are honest or dishonest men, and that the court should, by
refusing relief by way of judicial review, firmly discourage such attempted interference f
by other taxpayers. It follows that, in my view, taking all those matters into account, it
cannot be said that the federation had a 'sufficient interest' to justify its seeking the relief
claimed by way of judicial review.

I have already said that the court must not cross that boundary between administration
whether good or bad which is lawful, and what is unlawful performance of a statutory
duty. Much time was spent on considering the relevance of the Parliamentary g
Commissioner Act 1967. My Lords, I shall spend no time on its provisions, for it deals
with the injustices caused by maladministration. The remedy thereby accorded to the
individual citizen may be very effective in a proper case, but the existence of that remedy
seems to me irrelevant to the question now under consideration, which depends not on
allegations of maladministration leading to injustice but on allegations of illegality in the
performance of statutory duties. I doubt whether in considering whether legal redress h
by way of judicial review should be granted it is in any way relevant to consider the
existence of this other mode of redress of other grievances. Certainly, as at present
advised, I do not consider the existence of this other mode of redress can narrow the field
in which judicial review if otherwise proper is available. The latter is a remedy available
from Her Majesty's courts for the purpose of redressing legal wrongs. The former has a
wholly different origin and is designed to redress administrative wrongs not remediable j
in the courts.

I ought, however, to deal with the further question whether even if (contrary to my
opinion) the federation could show a 'sufficient interest' there is anything in the evidence
as a whole allowing the federation to interfere by way of obtaining an order of judicial
review. I have already considered the scope of the Revenue's duties and the nature of the

complaint which the federation makes. It is at this point that the answer to this
a complaint becomes relevant and ought to have been, but was not, considered by the
Divisional Court. To my mind it is clear beyond argument when one reads the affidavits
of Sir William Pile and Mr Hoadley that what was done was a matter of taxes
management, and I can see no shadow of dereliction of duty by the Revenue, or any
suggestion of improper or unlawful conduct on their part. On the contrary, what they
did seems to me to have been a matter of administrative common sense. Instead of
b wasting public time and money in seeking to collect taxes from persons whose names
were unknown and whose ability to pay was therefore equally unknown, they made an
arrangement which enabled taxes not hitherto able to be collected or in fact collected
collectable in the future at a cost to the general body of taxpayers of forgoing the
collection of that which in reality could never have been collected.

In my view the Divisional Court ought in the exercise of its discretion to have
c dismissed this application, not for want of jurisdiction to grant it, but because, on the
evidence as a whole, first no 'sufficient interest' was shown and second because in any
event the application could not possibly succeed. Since that court did not exercise its
discretion, and since the majority of the Court of Appeal was, in my view, wrong in law
in making the declaration which was there granted and therefore did not exercise the
discretion vested in that court, I think it open to your Lordships' House to exercise the
d discretion which ought to have been exercised in the first instance by the Divisional
Court. On that basis I would dismiss the application for judicial review, thus reaching
the same result as did Lawton LJ in his dissenting judgment in the Court of Appeal.

I would only add that counsel for the federation urged that something advantageous
to his client might emerge on discovery. He submitted that your Lordships ought not
to dispose of this appeal on the basis of the affidavit evidence alone. My Lords, the
e federation started these proceedings on the basis of an affidavit which was fully answered
by the two affidavits to which I have just referred. With all respect to counsel's argument
for the federation I can see no reason to allow what I am afraid I must necessarily regard
as a fishing expedition in the hope of obtaining on discovery something which might
counter that which appears so clearly from the affidavits filed on behalf of the Revenue.

My Lords, since preparing this speech, I have had the advantage of reading in draft the
f speeches of my noble and learned friends Lord Wilberforce and Lord Fraser. I am in full
agreement with what both my noble and learned friends have said.

Appeal allowed.

Solicitors: *Solicitor of Inland Revenue*; *Beachcroft, Hyman Isaacs* (for the federation).

Mary Rose Plummer   Barrister.

Burnes v Trade Credits Ltd

a

PRIVY COUNCIL

LORD DIPLOCK, LORD SIMON OF GLAISDALE, LORD EDMUND-DAVIES, LORD KEITH OF KINKEL AND
LORD SCARMAN

28th JANUARY, 4th MARCH 1981

b

*Guarantee – Discharge of guarantee – Variation of terms of principal contract – Guarantors
guaranteeing payment of principal and interest owing on mortgage – Guarantee including 'any
further advance' or any 'indulgence or consideration' made by mortgagee to mortgagor –
Mortgagor and mortgagee agreeing to variation of mortgage extending term and increasing
interest rate – Consent of guarantors to variation not obtained – Mortgagor defaulting –
Whether variation of mortgage amounting to 'further advance' or 'indulgence or consideration'
– Whether variation within scope of guarantee.*

c

*Mortgage – Advance – Further advances – Mortgage varied by extending term and increasing
rate of interest – Whether extension of term at increased rate of interest amounting to 'further
advances'.*

d

By a deed of guarantee executed in June 1972 the appellant and her husband guaranteed
the repayment of a mortgage of $100,000 at 9% interest repayable in October 1975.
Under the terms of the guarantee the appellant and her husband covenanted, inter alia,
(i) that 'any further advances' made by the mortgagee to the mortgagor were to be
included in the guarantee unless the guarantors gave notice in writing to the contrary
and (ii) that the mortgagee was entitled to grant the mortgagor time or 'any other
indulgence or consideration' without obtaining the guarantors' consent. When the
mortgage fell due for repayment in October 1975 the mortgagor and the mortgagee
entered into a memorandum of variation of mortgage extending the term for a year and
increasing the rate of interest to 16%. The guarantors were not asked to, and did not,
consent to the variation. The mortgagor defaulted in payment of the interest and the
mortgagee commenced proceedings against the guarantors claiming the sum of $8,583
unpaid interest. The district court judge dismissed the claim on the ground that the
variation of mortgage was a material variation which had been entered into without the
guarantors' consent and therefore had the effect of discharging their liability under the
guarantee. On appeal, the New South Wales Court of Appeal held that the guarantors
were liable for the unpaid interest on the ground that the variation of mortgage
amounted to a 'further advance' and was therefore within the scope of the guarantee.
The appellant appealed to the Privy Council.

e

f

g

Held – The appeal would be allowed for the following reasons—

(1) The term 'advance' normally meant the furnishing of money for a specified
purpose. Accordingly, the reference to 'further advances' in the guarantee referred to the
furnishing or lending of an additional principal sum by the mortgagee to the mortgagor
and did not include an extension of the term for repayment of the original principal sum
advanced (see p 124 *h j* and p 125 *h*, post).

h

(2) The increase in the rate of interest from 9% to 16% was not a liability which the
terms of the guarantee required the guarantors to undertake without their consent.
Furthermore, although the extension of the term of the mortgage might be an
'indulgence or consideration' which the mortgagee was entitled to make to the mortgagor
without affecting the validity of the guarantee, the increase in the rate of interest could
not be said to be an indulgence or consideration shown by the mortgagee to the
mortgagor. The purpose of that provision in the guarantee was merely to protect the
mortgagee if an indulgence granted by him to the mortgagor would otherwise have

j

released the guarantors from liability because it prejudiced the rights of the guarantors
a vis-à-vis the mortgagor, and it did not enable the mortgagee and mortgagor by agreement
between themselves to impose an additional liability on the guarantors without their
consent (see p 125 c to f and h, post); *Payton v S G Brookes & Sons Pty Ltd* [1977] WAR 91
distinguished.

Notes
b For discharge of a guarantee by variation of the terms of the principal contract, see 20
Halsbury's Laws (4th Edn) paras 253–258, and for cases on the subject, see 26 Digest
(Repl) 161, 1199–1210.
   For the effect of an agreement to give time to the principal debtor, see 20 Halsbury's
Laws (4th Edn) paras 261–262, and for cases on the subject, see 26 Digest (Repl) 181–182,
1340–1348.

c
Case referred to in judgment
Payton v S G Brookes & Sons Pty Ltd [1977] WAR 91.

Appeal
The appellant, Pauline Burnes, by leave of the Supreme Court of New South Wales, Court
d of Appeal, granted on 31st March 1980, appealed against the order of the Court of Appeal
(Street CJ, Samuels and Mahoney JJA) dated 7th August 1979 allowing an appeal by the
respondents, Trade Credits Ltd, against a judgment of the District Court of New South
Wales at Sydney (his Honour Judge Godfrey-Smith QC) dated 3rd February 1978 and
giving judgment for the respondents for the sum of $8,583·31 on their claim against the
appellant under a deed of guarantee. The facts are set out in the judgment of the Board.

e
P Flannery QC and *C E O'Connor* (both of the New South Wales Bar) for the appellant.
R C Southwell QC and *P J Moss* (of the New South Wales Bar) for the respondents.

LORD KEITH OF KINKEL. This appeal is concerned with the proper construction
of certain provisions in a deed of guarantee. On 12th July 1972 a company called D G
f Hogan Pty Ltd ('Hogan') contracted to sell certain land to Civic Private Hotel Pty Ltd ('the
hotel company'). It was agreed that the sum of $100,000, part of the purchase price,
should remain outstanding, being secured by a mortgage on the subjects of sale. So the
hotel company on 12th October 1972 executed in favour of Hogan a memorandum of
mortgage securing payment of $100,000, with interest at the rate of 9% per annum until
payment, payable monthly, the principal sum being repayable on 12th October 1975.
g On the same date the appellant and her then husband, who were associated with the
hotel company, executed in favour of Hogan a deed of guarantee of the debt. On 18th
October 1973 Hogan assigned the mortgage to the respondent in this appeal. The due
date for payment of the mortgage debt passed without such payment being made by the
hotel company, and on 25th November 1975 it and the respondent entered into a
memorandum of variation of the mortgage. This provided that the rate of interest
h payable under the mortgage should be increased from 9% to 16% per annum as from
12th October 1975, and that the term of the mortage should be extended to 12th October
1976. The appellant was not asked to, and did not, consent to this variation. Finally, on
25th March 1976 Hogan assigned to the respondent the benefit of the guarantee by the
appellant and her husband.
   It appears that the hotel company defaulted in the payment of interest under the
j mortgage as varied, and on 16th June 1976 the respondent commenced proceedings
against the appellant and her husband in the District Court at Sydney, claiming payment
by them as guarantors the sum of $8,583·31 by way of interest then due and unpaid by
the hotel company. Default judgment was entered against the appellant's husband, but
on 3rd February 1978 his Honour Judge Godfrey-Smith QC entered judgment for the

appellant. He held that the variation of the terms of the mortgage, which was agreed to be a material one, had been entered into without the consent of the appellant as *a* guarantor, that on a proper construction of the relevant conditions of the guarantee the variation was not such as might consistently therewith be entered into without her consent, and that accordingly its effect was to discharge the appellant's liability under the guarantee. The respondent appealed to the Supreme Court of New South Wales, and by order dated 7th August 1979 the Court of Appeal (Street CJ, Samuels and Mahoney JJA) set aside the order of Judge Godfrey-Smith and entered judgment against the present *b* appellant for the sum of $8,583·31. Against that judgment the appellant now appeals to Her Majesty in Council.

It is common ground between the parties that the variation of the term of the mortgage effected by the memorandum dated 25th November 1975 was a material one, and, if not authorised by some provision of the guarantee, of such a nature as to bring about the legal result of discharging the whole of the appellant's obligations *c* thereunder. The provision of the guarantee on which the respondent principally relies as having authorised the variation is cl 14. This provides, so far as material:

> 'It is hereby expressly provided that any further advance or advances which may be made by the Lender to the Borrower shall be included in this Guarantee unless the Guarantor shall have given to the Lender notice in writing . . . clearly stating that no further advances shall be covered under the terms of this Guarantee . . .' *d*

The main argument for the respondent, which was accepted by the Court of Appeal, was that the transaction embodied in the memorandum dated 25th November 1975 amounted in substance to a 'further advance' within the meaning of this provision. It was pointed out that cl 1 of the guarantee provided that it was to be a continuing one, while cl 5 contained reference to the guarantors' obligation to pay interest, in the event *e* of failure by the borrower, not only on the principal sum but also on 'any other moneys which may bear interest under the terms of the loan', and cl 11 mentioned 'any security or other document taken by the Lender'. The position was the same, so it was maintained, as if the original principal sum had been repaid and readvanced to the borrower.

In accepting this argument Mahoney JA, whose opinion was concurred in by the other *f* members of the Court of Appeal, said:

> 'In my opinion "further advance" as used in cl 14 should be held to include the subsequent transaction. I do not think that "advance" according to its ordinary meaning is limited to transactions under which money or goods are, as part of the particular transaction, handed over or delivered to the debtor. The term is, in my opinion, wide enough to include a transaction under which, money being already *g* available to a debtor, he becomes entitled to retain it for a period beyond that for which otherwise it would have been available to him. According to ordinary parlance, it would be proper to describe that money as having been "advanced" for a further term.'

In their Lordships' opinion that view is erroneous and the argument for the respondent *h* is unsound. While the meaning of the word 'advance' may be shaded somewhat by the context, it normally means the furnishing of money for some specified purpose. The furnishing need not necessarily be by way of loan, but clearly that is what was in contemplation here. When cl 14 refers to 'a further advance' it appears to their Lordships to be referring to the furnishing of an additional principal sum. Where the term for repayment of the original principal sum is extended, it is true to say that that sum *j* remains advanced for a further term, but it is a distortion of language to say that a further advance has been made. In reaching the conclusion which their Lordships have quoted, Mahoney JA referred to a considerable number of decided cases. Their Lordships have examined these, but have not found any of them to support his conclusion, or indeed to be of any assistance at all for present purposes.

In considering the true substance and effect of the memorandum dated 25th November
a 1975, it is important to keep in view the provisions of the first and second clauses of the
mortgage. These are:

'Firstly—That the mortgagor will pay to the mortgagee the principal sum, or so
much thereof as shall remain unpaid on the 12th day of October 1975.
'Secondly—That the mortgagor will pay interest on the principal sum or on so
much thereof as for the time being shall remain unpaid and upon any judgment or
b order in which this or the prceding covenant may become merged, at the rate of
nine (9) per centum per annum as follows, namely—By equal monthly payments
. . . until the principal sum shall be fully paid and satisfied . . .'

It is thus clearly agreed that the interest payable is to be at the rate of 9% per annum,
however long the principal sum may be outstanding.
c   Under the memorandum of 25th November 1975 it was agreed that the rate of
interest was to be increased to 16% from 12th October 1975. That cannot be regarded as
anything but an alteration of what was previously agreed, irrespective of the circumstance
that at the same time the term of the mortgage was extended for one year. Their
Lordships are unable to find anywhere in the provisions of the guarantee any indication
of an intention that the guarantors should be required to undertake, without their
d specific consent, liability for such increased interest as mortgagor and mortgagee might
subsequently agree on.
     The respondent relied on the subsidiary argument that what was agreed by the
memorandum of 25th November 1975 was authorised by cl 18 of the guarantee. This
provided for the lender, without the consent of the guarantor, granting to the borrower
time or 'any other indulgence or consideration', without thereby affecting the liability of
e the guarantors. Their Lordships are of opinion that, while the agreement for the
extension of the term of the mortgage might, if it stood alone, be authorised by this
provision, the superadded agreement for an increased rate of interest goes beyond
anything which was thereby contemplated. The granting of an indulgence to a debtor
may have the effect of prejudicing the rights of the guarantor vis-à-vis the debtor, and
accordingly, in the absence of a provision such as this one, it has the effect of releasing the
f guarantor from liability. The purpose and effect of the provision in question is merely
to safeguard the creditor against that eventuality. It does not enable the debtor and
creditor, by agreement between themselves, to require the guarantor to shoulder an
added liability.
     Their Lordships were referred on this branch of the appeal to the Western Australian
case of *Payton v S G Brookes & Sons Pty Ltd* [1977] WAR 91. This decision, which might
g at first sight appear to be in point, turns out on closer examination not to be so. The
granting of time to the debtor under a hire-purchase agreement was there held to be
covered by a provision similar to that presently under consideration, notwithstanding
that the agreement entered into had the result of the debtor being required to pay
additional sums by way of interest. That liability, however, arose from a provision of the
hire-purchase agreement itself, regarding the payment of interest on overdue instalments,
h and did not flow directly from the later agreement granting time. The case is therefore
distinguishable.
     For these reasons their Lordships will humbly advise Her Majesty that the appeal
should be allowed and the order of Judge Godfrey-Smith restored. The respondent will
be liable for costs before this Board and in the Court of Appeal.

Appeal allowed.

Solicitors: *Ingledew, Brown, Bennison & Garrett* (for the appellant); *Clifford-Turner & Co*
(for the respondent).

Mary Rose Plummer   Barrister.

A and another v C and others (No 2)   a

QUEEN'S BENCH DIVISION (COMMERCIAL COURT)
ROBERT GOFF J
22nd JANUARY, 5th FEBRUARY 1981

Injunction – Interlocutory – Danger that defendant may transfer assets out of jursdiction –   b
Injunction restraining removal of assets out of jurisdiction – Variation of injunction – Variation
to permit release of part of assets to pay defendant's legal costs of proceedings – Burden of proof
on defendant to obtain release of assets – Defendant adducing evidence that he was likely to incur
substantial legal costs but not that he had no other assets available to pay costs – Whether
injunction should be varied.

The defendants applied for the variation of a Mareva injunction granted against them in   c
proceedings brought by the plaintiffs, in order to permit them to pay out of the assets
which were subject to the injunction £65,000 for legal costs likely to be incurred by
them in the proceedings. The defendants placed evidence before the court that they
were likely to incur substantial costs in the proceedings but did not adduce any evidence
to show whether they had other assets available to pay the costs or, if they had, why they   d
were seeking to use the assets subject to the Mareva injunction.

Held – Although the court had jurisdiction to qualify a Mareva injunction where the
defendant satisfied the court that assets subject to the injunction were required for a
purpose which did not conflict with the policy underlying the Mareva jurisdiction, in
order to satisfy that burden the defendant had to go further than merely to state that he   e
owed money to someone, and had to show that he did not have any other assets available
out of which the debt would be paid. Since the defendants had failed to adduce evidence
to show that they had no other assets out of which they could pay the legal costs, their
application would be dismissed (see p 127 h to p 128 c, post).
    Iraqi Ministry of Defence v Arcepey Shipping Co SA (Gillespie Brothers & Co Ltd intervening)
[1980] 1 All ER 480 distinguished.   f

Note
For injunctions restraining the disposition of property, see 24 Halsbury's Laws (4th Edn)
para 1018.

Cases referred to in judgment   g
A v C [1980] 2 All ER 347, [1981] 2 WLR 629, [1980] 2 Lloyd's Rep 200.
Iraqi Ministry of Defence v Arcepey Shipping Co SA (Gillespie Brothers & Co Ltd intervening),
    The Angel Bell [1980] 1 All ER 480, [1980] 2 WLR 488, [1979] 2 Lloyd's Rep 491.

Summons
On 18th March 1980 the plaintiffs, on an ex parte application in their action against six   h
defendants, obtained a Mareva injunction against the first five defendants (see [1980] 2
All ER 347). By a summons dated 19th December 1980 the first and fifth defendants
applied for an order that the Mareva injunction be varied to permit payment to them of
£65,000 out of the assets subject to the injunction to enable them to pay legal expenses
likely to be incurred in the proceedings. The application was heard and judgment was
given by Robert Goff J in chambers on 22nd January 1981 but, with the parties' consent,   j
he repeated part of the judgment in open court because it raised a point of principle in
regard to Mareva injunctions. The facts are set out in the judgment.

Mark Waller QC and Richard Siberry for the plaintiffs.
Peter Sheridan QC and James Davies for the defendants.

5th February. **ROBERT GOFF J.** On 22nd January 1981 I heard an application by
a certain of the defendants in this case, in which they asked for an order varying a Mareva
injunction granted by this court on an earlier occasion (see *A v C* [1980] 2 All ER 347,
[1981] 2 WLR 629), the purpose of the proposed variation being to permit the payment
of £65,000 out of the assets now subject to the injunction in order to pay legal costs likely
to be incurred in the present proceedings. The application was heard in chambers; and
it was dismissed. But, having given my reasons in chambers for dismissing the
b application, I now propose (with the consent of the parties) to repeat part of my judgment
in open court, because it raises a point of principle with regard to Mareva injunctions,
which may be of general interest.

The argument before me in chambers was very largely directed to a detailed analysis
of certain very complicated transactions, which I do not propose to refer to in this
judgment in open court. But in the end the question at issue between the parties was
c reduced to one point, which was as follows. There was evidence before the court that the
defendants were likely to incur substantial costs in the forthcoming proceedings; and
they therefore applied, invoking the principle stated in *Iraqi Ministry of Defence v Arcepey
Shipping Co SA, The Angel Bell* [1980] 1 All ER 480, [1980] 2 WLR 488, for release of
money to pay those costs. But no evidence whatsoever was placed before the court
concerning any other assets of the defendants making the application; it was not therefore
d possible for the court to assess whether any other assets of these defendants were available
to pay the costs or, if they were so available, why the defendants were seeking to make
use of the assets which were subject to the Mareva injunction for this purpose. I had
therefore to consider whether it would be proper for the court, in such circumstances, to
accede to the defendants' application.

In *Iraqi Ministry of Defence v Arcepey* [1980] 1 All ER 480 at 485, [1980] 2 WLR 488 at
e 493 it was said that—

> 'the fundamental purpose of the Mareva jurisdiction is to prevent foreign parties
> from causing assets to be removed from the jurisdiction in order to avoid the risk
> of having to satisfy any judgment which may be entered against them in pending
> proceedings in this country.'

f From that statement of principle, of course the word 'foreign' has now to be deleted,
having regard to subsequent developments. However, it was also stated in the same case
that—

> 'it does not follow that, having established the injunction, the court should not
> thereafter permit a qualification to it to allow a transfer of assets by the defendant
> if the defendant satisfies the court that he requires the money for a purpose which
g > does not conflict with the policy underlying the Mareva jurisdiction.'

(See [1980] 1 All ER 480 at 486, [1980] 2 WLR 488 at 494.)

In the *Iraqi* case, the court did permit the release of money in order to make certain
payments bona fide in the ordinary course of business. However, that was a case where
the fund which was the subject of the Mareva injunction, viz the proceeds of insurance
h of the single ship of a one-ship company, was the defendants' only asset. There was no
question of the defendants having other funds from which the payment might be
made. It follows that the question which fell for decision in the present case did not arise
in that case.

In the present case, I have had to consider the position where the defendant has, or may
have, other assets from which the relevant payment may be made. I have still to apply
j the basic principle, ie that I can only permit a qualification to the injunction if the
defendant satisfies the court that the money is required for a purpose which does not
conflict with the policy underlying the Mareva jurisdiction. I do not consider that in
normal circumstances a defendant can discharge that burden of proof simply by saying,
'I owe somebody some money.' I put to the defendants' counsel, in the course of
argument, the example of an English-based defendant with two bank accounts, one

containing a very substantial sum which was not subject to the Mareva injunction, and
the other containing a smaller sum which was. I asked counsel: would it be sufficient for   *a*
the defendant simply to say, 'I owe somebody some money, please qualify the injunction
to permit payment from the smaller account, without giving any consideration to the
possibility of payment from the larger account'? Counsel was constrained to accept that
that would not be sufficient, because it would not satisfy the court that the payment out
of the small account would not conflict with the principle underlying the Mareva
jurisdiction. The whole purpose of selecting the smaller account might be to prevent the   *b*
money in that account from being available to satisfy a judgment in the pending
proceedings. In my judgment, a defendant has to go further than that; precisely what
he has to prove will depend, no doubt, on the circumstances of the particular case. At all
events, in the present case, if the defendants making the application have other assets,
freely available (and I do not know, on the evidence, whether they have or not), it would
be open to counsel for the plaintiffs to submit, on the evidence, that it would be wrong   *c*
for the court to vary the Mareva injunction. All I can say at present is that, on the
evidence before the court, the defendants have not discharged the burden of proof which
rests on them.

The application has therefore been dismissed with costs.

Application dismissed.

Solicitors: *Herbert Smith & Co* (for the plaintiffs); *Lorenz & Jones* (for the defendants).

K Mydeen Esq   Barrister.

a # R v Canterbury and St Augustine's Justices, ex parte Klisiak
R v Ramsgate Justices, ex parte Warren and others

b QUEEN'S BENCH DIVISION
LORD LANE CJ AND WEBSTER J
11th, 12th NOVEMBER 1980

c *Criminal law – Committal – Preliminary hearing before justices – Accused charged with offence entitling him to elect to be tried by a jury – Accused electing to be tried by jury – No evidence offered by prosecution – Lesser charge which is triable only summarily substituted by prosecution – Whether an abuse of process of court – Whether justices entitled to question prosecution decision to offer no evidence on original charge.*

d *Criminal law – Damage to property – Value – Value over certain sum giving defendant right to elect trial by jury – Court required to hear 'representations' as to value – Whether court bound to hear 'evidence' as to value – Criminal Law Act 1977, s 23(1).*

On 22nd November 1978 the applicant appeared before magistrates on a charge of damaging without lawful excuse 12 stem glasses, 12 glass tankards, 5 ashtrays, 5 stools, a table, a front door, a countertop and a wall at a public house on 21st July 1978, contrary
e to s 1 of the Criminal Damage Act 1971. The value of the damage was alleged to be £414·05. The magistrates informed him that, as the value of the damage involved was more than £200, the case need not be tried summarily and he could elect, under s 23(4)[a] of the Criminal Law Act 1977, to go for trial by jury at the Crown Court. The applicant, who intended to plead not guilty, elected to be tried by jury and the case was adjourned to 20th December 1978 to enable the prosecution to serve witness statements. On 8th
f December the prosecution informed him that they intended to prefer an amended charge against him, viz damaging without lawful excuse five ashtrays, five stools, a table, a countertop and a wall, together valued at £154·89, contrary to s 1 of the 1971 Act. That offence was triable only summarily. At the hearing on 20th December the prosecution informed the magistrates of the new charge and stated that they would be offering no evidence on the original charge. The applicant was discharged on the
g original charge and the magistrates then heard representations from the prosecution and the applicant as to the value of the damage concerned in the new charge. The applicant challenged the correctness of the prosecution's figure of £154·89 and submitted that it was unlikely that the value of the damage was under £200, that as the prosecution had alleged in the original charge that all the damage listed there had been done by him it was artificial to determine the nature and extent of the offence by reference to the
h limitation introduced by the new charge, and that the magistrates should hold that the new charge came within the exception provided by s 23(7) of the 1977 Act, so that he could elect to be tried by jury at the Crown Court. The magistrates refused to allow evidence to be admitted to prove the value of the damage and held that the new charge did not come within s 23(7), so that it had to be tried summarily. The applicant applied for a judicial review of the magistrates' decision, contending, inter alia, that they ought
j not to have acceded to the prosecution's offer of no evidence on the original charge, and that there had been an abuse of the process of the court.

---

a Section 23, so far as material, is set out at p 132 *c* to *g* and p 134 *j*, post

Held – The applications would be dismissed for the following reasons—
(1) The rule that when a prosecuting authority offered no evidence the court's consent *a* was required to that course being followed did not apply to committal proceedings because in such proceedings the magistrates did not have before them depositions or statements on which they could base their conclusion (see p 136 *c* and p 139 *g*, post); *R v Broad* (1979) 68 Cr App R 281 distinguished.

(2) Magistrates had inherent power to prevent an abuse of the process of their court but it was to be used very sparingly, ie only where there would otherwise be a blatant *b* injustice. Since the prosecution were entitled to decide not to proceed with a charge which was triable summarily or on indictment, even though the defendant had elected to go for trial at the Crown Court on that charge, and since the prosecution were entitled to prefer a lesser charge which was triable only summarily, it followed that there had not been an abuse of the process of the court (see p 136 *e f*, p 137 *c* to *f* and p 139 *g*, post); *R v Bennett* (1928) 20 Cr App R 188 and *R v Bodmin Justices, ex parte McEwen* [1947] 1 All ER *c* 109 considered.

(3) Magistrates were required under s 23(1) of the 1977 Act merely to have regard to 'representations' as to the value of the damage involved, which meant submissions, coupled with assertions of fact and sometimes production of documents. They were not bound to hear evidence as to the value of the damage, although they had a discretion to do so. Accordingly, there were no grounds for interfering with the magistrates' decision *d* not to hear evidence as to value (see p 137 *h* to p 138 *a* and p 139 *g*, post).

(4) The magistrates had rightly held that the substituted charge did not fall within s 23(7) because, although both the original and the substituted charges covered much the same items of damage, they did not form 'part of a series of offences' within s 23(7) (see p 138 *g* and p 139 *g*, post).

Per Curiam. Provided that the offences are not grave and that the powers of the *e* magistrates vis-à-vis sentence are appropriate, there is no reason why the prosecuting authority should not charge an offence which is not the gravest possible allegation on the facts. There may be many reasons for choosing a lesser charge, eg speed of trial, sufficiency of proof, and summary trial rather than a trial on indictment. It is necessarily a matter of discretion and careful choice, but if a prosecuting authority decides to prefer a lesser charge it should do so at the outset (see p 139 *g*, post). *f*

Notes

For committal proceedings generally, see 11 Halsbury's Laws (4th Edn) paras 136–164.

For damaging property, see ibid para 1306.

For the Criminal Damage Act 1971, s 1, see 41 Halsbury's Statutes (3rd Edn) 409.

For the Criminal Law Act 1977, s 23, see 47 ibid 703. *g*

Cases referred to in judgments

Connelly v Director of Public Prosecutions [1964] 2 All ER 401, [1964] AC 1254, [1964] 2 WLR 1145, 128 JP 418, 48 Cr App R 183, HL; *affg* [1963] 2 All ER 510, [1963] 3 WLR 839, CCA, Digest (Cont Vol B) 250, 472a.

Director of Public Prosecutions v Humphrys [1976] 2 All ER 497, [1977] AC 1, [1976] 2 WLR *h* 857, 140 JP 386, 63 Cr App R 95, HL, 14(1) Digest (Reissue) 315, 2427.

Mills v Cooper [1967] 2 All ER 100, [1967] 2 QB 459, [1967] 2 WLR 1343, 131 JP 349, 65 LGR 275, DC, Digest (Cont Vol C) 337, 472b.

R v Bennett (1928) 20 Cr App R 188, CCA, 33 Digest (Repl) 286, 1141.

R v Bodmin Justices, ex parte McEwen [1947] 1 All ER 109, [1947] KB 321, [1947] LJR 338, 111 JP 47, 45 LGR 74, DC, 33 Digest (Repl) 226, 602. *j*

R v Broad (1979) 68 Cr App R 281, CA.

R v Camberwell Green Magistrates, ex parte Prescott (11th June 1979, unreported), CA.

R v Crimlis [1976] Crim LR 693, CA.

R v Manchester City Stipendiary Magistrate, ex parte Snelson [1978] 2 All ER 62, [1977] 1 WLR 911, 142 JP 274, 66 Cr App R 44, DC, Digest (Cont Vol E) 134, 1700a.

Cases also cited

a *R v Metropolitan Police Comr, ex parte Blackburn* [1968] 1 All ER 763, [1968] 2 QB 118, CA.
R v Metropolitan Police Comr, ex parte Blackburn (No 2) [1968] 2 All ER 319, [1968] 2 QB 150, CA.
R v Metropolitan Police Comr, ex parte Blackburn (No 3) [1973] 1 All ER 324, CA.

Applications for judicial review

b   *R v Canterbury and St Augustine's Justices, ex parte Klisiak*

Mark Peter Klisiak applied, with the leave of the Divisional Court of the Queen's Bench Division granted on 7th September 1979, for (i) an order prohibiting the justices for the petty sessional division of Canterbury and St Augustines in the County of Kent from proceeding to hear a charge against him of damaging on 21st July 1978, without lawful
c excuse, five glass ashtrays, five stools, one table, one countertop and a wall belonging to John Hedigan, intending to damage such property or being reckless whether such property would be damaged, contrary to s 1 of the Criminal Damage Act 1971, and (2) an order of mandamus directing the justices to proceed on the charge in accordance with the provisions of s 23(3) or alternatively s 23(4) to (6) and/or ss 20 to 22 of the Criminal Law Act 1977. The facts are set out in the judgment of Lord Lane CJ.

d   *R v Ramsgate Justices, ex parte Warren and others*

Paul Richard Warren, David Michael Pain, John Terence Goulding and Karl William Elliott applied, with the leave of McNeill J granted on 11th August 1979, for (1) an order prohibiting the justices of the petty sessional division of Ramsgate in the County of Kent from proceeding to hear so called 'amended charges' against them that (i) the applicant
e Warren on 10th May 1980 assaulted Pc Frost in the execution of his duty, contrary to s 51(1) of the Police Act 1964, (ii) the applicant Pain on 10th May 1980 wilfully obstructed Pc O'Connell in the execution of his duty, contrary to s 51(3) of the 1964 Act, wilfully obstructed Pc Hunter in the execution of his duty, contrary to s 51(3) of the 1964 Act, and assaulted Wpc Giles in the execution of her duty, contrary to s 51(1) of the 1964 Act, (iii) the applicant Goulding on 10th May 1980 wilfully obstructed Pc Hunter in the
f execution of his duty, contrary to s 51(3) of the 1964 Act, and (iv) Karl William Elliott on 10th May 1980 wilfully obstructed Pc Hunter in the execution of his duty, contrary to s 51(3) of the 1964 Act, (2) an order of mandamus directed to the justices requiring them to proceed in accordance with the provisions of ss 20 to 22 of the Criminal Law Act 1977 on charges that (i) the applicant Warren on 10th May 1980 assaulted Pc Frost, thereby occasioning him actual bodily harm, contrary to s 47 of the Offences against the Person
g Act 1861, (ii) the applicant Pain on 10th May 1980 assaulted Pc O'Connell with intent to prevent the lawful detainer of Russel Edward Pittock and assaulted Pc Hunter with intent to prevent the lawful detainer of the applicant Warren and assaulted Wpc Giles thereby occasioning her actual bodily harm, (iii) the applicant Goulding on 10th May 1980 assaulted Pc Hunter with intent to prevent the lawful detainer of the applicant Warren, contrary to s 38 of the 1861 Act, and (iv) the applicant Elliott on 10th May 1980
h assaulted Pc Hunter with intent to prevent the lawful detainer of the applicant Warren, contrary to s 38 of the 1861 Act, and (3) an order of certiorari to quash an order made by the justices discharging the applicants in respect of the charges in respect of which mandamus was sought. The facts are set out in the judgment of Lord Lane CJ.

Anthony Speaight for the applicant in the first case.
j *Brian Prior* for the applicants in the second case.
David Pitman for the respondents in both cases.

LORD LANE CJ. These are two applications for judicial review directed respectively to the Canterbury and St Augustine's justices and to the Ramsgate justices. They raise very similar points and, at the request of the parties, we heard them together.

The points, if we may say so, have been argued with great skill, economy of words and charm by all the advocates, and we are very grateful for the assistance which has been *a* given to us in this matter.

I take the Klisiak case first. That arose out of an incident on 21st July 1978 in a public house at Westbere in the County of Kent. The result of that incident was a considerable amount of damage to the public house and its contents. On 19th October 1978 the applicant was charged under the Criminal Damage Act 1971 with criminal damage to eight items to a total value of £414·05. The items (and it is important to list them for *b* reasons which will be apparent in a moment) were these: 12 glasses, 12 tumblers, 5 ashtrays, 5 stools, a table, a door, a countertop and a wall. That was the original charge, and he will, if the question ever arises, plead not guilty to it at the trial.

On 22nd November 1978 he appeared before the justices at Canterbury on a charge under s 1 of the 1971 Act. Under the provisions of the Criminal Law Act 1977 that charge was triable either way, that is to say, either before the justices or at the Crown *c* Court. By s 23 of the 1977 Act, the following provisions are made:

'(1) If the offence charged by the information is one of those mentioned in the first column of Schedule 4 to this Act (in this section referred to as "scheduled offences") then, subject to subsection (7) below, the court shall, before proceeding in accordance with section 20 above, consider whether, having regard to any representations made by the prosecutor or the accused, the value involved (as *d* defined in subsection (10) below) appears to the court to exceed the relevant sum. For the purposes of this section the relevant sum is £200.

'(2) If, where subsection (1) above applies, it appears to the court clear that, for the offence charged, the value involved does not exceed the relevant sum, the court shall proceed as if the offence were triable only summarily, and sections 20 to 22 above shall not apply. *e*

'(3) If, where subsection (1) above applies, it appears to the court clear that, for the offence charged, the value involved exceeds the relevant sum, the court shall thereupon proceed in accordance with section 20 above in the ordinary way without further regard to the provisions of this section . . .'

Section 20 deals with the mode of trial and, in short, what those provisions mean, so *f* far as is material here, is that under £200 damage is tried summarily and over £200 damage means that the accused has the right of election to go to the Crown Court for trial by jury, if he so wishes.

Section 23(4) reads as follows:

'If, where subsection (1) above applies, it appears to the court for any reason not clear whether, for the offence charged, the value involved does or does not exceed *g* the relevant sum, the provisions of subsections (5) and (6) below shall apply.'

Again, in short, that means that where the value is not clear, the court must give the defendant the right to elect the mode of trial.

The applicant appeared before the justices on 22nd November 1978, and the court followed the procedure which is laid down in those sections. It was apparent, of course, that the value was over £200 because the charge sheet alleged it at £414·05. The court *h* accordingly offered the applicant the opportunity to elect for trial in the Crown Court if he so wished. The court then adjourned the case to enable the prosecution to serve witness statements in the usual way, because the applicant did elect for trial by jury.

No statements were, in fact, served, but on 8th December a letter was sent from the superintendent of the Kent County Constabulary to the applicant's solicitors which reads: *j*

'Dear Sir,
                              'Mark Peter Klisiak:
'I would refer to the case against the above-named and would inform you that prior to the court hearing on 20th December, 1978, it is intended to prefer an

a   amended charge upon your client. A copy of this charge is attached and I would
      draw your attention to the value which, as you of course will realise, precludes this
      case from a Crown Court hearing.'

      The charge reads as follows: it is headed with the name of the applicant and records his
b   address, his sex, his date of birth and his nationality. Then it is headed: 'Amended—
      Charge(s)'. Then it says:

          'You are charged with the offence(s) shown below. You are not obliged to say
          anything unless you wish to do so, but whatever you say will be taken down in
          writing and may be given in evidence.'

      Then there is typed:
c
          'On the 21st July, 1978, at Westbere in the County of Kent, without lawful excuse
          damaged five glass ashtrays, five stools, one table, one countertop and a wall,
          together valued at £154·89, belonging to John Hedigan, intending to damage such
          property or being reckless as to whether such property would be damaged.
          (Contrary to section 1 Criminal Damage Act, 1971).'
d
      It will be observed that that differed from the original charge because it omits the stem
      glasses, the damage to the door and the damage to the pint tankards. It adjusts the value
      accordingly from £414 to £154·89.
      On 20th December the applicant appeared before the Canterbury justices. The new
      charge was read over to him before the hearing and the matter was called on before the
e   justices. The story is then taken up in para 4 of the affidavit of the chairman to the
      justices, which reads as follows:

          'At the hearing on 20th December, 1978, before us, the prosecution offered no
          evidence upon the first charge on the basis that there was no evidence to support a
          charge alleging damage to all the items in that charge, and in particular there was
f   no evidence to support the allegation that the defendant caused damage to the
          twelve stem glasses, twelve pint glass tankards and one front door. The defendant,
          through his counsel, invited the court to reject the application. We accepted the
          submission by the prosecution that the police had insufficient evidence to proceed
          on the first charge and discharged the defendant in accordance with the provisions
          of section 7 of the Magistrates' Courts Act, 1952, upon that charge, and refused an
g   application by the defendant for costs both out of central funds and against the
          police.'

      No details of the evidence were given and the court accepted, as is apparent from that
      paragraph, the prosecution's submissions without further inquiry.
      Counsel for the applicant in this case submitted to us that the prosecution could have
h   operated by means of either of two methods, apart from the one they in fact adopted.
      First of all, they could have amended the original charge; secondly, they could have
      waited until the evidence in the committal proceedings had been given and then made
      submissions as to the appropriate charge because, he says, the charge does not have to be
      written down at the commencement of the proceedings. He submits that if a prosecutor
      at a committal is concerned with the weakness of his case, he can wait until the end of the
j   committal proceedings and put the matter right at that stage. He points out that the
      significance of the course which was actually adopted by the prosecution in this case is
      that the applicant did not have the right to elect trial by jury. On the other hand, he says
      that if the prosecution had taken either of the two alternative courses then the right of
      election would still have been open the applicant. The prosecution, on the other hand,
      applied to the magistrates to treat the new charge as entirely separate.

What happened then afterwards is again set out conveniently in the very helpful affidavit of the chairman of the magistrates, Mr Mount. The affidavit reads:

'5. We then proceeded to deal with the second charge and heard representations from both the prosecution and defence upon the value of the damage alleged in accordance with the provisions of section 23 of the Criminal Law Act, 1977. We were invited on behalf of the defendant to hear evidence as to the value involved, but we took the view that the statutory provisions permitted us merely to hear representations from either side and did not permit us to hear evidence upon this point.

'6. We heard details from the prosecution of the estimate for the replacement or repair of all the damaged items set out in the first charge, which amounted to £414·05. We were invited by the prosecution to deduct the estimated cost of the replacement of the twelve stem glasses and twelve pint glass tankards, which we were advised by the prosecution was £8·16, and the cost of the replacement of the front door which was £251, these items of damage no longer being alleged against the defendant, to reach the figure put forward by the prosecution in respect of the second charge of £154·89.

'7. The defendant through counsel submitted that there had been a major disturbance and a very large amount of damage had been done; that it was artificial to allege only parts of the damage and that the damage was not clearly under £200. He further submitted that the uncertain areas were the fact that there had been one big incident, that Value Added Tax had not been included in the estimate, that there was the possibility of the replacement of items by further items which were not identical with those damaged and that the defendant understood that the work done to the front door had been £215, £36 less than put forward.

'8. We indicated to the parties before retiring to consider the matter that if we were minded to rule against the defendant, before so doing we would ask the prosecution to make inquiries as to the actual cost of replacement and repairs as opposed to the estimates, as we were advised that the necessary replacements and repairs had already been undertaken.

'9. Having careful regard to the representations made, we were of opinion that it was clear that for the offence alleged, the value of damage involved did not exceed £200.

'10. We advised the parties of our opinion and requested the prosecution to inquire what the actual cost of the replacements and repairs had been. After a short adjournment, the prosecution advised us that the actual cost, including Value Added Tax, of replacement of the five glass ashtrays, five stools and one table had been £115·36, and that the cost, including Value Added Tax, of the repair of the countertop and wall had been £29·37, making a total of £146·73.

'11. We ruled that it appeared clear to the court that for the offence charged the value involved did not exceed £200, and we adjourned the case for a summary trial.'

On 9th May 1979 there was a further hearing before the magistrates' court at which counsel for the applicant invited the magistrates to consider whether the damage alleged under the new charges fell within the exceptions provided by s 23(7) of the Criminal Law Act 1977, which provides as follows:

'Subsection (1) above shall not apply where the offence charged—(a) is one of two or more offences with which the accused is charged on the same occasion and which appear to the court to constitute or form part of a series of two or more offences of the same or a similar character . . .'

I turn now to the facts of the Ramsgate case. They are as follows: the four applicants are Paul Richard Warren, David Michael Pain, John Terence Goulding and Karl William Elliot. On 10th May 1980 there was a disturbance on the sea front at Ramsgate. The two

applicants, and two other youths as well, were arrested as a result of those disturbances.
a On 11th May the four applicants were charged as follows: Warren was charged with a breach of the peace under s 5 of the Public Order Act 1936; with assault on a police constable in the execution of his duty under s 51 of the Police Act 1964, and assault occasioning actual bodily harm under s 47 of the Offences against the Person Act 1861. Pain was charged with a breach of the peace under s 5 of the Public Order Act 1936; assault with intent to prevent his lawful detainer under s 38 of the Offences against the *b* Person Act 1861, and another charge under the same section and, finally, assault occasioning actual bodily harm, apparently under s 47 of the 1861 Act.

Goulding was charged with a breach of the peace under s 5 of the Public Order Act 1936 and with assault with intent to prevent his lawful detainer under s 38 of the Offences against the Person Act 1861. Elliot was charged with breach of the peace under s 5 of the Public Order Act 1936, and an assault with intent to prevent his lawful detainer *c* under the 1861 Act. The other two youths, who I have already mentioned, were charged with offences triable summarily only.

On 2nd June 1980 Pain, Goulding and Elliot appeared before the justices, when the prosecution applied for an adjournment and made the suggestion that the applicants might be charged with more serious offences, in particular, possibly with affray. All three had been on bail. A similar suggestion had been made in respect of Warren, who *d* was remanded in custody, he having been on bail for another offence at the time of this incident (in which he is alleged to have been involved) took place.

On 30th June, the applicants again appeared before the justices, when each elected trial in the Crown Court in respect of those offences with which they had been charged which were triable either way, and the committal proceedings were then apparently adjourned. Meanwhile, it is clear that the police resolved that they would not proceed *e* with the offences which were triable either way, but would substitute similar charges which were triable only summarily. As a result of that determination, on 7th July 1980, and before the applicants appeared in the court, they were charged in the following manner. Warren was charged with an assault on a constable under s 51 of the Police Act 1964; Pain was charged with obstructing a police constable in the execution of his duty (there were two charges to that effect under the same section) and also with an assault on *f* a police constable under sub-s (1) of the same section; Goulding was charged with obstructing a police constable in the execution of his duty under s 51(3) of the 1954 Act, and Elliot was charged with a similar offence under the same Act.

When the applicants appeared before the justices later that day, on 7th July, the prosecution offered no evidence on the original offences, which had been triable either way, and consequently the justices discharged the applicants in respect of those offences *g* and adjourned the hearing of the offences which were only triable summarily. The chairman of the bench in this case too has filed a very helpful affidavit which is before us.

The way in which the matter was put was this (and I say in parenthesis that plainly very similar considerations arise in each of these two cases, although there are differences as will appear in a moment). The first submission made by counsel on behalf of the applicant Klisiak was that the justices ought not to have acceded to the prosecution *h* offering no evidence so far as the material allegations in the original charges were concerned. Secondly, he submits that the justices ought to have treated the new charges as an amendment rather than as a distinctly different charge. Thirdly, he submits that evidence ought to have been admitted as to the value of the damage done in the Klisiak case. Fourthly, he submits that if evidence was not admissible so far as the damage was concerned, the court ought to have regarded the damage either as being plainly over *j* £200 or as not being clearly established at all as to whether it was over £200 or not. Finally, the submission was that the provisions of s 23(7) of the Criminal Law Act 1977 should have been held to apply to this case.

The first submission was that when a prosecuting authority offers no evidence, the court's consent (and this, the submission goes, comprises magistrates as well as any other court) is required to that course being followed.

We will refer to the decision in *R v Broad* (1979) 68 Cr App R 281. All I need read
from that case is the headnote. It says:

> 'Where an accused person has been charged on indictment with an offence and
> counsel for the prosecution invites the trial judge to approve that the prosecution do
> not proceed, the judge is not a rubber stamp to approve a decision of counsel
> without further consideration; but may, having read the papers and formed the
> conclusion that there was very substantial evidence in the accused's case which a
> jury ought to consider, order the trial to proceed. Further, in the absence of an
> application that another judge should try the case, the judge is abundantly entitled
> to try the case himself.'

It seems to me that those considerations do not apply to committal proceedings and to
justices in committal proceedings. They only apply where there has already been a
committal as, in my view, it is not open to the justices to question the prosecution's
decision to offer no evidence. They have insufficient material before them on which to
come to a conclusion; they have not, like the judge at the Crown Court, depositions or
statements on which to base their conclusion. In any event, a refusal to commit by the
justices in these circumstances does not act as an acquittal or a bar to further proceedings.
If any authority is required for that, it is to be found in Lord Widgery CJ's judgment in
R v Manchester City Stipendiary Magistrate, ex parte Snelson [1978] 2 All ER 62 at 63–64,
[1977] 1 WLR 911 at 912.
    Next it is submitted that the justices always have a discretion to prevent an abuse of the
process of their court, and this, it is alleged, is what happened on both these occasions.
    We were referred to a number of authorities on the powers of courts to prevent an
abuse of the process before them. Principally the cases were *Connelly v Director of Public
Prosecutions* [1964] 2 All ER 401, [1964] AC 1254, *Mills v Cooper* [1967] 2 All ER 100 at
103, [1967] 2 QB 459 at 467 and *Director of Public Prosecutions v Humphrys* [1976] 2 All ER
497, [1977] AC 1.
    I am prepared to assume that there does exist in the justices, an inherent power to act
so as to prevent any flagrant abuse of the processes of their court, limited necessarily by
any relevant statutory obligation. This power, if it exists, would have to be exercised by
the justices very sparingly and only in the most obvious circumstances which disclose
blatant injustice. There must be, somewhere, some limit as to what can be done before
the court, and in that respect we were referred to *R v Bennett* (1928) 20 Cr App R 188, and
to *R v Bodmin Justices, ex parte McEwen* [1947] 1 All ER 109, [1947] KB 321. The passage
in the judgment of Lord Goddard CJ in *McEwen's* case ([1947] 1 All ER 109 at 111, [1947]
KB 321 at 324) is material. I will read the headnote in *McEwen's* case, which reads as
follows ([1947] KB 321):

> 'The accused, a soldier, was alleged, during a barrack-room quarrel, to have
> stabbed another soldier in the back with a bayonet, the injury being of so serious a
> nature that the doctors were of opinion that the injured man could not survive, and
> steps were taken to get his evidence by deposition. He, however, recovered, and at
> the trial before a court of summary jurisdiction, where the accused was charged
> under the Offences Against the Person Act, 1861, with "wounding with intent to do
> grievous bodily harm", the justices, at the request of both the prosecution and the
> defence, allowed the charge to be reduced to one of "unlawful wounding", and
> proceeded to deal with the case summarily. The accused pleaded guilty to the
> misdemeanor and the justices retired to their room to consider their sentence.'

There are then further matters which are not material. There was a further matter
which resulted in the conviction being quashed, and Lord Goddard LJ ([1947] 1 All ER
109 at 111, [1947] KB 321 at 324) said this:

> 'Here is a case in which a man's life has been seriously imperilled and if he had
> died the applicant would have been charged with murder. It was never intended

that justices should deal under that section with cases of this sort, where a man, whether under the influence of drink or not, takes a bayonet and stabs another in the back with the consequences which are disclosed here, and for justices to deal with it by treating it as nothing much more than common assault is a most extraordinary state of affairs. Justices should remember that they have to deal with matters of this sort judicially, and, although they must take into account what the prosecution and the defence say with regard to whether or not it is a proper case for the charge to be reduced, they are not bound, because the prosecution want to get the matter dealt with there and then without the necessity of going to the assizes (where this case undoubtedly should have been sent) to assent to dealing with it summarily.'

It seems to me, however, that in this particular case it cannot be said that there was any abuse of the process of the court. If this charge had originally been laid in the sum of under £200, in Klisiak's case, as it might well have been, and in the Ramsgate case, if the charges had originally been laid under s 51 of the Police Act 1964, there could have been no possible complaint that anyone had been deprived of his right to elect trial. It seems to me that to achieve this same result by the procedural course which, in fact, was adopted, cannot be said to have been oppressive or unjust or an abuse of the processes of the court. Indeed, what the prosecution have done is to lower the nature of the case against the defendant and the possible consequential penalties. We have a Gilbertian result here of applicants complaining that they are now charged with lesser offences than those which they originally had to face. The prosecution, it is conceded, acted in accordance with the statutory provision and, in my judgment, there was nothing in the result which was unfair.

In Klisiak's case, the new charge was headed 'Amended Charge(s)', and one of the planks of the argument of counsel for the applicant in that case was that the justices should have treated it as such, in which case the possibility of election would still have been open to his client. However, it seems to me that the justices were not bound by the heading which the prosecuting authority chose to put on the document. There is no doubt but that he was charged in new terms and, consequently, in my judgment, there is nothing in that point.

One comes next to the argument that the justices should have allowed evidence to be called on the question of value of the property damaged in the Klisiak case. For the purposes of clarity, I repeat the provisions of s 23(1) of the Criminal Law Act 1977, in so far as they are material. They are as follows:

'... the court shall, before proceeding in accordance with section 20 above, consider whether, having regard to any representations made by the prosecutor or the accused, the value involved (as defined in subsection (10) below) appears to the court to exceed the relevant sum.'

As I say, the argument is that the justices should have heard evidence. It is not altogether clear whether they decided they had no right to hear evidence, as seems to be the case in their own affidavit, or whether, as seems to appear from the applicant's affidavit, they elected not to hear evidence. It is a distinction which is of no importance on the facts of this case, as will appear.

The word 'representations' implies something less than evidence. It comprises submissions, coupled with assertions of fact and sometimes production of documents. The nearest analogy is that suggested by counsel who appears on behalf of the respondents in this case. The nearest analogy is, perhaps, the speech in mitigation after a finding or plea of guilty in a criminal trial. The justices did hear representations in the present case, as has already been made apparent from the passage of the affidavit by the chairman of the justices, Mr Mount, which I have read. They heard eventually an assertion of fact as to the value of the damage done, again as appears from the portion of the affidavit which I have read. They could, in my judgment, if they had in their discretion wished to do so,

have heard evidence but here there was no call for it and they came to the proper, if not
the only, conclusion on the matter which they had before them and on the representations a
which they had before them. Consequently, that point must fail.

Finally, counsel for the applicant Klisiak argues that the justices were wrong in not
coming to a conclusion in his favour on the terms of s 23(7) of the 1977 Act. Again, at
the risk of prolixity, I will repeat the terms of that subsection:

> 'Subsection (1) above shall not apply where the offence charged—(a) is one of two b
> or more offences with which the accused is charged on the same occasion and which
> appear to the court to constitute or form part of a series of two or more offences of
> the same or a similar character . . .'

The object of that subsection is plainly to prevent the prosecution from alleging, in the
case of criminal damage, a series of offences, each of them damaging property less than
£200 and thereby avoiding the chance of the accused to elect a trial by jury.   c

We were referred to an unreported decision of the Court of Appeal, by which, of
course, this Divisional Court is bound, in the case of R v Camberwell Green Magistrates, ex
parte Prescott (11th June 1979, unreported). It contains in the judgment of Ormrod LJ,
with which Browne LJ agreed, a judgment as to the meaning of the word 'series' in this
particular context:
                                                                                        d
> 'When one turns to the nature of the offences charged in this case, one is an
> offence of obstructing a police officer in the course of his duty, and the other is the
> offence of criminal damage to the officer's trousers. It seems to be plain beyond any
> question that the two offences are not of the same or similar character, nor can I see
> on the facts of this case how these two offences could possibly be described as a
> "series". There is no series. Miss Bedford gave us a definition of the word "series" e
> from the Oxford Dictionary as "a number of things of one kind or following one
> another in temporal succession". Here we have two offences of an entirely different
> kind which occurred simultaneously and so do not follow one another in temporal
> succession. It seems to me, therefore, perfectly plain that s 23(7) [of the Criminal
> Law Act 1977] does not apply in this case and consequently that the magistrate was
> correct in the conclusion to which he came.'   f

Counsel for the applicant Klisiak concedes that that judgment is in direct conflict with
the submissions he makes to this court, and with that we would agree, but on the other
hand it seems to us, independently of that judgment, that it cannot be said that the
earlier charge and the later charge in this case can possibly fall within the terms of s 23(7),
which I have just read. These two charges cover much of the very same items of damage, g
each of them. They cannot, by any stretch of the imagination, in my judgment, be
regarded as a series or part of a series.

That leaves the one additional point made by counsel on behalf of the four Ramsgate
applicants, he having adopted the arguments of counsel for the applicant in the other
case, in so far as those are arguments which fell to be considered in his own set of facts.
The point made by counsel was this, the evidence and affidavits in the Ramsgate case h
show that the decision to offer no evidence, so far as the first offences were concerned, was
not based on an assessment of the serious conduct of the accused but was to prevent the
case being tried on indictment. For that purpose he referred us to the affidavit filed by
Chief Superintendent Alan Harry Stuart, of the Margate police station.

Paragraph 5 of that affidavit reads as follows:
                                                                                        j
> 'The factors that influenced me in deciding not to charge the offences of affray
> and to seek to have the said four defendants summarily dealt with were (i) the view
> in the case of Regina v Crimlis ([1976] Crim L R 693) as to when affray should be
> charged; there being individual charges against each of those alleged offenders
> concerned in the indictment; (ii) that the said Russell Edward Pittock and David

a Alexander Murray were charged only with summary offences and it was desirable that all defendants be dealt with at the same court.'

I interpolate there to mention that Pittock and Murray were the other two youths I have mentioned, apart from the four applicants whose names appear at the head of these proceedings.

b '(iii) the state of cases listed for hearing in Crown Courts in Kent and the exceptional time certain cases take before being heard; (iv) the abnormal number of cases in the Isle of Thanet where defendants in the Petty Sessional Divisions of Margate and Ramsgate elect for trial at the Crown Court and plead to the charges on arraignment notwithstanding having been supplied with copies of statements prior to the committal proceedings; (v) the often-expressed view of High Court judges that whenever appropriate, criminal cases should be dealt with summarily and not *c* at the Crown Court, and I was satisfied that the Magistrates could deal with this matter adequately on a summary basis; (vi) public policy in as much as in a seaside town such as Ramsgate, it is appropriate to have summertime public disturbances on the seafront and harbour areas dealt with as speedily as possible to deter any possible recurrences.'

d It seems to me that having read that affidavit, the attitude and course adopted by the prosecuting authorities in this case fell within the principles which I have already endeavoured to state. The prosecuting authority never went beyond what was proper in the circumstances of this case. Before parting with this case, I should like to say this, if I may: providing that the offences are not grave ones and that the powers of the justices vis-à-vis sentence are appropriate, there is no reason why the prosecuting authority should not charge an offence which is not the gravest possible allegation on the facts. *e* There may be many reasons for choosing a lesser charge, amongst other ones, speed of trial, sufficiency of proof and trial summarily rather than on indictment. It is necessarily a matter of discretion and careful choice. It is not easy for a prosecuting authority to steer between Scylla and Charybdis, but it is a tolerably wide passage through which they have to navigate. Prosecuting authorities have the duty to exercise great care in selecting the proper charges to prefer in any case. Whilst they must obviously avoid the type of error *f* exemplified in *R v Bodmin Justices, ex parte McEwan*, to which reference has already been made, and in *R v Bennett*, nevertheless if, in reality, the offence is nothing more than can properly be dealt with summarily by the justices, then it is proper so to charge it, despite the fact that the defendant may thereby lose his right to trial by jury if, indeed, it is, on balance, properly to be described as a loss at all. It is, however, to be hoped that, where proper, the lesser charges will be preferred at the outset, and the sort of discussion we *g* have had in these two matters may thereby be avoided.

In the upshot, these applications will be refused.

WEBSTER J. I agree.

h *Applications refused.*

Solicitors: *Boxall & Boxall*, agents for *Godfrey Davis & Waitt*, Ramsgate (for the applicant in the first case); *Marsland & Barber*, Margate (for the applicants in the second case); *Richard A Crabb*, Maidstone (for the respondents in both cases).

April Weiss   Barrister.

Re Dennis (deceased)   a

CHANCERY DIVISION
BROWNE-WILKINSON J
7th, 10th NOVEMBER 1980

Family provision – Time for application – Extension – Exercise of court's discretion – Matters b
to which court is to have regard – Applicant required to satisfy court he has an arguable case of
entitlement to provision – Originating summons by son issued 19 months out of time – Part of
delay excusable but part unexplained – Son limiting claim for provision to amount of his liability
for capital transfer tax on inter vivos gift made to him by deceased – Deceased leaving large estate
– Son likely to be made bankrupt if unable to pay tax – Whether son entitled to payment of tax
out of father's estate – Whether payment of tax amounting to 'maintenance' – Inheritance c
(Provision for Family and Dependants) Act 1975, ss 1(2)(b), 4.

During his lifetime the father gave his son a gift of £90,000 and also other sums of
money which the son dissipated in spendthrift living. The father left a large estate, and
by his will gave the son a legacy of £10,000 duty free. He also gave £30,000 duty free
to the trustees of a settlement under which the son had a protected life interest. The will
made no other provision for the son. The father died in November 1977 and probate of
his will was granted on 17th January 1978. On 22nd February 1980, some 19 months
out of time, the son issued a summons seeking the permission of the court under s 4[a] of
the Inheritance (Provision for Family and Dependants) Act 1975 to bring proceedings
out of time for reasonable financial provision out of the father's estate. The son was aged
38 and because he had dissipated all his resources had no capital or income, and was   e
unemployed. The son's claim for provision out of the estate was limited to the amount
of the capital transfer tax, some £45,000 to £50,000, which he was liable to pay in
respect of the gift of the £90,000 made in the father's lifetime. The son claimed that he
had no assets to pay the tax and would be made bankrupt if he did not pay it. There was
no evidence that if he were made bankrupt he would be unable to earn a living. Part of
the long delay in bringing the application under the Act was excusable but a material f
part of the delay was unexplained.

Held – (1) In exercising its discretion under s 4 of the 1975 Act to grant or withold
permission to bring proceedings out of time under that Act, a factor to which the court
was required to have regard, in addition to other matters, was whether the applicant was
able to satisfy the court that he had an arguable case that he was entitled to reasonable
financial provision out of the estate. The criterion of an arguable case was the same as g
that applied by the court in deciding whether a defendant should have leave to defend
in proceedings for summary judgment (see p 144 j to p 145 a, post); Re Salmon (deceased)
[1980] 3 All ER 532 considered.
    (2) Since, under s 1[b] of the 1975 Act, a claim by a deceased's child for reasonable
financial provision out of the estate was limited to reasonable provision for his
'maintenance', which connoted only payments which would, directly or indirectly,   h

---

a   Section 4 is set out at p 143 e f, post
b   Section 1, so far as material, provides:
    '(1) Where after the commencement of this Act a person dies domiciled in England and Wales
    and is survived by any of the following persons . . . (c) a child of the deceased . . . that person may
    apply to the court for an order under section 2 of this Act on the ground that the disposition of the j
    deceased's estate effected by his will . . . is not such as to make reasonable financial provision for the
    applicant.
    '(2) In this Act "reasonable financial provision" . . . (b) in the case of [any application made by a
    child of the deceased] means such financial provision as it would be reasonable in all the
    circumstances of the case for the applicant to receive for his maintenance . . .'

enable the applicant to discharge the recurring costs of his living expenses, and since
a payment of the capital transfer tax would not, directly or indirectly, contribute to the
son's cost of living but would merely be the payment of a capital sum by the estate to pay
his creditors, it followed that the son's application for payment of the tax out of the
father's estate was not an application for maintenance within the 1975 Act. Therefore,
in addition to the long and partly unexplained delay in bringing the application, the
application failed because the applicant had failed to show that he had an arguable case
b that he was entitled under the 1975 Act to provision out of the father's estate.
Accordingly, the application for leave to bring proceedings out of time would be
dismissed (see p 145 *f* to *j* and p 146 *a* to *e*, post); *Re Coventry (deceased)* [1979] 3 All ER
815 and *Re Salmon (deceased)* [1980] 3 All ER 532 applied.
     Per Curiam. There may be cases where payment of the applicant's existing debts is
maintenance within the 1975 Act (see p 145 *j* to p 146 *a*, post).

c
Notes
For the time for applying for an order for financial provision out of a deceased's estate, see
17 Halsbury's Laws (4th Edn) para 1326, and for cases on the subject, see 24 Digest
(Reissue) 714–718, 7669–7712.
     For matters to which the court is to have regard on an application for financial
d provision from a deceased's estate, see 17 Halsbury's Laws (4th Edn) para 1337.
     For the Inheritance (Provision for Family and Dependants) Act 1975, ss 1, 4, see 45
Halsbury's Statutes (3rd Edn) 496, 503.

Cases referred to in judgment
Christie (deceased), Re [1979] 1 All ER 546, [1979] Ch 168, [1979] 2 WLR 102.
e *Coventry (deceased), Re* [1979] 2 All ER 408, [1980] Ch 461, [1979] 2 WLR 853; *affd*
     [1979] 3 All ER 815, [1980] Ch 461, [1979] 3 WLR 802, CA, Digest (Cont Vol E) 224,
     7680a.
Salmon (deceased), Re [1980] 3 All ER 532, [1980] 3 WLR 478.
Stone (deceased), Re (1969) 114 Sol Jo 36, CA.

f ### Originating summons
By a summons dated 22nd February 1980 the applicant, Charles Crispin Dennis, applied
for an order that he be granted permission to make an application under the Inheritance
(Provision for Family and Dependants) Act 1975, for reasonable financial provision out
of the estate of his father, Richard Frampton Dennis deceased, notwithstanding that the
period of six months from the date on which representation with respect to the deceased's
g estate was first taken out had expired. The respondents to the summons were Lloyds
Bank Ltd, Mary Dennis, Darby William Dennis and Toby Edward Drake Dennis, the
executors of the deceased's will. The facts are set out in the judgment.

P M Mottershead QC and *Jonathan Winegarten* for the applicant.
Jonathan Parker QC and *Jonathan Simpkiss* for the respondents.

h
BROWNE-WILKINSON J.   This is an application under s 4 of the Inheritance
(Provision for Family and Dependants) Act 1975 by Charles Christian Dennis ('the
applicant') for permission to bring proceedings under the Act out of time.
     The estate is a substantial one. It was sworn for probate at about £2·5 m, and I am
informed that, due to increases in value and other circumstances, it will probably be
j worth net after duty about the same sum. The testator died on 21st November 1977 and
probate of his will was granted on 17th January 1978. Under the Act proceedings had to
be brought within six months after the date of probate, ie by 17th July 1978. The
present summons by the applicant was issued on 22nd February 1980; that is to say,
some 19 months out of time. In order to be allowed to go forward with the application,
under s 4 of the Act the applicant has to obtain the permission of the court.

The testator, Richard Frampton Dennis, was twice married. His first wife was
Rosemary, and by that marriage there was one child, namely the applicant. He in turn a
has two infant children. The testator secondly married Mary; of that marriage there are
two children, namely Darby William Dennis and Toby Edward Drake Dennis.
   The testator made his will on 26th May 1977. He gave to the applicant certain small
personal chattels. He also bequeathed him a legacy of £10,000 free of duty. Finally, he
gave a sum of £30,000 free of duty to the trustees of a settlement under which the
applicant has a protected life interest. After the applicant's death the capital of that b
£30,000 will go to his children. He also gave legacies of £20,000 each to the applicant's
two children when they attain the age of 21. Subject to those gifts and certain other
small gifts, he gave his interest in two very substantial farming properties to the two sons
of his second marriage equally and left the residue of his estate on trust for his second
wife for life and after her death to the two children of the second marriage. By his will
he made no provision for his first wife. Within the time limited by the Act, the first wife c
made an application to the court that provision should be made for her out of the estate.
   The applicant sets out his life story and his circumstances in an affidavit in support.
I think it is fair to describe him as having been a 'rolling stone'. After saying that he had
had the benefit of a preparatory and public school education and of being sent to the
Sorbonne in Paris where he obtained a degree in French literature, from 1962 to 1964 he
first of all had a job in family companies which he held for about a year. He then went d
to live with his grandfather and worked as a director of another family company; that
lasted until some time in 1964 when he was 22 or 23 years old. He then went to Ceylon
and worked as a tea planter for 18 months at £35 a week. He went to Australia where
he worked for three months in a post office. He went to South Africa where he stayed
for a year working in a firm of estate agents. Then in 1968 he came back to England and
for six months ran a betting office. After that he moved to a house in Huntingdonshire e
where he was employed in another of his father's companies. He stayed there for six
years, which was the longest period he had remained fixed anywhere. During that
period he married and the two children were born. The marriage ended with a decree
absolute in November 1973. At about that time his father had bought him a farm called
Grove Farm, to which I will have to return. After the divorce he went to Spain for 12
months, selling property at a salary of about £40 a week. In 1975 he came back to f
England and lived in a small house which he rented where he trained coursing
greyhounds for a year and a half. Then he went to South Africa and worked in Durban
running variously a hotel and a restaurant. Then he went to Cape Town where he
managed a restaurant for six months. He came back to England briefly in July 1978 and
then back to South Africa in September 1978 where he worked as a representative for the
International Racing Bureau of South Africa and as a manager of a club. Then he g
returned permanently to England in July 1979. The word 'permanent' is his; but in
1980 he went to South Africa, working as a freelance journalist for a period. Then he
returned to this country, that work having finished. He says he lives in a flat belonging
to a friend of his where he has the use of a room. In his affidavit he said that he was
considering buying a small betting shop in Fulham but his application for a betting
permit and betting office licence was rejected.   h
   As is the case with many rolling stones, he has not gathered much moss; indeed he has
shed a good deal. His present position, he says, is that he has no capital, no income and
is unemployed. In the course of his life he has received substantial, but in his affidavit
unspecified, benefits from his family. Grove Farm cost something in the region of
£90,000, the money being a gift from his father. He says that he spent a further
£20,000 on it but notwithstanding that total expenditure of £110,000, he says it was j
sold after approximately one year for £70,000. The whole of the £70,000 has apparently
gone, although it is fair to say he was ordered to pay £10,000 to his wife on the
divorce. He attributes the failure of the farming venture to his inability to finance the
keeping-up of substantial stock on the farm (which he had bought at very high prices)

because of the rapid increase in the prices of feedstuff etc. That is quite difficult to
a reconcile with another part of his affidavit in which he apparently spent the 12 months
after the farm was purchased in Spain selling property. It is also notable that his own
solicitor, when instructing counsel on another matter, suggested that the reason for the¨
failure of the farm was that he 'ate the stock'. In this state of the evidence, I am quite
unable to reach any view as to why the farm proved to be such an unhappy financial
experience. But it does not affect the end result which is that the whole of the proceeds
b of sale, and therefore the whole of the proceeds of the gift, have gone.

In addition to that gift, he was a beneficiary under three trusts from which he received
capital over the years. I am not told how much the capital was in total and can form no
view about it. In addition, he has the settlement to which his father bequeathed £30,000
by the will under which he takes a protected life interest. As I understand it, there are
no funds in that settlement apart from what was bequeathed by the will.

c I inquired how it was that he was proposing to buy a small betting shop in Fulham in
Autumn 1979 since he had no assets. I was told that his source of funds was going to be
his mother and girlfriend. I am now told (but there is no evidence of it) that he has
obtained a bookmaker's licence.

None of this evidence has been tested by cross-examination but even on his own
evidence it is clear to me that he must emerge as a spendthrift drifter who has spent
d substantial periods of his life depending on, and dissipating, moneys provided by other
people.

Counsel for the applicant has specifically confined the applicant's claim to one point.
He is not asking that his father's estate should provide further moneys for his daily
living. He is only asking that the estate should provide the sum necessary to pay the
capital transfer tax on the gift of the £90,000 which he received from his father in order
e to finance the purchase of Grove Farm. The amount of that tax is estimated as being
between £45,000 and £50,000.

Section 4 of the Act provides as follows:

'An application for an order under section 2 of this Act shall not, except with the
permission of the court, be made after the end of the period of six months from the
date on which representation with respect to the estate of the deceased is first taken
f out.'

There is a recent decision of Sir Robert Megarry V-C in Re Salmon (deceased) [1980] 3
All ER 532, [1980] 3 WLR 748. In that case the Vice-Chancellor laid down certain
guidelines as to the basis on which the court should exercise its discretion in granting or
withholding its permission for proceedings under the Act to be brought out of time.
g The Vice-Chancellor laid down six guidelines. First, the discretion of the court, though
judicial, is unfettered. Second, the onus is on the applicant to show special reasons for
taking the matter out of the general six-month time limit; the Vice-Chancellor said that
this is not a mere triviality but a substantial requirement. Third, the court has to
consider how promptly and in what circumstances the application has been made after
the time has expired; one has to look at all the circumstances surrounding the delay.
h Fourth, the court has to see whether negotiations had started within the six months
period. Fifth, one has to consider whether or not the estate has been distributed before
the claim has been notified. Sixth, the court has to consider whether refusal of leave to
bring proceedings out of time will leave the applicant without recourse against anyone
else, eg if the failure to apply within the statutory time limit has been due to the default
of legal advisers.

j As to the first two of those guidelines, it is common ground that they apply to the
present case: I have an unfettered discretion and the burden lies on the applicant to show
a special case.

As to the third of those guidelines, the reasons for the delay are deposed to by the
applicant. He was in South Africa when his father died. He asked his mother to find out

from her solicitors whether he had any claim against his father's estate and was told that
he had no claim. He returned to England in July 1978, when he was again told, not by   *a*
his own solicitors but by his mother's solicitors, that he had no claim. He then went back
to South Africa in September 1978, where he stayed until July 1979, at all times acting
on the basis of the advice that his mother's solicitors had given. When he returned to
England in July 1979, that advice was repeated and it was not until he went to his own
solicitors in September 1979 that he discovered the existence of a possible claim. Counsel
were instructed and leading counsel eventually advised on 15th November 1979 that the   *b*
applicant had a claim under the Act. On 21st November the applicant's solicitors
informed the executors of an intention to make a claim but the originating summons
was not issued until 22nd February 1980 and was not served until 26th February.
Keeping up the same approach to speed in the matter, the applicant went off to South
Africa before the affidavit in support was sworn, as a result of which no affidavit in
support was sworn until 21st May 1980 when he returned from South Africa.   *c*
    Looking at these facts, on the assumption that the applicant has any claim against the
estate, his delay in bringing proceedings between July 1978 and September 1979 is, in
my judgment, explained by the advice which his mother's solicitors gave, namely that
he was not entitled to make a claim. I want to make it clear that I am in no sense saying
that that advice was erroneous. It is not clear to me whether they were saying he was not
eligible to make a claim at all or whether they were saying that, although eligible, he had   *d*
no hope of getting any award. On the assumption that the advice was erroneous, I think
that period of delay is explained. It is true to say he did not consult his own solicitors but
he was undoubtedly, on his evidence, acting under a misapprehension. But that is not
an end of the matter. Although he consulted his own solicitors in September 1979, it is
not explained why it was impossible to get advice from counsel until some two months
later in November. Nor is it explained why it took some three months more before the   *e*
originating summons starting these proceedings were served. On top of that, there is the
slightly lethargic approach he adopted in swearing the necessary evidence even when the
proceedings had been started.
    Therefore the position is that there is a long delay, a substantial part of which, in my
judgment, is excusable but another part of which, more than a trivial part, is neither
excusable nor indeed explained.   *f*
    Going back to the guidelines laid down by Sir Robert Megarry V-C, the fourth of them
has no application to this case.
    The fifth guideline is directly relevant and important. Certainly one of the prime
reasons for insisting on a time limit in bringing these proceedings is to enable an estate
to be distributed within a reasonable time. If the estate has been distributed before a
claim is made, either wholly or in part, or if the bringing of the claim is likely   *g*
substantially to postpone the date of distribution, that is obviously a factor which is
important for the court to take into account. But in this case the estate is a complicated
one to administer. There is the claim by the first wife pending in any event, and as no
distribution has taken place, the trying of the applicant's claim at the same time as his
mother's claim will not hold up any distribution. Therefore it is not possible to say that
the estate or the beneficiaries interested in it are going to be prejudiced by the delay as   *h*
such.
    As to the sixth of the Vice-Chancellor's guidelines, I have approached the case on the
basis that the applicant, not having consulted his own solicitors, can have no claim
against a third party if his application for an extension of time were to be refused.
    Sir Robert Megarry V-C was not purporting to lay down a comprehensive list of the
matters to which the court should have regard. A decision of the Court of Appeal in *Re*   *j*
Stone (deceased) (1969) 114 Sol Jo 36 was not drawn to his attention. In that case the Court
of Appeal allowed an appeal by a widow and enabled her to bring her application out of
time. Lord Denning MR said in the course of giving judgment that if the widow 'has an
arguable case or, as we say in the Ord 14 cases, if there is a triable issue, then permission
ought to be given'. In my judgment it is clear from that statement that a further

requirement which an applicant has to satisfy is to show that he has an arguable case, a
a case fit to go to trial, and that in approaching that matter the court's approach is rather
the same as it adopts when considering whether a defendant ought to have leave to
defend in proceedings for summary judgment.

What then will be the position in this case if the application goes forward? The
applicant will have to satisfy the court first that the will fails to make reasonable
provisions for his maintenance. If he succeeds in overcoming that, then the court will
b be able to make reasonable provision for his maintenance.

The court now approaches claims made by a son on the same basis as claims made by
any other applicant, though in the past it might be said that the court viewed such claims
with some disfavour. A son is in the same position as all other able-bodied applicants.
A person who is physically capable of earning his own living faces a difficult task in
getting provision made for him, because the court is inclined to ask: 'Why should
c anybody else make provision for you if you are capable of maintaining yourself?' The
applicant is 38 years old. There is no evidence that he is in any way unfit. Although at
present out of work he appears to have as much chance as anybody else of obtaining
employment and maintaining himself. In addition, the court is reluctant to make
further provision for someone for whom large sums of money have been provided and
which have been dissipated by him. It is no doubt for these reasons that the applicant has
d confined his claim to a claim to have the tax on the gift of the £90,000 paid and is not
asking that he should be given further benefits to keep himself alive. In addition, of
course, one would have to take into account the fact that the will does make some
provision for him; £10,000 outright plus a fund of £30,000 which he cannot dissipate
since he is prevented from getting at the capital.

The applicant's claim therefore amounts to this. He says: 'I have no assets to pay this
e tax. The tax will be due. If, as is the case, I cannot pay, I will be made bankrupt.
Therefore this will fails to make reasonable provision for me and the court should
provide a sum sufficient to pay the tax.' For myself, I do not necessarily accept that if the
tax is not paid he will be made bankrupt. If, as he says, he has no assets, I am myself
doubtful whether the Revenue would go to the trouble and expense of making him
bankrupt; but I will assume that bankruptcy is inevitable. Even on that assumption, the
f proposition must be that the court could hold that a father who has made a gift of
£90,000 to his son and seen it and much other money besides dissipated in spendthrift
living had failed to make provision for his 'maintenance' in failing to make a further gift
of £45,000 to £50,000 in order to pay the tax on the first gift. To my mind such an
application would have no chance of success, even bearing in mind, as I do, the fact the
father was an extremely wealthy man and the estate a very large one. To my mind the
g applicant is not really applying for 'maintenance'; he is asking for a capital sum to pay his
creditors.

It is now clearly established that claims under the Act by persons other than spouses are
limited to maintenance. The applicant has to show that the will fails to make provision
for his maintenance: see *Re Coventry (deceased)* [1979] 2 All ER 408, [1980] Ch 461; *affd*
[1979] 3 All ER 815, [1980] Ch 461. In that case both Oliver J at first instance and Goff
h LJ in the Court of Appeal disapproved of the decision in *Re Christie (deceased)* [1979] 1 All
ER 546, [1979] Ch 168, in which the judge had treated maintenance as being equivalent
to providing for the well-being or benefit of the applicant. The word 'maintenance' is
not as wide as that. The court has, up until now, declined to define the exact meaning
of the word 'maintenance' and I am certainly not going to depart from that approach.
But in my judgment the word 'maintenance' connotes only payments which, directly or
j indirectly, enable the applicant in the future to discharge the cost of his daily living at
whatever standard of living is appropriate to him. The provision that is to be made is to
meet recurring expenses, being expenses of living of an income nature. This does not
mean that the provision need be by way of income payments. The provision can be by
way of a lump sum, for example, to buy a house in which the applicant can be housed,
thereby relieving him pro tanto of income expenditure. Nor am I suggesting that there

may not be cases in which payment of existing debts may not be appropriate as a maintenance payment; for example, to pay the debts of an applicant in order to enable *a* him to continue to carry on a profit-making business or profession may well be for his maintenance.

But no such case is made here. It is not suggested that the payment of capital transfer tax will do anything to help the applicant's future maintenance. It may save him from bankruptcy, but there is no evidence that being made bankrupt is going to prevent the applicant from earning his living in the kinds of way he has sporadically chosen to do in *b* the past. I was told (although there is no evidence of this) that he has now got a bookmaker's licence and if made bankrupt he will lose it. In the circumstances of this case, I am reluctant to act on such information. But in any event, apart from evidence that some 12 years ago he ran a betting office for six months, there is nothing to suggest that being a bookmaker or the running of a betting shop is his chosen career. The truth of the matter is that he has not chosen any career. He has in the past drifted from one *c* occupation to another. Therefore, in my judgment, he has not shown an arguable case that he is making a claim for maintenance which the court could allow, since the payment of the capital transfer tax would not in any way, direct or indirect, contribute to the cost of his future living.

It follows that it has not, in my judgment, been shown that he has any arguable prospect of success if the application were to go forward. *d*

To sum up, I refuse my consent for the application to be made out of time, first, because there has been a long delay, of which a part is unexplained and, so far as one can see, inexcusable and, second, because the applicant has no arguable chance of success if the matter were to go forward. To my mind, these factors outweigh the fact that I am dealing with a large estate and that the delay which has occurred has not, and will not, hold up the distribution of the estate. It would in my judgment be wrong to allow costs *e* to be incurred in resisting a hopeless application which is long out of time.

Application dismissed.

Solicitors: *Edmonds, Bowen & Co* (for the applicant); *Roythorne & Co*, Spalding (for the respondents). *f*

Hazel Hartman   Barrister.

Customs and Excise Commissioners v Lord Fisher

QUEEN'S BENCH DIVISION

GIBSON J

16th, 17th, 24th FEBRUARY 1981

Value added tax – Supply of goods or services – Supply in course of a business – Business – Pheasant shoot – Invited guests making contributions to cost of shoot – Whether taxpayer carrying on a 'business' – Finance Act 1972, s 2(2)(b).

The taxpayer, whose main hobby was pheasant shooting, invariably invited friends and relations to join the shoot on his estate. The persons invited were asked to and did make contributions towards the cost of the shoot, but the taxpayer neither sought nor made any profit from the contributions, he himself making at least an equal contribution from his own pocket. The taxpayer was assessed to value added tax in respect of the contributions on the basis that they constituted consideration for the supply of services 'in the course of a business' carried on by the taxpayer within s 2(2)(b)[a] of the Finance Act 1972. A value added tax tribunal allowed an appeal by the taxpayer against the assessment on the ground that the supply of services by the taxpayer for which the contributions were received was made in the course of arranging a shoot for pleasure and social enjoyment and accordingly was not made in the course of a business within s 2(2)(b). The Crown appealed, contending that on the facts the tribunal could not reasonably conclude that the supplies made by the taxpayer were not made in the course of a business carried on by him. The Crown pointed to the facts that the contributions made were substantial in amount, that the shoots were conducted in a regular manner and were planned and efficiently run, and that shoots were commonly conducted by others as a business.

Held – Although the mere absence of a profit motive was not conclusive to exclude an activity from being a business, on its true meaning 'business' in s 2(2)(b) of the 1972 Act excluded any activity which was no more than an activity for pleasure and social enjoyment. There was a real difference between what was a business or trade and what was an activity for pleasure and social enjoyment, and, although that difference might sometimes be difficult to discern or prove, it was nevertheless a difference recognised by the 1972 Act, and the sharing of the costs of a sporting or other pleasure activity did not by itself turn such an activity into a business. The taxpayer's activities were in all respects indistinguishable from the private pleasure of a private shoot save for the matter of the contributions to expenses, and the fact that the taxpayer could not run his shoot as a private shoot without contributions towards the cost of it did not, on the facts, make the taking of contributions from those who joined the shoot the predominant concern or purpose of the taxpayer in organising it. The amount of money received by the taxpayer could not by itself be relevant to the question whether the activity was a business, since some pleasures and sports were very expensive and expense alone could not turn a pleasure into a business. Furthermore, the use of planning and the efficient running of the activity were part of the pleasure of running a large shoot and were necessary to make shooting enjoyable for the participants, but they could not turn the pleasure into a business. And it was irrelevant that others carried on such an activity as a business, since there were few pleasures which were not provided somewhere by people who carried on the business of providing them; the fact that others commonly supplied facilities for such pleasures for commercial profit could not turn a man's pleasure into a business. It

---

a   Section 2(2) is set out at p 150 b, post

followed that the tribunal had not made an error of law in deciding that the taxpayer's activities were not a business. Accordingly there was no supply of services by the *a* taxpayer in the course of carrying on a business. The appeal would therefore be dismissed (see p 155 *f* to p 156 *a* and h j, p 157 *a* to *e*, p 158 *h*, p 159 *e* to j, p 160 *d e g h* and p 161 *a* to *d*, post).

Re Wallis, ex parte Sully (1885) 14 QBD 950 applied.

Abernethie v A M & J Kleiman Ltd [1969] 2 All ER 790 followed.

Rolls v Miller [1881–5] All ER Rep 915, Rael-Brook Ltd v Minister of Housing and Local *b* Government [1967] 1 All ER 262, Town Investments Ltd v Department of the Environment [1977] 1 All ER 813 and Customs and Excise Comrs v Morrison's Academy Boarding Houses Association [1978] STC 1 distinguished.

Notes

For the charge of value added tax, see 12 Halsbury's Laws (4th Edn) para 870.

For the Finance Act 1972, s 2, see 42 Halsbury's Statutes (3rd Edn) 164.   *c*

Section 2 of the 1972 Act was substituted by the Finance Act 1977, s 14 and Sch 6, para 1, with effect from 1st January 1978.

Cases referred to in judgment

ACT Construction Ltd v Customs and Excise Comrs [1979] 2 All ER 691, [1979] 1 WLR 870, [1979] STC 358; affd [1981] 1 All ER 324, [1981] 1 WLR 49, [1980] STC 716, CA, *d* Digest (Cont Vol E) 512, 961b.

Abbott v Philbin (Inspector of Taxes) [1959] 3 All ER 590, [1960] Ch 27, [1959] 3 WLR 739, 39 Tax Cas 82, 38 ATC 284, [1959] TR 277, CA; affd on other grounds [1960] 2 All ER 763, [1961] AC 352, [1960] 3 WLR 255, 39 Tax Cas 82, 39 ATC 221, [1960] TR 171, 53 R & IT 487, HL, 28(1) Digest (Reissue) 345, 1249.

Abernethie v A M & J Kleiman Ltd [1969] 2 All ER 790, [1970] 1 QB 10, [1969] 2 WLR *e* 1364, 20 P & CR 56, CA, 31(2) Digest (Reissue) 951, 7747.

British Railways Board v Customs and Excise Comrs [1977] 2 All ER 873, [1977] 1 WLR 588, [1977] STC 221, [1977] TR 79, CA, Digest (Cont Vol E) 511, 961a.

Church of Scientology of California v Customs and Excise Comrs [1979] STC 297; affd [1981] 1 All ER 1035, [1981] STC 65, CA.

Customs and Excise Comrs v Morrison's Academy Boarding Houses Association [1978] STC 1, *f* Digest (Cont Vol E) 514, 968a.

Customs and Excise Comrs v Royal Exchange Theatre Trust [1979] 3 All ER 797, [1979] STC 728, Digest (Cont Vol E) 515, 973b.

Edwards (Inspector of Taxes) v Bairstow [1955] 3 All ER 48, [1956] AC 14, [1955] 3 WLR 410, 36 Tax Cas 207, 34 ATC 198, [1955] TR 209, 48 R & IT 534, HL, 28(1) Digest (Reissue) 566, 2089.

Hawes v Gardiner (Inspector of Taxes) (1957) 37 Tax Cas 671, 36 ATC 341, 51 R & IT 95, *g* 28(1) Digest (Reissue) 52, 209.

Jersey's (Lord) Executors v Bassom, Lord Derby v Bassom (1926) 10 Tax Cas 357, 135 LT 274, 28(1) Digest (Reissue) 235, 731.

National Water Council v Customs and Excise Comrs [1979] STC 157.

Pilkington v Randall (Inspector of Taxes) (1966) 42 Tax Cas 662, 45 ATC 32, [1966] TR 33, *h* CA, 28(1) Digest (Reissue) 94, 292.

Rael-Brook Ltd v Minister of Housing and Local Government [1967] 1 All ER 262, [1967] 2 QB 65, [1967] 2 WLR 604, 65 LGR 239, 18 P & CR 290, DC, Digest (Cont Vol C) 961, 3 ol.

Rolls v Miller (1884) 27 Ch D 71, [1881–5] All ER Rep 915, 53 LJ Ch 682, 50 LT 597, CA, 31(1) Digest (Reissue) 395, 3146.

Town Investments Ltd v Department of the Environment [1977] 1 All ER 813, [1978] AC 359, *j* [1977] 2 WLR 450, 34 P & CR 48, [1977] RVR 76, HL, Digest (Cont Vol E) 379, 7874a.

Wallis, Re, ex parte Sully (1885) 14 QBD 950, 4 Digest (Reissue) 20, 138.

Westward Television Ltd v Hart (Inspector of Taxes) [1968] 3 All ER 91, [1969] 1 Ch 202, [1968] 3 WLR 480, 45 Tax Cas 1, 47 ATC 200, [1968] TR 181, CA, 28(1) Digest (Reissue) 173, 528.

Case also cited

a *Inland Revenue Comrs v Marine Steam Turbine Co Ltd* [1920] 1 KB 193, 12 Tax Cas 174.

Appeal

The Customs and Excise Commissioners appealed against the decision of the London Value Added Tax Tribunal (chairman Mr Neil Elles) dated 11th December 1979 allowing an appeal by the Right Hon Lord Fisher ('the taxpayer') against an assessment to value

b added tax in respect of contributions by the taxpayer's guests to the expenses of maintaining the shooting over the taxpayer's estate. The facts are set out in the judgment.

Simon D Brown for the Crown.
David C Milne for the taxpayer.

c

Cur adv vult

24th February. **GIBSON J** read the following judgment: This is an appeal by the Customs and Excise Commissioners. They ask that the decision of a value added tax

d tribunal, given on 11th December 1979, be reversed.

The decision of the tribunal, of which Mr Neil Elles was chairman, was that certain payments received by Lord Fisher ('the taxpayer'), as contributions from a Mr C Matsas and from a Mr Martin and a Mr Gourlay towards the cost of running the taxpayer's shoot on his estate in Norfolk, were not received in the course of the taxpayer's business and thus the payments were not subject to payment of value added tax.

e The commissioners ask that this court should direct, as a matter of law, that those payments were received by the taxpayer for the taxable supply of services in the course of a business carried on by him, so that the payments would be subject to tax. The particular payments considered in this case were samples. Similar contributions were made by other relations and friends of the taxpayer who joined him in shooting at Kilverstone.

f An appeal from this tribunal is brought to the High Court under s 13 of the Tribunals and Inquiries Act 1971, which section is made applicable to decisions of value added tax tribunals by the Tribunals and Inquiries (Value Added Tax Tribunals) Order 1972, SI 1972 No 1210. This section provides:

g 'If any party to proceedings before any such tribunal . . . is dissatisfied in point of law with a decision of the tribunal he may, according as rules of court may provide, either appeal therefrom to the High Court or require the tribunal to state and sign a case for the opinion of the High Court.'

This appeal is not by case stated and accordingly the relevant rules of court are set out in RSC Ord 55. The powers of the court on hearing such an appeal are set out in Ord 55,

h r 7, and it is sufficient to refer to para (5) of that rule. That paragraph provides:

'The Court may give any judgment or decision or make any order which ought to have been given or made by the court, tribunal or person and make such further or other order as the case may require or may remit the matter with the opinion of the Court for rehearing and determination by it . . .'

There is, in short, an appeal on law only. The court cannot set aside or vary the

j decision of the tribunal on any issue of fact if that decision has been reached without any error of law.

Value added tax was first imposed by the Finance Act 1972. It is charged—

'on the supply of goods and services in the United Kingdom (including anything treated as such a supply) and on the importation of goods into the United Kingdom.'

That is s 1(1). This case is concerned only with the supply of services. The relevant law is that contained in the 1972 Act before the amendments made by the Finance Act *a* 1977. The scope of the tax is laid down by s 2 as follows:

'(1) Except as otherwise provided by this Part of this Act the tax shall be charged and payable as follows.
'(2) Tax on the supply of goods or services shall be charged only where—(*a*) the supply is a taxable supply; and (*b*) the goods or services are supplied by a taxable person in the course of a business carried on by him; and shall be payable by the *b* person supplying the goods or services . . .'

The taxpayer at all times was a taxable person being registered with reference to certain other activities which are agreed to have been business activities.

The provisions of s 5 determine what is a supply of services for the purposes of value added tax. It is sufficient to refer to parts of sub-s (2) and to sub-s (8) of that section. *c* Subsection (2) provides that '. . . supply of services does not include anything done otherwise than for a consideration', and sub-s (8) provides:

'Subject to the preceding provisions of this section, anything which is not a supply of goods but is done for a consideration (including, if so done, the granting, assignment or surrender of the whole or part of any right) is a supply of services.'
                                                                                                                    d
The tax is charged at the specified rate on the value of the supply of services. By s 10(2) it is provided:

'If the supply is for a consideration in money its value shall be taken to be such amount as, with the addition of the tax chargeable, is equal to the consideration.'

It is thus clear that a supply of services, made for a consideration within s 5(8), is not *e* a taxable supply unless it is supplied by a taxable person 'in the course of a business carried on by him'. It is with the meaning in law of this phrase that this case has been concerned.

It is provided by s 45(1) of the 1972 Act that:

'In this Part of this Act "business" includes any trade, profession or vocation; and—(*a*) the provision by the Independent Broadcasting Authority of broadcasting *f* services; and (*b*) the provision by a club or by an association to which this paragraph applies of the facilities available to its members; and (*c*) the provision by an organisation to which this paragraph applies of the advantages of membership; and (*d*) the admission, for a consideration, of persons to any premises; shall be deemed to be the carrying on of a business.'
                                                                                                                    g
The case for the commissioners before the tribunal was that the taxpayer, in organising his shoot at Kilverstone for himself, his friends and relations, made to them grants of a right to shoot, and that those grants were made for a consideration, namely the contribution paid. It was not there seriously contended by counsel for the taxpayer at the tribunal and in this court that the invitation by the taxpayer to his friends to join the shoot, and payment of the suggested sum by way of contribution to the cost, did not *h* constitute a supply of services under s 5(8) as being 'anything . . . done for a consideration', although counsel submitted that there was no grant of any right.

It was not submitted to the tribunal that the arrangements between the taxpayer and his friends and relations who joined the shoot were such that, because of its social or family nature, there was no intention thereby to give rise to any legal relationship.

In this court it was conceded by counsel that the arrangements made by the taxpayer *j* for his shoot did constitute the supply of services for a consideration within s 5(8), although of course counsel for the taxpayer said that the arrangements were plainly such as might be expected to be made among friends and relations for the sharing of the cost of a shoot in which they all wished to take part. In this appeal, therefore, the only

question has been whether the supply of services for a consideration by the taxpayer was
a   'in the course of a business carried on by him'.

Before the tribunal it was argued for the commissioners that the supply of services by
the taxpayer was made in the course of a business carried on by him, namely the business
of supplying shooting. In the alternative it was submitted that the taxpayer was carrying
on a business of running his estate at Kilverstone and that the taxable supplies relating to
the shooting at Kilverstone were made in the course of that business.

b   In this court that alternative submission has been abandoned. Counsel for the
commissioners has submitted that, on the facts found by the tribunal, the supply of
services by the taxpayer for a consideration, namely the invitation and receiving of
friends and relations as guests at his shoot, on terms that each should pay a stated
contribution to the cost, was a supply in the course of the activity of organising the
shooting on his estate, and that, as a matter of law, that activity was a business carried on
c   by him.

The tribunal heard the appeal against the decision of the commissioners on 30th
October 1979. Evidence was given by the taxpayer and his accountant, Mr Coote.
Documents and accounts were produced. That evidence was accepted by the tribunal
and, in their decision, the tribunal set out the facts which they found. The nature of this
case and the arguments submitted require that I set out the primary facts which the
tribunal found. Their decision is clear and detailed and shows the care with which they
d   determined the facts relevant to this issue. I can do no better than to set out their
findings in their own words, omitting only some matters of detail. I read then from the
decision:

'The Kilverstone estate near Thetford in Norfolk extends to approximately 3,000
e   acres. Of this estate approximately one-half is in the ownership of [the taxpayer]
and the other half is held upon trust for members of [the taxpayer's] family. [The
taxpayer] retains the shooting rights over the whole estate. As to that part of the
estate which remains in the ownership of [the taxpayer], approximately 50 acres
adjacent to the house form a wildlife park, and approximately 500 acres are in land
and are farmed by [the taxpayer]. The remaining part of the estate is let to tenant
f   farmers. [The taxpayer] lives at Kilverstone Hall and takes an active part in
managing the farm and also the wildlife park and generally in running his estate.
It is common ground that he carries on a business relating to the farm and also in
relation to the wildlife park and he is registered for value added tax ... The
Kilverstone estate account for the year ended 11th October 1978 ... gives a detailed
account of the receipts and expenses incurred in running this estate. [The taxpayer's]
g   main hobby is that of shooting and he has shot since he was 12 years of age. Before
the 1939–45 war the shoot at Kilverstone was run by his father. Friends were
invited to shoot on various days during the season, and no question of financial
contributions arose. During the late 1940s it was not possible to rear pheasants,
since food was rationed. During the early 1950s, however, while it became possible
once again to rear pheasants, the cost of running the shoot was too great for [the
h   taxpayer's] father to carry on his own account. The idea of running a syndicate was
rejected, but it was decided to ask friends who were invited to shoot to make
contributions. When [the taxpayer's] father died [the taxpayer] continued to run
the shoot on that basis. We find as a fact that the persons invited to join the shoot
at Kilverstone were invariably either friends of [the taxpayer] or his wife or close
friends of Mr Woolf who is [the taxpayer's] brother-in-law. There has never been
i   any question of seeking guns by advertisement or, with one exception, letting any
part of the shoot. We find that [the taxpayer's] object was to continue to run the
shoot as nearly as possible in the manner in which it had been run prior to the war,
but with the exception that it was necessary to ask friends and relations to make
contributions towards the cost of so doing. The one exception to which we have

referred above occurred in 1974 when on account of the acute degree of inflation, [the taxpayer] let the shooting to Rudolf Woolf & Co which is a metal broking firm *a* in which his brother-in-law is a partner. [The taxpayer] keeps an estate account of the Kilverstone estate which ends on 11th October in each year, and the purpose of keeping this estate account is, in the words of his accountant Mr Coote, "to ascertain the position at the end of the year to see if [the taxpayer] has drawn on capital, and to see generally what was going on in the estate". The estate account for the year ended 11th October 1978 . . . included all receipts and expenses arising in the *b* running of the estate except those concerning the farming activities and the wildlife park. These receipts included rents receivable from farming land let to tenant farmers, game shooting contributions, sales of game and broody hens, sale of woods, receipts from a refuse tip and extraction fees and various other matters.'

The expenses were also set out, including expenses relating to shooting, which included the wages of gamekeepers and beaters, and other expenses relating to the shoot. *c* Management expenses were dealt with in the same account under a separate heading, and included various items such as postage and stationery and professional fees:

'We find that this estate account was a personal account kept for the convenience of [the taxpayer] and those running the estate, and that it was not intended as a business account. Entirely separate accounts were kept in relation to the farming *d* activities and the wildlife park . . . It was [the taxpayer's] practice to write to his shooting friends and relations during April, by which time he had received the estate accounts for the previous year. When he wrote he asked each person whether he would like to join the shoot again in the coming year, stating on which date the shooting would begin, and that it would continue every Thursday and Friday at fortnightly intervals and telling them that the contribution for a full gun or a half *e* gun would be a particular sum. Full guns could expect ten days' shooting before Christmas, and a little further shooting was possible after Christmas, but this depended on the amount of game which remained. [The taxpayer] did not keep copies of such letters and no letter was available for production in evidence, but a bundle containing some replies for the current year 1979 was produced, and we have no doubt that on the receipt of affirmative replies, enclosing cheques for the *f* relevant contribution, [the taxpayer] would reply thanking them and acknowledging receipt of these cheques. Payments relating to any particular year were not necessarily completed by 11th October. For instance, an individual might have taken an extra gun or had some extra days shooting for which payment was made at a later date.'

I break off reading the decision at that point to say that the documents before the court *g* show that the contributions which were paid were in the sum of £1,350 per gun in 1975 and 1976, and £1,500 per gun in 1977 for an expected ten days' shooting. I return to the decision itself:

'The shooting at Kilverstone was conducted in the following manner. Guns meet at Kilverstone Hall and they are given refreshments. They come back to lunch at *h* the house and then again they are given tea at the end of the day. The cost of those meals and refreshments was included in the contributions. All the pheasants shot belonged to [the taxpayer] and at the end of the day he followed the usual custom of giving each gun a brace of pheasants. It is, however, possible for guns to purchase further pheasants from the head gamekeeper and [the taxpayer] has a game dealers' licence which makes it possible for this to be done. It is [the taxpayer's] practice to *j* sell the rest of the game in order to assist in defraying the cost of the shoot. [The taxpayer] employs one gamekeeper who is the head gamekeeper—whose father was head gamekeeper before him. There is also a part-time gamekeeper . . . [The taxpayer] pays for the beaters who take part in the shoot and for beaters' beer; he a also pays for the cartridges used by the keepers for shooting vermin, but each gun, including [the taxpayer], pays for his own cartridges. Any gun requiring a loader pays for him, although [the taxpayer] engages him for the gun concerned.'

That ends the extract from the decision.

During the hearing of this appeal reference was made to the Kilverstone estate accounts, and to the replies made by friends to the taxpayer's invitations to join the shoot b on payment. Those documents are before the court. It is common ground that from these contributions the taxpayer received substantial sums towards the high cost of an expensive sport. Contributions in all came to some £14,147 in 1977 and £10,443 in 1978. Sale of game produced £5,333 in 1977 and £3,569 in 1978. The taxpayer neither sought nor made any profit. His purpose was to cover the cost of the shoot while making at least an equal contribution to that cost from his own pocket, and for the most part his c contribution was substantial. It was not suggested for the commissioners that the taxpayer had intended, by the level at which he fixed the contributions, to get his own shooting free, or that he had done so in fact.

After considering various submissions made to them, and in particular the contentions made by the commissioners in writing to the advisers of the taxpayer, and certain authorities on the meaning of the phrase 'in the course of a business carried on by him' d the tribunal expressed their conclusions on this issue as follows: firstly they said that it was plain that the taxpayer did not make the supply of services, in inviting and receiving the guests to the shoot, 'in the course of the farming business admittedly carried on by [the taxpayer] and still less . . . in connection with the running of the wildlife park'. That conclusion has not been questioned in this court.

Next the tribunal said that the supply of services by the taxpayer, for which the e payment of contributions was received, was 'in the course of arranging a shoot for pleasure and social enjoyment', and they continued as follows:

'We have no doubt that this was done in a business-like manner, or there would have been confusion leading to inconvenience, but in our judgment this does not have the effect of turning the making of such arrangements into the carrying on of a business. We also have no doubt that the shoot was run in a competent and f business-like manner, but again this does not turn such a sport into the carrying on of a business. In our judgment it would also be straining the proper use of the English language to bring such an activity within the meaning of what Widgery J in *Rael-Brook Ltd v Minister of Housing and Local Government* [1967] 1 All ER 262 at 266, [1967] 2 QB 65 at 76 termed "a serious undertaking earnestly pursued" or within the words used by Lord Kilbrandon in *Town Investments Ltd v Department of* g *the Environment* [1977] 1 All ER 813 at 835, [1978] AC 359 at 402 "a serious occupation not necessarily confined to commercial or profit-making undertakings". Even if the sale of the pheasants is taken into account we regard this as entirely incidental to the shooting and was done because this was a sensible way of reducing the cost of what is nowadays a very expensive sport. For these reasons we will hold that the taxable supplies made by [the taxpayer] were not made in the h course of a business of supplying shooting.'

Finally the tribunal said that the arranging of shooting for pleasure and social enjoyment constituted a non-business activity, and that, having regard to the special circumstances of the case, the fact that those concerned made contributions to the expenses did not have the effect of turning what is essentially a non-business activity into a business.

For the Crown in this court counsel's submissions were as follows. The point of law arising in this appeal is formulated thus: on the true construction of the provisions of s 2(2) of the 1972 Act as applied to the undisputed facts of the case, could the tribunal reasonably conclude that the relevant taxable supplies were not made in the course of a

business carried on by the taxpayer? It is convenient to note that counsel for the taxpayer
accepted as correct that formulation of the question.   a

Counsel for the Crown referred to a number of authorities including *Customs and
Excise Comrs v Morrison's Academy Boarding Houses Association* [1978] STC 1, a decision of
the 24th February 1977 by the First Division of the Inner House of the Court of Session,
sitting as the Court of Exchequer in Scotland, consisting of the Lord President (Lord
Emslie) with Lord Cameron and Lord Johnston. An appeal from a value added tax
tribunal which, under s 13 of the Tribunals and Inquiries Act 1971 is provided to be   b
made to the High Court in England and Wales, must be made in Scotland to the Court
of Session. Counsel for the Crown placed much reliance on the principles which he says
were laid down in that decision.

He also referred to *Customs and Excise Comrs v Royal Exchange Theatre Trust* [1979] 3 All
ER 797, [1979] STC 728, a decision of Neill J on appeal from a value added tax tribunal,
and to *British Railways Board v Customs and Excise Comrs* [1977] 2 All ER 873, [1977] STC   c
221 in the Court of Appeal and to *ACT Construction Ltd v Customs and Excise Comrs*
[1981] 1 All ER 324, [1980] STC 716, again in the Court of Appeal.

Counsel's detailed submissions for the Crown were, to a large extent, advanced by
reference to the principles set forth in the judgments of their Lordships in the *Morrison's
Academy* case, and I shall append the references to those judgments in explaining the
submissions made.   d

Firstly, went the submission, it will never be possible or desirable to define exhaustively
the word 'business' within the meaning if s 2(2)(b) of the 1972 Act. By providing in
s 45(1) that 'business' includes any trade, profession or vocation it is clear that a wide
meaning of 'business' is intended: per the Lord President (see [1978] STC 1 at 6).

Secondly, in determining whether any particular activity constitutes a business it is
necessary to consider the whole of that activity as it is carried on in all its aspects: again   e
per the Lord President (at 5). The relevant activity, said counsel for the Crown, for
scrutiny in this way is the organising of his shooting by the taxpayer.

Thirdly, the aspects of that activity which are to be considered, as being indicia or
criteria for determining whether the activity is a business, are six in number and were
listed by counsel for the Crown as follows: (a) whether the activity is a 'serious
undertaking earnestly pursued', a phrase derived from the judgment of Widgery J in   f
Rael-Brook Ltd v Minister of Housing and Local Government [1967] 1 All ER 262 at 266,
[1967] 2 QB 65 at 76, or 'a serious occupation, not necessarily confined to commercial or
profit-making undertakings', a phrase derived from the speech of Lord Kilbrandon in
Town Investments Ltd v Department of the Environment [1977] 1 All ER 813 at 835, [1978]
AC 359 at 402, both of them cited to and referred to by the tribunal in their decision;
(b) whether the activity is an occupation or function actively pursued with reasonable or   g
recognisable continuity: per Lord Cameron in *Morrison's Academy* [1978] STC 1 at 8;
(c) whether the activity has a certain measure of substance as measured by the quarterly
or annual value of taxable supplies made: again per Lord Cameron (at 8); (d) whether the
activity was conducted in a regular manner and on sound and recognised business
principles: again per Lord Cameron (at 10); (e) whether the activity is predominantly
concerned with the making of taxable supplies to consumers for a consideration: per the   h
Lord President (at 6); (f) lastly, whether the taxable supplies are of a kind which, subject
to differences of detail, are commonly made by those who seek to profit by them: per the
Lord President (at 6) and per Lord Cameron (at 10).

Fourthly, in this submission, certain aspects of the activity are not to be considered as
relevant for determining whether the activity is a 'business', or are not decisive of that
question, namely whether the activity is pursued for profit or whether pursued for some   j
other private purpose or motive.

Fifthly and finally, if (as was submitted) all, or, alternatively a sufficient number, of
those indicia or criteria were satisfied in sufficient measure to override any contra-
indications which might be seen in the facts, then as a matter of law the activity must be
held to be a business.

For the taxpayer it was submitted by counsel that the one point in the case lay in the
a essential contrast between 'business', even in its widest meaning, and an activity which
is shown to be a true activity of and for pleasure and the company of friends. A hobby
or sport is not required to be defined as a business because it is expensive, and paid for by
the sharing of expenses, or because it requires planning and organisation. Counsel for
the taxpayer advanced examples of other sporting or holiday activities which may be run
by friends by sharing expenses of which he claimed that it would be ridiculous to say that
b they are 'businesses'.

Counsel for the taxpayer referred to the decisions in certain value added tax appeals by
Neill J, namely *Royal Exchange Theatre Trust v Customs and Excise Comrs*, cited above,
National Water Council v Customs and Excise Comrs [1979] STC 157 and *Church of Scientology
of California v Customs and Excise Comrs* [1979] STC 297, and to earlier decisions in
different contexts which, he said, supported the proposition that 'business' is seen as
c essentially different from 'pleasure'.

Counsel for the taxpayer advanced no criticisms of the first and second points in
counsel's submission for the Crown as to the undesirability of seeking any exhaustive
definition of 'business' in this context, as to the width of the meaning of the word and as
to the need to consider the activity in question in all its aspects.

As to the list of six indicia or criteria, again counsel for the taxpayer did not criticise
d them as being of no value for the purposes of analysing any activity in order to determine
whether it is a 'business' within s 2(2), but he asserted again that no principle of law
required that an activity, rightly determined to be an activity for pleasure and social
enjoyment, should or must be called 'a business' merely because it satisfied all or some of
those indicia.

Lastly counsel for the taxpayer submitted, after referring to such cases as *Edwards
e (Inspector of Taxes) v Bairstow* [1955] 3 All ER 48, [1956] AC 14, *Lord Jersey's Executors v
Bassom* (1926) 10 Tax Cas 357, *Hawes v Gardiner (Inspector of Taxes)* (1957) 37 Tax Cas 671
and *Pilkington v Randall (Inspector of Taxes)* (1966) 42 Tax Cas 662, that the court, in
exercising this jurisdiction on appeal on point of law, could only interfere in a case of this
nature if on the facts as found it is clear that the tribunal, applying the true construction
of the provisions of s 2(2) of the 1972 Act, could not reasonably reach the conclusion set
f out in its decision.

Having considered these submissions, I have reached the conclusion that no error in
point of law has been demonstrated in the decision of this tribunal.

The decision of the Court of Session in the *Morrison's Academy* case is clearly one which
I should follow as authoritative guidance on a revenue statute unless there should appear
some clear reason for differing from it: see *Westward Television Ltd v Hart (Inspector of
g Taxes)* [1968] 3 All ER 91, [1969] 1 Ch 202, 45 Tax Cas 1 and *Abbott v Philbin (Inspector of
Taxes)* [1959] 3 All ER 590 at 600–601, [1960] Ch 27 at 49, 39 Tax Cas 82 at 112. I see
no reason to differ from the decision and, moreover, respectfully agree with it. I do not,
however, consider that the decision in that case affords full support for the submissions
which counsel for the Crown has sought to found on it.

In that case, as I understand it, the taxpayer company, which had been formed to carry
h on boarding houses for students of Morrison's Academy, was in all respects carrying on
an activity within the ordinary meaning of the word 'business' save for one aspect of such
activity, namely that it was not carried on with the object of making a profit. The
company was carrying on the business of a boarding house keeper precisely as any good
and competent boarding house keeper would carry it on, save for the fact that it tried to
charge rates which would produce neither profit nor loss and reserved its accommodation
j for students of the academy. The value added tax tribunal held that the supply by the
taxpayer company of boarding house services was not made in the course of a business
carried on by the company on the sole ground that the activity of running the boarding
houses was not carried on with the object of making a profit.

The Court of Session held, on the true construction of s 2(2) of the 1972 Act, that the
tribunal was wrong in law in concluding that no activities carried on continuously by a

taxable person can ever be a 'business' if the profit motive is absent. The Lord President said that he could discover nothing in the natural meaning of the word 'business' so to *a* restrict its scope and that there was nothing in the context of the taxing provisions as a whole to require one to read 'business' in such a narrow way (see [1978] STC 1 at 6).

As I understand their judgments, the learned judges in the Court of Session did not thereafter set out to lay down principles which, if satisfied, would in all cases demonstrate that an activity must be regarded as a 'business' within those provisions. Those aspects of an activity, to which their Lordships drew attention, and on which counsel for the *b* Crown has relied in formulating the indicia listed above, plainly describe the main attributes of any activity which will be regarded as falling within the concepts of 'business' and 'trade, profession or vocation', and clearly they are useful tools, some perhaps more useful than others, for the analysis of an activity and for the comparing of it with other activities which are unarguably 'businesses'. The courts, however, cannot, by the formulation of tests and by the expounding of indicia, substitute any test or phrase *c* different from that set out in the statutory provision and I am sure that their Lordships had no intention of doing so.

The Lord President, having said that in his opinion it would never be possible or desirable to define exhaustively the word 'business' within the meaning of s 2(2)(b) of the 1972 Act, went on to say ([1978] STC 1 at 6):

> 'What one must do is to discover what are the activities of the taxable person in *d* course of which taxable supplies are made. If these activities are, as in this case, predominantly concerned with the making of taxable supplies to consumers for a consideration it seems to me to require no straining of the language of s 2(2)(b) of the 1972 Act to enable one to conclude that the taxable person is in the "business" of making taxable supplies, and that taxable supplies which he makes are supplies made in the course of carrying on that business, especially if, as in this case, the *e* supplies are of a kind which, subject to differences of detail, are made commercially by those who seek to profit by them. For my own part I consider that there is no justification in this case for holding that the activities deliberately and continuously pursued by the association in a business-like way are not a "business" for value added tax purposes merely because the underlying motive is to assist Morrison's Academy.' *f*

It was this passage which formed the basis of counsel's submissions for the Crown, coupled with the passage in the judgment of Lord Cameron to the effect that, since the making of a profit or gain is irrelevant to the issue of liability to value added tax, then it seemed to him that absence of such a purpose is equally irrelevant to the issue of whether the potential taxpayer carries on a 'business' in making the taxable supplies (see [1978] STC 1 at 9). Since, went the argument, the absence of the purpose of profit could not *g* prevent the running of the boarding houses from being a business in the *Morrison's Academy* case, so the presence of the purpose of running a private shoot for pleasure, coupled with the absence of the purpose of profit, could not prevent the organising of this shoot from being a business.

In my judgment it is essential to have in mind, in seeking to apply these statements to any other case, that their Lordships in the *Morrison's Academy* case were, as I have said, *h* dealing with an activity which was in all respects indistinguishable from the business of a boarding house keeper save for the matter of profit; they had, I believe, no intention of dealing with, or of laying down propositions applicable to, an activity as in this case which was in all respects indistinguishable from the private pleasures of a private shoot save for the matter of contributions to expenses.

I am moreover confident that Lord Cameron did not intend to say that in all cases the *j* absence of the purpose of gain is irrelevant to the issue whether the potential taxpayer is carrying on a business. It seems to me that there are many activities in which a potential taxpayer may supply services for a consideration within the meaning of s 5(8) of the 1972 Act and which will be so different from the ordinary concept of 'business' that the presence or absence of the purpose of gain would be highly relevant to the determination of the question whether he was carrying on a business.

a
I turn back to the words of the statute. This tax is to be charged only where a taxable supply is made 'by a taxable person in the course of a business carried on by him'. By s 45(1) '"business" includes any trade, profession or vocation'. It is clear, and there is much authority to support it, that 'business' is or may be in particular contexts a word of very wide meaning. Nevertheless, the ordinary meaning of the word 'business' in the context of this Act excludes, in my judgment, any activity which is *no more than* an activity for pleasure and social enjoyment.

b
The primary meaning of all these words, 'business, trade, profession and vocation', is an occupation by which a person earns a living. It is clear that all ordinary businesses, trades, professions and vocations can be carried on with differences from this standard and norm in regularity or seriousness of application, in the pursuit or disregard of profit or earnings, and in the use or neglect of ordinary commercial principles of organisation. As the decision in the *Morrison's Academy* case has shown, the absence of one common
c attribute of ordinary businesses, trades, professions or vocations, such as the pursuit of profit or earnings, does not necessarily mean that the activity is not a business or trade etc if in other respects the activity is plainly a 'business'.

Many people, however, carry on activities which are clearly 'business' but which have little to do with ordinary businesses or trades; thus a man may be a professional sportsman or make a business of his hobby, or make a trade of domestic hospitality. In this area, as
d it seems to me, the essential difference between what is 'business' or 'trade' and what is an activity for pleasure and social enjoyment may on occasions be difficult to discern or to prove, but no man, I believe, has any doubt that that essential difference is a real difference, and, in my judgment, that essential difference survives in the true construction in law of this word in this statute.

Counsel for the taxpayer was right, as I think, in his submission that this difference has
e always been recognised and contained in the use and meaning of this word 'business' as normally used in statutes such as the 1972 Act, and in other contexts. Thus Cave J in *Re Wallis* (1885) 14 QBD 950 held that a person who occupies a residential property and engages in farming and market gardening for his pleasure, and carries on the same at a profit, is not carrying on a 'trade or business' within the meaning of s 44 of the Bankruptcy Act 1883, even though he sells his surplus produce after supplying his
f household, but, if the primary intention is abandoned and the business is carried on with a view to profit as a means of livelihood, he will come within the section.

Next, in *Rolls v Miller* (1884) 27 Ch D 71, [1881–5] All ER Rep 915, the case was concerned with a covenant in a lease that the lessee should not carry on on the premises any trade or business. A charitable institution called a home for working girls, where the inmates were provided with board and lodging without payment, was held by the Court
g of Appeal to be within the restrictions of that covenant. Cotton LJ said (27 Ch D 71 at 85–86, [1881–5] All ER Rep 915 at 918–919):

'. . . receiving payment for what is done, using what you are doing as a means of getting payment with a view to profit . . . is certainly material in considering whether what was being done is, or is not, a business, yet, in my opinion, it is not
h essential that there should be payment in order to constitute a business. And the mere fact that there is payment under certain circumstances, does not necessarily make a thing a business which if there was no payment would not be a business . . . But what is done here? None of the Defendants are residing in the house, nor are they receiving into their house as their guests or friends, these girls who make their home there. The Defendants have a paid superintendent who manages the house for them, and it is the duty of that paid superintendent so to manage the house, and to see that the girls who are there conduct themselves properly, and in accordance with the rules and regulations of the charity, and provision is made as to the way in which they are to be accommodated. It is not that any particular individuals known to Defendants or whom they treat as their friends (except so far as they wish to be the friends of all those who are in distress) are admitted, but that all the public who are objects of this charity, on submitting to these regulations, are

admitted into the house which they occupy. It might well be that the Defendants if they liked to do this in a house which they occupied might do so, but when they do so in a house in which they pay a superintendent in order to receive the girls, these girls are really lodgers. They lodge there, and although the trustees are, with a most praiseworthy object, using this lodging-house for the purpose of charity, nevertheless, in my opinion, although the lodging is given gratuitously, what is being done must be considered as carrying on the business of a lodging-house.'

In the same case Lindley LJ said (27 Ch D 71 at 88, [1881–5] All ER Rep 915 at 920):

'When we look into the dictionaries as to the meaning of the word "business", I do not think they throw much light upon it. The word means almost anything which is an occupation, as distinguished from a pleasure—anything which is an occupation or duty which requires attention is a business.'

That statement by Lindley LJ was cited by Widgery J giving the judgment of the Divisional Court in *Rael-Brook Ltd v Minister of Housing and Local Government* [1967] 1 All ER 262, [1967] 2 QB 65. The question in that case was whether use by a local authority of premises for the purposes of a cooking centre in the provision of school meals was used for a process 'carried on in the course of trade or business' within the Town and Country Planning (Use Classes) Order 1950, SI 1950 No 1131. After observing that the arguments of counsel for the appellant and for the Minister recognised that the broad distinction desired to be drawn by the phrase under consideration was that between the amateur and the professional, the learned judge said that it did not follow that commercial motive provided the final and only test. He continued ([1967] 1 All ER 262 at 266, [1967] 2 QB 65 at 76):

'In our opinion neither the making of profit nor any commercial activity is an essential in order that a process may be carried on in the course of trade or business for the purpose of the definition of "industrial building" in the Use Class Order. Hence the activity of a local authority which exhibits all the other possible features of a business is not excluded on that account. Even on the meagre findings of fact in the present case it can be inferred that the provision of school meals by the local authority in possession of the building from 1940 to 1946 was an occupation as distinguished from a pleasure (to quote LINDLEY, L. J. [in *Rolls v Miller*]), that it was continuous rather than sporadic and that it was a serious undertaking earnestly pursued for the purpose of fulfilling a duty assumed by the occupier. Without attempting to decide that these features must necessarily all be present in order that an activity may amount to a business for present purposes, we are satisfied that they suffice in this case.'

It is to be observed that the phrase 'serious undertaking earnestly pursued', which appeared as part of the first indicium of counsel for the Crown, was used by Widgery J of an activity which, apart from profit, exhibited all the other possible features of a business. The full phrase 'serious undertaking earnestly pursued for the purpose of fulfilling a duty assumed by the occupier' is apt, in my judgment, to describe the sort of activity normally carried on by way of business or daily work, and not to describe an activity pursued for pleasure and social enjoyment.

Abernethie v A M & J Kleiman Ltd [1969] 2 All ER 790, [1970] 1 QB 10 was a case where the regular carrying on of a Sunday school by a tenant was alleged to be a 'business' within s 23 of the Landlord and Tenant Act 1954. In that Act also the word 'business' is defined as including a trade, profession or employment and any activity carried on by a body of persons, whether corporate or unincorporate. The Court of Appeal rejected that allegation. Widgery LJ said ([1969] 2 All ER 790 at 794, [1970] 1 QB 10 at 20):

'By and large, it seems to me that what a man does with his spare time in his home is most unlikely to qualify for the description "business" unless it has some direct commercial involvement in it, whether it be a hobby or a recreation or the

a
performance of a social duty, such as in this case. On the face of it these are matters which are not "business" matters at all; they go to a man's private life in his domestic surroundings.'

Lastly, *Town Investments Ltd v Department of the Environment* [1977] 1 All ER 813 at 835, [1978] AC 359 at 402 was the case from which came the second phrase set out in the first indicium of counsel for the Crown: 'a serious occupation, not necessarily confined to commercial or profit-making undertakings.' The case was concerned with the Counter-

b
Inflation (Business Rents) Order 1972, SI 1972 No 1850, in which restrictions were imposed on increases of rent under business tenancies. The definition of such a tenancy was similar to that under the Landlord and Tenant Act 1954. A question in the case was whether occupation and use of premises by government servants for government purposes on behalf of the Crown constituted occupation for the purposes of a business carried on by the Crown as tenant.

c
Lord Diplock referred to the word 'business' as an etymological chameleon in that it suited its meaning to the context in which it is found (see [1977] 1 All ER 813 at 819, [1978] AC 359 at 383). He quoted Lindley LJ's dictum in *Rolls v Miller* (1884) 27 Ch D 71 at 88, [1881–5] All ER Rep 915 at 920, in which business was contrasted with pleasure, and which I have already cited. Lord Diplock then proceeded to express the conclusion that the meaning of the word 'business' in the definition of 'business tenancy'

d
in the two orders was no less wide than that which it has been interpreted as having in covenants in leases restricting the use of demised premises.

Lord Kilbrandon said ([1977] 1 All ER 813 at 835, [1978] AC 359 at 402):

'As to the scope of the word "business" as defined in the statute I would be content to accept the submission for the department, namely that it denotes the carrying on

e
of a serious occupation, not necessarily confined to commercial or profit-making undertakings.'

In my judgment, the words 'serious occupation' in Lord Kilbrandon's speech were not intended to include a hobby, pleasure or pastime carried on by a man with no more serious application and organisation than the nature of the activity itself requires.

f
The conclusion which I have expressed that the true meaning of the word 'business' in the context of the 1972 Act excludes any activity which is not more than an activity for pleasure and social enjoyment does not mean that an activity carried on by a taxable person cannot in law be a business if it is carried on by him for pleasure and is one from which he derives social enjoyment. It is not difficult, for example, to imagine circumstances in which a man, controlling estates like those of the taxpayer, would so

g
organise his shooting activity that it would rightly be regarded as a business. A long-standing love and pursuit of the sport, and genuine delight in the society of other people who shoot, and no doubt shoot well, could not by themselves prevent the activity from being a 'business' if in other respects it is.

The running of the shoot for profit, the widening of the source of participants outside a genuine circle of friends and relations, the intensifying of the activity beyond what is

h
normal for a private shoot and the use of advertising to obtain customers or participants are examples of matters which, as it seems to me, would be relevant for consideration on the question whether the shoot is run as a business. For my part I find it difficult to think of a case in which the pursuit of profit from contributions by participants would not be decisive to show that it was a business. Parliament has entrusted to tribunals the task of examining the evidence and of determining the facts, and there need, I think, be no fear

j
that tribunals will be unable to detect a commercial enterprise or business which may be dressed up as no more than an activity of pleasure or social enjoyment.

Counsel's submission for the Crown in its final and shortest form on the primary facts of the case was that, although the taxpayer's shoot was genuinely a private shoot, yet the high cost of running it had forced the taxpayer to run it as a business. Thus, without questioning the validity of the tribunal's conclusion that the shoot was arranged for

pleasure and social enjoyment, the tests laid down in the listed indicia, and the true
meaning of the word 'business', must drive, he said, the court to the conclusion that in   *a*
law this shoot was a business. This submission was founded in particular, firstly, on the
fact that the right to take part in a shoot is something which is commonly the subject of
commercial dealing and, secondly, on that phrase in the judgment of the Lord President
in the *Morrison's Academy* case, namely that if the activities of the taxable person are
predominantly concerned with the making of taxable supplies to consumers for a
consideration it requires no straining of the language of the Act to conclude that the   *b*
taxable person is in the business of making taxable supplies (see [1978] STC 1 at 6).

This submission, if accepted, would lead in this case to a ruling that, as a matter of law,
the making of taxable supplies for a consideration causes the taxable person to be
carrying on the business of making those supplies provided that his concern for, or
purpose in, the making of those supplies is shown to be 'predominant', and provided, as
I understood counsel's submission for the Crown, that the turnover is substantial, and   *c*
that the activity is conducted with the necessary planning and efficiency, and that the
supplies are of a nature which other people do supply in the course of trade or business.

I am unable to accept that the true meaning of 'business' in the context of the 1972 Act
contains any such principle. As to the turnover being substantial, it does not seem to me
that, subject to the de minimis rule, the amount of money received can by itself be
relevant: some pleasures or sports are very expensive and expense alone cannot turn a   *d*
pleasure into a business. Again the use of planning and the efficient running of the
activity, or 'sound and recognised business principles', are, no doubt, both part of the
pleasure of running a large shoot and necessary to make shooting enjoyable for the
participants, but such matters again cannot turn a pleasure into a business. Lastly, there
are very few pleasures which are not also provided somewhere by people who carry on
the business of providing them; the fact that other people commonly supply facilities for   *e*
such pleasures for commercial profit cannot turn a man's pleasure into a business.

Counsel's submission for the Crown must, I think, on the facts of this case, be reduced
to this: if, in an activity which, in all other respects is or is consistent with being a
pleasure activity carried on for social enjoyment, the organiser of it receives contributions
towards the cost of running it on a basis that all participants, including the organiser,
make roughly equal contributions to the costs of each day's sport enjoyed, then that   *f*
activity must be regarded as 'predominantly concerned' with the making of taxable
supplies to consumers for a consideration and is therefore in law a business.

I understand, and am able to have some sympathy for, the preference of the
commissioners for simple rules which can be applied to all people who organise shooting
or similar activities and take payments from participants without there having to be an
inquiry into such matters as whether the payments are no more than contributions   *g*
towards costs and whether the participants have not only the true character of friends and
relations but also that of customers of a business.

I regard counsel's submission for the Crown, however, as unacceptable because it
would force into the category of 'business' many activities which, in my judgment, do
not fall within the true meaning of 'business' under the 1972 Act. The sharing of the
costs of a sporting or other pleasure activity does not by itself turn an activity of pleasure   *h*
and social enjoyment into a business. If Parliament had intended such an addition to or
extension of the meaning of the word 'business', it would, I think, have used express
words to say so.

I would add a further observation on the phrase 'activities ... predominantly
concerned with the making of taxable supplies to consumers for a consideration' on
which so much reliance was placed in supporting this appeal. The Lord President in the   *j*
Morrison's Academy case [1978] STC 1 at 6 used those words in a case where, as I have said,
the activities of a taxable person were indistinguishable from those of an ordinary
commercial boarding house keeper, save that instead of seeking profit he sought only to
make no loss. Apart from the special purpose of providing accommodation only for
students of the academy the activity which the taxpayer carried on was concerned solely

with, and directed at, and had no other purpose than, the making available of boarding
a house accommodation for a consideration; the word 'predominant' in the dictum is, in
my judgment, to be understood from that context.

If the task of the tribunal was to determine whether the organising by the taxpayer of
his shooting, in the year in which he received these contributions, was or was not
'predominantly concerned with the making of taxable supplies to consumers for a
consideration', then in my judgment their decision was a reasonable conclusion on the
b facts, namely that it was not so predominantly concerned.

The fact that he could not run his shoot as a private shoot for friends and relations
without contributions towards the cost of it did not, on the facts of this case, make the
taking of those contributions from those who joined the shoot the 'predominant concern'
or purpose of the taxpayer in organising it, nor did that fact cause the organising of the
shoot to be 'predominantly concerned' with the receipt of such contributions.

c The tribunal, as I understand their decision, saw their task, having determined the
primary facts, as deciding, in the light of the authorities cited to them, whether, after
considering the organising of the taxpayer's shoot in all its aspects, they found it to be a
business carried on by him or not. They found that it was not a business. In my
judgment, the tribunal are not shown to have committed any error of law in reaching
that conclusion, and, for the reasons which I have stated, this appeal must accordingly be
d dismissed.

Appeal dismissed.

Solicitors: *Solicitor for the Customs and Excise*; Greene & Greene, Bury St Edmunds (for the
taxpayer).

e

Evelyn M C Budd   Barrister.

Acrow (Engineers) Ltd v Hathaway

f EMPLOYMENT APPEAL TRIBUNAL
BROWNE-WILKINSON J, MRS M E SUNDERLAND AND MR D A C LAMBERT
27th FEBRUARY 1981

*Industrial tribunal – Decision – Finality – Dismissal of complaint – Complaint withdrawn by
complainant – Industrial tribunal formally dismissing complaint – Complainant making fresh
g complaint on same matter within time limit for making complaint – Complainant not seeking
review of tribunal's decision on original complaint – Whether fresh complaint vexatious –
Industrial Tribunals (Labour Relations) Regulations 1974 (SI 1974 No 1386), Sch, r 11(2)(e).*

*Vexatious proceedings – Industrial tribunal – Complaint – Complaint withdrawn by complainant
– Industrial tribunal formally dismissing complaint – Complainant making fresh complaint on
h same matter within time limit for making complaint – Whether fresh complaint vexatious –
Industrial Tribunals (Labour Relations) Regulations 1974 (SI 1974 No 1386), Sch, r 11(2)(e).*

An employee complained to an industrial tribunal that he had been constructively
dismissed. An appearance was entered by the employers and the case was set down for
hearing on 20th May 1980. On the day preceding the hearing a representative of the
j employee applied for an adjournment on the ground that the employee was too nervous
and depressed to attend alone and that his representative would not be available on 20th
May. The tribunal refused an adjournment and warned that costs might be awarded
against the employee. The representative then informed the tribunal that the complaint
was withdrawn. On 20th May the tribunal made a decision that the application was
dismissed, and that decision was registered on 21st May. Some weeks later and within

the time limit of three months specified by s 67(2) of the Employment Protection
(Consolidation) Act 1978 for lodging a complaint relating to the dismissal, the employee *a*
made a second complaint to the tribunal which, in all essential particulars, was similar to
the first. The employers applied to the tribunal to strike out the second complaint on the
ground that there was no jurisdiction to entertain the second complaint, or, alternatively,
that the second complaint was vexatious and ought not to be allowed to proceed. In the
meantime the employee applied for a review of the tribunal's decision of 20th May.
When the applications came on for hearing, the industrial tribunal, being differently *b*
constituted from the tribunal which had dealt with the matter on 20th May, held that it
had no jurisdiction to deal with the application for a review, but held that it had
jurisdiction to entertain the second complaint. The employers appealed to the
Employment Appeal Tribunal contending, inter alia, that the second complaint ought to
be dismissed under r 11(2)(e)*a* in the schedule to the Industrial Tribunals (Labour
Relations) Regulations 1974 as being vexatious.   *c*

Held – The appeal would be allowed, the employee's second complaint would be
dismissed as being vexatious and the employee's application for a review of the industrial
tribunal's decision of 20th May would be allowed to proceed, for the following reasons—
  (1) A decision on a complaint made by an industrial tribunal and entered in the
register was a final decision on the matters raised in the complaint, subject only to the *d*
correction of any accidental slip, review, revocation or variation of the decision under r 9*b*
in the schedule to the 1974 regulations or alteration of the decision by order of a superior
court. In view of the wide powers of an industrial tribunal to order a review of its
decision where it was satisfied that the interests of justice required such a review, the
appropriate course to adopt where it was alleged that a miscarriage of justice had
occurred by reason of a decision being entered was to apply to the industrial tribunal *e*
itself to review its decision, and it was vexatious to issue a fresh complaint, albeit in time,
without first seeking a review, since, if the second complaint were to proceed, the
respondent's costs of the first complaint would, in part at least, be thrown away and
irrecoverable (see p 164 *f* to *j* and p 165 *f*, post).
  (2) The employee did not have an absolute right to make a further complaint within
the three months' period specified in s 67(2) of the 1978 Act, similar to that in an action *f*
in the High Court, because a plaintiff in an action in the High Court had no right of
review in similar circumstances (see p 165 *b c* and *f*, post); *Birkett v James* [1977] 2 All ER
801 distinguished.

Notes
For complaints to an industrial tribunal in respect of unfair dismissal, see 16 Halsbury's *g*
Laws (4th Edn) para 639:3.
  For review of an industrial tribunal's decision, see ibid para 1027.
  For the Employment Protection (Consolidation) Act 1978, s 67, see 48 Halsbury's
Statutes (3rd Edn) 518.
  In relation to proceedings instituted on and after 1st October 1980 the Industrial
Tribunals (Labour Relations) Regulations 1974 have been replaced by the Industrial *h*
Tribunals (Rules of Procedure) Regulations 1980, SI 1980 No 884.

Case referred to in judgment
Birkett v James [1977] 2 All ER 801, [1978] AC 297, [1977] 3 WLR 38, HL, Digest (Cont
  Vol E) 666, 2698*b*.

_____ *j*

a Rule 11(2), so far as material, provides: 'A tribunal may, if it thinks fit . . . (*e*) at any stage of the
    proceedings order to be struck out or amended any originating application or notice of appearance
    or anything in such application or notice of appearance on the ground that it is scandalous,
    frivolous, or vexatious.'
b Rule 9, so far as material, is set out at p 164 *d*, post

Appeal

a Acrow (Engineers) Ltd ('the employers') appealed against the decision of an industrial
tribunal (chairman Mr R K Jones) sitting at Cambridge on 12th August 1980 whereby it
held that it had jurisdiction under s 67 of the Employment Protection (Consolidation)
Act 1978 to hear a complaint by Michael Benjamin Hathaway ('the employee') that he
had been unfairly dismissed by the employers notwithstanding that on 20th May a
differently constituted industrial tribunal (chairman Mr James Freeman) sitting at
b Cambridge had decided that the employee's complaint be dismissed. The facts are set
out in the judgment of the appeal tribunal.

Giles Harrap for the employers.
Jenny Fay for the employee.

c **BROWNE-WILKINSON J.** In this case the employee claims that he has been
constructively dismissed by his employers. The matter comes before us on a procedural
point.

The employee made an originating application to the Cambridge Industrial Tribunal
which was received in the tribunal office on 3rd April 1980. An appearance was entered
by the employers and the case was set down for hearing on 20th May 1980. So far as the
d tribunal were aware, on the day preceding the hearing (19th May) the employee, through
the medium of a representative, applied for an adjournment on the ground that he was
too nervous and depressed to attend alone, and that his chosen representative would not
be available on 20th May. The industrial tribunal refused that application and warned
the employee that costs might be awarded against him.

The representative of the employee then informed the tribunal that the application
was withdrawn, and by a letter of 19th May the application was withdrawn.
e
On that basis, on 20th May the tribunal made a decision that the application was
dismissed. That decision was duly registered on 21st May and copies sent to the parties.

Some weeks later the employee, who was dissatisfied with the position, made a further
application (in all essential particulars, similar to the first) to the tribunal which was
received by the tribunal on 19th June 1980, ie within the time limit for the lodging of
f a complaint relating to the dismissal.

That gave rise to an application by the employers to strike out the second complaint
to the industrial tribunal on the ground that there was no jurisdiction to entertain a
second application under the Employment Protection (Consolidation) Act 1978, or,
alternatively, that the second application was vexatious and ought not to be allowed to
proceed.

g On 5th August 1980 the employee asked for a review by the industrial tribunal of its
decision made on 20th May and, for that purpose, asked that the time limit for such a
review should be extended. The matter came before the Cambridge Industrial Tribunal
on those preliminary points only.

As to the application for a review of the decision of 20th May, the industrial tribunal,
being differently consitituted from the tribunal which had dealt with the matter on 20th
h May, held that it had no jurisdiction to deal with the application for a review. Therefore
that application for a review is still outstanding.

As to the rest, the industrial tribunal held that it had jurisdiction to entertain a second
application under s 67 of the 1978 Act, provided, of course, that the second application
was within the three months' time limit laid down by s 67(2). Unfortunately, in the
reasons given by the tribunal, although they advert to the fact that the employers were
j contending that the second application was vexatious, they do not in terms deal with that
claim. The industrial tribunal's decision is limited solely to the question: was there
jurisdiction or no? The tribunal having held that it did have jurisdiction to entertain a
second application, the employers now appeal to the Employment Appeal Tribunal.

Before this tribunal, the employers have argued three points. First, they argue that on
the true construction of the 1978 Act (and to an extent the attendant rules) only one

application can be made. Second and in the alternative, they argue that, since in this case the first application had led to a decision (albeit based on a withdrawal of the claim by the applicant), the existing decision of 20th May operates as an estoppel to prevent any further application being brought by the employee on the same subject matter. Third, they say that, even if they are wrong on both those points, to bring a second application in this way is vexatious and therefore that second application can properly be dismissed under r 11(2)(e) in the schedule to the Industrial Tribunals (Labour Relations) Regulations 1974, SI 1974 No 1386, on the ground that it is 'scandalous, frivolous or vexatious'.

On the view that we take of the matter, it is unnecessary for us to express any concluded view on the questions of statutory construction and of estoppel. Our conclusions will be limited to the third ground, ie whether in the circumstances of this case a second application is or is not vexatious. We should point out that we are in no sense saying that the employee's complaint is vexatious; what we are considering is whether the bringing of a second application is vexatious.

The 1978 Act and the 1974 rules plainly envisage one complaint, followed by a hearing, followed by a decision which is registered by the tribunal and copies of which are provided to the parties and others. The 1974 rules also provide that an entry of the decision in the register can be corrected, first, if there has been an accidental slip, second, if the decision has been reviewed under r 9, and, third, if the decision has been altered on appeal (see r 8(8)). The review provision in r 9 is that—

'(1) A tribunal shall have power to review and to revoke or vary by certificate under the chairman's hand any decision in which a county court has power to order a new trial on the grounds that . . . (c) the decision was made in the absence of a party or person entitled to be heard . . . or (e) the interests of justice require such a review . . .'

If such a review is permitted, the result of the review may be either a variation of the decision or a revocation of the decision and an order for rehearing. Such application for a review has to be made within 14 days after the date on which the decision was sent to the parties.

The application by the employee for a review in this case is out of time, not having been made until 5th August.

In our view, in the ordinary case (although there may be exceptions) under s 67 of the 1978 Act, where an industrial tribunal has made a decision on a complaint, that is a final decision on the matters raised in that complaint, subject only to correction in the three ways mentioned above. If it is said that some miscarriage of justice has occurred by a decision being entered, the normal course must be to apply to the industrial tribunal itself to review its decision. Its powers are exceptionally wide and it is able, if it is satisfied that the interests of justice require a review, to order a review.

In those circumstances, we cannot think that it is ordinarily right to issue a fresh application after a decision has been reached, without at least pursuing the remedy of review to set aside the wrong result which it is said has been achieved.

Counsel for the employee urges us that there is nothing vexatious here in the employee's behaviour. As we have said, we certainly accept that, so far as his general claim is concerned. But we do consider that for him to issue a fresh application, albeit in time, without pursuing a remedy of a review first, is a vexatious course to adopt. If the second application were to proceed, the employers' costs of the first application would, in part at least, be thrown away and irrecoverable.

Counsel presses us with the well-known decision of the House of Lords in Birkett v James [1977] 2 All ER 801, [1978] AC 297. In that case, the House of Lords was dealing with a case in which an action in the High Court had been struck out for want of prosecution, such striking out occurring within the six-year limitation period which was applicable. Lord Diplock, Lord Simon and Lord Edmund-Davies indicated that such a striking out was not appropriate since, if the original action is struck out for want of prosecution, there is normally nothing to stop the plaintiff whose claim has been struck

out from starting a second action within the six-year period, and that if he does in those
circumstances start a second action the court should not strike out that second action as
a being vexatious. So, says counsel, in this case, the employee's first complaint having been
dismissed, he has an absolute right to present a further complaint within the three
months' period and the tribunal should not strike out that second complaint as being
vexatious.

In our view that overlooks a critical distinction between proceedings in the High
b Court and proceedings in an industrial tribunal. In the High Court there is no review
procedure. Here what has gone wrong, according to the employee, is that there should
have been no refusal of the adjournment and that, if justice is to be done to his claim, he
ought to be allowed to go through to a hearing. In our judgment, the analogy with High
Court proceedings, where there is no right of review such as would cover the present
case, is not a close one; the question here is to decide what is the correct and fair
c procedure in pursuing claims under the 1978 Act.

We consider that the correct course, which is still open to the employee, is to pursue
his right to apply for a review. The merits of that course are that, in considering whether
or not to review the first decision, the chairman (or whoever makes the decision) can look
at all the facts of the case to see whether the interests of justice require such a review. He,
no doubt, will take into account any detriment which would be suffered by the employers
d if the existing decision were set aside, and would set against such detriment those factors
which the employee will seek to urge. We have no direct evidence at this stage what
those factors will be. We were told that he was, at a late stage, left without his anticipated
representation before the tribunal, his state of health was such that he felt unable to
present the case himself on 20th May and in the heat of the moment he either did give
or was thought to have given instructions to withdraw his application. It may well be
e that whoever has to consider whether a suitable case is shown here for a review (including
an extension of time) will feel that, in order to do justice between the parties in the light
of the evidence which we trust will be before him, the interests of justice require that the
employee should have his case fairly heard. But that is a matter for him to decide in the
light of all the circumstances. Our decision is simply that it is vexatious to pursue the
claim by a second complaint to the tribunal without having had recourse to the review
f procedure in relation to the first decision.

For those reasons we allow the appeal so as to enable the application to review to go
forward.

Appeal allowed.

Solicitors: *Heald, Son & Co,* Wigan (for the employers); *Wild, Hewitson & Shaw,* Saffron
Walden (for the employee).

K Mydeen Esq   Barrister.

Inland Revenue Commissioners v Metrolands (Property Finance) Ltd

CHANCERY DIVISION

NOURSE J

25th, 26th NOVEMBER, 11th DECEMBER 1980

Development land tax – Disposal of interest in land – Time of Disposal – Compulsory acquisition of interest in land – Taxpayer serving purchase notice on planning authority – Acceptance of purchase notice by planning authority – Parties subsequently agreeing amount of compensation – Deemed compulsory acquisition of interest in land – When interest in land disposed of for purposes of liability to tax – Town and Country Planning Act 1971, s 181(2) – Development Land Tax Act 1976, s 45(2)(4).

On 9th May 1974 a local authority ('the council') refused planning permission for houses to be built on land owned by the taxpayer. On 9th October the taxpayer served a purchase notice on the council under s 180 of the Town and Country Planning Act 1971 requiring the council to purchase the land. On 28th November the planning committee of the council resolved that the council was willing to comply with the purchase notice and the resolution was confirmed by the council at a meeting held on 11th December. By a letter dated 20th December the chief legal officer of the council informed the taxpayer that the council had determined to accept the purchase notice. At a meeting between the representatives of the taxpayer and the council on 16th September 1975 a figure of £64,650 was agreed as the appropriate amount of compensation, but the council's representative had no authority to bind the council to that figure. On 11th August 1976 that amount of compensation was finally approved by the council. The taxpayer was assessed to development land tax in the sum of £29,085 under s 1 of the Development Land Tax Act 1976 in respect of the disposal of the land to the council. The taxpayer appealed to the Special Commissioners against the assessment, contending that the service of the purchase notice and its acceptance, or the notification of its acceptance, by the council on 20th December 1974 constituted an enforceable contract for sale between the parties within s 45(2)ᵃ of the 1976 Act and that accordingly the interest in the land was disposed of before 1st August 1976, the date on which development land tax became chargeable. The Crown contended that once the council had accepted the purchase notice it was deemed by s 181(2)ᵇ of the Town and Country Planning Act 1971 to be authorised to acquire the interest of the taxpayer compulsorily and to have served a notice to treat in respect of such acquisition, that there was no enforceable contract between the parties until the amount of the compensation had been agreed between them and that since agreement as to compensation was not reached until 11th August 1976, when the council approved the compensation terms, s 45(4) of the 1976 Act applied, with the result that 11th August 1976 was the date on which the interest in the land had been disposed of, i e after the day appointed for the coming into force of the 1976 Act. The commissioners allowed the appeal, holding that there had been a contract between the parties when the council had informed the taxpayer that it had accepted the purchase notice on 20th December 1974 and that accordingly by virtue of s 45(2) of the 1976 Act the disposal by the taxpayer of its interest in the land occurred on that date with the result that no tax was chargeable. The Crown appealed.

Held – Since the purposes for which the statutory fiction created by the deeming provision in s 181(2) of the 1971 Act were either general or, at the lowest, not clear, and

---

a   Section 45, so far as material, is set out at p 177 *d* to *f*, post

b   Section 181(2) is set out at p 176 *c*, post

since its application for the purposes of s 45(4) of the 1976 Act would not lead to any
a unjust, anomalous or absurd result and was not clearly outside the purposes for which it
had been created, it followed that the deeming provision in s 181(2) was to be applied to
s 45(4). Applying s 181(2) of the 1971 Act to the facts of the case, the acquisition by the
council of the taxpayer's interest in the land following the purchase notice fell to be
treated as a compulsory acquisition of that interest by the council within s 45(4) of the
1976 Act and accordingly the disposal of the taxpayer's interest in the land did not take
b place until 11th August 1976 when the amount of the compensation was approved by
the council. The appeal would therefore be allowed (see p 181 *c* to *j*, p 182 *a* to *c* and *f* and
p 183 *e* to *j*, post).

Re Levy, ex parte Walton [1881–5] All ER Rep 548, East End Dwellings Co Ltd v Finsbury
Borough Council [1951] 2 All ER 587, Birmingham City Corpn v West Midland Baptist (Trust)
Association (Inc) [1969] 3 All ER 172 and Murphy v Ingram (Inspector of Taxes) [1974] 2 All
c ER 187 applied.

Notes
For the charge of development land tax, see Supplement to 5 Halsbury's Laws (4th Edn)
para 300A.1.
For deemed notice to treat on notice of compliance and the effect of a notice to treat,
d see 8 ibid paras 94, 136.
For the Town and Country Planning Act 1971, s 181, see 41 Halsbury's Statutes (3rd
Edn) 1790.
For the Development Land Tax Act 1976, s 45, see 46 ibid 1501.

Cases referred to in judgment
e Birmingham City Corpn v West Midland Baptist (Trust) Association (Inc) [1969] 3 All ER 172,
[1970] AC 874, [1969] 3 WLR 389, 133 JP 524, 67 LGR 571, 20 P & CR 1052, [1969]
RVR 484, HL, 11 Digest (Reissue) 149, 209.
Capital Investments Ltd v Wednesfield Urban District Council [1964] 1 All ER 655, [1965] Ch
774, [1964] 2 WLR 932, 128 JP 287, 62 LGR 566, 15 P & CR 435, Digest (Cont Vol B)
618, 925a.
f East End Dwellings Co Ltd v Finsbury Borough Council [1951] 2 All ER 587, [1952] AC 109,
49 LGR 669, 2 P & CR 135, HL, 45 Digest (Repl) 369, 169.
Harding v Metropolitan Railway Co (1872) 7 Ch App 154, 41 LJ Ch 371, 26 LT 109, 36 JP
340, LC, 11 Digest (Reissue) 235, 818.
Haynes v Haynes (1861) 1 Drew & Sm 426, 30 LJ Ch 578, 4 LT 199, 62 ER 442, 11 Digest
(Reissue) 208, 581.
g Hill v East and West India Dock Co (1884) 9 App Cas 448, 53 LJ Ch 824, 51 LT 163, 48 JP
788, HL, 5 Digest (Reissue) 1014, 8146.
Leitch v Emmott (Inspector of Taxes) [1929] 2 KB 266, [1929] All ER Rep 638, 98 LJKB 673,
141 LT 311, 14 Tax Cas 633, CA, 28(1) Digest (Reissue) 385, 1411.
Levy, Re, ex parte Walton (1881) 17 Ch D 746, [1881–5] All ER Rep 548, 50 LJ Ch 657, 45
LT 30, CA, 5 Digest (Reissue) 1005, 8062.
h Murphy v Ingram (Inspector of Taxes) [1973] 2 All ER 523, [1973] Ch 434, [1973] 2 WLR
983, [1973] STC 309, 49 Tax Cas 410; rvsd [1974] 2 All ER 187, [1974] Ch 363, [1974]
2 WLR 782, [1974] STC 205, 49 Tax Cas 410, 53 ATC 30, [1974] TR 33, CA, Digest
(Cont Vol D) 490, 1610a.
W & S (Long Eaton) Ltd v Derbyshire County Council (1975) 31 P & CR 99, CA; affg 29
P & CR 522, Lands Tribunal.

j
Cases also cited
Grice v Dudley Corpn [1957] 2 All ER 673, [1958] Ch 329.
Munton v Greater London Council [1976] 2 All ER 815, [1976] 1 WLR 649, CA.
Pollard v Middlesex County Council (1906) 95 LT 870.
Western Fish Products Ltd v Penwith District Council p 204, post, 77 LGR 185, CA.

Case stated

1. At a meeting of the Commissioners for the Special Purposes of the Income Tax Acts *a* held on 27th October and 10th November 1978, Metrolands (Property Finance) Ltd ('the taxpayer company') appealed against an assessment to development land tax in the sum of £29,085 made in respect of the disposal by it to the Metropolitan Borough Council of Bolton ('the council') of land at Westhoughton, near Bolton ('the land').

2. Shortly stated the question for decision was whether under s 45 of the Development Land Tax Act 1976 the land was disposed of before or after 1st August 1976, the date on *b* which development land tax first became chargeable.

[Paragraphs 3 and 4 listed the witnesses who gave evidence and the documents proved or admitted before the commissioners.]

5. As a result of the evidence both oral and documentary adduced before the commissioners they found the following facts proved or admitted. (1) On 9th October 1974 the taxpayer company served a purchase notice dated 8th October 1974 on the *c* council under s 180 of the Town and Country Planning Act 1971 in respect of the land (which comprised 4·31 acres being part of Hosker's Nook Farm and part of Eatocks Farm at Westhoughton near Bolton). On 9th May 1974 the council had refused planning permission for houses to be built on the land. After referring to the land and the refusal of planning permission the purchase notice proceeded as follows:

'WE SERVE NOTICE under section 180 of the Town and Country Planning Act 1971 *d* on the Council of the Bolton Metropolitan Borough that we claim (a) that the land has become incapable of reasonably beneficial use in its existing state, and (b) that it cannot be rendered capable of reasonably beneficial use by the carrying out of any other development for which permission has been granted or is deemed to be granted or for which the Local Planning Authority or the Secretary of State for the Environment have undertaken to grant permission, and WE HEREBY REQUIRE the *e* Council to purchase our interest in the said land namely the fee simple subject as to part thereof to the exceptions and reservations mentioned in a Conveyance dated the Twenty seventh day of April One thousand nine hundred and twenty one and made between Ada Mary Charlton of the first part the said Ada Mary Charlton Alice Marion Arnold and Thomas Butler Cato of the second part and William Alker of the third part and as to the remaining part thereof to the exceptions and reservations *f* grantees covenants and other matters contained and referred to in a Conveyance dated the Third day of March One thousand nine hundred and twenty made between The Right Honourable John Francis Granville Scrope Fourth Earl of Ellesmere of the first part the said Fourth Earl of Ellesmere The Honourable Thomas Henry Frederick Egerton and Claude Francis Arthur Egerton of the second part and James Riding of the third part so far only as such covenants and other *g* matters remain to be observed and performed and are capable of being enforced and relate to or affect the said land and subject to any such rights easements and appurtenances to which the said land is held subject.'

(2)(a) On 28th November 1974 the planning committee of the council considered the purchase notice and resolved that the council's director of administration be authorised *h* to service notice to the effect that the council was willing to comply with the purchase notice and that he also be authorised to enter into negotiations for the acquisition of the land. (b) The resolution was confirmed by the council at a meeting held on 11th December 1974. (c) By letter dated 20th December 1974 the chief legal officer of the council informed the company's solicitors, Messrs Henry Fallows & Co, that the council had determined to accept the purchase notice and enclosed with the letter a form of *j* claim 'for completion and return to me on behalf of your clients so that negotiations as to purchase price can begin'. (d) The form of claim was completed on 15th January 1975 and sent to the chief legal officer. It contained particulars of the company's interest in the land, its existing use and other necessary information to enable the negotiations to proceed. (e) By letter dated 20th January 1975 to Messrs Henry Fallows & Co the chief legal officer acknowledged receipt of the form of claim and by a further letter, dated 21st

January 1975, he informed them that the council's chief estate surveyor would be
a negotiating the compensation. (3)(a) On 21st May 1975 Mr Thornley, managing director
of the taxpayer company, had a preliminary meeting with Mr Disley, a senior estate
surveyor in the estates section of the council, at which they discussed the general level of
values and sought to reach some understanding on comparable properties. Mr Thornley
knew that Mr Disley was then an assistant in the office of the chief estate surveyor. (b)
A further meeting took place on 16th September 1975 by which time Mr Coane had
b taken over from Mr Disley (who had been promoted to take charge of a section in the
office of the chief estates surveyor) the negotiation of the compensation. At that meeting
Mr Thornley was accompanied by Mr Hopkins, a chartered surveyor, who had been
instructed on behalf of the taxpayer company. A figure of £64,650 was agreed to be the
appropriate amount of compensation. Mr Thornley was under the impression that Mr
Coane had power to bind, and had bound, the council to pay that sum. Neither Mr
c Coane nor any other officer of the council had said or done anything to imply that he
had, or was purporting to exercise, any such power, nor did the council hold out either
Mr Coane or any other officer as having any such power. (c) On 1st October 1975 the
chief estates surveyor wrote to the taxpayer company a letter which, so far as relevant,
read as follows:

d   'I refer to the recent meeting between Messrs Thornley and Hopkins and my
Assistant, Mr Coane, concerning the above land. I understand that the Director of
Administration is willing to comply with the Purchase Notices served by your
Company in respect of the land at Hoskers Nook and Eatocks Farm, Westhoughton
on the basis that the land is incapable of reasonable beneficial use. I further
understand that the two parcels of land are zoned for educational purposes on the
e   Westhoughton Master Plan and that you would have been granted planning
permission for residential development otherwise. Based on the above assumptions
I am prepared to recommend the Council to pay you the sum of £64,650 in full and
final settlement of all claims associated with the Purchase Notice served in respect
of 4·31 acres of land known as Hoskers Nook, subject to the following terms and
conditions:—(1) The area concerned of 4·31 acres is shown edged red on the
f   attached plan A. (2) The tenure of the land is freehold and free from chief rent.
(3) Vacant possession to be given on completion. (4) There are no restrictions,
easements, unusual covenants or burdens affecting the land. (5) There are no
outstanding charges registered against the land. (6) I understand a road is to be
constructed on the adjoining land by [the taxpayer company], and in return for full
rights of access to the Education land, Bolton MBC undertake to pay one half of the
g   "streetage costs" incurred in making up the stretch of road coloured blue on plan A,
which is co-extensive with the frontage of the land. [The taxpayer company] are to
make up the whole of this road to the satisfaction of the Local Authority within a
period of approximately two years of legal completion of the land. (7) The purchase
is subject to the approval of the Education Committee, the Council and any
Government Department concerned. (8) Each side to bear its own costs.'

h
(d) On 3rd December 1975 the taxpayer company wrote to the chief estates surveyor
acknowledging the letter of 1st October 1975 and accepting the terms set out therein.
(4)(a) On 23rd February 1976 the chief estates surveyor, on behalf of the council, applied
to the local planning authority under s 17 of the Land Compensation Act 1961, and s 47
of and Sch 9 to the Community Land Act 1975, for a certificate of alternative
j development for residential purposes in respect of that part of the land at Hosker's
Nook. (b) On 27th May 1976 a certificate of alternative development was granted to the
council and a copy was sent to the taxpayer company. The council, as planning authority,
certified in pursuance of s 17 that, in its opinion, if the land in question were not
proposed to be acquired by the council planning permission might reasonably have been
expected to be granted for residential development. (5)(a) On 27th July 1976 the
council's director of administration reported the compensation terms to the land sub-

committee of the council which duly approved them. The relevant minute of the proceedings of the sub-committee reads as follows:

'IX PURCHASE NOTICE—LAND AT HOSKER'S NOOK, WESTHOUGHTON
'The Director of Administration referred to the decision of the Council to accept a Purchase Notice served by Metrolands Ltd. in respect of approximately 4·31 acres of land at Hosker's Nook, Westhoughton, and submitted terms provisionally agreed as compensation for its acquisition. Resolved—That such terms be approved.'

(b) On 3rd August 1976 the proceedings of the land sub-committee were submitted to the council's management and finance committee which resolved that they be approved. (c) On 11th August 1976 the proceedings of the management and finance committee referred to in (b) above were put to a meeting of the council and were approved. (d) On 17th February 1977 the chief estates surveyor wrote to the taxpayer company informing it of the council's approval. (6)(a) Mr Disley informed the commissioners in evidence, which they accepted, that apart from certain powers delegated under the Community Land Act 1975 (which were not relevant to the question in issue in the case) the council's committees had no power to accept compensation terms on behalf of the council. The chief estates surveyor had delegated to him by the council power to agree compensation up to £5,000. All compensation in excess of £5,000 required the approval of the council. The practice was for compensation negotiated in excess of £5,000 to be reported to the land sub-committee of the management and finance committee; if the sub-committee approved the figure it would report it to its parent committee; if that committee approved the figure it would report it to the council for final approval. (b) Mr Disley's evidence was corroborated in material respects by such agreed documentary evidence as was before the commissioners. Thus (i) at the annual meeting of the council held on 19th May 1976 it was resolved, inter alia, under the heading 'Appointment of Committees and Standing Sub-Committees' as follows:

'(A) That Committees of the Council and Standing Sub-Committees be appointed for the current municipal year as set out below to exercise the powers and duties of the Council specified, subject to the acts and proceedings of such Committees being approved by the Council except in those matters which are subject to the Council's Scheme of Delegation . . .
'Managment and Finance Committee'

The resolution proceeded to name the members of that committee and to set out its powers and duties which included the following:

'1. General Management of the financial affairs of the Council . . .
'7. Through its Land Sub-Committee to:—(a) advise the Council on policies for the acquisition and disposal of land and to undertake the functions of the Council under the provisions of the Community Land Act 1975, to acquire, manage and dispose of land for private development; (b) to acquire and manage land acquired for general purposes of the Council until required for special functions of another Committee or until disposal of the land . . .'

(ii) At a meeting on 24th January 1974 (at which date a land sub-committee did not exist) the council confirmed a minute of the proceedings of its management and finance committee at the meeting of that committee on 27th December 1973. So far as relevant that minute was as follows:

'100 DELEGATIONS
'It was reported that pursuant to the decision of the Council on 28 June 1973, the various Committees had specified the functions which they considered should be the subject of delegation to either Committees, Chairmen, Officers, or otherwise, and the proposals of the various Committees were submitted. Resolved—That the delegations proposed by the Committees and contained in the lists now submitted be approved as amended with the exception that the delegations proposed by the

a
Planning Committee be referred back to such Committee for further consideration; and that a copy of the approved delegations be supplied to each Member of the Council.
'*Management and Finance Committee*
'*The Director of Administration*: . . . (c) Preliminary negotiations for land and property (without committing the Council) at the request of a Chief Officer or at the Director of Administration's discretion, and subject to report to the first succeeding meeting
b
of the appropriate Committee.'

(iii) In his letter of 10th January 1978 to the Development Land Tax Office the chief estate surveyor wrote as follows:

c
'I have delegated powers to negotiate acquisitions and compensation claims up to a figure of £5,000 but all settlements in excess have to be reported for the consideration of the appropriate Committee, whose decision is in turn considered by the full Council. A matter is only regarded as fully approved when the Council gives its ratification to the Committee Minutes, and such ratification is not automatic. In the case of Hoskers Nook a figure of £64,650 exceeded my delegated powers and after the Certificate of Alternative Development was issued by the Department of Planning to confirm the basis of valuation the matter was reported
d
for the consideration of the next available Land Sub-Committee which was held on 27 July 1976. Land Sub-Committee's Minutes were reported to, and approved, by the Management and Finance Committee on 3 August, 1976 and the full Council gave their approval at their meeting held on 11 August, 1976. Appropriate photocopies are enclosed as requested.'

(c) In Mr Disley's experience the council had never rejected out of hand any figure of
e
compensation which had been negotiated by one of its officers and reported to the council through the usual channels. If the council did not approve of anything reported to it its practice would be, in his experience, to refer the matter back to the appropriate committee. (d) Printed copies of the minutes of proceedings of the council and of its committees are deposited in the public library where they are available for inspection by
the public. (e) The 'Council's Scheme of Delegation' referred to in sub-para (b) above was
f
not a written document. Any powers delegated to officers would be set out in office instructions. The only delegated power brought to the commissioners' attention in these proceedings was the power conferred on the chief estates surveyor referred to in sub-para (a) and (b)(iii) above.

6. It was contended on behalf of the Crown: (a) that the service of the purchase notice and its acceptance, or the notification of its acceptance, by the council in December 1974
g
did not constitute an enforceable contract for sale and did not create the relationship of vendor and purchaser between the taxpayer company and the council; (b) that, by virtue of s 181(2) of the Town and Country Planning Act 1971, once the council had accepted the purchase notice it was to be 'deemed to be authorised to acquire the interest of [the taxpayer company] compulsorily in accordance with the relevant provisions, and to have served a notice to treat in respect thereof on the date of service of' notice of its acceptance;
h
(c) that the consequence of this provision was that the acquisition by the council of the land was to be treated as though it were a compulsory purchase initiated by the making of a compulsory purchase order and the service of a notice to treat; (d) that consequently there was no enforceable contract between the taxpayer company and the council until the amount of the compensation had been agreed between them; (e) that such agreement was not reached until 11th August 1976 when the council approved the compensation
j
terms; and (f) that for the purpose of s 45(4) of the Development Land Tax Act 1976 the taxpayer company disposed of the land on 11th August 1976 (ie after the appointed day for the coming into force of that Act) and the appeal hearing should be adjourned to enable the parties to agree figures on that basis.

7. It was contended on behalf of the taxpayer company: (a) that the service of the purchase notice and its acceptance, or the notification of its acceptance, by the council in

December 1974 constituted an enforceable contract for sale between the parties and
created between them the relationship of vendor and purchaser; (b) that the sole purpose   **a**
of s 181(2) of the Town and Country Planning Act 1971 was to incorporate into that Act
s 1 of the Land Compensation Act 1961 and s 6 of the Compulsory Purchase Act 1965
(which confer jurisdiction on the Lands Tribunal to determine the amount of the
compensation in the absence of agreement between the parties); (c)(i) that if there was no
enforceable agreement as contended for in (a) above, there was such an agreement when
the amount of the compensation was agreed between the parties; (ii) that such agreement   **b**
was reached *either* on 16th September 1975 at the meeting between Mr Thornley and Mr
Coane because Mr Coane's agreement to the figure of £64,650 was binding on the
council *or* on 3rd December 1975 when the taxpayer company wrote to the chief estates
surveyor the letter referred to in para 5(3)(d) above *or* on 27th July 1976 when the land
sub-committee approved the compensation terms; (iii) if neither Mr Coane nor the chief
estates surveyor for the land sub-committee was authorised to bind the council their   **c**
actions were ratified by the council when it approved the compensation terms on 11th
August 1976, and that that act of ratification placed the taxpayer company and the
council in exactly the position they would have been in if the relevant authority had
existed throughout; and (d) that on any view the diposal of the land took place before 1st
August 1976 (the appointed day for the purpose of s 1(2) of the Development Land Tax
Act 1976) and the assessment should be discharged.   **d**

    8. The following cases were cited in argument: *Barclays Bank Ltd v Inland Revenue
Comrs* [1960] 2 All ER 817, [1961] AC 509, HL; *Batcheller (Robert) & Sons Ltd v Batcheller*
[1945] 1 All ER 522, [1945] Ch 169; *Birmingham City Corpn v West Midland Baptist (Trust)
Association (Inc)* [1969] 3 All ER 172, [1970] AC 874, HL; *Brown v Gould* [1971] 2 All ER
1505, [1972] Ch 53; *East End Dwellings Co Ltd v Finsbury Borough Council* [1951] 2 All ER
587, [1952] AC 109, HL; *Harding v Metropolitan Railway Co* (1872) 7 Ch App 154, LC;   **e**
Haynes v Haynes (1861) 1 Drew & Sm 426, 62 ER 442; *Holloway v Dover Corpn* [1960] 2
All ER 193, [1960] 1 WLR 604, CA; *Lever (Finance) Ltd v Westminster Corpn* [1970] 3 All
ER 496, [1971] 1 QB 222, CA; *Murphy v Ingram (Inspector of Taxes)* [1973] 2 All ER 523,
[1973] STC 309; *affd* [1974] 2 All ER 187, [1974] STC 205, CA; *R v Norfolk County Council*
(1891) 60 LJQB 379, DC; *Southend-on-Sea Corpn v Hodgson (Wickford) Ltd* [1961] 2 All ER
46, [1962] 1 QB 416, DC; *Tomlin v Standard Telephones and Cables Ltd* [1969] 3 All ER 201,   **f**
[1969] 1 WLR 1378, CA; *Western Fish Products Ltd v Penwith District Council* p 204, post,
CA.

    9. The commissioners who heard the appeal took time to consider their decision and
gave it in writing on 7th December 1978 as follows:

    'On 9 October 1974 [the taxpayer company] served on [the council] a Purchase   **g**
Notice dated 8 October 1974 under section 180 of the Town and Country Planning
Act 1971 in respect of part of Hosker Nook Farm which the Company owned in fee
simple. That Purchase Notice was accepted by the Council on 11 December 1974
and notified to the Company accordingly by letter dated 20 December 1974.
Negotiations ensued about the amount of the compensation between Mr Coane of
the Office of the Chief Estates Surveyor of the Council and the Company. A figure   **h**
of £64,650 was eventually agreed upon and on 1 October 1975 the Chief Estates
Surveyor wrote to the Company saying that he was prepared to recommend the
Council to pay that sum in full and final settlement of all claims associated with the
Purchase Notice subject to certain terms and conditions therein set out. On 3
December 1975 the Company wrote to the Chief Estates Surveyor accepting the
terms set out in his letter. On 27 July 1976 the agreement regarding the   **j**
compensation was reported to the Land Sub-Committee of the Council which
resolved that the terms of the agreement be approved. On 3 August 1976 the
proceedings of the Land Sub-Committee were submitted to the Management and
Finance Committee of the Council and the terms were approved by that
Committee. On 11 August 1976 the Council approved the proceedings of its
Management and Finance Committee. The Company appeals against an assessment
to Development Land Tax made upon it in the sum of £29,085 under section 45(4)

of the Development Land Tax Act 1976 on the basis that the disposal and acquisition
was made on 11 August 1976 when the amount of the compensation was approved
by the Council at its meeting on that date. The Company contends that the relevant
date is 20 December 1974 when the Purchase Notice was accepted and, it submits,
the parties became contractually bound or, failing that, at some date prior to 1
August 1976 (when Development Land Tax first became chargeable) when, it
submits, the amount of the compensation had been agreed on behalf of the Council
by one of its officers or by one of its committees.

'It is contended on behalf of the Revenue that the parties did not become
contractually bound until the amount of the compensation received the approval of
the Council itself because by virtue of section 181(2) of the Town and Country
Planning Act 1971 the Council was, following acceptance of the Purchase Notice, to
be "deemed to be authorised to acquire the interest of the owner compulsorily . . . and
to have served a notice to treat in respect thereof on the date of service of the notice
[of acceptance]". The effect of that sub-section is, it is contended, to put the parties
in the same position as though the Council had served on the Company a notice to
treat following a compulsory purchase order from which it follows that sub-section
(4) of section 45 of the 1976 Act, which refers to the case "where an interest in land
is acquired compulsorily", applied and the relevant time is that at which the
compensation was agreed. Mr Hetherington-Sims for the Revenue referred us to
several authorities on the juridical nature of a notice to treat and, in particular, to
Haynes v Haynes (1861) 1 Drew & Sm 426, 62 ER 442 in which it was held that a
mere notice to treat did not constitute an enforceable contract. He also referred us
to the judgment of Megarry J in *Murphy v Ingram (Inspector of Taxes)* [1973] 2 All ER
523 at 534, [1973] STC 309 at 320 where the learned judge referred to the statement
of Lord Asquith in *East End Dwellings Co Ltd v Finsbury Borough Council* [1951] 2 All
ER 587 at 599, [1952] AC 109 at 132 that if one is bidden to treat an imaginary state
of affairs as real one must, unless prohibited from doing so, also imagine as real the
consequences and incidents which, if the putative state of affairs had in fact existed,
must inevitably have flowed from or accompanied it. Mr Hetherington-Sims
submitted that a necessary consequence of the imaginary notice to treat in the case
before us was to defer the formation of any contract between the parties to the time
when the compensation had been agreed between them.

'We are unable to accept Mr Hetherington-Sims' argument. There was in this
case no compulsory acquisition at all. By serving the Purchase Notice the Company
indicated its willingness to sell and by accepting that notice the Council indicated its
willingness to buy. It is common ground that neither party was able to withdraw
from that situation and that the only thing that remained to be done was the fixing
of the amount of compensation. It is also common ground between the parties that
there was no uncertainty as to this amount because it would be fixed either by
agreement or failing agreement by reference to the Lands Tribunal. We, therefore,
accept [counsel's] submission, on behalf of the Company, that there was a contract
between the parties as from 20 December 1974 and that their relationship under
that contract was that of vendor and purchaser. *Haynes v Haynes* is, in our view,
distinguishable because, as was pointed out by Kindersley V-C, in the case where all
that has happened is the service of a notice to treat there has only been a
communication of will by the acquiring authority; in the absence of any such
communication by the Landowner there can be no contract (see 1 Drew & Sm 426
at 433–435, 62 ER 442 at 445–446). In the case before us both the Council and the
Company had by 20 December 1974 expressed their willingness the one to acquire
and the other to dispose of the land at an ascertainable price. The essential
requirements for a contract had been satisfied.

'Mr Hetherington-Sims contends that even if there should be a contract between
the parties, that contract has no significance because the statutory hypothesis arising
out of the deeming provision in sub-section (2) of section 181 of the 1971 Act
requires one to assume that the only thing that had happened was the service of a
notice to treat following a compulsory purchase order. This we are unable to

accept. *Murphy v Ingram (Inspector of Taxes)* went to the Court of Appeal where Russell LJ observed that it had been remarked on high authority that in considering **a** "deeming" provisions in Statutes it is important to have in mind what appears to be the purpose of the enactment (see [1974] 2 All ER 187 at 190, [1974] Ch 363 at 370, [1974] STC 205 at 208). We are satisfied that [counsel for the taxpayer company] is right when he contends that the only purpose of the deeming provision was to incorporate into the 1971 Act section 1 of the Land Compensation Act 1961 and section 6 of the Compulsory Purchase Act 1965 which confer jurisdiction on the **b** Lands Tribunal to determine the amount of the compensation in the absence of agreement. In our view, there is no justification for the contention that we must, in view of sub-section (2), ignore the Purchase Notice and its acceptance and regard the transaction in question in this appeal as one of compulsory purchase pure and simple. That was not the purpose of the sub-section and was not a necessary consequence of it. We hold that the disposal and acquisition took place, as counsel **c** for the taxpayer company submits, as a result of the contract comprising the Purchase Notice and its acceptance and that by virtue of sub-section (2)(*b*) of section 45 of the 1976 Act, which deals with unconditional contracts, the relevant date is 20 December 1974. We discharge the assessment under appeal accordingly. We add that we have been helped in reaching our decision by the fact that in sub-section (8) of section 45 Parliament has expressly referred to a deemed service of a notice to **d** treat; if it had intended sub-section (4) to apply to a deemed compulsory acquisition we would have expected to find a similar express reference.

'If our decision should be wrong and the true view is that the land was acquired compulsorily so that the transaction does fall within sub-section (4) of section 45, then we hold that the disposal and acquisition did not take place until, as Mr Hetherington-Sims submits, 11 August 1976 when the amount of the compensation **e** received the approval of the Council. We find as a fact that Mr Coane did not have authority to commit the Council to pay the negotiated amount of the compensation, and that he did not hold himself out, and was not held out by the Council, as having any such authority. As to the powers of the Management and Finance Committee and of its Lands Sub-Committee it is specifically stated in the relevant minute of the Council . . . that the exercise of those powers was subject to approval by the Council **f** "except in those matters which are subject to the Council's Scheme of Delegation". On the evidence before us we find that the exercise by these Committees of their power to approve the amount of the compensation in this case was not subject to any such exception and that approval of the Council was therefore necessary.'

10. The Crown immediately after the determination of the appeal declared its dissatisfaction therewith as being erroneous in point of law and on 4th January 1979 **g** required the commissioners to state a case for the opinion of the High Court pursuant to s 56 of the Taxes Management Act 1970.

11. The question for the opinion of the court was whether the commissioners' decision was correct in law.

Robert Carnwath for the Crown.   **h**
D C Potter QC and *R M K Gray* for the taxpayer company.

Cur adv vult

11th December. **NOURSE J** read the following judgment: This is the first case in **j** which the court has been asked to decide a question on the development land tax which was introduced in 1976 by the Act of that name. The expressed intention of the Act was to impose a new tax on the realisation of the development value of land. That was the fifth occasion on which Parliament had sought to impose such a tax during the present century. Dealing only with more recent times, there was the betterment levy which was introduced by the Land Commission Act 1967. That was abolished in 1971. But in December 1973 the then Conservative administration made proposals, having immediate

effect, for the introduction of a tax on development gains. Those proposals had not been
a published in the form of a Bill before the change of government in March 1974, but a tax
which became known as development gains tax was brought into being by the Finance
Act 1974, and it remained in effect until replaced by the Development Land Tax Act
1976. Apart from a reduction in rates, there has been no significant change since that
date.

The new tax first became chargeable on 1st August 1976. It is not chargeable on
b disposals made before that date. In the present case the disposal was made under what
can broadly be described as the compulsory purchase legislation. But it was not the
normal case where the acquiring authority takes the land against the will of the owner.
It was a species of what are sometimes known as reverse compulsory purchases. The
owner, having been refused planning permission for the development of the land,
required the authority to purchase it pursuant to the provisions contained in Part IX of
c the Town and Country Planning Act 1971. The question which I have to decide is
whether in the light of those provisions and those of the 1976 Act the disposal took place
before or after 1st August 1976. If it took place before, no tax will be chargeable; if after,
the tax will be £29,085. This, then, is a case of a transitional nature. But it is likely to
result in a determination of the more general question: what is the time at which a
disposal is made in this type of reverse compulsory acquisition?

d The question comes to the court as an appeal by way of case stated from a decision of
the Special Commissioners dated 22nd August 1979. The land in question is 4·31 acres
at Westhoughton, near Bolton, and the owner is a company called Metrolands (Property
Finance) Ltd. The acquiring authority was the Metropolitan Borough Council of
Bolton. The Special Commissioners held that the disposal took place on 20th December
1974, before the tax became chargeable. They accordingly discharged an assessment
e which had been made on the company. But the Crown contends that the disposal and
acquisition took place on 11th August 1976, ten days too late from the company's point
of view, and that is the basis of its appeal to this court.

The facts are fully and carefully set out in the stated case. This was in part made
necessary so that the Special Commissioners might resolve a dispute of fact which is no
longer in issue. The facts which are still material can be stated with comparative brevity.
f On 9th May 1974 the council refused the company planning permission for houses to
be built on the land. That was because they themselves required it for educational
purposes. Accordingly, on 9th October 1974 the company served on the council a
purchase notice under s 180 of the 1971 Act claiming that the land had become incapable
of reasonably beneficial use in its existing state and that it could not be rendered capable
of such use by the carrying out of any other permissible development, and requiring the
g council to purchase it accordingly. On 20th December 1974 the council wrote to the
company's solicitors for the purpose of informing them that the council had determined
to accept the company's purchase notice. It is clear that that was a statement that the
council were willing to comply with the purchase notice within s 181(1)(a) of the 1971
Act. The letter enclosed a form of claim 'for completion and return to me on behalf of
your clients so that negotiations as to purchase price can begin'. As I have already
h indicated, the company contends and the Special Commissioners held that the council's
statement that they were willing to comply with the purchase notice effected a disposal
of the company's interest in the land for the purposes of the 1976 Act on that day.
Negotiations as to the purchase price did indeed take place subsequently, but they took
a long time to come to fruition. It was not until 11th August 1976, the date for which
the Crown contends, that a figure of £64,650 was finally approved by the council. It is
j now agreed that it was not until that approval was given that the purchase price (or, more
accurately, the compensation) was fixed. The Development Land Tax Act 1976 had
reached the statute book on 22nd July, and 1st August had been prescribed as the
appointed day for the purposes of the Act. If, contrary to the view of the Special
Commissioners, the company is liable for the tax, then it may be said that it is very hard
luck that the compensation was not fixed a fortnight or so earlier. But that is something
which cannot enter into a decision of this case.

I must now refer in greater detail to the material provisions of Part IX of the Town and

Country Planning Act 1971, to certain principles of the law of compulsory acquisition
and to the material provisions of the 1976 Act, and in particular to s 45.
    As to the 1971 Act, I have already sufficiently referred to s 180. Section 181(1), in
addition to enabling the council to state that they are willing to comply with the
purchase notice, gives them two other courses of action. Firstly, they can serve a notice
stating that another local authority or statutory undertakers have agreed to comply with
the purchase notice in their place. Secondly, they can serve a notice stating that, for
reasons which must be specified in the notice, they are not willing to comply with the
purchase notice, have not found anyone else who will agree to comply with it in their
place, and have transmitted a copy of it to the Secretary of State. I will return to him
later, but I must now read s 181(2), which is of great importance to the present case, in
full. It says:

> 'Where the council on whom a purchase notice is served by an owner have served
> on him a notice in accordance with subsection (1)(a) or (b) of this section, the council,
> or the other local authority or statutory undertakers specified in the notice, as the
> case may be, shall be deemed to be authorised to acquire the interest of the owner
> compulsorily in accordance with the relevant provisions, and to have served a notice
> to treat in respect thereof on the date of service of the notice under that subsection.'

That, then, is a deeming provision, the effect of which has been much debated in
argument before me.
    Section 182 sets out the procedure on transmission of a purchase notice to the Secretary
of State. Shortly stated, the position is that the Secretary of State can either confirm the
purchase notice or take certain other action of a kind which is specified in s 183. For
example, he can grant planning permission for the relevant development for which
permission has been refused by the council. The next section I should refer to is s 186,
which deals with cases where the Secretary of State either (1) confirms the purchase
notice or (2) neither confirms it nor takes any other action on it. In either of those events
there are deeming provisions similar to that contained in s 181(2). The only other
section of the 1971 Act to which I need refer at this stage is s 208, which provides that—

> 'the power conferred by section 31 of the Land Compensation Act 1961 to
> withdraw a notice to treat shall not be exercisable in the case of a notice to treat
> which is deemed to have been served by virtue of any of the provisions of this Part
> of this Act.'

I refer next to the principles of the law of compulsory acquisition relating to the effect
of a notice to treat. These are conveniently summarised in 8 Halsbury's Laws (4th Edn)
para 136. I will read that paragraph so far as material to the present case. The paragraph
heading is 'Relation of parties as vendor and purchaser after notice to treat'. It reads as
follows:

> 'The effect of serving a notice to treat is to establish a relation analogous in some
> respects to that of vendor and purchaser, a relation which binds the owner of the
> land to give up the land subject to his being paid compensation, and which binds
> the undertakers or acquiring authority to take the land, but there is no contract of
> sale until the price is ascertained and the land remains the property of the
> landowner. Both parties have the right to have the price ascertained and the
> purchase completed in manner provided by the Lands Clauses Acts or the
> Compulsory Purchase Act 1965 or any Acts modifying those Acts ... When the
> price has been ascertained the relationship of vendor and purchaser exists between
> the parties as if there had been an ordinary agreement for sale, and ... the parties'
> rights and duties are the same as those arising out of an ordinary contract for the sale
> of land including the right to have the contract enforced by specific performance,
> and the owner's interest then, but not before, becomes an interest in personalty.'

It is also material to note that where the landowner has notified the acquiring authority
of the amount he claims by way of compensation the authority has six weeks to
withdraw the notice to treat, if it wishes to do so. That power is given by s 31 of the Land

Compensation Act 1961, to which reference has already been made. I should also
a mention that the authority may normally enter on the land after service of a notice to
treat on not less than 14 days' notice. It is not necessary for the compensation to have
been agreed or assessed before entry is made.

I now come to the Development Land Tax Act 1976 itself. Section 1(1) provides that
the tax shall be charged in accordance with the provisions of the Act in respect of the
realisation of the development value of land in the United Kingdom. Subsection (2)
b provides that, subject to the provisions of the Act, a person shall be chargeable to the tax
on 'the realised development value', determined in accordance with the Act, which
accrues to him on the disposal by him on or after the appointed day of an interest in land
in the United Kingdom. Subsection (3) provides that, subject to s 13, the rate of the tax
should be 80%. Section 13 provides for a reduced rate of 66⅔% up to a certain limit, and
that is the rate which would be applicable in the present case. I can ignore ss 2 and 3.
c Sections 4 and 5 tell you how to get at the realised development value; and then I can go
straight to s 45.

I will read s 45(1), (2) and (4) in full, sub-s (3) being immaterial to the present case:

> '(1) The provisions of this section shall have effect for determining the time at
> which, for the purposes of liability to development land tax, an interest in land is to
> be taken to be disposed of or acquired.
d
> '(2) Subject to subsections (2) and (3) of section 3 above and the following
> provisions of this section, where under a contract an interest in land is disposed of
> and that interest or, in the case of a part disposal, the granted interest is acquired,
> then,—(a) if the contract is conditional (and, in particular, if it is conditional on the
> exercise of an option) the time at which the disposal and acquisition is made is the
> time when the condition is satisfied; and (b) in any other case, the time at which the
e > disposal and acquisition is made is the time the contract is made and not, if it is
> different, the time at which the interest is conveyed or transferred . . .
> '(4) Subject to subsections (5) and (8) below, where an interest in land is acquired
> compulsorily by an authority possessing compulsory powers, the time at which the
> disposal and acquisition is made is the time at which the compensation for the
> acquisition is agreed or otherwise determined (variations on appeal being disregarded
f > for this purpose) or, if earlier, the time when the authority enter on the land in
> pursuance of their powers . . .'

I must also read sub-s (8), which is in these terms:

> 'Subject to subsection (9) below, where an interest in land is disposed of on or after
> the appointed day to an authority possessing compulsory powers then, if notice to
g > treat in respect of that interest was (or is by virtue of any enactment deemed to have
> been) served before 13th September 1974 on the person making the disposal, the
> disposal shall be treated for the purposes of this Act as having been made before the
> appointed day.'

Shortly stated, the decision of the Special Commissioners was to the following effect.
Firstly, they rejected the Crown's contention that the disposal and acquisition fell within
h s 45(4). Secondly, they accepted the company's contention that the disposal and
acquisition fell within s 45(2)(b). The meat of their decision on these points was expressed
in these terms:

> 'There was in this case no compulsory acquisition at all. By serving the Purchase
> Notice the Company indicated its willingness to sell and by accepting that notice the
j > Council indicated its willingness to buy. It is common ground that neither party
> was able to withdraw from that situation and that the only thing that remained to
> be done was the fixing of the amount of compensation. It is also common ground
> between the parties that there was no uncertainty as to this amount because it would
> be fixed either by agreement or failing agreement by reference to the Lands
> Tribunal. We, therefore, accept [counsel's] submission, on behalf of the Company,
> that there was a contract between the parties as from 20 December 1974 and that
> their relationship under that contract was that of vendor and purchaser.'

The Special Commissioners then went on more particularly to reject the Crown's argument that the deeming provision in s 181(2) of the 1971 Act required an assumption *a* that the only thing that had happened was the service of a notice to treat following a compulsory purchase order. As to this, they expressed the view that there was no justification for the contention that they must ignore the purchase notice and its acceptance and regard the transaction in question as one of compulsory purchase pure and simple. They discharged the assessment accordingly. They then added that they had been helped in reaching their decision by the fact that s 45(8) expressly referred to *b* a deemed service of a notice to treat. In this connection they observed that if Parliament had intended sub-s (4) to apply to a deemed compulsory acquisition they would have expected to find a similar express reference in that subsection. Finally, they held, in case their decision should be wrong and the true view was that the transaction fell within s 45(4), that the disposal and acquisition did not take place until 11th August 1976 when the amount of the compensation received the approval of the council. That finding of *c* fact is the one from which there has been no appeal to this court.

Whatever else may be said about this case, it seems to me that once you have studied the material legislation and the relevant principles of the law of compulsory acquisition there is no obvious answer to the question what is the time at which, for the purposes of liability to development land tax, an interest in land is to be taken to be disposed of and acquired in the case of a purchase notice with which a council have stated that they are *d* willing to comply pursuant to s 181(1)(a) of the 1971 Act. On the arguments which I have heard, three possibilities have been suggested. Firstly, that the transaction falls within s 45(4). That is the contention of counsel for the Crown. Secondly, that it falls within s 45(2). That is the contention of counsel for the company. Thirdly, that it does not fall within s 45 at all. That is an alternative contention advanced by counsel for the Crown, and it is, I think, accepted that it would result in the question falling to be *e* determined by reference to the date of the 'disposal' for the purposes of s 1(2) of the Act.

Counsel for the Crown, in arguing for sub-s (4), says, first, that the transaction cannot fall within sub-s (2) because it is not a 'contract'. He says that, where a party, in this case the council, accepts the undertaking of a statutory obligation, that does not amount to a contract; and he says that the council's letter of 20th December 1974 was nothing more than an acceptance of that nature. He then refers to s 181(2) of the 1971 Act and points *f* out that a council which has accepted a purchase notice is deemed to have served a notice to treat. He says that the mere service of a notice to treat does not in itself create a contract, because at that stage the compensation has not been fixed. For that well-established proposition he refers amongst other cases to *Capital Investments Ltd v Wednesfield Urban District Council* [1964] 1 All ER 655 at 667, [1965] Ch 774 at 794 per Wilberforce J. He then says that, even if the transaction did amount to a 'contract' within *g* sub-s (2), it did not become such until, in accordance with the rule which was settled in cases of true compulsory purchase by the House of Lords in *Birmingham Corpn v West Midland Baptist (Trust) Association (Inc)* [1969] 3 All ER 172, [1970] AC 874, the amount of the compensation was fixed on 11th August 1976. And he points to the fact that the same rule has now been applied to transactions of this nature by the Court of Appeal in a case to which I will refer. *h*

Turning to sub-s (4), counsel for the Crown accepts that the sole question is whether the transaction was one by which it can be said that the land was acquired compulsorily. He accepts that it was not in reality so acquired. He relies entirely on the deeming provision in s 181(2) of the 1971 Act. He says that the effect of that provision is to transmute the transaction into one where the land is acquired compulsorily, not perhaps necessarily for all purposes, but at least for the purposes of sub-s (4). He also says that if *j* I were to hold that the transaction in the present case does not fall within sub-s (4) it would follow that a significant class of other reverse compulsory purchases under enactments containing similar deeming provisions would not fall within sub-s (4) either, and that at least one of them would by its nature be incapable of falling within sub-s (2). He therefore says that Parliament must have intended that sub-s (4) should apply to all cases of compulsory acquisition, both true and reverse. Finally, he says that it would

be very dangerous to attach, as the Special Commissioners did, too much weight to
a s 45(8).

Counsel for the company, in arguing for sub-s (2), says, first, that the events which
culminated in the council's letter of 20th December 1974 constituted a 'contract' within
the subsection. He says that many arrangements are entered into by statutory or other
bodies or individuals who owe duties to others, but that does not mean that those
arrangements do not have the consensual element necessary to constitute a contract. He
b relies on *Haynes v Haynes* (1861) 1 Drew & Sm 426, 62 ER 442 and on *Harding v
Metropolitan Railway Co* (1872) 7 Ch App 154. In the latter case Lord Hatherley LC,
sitting as the Court of Appeal in Chancery, said this in reference to a true compulsory
purchase (at 158):

> 'But the case is different when the price is ascertained, for you have then all the
> elements of a complete agreement, and, in truth, it becomes a bargain made under
c > legislative enactment between the railway company and those over whom they
> were authorized to exercise their power.'

Counsel for the company accepts that if the council had been bound to accept the
purchase notice the consensual element would have been lacking and there would have
been no contract. But he points to the various courses of action available to the council
d under s 181(1) and says that their decision to comply with the purchase notice was an act
of will which did give the transaction the necessary consensual element. He says that the
case is different from that where a notice to treat is served. He accepts that the notice
itself creates no consensus. If it is followed by an agreement as to compensation then at
that stage, but not before, there is a consensus. If, on the other hand, there is no such
agreement there is never a consensus at all. Although both parties are bound to proceed
e to an assessment by the Lands Tribunal and to carry out the other steps in the compulsory
purchase procedure, those are obligations originating not in a consensus but in statute.

Turning to sub-s (4), counsel for the company first examines the deeming provision in
s 181(2) of the 1971 Act. He says that the Crown's argument necessarily involves the
proposition that the provision undoes the whole effect of the previous service and
acceptance of the purchase notice. Counsel for the company says that that goes too far
f and that the provision is necessary only for the purpose of supplying the element which
is still lacking, namely the ascertainment of the compensation. Junior counsel for the
company, in following leading counsel, said that there was another reason for the
deeming provision, and that was to make it clear that in a case, like the present, where
planning permission had been refused because the council wanted the land for
educational purposes, the acquisition could and should be made under the compulsory
g purchase legislation and not under any other powers. Leading counsel then went on to
submit, both as a matter of common sense and on authority, that deeming provisions
must be construed to have effect only for the purposes for which they were enacted.
Those purposes were the two that he and junior counsel had mentioned. He said that it
would be absurd to think that Parliament intended to give to this transaction a character
which it would not otherwise own for the purposes of a taxing statute unheard of in
h 1971. He also relied on s 45(8) and on the point which appealed to the Special
Commissioners. He said that the express reference in sub-s (8) to a deemed service of a
notice to treat suggested that the exclusion of such a reference from sub-s (4) was
deliberate.

I have found this a difficult case, and my mind fluctuated from one side to the other
during the course of the arguments. Had it not been for their clarity and economy I
i would have had greater difficulty still in arriving at the clear conclusion to which I have
now come.

I will start with s 45(4). The general submission of counsel for the company that
deeming provisions must be construed to have effect only for the purposes for which
they were enacted is based on the judgment of the Court of Appeal in *Murphy v Ingram
(Inspector of Taxes)* [1974] 2 All ER 187, [1974] Ch 363, [1974] STC 205. In that case
Russell LJ, in delivering the judgment of the court, said that it had been remarked on

high authority that in considering 'deeming' provisions in statutes it was important to
have in mind what appeared to be the purpose of their enactment (see [1974] 2 All ER
187 at 190, [1974] Ch 363 at 370, [1974] STC 205 at 208). For that the court referred to
some earlier authorities to which I shall come in a moment. But it must first be noted
that the Court of Appeal expressed themselves to be of the view that not only anomalies
but also absurdities would follow if the deeming provisions which were there under
review were extended to the point for which the taxpayer had successfully argued before
Megarry J (see [1974] 2 All ER 187 at 191, [1974] Ch 363 at 371, [1974] STC 205 at
209). The Court of Appeal declined to go that far.

The earlier authorities on deeming provisions started with *Re Levy, ex parte Walton*
(1881) 17 Ch D 746, [1881–5] All ER Rep 548. That was a case on s 23 of the Bankruptcy
Act 1869 (the predecessor of s 54 of the 1914 Act), which enabled a trustee in bankruptcy
to disclaim, amongst other things, a lease belonging to the bankrupt, whereupon it was
deemed to have been surrendered on that date. It was held by the Court of Appeal that
such a disclaimer operated as a surrender only so far as was necessary to relieve the
bankrupt and his estate and the trustee from liability, and did not otherwise affect the
rights or liabilities of third parties in relation to the property disclaimed. There appears
this passage at the end of the judgment of James LJ (17 Ch D 746 at 756–757, [1881–5]
All ER Rep 548 at 553):

'When a statute enacts that something shall be deemed to have been done, which
in fact and truth was not done, the Court is entitled and bound to ascertain for what
purposes and between what persons the statutory fiction is to be resorted to. Now,
the bankruptcy law is a special law, having for its object the distribution of an
insolvent's assets equitably amongst his creditors and persons to whom he is under
liability, and, upon this *cessio bonorum*, to release him under certain conditions from
future liability in respect of his debts and obligations. That being the sole object of
the statute, it appears to me to be legitimate to say that, when the statute says that
a lease, which was never surrendered in fact (a true surrender requiring the consent
of both parties, the one giving up and the other taking), is to be deemed to have
been surrendered, it must be understood as saying so with the following
qualification, which is absolutely necessary to prevent the most grievous injustice,
and the most revolting absurdity, "shall, as between the lessor on the one hand, and
the bankrupt, his trustee and estate, on the other hand, be deemed to have been
surrendered".'

That passage was approved by all the members of the House of Lords in *Hill v East and
West India Dock Co* (1884) 9 App Cas 448, which was another case on the same section.
The first part of it was also relied on by Sankey LJ in *Leitch v Emmott (Inspector of Taxes)*
[1929] 2 KB 236 at 248, 14 Tax Cas 633 at 644. That was another case where the Court
of Appeal did not allow a deeming provision the extended effect contended for. But it
is not of much assistance in the present case. The deeming provision took the form of a
proviso to a substantive provision. The decision turned not on any injustice, anomaly or
absurdity which would have flowed from the contrary view but on a construction of the
enactment as a whole.

On the other side I was referred to *East End Dwellings Co Ltd v Finsbury Borough Council*
[1951] 2 All ER 587, [1952] AC 109, where the relevant enactment provided that in
ascertaining the appropriate payment under the War Damage Act 1943 the value of the
interest in question for the purposes of a compulsory purchase should 'be taken to be' the
value which it would have had if the whole of the damage had been made good before
the date of the notice to treat. In 1944 a block of dwellings let on rent controlled
tenancies was demolished by enemy action. In 1948, no rebuilding having been done,
a notice to treat was served. The House of Lords held that, the original building having
been totally destroyed, if the whole of the damage had been made good before the date
of the notice to treat the new building would have had a different identity and would not
have been subject to the Rent Acts; and that accordingly the value of the interest must
be arrived at on that basis (see [1951] 2 All ER 587 at 598–599, [1952] AC 109 at 132).
None of the earlier cases to which I have been referred appears to have been cited to their

Lordships, but nothing turns on that. Counsel for the Crown relies in particular on the
following passage in the speech of Lord Asquith ([1951] 2 All ER 587 at 599, [1952] AC
109 at 132–133):

> 'If you are bidden to treat an imaginary state of affairs as real, you must surely,
> unless prohibited from doing so, also imagine as real the consequences and incidents
> which, if the putative state of affairs had in fact existed, must inevitably have flowed
> from or accompanied it. One of these in this case is emancipation from the 1939
> level of rents. The statute says that you must imagine a certain state of affairs; it
> does not say that, having done so, you must cause or permit your imagination to
> boggle when it comes to the inevitable corollaries of that state of affairs.'

Those were the only authorities to which I was referred on the extent to which
deeming provisions or the like can be carried. From them I deduce these principles.
When considering the extent to which a deeming provision should be applied, the court
is entitled and bound to ascertain for what purposes and between what persons the
statutory fiction is to be resorted to. It will not always be clear what those purposes are.
If the application of the provision would lead to an unjust, anomalous or absurd result
then, unless its application would clearly be within the purposes of the fiction, it should
not be applied. If, on the other hand, its application would not lead to any such result
then, unless that would clearly be outside the purposes of the fiction, it should be applied.

In order to apply these principles to the present case I must start by examining s 181(2)
of the 1971 Act with some care. That which is to be deemed in the case of a purchase
notice accepted by the council is, firstly, that they are 'authorised to acquire the interest
of the owner compulsorily in accordance with the relevant provisions', and, secondly,
that they 'have served a notice to treat in respect thereof' on the date of service of the
purchase notice. The relevant provisions are defined by s 181(4) to mean those of Part VI
of the Act. That Part is entitled 'Acquisition and Appropriation of Land and Related
Provisions', and it is clear that, as with other similar provisions in other Acts, they must
themselves be supplemented by resort to the general principles of the law of compulsory
acquisition. It seems to me, therefore, that the arguments of counsel for the company
that the purposes of the deeming provision are at the most twofold cannot be right.
Indeed, it might have been enough for the main purpose of ascertaining the compensation
if the second part of s 181(2) had merely said 'shall be deemed to have served a notice to
treat in respect thereof on the date of service of the notice under that subsection', but I
do not attach much weight to that as an individual point. What does seem clear to me
is that it was intended that the statutory fiction should be resorted to at least for all the
purposes of the law of compulsory acquisition. Having got that far, I observe that there
is nothing in the provision itself which requires that resort should be made to it for those
purposes and for none other. And so it can be said that resort should prima facie be made
to it for all purposes. At the lowest it seems to me that it is a provision where the
purposes for which the statutory fiction is to be resorted to are not clear.

I must next consider whether the application of the deeming provision for the purposes
of s 45(4) would lead to any of the results to which I have referred. Counsel for the
company said that it would be absurd to apply it for the purposes of a taxing statute
unheard of in 1971. But is that so? On one view there is a big step to be taken between
the two Acts. And it must be said that in all the earlier cases what was in question was
whether a deeming provision or the like should be applied to a state of affairs which did
not involve the application of a later statute dealing with a different subject matter,
whereas what I have to decide is whether a deeming provision in the compulsory
purchase legislation should be applied for the purposes of a later statute which is not part
of that legislation. In spite of these objections, I cannot on consideration see that any
unjust, anomalous or absurd result would follow from applying the deeming provision
in s 181(2) for the purposes of s 45(4). The object of s 45 is to determine the time at
which, for the purposes of the tax, an interest in land is to be taken to be disposed of or
acquired. It may be that its provisions are not exhaustive. Counsel for the Crown gave
the example of a case where the parties to a sale by private treaty proceeded to conveyance
without a prior contract. In that case it would appear that the matter would be governed

by the general provision in s 1(2), and that the disposal would occur on the execution of
the conveyance. Nevertheless, I think I ought to proceed on the assumption that s 45 was
intended to be exhaustive so far as concerns cases where the parties become subject to an
obligation to complete, contractual or otherwise, prior to conveyance. On that footing
I can see nothing unjust, anomalous or absurd in saying that the transaction in this case
falls within sub-s (4) rather than within sub-s (2). If it is right to assume that it falls
within one or the other, there is no a priori reason for preferring either.

I can at this stage summarise my provisional view of sub-s (4) as follows. The purposes
for which the statutory fiction created by the deeming provision in s 181(2) are to be
resorted to are either general or, at the lowest, not clear. Since its application for the
purposes of s 45(4) would not lead to any unjust, anomalous or absurd result, and since
its application would not clearly be outside the purposes of the fiction, it should be so
applied. I must now see whether my provisional view of sub-s (4) is either confirmed or
displaced by a consideration of three other matters.

Firstly, I will consider the other reverse compulsory purchases under enactments
containing similar deeming provisions. Counsel for the Crown referred me to two of
these: s 196(1) of the 1971 Act (blight notices) and s 11 of the New Towns Act 1965. He
also told me that there were similar provisions in the current legislation dealing with
forestry, agriculture and housing. I think it important that I should say as little as
possible about these other provisions, which were not fully explored or debated in
argument. Nevertheless, counsel for the Crown has I think shown clearly enough,
firstly, that the decision in this case may have wide results for the purposes of s 45, and,
secondly, that his argument would have the virtue of applying sub-s (4) to most, and
perhaps all, of the reverse compulsory purchase cases, whereas the argument of counsel
for the company might leave some of them in a no man's land between sub-ss (2) and
(4). In regard to the latter point, I will mention s 11 of the New Towns Act 1965. That
is a provision which *obliges* the acquiring authority to accept the landowner's purchase
notice. Even though, as I believe to be the position, the power conferred by s 31 of the
Land Compensation Act 1961 to withdraw the deemed notice to treat would there be
available to the acquiring authority, I understood counsel for the company to accept that
that was a case where the consensus necessary to bring the transaction within sub-s (2)
was lacking. On the argument of counsel for the company that would be a transaction
which fell within neither subsection. On the whole, therefore, it seems to me that a
consideration of this point confirms my provisional view of sub-s (4).

Secondly, I must look more closely at sub-s (2). I find it helpful to approach it in this
way. I start by assuming that sub-s (4) was not there. If that were the position, then,
applying *Haynes v Haynes* and *Harding v Metropolitan Railway Co*, I would have little
difficulty in concluding that a true compulsory acquisition where the compensation had
been agreed fell at that stage within sub-s (2)(*b*). And, limiting myself only to the case of
a purchase notice accepted by a council under s 181(1)(*a*), I can see a strong case for saying
that the same could be said of that transaction, even though the compensation remained
to be agreed or assessed. However, on the authorities, such as they are, that latter
proposition is by no means established. It appears that the only authority which touches
on this point is *W & S (Long Eaton) Ltd v Derbyshire County Council* (1974) 29 P & CR 522;
affd 31 P & CR 99, which was the case which applied the rule settled in *Birmingham City
Corpn v West Midlands Baptist (Trust) Association (Inc)* [1969] 3 All ER 172, [1970] AC 874
to transactions of this nature. But in the judgments both of the Lands Tribunal, of which
Sir Douglas Frank QC was a member, and of the Court of Appeal (Buckley and Orr LJJ)
there are passages which bear on the question whether the transaction constitutes a
contract or not. In the judgment of the Lands Tribunal there is this passage (29 P & CR
522 at 524–525):

> 'In our view the two notices, coupled with the statutory procedures for
> determining the price, do constitute a contract for sale. But is the contract, at that
> stage, an enforceable one? We think not. It is well settled that the court does not
> order specific performance of a contract until the price is fixed.'

As I read that passage the Lands Tribunal were saying that the transaction constituted a

contract in the sense that there were mutual obligations which had originated in a
a consensus, but that the contract was not at that stage enforceable by specific performance.
I do not, however, read the passage as meaning that the Lands Tribunal were necessarily
of the view that the contract was not enforceable in damages. For example, in a case
where a council went back on their acceptance of the purchase notice and the landowner
had in the meantime lost an opportunity for a private sale to a third party at a favourable
price, it might be (I do not know) that the landowner would have an action for damages
b in contract. But whether that is right or not I would myself think that there was a lot to
be said for the view that a transaction of this nature would fall within sub-s (2) if sub-s
(4) was not there. However, in *W & S (Long Eaton) Ltd v Derbyshire County Council* 31 P
& CR 99 at 104 the Court of Appeal said:

> 'It is also true that, when the acquiring authority accepts the purchase notice, a
> consensual situation arises. The Lands Tribunal expressed the opinion that this,
c > coupled with the statutory procedures for determining the price, constitutes a
> contract for sale, but not, at that stage, an enforceable one. We do not think that it
> is necessary for us to decide that question. We are inclined to doubt whether the
> consensual situation amounts to more than an agreement that the case is a proper
> one for a purchase notice. At any rate, it is clear that ownership of the land and the
> title to it remain at that stage both at law and in equity in the party serving the
d > purchase notice.'

Although the court did not think it necessary to decide the question, that passage shows
that it is by no means clear that the transaction would fall within sub-s (2) if sub-s (4) was
not there. And, more important, it does I think show that even if it could be a contract
for the purposes of sub-s (2) it is one which would not sit there with any great comfort.
e And that returns me from the hypothetical to the actual contents of s 45, and to the
conclusion that a consideration of sub-s (2) does not displace my provisional view of
sub-s (4).

Thirdly and finally, I must consider s 45(8). One thing which is clear about sub-ss (4)
and (8) is that the former is a permanent provision and the latter is a transitional one. On
a superficial level I can see the attractions of the argument which appealed to the Special
f Commissioners. But I think that it would be very dangerous, in trying to get to the
effect of the permanent provision, to attach too much weight to the particular wording
of the transitional one. The 13th September 1974 was the date on which the White
Paper was published. That, then, was a crucial date for the purposes of the new tax. It
seems to me that the probable explanation of the express reference to a deemed notice to
treat in subsection (8) is that it was intended to make it absolutely clear that the crucial
g date was to be the same in the cases of both actual and deemed such notices. In my
judgment there is nothing in sub-s (8) which displaces my provisional view of subsection
(4).

In the result my clear conclusion is that the transaction did fall within sub-s (4). I
derive great comfort from the fact that this means that sub-ss (2) and (4) ought for the
most part to have a tidy working relationship between them. That may be something
h which will make the answer to the question in this case appear more obvious to some
minds than it has to mine. But it will, I think, be clear from the lengthy, perhaps
laborious, process of reasoning by which I have arrived at my conclusion that it is a
consideration on which I have not found it necessary to rely.

It follows that the disposal and acquisition in the present case did not take place until
11th August 1976 when the amount of the compensation received the approval of the
j council. That means that the Crown's appeal must be allowed.

*Appeal allowed. Certificate granted to the taxpayer company, under s 12 of the Administration
of Justice Act 1969, to apply to the House of Lords for leave to appeal directly to the House.*

Solicitors: *Solicitor of Inland Revenue; Henry Fallows & Co,* Bolton (for the taxpayer
company).

Edwina Epstein   Barrister.

Coventry City Council v Doyle
and other appeals

QUEEN'S BENCH DIVISION

DONALDSON LJ AND HODGSON J

24th NOVEMBER, 17th DECEMBER 1980

Nuisance − Statutory nuisance − Nuisance order − Date to be considered by justices in deciding whether nuisance exists − Whether relevant date is date of complaint or date of hearing by justices − Public Health Act 1936, s 94(2).

Nuisance − Statutory nuisance − Complaint to justices − Proceedings against local authority − Expenses of complainant − Nuisance abated at date of hearing of complaint − Whether complainant entitled to reasonable expenses − Public Health Act 1936, ss 94(3), 99.

Nuisance − Statutory nuisance − Premises in such a state as to be prejudicial to health or a nuisance − Unoccupied premises − Relevance of fact that premises unoccupied − Public Health Act 1936, s 92(1)(a).

On the true construction of s 94(2)[a] of the Public Health Act 1936 the relevant date on which justices are to consider whether a statutory nuisance within s 92(1) of that Act exists or, although abated, is likely to recur is the date of the hearing before the justices and not the date on which the information alleging the nuisance is laid (see p 190 *b* to *e* and p 192 *e*, post); *Northern Ireland Trailers Ltd v Preston Corpn* [1972] 1 All ER 260 followed; *London Borough of Lambeth v Stubbs* (1980) Times, 15th May explained.

On the true construction of s 94(3)[b] of the 1936 Act, read in conjunction with s 99[c] of that Act, where the local authority is the defendant in proceedings for the abatement of an alleged statutory nuisance which at the date of the hearing of the complaint has been abated, the complainant, if he establishes that at the date of the information the nuisance alleged therein did in fact exist, is entitled to payment of his reasonable expenses (see p 190 *g h* and p 192 *e*, post).

Where a statutory nuisance under s 92(1)(a)[d] of the 1936 Act exists by virtue of premises being in such a state as to be prejudicial to health or a nuisance, the fact that the premises are empty is irrelevant and in the circumstances the removal of the occupants from such premises does not constitute an abatement of the nuisance. Different considerations might apply, however, where the premises have been effectively rendered incapable of being occupied (see p 191 *e f* and p 192 *e*, post).

Notes
For proceedings to abate a statutory nuisance, see 31 Halsbury's Laws (3rd Edn) 374–378, paras 551–556.

For the Public Health Act 1936, ss 92, 94 and 99, see 26 Halsbury's Statutes (3rd Edn) 270, 272, 275.

Cases referred to in judgments
London Borough of Lambeth v Stubbs (1980) Times, 15th May, DC.
Northern Ireland Trailers Ltd v Preston Corpn [1972] 1 All ER 260, [1972] 1 WLR 203, 136 JP 149, DC, Digest (Cont Vol D) 629, 387d.

---

a   Section 94(2) is set out at p 188 *a* to *c*, post
b   Section 94(3) is set out at p 188 *d*, post
c   Section 99 is set out at p 188 *g h*, post
d   Section 92(1), so far as material, is set out at p 187 *f*, post

Nottingham Corpn v Newton, Nottingham Friendship Housing Association Ltd v Newton [1974]
a   2 All ER 760, [1974] 1 WLR 723, 72 LGR 535, DC, 36(1) Digest (Reissue) 436, 276.
R v Epping (Waltham Abbey) Justices, ex parte Burlinson [1947] 2 All ER 537, [1948] 1 KB
79, [1948] LJR 298, 112 JP 3, 46 LGR 6, DC, 33 Digest (Repl) 27, 123.
R v Newham Justices, ex parte Hunt, R v Oxted Justices, ex parte Franklin [1976] 1 All ER
839, [1976] 1 WLR 420, 74 LGR 305, DC, Digest (Cont Vol E) 465, 273a.

b **Case also cited**
Salford County Council v McNally [1975] 1 All ER 597, [1975] 1 WLR 365, DC; *affd* [1975]
2 All ER 860, [1976] AC 379, HL.

Cases stated
Coventry City Council v Doyle
c Coventry City Council appealed by way of case stated by the justices for the City of
Coventry in respect of their adjudication as a magistrates' court sitting at St Mary's Hall,
Coventry on 30th May and 20th June 1979 whereby, on an information laid by John
William Doyle ('the tenant') on 22nd February 1979, they decided that certain premises
at 12 Mason Road, Coventry occupied by the tenant and his family and of which the
council was the owner or leaseholder constituted a statutory nuisance within the meaning
d of s 92(1)(a) of the Public Health Act 1936 notwithstanding that on 9th April 1979 the
tenant and his family had moved out of the premises. The questions on which the
opinion of the High Court was sought were, inter alia, whether the justices were correct
as a matter of law in deciding that the material date for determining whether the
premises were in a state prejudicial to health was the date the information was laid and
whether the justices were correct as a matter of law in making a nuisance order when at
e the date of the hearing the tenant had ceased to reside in or near the premises.

Coventry City Council v Quinn
Coventry City Council appealed by way of case stated by the justices for the City of
Coventry in respect of their adjudication as a magistrates' court sitting at St Mary's Hall,
Coventry on 19th and 28th November and 3rd December 1979 whereby, on an
f information laid by Catherine Patricia Quinn ('the tenant') on 22nd February 1979, they
decided that certain premises at 71 Foleshill Road, Coventry occupied by the tenant and
her family and of which the council was the owner or leaseholder constituted a statutory
nuisance within the meaning of s 92(1)(a) of the Public Health Act 1936 notwithstanding
that on 2nd December 1979 the tenant and her family had moved out of the premises.
The questions on which the opinion of the High Court was sought were, inter alia,
g whether the justices were correct as a matter of law in deciding that the material date for
determining whether the premises were in a state prejudicial to health was the date the
information was laid and whether the justices were correct as a matter of law in making
a nuisance order when at the date of the hearing the tenant and her family had ceased to
reside in or near the premises.

Clarke v Coventry City Council
h Edna May Clarke ('the tenant') appealed by way of case stated by the Crown Court at
Coventry (Mr William B Moran, sitting as a deputy circuit judge, with Mr H R Powles
JP) in respect of its adjudication on an appeal by Coventry City Council against the
adjudication as a magistrates' court on 22nd August and 5th and 11th September 1979
of the justices for the City of Coventry whereby, on an information laid by the tenant on
22nd February 1979, they decided that on 22nd February 1979 certain premises at 133
Windmill Road, Coventry occupied by the tenant and her family and of which the
council was the owner or leaseholder constituted a statutory nuisance within the meaning
of s 92(1)(a) of the Public Health Act 1936. The justices also awarded the tenant £415.80
in respect of her reasonable expenses in connection with the making of the complaint
and the proceedings in the magistrates' court under s 94(3) of the 1936 Act. The Crown

Court heard the appeal on 17th, 18th and 19th December 1979. It found that the
nuisance had been abated by the council prior to the hearing of the case before the *a*
magistrates and dismissed the information. The Crown Court reduced to £100 the
award of expenses payable to the tenant. The questions on which the opinion of the
High Court was sought were, inter alia, whether the Crown Court was correct as a matter
of law in determining that the material date for establishing whether the premises were
prejudicial to health and therefore that an offence had been committed under s 92(1)(a)
of the 1936 Act was the date of the hearing before the magistrates' court and not the date *b*
of the laying of the information before that court, and whether, having found that a
statutory nuisance existed at the date of the laying of the information before the
magistrates, the Crown Court was correct in law in depriving the tenant of the reasonable
expenses incurred by her in connection with the hearing before the magistrates' court
and awarded to her by that court under s 94(3) of the 1936 Act.

c

Keith Simpson for the council.
Stephen Sedley for the tenants.

Cur adv vult

17th December. The following judgments were read.   *d*

HODGSON J (delivering the first judgment at the invitation of Donaldson LJ). These
three appeals arise out of litigation between council house tenants and their landlord, the
Coventry City Council. Two of them, *Coventry City Council v Doyle* and *Coventry City
Council v Quinn*, are appeals from decisions of the Coventry City magistrates who have *e*
stated cases; these are brought by the council. The third, *Clarke v Coventry City Council*,
is an appeal by case stated from the Crown Court at Coventry; this is brought by the
tenant from the Crown Court decision to allow the council's appeal from the adjudication
of the magistrates. We heard these cases together. They raise questions of some
difficulty and importance.

The council owns a number of houses which are designated as temporary *f*
accommodation to be used by homeless families or others who do not qualify for a
regular tenancy. The houses in these cases were short life property, so that the council
was naturally reluctant to spend its scarce resources on them. The tenants were members
of the Coventry Temporary Tenants Association. Prior to 22nd February 1979 each had
made numerous complaints to the council about the condition of their property. On
that date all three preferred informations with the city magistrates against the council *g*
under s 99 of the Public Health Act 1936, alleging that the houses they occupied
constituted statutory nuisances within the meaning of s 92(1)(a) of the Act, namely that
they were in such a state as to be prejudicial to health.

The magistrates heard the informations on the following dates: *Doyle* on 30th May and
20th June; *Clarke* on 22nd August, 5th September and 11th September; and *Quinn* on
19th November and 3rd December. The appeal from the magistrates in *Clarke's* case was *h*
heard at the Crown Court on 17th, 18th and 19th December 1979.

The magistrates found in respect of each house that a statutory nuisance existed at the
date of the preferring of the informations, ie 22nd February 1979. The Doyle family
were moved out of their house on 9th April 1979, as the council had decided to extend
and modernise their house; at the dates of the hearing work on the house had begun but
was not completed. The Clarke family was still in occupation at the date of the hearing *j*
before the magistrates, but the Crown Court found that at that date the nuisance had
been abated. The Quinn family were offered alternative accommodation a week or two
before the date (19th November) fixed for the hearing; they moved to alternative
accommodation on 2nd December, the day before the third and final hearing day.

In each case the tenants contended that, if they established that a statutory nuisance

existed at the date the information was laid, then the magistrates would have to find that
a an offence under s 94 had been committed, whether or not the nuisance had been abated
at the date of the hearing. The council contended that the date on which the magistrates
had to find that a nuisance existed was the date of the hearing and that, if no nuisance
existed on that date, then the magistrates could not find that an offence had been
committed, or make an order unless (and for the purpose of these appeals this is not
relevant) there was a danger of recurrence. The only order the court could make, if the
b nuisance no longer existed at the date of hearing, was, contended the council, an order as
to costs.

Two other questions of law are raised. First, whether, when the defendant is the
council itself, the mandatory provisions as to costs in s 94(3) apply or whether the award
of costs in such cases is within the discretion of the magistrates. Second, whether
premises can be prejudicial to health if there is no one living in them (and therefore no
c actual prejudice) at the date of hearing.

We were also invited to give some guidance as to the considerations which magistrates
should take into account in deciding on the terms of an enforcement order particularly
when made against the local authority itself.

So far as the first and most important question is concerned, the magistrates' view was
that the material date was the date when the information was preferred; if a statutory
d nuisance existed at that date, then the council was guilty of an offence under s 94. In the
case that went to appeal to the Crown Court (*Clarke*), the Crown Court took the opposite
view.

It is with ss 91 to 100 of the 1936 Act that these cases are concerned. These sections are
primarily concerned with making provision for local authorities to comply with the
duty placed on them by s 91—

e
'to cause their district to be inspected from time to time for the detection of
matters requiring to be dealt with . . . as being statutory nuisances . . .'

With the exception of s 99, to which I shall return, the scheme of this part of the 1936
Act is, I think, clear. By s 92(1) it is provided:

f
'Without prejudice to the exercise by a local authority of any other powers vested
in them by or under this Act, the following matters may, subject to the provisions
of this Part of this Act, be dealt with summarily, and are in this Part of this Act
referred to as "statutory nuisances", that is to say:— (*a*) any premises in such a state
as to be prejudicial to health or a nuisance . . .'

There then follow a number of other 'statutory nuisances' in paras (*b*) to (*f*). The
g remaining subsections of s 92 are not relevant to these cases.

Section 93 provides for the service of abatement notices by the local authority:

'Where a local authority are satisfied of the existence of a statutory nuisance, they
shall serve a notice (hereafter in this Act referred to as "an abatement notice") on the
person by whose act, default or sufferance the nuisance arises or continues, or, if that
h person cannot be found, on the owner or occupier of the premises on which the
nuisance arises, requiring him to abate the nuisance and to execute such works and
take such steps as may be necessary for that purpose . . .'

Section 94 deals with the situation which arises if the abatement notice is not complied
with and adds a judicial dimension to the administrative action the local authority is
empowered to take under s 93. Section 94 reads:
j
'(1) If the person on whom an abatement notice has been served makes default
in complying with any of the requirements of the notice, or if the nuisance,
although abated since the service of the notice, is, in the opinion of the local
authority, likely to recur on the same premises, the authority shall cause a complaint
to be made to a justice of the peace, and the justice shall thereupon issue a summons

requiring the person on whom the notice was served to appear before a court of summary jurisdiction.

'(2) If on the hearing of the complaint it is proved that the alleged nuisance exists, or that although abated it is likely to recur on the same premises, then, subject to the provisions of subsections (4) and (5) of this section the court shall make an order (hereinafter in this Act referred to as "a nuisance order") for either, or both, of the following purposes—(a) requiring the defendant to comply with all or any of the requirements of the abatement notice, or otherwise to abate the nuisance, within a time specified in the order, and execute any works necessary for that purpose; (b) prohibiting a recurrence of the nuisance, and requiring the defendant, within a time specified in the order, to execute any works necessary to prevent a recurrence; and may also impose on the defendant a fine not exceeding £200. Where a nuisance proved to exist is such as to render a building, in the opinion of the court, unfit for human habitation, the nuisance order may prohibit the use of the building for that purpose until a court of summary jurisdiction, being satisfied that it has been rendered fit for human habitation, withdraws the prohibition.

'(3) Where on the hearing of a complaint under this section it is proved that the alleged nuisance existed at the date of the service of the abatement notice and that at the date of the making of the complaint it either still existed or was likely to recur, then, whether or not at the date of the hearing it still exists or is likely to recur, the court shall order the defendant to pay to the local authority such reasonable sum as the court may determine in respect of the expenses incurred by the authority in, or in connection with, the making of the complaint and the proceedings before the court . . .'

There is no doubt that s 94 creates an offence: see *Northern Ireland Trailers Ltd v Preston Corpn* [1972] 1 All ER 260, [1972] 1 WLR 203. Therefore proceedings are properly begun by information, although the 1936 Act provides for the institution of proceedings by complaint (see the Magistrates' Courts Act 1952, s 42, and, now, the Magistrates' Courts Act 1980, s 50). It is however the tenants' contention that it is s 94(1) and not s 94(2) which is the offence-creating subsection.

Section 95 provides for penalties for failure to comply with a nuisance order and empowers the local authority to abate a nuisance itself where a nuisance order has not been obeyed, and s 96 provides for the recovery by the local authority of its expenses in abating or preventing the recurrence of a nuisance. Sections 97 and 98 are not relevant to these cases.

Section 99 provides:

'Complaint of the existence of a statutory nuisance under this Act may be made to a justice of the peace by any person aggrieved by the nuisance, and thereupon the like proceedings shall be had, with the like incidents and consequences as to the making of orders, penalties for disobedience of orders and otherwise, as in the case of a complaint by the local authority, but any order made in such proceedings may, if the court after giving the local authority an opportunity of being heard thinks fit, direct the authority to abate the nuisance.'

It was held in *R v Epping (Waltham Abbey) Justices, ex parte Burlinson* [1947] 2 All ER 537, [1948] 1 KB 79 that under this section a local authority may be made a defendant. When one comes to look carefully at the interaction between this section and the other sections in this part of the 1936 Act one is led to suspect that this decision probably came as a surprise to the draftsman. It was under this subsection that the tenants laid informations against the council.

The submissions made on behalf of the tenants are succinctly set out in the case stated by the Crown Court. For the tenants it was contended that, following the decisions in *R v Newham Justices, ex parte Hunt, R v Oxted Justices, ex parte Franklin* [1976] 1 All ER 839, [1976] 1 WLR 420, proceedings brought under s 99 of the 1936 Act were criminal proceedings. Hence, in this case, proceedings were commenced by the laying of

a information and the issue of a summons. Both the summons and information alleged that a criminal offence had taken place and the date of this offence was the day on which the information was laid. *R v Oxted Justices, ex parte Franklin* stated that it was not necessary for a person taking proceedings under s 99 of the 1936 Act to serve an abatement notice before laying information before magistrates. The matter for the court to decide was not whether the respondents had failed to comply with an abatement

b notice but whether 'there was a nuisance in existence in fact' (see [1976] 1 All ER 839 at 843, [1976] 1 WLR 420 at 425). It was argued by the tenants therefore that the question in this case was whether at the date of the issue of proceedings there existed in fact a statutory nuisance at the houses which they occupied.

It was further contended by the tenants that, although the law might impose a heavy burden on local authorities against whom persons issued proceedings under s 99, such a

c burden was justified, given the statutory duties and responsibilities of such authorities in relation to housing. It was argued, furthermore, that to reject the tenants' submission as to the appropriate date and to accept as an alternative the date of the hearing before the magistrates would be in effect to treat the summonses as abatement notices. This would mean that local authorities could escape criminal liability by carrying out repairs or rehousing the occupier between the date proceedings were issued and the date of the

d hearing. This would be analogous to allowing a burglar to escape criminal liability provided he returned the goods he had stolen before the hearing of his case.

That, I think, also fairly summarises the submissions made to us by counsel for the tenants. He further pointed out that, if his argument was rejected, it would mean that a local authority would be able, by delaying the hearing as much as possible, to give itself more time to escape liability.

e Counsel for the council relied on the wording of s 94(2) and submitted that the plain meaning is that the nuisance must exist at the date of the hearing before the magistrates and that, unless it does exist or, being temporarily abated, is likely to recur, the magistrates can neither make an order nor impose a fine.

In *Northern Ireland Trailers Ltd v Preston Corpn* the question was whether quarter sessions, when hearing an appeal from magistrates, had to have regard to the situation as

f it was at the date of the hearing before the magistrates or the date they heard the appeal. The court held that the relevant date was the date of the hearing before the magistrates.

In dealing with this part of the case Lord Widgery CJ said ([1972] 1 All ER 260 at 264–265, [1972] 1 WLR 203 at 208):

g > 'The second point . . . arises in this way: there had . . . been a substantial interval of time between the date when the justices made the nuisance order . . . and the date when quarter sessions considered the appeal . . . It was not disputed below or before us that when the matter was before the magistrates' court it was essential for the respondents to show that the alleged nuisance still existed at that time. The phrase in s 94(2) is: "If on the hearing of the complaint it is proved that the alleged nuisance

h > exists", and accordingly when the matter was before the magistrates' court, proof was directed to the existence of the nuisance at that date.'

The same point arose in *London Borough of Lambeth v Stubbs* (1980) Times, 15th May. In that case the tenant was in occupation at the date of the hearing before the magistrates but had been rehoused by the time the appeal was heard. At that date the house was no longer occupied. The court decided that the mere fact that the house was empty did not

j mean that the nuisance had been abated (as to this aspect of the case I shall have to return) but, in giving judgment, Stephen Brown J used these words:

> 'The specific ground of appeal which might have resulted, if successful, in the nuisance order being quashed related to the time at which the nuisance was alleged to have existed. I think it is clear from the decision in *Northern Ireland Trailers Ltd*

v Preston Corpn that the relevant date is the date of the information. Accordingly
the Crown Court was bound to consider the state of affairs at that date. Of course *a*
it was open to them, and indeed they acted on, the changed circumstances which
had occurred since the original hearing before the justices.'

The reference to the *Northern Ireland Trailers* case, the fact that it had not been
contended that the relevant date was the preferring of the information and the reference
at the end of the sentence to the 'original hearing before the justices' convinces me that *b*
the reference to 'the date of the information' was an understandable slip of the tongue
and that what the judge meant was 'the date of the hearing of the information'.

I find it a strange argument that the words in an offence-creating statute should be
construed in a way which is not their natural meaning so as to enlarge the ambit of the
offence. In their plain and ordinary meaning the words of s 94(2) say that the relevant
date for the magistrates to consider is the date of the hearing before them. In the usual *c*
case where it is the local authority which is bringing the proceedings there is not the
slightest difficulty involved in giving them their natural meaning and the fact that s 99
was badly drafted does not in my judgment warrant giving the words in s 94 the strained
meaning for which the tenants contend.

I am fortified in my view by the provisions of s 94(3) which make an award of
expenses to the local authority mandatory in cases where the nuisance has been abated at *d*
the date of hearing. If the relevant date were the date of the information, no such
provision would be necessary. I think it is clear that it was just because the draftsmen
realised that if the nuisance was abated at the time of the hearing the magistrates could
make no order nor convict of any offence that this provision for payment of the council's
costs was included.

I have no hesitation in finding that the relevant date is the date of the hearing before *e*
the magistrates. It is true that s 99 makes no provision for the prior service of an
abatement notice and that therefore its provisions do not fit neatly into the principal
scheme, but this does not seem to me in any way to warrant the forced construction of
the plain words of s 93 and 94 for which counsel for the tenants contends.

The second question we are asked to consider is whether, where the council is
defendant, the mandatory provision as to costs in s 94(3) applies. Section 94(3) in terms *f*
refers to an order that 'the defendant . . . pays to the local authority such reasonable sum
as the court may determine in respect of the expenses incurred by the authority'. Section
99 refers to 'the like proceedings' with the like incidents and consequences as to the
making of orders, penalties for disobedience of orders and otherwise, as in the case of a
complaint by the local authority. Obviously these two provisions cannot sensibly be read
together. The position contemplated by s 94(3) is, as I have pointed out, one where, *g*
because the nuisance has been abated at the date of hearing, there is no order or
conviction on which the magistrates could hang an order for costs. I think s 99 was
intended to put 'any person aggrieved' as nearly as possible in the same position as the
local authority when the authority brings proceedings, and accordingly I would hold that
the mandatory provisions as to payment of expenses applies to 'a person aggrieved' who
establishes that at the date of the information the nuisance (since abated) existed. *h*

The last question, whether the premises can be prejudicial to health if there is no one
living in them and therefore no actual prejudice to health at the time of the hearing,
arose for consideration in *London Borough of Lambeth v Stubbs* to which I have referred. In
that case at the relevant date, which was the hearing of the Crown Court appeal, the
house was no longer occupied by anyone (it was in fact demolished within four months
of the hearing). Nevertheless no order had been made under s 94(2) of the 1936 Act *j*
prohibiting the use of the house for human habitation. Waller LJ in his judgment said
that 'theoretically', therefore, 'it was possible at any time for the house to be relet, though
of course it is not suggested . . . that Lambeth Borough Council, as a responsible
authority, would have done such a thing. But the theoretical position was that it would
have been a possibility'. Waller LJ continued:

'We have been referred to a number of cases dealing with the various problems that have arisen under these sections. As I see it, on that very first submission that [counsel for the local authority] has made, it is not a question of authority, but a question of the words of the section. [Counsel] on behalf of the respondents has submitted that there are two sides to the problem which preserve the position of the local authority in a case of this sort without any of the extreme results for which [counsel for the local authority] was contending. In my opinion it is not sufficient to say that a nuisance has been abated because the dwelling house has been vacated. [Counsel for the respondents] submits that the whole purport of these sections is to order work to be done; and the words of s 93 of the Public Health Act 1936, which I have already quoted, "requiring [the owner] to abate the nuisance and to execute such works and take such steps as may be necessary for that purpose" indicate that that is the purpose of these provisions. As it seems to me the original finding was that the premises were in such a state as to be prejudicial to health, and if the tenants are removed nothing has been done to alter the state of the premises. They remain prejudicial to health even if nobody goes and lives in those premises. I should quote one other subsection in dealing with the question of "prejudicial to health", because "prejudicial to health" is defined in s 343 as meaning "injurious, or likely to cause injury, to health". All that is being done by removing the tenant from the house is to reduce the likelihood of injury, but at any time if anybody went back into the house the likelihood of injury would increase and there would be somebody whose health would be likely to be prejudiced by the state of the house. As it seems to me, in order to abate the statutory nuisance, something must be done to the house. So I would be against [counsel's] main submission [for the local authority]. Prohibiting occupation simply avoids actual injury to health; the danger remains and therefore the nuisance is not affected.'

In that case it seems that the house, though empty, had had nothing done to it, and the case is clear authority for the proposition that in those circumstances the nuisance has not been abated. If the case ever arises where a house has been effectively rendered incapable of being occupied, e g having all services permanently cut off and being boarded up prior to eventual demolition, I think different considerations might apply. But that is not the situation in any of these cases.

As to the considerations which should influence justices in making orders under the 1936 Act, I do not think I can do better than refer to the words of Lord Widgery CJ in *Nottingham District Council v Newton* [1974] 2 All ER 760, [1974] 1 WLR 923. That was a case where there were difficulties as to the precise order which should be made when the final disposition of the house under a clearance order had not been decided at the time of the hearing by the court. Lord Widgery CJ after referring to the wide discretion in the court as to the order that it made, said [1974] 2 All ER 760 at 766, [1974] 1 WLR 923 at 930):

'In deciding within that wide ambit of detailed discretion just what the terms of the nuisance order should be, I have no doubt it is the duty of the justices, as common sense dictates, to look at the whole circumstances of the case and to try and make an order which is in its terms sensible and just having regard to the entire prevailing situation. They were wrong in my judgment in closing their eyes to the Housing Act proceedings and the imminence of demolition, and had they had regard to those factors as well as all the other relevant factors, it may be that they would have provided for the nuisance to be abated by perhaps March 1974 so that if the demolition proceedings had taken effect meanwhile, the danger of money being spent on the house abortively in view of the subsequent demolition would be avoided. I think the justices were very nearly right in this case, but I conclude that they were wrong in restricting the factors to which they had regard, and I think this appeal should be allowed to the extent that the case should be sent back to the justices asking them to reconsider their decision in the light of the discretion within

the precise terms of s 94(2), and in the light of all the prevailing circumstances, and
endeavour to come to what seems to them to be a sensible and just conclusion.'   *a*

As Waller LJ said of this passage in the *Lambeth* case:

'Lord Widgery CJ was stressing at the beginning of that passage what common
sense dictates. He was stressing that justices should have in mind a decision which
will avoid the possibility of public money being wasted because of the subsequent
demolition and saying that the conclusion should be a sensible and just one.'   *b*

[His Lordship then turned to answer the specific questions asked in each of the cases.
He held, inter alia, that in *Doyle's* case the magistrates were not correct as a matter of law
in deciding that the material date for determining whether the premises were in a state
prejudicial to health was the date the information was laid, that in *Clarke's* case the
Crown Court was correct as a matter of law in determining that the material date for
establishing whether the premises were prejudicial to health was the date of the hearing   *c*
before the magistrates' court and not the date of the laying of the information before that
court, and that, having found that a statutory nuisance existed at the date of the laying
of the information before the magistrates, the Crown Court was wrong in law in
depriving the tenant of the reasonable expenses incurred by her in connection with the
hearing before the magistrates' court and awarded to her by that court under the
provisions of s 94(3) of the 1936 Act, and that in *Quinn's* case the magistrates were not   *d*
correct, as a matter of law, in deciding that the relevant date for determining whether the
premises were in a state prejudicial to health was the date the information was laid, but,
as the premises were still in a defective condition and prejudicial to health at the
conclusion of the proceedings, the magistrates were correct as a matter of law in deciding
that the premises constituted a statutory nuisance within the meaning of s 92 of the 1936
Act, despite the fact that the premises were no longer occupied.]   *e*

DONALDSON LJ. I agree.

Orders accordingly.

*The court refused leave to appeal to the House of Lords but certified under s 1(2) of the
Administration of Justice Act 1960 that the following point of law of general public importance
was involved in the decision: whether on a prosecution under ss 94 and 99 of the Public Health Act
1936 the date at which the existence of a statutory nuisance must be proved in order to justify a
finding of guilt is the date to which the information relates or the date of the hearing.*

Solicitors: *Andrew H Pitts*, Coventry (for the council); *Michael J King*, Leamington Spa (for
the tenants).

Jacqueline Charles   Barrister.

a

Ajodha v The State
and other appeals

PRIVY COUNCIL

LORD KEITH OF KINKEL, LORD SIMON OF GLAISDALE, LORD BRIDGE OF HARWICH AND SIR WILLIAM
b DOUGLAS

2nd, 3rd, 4th, 5th MARCH, 1st APRIL 1981

*Criminal evidence – Admissions and confessions – Voluntary statement – Issue of voluntariness
– Accused admitting signature is his but claiming it was improperly obtained – Accused claiming
signature was obtained by threats or inducement – Whether voluntary character of statement put
c in issue.*

*Criminal evidence – Admissions and confessions – Voluntary statement – Issue of voluntariness
– Accused admitting signature is his but claiming it was improperly obtained – Accused claiming
document he signed was fraudulently misrepresented to him as being of entirely different character
– Whether voluntary character of statement put in issue.*

d

*Criminal evidence – Statement by accused – Incriminating statement – Admissibility – Functions
of judge and jury – Procedure to be adopted.*

*Privy Council – Fresh point – Point not taken in court of first instance because that court bound
by authority to overrule it – Whether point may be taken by appellant on appeal.*

e

When the prosecution proposes to tender in evidence a written confession statement
signed by the accused, it is relying on the signature as the acknowledgment and
authentication by the accused of the statement as his own. Accordingly, if the accused
denies that he is the author of the statement but admits that the signature on the
f document is his and claims that it was improperly obtained by threats or inducement, he
puts in issue the voluntary character of the signature and thus of the statement itself, and
thereby raises a question of law for decision by the judge as to the admissibility of the
statement. Furthermore, if the accused claims that his signature to what was in fact a
confession statement was obtained by the fraudulent misrepresentation that he was
signing a document of an entirely different character, that also raises an issue whether the
g statement was the voluntary statement of the accused and therefore goes to admissibility
(see p 200 *g* to p 201 *g*, post); dictum of Lord Sumner in *Ibrahim v R* [1914–15] All ER
Rep at 877 applied.

Observations on the respective functions of judge and jury in relation to incriminating
statements tendered in evidence by the prosecution and the procedure to be adopted at
a jury trial where a question of the admissibility of a confession statement arises (see
h p 201 *g* to p 202 *c* and *h* to p 203 *d*, post).

Where a point of law is not taken in the court of first instance because that court is
bound by authority to overrule it, that is not by itself a ground for the Judicial Committee
of the Privy Council refusing to allow the point to be taken on appeal (see p 202 *d* to *g*,
post).

j **Notes**

For confessions to persons in authority and the duty of the trial judge in relation to
admissibility, see 11 Halsbury's Laws (4th Edn) paras 411, 413, and for cases on the
subject, see 14(2) Digest (Reissue) 562–565, 4578–4601.

For raising new points in appeals to the Privy Council, see 10 Halsbury's Laws (4th
Edn) para 820, and for cases on the subject, see 16 Digest (Reissue) 197–202, 1965–2008.

Cases referred to in judgment

Director of Public Prosecutions v Ping Lin [1975] 3 All ER 175, [1976] AC 574, [1975] 3   **a**
    WLR 419, 139 JP 651, HL, Digest (Cont Vol D) 181, 4522a.
Gransaul and Ferreira v The Queen (9th April 1979, unreported), PC.
Harper v The State (1970) 16 WIR 353, CA of Guyana.
Herrera and Dookeran v R (1966) 11 WIR 1, CA of Trinidad and Tobago.
Ibrahim v R [1914] AC 599, [1914–15] All ER Rep 874, 83 LJPC 185, 111 LT 20, 24 Cox
    CC 174, PC, 14(2) Digest (Reissue) 562, 4583.   **b**
R v Anderson (1929) 142 LT 580, 21 Cr App R 178, 29 Cox CC 102, CCA, 22 Digest
    (Reissue) 512, 5198.
R v Watson (1975) 24 WIR 367, CA of Jamaica.
The State v Fowler (1970) 16 WIR 452, CA of Guyana.
The State v Gobin and Griffith (1976) 23 WIR 256, CA of Guyana.
The State v Ramsingh (1973) 20 WIR 138, CA of Guyana.   **c**
Williams v Ramdeo and Ramdeo (1966) 10 WIR 397, CA of Trinidad and Tobago.

Appeals

Ajodha v The State

Seeraj Ajodha appealed by special leave granted on 27th March 1980 against the **d**
judgment of the Court of Appeal of Trinidad and Tobago (Hyatali CJ, Phillips and Rees
JJA) dated 18th July 1977 which dismissed his appeal against his conviction on 17th
January 1975 in the High Court of Justice for Trinidad and Tobago (McMillan J and a
jury) for murder in respect of which he was sentenced to death.

Chandree v The State, Fletcher v The State, Noreiga v The State   **e**

Peter Chandree and Dennis Fletcher appealed by special leave granted on 27th March
1980 and Lincoln Noreiga appealed by special leave granted on 27th November 1980
against the judgment of the Court of Appeal of Trinidad and Tobago (Hyatali CJ, Corbin
and Scott JJA) dated 15th July 1977 dismissing their appeals against their conviction on
3rd June 1976 at the Port of Spain Assizes (Braithwaite J and a jury) for murder in respect **f**
of which Chandree and Fletcher were sentenced to death and Noreiga was ordered to be
detained during Her Majesty's (now the State's) pleasure.

By consent of all the parties the appeals were heard together. The facts are set out in
the judgment of the Board.

Barbara Calvert QC and *Aditya-Kumar Sen* for the appellant Ajodha.   **g**
Barbara Calvert QC and *Derek Zeitlin* for the appellant Chandree.
Barbara Calvert QC and *Michael J Burton* for the appellant Fletcher.
Barbara Calvert QC and *John Dickson* for the appellant Noreiga.
Stuart McKinnon QC, Jonathan Harvie and *Lionel Jones* (of the Trinidad and Tobago Bar) for
    the respondent.   **h**

At the conclusion of the arguments the Board announced that in each case the appeal
would be allowed, the conviction quashed and a verdict of acquittal entered for reasons
to be given later.

1st April. **LORD BRIDGE OF HARWICH.** These four appellants were each tried **j**
and convicted of murder. Ajodha, Chandree and Fletcher were sentenced to death.
Noreiga, being under 18 years of age at the date of the offence, was ordered to be detained
during Her Majesty's (now the State's) pleasure. Ajodha was tried before McMillan J at
the San Fernando Assizes in January 1975. Chandree, Fletcher and Noreiga were jointly

tried before Braithwaite J at the Port of Spain Assizes in May and June 1976. There was
a no connection between the two trials save that the same point of law arose in both and
affected each of the four appellants. All four appealed against their convictions to the
Court of Appeal of Trinidad and Tobago. The appeals of Chandree, Fletcher and Noreiga
were dismissed on 15th July 1977, and that of Ajodha on 18th July 1977. Special leave
to appeal to the Judicial Committee of the Privy Council was granted to Ajodha, Chandree
and Fletcher on 27th March 1980 and to Noreiga on 27th November 1980. By consent
b of the parties their Lordships heard the appeals together on 2nd, 3rd, 4th and 5th March
and announced at the conclusion of the arguments their decision that in each case the
appeal would be allowed, the conviction quashed and a verdict of acquittal entered for
reasons to be given later. This judgment set out the reasons for their Lordships' decision.

The appellant Ajodha was tried jointly with one Tahaloo on an indictment charging
both with counts of murder, robbery and rape. The case for the prosecution was that a
c man named Gosine, the murder victim, and his girlfriend were, on 9th January 1973,
sitting in a parked van when they were set on by two masked men, both armed. Gosine
ran away, pursued by one of the masked men, who caught up with him and inflicted on
him injuries from which he died. Meanwhile the other masked man robbed and raped
the girlfriend. Before he had completed the act of intercourse, Gosine's assailant rejoined
him and they left together.

d The only evidence relied on by the prosecution connecting Ajodha and Tahaloo with
these crimes were signed confession statements which it was alleged that each had made
to police officers investigating the matter. The purported statement of Ajodha is a
document signed by him in four places. The first two signatures are appended to
acknowledgments in two different forms, at the beginning of the document, that he had
been duly cautioned, then follows the substance of the statement signed at the foot and
e finally the familiar caption, 'I have read the above statement and I have been told that I
can correct, alter or add anything I wish. This statement is true. I have made it of my
own free will', followed by a further signature. The prosecution alleged that the caption
was in Ajodha's handwriting. This was disputed by the defence but the signatures were
accepted as being the appellant's. The case for the appellant as presented both in cross-
examination and in his own evidence was that he was in no way responsible for the
f contents of the statement, that it had been previously prepared by the police, that he had
had no opportunity to read it, but that he had been forced to sign it by being beaten by
the police and threatened with further beatings if he did not do so.

In the event Ajodha was convicted of murder and acquitted of robbery and rape;
Tahaloo was acquitted of murder and convicted of robbery and rape.

The case for the prosecution against Chandree, Fletcher and Noreiga was that they
g were three of four men who on 24th May 1974 robbed one Shah, a paymaster of the
Ministry of Finance, of $24,000. Three of the robbers were armed with shot guns, Shah
was escorted by two armed police officers, and in the course of the robbery one of the
police officers, Corporal Britto, was shot dead by one of the robbers.

In this case there was some evidence of identification of each of the appellants as one
of the robbers but the way in which this was reviewed by the learned judge in summing
h up strongly suggests that he was inviting the jury to treat the evidence as unreliable.
Here again the corner-stone of the prosecution's case against each appellant was a written
and signed confession statement, supplemented in Chandree's case by a prior oral
confession to the like effect. The form of the written statement in each case was similar
to that which has been described in the case of Ajodha in that each embodied two initial
signatures acknowledging the caution, a signature to the substance of the statement and
j a signature to the concluding caption.

The case for the defence of all three appellants was conducted on the footing that they
were not the authors of the confession statements they had signed and in Chandree's case
that he had not made the oral confession attributed to him. The case for Chandree and
Noreiga was that they had been forced by violence and threats of further violence to sign

the statements in ignorance of their contents. The case for Fletcher was that he had been tricked into signing his statement, having been falsely led by police officers to believe *a* that it was a statement of the evidence he could give for the prosecution in connection with an incident in which he himself had been wounded and which was wholly unrelated to the incident in which Corporal Britto was killed. These defence allegations were made clear in cross-examination of the prosecution witnesses concerned. Chandree and Fletcher did not give evidence but made unsworn statements from the dock in support of what had been put by counsel on their behalf. Noreiga gave evidence on oath to like *b* effect.

The primary question for their Lordships' decision in these appeals can be stated in its simplest form as follows. When the prosecution proposes to tender in evidence a written statement of confession signed by the accused and the accused denies that he is the author of the statement but admits that the signature or signatures on the document are his and claims that they were obtained from him by threat or inducement, does this raise a *c* question of law for decision by the judge as to the admissibility of the statement? This question has provoked the keenest judicial controversy in a number of Caribbean appellate courts and a great amount of erudition has been devoted to the lengthy judgments which have been written answering the main question in one way or the other and expressing different shades of opinion on a number of related questions. Their Lordships propose to refer to what seem to be the main cases in the development of the *d* controversy and to cite from these so far as necessary to indicate in broad outline the rival contentions, but hope they will be acquitted of disrespect if they do not examine the authorities in great detail since it appears to them that neither the principles to be applied in this field nor the results of their application to any one of a number of commonly encountered situations, including that under immediate consideration, are seriously in doubt. Their Lordships find some confirmation of this opinion in the circumstance that *e* counsel for the respondent did not feel able to advance any argument in support of the view which commended itself to the Court of Appeal of Trinidad and Tobago.

The first important decision is that of the Court of Appeal of Trinidad and Tobago (Wooding CJ, McShine and Fraser JJA) in *Williams v Ramdeo and Ramdeo* (1966) 10 WIR 397. The nature of the issue and the court's decision sufficiently appear from the following passage from the judgment of the court delivered by Fraser JA (at 398): *f*

'In the course of his evidence Cpl. Williams tendered the written statement allegedly given by Harrilal. His counsel objected to its admission on the ground that it was not given voluntarily but was obtained by force and threats. Accordingly, the magistrate proceeded to hear evidence as regards the taking of the statement. It turned out, however, that Harrilal was alleging, not that he had given the *g* statement under duress, but that he had been beaten into signing a piece of paper and that he had in fact given no statement at all. Immediately after hearing the evidence the magistrate rejected the statement and refused to allow it in. He then continued the trial at the end of which, as we have said, he acquitted Harrilal. In view of the course we propose, we refrain from commenting on Harrilal's defence. We content ourselves with saying that the magistrate was wrong in *h* refusing the admission of the statement into evidence and that he thereby rejected legal evidence substantially affecting the merits of the case. In our judgment, a clear distinction falls to be drawn between an objection that a statement made by a person charged with an offence was not made voluntarily and an allegation that he never made any statement at all. In the case of an objection that a statement was not made voluntarily, a judge sitting with a jury or a magistrate sitting without one must hear *j* the relevant evidence and on it decide whether or not to admit the statement: if admitted, it will then have to be weighed along with the rest of the evidence in order to find whether the person charged is guilty or not. In the case of an allegation by the person charged that he made no statement at all, the statement must be admitted and the allegation will fall to be considered along with the rest of

a   the evidence in the case and a verdict must be reached after consideration of the
whole.'

Presumably the signature which the defendant Harrilal Ramdeo alleged he was beaten
into giving was annexed to the written statement tendered by the prosecution. It does
not clearly appear from the report whether the 'piece of paper' was, according to the
defendant, blank when signed and subsequently completed by the police or whether it
already had the statement on it and the defendant was saying that he was beaten into
b   signing it unread. This distinction, however, makes no difference to the principle
applicable.

In *Herrera and Dookeran v R* (1966) 11 WIR 1 the Court of Appeal of Trinidad and
Tobago, similarly constituted as in the *Ramdeo* case, followed their own earlier decision
in holding that no issue arose as to the admissibility of a written statement made by
Dookeran. The statement was challenged on the ground that Dookeran had been beaten
c   and then tricked into copying in his own handwriting a document handed to him by the
police and signed it as a statement of his own. Wooding CJ, delivering the judgment of
the court, said (at 5):

> 'Further, we agree with the learned judge that the issue raised did not go to the
> admissibility of the statement but rather to its acceptability as being genuine. In
d   > effect, Dookeran was alleging that he never gave the police a statement, he merely
> copied a document as they required him to do. On the other hand, Inspector
> George was saying that the statement was Dookeran's, so much so that he actually
> wrote it himself. That issue, the judge quite rightly held, was not for him but for
> the jury to resolve . . .'

The next relevant decision was that of the Court of Appeal of Guyana (Bollers AC,
e   Persaud ACJ and Cummings JA) in *Harper v The State* (1970) 16 WIR 353. The nature of
the decision sufficiently appears from the headnote:

> 'The appellant was charged with uttering a forged order for the payment of
> money. During the course of the trial, he objected to the admission in evidence of
> a statement alleged to have been made by him on the ground that he had been
f   > induced to do so. Upon the issue being tried at the *voir dire*, the appellant in his
> evidence said that the statement was not his, that what was written therein had
> never occurred, that he had only signed it because of an inducement held out to
> him. The judge refrained from determining the issue of voluntariness, and instead
> left it to the jury to determine whether or not the accused had in fact made the
> statement. *Held* [Persaud, CJ(Ag) dissenting]: that it was the duty of the judge,
g   > having tried the issue on the *voir dire* to have ruled whether the statement was a free
> and voluntary one, and if he had found it to be free and voluntary, to have admitted
> it into evidence, and then left it to the jury to say what weight should be attached
> to it.'

It does not appear that the decisions of the Court of Appeal of Trinidad and Tobago in
Ramdeo and *Herrera* were cited to the court. Bollers AC said (at 355):

h   > 'In my view the judge misinterpreted the evidence of the appellant on the issue
> and misunderstood what the appellant was saying. The appellant was admitting
> that he had signed the statement, and in my view where an accused person admits
> that he has signed a statement, it must follow that he is adopting what is written,
> but in those circumstances what the accused person would be saying is that although
> he signed the statement, it was not a free and voluntary statement because he had
i   > been induced to sign it because of the promise made to him.'

Persaud ACJ said in his dissenting judgment (at 358):

> 'My understanding of the appellant's evidence on the *voir dire*, even though he
> did say that he did not make the statement of his own free will, was that the

statement was not his, that he had merely signed it and that he had done so because
of the inducement. He was not, in my opinion, saying that he had made the
statement but that he did so because of the inducement—a clear distinction which,
in my opinion, must be borne in mind, because upon that distinction rests the duty
of the judge. The authorities are clear that if an appellant is challenging the
voluntariness of a statement, that issue must be tried by the judge on a *voir dire*, but
if he is alleging that he did not make the statement, then that is a question of fact
which must be left with the jury. With great respect I cannot understand the
appellant to have been saying that by affixing his signature to the statement he was
accepting the authorship of the contents thereof; indeed, he was contending for the
contrary, and no amount of verbal refinement can lead me to any other view.'

Shortly after the decision in *Harper's* case the same issue arose for decision by a
differently constituted Court of Appeal of Guyana (Luckhoo C, Bollers CJ and Cummings
JA) in *The State v Fowler* (1970) 16 WIR 452. Again the accused had challenged the
admissibility of a written statement incriminating him on the ground that his signature
on the document had been improperly obtained but had said in effect, on the voir dire,
that he was not the author of the contents of the statement, whereupon the trial judge
had declined to rule on admissibility and had left the issue to the jury. The majority of
the court (Cummings JA dissenting) approved the course taken by the judge and upheld
the conviction. Bollers CJ said (at 462):

'The question therefore now in the present appeal is whether the appellant's
evidence on the *voir dire* is to be interpreted as meaning that he was objecting to the
admissibility of the statement on the ground that it was not a free and voluntary
statement, in which case it would be an issue for the judge to try, or whether he was
objecting to the admission of the statement on the ground that it was not his
statement, in which case that issue would be for the jury. For my part, I find the
circumstances of this case indistinguishable from the Trinidad cases of *Herrera and
Dookeran v. R.* and *Williams v. Ramdeo and Ramdeo.*'

He later sought to distinguish his own earlier opinion as expressed in the passage cited
above from *Harper's* case and added (at 465):

'I need hardly say that an accused person cannot raise a double-barrelled attack on
a statement on the grounds that (a) it is not free and voluntary, and (b) it is not made
by him, for, as PERSAUD, J.A. in the *Harper* appeal pointed out, it would be most
illogical for him to say, if the order is reversed: "I made the statement but I did so
under an inducement or a threat, but if it is found that there is no inducement or
threat, then I say I did not make the statement."'

Cummings JA said in his dissenting judgment (at 471):

'I am unable to appreciate the difference between adopting a statement under
duress and dictating or writing it under duress. The issue of voluntariness is
involved in all three operations, and once that issue is raised, the onus is on the
prosecution to show that whether by dictation, express writing by the accused, or
adoption by signature of the accused, the statement was voluntary.'

The identical issue arose yet again for decision by the Court of Appeal of Guyana in *The
State v Ramsingh* (1973) 20 WIR 138. Five judges sat (Luckhoo C, Bollers CJ, Persaud,
Cummings and Crane JJA), no doubt intending that the question should be resolved once
and for all. As the headnote indicates, it was held by a majority (Cummings and Crane
JJA dissenting) that an accused person is not entitled to raise on the voir dire both the
question of the voluntariness of his statement and the question of fact whether or not he
had made the statement; that 'once it becomes apparent that an accused person is in truth
raising the latter issue it becomes a matter of fact for the jury to determine'.

It is pertinent to observe that at the date when the present appellant Ajodha was tried
a the decisions referred to above must have appeared both to the trial judge and to all
counsel involved to have settled the law in the sense that Ajodha's version of the
circumstances in which his disputed statement came into existence gave rise to no issue
for decision by the judge as to its admissibility but only to an issue of fact for decision by
the jury. The same was almost certainly thought to be the position when Chandree,
Fletcher and Noreiga were tried, for, although the judgments of the Court of Appeal of
b Guyana in *The State v Gobin and Griffith* (1976) 23 WIR 256 were delivered on 31st March
1976, they were not reported until much later and this decision is unlikely to have been
known to practitioners in Trinidad and Tobago in May and June 1976.

In *Gobin's* case the Court of Appeal of Guyana again sat a full court of five (Haynes C,
Bollers CJ, Crane, R H Luckhoo and Jhappan JJA) to review their own earlier decisions in
Fowler and *Ramsingh*. It appears from an editorial note to the report that these cases had
c caused difficulties in practice. Moreover, since those decisions, the House of Lords had
given its decision in *Director of Public Prosecutions v Ping Lin* [1975] 3 All ER 175, [1976]
AC 574. The upshot of *Gobin's* case was that the Court of Appeal of Guyana by a majority
of four to one (Bollers CJ dissenting) overruled its own earlier decisions in the cases of
Fowler and *Ramsingh*. The judgments are extremely long (they cover 59 pages in the
report) and the reasoning of the four judges in the majority is not the same. Their
d Lordships will content themselves with quoting two sentences from the leading
judgment of Haynes C which seem to them best to epitomise the main ground of the
decision. The learned Chancellor said (at 278):

> 'If the confession of an accused in writing must be voluntary, then the signature
> that makes it his must be voluntary also. For, when the prosecution puts in a signed
> statement, what they seek to rely on is not the words of oral confession spoken to the
e> recording policeman; it is what is adopted as true and correct "in black-and-white"
> by the signature.'

When the appeals of Chandree, Fletcher and Noreiga reached the Court of Appeal of
Trinidad and Tobago, the decision of the Court of Appeal of Guyana in *Gobin's* case was
relied on as the basis of an invitation to the court to overrule its own earlier decisions in
f *Ramdeo* and *Herrera*. The court declined this invitation, not, as it might have done, on
the principle of stare decisis, but on the basis of reasoned argument that the earlier
decisions were to be preferred to the latest decision of the Court of Appeal of Guyana.
Especially since counsel, as mentioned earlier, did not feel able to support the Court of
Appeal's reasoning, it seems to their Lordships right to quote in full the main passage
from the careful judgment of the court, delivered by Hyatali CJ. He said:

g> 'It is clear to us that the controversy which has developed in the courts of the West
> Indies and Guyana is not one over the principles governing the admissibility of
> confessions, since all the courts agree, and rightly so, that whenever an issue is raised
> whether or not an accused made a confession voluntarily it is the duty of the trial
> judge to determine that issue on the voir dire. The essential point of the controversy
> poses the question whether an issue of voluntariness is raised when an accused
h> alleges that he was beaten and forced to append his signature to a statement which
> he alleges he did not make. It is, in our judgment, a pure question of the
> interpretation of the objection made. If the true and correct answer to that question
> is in the affirmative then the decision in *Gobin's* case cannot, in our judgment, be
> faulted. It is otherwise, however, if the answer is in the negative, because if
> voluntariness is not in issue for the reason that the prosecution's evidence in support
j> of it is not challenged or contested then there is nothing for the trial judge to
> determine on the voir dire. With the utmost respect to the Court of Appeal of
> Guyana, we find ourselves unable to agree with the proposition that the allegation
> of an accused that he was forced to append his signature to a confessional statement
> which he did not make is tantamount to an allegation that *he was forced to accept as*

true and correct a confessional statement which he did not make. That proposition, in our judgment, is self-contradictory. It is founded, if we may say so with respect, *a* on a strained and illogical construction of the objection which cannot be justified. It is of vital importance to note that an objection in the terms under reference does not allege that the accused by duress was *forced to say* what is contained in the statement, and further that by duress he *was forced to append his signature* to what he was *forced to say* in the statement, but rather he was forced by duress to sign a statement containing facts which were fabricated and of which he is not the *b* author. Accordingly, if his allegations are true, his mind did not go with his signature on the statement nor his signature with its contents. In contemplation of law therefore he did not sign the statement nor accept its contents as his. In other words, whenever an accused alleges that a confessional statement purporting to be his was in fact a fabrication, it is immaterial for the purposes under consideration that he alleges in addition that he was forced to append his signature to it. The two *c* situations referred to are, in our judgment, fundamentally different from each other. Indeed the first is the antithesis of the second and vice versa. In the first example, the accused was forced to confess and in fact did so; but in the second he never did. This fundamental difference, it seems to us, was not sufficiently appreciated by the Guyana Court of Appeal in *Gobin*'s case. The instant case clearly falls within the second example, and we are therefore unable to agree that the *d* objection under reference raised the issue of the voluntariness of Chandree's confession. In our judgment, the interpretation placed on the objections made in *Williams v Ramdeo and Ramdeo, Dookeran and Herrera v R* and *The State v Ramsingh* was correct, and the conclusions at which the respective courts arrived in consequence thereof in those cases were clearly right.' (Emphasis Hyatali CJ's.)

Three days later, in dismissing the appeal of Ajodha, the court simply followed its own *e* earlier decision.

A sound starting point for the consideration of any question of the admissibility of confessions is the dictum of Lord Sumner, giving the judgment of this Board in *Ibrahim v R* [1914] AC 599 at 609, [1914–15] All ER Rep 874 at 877 as follows:

> 'It has long been established as a positive rule of English criminal law, that no *f* statement by an accused is admissible in evidence against him unless it is shewn by the prosecution to have been a voluntary statement, in the sense that it has not been obtained from him either by fear of prejudice or hope of advantage exercised or held out by a person in authority.'

As Lord Hailsham pointed out in *Director of Public Prosecutions v Ping Lin* [1975] 3 All ER *g* 175 at 180, [1976] AC 574 at 597, the word 'exercised' in this passage is probably a misreading for 'excited'.

Given this deeply entrenched and quite unequivocal principle it seems to their Lordships clear beyond argument that, if the prosecution tender in evidence a statement in writing signed in one or more places by the accused, they are relying on the signature as the acknowledgment and authentication by the accused of the statement as his own, *h* and that from this it must follow that, if the voluntary character of the signature is challenged, this inevitably puts in issue the voluntary character of the statement itself.

The fallacy which in their Lordships' respectful opinion, underlies the reasoning of the judgments in the cases considered above which have arrived at a contrary conclusion is to suppose that a challenge by an accused person to a statement tendered in evidence against him on the ground that he never made it and a challenge on the ground that the *j* statement was not voluntary are mutually exclusive, so as to force on the judge a choice between leaving an issue of fact to the jury and deciding an issue of admissibility himself. In all cases where the accused denies authorship of the contents of a written statement but complains that the signature or signatures on the document which he admits to be his own were improperly obtained from him by threat or inducement, he

is challenging the prosecution's evidence on both grounds and there is nothing in the
a least illogical or inconsistent in his doing so.

It has to be remembered that the rule requiring the judge to be satisfied that an
incriminating statement by the accused was given voluntarily before deciding that it is
admissible in evidence is anomalous in that it puts the judge in a position where he must
make his own findings of fact and thus creates an inevitable overlap between the fact-
finding functions of judge and jury. In a simple case, where the sole issue is whether the
b statement, admittedly made by the accused, was voluntary or not, it is a commonplace
that the judge first decides that issue himself, having heard evidence on the voir dire,
normally in the absence of the jury. If he rules in favour of admissibility, the jury will
then normally hear exactly the same evidence and decide essentially the same issue albeit
not as a test of admissibility but as a criterion of the weight and value, if any, of the
statement as evidence of the guilt of the accused.

c   In the case presently under consideration, where the accused denies authorship of the
statement but admits signing it under duress, the overlap of functions is more
complex. Hearing evidence on the voir dire, the judge will of necessity examine all the
circumstances and form his own view of how the statement came to be written and
signed. In practice the issue of authorship and that of whether the signature was
voluntary are likely to be inseparably linked. One can hardly envisage a case where a
d judge might decide that an accused was not responsible for the contents of the statement
but had signed it voluntarily. A purist might say that, in considering the issue of
authorship, the judge was usurping the function of the jury; but, if it is necessary to
consider the issue of authorship before the judge can be satisfied that the statement was
signed voluntarily, there is in truth no usurpation but only a discharge by the judge of
his necessary function in deciding the question of admissibility. If the judge rules the
e statement to have been signed voluntarily and therefore admissible, in this, as in the
simple case, the issues both of authorship and of the manner in which the signature was
obtained will again have to be canvassed before and left for consideration by the jury.

In the instant appeals there can be no doubt that the case presented in cross-
examination on behalf of the accused and what was said by the accused either in evidence
or in a statement from the dock in the case of the appellants Ajodha, Chandree and
f Noreiga raised in each case an issue as to the voluntariness of their signatures and thus of
their statements, on the simple ground that they were beaten into signing. Fletcher's
case was slightly different in that he was claiming that his signatures to what in fact was
a confession statement were obtained by the fraudulent misrepresentation that he was
signing a document of an entirely different character. But it is conceded by counsel for
the respondent, as their Lordships think quite rightly, that this equally raises an issue
g whether this statement was the voluntary statement of the accused and therefore goes to
admissibility.

The arguments before their Lordships, like the lengthy judgments in the two Guyana
cases of *Ramsingh* and *Gobin*, ranged over a wide variety of situations in which a question
may arise as to the respective functions of judge and jury in relation to incriminating
statements tendered in evidence by the prosecution. It may be helpful if their Lordships
h indicate their understanding of the principles applicable by considering how the question
should be resolved in four typical situations most likely to be encountered in practice.

1. The accused admits making the statement (orally or in writing) but raises the issue
that it was not voluntary. This is a simple case where the judge must rule on
admissibility, and, if he admits the evidence of the statement, leave to the jury all
questions as to its value and weight.

j   2. The accused, as in each of the instant appeals, denies authorship of the written
statement but claims that he signed it involuntarily. Again, for the reasons explained,
the judge must rule on admissibility, and, if he admits the statement, leave all issues of
fact as to the circumstances of the making and signing of the statement for the jury to
consider and evaluate.

3. The evidence tendered or proposed to be tendered by the prosecution itself indicates

that the circumstances in which the statement was taken could arguably lead to the conclusion that the statement was obtained by fear of prejudice or hope of advantage *a* excited or held out by a person in authority. In this case, irrespective of any challenge to the prosecution evidence by the defence, it will be for the judge to rule, assuming the prosecution evidence to be true, whether it proves the statement to have been made voluntarily.

4. On the face of the evidence tendered or proposed to be tendered by the prosecution, there is no material capable of suggesting that the statement was other than voluntary. *b* The defence is an absolute denial of the prosecution evidence. For example, if the prosecution rely on oral statements, the defence case is simply that the interview never took place or that the incriminating answers were never given; in the case of a written statement, the defence case is that it is a forgery. In this situation no issue as to voluntariness can arise and hence no question of admissibility falls for the judge's decision. The issue of fact whether or not the statement was made by the accused is *c* purely for the jury. In so far as the dissenting judgment of Crane JA in *Ramsingh*, the concurring judgments of Crane and Luckhoo JJA in *Gobin* and the judgment of the Court of Appeal of Jamaica in *R v Watson* (1975) 24 WIR 367 are at variance with the propositions set forth in this paragraph, their Lordships are respectfully unable to agree with them.

Counsel for the respondent invited the Board to uphold the convictions of the present *d* appellants on the sole ground that no formal objection to the admissibility of the confession statements was taken by defending counsel in any of the four cases. Their Lordships are satisfied that it would be quite wrong to accede to this invitation. Even if, in the normal case, a point of law is only open to an appellant if the point has been duly taken in the court of first instance, the almost irresistible inference here is that the only reason why no formal objection to admissibility was taken at either of these trials was *e* because judge and counsel all supposed, rightly as matters stood, that, if any such objection had been taken, the court would have been bound by authority to overrule it. Thus, in the event, each of these four appellants has been deprived, through no significant fault of his own or his advisers, of the all-important safeguard of a judge's ruling as to the admissibility of the central (in Ajodha's case the only) evidence relied on by the prosecution against him. This was, in their Lordships' view, an injustice of such *f* a substantial character, especially in a capital case, that no appellant should be disentitled to rely on it on the narrow technical ground that his advisers omitted what would have been, in the circumstances, the pure formality of taking the point in order to keep it open on appeal.

As in relation to the substantive law governing the admissibility of confession statements, so also in relation to the proper procedure to be adopted at a jury trial in *g* various circumstances in which a question as to admissibility may arise, the argument before their Lordships ranged over a wide field. Their Lordships would certainly not attempt to lay down an exhaustive code of procedure intended to cover every contingency, but here again it may be helpful to practitioners in some jurisdictions where difficulties seem to have been encountered if they indicate their understanding of the appropriate procedure in a number of not uncommon situations. *h*

1. In the normal situation which arises at the vast majority of trials where the admissibility of a confession statement is to be challenged, defending counsel will notify prosecuting counsel that an objection to admissibility is to be raised, prosecuting counsel will not mention the statement in his opening to the jury, and at the appropriate time the judge will conduct a trial on the voir dire to decide on the admissibility of the statement; this will normally be in the absence of the jury, but only at the request or *j* with the consent of the defence: see *R v Anderson* (1929) 21 Cr App R 178.

2. Though the case for the defence raises an issue as to the voluntariness of a statement in accordance with the principles indicated earlier in this judgment, defending counsel may for tactical reasons prefer that the evidence bearing on that issue be heard before the jury, with a single cross-examination of the witnesses on both sides, even though this

means that the jury hear the impugned statement whether admissible or not. If the
a defence adopts this tactic, it will be open to defending counsel to submit at the close of
the evidence that, if the judge doubts the voluntariness of the statement, he should direct
the jury to disregard it, or, if the statement is essential to sustain the prosecution case,
direct an acquittal. Even in the absence of such a submission, if the judge himself forms
the view that the voluntariness of the statement is in doubt, he should take the like action
proprio motu.

b   3. It may sometimes happen that the accused himself will raise for the first time when
giving evidence an issue as to the voluntariness of a statement already put in evidence by
the prosecution. Here it will be a matter in the discretion of the trial judge whether to
require relevant prosecution witnesses to be recalled for further cross-examination. If he
does so, the issue of voluntariness should be dealt with in the same manner as indicated
in para 2 above.

c   4. Particular difficulties may arise in the trial of an unrepresented defendant, when
the judge must, of course, be especially vigilant to ensure a fair trial. No rules can be laid
down, but it may be prudent, if the judge has any reason to suppose that the voluntary
character of a statement proposed to be put in evidence by the prosecution is likely to be
in issue, that he should speak to the defendant before the trial begins and explain his
rights in the matter.

d   A further ground of appeal was raised on behalf of Ajodha that he was prejudiced by
the joinder of the counts of robbery and rape with the count of murder. Section 16 of
the Jury Ordinance of Trinidad and Tobago requires trials for murder or treason to be by
a jury of 12, and those for lesser offences by a jury of nine. It is settled that a trial before
a jury of 12 of an indictment in which counts for lesser offences are misjoined with a
count for murder invalidates any conviction of the lesser offences, but not the conviction
e for murder: see *Gransaul and Ferreira v The Queen* (9th April 1979), an unreported
decision of this Board. It was conceded in the instant case by counsel for Ajodha that the
evidence relevant to the counts of robbery and rape was relevant and admissible also on
the count of murder and could properly have been led even if the lesser charges had been
omitted from the indictment. Their Lordships respectfully agree with the Court of
Appeal that in these circumstances there was no prejudice.

f   Their Lordships were invited by the respondent, if minded to allow the appeals, to
remit them to the Court of Appeal of Trinidad and Tobago to enable that court to
consider whether to order new trials, as it has power to do under s 6(2) of the Criminal
Appeal Ordinance. Their Lordships were satisfied that it would be inappropriate to
order new trials in cases in which so long a time has elapsed since the commission of the
alleged offences, scilicet over eight years in Ajodha's case and nearly seven years in the
g case of the other three appellants.

It was for these reasons that their Lordships decided to allow the appeals in the terms
of the order indicated in the first paragraph of this judgment.

Appeals allowed. Convictions quashed. Verdicts of acquittal entered.

Solicitors: *Gasters* (for the appellants Ajodha and Fletcher); *Ingledew, Brown, Bennison &*
Garrett (for the appellants Chandree and Noreiga); *Charles Russell & Co* (for the
respondent).

Mary Rose Plummer Barrister.

Western Fish Products Ltd v Penwith District Council and another

COURT OF APPEAL, CIVIL DIVISION

MEGAW, LAWTON AND BROWNE LJJ

27th, 28th FEBRUARY, 1st–3rd, 6th–9th, 13th–17th, 20th–22nd MARCH, 4th–7th, 10th–13th, 17th–19th APRIL, 22nd MAY 1978

Estoppel – Proprietary estoppel – Conduct leading representee to act to his detriment – Expectation of acquiring right over land – Plaintiff obtaining assurance from council that planning permission would be granted for development of his land – Plaintiff spending money in expectation of obtaining planning permission – Plaintiff not expecting to obtain rights over another's land – Council refusing planning permission – Whether council estopped from refusing permission.

Estoppel – Statutory body – Local planning authority – Exercise of discretion – Whether local planning authority can be estopped from exercising statutory discretion.

In April 1976 the plaintiffs bought an industrial site on which there was a disused factory that had previously been used for the production of fertiliser from fish and fishmeal. That business had closed down in 1975. The plaintiffs intended to use the site for the manufacture of fish oil and fishmeal, for use as animal food, and to prepare and pack fresh fish for human consumption, and wished to demolish some of the old buildings, repair, alter or rebuild others, and build substantial new buildings. On 7th April 1976 at a meeting between the plaintiffs' chairman and a planning officer representing the defendant council, the chairman explained the intended project and asserted that the plaintiffs had an established use right arising out of the previous use of the factory and the site and were entitled to carry on their intended processes without the necessity of obtaining planning permission. The planning officer asked the chairman to supply information supporting the assertion of an established use right. The planning officer further stated that if the plaintiffs satisfied him that they had an established use right the council would do everything possible to assist the plaintiffs and would not obstruct them. The plaintiffs wrote two letters on 8th and 17th April supplying the information requested. On 26th April the planning officer replied by letter stating that 'it is confirmed that the limits of the various component parts of the commercial undertaking as now existing appear to be established'. The plaintiffs forthwith proceeded to renovate or rebuild the old buildings, to start erecting new buildings and to prepare for the installation of expensive machinery. That work was carried on without protest by the council's representatives although planning permission had not been obtained. On 6th July the planning officer asked the plaintiffs' architects to submit planning applications and also an application for an established use certificate under s 94 of the Town and Country Planning Act 1971 and stated that the application for an established use certificate was purely a formality. Four applications in respect of the various operations were submitted as well as an application for the established use certificate. On 26th August a full meeting of the council refused all the applications and authorised the service of enforcement and stop notices in respect of the building works which were in progress. In September enforcement notices were issued and all work on the site stopped. The plaintiffs brought an action against the council, seeking declarations that they were entitled to existing use rights entitling them to use the factory for the purposes they intended or that they were entitled to be treated as having planning permission, an injunction restraining the council from enforcing the stop order and enforcement notices, an order requiring the council to withdraw the enforcement notices, and damages. The judge dismissed the plaintiffs' action. The plaintiffs appealed, contending,

inter alia, (i) that the statements made on 7th April by the planning officer and in his
a letter of 26th April amounted to a representation that the plaintiffs had an existing use
right in respect of the site and that once the existing use right was established the council
would grant planning permission for the new buildings, and that under the doctrine of
proprietary estoppel the council was estopped from deciding on the plaintiffs' applications
in a manner contrary to the planning officer's representations, (ii) that the letter of 26th
April was either a determination under s 53ᵃ of the 1971 Act that planning permission
b was not required for the site or an established use certificate under s 94 of that Act, and
(iii) that the plaintiffs had an existing use right which entitled them to erect new
buildings to enable them to exploit that right.

Held – The appeal would be dismissed for the following reasons—
(1) The principle of proprietary estoppel only applied where the plaintiff, encouraged
c by the defendant, acted to his detriment in relation to his own land in the expectation of
acquiring a right over the defendant's land. Even if the plaintiffs had to their detriment
spent money on their own land at the encouragement of the council, they had not done
so in the expectation of acquiring any rights in relation to the council's or any other
person's land and they could not therefore rely on the principle of proprietary estoppel
(see p 217 *e* to *j* and p 219 *a b*, post); *Crabb v Arun District Council* [1975] 3 All ER 865
d applied; *Hammersley v Baron de Biel* (1845) 12 Cl & Fin 45 and *Evenden v Guildford City
Association Football Club Ltd* [1975] 3 All ER 269 distinguished.
(2) In any event, an estoppel could not be raised to prevent a statutory body exercising
its statutory discretion or performing its statutory duty, and therefore, even if the
council's officers while acting in the apparent scope of their authority had purported to
determine the plaintiffs' planning applications in advance, that was not binding on the
e council because it alone had power under the 1971 Act to determine the applications.
Furthermore, although a planning authority might be bound by the decisions of an
officer if the power to decide the particular matter had been, or appeared to be, delegated
to the officer, for an estoppel to arise in such circumstances there had to be some
evidence, over and above the mere fact of the officer's position, on which the applicant
was justified in thinking that the officer's statements would bind the council. Since there
f was nothing, apart from the position held by the planning officer, on which the plaintiffs
could have assumed that the officer could bind the council, the council was not estopped
by anything the planning officer had said from refusing the plaintiffs' applications for
planning consent (see p 217 *e f*, p 219 *b c f* to *h*, p 220 *g h* and p 221 *b d*, post); *Maritime
Electric Co Ltd v General Dairies Ltd* [1937] 1 All ER 748 and *Southend-on-Sea Corpn v
Hodgson (Wickford) Ltd* [1961] 2 All ER 46 applied; *Lever (Finance) Ltd v Westminster Corpn*
g [1970] 3 All ER 496 explained; dicta of Lord Denning MR and Sachs LJ in *Lever (Finance)
Ltd v Westminster Corpn* [1970] 3 All ER at 501, 503–504 criticised.
(3) Furthermore, the letter of 26th April was not a representation because it was not
confirmation that the plaintiffs had existing use rights entitling them to use the site for
the purposes they proposed; but, even if it was, the plaintiffs had not acted on it to their
detriment since they had relied not on any representation but on their own belief that
h they had an existing use right when carrying out their building works without planning
permission. Accordingly, on the facts no estoppel arose, and even if one did the plaintiffs
could not rely on it (see p 216 *f* to p 217 *d*, post).
(4) Although it was not necessary for a person to make a formal written application
for a determination under s 53 of the 1971 Act that planning permission was not
required if an application for planning permission had already been submitted, since the
j application for permission impliedly invited the authority to determine that permission
was not required, a formal written application under s 53 could only be dispensed with
if an application for permission had been made. Since the plaintiffs had not made an
application for planning permission their letters of 8th and 17th April could not be

treated as informal applications under s 53 and neither could the planning officer's letter of 26th April be construed as a determination under s 53 (see p 224 *a* to *d*, post); *Wells v Minister of Housing and Local Government* [1967] 2 All ER 1041 explained; dictum of Sachs LJ in *Lever (Finance) Ltd v Westminster Corpn* [1970] 3 All ER at 503–504 criticised.

(5) An established use certificate under s 94 of the 1971 Act was required to be a formal document in the form set out in Part II of Sch 6 of the Town and Country Planning General Development Order 1973, and since the planning officer's letter of 26th April was not in that form it could not be treated as a certificate under s 94; but in any event even if the formal defects were disregarded the letter of 26th April could not in the circumstances be construed as a certificate under s 94 (see p 224 *d* to *h*, post).

Per Curiam. Consideration should be given to the making of provision, either administratively or by rules of court, to ensure that the Department of the Environment is apprised of litigation on matters affecting the powers and duties of the Secretary of State in respect of his functions relating to town and country planning (see p 216 *d e*, post).

Notes

For proprietary estoppel, see 16 Halsbury's Laws (4th Edn) para 1511, and for cases on the subject, see 21 Digest (Repl) 452–455, *1542–1568*.

For a planning authority's powers in relation to existing uses, see 37 Halsbury's Laws (3rd Edn) 375–379, paras 478–479.

For the Town and Country Planning Act 1971, ss 53, 94, see 41 Halsbury's Statutes (3rd Edn) 1650, 1702.

As from 29th March 1977 the Town and Country Planning General Development Order 1973, Sch 6, Part II, has been replaced by the Town and Country Planning General Development Order 1977, SI 1977 No 289, Sch 6, Part II.

Cases referred to in judgment

Brooks and Burton Ltd v Secretary of State for the Environment (1976) 75 LGR 285, 35 P & CR 27; *rvsd* [1978] 1 All ER 733, [1977] 1 WLR 1294, 76 LGR 53, 35 P & CR 27, [1977] RVR 211, CA, Digest (Cont Vol E) 599, *101b(i)*.

Campbell Discount Co Ltd v Bridge [1961] 2 All ER 97, [1961] 1 QB 445, [1961] 2 WLR 596, CA; *rvsd* [1962] 1 All ER 385, [1962] AC 600, [1962] 2 WLR 439, HL, Digest (Cont Vol A) 648, *39a*.

Crabb v Arun District Council [1975] 3 All ER 865, [1976] 1 Ch 179, [1975] 3 WLR 847, CA, Digest (Cont Vol D) 312, *1250a*.

Evenden v Guildford City Association Football Club Ltd [1975] 3 All ER 269, [1975] QB 917, [1975] 3 WLR 251, [1975] ICR 367, CA, Digest (Cont Vol D) 677, *816Add(i)*.

Hammersley v Baron de Biel (1845) 12 Cl & Fin 45, 8 ER 1312, HL; *affg* 12 Cl & Fin 61n, 8 ER 1320n, LC; *affg* sub nom *De Biel v Thomson* (1841) 3 Beav 469, 49 ER 184, 35 Digest (Repl) 57, *505*.

Inwards v Baker [1965] 1 All ER 446, [1965] 2 QB 29, [1965] 2 WLR 212, CA, Digest (Cont Vol B) 242, *1552a*.

Lever (Finance) Ltd v Westminster Corpn [1970] 3 All ER 496, [1971] 1 QB 222, [1970] 3 WLR 732, 134 JP 692, 21 P & CR 778, CA, Digest (Cont Vol C) 967, *51c*.

Maritime Electric Co Ltd v General Dairies Ltd [1937] 1 All ER 748, [1937] AC 610, 106 LJPC 81, 156 LT 444, PC, 20 Digest (Repl) 228, **54*.

Moorgate Mercantile Co Ltd v Twitchings [1975] 3 All ER 314, [1976] QB 225, [1975] 3 WLR 286, [1975] RTR 528, CA; *rvsd* [1976] 2 All ER 641, [1977] AC 890, [1976] 3 WLR 66, [1976] RTR 437, HL, Digest (Cont Vol E) 211, *1109a*.

Plimmer v Wellington Corpn (1884) 9 App Cas 699, 53 LJPC 105, 51 LT 475, PC, 11 Digest (Reissue) 129, **98*.

Ramsden v Dyson (1866) LR 1 HL 129, 12 Jur NS 506, HL, 21 Digest (Repl) 453, *1551*.

Southend-on-Sea Corpn v Hodgson (Wickford) Ltd [1961] 2 All ER 46, [1962] 1 QB 416, [1961] 2 WLR 806, 125 JP 348, 59 LGR 193, DC, 21 Digest (Repl) 371, *1113*.

a *Wells v Minister of Housing and Local Government* [1967] 2 All ER 1041, [1967] 1 WLR
   1000, 131 JP 431, 65 LGR 408, 18 P & CR 401, CA, Digest (Cont Vol C) 965, 49a.

Cases also cited

Abbott v Sullivan [1952] 1 All ER 226, [1952] 1 KB 189, CA.

Acland v Buller (1848) 1 Exch 837, 154 ER 357.

Acrow (Automation) Ltd v Rex Chainbelt Inc [1971] 3 All ER 1175, [1971] 1 WLR 1676, CA.

b *Adams v Adams (Attorney General intervening)* [1970] 3 All ER 572, [1971] P 188.

Anisminic Ltd v Foreign Compensation Commission [1969] 1 All ER 208, [1969] 2 AC 147,
   HL.

Anns v London Borough of Merton [1977] 2 All ER 492, [1978] AC 728, HL.

Ayr Harbour Trustees v Oswald (1883) 8 App Cas 623, HL.

Barker v Furlong [1891] 2 Ch 172.

c *Brasyer v Maclean* (1875) LR 6 PC 398.

Brayhead (Ascot) Ltd v Berkshire County Council [1964] 1 All ER 149, [1964] 2 QB 303, DC.

Bulmer (HP) Ltd and Showerings Ltd v J Bollinger SA and Champagne Lanson Père et Fils [1978]
   RPC 79, CA.

Bunge SA v Kruse [1977] 1 Lloyd's Rep 492, CA.

Burdle v Secretary of State for the Environment [1972] 3 All ER 240, [1972] 1 WLR 1207,
d DC.

Byrne v Kinematograph Reuters Society [1958] 2 All ER 579, [1958] 1 WLR 762.

Canadian Pacific Railway Co v R [1931] AC 414, [1931] All ER Rep 113, PC.

Cannock Chase District Council v Kelly [1978] 1 All ER 152, [1978] 1 WLR 1, CA.

Congreve v Home Office [1976] 1 All ER 697, [1976] QB 629, CA.

Crabb v Arun District Council (No 2) [1976] Court of Appeal Transcript 447B.

e *Crittenden (Warren Park) Ltd v Surrey County Council* [1965] 3 All ER 917, [1966] 1 WLR
   25.

Daily Mirror Newspapers Ltd v Gardner [1968] 2 All ER 163, [1968] 2 QB 762, CA.

David (Asoka Kumar) v M A M M Abdul Cader [1963] 3 All ER 579, [1963] 1 WLR 834, PC.

Davis v Bromley Corpn [1908] 1 KB 170, CA.

Dowty Boulton Paul Ltd v Wolverhampton Corpn [1971] 2 All ER 277, [1971] 1 WLR 204;
f subsequent proceedings [1973] 2 All ER 491, [1976] Ch 13, CA.

Drewe v Coulton (1787) 1 East 563, 102 ER 217.

Eastham v Newcastle United Football Club Ltd [1963] 3 All ER 139, [1964] Ch 413.

Everett v Griffiths [1921] 1 AC 631, HL.

Fairmount Investments Ltd v Secretary of State for the Environment [1976] 2 All ER 865,
   [1976] 1 WLR 1255, HL.

g *Farrington v Thomson and Bridgland* [1959] VR 286.

Francis v Yiewsley and West Drayton Urban District Council [1957] 3 All ER 529, [1958] 1
   QB 478, CA.

Gouriet v Union of Post Office Workers [1977] 3 All ER 70, [1978] AC 435, HL.

HTV Ltd v Price Commission [1976] ICR 170, CA.

Hamilton v West Sussex County Council [1958] 2 All ER 174, [1958] 2 QB 286.

h *Hoffmann-La Roche (F) & Co AG v Secretary of State for Trade and Industry* [1974] 2 All ER
   1128, [1975] AC 295, HL.

Holiday Inns Inc v Broadhead, Same v Yorkstone Properties (Harlington) Ltd (1974) 232 Estates
   Gazette 951.

Hopgood v Brown [1955] 1 All ER 550, [1955] 1 WLR 213, CA.

Howard v Secretary of State for the Environment [1974] 1 All ER 644, [1975] QB 235, CA.

j *Howell v Falmouth Boat Construction Ltd* [1951] 2 All ER 278, [1951] AC 837, HL.

Hussain v Secretary of State for the Environment (1971) 23 P & CR 330, DC.

Hutchison v Firetto [1973] JPL 314.

Jeary v Chailey Rural District Council (1973) 26 P & CR 280, CA.

Jones (A E) v Jones (F W) [1977] 2 All ER 231, [1977] 1 WLR 438, CA.

Kammins Ballrooms Co Ltd v Zenith Investments (Torquay) Ltd [1970] 2 All ER 871, [1971] AC 850, HL.

a

LTSS Print and Supply Services Ltd v London Borough of Hackney [1976] 1 All ER 311, [1976] QB 663, CA.

Laker Airways Ltd v Department of Trade [1977] 2 All ER 182, [1977] QB 643, CA.

London Borough of Southwark v Williams, London Borough of Southwark v Anderson [1971] 2 All ER 175, [1971] Ch 734, CA.

Minister of Agriculture and Fisheries v Matthews [1949] 2 All ER 724, [1950] KB 148.   *b*

Norfolk County Council v Secretary of State for the Environment [1973] 3 All ER 673, [1973] 1 WLR 1400, DC.

O'Connor v Isaacs [1956] 2 All ER 417, [1956] 2 QB 288, CA.

Parker v Clark [1960] 1 All ER 93, [1960] 1 WLR 286.

Partridge v General Council of Medical Education and Registration of the United Kingdom (1890) 25 QBD 90, CA.   *c*

Prenn v Simmonds [1971] 3 All ER 237, [1971] 1 WLR 1381, HL.

Price v Strange [1977] 3 All ER 371, [1978] Ch 337, CA.

Punton v Ministry of Pensions and National Insurance (No 2) [1964] 1 All ER 448, [1964] 1 WLR 226, CA.

Pyx Granite Co Ltd v Ministry of Housing and Local Government [1959] 3 All ER 1, [1960] AC 260, HL.   *d*

R v Liverpool Corpn, ex parte Liverpool Taxi Fleet Operators' Association [1972] 2 All ER 589, [1972] 2 QB 299, CA.

R v London Borough of Hillingdon, ex parte Royco Homes Ltd [1974] 2 All ER 643, [1974] QB 720, DC.

R v Secretary of State for the Environment, ex parte Ostler [1976] 3 All ER 90, [1977] QB 122, CA.   *e*

R v Yeovil Corpn, ex parte Trustees of Elim Pentecostal Church, Yeovil (1971) 70 LGR 142, DC.

Redbridge London Borough Council v Perry (1976) 75 LGR 90, CA.

Rhyl Urban District Council v Rhyl Amusements Ltd [1959] 1 All ER 257, [1959] 1 WLR 465.

Roncarelli v Duplessis [1952] 1 DLR 680; rvsd [1956] Que QB 447; rvsd (1959) 16 DLR (2d) 689, Can SC.

Sarat Chunder Dey v Gopal Chunder Lala (1892) LR 19 Ind App 203.   *f*

Shaw v Applegate [1978] 1 All ER 123, [1977] 1 WLR 970, CA.

Shemara Ltd v Luton Corpn (1967) 18 P & CR 520.

Slough Estates Ltd v Slough Borough Council (No 2) [1969] 2 All ER 988, [1969] 2 Ch 305, CA; affd [1970] 2 All ER 216, [1971] AC 958, HL.

Smith v East Elloe Rural District Council [1956] 1 All ER 855, [1956] AC 736, HL.

Smith v King (1970) 21 P & CR 560.   *g*

Spartan Steel and Alloys Ltd v Martin & Co (Contractors) Ltd [1972] 3 All ER 557, [1973] QB 27, CA.

Square Meals Frozen Foods Ltd v Dunstable Corpn [1974] 1 All ER 441, [1974] 1 WLR 59, CA.

Tessier v Secretary of State for the Environment (1975) 74 LGR 279, 31 P & CR 161, DC.

Trentham (G Percy) v Gloucestershire County Council [1966] 1 All ER 701, [1966] 1 WLR 506, CA.   *h*

Whitelegg v Richards (1823) 2 B & C 45, 107 ER 300.

Willmott v Barber (1880) 15 Ch D 96.

Appeal

By a writ issued on 22nd December 1976 the plaintiffs, Western Fish Products Ltd, *j* brought an action against the defendants, Penwith District Council, claiming by their re-amended statement of claim (1)(a) a declaration that they were entitled to established user rights to class IX of the Town and Country Planning (Use Classes) Order 1972, SI 1972 No 1385, and/or to use of their property at Stable Hobba, Newlyn, Cornwall, as a factory for processing fish, warehousing and ancillary functions, (b) a declaration that

a
they were entitled to all necessary planning permissions for all necessary works for the factory, (2) an injunction restraining the defendants from enforcing a stop order and enforcement notices served by them, (3) an order that the defendants do forthwith withdraw the stop order and enforcement notices, and (4) damages in addition to or in lieu of such injunction. On 19th November 1977 Walton J dismissed their action and the plaintiffs appealed. By a respondent's notice the defendants contended that Walton J's judgment should be affirmed and further challenged his finding that the pre-existing

b
use was a class IX use. Shortly after the commencement of the hearing of the appeal the court allowed an application by the Department of the Environment to be added as an additional respondent to the appeal on an undertaking not to ask for costs. During the hearing of the appeal the statement of claim was further amended by leave of the court by substituting for head (1) of the prayer a claim (a) for a declaration that the plaintiffs were entitled to use rights enabling them to use the property as a factory for the purposes

c
of fresh fish preparation and fish oil and fishmeal manufacture and (b) a declaration that the plaintiffs were entitled to be treated as having planning permission in respect of the four applications which were before the defendants on 26th August 1976. The facts are set out in the judgment of the court.

Charles Sparrow QC and *Gavin Lightman* for the plaintiffs.

d
Bernard Marder QC and *Konrad Schiemann* for the defendant council.
Harry Woolf and *Jeremy Sullivan* for the Department of the Environment.

Cur adv vult

e
22nd May. **MEGAW LJ** delivered the following judgment of the court: The appeal is dismissed for the reasons now being handed down. This is an appeal by the plaintiffs, Western Fish Products Ltd, from the dismissal of their action by Walton J in a judgment delivered on 19th November 1977. The defendants are Penwith District Council. In this court, in circumstances to be mentioned hereafter, leave was given for the Department of the Environment to be joined as a respondent to the appeal. The action arose out of the refusal by the defendant council of planning permissions sought by the

f
plaintiffs in respect of a factory which they had planned to bring into production at Stable Hobba in Penwith, Cornwall, in the area for which the defendant council were the local planning authority; the refusals were followed by the issue of enforcement notices and stop notices.

Outline of issues

g
This appeal raises points which may, very broadly, be stated as follows.
(A) Did the defendant council make representations to the plaintiffs as to what the plaintiffs were permitted to do on the Stable Hobba site in such circumstances that the defendant council became estopped from making decisions contrary to the representations, and so that, the defendant council having made or purported to make such decisions, the plaintiffs are entitled to damages and other relief?

h
(B) Did the defendant council make any determination under s 53 or s 94 of the Town and Country Planning Act 1971, and, if so, what is the effect?
(C) Did the defendant council act in abuse of their statutory powers, or act negligently, so as to give the plaintiffs the right by action in a court of law to claim damages or any other remedy?
The hearing before Walton J lasted 19 days. The hearing of the appeal, which was

j
expedited by order of another division of the court, took 28 days. The issues which were raised were multifarious and in many respects interlocking, that is, the question whether a particular issue required decision for the purpose of the decision of the appeal and, if so, on what basis it had to be approached depended on the decision of another issue or issues. In the end it is not necessary for us to deal with all the points which were argued. As to a number of them which it is necessary or desirable for us to consider in

this judgment, we shall, without disrespect to counsel's arguments, express our conclusions on fact or law without elaboration, and without attempting to set out counsel's arguments in anything like the fullness with which they were helpfully presented.

We shall first set out, as briefly as is practicable, an outline of the events giving rise to the action. We shall then summarise the pleadings. It will be necessary thereafter to fill in further detail of facts in respect of some of the issues.

Outline of facts

The plaintiff company, the appellants in this court, are Western Fish Products Ltd. They are a member company of a group of companies called the Duncan Tucker Group. Mr John de Savary is chairman and managing director of the parent company, Duncan Tucker Ltd. He was also the chairman of the plaintiff company and their principal representative in their activities relevant to the present case.

The site at Stable Hobba, with the buildings of a disused factory on the site, were bought by or on behalf of the plaintiff company in April 1976. The use which the plaintiffs intended to make of the property was to establish and carry on there a business of manufacture of fish oil and fishmeal, the fishmeal for use as animal food, and of the preparation and packing of fresh fish for human consumption. This project involved the demolition of some of the old buildings, the repair or alteration of others of the old buildings and, in some instances, rebuilding where demolition became necessary. It also involved substantial new buildings, including a tall chimney. It also involved the installation of machinery. Arrangements for the intake of water and the outfall of effluent and sewage were also necessary, as well as provision for access of transport. It was contemplated that a very large sum of money would be spent, and a very large sum was in fact spent. It was hoped that it would be possible to start the new business by the late summer or autumn of 1976. It was hoped that it would prove very profitable. As the action was by consent limited to liability, any issue as to the amount of damages remaining over, the court has not been concerned with figures. But it would seem that the figure which the plaintiffs have indicated as being their potential claim for damages, including loss of anticipated profits, is very large indeed. A figure running into millions of pounds has been mentioned.

In addition to Mr de Savary, the person who was most concerned on behalf of the plaintiffs with the relevant events and discussions was Mr Smithies, an employee of a firm of architects who acted on behalf of the plaintiffs.

The action is concerned with the relationship between the plaintiff company and the defendants, Penwith District Council, in their capacity as the local planning authority. Their representatives who were primarily concerned with the relevant events are Mr Giddens, who was deputy to the chief planning officer, Mr Smith, and Mr Rowland, the solicitor to the defendant council.

The factory at Stable Hobba had been used in the past by its previous owners, Cornish Fish Fertilisers Ltd, for the production of fertiliser. From 1965 until 1972 the manufacture had been by a process of composting a mixture of fish and cocoa waste. In 1972 the composting process ceased. From then until 1975 different materials and different processes were used. Fishmeal was bought from outside and brought to the factory. There it was mixed with various chemicals. In 1975 the business had ceased to be profitable and it was closed down. The machinery was out of date. Many of the buildings were in need, at least, of substantial repair if they were to be used for any purpose. The staff had been paid off in April 1975, the plant and machinery had been removed and by the end of December 1975 the company had ceased trading. The factory premises were put on the market. They were bought by, or for, the plaintiff company in April 1976 for the purpose which we have mentioned.

At a meeting on 7th April 1976 between Mr de Savary and Mr Smithies, for the plaintiffs, and Mr Giddens representing the defendant council's chief planning officer,

Mr de Savary explained to Mr Giddens the intended project and asserted that there existed an 'established user right' as a result of the processes which had been carried on in the factory by its previous owners. Therefore, according to Mr de Savary, the plaintiffs were entitled to carry on their intended processes without the necessity for obtaining planning permission in respect of the intended use. Mr Giddens said that plaintiffs must satisfy him of their entitlement and should supply information in writing. Mr Giddens said that if the plaintiffs did so satisfy him, the defendant council would do everything that they could to assist the plaintiffs, and would not obstruct them.

The plaintiffs wrote two letters, on 8th and 17th April, supplying information. In reply, on 26th April, Mr Giddens, on behalf of the chief planning officer, wrote a letter as follows:

> 'Thank you for your letter of 17th April 1976. Details of the floor areas allocated for the various commercial uses on the site when last so used have now been supplied by your architects. These figures have been checked and it is agreed that these accurately reflect site conditions. Accordingly it is confirmed that the limits of the various component parts of the commercial undertaking as now existing appear to be established.'

That letter in conjunction with what had been said on 7th April, according to the plaintiffs' case, when acted on by the plaintiffs by the expenditure of money, constituted, or gave rise to, a 'proprietary estoppel'. That, coupled with the further estoppel, or other part of the estoppel, which is said to have arisen from Mr Giddens's verbal assurances about co-operation with the plaintiffs, is the principal basis of the plaintiffs' case. These estoppels were, it is contended, confirmed by the subsequent conduct of the defendant council, which, it is said, stood by while the plaintiffs to their knowledge continued to act on the faith of the representations. The plaintiffs proceeded with all possible expedition to renovate, and in some cases to rebuild, parts of the old buildings, to start the erection of some new buildings and to prepare to install expensive machinery from Norway. Some of these operations unquestionably required planning permission. The work was started and carried on, to the knowledge of the defendant council's representatives, without planning permission having been obtained.

On 6th July 1976 in a telephone call Mr Giddens asked Mr Smithies to submit outstanding planning applications and also an application for an established use certificate (under s 94 of the 1971 Act). Walton J found that in the course of that telephone conversation Mr Giddens told Mr Smithies that the application for the established use certificate was purely a formality. As a result Mr Smithies caused that application to be submitted, in addition to the planning applications.

By a letter of 7th July, following the telephone call, the chief planning officer, in a letter drafted by Mr Giddens, asked that the outstanding planning applications should be submitted as soon as possible, 'in order that your proposals could be viewed comprehensively' and 'in order that the necessary advertising and consultation procedures may be put in hand'. By its second paragraph the letter invited the submission of an application for the established use certificate.

Four planning applications in respect of various operations were submitted. (One of them was already before the committe on 5th July.) The application for the established use certificate was also submitted.

On 20th July 1976 Mr Rowland wrote to the plaintiffs' architects, Mr Smithies's firm, a letter which he began by saying: 'I regret to say that on the evidence which you have provided I am unable to recommend the Council to issue such a Certificate'. On 13th August he wrote again saying that the application for the established use certificate was rejected and giving warnings with regard to the work which had been carried out in breach of planning control. The plaintiffs were invited to submit 'a comprehensive planning application for the totality of the development proposed at Stable Hobba, including the change of use, by 30th August 1976'.

Between then and 26th August there was correspondence between the plaintiffs and the defendant council and there were a number of meetings. At a meeting of the special   *a* sub-committee which had been concerned with these matters since early July, Mr de Savary was given the opportunity to state his case and to express his views. He took advantage of the opportunity. A special meeting of the full council was held on 26th August. There is no justification for the suggestion, if it was intended to be made, that there was withheld from the sub-committee or from the full council any material documents or information, whether deliberately or by inadvertence.   *b*

At the full meeting of the council it was resolved that the four planning applications be refused, and that the application for the established use certificate be refused; and authorisation was given for the service of enforcement notices and stop notices 'in relation to the building works which are proceeding on site without planning permission'. The necessary consents of other authorities in respect of highway access, water provision and effluent disposal had not been given by the other authorities   *c* concerned by 26th August 1976. It was not until the following December that such consents were given.

On 1st and 3rd September 1976 enforcement notices and stop notices were issued. Notices of appeal to the Secretary of State by the plaintiffs against the enforcement notices were served, but they were one day out of time, and the Secretary of State had no jurisdiction to extend the time or entertain the appeals. The enforcement notices having   *d* taken effect, the stop notices ceased to have force. All work on the site stopped and has not since been resumed. The plaintiffs say they have suffered grave loss and that the defendant council are liable to them for that loss.

Discussions took place between the plaintiffs and the defendant council as to possible 'agreement under s 52 of the 1971 Act. Those discussions had not produced an agreement when the plaintiffs issued their writ in this action on 22nd December 1976.   *e*

The pleadings summarised

The reamended statement of claim is a lengthy document. We shall summarise it, and, where it seems convenient to do so at this stage, we shall express our conclusions on certain of the issues in the course of the summary.   *f*

Paragraph 3 of the reamended statement of claim asserts that the property, the Stable Hobba site, has 'at all material times enjoyed established right to class IX user and in particular established use right to user for a factory for processing fish and fishmeal'. The defendant council contended that from 1972 until the cessation of the use of the factory by the previous owners the use, and the use right, had been a class IV use. (The reference to classes of use is a reference to the classes specified in the schedule to the Town and   *g* Country Planning (Use Classes) Order 1972, SI 1972 No 1385 ('the Use Classes Order').) On that issue the answer depends on the effect to be given to the word 'putrescible' in relation to fishmeal. Walton J on that issue decided in favour of the plaintiffs' contention. His decision on it is challenged in the cross-notice of appeal. We agree with the learned judge. So the pre-existing use was a class IX use, which the judge rightly held had begun before 1st July 1948. The defendant council did not assert at the trial that   *h* there had been an abandonment of that use.

However, another issue was raised under the Use Classes Order. The plaintiffs' project involved the use of the site, not only for the fishmeal manufacture, but also for the preparation of fresh fish for human consumption. The site had not previously been used for that latter purpose. That use, by itself, would be a class IV use, not a class IX use. If, however, the fresh fish process was 'ordinarily incidental to and included in' the fishmeal   *j* process, the fresh fish process would, as a result of art 3(3) of the Use Classes Order, not constitute a separate, class IV, use. It would be treated as a part of the class IX use. The plaintiffs contended that that was the true view. The defendant council contended the contrary. Walton J accepted the defendant council's submission. We have no doubt that

he was right. There was no satisfactory evidence sufficient to support a different
conclusion on the meaning properly to be given to the words 'ordinarily incidental to
and included in'. It follows that, even though the parties may not have realised this, as
a matter of planning law planning permission was required for the plaintiffs' intended
development.

Paragraphs 4 to 24 of the reamended statement of claim set out the plaintiffs' version
(much of which, so far as it is an assertion of facts, was not challenged by the defendant
council at the trial) of the events and correspondence between 24th March and 26th
August 1976. Here arise various issues which we shall consider later, such as whether
any oral statements which were made could be treated as giving rise to an estoppel, and
if so, an estoppel as to what, whether the letter of 26th April 1976 from Mr Giddens
constitutes a relevant representation of anything, and if so, what, and whether the
plaintiffs did rely on any representation which may be contained, or which they thought
was contained, in that letter.

It is desirable that we should set out paras 23 and 24 of the statement of claim in
full. Paragraph 23 reads:

> 'At some date in or about July or August 1976 the Defendants determined to
> acquire and obtain from the Plaintiffs an agreement under Section 52 of the 1971
> Act in respect of the property, and for the purpose of compelling or inducing the
> Plaintiffs to enter into the same or for some other improper and/or unlawful reason
> determined to challenge the Plaintiffs' established use right and to refuse the
> Plaintiffs' outstanding application for planning permission.'

The defendant council asked the plaintiffs to give by way of further particulars each
fact on which the plaintiffs relied for the allegation 'some other improper and/or
unlawful reason'. The answer was: 'The best particulars which the Plaintiffs can give is
the absence of any proper or lawful reasons.' The defendant council say that that
allegation, so partcularised, is, at best, obscure; its defects are in no way remedied, they
say, by the further pleading in the reply to which we shall refer later.

Paragraph 24 reads (with a correction of date):

> 'On 6th July 1976, Mr. Giddens telephoned Mr. Smithies and told him (1) that all
> outstanding planning applications had to be got in immediately and (2) that the
> Defendants wished the Plaintiffs to apply for an Established Use Certificate, but that
> this was a pure formality. Pursuant to the request so made and made by a letter
> dated 7th July 1976, on 8th July 1976 the Plaintiffs submitted the outstanding
> planning applications and made application to the Defendants for an Established
> Use Certificate in respect of the property for the purposes of a factory for processing
> fish, warehousing, offices and ancillary functions, believing the same by reason of
> the foregoing to be a formality only.'

No application has been made at any stage to amend that paragraph. Yet that
paragraph, coupled with para 23, was relied on before us as founding the assertion, said
to have been accepted by Walton J in his judgment, that Mr Giddens, with the connivance
of Mr Smith, the chief planning officer, and Mr Rowland, the solicitor, was guilty of a
fraudulent misrepresentation.

Paragraph 25 set out the refusal on 26th August 1976 of the plaintiffs' application for
the established use certificate and the refusal of all the outstanding applications for
planning permission 'on the ground that the Plaintiffs did not have such established user
right'. It is averred that these refusals were made 'wrongfully and further or alternatively
for the unlawful reason pleaded in paragraph 23 hereof and/or in abuse of their
powers'. The paragraph then sets out the facts as to the issue of the enforcement notices
and stop notices 'preventing any continuation of the work thereby causing loss and
damage to the Plaintiffs'.

Further particulars were asked for on behalf of the defendant council of the allegations of 'wrongfully' and 'in abuse of their powers'. The plaintiffs were asked to 'state the nature of the case on which the Plaintiffs rely'. The particulars given add nothing.

Paragraph 26 formulates claims by the plaintiffs in two other ways. It reads:

'By reason of the facts and matters hereinbefore pleaded, the Defendants have or are to be taken to have granted all (if any) necessary planning permissions for the intended use of the property and the intended work and/or are estopped from denying that the property is entitled to such established user rights and planning permissions.'

This contains the pleading of two heads of the plaintiffs' claim. First, it is said that Mr Giddens's letter of 26th April was a statutory determination by the defendant council under s 53, or that it constituted a certificate under s 94 of the 1971 Act from which the defendant council may not resile, as to the existing user right enjoyed by the plaintiffs, which, the plaintiffs say, having regard to the terms of the letter of 26th April 1976 in its context, was a right, so far as use was concerned, to carry on the processes envisaged by their project. Second the defendant council are by reasons of the matters pleaded in paras 4 to 25, estopped from contending that the plaintiffs do not have such existing use rights, even if in law they do not have such rights. The estoppel alleged goes further. It is accepted that various planning permissions were required, including permission for some of the building works which had already been carried out by 26th August 1976; but, it is said, the assurances given by or on behalf of the defendant council as to the co-operation which they would give once the existing use right for the new project was satisfactorily established bound the defendant council so as at least severely to limit the lawful use by them of their statutory discretion to refuse such permissions.

Paragraph 27 of the reamended statement of claim contains an allegation of negligence. There is also an allegation of the existence of a duty on the part of the defendant council to exercise their powers 'in a bona fide and reasonable manner' and not to cause damage to the plaintiffs by misleading them as to the existence of any established rights. When it comes to the part of the paragraph where breach of the alleged duties is intended to be pleaded, there is no plea of bad faith or of any 'misleading'. The assertion is that the defendant council have acted 'contrary to the legitimate and reasonable expectations induced by them'.

The relevant paragraphs of the prayer, as to the relief claimed, as they stood when the action was heard by Walton J were:

'(1) (a) A declaration that they [the Plaintiffs] are entitled to established user rights to Class IX and/or to use of the property as a factory for processing fish, warehousing and ancillary functions. (b) A declaration that the Plaintiffs are entitled to all necessary planning permissions for all necessary works for the said factory.

'(2) An injunction restraining the Defendants from enforcing the said Stop Order and Enforcement Notices.

'(3) An order that the Defendants do forthwith withdraw the said Stop Order and Enforcement Notices.

'(4) Damages in addition (to) or in lieu of such Injunction.'

The terms of the declaration in head (1) of the prayer were amended by the leave of this court on the application of the plaintiffs at a late stage of the hearing before us. The defendant council objected to such leave being given. As amended, this part of the prayer reads:

'(1) (a) A declaration that the Plaintiffs are entitled to use rights enabling them to use the property as a factory for the purposes of fresh fish preparation and fish oil and fishmeal manufacture. (b) A declaration that the Plaintiffs are entitled to be treated as having planning permission in respect of the four applications which were before the Defendants on 26th August 1976.'

As to heads (2) and (3), it is, as we understand it, conceded (and, if it is not conceded, it must be the law) that the stop notices ceased to have effect when the enforcement notices, in the absence of valid notices of appeal against them to the Secretary of State, became effective. So there could be no question of the court making orders as to extinct stop notices.

One basis on which the claim for damages is founded is the alleged failure to give effect to the alleged 'proprietary estoppel'. Another ground is the alleged 'abuse of powers'. That claim is also based on the alleged negligence.

The amended defence included both denials of certain facts pleaded by the plaintiffs and assertions of other facts, none of which the defendant council sought to support at the trial by oral evidence called on their behalf. It was denied that any relevant representations to found an estoppel were made or were relied on, or that there could be any operative estoppel affecting the defendant council in the discharge of their duties, or that there was any abuse of powers or negligence on their part. By para 36 of the defence it was contended that the validity of the enforcement notices may not be questioned in these proceedings, having regard to s 243(1) of the 1971 Act. It was denied that damages are recoverable or that the court had jurisdiction to grant the relief sought in heads (2), (3) or (4) of the prayer in the statement of claim.

Early in the hearing before Walton J the plaintiffs by leave served a reply in respect of para 36 of the defence. They say that they do not question the validity of the enforcement notices as such, but assert a personal right against the defendant council to have them withdrawn or nullified. They deny the applicability of s 243(1) of the 1971 Act on the ground that the plaintiffs 'are concerned only with ground (a) of section 88(1) of the Act'. They contend by para (3) of the reply that the enforcement notices are 'a nullity' because (a) the defendant council acted in disregard of the plaintiffs' rights by estoppel, (b) the defendant council served the notices 'for a purpose other than planning control', namely to obtain an agreement in respect of the property as pleaded in para 23 of the reamended statement of claim, (c) the defendant council served such notices for a purpose 'to discipline the plaintiffs for their supposed intransigence'. (Mr Giddens, Mr Rowland and the chief planning officer (Mr Smith) were the persons to whom 'such purpose was ascribed'), (d) the defendants acted on 'the factual misapprehension that fishmeal was not a putrescible substance', (e) the defendants 'failed to honour in a fair way or at all the undertaking voluntarily given to the plaintiffs that they should have until 30th August to make an application as sought by the defendants. The plaintiffs do not hereby allege fraud or malice.'

No fraud or malice

[The court then considered the assertions of fraud and malice on the part of officers and agents of the council and on the part of the council themselves and found that fraud and malice were not pleaded and that the allegations were without foundation. His Lordship continued:]

In his concluding address, counsel for the plaintiffs referred to the fact that in some authorities and textbooks the phrase 'bad faith' is used to describe cases in which a statutory authority has, in what would ordinarily be called good faith, made a mistake as to the extent of its powers or, without any dishonesty or malice, acted in a way that was not permitted by its powers and in a way that infringed someone's legal rights. We regret that there should be that debasement of the currency of language. It is not fair to a public authority or its members or its servants that the public, not versed in the technical jargon, should read that a court has held them to be guilty of 'bad faith' when they have made an honest mistake. Nor is the use of the phrase in such a technical sense conducive to preserving the seriousness of a finding of bad faith where there has been dishonesty. But, if and in so far as 'bad faith' may properly be used to describe the acts of a public authority where, without dishonesty or malice, it has made errors of fact or

law, then it is open to the plaintiffs in this case to allege 'bad faith'. But let it be clear, in
that sense only.

The intervention of the Secretary of State for the Environment
    Counsel for the plaintiffs, in his opening address, divided his submissions, broadly,
into two main heads. The first was 'proprietary estoppel'; the second was 'the statutory
position'. But under these main heads there have been canvassed before us many issues
and sub-issues, extending, as it appeared at times in the argument, over almost the whole
field of administrative law, as well as other branches of the law. It was the likelihood of
the emergence of such matters which led to the application on the first day of the hearing
by counsel for the Department of the Environment that the department should be joined
as a respondent to the appeal. Through no fault of his or of his advisers, the department
had not been aware of this litigation until the last moment before the appeal was due to
be heard. Since it was apparent that there were likely to be arguments on matters
affecting, possibly in important respects, the powers and duties of the Secretary of State
in the functions entrusted to him by Parliament in the field of town and country
planning legislation, we granted the application that the department be joined as a
respondent to the appeal. It would obviously have been preferable, if it be right that the
department should be heard in the appeal, that it should have had the opportunity to
have been heard before Walton J. At present there appears to be no provision, either
administratively or by rules of court, to ensure that the department is apprised of
litigation such as the present case. We think consideration should be given by those
concerned to that question, so as to lessen the risk of a similar position arising in the
future. *Lever (Finance) Ltd v Westminster Corpn* [1970] 3 All ER 496, [1971] 1 QB 222,
which we shall have to consider later, is another instance where the intervention of the
department might have been of assistance.
    The issues relating to proprietary estoppel and in some respects also the issues as to the
statutory position have their foundation in events which took place between 24th March
and 26th April 1976. We shall therefore summarise the relevant events relating to that
period in more detail than has been done in our earlier brief outline.

Was the letter of 26th April a representation and, if so, of what?
    [The court then considered the evidence in more detail and considered whether the
letter of 26th April written by Mr Giddens to the plaintiffs was a representation and, if
so, of what. His Lordship continued:]
    We are unable to accept that a person familiar with the relevant facts known to both
the writer and the recipient of the letter, reading the letter with reasonable care, could
reasonably have read it as giving the plaintiffs confirmation that there was an existing use
right which would cover the uses contemplated by the plaintiffs' scheme without the
necessity for planning permission in respect of use. Whether Mr de Savary's belief that
the letter contained that confirmation was because he was so firmly convinced of the
'incontrovertible right' that he did not read the letter with due care, or whether it was for
some other reason, we are unable to see how, taking full account of the relevant
circumstances and of the context of the letter itself and of the letters and conversations
which had led up to it, the words 'Accordingly it is confirmed that the limits of the
component parts of the commercial undertaking as now existing appear to be established'
could reasonably be understood to be a confirmation of that which the plaintiffs allege it
did confirm.
    At the most the letter means that Mr Giddens on behalf of the defendant council was
satisfied that the buildings on the site had been used previously for the purposes written
on the plan and that the dimensions of the respective buildings used for those various
purposes were correctly shown. If and in so far as it could be interpreted as confirming
any use right, it was no more than a use right for the purposes for which the site had
previously been used.

It follows that no relevant estoppel, 'proprietary' or otherwise, can be founded on any
a representation contained in that letter.

Did the plaintiffs rely on such representation as they allege?
Even if it were to be construed as having the meaning which the plaintiffs placed on
it, it would still, in our judgment, not avail the plaintiffs as an estoppel. They did not act
on it to their detriment.
b   The judge, as we understand his judgment, has held that the plaintiffs, through Mr de
Savary, did rely on what he understood to be the representation. 'I think', says the judge,
'he acted on that assurance, by going ahead with his projects as a whole'; and again, 'He
regarded it as all important, and considered that, having obtained that confirmation, all
his troubles were over.' The defendant council submit that the judge did not intend so
to hold; but they also contend, by cross-notice, that, if he did so hold, he was wrong in
c so holding.
We regard the evidence provided by the contemporary documents and by Mr de
Savary himself in the witness box as being overwhelmingly in support of the conclusion
that, if the plaintiffs had not received the letter of 26th April, or had not construed it as
they did, they would have gone ahead with their planned project as they did go ahead
with it, both in timing and other respects. Mr de Savary's absolute conviction of the
d incontrovertible status of his user rights in respect of his planned operations was such
that he would not have been deterred by the absence of a confirmation from Mr
Giddens.
[The court then considered in more detail the evidence leading to the conclusion that
the plaintiffs acted on Mr de Savary's conviction that they had an existing use right rather
than any representation made by Mr Giddens. His Lordship continued:]

e
Proprietary estoppel. The law
Even if we had been satisfied that the defendant council through their officers had
represented to the plaintiffs that all they wanted to do on the Stable Hobba site could be
done because of the existing uses, planning permission being required only for new
buildings and structures, and that they had acted to their detriment to the knowledge of
f the defendant council because of their representations, their claim would still have failed.
There are two reasons for this: first, because they did not have the equitable right which
has come to be called proprietary estoppel; and, second, because in law the defendant
council could not be estopped from performing their statutory duties under the 1971
Act.
Counsel for the plaintiffs submitted that the equitable principle applied by this court
g in *Crabb v Arun District Council* [1975] 3 All ER 865, [1976] 1 Ch 179, should be applied
in this case. What was this principle? In our judgment what was decided in that case
was this: when A to the knowledge of B acts to his detriment in relation to his own land
in the expectation, encouraged by B, of acquiring a right over B's land, such expectation
arising from what B has said or done, the court will order B to grant A that right on such
terms as may be just. This principle is a development of what was stated in *Ramsden v
h Dyson* (1866) LR 1 HL 129 at 144, 168, 170, per Lord Cranworth LC, Lord Wensleydale
and Lord Kingsdown. There have been a number of reported cases since then in which
the principle enunciated in *Ramsden v Dyson* has been applied (see, for example, *Plimmer
v Wellington Corpn* (1884) 9 App Cases 699 and *Inwards v Baker* [1965] 1 All ER 446,
[1965] 2 QB 29). In all these cases the court was concerned with the creation by estoppel
of rights and interests in or over land. In the course of argument counsel for the
j plaintiffs was asked if he had found any cases of the court enforcing a right created by
estoppel other than one in or over land. He said he had, namely *Evenden v Guildford City
Association Football Club Ltd* [1975] 3 All ER 269, [1975] QB 917 and *Hammersley v Baron
de Biel* (1845) 12 Cl & Fin 45, 8 ER 312. In our judgment the first of these cases was not
one in which the court had enforced a right: it was one of promissory estoppel arising out

of a contract. Employers were estopped from relying on a defence which was inconsistent
with what they had agreed with their employee when he entered their service.

The second case (which is not mentioned in the current editions of either Snell's
Principles of Equity (27th Edn, 1973) or Spencer Bower and Turner on Estoppel by
Representation (3rd Edn, 1977), both commenting on proprietary estoppel) was a
decision of the House of Lords on appeal from an order of Lord Cottenham LC affirming
a decree of Lord Langdale MR (sub nom *De Biel v Thomson* (1841) 3 Beav 469, 49 ER
184). In the course of his judgment Lord Cottenham LC had said 12 Cl & Fin 61n, 8 ER
1320):

> 'A representation made by one party for the purpose of influencing the conduct
> of the other party, and acted on by him will in general be sufficient to entitle him
> to the assistance of this Court for the purpose of realizing such representation.'

The House of Lords affirmed Lord Cottenham LC's order. This means, submitted
counsel for the plaintiffs, that the House accepted what Lord Cottenham LC had said and
that which he had said should be applied to this case with the same kind of result, viz that
this court should adjudge that the plaintiffs had an equitable right to receive a money
payment from the defendant council. The House of Lords decided as they did because
they were satisfied that the plaintiff's father, B, had agreed with one T that he would
marry T's daughter and provide a jointure for her in consideration of T's undertaking to
leave a sum of £10,000 in his will to his daughter to be settled on her and her children.
B married T's daughter and provided her with a jointure, but T did not leave his
daughter in his will the £10,000 which he had promised. B's son asked the Court of
Chancery to order T's executors to pay the money. Running through the case at all its
stages was a submission that there never had been more than 'a rough sketch of the
proposals expressly subject to revision' (see 12 Cl & Fin 45 at 62–63, 8 ER 1312 at
1321). The House of Lords found against this submission, adjudging that there had been
a binding agreement. Lord Lyndhurst, who had succeeded Lord Cottenham as Lord
Chancellor, said (12 Cl & Fin 45 at 78–79, 8 ER 1312 at 1327):

> 'But the principle of law, at least of equity, is this—that if a party holds out
> inducements to another to celebrate a marriage, and holds them out deliberately
> and plainly, and the other party consents, and celebrates the marriage in consequence
> of them, if he had good reason to expect that it was intended that he should have the
> benefit of the proposal which was so held out, a Court of Equity will take care that
> he is not disappointed, and will give effect to the proposal. This is stated as a part of
> the arrangement; it is stated as the proposal.'

Lord Brougham, in his speech, made it clear that he based his concurring opinion on
the existence of a binding agreement; and Lord Campbell in his speech set out what Lord
Cottenham LC had said and added (12 Cl & Fin 45 at 88, 8 ER 1312 at 1331): 'Of course
Lord Cottenham is here speaking of negotiations in reference to marriage . . .' In our
judgment this case had nothing to do with proprietary estoppel; it was concerned with
the enforcement in equity of a binding agreement made by a father in contemplation of
his daughter's marriage.

We know of no case, and none has been cited to us, in which the principle set out in
Ramsden v Dyson and *Crabb v Arun District Council* has been applied otherwise than to
rights and interests created in and over land. It may extend to other forms of property:
see per Lord Denning MR in *Moorgate Mercantile Co Ltd v Twitchings* [1975] 3 All ER 314
at 323–324, [1976] QB 225 at 242. In our judgment there is no good reason for
extending the principle further. As Harman LJ pointed out in *Campbell Discount Co Ltd
v Bridge* [1961] 2 All ER 97 at 103, [1961] 1 QB 445 at 459, the system of equity has
become a very precise one. The creation of new rights and remedies is a matter for
Parliament, not the judges.

In his reply counsel for the plaintiffs seemed to recognise that the reported cases did
put limits to the application of the so-called concept of proprietary estoppel. He

submitted that the plaintiffs' case was within that concept because what the defendant
a council, by their officers, had represented had, to their knowledge, caused the plaintiffs
to spend money on or in connection with their own land which they would not
otherwise have spent. On their own case they have spent money in order to take
advantage of existing rights over their own land which the defendant council by their
officers had confirmed they possessed. There was no question of their acquiring any
rights in relation to any other person's land, which is what proprietary estoppel is
b concerned with.

The second reason why the plaintiffs' own case cannot succeed is this. The defendant
council's officers, even when acting within the apparent scope of their authority, could
not do what the 1971 Act required the defendant council to do; and if their officers did
or said anything which purported to determine in advance what the defendant council
themselves would have to determine in pursuance of their statutory duties, they would
c not be inhibited from doing what they had to do. An estoppel cannot be raised to
prevent the exercise of a statutory discretion or to prevent or excuse the performance of
a statutory duty (see Spencer Bower and Turner on Estoppel by Representation (3rd Edn,
1977, p 141) and the cases there cited). The application of this principle can be illustrated
on the facts of this case: under s 29 of the 1971 Act the defendant council as the planning
authority had to determine applications for planning permission, and when doing so had
d to have regard to the provision of the development plan and 'to any other material
considerations'. The plaintiffs made an application for planning permission to erect a tall
chimney on the site. When considering this application the defendant council had to
'take into account any representations relating to that application' which were received
by them following the publishing and posting of notices: see ss 26 and 29(2). This
requirement was in the interests of the public generally. If any representations made by
e the defendant council's officers before the publication or posting of notices bound the
council to act in a particular way, the statutory provision which gave the public
opportunities of making representations would have been thwarted and the defendant
council would have been dispensed from their statutory obligation of taking into account
any representation made to them. The officers were appointed by the defendant council
but the council's members were elected by the inhabitants of their area. Parliament by
f the 1971 Act entrusted the defendant council, acting through their elected members, not
their officers, to perform various statutory duties. If their officers were allowed to
determine that which Parliament had enacted the defendant council should determine
there would be no need for elected members to consider planning applications. This
cannot be. Under s 101(1) of the Local Government Act 1972 (which repealed s 4 of the
1971 Act, which re-enacted in an amended form s 64 of the Town and Country Planning
g Act 1968), a local authority may arrange for the discharge of any of their functions by an
officer of the authority. This has to be done formally by the authority acting as such. In
this case the defendant council issued standing orders authorising designated officers to
perform specified functions including those arising under ss 53 and 94 of the 1971 Act.
Their officers had no authority to make any other determinations under the 1971 Act.
We can see no reason why Mr de Savary, acting on behalf of the plaintiffs, and having
h available the advice of lawyers and architects, should have assumed, if he ever did, that
Mr Giddens could bind the defendant council generally by anything he wrote or said.

Counsel for the plaintiffs submitted that, notwithstanding the general principle that
a statutory body could not be estopped from performing its statutory duties, there are
exceptions recognised by this court. This case, he asserted, came within the exceptions.

There seem to be two kinds of exceptions. If a planning authority, acting as such,
j delegates to its officers powers to determine specific questions, such as applications under
ss 53 and 94 of the 1971 Act, any decisions they make cannot be revoked. This kind of
estoppel, if it be estoppel at all, is akin to res judicata. Counsel for the Department of the
Environment accepted that there was this exception, as did counsel for the defendant
council in his final submissions. *Lever (Finance) Ltd v Westminster Corpn* [1970] 3 All ER
496, [1971] 1 QB 222 can, we think, be considered as an application of this exception.

The trial judge had found that it was a common practice amongst planning authorities, including the defendants, for planning officers to sanction immaterial modifications to plans sent with successful applications for planning permission. This is what one of the defendants' planning officers thought he was doing when he agreed with the plaintiffs' architect that they could make a modification to the plans of some houses which were being errected; but Lord Denning MR thought that what he had agreed to was not an immaterial modification: it was a material one. He should have told the plaintiffs that they required planning permission to make it. When the defendants found out what had happened as a result of complaints made by members of the public who were likely to be affected by the modification, they suggested to the plaintiffs that they should apply for planning permission. They did; and their application was refused. This court affirmed the declaration made by the trial judge that there was a valid planning permission for the modification. The members of this court gave different reasons for finding as they did. Sachs LJ stated that the combined effect of the past practice, taken with the powers of delegation under s 64 of the 1968 Act, was that the oral agreement made between the plaintiffs' architect and the defendants' planning officer operated as if all the formalities of s 43 of the Town and Country Planning Act 1962 (now s 53 of the 1971 Act) had been complied with. The other members of the court (Lord Denning MR and Megaw LJ) made no mention of this reasoning. It follows that it was not the ratio decidendi of the judgment. We do not agree with it, as appears later in this judgment. Lord Denning MR rested his judgment on estoppel and delegation. After referring to the authorities setting out the general rule that planning authorities cannot be estopped from doing their public duty, he went on as follows ([1970] 3 All ER 496 at 500, [1971] 1 QB 222 at 230):

> 'But those statements must now be taken with considerable reserve. There are many matters which public authorities can now delegate to their officers. If an officer, acting within the scope of his ostensible authority, makes a representation on which another acts, then a public authority may be bound by it, just as much as a private concern would be.'

He went on to refer by way of illustration to *Wells v Minister of Housing and Local Government* [1967] 2 All ER 1041, [1967] 1 WLR 1000, which was concerned with what this court adjudged to be an informal application made under s 43 of the 1962 Act. It is pertinent to note too that Lord Denning MR used the words 'may be bound'. Megaw LJ said that he agreed with the reasons for judgment given by Lord Denning MR. This case, of course, binds us unless there is in the reasoning an element which can be said to be 'per incuriam'. In our judgment it is not an authority for the proposition that every representation made by a planning officer within his ostensible authority binds the planning authority which employs him. For an estoppel to arise there must be some evidence justifying the person dealing with the planning officer for thinking that what the officer said would bind the planning authority. Holding an office, however senior, cannot, in our judgment, be enough by itself. In the *Lever (Finance) Ltd* case there was evidence of a widespread practice amongst planning authorities of allowing their planning officers to make immaterial modifications to the plans produced when planning permission was given. Lever (Finance) Ltd's architect presumably knew of this practice and was entitled to assume that the practice had been authorised by the planning authorities in whose areas it was followed. The need for some evidence of delegation of authority can be illustrated in this way. Had Lever (Finance) Ltd's architect produced plans showing material and substantial modifications to the planning permission for a large development in Piccadilly Circus already granted, he could not sensibly have assumed that the planning officer with whom he was dealing had authority to approve the proposed modifications without putting them before the planning authority. Whether anyone dealing with a planning officer can safely assume that the officer can bind his authority by anything he says must depend on all the circumstances. In the

Lever (Finance) Ltd case [1970] 3 All ER 496 at 501, [1971] 1 QB 222 at 231 Lord Denning
a MR said: 'Any person dealing with them [ie officers of a planning authority] is entitled
to assume that all necessary resolutions have been passed.' This statement was not
necessary for the conclusion he had reached and purported to be an addendum. We
consider it to be obiter; with all respect, it stated the law too widely.

In this case there was no evidence of any relevant delegations of authority save in
relation to applications under ss 53 and 94. We deal later in this judgment with the
b plaintiffs' submissions about the operation of those sections.

We can deal with the second exception shortly. If a planning authority waives a
procedural requirement relating to any application made to it for the exercise of its
statutory powers, it may be estopped from relying on lack of formality. Much, however,
will turn on the construction of any statutory provisions setting out what the procedure
is to be. *Wells v Minister of Housing and Local Government* is an example of the
c exception. Both counsel for the Department of the Environment and counsel for the
defendant council submitted that this case was wrongly decided. Counsel for the
Department of the Environment said that the dissenting judgment of Russell LJ was to
be preferred and both he and counsel for the defendant council reserved the right to
argue this point elsewhere. Save in relation to the plaintiffs' submissions as to the
operation of ss 53 and 94 on the facts of this case, this exception cannot have any
d application to this case.

The extension of the concept of estoppel beyond these two exceptions, in our
judgment, would not be justified. A further extension would erode the general principle
as set out in a long line of cases of which the decision of the Privy Council in *Maritime
Electric Co Ltd v General Dairies Ltd* [1937] 1 All ER 748, [1937] AC 610 and the judgment
of the Divisional Court in *Southend-on-Sea Corpn v Hodgson (Wickford) Ltd* [1961] 2 All ER
e 46, [1962] 1 QB 416 are notable examples. Parliament has given those who are aggrieved
by refusals of planning permission or the serving of enforcement notices a right of appeal
to the Secretary of State: see ss 36 and 88 of the 1971 Act. He can hear evidence as to the
merits and take into account policy considerations. The courts can do neither. The
application of the concept of estoppel because of what a planning officer had represented
could result in a court adjudging that a planning authority was bound to allow a
f development which flouted its planning policy, with which the courts are not concerned.

There is another objection to any extension of the concept of estoppel which is
illustrated by the facts of the *Lever (Finance) Ltd* case. If the modifications which were
permitted by the planning officer in that case had been properly to be regarded as
immaterial, no problem of general principle would arise. But the court regarded itself
as competent to decide as to the materiality and, despite the submission to the contrary
by the successful plaintiffs, held that the modifications were material. On what basis of
g evidence or judicial notice the court reached that conclusion, we need not stay to
consider. We assume both that the court had jurisdiction to decide that question, and
that, on the facts of that case, their decision as to materiality was right. But then comes
the difficulty, and the real danger of injustice. To permit the estoppel no doubt avoided
an injustice to the plaintiffs. But it also may fairly be regarded as having caused an
h injustice to one or more members of the public, the owners of adjacent houses who
would be adversely affected by this wrong and careless decision of the planning officer
that the modifications were not material. Yet they were not, and it would seem could
not, be heard. How, in their absence, could the court balance the respective injustices
according as the court did or did not hold that there was an estoppel in favour of the
plaintiffs? What 'equity' is there in holding, if such be the effect of the decision, that the
i potential injustice to a third party, as a result of the granting of the estoppel is
irrelevant? At least it can be said that the less frequently this situation arises the better
for justice.

In *Brooks and Burton Ltd v Secretary of State for the Environment* (1976) 75 LGR 285 at 296
Lord Widgery CJ adverted to extending the concept of estoppel. He said:

'There has been some advance in recent years of this doctrine of estoppel as applied to local authorities through their officers, and the most advanced case is the one referred to by the inspector, namely *Lever Finance Ltd.* v. *Westminster (City) London Borough Council.* I do not propose to read it. It no doubt is correct on its facts, but I would deprecate any attempt to expand this doctrine because it seems to me, as I said a few minutes ago, extremely important that local government officers should feel free to help applicants who come and ask them questions without all the time having the shadow of estoppel hanging over them and without the possibility of their immobilising their authorities by some careless remark which produces such an estoppel.'

We agree with what he said.

The statutory position

We turn now to 'the statutory position'. Counsel for the plaintiffs submits that besides their claims based on estoppel the plaintiffs have rights and remedies arising from the planning legislation and the decisions of the courts as to the exercise by statutory authorities of their powers and duties. The consideration of these rights and remedies overlaps at one point with the estoppel claim, but the plaintiffs could succeed on the 'statutory position' even if they fail on estoppel. The essence of this part of the plaintiffs' case is that the decisions made by the defendant council on 26th August were invalid, a 'nullity', an 'abuse of their powers' and 'unlawful'. We have already said that there was no fraud or malice on the part of the defendant council or their officers. In this part of the case, therefore, the phrase 'abuse of powers' means no more than that the defendant council have mistakenly acted in a way which was not permitted by their powers.

Sections 53 and 94 of the 1971 Act

In addition or in the alternative to their contention that the letter of 26th April is the foundation of an estoppel, the plaintiffs contend that it was a 'determination' under s 53 of the 1971 Act, or alternatively an 'established use certificate' under s 94 of that Act. Counsel for the defendant council accepts that if it was such a determination or certificate the council would be bound by it; under their standing orders the power to make such decisions is delegated to their officers.

Section 53(1) provides as follows:

'If any person who proposes to carry out any operations on land, or to make any change in the use of land, wishes to have it determined whether the carrying out of those operations, or the making of that change, would constitute or involve development of the land, and, if so, whether an application for planning permission in respect thereof is required under this Part of this Act, having regard to the provisions of the development order, he may, either as part of an application for planning permission, or without any such application, apply to the local planning authority to determine that question.'

Section 53(2) applies in relation to applications and determinations under this section a number of other provisions of the 1971 Act, relating to development orders (ss 24 and 31(1)), determinations by local planning authorities (s 29(1)), the power of the Secretary of State to give directions to local planning authorities (s 31(1)), the keeping of registers of applications which are open for inspection by the public (s 34(1) and (3)), the powers of the Secretary of State to call in applications (s 35) and the right of appeal to the Secretary of State (ss 35 and 36).

The Town and Country Planning General Development Order 1973, SI 1973 No 31 (which in these respects is substantially reproduced in the Town and Country Planning General Development Order 1977, SI 1977 No 289), makes provision for the procedure to be followed on s 53 applications and determinations. Articles 6(2) and 7(2), (3) and (4)

provide for the steps to be taken, the provision in each case being governed by the word
a 'shall'.

It is pleaded in para 3 of the amended defence that on 24th March 1976 Mr Giddens invited Mr Bushell, the managing director of the plaintiff company, to submit an application under s 53, but neither Mr Giddens nor Mr Bushell was called and there was no other evidence of such an invitation. We think that paras 5 and 9 of the statement of claim can be treated as alleging that the letters of 8th and 26th April were an application
b and determination under s 53, but there is no claim for any declaration relating to that section. The judge did not deal with this in his judgment and the point is not raised in the notice of appeal. However, we allowed it to be argued. Counsel for the plaintiffs does not contend that the letter of 26th April amounted to a determination that no planning permission was required in respect of the plaintiffs' building operations, but he contends that it was a determination either that the user contemplated by the plaintiffs'
c project did not constitute development or that no planning permission was required for such development.

It seems to us that s 53(2) of the 1971 Act and arts 6(2) and 7(2), (3) and (4) of the 1973 order contemplate a considerable degree of formality in applications and determinations under s 53. But counsel for the plaintiffs relied on the decision of the majority of this court in *Wells v Minister of Housing and Local Government* [1967] 2 All ER 1041, [1967] 1
d WLR 1000 and on the judgment of Sachs LJ in *Lever (Finance) Ltd v Westminster Corpn* [1970] 3 All ER 496, [1971] 1 QB 222 as establishing that no particular formalities are required.

In the *Wells* case the plaintiffs had applied for planning permission for the erection of a concrete batching plant 27'6" in height. The council engineer and surveyor replied by letter saying: 'I am now instructed to inform you that the works proposed can be
e regarded as "permitted development" under Class VIII of the . . . Development Order . . . and it is therefore not proposed to take any further action on your application.' The plaintiffs then changed their minds and decided to build a plant 48' high. Their architect assumed that this new proposal would be covered by the council's letter in respect of the 27'6" plant and applied for byelaw consent in respect of the 48' plant. The council granted byelaw consent on a form which contained the words: 'No action should be
f taken hereunder till the approval of the town planning and licensing authority have been obtained' (sic); these words had been struck out but were still legible. The majority of the court (Lord Denning MR and Davies LJ, Russell LJ dissenting) held that there had been a valid application and determination under s 43 of the 1962 Act (now s 53) that planning permission was not required for the 27'6" plant, but the court held unanimously that there had been no application for planning permission, nor any application or
g determination under s 43 in respect of the 48' plant.

In the *Lever (Finance) Ltd* case (the facts of which have already been stated) Sachs LJ took the view that what had happened could and should be treated as a valid application and determination under s 43 of the 1962 Act that no further planning permission was needed for the change in the position of the house (see [1970] 3 All ER 496 at 503–504, [1971] 1 QB 222 at 234). But the majority of the court (Lord Denning MR and Megaw
h LJ) put their decision on different grounds, which have been considered earlier in this judgment.

This court is, of course, bound by the ratio of the decision of the majority in the *Wells* case, though if we may respectfully say so we find the dissenting judgment of Russell LJ very powerful. In our view, the ratio on which Lord Denning MR and Davies LJ were agreed was that a formal written application for a determination under s 43 (now s 53)
j was not necessary and that an application for planning permission impliedly contains an invitation to determine under s 43 that planning permission is not required (see [1967] 2 All ER 1041 at 1045, 1046, [1967] 1 WLR 1000 at 1008, 1010 per Lord Denning MR and Davies LJ). But all three members of the court held that there was no application or determination under s 43 in respect of the 48' plant, Lord Denning MR saying ([1967] 2 All ER 1041 at 1045, [1967] 1 WLR 1000 at 1008):

'Ready as I am to waive irregularities and procedural defects, I think that to satisfy s. 43 there must be at least a positive statement in writing by or on behalf of the planning authority that no planning permission is necessary.'

If we are right in our understanding of the ratio of the majority in the *Wells* case, it does not bind us to hold that there was in the present case an application under s 53: there was in April 1976 no application for planning permission. Although the judgment of Sachs LJ in the *Lever (Finance) Ltd* case would, we think, greatly extend beyond the *Wells* case the permitted degree of informality in applications and determinations under s 53, it is, as we have already said, not binding on this court. In our judgment, the decision of the majority in the *Wells* case as to the 27'6" plant should not be extended beyond cases in which there has been an application for planning permission; we feel supported in this view by the unanimous decision as to the 48' plant.

But even if this is wrong, and some communications from a proposed developer to a planning authority other than an application for planning permission can constitute an application under s 53, we should find it impossible to hold as a matter of construction of the letters of 8th and 26th April that they constituted an application or a determination under s 53. As to the latter, we refer again to what Lord Denning MR said in the *Wells* case [1967] 2 All ER 1041 at 1045, [1967] 1 WLR 1000 at 1008, which we have already quoted.

We also reject the alternative contention that the letter of 26th April was an established use certificate under s 94 of the 1971 Act. This, too, is not pleaded in or raised in the notice of appeal. Mr de Savary emphatically (indeed explosively) denied the allegations in the amended defence that the plaintiffs had been asked by Mr Giddens in April and May to apply for a s 94 certificate (which he called 'the second great lie'); he said that if he had been asked then he would have refused, and would have refused in July if he had not been told that it was a pure formality. But even if he did not intend that his letter of 8th April should be an application under s 94 we will assume that in law it could be capable of being such an application. The purpose and effect of a s 94 certificate is that it is conclusive evidence 'as respects any matters stated therein' for the purposes of an appeal to the Secretary of State against an enforcement notice served in respect of any land to which it relates (s 94(7)); the benefit of the certificate runs with the land. One would therefore expect that it would be required to be a formal document, and Sch 14 to the 1971 Act and art 18 of the Town and Country Planning General Development Order 1973 contain provisions to that effect as to the application and the certificate. We do not think we need refer to them in detail. But they include provisions that an application 'shall not be entertained' unless it is accompanied by a certificate containing the prescribed particulars (see para 3(1) of Sch 14 and art 18(2)), which the letter of 26th April was not, and that established use certificates 'shall be issued' in the form set out in Part II of Sch 6 to the 1973 order, which of course does not bear the slightest resemblance to the letter of 26th April. Even if these formal defects are not in themselves a complete answer to this contention, as in our view they are, we think it is impossible to construe the letter of 26th April as a certificate under s 94. We cannot see that it is capable of being conclusive evidence of anything.

Existing use rights

But even if the letter of 26th April was not a determination under s 53 or an established use certificate under s 94 the plaintiffs were entitled to the benefit of whatever were in fact and in law the existing use rights in respect of the Stable Hobba site. We accept the definition of 'existing use right' formulated by counsel for the defendant council which counsel for the plaintiffs said he did not contest: the right to continue using land or buildings immune from enforcement action, whether the use is lawful or unlawful, but subject to abrogation on payment of compensation, and including no right to carry out development, whether by operations or change of use (except as stated below).

Although no industrial operations had been carried on at the site for a year before the
a plaintiffs bought it, they were entitled to resume the use which Cornish Fish Fertilisers
Ltd had made of it; Walton J found that there was insufficient evidence of abandonment,
and counsel for the defendant council accepts this finding.

We have already stated the facts as to the use by Cornish Fish Fertilisers Ltd and said
that we agree with Walton J's conclusions that it was a class IX use and that it did not
include the plaintiffs' proposed fresh fish process, which would have been a class IV use.

b This existing use entitled the plaintiffs to various rights. As to use, they could resume
the use made of the site by Cornish Fish Fertilisers Ltd, or change that use to another use
within class IX, or intensify it within that class to an extent which would otherwise
amount to a change of use. As to building or other 'operations', they were only entitled
to do what is permitted by s 22(2)(a) of the 1971 Act or by art 3 of, and Sch 1 to, the 1973
order, which only allow minor works of maintenance, improvement or alteration.
c There is no doubt that the carrying out of the plaintiffs' project required 'operations',
including new buildings, amounting to 'development' going beyond what is so
permitted, and for which planning permission was required.

On the second day of the hearing before this court counsel for the plaintiffs accepted
that nobody has a right to a planning permission, but said that what a person does have
is a right to a proper adjudication. He said that in a case where there is an existing use
d right this right to a proper adjudication can produce an effect 'approximating' to a right
to planning permission: 'The local planning authority must decide responsibly and for
good reason, in short, lawfully.' He said that where there is an application for planning
permission for a building to exploit an existing use the planning authority is not entitled
to refuse it because it objects to the use; it is only entitled to object to the building on
matters of detail. He suggested that the position was analogous to a grant of outline
e planning permission, leaving only matters of detail to be considered. He said that a
planning authority is not entitled to revoke or nullify an existing use right without
compensation by saying 'No' to every one of a series of detailed designs. He repeated that
'in the end the applicant will have something approximating to a right to permission'.
In his reply, he said that on a true analysis an existing use right is a right to use the land
in question for a building of whatever kind is being used on the land in the particular
f case, in this case for a factory for the manufacture of manure within class IX. The
existing use right therefore includes a right to have a building (in this case a factory), and
the local planning authority is bound to give permission for the same sort of building (e g
a house or a factory), subject only to matters of detail. An existing use right is thus
analogous to an outline planning permission. He said that the plaintiffs' four applications
for planning permission were refused only on the ground of use, that it should be
g inferred that the council had no objection to the buildings as such, and that 'there was in
truth an approval of the four applications which the court can recognise'.

Counsel for the defendant council described this submission as a 'fundamental
misconception'. Counsel for the Department of Environment, too, invited us to reject
it. It is clear that Mr de Savary was firmly convinced that it was right. As Walton J said:

h
> 'Having seen Mr de Savary in the witness box, it is quite evident that he was from
> first to last under the firm impression that once he had obtained confirmation of the
> existing use right nothing else mattered, that once he had obtained clearance of class
> IX rights he was entitled to all planning permissions necessary to enable him to
> exploit that right, and that they could not be withheld save perhaps on unimportant
> matters such as siting and finishes.'

In our judgment the submission of counsel for the plaintiffs is wrong. We think it
would be surprising if it was right. In whichever 'species' described by counsel for the
defendant council an existing use right has its origin, it has been begun without the grant
of planning permission, so that the planning authority has never had the opportunity of
considering its merits or demerits from a planning point of view. Its effect is to confer

a 'status of unenforceability'; although it is called a 'right' it is really an immunity, a protection against enforcement action to stop it. In our view, it does not confer any positive rights in relation to an application for permission for development which needs such permission. We reject the analysis of counsel for the plaintiffs in his reply of the nature of such rights (which seems to ignore the fundamental distinction between development by 'use' and development by 'operations') and his analogy with the grant of an outline planning permission for 'operations'. The 'right' is to use an existing building for a particular purpose, not to have another building for that use. An existing use is obviously one of the 'material considerations' to which a planning authority is required by s 29(1) of the 1971 Act to have regard when considering an application for permission for buildings, and it may be a very important one. The planning authority must take into account all the relevant considerations, including any existing use, but it is not bound to treat the existing use as decisive of an application for permission for buildings to exploit that use. The authority is, we think, entitled to say in its discretion: 'We cannot stop this use (except with compensation), but on planning considerations we do not like it and we do not wish to encourage or extend it either in nature or in duration; the applicant can go on exercising it in his existing buildings, with the benefit of the rights given to him by s 22(2)(a) and the 1973 order, but we are not going to permit him to put up any new buildings.' Suppose the applicant has an existing class IX use. He is entitled (in the sense that he is immune from enforcement action to stop it) to change to another, more objectionable, class IX use or to intensify his present use to an extent which would otherwise constitute development, but to enable him to do so he needs new buildings. We can see nothing wrong in a planning authority refusing permission for the new buildings because they object (eg on amenity grounds) to the proposed change of use or intensification which the applicant is entitled to make but for which the new buildings are necessary or desirable. The applicant can go on using his old buildings, and if they get into such a state that they can no longer be patched up and planning permission is still refused, he may be entitled to exercise the rights given by Part IX of the 1971 Act (purchase notices).

[The court then considered whether the defendant council's decision of 26th August 1976 was an abuse of the council's powers and therefore a nullity and held on the facts that the council were entitled to decide on the plaintiffs' applications in the way they did and had not abused their powers in doing so. His Lordship continued:]

Remaining questions

In view of our conclusions on the points with which we have already dealt, several other questions which were fully argued do not arise: the remedies which should have been granted if we had decided otherwise on some or all of these points; the effect of ss 88 and 243 of the 1971 Act; and the effect of s 177. These points, and especially the arguments of counsel for the Department of the Environment on them, raise important and difficult questions, and we think it better to leave decisions on them until they do arise in some other case rather than to express opinions about them in the form of obiter dicta.

We can deal very shortly with the plaintiffs' claims for damages based on 'misfeasance' or 'abuse of powers', negligence or the 'innominate tort'.

We have held that there was no 'abuse of powers' by the defendant council in the only sense in which that phrase can be used in this case. Further, we are very far from satisfied that 'abuse of powers' would give rise to a cause of action in the absence of fraud or malice.

As to negligence, it was never made clear to us what was the negligence alleged; para 27 of the reamended statement of claim seems to us hopelessly vague and obscure. In our judgment, there is no justification for any claim in negligence.

The so-called 'innominate tort' is said to be the causing of economic damage by

unlawful means. In the present case, this head of claim seems to us indistinguishable
a from the claim based on 'abuse of powers'.
Accordingly, we dismiss the appeal.

Appeal dismissed.

Solicitors: *Lewis, Lewis & Co* (for the plaintiffs); *Sharpe, Pritchard & Co*, agents for *Lyn*
b Rowland, Penzance (for the defendant council); *Treasury Solicitor.*

Mary Rose Plummer   Barrister.

Rootkin v Kent County Council

COURT OF APPEAL, CIVIL DIVISION
LAWTON, EVELEIGH LJJ AND SIR STANLEY REES
24th, 25th APRIL 1980

Education – Local education authority – Provision of transport for pupils – Transport to and
from school – Discretion – Exercise of discretion to pay fares of pupil living more than three miles
d from school – Council paying pupil's fares in belief that he lived more than three miles from school
– Pupil subsequently found to be living nearer than three miles from school – Whether authority
entitled to change decision and refuse to pay fares – Education Act 1944, ss 39(2), 55(2).

Estoppel – Statutory body – Local education authority – Exercise of discretion – Whether local
education authority can be estopped from exercising statutory discretion.

The plaintiff's daughter was allocated a place in a secondary school which, according to
measurements made by the local authority, was a little over three miles from the
plaintiff's home. The local authority was therefore under a duty, by virtue of s 39(2)ᵃ of
the Education Act 1944, to provide transport for, or reimburse the travelling expenses of,
the plaintiff's daughter to and from school. The authority accordingly decided, in the
exercise of the discretion conferred on it by s 55(2)ᵇ of the 1944 Act to 'pay the whole or
any part, as the authority think fit, of the reasonable travelling expenses' of a school
pupil, to issue a bus pass to the plaintiff's daughter entitling her to free bus travel to and
from the school at the authority's expense. A short time later the authority made a more
precise measurement of distance between the plaintiff's house and the school and found
the distance to be less than three miles. The authority withdrew the bus pass in
f accordance with its policy that if the distance was less than three miles and there were no
special circumstances the child should walk to school or pay his own fare. The plaintiff
applied to the Divisional Court for a judicial review of the authority's decision to
withdraw the bus pass but that was refused. She appealed to the Court of Appeal,
contending (i) that the authority was not entitled to rescind its determination that a bus
pass should be issued once it had made that determination, and (ii) that the authority was,
g in the circumstances, estopped from revoking its decision.

Held – The appeal would be dismissed for the following reasons—
(1) If, on determining facts, a local authority had a discretion to confer a benefit on a
citizen rather than a duty to confer a right, a decision exercising that discretion was not
irrevocable and, where it exercised that discretion in favour of the citizen, but
subsequently found the decision to have been based on wrong or mistaken facts, it then

---

a Section 39(2), so far as material, is set out at p 232 *d*, post
b Section 55(2) is set out at p 231 *j*, post

came under a duty to review the decision and alter it if necessary. Accordingly, once the local authority discovered that the exercise of its discretion under s 55(2) of the 1944 Act to issue a bus pass to the plaintiff's daughter was based on a misconception as to the distance between the plaintiff's home and the school, it was bound to review the exercise of its discretion and was entitled to revoke the pass (see p 233 c to g, p 234 g to p 235 b and p 237 g h, post); *Livingston v Westminster Corpn* [1904] 2 KB 109 and *Re 56 Denton Road, Twickenham* [1952] 2 All ER 799 distinguished.

(2) The doctrine of estoppel could not be used to prevent the local authority from exercising a discretion which it was required by statute to exercise. But, even if it could be so used, the plaintiff had not altered her position so as to entitle her to rely on that doctrine (see p 233 j to p 234 d g and j, p 235 b and p 237 g h, post); *Southend-on-Sea Corpn v Hodgson (Wickford) Ltd* [1961] 2 All ER 46 applied.

(3) In all the circumstances, the local authority's policy was not unreasonable and it could not be said to have exercised its discretion under s 55(2) unreasonably (see p 233 a, p 234 e to g, p 235 b and p 237 g h, post).

Notes

For the principles on which a statutory discretion must be exercised, see 1 Halsbury's Laws (4th Edn) paras 20, 60–62, and for cases on the subject, see 1(1) Digest (Reissue) 102–104, 599–606.

For a local education authority's duty to provide transport or to pay travel expenses to schools, see 15 Halsbury's Laws (4th Edn) para 171.

For the Education Act 1944, ss 39, 55, see 11 Halsbury's Statutes (3rd Edn) 198, 217.

Cases referred to in judgments

Associated Provincial Picture Houses Ltd v Wednesbury Corpn [1947] 2 All ER 680, [1948] 1 KB 223, [1948] LJR 190, 177 LT 641, 112 JP 55, 45 LGR 635, CA, 45 Digest (Repl) 215, 189.

Denton Road (56), Twickenham, Middlesex, Re [1952] 2 All ER 799, [1953] Ch 51, 17 Digest (Reissue) 544, 337.

Lever (Finance) Ltd v Westminster Corpn [1970] 3 All ER 496, [1971] 1 QB 222, [1970] 3 WLR 732, 134 JP 692, 68 LGR 757, 21 P & CR 778, CA, Digest (Cont Vol C) 967, 51c.

Livingston v Westminster Corpn [1904] 2 KB 109, 73 LJKB 434, 68 JP 276, 2 LGR 581, 38 Digest (Repl) 79, 540.

Southend-on-Sea Corpn v Hodgson (Wickford) Ltd [1961] 2 All ER 46, [1962] 1 QB 416, [1961] 2 WLR 806, 125 JP 348, 12 P & CR 165, 59 LGR 193, DC, 21 Digest (Repl) 371, 1113.

Surrey County Council v Ministry of Education [1953] 1 All ER 705, [1953] 1 WLR 516, 117 JP 194, 51 LGR 319, 19 Digest (Repl) 609, 112.

Western Fish Products Ltd v Penwith District Council p 204, ante, 77 LGR 185, 38 P & CR 7, [1978] JPL 623, CA.

Appeal

Mrs Pamela Patricia Rootkin appealed against the decision of the Divisional Court of the Queen's Bench Division (Waller LJ and Park J) on 20th November 1979 refusing her application for leave to apply for judicial review of the decision of the Kent County Council on 18th November 1976 to revoke an earlier decision by the council on 27th July 1976 whereby the council undertook to provide the cost of travel by the appellant's daughter to and from her school. The facts are set out in the judgment of Lawton LJ.

John Powles for the appellant.
Gregory Stone for the council.

LAWTON LJ. In form this is an appeal by the leave of this court by the appellant against a refusal of the Divisional Court for leave to move for a judicial review of a decision made by the Kent County Council whereby that local authority refused to grant the appellant an allowance for the cost of the transport for her daughter from home to school. It is accepted by both parties that on the hearing of this appeal this court has jurisdiction to consider the merits of the appeal.

The appellant claims that she is entitled to be given a grant for the cost of transport from home to school for her daughter Helen. She says that when she first applied for the cost of transport, the council refused; then they said she could have it and they issued a yearly season ticket for her daughter; after about three months they purported to withdraw that season ticket; and thereafter they refused to grant any other season ticket or to reimburse the appellant in any other way for the cost of transport.

The council say that they issued a season ticket under a mistake of fact believing that they had a duty to issue one. When they discovered they were wrong on the facts as they became known to them, they exercised their right to withdraw the season ticket and thereafter, in the proper exercise of their discretion, they refused to grant any other season ticket or to reimburse the appellant for the cost of transport for her daughter.

The appellant through her counsel says that once the council had decided to issue a season ticket they could not go back on that decision. Alternatively, as a result of what they did, the appellant altered her position with the consequence that the council are estopped from saying that they were entitled to refuse the grant of a season ticket. Alternatively that in any event they exercised their statutory powers unreasonably.

The council for their part say that once they discovered they had made a mistake of fact they were entitled to revoke their earlier decision and they have in no way acted unreasonably, and that the doctrine of estoppel would not apply in this case, firstly because the law does not allow estoppel to be used to prevent a local authority exercising their statutory discretion and, in any event, there was not such a change in circumstances on the part of the appellant on the wrong decision of the council as to justify the doctrine of estoppel being brought into operation. Those are the broad issues in this case.

The appellant is what has come to be known as the head of a one-parent family. She is divorced; she has two children, of whom one is the girl Helen, who is now 15 years of age. In 1976 that child was 12. The appellant was living with her children in the Gillingham area. Helen had been to a primary school and at the age of 12 the time had come for her to move from primary education to secondary education. In the spring of 1976 the Kent County Council, as the local education authority, had the task of allocating a secondary school for Helen. They also had the duty, as far as was practicable, to comply with the wishes of her parent. As a result, in the spring of 1976, the appellant, in common with a number of other parents in a similar situation, was told what facilities were available for the children and she was asked what school she would like her daughter to go to. The appellant returned a form which she had been sent, saying that her first choice was for the Rainham Girls Secondary School and her second choice was for the Upbury Manor Secondary School. On the back of the form she said: 'I have selected one school for Helen as the other schools are some distance from our home and would mean also using public transport, and being a one parent family it would mean extra expenses for travelling.'

I do not myself think it necessary to go into the details of the appellant's finances; they are very personal to her. It suffices to say that she is in straitened circumstances and for my part I readily appreciate that every single penny is of importance to her and, if she could save money in bus fares for Helen, then she was being prudent in trying to do so.

Her choice, however, could not be met. Rainham Girls Secondary School, which was near the appellant's house, was over-subscribed. It followed that her second choice had to be considered. There was a vacancy in the Upbury Manor School, and the appellant was told that. Under the arrangements made by the Kent County Council in these sorts of circumstances, parents are given an opportunity of appealing against any decision about the allocation of schools. The appellant exercised her right of appeal and she appeared before an appeal panel. In the course of the presentation of her case she said that one of the reasons why she had chosen Upbury Manor School was that she understood it was more than three miles from her home, and in those circumstances, she would be entitled, as of right, to be reimbursed the cost of travel by public transport for Helen from home to school. She went on to say, rather surprisingly in the circumstances, that although there was another school, Woodlands, which was nearer her home and to which Helen could have gone, she did not want her to go to that school because she felt she would have to pay bus fares as that school was about one mile from Helen's home. There is no reason to think there were any particular hazards about the route from home to Woodlands School, so it seems a little unreasonable at first sight for the appellant to have taken the view that Helen could not be expected to walk a mile to school. However, that was her attitude.

She was then told by the divisional education officer, Mr Evans, that Upbury Manor School was not more than three miles from her home and she would not in those circumstances, for reasons to which I shall refer later in this judgment, be entitled to reimbursement for the cost of transport from home to school. She seems, however, to have been content at that stage with sending Helen to Upbury Manor School.

Shortly afterwards, the divisional education officer caused the route from Helen's home to the school to be measured by being driven over by somebody in a motor car with the distance measured on the ordinary car speedometer. When this was done, the reading showed that the difference from home to school was just over three miles. That would have entitled the appellant to be reimbursed for the cost of transport. She was so informed by letter dated 30th July.

At the beginning of September, Helen started attending the Upbury Manor School and, because it was more than three miles from her home, the Kent County Council issued her with a bus season ticket which was valid until the end of July 1977. Helen seems to have been one of a number of girls who lived in the same area of Gillingham and they too had been granted season tickets on the basis that their homes were more than three miles from the school. But another pupil at the school had been refused a season ticket on the ground that his home was less than three miles away. Inevitably the parent of that pupil complained, pointing out that some children in the neighbourhood were getting bus season tickets and others were not. The inference was that a mistake had been made by someone. As a result, the divisional education officer decided that the proper course would be to have the distance properly measured in respect of pupils who had been given bus season tickets. That was done with an instrument known as a Trumeter, and when it was done the measurement in Helen's case was found to be 175 yards less than three miles. As a result of that discovery, the divisional education officer decided that Helen was not entitled under the law, as he understood it, to be granted a bus season ticket. By letter dated 16th November he informed the appellant and said that the bus season ticket was withdrawn.

The appellant, understandably, was both upset and annoyed by this. She was upset because the cost of transport at that time was at about the rate of £120 per annum and she felt that she could not afford it. Secondly, she was annoyed because there had been a reversal of a decision by the local authority and she did not think that was right. She had an interview with the divisional education officer about the reversal of the decision. It is not clear from the affidavit what was discussed at that interview. It suffices to say that she was invited to think over the situation which had arisen and there was evidence before this court that at mid-November Helen could have been transferred from the Upbury Manor School to Woodlands School. Whether that was specifically put to the appellant at the meeting with the divisional education officer in November 1976 is not clear. The appellant did consider the matter and she felt aggrieved. She then consulted solicitors, and from November 1976 right up to the present time she has been represented by solicitors. From time to time they made representations on her behalf to the council.

One of the reasons why the appellant felt that Helen had to go to school by public
a transport and not have to walk a distance of just under three miles was that Helen had
had bronchitis and the appellant thought with a tendency towards bronchitis a long walk
to and from school, certainly in the winter months, would not be in Helen's interests.
She consulted her doctor just before the beginning of the school term in 1977. The
doctor wrote a report dated 2nd September 1977, the effect of which was that he
recommended that Helen should not walk to school. That report was sent to the
b council. The council asked a doctor in their employment to examine Helen. He came
to the conclusion, and so advised the council, that Helen's physical condition was
satisfactory and there was no reason, from a health point of view, why she should not
walk three miles to and from school.

The result of all that was that the council decided not to issue a season ticket to Helen
and she has never since had one.

c The appellant's solicitors continued to press for a review of Helen's case. In May 1978
her case was reviewed by the appropriate committee of the council and it was decided not
to issue any season ticket to her.

It is against that background of fact that the appellant applied for leave for a judicial
review. She was somewhat tardy in making her application to the Divisional Court. She
had learned of the decision of the committee of the council in May 1978, but she made
d no attempt to apply to the Divisional Court until August 1979. When she did apply it
was during the long vacation, and the vacation judge decided that her application did not
amount to vacation business and stood it over to be dealt with by the Divisional Court in
the Michaelmas term. It was heard by this court in November 1979 and leave to move
for a judicial review was refused; we have been informed by counsel that one of the
factors which was mentioned as being a ground for refusing leave was the tardiness with
e which the application had been made. The appellant at once applied to this court for
leave to appeal against the refusal and this court granted leave in December 1979.

Counsel for the council, without pressing the matter, invited our attention to the
tardiness in which the application had been made. Counsel for the appellant has invited
our attention to the provisions of RSC Ord 53, r 4, which deals with delay in applying for
relief. It seemed to us that under the terms of that rule we ought not to deal with this
f matter on the basis of delay unless we were satisfied that the delay would be detrimental,
and I use the words of the order, 'to good administration'. There is nothing in this case
to lead me to think that the tardiness of the application in any way puts the council in a
difficulty. I approach this case solely on the general merits and on the law applicable.

The law applicable is to be found in the Education Act 1944 as amended. Section 55
is the governing provision which enables local educational authorities to make payments
g for transport for pupils attending school. Subsection (1) reads as follows:

> 'A local education authority shall make such arrangements for the provision of
> transport and otherwise as they consider necessary or as the Secretary of State may
> direct for the purposes of facilitating the attendance of pupils at schools or county
> colleges or at any course or class provided in pursuance of a scheme of further
> education in force for their area, and any transport provided in pursuance of such
> *h* arrangements shall be provided free of charge.'

That is the statutory provision which enables local education authorities to provide
school buses. The provision of school buses is sometimes inconvenient, and it is found
better to provide money so that the pupils can get to school and have their bus fares or
train fares provided for by the local education authority. The enabling power for such
j payment is contained in sub-s (2) which reads as follows:

> 'A local education authority may pay the whole or any part, as the authority
> thinks fit, of the reasonable travelling expenses of any pupil in attendance at any
> school or county college or at any such course or class as aforesaid for whose
> transport no arrangements are made under this section.'

It is relevant to bear in mind that sub-s (2) gives the local authority a discretion and a wide one. They are not bound, on the face of that subsection, to pay anybody anything. *a* It is an enabling section and, when they do decide to pay, they can use their discretion whether they shall pay the whole or any part of the reasonable travelling expenses. It is the exercise of that discretion in the circumstances of this case which we have to review.

Oddly, the provision which has attracted a good deal of public attention about the distance children have to walk to school comes under a penal section of the statute, namely s 39. A local education authority are bound by statute to provide educational *b* facilities for children, and parents are bound to take advantage of those educational facilities for the benefit of their children, and if they do not do so they become subject to penalties under the provisions of s 39.

Section 39, in its relevant parts, reads as follows:

> '(1) If any child of compulsory school age who is a registered pupil at a school fails to attend regularly thereat, the parent of the child shall be guilty of an offence *c* against this section.

> '(2) In any proceedings for any offence against this section in respect of a child who is not a boarder at the school at which he is a registered pupil, the child shall not be deemed to have failed to attend regularly at the school by reason of his absence therefrom with leave or [and then come paras (*a*) and (*b*) which are irrelevant] (*c*) if the parent proves that the school at which the child is a registered pupil is not within *d* walking distance of the child's home, and that no suitable arrangements have been made by the local education authority either for his transport to and from school or for boarding accommodation for him at or near the school or for enabling him to become a registered pupil at a school nearer to his home . . .'

Subsection (5) defines what is meant by 'walking distance', and the relevant parts of *e* that subsection are as follows:

> '. . . the expression "walking distance" means, in relation to a child who has not attained the age of eight years two miles, and in the case of any other child three miles, measured by the nearest available route.'

This is why the three miles limit is so important because if the child lives more than *f* three miles from the school, then the parents are provided with a defence under s 39(2). It is because there was the defence based on distance from the school that in *Surrey County Council v Ministry of Education* [1953] 1 All ER 705, [1953] 1 WLR 516 it was adjudged that the effect of s 39 of the 1944 Act was to impose a duty on a local education authority to provide transport or to reimburse the cost of reasonable travelling expenses for any child who lived more than three miles from a school.

This provision seems to have been known to the appellant, and probably to many *g* other parents, and is what led her, when she appeared before the appeal panel which heard applications for review of allocations, to say that she wanted the child to go to Upbury Manor School because it was more than three miles from her home and that Helen would thereby become entitled to have her travelling expenses paid by the council.

The council accept, for the purposes of this appeal, that in any case where the child *h* lives more than three miles from a school they must pay the reasonable travelling expenses. On the other hand they submit that where the child lives less than three miles from the school there is a rebuttable presumption that the child is capable of walking to school and does not require to be reimbursed for the cost of travelling by public transport. They accept that they must look at the circumstances of each child. If the *j* child has to walk less than three miles but by a hazardous route, then it may be appropriate to exercise the discretion given by s 55(2) to pay reasonable travelling expenses. Similarly, if the child is of a weak constitution and is physically incapable of walking up to three miles from home to school, that is another reason for paying reasonable travelling expenses.

But, say the council, as a matter of policy, as long as the child is physically capable of

walking up to three miles and there are no special circumstances, such as a hazardous
a route in getting to school, then the child should walk.

Counsel for the council has informed this court that that is a policy which is followed
not only by the Kent County Council but by many other county councils. For my part
I can see nothing wrong in the council following that policy.

In this case there is evidence that, when it was submitted to them that it might be a
strain for Helen to walk to school because of her previous attack of bronchitis, they did
b reconsider the matter but came to the conclusion that the evidence before them was
insufficient to justify their changing their policy on that ground.

It is against that background that I now have to look at what happened in this case.
The council, at the end of July 1976, did decide to exercise their discretion under
s 55(2). It is accepted that the divisional education officer was duly authorised by them
to make the decision. He made his decision under a mistake of fact, namely that the
c difference from Helen's home to the school was more than three miles. On the basis of
that mistake of fact, and pursuant to the decision in *Surrey County Council v Ministry of
Education*, he, as an officer of the council authorised to exercise his discretion, was bound
to authorise the reimbursement to the appellant of the cost of travelling. He performed
his duty by authorising the issue of a yearly bus ticket. But when the mistake of fact was
discovered in November 1976 he was duty bound, as I see it, to the council to reconsider
d the matter because on the facts as he knew them in November 1976 there was no duty
to issue a bus season ticket to Helen. I can see no reason in law why he should not have
reconsidered the matter when he found that a mistake had been made about the distance.

It was submitted to us on the authority of a number of cases, of which the last in order
of time was *Re 56 Denton Road, Twickenham, Middlesex* [1952] 2 All ER 799, [1953] Ch 51,
that what the divisional education officer was doing was making a determination and,
e having once made a determination, he was not entitled to go back on it. In my
judgment, that is a misconception.

It is the law that if a citizen is entitled to payment in certain circumstances and a local
authority is given the duty of deciding whether the circumstances exist and if they do
exist of making the payment, then there is a determination which the local authority
cannot rescind. That was established in *Livingston v Westminster Corpn* [1904] 2 KB
f 109. But that line of authority does not apply in my judgment to a case where the citizen
has no right to a determination on certain facts being established, but only to the benefit
of the exercise of a discretion by the local authority. The wording of s 55(2) of the 1944
Act is far removed from the kind of statutory wording which was considered in *Re 56
Denton Road, Twickenham* and *Livingston v Westminster Corpn*. I cannot, for my part, see
any basis for the submission that the decision of the divisional education officer in July
g 1976 was irrevocable when he found out what the true facts were.

I turn now to the second head of the submission on behalf of the appellant, namely
that the local authority were estopped from revoking their decision. The way that
argument was put was as follows. It was said that the appellant was put into a false
position in July 1976 when she was told that Helen's travelling expenses would be paid.
At that time she decided to abandon any further rights of appeal she might have against
h the allocation of Helen to Upbury Manor School. She could have appealed to the
education officer of the county council and if she got no satisfaction out of him she had
statutory rights of appeal to the Secretary of State for Education under the provisions of
ss 68 and 99 of the 1944 Act.

It was said that, relying on the assurance given to her about reimbursement of
travelling expenses, she decided not to exercise any other rights she might have had.
j Further, it is said that in September 1976 Helen started at this school on the assurance
that her travelling expenses would be paid, but by mid-November 1976 she had settled
into the school and it would have been unreasonable for the appellant to have taken
Helen away from a school which she liked and had settled into and put her, half-way
through the term, into another school. One can see the human side of this. Children do
not like being uprooted from one school to another.

It seems to me that there are two answers to the submission based on estoppel. First, it is a general principle of law that the doctrine of estoppel cannot be used against local authorities for the purpose of preventing them from using the statutory discretion a which an Act of Parliament requires them to use. That principle was established clearly in *Southend-on-Sea Corpn v Hodgson (Wickford) Ltd* [1961] 2 All ER 46, [1962] 1 QB 416.

The cases relating to estoppel as against local authorities were reviewed by this court in *Western Fish Products Ltd v Penwith District Council* p 204, ante. In the course of that judgment it was pointed out that the principle in the *Southend-on-Sea* case was generally applicable. Again, for the reasons I have already given, in my judgment there was no b determination in the sense used in the *Western Fish Products* case by the divisional education officer when he decided to issue a yearly bus season ticket to Helen.

But, even if that were not the position in law, it seems to me that the appellant had not so altered her position as to entitle her to rely on the doctrine of estoppel. She had the benefit of legal advice from November 1976 onwards and no doubt she was well advised not to attempt to exercise any statutory rights of appeal which she had to the Secretary c of State. She was probably advised that the minister was not likely to interfere with the discretion exercised by a local authority about a matter of this kind. In addition, as I have already said, there was not much likelihood of upset so far as Helen was concerned. True it would have been more satisfactory for Helen to have remained at Upbury Manor School. On the other hand, it is difficult to see how she would have been prejudiced in any real way by being moved, if the appellant had decided to move her, to Woodlands d School.

This case in my judgment is a very long way away from the kind of situation where there is prejudice such as to bring into operation the doctrine of estoppel.

Finally, I come to the question whether in all the circumstances of this case the council can be said to have used their statutory powers under s 55(2) in an unreasonable way, so as to entitle this court to interfere. This court can only interfere with the exercise of e discretion by statutory bodies on the grounds set out and recognised as being good in law in *Associated Provincial Picture Houses Ltd v Wednesbury Corpn* [1947] 2 All ER 680, [1948] 1 KB 223. Here the Kent County Council had a policy which, as I have already stated, cannot be faulted. They were entitled to take the view that there was a rebuttable statutory presumption that a child of 12 and upwards could walk to and from school a distance of up to three miles. There was nothing wrong physically with Helen, there f were no particular hazards about the route which she took, and the fact that her mother was apprehensive and would have preferred her to go by public transport than to walk was an irrelevant consideration. I can see nothing unreasonable about the way the council exercised their discretion. For my part, I can see no reason why this court should interfere.

Accordingly, I would dismiss the appeal. g

EVELEIGH LJ. I agree. This appeal does in the end come down to an attempt to control the discretion of the education authority of estoppel.

If the distance was over three miles, then the Education Act 1944 in effect creates a duty to provide transport: see *Surrey County Council v Ministry of Education* [1953] 1 All ER 705, [1953] 1 WLR 516. Therefore, if an authority had provided the cost of transport h for one year because the distance was in fact over three miles, it would inevitably renew the grant for the next year because it would be under a duty so to do.

In the present case, it could not be said that there was a duty to renew the grant, for the distance was under three miles, and the authority cannot impose on itself a duty by a mistaken assumption about the facts when that duty arises only if in truth the distance is over three miles. j

There was no doubt a discretion in this case, under s 55(2) of the 1944 Act; that discretion must be exercised freely and cannot be thwarted by estoppel: see *Southend-on-Sea Corpn v Hodgson (Wickford) Ltd* [1961] 2 All ER 46, [1962] 1 QB 416.

Counsel has argued that the decision to pay the fare was irrevocable, even if mistaken, and he has relied on the principle in *Livingston v Westminster Corpn* [1904] 2 KB 109.

a That principle of irrevocability may well be applicable when there is a power or a duty to decide questions affecting existing legal rights. In the *Livingston* case itself the council were concerned to assess compensation for loss of office, to which compensation the plaintiff had a right under the Local Government Act 1899. Generally speaking, however, a discretionary power may be exercised from time to time unless a contrary intention appears. I can see nothing in the 1944 Act to prevent the education authority

b from reviewing its decisions from time to time, when the decision is under s 55(2), which is claimed to be applicable in this case.

I too would dismiss this appeal.

SIR STANLEY REES. In view of the judgments which have been delivered by Lawton and Eveleigh LJJ, I can state my views very shortly. When the question arose in

c April 1976 as to the choice of secondary school for the child Helen, the mother, the appellant in this case, made her position very clear in early 1976 in a document which was dispatched to the school and which has been read by Lawton LJ. It is plain from that document and from the evidence that this mother took a very strong view on two points. The first was that it was undesirable for this child Helen to walk a distance of three miles, or even up to one and a half miles as appeared from other evidence in the

d case, and that she attached great importance to that point. The medical evidence of the family doctor has already been read in the judgment of Lawton LJ, and it is plain that both the mother and the family doctor took the view that there was a bronchitic condition affecting this child which made it desirable that she should not walk a distance of three miles or any distance of that order.

The second was that it was plain to all concerned that this mother, being a mother

e having the care and control of two daughters who were then aged about 11 and 9, was attempting to keep herself and the two daughters on an extremely small allowance, and indeed was seeking to supplement that income by working part-time herself as a school meals attendant. Those factors run throughout this case and accordingly, for the reasons which she made plain, she would prefer the child to go to a school at Rainham very close to the home, but if that were not possible then to Upbury Manor School which was, as

f she was led to believe, about three miles away and therefore would qualify for a grant towards the bus fare.

When she learned of the decision in May 1976 that her request that the child should go to the school at Rainham had been turned down and she had been offered her second choice, the appellant was content with the second choice, provided that transport could be paid for by the council, and she accordingly appealed. She lost her appeal on 29th July

g 1976 and she was handed a letter on that date, which I need not read, indicating that the child would go to Upbury Manor School.

Up to that stage the distance to the school had been calculated on a map as being, as I think, within three miles. It was recalculated by means of a trip in a motor car, and as a result the school authorities then accepted that the distance was over three miles. As a result the divisional education officer wrote the letter of 30th July 1976, in which this

h sentence appears:

> 'A further distance check has been made from your home to the Upbury Manor Secondary School gates, and as the distance has been confirmed as three miles, you will qualify for free travel for Helen.'

Now that letter and the decision in it, which was conveyed to the mother, was made

j by the divisional education officer, and it is plain from the evidence, and is conceded by counsel for the council, that the divisional education officer had had delegated to him the power under s 55(1) of the 1944 Act to make the grant of the payment of the fare for the child.

I venture to express the view that that letter did not in fact purport to be in the exercise

of a discretion under s 55(2) but was an acceptance of the statutory obligation on behalf
of the council to pay the fare of this child on the basis that the council were obliged to do   *a*
so because the distance exceeded three miles, which is referred to in s 39.

Accordingly, on the receipt of that letter there was, as I venture to think, an exercise
of a power in pursuance of a duty on the basis that the distance involved exceeded three
miles. So that in my respectful view the officer was exercising the power delegated to
him, and he accepted that once the distance exceeded three miles he was bound to grant
payment to the mother for this child. There can be no doubt at all that he knew from   *b*
all that had passed that the appellant would take the view, as plainly he did also, that so
long as the child resided at that address, and remained at Upbury Manor School, the
council would be obliged, in pursuance of their duty under s 55(1) (and not under
s 55(2)), to pay the bus fare of this child.

In these circumstances, having received that letter and having taken the view that the
problem with which she had been faced since April 1976 had at last been resolved in her   *c*
favour, and before the child went to the school, the appellant abandoned all further
efforts to have the child moved to a school nearer to Rainham and accepted the offer
which had been made. As a result, it is strongly argued that she altered her position.

Then the letter of 18th November 1976 came and she learnt that the distance had been
measured for a third time, on this occasion by means of a meter, and found to be between
300 and 175 yards less than three miles. The council then required the appellant to   *d*
return the ticket which had been issued to her. She was obviously very upset, but she
took the view that, since she had been misled by the offer made to her that the school fare
would be paid for the whole time that the child was at the school and since the child had
gone to the school and was settling in it, she was entitled in the child's interests to allow
her to continue at Upbury Manor School. Therefore she perfectly understandably refused
to return the season ticket which lasted for one year and the child continued to attend the   *e*
school.

There is the factor which disclosed the vital importance she attached to protecting
Helen from a 5½ mile walk to and from school, that despite her exiguous income which
ranged over the material time between about £32 a week to about £39 a week, for three
people to live on, she somehow managed to pay for the fares for her child to travel to
school after the period of the season ticket expired. We were not given precise figures,   *f*
but over the whole period, excluding the first year, it seems that the amount of money
involved is something between £400 and £500. Somehow this mother managed to find
that money.

She continued with her efforts to enable the child to receive a free ticket. I need not
go at any length into what she did, because the evidence before us is very clear: that she
appealed to the council and the council then of course were only able to grant the ticket   *g*
to the appellant if they could properly do so under s 55(2) as a matter of discretion. That,
as Lawton LJ has pointed out, is a matter with which this court would only interfere in
the most exceptional circumstances.

Accordingly, the case put by counsel for the appellant is on the ground that the
decision to grant the ticket and to pay the fare during the whole of the school life of the
child at this particular school was the exercise of a statutory duty arising under a   *h*
combination of s 55(1) and the provisions of s 39 of the 1944 Act. He put the case in its
simplest form on behalf of the appellant in this way: that the council, through their
proper delegated officer, decided that as a matter of duty, they were obliged to pay the
fares of this child. That was communicated to the appellant, and the appellant rightly
understood that that was a decision binding on the council, and accordingly she acted on
it to her detriment, as it subsequently turned out. Despite all efforts by way of appeal to   *j*
the council she was not able to achieve the result she thought right for her child, as a
matter of discretion, and accordingly in those circumstances she came to this court and
did not choose to exercise her right of appeal to the Secretary of State under ss 68 and 99
of the 1944 Act which we are considering.

Counsel for the appellant relied on the decision of this court in *Lever (Finance) Ltd v*
a *Westminster Corpn* [1970] 3 All ER 496, [1971] 1 QB 222, and in particular to a passage
in the judgment of Lord Denning MR, to which I shall refer in a moment. In the
headnote to this case Lord Denning MR's utterance is summarised in these words ([1971]
1 QB 222 at 223):

b 'A public authority may be bound by a representation made by one of its officers
within the scope of his ostensible authority on which another acts. As in the case of
a company, a person dealing with a local authority is entitled to assume that all
necessary internal resolutions have been passed.'

In the instant case the question of ostensible authority did not arise because the
authority was accorded to the divisional education officer by his council and he exercised
it, and the appellant sent her child to this school in the firm belief that he had the power
c to grant payment of the fare for the whole time that the child went to this school and for
so long as she resided at her present address.

Lord Denning MR referred to the facts of the *Lever (Finance) Ltd* case, which was a
planning matter, and said ([1970] 3 All ER 496 at 500, [1971] 1 QB 222 at 230):

'Things may arise which were not foreseen. It should not be necessary for the
developers to go back to the planning committee for every immaterial variation.
d The permission covers any variation which is not material. But then the question
arises: who is to decide whether a variation is material or not? In practice it has been
the planning officer. This is a sensible practice and I think we should affirm it. If
the planning officer tells the developer that a proposed variation is not material, and
the developer acts on it, then the planning authority cannot go back on it. I know
that there are authorities which say that a public authority cannot be estopped by
e any representations made by its officers. It cannot be estopped from doing its public
duty. See, for instance, the recent decision of the Divisional Court in *Southend-on-Sea*
Corpn v Hodgson (Wickford) Ltd [1961] 2 All ER 46, [1962] 1 QB 416. But those
statements must now be taken with considerable reserve. There are many matters
which public authorities can now delegate to their officers. If an officer, acting
within the scope of his ostensible authority, makes a representation on which
f another acts, then a public authority may be bound by it, just as much as a private
concern would be.'

And, says counsel for the appellant, the present case is stronger than that, as the
divisional education officer had the actual authority delegated to him and he granted the
right for this child's transport to be covered. In those circumstances, he argues that the
g council are bound by that decision.

Unhappily, for the reasons which have been given by Lawton and Eveleigh LJJ, I am
unable to differ from them. I am convinced by the arguments which they have so clearly
set out that this court has no power (despite the strength of the case as I see it which has
been placed before us by counsel for the appellant) to do otherwise than to act in
accordance with the judgments which have been given by them.

h
Appeal dismissed.

Solicitors: *Robbins, Olivey & Lake*, agents for *Booth, Hearn, Stratton & Roberts*, Chatham (for
the appellant); *W G Hopkin*, Maidstone (for the council)

William Hoskins Esq   Barrister.

Tebbutt v Haynes and another   *a*

COURT OF APPEAL, CIVIL DIVISION
LORD DENNING MR, BRIGHTMAN AND GRIFFITHS LJJ
23rd, 24th OCTOBER 1980

Divorce – Property – Adjustment order – Matters to be considered – Jursidiction to determine **b**
interest in property of third party on spouse's application for adjustment order – Whether judge
of Family Division having jurisdiction to determine rights and interests of third party in property
before making order between spouses – Matrimonial Causes Act 1973, s 24(1).

Estoppel – Issue estoppel – Proceedings in Family Division for transfer of property order – Third
party intervening in proceedings to claim interest in property – Family Division judge **c**
determining after full hearing that equitable interest in property belonging to third party and that
husband having no interest in property – Judge therefore finding wife not entitled to any interest
– Prior to judgment in Family Division third party bringing proceedings in Chancery Division
against husband and wife claiming interest in house – Wife counterclaiming in those proceedings
that she was entitled to a beneficial interest in the property – Whether wife estopped by findings
of Family Division judge from asserting interest in property – Matrimonial Causes Act 1973, **d**
s 24(1).

When they married in 1968 the husband and wife went to live at the husband's mother's
house where his aunt also lived. Later it was arranged that the house should be sold, that
the husband should carry out certain alterations before the sale to increase the price and
that a larger house should be purchased out of the proceeds of sale where they could all **e**
live. The husband carried out the alterations to the old house and it was sold in 1971.
A new house was purchased using the proceeds from the old house but in the husband's
name to facilitate the grant of a mortgage. The husband and wife only stayed in the new
house for a short time and left in 1972 to live elsewhere. The husband's mother and aunt
continued to reside there. In 1973 the husband disappeared and in the same year the
wife obtained a divorce. She then applied in the Family Division for a transfer of **f**
property order against the husband, under s 24(1)ᵃ of the Matrimonial Causes Act 1973,
seeking the transfer to herself of the legal and equitable interest in the new house. The
registrar gave leave to the husband's mother and aunt to intervene in the wife's
application, and on the hearing of the application ordered that the husband's legal and
beneficial interest in the house be transferred to the wife. The husband's mother
appealed and on 29th April 1975 Hollings J, having heard oral evidence from the wife **g**
and the mother and having considered documentary evidence produced by the mother,
held, in effect, that the mother was entitled to the equitable interest in the house in view
of an oral agreement made in or about October 1970 between her and the husband to the
effect that the legal title to the house should be vested in him, that she would pay the
necessary sum towards the purchase price and the mortgage instalments on the house
and that when the mortgage was paid off she would be entitled to an absolute interest in **h**
it. But the judge also found that the husband had contributed to the purchase of the
house by the amount he had expended on alterations to the old house and possibly by
contributing to the purchase price of the new house. In effect, therefore, he found that
the wife had no claim through the husband to the house except to the extent that he had
contributed to its purchase. A few days before Hollings J's judgment the husband's

                                                                                                  j
_____

a   Section 24(1), so far as material, provides: 'On granting a decree of divorce . . . or at any time
     thereafter . . . the court may make any one or more of the following orders, that is to say—(a) an
     order that a party to the marriage shall transfer to the other party . . . such property as may be so
     specified, being property to which the first-mentioned party is entitled, either in possession or
     reversion . . .'

a mother issued a writ in the Chancery Division against the husband and wife claiming an interest in the house. In those proceedings the wife counterclaimed for a declaration that she was entitled to a 90% beneficial interest in the house or to such interest as the court thought fit. The master ordered the trial of a preliminary issue whether, by reason of the findings of Hollings J, the wife was estopped from asserting that she was entitled to an equitable interest in the house. That issue was determined by Vinelott J who held that Hollings J's findings did not give rise to an estoppel against the wife because, as had been

b conceded before Vinelott J, the Family Division had no jurisdiction on an application under s 24 of the 1973 Act to determine property rights between a spouse and a third party. If that decision were correct the Chancery action had to be fought out to determine the interests in the house of the husband and wife and the mother. The mother appealed.

c **Held** – The appeal would be allowed for the following reasons—
    (1) On an application by a spouse under s 24 of the 1973 Act for a transfer of property order the court had jurisdiction to determine not only the rights and interests of the husband and wife in the property but also the rights and interests of third parties who had intervened in the application to claim an interest in the house, for it was fundamental to the jurisdiction under s 24 that the judge should know over what property he was

d entitled to exercise his discretion, and, if there was a dispute between a respondent spouse and a third party as to the ownership of the property, that dispute had to be resolved before the judge could make an effective order under s 24. Accordingly, Hollings J had had jurisdiction to determine the mother's interest in the house, as well as the interests of the husband and wife, and the concession before Vinelott J on which he had based his decision was erroneous (see p 242 b to f, p 243 b and p 245 c to h, post).

e   (2) Since the issue of the rights and interests of the husband and wife and the mother in the house had been fully and fairly inquired into and dealt with by Hollings J, who in effect had found that the husband and wife had no claim to an equitable interest in the house (subject only to any charge the wife might have in right of the husband in respect of his contributions towards the purchase of the house), it followed that that finding was conclusive as between the wife and the mother and that the wife was estopped from

f reopening in the Chancery action the issue of her and the mother's interests in the house, unless there were circumstances which made it fair and just that the issue should be reopened. Since there were no such circumstances, the mother was entitled to a declaration that the wife was estopped from claiming that she or the husband had any equitable interest in the house, but without prejudice to the wife's right to claim a charge in respect of money spent by the husband in respect of either the old or the new house

g (see p 242 g to p 243 b, p 244 b c and p 245 b d g h, post); McIlkenny v Chief Constable of West Midlands Police Force [1980] 2 All ER 227 applied.

Notes
For the court's power to order transfer of property on granting a decree of divorce, see 13 Halsbury's Laws (4th Edn) para 1116.

h   For issue estoppel generally, see 16 ibid para 1530.
    For the Matrimonial Causes Act 1973, s 24, see 43 Halsbury's Statutes (3rd Edn) 566.

Case cited in judgment
McIlkenny v Chief Constable of West Midlands Police Force [1980] 2 All ER 227, [1980] QB 283, [1980] 2 WLR 689, CA.

j **Appeal**
In an action brought in the Chancery Division by the plaintiff, Mrs Edna Evelyn Tebbutt, against the first defendant, Haydn Sandy Haynes ('the husband'), and the second dependant, Susan Haynes ('the wife'), claiming, in effect, a declaration that Mrs Tebbutt was entitled to have conveyed to her a property known as 160 Hoppers Road, London,

N21 and that the husband and wife had no interest in it, the master ordered that the following point of law raised by a defence and counterclaim put in by the wife should be *a* disposed of before the trial of the action, namely whether the wife was estopped by reason of the judgment given and/or the findings of fact made by Hollings J on 29th April 1975 in proceedings in the Family Division of the High Court entitled *Haynes v Haynes (Tebbutt and Haynes intervening)* from denying (1) that the property was purchased by the husband pursuant to an oral agreement of October 1970 made between himself and Mrs Tebbutt, (2) that Mrs Tebbutt was entitled on paying off the mortgage affecting *b* the property to have the legal and beneficial title thereto transferred to her, and (3) that the sum of £2,666·98 was paid by Mrs Tebbutt to the husband to discharge the mortgage instalments on the property out of her own moneys. On 12th June 1980 Vinelott J determined the preliminary issue and held that the wife was not estopped by the judgment of Hollings J from denying the foregoing facts and matters but gave Mrs Tebbutt liberty to appeal. Mrs Tebbutt appealed on the grounds (1) that Vinelott J *c* misdirected himself in holding that there was no relevant issue capable of being finally determined in the action before Hollings J by reason of the fact that the Family Division of the High Court had no jurisdiction to determine property rights between a spouse and third parties, and ought to have held that Hollings J had jurisdiction to make the findings of fact in question and that those findings gave rise to issue estoppel in the Chancery action, which was between the same parties, in so far as they related to the same matters *d* in dispute between the parties and that they constituted a judgment in personam and not in rem and, (2) that Vinelott J misdirected himself in holding that those findings of fact by Hollings J were not necessary or essential in order for him to reach his decision and did not therefore constitute issue estoppel, and ought to have held that it was essential for Hollings J to determine the issues of fact raised by Mrs Tebbutt as intervenor in the wife's application under s 24 of the 1973 Act in order to determine what property the husband *e* held, whether to transfer such property to the wife and whether to accede to the wife's application to have 160 Hoppers Road sold and the proceeds of sale paid to her. The facts are set out in the judgment of Lord Denning MR.

John Penry for Mrs Tebbutt.
C P L Braham for the wife.   *f*

LORD DENNING MR. Mr and Mrs Haynes married in January 1968. He was 24 and she was 19. They had two children. In 1973 the marriage broke down completely. The husband disappeared with the two children. He went from Southampton. We do not know where. He has never been heard of since. The wife has been left on her own. Even so, she is able to earn and look after herself quite well. She *g* is not on social security.

The issue is whether she has any interest in the house. I will not call it the matrimonial home, but 'the house'. It is at 160 Hoppers Road, London. After the divorce, the wife took out transfer of property proceedings under s 24 of the Matrimonial Causes Act 1973. She said that the house was in her husband's name. She wanted it transferred to her. An order was made for it to be transferred to her. The house has been transferred *h* to her. So in law she has legal title to it.

The house is at present occupied by the husband's mother (Mrs Haynes) and the husband's aunt (Mrs Tebbutt). The question is whether, in law, the wife can now turn out the husband's mother and aunt from the house. She says that she can turn them out. As long ago as 1975 she made an application to the court asking that she should be able to return to the house, and that the husband's mother and aunt should vacate it *j* forthwith. She failed at that time. Now she wants to litigate it all over again.

As I said, the husband and wife married in 1968. At that time the husband's mother (Mrs Haynes) and her sister (Mrs Tebbutt) lived together in a house known as Whetstones in North London. When the husband and wife married, they went to stay at that house. But later, by arrangement, that house was sold, and the house at 160 Hoppers

Road was bought. Whetstones had been in Mrs Tebbutt's name. It was sold in order to
a facilitate the purchase of 160 Hoppers Road. 160 Hoppers Road was put in the husband's
name because a mortgage had to be obtained. In those days, building societies or
mortgagees often required a man to be the holder of the mortgage. So 160 Hoppers
Road was not put in the name of Mrs Tebbutt, although she had done a great deal
towards getting it by selling her own house Whetstones.

Mrs Tebbutt and Mrs Haynes went to live at 160 Hoppers Road. In addition the
b young couple lived there for a while. But soon afterwards the young couple left. They
went to other houses. They went overseas. They lived in Australia for a time, and in
other places. So they were not much at 160 Hoppers Road. But, in 1973 after the
husband disappeared, there was much controversy. The wife said: 'This is my husband's
house. It should be mine now that he has gone and I do not know where he is.' She
claimed that the house should be transferred to her. She also claimed the whole equitable
c interest in the property, and that she should be able to turn out Mrs Tebbutt and Mrs
Haynes.

There was a three-day hearing before a registrar in which he seems to have held in
favour of the wife. Then, on appeal from him, there was a three-and-a-half-day hearing
before Hollings J. I may say that this was all being done by both sides on legal aid. On
29th April 1975 the judge, having heard all the evidence, gave a judgment of 26 pages
d in length. He went into the history in great detail. He described what had happened to
the property; what had happened to the parties; what had happened to the mortgage,
repairs, and so forth. He took a poor view of Mrs Tebbutt. He thought that she was
unfairly hostile to the wife. But nevertheless he felt compelled on the evidence to find
that there was—

e
'an agreement in about October 1970 on the basis that although the husband
would be the legal owner of the property [160 Hoppers Road] the intervenor, at
least Mrs Tebbutt, that is, would pay all that was necessary in the way of purchase
price, [she would be liable for the] mortgage instalments, that if and when she paid
off the mortgage then she would be entitled to call for the transfer of the full legal
and beneficial ownership to her, but only then.'

f   That finding is clear. It amounts to this: that the legal title would be in the
husband. But the full equitable title was in Mrs Tebbutt inasmuch as, when the
mortgage instalments had been paid off, the house would belong to her. But the judge,
having made that finding, went on to consider the contributions the husband had made
in two respects: first, in doing work on Whetstones which had cost him £2,000, although
he did receive some rent towards it; and, second, that the husband may have contributed
g some money towards the acquisition of 160 Hoppers Road. The judge did not decide it
finally; but he did make it quite clear that that was his view. At the end of his judgment
he said:

h
'. . . so long as Mrs Tebbutt maintains the mortgage payments and so long as the
contract remains in full agreement, remains in existence, is not terminated by the
other party to the bargain, whether it be the husband or wife, properly, then, not
only Mrs Tebbutt but also Mrs Haynes is entitled to live in Hoppers Road.'

On those findings, it is clear that Mrs Tebbutt has the equitable interest in the house.
The wife has no claim in respect of her former husband except in so far as he has spent
money in relation to the two properties and was not repaid.

Those were the findings of Hollings J in April 1975. But the order of the court was not
j properly drawn up. It reads as if the wife had succeeded altogether, and that the claim
of Mrs Tebbutt had been dismissed. That was wrong. It ought to have been corrected
under the 'slip' order and should be corrected now.

Now I must draw attention to a most deplorable state of affairs. Just a few days before
Hollings J gave his judgment, on 21st April 1975, a writ had been issued in the Chancery
Division by Mrs Tebbutt claiming that she was entitled to an interest in the property

against the husband and the wife. Those proceedings went on interminably. A defence
and counterclaim were put in by the wife. She claimed that she was entitled to 90% of   *a*
the property. Long pleadings were delivered. Eventually the master said that there
ought to be a preliminary issue to see whether all these matters could be canvassed again
or not. He made an order for a preliminary issue to decide it.

The preliminary issue came before Vinelott J on 12th June 1980. He held that the
findings of Hollings J did not give rise to an estoppel; and that the case had to be fought
out again between Mrs Tebbutt and the wife to see what the interests in the property   *b*
were. All had to be canvassed again, all the matters which had been dealt with by
Hollings J. Not on the old evidence but, as counsel for the wife told us this morning, the
wife would like to bring in a great deal of new evidence so as to get different findings
from those made by Hollings J.

I am afraid that Vinelott J was misled by a concession which was made before him.
Counsel seems to have conceded that Hollings J had no jurisdiction to determine the   *c*
existence or otherwise of the proprietary right claimed by Mrs Tebbutt. I think that
concession was erroneous.

The wife's claim before Hollings J was a claim under s 24 of the Matrimonial Causes
Act 1973. It was for a transfer of property as between husband and wife. Nevertheless
in this case, unlike most other cases, there was an intervenor. Mrs Tebbutt claimed that
'160 Hoppers Road is a house in which I have a considerable interest'. Because she made   *d*
that claim, she was quite rightly brought in as an intervenor. It seems to me that, under
s 24 of the 1973 Act, if an intervenor comes in making a claim for the property, then it
is within the jurisdiction of the judge to decide on the validity of the intervenor's
claim. The judge ought to decide what are the rights and interests of all the parties, not
only of the intervenor, but of the husband and wife respectively in the property. He can
only make an order for the transfer, to the wife, of property which is the husband's   *e*
property. He cannot make an order for the transfer to the wife of someone else's
interest. So, in order to make an order under s 24, it must be within the jurisdiction of
the judge to determine what are the various rights and interests in the property not only
of husband and wife but also of any other persons who claim an interest.

So the matter was not put properly before Vinelott J and that led him into error. It
seems to me that Hollings J had ample jurisdiction; and that it was quite proper for him   *f*
to determine the interests, as he did, of the intervenor as well as of husband and wife.

The next point is whether there is an issue estoppel. These matters were decided by
Hollings J after full inquiry and evidence. Can they be reopened again in subsequent
Chancery proceedings? The case was decided by Hollings J in 1975. If it is to be fought
out again in Chancery proceedings, goodness knows when the action will come for
trial. It is not anywhere near trial at the moment. And just think of the expense, all on   *g*
legal aid.

We considered the question of issue estoppel recently in *McIlkenny v Chief Constable of
West Midlands Police Force* [1980] 2 All ER 227, [1980] QB 283. I ventured to suggest this
principle: if there has been an issue raised and decided *against* a party in circumstances in
which he has had a full and fair opportunity of dealing with the whole case, then that
issue must be taken as being finally and conclusively decided *against* him. He is not at   *h*
liberty to reopen it unless the circumstances are such as to make it fair and just that it
should be reopened.

Counsel for the wife has sought before us this morning to say that there are
circumstances here in which it would be fair and just for it to be reopened. But I must
say that none of them is of any weight. This case was fully tried out in 1975. It should
not be reopened in 1980 on the suggestion of fresh evidence or the like. The issues as to   *j*
the rights and interests of the parties in the house at Hoppers Road were decided by
Hollings J in 1975. That decision is conclusive between them. The only difficulty is that
it is not entirely easy to spell out exactly what Hollings J decided; but Brightman LJ has
drafted a few words which seem to me to express the effect of Hollings J's decision. It is:

'The wife is estopped from claiming that she or her former husband has any claim to a share in the equity of 160 Hoppers Road, but without prejudice to her right to claim that she is entitled in right of her husband to a charge on the property for money spent by him on or in relation to Whetstones or 160 Hoppers Road, save in so far as it has already been repaid to or recouped by the husband.'

I would therefore allow the appeal and hold that there is an estoppel to the extent drafted by Brightman LJ in the passage that I have just read.

BRIGHTMAN LJ. I agree. The question arising on this appeal is whether the wife is entitled to raise for a second time an issue which was decided against her as long ago as April 1975 in proceedings in the Family Division. That issue is whether her divorced husband or she herself owned the whole or any part of the equity in a house known as 160 Hoppers Road, London.

The husband and wife married in 1968. At that time the husband's mother (whom I will call 'Mrs Haynes') and his aunt, Mrs Tebbutt, lived in a house in North London which was known as 'Whetstones', together with the husband's grandmother. Whetstones belonged to Mrs Tebbutt. The grandmother died in September 1970. Mrs Haynes and Mrs Tebbutt at once moved out of Whetstones, which apparently they could not bring themselves to occupy any longer, and they lived for the time being in certain rented accommodation which was occupied by the husband and the wife. On 26th October 1970 a large house nearby, that is 160 Hoppers Road, was bought in the name of the husband. The price was £8,700. £1,500 was paid by the husband, and the balance of £7,200 was provided by a building society mortgage. All four members of the family then moved into the house.

Certain alterations were made to Whetstones to convert it into bed-sitting rooms, with a view to an advantageous sale. By arrangement between the husband and Mrs Tebbutt, the husband carried out certain alterations. Whetstones was ultimately sold in July 1971 for some £8,500 after repaying the mortgage.

In September 1973 the husband, who had clearly treated the wife quite appallingly, disappeared, taking with him the two children of the marriage. None of them has since been traced by the wife. In October 1973 the wife presented a divorce petition, and a decree nisi was made in May 1974. The wife then applied for a property adjustment order. On the hearing of that application, the registrar ordered that notice be given to Mrs Tebbutt, who was still living at 160 Hoppers Road with Mrs Haynes. The wife had not lived there since early in 1972, as I understand the findings of the judge. In the result, the registrar gave Mrs Tebbutt and Mrs Haynes leave to intervene in the wife's application. On 26th January 1975, after what seems to have been a very full hearing, the registrar made an order directing that the legal and beneficial interest of the husband in 160 Hoppers Road be transferred to the wife, and that transfer was effected under a court order. There was then an appeal which came before Hollings J in April. He had the oral evidence of the wife and Mrs Tebbutt, and a certain amount of documentary evidence produced by Mrs Tebbutt. We have seen a copy of the order which was drawn up following the decision of Hollings J, but it does not quite accord with what he said in his judgment. What he said in his judgment was that he dismissed the appeal of Mrs Tebbutt and Mrs Haynes, but he would vary the registrar's order by directing that the husband should transfer to the wife, not the legal and beneficial ownership, but such rights as the husband might have in 160 Hoppers Road. I will come later to the reason for that change.

On 21st April 1975, just a few days before the judgment of Hollings J, Mrs Tebbutt issued a writ in the Chancery Division. She claimed, in effect, a declaration that she was entitled to have 160 Hoppers Road conveyed to her and that the husband and wife had no interest therein. This Chancery action has proceeded at a pace which would put a snail to shame.

In March 1980 an order was made in the Chancery Division for the trial of a preliminary issue. The preliminary issue was whether the wife was estopped by reason of certain findings of fact made by Hollings J from denying that 160 Hoppers Road was

purchased by the husband pursuant to an oral agreement made in October 1970 between
the husband and Mrs Tebbutt. This formulation of the preliminary issue does not, in   *a*
my view, sufficiently explain it. The real question was whether the wife was estopped
from asserting that she was entitled to a share in the equity of the house. She
counterclaimed for a declaration that the beneficial interest was held as to 90% in trust
for herself and 10% in trust for Mrs Tebbutt; or, alternatively, in such proportions as the
court thought fit having regard to the contributions made by the husband and herself.

   The principle involved is that of issue estoppel. A person should not have to fight all   *b*
over again the selfsame issue that has been decided before, provided that the party *against*
whom the estoppel is raised has had a fair and full opportunity to contest the issue, so that
it would not be just to allow him to reopen the matter in subsequent proceedings.

   So it is necessary to turn to the judgment of Hollings J to see exactly what issue was
before him and how he decided the issue.

   The two issues before the judge were these. First, what property did the husband own   *c*
on which s 24 of the Matrimonial Causes Act 1973 could operate? Second, should any
of such property be transferred to the wife?

   The only property in dispute was 160 Hoppers Road. The only claimants to that
property were the wife, apparently partly in her own right but substantially in the right
of the husband, and Mrs Tebbutt. So the judge was compelled to decide whether the
husband owned the house, or whether Mrs Tebbutt owned it, or possibly whether the   *d*
wife owned it, or whether they owned it between themselves in some shares, before he
could approach the second issue and determine what should be transferred from the
husband to the wife under the 1973 Act.

   There was no dispute that Mrs Tebbutt had arranged with the husband that he would
see to the alterations to Whetstones and recoup himself from the rents, so far as the rents
would extend. The judge found that he must have spent at least £2,000 on that. Mrs   *e*
Tebbutt also claimed that during the last illness of the grandmother, and during the
period which elapsed before the new house was bought, she made an agreement with the
husband about the new house. She said that it was to be bought in the husband's name,
no doubt to facilitate the raising of a mortgage, that when Whetstones was sold, the
proceeds of sale should be used in order to recoup to the husband what he had to pay out
in buying the new house, and that when she had paid off everything and the mortgage   *f*
was cleared, the property should be transferred into her own name as her absolute
property. That was the agreement alleged by Mrs Tebbutt. In the meantime, the new
house was to be available as a family home for all four to live in. Under the arrangement
asserted by Mrs Tebbutt, it is plain that the husband would have taken no share of the
equity in the house.

   For reasons which Hollings J makes clear in his judgment, he approached the evidence   *g*
of Mrs Tebbutt with a great degree of scepticism, and he examined and assessed it very
critically. The conclusion he reached was this:

   'I find that the evidence of Mrs Tebbutt with regard to the arrangements in
   respect of Hoppers Road is broadly correct . . . I am driven to the conclusion that
   what transpired was . . . an agreement in about October 1970 on the basis that   *h*
   although the husband would be the legal owner of the property . . . Mrs Tebbutt
   . . . would pay all that was necessary in the way of purchase price [and] mortgage
   instalments, that if and when she paid off the mortgage then she would be entitled
   to call for the transfer of the full legal and beneficial ownership to her, but only
   then.'

He added this, referring to the husband: *j*

   'In addition to that, he may well (I put it that way because I am not deciding this)
   have a claim for a charge on the property even after Mrs Tebbutt has discharged the
   mortgage. That is in respect of the moneys that he has laid out on Whetstones,

some £2,000 less such rent, if any, as he received in respect of Whetstones. I am satisfied on the evidence that that was an expenditure which he was entitled under this agreement to bring into account, and it may well be that before or as a condition of the transfer of the legal ownership to Mrs Tebbutt she may have to pay that sum, whatever it is. So, there is a right, or a potential right, in the husband here, which is a right which the wife is entitled to ask me to transfer.'

I find it unnecessary to refer to the numerous and complicated financial dealings which the judge examined with great care during the course of his judgment. The main issue was clear: did the husband have any share of the equity in the house? This involved inevitably the issue whether the wife had any claim in her own right. The judge's decision on that issue was clear, that neither he nor the wife had any such interest. But the judge left open the question whether the husband had any claim in respect of expenditure on Whetstones.

Vinelott J decided the preliminary point against the wife because, as he said in relation to the proceedings before Hollings J: 'There is no estoppel because there is no lis in which any issue for proprietary right falls to be decided.' I respectfully differ. It seems to me that it was absolutely essential for Hollings J to adjudicate on Mrs Tebbutt's claim and the wife's claim in her own right because, only by reaching a decision on that issue, could he discover over what property he had any jurisdiction for the purposes of s 24 of the 1973 Act. That issue has now been disposed of to the extent of determining that the husband has no equity in the house but at most a charge, and that the wife has no interest, and there the matter must stand. It is not open to the wife in the Chancery proceedings to assert that she or the husband has any interest in the equity.

It was canvassed before us that the Family Division had no jurisdiction to decide property rights under s 24, and I think that Vinelott J accepted that submission. I cannot think it is right. It is fundamental to the s 24 jurisdiction that the judge should know over what property he is entitled to exercise his discretion. If there is a dispute between a respondent spouse and a third party as to the ownership of a particular item of property which stands in the respondent spouse's name, that dispute must be resolved before the judge can make an effective final order under s 24. There are only two ways of resolving such a dispute. Either the Family Division proceedings must be adjourned pending the trial of the claim in other proceedings, or the dispute must be decided in the s 24 proceedings by allowing the third party to intervene. The latter course was adopted in the instant case. It has not been suggested, and I do not think it would be right to suggest, that the court had no jurisdiction to permit Mrs Tebbutt to intervene. There could be no purpose in her intervention except to decide the dispute. I think that in a case like the present the Family Division has jurisdiction under s 24 to decide property rights.

I would therefore answer the preliminary issue by a declaration in the form that has been read out by Lord Denning MR and I would allow the appeal accordingly.

GRIFFITHS LJ. I agree that this appeal should be allowed for the reasons contained in the judgments of Lord Denning MR and Brightman LJ. I do not wish to add any observations of my own.

Appeal allowed; declaration accordingly.

Solicitors: *Duke-Cohan & Co* (for Mrs Tebbutt); *Dixon, Ward & Co* (for the wife).

Frances Rustin Barrister.

R v Raymond

COURT OF APPEAL, CRIMINAL DIVISION
WATKINS LJ, BOREHAM AND HODGSON JJ
22nd MAY, 16th OCTOBER 1980

Criminal law – Bill of indictment – Preferment – No committal for trial – Application to judge for leave to prefer bill of indictment – Discretion of judge – Whether defendant having right to be heard on application – Whether judge having discretion to hear representations from defendant – Administration of Justice (Miscellaneous Provisions) Act 1933, s 2.

The appellant was charged with theft. At an early stage in the committal proceedings it became obvious that he intended to disrupt them in a way which would make a mockery of them. The proceedings were abandoned and counsel for the Crown notified the appellant that he was applying to a High Court judge for leave to prefer a bill of indictment. The appellant's solicitor wrote to the courts administrator informing him that the appellant intended to oppose the application and asking for leave to instruct counsel to attend the hearing of the application so that he could press for the reinstatement of the committal proceedings. The solicitor was told that his observations would be made known to the judge. The judge, after giving full consideration to the solicitor's letter, decided that in the interests of justice he should give leave to prefer the bill of indictment and that there was no reason for him to depart from the usual practice of dealing with an application for leave on the documents without hearing counsel for the Crown or for the defendant. At his trial the appellant applied to have the indictment quashed. The trial judge rejected the application, and the appellant was eventually convicted. He appealed against conviction, contending (i) that the trial was a nullity because the bill of indictment preferred against him had been obtained otherwise than in accordance with s 2(2)[a] of the Administration of Justice (Miscellaneous Provisions) Act 1933, in that the High Court judge had granted leave without hearing the appellant or counsel on his behalf, and (ii) that the trial judge had wrongly refused to quash the bill of indictment under s 2(3) of the 1933 Act either because the observance of the audi alteram partem rule for the determination of any issue in legal proceedings was, in the absence of any express statutory authority to the contrary, mandatory, and in so far as the Indictments (Procedure) Rules 1971, which were made under s 2(6)[b] of the 1933 Act, permitted an ex parte determination of the question of leave to prefer a bill of indictment they were ultra vires that Act, or because, by delegating in s 2(6) to the Lord Chancellor the power to determine the manner in which bills of indictment should be preferred, the 1933 Act was to be interpreted to mean that such rules would be made subject to the audi alteram partem rule.

Held – The appeal would be dismissed for the following reasons—
(1) A defendant had no right to be heard or to make representations to a High Court judge on an application for leave to prefer a bill of indictment because—
(a) the 1933 Act and the 1971 rules, rather than changing the ex parte method of obtaining leave which had been used since 1859, had in fact deliberately perpetuated it (see p 250 *e f*, p 251 *g h*, p 252 *c*, p 255 *c* and p 256 *d*, post); *R v Rothfield* [1937] 4 All ER 320 and *Public Prosecutor v Fan Yew Teng* [1973] AC 846 considered;
(b) the audi alteram partem rule was inapplicable to the process of preferring a bill of indictment; there was nothing unjust in the ex parte nature of the procedure because the defendant would undoubtedly have a right to be heard at the trial, and the courts would not go against the clear intention of the 1933 Act and the 1971 rules to exclude the operation of the audi alteram partem rule (see p 254 *c* and *f* to *h* and p 256 *d*, post);

---

a Section 2(2), so far as material, is set out at p 250 *d*, post
b Section 2(6) is set out at p 250 *g h*, post

Wiseman v Borneman [1969] 3 All ER 275 and *Dyson Holdings Ltd v Fox* [1975] 3 All ER
a 1030 considered.

(2) A High Court judge might, however, have a discretion to receive representations
from the defendant with regard to an application for leave to prefer a bill of indictment,
but that discretion would be exercisable only in very exceptional circumstances (see
p 255 *d* and p 256 *d*, post).

(3) It was probable that only the Court of Appeal could review a decision made by a
b High Court judge on an application made to him for leave to prefer a bill of indictment;
but, in any event, in the circumstances the trial judge had rightly rejected the appellant's
application to quash the indictment. The High Court judge had acted within his
jurisdiction in granting leave to prefer the bill of indictment without hearing the
appellant or counsel on his behalf, and there were no grounds for interfering with his
decision (see p 253 *c*, p 255 *a* to *c* and p 256 *c d*, post); *R v Rothfield* [1937] 4 All ER 320
c applied.

Notes

For preferring an indictment, see 11 Halsbury's Laws (4th Edn) paras 193–201, and for
cases on the subject, see 14 (1) Digest (Reissue) 265–267, 1993–2014.

For the Administration of Justice (Miscellaneous Provisions) Act 1933, s 2, see 8
d Halsbury's Statutes (3rd Edn) 308.

For the Indictments (Procedure) Rules 1971, r 10, see 6 Halsbury's Statutory
Instruments (Third Reissue) 26.

Cases referred to in judgment

Archer, HMS [1919] P 1, 88 LJP 3, 42 Digest (Repl) 929, 7209.
e *Connelly v Director of Public Prosecutions* [1964] 2 All ER 401, [1964] AC 1254, [1964] 2
WLR 1145, 128 JP 418, 48 Cr App R 183, HL, Digest (Cont Vol B) 250, 472a.
Cooper v Wandsworth Board of Works (1863) 14 CBNS 180, 2 New Rep 31, 32 LJCP 185,
8 LT 278, 9 Jur NS 1155, 143 ER 414, 26 Digest (Repl) 585, 2450.
Dyson Holdings Ltd v Fox [1975] 3 All ER 1030, [1976] QB 503, [1975] 3 WLR 744, CA,
Digest (Cont Vol D) 592, 7946a.
f *Public Prosecutor v Fan Yew Teng* [1973] AC 846, [1973] 2 WLR 1053, PC.
R v Rothfield [1937] 4 All ER 320, 26 Cr App R 103, CA, 14(1) Digest (Reissue) 267, 2011.
Wiseman v Borneman [1969] 3 All ER 275, [1971] AC 297, [1969] 3 WLR 706, 45 Tax Cas
540, [1969] TR 279, 48 ATC 278, HL, 28(1) Digest (Reissue) 493, 1760.

Appeal

g On 10th October 1978 at the Central Criminal Court Stephen Patrick Raymond was
convicted on three counts of theft and sentenced by his Honour Judge Gibbens to 10
years' imprisonment on each count (concurrent). In addition restitution and criminal
bankruptcy orders were made against him. He appealed against his conviction. The
facts are set out in the judgment of the court.

h *Louis Blom-Cooper QC* and *Geoffrey Robertson* for the appellant.
Henry Pownall QC and *Alan Suckling* for the Crown.

Cur adv vult

16th October. **WATKINS LJ** read the following judgment of the court: On 10th
i October 1978 at the Central Criminal Court the appellant, who raises points of law in this
court, was convicted of three counts of theft and sentenced by his Honour Judge Gibbens
to 10 years' imprisonment on each count, to run concurrently. In addition, a restitution
order was made against him for a camera, a briefcase, and 12,072·85 Swiss francs, in
favour of the Trade Development Bank, London, and a criminal bankruptcy order in the
sum of £78,000 was made.

The appellant's trial lasted almost four weeks. During much of it he defended
himself. At the close of the prosecution case he asked for, and was granted, the assistance
of leading counsel. Thereafter counsel appeared for him and made detailed submissions
in applying to quash the indictment. The judge rejected this submission and refused the
application. Counsel then departed, leaving the appellant, of his own choice, to resume
his defence by himself.

At the outset of the trial he denied that he had stolen any of the money contained in
the three counts of which he was convicted. Later he admitted taking the money, but
contended that he had done so only because he had been the victim of duress. This
defence eventually became the only issue remaining in the trial. The duress relied on
was a threat made by a number of desperate criminals to shoot the appellant if he did not
do what they asked of him. The threats were said to have been made in a gravel pit at
Tunbridge Wells and also in the back of a motor car. The appellant, who is a highly
intelligent and very articulate man, was obviously disbelieved by the jury, though not
before he had extended almost to the limit the vast patience of the judge, who handled
a most difficult trial with consummate skill. The appellant appeals against his convictions
on the following grounds:

'1. The trial was a nullity in that the bill of indictment preferred against the
appellant had been obtained otherwise than in accordance with section 2 (2) of the
Administration of Justice (Miscellaneous Provisions) Act 1933—namely, that leave
to prefer a Bill of Indictment on the written application of 5th October 1977 of the
Director of Public Prosecutions, in accordance with rule 8 of the Indictments
(Procedure) Rules 1971 (SI 1971 No 2084) was granted by the Hon. Mr. Justice
Michael Davies, in chambers on 25th October 1977 without the learned Judge
hearing the defendant or counsel on his behalf.
'2. The learned trial Judge wrongly refused to quash the Bill of Indictment in
accordance with section 2 (3) of the Administration of Justice (Miscellaneous
Provisions) Act 1933 on the grounds that either (a) that in the absence of any express
statutory authority to the contrary, the courts will always insist on the observance
of the rule *audi alteram partem* for the determination of any issue in legal
proceedings, particularly in criminal proceedings . . . and that, to the extent that the
1971 Rules permit an ex parte determination of the question of leave to prefer a Bill
of Indictment the Rules are ultra vires of the 1933 Act, or (b) the 1933 Act by virtue
of section 2 (6), in delegating the power to the Lord Chancellor to determine the
manner in which Bills of Indictment shall be preferred, is to be interpreted to mean
that such Rules will be made subject to the rule of *audi alteram partem*.'

Those grounds of appeal were drafted by counsel. The appellant has himself drafted
many other grounds of appeal. He has abandoned all of them, and is content to rely now
on those drafted by counsel, which have been argued for him in this court by counsel.

The thefts committed by the appellant were the result of a carefully conceived plan
which was most skilfully executed by him with the assistance of a number of other
people. The facts, very briefly stated, are as follows. A company called Puralator
(Services) Ltd specialises in the carriage of currency and other valuable articles. One of its
clients is the Trade Development Bank. At the beginning of May 1976 Puralator
advertised in the well-known newspaper, the Evening News, for a person who was fully
experienced in the import and export business through Heathrow airport. This job
provided, so it was stated, an excellent opportunity for the right person. The
advertisement caught the eagle eye of the appellant, who soon became a trusted servant
of Puralator.

The strongrooms at Heathrow contain from time to time much valuable cargo. On
26th June 1976, 48 days after the appellant had become employed by Puralator, that
cargo included about £2¼ m worth of currency in sterling and French francs. All of it
was contained in packages which could be carried away with comparative ease by one or
two men. The strongrooms are heavily and carefully guarded. However, by the use of

forged documents and other stratagems and his position as an employee of Puralator, the
a appellant on 26th June was enabled to enter a strongroom and steal from there the whole
of the two and a quarter million pounds' worth of currency which was the property of
the Trade Development Bank.

He then left Heathrow airport to join his collaborators. Soon afterwards he travelled
to Zurich via Dublin. The alertness of a shop assistant in Zurich brought about his
downfall. She had read of the Heathrow theft. One day the appellant whom she did not,
b of course, know, entered the shop where she worked and immediately began spending
a great deal of money; so much that she became suspicious of him and informed the local
police about his activities. As a result he was arrested, and in June 1977 extradited from
Switzerland and brought back to this country under escort. In his prolonged absence
abroad those others who had in one way and another allegedly participated in the crime
were arrested, tried and, all save one, convicted of theft or of handling stolen property.

c Thus it was that the appellant alone appeared for committal for trial at the Crown
Court at Staines Magistrates' Court on 29th September, 1977. There he gave such
unmistakable indications of an intention seriously to disrupt the committal proceedings
as to make a mockery of them that counsel for the Crown decided to abandon them and
to seek leave to prefer a bill of indictment from a High Court judge. He informed the
appellant's solicitor, who seems to have been in sympathy at the time with what he
d meant to do. The committal proceedings were thereupon abandoned, and leave to
prefer a bill of indictment was sought.

The appellant's solicitor on 17th October 1977 wrote to the courts administrator at the
Central Criminal Court informing him that it was the appellant's intention to oppose the
application; and he asked leave to instruct counsel to attend on the occasion when a High
Court judge would consider the application to prefer a bill of indictment, in order to
e oppose it with the object of reinstating the committal proceedings. The solicitor was
informed that his observations would be made known to the High Court judge who
would be invited to consider the application.

The application, together with the solicitor's letter and the reply to it, were placed
before Michael Davies J, whose own observations were, at his request, afterwards made
known to the appellant's solicitor. The judge stated:

f   'I have given full consideration to the defendant's solicitor's letter of 17th October
        1977 but in all the circumstances I am satisfied that the interests of justice require
        me to grant leave to prefer. Furthermore, there would have been no justification
        for me to have departed from the usual practice of dealing with the application on
        the documents without hearing counsel for the prosecution or the defendant.'

g Counsel for the appellant submits that, since the appellant, by himself or by someone
on his behalf, had a right to be heard on the application if he wished to do so, the judge
was wrong to deny him that right. Accordingly, in giving leave to the Crown to prefer
the bill of indictment, he acted without jurisdiction. So the indictment is, and always
has been, a nullity, for which good reason it should have been quashed by his Honour
Judge Gibbens at the trial at the Central Criminal Court at the end of the prosecution's
h case, if not sooner.

In order to deal comprehensively with the submissions it is necessary to trace in
outline the historical development of the creation of a bill of indictment.

Prior to the enactment of the Administration of Justice (Miscellaneous Provisions) Act
1933 a grand jury was responsible for deciding whether a bill of indictment preferred
against a person accused of crime was a true bill on which an accused should stand trial.
j If the grand jury found a true bill the accused faced trial at assizes or quarter sessions on
that indictment. If it did not find a true bill the grand jury threw the bill out, and the
accused was thereupon discharged.

A bill presented to a grand jury could emanate from any one of the following lawful
sources. (a) From a committal for trial of an accused by magistrates at which the accused
was present with a right to be heard. The finding of a true bill by a grand jury from a
committal by magistrates had by the year 1933 become a formality, since by that time

committal proceedings had become the common form of producing a bill of indictment. (b) By the presentation of a voluntary bill of indictment, private persons *a* could prefer such bills. Statutory inroads into their rights to do this were made by the Vexatious Indictments Act 1859, since the right was found to be open to abuse and capable of producing injustice and hardship to an accused, who had no right to appear before and to be heard by a grand jury, which gave heed to the evidence of the accuser only. By 1933 the presentation of a voluntary bill by one private person against another was a rarity. (c) By the presentation of a voluntary bill of indictment with the consent *b* of a High Court judge or the Attorney General or the Solicitor General (see the Vexatious Indictments Act 1859). On this kind of presentation the findings of a true bill by a grand jury was also a formality. An accused person did not appear before and had no right to be heard by the grand jury in any manner. Nor had he the right to appear before a High Court judge or the Attorney General or Solicitor General. The procedures before them were always ex parte. (d) By a presentation resulting from an order made under the *c* provisions of s 9 of the Perjury Act 1911.

One of the main designs of the 1933 Act was to abolish the grand jury. It also disposed of the roles of the Attorney General and Solicitor General. Thus an accused person could thereafter be brought to trial only at assizes or quarter sessions as a consequence of s 2(2) of the 1933 Act, the provisions of which, so far as they need to be stated, are:

> '. . . no bill of indictment charging any person with an indictable offence shall be *d* preferred unless either—(a) the person charged has been committed for trial for the offence; or (b) the bill is preferred . . . by the direction or with the consent of a judge of the High Court or pursuant to an order made under section nine of the Perjury Act 1911 . . .'

Neither by this provision nor by any other section in the 1933 Act was there introduced *e* a new system of bringing about a trial on indictment. The Act merely did away with a virtually useless anachronism, the grand jury, and with the powers of the Attorney General and Solicitor General. It perpetuated the other existing procedures along with the existing powers of a High Court judge and magistrates.

We reject the submission that the 1933 Act did not have this effect, and disagree with the proposition that a precise effect of it was to substitute the High Court judge for the *f* grand jury. The powers of a High Court judge, be it noted, find identical expression in the 1859 and 1933 Acts.

It would, we think, be proper to assume that Parliament was aware that prior to the 1933 Act, High Court judges had been using their powers under the 1859 Act by a procedure which was exclusively ex parte. That being so, was anything done thereafter by statute or rule to change that procedure? The 1933 Act was silent on the matter. By *g* s 2(6) the Lord Chancellor was given rule-making power as follows:

> 'The Lord Chancellor may make rules for carrying this section into effect and in particular for making provision as to the manner in which and the time at which bills of indictment are to be preferred before any court and the manner in which application is to be made for the consent of a judge of the High Court or of a *h* commissioner of assize for the preferment of a bill of indictment.'

The rules made under this subsection are now known as the Indictments (Procedure) Rules 1971, SI 1971 No 2084. Those of them which are material to this appeal provide:

> '**6.** An application under section 2(2)(b) of the Act for consent to the preferment of a bill of indictment may be made to a judge of the High Court.   *j*
> '**7.** Every such application shall be in writing, shall be signed by the applicant or his solicitor.
> '**8.** Every such application—(a) shall be accompanied by the bill of indictment which it is proposed to prefer and, unless the application is made by or on behalf of

a
the Director of Public Prosecutions, shall also be accompanied by an affidavit by the applicant, or, if the applicant is a corporation, by an affidavit by some director or officer of the corporation, that the statements contained in the application are, to the best of the deponent's knowledge, information and belief, true; and (b) shall state whether or not any application has previously been made under these Rules or any Rules revoked by these Rules and whether there have been any committal proceedings, and the result of any such application or proceedings.

b
'**9.**—(1) Where there have been no committal proceedings, the application shall state the reason why it is desired to prefer a bill without such proceedings and—(a) there shall accompany the application proofs of the evidence of the witnesses whom it is proposed to call in support of the charges; and (b) the application shall embody a statement that the evidence shown by the proofs will be available at the trial and that the case disclosed by the proofs is, to the best of the knowledge, information and belief of the applicant, substantially a true case.

c
'(2) Where there have been committal proceedings, and the justice or justices have refused to commit the accused for trial, the application shall be accompanied by—(a) a copy of the depositions; and (b) proofs of any evidence which it is proposed to call in support of the charges so far as that evidence is not contained in the depositions; and the application shall embody a statement that the evidence shown by the proofs and (except so far as may be expressly stated to the contrary in the application) the evidence shown by the depositions, will be available at the trial and that the case disclosed by the depositions and proofs is, to the best of the knowledge, information and belief of the applicant, substantially a true case.

d

'(3) Where the accused has been committed for trial the application shall state why the application is made and shall be accompanied by proofs of any evidence which it is proposed to call in support of the charges, so far as that evidence is not contained in the depositions, and, unless the depositions have already been transmitted to the judge to whom the application is made, shall also be accompanied by a copy of the depositions; and the application shall embody a statement that the evidence shown by the proofs will be available at the trial, and that the case disclosed by the depositions and proofs is, to the best of the knowledge, information and belief of the applicant, substantially a true case.

e

f
'**10.** Unless the judge otherwise directs in any particular case, his decision on the application shall be signified in writing on the application without requiring the attendance before him of the applicant or of any of the witnesses, and if the judge thinks fit to require the attendance of the applicant or of any of the witnesses, their attendance shall not be in open court. Unless the judge gives a direction to the contrary, where an applicant is required to attend as aforesaid, he may attend by a solicitor or by counsel.'

g

Those rules are notable for their total lack of reference to an accused, or a defendant as he is now called. Altogether they may be taken as an acknowledgment of the fact that when a High Court judge considers an application to prefer a bill of indictment he does so by an ex parte procedure, as he has been doing since 1859, a defendant having no right to be heard by him or otherwise to make representations to him. Moreover they may be taken as a determination to perpetuate that procedure. This view of the matter seems to have been universally accepted until lately. It has taken an almost immeasurably long time for an attempted demolition of this ex parte procedure to commence via the grounds of appeal in the present case. However, the attempt may be none the worse for its very recent origins.

h

j
We accept, of course, that, especially since the 1933 Act came into force, the principal means of bringing a defendant to trial on indictment is by committal by magistrates, which since the coming into force of the Criminal Justice Act 1967 is usually performed by use of the provisions of s 1 of that Act, which allows in given circumstances a committal for trial without consideration of the evidence. To avoid this procedure by

seeking the leave of a High Court judge to prefer a bill of indictment (the word 'voluntary' does not appear in modern legislation) is undoubtedly to take a very *a* exceptional step.

In the forefront of his submissions counsel for the appellant contends that (1) the issue confronting a High Court judge on receipt by him of an application for leave to prefer a bill of indictment is not whether the statements or other evidence which support the application for leave to prefer disclose a prima facie case, but whether that vital decision should be taken by magistrates or exceptionally by preferment of a bill by the judge's *b* leave, and (2) that the 1933 Act requires that the defendant should be heard on the application if he wishes.

We find no difficulty in accepting that, if a defendant has a right to be heard and exercises it, or is heard only because the judge in his discretion has agreed to hear him or to receive written representations from him, the only issue on which he can be heard is whether the judge should determine the application for leave to prefer a bill of *c* indictment, or whether in the circumstances committal proceedings should be undertaken. But with the bold assertion that the 1933 Act gave a right to a defendant to be heard by, or otherwise to make representation to, a judge we cannot agree.

Support for this assertion is said to be derived from the elimination of the roles of the Attorney General and Solicitor General, which is said to be an indication that the executive element prior to the 1933 Act was dispensed with, leaving only procedures in *d* which the High Court judge and magistrates take decisions by acting judicially. The 1971 rules, especially r 10, if they are to be taken as referable only to an ex parte procedure, are ultra vires of the 1933 Act, by the passing of which Parliament must have intended to give the right contended for, regardless of whether a defendant could show prejudice to himself by denial of the right.

In this behalf much reference was made to the Privy Council case of *Public Prosecutor* *e* *v Fan Yew Teng* [1973] AC 846. In giving the judgment of the Board, Lord Salmon stated (at 852):

'On the particular facts of the present case the respondent has not suffered one iota of prejudice. It was he who made the application for transfer. None of the facts was in dispute. If there had been committal proceedings, he must have been committed for trial and the result of the trial would have depended solely upon the difficult *f* points of law in issue. Moreover at the trial he never took the point that the court lacked jurisdiction to try him because he had not been committed for trial. No question of waiver however has or could successfully have been argued before this Board. Everything depends upon the true construction of the statute, which has a much wider application than to the special facts of this particular case. It may be that an amendment to the statute is desirable in order to make committal *g* proceedings unnecessary in such very special circumstances as these. But this is irrelevant; the Board must apply the law as it now exists and their Lordships are of the opinion that section 138 [of the Malaysian Criminal Procedure Code] applies to all trials in the High Court including those following an order made under section 417.'

h
As guidance on the relevance of prejudice to the exercise of a legal right what Lord Salmon said is obviously of particular interest and value. We respectfully agree with all he said in the above passage, and would apply the principles he expounded if they were applicable to the present case. In our judgment they have no bearing on the effect of the 1933 Act. In *Teng's* case, as Lord Salmon's judgment in its totality clearly demonstrates, the appropriate legislation of Malaysia lays down in plain terms that no person shall be *j* tried before the High Court unless he has been committed for trial after a preliminary inquiry before a magistrate. Therefore a trial in the High Court in Malaysia without committal proceedings would be unlawful, since no one, a defendant included, has the right to dispense with committal proceedings.

As we have no corresponding legislation, we fail to see how the decision in *Teng* assists

a counsel for the appellant in what he submits is the effect of the 1933 Act, if that was one of the reasons why he laid so much stress on this decision.

We have considered also the submission, for which *R v Rothfield* [1937] 4 All ER 320 is claimed to provide some authority, that, when a judge is exercising in criminal proceedings a discretion, the discretion has to be exercised judicially, which means that a defendant must have the right to be present. The real discretion discussed in *Rothfield's*

b case was that which a judge exercises on the merits of an application to prefer a bill of indictment. This discretion, which has been exercised ever since the 1859 Act, could, it was said, be exercised providing there had been essential compliance with the Indictments (Procedure) Rules. The case involved an alleged failure to comply with r 5(a) of the 1933 rules (SR & O 1933 No 745). We observe that in *Rothfield's* case it was exercised without representation by the defendant, and no point was taken about this during the hearing

c of the appeal in this court. Finally, it is not inappropriate to note that *Rothfield's* case is authority for the proposition that this court will not interfere with the exercise by the judge of his discretion, providing he had jurisdiction to entertain the application for leave to prefer the bill. We cannot regard it as an authority which helps to show that the 1933 Act conferred the right contended for in the present case.

The next submission argued in a number of ways, to not all of which do we feel called

d on to make special reference, relates to the rules of natural justice, in particular the audi alteram partem rule.

The 1933 Act being silent about the matter, the court, so it is argued, is enabled, indeed required, so to exercise its inherent jurisdiction as to allow a defendant to have his say on an application for leave to prefer a bill of indictment; fairness requires also that he should have formal notice of the application and be told the ground on which it is based.

e It is further argued that there has been a revolution in judicial practice with regard to natural justice, that judges are far more sensitive than they used to be to the necessity for an inter partes hearing to take place where once upon a time an ex parte hearing was deemed to meet the requirements of justice and that this current attitude should induce a fresh construction of the 1933 Act: see *Dyson Holdings Ltd v Fox* [1975] 3 All ER 1030, [1975] QB 503.

f The audi alteram partem rule was dealt with extensively in *Wiseman v Borneman* [1969] 3 All ER 275 at 277, [1971] AC 297 at 308 where Lord Reid stated:

> 'Natural justice requires that the procedure before any tribunal which is acting judicially shall be fair in all the circumstances, and I would be sorry to see this fundamental general principle degenerate into a series of hard and fast rules. For a
>
g > long time the courts have, without objection from Parliament, supplemented procedure laid down in legislation where they have found that to be necessary for this purpose. But before this unusual kind of power is exercised it must be clear that the statutory procedure is insufficient to achieve justice and that to require additional steps would not frustrate the apparent purpose of the legislation.'

h Lord Morris stated ([1969] 3 All ER 275 at 278, [1971] AC 297 at 308–309):

> 'My Lords, that the conception of natural justice should at all stages guide those who discharge judicial functions is not merely an acceptable but is an essential part of the philosophy of the law. We often speak of the rules of natural justice. But there is nothing rigid or mechanical about them. What they comprehend has been
>
i > analysed and described in many authorities. But any analysis must bring into relief rather their spirit and their inspiration than any precision of definition or precision as to application. We do not search for prescriptions which will lay down exactly what must, in various divergent situations, be done. The principles and procedures are to be applied which, in any particular situation or set of circumstances, are right

and just and fair. Natural justice, it has been said, is only "fair play in action". Nor do we wait for directions from Parliament. The common law has abundant riches; there may we find what BYLES, J., called "the justice of the common law" (*Cooper v. Wandsworth Board of Works* ((1863) 14 CBNS 180 at 194)).'

In a large number of other recent cases judicial comment of similar kind has been expressed, but those two outstanding commentaries on natural justice surely suffice to illustrate the great importance our courts attach to providing a right to be heard to persons who become involved in civil or criminal matters. The audi alteram partem rule is also instructively and helpfully discussed in de Smith's Judical Review of Administrative Action (4th Edn, 1980). But this rule is not unfailingly to be invoked in every conceivable kind of court proceeding or initiation of court proceedings such as the laying of an information, merely because a person asserts that he has a right to be heard. Ex parte proceedings still take place in our courts regularly for a multiplicity of reasons and purposes. There are many exclusions from the rule, as de Smith's work shows. In that work it is asserted (with justification, we think) that the courts should not fly in the face of a clearly evinced Parliamentary intention to exclude the operation of the rule (see p 179); and later it is stated (p 199):

'Where an act or proposal is only the first step in a sequence of measures which may culminate in a decision detrimental to a person's interests the courts will generally decline to accede to that person's submission that he is entitled to be heard in opposition to this initial act, particularly if he is entitled to be heard at a later stage.'

Moreover, Lord Reid went on in his speech in *Wiseman's* case [1969] 3 All ER 275 at 277–278, [1971] AC 297 at 308 to state:

'It is, I think, not entirely irrelevant to have in mind that it is very unusual for there to be a judicial determination of the question whether there is a prima facie case. Every public officer who has to decide whether to prosecute or raise proceedings ought first to decide whether there is a prima facie case, but no one supposes that justice requires that he should first seek the comments of the accused or the defendant on the material before him. So there is nothing inherently unjust in reaching such a decision in the absence of the other party.'

To that we would add, with respect, that there is nothing inherently unjust in a High Court judge deciding whether he will entertain an application to prefer a bill of indictment without seeking the comments of the defendant, who will undoubtedly have the right to be heard at his trial.

We believe that the audi alteram partem rule is inapplicable to the process of the preferment of a bill of indictment. There is nothing unjust in the ex parte nature of this procedure, which is undertaken in exceptional circumstances. Furthermore, we take the view that by the 1933 Act Parliament intentionally denied to a defendant a right to be heard.

Consequently, we decline to undertake a fresh construction of the 1933 Act on the basis that the audi alteram partem rule should apply to the present case. In any case, we doubt that even in that circumstance it would be open to us to do so. The decision in *Dyson's* case turned on very special facts and is not, we think, of general application.

We were reminded that some courts may at any time set aside an order made ex parte: see RSC Ord 32, r 6, and *HMS Archer* [1919] P 1.

Whether a criminal court has the power in its undoubted inherent jurisdiction (as to which see what Lord Morris said in *Connelly v Director of Public Prosecutions* [1964] 2 All ER 401 at 409, [1964] AC 1254 at 1301) to set aside leave to prefer a bill of indictment granted ex parte, we do not now in disposing of this appeal have to decide. But we think it right to say that we know of no instance of this power having been used in the past, and cannot envisage a circumstance in which a court would be called on to invoke it in the future, having regard to the view that we take of the construction to be placed on the provisions of the 1933 Act and the 1971 rules.

The trial judge was doubtful whether he could entertain an application to quash an indictment, leave to prefer which had been granted by a High Court judge. Nevertheless he acted on the assumption that he had the right to do so, before rejecting the submissions made to him in this respect. This point was not argued before us, except possibly in a cursory way; and, since our views on it can have no influence on the decisions we have reached on the main grounds of appeal, we say nothing of them, beyond expressing a tentative belief that it is for this court, and not another High Court judge or circuit judge, to review a decision made by a High Court judge on an application to him for leave to prefer a bill of indictment. Obviously, under the present appellate system this would involve a trial of the indictment, before an appeal from any consequence of the trial could be made to this court. In any event, we have no doubt that the trial judge here rightly rejected the motion to quash the indictment.

In our judgment, a defendant has no right to appear by himself or by someone on his behalf before a High Court judge who is considering an application for leave to prefer a bill of indictment against him. He has no right to make any kind of representation whatever to that judge.

There may well be a discretion vested in the judge to agree to receive written representations with regard to an application for leave to prefer a bill from, or on behalf of, a defendant. That discretion, exercisable, we think, only in very unusual circumstances, does not extend, in our opinion, to hearing oral representations. But if, contrary to our opinion, the discretion does go that far, we are further of the opinion it is only in an extraordinary circumstance that it should be exercised in favour of a defendant.

In the present case Michael Davies J in his discretion seems merely to have agreed to look at the representations made on behalf of the appellant in the letter written by his solicitor to the courts administrator at the Central Criminal Court on 17th October, 1977. These representations were as follows:

'1. The charges involved the theft or dishonest obtaining of a sum in excess of £2,000,000. The defendant should have the opportunity to test and probe the evidence at committal proceedings in such a serious matter.

'2. The defendant should have the opportunity to call witnesses for the defence at committal proceedings especially as there are a number of relevant witnesses who gave evidence in the spring of 1977 at another trial relating to this matter [see *R v Franciosy* (1978) 68 Cr App R 197] who are not relied upon against this defendant.

'3. The defendant was extradited to this country in July, 1977 after spending one year in custody in Switzerland. After this lapse of time the preparation of his defence may be more difficult if he is disallowed the opportunity of hearing the evidence of the prosecution at committal proceedings.

'4. This is not a case where a Bill is necessary because other defendants have already been committed for and are awaiting trial. In fact the other defendants have been tried as indicated above, and in four cases convicted.

'5. It is not an abuse of the process of the courts for the defendant to require the attendance of the prosecution witnesses at committal proceedings; this is a common feature of fraud cases or cases of a serious nature such as this.

'6. This particular defendant instructs us that if a Bill is granted he will feel that he has been deprived of his rights and treated unjustly.'

Having considered them, he rejected them totally, as appears from his already quoted observations, and declared his intention of following the 'usual practice'.

It is the usual practice for applications to prefer bills of indictment to be dealt with on the documents which accompany the application, and on nothing else. Departures from this practice have been extemely rare. We refer to an instance of it in which this appellant was again concerned.

Early in 1979 he and others appeared in committal proceedings on a charge of conspiracy to pervert the course of justice. His behaviour over a protracted period in those proceedings seriously disrupted them. The Director of Public Prosecutions therefore decided to seek leave to prefer a bill of indictment against him. The application came before Talbot J on 15th March 1979. He allowed the appellant to appear before him and to make representations that the bill be not preferred and that the committal proceedings be allowed to continue. The judge granted the application for leave to prefer, since he was satisfied that the appellant had abused the processes of the magistrates' court at St Albans, where the committal proceedings were taking place, and the documents before him showed a prima facie case against the appellant.

We do not doubt that, had Michael Davies J permitted this appellant to appear before him by himself or by someone on his behalf to make oral representations, in the circumstances known to us of this appellant's behaviour and threatened behaviour at the Staines Magistrates' Court, he would inevitably have rejected the application for committal proceedings to take place, and would have granted the application for leave to prefer a bill of indictment. That decision would not have been open to review by this court. No injustice whatever was done to this appellant by the granting of leave. The indictment on which he was convicted was not, and is not, a nullity. There can be no doubt that the appellant is becoming, if has not already become, a practised disturber of court proceedings. In agreeing to receive and consider the written representations made by his solicitor on the appellant's behalf, Michael Davies J probably paid him much more regard than he ever deserved.

For those reasons this appeal is dismissed.

Appeal dismissed. Leave to appeal to the House of Lords refused.

Solicitors: *Hallinan, Blackburn Gittings & Co* (for the appellant); *R E T Birch* (for the Crown).

Sepala Munasinghe Esq   Barrister.

Gold Star Publications Ltd v Director of Public Prosecutions

HOUSE OF LORDS

LORD WILBERFORCE, LORD SIMON OF GLAISDALE, LORD RUSSELL OF KILLOWEN, LORD KEITH OF KINKEL AND LORD ROSKILL

9th, 10th MARCH, 7th MAY 1981

Criminal law – Obscene publications – Forfeiture – Obscene articles intended for export and publication overseas – Whether English court entitled to hold that articles obscene and to order forfeiture – Obscene Publications Act 1959, s 3.

The appellants kept crates of obscene magazines in a warehouse prior to exporting them for sale overseas. The magazines were seized by the police under s 3(1)[a] of the Obscene Publications Act 1959 as being 'obscene articles ... kept for publication for gain'. An order for the forfeiture of the magazines was made by magistrates under s 3(3). On appeal, that order was confirmed by the Crown Court which, having perused the articles and having found that they were destined for Europe, America, Africa and elsewhere abroad, held that they were intended for publication to persons who would have some standard of literacy in English and who would therefore be able to comprehend them, and that the effect of the articles would be to tend to deprave and corrupt those persons. The Divisional Court of the Queen's Bench Division affirmed the Crown Court's decision. The appellants appealed to the House of Lords against the forfeiture order, contending that the 1959 Act did not apply to articles destined for export and publication overseas and that there was no evidence that the eventual readers overseas, who might well have different attitudes and moral standards, would be corrupted or depraved by the magazine.

Held (Lord Simon dissenting) – The appeal would be dismissed for the following reasons—

(1) On the true construction of s 3(1) of the 1959 Act the police, acting under a warrant issued by a magistrate, were empowered to seize an obscene article kept for publication for gain and the courts were entitled to hold that such an article was obscene even though the article was kept for publication outside the jurisdiction of the English courts (see p 259 *e*, p 260 *b*, p 262 *g h* and p 265 *h* to p 266 *a* and *f*, post).

(2) Whether an article tended to deprave and corrupt persons who were likely to read it, and so was obscene by virtue of s 1(1)[b] of the 1959 Act, when the likely readers were in foreign countries was a matter to be decided by the magistrates hearing the summons for a forfeiture order according to the evidence that the article would or would not tend to deprave or corrupt likely readers in the country of destination. Although the magistrates were not entitled simply to apply English standards of morality to the article, they were entitled to form the opinion, from their own knowledge and without evidence, that, having regard to the likely readers, the article was so clearly obscene as to be likely to deprave and corrupt. Since the Crown Court had correctly adopted that approach to the seized articles its decision to confirm the forfeiture order was rightly upheld by the Divisional Court (see p 259 *g h*, p 260 *b*, p 262 *g h* and p 266 *b* to *f*, post).

Notes

For the power to search for and seize obscene articles kept for publication, see 11

---

a   Section 3, so far as material, is set out at p 263 *g* to p 264 *c*, post
b   Section 1(1) is set out at p 263 *e f*, post

Halsbury's Laws (4th Edn) para 1020, and for cases on indecent publications, see 15
Digest (Reissue) 1034–1043, 8969–9023.   a
    For the Obscene Publications Act 1959, ss 1, 3, see 8 Halsbury's Statutes (3rd Edn) 479,
482.

Cases referred to in opinions
Attorney General's Reference (No 2 of 1975) [1976] 2 All ER 753, [1976] 1 WLR 710, 62 Cr
    App R 255, CA, 15 Digest (Reissue) 1037, 8984.   b
Director of Public Prosecutions v Jordan [1976] 3 All ER 775, [1977] AC 699, [1976] 3 WLR
    887, 141 JP 13, HL, 15 Digest (Reissue) 1042, 9023.
Director of Public Prosecutions v Whyte [1972] 3 All ER 12, [1972] AC 849, [1972] 3 WLR
    410, 136 JP 686, HL, 15 Digest (Reissue) 1036, 8978.
Handyside (7th December 1976, Series A No 24), European Court of Human Rights.
R v Henn, R v Darby [1980] 2 All ER 166, [1980] 2 WLR 597 [1979] ECR 3795, [1980] 1   c
    CMLR 246, CJEC and HL.
Transport Publishing Co Pty Ltd v Literature Board of Review (1956) 99 CLR 111, H Ct of
    Aust.

Appeal
On 12th December 1978 the justices for the petty sessional division of Croydon sitting   d
as a magistrates' court at Croydon made an order under s 3(3) of the Obscene Publications
Act 1959 ordering forfeiture of 151,877 magazines published by the appellants, Gold
Star Publications Ltd, which were seized on 21st April 1978 in the appellants' warehouse
pursuant to a warrant issued under s 3(1) of the 1959 Act on 18th April 1978. On 2nd
May 1979 the Crown Court at Croydon (his Honour Judge Thomas sitting with justices)
dismissed an appeal by the appellants against the order. On 2nd April 1980 the Divisional e
Court of the Queen's Bench Division (Eveleigh LJ and Watkins J) dismissed the appellants'
appeal by way of case stated from that decision. On 30th April 1980 the Divisional Court
refused an application by the appellants for leave to appeal to the House of Lords but
certified, under s 1(2) of the Administration of Justice Act 1960, that the following point
of law of general public importance was involved in its decision: whether, in proceedings
for forfeiture under s 3 of the 1959 Act where articles had been seized in a warehouse in   f
England but were destined for export and publication overseas, having regard to the
definition of obscenity in s 1(1) of that Act, an English court was both competent and
entitled in law to hold that those articles were obscene. On 3rd July the House of Lords
granted the appellants leave to appeal. The facts are set out in the opinion of Lord
Roskill.

                                                                                          g
Louis Blom-Cooper QC and *Geoffrey Robertson* for the appellants.
David Tudor Price and *Timothy Davis* for the respondent.

Their Lordships took time for consideration.

7th May. The following opinions were delivered.   h

LORD WILBERFORCE. My Lords, s 3 of the Obscene Publications Act 1959 entitles
the police, on warrant issued by a magistrate, to seize and remove obscene articles from
premises in which they are 'kept for publication for gain'. By subsequent proceedings,
the articles so seized may be forfeited. In the appellants' export warehouse at Whyteleafe,
Surrey, the police found a large number of magazines which were, according to standards
applied in England, undoubtedly 'obscene articles', viz hard pornography. Of these the
great majority, some 150,000 in all, were, according to the appellants' contentions, which
the justices and the Crown Court must have accepted, for export to Europe, America,
Africa and elsewhere abroad, though there were a few destined for sale in this country by
mail order. This has given rise to the certified question of law whether the Act applies
not only to material published in this country but to material destined for publication

overseas. The issue depends entirely on the scope to be given to the words 'kept for
a publication for gain', in, of course, their context. I do not think, though the contrary was
submitted, that the case raises any question as to the territoriality or extra-territoriality
of United Kingdom legislation: the property in question is located in this country, and
the disposal of it by the police is to take place in this country. Nor are authorities as to
composite crimes, that is crimes of which some elements may occur within and some
outside the jursisdiction, of any help or relevance. Nor is the fact, if it be so, that
b property interests of foreigners may be affected by the seizure of any relevance.
Foreigners may be, and commonly are, interested as importers, or indeed as publishers,
of obscene literature or articles, but within the United Kingdom they are totally subject
to our laws against obscenity.

The relevant words are quite general, but it is necessary to consider the implications
of holding that they apply to articles intended for export. The question is a quite
c legitimate one of whether Parliament intended this piece of legislation to apply to
articles which could not deprave or corrupt the British public, but were sent to places
outside the jurisdiction of English courts.

There were two objections against ascribing this intention to Parliament. First it may
be said that to do so would be a kind of moral imperialism, or at least paternalism. The
answer to this is that Parliament's intentions cannot be limited in this way. Parliament
d may well have desired to prevent this country becoming the source of a flourishing
export trade in pornography, and may have thought that profits made by exports could
help to sustain domestic trade. The words 'for gain' seem to me significant. Further, the
Act does not apply to Scotland or Northern Ireland, so it would follow from the appellants'
argument that articles destined for those parts of the United Kingdom could not be
seized. It seems to me most unlikely that Parliament can have intended this, and, if not,
e it must follow that articles destined for export to other countries must be capable of
seizure. One may add that to exempt articles intended for export would offer an easy
pretext for avoiding the application of the section. So I cannot accept that Parliament
must be supposed to have intended to confine this power to articles intended for
publication in England or Wales.

But, second, it may be said that to extend the Act to articles destined for export would
f make the Act unworkable. Obscenity, viz tendency to deprave or corrupt persons likely
to read the relevant matter (see s 1 of the Act), is relative: what may deprave or corrupt
some may have no effect, or, theoretically a beneficial effect, on others: see *Director of
Public Prosecutions v Whyte* [1972] 3 All ER 12, [1972] AC 849, *Director of Public Prosecutions
v Jordan* [1976] 3 All ER 775, [1977] AC 699 and the *Handyside* case (7th December 1976,
Series A No 24), decided by the European Court of Human Rights. How, it may be
g asked, can magistrates decide on the likely effect of this material on foreigners of
different attitudes and mores? How (still less) can they decide on a defence of the public
good if this is raised under s 4 of the Act?

In my opinion it has to be accepted that in some cases the magistrates will not be able
to form any opinion on this matter. In such cases, since the court has to be satisfied that
the articles are obscene (see s 3(3)), it would have to release them. In other cases there
h might be evidence before them either way: that the articles would not tend to deprave
or corrupt likely readers in the country of destination, or that they would. Then they
would have to decide on the evidence. In still other cases they would be justified in
taking the view that, having regard to the likely readers, the articles were so clearly
obscene that evidence was not needed. As was said in *Transport Publishing Co Pty Ltd v
Literature Board of Review* (1956) 99 CLR 111 at 118 there is such a thing as ordinary
human nature which is not a subject for proof by evidence. If a defence of public good
is raised, they must deal with it on the evidence.

In the present case, the Crown Court took the view that the articles were clearly
obscene. The decision shows that the members of the court perused agreed samples;
they found that they consisted of photographs and written matter in the English
language, the price of the articles was given in United States, Canadian or Australian
dollars:

'They are plainly not intended for publication to some remote and primitive tribe who would not comprehend them. We can properly infer and do infer that they *a* were intended to be published to persons . . . who have some standard of literacy in English and who would comprehend them and that the effect of them would be such as to tend to deprave and corrupt those persons.'

These findings to my mind show both that the Act is workable as regards exports, and that the court properly applied its mind to the probable effect of the articles on likely readers. The Divisional Court so found, and I agree with their judgment. In my *b* opinion, therefore, the certified question should be answered in the affirmative with the rider that the word 'overseas' should properly be 'outside the jurisdiction of the English courts', and the appeal dismissed.

LORD SIMON OF GLAISDALE. My Lords, I have the misfortune to differ from *c* my noble and learned friends. I venture a few words in deference to the argument by which I was convinced and because consideration of the Report of the Committee on Obscenity and Film Censorship (chairman, Professor Bernard Williams) (Cmnd 7772 (1979)) might embrace the question how far English law really wishes to concern itself with the morals of foreign nationals.

I do not think that the instant issue can be resolved merely by fastening on the words *d* 'publication for gain': 'publication' cannot here be construed as an abstraction. With publication to whom was Parliament concerned? It seems to me inherently unlikely that Parliament was concerned with the effect of obscene publications on anyone outside the United Kingdom. It would be mere officiousness in any case to seek to impose our own rules and standards and forensic judgments for the moral welfare of foreign nationals. And this is a field in which cultural standards and legislative policies are *e* notoriously diverse.

The inherent unlikelihood of Parliament being concerned with the morals of foreign nationals, and therefore with publication abroad, is borne out when the 1959 Act is purposively construed. It had two objectives: first, to enable serious literary, artistic, scientific or scholarly work to draw on the amplitude of human experience without fear of allegation (which was implicit in the previous law) that it could conceivably have a *f* harmful effect on persons other than those to whom it was in truth directed; and, second, by hiving off such work, to enable effective action to be taken against the exploitation of 'hard pornography', obscene articles without pretension to any literary, artistic, scientific or scholarly value.

These twin objectives are, indeed, indicated in the long title of the Act: '. . . to amend the law relating to the publication of obscene matter; to provide for the protection of *g* literature; and to strengthen the law concerning pornography.'

It is, incidentally, a mistake to suppose that the phrase 'strengthen the law concerning pornography' in the long title involves any artificial construction of the powers of search, seizure and forfeiture in s 3 of the Act. There were such powers in the Obscene Publications Act 1857. The changes made in 1959 as regards such powers were as follows: (1) certain interested persons other than the person summoned became entitled *h* to be heard by the court; (2) the operation of the powers was extended to cover articles on a stall or vehicle; (3) a search warrant empowered the police to seize documents related to a business; (4) it was no longer necessary for the complainant to swear that there had already been a publication; (5) the defence of 'public good' under s 4 became available in forfeiture proceedings. These changes sufficiently explain everything in the long title so far as it relates to the powers of search, seizure and forfeiture. They give no *j* warrant to construction of s 3 to protect the morals of foreign nationals living in foreign countries. I can well believe that not a few people hold that, notwithstanding any difficulty in defining internationally acceptable standards of what is obscene, it is the moral duty of the British legislature to inhibit international trade in pornographic material. But, if so high-minded an objective had really been one of the purposes of the

1959 Act, it would certainly have been stated in the long title. Its absence is clamant
a when it comes to a purposive interpretation of the enacting provisions.

The inherent unlikelihood of Parliament legislating to safeguard from moral pollution
foreign nationals in foreign countries, regardless of the policies of their own respective
legislatures, the confirmation of such self-restraint by scrutiny of the long title, and the
absence of any contra-indication in the enacting provisions, these considerations are
borne out by a further one: the nature of the tasks imposed on the justices in the
b forfeiture jurisdiction. They have in the first place to determine whether the material
liable to forfeiture is likely to deprave and corrupt a significant proportion of the persons
likely to be exposed to it. They have, second, to determine whether publication was
nevertheless justified as being for the public good on the grounds of its literary etc
value. English justices are capable of making such judgments in respect of their fellow
citizens in the United Kingdom. To form such a judgment for the benefit of, say, Danes
c (even those who can read English), not to mention the Ik people of East Africa or
Rastafarians in the Caribbean (who, incidentally, can presumably read English), seems an
unlikely task to be imposed by Parliament.

In my respectful submission the argument reduced itself to absurdity when counsel
for the respondent candidly accepted that in principle it had to extend to a publication
in Arabic for export to an Arab-speaking country, and presumably even if the owner of
d the material and prospective publisher was himself a national of the country to which the
export was proposed.

But the difficulty facing the justices on the construction contended for by the
respondent is not limited to the task of determining what will deprave and corrupt
people with whom they might well have no cultural standards in common. By s 4 of the
1959 Act they have to go on to determine in respect of such people whether the
e deleterious tendency of the material is outweighed by the benefits conferred by its
literary, artistic, scientific etc value. This balancing task is difficult enough of
performance by English justices as regards fellow citizens; it seems to me so impossible
of performance as regards exotic peoples as to constitute yet further indication that
Parliament was not concerned at all with publication in foreign countries.

Counsel for the appellants put in the forefront of his argument the undoubted
f principle that it is only exceptionally (and then by clear words) that United Kingdom
legislation operates extra-territorially. I do not think that this rule assists the appellants'
case directly, since, although the material in question was destined for abroad, it was
seized and declared to be forfeited within the jurisdiction. But two concepts lie behind
this rule. First, that Parliament does not legislate where it has no effective power of
enforcement; this does not assist the appellants, since enforcement here is within the
g jurisdiction. But the second concept does indeed further the appellants' argument: the
rule is also based on international comity. Other than quite exceptionally, sovereigns do
not meddle with the subjects of foreign sovereigns within the jurisdiction of those
foreign sovereigns, a consideration inherently potent in matters where international
standards vary greatly. It is in this indirect way that the presumption against extra-
territoriality avails the appellants.

h   Counsel for the appellants sought to support his argument based on extra-territoriality
by reference to the fact that the Act does not extend to Scotland or Northern Ireland. I
do not think this helps the appellants. In so far as the presumption against extra-
territoriality assists the appellants, it is because sovereigns do not legislate for foreign
subjects; and Scots and Northern Irish are not foreign subjects. But if the argument that
the Act does not extend to Scotland or Northern Ireland does not help the appellants,
j neither does it avail the respondent. It is said that, if the forfeiture provisions of the Act
do not extend to material destined for publication in foreign countries, neither can they
apply to material designed for publication in Scotland or Northern Ireland. I do not
think that this follows at all. Legislation of this type is characteristically cast in separate
English and Scottish (and sometimes Northern Irish) enactments; this merely reflects the
several systems of law which operate within the United Kingdom. But an Act which

does not extend beyond England and Wales (or Scotland) is still passed by a Parliament consisting of representatives of England, Wales, Scotland and Northern Ireland. If such *a* a Parliament passes an Act limited to England and Wales it does not imply that Scotland is regarded as a foreign country. A Parliament in which the people of Scotland and Northern Ireland are represented may be legitimately concerned with material in England which would deprave and corrupt people in Scotland or Northern Ireland, without its being an inevitable conclusion that such a Parliament legitimately has an equivalent concern to impose its domestic standards of morality on foreign people. *b* Equally, the fact that Parliament does not concern itself with the morals of the people of Denmark does not imply that it must necessarily show unconcern for the welfare of the people of Scotland.

As for 'export', which is the word which appears in the point of law certified for your Lordships' consideration, not since the Union with Scotland Act 1706 has the traffic of goods across the Scottish border been described as 'export'; and not since the days of *c* Canute has traffic from England to Denmark been otherwise described. This is no mere verbal point: it indicates the fallacy of arguing that, if Parliament did not intend 'publication' to extend to publication to persons for whom it has no political concern, then Parliament must equally be credited with unconcern as to the effect of publication in Scotland or Northern Ireland.

There is one further matter which I think reinforces the interpretation I venture to put *d* on the Act, namely that 'publication' was not intended to extend to publication in foreign countries. Parliament has not only legislated generally in this field by the Obscene Publications Act 1959; it has also legislated particularly within the field by the Protection of Chidren Act 1978. That is an Act to prevent the exploitation of children by making indecent photographs of them; and to penalise the distribution, showing and advertisement of such indecent photographs. The Act contains provisions for entry, *e* search, seizure and forfeiture similar to those in the Obscene Publications Act 1959. But the significant feature of the Protection of Children Act 1978, in contrast to the 1959 Act, is that it contains a provision whereby offences under the Act are to be included in the list of extradition crimes contained in Sch 1 to the Extradition Act 1870. The effect of this is that the British government can negotiate treaties with foreign powers providing for the mutual extradition of persons who have committed the extradition crime. The 1978 *f* Act thus shows the different way in which Parliament proceeds when it evinces concern for offences against decency which might affect the nationals of foreign powers.

For these reasons I would allow the appeal, holding that s 3 of the Obscene Publications Act 1959 does not apply in respect of articles which are 'destined for export and publication overseas'.

g

LORD RUSSELL OF KILLOWEN. My Lords, I have had the advantage of reading in draft the speeches prepared by my noble and learned friends Lord Wilberforce and Lord Roskill. I agree with them and concur in the answer proposed to the question posed and the dismissal of this appeal.

LORD KEITH OF KINKEL. My Lords, I have had the benefit of reading in draft the *h* speech of my noble and learned friend Lord Wilberforce. I agree with it, and for the reasons which he gives I too would answer the certified question in the manner which he proposes, and dismiss the appeal.

LORD ROSKILL. My Lords, the appellants appeal to your Lordships' House against an order of the Divisional Court (Eveleigh LJ and Watkins J) made on 2nd April 1980 *j* dismissing an appeal by way of case stated from an order made by the Crown Court at Croydon (his Honour Judge Thomas sitting with justices) on 2nd May 1979. The Crown Court had dismissed an appeal by the appellants from an order made by justices sitting at Croydon Magistrates' Court on 12th December 1978 pursuant to the powers conferred on them by s 3(3) of the Obscene Publications Act 1959. That order was for the

forfeiture of no less than 151,877 magazines published by the appellants and seized on
a 21st April 1978 in the appellants' export warehouse, pursuant to a warrant issued under
s 3(1) of the 1959 Act on 18th April 1978. The total market value of those magazines is
found by the Crown Court to have been of the order of £150,000. The Divisional Court
certified this question for your Lordships' House as a point of law of general public
importance:

b   'Whether in proceedings for forfeiture under Section 3 of the Obscene Publications
Act 1959 where articles have been seized in a warehouse in England but are destined
for export and publication overseas having regard to the definition of obscenity in
Section 1(1) of the Act, an English Court is both competent and entitled in law to
hold that these articles are obscene.'

The Divisional Court refused leave to appeal to your Lordships' House but that leave was
c granted on 3rd July 1980.

The appeal indeed raises a point of general importance under the 1959 Act in relation
to magazines and the like found by justices to be 'obscene' but which are destined for
export and thus for publication overseas, for it is submitted on the appellants' behalf that
in such a case it is not within the power of an English court of otherwise competent
jurisdiction to make a forfeiture order such as was made in the present case. Whether
d this submission is well founded depends solely on the true construction of the 1959
Act. For ease of reference I set out in full the several relevant parts of that statute. The
long title reads thus:

'An Act to amend the law relating to the publication of obscene matter; to
provide for the protection of literature; and to strengthen the law concerning
e   pornography.'

The following sections are the most relevant:

'**1.**—(1) For the purposes of this Act an article shall be deemed to be obscene if its
effect or (where the article comprises two or more distinct items) the effect of any
one of its items is, if taken as a whole, such as to tend to deprave and corrupt persons
f   who are likely, having regard to all relevant circumstances, to read, see or hear the
matter contained or embodied in it.

'(2) In this Act "article" means any description of article containing or embodying
matter to be read or looked at or both . . .

'(3) For the purposes of this Act a person publishes an article who—(a) distributes,
circulates, sells, lets on hire, gives, or lends it, or who offers it for sale or for letting
g   on hire . . .

'**3.**—(1) If a justice of the peace is satisfied by information on oath that there is
reasonable ground for suspecting that, in any premises in the petty sessions area for
which he acts, or on any stall or vehicle in that area, being premises or a stall or
vehicle specified in the information, obscene articles are, or are from time to time,
kept for publication for gain, the justice may issue a warrant under his hand
h   empowering any constable to enter (if need be by force) and search the premises, or
to search the stall or vehicle, within fourteen days from the date of the warrant, and
to seize and remove any articles found therein or thereon which the constable has
reason to believe to be obscene articles and to be kept for publication for gain . . .

'(3) Any article seized under subsection (1) of this section shall be brought before
a justice of the peace acting for the same petty sessions area as the justice who issued
j   the warrant, and the justice before whom the articles are brought may thereupon
issue a summons to the occupier of the premises or, as the case may be, the user of
the stall or vehicle to appear on a day specified in the summons before a magistrates'
court for that petty sessions area to show cause why the articles or any of them
should not be forfeited; and if the court is satisfied, as respects any of the articles,
that at the time when they were seized they were obscene articles kept for

publication for gain, the court shall order those articles to be forfeited: Provided that if the person summoned does not appear, the court shall not make an order unless service of the summons is proved.

'(4) In addition to the person summoned, any other person being the owner, author or maker of any of the articles brought before the court, or any other person through whose hands they had passed before being seized, shall be entitled to appear before the court on the day specified in the summons to show cause why they should not be forfeited . . .

'(7) For the purposes of this section the question whether an article is obscene shall be determined on the assumption that copies of it would be published in any manner likely having regard to the circumstances in which it was found, but in no other manner . . .

'**4.**—(1) A person shall not be convicted of an offence against section two of this Act, and an order for forfeiture shall not be made under the foregoing section, if it is proved that publication of the article in question is justified as being for the public good on the ground that it is in the interests of science, literature, art or learning, or of other objects of general concern.

'(2) It is hereby declared that the opinion of experts as to the literary, artistic, scientific or other merits of an article may be admitted in any proceedings under this Act either to establish or to negative the said ground.

'**5** . . . (3) This Act shall not extend to Scotland or to Northern Ireland.'

My Lords, it is important to observe that, as already mentioned, the present proceedings arise under s 3 of the 1959 Act. That section, unlike s 2(1) which was later amended by s 1 of the Obscene Publications Act 1964, does not create a criminal offence and a person whose property is seized or forfeited under s 3 is not for that reason alone guilty of a criminal offence. Section 3 is concerned with prevention and not with punishment and is one of the provisions in the 1959 Act which is designed, as the long title of that Act shows, 'to strengthen the law concerning pornography'. No prosecution of the appellants has taken place. My Lords, the Crown Court made the following findings of fact relevant to the present appeal:

'The forfeited magazines fall into three groups. (1) In the first group are 391 magazines which were found in the mail order department of the appellants' premises. These were destined for home consumption. (2) The second group consists of 6,609 magazines which were packed in crates ready for export to the USA. (3) The third group consists of 144,877 magazines. These were found in the export warehouse at the appellants' premises. We do not know the precise destination of any of them, but we have been told that the appellant company exports its publications to Europe, America, Africa and elsewhere abroad.'

Nothing turns in the present appeal on the first of those three groups.

My Lords, the first question to determine is the true construction of the relevant words in s 3(1) of the 1959 Act. The condition precedent to the right of a justice to issue a warrant is that he is satisfied that in the area in question 'obscene articles are, or are from time to time, kept for publication for gain . . .' It was strenuously argued that these words mean 'kept for publication in England and Wales for gain in England and Wales' and that any other construction would involve giving extra-territorial effect to these provisions of the 1959 Act when not only was there no clear provision to that effect but it could not have been the intention of Parliament in this statute to concern itself with the morals of persons outside the jurisdiction. It was further argued that the construction contended for by the respondent could not be correct since to accept that construction would or might involve the forfeiture of property, rights or interests within the jurisdiction of persons outside the jurisdiction. My Lords, this last point though argued first may be quickly disposed of. Not only is there no finding that any property, rights or interests within the jurisdiction of persons outside the jurisdiction are presently

involved, but even if there were such a finding there could be no objection to such
a property, rights or interests being subjected to legislative control by Parliament.

My Lords, there are no express words of limitation on the relevant words in s 3(1).
Moreover the 1959 Act has no application to Scotland or Northern Ireland. Though the
certified question is stated to relate to export 'overseas', the appellants' argument if sound
must apply equally to obscene articles (as defined in s 1(2)) kept in England not for export
overseas, as in the present case, but for dispatch ('export' is hardly the right word) to
b Scotland or Northern Ireland. My Lords, there being no express words of limitation in
s 3(1), the limitation contended for by the appellants must be deduced, if at all, from
other provisions of the 1959 Act. In my view no question of the extra-territorial effect
of legislation in the proper understanding of that phrase arises in this appeal. The
magazines in question are within the jurisdiction. The place of their seizure was within
the jurisdiction. The appellants are a limited company amenable to the jurisdiction. No
c question of extra-territoriality arises in connection with s 3.

The crucial question is whether, because of the definition of obscenity in s 1(1) and also
because of the provisions of s 4, a narrow meaning must be given to the all important
words in s 3(1), notwithstanding the absence of any words of limitation in that
subsection. The strongest way in which the appellants' case can be put arises from the
fact that, since the passing of the 1959 Act, there is no longer any 'abstract' concept of
d obscenity. As Lord Wilberforce pointed out in Director of Public Prosecutions v Whyte
[1972] 3 All ER 12 at 17, [1972] AC 849 at 860 and again in Director of Public Prosecutions
v Jordan [1976] 3 All ER 775 at 778, [1977] AC 699 at 717, s 1 is directed to 'relative
obscenity', that is, obscenity relative to likely readers or other likely recipients of the
article in question. It has thus become important in these cases to determine who are the
likely readers or customers, for it is only when that class or those classes have been
e sufficiently identified that the next question arises, namely whether the allegedly
offending article will 'tend to deprave and corrupt persons' who form a significant part
of that class or of those classes. Only if that further condition is satisfied will the article
in question then be 'obscene' within s 1(1). This being the true construction of this
subsection, the question is naturally forcefully asked on the appellants' behalf how an
English magistrates' court can possibly answer these questions in relation to persons of no
f known or readily identifiable class or propensity in different countries throughout the
world. It is further asked why Parliament should have concerned itself with the
protection of the morals of such persons whoever they may be. Standards of morality
vary immensely in different countries and what is forbidden or is obscene in one country
may even be thought to be therapeutic in another. Reliance was placed in this connection
on the opinion of the Advocate-General (J-P Warner) in R v Henn, R v Darby [1980] 2 All
g ER 166 at 180, [1980] 2 WLR 597 at 604, quoting from the judgment of the European
Court of Human Rights in the Handyside case (7th December 1976, Series A No 24, paras.
48–49), and also on the passage in the judgment of the Court of Justice of the European
Communities in Henn [1980] 2 All ER 166 at 191, [1980] 2 WLR 597 at 629: 'In
principle, it is for each member state to determine in accordance with its own scale of
values and in the form selected by it the requirements of public morality in its territory.'
h   My Lords, these are powerful arguments and they can be reinforced by consideration
how the defence of 'public good' introduced by s 4 of the 1959 Act could be effectively
raised in such circumstances as those now under consideration. But, powerful as these
arguments are, they seem to me to overlook the fact that the 1959 Act was concerned
amongst other matters to strengthen the law concerning pornography and that one of its
objectives in s 3(1) is to stop persons in England and Wales 'publishing for gain'.
j 'Publish', so far as presently relevant, is defined in s 1(3)(a) and if a person in this country,
for example, offers an article for sale he is publishing that article. If that article is obscene
he is publishing an obscene article for sale, and if he does so for valuable consideration he
is publishing an obscene article for gain. On a fair reading of s 3(1) I am unable to see
why he ceases so to publish an obscene article for gain because its ultimate destination is
in Scotland, Northern Ireland or anywhere else in the world, for Parliament may very

well have intended that England and Wales should not become a source from which
unrestricted supplies of obscene articles should flow unchecked not only to other parts of   *a*
the United Kingdom but also to other countries throughout the world.

My Lords, I fully recognise that this conclusion may face a magistrates' court with
difficult practical and evidential problems. But their task in administering the 1959 Act
and the later amending legislation on this subject has long been recognised as difficult,
unenviable and a matter for sympathy. It is not correct to say that a magistrates' court
grappling with this problem will be asked to apply English standards of morality to   *b*
allegedly offending articles destined elsewhere. The court will be asked to do its best to
decide whether those articles will have a tendency to deprave or corrupt a significant
number of people in the country to which they are destined. It would be open to those
objecting to forfeiture, and thus exercising their rights under s 3(3) and (4), to adduce
evidence to show that the conditions specified in s 1(1) have not in relation to the
particular destination in question been satisfied. Moreover, I see no reason in principle   *c*
why, if it is desired in a particular case to raise the 'public good' defence, it should not be
possible to do so. In principle I see no objection to seeking to show by admissible
evidence that a particular article is to be regarded in a particular country to which it is
destined as of (for example) literary merit even though it might not be so regarded in this
country.

Two other matters shall be mentioned for the sake of completeness. First, reliance was   *d*
placed on the appellants' behalf on the Protection of Children Act 1978 and in particular
on the extradition conditions in s 1(6) of that statute, a provision omitted from the 1959
Act. My Lords it cannot be right to interpret the 1959 Act by reference to another Act
passed nearly twenty years later on a different subject matter. The presence of an
extradition provision in the 1978 Act or the absence of such a provision in the 1959 Act
are not aids to the construction of s 3(1) of the latter statute. Second, much reliance was   *e*
placed on the decision of the Court of Appeal in *Attorney General's Reference (No 2 of 1975)*
[1976] 2 All ER 753, [1976] 1 WLR 710. With respect, I have not found that decision of
assistance in determining the present appeal.

In the result I would answer the certified question in the affirmative, subject to the
amendment proposed by my noble and learned friend Lord Wilberforce, and I would
dismiss this appeal for substantially the same reasons as those given in the Crown Court   *f*
and in the Divisional Court in their clear and succinct judgments.

*Appeal dismissed. Order appealed from affirmed and certified question answered in the
affirmative with the qualification that 'overseas' means 'outside the jurisdiction of the English
courts'.*

Solicitors: *Offenbach & Co* (for the appellants); *Director of Public Prosecutions (for the
respondent).*

Mary Rose Plummer   Barrister.

Finnigan v Sandiford
Clowser v Chaplin

HOUSE OF LORDS

LORD HAILSHAM OF ST MARYLEBONE LC, LORD DIPLOCK, LORD KEITH OF KINKEL, LORD SCARMAN
AND LORD ROSKILL

13th APRIL, 14th MAY 1981

Road traffic – Breath test – Failure to provide specimen – Validity of arrest – Constable entering
private premises to effect arrest without invitation and as a trespasser following refusal of lawful
request to provide specimen of breath – Whether arrest lawful – Road Traffic Act 1972, s 8(5).

Where a statute confers a power of arrest without warrant, but does not contain a specific
power of entry onto private premises for the purpose of effecting the arrest, it is rarely,
if ever, possible to conclude that the power of arrest implies a power of entry, since
Parliament is not to be taken to authorise inroads into the rights of private citizens other
than those that it expressly enacts. Accordingly, the power to arrest without warrant
conferred on a constable by s 8(5)[a] of the Road Traffic Act 1972 where he has lawfully
made a request for a breath test and wishes to effect an arrest under s 8(5) following a
failure to provide a specimen of breath does not empower him to enter onto the property
of the person to whom he has made the request if he has no invitation to enter and would
be trespassing on the property (see p 268 *f* to *h*, p 270 *d g j* to p 271 *e*, post).

Morris v Beardmore [1980] 2 All ER 753 applied.

Notes

For the power to require a specimen of breath for a breath test and the power of arrest
following refusal to provide a specimen, see Supplement to 33 Halsbury's Laws (3rd Edn)
para 1061A.3,6.

For the Road Traffic Act 1972, s 8, see 42 Halsbury's Statutes (3rd Edn) 1651.

Case referred to in opinions

Morris v Beardmore [1980] 2 All ER 753, [1980] 3 WLR 283, [1980] RTR 321, HL.

Appeals

Finnigan v Sandiford

On 16th September 1980 justices for the county of Cheshire acting in and for the petty
sessional division of Ellesmere Port and Neston sitting as a magistrates' court dismissed
an information preferred by the appellant, Dennis Finnigan, against the respondent,
Anthony Victor Sandiford, that he, on 10th May 1980 at Whitby, Ellesmere Port, did
drive a motor car on Chester Road having consumed alcohol in such a quantity that the
proportion thereof in his blood exceeded the prescribed limit, contrary to s 6(1) of the
Road Traffic Act 1972, on the ground that the arrest of the respondent under s 8(5) of the
1972 Act, following his refusal to provide a specimen of breath, was unlawful and
therefore that the charge under s 6 should be dismissed. The appellant appealed by way
of case stated to the Divisional Court of the Queen's Bench Division. On 20th February
1981 the Divisional Court (Donaldson LJ and Bingham J) dismissed the appeal and
refused leave to appeal to the House of Lords but certified, pursuant to s 1(2) of the
Administration of Justice Act 1960, that a point of law of general public importance was
involved in the decision. On 19th March 1981 the House of Lords gave the appellant
leave to appeal against the decision. The facts are set out in the opinion of Lord Keith.

---

a Section 8(5) is set out at p 270 *a b*, post

Clowser v Chaplin

On 23rd May 1980 informations were preferred by the appellant, Bruce John Clowser, **a** against the respondent, Clive Norman Chaplin, (1) that he, on 18th May 1980, at Brighton, being a person driving a motor car on a road or public place, on being required by a constable in uniform, failed without reasonable excuse to provide a specimen of breath for a breath test contrary to s 8 of the Road Traffic Act 1972, and (2) that he, on 18th May 1980, at Brighton, being a person driving a motor car on a road called the A23 London to Brighton road and having been required by a constable at the Brighton police **b** station to provide a specimen of blood or urine for a laboratory test did without reasonable excuse fail to provide such a specimen contrary to s 9 of the 1972 Act. On 22nd December 1980 justices for the county of East Sussex acting in and for the petty sessional division of Brighton, sitting as a magistrates' court, dismissed the informations. The appellant appealed by way of case stated to the Divisional Court of the Queen's Bench Division. On 20th February 1981 the Divisional Court (Donaldson LJ **c** and Bingham J) allowed the appeal in respect of the charge under s 8 but dismissed it in respect of the charge under s 9. The court refused the appellant leave to appeal to the House of Lords but certified, pursuant to s 1(1) of the Administration of Justice Act 1960, that points of law of general public importance were involved in the decision. On 19th March 1981 the House of Lords gave the appellant leave to appeal against the decision. The facts are set out in the opinion of Lord Keith. **d**

Desmond Fennell QC and *Rodger Bell* for the appellant Finnigan.
Benet Hytner QC and *D M Evans* for the respondent Sandiford.
Desmond Fennell QC and *R Carr* for the appellant Clowser.
Michael Beckman QC and *C Taylor* for the respondent Chaplin.

e

Their Lordships took time for consideration.

14th May. The following opinions were delivered.

LORD HAILSHAM OF ST MARYLEBONE LC. My Lords, having read in draft **f** the opinion about to be delivered by my noble and learned friend Lord Keith, I find its reasoning to be unanswerable, and it therefore follows that, for the reasons he gives, these two appeals must be dismissed. Whether, from the point of view of policy, the results of these or several of the earlier decisions arrived at by the courts under the peculiar jurisprudence of the breathalyser are desirable in the public interest is something which only Parliament in its legislative capacity can now determine.

In my view, the analysis of the law contained in the speeches in *Morris v Beardmore* **g** [1980] 2 All ER 753, [1980] 3 WLR 283 is clearly correct, and I agree with my noble and learned friend that this analysis implies a general principle, and that the exact point in these appeals, although technically left open in *Morris v Beardmore*, is covered by that principle. The conclusion is therefore inescapable.

h

LORD DIPLOCK. My Lords, the reasoning in the speech of my noble and learned friend Lord Keith, which I find unanswerable, leads ineluctably to the conclusion that once again the way in which the 'breathalyser' provisions of the Road Traffic Act 1972 are drafted has enabled motorists to 'cock a snook' at the law.

These provisions, as first enacted in the Road Safety Act 1967, were controversial. They represented a novel intrusion on the liberty of the motorist to drive a potentially **j** lethal vehicle on a public road when there was a risk that his judgment or co-ordination had been impaired by the alcohol he had consumed, and consequently the means available to a constable to ascertain whether such was the case were hedged around with restrictions. The many loopholes in the law that the ingenuity of defence lawyers has a brought to light are, in my view, doing more to bring the criminal law of this country into disrepute than any other legislation.

The revision of the 'breathalyser' provisions is under consideration in the Transport Bill now before Parliament. It is for Parliament to make up its mind whether it wants this lamentable state of affairs to continue.

b **LORD KEITH OF KINKEL.** My Lords, these appeals represent a sequel to the decision of this House in *Morris v Beardmore* [1980] 2 All ER 753, [1980] 3 WLR 283. It was there held, on a consideration of s 8(2) of the Road Traffic Act 1972, that Parliament had not thereby authorised a police constable in uniform lawfully to require a person to undergo a breath test under circumstances where the constable was in a position to make the requirement only because he was present, without any right to be so, on premises c occupied by the person concerned. Accordingly, a person who refused to comply with a requirement made under such circumstances was not guilty of an offence under s 8(3).

The two instant cases present the common feature that in each of them the requirement to undergo a breath test was lawfully made. In Mr Sandiford's case it was made under s 8(1) and in Mr Chaplin's case under s 8(2). The police officer in each case was lawfully present just outside the main door of the defendant's dwelling house, and d the defendant was standing just inside the main door. The defendant heard and understood the requirement, but he refused to comply with it and retreated further inside the house. Police officers advanced inside after the defendant, although they had no permission to enter the house, arrested him and took him to a police station. Mr Sandiford there supplied a specimen of blood which proved positive, and in due course he was charged with a contravention of s 6(1) of the 1972 Act. Mr Chaplin, having e subsequently refused to supply a specimen of blood or urine for laboratory test, was charged with offences under ss 8(3) and 9(3) of the Act. In each case the justices dismissed the information on the ground that the arrest of the defendant, following his refusal to undergo a breath test, was unlawful. The respective prosecutors appealed by way of stated case, and both appeals came before a Divisional Court consisting of Donaldson LJ and Bingham J. As regards Mr Chaplin's appeal, they held that he should have been f convicted of the offence under s 8, in respect that nothing which happened after his failure to comply with the requirement to undergo a breath test invalidated the legality of the requirement, but they dismissed the appeal in respect of the s 9 charge, on the ground that the police officers were trespassing in Mr Chaplin's house where they arrested him, and that this invalidated all that followed. The court dismissed the appeal in Mr Sandiford's case for the same reason.

g In relation to each appeal the Divisional Court, while refusing leave to the prosecutor to appeal to this House, certified that their decision involved the following point of law of general importance:

'Whether a constable in uniform who is lawfully within the curtilage of a house and at the door of such premises being the home of a person to whom the constable h makes a lawful requirement for a specimen of breath pursuant to section 8(1) [s 8(2) in Mr Chaplin's case] Road Traffic Act 1972 is empowered to enter the said house without invitation and as a trespasser and effect an arrest under section 8(5) Road Traffic Act 1972 following a failure to provide a specimen of breath.'

In connection with the appeal in Mr Chaplin's case the Divisional Court certified a j further question relating to the effect, on the legality of the requirement to undergo a breath test, of excessive force employed by the police officers in arresting Mr Chaplin. In view of the course which the hearing on the main question followed before your Lordships, no argument was advanced on this second question, and it need not be considered.

So the only issue which your Lordships have to decide turns on the proper construction of s 8(5) of the 1972 Act, which provides:

'If a person required by a constable under subsection (1) or (2) above to provide a specimen of breath for a breath test fails to do so and the constable has reasonable cause to suspect him of having alcohol in his body, the constable may arrest him without warrant except while he is at a hospital as a patient.'

The procedures prescribed by s 9 of the Act as regards the making of a requirement to provide a specimen of blood or urine for laboratory test, which, on compliance, may lead to a charge under s 6(1) or, on non-compliance, to a charge under s 9(3), are applicable only to a person who has been arrested under s 8 (or possibly under s 5(5), relating to driving when unfit to drive through drink or drugs). It follows that, if a person has not been lawfully arrested under the relevant enactment, the s 9 procedures cannot validly be applied to him and the results of the purported application are inept to form the basis of any conviction. Counsel for the appellants, quite rightly, made no attempt to argue the contrary. The question accordingly comes to be whether the power to arrest without warrant conferred by s 8(5) carries with it the power lawfully to enter, by force if need be, the dwelling house of the person whom it is intended to arrest, for the purpose of carrying out that intention.

It may confidently be stated as a matter of general principle that the mere conferment by statute of a power to arrest without warrant in given circumstances does not carry with it any power to enter private premises without the permission of the occupier, forcibly or otherwise. Section 2 of the Criminal Law Act 1967 creates a category of 'arrestable offences' in respect of which the power of arrest without warrant may be exercised. Such offences are extremely serious, being those punishable by five years' imprisonment on first conviction, and attempts thereat. Subsection (6) specifically provides:

'For the purpose of arresting a person under any power conferred by this section a constable may enter (if need be, by force) and search any place where that person is or where the constable, with reasonable cause, suspects him to be.'

Apart from the category of arrestable offences, there are a considerable number of instances where a specific power of arrest without warrant is conferred in relation to particular statutory offences. In some instances power of entry is also conferred, for example by s 50(2) of the Firearms Act 1968. In a great many others, no power of entry is conferred. The proper inference, in my opinion, is that, where Parliament considers it appropriate that a power of arrest without warrant should be reinforced by a power to enter private premises, it is in the habit of saying so specifically, and that the omission of any such specific power is deliberate. It would rarely, if ever, be possible to conclude that the power had been conferred by implication. Counsel for the appellants maintained that in the present case such an implication was properly to be drawn from the circumstance that the penalty under s 8(3) for failing to provide a specimen of breath was a minor one compared with that under s 9(3) for failing to provide a specimen of blood or urine, or under s 6(1) in the event of the specimen proving positive. It was therefore to be inferred, so it was argued, that Parliament did not contemplate the possibility of any interruption in the sequence of events from the making of a lawful requirement for a breath test to the formulation of charges under s 6(1) or s 9(3). But that consideration does not offer any sufficient foundation for the implication claimed to be necessary. There can be no question of the legislative scheme being unworkable in its absence. It is also to be observed that, as noticed above, s 9 is tied in with s 5(5) as well as with s 8(5). It would be strange if the latter were held to confer power to enter for the purpose of effecting an arrest, but not the former. The proper conclusion, in my opinion, is that Parliament did not intend to confer such power in either case.

a This conclusion is consistent with the principle on which the decision in *Morris v Beardmore* proceeded, namely that in this particular piece of legislation Parliament cannot be taken to have authorised any further inroads on the rights of individual citizens than it specifically enacted. The conclusion does, however, have a wider significance, in respect that it must be of general application in cases where a statute has conferred a power of arrest without warrant, but no specific power of entry on private premises for the purpose of effecting the arrest.

b My Lords, for these reasons I would deal with each of these appeals by answering the certified question in the negative and dismissing the appeal.

LORD SCARMAN. My Lords, I have had the advantage of reading in draft the speech delivered by my noble and learned friend Lord Keith. I agree with it, and would dismiss each appeal.

c I also agree with his comment that the House's conclusion has a wider significance than the mere interpretation of s 8(5) of the Road Traffic Act 1972. It is that, as a general rule, the courts will not construe an enactment conferring a power of arrest without warrant as impliedly authorising a power of entry into private premises for the purpose of effecting the arrest. If it be Parliament's intention to confer a power of entry, the draftsman must ensure that the power is expressly conferred. Parliament is to not be

d presumed, in the absence of express words, so to intend, unless the implication is irresistible, which would be rare indeed.

LORD ROSKILL. My Lords, I too have had the advantage of reading in draft the speech of my noble and learned friend Lord Keith. For the reasons which are there set out, I agree that these appeals must be dismissed. It would seem that the problems to

e which the decision of your Lordships' House in *Morris v Beardmore* [1980] 2 All ER 753, [1980] 3 WLR 283 and the instant appeals have given rise had not previously been appreciated. I venture to echo the hope that in the light of these decisions the matter may now be reviewed by Parliament.

Certified questions answered in the negative. Appeals dismissed. Orders appealed from affirmed.

f Solicitors: *Sharpe, Pritchard & Co*, agents for *E C Woodcock*, Chester (for the appellant Finnigan); *Kenwright & Cox*, agents for *Blain Boland & Co*, Ellesmere Port (for the respondent Sandiford); *Sharpe, Pritchard & Co*, agents for *T Lavelle*, Lewes (for the appellant Clowser); *David M Laing & Co*, Brighton (for the respondent Chaplin).

Mary Rose Plummer   Barrister.

Grappelli and another v Derek Block (Holdings) Ltd and another

COURT OF APPEAL, CIVIL DIVISION

LORD DENNING MR, TEMPLEMAN AND DUNN LJJ

19th, 20th JANUARY 1981

Libel and slander – Innuendo – Extrinsic facts – Facts coming to light after publication complained of – Whether such facts capable of supporting innuendo.

Libel and slander – Publication – Limited publication – Innuendo – Extrinsic facts supporting innuendo – Identification of persons knowing extrinsic facts – Whether plaintiff must identify persons knowing extrinsic facts when publication complained of is limited.

The plaintiff was a well-known professional musician with an international reputation who employed the defendants as his managers or agents. In June 1976 the defendants arranged for the plaintiff to give concerts at various venues in England on certain specified dates. However the bookings were made without the plaintiff's authority and accordingly had to be cancelled. When informing the managers of concert halls in September that the plaintiff's concerts had to be cancelled a representative of the defendants falsely stated that the plaintiff was very seriously ill and it was doubtful if he would ever tour again. That reason for the cancellation was passed on to members of the public who inquired about the cancelled concerts. On 28th November a notice appeared in a national newspaper and other newspapers giving the dates of forthcoming concerts by the plaintiff during a concert tour of England. The forthcoming concerts included concerts on the same dates as the cancelled ones but in different towns. The plaintiff brought an action against the defendants alleging, inter alia, that the false statement made by the defendants that he was seriously ill and would never tour again was a slander on him since, having regard to the announcement on 28th November of a different series of concerts, it gave rise to an innuendo that the plaintiff had given a reason in September for cancelling concerts which he knew to be false. The defendants applied to have the claim struck out as disclosing no cause of action in defamation because (i) the subsequent publication of certain facts which enabled a person to read a defamatory meaning into otherwise innocent material did not make the writer of the material liable in defamation and (ii) the plaintiff had not identified in his pleadings any members of the public who were alleged to have put a defamatory meaning on the statement when they read the announcement of 28th November. The registrar and the judge dismissed the defendants' application and they appealed.

Held – The appeal would be allowed for the following reasons—

(1) Since the cause of action in defamation arose as soon as the words complained of were published, any extrinsic facts which were relied on to support a legal innuendo had to be known at the time of publication by the person to whom the words were published. Accordingly, inferences put on the words complained of as a result of facts coming to light after the publication did not make the words defamatory (see p 274 *g* to p 275 *c* and *f* to *h*, p 278 *b h* and p 279 *g h*, post); *Simons Pty Ltd v Riddell* [1941] NZLR 913 applied.

(2) Where there was limited publication to a limited number of persons a plaintiff pleading a legal innuendo in a defamation action was required to identify in his pleading the person or persons who knew of the special facts which enabled them to understand the innuendo (see p 275 *d* to *h* and p 278 *b* and *g* to p 279 *a*, post); dicta of Lord Denning MR in *Fullam v Newcastle Chronicle and Journal Ltd* [1977] 3 All ER at 35, 37 applied.

Notes

For pleadings in defamation actions, see 28 Halsbury's Laws (4th Edn) paras 171–172, 179–180, and for cases on the subject, see 32 Digest (Reissue) 158–161, 1394–1414.

For particulars required in support of an innuendo, see 28 Halsbury's Laws (4th Edn) paras 175–178, and for cases on the subject, see 32 Digest (Reissue) 166–171, 1460–1491.

Cases referred to in judgments

Astaire v Campling [1965] 3 All ER 666, [1966] 1 WLR 34, CA, 32 Digest (Reissue) 166, 1458.

Bata v Bata [1948] WN 366, CA, 50 Digest (Repl) 353, 770.

Cassidy v Daily Mirror Newspapers Ltd [1929] 2 KB 331, [1929] All ER Rep 117, 98 LJKB 595, 141 LT 404, CA, 32 Digest (Reissue) 157, 1390.

Consolidated Trust Co Ltd v Browne (1948) 49 SR (NSW) 86.

Fullam v Newcastle Chronicle and Journal Ltd [1977] 3 All ER 32, [1977] 1 WLR 651, CA, 32 Digest (Reissue) 161, 1414.

Hayward v Thompson (1978, unreported).

Hough v London Express Newspapers Ltd [1940] 3 All ER 31, [1940] 2 KB 507, 109 LJKB 524, 163 LT 162, CA, 32 Digest (Reissue) 161, 1413.

Russell v Kelly (1872) 13 Amer 169, 44 Cal 641.

Sadgrove v Hole [1901] 2 KB 1, 70 LJKB 455, 84 LT 647, CA, 32 Digest (Reissue) 235, 1977.

Simons Pty Ltd v Riddell [1941] NZLR 913.

Tolley v J S Fry & Sons Ltd [1931] AC 333, [1931] All ER Rep 131, 100 LJKB 328, 145 LT 1, HL, 32 Digest (Reissue) 119, 717.

Cases also cited

Chubb v Westley (1834) 6 C & P 436, 172 ER 1309, NP.

Hulton (E) & Co v Jones [1910] AC 20, [1908–10] All ER Rep 29, HL.

Lewis v Daily Telegraph Ltd [1963] 2 All ER 151, [1964] AC 234, HL.

Interlocutory appeal

The defendants, Derek Block (Holdings) Ltd and Ray Nedas, appealed against the decision of Hodgson J on 1st December 1980 dismissing their appeal from the refusal of Master Waldman to strike out those paragraphs alleging libel and slander in the statement of claim served on the defendants by the plaintiffs, Stephane Grappelli and William Charles Disley. The facts are set out in the judgment of Dunn LJ.

Peter Bowsher QC and *Adrienne Page* for the defendants.
Richard Rampton for the plaintiffs.

LORD DENNING MR. Mr Grappelli is a professional jazz violinist with an international reputation. Mr Disley is a professional guitarist. He is the leader of a trio which accompanied Mr Grappelli as part of his team. It appears that they had as their managers or agents at one time a company called Derek Block (Holdings) Ltd. About June 1976 these managers or agents purported to book concerts for Mr Grappelli and his team at various places in England. They were fixed for some months ahead. For instance, in June a concert was fixed at Milton Keynes to be held on 4th December 1976. At Huddersfield an arrangement was made for a concert to be held on 10th December 1976. And so forth.

Mr Grappelli says that the agents acted without his authority when they booked him for those engagements. The agents had to cancel the bookings they had made. So on 21st September 1976 they telephoned the people concerned, and put forward this excuse: 'The Stephane Grappelli concert has been cancelled because Stephane Grappelli is very seriously ill in Paris and I would be surprised if he ever toured again.'

Mr Grappelli says that that was an entirely false statement about his health: it was known by the agents to be false. They put it forward as an excuse to get themselves out of the unauthorised engagements. If it was a false statement, maliciously made, which would cause damage, it would give rise to a cause of action for injurious falsehood. A cause of action has been brought accordingly.

Not content with a cause of action for injurious falsehood, Mr Grappelli and Mr Disley also allege that the statement was a slander as being defamatory of Mr Grappelli. It is obviously not defamatory as it stands. It is not defamatory of a person to say that he is seriously ill. But Mr Grappelli says that it became actionable thereafter. He says that late in November there was a notice in the Sunday Times (and other papers) saying that Mr Grappelli was performing in various concert halls. Not at the concert halls previously arranged but at others. For instance, the notice in the Sunday Times said that he was going to appear at St Albans on 4th December. Not at Milton Keynes. It also said that he was going to appear somewhere else on 10th December. Not at Huddersfield.

It is said on behalf of Mr Grappelli that when people read in November 1976 in the Sunday Times that these other new engagements had been made for him, they would read an innuendo into the statement made in September 1976. They would say to themselves, 'That was a put-up job. He was not really ill. He gave a reason which he knew to be false.' It is said that that subsequent knowledge would lead people to think that the original statement about Mr Grappelli being ill was a put-up job. The plaintiffs allege a legal innuendo that the words were understood to mean that the plaintiffs had given a reason for cancelling the concerts which they knew to be false.

That is the pleading as it stands. An application was made by the defendants, not to strike out the malicious falsehood part of the claim, but to strike out the claim in regard to slander on the ground that there was no cause of action in defamation.

The case raises two quite interesting points on the law of libel. I summarised the law about innuendo in *Fullam v Newcastle Chronicle and Journal Ltd* [1977] 3 All ER 32, [1977] 1 WLR 651. There is a cause of action for words in their natural and ordinary meaning. That is not alleged here. The other cause of action is one which is based on a legal innuendo. In it the plaintiff relies on special circumstances which convey to some particular person or persons, knowing those circumstances, a special defamatory meaning other than the natural and ordinary meaning. That is a separate cause of action.

The question which arises in this case is as to legal innuendo. When the plaintiff relies on special circumstances known to another person, have those special circumstances to be in his knowledge *at the time* when he reads or hears the words? Or is it sufficient that, because of some later facts, he puts a defamatory meaning on them?

On this point we heard an interesting discussion on both sides. I would go by the principle, which is well established, that in defamation, be it libel or slander, the cause of action is the *publication* of defamatory words of and concerning the plaintiff. The cause of action arises when those words are *published* to the person by whom they are read or heard. The cause of action arises then, and not later.

Counsel for the plaintiffs urged us to say that in slander it may be different. He suggests that the cause of action there does not arise until there is damage, like actions in negligence and the like.

I prefer to go by the principle that in defamation a cause of action arises (and a writ can be issued) as soon as the words are published to a person *then* knowing all the material facts. If there are extrinsic facts, he must know them *then*, at the time of publication. That is when a cause of action arises. It cannot be made into a cause of action by reason of facts subsequently coming to the knowledge of the reader or hearer.

We were referred to a New Zealand case, which was not cited to the judge below. It is *Simons Pty Ltd v Riddell* [1941] NZLR 913. Blair J seems to me to put the position quite accurately when he said (at 932):

'On the authorities—see *Cassidy* v. *Daily Mirror Newspapers* ([1929] 2 KB 331, [1929] All ER Rep 117) and *Tolley* v. *J. S. Fry and Sons, Ltd.* ([1931] AC 333, [1931]

All ER Rep 131)—innocent matter may be given a defamatory meaning by readers with knowledge of facts not known to the writer. But those cases do not lay down that a writer of innocent matter can by reason of certain facts coming into existence *subsequent* to publication of his innocent matter become liable in damages for libel because persons learning of that subsequent material are able to read into the innocent matter a defamatory meaning.' (My emphasis.)

That seems to me to be correct. He emphasised it by saying that, if the person was liable in damages in those circumstances, it would mean a great extension in the law of libel. He sàid it would be extending it much too far—

'to ascertain whether the next day or the next week or the next year some one may not say or do something that will enable a defamatory meaning to be given to otherwise innocent statements.'

That principle seems to me to be applicable here. The inferences which were put on the statements *after* the publication (by facts subsequently learnt) do not render them defamatory in the beginning.

The second point arises on the pleadings. The plaintiffs do not identify any of the readers of the Sunday Times, or other publications, who, by reason of the later facts, may have put a defamatory meaning on the statement. The question is whether particulars should be given identifying the persons concerned. Again, on this point it seems to me that it can be dealt with in principle. I ventured to put it myself in *Fullam v Newcastle Chronicle and Journal Ltd* [1977] 3 All ER 32 at 35, [1977] 1 WLR 651 at 655 in the case of secondary meanings:

'... he must in his statement of claim specify the particular person or persons to whom they were published and the special circumstances known to that person or persons ... there is no exception in the case of a newspaper ...'

It seems to me that that general principle of pleading applies here. In the case of these secondary meanings, even innuendos, the plaintiff ought to specify the persons who have the particular knowledge from which they drew a defamatory meaning.

So on both these points it seems to me that we ought to give leave to appeal. I can understand the judge's difficulty: he was not referred to all the cases to which we were referred. He was referred to a ruling of O'Connor J at first instance (in *Hayward v Thompson* (1978), unreported). That seems to me to be understandable on other grounds, but of no assistance here. I would give leave to appeal, allow the appeal and strike out the causes of action in so far as they rely on defamation, but leave intact completely the causes of action in relation to malicious or injurious falsehood, because it seems to me that that is really what the plaintiffs should depend on.

I would allow the appeal accordingly.

TEMPLEMAN LJ. I have had the advantage of some discussion with Lord Denning MR and Dunn LJ. For the reasons given by Lord Denning MR and for the reasons which Dunn LJ is about to give, I too would allow the appeal, and cannot usefully add anything.

DUNN LJ. I agree that the appeal should be allowed. The learned judge, in giving leave to appeal, said that this appeal raised a novel point of law. The principal question of law is whether, when extrinsic facts are relied on in support of an innuendo which arose after the publication, the original words, not defamatory in their ordinary and natural meaning, can have the defamatory meaning alleged in the innuendo. Both the master and the judge held that they could. The defendants in this appeal have submitted that they could not.

For the purposes of the appeal we must assume that all the facts alleged in the statement of claim are proved. The statement of claim is complicated and only parts of it are material to this appeal. The plaintiff is a well-known jazz violinist with an international reputation. The first defendants are promoters of concerts. In May or June 1976, without the authority of the plaintiffs, they purported to arrange a number of concerts by the first plaintiff and the second plaintiff, his accompanist. The only concerts to which I need refer in this judgment are those fixed at Milton Keynes eventually on 4th December 1976 and at Tameside fixed for 26th November 1976.

On 21st September, or perhaps just before, the second defendant, who was an employee of the first defendants, told a Miss Collard, who was the manager of the Milton Keynes entertainment authority, that (and I quote from para 4 of the statement of claim): 'The Stephane Grappelli concert has been cancelled because Stephane Grappelli is very seriously ill in Paris and I would be surprised if he ever toured again.' Miss Collard passed on that information to a subordinate of hers, a Mrs Gormly; and between 21st September and 4th December 1976 Mrs Gormly informed over the telephone a large number of members of the public both of the cancellation and the reason for it. A substantial number of members of the public were informed before 28th November and some after. The importance of the date, 28th November, will appear in a moment. According to a letter sent by the plaintiffs' solicitors to the defendants' solicitors on 18th November 1980, between the end of September 1976 and the date of the concert, 4th December 1976—

> 'Mrs Gormly answered no less than 100 and possibly as many as 250 enquiries from members of the public about the concert. On each occasion, she told the person concerned that the concert had been cancelled because Stephane Grappelli was seriously ill and would probably never tour again. She was still answering enquiries in that way during the week before the concert (i.e. the week beginning the 28th November 1976), but she is unable to be precise about the number of enquiries she received during that week.'

The relevance of the date, 28th November, is that on that day there appeared in the issue of the Sunday Times an advertisement announcing that concerts would be given by 'the legendary Stephane Grappelli with the Diz Disley trio' led by the second plaintiff 'at the following venues on the following dates: Odeon Theatre, Hanley, 2nd December 1976, [and this is the material one] Royal Exchange Theatre, Manchester, 3rd December 1976'. Then there were other concerts advertised: at the City Hall, St Albans on 4th December, the Central Hall, Chatham on 5th December, and the Civic Hall, Guildford on 6th December.

What is alleged in the action as a result of those facts is that they give rise to an innuendo that the plaintiffs had given a reason for cancelling the concert which they knew to be false. That is the allegation which is claimed to be defamatory and on which this action so far as it relates to slander and libel is based.

It will be observed that in the case of Milton Keynes some members of the public were informed of the cancellation before the Sunday Times advertisement and others after the Sunday Times advertisement, and consequently different considerations may apply to each of those two categories.

The other concert which illustrates the points of law which arise in the case is the Tameside concert. In that case the same words, namely that the concert had been cancelled because Stephane Grappelli was very seriously ill and the second defendant would be surprised if he ever toured again, were published to a Mr Booth, who was the manager of the Tameside Theatre in Ashton-under-Lyne on or before 21st September. Mr Booth republished those words to a Mr Clark, who was his assistant manager, and Mr Clark passed on the information to a number of members of the public who had inquired when the concert was going to take place.

The plaintiffs' concert at the Royal Exchange Theatre, Manchester, for 3rd December had been advertised in the weeks prior to that concert by posters in Manchester, by a press release dated 15th November, and in programmes for forthcoming events in Manchester, which of course is quite close to Tameside and Ashton-under-Lyne, for the

four weeks before the concert. There had also been advertisements in the Manchester
Evening News of 12th, 18th and 19th November and 3rd December.

a The relevance of the Tameside example is that knowledge of the special circumstances
about the Ashton-under-Lyne slander existed, it is said, before the Sunday Times
advertisement and probably from early November. In that respect, by further and better
particulars, which were subsequently delivered, of the innuendo, it was said that on a
date in November one of the members of the public to whom Mr Clark had republished
b the words informed Mr Clark—

> 'that she had seen an advertisement in the Manchester Evening News for a
> concert by the Plaintiffs at the Royal Exchange Theatre on the 3rd December
> 1976. Thereafter, Mr Clark republished the said words to members of the public on
> about six occasions and on each occasion he informed the member of the public
> concerned that, although the Plaintiffs' concert at Tameside had been cancelled for
c > the reason given, it nonetheless appeared that the Plaintiffs were due to give a
> concert at the Royal Exchange Theatre on the 3rd December.'

And the same innuendo was alleged as for the previous allegation.

On that basis of fact counsel for the defendants submitted, first, that at the time of the
publication or republication to Mrs Gormly and Mr Clark there was no slander because
d the extrinsic facts constituting the innuendo were not known to the public. Second, he
submitted that any republication by Mrs Gormly or Mr Clark to members of the public
at the time before information was available that the reason given by the plaintiffs for
cancelling the concert was false was likewise no slander in the case of Milton Keynes
before 28th November and in the case of Tameside before early November when the
Royal Exchange concert was first publicised. He submitted accordingly that the
e paragraphs alleging libel and slander based on those new publications before those dates
should be struck out.

He submitted in the alternative, and in any event, that the paragraphs alleging libel
and slander should be struck out because the pleadings did not identify those members
of the public who were alleged to have knowledge of the extrinsic facts supporting the
innuendo. He submitted that the plaintiffs should be left to their remedy for damages for
f injurious falsehood in respect of the false statement by the defendants.

As to his first submission, counsel for the defendants submitted that publication was
an essential ingredient of the torts of libel and slander. Once there was publication, he
submitted, the cause of action was complete and the relevant knowledge of the publishees
to support the innuendo was their knowledge at the date of the publication and not
thereafter acquired knowledge. In support of that submission he cited to us the cases of
g Bata v Bata [1948] WN 366, Sadgrove v Hole [1901] 2 KB 1, Astaire v Campling [1965] 3 All
ER 666 at 668–669, [1966] 1 WLR 34 at 41 per Diplock LJ, and in particular a New
Zealand case, Simons Pty Ltd v Riddell [1941] NZLR 913. That was a case in which the
appellants were a brewery company, and the manager published in a newspaper on 6th
June an advertisement that H and R 'are no longer in our employ and are not authorized
to canvass for us or collect cash or empties on our behalf'. Then in a later issue, a week
h later, there was a report of the conviction of H on a charge of issuing a valueless cheque
with intent to defraud. It was held by the whole Court of Appeal firstly that the words
of the advertisement were not by themselves capable of a defamatory meaning. It was
also held by the whole court that the news item published a week later was inadmissible,
and accordingly they ordered a new trial. Lord Denning MR has read extracts from the
judgment of Blair J, who dealt with the matter most fully and who concluded his
i judgment with these words (at 932–933):

> 'If that be a correct summary of the law as it now stands, then, with respect, I
> venture to say that it would be widening the net of liability of writers too far by
> enunciating the doctrine that the inquiry . . . must go still further by looking into
> the future to ascertain whether the next day or the next week or the next year some

one may not say or do something that will enable a defamatory meaning to be given
to otherwise innocent statements.'

    As to his second point, the pleading point, counsel for the defendants adopted as part
of his argument a statement in Duncan and Neill on Defamation (1978, p 37, para 8.04),
where it is said:

> 'Where the plaintiff relies on a true innuendo meaning [sometimes called a legal
> innuendo] the general rule is that it is necessary for the plaintiff to plead and prove:
> (a) that the words were published to a specific publishee or to specific publishees;
> and (b) that the publishee or publishees knew of specific facts which would enable
> them to understand the words in the innuendo meaning or to understand the words
> to refer to the plaintiff.'

He relied on two cases mentioned in Duncan and Neill: *Hough v London Express
Newspapers Ltd* [1940] 3 All ER 31, [1940] 2 KB 507, and an Australian case, *Consolidated
Trust Co Ltd v Browne* (1948) 49 SR (NSW) 86. He submitted accordingly that, the
plaintiffs having said in the statement of claim in terms that they could not identify the
members of the public with the special knowledge, those paragraphs should be struck
out.

    As to that second point, counsel for the plaintiffs has said, firstly that *Fullam v Newcastle
Chronicle and Journal Ltd* [1977] 3 All ER 32, [1977] 1 WLR 651, to which Lord Denning
MR has referred, was a very special case, and that, in any event, this case falls within the
exception stated by Scarman LJ when he said ([1977] 3 All ER 32 at 39, [1977] 1 WLR
651 at 659):

> '. . . the facts may be very well known in the area of the newspaper's distribution—
> in which event I would think it would suffice to plead merely that the plaintiff will
> rely on inference that some of the newspaper's readers must have been aware of the
> facts which are said to give rise to the innuendo.'

Counsel for the plaintiffs submitted that that was this case; that there was the allegation
that Mr Clark had passed on the information to a number of persons who had rung up
asking for the date of the original Ashton-under-Lyne concert, and from the pleading
point of view that was sufficient. Difficult questions might arise on questions of
admissibility of evidence when it came to trial, but counsel for the plaintiffs submitted
that this court should not adopt the draconian course of striking out the allegations at this
stage because he was unable to identify the persons with special knowledge.

    I agree with Lord Denning MR that the law is fully set out in *Fullam v Newcastle
Chronicle and Journal Ltd*, especially in the passage of the judgment to which he has
referred and later where he said ([1977] 3 All ER 32 at 37, [1977] 1 WLR 651 at 656):

> 'In such cases as those [that is to say, cases of legal innuendo] the identity of the
> person (who has knowledge of the special circumstances) is a most material fact in
> the cause of action. It is the publication to him which is the very foundation of the
> cause of action. So he should be identified in the pleading itself or in particulars
> under it.'

I agree that that is the general rule as stated by Duncan and Neill in the passage which
I have quoted from their book on defamation.

    I would only add this, that I agree also with Scarman LJ that there may be cases which
are exceptions to that rule, such as the cases that he refers to where the publication is in
a national newspaper with a very wide circulation, and the only reasonable inference is
that some of the readers of that newspaper must have knowledge of the facts which are
said to give rise to the innuendo.

    But that is not this case. In this case there was a very much more limited publication
to a very much more limited number of publishees. It involved them connecting up in
the first instance the reason given for the cancellation with either the advertisement in
the Sunday Times or one of the advertisements which appeared in Manchester. In

circumstances of that kind, I agree with Lord Denning MR that the general rule should prevail and that those persons should be identified in the pleadings.

That would be sufficient to dispose of this case by allowing the appeal; but, so far as the general question is concerned, counsel for the plaintiffs submitted that the cause of action for libel or slander was complete when all the facts were in existence and not before. He submitted that it was one thing to say that once all the facts were in existence the cause of action was complete, but another thing to say that once there was publication the cause of action was complete and that it was impossible for further facts to arise which might give rise to a cause of action subsequent to publication. He pointed out that there are three elements in a cause of action. There must be publication; the publication must refer to the plaintiff; and the words must have a defamatory meaning. Counsel for the plaintiffs submitted that there was no cause of action until the necessary meaning had been supplied. Once that occurred, then the cause of action was complete.

He relied in support of that submission on the American case of *Russell v Kelly* (1872) 13 Amer 169. That was a case in which in the original publication the name of the plaintiff had not been mentioned. Evidence was called, including a subsequent publication by the defendant, in which the plaintiff's name was mentioned; and it was held that that evidence was admissible so as to make the original publication referable to the plaintiff and so defamatory. Crockett J (at 171) referred to the rule as laid down in Starkie on Slander (vol 2, p 51)—

> 'that the application of the slanderous words to the plaintiff, and the extrinsic matters alleged in the declaration, may be shown "by the testimony of witnesses who knew the parties and circumstances, and who can state their judgement and opinion on the application and meaning of the terms used by the defendant".'

Holding that the evidence was admissible, he said: 'It is equally clear that the subsequent publication was admissible for the same purpose, and this was the only purpose for which it was offered or admitted.'

Counsel for the plaintiffs said that there was no English authority directly in point, apart from a ruling of O'Connor J in the very recent case of *Hayward v Thompson* (1978, unreported) in which, in the course of the trial before the jury, he allowed to stand an allegation that a second article had been published referring by name to the plaintiff, who had been the subject of an article the previous week which did not refer to him by name. The learned judge appears to have relied on *Russell v Kelly* (he referred to it as the most useful case which had been cited to him), but at the end of the notes of his judgment, with which we have been helpfully provided, he appears to have dealt with the case as a republication of the original defamatory statement; and certainly it appears from the transcript of his summing up to the jury that that indeed was how he dealt with it. Speaking for myself, I do not derive a great deal of assistance from that case.

Like Lord Denning MR, I would prefer to deal with this on principle. I agree that a publication is an essential part of the case of action; that once there is publication the cause of action is complete, and there is no room for the doctrine that the cause of action can, so to speak, be allowed to be inchoate or lie dormant until such time as some fact emerges which would transform an otherwise innocent statement into a defamatory one. That I believe to be the principle underlying the judgment of Blair J in the New Zealand case of *Simons Pty Ltd v Riddell* [1941] NZLR 913; and on that ground I too would hold that these paragraphs alleging libel and slander cannot stand. I think the plaintiffs should rely on the allegation of injurious falsehood, and I would allow the appeal.

Appeal allowed.

Solicitors: *Ingledew, Brown, Bennison & Garrett* (for the defendants); *Marsh, Regan* (for the plaintiffs).

Sumra Green Barrister.

A Lambert Flat Management Ltd v Lomas

QUEEN'S BENCH DIVISION
ACKNER LJ AND SKINNER J
19th DECEMBER 1980

Nuisance – Statutory nuisance – Abatement notice – Noise – Noise emitted by lift and motor in block of flats – Complaint by tenants of flats adjoining lift shaft – Abatement notice served by local authority on managers of flats – Right of appeal given by statute where notice alleged to be invalid – No notice of appeal given by managers – No steps taken by managers to abate nuisance – Managers charged with failure to comply with abatement notice – Managers pleading by way of defence that by signing leases the tenants had assented to noise from lift – Whether that defence available in criminal proceedings – Whether managers had a 'reasonable excuse' for not complying with abatement notice – Control of Pollution Act 1974, s 58.

The respondents managed a block of 24 self-contained flats which were leased to tenants. Each lease contained a covenant by the respondents to keep those parts of the building which were not demised to the tenants, eg the stairs, lifts etc, clean and in good order. The tenants of flats adjoining the lift shaft complained to the local authority that they were seriously disturbed by the noise emitted by the lift and its motor. The local authority investigated the matter under s 57 of the Control of Pollution Act 1974 and, being satisfied that a noise amounting to a nuisance existed, served on the respondents, as the persons responsible within the meaning of s 73(1)^a of that Act, notices under s 58(1)^b requiring them to abate the nuisance within six months and for that purpose to execute certain specified works. Section 58(3) gave the respondents 21 days in which to appeal to a magistrates' court against the notices if they so wished, and reg 4^c of the Control of Noise (Appeals) Regulations 1975 set out the permissible grounds of appeal (which included the ground that the notice was not justified by the terms of s 58) and the powers of the magistrates' court on the hearing of such an appeal. The respondents did not appeal against the notices and did not take any steps to abate the nuisance in accordance with the terms of the notices. The appellant, a representative of the local authority, laid informations before the magistrates alleging that the respondents had contravened the requirements of the notices, contrary to s 58(4). The magistrates convicted the respondents, who appealed to the Crown Court contending that the defence which would have been open to them if the tenants of the flats affected by the noise had brought a civil action against them (viz that the tenants had full knowledge of the existence of the lifts before entering into their respective leases and therefore were to be taken to have impliedly consented to the presence of the lifts) was also a valid defence to the proceedings under s 58, and that, as the notices were not justified by the terms of s 58, they accordingly had a 'reasonable excuse' within s 58(4) for not complying with them and were exempt from liability. The Crown Court found that the noise from the lift and the motor was excessive and caused the tenants distress, but accepted the respondents' contention that they had a valid defence and allowed the appeal. At the request of the local authority's representative, however, the court stated a case for the opinion of the High Court.

Held – (1) The 1974 Act was concerned with statutory nuisance and created its own code with regard to the institution of proceedings, liability and the availability of defences. The common law as to nuisance was relevant in proceedings under s 58 of that Act only for the purpose of establishing the level of noise that existed, ie whether it amounted to

---

a Section 73(1), so far as material, is set out at p 283 *d*, post
b Section 58 is set out at p 282 *j* to p 283 *b*, post
c Regulation 4, so far as material, is set out at p 283 *d*, post

a nuisance within the meaning of s 58(1) by constituting an undue interference with the use and enjoyment of the land of another. Accordingly, in proceedings under s 58 it did not have to be shown that the nuisance would be actionable at the suit of the party aggrieved, and in proceedings under s 58 a defendant could not rely on any defence based on his duties in tort or contract to the person affected by the noise (see p 285 a to j, post).

(2) The 1974 Act and the 1975 regulations made comprehensive provision for appeals, and the respondents were trying to use one of the permissible grounds of appeal (ie that the notice was not justified by the terms of s 58 of the 1974 Act) as an excuse for not complying with the notices. However, since they had not put forward any special reason, such as illness, for not appealing against the notices within the prescribed time limit, they could not be permitted to rely on the defence of 'reasonable excuse' in s 58(4), which was designed not to give the recipient of the notice a choice of forum in which to attack a notice served under s 58(1) but to cover the case where there was some special difficulty in relation to complying with the notice. The Crown Court had therefore erred in allowing the respondents' appeal. Accordingly the case would be remitted to the Crown Court with a direction to restore the convictions (see p 284 c to e, p 285 b c and p 286 b to g, post).

Notes

For nuisance by noise, see 34 Halsbury's Laws (4th Edn) para 324, and for cases on the subject, see 36(1) Digest (Reissue) 417–419, 92–119.

For the Control of Pollution Act 1974, s 58, see 44 Halsbury's Statutes (3rd Edn) 1239.

For the Control of Noise (Appeals) Regulations 1975, reg 4, see 18 Halsbury's Statutory Instruments (Third Reissue) 113.

Cases referred to in judgments

Ager v Gates (1934) 151 LT 98, [1934] All ER Rep 566, 98 JP 223, 32 LGR 167, 30 Cox CC 105, DC, 36(1) Digest (Reissue) 517, 862.

Francis v Yiewsley and West Drayton Urban District Council [1957] 3 All ER 529, [1958] 1 QB 478, [1957] 3 WLR 919, 122 JP 31, 56 LGR 1, 9 P & CR 38, CA, 45 Digest (Repl) 346, 74.

Kiddle v City Business Premises Ltd [1942] 2 All ER 216, [1942] 1 KB 269, 111 LJKB 196, 166 LT 302, 36(1) Digest (Reissue) 463, 432.

Cases also cited

Sedleigh-Denfield v O'Callagan [1940] 3 All ER 349, [1940] AC 880, HL.

Mason v Smith [1953] CPL 493, CA.

Case stated

Keith Lomas, the chief executive and town clerk of Bournemouth Borough Council, appealed by way of case stated by the Crown Court at Bournemouth (his Honour Judge Blaker QC and two justices) against the decision of that court whereby it allowed an appeal by the respondent, A Lambert Flat Management Ltd, against its conviction in the Bournemouth Magistrates' Court on 15th March 1979 of ten offences under s 58 of the Control of Pollution Act 1974 in respect of premises known as Kernella Court, 51–53 Surrey Road, Bournemouth, Dorset. The questions for the decision of the High Court were: (i) whether the implied consent to taking premises as one found them was a valid defence to proceedings for an offence under the 1974 Act; (ii) whether volenti non fit injuria could be a defence in such proceedings on the grounds that (a) there was then no nuisance or (b) there was then a reasonable excuse, and, if so, whether on the facts found that defence had been made out; (iii) whether there could be a legal nuisance within the meaning of the 1974 Act when (a) the activities complained of were undertaken in a block of flats by a management company in pursuance of a covenant between the management company and the lessees of the flats in the block and (b) the noise caused by the activities was experienced only in the flats in the block; (iv) whether proof of the facts set forth in question (iii) (a) and (b) could amount to a reasonable excuse within s 58 of

the 1974 Act and, if not, whether such proof together with proof that the cost of
complying with the statutory notices would ultimately fall on the lessees of each flat
could amount to such reasonable excuse; (v) whether the provisions of s 58 of the 1974
Act applied where, as in the case of Kernella Court, the property was divided into flats on
the one part and property reserved to the management on the other part, so that there
were a number of separate legal entities within the exterior walls of the building; and
(vi) whether the Crown Court was wrong in allowing the appeal of the respondent.

David Keene QC and *Deirdre McKinney* for the appellant.
Michael Norman for the respondent.

SKINNER J delivered the first judgment at the invitation of Ackner LJ. This is an
appeal by way of case stated from a decision of the Crown Court at Bournemouth
presided over by his Honour Judge Blaker QC. The Crown Court allowed an appeal
from the Bournemouth Magistrates' Court against convictions of the respondent
company on ten summonses alleging contraventions of s 58 of the Control of Pollution
Act 1974 in respect of a block of flats known as Kernella Court in Bournemouth.

The Crown Court found that Kernella Court consisted of a block of 24 self-contained
flats owned by A Lambert (Investment) Ltd, the freeholders. All the flats were leased on
99-year leases to which the respondent company, A Lambert Flat Management Ltd, were
a party. In each lease the hall, stairs, lifts, landings and passages were referred to as
'reserved premises' and the respondent company covenanted both with the freeholder
and the lessees to keep the reserved property clean and in good order. Subsequently in
1976 the freeholder granted the respondent company a lease of the whole building at a
peppercorn rent for 99 years.

In the block of flats were two lifts. At the top of each lift was one flat and above each
flat was the lift motor. It is these flats, nos 11 and 23, which are the subject of the
proceedings in this case. The Crown Court found:

'In the case of flat 23 the lessees were seriously disturbed by a shrieking noise each
time the lift was used, followed by a hum as the lift travelled, and a banging each
time the landing gates opened and shut, with rattling and vibration in the lift
doors. The lessee of flat 11 was seriously disturbed by a shrieking noise each time
the lift was used followed by a clattering when the landing gates opened and shut.'

The residents complained, the local authority investigated the matter, and on 23rd
January 1978 served notices under s 58 of the Control of Pollution Act 1974 on the
respondent company.

Section 58 lies in Part III of the Act, which provides an entirely new code for the
control of noise. Previous legislation had been contained in the Noise Abatement Act
1960 which had applied the provisions of the Public Health Act 1936 to noise as a
'statutory nuisance'.

Section 57 of the 1974 Act provides:

'It shall be the duty of every local authority to cause its area to be inspected from
time to time—(a) to detect anything which ought to be dealt with under the
following sections . . .'

Section 58 provides:

'(1) Where a local authority is satisfied that noise amounting to a nuisance exists,
or is likely to occur or recur, in the area of the local authority, the local authority
shall serve a notice imposing all or any of the following requirements—(a) requiring
the abatement of the nuisance or prohibiting or restricting its occurrence or
recurrence; (b) requiring the execution of such works, and the taking of such other
steps, as may be necessary for the purpose of the notice or as may be specified in the
notice; and the notice shall specify the time or times within which the requirements
of the notice are to be complied with.

'(2) The notice shall be served on the person responsible for the nuisance or, if that person cannot be found or the nuisance has not yet occurred, on the owner or occupier of the premises from which the noise is emitted or would be emitted.

'(3) The person served with the notice may appeal against the notice to a magistrates' court within twenty-one days from service of the notice.

'(4) If a person on whom a notice is served under this section without reasonable excuse contravenes any requirement of the notice, he shall be guilty of an offence against this Part of this Act.'

The procedure on appeals under s 58(3) is contained in s 70 of the 1974 Act which provides that they shall be made by way of complaint and gives the Secretary of State power to make regulations as to appeals under Part III of that Act. These regulations are contained in the Control of Noise (Appeals) Regulations 1975, SI 1975 No 2116, which came into force on the same day as Part III of the Act, ie 1st January 1976.

Regulation 4 (2) deals comprehensively with the grounds of appeal available, including at para (a): 'the notice is not justified by the terms of section 58.' Regulation 4(5) gives the magistrates' court wide powers on the hearing of the appeal, to quash the notice, vary it in favour of the appellant or to dismiss the appeal, and goes on to provide: '. . . a notice which is varied . . . shall be final and shall otherwise have effect, as so varied, as if it had been so made by the local authority.' Section 73(1) of the Act defines the 'person responsible' for the purpose of s 58(2) as 'in relation to the emission of noise, means the person to whose act, default or sufferance the noise is attributable'.

Returning to the history, the effect of the notices served on the respondent company was to require them within six months to abate the noise and for that purpose to isolate acoustically the motors and associated equipment of the lift from the building structure, to modify the landing gate mechanism in such a manner as to prevent noise amounting to a nuisance arising, and to carry out such works necessary to prevent noise from the lift motors and other associated equipment from generating noise amounting to a nuisance in the living accommodation concerned. They also required the respondent company to take similar steps to prevent the recurrence of the nuisance.

The respondent company did not appeal against the notices under s 58(3) nor did it do anything to abate the nuisance in accordance with the notices or at all. Thus on 13th December 1978 the present appellant laid informations in the magistrates' court alleging 'contraventions' of the s 58 notices contrary to sub-s (4). The magistrates convicted. The respondent company appealed to the Crown Court and the Crown Court found, in addition to the facts I have already mentioned, that the noise level emanating from the two lifts was excessive and caused the residents of the two flats, nos 11 and 23, distress and would amount to a nuisance by noise, and further that no work had been done by the respondent company to comply with the s 58 notices and/or to abate the nuisance. The court went on to hold that it was bound by certain authorities which had been quoted to it and, in particular, *Kiddle v City Business Premises Ltd* [1942] 2 All ER 216, [1942] 1 KB 296, which in effect meant that the lessees at Kernella Court had to take the premises as they found them. The Crown Court thereupon allowed the appeal.

The basis of the Crown Court's decision was that any defence that would have been open to the respondent company if sued by the occupier of premises affected by the nuisance in a civil action was available to it in proceedings brought by the local authority under s 58(4). This the local authority challenge. It was common ground before this court that, on the Crown Court findings, the respondent company had contravened requirements of the notices and the only question this court has to consider is whether, in law, the facts disclosed could amount to 'a reasonable excuse' which would exempt it from liability under s 58(4).

Counsel for the appellant, in his clear and helpful argument, submitted that a reasonable excuse must be limited to an excuse for non-compliance with the notice and cannot include a challenge to its validity. He gave as an instance an owner who was not an occupier who had difficulty in gaining access to the premises. An excuse cannot be reasonable, he went on to submit, if it involves matters which could have been raised on appeal under s 58(2). He cited in support of that proposition *Ager v Gates* (1934) 151 LT 98, [1934] All ER Rep 566, a decision under the Public Health Act 1875, where the question at issue was whether a person served with a nuisance order under that Act had acted with due diligence. Against that counsel for the respondent company cited *Francis v Yiewsley and West Drayton Urban District Council* [1957] 3 All ER 529, [1958] 1 QB 478, a decision under the provisions of the Town and Country Planning Act 1947, ss 23 and 24.

Counsel for the respondent company objected that since s 58 of the 1974 Act involves an invasion into private rights of property, and creates criminal offences, Parliament cannot have intended that the onus of challenging the local authority's right to interfere should be placed on the 'person liable' and that, since there is no provision for extension of the time for appealing, he should lose his right of challenge after 21 days. What, he asked, if the 'person liable' did not receive the notice because he was ill or abroad? The answer, says counsel for the appellant, and I agree with him, is that these are matters which can, and would, constitute 'a reasonable excuse' within s 58(4); the contravention proceedings would be defeated and the local authority could then, if it wished, commence fresh proceedings in which the 'person liable' would have his right of appeal.

For my part I do not derive assistance from either of the cases cited by counsel; each is a decision on its own special facts and its own special statute. I prefer to look at the scheme laid down in the 1974 Act and its associated regulations. A comprehensive right of appeal is given by s 58(3) which was not available under the 1960 Act. Regulation 4(2)(*a*) of the 1975 regulations permits an appeal on the ground that the notice is not justified by the terms of s 58. In my judgment an excuse cannot be 'reasonable' under s 58(4) if it involves matters which could have been raised on appeal under s 58(2) unless such matters arose after the appeal was heard or, if there was no appeal, after the time for appeal had expired.

Counsel for the appellant next submitted that the Crown Court was wrong in holding in any event that a defence inter partes in a civil action based on the tort of nuisance could be a defence to a charge under s 58(4). The burden of this submission was that, save in one respect, the concepts involved in a civil action in tort are foreign to ss 57 and 58. He makes four points.

First the one respect in which the tort of nuisance is relevant is in dealing with the question whether 'noise amounting to a nuisance' exists within s 58(1). The subsection does not require that noise amounting to a nuisance actionable at common law by a party who has suffered damage should exist. Counsel for the respondent company replies that to be 'noise amounting to a nuisance' it must be tortious, ie wrongful and unlawful, and it cannot be wrongful or unlawful if a defence at common law is available.

Counsel for the appellant countered that argument in advance by his third submission, viz the defences upheld by the Crown Court only exist between certain identifiable parties who are ex hypothesi different from the parties to proceedings under s 58. What is more, whereas liability at common law rests with the person who created the nuisance, or the landowner if he knew or ought to have known the facts constituting the nuisance, liability under the statute is determined by s 58(2) and the definition of 'person responsible' in s 73(1). I need not repeat the words of s 58(2). Suffice it to say that a notice requiring the abatement of the nuisance and the execution of works may be served on the owner of the premises from which the noise is emitted even though he is not the 'person liable' and may know nothing about it. The Act, says counsel for the appellant, has its own code of who takes proceedings, who is liable and what are the defences available and the only relevance of the common law is in deciding the question whether the noise amounts to a nuisance. He justifies this interpretation in part by his second submission, viz this is an Act concerned with the public good and the cure of nuisances at the initiative of the local authority under the duty imposed by s 57. It is not concerned with the consents of individuals or the complex questions which can arise in

actions between individuals. Finally he submitted that, on the facts of the present case,
a the Crown Court had no difficulty in concluding that 'a noise amounting to a nuisance'
existed within s 58(1) and that was the only relevant question for them to decide.

I accept counsel for the appellant's submissions. The only relevance of the tort of
nuisance in proceedings under s 58 is to establish the level of noise which exists; it is a
measure or standard. Once that level has been established to the satisfaction of the local
authority, the procedure laid down by s 58 comes into play. The 'person liable' may
b contest that the noise amounts to a nuisance under reg 4(2)(*a*) of the 1975 regulations,
but any defence based on his duties in tort or contract to any person affected by the
nuisance is not open to him.

This last sentence answers the first five questions raised in this case. The sixth and last
asked whether the Crown Court was wrong in allowing the appeal of the respondent. In
my judgment it was and I would remit the case to the Crown Court with a direction to
c restore the convictions.

ACKNER J. I agree. On 1st January 1976 Part III of the Control of Pollution Act 1974
was brought into operation. There was also brought into operation on the same day the
Control of Noise (Appeals) Regulations 1975, SI 1975 No 2116, made by the Secretary of
State for the Environment in the exercise of the powers conferred on him by s 70(2) of
d the 1974 Act. Thus from the date mentioned above it became the duty of every local
authority under s 57 of the Act to inspect its area from time to time and to detect
anything which ought to be dealt with under s 58. Section 58(1) provides that where a
local authority is satisfied that noise amounting to a nuisance exists, it shall serve a notice
which may require the abatement of the nuisance or the execution of necessary works.

The first question to decide is the proper interpretation of the words 'noise amounting
e to a nuisance'. It is common ground that the noise must amount to a nuisance in the
ordinary legal sense. Counsel for the appellant contends that although this must mean
that the noise must amount to the undue interference with the use or enjoyment of the
relevant flats, the local authority does not have to be satisfied that a civil action in respect
of such nuisance would necessarily succeed.

Counsel for the respondents contends that the local authority must be satisfied that the
f noise constitutes an actionable nuisance at common law. In my judgment it is clear that
s 58 is not concerned, given that the noise unduly interferes with the use or enjoyment
of land, with whether or not there is a sound cause of action in respect of that noise.
Section 58(2) provides that the notice shall be served on the person responsible for the
nuisance or, if he cannot be found, on the owner or occupier of the premises from which
the noise is emitted. The 'person responsible' in relation to the emission of noise is
g defined by s 73(1) as meaning 'a person to whose act, default or sufferance the noise is
attributable'. It by no means follows that he must of necessity be a tortfeasor.

Moreover, if the legislature was concerned to restrict the local authority's activities to
actionable nuisances, then it seems odd indeed that the owner or occupier, who ex
hypothesi, on the wording of sub-s (2), is not the 'person responsible for the nuisance',
should be a proper recipient of the notice. To make such a person who is innocent of all
h civil liability guilty of a criminal offence for not complying with the notice would seem
an odd result indeed to achieve, if an actionable nuisance, ie one to which there was no
defence, has to be established before the notice could issue.

To my mind s 58 is concerned with what can conveniently be labelled a statutory
nuisance, that is a nuisance where the conduct complained of unduly interferes with the
use or enjoyment of the land of another, but in regard to which the various common law
i defences are irrelevant.

The person served with a notice may appeal against the notice to a magistrates' court
within 21 days of the service of the notice (s 58(3)). The regulations to which I have
referred at the outset of this judgment make detailed provision for such appeal. They
provide for the grounds of appeal, which are many and various, they also provide for the

quashing or variation of the notice as well as, of course, for the dismissal of the appeal. On the hearing of the appeal the court may make such order as it thinks fit with respect to the person by whom any work is to be executed and the contribution to be made by any person towards the cost of the work, or as to the proportions in which any expenses which may become recoverable by the local authority are to be borne by the appellant and any other person. The magistrates' courts are specifically enjoined, in exercising the power to which I have just referred, to have regard as between an owner and an occupier to the terms and conditions, whether contractual or statutory, of any relevant tenancy in the nature of the work required. There are, of course, the ordinary rights of appeal from the magistrates' court to the Crown Court or to this court by case stated.

Section 58(4) provides that if a person on whom a notice is served under the section *without reasonable excuse* contravenes any requirement of the notice, 'he shall be guilty of an offence against this Part of this Act'. In this case no appeals were lodged against the notices and no work of modification or otherwise was carried out to the lift machinery or allied equipment or to the landing gate mechanism of flat 11. In those circumstances can the respondents urge, as a reasonable excuse for failing to comply with the notice, that the same was invalid for one or more of the reasons provided by the regulations as permissible grounds of appeal? I am assuming, which assumption is wholly justified on the facts of this case, that there was no special reason such as illness, non-receipt of the notice or other potential excuse for not entering an appeal.

The answer to my mind is clearly in the negative. As stated above, not only is the right of appeal given by the statute but very detailed provisions have been made by the regulations for the prosecution of such appeals. Section 58(4) was not designed, in my judgment, to give the recipient of the notice a choice of forum in which to mount his attack on the notice. It was designed to provide a defence to a criminal charge where he had some reasonable excuse, such as some special difficulty in relation to compliance with the notice. It does not provide an opportunity, when prosecuted, to challenge the correctness and justification of the notice where the defendant has not availed himself of his statutory opportunity to do this by way of appeal.

In my judgment the Crown Court had no jurisdiction to inquire into the question whether the noise amounted to a nuisance. However, if I am wrong about that, the Crown Court having found that the noise level emanating from the two lifts was excessive and caused the residents of the two flats distress, and that no work had been done by the respondents to comply with the notices, had no alternative but to dismiss the appeals against the convictions by the Bournemouth magistrates on 15th March 1979. The Crown Court were therefore wrong in allowing the appeal and I accordingly agree with the order proposed.

Appeal dismissed.

Solicitors: *Stephen J C Chappell*, Bournemouth (for the appellant); *E W Marshall Harvey & Dalton*, Bournemouth (for the respondent).

Dilys Tausz   Barrister.

R v Hussain

COURT OF APPEAL, CRIMINAL DIVISION
EVELEIGH LJ, CANTLEY AND LLOYD JJ
30th OCTOBER, 19th NOVEMBER 1980

Firearms – Possession – Possession of firearm without a certificate – Mens rea – Whether necessary to prove that accused knew that article in his possession was a firearm – Firearms Act 1968, s 1(1)(a).

Section 1(1)(a)[a] of the Firearms Act 1968 creates an absolute offence and all that the Crown need to prove to establish the offence is that the accused was knowingly in possession of an article which, on the evidence, is a firearm. The Crown does not have to prove that the accused knew that the article was a firearm (see p 289 *a* to *e, post*).

Warner v Metropolitan Police Comr [1968] 2 All ER 356 applied.

Notes
For the offence of possessing a firearm without a certificate, see 11 Halsbury's Laws (4th Edn) para 875.

For the Firearms Act 1968, s 1, see 8 Halsbury's Statutes (3rd Edn) 729.

Cases referred to in judgment
R v Howells [1977] 3 All ER 417, [1977] QB 614, [1977] 2 WLR 716, 141 JP 641, 65 Cr App R 86, CA, Digest (Cont Vol E) 150, 8057*b*.
Warner v Metropolitan Police Comr [1968] 2 All ER 356, [1969] 2 AC 256, [1968] 2 WLR 1303, 132 JP 378, 52 Cr App R 373, HL, 15 Digest (Reissue) 1069, 9156.

Cases also cited
Director of Public Prosecutions v Morgan [1975] 2 All ER 347, [1976] AC 182, HL.
R v Freeman [1970] 2 All ER 413, [1970] 1 WLR 788, CA.
Sweet v Parsley [1969] 1 All ER 347, [1970] AC 132, HL.
Thorne v Motor Trade Association [1937] 3 All ER 157, [1937] AC 797, HL.

Appeal
The defendant, Iftikhar Hussain, was charged with possessing a firearm without holding a firearm certificate, contrary to s 1(1) of the Firearms Act 1968. His defence, inter alia, was that he did not know that the article in his possession was a firearm. He was convicted of the offence on 10th July 1979, in the Crown Court at Snaresbrook, and fined £100 and ordered to pay the full costs of his defence. He appealed against the conviction on the ground, inter alia, that the trial judge misdirected the jury in telling them that it was not necessary for the Crown to prove that he knew that the article in his possession was a firearm and that he was guilty of the offence if the jury were satisfied that he was in possession of the article. The facts are set out in the judgment of the court.

Nina Stanger for the defendant.
Christopher Nutt for the Crown.

Cur adv vult

19th November. **EVELEIGH LJ** read the following judgment of the court: On 10th July 1979 in the Crown Court at Snaresbrook the defendant was convicted of possessing

---

a   Section 1, so far as material, is set out at p 288 *f, post* a firearm without holding a firearms certificate. He was fined £100 and was ordered to pay the full costs of his defence. He now appeals against conviction.

On 22nd March 1978 a police officer went to the defendant's house and in a box containing motor cycle parts he found an article which the prosecution alleged was a firearm. The appellant did not have a certificate. The article was a metal tube about 8 inches long. It had a striker pin which was activated by a spring. The appellant said: 'It is a small gun. Kids use them in my country.'

An expert witness from the Metropolitan Police forensic science laboratory gave evidence that he clamped the tube to a table and fired from it .32 Smith and Wesson cartridges. A London telephone directory was penetrated to about three-quarters of its thickness, indicating a potentially lethal force. The defence called an expert witness who expressed the opinion that the article was not an effective firearm. He said that if held in the hand the penetration would be considerably less than when clamped to the table, that it would not fire certain cartridges, and that if the tube was held in the hand it would penetrate ¼ inch of wood at 15 inches whereas a standard Smith and Wesson revolver would go through something like three and a half ⅞ inch boards.

The defendant himself said that the article was a toy which his son had once used to fire corks.

Section 57 of the Firearms Act 1968 reads:

'(1) In this Act, the expression "firearm" means a lethal barrelled weapon of any description from which any shot, bullet or other missile can be discharged . . .'

In summing up to the jury the judge told them the meaning of the expression 'firearm' and in effect directed them that if the article was a firearm the accused would be guilty of the offence if they found that he was in possession of that article, even though he might not know that it was a firearm. On behalf of the defendant it is submitted that this direction was wrong and that, as counsel put it, it is necessary for the Crown to prove that the accused had knowledge of the nature of the article in order to establish the mens rea required for the offence.

Section 1 (1) of the 1968 Act provides:

'Subject to any exemption under this Act, it is an offence for a person—(a) to have in his possession, or to purchase or acquire, a firearm to which this section applies without holding a firearm certificate in force at the time, or otherwise than as authorised by such a certificate . . .'

The subsection makes no reference to the state of knowledge of the accused. It is drafted in absolute terms and can be contrasted with other sections of the Act where the accused's state of mind is specifically referred to. For example, s 24(1) provides: 'It is an offence to sell or let on hire any firearms or ammunition to a person under the age of 17', but in s 24(5) it is stated: 'In proceedings for an offence under any provision of this section it is a defence to prove that the person charged with the offence believed the other person to be of or over the age mentioned in that provision and had reasonable ground for the belief.'

Again, s 25 reads:

'It is an offence for a person to sell or transfer any firearm or ammunition to, or to repair, prove or test any firearm or ammunition for, another person whom he knows or has reasonable cause for believing to be drunk or of unsound mind.'

However, we do not think it is necessary to deal with this matter at length, for in our opinion the reasoning of their Lordships in *Warner v Metropolitan Police Comr* [1968] 2 All ER 356, [1969] 2 AC 256, which case was referred to in *R v Howells* [1977] 3 All ER 417, [1977] QB 614 in relation to s 1 of the Drugs (Prevention of Misuse) Act 1964, is applicable to this case. That section provides: '(1) . . . it shall not be lawful for a person to have in his possession a substance . . . specified in the Schedule to this Act . . .' It was held that the offence created by that subsection is an absolute offence and proof of mens

rea is not required. In *Warner v Metropolitan Comr* [1968] 2 All ER 356 at 380, [1969] 2
a AC 256 at 295 Lord Morris stated the way in which the construction of the Act should
be approached and said:

> 'For the reasons that I have earlier given I think that, before the prosecution can
> succeed, they must prove that a person knowingly had in his possession something
> which in fact was a prohibited substance.'

b In the present case the prosecution proved that the defendant knowingly had in his
possession an article which was in fact a lethal weapon, in other words a firearm. Lord
Morris went on to say:

> 'Was it, however, for the prosecution to prove that the appellant knew the nature
> and quality of that which he had? In my view, it was not. The evidence proved
> that what the appellant had in his possession was B-aminopropylbenzine or a salt of
c that substance.'

Lord Guest said ([1968] 2 All ER 356 at 385, [1969] 2 AC 256 at 301):

> 'Absolute offences are by no means unknown to our law and have been created
> inter alia in relation to firearms (Firearms Act 1937) and shotguns (Criminal Justice
> Act 1967, s 85), which Acts create serious offences. A common feature of these Acts
d and the Drugs Act is that they all deal with dangerous substances where the object
> is to prevent unauthorised possession and illegal trafficking in these articles.'

In our opinion *Warner v Metropolitan Police Comr* provides a short answer to the
defendant's submission.

It was also submitted that the judge wrongly influenced the jury in relation to the
e question whether the article was a lethal weapon. It is true that during the examination
of the expert witnesses for the Crown he used expressions which indicated that the article
appeared to be a lethal weapon but in this he was in no way misrepresenting the effect
of the Crown evidence. It is also true that he used expressions which indicated that he
considered the article to be lethal, but in summing up to the jury he said:

> 'Counsel was absolutely right when she said to you last evening and today that if
f I, as presiding judge, in the course of the case make any comment about it, or in the
> course of this summing up make any comment about it, and those comments relate
> to the facts, which are your province, you must disregard entirely what I say unless
> the comments I have made and the views I have expressed happen to tally with your
> views because this case, so far as the facts are concerned, is being tried by you, the
> jury, no one else.'
g
We do not think that the jury were wrongly influenced. This appeal is dismissed.

*Appeal dismissed. Application by the defendant for a certificate that a point of law of general
public importance was involved in the decision refused.*

Solicitors: *Maurice Nadeen & Co* (for the defendant); *R E T Birch* (for the Crown).

April Weiss   Barrister.

Allnatt London Properties Ltd v Newton   a

CHANCERY DIVISION
SIR ROBERT MEGARRY V-C
17th, 20th NOVEMBER 1980

Landlord and tenant – Business premises – Surrender of tenancy – Restriction on agreements b
purporting to preclude tenant from applying for new tenancy – Purporting to preclude – Lease
requiring tenant to offer to surrender lease before he is entitled to consent to assign – Tenant
offering to surrender lease and offer accepted by landlord but tenant subsequently withdrawing
offer because sum offered by landlord for surrender insufficient – Landlord suing tenant to enforce
agreement – Whether agreement void as 'purporting to preclude' tenant from applying for new
tenancy at end of term – Whether if agreement void provisions in lease for surrender also void c
and tenant entitled to consent to assign without first offering to surrender lease – Landlord and
Tenant Act 1954, s 38(1).

By a lease made in 1972 the landlords demised certain business premises to the tenant for
21 years from 25th March 1972. The lease provided that if the tenant desired to assign
the premises he had first to make the landlords 'an offer in writing . . . to surrender the d
lease with vacant possession . . . in consideration of the payment by the Landlords . . . of
a sum representing the net premium value (if any) of the lease for the unexpired residue
of the term', and further provided that if the landlords refused the offer or did not accept
it within a certain period the tenant could within one month after the refusal or
otherwise within two months after the offer was made 'apply to the Landlords in writing
for consent to assign . . . and such consent shall not be unreasonably witheld'. Seven e
years after the commencement of the lease the tenant wished to assign the premises and
approached the landlords for consent to assign. The landlords refused their consent and
required the tenant to offer to surrender the lease. By a letter dated 20th December 1979
the tenant offered to surrender the lease 'in accordance with the terms of the lease' and
on 9th January 1980 the landlords accepted the offer. Subsequently the tenant withdrew
his offer to surrender because the sum offered by the landlords for the surrender was f
considered by the tenant to be too low. The landlords issued a writ against the tenant,
seeking (i) a declaration that there was an enforceable contract for the surrender of the
lease, (ii) specific performance of the contract and (iii) damages. The tenant submitted
that the agreement to surrender was rendered void by s 38(1)[a] of the Landlord and
Tenant Act 1954 because Part II of that Act applied to the tenancy and the agreement
'purported to preclude the tenant from making an application or request' for a new g
tenancy under Part II of the Act. The tenant counterclaimed (i) for a declaration to that
effect and (ii) for a declaration that so long as his tenancy was subject to Part II of the 1954
Act he was entitled to assign the premises, with the landlords' consent, without first
offering to surrender the lease to them, because the provisions for surrender in the clause
in the lease were also rendered void by s 38(1) but as they were merely a condition
precedent to the provisions for assignment the latter provisions remained in force. The h
landlords submitted that, if s 38(1) invalidated the agreement to surrender, it also
invalidated the provisions for assignment.

Held – (1) An agreement 'purported to preclude' a tenant from making an application
or request for a new tenancy, and was contrary to s 38(1) of the 1954 Act, if it in fact
operated so to prevent him, even though it may not in terms have prevented him from j
making an application or request for a new tenancy. Since the effect of the agreement
to surrender, if carried out, would be to preclude the tenant from applying at the end of
the tenancy for a new tenancy under Part II of the 1954 Act, the agreement was void

---

a   Section 38(1) is set out at p 292 f g, post

under s 38(1). Accordingly, the landlords were not entitled to the relief they sought and
a the tenant was entitled to a declaration that the agreement to surrender was void (see p
294 *a* to *c* and *g h*, post); *Joseph v Joseph* [1966] 3 All ER 486 followed.

(2) However, s 38(1) of the 1954 Act did not apply to the clause in the lease so as to
invalidate any part of it, because the provisions for surrender constituted merely the
machinery for producing an offer to surrender and were not themselves an agreement to
surrender precluding the tenant from making an application or request for a new
b tenancy, since an agreement to surrender came into existence only if and when the
landlords accepted an offer to surrender made under the clause. Moreover, to guard
against the mischief envisaged by s 38(1) it was sufficient for the actual agreement to
surrender to be struck down as void and there was no need for s 38(1) to extend to the
provisions for surrender in the clause. Furthermore, the provisions for surrender were
not merely conditions precedent to the provisions for assignment but were so
c interdependent with the latter as not to be severable from them, so that the whole clause
would have had to be invalidated if the provisions for surrender were held to be
invalidated by s 38(1). It followed that the whole of the clause remained valid and that
the tenant was still required to offer to surrender the lease before he could obtain the
landlords' consent to an assignment. Accordingly, he was not entitled to the second
declaration he sought (see p 295 *a* to p 296 *a*, post).

d

Notes
For the prohibition against contracting out of Part II of the Landlord and Tenant Act
1954, see 23 Halsbury's Laws (3rd Edn) 883, para 1705.
For the Landlord and Tenant Act 1954, s 38, see 18 Halsbury's Statutes (4th Edn) 578.
e

Cases referred to in judgment
Gaskell v King (1809) 11 East 165, 103 ER 967, 31(2) Digest (Reissue) 578, 4718.
Jones v Wrotham Park Settled Estates [1979] 1 All ER 286, [1980] AC 74, [1979] 2 WLR
132, 38 P & CR 77, HL; *rvsg* [1978] 3 All ER 527, [1978] 3 WLR 585, CA, Digest (Cont
f Vol E) 359, 1497*a*.
Joseph v Joseph [1966] 3 All ER 486, [1967] Ch 78, [1966] 3 WLR 631, CA, 31(2) Digest
(Reissue) 940, 7707.
Pickering v Ilfracombe Railway Co (1868) LR 3 CP 235, [1861–73] All ER Rep 773, 37 LJCP
118, 17 LT 650, 10 Digest (Reissue) 1369, 8789.

g

Action
By a writ dated 11th April 1980 the plaintiffs, Allnatt London Properties Ltd ('the
landlords'), sought as against the defendant, Ronald James Newton ('the tenant'), a
declaration that there existed an enforceable contract for the surrender by the tenant to
the landlords of the tenant's lease, dated 20th April 1972, of business premises known as
h Building 665, Pulborough Way, Green Lane, Hounslow, and also specific performance
of the contract; and damages in addition to or in lieu of specific performance. By his
defence the tenant contended that the purported contract to surrender was void as being
contrary to s 38 of the Landlord and Tenant Act 1954, and counterclaimed for (i) a
declaration to that effect and (ii) a declaration that so long as the tenancy was subject to
Part II of the 1954 Act, the tenant was entitled to assign and/or sublet the whole of the
premises, with the landlords' consent, such consent not to be unreasonably withheld,
without first offering to surrender the residue of the term to the landlords. The facts are
set out in the judgment.

J H G Sunnucks for the landlords.
Paul de la Piquerie for the tenant.

Cur adv vult

20th November. **SIR ROBERT MEGARRY V-C** read the following judgment: This
action raises two points on business tenancies under the Landlord and Tenant Act 1954,
Part II. Under a lease dated 20th April 1972 the plaintiffs, the landlords, demised
business premises to the defendant, the tenant, for a term of 21 years from 25th March
1972. The lease contained an elaborate clause, cl 3(21)(b), which I will set out in due
course. This prohibited any assignment of the premises as a whole, though if the tenant
wished to assign them and first offered to surrender the lease to the landlords on certain
terms, and the landlords either refused the offer or failed to accept it within 21 days, the
tenant was free to assign the premises within a stated time, and the landlords were not
to withhold their consent unreasonably.

What happened was that after the lease had been running for nearly seven years the
tenant wished to assign it, and he approached the landlords for consent. They refused
this, and required the tenant first to offer to surrender his lease. This he did by a letter
dated 20th December 1979, which offered to surrender the lease 'in accordance with the
terms of the Lease'; and on 9th January 1980 the landlords accepted the offer. An
exchange of letters in February and March showed that whereas the tenant expected to
receive £45,000 for the surrender, the landlords were willing to pay only £10,000. The
difference, I was told, was in the main due to the landlords' offer being based on the value
of the unexpired term, with nothing for goodwill, whereas the tenant's value included
what an assignee would be expected to pay for goodwill. When this emerged, the tenant
withdrew his offer to surrender. This was on March 6th 1980: and on 11th April the
landlords issued the writ. This claims a declaration that the contract for surrender was
enforceable, specific performance of the contract, and damages. The tenant's defence
and counterclaim, as amended and re-served on 8th July, is that s 38 of the Landlord and
Tenant Act 1954 renders the agreement to surrender void; and the tenant seeks a
declaration to this effect, and also a declaration that so long as the tenancy is subject to
Part II of the 1954 Act the tenant is entitled to assign or sublet the whole of the premises
with the landlords' consent (such consent not to be unreasonably withheld) without first
offering any surrender.

In the 1954 Act, as amended by the Law of Property Act 1969, s 38(1) runs as follows:

'Any agreement relating to a tenancy to which this Part of this Act applies
(whether contained in the instrument creating the tenancy or not) shall be void
(except as provided by subsection (4) of this section) in so far as it purports to
preclude the tenant from making an application or request under this Part of this
Act or provides for the termination or the surrender of the tenancy in the event of
his making such an application or request or for the imposition of any penalty or
disability on the tenant in that event.'

I pause to say that it became common ground that the second part of that provision,
beginning with 'or provides for the termination', did not arise in the present case, for
there was nothing which provided for the termination or surrender of the tenancy 'in the
event of his making such an application or request'. What is at the heart of the matter
is the provision 'in so far as it purports to preclude the tenant from making an application
or request under this Part of this Act'.

In sub-s (4) of s 38, para (a) admittedly does not apply, and so I read it without that
paragraph; and for the errant semi-colon after the words 'so specified' I have substituted
the comma that lucidity demands:

'The court may . . . (b) on the joint application of the persons who are the landlord
and the tenant in relation to a tenancy to which this Part of this Act applies,
authorise an agreement for the surrender of the tenancy on such date or in such
circumstances as may be specified in the agreement and on such terms (if any) as

a
may be so specified, if the agreement is contained in or endorsed on the instrument creating the tenancy or such other instrument as the court may specify; and an agreement contained in or endorsed on an instrument in pursuance of an authorisation given under this subsection shall be valid notwithstanding anything in the preceding provisions of this section.'

It is common ground that the agreement for the surrender is not contained in or indorsed on the lease, or in 'such other instrument as the court may specify'; no
b application to the court on this point has been made. Accordingly, sub-s (4) does not apply, and the case turns on the first limb of sub-s (1).

With that, I can come to the terms of the lease itself. Clause 3 contains the tenant's covenants. The lease refers to 'tenants' in the plural because, I think, the tenant was contemplating the incorporation of his business, though in fact he never did this. Clause 3(21) begins by imposing an absolute prohibition on any assignment of part of the
c demised premises: '(a) Not to assign underlet or part with the possession or occupation or share the occupation of any part (as a part) of the demised premises.' Nothing directly arises under that. There is then sub-cl (b), which is at the heart of the matter. It is an ungainly bit of drafting, with three provisos, and it shuttles to and fro between the first stage, that of the offer to surrender, and the second, that of an assignment if the offer is not accepted. For ease of reference I have inserted numerals which divide the sub-clause
d up into separate limbs, though of course this subdivision cannot affect the construction of the sub-clause. So divided, it reads as follows:

'(1) Not (subject to the proviso to this clause) to assign underlet part with the possession or occupation of the demised premises as a whole (2) Provided Always that if at any time and so often as the Tenants shall desire to assign or underlet the demised premises as a whole the Tenants shall make to the Landlords an offer in
e writing in the terms hereinafter mentioned (3) then if the Landlords shall refuse such offer or shall not within twenty-one days after the receipt by the Landlords of such offer accept the same (4) the Tenants shall be at liberty within one month after such refusal or otherwise within two months after the making of such offer to apply to the Landlords in writing for consent to assign or underlet the demised premises as a whole (5) and such consent shall not be unreasonably withheld (6) Any such
f offer shall be in the terms following namely the Tenants shall offer to surrender the Lease with vacant possession and otherwise free from encumbrances on a date three months from the date of the said written offer in consideration of the payment by the Landlords to the Tenants of a sum representing the net premium value (if any) of this Lease for the unexpired residue of the term such value to be agreed upon by
g the parties or in default of agreement as may be determined by a surveyor to be appointed upon the application of either party by the President for the time being of the Royal Institution of Chartered Surveyors (7) Provided further that any acceptance by the Landlords of any such offer so made to them shall be without prejudice to the rights and remedies of the Landlords in respect of any rent in arrear or any breach of any of the covenants herein contained and on the part of the
h Tenants to be observed (8) Provided further that if the Landlords shall agree to give consent for the Tenants to assign this Lease then it shall be a condition of any such consent that the Assignee shall enter into a direct covenant with the Landlords to pay the rents hereinbefore reserved and to observe and perform the covenants herein contained during the residue of the term hereby created.'

i
It will be seen that limb (1) imposes the prohibition, limbs (2), (3), (6) and (7) refer to stage 1, and limbs (4), (5) and (8) relate to stage 2.

With that in mind, I return to the accepted offer to surrender. This is plainly an agreement relating to a tenancy to which Part II of the 1954 Act applies, within the opening words of s 38(1). That agreement does not fall within s 38(4), and so by sub-s

(1) it is void 'in so far as it purports to preclude the tenant from making an application or request under this Part of this Act'. Does it so purport?

Whatever might be thought about the meaning of the word 'purport' in the abstract, that word has to be construed in its context: and this was done in *Joseph v Joseph* [1966] 3 All ER 486, [1967] Ch 78. There, the Court of Appeal unanimously held that the phrase 'purports to preclude', in its context, meant not 'professes to preclude' but 'has the effect of precluding'. The question is not so much whether there is an agreement which in terms prevents the tenant from making an application or request, but whether, whatever the agreement says, it in fact operates to prevent the tenant from doing this. In *Joseph v Joseph* there was an agreement for a lease for ten years, and after this had run for some two years, an agreement was made to surrender the tenancy within the next two years. The inevitable effect of the agreement to surrender the tenancy, if carried out, would be to preclude the tenant from applying for a new tenancy when the tenancy agreement ran out some six years after the date of the agreement to surrender: for by s 24(2), s 24(1) would not operate to prolong a tenancy which had actually been surrendered. Section 38(1) invalidated that agreement to surrender, and therefore the landlord could not obtain any damages for the tenant's breach of the agreement.

Joseph v Joseph, of course, binds me: and I have heard nothing to detract from its authority. It was followed by the Court of Appeal in *Jones v Wrotham Park Settled Estates* [1978] 3 All ER 527, [1980] AC 74, and although it was challenged on appeal, the House of Lords found it unnecessary to decide anything on it, and said nothing one way or the other to affect its authority (see [1979] 1 All ER 286 at 295, [1980] AC 74 at 114). Certain other authorities were cited to me, but I do not think any of them affect what I have to decide. Counsel for the landlords had a point on the lease not being assignable by reason of the parties' clause at the beginning referring to the parties only by name, without mentioning assigns. Counsel for the tenant met this by invoking the Law of Property Act 1925, s 79; but then the point blew up in counsel for the landlords' hands when, very properly, he drew attention to cl 5(c) of the lease, which provided, inter alia, that 'the Tenants', where the context so required or admitted, included their assigns. Counsel for the landlords also had a point on the contrast in s 38(1) of the 1954 Act between 'tenant' and 'tenancy', and he contended that the subsection gave no protection to a tenant who did not want his tenancy to continue but instead wished to terminate it. I did my best to follow his submissions, but in the end I was quite unable to see anything in them which could suffice to exclude the operation of s 38(1) as construed in *Joseph v Joseph*, or to distinguish that case.

In the result, it appears to me that I must hold that the agreement to surrender is rendered void by s 38(1). It follows that the landlords' claim must fail. I cannot declare that the agreement is an enforceable contract, nor decree specific performance of it or award damages for its breach. On the counterclaim, the tenant has made out a sufficient case to support his claim to a declaration that the agreement to surrender is void by virtue of s 38; and in the absence of any reason why I should exercise my discretion to refuse to grant declaratory relief, I propose to make a declaration to that effect.

That leaves the tenant's further claim to a declaration that so long as the tenancy is within Part II of the 1954 Act the tenant is entitled to assign or sublet the whole of the demised premises with the consent of the landlords (such consent not to be unreasonably withheld) without first offering to surrender the residue of the term. That is the second point in the case. Relatively little was said about it during the argument, though it seems to me the most difficult part of the case. Counsel for the landlords contended that if (contrary to his main contention) s 38(1) harmed him, it did not merely avoid the contract to surrender, but also rendered void or ineffective the machinery in cl 3(21)(b) of the lease for the tenant having to make an offer to surrender the lease before seeking to assign; and if it did that, it made the whole of cl 3(21)(b) void or ineffective. Counsel for the tenant, on the other hand, argued that the provision for a surrender was merely a condition precedent to an assignment; and if the condition precedent was void, as he said it was, that left the provision for assignment in full operation.

I think the starting point must be to consider whether s 38(1) invalidates any of cl
a 3(21)(b), and if so, how much of it. What s 38(1) invalidates is an agreement in so far as
it has the effect of precluding the tenant from making an application or request under
Part II of the 1954 Act. Is there anything in cl 3(21)(b) which does this? If one takes the
sub-clause as it stands, without applying s 38(1), I cannot see that, without more, there is
anything which has the effect of precluding the tenant from making an application or
request. Limb (2) requires the tenant to make an offer to surrender: but an offer is not
b an 'agreement', nor does an agreement to make an offer to surrender, by itself, preclude
the tenant from making an application or request. If the landlords reject the offer, there
is still no such precluding, and the tenant is free to assign under the conditions stated.
If on the other hand the landlords accept the offer, then the resulting agreement to
surrender (if enforceable) would have the effect of precluding the tenant from making
an application or request: and then at that point s 38(1) would make that agreement
c void. In short, until it is known whether the landlords have accepted or rejected the offer
to surrender it cannot be known whether there is any agreement which will preclude an
application or request, within the meaning of the subsection: there may or may not be.
It will be observed that all that cl 3(21)(b) does is to require an offer to be made; it
depends on what happens to that offer whether there ever comes into being an agreement
which offends against the subsection. It is not as if the sub-clause gave the landlords an
d option or other right to require the tenant to surrender the lease. In my view, the sub-
clause does not fall within the subsection, but stands at one remove from anything that
does. It seems to me that the subsection, as construed in *Joseph v Joseph*, is perfectly
adequate to guard against the mischief which it envisages if it strikes down the actual
agreement to surrender, and that there is no need to construe the subsection so as to
make it extend to the mechanism for producing an offer which, if accepted, would be
e invalidated. Nor do I feel any more enthusiasm than was felt by the Court of Appeal in
Joseph v Joseph for enabling either party to a lease to escape from his bargain further than
is necessary to give effect to the subsection and its manifest purpose.
There is a further consideration. The subclause represents a bargain in which the
rights of the parties depend on a balance of advantages and disadvantages to each. If
statute declares void part of such a subclause which operates for the benefit of one party,
f I should hesitate to hold that the other party could thereupon obtain the benefit of the
rest of the clause without suffering the burden of what has been declared void, unless the
provisions were clearly severable. Limbs (2) to (8) of the sub-clause seem to me to be so
interdependent that it would be making a different contract for the parties if the
provisions for the offer to surrender were to be disregarded as being void and the rest of
the limbs were then revised so as to put them into an intelligible and enforceable form.
g I certainly would not regard the provisions for the offer to surrender as being a mere
condition precedent. This is not a case of independent provisions such as there were in
Gaskell v King (1809) 11 East 165, 103 ER 967; and see *Pickering v Ilfracombe Railway Co*
(1868) LR 3 CP 235 at 250, [1861–73] All ER Rep 773 at 777. Accordingly, if I am
wrong in thinking that the sub-clause is not affected by the subsection, then I would hold
that limbs (2) to (8) all fall together.
h Limb (1), which prohibits the whole of the premises from being assigned, and so on,
seems to me to be in a somewhat different position. It is, of course, in terms made
'subject to the proviso to this clause', which presumably means all three provisos, and
thus includes limbs (2) to (8). If all those limbs fall by virtue of the subsection, then limb
(1) remains perfectly intelligible and capable of operation, though it then ceases to be
subject to anything. Limb (1) seems to me to be severable from limbs (2) to (8) in a way
j that is not possible for the latter limbs inter se. However, none of this was argued before
me, and I hesitate to reach a firm conclusion on it. For the reasons that I have given I base
my decision on the subsection not having any application to the sub-clause.
In the result, it seems to me that the second declaration sought by the counterclaim
ought to be refused. I do not think that the effect of the subsection is to permit
assignments or sublettings of the whole with the consent of the landlords which must

not unreasonably be withheld, without the prior offer of a surrender. In the result, the
counterclaim fails save as to the declaration which merely reflects the failure of the claim.   *a*

Action dismissed ; declaration on counterclaim accordingly.

Solicitors: *Marshall, Shortland & Co* (for the landlords); *Paul Gromett & Co* (for the tenant).

Azza M Abdallah   Barrister.   *b*

Thompson v Brown Construction (Ebbw Vale) Ltd and others

HOUSE OF LORDS   *c*
LORD DIPLOCK, LORD ELWYN-JONES, LORD FRASER OF TULLYBELTON, LORD SCARMAN AND LORD
BRIDGE OF HARWICH
17th, 18th MARCH, 7th MAY 1981

Limitation of action – Court's power to override time limit in personal injury or fatal accident   *d*
claim – Exercise of discretion – Plaintiff having incontestable case in negligence against own
solicitor equal to claim against defendant – Whether discretion unfettered – Whether plaintiff
prejudiced by expiry of limitation period – Limitation Act 1939, s 2D (as inserted by the
Limitation Act 1975, s 1(1)).

The appellant was injured when scaffolding on which he was working collapsed, the   *e*
accident being caused entirely by the negligence of the firm of scaffolders which erected
the scaffolding. The appellant instructed solicitors with a view to claiming damages
against the scaffolders but the solicitors negligently allowed the three-year limitation
period prescribed by s 2A(4)[a] of the Limitation Act 1939 to expire before issuing the
writ. When the writ was issued the scaffolders pleaded by way of defence that the action
was out of time. At the trial of a preliminary issue whether it would be equitable to   *f*
allow the appellant's action to proceed and whether a direction to that effect ought to be
given under s 2D[b] of the 1939 Act, the judge held that he was bound by authority to hold
that he had no jurisdiction to make a direction, because the appellant would not be
prejudiced if the statutory limitation imposed by s 2A continued to apply to his action
since he had an incontestable case in negligence against his own solicitors by which he
would recover at least as much as he would have recovered against the scaffolders. The
appellant appealed to the House of Lords against the judge's refusal to make a direction   *g*
under s 2D.

Held – The court's discretion to make or refuse a direction under s 2D of the 1939 Act
that s 2A of that Act should not apply to a particular cause of action was unfettered. The
conduct of the parties as well as the prejudice one or other would suffer if a direction was   *h*
or was not given were all matters to be put into the balance in deciding under s 2D
whether it would be equitable to allow the plaintiff's action to proceed. Furthermore,
although a plaintiff's potential claim against his solicitor in the event of his not being
permitted to proceed against the defendant was a highly relevant factor to be put into the
balance, it was to some extent offset by the fact that he would nevertheless be prejudiced
to some degree by having to bring a fresh action against his solicitor. It followed that the   *j*
judge had been wrong to treat the appellant's potential claim against his solicitors as a
reason for not exercising his jurisdiction rather than as merely one of the circumstances
to be considered in exercising his discretion. The appeal would accordingly be allowed

a   Section 2A, so far as material, is set out at p 299 *f* to p 300 *c, post*
b   Section 2D, so far as material, is set out at p 300 *c* to *j, post*

a
and the case remitted to the judge for further consideration (see p 299 *b c*, p 301 *g* to p 302 *d* and p 303 *b* to p 304 *c*, post).

    Browes v Jones & Middleton (1979) 123 Sol Jo 489 disapproved.

    Per Curiam. When deciding whether to make a direction under s 2D of the 1939 Act, the court is to have regard not only to the degree of prejudice to the plaintiff and the defendant respectively but also to the matters referred to in s 2D(6) (see p 301 *d e*, p 302 *c d* and p 303 *j* to p 304 *c*, post).

b
    Dictum of Lord Diplock in *Walkley v Precision Forgings Ltd* [1979] 2 All ER at 559 qualified.

Notes

For the court's power to override the limitation period in personal injury actions, see 28 Halsbury's Laws (4th Edn) para 694.

c
    For the Limitation Act 1939, ss 2A, 2D (as inserted by the Limitation Act 1975, s 1), see 45 Halsbury's Statutes (3rd Edn) 848, 850.

    As from 1st May 1981 ss 2A and 2D of the 1939 Act have been replaced by ss 11 and 14 and by s 33 of the Limitation Act 1980.

Cases referred to in opinions

d
Browes v Jones & Middleton (1979) 123 Sol Jo 489, CA.

Central Asbestos Co Ltd v Dodd [1972] 2 All ER 1135, [1973] AC 518, [1973] 3 WLR 333, [1972] 2 Lloyd's Rep 413, HL, Digest (Cont Vol D) 618, *2022Ae.*

Firman v Ellis [1978] 2 All ER 851, [1978] QB 886, [1978] 3 WLR 1, CA, 32 Digest (Reissue) 742, *5341.*

Walkley v Precision Forgings Ltd [1979] 2 All ER 548, [1979] 1 WLR 606, HL, Digest (Cont
e
    Vol E) 390, *5341a.*

Interlocutory appeal

On 4th March 1976 the appellant, James Thompson, sustained personal injuries in the course of his employment with the first respondents, Brown Construction (Ebbw Vale) Ltd (sued as George Albert Brown, trading as George Albert Brown (Builders) & Co (a
f
firm)) when scaffolding erected by the second respondents, S G B Scaffolding (Great Britain) Ltd, collapsed. On 10th April 1979, after the three-year limitation period prescribed for personal injury actions by s 2A of the Limitation Act 1939 expired, the appellant's solicitors issued a writ on his behalf claiming damages for personal injuries against the respondents in respect of the accident, alleging negligence and breach of the Construction (Working Places) Regulations 1966. The respondents each denied liability and alleged that the fault of the other had caused the accident and pleaded that, in any
g
event, the appellant's claim was statute barred by the provisions of the 1939 Act. On 18th October 1979 Master Warren ordered that the question raised by the defence of the second respondents whether the claim was statute barred and/or whether it would be just and equitable for the appellant's claim to be allowed to proceed under the provisions of s 2D of the 1939 Act should be tried as a preliminary issue. At the trial of the preliminary
h
issue on 16th May 1980 Phillips J dismissed the appellant's action against both respondents on the ground that he was bound by the decision of the Court of Appeal in *Browes v Jones & Middleton* (1979) 123 Sol Jo 489 to hold that the appellant had not, for the purposes of s 2D of the 1939 Act, been prejudiced by the provisions of s 2A of that Act because he had an unanswerable claim for damages against his solicitors for negligently failing to issue the writ in time, and that therefore the court had no jurisdiction to direct that s 2A should not apply to his cause of action. Pursuant to a certificate granted by Phillips J under s 12(1) of the Administration of Justice Act 1969 and leave granted by the Appeal Committee of the House of Lords, the appellant appealed directly to the House in respect of his action against the second respondents. The facts are set out in the opinion of Lord Diplock.

Michael Turner QC and *C Welchman* for the appellant.
Piers Ashworth QC and *Roderick Denyer* for the second respondents.

Their Lordships took time for consideration.

7th May. The following opinions were delivered.

LORD DIPLOCK. My Lords, on 4th March 1976 scaffolding that had been erected by the second respondents ('the scaffolders') at the Ebbw Vale works of the British Steel Corpn collapsed and injured the appellant, a bricklayer's labourer employed by the first respondents ('the builders'). Through his trade union the appellant was put in touch with solicitors who took up his claim against the scaffolders and the builders for damages for personal injuries caused by their negligence. The solicitors acted promptly; as early as 27th April 1976 the claim was notified to both intended defendants who referred it to their respective insurers. The scaffolders were clearly liable to the appellant, so it was their insurers who conducted the negotiations for settling the case. On 17th March 1977 these insurers wrote to the appellant's solicitors saying that they had completed their inquiries and were prepared to put forward an offer in settlement of the case. They asked for particulars of the appellant's earnings and a medical report. The solicitors encountered considerable delay in obtaining the medical report and, at some date after August 1977, their file dealing with the appellant's claim became mislaid and forgotten. It was not rediscovered until the spring of 1979, and the writ was not issued until 10th April 1979, 37 days after the expiration of the three-year limitation period under s 2A of the Limitation Act 1975. The sections of that Act that fall to be construed in this appeal have since been replaced by ss 11 to 14 and 33 of the Limitation Act 1980, but the relevant words remain the same.

The statement of claim followed three days after the writ. The builders as well as the scaffolders were made defendants; but, since it is undisputed that the accident was entirely due to the negligence of the scaffolders, the fact that the builders are also parties to the action may now be ignored. In their defence the scaffolders pleaded the Limitation Act 1939 and denied that it would be equitable to allow the action to proceed under s 2D notwithstanding the expiry of the three-year limitation period under s 2A. The issue raised by this defence was tried as a preliminary issue by Phillips J on 16th May 1980. That learned judge was of opinion that if the action were not allowed to proceed the appellant would have a 'cast-iron' case in an action for negligence against his own solicitors in which the damages recoverable would be at least as much as, and, it may be, more than, those which would have been recoverable against the scaffolders if the action against them had been allowed to proceed. Although it was disputed by counsel for the appellant at the hearing before Phillips J it has been conceded before your Lordships' House that this is indeed so.

The judge was of opinion that in these circumstances he was bound by an unreported decision of the Court of Appeal in *Browes v Jones & Middleton* (1979) 123 Sol Jo 489 to hold as a matter of law that the provisions of s 2A had not prejudiced the appellant and that the court had no jurisdiction under s 2D to direct that those provisions should not apply to his cause of action against the scaffolders. So he gave the appropriate certificate under s 12 of the Administration of Justice Act 1969 to enable an appeal from his decision to come direct to your Lordships' House by the 'leapfrog' procedure.

My Lords, the unreported case of *Browes* was one in which the early history of the matter was similar to the instant case. The plaintiff, Browes, had been injured in a traffic accident by the undoubted negligence of a lorry driver employed by H Camm Ltd. He went to solicitors, Jones & Middleton, who conducted negotiations with Camm's insurers but allowed the three-year limitation period under s 2A to expire before they had issued a writ. On learning that the limitation point would be relied on by Camm if a writ should be issued, Jones & Middleton advised Browes to consult other solicitors. He did so and, on their advice, started an action against Jones & Middleton claiming damages for their negligence as solicitors. That action had gone on for a year against Jones & Middleton alone before Camm was added as a second defendant. Camm pleaded s 2A of the Limitation Act 1939 as a defence and this was tried as a preliminary issue.

a Paradoxically notwithstanding that it was the plaintiff, Browes, who had joined Camm as a defendant it was his counsel who was arguing strenuously that the plaintiff had *not* been prejudiced by his former solicitors' failure to issue the writ within the time limited by s 2A, and it was counsel for his former solicitors who was arguing strenuously that he had. There were additional complications into which it would not be profitable to go. Suffice it to say that the Court of Appeal felt compelled by the reasoning in the speeches of Viscount Dilhorne and myself in *Walkley v Precision Forgings Ltd* [1979] 2 All ER 548,
b [1979] 1 WLR 606 to hold that s 2D did not apply in the circumstances of that case.

My Lords, I shall have to refer briefly to *Walkley* in connection with the construction of ss 2A and 2D; but in view of the very special facts of *Browes* and the bizarre course that the argument took, the law reporters, in my opinion, exercised a wise discretion in consigning it to the limbo of unreported cases. For reasons I shall endeavour to develop it ought not to be treated as authority for the proposition of law that Phillips J treated it
c as laying down.

In approaching the construction of ss 2A and 2D of the Limitation Act 1939 (now ss 11 and 14 and s 33 of the Limitation Act 1980) account must be taken of the legislative history of these sections. The Limitation Act 1939 by s 2 re-enacted the limitation period of six years from the date on which the cause of action accrued for actions founded in tort. The Law Reform (Limitation of Actions &c) Act 1954, s 2(1) reduced this period
d to three years in actions for damages for personal injuries. This shortened period led to what was felt to be injustice, particularly in cases of long-maturing industrial diseases; and the somewhat complicated provisions of Part I of the Limitation Act 1963 were passed in the hope that they would provide an equitable solution. These proved to be unsatisfactory in application and gave rise to considerable differences of judicial opinion as to their true interpretation, particularly whether a plaintiff's ignorance that acts or
e omissions by the defendant that were known to him and gave him in law a cause of action, had the effect of extending the limitation period: cf *Central Asbestos Co Ltd v Dodd* [1972] 2 All ER 1135, [1973] AC 518.

Section 1 of the Limitation Act 1975 represented the next attempt by Parliament to solve the problem. It did so by adding four new sections, ss 2A, 2B, 2C and 2D, to the Limitation Act 1939. The sections relevant to the instant case were ss 2A and 2D, and, for
f the purpose of seeing how they apply to it, it is convenient to set out most of their provisions in extenso leaving out only those which deal with cases when the person injured has died:

'2A.—(1) This section applies to any action for damage [sic] for negligence, nuisance or breach of duty (whether the duty exists by virtue of a contract or of
g provision made by or under a statute or independently of any contract or any such provision) where the damages claimed by the plaintiff for the negligence, nuisance or breach of duty consist of or include damages in respect of personal injuries to the plaintiff or any other person.

'(2) Section 2 of this Act shall not apply to an action to which this section applies.

'(3) Subject to section 2D below, an action to which this section applies shall not
h be brought after the expiration of the period specified in subsections (4) and (5) below.

'(4) Except where subsection (5) applies, the said period is three years from—(a) the date on which the cause of action accrued, or (b) the date (if later) of the plaintiff's knowledge . . .

'(6) In this section, and in section 2B below, references to a person's date of
j knowledge are references to the date on which he first had knowledge of the following facts—(a) that the injury in question was significant, and (b) that that injury was attributable in whole or in part to the act or omission which is alleged to constitute negligence, nuisance or breach of duty, and (c) the identity of the defendant, and (d) if it is alleged that the act or omission was that of a person other than the defendant, the identity of that person and the additional facts supporting

the bringing of an action against the defendant, and knowledge that any acts or
omissions did or did not, as a matter of law, involve negligence, nuisance or breach *a*
of duty is irrelevant.

'(7) For the purposes of this section an injury is significant if the plaintiff would
reasonably have considered it sufficiently serious to justify his instituting proceedings
for damages against a defendant who did not dispute liability and was able to satisfy
a judgment.

'(8) For the purposes of the said sections a person's knowledge includes knowledge *b*
which he might reasonably have been expected to acquire—(*a*) from facts observable
or ascertainable by him, or (*b*) from facts ascertainable by him with the help of
medical or other appropriate expert advice which it is reasonable for him to seek,
but a person shall not be fixed under this subsection with knowledge of a fact
ascertainable only with the help of expert advice so long as he has taken all reasonable
steps to obtain (and, where appropriate, to act on) that advice . . .   *c*

'2D.—(1) If it appears to the court that it would be equitable to allow an action to
proceed having regard to the degree to which—(*a*) the provisions of section 2A or 2B
of this Act prejudice the plaintiff or any person whom he represents, and (*b*) any
decision of the court under this subsection would prejudice the defendant or any
person whom he represents, the court may direct that those provisions shall not *d*
apply to the action, or shall not apply to any specified cause of action to which the
action relates . . .

'(3) In acting under this section the court shall have regard to all the circumstances
of the case and in particular to—(*a*) the length of, and the reasons for, the delay on
the part of the plaintiff; (*b*) the extent to which, having regard to the delay, the
evidence adduced or likely to be adduced by the plaintiff or the defendant is or is *e*
likely to be less cogent than if the action had been brought within the time allowed
by section 2A or as the case may be 2B; (*c*) the conduct of the defendant after the
cause of action arose, including the extent if any to which he responded to requests
reasonably made by the plaintiff for information or inspection for the purpose of
ascertaining facts which were or might be relevant to the plaintiff's cause of action
against the defendant; (*d*) the duration of any disability of the plaintiff arising after *f*
the date of the accrual of the cause of action; (*e*) the extent to which the plaintiff
acted promptly and reasonably once he knew whether or not the act or omission of
the defendant, to which the injury was attributable, might be capable at that time
of giving rise to an action for damages; (*f*) the steps, if any, taken by the plaintiff to
obtain medical, legal or other expert advice and the nature of any such advice he
may have received.   *g*

'(4) In a case where the person injured died when, because of section 2A, he could
no longer maintain an action and recover damages in respect of the injury, the court
shall have regard in particular to the length of, and the reasons for, the delay on the
part of the deceased.

'(5) In a case under subsection (4) above, or any other case where the time limit,
or one of the time limits, depends on the date of knowledge of a person other than *h*
the plaintiff, subsection (3) above shall have effect with appropriate modifications,
and shall have effect in particular as if references to the plaintiff included references
to any person whose date of knowledge is or was relevant in determining a time limit
. . .

'(7) In this section "the court" means the court in which the action has been
brought . . .'   *j*

At common law there was no time limit on a person's right to bring an action for
tort. So a Limitation Act takes the form of a statutory prohibition on bringing an action
after the expiry of a specified time. In the case of actions for damages for personal
injuries s 2A(3) imposes such a prohibition after the expiry of a period of three years from

the date of the accrual of the plaintiff's cause of action, or his knowledge of the material
a facts specified in sub-s (6) if that is later. But the prohibition is not absolute; it is
expressed to be subject to s 2D, which creates exceptions to the general rule laid down in
s 2A(4). During this primary limitation period the plaintiff has an indefeasible right to
bring his action; until it has expired s 2A has no effect on him or his cause of action at all.

Section 2A(6) provides a statutory answer to the question that divided this House in
Central Asbestos Co Ltd v Dodd under the 1963 Act. A plaintiff's ignorance that in law he
b had a cause of action against the defendant is not to prevent the limitation period from
starting if he knows the other facts referred to in sub-ss (6) and (7) or has imputed
knowledge of them under sub-s (8). In s 2D(3)(*e*), when one comes to it, will be found an
indication that the draftsman contemplated that such ignorance of law on the plaintiff's
part might be a common reason why he would need to have recourse to s 2D.

Walkley v Precision Forgings Ltd was a case in which the plaintiff had issued and served
c his writ within the primary limitation period; so s 2A had not affected him at all. No
further steps were taken in the action within the primary limitation period and it was
ripe to be dismissed for want of prosecution. In an attempt to avoid this fate a second
writ founded on the same cause of action was issued by the plaintiff's new solicitors.
Considerable procedural manoeuvring by both parties followed, in the course of which
application was made under s 2D to allow the action started by the second writ to
d proceed. This House took the view that, the plaintiff having brought within the primary
limitation period an action for damages for the very negligence which constituted the
cause of action in the second writ, he had not been affected by s 2A at all, let alone
prejudiced by it. In my own speech in that case, however, there is a sentence (see [1979]
2 All ER 548 at 559 *bc*, [1979] 1 WLR 606 at 618H) that needs to be amended in the light
of the arguments addressed to the House in the instant case.

e Section 2D empowers the court to direct that the primary limitation period shall not
apply to a particular action or cause of action. This is by way of exception, for unless the
court does make a direction the primary limitation period will continue to apply. The
effect of such a direction, and its only effect, is to deprive the defendant of what would
otherwise be a complete defence to the action, viz that the writ was issued too late. A
direction under the section must therefore always be highly prejudicial to the defendant,
f for even if he also has a good defence on the merits he is put to the expenditure of time
and energy and money in establishing it, while if, as in the instant case, he has no defence
as to liability he has everything to lose if a direction is given under the section. On the
other hand if, as in the instant case, the time elapsed after the expiration of the primary
limitation is very short, what the defendant loses in consequence of a direction might be
regarded as being in the nature of a windfall.

g Section 2D appears to be drafted on the further assumption that the expiry of a
limitation period before his action has been started must always prejudice the plaintiff in
some degree. With great respect to the opposite view taken by the Court of Appeal in
Browes, this too seems to me self-evident, unless the plaintiff's prospects of success in the
action if it is allowed to proceed are so hopeless as to deprive it even of nuisance value,
which is very far from being the instant case. The degree to which the plaintiff would
h be prejudiced by being prevented from proceeding with his action will be affected by
how good or bad would have been his prospects of success; so too it will be affected by the
extent to which the plaintiff will be able to recover in an action for negligence against his
own solicitor the value of his lost prospects of success. But, even where, as in the instant
case, and as in *Browes*, if the action were not allowed to proceed the plaintiff would have
a cast-iron case against his solicitor in which the measure of damages will be no less than
j those that he would be able to recover against the defendant if the action were allowed
to proceed, some prejudice, although it may be only minor, will have been suffered by
him. He will be obliged to find and to instruct new and strange solicitors; there is bound
to be delay; he will incur a personal liability for costs of the action up to the date of the
court's refusal to give a direction under s 2D; he may prefer to sue a stranger who is a
tortfeasor with the possible consequences that may have on the tortfeasor's insurance

premiums rather than to sue his former solicitors with corresponding consequences on their premiums. It was suggested that it might be more advantageous to a plaintiff to sue his own solicitor rather than the original tortfeasor since he could recover in an action against the solicitor interest on damages from the date on which the writ against the tortfeasor would have been issued if reasonable diligence had been shown, whereas against the tortfeasor he could only recover interest on damages from the later date, after the expiry of the primary limitation period, at which the writ was actually issued. This, however, is fallacious; he can recover the difference in the interest on damages between the earlier and the later date in a separate action against his solicitor for negligence even if the action against the first tortfeasor is allowed to proceed.

In *Walkley* the primary period of limitation had not expired when the plaintiff had started his action against the tortfeasor. That was the only reason why s 2D did not apply to his case. Whenever s 2D does apply, however, what the court has to decide is whether it would be 'equitable' to allow the action to proceed. The section goes on to specify the matters to which the court must have regard in deciding whether it would be equitable. Those matters are contained not only in sub-s (1) itself but also, and importantly for the purposes of the instant case, in sub-s (3). In *Walkley* I referred incorrectly to the degree of prejudice to plaintiff and defendant respectively which is referred to in sub-s (1) as the only two matters to which the court must have regard. Although reference to these two matters was all that was necessary for the decision that in *Walkley* s 2D did not apply, I ought either to have omitted the word 'only' or to have mentioned the matters referred to in sub-s (3) as other matters to which the court would also have had to have regard if s 2D had applied.

Subsection (3) requires the court to have regard to 'all the circumstances of the case', but singles out six matters for particular mention. These six present a curious hotchpotch. 'The delay' referred to in para (*a*) must be the same delay as in para (*b*); so it means the delay after the primary limitation period has expired. It is the length of this delay (in the instant case 37 days), and the reasons for it, that matter under para (*a*). Paragraph (*b*) refers to the extent to which the cogency of evidence likely to be adduced by either the plaintiff or the defendant is likely to be less as a result of the delay. So far as the diminished cogency affects the defendant's evidence it increases the degree of prejudice he will suffer if the action is allowed to be brought despite the delay; but so far as diminished cogency affects the plaintiff's evidence and so reduces his chances of establishing cause of action if the action is allowed to be brought it lessens the degree of prejudice the plaintiff will suffer if he is not allowed to bring the action at this late stage.

Paragraphs (*a*) and (*b*) are the only two paragraphs which appear to be dealing with matters that affect the extent to which the plaintiff and the defendant will be prejudiced according to whether or not the action is allowed to proceed. Paragraphs (*c*), (*e*) and (*f*), on the other hand, deal with the conduct of the parties, a matter that is always relevant when considering whether it is 'equitable' to give a direction granting a benefit to one party at the expense of the other party. Paragraph (*d*) is restricted to cases where plaintiffs have been under a disability, a class of persons that equity has always been zealous to protect.

Paragraph (*c*) requires the court to take into account the defendant's conduct ever since the action arose, not, be it noted, from what in the absence of knowledge by the plaintiff of material facts may be the later date when the primary limitation period started to run. The reference in this paragraph to response to reasonable requests by the plaintiff for information, recognises an obligation on a potential defendant not to be obstructive in enabling a potential plaintiff to obtain relevant information, though not imposing any obligation to volunteer such information; but in this paragraph the conduct of the defendant must, I think, be understood as including the conduct of his solicitors and his insurers by whom in the ordinary course of things any requests for information will be dealt.

Paragraphs (*e*) and (*f*), which deal with the conduct of the plaintiff, appear to be chronologically in the wrong order, at any rate so far as the latter deals with the obtaining

of legal advice. Until he has obtained legal advice a plaintiff (unless he is himself a
a barrister or solicitor) will not know whether or not he has a cause of action for damages
against the defendant, although under s 2A(6) the lack of this knowledge will not prevent
the primary limitation from starting to run. The steps he has taken up to the point when
he receives advice that he has a possible cause of action are dealt with in para (*f*), whereas
how promptly and reasonably he acted after receiving that advice is dealt with in para
(*e*).

b   In contrast to para (*c*) I think it is apparent that paras (*e*) and (*f*) are referring to the
conduct of the plaintiff himself, as well as that of his lawyers after he has consulted them
for the first time. If he has acted promptly and reasonably it is not to be counted against
him, when it comes to weighing conduct, that his lawyers have been dilatory and
allowed the primary limitation to expire without issuing a writ. Nevertheless, when
weighing what degree of prejudice the plaintiff has suffered, the fact that if no direction
c is made under s 2D he will have a claim over against his solicitor for the full damages that
he could have recovered against the defendant if the action had proceeded must be a
highly relevant consideration.

My Lords, when the court makes a direction under s 2D that the provisions of s 2A
should not apply to a cause of action, it is making an exception to a general rule that has
already catered for delay in starting proceedings that is due to excusable ignorance of
d material facts by the plaintiff as distinct from his lack of knowledge that the facts which
he does know may give him a good cause of action in law. The onus of showing that in
the particular circumstances of the case it would be equitable to make an exception lies
on the plaintiff; but, subject to that, the court's discretion to make or refuse an order if
it considers it equitable to do so is, in my view, unfettered. The conduct of the parties
as well as the prejudice one or other will suffer if the court does or does not make an order
e are all to be put into the balance in order to see which way it falls. I do not think that this
House with its minimal experience of appeals which have involved directions under s 2D
ought to attempt itself to lay down guidelines for the High Court judges who are
familiar with the typical kinds of circumstances in which applications are made. In
matters of practice and discretion if guidelines are needed they are better laid down by
the Court of Appeal.

f   It follows that I agree with what was said about the unfettered nature of the discretion
by the Court of Appeal in *Firman v Ellis* [1978] 2 All ER 851, [1978] 1 QB 886, although
the actual decision in that case must be regarded as having been overruled by *Walkley*.
The writ in *Firman v Ellis* and in the other three cases that were heard with it had been
issued before the expiry of the primary limitation period. The trouble was that they had
been neither served nor renewed within a year. It may seem anomalous that a defendant
g should be better off where, unknown to him, a writ has been issued but not served, than
he would be if the writ had not been issued at all; but this is a consequence of the greater
anomaly too well established for this House to abolish that, for the purposes of a
limitation period, an action is brought when a writ or other originating process is issued
by the Central Office of the High Court and not when it is brought to the knowledge of
the defendant by service on him.

h   Phillips J considered that as a matter of law he had no jurisdiction to make a direction
under s 2D. He accordingly did not exercise his discretion, nor did he say how he would
have exercised it if he had felt free to do so. Since for the reasons I have given I am of
opinion that he had an unfettered discretion, I would allow the appeal and remit the case
to Phillips J for further consideration whether it would be equitable to direct that the
provisions of s 2A of the 1939 Act shall not apply to this action.

j

LORD ELWYN-JONES. My Lords, I have had the advantage of reading in draft the
speech prepared by my noble and learned friend Lord Diplock and I agree with it.
For the reasons he gives, I would allow the appeal and remit the case to Phillips J for
further consideration, as Lord Diplock has proposed.

LORD FRASER OF TULLYBELTON. My Lords, I have had the advantage of reading in draft the speech prepared by my noble and learned friend Lord Diplock and I agree with it.

    For the reasons given by him, I would allow the appeal and remit the case to Phillips J for further consideration, as Lord Diplock has proposed.

LORD SCARMAN. My Lords, I have had the advantage of reading in draft the speech of my noble and learned friend Lord Diplock. I agree with it. For the reasons he gives I would allow the appeal and remit the case to the judge for further consideration, as my Lord proposes.

LORD BRIDGE OF HARWICH. My Lords, I have had the advantage of reading in draft the speech of my noble and learned friend Lord Diplock. I agree with it and with the order he proposes.

Appeal allowed. Case remitted to Phillips J for further consideration.

Solicitors: *O H Parsons & Partners* (for the appellant); *Hextall, Erskine & Co*, agents for *Cartwights*, Bristol (for the second respondents).

Mary Rose Plummer   Barrister.

Veater v G and others

QUEEN'S BENCH DIVISION
LORD LANE CJ AND LLOYD J
26th, 27th JANUARY, 16th FEBRUARY 1981

Magistrates – Binding over – Binding over to keep the peace – Refusal to enter into recognisance – Young person under 17 – Whether power to imprison for refusing to enter into recognisance – Whether prohibition on imprisonment of persons under 17 applying to power to bind over – Whether binding over order can be made unilaterally by the court without defendant's consent to be bound over in sum fixed by court – Justices of the Peace Act 1361 – Powers of Criminal Courts Act 1973, s 19(1).

The police preferred a complaint against the defendants, six youths all under the age of 17, alleging that they had behaved in a manner whereby a breach of the peace was likely to be occasioned. At the hearing of the complaint the defendants admitted the facts alleged against them. The magistrates wished to exercise their preventive power under the Justices of the Peace Act 1361[a] to bind over the defendants in their own recognisances to keep the peace, and asked each defendant if he would consent to be bound over in his own recognisance of £100 to keep the peace for a year. The defendants refused to enter into a recognisance and were released because the magistrates took the view that they could not exercise their common law power to imprison for refusal to enter into a recognisance, because s 19(1)[b] of the Powers of Criminal Courts Act 1973 prohibited the imprisonment of persons under 17 in such circumstances, that they had no power to impose any other custodial sentence, such as a detention order, for the refusal to enter into the recognisances, and that they had no power to impose a binding-over order

---

a   The 1361 Act, so far as material, provides: '... [justices] shall have power ... to take of all them that be not of good fame, where they shall be found, sufficient surety and mainprise of their good behaviour towards the King and his people ... to the intent that ... the peace [be not] blemished ...'

b   Section 19(1) is set out at p 307 g, post

unilaterally, ie without the defendant's consent to enter into a recognisance. The
a prosecutor appealed, contending (i) that the power to bind over in the 1361 Act was part
of the civil jurisdiction of magistrates and as such was excepted from the prohibition on
imprisonment of persons under 17 in s 19(1) of the 1973 Act and that, accordingly, the
magistrates were entitled to send the defendants to prison until they agreed to be bound
over in their own recognisances, and (ii) that, in any event, the magistrates were entitled
to impose a binding-over order unilaterally.

b
Held – The appeal would be dismissed for the following reasons—
(1) Assuming that the power of magistrates to bind over under the 1361 Act was part
of their civil, as opposed to their criminal, jurisdiction (which was doubtful), there was
nothing in the 1973 Act which made that Act, even though it was a criminal statute,
inapplicable to the power to bind over, and, since s 19(1) of the 1973 Act, where
c applicable, was comprehensive and imperative in its prohibition on imprisonment of
persons under 17 and therefore applied to magistrates' civil jurisdiction as well as to their
criminal jurisdiction, it followed that, by virtue of s 19(1), the magistrates had no power
to impose a sentence of imprisonment on the defendants for their refusal to enter into
the required recognisances (see p 307 *j* to p 308 *b*, p 309 *d e* and p 310 *h*, post); *Morris v
Crown Office* [1970] 1 All ER 1079 distinguished.
d (2) Since acknowledgment by the person bound over of his indebtedness to the
sovereign in the sum of the recognisance fixed by the court was the essence of a binding-
over order, the court could not unilaterally, without the defendant's consent to enter into
the recognisance, impose a binding-over order, and the only remedy where a person
refused to enter into a recognisance for the purpose of a binding-over order was to
imprison him until he did so. That remedy was only available, however, if the person
e was over 17 (see p 309 *j* and p 310 *f* to *j*, post).
Per Curiam. Detention in a detention centre or remand home is not available as an
alternative sanction for failure by a person under 17 to enter into a recognisance (see
p 309 *g*, post).

Notes
f For binding-over orders, see 29 Halsbury's Laws (4th Edn) para 402, and for cases on the
subject, see 33 Digest (Repl) 257–261, 841–886.
For restrictions on imposing prison sentences on young offenders, see 29 Halsbury's
Laws (4th Edn) para 418.
For the Justices of the Peace Act 1361, see 21 Halsbury's Statutes (3rd Edn) 17.
For the Powers of the Criminal Courts Act 1973, s 19, see 43 ibid 313.

g **Cases referred to in judgment**
Everett v Ribbands [1952] 1 All ER 823, [1952] 2 QB 198, 116 JP 221, 50 LGR 389, CA, 33
Digest (Repl) 135.
Lansbury v Riley [1914] 3 KB 229, [1911–13] All ER Rep 1059, 83 LJKB 1226, 109 LT
546, 77 JP 440, 23 Cox CC 582, DC, 33 Digest (Repl) 258, 855.
h *Morris v Crown Office* [1970] 1 All ER 1079, [1970] 2 QB 114, [1970] 2 WLR 792, CA, 16
Digest (Reissue) 14, 136.
R v Aubrey-Fletcher, ex parte Thompson [1969] 2 All ER 846, [1969] 1 WLR 872, 133 JP
450, 53 Cr App R 380, DC, Digest (Cont Vol C) 658, 843a.
R v County of London Quarter Sessions Appeals Committee, ex parte Metropolitan Police Comr
[1948] 1 All ER 72, [1948] 1 KB 670, [1948] LJR 472, 112 JP 118, 46 LGR 183, DC, 33
j Digest (Repl) 290, 1169.
R v Greenwich Justices, ex parte Carter [1973] Crim LR 444, DC.
R v Southampton Justices, ex parte Green [1975] 2 All ER 1073, [1976] QB 11, [1975] 3
WLR 277, 139 JP 667, CA, 14(1) Digest (Reissue) 237, 1709.

Cases also cited
R v Cork Justices (1882) 15 Cox CC 149.
R v Woking Justices, ex parte Gossage [1973] 2 All ER 621, [1973] QB 448, DC.

Case stated

On 25th and 31st July 1980 the justices for the county of Avon acting in and for the petty a
sessional division of Bristol sitting as a magistrates' court at Bristol heard complaints
preferred by the prosecutor on 11th April 1980 against the defendants, G, M, L, W, P and
J, who were all juveniles, that on 22nd February 1980 in the City of Bristol they behaved
in a manner whereby a breach of the peace was likely to be occasioned contrary to
common law.   In the light of the defendants' conduct and demeanour on 22nd February
1980 the prosecutor applied to the magistrates to exercise their powers of preventive b
justice to bind over each defendant to keep the peace for the future in some suitable sum
for a suitable period.   The defendants admitted that their behaviour was such that a
breach of the peace was likely to have been occasioned, but when each was asked if he
would enter into his own recognisance of £100 to keep the peace for one year he
refused.   The magistrates were of the opinion that, since they were exercising their
powers of preventive justice, they were acting not under their statutory powers given by c
s 91 of the Magistrates' Courts Act 1952 (which gave a magistrates' court power to bind
over persons to keep the peace) but under their common law powers derived from the
Justices of the Peace Act 1361 and the commission of the peace, and that accordingly,
having regard to the terms of the 1361 Act and the commission, they could not bind over
a person who refused to acknowledge himself to be bound.   They were further of the
opinion that when dealing with juveniles no sanctions were available if the juveniles d
refused to acknowledge themselves bound in their own recognisance to keep the peace,
and that, since they were exercising their powers of preventive justice, they were not
passing sentence on the defendants and therefore, in view of s 4 of the Criminal Justice
Act 1961 and s 19(1) of the Powers of Criminal Courts Act 1973, they had no power to
commit the defendants to custody.   The magistrates accordingly felt that they had no
alternative but to order the defendants to leave the court.   At the request of the prosecutor e
the magistrates stated a case for the opinion of the High Court.   The questions of law for
the opinion of the court were (i) whether the magistrates were correct in holding that a
defendant had to acknowledge the recognisance before they could bind him over to keep
the peace under the 1361 Act or their commission, (ii) whether they were correct in
holding that they had no power to order unilaterally that a defendant (whether adult or
juvenile) be bound over to keep the peace in a specified sum when acting under the 1361 f
Act or their commission, and (iii) whether they had power where a juvenile refused to
acknowledge the recognisance to order him to be detained in a remand or detention
centre pending his entering into that recognisance, analogous to the power to imprison
an adult.   The facts are set out in the judgment of the court.

James Black QC and *Ian Glen* for the prosecutor. g
Ian Bullock for the defendant W.
The other defendants did not appear.

Cur adv vult

16th February.   **LORD LANE CJ** read the following judgment of the court: This is an h
appeal by way of case stated from a decision of the Bristol magistrates given on 31st July
1980.
    The facts are very simple.   On 22nd February 1980 six youths aged 14 and 15 were
reported as behaving in a disorderly manner in Park Road, Stapleton, Bristol.   When the
police arrived on the scene they found two of the youths carrying sticks and a third
wearing a stocking mask.   All six were arrested, and taken to the police station. j
Subsequently they all made statements in which they admitted that they had been on an
expedition with the object of assaulting pupils at the neighbouring school, but had not
been able to find them.   They had all at some stage been armed with sticks.   The police
preferred a complaint against them that they were behaving in a manner whereby a
breach of the peace was likely to be occasioned, contrary to common law.
    When the matter came before the magistrates, the facts were admitted.   The
magistrates were minded to bind over each of the defendants in his own recognisance of

£100 to keep the peace for one year. They asked each of the defendants whether he
a would acknowledge himself bound, and each refused. The magistrates then heard legal
argument as to their powers. They took the view that they could not, in law, impose a
binding-over order unilaterally. To be effective each of the defendants had to
acknowledge his indebtedness in the amount fixed. So the magistrates asked them all
once again whether they would acknowledge their indebtedness. Once again they all
refused. The magistrates then found themselves in what they described as a humiliating
b position. They felt that they had no sanction to secure compliance with their order; that
they had no alternative but to let the defendants go, which they did. The question for
the court is whether they were right.

Counsel for the prosecutor took two main points. In the first place he argued that the
magistrates were wrong to conclude that they had no sanction. They were entitled to
send the defendants to prison until they agreed to be bound. Second, he argued that the
c magistrates were in any event entitled to impose a binding-over order unilaterally. Such
an order would have had exactly the same effect as if the defendants had acknowledged
their indebtedness, and entered into their own recognisance in the amount fixed. It is
convenient to take each of these points in turn.

By s 91(1) of the Magistrates' Courts Act 1952 a magistrates' court has power, on
complaints, to order a person to enter into a recognisance, with or without sureties, to
d keep the peace or to be of good behaviour. If the person fails or refuses to comply with
the order, then by s 91(3) of the Act the court may commit him to prison for a period not
exceeding six months, or until he sooner complies. The power under s 91 must be
distinguished from the somewhat similar power under the Justices of the Peace Act
1361. Unlike the powers under the 1952 Act, the powers under the 1361 Act are
exercisable by a single magistrate; and they are exercisable not by reason of any offence
having been committed, but as a measure of preventive justice, that is to say, where the
e person's conduct is such as to lead the magistrate to suspect that there may be a breach of
the peace, or that he may misbehave; see 4 Bl Comm 251, *Lansbury v Riley* [1914] 3 KB
229, [1911–13] All ER Rep 1059, *R v County of London Quarter Sessions Appeals Committee*
[1948] 1 All ER 72, [1948] 1 KB 670, and *R v Aubrey-Fletcher* [1969] 2 All ER 846, [1969]
1 WLR 872; see also *Everett v Ribbands* [1952] 1 All ER 823 at 826, [1952] 2 QB 198 at
f 205, per Denning LJ. The sanction in the case of a failure or a refusal to enter into a
recognisance under the 1361 Act is the same as under the 1952 Act, namely
imprisonment.

By s 19(1) of the Powers of Criminal Courts Act 1973 Parliament provided that
'Neither the Crown Court nor a magistrates' court shall impose imprisonment on a
person under 17 years of age'. Section 19(4) is a definition section. It provides as follows:

g   'In this section "impose imprisonment" means pass a sentence of imprisonment
or commit to prison in default of payment of any sum of money, or for want of
sufficient distress to satisfy any sum of money, or for failure to do or abstain from
doing anything required to be done or left undone.'

On the face of it, s 19(1) of the 1973 Act has taken away the power of a magistrate to
h impose imprisonment on a person under 17 who has failed to enter into a recognisance
when required. Counsel for the prosecutor submits that that is not so. He submits that
the powers of magistrates under the 1361 Act are part of their civil jurisdiction, and have
been left intact by subsequent criminal legislation, including s 19 of the 1973 Act. He
argues that Parliament cannot have intended to take away from magistrates their only
sanction under the 1361 Act.

j We cannot accept that argument. Even if one assumes that the power of magistrates
to bind over under the 1361 Act is part of their civil, and not their criminal, jurisdiction,
we would still hold that the prohibition on imprisonment of persons under 17 years of
age applies. The language of s 19(1) of the 1973 Act is clear, comprehensive and
imperative. We see no reason to suppose that Parliament intended to make an exception
in the case of the magistrates' civil jurisdiction. It would indeed be an odd result if, in the
case of persons under 17, Parliament had intended to take away the power to commit
under s 91 of the 1952 Act, where an offence had actually been committed, but had left

unaffected the power to commit under the 1361 Act where no offence had been committed.

It is therefore unnecessary to decide whether the premise to the argument of counsel for the prosecutor is correct. At first sight however there is much to be said for the view, contrary to his argument, that the power to bind over to keep the peace is part of the magistrates' criminal jurisdiction. Certainly the occasion on which it was exercised in the present case was a criminal proceeding. R v Southampton Justices, ex parte Green [1975] 2 All ER 1073, [1976] QB 11 was a very different case. In that case a man was granted bail on terms that he provide sureties. One of his sureties was his wife, who duly entered into a recognisance. The man failed to appear at the committal proceedings, and the magistrates estreated the wife's recognisance. She applied for leave to move the Divisional Court, but her application was refused. On appeal to the Court of Appeal it was held that the court had jurisdiction, because it was not a criminal cause or matter. The debt created by the recognisance was a civil debt. But in that case there was no question of the exercise of any powers under the 1361 Act. The facts of the case are so removed from the present that it affords no real help.

Counsel for the prosecutor submitted as a last resort that there had not been a 'failure' to do anything here within s 19(4) of the Act, merely an outright refusal. That is a distinction without a difference.

Counsel further relied heavily on a decision of the Court of Appeal in Morris v Crown Office [1970] 1 All ER 1079, [1970] 2 QB 114. In that case a number of Welsh students created a disturbance in the High Court in the course of a hearing of a libel action. Eleven of them refused to apologise and were sentenced to three months' imprisonment for contempt of court. They were all, save one, under 21. They appealed to the Court of Appeal. There were two points. First, it was said that a sentence of imprisonment should not have been imposed on those under 21 by reason of s 17(2) of the Criminal Justice Act 1948, which corresponds to s 19(2) of the 1973 Act. The Court of Appeal held that the judge was entitled to take the view that no other method of dealing with the students was appropriate, and that the second half of s 17(2) is directory and not mandatory. What was said on that point does not help the prosecutor.

But there was a second point. It was argued that the sentence of imprisonment, being for only three months, should have been suspended under s 39(3) of the Criminal Justice Act 1967. It was held by the Court of Appeal that s 39 of the 1967 Act did not apply to a sentence of imprisonment for contempt. Davies LJ said ([1970] 1 All ER 1079 at 1085, [1970] 2 QB 114 at 126–127):

'What may loosely be called the criminal law statutes apply in my view to the ordinary process of criminal prosecution, whether in a court of summary jurisdiction or at assizes or quarter sessions. Quite apart from the difficulty, to which Lord Denning MR adverted, in the way of enforcing a suspended sentence, if such were passed for a criminal contempt, there are a number of provisions in the criminal law statutes, as I am calling them, which obviously have no application whatsoever to proceedings for contempt. Take probation; it would be quite impossible, I think, for a judge dealing with a case of contempt to make a probation order. Yet such a course is possible in all criminal cases. I cannot see for myself that it would be possible for the judge committing for contempt to send the offender, if he were of the appropriate age, to a detention centre. What it comes to, in my mind, is that the code—the procedure, if that is the apt expression—is entirely different in cases of criminal contempt from that which applies in ordinary criminal cases.'

Salmon LJ said ([1970] 1 All ER 1079 at 1087, [1970] 2 QB 114 at 129):

'This power to commit for what is inappropriately called "contempt of court" is sui generis and has from time immemorial reposed in the judge for the protection of the public. Although the point is by no means free from difficulty, I agree with my Lords that Parliament cannot be taken to have intended that his power should be fettered by the Criminal Justice Acts of 1948 and 1967. To my mind it is plain that Parliament never intended these Acts to apply to proceedings such as these. For a one thing, the 1967 Act supplied no machinery whereby a suspended sentence for contempt of court could ever be made effective if the culprit repeated his offence. Therefore the point that the judge's power was limited by s 39(3) of the 1967 Act to imposing only suspended sentences fails.'

Counsel for the prosecutor argued that by the same process of reasoning the 'criminal law statutes' do not apply to the power of magistrates to commit to prison for refusal to enter into a recognisance under the 1361 Act.

b There are two reasons why we cannot accept that argument. In the first place the Court of Appeal clearly regarded the power to commit for contempt as sui generis: see the successful argument of counsel as amicus curiae ([1970] 2 QB 114 at 118) and the judgment of Salmon LJ ([1970] 1 All ER 1079 at 1086, [1970] 2 QB 114 at 129). If the powers of the court in the case of contempt are indeed sui generis, it follows that they cannot provide any useful analogy in any other case. The powers of magistrates under c the 1361 Act may also be regarded as sui generis. But that does not make them ejusdem generis.

Secondly, the ratio of Lord Denning MR's judgment (with which Davies LJ agreed) is the quite narrow ground that the 1967 Act read as a whole does not contain any provision for giving effect to a suspended sentence in the case of contempt. Therefore s 39 cannot have been intended to apply to such a case. There is nothing in s 19 of the 1973 Act, or d anywhere else, which makes it inapplicable to the power of magistrates to commit under the 1361 Act.

For the reasons which we have given we hold that magistrates have no power to impose a sentence of imprisonment for failure or refusal to enter into a recognisance in the case of persons under 17.

We note in passing that in *R v Greenwich Justices, ex parte Carter* [1973] Crim LR 444 e the Divisional Court seems to have assumed that magistrates would likewise have no power to impose a sentence of imprisonment on a person under 17 for failing to comply with a witness summons.

It was common ground that the magistrates had no power to impose any other custodial sentence. The reason is that the power to order a person under 21 to be detained in a detention centre or remand home is purely statutory. By s 4 of the f Criminal Justice Act 1961 the court is given power to make a detention order in the case of a person under 21 in lieu of passing a sentence of imprisonment. But it only applies in the case of 'an offender', which these persons, ex hypothesi, were not. Moreover, by s 38(1) a 'sentence' is defined as excluding committal for default, which is in turn defined by s 39(1) as including a failure to do anything required to be done. So it is clear that detention in a detention centre or remand home is not available as an alternative sanction g in the case of a failure by a person under 17 to enter into a recognisance.

We now turn to the second main submission of counsel for the prosecutor. Were the magistrates entitled to impose a binding-over order unilaterally?

At first sight there is much to be said for the view that an order that a person be bound over to keep the peace or to be of good behaviour is like any other order imposed by a court. To suggest that such an order requires consent before it is effective is almost a h contradiction in terms. Moreover, a consent which can be compelled, in the case of a person over 17, by the threat of imprisonment, is hardly the sort of consent which, in other circumstances, the court looks on with favour. But counsel has taken us through the whole history of the matter, starting with Dalton's Countrey Justice (1697), described by Lord Goddard CJ in *R v County of London Quarter Sessions* [1948] 1 All ER 72 at 74, [1948] 1 KB 670 at 675 as a work of the highest authority. As a result we have been j convinced first, that the essence of a binding over is that the person bound over acknowledges his indebtedness to the Queen, and thereby becomes bound in the sum fixed by the court, and second, that the court cannot, as it were, force such an acknowledgment on a person behind his back, or treat him as being bound when he is not. The court's only remedy where a person refuses to acknowledge his indebtedness, and thereby becomes bound, is put him in prison until he does.

The process of binding over to keep the peace is described in Dalton's Countrey Justice (1697, p 263) as follows:

'Surety for the Peace, is the acknowledging of a Recognizance (or Bond) to the King (taken by a competent Judge of Record) for the keeping of the Peace: And it is called Surety, of the word *Securitas*, because the party that was in fear, is thereby the more secure and safe.'

From this, and subsequent passages, it appears that the 'security' offered by the process of binding over consists in the recognisance, or bond, entered into either by the principal or by his sureties or both.   In Blackstone's Commentaries there is this passage (4 Bl Comm 252–253):

'This security consists in being bound, with one or more sureties in a recognizance or obligation to the King, entered on record, and taken in some court and by some judicial officer; whereby the parties acknowledge themselves to be indebted to the Crown in the sum required, (for instance £100) with condition to be void and of none effect, if the party shall appear in court on such a day, and in the meantime shall keep the peace; either generally, towards the King, and all his liege people; or particularly also, with regard to the person who craves the security.'

Then (at p 253):

'Wives may demand [such security] against their husbands: or husbands, if necessary, against their wives. But feme covert, and infants under age, ought to find security by their friends only, and not to be bound themselves: for they are incapable of engaging themselves to answer any debt; which, as we observed, is the nature of these recognizances or acknowledgments.'

A similar point is made in Hawkin's Pleas of the Crown (16th Edn, 1824, vol 1, p 479) as follows: 'But infants and femes covert ought to find security by their friends, and not to be bound themselves.'

These last passages seem to us particularly significant, for they show that the essential element in the process of binding over is that the person binds himself. If the court could impose an obligation to be bound, then there would be no difference between the case of femes coverts and infants and any other case.

There is nothing in any of the books to which we were referred which suggests that justices have any power to impose an obligation to be bound, except indirectly by threatening imprisonment. If they have such a power, then it seems strange that the much more drastic sanction of imprisonment should have become so firmly rooted in our law at such an early stage. The form of recognisance into which a person is required to enter has remained in substantially the same language for centuries. By that language the person acknowledges that he is indebted to the Queen in the sum fixed. In our judgment, it is now far too late to argue that the acknowledgment can be treated as a mere formality, which can be dispensed with when occasion demands. Acknowledgment of the indebtedness is an essential ingredient in the binding-over process. We would therefore reject counsel for the prosecutor's second main submission.

That disposes of the present appeal. Though we have every sympathy with the magistrates in the position in which they found themselves, they reached the right conclusion in law. The appeal is accordingly dismissed.

We would add this. It is clear from what we have said that the law is in an unsatisfactory state. The magistrates should not be left as powerless as they are.

Appeal dismissed.

Solicitors: *Blyth, Dutton, Holloway*, agents for *R O M Lovibond*, Bristol (for the prosecutor); *Gerald Davey & Co*, Bristol (for the defendant W).

N P Metcalfe Esq   Barrister.

R v St Albans Juvenile Court, ex parte Godman

QUEEN'S BENCH DIVISION
ACKNER LJ AND SKINNER J
8th, 12th DECEMBER 1980

Magistrates – Summary trial – Offence triable summarily or on indictment – Determination of mode of trial of person attaining age of 17 after pleading to charge – Trial by juvenile court or in magistrates' court with right to elect trial by jury – Date when defendant's age relevant for determining mode of trial – Defendant attaining 17 before commencement of trial but after pleading to charge – Whether defendant entitled to elect trial by jury on attaining 17 – Whether magistrates' decision to try case summarily when plea taken a final decision as to mode of trial – Whether juvenile court having discretion as to mode of trial after defendant attaining 17 – Children and Young Persons Act 1963, s 29 (as amended by the Children and Young Persons Act 1969, Sch 5, para 49, Sch 6) – Criminal Law Act 1977, ss 19(1), 21.

In July 1979 when the applicant was aged 16 he was charged on an information with theft. On 9th October 1979 when he was still 16 he appeared before a juvenile court to enter a plea to the charge and pleaded not guilty. The magistrates adjourned the case for summary hearing on 13th November. By the date of the adjourned hearing on 13th November the applicant had turned 17. His counsel took the view that a jury trial was in the applicant's best interests and submitted to the juvenile court that as the applicant was by then 17, s 19(1)[a] of the Criminal Law Act 1977 entitled him to elect trial by jury. Alternatively counsel submitted that the juvenile court had a discretion as to the mode of trial and should exercise it by allowing the applicant to elect for jury trial. The magistrates decided that the decision on 9th October to try the charge summarily was a final decision as to the mode of trial which could not be reversed when the applicant attained 17 and that accordingly on 13th November he had no right to elect for trial by jury; if, however, they had a discretion in the matter they would have exercised it by requiring a summary trial. The applicant applied for judicial review of that decision seeking an order of certiorari to quash the decision, an order of prohibition forbidding the juvenile court from proceeding with the hearing of the charge and an order of mandamus requiring them to permit the applicant to elect for trial by jury. On the hearing of the application it was submitted for the juvenile court that where there was a right of election between summary trial and trial by jury under the 1977 Act, s 21(2)[b] of that Act required the mode of trial to be decided before a plea was entered and accordingly it was too late on 13th November for the applicant to exercise any right of election.

Held – Although s 21(2) of the 1977 Act indicated that, generally, the mode of trial for an offence triable either way was to be decided before a plea was taken, s 19(1) of that Act

---

a   Section 19, so far as material, is set out at p 313 *h*, post
b   Section 21, so far as material, provides:
   '(1) If, where the court has considered as required by section 20(1) above, it appears to the court that the offence is more suitable for summary trial, the following provisions of this section shall apply (unless excluded by section 24 below).
   '(2) The court shall explain to the accused in ordinary language—(*a*) that it appears to the court more suitable for him to be tried summarily for the offence, and that he can either consent to be so tried or, if he wishes, be tried by a jury; and (*b*) that if he is tried summarily and is convicted by the court, he may be committed for sentence to the Crown Court under section 29 of the Magistrates' Courts Act 1952 if the convicting court, on obtaining information about his character and antecedents, is of opinion that they are such that greater punishment should be inflicted than the convicting court has power to inflict for the offence . . .'

gave a defendant who attained the age of 17 the right in certain circumstances to elect for
jury trial and that right could, by virtue of s 19(2), be exercised up to the time when the *a*
evidence in the case was called, since that point of time and not the time when the plea
was taken was the relevant point of time for deciding on the mode of trial. Accordingly,
even though the applicant had pleaded to the charge when he was 16, he was entitled to
elect for jury trial on 13th November (for he had then attained the age of 17 and the
evidence in the case had not at that time been called). It followed that the application
would be granted (see p 314 *a* to *e* and *j* and p 315 *c*, post).　　　　　　　　　　　　*b*
　　Per Skinner J. Section 29ᶜ of the Children and Young Persons Act 1963 applies only
to sentencing and does not confer on magistrates a discretion in regard to the mode of
trial of a defendant who has attained the age of 17 (see p 315 *a*, post).

Notes
For summary trial of a young person and the power to change from summary trial to　*c*
committal proceedings, see 24 Halsbury's Laws (4th Edn) paras 898:9, 10.
　　For presumption and determination of age of a person charged with an offence, see
ibid para 898:6.
　　For the mode of trial for offences triable either way, see 29 ibid para 303.
　　For the Children and Young Persons Act 1963, s 29, see 17 Halsbury's Statutes (3rd
Edn) 719.　　　　　　　　　　　　　　　　　　　　　　　　　　　　　　　　　　　*d*
　　For the Criminal Law Act 1977, ss 19, 21, see 47 ibid 700, 702.

Application for judicial review
Nigel John Godman, by his next friend and father, John Harry Godman, applied with the
leave of the Divisional Court of the Queen's Bench Division granted on 28th February
1980, for orders of (i) certiorari to quash a decision of the St Albans Juvenile Court given　*e*
on 13th November 1979 refusing to allow him to elect for trial by jury, (ii) prohibition
forbidding the juvenile court from further hearing and adjudicating on the information
against the applicant, and (iii) mandamus directing the juvenile court to permit the
applicant to exercise his right to choose trial by jury. The ground of the application was
that although the applicant when he first appeared in court on the information was aged
16, he had attained 17 before the adjourned hearing on 13th November and accordingly　*f*
on that date the juvenile court had no jurisdiction to refuse his application to elect for
trial by jury. The facts are set out in the judgment of Ackner LJ.

Geoffrey Ames for the applicant.
William Boyce for the magistrates.

　　g

　　　　　　　　　　　　　　　　　　　　　　　　　　　　　　　Cur adv vult

12th December. The following judgments were read.

ACKNER LJ. The applicant was born on 27th October 1962. In July 1979, when he　*h*
was of course 16, he was served with a summons to answer an information that he stole
£232 cash, the propery of the St Albans Co-operative Society Ltd. On 9th October 1979,
when he was still 16, he appeared before the St Albans Juvenile Court and pleaded not
guilty. Apparently his case was listed only for plea and once he had pleaded, the case was
adjourned to 13th November.　　　　　　　　　　　　　　　　　　　　　　　　　　　*j*

---

　c　Section 29 provides: 'Where proceedings in respect of a young person are begun under section 1
　　　of the Children and Young Persons Act 1969 or for an offence and he attains the age of seventeen
　　　before the conclusion of the proceedings, the court may deal with the case and make any order
　　　which it could have made if he had not attained that age.'

By 13th November he had become 17. His counsel had advised him that it was in his interests to be tried by judge and jury in the Crown Court and he applied for him to be put to his election. He submitted (i) as the defendant was now 17 years of age, the provisions of s 19 of the Criminal Law Act 1977 required that he be given the opportunity to elect for trial by jury and that the justices had no discretion to refuse him that opportunity and alternatively, (ii) if it was a matter of discretion, then discretion should be exercised in his client's favour.

The justices, in an affidavit provided by their chairman, have stated that they were of the opinion that the relevant point in time for the court to decide whether the hearing is to proceed in accordance with the provisions of s 6 of the Children and Young Persons Act 1969, or in accordance with the provisions of s 19 of the 1977 Act, is when the juvenile first appears in court charged with the offence, and the relevant age for the purpose of these sections is the age of the juvenile at that time. They felt that decision to be a once and for all decision and that the court had no discretion to reverse it on the defendant attaining the age of 17 years. The chairman went on to say that if the matter had been discretionary, they would have insisted on summary trial 'bearing in mind that offences of this nature were frequently tried summarily, and that the factors present did not make it desirable that the case be heard before a jury'.

The applicant accordingly applies for orders of judicial review, namely certiorari to remove the decision into this court for the purpose of it being quashed, prohibiting the justices from further hearing and adjudicating on the information against him, and mandamus directing the justices to permit him to exercise his right to choose trial by jury.

The relevant statutory provisions are:
(i) s 48(1) of the Children and Young Persons Act 1933:

> 'A juvenile Court sitting for the purpose of hearing a charge against . . . a person who is believed to be a child or young person may, if it thinks fit to do so, proceed with the hearing and determination of the charge . . . notwithstanding that it is discovered that the person in question is not a child or young person.'

(ii) Section 6 of the Children and Young Persons Act 1969:

> 'Where a person under the age of seventeen appears or is brought before a magistrates' court on an information charging him with an offence, other than homicide, which is an indictable offence within the meaning of the Magistrates' Courts Act 1952, he shall be tried summarily unless—(a) he is a young person and the offence is such as is mentioned in subsection (2) of section 53 of the Act of 1933 . . . and the court considers that if he is found guilty of the offence it ought to be possible to sentence him in pursuance of that subsection; or (b) he is charged jointly with a person who has attained the age of seveteen and the court considers it necessary in the interests of justice to commit them both for trial . . .'

(iii) Section 19(1) of the Criminal Law Act 1977:

> 'Sections 20 to 24 . . . shall have effect where a person who has attained the age of seventeen appears or is brought before a magistrates' court on an information charging him with an offence triable either way.'

Sections 20 to 24 deal with the procedure for determining the mode of trial of offences which can be tried either summarily or by trial before judge and jury.

It is clear from the facts set out above that the applicant has not as yet begun to be tried for the offence alleged against him. All he has done is to enter a plea of not guilty. Accordingly the question that had to be decided on 13th November was: how was this young man of 17 to be tried? To this question the short answer would appear to be: in accordance with the procedure laid down by ss 20 to 24 of the Criminal Law Act 1977, having regard to the provisions of s 19(1) as set out above. To this counsel for the justices makes but one short submission. Under s 21(2) it is clear that the mode of trial is decided before the plea is entered. Here, the plea having been entered, it is too late to seek to alter the mode of trial.

Counsel is of course perfectly correct in his submission that s 21 presupposes in the ordinary case that the mode of trial will be decided before the plea is taken. But this is no ordinary case. Parliament has given to those who have attained the age of 17 a statutory right in certain circumstances, of which this is an example, to be tried by a jury. Of course Parliament could have provided that, if the applicant is 16 when charged, he has no entitlement to trial by jury even though he attains 17 before his trial commences. However, very clear words would be needed to enact such a provision. I would not accept that it could be achieved by the sidewind on which counsel for the justices relies. It must not be overlooked that there was a common law right to be tried by jury and such a right is not to be lightly removed. The procedural difficulty which is pinpointed by counsel's submission can be simply dealt with by the accused, who has pleaded but has not yet been tried, being asked, in the event of his reaching 17 years, whether he still consents to be tried summarily. The court will at the same time, pursuant to its statutory obligation under s 21(2), provide the explanation there stipulated.

I have been at pains to stress that at no material time had the trial of the applicant been embarked on. If on 9th October, in addition to taking his plea, the court had heard evidence and then adjourned the case part heard, then I would certainly tend to the view that the matter then became one for the exercise of the justices' discretion under s 48 of the 1933 Act. It is however not necessary finally to determine that point on this application.

I would accordingly grant the application for the orders referred to above.

SKINNER J. I agree. On the facts which have been outlined by Ackner LJ, two questions arise on this application. (1) Had the applicant a right at that stage to elect trial by jury? (2) If not, had the justices a discretion to allow him to elect for trial by jury? The answers to these questions lie wholly in the statutory provisions which have already been referred to by Ackner LJ.

In my judgment the decisive provision is s 19 of the Criminal Law Act 1977. That Act deals with a fundamental right of any citizen over 17 charged with a serious offence. It is mandatory in its terms. Sections 19(1) reads: 'Sections 20 to 24 . . . shall have effect where a person who has attained the age of seventeen appears or is brought before a magistrates' court on an information charging him with an offence triable either way.' The applicant in this case had attained the age of 17. He did appear before the magistrates' court, charged with an offence triable either way.

Section 19(2) provides that everything the court is required to do by ss 20 to 23 must be done before any evidence is called. Sections 20 to 23 lay down the familiar procedure followed when an offence triable either way normally comes before the courts.

Counsel for the justices in his short, but nevertheless effective, argument submitted that once the plea had been taken in the magistrates' court or the juvenile court that determined the court of trial once for all and he drew our attention to the provisions of s 21(2)(b). This deals with the position if the magistrates have decided that an offence triable either way may be tried summarily and goes on to give the accused his right of election between summary trial and trial by jury. Counsel points out that if the accused had already pleaded, and had pleaded guilty, then it would seem inappropriate to give him the warning set out in the subsection.

That was the only real anomaly that he could point to if the argument advanced on behalf of the applicant were to succeed. It is not enough, in my judgment, to displace the clear meaning of s 19 which itself provided the point of no return in sub-s (2). The watershed, or point of no return, for the purpose of the problem which arises in this case, is the calling of evidence and not the taking of the plea.

Thus the answer to the first question which I have posed earlier is that the applicant had a right to trial by jury at the stage at which he claimed it on 13th November 1979.

Turning to the second question, if I am right in the above, I would accept the submission by both counsel that s 29(1) of the Children and Young Persons Act 1963 applies only to questions of disposal and not to questions of trial. Until it was amended by the Children and Young Persons Act 1969 that section merely dealt with what are broadly called 'care proceedings' and the amendment in 1969 would, for example, allow a court which had made a finding of guilt against a 16-year old and adjourned the case for reports to resume the hearing and pass sentence if he attained 17 years during the adjournment.

However, if I am wrong in my interpretation of s 19 of the 1977 Act, then the scheme of the statutory provisions has to be looked at again from a different angle. In view of the conclusion I have reached on the first question. it is neither necessary nor desirable to do this now.

For the reasons I have given I agree with the orders proposed by Ackner LJ.

Application granted.

Solicitors: *Kingsley Wood & Co*, agents for *Anderson-Davis & Metcalfe*, St Albans (for the applicant); *Woolley & Weston*, St Albans (for the justices).

Sepala Munasinghe Esq   Barrister.

R v Amersham Juvenile Court, ex parte Wilson

QUEEN'S BENCH DIVISION
DONALDSON LJ AND BINGHAM J
13th FEBRUARY 1981

Magistrates – Summary trial – Offence triable summarily or on indictment – Determination of mode of trial of person attaining age of 17 after pleading to charge – Trial by juvenile court or in magistrates' court with right to elect trial by jury – Date when defendant's age relevant for determining mode of trial – Defendant attaining 17 before commencement of trial but after pleading to charge – Whether defendant entitled to elect trial by jury on attaining 17 – Whether magistrates' decision to try case summarily when plea taken a final decision as to mode of trial – Whether juvenile court having discretion as to mode of trial after defendant attaining 17 – Children and Young Persons Act 1963, s 29 (as amended by the Children and Young Persons Act 1969, Sch 5, para 49, Sch 6) – Children and Young Persons Act 1969, s 6(1) – Criminal Law Act 1977, s 19(1).

By virtue of s 6(1)[a] of the Children and Young Persons Act 1969 and s 19(1)[b] of the Criminal Law Act 1977 the mode of trial of an accused charged with an offence triable only on indictment (eg robbery) who is on the borderline between being a juvenile and an adult, thus raising the question whether he is to be classified as a juvenile or an adult, is to be determined by his age when he first has to appear or is brought before the court, in response to a summons, to surrender to his bail or is brought from police custody. If he will be 17 when he first has to appear in court he is to be treated as an adult and dealt with in an adult magistrates' court and that court will proceed as examining justices with a view to committal to the Crown Court. But if he will not be 17 when he first has to appear he is to be treated as a juvenile and dealt with in a juvenile court, with the consequence that the offence will be tried summarily; and if he attains 17 before the

---

a   Section 6(1), so far as material, is set out at p 317 *d*, post
b   Section 19(1) is set out at p 317 *e*, post

conclusion of the proceedings in the juvenile court he will not be entitled to elect for trial by jury under s 19(1) of the 1977 Act, because s 29^c of the Children and Young Persons *a* Act 1963, by empowering the juvenile court to 'deal with the case,' thereby empowers that court, if the case was begun in the juvenile court, to continue to try the case summarily as if he had not attained 17, since the power to 'deal with the case' is in contradistinction to the later power in s 29 to 'make any order' and therefore refers to questions of trial as opposed to questions of disposal (see p 317 *f g*, p 318 *a b* and p 320 *a* to *d*, post).

> *R v St Albans Juvenile Court, ex parte Godman* p 311, ante, not followed. *b*

Observations on the procedure to be followed where there is doubt about an accused's age (see p 320 *d e*, post).

Notes

For summary trial of a young person and the power to change from summary trial to *c* committal proceedings, see 24 Halsbury's Laws (4th Edn) paras 898: 9, 10.

For presumption and determination of age of a person charged with an offence, see ibid para 898: 6.

For the mode of trial for offences triable either way, see 29 ibid para 303.

For the Children and Young Persons Act 1963, s 29, see 17 Halsbury's Statutes (3rd Edn) 719.

For the Children and Young Persons Act 1969, s 6, see 40 ibid 860. *d*

For the Criminal Law Act 1977, s 19, see 47 ibid 700.

Cases referred to in judgment

R v Brentwood Justices, ex parte Jones (1978) 143 JP 211, [1979] Crim LR 115, DC, Digest (Cont Vol E) 399, 825Aa. *e*

R v St Albans Juvenile Court, ex parte Godman p 311, ante.

Application for judicial review

Dean Edward Wilson applied, with the leave of the Divisional Court of the Queen's Bench Division granted on 19th December 1980, for an order of certiorari to quash an order of the Amersham Juvenile Court made on 9th December 1980 convicting him of *f* the offence of robbery and sentencing him to three months in a detention centre. The grounds of the application were that the court acted without jurisdiction in trying the applicant on 9th December 1980 because although he was under the age of 17 when he was charged with the offence, he attained 17 on 6th November 1980, prior to the trial, and accordingly the juvenile court should have directed that the case be heard by an adult magistrates' court with a view to committal to the Crown Court for trial. The facts are *g* set out in the judgment of the court.

C J M Tyrer for the applicant.
Philip Shears for the prosecutor.

DONALDSON LJ read the following judgment of the court: The applicant applies for *h* judicial review of a decision of the Amersham Juvenile Court which, on 9th December 1980, convicted him of robbery and sentenced him to three months' detention. Within a few days he was released on bail.

His grievance is that he was denied a trial by judge and jury, but was instead tried and sentenced by the justices sitting as a juvenile court. Both at the time when the offence *j* is alleged to have been committed and at the time when he was charged, Wilson was under the age of 17. After being charged on 31st October 1980, he was remanded on

---

c Section 29 is set out at p 317 *j*, post

police bail to appear before the juvenile court on 11th November 1980. Meanwhile on 6th November 1980, he attained the age of 17 and thus, for the purposes of the criminal law, became an adult instead of a young person.

The juvenile court justices thought that they could treat him as a juvenile in reliance on s 29 of the Children and Young Persons Act 1963. We have to decide whether they were right.

The powers and duties of adult and juvenile magistrates' courts are quite different. In the case of magistrates' courts concerned with charges against adults, there are a number of offences which can only be tried on indictment, that is to say by judge and jury, a number which can only be tried summarily and a number which may be tried 'either way', that is summarily or on indictment. A charge of robbery is one which in the case of an adult can only be tried on indictment and the magistrates' duty is to inquire into it as examining magistrates with a view to deciding whether there is a case fit for trial. If there is, they commit the accused to the Crown Court.

In the case of juvenile courts, magistrates are in general required to try all charges summarily unless the charge is one of homicide.

The dividing line between those who are the concern of the juvenile court magistrates and those who are the concern of the adult court magistrates emerges most clearly from two statutory provisions. The first is s 6(1) of the Children and Young Persons Act 1969, which provides that: 'Where a person under the age of seventeen appears or is brought before a magistrates' court on an information charging him with an offence, other than homicide, which is an indictable offence . . . he shall be tried summarily unless' he is charged with a grave offence or he is charged with an adult and a joint trial is necessary in the interests of justice.

The second is s 19 of the Criminal Law Act 1977, which deals with the procedure to be adopted when an adult is charged with an 'either way' offence, and is in the following terms:

'(1) Sections 20 to 24 below shall have effect where a person who has attained the age of seventeen appears or is brought before a magistrates' court on an information charging him with an offence triable either way . . .'

These statutes show that the dividing line is the age of the accused when he 'appears or is brought before a magistrates' court'. In context this must mean when he first appears or is brought before such a court in connection with the offence charged. This first appearance may, as in this case, be when the accused surrenders to police bail. In other cases it may be when he appears in response to a summons or when he is brought before the court from police custody, the police not having granted bail.

There are also statutory provisions to cover the situation in which the precise age of the accused is in doubt and it is accordingly uncertain whether he is a young person and, as such, the concern of the juvenile court, or whether he is an adult and the concern of an adult court (see, for example, ss 48 and 99 of the Children and Young Persons Act 1933, s 80(3) of the Criminal Justice Act 1948, s 126(5) of the Magistrates' Courts Act 1952, and s 70(3) of the Children and Young Persons Act 1969). However, in the present case the applicant's age was known.

Section 29 of the Children and Young Persons Act 1963, as amended by the 1969 Act, is concerned with a quite different problem, namely what is to happen if a young person attains the age of 17 and so becomes an adult and the concern of the adult magistrates' court before the end of the proceedings against or concerning him in a juvenile court. It is in the following terms:

'*Provisions as to persons between the ages of 17 and 18.* (1) Where proceedings in respect of a young person are begun under section 1 of the Children and Young Persons Act 1969, or for an offence and he attains the age of seventeen before the conclusion of the proceedings, the court may deal with the case and make any order which it could have made if he had not attained that age.'

This section is wholly consistent with the statutory approach of classifying offenders as adult or juvenile by reference to their age when they first appear or are brought before a magistrates' court, provided that on the true construction of the section proceedings are 'begun' at that time and not at the earlier time when an information is laid or a charge preferred. We have no doubt that it should be so construed, particularly bearing in mind the manner in which care proceedings are begun. It is on the defendant first appearing or being brought before a court that his age is fixed for the purpose of all these provisions. In so holding, however, we must make mention of two decisions which might suggest a different approach.

The first is *R v Brentwood Justices, ex parte Jones* (1978) 143 JP 211. There the Divisional Court was concerned to construe a transitional provision contained in Sch 14 of the Road Traffic Act 1972, whereby certain parts of the Act did not apply 'in relation to proceedings commenced before the coming into force of that provision'. This court held that proceedings were 'commenced' when a charge was preferred. It is sufficient to say that the court was concerned with a different statute in a different context.

The second authority is the very recent decision of this court in *R v St Albans Juvenile Court, ex parte Godman* p 311, ante. The offence charged was theft which, in the case of an adult, is an 'either way' offence. The justices considered that—

> 'the relevant point of time to decide whether the hearing is to proceed in accordance with the provisions of s 6 of the Children and Young Persons Act 1969, or in accordance with the provisions of s 19 of the Criminal Law Act 1977 is when the juvenile first appears in court charged with the offence and the relevant age for the purpose of these sections is the age of the juvenile at that time.'

When Godman first came before the juvenile court magistrates he was still 16 and he was asked to plead to the charge. Having pleaded 'Not guilty', the further hearing of the case was adjourned until a later day by which time he was 17. Ackner LJ said (at pp 313–314, ante):

> 'It is clear from the facts set out above that the applicant has not as yet begun to be tried for the offence alleged against him. All he has done is to enter a plea of not guilty. Accordingly the question that had to be decided on 13th November was: how was this young man of 17 to be tried? To this question the short answer would appear to be: in accordance with the procedure laid down by ss 20 to 24 of the Criminal Law Act 1977, having regard to the provisions of s 19(1) as set out above. To this counsel for the justices makes but one short submission. Under s 21(2) it is clear that the mode of trial is decided before the plea is entered. Here, the plea having been entered, it is too late to seek to alter the mode of trial. Counsel is of course perfectly correct in his submission that s 21 presupposes in the ordinary case that the mode of trial will be decided before the plea is taken. But this is no ordinary case. Parliament has given to those who have attained the age of 17 a statutory right in certain circumstances, of which this is an example, to be tried by a jury. Of course Parliament could have provided that, if the applicant is 16 when charged, he has no entitlement to trial by jury even though he attains 17 before his trial commences. However, very clear words would be needed to enact such a provision. I would not accept that it could be achieved by the sidewind on which counsel for the justices relies. It must not be overlooked that there was a common law right to be tried by jury and such a right is not to be lightly removed. The procedural difficulty which is pinpointed by counsel's submission can be simply dealt with by the accused, who has pleaded but has not yet been tried, being asked, in the event of his reaching 17 years, whether he still consents to be tried summarily. The court will at the same time, pursuant to its statutory obligation under s 21(2), provide the explanation there stipulated. I have been at pains to stress that at no material time had the trial of the applicant been embarked on. If on 9th October, in addition to taking his plea, the court had heard evidence and then

adjourned the case part heard, then I would certainly tend to the view that the matter then became one for the exercise of the justices' discretion under s 48 of the 1933 Act. It is however not necessary finally to determine that point on this application.'

Skinner J said (see pp 314–315, ante):

'I agree. On the facts which have been outlined by Ackner LJ, two questions arise on this application. (1) Had the applicant a right at that stage to elect trial by jury? (2) If not, had the justices a discretion to allow him to elect for trial by jury? The answers to these questions lie wholly in the statutory provisions which have already been referred to by Ackner LJ. In my judgment the decisive provision is s 19 of the Criminal Law Act 1977. That Act deals with a fundamental right of any citizen over 17 charged with a serious offence. It is mandatory in its terms. Section 19(1) reads: "Sections 20 to 24 . . . shall have effect where a person who has attained the age of seventeen years appears or is brought before a magistrates' court on an information charging him with an offence triable either way." The applicant in this case had attained the age of 17. He did appear before the magistrates' court, charged with an offence triable either way. Section 19(2) provides that everything the court is required to do by ss 20 to 23 must be done before any evidence is called. Sections 20 to 23 lay down the familiar procedure followed when an offence triable either way normally comes before the courts. Counsel for the justices in his short, but nevertheless effective, argument submitted that once the plea had been taken in the magistrates' court or the juvenile court that determined the court of trial once for all and he drew our attention to the provisions of s 21(2)(b). This deals with the position if the magistrates have decided that an offence triable either way may be tried summarily and goes on to give the accused his right of election between summary trial and trial by jury. Counsel points out that if the accused had already pleaded, and had pleaded guilty, then it would seem inappropriate to give him the warning set out in the subsection. That was the only real anomaly that he could point to if the argument advanced on behalf of the applicant were to succeed. It is not enough, in my judgment, to displace the clear meaning of s 19 which itself provided the point of no return in sub-s (2). The watershed, or point of no return, for the purpose of the problem which arises in this case, is the calling of evidence and not the taking of the plea. Thus the answer to the first question which I have posed earlier is that the applicant had a right to trial by jury at the stage at which he claimed it on 13th November 1979. Turning to the second question, if I am right in the above, I would accept the submission by both counsel that s 29(1) of the Children and Young Persons Act 1963 applies only to questions of disposal and not to questions of trial. Until it was amended by the Children and Young Persons Act 1969 that section merely dealt with what are broadly called "care proceedings" and the amendment in 1969 would, for example, allow a court which had made a finding of guilt against a 16-year-old and adjourned the case for reports to resume the hearing and pass sentence if he attained 17 years during the adjournment. However, if I am wrong in my interpretation of s 19 of the 1977 Act, then the scheme of the statutory provisions has to be looked at again from a different angle. In view of the conclusion I have reached on the first question, it is neither necessary nor desirable to do this now.'

We have quoted the relevant parts of the judgments in full because they show that (i) counsel for the justices placed no reliance on s 29 of the 1963 Act, (ii) both counsel were agreed that it related only to questions of disposal and not to questions of trial and (iii) the court did not really consider s 29 which was not even mentioned in the judgment of Ackner LJ.

In the present case both counsel are equally agreed but in a contrary sense, namely that s 29 does relate both to questions of trial and of disposal. As they point out, the section in its original unamended form read 'the court may continue to deal', but Parliament when adding the words 'or for an offence' in 1969 deleted the words 'continue to'. This suggests that it now applies to the proceedings ab initio. Furthermore, the words 'deal with the case' stand as a phrase on their own and are used in contradistinction to the words 'make any order', the latter clearly covering all questions of disposal and leaving the earlier words as only really referable to questions of trial.

In the circumstances we feel free to give effect to our own view of the construction of s 29. We do not for one moment dissent from the proposition that the common law right to trial by jury is not to be lightly removed, but in our judgment s 29 has this effect where it applies. In fact, on our construction the section has no application to the case of the applicant, since he first appeared before the juvenile court after he had attained the age of 17, but it would have applied in *Godman's* case where the applicant appeared before the court whilst he was still 16, albeit only for a plea to be taken. However, in the light of the joint submissions of counsel in that case, it is perhaps not surprising that our construction of s 29 was not adopted and that the section was virtually ignored.

In our view, those who arrest and charge or lay informations against persons who are in the juvenile/adult borderline age group should take all reasonable steps to find out exactly when they will attain the age of 17. If they are to be brought or summoned to appear before a court for the first time on a date when they will have attained the age of 17, the court selected or specified in the summons should be an adult court. If they will not have attained the age of 17, it should be a juvenile court. If the accused is properly brought before a juvenile court and thereafter attains the age of 17, s 29 will apply.

If those concerned have doubts about the age of the accused, they can bring him or summon him to appear before either type of court. If it is the juvenile court and that court agrees that the accused appears to be under the age of 17, but it subsequently emerges that he was 17 or over, no harm will have been done because the court will be able to rely on s 48 of the Children and Young Persons Act 1933. If it is the adult court, the court can, on learning the true facts, remit the case to a juvenile court or retain it (see s 56(1) of the 1933 Act, and s 7(8) of the 1969 Act).

So far as the applicant is concerned, in our view he should have been bailed to appear before an adult court and that court should and no doubt would have proceeded to investigate the charge as examining magistrates. We will therefore make an order quashing the proceedings before the juvenile court.

Application granted.

Solicitors: *Geoffrey Wicks & Co*, Chesham (for the applicant); *C S Hoad*, Reading (for the prosecutor).

Dilys Tausz   Barrister.

Schering Chemicals Ltd v Falkman Ltd and others

COURT OF APPEAL, CIVIL DIVISION

LORD DENNING MR, SHAW AND TEMPLEMAN LJJ

8th, 9th, 11th, 12th, 15th, 16th DECEMBER 1980, 27th JANUARY 1981

Equity – Breach of confidence – Injunction – Information obtained by journalist during employment as professional adviser – Information available from public sources – Journalist employed by intermediary to give professional advice to company on how best to refute criticism and adverse publicity – Company imparting confidential information which was made available to journalist – No contract between company and journalist – Journalist later making television film about company – Journalist claiming information imparted by company also available from public sources – Whether duty of confidentiality existing between company and journalist in absence of contract – Whether confidentiality attaching to information even though available from public sources – Whether company entitled to injunction to prevent film being shown.

The plaintiffs, a reputable international drug manufacturing company, manufactured and marketed a drug which was widely prescribed and used for pregnancy testing for some ten years. It was then suggested in medical circles that the drug could have harmful effects on unborn children if taken during pregnancy. Actions were brought against the plaintiffs by mothers of children born with deformities alleging that the deformities were caused by the drug and that the plaintiffs were negligent in manufacturing and marketing a drug with the potential to cause such deformities. The drug, and consequently the plaintiffs also, became the subject of considerable adverse publicity in the press and on television and the plaintiffs withdrew the drug from the market. In an effort to counter the adverse publicity the plaintiffs engaged the first defendant, who specialised in television training, to train their executives to refute criticism of the plaintiffs and put across the plaintiffs' point of view effectively when interviewed on television. In turn the first defendant hired the second defendant, an experienced broadcaster, on a freelance basis to carry out part of the training. The plaintiffs supplied a large amount of information on the drug to the first defendant for use in the training courses and that information was in turn passed on to the second defendant. The first defendant acknowledged that the information was received in confidence and would not be used for any other purpose, but it was not established whether that was expressly made known to the second defendant. Shortly after the training course finished, the second defendant, prompted by what he had discovered on the training course (as he readily admitted), conceived the idea of making a television documentary about the drug and put forward detailed proposals for a film to the third defendants, a television company. Both the second and third defendants attempted to persuade the plaintiffs to take part in the film but the plaintiffs refused to do so and intimated that if any of the information used on the training course was used in the film they would seek an injunction. The first and second defendants nevertheless went ahead and made the film, which was a fair and balanced account of the issues involved. The plaintiffs sought injunctions preventing the film being shown, on the grounds (i) that the making of the film by the second defendant was a breach of confidence of which the third defendants were aware, and (ii) that the showing of the film would amount to a contempt of court because it would prejudice the trial of the actions brought against the plaintiffs on behalf of the deformed children.

Held – (1) The showing of the film would not amount to a contempt of court since the trial of the pending actions would be by a judge alone and a fair trial of the issues would not be hampered or adversely affected (see p 328 *b*, p 331 *j* to p 332 *b*, p 333 *a* to *c*, p 339 *g* to p 340 *b* and p 347 *j* to p 348 *b*, post).

(2) However, (Lord Denning MR dissenting), the showing of the film was a breach of confidence and there should be an injunction to restrain the showing of it (see p 338 *d*, p 339 *b* to *d*, p 345 *b* to *d f* to *h*, p 346 *a* to *c*, p 347 *f* to *j* and p 348 *b*, post).

Per Shaw LJ. The communication in a commercial context of information which at the time is regarded by the giver and recognised by the recipient as confidential, and the nature of which has a material connection with the commercial interests of the party confiding that information, imposes on the recipient a fiduciary obligation to maintain that confidence thereafter unless the giver consents to relax it (see p 337 *h*, post).

Notes

For injunctions restraining breach of confidence, see 24 Halsbury's Laws (4th Edn) para 1014 and 16 ibid para 1455, and for cases on the subject, see 28(2) Digest (Reissue) 1081–1091, 868–917.

Cases cited in judgments

American Cyanamid Co v Ethicon Ltd [1975] 1 All ER 504, [1975] AC 396, [1975] 2 WLR 316, [1975] RPC 513, HL, Digest (Cont Vol D) 536, *152a*.

Argyll (Margaret) (Duchess) v Duke of Argyll [1965] 1 All ER 611, [1967] Ch 302, [1965] 2 WLR 790, 28 (2) Digest (Reissue) 1089, *916*.

Attorney General v British Broadcasting Corpn [1980] 3 All ER 161, [1980] 3 WLR 109, HL; *rvsg* [1979] 3 All ER 45, [1979] 3 WLR 312, CA

Attorney General v Times Newspapers Ltd [1973] 3 All ER 54, [1974] AC 273, [1973] 3 WLR 298, HL, 16 Digest (Reissue) 23, *221*.

Bonnard v Perryman [1891] 2 Ch 269, [1891–4] All ER Rep 965, 60 LJ Ch 617, 65 LT 506, CA, 22 Digest (Reissue) 601, *6270*.

British Steel Corpn v Granada Television Ltd [1981] 1 All ER 417, [1980] 3 WLR 774, CA and HL.

Coco v A N Clark (Engineers) Ltd [1969] RPC 41, 28(2) Digest (Reissue) 1088, *914*.

Fraser v Evans [1969] 1 All ER 8, [1969] 1 QB 349, [1968] 3 WLR 1172, CA, 28(2) Digest (Reissue) 1090, *917*.

Initial Services Ltd v Putterill [1967] 3 All ER 145, [1968] 1 QB 396, [1967] 3 WLR 1032, CA, 28(2) Digest (Reissue) 1087, *907*.

N W L Ltd v Woods [1979] 3 All ER 614, [1979] 1 WLR 1294, [1979] ICR 867, [1980] 1 Lloyd's Rep 1, HL, Digest (Cont Vol E) 612, *1457a*.

Near v Minnesota (1931) 283 US 697.

Quartz Hill Consolidated Gold Mining Co v Beall (1882) 20 ChD 501, 51 LJ Ch 874, 46 LT 746, CA, 22 Digest (Reissue) 601, *6286*.

Seager v Copydex Ltd [1967] 2 All ER 415, [1967] 1 WLR 923, [1967] RPC 349, CA, 28(2) Digest (Reissue) 1019, *453*.

Cases also cited

Attorney General v London Weekend Television Ltd [1972] 3 All ER 1146, [1973] 1 WLR 202, DC.

Boardman v Phipps [1966] 3 All ER 721, [1967] 2 AC 46, HL.

Coomber, Re, Coomber v Coomber [1911] 1 Ch 723, CA.

Cranleigh Precision Engineering Ltd v Bryant [1964] 3 All ER 289, [1965] 1 WLR 1293.

Crofter Hand Woven Harris Tweed Co Ltd v Veitch [1942] 1 All ER 142, [1942] AC 435, HL.

Emerald Construction Co Ltd v Lowthian [1966] 1 All ER 1013, [1966] 1 WLR 691, CA.

Hamilton v Wright (1842) 9 Cl & Fin 111, 8 ER 357, HL.

Hivac v Park Royal Scientific Instruments Ltd [1946] 1 All ER 350, [1946] Ch 169, CA.

Jasperson v Dominion Tobacco Co [1923] AC 709, PC.

Lewis v British Broadcasting Corpn [1979] Court of Appeal Transcript 193.

Lumley v Gye (1853) 2 E & B 216, 118 ER 749.

Mustad (O) & Son v S Allcock & Co Ltd (1928) [1963] 3 All ER 416, [1964] 1 WLR 109, HL.

Quinn v Leathem [1901] AC 495, [1900–3] All ER Rep 1, HL.

Rakusen v Ellis, Munday and Clarke [1912] 1 Ch 831, [1911–13] All ER Rep 813, CA.
Reading v Attorney General [1951] 1 All ER 617, [1951] AC 507, HL.
Scruttons Ltd v Midland Silicones Ltd [1962] 1 All ER 1, [1962] AC 446, HL.
Thompson, Re, Thompson v Allen [1930] 1 Ch 203.
Thompson (D C) & Co Ltd v Deakin [1952] 2 All ER 361, [1952] Ch 646, CA.
Thomson (Inspector of Taxes) v Gurneville Securities Ltd [1971] 3 All ER 1071, [1972] AC 661, HL.
Torquay Hotel Co Ltd v Cousins [1969] 1 All ER 522, [1969] 2 Ch 106, CA.
Vine Products Ltd v Mackenzie & Co Ltd [1965] 3 All ER 58, [1966] Ch 484.

Appeal and Cross-appeal
The second defendant, David Elstein, and the third defendants, Thames Television Ltd, who were defendants to an action brought against them and the first defendants, Falkman Ltd, by the plaintiffs, Schering Chemicals Ltd, appealed against the order made by McNeill J in chambers on 27th August 1980 granting the plaintiffs an injunction restraining the second and third defendants from publishing a television film entitled 'The Primodos Affair' on the ground that publication of the film would be, inter alia, a breach of confidence owed to the plaintiffs by the second and third defendants. By a respondent's notice the plaintiffs cross-appealed against McNeill J's refusal to grant an injunction to restrain the showing of the film as being in contempt of court. The facts are set out in the judgment of Lord Denning MR.

Roy Berdam QC, Gavin Lightman QC and *John Powles* for Schering Chemicals Ltd.
Alan Bishop for Falkman Ltd.
O B Popplewell QC and *Christopher Sumner* for Mr Elstein and Thames Television Ltd.

Cur adv vult

27th January. The following judgments were read.

LORD DENNING MR. Thames Television have made at much expense a film called 'The Primodos Affair'. It is about a matter of great public interest, the use of a drug called 'Primodos'. The makers of the drug want to stop the showing of the film. On the ground that it would be a contempt of court or a breach of confidence. The question for the court is: should it be stopped or not? Or would the stopping of it be an unwarranted restraint on freedom of the press? In which I include, of course, television. It is an important question on which the law is not yet settled. But first, the facts.

1. THE FACTS
(i) *The 'Yellow Warning'*
    It often happens that, when a woman misses her period, she is anxious to know if she is pregnant or not. If she does not want a baby, she takes something which, she hopes, will bring on her period. In 1958 the word went round that a drug was available for the purpose. It was called Primodos. It was produced in Germany by Schering Chemicals and marketed in England by a subsidiary at Burgess Hill. Doctors prescribed it. Women took it. For nearly ten years it was considered safe. But in 1967 a lady doctor, Dr Isabel Gal, threw doubt on it. She examined the children of 100 women who had taken the drug as a pregnancy test and the children of 100 women who had not. On her reading of the statistics, she thought that the children of the women who had taken the drug were liable to have incurable ills like heart disease or spinal trouble. Her researches led to many investigations by many specialists. Research papers appeared in many scientific journals. Finally, in June 1975, the Committee on the Safety of Medicines in London issued a 'yellow warning' against it. They thought it possible that the use of Primodos and similar drugs could on occasion cause abnormalities in the unborn child. They advised that a urine test should be used for pregnancy testing, in which there was then

no risk to the unborn child. As a result of these warnings, the makers gradually gave up the drug and in January 1978 withdrew it altogether.

(ii) *It is given full coverage*

This was a subject of the greatest public interest. The newspapers and television companies gave it full coverage. The Sunday Times was particularly active. It had a medical correspondent, Oliver Gillie. He did much research himself. He got hold of a file of the internal correspondence of Scherings. (They said it had been stolen from them.) It contained a letter from their medical director in England to their German headquarters, saying: 'I would like to call your attention to the fact that there is very little justification for the use of Primodos when a more rapid diagnosis may be made by means of the slide or tube test.'

The Sunday Times published this letter and much other information. It did so in several issues in 1975 and 1977. These carried big headlines: 'These drugs can deform babies but mothers are not warned'; 'Hazard drug still sold in Britain'; 'Drug Company ignored deformity risk for ten years'. Other newspapers followed suit.

(iii) *A campaign is launched*

Many parents of deformed children read these articles. They jumped to conclusions. One mother after another came forward and said such things as: 'My child has a congenital heart. I took Primodos. I claim compensation.' Campaigns were launched to support these parents. 172 claims were notified. Newspapers came out with headlines: 'Two tiny tablets led to heartbreak'; 'Help these heartbreak kids'; '200 may sue over baby pills'. The redoubtable campaigner, Mr Jack Ashley MP, took up their cause, just as he did in the thalidomide cases.

(iv) *Actions are started*

Legal aid was obtained. Actions were started against Scherings. On 19th September 1977 by Williams; on 21st March 1978 by Hudd; on 21st March 1978 by Fletcher; on 19th May 1978 by Adams; on 9th December 1978 by Hyman. In two of these actions pleadings were delivered. On 29th October 1979 they were ordered to be set down for trial. The trial has been fixed for October 1981 and is estimated to last for six months. One of the principal issues is causation. These deformities are all to be found in children whose mothers did not take any of these drugs. Some of the complaining mothers may be deluding themselves in saying they took them. Another issue is negligence. Scherings deny that they were guilty of any want of care.

(v) *Television programmes are shown*

In addition to the newspapers, there were the television companies. On 16th April 1978 London Weekend Television showed a most informative documentary. It lasted about three-quarters of an hour. They had pictures of parents, Mrs Hyman, Mrs Wheeler and Mrs Williams, and of their deformed children. These parents made statements of their belief that Primodos was responsible. The television showed experts, Dr Isabel Gal and Professor Graham Dukes and two from the Pregnancy Advisory Service. They showed Mr Jack Ashley CH, MP. They had also the Rt Hon Roland Moyle MP, the Minister of State for the Health Service. In October 1978 Granada Television had a documentary. It again showed parents and children on much the same lines.

(vi) *Scherings engage specialists*

All this publicity was very adverse to Scherings. Yet they took no proceedings to stop it. Much of it was defamatory of Scherings but they issued no writ for libel. Some of it (such as the stolen correspondence) may have been an infringement of copyright or a breach of confidence by someone, but they issued no writ for infringement of copyright or breach of confidential information. Actions had been started on behalf of parents and children but Scherings did not suggest that these publications would prejudice the fair trial of those actions or were a contempt of court. No doubt Scherings considered (perhaps they were advised) that proceedings of those kinds would be unlikely to succeed.

The one thing that Scherings did was to try to mitigate the effect of the publicity. They decided to get their own executives trained in the techniques of television so that they could put their point of view to the public. They approached a firm which specialised in training company executives. This firm was called Executive Television Training but it was really Falkman Ltd run by Mr Bernard Falk. They ran courses which were attended by the executives under training; and these were taught by professional broadcasters.

(vii) *Confidentiality is assured*

Scherings handed to Mr Falk a great deal of information relating to Primodos. Mr Falk studied it and made his own inquiries about it. He prepared a paper containing specific proposals for training the Schering executives. These proposals were accepted by Scherings on 15th December 1978. The fee payable was £10,750 plus VAT at 8 per cent. The course was to be held at the ICI Studios at Welwyn Garden City. The proposals contained this provision:

> 'We [Falkman Ltd, alias ETT] have received information on the company [Scherings] and in particular this deals with the product PRIMODOS. We wish to stress that this information, some of which is public and some of which is private, remains STRICTLY CONFIDENTIAL to E.T.T. and will remain so whether a training programme is accepted or not. We also guarantee that it will never be used in the future by any broadcasting associate of E.T.T. According to the strict code of ethics laid down by the National Union of Journalists, of which our associates are members, the use of such information would be a severe breach of confidence.'

(viii) *The training course is held*

The course was held on 28th February, 1st March and 27th April 1979. A training programme was prepared in which it was stated: 'Both the E.T.T. panel and I.C.I. studio staff have been informed of the CONFIDENTIALITY of the course and this requirement is fully respected.'

Falkman Ltd engaged several professional broadcasters to train the executives of Schering. The training took many forms. One was to put an executive through a 'mock' television interview. Such as to ask him: 'What action did the company take once suspicion was cast on Primodos?' The professional broadcasters necessarily acquired much information about the drug Primodos and all that had happened about it.

(ix) *Elstein has an idea*

One of the professional broadcasters was David Elstein. He got to know so much about this drug that an idea occurred to him: 'Why not make a documentary film on the subject and call it "The Primodos Affair"?' He got out a synopsis in May 1979 in which he outlined the contents of the film. On 23rd May 1979 he put it up to Thames Television Ltd and suggested that they might make such a film and show it on Thames Television. He hoped that Scherings would co-operate in the making of it. Thames were receptive of the idea.

(x) *The idea is put to Scherings*

On 4th July 1979 David Elstein wrote on the notepaper of Thames Television to Scherings. He enclosed the synopsis headed 'The Primodos Affair' and said:

> 'This is the idea that I have put up to Thames. As you can see, it is a confidential document, which only the Executive Producer has seen. The reason for this is that the treatment rests heavily on privileged information, and the Executive Producer understands that the only basis on which we could make the film as proposed would be if Schering were to co-operate fully, and so render much of that information "unprivileged". At Thames, we have no anxiety at all about the issue of sub judice . . . I have taken particular care to relegate the issue or liability to a position where it does not dominate the film, nor does the film have to pre-empt the verdict of the

courts. However, it would be impossible to make any kind of programme about Primodos which didn't include the elements of the material on which liability will finally be judged . . . And remember that the film gives you a chance to discover the parents' best case!'

At a meeting in August 1979 Scherings did not turn down the idea but they were still nervous that such a programme might be in contempt of court. David Elstein said he thought that he could obtain counsel's opinion that it would not be a contempt.

(xi) *Elstein does research*

Hoping that Scherings would agree, David Elstein got Sharon Goulds to do research for the programme. She assembled a great mass of material: research papers, periodicals, other publications, newspapers and magazines, and television programmes. She consulted many individuals. David Elstein went into it and made up a programme, all of material which had been made public already in the newspapers and on television.

As it turned out, however, Scherings never did agree. The decisive point came on 29th October 1979 when an order was made by the court that the actions by the parents be set down for trial.

(xii) *Scherings turn down the idea*

On 5th November 1979 Scherings wrote to David Elstein making it clear that they would not co-operate in the proposed programme. This is the crucial paragraph in their letter:

'I share the view expressed by yourself at the end of paragraphs one and two of your letter dated 4 July 1979, and therefore I cannot see how such a programme could be produced without there being a serious risk of prejudice to the pending litigation. We have been advised not to participate in any programmes of this nature and in the circumstances we would naturally be concerned that none of the information supplied to you in confidence should be utilised.'

(xiii) *But Elstein goes on*

In reply on 9th November 1979 David Elstein for Thames Television said that they were advised by counsel that there was no danger of the programme as outlined being a contempt. He still hoped that Scherings might co-operate, but he made it clear that, even if they did not do so, Thames would go ahead with the programme. The important passage in that letter is:

'I now believe that a balanced and temperate account of the issues involved in the story of Primodos is possible even without Schering's participation, and that such a programme would be worth making. Certainly, we intend to make the effort, and I will keep you informed as to our progress, whether or not you eventually decide to participate. There is, of course, no question of my using any information supplied to me in confidence in other circumstances.'

Thereafter David Elstein sought the opinion of counsel who advised that it would be possible without too much difficulty to produce a programme which would not offend. He gave a copy of this opinion to Scherings. But he did not succeed in getting them to change their mind. On the 20th December 1979 the solicitors for Scherings wrote to the managing director of Thames Television: 'Should the proposed programme go ahead, our clients will take every step open to them to prevent both the proposed abuse of their confidences and the risk of prejudice.'

(xiv) *Elstein prepares the programme*

So the lines of battle were drawn. David Elstein went ahead with the preparation of a programme for Thames Television. He worked on it from January to May 1980. He saw parents and children, experts and academics. He made the programme, he says, 'not out of anything I was told during the training courses but as a result of the independent research carried out by Sharon Goulds and myself'.

Scherings knew that David Elstein was going ahead with the programme: but they made no move to stop it. In a letter of the 8th February 1980 their solicitors said:

> 'We must reserve our clients' position until we have had an opportunity to see the finished programme . . . We still feel that it should be possible for a programme on the matter of public concern . . . to be presented, without prejudicing the fair trial of the actions in which our clients are concerned. For obvious reasons we have advised them that they should neither participate in the programme or put forward proposals for the programme, but equally you may rest assured that our instructions do permit us to try to seek a satisfactory solution with you.'

(xv) *Scherings issue a writ*

So the matter was left over until Scherings saw the programme. The text of it was provided on 24th July 1980. On 1st August 1980 it was seen by Scherings' counsel. It was to be broadcast on 16th September 1980. But on the 12th August 1980 Scherings issued a writ and moved for an injunction to prevent the broadcasting of the film. On 27th August 1980 McNeill J granted an injunction, not on the ground of contempt of court, but on the ground of breach of confidence. There is now an appeal to this court.

(xvi) *We see the film*

We ourselves have seen the television films shown by London Weekend and Granada. We have seen the film 'The Primodos Affair' produced by David Elstein and Thames Television. We have also seen the script. I will describe it.

The film is called 'The Primodos Affair'. It takes 52 minutes. In his introduction the commentator says:

> 'Thalidomide taught us that drugs can damage the unborn child. But are we right to treat every suspect drug as if it were Thalidomide, however ambiguous the evidence? Today, hundreds of mothers around the world are convinced that pills they took to find out if they were pregnant caused their children to be born malformed. Two test cases will be heard in the High Court in October 1981, and will involve highly complex and technical arguments, on which we cannot comment. This programme asks what are the wider implications for society of cases such as the Primodos Affair.'

Early in the film there appear the parents of three children, Mr and Mrs Hayes, Mrs Wheeler and Mrs Stern. Each woman says that she believes she took the drug and that her baby was born malformed. Pictures are shown of the babies. But Mrs Wheeler admits that she has dropped her case because the records do not show that she took Primodos. Those parents take up about 16 minutes of the film. None of them have any actions pending against Scherings.

A considerable part of the film (about 9 minutes) is taken up by Dr Michael Briggs. He is now a professor in Australia but he was formerly Scherings' director of research in the United Kingdom. He talks of the investigations which he and other members of the company made and of the steps they took when the drug came under suspicion. He was very reasonable and said nothing unfair to Scherings. For instance, when it was put to him that the Sunday Times said that the number of deformed children born as a consequence is estimated to run into thousands, Dr Briggs said: 'I think that's a most irresponsible statement. On the basis of the evidence that we have, there are no grounds for making that statement.'

Next in turn is Professor Atiyah of Oxford University. He spent about five minutes talking about the legal position. All very sensible and straightforward.

Then there was Dr Isabel Gal. She spoke of her researches. Professor Nora of Denver University who talked about American experience; Mr Cooks, a statistician; and one or two others. All very reasonable.

Then there was, of course, the commentator. He was the leader of the discussion. He introduced the participants, led them by questions to speak of their particular knowledge, and he connected the whole into one running sequence. Added up, I expect his piece would amount to about 16 minutes.

(xvii) *Its effect*

When I saw the film, and now again when I read the script, I would like to pay tribute to its fairness. It seems to me that it contains nothing whatever to prejudge the pending cases. It leaves the issue wide open for consideration at the trial. I do not suppose for one moment that the trial judge (whoever he is) will have seen the film. Care would be taken to select a judge who had not done so. But even if he had, I am sure that his judgment would not be influenced by it in the slightest.

Nor can I see that any witness would be put in any difficulty at the trial. It was suggested that Dr Michael Briggs might be embarrassed if he was called as a witness. I do not think so. The commentator was most considerate to him. No trace of his being bullied or treated unfairly. No element whatever of 'trial by television'.

Nor can I find any single piece of confidential information which was, or might have been, gleaned by David Elstein from the course. Scherings have not pointed to a single item. No fact, no comment, no incident was taken from the course. Everything said by the parents (16 minutes) was new in the film. Everything said by the professors and other participants (20 minutes) was new. The commentator in his 16 minutes made only general statements such as was public knowledge already, owing to the publicity that had been given by the Sunday Times and others. It had been gathered together by Sharon Goulds and David Elstein independently of the course.

The only thing that was taken from the course, so far as I can see, was the idea, the theme, the story of the Primodos affair. Just as Shakespeare used Holinshed's Chronicles, and Tennyson used Malory's Morte d'Arthur, so David Elstein used the information in the course. In each case the previous work was the launching pad from which the new work took off. But no one would dispute the originality of the new work.

Such being the facts, I turn to the law.

2. THE LAW

(i) *The cause of action against Elstein*

Scherings do not suggest that they had any contract with David Elstein himself. Nor do they suggest that the programme contains anything which could be the subject of an action for defamation or for infringement of copyright. They say, however, that they have one or other of a number of other causes of action against David Elstein. These were set out for us by counsel for Scherings in a useful note:

(a) Threatening to bring about or induce a breach by Falkman of its contract with Scherings for confidentiality.

(b) Falkman gave the promise of confidentiality as agent for David Elstein.

(c) David Elstein was under a fiduciary duty towards Scherings.

(d) David Elstein owed a duty to Scherings to respect confidence.

(e) The information imparted by Scherings had the necessary quality of confidence about it, even though some of it was available in the public domain.

(f) David Elstein should be restrained from making use of witnesses of whom he heard in confidence, or making use of documents improperly obtained from Scherings.

I do not propose to go through each of those propositions or the cases on which they were founded. Suffice it to say that the common thread is that David Elstein was under a duty of confidence towards Scherings. This I agree. I would myself put it now just as I put it in *Seager v Copydex* [1967] 2 All ER 415 at 417, [1967] 1 WLR 923 at 931–932:

'The law on this subject does not depend on any implied contract. It depends on the broad principle of equity that he who has received information in confidence shall not take unfair advantage of it. He must not make use of it to the prejudice of him who gave it without obtaining his consent. The principle is clear enough when the whole of the information is private. The difficulty arises when the information is in part public and in part private . . . then the recipient must take special care to use only the material which is in the public domain. He should go to the public source and get it: or, at any rate, not be in a better position than if he had gone to the public source. He should not get a start over others by using the information which he received in confidence. At any rate, he should not get a start without paying for it. It may not be a case for an injunction or even for an account, but only for damages depending on the worth of the confidential information to him in saving him time and trouble.'

(ii) *Was Elstein in breach of his duty?*

In considering whether David Elstein was in breach of his duty, it is important to remember that this is an interlocutory application in which it is not possible to know the full facts. Suffice it to say that there is no evidence, or, at any rate, no sufficient evidence, to show that David Elstein knew anything about the terms on which Falkman were engaged by Scherings, except that the course was confidential and that he would be expected to respect that confidence. Not that Thames Television knew any more either. In these circumstances I would go with Scherings to this extent: neither Elstein nor Thames Television were at liberty to use any *private* information without the consent of Scherings. Nor to use any *public* information (this was recognised in the letter of 4th July 1979) unless they did the research and collected it themselves. But they were at liberty to use public information by going and collecting it themselves. As they said they did. And they were at liberty to use any ideas which came into their heads by reason of the course; and, in particular, the idea of making a documentary on the story of the Primodos affair. As they said they did. Ideas are not the subject of copyright. Nor of breach of confidence. So on the evidence as it stands, it seems to me very arguable that, although David Elstein was under a duty of confidence to Scherings, he was not in breach of that duty. It is, to my mind, quite unfair to accuse him, on the present evidence, of a flagrant breach of duty, or of being a traitorous adviser seeking to make money out of his misconduct, or to base any decision against him on that assumption. I look at it in this way: the correspondence shows that if Scherings had approved of the film, if it had been good publicity for them, they would gladly have let it be shown. But, because they disapproved of it, thinking it was bad publicity, they claim to be entitled to ban the showing of it indefinitely, the whole of it. In short, the breach of confidence, whatever it was (it has never been specified), gave them a veto on the showing of the film. Even though, as I think, it was a balanced and impartial presentation and was fair comment on a matter of public interest and could not be the subject of an action for defamation; and that was not suggested. This claim raises a point of the first importance.

(iii) *The remedy by injunction*

The remedy sought by Scherings is an injunction. They want to stop the showing of the film altogether. How far is it proper for the court to grant an injunction to restrain publication by the press and television? Such an injunction falls into a special category because it encroaches on one of our most fundamental freedoms, the freedom of the press. So I put on one side the *American Cyanamid* case (*American Cyanamid Co v Ethicon Ltd* [1975] 1 All ER 504, [1975] AC 396), a patent case which has given us an infinity of trouble, and the *Nawala* case (*NWL Ltd v Woods* [1979] 3 All ER 614, [1979] 1 WLR 1294), a trade dispute case which was of more help. And I turn to the press and television cases. Of these the most important are the *Sunday Times* case (*Attorney General v Times Newspapers Ltd* [1973] 3 All ER 54, [1974] AC 273) and the *Granada* case (*British Steel Corpn v Granada Television Ltd* [1981] 1 All ER 417, [1980] 3 WLR 774). None of these, however, contains any discussion of the principle about injunctions. So I go back to first principles.

(iv) *Prior restraint*
    The freedom of the press is extolled as one of the great bulwarks of liberty. It is *a*
entrenched in the constitutions of the world. But it is often misunderstood. I will *first*
say what it does *not* mean. It does not mean that the press is free to ruin a reputation or
to break a confidence, or to pollute the course of justice or to do anything that is
unlawful. I will *next* say what it *does* mean. It means that there is to be no censorship.
No restraint should be placed on the press as to what they should publish. Not by a
licensing system. Nor by executive direction. Nor by court injunction. It means that *b*
the press is to be free from what Blackstone calls 'previous restraint' or what our friends
in the United States, co-heirs with us of Blackstone, call 'prior restraint'. The press is not
to be restrained *in advance* from publishing whatever it thinks right to publish. It can
publish whatever it chooses to publish. But it does so at its own risk. It can 'publish and
be damned'. Afterwards, after the publication, if the press has done anything unlawful
they can be dealt with by the courts. If they should offend by interfering with the course *c*
of justice they can be punished in proceedings for contempt of court. If they should
damage the reputation of innocent people, by telling untruths or making unfair
comment, they may be made liable in damages. But always afterwards. Never
beforehand. Never by previous restraint.

(v) *Blackstone speaks*   *d*
    Such is the meaning of freedom of the press as enunciated by Blackstone. He put it so
well in his Commentaries in the year 1765 that I would set out the passage in full (4 Bl
Com 151–152):

> 'In this, and the other instances which we have lately considered, where
> blasphemous, immoral, treasonable, schismatical, seditious, or scandalous libels are
> punished by the English law, some with a greater, others with a less degree of *e*
> severity; the *liberty of the Press*, properly understood, is by no means infringed or
> violated. The liberty of the Press is indeed essential to the nature of a free state: but
> this consists in laying no *previous* restraints upon publications, and not in freedom
> from censure for criminal matter when published. Every freeman has an undoubted
> right to lay what sentiments he pleases before the public: to forbid this, is to destroy
> the freedom of the Press: but if he publishes what is improper, mischievous, or *f*
> illegal, he must take the consequences of his own temerity. To subject the Press to
> the restrictive power of a licenser, as was formerly done, both before and since the
> revolution, is to subject all freedom of sentiment to the prejudices of one man, and
> make him the arbitrary and infallible judge of all controverted points in learning,
> religion, and government. But to punish (as the law does at present) any dangerous
> or offensive writings, which, when published, shall on a fair and impartial trial be *g*
> adjudged of a pernicious tendency, is necessary for the preservation of peace and
> good order, of government and religion, the only solid foundations of civil liberty.
> Thus the will of individuals is still left free; the abuse only of that free will is the
> object of legal punishment.'

    That passage of Blackstone is the origin of the doctrine of 'prior restraint' which is so *h*
well known in the United States. It was quoted by Hughes CJ and the doctrine
summarised in the classic case in the Supreme Court of *Near v Minnesota* (1931) 283 US
697 at 713–720.

(vi) *An exception*
    Since Blackstone's day there has been some relaxation of this doctrine. In exceptional *j*
cases, where the intended publication is plainly unlawful and would inflict grave injury
on innocent people or seriously impede the course of justice, then the court may issue a
prior restraint. It may grant an interim injunction to restrain the proposed
publication. The general rule, and the narrowness of the exception, is well illustrated by

a

our practice in libel cases. On many occasions we have had cases where a plaintiff seeks an interim injunction to prevent the publication of a libel. We never grant the application when the defendant says that he intends to justify, no matter how improbable that he will succeed. We go by the ruling of this court in *Bonnard v Perryman* [1891] 2 Ch 269, [1891–4] All ER Rep 965. In all but the most exceptional cases we will not grant an interim injunction to restrain the publication of a libel. Such an exceptional case was instanced by Jessel MR. It was in *Quartz Hill Consolidated Gold Mining Co v Beall* (1882) 20 Ch D 501 at 508: '. . . an atrocious libel wholly unjustified and inflicting the most serious injury on the Plaintiff.' Except in such a case we never grant an interim injunction.

b

(vii) *The European Convention*

The same principle is contained in the European Convention on Human Rights (TS 71 (1953); Cmd 8969). We are here concerned with a question of policy. What should be the policy of the law in restraining publication? On such a question, I take it that our law should conform as far as possible with the provisions of the European Convention on Human Rights. As Lord Scarman said in the *Exclusive Brethren* case (*Attorney General v British Broadcasting Corpn* [1980] 3 All ER 161 at 178, [1980] 3 WLR 109 at 130): 'If the issue should ultimately be, as I think in this case it is, a question of legal policy, we must have regard to the country's international obligation to observe the European Convention as interpreted by the European Court of Human Rights.'

c

d

Now we do know the views of the European Court of Human Rights on this subject. It is contained in art 10 of the convention as interpreted in the *Sunday Times* case in the official report, para 65, pp 40–41. The court stressed the importance of the general principle that 'everyone has the right to the freedom of expression' and deliberately cut down the exceptions to it. It said that the exceptions 'must be narrowly interpreted'. The relevant exception in the *Sunday Times* case and here is that the freedom of expression may be subject to such restrictions as are 'necessary in a democratic society'. That was interpreted by the European Court to mean that there must be 'a social need sufficiently pressing to outweigh the public interest in freedom of expression': see the judgment, para 67, p 42.

e

f (viii) *Lord Scarman's dictum*

All this was well summed up by Lord Scarman in the *Exclusive Brethren* case [1980] 3 All ER 161 at 183, [1980] 3 WLR 109 at 138:

> '. . . the prior restraint of publication, though occasionally necessary in serious cases, is a drastic interference with freedom of speech and should only be ordered where there is a substantial risk of grave injustice. I understand the test of "pressing social need" as being exactly that.'

g

By that one sentence Lord Scarman has brought back into English law the doctrine of prior restraint which has been forgotten for too long. It applies not only in libel cases (as I have said) but also in all other cases where it is sought to restrain publication in the press, or on television. Such as in this case where there is an attempt to restrain publication on the ground that it would be a contempt of court or a breach of confidence. To these I now turn.

h

(ix) *Contempt of court*

We find no discussion about interim injunctions in the cases on contempt of court. In most cases the article has already been published by the newspaper. The application was made *after* the application to commit the editor and publisher for contempt for *having* published. It was tried summarily by the court, not by a jury. If guilty, punishment was inflicted of a fine or imprisonment and payment of costs. No damages could be or were awarded. No injunction was granted except that, as an alternative to committal, the court might in its discretion adopt the more lenient course of granting an injunction to

j

restrain *repetition* of the act of contempt: see 9 Halsbury's Laws (4th Edn) para 100. That
was not 'prior restraint', because the contempt had already been proved. The court said   *a*
in effect: 'Don't do it again or we will commit you.' I cannot believe that an injunction
would be granted beforehand, when nothing had been published, unless it was a case in
which it was clear beyond doubt that the article, when published, would be a grave
contempt and would seriously impede the course of justice. I gave my reasons in full in
the *Exclusive Brethren* case [1979] 3 All ER 45 at 51, [1979] 3 WLR 312 at 318 and I am
gratified to find that my conclusion was approved by Lord Edmund-Davies in the House   *b*
of Lords ([1980] 3 All ER 161 at 172, [1980] 3 WLR 109 at 123). I said:

> 'To my mind, the courts should not award [the Attorney General] such an
> injunction except in a clear case where there would manifestly be a contempt of
> court for the publication to take place. The same reasoning applies here as in the
> cases where a party seeks to restrain the publication of a libel.'

c
(x) *The Sunday Times case*
The *Sunday Times* case is no authority against the proposition. It was a remarkable
case. Not least because it elevated the Attorney General to an exceptional height. The
House said that it was—

> 'most desirable that in civil as well as in criminal cases anyone who thinks that a
> criminal contempt of court has been or is about to be committed should, if possible,   *d*
> place the facts before the Attorney-General for him to consider whether or not those
> facts appear to disclose a contempt of court of sufficient gravity to warrant his
> bringing the matter to the notice of the court'

because—

> 'He is the appropriate public officer to represent the public interest in the   *e*
> administration of justice.'

(See [1973] 3 All ER 54 at 87, 74, [1974] AC 273 at 326, 311.)
If the Attorney General thought the facts were of sufficient gravity, it was his duty to
move the court for committal or for an injunction, as the case may be (see [1973] 3 All
ER 54 at 76, [1974] AC 273 at 314). If he did not think it of sufficient gravity, then he   *f*
would not bring proceedings against the newspaper. He would leave it at liberty to
publish the article.
The Attorney General regarded those observations as making him in practice the
guardian of the public interest. It was for him, his ipse dixit, to decide whether the
proposed publication would be a contempt of court or not. Fortunately, however, he was
cut down to size by Lord Edmund-Davies in the *Exclusive Brethren* case [1980] 3 All ER   *g*
161 at 172, [1980] 3 WLR 109 at 123. It is not for the Attorney General, but for the
judges to be the guardians of the public interest.
Next, the *Sunday Times* case was remarkable in that it was all so friendly. Lord
Rawlinson explained it during the debate on the Contempt Bill on the 9th December
1980. The Sunday Times were anxious not to break the law. So they submitted the draft
article to the Attorney General and asked for his advice. He advised them that, if   *h*
published, it would be a contempt of court. The Sunday Times said: 'Let us have a
friendly action to see if it would be a contempt or not.' That was done. The only point
at issue was whether it would be a contempt of court or not. If it would be, then by
agreement there would be an injunction. Otherwise not.
But when the case was taken to the European Court of Human Rights, the propriety
of granting an injunction ran throughout the judgment. The European Court of Human   *j*
Rights stated that they took a different approach from the House of Lords. They
concluded that 'the interference complained of', that is, the injunction, ought not to have
been granted. It was too great an intereference with the freedom of the press.

(xi) *Application to this case*
This case differs from the *Sunday Times* case in this important respect. It is not brought

by the Attorney General as the guardian of the public interest. So far as we know, he has
a not been consulted about it, despite the advice of the Law Lords that it was most
desirable. It is brought by Schering Chemicals in their own interest. They assert that it
is also in the interest of the public generally that the programme should not be
broadcast. But they are not the judges of that. We are. Having seen the film, I do not
see that there is any risk that the course of justice in the pending actions will be impeded
or prejudiced in the least. The judge who tries the actions will be one who has not seen
b the broadcast. That is easily arranged. The witnesses may be cross-examined about
statements they have made in the broadcast but there is nothing unfair about that being
done; in any event they can be cross-examined now from the script, which Scherings
have already in their hands, before the broadcast. There is nothing here prejudging the
issues or bringing undue pressure on a party to settle. It is not nearly so objectionable as
the article in the thalidomide case (the *Sunday Times* case) of the 24th September 1972 as
c to which Lord Reid said ([1973] 3 All ER 54 at 64, [1974] AC 273 at 299): 'I see no offence
against public policy and no pollution of the stream of justice by its publication.'
   In all the circumstances I do not think this would be a contempt of court at all,
certainly not so clear as to warrant an injunction to restrain the publication of the film.

(xii) *Breach of confidence*
d   In some respects breach of confidence is different. Whilst freedom of expression is a
fundamental human right, so also is the right of privacy. Everyone has the right to
respect for his private life and his correspondence (see art 8 of the European
Convention). This includes a right to have his confidential information kept
confidential. This right may in some circumstances be so important that it takes priority
over the freedom of the press. An injunction may be granted restraining the newspapers
e from breaking the confidence. The principle is well expressed in art 10(2) of the
European Convention. It recognises that the freedom of expression may be restricted
whenever a restriction is 'necessary in a democratic society ... for preventing the
disclosure of information received in confidence'.

(xiii) *When no injunction should be granted*
   But there are other cases when the right of the press to inform the public, and the
corresponding right of the public to be properly informed, takes priority over the right
of privacy: see paras 65–66 of the judgment of the European Court of Human Rights in
the *Sunday Times* case. In such a case no injunction should be granted against the
newspapers and television to prevent them from publishing the information, even
g though it originated in confidence: see the discussion in *Initial Services Ltd v Puttrill* [1967]
3 All ER 145, [1968] 1 QB 396.
   On which side of the line did the confidential information fall in the *Granada* case?
The matter never fell for decision. It was never argued out, because it *was not disputed by
Granada* that British Steel could, if they had acted in time, have obtained from the court
an injunction against publishing or reproducing any of the contents of the documents
h (see [1981] 1 All ER 417 at 455, [1980] 3 WLR 774 at 821 per Lord Wilberforce). But
Lord Salmon thought that, if the matter had been argued out, an interim injunction
might have been lifted (see [1981] 1 All ER 417 at 468–469, [1980] 3 WLR 774 at 838).
And I myself said that if a newspaper—

   'gets hold of a trustworthy informant, who gives information of which the public
   ought to know, then, even though it originated in confidence, the newspaper may
   well be held to act with a due sense of responsibility in publishing it. It should not
   be compelled to divulge its source.'

(See [1981] 1 All ER 417 at 441, [1980] 3 WLR 774 at 805.)
   Nor, may I now add, be subjected to an injunction restraining it from use of the
information.
   On which side of the line does the present case fall? If Thames Television were about

to publish important private information which was highly confidential and very properly confined to Scherings, I have no doubt that an injunction should be granted to *a* prevent its publication in the film. But this information was not highly confidential. It was not confidential at all. It was not private. It was all in the public domain. Any stranger starting from scratch, and studying the old issues of the Sunday Times and so forth, could have got all this information together and published it without breaking any confidence at all. Is an injunction to be granted simply because David Elstein did not start from scratch, but got the idea of doing it from the course? I am clearly of opinion *b* that no injunction ought to be granted to prevent the publication of this information, even though it did originate in confidence. It dealt with a matter of great public interest. It contained information of which the public has a right to know. It should not be made the subject of an injunction.

3. DELAY   *c*
   It was in November 1979 that David Elstein told Scherings that he was going ahead to make the film 'The Primodos Affair' without their consent. Yet they did not move to stop him. They decided to wait until they had seen the finished film. If they approved it, they would agree to it being shown. If they did not approve, they would stop it.
   I do not consider they were entitled to stand by in this way, knowing all the expense involved in making this film, and yet render it valueless, at their own option. At any *d* rate, not unless it was highly objectionable. I do not think it was. It seems to me that it was a very balanced and fair presentation to which no reasonable objection could be made.

4. CONCLUSION
   Freedom of the press is of fundamental importance in our society. It covers not only *e* the right of the press to impart information of general interest or concern, but also the right of the public to receive it. It is not to be restricted on the ground of breach of confidence unless there is a 'pressing social need' for such restraint. In order to warrant a restraint, there must be a social need for protecting the confidence sufficiently pressing to outweigh the public interest in freedom of the press. No injunction forbidding publication should be granted except where the confidence is justifiable on moral or *f* social grounds (*Duchess of Argyll v Duke of Argyll* [1965] 1 All ER 611, [1967] Ch 302); or, I will add, on industrial grounds (the *Granada* case): and, in addition, where the *private* interest in maintaining the confidence outweighs the *public* interest in making the matter known to the public at large.
   A neat problem was set out in the Report of the Committee on Privacy (Cmnd 5012 (1972) p 298):   *g*

   'Suppose a newspaper comes into possession of information, which it knows to be confidential and obtained surreptitiously by the newspaper's informant, that a particular firm is about to discharge 10,000 employees. It approaches the firm who will neither confirm nor deny the report but immediately proceeds to apply for an injunction to prevent publication of the information. Perhaps the newspaper would have a defence, but it cannot be asserted with certainty.'   *h*

   I hope that the courts in such cases would refuse an injunction. The public interest in receiving the information would outweigh the private interest of the firm in keeping it secret. So in our present case, the *public* interest in the drug Primodos and its effects far outweighs the *private* interest of the makers in preventing discussion of it. Especially when all the information in the film is in the public domain, and where there has already *j* been considerable coverage in newspapers and on television; and when the publication cannot in any way affect the course of justice in the pending action. Nor affect the sales of Primodos, because it has long been withdrawn from the market.
   It comes back to this. Prior restraint is such a drastic intereference with freedom of the

press that it should only be ordered when there is a substantial risk of grave injustice. I stand as ever for the freedom of the press, including television, except when it is abused. I thought it was abused in the *Granada* case: but I see no abuse here. Even if there was any abuse, it was not such as to warrant the injunction of a prior restraint. I think that the judge ought to have refused the injunction on 27th August 1980. I would allow the appeal accordingly.

SHAW LJ. The material history of this litigation can be concisely stated. Schering Chemicals Ltd ('Schering') are manufacturing chemists with an international market and reputation. In recent times one of their important products has been a drug called Primodos which was designed as a contraceptive pill. It was extensively sold and had a wide vogue. The time came when it was thought that Primodos could also serve the function of a pregnancy test, and its sale was promoted on this basis. After a time misgivings arose in some quarters of the medical and scientific world. Articles in learned journals suggested a connection between the use of Primodos as a pregnancy test and the birth of infants suffering from serious physical and physiological defects. In the spring of 1975 the popular press took up the theme. The Sunday Times printed a pungent article in May of that year. It contained the plain implication that if Primodos was used as a pregnancy test with a subject who was pregnant at the time of the test, the child when born might be afflicted by some defect or abnormality induced by the drug because the foetus had been damaged. Other newspapers followed suit.

Schering were naturally much concerned. Their reputation was involved as well as their commercial interest, though both did not at all times walk easily and naturally hand in hand. In 1977 the Sunday Times published a second article on the topic. Not long afterwards Primodos was withdrawn from sale. When in April 1978 London Weekend Television produced a documentary devoted to the by then contentious topic of the relation between the use of Primodos and defective births, and this was followed by a similar showing in October of that year by Granada Television, Schering were left in no doubt that they had to regard themselves as being on the defensive. The onslaught had gathered such a momentum that it could not be ignored. By this time an association had been formed by parents of children who had been born with grave afflictions which were alleged to have resulted from the use by their mothers of Primodos as a test in the early stages of pregnancy. By December 1978 actions had been instituted on behalf of some of those children. In the same month in the face of this succession of adverse and hostile events, Schering were in touch with Falkman Ltd, the first defendant. That organisation (Falkman) operated as 'Executive Television Training' and was under the direction of Mr Bernard Falk. He put forward on behalf of his company proposals for the training of selected executives of Schering to appear on television and to speak effectively on that medium or on the radio in support or in defence of their marketing and application of Primodos before it was withdrawn, and in repudiation of the criticisms and attacks which had been levelled against the plaintiffs.

To construct an appropriate and effective course it was clearly necessary for Falkman to be put in possession of all the information Schering could offer in relation to the manufacture and marketing of Primodos, and to be told of any doubts expressed in any quarter, internal or external, as to its use as a hormone pregnancy test. This was done by Schering and acknowledged by Falkman. The information so provided necessarily included much that was then justifiably regarded as confidential.

A training programme was devised. It was to consist of four sessions designed to cover every aspect of Schering's situation in regard to Primodos. The first session was held at the end of February 1979 and the second at the beginning of March. The administrative and commercial attitudes of Schering as well as their scientific approach to the problems arising from the sale of Primodos were revealed, investigated and considered. The appropriate answers to the doubts and criticisms which had been expressed and might

still come were debated and decided on. At the end of April 1979, the third session took
place. The course did not, in the event, extend to a fourth session.			*a*

The terms of Schering's contract with Falkman expressly imposed on that company
the obligation to preserve the confidentiality of the information imparted to them by
Schering. The obligation to maintain that confidentiality would have existed by
implication between the parties even if there had been no express provision in that
regard. In the proposal for the course, Falkman referred to the fact that they had
received information on Schering and in particular in regard to Primodos. It was also *b*
stated that 'according to the strict code of ethics laid down by the National Union of
Journalists, of which our associates are members the use of such information would be
a severe breach of confidence'.

Mr Elstein was recruited by Falkman to take part in the course as one of the mentors.
He was called 'an interviewer' and fell within the term 'associates' in the passage cited
from the proposal. He was an important member of the training panel for he was *c*
employed by Thames Television (the third defendant) so that he knew the ropes as
regards television and broadcasting. He was just the sort of person who would, in a given
situation, be able to advise how best to parry or to deflect adverse publicity on those
media. His guidance and advice were to be relied on. What he imparted might be
invaluable especially to a company like Schering in a situation in which their standing
and repute were threatened.			*d*

No wonder then that Schering agreed to pay very nearly £11,000 for the planned
course with Falkman; and small wonder that Mr Elstein, who in this regard acted as a
freelance, was paid a fee of £200 (exclusive of VAT and expenses) for each of the three
days that he attended to give his guidance and the benefit of his knowledge and
experience in Schering's interests.

Mr Elstein was not directly employed by Schering. The implied obligation to *e*
maintain confidentiality as to matters which he learned as an interviewer on the course
would not arise from any contract between him and the plaintiff. According to Mr Falk,
he told Mr Elstein 'that he must not use any confidential information the source of which
[was any] training session in which he participated'. Mr Falk averred that 'this was
accepted by the second defendant'.

Mr Elstein himself has deposed that he knew at the outset of the training course about *f*
'the controversy surrounding the plaintiff's pregnancy testing drug Primodos' and that
he 'learned during the course that the plaintiff had an interesting and robust defence
with which [he] was not familiar'.

Mr Elstein thus acquired the knowledge which it was necessary that he should have if
he was to fulfil his function of advising Schering how best to protect themselves if there
arose further criticism or attack via television or broadcasting.			*g*

Within a month or so of the last training session in which Mr Elstein performed his
role he submitted what he has described as 'a confidential proposal' to the third defendant,
Thames Television. The subject matter was to be a documentary 'based largely on my
memory of the courses'. I find it very remarkable that Mr Elstein should have thought
fit to make any such suggestion to any outside party, let alone a powerful purveyor of
publicity, without first consulting Schering and obtaining their permission. At the very *h*
least he might have sought the view of his ad hoc employer Falkman. No considerations
of loyalty or good faith seem to have arisen in Mr Elstein's mind. If they did they were
completely submerged by his professional zeal as a publicist. When he did condescend
to tell Schering of his idea, he wrote on 4th July 1979 that 'the treatment rests heavily on
privileged information and . . . the only basis on which we could make the film as
proposed would be if Schering were to co-operate fully and so render much of that *j*
information "unprivileged"'.

It is clear from the context that Mr Elstein was using the word 'privileged' as meaning
'not to be revealed to anyone else without Schering's consent'. That is to say, he was
recognising that what he had learned from his participation in the Falkman course for
Schering was confidential to him, and was not to be passed on without their assent.

That assent was not forthcoming. Mr Elstein had, however, got the bit between his
a teeth. He was not to be stopped. A protest from Schering about the utilisation of
information supplied in confidence evoked a response by letter dated 9th November
1979, which contained the passage: '. . . such a programme would be worth making.
Certainly, we intend to make the effort and I will keep you informed as to our progress,
whether or not you eventually decide to participate.' This apparently represented the
limit of Mr Elstein's condescension to any canon of loyalty or standard of good faith and
b simple integrity. The letter continued: 'There is, of course, no question of my using any
information supplied to me in confidence in other circumstances.' I find this piece of
equivocation baffling. I doubt if Mr Elstein can explain satisfactorily what he meant to
convey by it.

On 29th November 1979 solicitors acting for Schering wrote to Mr Elstein stating that
they had advised their clients 'that it would be a flagrant breach of confidence by (him)
c if (he) were to use for the purpose of (his) programme information given to (him) in the
course of [Falkman's] service'. The letter went on to deal with Schering's intention, if the
proposed programme was not abandoned, to seek an injunction on the grounds of breach
of confidence and contempt of court. On 20th December following, a letter of similar
import was addressed by Schering's solicitors to Thames Television. That institution
wrote in reply on 17th January 1980 enclosing a synopsis of the contemplated
d programme. They asserted that it would contain no material not freely available from
other sources (that is, other than the training course via Mr Elstein). It followed, so they
contended, that no breach of confidence could arise from putting out the programme on
television. They offered in due course to provide a view of the finished programme but
pointed out that by the time it became available great expense would have been
incurred. Schering's solicitors' response on 8th February was to reserve their clients'
e position until the finished programme had been seen by them and to reiterate their
intention to seek the court's protection against a breach of confidence or interference
with the administration of justice. They could hardly have stated the attitude of their
clients more plainly or more promptly.

This history set the stage for the submissions addressed to McNeill J and to this court
in regard to the issue of confidentiality.
f The first proposition contended for on behalf of the second and third defendants was
that at no time was there any direct contractual connection between them and the
plaintiff from which a duty of confidentiality could derive.

McNeill J, to whose judgment I would pay respectful tribute, disposed of this argument
summarily but incisively in these terms:

g 'I would grant the injunction against the second defendant on two grounds.
First, on the grounds of breach of the duty of confidence arising out of the trust the
plaintiffs placed in him, in the course of his remunerated employment to advise
them professionally . . .'

I agree with him. As I see the position, the communication in a commercial context
of information which at the time is regarded by the giver and recognised by the recipient
h as confidential, and the nature of which has a material connection with the commercial
interests of the party confiding that information, imposes on the recipient a fiduciary
obligation to maintain that confidence thereafter unless the giver consents to relax it.

The obligation of confidentiality may in some circumstances be overborne. If the
subject matter is something which is inimical to the public interest or threatens
individual safety, a person in possession of knowledge of that subject matter cannot be
j obliged to conceal it although he acquired that knowledge in confidence. In some
situations it may be his duty to reveal what he knows. No such consideration has existed
in this case since the time that Primodos was withdrawn from the market. Neither the
public nor any individual stands in need of protection from its use at this stage in the
history. There is no occasion to beat the drum again. As to any rights or liability which
may have arisen from the use of Primodos in the past, these will be determined by the

outcome of the pending litigation. Mr Elstein and Thames Television can offer no valid or effective assistance in this regard; they are without any legitimate justification for *a* canvassing the issues in flagrant breach of an elementary duty to honour confidences acquired by Mr Elstein in the guise of a professional adviser. The law of England is indeed, as Blackstone declared, a law of liberty; but the freedoms it recognises do not include a licence for the mercenary betrayal of business confidences.

The judge added a second reason for granting the injunction against Mr Elstein, namely that 'he is the person whose conduct caused the first defendant to be in breach of *b* contract'.

Falkman would of course be palpably in breach. Mr Falk protested strongly on its behalf against Mr Elstein's proposals, but the first defendant has refrained from taking steps against the second defendant because of the prospective burden of costs. I do not myself think that recourse to the second ground is necessary and make no comment in regard to it.

c

While it is true that Thames Television were not the direct recipients of confidential information conveyed in a fiduciary situation, it is not in controversy that they were at all times aware of the circumstances in which Mr Elstein first became possessed of it. If Mr Elstein was in breach of duty in seeking to use it at all, Thames Television cannot be entitled to collaborate with him by taking advantage of his repudiation of his fiduciary obligations. I agree with McNeill J, when he said: 'As far as the third defendants are *d* concerned, they should be enjoined from publishing any material that was produced consequent on the second defendant's breach of the duty of confidentiality and the first defendant's breach of contract.'

The second proposition put forward on behalf of Mr Elstein and Thames Television was to this effect. When Mr Elstein undertook as an associate of Falkman to participate in the course for Schering, he had no intimate knowledge of the controversy and *e* contention which surrounded Primodos. By that time there had been numerous articles in scientific papers and journals and the first Sunday Times article had given publicity to the matter in the popular press. Mr Elstein's mind had, however, not been prompted to look in that direction. What he learned at the course came new to him.

It is now said that all the information on which the programme of the projected documentary is based could have been derived from sources available to the public *f* before the Schering course with Executive Television Training. It is asserted also that Mr Elstein with the assistance of a colleague in Thames Television has assiduously explored and collated all those sources. The relevant facts and opinions are all to be found in what has been described as 'the public domain' or 'the public sector'. No principle of confidentiality can apply, so it is contended, to matters which have become notorious. Whatever may have been the fiduciary duty on the part of Mr Elstein not to disclose *g* anything of a confidential nature that he had learned on the course, it had been entirely dissipated when the Primodos affair emerged into public view. What obligation of reticence can apply to what has long been an open secret? So the argument ran.

It is an argument which at best is cynical; some might regard it as specious. Even in the commercial field, ethics and good faith are not to be regarded as merely opportunist or expedient. In any case, though facts may be widely known, they are not ever present *h* in the minds of the public. To extend the knowledge or to revive the recollection of matters which may be detrimental or prejudicial to the interests of some person or organisation is not to be condoned because the facts are already known to some and linger in the memories of others. It is worth recalling that the London Weekend and Granada documentaries had been shown before the Executive Television Training course for Schering was devised by Falkman. A good deal of infromation about Primodos was *j* already 'in the public domain'. Schering's intention was to get what assistance could be given by Falkman to contain or to repudiate further public criticism and debate on a topic the discussion of which could only cause prejudice to Schering. Mr Elstein knew this as well as anybody. His claim that he wished to provide a debating ground in which

the factors favourable to Schering could be effectively demonstrated is sheer sophistry.
a The importation into the programme of Professor Michael Briggs, who, from 1966 until
1969 had been Schering's research director in the United Kingdom, is said to demonstrate
the even-handed treatment of the theme. I refrain from comment. Suffice it to say that
. Schering is naturally not eager to enter the lists and does not seek a champion for a
jousting match contrived by one of their confidential advisers.

It is not the law that where confidentiality exists it is terminated or eroded by
b adventitious publicity. Nor is the correlative duty to preserve that confidentiality. The
public interest may demand that the duty be gainsaid; but it cannot be arbitrarily cast
aside. An order of a court of law may relieve the confidant of the burden of secrecy and
may, after due inquiry, require him to reveal the subject matter of the confidence; but
it is not to be sloughed off at will for self-interest. I therefore come to the same
conclusion as McNeill J on the issue of confidence.

c   There remains the question whether the plaintiff's remedy should sound only
damages. This is a case in which the injury to Schering's interests might well be
irreparable. They are a substantial organisation pursuing a legitimate and important
enterprise as manufacturing pharmacists. They are entitled to be protected from
gratuitous onslaughts even when they assume the guise of public crusades. The judge
was, in my judgment, right to grant an injunction against breach of confidence. I would
d accordingly dismiss the appeal.

This renders almost academic the cross-appeal against his refusal to grant an injunction,
on the ground of contempt, to restrain the second and third defendants from showing
the programme. However, as much argument was directed to this issue, I think it right
to state the view that I have formed in the circumstances of this case having regard to the
pending actions by parents against Schering. The hearing of those actions has been fixed
e for October of this year. If 'The Primodos Affair' is allowed to be shown it will appear on
television early this spring. Will that conjunction of events bring about a contempt of
court in the sense that the fair trial of the issues in the actions will be hampered or
threatened or in the sense that the authority and status of the court will be impaired or
flouted? In this regard McNeill J adopted what he will forgive me for describing as an
· ambivalent stance. Judicial pronouncements on the topic of contempt may make it
f difficult to escape such a posture save in the plainest cases; and the present case does not,
on this aspect, fall within that category.

The judge stated his conclusion in these terms: 'Doing the best I can, I say that
although there is material which falls within the definition of contempt, there is not such
contempt as would justify making the order on that ground.' This expression of view
finds a parallel in the possible verdict of not proven in a criminal trial in Scotland. If one
g is driven to say contempt or no, my answer on the facts of the present case is the negative
one.

I cannot see that the fair trial of the issues in the pending actions would be in any way
hampered or adversely affected if the programme were shown. The trial is to be by a
judge alone; it is safe to assume he will not be improperly influenced in any way should
he see the programme or read the transcript. If among the witnesses to be called are
h some who have a part in the documentary, there is no reason to suppose that the
substance of their evidence or their readiness to contribute it will be affected or in any
way impaired. Witnesses in an action are credible and reliable or they are not. Our
system of trial in which evidence is elicited by examination and cross-examination
provides the means of demonstrating the character and quality of a witness.

It has been suggested that prospective or potential witnesses may be deterred or
j discouraged from contributing their testimony if the documentary contains material
which appears to be at variance with, or in contradiction of, what they would have been
prepared to say from their actual knowledge. I regard this as an insubstantial objection
to producing the documentary. This court has been afforded a view of the programme
and I am left with no impression of lurking dangers of the kind I have mentioned.

There is the larger question as to the undesirability of presenting simulated trials of the subject matter of pending or prospective litigation on so influential a medium of *a* publicity as television. This must be a matter of degree. Where the presentation appears to encroach on the function and authority of the judicature, the limits of tolerance are clearly exceeded.

In other circumstances the opportunity for free public discussion of topics of general concern should, in general and always subject to legitimate private rights, not be unduly curtailed. In the present case I see no challenge or threat to the due administration of *b* justice in the production of 'The Primodos Affair'. I would refuse the injunction sought on this ground.

TEMPLEMAN LJ. The first question which arises in this appeal is whether the showing of the television programme called 'The Primodos Affair' will constitute a breach of a duty of confidence owed by Mr Elstein to Scherings. *c*

From at least May 1975 Scherings have been under attack in the press and television and are being sued for producing and selling Primodos which, it is alleged, resulted in damage to unborn babies causing them to be born with crippling and distressing mental and physical handicaps. Scherings have no right to restrain any such attacks, subject always to the limited protection afforded by the law of contempt.

Falkman Ltd, trading under the name Executive Television Training or ETT, specialise *d* in training businessmen to give a good account of themselves on the radio or television, to defend themselves against their critics and to put forward positive justifications for their conduct and actions in a convincing and coherent manner.

In December 1978 Falkman submitted written proposals to Scherings. These proposals acknowledged that Falkman had received information from Scherings dealing in particular with Primodos. The proposals contained this assurance: *e*

'We wish to stress that this information, some of which is public and some of which is private, remains STRICTLY CONFIDENTIAL ... and will remain so whether a training programme is accepted or not. We also guarantee that it will never be used in the future by any broadcasting associate of E.T.T.'

The proposals recommended the employment of certain specified associates, including *f* Mr Elstein for the purpose of training senior company executives of Scherings in the art of communication.

The proposals referred to a television programme which was extremely damaging to Scherings and forecast that the Primodos issue was not going to disappear and that the level of anti-Schering publicity would increase. Falkman recommended a series of courses on how to handle interviews on radio and television and 'to assist Scherings to *g* spotlight the strongest arguments in the company's defence'. The final paragraph of the proposals stated: 'A training programme does not commit a company to participation in live broadcasting. What it can do is to ensure that the company does have people trained and available if Scherings decide to enter the public debate.' These proposals were followed by a memorandum which recommended that training courses should take place at certain studios belonging to ICI. Paragraph 1 of the memorandum stated: *h*

'Our recommendation is that due to sensitivity of editorial content in training programmes all Scherings courses should take place "in house" at a studio and with personnel conscious of the need for total confidentiality in dealing with the company's affairs.'

Under a separate confidentiality heading the memorandum stated that: *j*

'Although I.C.I. and Scherings are two separate companies their interests are similar. I.C.I. public relations department is fully aware of Scherings' specific needs for immediate training and recommend E.T.T. as suitable to carry out a training programme. The studio staff and E.T.T. panel are familiar with courses held to deal

a with sensitive issues and guarantee as we do that there will be no breach of confidence.'

The ETT panel recommended in the memorandum again included Mr Elstein. The memorandum offered a training course spread over four days for the sum of £10,750. On 15th December 1978 Scherings confirmed acceptance of the offer. For the purpose of enabling members of the panel to train executives of Scherings in the art of

b participating in radio and television interviews concerning Primodos, there were furnished by Scherings to Falkman press cuttings, copies of articles in medical and other journals, transcripts of television programmes which had already taken place and a good deal of other information concerning the controversy surrounding Primodos, the criticisms of Scherings which had already been made and the lines of defence available to Scherings.

c Falkman provided Schering with a training course programme which stated, inter alia: 'Both the E.T.T. panel and I.C.I. studio staff have been informed of the CONFIDENTIALITY of the course and this requirement is fully respected.' Mr Elstein was billed as the ETT analyst and panel chairman for the first day of the training course. The training programme gave details of the proposed training interviews which must have been based on the information supplied by Scherings. Interviews were projected

d covering the history, research programme and safety standards of Scherings, the reaction of Scherings to attacks made on Primodos, the precautions taken by Scherings for the testing of their products, the actions taken by Scherings in response to medical and other criticisms and discussions of medical arguments for and against Primodos. The training programme advised:

e   'Prior to the start of the course Schering executives taking part should brief themselves fully on all aspects of the company's operations both in Britain and worldwide. In particular they must know the background to the "Primodos Affair" and what action the company has taken since it first became a controversial issue.'

The first training sessions took place on 28th February 1979 and 1st March 1979. These two sessions raised a number of queries concerning Scherings' actions regarding

f Primodos in the light of criticisms of that product. Scherings' executives prepared themselves with answers to the queries raised in preparation for the third session. The third session took place on 27th April 1979. Mr Elstein attended all three sessions and was paid by Falkman £200 per session for his services. The projected fourth session never took place.

There are at present conflicts of fact, recollection and impression between Mr Elstein

g on the one hand and Scherings on the other hand. Mr Elstein avers that he has no recollection of studying the proposals, the memorandum, the training programme or the documentary information supplied by Scherings save for two newspaper cuttings. He was, he says, unaware of the express promises of confidentiality made by Falkman and as a journalist assumed that he could subsequently use information which was not confidential. At the outset of the training course he was aware that there was a

h controversy surrounding Primodos but 'learned during the course that the plaintiffs had an interesting and robust defence, with which I was not familiar as it had not appeared in the British media'. As a result of the training course he conceived an idea for the production of a television documentary about Scherings' product Primodos. He said: 'The idea for the production of a television documentary about the plaintiffs' product Primodos came out of my involvement in the training of the plaintiffs' personnel.' In

j May 1979 Mr Elstein submitted a confidential proposal in the form of a synopsis of a film to the third defendants Thames Television—

    'based largely on my memory of the courses. This proposal was written on the assumption that the plaintiffs would be willing to take part in and assist in the

making of the programme and that the information acquired in confidential
circumstances would thereby be available for the programme.'   *a*

The synopsis is entitled 'The Primodos Affair', 'an idea for a documentary film'.
Paragraph 2 of the synopsis sets out in chronological form the history of Primodos, the
research, articles, reports and official action which cast doubt on Primodos and Scherings'
reactions to and defences raised against the criticisms made of Primodos. Paragraph 3
gives case histories of some of the children on whose behalf it is claimed that Primodos
was reponsible for their handicaps. Paragraph 4 sets out certain questions which remain   *b*
to be answered. Paragraph 5, which was not sent to Scherings, intimated that Scherings
were willing for the first time to participate in a documentary film and submitted that
Scherings' participation—

> 'together with the other doctors, the parents, the children and the documentation
> of events (including anti-Schering demonstrations in various countries), should   *c*
> provide a fascinating 52 minute film, which lays out the issues without attempting
> to judge them.'

In general the synopsis proposed that the training course sessions should be transferred
to a documentary film and the dramatic effect heightened by the introduction of
Scherings' opponents. It could well have been fascinating. The contents of the synopsis
prove that during the training programme Scherings taught and imparted a good deal of   *d*
information and that Mr Elstein proved an apt pupil with a formidable memory.

After Mr Elstein had submitted his synopsis to Thames Television, he submitted it also
to Scherings. In an accompanying letter dated 4th July 1979 addressed to a director of
Scherings, the then views of Mr Elstein on confidentiality are spelled out. He said:

> 'This is the idea that I have put up to Thames. As you can see it is a confidential   *e*
> document, which only the Executive Producer [of Thames] has seen. The reason
> for this is that treatment relies heavily on privileged information and the Executive
> Producer understands that the only basis on which we could make the film as
> proposed would be if Schering were to co-operate fully, and so render much of that
> information "unprivileged" . . . At this stage I have not made any contact with the
> parents, as there would be no point unless Schering were prepared to co-operate. So   *f*
> the first decision is yours . . .'

In that letter Mr Elstein recognised a duty of confidentiality to Scherings which precluded
him from making a television film on the lines suggested in his synopsis unless Scherings
consented.

In October 1979 two actions against Scherings on behalf of a child, claiming that
physical and mental handicaps present since birth were due to Primodos and that   *g*
Scherings were liable in damages, were ordered to be set down for trial. Other actions
were in their preliminary stages.

On 5th October 1979 a director of Scherings wrote on their behalf to Mr Elstein. He
said:

> '. . . nothing has happened between the beginning of July, when you wrote to us,   *h*
> and now, which might have caused us to change our view that a programme was
> inappropriate . . . we have been advised not to participate in any programmes of this
> nature and in the circumstances we would naturally be concerned that none of the
> information supplied to you in confidence should be utilised.'

In a reply dated 9th November 1979 Mr Elstein sought to remove the fear of Scherings   *j*
that a programme might be in danger of contempt of court having regard to the
proceedings which had been instituted against Scherings and he resiled from the view
expressed in his letter dated 4th July 1979 that 'the only basis on which we could make
the film as proposed would be if Schering were to co-operate fully, and so render much

of that information "unprivileged"'. In his letter of 9th November 1979 Mr Elstein said
a this:

'I remain of the opinion that a programme which does not include the company
would be less than the best we could offer the public. But I now believe that a
balanced and temperate account of the issues involved in the story of Primodos is
possible even without Scherings' participation and that such a programme would be
b worth making. Certainly, we intend to make the effort and I will keep you
informed as to our progress, whether or not you eventually decide to participate.
There is of course no question of my using any information supplied to me in
confidence in other circumstances. If it turns out that the responsibility of putting
the views of Scherings falls on me, I will naturally seek advice from you as to how
to express those views.'

c   Scherings then instructed solicitors, McKenna & Co, who wrote to Mr Elstein on 29th
November 1979. They said that they had advised Scherings that the programme
proposed by Mr Elstein would be a 'flagrant breach of confidence by you if you were to
use for the purpose of your programme information given to you in the course of the
executive television service to our clients'. They were also worried that the programme
might constitute a contempt of court. They warned: '. . . accordingly our clients wish it
d to be known that if a programme based on your existing synopsis were prepared for
broadcasting they would have no option but to seek an injunction forthwith on the
grounds of breach of confidence and contempt of court.'
     On 30th November 1979 Mr Elstein wrote to Scherings' public relations director
enclosing the opinion of counsel that a programme could be made without involving
contempt of court. On the same day Mr Elstein replied to McKenna & Co admitting—
e

'My participation in the E.T.T. course alerted me to the strength of Scherings'
expression on the Primodos question of which I had been previously less than fully
informed.'

As a result of reading up the subject he discovered—

f   'that there are only a few trivial details of a personal nature which emerged in the
course that are not also available in the extensive scientific and journalistic reporting
on Primodos.'

McKenna & Co wrote to Thames Television on 20th December 1979 saying that they
had learned that Mr Elstein was making a programme on behalf of Thames Television
g called 'The Primodos Affair' and that they understood that Thames Television intended
to show the programme in April 1980. After detailing the circumstances by which Mr
Elstein had become interested in the Primodos question and stating the position of
Scherings with regard to confidentiality and contempt of court, McKenna & Co
concluded:

h   'We felt it only fair to write to tell you that should the proposed programme go
ahead, our clients will take every step open to them to prevent both the proposed
abuse of their confidence and the risk of prejudice. We hope, however, that now we
have informed you of the background to these matters, legal proceedings by our
clients will be unnecessary and that you will agree that in all the circumstances this
programme should not be shown.'

j   On 17th January 1980 Thames Television replied to McKenna & Co and sent them a
revised synopsis but concluded:

'We accept that it is the programme rather than the synopsis which has to be
considered; you may wish to reserve your position until you have had an

opportunity to view the finished programme, but obviously we would prefer to
receive your comments at this stage before any great expense is incurred.'   *a*

On 8th February 1980 McKenna & Co replied to Thames Television. They said inter
alia:

'Of course we must reserve our clients' position until we have had an opportunity
to see the finished programme. It seemed to us that by telling you at the outset of   *b*
our concern we might not only avoid the need for legal proceedings but also save
you and your company time and expense. Equally, however, we must tell you that
our clients will have no hesitation in applying to the court to prevent a breach of
confidence by Mr. Elstein or to prevent interference with the due administration of
justice.'

They argued that the new synopsis still rested heavily on privileged information and   *c*
that there was a real risk of prejudice to the fair trial of the actions in which Scherings
were concerned. Finally they said:

'But we have tried to be constructive by indicating to you in general terms the
objections we have to the proposed programme. We still feel that it should be
possible for a programme on the matter of public concern to which we have   *d*
referred to be presented, without prejudicing the fair trial of the actions in which
our clients are concerned. For obvious reasons we have advised them that they
should neither participate in the programme or put forward proposals for the
programme, but equally you may rest assured that our instructions do permit us to
try to seek a satisfactory solution with you.'

After some further correspondence McKenna & Co reserved their clients' position and   *e*
waited to see the film. The film was in fact seen on 24th July 1980 when a copy of the
script was handed over and there was a further showing to Scherings' counsel on 1st
August. The writ in these proceedings was issued on 12th August and on 27th August
1980 McNeill J granted an injunction against the showing of the film until trial or
further order. Mr Elstein and Thames Television now appeal to this court against the   *f*
granting of that interlocutory injunction.

The film 'The Primodos Affair' contains as did the original synopsis, a large amount of
information which was supplied by Scherings to Mr Elstein in the course of, and for the
purposes of, the training course in which he participated and for which participation he
was paid. That information could have been obtained by Mr Elstein from public sources
but was in the first instance obtained in fact from Scherings. If Mr Elstein had not taken   *g*
part in the training course, he would not have made the film.

On behalf of Mr Elstein it was submitted that there is no power in the court to restrain
publication of information which is not confidential information but is available from
public sources. For this purpose reliance was placed on *Seagar v Copydex* [1967] 2 All ER
415, [1967] 1 WLR 923, *Fraser v Evans* [1969] 1 All ER 8, [1969] 1 QB 349 and in
particular *Coco v A N Clark (Engineers) Ltd* [1969] RPC 41 at 46–50.   *h*

It was conceded on behalf of Mr Elstein that if Mr Elstein had promised Scherings not
to make use for his own purposes of information, whether confidential or not, which he
received from Scherings for the purposes of the training course, then he would be bound
by that promise. It was also conceded that if Mr Elstein was aware that Falkman had
promised Scherings on behalf of Mr Elstein that Mr Elstein would not make use for his
own purposes of information, whether confidential or not, which he received from   *j*
Scherings for the purposes of the training course, then again Mr Elstein would be bound
to observe that promise. It is said by Mr Elstein that he made no promise, he knew
nothing of Falkmans' promise and therefore he is not bound. There is a triable issue as
to whether Mr Elstein saw the proposals made in December 1978 whereby Falkman

acknowledged that information which they had received from Scherings 'some of which
a is public and some of which is private remains STRICTLY CONFIDENTIAL' and guaranteed
that such information 'will never be used in the future by any broadcasting associate of
E.T.T.'. There is a triable issue whether Mr Elstein, if he did not see the proposals, saw
any other document which disclosed the promise made by Falkman on his behalf or
whether by reason of earlier employment by Falkman he was aware that such a promise
would be made.   On these grounds alone, subject to the question of balance of
b convenience, Scherings are entitled to an injunction against Mr Elstein pursuant to the
principles established by *American Cyanamid Co v Ethicon Ltd* [1975] 1 All ER 504, [1975]
AC 396.

In any event, even if Mr Elstein did not make an express promise himself to Scherings
and did not know that Falkman had made an express promise to Scherings on his behalf
that he would not make use in the future of information public or private supplied by
c Scherings for the purposes of the training programme, he nevertheless, in my judgment,
impliedly made such a promise to Scherings when he agreed to take part in the training
programme, accepted information supplied by Scherings for that purpose and took part
in the training programme in which further information was supplied to him.   Scherings'
information formed the basis of the training.   The fact that Mr Elstein was not employed
and paid by Scherings but by Falkman does not prevent the implication of such a
d promise.

When Mr Elstein agreed to take part in the training programme and did take part in
the training programme and received information from Scherings, it was obvious to Mr
Elstein that Scherings were supplying the information in order that Mr Elstein might be
able to advise and train Scherings' representatives because Scherings had received bad
publicity in the past and hoped that Mr Elstein would assist them to avoid or at least
e mitigate bad publicity in the future.   It was obvious to Mr Elstein that the information
supplied by Scherings was given to Mr Elstein for one purpose and one purpose only,
namely to enable Mr Elstein to advise Scherings how to avoid or mitigate bad publicity
in the future.   It was obvious to Mr Elstein, and the synopsis dated May 1979 and the
film 'The Primodos Affair' amply illustrate, that the information supplied by Scherings
for one purpose, namely to enable Mr Elstein to assist Scherings, was capable of being
f used for another purpose, namely for preparing bad publicity for Scherings in the future.

In my judgment, when Mr Elstein agreed for reward to take part in the training
course and received and absorbed information from Scherings, he became under a duty
not to use that information and impliedly promised Scherings that he would not use that
information for the very purpose which Scherings sought to avoid, namely bad publicity
in the future including publicity which Scherings reasonably regarded as bad publicity.
g Scherings reasonably regard the film 'The Primodos Affair' as bad publicity based on
information which they supplied to Mr Elstein to enable him to advise Scherings.   Mr
Elstein could have made a film based on Primodos if he had not taken part in the training
programme, but 'The Primodos Affair' film only came into existence because Mr Elstein
received from Scherings information for one purpose and used that information for
another purpose, for his own gain and to the detriment, as they reasonably believe, of
h Scherings.

The information supplied by Scherings to Mr Elstein had already been published, but
it included information which was damaging to Scherings when it was first published
and which could not be republished without the risk of causing further damage to
Scherings.   Any republication and recycling by Mr Elstein of any of the information
supplied to him by Scherings could be unwelcome to Scherings, could be inimical to the
j best interests of Scherings and could reasonably be regarded by Scherings as further bad
publicity.   Mr Elstein must have realised that if he revived and recycled and republished
information which he received from Scherings, that action on his part was liable to be
damaging.   Mr Elstein must have realised that Scherings would not supply Mr Elstein
with any information at all if they thought for one moment that there was any possibility

that he might make use of that information for his own purposes and in a manner which
Scherings might find unwelcome or harmful. That Mr Elstein realised and accepted this   *a*
is shown by his letter dated 4th July 1979. As between Scherings and Mr Elstein, if Mr
Elstein had obtained information from sources other than Scherings, then it would of
course not have been confidential in his hands, but, by agreeing to advise Scherings and
by accepting information from them to enable him to advise Scherings, Mr Elstein
placed himself under a duty, in my judgment, not to make use of that information
without the consent of Scherings in a manner which Scherings reasonably considered to   *b*
be harmful to their cause. As between Scherings and Mr Elstein, the information which
Mr Elstein received from Scherings was confidential and cannot be published by Mr
Elstein in the film 'The Primodos Affair'. Thames Television made the film 'The
Primodos Affair' with full knowledge of all the circumstances and with knowledge of the
claim by Scherings that the film would constitute a breach of confidentiality and could
not be broadcast without the prior consent of Scherings.   *c*

Thames Television submit that, if the information was confidential and Thames
Television were made aware of that confidentiality, nevertheless Scherings are not
entitled to an injunction because Scherings did not intervene at an earlier stage to prevent
the film being made. Thames Television have spent money in making the film. This
argument has been raised very late in the day and ignores three facts. First, Scherings by
the letter dated 20th December 1979 from McKenna & Co made their position quite   *d*
clear and asked Thames Television to agree that the programme should not be shown.
Thereafter Scherings never abandoned their rights and Thames Television made the film
at their own risk and with full knowledge that if Scherings did not consent to the
showing of the film then Scherings would take action. Second, in their letter dated 2nd
January 1980 Thames Television themselves invited Scherings to reserve their position
until they had had an opportunity to view the finished programme. Third, in their   *e*
letter dated 8th February 1980 McKenna & Co while accepting the invitation to reserve
Scherings' position until they had an opportunity to see the finished programme, made
it clear that Scherings would have no hesitation in applying to the court to prevent a
breach of confidence. At the same time in the same letter Scherings, through McKenna
& Co, took much the same attitude as Thames Television, namely that there was still a
possibility that the film might be shown with Scherings' approval. That of course   *f*
depended on the content of the film and, when Scherings saw the film, they took action
within an admittedly reasonable period to register and enforce their disapproval of the
film by bringing these proceedings and seeking the present injunction. In the
circumstances Thames Television, who chose to employ Mr Elstein in making the film
with full knowledge of all the circumstances, are in no better position than Mr Elstein
himself. The confidentiality which attaches to Mr Elstein attaches likewise to Thames   *g*
Television.

There remains to be considered the balance of convenience. If the film 'The Primodos
Affair' was shown, damages would be a grossly inadequate remedy for Scherings. It is
impossible to quantify the damage caused by bad publicity. It is said, however, that Mr
Elstein is immune from the remedy of an injunction because he is a journalist and that
Thames Television are immune from the remedy of an injunction because the showing   *h*
of 'The Primodos Affair' is not part of the business of the production of entertainment for
profit but part of a function of supplying information to the public.

It is not abundantly clear that Mr Elstein is to be regarded as a part-time or full-time
journalist for present purposes. He resists compliance with a rule of professional conduct
laid down by the National Union of Journalists for the purposes of maintaining high
professional standards amongst journalists on the grounds that he is not a member of the   *j*
union. When Mr Elstein took part in the training programme, he was not acting as a
journalist but as a confidential adviser. But, assuming for present purposes that Mr
Elstein is entitled to cast over himself the cloak and protection of journalism, he is
claiming an immunity from the remedy of an injunction in circumstances in which

other persons not claiming to be journalists would not be immune. The associates
a employed by Falkman in their business or employed by Falkman for the specific purpose
of advising Scherings were not necessarily all journalists. They could include actors,
retired journalists, broadcasters and others who do not claim to be journalists. Similarly
Thames Television are claiming an immunity which would not be extended to the
authors or publishers of a book. Mr Elstein asserts the independence of a journalist in
connection with information which he received as a hired confidential adviser.

b   Notwithstanding the difficulties caused by the claims to journalist and press status put
forward in the context of the present facts, I am content to consider this appeal on the
footing that Mr Elstein is entitled to all the protection afforded a journalist and that
Thames Television are entitled to all the protection afforded to a newspaper. The
questions then arise whether a journalist or a newspaper is entitled as of right to
immunity from an injunction against publication and whether, if there is no absolute
c immunity, nevertheless in the circumstances of the present case the court should in the
exercise of its discretion decline to grant an injunction.

It is not contended that journalists and the press are entitled to absolute immunity
from injunctions to restrain the publication of confidential information. Any such
contention must fail in the light of the decision of the House of Lords in *British Steel
Corpn v Granada Television Ltd* [1981] 1 All ER 417, [1980] 3 WLR 774. In that case
d Granada were ordered to disclose the name of the informant who supplied confidential
information and that decision is only consistent with the view that journalists and the
press are not immune from any of the remedies or processes of the common law. The
press is not above the law. Blackstone was concerned to prevent government interference
with the press. The times of Blackstone are not relevant to the times of Mr Murdoch.

It has been suggested that an injunction restraining breach of confidentiality should
e only be granted in circumstances in which the right to preserve confidentiality is so
important that it takes priority over the freedom of the press. If this means that the
court should consider the consequences to the public of withholding or granting an .
injunction, then I fully agree. In the *Granada* case it was important to the public that, if
the injunction was withheld, the court would protect a disloyal employee. It is important
in the present case that, if the injunction is withheld, the court will enable a trusted
f adviser to make money out of his dealing in confidential information. These
consequences must be weighed against the argument that, if an injunction is granted, the
public will be deprived of information.

I do not consider that the injunction in the present case does interfere with the
freedom of the press to inform the public or any other freedom of the press. Mr Elstein
voluntarily placed himself under a duty to refrain from using information which he
g received from Scherings. By composing the film 'The Primodos Affair' Mr Elstein acted
in breach of that duty. Thames Television cannot knowingly take advantage of that
breach of duty by Mr Elstein. There is nothing to prevent any journalist or television
company, including Thames Television, from making a film about Primodos provided
that they do not employ the services of Mr Elstein who can only give those services by
making use of information which he received from Scherings. If Mr Elstein is restrained
h from breach of his duty to Scherings and if Thames Television are restrained from
exploiting any breach of duty on the part of Mr Elstein, there will be no concealment of
any fact from the public. Those facts have already been made available to the public and
may again be made available to the public but not through the medium of Mr Elstein
who engaged himself to advise Scherings, received relevant information from Scherings
to enable him to advise Scherings and thus voluntarily debarred himself from making
j use of that information for his own purposes.

As an alternative to their claim for an injunction based on confidentiality, Scherings
suggest that the film 'The Primodos Affair' will, if now shown, constitute a contempt of
court in that the film involves the discussion of the issues and evidence relating to an
action which has been set down for trial and is due for hearing in October 1981. The trial

will be before a single judge and will involve a battle dominated by medical experts and statisticians. In my judgment, the film cannot affect the result of the action and the *a* court should not be anxious to accept submissions that discussions of a pending action' must necessarily be unseemly or harmful to the administration of justice. Each case must be judged on its own merits and, so far as this case is concerned, the fear of harm does not justify the grant of an injunction. The showing of the film would be unwelcome to Scherings and contains harmful publicity for Scherings, but if the film had not been made in breach of confidence by Mr Elstein there would not, in my view, be adequate *b* grounds for the grant of an injunction. For the reasons which I have given, however, which are substantially the reasons advanced by the learned judge, I would dismiss the appeal.

Appeal and cross-appeal dismissed.

                                                                c

Solicitors: *McKenna & Co* (for Schering Chemicals Ltd); *Roiter, Zucker,* Hampstead (for Falkman Ltd); *Anthony M Gostyn* (for Mr Elstein and Thames Television Ltd).

                                               Frances Rustin   Barrister.

Home Office v Harman

QUEEN'S BENCH DIVISION
PARK J
19th, 20th, 21st, 27th NOVEMBER 1980

COURT OF APPEAL, CIVIL DIVISION
LORD DENNING MR, TEMPLEMAN AND DUNN LJJ
28th, 29th, 30th JANUARY, 6th FEBRUARY 1981

Contempt of court – Publications concerning legal proceedings – Documents disclosed on discovery in action – Undertaking not to use documents disclosed for purposes other than action – Duty of solicitor – Litigant obtaining discovery of documents – Documents quoted in court in action – Litigant's solicitor allowing journalist access to quoted documents – Whether solicitor released from implied undertaking not to use documents for purposes other than action because documents quoted in court – Whether solicitor guilty of contempt.

A long-term prisoner brought an action claiming damages against the Home Office in respect of his detention in an experimental 'control unit' isolated from the rest of the prison system. The prisoner was represented by the respondent, a solicitor who was also a legal officer for the National Council of Civil Liberties ('the NCCL'). In the course of discovery in the action, the respondent, acting on behalf of the prisoner, obtained discovery of documents amounting to some 6,800 pages relating, inter alia, to the setting up of the control unit and the treatment of its inmates. At the request of the Home Office the respondent gave an express undertaking that the documents obtained on discovery would 'not be used for any other purpose except for the case in hand'. At the trial of the action the material parts of some 800 documents were read out in open court by counsel for the prisoner. Some days after the trial the respondent allowed a journalist to have access to the 800 documents referred to in court. The journalist later wrote and published an article, based on the documents, which was highly critical of the Home Office and the setting up of the control unit. The Home Office applied for an order that the respondent was in contempt of court in breaching the implied obligation imposed on a party to whom documents were disclosed on discovery that the documents would not be used for any purpose other than the purposes of the action in which they were disclosed. The judge held that the respondent was guilty of a serious contempt. The respondent appealed, contending (i) that as part of the principle of justice being done in public a party to an action was released from any undertaking in regard to the other party's documents once they were quoted in open court, (ii) that the journalist could himself have obtained access to the contents of the documents if he had attended court when they were read out or if he obtained a transcript, and would not have been in contempt had he done so, and (iii) that to ensure the reports and comments on cases were accurate it was convenient for a litigant to be entitled to disclose to reporters and journalists all documents read out in open court.

Held – The appeal would be dismissed for the following reasons—
(1) The law requiring disclosure of documents on discovery in litigation was a restriction, in the interests of justice, on the right which the owner of any document had to keep the document and its contents private and confidential, and being limited to requiring disclosure in the public interest of doing justice it did not mean that further use could be made of documents so disclosed or that their contents could be disseminated elsewhere without the consent of the owner, or that because the documents were quoted in open court a party or his solicitor was freed from the undertaking implied by law that he would not make use of documents disclosed on discovery except for the purposes of

the action (see p 363 g to j, p 364 g to j, p 365 d, p 366 f to h and p 367 e j, post); dictum of Lord Denning MR in *Riddick v Thames Board Mills Ltd* [1977] 3 All ER at 687 applied. *a*

(2) Even though the contents of documents read out in court were readily available to others, that was not a reason for allowing a litigant who had had the benefit of obtaining such documents by discovery for the purpose of assisting him in obtaining justice in the action to use the documents or the weapon of discovery for any other purpose. Furthermore (per Templeman and Dunn LJJ), if the accuracy of a document read out in court needed to be checked by a journalist or a reporter there was no reason why *b* permission to see the document should not be sought from the party that owned the document rather than from the other side, and (per Dunn LJ) there was a distinction between checking the date or exact wording of a document referred to in evidence and allowing a journalist access to the quantity of documents in the instant case (see p 363 g h, p 366 j to p 367 a and c to j and p 368 a to c, post).

(3) It was to be inferred that the respondent had not confined her use of the discovered *c* documents to use in her position as solicitor for the prisoner but had used them for the purposes of the NCCL. In doing so the respondent had breached the express undertaking given to the Home Office and the undertaking to the court implied by law and was thus guilty of a serious contempt (see p 359 f, p 362 j to p 363 c, p 364 b to f, p 367 d e and p 368 f, post).

d

Notes
For the undertaking not to use documents produced on discovery for collateral or ulterior purposes, see 13 Halsbury's Laws (4th Edn) para 66, and for cases on the subject, see 18 Digest (Reissue) 62, 70, 426, 492–495.

e

Cases referred to in judgments
Alterskye v Scott [1948] 1 All ER 469, 18 Digest (Reissue) 62, 426.
Attorney General v New Statesman and Nation Publishing Co Ltd [1980] 1 All ER 644, [1981] QB 1, [1980] 2 WLR 246, 69 Cr App R 193, DC.
Baker v Bethnal Green Corpn [1945] 1 All ER 135, 109 JP 72, 43 LGR 75, CA, 17 Digest (Reissue) 546, 344. *f*
Burmah Oil Co Ltd v Bank of England (Attorney General intervening) [1979] 3 All ER 700, [1980] AC 1090, [1979] 3 WLR 722, HL; affg [1979] 2 All ER 461, [1979] 2 WLR 473, CA, Digest (Cont Vol E) 184, 1277a.
Church of Scientology of California v Department of Health and Social Security [1979] 3 All ER 97, [1979] 1 WLR 723, CA, Digest (Cont Vol E) 181, 495c.
Conway v Rimmer [1968] 1 All ER 874, [1968] AC 910, [1968] 2 WLR 998, HL; subsequent *g* proceedings [1968] 2 All ER 304 n, [1968] AC 996, [1968] 2 WLR 1535 n, HL, 18 Digest (Reissue) 155, 1273.
Gammell v Wilson [1981] 1 All ER 578, [1981] 2 WLR 248, HL; affg [1980] 2 All ER 557, [1980] 3 WLR 591, CA.
Halcon International Inc v Shell Transport and Trading Co [1979] RPC 97, CA.
Pickett v British Rail Engineering Ltd [1979] 1 All ER 774, [1980] AC 136, [1978] 3 WLR *h* 955, [1979] 1 Lloyd's Rep 519, HL, Digest (Cont Vol E) 459, 1314b.
R v Wilkes (1770) 4 Burr 2527, [1558–1774] All ER Rep 570, 19 State Tr 1075, 4 Bro Parl Cas 360, Wilm 322, 2 ER 244, 98 ER 327, HL, 11 Digest (Reissue) 676, 121.
Riddick v Thames Board Mills Ltd [1977] 3 All ER 677, [1977] QB 881, [1977] 3 WLR 63, CA, Digest (Cont Vol E) 180, 495b.
Schering Chemicals Ltd v Falkman Ltd p 321, ante. *j*
Scott v Scott [1913] AC 417, [1911–13] All ER Rep 1, 82 LJP 74, 109 LT1, HL, 16 Digest (Reissue) 42, 426.
Williams v Home Office [1981] 1 All ER 1151.
Williams v Home Office (No 2) [1981] 1 All ER 1211.

Cases also cited

a *Association of Licensed Aircraft Engineers v British European Airways* [1973] ICR 601, NIRC.
Distillers Co (Biochemicals) Ltd v Times Newspapers Ltd [1975] 1 All ER 41, [1975] QB 613.

Motion

The Home Office applied by motion dated 12th June 1980 for an order under RSC Ord
52, r 9 that the court grant relief other than committal to prison against the respondent,
b Harriet Harman, a solicitor, in respect of Miss Harman's contempt of court in supplying
to the Guardian newspaper copies of documents disclosed by the Home Office to her in
her capacity as solicitor for the plaintiff in the action *Williams v Home Office (No 2)* [1981]
1 All ER 1211 in breach of an undertaking implied by law and affirmed by her in a letter
dated 17th October 1979 to the Treasury Solicitor that the documents disclosed on
discovery in the action would not be used for any purpose other than the purposes of the
c action. The facts are set out in the judgment of Park J.

Simon D Brown and *Philip Vallance* for the Home Office.
Leolin Price QC and *Geoffrey Robertson* for Miss Harman.

d   *Cur adv vult*

27th November. **PARK J** read the following judgment: In these proceedings counsel
on behalf of the Home Office moves for an order against the respondent, Harriet
Harman, a solicitor, under RSC Ord 52, r 9, for relief, other than committal to prison, for
contempt of this court in supplying to the Guardian newspaper copies of 800 pages of
e documents disclosed to her in her capacity as the solicitor for her client Mr Williams, in
his action against the Home Office.
    The basis of the case against her is that in supplying these documents, in the
circumstances about to be related, to a Mr David Leigh, who is an experienced reporter
and writer of feature articles for the Guardian newspaper, she broke the undertaking
which, as a matter of law, is impliedly given by all those to whom documents are
f vouchsafed by discovery in legal proceedings, that undertaking being not to make use of
such documents except for the purposes of the action in which they have been disclosed.
    The matter came to light on the publication of the edition of the Guardian newspaper
for 8th April 1980. It contained an article by Mr David Leigh entitled, 'How Ministry
hardliners had their way over prison units'. The article made quotations from, or
references to, a number of Home Office internal documents which had been disclosed in
g *Williams v Home Office (No 2)* [1981] 1 All ER 1211. That action had lasted for five weeks
from 25th February to 25th March 1980. Mr Williams's counsel took five days to open
the case and, in the course of doing so, all the 800 documents were read out in court.
    The questions to be decided in the present proceedings are whether the reading out of
the documents operated to destroy the undertaking implied by law and, if not, whether
what was done by the respondent nevertheless constituted a breach of the undertaking.
h The contempt alleged is a civil contempt not a criminal contempt. Accordingly, it is
not suggested that the respondent's conduct prejudiced a fair trial of the action or
interfered with the course of justice either in the action or as a continuing process, or that
the judge could have been in any way affected by the article which appeared before he
had delivered his judgment. Further, it is accepted that reporters from the Guardian
newspaper, or anyone else who happened to be in court during the hearing and had the
j facilities for doing so, could have made such notes as they were able to make or obtained
a transcript and that, had such material been used for the writing of the article, no
contempt would have been committed.
    The facts are these. In the action Mr Williams claimed damages because he had spent
six months of a substantially longer prison sentence in what was called a special control

unit, that being a form of imprisonment for particularly disruptive prisoners. As a result of three separate orders for discovery, the Home Office disclosed a total of 6,800 pages of *a* documents. Because of the volume of disclosed minutes and memoranda relating to the formulation and discussion of policy, the Home Office was concerned that the plaintiff and his expert witnesses should be aware of the rule of law that documents offered on discovery should not be used for any other purpose than that of the action in which they were disclosed. The Home Office was also concerned that documents so obtained should not inadvertently be allowed to be put to some other use at some future date.   *b*

So just before the second order for discovery on 25th October 1979 there was some correspondence between the Treasury Solicitor and the respondent, beginning with a letter dated 17th October 1979. In that letter the Treasury Solicitor sought assurances that the documents disclosed would be used solely for the purposes of the action. The letter concludes:

> 'My client does, however, require that inspection of the disclosed documents and *c* dissemination of their contents should be limited to the legal officers of the N.C.C.L. and their assistants at any time concerned with the conduct of this action, except insofar as wider inspection or dissemination is strictly necessary for the conduct of the action. In other words, my client would not wish the documents to be used for the general purpose of the N.C.C.L. outside your function as solicitor for the *d* Plaintiff.'

In the last two paragraphs of her reply the respondent wrote:

> 'As far as the documents which have been shown to potential expert witnesses are concerned, we have in the normal way warned those witnesses that the only purpose for which the documents are to be used is for preparing their evidence in this case. *e* As far as "the general purposes of N.C.C.L." is concerned you may rest assured that, as a solicitor, I am well aware of the rule that requires that documents obtained on Discovery should not be used for any other purpose except for the case in hand.'

Her assurance did not differ in any material respect from the undertaking implied by law. The Treasury Solicitor's answer included these sentences: *f*

> 'As to your last paragraph my client Department is happy to accept the assurance which you give and I shall accordingly not pursue the matter further. So far as the potential expert witnesses are concerned, I have noted the warning which you have given them as to the use of the documents and am grateful for this. I am not, in any way, doubting their good faith in adhering to the warning. However, with the best will in the world it is possible for other people to forget the purpose for which the *g* documents were originally supplied; entirely without blameworthiness on the part of the original recipients, it is possible for these documents to change hands and as a result fall into the custody of people who may be entirely ignorant of the background. In these circumstances I still require an assurance that the documents supplied to potential expert and other witnesses should be returned as soon as reasonably practical after the trial.'   *h*

By her letter dated 18th December 1979 that assurance was given by the respondent:

> 'As far as the documents that have been disclosed in this case are concerned I undertake to ask the expert witnesses who have been sent copies of the documents to return them to me when the action has been completed,'

At the time of this correspondence public interest immunity was claimed in respect of *j* 23 disclosed documents. On the plaintiff's application, McNeill J, on 29th January 1980, ordered production of five of those documents, which included a submission to Sir Arthur Peterson and Minister of State, Lord Colville; a submission to the Secretary of

State and others, and a note of a meeting with the Secretary of State. Mr David Leigh's article contained quotations from these documents.

The respondent was present when McNeill J delivered a careful judgment in *Williams v Home Office* [1981] 1 All ER 1151. At one point in his judgment McNeill J cited the passage in the speech of Lord Reid in *Conway v Rimmer* [1968] 1 All ER 874 at 888, [1968] AC 910 at 952 where he said:

> 'The business of government is difficult enough as it is and no government could contemplate with equanimity the inner workings of the government machine being exposed to the gaze of those ready to criticise without adequate knowledge of the background and perhaps with some axe to grind.'

Towards the end of his judgment, McNeill J said ([1981] 1 All ER 1151 at 1160–1161):

> 'The risks attendant on inspection and production as postulated by Lord Reid are in any event minimised in two ways. Firstly, if after inspection the court orders production, the order may provide for production of part only of a document, the remainder being sealed up or otherwise obscured. Secondly, it is plain from the decision of the Court of Appeal in *Riddick v Thames Board Mills* [1977] 3 All ER 677, [1977] QB 881 if it was not plain before, that a party who disclosed a document was entitled to the protection of the court against any use of the document otherwise than in the action in which it is disclosed. As Lord Denning MR put it ([1977] 3 All ER 677 at 687, [1977] QB 881 at 896): "The courts should, therefore, not allow the other party, or anyone else, to use the documents for any ulterior or alien purpose ... In order to encourage openness and fairness, the public interest requires that documents disclosed on discovery are not to be made use of except for the purposes of the action in which they are disclosed." Undoubtedly this applies to litigants and their legal advisers: see also the references in *Church of Scientology of California v Department of Health and Social Security* [1979] 3 All ER 97 at 101–102, 116, [1979] 1 WLR 723 at 729, 746. Much of the reservation expressed by Lord Reid to which I have referred would in my view be met by adherence to what was said by the Court of Appeal in *Riddick's* case, reasserting what indeed had been the law previously. Having weighed all these various factors in the balance, I have come to the conclusion that the public interests of justice, including as they do here the rights of the citizen, and that liberty of a prisoner preserved for him by the statute and rules, must be the prevailing interest and that I should inspect the withheld documents. Accordingly I have asked the Treasury Solicitor to provide the documents for that purpose.'

Counsel for the Home Office referred to these letters and to the subsequent history for the purpose of underlining two things: first, the great importance attached by the Home Office to compliance with the implied undertaking and, second, the respondent's awareness of the importance being attached to it and of their reliance on her good faith. In her affidavit the respondent says that following press reports of the decision of McNeill J she received a number of inquiries from persons describing themselves as reporters, requesting either a sight of the documents or general information as to their contents. She denied each request saying that she was not at liberty to make any such disclosures.

Mr David Leigh was known to her as an experienced and respected reporter who had specialised in Home Affairs features for the Times and, more recently, the Guardian newspapers. During the hearing he had attended the court on some occasions when documentary exhibits were being read and he had written news stories about the action. Shortly before the hearing concluded Mr Leigh approached her and told her that he was writing a feature article about some of the issues raised in the course of the case. He explained that he had not been in court throughout the whole of the proceedings and asked whether he could inspect the documents which had been read out in open court

in order to refresh his memory and to obtain an accurate note of their contents. She did
not think that Mr Leigh's request was either unusual or inappropriate and saw no reason
why she should refuse it.

Accordingly, at some date between 28th March and 8th April 1980, Mr Leigh called
by appointment at her office. She does not say on how many occasions he called. She
permitted him under her surveillance to inspect and makes notes of the contents of the
two bundles comprising the 800 documents. Shortly before taking his leave Mr Leigh
asked about two photographs of the control unit produced by the Home Office for the
convenience of the court and the parties. She allowed Mr Leigh to take away the
photographs, which do not form part of the contempt, because they were not disclosed
documents.

The respondent says that she played no part in the writing of Mr Leigh's article nor did
she see it prior to its publication. On the other hand, it is contended, rightly as I think,
that her conduct has to be judged in the light of all the circumstances in which the
disclosure of the 800 documents came to be made, namely (i) the correspondence with
the Treasury Solicitor between October and December 1979, (ii) the fact that the sensitive
category of the five documents disclosed in consequence of the order of McNeill J was not
thereby altered, (iii) her acquiescence in arrangements for a reporter, who had been only
occasionally in court, to inspect and take notes from a very large number of documents
at her office, not for the purpose of preparing a law report or an account of the trial but
for the purpose of a feature article which she must have known would have little concern
with the legal issues which had arisen in the *Williams* action; it would be a spin-off from
those proceedings, and (iv) her failure to seek the consent of the Home Office to the
proposed disclosure, unquestionably due to the fact that she knew that any hint of her
intention would have resulted in an immediate application to the trial judge for an
injunction which would have been granted.

There is no dispute that at least until the hearing of this motion the law has been that
a party to whom documents are disclosed on discovery in an action is under an implied
obligation not to make use of them except for the purposes of the action in which they
have been disclosed (see *Alterskye v Scott* [1948] 1 All ER 469 and, more recently, *Riddick
v Thames Board Mills Ltd* [1977] 3 All ER 677, [1977] QB 881, cited by McNeill J in the
passages from his judgment to which I earlier referred).

Counsel for the respondent, however, contends that in the absence of any previous
decision of the court as to the duration of the obligation, the words 'for the purposes of
the action' in this statement of the law have to be qualified to the extent that, as regards
any document read out in open court, the ordinary implied obligation to protect the
confidentiality of that document is at an end because of the publicity necessarily attendant
on the proceedings. What is said in open court can be reported without infringing the
implied obligation.

I can summarise his argument in this way. Discovery is an invasion of a person's
private right to keep his documents to himself. The effect of the implied obligation is to
protect the confidentiality and privacy of such documents pendente lite. But in the
words of Lord Halsbury in *Scott v Scott* [1913] AC 417 at 440, [1911–13] All ER Rep 1 at
11 'every Court of Justice is open to every subject of the King'. Thus, the public has an
interest in the openness of justice in our courts. In those circumstances, once a document,
however private or confidential, is read out in court there is, as he put it, something
comical about the proposition that there is still some confidentiality attaching to it. So
from that moment confidentiality is at an end. He cited a passage from Goff and Jones
on the Law of Restitution (2nd Edn, 1978, p 512):

'The courts will not restrain a confidant from making use of information which
is not confidential. "Something which is public property and public knowledge"
cannot *per se* provide any foundation for proceedings for breach of confidence
. . . . (T)here can be no breach of confidence in revealing to others something which

is already common knowledge." It is irrelevant how the information became common knowledge . . .'

Counsel for the respondent points out that the courts provide ample protection for a party who wishes to ensure that the confidentiality of his documents will not be damaged at the trial. He can apply to a master or to a judge for a special order to ensure non-disclosure of a document's contents. For example, the document can be kept out of the bundle to be read in open court so that the judge and counsel can read it to themselves; or the judge can hear part of the case in camera; or special orders on the lines of those sometimes made in trade-secrets cases and the like can be made. Counsel for the respondent relies on the fact that no such application was made on behalf of the Home Office in the *Williams* action.

For these reasons counsel says that as all the 800 documents were read out in open court they all lost their confidentiality and, in those circumstances, the respondent was at liberty to re-publish their contents without infringing the implied obligation.

It may at first seem absurd that, although the confidentiality of a disclosed document has been destroyed by the measure of publicity given to it when it is read in open court, yet the party obtaining a copy of it for the purposes of the civil action may not thereafter publish it again outside the court without committing a contempt. But I think that the explanation for the apparent absurdity is to be found by examining the reason for an order for discovery and its consequences. The reason was spelt out by Lord Denning MR in the *Riddick* case in one sentence ([1977] 3 All ER 677 at 687, [1977] QB 881 at 895):

'The reason for compelling discovery of documents in this way lies in the public interest in discovering the truth so that justice may be done between the parties.'

Therefore documents disclosed on discovery are those to be used by one party or the other in support of his claim or in support of his defence to a claim or in any other way thought right for the purpose of determining or assisting in the determination of the issues between them and discovering where the truth lies so that justice may be done. It is as if each document disclosed bears a warning in some such words as: 'Disclosed in the action A v B NOT to be used for any other purpose except with the leave of the court or the owner.' All the objects of discovery have been achieved by the time disclosed documents have been produced, put in evidence and read in open court.

The question in these proceedings is, when once a document has been read in open court is the party who did not disclose it free to make such use of it as he likes, subject only to the restraints imposed by the law of defamation or of copyright and the like?

As I have said, I think that the answer to the question is to be found in the reason why he had possession of it in the first place, that is, by virtue of an order for discovery made for the purpose of determining the issues between himself and his opponent and of discovering where the truth lies. In my judgment that reason for his possession of it never changes. It must continue throughout the period of his possession of the document however long that may be. If, during that period, he were to be asked how the document came to be in his possession he would have to reply that he received it by virtue of an order for discovery in the proceedings against its owner. In those circumstances, is it necessary in the interests of justice that the implied obligation in relation to the documents should run concurrently with his possession of it?

Counsel for the Home Office draws attention to the consequences if the obligation ceased at the moment when the document was read in open court. In that event there would be nothing to prevent him from sending to the press or to anyone else not only that document but all the documents of his opponent read out in court. In the instant case the respondent would be able to make available, whenever she pleased and to whomsoever she pleased, the contents of the highly confidential documents in her possession. Indeed, judging from remarks alleged to have been made by her to a Frances

Gibb, a writer of an article in the Times of 10th May 1980, that is what she probably intends to do.

Of course, a litigant in a civil action has to accept the possibility that his confidential documents, if read out in court in the proceedings, might well receive much wider publicity than he foresaw. If his case happened to raise some interesting point of law, they might be recorded in a law report; if the case aroused public interest newspaper reporters would be present in court throughout most of the proceedings for the purpose of reporting on the facts which might well include references to confidential documents. But in the ordinary way the risk of publicity outside the court to the contents of documents read inside the court is small. That risk, however, would be immeasurably increased if his opponents were able to publish his documents once they had been read in open court. In *Riddick's* case [1977] 3 All ER 677 at 687, [1977] QB 881 at 896 Lord Denning MR said:

> 'Compulsion is an invasion of a private right to keep one's documents to oneself. The public interest in privacy and confidence demands that this compulsion should not be pressed further than the course of justice requires.'

I think that if one of the consequences of an order for discovery were to make it possible for a party to make free use of his opponent's documents once such documents had been read in court, the fact that such a right existed would convert the order into an even greater invasion of privacy than it now is and would also operate as a powerful disincentive to the making of proper discovery, for at this stage there could be no certainty that the court would later make any order giving special protection to confidential documents.

The most recent case to which I was referred on this subject was *Halcon International Inc v Shell Transport and Trading Co* [1979] RPC 97. Of the somewhat complicated facts I need say only that the documents referred to in the judgment had not been read in court. I read the whole of the passage from the judgment of Megaw LJ because it summarises the effect of all the cases cited to me in argument and, in addition, refers to the fact that there is no breach of the implied obligation if the court permits a party who has obtained documents on discovery to use them for a purpose other than the purposes for which they have been produced. Megaw LJ said (at 121):

> 'The general provision of English law with regard to the use of documents which have been made available by a party in discovery in an English action is, I think, not in dispute. I am quite content to accept it as it is set out in passages in Bray on The Principles and Practice of Discovery. It is an old book, published in 1885; but, so far as concerns the principles which I am going to quote, they are, in my judgment, still applicable and they are accurately set out. At page 238 it is said: "A party who has obtained access to his adversary's documents under an order for production has no right to make their contents public or communicate them to any stranger to the suit." The reasons for that have been stated in a number of cases in the courts. One of them is, to my mind, an obvious reason: documents belonging to a party are their own property. It is perfectly right, in accordance with English procedure, that, where litigation is involved in which that party is either the plaintiff or the defendant, he should be obliged to disclose documents which are in his possession, even though they may tell against his own interest, subject always, of course, to particular rules as to certain documents being privileged (which does not arise in this case). But it is in general wrong that one who is thus compelled by law to produce documents for purposes of particular proceedings should be in peril of having these documents used by the other party for some purpose other than the purpose of those particular legal proceedings and, in particular, that they should be made available to third parties who might use them to the detriment of the party who has produced them on discovery. And there is the further, practical, reason

which has been stressed recently in the case of *Riddick* v *Thames Board Mills Limited* ([1977] 3 All ER 677, [1977] 1 QB 881) by the Master of the Rolls, Lord Denning: that it is important, for the administration of justice, that there should not be a disincentive to parties to make proper discovery, so that they are minded to hold back, and seek to avoid the disclosure of documents which may tell against themselves in litigation. One substantial disincentive would be if there was the danger that those documents, being disclosed, might be used for purposes outside the purposes of the particular action. Mr. Bray in his book at page 239 says: "The principle, however"—that is, the principle in the passage which I have recently quoted—"is not that the party cannot be compelled to divulge them for any other reason even if the court should in any case so think fit, but that they cannot be used except under the authority of the court." It is open to the court, if the court sees fit, to give permission to a party who has obtained documents or copies of documents on discovery in an action, to use those documents for a purpose other than the purposes of the action in respect of which they have been produced.'

To the instance referred to in the last paragraph there can be added another: there would be no breach by a party who used his opponent's documents for another purpose with his consent.

For these reasons I have come to the conclusion that the implied obligation binds the party throughout the period his opponent's documents are in his possession. That period will vary considerably from case to case. In some cases the documents may not be preserved for long after the final hearing in the court; in other cases, such as matrimonial causes and actions in the Chancery Division relating to wills and trusts, they may well have to be kept for a very long time indeed.

Counsel for the respondent says that if his first submission goes too far, then he submits in the alternative that the implied obligation is subject to the limitation that any disclosed document which at the trial is read out in open court can be disclosed to reporters, journalists and others for the purpose of reporting or commenting on the trial or the matters in issue in the proceedings.

As I have said earlier, documents are disclosed for the purpose of assisting in the determination of the issues between the parties. They are not disclosed for the purpose of assisting reporters, journalists and others in the business of reporting or commenting on the trial or the matters in issue in the proceedings. In my view, the implied obligation is not subject to the limitation contended for by counsel for the respondent in his alternative submission.

On the other hand, a person who permits a reporter or a journalist to study a disclosed document read out in open court does not thereby inevitably commit a contempt (see *Alterskye* v *Scott* [1948] 1 All ER 469 at 471). His conduct would certainly be capable of constituting a contempt but whether it was in fact a contempt would have to be judged in the light of all the circumstances in which the disclosure was made (see *Attorney General* v *New Statesman* [1980] 1 All ER 644 at 649, [1981] QB 1 at 10).

In my opinion it is very unlikely that a person who disclosed the document, for example, to a reporter or a journalist or the writer of an article for a law journal so that he might use it in the ordinary way for the purposes of his work would commit a contempt of court. But in deciding whether any disclosure amounted to a contempt the court would have to take into consideration all the circumstances, including such matters as the purposes and the extent of the disclosure; its date in relation to the trial and the action; whether the opposite party's consent to the disclosure was sought and, if so, the reason for the refusal; whether leave of the court should have been obtained before the disclosure was made, and generally all the circumstances surrounding the making of the request for disclosure and the compliance therewith.

In the present case the respondent was bound by the implied obligation at the time when she disclosed the Home Office documents to Mr Leigh. In thus disclosing them she was not making use of them for the purpose of the action by Mr Williams against the Home Office. Having regard to all the circumstances in which she made the disclosure, *a* I have no doubt that she was guilty of a serious contempt of court.

The Home Office believes that she acted in good faith. I am willing to regard myself as bound by that opinion. For these reasons I will impose no penalty, but she will pay the costs of these proceedings.

Order accordingly.   *b*

K Mydeen Esq   Barrister.

Appeal
Miss Harman appealed to the Court of Appeal.

c

Leolin Price QC, Geoffrey Robertson and *Andrew Nicol* for Miss Harman.
Simon D Brown and *Philip Vallance* for the Home Office.

Cur adv vult

d

6th February. The following judgments were read.

LORD DENNING MR. Miss Harriet Harman is a solicitor of the Supreme Court. The judge made a finding of grave import against her. He found that she had been guilty of a 'serious contempt of court'. His decision was at once criticised in the press. The Times next morning flatly contradicted the judge. It said that her offence was *e* 'extremely trivial'. Later on Lord Gifford, the sixth baron, whose ancestor, the first Lord Gifford, was the Master of the Rolls in 1824, thought that the decision was so wrong that he moved an amendment to the Contempt of Court Bill on 20th January 1981 (see 416 HL Official Report (5th series) col 351). He added that 'if in the course of the discussion, the Court of Appeal may be in no doubt about what I think they ought to do in the particular case, that will be merely incidental to the discussion'. Other peers followed *f* suit. They felt no inhibitions about sub judice. Nor did the Lord Chancellor advise them to desist. Nor can we question their proceedings. It is so declared in the Bill of Rights. In answer to all these protestations I would say with Lord Mansfield in *R v Wilkes* (1770) 4 Burr 2527 at 2562, 98 ER 327 at 347:

> 'We are to say, what we take the law to be: if we do not speak our real opinions, we prevaricate with God and our own consciences ... Once for all, let it be *g* understood, that no endeavour of this kind will influence any man who at present sits here.'

I wish that people who criticise the decisions of the judges would study the facts first; because every rule of law is stated in relation to the facts of the instant case. It is by their application to the facts that the rule is to be justified or condemned. That was shown *h* strikingly only yesterday when the Lords in *Gammell v Wilson* [1981] 1 All ER 578, [1981] 2 WLR 248 deplored the effect of their decision the previous year in *Pickett v British Rail Engineering Ltd* [1979] 1 All ER 774, [1980] AC 136.

A dedicated troublemaker
The story starts with an arch-criminal, Michael Williams. He was guilty of the armed robbery of a bank in Cardiff. In 1971 he was sentenced to 14 years' imprisonment. He *j* was placed in 'Category A' as being a man whose escape would be highly dangerous to the public or the police. After three years, the Governor of Hull Prison described him as a 'high notoriety Category A prisoner' and as 'a totally subversive and dedicated

troublemaker'. He used to move from group to group of prisoners sowing seeds of
a discontent. It was he who 'contributed largely to changing a composed wing to a
seething mass of resentment and rebellion'.

Such being his character, he was the very man to qualify for entry to a newly-formed
'control unit'. This had been recommended by a highly qualified committee and
approved by the Secretary of State. One of the objects was to remove a troublemaker
from ordinary prison routine and put him in a separate unit on his own where he would
b not be able to exert an evil influence on other prisoners. The first of such units was at
Wakefield. Michael Williams was a very suitable candidate. He was transferred to that
unit on 23rd August 1974. He left it after 180 days on 18th February 1975 and was
transferred to another prison.

Now here is the point. The control unit was found not to have been a success. It was
closed in October 1975. The experiment, however well intentioned, had failed. This
c gave the 'dedicated troublemaker' a grand opportunity to make further trouble for many
innocent people. He made complaints against the Home Office and the prison service.
With the assistance of lawyers, he asserted that the setting up of the control unit was
illegal. He alleged that he had been subjected to 'cruel and unusual punishments'
contrary to the Bill of Rights, art 10. He said that he had been unfairly treated contrary
to the dictates of natural justice. Those complaints did not come well from his mouth,
d seeing that he had been such an enemy of society himself. His complaints were taken up
by the National Council for Civil Liberties ('NCCL'). He got legal aid; he sued the Home
Office for damages. The writ was issued in 1975 whilst he was still in prison. The case
was tried for four and a half weeks by Tudor Evans J. On 9th May 1980 the judge gave
a judgment covering 132 pages. He rejected the evidence of Michael Williams. He held
that the control unit was not unlawful; that Michael Williams was transferred to it quite
e properly; that the punishments were not cruel and unusual; and that the action for
damages failed (see *Williams v Home Office (No 2)* [1981] 1 All ER 1211).

Legal representation

Here I must mention a point which lies at the root of his case. Michael Williams got
legal aid. All the fees and expenses were being paid for by the legal aid fund, that is, by
f the taxpayers of this country. Miss Harman took over the case on his behalf in 1978; at
the same time as she entered the employment of the NCCL as their solicitor. But in the
action she was solicitor only for Michael Williams. If and in so far as she acquired
information in confidence for the purposes of this action, she was *not* at liberty to use it
for the purposes of the NCCL. I would emphasise 'not'.

Discovery in the action
g It is one of the rules of our English law that a party to litigation must disclose to the
other all his confidential documents relevant to the issue in the case. This is done so that
the trial judge can get at the truth and do justice between the parties. In the action
brought by Michael Williams his solicitor, Miss Harman, took advantage of this rule.
She required the Home Office to disclose all their documents relating to the setting up
of the control unit and to the treatment of Michael Williams and other prisoners in it,
h and many other matters. The Treasury Solicitor for the Home Office tried to limit the
scope of discovery but without much success. The documents were in a huge pile of
6,800 pages, over a foot high. The Treasury Solicitor was very concerned that these
documents should be kept confidential and should not be used for any collateral or
ulterior purpose. On 17th October 1979 he wrote to Miss Harman:

i 'However, having regard to the very large number of policy documents intended
for internal use which have been disclosed, my client [the Home Office] is concerned
at the risk of improper use of the documents ... my client would not wish the
documents to be used for the general purposes of the N.C.C.L. outside your function
as solicitor for the Plaintiff.'

On 17th October, 1979 Miss Harman replied:

'As far as "the general purposes of N.C.C.L." is concerned you may rest assured *a* that, as a solicitor, I am well aware of the rule that requires that documents obtained on discovery should not be used for any other purpose except for the case in hand.'

On 23rd October 1979 the Treasury Solicitor replied: 'My client Department is happy to accept the assurance which you give . . .'

Besides that big pile of documents, there was however a small bundle of special *b* documents in respect of which the Home Secretary gave a certificate that 'the production of them would be injurious to the public interest'. This certificate was challenged by the legal adviser for Michael Williams. The point was fully argued before McNeill J and he gave a considered judgment on 29th January 1980 (see *Williams v Home Office* [1981] 1 All ER 1151). He inspected the documents and ordered the production of six of them. These were records of high-level meetings reporting to the Secretary of State or the *c* Minister of State for decision. I have no doubt that until very recently these documents would have been held privileged from production. They come within the words of Lord Reid in *Conway v Rimmer* [1968] 1 All ER 874 at 888, [1968] AC 910 at 952:

'To my mind the most important reason [for the privilege] is that such disclosure would create or fan ill-informed or captious public or political criticism. The business of government is difficult enough as it is and no government could *d* contemplate with equanimity the inner workings of the government machine being exposed to the gaze of those ready to criticise without adequate knowledge of the background and perhaps with some axe to grind. And that must, in my view, also apply to all documents concerned with policy making within departments . . .'

Although these six documents came within that category, nevertheless McNeill J *e* ordered production of them. He did this because of the more recent ruling of this court in *Riddick v Thames Board Mills* [1977] 3 All ER 677 at 687, [1977] QB 881 at 896. We there held that '. . . documents disclosed on discovery are not to be made use of except for the purposes of the action in which they are disclosed'. McNeill J thought that, if confined to use in the action, they could not be used (in the way feared by Lord Reid) 'to create or fan ill-informed or captious public or political criticism'. *f*

So the judge ordered disclosure of these documents, relying on the implied undertaking of Miss Harman that the documents would not be used for any other purpose than the case in hand, an undertaking of which, on her own showing, she was well aware.

The use at the hearing

One week before the trial commenced, Miss Harman selected 800 pages and bound *g* them in two bundles and made nine copies for the use of the judge and counsel. She says that 'all material parts of the documents in the said two bundles were read out in open Court by Counsel for the Plaintiff . . .' Note her words 'all material parts'. She does not identify those parts. Probably she does not know what they were. She was not in the court all the time. I should imagine that no one except the shorthand writer or the tape *h* could tell what parts were read and what were not. I should be very surprised if every word of every one of the 800 documents was read out. Counsel would himself select what parts to read. He would say, 'I do not think it necessary to read this page or this paragraph.' Or the judge would say, 'I have already read it. Do get on.' The reading of documents is very much a selective process in which all concerned take part.

The use after the hearing

Now I come to the crucial part of the case. A day or two after the hearing Miss Harman allowed Mr David Leigh to have access to all the documents in the two bundles. I feel it desirable to let her describe her part in it in her own words:

a
'One of the reporters who had attended Court on some occasions when the documentary exhibits were being read and who had written news stories about the Action was a Mr. David Leigh: Mr. Leigh is known to me as an experienced and respected reporter who has specialised in "Home Affairs" features for "the Times" and more recently "the Guardian". On a day shortly before the case concluded after all the exhibits had been read out, Mr. Leigh approached me in the Court room and informed me that he was writing a feature article about some of the issues raised in

b
the course of the case: I Ie explained that he had not been in Court throughout all the Proceedings and asked whether he could inspect the documents which had been read out in open Court in order to refresh his memory and to obtain an accurate note of their contents: I saw no reason at all subject to considerations of my own convenience to refuse this reasonable and limited request: It seemed to me to be in the interests of Justice that the case should be reported fully and accurately while it

c
was fresh in the public mind: I was of course aware that Mr. Leigh could achieve his purpose by ordering transcripts of the evidence but it seemed unreasonable to put him to the expense and delay involved in adopting that course: I was aware of other cases in which press reporters had been shewn exhibits by Counsel or instructing Solicitors in order to make a full and complete note of evidence delivered inaudibly or at speed or in order to record material introduced into evidence in their absence:

d
Mr. Leigh's request was neither unusual nor inappropriate and I saw no reason why I should refuse it. At some time after the evidence had been concluded and 8th of April (when the article appeared) Mr. Leigh called by appointment at my office: I permitted him at all times under my surveillance to inspect and to make notes of the contents of documents in exhibit bundles P1 and P2 which had been read out in open Court . . . at no time did I supply any of these documents to Mr. Leigh nor

e
did I permit Mr. Leigh to make photocopies of any of these documents . . . at no time did I surrender possession of any copy of the documents referred to in the "Guardian" article by handing them over to Mr. Leigh: At no time when Mr. Leigh was in my office or at any other time did I give him any access to the master set of 17 files containing some 6,600 pages of documents which had not been placed in evidence. Shortly before taking his leave Mr. Leigh asked about photographs which

f
he had seen in Court during the Hearing. These photographs of the site of the control unit at H.M. Prison Wakefield . . . were the only documents which I allowed Mr. Leigh to take out of my office.'

In what capacity did Miss Harman act?
Such being her own account, I would ask: in what capacity was Miss Harman acting

g
when she allowed Mr Leigh to have access to these documents? Was she acting as solicitor for Michael Williams? Or as solicitor for the NCCL? She does not say herself. But she certainly led Mr Leigh to believe that she was acting as solicitor for the NCCL. Indeed he believed that, in conducting this very action, she was acting as solicitor for the NCCL. On this point I let Mr Leigh speak for himself. He wrote an article which was published in the Guardian newspaper on 8th April 1980, ten days after the hearing

h
concluded, and four and a half weeks before the judge gave judgment. The article throws such a light on the use of these documents that I set out here some extracts from it.

The article
At the top there are the two photographs of Wakefield control unit which had been

j
handed by Miss Harman to Mr Leigh. The article was headed:

'HOW MINISTRY HARDLINERS HAD THEIR WAY OVER PRISON UNITS

'Papers released through a court case—brought by a civil rights group and in which judgment is awaited—have raised questions about the running of the Home

Office after its blunder in setting up in secrecy control units for inmates. David
Leigh reports.

'A MAJOR Whitehall blunder, involving internal bureaucratic intrigue and
ministerial attempts to prevent disclosure, has been revealed in rare detail by
documents released to the National Council for Civil Liberties by a court order. It
is the story of how the Home Office invented special "control units" for prisoners;
set one up amid bureaucratic infighting; swept aside all protests; hastily altered it
when its apparently harsh and pointless regime was exposed; and finally abandoned
the whole notion, admitting its ineffectiveness. It is a story of muddle and
recriminations, in which civil servants experimented with psychological techniques
for punishing "subversives" which were quite different from those originally
approved by ministers. A prison regime was established which was arguably illegal
and which is now, five years later, awaiting judgment after a long and expensive
High Court case which finished last week . . . The documents were obtained, despite
protests by ministers that disclosure was not in the public interest, by the NCCL
who used them in evidence in the court case brought through them by one of the
control unit inmates, Michael Williams, against the Home Office . . . And the
documents obtained by the NCCL—including minutes, reports, and advice to
ministers containing normally well-guarded official secrets—raise further questions
about the way the Home Office is administered.'

The article goes on to give extracts from top level documents and to use them for
criticising Ministers of the Crown and high civil servants. These are named in the
article. Contrary to the well-understood convention in Parliament that civil servants
should not be attacked individually but only the minister who is responsible for them.
Civil servants cannot answer back.

Note that when the article was published the case was still sub judice, whilst the judge
was considering his judgment. But that does not seem to have produced any inhibitions
in Mr Leigh or the newspaper.

The position of Miss Harman

Counsel for Miss Harman told us that Mr Leigh had got it all wrong when he said in
the article that 'the documents were released to the NCCL by a court order'. He said that
Mr Leigh said this without the authority of Miss Harman at all. But if so, The Times
reporter, Frances Gibb, got it wrong also. For on the day after the judgment was given
The Times said (10th May 1980):

'The National Council for Civil Liberties (NCCL) took up the case of one of the
prisoners who had been in the control unit, Mr Michael Williams, and embarked on
a five-year struggle to obtain the necessary documents to enable it to bring an
action. The Home Office unsuccessfully resisted handing over the papers. "Quite
apart from the case", Miss Harriet Harman, NCCL's legal officer, says, "we achieved
a milestone ruling when the court said it was in the public interest for us to have
those papers. There has been no previous case involving the disclosure of papers at
that level of decision-making and we now have a case study as to how such high-
level policy is arrived at". The papers, which provide details of discussions between
Home Office officials, showed how the idea of a control unit came about.'

The inference

It is all very well for Miss Harman to disclaim the statements made by those reporters,
but I draw the inference that she led them to believe that she, on behalf of the NCCL, had
obtained the disclosure of these documents, that it was a legal milestone on disclosure,
that it was 'in the public interest' for the NCCL to have them and that the NCCL could
use them as 'a case study as to how such high-level policy is arrived at'.

Note that there is no hint in the newspapers that the documents were read out in open

court. The reporters inferred that, by the disclosure, the NCCL were at liberty to use the
a documents as they wished, by showing them to reporters or by using them themselves
as a case study.

Now if that be the right inference it seems to me that Miss Harman was under a grave
misapprehension. She treated herself as bringing this action for the NCCL whereas she
was bringing it for Michael Williams. She was being paid by the legal aid fund. The
documents were disclosed to her, as solicitor for Michael Williams, not as solicitor for the
b NCCL. She ought to have confined the use of the documents to him and his action and
not to have handed them over, from herself as his solicitor, to herself as solicitor to the
NCCL. It was the very thing that the Treasury Solicitor had feared in his letter of 17th
October 1979: 'My client would not wish the documents to be used for the general
purposes of the N.C.C.L. outside your function as a solicitor for the plaintiff.'

On the facts thus far I am clearly of opinion that Miss Harman did not confine her use
c of the documents to use in the action: she used or authorised their use for the purposes
of reproduction in the press.

Her defence

The defence of Miss Harman is simple. These documents were read out in open court
by counsel whom she instructed for the plaintiff. Once read out in court, they became
d in the public domain. If the shorthand writer had taken down the words and reproduced
them in a transcript, they would have been available for all the world to use. So why
should they not be available from the documents themselves in her office?

That is the argument which has been put forward by the press and by some peers in
the House of Lords. It has been reinforced by affidavits by some of the most
distinguished men of our time: Lord Goodman, the Master of University College,
e Oxford; Lord Hutchinson of Lullington whom we all hold in high esteem; and Mr
Harold Evans, the editor of the Sunday Times. Each says that there is a long-standing
practice of showing documents to members of the press which have been read out in
open court so as to verify what has been said or to assist accurate reporting.

This contention is said to be derived from the principle stated by Lord Halsbury in
Scott v Scott [1913] AC 417 at 440, [1911–13] All ER Rep 1 at 11: '... every Court of
f Justice is open to every subject of the King.' So it is said that every document read out
aloud in a court of justice is available to every subject of the Queen, in the court at the
time, or outside it anywhere at any time thereafter; or if not to everyone, at any rate to
every reporter or journalist. The document, however confidential beforehand, loses all
confidentiality once it is read aloud in court. The owner of it retains his copyright; and
any person defamed retains his action for libel. But the owner of the confidentiality loses
g all claim for breach of confidence.

I cannot accept this argument for one moment. It is one of our fundamental human
rights that everyone has a right to privacy, included in which is a right to respect for his
confidential documents. This can be overridden in the interests of justice. It was so
overridden in our present case when the court ordered the Home Office to disclose these
thousands of documents to Michael Williams so that justice might be done in the action
h he had brought. This overriding meant that the documents could be read in open court
to the judge who had to try the case. It meant that those present could listen; that the
reporters could take down what was said; and could make from their notes a fair and
accurate report of the proceedings. But nothing more. It did *not* mean that there could
be any further use of the confidential documents or any further dissemination of their
contents without the consent of the owner. It is of no use to plead the freedom of the
j press. That freedom is itself subject to restriction. The press is not free to publish
confidential documents without the consent of the owner. Save when the interest of the
owner in keeping them confidential is outweighed by the public interest in having the
matter made public (see the recent case of the Primodos affair, *Schering Chemicals Ltd v
Falkman Ltd* p 321, ante). I can see no public interest whatever in having these highly

confidential documents made public. Quite the other way. It was in the public interest
that these documents should be kept confidential. They should not be exposed to the *a*
ravages of outsiders. I regard the use made by the journalist in this case of these
documents to be highly detrimental to the good ordering of our society. They were used
so as to launch a wholly unjustified attack on Ministers of State and high civil servants,
who were only doing their very best to deal with a wicked criminal who had harassed
society and was serving a long sentence for armed robbery. For this use I think that Miss
Harman was herself responsible. It was a gross breach of the undertaking which she *b*
impliedly gave to the court and affirmed in writing to the Treasury Solicitor. That
undertaking was to use the documents solely for the purpose of the action of Michael
Williams against the Home Office. Instead, she used them for the purposes of this
organisation called the National Council for Civil Liberties: and that organisation made
them available for use by a journalist; and he, whilst the case was still sub judice, wrote
an article prejudging the outcome most unfairly. It makes me regret that the court ever *c*
ordered disclosure of the documents. The 'legal milestone' will have to be taken up and
set back a bit.

Conclusion

I would follow the wise words of Lord Wilberforce in *Burmah Oil Co Ltd v Bank of
England* [1979] 3 All ER 700 at 707, [1980] AC 1090 at 1112. When ministers and high *d*
civil servants are forming important governmental policy, their discussions and their
memoranda are, and should be, treated as highly confidential. No court should order the
disclosure of these confidential documents to outsiders, even in the interests of justice,
except under the most stringent safeguards against abuse. The danger of disclosure is
that critics of one political colour or another will seize on this confidential information
so as to seek changes in governmental policy, or to condemn it. So the machinery of *e*
government will be hampered or even thwarted. In our present case it was thought that
the implied undertaking, as confirmed in *Riddick's* case, provided a sufficient safeguard
against abuse. Unfortunately events have proved otherwise. The disclosure of
confidential documents was abused. It was abused by Miss Harman. She allowed a
journalist to have free access to the confidential documents, not caring how he would use
them. To my mind her part in this, her conduct, was not 'extremely trivial' as The Times *f*
described it. It was a 'serious contempt', as the judge said. It was a serious contempt by
a solicitor of the Supreme Court, which is much to be regretted. The criticisms directed
against the judge and his judgment were quite unfounded. I would dismiss the appeal.

TEMPLEMAN LJ. A person who owns a document may keep that document and its
contents secret and private. A person who owns the copyright in the contents of a *g*
document may prevent the republication of those contents. The owner of the document
and the owner of the copyright are not necessarily the same person. Both the right to
privacy and copyright are only exercisable subject to laws of disclosure which, for
example, require publication of copies of the accounts of limited companies, and copies
of wills which have been proved, and copies of minutes of certain public authorities.

The laws of procedure relating to litigation also require limitations on the right to *h*
privacy and copyright. Every party to an action must disclose all documents in his
possession or power relating to the matters in issue in the action, must allow the other
parties to inspect those documents and to take copies of them and to make use of the
documents and the copies and the contents for the purposes of the action in which they
are revealed. As Lord Denning MR said in *Riddick v Thames Board Mills* [1977] 3 All ER
677 at 687, [1977] QB 881 at 895: *j*

> 'The reason for compelling discovery of documents . . . lies in the public interest
> in discovering the truth so that justice may be done between the parties. That
> public interest is to be put into the scales against the public interest in preserving

privacy and protecting confidential information. The balance comes down in the
ordinary way in favour of the public interest of discovering the truth, ie in making
full disclosure.'

But, Lord Denning MR went on, once discovery has enabled the relevant action to be
disposed of, the public interest 'has served its purpose'. Discovery, Lord Denning MR
said—

'was obtained by compulsion. Compulsion is an invasion of a private right to
keep one's documents to oneself. The public interest in privacy and confidence
demands that this compulsion should not be pressed further than the course of
justice requires. The courts should, therefore, not allow the other party, or anyone
else, to use the documents for any ulterior or alien purpose. Otherwise the courts
themselves would be doing injustice ... In order to encourage openness and
fairness, the public interest requires that documents disclosed on discovery are not
to be made use of except for the purposes of the action in which they are disclosed.'

The court therefore implies an undertaking by a litigant that he will make use of his
opponent's documents only for the purpose of the action and for no other purpose: see
Riddick's case and the authorities there cited ([1977] 3 All ER 677 at 687–688, [1977] QB
881 at 895–896).

The question raised on this appeal is whether the undertaking by a litigant not to
make use of his opponent's documents save for the purposes of the action in which they
are revealed ceases to bind the litigant if and as soon as and to the extent that the contents
of a document thus disclosed are spoken aloud in open court.

Mr Williams sued the Home Office for false imprisonment and other torts. The
Home Office disclosed 6,800 pages of documents. The material parts of some 800 pages
were quoted in the course of the trial. So far as the 6,000 pages which were not quoted
are concerned, it is conceded that any copies made to assist Mr Williams in the course of
the action must be returned to the Home Office or must be destroyed or at any rate must
be kept safely so that the contents can never be referred to or summarised or used in any
way by anybody without the permission of the Home Office. So far as the 800 pages are
concerned, it is contended that the copies in the possession of Mr Williams may, subject
to the law of copyright and defamation, be used by anybody for any purpose.

It is common ground that the 800 pages of documents have been used for purposes
other than use in Mr Williams's action. If the appellant's submissions are correct, the
purpose for which the copies of the 800 Home Office pages obtained by Mr Williams
could be used or were used are quite irrelevant. It does not matter that Mr Williams to
whom discovery was made was a former convict, or that the defendants to that action
who gave discovery were the Home Office, or that the documents disclosed included
official memoranda and not love letters, or that Miss Harman the solicitor acting for Mr
Williams was also legal adviser to the NCCL, or that Miss Harman, with or without the
consent of her client, showed copies of the 800 pages to a journalist with or without the
hope or expectation that the journalist would write an article attacking the Home Office,
or that the journalist wrote an article without waiting to see the judgment then
undelivered in the action, or that Mr Williams failed in the action.

If the undertaking was automatically released when the contents of the documents
were spoken aloud in court, then, subject to the laws of copyright and defamation, Mr
Williams can do as he pleases with the copies of the relevant Home Office documents
obtained on his behalf for the purposes of the action and quoted in court. Mr Williams
could, for example, sell his copies to the highest bidder and that possibility is also
irrelevant if the undertaking ceased to have effect when the documents were read. If
quotation in open court totally destroys privacy, the result must be the same in any
action and in any circumstances, subject to the right of the court to forbid the

dissemination of any particular piece of information which on grounds of national
security or on any other exceptional grounds the court decides to conceal.   *a*

On behalf of Miss Harman it is submitted that the undertaking implied by a litigant
who receives copies of his opponent's documents on discovery is that 'I will only use this
document and its contents for the purposes of this action unless and until and to the
extent that the contents are read out in open court'.

It is not contended that the undertaking is released in respect of any document which
is not read out in open court or in respect of any part of a document which is not read out *b*
in open court. If the judge reads the whole or part of a document to himself, the
undertaking is not thereby released. The undertaking, it is said, ceases to apply, but only
ceases to apply, to every word which is spoken aloud in court by counsel, witness or judge
and which consists of a direct quotation from a document disclosed on discovery.

This submission is sought to be justified by three alternative but cumulative reasons,
firstly on idealistic grounds, secondly on cynical grounds, and thirdly on grounds of *c*
convenience.

The idealistic ground is based on the undoubted principle that, subject to limited
exceptions not here relevant, it is a cardinal rule of the administration of justice in this
country that trials should be held in public: see *Scott v Scott* [1913] AC 417 at 441–442,
[1911–13] All ER Rep 1 at 11–12 and *Baker v Bethnal Green Corpn* [1945] 1 All ER 135 at
143–144. Proceedings in open court ensure that justice is done and is seen to be done and *d*
that the public may be able to ponder whether justice has in fact been done. Not only are
proceedings held in open court but, for similar reasons, anyone can attend and memorise
and make notes and obtain transcripts of the proceedings if any be available. The court
does not, save in exceptional circumstances, impose any restrictions on publicity, or
dissemination of information or comment, good or bad.

Therefore, it is said, a party to an action is freed from any undertaking with regard to *e*
his opponent's documents once they have been quoted in open court. It is not suggested
that a litigant is under a duty to make freely available documents or copies of documents
to to give any information concerning documents which are quoted in open court,
whether those documents belong to the litigant himself or to his opponent. Quotation
of a document in open court, it is said, confers a power but not a duty on a litigant to
make his opponent's documents available to the public and also confers on the litigant, *f*
subject to the limitations of defamation and copyright, powers to exploit his copies of his
opponent's documents for purposes far removed from the administration of justice.

In my judgment, if the public interest does not require the parties to private litigation
to make their documents freely available, then the public interest does not require a
party to private litigation to be freed from an undertaking that he will not use his
opponent's documents save for the purposes of the action. The rule that court *g*
proceedings must be held in public should not be exploited for purposes which have
nothing to do with the administration of justice, even if an air of respectability is claimed
for that exploitation by the argument, good or bad, that the public interest requires the
invention of some method of enforcing the principle of freedom of information against
public authorities. That is an argument for Parliament, not for the courts.

The cynical ground is based on the undoubted fact that the contents of any document *h*
quoted in court may, so far as they are quoted in court, be obtainable by personal
attendance or by means of a transcript. Therefore, it is said, there is no point in
continuing the undertaking by a litigant that he will not use that document save for the
purposes of the action. But in my judgment the litigant is in a special position.
Successful or unsuccessful, he has been enabled to break down the barriers of privacy for
one limited purpose only, namely to assist him in obtaining justice in the action. For *j*
that purpose and for no other purpose he has been able to obtain copies of documents and
he should not be able to exploit those documents for his own purposes. He is entitled at
his discretion to read documents in open court even though they may later be held to be
irrelevant or inadmissible. He is given a powerful weapon which enables him to invade

privacy in the interests of justice. He should not be free to use that weapon himself for
a any other purpose. Once a document has been used to win or lose an action, a litigant
should be in no different position from any other member of the public.

The ground of convenience is limited to journalists and reporters. It is suggested that,
in the interests of ensuring that accurate information is available to journalists and
reporters to enable them to inform and comment, a litigant should be entitled but not
bound to disclose his own and his opponent's documents, limited, so far as the opponent's
b documents are concerned, to such of them or such parts of them as have been read in
open court. In the course of the argument in this court a distinction was sought to be
drawn between journalists and reporters in general, and feature writers and law reporters
in particular. For present purposes I find it impossible to make any logical or identifiable
distinction. Again it is accepted that no party to litigation can be obliged to assist a
journalist or a reporter. If permission to use a document or a copy of a document must,
c as is conceded, be obtained from one party to the litigation, I see no reason why
permission should not be required from the party who owns the document. Permission
will rarely be refused, especially if the information can be obtained from a transcript;
but, if the permission of the owner of the document is withheld, I cannot accept that
permission can be granted by his opponent who is only in possession of a copy of the
document for a limited purpose which has been fulfilled.

d I have dealt with this appeal as a matter of principle; but, on the merits of this
particular appeal, I agree with Lord Denning MR that this was a serious contempt
especially in the light of the earlier correspondence with the Home Office. I think Miss
Harman ought to have consulted the Home Office and taken advice before acting as she
did. She presented the Home Office with a fait accompli. I too would dismiss the appeal.

e **DUNN LJ.** I agree with both judgments. To my mind this case has nothing whatever
to do with the freedom of the press or the freedom of communication. The *Williams* trial
was a public trial, and anything said in open court was available for publication or
comment subject to the law. Every word was recorded and the public including the
press were fully entitled to be present, to take notes and to buy a copy of the transcript
of the whole trial if they wished. This case is, however, very much concerned with the
f conduct of a solicitor engaged in litigation on behalf of a client. Such a solicitor is in a
powerful and privileged position. He or she has in his possession private and confidential
documents belonging to the other party to the litigation, which have only come into his
possession in his capacity as an officer of the court because of the Rules of the Supreme
Court, or because the court has ordered that they shall be disclosed. The fact that some
or all of those documents may be read out in open court is neither here nor there so far
g as the solicitor is concerned. It is no part of the duty of a solicitor to assist the press or
anyone else by providing information from documents which have been disclosed to
him in his capacity as a solicitor. He is the agent of his client and the documents came
into the possession of the client on the same basis and for the same reason.

If after documents have been read out in open court the client to whom they have
been disclosed or his solicitor were free to make such use of them as he pleased the public
h would soon lose confidence in the administration of justice, and the process of discovery,
an essential adjunct to civil proceedings in this country, would be likely to fall into
disrepute and become more difficult and less effective. Parties would have a strong
disincentive to disclose their own documents.

None of this affects the right of any member of the public, including the press, if they
are sufficiently interested, to take notes of documents read out in court, or, as I have said,
i to buy a copy of the transcript. But the party to whom they are disclosed and his solicitor
in return for their special right to the disclosure of the documents in the first place have
the corresponding obligation not to use them at any time except for the purposes of the
action.

It is said that the rulings of Park J as to the extent of the implied obligation on the person to whom the discovery is given would inhibit law reporting and the bona fide reporting of fair and accurate reports of the trial. I do not believe that for one moment, *a* and I think that this part of the case has been much exaggerated in the affidavits we have read and at the bar. If a reporter wishes to check the date of a document referred to in evidence, or the exact wording of a document, he or she can always ask the counsel or solicitor for the party who has disclosed the document. I have never known such a request to be refused even in respect of private and confidential documents. And there is no reason why such a request should be refused. It is said that it would be undesirable *b* and confusing if counsel or solicitor for the person to whom a document had been disclosed were by showing it to a law reporter to commit a contempt of court. I do not foresee any such problem in practice. The mere showing of a document which had been used in court to a reporter for the purpose of checking it would in my view either be subject to the de minimis principle or would at most be a technical contempt. But that is not what we are dealing with. We are dealing here with a solicitor who quite *c* deliberately allowed a journalist to inspect and make notes of 800 documents.

The Home Office believe Miss Harman acted in good faith in disclosing the documents to Mr Leigh, and the judge was willing to regard himself as bound by that opinion, although in contempt proceedings all matters are for the court and not for the party bringing the contempt proceedings. It depends of course what one means by good faith. If in the context of this case it means that when she gave the assurance in her letter *d* of 17th October 1979 Miss Harman honestly believed that the assurance was limited to documents which were not read out in court, and ceased to operate as soon as any document was read out in court, then I find it extraordinarily naive. I agree with the finding of the judge. He said:

'[Miss Harman's] failure to seek the consent of the Home Office to the proposed disclosure [was] unquestionably due to the fact that she knew that any hint of her *e* intention would have resulted in an immediate application to the trial judge for an injunction which would have been granted.'

I agree with the judge that this was a serious contempt of court by a solicitor in breach not only of the implied obligation relating to discovery but also of an express assurance that she had given in her capacity as a solicitor. She acted unprofessionally and *f* irresponsibly. I would dismiss this appeal.

Appeal dismissed. Leave to appeal to the House of Lords refused.

19th February. The Court of Appeal (Lord Denning MR, Templeman and Dunn LJJ) certified, under ss 1(2) and 13(1), (2)(c) and (4) of the Administration of Justice Act 1960, that the *g* *following point of law of general public importance was involved in the decision: whether a litigant's obligation or undertaking, implied by law in respect of the use which may be made of any of his opponent's documents disclosed on discovery in the action, is correctly defined as terminating if and when and to the extent that any such document is read out in open court in the course of proceedings in that action, or is otherwise affected by such reading out.*

9th April. The Appeal Committee of the House of Lords granted Miss Harman leave to appeal.

Solicitors: *Seifert, Sedley & Co* (for Miss Harman); *Treasury Solicitor.*

Frances Rustin   Barrister.

a

Nickerson v Barraclough and others

COURT OF APPEAL, CIVIL DIVISION

BUCKLEY, EVELEIGH AND BRIGHTMAN LJJ

8th, 9th, 10th, 11th, 12th, 15th DECEMBER 1980

b *Easement – Way of necessity – Express term in grant of land excluding any right of way – Sale of building plot – Plot part of building estate – Plan to conveyance of plot showing proposed estate roads – Plot adjoining unmade lane shown on conveyance plan as proposed road – Conveyance stipulating that no right of way over any proposed road until made up – Whether public policy preventing exclusion of way of necessity over unmade lane for building purposes – Whether right of way over lane ought to be implied into conveyance.*

c

Easement – Right of way – Creation – Right of way to one plot of land used as means of access to another plot lying beyond it – First plot intended as estate road servicing building plot lying beyond it – Implied grant of right of way over lane to first plot – Whether implied grant including grant of right of way to plot lying beyond it because first plot forming means of access to second d *plot – Whether implied grant of right of way to first plot including grant to second plot because intended purpose of first plot was to service second plot – Law of Property Act 1925, s 62(1).*

In 1900 a building estate which had been divided into individual building plots was put up for sale by auction. The plan attached to the auction particulars and conditions showed the estate as being intersected by several proposed roads. By a conveyance made e in 1900 X acquired five of the plots, including plot 77 which adjoined the site of the proposed east-west estate road. The conveyance contained an express grant to X of a right of way for all purposes over the east-west road. In 1901 X acquired plot 78 which was alongside plot 77. By a further conveyance made in 1906 X acquired plot 78A which lay between plot 78 to the west and an unmade lane belonging to the vendor (the estate f owner) to the east. The lane, which ran northwards into a public highway, was shown on the plan to the 1906 conveyance as a proposed north-south estate road. The 1906 conveyance recited the auction particulars and conditions and contemplated that X would build on plot 78A. Although plot 78A was bounded to the north by the site of the proposed east-west road and to the east by the lane, and was divided from the lane by a ditch over which there was, in the north-east corner of plot 78A, an eight foot sleeper g bridge leading to the lane, the 1906 conveyance did not expressly grant any rights of way giving access to plot 78A. Furthermore, the conveyance contained an express stipulation that the vendor 'did not undertake to make any of the proposed new roads shewn on the [plan to the conveyance] nor did he give any rights of way over the same until the same should (if ever) be made'. X did not build on plot 78A and it remained a field and was used for agricultural purposes and as a sports ground. From at least 1921 the lane and h bridge were used as a means of access to plot 78A for those purposes. The site of the unmade east-west road was also used as a means of access from the lane and as a means of access to plot 78A. By a conveyance made in 1922 X acquired the site of the east-west road ('the strip') to add to plot 78A. By subsequent conveyances the enlarged plot 78A became vested in the plaintiff. The lane, which remained unmade, became vested in the defendants. They attempted to prevent the plaintiff from exercising any right of way j from the enlarged plot 78A over the bridge and the lane. The plaintiff brought an action against them claiming that she was entitled to a right of way for all purposes over the bridge and the lane to the highway. Although she did not plead that plot 78A had become landlocked by virtue of the 1906 conveyance, she claimed that she was entitled to such a right of way because (i) such a right ought to be implied as a matter of necessity into the 1906 conveyance or (ii) alternatively, such a right had become vested in her by

virtue of the 1922 conveyance and s 62(1)^a of the Law of Property Act 1925 since, by
virtue of s 62(1), a right of way from the lane onto the strip was deemed to be granted by *a*
the 1922 conveyance because at the time of that conveyance such a right appertained to,
or was reputed to appertain to, or was enjoyed with, the strip, and, as the strip was used
as a means of access to plot 78A, the deemed right of way could be used also for the
benefit of plot 78A. The judge ([1979] 3 All ER 312) held (i) that for public policy
reasons, namely that land should not be made unusable, the prohibition on the grant of
rights of way over the proposed new roads until they were made up contained in the *b*
stipulation in the 1906 conveyance did not negative the implication in that conveyance
of the grant of a right of way over the lane to plot 78A and that, in the circumstances,
based on necessity, public policy required the implication of the grant of a right of way
over the lane for building purposes to give effect to the parties' intention that plot 78A
was to be used to build on, and (ii) that the 1922 conveyance of the strip carried with it,
by virtue of s 62(1), a right of access to the lane for the benefit of the strip for agricultural *c*
and sporting purposes, and as the strip was itself used as a means of access to plot 78A the
1922 conveyance also carried with it by virtue of s 62(1) a similar right for the benefit of
plot 78A. The defendants appealed. They conceded that the plaintiff was entitled to a
limited right of way, namely for agricultural and sporting purposes, over the bridge and
the lane to the highway, but sought to confine it to a right of way for those purposes only,
and over a bridge limited to a width of eight feet, which thus precluded a right of way *d*
for other purposes such as the transport of building materials to the enlarged plot 78A or
as an accommodation road when that plot was built on. By a respondent's notice the
plaintiff sought to contend on the appeal that the enlarged plot 78A was, by virtue of the
1922 conveyance and s 62(1), entitled to a right of way for all purposes over the bridge
and lane to the highway (i) because the 1922 conveyance and s 62(1) had the effect of
impliedly granting such a right for the benefit of plot 78A as well as for the strip, since *e*
the strip was used as a means of access to plot 78A at the time of the conveyance, or (ii)
alternatively, because one of the purposes of the strip, as a proposed road, was to service
the building estate of which plot 78A formed part and therefore, when the lane became
available, by virtue of the 1922 conveyance and s 62(1), as a right of way for the purposes
of the strip, it also became available for the building purposes of plot 78A since those were
purposes of the strip. *f*

Held – (1) The doctrine of a way of necessity was not founded on public policy but on
implication into the document granting the land from the circumstances, namely that
the parties intended that a way giving access to the land conveyed should be granted
because, unless it was, the land would be inaccessible. Moreover, since the construction
of the document granting the land (with which the implication of a way of necessity had *g*
to be associated) depended on ascertaining the parties' intentions, public policy was not
relevant to the construction of the document unless the court was required to frustrate
the parties' intention because it was against public policy. It followed that public policy
could not influence the construction of the 1906 conveyance in regard to any implied
grant of a right of way (see p 379 *b* to *f*, p 383 *j* and p 384 *a* to *d* and *f*, post); *Proctor v
Hodgson* (1855) 10 Exch 824, *Wilkes v Greenway* (1890) 6 TLR 449 and *North Sydney* *h*
Printing Pty Ltd v Sabemo Investments Corpn Pty Ltd [1971] 2 NSWLR 150 applied.
    (2) Since the pleadings did not allege that plot 78A became landlocked on the occasion
of the 1906 conveyance (and in the absence of such an allegation the action was not
concerned with a way of necessity strictly so called), the question for decision in regard
to the 1906 conveyance was what rights of way it was necessary to imply into the *j*

---

a Section 62(1), so far as material, provides: 'A conveyance of land shall be deemed to include and
    shall by virtue of this Act operate to convey, with the land, all . . . easements, rights, and
    advantages . . . appertaining or reputed to appertain to the land, or any part thereof, or, at the time
    of conveyance, demised, occupied, or enjoyed with or reputed or known as part or parcel of or
    appurtenant to the land or any part thereof.'

conveyance, as a matter of construction, against the background of the sale of a large

a number of individual building plots and the consequent inference that the purchaser of any plot should have access to a proposed estate road, and having regard to the purpose of the 1906 conveyance, which was to enable plot 78A to be developed. Accordingly, despite the express stipulation in the conveyance that X was not to have any right of way over the lane until it was made into a road, there was to be implied into the conveyance, in view of the background to and purpose of the conveyance, some provision for access

b to plot 78A. However (per Brightman and Buckley LJJ), in view of the stipulation, the implication to be made had to be that which involved the least incursion onto the lane as a proposed road not yet made up, and accordingly a provision was to be implied into the 1906 conveyance that X should have the right to use his existing easement of way over the site of the east-west road, granted to him as the purchaser of plot 77 by the 1900 conveyance, for the benefit of plot 78A as an additional dominant tenement in regard to

c that easement, but a provision could not be implied into the 1906 conveyance granting a right of way for all purposes over the lane because that would involve a major incursion onto a proposed new road which had not been made up, and (per Eveleigh LJ) the route to be implied had to be indicated by the grantor, but, in view of the limited user of the land for agricultural and sporting purposes, a right of way for wider purposes, ie for building operations, had not been impliedly granted by the 1906 conveyance. It

d followed that the plaintiff's right over the lane was limited to the right of way conceded, namely for the purposes of agriculture and sport only. The appeal would accordingly be allowed (see p 376 b to d and j to p 377 a, p 379 g h, p 380 a to j, p 382 g to p 383 e and p 384 a and d to f, post).

(3) Furthermore, the plaintiff's submission in her respondent's notice that she had a right of way for all purposes over the lane by virtue of the 1922 conveyance and s 62(1)

e of the 1925 Act also failed because (a) s 62(1) could not have the effect of making land which was not the subject matter of a conveyance a dominant tenement in relation to an easement deemed by s 62(1) to have been granted by the conveyance, and accordingly the right of way over the lane deemed to be granted by the 1922 conveyance for the benefit of the strip could not be deemed to be granted also for the benefit of plot 78A since plot 78A was not comprised in the 1922 conveyance, and (per Eveleigh LJ) as s 62(1) only

f passed that which actually existed at the time of the conveyance, and the way proved to exist at the time of the 1922 conveyance was limited to a way for agricultural and sporting purposes, a wider right of way for all purposes could not pass by virtue of the 1922 conveyance and s 62(1), and (b) s 62(1) was concerned only with an advantage which could properly be regarded as appertaining or reputed to appertain to or enjoyed with the land conveyed at the time of the conveyance and not with the grantor's future purposes

g in regard to the land conveyed, and therefore, because in 1922 the strip had not been laid out as a road and plot 78A had not been built on, it could not be contended that the right of way over the lane for the purposes of the strip, deemed to be granted by the 1922 conveyance, also became available, by virtue of the 1922 conveyance, for the purposes of plot 78A (see p 381 j to p 382 g, p 383 g to j and p 384 a and f, post).

Per Eveleigh LJ. Public policy can, in rare cases, aid in the construction of a

h conveyance, namely where the scales are equally balanced between two different meanings of the conveyance, for then it is right to attribute to the intention of the parties that meaning which offends least against public policy (see p 383 j to p 384 a, post).

Decision of Sir Robert Megarry V-C [1979] 3 All ER 312 reversed.

Notes

j For easements of necessity, for non-derogation from grant, for ascertainment of the extent and nature of an easement and for the effect of s 62 of the Law of Property Act 1925 on conveyances, see 14 Halsbury's Laws (4th Edn) paras 29, 37, 54, 55, and for cases on those subjects, see 19 Digest (Repl) 106–110, 114–117, 38–40, 637–674, 708–723, 202–205.

For the Law of Property Act 1925, s 62, see 27 Halsbury's Statutes (3rd Edn) 438.

Cases referred to in judgments

Gayford v Moffatt (1868) 4 Ch App 133, 33 JP 212, LC, 19 Digest (Repl) 47, 249.

Harris v Flower (1904) 74 LJ Ch 127, 91 LT 816, CA, 19 Digest (Repl) 119, 738.

North Sydney Printing Pty Ltd v Sabemo Investments Corpn Pty Ltd [1971] 2 NSWLR 150.

Proctor v Hodgson (1855) 10 Exch 824, 3 CLR 755, 24 LJ Ex 195, 156 ER 674, 19 Digest (Repl) 57, 312.

Wilkes v Greenway (1890) 6 TLR 449, CA, 19 Digest (Repl) 107, 649.

Cases also cited

Barry v Hasseldine [1952] 2 All ER 317, [1952] Ch 835.

Brown v Alabaster (1887) 37 Ch D 490.

Brown v Burdett (1882) 21 Ch D 667.

Crabb v Arun District Council [1975] 3 All ER 865, [1976] Ch 179, CA.

Dutton v Tayler (1700) 2 Lut 1487, 125 ER 819.

Egerton v Earl Brownlow (1853) 4 HL Cas 1, [1843–60] All ER Rep 970, HL.

Gerard (Lord) and London and North Western Railway Co's arbitration, Re [1895] 1 QB 459, [1895–9] All ER Rep 1144, CA.

Holmes v Goring (1824) 2 Bing 76, 130 ER 233.

Jorden v Attwood (1605) Owen 121, 74 ER 945.

Keefe v Amor [1964] 2 All ER 517, [1965] 1 QB 334, CA.

London Corpn v Riggs (1880) 13 Ch D 798.

Menzies v Breadalbase (No 2) (1901) 4 F (Ct of Sess) 59.

Midland Railway Co v Miles (1886) 33 Ch D 632.

Newcomen v Coulson (1877) 5 Ch D 133, CA.

Packer v Welstead (1658) 2 Sid 111, 82 ER 1284.

Parry and Daggs, Re (1885) 31 Ch D 130, CA.

Pearson v Spencer (1863) 3 B & S 761, 122 ER 285, Ex Ch.

Pinnington v Galland (1853) 9 Exch 1, 156 ER 1.

Pomfret v Ricroft (1669) 1 Wms Saund 321, 85 ER 454.

Pwllbach Colliery Co Ltd v Woodman [1915] AC 634, [1914–15] All ER Rep 124, HL.

Reignolds v Edwards (1741) Willes 282, 125 ER 1173.

Serff v Acton Local Board (1886) 31 Ch D 679.

Shannon Ltd v Venner Ltd [1965] 1 All ER 590, [1965] Ch 682, CA.

Thorpe v Brumfitt (1873) 8 Ch App 650, LJJ.

Wheeldon v Burrows (1879) 12 Ch D 31, [1874–80] All ER Rep 669, CA.

Williams v James (1867) LR 2 CP 577.

Wong v Beaumont Trust Ltd [1964] 2 All ER 119, [1965] 1 QB 173, CA.

Appeal

The defendants, Terence Alfred Joseph Barraclough, John Letten Mountain and John Thomas Roberts, appealed against that part of the order of Sir Robert Megarry V-C ([1979] 3 All ER 312, [1980] Ch 325) made on 19th March 1979, which declared that the plaintiff, Mrs Erna Nickerson, was entitled to a right of way from her land ('the pink land') in the Parish of New Waltham in the county of Lincoln, over a bridge across a ditch at the corner of her land and over a road known as Scouts Lane to the point at which it joined a public highway, Humberston Avenue, for herself and her servants and licensees on foot and with horses and other animals, carriages, motor vehicles or other conveyances at all times and for all purposes. The grounds of the appeal were (1) that on the true construction of a conveyance dated 8th December 1906 there was no implied grant to the plaintiff's predecessor in title of any right of way over Scouts Lane, (2) that by para 7 of Sch 1 to the 1906 conveyance the grant of any such right of way was expressly negatived, (3) that the judge erred in law in holding that public policy was relevant to the question whether a right of way over Scouts Lane was granted by the 1906 conveyance, (4) that in particular the judge erred in law in holding that public policy (i) required that the conveyance should not be treated as depriving the plaintiff's land of a suitable means of

access or (ii) required or justified that the conveyance be construed in a sense other than
a that in which it would be construed without resort to the principle of public policy or
(iii) required that para 7 of Sch 1 to the conveyance should not take effect so as to negative
the implied grant of a way of necessity, (5) that the judge erred in law in holding that if
the conveyance resulted in the pink land being conveyed to the plaintiff's predecessor in
title without the benefit of a means of access to it, that constituted a derogation from
grant on the part of the vendor in the 1906 conveyance, and (6) that, accordingly, the
b plaintiff was entitled only to such a right of way over Scouts Lane as had been acquired
by her predecessors in title by prescription, or by virtue of a conveyance dated 28th April
1922 and s 62 of the Law of Property Act 1925, namely a right of way from the pink land
over a bridge confined to the width of eight feet to Scouts Lane and over the lane only as
a means of access to and from the pink land for ordinary agricultural purposes and as a
sports ground for amateur sports. By a respondent's notice the plaintiff gave notice that
c on the hearing of the appeal she would submit that by virtue of the 1922 conveyance and
s 62(1) of the 1925 Act there was a right of way for all purposes over the bridge and Scouts
Lane to Humberston Avenue which became vested in the plaintiff as if the right had
been expressly conveyed to her. The facts are set out in the judgment of Brightman LJ.

Peter Millett QC and *F M Ferris QC* for the defendants.
d *Paul V Baker QC* and *Spencer G Maurice* for the plaintiff.

BRIGHTMAN LJ delivered the first judgment at the invitation of Buckley LJ. This
is an appeal by the first defendant from a decision of Sir Robert Megarry V-C ([1979] 3
All ER 312, [1980] Ch 325) relating to a claim by the plaintiff to a right of way over the
defendant's land. The plaintiff is the owner of a field at New Waltham in Lincolnshire.
e According to the pleadings the field is at present used by the plaintiff as a paddock. A
ditch runs along the east side of the field; the ditch is spanned by a bridge at the north-
east corner of the field. The bridge was constructed in or before 1908. It was first made
of old railway sleepers and was 8 feet wide. It was replaced by a more substantial
structure in the early 1970s. The bridge gives access to a road known as Scouts Lane,
which runs parallel to the ditch and to the side of the field. Scouts Lane belongs to the
f defendants. The lane goes northwards and joins the public highway, Humberston
Avenue, at a distance of about 150 yards from the corner of the field; Humberston
Avenue runs east and west. Sir Robert Megarry V-C held that there was, appurtenant to
the field, a right of way for all purposes over the bridge and along Scouts Lane.
    I shall call the field 'the pink land'. The defendants do not, so far as this appeal is
concerned, seek to challenge the existence of a right of way. They seek to limit it in two
g respects, by confining the width of any bridge to 8 feet and by restricting user to a means
of access to the pink land 'for ordinary agricultural purposes and as a sports ground for
the playing of amateur sports and games'. The limitation sought to be imposed would,
for example, preclude the use of Scouts Lane for the transport of building materials to the
pink land or the use of Scouts Lane as an accommodation road to the pink land once it
was built on.
h   None of the conveyancing documents contain any express grant of a right of way over
Scouts Lane for the benefit of the pink land. The right of way, whatever may be its
extent, must depend on implication or prescription in some form.
    The pink land and Scouts Lane originally formed part of the Carrington Settled
Estates. At the beginning of this century an area to the north and south of Humberston
Avenue began to be laid out in building plots. We are concerned only with the plots
i which lie to the south of Humberston Avenue. The western boundary of this part of the
area was delineated as a proposed 36 foot road running north and south, which later
became Enfield Avenue. The plots numbered 7 to 28 fronted on Humberston Avenue,
extending eastwards from the future Enfield Avenue. Immediately to the south of plots
7 to 28, in line with such plots so that they were back to back, were plots 45 to 66.
Immediately to the south of plots 45 to 66 and forming the southern boundary thereof,

there was delineated another 36 foot road, which I shall call 'the proposed east-west road'. Fronting on the southern verge of the proposed east-west road and lying immediately beneath plots 45, 46 and 47, plots 77 and 78 were later laid out. Plot 77, which tapered to the southward, was directly in line with plots 45 and 46. Plot 78 was in line with plot 47. Between plots 14 and 52 on one side and plots 15 and 53 on the other side, there was delineated a third proposed 36 foot road, which I shall call 'the original proposed north-south road'. This intersected the proposed east-west road. Between plot 78 and the proposed north-south road, in line with plots 48, 49, 50 and 51, was a field out of which the pink land was ultimately carved. There appears from the plan of the whole of the building estate to have been a total of seven proposed roads intersecting the estate.

I turn now to the conveyancing documents, the first of which was a conveyance of 20th September 1900. The owner of the Carrington Estates sold and conveyed to Mr George Alward plots 7 and 8, which lay in the corner between Humberston Avenue and the future Enfield Avenue, plots 45 and 46, which were to the south of, and in line with, plots 7 and 8, and plot 77, on the other side of the proposed east-west road, which was in the corner between that road and the future Enfield Avenue and in line with plots 45 and 46. This conveyance contained a grant of a right of way for all purposes 'over and along the proposed streets or roads adjoining the premises thereby conveyed shewn on the said Plan'. That is taken from an abstract which is marked as having been examined with the original in 1936. 'The said Plan' appears to have meant the plan to the particulars of sale which covered the whole area, and not the smaller plan which was drawn on the conveyance. In the result I apprehend that Mr Alward clearly acquired a right of way for all purposes over the future Enfield Avenue and the proposed east-west road, or at any rate the adjoining parts thereof, in connection with his enjoyment of the five plots conveyed to him. I think it is arguable that the right of way extended to the original proposed north-south road, since the expression 'all the proposed streets or roads' might be thought to apply to more proposed roads than two, in which case the word 'adjoining' would have been used in the broader sense of proximity. I mention this point only to dismiss it, because it need not be pursued. The site of the future Scouts Lane, which is the road we are concerned with, did not at the end of the day coincide with the site of the original proposed north-south road; that is a point which will become clearer a little later.

The next conveyancing document is dated 18th April 1901. By that conveyance Mr Alward acquired from the Carrington Estates plots 47 and 78, which were alongside plots 46 and 77, which he had previously acquired. This conveyance contained an identical grant of a right of way for all purposes over all the adjoining streets or roads, save that the examined abstract records the addition of the words 'when and so soon as the same shall have been made'. On the face of the conveyance that formulation purported to leave Mr Alward as the owner of plots 47 and 78, without any means of access thereto, for an undefined period. Admittedly he could pass on to such plots from plots 46 and 77 respectively, but he could not properly use plots 46 and 47 as a means of access to Humberston Avenue via the easement granted by the 1900 conveyance in the absence of an express or implied grant to that effect, because no conveyance expressly made plots 47 and 78 dominant tenements quoad such easement: see *Harris v Flower* (1904) 74 LJ Ch 127. Some implication needs to be made in the 1900 conveyance as a matter of business necessity in order to give a sensible meaning to the conveyance. Exactly what that implication should be does not arise for decision in this case. In fact, the grant by the 1901 conveyance of a contingent future easement of way was probably void for perpetuity, but that problem does not have any added significance.

Next comes the most important conveyance, which is dated 8th December 1906. Before I turn to its contents, it will be convenient to refer to the plan attached to it. This indicates the happening of two intermediate events: first, it seems that Mr Alward had acquired plot 9, fronting on to Humberston Avenue; secondly it indicates that the original proposed north-south road had been moved one plot westwards so as to run between plots 13 and 51 on one side and plots 14 and 52 on the other side. The proposed

north-south road in its new location came to be known as Scouts Lane, and it will be
convenient to refer to it by that name hereafter. Scouts Lane did not become a properly
made up road until 1963. In its early days it was a mere track; in the 1930s it was
roughly surfaced with clinker.

By the 1906 conveyance Mr Alward acquired the land lying between plot 78 to the
west and Scouts Lane to the east, known as plot 78A. The proposed east-west road formed
the northern boundary of the land and was not included in it. The southern boundary
of the land was in line with the southern boundaries of plots 77 and 78. There was also
conveyed to Mr Alward a strip of land 4 feet wide, going from the south-east corner of
plot 78A to the south-west corner of that plot and then along the southern boundaries of
plots 77 and 78, until it joined the future Enfield Avenue. The conveyance did not
expressly grant any rights of way for the benefit of plot 78A. The narrow strip 4 feet wide
plays no part in this case and can be ignored; it did not form a practical access to plot 78A.

I said that the conveyance did not grant any express rights of way. In fact it did the
reverse, because stipulation 7 in the first schedule to the conveyance (according to the
oratio obliqua of the examined abstract) said: 'The Vendor did not undertake to make
any of the proposed new roads shewn on the said Plan nor did he give any rights of way
over the same until the same should (if ever) be made.' 'The said Plan' here is the plan
to the conveyance. That is the stipulation which causes most of the trouble in this case.
Obviously the Carrington Estates did not mean to sell and Mr Alward did not mean to
buy, a piece of land with no access to it. The question is: what right of way ought to be
implied? Before attempting to answer that question I must complete the conveyancing
history.

By a conveyance dated 22nd April 1922 the Carrington Estates conveyed to Mr Alward
the site of the future Enfield Avenue and also the proposed east-west road. It was
expressed to be 'subject to all rights of way affecting the same, whether public or private
and whether expressly granted by the vendor or being rights of way of necessity'; I think
nothing is going to turn on that.

The next conveyance is dated 11th February 1935. The executors of Mr George
Alward, who had died in 1933, conveyed to Mr Philip Alward plot 78A, together with,
first, the adjoining length of the proposed east-west road, and secondly a strip of land
which I shall call the green land. The green land was expressed in the conveyance to be
the site of a proposed 22 foot road, leading from the west side of plot 78A to the future
Enfield Avenue, and running directly to the south of the part of the proposed east-west
road which bordered plots 45, 46 and 47.

In the result it seems clear that the position at this time was that the access available to
plot 78A, ignoring the 4 foot strip, consisted of, or included, the green strip which was in
the same ownership, plus a right of way by implication over the future Enfield Avenue.

By a conveyance dated 20th November 1936, Mr Philip Alward conveyed plot 78A to
Mr Little, without the green strip or any right of way over the green strip, but including
the site of the east-west road to the north of plot 78A which had in effect been thrown
into it. The reason for this omission may have been that Mr Little did not require the
green strip or any right of way thereover in order to gain access to plot 78A. It appears
from the assent, which is the next document that I shall mention, that Mr Little was the
owner of parts of plots 12 and 50, which gave access to plot 78A.

Mr Little died in 1944. On 30th April 1946 his executors assented to the vesting of
parts of plots 12 and 50 and plot 78A (including the adjoining east-west proposed road)
in his widow. On 12th November 1973 she conveyed most of plot 78A (that was to say,
the eastern three-quarters) to a Mr Marvin and he simultaneously conveyed it onwards
to Mrs Nickerson, the plaintiff. The three-quarters of plot 78A thereby conveyed is what
I termed earlier the pink land. Such conveyances also granted, so far as the vendors had
power to do so, a right of way for all purposes over Scouts Lane.

Most unfortunately, a dispute then arose between the plaintiff and Mr Barraclough,
who was thought to be the owner of Scouts Lane. The plaintiff claimed that she was
entitled to a right of way for all purposes over the bridge in the north-east corner of the

pink land and so on to Scouts Lane and to Humberston Avenue. Mr Barraclough
asserted that Scouts Lane was vested in the trustees of a settlement made by him, who   *a*
were subsequently added as defendants. The defendants denied the existence of any
right of way over Scouts Lane.

In argument in the court below the plaintiff's claim to a right of way over Scouts Lane
was based on four foundations: first, implied grant of an easement by the 1906
conveyance; second, prescription under the Prescription Act 1832; third, lost modern
grant; fourth, s 62 of the Law of Property Act 1925 read with the 1922 conveyance.   *b*

I shall deal first with the implied grant under the 1906 conveyance. As I have already
said, it could not possibly have been the intention of the Carrington Estates to sell, or of
Mr George Alward to buy, plot 78A without an appropriate means of access thereto. It
is absolutely clear from the contents of the conveyance that it was within the
contemplation of the parties that Mr Alward should be at liberty to build on plot 78A if
he so wished, subject to certain restrictions with regard to density, building lines and so   *c*
on. It therefore becomes necessary to decide what right, or rights, of way have to be read
into the 1906 conveyance as a matter of necessary implication in order to give effect to
the apparent purposes of the conveyance and the contemplated use to which the land
might be put. That decision, what implication should be made, has to be taken in the
light of the express stipulation, which I repeat because it is of prime importance, that the
vendor did not give any rights of way over the proposed new roads shown on the plan to   *d*
the conveyance 'until the same should (if ever) be made'. That stipulation, one would
think, was inserted in order to reserve for the Carrington Estates the maximum freedom
to move the route of a proposed road to a more convenient location, as had already been
done on one occasion in relation to the future Scouts Lane, or to throw the site of a
proposed road into the adjacent plots if the road could be dispensed with, as was later
done in 1935 in reference to the eastern part of the east-west road, or perhaps to change   *e*
altogether the layout of unsold lots.

There are five different possible implications which can usefully be considered. A
choice needs to be made between them. I shall distinguish them as follows. Implication
A, the broadest of all, is a right of way over all the strips designated on the 1906
conveyance plan as proposed new roads. This implication would have given a right of
way over the designated routes of the future Enfield Avenue, the east-west road and   *f*
Scouts Lane, right up to its junction with Humberston Avenue. Implication B: a right
of way over the whole of Scouts Lane and over the parts of the proposed east-west road
adjacent to plot 78A, so as to give access to the public highway by the shortest and most
convenient route. Implication C: a right of way along the designated routes of such of
the proposed roads as were then adjacent to plot 78A and the plots previously purchased
by Mr George Alward, so far as necessary to give access from plot 78A to Humberston   *g*
Avenue; in other words, the owner or occupier of plot 78A could make use of the
southern part of Scouts Lane but not the northern part, and could use the route of the
proposed east-west road to get into the future Enfield Avenue and thence into
Humberston Avenue. Implication D: a right of way at some convenient point across the
route of the proposed east-west road, so as to give access from plot 78A to Humberston
Avenue by proceeding over Mr Alward's other land westwards and northwards; that is   *h*
to say, from plot 78A to plot 78 and thence to plots 47 and 9 and so into Humberston
Avenue. The only right of way needed would be a crossing point over the east-west
road. Implication E: plot 78 was to become a dominant tenement for the purpose of
enabling the owner or occupier of plot 78A to make use of the existing right of way
which was already appurtenant to plot 77 by virtue of the 1900 conveyance. The owner
or occupier of plot 78A could then proceed from that plot over plot 78 and on to plot 77,   *j*
then making use of the right of way originally appurtenant only to plots 77, 45 and 7.

Before considering these possibilities, I should mention that the plaintiff did not plead
that plot 78A was landlocked at the time of the 1906 conveyance, and at the trial her
counsel expressly disclaimed any reliance on the doctrine of a way of necessity. What the
plaintiff's counsel did submit (and this was made perfectly clear in the course of the

argument below) was that a right of way ought to be implied over the proposed east-west
a road and Scouts Lane as a matter of necessary implication in order to give effect to the
purpose of the 1906 conveyance, namely the development of the plot by building houses
thereon. The plaintiff relied not on a way of necessity in the strict sense but on the
implication of a right of way as a matter of construction.

In the court below the plaintiff was successful in establishing a right to an easement of
way for all purposes over the bridge at the north-east corner of the pink land and over
b Scouts Lane to its junction with Humberston Avenue as appurtenant to the pink land.
This was described in the second judgment of Sir Robert Megarry V-C as 'a way implied
from the common intention of the parties, based on a necessity apparent from the deeds'
(see [1979] 3 All ER 312 at 324, [1980] Ch 325 at 336). It is the implication lettered B in
the different forms of implication which I indicated earlier for consideration.

A problem that has to be surmounted when selecting Scouts Lane as the easement to
c be implied under the 1906 conveyance is that the conveyance negatives the grant of any
right of way over the proposed new roads until they should be made, the obvious
intention being, as I have said, to preserve for the Carrington Estates the ability to alter
or abandon proposed roads unless their existence had in effect been decided on because
they were made, or because houses had been built which were dependent on them. Sir
Robert Megarry V-C felt able to minimise the prohibition imposed by the second part of
d stipulation 7 by taking into account considerations of public policy.

I must go through certain passages in the judgment; I shall indicate the starting points,
but for brevity I shall leave out certain sentences which are not essential for present
purposes. In his first judgment, Sir Robert Megarry V-C said ([1979] 3 All ER 312 at
316–317):

e   'In the present case the land conveyed was plainly intended to be used for
building purposes, and of course it plainly needed access for building materials and
for the occupants of the houses when constructed: yet there was the express
negativing of the grant of any way in the second limb of para 7 of Sch 1, despite the
need for some grant of a way that appeared from the surrounding circumstances as
disclosed by the conveyance itself . . . I find great difficulty in holding that there has
been granted by implication something that the grant expressly negatives . . . I find
f it almost impossible to imply a grant in the teeth of the express negation of any
grant; and the grant of a way of necessity seems plainly to be one form of implied
grant. There is, however, one consideration that is peculiar to ways of necessity that
seems to be in point. During argument, I was referred to a sentence in Gale on
Easements (14th Edn, 1972, p 117) on the subject of ways of necessity, which runs:
"The principle appears to be based on the idea that the neglect of agricultural land
g is contrary to public policy": and for this two old decisions are cited.'

Then, a little later:

        'This seems to me to raise a novel point of some difficulty and importance. Put
shortly, it is whether on a grant of land in circumstances which otherwise would
h create a way of necessity or a way implied from the common intention of the parties
based on a necessity apparent from the deeds, it is open to the parties to negative the
creation of such a way by some express term in the conveyance. I cannot think that
the point is in any way confined to agricultural land: whatever the actual or
prospective use of the land, the question arises whether in the absence of special
circumstances public policy will permit the parties to a conveyance to make land
j inaccessible save by air transport and thus unusable. As applied to the present case,
the question would be whether the court should impose on the second limb of para
7 of Sch 1 a qualification which would exclude from its operation any way required
for access for building purposes which would otherwise be implied. As the evidence
stands, apart from para 7 I would have no hesitation in holding that in the
circumstances of the 1906 conveyance there was an implied grant of a way to plot

78A for building purposes; for the contemplated use of the plot was for those
purposes, and so the extent of the way is to be measured by those purposes: see
Gayford v Moffatt (1868) 4 Ch App 133 at 136. As for the line of the way, since no
express allocation of a line by the grantor appears to have been made, I think the
tacit allocation of a way over the future Scouts Lane which has emerged from the
user that I shall describe in due course would suffice as an allocation . . . However,
in the absence of full argument on the point I do not think that I ought to decide
it . . .'

That is the end of the quotation from the first judgment.

I turn now to the second judgment, which was given after further argument. Sir
Robert Megarry V-C said ([1979] 3 All ER 312 at 320, [1980] Ch 325 at 331):

'. . . if land is conveyed in circumstances which otherwise would create a way of
necessity, or a way implied from the common intention of the parties based on a
necessity apparent from the deeds, does public policy prevent the creation of such
a way from being negatived by an express term in the grant?'

Sir Robert Megarry V-C then discussed a number of reported cases and an article on
the point of public policy in the Law Quarterly Review ((1973) 89 LQR 87). He
continued ([1970] 3 All ER 312 at 322–324, [1980] Ch 325 at 334–336) and again I shall
not read the entire narrative of the judgment:

'If such a head of public policy exists, as I think it does, the question is what its
bounds are. I do not think it can be said that, whatever the circumstances, a way of
necessity will always be implied whenever a close of land is made landlocked. One
can conceive of circumstances where there may be good reason why the land should
be deprived of all access . . . Accordingly, I would not go beyond saying that there
is a rule of public policy that no transaction should, without good reason, be treated
as being effectual to deprive any land of a suitable means of access. Alternatively,
the point might be put as a matter of construction: any transaction which, without
good reason, appears to deprive land of any suitable means of access should, if at all
possible, be construed as not producing this result . . . Now the wording of the
clause in question, para 7 of Sch 1 to the 1906 conveyance, as it appears in the
examined abstract and with the contractions expanded, runs as follows: "The Vendor
did not undertake to make any of the proposed new roads shewn on the said Plan
nor did he give any rights of way over the same until the same should (if ever) be
made" . . . This clause of the schedule seems primarily concerned to relieve the
vendor of any obligation to make any of the proposed new roads, in the sense of
constructing roadways over the routes shown on the plan. If one disregards public
policy and the doctrine of derogation from grant, I think the natural meaning of the
second limb of the clause is that until roadways had been constructed on the routes
shown on the plan, the purchaser was to have no right of way over the routes along
which those roadways were to be constructed. I think, however, that it is also
possible, though less natural, to read the second limb as in effect merely reinforcing
the first limb. The first limb simply negatives any undertaking by the vendor to
make up the new roads; the second limb goes on to prevent the conveyance giving
any rights of way over the new roads which might enable the purchaser to claim
that, having been granted a right of way over the new roads, he can, by virtue of that
right, require the vendor to construct them. On that footing, the second limb does
not negative any way of necessity over the unmade sites of the proposed new
roads. All that is negatived is any rights of way over the proposed new roads until
they are constructed . . . Nothing, however, was done to negative any way of
necessity . . . I readily accept that this may be regarded as a somewhat strained
interpretation of para 7 of Sch 1; but I do not think that it is so impossible that I
must reject it. If, then, in construing this provision I give proper weight to the
doctrine against derogation from grant and the rule of public policy, I think that I

can construe para 7 in this particular way, and that I ought in fact to do so. If I am
a wrong in this, then I would hold, though with some hesitation, that public policy
requires that para 7 should not take effect so as to negative the implied grant of a
way of necessity. As I have already held, I think that there has been a tacit allocation
by user of a way over what is now Scouts Lane, and that the way granted by implied
grant is a way for building purposes.'

b Then Sir Robert Megarry V-C explained exactly what he meant by a 'way of necessity' in
that passage: 'a way implied from the common intention of the parties, based on a
necessity apparent from the deeds'.

In this court we have heard a great deal of argument about ways of necessity: what is
their basis, how they can be acquired and whether they can be lost. With the utmost
respect to Sir Robert Megarry V-C, I have come to the conclusion that the doctrine of way
c of necessity is not founded on public policy at all but on an implication from the
circumstances. I accept that there are reported cases, and textbooks, in which public
policy is suggested as a possible foundation of the doctrine, but such a suggestion is not,
in my opinion, correct. It is well established that a way of necessity is never found to
exist except in association with a grant of land: see *Proctor v Hodgson* (1855) 10 Exch 824
where it was held that land acquired by escheat got no way of necessity; and *Wilkes v*
d *Greenway* (1890) 6 TLR 449 where land acquired by prescription got no way of
necessity. If a way of necessity were based on public policy, I see no reason why land
acquired by escheat or by prescription should be excluded. Furthermore, there would
seem to be no particular reason to father the doctrine of way of necessity on public policy
when implication is such an obvious and convenient candidate for paternity. There is an
Australian case, *North Sydney Printing Pty Ltd v Sabemo Investments Corpn Pty Ltd* [1971] 2
e NSWLR 150, where that conclusion was reached. Furthermore, I cannot accept that
public policy can play any part at all in the construction of an instrument; in construing
a document the court is endeavouring to ascertain the expressed intention of the
parties. Public policy may require the court to frustrate that intention where the
contract is against public policy, but in my view public policy cannot help the court to
ascertain what that intention was. So I reach the view that a way of necessity is not
f founded on public policy, that considerations of public policy cannot influence the
construction of the 1906 conveyance, and that this action is not concerned with a way of
necessity strictly so called; nor, I think, did Sir Robert Megarry V-C intend to suggest
otherwise.

I return to the real problem which, at the end of the day, strikes me as being a
relatively short question of construction. On the basis of the terms of the 1906 conveyance
g and the previous history, and bearing in mind the indisputable fact that some implication
has to be made into the conveyance, what implication ought to be made in order to
resolve the question of access?

As I have indicated earlier, there are at least five methods of solving the question of
access. No one so far has suggested that there are any other than those. The problem is
to decide which of the five will best answer the circumstances; what is the court to infer
h that the parties intended? That question must be answered by examining the conveyance
against past history and then deciding which implication will best meet the circumstances
of the situation. Some things point to a broad implication in favour of the purchaser of
plot 78A. There is the recital in the 1906 conveyance that the Humberston building
estate had been put up for sale by auction in building plots. There is a reference to the
printed particulars and conditions of sale used at the auction. We have a copy of those
j particulars and conditions. They refer to a plan, and we have a copy of that plan. It
shows a compact building estate of 66 plots grouped round a mansion house known as
Humberston Grange, laid out in four lines consisting of two double lines of back-to-back
plots. Between the double line is Humberston Avenue and there is shown a proposed
new road along the north side of one of the double lines of plots and along the south side
of the other double line, the whole being intersected by proposed roads running north

and south. Plot 78A, as I have indicated earlier, is outside this compact area, but is in connection with it to the southwest. The plan to the 1906 conveyance amounts to an extension of the auction plan.

It is legitimate to look at the auction plan to construe the 1906 conveyance, because the parties show in the conveyance that they have the auction particulars and conditions in mind, and the auction plan is an integral part of the auction particulars. If a conveyance of a building plot is silent about any easement of way, it is easy to imply the grant of an easement over all the strips which are shown on the plan as proposed new roads. The obvious inference is that the purchaser of a plot is to have access to the proposed road on to which his house fronts and is to be allowed to proceed along any of the proposed roads until he reaches a highway over which all have a right of way. Except for the stipulation in the 1906 conveyance, I would not have felt any difficulty at all in implying a right of way over Scouts Lane for the benefit of plot 78A to enable access to be had to the public highway. But we are faced with stipulation 7. This states in clear terms that the vendor is not obliged to make (not make up, but make) any of the proposed new roads shown on the plan to the conveyance. Scouts Lane is one of such roads, so the vendor is not obliged to make it a road servicing the estate. Also, the vendor did not give any rights of way, until some indefinite future date, over any of the proposed new roads shown on the plan, of which Scouts Lane is one. So the stipulation is in terms a distinct and direct negation of any right of way over, inter alia, Scouts Lane. There is, on the face of the conveyance, a head-on collision between two opposing conceptions. Some immediate access has to exist; the conveyance says that no immediate easement is to exist over any proposed road, but, if an immediate access is to exist, there must at some point be an incursion onto a proposed road.

So I ask myself: what is the reconciliation? There are, as it seems to me, only two ways of resolving the impasse. One method is to strike out altogether the second limb of stipulation 7, which would let in implication A, as I called it earlier in my judgment. The other method is to make that implication which involves the least incursion on to any proposed new roads.

As regards the first approach, the deletion of the second limb of stipulation 7 would in my judgment do unjustifiable violence to the language of the conveyance. So I feel driven to the other method of reconciliation; that is to say, to consider which of implications B to E involves the least incursion on to any of the proposed new roads. Implication B, giving a right of way over the whole of Scouts Lane, is not in my view the answer to the question which I have posed. It would be a major incursion on to a proposed new road. That proposed new road had not been made; we know of no earlier easements which had been granted over it; and there is no evidence that the line of the northern part of the proposed road had become fixed because of building operations. The 1920 auction particulars merely stated that Scouts Lane and other proposed roadways were subject to rights of way if and when they should ever be made.

In my opinion the least incursion would be made if the implication in the 1906 conveyance were that Mr Alward should have the right to use his existing easement of way for the purposes of his new purchase; or, to put the matter in more precise legal language, if it were implied that plot 78A was to become an additional dominant tenement in relation to the existing easement of way owned by Mr Alward as the purchaser of plot 77 under the 1900 conveyance, a solution which would be equally applicable to the needs of plot 78. However, I quite see the merits of implications C and D. It is not strictly necessary for us to decide between C, D and E, since none of them will yield a right of way over Scouts Lane.

I have therefore reached the conclusion that there ought not to be implied into the 1906 conveyance any right of way over Scouts Lane in the face of the express terms of stipulation 7.

That is the end of the appeal, except for a short point arising under the respondent's notice. Before I come to that, I should, for clarity, mention that Sir Robert Megarry V-C also found that the plaintiff was entitled to a right of way over Scouts Lane and the

bridge, in order to make use of the pink land for agricultural purposes. and as a sports
a ground for amateur sports. This finding was based on s 62 of the Law of Property Act
1925 and equally, as I understand it, on prescription and on lost modern grant. Nothing
turns on it on this appeal, because the existence of that limited right of way is not
challenged by the defendants.

The respondent's notice arises under the 1922 conveyance, read with s 62 of the 1925
Act. Paragraph 3 of the amended statement of claim pleaded that at the time of the 1922
b conveyance there was appertaining to, or reputed to appertain to, or enjoyed with, or
reputed to or known as part or parcel of or appurtenant to the pink land, a right of way
for all purposes across the bridge and over Scouts Lane to Humberston Avenue, and it
was pleaded that by virtue of the 1922 conveyance and s 62, the right to use the way
became vested in the plaintiff as if the same had been expressly conveyed. Sir Robert
Megarry V-C found as a fact that Scouts Lane was used as a means of access to the pink
c land from at least 1921 and until the interruptions of 1972 or 1973 to which he referred,
but that there was no appreciable user except for the purposes of agriculture and amateur
sports. He held that the conveyance of the proposed east-west road in 1922 carried with
it, by virtue of s 62, a right of access to Scouts Lane, and that as the east-west road was
itself used as an access to the pink land, the effect of the 1922 conveyance was to grant to
the purchaser of the east-west road a right of way to Scouts Lane, not only for the
d purposes of the east-west road, but also for the purposes of plot 78A.

Sir Robert Megarry V-C said ([1979] 3 All ER 312 at 324, [1980] Ch 325 at 336):

'In my previous judgment I set out the view that I provisionally took, the point
not having been argued then. That view was that although the general rule was
that the grant of a right of way to reach plot A cannot be used as a means of access
to plot B, which lies beyond, this rule would not apply if, at the time of the grant,
e   plot A forms a means of access to plot B . . . Let me take as an example a case where
plot A consists of a footpath some three feet wide and a hundred yards long, running
from land near a public highway up to plot B. If there is an express grant of a right
of way to plot A over land which lies between plot A and the highway, it seems to
me that the grant would, subject to any language to the contrary, be construed in
the light of the nature and user of plot A at the time of the grant. Since that nature
f   and user is as a footpath which constitutes a means of access to plot B, then I would
have thought that the grant would be construed as authorising the dominant owner
to use the way as a means of access to plot A for the purposes for which plot A is
used, namely, as a means of access to plot B. In the result, the way can be used as a
means of access to plot B via plot A, notwithstanding Harris v Flower (1904) 74 LJ
Ch 127. If plot A is not used as an actual means of access to plot B but as between
g   the parties to the transaction it is intended to be used thus, I think that the same rule
would apply.'

One must look first at the wording of s 62 of the 1925 Act. Omitting words which are
not of immediate significance for present purposes, I can read it as follows:

'(1) A conveyance of land shall . . . by virtue of this Act operate to convey, with
h   the land, all . . . advantages whatsoever, appertaining or reputed to appertain to the
land, or any part thereof, or, at the time of conveyance . . . enjoyed with . . . the land
or any part thereof . . .'

Then sub-s (6): 'This section applies to conveyances made after the thirty-first day of
December, eighteen hundred and eighty-one.'

j   It is common ground that the words in the full text of the subsection, 'ways, easements
and rights', have no application here, and that the plaintiff can only rely on the word
'advantages'. I should also add that immediately before the 1922 conveyance Mr Alward
was not only the owner of plot 78A, but also the tenant of the proposed east-west road, so
that such proposed road and Scouts Lane were not at the time in the same occupation.

In effect s 62 states that a conveyance of a piece of land operates to convey with that land all advantages appertaining to, or, at the time of the conveyance, enjoyed with, the land, so as to convert such advantages into legally enforceable rights. If, therefore, the *a* advantage is a roadway or pathway, or access from the land granted by the conveyance over land retained by the grantor and so to a public highway, that roadway or pathway or access gives rise to a legal easement by way of a deemed grant, in relation to which easement the land conveyed is the dominant tenement and the land retained is the servient tenement. What s 62 does not, I think, do is to make a piece of land which is not the subject matter of the grant the dominant tenement in relation to an easement *b* deemed to have been granted by the conveyance. At the same time we do know from the findings of the judge that the bridge and Scouts Lane were being used for certain limited purposes of plot 78A, namely agriculture and amateur sports. So I think the true analysis of the situation is this: (1) the 1922 conveyance was deemed to grant to Mr Alward, as the purchaser of the site of the proposed east-west road, a right of way over Scouts Lane for the purposes of that site; and (2) after the 1922 conveyance Mr Alward, *c* as the owner and occupier of plot 78A, continued to have the same right to use Scouts Lane for the purpose of plot 78A as he enjoyed before the 1922 conveyance; but (3) the 1922 conveyance did not have the effect of making land which was not comprised in that conveyance the dominant tenement in respect of a servitude over land retained by the vendor.

Counsel for the plaintiff sought to argue that one of the purposes of the proposed east- *d* west road in and after 1900 had been the servicing of a building estate, and plot 78A was part of that building estate; that there was no evidence that Mr Alward had abandoned that purpose in relation to plot 78A; that therefore the exploitation of plot 78A as a building site was one of the purposes of the proposed east-west road; and that therefore Scouts Lane, when it became available for the purposes of the proposed east-west road, became available for building on plot 78A as one of such purposes. *e*

In my opinion, s 62 is not concerned with the future purposes of the grantor. It is only concerned with an advantage that can properly be regarded as appertaining, or reputed to appertain, to the land granted or, at the time of the conveyance, enjoyed with it. In 1922 the proposed east-west road had not been laid out as a road to any buildings on plot 78A, nor had it been used for the transport of any building materials to the plot, or as an accommodation road for any houses on the plot, for none had been built. So I do not *f* think the facts will support the plaintiff's argument.

Furthermore, I have some difficulty in seeing how land which is not included in the grant can become the dominant tenement in relation to an easement deemed to be created by the grant.

I would therefore allow the appeal, subject to one minor point. The order below declared the existence of a right of way over the bridge, without limitation of width. *g* The notice of appeal seeks to confine the width of any bridge to 8 feet. There is a finding of fact that the bridge consisted originally of sleepers and that it was 8 feet wide. We have not heard much argument on this point. Unless counsel take the view that this is not a live issue, or that it is a live issue but has not yet been fully argued, I would be disposed to accept that the limitation to 8 feet sought by the notice of appeal is correct.

I desire to conclude by saying that I have much sympathy for the plaintiff in this *h* action. She clearly bought the land in reliance on a statutory declaration by a previous occupier, which seemed to make it clear that a right of way existed for all purposes along Scouts Lane. But nevertheless, as I have said, I feel constrained to take the view that the appeal should be allowed.

EVELEIGH LJ. Paragraph 7 of the first schedule to the 1906 conveyance makes it *j* clear that there will not be a right to go over all the proposed roads, at least until they are made up and thus finally determined. But the building of houses is contemplated along the east-west road and round the corner on the north-south road. Against the background of the sale of a large number of individual plots, and contemplating therefore a large number of different owners, I think that access in order to build on them would

normally be implied. Moreover, it would be access to each plot individually, because not
a only could one plot be sold to a single purchaser, but where a purchaser himself buys a
large number of plots, it would generally be in order to sell the individual plots as and
when houses were built, or indeed as vacant building land. The fact that Mr Alward
possessed a right of access to another plot does not in my opinion require a different
conclusion in relation to his purchase of plot 78A. He had bought a building plot; he
may decide not to build, but that is his choice. His right is to build and to sell individual
b sites or houses.

In my view it would be quite unreasonable to expect him to build using plot 77 as
access. The work would have to be planned so that a completed house did not obstruct
access to another site not yet completed, and he could not sell a site which had to be
crossed in order to reach another site unless that other site had already been completed.

I think, therefore, that there is an implied provision for access, but that it is for the
c grantor to choose the actual route. Sir Robert Megarry V-C said ([1979] 3 All ER 312 at
317):

> 'As for the line of the way, since no express allocation of a line by the grantor
> appears to have been made, I think the tacit allocation of a way over the future
> Scouts Lane which has emerged from the user that I shall describe in due course
> would suffice as an allocation.'

d
The user to which he then referred, and as proved in evidence, was user for sporting
and agricultural purposes. As there never were building operations, I do not see how any
user of the way can be said to indicate a route designated or allocated by the grantor for
such operations. The user was for a quite different purpose. Therefore, whilst I agree
that para 7 does not deny the purchaser any right of way at all to the plot, Scouts Lane is
e not shown, in my judgment, to be a right of way granted in pursuance of the conveyance.

As to s 62 of the Law of Property Act 1925, counsel for the defendants said that he
would be prepared to argue that no right of way of any kind was conveyed by virtue of
s 62 of the 1925 Act; but as Sir Robert Megarry V-C had found a way by virtue
of prescription he, counsel, saw no point in arguing that, unless driven to it in support
of his further argument.

f On behalf of the plaintiff, it was argued that if a right of way was exercised over Scouts
Lane through the strip to plot 78A, a right of way is deemed to be included in the
conveyance and passes under s 62; and it is said, by a step which I find difficult to follow,
that as a right of way passes, reference to a right of way must be to a right of way for all
purposes. It is that step that I find difficult.

Section 62 is a conveyancing section; it passes only that which actually exists already,
g be it, for example, a right of easement, or be it an advantage actually enjoyed. In some
cases that which is enjoyed is enjoyed by the exercise of the general right of ownership,
and may become a particular legal right of some kind in the purchaser. None the less,
the section envisages something which exists and is seen to be enjoyed either as a specific
right in itself, or as an advantage in fact.

Section 62 says: '(1) A conveyance of land shall be deemed to include' a number of
h things, all of which are clearly shown to be in actual existence either, as I say, as a right
or as a factual advantage. It conveys that which is there to be conveyed, and from this it
follows that that which is conveyed can be described, and by s 62 is deemed to be
conveyed and consequently described. That means it is described accurately.

The way proved in this case was for a limited object, sporting and agricultural, and a
conveyance intended to include it would so describe it. It could not accurately be
j described as a right of way for all purposes, for that it never was.

For those reasons, and for those given by Brightman LJ, I would reject the argument
that the wider right of way passes by virtue of s 62.

On the question of public policy, I agree with what Brightman LJ has said. I would
add, however, that I could see possibly a case where public policy could aid in the
construction of an agreement. It would be a rare case, but where the scales are equally

balanced between two different meanings, I would think it right to attribute to the intention of the parties that which offends least against public policy.

I agree that this appeal should be allowed to the extent indicated by Brightman LJ.

BUCKLEY LJ. I entirely agree with the judgment which has been delivered by Brightman LJ. In particular, in my judgment the law relating to ways of necessity rests, not on a basis of public policy but on the implication to be drawn from the fact that unless some way is implied, a parcel of land will be inaccessible. From that fact the implication arises that the parties must have intended that some way giving access to the land should have been granted.

I agree, also for the reasons given by Brightman LJ, that public policy can play no part in the process of ascertaining the intention of the parties as a matter of construction of a written document, in particular in this case the conveyance of 8th December 1906. Public policy may inhibit the parties from carrying their intention into effect, but I cannot see how public policy can have a bearing on what their intention was. In my judgment, that must be ascertained in accordance with the ordinary principles of construction, the language used and relevant admissible evidence of surrounding circumstances.

In the present case the pleadings contain no allegation of fact that plot 78A became landlocked on the occasion of the conveyance of 8th December 1906, and in the absence of such an allegation it seems to me impossible to say that a case has been pleaded of circumstances which would give rise to the implication of a way as a way of necessity. Moreover, before Sir Robert Megarry V-C counsel abjured any intention of relying on a factual situation that plot 78A became physically landlocked as the result of the 1906 conveyance. Accordingly this is not, in my judgment, a case in which the law of ways of necessity is applicable.

It is not in my view a case which depends on any allocation by the grantor under the 1906 conveyance of any particular way. In my view it is a case which depends on the proper interpretation, and the proper implications, to be attached to the conveyance of 8th December 1906.

I agree with the reasons which Brightman LJ has given for reaching the conclusion which he has reached, and I agree with those other reasons, dealing with other aspects of the case, which he has given in the course of his judgment. For these reasons I also would allow this appeal.

Appeal allowed. Declaration in terms of second schedule to notice of appeal. Leave to appeal to House of Lords refused.

9th April. The Appeal Committee of the House of Lords (Lord Russell of Killowen, Lord Scarman and Lord Bridge of Harwich) dismissed a petition by the plaintiff for leave to appeal.

Solicitors: *Sharpe, Pritchard & Co*, agents for *Bates & Mountain*, Grimsby (for the defendants); *Lee, Bolton & Lee*, agents for *Roythorne & Co*, Spalding (for the plaintiff).

Diana Brahams   Barrister.

A v Liverpool City Council and another

HOUSE OF LORDS

LORD WILBERFORCE, LORD DIPLOCK, LORD FRASER OF TULLYBELTON, LORD KEITH OF KINKEL AND LORD ROSKILL

8th, 9th APRIL, 20th MAY 1981

Child – Care – Local authority – Wardship proceedings – Jurisdiction of court to review decisions of local authority – Wardship proceedings by natural parent – Decision of local authority to limit mother's access to child – Proceedings brought by mother to challenge local authority's decision – Whether jurisdiction to review merits of decision where wardship proceedings invoked by natural parent – Children and Young Persons Act 1969, s 1.

In March 1980 a local authority obtained a care order under s 1(2)(a) and (3) of the Children and Young Persons Act 1969 in respect of the mother's infant son. Thereafter the child was placed with foster parents but the mother was allowed weekly access. In June 1980 the local authority decided to limit the mother's access to monthly visits of one hour under supervision because in its opinion rehabilitation of the mother and the child was not in the child's best interest and consequently that regular access by the mother was undesirable. When the local authority refused to reconsider its decision, the mother issued a wardship summons to have her son made a ward of court for the purpose of challenging the local authority's decision and also issued an interim summons asking for care and control. On the hearing of the summonses the judge, without investigating the merits, held that he was bound by authority to discharge the wardship proceedings because the court could not exercise its wardship jurisdiction to review the discretionary power of a local authority under a care order. He accordingly discharged the wardship proceedings. The mother appealed directly to the House of Lords.

Held – Because Parliament had by statute entrusted to local authorities the power and duty to make decisions as to the welfare of children without reserving to the courts any right of review on the merits (subject to certain limited rights of appeal in relation to care orders), the courts had no jurisdiction to review a local authority's discretionary powers under a care order except under the supervisory jurisdiction to review the legality of administrative decisions. Since the mother's application was no more than an attempt to persuade the court to exercise its wardship jurisdiction to interfere in matters which were within the local authority's province, the judge had been right to decline jurisdiction. The mother's appeal would therefore be dismissed (see p 388 *e* to *h*, p 389 *c* to *f* and *j*, p 392 *b* to *f* and p 393 *f* to *j*, post).

Re A B (an infant) [1954] 2 All ER 287, *Re M (an infant)* [1961] 1 All ER 788 and *Re W (minors) (wardship: jurisdiction)* [1979] 3 All ER 154 approved.

Notes

For the care of a child by a local authority, see 24 Halsbury's Laws (4th Edn) para 787, for the assumption of parental rights by a local authority, see ibid paras 790–793, and for cases on the subject, see 28(2) Digest (Reissue) 940–943, 2432–2442.

For wardship jurisdiction, see 24 Halsbury's Laws (4th Edn) paras 576–583, and for cases on the subject, see 28(2) Digest (Reissue) 911–916, 2220–2247.

For the Children and Young Persons Act 1969, s 1, see 40 Halsbury's Statutes (3rd Edn) 849.

Cases referred to in opinions

A B (an infant), Re [1954] 2 All ER 287, [1954] 2 QB 385, [1954] 3 WLR 1, 118 JP 318, 52 LGR 421, DC, 28(2) Digest (Reissue) 940, 2432.

Associated Provincial Picture Houses Ltd v Wednesbury Corpn [1947] 2 All ER 680, [1948] 1
    KB 223, [1948] LJR 190, 177 LT 641, 112 JP 55, 45 LGR 637, CA, 45 Digest (Repl) 215, *a*
    189.
Attorney General v De Keyser's Royal Hotel Ltd [1920] AC 508, [1920] All ER Rep 80, 89 LJ
    Ch 417, 122 LT 691, HL, 17 Digest (Reissue) 485, 100.
B (a minor) (wardship: child in care), Re [1974] 3 All ER 915, [1975] Fam 36, [1975] 2 WLR
    302, 139 JP 87, 72 LGR 691, Digest (Cont Vol D) 529, 2239a.
D (a minor) (justices' decision: review), Re [1977] 3 All ER 481, [1977] Fam 158, [1977] 2 *b*
    WLR 1006, 141 JP 669, 75 LGR 845, Digest (Cont Vol E) 326, 2247a.
H (a minor) (wardship: jurisdiction), Re [1978] 2 All ER 903, [1978] Fam 65, [1978] 2 WLR
    608, 142 JP 474, 76 LGR 254, CA, Digest (Cont Vol E) 324, 2239b.
J v C [1969] 1 All ER 788, [1970] AC 668, [1969] 2 WLR 540, HL, 28(2) Digest (Reissue)
    800, 1230.
M (an infant), Re [1961] 1 All ER 788, [1961] Ch 328, [1961] 2 WLR 350, 125 JP 278, 59 *c*
    LGR 146, CA, 28(2) Digest (Reissue) 940, 2433.
T (AJJ)(an infant), Re [1970] 2 All ER 865, [1970] Ch 688, [1970] 3 WLR 315, 134 JP 611,
    CA, 28(2) Digest (Reissue) 913, 2239.
W (minors) (wardship: jurisdiction), Re [1979] 3 All ER 154, [1980] Fam 60, [1979] 3 WLR
    252, CA.
Ward v Laverty [1925] AC 101, [1924] All ER Rep 319, 94 LJPC 17, 131 LT 614, HL, *d*
    28(2) Digest (Reissue) 846, 1431.

Appeal
The mother appealed directly to the House of Lords, pursuant to a certificate granted by
Balcombe J under s 12 of the Administration of Justice Act 1969 and with leave of the
House granted on 3rd December 1980, against an order of Balcombe J dated 14th *e*
October 1980 made on the hearing of a wardship summons issued by the mother on
27th August 1980 and an interim summons dated 1st September 1980 applying for care
and control of her infant son who was in the care of the Liverpool City Council ('the local
authority'), whereby the judge refused to exercise the prerogative jurisdiction in
wardship and discharged the wardship on the ground that he had no jurisdiction. The
judge certified under s 12 of the 1969 Act that the following point of law of general *f*
importance was involved in the decision: whether, and if so, to what extent, the
prerogative jurisdiction of the High Court in wardship should be invoked or exercised
when there is in force at the material time in relation to the ward a statutory care order;
he further certified that the point of law was one in respect of which he was bound by a
decision of the Court of Appeal in previous proceedings and was fully considered in
judgments given by the Court of Appeal in those previous proceedings. The second *g*
respondent to the appeal, the father of the infant, took no part in the proceedings. The
facts are set out in the opinion of Lord Roskill.

Michael Morland QC and *Judith Daley* for the mother.
J Hugill QC and *Mark Hedley* for the local authority.

Their Lordships took time for consideration.

20th May. The following opinions were delivered.

LORD WILBERFORCE. My Lords, this appeal comes to this House in accordance
with s 12 of the Administration of Justice Act 1969 from a decision of Balcombe J in the
Family Division of the High Court. He decided that he had no jurisdiction to continue
the wardship sought by the mother of a young boy who was in the care of the respondent
local authority. The child was the subject of a care order made by a juvenile court in
Liverpool on 10th March 1980 under the Children and Young Persons Act 1969 as the
result of which he was placed with foster parents with whom he now resides. The
mother, though formally seeking the care and control of the child, is not asking that this

should immediately be given to her but she does wish to oppose restrictions on her access to him imposed by the council, they having taken the view that 'rehabilitation' (which means restoration to his mother's care) was not in the child's best interest and consequently that regular access by the mother was not desirable. The father takes no part in these proceedings.

The learned judge decided as he did following two decisions of the Court of Appeal, namely *Re M (an infant)* [1961] 1 All ER 788, [1961] Ch 328 (approving *Re A B (an infant)* [1954] 2 All ER 287, [1954] 2 QB 385) and *Re W (minors) (wardship: jurisdiction)* [1979] 3 All ER 154, [1980] Fam 60; the former case has been consistently followed. The mother thus invites the House to overrule a consistent line of authority over a period of twenty years. The main contention is that the welfare of the child being the 'first and paramount consideration' (under the Guardianship of Infants Act 1925, s 1) the High Court has an overriding power and duty to apply this fundamental principle, and that this jurisdiction is not to be cut down, or considered as diminished by the legislation which has been passed as to the care of infants or minors.

At the present time, responsibility for jurisdiction over minors is divided between a large number of courts and authorities and is regulated by a number of Acts of Parliament as well as by principles of equity and law. There are many different strands which it is difficult to disentangle, and any statement of principle is liable to be complicated or confused by exceptions and qualifications. I do not therefore attempt to survey the whole field. The principles which govern the present case, however, are comparatively simple to state.

The welfare of the child has always been the yardstick by which courts of equity, exercising their ancient jurisdiction over minors (or infants as they were historically described), were guided. But naturally the considerations by which they were guided in reaching their decisions as to a child's welfare, or his best interests, have varied. This was particularly so in relation to the claims of parents. I need not repeat in this context the very full historical analysis present by the speeches in *J v C* [1969] 1 All ER 788, [1970] AC 668 showing the progressive evolution of the present law through the Victorian era to ours. This culminated in the passing of the Guardianship of Infants Act 1925, s 1, with its statement that in any proceedings involving the custody or upbringing of an infant the court should regard the welfare of the infant as the first and paramount consideration. No doubt this section was in the main a 'sex equality' enactment putting the mother on an equality with the father. No doubt also it applied generally beyond cases of disputes between parents, but in so far as it did so it was little more than a reminder, unnecessary to the Chancery courts which had always acted on this principle, as to the ultimate test to be applied. I shall not take time by commenting on the word 'paramount', clearly taken from the opinion of Viscount Cave LC in *Ward v Laverty* [1925] AC 101 at 108, [1924] All ER Rep 319 at 323, where he related this test to 'rules which are now well accepted', so clearly not intended as a new or even talismanic word. The speeches in *J v C* provide authoritative guidance which I should not wish to repeat or to gloss. The point which I desire to emphasise is that, against a background of continual social changes, within and beyond the family, the object of intervention by the courts, whether the courts of Chancery, or their predecessor the Court of Wards and Liveries, or their present successors, the courts of the Family Division of the High Court, is to promote the welfare of the child.

I have not available any reliable statistics as to the number of children whose cases, in the nineteenth century, or even before the 1939–45 war, had to be considered by the courts, including county courts and magistrates' courts. What is undoubted is that the number of those in need of some supervision or assistance is now very large: 90,000 was the figure given us for the number of children in care, of which over 65,000 are cases where the local authority have full responsibility under care orders or parental rights resolutions. The respondent authority alone has 1,500 such cases. It is obvious that this situation called for a large delegation of power to local authorities and a large measure of discretion for them, and this has been conferred by the (consolidating) Child Care Act 1980 and by the surviving portion of the Children and Young Persons Act 1969. When

one asks what is the principle by which these authorities are to be guided there can only
be one general answer: the welfare of the child. I add the word 'general' in order to leave *a*
room for the jurisdiction exercisable for the protection of the public. As regards children
in voluntary care, this is quite explicitly stated in the Child Care Act 1980, ss 1 and 2 (I
need not retrace the earlier enactments); as regards those the subject of care orders this
appears no less clearly from the Children and Young Persons Act 1969, s 24; as regards
juvenile courts the same is true: see *Re H (a minor) (wardship: jurisdiction)* [1978] 2 All ER
903 at 910, [1978] Fam 65 at 77 per Ormrod LJ. To the argument, therefore, that the *b*
High Court has a special and overriding jurisdiction because only there can the welfare
of the child be assigned its proper place, the answer is clear: that there is no other
principle on which any court or administrative body can (with the exception of public
protection cases, and even there considerations must be mixed) act than that which is best
for the child's welfare. It must, however, be borne in mind that, whereas the duties and
powers of local authorities and of juvenile courts are defined and limited by statute, there *c*
is no similar limitation on those of the High Court.

   This leads to the next and decisive question: given that both the High Court and the
local authority have responsibilities for the welfare of the child, what is the relationship,
or dividing line, between them? I think that there is no doubt that the appellant, the
child's mother, is arguing for a general reviewing power in the court over the local
authority's discretionary decision; she is, in reality, asking the court to review the *d*
respondents' decision as to access and to substitute its own opinion on that matter.
Access itself is undoubtedly a matter within the discretionary power of the local
authority.

   In my opinion the court has no such reviewing power. Parliament has by statute
entrusted to the local authority the power and duty to make decisions as to the welfare
of children without any reservation of reviewing power to the court. There are, indeed, *e*
certain limited rights of appeal as to the care order itself: under s 2(12) of the 1969 Act
there is an appeal to the Crown Court against the care order; the appellant did not
exercise this right and is now long out of time. Or the appellant could apply to the
juvenile court under s 21 of the 1969 Act to discharge the care order or to vary it; this she
has not done, and any such application would not be likely to succeed. Furthermore, if
the facts so permitted, she could apply to the High Court for judicial review of the care *f*
order or the local authority's actions under it; there is no suggestion of any ground on
which this would be possible in the present case. Nowhere is there any suggestion in the
legislation that the High Court was to be left with a reviewing power as to the merits of
local authorities' decisions.

   It was suggested that, as the local authority is put effectively in the position of the
natural parent (see s 24(2) of the 1969 Act), the High Court must have the same power *g*
in the interest of the infant, to review and control its actions, as it undoubtedly has over
those of the natural parent. But I can see no parallel between the responsibilities of a
natural parent and those entrusted by Parliament by statute to a public authority
possessed of the necessary administrative apparatus to form and to carry out, if necessary
against the wishes of the natural parent, its discretionary decisions. In my opinion
Parliament has marked out an area in which, subject to the enacted limitations and *h*
safeguards, decisions for the child's welfare are removed from the parents and from
supervision by the courts.

   This is not to say that the inherent jurisdiction of the High Court is taken away. Any
child, whether under care or not, can be made a ward of court by the procedure of s 9(2)
of the Law Reform (Miscellaneous Provisions) Act 1949. In cases (and the present is an
example) where the court perceives that the action sought of it is within the sphere of *j*
discretion of the local authority, it will make no order and the wardship will lapse. But
in some instances there may be an area of concern to which the powers of the local
authority, limited as they are by statute, do not extend. Sometimes the local authority
itself may invite the supplementary assistance of the court. Then the wardship may be
continued with a view to action by the court. The court's general inherent power is

always available to fill gaps or to supplement the powers of the local authority; what it will not do (except by way of judicial review where appropriate) is to supervise the exercise of discretion within the field committed by statute to the local authority.

Because they conform to those principles of law which I have endeavoured to state, I am of opinion that Re M and Re W were correctly decided. Indeed, the principles which I have endeavoured to state were clearly laid down by Lord Evershed MR in Re M [1961] 1 All ER 788 at 795, [1961] Ch 328 at 345 in terms which have guided the courts ever since. Intervening cases have been fully discussed by my noble and learned friend Lord Roskill and I am more than content to accept his analysis. As regards Re H, this is a type of case very familiar to anyone concerned with the insoluble syndromes of infancy cases in which the decision, made in most difficult circumstances, appears a wise one but, if taken to appeal, might be hard to sustain, at least on the grounds assigned. I have no inclination to criticise such decisions even if they make doubtful precedents. I prefer to say no more on it.

In this case the judge, in my opinion, was clearly right and the appeal must be dismissed.

LORD DIPLOCK. My Lords, I have had the advantage of reading in draft the speech prepared by my noble and learned friend Lord Wilberforce, with which I agree. I too would therefore dismiss the appeal.

LORD FRASER OF TULLYBELTON. My Lords, I have had the advantage of reading in draft the speeches of my noble and learned friends Lord Wilberforce and Lord Roskill. I agree with them, and, for the reasons stated by them, I would dismiss this appeal.

LORD KEITH OF KINKEL. My Lords, having had the benefit of reading in draft the speeches prepared by my noble and learned friends Lord Wilberforce and Lord Roskill, I agree that, for the reasons there stated, the appeal should be dismissed.

LORD ROSKILL. My Lords, this appeal from an order of Balcombe J made in Liverpool on 14th October 1980 comes directly to your Lordships' House pursuant to the provisions of s 12 of the Administration of Justice Act 1969, the learned judge having granted the appropriate certificate and leave having been subsequently given by your Lordships' House. By his order the learned judge discharged wardship proceedings which the appellant (whom I shall call 'the mother') had begun on 29th August 1980 pursuant to s 9 of the Law Reform (Miscellaneous Provisions) Act 1949. Those proceedings related to her son, to whom in order to avoid further identification I shall refer as K, then some two years of age and now 2½. The first respondent to that summons were the present respondents, the Liverpool City Council ('the local authority'). The second respondent was K's father who has not appeared or taken part in these proceedings.

My Lords, it cannot be doubted that the learned judge was bound by authorities of long standing to discharge the wardship proceedings which the mother had begun. Those authorities start with Re A B (an infant) [1954] 2 All ER 287, [1954] 2 QB 385. That decision was expressly approved by the Court of Appeal in Re M (an infant) [1961] 1 All ER 788, [1961] Ch 328. It has been repeatedly followed both in the Court of Appeal and by judges of first instance in the ensuing twenty years, as for example in Re T (AJJ) (an infant) [1970] 2 All ER 865, [1970] Ch 688 and most recently in Re W (minors) (wardship: jurisdiction) [1979] 3 All ER 154, [1980] Fam 60. The effect of those and other decisions is clear and is well summarised by the learned judge in his judgment in the present case:

> 'The court will not, indeed should not, exercise its wardship jurisdiction when what is sought to be done is to question the manner in which a local authority in whose favour a care order has been made is exercising its statutory jurisdiction.'

But your Lordships' House has not previously considered the problems arising from the coexistence of the wardship jurisdiction of the court and the statutory jurisdiction of *a* local authorities in relation to the care and control of children which is exercised by those authorities. It was to enable that consideration to be given that leave to appeal was given in the instant case.

The relevant facts can be shortly stated. On 10th March 1980 the local authority obtained a care order pursuant to s 1(2)(a) and (3) of the Children and Young Persons Act 1969 in respect of K. He was then placed with foster parents but the mother was allowed *b* weekly access. That access continued until 16th June 1980 when the mother was told that henceforth only monthly supervised access would be allowed. That access was to take place at a day nursery and was to be limited to one hour. The local authority's stated reason was that 'rehabilitation' of the mother and K was not in K's best interest. Accordingly there was no point in maintaining regular access when no such 'rehabilitation' was still planned.   *c*

The local authority refused to reconsider its decision and it was with the intention of challenging that decision as 'wholly unreasonable' and 'arbitrary' that the present wardship proceedings were begun. The summons issued by the mother not only sought from the court an order for defined access but also care and control of K. The learned judge, rightly in my view, declined to express any view on the facts, being of the opinion as already stated that he was bound by authority to discharge the wardship proceedings. *d*

An attempt was made on behalf of the mother before the learned judge to challenge the decision of the local authority on the basis of the well-known decision of the Court of Appeal in *Associated Provincial Picture Houses Ltd v Wednesbury Corpn* [1947] 2 All ER 680, [1948] 1 KB 223. There was no evidence which could possibly justify this attempted challenge and the learned judge rightly rejected it. This challenge was not renewed in argument before your Lordships' House.   *e*

Counsel for the mother rightly accepted that the mother's appeal could not succeed unless your Lordships were prepared to overrule the long-standing decisions to which I have already referred of *Re A B* and *Re M*, and he invited your Lordships to do so. His basic challenge to those decisions was that each was wrong in so far as it asserted that the wardship jurisdiction of the court was curtailed or restricted by the relevant legislation, at the time of the former case the Children Act 1948 and at the time of the latter the 1969 *f* Act, both of which statutes had been later amended by the Children Act 1975. Those cases and also *Re T (A J J)* had been decided before the decision of your Lordships' House in *J v C* [1969] 1 All ER 788, [1970] AC 688 which authoritatively determined that under the Guardianship of Infants Act 1925, since replaced by the Guardianship of Minors Act 1971 as later amended, it was the welfare of the child which was the first and paramount consideration, a statutory provision seemingly ignored, so counsel claimed, both in the *g* arguments and in the judgments in those three cases to which I have just referred. Once it was accepted that the welfare of the child was the paramount consideration the court should freely exercise its wardship jurisdiction in any case where it could be shown that the decision taken by the local authority did not satisfy what the court might think was in the best interest of the welfare of the child concerned.

Though a right of appeal to quarter sessions, now to the Crown Court, had been given *h* to a child under s 2(12) of the 1969 Act against (subject to a single exception) an order made under s 1 of that Act, and a wholly new right of appeal to the High Court was given by s 58 of the 1975 Act, which added s 4A to the 1948 Act so as to permit appeals to the High Court from a juvenile court which had made or refused to make orders under s 2(5) or s 4(3) of that Act, no statutory right of appeal had even been accorded to a person aggrieved by the exercise of the day-to-day performance of its statutory duties in relation *j* to child care by a local authority. It was therefore essential, so counsel for the mother submitted, to the welfare of the child that the court should retain and be prepared to exercise its wardship jurisdiction so as to ensure that the child's welfare always remained the paramount consideration.

Counsel for the mother also pointed to the powers given to the court under s 7(2) of the Family Law Reform Act 1969 which enabled the court in the exercise of wardship jurisdiction to commit a child to the care of a local authority and to the encouragement which in recent years had been given by the courts and particularly by the Court of Appeal to local authorities themselves to invoke the wardship jurisdiction of the court so as to supplement their own sometimes inadequate statutory powers by adding to them the powers which the court could exercise in its own jurisdiction. It was, counsel for the mother contended, illogical that when in these respects the two jurisdictions were complementary there should be objection to the wardship jurisdiction being made available not as (he claimed) a means of appeal against or review of the day-to-day administrative decisions of the local authority but as a means of ensuring that the welfare of the child was always the paramount consideration in reaching whatever decision was taken in accordance with the requirements of the 1925 and 1971 Acts to which I have already referred.

My Lords, I do not think it necessary to review the authorities on the interrelationship between prerogative and statutory powers. The basic principles were authoritatively determined by your Lordships' House in *Attorney General v De Keyser's Royal Hotel Ltd* [1920] AC 508, [1920] All ER Rep 80: see especially the speech of Lord Sumner ([1920] AC 508 at 561, [1920] All ER Rep 80 at 103). My Lords, I do not doubt that the wardship jurisdiction of the court is not extinguished by the existence of the legislation regarding the care and control of deprived children, a phrase I use to include children whose parents have for some reason failed to discharge their parental duties towards them. I am not aware of any decision which suggests otherwise. It is helpful to examine the unsuccessful submissions in *Re A B* [1954] 2 QB 385 at 389–390 of J E Simon QC for the foster parents and the successful submissions of R J Parker for the local authority. Mr Parker argued that 'the court's powers as parens patriae are limited by the Children Act, 1948 by which Parliament has committed, in certain cases, the task and the right of the supervision of the welfare of children to local authorities'. It was this argument which Lord Goddard CJ was accepting (see [1954] 2 All ER 287 at 291, [1954] 2 QB 385 at 398). Indeed, Donovan J concurring on this point said ([1954] 2 All ER 287 at 293, [1954] 2 QB 385 at 401):

'Thus far, at any rate, Parliament has entrusted the welfare of the child to the local authority, and to that extent the prerogative right to secure the welfare of the child is, in my view, by necessary implication, restricted. Accordingly ... the court cannot intervene simply because it differs from the local authority as to what is best for the child.'

It was this view which found favour with the Court of Appeal in *Re M*. Lord Evershed MR, with whom Upjohn and Pearson LJJ expressly concurred, stated his first two conclusions thus ([1961] 1 All ER 788 at 795, [1961] Ch 328 at 345):

'(i) The prerogative right of the Queen as parens patriae in relation to infants within the realm is not for all purposes ousted or abrogated as the result of the exercise of the duties and powers by local authorities under the Children Act, 1948: in particular the power to make an infant a ward of court by invocation of s. 9 of the Act of 1949 is unaffected. (ii) But even where a child is made a ward of court by virtue of the Act of 1949, the judge in whom the prerogative power is vested will, acting on familiar principles, not exercise control in relation to duties or discretions clearly vested by statute in the local authority, and may, therefore, and in a case such as the present normally will, order that the child cease to be a ward of court.'

The statutory codes which existed in 1958 and in 1961 have been elaborated and extended and amended several times since these decisions as the social needs of our society have changed and, unhappily, the number of deprived children in the care of local authorities has tragically increased. It cannot possibly be said that the massive volume of legislation since 1961 culminating in the Child Care Act 1980, a consolidating Act which, though repealing the whole of the 1948 Act, left intact the early part of the 1969 Act has lessened the responsibilities of local authorities. This hardly suggests an intention by Parliament to restrict the scope of the statutory control by local authorities of child welfare in favour of the use by the courts of the prerogative wardship jurisdiction. On the contrary, the plain intention of this legislation is to secure the *a* continued expansion of that statutory control.

I do not think that the language of s 1 of the Guardianship of Infants Act 1925 and of its statutory successor in any way points in a contrary direction. The former statute, as its preamble shows, was largely designed to secure equality of rights as between father and mother in relation to their children and making the welfare of those children paramount in relation to those two henceforth equal interests. Nor do I think that the *b* emphasis laid on that section in your Lordships' House in *J v C* casts any doubt on the correctness of the several earlier decisions to which I have already referred.

I am of the clear opinion that, while prerogative jurisdiction of the court in wardship cases remains, the exercise of that jurisdiction has been and must continue to be treated as circumscribed by the existence of the far-ranging statutory code which entrusts the care and control of deprived children to local authorities. It follows that the undoubted *c* wardship jurisdiction must not be exercised so as to interfere with the day-to-day administration by local authorities of that statutory control.

My Lords, to say that is not to suggest that local authorities are immune from judicial control: in an appropriate case, as Lord Evershed MR himself said in *Re M*, the *Wednesbury* principle is available. The remedy of judicial review under RSC Ord 53 is also available in an appropriate case. Moreover, there are the specific, if limited, rights *d* of appeal to which I have already drawn attention.

My Lords, I think this conclusion is strongly reinforced by the consideration that, though the law as laid down by the courts has been clear since 1961 when *Re M* was decided and though there have been many legislative changes since that date, noticeably in 1969 and again in 1975 when the new right of appeal or review to the High Court already mentioned was first created, no right of appeal or review such as the mother has in effect now *e* seeks to achieve by invocation of the wardship jurisdiction of the court has ever been accorded by Parliament. The inference that I would draw from that fact is that Parliament was satisfied with the restriction on the remedies available to a person aggrieved by a discretionary administrative decision of the local authority, declared by the cases to which I have referred, and decided to leave the law as thus laid down unaffected.   *f*

Much reliance on the mother's behalf was placed on the decision of the Court of Appeal affirming Balcombe J in *Re H (a minor) (wardship: jurisdiction)* [1978] 2 All ER 903, [1978] Fam 65, where that court, in agreement with the learned judge, exercised its wardship jurisdiction so as to enable the Pakistani parents of a child in respect of whom a care order had been made under s 1 of the 1969 Act to remove that child from this country, notwithstanding the existence of that care order. The juvenile court concerned *g* was precluded from discharging that care order because of the amendment to the 1969 Act effected by the introduction into that Act of s 21(2A) by the 1975 Act (see [1978] 2 All ER 903 at 910, [1978] Fam 65 at 77). The judgment of the Court of Appeal delivered by Ormrod LJ contains (if I may respectfully say so) a most valuable review of all the relevant statutory provisions and judicial decisions in this field as they stood at the date of that decision. Moreover the judgment drew attention to the anomalies which exist *h* between those cases where a statutory right of appeal existed and those where it did not (see [1978] 2 All ER 903 at 909–910, [1978] Fam 65 at 76–77). As I have already said, however unfortunate it may seem that these anomalies exist, the recent legislative history suggests that their retention has not been accidental. In *Re H* the Court of Appeal felt able to exercise wardship jurisdiction because 'the challenge is directed, not to the exercise of a discretionary power, but to the source of that power' (see [1978] 2 All ER 903 at 909, [1978] Fam 65 at 76). Since it is the exercise of a discretionary administrative *j* power of which the mother now seeks to complain in the instant case, the decision in *Re H* is of no assistance to her. But I confess, with all respect to the judgment of the Court of Appeal, I find the suggested distinction by Ormrod LJ of *Re M* and the other cases, which he himself described as 'slim' (see [1978] 2 All ER 903 at 908, [1978] Fam 65 at 74–

75), difficult to justify in principle. The decision in *Re H* is, if I may respectfully say so,
obviously sensible: whilst acknowledging the possibility of some risk to the child, this
was the lesser of the only two possible courses which it was open to a court to take, the
other being to leave the child behind in this country after its parents had returned to
Pakistan.

I venture to think that the decision can perhaps be better supported on the ground that
the wardship jurisdiction of the court could properly be invoked in addition to the
statutory jurisdiction of the local authority because it was only in this way that the result
which was best in the paramount interest of the child could be achieved, the local
authority and juvenile court being unable within the limits of their powers to achieve
that result.

Lane J in *Re B (a minor) (wardship: child in care)* [1974] 3 All ER 915, [1975] Fam 36
drew attention to the positive advantages which could flow from the invocation of
wardship jurisdiction in cases of child abuse from the point of view of local authorities.
Though the learned judge refused the grandmother's application for care and control of
the child in the wardship proceedings which the grandmother had begun, she continued
those proceedings so that if required the local authority could apply for an injunction
restraining the child's undesirable stepfather from any contact or attempted contact with
the child. A local authority may often be powerless to stop attempted interference by
third parties. The exercise of wardship jurisdiction affords a simple method of attaining
a result much to be desired in such cases.

Re D (a minor) (justices' decision: review) [1977] 3 All ER 481, [1977] Fam 158 affords
another illustration of the utility of wardship jurisdiction which in that case was invoked
by the local authority and accepted by Dunn J. But, with respect, I cannot agree with the
learned judge's suggested distinction between the welfare of the child always being
paramount in wardship proceedings but not in cases under the 1969 Act. It is true that
the language of the relevant parts of the 1969 and the 1925 Acts is somewhat different.
But I agree with the comment of Ormrod LJ on this statement in *Re H* [1978] 2 All ER
903 at 910, [1978] Fam 65 at 77 because, as the learned Lord Justice there said, juvenile
courts always do act in the best interests of the child so far as their powers permit.

In the result I am clearly of the opinion that the earlier cases to which I have referred
were rightly decided, and should now be affirmed by your Lordships' House. On any
view, had I felt doubts on this matter, which I do not, I would have been reluctant to
suggest to your Lordships that those cases should, after twenty years and more, be
disturbed for they have been acted on many times, both in the Court of Appeal and by
judges at first instance. But the wardship jurisdiction of the court is never extinguished
merely because the child is in the care of a local authority. Its exercise must, however,
be closely circumscribed. I do not think that any useful purpose would be served by your
Lordships attempting to define the limits within which that circumscription must exist,
for cases of this class vary infinitely. Clearly the jurisdiction can be invoked by a local
authority when its own powers are inadequate to make the welfare of the child
paramount or when it is necessary to this end to take action against some stranger. But
the courts must not, in purported exercise of wardship jurisdiction, interfere with those
matters which Parliament has decided are within the province of a local authority to
whom the care and control of a child has been entrusted pursuant to statutory
provisions. That is what the mother seeks in the present case. I think the learned judge
was entirely right in the order he made and I would dismiss the appeal and answer the
certified question in accordance with what I have already said.

Appeal dismissed.

Solicitors: *Bulcraig & Davis*, agents for *E Rex Makin & Co*, Liverpool (for the mother);
Howlett & Clarke, Cree & Co, agents for *K M Egan*, Liverpool (for the local authority).

Mary Rose Plummer   Barrister.

Inland Revenue Commissioners v Stype Investments (Jersey) Ltd

CHANCERY DIVISION

GOULDING J

23rd, 24th, 25th, 26th, 27th FEBRUARY, 12th MARCH 1981

Capital transfer tax – Liability for tax – Persons liable as executor or trustee – Executor de son tort – Intermeddling – Company selling land as bare nominee for beneficial owner – Company resident in Jersey – Owner dying before completion of sale – Steps not taken to obtain grant of representation – Company remitting purchase money to its own bank account in Jersey – Whether company intermeddling – Whether company acting as executor de son tort – Finance Act 1975, s 25(6)(a).

The defendant, a company resident in Jersey, held land in England as a nominee for C. In 1979 the defendant, at the request of C, sold the land to P Ltd. C died on 26th July 1979 and when the sale was completed in September no grant of representation had been obtained in respect of his estate. In the circumstances, the defendant was obliged to hold the net proceeds of sale on behalf of C's estate, which it did by transferring them to its own bank account in Jersey. Subsequently, when still no personal representative had been constituted in respect of C's estate, the Inland Revenue Commissioners, taking the view that the defendant, by transferring the proceeds of sale to Jersey, had intermeddled with C's property and had thus become liable as an executor within s 25(6)(a)[a] of the Finance Act 1975, obtained an order giving leave under RSC Ord. 11 to issue and serve an originating summons against the defendant in Jersey claiming, inter alia, (i) delivery by the defendant of an account for the purposes of capital transfer tax of all property comprised in C's estate at his death and (ii) an injunction restraining the defendant from removing or dealing with its own assets within the jurisdiction of the court until the account had been delivered and any tax and interest due from the defendant had been paid. The defendant applied to have the order set aside, contending that it was not an executor within the meaning of s 25(6)(a) of the 1975 Act.

Held – If a person appointed a foreign resident to receive money about to fall due to the appointor in England and the appointor died before the money was payable, the foreign resident was not liable as an executor de son tort merely by taking the money to his place of residence before a grant of representation was made by the English court. Accordingly, the defendant was not liable as executor within s 25(6)(a) of the 1975 Act. It followed therefore that the case was not a proper one for service out of the jurisdiction and the order made pursuant to RSC Ord 11 would be set aside (see p 400 a b and d to j, post).

Notes

For the executor de son tort and intermeddling with the estate, see 17 Halsbury's Laws (4th Edn) paras 753–762, and for cases on the subject, see 23 Digest (Reissue) 69–76, 846–930.

For the Finance Act 1975, s 25, see 45 Halsbury's Statutes (3rd Edn) 1805.

Cases referred to in judgment

Hooper v Summersett (1810) Wight 16, 145 ER 1157, 23 Digest (Reissue) 73, 902.

New York Breweries Co v Attorney General [1899] AC 62, 68 LJQB 135, 79 LT 568, HL; *affg* [1898] 1 QB 205, CA, 23 Digest (Reissue) 78, 967.

Serle v Waterworth (1838) 4 M & W 9, 6 Dowl 684, 1 Horn & H 281, 7 LJ Ex 202, 150 ER 1321, 2 Jur 745, 23 Digest (Reissue) 73, 899.

---

a   Section 25(6), so far as material, is set out at p 396 e, post

Cases also cited

a Bayne v Slack (1857) 3 CBNS 363, 140 ER 781.
Bird, Re, ex parte the Debtor v Inland Revenue Comrs [1962] 2 All ER 406, [1962] 1 WLR 686, CA.
Dodd's Case (1857) 2 De G & J 510, 44 ER 1087.
Jay v Budd [1898] 1 QB 12, CA.
R v Gardner (1774) 1 Cowp 79, 98 ER 977.
b Siskina, The [1977] 3 All ER 803, [1979] AC 210, HL.
Tyne Improvement Comrs v Armement Anversois SA, The Brabo [1949] 1 All ER 294, [1949] AC 326, HL.
Vitkovice Horni a Hutni Tezirstvo v Korner [1951] 2 All ER 334, [1951] AC 869, HL.

Motion

c By a notice of motion dated 14th November 1980 the defendant, Stype Investments (Jersey) Ltd, moved to set aside an order made on 12th September 1980 by which the Commissioners of Inland Revenue obtained leave to issue an originating summons against the defendant and leave to serve the summons on the defendant in Jersey. The facts are set out in the judgment.

d Leolin Price QC and P W E Taylor for the defendant.
Peter Gibson for the Crown.

Cur adv vult

e 12th March. GOULDING J read the following judgment: The late Sir Charles Clore died in London on 26th July 1979. I shall refer to him simply as 'Sir Charles'. It is common ground that he was a very rich man. Unfortunately, his testamentary dispositions are under attack in the courts both of Monaco and of Jersey, and those who claim to be the executors of his last will have, as yet, been unable to proceed very far with the administration of his estate. The plaintiffs in this action, namely the Commissioners f of Inland Revenue, find that, more than 18 months after his death, no steps have yet been taken to constitute a legal personal representative of Sir Charles in England or elsewhere in the United Kingdom. The commissioners are thus impeded in the performance of their duty to determine the amount, and to exact payment, of any capital transfer tax chargeable on his death. Their anxiety is all the greater because it seems probable on the facts that (subject to specific statutory exemptions) the value of all Sir Charles's unsettled g estate, wherever situate, is chargeable to capital transfer tax, yet a large part of such estate, as well as other assets that may be so taxable on his death, is located outside the United Kingdom. It is said by the commissioners that Sir Charles's outstanding liabilities to creditors in the United Kingdom exceed in value the assets of his estate at present within the Kingdom.

The defendant to the action is a company which was incorporated, and has at all h material times been resident, in Jersey. The defendant is possessed, in circumstances which I shall soon have to narrate, of a large sum of money which forms part, probably the greater part, of Sir Charles's unsettled estate.

Because of the litigation I have mentioned the defendant is, as yet, unable to get a good receipt for that money from duly constituted personal representatives of Sir Charles. In those circumstances the commissioners obtained leave, pursuant to RSC Ord 11, to issue an originating summons and to serve it on the defendant in Jersey. By the motion on which I am about to give judgment the defendant applies to the court to set aside the order authorising the commissioners to issue and serve the originating summons and all the subsequent proceedings.

By the originating summons the commissioners claim three heads of relief. Put shortly they are as follows: (1) delivery by the defendant of an account for purposes of

capital transfer tax of all property comprised in Sir Charles's estate at his death; (2)
delivery by the defendant on oath of documents in support of such account; and (3) an *a*
injunction restraining the defendant from removing or dealing with its own assets
within the jurisdiction of the court until the account has been delivered and any tax and
interest due from the defendant has been paid.

Leave to serve the summons out of the jurisdiction was given under Ord 11, r 9. I
need not consider whether or not the case falls within para (2) of the rule, since counsel
for the Crown agrees that he must show the commissioner's claim is within one or other *b*
of the cases enumerated in r 1(1) of Ord 11. He relies principally on case (*o*), saying that
the action is brought in respect of a claim by the commissioners for capital transfer tax.
He relies also on case (*i*), submitting that all three heads of the relief claimed seek an
order requiring the defendant to do or refrain from doing something within the
jurisdiction. Counsel for the defendant took a preliminary objection that there is as yet
no actual claim by the commissioners for capital transfer tax. All they are seeking at *c*
present is the performance of statutory obligations, alleged to be binding on the
defendant, intended to enable the commissioners to formulate and quantify a claim for
tax. Therefore, it is argued, the present action is not brought in respect of a claim for
tax. This contention, although to me attractive, requires, in my judgment, too pedantic
a construction of the material part of Ord 11, and I reject it. In any case the
commissioners, in my opinion, bring themselves within case (*i*). *d*

I proceed, therefore, to examine the basis of the commissioners' claim against the
defendant. I need not take time to go through the relevant provisions of the Finance Act
1975, for it is common ground that to obtain the relief they seek the commissioners
must, on the hearing of the originating summons, show that the defendant is, in relation
to Sir Charles, within the definition of personal representatives contained in s 51(1) of
that Act by reason of being such a person as is mentioned in s 25(6)(*a*) thereof. Section *e*
25(6)(*a*) is in these terms:

'any person who takes possession of or intermeddles with, or otherwise acts in
relation to, property so as to become liable as executor or trustee (or, in Scotland, any
person who intromits with property or has become liable as a vitious intromitter) . . .'

The primary facts whereby the defendant is alleged so to have intermeddled with *f*
property of Sir Charles as to become liable as an executor are not in dispute, save that (as
will appear) the commissioners do not accept the defendant's evidence regarding its
motives in effecting the material transaction and intend to challenge it in the course of
the proceedings if they are allowed to go ahead. In my view (as will also appear) there is
enough before the court at this stage to enable me to decide whether the commissioners
are right in law in treating the defendant as a person within s 25(6)(*a*) of the 1975 Act, *g*
and on the authorities relating to Ord 11 I conceive that it is my duty to do so. I must,
therefore, set out shortly the history on which the commissioners base their case. It is
common ground that the test to be applied is that of the general law relating to the
character of an executor de son tort.

The defendant was very closely connected with Sir Charles during his life and is *h*
equally closely connected with his estate. Its share capital is held on the trusts of a
settlement made by Sir Charles in February 1979 under the laws of Jersey. Sir Charles
retained a life interest under the settlement, with remainder on trust for the benefit of
charitable institutions, though not necessarily charitable in the technical sense of English
law. The directors of the defendant during Sir Charles's lifetime were himself, three
professional friends or advisers of his, and the manager of Lloyds Bank Trust Co (Channel *j*
Islands) Ltd, Mr J K Dobbs. None of them was resident in the United Kingdom and only
Mr Dobbs was resident in Jersey. Mr Dobbs's employer, Lloyds Bank Trust Co (Channel
Islands) Ltd, was and is secretary of the defendant. The day-to-day conduct of its affairs
has clearly rested at all material times very largely in the hands of Mr Dobbs. The three
professional gentlemen I have mentioned are the executors named in what is alleged to

be the last will of Sir Charles dealing with all his property, wherever situate, outside the
a Principality of Monaco. One of them, counsel has stated, has since renounced the office
of executor and resigned as a director of the defendant.

In 1961 Sir Charles acquired a large landed estate in Herefordshire from the board of
governors of Guy's Hospital. As enlarged by certain subsequent acquisitions by Sir
Charles, and diminished by certain sales or other dispositions on his part, that property
appears to have been known to his advisers as the 'Guy's estate' and I shall so refer to it.
b By a conveyance dated 23rd May 1979 Sir Charles conveyed the Guy's estate to the
defendant in fee simple. The conveyance discloses no consideration, except certain
covenants by the defendant to indemnify Sir Charles from liabilities affecting the
property, and declares no express trust. By a contemporaneous deed, however, made
between the defendant and Sir Charles, an intention was declared that no beneficial
interest in the property should pass to the defendant and that the defendant should hold
c it as a bare nominee for Sir Charles. This instrument contained an acknowledgment by
the defendant of Sir Charles's beneficial ownership and its undertaking to convey the
property as he should direct and to account for the future net proceeds of sale and net
rents and profits thereof, subject to the defendant's right to pay outgoings from the
rents. Sir Charles, however, requested the defendant itself to sell the Guy's estate to the
Prudential Assurance Co Ltd. The defendant acceded to that request and effected the sale
d in its own name as the legal landowner. For convenience the contract between the
defendant and the Prudential was contained in two documents, each referring to the
other, relating to different parts of the Guy's estate. The aggregate purchase money was
£20,500,000 and a deposit of £1,025,000 was paid by the Prudential to the defendant's
solicitors in London as stakeholders. The completion date stipulated in each document
was 28th September 1979. I may observe that, after the sale to the Prudential, it was, in
e my opinion, no longer accurate to describe the defendant as a bare nominee for Sir
Charles. The defendant had now assumed the active duty of completing for the benefit
of Sir Charles the contract which it had entered into in its own name at his request.

Completion took place on or about the stipulated date. Sir Charles, of course, had by
then been dead for two months, and no grant had been obtained in respect of his
estate. The defendant was thus obliged to receive the purchase money and to retain it for
f the time being. Shortly before the completion date the defendant through its London
solicitors arranged with the Prudential that the money payable on completion should be
remitted direct by the Prudential to the defendant's account with a bank in Jersey. The
defendant also instructed its solicitors to transfer to the same account the balance of the
deposit held by them, after retaining their costs and expenses. The whole net proceeds
of sale of the Guy's estate thus came to be deposited in Jersey. The defendant has since
g been restrained from disposing of them by interlocutory injunctions of the Royal Court
of Jersey, in proceedings instituted by Sir Charles's son.

The commissioners suggest that the motive of the defendant's instructions to transmit
the money to Jersey was to enable the defendant to pay it hereafter to Sir Charles's
executors under the authority of a grant of probate in the court of the island, thus eliding
the necessity for an English grant, and avoiding the payment of capital transfer tax. An
h officer of the commissioners, in an affidavit, put the matter as follows:

> 'It must have been known to the Defendant when deciding two months after the
> Deceased's death to transfer the proceeds of sale of the Guy's Estate out of the
> jurisdiction to Jersey that the Deceased's interest in the Guy's Estate and the proceeds
> of sale formed part of the Deceased's estate at his death and that capital transfer tax
> was chargeable in respect thereof, that an English grant of probate or letters of
i > administration would be needed to establish the title of the Deceased's personal
> representatives to the net proceeds of sale if left within the jurisdiction and that to
> transfer the proceeds out of the jurisdiction to Jersey would prevent English personal
> representatives from establishing title thereto and would entitle Jersey personal
> representatives to establish title thereto.'

The defendant does not accept that allegation. Mr Dobbs swears that the defendant's bank accounts had always been where its day-to-day management took place, namely at St Helier, and that until the summer of 1980 it never had any bank account in the United Kingdom. He also says it was thought that a higher rate of interest, after payment of any tax, could be obtained on a bank deposit in Jersey than in the United Kingdom.

The commissioners suggest further that the defendant wanted to have the money in Jersey with a view to providing financial assistance to the persons claiming to be executors of Sir Charles's will during the early stages of their administration of his estate, that is for necessary expenses before probate. The defendant, however, says that it was largely indebted to Sir Charles at the time of his death, and that the advances it has made to his executors come from its own funds. In general answer to the commissioners' suspicions, Mr Dobbs has sworn as follows:

'None of these considerations in fact entered into the remitting of the proceeds to Jersey. At the time I and, I believe, my co-Directors of the Defendant Company were unaware that it would make any significant difference to the subsequent disposal of the proceeds. It was not then appreciated that there might be long delays in obtaining a grant of probate in England or Jersey, or in resealing a grant in one of these countries in the other, or that there would be any capital transfer tax issues raised by the remittance of the proceeds belonging to the Defendant Company. I then thought, and still believe, that the Executors would, and should, look for payment of the net proceeds of sale from the seat of the Defendant Company in Jersey after the Company had retained its expenses of the sale out of the proceeds.'

It is correct to say, as counsel for the defendant insists, that the evidence of motive from the commissioners' side necessarily consists of inference, while Mr Dobbs is giving direct testimony of things within his own knowledge. Counsel for the defendant has also pointed out in argument that if the defendant's motive was to escape from the clutches of the commissioners it did not do so very cleverly, for it left several million pounds' worth of the defendant's own assets invested in United Kingdom government stocks registered at the Bank of England. Those holdings are now the subject of an interlocutory order in these proceedings, restraining the defendant from removing or disposing of them until the determination of the originating summons or further order. However, the commissioners (as I have already indicated) do not accept Mr Dobbs's statements, and desire to test them by the processes of discovery, and by cross-examination on the hearing of the originating summons. I have considered whether I ought not, even on that ground alone, to allow the proceedings to go forward. On the whole, however, I find it insufficient by itself. Neither side in argument treated the question of motive as crucial, and I think I am bound to decide generally, on the material before me, whether the commissioners have shown such a case as justifies the exercise of the court's discretion to allow service in another jurisdiction. I turn therefore to the law of executor de son tort.

On that topic three authorities have been cited. The oldest is *Hooper v Summersett* (1810) Wight 16, 145 ER 1157, a decision of the Court of Exchequer. There the defendant was held liable for a debt of his deceased mother-in-law, a publican, on the ground that he had lived in the house and carried on the business, in the same manner as in her lifetime. The judgment of the court, delivered by Macdonald CB, said (Wight 16 at 21, 145 ER 1157 at 1159): 'The authorities to shew, that this is a sufficient intermeddling, are too strong to be got over', but the court did not find it necessary to formulate any criterion in general terms. The case was indeed, I think, a clear one. Counsel for the plaintiff had argued (Wight 16 at 20–21, 145 ER 1157 at 1159): '. . . he was in fact living in the house, and using the goods exactly as his own, and if that does not constitute him an Executor de son tort, nothing will.'

The next case is *Serle v Waterworth* (1838) 4 M & W 9, 150 ER 1321 in the Court of Exchequer. The defendant, though alleged to be chargeable as executrix de son tort, was held liable on an alternative ground, and the judgments really throw no light on the former question.

The third, and the principal, authority debated before me was *New York Breweries Co*
v Attorney General [1899] AC 62. The appellant company was there held by the House of
Lords to have made itself an executor de son tort by transferring shares on its share
register from the name of a deceased American member into the names of executors who
had proved his will in New York but had not obtained, and had no intention of
obtaining, a grant in England. The company was held to have intermeddled with an
asset of the deceased's estate and to have performed without lawful authority an act of
administration, because in the words of Lord Halsbury LC (at 69) it 'did an act whereby
the title to the property belonging to the deceased person became vested in somebody
else', and therefore prima facie was an executor de son tort. Lord Shand said (at 76):

> 'The right could never have been transferred if they had not interposed or
> intervened and, to that extent, intromitted in this estate. I think, therefore, that the
> result was that they became executors de son tort.'

Lord Davey said (at 77):

> 'If a man who owes money to a deceased person takes upon himself to pay that
> money to some one who has no authority to receive it, I think he does an act which
> is an appropriation in his own hands, and asserts a right to exercise control and
> dominion over the debt.'

In addition to the authorities, I have been referred by counsel to two or three recent
textbooks. They draw attention to the provisions of s 28 of the Administration of Estates
Act 1925, which is in the following terms:

> 'If any person, to the defrauding of creditors or without full valuable consideration,
> obtains, receives or holds any real or personal estate of a deceased person or effects
> the release of any debt or liability due to the estate of the deceased, he shall be
> charged as executor in his own wrong to the extent of the real and personal estate
> received or coming to his hands, or the debt or liability released, after deducting—
> (*a*) any debt for valuable consideration and without fraud due to him from the
> deceased person at the time of his death; and (*b*) any payment made by him which
> might properly be made by a personal representative.'

The learned author of Williams and Mortimer on Executors, Administrators and
Probate (15th and 3rd Edns, 1970, pp 40–41) takes the view that the foregoing section
now defines the liability of an executor de son tort and that it is wide enough to cover all
cases in which liability could, in practice, arise, so that it would be difficult to contend
that there survives a concurrent and independent liability at common law. 17 Halsbury's
Laws (4th Edn) para 753 sets out the terms of the section without suggesting that it
replaces common law liability. The next paragraph, para 754, purports to state the
principle as follows:

> 'The slightest circumstance may make a person executor de son tort if he
> intermeddles with the assets in such a way as to denote an assumption of the
> authority or an intention to exercise the functions of an executor or administrator.'

The commissioners do not now assert that the defendant became an executor de son
tort merely by completing the sale of the Guy's estate and receiving the purchase
money. That concession, I think, is right, for the defendant was contractually bound to
the Prudential to convey the land at the completion date and was under a fiduciary duty
to secure the money for the benefit of Sir Charles's estate. The commissioners' claim is
put on the single act of causing the money to be removed out of the jurisdiction of the
English court. Counsel for the Crown submitted that where a person who is not a
lawfully appointed executor or administrator by his own act intrudes on the affairs of the
deceased he may be treated as an executor de son tort, secondly, that any act which, if
done by an executor named in the will of the deceased, would preclude him from
renouncing probate, will make a person not so named an executor de son tort, and,
thirdly, that the slightest intermeddling with the assets of the deceased is, in principle,

sufficient to create such liability. To take money to a bank beyond the seas, with whatever motive, counsel argued, is plainly such an intrusion, act or intermeddling, *a* because it exposes the asset to the operation of a different legal system and may gravely prejudice the rights of English creditors of the estate.

The question is therefore this: if an individual A appoints a foreign resident B to receive money about to arise to A in England, and A dies before the money is payable, and B, lawfully in the circumstances of the case, receives it after A's death and before a grant of representation has been made by the English court, does B make himself liable *b* as an executor de son tort merely by taking the money to his own place of residence?

There is no direct authority on the question. *Hooper v Summersett* throws no light on it. The transmission of the money does not effect any such change of title as founded the decision in the *New York Breweries* case. Nor, to my mind, on a fair reading of the language of s 28 of the Administration of Estates Act 1925, is it any of the acts there struck at. Nor, if I take the test from Halsbury's Laws, does it in my judgment denote *c* an assumption of the authority, or an intention to exercise the functions, of an executor or administrator.

I must not anticipate a case that has not yet arisen, and may never arise, but I must make it clear that I do not think the liability of the defendant to Sir Charles's estate is in the least affected by the local situation of the money. The asset is one to which Sir Charles's personal representative in England, when duly constituted, will be entitled, *d* and, if the defendant, in whatever part of the world, should part with it without the authority of an English grant, it must not be surprised if it is alleged to have made itself an executor de son tort on the principle of the *New York Breweries* case. But that is not to say that the natural act of taking the money to be held in suspense at the place where the defendant resides is to have the like result. The liabilities of an executor de son tort are onerous, and it would in my judgment be wrong to impose them over a wider field than *e* heretofore in order to meet the difficulties of the commissioners in the present case. The possibility, and on the evidence it is no more than a possibility, of a fraud on English creditors of Sir Charles's estate, or on the Revenue, arises essentially not from the location of the bank account but from the place of residence of the defendant, in whose name the money stands as a result of Sir Charles's dispositions during his lifetime.

For the foregoing reasons, I am of opinion that I am not bound by authority to hold, *f* and ought not without authority to hold, that the defendant is brought within the language of s 25(6)(a) of the Finance Act 1975. It follows that in my judgment the commissioners have not shown to my satisfaction that their case is a proper one for service out of the jurisdiction.

The defendant put forward an alternative and independent objection to the present proceedings by the commissioners. It is founded on the immunities from English *g* process and from taxation in aid of the Crown that have been granted by the Crown, subject to certain exceptions and reservations, to the inhabitants of Jersey. The privileges in question, at least in part, are of ancient origin: in their modern form they may be found in charters of 4 Elizabeth 1 and of 3 James 2. Their true construction and their legal effect at the present day are plainly matters of substantial concern, both to the commissioners and to the inhabitants of Jersey as a class. Accordingly, I think it is better *h* that the English court should make no observations about those matters until it becomes necessary to do so for the purpose of an actual decision.

For the reasons I have already given, accepting the primary submission of the defendant, I set aside the order of 12th September 1980 authorising the issue and service of the concurrent originating summons, and likewise the consequent proceedings. The exact form of the order can, no doubt, be agreed between junior counsel. *j*

Order accordingly.

Solicitors: *Titmuss, Sainer & Webb* (for the defendant); *Solicitor of Inland Revenue.*

Evelyn M C Budd   Barrister.

Wadsworth v Lydall

COURT OF APPEAL, CIVIL DIVISION

ORMROD, BRIGHTMAN LJJ AND REEVE J

15th, 16th JANUARY 1981

b   *Contract – Damages for breach – Foreseeable consequence of breach – Special loss incurred as consequence of non-payment of contract price – Interest charges – Parties dissolving farming partnership – Defendant agreeing to make payment to plaintiff on dissolution – Plaintiff purchasing another farm in anticipation of receiving payment – Defendant defaulting in making payment – Plaintiff incurring interest charges because of delay in completion of purchase of new farm – Whether interest charges too remote – Whether plaintiff entitled to recover interest* *c*   *charges from defendant.*

The plaintiff and the defendant went into partnership to farm a property owned by the defendant. Three years later when the defendant wished to sell the property the parties agreed to dissolve the partnership in consideration of the defendant paying £10,000 to the plaintiff in return for receiving vacant possession of the property. The plaintiff, *d*   anticipating the receipt of the £10,000 from the defendant, entered into an agreement to purchase another property for £16,000, £10,000 to be paid on completion and the balance three years later. The plaintiff vacated the defendant's farm in accordance with the dissolution agreement but the plaintiff failed to pay the £10,000 as agreed. Instead he paid £7,200 some months later and the plaintiff was forced to take out a second mortgage for £2,861 to complete the purchase of the new property. The plaintiff *e*   brought an action against the defendant claiming, inter alia, £2,800, being the balance of the £10,000, £335 in respect of interest incurred because of the delay in the completion of the purchase of the new property and £16·20 legal costs of the second mortgage. The judge found that the defendant owed the plaintiff £2,800 but dismissed the claim for interest and legal costs on the ground that they were too remote. The plaintiff appealed.

f

Held – Where the circumstances were such that there was a special loss, including the incurring of interest charges, as a consequence of non-payment of money under a contract and the loss was foreseeable at the time of the contract, the loss was recoverable from the defaulting party. Since the defendant knew at the time of the dissolution agreement that the plaintiff would need to buy another farm and would need the *g*   £10,000 to do so and would have to pay interest if it was not forthcoming, the plaintiff was entitled to recover the interest and charges incurred as a result of the defendant's default. The plaintiff's appeal would accordingly be allowed (see p 405 *a* to *c* and *j* to p 406 *a f g j* and p 407 *a* and *h* to p 408 *a*, post).

Dicta of Denning and Romer LJJ in *Trans Trust SPRL v Danubian Trading Co Ltd* [1952] 1 All ER at 977, 978 applied.

h   *London, Chatham and Dover Railway Co v South Eastern Railway Co* [1893] AC 429 distinguished.

Notes

For remoteness of damage in contract and tort, see 12 Halsbury's Laws (4th Edn) paras 1127, 1133, and for cases on the subject, see 17 Digest (Reissue) 135–143, 312–371.

j   **Cases referred to in judgments**

Hadley v Baxendale (1854) 9 Exch 341, [1843–60] All ER Rep 461, 23 LJ Ex 179, 23 LTOS 69, 18 Jur 358, 2 CLR 517, 156 ER 145, 17 Digest (Reissue) 101, 109.

London, Chatham and Dover Railway Co v South Eastern Railway Co [1893] AC 429, 63 LJ Ch 93, 69 LT 637, 58 JP 36, 1 R 275, HL, 35 Digest (Repl) 209, 159.

Parsons (H) (Livestock) Ltd v Uttley Ingham & Co Ltd [1978] 1 All ER 525, [1978] QB 791, [1977] 3 WLR 990, [1977] 2 Lloyd's Rep 522, CA, Digest (Cont Vol E) 172, 110a.

Trans Trust SPRL v Danubian Trading Co Ltd [1952] 1 All ER 970, [1952] 2 QB 297, [1952]
1 Lloyd's Rep 348, CA, 39 Digest (Repl) 781, 2557.   *a*

Appeal
The plaintiff, David Howard Wadsworth, appealed against the judgment of Smith J
given in the Queen's Bench Division at Leeds on 7th December 1979 dismissing part of
the plaintiff's claim in an action to recover money from the defendant, Frank B Lydall.
The facts are set out in the judgment of Brightman LJ.
                                                                                               b

John Behrens for the plaintiff.
Timothy Hirst for the defendant.

BRIGHTMAN LJ delivered the first judgment at the invitation of Ormrod LJ. This
is an appeal from an order made by Smith J in an action by one partner to recover money   *c*
said to be due from the other partner on the dissolution of the partnership.
   In 1972 the defendant bought a dairy farm known as Cherry Tree Farm, near
Sheffield. His purpose was to accommodate his racehorses rather than to farm the land
himself. He entered into an informal partnership agreement with the plaintiff under
which the partnership was granted an agricultural tenancy by the defendant and the
farm was to be run by the plaintiff and his wife at a salary for each of them. The capital
of the partnership was £6,000 contributed by them in equal shares in cash or kind. The *d*
net profits of the partnership business were to be divided between the two partners
equally.
   Three years later the defendant decided to determine the partnership so that he could
sell the farm, as he was entitled to do. The plaintiff had nowhere else to live and no other
occupation and, not unnaturally, sought to protect his position. He had the advantage
of a partnership share in an agricultural tenancy, and that no doubt gave him a bargaining *e*
counter. Negotiations ensued between the plaintiff and the defendant. The defendant
made arrangements to sell the farm by auction on 22nd January 1976. The first
dissolution agreement made between the parties proved abortive because the farm did
not sell at the auction.
   A second bargain was struck. It is contained in a letter dated 16th January 1976   *f*
written by the defendant's solicitors to the plaintiff's solicitors and altered in manuscript
by the plaintiff and the defendant shortly after the auction. The agreement as recorded
in this letter was as follows:

   '1. [The defendant] will pay £10,000 to [the plaintiff] on vacant possession, on or
   before May 15th 1976, being given of Cherry Tree Farm, house, land and buildings,
   time being of the essence. 2. [The plaintiff] will do all that is necessary to facilitate *g*
   the giving up of possession of the land and farm buildings (other than the house
   itself) prior to May 15th 1976, if so required. 3. [The plaintiff] will be entitled to
   no part of the partnership assets or the proceeds of sale thereof, all of which shall
   belong to [the defendant]. 4. The partnership now subsisting between our respective
   clients shall be treated as determined on the 22nd instant, the date of the auction sale
   of the farm. 5. Notwithstanding the contents of paragraph 4 above, [the plaintiff] *h*
   shall be entitled (a) To his salary of £35 per week until the sale of the live and dead
   stock, which is to be agreed himself and [the defendant], but is anticipated to be
   around February 1976. (b) To any underdrawn salary from the date of the
   commencement of the partnership current financial year to the above mentioned
   date of termination, the 22nd instant, but if such salary (at the rate of £35 per week)
   shall have been overdrawn, [the plaintiff] shall repay to [the defendant] the amount *j*
   overdrawn. 6. [The defendant's] prior approval shall be required to the sale prices
   of all partnership assets sold.'

   That agreement was subject to a term arranged between the parties themselves that
the amount due to the plaintiff under para 5 (b) should be referred to the parties'

respective accountants for agreement. That is set out in the letter of 19th January

a 1976. In fact I understand that one firm of accountants acted for both sides. The partnership business continued down to 31st March, and not to the date referred to in the agreement which I have read.

The plaintiff scrupulously fulfilled his part of the agreement. On 15th May he gave up possession of the farmhouse as the agreement required. At about the same time a bargain was struck between the plaintiff and the defendant that the plaintiff should take

b over from the partnership five items of farm equipment at an agreed total sum of £1,563. They consist of a pump valued at £1,015, a bottle filler valued at £140, a chain saw valued at £18, a tractor valued at £190 and a van valued at £200.

On 10th May the plaintiff, in anticipation of the receipt in five days' time of £10,000 from the defendant under the express terms of the contract, entered into an agreement to purchase a property known as Overton Farmhouse, near Wakefield, from a Mr

c Gascoyne. I take the details from the correspondence, the contract not being before us. The price was £16,000. £10,000 was to be paid on completion. The balance of £6,000 was to be paid three years later.

Unfortunately the defendant defaulted on his obligation to pay the £10,000 on 15th May under cl 1 of the agreement. On 16th July the plaintiff's solicitors wrote to the defendant's solicitors demanding payment, which they correctly stated was then already

d two months overdue. On 21st July Mr Gascoyne's solicitors served on the plaintiff a 28-day notice to complete in accordance with the general conditions of sale incorporated in the contract for the purchase of Overton Farmhouse. The defendant was informed of this. The effect of the notice to complete was that, on the plaintiff's default, Mr Gascoyne would be entitled to forfeit the deposit paid under the contract, to resell the property and to charge the plaintiff with any loss on the resale. The defendant remained in default.

e The plaintiff's position became desperate.

In October the plaintiff succeeded in extracting £7,200 from the defendant. This sum was immediately paid over to Mr Gascoyne. Mr Gascoyne had stayed his hand under the notice to complete. The sale was completed on 18th October on the basis that the balance shown due by the completion statement, namely £2,861·20, should remain outstanding on second mortgage until 1st December 1976. The first mortgage comprised the balance

f of £6,000 to which I have already referred and which was to remain outstanding for three years. The figure of £2,861·20, which I mentioned as due on the completion date, included a sum of £16·20 representing the legal costs of the second mortgage.

The defendant declined to pay the balance of £2,800 due under the agreement until the partnership accounts to 31st March 1976 were signed. It was not until October 1977 that the accountants were able, for some reason or another, to complete the accounts.

g These showed that a sum of £246·33 was due to the plaintiff as at 31st March 1976. Accordingly, on 20th October, the plaintiff's solicitors wrote to the defendant's solicitors asking for payment by the defendant of the outstanding £2,800 plus interest, and the amount of £246·33 shown by the accounts as due to the plaintiff. By this time the plaintiff was almost ten months in arrear in discharging the second mortgage and he was threatened with legal proceedings.

h On 24th May 1978 the plaintiff, having exhibited exemplary patience, issued a writ against the defendant. He claimed: £2,800, the balance of the £10,000; £246·33, the balance shown as due to him on the partnership accounts; £335 in respect of interest payable by the plaintiff to Mr Gascoyne by reason of the delayed completion of the purchase of Overton Farmhouse; and £16·20 legal costs of the second mortgage.

The plaintiff succeeded in the action to the extent that the judge found that the

i plaintiff was entitled to receive £10,000 under the terms of the dissolution agreement, whereas he had only been paid £7,200. The judge expressed himself as follows:

'In my judgment the defendant was liable by the terms of the agreement to pay £10,000, to which must be added an agreed sum of £200 in respect of the electric cooker which is referred to in the letter of 28th April 1976. To the total I should add

to that a further agreed sum of £246·33 for profits, a figure which has been agreed
and which emerges from the accounts which have been exhibited in the annex in
this case. From the total of £10,446·33 is to be deducted the payment of £7,200
and from the balance is to be deducted the aforementioned sum of £1,563 in
respect of the items of equipment which the plaintiff bought from the defendant.
If my mathematics are correct the plaintiff is accordingly entitled to judgment for
£1,683·33.'

That paragraph contains the error which the plaintiff submits has been made by the
judge. It is the principal matter arising on this appeal. The plaintiff submits that the
sum of £1,563·00 ought not to be treated as a deduction because it had already been
taken into account by the accountants in arriving at the figure of £246·33.

In my view the plaintiff is correct in his submission. To demonstrate this I must refer
to the accounts and I shall endeavour to do so in a way which will enable a reader to
follow the point without having the actual accounts before him. The figure of £246·33
is an agreed figure between the parties, subject only to a small qualification relating to
milk sales which is irrelevant at this point of my judgment. The sum of £246·33 is the
credit balance on the plaintiff's current account with the partnership as at 31st March
1976. It is made up to £49·23 debit balance on the current account at 1st July 1975, plus
drawings since 1st July 1975 of £1,862·97, making a total of £1,912·20. The plaintiff's
current account is then credited with his salary of £1,365 and his share of the profits for
the last period of the partnership, amounting to £793·53, making a total credit of
£2,158·53. This produces in the plaintiff's favour an ultimate credit balance of £246·33
which, as I have said, is an agreed sum subject only to the qualification that I have
mentioned. The important figure in that computation is the sum of £1,862·97 expressed
as 'drawings'. In the record there is a long and detailed computation headed 'Partners'
Drawings 9 months to 31st March 1976'. The page on which it appears forms a part of
the agreed and signed accounts. Included in that computation is a sum of £1,563 in
respect of the five items of equipment. That sum is charged to the plaintiff as if it had
been a drawing by him. I return to the balance sheet. The plaintiff's total drawings for
the final period of the partnership are shown as £1,862·97, whereas the drawings in the
record are given as £1,844·88. That is a difference or discrepancy of £18·09. Counsel
has explained to us the reason for the difference in the figures; put shortly, there was a
small omission from the computation in the record. The two figures of £1,862 and
£1,844 can be treated for present purposes as identical because the discrepancy does not
in any way affect the conclusion, namely that the sum of £246·33 balance due to the
plaintiff on the partnership accounts was struck after debiting the plaintiff with the sum
of £1,563 due for the equipment.

In my view the accounting position is absolutely clear beyond any possibility of
doubt. It must follow therefore that the judge was mistaken when he deducted the sum
of £1,563 from the balance which he was calculating in his judgment as due to the
plaintiff. On this issue of the appeal (which is the primary issue) it seems to me clear that
the plaintiff is entitled to succeed.

The second question on the appeal is a little more difficult. It is whether the plaintiff
is entitled to recover as special damages the loss which he has suffered as a result of the
defendant's failure to pay his debt under the contract on the due date. To put the matter
shortly, the plaintiff incurred under his contract with Mr Gascoyne an interest charge of
£335 as a result of the delayed completion, the interest being calculated for the period
from the date fixed for completion until actual completion on 18th October 1976. He
also incurred an expenditure of £16·20 legal costs of the second mortgage for the sum of
£2,800 (odd) balance due on completion. Neither of those charges would have been
incurred if the defendant had fulfilled his part of the contract by paying £10,000 on the
due date namely, 15th May 1976. The judge dismissed this claim on the ground that it
was too remote. He made an award of interest on the amount recovered under the
judgment.

In my view the damage claimed by the plaintiff was not too remote. It is clearly to be inferred from the evidence that the defendant well knew at the time of the negotiation of the contract of January 1976 that the plaintiff would need to acquire another farm or smallholding as his home and his business, and that he would be dependent on the £10,000 payable under the contract in order to finance that purchase. The defendant knew or ought to have known that if the £10,000 was not paid to him the plaintiff would need to borrow an equivalent amount or would have to pay interest to his vendor or would need to secure financial accommodation in some other way. The plaintiff's loss in my opinion is such that it may reasonably be supposed that it would have been in the contemplation of the parties as a serious possibility had their attention been directed to the consequences of a breach of contract.

The defendant sought to escape from this conclusion by relying on the decision of the House of Lords in *London, Chatham and Dover Railway Co v South Eastern Railway Co* [1893] AC 429. In that case the appellants had brought an action against the respondent for an account of money due under a joint traffic agreement. The account was taken before an official referee who found that a considerable sum was due to the appellants. He included in the sum found due £36,000 interest under Lord Tenterden's Act (the Civil Procedure Act 1833). To recover interest under that Act, so far as material for present purposes, it was necessary to show that there was a debt or sum certain payable at a certain time by virtue of some written instrument. It was held by the Court of Appeal and by the House of Lords that the claim did not satisfy that condition. So the appellants sought interest by way of damages as alternative relief. Lord Herschell LC said (at 437):

'... the appellants contended that even although they might not under the terms of Lord Tenterden's Act be entitled to interest, yet interest might be given by way of damages in respect of the wrongful detention of their debt. I confess that I have considered this part of the case with every inclination to come to a conclusion in favour of the appellants, to the extent at all events, if it were possible, of giving them interest from the date of the action; and for this reason, that I think that when money is owing from one party to another and that other is driven to have recourse to legal proceedings in order to recover the amount due to him, the party who is wrongfully withholding the money from the other ought not in justice to benefit by having that money in his possession and enjoying the use of it, when the money ought to be in the possession of the other party who is entitled to its use. Therefore, if I could see my way to do so, I should certainly be disposed to give the appellants, or anybody in a similar position, interest upon the amount withheld from the time of action brought at all events. But I have come to the conclusion, upon a consideration of the authorities, agreeing with the Court below, that it is not possible to do so, although no doubt in early times the view was expressed that interest might be given under such circumstances by way of damages.'

The defendant contends that we are bound to follow that principle and that, although interest can be awarded nowadays under the Law Reform (Miscellaneous Provisions) Act 1934, damages cannot be awarded in respect of unpaid indebtedness. The plaintiff is confined, the defendant says, to such interest as he is able to claim under the Act, but is not entitled to damages. The interest which can be claimed under the Act is not sufficient to cover the damage suffered by the plaintiff if as the plaintiff concedes it cannot be awarded on the sum of £7,200 paid before the action was started.

In my view the court is not so constrained by the decision of the House of Lords. In *London, Chatham and Dover Railway Co v South Eastern Railway Co* the House of Lords was not concerned with a claim for special damages. The action was an action for an account. The House was concerned only with a claim for interest by way of general damages. If a plaintiff pleads and can prove that he has suffered special damage as a result of the defendant's failure to perform his obligation under a contract, and such damage is not too remote on the principle of *Hadley v Baxendale* (1854) 9 Exch 341, [1843–60] All ER Rep 461, I can see no logical reason why such special damages should be irrecoverable *a* merely because the obligation on which the defendant defaulted was an obligation to pay money and not some other type of obligation. I derive support for this view from obita dicta in *Trans Trust SPRL v Danubian Trading Co Ltd* [1952] 1 All ER 970, [1952] 2 QB 297. I refer first to a paragraph in the judgment of Denning LJ ([1952] 1 All ER 970 at 977, [1952] 2 QB 297 at 306):

> 'It was said that the breach here was a failure to pay money and that the law has *b* never allowed any damages on that account. I do not think that the law has ever taken up such a rigid standpoint. It did undoubtedly refuse to award interest until the introduction of the Law Reform (Miscellaneous Provisions) Act, 1934, s. 3(1): see *London, Chatham & Dover Ry. Co. v. South Eastern Ry. Co.*; but the ground was that interest was "generally presumed not to be within the contemplation of the parties": see BULLEN & LEAKE (Precedents of Pleadings (3rd Edn, 1868) p 51, note (a)). That *c* is, I think, the only real ground on which damages can be refused for non-payment of money. It is because the consequences are as a rule too remote. But when the circumstances are such that there is a special loss foreseeable at the time of the contract as the consequence of non-payment, then I think such loss may well be recoverable. It is not necessary, however, to come to a firm conclusion on this point, because I regard the provision of a credit as different from the payment of money *d* and not subject to the special rules, if any there are, relating thereto.'

Romer LJ said ([1952] 1 All ER 970 at 978, [1952] 2 QB 297 at 307):

> '. . . I am not, as at present advised, prepared to subscribe to the view that in no case can damages be recovered for non-payment of money; I agree with DENNING, L.J., that in certain circumstances such damages might well be recoverable provided *e* that the loss occasioned to the plaintiff by the defendant's default was reasonably within the contemplation of the parties when the bargain between them was made.'

In my view the plaintiff in the instant case ought to have been allowed the £335 and £16·20 damages which he claimed. Those damages are pleaded as special damages. They are not, for the reasons which I have given, too remote. I think that they are *f* recoverable under the ordinary principles on which this court proceeds in the case of damages. I do not think that the present case is concluded by the *London, Chatham and Dover Railway Co* case. I would adopt as the law the view tentatively expressed by Denning and Romer LJJ in the passages I have read.

The last issue on the appeal is whether this court ought to interfere with the trial judge's decision to reserve the costs of the trial to the district registrar. The basis of the *g* judge's decision was that, by agreement between the parties, one item on the partnership accounts which related to milk sales receipts was to be referred to the district registrar. The judge thought that the result of that inquiry might deprive the plaintiff of any substantial benefit from the judgment. I do not myself think that the judge was justified in delegating that decision to the registrar. He ought, in my view, to have dealt with the costs himself and he ought to have awarded them to the plaintiff. The judge's conclusion *h* was that the defendant was liable, by the terms of the agreement of January 1976, to pay £10,000 to the plaintiff. That was the principal claim of the plaintiff when he started his action. It seems to me that the plaintiff clearly succeeded in his action. He obtained the major part of the relief he sought. The fact that the taking of an account on one particular aspect of the partnership might lead to a cross-payment by the plaintiff to the defendant was not, in my opinion, any sufficient reason for omitting to give the plaintiff *j* the costs of the action there and then. All that ought to have been referred to the district registrar was the costs of the inquiry relating to the milk sales.

In the result, I would allow the appeal on all the points.

REEVE J. I agree.

ORMROD LJ. I too agree, but, as we are differing from the judge, I shall add a few
a words of my own.

So far as the main point is concerned, it is conceded by the defendant that, as the
judge's judgment stands, the plaintiff has been debited twice over in the sum of £1,563,
namely the price of the equipment he purchased from the partnership. What is said, as
I understand it, on behalf of the defendant is that, by a later agreement which is recorded
(or said to be recorded) in a letter written by himself on 28th April 1976, there was a
b subsequent arrangement made between these two people that the price of the equipment
was to be deducted from the £10,000.

It is by standing on the letter of that agreement that counsel for the defendant seeks
to support the judge's judgment. He concedes that, as a consequence of that, the figure
taken as the plaintiff's share of the profits, namely £246·33, was much too low and that
figure would have to be increased by the figure of £1,563 for the reasons explained by
c Brightman LJ. So one way or the other the plaintiff must succeed in respect of that
sum. In the background I think is some feeling on the part of the defendant that, if he
had thought the plaintiff's case was going to be put that way, he would not have
admitted the partnership accounts to the extent that he did, but just how far he could
have disputed the partnership accounts, he having signed them and they having been
prepared by the parties' accountants, I do not for my part understand. What I do
d understand is that the present answer to the plaintiff's claim is of the most abject
technicality and is certainly not one to which, in these days, a court should pay any
attention at all. It is perfectly plain that the plaintiff is owed, one way or the other, the
sum of £1,563. I would allow the appeal on that item for those reasons as well as for
those much more fully given by Brightman LJ.

On the interesting question of damages for the cost to which the plaintiff was put as
e a result of the non-payment of the £10,000, I would just say this. The first question it
seems to me is: is this alleged damage too remote? The test as set out in the judgments
of this court in *H Parsons (Livestock) Ltd v Uttley Ingham & Co Ltd* [1978] 1 All ER 525,
[1978] QB 791 gives the test for remoteness. Taking it very shortly, Lord Denning MR
said ([1978] 1 All ER 525 at 531, [1978] QB 791 at 801):

> 'In the case of a *breach of contract*, the court has to consider whether the
> *f* consequences were of such a kind that a reasonable man, at the time of making the
> contract, would *contemplate* them as being of a very substantial degree of
> probability.' (Lord Denning MR's emphasis.)

Scarman LJ made the same point in a slightly different way ([1978] 1 All ER 525 at 537,
[1978] QB 791 at 807):

> *g* 'The court's task, therefore, is to decide what loss to the plaintiffs it is reasonable
> to suppose would have been in the contemplation of the parties as a serious
> possibility had they had in mind the breach when they made their contract.'

To use the language of objective/subjective, it is an objective test. The court has to
look not at what this particular defendant knew or contemplated but what a reasonable
h person in his position would have contemplated. I find it inconceivable that this
particular defendant did not contemplate and fully understand the plaintiff's position.
He must have known as a fact that the plaintiff was dependent on this £10,000 to make
arrangements for alternative accommodation for himself and his family. Moreover, if
he did not know, no reasonable person in 1976 looking at the facts could come to any
other conclusion but that £10,000 was vital to the plaintiff and that, if he could not get
j the £10,000 immediately, he was bound to be put to expense in arranging alternative
sources of finance, assuming that he could do so.

On remoteness, I find no difficulty in disagreeing with the judge. A more important
and more difficult point arises on *London, Chatham and Dover Railway Co v South Eastern
Railway Co* [1893] AC 429. As to that, I entirely agree with all that Brightman LJ has said
and I do not find it necessary to say anything more than that. It would seem to me the

most extraordinary conclusion to reach, and one has the advantage of knowing that in
1893 Lord Herschell LC regarded the statement of the law he felt obliged to make as   *a*
profoundly unsatisfactory. This case is not on all fours, and can be distinguished from,
the *London, Chatham and Dover Railway Co* case and clearly ought to be so distinguished.
I agree that this appeal should be allowed.

Appeal allowed.

b

Solicitors: *Dransfield & Hodgkinson*, Penistone (for the plaintiff); *Eaton Smith & Downey*,
Huddersfield (for the defendant).

Avtar S Virdi Esq   Barrister.

c

Lamb and another v London Borough of Camden and another

d

COURT OF APPEAL, CIVIL DIVISION
LORD DENNING MR, OLIVER AND WATKINS LJJ
4th, 5th, 6th FEBRUARY, 18th MARCH 1981

Damages – Remoteness of damage – Foreseeability – Novus actus interveniens – Likelihood of   *e*
intervening human action – Defendants breaching water main outside plaintiff's house while
repairing sewer – Water from main undermining foundations of house causing it to subside –
House becoming unsafe to live in and left unoccupied by plaintiff – Squatters invading unoccupied
house and causing damage – Whether defendants liable for damage caused by squatters –
Whether damage caused by squatters too remote.

In 1972 the plaintiff let her house while she was away in America. In 1973, while   *f*
replacing a sewer pipe in the road outside the plaintiff's house, contractors employed by
the local council breached a water main causing the foundations of the house to be
undermined and the house to subside. The house became unsafe, the tenant moved out,
and the plaintiff moved her furniture into storage. The house was then left unoccupied
to await repair. In 1974 squatters moved in but were evicted. The house was boarded
up and the plaintiff returned to America. In 1975 squatters again moved in and caused   *g*
substantial damage to the interior of the house before being evicted. The plaintiff
brought an action against the council claiming, inter alia, damages in nuisance and
negligence for the damage caused by the squatters. The official referee held that,
although squatting was at the time a reasonably foreseeable risk, it was not likely to occur
in the locality of the plaintiff's house and was therefore too remote for the plaintiff to be   *h*
able to recover damages. The plaintiff appealed.

Held – The appeal would be dismissed for the following reasons—
  (1) Although the primary test of remoteness of damage in negligence and nuisance
was reasonable foreseeability of damage, that was not conclusive of the issue of
remoteness in all circumstances. However, where the damage was caused by intervening   *j*
human action, it was not sufficient to limit the liability for damage to that which was
'likely' or even 'very likely', since that could still extend the defendant's liability beyond
all reason and lead to bizarre or ludicrous results (see p 412 *e f*, p 413 *b c*, p 417 *d*, p 419
b to *f*, p 421 *c* to *f* and p 422 *b*, post); dictum of Lord Reid in *Home Office v Dorset Yacht Co*
Ltd [1970] 2 All ER at 300 criticised.

(2) (Per Lord Denning MR) The range and limits of liability for negligence or nuisance
a were to be determined as a matter of judicial policy, and, applying that approach, the fact
that the plaintiff rather than the council was responsible for keeping the squatters out
and evicting them when they got in meant that the council was not liable for the
damage, which in any event was damage against which the plaintiff herself should have
taken precautions (see p 414 *a* to p 415 *d*, post).

(3) (Per Oliver LJ) Where the consequence of a negligent act or a nuisance resulted
b from, or would not have occurred but for, the intervention of an independent human act
over which the tortfeasor had no control and for which he was not responsible or was not
employed to prevent, the tortfeasor was not liable for that damage which was foreseeable
merely as a possibility, because, given the unpredictability of human behaviour, the bare
possibility of the damage that occurred, however unpredictable, was always likely to be
foreseeable. Instead, the tortfeasor was only liable for that damage which a reasonable
c man in the position of the tortfeasor would have foreseen if he had thought about it,
which, in turn, was only damage resulting from behaviour which, viewed objectively,
was very likely to occur. Since a reasonable man would not reasonably have foreseen that
by breaking a water pipe when working on the road he would cause the plaintiff's house
to be invaded by squatters, the damage was too remote (see p 418 *a* to *e* and *g* to p 419 *b*,
post); dictum of Lord Reid in *Home Office v Dorset Yacht Co Ltd* [1970] 2 All ER at 300
d applied.

(3) (Per Watkins LJ) In those cases where the very features (eg the nature, time and
place of the act, the person committing it, his intentions and his responsibility for
avoiding it) of an event or act for which damages were claimed or where public policy
suggested that the event or act was not, on a practical view, in any way connected with
the tortfeasor's negligence, the court was entitled, and should, adopt the practical view
e that the event or act was too remote to make the tortfeasor liable for it. Applying that
approach, the damage caused by the squatters was too remote for the council to be liable
for it, even though it was reasonably foreseeable (see p 421 *g* to p 422 *b*, post).

Per Oliver LJ. It may be that a more stringent test requiring a degree of likelihood
amounting almost to inevitability is required for determining the liability of a tortfeasor
for the act of a third person over whom he has and can have no control (see p 419 *f g*,
f post).

Per Watkins LJ. The test of reasonable foreseeability, when applicable, should always
be applied without any gloss (see p 421 *e f*, post).

Notes
For remoteness and foreseeability of damages in tort, see 12 Halsbury's Laws (4th Edn)
g paras 1127, 1131, 1133, 1138–1143, and for cases on the subject, see 36(1) Digest
(Reissue) 63–65, 227–236.

For the tests of foreseeability and proximity in relation to a duty of care, see 34
Halsbury's Laws (4th Edn) para 5, and for cases on the subject, see 36(1) Digest (Reissue)
27–31, 93–101.

h ### Cases referred to in judgments
Anns v London Borough of Merton [1977] 2 All ER 492, [1978] AC 728, [1977] 2 WLR 1024,
    141 JP 526, 75 LGR 555, HL, Digest (Cont Vol E) 449, 99*b*.
Chomentowski v Red Garter Restaurant Pty Ltd (1970) 92 WN (NSW) 1070, NSW CA;
    appeal dismissed (1971) 45 ALJR 713(note), HC of Aust.
Compania Financiera Soleada SA v Hamoor Tanker Corpn Inc, The Borag [1981] 1 All ER 856,
j   [1981] 1 WLR 274, CA.
Dutton v Bognor Regis United Building Co Ltd [1972] 1 All ER 462, 136 JP 201, [1972] 1
    Lloyd's Rep 227, sub nom *Dutton v Bognor Regis Urban District Council* [1972] 1 QB 373,
    [1972] 2 WLR 299, 70 LGR 57, CA, 36(1) Digest (Reissue) 30, 98.
Home Office v Dorset Yacht Co Ltd [1970] 2 All ER 294, [1970] AC 1004, [1970] 2 WLR
    1140, [1970] 1 Lloyd's Rep 453, HL, 36(1) Digest (Reissue) 27, 93.

Koufos v C Czarnikow Ltd, The Heron II [1967] 3 All ER 686, [1969] 1 AC 350, [1967] 3
WLR 1491, [1967] 2 Lloyd's Rep 457, HL, Digest (Cont Vol C) 882, *1754a.*   *a*
McKew v Holland & Hannen & Cubbitts (Scotland) Ltd [1969] 3 All ER 1621, HL, 17 Digest
(Reissue) 115, *187.*
McLoughlin v O'Brian [1981] 1 All ER 809, CA.
Photo Production Ltd v Securicor Transport Ltd [1980] 1 All ER 556, [1980] AC 827, [1980]
2 WLR 283, [1980] 1 Lloyd's Rep 545, HL.
Polemis and Furness Withy & Co Ltd, Re [1921] 3 KB 560, [1921] All ER Rep 40, 90 LJKB   *b*
1353, 126 LT 154, 15 Asp MLC 398, 27 Com Cas 25, CA, 36(1) Digest (Reissue) 64,
232.
Stansbie v Troman [1948] 1 All ER 599, [1948] 2 KB 48, [1948] LJR 1206, 46 LGR 349,
CA, 36(1) Digest (Reissue) 37, *107.*
Wagon Mound, The (No 1), Overseas Tankship (UK) Ltd v Morts Dock & Engineering Co Ltd
[1961] 1 All ER 404, [1961] AC 388, [1961] 2 WLR 126, [1961] 1 Lloyd's Rep 1, [1961]   *c*
ALR 569, PC, 36(1) Digest (Reissue) 63, *227.*
Wagon Mound, The (No 2), Overseas Tankship (UK) Ltd v Miller Steamship Co Pty Ltd [1966]
2 All ER 709, [1967] 1 AC 617, [1966] 3 WLR 498, [1966] 1 NSWR 411, [1967] ALR
97, [1966] 1 Lloyd's Rep 657, PC, 36(1) Digest (Reissue) 65, *236.*

Cases also cited   *d*
Bolton v Stone [1951] 1 All ER 1078, [1951] AC 850.
Cobb v Great Western Railway Co [1893] 1 QB 459, CA; *affd* [1894] AC 419, HL.
Davies v Liverpool Corpn [1949] 2 All ER 175, CA.
Donoghue (or M'Alister) v Stevenson [1932] AC 562, [1932] All ER Rep 1, HL.
Dodd Properties (Kent) Ltd v Canterbury City Council [1980] 1 All ER 928, [1980] 1 WLR
433, CA.   *e*
Engelhart v Farrant & Co [1897] 1 QB 240, CA.
Haynes v Harwood [1935] 1 KB 146, [1934] All ER Rep 103, CA.
Hughes v Lord Advocate [1963] 1 All ER 705, [1963] AC 837, HL.
Iron and Steel Holding and Realisation Agency v Compensation Appeal Tribunal [1966] 1 All
ER 769, [1966] 1 WLR 480, DC.
Liesbosch Dredger (Owners) v Owners of Steamship Edison [1933] AC 449, sub nom *The*   *f*
Edison [1933] All ER Rep 144, CA.
McDowall v Great Western Railway Co [1903] 2 KB 331, [1900–3] All ER Rep 593, CA.
Monarch Steamship Co Ltd v A/B Karlshamns Oljefabriker [1949] 1 All ER 1, [1949] AC 196,
HL.
Oropesa, The [1943] 1 All ER 211, [1943] P 32, CA.
Parsons (H) (Livestock) Ltd v Uttley Ingham & Co Ltd [1978] 1 All ER 525, [1978] QB 791, *g*
CA.
Radford v De Froberville [1978] 1 All ER 33, [1977] 1 WLR 1262.
Rouse v Squires [1973] 2 All ER 903, [1973] QB 889, CA.
Ruoff v Long & Co [1916] 1 KB 148, DC.
Scott v Shepherd (1773) 2 Wm Bl 892, [1558–1774] All ER Rep 295.
Scott's Trustees v Moss (1889) 17 R (Ct of Sess) 32, 27 Sc LR 30.   *h*
Steamship Singleton Abbey (Owners) v Steamship Paludina (Owners), The Paludina [1927] AC
16, [1926] All ER Rep 220, HL.
Taupo Borough Council v Birnie [1978] 2 NZLR 397.
Victoria Laundry (Windsor) Ltd v Newman Industries Ltd (Coulson & Co Ltd (Third Party))
[1949] 1 All ER 997, [1949] 2 KB 528.
Weld-Blundell v Stephens [1920] AC 956, [1920] All ER Rep 32, HL.   *j*

Appeal
The plaintiffs, Mrs Rosemary Joyce Wittman Lamb and her father, Gustav Rudolph
Wittman, appealed against the decision of his Honour Judge Edgar Fay QC, sitting as an

a official referee of the Supreme Court, given on 5th April and 12th October 1979 whereby he held that they were not entitled to damages against the defendants, the London Borough of Camden ('the council') and J Murphy & Sons Ltd, in respect of damage caused to the plaintiffs' property at 6 Villas on the Heath, Vale of Health, Hampstead, London, by squatters between 1974 and 1976. The facts are set out in the judgment of Lord Denning MR.

b Louis Blom-Cooper QC and John Dyson for the plaintiffs.
G Bruce Laughland QC and Richard Woodhouse for the defendants.

Cur adv vult

18th March. The following judgments were read.

c

LORD DENNING MR.

The facts
Off Hampstead Heath there is a terrace of houses of quality built in the early nineteenth century. They are called 'the Villas on the Heath'. One of them belonged to Mrs Lamb. In 1972 she went to New York and let the house to a tenant. Whilst she was away *d* the local council decided to replace the sewer in the road next to the house. In October 1973 they dug a deep trench a few feet from the front wall of the house. In doing it, they broke into a water main. The water burst out and washed out soil from the foundations of the house. There was subsidence. The walls cracked. It became unsafe to live in. The tenant moved out. Mrs Lamb, still in America, got her father, her solicitors and her agents to look after her interests. In the summer of 1974 she herself came back for six *e* weeks and made preliminary arrangements for repairs to be done. The work was so extensive that she had her furniture removed and put into store in Harrods' repository. Then she went back to America.

The house, being then left unoccupied and unfurnished, was a sitting target for squatters. In October 1974 they invaded it. Mrs Lamb returned for three weeks at Christmas. She found the squatters still there. She was appalled at the state of the *f* place. Her solicitors issued a summons under RSC Ord 113 and managed to get them out. After those squatters had gone, her father got some building labourers to put up a few boards at a cost of £10. The neighbours helped too.

But a few months later, in the summer of 1975, there was a second invasion of squatters. A shifting population. As some went out, others came in. Mrs Lamb's agents did what they could to get them out. The electricity and gas were cut off. But to no *g* avail. The squatters pulled off the panelling for fuel. They ripped out the central heating and other installations. They stole them. Eventually the police arrested the squatters on a charge of larceny. Whilst they were at the police station, Mrs Lamb's agents got in and made the premises secure with elaborate reinforced defences. That was in May 1977. The end of the squatters.

Then at last the work of repair was started. It was finished in 1979. The house was put *h* in first class order and let once again. Mrs Lamb then sent the bill in to the council. She said the expense was all due to their negligence or to a nuisance created by them in the course of their work on the sewer. Eventually the council admitted liability for nuisance. The damages were left to an official referee. Over £50,000 was expense due to the subsidence. But nearly £30,000 was the cost of repairing the malicious damage done by the squatters and their thefts.

j

Lord Reid's test
On those facts this point of law arises: can Mrs Lamb recover from the council the £30,000 due to the squatters' damage? The official referee found that it was too remote and was not recoverable. He cited the speech of Lord Reid in *Home Office v Dorset Yacht*

Co Ltd [1970] 2 All ER 294 at 300, [1970] AC 1004 at 1030, especially the passage where Lord Reid said:

'These cases show that, where human action forms one of the links between the original wrongdoing of the defendant and the loss suffered by the plaintiff, that action must at least have been something very likely to happen if it is not to be regarded as novus actus interveniens breaking the chain of causation. I do not think that a mere foreseeable possibility is or should be sufficient, for then the intervening human action can more properly be regarded as a new cause than as a consequence of the original wrongdoing. But if the intervening action was likely to happen I do not think that it can matter whether that action was innocent or tortious or criminal. Unfortunately, tortious or criminal action by a third party is often the "very kind of thing" which is likely to happen as a result of the wrongful or careless act of the defendant. And in the present case, on the facts which we must assume at this stage, I think that the taking of a boat by the escaping trainees and their unskilful navigation leading to damage to another vessel were the very kind of thing that these borstal officers ought to have seen to be likely.'

In our present case the official referee applied that passage in these words:

'... I would feel disposed, if it were relevant, to hold that squatting was at the material time a *reasonably foreseeable* risk, but I am quite satisfied that no one familiar with the house and the locality would at any time between the accident in the autumn of 1973 and the first invasion about a year later have said that squatting was *likely*. It follows that in my judgment the extensive damage caused by the squatters is too remote and cannot form part of the damage payable by the defendants.' (My emphasis.)

Was Lord Reid right or wrong?

Counsel for Mrs Lamb (who was himself counsel in the *Dorset Yacht* case) submitted that Lord Reid was in error in that passage. For once Homer nodded. Presumptuous as it is, I agree.

In the first place the saying of Lord Reid was an obiter dictum. The *Dorset Yacht* case came up for decision on a preliminary issue. It was whether the Home Office 'owed any duty of care to the plaintiffs [the owners of the yacht] capable of giving rise to a liability in damages' (see [1970] 2 All ER 294 at 296, [1970] AC 1004 at 1008). So the question was only as to the duty of care. It was not as to remoteness of damage or as to causation.

Yet, as I have often said, the three questions, duty, causation and remoteness, run continually into one another. So it was natural for the Law Lords to run them together. As I read the speeches they were much concerned to limit the extent of the liability of the Home Office. But they did it in different ways. Three of them did it by restricting the range of persons to whom the duty was owed. Lord Morris said the duty was owed 'to the *owners of the nearby yachts*' (see [1970] 2 All ER 294 at 303, [1970] AC 1004 at 1034). Lord Pearson said that the duty was owed to the *boatowners*; he said that 'the respondents as boatowners were in law "neighbours" of the defendants' (see [1970] 2 All ER 294 at 321, [1970] AC 1004 at 1054). Lord Diplock said that the duty of the borstal officer was—

'owed *only* to persons whom he could reasonably foresee had property situate *in the vicinity of* the place of detention of the detainee which the detainee was likely to steal or to appropriate and damage in the course of eluding immediate pursuit and recapture.' (My emphasis.)

(See [1970] 2 All ER 294 at 334, [1970] AC 1004 at 1070–1071.)

Now I would test the rulings of the Law Lords by asking: suppose that by some negligence of the staff, a borstal boy, or an adult prisoner, escapes over the wall, or from a working party. It is not only reasonably foreseeable, it is, as we all know, *very likely*, that he will steal a car in the immediate vicinity. He will then drive many miles,

abandon the car, break into a house and steal clothes, get a lift in a lorry, and continue his
a depredations. On Lord Diplock's test, and I fancy on that of Lord Morris and Lord
Pearson also, the Home Office would owe a duty of care to the owner of the stolen car but
to none of the others who suffered damage. So the owner of the car could sue, but the
others could not.

But on Lord Reid's test of 'very likely' to happen, the Home Office would be liable not
only to the owner of the stolen car but also to all the others who suffered damage: because
b it was very likely to happen.

That illustration convinces me that Lord Reid's test was wrong. If it were adopted, it
would extend the liability of the Home Office beyond all reason. The Home Office
should not be liable for the depredations of escaped convicts. The householders should
recover for the damage not against the Home Office but on their insurance policies. The
insurers should not by subrogation be able to pass it on to the Home Office.

c Another reason why I would reject Lord Reid's test is that I find it difficult to reconcile
with the decision in *Stansbie v Troman* [1948] 1 All ER 599, [1948] 2 KB 48. The
decorator was held to be under a duty of care to the householder to lock the door, but no
one could suggest that it was *very likely* that a thief would walk in and steal the diamond
bracelet. Tucker LJ said that the decorator was liable because it was 'as a direct result of
his negligence that the thief entered by the front door'. He was obviously applying *Re
d Polemis* [1921] 3 KB 560, [1921] All ER Rep 40 which had not then been overruled. If the
decision in *Stansbie v Troman* is to be justified nowadays, it can only be because it was
reasonably foreseeable that a thief might walk in, nor that it was at all *likely*.

The third reason is that I find the test of 'very likely' very difficult to reconcile with *The
Wagon Mound (No 1)* [1961] 1 All ER 404, [1961] AC 388 and *The Wagon Mound (No 2)*
[1966] 2 All ER 709, [1967] 1 AC 617 which were summarised by Lord Upjohn in *The
e Heron II, Koufos v C Czarnikow Ltd* [1967] 3 All ER 686 at 716, [1969] 1 AC 350 at 422:

'. . . the tortfeasor is liable for any damage which he can reasonably foresee may
happen as a result of the breach, *however unlikely it may be*, unless it can be brushed
aside as far fetched. See *The Wagon Mound* cases.' (My emphasis).

The alternative test
f If Lord Reid's test is wrong, what is the alternative test? Logically, I suppose that
liability and compensation should go hand in hand. If reasonable foresight is the
criterion in negligence, so also it should be in remoteness of damage. That was the test
for which counsel for Mrs Lamb contended. He supported it by reference to the case in
New South Wales of *Chomentowski v Red Garter Restaurant Pty Ltd* (1970) 92 WN (NSW)
1070, where a head waiter was hit over the head by a robber. The management were
g negligent in not taking sufficient precautions. They were held liable because the attack
might reasonably have been foreseen, though not very likely.

To my mind that alternative test is also not acceptable. It would extend the range of
compensation far too widely. Take the *Chomentowski* case itself. In England the head
waiter would be able to get full compensation for his injuries from the Criminal Injuries
h Compensation Board which provides compensation for victims of violent crimes. That
would be preferable to making the manager liable for his pardonable want of foresight.
Take next the illustration I took from the *Dorset Yacht* case of the criminal who escapes
(owing to the negligence of the prison staff) and breaks into people's houses. Although
it could reasonably be foreseen, the Home Office are not liable for his depredations.

Take next the recent case in this court of the wife who suffers nervous shock by being
j told of the motor accident in which her family were dead or dying (*McLoughlin v O'Brian*
[1981] 1 All ER 809). It could reasonably be foreseen. But the negligent driver is not
liable in damages for her shock.

The truth
The truth is that all these three, duty, remoteness and causation, are all devices by
which the courts limit the range of liability for negligence or nuisance. As I said recently

in *Compania Financiera Soleada SA v Hamoor Tanker Corpn Inc, The Borag* [1981] 1 All ER
856 at 861, [1981] 1 WLR 274 at 281: '... it is not every consequence of a wrongful act   *a*
which is the subject of compensation. The law has to draw a line somewhere.'
    Sometimes it is done by limiting the range of the persons to whom duty is owed.
Sometimes it is done by saying that there is a break in the chain of causation. At other
times it is done by saying that the consequence is too remote to be a head of damage. All
these devices are useful in their way. But ultimately it is a question of policy for the
judges to decide. I venture to repeat what I said in *Dutton v Bognor Regis United Building*   *b*
Co Ltd [1972] 1 All ER 462 at 475, [1972] 1 QB 373 at 397:

> 'It seems to me that it is a question of policy which we, as judges, have to
> decide. The time has come when, in cases of new import, we should decide them
> according to the reason of the thing. In previous times, when faced with a new
> problem, the judges have not openly asked themselves the question: what is the best
> policy for the law to adopt? But the question has always been there in the   *c*
> background. It has been concealed behind such questions as: Was the defendant
> under any duty to the plaintiff? Was the relationship between them sufficiently
> proximate? Was the injury direct or indirect? Was it foreseeable or not? Was it
> too remote? And so forth. Nowadays we direct ourselves to considerations of
> policy.'

    When *Dutton's* case reached the House of Lords by way of *Anns v London Borough of*   *d*
Merton [1977] 2 All ER 492, [1978] AC 728, our decision was upheld. This approach, on
grounds of policy, was adopted by the Court of Appeal in the recent case about nervous
shock, *McLoughlin v O'Brian* [1981] 1 All ER 809. Liability for nervous shock is limited
to those at or near the highway at the time of the accident. It does not extend to those
further away.
                                                                                              e
A question of policy—return to the present case
    Looking at the question as one of policy, I ask myself: whose job was it to do
something to keep out the squatters? And, if they got in, to evict them? To my mind
the answer is clear. It was the job of the owner of the house, Mrs Lamb, through her
agents. That is how everyone in the case regarded it. It has never been suggested in the
pleadings or elsewhere that it was the job of the council. No one ever wrote to the   *f*
council asking them to do it. The council were not in occupation of the house. They had
no right to enter it. All they had done was to break the water main outside and cause the
subsidence. After they had left the site, it was Mrs Lamb *herself* who paved the way for
the squatters by moving out all her furniture and leaving the house unoccupied and
unfurnished. There was then, if not before, on the judge's findings, a reasonably
foreseeable risk that squatters might enter. She ought to have taken steps to guard   *g*
against it. She says that she locked the doors and pulled the shutters. That turned out to
be insufficient, but it was her responsibility to do more. At any rate, when the squatters
did get in on the first occasion in 1974, it was then her agents who acted on her behalf.
They got the squatters out. Then, at any rate, Mrs Lamb or her agents ought to have
done something effective. But they only put up a few boards at a cost of £10. Then
there was the second invasion in 1975. Then her agents did recognise her   *h*
responsibility. They did what they could to get the squatters out. They eventually
succeeded. But no one ever suggested throughout that it was the responsibility of the
council.
    In her evidence Mrs Lamb suggested that she had not the money to do more. I do not
think the judge accepted the suggestion. Her agents could well have made the house
secure for a modest sum which was well within her capabilities.   *j*
    On broader grounds of policy, I would add this: the criminal acts here, malicious
damage and theft, are usually covered by insurance. By this means the risk of loss is
spread throughout the community. It does not fall too heavily on one pair of shoulders
alone. The insurers take the premium to cover just this sort of risk and should not be

allowed, by subrogation, to pass it on to others. Just as in *Stansbie v Troman* [1948] 1 All
a ER 599, [1948] 2 KB 48, the householder was no doubt insured against theft of the
diamond bracelet. She should have recovered its value from the insurers and not from
the decorator whose only fault was that he forgot to put the latch down. It might be
decided differently today. It is commonplace nowadays for the courts, when considering
policy, to take insurance into account. It played a prominent part in *Photo Production Ltd
v Securicor Transport Ltd* [1980] 1 All ER 556, [1980] AC 827. The House of Lords clearly
b thought that the risk of fire should be borne by the fire insurers, who had received the
full premium for fire risk, and not by Securicor's insurers, who had only received a tiny
premium. That, too, was a policy decision. It was a direct consequence of the Unfair
Contract Terms Act 1977. Before that Act, the doctrine of fundamental breach was an
essential part of our legal system: so as to protect the small consumer from unjust
exemption clauses.
c   So here, it seems to me that, if Mrs Lamb was insured against damage to the house and
theft, the insurers should pay the loss. If she was not insured, that is her misfortune.
    Taking all these policy matters into account, I think the council are not liable for the
acts of these squatters.
    I would dismiss this appeal.

d **OLIVER LJ.** The relevant facts have already been recited in the judgment of Lord
Denning MR and were never seriously in dispute. At the time when the nuisance
occurred the plaintiff was living in the United States and the house had been let to some
tenants. They continued to live in the house for a few months after the disaster but
moved out in January 1974 thinking, no doubt correctly, that the house was no longer
safe for occupation. Fortunately, although the house was unoccupied, the plaintiff's
e furniture remained intact and in July 1974 she returned to England in order, among
other things, to cope with the emergency. Being then of the view that work on restoring
the house would be undertaken in the near future, she removed her furniture into store
and the house was from then on empty and unoccupied until it was invaded by squatters
in the latter part of 1974. The evidence of one of the neighbouring householders was
that the house was well protected. It had shutters, was well locked and bolted and had
f secure glass. It was not, he said, particularly vulnerable compared with most houses.
    When the squatters broke in, the neighbours communicated with the plaintiff and
she, through her then solicitors, started proceedings to evict them under RSC Ord 113.
Those proceedings were duly served but it proved unnecessary to obtain an order since
the squatters left in January 1975 of their own accord. Thereafter the house was
resecured, although perhaps not very effectively. The plaintiff's father, who was looking
g after her affairs in England, she having returned to New York before the squatters
arrived, arranged with some builders working nearby to board up some of the lower
windows with hardboard nailed to the frames, and some further boarding was affixed by
neighbours, who were naturally concerned at the arrival of squatters in their midst.
These measures proved ineffective, and at some time in the spring or summer of 1975 a
fresh lot of squatters broke in. Thereafter, until May 1977, the house was occupied by
h a shifting population of trespassers. No proceedings were taken to evict them, but an
attempt was made to encourage them to leave by cutting off services. The only result of
that was that they took retaliatory action, by stripping everything in the house and either
selling it or burning it. No doubt that contributed substantially to the staggering figure
of £36,000 for making good the damage caused. Finally in May 1977 the plaintiff's
agents managed to secure possession of the house by a combined operation with the local
police and thereafter most elaborate precautions were taken to prevent further break-in
until the builders arrived on the scene and started the work of repair. Even these do not
appear to have been 100% successful, but at least there was no further occupation by
squatters.
    We are not concerned in this appeal with any question of contributory negligence or

failure by the plaintiff to mitigate. These were matters which were canvassed extensively before the official referee, although the only case pleaded was that the damage suffered *a* from squatters was too remote. In the course of his judgment he posed a number of questions with regard to the plaintiff's responsibility in leaving a house empty, but he felt it unnecessary to answer them because of the view which he took on the question of remoteness. In the result, there are no findings of fact on these matters on which this court can act, if it takes a contrary view on the question of remoteness. That therefore is and remains the only question: is the damage which was undoubtedly caused as a *b* result of the successive incursions of squatters into this empty house damage for which the council, as the authors of the condition of the house, must be held responsible or is it an alien misfortune which the plaintiff must bear herself as one of the uncompensatable hazards of living in a modern society?

The plaintiff's case is a very simple one. She says that here was a house rendered unfit for occupation by the fault of the council. It needed little imagination to foresee that if *c* a tortfeasor causes such serious damage to a house that it can no longer be occupied that house must inevitably be vacated and cleared and will remain empty for such period as is necessary for the necessary remedial work to be identified, specified, financed and undertaken. That period will almost inevitably be lengthened in the case of very serious damage such as occurred here, damage which in fact exceeded the value of the original building, if the tortfeasor persists, as the council did, in resisting any liability at all right *d* up to the last moment. If, at the time when this disaster occurred, you left a house empty for any length of time in the area of Greater London, at any rate empty without a 'For sale' board outside it, the most likely thing in the world was that it would be entered by casual trespassers of one sort or another and probably by regular squatters, and it is notorious that squatters cause just the sort of damage that was caused here. Thus, the argument proceeds, the precise type of damage which has in fact occurred, although not *e* perhaps the severity of it, was a reasonably foreseeable result of the council's original wrongful act.

The council, on the other hand, argue that although damage which is not reasonably foreseeable is too remote, foreseeability is only one ingredient of remoteness. It is necessary, so it is argued, to demonstrate in addition a further ingredient of a sufficient nexus between the wrongful act and the injury sustained. What is referred to as the *f* 'chain of causation' may be broken, and the most common example of a break in the chain is the intervening act of a third person over whom the tortfeasor can exercise no control. Such an intervention does not always break the chain and, in particular, it will not do so where the very breach of duty relied on is the duty of the defendant to prevent the sort of intervention which has occurred, or where, at the date of the commission of the tortious act, the act of the third party which has given rise to the damage was likely *g* to occur (as opposed to being merely foreseeable).

It was this argument which appealed to the official referee. He based himself on the analysis contained in the speech of Lord Reid in *Home Office v Dorset Yacht Co Ltd* [1970] 2 All ER 294 at 298–300, [1970] AC 1004 at 1027–1030, and he concluded that, in cases where what has brought about the damage complained of is the free act of an independent third party, whether that act be innocent or tortious, it is not enough to *h* demonstrate that the act of the third party was reasonably foreseeable. It is necessary to go further and to show that the act was *likely* to occur. In the light of his findings of fact, he held that the damage was too remote, but in making his findings of fact he had in mind the test which he had just propounded. No complaint can be made about that, if the test is right, but there is a considerable difficulty if the test in the light of which the findings are made is not the right test.

The only relevant evidence on this aspect of the case before the official referee was that *j* of two neighbours of the plaintiff, which was to the effect that they were aware that there had been problems with squatters in Hampstead, in particular in the Malden Road area about a mile away. That was, however, an area of a very different character from that in

which the plaintiff's house was situate, and there had been no previous experience of
squatters in the Vale of Health. The first witness, Mr Landon Mills, added: 'I think we
were all very shocked and surprised when it happened.'

What the learned official referee found was this:

'There had been no squatters before this case in the better class parts of
Hampstead. In the light of this evidence I think I would feel disposed, if it were
relevant, to hold that squatting was at the material time a reasonably foreseeable
risk, but I am quite satisfied that no one familiar with the house and the locality
would at any time between the accident in the autumn of 1973 and the first
invasion about a year later have said that squatting was likely. It follows that in my
judgment the extensive damage caused by the squatters is too remote and cannot
form part of the damage payable by the defendants.'

The difficulty about this is that if, as counsel for the plaintiff submits, the test of
likelihood was a wrong test then there is no clear finding about whether the risk was a
reasonably foreseeable one, for the official referee merely states what he thinks that he
would have been disposed to find if, contrary to the view which he took, it had been
relevant to make a finding on the point. But leaving this difficulty aside for the
moment, was the test the right one? I think that it was, or that, if it was not, the error
lay not in qualifying the general test of foreseeability but in not qualifying it sufficiently.

Speaking for myself, I am not able to accept the submission of counsel for the council
in the form in which he put it, namely that reasonable foreseeability is but one ingredient
in a composite test of remoteness, which involves a further ingredient which he has
described as 'nexus'. This seems to me to be restoring that very fallacy which was
exemplified in Re Polemis [1921] 3 KB 560, [1921] All ER Rep 40 and was so decisively
rejected in The Wagon Mound (No 2) [1966] 2 All ER 709, [1967] 1 AC 617. That case
established that the test of causation is reasonable foreseeability, and I can find no room
for the suggestion that, even though a particular result may be reasonably foreseen as the
consequence of an act, yet the result may be too remote a consequence because of a lack
of 'nexus'. Nexus, after all, means only 'connection' and it must be comprehended in the
very concept of foreseeability itself. If there is, as a matter of fact, no connection between
the act and the result, it is difficult to see how the result could be foreseen by any
reasonable man *as a consequence* of the act.

Counsel for the council advances his submission as the groundwork for the further
submission that, where one of the links in the chain between act and result is the act of
an independent third person, the nexus is broken, unless that act is not merely foreseen
but is either 'likely' or 'very likely'. This concept is reflected in the judgment of the
official referee in the passage to which I have referred and is based on the analysis in the
speech of Lord Reid in Home Office v Dorset Yacht Co Ltd [1970] 2 All ER 294 at 300, [1970]
AC 1004 at 1030. His analysis is summarised in the following passage:

'These cases show that, where human action forms one of the links between the
original wrongdoing of the defendant and the loss suffered by the plaintiff, that
action must at least have been something very likely to happen if it is not to be
regarded as novus actus interveniens breaking the chain of causation. I do not think
that a mere foreseeable possibility is or should be sufficient, for then the intervening
human action can more properly be regarded as a new cause than as a consequence
of the original wrongdoing. But if the intervening action was likely to happen I do
not think it can matter whether that action was innocent or tortious or criminal.
Unfortunately tortious or criminal action by a third party is often the "very kind of
thing" which is likely to happen as a result of the wrongful or careless act of the
defendant.'

The views which Lord Reid there expressed are not reflected in the speeches of the
others of their Lordships in the case, and were, I think, obiter, since there was no scope

for argument on the assumed facts that the damage which occurred was not the very thing that was likely to happen. But, obiter or no, Lord Reid's opinion must be at least *a* of the very highest persuasive authority. For my part, however, I very much doubt whether he was, in what he said regarding the likelihood of the act of a third party, intending to bring back into the test of remoteness some further philosophical consideration of nexus or direct or indirect causation. As it seems to me, all that Lord Reid was saying was this, that, where as a matter of fact the consequence which the court is considering is one which results from, or would not have occurred but for, the *b* intervention of some independent human agency over which the tortfeasor has no control it has to approach the problem of what could be reasonably foreseen by the tortfeasor, and thus of the damage for which he is responsible, with particular care. The immediate cause is known: it is the independent human agency; and one has therefore to ask: on what basis can the act of that person be attributed back to the tortfeasor? It may be because the tortfeasor is responsible for his actions or because the third party act *c* which has precipitated the damage is the very thing that the tortfeasor is employed to prevent. But what is the position in the absence of some such consideration? Few things are less certainly predictable than human behaviour, and if one is asked whether in any given situation a human being may behave idiotically, irrationally or even criminally the answer must always be that that is a possibility, for every society has its proportion of idiots and criminals. It cannot be said that you cannot foresee the possibility that people *d* will do stupid or criminal acts, because people are constantly doing stupid or criminal acts. But the question is not what is foreseeable merely as a possibility but what would the reasonable man actually foresee if he thought about it, and all that Lord Reid seems to me to be saying is that the hypothetical reasonable man in the position of the tortfeasor cannot be said to foresee the behaviour of another person unless that behaviour is such as would, viewed objectively, be very likely to occur. Thus, for instance, if by my *e* negligent driving I damage another motorist's car, I suppose that theoretically I *could* foresee that, whilst he leaves it by the roadside to go and telephone his garage, some ill-intentioned passer-by may jack it up and remove the wheels. But I cannot think that it could be said that, merely because I have created the circumstances in which such a theft might become possible, I ought reasonably to foresee that it would happen.

Now if this is right, it does raise a difficulty over the official referee's finding. If the *f* likelihood of human behaviour is an element in reasonable foreseeability the official referee's disposition to say that the invasion of squatters was reasonably foreseeable is inconsistent with his actual finding of fact that squatting was unlikely, and that is the only actual finding. What I think, with respect, he was doing in this passage of his judgment was confusing 'foreseeable' with 'reasonably foreseeable'. That indeed would be consistent with the passage from Lord Reid's speech on which he was relying as stating *g* the principle. Lord Reid said in terms that foreseeability 'as a possibility' was not sufficient and I think that what the official referee has done is to treat that as meaning, in the context, '*reasonable* foreseeability as a possibility'. In the context in which, as I think, Lord Reid was using the expression 'as a possibility' (that is to say, as meaning '*only* a bare possibility and no more') that seems to me to be a contradiction in terms, and for the reasons which I have endeavoured to explain it was not what Lord Reid intended and *h* it was not what he said. The critical finding here is, to my mind, that the incursion of squatters was in fact unlikely.

Given this finding, it seems to me that, accepting Lord Reid's test as correct (which counsel for the plaintiff challenges), it must be fatal to the plaintiff's contentions on this appeal, because it constitutes in effect a finding that the damage claimed is not such as could be reasonably foreseen. And that, indeed, seems to me to accord with the common *j* sense of the matter.

The test of remoteness is said to be the same as the test of duty in negligence (see *The Wagon Mound (No 1)* [1961] 1 All ER 404, [1961] AC 388). If the instant case is approached as a case of negligence and one asks the question, did the defendants owe a

duty not to break a water pipe so as to cause the plaintiff's house to be invaded by
a squatters a year later, the tenuousness of the linkage between act and result becomes
apparent. I confess that I find it inconceivable that the reasonable man, wielding his pick
in the road in 1973, could be said reasonably to foresee that his puncturing of a water
main would fill the plaintiff's house with uninvited guests in 1974. Whilst, therefore,
I am not altogether in accord with the official referee's reasoning, I think that he came to
the right conclusion in the light of his finding of fact, which has not been challenged.
b Accordingly, the appeal should, in my judgment, be dismissed.

   I should perhaps add that I do not dissent from the view of Lord Denning MR that the
test expressed by Lord Reid (with, as I think, the intention of restricting the ambit of the
duty in tort) was incorrect, in that it was not exhaustive and did not go far enough in that
direction. To apply a straight test of foreseeability or likelihood to hypothetical
circumstances which could arise in relation to the acts of independent third parties in the
c case of, for instance, carelessness on the part of servants of the Home Office does, as Lord
Denning MR points out, produce some astonishing results. Suppose that as a result of
the carelessness of a prison officer a prisoner escapes and commits a crime of the same
type as that for which he is in custody a fortnight later and 400 miles away from the place
at which he escaped. Is it any less foreseeable that he will do so than that he will steal his
rail fare from a house adjoining the prison? And is the Home Office to be liable without
d limit until the prisoner is apprehended? Does it make any difference if he is, at the date
of his escape, on remand or due for parole? Happily, such hypothetical questions do not,
on the view that I take, have to be answered in the instant case, but whether or not it is
right to regard questions of remoteness according to some flexible test of the policy of the
law from time to time (on which I prefer at the moment to express no view) I concur
with Lord Denning MR in regarding the straight test of foreseeability, at least in cases
e where the acts of independent third parties are concerned, as one which can, unless
subjected to some further limitation, produce results which extend the ambit of liability
beyond all reason. Speaking for myself, I would respectfully regard Lord Reid's test as a
workable and sensible one, subject only to this, that I think that he may perhaps have
understated the *degree* of likelihood required before the law can or should attribute the
free act of a responsible third person to the tortfeasor. Such attribution cannot, as I think,
f rationally be made simply on the basis of some geographical or temporal proximity, and
even 'likelihood' is a somewhat uncertain touchstone. It may be that some more
stringent standard is required. There may, for instance, be circumstances in which the
court would require a degree of likelihood amounting almost to inevitability before it
fixes a defendant with responsibility for the act of a third party over whom he has and
can have no control. On the official referee's finding, however, that does not arise here,
g and the problem can be left for a case in which it directly arises.

WATKINS LJ. 'This doctrine of remoteness of damage is one of very considerable
obscurity and difficulty.' So wrote the editor of Salmond on the Law of Torts (17th Edn,
1977, p 38). If I did not consciously share that opinion previously from a fairly long
acquaintance with the subject, I have, since hearing the able submissions made to this
h court, to confess to feelings of apprehension of never emerging out of the maze of
authorities on the subject of remoteness into the light of a clear understanding of it. On
my way to providing an answer to the question raised in this appeal I have sometimes felt
like Sir Winston Churchill must have done when he wrote:

   'I had a feeling once about mathematics—that I saw it all. Depth beyond depth
   was revealed to me—the byss and abyss. I saw—as one might see the transit of
   Venus or the Lord Mayor's Show—a quantity passing through an infinity and
   changing its sign from plus to minus. I saw exactly how it happened and why the
   tergiversation was inevitable—but it was after dinner and I let it go.'

This appeal involves but a single issue. Was the damage done to Mrs Lamb's house by squatters too remote to be a consequence of the council's initial negligent and damaging act which partly destroyed support for the house and for which they have to compensate *a* her?

Counsel for the plaintiffs contends that, since the official referee intimated in his judgment that if thereby he was applying the only relevant and correct test he would be disposed to hold that an invasion of the undermined house by squatters was a risk reasonably foreseeable by the defendants, the case should go back to him so that he can positively make that finding and give judgment for Mrs Lamb for the sum claimed in *b* respect of the squatters' damage. For, he says, reasonable foreseeability simpliciter of the fresh kind of damage done is, since *The Wagon Mound (No 2)* [1966] 2 All ER 709, [1967] 1 AC 617, the sole test which determines whether fresh damage caused by an act which is independent of and committed later than the initial tortious act is too remote: whether, in other words, it is truly a novus actus interveniens for the damage caused by which a defendant is not liable. *c*

He submits that Lord Reid was out of step with the *Wagon Mound* test which should always be followed nowadays when in *Home Office v Dorset Yacht Co Ltd* [1970] 2 All ER 294 at 300, [1970] AC 1004 at 1030 he said:

> '. . . where human action forms one of the links between the original wrongdoing of the defendant and the loss suffered by the plaintiff, that action must at least have *d* been something very likely to happen if it is not to be regarded as novus actus interveniens breaking the chain of causation. I do not think that a mere foreseeable possibility is or should be sufficient, for then the intervening human action can more properly be regarded as a new cause than as a consequence of the original wrongdoing. But if the intervening action was likely to happen I do not think that it can matter whether that action was innocent or tortious or criminal. *e* Unfortunately, tortious or criminal action by a third party is often the "very kind of thing" which is likely to happen as a result of the wrongful or careless act of the defendant.'

So by adopting, as he did, the opinion of Lord Reid the official referee was also out of step with *The Wagon Mound (No 2)* and applied the wrong test to the issue of remoteness. *f* If he had allowed himself to be governed by *The Wagon Mound (No 2)* he would inevitably have found for Mrs Lamb for the considerable damage deliberately and criminally caused by the squatters.

I feel bound to say with respect that what Lord Reid said in the *Dorset Yacht* case does nothing to simplify the task of deciding for or against remoteness, especially where the fresh damage complained of has been caused by the intervening act of a third party. It *g* may be that in respect of such an act he is to be understood as saying, without using his remarkable and usual clarity of expression, that damage is inevitably too remote unless it can reasonably be foreseen as likely to occur. If that be so, it could be said that he was not intending to depart from the *Wagon Mound* test save in cases involving intervening human action to which he would apply a rather stricter than usual test by placing acts which are *not likely to occur* within the realm of remoteness. *h*

In *McKew v Holland & Hannen & Cubitts (Scotland) Ltd* [1969] 3 All ER 1621 at 1623 he had given more than a hint of this when he said:

> 'A defender is not liable for a consequence of a kind which is not foreseeable. But it does not follow that he is liable for every consequence which a reasonable man could foresee. What can be foreseen depends almost entirely on the facts of the case, and it is often easy to foresee unreasonable conduct or other novus actus interveniens *j* as being quite likely. But that does not mean that the defender must pay for damage caused by the novus actus. It only leads to trouble that if one tries to graft on to the concept of foreseeability some rule of law to the effect that a wrongdoer is not bound to foresee something which in fact he could readily foresee as quite likely

to happen. For it is not at all unlikely or unforseeable that an active man who has
suffered such a disability will take some quite unreasonable risk. But if he does he
cannot hold the defender liable for the consequences.'

From the foregoing it is also obvious that Lord Reid would regard some kinds of
intervening acts done by third parties as too remote even though they could reasonably
be foreseen as likely or quite likely to occur.

The plaintiff McKew had caused fresh damage to himself as a result of taking an
unreasonable risk. That he would be likely or quite likely to do this was said to have
been reasonably foreseeable. Yet, because he had behaved unreasonably in the doing of
it, his act was found to be a novus actus interveniens which freed the defendants from all
liability for it. This decision has in some quarters been criticised on the basis that it
would have been more in accordance with principle to have treated the plaintiff's
unreasonable conduct as contributory negligence. I do not agree. I prefer to regard the
decision in *McKew* as a good example of a determination to bring realistic consideration
to bear on the question of fresh damage arising from an event or act occurring
subsequently to the initial negligent act in the context of remoteness of damage.

It seems to me that if the sole and exclusive test of remoteness is whether the fresh
damage has arisen from an event or act which is reasonably foreseeable, or reasonably
foreseeable as a possibility, or likely or quite likely to occur, absurd, even bizarre, results
might ensue in actions for damages for negligence. Why, if this test were to be rigidly
applied to the facts in the *Dorset Yacht* case, one can envisage the Home Office being
found liable for the damage caused by an escaped borstal boy committing a burglary in
John o' Groats. This would plainly be a ludicrous conclusion.

I do not think that words such as, among others, 'possibility', 'likely' or 'quite likely'
assist in the application of the test of reasonable foreseeability. If the crisply stated test
which emanates from *The Wagon Mound (No 2)* is to be festooned with additional words
supposedly there for the purpose of amplification or qualification, an understandable
application of it will become impossible.

In my view the *Wagon Mound* test should always be applied without any of the gloss
which is from time to time being applied to it.

But when so applied it cannot in all circumstances in which it arises conclude
consideration of the question of remoteness, although in the vast majority of cases it will
be adequate for this purpose. In other cases, the present one being an example of these
in my opinion, further consideration is necessary, always providing, of course, a plaintiff
survives the test of reasonable foreseeability.

This is because the very features of an event or act for which damages are claimed
themselves suggest that the event or act is not on any practical view of it remotely in any
way connected with the original act of negligence. These features will include such
matters as the nature of the event or act, the time it occurred, the place where it occurred,
the identity of the perpetrator and his intentions, and responsibility, if any, for taking
measures to avoid the occurrence and matters of public policy.

A robust and sensible approach to this very important area of the study of remoteness
will more often than not produce, I think, an instinctive feeling that the event or act
being weighed in the balance is too remote to sound in damages for the plaintiff. I do not
pretend that in all cases the answer will come easily to the inquirer. But that the question
must be asked and answered in all these cases I have no doubt.

To return to the present case, I have the instinctive feeling that the squatters' damage
is too remote. I could not possibly come to any other conclusion, although on the
primary facts I, too, would regard that damage or something like it as reasonably
foreseeable in these times.

We are here dealing with unreasonable conduct of an outrageous kind. It is notorious
that squatters will take the opportunity of entering and occupying any house, whether
it be damaged or not, which is found to be unoccupied for more than a very temporary
duration. In my opinion this kind of antisocial and criminal behaviour provides a

glaring example of an act which inevitably, or almost so, is too remote to cause a
defendant to pay damages for the consequences of it.

Accordingly, I would hold that the damage caused by the squatters in the present case
is too remote to be recovered from these defendants.

The reasons I have explained for arriving at this conclusion are, of course, dissimilar
from those which led the official referee to a similar one. His approach to the matter was
I feel bound to say wrong in my opinion but, since it produced what I believe to be a
correct answer to the question posed in the appeal, he cannot be called on to reconsider
his judgment.

I would dismiss this appeal.

Appeal dismissed.

Solicitors: *Bernard Sheridan & Co* (for the plaintiffs); *Wilkinson, Kimbers & Staddon* (for the
defendants).

Sumra Green   Barrister.

R v Malcherek
R v Steel

COURT OF APPEAL, CRIMINAL DIVISION
LORD LANE CJ, ORMROD LJ AND SMITH J
17th MARCH 1981

*Criminal law – Homicide – Causation – Cause of death – Act breaking chain of causation –
Victim's injuries requiring treatment on life support machine – Machine disconnected when
doctors concluding by application of accepted medical criteria that victim dead – Defendant
convicted of murder – Whether disconnection of life support machine breaking chain of causation
– Whether medical evidence that treatment by life support machine would have been administered
differently by other medical practitioners admissible.*

In the first case the appellant, on 26th March 1979, stabbed his wife causing a deep
wound in her abdomen which made hospital treatment necessary. After treatment the
wife appeared to be recovering but on 1st April she collapsed in hospital and shortly
afterwards, her heart stopped beating. Surgery was performed to remove a blood clot
from the pulmonary artery and thereafter the heart, after not beating for 30 minutes,
started to beat again. Because of the danger of brain damage resulting from the period
when the heart was not beating, the wife was put on a life support machine. By 4th
April she appeared to have suffered irretrievable brain damage. After tests were carried
out to confirm that that was the position it was decided, on 5th April, to disconnect the
life support machine and shortly afterwards the wife was declared to be dead. In the
second case the applicant, on 10th October 1977, attacked a girl causing her grave head
injuries. On the same day she was taken to hospital and put on a life support machine.
On 12th October the doctors concluded that her brain had ceased to function and the
machine was disconnected. Shortly afterwards she was declared to be dead. In each case
the medical treatment given to the victim was normal and conventional. The appellant
and the applicant were each charged with murder. At each trial the judge, after hearing
submissions from counsel, decided to withdraw from the jury the issue of the cause of
the victim's death, on the ground that at the time of death the original injuries inflicted
on the victim were an operating cause of death and that it was not open to the jury to
conclude that the accused had not caused the death of his victim. The appellant and the

applicant were each convicted of murder. The appellant appealed, and the applicant
a applied for leave to appeal, against conviction, on the ground that the judge had been
wrong to withdraw the issue of causation from the jury because there was evidence that
the cause of death in each case was the switching off of the life support machine and the
jury in each case should have been allowed to consider that evidence. The applicant also
applied for leave to adduce further medical evidence regarding withdrawal of the life
support machine from his victim.

b
Held – The appeal and applications would be dismissed for the following reasons—
    (1) Where competent and careful medical treatment given to a victim for an injury
inflicted by an assailant included putting the victim on a life support machine, the
decision by the medical practitioners concerned to disconnect the machine because, by
generally accepted medical criteria, the victim was dead could not exonerate the assailant
c from responsibility for the death if at the time of death the original injury was a
continuing or operating cause of the death, for then the disconnection of the machine
did not break the chain of causation between the infliction of the original injury and the
death. Since there was no evidence that the original injury inflicted on each victim had
ceased to be a continuing or operating cause of death at the time of the victim's death
following disconnection of the life support machine, it followed that the issue of
d causation was, in each case, properly withdrawn from the jury (see p 428 h to p 429 g,
post); R v Smith [1959] 2 All ER 193 applied; R v Jordan (1956) 40 Cr App R 152
distinguished.
    (2) In the ordinary case, where treatment by a life support machine was given in good
faith by competent and careful medical practitioners, evidence was not admissible to
show that that treatment would have been administered differently by other medical
e practitioners. Since the applicant's actions continued to be an operating cause of his
victim's death and the medical evidence which the applicant sought to adduce could not
alter that fact, it was neither necessary, under s 23(2) of the Criminal Appeal Act 1968,
nor desirable or expedient, under s 23(1) of that Act, to receive the proposed medical
evidence. Accordingly the application to adduce further evidence would be refused (see
p 428 j and p 429 a to c and f, post).

f
Notes
For causation in homicide, see 11 Halsbury's Laws (4th Edn) para 1156, and for cases on
cause of death, see 15 Digest (Reissue) 1114–1117, 9355–9392.

Cases referred to in judgment
g R v Blaue [1975] 3 All ER 446, [1975] 1 WLR 1411, 61 Cr App R 271, sub nom R v Blaub
    139 JP 841, CA, 15 Digest (Reissue) 1116, 9384.
R v Jordan (1956) 40 Cr App R 152, CCA, 14(2) Digest (Reissue) 785, 6676.
R v Smith [1959] 2 All ER 193, [1959] 2 QB 35, [1959] 2 WLR 623, 123 JP 295, 43 Cr App
    R 121, C-MAC, 14(2) Digest (Reissue) 562, 4588.

h **Cases also cited**
R v Harding (1936) 25 Cr App R 190, CCA.
R v Lomas [1969] 1 All ER 920, [1969] 1 WLR 306, CA.

Appeal and applications
                                    R v Malcherek
j On 26th March 1979 the appellant, Richard Tadeusz Malcherek, stabbed his wife, one of
the stabs resulting in a deep wound to her abdomen. She was taken to hospital and
subsequently it became necessary to put her on a life support machine, namely a
ventilator; but later on, when she was found to have irreversible brain damage, the
ventilator was disconnected and shortly after that she died. At Malcherek's trial for her
murder, in the Crown Court at Winchester, the trial judge, Willis J, withdrew the issue

of causation from the jury after hearing submissions from counsel and the only issue left
to the jury was that of intent. On 12th November 1979 Malcherek was convicted of **a**
murder and sentenced to life imprisonment. He appealed against the conviction by
leave of the single judge on the ground that the judge ought to have left the issue of
causation to the jury. The facts are set out in the judgment of the court.

R v Steel

On 10th October 1977 the applicant, Anthony Steel, attacked a girl called Carol **b**
Wilkinson causing her multiple skull fractures and severe brain damage. She was taken
to hospital and almost immediately put on a life support machine, namely a ventilator,
but on 12th October the doctors in charge of her concluded that her brain had ceased to
function and disconnected the machine and shortly after all her bodily functions
ceased. At Steel's trial for murder, in the Crown Court at Leeds, the trial judge, Boreham
J, withdrew the issue of causation from the jury after hearing submissions from **c**
counsel. Steel was convicted of murder and sentenced to life imprisonment. He applied
to the court for leave to appeal against the conviction on the grounds that the judge was
wrong to withdraw the issue of causation from the jury, and, that the jury's verdict was,
for various reasons, unsafe or unsatisfactory. He also applied for leave to call medical
evidence. The facts are set out in the judgment of the court.

     d

T G Field-Fisher QC and *Anthony Bailey* for Malcherek.
Wilfred Steer QC and *J S H Stewart* for Steel.
John J Smyth QC, Donald Gordon and *J M Meredith* for the Crown.

LORD LANE CJ delivered the following judgment of the court: These two appeals,
one an appeal and the other an application, raise similar points and it was accordingly **e**
thought convenient that they should be dealt with together, and that is what has
happened.

    The facts of the two cases are as follows. I start with the applicant Steel. This man, on
13th December 1979, in the Crown Court at Leeds before Boreham J and a jury, was
convicted of murder, and he now applies to this court for leave to appeal against
conviction and also to call certain witnesses, two medical men. **f**

    The victim of the attack was a girl called Carol Wilkinson. She was 20 years of age at
the time. She lived in the Ravenscliffe area of Bradford with her fiancé and worked at a
bakery which was situated about half a mile away from her home. Steel was then aged
21. He lived not far away in another house on the same Ravenscliffe estate. He was
sharing accommodation with a girl named Pamela Ward, but at the same time he was
carrying on an association with another girl whom he eventually married. Steel was **g**
employed by the local council as a gardener.

    It was on 10th October 1977, at about 9 am, that Carol Wilkinson was walking to
work from her home to the bakery. At some time on that morning, between about 9.00
and 9.30, she was savagely attacked by someone who stripped off the greater part of her
clothing, and then battered her about the head with a 50 lb stone which was found
nearby. She was found shortly afterwards, in a field by the road, unconscious. She was **h**
taken as rapidly as could be to hospital. She had multiple fractures of the skull and severe
brain damage as well as a broken arm and other superficial injuries which need not
concern us. She was put almost immediately on a life support machine in the shape of
a ventilator.

    On 12th October the medical team in whose charge she was, after a number of tests,
came to the conclusion that her brain had ceased to function and that, accordingly, the **j**
ventilator was in effect operating on a lifeless body. The life support machine was
switched off and all bodily functions ceased shortly afterwards.

    The judge withdrew the issue of causation from the jury on the fifth day of that trial,
and the jury were accordingly left to decide the issue, hotly contested, of whether they
were sure that it was Steel who had been the girl's assailant.

The case for the Crown depended very largely, though not entirely, on admissions
a which were said to have been made by Steel, both orally and in writing, to the police
during the time in April 1979 when he was being questioned about the events of 10th
October 1977. Part of the grounds of appeal are based on the allegation that those
admissions were wrongly allowed to go before the jury by the judge when the admissions
had, it is said, been extracted from Steel by threats or by oppression or possibly in
contravention of the Judges' Rules. That aspect of the application has been left in
b abeyance until the problem of causation, with which we are concerned now, has been
concluded.

So far as that issue is concerned, namely the issue of causation, the following facts are
material. On admission to the casualty department of the Bradford Royal Infirmary at
about 10.15 am on Monday, 10th October, Carol was seen by a Dr Nevelos, who found
her to be deeply unconscious with no motor activity, her eyes open and the pupils
c fixed. She was breathing only with the aid of the ventilator. An hour later she was
admitted to the intensive care unit of the Royal Infirmary and during the whole of that
day she remained deeply unconscious and unresponsive. At 10.00 pm the consultant
neuro-surgeon, a Mr Price, examined her. He found her to be in a deep coma,
unresponding to any stimulus. He carried out a test for electrical activity in the brain
which proved negative. The total absence of any motor activity since the girl had been
d admitted to hospital and the early fixation of the pupils, which I have already mentioned,
led him to the conclusion that there had been a devastating impact injury to the brain.

The cerebral function monitor showed no activity. Her eyes were too occluded, so it
is said, to allow any caloric testing. The suggestion was made by Mr Price that her
temperature should be raised and that if by the morning her cerebral function remained
as it had been up to date, namely zero, they should declare her brain to be dead. In fact,
e shortly after 10.00 am the next day, a cerebral blood flow test was carried out which
indicated that there was no blood circulating in the brain. Several electroencephalogram
tests were made during that day. None of them had any positive result.

On Wednesday, 12th October, two days after the injuries had been inflicted, another
electroencephalogram test was made in the morning and another one at 6.00 pm but
none of these tests showed any signs of electrical activity at all. After that there was a
f consultation between the doctors who were in charge of the patient, and it was agreed
amongst them that the continued use of the ventilator was without any purpose. At
6.15 pm the patient was withdrawn from the ventilator, and at 6.40 pm she was declared
to be dead. There is an indication, though we are told it was not part of the evidence at
the trial, that on post-mortem 50 minutes later it was found that her brain was already
in the process of decomposition. Much of the cross-examination of the medical men was
g taken up with suggestions that they had failed to conform to certain criteria which have
been laid down by the Royal Medical Colleges on the subject of the ascertainment of
brain death.

The matter which counsel for Steel invites this court to take into consideration as
possibly differentiating the case of Steel from that of Malcherek is that he says that two
of the suggested tests were not carried out properly, namely the corneal reflex test and
h the vestibulo-ocular reflex test. The corneal reflex test consists of touching the cornea of
the eye with a piece of cotton wool to see if that creates any reaction in the patient and,
as we understand it, the vestibulo-ocular reflex test consists of putting ice cold water into
the aperture of the ear, again to see if that produces any reflex in the patient. Reasons
were given for neither of those tests having been carried out.

We now turn to the facts in the case of Malcherek. On 12th November 1979, this time
j in the Crown Court at Winchester before Willis J and a jury, Malcherek was convicted of
murder. He appeals against the conviction by leave of the single judge. The victim was
Christian Malcherek, his wife, who was then aged 32. It seems that in November 1978
she left Malcherek in order to go and live with her daughters at Poole. There was a non-
molestation order in force, directed at Malcherek, but on the evening of 26th March
1979 he went to her flat where she was living. There was a quarrel and, to cut a long

story short, he stabbed his wife nine times with a kitchen knife. One of the stabs resulted
in a deep penetrating wound to Mrs Malcherek's abdomen.   *a*

She was taken to Poole General Hospital and there was preliminary treatment in order
to try to rectify her very low blood pressure, which was ascertained on admission. The
surgical registrar then performed a laparotomy and removed rather more than one and
a half litres of blood from the abdomen. There was a section of the intestine which was
damaged, and he excised that and joined up the two ends. For several days it seemed as
though Mrs Malcherek was making an uneventful recovery. Indeed, she was clearly *b*
confidently expected to survive. However, on 1st April she collapsed and the preliminary
diagnosis was that she had suffered a massive pulmonary embolism. She was resuscitated
and arrangements were made for her admission to the Western Hospital at Southampton,
which was equipped to deal with this type of emergency. She arrived there shortly
before midnight. A couple of hours later her condition suddenly deteriorated and her
heart stopped. She was taken straight away to the operating theatre and given cardiac *c*
massage. The surgeon then opened her chest. He found that her heart was distended
and not beating. He made an incision into the pulmonary artery and extracted from the
pulmonary artery a large clot of blood some twelve inches long, which had plainly
formed in one of the veins of the leg (which, we are told, is a common complication of
major abdominal surgery), and had then moved on from the leg to the pulmonary artery
with the results already described.   *d*

When the clot was removed the heart started again spontaneously. It will be
appreciated that since the heart was not beating for a period of something like thirty
minutes there was a grave danger of anoxic damage to the brain. She was returned to the
ward and connected to a ventilator. Throughout the Monday she remained on that
machine receiving intensive care, but in the afternoon an electroencephalogram showed
that there were indeed symptoms of severe anoxic damage to the brain. The prognosis *e*
was poor.

The consultant neurologist saw her at 7.00 pm. She was unresponsive to any stimulus
save that her pupils did react to light. He suggested a further electroencephalogram
because at that stage it was not clear how much brain damage had been suffered. On the
morning of Tuesday, Dr Manners decided to dispense with the ventilator if that could
possibly be done. When that was done she was able, first of all, to breathe adequately by *f*
herself, but towards midday she suffered a sharp and marked deterioration and the
diagnosis was that she had suffered a cerebral vascular accident, possibly a ruptured blood
vessel, possibly a clot, causing further brain damage. In any event, by quarter to two in
the afternoon her attempts to breathe were inadequate and she was put back onto the
ventilator. There was a continued deterioration and by the following day she was deeply
unconscious and seemed to have irreversible brain damage. There was less electrical *g*
activity than before when a further electroencephalogram was carried out.

On 5th April the situation had deteriorated still more, and it was quite obvious at
1.15 pm on that day, when Dr Lawton made an examination, that her brain was
irretrievably damaged. He carried out five of the six Royal Medical Colleges'
confirmatory tests. The one he omitted was the 'gag reflex' test, again for reasons which
he explained. The patient's relations were consulted and a decision was made to *h*
disconnect the ventilator, which was done at half past four. A supply of oxygen was fed
to her lungs in case she should make spontaneous efforts to breathe but she did not, and
shortly after 5.00 pm she was certified to be dead.

In these circumstances, as in the earlier case, the judge decided that the question of
causation should not be left for the jury's consideration. Consequently, the only issue
they had to decide was the one of intent, there being no argument but that Malcherek *j*
had in fact inflicted the knife wound or wounds on Mrs Malcherek.

In this case the principal and, in effect, the only ground of appeal, as counsel for
Malcherek has told us, is that the judge should have left the issue of causation to the jury.

This is not the occasion for any decision as to what constitutes death. Modern
techniques have undoubtedly resulted in the blurring of many of the conventional and

traditional concepts of death. A person's heart can now be removed altogether without
a death supervening; machines can keep the blood circulating through the vessels of the
body until a new heart can be implanted in the patient, and even though a person is no
longer able to breathe spontaneously a ventilating machine can, so to speak, do his
breathing for him, as is demonstrated in the two cases before us. There is, it seems, a
body of opinion in the medical profession that there is only one true test of death and
that is the irreversible death of the brain stem, which controls the basic functions of the
b body such as breathing. When that occurs it is said the body has died, even though by
mechanical means the lungs are being caused to operate and some circulation of blood is
taking place.

We have had placed before us, and have been asked to admit, evidence that in each of
these two cases the medical men concerned did not comply with all the suggested criteria
for establishing such brain death. Indeed, further evidence has been suggested and
c placed before us that those criteria or tests are not in themselves stringent enough.
However, in each of these two cases there is no doubt that whatever test is applied the
victim died; that is to say, applying the traditional test, all body functions, breathing and
heartbeat and brain function came to an end, at the latest, soon after the ventilator was
disconnected.

The question posed for answer to this court is simply whether the judge in each case
d was right in withdrawing from the jury the question of causation. Was he right to rule
that there was no evidence on which the jury could come to the conclusion that the
assailant did not cause the death of the victim?

The way in which the submissions are put by counsel for Malcherek on the one hand
and by counsel for Steel on the other is as follows: the doctors, by switching off the
ventilator and the life support machine, were the cause of death or, to put it more
e accurately, there was evidence which the jury should have been allowed to consider that
the doctors, and not the assailant, in each case may have been the cause of death.

In each case it is clear that the initial assault was the cause of the grave head injuries in
the one case and of the massive abdominal haemorrhage in the other. In each case the
initial assault was the reason for the medical treatment being necessary. In each case the
medical treatment given was normal and conventional. At some stage the doctors must
f decide if and when treatment has become otiose. This decision was reached, in each of
the two cases here, in circumstances which have already been set out in some detail. It
is no part of the task of this court to inquire whether the criteria, the Royal Medical
College confirmatory tests, are a satisfactory code of practice. It is no part of the task of
this court to decide whether the doctors were, in either of these two cases, justified in
omitting one or more of the so called 'confirmatory tests'. The doctors are not on trial:
g Steel and Malcherek respectively were.

There are two comparatively recent cases which are relevant to the consideration of
this problem. The first is *R v Jordan* (1956) 40 Cr App R 152. That was a decision of the
Court of Criminal Appeal, presided over by Hallett J. There the appellant stabbed his
victim on 4th May 1956. The victim died in hospital on 12th May. At the trial the
pathologist who carried out the autopsy gave evidence that the cause of death was
h bronchopneumonia following a penetrating abdominal injury. The main burden of the
appeal was whether fresh medical evidence, which was not called at the trial, should be
admitted and considered by the Court of Criminal Appeal. In due course, in what was
described as the exceptional or the exceedingly unusual circumstances of the case, that
evidence was admitted. Evidence was given, accordingly, by two pathologists who said
that in their opinion death had not been caused by the initial stab wound, which had
j almost healed at the time of the death, but by the introduction of terramycin after the
deceased man had shown himself to be intolerant to that drug, and also by the
intravenous introduction of huge quantities of liquid, which was an abnormal medical
treatment and which, in these circumstances, was quite wrong. The conviction was
quashed because the court came to the conclusion, in effect, that the further evidence
demonstrated that the death of the victim might not have resulted from normal

treatment employed to cope with a felonious injury but that the treatment administered, the terramycin and the intravenous fluid, was an abnormal treatment which was palpably *a* wrong which, in its turn, caused the death at a time when the original wound was in the process of healing and indeed had practically healed.

The other decision is *R v Smith* [1959] 2 All ER 193, [1959] 2 QB 35. In that case the appellant had stabbed a fellow soldier with a bayonet. One of the wounds had pierced the victim's lung and had caused bleeding. Whilst being carried to the medical hut or reception centre for treatment, the victim was dropped twice and then, when he reached *b* the treatment centre, he was given treatment which was subsequently shown to have been incorrect. Lord Parker CJ, who gave the judgment of the court, stressed the fact, if it needed stressing, that *R v Jordan* was a very particular case depending on its own exact facts, as indeed Hallett J himself had said in that case.

In *R v Smith* counsel for the appellant argued that if there was any other cause, whether resulting from negligence or not, operating, if something happened which impeded the *c* chance of the deceased recovering, then the death did not result from that wound.

A very similar submission to that has been made to this court by counsel in the instant case. The court in *R v Smith* was quite unable to accept that contention. Lord Parker CJ said ([1959] 2 All ER 193 at 198, [1959] 2 QB 35 at 42–43):

'It seems to the court that, if at the time of death the original wound is still an operating cause and a substantial cause, then the death can properly be said to be the *d* result of the wound, albeit that some other cause of death is also operating. Only if it can be said that the original wounding is merely the setting in which another cause operates can it be said that the death does not result from the wound. Putting it in another way, only if the second cause is so overwhelming as to make the original wound merely part of the history can it be said that the death does not flow from the wound.' *e*

In the view of this court, if a choice has to be made between the decision in *R v Jordan* and that in *R v Smith*, which we do not believe it does (*R v Jordan* being a very exceptional case), then the decision in *R v Smith* is to be preferred.

The only other case to which reference has been made, it having been drawn to our attention by counsel for Steel, is *R v Blaue* [1975] 3 All ER 446, [1975] 1 WLR 1411. That *f* was the case where the victim of a stabbing incident was a Jehovah's Witness who refused to accept a blood transfusion although she had been told that to refuse would mean death for her, a prophecy which was fulfilled. The passage that has been drawn to our attention in that case is the last paragraph of the judgment of Lawton LJ ([1975] 3 All ER 446 at 450, [1975] 1 WLR 1411 at 1416):

'The issue of the cause of death in a trial for either murder or manslaughter is one *g* of fact for the jury to decide. But if, as in this case, there is no conflict of evidence and all the jury has to do is apply the law to the admitted facts, the judge is entitled to tell the jury what the result of that application will be. In this case the judge would have been entitled to have told the jury that the appellant's stab wound was an operative cause of death. The appeal fails.'

h

There is no evidence in the present case here that at the time of conventional death, after the life support machinery was disconnected, the original wound or injury was other than a continuing, operating and indeed substantial cause of the death of the victim, although it need hardly be added that it need not be substantial to render the assailant guilty. There may be occasions, although they will be rare, when the original injury has ceased to operate as a cause at all, but in the ordinary case if the treatment is *j* given bona fide by competent and careful medical practitioners, then evidence will not be admissible to show that the treatment would not have been administered in the same way by other medical practitioners. In other words, the fact that the victim has died, despite or because of medical treatment for the initial injury given by careful and skilled medical practitioners, will not exonerate the original assailant from responsibility for the

death. It follows that so far as the ground of appeal in each of these cases relates to the
a direction given on causation, that ground fails. It also follows that the evidence which
it is sought to adduce now, although we are prepared to assume that it is both credible
and was not available properly at the trial (and a reasonable explanation for not calling it
at the trial has been given), if received could, under no circumstances, afford any ground
for allowing the appeal.

The reason is this. Nothing which any of the two or three medical men whose
b statements are before us could say would alter the fact that in each case the assailant's
actions continued to be an operating cause of the death. Nothing the doctors could say
would provide any ground for a jury coming to the conclusion that the assailant in either
case might not have caused the death. The furthest to which their proposed evidence
goes, as already stated, is to suggest, first, that the criteria or the confirmatory tests are not
sufficiently stringent and, second, that in the present case they were in certain respects
c inadequately fulfilled or carried out. It is no part of this court's function in the present
circumstances to pronounce on this matter, nor was it a function of either of the juries
at these trials. Where a medical practitioner adopting methods which are generally
accepted comes bona fide and conscientiously to the conclusion that the patient is for
practical purposes dead, and that such vital functions as exist (for example, circulation)
are being maintained solely be mechanical means, and therefore discontinues treatment,
d that does not prevent the person who inflicted the initial injury from being responsible
for the victim's death. Putting it in another way, the discontinuance of treatment in
those circumstances does not break the chain of causation between the initial injury and
the death.

Although it is unnecessary to go further than that for the purpose of deciding the
present point, we wish to add this thought. Whatever the strict logic of the matter may
e be, it is perhaps somewhat bizarre to suggest, as counsel have impliedly done, that where
a doctor tries his conscientious best to save the life of a patient brought to hospital in
extremis, skilfully using sophisticated methods, drugs and machinery to do so, but fails
in his attempt and therefore discontinues treatment, he can be said to have caused the
death of the patient.

For these reasons we do not deem it either necessary under s 23(2) of the Criminal
f Appeal Act 1968 nor desirable or expedient under s 23(1) to receive the proposed
evidence of the doctors which, in statement form, has been placed before us. Likewise,
there is no ground for saying that the judge in either case was wrong in withdrawing the
issue of causation from the jury. It follows that the appeal of Malcherek is dismissed. It
now remains to consider the application in the case of Steel in so far as it relates to the
matters other than causation.

g [The court then considered the other ground of Steel's application for leave to appeal
against conviction on the grounds that the jury's verdict was unsafe or unsatisfactory, and
concluded that the verdict was not unsafe or unsatisfactory and accordingly refused the
application.]

Appeal and applications dismissed.

Solicitors: *Trevanion & Curtis*, Parkstone (for Malcherek); *T I Clough & Co*, Bradford (for
Steel); *Director of Public Prosecutions*.

N P Metcalfe Esq   Barrister.

Dip Kaur v Chief Constable for Hampshire

QUEEN'S BENCH DIVISION
LORD LANE CJ AND LLOYD J
29th JANUARY 1981

Criminal law – Theft – Property belonging to another – Sale of goods – Shoes displayed in supermarket in two racks one containing more expensive shoes and one containing less expensive shoes – Defendant selecting pair of shoes from more expensive rack one of which incorrectly labelled at less expensive price – Defendant presenting shoes to cashier without concealing price labels intending to take advantage of incorrect pricing of shoes – Cashier wrongly charging less expensive price for pair – Defendant taking shoes out of shop – Whether contract of sale void by reason of cashier's mistake as to price – Whether property in shoes passing to defendant so that she did not appropriate property belonging to another – Whether defendant guilty of theft – Theft Act 1968, s 1(1).

Shoes were displayed in a supermarket in two adjoining racks, one rack containing shoes priced at £6·99 and the other shoes priced at £4·99. The appellant took a pair of shoes from the £6·99 rack one of which she noticed was labelled with the price £4·99 (the other being correctly labelled £6·99) and hoped that the cashier would charge her only £4·99 for the pair. She placed both shoes on the cashier's desk without concealing the labels but intending, if possible, to take advantage of the mistaken pricing. The cashier asked her to pay £4·99, the appellant paid that amount, the shoes were handed to her in a bag and she walked out of the shop carrying the shoes. She was stopped outside the shop by a store detective and was later charged with theft of the shoes contrary to s 1(1)[a] of the Theft Act 1968. The magistrates decided that she had dishonestly appropriated shoes belonging to another, and was therefore guilty of theft, because (i) she believed it was wrong, in the circumstances, to take the shoes out of the shop but nevertheless did so and therefore acted dishonestly, and (ii) the apparent contract of sale made at the cash desk was void by reason of the cashier's mistake and because the cashier had no authority to charge only £4·99 for the shoes, and therefore the shoes remained in the ownership of the shop, and the appellant, when she took them away, appropriated them with the intention of permanently depriving the shop of them. The appellant appealed against her conviction.

Held – There was a valid contract between the appellant and the shop for the sale of the shoes because the cashier's mistake as to the proper price, induced by the wrong labelling, was not a fundamental mistake which destroyed the validity of the contract, since it was in essence similar to a mistake as to quality, the cashier having thought in effect that the shoes were £4·99 quality shoes when they were in fact £6·99 quality shoes. Furthermore, the cashier had authority to charge £4·99 for the shoes as that was a price marked on them. Accordingly, the prosecution had not proved that the contract was void; and, if it was merely voidable, it had not been avoided by the time the appellant had taken the shoes and left the shop. It followed that the property in the shoes had passed to the appellant before she left the shop and that she had not appropriated property belonging to another. Accordingly, she was not guilty of theft, and the appeal would be allowed and the conviction quashed (see p 432 g, p 433 c d f to h and p 434 a b, post).

Per Curiam. The court should not be astute to find that a theft has taken place where so to find would strain the language of the statute or where the ordinary person would not regard the defendant's acts, although morally reprehensible, as theft (see p 433 d e and p 434 a b, post).

---

a   Section 1(1), so far as material, provides, 'A person is guilty of theft if he dishonestly appropriates property belonging to another with the intention of permanently depriving the other of it . . .'

Notes

a For the definition of theft, see 11 Halsbury's Laws (4th Edn) para 1262, and for Cases on the subject, see 15 Digest (Reissue) 1262–1264, 10,824–10,830.

For the Theft Act 1968, s 1, see 8 Halsbury's Statutes (3rd Edn) 783.

Cases referred to in judgments

Anderton v Wish [1980] Crim LR 319, DC.

b Hartog v Colin and Shields [1939] 3 All ER 566, 35 Digest (Repl) 115, 148.

Lacis v Cashmarts [1969] 2 QB 400, [1969] 2 WLR 329, DC, 15 Digest (Reissue) 1282, 11,030.

Lawrence v Comr of Police for the Metropolis [1971] 2 All ER 1253, [1972] AC 626, [1971] 3 WLR 225, 135 JP 481, 55 Cr App 471, HL, 15 Digest (Reissue) 1262, 10,825.

Pilgram v Rice-Smith [1977] 2 All ER 658, [1977] 1 WLR 671, 15 Digest (Reissue) 1263,
c 10,828.

Case stated

Dip Kaur appealed by case stated from a decision of the justices for the County of Hampshire in respect of their adjudication as a magistrates' court sitting at Southampton whereby they convicted the appellant on a charge of stealing a pair of shoes valued at
d £6·99, the property of British Home Stores Ltd, contrary to s 1(1) of the Theft Act 1968, and fined her £25. The charge was preferred by the Chief Constable for Hampshire ('the prosecutor'). At the hearing of the charge the magistrates were referred to Anderton v Wish [1980] Crim LR 319, Hartog v Colin and Shields [1939] 3 All ER 566 and Pharmaceutical Society of Great Britain v Boots Cash Chemists (Southern) Ltd [1953] 1 All ER 482, [1952] 2 QB 795. The facts found by the magistrates, the magistrates' conclusions
e and the question for the opinion of the court are set out in the judgment of Lord Lane CJ.

Stephen Alexander for the appellant.
Nigel Mylne for the prosecutor.

f **LORD LANE CJ.** This is an appeal by way of case stated from the justices for the County of Hampshire acting for the petty sessional division of Southampton. It arises in this way. On 18th October 1979 the respondent ('the prosecutor') preferred a charge against the appellant, that she had stolen a pair of shoes in September 1979, valued at £6·99, the property of British Home Stores Ltd.

The facts of the alleged theft were these. On 1st September 1979 the appellant went
g to British Home Stores at Southampton. Amongst other goods displayed, there were two racks of shoes, one alongside the other. One of the racks contained shoes which were said to be priced at £6·99 and the other adjacent rack contained shoes marked at £4·99. The appellant took a pair of shoes from the £6·99 rack and noticed that the pair were not identically marked: one of the shoes was marked £6·99 and the other was marked £4·99. The correct price in fact of the shoes she had selected was £6·99 and the justices
h found as a fact that the appellant realised this. She did not, as is regrettably sometimes done, interfere in any way with the price labels on the shoes.

She took the pair of shoes to the check-out. She placed them on the desk in front of the cashier. She made no attempt to conceal either of the price labels, but she hoped that the cashier would select the wrong label and would charge her £4·99 instead of £6·99. She was going to buy the shoes whichever price was demanded.
j She was lucky. She must have thought so, at any rate, because the cashier rang up £4·99. That sum was handed over by the appellant to the cashier, who put it in the till and, all that having happened, the shoes were then placed in a bag. They were handed to the appellant who left to go home.

The justices found as a fact that 'The appellant believed that it would be wrong to take the shoes out of the shop in these circumstances, but nevertheless did so, and was accosted by a store detective'. These proceedings were then launched. It seems, from what we have been told, that initially the suspicion was that the appellant had in fact switched the labels on the shoes, but that was not the case.

The justices came to the conclusion that the cashier had no authority to accept, on behalf of the retailer, an offer by the appellant to buy the shoes for £4·99, and, since the appellant knew that this was not the correct price, the apparent contract made at the cash point was void. Secondly, they were of the opinion that the transaction at the cash point did not convey ownership to the appellant, so that on leaving the shop she appropriated the property belonging to British Home Stores Ltd. Finally, they concluded, it was right to describe as dishonest the state of mind with which the appellant appropriated the shoes. Accordingly the justices convicted the appellant on the charge and adjudged that she be fined £25. They ask this court to say:

'Whether on the facts found by us we were right in law to conclude that the appellant had dishonestly appropriated property belonging to British Home Stores Limited so as to be guilty of theft contrary to section 1(1) of the Theft Act 1968.'

It is sometimes of advantage to reduce this sort of problem to its ingredients. In order to bring the charge home to the appellant the prosecution had to prove the following matters: first of all, that the appellant acted dishonestly; second, that she appropriated the shoes, that is to say she assumed over the shoes the rights of an owner; third, that at that moment those shoes belonged to somebody else; and fourth and finally, that she intended permanently to deprive the owner of them.

It was found by the justices that she realised that the correct price of the shoes selected by her was £6·99, and that she believed it would be wrong to take the shoes out of the shop in the circumstances. They came to the conclusion that it was right to describe that as dishonest. She certainly assumed the rights of an owner when, having paid, she took the shoes in the paper bag from the cashier in order to go home. I do not pause to inquire at the moment whether 'appropriation' is an accurate description of what she did. There is no doubt that she intended permanently to deprive the owner of the shoes. So the only matter in issue in this case is whether the prosecution had proved that at the moment she took the shoes out of the shop the ownership of the shoes was still in the shop. If so, the offence was proved; if not, it was not proved.

There is ample authority for the proposition that so far as supermarkets at any rate are concerned, and in so far as an ordinary transaction in a supermarket is concerned, the intention of the parties, under s 18 of the Sale of Goods Act 1979, is that the ownership of the goods should pass on payment by the customer of the price to the cashier. It also seems to accord with good sense, and if any authority is needed for that it is to be found in *Lacis v Cashmarts* [1969] 2 QB 400.

Prima facie, then, when the appellant picked up the shoes to take them home, she was already the owner of the shoes. They did not then belong to somebody else, and she was not intending to deprive the owner of them.

But the prosecutor contends that the apparent contract between the shop and the appellant was no contract at all, was void, and that therefore, despite the payment made by the appellant, the ownership of the shoes never passed to the appellant, and the offence was accordingly made out. Counsel for the prosecutor puts it with very great simplicity: she never paid the price, he says, and so there was never any contract at all. He went so far as to suggest that if the appellant had been given 10p too much by way of change and realised that she had been given 10p too much by way of change and had walked out of the shop with the shoes, in those circumstances she would likewise have been guilty of theft of the shoes.

The first thing to note, as indeed the justices did, is that this was not a case where there was any deception at all perpetrated by the appellant. She had not switched the price labels, as happened in *Anderton v Wish* [1980] Crim LR 319 in which it was held that the property was appropriated when the price tickets were changed. There is no need to comment on that decision, although it has been the subject of adverse criticism.

The prosecutor, before the justices, as he did here, relied on the decision in *Hartog v
Colin and Shields* [1939] 3 All ER 566.

In that case there had been extensive negotiations between the parties, both oral and
in writing, about the sale by the defendants to the plaintiffs of hare skins. All those
negotiations had been based on a price of so many pence per piece. The final offer by the
defendants to sell was mistakenly quoted as so many pence per pound. Skins worth 10¾d
each were on this basis being offered at 3¾d. On discovering their obvious mistake, the
defendants refused to deliver the skins and the plaintiffs claimed damages. The report
of the ex tempore judgment of Singleton J is not altogether clear, but the facts are so far
divorced from those on the present case that they provide little assistance. We were also
referred to *Pilgram v Rice-Smith* [1977] 2 All ER 658, [1977] 1 WLR 671. That was a case
where the shop assistant and the customer agreed together to defraud the shop owners,
and likewise does not provide any guidance.

The justices based their conclusion primarily on the fact that the cashier had no
authority to accept on behalf of the retailer an offer by the appellant to buy the shoes for
£4·99. In my judgment they were in error. The cashier had the authority to charge the
price which was marked on the ticket on the goods. The fact that there were two
different prices marked and that she chose the lower one does not mean that she was
acting without authority. No false representation was made by the purchaser. This is
not one of those cases where the true offence was really obtaining by deception under
s 15 of the 1968 Act, and where the prosecution should accordingly have alleged that
offence, and have resisted the temptation to charge theft. This was either theft or
nothing.

It seems to me that the court should not be astute to find that a theft has taken place
where it would be straining the language so to hold, or where the ordinary person would
not regard the defendant's acts, though possibly morally reprehensible, as theft. In
essence here, as I have already said, the problem is: did the ownership of the shoes pass
to the appellant, or was the apparent contract void by reason of mistake? Where
questions of mistake are involved there will always be great difficulty in deciding where
the line is to be drawn and what renders a contract void and what renders a contract
merely voidable.

The mistake here was the cashier's, induced by the wrong marking on the goods as to
the proper price of those goods. It was not as to the nature of the goods or the identity
of the buyer. Speaking for myself, I find it very difficult to see how this could be
described as the sort of mistake which was so fundamental as to destroy the validity of the
contract. It was in essence, as Lloyd J pointed out in argument, very little, if at all,
different from a mistake as to quality. A mistake as to quality has never been held
sufficiently fundamental so as to avoid a contract. The cashier was in effect thinking that
these were £4·99 quality shoes, when in fact they were £6·99 quality shoes.

Consequently in my judgment the prosecution failed to prove that this alleged contract
was void. If it was merely voidable it had certainly not been avoided when the time
came for the appellant to pick up the shoes and go.

Happily in this case we are not concerned with the difficulties raised by the decision
in *Lawrence v Comr of Police for the Metropolis* [1971] 2 All ER 1253, [1972] AC 626
because here the ownership of the goods had passed on payment, and the appropriation
was at a later stage, when the shoes were put in the bag and carried away by the
appellant. Nor is it necessary to discuss the vexed question of whether the true owner,
albeit in a voidable contract, can properly be said to 'appropriate' his own property or to
'assume the rights of an owner' over it when he takes possession of it. At first sight those
words would appear to imply some action which was adverse to the interests of
another. Nor do I pause to consider whether the justices' finding of dishonesty on the
part of the appellant can be justified; whether in other words this is the sort of dishonesty
which is envisaged by the Theft Act 1968. I should also add, for the sake of completeness,
that s 5(4) of the 1968 Act has no application here, because the appellant was not under
an obligation to make restitution of the shoes at the material time.

For these various reasons I would allow this appeal and would answer the justices' question, namely whether on the facts found by them they were right in law to conclude *a* as they did, in the negative. It follows that the conviction will be quashed.

LLOYD J. I agree.

Appeal allowed ; conviction quashed.

Solicitors: *Plumer Price & Beswick*, Southampton (for the appellant); *R N Bourne*, Winchester.

Jacqueline Charles   Barrister.

Worringham and another v Lloyds Bank Ltd

(Case 69/80)

COURT OF JUSTICE OF THE EUROPEAN COMMUNITIES

JUDGES MERTENS DE WILMARS (PRESIDENT), PESCATORE, LORD MACKENZIE STUART, KOOPMANS (PRESIDENTS OF CHAMBERS), O'KEEFFE, BOSCO AND TOUFFAIT

ADVOCATE-GENERAL J-P WARNER

29th OCTOBER, 11th DECEMBER 1980, 11th MARCH 1981

European Economic Community – Equality of treatment of men and women – Equal pay for equal *f* *work – Pay – Whether 'pay' includes contributions paid by employer to retirement benefits scheme in name of employees – EEC Treaty, art 119.*

European Economic Community – Treaty provisions – Direct application in member states – Social policy – Men and women to receive equal pay for equal work – Court's duty to protect rights of individuals to equal pay for equal work – Whether rights directly enforceable in national *g* *courts – EEC Treaty, art 119.*

European Economic Community – Reference to European Court – Decision of court – Temporal effect of decision – Circumstances in which court may restrict effect of decision to future only – Decision of court not having effect on parties other than parties to action – Information available which would have shown that respondent was in breach of Treaty provisions – Whether *h* *appropriate to restrict effect of decision to future conduct.*

Two women, who were under the age of 25 and had been employed by a bank as clerical officers, complained to an industrial tribunal that the bank was in breach of the Equal Pay Act 1970 in that it had not paid its female staff under 25 years of age the same gross salary as that of male staff of the same age engaged in the same work. The difference *j* arose because the bank operated a compulsory contributory pension scheme whereby, with the exception of women under the age of 25, all employees were required to contribute 5% of their gross salary to one of two pension funds, one of which was for men and the other for women. The 5% contribution was deducted at source and paid over by the employer into the fund. In order that the actual take home pay of all employees should be the same, the gross salary of male employees and of female employees over 25 was credited with an additional 5% to cover the amount of the pension contribution. Since redundancy payments, unemployment benefits and family allowances were determined by reference to gross pay, female employees who left before the age of 25 were at a disadvantage when compared with their male counterparts. Such females were similarly disadvantaged in respect of mortgage and credit facilities made available to the bank's employees. Furthermore, male employees who left the pension scheme could either transfer their accrued benefits to other schemes or, if they joined the state's pension scheme, receive back a part of their contributions, including the 5% contribution paid in their name by the bank, with interest. The industrial tribunal dismissed the complaint on the ground that the difference in gross pay was the result of a difference in the rules of the pension schemes and was therefore within the exception contained in s 6(1A)(b)[a] of the 1970 Act. On appeal the Employment Appeal Tribunal allowed the appeal on the grounds that, inter alia, the terms of the contracts of employment relating to pay were to be kept separate from those relating to pensions and that the relevant clause in the contracts was not a provision made in connection with death or retirement within s 6(1A)(b). The bank appealed to the Court of Appeal, which referred certain questions on the interpretation of Community law to the Court of Justice of the European Communities, including the questions (i) whether contributions paid by an employer to a retirement benefits scheme or rights and benefits of a worker under such a scheme were 'pay' within art 119[b] of the EEC Treaty, and (ii) whether art 119 had direct effect in member states so as to confer enforceable Community rights on individuals. The bank asked the court, in the event of a decision against it, to limit the temporal effect of its judgment so that it could not be relied on in order to support claims concerning pay periods prior to the date of the judgment.

Held – (1) A contribution to a retirement benefits scheme paid by the employer in the name of the employee by means of an addition to his gross salary and which helped to determine the amount of that salary was 'pay' for the purposes of the second paragraph of art 119 of the EEC Treaty (see p 446 *f* to *j* and p 448 *h*, post).

(2) The payment by the employer of contributions to such a scheme in the name of male employees but not in the name of female employees of the same age who did the same work or work of equal value was a source of discrimination contrary to art 119 which a national court could directly establish with the aid of the pay components in question and the criteria laid down in art 119. It followed that an individual was entitled to rely on art 119 before a national court and that that court had a duty to ensure the protection of the rights conferred on individuals by that article (see p 447 *c* to *j* and p 448 *h j*, post); *Defrenne v Sabena* [1981] 1 All ER 122 and *Macarthys Ltd v Smith* [1981] 1 All ER 111 applied.

(3) Although the consequences of any judicial decision were to be carefully taken into account, it would be impossible to go so far as to diminish the objectivity of the law and thus compromise its future application on the ground of the repercussions which might result, as regards the past, from that decision. Since there had been no conduct on the part of the member states or of the Commission of the European Communities which had led the bank to believe it could continue with a practice which was contrary to art 119 and since questions of legal certainty did not affect a whole series of interests both

---

a   Section 6(1A), so far as material, provides: 'An equality clause . . . (b) . . . shall not operate in relation to terms related to death or retirement, or to any provision made in connection with death or retirement.'

b   Article 119 is set out at p 442 *b c*, post

public and private beyond those of the parties to the action, it was not a case in which it
was appropriate for the court to restrict the effect of its decision to future conduct,   *a*
particularly in the light of the information which had been available to the parties
concerning art 119, the court's previous decisions on the subject and the number of cases
which would be affected (see p 448 *b* to *f*, post); *Defrenne v Sabena* [1981] 1 All ER 122
distinguished.

Notes   *b*

For equal treatment of men and women as regards terms and conditions of employment,
see 16 Halsbury's Laws (4th Edn) para 767.

For enforcement of Community law, see 39A Halsbury's Laws (3rd Edn) paras 29–32,
54.

For the Equal Pay Act 1970, s 6 (as amended by the Sex Discrimination Act 1975), see
45 Halsbury's Statutes (3rd Edn) 295.   *c*

For the EEC Treaty, art 119, see 42A ibid 779.

Cases cited

Caisse Régionale d'Assurance Maladie (CRAM), Lille v Diamante Palermo, née Toia Case
237/78 [1979] ECR 2645, [1980] 2 CMLR 31, CJEC.

de Cavel (Luise) v de Cavel (Jaques) Case 120/79 [1980] ECR 731, [1980] 3 CMLR 1, CJEC.   *d*

Defrenne (Gabrielle) v Belgian State Case 80/70 [1971] ECR 445, [1974] 1 CMLR 494, CJEC.

Defrenne v Sabena Case 43/75 [1981] 1 All ER 122, [1976] ICR 547, [1976] ECR 455,
[1976] 2 CMLR 98, CJEC.

Defrenne (Gabrielle) v Sabena Case 149/77 [1978] ECR 1365, [1978] 3 CMLR 312, CJEC,
Digest (Cont Vol E) 409, 72Ae.

EC Commission v Ireland Case 61/77 [1978] ECR 417, [1978] 2 CMLR 466, CJEC.   *e*

Garland v British Rail Engineering Ltd [1979] 2 All ER 1163, [1979] 1 WLR 754, [1979] ICR
558, [1979] IRLR 244, CA, Digest (Cont Vol E) 408, 72Ad.

Macarthys Ltd v Smith Case 129/79 [1981] 1 All ER 111, [1980] 3 WLR 929, [1980] ECR
1275, [1980] 2 CMLR 205, CJEC.

Sotgiu (Giovanni Maria) v Deutsche Bundespost Case 152/73 [1974] ECR 153, CJEC.
                                                                                             f
Reference

The Court of Appeal, Civil Division, referred certain questions (set out at pp 439 *j* to
p 440 *b*, post) as to the interpretation of art 119 of the EEC Treaty and EEC Council
Directives 75/117 and 76/207, to the Court of Justice of the European Communities for
a preliminary ruling under art 177 of the Treaty. The questions arose as result of the
decision of the Court of Appeal (Lord Denning MR, Shaw and Templeman LJJ) on 5th   *g*
October 1979 in an appeal by the applicant, Lloyds Bank Ltd ('the bank'), against the
decision of the Employment Appeal Tribunal (Kilner Brown J, Mr S C Marley and Mrs
M E Sanderland) dated 9th November 1978 allowing the appeal of the respondents,
Susan Jane Worringham and Margaret Humphreys, against the decision of an industrial
tribunal (chairman Mr G E Heggs) sitting in London on 19th September 1977 dismissing
the consolidated complaints of the respondents that the bank was in breach of the clause *h*
guaranteeing equal pay for men and women incorporated by virtue of s 1(2)(*a*) of the
Equal Pay Act 1970 in their contracts of employment with the bank. The United
Kingdom and the Commission of the European Communities submitted observations to
the European Court. The language of the case was English. The facts are set out in the
opinion of the Advocate-General.

Anthony Lester QC and *Christopher Carr* for the respondents.   *j*
D S Hunter QC for the bank.
Peter Scott QC for the United Kingdom.
Michael Beloff for the Commission.

11th December. **The Advocate–General (J-P Warner)** delivered the following
a opinion: My Lords, this case comes before the court by way of a reference for a
preliminary ruling by the Court of Appeal of England and Wales. It raises questions as
to the scope and effect, in relation to sex discrimination in pension schemes, of art 119 of
the EEC Treaty and of certain Council directives.

The appellant in the proceedings before the Court of Appeal is Lloyds Bank Ltd, which
is one of the 'big four' English clearing banks. The respondents are two young women
b who were employed by Lloyds Bank as clerical officers but who left its employment
while they were still under 25, namely Mrs Susan Jane Worringham and Miss Margaret
Humphreys. No secret has been made of the fact that, in this litigation, Mrs Worringham
and Miss Humphreys are supported by the Equal Opportunities Commission, which is
a body established by a British statute, the Sex Discrimination Act 1975, with the duty
of working towards the elimination of discrimination between men and women, and
c with the power (under s 75 of that Act) to provide assistance in legal proceedings having
that purpose.

It is common ground that male and female clerical officers employed by Lloyds Bank
perform, in their respective grades, 'equal work' within the meaning of that expression
in art 119. The arrangements made to provide them with pensions differ however in
some respects.

d All permanent staff of the bank are, on entering its employment, required to become
members of a retirement benefits scheme. There are two such schemes, one for men and
one for women. Both schemes are funded schemes managed by trustees. There are six
trustees, the chairman, the deputy chairman, the chief general manager and the deputy
chief general manager of the bank, a trustee nominated by the Lloyds Bank Staff
Association and one nominated by the Banking, Insurance and Finance Union, which is
e a trade union. The trustees are obliged to, and do, carry out their duties as trustees
independently of and without reference to their respective positions as officers of the
bank and nominees of the staff association and union.

The two funds are fed by contributions made by the members and by the bank.

Each member, with the exception of women under 25, is required to contribute 5%
of his or her salary to the appropriate fund. Contributions are deducted from a member's
f salary at source and paid by the bank directly to the trustees.

Since 1968 the salary scales of all clearing bank employees in the United Kingdom, in
the grades that matter in this case, have been agreed nationally in the Joint Negotiating
Council for Banking ('the JNC'). The JNC has recommended that in the case of banks
with contributory pension schemes (ie schemes under which the employees are required
to contribute) the nationally agreed salary scales should be adjusted to provide for the
g employees' contributions. Of the four major clearing banks only Lloyds Bank operates
a contributory scheme. Accordingly Lloyds Bank has instituted salary scales under
which its female staff under 25 are paid at the rates agreed in the JNC, while all other staff
(ie females over 25 and males of all ages) are paid at those rates plus 5%. The object is to
achieve equality in 'take-home' pay, but we were told that in practice the take-home pay
of a man under 25 is slightly less than that of a woman of the same age and grade. We
h were not told why.

By the rules of the two schemes, Lloyds Bank is required to pay annually to the trustees
of each fund sums calculated by an actuary on the basis of current and anticipated
demands on the fund, in the light of such factors as the number, age, seniority and
marital status of present and of retired staff, and the effects of inflation both current and
prospective. Those factors differ from year to year and as between the two funds. The
j result of the actuary's calculation is expressed as a percentage of the aggregate of the
salaries of all the members of the scheme. No part of the bank's contribution is ascribed
to any particular member.

There is no fixed mathematical relationship between the proportion of the funds
representing employees' contributions and the proportion representing the bank's annual

contributions; but the former account for the smaller part. For example, in the year ended 30th June 1979, which was, I understand, a typical year, the total of members' **a** contributions was about £6m whilst that of the bank was nearly £36m.

Benefits are paid out of each fund by the trustees according to its rules. Some benefits are mandatory; some lie in the trustees' discretion. Some are payable to the member; others to his or her dependents. Since 1st July 1974 the major benefits under both schemes have been substantially the same for men and women. In either case a member qualifies for benefit after completing five years' service or attaining the age of 26. The **b** retirement age is 60 in both cases and retired employees of both sexes are entitled to pensions of $\frac{1}{720}$ of their annual salary at retirement for each completed month of service, with a maximum pension of $\frac{2}{3}$ of final remuneration. There are, however, some differences between the terms of the men's and the women's schemes. For example, the men's scheme provides for the payment of pensions to the surviving spouse and dependent children of a member who dies after retirement, whereas the women's **c** scheme makes no such provision; and there are differences between the two schemes as regards payments made to dependents on the death of a member in service.

We are told that both schemes have been 'certified' by the Occupational Pensions Board under Part III of the Social Security Pensions Act 1975 and 'approved' by the Board of Inland Revenue under ss 19 and 20 of the Finance Act 1970. That calls for explanation.

The legislation governing the British social security system (principally the Social **d** Security Act 1975 and the Social Security Pensions Act 1975) provides for retirement pensions to consist of two elements, a basic component, which is the same for everyone, and a variable earnings-related component. Such pensions are payable out of the National Insurance Fund, which is fed by contributions from earners, employers and the Treasury. The principle of the earnings-related component is that the more a person earns the more he and his employer contribute and the more he receives by way of **e** pension on retirement. Part III of the Social Security Pensions Act 1975 provides for what has been described as a 'partnership' between the state social security scheme and independent occupational pension schemes such as those here in question. Where an occupational pension scheme fulfils requirements laid down in the Act, its members may be 'contracted out' of the earnings-related part of the state scheme. Among those requirements are requirements as to the minimum annual rate of pension (calculated by **f** reference to the member's salary and period of service with the employer), as to benefits for widows, as to the transfer of accrued rights by members who cease working for the employer before reaching pensionable age, as to the rules governing the commutation and surrender of pensions, and so forth. On the issue by the Occupational Pensions Board, which is a statutory body responsible for the oversight of occupational pensions schemes, of a 'contracting-out certificate' the members of the scheme to which the **g** certificate relates cease to belong to the earnings-related part of the state scheme. They and their employer then pay reduced rates of contribution to the state scheme and the members are eligible only for the basic component of the state pension.

Approval of a retirement benefits scheme under the Finance Act 1970 is a different matter. Under s 19 ff of that Act the Board of Inland Revenue may, and in some circumstances must, 'approve' such a scheme if it fulfils certain elaborately prescribed **h** conditions. Approval entails fiscal advantages. For instance, the employer's contributions to the scheme are deductible in computing its profits for corporation tax purposes and excluded from the computation of the members' emoluments for income tax purposes. Members' contributions are deductible in computing their emoluments. Counsel for the bank told us at the hearing that those tax savings covered about half the total cost of the contributions. **j**

The rules of Lloyds Bank's two schemes governing the rights of members who leave the service of the bank before normal retirement age are similar. In order to comply with Part III of the Social Security Pensions Act 1975 they provide that there shall be either (i) a payment to another 'contracted-out' scheme transferring that person's accrued rights to that scheme or (ii) a payment to the state scheme of what is called a 'contributions

equivalent premium', buying the person back into that scheme. Where a contributions
a equivalent premium is paid, the person concerned is entitled to a refund of his or her past
contributions, with interest, but subject to deductions in respect of part of the cost of the
contributions equivalent premium and in respect of income tax. Since a female
employee of the bank who is under 25 has made no contributions, she receives no
refund.

The fact that, under Lloyds Bank's salary scales, a man under 25 is nominally paid 5%
b more than a woman of the same age results in other incidental disadvantages to the
woman. In particular any redundancy payment and any unemployment benefit to
which she may become entitled will be less than the man's, because such payments and
benefits are calculated by reference to gross earnings. For the same reason, she has access
to lesser mortgage and credit facilities.

It appears to be recognised by everyone concerned that the position is unsatisfactory.
c We have been told in outline of the negotiations that have taken place between the
management of the bank, the staff association and the union, with a view to resolving it,
preferably by the formation of a single scheme covering both men and women, and of
the difficulties in the way of the adoption of that course. We have been told also that
those negotiations have been suspended pending the outcome of this litigation.

The litigation was initiated by applications made by Mrs Worringham on 19th May
d 1977 and by Miss Humphreys on 12th September 1977 for the hearing by an industrial
tribunal of their complaints about the salary scales fixed for male and female clerical staff
of Lloyds Bank under the age of 25. Their cases were, by consent, consolidated and were
heard by an industrial tribunal at London on 19th September 1977. On 30th September
the tribunal gave its decision. The tribunal, whilst recognising that 'the arrangements
now in force are in certain limited areas inequitable to the female employees', held that
e the differences in those salary scales were covered by s 6(1A)(b) of the Equal Pay Act 1970,
which exempts from the provisions of that Act 'any provision made in connection with
death or retirement'.

The applicants appealed to the Employment Appeal Tribunal. They contended that
the payment of an additional 5% gross salary to male employees of Lloyds Bank aged
under 25 was not within the exception in s 6(1A)(b) of the Equal Pay Act 1970. In
f support of that contention they relied on Community law, in particular art 119 of the
EEC Treaty. By a judgment delivered on 9th November 1978 the Employment Appeal
Tribunal allowed the appeal. It based its decision exclusively on the interpretation of
s 6(1A)(b) of the 1970 Act. It held that, although the purpose of paying an extra 5% to the
men was connected with the pension arrangements, the terms of the contract of
employment as to pay must be kept separate from terms or provisions as to pensions, and
g that there was an inequality of pay. The tribunal accordingly left unresolved the
argument about Community law.

The bank now appeals to the Court of Appeal.

Before the Court of Appeal, it was conceded on behalf of the applicants, in view of the
decision of that court in a case heard in the meantime (*Garland v British Rail Engineering
Ltd* [1979] 2 All ER 1163, [1979] 1 WLR 754), that the salary differential was exempted
h from the scope of the Equal Pay Act 1970 by s 6(1A)(b), and that the applicants could
therefore succeed only on the strength of Community law. They relied on art 119 of the
EEC Treaty and on art 1 of EEC Council Directive 75/117 of 10th February 1975 ('the
equal pay directive') and, in the alternative, on arts 1(1) and 5(1) of EEC Council Directive
76/207 of 9th February 1976 ('the equal treatment directive'). They contended that, by
virtue of those provisions, they were entitled to (a) an additional 5% by way of salary and
j (b) a refund of pension contributions on leaving the employment of the bank.

Such are the circumstances in which the Court of Appeal has referred to this court four
questions, which, in slightly abbreviated terms, are as follows:

1. Are (a) contributions paid by an employer to a retirement benefits scheme or (b)
rights and benefits of a worker under such a scheme, 'pay' within the meaning of art 119
of the EEC Treaty?

2. Are (a) such contributions or (b) such rights and benefits 'remuneration' within the meaning of art 1 of the equal pay directive?

3. If the answer to question 1 or 2 is in the affirmative, does art 119 of the Treaty or art 1 of the equal pay directive, as the case may be, have direct effect in member states so as to confer enforceable rights on individuals in the circumstances of the present case?

4. If the answers to questions 1 and 2 are in the negative, (i) are (a) contributions paid by an employer to a retirement benefits scheme or (b) rights and benefits of a worker under such a scheme, within the scope of the principle of equal treatment for men and women as regards 'working conditions' contained in arts 1(1) and 5(1) of the equal treatment directive? and (ii) if so, does that principle have direct effect in member states so as to confer enforceable rights on individuals in the circumstances of the present case?

Your Lordships observe that those questions make no reference to the 5% salary differential, or to any consequent inequality in redundancy payments, unemployment benefits or mortgage or credit facilities. This court is not therefore concerned with those matters. The Court of Appeal has clearly taken the view that the outcome of this case depends on whether or not the provisions of Community law relied on by the applicants apply to retirement benefits schemes of the kind here in question. That, it seems to me, involves a decision by that court as to the nature of the arrangements from which the relevant discrimination arises. This court cannot, in my opinion, on a reference under art 117 of the EEC Treaty, go behind such a decision of the national court. I say that because arguments were addressed to us on those matters.

Two further propositions were, as it seemed to me, clearly established as a result of the argument before this court. The first is that the concept of equality between men and women cannot be applied to contributions paid by an employer to such a retirement benefits scheme. The reason is that they are global contributions, no particular part of which is attributable to any individual member of the scheme. The second proposition is that that concept cannot be applied to the benefits actually received by members from the scheme. That is because the amount of the benefits to be eventually drawn by a member from the scheme must inevitably depend on factors personal to him or to her, such as the age at which he or she dies, whether he or she leaves a surviving spouse or other dependents, and so forth.

Therefore, as counsel for the bank submitted, and as I think counsel for the applicants accepted, the only matter over which equality can be achieved is rights to benefits under the scheme, what counsel for the bank called 'identity of scheme terms'.

So, in my opinion, the first point for consideration is whether art 119 of the EEC Treaty, taken by itself, requires a pension scheme of the kind here in question to confer the same rights on a man and on a woman, and whether, if so, art 119 has in that respect direct effect, in the sense of conferring on individuals such as the applicants rights enforceable in the courts of member states. I take those questions together because, manifestly, even if rights to benefits under such a pension scheme are 'pay' within the meaning of art 119, it will avail the applicants nothing if that article does not, in relation to such rights, have direct effect.

The authorities in this court about art 119 do not afford clear answers to those questions.

From the judgment in the first *Defrenne* case, *Defrenne v Belgian State* [1971] ECR 445, one can deduce that, whilst pension rights may constitute 'pay' as defined by art 119, that concept does not include rights under social security schemes established by legislation and partly financed from public funds, whether they be established for the benefit of workers generally or for the benefit of special categories of workers. That excludes, of course, from the ambit of art 119 pension rights under the British state scheme, but it throws little further light on the problem. The opinion of the Advocate-General (A Dutheillet de Lamothe) in that case affords some additional help. He too thought that schemes established by national social security legislation, whether general or special, were outside the scope of art 119. He thought on the other hand that retirement pensions paid directly by an employer to his former employees (sometimes called

'deferred pay') were undoubtedly within its scope. He had more hesitation about what
a he called 'supplemental schemes' ('régimes complémentaires'), but came down in favour
of the view that art 119 did apply to them. His description of such schemes would cover
the schemes here in question but for one feature of them, their link with the state
scheme through the contracting-out system. The Advocate-General did not consider
such a case, presumably because no such system existed at the time in any of the member
states.

b   From the judgment in the second *Defrenne* case, *Defrenne v Sabena* [1981] 1 All ER 122,
one may deduce three general propositions.

The first had already been briefly stated by the Advocate-General in the first *Defrenne*
case. It is that art 119 has two purposes, first to avoid a situation in which undertakings
established in member states with advanced legislation on the equal treatment of men
and women suffer a competitive disadvantage as compared with undertakings established
c in member states that have not eliminated discrimination against female workers as
regards pay, and second to pursue the social objectives of the Community as expressed in
the preamble to the EEC Treaty and in art 117 of it.

The second general proposition laid down in that judgment is that, having regard to
the context in which art 119 is to be read, in particular that of the improvement of
working conditions and of the improvement of the standard of living of workers
d referred to in art 117, effect can be given to art 119 only by 'raising the lowest salaries'.
The option of lowering the higher ones is not open (see para 15 of the judgment [1981]
1 All ER 122 at 133).

Thirdly the judgment makes it clear that there is an area within which art 119 has
direct effect and an area within which it does not. As to that the judgment draws a
distinction between 'direct and overt' discrimination and 'indirect and disguised'
e discrimination. The first can be identified by reference to the simple criteria of 'equal
pay' and 'equal work' that are to be found in art 119 itself. The second can be identified
only by reference to implementing legislation enacted either at Community level or at
national level.

I confess that I find the distinction thus made puzzling. I understand, of course, that
art 119 has direct effect in some areas and not in others, that it has direct effect in those
f areas where a court can apply its provisions by reference to the simple criteria that those
provisions themselves lay down, and that it can have no direct effect where implementing
legislation is necessary to lay down the relevant criteria. What puzzles me is why the
concepts of 'direct and overt' discrimination as distinct from 'indirect and disguised'
discrimination should be relevant in that connection. We are all familiar with the cases
in this court that establish that covert discrimination is just as much discrimination as
g overt discrimination: *Sotgiu v Deutsche Bundespost* [1974] ECR 153, *EC Commission v
Ireland* [1978] ECR 417 and *CRAM v Palermo (née Toia)* [1979] ECR 2645. In none of
those cases, however, was it suggested, or could it sensibly have been suggested, that the
distinction between overt and covert discrimination affected the question whether the
relevant provision of Community law had direct effect or not. In the present case there
is nothing indirect, covert or disguised about the different treatment of men and women
h under Lloyds Bank's pension arrangements. Yet, if such arrangements are within the
scope of art 119, the question manifestly arises whether that difference in treatment is a
matter that can be dealt with directly by the courts under art 119 itself or whether it can
be dealt with only on the basis of legislation implementing it. At all events the decision
of the court in the second *Defrenne* case did not turn on the distinction, which is not
mentioned in the actual ruling.

j   In the third *Defrenne* case, *Defrenne v Sabena* [1978] ECR 1365, the court drew the
distinction between equal pay, to which art 119 applies, and the equal treatment of men
and women in other respects which is to be achieved pursuant to arts 117 and 118 of the
Treaty. The judgment contains a passage (in para 23) which could even be interpreted
as meaning that there is no overlap between the spheres of application of arts 117 and 118
and the sphere of application of art 119.

Lastly, in *Macarthys Ltd v Smith* [1981] 1 All ER 111, [1980] 3 WLR 929 the court reiterated and further explained the difference between the type of situation in which art *a* 119 has direct effect and the type of situation where it does not, but again by reference to the test of direct and overt as opposed to indirect and disguised discrimination. No more, however, than in the second *Defrenne* case, did the decision of the court turn on that distinction or was it mentioned in the ruling.

I turn to consider the language of art 119. It is as follows:

'Each Member State shall during the first stage ensure and subsequently maintain *b* the application of the principle that men and women should receive equal pay for equal work.

'For the purpose of this Article, "pay" means the ordinary basic or minimum wage or salary and any other consideration, whether in cash or in kind, which the worker receives, directly or indirectly, in respect of his employment from his *c* employer.

'Equal pay without discrimination based on sex means: (*a*) that pay for the same work at piece rates shall be calculated on the basis of the same unit of measurement; (*b*) that pay for work at time rates shall be the same for the same job.'

In my opinion one must not attach too much importance to the precise meaning of the words used in the English text of that article. As was pointed out by the Advocate- *d* General (A Trabucchi) in the second *Defrenne* case [1981] 1 All ER 122 at 125, art 119 is the 'translation' into Community law of the International Labour Organisation convention concerning equal remuneration for men and women workers for work of equal value (ILO Convention no 100 (Geneva, 29th June 1951, TS 88 (1972), Cmnd 5039)), which all the member states of the Community have ratified. It is noteworthy that, whilst the French text of art 119 uses, where the two texts correspond, the same *e* words as art 1 of the convention, the English text use different words. Thus, where the English text of the convention has 'remuneration', art 119 has 'pay', and where the English text of the convention has 'any additional emoluments whatsoever payable directly or indirectly, whether in cash or in kind, by the employer to the worker and arising out of the worker's employment', art 119 has the phrase that I read a moment ago, which uses the words 'consideration' and 'in respect of his employment'. 'Consideration' *f* has of course a technical meaning in the English law of contract, which it cannot bear here, where the corresponding French word is 'avantage'; and an argument was addressed to us on 'in respect of his employment' which could hardly have been sustained on 'arising out of' his employment or on the French 'en raison de l'emploi de ce dernier'.

There are two respects in which the English and French texts of art 119 both differ from the texts of the ILO convention. One is that in the convention the definition of *g* 'remuneration' is introduced by the word 'includes' ('comprehend' in French), whereas in art 119 it is introduced by 'means' ('il faut entendre' in French). The other is that the convention does not contain the tailpiece in art 119 defining 'discrimination based on sex' in the case of work at piece rates and work at time rates respectively. As to that tailpiece, however, it is to be observed that, whilst the English text of it uses the word 'means', the French uses 'implique', which has no restrictive effect. *h*

I will spare your Lordships a discussion of the other four authentic texts of art 119, and say only that their wording is closer to that of the French text.

Viewing the language of art 119 in that light, it seems to me perfectly capable of extending to rights under a retirement benefits scheme. The phrase 'consideration, whether in cash or in kind' seems to me one of wide import. It was suggested to us that it would not cover anything to which the worker concerned was not entitled under his *j* or her contract of employment. Perhaps that suggestion was based on the meaning of the word 'consideration' in English law. At all events it is in my opinion wrong. Let me give an example. An employer may, in prosperous times, voluntarily distribute Christmas bonuses to his staff. No employee has a contractual right to such a bonus. But art 119 would, in my opinion, clearly preclude an employer from discriminating between men and women in the distribution of it.

It was also submitted that rights under such a scheme were not received, even indirectly, from the employer. Others were concerned in their elaboration and in their financing: the trustees, the Occupational Pensions Board and the Inland Revenue. In my view the circumstances that the terms of a scheme have to be discussed with and to be approved by others does not detract from the fact that, at the end of the day, its adoption is the act of the employer. Nor is the element of tax saving in my opinion relevant. Wages and salaries, which are undoubtedly 'pay', are also deductible in computing the employers' profits for tax purposes; and I hardly think that the circumstances that a member of the scheme is taxable on benefits he receives from it and not on contributions he makes to it can affect the issue. It was also pointed out that some of the benefits under the scheme were payable not to the member but to his dependants. The conferment of the right to those benefits on his dependants can, however, in my opinion, properly be regarded as an advantage to the member arising from his employment.

Thus I would, but for one factor, have come to the conclusion that rights under pension schemes such as those here in question were 'pay' within the extended meaning given to that word by art 119.

That factor is the link between such schemes and the state social security scheme created by the contracting-out system. To hold that art 119 applied in relation to those schemes would mean holding that ever since that article took effect (ie since the end of the first stage of the transitional period in the case of the original member states and since 1st January 1973 in the case of the new member states) a member state operating such a system was under an obligation to ensure that a contracted-out scheme afforded equal rights for men and women whilst it was under no such obligation as regards its state scheme. That would, it seems to me, be an unbalanced result to reach, as well as one calculated to deter contracting out. In my opinion, where a privately established pension scheme is designed not as a supplement to the state social security scheme (as was envisaged by Mr Advocate-General Dutheillet de Lamothe) but as a substitute for it or for part of it, it must be regarded as outside the scope of art 119 and as falling to be dealt with under the broader headings in art 118.

Lest, however, your Lordships should differ from me on that point, I will add that, in my opinion, if art 119 does apply to rights under such schemes, it cannot have direct effect in relation to them. I do not say that because of the different expectations of life of men and women, a factor on which the bank laid much stress. That, so far as I can see, merely affects the cost of providing the same pensions for women as for men, without giving rise to the sort of choice of method that only a legislature can make. Unequal contributions by men and women would themselves be a breach of the principle of equal pay, so that the extra cost can only be borne by the employer. I say it because, as appears from a report of the Occupational Pensions Board to which we were referred (Equal Status for Men and Women in Occupational Pensions Schemes (Cmnd 6599 (1976)) the conferment of equal rights on men and women under such schemes gives rise to some problems that can be solved only by legislation. A court cannot decide, for instance, on the basis of a general provision like art 119, whether a period of maternity leave should or should not be treated as pensionable service. In the case of the United Kingdom a problem arises for contracted-out schemes from the circumstance that the state scheme is based on different retirement ages for men and women, 65 and 60 respectively, and that a scheme cannot be contracted out unless it provides benefits at least as good as those provided by the state scheme. In the case of Lloyds Bank that problem is solved by the fact that both men and women retire from its service at 60. But, for an employer from whose service the normal retiring age was 65, only legislation could resolve the conflict between the requirement that men and women should be treated equally and the requirement that they should receive not less than they would under the state scheme.

I will not detain your Lordships for so long on the directives relied on by the applicants. The considerations that lead me to think that the applicants cannot succeed on art 119 lead me to the same conclusion as regards those directives.

The provision in the equal pay directive on which the applicants rely is the first paragraph of art 1, which reads:

'The principle of equal pay for men and women outlined in Article 119 of the Treaty, hereinafter called "principle of equal pay", means, for the same work or for *a* work to which equal value is attributed, the elimination of all discrimination on grounds of sex with regard to all aspects and conditions of remuneration.'

Nothing turns on the change from the use of the word 'pay' in art 119 to the use of the word 'remuneration' in the directive. That is a feature of the English texts only. In all the other texts the same word is used in art 119 and in the directive: 'rémunération' in French, 'Entgelt' in German, and so forth. Bearing that in mind, it does not seem to me *b* that, for present purposes, the directive adds anything to art 119.

Article 9 of the equal treatment directive provides that member states are to put into force the laws, regulations and administrative provisions necessary in order to comply with the directive within 30 months of its notification. Notification took place in February 1976, so that the directive cannot on any view be invoked in these proceedings, which were started in 1977. The court has been pressed none the less to answer the *c* question that the Court of Appeal has asked about it, so that the bank should know what its obligations are. I think that the court can properly respond to that request, as it responded to a somewhat similar request of the Bundesgerichtshof in *de Cavel v de Cavel* [1980] ECR 731.

Article 1(1) of the directive provides:

'The purpose of this Directive is to put into effect in the Member States the *d* principle of equal treatment for men and women as regards access to employment, including promotion, and to vocational training and as regards working conditions and, on the conditions referred to in paragraph 2, social security. This principle is hereinafter referred to as "the principle of equal treatment."'

Article 2(2), read in conjunction with the preamble, makes it clear that, although the *e* principle of equal treatment is to apply to social security, the manner of its application in that field is not covered by the directive but is to be the subject of subsequent instruments.

Article 5(1) provides:

'Application of the principle of equal treatment with regard to working *f* conditions, including the conditions governing dismissal, means that men and women shall be guaranteed the same conditions without discrimination on grounds of sex.'

That language does not appear to me apt to cover the terms of a pension scheme, at all events one linked to the national social security scheme. But, if I am wrong about that, there are, in my opinion, the same obstacles in the way of giving direct effect to it as there *g* are in the case of art 119. That being so, I refrain from discussing the wider and more difficult question whether a directive can directly impose obligations on private persons.

In the result I am of the opinion that, in answer to the questions referred to the court by the Court of Appeal, your Lordships should rule that, where a retirement benefits scheme is designed as a substitute for all or part of a state social security scheme, neither contributions paid by the employer to it nor the rights or benefits of a worker under it *h* are 'pay' within the meaning of art 119 of the EEC Treaty, or 'remuneration' within the meaning of art 1 of EEC Council Directive 75/117, or within the scope of any provision of EEC Council Directive 76/207.

11th March. **THE COURT OF JUSTICE** delivered its judgment which, having *j* summarised the facts, procedure and submissions of the parties, dealt with the law as follows:

1. By order of 19th February 1980, which was received at the court on 3rd March 1980, the Court of Appeal, London, referred to the Court of Justice under art 177 of the

EEC Treaty several questions for a preliminary ruling on the interpretation of art 119 of
a the EEC Treaty, EEC Council Directive 75/117 of 10th February 1975 on the
approximation of the laws of the member states relating to the application of the
principle of equal pay for men and women and EEC Council Directive 76/207 of 9th
February 1976 on the implementation of the principle of equal treatment for men and
women as regards access to employment, vocational training and promotion, and
working conditions.

b   2. These questions have been raised within the context of proceedings between two
female workers and their employer, Lloyds Bank Ltd (hereinafter referred to as 'Lloyds'),
which they complain was in breach of the clause guaranteeing equal pay for men and
women incorporated in their contracts of employment with the bank by virtue of the
provisions of s 1(2)(*a*) of the Equal Pay Act 1970. The plaintiffs in the main action have
claimed in particular that Lloyds has failed to fulfil its obligations under the Equal Pay
c Act 1970 by not paying female staff under 25 years of age the same gross salary as that of
male staff of the same age engaged in the same work.

       3. It is clear from the information contained in the order making the reference that
Lloyds applies to its staff two retirement benefit schemes, one for men and one for
women. Under these retirement benefits schemes, which are the result of collective
bargaining between the trade unions and Lloyds and which have been approved by the
d national authorities under the Finance Act 1970 and certified under the Social Security
Pensions Act 1975, the member contracts out of the earnings-related part of the state
pension scheme and this part is replaced by a contractual scheme.

       4. It follows from the same order that, although the two retirement benefits schemes
applied by Lloyds do not essentially involve a difference in the treatment of men and
women as regards the benefits relating to the retirement pension, they lay down different
e rules as regards other aspects not related to that pension.

       5. The unequal pay alleged in this case before the national court originates, according
to the plaintiffs in the main action, in the provisions of these two retirement benefits
schemes relating to the requirement to contribute applicable to staff who have not yet
attained the age of 25. In fact, it is clear from the order making the reference that men
under 25 years of age are required to contribute 5% of their salary to their scheme
f whereas women are not required to do so. In order to cover the contribution payable by
the men, Lloyds adds an additional 5% to the gross salary paid to those workers which is
then deducted and paid directly to the trustees of the retirement benefits scheme in
question on behalf of those workers.

       6. The order making the reference also shows that workers leaving their employment
who consent to the transfer of their accrued rights to the state pension scheme receive a
g 'contributions equivalent premium' which entitles them to the refund, subject to
deductions in respect of a part of the cost of the premium and in respect of income tax,
of their past contributions to the scheme of which they were members, with interest;
that amount includes, in the case of men under the age of 25, the 5% contribution paid
in their name by the employer.

       7. Finally, as follows from the information provided by the national court, the amount
h of the salary in which the above-mentioned 5% contribution is included helps to
determine the amount of certain benefits and social advantages such as redundancy
payments, unemployment benefits and family allowances, as well as mortgage and credit
facilities.

       8. The industrial tribunal, before which an action was brought at first instance,
dismissed by decision of 19th September 1977 the applicants' claim on the ground in
i particular that the unequal pay for men and women complained of in this instance was
the result of a difference in the rules of the bank's retirement benefits schemes for men
and women and therefore fell within the exception contained in s 6(1A)(*b*) of the Equal
Pay Act 1970, which excludes from the operation of the principle of equal pay for men
and women terms related to death or retirement or any provision made in connection
with death or retirement.

       9. The plaintiffs in the main action appealed to the Employment Appeal Tribunal,

contending that the payment of an additional 5% gross salary to male employees of Lloyds aged under 25 raised a problem of discrimination between men and women in respect of pay which fell outside the exception contained in s 6(1A)(b) of the 1970 Act. They also argued that in any case that section could not be interpreted and applied so as to be contrary to Community law, which overrides the provisions of the 1970 Act.

10. The Employment Appeal Tribunal allowed the appeal on the grounds that (a) there was inequality of pay for men and women under the age of 25 in that instance, (b) the terms or provisions in the contract of employment with reference to pay had to be kept separate from terms or provisions with reference to pensions, and (c) the relevant clause in the contract of employment was not a provision relating to death or retirement as contemplated by s 6(1A)(b) of the 1970 Act.

11. In view of this legal problem, the Court of Appeal, before which an appeal was brought by Lloyds against the decision of the Employment Appeal Tribunal, decided to refer to the Court of Justice questions on the interpretation of art 119 of the EEC Treaty, art 1 of EEC Council Directive 75/117 and arts 1 and 5 of EEC Council Directive 76/207.

The first question

12. The first question submitted by the national court is worded as follows: 'Are (a) contributions paid by an employer to a retirement benefits scheme or (b) rights and benefits of a worker under such a scheme, "pay" within the meaning of art 119 of the EEC Treaty?'

13. It is clear from the information supplied by the national court that the first question asks essentially, first, under (a), whether sums of the kind in question paid by the employer in the name of the employee to a retirement benefits scheme by way of an addition to the gross salary come within the concept of 'pay' within the meaning of art 119 of the Treaty.

14. Under the second paragraph of art 119 of the EEC Treaty, 'pay' means, for the purpose of that provision, 'the ordinary basic or minimum wage or salary and any other consideration, whether in cash or in kind, which the worker receives, directly or indirectly, in respect of his employment from his employer'.

15. Sums such as those in question which are included in the calculation of the gross salary payable to the employee and which directly determine the calculation of other advantages linked to the salary, such as redundancy payments, unemployment benefits, family allowances and credit facilities, form part of the worker's pay within the meaning of the second paragraph of art 119 of the Treaty even if they are immediately deducted by the employer and paid to a pension fund on behalf of the employee. This applies a fortiori where those sums are refunded in certain circumstances, and subject to certain deductions, to the employee as being repayable to him if he ceases to belong to the contractual retirement benefits scheme under which they were deducted.

16. Moreover, the argument mentioned by the British government that the payment of the contributions in question by the employer does not arise out of a legal obligation towards the employee is not in point since that payment is in fact made, it corresponds to an obligation by the worker to contribute and is deducted from his salary.

17. In view of all these facts, it is therefore necessary to reply to question 1(a) that a contribution to a retirement benefits scheme which is paid by the employer in the name of the employees by means of an addition to the gross salary and which helps to determine the amount of that salary is 'pay' within the meaning of the second paragraph of art 119 of the EEC Treaty.

18. In view of this reply, there is no need to examine the second part of the first question, question 1(b), which is subsidiary to question 1(a).

The second question

19. In its second question, which is almost identical to the first, the national court puts the same problem to the court with reference to art 1 of EEC Council Directive 75/117.

20. Since the interpretation of Directive 75/117 was requested by the national court merely subsidiarily to that of art 119 of the EEC Treaty, examination of the second question is purposeless, having regard to the interpretation given to that article.

21. Moreover, Directive 75/117, whose objective is, as follows from the first recital of
a the preamble thereto, to lay down the conditions necessary for the implementation of
the principle that men and women should receive equal pay, is based on the concept of
'pay' as defined in the second paragraph of art 119 of the Treaty. Although art 1 of the
directive explains that the concept of 'same work' contained in the first paragraph of art
119 of the Treaty includes cases of 'work to which equal value is attributed', it in no way
affects the concept of 'pay' contained in the second paragraph of art 119 but refers by
b implication to that concept.

The third question

22. The national court asks further in its third question whether, if the answer to
question 1 is in the affirmative, 'art 119 of the EEC Treaty . . . [has] direct effect in the
c member states so as to confer enforceable Community rights on individuals in the
circumstances of the present case'.
23. As the court has stated in previous decisions (*Defrenne v Sabena* [1981] 1 All ER 122
and *Macarthys Ltd v Smith* [1981] 1 All ER 111, [1980] 3 WLR 929) art 119 of the Treaty
applies directly to all forms of discrimination which may be identified solely with the aid
of the criteria of equal work and equal pay referred to by the article in question, without
d national or Community measures being required to define them with greater precision
in order to permit of their application. Among the forms of discrimination which may
be thus judicially identified, the court mentioned in particular, cases where men and
women receive unequal pay for equal work carried out in the same establishment or
service, public or private. In such a situation the court is in a position to establish all the
facts enabling it to decide whether a woman receives less pay than a man engaged in the
e same work or work of equal value.
24. This is the case where the requirement to pay contributions applies only to men
and not to women and the contributions payable by men are paid by the employer in
their name by means of an addition to the gross salary the effect of which is to give men
higher pay within the meaning of the second paragraph of art 119 than that received by
women engaged in the same work or work of equal value.
f 25. Although, where women are not required to pay contributions, the salary of men
after deduction of the contributions is comparable to that of women who do not pay
contributions, the inequality between the gross salaries of men and women is nevertheless
a source of discrimination contrary to art 119 of the Treaty since because of that
inequality men receive benefits from which women engaged in the same work or work
of equal value are excluded, or receive on that account greater benefits or social
g advantages than those to which women are entitled.
26. This applies in particular where, as in this instance, workers leaving their
employment before reaching a given age are, in certain circumstances, refunded in the
form of a 'contributions equivalent premium' at least a proportion of the contributions
paid in their name by the employer and where the amount of the gross salary paid to the
worker determines the amount of certain benefits and social advantages, such as
h redundancy payments or unemployment benefits, family allowances and mortgage or
credit facilities, to which workers of both sexes are entitled.
27. In this case the fact that contributions are paid by the employer solely in the name
of men and not in the name of women engaged in the same work or work of equal value
leads to unequal pay for men and women which the national court may directly establish
with the aid of the pay components in question and the criteria laid down in art 119 of
i the Treaty.
28. For those reasons, the reply to the third question should be that art 119 of the
Treaty may be relied on before the national courts and that these courts have a duty to
ensure the protection of the rights which this provision vests in individuals, in particular
in a case where, because of the requirement imposed only on men or only on women to
contribute to a retirement benefits scheme, the contributions in question are paid by the
employer in the name of the employee and deducted from the gross salary whose
amount they determine.

The temporal effect of this judgment

29. In its written and oral observations, Lloyds has requested the court to consider the *a* possibility, if the answer to the third question is in the affirmative, of limiting the temporal effect of the interpretation given by this judgment to art 119 of the Treaty so that this judgment 'cannot be relied on in order to support claims concerning pay periods prior to the date of the judgment'.

30. It maintains for this purpose, first, that the problem of the compatibility of the national law with Community law was raised only at the stage of the appeal brought *b* before the Employment Appeal Tribunal and, second, that acknowledgment by the court of the direct effect of art 119 of the Treaty would lead, in a case such as the present, to 'claims for the retrospective adjustment of pay scales covering a period of years'.

31. As the court acknowledged in *Defrenne v Sabena* [1981] 1 All ER 122, although the consequences of any judicial decision must be carefully taken into account, it would be impossible to go so far as to diminish the objectivity of the law and thus compromise its *c* future application on the ground of the repercussions which might result, as regards the past, from such a judicial decision.

32. In the same judgment the court admitted that a temporal restriction on the direct effect of art 119 of the Treaty might be taken into account exceptionally in that case having regard, first, to the fact that the parties concerned, in the light of the conduct of several member states and the views adopted by the Commission and repeatedly brought *d* to the notice of the circles concerned, had been led to continue, over a long period, with practices which were contrary to art 119 and having regard, second, to the fact that important questions of legal certainty affecting not only the interests of the parties to the main action but also a whole series of interests, both public and private, made it undesirable in principle to reopen the question of pay as regards the past.

33. In this case neither of these conditions has been fulfilled, either in respect of the *e* information available at present to the circles concerned as to the scope of art 119 of the Treaty, in the light in particular of the decisions of the court in the meantime on this subject, or in respect of the number of the cases which would be affected in this instance by the direct effect of that provision.

The fourth question

34. As the fourth question was only submitted to the Court of Justice by the national *f* court in case the first two questions were answered in the negative, examination of it has become purposeless.

Costs

The costs incurred by the government of the United Kingdom and the Commission of the European Communities, which have submitted observations to the court, are not recoverable. As these proceedings are, in so far as the parties to the main action are *g* concerned, in the nature of a step in the action pending before the national court, the decision on costs is a matter for that court.

On those grounds, the court in answer to the questions referred to it by the Court of Appeal, London, by order of 19th February 1980 hereby rules: (1) a contribution to a retirement benefits scheme which is paid by an employer in the name of employees by *h* means of an addition to the gross salary and which therefore helps to determine the amount of that salary constitutes 'pay' within the meaning of the second paragraph of art 119 of the EEC Treaty; (2) art 119 of the Treaty may be relied on before the national courts and these courts have a duty to ensure the protection of the rights which this provision vests in individuals, in particular in a case where, because of the requirement imposed only on men or only on women to contribute to a retirement benefits scheme, *j* the contributions in question are paid by the employer in the name of the employee and deducted from the gross salary whose amount they determine.

Agents: *Lawford & Co* (for the respondents); *Geoffrey Johnson* (for the bank); *A D Preston*, Treasury Solicitor's Department (for the United Kingdom); *A Toledano-Laredo* (for the Commission).   Andrew Durand Esq   Barrister

a Swiss Bank Corpn v Lloyds Bank Ltd and others

HOUSE OF LORDS
LORD WILBERFORCE, LORD RUSSELL OF KILLOWEN, LORD KEITH OF KINKEL, LORD SCARMAN AND
b LORD BRIDGE OF HARWICH
30th, 31st MARCH, 1st APRIL, 14th MAY 1981

Equity – Equitable interest – Loan – Money lent by Swiss bank to English company to acquire securities in Israeli company – Covenant by English company to observe Bank of England conditions for loan – Bank of England conditions requiring loan to be repaid out of securities
c acquired with loan and requiring securities to be kept in separate account – Whether Swiss bank having equitable charge on securities – Whether parties evincing intention in loan agreement that loan should be repaid out of fund constituted by proceeds of securities.

Currency control – Exchange control – Transfer of foreign currency security – Transfer by person other than authorised depositary to authorised depositary – Transfer without specific Bank
d of England permission – Whether transaction illegal – Exchange Control Act 1947, s 17(2).

An English company, IFT, a subsidiary of another English company, Triumph, sought Bank of England permission under the Exchange Control Act 1947 to borrow Swiss francs from a Swiss bank ('SBC') to acquire securities in an Israeli bank ('FIBI'). On 22nd October 1971 the Bank of England gave permission for the borrowing subject to
e conditions which included, inter alia, that the scrip of the FIBI securities be held by an authorised depositary, that no security acquired be sold for sterling, that the interest and charges in respect of the loan be paid out of the income from the FIBI securities, and that the proceeds of the FIBI securities ('the loan portfolio') be the primary source for repayment of the loan. The conditions also required the FIBI securities to be kept by IFT in a separate account. On 11th January 1973 SBC and IFT entered into a written
f agreement for the loan to IFT of up to 10·5m Swiss francs. By cl 3(b) of the loan agreement IFT warranted and covenanted that 'All necessary consents and authorisations for the service maintenance and repayment of the Loan have been obtained . . . and all conditions thereof will be observed by [IFT] during the continuance of this Agreement'. The agreement provided for a sterling cash deposit to be made by IFT with SBC, and by cl 8 IFT expressly charged the sterling cash deposits as 'a continuing security
g for the principal moneys and interest and all other sums payable by [IFT] under this Agreement'. The loan was repayable on demand and also in a number of specified events including breaches by IFT of any condition of the loan. Pursuant to the agreement SBC advanced some 9m Swiss francs to IFT which IFT used to acquire the FIBI securities. The relevant scrip was deposited with Triumph as an authorised depositary under the 1947 Act. The Triumph group encountered financial difficulties and sought credit facilities
h from an English bank ('Lloyds') who agreed to give Triumph facilities if, inter alia, charges over the group's securities, including the FIBI securities, were executed in Lloyds' favour. By a written memorandum signed by IFT and dated 24th September 1974, IFT charged to Lloyds all securities 'lodged with or held by' Lloyds. Prior to the signing of the memorandum Triumph had lodged the scrip for the FIBI securities with Lloyds (who were also an authorised depositary) without specific Bank of England permission. Triumph went into liquidation. SBC, being then entitled to do so, demanded repayment of the loan from IFT. IFT sold the FIBI securities for dollars (with Lloyds' consent) and Lloyds sold the dollars for sterling which they held in a separate account. It was doubtful if IFT could discharge its debts to SBC and Lloyds. SBC brought an action against Lloyds and IFT asserting that in the circumstances SBC had acquired an equitable interest by way of equitable charge in the FIBI securities and their proceeds to secure payment of

IFT's loan, and sought declarations that it was entitled to require repayment of the loan
out of the sale proceeds of the FIBI securities. The judge held ([1979] 2 All ER 853) (i) *a*
that the loan agreement gave rise to an equitable charge over the FIBI securities and their
proceeds in favour of SBC, by virtue of cl 3(b) of the agreement, because that clause read
with the Bank of England conditions bound IFT, by a specifically enforceable obligation,
to repay the loan out of the proceeds of the FIBI securities, but (ii) that the equitable
charge did not extend to the additional securities for the loan and (iii) that Lloyds' charge
was void under s 17(2)^a of the 1947 Act since it was excluded, by para 88^b of the Bank of *b*
England's notice EC7, from the general permission contained in para 87^c of notice EC7
for the transfer of foreign currency securities to an authorised depositary. The judge
accordingly declared (i) that SBC was entitled to require the sterling proceeds of the FIBI
securities to be applied towards repayment of the loan, (ii) that Lloyds' charge was void
and (iii) that SBC's equitable charge did not extend to a charge over the additional
securities for the loan. Lloyds appealed against declarations (i) and (ii), and IFT (which *c*
was by then in liquidation) against declaration (ii). SBC cross-appealed contending that
the equitable charge should extend to the additional securities and their proceeds. The
Court of Appeal ([1980] 2 All ER 419) allowed the appeals and dismissed the cross-appeal
holding that SBC was not entitled to an equitable charge on the FIBI securities or their
proceeds. SBC appealed to the House of Lords.

d

Held – The appeal would be dismissed for the following reasons—

(1) Whether a valid equitable charge was created over a specified fund in favour of a
creditor depended on whether there was an agreement between the debtor and the
creditor which imposed an obligation in favour of the creditor to pay the debt out of that
specified fund. Since it was impossible to extract from the loan agreement and the
conditions on which permission for the loan was granted any agreement with SBC on the *e*
part of IFT to repay the loan out of the FIBI securities SBC's claim to be entitled to any
charge over or proprietary interest in the FIBI proceeds of sale failed (see p 453 *g* to p 454
d and p 455 *h* to p 456 *b*, post); dictum of Lord Wrenbury in *Palmer v Carey* [1926] All
ER Rep at 651–652 applied.

(2) Lloyds' charge extended to the FIBI securities, notwithstanding that the transfer of
those securities to Lloyds by Triumph might have been in breach of s 16 of the 1947 Act, *f*
because they were securities incontestably 'held' by Lloyds and so within the scope of the
memorandum of deposit (see p 454 *g h* and p 455 *h* to p 456 *b*, post).

(3) Furthermore, the charge created by IFT over the FIBI securities was valid
notwithstanding that IFT did not have specific Bank of England permission to transfer
the securities to Lloyds, because the transfer to Lloyds was authorised by the general
permission in notice EC7 and was not excluded therefrom by para 88 thereof, by reason *g*
of the following matters—

(a) although the execution of the charge effected a transfer of a foreign currency
security within the meaning of para 9 of notice EC7 the charge did not create a change
in beneficial ownership within the meaning of para 88(*a*), because in relation to a given
security there could only be one beneficial owner for the purposes of the 1947 Act, ie the
person for whom the authorised depositary held the securities and from whom he took *h*
instructions, and a chargee as such became neither the beneficial owner nor a beneficial
owner (see p 455 *a b* and *e* to p 456 *b*, post);

(b) the word 'custody' in para 88(*b*) and (*c*) connoted physical possession and nothing
else, and accordingly since at the date of the charge the FIBI securities were in the
physical possession of Lloyds, the charge was a transfer of those securities to an authorised

j

---

a Section 17(2), so far as material, provides: 'Except with the permission of the Treasury, no person
    shall, in the United Kingdom . . . transfer, or do anything which affects his rights or powers in
    relation to, any security to which this section applies.'
b Paragraph 88 is set out at p 455 *d*, post
c Paragraph 87 is set out at p 455 *b*, post

depositary (Lloyds) in whose custody those securities were, within para 88(b), and accordingly the charge was not excluded from para 87 by para 88(b). Paragraph 88(c) was not applicable because the securities were in the possession of an authorised depositary (see p 455 f to p 456 b, post).
Decision of the Court of Appeal [1980] 2 All ER 419 affirmed.

Notes
For equitable interests under contracts, see 16 Halsbury's Laws (4th Edn) para 1341.
For exchange control, see 32 ibid paras 272–324.
For the Exchange Control Act 1947, s 17, see 22 Halsbury's Statutes (3rd Edn) 917.
As from 13th December 1979 all exchange control restrictions have been removed (see the Exchange Control (General Exemptions) Order 1979, SI 1979 No 1660).

Cases referred to in opinions
Palmer v Carey [1926] AC 703, [1926] All ER Rep 650, 95 LJPC 146, 135 LT 237, [1926] B & CR 51, PC, 8(2) Digest (Reissue) 532, *297*.
Rodick v Gandell (1852) 1 De GM & G 763, 42 ER 749, LC, 8(2) Digest (Reissue) 525, *243*.

Appeal
The plaintiffs, Swiss Bank Corpn ('SBC'), appealed with leave of the Court of Appeal against the judgment of the Court of Appeal (Buckley, Brandon and Brightman LJJ) ([1980] 2 All ER 419, [1980] 3 WLR 457) dated 1st February 1980 whereby the court allowed appeals by the first defendants, Lloyds Bank Ltd ('Lloyds'), and the third defendants, Israel Financial Trust Ltd ('IFT'), against the judgment of Browne-Wilkinson J ([1979] 2 All ER 853, [1979] Ch 548) given on 8th May 1978 and dismissed the cross-appeal of SBC. The action was commenced by writ dated 26th February 1975 against the first three defendants (Lloyds, Barclays Bank Ltd and IFT) and the fourth defendants, Triumph Investment Trust Ltd ('Triumph'), who were added as defendants pursuant to leave granted by Master Chamberlain on 29th April 1975. By notice dated 24th April 1975 the proceedings were discontinued against the second defendants, Barclays Bank Ltd, who had sought interpleader relief in other proceedings. IFT and Triumph, who were now in liquidation and insolvent, took no part in the proceedings in the House of Lords. The action concerned the competing claims of SBC and Lloyds to a fund of £828,066·84 which represented the proceeds of sale of securities issued by a company incorporated in Israel, FIBI Holding Co Ltd, to IFT. The facts are set out in the opinion of Lord Wilberforce.

Richard Scott QC and *Timothy Lloyd* for SBC.
Peter Millett QC and *Richard Sykes* for Lloyds.

Their Lordships took time for consideration.

12th May. The following opinions were delivered.

LORD WILBERFORCE. My Lords, this appeal is concerned with competing claims to a fund of £828,066 held on deposit by Lloyds Bank Ltd ('Lloyds'). It represents the proceeds of sale of securities issued by a company incorporated in Israel, FIBI Holding Co Ltd, to the respondent Israel Financial Trust Ltd ('IFT'). These securities are referred to as 'the FIBI securities'. There are three issues: (1) whether the appellants, Swiss Bank Corpn ('SBC'), had a charge over or a proprietary interest in the FIBI securities and, if so, what the nature of that charge or interest is; (2) whether a charge created by IFT over the FIBI securities in favour of Lloyds is valid; (3) (depending on the answers to questions (1) and (2)) whether the interest of SBC has priority over the charge to Lloyds.
The only effective parties to the appeal are SBC and Lloyds, the fourth and fifth respondents being insolvent.

The answer to the first question depends on two documents. The first is a letter of consent under the Exchange Control Act 1947 given by the Bank of England to G T Whyte & Co Ltd (on behalf of IFT) on 22nd October 1971, for a loan to IFT of up to 10·5m Swiss francs. The Bank of England granted consent for this loan subject to various conditions set out in the letter and an accompanying memorandum. It was contemplated that the loan was to be used in order to take up what became the FIBI securities; under the terms of the consent these securities had to be deposited with an authorised depositary, and held on a separate account distinguished from any other foreign securities belonging to IFT. The memorandum set out eight conditions, evidently designed to protect sterling. Those most relevant are the following:

'(iv) No security acquired is sold for sterling and no foreign currency sale/redemption etc., proceeds thereof are sold for sterling in the investment currency market . . . (vi) Interest and other charges in respect of the borrowing and management expenses are paid out of the income arising from the foreign currency securities acquired, any shortfall being met from the sale proceeds of such securities, or from any part of the borrowing then held in liquid form or, subject to the Bank of England's prior permission being obtained, with investment currency or by an increase in the borrowing . . . (vii) Repayment of the borrowing is made from the sale proceeds of foreign currency securities held by the above-named borrower in the relative "loan portfolio" or, in the event of a shortfall and subject to the Bank of England's prior permission being obtained, with investment currency . . . In view of the terms of sub-paragraphs (iv) and (vi) above, it will be appreciated that the securities acquired with the foreign currency borrowing will need to be kept on a separate account to distinguish them from any other foreign currency securities owned by the borrower.'

The agreement for the loan by SBC was made on 11th January 1973 between SBC and IFT. It provided for a loan of up to 10·5m Swiss francs to be taken up by IFT not later than 31st March 1974. It contained a number of provisions designed to ensure that the loan should be in conformity with exchange control regulations and that all necessary consents would be obtained by IFT. The critical clause is cl 3 which reads:

'THE Company hereby warrants to and covenants with the Bank as follows:—(a) This Agreement will when executed constitute a valid and enforceable obligation of the Company which has the necessary authority to enter into it. Nothing hereby contained contravenes any statutory requirement or contractual obligation binding upon the Company or any provision of its Memorandum and Articles of Association. (b) All necessary consents and authorisations for the service maintenance and repayment of the Loan have been obtained by or on behalf of the Company and all conditions thereof will be observed by the Company during the continuance of this Agreement.'

The agreement provided for a sterling cash deposit to be made by IFT with SBC of an amount which IFT agreed to maintain at 95% of the sterling equivalent of the amounts advanced, and with regard to this deposit it was agreed as follows:

'8. (a) As a continuing security for the principal moneys and interest and all other sums payable by the Company under this Agreement and the performance and observance of all the terms and conditions set out herein the Company hereby charges with effect from each of the relevant Advance Dates the Sterling Cash Deposits on the terms set out below and undertakes to execute on demand any further documents which may reasonably be required by the Bank to give effect to this Clause 8.'

The loan was repayable on demand and also in a number of specified events including breaches by IFT of any condition of the loan.

In due course, SBC advanced to IFT a total of 9,352,833 Swiss francs, which IFT used in acquiring the FIBI securities. These securities were deposited with Triumph

Investment Trust Ltd ('Triumph') as authorised depositary; Triumph was the parent company of IFT.

In 1974 the Triumph group of companies ran into financial difficulties, to meet which Lloyds agreed to lend Triumph some £27·5m, on terms that IFT, and other subsidiaries, should guarantee this loan, and grant charges over various assets. IFT accordingly executed a memorandum of deposit in favour of Lloyds on 24th September 1974; I explain the transaction in greater detail below. Later in 1974 the FIBI securities were sold by agreement with Lloyds, and the dollar proceeds of the sale converted into sterling, realising the above-mentioned sum of £828,066.

On the first question, it is contended by SBC that the effect of cl 3(b) of the loan agreement, taken together with the conditions on which permission for the loan was granted, in particular condition (vii), was to confer on SBC an equitable charge, or some other equitable interest of a proprietary nature. Browne-Wilkinson J accepted this contention and he held that SBC was contractually entitled to have the loan repaid out of the proceeds of sale of the FIBI securities, that the agreement to this effect was specifically enforceable by SBC, and that consequently SBC acquired an equitable interest of a proprietary character in those proceeds (see [1979] 2 All ER 853, [1979] Ch 548). The Court of Appeal took the opposite view that SBC was not entitled to any charge or other proprietary interest (see [1980] 2 All ER 419, [1981] 2 WLR 893). In my opinion it was right.

I do not doubt the correctness of the principles of law on which the appellants, SBC, rely and which were stated by the learned judge. These are best summed up in the well-known passage from the judgment of the Privy Council in *Palmer v Carey* [1926] AC 703 at 706–707, [1926] All ER Rep 650 at 651–652 delivered by Lord Wrenbury:

> 'The law as to equitable assignment, as stated by Lord Truro in *Rodick v. Gandell* ((1852) 1 De GM & G 763 at 777–778, 42 ER 749 at 754), is this: "The extent of the principle to be deduced is that an agreement between a debtor and a creditor that the debt owing shall be paid out of a specific fund coming to the debtor, or an order given by a debtor to his creditor upon a person owing money or holding funds belonging to the giver of the order, directing such person to pay such funds to the creditor, will create a valid equitable charge upon such fund, in other words, will operate as an equitable assignment of the debts or fund to which the order refers." An agreement for valuable consideration that a fund shall be applied in a particular way may found an injunction to restrain its application in another way. But if there be nothing more, such a stipulation will not amount to an equitable assignment. It is necessary to find, further, that an obligation has been imposed in favour of the creditor to pay the debt out of the fund. This is but an instance of a familiar doctrine of equity that a contract for valuable consideration to transfer or charge a subject matter passes a beneficial interest by way of property in that subject matter if the contract is one of which a court of equity will decree specific performance.'

But I find it impossible to extract from the documents any agreement with SBC on the part of IFT to repay the loan out of the FIBI securities.

In my opinion:

1. Condition (vii) is perhaps capable of two meanings. It might create an obligation to apply the loan portfolio to repayment of the loan and for no other purpose. Or it might create an obligation to repay the loan only out of the loan portfolio and not from any other fund unless authorised. Which of these it is to bear must depend on the nature of the document in which the condition appears. In a commercial contract, between lender and borrower, the first meaning would be appropriate, possibly the more appropriate of the two. But in a document emanating from the Bank of England, in a context of exchange control, the second is the only one possible. The Bank of England would have no interest whatever in protecting a foreign lender: its concern would be, and certainly was, to prevent foreign currency (Swiss francs) acquired at the official rate from being sold with the investment currency premium. In my opinion condition (vii) imposes nothing more than a negative restriction preventing IFT from repaying the loan

otherwise than out of the sale proceeds of the FIBI securities or other investment currency if approved by the Bank of England.

    2. As a matter of contract between SBC and IFT, cl 3(b) of the loan agreement is nothing more than a clause, usual in such agreements, designed to ensure that the lender complies with all necessary exchange and control regulations. It cannot convert condition (vii) from an exchange control negative stipulation into one of a different character. There is in fact no agreement with SBC as to the manner of repayment of the loan except that it will be repaid in conformity with Bank of England consent and exchange control *b* regulations.

    3. The condition, stated after the numbered conditions, that the FIBI securities had to be kept on a separate account, was imposed solely for exchange control purposes and to prevent securities acquired at the official exchange rate from being used without permission.

    4. The fact that the loan agreement (cl 8) contains an express charge on the sterling *c* deposits argues strongly against any intention to create a charge on the FIBI securities through the very different language used in cl 3(b). As pointed out by Buckley LJ, under the terms of cl 3(b) read together with condition (vii), any charge which these provisions might be thought to create would be so precarious that no such intention ought to be imputed to the contracting parties in the context of the elaborate agreement they thought fit to make.

    I therefore conclude that SBC's claim to any charge over or proprietary interest in the FIBI proceeds of sale fails.

    The second question, however, still requires decision, for it is in the interest of SBC to contend that Lloyds too have no effective charge over the FIBI securities, so as to rank, together with SBC, as unsecured creditors of IFT. I deal now with that question. The relevant facts are the following. In 1974 Lloyds agreed to lend Triumph, then in *e* financial difficulty, a sum of about £27·5m, repayment to be guaranteed by the subsidiaries of Triumph, including IFT. These guarantees in turn were to be secured by charges over certain assets. On 26th February 1974 Triumph, who, as authorised depositary, were holding the FIBI securities for IFT, forwarded them to Lloyds. This transfer, it is said and apparently accepted by Lloyds, though I should have thought it doubtful, was in breach of the Exchange Control Act 1947, s 16. On 4th March 1974 IFT *f* guaranteed repayment of Lloyds' loan to Triumph and on 24th September 1974 executed in favour of Lloyds a memorandum of deposit by way of charge. This extended to all securities 'lodged with or held by you [sc Lloyds] . . . (whether lodged held transferred or registered for safe custody collection security or for any specific purpose or generally . . .)'. No specific consent was obtained by the Bank of England for the creation of a charge in favour of Lloyds.

    The first question is whether the memorandum of deposit can be taken to extend to the FIBI securities. SBC contend that it cannot because the transfer of those securities to Lloyds by Triumph was unlawful, and consequently Lloyds cannot be allowed to say that they 'held' these securities. I have no difficulty in rejecting this contention. Lloyds in fact 'held' the securities. In order to establish this factual situation they did not have to rely on any illegal act: the FIBI securities were simply and uncontestably 'held' by them *h* and so within the scope of the memorandum of deposit.

    The second question is whether the charge itself was illegal. This depends on the construction to be placed on provisions of the Exchange Control Act 1947 and of a document issued by the Bank of England under that Act known as EC7. This, as appears on its face, is in part an administrative document designed to draw attention to the law relating to exchange and control and in part a legislative document designed to grant *j* certain exemptions, permissions and consents. 'It is to be construed accordingly', so the draftsman blandly says, but that is easier said than done.

    It first has to be considered whether charges, or at least charges by deposit which do not involve any change in legal ownership, require permission under the 1947 Act at all. Neither the Act nor EC7 deals specifically with charges, and it does not seem to me at all inconceivable that, unless charges do involve a change in legal ownership, they should be left outside the Act so that they can be created without permission. However, the language of EC7, para 9, is extremely wide. It defines a 'transfer' (and any 'transfer' requires permission under s 17(2) of the Act) as the doing of anything by the legal or beneficial owner which affects his rights or powers in relation to any foreign currency security. I am unable to say that this language does not extend to a charge, including one by deposit, so that it becomes necessary to inquire whether any permission was given. There was no specific permission, but Lloyds invoke EC7, para 87, as conferring a general permission:

> 'Permission is hereby given (subject to the exceptions contained in paragraph 88) for transfers of foreign currency securities by persons other than Authorised Depositaries to Authorised Depositaries and to the nominees of Authorised Depositaries.'

This and the contrary, was not seriously argued, is capable of covering the case since IFT were not an authorised depositary but Lloyds were. However, SBC contend that the case is taken out of para 87 by para 88, which creates three exceptions:

> 'The following transfers are excluded from the permission given in paragraph 87:— (a) any transfer which involves a change of beneficial ownership; and (b) any transfer of a security which is in the custody of an Authorised Depositary other than a transfer to that Authorised Depositary or his nominee; and (c) any transfer of a security which is not in the custody of an Authorised Depositary other than a transfer to the Authorised Depositary who is to have custody of the security or to the nominee of that Authorised Depositary.'

These provisions are not easy to interpret. However, I have reached the following conclusions, and in this I have been much assisted by the full and clear argument in the judgment of Buckley LJ: (i) that exception (a) does not apply because the charge did not create a change in beneficial ownership. I think it is clear that in relation to a given security there can, for the purposes of the 1947 Act, only be one beneficial owner, that is the person for whom the authorised depositary holds the securities and from whom he takes instructions (cf s 15(3) of the Act). In my opinion a chargee as such becomes neither the beneficial owner nor a beneficial owner; (ii) that exception (b) does not apply because the securities were in the custody of Lloyds and the charge was a 'transfer' to Lloyds. That the charge was a transfer results from the definition of transfer which I have already quoted, so it only remains to consider whether the securities were in the custody of Lloyds. In my opinion they were, even if in accepting them Lloyds may have committed a breach of the 1947 Act. 'Custody', to my mind, connotes a physical situation and nothing else: the alternative to holding that Lloyds had 'custody' is to suppose either that Triumph had custody or that nobody had custody and I cannot believe that the Act aims at producing either of these results; (iii) that exception (c) does not apply because the securities were in custody of an authorised depositary, viz Lloyds, for the same reason as stated under (ii).

In my opinion, therefore, none of the exclusions of EC7, para 88 apply, the charge was authorised, if authorisation was needed, by para 87, and the contention of illegality fails.

In view of these conclusions, other points as to priorities as between SBC and Lloyds do not arise. I would dismiss the appeal.

LORD RUSSELL OF KILLOWEN. My Lords, I have had the advantage of reading in draft the speech delivered by my noble and learned friend Lord Wilberforce. I agree with it and would dismiss this appeal.

LORD KEITH OF KINKEL. My Lords, I agree with the speech of my noble and learned friend Lord Wilberforce, which I have had the benefit of reading in draft, and to which I cannot usefully add. I too would dismiss the appeal.

LORD SCARMAN. My Lords, I have had the advantage of reading in draft the speech delivered by my noble and learned friend Lord Wilberforce. I agree with it, and would *a* dismiss the appeal.

LORD BRIDGE OF HARWICH. My Lords, I have had the advantage of reading in draft the speech of my noble and learned friend Lord Wilberforce. I agree with it and would dismiss this appeal.

b

Appeal dismissed. Order appealed from affirmed.

Solicitors: *Simmons & Simmons* (for SBC); *Linklaters & Paines* (for Lloyds).

Mary Rose Plummer   Barrister.

c

Lonrho Ltd and others v Shell Petroleum Co Ltd and others

HOUSE OF LORDS

d

LORD DIPLOCK, LORD EDMUND-DAVIES, LORD KEITH OF KINKEL, LORD SCARMAN AND LORD BRIDGE OF HARWICH

5th, 6th MAY, 4th JUNE 1981

Statutory duty – Breach – Civil liability – Circumstances in which breach will give rise to cause of action – Statute passed to prohibit British subjects from trading with overseas country – Statute *e* *not passed to benefit or protect particular class of persons or to create public right to be enjoyed by all citizens – Whether contravention of statute giving rise to cause of action in person suffering loss consequent on contravention.*

Tort – Conspiracy – Scope of tort – Tort restricted to acts done in execution of agreement to injure plaintiff – Tort not extending to acts done by defendants in protecting their own interests. *f*

Tort – Action on the case – Unlawful act – Action for loss or harm suffered as inevitable consequence of defendant's unlawful, intentional and positive act – Whether tort part of English law.

The appellants were the owners of a crude oil pipeline running from the ocean port of *g* Beira in Mozambique to a refinery near Umtali in Southern Rhodesia. The refinery was owned and operated by a Rhodesian company, the shares in which were owned by the respondents and other major oil companies. The pipeline was operated under an agreement made between the appellants and the major oil companies, including the respondents. On 11th November 1965 the government of Southern Rhodesia made a unilateral declaration of independence ('UDI') and in consequence the United Kingdom *h* Parliament, by the Southern Rhodesia Act 1965 and an Order in Council ('the sanctions order') made thereunder, prohibited anyone from supplying or delivering any crude oil or petroleum products to Southern Rhodesia on a penalty of a fine or imprisonment. As a result from December 1965 no oil was shipped to the Beira terminal of the pipeline and it ceased to be used. Consequently the appellants' revenue from operating the pipeline ceased. The appellants brought an action against the respondents claiming damages, *j* alleging that before the making of the sanctions order the respondents assured the illegal regime in Southern Rhodesia that an adequate supply of petroleum products would reach that country after UDI and thereby influenced the regime to declare UDI, and that after the sanctions order was made the respondents supplied petroleum products to Southern Rhodesia by other means and thereby prolonged the period during which the pipeline was prevented by the sanctions order from operating. The matter was referred

to arbitration where the arbitrators and the umpire, before deciding the facts in issue,
a decided that the appellants' points of claim disclosed no cause of action against the
respondents. That finding was upheld by both the judge at first instance and the Court
of Appeal. The appellants appealed to the House of Lords, contending, inter alia, that
contravention of the sanctions order, if proved, would amount to breach of statutory
duty by the respondents severally, giving the appellants a right of action in tort, or a
conspiracy by the respondents jointly.

b
Held – The appeal would be dismissed for the following reasons—
(1) The purpose of the sanctions order being to stop the supply and delivery of oil to
Southern Rhodesia by withdrawing the previously existing right of British citizens and
companies to trade in oil to that country, the order could not be said to have been
imposed for the benefit or protection of the particular class of persons who were engaged
c in supplying or delivering oil to that country or to create a public right to be enjoyed by
all subjects of the Crown who wished to avail themselves of it. In those circumstances
contravention of the sanctions order by the respondents could not amount to a breach of
statutory duty which would give the appellants a right to recover in tort any loss caused
by such contravention (see p 462 *c* to *g*, p 463 *f* and p 464 *h* to p 465 *b*, post).
(2) The scope of the tort of conspiracy was restricted to acts done in the execution of
d an agreement between two or more persons for the purpose of injuring the plaintiff's
interest and did not extend to acts done by such persons merely for the purpose of
protecting their own interests. Since the purpose of the respondents in entering into any
agreement to contravene the sanctions order would have been to further their own
commercial interests rather than to injure the appellants, there could be no claim against
the respondents in conspiracy (see p 463 *j* and p 464 *c d* and *g* to p 465 *b*, post); *Crofter*
e *Hand Woven Harris Tweed Co Ltd v Veitch* [1942] 1 All ER 142 applied.
Per Curiam. An innominate tort in the nature of an action on the case for damages
at the suit of a person who suffers harm or loss as the inevitable consequence of the
unlawful, intentional and positive acts of another is not part of English law (see p 463 *c*
to *f* and p 464 *h* to p 465 *b*, post); *Beaudesert Shire Council v Smith* (1966) 120 CLR 145 not
followed.

f **Notes**
For construction of a statute to ascertain whether a civil action lies in respect of a breach
of a duty imposed by the statute, see 36 Halsbury's Laws (3rd Edn) 451–455, paras 687–
692, and for cases on the subject, see 44 Digest (Repl) 354–357, *1912–1938*.
For the tort of conspiracy, see 37 Halsbury's Laws (3rd Edn) 127–131, paras 221–222,
and for cases on the subject, see 45 Digest (Repl) 299–302, *162–191*.
g For actions on the case, see Supplement to 30 Halsbury's Laws (3rd Edn) para 549A.22.
For the Southern Rhodesia Act 1965, see 4 Halsbury's Statutes (3rd Edn) 573.

Cases referred to in opinions
Beaudesert Shire Council v Smith (1966) 120 CLR 145, HC of Aust.
Benjamin v Storr (1874) LR 9 CP 400, 43 LJCP 162, 30 LT 362, 36(1) Digest (Reissue) 481,
h   602.
Black v Fife Coal Co Ltd [1912] AC 149, 81 LJPC 97, 106 LT 161, 5 BWCC 217, HL, 33
Digest (Repl) 892, *1287*.
Boyce v Paddington Borough Council [1903] 1 Ch 109, 72 LJ Ch 28, 87 LT 564, 67 JP 23, 1
LGR 98; *rvsd* [1903] 2 Ch 556, 72 LJ Ch 695, 89 LT 383, 68 JP 49, 1 LGR 696, CA; *on*
appeal sub nom *Paddington Corpn v Attorney General* [1906] AC 1, [1904–7] All ER Rep
j   362, 75 LJ Ch 4, 93 LT 673, 70 JP 41, 4 LGR 19, HL, 16 Digest (Reissue) 274, 2603.
Crofter Hand Woven Harris Tweed Co Ltd v Veitch [1942] 1 All ER 142, [1942] AC 435, 111
LJPC 17, 166 LT 172, HL, 45 Digest (Repl) 534, *1175*.
Cutler v Wandsworth Stadium Ltd [1949] 1 All ER 544, [1949] AC 398, [1949] LJR 824,
HL, 25 Digest (Reissue) 504, *4396*.
Doe d Bishop of Rochester v Bridges (1831) 1 B & Ad 847, [1824–34] All ER Rep 167, 9
LJOSKB 113, 109 ER 1001, 44 Digest (Repl) 346, *1813*.

Dunlop v Woollahra Municipal Council [1981] 1 All ER 1202, [1981] 2 WLR 693, PC.
Island Records Ltd, Ex parte [1978] 3 All ER 824, [1978] Ch 122, [1978] 3 WLR 23, CA, *a*
Digest (Cont Vol E) 339, 1238e.
Kitano v Commonwealth of Australia (1974) 129 CLR 151, HC of Aust.
Mogul Steamship Co v McGregor, Gow & Co (1888) 21 QBD 544, 57 LJQB 541, 59 LT 514;
affd (1889) 23 QBD 598, 58 LJQB 465, 61 LT 820, 53 JP 709, 6 Asp MLC 455, CA; *affd*
[1892] AC 25, [1891–4] All ER Rep 263, 61 LJQB 295, 66 LT 1, 56 JP 101, 7 Asp MLC
120, HL, 45 Digest (Repl) 275, 6.   *b*
Quinn v Leathem [1901] AC 495, [1901–3] All ER Rep 1, 70 LJPC 76, 85 LT 289, 65 JP 708,
HL, 45 Digest (Repl) 280, 33.

Interlocutory appeal

Lonrho Ltd ('Lonrho'), an English company, and Companhia Do Pipeline Moçambique
Zimbabwe SARL, formerly known as Companhia Do Pipeline Moçambique Rodesia
SARL ('CPMR'), a company incorporated under the laws of Mozambique, appealed with *c*
the leave of the Court of appeal against a decision of the Court of Appeal (Lord Denning
MR, Eveleigh and Fox LJJ) given on 6th March 1981 dismissing the appellants' appeal
from a decision of Parker J dated 1st December 1980 in favour of the respondents, Shell
Petroleum Co Ltd ('Shell') and British Petroleum Co Ltd ('BP'), on a consultative case
stated by the umpire (Lord Cross of Chelsea) and the arbitrators (Hon Sir Henry Fisher
and Dr Jorge Mota) under s 21(1)(a) of the Arbitration Act 1950 in an arbitration between *d*
the appellants as claimants and the respondents. The case stated raised for the
determination of the court a number of questions of law, on assumed facts, arising in the
course of the arbitration which was still pending between the appellants and the
respondents. The facts are set out in the opinion of Lord Diplock.

Jonathan Parker QC and *Timothy Lloyd* for Lonrho and CPMR.   *e*
Peter Curry QC, Brian Davenport QC and *Gordon Langley* for Shell.
Robert Alexander QC, Roger Buckley QC and *Jonathan Sumption* for BP.

At the conclusion of the argument their Lordships dismissed the appeal, stating that
their reasons for so doing would be given at a later date.
     f
4th June. The following opinions were delivered

LORD DIPLOCK. My Lords, this appeal arises out of a consultative case stated under
s 21(1)(a) of the Arbitration Act 1950 by the umpire (Lord Cross of Chelsea) and the
arbitrators (Hon Sir Henry Fisher and Dr Jorge Mota) in an arbitration between the
appellants (to which I shall refer together as 'Lonrho') and the respondents (to which I *g*
shall refer together as 'Shell and BP'). Lonrho were the claimants in the arbitration. The
facts which they alleged and on which they relied as the foundation of their claim to
recover damages in excess of £100m against Shell and BP are disputed by the latter who
also contend that even if the facts alleged in Lonrho's points of claim, which runs to 93
pages, were true they would not disclose any cause of action in law against Shell and BP.
If those facts that were in issue had to be decided in the arbitration the cost in time and *h*
money would have been immense; the parties accordingly agreed as a first step in the
reference to invite the umpire and the arbitrators, who for this purpose sat together, to
answer nine questions of law on the assumption that all the allegations of fact in the
points of claim were true. If all of them were answered in the negative Lonrho's claim
in the arbitration would be doomed to fail.

Lonrho's claim arose out of the construction and operation of an oil refinery near *j*
Umtali in Southern Rhodesia by a company ('the refinery company') of which Shell and
BP, and other major oil companies (to which I will refer collectively as 'the participant
companies'), held all the shares, and the construction and operation by Lonrho of a
pipeline connecting the refinery with an ocean terminal near the port of Beira in
Mozambique. The construction and operation of the refinery and the pipeline were the
subject of a number of complicated interconnected contracts and concessions entered
into in 1962 between various parties which included the governments of Mozambique .

and of what was then the Federation of Rhodesia, the refinery company, the participating
a companies and Lonrho. The refinery on completion would be the only producer of
petroleum products situated in the Federation of Rhodesia and the commercial
expectation of all the parties to these agreements and concessions was that the refinery
would obtain its requirements of crude oil for refining from supplies shipped by sea to
the ocean terminal of the pipeline by participating companies or other companies
forming part of their respective 'groups', and thence transported through the pipeline to
b Umtali. The terms on which this was to be done were contained in an agreement of 30th
October 1962, made between Lonrho and the participating companies, which in these
proceedings has been referred to as 'the shippers' agreement'.

The refinery and pipeline were completed and came into operation in January 1965;
thereafter all proceeded according to expectations until on 11th November 1965 the
government of Southern Rhodesia unilaterally declared independence ('UDI'). Five days
c later the United Kingdom Parliament passed the Southern Rhodesia Act 1965, and
pursuant to that Act on 17th December 1965 the Southern Rhodesia (Petroleum) Order
1965, SI 1965 No 2140, was made, in terms which I shall have to set out later, prohibiting
Shell and BP, as companies incorporated in the United Kingdom, from supplying any
crude oil or petroleum products to Southern Rhodesia. This was replaced in 1968 by a
more comprehensive order (the Southern Rhodesia (United Nations Sanctions) (No 2)
d Order 1968, SI 1968 No 1020) which made no significant change so far as crude oil and
petroleum products were concerned. I will refer to the 1965 and 1968 orders together
as 'the sanctions orders'.

From the beginning of December 1965 no further oil was shipped to the ocean
terminal of the pipeline at Beira by Shell and BP or, for that matter, by any other of the
participating companies. The pipeline remained unused throughout the period of UDI
e and consequently Lonrho received no fees under the shippers' agreement for transporting
oil and no return on its investment in the pipeline.

For the purpose of disposing of this appeal the alleged conduct of Shell and BP on
which Lonrho rely as constituting their cause of action can be stated in a couple of
sentences: (1) before the making of the 1965 sanctions order Shell and BP, by assuring the
illegal regime that an adequate supply of petroleum products would reach Southern
f Rhodesia even if sanctions were imposed by other nations, influenced the regime to
declare and to continue to give effect to UDI; and (2) after the sanctions order had been
made, Shell and BP themselves and through associated companies which they controlled,
supplied petroleum products to Southern Rhodesia and thereby prolonged the period for
which the pipeline was prevented from operating, owing to UDI and the sanctions
imposed by the United Kingdom and other nations in consequence of it. Those, in a
g nutshell, are the facts which must be assumed to be true for the purposes of answering
the questions of law that come before your Lordships on the consultative case.

Not all of the original nine questions which the umpire and arbitrators were invited
by the parties to answer found their way into the case stated for the opinion of the High
Court. Of those that did questions 1 and 2 were directed to determining whether on the
true construction of the shippers' agreement which was governed by English law the
h conduct alleged would constitute a breach by Shell and BP of any of its express or implied
terms. The shippers' agreement was tailor-made by expert legal draftsmen in 1962 to
meet the peculiar circumstances of the case, which are unlikely ever to occur again. To
ascertain its meaning calls for the application to the actual language used by the
draftsmen of well-known canons of construction as to which there can be no real
dispute. It is of great importance to the parties but of no wider legal interest whatever.
j Your Lordships have had the benefit of reading no less than five meticulous analyses of
the language of the agreement and of the surrounding circumstances which accompanied
its making, one by Lord Cross, the umpire, one by Parker J by whom the stated case was
first heard in the Commercial Court, and one each by Lord Denning MR, Eveleigh and
Fox LJJ in the Court of Appeal. They are unanimous, and without repeating any of them
or adding yet a sixth analysis in words of my own choosing, I am content to say that I
agree with them and for the reasons that they give I too would hold that the matters
pleaded in Lonrho's points of claim disclose no cause of action for breach of contract.

The next two questions for your Lordships, numbered 5(a) and (b), are directed to determining whether, notwithstanding that no breach of contract was involved, delivery a to Southern Rhodesia by Shell and BP of petroleum products contrary to the sanctions orders gives to Lonrho a right of action in tort against them, assuming that Lonrho did suffer loss in consequence of what they did. The claim is put in the alternative: either as an innominate tort, committed by Shell and by BP severally, of causing foreseeable loss by an unlawful act; or as a joint tort of conspiring together to do an unlawful act which caused damage to Lonrho.   b

The phrasing of these questions is as follows:

> '5. Even if there were breaches by the Respondents of the 1965 and 1968 Orders [sc the sanctions orders]: (a) Whether breaches of those Orders would give rise to a right of action in the Claimants for damage alleged to have been caused by those breaches; and (b) Whether the Claimants have a cause of action for damage alleged to have been caused by such breaches by virtue only of the allegation that there was c an agreement to effect them.'

My Lords, it is well settled by authority of this House in Cutler v Wandsworth Stadium Ltd [1949] 1 All ER 544, [1949] AC 398 that the question whether legislation which makes the doing or omitting to do a particular act a criminal offence renders the person guilty of such offence liable also in a civil action for damages at the suit of any person who d thereby suffers loss or damage is a question of construction of the legislation.

So first it is necessary to set out the relevant provisions of the Southern Rhodesia Act 1965 and of the 1965 sanctions order.

The Act

> '1. It is hereby declared that Southern Rhodesia continues to be part of Her e Majesty's dominions, and that the Government and Parliament of the United Kingdom have responsibility and jurisdiction as heretofore for and in respect of it.
>
> '2.—(1) Her Majesty may by Order in Council make such provision in relation to Southern Rhodesia, or persons or things in any way belonging to or connected with Southern Rhodesia, as appears to Her to be necessary or expedient in consequence of any unconstitutional action taken therein.   f
>
> '(2) Without prejudice to the generality of subsection (1) of this section an Order in Council thereunder may make such provision ... (c) for imposing prohibitions, restrictions or obligations in respect of transactions relating to Southern Rhodesia or any such persons or things, as appears to Her Majesty to be necessary or expedient as aforesaid; and any provision made by or under such an Order may apply to things done or omitted outside as well as within the United Kingdom or other country or g territory to which the Order extends ...'

The sanctions order

> 'Restriction on supply of petroleum to Southern Rhodesia
>
> '1.—(1) Except under the authority of a licence granted by the Minister, no person shall—(a) supply or deliver or agree to supply or deliver to or to the order of h a person in Southern Rhodesia any petroleum which is not in that country; (b) supply or deliver or agree to supply or deliver such petroleum to any person knowing or having reasonable cause to believe that it will be supplied or delivered to or to the order of a person in Southern Rhodesia; or (c) do any act calculated to promote the supply or delivery of petroleum in contravention of the foregoing provisions of this paragraph.   j
>
> '(2) Any person who contravenes the foregoing provisions of this Article shall be guilty of an offence against this Order and, in the case of a person who—(a) is a body incorporated under the law of the United Kingdom; or (b) is a citizen of the United Kingdom and Colonies or a British protected person and is ordinarily resident in the United Kingdom shall be guilty of such an offence wherever the contravention takes place ...'

'Penalties and proceedings

a   '**4.**—(1) Any person guilty of an offence under this Order shall be liable—(*a*) on conviction on indictment to imprisonment for a term not exceeding two years or to a fine or to both; or (*b*) on summary conviction to imprisonment for a term not exceeding six months or to a fine not exceeding £500 or to both.

'(2) Where any body corporate is guilty of an offence under this Order and that offence is proved to have been committed with the consent or connivance, or to be

b   attributable to any neglect on the part of, any director, manager, secretary or other similar officer of the body corporate or any person who was purporting to act in any such capacity he, as well as the body corporate, shall be guilty of that offence and shall be liable to be proceeded against and punished accordingly . . .

c   *'Interpretation*

'**6.**—(1) . . . "petroleum" means mineral oil and natural gas and hydrocarbons derived wholly or mainly therefrom or from coal, bituminous shale or other mineral but excludes pharmaceutical, insecticide and pesticide products . . .'

The sanctions order thus creates a statutory prohibition on the doing of certain classes of acts and provides the means of enforcing the prohibition by prosecution for a criminal

d   offence which is subject to heavy penalties including imprisonment. So one starts with the presumption laid down originally by Lord Tenterden CJ in *Doe d Bishop of Rochester v Bridges* (1831) 1 B & Ad 847 at 859, [1824–34] All ER Rep 167 at 170, where he spoke of the 'general rule' that 'where an Act creates an obligation, and enforces the performance in a specified manner . . . that performance cannot be enforced in any other manner', a statement that has frequently been cited with approval ever since, including on several

e   occasions in speeches in this House. Where the only manner of enforcing performance for which the Act provides is prosecution for the criminal offence of failure to perform the statutory obligation or for contravening the statutory prohibition which the Act creates, there are two classes of exception to this general rule.

The first is where on the true construction of the Act it is apparent that the obligation or prohibition was imposed for the benefit or protection of a particular class of

f   individuals, as in the case of the Factories Acts and similar legislation. As Lord Kinnear put it in *Black v Fife Coal Co Ltd* [1912] AC 149 at 165, in the case of such a statute:

'There is no reasonable ground for maintaining that a proceeding by way of penalty is the only remedy allowed by the statute . . . We are to consider the scope and purpose of the statute and in particular for whose benefit it is intended. Now

g   the object of the present statute is plain. It was intended to compel mine owners to make due provision for the safety of the men working in their mines, and the persons for whose benefit all these rules are to be enforced are the persons exposed to danger. But when a duty of this kind is imposed for the benefit of particular persons there arises at common law a correlative right in those persons who may be injured by its contravention.'

h   The second exception is where the statute creates a public right (ie a right to be enjoyed by all those of Her Majesty's subjects who wish to avail themselves of it) and a particular member of the public suffers what Brett J in *Benjamin v Storr* (1874) LR 9 CP 400 at 407 described as 'particular, direct and substantial' damage 'other and different from that which was common to all the rest of the public'. Most of the authorities about

j   this second exception deal not with public rights created by statute but with public rights existing at common law, particularly in respect of use of highways. *Boyce v Paddington Borough Council* [1903] 1 Ch 109 is one of the comparatively few cases about a right conferred on the general public by statute. It is in relation to that class of statute only that Buckley J's oft-cited statement (at 114) as to the two cases in which a plaintiff, without joining the Attorney General, could himself sue in private law for interference with that public right must be understood. The two cases he said were:

'first, where the interference with the public right is such as that some private right of his is at the same time interfered with . . . and, secondly, where no private *a* right is interfered with, but the plaintiff, in respect of his public right, suffers special damage peculiar to himself from the interference with the public right.'

The first case would not appear to depend on the existence of a public right in addition to the private one; while to come within the second case at all it has first to be shown that the statute, having regard to its scope and language, does fall within that class of statutes *b* which create a legal right to be enjoyed by all of Her Majesty's subjects who wish to avail themselves of it. A mere prohibition on members of the public generally from doing what it would otherwise be lawful for them to do is not enough.

My Lords, it has been the unanimous opinion of the arbitrators with the concurrence of the umpire, of Parker J and of each of the three members of the Court of Appeal that the sanctions orders made pursuant to the Southern Rhodesia Act 1965 fell within neither of these two exceptions. Clearly they were not within the first category of *c* exception. They were not imposed for the *benefit* or *protection* of a particular class of individuals who were engaged in supplying or delivering crude oil or petroleum products to Southern Rhodesia. They were intended to put an end to such transactions. Equally plainly they did not create any public right to be enjoyed by all those of Her Majesty's subjects who wished to avail themselves of it. On the contrary, what they did was to withdraw a previously existing right of citizens of, and companies incorporated in, the *d* United Kingdom to trade with Southern Rhodesia in crude oil and petroleum products. Their purpose was, perhaps, most aptly stated by Fox LJ. He said:

'I cannot think that they were concerned with conferring rights either on individuals or the public at large. Their purpose was the destruction, by economic pressure, of the UDI regime in Southern Rhodesia; they were instruments of state *e* policy in an international matter.'

Until the United Nations called on its members to impose sanctions on the illegal regime in Southern Rhodesia it may not be strictly accurate to speak of it as an international matter, but from the outset it was certainly state policy in affairs external to the United Kingdom. *f*

In agreement with all those present and former members of the judiciary who have considered the matter I can see no ground on which contraventions by Shell and BP of the sanctions orders, though not amounting to any breach of their contract with Lonrho, nevertheless constituted a tort for which Lonrho could recover in a civil suit any loss caused to them by such contraventions.

Briefly parting from this part of the case, however, I should mention briefly two cases, *g* one in the Court of Appeal of England, *Ex parte Island Records Ltd* [1978] 3 All ER 824, [1978] Ch 122, and one in the High Court of Australia, *Beaudesert Shire Council v Smith* (1966) 120 CLR 145, which counsel for Lonrho, as a last resort, relied on as showing that some broader principle has of recent years replaced those long-established principles that I have just stated for determining whether a contravention of a particular statutory prohibition by one private individual makes him liable in tort to another private *h* individual who can prove that he has suffered damage as a result of the contravention.

Ex parte Island Records Ltd was an unopposed application for an Anton Piller order against a defendant who, without the consent of the performers, had made records of musical performances for the purposes of trade. This was an offence, punishable by a relatively small penalty under the Dramatic and Musical Performers' Protection Act 1958. The application for the Anton Piller order was made by performers whose *j* performances had been 'bootlegged' by the defendant without their consent and also by record companies with whom the performers had entered into exclusive contracts. So far as the application by performers was concerned, it could have been granted for entirely orthodox reasons. The Act was passed for the protection of a particular class of individuals, dramatic and musical performers; even the short title said so. Whether the record companies would have been entitled to obtain the order in a civil action to which

the performers whose performances had been bootlegged were not parties is a matter
a which for present purposes it is not necessary to decide. Lord Denning MR, however,
with whom Waller LJ agreed (Shaw LJ dissenting) appears to enunciate a wider general
rule, which does not depend on the scope and language of the statute by which a criminal
offence is committed, that whenever a lawful business carried on by one individual in
fact suffers damage as the consequence of a contravention by another individual of any
statutory prohibition the former has a civil right of action against the latter for such
b damage.

My Lords, with respect, I am unable to accept that this is the law; and I observe that
in his judgment rejecting a similar argument by the appellants in the instant appeal Lord
Denning MR accepts that the question whether a breach of sanctions orders gives rise to
a civil action depends on the object and intent of those orders, and refers to *Ex parte Island
Records Ltd* as an example of a statute passed for the protection of private rights and
c interests, viz those of the performers.

Beaudesert Shire Council v Smith is a decision of the High Court of Australia. It appeared
to recognise the existence of a novel innominate tort of the nature of an 'action for
damages upon the case' available to 'a person who suffers harm or loss as the inevitable
consequence of the unlawful, intentional and positive acts of another'. The decision,
although now 15 years old, has never been followed in any Australian or other common
d law jurisdiction. In subsequent Australian cases it has invariably been distinguished,
most recently by the Privy Council in *Dunlop v Woollahra Municipal Council* [1981] 1 All
ER 1202, [1981] 2 WLR 693, on appeal from the Supreme Court of New South Wales.
It is clear now from a later decision of the Australian High Court in *Kitano v Commonwealth
of Australia* (1974) 129 CLR 151 that the adjective 'unlawful' in the definition of acts
which give rise to this new action for damages on the case does not include *every* breach
e of statutory duty which in fact causes damage to the plaintiff. It remains uncertain
whether it was intended to include acts done in contravention of a wider range of
statutory obligations or prohibitions than those which under the principles that I have
discussed above would give rise to a civil action at common law in England if they are
contravened. If the tort described in *Beaudesert* was really intended to extend that range,
I would invite your Lordships to declare that it forms no part of the law of England.
f I would therefore answer question 5(a) No.

Question 5(b), to which I now turn, concerns conspiracy as a civil tort. Your Lordships
are invited to answer it on the assumption that the purpose of Shell and BP in entering
into the agreement to do the various things that it must be assumed they did in
contravention of the sanctions order was to forward their own commercial interests, *not*
to injure those of Lonrho. So the question of law to be determined is whether an intent
g by the defendants to injure the plaintiff is an essential element in the civil wrong of
conspiracy, even where the acts agreed to be done by the conspirators amount to criminal
offences under a penal statute. It is conceded that there is no direct authority either way
on this question to be found in the decided cases; so if this House were to answer it in the
affirmative, your Lordships would be making new law.

My Lords, conspiracy as a criminal offence has a long history. It consists of 'the
h agreement of two or more persons to effect any unlawful purpose, whether as their
ultimate aim, or only as a means to it, and the crime is complete if there is such
agreement, even though nothing is done in pursuance of it'. I cite from Viscount Simon
LC's now classic speech in *Crofter Hand Woven Harris Tweed Co Ltd v Veitch* [1942] 1 All
ER 142 at 146, [1942] AC 435 at 439. Regarded as a civil tort, however, conspiracy is a
highly anomalous cause of action. The gist of the cause of action is damage to the
i plaintiff; so long as it remains unexecuted, the agreement, which alone constitutes the
crime of conspiracy, causes no damage; it is only acts done in execution of the agreement
that are capable of doing that. So the tort, unlike the crime, consists not of agreement
but of concerted action taken pursuant to agreement.

As I recall from my early years in the law, first as a student and then as a young
barrister, during its chequered history between Lord Coleridge CJ's judgment at first
instance in *Mogul Steamship Co v McGregor, Gow & Co* (1888) 21 QBD 544 and the *Crofter*

case, the civil tort of conspiracy attracted more academic controversy than success in practical application. Why should an act which causes economic loss to A but is not *a* actionable at his suit if done by B alone become actionable because B did it pursuant to an agreement between B and C? An explanation given at the close of the nineteenth century by Bowen LJ in the *Mogul* case 23 QBD 598 at 616 when it was before the Court of Appeal was: 'The distinction is based on sound reason, for a combination may make oppressive or dangerous that which if it proceeded only from a single person would be otherwise . . .' But to suggest today that acts done by one street-corner grocer in concert *b* with a second are more oppressive and dangerous to a competitor than the same acts done by a string of supermarkets under a single ownership or that a multinational conglomerate such as Lonrho or oil company such as Shell or BP does not exercise greater economic power than any combination of small businesses is to shut one's eyes to what has been happening in the business and industrial world since the turn of the century and, in particular, since the end of the 1939–45 war. The civil tort of conspiracy to injure *c* the plaintiff's commercial interests where that is the predominant purpose of the agreement between the defendants and of the acts done in execution of it which caused damage to the plaintiff must I think be accepted by this House as too well-established to be discarded, however anomalous it may seem today. It was applied by this House eighty years ago in *Quinn v Leathem* [1901] AC 495, [1900–3] All ER Rep 1, and accepted as good law in the *Crofter* case in 1942, where it was made clear that injury to the plaintiff *d* and not the self-interest of the defendants must be the predominant purpose of the agreement in execution of which the damage-causing acts were done.

My Lords, in none of the judgments in decided cases in civil actions for damages for conspiracy does it appear that the mind of the author of the judgment was directed to a case where the damage-causing acts, although neither done for the purpose of injuring the plaintiff nor actionable at his suit if they had been done by one person alone, were *e* nevertheless a contravention of some penal law. I will not recite the statements in those judgments to which your Lordships have been referred by Lonrho as amounting to dicta in favour of the view that a civil action for conspiracy does lie in such a case. Even if the authors' minds had been directed to the point, which they were not, I should still find them indecisive. This House, in my view, has an unfettered choice whether to confine the civil action of conspiracy to the narrow field to which alone it has an established claim *f* or whether to extend this already anomalous tort beyond those narrow limits that are all that common sense and the application of the legal logic of the decided cases require.

My Lords, my choice is unhesitatingly the same as that of Parker J and all three members of the Court of Appeal. I am against extending the scope of the civil tort of conspiracy beyond acts done in execution of an agreement entered into by two or more persons for the purpose not of protecting their own interests but of injuring the interests *g* of the plaintiff. So I would answer question 5(b) No.

The only remaining question, question 9, is whether the answers to the previous questions, now reduced to questions 1, 2 and 5(a) and (b), lead to the conclusion that any cause of action is disclosed by the points of claim. Since I would give negative answers to each of those four questions, it follows that I would also answer question 9 No and would dismiss the appeal. *h*

LORD EDMUND-DAVIES. My Lords, I have had the advantage of reading in draft the speech prepared by my noble and learned friend Lord Diplock. I am in respectful and complete agreement with him and cannot usefully add any observations of my own. For the reasons he gives, I would uphold the unanimous judgments of the Court *j* of Appeal and dismiss this appeal.

LORD KEITH OF KINKEL. My Lords, I have had the benefit of reading in draft the speech prepared by my noble and learned friend Lord Diplock. I agree with it entirely, and for the reasons which he gives I too would dismiss the appeal.

LORD SCARMAN. My Lords, I have had the advantage of reading in draft the speech
a of my noble and learned friend Lord Diplock. For the reasons he gives I would dismiss
the appeal.

LORD BRIDGE OF HARWICH. My Lords, I have had the advantage of reading in
draft the speech of my noble and learned friend Lord Diplock. I entirely agree with it
and accordingly would dismiss the appeal.

b
Appeal dismissed. Order appealed from affirmed.

Solicitors: *Cameron Markby* (for Lonrho and CPMR); *Slaughter & May* (for Shell); *Linklaters
& Paines* (for BP).

c   Mary Rose Plummer   Barrister.

Purse v Purse

COURT OF APPEAL, CIVIL DIVISION
d ARNOLD P, ORMROD AND DUNN LJJ
1st, 2nd, 3rd, 19th DECEMBER 1980

*Divorce – Appeal – Decree absolute – Death of party to suit after decree granted – Death of
petitioner – Jurisdiction of court to entertain appeal by respondent – Decree voidable because of
irregularity in service of petition – Whether death abating suit – Whether jurisdiction to entertain
e respondent's appeal against decree after death of petitioner.*

*Divorce – Practice – Service – Petition – Dispensing with service – Impracticable to serve
respondent – Whereabouts unknown – All reasonable inquiries to be made by petitioner before
applying for order dispensing with service – Registrar requiring petitioner's attendance on
application if all reasonable lines of inquiry not fully explored – Irregularity in service –
f Registrar failing to require petitioner's attendance on application – Decree of divorce granted –
Whether court should set aside order dispensing with service and decree – Matrimonial Causes
Rules 1977 (SI 1977 No 344), r 14(11).*

The husband and wife were married in 1933 but separated in 1966. The wife moved to
Bristol where the parties' only child, a married daughter, was living. In 1970 the
g husband wished to attempt a reconciliation and employed a private detective to find the
wife. He instructed the private detective to get in touch with the daughter and her
husband in Bristol but the private detective, after making inquiries, reported that the
wife had left her accommodation in Bristol and that her whereabouts were unknown and
that the daughter and her husband had moved to Colchester in 1967 and that their
whereabouts were also unknown. The husband did not follow up other lines of inquiry
h available to him, eg through the Department of Health and Social Security or through
the wife's bank, and made no other attempt to trace the wife or his daughter. In 1977
he filed a divorce petition in the county court based on five years' separation from the
wife. He applied to the registrar of the court for an order dispensing with service of the
petition and stated in his affidavit in support that he had not seen the wife since 1966 and
had been unable to establish her whereabouts. The private detective's report was
j exhibited to the affidavit. On the basis of the affidavit, and without requiring the
husband to attend before him, the registrar made an order dispensing with service of the
petition. On 24th October 1977 the judge granted the husband a decree nisi which was
made absolute on 7th December 1977. The husband died in April 1979. The wife
learned of his death in December 1979 and applied to his employers for a widow's
pension. She then learned from them that her marriage had been dissolved. The wife

would have had a strong case, on the ground of financial hardship, for resisting the husband's petition. She appealed to the Court of Appeal, out of time but with leave, to *a* set aside the order dispensing with service of the petition, on the grounds of irregularity, and also to set aside the decrees nisi and absolute on the ground that they were voidable because of the irregularity of service.

Held – The appeal would be allowed for the following reasons—

(1) Although the death of a party to a divorce suit before a decree was pronounced deprived the court of jurisdiction to grant a decree in the suit, because the death itself *b* ended the marriage, there was no general rule that a divorce suit automatically abated on the death of one of the parties so as to deprive the court of further jurisdiction in the suit. Where the death occurred after the decree absolute in circumstances in which, apart from the death, the court in the exercise of its discretion would have set aside the decree because it was voidable, the court retained jurisdiction in the suit notwithstanding the death, because the decree absolute was to be regarded as a res which *c* was under the court's control and the court had an inherent jurisdiction to set it aside, or alternatively (per Arnold P) because the wife had a statutory right of appeal, or (per Ormrod LJ) because the wife could be regarded as having an enforceable claim or right to have the decree set aside which had accrued before the husband's death. It followed that the court had jurisdiction to entertain the wife's appeal (see p 471 *a* to *e*, p 472 *a* to *e*, p 473 *h j*, p 474 *b c*, p 475 *b c f* and p 476 *e* to *h*, post); *Mosey v Mosey and Barker* [1955] *d* 2 All ER 391 and dictum of Denning LJ in *Sugden v Sugden* [1957] 1 All ER at 302 applied; dicta of Shearman J in *Maconochie v Maconochie* [1916] P at 328 and of Lord Hanworth MR in *Beaumont v Beaumont* [1932] All ER Rep at 618 considered.

(2) A person claiming the privilege afforded by r 14(11)[a] of the Matrimonial Causes Rules 1977 (and similar rules previously in force) of being allowed to dispense with service of a petition had to make every inquiry which it was reasonable for him to make *e* in the light of his knowledge which might lead to service of the petition in accordance with r 14(1) of the 1977 rules before applying for an order dispensing with service, and, if he did not, he had not sufficiently demonstrated that service was impracticable within r 14(11). In the circumstances the husband's efforts to discover his wife's whereabouts were inadequate to comply with that obligation, and the registrar ought to have required the husband to attend before him and should not have relied solely on the affidavit in *f* ordering service to be dispensed with. It followed that the order dispensing with service had been irregularly obtained and, having regard to the wife's strong case for resisting the petition and the fact that the petition had never been brought to her notice, the court would exercise its discretion to set aside the order dispensing with service and the decrees nisi and absolute (see p 470 *a* to *h*, p 471 *e*, p 474 *g* to *j* and p 475 *b* to *g*, post); *Wiseman v Wiseman* [1953] 1 All ER 601 applied. *g*

Per Curiam. Solicitors applying for, and registrars making, an order dispensing with service of a petition have a duty to take great care to ensure that all practical steps to contact the respondent have been taken (see p 470 *c d*, p 474 *f* and p 475 *g*, post).

Per Ormrod and Dunn LJJ. Where it is sought to set aside a decree absolute after the death of one of the parties, notice of the application ought to be given to any person *h* likely to be affected by the setting aside of the decree (see p 474 *d e* and p 476 *h j*, post).

Notes

For the effect of the death of a party to a divorce suit, see 13 Halsbury's Laws (4th Edn) paras 891–893, and for cases on the subject, see 27(2) Digest (Reissue) 714–716, 5513–5536.

---

a Rule 14(11) provides: 'Where in the opinion of the registrar it is impracticable to serve a party in *j* accordance with any of the foregoing paragraphs or it is otherwise necessary or expedient to dispense with service of a copy of a petition on the respondent or on any other person, the registrar may make an order dispensing with such service. An application for an order under this paragraph shall, if no notice of intention to defend has been given, be made in the first instance ex parte by lodging an affidavit setting out the grounds of the application, but the registrar may, if he thinks fit, require the attendance of the petitioner on the application.'

For service of the petition, see 13 Halsbury's Laws (4th Edn) para 739, and for setting
a aside a decree absolute for irregularity of service, see ibid paras 684, 985.
For the Matrimonial Causes Rules 1977, r 14, see 10 Halsbury's Statutory Instruments
(4th Reissue) 241.

Cases referred to in judgments

Balloqui v Balloqui [1963] 3 All ER 989, [1964] 1 WLR 82, CA, 27(2) Digest (Reissue) 790,
b   6348.

Beaumont v Beaumont [1933] P 39, [1932] All ER Rep 615, 102 LJP 4, 148 LT 247, CA,
27(2) Digest (Reissue) 715, 5532.

Bevan v McMahon and Bevan (falsely called McMahon) (1859) 2 Sw & Tr 58, 28 LJP & M
127, 2 LT 255, 23 JP 472, 5 Jur NS 686, 164 ER 913, 27(2) Digest (Reissue) 714, 5516.

Brydges v Brydges and Wood [1909] P 187, 78 LJP 97, 100 LT 744, CA, 27(2) Digest
c   (Reissue) 924, 7427.

Burroughes v Abbot [1922] 1 Ch 86, [1921] All ER Rep 709, 91 LJ Ch 157, 126 LT 354,
28(1) Digest (Reissue) 269, 876.

Coleman v Coleman and Simpson [1920] P 71, 27(2) Digest (Reissue) 716, 5535.

D (J) v D (S) [1973] 1 All ER 349, sub nom *D'este v D'este* [1973] Fam 55, [1973] 2 WLR
183, Digest (Cont Vol D) 430, 7008a.

d *Dipple v Dipple* [1942] P 65, 111 LJP 18, 166 LT 120, 27(2) Digest (Reissue) 817, 6569.

Dryden v Dryden [1973] 3 All ER 526, [1973] Fam 217, [1973] 3 WLR 524, Digest (Cont
Vol D) 435, 7590c.

Everitt v Everitt [1948] 2 All ER 545, CA, 27(2) Digest (Reissue) 789, 6344.

F (infants), Re [1977] 2 All ER 777, [1977] Fam 165, [1977] 2 WLR 488, CA, Digest (Cont
Vol E) 322, 1415d.

e *Maconochie v Maconochie, Maconochie v Maconochie and Blake* [1916] P 326, 86 LJP 10, 115
LT 790, 27(2) Digest (Reissue) 716, 5534.

Mosey v Mosey and Barker [1955] 2 All ER 391, [1956] P 26, [1955] 2 WLR 1118, 27(2)
Digest (Reissue) 821, 6585.

Richards v Richards and Flocton (1940) [1942] P 68n, 111 LJP 2n, 27(2) Digest (Reissue)
761, 6048.

f *Roberts, Re, Roberts v Roberts* [1978] 3 All ER 225, [1978] 1 WLR 653, CA, Digest (Cont
Vol E) 649, 1421a.

Seaford, Re, Seaford v Seifert [1968] 1 All ER 482, [1968] P 53, [1968] 2 WLR 155, CA,
Digest (Cont Vol C) 355, 1647a.

Stanhope v Stanhope (1886) 11 PD 103, 55 LJP 36, 54 LT 906, 50 JP 276, CA, 27(2) Digest
(Reissue) 714, 5518.

g *Sugden v Sugden* [1957] 1 All ER 300, [1957] P 120, [1957] 2 WLR 210, 121 JP 121, CA,
27(2) Digest (Reissue) 817, 6570.

Thomson v Thomson and Rodschinka [1896] P 263, 65 LJP 80, 74 LT 801, CA, 27(2) Digest
(Reissue) 876, 6993.

Wiseman v Wiseman [1953] 1 All ER 601, [1953] P 79, [1953] 2 WLR 499, CA, 27(2)
Digest (Reissue) 789, 6345.

h *Woolfenden (otherwise Clegg) v Woolfenden (otherwise Clegg)* [1947] 2 All ER 653, [1948] P
27, [1948] LJR 622, 27(2) Digest (Reissue) 941, 7604.

Cases also cited

Brocas v Brocas (1861) 30 LJPM & A 172.

j *Craig v Kanssen* [1943] 1 All ER 108, [1943] KB 256, CA.

Elliott v Gurr (1812) 2 Phill 16.

Kelly v Kelly and Brown [1960] 3 All ER 232, [1961] P 94.

Kent v Atkinson [1923] P 142, [1923] All ER Rep 28.

M v M and A (1910) 26 TLR 305.

Whitehead v Whitehead (otherwise Vasbor) [1962] 3 All ER 800, [1963] P 117, CA.

Wright v Wright [1976] 1 All ER 796, [1976] Fam 114.

Appeal

In 1977 William Allever Purse ('the husband') filed a petition for divorce in the Brighton   *a*
County Court against Joy Patricia Marie Purse, his wife, and applied for an order
dispensing with service of the petition on her because he had not seen her since 1966 and
did not know where she lived. On 20th September 1977 the registrar of the county court
made an order dispensing with service of the petition. On 25th October 1977 his
Honour Judge Grant sitting at the Brighton County Court granted the husband a decree
nisi on his petition and on 7th December 1977 the decree was made absolute. The   *b*
husband died on 26th April 1979 and Mrs Purse first learned of his death in December
1979. Mrs Purse, who wished to set aside the divorce on financial grounds, appealed out
of time, with leave of the Court of Appeal, for an order that the registrar's order
dispensing with service of the petition on her be set aside and that the decree nisi and
decree absolute also be set aside. The ground of the appeal was that the registrar wrongly
exercised his discretion to dispense with service of the petition. The facts are set out in   *c*
the judgment of Arnold P.

Margaret Windridge for Mrs Purse.
E James Holman as amicus curiae.

d

Cur adv vult

19th December. The following judgments where read.

ARNOLD P. By this appeal Mrs Joy Patricia Purse seeks to set aside an order made on
20th September 1977 by the registrar of Brighton County Court dispensing with service   *e*
of a petition for divorce filed by her husband, William Allever Purse, the decree nisi of
dissolution of marriage granted on that petition by his Honour Judge Brian Grant at
Brighton County Court on 25th October 1977 and the decree absolute appertaining to
the latter granted on 7th December 1977. Leave for this appeal out of time has already
been granted.

Mr and Mrs Purse were married in 1933 and separated in 1966. They had one child,   *f*
Unity Edith Angela, who in 1963, married Jeremy John Heath. After the separation Mrs
Purse went to live in Bristol where her daughter was living and she never again met or
corresponded directly with her husband, who died on 26th April 1979. Mr Purse knew
that his wife took up residence in Bristol and there was some correspondence during
1966 and 1967 between their respective solicitors. In 1970 Mr Purse was anxious to get
into touch with his wife, apparently with a view to a possible reconciliation, and he   *g*
employed a private detective to ascertain her whereabouts. He informed the detective
of the address in Bristol at which he knew his wife to have been living in 1966 and that
a likely source of information would be Mr and Mrs Heath since he surmised correctly
that his wife would be in touch with them. The detective reported to Mr Purse in
December 1970 that he had ascertained that Mrs Purse had been replaced as the occupant
of the Bristol premises by other occupants and that he had been unable to discover her   *h*
present whereabouts or those of Mr and Mrs Heath, save that the latter had, about three
years previously, moved to the Colchester area. The detective offered, in case Mr Purse
should not have any further knowledge of relevance to the inquiry, to continue his
investigations and submit a further report. So far as appears, however, Mr Purse did not
pursue this suggestion or make any other attempt to obtain contact either with his wife
or his daughter and son-in-law. In 1977 Mr Purse, who by this time had been separated   *j*
from his wife for about 11 years, was minded to obtain the dissolution of his marriage,
and, on 19th May 1977, he filed a petition for dissolution based on the irretreivable
breakdown of the marriage and five years' separation. He did not have any information
to enable the petition to be served in accordance with the primary requirements of the
Matrimonial Causes Rules and he therefore applied for an order dispensing with service.
It is evident that before this application was made, Mr Purse's solicitors had attempted to

discover Mrs Purse's whereabouts by inquiry of the solicitors who had been representing
her soon after the separation, but had been informed by them that they had lost contact
with Mrs Purse in 1969. In support of his application to the court, Mr Purse swore an
affidavit on 15th September 1977 stating that he had not seen his wife since she left the
matrimonial home on 27th May 1966, giving the last address which he had for her,
namely that in Bristol, relating the facts of his instruction of the detective and exhibiting
the latter's report and stating that since the date of that report he had been unable to
establish the whereabouts of his wife. On the basis of the contents of those documents,
and without further inquiry, the registrar made the order on 20th September 1977
dispensing with service. On 24th October 1977 the judge pronounced the decree nisi
and this was made absolute on 7th December 1977. Of all of these events concerning the
petition and application of Mr Purse and the proceedings of the court thereon, Mrs Purse
was of course wholly in ignorance.

In 1967 Mr and Mrs Heath left Bristol and went to live in Colchester where he was
employed as curator of the Colchester Natural History Museum. This was a field in
which Mr Heath had been employed at all times since before his marriage to his wife and
this was known by Mr Purse to have been the case at about the time of that marriage.
From the time of their move to Colchester until 1973 the Heaths lived in rented
accommodation there and apparently did not have an entry under their name in the local
telephone directory but in 1973 they bought their own house in Colchester and from
then onwards there was such an entry. In 1972 Mrs Purse followed her daughter and
son-in-law to the Colchester area, at first residing in a flat at Frinton and in 1975 moving
to an address in Colchester where she has ever since resided.

By his will dated 15th March 1978 Mr Purse gave some pecuniary legacies and made
a residuary gift to charity but made no provision for Mrs Purse. His will was proved on
20th July 1979 by Lloyds Bank Ltd. His net estate is of the order of £30,000 in value.
By an originating summons dated 18th July 1980 Mrs Purse has commenced proceedings
under the Inheritance (Provision for Family and Dependants) Act 1975 which have been
adjourned to await the outcome of this appeal.

The basis of Mrs Purse's case is that there were various channels through which
inquiries could have been made as to her whereabouts by her husband in 1977 which
would, in all probability, have been successful in their object but that none of these were
undertaken and no sufficient investigation was made by the registrar about the making
of any such inquiries although the information available to him suggested, she alleges,
the possibility of such inquiries being useful. She further says that if she had known by
service of the petition on her personally of its existence as, she says, would probably have
been effected after the appropriate inquiries, she had ample ground for opposing the
petition on the ground of grave financial hardship under s 5 of the Matrimonial Causes
Act 1973 and, if that defence had been unsuccessful, the possibility of obtaining
appropriate financial provision under s 10 of that Act.

In support of the first part of that claim she says that Mr Purse knew of the address of
her bank in 1966 and that an inquiry there would have resulted in the transmission to
her of any correspondence sent to the bank, that it would have been easy to have traced
Mr Heath, and through him Mrs Purse herself, by inquiry in the Colchester area directed
to the possibility of his employment at a museum, and that inquiry for her or Mr Heath
through the Department of Health and Social Security would be likely to have revealed
her whereabouts. She also referred to her friendship with a family called Randal with
whom her husband was acquainted and whose address he knew, as being a point of
contact with her which he should have investigated, but it appears that he supposed the
family to have been called Randall so that this line of inquiry was less obviously useful
than might have been the case. Mr Purse was a ship's engineer and served in the ships
of the Union Castle Mail Steamship Co rising to the post of chief engineer. Under the
terms of his employment, any wife who survived him would receive a pension, in the
event, of £1,648·25 per annum which would not, however, be payable to a woman who
was his ex-wife and this circumstance would have been the foundation for Mrs Purse's
resistance to the petition under s 5 of the 1973 Act.

There is not, in my judgment, any material from which it would be proper to derive
the conclusion that there was any dishonest concealment from the court of material a
which might have led to the discovery of the whereabouts of Mrs Purse at the date of Mr
Purse's application to dispense with service of the petition, but the efforts of Mr Purse to
discover his wife's whereabouts were, in my view, quite inadequate to comply with his
obligations as a person claiming the privilege afforded by the relevant rule, now r 14(11)
of the Matrimonial Causes Rules 1977, SI 1977 No 344, which is in similar terms to that
in force at the date of Mr Purse's application. A party applying under that paragraph b
ought in my judgment to make every inquiry which it is reasonable to make in the light
of the knowledge of that person which might lead to his ability to serve the process in
accordance with para (1), and if he does not do that he has not demonstrated sufficiently
the impracticability of such service. It is specifically provided in the paragraph that after
the lodging of the affidavit of the applicant, the registrar may, if he thinks fit, require the
attendance of the applicant on the application. The registrar in this case knew that it was c
thought likely that the discovery of the whereabouts of Mr and Mrs Heath would lead to
the discovery of the whereabouts of Mrs Purse, that it was known that Mr and Mrs Heath
had moved to the Colchester area in 1967 and that apparently no inquiry for them had
been made in that area since December 1970. In my judgment the power to require the
attendance of the applicant should be used by a registrar when dealing with an application
of this sort whenever it appears from the available material that lines of inquiry have not d
been fully explored, and in this case there was certainly, in my view, sufficient material
to have justified that course.
    Where there is alleged to be a defect in service of a petition and it is sought for that
reason to set aside the decree made thereon where it has been made absolute, an
appropriate process for the purpose is an appeal to this court. In *Everitt v Everitt* [1948]
2 All ER 545 in which there was no service at all of the petition so that the decree was e
void, it was held that an appropriate process was by the way of an appeal to the Court of
Appeal to have the decree nisi and the decree absolute set aside. In *Wiseman v Wiseman*
[1953] 1 All ER 601, [1953] P 79 where an order for substituted service had been
obtained, not fraudulently but on inadequate disclosure, so that the decree was not void
but voidable, it was again held that a proper mode of avoidance was by way of an appeal
and in that case in the exercise of its discretion this court set aside the decree nisi and the f
decree absolute. The view which I take is that the present case is in every respect
comparable to *Wiseman v Wiseman*, there being no relevant difference between an order
for substituted service and an order dispensing with service, that the decrees in this case
are voidable and that whether they should be set aside depends on the exercise of this
court's discretion. In my judgment, since the petition never came to the notice of Mrs
Purse by reason of service being dispensed with on inadequate disclosure and after g
inadequate inquiry both by Mr Purse and the registrar, and since Mrs Purse would have
had a serious prospect of resisting the decree nisi under s 5 and the decree absolute under
s 10, of the Matrimonial Causes Act 1973, this is a case in which the discretion of the
court should be exercised in favour of setting the decrees aside.
    It is, however, objected that this process is barred by the death of Mr Purse. It is well
established that as between husband and wife no step in a divorce proceeding can be h
taken after the death of either of them. This was laid down in very general terms in
Maconochie v Maconochie and Blake [1916] P 236 by Shearman J at first instance, and this
decision received the approbation of this court in *Beaumont v Beaumont* [1933] P 39, [1932]
All ER Rep 615. In neither of those cases, nor indeed in any other case which the very
great industry of counsel in this case has revealed, has the question been considered what
is the effect of the death of a spouse on the power of the Court of Appeal to reverse or vary j
an order made in a divorce suit. There would be many cases in which the fact of death
rendered the process meaningless by reason of the circumstance that a marriage brought
to an end by death could no longer be dissolved by an act of the court and indeed in many
of the cases this consideration is put forward as decisive for the conclusion that the
process cannot survive the death: see, e.g., *Stanhope v Stanhope* (1886) 11 PD 103. This
consideration would be decisive in a case in which the Court of Appeal was asked, in the

exercise of its discretion, after the death of a spouse, to reverse or to set aside an order
a refusing a decree and to order a new trial. The question in this case however is whether
there is anything in the authorities which destroys the power of this court to exercise its
appellate function in a case in which a decree has been made, and in circumstances in
which this court would otherwise interfere, merely because of the intervening death of
one of the parties or, if there be nothing in the authorities to lead to that consequence,
whether there is some principle which should have the same result. There are certainly
b to be found in some authorities dicta which point to a more extensive result of the
abatement of matrimonial proceedings by the death of a party than the recognition by
the court of its inability to dissolve a marriage already ended by death. These however,
in my judgment, support no more than the proposition that the personal representative
of a deceased party to proceedings under the Matrimonial Causes Acts is unable to invoke
on behalf of his estate a jurisdiction afforded by those Acts which does not confer a cause
c of action on the deceased party which can fairly be regarded as separate from the divorce
proceedings: see *Sugden v Sugden* [1957] 1 All ER 300, [1957] P 120 and *D(J) v D (S)* [1973]
1 All ER 349, [1973] Fam 55.

If the error in the present case be regarded as an error in point of law, the right of Mrs
Purse to appeal to this court is granted to her under s 108 of the County Courts Act 1959
and is to be exercised in such manner, and subject to such conditions, as may be for the
d time being provided by the Rules of the Supreme Court and, if the error is to be regarded
as involved in a determination of any question of fact, the right is a similar right under
s 109 of that Act as amended by s 6 of the Matrimonial Causes Act 1967, but there is not,
in my judgment, anything in the Rules of the Supreme Court to destroy Mrs Purse's
right of appeal to this court, nor can I find anything in the authorities or in principle
which should cause this court to decline to entertain the statutory right of appeal given
e to Mrs Purse.

I would therefore allow this appeal and set aside the order of the registrar and the
decree nisi and the decree absolute.

ORMROD LJ. There is no doubt that the appellant in this case, Mrs Purse, has suffered
a serious injustice, in that she has been divorced by her husband without her knowledge
f and, in consequence, has lost her rights to a widow's pension under the occupational
pension scheme of her husband's former employers, the Union Castle Line. The husband
obtained a decree nisi on 24th October 1977, under s 1(2)(e) of the Matrimonial Causes
Act 1973, ie on five years' separation. The decree was made absolute on 7th December
1977. It is obvious, having regard to the length of the marriage (44 years), the ages of the
parties (Mrs Purse was then 64 and her husband a little older) and the financial position
g of the parties, that Mrs Purse would have had a strong case for resisting the making of the
decree either under s 5 of the 1973 Act, on the ground of grave financial hardship, or
under s 10 of that Act if the husband had not provided her with adequate compensation
for the loss of her right to a widow's pension if she survived him.

The husband died on 26th April 1979. Mrs Purse had first learned of her husband's
death in December 1979, and applied to the Union Castle Line superannuation scheme
h for her pension as a widow, only to be informed, for the first time, that her marriage had
been dissolved on 7th December 1977.

Mrs Purse now appeals to this court asking that the decree absolute be set aside. The
question, and it is a difficult one, is whether, the husband being dead, this or any other
court has jurisdiction to entertain her application. It is a purely procedural problem and
the court is greatly indebted to the Queen's Proctor, and particularly to counsel, who
i appeared at the request of the court as amicus curiae, for his exhaustive research, the decree
able argument, which have been of great assistance.   , could not be
Counsel for Mrs Purse made it clear that she was challenging the 20th September
absolute on the ground of irregularity of service. Non-support on the part of the
relied on because the husband obtained an order of   such an allegation,
1977, under r 14(11) of the Matrimonial C
husband is not relied on because there

but it is alleged that this order was obtained or granted irregularly. The case, therefore, falls within the decision of this court in *Wiseman v Wiseman* [1973] 1 All ER 601, [1953] P 79, which is authority for two propositions, namely that in such circumstances the decree absolute is voidable but not void, and that the Court of Appeal has jurisdiction to inquire into, make the necessary findings of fact in relation to the validity of, and set aside, a decree absolute, notwithstanding that an application to set aside such a decree may also be made to a judge at first instance: see *Woolfenden v Woolfenden* [1947] 2 All ER 653, [1948] P 27 and *Dryden v Dryden* [1973] 3 All ER 526, [1973] Fam 217.

Counsel's difficulties on behalf of Mrs Purse would have been very much less had she been able to show that the decree in this case was void, because the court would have had power to grant the necessary declaration in any proceedings in which the validity of the decree was in question, eg in an action against the Union Castle Line superannuation scheme for a declaration that Mrs Purse was the widow of Mr Purse and as such a beneficiary under the pension scheme. But, the decree being voidable only, the court has a discretion to set aside or to refuse to set it aside, in which case the decree would be valid. A judicial act going beyond a mere declaration is, therefore, required, and such an order, it seems, could only be made in the divorce suit. But, it is often said that a divorce suit automatically 'abates' on the death of either party to the marriage and cannot be revived. Counsel appearing as amicus curiae set himself the arduous, but in this case the essential, task of investigating the soundness of this doctrine and has submitted, as a result of his researches, that there is no such general rule. On the contrary, the statement that a divorce suit abates on the death of either party is, in truth, and in fact, a generalisation from a large number of cases, each holding for a specific reason or reasons that the court had no jurisdiction after the death of one of the parties to grant the particular kind of relief sought. Detailed examination of the authorities supports this submission. The following are some examples.

Claims by personal representatives

The personal representatives of a husband who dies after decree nisi but before decree absolute cannot revive the suit in order to apply for a decree absolute, because the marriage has already been finally dissolved by death: *Stanhope v Stanhope* (1886) 11 PD 103. Personal representatives cannot apply for variation of a settlement after the death of a husband or for any other kind of matrimonial relief, because, as a matter of construction of the relevant statutory provisions, only a party to the marriage or, in some cases, the children can rely on them: *Thomson v Thomson and Rodschinka* [1896] P 263, and *D (J) v D (S)* [1973] 1 All ER 349, [1973] Fam 55.

Claims against personal representatives

Until the Law Reform (Miscellaneous Provisions) Act 1934 came into force, attempts to obtain relief under the Matrimonial Causes Acts against the personal representatives of a husband who had died during the pendency of a divorce suit failed. The reason usually given was that the claim was caught by the common law rule actio personalis cum persona moritur. Sometimes it was said that the jurisdiction in divorce was purely statutory and that the statute contained no provision under which the personal representatives could be made parties to the suit, with the result that the court had no jurisdiction over them. An award of damages for adultery against a co-respondent did not create a judgment debt, because the order required the co-respondent to pay the money into court. Such an order could only be enforced by attachment, a remedy which clearly could not be used against an executor. To avoid this difficulty the Divorce Court ~~sometimes varied the order and directed that the damages be paid to the husband~~ ~~on his undertaking to pay the money into court to enable execution by way of~~ ~~there was no jurisdiction to make such an order against the executor of the~~ ~~successful against~~ *es v Brydges and Wood* [1909] P 187.
                in which alternative procedures were available claims were
                representatives. In *Burroughs v Abbott* [1922] 1 Ch 86, [1921]

All ER Rep 709 the court made an order after the death of the husband for rectification
a of a deed executed by the husband in compliance with an order for secured
maintenance. In *Beaumont v Beaumont* [1933] P 39, [1932] All ER Rep 615 the husband
had been ordered to pay £200 into court as security for the wife's costs. After payment
into court the husband died before the suit was heard. It was held that there was
jurisdiction in rem over the fund in court to order taxation and payment of the wife's
costs out of the fund in court.

b After the 1934 Act came into force the position was slightly eased. In *Mosey v Mosey
and Barker* [1955] 2 All ER 391, [1956] P 26 Sachs J rejected the submission made on
behalf of the executor that there was no jurisdiction to deal with a matter arising in a
divorce suit after the death of one of the parties because there was no fund in court or
other res on which to found that post-death jurisdiction. He held that the test was: does
the order create an enforceable claim? Applying that test, an order to secure an annual
c sum of £300 'upon part of the real property' of the husband was enforceable after his
death against his estate. Similarly in *Richards v Richards and Flockton* [1942] P 68n
taxation of costs against a co-respondent was allowed to proceed after his death as it was
an 'enforceable claim'. On the contrary, a wife could not proceed with an application
(not yet adjudicated on) for secured maintenance after the death of her husband because
she had not got an 'enforceable claim', but merely a right to ask the court to exercise its
d discretionary powers in her favour: *Dipple v Dipple* [1942] P 65. In *Sugden v Sugden*
[1957] P 120 at 135, cf [1957] 1 All ER 300 at 302, Denning LJ said:

> 'I would add that, in divorce proceedings, in order that the cause of action should
> subsist at the death, the right under the order must itself have accrued at the time
> of death.'

e There, is, however, another line of cases. It begins with the judgment of Shearman J
in *Maconochie v Maconochie* [1916] P 326 at 328, where he said:

> 'The result then is that where one of these parties dies the action abates: it comes
> to an end, it is dead and done with. These personal actions then having abated, no
> one can come to the court and make an application in these actions. There is one
> *f* exception to this rule, and that is where there are already funds in court.'

That case was followed in *Coleman v Coleman and Simpson* [1920] P 71 and both cases were
approved in the result by this court in *Beaumont v Beaumont* [1933] P 39, [1932] All ER
Rep 615 'but Lord Hanworth MR commented on the use of the word 'abated', which he
said, is really a metaphorical term and does not mean that the Court itself has taken the
suit off the file' (see [1933] P 39 at 48, [1932] All ER Rep 615 at 618). Lawrence LJ said
g ([1933] P 39 at 53, [1932] All ER Rep 615 at 621):

> 'As regards the exercise of the jurisdiction to order taxation of costs and payment
> out, I think this jurisdiction should preferably be exercised in the suit in which the
> money has been paid into Court ... In my opinion this suit is not abated for the
> purpose of the distribution of the fund in Court ...'

h In my judgment, Shearman J's dictum goes too far. To say that the court has no
jurisdiction in a divorce suit after the death of one of the parties to the marriage because
the suit has been abated by the death is to confuse cause and effect. The death may, for
various reasons, deprive the court of jurisdiction; the effect may then be described,
loosely, as abatement of the suit. In each case, therefore, it is necessary to consider
whether the death has deprived the court of jurisdiction to grant the relief claimed.

j There appears to be no authority on the effect on a pending appeal of the death of one
party to the marriage during the pendency of the appeal. If the doctrine of abatement
of the suit on death is sound, an appeal must also abate because the suit is at an end.
When the appeal is against the granting or refusing of a decree nisi, the death of either
party before judgment will bring the appeal to an end on the principle of *Stanhope v
Stanhope* because the marriage will have been dissolved in any event. Similarly, an appeal

against an order for periodical payments, because the order will have lapsed already. But an appeal against an order for a lump sum or a property adjustment order (ss 23 and 24 of the 1973 Act) will have to be dealt with because important property rights are at stake, and it would be manifestly unjust to either the surviving spouse or to the estate of the deceased if the order under appeal was, as it were, frozen by the death, regardless of the justice of the case.

In my judgment, therefore, we are free to consider whether Mrs Purse's appeal is barred by the death of her husband. The first point to be made is that the relief which she is claiming does not depend on any statutory provision; she is appealing to the inherent jurisdiction of the court over its own process. Alternatively, the decree absolute might be regarded as a res, something which is under the control of the court, or the wife might be regarded as having an enforceable claim or right which had accrued before the death.

For these reasons I am prepared to hold that there is jurisdiction to entertain Mrs Purse's appeal. There are, however, some procedural problems. Although leave was given in this case to substitute the husband's executors in the title of the suit, it was an unnecessary step because the estate is not concerned in any way in this case. It would be otherwise if the appeal concerned a lump sum or property adjustment order. Directions were also given to serve the Union Castle Line superannuation scheme with notice of the appeal in order to give them an opportunity to apply for leave to intervene if so advised. Where a decree absolute is involved notice ought to be given to any person likely to be affected by the setting aside of the decree. In this case neither the executors nor the Union Castle Line superannuation scheme sought to be heard.

I turn now to the merits of the appeal. The power given by r 14(11) of the Matrimonial Causes Rules 1977, SI 1977 No 344, to dispense with service of a petition on the respondent has no parallel in other types of litigation, but in family cases it can be of great value. It enables a spouse who is unable to serve the other spouse to obtain a dissolution of the marriage, and so to escape from what has become a meaningless tie, without waiting indefinitely to discover that spouse's whereabouts. But it is also, as this case shows, a potentially dangerous weapon. For this reason, formerly only a judge could make such an order and experience showed that, in practice, it was only made after careful and thorough inquiry to exhaust the possibilities of effecting proper service. In my judgment, that salutory practice should still be followed. Solicitors who apply for, and registrars who can now make, such an order have a duty to take great care to ensure that all practical steps to contact the respondent have been taken. If they have not been taken *Wiseman v Wiseman* demonstrates the lengths to which this court may go to right the wrong done to a respondent who has not been served.

The affidavit of the husband which was sworn in support of the application to dispense with service was little more than a formality and quite inadequate to justify the order which was made. As Arnold P has demonstrated, there were a number of inquiries which could and should have been made in this case which would probably have resulted in obtaining Mrs Purse's address, which was in Frinton-on-Sea. An important omission was the failure to make use of the arrangement under which the Department of Health and Social Security will forward, at the request of the petitioner's solicitors, a letter addressed to the respondent at the last known address: see Practice Direction [1973] 1 All ER 61, [1973] 1 WLR 60. Since Mrs Purse was employed at the material time, it is very probable that such a letter would have reached her.

I, therefore, have no difficulty in holding that the order dispensing with service was irregularly obtained and irregularly made and can be set aside by this court if it thinks fit to do so.

On the question of discretion I again have no difficulty in holding that this order and all subsequent proceedings ought to be set aside. To do so will hurt no one and will correct a grave injustice to Mrs Purse.

The only consideration which makes me hesitate is the importance, as a matter of public policy, of maintaining confidence in the integrity of decrees absolute. For this reason I would like to try to clarify the semantic morass which surrounds the words 'void'

and 'voidable'. Analogies with the law of contract are most misleading when these words
a are used in relation to orders or decrees made by the court. A voidable order is an order
which the court has a discretion to set aside. The option is in the court, not in the
parties. A void order is an order which the court must set aside ex debito justitiae if
requested to do so by any person concerned. Such an order, however, is to be acted on
as if it were valid unless and until it is set aside by a competent court. The term 'nullity'
should be confined to cases where the order is bad on its face, e g if it purports to be made
b by a court which is incompetent to make an order of the type in question. The matter
is dealt with in more detail in *Re F (infants)* [1977] 2 All ER 777, [1977] Fam 165.

I would allow the appeal and set aside the decree absolute.

DUNN LJ. The question of law raised in this appeal is whether this court has
c jurisdiction to set aside the decree absolute after the death of the husband.

If the court has jurisdiction I agree with Arnold P and Ormrod LJ that the wife has a
strong case for setting the decree aside. She had no knowledge that the petition had been
filed and as a result she lost the opportunity of relying on s 5 of the Matrimonial Causes
Act 1973 to resist the grant of a decree nisi, and also on s 10 of that Act to resist the grant
of a decree absolute if a decree nisi had been granted. As the effect of the decree absolute
d was that she lost the right to a widow's pension from her husband's former employers,
it is virtually certain that even if the decree nisi had been granted it would not have been
made absolute unless the court had been satisfied that the petitioner had made reasonable
financial provision to compensate her for such loss.

If the husband were still alive there is no dispute that the court would have had the
power to set the decree aside if it thought fit: see *Wiseman v Wiseman* [1953] 1 All ER 601,
e [1953] P 79 and *Balloqui v Balloqui* [1963] 3 All ER 989, [1964] 1 WLR 82. The
inadequacy of the steps taken by the husband and his solicitors to trace the wife should
have put the registrar on inquiry, and the lack of inquiry by the registrar as to her
whereabouts provides strong grounds for setting aside the order for dispensing with
service. If that were done, there being no evidence of fraud by the petitioner, the decree
absolute would be voidable, that is to say it would be valid until such time as it was set
f aside.

Without reciting the facts, which have already been dealt with by Arnold P and
Ormrod LJ, I agree that if the court has jurisdiction the order dispensing with service and
the decree absolute should be set aside. In these days, especially with the special
procedure, practitioners should take all reasonable steps to discover the whereabouts of
respondents, including the steps specifically referred to by Arnold P and Ormrod LJ,
g before applying to dispense with service of a petition. And registrars should be careful
not to make such orders unless quite satisfied that all such steps have been taken. If in
doubt they should use the power vested in them by r 14(11) of the Matrimonial Causes
Rules 1977, SI 1977 No 344, to require the presence of a petitioner before them in person
so that they may explore all possible avenues of inquiry. The facts of this case show the
injustice which may result if these steps are not taken, and a party's status is changed
h without her knowledge and to her detriment.

The question whether or not this court has jurisdiction depends on whether or not the
suit has abated by reason of the death of the husband. Having taken us through all the
relevant authorities relating to the doctrine of abatement, counsel appearing as amicus
curiae, for whose researches, assisted by the Queen's Proctor, I am personally much
indebted, advanced five propositions. (1) The term 'abate' or 'abatement' is not a precise
i term, and one must look at the decided cases and see the circumstances in which the term
has been used, and whether there is any principle or rationale for its use. (2) The most
general statement of the principle and effect of the word 'abatement' is to be found in
Maconochie v Maconochie [1916] P 326 at 328 per Shearman J in the passage read by
Ormrod LJ. This statement was applied by this court in *Beaumont v Beaumont* [1933] P 39
at 51, [1932] All ER Rep 615 at 620 by Lord Hanworth MR. But Lord Hanworth said
([1933] P 39 at 48, [1932] All ER Rep 615 at 618):

'I have commented on the use of the word "abated" in the course of the argument. It is really a metaphorical term and does not mean that the Court itself has taken the suit off the file. The suit is in reality sterilized by the death of one of the spouses.'

Beaumont v Beaumont and the cases there cited provide no clear rationale of the word 'abatement'. (3) The only clear rationale of the term is to be found in *Stanhope v Stanhope* (1886) 11 PD 103 at 108 by Bowen LJ:

'A man can no more be divorced after his death than he can after his death be married or sentenced to death. Marriage is a union of husband and wife for their joint lives unless it be dissolved sooner, and the Court cannot dissolve a union which has already been determined.'

See also *Re Seaford, Seaford v Seifert* [1968] 1 All ER 482 at 489, [1968] P 53 at 70 per Willmer LJ. The principle is summarised in Latey on Divorce (15th Edn, 1973, p 697) in these words: 'On the death of a petitioner at any time before the decree absolute is made, the suit abates.' There is no case in which the doctrine has been applied to the death of a party pending an appeal, and although an appeal against the grant of a decree nisi would abate on the principle of *Stanhope v Stanhope* there is no reason in principle why certain other appeals should not, and injustice would be caused if they did. (4) The doctrine of abatement has also been applied to nullity suits (see *Bevan v McMahon and Bevan* (1859) 2 Sw and Tr 58) which before 1971 was not explicable on the *Stanhope* rationale, since before that date a decree of nullity of a voidable marriage related back to the date of the marriage. Since 1971 a voidable marriage is void only from the date of the decree (see *Re Roberts, Roberts v Roberts* [1978] 3 All ER 225, [1978] 1 WLR 653). There is no nullity case analogous to *Stanhope*. (5) All the cited cases were concerned with death before decree absolute. After decree absolute the object of the suit has been achieved and cannot be affected by a subsequent death. But the suit itself has not ceased to exist and for certain purposes the court still retains jurisdiction: see *Mosey v Mosey and Barker* [1955] 2 All ER 391, [1956] P 26.

I accept the helpful analysis of the cases presented by counsel appearing as amicus curiae in his five propositions. In my judgment Shearman J's dictum in *Maconochie v Maconochie* [1916] P 326 at 328 is too wide. The use of the word 'abate' seems to me to confuse the situation which arises on the death of a party to divorce proceedings. The question rather is whether by reason of the death the court is deprived of jurisdiction to grant the particular remedy prayed.

It was suggested by counsel as amicus curiae that the status of a person crystallises after his death and that perhaps the court should not intervene to change a person's status thereafter. He cited no authority for that proposition and I can find no necessary reason why the death of one of the parties to a divorce suit should affect proceedings going to the validity of a decree granted in those proceedings, even if that involves changing the status of a party after death. I agree with Ormrod LJ that the decree absolute is itself a res under the control of the court, and that the court has an inherent jurisdiction to set aside that decree in its discretion if it is just in all the circumstances to do so. I would therefore hold that the court has jurisdiction to set aside the decree and would make the necessary orders accordingly.

I would only add that I agree with Ormrod LJ that where it is sought to set aside a decree absolute after the death of one of the parties, notice of the application should be given to all persons likely to be affected by the order.

Appeal allowed.

Solicitors: *Greenwood, Page & Ward*, Colchester (for the wife); *Queen's Proctor*.

Avtar S Virdi Esq   Barrister.

Re Thompson & Riches Ltd

CHANCERY DIVISION
SLADE J
12th, 16th JANUARY 1981

Company – Dissolution – Application to have dissolution declared void – Dissolution after date of winding-up petition but before winding-up order made – Petitioner and court ignorant of dissolution – Official Receiver as liquidator of company discovering dissolution before winding-up order perfected and informing petitioner of dissolution – Petitioner failing to apply to court before winding-up order perfected – Petitioner applying after order perfected for order declaring dissolution void – Official Receiver and Treasury Solicitor on behalf of Crown not objecting to order – Whether court should make declaration that dissolution void – Companies Act 1948, s 352(1).

On 14th August 1979 the petitioner, a contributory of a company, in ignorance of the fact that the Registrar of Companies was taking steps to dissolve the company as being defunct, presented a petition to wind up the company. On 21st August, unknown to the petitioner or his solicitor, the company was dissolved pursuant to s 353(5)[a] of the Companies Act 1948, and, in ignorance of the dissolution, the judge made a winding-up order on the petition and appointed the Official Receiver as the provisional liquidator of the company. The Official Receiver then discovered that the company had been dissolved before the winding-up order was made and, about three weeks before the winding-up order was perfected, he notified the court and the petitioner's solicitor of the dissolution. The petitioner failed to take any action until some eight months after the winding-up order was perfected, when he issued a notice of motion, addressed only to the Official Receiver as respondent, seeking an order under s 352(1)[b] of the 1948 Act declaring that the dissolution was void. On 11th November 1980 the petitioner issued a second notice of motion to which the company, the Official Receiver and the Treasury Solicitor (representing the Crown's interest in the company's assets under s 354[c] of the 1948 Act) were the respondents, seeking (i) liberty to amend the petition under the slip rule, in order to pray that the dissolution of the company be declared void, and (ii) an order amending the winding-up order by adding an order declaring that the dissolution of the company was void immediately prior to the winding-up of the company. Neither the Official Receiver nor the Treasury Solicitor objected to the grant of the declaration claimed on the first motion. The motions were heard together.

Held – Although it had been open to the petitioner to apply under s 353(6)[d] of the 1948 Act for restoration of the company to the register, he was entitled in the alternative to apply under s 352(1) of that Act for an order declaring the dissolution to be void, and, since such an application had been made by him in the first motion as a 'person interested' within s 352(1) (ie as a contributory of the company) within two years of the dissolution, the court had jurisdiction to make the order sought on that motion. Furthermore, since the company was already in liquidation when the first motion was issued, joinder of the Registrar of Companies as a respondent to the motion was unnecessary either in his interest or in the public interest. Since the Official Receiver and the Treasury Solicitor did not object to the order sought on the first motion, the matter was in the court's discretion, and, in all the circumstances and notwithstanding that the winding-up order had been perfected several months before, the court would declare on

---

a   Section 353(5), so far as material, is set out at p 479 *b*, post
b   Section 352(1) is set out at p 479 *d*, post
c   Section 354 is set out at p 479 *g*, post
d   Section 353(6) is set out at p 479 *e f*, post

the first motion that the dissolution was void. Accordingly, it was unnecessary for the court to consider the second motion (see p 482 *j*, p 483 *a b d* and p 484 *b c*, post).

Re Test Holdings (Clifton) Ltd [1969] 3 All ER 517 followed.

Per Curiam. (1) Relief will not automatically be granted under s 352(1) whenever the petitioner brings himself within the wording of the subsection, and circumstances can arise, e g where the application is opposed on reasonable grounds by the Official Receiver, the Treasury Solicitor or other persons, where the court may feel bound, notwithstanding that the petitioner brings himself within s 352(1), to refuse to exercise its discretion to declare a dissolution void. Furthermore, in view of the risk of embarassment to the Official Receiver the longer uncertainty about a company exists, a petitioner should apply for relief under s 352(1) or under s 353(6) as soon as reasonably practicable after he becomes aware of the company's dissolution, whether he becomes aware of it before the winding-up order is perfected or afterwards, for if he delays he will face greater difficulties on his application (see p 483 *e* to *j*, post).

(2) Although the Official Receiver may have locus standi to make an application under s 352(1) as a 'person interested' within that subsection, in all but the most exceptional cases the primary responsibility for making the application falls on the petitioner (see p 483 *j* to p 484 *a*, post).

Notes

For the power of the court to declare the dissolution of a company void, see 7 Halsbury's Laws (4th Edn) para 1452, and for cases on the subject and on restoration of a company to the register, see 10 Digest (Reissue) 1233–1235, 7757–7777.

For the Companies Act 1948, ss 352, 353, 354, see 5 Halsbury's Statutes (3rd Edn) 372, 373, 374.

Cases referred to in judgment

Cambridge Coffee Room Association Ltd, Re [1952] 1 All ER 112, [1951] 2 TLR 1155, 10 Digest (Reissue) 1233, 7764.

Pritchway Ltd, Re (20th October 1980, unreported), Ch D.

Test Holdings (Clifton) Ltd, Re, Re General Issue and Investment Co Ltd [1969] 3 All ER 517, [1970] Ch 285, [1969] 3 WLR 606, 10 Digest (Reissue) 1234, 7771.

Motions

By a notice of motion dated 22nd August 1980 the petitioner, Michael Frederick John Thompson, a creditor and contributory of Thompson & Riches Ltd ('the company'), sought a declaration under s 352(1) of the Companies Act 1948 that the dissolution of the company on 21st August 1979 was void. The Official Receiver was the respondent to the motion. By a second motion dated 11th November 1980 the petitioner sought an order that he be at liberty to amend his petition to wind up the company to pray that the dissolution of the company be declared void, and amendment of the winding-up order made on his petition (which was perfected on 5th December 1979) by the addition of an order declaring that immediately before the winding up of the company the dissolution of the company was void. The company, the Official Solicitor and the Treasury Solicitor were the respondents to the second motion. The facts are set out in the judgment.

Richard Hacker for the petitioner.
John Lindsay for the Official Receiver.

Cur adv vult

16th January. **SLADE J** read the following judgment: There are before me two motions issued in somewhat unusual circumstances. In each of them the applicant is Mr M F J Thompson ('the petitioner') who is a contributory of a company known as Thompson & Riches Ltd. The first seeks a declaration under s 352(1) of the Companies Act 1948, that the dissolution of the company is void. The second seeks an order that the petitioner may be at liberty to amend a petition for the winding up of the company which was presented by him on 14th August 1979, and that a winding-up order made by the court in respect of the company and perfected on 5th December 1979 may be amended by the addition of an order that the dissolution of the company may be declared void immediately prior to its winding up.

The company has been struck off the register of companies and dissolved by virtue of s 353(5) of the 1948 Act. For ease of subsequent reference, I shall begin by setting out the relevant statutory provisions. Section 353(5), so far as material for present purposes, provides:

> 'At the expiration of the time mentioned in the notice the registrar may, unless cause to the contrary is previously shown by the company, strike its name off the register, and shall publish notice thereof in the Gazette, and on the publication in the Gazette of this notice the company shall be dissolved: Provided that ... (b) nothing in this subsection shall affect the power of the court to wind up a company the name of which has been struck off the register.'

Section 352(1) of the 1948 Act provides:

> 'Where a company has been dissolved, the court may at any time within two years of the date of the dissolution, on an application being made for the purpose by the liquidator of the company or by any other person who appears to the court to be interested, make an order, upon such terms as the court thinks fit, declaring the dissolution to have been void, and thereupon such proceedings may be taken as might have been taken if the company had not been dissolved.'

Section 353(6) provides:

> 'If a company or any member or creditor thereof feels aggrieved by the company having been struck off the register, the court on an application made by the company or member or creditor before the expiration of twenty years from the publication in the Gazette of the notice aforesaid may, if satisfied that the company was at the time of the striking off carrying on business or in operation, or otherwise that it is just that the company be restored to the register, order the name of the company to be restored to the register, and upon an office copy of the order being delivered to the registrar for registration the company shall be deemed to have continued in existence as if its name had not been struck off; and the court may by the order give such directions and make such provisions as seem just for placing the company and all other persons in the same position as nearly as may be as if the name of the company had not been struck off.'

Finally, section 354 provides:

> 'Where a company is dissolved, all property and rights whatsoever vested in or held on trust for the company immediately before its dissolution (including leasehold property but not including property held by the company on trust for any other person) shall, subject and without prejudice to any order which may at any time be made by the court under the two last foregoing sections, be deemed to be bona vacantia and shall accordingly belong to the Crown, or to the Duchy of Lancaster or to the Duke of Cornwall for the time being, as the case may be, and shall vest and may be dealt with in the same manner as other bona vacantia accruing to the Crown, to the Duchy of Lancaster or to the Duke of Cornwall.'

In the present case the company was incorporated in March 1965 under the Companies Act 1948 as a private company limited by shares. Its nominal capital is £15,000 divided into 15,000 shares of £1 each. The amount of its capital paid up or credited as paid up is £14,600. The petitioner holds 5,000 fully paid-up shares in the company, of which he holds one as the administrator of his late mother. According to his evidence, he has never been an active participant in the business of the company. The history of the matter up to 22nd February 1978 is conveniently summarised as follows in paras 7 to 13 of the winding-up petition, which the petitioner has verified on oath:

'7. The company was formed to carry on the business of retail dealers in milk. The company ceased to carry on business in or about early 1973. It has not carried on business since and it would appear unlikely that it will ever resume business. 8. Certain of the milk rounds which were the company's undertaking were sold on or about the 9th day of March 1973, the 8th day of April 1974, and the 12th day of March 1975, for £5,000, £3,500 and £5,033 respectively. The company has sold and/or is in the process of selling off its commercial vehicles. 9. No annual return has been made by the company under section 124 of the Companies Act 1948 since the return for 1973, which said return was made up to the 10th day of May, 1973. The annual returns of the company for the years 1970, 1971 and 1972 were, however, made up to the end of December or thereabouts of each said year. 10. The company has failed to hold annual general meetings since in or about 1973 or has failed to give your petitioner notice of any such meetings as may have been held. 11. On numerous occasions in 1975, 1976 and 1977 your petitioner made written and oral requests by himself and by his solicitors to directors of the company for information about the general and financial position of the company and of the application of proceeds of sale of the company's undertaking. The company has failed or omitted to furnish any or any adequate information and has not made up accounts to any date later than 31st January 1972. 12. On the 22nd day of February 1978 your petitioner gave notice that he required to be allowed to inspect the register of, and copies of instruments creating, charges over the company, and books containing the minutes of the proceedings of any general meetings of the company, to be sent copies of certain said documents, and that he required the directors to hold an extraordinary general meeting under section 132 of the Companies Act 1948. 13. On the 22nd day of February 1978 the petitioner's agent was informed by one W Joice, a director of the company, that all documents referred to in paragraph 12 hereof had been destroyed by fire, and the company has failed to provide your petitioner with copies of them. The directors have failed to hold the extraordinary general meeting referred to in paragraph 12 hereof, or have failed to give your petitioner notice of any such meeting.'

On the basis of these facts the petitioner presented a winding-up petition to the court on 14th August 1979. Some months before that date, the Registrar of Companies had taken steps with a view to the dissolution of the company under the powers conferred on him by s 353 of the 1948 Act, enabling him to take action in regard to defunct companies. The petitioner and his solicitors had no knowledge that such steps had been taken. On 21st August 1979 the company was dissolved under s 353(5) of the 1948 Act. The fact of the dissolution still did not for the time being come to the notice of the petitioner or his solicitors. He therefore proceeded with his winding-up petition in the ordinary way.

In a situation such as this, there is no procedure by which, before the making of a winding-up order, the court will gain knowledge of a prior dissolution of the company concerned, unless this is brought to its attention by the parties. Accordingly on 12th November 1979, no doubt in ignorance of the prior dissolution, Oliver J made the usual compulsory winding-up order in respect of the company under which, inter alia, one of the official receivers attached to the court was constituted provisional liquidator of the company's affairs.

In the absence of any authority, it might perhaps have appeared open to possible question whether the court had power to wind up a company the name of which had previously been struck off the register. The existence of such power is, however, clearly recognised both by statute and at least one reported decision of the court. Section 353(5)(b) of the 1948 Act expressly provides that 'nothing in this subsection shall affect the power of the court to wind up a company the name of which has been struck off the register'. Furthermore, in *Re Cambridge Coffee Room Association Ltd* [1952] 1 All ER 112 the name of a company limited by guarantee had been struck off the register of a companies and the company itself had been dissolved pursuant to s 353(5). Subsequently two of the directors presented a petition to the court asking (i) that the name of the company might be restored to the register pursuant to s 353(6) and (ii) that the company might be wound up. Wynn-Parry J in his judgment pointed out that the only question for decision was whether or not it was more convenient to restore the name of the company to the register before making a winding-up order. He said (at 112):

b   'In my judgment, it is more convenient to do so, but I do not intend to cast doubt on past cases where a compulsory winding-up order has been made without the name of the company having been restored to the register.'

In these circumstances I conclude that the winding-up order of 12th November 1979 was a valid order, even though the name of the company had not previously been restored to the register, and I shall for the rest of this judgment proceed on that footing.

c   However, before leaving *Re Cambridge Coffee Room Association Ltd*, it should be observed that Wynn-Parry J reached his decision because he considered that doubt existed whether a compulsory winding-up order alone would amount to an order 'made by the court under the two last foregoing sections', within the meaning of s 354 of the 1948 Act, so as to divest the Crown of the interest in the company's assets which the Crown would otherwise have under that section, and so as to revest it in the company (see at 114). The d essential purpose of the present applications is to resolve the difficulties that would otherwise arise from the existence of such doubt.

After the making of the winding-up order in the present case, the registrar of the court sent to the Official Receiver a notice informing him of it, pursuant to r 38 of the Companies (Winding-Up) Rules 1949, SI 1949 No 330. As is his practice, the Official Receiver then proceeded to check the facts asserted in the petition. This, as in other e similar cases, was the first independent investigation of these facts. During the course of it, he discovered that the company had been dissolved on 21st August 1979, that is after the date of the presentation of the petition but before the making of the winding-up order. Counsel who has appeared on his behalf tells me on instructions that, where the Official Receiver, during the investigations following the making of a winding-up order, discovers that the company in question has already been dissolved before the making of f such order, it is his practice to communicate this information both to the court and to the petitioner's solicitors. He tells me on instructions that this was done in the present case.

The evidence sworn on behalf of the petitioner in support of his present application suggested that neither he nor his solicitors knew of the dissolution until after the winding-up order was perfected. However, counsel for the petitioner now tells me that his instructing solicitors, after a further search of their files, have discovered that the g Official Receiver in fact informed them of the dissolution on or about 15th November 1979, that is about three weeks before the perfection of the winding-up order.

Following such communication, the course ordinarily adopted by petitioners in such cases (which I think are not uncommon) is to come to the court as soon as possible before the winding-up order is perfected, for the purpose of ensuring that the company's assets are vested in it and not in the Crown, and that the liquidator will be able effectively to h act as such. If a petitioner follows the common practice which has been adopted in the light of the decision in *Re Cambridge Coffee Room Association Ltd* he will ask for (1) rescission of the existing winding-up order, (2) liberty to amend his petition, so as to include an application for restoration of the name of the company to the register, (3) an order for such restoration, and (4) a new winding-up order. In my experience this course usually gives rise to few difficulties.

Regrettably, I think, for reasons which are not entirely clear to me, this was not the course adopted by the petitioner's legal advisers in the present case. This is the factor which makes it an unusual one. Instead, without making any further application to the court, they allowed the winding-up order to be perfected in the ordinary way and in the common form on 5th December 1979. The subsequent course of events, so far as material for present purposes, was as follows. On 22nd August 1980 the petitioner

issued the first notice of motion which is now before me, seeking a declaration that the
dissolution of the company is void, the notice being addressed to the Official Receiver as *a*
respondent. This motion came on for hearing for the first time on 20th October.
Counsel for the petitioner has reminded me that, earlier that day, I made an order in a
somewhat similar case, Re Pritchway Ltd (unreported), granting relief to a petitioner by
way of an amendment of a winding-up order under the 'slip rule' (RSC Ord 20, r 11). I
recollect making some such order, but do not recall any other particulars of the case.

On 20th October counsel for the petitioner in the present case informed me that the *b*
notice of motion had not yet been served on the Official Receiver. He asked for, and
obtained, an adjournment of 28 days for the purpose of such service, and of considering
whether relief should be sought in the alternative under the slip rule.

On 11th November the petitioner issued the second notice of motion which is now
before me. The persons named as respondents to it are the company, the Official
Receiver and the Treasury Solicitor. It seeks liberty for the petitioner to amend the *c*
petition in accordance with the terms of the draft annexed to it, and an order that the
winding-up order may be amended by the addition of an order that the dissolution of the
company may be declared void immediately prior to its winding up.

On 17th November both motions came before me, and the Official Receiver appeared
for the first time, on this occasion in person. I then suggested to him, in effect, that,
because the points raised by the motions raised points of law and practice which appeared *d*
to be somewhat novel, and not without difficulty, and because my decision might affect
similar cases in the future with which he might be concerned, he might like to consider
instructing counsel. As a result, on his application, the motions were adjourned, without
opposition from the petitioner. Counsel appeared for the Official Receiver on their final
hearing last Monday, 12th January. He has given me very valuable assistance for which
I am grateful. *e*

I shall deal first with the first motion. As Megarry J said in Re Test Holdings (Clifton) Ltd
[1969] 3 All ER 517 at 518, [1970] Ch 285 at 287:

'Prima facie the appropriate mode of proceeding in respect of a company struck
off under s. 353 [of the Companies Act 1948] is by an application under s. 353(6).'

The declaration sought by the petitioner in the first motion is sought not under that *f*
subsection but under s 352(1). In the last-mentioned case it was submitted, inter alia,
that any application which can be made under s 353(6) ought to be made under that
subsection, even if it could also be made under s 352(1). Megarry J rejected this
argument. As he said ([1969] 3 All ER 517 at 518, [1970] Ch 285 at 288):

'If on the true construction of the Act the applicant is entitled to proceed under
either subsection, it is not for the court to say that he ought to have proceeded under *g*
what that court considers to be the more suitable subsection instead of under what
the court considers to be the less suitable subsection. It would be wrong for the
courts to seek to take away a choice which the legislature has decided that the
applicant should have.'

In the light of that decision counsel for the Official Receiver accepted that the petitioner
in the present case could not properly be criticised for applying to the court under *h*
s 352(1) rather than adopting the alternative course, which he submitted would have
been open to the petitioner, that is an application under s 353(6). Furthermore, he
accepted, in my judgment correctly, that s 352(1) by its terms gives the court the
jurisdiction to make the order which is sought by the first motion. The application has
been duly made within two years of the date of the dissolution. It is made by a person
who is manifestly 'interested' within the subsection, as being a contributory of the
company. *j*

Megarry J in Re Test Holdings (Clifton) Ltd held that where it is sought under s 352(1) to
revive a company which has been struck off under s 353, but which is not in liquidation,

the Registrar of Companies ought normally to be made a respondent to the notice of
motion, to this extent assimilating the practice to that under s 353(6). Megarry J,
however, expressly excepted from this general statement of principle other applications
under s 352(1) (see [1969] 3 All ER 517 at 522, [1970] Ch 285 at 292).

I myself can see no factors which ordinarily would make the joinder of the Registrar
of Companies necessary, either in his own or in the public interest, in a case where the
company concerned is already in liquidation. I accept the submission of counsel for the
Official Receiver that his joinder is not necessary in the present case.

The Treasury Solicitor has written a letter stating in effect that no objection is taken on
his behalf to the grant of the declaration sought, so that no difficulty arises on account of
the Crown's possible interest.

Accordingly, the question on the first motion resolves itself into one for the court's
discretion. In the particular circumstances, counsel for the Official Receiver has told me
that the Official Receiver does not feel able to resist the making of the order sought on
this motion. If and when it is made, the Official Receiver will be in a position for the
first time effectively to exercise his functions without any doubt as to his powers in
regard to the company's assets. Furthermore, on the particular facts, I am told he will be
able to do so without embarrassment, particularly since the company ceased trading
many years ago.

In all the circumstances, I can see no remaining obstacle to the making of the order
sought on the first motion and I propose to make such order. This makes it unnecessary
to consider the second motion, and I do not propose to do so. I should, however, mention
that, in relation to that motion, counsel for the Official Receiver submitted that on the
particular facts of the present case, the court would have no jurisdiction to make the
order sought, essentially on the grounds that the slip rule cannot apply in relation to the
winding-up order, because, though the court which made it was under a misapprehension
of fact, the order made by it duly gave effect to its actual intention, which was to wind
up the company.

Before leaving the substance of the matter I would make these observations. First,
although the petitioner has now succeeded in obtaining relief under s 352(1), even
though the winding-up order was perfected many months ago, it should not be
concluded that such relief will always be available for the asking in any similar case in the
future. The court is given a discretion by s 352(1). I conceive that circumstances could
arise in which it would feel bound to refuse to exercise its discretion even in favour of a
petitioner who brought himself within the wording of the subsection, for example, if
there were to be opposition to the application on reasonable grounds by the Official
Receiver or the Treasury Solicitor, or other persons. Particularly in view of the risk of
potential embarrassment to the Official Receiver, which may increase the longer the
period of uncertainty subsists, a petitioner who seeks relief under s 352 or s 353 in a case
such as the present, after a winding-up order has been made, should, in my judgment,
apply to the court promptly, as soon as reasonably practicable after he becomes aware of
the dissolution. If, as will normally be the case, he becomes so aware before the winding-
up order has been perfected, he will still be well advised, without any delay and before
the winding-up order is perfected, to apply to the court for relief, in accordance with the
common practice adopted in the light of the decision in Re Cambridge Coffee Room
Association Ltd; I have outlined the form of appropriate relief earlier in this judgment.
If he fails to take this course, he could be faced with much greater difficulties on a
subsequent application.

Second, I have already referred to the possible difficulties which could face the Official
Receiver during the awkward twilight period occurring after the making of a winding-
up order but before the making of any order under s 352 or s 353, and, indeed, after the
latter order has been made, particularly if it was long delayed. I conceive that he himself
might well have the locus standi to make an application under s 352(1), though not
s 353, as being a 'person interested' within the former subsection. However, in all but
the most exceptional cases, the primary responsibility for making any such application

will, I conceive, fall on the petitioner rather than the Official Receiver. If the petitioner wishes practical effect to be given to the winding-up order obtained at his instance, it will *a* ordinarily be incumbent on him to take all necessary steps to enable this to be done. If, however, he is in any doubt as to the course which he should adopt, the Official Receiver can always apply to the court for directions under s 246(3), as indeed, I understand, he did in the present case.

It remains to consider the matter of costs which has already been argued before me. In my judgment, the fair order in all the circumstances will be that the petitioner pay the *b* Official Receiver's costs of both motions, other than the costs of the adjourned hearing on 12th January, as to which there will be no order. There will be no further order on the second motion. On the first motion there will be an order that the dissolution of the company is void. I propose also to give the petitioner, and any other creditor or contributory of the company, liberty to apply. It will be the duty of the petitioner to deliver to the Registrar of Companies, for registration, an office copy of the order under *c* s 352: see sub-s (2). I propose, however, to extend the time for such delivery to 21 days from the making of this order.

[After discussion his Lordship continued:] I say nothing as to the course which should be followed by the court on a similar application in the future, in the light of my present judgment. But, on the particular facts of this case, I do not think that there is sufficient justification for making an order against the petitioner more burdensome than an order *d* on the ordinary party-and-party basis, and that is the order which I propose to make.

[After further discussion his Lordship continued:] I have now heard further argument in relation to the question of costs at the instance of counsel for the Official Receiver. Among the points which he has made is one that seems to me important but was not, I think, made when the matter was previously argued before me. It is this. If the Official Receiver had chosen to instruct counsel at the hearing on 17th November 1980, the *e* petitioner could not reasonably have submitted that such instruction of counsel was unnecessary, in the light of the difficult problems of law and practice posed by the existence of the two alternative notices of motion. Furthermore, if the Official Receiver had instructed counsel for the hearing on 17th November 1980, and, immediately following the hearing, the petitioner had obtained the relief which, in the event, he has obtained under the first motion, he would doubtless have been ordered to pay the costs *f* of the Official Receiver of both motions, such costs, as a matter of course, to include the costs incurred by the Official Receiver in instructing counsel.

On this hypothesis, counsel for the Official Receiver does not, I think, dispute that, because the Official Receiver did not in fact instruct counsel on 17th November and then sought an adjournment for this purpose, it might be right that he should have to pay the costs of the petitioner thrown away by the adjournment. Subject to this, however, *g* counsel submits that the proper order in all the circumstances is that the petitioner should pay the Official Receiver's costs of both motions.

It appears to me that counsel's new submissions in this context are well founded and that accordingly, in the exercise of the court's discretion, the proper order to make in relation to costs is that envisaged in his argument, namely first, that the Official Receiver should pay the petitioner's costs occasioned by the adjournment of the hearing from 17th *h* November 1980 to 12th January 1981, but that subject to this, the petitioner should pay the Official Receiver's costs of both motions on a party and party basis.

Declaration accordingly.

Solicitors: *Turner, Peacock,* agents for *Basil D Laitner & Smythe,* Sheffield (for the petitioner); *Treasury Solicitor.*

Jacqueline Metcalfe   Barrister.

Great Atlantic Insurance Co v Home Insurance Co and others

COURT OF APPEAL, CIVIL DIVISION

TEMPLEMAN AND DUNN LJJ

14th, 15th, 28th JANUARY 1981

Discovery – Privilege – Waiver of privilege – Disclosure of part of document in open court – Whether disclosure waiving privilege in respect of rest of document.

The plaintiffs, who were insurers, entered into reinsurance agreements with the defendants who later repudiated the agreements. The plaintiffs brought an action against the defendants claiming a declaration that the defendants were bound by the agreements. When preparing their case the plaintiffs received a memorandum from their American attorneys relating to the action. The first two paragraphs of the memorandum consisted of an account of a discussion between the attorneys and a third party and in the course of discovery before trial the plaintiffs' solicitors disclosed only those two paragraphs of the memorandum. The solicitors intended to claim privilege for the remainder but omitted to do so. At the trial the plaintiffs' counsel read out in open court the first two paragraphs of the memorandum under the impression that it was complete as it stood. When counsel on both sides became aware some days later that the memorandum as read out was incomplete, the defendants' counsel asked for disclosure of the additional matter on the ground that even if the whole document was privileged the disclosure of part of it to the court amounted to a waiver of privilege. The judge upheld that claim and the plaintiffs appealed.

Held – (1) Even though the first two paragraphs of the memorandum contained information obtained by the American attorneys from a third party the whole of the memorandum was privileged since the memorandum itself was a communication between solicitor and client. Furthermore, the memorandum dealt throughout with the same subject matter and it was therefore not possible for the plaintiffs to sever the document by claiming privilege for part and waiving privilege for the remainder (see p 489, *a b*, p 490 *d* to *j*, p 492 *g* to *j* and p 494 *h j*, post); *Churton v Frewen* (1865) 2 Drew & Sm 390, *Wilson v Northampton and Banbury Junction Railway Co* (1872) LR 14 Eq 477 and *Wheeler v Le Marchant* (1881) 17 Ch D 675 applied.

(2) However, the introduction by the plaintiffs of part of the memorandum into the trial record waived privilege in regard to the whole document, since a party was not entitled to disclose only those parts of a document that were to his advantage, and both the court and the opposing party were entitled to know whether the material released from privilege represented the whole of the material relevant to the issue in question. The fact that the waiver had been made by the plaintiffs' counsel without the plaintiffs agreeing to it was irrelevant, since counsel had ostensible authority to bind the plaintiffs in any matter arising in, or incidental to, the litigation, and when counsel introduced into the record part of the document he thereby effectively waived any privilege attaching to the document that could be asserted by the plaintiffs. The whole of the memorandum was therefore required to be disclosed, and the plaintiffs' appeal would be dismissed (see p 492 *j* and p 494 *a* and *h j*, post); *Matthews v Munster* [1886–90] AELR Rep 251, *Goldstone v Williams, Deacon & Co* [1899] 1 Ch 47, dictum of Denning LJ in *Griffiths v Evans* [1953] 2 All ER at 1371 and *Burnell v British Transport Commission* [1955] 3 All ER 822 applied.

Notes

For legal professional privilege in respect of communications between a legal adviser and his client and for waiver of that privilege, see 13 Halsbury's Laws (4th Edn) paras 71–76, 84, and for cases on the subject, see 18 Digest (Reissue) 105–115, 163, 774–874, 1303–1308.

Cases referred to in judgments

Anderson v Bank of British Columbia (1876) 2 Ch D 644, [1874–80] All ER Rep 396, 45 LJ *a*
Ch 449, 35 LT 76, 3 Char Pr Cas 212, CA, 18 Digest (Reissue) 114, 867.

Ashburton (Lord) v Pape [1913] 2 Ch 469, [1911–13] All ER Rep 708, 82 LJ Ch 527, 109
LT 381, CA, 22 Digest (Reissue) 236, 2033.

Belsham v Harrison (1846) 15 LJ Ch 438, 10 Jur 772, sub nom *Belcham v Percival* 7 LTOS
300, 18 Digest (Reissue) 109, 818.

Burnell v British Transport Commission [1955] 3 All ER 822, [1956] 1 QB 187, [1956] 2 *b*
WLR 61, [1955] Lloyd's Rep 549, CA, 22 Digest (Reissue) 513, 5215.

Butler v Board of Trade [1970] 3 All ER 593, [1971] Ch 680, [1970] 3 WLR 822, 22 Digest
(Reissue) 454, 4524.

Buttes Gas and Oil Co v Hammer (No 3) [1980] 3 All ER 475, [1980] 3 WLR 668, CA.

Causton v Mann Egerton (Johnsons) Ltd [1974] 1 All ER 453, [1974] 1 WLR 162, [1974] 1
Lloyd's Rep 197, CA, 18 Digest (Reissue) 126, 962.   *c*

Churton v Frewen (1865) 2 Drew & Sm 390, 12 LT 105, 62 ER 669, 18 Digest (Reissue)
169, 1371.

Doland (George) Ltd v Blackburn Robson Coates & Co (a firm) [1972] 3 All ER 959, [1972] 1
WLR 1338, 22 Digest (Reissue) 456, 4557.

Goldstone v Williams, Deacon & Co [1899] 1 Ch 47, 68 LJ Ch 24, 79 LT 373, 18 Digest
(Reissue) 103, 764.   *d*

Griffiths v Evans [1953] 2 All ER 1364, [1953] 1 WLR 1424, CA, 43 Digest (Repl) 116,
1050.

Lyell v Kennedy (No 3) (1884) 27 Ch D 1, [1881–5] All ER Rep 814, 53 LJ Ch 937, 50 LT
730, CA, 18 Digest (Reissue) 59, 404.

Macfarlan v Rolt (1872) LR 14 Eq 580, 41 LJ Ch 649, 27 LT 305, 18 Digest (Reissue) 107,
796.   *e*

Matthews v Munster (1887) 20 QBD 141, [1886–90] All ER Rep 251, 57 LJQB 49, 57 LT
922, 52 JP 260, CA, 3 Digest (Reissue) 766, 4654.

Minter v Priest [1930] AC 558, [1930] All ER Rep 431, 99 LJKB 391, 143 LT 57, HL, 22
Digest (Reissue) 449, 4474.

Nea Karteria Maritime Co Ltd v Atlantic and Great Lakes Steamship Corpn (11th December
1978, unreported), QBD.   *f*

Procter v Smiles (1886) 55 LJQB 527, CA, 18 Digest (Reissue) 249, 1963.

Wheeler v Le Marchant (1881) 17 Ch D 675, 50 LJ Ch 793, 44 LT 632, 45 JP 728, CA, 18
Digest (Reissue) 99, 741.

Wilson v Northampton and Banbury Junction Railway Co (1872) LR 14 Eq 477, 27 LT 507,
18 Digest (Reissue) 117, 901.

g

Cases also cited

Calcraft v Guest [1898] 1 QB 759, [1895–9] All ER Rep 346.

Cameron's Coalbrook etc Railway Co (1857) 25 Beav 1, 53 ER 535.

Davis v Spurling (1829) 1 Russ & M 64, 39 ER 25.

Humpherey v Humpherey and Wake (1917) 33 TLR 433.

Jones v Jones [1970] 3 All ER 47, [1970] 2 QB 576, CA.   *h*

Lodge v Prichard (1851) 4 De G & Sm 587, 64 ER 969.

Prince v Samo (1838) 7 Ad & El 627, 112 ER 606.

Randle v Blackburn (1813) 5 Taunt 245, 128 ER 683.

Science Research Council v Nassé, BL Cars Ltd (formerly Leyland Cars) v Vyas [1979] 3 All ER
673, [1980] AC 1028, HL.

Waugh v British Railways Board [1979] 2 All ER 1169, [1980] AC 521, HL.   *j*

Interlocutory appeal

The plaintiffs, Great Atlantic Insurance Co, appealed against the order of Lloyd J made on
16th December 1980 granting, inter alia, an application by the third defendants, C E
Heath & Co (International) Ltd, for disclosure of a document for which the plaintiffs
claimed privilege. The facts are set out in the judgment of Templeman LJ.

Patrick Phillips QC and *Paul Walker* for the plaintiffs.
a *Johan Steyn QC* and *Jeffrey Gruder* for the third defendants.

At the conclusion of the arguments Templeman LJ announced that the appeal would be dismissed for reasons to be given later.

28th January. The following judgments were read.

b
TEMPLEMAN LJ. This is an appeal from an order made by Lloyd J on the fourteenth day of a trial which is still progressing whereby he ordered the plaintiffs to give discovery of parts of a memorandum for which the plaintiffs claim privilege. In granting leave to appeal the judge made observations deprecating any appeal in the course of a trial but he considered that he was constrained in the exceptional circumstances to grant leave. I
c agree wholeheartedly that appeals in the course of a trial should be firmly prevented or discouraged save in the most exceptional circumstances. Such appeals cause difficulties for the litigants, for the trial judge and for this court. In the present case, for example, this court has been inevitably hampered, notwithstanding the assistance of experienced counsel, by a necessarily brief and incomplete recital of the facts, some of which remain in dispute, and by the necessity for a speedy resolution of this appeal. I intend no
d criticism. Indeed it is a credit to all concerned that the plaintiffs' cause of action in a matter of great complexity with large sums of money at stake only arose on 11th June 1980 and trial of the action began before Lloyd J on 24th November 1980.

By an underwriting agency agreement dated 2nd June 1977 the second defendants, Afia, authorised the third defendants, C E Heath & Co (International) Ltd ('Heath'), to enter into reinsurance agreements as agents for and on behalf of the first defendants,
e Home Insurance Co ('Home'). In November 1977, in exercise or in purported exercise of their authority, Heath entered into an agreement with the plaintiffs, Great Atlantic Insurance Co, who are insurers, and the fourth to eighth defendants, who are companies carrying on marine insurance broking business under the inspiration of a Mr Elger. The agreement of 1977 was replaced by a quota share marine and aviation reinsurance agreement dated 9th January 1978 whereby marine insurance sought by clients of and
f negotiated by Elger and his companies would be accepted by the plaintiffs while Home would reinsure to the extent of 90% of the risk. On 29th March 1978 Heath confirmed to the plaintiffs that the reinsurance agreement made on 9th January 1978 was effective and was binding on Home by reason of the authority vested in Heath by the underwriting agency agreement dated 2nd June 1977.

In 1980 the plaintiffs became worried about the results of insurance business negotiated
g by Elger, accepted by the plaintiffs and reinsured by Home. The plaintiffs sent out an insurance expert, a Mr Alexander, to investigate Elger's business, and he made a written report commenting very adversely on the conduct and results of Elger's business. This report is not a document for which privilege against disclosure in legal proceedings can be claimed by the plaintiffs or has been claimed by the plaintiffs.

About the same time as he made his report, Mr Alexander orally reported the results
h of his investigation and discussed the results of his visit to Elger's offices with a representative of the firm of American attorneys who were acting for the plaintiffs as their lawyers. No privilege can be claimed for what Mr Alexander said to the American representative because litigation was not at the time in prospect in the present proceedings: see *Wheeler v Le Marchant* (1881) 17 Ch D 675. Heath could for example subpoena Mr Alexander and the American representative to give evidence of what was
j said between them.

By a memorandum dated 2nd May 1980 the American attorneys wrote to the plaintiffs setting out in the first two paragraphs of that memorandum an account of the discussions between Mr Alexander and the representative of the American attorneys. The memorandum then continued with additional matter which, according to the sworn affidavit of a partner in the plaintiffs' English firm of solicitors, dealt with 'questions of strategy affecting both the Elger and Marlow matters'. For present purposes the 'Marlow matters' need no explanation; they are connected with the difficulties which had arisen over the Elger matters.

In this appeal the plaintiffs argue that the first two paragraphs of the memorandum are not privileged because they are merely an account of a discussion which was itself not privileged. They argue that the additional matter was privileged. Heath claim that the whole of the memorandum was privileged and that the privilege has been waived in the circumstances which I shall shortly narrate and that Heath are entitled to see the whole of the memorandum including the additional matter for which privilege is asserted. The judge agreed with Heath.

In June 1980 Home and Afia repudiated the 1977 reinsurance agreement and also the substituted reinsurance agreement dated 9th January 1978. Home and Afia denied that Heath had authority to bind either Home or Afia to the 1978 agreement. The plaintiffs in the present proceedings are seeking a declaration that both Home and Afia are bound by the 1977 and 1978 agreements. If the plaintiffs fail in any respect because Heath did not possess the necessary authority to bind Home and Afia, then in the same action the plaintiffs seek damages from Heath for breach of warranty of authority.

It is part of Heath's reamended defence that the plaintiffs connived with Home and Afia in connection with the repudiation by Home and Afia of the 1977 and 1978 reinsurance agreements. The report by Mr Alexander and the memorandum from the plaintiffs' American attorneys dated 2nd May 1980 are said to be relevant to this defence in that they support the plaintiffs' case as to the reason for a meeting held in London in June 1980 between representatives of the plaintiffs and Afia at which it is said by Heath that the connivance between the plaintiffs and Home and Afia took place.

The plaintiffs' English solicitors intended to give discovery of the first two paragraphs of the memorandum dated 2nd May 1980 and intended to claim privilege for the additional matter contained in that memorandum. The plaintiffs' solicitors did not intend and the plaintiffs did not intend to waive any privilege in respect of any document. By mishap, no doubt due to the speed with which this litigation has been conducted, the plaintiffs' solicitors failed to claim privilege or to make clear that they were claiming privilege in respect of the additional matter contained in the memorandum. The plaintiffs' solicitors, however, only provided to the defendants and for use in the trial copies of the memorandum limited to the first two paragraphs and excluded the additional matter for which privilege was intended to be claimed and is now claimed. In the result none of the defendants are aware of the contents and terms of the additional matter.

In the course of his opening speech in the first days of the trial which began on 24th November 1980 the plaintiffs' counsel read to the judge in open court the first two paragraphs of the memorandum dated 2nd May 1980 which formed part of a bundle of agreed documents. At that stage the plaintiffs' counsel was not aware that the two paragraphs represented only part of the contents of the memorandum and he had no knowledge of the additional matter and he had no intention of waiving privilege in respect of the whole or part of the memorandum or any other privileged document.

A few days later the plaintiffs' counsel and Heath's counsel discovered that the memorandum as read to the judge was incomplete and did not include the additional matter which the plaintiffs' solicitors believed to be privileged and for which they intended to claim privilege. Heath's counsel on behalf of Heath asked for disclosure of the additonal matter on the grounds that part of a document having been put before the court by the plaintiffs Heath were entitled to see the whole of the document whether or not that document had originally been privileged. The plaintiffs declined to disclose the additional matter in the memorandum on the grounds that the first two paragraphs were not priviliged and had been disclosed for that reason, but that the additional matter was privileged and that privilege had not been waived. Lloyd J decided in favour of Heath, and ordered disclosure of the whole of the memorandum. With leave of the judge, the plaintiffs appeal to this court.

The first question is whether the whole of the memorandum dated 2nd May 1980 was privileged or, as the plaintiffs' English solicitors thought, the first two paragraphs were

not privileged and therefore were bound to be disclosed. In my judgment, the whole of
a the memorandum was privileged because it was a communication by the plaintiffs'
American attorneys to the plaintiffs relating to a matter, namely the Elger matter, on
which the American attorneys were instructed to act as legal advisers to the plaintiffs.
The fact that the memorandum included an account of a conversation between Mr
Alexander and a representative of the American attorneys, which conversation was not
privileged, does not alter the confidentiality attaching to the memorandum as a whole by
b virtue of the relationship between the American attorneys in their capacity as legal
advisers and the plaintiffs in their capacity as clients of those legal advisers.

In *Anderson v Bank of British Columbia* (1876) 2 Ch D 644 at 658, [1874–80] All ER Rep
396 at 400 Mellish LJ drew a distinction between privileged communications between
solicitor and client and information which is obtained by a solicitor from a third party,
which information is not necessarily connected with litigation, is not obtained for the
c purpose of litigation and is not privileged.

In *Wheeler v Le Marchant* (1881) 17 Ch D 675 at 681 this distinction was affirmed.
Jessel MR said that information obtained by a solicitor from a third party was only
protected where it had 'come into existence after litigation commenced or in
contemplation . . .' But the protection afforded to communications between a solicitor
and his client is wider. The protection is applied and is, said Jessel MR (at 682):

d
> '. . . restricted to the obtaining the assistance of lawyers, as regards the conduct of
> litigation or the rights to property. It has never gone beyond the obtaining legal
> advice and assistance, and all things reasonably necessary in the shape of
> communication to the legal advisers are protected from production or discovery in
> order that that legal advice may be obtained safely and sufficiently . . . a
> communication with a solicitor for the purpose of obtaining legal advice is protected
e
> though it relates to a dealing which is not the subject of litigation, provided it be a
> communication made to the solicitor in that character and for that purpose . . . It
> is a rule established and maintained solely for the purpose of enabling a man to
> obtain legal advice with safety.'

Similarly Brett LJ said (at 683):

f
> 'The rule as to the non-production of communications between solicitor and
> client is a rule which has been established upon grounds of general or public
> policy. It is confined entirely to communications which take place for the purpose
> of obtaining legal advice from professional persons.'

In *Minter v Priest* [1930] AC 558, [1930] All ER Rep 431 the House of Lords affirmed
g that a communication between a solicitor and his client is privileged provided that the
relationship of solicitor and client is established and that the communication is such as
'within a very wide and generous ambit of interpretation, must be fairly referable to the
relationship . . .' (see [1930] AC 558 at 568, [1930] All ER Rep 431 at 434 per Lord
Buckmaster).

The clearest authority relevant to the present point is to be found in *Wilson v*
h *Northampton and Banbury Junction Railway Co* (1872) LR 14 Eq 477 where in a specific
performance action the plaintiffs sought disclosure of, inter alia, correspondence between
the defendants and their solicitors subsequent to the contract but previous to the
commencement of litigation and before the litigation was in contemplation. Malins V-C
in his judgment said (at 482–483):

j
> 'I think cases of this kind are better decided upon principle. Here is a contract
> entered into which has led to litigation, and how is it possible for anybody to point
> out the precise moment between the date of the contract and the filing of the bill
> when the dispute arose? . . . It is of the highest importance . . . that all
> communications between a solicitor and his client upon a subject which may lead
> to litigation should be privileged, and I think the Court is bound to consider that
> . . . almost any contract entered into between man and man . . . may lead to
> litigation before the contract is completed. Any correspondence passing between

the date of the contract which afterwards becomes the subject of litigation and the
litigation itself is, in my opinion, on principle, within the privilege extended to the *a*
non-production of communications between solicitors and clients . . . it is absolutely
essential to the interests of mankind that a person should be free to consult his
solicitor upon anything which arises out of a contract which may lead to litigation;
that the communications should be perfectly free, so that the client may write to the
solicitor, and the solicitor to the client, without the slightest apprehension that those
communications will be produced if litigation should afterwards arise on the subject *b*
to which the correspondence relates.'

Finally (at 484) Mallins V-C repeated the principle that—

'all correspondence between solicitors and clients relating to the subject-matter of
a contract which has been entered into, and which may lead to litigation—whether
it has done so or may do so, whether it is probable or improbable that it will do so— *c*
ought certainly to be privileged.'

In the present case the correspondence between the American attorneys and the
plaintiffs related to the Elger matter and to the reinsurance contract which had been
entered into and which, as history relates, have led to litigation. Such correspondence
'ought certainly to be privileged'.   *d*

In the present case the relationship of solicitor and client between the American
attorneys and the plaintiffs is undoubted. The plaintiffs were seeking and the American
attorneys were proffering advice in connection with a business transaction. The fact that
litigation was not then contemplated is irrelevant. This appeal may serve a useful
purpose if it reminds the profession that all communications between solicitor and client
where the solicitor is acting as a solicitor are privileged subject to exceptions to prevent *e*
fraud and crime and to protect the client and that the privilege should only be waived
with great caution. This principle applies equally to communications between a client
and his foreign lawyers or attorneys (see *Macfarlan v Rolt* (1872) LR 14 Eq 580).

The second question is whether, the whole of the memorandum being a privileged
communication between legal adviser and client, the plaintiff may waive the privilege
with regard to the first two paragraphs of the memorandum but assert privilege over the *f*
additional matter. In my judgment severance would be possible if the memorandum
dealt with entirely different subject matters or different incidents and could in effect be
divided into two separate memoranda each dealing with a separate subject matter. The
judge with the experience of 14 days of the trial and after reading the whole of the
memorandum came to the conclusion that the first two paragraphs of the memorandum
and the additional matter dealt with the same subject matter. Knowing far less about the *g*
circumstances, I would be slow to come to a different conclusion. Having read the whole
memorandum, I agree with him. Indeed the affidavit of the plaintiffs' English solicitors
makes this plain.

Counsel for the plaintiffs argued that severance is permissible where the part disclosed
is only an account of a discussion which itself is not privileged. But, once it is decided
that the memorandum deals with only one subject matter, it seems to me that it might *h*
be or appear dangerous or misleading to allow the plaintiffs to disclose part of the
memorandum and to assert privilege over the remainder. In the present case the
suspicions of Heath which have not unnaturally been aroused by the disclosure of only
part of the memorandum can only be justified or allayed by disclosing the whole. It
would be undesirable for severance to be allowed in these circumstances. In my
judgment, the simplest, safest and most straightforward rule is that if a document is *j*
privileged then privilege must be asserted, if at all, to the whole document unless the
document deals with separate subject matters so that the document can in effect be
divided into two separate and distinct documents each of which is complete.

Support for this simple method of dealing with the matter is to be found in *Churton v
Frewen* (1865) 2 Drew & Sm 390, 62 ER 669. In that case a privileged report contained
copies of, extracts from and references to documents and records which had been culled

from a public registry and for which no privilege could be asserted. The plaintiffs sought
a discovery of so much of the report as consisted of 'copies or abstracts from or references
to documents or records in the Bishop's Registry at Lewes . . .' Disclosure was refused on
the grounds stated that—

> *b* 'it would be very dangerous, and trench very much upon the principle which
> protects the report itself, if that were permitted; for it would be hardly possible to
> seal up and effectually protect from inspection those parts which constitute the
> report, and which it is admitted there is no right to see. Such a report would most
> probably (indeed, from its nature, almost necessarily) be not merely a collection of
> extracts from, and copies of, ancient records, with a distinct and separate report
> referring to them; but the extracts and copies would be so interspersed with . . .
> observations and comments . . . as to render it quite impossible to separate the
> different portions.'

c

(See 2 Drew & Sm 390 at 394, 62 ER 669 at 671).

It is true that in the present case the first two paragraphs can be divided from the
remainder of the memorandum but they deal with the same subject matter. Waiver of
part of a document is bound to lead to grave difficulties for all parties and to many
unjustified suspicions.

d   Counsel for the plaintiffs relied on *Belsham v Harrison* (1846) 15 LJ Ch 438. In that case
the personal representative of a deceased defendant filed a defence referring to a draft
answer prepared for the deceased and setting out parts of the contents of the draft
answer. The plaintiffs were refused disclosure of the whole of the draft answer. No
reasons were given for the decision which may be bound up with the niceties of
pleading. I derive no assistance from this case. Counsel referred to *Lyell v Kennedy* (No
e 3) (1884) 27 Ch D 1 at 24, [1881–5] All ER Rep 814 at 823–824 and to *Buttes Gas and Oil
Co v Hammer (No 3)* [1980] 3 All ER 475 at 486, 490, 502, [1980] 3 WLR 668 at 683, 688,
703, but these citations do not assist him to show that where a document refers to one
subject matter privilege may be waived with regard to part of that document and
asserted with regard to the remainder.

The third question is whether privilege in respect of the memorandum dated 2nd May
f 1980 was in fact waived by or on behalf of the plaintiffs. Neither the plaintiffs nor any
of the plaintiffs' legal advisers intended to waive any privilege. The plaintiffs' English
solicitor intended to disclose the first two paragraphs of the memorandum which he
wrongly but excusably considered must be disclosed. The plaintiffs' counsel, who read
the memorandum in open court, did not know that the memorandum which he read
was an incomplete part of a document. The plaintiffs in so far as they were in attendance
g by their directors and officers knew nothing of what was going on. The plaintiffs and all
their legal advisers never intended to waive any privilege.

The plaintiffs' legal advisers introduced and intended to introduce before the judge in
open court during the trial a document which proved to be part of the memorandum.
It is true that the plaintiffs now say that the first two paragraphs of the memorandum are
of no assistance to them and of no harm to the defendants and could have been omitted
h and would have been omitted if they had realised that they were introducing part of a
privileged document. But the plaintiffs' legal advisers did not read the first two
paragraphs of the memorandum as a result of a mistake induced by any of the defendants,
and it is difficult to see how the mistake which the plaintiffs did make could fairly be
rectified after the first two paragraphs of the memorandum had been read to the judge.

In interlocutory proceedings and before trial it is possible to allow a party who discloses
j a document or part of a document by mistake to correct the error in certain
circumstances. Where a document has been disclosed as a result of misconduct by the
defendants, against the will of the plaintiffs and in any event not by the deliberate act of
the plaintiffs, then remedial action both before and during the trial may be possible. But
in my judgment the plaintiffs deliberately chose to read part of a document which dealt
with one subject matter to the trial judge, and must disclose the whole. The deliberate
introduction by the plaintiffs of part of the memorandum into the trial record as a result

of a mistake made by the plaintiffs waives privilege with regard to the whole document.
I can see no principle whereby the court could claim to exercise or could fairly and *a*
effectively exercise any discretion designed to put the clock back and to undo what has
been done.

In *Burnell v British Transport Commission* [1955] 3 All ER 822, [1956] 1 QB 187 counsel
for the defendant, cross-examining a witness, put to the witness certain observations
made by the witness in a written statement. Denning LJ said ([1955] 3 All ER 822,
[1956] 1 QB 187 at 190):   *b*

'. . . although this statement may well have been privileged from production and
discovery in the hands of the defendants at one stage, nevertheless, when it was used
by cross-examining counsel in this way, he waived the privilege, certainly for that
part which was used; and in a case of this kind, if the privilege is waived as to the
part, it must, I think, be waived also as to the whole. It would be most unfair that
cross-examining counsel should use part of the document which was to his *c*
advantage and not allow anyone, not even the judge or the opposing counsel, a sight
of the rest of the document, much of which might have been against him.'

In *George Doland Ltd v Blackburn Robson Coates & Co* [1972] 1 All ER 959, [1972] 1 WLR
1338 the deliberate waiver of privilege of certain communications between solicitor and
client relating to two particular subject matters before litigation became pending or *d*
contemplated involved waiver of any other communications relating to those two subject
matters but did not involve waiver of the further privilege which applied to documents
which were brought into existence after litigation was pending or contemplated. In *Nea
Karteria Maritime Co Ltd v Atlantic and Great Lakes Steamship Corpn* (11th December 1978,
unreported) decided by Mustill J the judge succinctly summarised the position as follows:

'I believe that the principle underlying the rule of practice exemplified by *Burnell* *e*
v British Transport Commission is that, where a party is deploying in court material
which would otherwise be privileged, the opposite party and the court must have
an opportunity of satisfying themselves that what the party has chosen to release
from privilege represents the whole of the material relevant to the issue in
question. To allow an individual item to be plucked out of context would be to risk
injustice through its real weight or meaning being misunderstood. In my view, the *f*
same principle can be seen at work in *George Doland Ltd v Blackburn Robson Coates
& Co* in a rather different context.'

I agree and would only add that it would not be satisfactory for the court to decide that
part of a privileged document can be introduced without waiving privilege with regard
to the other part in the absence of informed argument to the contrary, and there can be *g*
no informed argument without the disclosure, which would make argument
unnecessary.

Counsel for the plaintiffs attempted to distinguish the decisions in *Burnell v British
Transport Commission* and *George Doland Ltd v Blackburn Robson Coates & Co* on the
grounds that it was necessary in those cases for the whole statement to be disclosed in
order that the consistency of the testimony of a witness could be scrutinised. In my *h*
judgment, however, the rule that privilege relating to a document which deals with one
subject matter cannot be waived as to part and asserted as to the remainder is based on the
possibility that any use of part of a document may be unfair or misleading, that the party
who possesses the document is clearly not the person who can decide whether a partial
disclosure is misleading or not, nor can the judge decide without hearing argument, nor
can he hear argument unless the document is disclosed as a whole to the other side. Once *j*
disclosure has taken place by introducing part of the document into evidence or using it
in court it cannot be erased.

The fourth question is whether the introduction of the memorandum into the trial
record by the plaintiffs' counsel was effective to waive the privilege which belonged to
the plaintiffs personally and which the plaintiffs did not wish to waive.

The general principle is that 'a solicitor is the agent of his client in all matters that may
reasonably be expected to arise for decision in the cause': per Denning LJ in *Griffiths v*

Evans [1953] 2 All ER 1365 at 1371, [1953] 1 WLR 1424 at 1431. In *Matthews v Munster*
a (1887) 20 QBD 141, [1886–90] All ER Rep 251 the defendant's counsel in the absence of
the defendant and without his express authority in open court consented to a verdict for
the plaintiff for £350 and costs and agreed that all imputations should be withdrawn
against the plaintiff. This settlement was held to be a matter within the apparent general
authority of the counsel and was binding on the defendant. Lord Esher MR said (20
QBD 141 at 143, [1886–90] All ER Rep 251 at 252):

b   'But when the client has requested counsel to act as his advocate . . . he thereby
    represents to the other side that counsel is to act for him in the usual course, and he
    must be bound by that representation so long as it continues, so that a secret
    withdrawal of authority unknown to the other side would not affect the apparent
    authority of counsel. The request does not mean that counsel is to act in any other
    character than that of advocate or to do any other act than such as an advocate
c   usually does. The duty of counsel is to advise his client out of court and to act for
    him in court, and until his authority is withdrawn he has, with regard to all matters
    that properly relate to the conduct of the case, unlimited power to do that which is
    best for his client.
        'I apprehend that it is not contended that this power cannot be controlled by the
    Court. It is clear that it can be, for the power is exercised in matters which are
d   before the Court, and carried on under its supervision. If, therefore, counsel were
    to conduct a cause in such a manner that an unjust advantage would be given to the
    other side, or to act under a mistake in such a way as to produce some injustice, the
    Court has authority to overrule the action of the advocate.'

    The provisions of the last paragraph of Lord Esher MR's judgment do not avail the
e plaintiffs in the present case because the action of the plaintiffs' counsel in disclosing part
of the memorandum in open court cannot be overruled. What is done is done.
    To this general rule, there is, according to counsel for the plaintiffs, an exception in the
case of waiver because the privilege belongs to the client and not to the solicitor. For this
proposition he cited *Procter v Smiles* (1886) 55 LJQB 527 and other authorities which
establish that a solicitor in an action to which a client is not a party or in which the
f solicitor is not representing a client cannot waive the client's privilege. In *Procter v Smiles*
the client was not a party to the action and did not confer any express or implied
authority on the solicitor to waive privilege. The solicitor was a defendant to a libel
action and pleaded justification. The solicitor objected to answering certain interrogatories administered by the plaintiff on the grounds that the answers would involve the
solicitor in disclosing information of a confidential nature procured by the solicitor as
g solicitor for a third party for the purpose of litigation pending or threatened against that
third party. Lord Esher MR refused to order the solicitor to disclose the privileged
information notwithstanding that the solicitor might already have disclosed part.
Different considerations apply in the present case in which, as in *Matthews v Munster*, the
plaintiffs who are entitled to the privilege have instructed solicitors and counsel to
represent them for all the purposes of the action and are bound by the decisions made by
h their legal advisers within the scope of their ostensible authority including authority to
conduct the case in such manner as they think in the interests of the clients, involving
decisions as to waiver of privilege and other matters connected with the proceedings.
    In *Causton v Mann Egerton (Johnsons) Ltd* [1974] 1 All ER 453, [1974] 1 WLR 162 Lord
Denning MR, in a dissenting judgment, held that the defendants' solicitors had entered
into a binding agreement with the plaintiff's solicitors for the exchange of certain
j medical reports including medical reports for which the defendants could claim
privilege. This agreement amounted to waiver of privilege and came within the
authority of the solicitor to conduct litigation on behalf of his client. Stamp and Roskill
LJJ decided that there was no agreement. In the absence of such an agreement it was not
necessary for them to express and they reserved their views on the question of whether
a waiver can be affected by a solicitor without the authority of his client. In my
judgment this authority does not assist the plaintiffs in the present case. It certainly does
not establish the principle for which counsel for the plaintiffs contends, that the waiver

of privilege is an exception to the general rule that the legal advisers of a client have ostensible authority to bind him in any matter which arises in or is incidental to *a* litigation. In my judgment when counsel in the course of a trial introduces into the record a document or part of a document he thereby effectively waives any privilege attaching to that document which could otherwise be asserted by his client.

That proposition is supported by *Goldstone v Williams, Deacon & Co* [1899] 1 Ch 47 to which Dunn LJ referred in the course of argument. Stirling LJ said (at 52):

> 'It has been decided that notes of proceedings in open court . . . are, as a rule, not *b* privileged, but must be produced . . . on the ground . . . that the administration of justice in this country is a matter of public interest, and to be conducted (again as a general rule) in public, and, consequently, that there can be nothing privileged or confidential which passes in open court.'

The fifth question is whether there is any general or special discretion equitable or *c* otherwise which will enable the court in this instance to restore and enable the plaintiffs to assert privilege in respect of the whole of the memorandum or in respect of that part which has not been introduced in evidence so far. In the instant case Lloyd J decided that if there was such a discretion it would not be proper for him to exercise it in favour of the plaintiffs. The learned and experienced judge who, as I have said, had already endured 14 days of the trial and who had read the whole of the memorandum decided that this *d* was not a case in which he should exercise any discretion vested in him. There being no grounds for saying that the judge did not properly consider the exercise of his discretion, this court will not interfere.

In any event I am not persuaded that any discretion exists. Counsel for the plaintiffs relied on *Lord Ashburton v Pape* [1913] 2 Ch 469, [1911–13] All ER Rep 708. The court granted an injunction to restrain the use of stolen privileged documents. A man who is *e* entitled to assert privilege over a document does not waive that privilege by suffering the misfortune of the theft of those documents from his custody or from the custody of his solicitor. In *Butler v Board of Trade* [1970] 3 All ER 593, [1971] Ch 680 the Board of Trade through the Official Receiver obtained a copy of a letter written by the plaintiff's solicitor to the Official Solicitor in connection with the affairs of a company which subsequently went into compulsory liquidation. The Board of Trade were therefore *f* innocent recipients of privileged information. Goff J was of the opinion that the principles to be found in *Lord Ashburton v Pape* applied not only where documents were stolen but where documents were innocently conveyed in breach of confidence. He nevertheless held ([1970] 3 All ER 593 at 599, [1971] Ch 680 at 690):

> '. . . it would not be a right or permissible exercise of the equitable jurisdiction in confidence to make a declaration at the suit of the accused in a public prosecution *g* in effect restraining the Crown from adducing admissible evidence relevant to the crime with which he is charged.'

These two authorities have no relevance to the present case. The court has no jurisdiction to relieve the plaintiffs from the consequences of their own mistakes particularly as those consequences cannot be wholly eradicated; part of the memorandum *h* has in fact been read to the trial judge.

For these reasons I would dismiss the appeal.

DUNN LJ. I entirely agree with the judgment of Templeman LJ and have nothing to add.

j

Appeal dismissed.

Solicitors: *McKenna & Co* (for the plaintiffs); *Ince & Co* (for the third defendants).

Frances Rustin   Barrister.

a Exxon Corpn and others v Exxon Insurance Consultants International Ltd

CHANCERY DIVISION
GRAHAM J
13th, 16th, 22nd JANUARY 1981

b

Copyright – Literary work – Original literary work – Single invented word – Time and labour spent on inventing word – Word forming part of plaintiff company's name – Defendant company incorporating word in its name – Whether infringement of copyright – Whether word an 'original literary work' – Copyright Act 1956, s 2(1).

c *Company – Name – Use of name – Restraining use of name by company – Injunction restraining passing off by continued use of word in corporate name – Injunction restraining company from allowing its name incorporating word to remain on register.*

The first plaintiff, a company which dealt in petroleum and similar products, decided to devise a new corporate name and trade mark for itself and its associated companies. The *d* plaintiff was looking for an invented name which was short, distinctive, devoid of meaning and easily memorised. After spending considerable time and effort on the matter the plaintiff selected the word 'Exxon' and used it as part of the corporate names of itself and, inter alios, the second and third plaintiffs who were two of its associated companies, and as their main trade mark. The defendant company, which had no connection with the plaintiffs, adopted the word 'Exxon' as part of its corporate name *e* without the plaintiffs' licence or consent. The plaintiffs brought an action against the defendant claiming an injunction to restrain infringement of their copyright in the name 'Exxon' on the ground that the word 'Exxon' was an 'original literary work' within s 2(1)*ᵃ* of the Copyright Act 1956. The plaintiffs also sought an injunction to restrain the defendant from passing off its goods as the plaintiffs' goods by using the word 'Exxon'. The defendant failed to serve a defence to the action and the plaintiffs moved for *f* judgment in default of defence pursuant to RSC Ord 19, r 7(1)*ᵇ*.

Held – (1) The mere fact that a single word was invented and that research and labour had been involved in its invention did not by itself make it an original literary work within s 2(1) of the 1956 Act, and for a single word used as a title to qualify as an original literary work it had to have some meaning or significance in itself (other than merely *g* being an invented word) justifying its recognition as an original literary work. Since the word 'Exxon' only took on meaning or significance when it was used with other words, i e as part of the plaintiffs' corporate names, or in particular juxtapositions as, for example, to their goods, and in itself had no meaning or significance, it was not an 'original literary work' within s 2(1), even though it was an invented and original word. It followed that the plaintiffs were not entitled to copyright in the word and that the claim for an *h* injunction restraining infringement of copyright failed (see p 503 *e* to *j* and p 504 *f g*, post).

(2) However, the plaintiffs were entitled to an injunction and ancillary relief restraining passing off by the defendant by its continued use of the word 'Exxon', and

a   Section 2(1), so far as material, provides: 'Copyright shall subsist, subject to the provisions of this Act, in every original literary ... work which is unpublished, and of which the author was a
j   qualified person at the time when the work was made ...'
b   Rule 7(1), so far as material, provides: 'Where the plaintiff makes against a defendant ... a claim of a description not mentioned in Rules 2 to 5, then, if the defendant ... fails ... to serve a defence on the plaintiff, the plaintiff may, after the expiration of the period fixed by or under these Rules for service of the defence, apply to the Court for judgment, and on the hearing of the application the Court shall give such judgment as the plaintiff appears entitled to on his statement of claim.'

they were also entitled to an injunction against the defendant restraining it from allowing
its name in a form incorporating the word 'Exxon' to remain on the companies' register, *a*
because it would be unlawful and damaging to the plaintiffs to allow the name to remain
on the register (see p 504 *h* to 505 *b*, post); *Société Anonyme des Anciens Etablissements
Panhard et Levassor v Panhard Levassor Motor Co Ltd* [1900–3] All ER Rep 477 applied.

Per Curiam. The court has a discretion under RSC Ord 19, r 7(1) whether to give
judgment in default of defence, and where only the party asking for the relief is present
and the relief is far-reaching in its consequences and may, if granted, affect the public *b*
interest adversely in other cases the court, before giving judgment in default, is entitled
to hear full and proper argument for and against the correctness of the law on which the
statement of claim is founded and as to the propositions alleged to establish the relief
asked for (see p 498 *a* to *c*, post); dicta of Lord Denning MR and of Scarman LJ in
Wallersteiner v Moir [1974] 3 All ER at 232, 252 applied.

Notes   *c*
For copyright in an original literary work, see 9 Halsbury's Laws (4th Edn) para 934, and
for cases on the subject, see 13 Digest (Reissue) 54–56, 572–581.

For the Copyright Act 1956, s 2, see 7 Halsbury's Statutes (3rd Edn) 132.

Cases referred to in judgment
Anderson (D P) & Co Ltd v Lieber Code Co [1917] 2 KB 469, 86 LJKB 1220, 117 LT 361, 13 *d*
    Digest (Reissue) 55, 579.
Charles v Shepherd [1892] 2 QB 622, 61 LJQB 768, 67 LT 67, CA, 50 Digest (Repl) 168,
    1445.
Dicks v Yates (1881) 18 Ch D 76, 50 LJ Ch 809, 44 LT 660, CA, 13 Digest (Reissue) 77, 693.
Francis, Day and Hunter Ltd v Twentieth Century Fox Corpn Ltd [1939] 4 All ER 192, [1940]
    AC 112, 109 LJPC 11, 161 LT 396, [1939] 4 DLR 353, PC, 13 Digest (Reissue) 130, *e*
    1079.
Gibbings v Strong (1884) 26 Ch D 66, 50 LT 578, CA, 50 Digest (Repl) 159, 1377.
Graves v Terry (1882) 9 QBD 170, 51 LJQB 464, DC, 50 Digest (Repl) 258, 102.
Ladbroke (Football) Ltd v William Hill (Football) Ltd [1964] 1 All ER 465, [1964] 1 WLR 273,
    HL, 13 Digest (Reissue) 62, 623.
Life Music Inc v Wonderland Music Co (1965) 241 Fed Supp 653.   *f*
*Panhard et Levassor (Société Anonyme des Anciens Etablissements) v Panhard Levassor Motor Co
    Ltd* [1901] 2 Ch 513, [1900–3] All ER Rep 477, 70 LJ Ch 738, 85 LT 20, 28(2) Digest
    (Reissue) 1063, 789.
Suhner & Co AG v Suhner Ltd [1967] FSR 319.
University of London Press Ltd v University Tutorial Press Ltd [1916] 2 Ch 601, 86 LJ Ch 107,
    115 LT 301, 13 Digest (Reissue) 55, 578.   *g*
Wallersteiner v Moir, Moir v Wallersteiner [1974] 3 All ER 217, [1974] 1 WLR 991, CA,
    Digest (Cont Vol D) 1042, 1455b.
Walter v Lane [1900] AC 539, 69 LJ Ch 699, 83 LT 289, HL, 13 Digest (Reissue) 87, 750.

Cases also cited
Burberrys v J C Cording & Co Ltd (1909) 26 RPC 693.   *h*
Day v Brownrigg (1878) 10 Ch D 294, CA.
Taverner Rutledge Ltd v Trexapalm Ltd [1977] RPC 275.
Wombles Ltd v Wombles Skips Ltd [1977] RPC 99.

Motion for judgment
The plaintiffs, Exxon Corpn, Esso Petroleum Co Ltd, Exxon Ltd and Exxon International *j*
Ltd, by a writ dated 21st March 1980, brought an action against the defendants, Exxon
Insurance Consultants Ltd, claiming, inter alia, an injunction to restrain the defendants
from infringing the plaintiffs' copyright in the name Exxon, an order that the defendants
be directed to change their corporate name to omit the word Exxon therefrom and an
injunction to restrain the defendants from using the word Exxon or any name

confusingly similar thereto so as to pass off their business goods or services as and for
a those of the plaintiffs or as being connected or associated with the plaintiffs. The
defendants failed to serve a defence to the action and by a notice of motion dated 24th
July 1980 the plaintiffs applied for judgment in default of defence under RSC Ord 19,
r 7. The facts are set out in the judgment.

Vivian Price QC and *J V Fitzgerald* for the plaintiffs.
b *John Mummery* for the Attorney General as amicus curiae.
The defendants were not represented.

Cur adv vult

22nd January. **GRAHAM J** read the following judgment: This is a motion for
c judgment against the defendants in default of defence. Only the plaintiffs were
represented at the hearing.

The principles applicable are to be found in RSC Ord 19, and particularly in r 7 of that
order. No evidence is permissible and judgment must be given in accordance with the
pleadings alone; and the court will give such judgment as the plaintiffs appear entitled
to on the statement of claim.

d At the same time, the note to r 7 in the Supreme Court Practice 1979 (vol 1, para
19/7/11, p 333) states that, although expressed to be mandatory, the rule is that the
judgment on the motion is in fact discretionary, as for example when, instead of giving
judgment, the court extends the defendant's time for pleading.

The leading case is *Wallensteiner v Moir* [1974] 3 All ER 217, [1974] 1 WLR 991 and
there are two passages in that case which I would like to mention. First of all, Lord
e Denning MR said ([1974] 3 All ER 217 at 232, [1974] 1 WLR 991 at 1007):

'According to RSC Ord 19, r 7(1), "on the hearing of the application the Court
shall give such judgment as the plaintiff appears entitled to on his statement of
claim". Likewise with a counterclaim: see RSC Ord 19, r 8. Although the word
"shall" is used in that rule, it is clear from the authorities that it is not imperative but
directory. The court will not enter a judgment which it would afterwards set aside
f on proper grounds being shown: see *Graves v Terry* (1882) 9 QBD 170; *Gibbings v
Strong* (1884) 26 Ch D 66. A judge in chambers has a discretion which he will
exercise on the same lines as he will set aside a judgment in default. He will require
the party to show that he has a good defence on the merits.'

The second passage is in the judgment of Scarman LJ. (This was an appeal from
g Geoffrey Lane J.) After referring to the cases, Scarman LJ said ([1974] 3 All ER 217 at
252, [1974] 1 WLR 991 at 1029–1030):

'In my opinion, the judge went too far. RSC Ord 19 declares the consequences of
a default of pleading'. [He then dealt with rr 2 to 6; and when he got to r 7, he
said:] Rule 7 makes provision for all other descriptions of claim (of which claims
for declaratory relief are one). Paragraph (1) of the rule provides that in all such
h cases the consequence of a failure to serve a defence within the proper time shall be
that the claimant "may . . . apply to the Court for judgment, and . . . the Court shall
give such judgment as [he] appears entitled to on his statement of claim".
Notwithstanding the word "shall", the case law has established that the court retains
the right to refuse the claimant judgment even when on his pleading he appears
entitled to it. If the court "should see any reason to doubt whether injustice may
j not be done by giving judgment", it may refuse judgment at this stage: [Then there
is a reference to *Charles v Shepherd*, and to the judgment of Lord Esher MR in that
case ([1892] 2 QB 622 at 624). Then Scarman LJ went on:] 'This discretion is a
valuable safeguard in the hands of the court.'

Then he took the case and explained why in that case the judge in the court below had gone too far. The cases of *Gibbings v Strong* and *Graves v Terry*, referred to by Scarman LJ, were cases where time for pleading was extended.

As I read it, *Wallersteiner v Moir* is deciding that the rule means that the court should prima facie give judgment if justified on the pleadings, but there may be some good reason why it should not do so, such as doubt whether injustice may not be done by doing so, and in such a case there is clear discretion to refuse. Now, in a case where, as here, only the party asking for relief is present, it seems to me that, if the relief claimed is far-reaching in its consequences and may, if granted, affect the public interest adversely in other cases, before giving judgment the court is entitled to be sure that it has heard full and proper argument both for and against the correctness of the law on which the statement of claim is founded and as to the propositions alleged to establish the relief asked for.

Here, if the plaintiffs' argument is right, all invented words which might be registrable as trade marks could be argued to be the subject of copyright whether they were also registered or not. The consequences would be far-reaching and probably in many cases objectionable, as will be seen hereafter; and in such circumstances it seemed right to me to ask for the assistance of the Attorney General so that I could be sure that I received argument on both sides. I am grateful to the Attorney General for nominating counsel to represent him here and to help the court in its task; but I should also make it clear that, as one would expect, there is no question that counsel for the plaintiffs, in the first instance did not deal with the case fully and fairly in the absence of any opponent.

The facts are very simple as disclosed in the statement of claim. Paragraphs 2 to 7 are not relied on and need not be referred to, but I think that I should read some of the following paragraphs, starting with para 8:

'8. Further and/or alternatively to the matters set out in paragraphs 2 to 7 above, the plaintiffs allege that until the 1st November 1972 the first plaintiff was known as the Standard Oil Company (New Jersey), which is directly and/or through its associates or subsidiaries concerned in the business of production, transportation and marketing of petroleum and petroleum products and other energy resources, together with all goods and services connected therewith and incidental thereto. Moreover it is concerned as aforesaid in the promotion and sale of a wide variety of goods including electronic equipment, office machines, sporting products and in the manufacture, promotion and sale of numerous chemical products.

'9. Prior to 1970, the first plaintiff set up a committee to devise and select a new name and trade mark for itself and which could also be used by overseas associates and subsidiary companies when appropriate. The said committee concluded that the said new name must satisfy the following three basic conditions, namely: (a) was capable of being readily identified with the first plaintiff and its associates or subsidiary companies, their goods and services, (b) was invented and was devoid of any meaning in English or in any other language spoken in any place in which the goods and/or services of the first plaintiff and/or its associates and/or subsidiary companies were marketed or likely to be marketed, (c) was short, distinctive and easily memorised.

'10. Following considerable research and testing the said committee selected the word Exxon, devised by them.

'11. Accordingly, on the 1st November 1972, the first plaintiff adopted the name Exxon and the name of Standard Oil Company (New Jersey) was formally changed to Exxon Corporation. A number of its associate or subsidiary companies similarly adopted Exxon as their company or trade name.

'12. The first plaintiff carries on business throughout the United States of America and has associate or subsidiary companies in almost 100 countries. All or almost all of the said associates or subsidiary companies used the word Exxon as a trade mark. In particular and by way of example, firstly a United Kingdom subsidiary of the first plaintiff, namely Esso Chemical Limited, carries on the

business of manufacturing and marketing in the United Kingdom and exporting
therefrom chemical goods, the majority of which are sold under the plaintiffs' Esso
and Exxon brand names; secondly, a Bermudan (associate) company of the first
plaintiff, namely Exxon Insurance Services Limited carries on the business of
performing management services, in the field of insurance for associate or affiliated
companies of the plaintiffs.

'13. The second plaintiff is engaged inter alia in the business of producing,
transporting, refining and marketing through inter alia motor garage outlets,
petroleum products in all parts of the United Kingdom, together with all goods and
services connected therewith and a wide variety of other goods displaying the name
Exxon together with the name Esso.

'14. The first plaintiff is the registered proprietor of the trade mark Exxon in Part
A of the Register in the United Kingdom in respect of goods in every class and in
each case the second plaintiff is the registered user thereof. Further, the first
plaintiff is the registered proprietor of the trade mark Exxon in many other
countries throughout the world.

'15. The third plaintiff was incorporated on the 25th day of February 1969 to
carry on business as set out in the Memorandum and Articles of Association of the
said third plaintiff.

'16. The fourth plaintiff was incorporated on the 14th day of May 1973 to carry
on business as set out in the Memorandum and Articles of Association of the said
fourth plaintiff.

'17. The plaintiffs have either by themselves or through their associated or
subsidiary companies made extensive and considerable use of the name Exxon in
numerous countries throughout the world in connection with their business and
numerous goods have been sold and services have been supplied under or by
reference to the name Exxon.

'18. The plaintiffs have either by themselves or through their subsidiaries and
associated companies expended considerable sums on promoting their diverse
business activities, goods and services by reference to the name Exxon in numerous
countries of the world including the United Kingdom by almost every promotional
means. Moreover the business goods and/or services of the plaintiffs or their
associated companies and subsidiaries have under the name Exxon been the subject
of numerous references on radio, television and in the press in many countries of
the world, including the United Kingdom.'

The statement of claim then comes to the question of copyright, and reads:

'19. The word Exxon is an original literary work falling within the provisions of
section 2(1) of the Copyright Act 1956 and the first plaintiff is the owner of the
copyright therein and the second, third and fourth plaintiffs licensees thereof.

'20. Further by reason of the matters referred to above the plaintiffs have acquired
a substantial reputation and goodwill in the name Exxon inter alia amongst the
relevant trade and public in the United Kingdom so that, when used in relation to
any business, goods or services, the word Exxon means the business goods or
services of the plaintiffs and none other. Further and/or alternatively, the name
Exxon when used in connection with any business, goods or services indicates to the
relevant trade and public a connection or association with the plaintiffs' large and
substantial multinational business and related goodwill.'

and the statement of claim then goes on to deal with the formation of the defendant, and
says in para 22 that—

'the defendant has, without the licence or consent of the plaintiffs, reproduced
and/or authorised the reproduction of the plaintiffs' copyright work Exxon in the
defendants' corporate name,'

that it has adopted the name Exxon, and—

'23. By reason of the matters referred to in paragraphs 1 and 8–22 the defendant *a* has infringed the plaintiffs' copyright in the word Exxon, and threatens to continue to do so.

'24. Further and/or alternatively, the defendant has, by reason of matters referred to in paragraphs 1 and 8 to 22 above, used the word Exxon in connection with its business so as to be likely to cause confusion and deception and pass off its business and/or services as and for the business and/or services of the plaintiffs and further or *b* alternatively as being connected or associated with the business or services of the plaintiffs.'

From the statement of claim, it is seen that the Exxon Corpn came into being as a result of the change of name by the Standard Oil Co in the USA in November 1972. There are no reasons given for this change and it is, I think, anyway irrelevant for present *c* purposes. After the change of the corporation's name in the USA and of its adoption by many subsidiaries throughout the world, Exxon appears to have become their main trade mark and it is registered for goods in every class of the classification of goods in the register.

It seems, however, that the plaintiffs' previous trade mark Esso, which was also part of their name in many of their companies, is still being used, certainly in this country; and *d* that the word Exxon is really a substitute for wider use throughout the world in place of the previous mark Esso.

The defendants have no connection with the plaintiffs or any of them, but none the less they have adopted the plaintiffs' name Exxon as part of their corporate name.

It will be seen from the statement of claim that the plaintiffs make two claims for relief and say that they have two independent rights of action against the defendants. *e* The first is passing off, and as to this the statement of claim alleges, inter alia, that the use by the defendants of Exxon is bound to lead to passing off and in particular to suggest that the defendant company has some connection with, or is a subsidiary of, the plaintiffs and in particular the parent corporation. This I think must be so; and I have already indicated in argument, and I now confirm, that the plaintiffs are, in my judgment, entitled to an injunction and ancillary relief to restrain such passing off by continued use *f* by the defendants of the word Exxon.

In addition, however, the plaintiffs claim to have copyright in the name Exxon and to be entitled to an injunction to restrain infringement of such copyright. This, if correct, would give a number of advantages to the plaintiffs in establishing their rights in their name and mark. The argument in support is short and simple. It is said, first, that considerable time and labour was expended in arriving at the name Exxon, which had *g* to fulfil all the special requirements set out in para 9 of the statement of claim. Though I must accept this for present purposes, I do so with some reservation as to the extent and nature of the literary or research work involved. Second, it is said that the word having been devised after the expenditure of such effort, qualified therefore as an 'original literary work' within the meaning of s 2 of the Copyright Act 1956.

It was argued strongly that it is, and it was said that the size of a literary work is *h* immaterial; there is logically no reason why one word which is written should not be a literary work just as much as a work of greater length; if otherwise qualified because of labour expended on it, then it can be a literary work. The definition of 'literary' in the Shorter Oxford Dictionary is: 'Pertaining to the letters of the alphabet [that is an earlier meaning]. Of or pertaining to, or of the nature of, literature . . . or books . . .'

A number of cases were referred to by counsel for the plaintiffs. In *University of London* *j* *Press Ltd v University Tutorial Press Ltd* [1916] 2 Ch 601 he referred in particular to an important passage in the judgment of Peterson J. That passage comes at the start of the judgment and reads (at 608):

'The first question that is raised is, Are these examination papers subject of copyright? Sect. 1, sub-s. 1, of the Copyright Act of 1911 provides for copyright in "every original literary dramatic musical and artistic work," [the relevant words are therefore the same as in the 1956 Act] subject to certain conditions which for this purpose are immaterial, and the question is, therefore, whether these examination papers are, within the meaning of this Act, original literary works. Although a literary work is not defined in the Act, s. 35 states what the phrase includes; the definition is not a completely comprehensive one, but the section is intended to show what, amongst other things, is included in the description "literary work," and the words are "'Literary work' includes maps, charts, plans, tables, and compilations." It may be difficult to define "literary work" as used in this Act, but it seems to be plain that it is not confined to "literary work" in the sense in which that phrase is applied, for instance, to Meredith's novels and the writings of Robert Louis Stevenson. In speaking of such writings as literary works, one thinks of the quality, the style, and the literary finish which they exhibit. Under the [Copyright] Act of 1842, which protected "books," many things which had no pretensions to literary style acquired copyright; for example, a list of registered bills of sale, a list of foxhounds and hunting days, and trade catalogues; and I see no ground for coming to the conclusion that the present Act was intended to curtail the rights of authors. In my view the words "literary work" cover work which is expressed in print or writing, irrespective of the question whether the quality or style is high. The word "literary" seems to be used in a sense somewhat similar to the use of the word "literature" in political or electioneering literature and refers to written or printed matter. Papers set by examiners are, in my opinion, "literary work" within the meaning of the present Act.'

It is clear from that definition that Peterson J, dealing with the matter in 1916, felt that the words 'literary' and 'original' must be treated reasonably broadly; and I think it follows from what he said that, if a word is invented, it must, for practical purposes, be considered as original.

I also, while I have the report before me, should refer to a short statement where he says (at 609–610):

'The objections with which I have dealt do not appear to me to have any substance, and, after all, there remains the rough practical test that what is worth copying is prima facie worth protecting.'

The longer passage in the judgment of Peterson J which I have just read was quoted with approval by Lord Pearce in *Ladbroke (Football) Ltd v William Hill (Football) Ltd* [1964] 1 All ER 465 at 479, [1964] 1 WLR 273 at 291 where he says:

'My Lords, the question whether the plaintiffs are entitled to copyright in their coupon [this was a football coupon case] depends on whether it is an original literary work. The words "literary work" include a compilation. They are used to describe the work which is expressed in print or writing irrespective of whether it has any excellence of quality or style of writing.'

Then he refers to what Peterson J said in *University of London Press Ltd v University Tutorial Press Ltd* and continues:

'The word "original" does not demand original or inventive thought, but only that the work should not be copied and should originate from the author. In deciding therefore whether a work in the nature of a compilation is original, it is wrong to start by considering individual parts of it apart from the whole, as the appellants in their argument sought to do. For many compilations have nothing original in their parts, yet the sum total of the compilation may be original.'

Then he refers as an example to Palgrave's Golden Treasury, and goes on:

'In such cases the courts have looked to see whether the compilation of the

unoriginal material called for work or skill or expense. If it did, it is entitled to be
considered original and to be protected against those who wished to steal the fruits *a*
of the work or skill or expense by copying it without taking the trouble to compile
it themselves. So the protection given by such copyright is in no sense a monopoly,
for it is open to a rival to produce the same results if he chooses to evolve it by his
own labours.'

Lord Reid in the same case, in dealing with the question of infringement referred *b*
([1964] 1 All ER 465 at 471, [1964] 1 WLR 273 at 279) to the 'rough practical test' of
Peterson J with approval.

However, I still have to come back to the basic question whether it is proper to
construe 'original literary work' in s 2 of the Copyright Act 1956 as covering a single
invented word even if considerable time and work were expended on it and, if so,
whether the word Exxon here is such a work. There are, I think, no decided cases which *c*
deal specifically with the precise point that I have to decide. The answer, therefore, must
in the end depend on the proper construction of the words in the 1956 Act according to
general principles and the facts of the case.

The history of copyright legislation shows that prior to 1911, when the Act of that year
was passed and in s 1 first used the words 'original literary work', the protection given by
copyright before that time was limited to books; and the 1842 Act did not require *d*
originality as a necessary qualification: see *Walter v Lane* [1900] AC 539. Cases before
1911 and also *Francis, Day and Hunter Ltd v Twentieth Century Fox Corpn Ltd* [1939] 4 All
ER 192, [1940] AC 112, a Privy Council appeal from Canada, must be read with these
qualifications in mind. In 1911 and again in the present 1956 Act, the words used are
'original literary work', but there is no definition in the Act of what is meant by this
phrase though s 48 does specify that 'literary work' includes any written table or *e*
compilation.

On general principles of construction, the words must be treated as having their
ordinary English meaning as applied to the subject matter with which they are
dealing. There is, as I see it, no necessity to read the words in any sense which is not their
ordinary sense in the English language as so applied, though the definition in s 48 and
cases such as *University of London Press Ltd v University Tutorial Press Ltd* and *Ladbroke* *f*
(Football) Ltd v William Hill (Football) Ltd show that the word 'literary' is not to be read in
the Act in a narrow sense so as to be confined, for example, to material having a high
intellectual quality or style of writing. The words of Peterson J in the *University of London*
case were, as I have shown, approved, and the 'rough practical test' is prayed in aid by
counsel for the plaintiffs as a justification for the plaintiffs' contention.

Counsel for the plaintiffs also referred to the so-called 'code' cases, of which *D P* *g*
Anderson & Co Ltd v Lieber Code Co [1917] 2 KB 469 is perhaps the best example, as
showing that meaningless words can be the subject of copyright. In these cases, however,
it is of course the whole compilation of many thousands of such words designed for use
in coded messages which is the subject of copyright and the question whether a particular
meaningless word infringed the copyright is a different question, which was not
considered. It is fair to say that counsel for the plaintiffs did not put the case forward as *h*
establishing that a single word qualified as a 'literary work'.

He did emphasise, of course, that in the *Francis, Day and Hunter* case, it was the title of
the song, 'The Man who Broke the Bank at Monte Carlo', for which copyright was
claimed, and that Lord Hodson in the *Ladbroke* case [1964] 1 All ER 465 at 476, [1964]
1 WLR 273 at 286 had made it clear that the appellants' submission in the case before
him that 'titles could not be protected' was based on the *Dick v Yates* (1881) 18 Ch D 76 *j*
and *Francis, Day and Hunter* cases, neither of which supported the proposition as a matter
of law. The primary reason was no doubt because the question in those cases was not
whether a title was a 'literary work', but whether it came within the definition of 'book'
within the 1842 Act.

The argument of counsel appearing as amicus curiae was similarly short and to the point. He contended that a single word such as Exxon here could not fairly and properly be considered to be a 'literary work' within s 2 of the Copyright Act 1956. Even if such a word were invented so as to qualify for originality, it could not in any normal English sense be considered as 'a literary work'. It was, of course, capable of being written and in that sense is literary, as being something identified by letters and the subject of writing. This meaning, incidentally, corresponds with the early meaning of 'literary', in the Shorter Oxford Dictionary already mentioned. It was not, however, a work which was literary in the normal sense of constituting or concerned with literature or books.

He also pointed out, and I agree that there is force in the contention, that, if the plaintiffs are right, it would have extremely inconvenient consequences as far as the public are concerned, in that no one could refer to any of the plaintiff companies or to any of their goods bearing the name Exxon without having the plaintiffs' licence expressly or impliedly to do so. There is nothing in s 6, which deals with general exceptions from protection, which would exclude the necessity for such a licence, since the exceptions relate only to literary, reporting and similar more specialised activities. One may well ask also whether the Bishop of Exeter can continue to use the Exon as part of his name, albeit when spelt with one 'x'.

Counsel appearing as amicus curiae also contended that, on a fair reading of the Act, it cannot really have been intended to give further rights of property in words or names which would naturally and properly qualify for excellent protection as registered trade marks or as the subject of passing-off actions. There was no need to give any further protection, which, though it might assist a plaintiff in proving his case against a user of his name or mark, would be limited to the period of copyright, a thing quite inappropriate to a trade mark or name, whether registered or a common law mark, neither of which are so limited. Such protection as such is inappropriate to a single word or name such as Exxon, having no meaning in itself.

The counter-argument is thus equally short and simple, and neither of them admits of much elaboration.

As I have already stated, the question that I have to decide is, shortly stated, whether Exxon is an 'original literary work' within s 2 of the 1956 Act? I do not think it is. What is it then, one may ask. It is a word which, though invented and therefore original, has no meaning and suggests nothing in itself. To give it substance and meaning, it must be accompanied by other words or used in a particular context or juxtaposition. When used as part of any of the plaintiffs' corporate names, it clearly has a denominative characteristic as denoting the company in question. When used, as I assume it is, with the plaintiffs' goods, it would clearly have the effect of denoting origin or quality. It is in fact an invented word with no meaning, which is a typical subject for trade mark registration, and which no doubt, with adequate user, is capable also of becoming, if it has not already become, distinctive of the plaintiffs and their goods at common law. It is not in itself a title or distinguishing name and, as I have said, only takes on meaning or significance when actually used with other words, for example indicating that it is the name of a company, or in a particular juxtaposition as, for example, on goods.

Nothing I have said above is intended to suggest that I consider that a word which is used as a title can, as a matter of law, never in any circumstances be the subject of copyright, and I would disagree with dicta in previous cases to the contrary effect. Such a word would, however, I think have to have qualities or characteristics in itself, if such a thing is possible, which would justify its recognition as an original literary work rather than merely as an invented word. It may well turn out not to be possible in practice but as at present advised I consider that the mere fact that a single word is invented and that research or labour was involved in its invention does not in itself in my judgment necessarily enable it to qualify as an original literary work within s 2 of the 1956 Act.

By analogy, nobody really would suggest that there would be an infringement of Edward Lear's copyright (ignoring the fact that the author of Nonsense Songs died in 1888 and copyright no longer subsists) in calling one's home 'Chankly Bore' or in selling new toy products called 'Jumblies', even if the latter had green heads and blue hands.

The point is a narrow one, and it may well be thought difficult to decide between the two arguments, but my view is clear. At the risk of losing my way in the 'tulgey wood' *a* and becoming bogged in the 'slithy toves', my view can perhaps best be illustrated by consideration of Lewis Carroll's fantasy 'Jabberwocky'. The whole poem was, during the appropriate period, undoubtedly properly part of Lewis Carroll's copyright in the book 'Through the Looking-Glass'. As such, the poem itself, if copied, would certainly be regarded as an infringement of the copyright in the book. The poem, it will be remembered, 'seemed very pretty' to Alice, but was 'rather hard to understand'. The *b* subject, as illustrated so vividly in John Tenniel's drawings, was the awesome Jabberwock, an invented monster with an invented name. The title of the poem, 'Jabberwocky' with a 'y' at the end, seems to be used by the author adjectivally to mean a story about a Jabberwock. Undoubtedly the whole composition of the poem and the suggestive and invented words which form its essence and make it so memorable is, just as in the 'code' cases, worthy of copyright, and that copyright could properly be held to be infringed by *c* the copying to a greater or lesser extent, as the case might be, of its invented words.

Assuming the poem had been recently written and was the subject of the 1911 Act or the 1956 Act, it is I suppose just conceivable that the use in some literary context of either of the single words 'Jabberwock' or 'Jabberwocky' alone might also be held to be an infringement as being a substantial part of the whole poem. But could Lewis Carroll, if he had merely invented the word 'Jabberwock' and had never written the poem of which *d* it is a part, have successfully contended that he had copyright in the word alone? In the absence of its registration as a trade mark, could he, by virtue of copyright, prevent a commercial company adopting it as part of such company's corporate name? I think not, the legal reason being that the word alone and by itself cannot properly be considered as a 'literary *work*', the subject of copyright under the Act. It becomes part of a 'literary work' within the Act when it is embodied in the poem, but it is the poem as a *e* composition which is a work within the Act and not the word itself. The American case *Life Music Inc v Wonderland Music Co* (1965) 241 Fed Supp 653 was referred to by counsel appearing as amicus curiae. Copyright was claimed in the word 'supercalafajalistickes-peealadojus', but the case does not really carry the matter any further. The refusal there of an interlocutory injunction turned on the failure of the plaintiff to make out a prima facie case of infringement and, although it could be said that the possibility of copyright *f* in the word was assumed, there was no real argument on the copyright aspect of the matter and the case has really no persuasive authority on this point.

I therefore conclude that the plaintiffs cannot, for the reasons given above, succeed on the ground of copyright in their word Exxon.

[Counsel addressed his Lordship on whether an order could be made directing the defendants to change their corporate name by omitting the word 'Exxon' therefrom. *g* His Lordship continued:] As a result of the judgment which I gave this morning the plaintiffs ask me, inter alia, to grant an injunction in the form for which they ask in their statement of claim, which reads: '(4) An order that the defendant be directed to change its corporate name and omit the word Exxon therefrom.' Having listened to the arguments on both sides and having been referred to *Société Anonyme des Anciens Etablissements Panhard et Levassor v Panhard Levassor Motor Co Ltd* [1901] 2 Ch 513, *h* [1900–3] All ER Rep 477 and to *Suhner & Co AG v Suhner Ltd* [1967] FSR 319, where Plowman J, who had also been referred to the *Panhard et Levassor* case, decided that the injunction should be in the form of that granted by Farwell J in the *Panhard* case, I agree that, in the circumstances, that is the right injunction to make, namely an injunction to restrain the company from allowing its name to remain on the register in its present form, using the word Exxon.

This case is slightly different from the two previous cases, because there is no defendant *j* here except the company itself. Under s 18(1) of the Companies Act 1948, a company is empowered to change its name by special resolution, employing the mechanism that is there set out; and therefore it does seem to me that there is nothing wrong in preventing it continuing to have its name on the register if the conclusion is that the company is

doing something which is unlawful by so doing. If it continues to do it, the act of so
doing, if not fraudulent, is at least more unlawful and is clearly damaging to the
plaintiffs. If that is the situation, I think that a court would be shutting its eyes to
realities unless it did the best that it can to prevent any such thing happening in the
future.

For my own part, I am prepared therefore to grant an injunction against the company
itself in the terms of the *Panhard* case, as near as may be.

*Injunction restraining infringement of copyright refused. Injunctions granted to restrain passing
off by defendants by use of the word 'Exxon' and to restrain the defendants from allowing any
name containing the word 'Exxon' to remain on the register as the name of their company.*

Solicitors: *Needham & Grant* (for the plaintiffs); *Treasury Solicitor.*

Evelyn M C Budd   Barrister.

Van Boeckel v Customs and Excise Commissioners

QUEEN'S BENCH DIVISION
WOOLF J
17th, 18th DECEMBER 1980

*Value added tax – Assessment in default of proper returns by taxpayer – Sum assessed deemed
to be amount of tax due from him – Appeal against assessment – Taxpayer a licensee of a public
house – Assessment for period of three years based on material made available by taxpayer and
on takings for a test period of five weeks – Commissioners not taking account of pilferage –
Whether commissioners' assessment 'to the best of their judgment' – Finance Act 1972, s 31(1).*

The taxpayer, a licensee of a public house, relied on a manager to run the establishment
and based his value added tax returns on the takings handed to him by the manager.
Officers of the Commissioners of Customs and Excise visited the taxpayer's premises and
inspected the relevant documents. As a result of the inspection it appeared to them that
the taxpayer's value added tax returns for the period 1st August 1973 to 31st July 1976
were incorrect in that he had failed to declare and account for tax accurately on the full
value of supplies made by him. When questioned, the taxpayer suggested pilferage as a
possible cause of the deficiency. The officers did not interview the manager or visit the
premises during opening hours, but they noted the takings of the public house during
a test period of five weeks. On that basis, and pursuant to the powers conferred on them
by s 31(1)[a] of the Finance Act 1972, the commissioners assessed the amount of tax due.
The taxpayer appealed to a value added tax tribunal, contending that the commissioners
had taken insufficient steps to ascertain the amount of tax due, that five weeks was too
short a period on which to base an assessment covering three years and that no account
had been taken of pilferage. The tribunal held that, on balance, the assessment had been
made by the commissioners to the best of their judgment as required by s 31(1), but it
reduced the amount of the assessment to take account of pilferage. The taxpayer
appealed against the tribunal's decision contending that in making the assessment the
commissioners had failed to act to the best of their judgment as required by s 31(1) and
that, if in the view of the tribunal the commissioners should have taken account of
pilferage, then the assessment was invalidly made and should be set aside.

a Section 31(1) is set out at p 507 c, post

Held – The appeal would be dismissed for the following reasons—

(1) In assessing the amount of tax due 'to the best of their judgment' within s 31(1) of *a* the 1972 Act, the commissioners were required to consider fairly all material put before them by the taxpayer and on that material make a decision which was reasonable as to the amount of tax due. They were not required to make investigations as long as there was some material on which they could reasonably base an assessment, although if they did make any investigation they had to take into account the material disclosed by that investigation. In the circumstances it was perfectly proper for the commissioners to *b* make a test over a limited period such as five weeks and to take the results of the test into account in making the assessment. It followed therefore that the assessment had been made by the commissioners to the best of their judgment as required by s 31(1) (see p 508 *a* to *d*, p 509 *d e*, p 511 *b* to *f* and *j* and p 512 *b* and *g*, post); dicta of Lord Russell in *Income Tax Comr, United and Central Provinces v Badridas Ramrai Shop* (1937) LR 64 Ind App at 114–115 and of Lord Donovan in *Argosy Co Ltd v Inland Revenue Comr* [1971] 1 *c* WLR at 516–517 applied.

(2) The tribunal was entitled to come to the view that some reduction should be made in the amount of the assessment to take account of pilferage, but the fact that it came to that conclusion and rejected the view of the commissioners to that extent did not call into question the validity of the assessment (see p 512 *c* to *g*, post).

Notes
d
For assessments to value added tax in default of proper returns by taxpayer, see 12 Halsbury's Laws (4th Edn) para 955, and for appeals generally in respect of value added tax, see ibid paras 975–990.

For the Finance Act 1972, s 31, see 42 Halsbury's Statutes (3rd Edn) 190.

Cases referred to in judgment *e*
Argosy Co Ltd v Inland Revenue Comr (or Guyana Inland Revenue Comr) [1971] 1 WLR 514, 50 ATC 49, [1971] TR 29, PC, Digest (Cont Vol D) 502, *1310a*.
Income Tax Comr, United and Central Provinces v Badridas Ramrai Shop (1937) LR 64 Ind App 102, PC, 28(1) Digest (Reissue) 542, *1310*.

Appeal *f*
By a notice of appeal dated 6th December 1977 C P M Van Boeckel ('the taxpayer') appealed against a decision of the London Value Added Tax Tribunal given on 7th November 1977 on the ground that an assessment as to the amount of tax due made on him by the Customs and Excise Commissioners had not been made 'to the best of their judgment' within s 31(1) of the Finance Act 1972 since (1) the commissioners made no sufficient attempt to investigate the possibility of pilferage of stock and (2) the assessment *g* was based on an insufficiently long and representative period of the taxpayer's business. The facts are set out in the judgment.

Walter Aylen for the taxpayer.
David Latham for the Crown.

h
WOOLF J. This is an appeal by the taxpayer from a decision of the London Value Added Tax Tribunal given on 7th November 1977. On that appeal before the tribunal it was decided that the assessment of value added tax made by the Commissioners of Customs and Excise on the taxpayer on 15th November 1976 in the sum of £2,656 should be recomputed on the basis that an allowance should be made of £50 per week throughout the period of assessment for pilferage of stock. In this court it is contended *j* that the assessment which led to the appeal to the value added tax tribunal is an assessment which should be quashed as being one which is, in effect, made ultra vires.

An appeal to this court from the decision of the value added tax tribunal is an appeal confined to a point of law. However, if on the facts of the matter which were before the value added tax tribunal, it was shown that the assessments were in fact ones which the

the commissioners had no authority to make then that is a matter which can be properly
a questioned on the appeal to this court.

The right of appeal against an assessment made by the commissioners in respect of
value added tax to the tribunal is governed by s 40 of the Finance Act 1972. Section 40(1)
so far as relevant, provides:

> 'An appeal shall lie to a value added tax tribunal . . . against the decision of the
> Commissioners with respect to . . . (b) an assessment under section 31 of this Act or
b > the amount of such an assessment . . .'

That provision dealing with the right of appeal makes it clear that, before the tribunal,
not only can the amount of the assessment be challenged but also the actual making of
the assessment itself. The power of the commissioners to assess value added tax which
is due is contained in s 31(1) in these terms:

c
> 'Where a taxable person has failed to make any returns required under this Part
> of this Act or to keep any documents and afford the facilities necessary to verify such
> returns or where it appears to the Commissioners that such returns are incomplete
> or incorrect they may assess the amount of tax due from him to the best of their
> judgment and notify it to him.'

d Section 31(1) sets out various conditions which have to be fulfilled before the right to
assess arises. Some of those conditions are ones which depend on an objective state of
affairs such as the taxable person failing to make returns. Others are ones which depend
on the judgment of the commissioners, for example, the judgment of the commissioners
when it appears to them that the returns which were made were incomplete. If the
conditions or one of the conditions are fulfilled which give the right to make an
assessment, then the power of the commissioners is to make an assessment of the amount
e of tax due from the taxpayer to the best of the commissioners' judgment.

The issue which arises on the appeal before this court is whether or not the
commissioners, in making their assessment, complied with the requirement that the
assessment must be for the amount of tax which, to the best of the commissioners'
judgment, is due from the taxpayer. There is no issue as to the compliance with the
f conditions which have to be fulfilled before the right to make an assessment arises.

The provisions of s 31(1) of the 1972 Act are very similar to provisions which have
appeared in revenue legislation in this country and in the legislation of Dominions. So
far as this country is concerned, the power to assess for income tax is dealt with in s 29(1)
of the Taxes Management Act 1970; and in the appropriate circumstances the inspector
of taxes, under that legislation, may make an assessment to tax to the best of his
g judgment.

Both in relation to the income tax legislation and the value added tax legislation, the
power to make an assessment is an important element in the Revenue's machinery for
the recovery of tax. Value added tax, in the first instance, relies on the taxpayer making
a return which is a form of self assessment of the tax which is due. If the taxpayer does
not perform that function properly then the commissioners are dependent on the powers
h contained in the 1972 Act, including s 31(1), to enforce their right to recover the amount
of tax which is payable from a taxpayer.

The contentions on behalf of the taxpayer in this case can be summarised by saying
that on the facts before the tribunal it is clear, so it is contended, that the assessment in
question was not valid because the commissioners had taken insufficient steps to ascertain
the amount of tax due before making the assessment. Therefore it is important to come
to a conclusion as to what are the obligations placed on the commissioners in order
j properly to come to a view as to the amount of tax due to the best of their judgment. As
to this, the very use of the word 'judgment' makes it clear that the commissioners are
required to exercise their powers in such a way that they make a value judgment on the
material which is before them. Clearly they must perform that function honestly and
bona fide. It would be a misuse of that power if the commissioners were to decide on a

figure which they knew was, or thought was, in excess of the amount which could
possibly be payable, and then to leave it to the taxpayer to seek, on appeal, to reduce that   **a**
assessment.

Secondly, clearly there must be some material before the commissioners on which
they can base their judgment. If there is no material at all it would be impossible to form
a judgment as to what tax is due.

Thirdly, it should be recognised, particularly bearing in mind the primary obligation
to which I have made reference, of the taxpayer to make a return himself, that the   **b**
commissioners should not be required to do the work of the taxpayer in order to form
a conclusion as to the amount of tax which, to the best of their judgment, is due. In the
very nature of things frequently the relevant information will be readily available to the
taxpayer, but it will be very difficult for the commissioners to obtain that information
without carrying out exhaustive investigations. In my view, the use of the words 'best
of their judgment' does not envisage the burden being placed on the commissioners of   **c**
carrying out exhaustive investigations. What the words 'best of their judgment'
envisage, in my view, is that the commissioners will fairly consider all material placed
before them and, on that material, come to a decision which is one which is reasonable
and not arbitrary as to the amount of tax which is due. As long as there is some material
on which the commissioners can reasonably act then they are not required to carry out
investigations which may or may not result in further material being placed before   **d**
them.

Some support for this approach to the relevant provisions of s 31(1) are to be found in
two decisions of the Privy Council. The first is the case of the *Income Tax Comr, United and
Central Provinces v Badridas Ramrai Shop* (1937) LR 64 Ind App 102. In giving the
opinion of the Privy Council in that case, Lord Russell said, in relation to a similar
provision in the relevant Indian legislation (at 114–115):   **e**

'There remains for consideration the point whether the assessment can be attacked
on the ground that it was not made by the officer to the best of his judgment within
the meaning of s. 23, sub-s. 4. The Judicial Commissioners have laid down two
rules which impose upon the officer the duty of (i.) conducting some kind of local
inquiry before making the assessment under s. 23, sub-s. 4, and (ii.) recording a note   **f**
of the details and results of such inquiry. Their Lordships find it impossible to
extract these requirements from the language of the Act, which after all is, in such
matters, the primary and safest guide. The officer is to make an assessment to the
best of his judgment against a person who is in default as regards supplying
information. He must not act dishonestly, or vindictively or capriciously, because
he must exercise judgment in the matter. He must make what he honestly believes
to be a fair estimate of the proper figure of assessment, and for this purpose he must,   **g**
their Lordships think, be able to take into consideration local knowledge and repute
in regard to the assessee's circumstances, and his own knowledge of previous returns
by and assessments of the assessee, and all other matters which he thinks will assist
him in arriving at a fair and proper estimate: and though there must necessarily be
guess-work in the matter, it must be honest guess-work. In that sense, too, the   **h**
assessment must be to some extent arbitrary. Their Lordships think that the section
places the officer in the position of a person whose decision as to amount is final and
subject to no appeal; but whose decision, if it can be shown to have been arrived at
without an honest exercise of judgment, may be revised or reviewed by the
Commissioner under the powers conferred upon that official by s. 33.'

The reference by Lord Russell to the assessment being to some extent arbitrary must   **j**
be considered in the context in which it is used, and as in no way derogating from what
he had said earlier about the assessment not being made capriciously.

The other decision of the Privy Council was in *Argosy Co Ltd v Inland Revenue Comr*
[1971] 1 WLR 514. The legislation which was there under consideration was the Income
Tax Ordinance of Guyana in which again the words 'to the best of his judgment'

appear. As in the case of s 31 of the 1972 Act there was a condition, precedent to the
a right to assess, to be fulfilled before it was open to the commissioner to assess to the best
of his judgment. Dealing with the exercise of the assessing process once the condition
had been fulfilled, Lord Donovan, giving the judgment of their Lordships, said this (at
516–517):

b
'Once a reasonable opinion that liability exists is formed there must necessarily be
guess-work at times as to the quantum of liability. A resident may be known to be
living well above the standard which his declared income would support. The
commissioner must make some estimate, or guess, at the amount by which the
person has understated his income. Or reliable information may reach the
commissioner that the books of account of some particular taxpayer have been
falsified so as to reduce his tax. Again the commissioner may have to make some
c
guess of the extent of the reduction. Such estimates or guesses may still be to the
best of the commissioner's judgment—a phrase which their Lordships think simply
means to the best of his judgment on the information available to him. The
contrast is not between a guess and a more sophisticated estimate. It is between, on
the one hand, an estimate or a guess honestly made on such materials as are available
to the commissioner, and on the other hand some spurious estimate or guess in
d
which all elements of judgment are missing. The former estimate or guess would
be within the power conferred by section 48(4): the latter without.'

I draw attention to that passage, particularly because of the fact that Lord Donovan
stresses the requirement that the guess should be made honestly on the material which
is available to the commissioner.
Turning to the facts of the present case they are conveniently set out in the decision of
e the tribunal in these terms:

'[The taxpayer] for many years ran a public house in Putney Bridge Road,
Wandsworth, known as the Hop Pole. It is not an issue that this public house was
well managed and that it had a good clientele. In August 1970, however, [the
taxpayer] had the misfortune to have a stroke which paralysed his right-hand side
f and he was unable to take any part in running this public house for a period of two
years. During this period he had no control of the business whatsoever and had to
rely on managers and staff. By the end of 1972, however, he had recovered
sufficiently to go to the Hop Pole on Mondays and Fridays so as to collect and bank
money, but, except for rare occasions when he paid a visit in the early evening, he
was not at the public house when it was open, since this would have been too much
of a strain for him. He was never there in the later evening or at night. During the
g whole of this period [the taxpayer] was compelled to rely on managers and staff. He
finally gave up his tenancy on 30th November 1976, and he now has no connection
with the business. Not only did [the taxpayer], during the period to which the
assessment relates, bank the money which he collected on Mondays and Fridays, but
he also made out the value added tax returns which were based on the cash received
by him from his manager. [The taxpayer], who was in the circumstances compelled
h to rely on the managers and trusted them until he had reason to do otherwise,
treated this cash as reflecting the total gross takings of the Hop Pole in relation to
each return made by him. As to input tax he was in possession of all the invoices
and the total inputs were made out from these. There were two bars at the Hop
Pole, but only one till which was of a type which did not use till rolls. In the
j circumstances of the case [the taxpayer] was unable to check the till totals against the
cash, but was compelled to rely on his managers to do this, and the managers set the
till at zero at the end of each day. On 18th October 1976 [the taxpayer] was visited
at the Hop Pole by two officers of the commissioners, namely Mr Cannen and Mr
Scott. On their first visit they noted down the prices which were advertised in the
public house and proceeded on the basis that one-third of the sales took place in the

saloon bar and two-thirds in the public bar. [The taxpayer] gave them all the papers for which they asked, including account books and stocktakers' sheets. What the *a* officers of the commissioners did was over a trial period of five weeks to take a total of each line and thus calculate the percentage mark-up relating to each and divide the estimated gross takings as between the saloon bar and the public bar on the basis of one-third to two-thirds. In this manner they reached a total figure of what they considered the gross takings of the Hop Pole ought to have been. They then made various allowances in respect of off-sales and staff entertainment. They made *b* marginal reductions in the mark-up of minerals and soft drinks, and also in relation to some spirits. In this connection they assumed that 32 tots could be taken from a 26⅔ oz bottle, but they considered it fair to make a marginal allowance in the mark-up to take in small allowances for wastage. In relation to draught beer they allowed a figure of 3% for wastage. The [taxpayer] does not really seek to challenge the mathematical calculations made by these officers, although they made some *c* submissions as to both the off-sale and staff entertainment allowances to which reference is made below. The computations made by the officers were based on a five-week period from 26th June to 3rd August 1976, which they applied to the whole period for which the assessment was made [and I interpose, that is a period of three years]. The same officers of the commissioners returned to the 'Hop Pole' on 2nd November 1976 and had a conversation with [the taxpayer]. At this second *d* interview the commissioners stated that they found that there was an under-declaration of between £20,000 and £30,000 and they asked [the taxpayer] for an explanation. [The taxpayer] could not give any detailed explanation but told them that if you did not run a public house yourself you were bound to accept what your manager told you, and that it was not possible to go by anything else. [The taxpayer] had been aware that the gross profit was too low, but he felt unable in his *e* state of health to make any detailed investigations at the Hop Pole to find out what the cause of this might be. He did not feel well enough to have discussions with his manager or staff in which he might have to challenge them on matters such as stock pilferage. In fact, [the taxpayer] was not satisfied with the way in which the managers were conducting the business, and he changed managers three times. The last change took place on 1st January 1976, but despite this change the gross *f* profit became progressively lower. He was compelled to leave the running of the Hop Pole completely in the hands of this manager, so that [the taxpayer] decided that he had to terminate his tenancy. Things had been getting gradually worse over the latter part of the period to which the assessment relates, and he was convinced that considerable quantities of stocks were disappearing, and were consequently not reflected in the gross takings, but once again, on account of his health, he was unable *g* to make detailed investigations on the spot. He took this matter up with the stock-takers employed by him, but they were also unable to explain why stocks from time to time were considerably lower than they should have been. [The taxpayer] agreed that some of the deficiencies could have arisen from the stealing of cash, but he had no proof thereof or the extent to which it might be taking place. The stocktakers were not called to give evidence, and we understand from [the taxpayer] that he had *h* lost confidence in their ability to assist him. During the conversations which [the taxpayer] had with the officers who visited the Hop Pole, we are satisfied that he drew attention to the possibility of substantial pilferage of stock. [The taxpayer] also told us, and we accept his evidence, and this is confirmed by the evidence of the officers themselves, that they did not speak to any of the managers or the staff about the manner in which the business was conducted. Nor did they visit the bars of the *j* Hop Pole when the public house was open. During the conversation which took place, [the taxpayer] was asked by the officers about the amounts which might be allowed for staff entertaining and off-sales. Figures were put to [the taxpayer] by the officers, which [the taxpayer] did not seriously dispute, but we do not think he positively agreed with these figures, because he was not in a position to know what

a
was happening. He merely thought that the figures put to him by the officers
might be about right. In evidence before us he doubted the correctness of these
figures.'

In respect of those facts as found by the tribunal it was submitted on the taxpayer's
behalf before the tribunal that the assessment should be set aside. In the first place it was
not made to the best of the judgment of the commissioners since it was based on a five-
b
week period which was arbitrarily applied to the whole period of assessment.

Pausing there, it seems to me that the criticism which is there made of the
commissioners is one which is entirely without foundation. It is perfectly proper for the
commissioners, if they choose to do so, to make a test over a limited period such as five
weeks, and take the results which are thrown up by that test period of five weeks into
account in performing their task of making an assessment in accordance with the
c
requirements of s 31 of the 1972 Act.

The second contention which was made before the tribunal was that the commissioners
made no real investigations into the manner in which the Hop Pole was run, either by
interviewing a manager or by visiting the public house when it was open. In view of the
taxpayer's state of health and the fact that the officers well knew that he played no active
part in the actual running of the Hop Pole this was an omission so serious as went to the
d
root of the whole assessment.

With regard to that second contention, the approach to the provisions of s 31 which I
have indicated earlier in this judgment again, in my view, makes it clear that the
criticisms of the commissioners were not justified. In fact, quite clearly on the material
which was before the tribunal the commissioners had made substantial investigations in
this case. As I have indicated, unless the situation is one where no material is before the
commissioners on which they can reasonably base an assessment, the commissioners are
e
not required to make investigations. If they do make investigations then they have got
to take into account the material disclosed by those investigations. Obviously, as a
matter of good administrative practice, it is desirable that the commissioners should
make all reasonable investigations before making an assessment. If they do that it will
avoid, in many cases, the necessity of appeals to the tribunal. However to try and say that
in a particular case a particular form of investigation should have been carried out is a
f
contention which, in my view, as a matter of law, bearing in mind the wording of
s 31(1), is difficult to establish.

What the tribunal said about the contentions to which I have just made reference is as
follows:

g
'In our view this case is near the borderline, first because the commissioners
applied to the whole three-year period under assessment a trial period so short as five
weeks, and second because the officers did not make any attempt to discuss with the
manager of the Hop Pole the manner in which the business of this public house was
carried on, nor did they on any occasion visit the bars of this public house to see the
way in which it was conducted on a day-to-day basis. The way in which a public
house is actually conducted may be of the greatest importance in cases of assessments,
h
and a mere exercise in mathematics, however fairly carried out, may sometimes be
very wide of the mark. On the other hand, the officers who visited the Hop Pole,
the bona fides of whom does not stand in any doubt, formed the view that [the
taxpayer], although they were aware that he had been ill, was fully conversant with
the business and was able to give them figures on which they thought they could
rely in making an assessment. We are in no doubt that it would have been
j
preferable if they had interviewed the current manager and actually visited the bars
at the Hop Pole when they were open; nonetheless we reach the conclusion, on
balance, that they made this assessment to the best of their judgment.'

In so far as the tribunal came to the conclusion that the assessment was made to the
best of the judgment of the commissioners, I agree with what the tribunal has said.

In relation to this case being on the borderline, it was urged before me on behalf of the
taxpayer that I should come to the conclusion that in fact the case is on the other side of   a
the borderline from that indicated by the tribunal. As I have already made clear, I do not
accede to that submission. Indeed, I am bound to say that I do not, on the material which
is before me, regard this case as being near the borderline. I do not think, looking at the
matter from the question of whether or not the requirements of s 31 have been complied
with, that this was a case which was close to the borderline. It seems to me that it would
be impossible to find, on the material put before the tribunal, that the commissioners   b
had not exercised their judgment as required by s 31.

A specific argument which was advanced with considerable force before me depended
on the fact that, having rejected the argument as to the validity of the assessment, the
tribunal went on to find that there should be a reduction made in the amount of the
assessment to make an allowance for pilferage. Quite clearly that was a view which the
tribunal could properly come to; but the fact that they came to that conclusion as to the   c
amount of the assessment and rejected the view of the commissioners to that extent does
not mean that the validity of the assessment was called into question. What the tribunal
were doing when they decided to reduce the assessment was making a decision on the
material before them as to the proper amount of tax in fact due. It was quite open to the
tribunal, on the balance of probabilities, to come to the conclusion that there had been
in fact pilferage which had to be taken into account in arriving at the amount of tax   d
which was in fact due. But that does not mean that you can challenge the validity of the
exercise performed by the commissioners, through their officers, in making the
assessment. Just as the tribunal, on the material before them, were entitled to come to
a conclusion as to the likelihood of pilferage being an explanation for part of the
deficiency, so it was open to the commissioners, having heard what the taxpayer said, to
have come to a conclusion that this was not a case where it was proper on the material   e
before them to make a reduction. There could be many reasons for this. There was no
positive evidence of pilferage placed before the commissioners, according to the facts as
found by the tribunal. All that happened was that the taxpayer was putting this forward
before the commissioners' officers as being a possible cause for the deficiency. It was no
doubt one which the taxpayer fairly believed should be taken into account; but equally
it was open to the officers to reject that as an explanation and to not take it into account   f
in making the assessment to the best of their judgment. Their bona fides were not being
challenged, and on the material put before the tribunal there was no way it could be said
that it was wholly unreasonable for the officers not to make further investigations into
the question of pilferage nor to come to a conclusion that there was pilferage in this case
which had to be taken into account.

Accordingly, it seems to me that this is a case where the appeal must fail, the tribunal's   g
decision being one which was a proper one on the material which was before them.

Appeal dismissed.

Solicitors: *Davies, Topping & Watkins* (for the taxpayer); *Solicitor for the Customs and Excise.*

Evelyn M C Budd   Barrister.

Bunge Corpn v Tradax SA

QUEEN'S BENCH DIVISION (COMMERCIAL COURT)
PARKER J
21st, 22nd, 23rd MARCH, 11th APRIL 1979

COURT OF APPEAL, CIVIL DIVISION
MEGAW, BROWNE AND BRIGHTMAN LJJ
13th, 14th, 15th, 16th, 19th, 20th NOVEMBER, 14th DECEMBER 1979

HOUSE OF LORDS
LORD WILBERFORCE, LORD FRASER OF TULLYBELTON, LORD SCARMAN, LORD LOWRY AND LORD ROSKILL
23rd, 24th, 25th, 26th FEBRUARY, 7th MAY 1981

Contract – Condition – Breach – Effect – Right of other party to terminate contract forthwith – Stipulation as to time – Condition or intermediate or innominate term – Term in shipping contract that buyers to give 15 days' notice of readiness of vessel – Buyers giving only 10 days' notice – Breach not sufficiently serious to entitle sellers to rescind contract if term not a condition – Whether effect of breach depending on gravity of breach – Whether term as to notice a condition or intermediate term – Whether sellers entitled to rescind contract – GAFTA form 119, cl 7.

Contract – Damages for breach – Default in shipment or delivery – Damages to be computed on mean contract quantity – Failure to ship because of buyers' breach – Whether 'default in shipment or delivery' referring only to sellers' breach or including buyers' breach – Whether damages to be computed on mean contract quantity or minimum quantity buyers required to accept – GAFTA form 119, cl 22.

Under a contract which incorporated GAFTA form 119 the buyers agreed to purchase from the sellers 15,000 tons of soya bean meal, 5% more or less, for shipment from the United States. It was the practice in the trade for a string of contracts to be made in which the shipment contract was merely an intermediate contract made in the course of the passage of the goods from the supplier to the eventual receiver. The terms of the parties' contract required three shipments of 5,000 tons fob from an American port in the Gulf of Mexico nominated by the sellers. By agreement between the parties one of the shipments was to be during June 1975. The buyers were to provide a vessel at the nominated port and by virtue of cl 7 of form 119 as completed by the parties they were required to 'give at least 15 consecutive days' notice' of the probable readiness of the vessel. If the goods were to be shipped during June the buyers were therefore required to give notice of their vessel's readiness by 13th June. In fact the buyers did not give notice until 17th June. The sellers claimed that the late notice was a breach of contract amounting to a repudiation and claimed damages from the buyers on the basis that by then the market price had fallen by over $US60 a ton. The dispute was referred to arbitration where the sellers were awarded $US317,500 damages. Those damages were computed on the basis that the quantity involved was 5,000 tons, having regard to cl 22 of form 119 which stipulated, inter alia, that 'In the event of default in shipment or delivery, damages [were to] be computed upon the mean contract quantity' (ie 5,000 tons). On appeal to the Commercial Court the judge reversed that award on the ground that the term as to time when notice was required to be given was not a condition but an intermediate term and the lateness of the notice did not amount to a breach of contract. The Court of Appeal reversed that finding on the ground that the term was a condition, and restored the award of damages. The Court of Appeal, however, reduced the award on the ground that cl 22 of form 119 was restricted to default by the sellers and did not therefore apply to the award which was, on ordinary principles, to be computed on the minimum quantity the buyers were required to take, namely 4,750 tons (ie 5,000 tons less 5%). The buyers appealed to the House of Lords, contending that the term as to notice was an intermediate term, that the effect of a breach of the term depended on the gravity of the breach, and that (as the sellers conceded) if the term was not a condition but merely an intermediate term the breach was not sufficiently serious to entitle the sellers to treat the contract as being repudiated. The sellers cross-appealed, contending cl 22 of form 119 applied to the award and therefore the damages ought to be based on a quantity of 5,000 tons.

Held – (1) The buyers' appeal would be dismissed for the following reasons—
(a) Stipulations as to time in mercantile contracts were generally to be treated as conditions (breach of which, no matter how minor, entitled the innocent party to treat the contract as at an end) and not as intermediate or innominate terms, because the reason for such a clause was to enable each party to organise his affairs to meet obligations arising in the future under the contract and not merely to determine, with the benefit of hindsight, the appropriate remedy when a breach occurred. Furthermore, the need for certainty, especially when there was a string of contracts involved, required such a clause to be strictly adhered to (see p 540 j, p 541 f to j, p 542 a b d to j, p 543 j to p 544 c and j to p 545 b and g to p 546 e, p 549 h to p 550 e, p 551 d to g and p 554 d, post); dictum of Diplock LJ in *Hong Kong Fir Shipping Co Ltd v Kawasaki Kisen Kaisha Ltd* [1962] 1 All ER at 485–489 distinguished.
(b) Whether a stipulation in a contract, including a stipulation as to time, was either expressly or impliedly a condition depended on the construction of the contract as at the time it was made and in the light of the surrounding circumstances, including, in the case of an obligation as to time, the nature of the subject matter and whether there was an express clause or notice that time was of the essence. Furthermore, when performance by one party of a stipulation in a mercantile contract was a condition precedent to the ability of the other party to perform his obligations, a stipulation as to time of performance by the first party was generally to be treated as a condition. In the light of the surrounding circumstances and the fact that the sellers could not nominate the port of loading until they received notice from the buyers of their vessel's readiness, the stipulation in cl 7 of form 119 that the buyers were to give at least 15 days' notice of readiness was a condition, and the sellers were therefore entitled to treat the contract as repudiated when the buyers failed to give the requisite 15 days' notice and to claim damages (see p 540 j, p 542 h j, p 544 b c, p 546 e f, p 553 c to e and p 554 d, post); dictum of Bowen LJ in *Bentsen v Taylor, Sons & Co (No 2)* [1893] 2 QB at 281 applied; dictum of Lord Diplock in *United Scientific Holdings v Burnley Borough Council* [1977] 2 All ER at 70–71 distinguished.
(2) The sellers' cross-appeal would be dismissed because 'default in shipment or delivery' in cl 22 of form 119 referred not to non-performance for whatever reason but to a failure to supply arising out of a breach of contract by the sellers. Since the failure to deliver had been caused by the buyers' and not the sellers' breach, cl 22 did not apply to the assessment of damages which were therefore to be assessed according to ordinary principles (see p 540 j, p 542 h j, p 544 b c, p 546 e f and p 554 j to p 555 a, post); *Toprak Mahsulleri Ofisi v Finagrain Compagnie Commerciale Agricole et Financière SA* [1979] 2 Lloyd's Rep 98 applied.
Per Lord Wilberforce. Time clauses are not susceptible of analysis according to the nature of breach, since there is only one kind of breach possible, namely to be late (see p 541 e f, post).

Cases referred to in judgments and opinions
Behn v Burness (1863) 3 B & S 751, 2 New Rep 184, 32 LJQB 204, 8 LT 207, 9 Jur NS 620, 1 Mar LC 329, 122 ER 281, Ex Ch, 12 Digest (Reissue) 522, *3612*.
Bentsen v Taylor, Sons & Co (No. 2) [1893] 2 QB 274, 63 LJQB 15, 69 LT 487, 4 R 510, 7 Asp MLC 385, CA, 12 Digest (Reissue) 431, *3114*.

Boone v Eyre (1779) 1 Hy Bl 273n, 1 Wms Saund 320c, 2 Wm Bl 1312, 126 ER 160, 12
Digest (Reissue) 524, *3630*.
Bowes v Shand (1877) 2 App Cas 455, 46 LJQB 561, 36 LT 857, 5 Asp MLC 461, HL, 39
Digest (Repl) 519, *598*.
Bremer Handelsgesellschaft mbH v J H Rayner & Co Ltd [1978] 2 Lloyd's Rep 73; *rvsd in part*
[1979] 2 Lloyd's Rep 216, CA.
Bremer Handelsgesellschaft mbH v Vanden Avenne-Izegem PVGA [1978] 2 Lloyd's Rep 109,
HL; *rvsg* [1977] 2 Lloyd's Rep 329, CA.
Carapanayoti & Co Ltd v Comptoir Commercial Andre & Cie SA [1972] 1 Lloyd's Rep 139,
CA, Digest (Cont Vol D) 825, *2046a*.
Cassell & Co Ltd v Broome [1972] 1 All ER 801, [1972] AC 1027, [1972] 2 WLR 645, HL,
17 Digest (Reissue) 82, *17*.
Cehave NV v Bremer Handelsgesellschaft mbH, The Hansa Nord [1975] 3 All ER 739, [1976]
QB 44, [1975] 3 WLR 447, [1975] 2 Lloyd's Rep 445, CA, Digest (Cont Vol D) 784,
510a.
Comptoir Commercial Anversois & Power, Son & Co, Re [1920] 1 KB 868, [1918–19] All ER
Rep 661, 89 LJKB 849, 122 LT 567, CA, 39 Digest (Repl) 570, *975*.
Davis Contractors Ltd v Fareham Urban District Council [1956] 2 All ER 145, [1956] AC 696,
[1956] 3 WLR 37, 54 LGR 289, HL, 12 Digest (Reissue) 507, *3518*.
Hong Kong Fir Shipping Co Ltd v Kawasaki Kisen Kaisha Ltd [1962] 1 All ER 474, [1962] 2
QB 26, [1962] 2 WLR 474, [1961] 2 Lloyd's Rep 478, CA, 41 Digest (Repl) 363, *1553*.
Jackson v Union Marine Insurance Co Ltd (1874) LR 10 CP 125, [1874–80] All ER Rep 317,
44 LJCP 27, 31 LT 789, 2 Asp MLC 435, Ex Ch, 12 Digest (Reissue) 484, *3435*.
Maredelanto Compania Naviera SA v Bergbau-Handel GmbH [1970] 3 All ER 125, [1971] 1
QB 164, [1970] 3 WLR 601, [1970] 2 Lloyd's Rep 43, CA, 12 Digest (Reissue) 420,
3059.
McDougall v Aeromarine of Emsworth Ltd [1958] 3 All ER 431, [1958] 1 WLR 1126, [1958]
2 Lloyd's Rep 345, 39 Digest (Repl) 615, *1281*.
Moorcock, The (1889) 14 PD 64, [1886–90] All ER Rep 530, 58 LJP 73, 60 LT 654, 6 Asp
MLC 373, CA, 12 Digest (Reissue) 751, *5395*.
Oppenheim v Fraser (1876) 34 LT 524, 3 Asp MLC 146, 39 Digest (Repl) 507, *510*.
Photo Production Ltd v Securicor Transport Ltd [1980] 1 All ER 556, [1980] AC 827, [1980]
2 WLR 283, HL; *rvsg* [1978] 3 All ER 146, [1978] 1 WLR 856, [1978] 2 Lloyd's Rep
172, CA, Digest (Cont Vol E) 111, *3407a*.
Reardon Smith Line Ltd v Hansen-Tangen [1976] 3 All ER 570, [1976] 1 WLR 989, [1976]
2 Lloyd's Rep 621, HL, 545, *183a*.
Reuter v Sala (1879) 4 CPD 239, 48 LJQB 492, 40 LT 476, 4 Asp MLC 121, CA, 12 Digest
(Reissue) 382, *2769*.
Stach (Ian) Ltd v Baker Bosly Ltd [1958] 1 All ER 542, [1958] 2 QB 130, [1958] 1 Lloyd's
Rep 127, 39 Digest (Repl) 733, *2125*.
Suisse Atlantique Société d'Armement Maritime SA v NV Rotterdamsche Kolen Centrale [1966]
2 All ER 61, [1967] 1 AC 361, [1966] 2 WLR 994, [1966] 1 Lloyd's Rep 529, HL,
Digest (Cont Vol B) 652, *2413a*.
Tarrabochia v Hickie (1856) 1 H & N 183, 26 LJ Ex 26, 156 ER 1168, 41 Digest (Repl) 181,
216.
Toepfer v Lenersan-Poortman NV [1978] 2 Lloyd's Rep 555; *affd* [1980] 1 Lloyd's Rep 143,
CA.
Toprak Mahsulleri Ofisi v Finagrain Compagnie Commerciale Agricole et Financière SA [1979]
2 Lloyd's Rep 98, CA, 12 Digest (Reissue) 111, *3344a*.
Tradax Export SA v Andre & Cie SA [1976] 1 Lloyd's Rep 416, CA.
Tsakiroglou & Co Ltd v Noblee & Thorl GmbH [1961] 2 All ER 179, [1962] AC 93, [1961]
2 WLR 633, [1961] 1 Lloyd's Rep 329, HL, 12 Digest (Reissue) 497, *3488*.
Turnbull (Peter) & Co Pty Ltd v Mundas Trading Co (Australasia) Pty Ltd [1954] 2 Lloyd's
Rep 198, 28 ALJ 162, Digest (Cont Vol B) 631, *491a*.
United Scientific Holdings Ltd v Burnley Borough Council [1977] 2 All ER 62, [1978] AC 904,
[1977] 2 WLR 806, 75 LGR 407, 33 P & CR 220, HL, Digest (Cont Vol E) 364, *3952ba*.

Wathes (Western) Ltd v Austins (Menswear) Ltd [1976] 1 Lloyd's Rep 14, CA.
White & Carter (Councils) Ltd v McGregor [1961] 3 All ER 1178, [1962] AC 413, [1962] 2 **a**
WLR 17, HL, 12 Digest (Reissue) 433, 3126.

Special case stated
By an award dated 7th November 1978 in the form of a special case stated by the Board
of Appeal of the Grain and Feed Trade Association Ltd in a dispute between Bunge Corpn
of New York ('the buyers') and Tradax Export SA of Panama ('the sellers') over the **b**
shipment of 15,000 long tons of US soya bean meal, the board upheld the award of the
umpire awarding the sellers damages of $US317,500. The question of law raised in the
special case for the court's decision was whether on the facts found, and on the true
construction of the contract, (1) the sellers were entitled by a telex sent on 20th June 1975
to hold the buyers in default of fulfilment, (2) the sellers were entitled to any, and if so
what, sum or sums by way of (a) damages and (b) carrying charges. The facts are set out **c**
in the judgment.

Nicholas Merriman for the buyers.
Christopher Staughton QC and *A M Havelock-Allan* for the sellers.

Cur adv vult **d**

11th April. **PARKER J** read the following judgment: This special case raises a number
of points in connection with the Grain and Feed Trade Association Ltd's contract no 119
being the 'General Contract F.O.B. Terms for Goods or Bags in Bulk'. I shall refer to it
hereafter as 'GAFTA 119'.

In January 1974, Bunge Corpn of New York, the appellants, agreed to buy from **e**
Tradax Export SA Panama, the respondents, 15,000 long tons 5% more or less of US soya
bean meal, shipment of 5,000 long tons in each of May, June, and July 1975 at $US199·50
per metric ton fob one US Gulf port at sellers' option, stowed and trimmed. The
contract was written and was made through Peter Marcy Inc of Rotterdam (Marcy) and
Bunge SA of Antwerp (Bunge Antwerp). It incorporated the terms of GAFTA 119. This
written contract was issued by Bunge Antwerp on behalf of the appellants. The **f**
respondents, as was their normal custom, issued a separate contract in respect of the May
shipment.

The contract for the full quantity, the separate contract for May, and GAFTA 119 are
annexed to the special case.

The dispute between the parties relates to the May shipment which, as a result of an
extension claimed under cl 8 of GAFTA 119 became a June shipment.

The May shipment was sold on by the appellants to Warinco AG of Zurich, who sold **g**
on to Fribesco SA of Lausanne who in turn sold to Sosimage SPA of La Spezia. Extensions
under all these subcontracts were also claimed under cl 8 of GAFTA 119.

Clause 7 of GAFTA 119 provides:

'PERIOD OF DELIVERY—During   at Buyers' call. Buyers shall
give at least   consecutive days' notice of probable readiness of **h**
vessel(s), and of the approximate quantity required to be loaded. Buyers shall keep
Sellers informed of any changes in the date of probable readiness of vessel(s).'

Both the contract issued by Bunge Antwerp and the separate contract issued for the
May shipment provided for the quantity within the permitted range to be declared at
latest when nominating the vessel. The overall contract provided that buyers should **j**
give '15 days pre-advice of readiness of steamer'. The May contract stated 'buyers to give
15 days loading notice'.

In the result the appellants were obliged to take delivery by the end of June 1975 of
5,000 tons 5% more or less and to give a minimum of 15 days notice of probable
readiness to load, which notice had also to declare the quantity within the permitted
range which the appellants intended to take.

As June has 30 days, the last day for giving notice under cl 7 was either Saturday, 14th
a June, or Sunday, 15th June, according to whether the obligation under the clause to give
consecutive days notice should be construed as providing for clear days notice or not. For
reasons which will hereafter appear, that point is academic in the present case. I mention
it only because counsel for the respondents did not wish to be taken to be accepting as
necessarily correct in law the view of the board of appeal that, apart from difficulties
caused by the 15th day of a 30-day month being a Sunday or other non-business day, a
b notice could, in such a month, be given up to and including the 15th of the month.

No notice pursuant to cl 7 was initiated by the appellants or any sub-buyer until
1429 hrs on 16th June when Sosimage despatched a telex to the brokers between Fribesco
and Warinco containing the following: 'For the contract in object we nominate SS
Sankograin ETA US Gulf 23/25 June 1975 for T. 5,000 5% M/L US soyabean meal.
Waiting for shippers name/loading port.'

c The essential subsequent history of this notification is (i) that it reached the appellants
in New York on the same day, (ii) that also on the same day, the appellants dispatched it
from New York at 1103 hrs edt to Bunge Antwerp, (iii) that on 17th June, Bunge
Antwerp sent it to Marcy who received it at 0846 hrs.

The board of appeal have found and the respondents accept that notification was given
to the respondents when it was received by Marcy on 17th June. The board of appeal
d have also found that on its way to Marcy from Sosimage it was passed on without
delay. This too is accepted by the respondents.

On 20th June at 1225 hrs the respondents sent a telex to the appellants in the following
terms:

'Contract hgs 8603 dd 1/30/74 5000 lt US sbm fob Gulf
e 'We refer to your telex of 18th June by which you nominated the vessel
Sankograin expected to arrive at the US Gulf on 23/25 June. We ask you to note that
under the above contract you have the obligation to give a 15 days loading notice.
On the other hand the extended period of shipment will expire on 30th June.
Under the circumstances your loading notice is late and we consider that you are in
breach of the above contract in accordance with the default clause of the GAFTA
f form No 119. We hereby declare you in default and hold you responsible for any
and all losses damages costs and expenses which we may suffer as a result of your
default.

'TradaxSA.'

The references to the buyers' telex of 18th June is, as the board of appeal have found,
a mistaken reference to their telex of 17th June.

g The first question of law raised in this special case is whether on the facts found and on
the true construction of the contract the respondents were entitled by the telex sent on
20th June 1975 to hold the appellants in default of fulfilment.

This question involves the determination of the following principal issues: 1. Did the
appellants give notice under cl 7 in time? 2. Was the notice valid in content? 3. If the
notice given was out of time, was the breach such as to entitle the respondents to hold the
h appellants in default? 4. If the notice was not valid in content was the breach such as to
entitle the respondents to hold the appellants in default? 5. If the appellants' notice was
such as to entitle the respondents to hold the appellants in default, have the respondents
lost that right before they, on 20th June, sought to exercise it?

Principal issue 1—Did the appellants give notice in time?
j This issue involves no less than four sub-issues.

Sub-issue (i)
Were the appellants obliged to give notice to Marcy or was notice to Bunge Antwerp
sufficient?

Clause 20 of GAFTA 119 provides that: 'A Notice to the Broker of Agent shall be
deemed a Notice under this contract.' Paragraph 2 of the special case begins as follows:

'The Contract was made through (Marcy) and (Bunge Antwerp) who acted as brokers and who received commission.' The appellants therefore submit that notice to either Bunge Antwerp or Marcy was sufficient.

Paragraph 11 of the special case however finds that: 'The telex from Bunge New York to Bunge Antwerp on the 16th June did not constitute giving notice to the Sellers since Bunge Antwerp were not "brokers" for the purposes of the contract.'

The respondents submit that this is correct since the contract for the May shipment issued by the respondents states that the brokers are Peter Marcy Inc, gives their address, and bears the appellants' receipt stamp. Marcy must therefore, it is said, be taken to be the brokers for the purposes of cl 20 to the exclusion of Bunge Antwerp.

I accept this submission. The appellants' reliance on the opening sentence of para 2 of the special case is, in my judgment, misplaced. The contract issued by Bunge Antwerp named no brokers and is found in para 2 itself to have been issued by Bunge Antwerp on behalf of Bunge New York. This indicates agency rather than brokerage and, Marcy having been named in the documents, the finding of the board of appeal that they were, together with Bunge Antwerp, brokers in the making of the contract cannot in my judgment prevail over the documents. Furthermore, when there are two brokers, one for each party, the reference in cl 20 to *the* broker can only sensibly mean the broker for the party to whom the notice is to be given, just as the reference to *the* agent must mean either a common agent or the agent of the party to whom notice is to be given and not the agent of the giver of the notice; for a notice to a party's own agent, unless he acts also for the other party, cannot sensibly be regarded as giving notice to the other party.

Accordingly, I hold that notice to Bunge Antwerp was not notice to the respondents and that, in order to comply with the contract, the appellants were obliged to give notice either to the respondents themselves or to Marcy.

Sub-issue (ii)

Is a notice under cl 7 of GAFTA 119 given when it is dispatched or when it is received? Clause 7 itself gives little guidance as to the meaning of 'give' or 'given' save that, in a case where the buyer has to a give a minimum notice, it seems a little odd if the parties intended that he might be faced with the position of being unable to tell whether he was in time when he performed the act of dispatch but must wait to see whether the wire services had functioned efficiently.

Clause 20 of GAFTA 119, however, does afford assistance. It provides:

'NOTICES—Any Notices received after 1600 hours on a business day shall be deemed to have been received on the business day following. A Notice to the Broker or Agent shall be deemed a Notice under this contract. All Notices given under this contract shall be given by letter or by telegram or by telex or by other method of rapid written communication. In case of resales all Notices shall be passed on without delay by Buyers to their respective Sellers or vice versa.'

The clause is in terms dealing with receipt of notices, the effect of notices given to brokers, the methods of giving of notices and the passing on of notices. The methods listed for the giving of notices, the emphasis on rapidity and the requirement for passing on of notices without delay, point to the giving of the notice meaning the dispatch of the notice. If a notice is not 'given' until it is received, rapidity appears to be unimportant. If a notice must be passed on without delay and a recipient dispatches a telegram without delay, it appears unlikely that the parties would have intended that the party dispatching the telegram should be held to have delayed because there was subsequently some delay in the cable service. The provision as to receipt does not in my judgment indicate that giving and receipt were intended to be the same thing, but the opposite. They are, as a matter of language, different and there is good reason for the provision as to receipt in that the recipient has to pass on without delay. The provision protects the receiver of a notice from the charge of having delayed a day when a notice reaches his offices after normal business hours.

a   Indications in the clause itself are therefore that a notice is 'given' when dispatched by proper means. This is in accord with the decision of the House of Lords in *Bremer Handelsgesellschaft mbH v Vanden Avenne-Izegem PVBA* [1978] 2 Lloyd's Rep 109. That decision concerned the giving of notice under the force majeure clause of GAFTA 100 and turned largely on the language of that clause which is not present in GAFTA 119. The GAFTA contract there in question did however contain a clause similar to cl 7 of GAFTA 119, and Lord Salmon said (at 125):

b   'It has been argued on behalf of the buyers that the notice was given too late, having been given at 1750 hours on July 3 whereas it should have been given before 1600 hours on that day. Clause 23 was said to support this argument since it provided that: "Any notices received after 1600 hours on a business day shall be deemed to have been received on the business day following ... All notices given under this contract shall be given by letter or by telegram or by telex or by other
c   method of rapid written communication ..." I cannot accept the argument that the notice was given too late. Clause 23 itself illustrates the difference which this contract draws between giving and receiving notice. The first sentence of the clause deals with the receipt of a notice. The second sentence deals with the giving of a notice. There is a clear distinction drawn between the meaning of giving notice and the receiving notice. Giving notice means the sending of the notice and this may,
d   and usually does, occur before it is received.'

That passage applies equally to the present case and I hold that a notice under cl 7 is given when dispatched.

Sub-issue (iii)
e   If the last day for giving a notice under cl 7 expires on a non-business day, is the time extended by virtue of cl 21? Clause 21 provides:

'NON-BUSINESS DAYS—Saturdays, Sundays and the officially recognised and/or legal holidays of the respective countries and any days which The Grain and Feed Trade Association Limited may declare as Non-Business Days for specific purposes shall be Non-Business Days. Should the time limit for doing any act or giving any notice
f   expire on a Non-Business Day, the time so limited shall be extended until the first Business Day thereafter. The period of shipment shall not be affected by this clause.'

It was submitted for the respondents that the clause has no application where the last day for giving the notice is only ascertainable by working backwards from a reference point and only applies to cases where the notice has to be given not later than so many
g   days after a reference point. To provide, it is said, that a 15-day notice of shipment is to be given does not give a time limit for the giving of the notice at all. This, so far as it goes, is plainly correct, but it is equally true that, if the last day for loading is the last day of the month, then the time limit for giving a 15-day notice expires 15 days earlier. Since the clause is of general application I can see, even looking at the clause by itself, no reason to construe it narrowly as the respondents suggest. Other clauses however show
h   in my judgment that the wider construction is right. The only clauses which specifically provide for notice are cl 7 itself and cl 8. Clause 8 provides for a notice 'not later than the next business day following the last day of the delivery period'. There is here plainly a time limit forward from a reference point but the time limit necessarily expires on a business day. Hence cl 21 can have no application to a notice under that clause. If therefore it is to have any content so far as notices are concerned it must apply to notices
i   under cl 7, for, as GAFTA 119 is printed, there is no other notice provided for to which it could apply. It is of course true that notices might be provided for in whatever force majeure clause was inserted or in other special clauses, but it would be strange if cl 21 was intended not to apply to either of the two forms of notice specifically provided for and to be there merely to cover the eventuality that some specific agreement outside the printed form might provide for a notice with a time limit running forward from a

reference point. Moreover, cl 21 also deals with expiry of the time limit for doing any act. Neither the appellants nor respondents were able to point to a time limit for doing any act running forward from a reference point. The nearest to such a provision is the *a* obligation on sellers under cl 18 to advise buyers without delay in the event of shipment proving impossible in the contract period. Only one case of an act to be done within a time calculated backwards from a reference point was found. That is in cl 17 where buyers are obliged to confirm to sellers that they have effected insurance at least five consecutive days before expected readiness of vessel and, on failure, sellers are given the right to effect insurance at buyers' expense. On the appellants' construction of cl 21 it *b* would not apply in that case and as a result would apply to no notice and no act provided for in the printed form. I decline to give it any such construction and I hold that it does operate to extend the time in the case of the last day for giving notice under cl 7 being a non-business day.

In the present case the last day for giving notice was either Saturday, 14th June, or Sunday, 15th June. As both are non-business days time was therefore on either view *c* extended to Monday, 16th June. Notice was initiated on that day but was not dispatched to Marcy until 17th June. Accordingly, unless saved by the provisions of cl 20, it was still a day late. This leads me to sub-issue (iv).

Sub-issue (iv)   *d*

Notwithstanding that notice was not given until 17th June, was it nevertheless in time?

It was sought to be argued, but in the end only faintly, that the delay from midnight on the 16th/17th to 0846 hrs on the 17th fell within the de minimis principle, but I cannot accept this. Time provisions are important and although the rule might possibly operate in the event of a delay of a very short space of time the delay here was in my *e* judgment not trivial. The original notice from Sosimage was passed on within 14 minutes of receipt and even if the time from midnight to 0800 hrs should be ignored on the basis that offices were unlikely to open until then, subsequent delay could not be regarded as trifling.

If therefore the notice given to Marcy on the 17th is to be regarded as being in time, it can only be by virtue of cl 20. Paragraph 5 of the special case states: *f*

'Moreover, an FOB buyer cannot rely on the notices clause of GAFTA 119 and thereby give a lesser notice by reason only that a notice which was given in time by a subsequent sub-buyer has, although passed on without delay, reached him too late to pass onto the seller in time.'

This must depend on the construction of the clause and whilst due weight must be *g* given to the views of the board of appeal, the question is one for the court to decide. In my judgment, cl 20 means that provided the intitial notice is in time and is passed on without delay it will be good as between first buyer and seller notwithstanding that as between them alone and in the absence of sub-sales it would have been late. The obligation to pass on without delay indicates both that what is to be passed on is the original notice and that speed in doing so is important. Speed would be of comparatively *h* little importance if, as between each buyer and seller, the full period had to be given. It would however clearly be vital if the first seller was to be deprived of the time it takes to pass a notice up the chain. The requirement of speed appears to me to show that, in the case of string contracts, the seller was prepared to accept an originally good notice provided it reached him without delay and therefore deprived him of only a small part *j* of the originally stipulated period in which to get the goods ready for shipment. Such a construction need cause no difficulty, for sellers can, if they wish to, stipulate for a time which will allow a margin for the mechanics of passing an originally good notice up the chain.

Since in the present case it is found that there was no delay and since the initial notice

was, as a result of the operation of cl 21, in time, I hold that the notice given to Marcy was
a in time.

Principal issue 2—Was the notice valid in content?
The notice was required to be a notice of probable readiness to load, to state the
quantity and, subject to the matters of abridgment already considered, was to be for 15
days. It was on the face of it defective in that it was not a notice of readiness to load but
b of eta US Gulf, and it did not declare the quantity. Further, if it is to be regarded as a
notice of readiness to load, it was too short, for it specified 23rd/25th June.
During the course of the argument it was accepted by both parties that if it became
necessary to determine the notice's validity as to content, the case would have to go back
to the board of appeal, for it appears that there is an existing practice in the trade that the
seller does not nominate the port until he has received a cl 7 notice and that by reason of
c this, cl 7 notices specify not expected readiness to load, but eta Gulf. Neither party was
clear as to the precise limits of this practice and whatever its limits it does not follow that
they have contractual force. There are many possibilities as to this practice. It may for
example be to give 15 days' notice of arrival in the US Gulf; or to give some shorter
period with some standard allowance for the time from arrival in the Gulf to readiness
to load in port; or for notices of arrival in the Gulf in less than the stipulated days to be
d treated as notices of readiness in the stipulated days. These matters will all have to be
investigated if the matter becomes material. I can therefore reach no conclusion on this
issue.

*Principal issue 3—If the notice was out of time was the breach such as to entitle the respondents
to hold the appellants in default?*
e As I have already concluded that the notice given was in time, it is unnecessary to reach
a conclusion on this matter but it was fully argued before me and both parties considered
it to be the most important point in the case. In view of this and the fact that my
conclusion that the notice was in time may not survive, I consider it right to express my
views on it. It involves the following questions: (a) Was the obligation as to time a
'condition', ie, a term, any breach of which would entitle the seller to rescind the
f contract? (b) If not, was it an innominate term or a warranty? (c) If it was an innominate
term, was the breach sufficiently serious to amount to a repudiation?
In his argument that the clause was a condition, counsel for the respondents made the
following four principal points: 1. Clauses specifying time limits should be regarded as
conditions. In this connection he relied on the observations of Donaldson J in *Toepfer v
Lenersan-Poortman NV* [1978] 2 Lloyd's Rep 555 at 558–559. 2. A similar clause has been
g held by Mocatta J in *Bremer Handelsgesellschaft mbH v J H Rayner & Co Ltd* [1978] 2 Lloyd's
Rep 73 to be a condition; the decision in the case has been over-ruled by the Court of
Appeal on another ground and the Court of Appeal has expressly refrained from dealing
with the point. There was however at least one observation in the Court of Appeal
judgments which appears to favour Mocatta J's judgment on the point. 3. In other cases,
successive courts and counsel have proceeded on the basis that such a clause was clearly
h a condition. An example was *Carapanayoti & Co Ltd v Comptoir Commercial Andre & Cie
SA* [1972] 1 Lloyd's Rep 39. 4. The board of appeal found in the special case, in para 5:
'This term in an FOB contract is regarded in the trade as of such great and fundamental
importance that any breach thereof goes to the root of the contract.'
For the appellants counsel submitted: 1. That whether such a clause is or is not a
condition must depend on the construction of the clause in the context of the contract as
i a whole. Decisions even on identical clauses under other contracts must therefore be
viewed with caution. 2. The decision of Mocatta J was wrong and should not be
followed. 3. Clause 7 of GAFTA 119 is not on its true construction a condition but is an
innominate term within the principles established in recent cases.
Counsel for the respondents has two principal difficulties. In the first place he was
constrained to admit that the effect of cl 8 is that the clause cannot be regarded as a

condition during the initial delivery period, for the buyer may claim an extension after the end of that period. This indeed is the effect of the Court of Appeal decision in *Bremer v Rayner* [1979] 2 Lloyd's Rep 216. Secondly, that decision pro tanto overrules or makes inapplicable the decision of Mocatta J which was based on the incorrect view that the extension clause was not applicable in the contract there under consideration.

The effect of cl 8 is of importance. Suppose that no notice has been given by what will transpire to have been the last day if the buyer does not claim an extension. The seller cannot hold the buyer in default and will not be able to do so until the next business day following the end of the initial period has come to an end without any claim to extension having been given. This does not suggest that the clause was regarded as being or intended to be of fundamental importance. It suggests rather that it was intended to produce the result, also found by the board of appeal in para 5, that 'if a seller is not given the full 15 consecutive days notice the buyer cannot complain if the seller is thereby unable to deliver the goods on the date indicated', a finding which was also present in the special case in *Bremer v Rayner*: see [1978] 2 Lloyd's Rep 73 at 89. Furthermore, there is a certain difficulty in construing the clause as not being a condition in the initial period but converting itself into a condition in the extended period. Indeed, it is in my judgment impossible to do so. If a bad notice in the initial period is not a breach of condition, it must follow that a bad notice in the extended period is not a breach of condition, at all events so long as there is still time to replace it with a good notice.

The problem therefore reduces itself to this: was it a condition that a notice be given by the last possible day of the extended period notwithstanding that it was not a condition that a notice be given by the last possible day of the initial period? With clear words this is no doubt possible but the terms of the contract point to the opposite conclusion. Suppose the last day for giving the notice is Good Friday, then even if 'give' equals 'receipt', the time will be extended to the following Tuesday and the seller will then get less than his full 15 days.

In addition the fact that the notice is to be of 'probable readiness' and may be changed, the provisions as to passing on of notices already mentioned and the fact that the sellers might in any event have to forego some part of the full 15 days waiting for their brokers or agents to pass a notice to them (see the special case para 23), in my judgment tend to indicate that the clause was not intended to be one for the breach of which, however slight, the sellers were to be entitled to rescind.

In *Cehave NV v Bremer Handelsgesellschaft mbH, The Hansa Nord* [1975] 3 All ER 739 at 755, [1976] QB 44 at 70–71 Roskill J said:

'In my view, a court should not be over ready, unless required by statute or authority so to do, to construe a term in a contract as a "condition" any breach of which gives rise to a right to reject rather than as a term any breach of which sounds in damages ... In principle, contracts are made to be performed and not to be avoided according to the whims of market fluctuation and where there is a free choice between two possible constructions I think the court should tend to prefer that construction which will ensure performance and not encourage avoidance of contractual obligations.'

I am not bound either by statute or authority. There are neither express words nor, in my judgment, clear indications that the provision as to notice was intended to be a condition even to the limited extent under consideration and, following the passage cited above, I hold that the clause is not a condition even to such limited extent. To do so appears to me to be in accordance not only with that passage but with the general principles established in *Hong Kong Fir Shipping Co Ltd v Kawasaki Kisen Kaisha Ltd* [1962] 1 All ER 474, [1962] 1 QB 26, *The Hansa Nord* itself and *Reardon Smith Line Ltd v Hansen-Tangen* [1976] 3 All ER 570, [1976] 1 WLR 989.

As between an innominate term and a warranty I have no doubt that the term was an innominate term and the contrary was not argued. Whether the breach, qua time, was sufficiently serious to justify the respondents in rescinding must depend on the delay

involved if delay there was. If, as the board of appeal have held, the notice should have
a been given on Friday the 13th, the delay appears at first sight to be considerable but this
is not really so. The object of the notice is principally to give the seller time in which to
assemble the goods for shipment. The gravity of a breach must therefore be judged by
the extent to which he is deprived of that time. Notice having been given at 0846 hrs on
17th June he was left with 12 clear days or four-fifths of the longest stipulated period.
In my judgment this cannot, within the principles established in the *Hong Kong Fir* case
b and *The Hansa Nord*, be regarded as sufficient to justify the respondents in rescinding. It
did not come near to depriving the sellers of 'substantially the whole benefit which it was
intended they should obtain from the contract' (see the *Hong Kong Fir* case [1962] 1 All
ER 474 at 487, [1962] 2 QB 26 at 69 per Diplock LJ).
    At most it deprived them of some small part of the time in which to assemble the
goods and they might, without breach, be deprived of some part of this time in any
c event.

*Principal issue 4—If the notice was invalid as to content was the breach such as to entitle the
respondents to hold the appellants in default?*
    I have no doubt that the provisions as to content do not amount to a condition of the
contract. As counsel for the respondents conceded that if the time for the giving of the
d notice was not a condition, as was in my judgment the case, it would follow that
provisions as to content were not either. I need say no more on the point.
    Was it then an innominate term or a warranty? Again, it was not suggested that it was
no more than a warranty and I hold that it was an innominate term. As, at present, the
only certain breach as to content lies in the failure to specify quantity and as to reach a
conclusion involves assessing the gravity of the breach, I can only come to a conclusion
e on this issue if either a) the breach as to quantity was itself such as to warrant rescission,
or b) albeit that it was not, there would be no sufficient breach even if the position is
assumed to be the worst possible against the appellants.
    As to quantity the failure to specify does not in my judgment by itself justify rescission
and it was not argued that it did. This is hardly surprising in view of the limited effect
of the option clause. At worst against the appellants the notice could be taken to be a
f notice of readiness to load on 25th June and thus plainly short by a considerable
amount. It would give 8 instead of 15 days notice. However, as the board of appeal
states in para 5 of the case—'if a seller is not given the full fifteen . . . days notice then the
buyer cannot complain if the seller is . . . unable to deliver the goods on the date
indicated.' He can, therefore, in substance treat a short notice as being for the full
period. Furthermore, under the extension clause he has the option, if delivery is not
g taken by the end of the period, to demand the price against tender of warehouse
warrants. I cannot therefore see that, even at its worst against the appellants, the breach
would be of the gravity required to justify rescission.
    I conclude therefore that, even assuming the worst possible position against the
appellants, breaches as to content would not justify the respondents in holding the
appellants in default. Before leaving this matter I should perhaps add a word of
h caution. When I use the word 'possible' I do not intend to indicate that I accept that the
appellants could be legally obliged to give 15 days notice of arrival in the Gulf. There
would clearly be great difficulty about this since the obligation is to give notice of
probable readiness to load and it seems highly improbable that a vessel could always be
ready to load contemporaneously with her arrival in the Gulf. I include it as a possibility
merely because counsel for the respondents submitted that 15 days' notice of eta US Gulf
j was required.

*Principal issue 5—If there was a breach entitling the respondents to hold the appellants in default,
was the right lost by the time the respondents sought to exercise it?*
    This does not arise in view of my earlier conclusions but assuming those conclusions
are wrong and that there was a breach justifying the respondents in holding the appellants

in default, they had not in my judgment lost it. In order to establish that they had, counsel for the appellants accepted that he would have to show that the only possible *a* conclusion in law from the lapse of time between breach and purported exercise of the right was that the respondents had decided to affirm the contract despite the breach. He did not establish this to my satisfaction. The board of appeal clearly approached the matter in the right way and they were in my judgment entitled to hold as they did that there was no unreasonable delay and thus no evidence that the respondents had decided to accept the nominations and thereby affirm the contract.   *b*

In the result, I answer the first question of law in the negative.

The conclusion on the second question, namely: 'Whether . . . (the Respondents) are entitled to any, and if so what sum or sums by way of (a) damages and (b) carrying charges?' must as a result also be answered in the negative; but again I shall consider the arguments which were presented on the assumption that my earlier conclusions are wrong.   *c*

Counsel for the appellants submitted that, even on that assumption, the respondents had suffered no damage for they had failed in their duty to mitigate by, in effect, failing to wait till the end of the extension period and then demanding price against warrants which the appellants would then have been obliged to pay. This argument appears to me unsustainable for it is in effect saying that the respondents were not entitled to hold the appellants in default whilst for present purposes it is assumed that they were so entitled. *d* It is true that in commercial contracts it may be unreasonable for an innocent party to refuse an offer from a defaulter which will have the effect of reducing the damage, but to take advantage of this principle the appellants would require findings both that they had made an offer after the respondents had declared default and that the respondents had unreasonably refused that offer. They had no such findings.

Counsel for the appellants submitted, secondly, that if the respondents were entitled *e* to damages on the basis of the difference between market price and contract price, as the board of appeal have held, such damages should be assessed on the minimum quantity and not on the mean quantity. In my judgment this is correct. As against a wrongdoer damages should be assessed on the basis that he would, had he not defaulted, have performed the contract in the manner which would result in the lowest damages for the breach. Since the appellants could have opted for the minimum quantity without being *f* in breach, it is on that quantity that damages should in my judgment be assessed. Counsel for the defendants argued that, since the appellants had not exercised their option and since any option subsequently exercised would have been too late, the principle has no application, but this argument appears to me to beg the question. The principle is that the innocent party can recover no more than would result from breach if the contract had been performed in the most favourable way to the defaulter. Since, *g* ex hypothesi, the contract has not been performed, the fact that the defaulter has not taken advantage of the option does not appear to me to arise.

In the result I answer both questions in the special case in the negative.

Order accordingly. Award remitted to board of appeal to give effect to judgment. Leave to appeal granted.   *h*

K Mydeen Esq   Barrister.

j

Appeal
The sellers appealed to the Court of Appeal.

Christopher Staughton QC and *A M Havelock-Allan* for the sellers.
Roger Buckley QC and *Nicholas Merriman* for the buyers.

Cur adv vult

a
14th December. The following judgments were read.

MEGAW LJ. By a contract made on 30th January 1974, Tradax Export SA, Panama, whom I shall call the sellers, agreed to sell and Bunge Corpn, New York, whom I shall call the buyers, agreed to buy 15,000 long tons, 5% more or less at buyers' option, of US soya
b bean meal, with shipment of 5,000 tons in each of the months of May, June and July 1975. So the contract provided for delivery and shipment more than a year after the contract date. The sale, at $US199·50 per metric ton, was f o b one US Gulf port at sellers' option. The contract incorporated the terms of the Grain and Feed Trade Association Ltd's standard form of contract no 119. I shall call the association GAFTA and the contract form GAFTA 119.
c   A dispute arose under the contract which was referred to arbitration in accordance with the GAFTA rules. The sellers claimed, and the buyers denied, that the buyers were in breach of contract by reason of the buyers' failure to give to the sellers a proper and timeous notice nominating the carrying vessel and stating its anticipated date of readiness for loading. The dispute related to the shipment which, under the contract, was due to be made in May 1975. No question arose as to the contractual obligations relating to the
d other two months' shipments. It has been assumed, and I shall assume, that the question whether or not there was a repudiation by the buyers could, and should, be decided by reference to the one month's shipment, as though the relevant contract did not provide for further shipments. Whether that assumption is right or wrong in law, I do not need to consider, since the House of Lords found it unnecessary to consider a similar point which had been raised, and on which there had been a difference of opinion in this court,
e in *Bremer Handelsgesellschaft mbH v Vanden Avenne-Izegem PVBA* [1978] 2 Lloyd's Rep 109.
    The umpire appointed by the arbitrators found in favour of the sellers and awarded them damages against the buyers which included as its principal element $US317,500, being the difference between the contract price and the market price at the date of the default by the buyers which the umpire held had occurred. The market had dropped substantially between January 1974 and June 1975. The buyers appealed to the board of
f appeal of GAFTA. The board of appeal, subject to the decision of the court on questions of law in a special case stated at the request of the buyers, upheld the umpire's award. The board of appeal's award is dated 7th November 1978. The special case was heard by Parker J in the Commercial Court. He was invited to decide, and did decide, a large number of issues and sub-issues. He answered the questions in the special case in such a way as to reverse the board of appeal's decision. He held that the buyers had not been
g in breach of contract, and, if they had been, that the breach was not a breach of a condition of the contract in the Sale of Goods Act sense of the word 'condition'. Hence the sellers, even if the contract had been broken by the buyers, would not have been entitled to do as they purported to do, that is to treat the alleged breach or breaches by the buyers as entitling the sellers to treat the contract as repudiated. In consequence, he held the sellers were not freed from their obligation to perform their remaining obligations
h under the contract in accordance with its terms, nor were they entitled to recover damages for default by the buyers.
    From that judgment of Parker J, delivered on 11th April 1979, the sellers appeal. The buyers have served a cross-notice asking this court to hold in their favour on a number of issues on which the judge decided against them.
    The contract of sale, as I have said, was made on 30th January 1974. Two documents,
j purporting to contain or evidence the terms of the contract, or of part of it, were issued, both dated 30th January 1974, one by the sellers' brokers or agents, the other by the buyers' brokers or agents. The board of appeal does not appear to have thought that anything turned on any difference in the wording of the two documents. Neither do I.
    The sellers' form of contract related only to the May 1975 shipment; no doubt the sellers issued similar forms to cover the remaining two months' shipments. The buyers'

form covered all three months, the whole 15,000 tons, in one document. I shall take the
contract terms from the buyers' form. It included, or incorporated, the terms which I
now set out:

'QUANTITY: 15,000 LT ... 5% more or less at vessels' option ... quantity to be
declared latest when nominating vessel.
'SHIPMENT: May/June/July 1975 (5,000 LT. each).
'PRICE: US $.199·50 per 1,000 Kilos FOB. stowed trimmed one gulf port in sellers'
option.
'OTHER CONDITIONS: vessel to be loaded at the rate of 2,000 L.T. per weather
working day of 24 consecutive hours Sundays and holidays excepted (Saturday as
per Baltimore form C Saturday Clause) provided vessel is able to receive at this rate
... Buyers to give 15 days preadvice of readiness of steamer. Additional conditions
as per GAFTA contract 119.'

A number of clauses of GAFTA 119 are, or are said to be, relevant to one or more of the
issues before us. I set out clls 7, 8, 20 and 21:

'7. PERIOD OF DELIVERY: During   at Buyers' call. Buyers shall
give at least   consecutive days' notice of probable readiness of
vessel(s), and of the approximate quantity required to be loaded. Buyers shall keep
Sellers informed of any changes in the date of probable readiness of vessel(s).

'8. EXTENSION OF DELIVERY: The contract period of delivery shall, if desired by
Buyers, be extended by an additional period of one calendar month, provided that
Buyers give notice in accordance with the Notices Clause not later than the next
business day following the last day of the delivery period. In this event Sellers shall
carry the goods at Buyers' account and all charges for storage, interest, insurance and
other such normal carrying expenses shall be for Buyers' account. Should Buyers
not have taken delivery by the end of this extension period, Sellers shall have the
option of declaring the Buyers to be in default or shall be entitled to demand
payment at contract price plus such charges as stated above, less current f.o.b.
charges, against warehouse warrants and such tender of warehouse receipts shall be
considered complete performance of the contract on the part of the Sellers.

'20. NOTICES: Any Notices received after 1600 hours on a business day shall be
deemed to have been received on the business day following. A Notice to the
Broker or Agent shall be deemed a Notice under this contract. All Notices given
under this contract shall be given by letter or by telegram or by telex or by other
method of rapid written communication. In case of resales all Notices shall be
passed on without delay by Buyers to their respective Sellers or vice versa.

'21. NON-BUSINESS DAYS: Saturdays, Sundays and the officially recognised and/or
legal holidays of the respective countries and any days which The Grain and Feed
Trade Association Limited may declare as Non-Business Days for specific purposes
shall be Non-Business Days. Should the time limit for doing any act or giving any
notice expire on a Non-Business Day, the time so limited shall be extended until the
first business day thereafter. The period of shipment shall not be affected by this
clause.'

The board of appeal, in para 5 of the award, said that there was a contractual obligation
on the buyers 'to give 15 days loading notice, which', says the board of appeal, 'we find
(so far as it is a question of fact) meant buyers were to give at least 15 consecutive days
notice of probable readiness of vessel(s)'. I see no reason to disagree with this view as to
what the relevant contractual term was. In the latter part of para 5, the board of appeal
express views to which I shall have to return later.
There is no contractual provision, whether in the specific terms or in the terms
incorporated through the incorporation of GAFTA 119, whereby the sellers are obliged
to notify the buyers of the 'one US Gulf port' which they have chosen as the selected

loading port at any time before they, the sellers, have received the buyers' 15 days' notice

a of probable readiness to load. It was accepted on behalf of the buyers at the hearing before the judge that in such a contract as this the sellers' duty to nominate to the buyers the particular loading port in the Gulf arises upon, but not before receipt by the sellers of, the buyers' 15 days' notice of probable readiness of vessel. We are told that the judge felt considerable doubt about the commercial sense of such a contractual requirement. With all respect to him, I can see nothing in this which is inconsistent either with the

b express terms of the contract or with commercial good sense. There may be excellent reasons why the parties should agree that the sellers shall know the probable date of readiness of the vessel before they are required to decide at which port, on or about what date, loading will be possible or will be most convenient. There does not appear to be any practical difficulty, because of the relatively short sailing time (one day or at the most two days) between any one and any other of the potentially relevant ports. As will be

c seen later, the notice given in this case was expressed as '23/25 June'. No complaint has been made on behalf of the sellers that the notice contains a spread of three days, which spread would amply cover any variance in sailing time to reach whatever port the sellers might nominate.

I return to a summary of such of the facts as appear to me to be relevant to the issues which, at the end of the submissions before us, we are required to decide.

d The buyers were themselves, in their turn, sellers of the same quantity and description of goods, for shipment in the same month, as were covered by the May shipment part of the contract which the buyers had made with the sellers. The sub-buyers from the buyers in their turn had sold similar goods. There were at least three, probably more, sub-buyers below the buyers. All the contracts were in identical terms. As a result of decisions made by the various sub-buyers when the time came, giving notices to their

e immediate sellers, a so-called 'string' was created.

Under cl 8 of GAFTA 119, the buyers were entitled, at any time up to the first business day after the last day of the delivery period, to claim a calendar month's extension of the shipment period. They did so, on a date not disclosed in the award. Hence the delivery period which had originally been the month of May 1975 became the month of June 1975. No issue arises as to the buyers' entitlement to claim that extension, though the

f judge regards the existence of that term as relevant to one of the issues in a way which I shall have to consider later. Having claimed it, their obligation was, by the terms of the contract itself, varied so as to become an obligation to provide a vessel at the nominated loading port in time to be loaded with the 5,000 tons, 5% more or less, before the end of June. On the face of the contract, subject to arguments on various issues, at least 15 days' notice of readiness to load had to be given by the buyers to the sellers, leaving time, from

g the expiry of that notice, for the 5,000 tons to be loaded before 30th June.

No notice of probable readiness was given, or purported to be given, to the sellers or to anyone representing the sellers, by the buyers, or by anyone else, earlier than 1429 hrs on Monday, 16th June 1975. At that time on that date, the third sub-buyers down the string below the buyers (the string came into existence through the consecutive passing on of notices, ultimately reaching the sellers) sent a telex, the contents of which were

h passsed on up the thus developing string.

The text of the telex, so far as it need be recorded, reads:

'For the contract in object we nominate SS Sankrograin ETA US Gulf 23/25 June 1975 for T5000 5% M/L US soyabean meal. Waiting for shippers name/loading port.'

j

That nomination, passing up the string, reached the buyers' brokers in Antwerp at 1603 hrs local time on Monday, 16th June. It was passed on by them to the sellers' brokers at 0846 hrs on the following day, Tuesday, 17th June.

On 20th June the sellers sent a telex to the buyers rejecting their nomination. They said, amongst other things:

'We ask you to note that under the above contract you have the obligation to give a 15 days loading notice. On the other hand the extended period of shipment will expire on 30th June. Under the circumstances your loading notice is late and we consider that you are in breach of the above contract in accordance with the default clause of the GAFTA form No. 119. We hereby declare you in default . . .'

(I have punctuated this extract from the telex in the way in which I think it would have been understood.)

So the sellers treated the contract, or rather the part of it originally intended for May shipment, as having been wrongfully repudiated by the buyers. The GAFTA arbitration followed, in which both the umpire and the board of appeal held that the sellers were right and were entitled to damages on the basis that the contract had been wrongfully repudiated. Parker J has held the contrary.

Two main issues arise in the appeal. The first main issue is whether or not the buyers were in breach of the contract. The board of appeal held that they were. The judge, subject to one qualification which I shall describe later, held that they were not. The second main issue, which requires to be decided only if the buyers are wrong on the first main issue, is whether, if the buyers were in breach of contract, that breach, or those breaches, was or were in respect of a term of the contract which is a condition, in the Sale of Goods Act sense of that term. Parker J, expressing his conclusion on the second issue, held that the breach or breaches, if there had been any such, would not have been a breach or breaches of a condition, but only of what is now known, somewhat unhappily, as an 'innominate' or an 'intermediate' term.

He went on to express the view that if there had been a breach or breaches of an 'intermediate' term of the contract, the consequences would not have been such as to give the sellers the right to treat the contract as having been repudiated and themselves to be freed from the performance of any further obligation under the contract. The sellers do not, in this court, challenge that part of the judge's decision. But they do strongly challenge his decision that the relevant contractual term is not a condition.

I turn to the first main issue. Was there any breach of contract by the buyers in respect of the contractual term as to giving notice of readiness of the vessel? We are not at this stage concerned with the quality of the contractual term or the seriousness of any such breach. We are concerned with whether there was or was not a breach. The question of the quality of the term, condition or 'intermediate' term, is reserved for the second main issue, if it arises.

The sellers assert that there were three respects in which the buyers broke the contract in what they did, or failed to do, as regards the notice of readiness. First, the notice was given too late, later than the last date permissible under the contract. Second, the notice was a notice of substantially less than 15 days, whereas the contractual term expressly prescribed 15 days. Third, the buyers failed to declare the quantity to be loaded, which by the contract they were required to do at the 'latest when nominating vessel'.

As to the second of the alleged breaches, at first sight it is hard to see how this was not a breach of contract. The contract said '15 days' notice'. The notice was, at the earliest, given on 16th June, and it specified 'ETA US Gulf 23/25 June'. From 16th to 25th June is not 15 days. But the judge thought that there might be some usage of the trade which would have made this conform with the contract terms. This is the judge's one qualification as to whether or not there was a breach of contract, to which I referred earlier. I think this involved treating 'eta US Gulf' in the notice as indicating the arrival of the vessel in the Gulf of Mexico, not at a port in the Gulf of Mexico. That in itself, if it were right, would seem to be a breach of the express term of the contract which provided for notice of probable readiness, meaning readiness to load at a port. However that may be, the judge said that if he had thought that on the second main issue there might in this respect have been a breach of condition, he would have remitted the award to the board of appeal to make findings as to the supposed usage. But, in the light of the conclusion which he reached on the second main issue, he did not find it necessary to remit.

a With great respect to the judge, I have difficulty in seeing how the kind of trade usage on which he speculates in his judgment could be anything other than inconsistent with the express term of the contract. On that basis, remission for further findings would be inappropriate and abortive. But the judge clearly thought that the parties, through their counsel, had agreed that remission would be a proper course. I think, from what we have been told, that there may have been a misunderstanding as to the basis on which counsel for the sellers accepted that a remission would be necessary. However, I do not

b find it necessary to pursue this question further, because I am content to assume in favour of the buyers, in the light of my conclusion on other matters, that this particular allegation of a breach should be left on one side.

The third of the alleged breaches appears to me to have been unquestionably a breach of contract (the first alleged breach) if the notice was given too late. For the contract said 'quantity to be declared latest when nominating vessel'. As the buyers had an option of

c 5% more or less, the sellers, until the quantity was declared, would not know whether their contractual obligation was to ensure that 4,750 tons were available for loading, or 5,250 tons, or somewhere between the two. That this is the purpose of the required declaration of quantity is accepted by the judge. In the judgment he says: '. . . which notice had also to declare the quantity within the permitted range which the [buyers] intended to take'.

d The alleged breach with which the judge concerned himself was the lateness in the notice nominating the vessel and giving the probable date of readiness for loading. Before the judge, there were no less than five sub-issues which were argued by the parties in relation to the question whether there was a breach in this respect. I do not find it necessary to go into all those sub-issues.

There is no doubt but that the buyers were under a contractual obligation to give

e notice of readiness at least 15 days before the expiry of the shipment period, as extended, that is 30th June. I say 'at least 15 days' because for the moment I am leaving out of account the need for further time for the actual loading, after the vessel is ready to load at the expiry of the 15 days. That question of loading time will fall to be considered as the next step in this judgment.

So, for the moment, I treat the obligation as being merely one of 15 days' advance

f notice. Even so, the notice received by the sellers' brokers on Tuesday, 17th June was prima facie too late. But if the time of the giving of the notice could be ante-dated to Monday, 16th June, then, because of certain provisions of the contract as to 'non-business days', the buyers might be able to treat the notice as though it had been, in effect, given on Friday, 13th June. The buyers sought to persuade the judge that that was the true view.

g The first way in which they sought to put it, described by the judge in his judgment as sub-issue (i), was that under a provision of the contract a notice given to the buyers' brokers was an effective giving of notice to the sellers. For the reasons given by the judge, which I regard as unanswerable, I agree that the buyers' submissions cannot be accepted.

The second way in which the buyers sought to put it, which was accepted by the judge

h in dealing with what he called sub-issue (iv), was that the notice which in fact reached the sellers' brokers on Tuesday, 17th June, was to be treated by virtue of cl 20 of GAFTA 119 as having been given on Monday, 16th June. On that day a notice was put in a telex by a sub-buyer down the string and thus, as a result of the judge's view on another of the sub-issues, it had, as it were, the advantage of the two preceding 'non-business' days, the Saturday and the Sunday, so that it could be treated as though it had been sent on Friday,

j 13th June.

With all respect to the judge, I am unable to accept the validity of his construction of the relevant contractual provisions as enabling the date of someone else's notice to be treated as the date of the buyers' notice. The buyers' own contract form said 'Buyers to give 15 days preadvice of readiness of steamer'. That is not fulfilled by the buyers giving a 'preadvice of readiness of steamer' which is less than 15 days' preadvice when they, the buyers, gave it to the sellers. It is not fulfilled merely because the 'preadvice' may consist of passing on a 'preadvice' emanating from someone unknown to the sellers, in no contractual relationship with the sellers, at some unknown distance down a newly created string, which, when it was first given as a notice by the unknown sub-buyer to his unknown seller, gave to the latter '15 days' preadvice'. I see nothing in the GAFTA 119 terms, including therein the last sentence of cl 20, which could on a fair construction be treated as so providing.

While this, being a question of construction, is a question of law for the court, I am encouraged as to the correctness of my view by observing that the board of appeal, with their much greater understanding of the practical working of these contracts and of how they are understood in the trade, take the same view as I have expressed. In the last sentence of para 5 of the award they say:

'Moreover, an FOB buyer cannot rely on the notices clause of GAFTA 119 and thereby give a lesser notice by reason only that a notice which was given in time by a subsequent sub-buyer has, although passed on without delay, reached him too late to pass on to the seller in time.'

To make sense of the contract, as the board of appeal thinks, the relevant time of the giving of notice is the time when it is given by the buyers, or their agents, to the sellers, or their agents; not when it is first given by someone other than the buyers, by persons of whose existence and identity the sellers are unaware and have no means of ascertaining, and with no information to the sellers, or any means for them to find out, on what date the notice has been given as between two persons who are in contract with one another but neither of whom is in any relevant contractual relationship with the sellers.

The sellers have raised, further, before this court another submission, not taken in the court below, which, if right, is also in my view conclusive as deciding the first main issue, breach of contract by the buyers, in the sellers' favour. When counsel for the sellers sought our leave to introduce this argument before us, it was not opposed by counsel for the buyers, 'so far as it does not involve any further investigation of facts'. I am satisfied that it is a point of law not involving, or requiring the investigation of, any additional facts.

This fresh submission as defined by counsel is: must the notice be such that after it has expired there is time within the shipment period for the goods to be loaded at the loading rate specified in the contract?

In my judgment, the answer to that question is 'Yes'. If that be right then, in addition to the 15 days which falls to be provided by virtue of the notice of readiness itself, the notice must be given by, at latest, such date as will provide for the loading, before the end of the day on 30th June, of 5,000 tons (5% more or less) of soya bean meal at 2,000 tons per day (being the contractual loading rate), that is a further 2½ days, not to include Sundays. On that basis, the notice given in this case was clearly too late. The loading would have had to have started not later than Friday, 27th June, with 15 days' advance notice expiring by that day.

There is no doubt that the sellers cannot be obliged to load cargo in July when the contract, as extended, provides for June shipment. There is no doubt that the sellers, without breach of contract by the buyers, cannot be required to be ready to provide goods for loading earlier than the expiry of the 15 days stated by the buyers in their notice of probable readiness. The giving of the notice must be geared to the enabling of the sellers to perform their contractual obligations, as provided by the contract, and not in some more onerous way. It cannot be such as to put on them an obligation, at peril of not completing the loading of the contract goods before the end of June, to do more than they are obliged by their contract to do.

I do not accept the submission of the buyers that there is any doubt or ambiguity as to the contractual terms in this respect. I do not accept that the sellers' form of contract (on which the buyers seek to rely in this context) can be construed as imposing on the sellers an obligation to load at a greater rate than an average loading rate of 2,000 long tons per

weather working day. The suggestion of the buyers, as I understand it, is that the words
a in the sellers' form of contract 'Sellers guarantee average loading of 2,000 long tons per
weather working day' would involve an obligation on the sellers to load at, say, 5,000 tons
per day if the custom of the particular port at which loading took place was that loading
should be carried out at that rate. I do not think that the words are capable of putting on
the sellers any such obligation. It would involve construing the word 'guarantee' as
having the effect of making the obligation that which it would have been if the
b contractual term had been expressed as 'an average loading rate of a minimum of
2,000 long tons . . .'

I should mention, in passing, that we have been told that, at the hearing before the
board of appeal, the buyers asked the board to make a finding that 'a rate of about
5,000 tons per day can easily be achieved at Gulf ports'. The finding made by the board
in response to that invitation was (para 23 of the award): '. . . some Ports in the Gulf can
c load vessels at the rate of 5,000 long tons in one day'.

In the result, then, the notice had to be given not later than, at best for the buyers, 13th
June. It was not given until 17th June.

For both the reasons which I have given, one of which is based on a submission not
made before Parker J and therefore not considered by him, I have reached the conclusion,
on the first main issue, that the buyers have been shown to have been in breach of
d contract in having failed to give the notice of probable readiness by the latest date when,
under the contract, it was required to have been given. I do not find it necessary to go
into the other sub-issues which were debated before the judge and before us on this issue.

I come to the second main issue: is the term of the contract which has been broken by
the buyers a condition or an intermediate term? The sellers have, before us, made it clear
that if the term is not a condition, but is an intermediate term, they will not seek to
e contend that they can discharge the burden of showing that they were entitled to treat
the contract as having been repudiated by the buyers.

The contract is, by its express terms, governed by English law. That is the effect of
cl 25 of GAFTA 119.

It is an accepted principle of English law that in a mercantile contract for the sale of
goods 'prima facie a stipulated time of delivery is of the essence'. This long-standing
f principle has recently been re-stated by Lord Diplock in *United Scientific Holdings Ltd v
Burnley Borough Council* [1977] 2 All ER 62, [1978] AC 904 in a passage which I shall cite
later.

In the present case, then, there can be no doubt but that the obligation of the sellers to
deliver the soya bean meal not later than 30th June 1975 was a condition of the
contract. They had an obligation to tender the contractual quantity of the goods at the
g ship's rail so that they could be loaded in accordance with the contractual provisions as to
rate of loading, on or before that date. If they failed, in breach of contract, to carry out
that obligation, and if the buyers thereupon were to treat the contract as having been
wrongfully repudiated by the sellers, it would be no answer for the sellers to say that the
buyers had not proved that they, the buyers, had suffered any loss or would suffer any
loss, if loading were to take place on 1st July. It would be unreal to suggest that one day's
h lateness in delivery would necessarily be a matter of serious consequence to the buyers.
The lateness might or might not have such consequences. But the buyers' right to treat
the contract as repudiated, and to treat themselves as freed from the performance of any
further contractual obligations which they would otherwise have been required to
perform under the contract, does not depend on the buyers being able to prove any such
thing.

j No one, so far as I know, has suggested that the House of Lords' decision in *Bowes v
Shand* (1877) 2 App Cas 445 which has stood now for 102 years as an integral part of the
English law of mercantile contracts, has been, or should be, overruled by the House of
Lords or abrogated by legislation. So far as this court is concerned, we are certainly
bound by it. So far as I know, this rule of law that, in the absence of provision to the
contrary in the contract, the date by which, or the period within which, shipment is to

be made is a condition, has not been regarded by the mercantile community as failing to
conform with what is commercially desirable and appropriate.

Since the obligation of the sellers to deliver the goods so that they could be shipped by a
30th June at latest was a condition of the contract, why should the buyers' contractual
obligation to give the sellers notice of a length which the parties had agreed to be the
reasonable time for the purpose of enabling the sellers to perform that condition,
binding on them, be any the less a condition, binding on the buyers?

That this is the purpose of the term as to notice of probable readiness is, I think, not in b
doubt. I refer again here to para 5 of the award. A question of the construction of the
contract is a question of law for the court. But the business purpose for the introduction
of a clause into a mercantile contract is, in my opinion, a question of fact. Even if it is
not, the view of commercial arbitrators on such a question must be of great weight. I
refer to what Lord Radcliffe said in *Tsakiroglou & Co Ltd v Noblee & Thorl GmbH* [1961] 2
All ER 179 at 189, [1962] AC 93 at 124 in relation to a finding of commercial arbitrators c
on a question of frustration, a mixed question of fact and law: 'The ultimate conclusion
is a conclusion of law, but, in a case of this sort that conclusion is almost completely
determined by what is ascertained as to mercantile usage and the understanding of
mercantile men.'

In para 5 of the award the board of appeal, having said that the term means 'Buyers
were to give at least 15 consecutive days notice of probable readiness of vessel(s)', went d
on: 'Such a provision is customarily treated in the trade as being for the purpose of giving
to sellers sufficient time to make necessary arrangements to get the goods to the port for
loading on board the nominated vessel.' In other words, the parties have agreed, by
acceptance of this term, that 15 days is the time which is reasonably required by the
sellers, for the purpose of this particular contract, to enable them to make the
arrangements necessary for the fulfilment by them of their contractual duty to deliver e
the goods by the due time. It would, in my view, be impossible for a court to hold that
that was not the parties' intention in agreeing this term. There is no question here of the
parties not being in an equal bargaining position. It would, in my opinion, be arrogant
and unjustifiable for a court to substitute any view of its own for the view of the parties
themselves as to what was a reasonable time for this purpose.

Unless there is some principle of law, or some authority binding on us, which leads f
necessarily to a contrary conclusion, it appears to me to follow that, just as the contractual
time for delivery of the goods is a condition binding on the sellers, so the contractual
time by which the notice has to be given for the purpose of enabling the sellers to
perform that condition should be regarded as a condition binding on the buyers. There
is no more, and no less, reason to suppose that a breach of the time provision in the sellers'
obligation will necessarily or probably lead to serious loss to the buyers than there is to g
suppose that a breach of the notice of readiness provision will necessarily or probably lead
to serious loss to the sellers.

I should refer to the remainder of para 5 of the award. It reads:

> '. . . if a seller is not given the full 15 consecutive days notice then the buyer
> cannot complain if the seller is thereby unable to deliver the goods on the date h
> indicated. This term in an FOB contract is regarded in the trade as of such great and
> fundamental importance that any breach thereof goes to the root of the contract.'

It is suggested that the first proposition in that passage is inconsistent with the second
proposition. I do not think it is. The first proposition may well refer to the sellers' right j
to elect to treat the contract as repudiated. However that may be, while normally very
great weight would properly be given to the opinion of the board of appeal as to the trade
view of the fundamental importance of the term, in the special circumstances I think
that it is better not to found anything on the opinion expressed on that particular
question in this case. The reason is that in May 1977 the board of appeal of GAFTA,
differently constituted in membership, expressed the contrary view. That was in their

award, considered by Mocatta J in *Bremer Handelsgesellschaft mbH v J H Rayner & Co Ltd*
a [1978] 2 Lloyd's Rep 73. I shall refer further to that case later.
   I come back to the purpose of the notice of probable readiness term in the present
contract. The commercial reasons why advance notice is required are, I think, obvious.
The sellers have to nominate the loading port. Is loading going to be possible, and if
possible convenient, at port A, or port B, or port C? Until the probable date of readiness
is known, it may be impossible to answer those questions. Until they are answered, the
b sellers cannot perform their contractual duty of nominating the port. When the port is
decided, arrangements have to be made to have the contract quantity (to be defined by
the buyers by reference to '5% more or less') of the contract goods available when the
vessel is ready. What is involved in making such arrangements? It may involve, or
include, buying goods, arranging for them to be moved by road, rail or water from
wherever they may be; for warehousing them or moving them from one warehouse to
c another. Of course, in any given case, some or all of these tasks may be simply achieved,
or their achievement may be possible in less than 15 days, in order to have the goods
ready for loading where and when the vessel is ready for loading. It obviously cannot be
predicated that 14 days' notice, instead of 15 days', would necessarily and in all
circumstances cause sellers serious difficulties in respect of a contract containing these
terms. What can and should be accepted is that the parties have agreed that, for the
d purposes of this contract, the reasonable time required to enable the sellers to perform
their contractual obligations as to delivery of the goods is 15 days' notice of the probable
readiness of the vessel to load.
   The first, and as I understand it, the principal reason which Parker J gave for holding
that this term was not a condition was because the contract included the provision for
extension of the time of shipment by one calendar month (GAFTA 119, cl 8). I do not
e think that counsel for the buyers in this court placed, at any rate great, reliance on that
point. With all respect to the judge, I do not think that the inclusion of the extension
provision in the contract is relevant to the question whether the term as to notice is a
condition or an intermediate term. The sellers, it is true, could not assert that a failure
during the month of May to give any notice, or any proper notice, of probable readiness
would enable them at that stage to treat the contract as having been broken. The
f question as to the nature of any breach thus could not arise. They could not, until the
first business day in the month of June had passed, treat the absence of notice of probable
readiness as being a breach of contract at all. If no claim for extension had been made on
the first business day of June, then there would, retrospectively, have been a breach of
contract by the failure to give notice of probable readiness. The nature of that term is not
in any way affected or altered. If the term would otherwise be a condition, it is no less
g a condition because it cannot be said until the beginning of June that there has been a
breach of it.
   Apart from that particular reason, relating to the extension of shipment clause, Parker
J was of the opinion that the term could not be a condition because of what he regarded
as being 'the principles established in the *Hong Kong Fir* case' (*Hong Kong Fir Shipping Co
Ltd v Kawasaki Kisen Kaisha Ltd* [1962] 1 All ER 474, [1962] 2 QB 26) and *The Hansa Nord*,
h *Cehave NV v Bremer Handelsgesellschaft mbH* [1975] 3 All ER 739, [1976] QB 44. In the
latter case, Roskill LJ, while recognising that some terms of a contract of sale may be
conditions, expressed the view that 'a court should not be over ready, unless required by
statute or authority so to do, to construe a term in a contract as a "condition". . .' (see
[1975] 3 All ER 739 at 755, [1976] QB 44 at 70).
   The passage in the *Hong Kong Fir* case, to which Parker J referred, was that where
j Diplock LJ said this ([1962] 1 All ER 474 at 487, [1962] 2 QB 26 at 69):

'No doubt there are many simple contractual undertakings, sometimes express,
but more often because of their very simplicity ("It goes without saying") to be
implied, of which it can be predicated that every breach of such an undertaking
must give rise to an event which will deprive the party not in default of substantially
the whole benefit which it was intended that he should obtain from the contract.

And such a stipulation, unless the parties have agreed that breach of it shall not entitle the non-defaulting party to treat the contract as repudiated, is a "condition".' **a**

If that statement is intended to be a definition of the requirements which must always be satisfied, in all types of contract and all types of clauses, in order that a term may qualify as a condition, I would very respectfully express the view that it is not a correct statement of the law. I am confirmed in the view that it was not so intended because of what was recently said by Lord Diplock in a passage which I shall cite hereafter from his speech in *United Scientific Holdings Ltd v Burnley Borough Council* [1977] 2 All ER 62 at 67, **b** [1978] AC 904 at 924 in relation to time being 'of the essence' in certain commercial contracts. I shall return to the *Hong Kong Fir* case at the end of this judgment.

If time is of the essence of a contract, then that provision as to time has effect as a condition. It is possible that somewhat different considerations may apply, when the question arises as to condition or 'intermediate' term, as regards, on the one hand, provision as to time and, on the other hand, provisions unrelated to time. As the **c** contractual term with which we are concerned is a time provision, I propose to consider the authorities as to time being of the essence, for it is those authorities which must be most directly relevant. In this context, I propose to confine myself to mercantile contracts in which I include, of course, a contract such as the present, an fob contract for the sale of goods.

I start with two textbooks which may, I think, be taken as typical of the opinions **d** generally expressed. In Chalmers' Sale of Goods (17th Edn, 1975, p 107) it is said:

'As regards stipulations other than those relating to the time of payment, time is of the essence of the contract, in most mercantile transactions and in some non-mercantile transactions.'

9 Halsbury's Laws (4th Edn) para 481 says:　　　　　　　　　　　　　　　　　　**e**

'The modern law, in the case of contracts of all types, may be summarised as follows. Time will not be considered of the essence unless: (1) the parties expressly stipulate that conditions as to time must be strictly complied with; or (2) the nature of the subject matter of the contract or the surrounding circumstances show that time should be considered to be of the essence . . .'　　　　　　　　　**f**

The footnote (6), applicable to the proposition numbered (2) in the passage cited above, refers to paras 482–484. Paragraph 482 contains this sentence: 'Broadly speaking, time will be considered of the essence in "mercantile" contracts . . .' The footnote to that proposition refers to *Reuter v Sala* (1879) 4 CPD 239, a decision of the Court of Appeal, and to *Bowes v Shand* (1877) 2 App Cas 455 to which I have already referred, and to other cases.　　　　　　　　　　　　　　　　　　　　　　　　　　　　**g**

In *United Scientific Holdings Ltd v Burnley Borough Council* [1977] 2 All ER 62 at 67, [1978] AC 904 at 924 Lord Diplock says:

'In some stipulations in commercial contracts as to the time when something must be done by one of the parties or some event must occur, time is of the essence; in others it is not. In commercial contracts for the sale of goods prima facie a **h** stipulated time of delivery is of the essence, but prima facie a stipulated time of payment is not (Sale of Goods Act 1893, s 10(1)); in a charterparty a stipulated time of payment of hire is of the essence.'

Viscount Dilhorne agrees that the law in relation to such stipulations in contracts is correctly stated in 9 Halsbury's Laws (4th Edn) para 481. I assume that that approval **j** applies to the further reference which I have cited in para 482, introduced by the footnote to para 481. In the same case, Lord Simon expresses approval of the passage which I have cited from para 481. Lord Salmon, treating the lease there in question as being 'fairly described as a commercial transaction', says: 'In commercial transactions, provisions as to time are usually but not always regarded as being of the essence of the

contract.' Lord Fraser accepts the correctness of the summary in 9 Halsbury's Laws (4th
a Edn) para 481: see [1977] 2 All ER 62 at 78, 81, 88, 94, [1978] AC 904 at 937, 944, 950,
953.

In the light of what was said by their Lordships in that case, I think it can fairly be said
that in mercantile contracts stipulations as to time not only may be, but usually are, to
be treated as being 'of the essence of the contract', even though this is not expressly stated
in the words of the contract. It would follow that in a mercantile contract it cannot be
b predicated that, for time to be of the essence, any and every breach of the term as to time
must necessarily cause the innocent party to be deprived of substantially the whole of the
benefit which it was intended that he should have.

I go back now to some of the earlier authorities. I do not find it necessary to consider
further *Bowes v Shand* or *Reuter v Sala*, to which I have already referred.

Before I refer to three authorities which can be said to have a direct bearing on a
c contractual clause of the type with which we are concerned, I should mention, by way of
example, two other cases which I think are representative of the attitude of the courts to
time provisions in mercantile contracts.

In *McDougall v Aeromarine of Emsworth Ltd* [1958] 3 All ER 431 at 439, [1958] 1 WLR
1126 at 1132 Diplock J said:

d   'In my view the obligation to deliver within a reasonable time of May 1, 1957, is
        a condition. It was conceded by counsel for the defendants that this is so as a general
        rule in mercantile transactions . . .'

That was a case in which the express terms of the contract, while specifying 1st May
as the date for the delivery of a pleasure yacht under a contract of sale, made it clear that
e that date was not 'of the essence'. Therefore the defendant was entitled to a reasonable
time thereafter before the plaintiff could treat non-delivery as a repudiation. But where,
as in the present case, the inevitable implication is that the parties have themselves agreed
on the time which is reasonable, it would seem to follow that the 'general rule in
mercantile transactions' should apply. It would be odd, indeed, if, when the parties to a
contract have agreed upon a time which is reasonable for the particular contract, the
f court thereafter had to undertake the task of deciding what extension beyond a reasonable
time is itself reasonable.

In the recent judgment of this court delivered by Brandon LJ in *Toepfer v Lenersan-
Poortman NV* [1980] 1 Lloyd's Rep 143 it was decided that a provision in a cif contract as
to the time for the tender of documents was a condition. There are numerous other
cases, older and more recent, to the same effect in respect of time provisions in various
g aspects of mercantile contracts.

I now turn to the three authorities which were concerned with terms of the same
nature as the term with which we are here concerned.

The first of these authorities is *Peter Turnbull & Co Ltd v Mundas Trading Co (Australasia)
Pty Ltd* [1954] 2 Lloyd's Rep 198. That was a decision of the High Court of Australia.
The majority judgment was delivered by Dixon CJ. (Taylor J dissented on a point not
h material for present purposes.) A term of a sale contract which stipulated that the buyer
was to give the seller '14 days' notice of ship and shipping date' was treated as being a
condition. It may be that the contrary was not argued. Nevertheless I regard it as of no
slight significance that it did not occur to Dixon CJ to doubt the status of the contractual
term as a condition. It is indistinguishable from the term with which we are concerned.

The second authority is *Carapanayoti & Co Ltd v Comptoir Commercial Andre & Cie SA*
j [1972] 1 Lloyd's Rep 139. Again the question 'condition or intermediate term?' does not
appear to have been argued. But the decision of this court is not consistent with the term
being other than a condition; for if it had been an 'intermediate' term, the decision must
have been different. The relevant term was '. . . the port of destination shall be declared
by the last buyer to his seller not later than 21 days before commencement of shipment
period'. The shipment period was 'February/March 1968'. The nomination of the port

of destination was given on 11th January 1968. The sellers, saying that this was a day too late, treated it as a breach of a condition. The question argued was whether, to comply with the contract term, the declaration should have been given a day earlier. It did not occur to very experienced counsel to argue at any stage, nor to the arbitral tribunal, nor to Donaldson J, nor to any of the members of this court to suggest, that this might be an 'intermediate' term. We are told that an application for leave to appeal to the House of Lords was refused by a committee of three of their Lordships.

The third authority, though not binding on this court, is not merely an inferential but a direct decision which, if right, is conclusive on this issue. In *Bremer Handelsgesellschaft mbH v J H Rayner & Co Ltd* [1978] 2 Lloyd's Rep 73 Mocatta J held that a contractual term, indistinguishable from the term with which we are here concerned, was a condition. It was in that case, as I have previously mentioned, that a board of appeal of GAFTA had expressed the view, contradictory of the view expressed by the board of appeal in the present case, that ' a term such as this in a fob contract is not regarded in the trade as a matter of great or fundamental importance'. Mocatta J, as he was entitled to do on this question of law, did not regard himself as bound by that finding or expression of opinion. He held that the term was a condition. On appeal to this court, the actual decision was reversed, but on a ground which did not reflect on the judge's decision on the question whether the term was a condition. Bridge LJ, delivering the leading judgment in this court said ([1979] 2 Lloyd's Rep 216 at 224):

> 'I find it unnecessary to express a concluded opinion on that matter. I content myself with saying simply that as at present advised I am not persuaded by (appellant counsel's) argument that the learned Judge was wrong in the conclusion he reached on the point.'

Having had the further advantage of the submissions made in the present case, I am persuaded that Mocatta J was right in his view that the contractual term was a condition.

In my opinion in the term with which we are concerned the provision as to time is of the essence of the contract. The term is a condition.

It is, I believe, a factor which is not without weight in that conclusion that, at least, it tends towards certainty in the law. Lord Hailsham LC has said: '. . . in legal matters, some degree of certainty is at least as valuable a part of justice as perfection'. (See *Cassell & Co Ltd v Broome* [1972] 1 All ER 801 at 809, [1972] AC 1027 at 1054.) I adhere to what I said in that respect in *Maredelanto Compania Naviera SA v Bergbau-Handel Gmbh, The Mihalis Angelos* [1970] 3 All ER 125 at 138, [1971] 1 QB 164 at 205. The parties, where time is of the essence, will at least know where they stand when the contractually agreed time has passed and the contract has been broken. They will not be forced to make critical decisions by trying to anticipate how serious, in the view of arbitrators or courts, in later years, the consequences of the breach will retrospectively be seen to have been, in the light, it may be, of hindsight.

I must, however, return to the *Hong Kong Fir* case [1962] 1 All ER 474, [1962] 2 QB 26. No one now doubts the correctness of that decision: that there are 'intermediate' terms, breach of which may or may not entitle the innocent party to treat himself as discharged from the further performance of his contractual obligation. No one now doubts that a term as to seaworthiness in a charterparty, in the absence of express provision to the opposite effect, is not a condition, but is an 'intermediate' term. The question arising on that case which I think we are compelled to examine in the present case is the test by which it falls to be decided whether a term is a condition.

I have previously quoted a passage from the judgment of Diplock LJ ([1962] 1 All ER 474 at 487, [1962] 2 QB 26 at 29). In its literal sense, the words there used would mean that the test whether a term is a condition is whether *every* breach of such an undertaking *must* give rise to an event which will deprive the party not in default of *substantially the whole benefit which it was intended that he should obtain from the contract.* If this is a definition of the requirements which, in English law, must always be fulfilled before any contractual term (in the absence, of course, of express words) can achieve the legal status *a* of a condition, then the term with which we are here concerned would not pass the test. The view which I have expressed that it is a condition would necessarily be wrong.

There are various reasons why I do not think that this was intended to be a literal, definitive and comprehensive statement of the requirements of a condition; and also, if it were, why, with great respect, I do not think that it represents the law as it stands today.

b First, if it were intended to cover terms as to time in mercantile contracts, how could the requirements be said to be met in respect of stipulations in contracts of types in which, as Lord Diplock has recently said, time may be of the essence (see [1977] 2 All ER 62 at 67, [1978] AC 904 at 924): for example, in respect of a stipulated time for delivery? It could never be said, as I see it, in any real sense, that *any* breach of such a stipulation *must necessarily cause the innocent* party to be deprived of *substantially all the benefit.*

c Second, and following on what I have just said, I do not see how any contractual term, whether as to time or otherwise, could ever pass the test. Conditions would no longer exist in the English law of contract. For it is always possible to suggest hypothetically some minor breach or breaches of any contractual term which might, without undue use of the imagination, be wholly insufficient to produce serious effects for the innocent party, let alone the loss of substantially all the benefit.

d Third, English law does recognise as conditions contractual terms which do not pass that test. For example, *Bowes v Shand* (1877) 2 App Cas 455 and, I think, a substantial number of other cases which are binding, at least on this court.

Fourth, it is clear law, reaffirmed by the House of Lords since *Hong Kong Fir* was decided, that where there has been a breach of a condition the innocent party is entitled to elect whether or not to treat the contracts as repudiated. Recent examples where the

e courts recognise this right to elect include *White and Carter (Councils) Ltd v McGregor* [1961] 3 All ER 1178, [1962] AC 413; *Suisse Atlantique Société d'Armement Maritime SA v NV Rotterdamshe Kolen Centrale* [1966] 2 All ER 61, [1967] AC 361; *Wathes (Western) Ltd v Austins (Menswear) Ltd* 1 Lloyd's Rep 14.

In *White and Carter v McGregor* Lord Reid said ([1961] 3 All ER 1178 at 1181, [1962] AC 413 at 427): 'He may accept that repudiation and sue for damages for breach of

f contract . . . or he may if he chooses disregard or refuse to accept it and then the contract remains in full effect.' See also what Lord Upjohn said in *Suisse v Atlantique* [1966] 2 All ER 61 at 86, [1967] 1 AC 361 at 422. How could this right of election be anything other than a legal fiction, a chimera, if the election can arise only in circumstances in which, as a result of the breach, an event has happened which will deprive the innocent party of substantially the whole benefit which it was intended that he should receive? This test,

g it is to be observed, is regarded (*Hong Kong Fir* [1962] 1 All ER 474 at 489, [1962] 2 QB 26 at 72) as applying also where the term is an intermediate term, except that you then look to what has actually happened in order to see if the innocent party has lost substantially all the benefit. So, again, if the test be right, the former principle of English law that the innocent party has the right to elect is no longer anything but an empty shadow. For a right to elect to continue a contract, with the result that the innocent

h party will be bound to continue to perform his own contractual obligations, when he will, by definition, have lost substantially all his benefit under the contract, does not appear to me to make sense.

Fifth, the same considerations as I have set out in the previous paragraph apply if the test be that a breach of contract gives a right to the innocent party to treat it as a repudiation only if the events which in fact have flowed from the breach would, if they

j had come about otherwise than by a breach of contract, amount to frustration of the contract. Lord Radcliffe's classical definition of frustration in *Davis Contractors Ltd v Fareham Urban District Council* [1956] 2 All ER 145 at 160, [1956] AC 696 at 729 is—

'without default of either party, a contractual obligation has become incapable of being performed because the circumstances in which performance is called for would render it a thing radically different from that which was undertaken by the contract. Non haec in foedera veni. It was not this that I promised to do . . . There must be . . . such a change in the significance of the obligation that the thing undertaken would, if performed, be a different thing from that contracted for.'

If that, with the substitution of 'default' for 'no default' as being the cause of 'the different thing', were the universal test which must be applied before there can be a condition or a breach of condition, then there can never be an election by the innocent party to proceed with the contract, despite the other party's default. For, as appears dramatically in the Virgilian quotation, it would not be the same contract. Yet the law has never ceased to recognise that there may be a right of election, when the innocent party is faced with a repudiatory breach, to keep the contract alive: the same contract, not a different one, as it would, necessarily and invariably, be on the frustration test.

Counsel for the sellers submitted that the test of a condition suggested in the paragraph which I have quoted, at least if it fell to be treated in its literal sense and as a comprehensive definition of the requirements of a condition, in all types of contracts and all types of contractual stipulations, is not a part of the ratio decidendi of the *Hong Kong Fir* case. I would, with very great respect, feel obliged to agree. Upjohn LJ, in the opening words of his judgment said that he 'entirely agreed with the judgment which has just been delivered'. That judgment was the judgment of Sellers LJ. As I understand it, the ratio of the judgment of Sellers LJ, as to the test of a condition is to be found in the paragraph in which he said ([1962] 1 All ER 474 at 481, [1962] 2 QB 26 at 60):

'The formula for deciding whether a stipulation is a condition or a warranty is well recognised; the difficulty is in its application. It is put in a practical way by BOWEN, L.J. in *Bentsen* v. *Taylor Sons & Co.* ([1893] 2 QB 274 at 281): "There is no way of deciding that question except by looking at the contract in the light of the surrounding circumstances, and then making up one's mind whether the intention of the parties, as gathered from the instrument itself, will best be carried out by treating the promise as a warranty sounding only in damages, or as a condition precedent by the failure to perform which the other party is relieved of his liability."'

Applying that test, for the reasons which I have sought to give, I would hold that the term here in question is a condition.

I would allow the appeal and, subject to any questions of detail which may arise as to the form of the order, I would restore the decision of the board of appeal.

BROWNE LJ. I agree that this appeal should be allowed, for the reasons given by Megaw LJ, with which I entirely agree.

As he has said, the appeal raises two main issues—(1) whether or not the buyers were in breach of the contract; (2) whether, if the buyers were in breach of contract, that breach was of a stipulation which was a 'condition', in the sense that any breach of it entitled the sellers to cancel the contract, as they did on 20th June 1975.

I find nothing I can usefully add on the first issue, but I wish to add something on the second issue in deference to the admirable argument of counsel for the buyers.

Counsel's argument concentrated on the nature of the breach. He submitted that in deciding whether a term of a contract is a 'condition' (in the sense that any breach of it entitles the innocent party to treat this as a repudiation by the other party), the inquiry is whether the stipulation in question goes to the root of the contract, in the sense that any breach of it will deprive the other party of substantially the whole of the benefit for which he has bargained. He said, 'It all comes down to what has happened in the event. Has it seriously prejudiced the seller, or is it utterly trivial?' He then submitted that if it is seen that some breaches would only have a trifling effect, it follows that the term in question is only an 'innominate' or 'intermediate' term and not a condition.

Attractively as this argument was presented, it seems to me that it puts the cart (that is the breach) before the horse (that is the contract) and confuses two quite separate and

different questions: (1) As a matter of interpretation of the contract, is the term in
a question a condition (in the sense set out above), or an intermediate term, or a
warranty? (2) When it has been decided that the term in question is an intermediate
term, is a breach which has happened such as to entitle the innocent party to treat it as
a repudiation and cancel the contract?

As I understand what Lord Upjohn said in *Suisse Atlantique Société d'Armement Maritime
SA v Rotterdamsche Kolen Centrale* [1966] 2 All ER 61 at 85–86, [1967] 1 AC 361 at 421–
b 422, it was the distinction between these two questions which he had in mind.

The only question which is relevant in this case is question (1). Counsel has not argued
that if the term here in question was an intermediate term, the breach was such as to
justify the sellers in cancelling the contract on 20th June. In a case where the second
question does arise, I confess that I share Megaw LJ's difficulty in seeing how the
suggested test, that the breach must be such as to deprive the innocent party of
substantially the whole benefit for which he has bargained, can be reconciled with the
c principle that the innocent party has an option to elect whether to cancel the contract or
to affirm it.

It is clear that the parties to a contract can expressly make a time clause of the essence
of the contract, and so a condition, any breach of which will justify the innocent party in
cancelling. I think it is also clear that time can be made of the essence by necessary
d implication (see, for example, *Hong Kong Fir Shipping Co Ltd v Kawasaki Kisen Kaisha Ltd*
[1962] 1 All ER 474 at 481, 482, 483, [1962] 2 QB at 60, 61, 63 per Sellers LJ in the
passage already quoted by Megaw LJ, and per Upjohn LJ (agreeing with Sellers LJ)) and
'expressly or by necessary implication': see also exception (2) in 9 Halsbury's Laws (4th
Edn) paras 481–482, already quoted by Megaw LJ, *United Scientific Holdings Ltd v Burnley
Borough Council* [1977] 2 All ER 62 at 78, 88, 94, [1978] AC 904 at 937, 950, 958, per
e Viscount Dilhorne quoting Lord Romilly MR, Lord Salmon, and Lord Fraser quoting
Fry on Specific Performance.

The question whether or not a time clause is as a matter of necessary implication 'of
the essence of the contract', and so a condition, must depend on the presumed intention
of the parties at the time when the contract was made. If it would then have been
foreseen by any reasonable person in the position of the contracting parties that any
f breach of some term would 'deprive the party not in default of substantially the whole
benefit which it is intended that he should obtain from the contract', it would be very
easy, and probably inevitable, for a court to hold that by necessary implication that term
was a condition. But I agree with Megaw LJ that, at any rate in relation to time clauses
in mercantile contracts, this cannot be the only test of whether or not such clauses are
conditions. If it was, it would, as he says, be difficult to imagine any stipulation which
g would be a 'condition'.

So far as time clauses in mercantile contracts are concerned, it is established by the
authorities to which Megaw LJ has referred that this is not the test. If goods are shipped,
or notice of appropriation is given, or documents are tendered one day after the time
stipulated by the contract, this may cause no damage at all to the buyer, still less 'deprive
him of substantially the whole benefit which it is intended he should obtain from the
h contract', but it is well-established that such stipulations as to time are conditions on
breach of which the innocent party is entitled to cancel: see, for example, *Bowes v Shand*
(1877) 2 App Cas 455 and *Reuter v Sala* (1879) 4 CPD 239; *Toepfer v Lenersan-Poortman NV*
[1980] 1 Lloyd's Rep 143.

In my judgment, for the reasons given by Megaw LJ, time was of the essence of the
stipulation, 'Buyers to give 15 days preadvice of readiness of steamer', and that stipulation
j was a condition. I will not attempt to repeat or summarise the reasons given by Megaw
LJ, with which I entirely agree. They are: (a) The statements of principle as to time
provisions in mercantile contracts to which he refers. I am especially impressed by the
importance of certainty (see *Maredelanto Compania Naviera SA v Bergbau-Handel GmbH,
The Mihalis Angelos* [1970] 3 All ER 125 at 138, [1971] 1 QB 164 at 205 and *Toepfer v
Lenersan-Poortman NV* [1980] 1 Lloyd's Rep 143 at 147–148. If less than 15 days' notice

of readiness to load is given, and time is not of the essence, a seller would be placed in a very difficult position: he would have to make an immediate decision whether or not an arbitrator or a court would decide, perhaps years afterwards, that the notice was given so *a* late that it made it impossible for him to fulfil his obligation to deliver within the contract time. (b) The authorities in which it has been assumed, and in one case held, that provisions indistinguishable from the provision with which we are concerned are conditions. Counsel for the buyers submitted that the decision of Mocatta J in *Bremer Handelsgesellschaft mbH v J H Rayner & Co Ltd* [1978] 2 Lloyd's Rep 73 was wrong because *b* the statement of Lord Denning MR in *Tradax Export SA v Andre & Cie SA* [1976] 1 Lloyd's Rep 416 that 'without delay' in cl 21 of GAFTA 100 was a condition, on which (among other authorities) Mocatta J relied, had been overruled by the House of Lords in *Bremer Handelsgesellschaft mbH v Vanden Avenne-Izegem* [1978] 2 Lloyd's Rep 109 at 113, 121, 128, 130 (per Lord Wilberforce, Viscount Dilhorne, Lord Salmon and Lord Russell). *Tradax v Andre* and *Bremer v Vanden* were concerned with cl 21 of GAFTA 100, *c* of which the wording is very different from that of the provision with which we are concerned; Lord Salmon (at 125) thought that time was of the essence of cl 22 of GAFTA 100. I do not think this submission is enough to vitiate the correctness of Mocatta J's decision. (c) The essential link between the seller's obligation to deliver within the contract period (which is a condition) and the buyer's obligation to give at least 15 days' notice of readiness to load, which is established by the findings of fact in para 5 of the *d* award. (Like Megaw LJ, I ignore the sentence which is in conflict with the finding in *Bremer v Rayner*.) I think that this point alone would be enough to establish that in this particular contract this time provision is, as a matter of necessary implication, of the essence and a condition.

Finally, I would add that I also agree entirely with Megaw LJ's analysis of the *Hong Kong Fir* case and its ratio decidendi.

e

MEGAW LJ. Brightman LJ, who is not able to be present this morning, has asked me to say that he agrees with both judgments that have been delivered.

Appeal allowed. Case to be remitted to board of appeal to reduce award by 5%. Leave to appeal to the House of Lords granted.

f

Mary Rose Plummer   Barrister.

Appeal and cross-appeal
The buyers appealed to the House of Lords and the sellers cross-appealed to the House in respect of the 5% reduction in the amount of the award ordered by the Court of Appeal. *g*

Roger Buckley QC and *Nicholas Merriman* for the appellants.
Christopher Staughton QC and *A M Havelock-Allan* for the respondents.

Their Lordships took time for consideration.

h

7th May. The following opinions were delivered.

LORD WILBERFORCE. My Lords, I have had the advantage of reading in advance the speech to be delivered by my noble and learned friend Lord Roskill. I agree entirely with it and desire only to add a few observations on some general aspects of the case. *j*
The appeal depends on the construction to be placed on cl 7 of GAFTA form 119 as completed by the special contract. It is not expressed as a 'condition' and the question is whether, in its context and in the circumstances, it should be read as such.
Apart from arguments on construction which have been fully dealt with by my noble and learned friend, the main contention of counsel for the appellants was based on the

decision of the Court of Appeal in *Hong Kong Fir Shipping Co Ltd v Kawasaki Kisen Kaisha*
a *Ltd* [1962] 1 All ER 474, [1962] 2 QB 26, as it might be applied to cl 7. Diplock LJ in his
seminal judgment illuminated the existence in contracts of terms which were neither,
necessarily, conditions nor warranties, but, in terminology which has since been applied
to them, intermediate or innominate terms capable of operating, according to the
gravity of the breach, as either conditions or warranties. Relying on this, counsel's
submission was that the buyer's obligation under the clause, to 'give at least [15]
b consecutive days' notice of probable readiness of vessel(s), and of the approximate
quantity required to be loaded', is of this character. A breach of it, both generally and in
relation to this particular case, might be, to use counsel's expression, 'inconsequential', i e
not such as to make performance of the seller's obligation impossible. If this were so it
would be wrong to treat it as a breach of condition: *Hong Kong Fir* would require it to be
treated as a warranty.
c   This argument, in my opinion, is based on a dangerous misunderstanding, or
misapplication, of what was decided and said in *Hong Kong Fir*. That case was concerned
with an obligation of seaworthiness, breaches of which had occurred during the course
of the voyage. The decision of the Court of Appeal was that this obligation was not a
condition, a breach of which entitled the charterer to repudiate. It was pointed out that,
as could be seen in advance, the breaches which might occur of it were various. They
d might be extremely trivial: the omission of a nail; they might be extremely grave: a
serious defect in the hull or in the machinery; they might be of serious but not fatal
gravity: incompetence or incapacity of the crew. The decision, and the judgments of the
Court of Appeal, drew from these facts the inescapable conclusion that it was impossible
to ascribe to the obligation, in advance, the character of a condition.
      Diplock LJ then generalised this particular consequence into the analysis which has
e since become classical. The fundamental fallacy of the appellants' argument lies in
attempting to apply this analysis to a time clause such as the present in a mercantile
contract, which is totally different in character. As to such a clause there is only one kind
of breach possible, namely to be late, and the questions which have to be asked are: first,
what importance have the parties expressly ascribed to this consequence? and, second, in
the absence of expressed agreement, what consequence ought to be attached to it having
f regard to the contract as a whole?
      The test suggested by the appellants was a different one. One must consider, they said,
the breach actually committed and then decide whether that default would deprive the
party not in default of substantially the whole benefit of the contract. They even
invoked certain passages in the judgment of Diplock LJ in *Hong Kong Fir* to support it.
One may observe in the first place that the introduction of a test of this kind would be
g commercially most undesirable. It would expose the parties, after a breach of one, two,
three, seven and other numbers of days, to an argument whether this delay would have
left time for the seller to provide the goods. It would make it, at the time, at least
difficult, and sometimes impossible, for the supplier to know whether he could do so.
It would fatally remove from a vital provision in the contract that certainty which is the
most indispensable quality of mercantile contracts, and lead to a large increase in
h arbitrations. It would confine the seller, perhaps after arbitration and reference through
the courts, to a remedy in damages which might be extremely difficult to quantify.
These are all serious objections in practice. But I am clear that the submission is
unacceptable in law. The judgment of Diplock LJ does not give any support and ought
not to give any encouragement to any such proposition; for beyond doubt it recognises
that it is open to the parties to agree that, as regards a particular obligation, any breach
j shall entitle the party not in default to treat the contract as repudiated. Indeed, if he were
not doing so he would, in a passage which does not profess to be more than clarificatory,
be discrediting a long and uniform series of cases, at least from *Bowes v Shand* (1877) 2
App Cas 455 onwards, which have been referred to by my noble and learned friend Lord
Roskill. It remains true, as Roskill LJ has pointed out in *Cehave NV v Bremer
Handelsgesellschaft mbH* [1975] 3 All ER 739 at 755, [1976] QB 44 at 70–71, that the courts

should not be too ready to interpret contractual clauses as conditions. And I have myself commended, and continue to commend, the greater flexibility in the law of contracts to **a** which *Hong Kong Fir* points the way (see *Reardon Smith Line Ltd v Hansen-Tangen* [1976] 3 All ER 570 at 576, [1976] 1 WLR 989 at 998). But I do not doubt that, in suitable cases, the courts should not be reluctant, if the intentions of the parties as shown by the contract so indicate, to hold that an obligation has the force of a condition, and that indeed they should usually do so in the case of time clauses in mercantile contracts. To such cases the 'gravity of the breach' approach of *Hong Kong Fir* would be unsuitable. I **b** need only add on this point that the word 'expressly' used by Diplock LJ in *Hong Kong Fir* [1962] 1 All ER 474 at 487, [1962] 2 QB 26 at 70 should not be read as requiring the actual use of the word 'condition'; any term or terms of the contract, which, fairly read, have the effect indicated, are sufficient. Lord Diplock himself has given recognition to this in this House (see *Photo Production Ltd v Securicor Transport Ltd* [1980] 1 All ER 556 at 566–567, [1980] AC 827 at 849). I therefore reject that part of the appellants' **c** argument which was based on it, and I must disagree with the judgment of the trial judge in so far as he accepted it. I respectfully indorse, on the other hand, the full and learned treatment of this issue in the judgment of Megaw LJ in the Court of Appeal.

I would add that the argument above applies equally to the use which the appellants endeavoured to make of certain observations in *United Scientific Holdings Ltd v Burnley Borough Council* [1977] 2 All ER 62, [1978] AC 904, a case on which I do not need to **d** comment on this occasion.

In conclusion, the statement of the law in 9 Halsbury's Laws (4th Edn) paras 481–482, (including the footnotes to para 482) (generally approved in the House in the *United Scientific Holdings* case) appears to me to be correct, in particular in asserting (1) that the court will require precise compliance with stipulations as to time wherever the circumstances of the case indicate that this would fulfil the intention of the parties, and **e** (2) that broadly speaking time will be considered of the essence in 'mercantile' contracts, with footnote reference to authorities which I have mentioned.

The relevant clause falls squarely within these principles, and such authority as there is supports its status as a condition (see *Bremer Handelsgesellschaft mbH v J H Rayner & Co Ltd* [1978] 2 Lloyd's Rep 73 and cf *Peter Turnbull & Co Pty Ltd v Mundas Trading Co (Australasia) Pty Ltd* [1954] 2 Lloyd's Rep 198. In this present context it is clearly **f** essential that both buyer and seller (who may change roles in the next series of contracts, or even in the same chain of contracts) should know precisely what their obligations are, most especially because the ability of the seller to fulfil his obligation may well be totally dependent on punctual performance by the buyer.

I would dismiss the appeal and, for the reasons given by my noble and learned friend Lord Roskill, the cross-appeal.

g

LORD FRASER OF TULLYBELTON. My Lords, I have had the advantage of reading in draft the speeches of my noble and learned friends Lord Wilberforce and Lord Roskill, and I agree with them. For the reasons stated by them I would dismiss the appeal and cross-appeal.

h

LORD SCARMAN. My Lords, I have the advantage of reading in draft the speeches of my noble and learned friends Lord Wilberforce and Lord Roskill. I agree with both of them, and would, therefore, dismiss the appeal and the cross-appeal.

I wish, however, to make a few observations on the topic of 'innominate' terms in our **j** contract law. In *Hong Kong Fir Shipping Co Ltd v Kawasaki Kisen Kaisha Ltd* [1962] 1 All ER 474, [1962] 2 QB 26 the Court of Appeal rediscovered and reaffirmed that English law recognises contractual terms which, on a true construction of the contract of which they are part, are neither conditions nor warranties but are, to quote Lord Wilberforce's words in *Bremer Handelsgesellschaft mbH v Vanden Avenne-Izegem* [1978] 2 Lloyd's Rep 109 at 113,

'intermediate'. A condition is a term the failure to perform which entitles the other
a party to treat the contract as at an end. A warranty is a term breach of which sounds in
damages but does not terminate, or entitle the other party to terminate, the contract. An
innominate or intermediate term is one the effect of non-performance of which the
parties expressly or (as is more usual) impliedly agree will depend on the nature and the
consequences of breach. In the *Hong Kong Fir* case the term in question provided for the
obligation of seaworthiness, breach of which it is well known may be trivial (eg one
b defective rivet) or very serious (eg a hole in the bottom of the ship). It is inconceivable
that parties when including such a term in their contract could have contemplated or
intended (unless they expressly say so) that one defective rivet would entitle the charterer
to end the contract or that a hole in the bottom of the ship would not. I read the *Hong
Kong Fir* case as being concerned as much with the construction of the contract as with
the consequences and effect of breach. The first question is always, therefore, whether,
c on the true construction of a stipulation and the contract of which it is part, it is a
condition, an innominate term, or only a warranty. If the stipulation is one which on the
true construction of the contract the parties have not made a condition, and breach of
which may be attended by trivial, minor or very grave consequences, it is innominate,
and the court (or an arbitrator) will, in the event of dispute, have the task of deciding
whether the breach that has arisen is such as the parties would have said, had they been
d asked at the time they made their contract, 'It goes without saying that, if that happens,
the contract is at an end.'

Where, therefore, as commonly happens, the parties do not identify a stipulation as a
condition, innominate term or warranty, the court will approach the problem of
construction in the way outlined by Upjohn LJ ([1962] 1 All ER 474 at 484, [1962] 2 QB
26 at 63–64):

e   'Where, however, on the true construction of the contract, the parties have not
      made a particular stipulation a condition, it would be unsound and misleading to
      conclude that, being a warranty, damages is a sufficient remedy.'

Unless the contract makes it clear, either by express provision or by necessary implication
f arising from its nature, purpose and circumstances ('the factual matrix' as spelt out, for
example, by Lord Wilberforce in his speech in *Reardon Smith Line Ltd v Hansen-Tangen*
[1976] 3 All ER 570 at 573–575, [1976] 1 WLR 989 at 995–997), that a particular
stipulation is a condition or only a warranty, it is an innominate term the remedy for a
breach of which depends on the nature, consequences and effect of the breach.

When the Court of Appeal had taken the logical step of declaring that the *Hong Kong
g Fir* analysis applied to contracts generally (see *Cehave NV v Bremer Handelsgesellschaft mbH*
[1975] 3 All ER 739, [1976] 1 QB 44), the law was back where it had been left by Lord
Mansfield in *Boone v Eyre* (1779) 1 Hy Bl 273n, 126 ER 160 and the judgment of
Bramwell B in *Jackson v Union Marine Insurance Co Ltd* (1874) LR 10 CP 125, [1874–80]
All ER Rep 317. Section 11(1)(b) of the Sale of Goods Act 1893 can now be seen to be no
more than a statutory guide to the use of the expressions 'condition' and 'warranty' in
h that Act. It is not to be treated as an indication that the law knows no terms other than
conditions and warranties. This fallacy was exposed in the *Hong Kong Fir* case. To read
the subsection as a guide to a comprehensive classification of contractual terms is to
convert it into a will-o'-the-wisp leading the unwary away from the true path of the law.

The difficulty in the present case is, as counsel's excellent argument for the appellants
revealed, to determine what the true construction is of the completed cl 7 of GAFTA
j form 119, which the parties incorporated in their contract. After some hesitation, I have
concluded that the clause was intended as a term the *buyer's* performance of which was
the necessary condition to performance by the seller of his obligations. The contract,
when made, was, to use the idiom of Diplock LJ (in *Hong Kong Fir* [1962] 1 All ER 474
at 485, [1962] 2 QB 26 at 65 and Demosthenes (Oratt, Attici, Reiske 867.11),
'synallagmatic', ie a contract of mutual engagements to be performed in the future, or,

in the more familiar English/Latin idiom, an 'executory' contract. The seller needed sufficient notice to enable him to choose the loading port; the parties were agreed that the notice to be given him was 15 days; this was a mercantile contract in which the parties required to know where they stood not merely later with hindsight but at once as events occurred. Because it makes commercial sense to treat the clause in the context and circumstances of this contract as a condition to be performed before the seller takes his steps to comply with bargain, I would hold it to be not an innominate term but a condition.

LORD LOWRY. My Lords, I have had the advantage of reading in draft the speeches of my noble and learned friends Lord Wilberforce and Lord Scarman, as well as the comprehensive review of the facts and the relevant law contained in the speech about to be delivered by my noble and learned friend Lord Roskill. I respectfully agree with their opinions, which taken together leave little of value to be said.

If I venture to add a few words of my own (which gives me an opportunity to acknowledge the excellent arguments on both sides), it is because I wish to refer to two points of general interest and then to state shortly why I would hold the term breached by the buyers to have been a condition.

As your Lordships have observed, the appellants based themselves on *Hong Kong Fir Shipping Co Ltd v Kawasaki Kisen Kaisha Ltd* [1962] 1 All ER 474, [1962] 2 QB 26, but they sought from that case a degree of support, which it could not give them, by citing it for the proposition that a term of a contract is not a condition unless a breach of it is seen to have deprived the party not in default of substantially the whole benefit which he was intended to obtain from the contract. By this argument the appellants were saying that in *Hong King Fir* Diplock LJ had adopted a new criterion for deciding by means of hindsight whether a term was a condition or not.

This was wrong. In the first place, the term in question in *Hong Kong Fir* was one relating to seaworthiness, and the entire court agreed that it was not a condition but a term the remedy for a breach of which might be rescission (with or without damages) or merely damages for the breach. Secondly Diplock LJ introduces the discussion by saying that there are many contractual undertakings of a more complex character which cannot be categorised as being conditions or warranties (see [1962] 1 All ER 474 at 487, [1962] 2 QB 26 at 70). And the description which has since been applied to this kind of term provides a conclusive answer to the appellants' contention. It is 'intermediate' because it lies in the middle *between* a condition and a warranty (just as the remedy for its breach lies somewhere between the remedies for breach of a condition and breach of a warranty), and it is 'innominate' because it is not *called* a condition or a warranty but assumes the character of each in turn.

It is by construing a contract (which can be done as soon as the contract is made) that one decides whether a term is, either expressly or by necessary implication, a condition, and not by considering the gravity of the breach of that term (which cannot be done until the breach is imminent or has occurred). The latter process is not an aid to construing the contract, but indicates whether rescission or merely damages is the proper remedy for a breach for which the innocent party might be recompensed in one way or the other according to its gravity. The approach of Diplock LJ in *Hong Kong Fir* [1962] 1 All ER 474 at 497, [1962] 2 QB 26 at 69–70 is absolutely consistent with the classic statement of Bowen LJ in *Bentsen v Taylor, Sons & Co (No 2)* [1893] 2 QB 274 at 281 which Sellers LJ cited (see [1962] 1 All ER 474 at 481, [1962] 2 QB 26 at 60).

The 'wait and see' method, or, as my noble and learned friend Lord Wilberforce has put it, the 'gravity of the breach' approach, is not the way to identify a condition in a contract. This is done by construing the contract in the light of the surrounding circumstances. By his illuminating analysis Diplock LJ shed a new light on old and accepted principles; he did not purport to establish new ones.

The second general point which I desire to mention concerns stipulations as to time in mercantile contracts, in regard to which it has been said that, broadly speaking, time will

be considered to be of the essence. To treat time limits thus means treating them as
a conditions, and he who would do so must pay respect to the principle enunciated by
Roskill LJ in *Cehave NV v Bremer Handelsgesellschaft mbH* [1975] 3 All ER 739 at 755,
[1976] QB 44 at 71, [1976] QB 44 at 71 that contracts are made to be performed and not
to be avoided.

The treatment of time limits as conditions in mercantile contracts does not appear to
me to be justifiable by any presumption of fact or rule of law, but rather to be a practical
b expedient founded on and dictated by the experience of businessmen, just the kind of
thing which Bowen LJ could have had in mind when framing his classic observations on
the implied term in *The Moorcock* (1889) 14 PD 64 at 68:

'Now, an implied warranty, or, as it is called, a covenant in law, as distinguished
from an express contract or express warranty, really is in all cases founded on the
presumed intention of the parties, and upon reason. The implication which the law
c draws from what must obviously have been the intention of the parties, the law
draws with the object of giving efficacy to the transaction and preventing such a
failure of consideration as cannot have been within the contemplation of either side;
and I believe if one were to take all the cases, and they are many, of implied
warranties of covenants in law, it will be found that in all of them the law is raising
an implication from the presumed intention of the parties with the object of giving
d to the transaction such efficacy as both parties must have intended that at all events
it should have. In business transactions such as this, what the law desires to effect
by the implication is to give such business efficacy to the transaction as must have
been intended at all events by both parties who are business men; not to impose on
one side all the perils of the transaction, or to emancipate one side from all the
chances of failure, but to make each party promise in law as much, at all events, as
e it must have been in the contemplation of both parties that he should be responsible
for in respect of those perils or chances. Now what did each party in a case like this
know? For if we are examining into their presumed intention we must examine
into their minds as to what the transaction was.'

This passage has stood the test of time and I commend it to all lawyers who undertake to
f advise their clients on mercantile affairs.

In order to identify an implied term (concerning which both parties to the contract,
being men of business, would say, 'Of course; it goes without saying') one must construe
the contract in the light of the surrounding circumstances and, to understand how that
is done, we cannot do better than read the passage from Lord Wilberforce's speech in
Reardon Smith Line Ltd v Hansen-Tangen [1976] 3 All ER 570 at 573–575, [1976] 1 WLR
g 989 at 995–997 to which my noble and learned friend Lord Scarman has already referred
your Lordships.

The law having been established, why should we regard the term here in question as
a condition? I start by expressing my full agreement with the reasons given in your
Lordships' speeches. Among the points which have weighed with me are the following.
1. There are enormous practical advantages in certainty, not least in regard to string
h contracts where today's buyer may be tomorrow's seller. 2. Most members of the string
will have many ongoing contracts simultaneously and they must be able ~~~~~~ business
with confidence in the legal results of their actions. 3. Decisions would be too difficult
if the term were innominate, litigation would be rife and years might elapse before the
results were known. 4. The difficulty of assessing damages is an indication in favour of
condition: see *McDougall v Aeromarine of Emsworth Ltd* [1958] 3 All ER 431 at 439, [1958]
i 1 WLR 1126 at 1133. 5. One can at least say that recent litigation has provided
indications that the term is a condition. Parties to similar contracts should (failing a
strong contra-indication) be able to rely on this: see *Maredelanto Compania Naviera SA v
Bergbau-Handel GmbH* [1970] 3 All ER 125 at 133, [1971] 1 QB 164 at 199 per Edmund
Davies LJ. 6. To make 'total loss' the only test of a condition is contrary to authority and
experience, when one recalls that terms as to the date of sailing, deviation from a voyage

and the date of delivery are regarded as conditions, but that failure to comply with them does not always have serious consequences. 7. Nor need an implied condition pass the *a* total loss test: see 6 above. 8. If the consequences of breach of condition turn out to be slight, the innocent party may treat the condition as an innominate term or a warranty. 9. While the sellers could have made time of the essence, if it were not so already, this would require reasonable notice, which might well not be practical either in a string contract or at all. 10. In *Tarrabochia v Hickie* (1856) 1 H & N 183 at 188, 156 ER 1168 at 1170, on which case the appellants strongly relied, Bramwell B said: *b*

> 'No doubt it is competent for the parties, if they think fit, to declare in express terms that any matter shall be a condition precedent, but when they have not so expressed themselves, it is necessary for those who construe the instrument to see whether they intended to do it. Since, however, they could have done it, those who construe the instrument should be chary in doing for them that which they might, but have not done for themsleves.' *c*

But in that very case both Pollock CB and Bramwell B, without the benefit of any express term, said that, where the agreement was that a ship should sail on a particular day, that was a condition precedent. 11. To accept the argument that conditions ought not to be implied 'because the parties themselves know how to describe a term' would logically condemn the entire doctrine of implied terms. 12. Arbitrators and courts might, if the *d* term were innominate, give different answers concerning the effect of a breach in very similar transactions, and parties could never learn by experience what was likely to happen in a given situation. So-called string contracts are not made, or adjudicated on, in strings.

The only arguments against treating the term as a condition appear to me to be based on generalities, whereas the considerations which are peculiar to this contract and similar *e* contracts tell in favour of its being a condition.

For these reasons, and for the reasons given by my noble and learned friends, I would concur in dismissing both the appeal and the cross-appeal.

LORD ROSKILL. My Lords, the appellants were the buyers and the respondents the sellers under a contract concluded on 30th January 1974 through their respective brokers *f* in Antwerp and Rotterdam for the sale and purchase of 15,000 long tons, 5% more or less in vessel's option of US soya bean meal, shipment of 5,000 long tons in each of May, June and July 1975 at a price of $US199·50 per metric ton, fob one US Gulf port at sellers' option. The respondents through their associated German company issued a contract note bearing that date for 5,000 long tons, 5% more or less for May 1975 shipment and the present appeal arises out of that May 1975 shipment. The appellants' brokers in *g* Antwerp issued a single contract note for the entire quantity of 15,000 tons already referred to. The two contract notes were not in identical terms but nothing now depends on the differences.

The contract incorporated the terms and conditions of GAFTA form 119. The relevant extracts the two contract notes are as follows.

The respondents' contract note: *h*

> 'QUANTITY: 5,000 (five thousand) tons of 2,240 lbs, 5% more or less in vessels option at contract price, to be declared latest when nominating the vessel . . .
> 'SHIPMENT: May, 1975—buyers to give 15 days loading notice Fob one Gulf port at seller's option, stowed/trimmed.'

The appellants' contract note: *j*

> 'QUANTITY: 15.000 LT. of 1.016 Kos 5% more or less at vessels' option at contract price, quantity to be declared latest when nominating vessel . . .
> 'OTHER CONDITIONS . . . Buyers to give 15 days preadvice of readiness of steamer.'

The most relevant clauses in form 119 are as follows:

'7. PERIOD OF DELIVERY—During   at Buyers' call.
Buyers shall give at least   consecutive days' notice of
probable readiness of vessel(s), and of the approximate quantity required to be
loaded. Buyers shall keep Sellers informed of any changes in the date of probable
readiness of vessel(s).

'8. EXTENSION OF DELIVERY—The contract period of delivery shall, if desired by
Buyers, be extended by an additional period of one calendar month, provided that
Buyers give notice in accordance with the Notices Clause not later than the next
business day following the last day of the delivery period. In this event Sellers shall
carry the goods at Buyers account and all charges for storage, interest, insurance and
other such normal carrying expenses shall be for Buyers' account. Should Buyers
not have taken delivery by the end of this extension period, Sellers shall have the
option of declaring the Buyers to be in default or shall be entitled to demand
payment at contract price plus such charges as stated above, less current f.o.b.
charges against warehouse warrants and such tender of warehouse receipts shall be
considered complete performance of the contract on the part of the Sellers . . .

'20. NOTICES—Any Notices received after 1600 hours on a business day shall be
deemed to have been received on the business day following. A Notice to the
Broker or Agent shall be deemed a Notice under this contract. All Notices given
under this contract shall be given by letter or by telegram or by telex or by other
method of rapid written communication. In case of resales all Notices shall be
passed on without delay by Buyers to their respective Sellers or vice versa . . .

'22. DEFAULT—In default of fulfilment of contract by either party, the other, at
his discretion shall, after giving notice by letter, telegram, or telex, have the right to
sell or purchase, as the case may be, against the defaulter and the defaulter shall
make good the loss, if any, on such purchase or sale on demand. If the party liable
to pay be dissatisfied with the price of such sale or purchase or if the above right is
not exercised and damages cannot be mutually agreed, any damages, payable by the
party in default, shall be settled by arbitration. In the event of default by Sellers
entitling Buyers to damages, such damages shall be based upon the actual or
estimated value of the goods on date of default, to be fixed by arbitration unless
mutually agreed, and nothing contained in or implied under this contract shall
entitle Buyers to recover any damages in respect of loss of profit upon any subcontracts made by themselves or others unless the Arbitrators or Board of Appeal,
having regard to any special circumstances, shall in their sole and absolute discretion
award such damages. In the event of default in shipment or delivery, damages, if
any, shall be computed upon the mean contract quantity . . .'

My Lords, since it was agreed that there was no material difference between the two
important clauses regarding the giving of the 15 days' notice to which those clauses refer,
it is clear that the two blanks in cl 7 of form 119 have to be treated as completed with the
words 'May 1975' in the first blank and the figures '15' in the second blank, so that cl 7
thus completed reads:

'PERIOD OF DELIVERY—During May 1975 at Buyers' call. Buyers shall give at least
15 consecutive days' notice of probable readiness of vessel(s), and of the approximate
quantity required to be loaded. Buyers shall keep Sellers informed of any changes
in the date of probable readiness of the vessel(s).'

It was found by the Board of Appeal of GAFTA, in para 6 of the special case, that
extensions were claimed under cl 8 of form 119 so that the relevant period became June
1975. The board of appeal also found, in para 11 of the special case, that the appellants'
nomination of the vessel concerned to load what had thus become a June shipment was
given to the respondents at 0846 on 17th June 1975 when it was received by the
respondents' brokers in Rotterdam, less than 15 consecutive days before the end of the
extended shipment period. It is not necessary to detail the passing on of this notice until

it reached the respondents on 18th June. On 20th June the respondents claimed default because of the alleged lateness of the appellants' notice. The relevant details will be found in paras 12, 13, and 14 of the special case. As is found in para 19 of the special case, the market price had by then fallen by over $US60 per metric ton. The respondents claimed damages from the appellants. The dispute was referred to arbitration in accordance with cl 26 of form 119. The umpire awarded the respondents $US317,500 as damages, this figure being based on the mean contract quantity of 5,000 long tons together with certain other sums not now immediately relevant. The appellants appealed to the Board of Appeal of GAFTA and that board consisting of five members dismissed their appeal in all respects but stated a special case for the decision of the court. On the hearing of that special case by Parker J, that judge reversed the decision of the board of appeal and upheld their alternative award. The respondents thereupon appealed to the Court of Appeal (Megaw, Browne and Brightman LJJ) who restored the award of the board of appeal on liability but varied the quantum of damages holding that these should measured by the minimum quantity the appellants would have been obliged to take. Leave to appeal to your Lordships' House was granted by the Court of Appeal.

My Lords, your Lordships' House is the fifth tribunal before whom this dispute has been heard. I understand all your Lordships are agreed that the appeal and also the cross-appeal on quantum fail in substance for the reasons given by Megaw LJ in, if I may respectfully say so, a powerful and closely reasoned judgment in the Court of Appeal. It follows that the same view on the main issue involved in this dispute has been formed by six members of GAFTA, three Lords Justices and five members of your Lordships' House, a total of fourteen with only the judge taking the opposite view on that main issue. My Lords, I intend no disrespect to the judge in pointing this out. I do so merely for the purpose of expressing regret that, notwithstanding repeated adverse comments in your Lordships' House, in a simple case of this kind there should be a succession of no less than four appeals from the decision of an umpire well versed in disputes of this kind and that this is still possible. I derive some comfort, however, from the fact that with the passing of the Arbitration Act 1979 this multiplicity of appeals should soon be a thing of the past.

My Lords, the central question in this appeal is whether the appellants' obligation under cl 7 completed as I have completed it are of such a character that a breach of them by the appellants such as, in my view, undoubtedly took place entitled the respondents forthwith to rescind and claim damages. Put into lawyers' language: is the appellants' obligation to give the required 15 days' notice a condition or not? If it is, this appeal fails. If it is not, this appeal must succeed. As already stated, at all stages of these proceedings, save one, this obligation has been held to be a condition. The judge not only held that it was not a condition but also held that there was no breach by the appellants of cl 7. The Court of Appeal disagreed, and this latter submission which found favour with the judge was not, rightly in my view, pursued in argument before your Lordships' House.

My Lords, the relevant phrase 'give at least 15 consecutive days' notice' consists only of six words and two digits. But the able arguments of which your Lordships have had the benefit have extended over three full days. The appellants' arguments may be summarised thus. They submitted that this term was not a condition but was what has come to be described since Hong Kong Fir Shipping Co Ltd v Kasawaki Kisen Kaisha Ltd [1962] 1 All ER 474, [1962] 2 QB 26 as an 'innominate' obligation (neither a condition nor a warranty), and that when a term is an innominate obligation the question whether or not a breach gives the innocent party the right to rescind depends on whether the innocent party was thereby deprived 'of substantially the whole benefit which it was intended he should obtain from the contract'. This last quotation is from the judgment of Diplock LJ in the Hong Kong Fir case [1962] 1 All ER 474 at 487, [1962] 2 QB 26 at 70. It was further argued that since the respondents accepted that they could not show that admitted breach by the appellants in giving a late notice had deprived them of substantially the whole benefit which it was intended they should obtain from the contract, the respondents had no right to rescind on account of that late notice. Much reliance was also placed by counsel for the appellants on the ensuing passage in Diplock LJ's judgment: 'and the legal consequences of a breach of such an undertaking, *unless provided for expressly in the contract*, depend on the nature of the event to which the breach gives rise ...' (my emphasis). There was, counsel argued, no such 'express' provision in this contract. Counsel also placed reliance on the application of the principle enunciated in the *Hong Kong Fir* case, which was a case of a time charterparty relating to an unseaworthy ship, to contracts for the sale of goods, such as the present, by the Court of Appeal in *Cehave NV v Bremer Handelsgesellschaft mbH* [1975] 3 All ER 739, [1976] QB 44, a decision approved in your Lordships' House in *Reardon Smith Line Ltd v Hansen-Tangen* [1976] 3 All ER 570, [1976] 1 WLR 989. The principles enunciated in the first two cases mentioned were, he said, of general application and pointed the way to a new and now correct approach to the question how a term in a contract alleged on the one hand to be a condition and on the other hand to be an 'innominate term' should be approached.

My Lords, it is beyond question that there are many cases in the books where terms the breach of which do not deprive the innocent party of substantially the whole of the benefit which he was intended to receive from the contract were nonetheless held to be conditions any breach of which entitled the innocent party to rescind. Perhaps the most famous is *Bowes v Shand* (1877) 2 App Cas 455. *Reuter v Sala* (1879) 4 CPD 239 is another such case. Both these cases were decided before the Sale of Goods Act 1893 was enacted. But that Act only codified the relevant common law. I think counsel was entitled to say that these two, and other similar cases, largely turned on the fact that the breach complained of was part of the description of the goods in question, and that would therefore today be a statutory condition under s 13 of the 1893 Act. But there are many other cases, modern and less modern, where terms in contracts for the sale of goods have been held to be conditions any breach of which will give rise to a right to rescind. Though s 10(1) of the 1893 Act provides that, unless a different intention appears, terms as to the time of payment are not deemed to be of the essence of a contract of sale, there are many cases, notably those in connection with the opening of bankers' credits and the payment against documents, where the relevant obligations have been held to be a condition a breach of which will entitle the innocent party to rescind. No useful purpose will be served by listing all those cases cited in argument on either side. Many are usefully collected in the judgment of Diplock J in *Ian Stach Ltd v Baker Bosly Ltd* [1958] 1 All ER 542 at 546–549, [1958] 2 QB 130 at 139–144, and I would emphasise in this connection the need for certainty in this type of transaction to which that judge referred (see [1958] 1 All ER 542 at 546–548, [1958] 2 QB 130 at 143–144). Parties to commercial transactions should be entitled to know their rights at once and should not, when possible, be required to wait on events before those rights can be determined. Of course, in many cases of alleged frustration or of alleged repudiatory delay it may be necessary to await events on the happening or non-happening of which rights may well crystallise. But your Lordships' House has recently reiterated in a series of cases arising from the withdrawal of ships on time charter for non-payment of hire the need for certainty where punctual payment of hire is required and has held that the right to rescind automatically follows a breach of any such condition.

My Lords, I find nothing in the judgment of Diplock LJ in the *Hong Kong Fir* case which suggests any departure from the basic and long-standing rules for determining whether a particular term in a contract is or is not a condition and there is much in the judgment of Sellers LJ, with which Upjohn LJ expressly agreed, to show that those rules are still good law and should be maintained. They are enshrined in the oft-quoted judgment of Bowen LJ in *Bentsen v Taylor, Sons & Co (No 2)* [1893] 2 QB 274 at 281:

'There is no way of deciding that question except by looking at the contract in the light of the surrounding circumstances, and then making up one's mind whether

the intention of the parties, as gathered from the instrument itself, will best be
carried out by treating the promise as a warranty sounding only in damages, or as   a
a condition precedent by the failure to perform which the other party is relieved of
his liability.'

That well-known passage will be found quoted by Sellers LJ in the *Hong Kong Fir* case
[1962] 1 All ER 474 at 481, [1962] 2 QB 26 at 60. I would add a reference in this
connection to the judgment of Scrutton LJ in *Re Comptoir Commercial Anversois & Power,
Son & Co* [1920] 1 KB 868 at 899, [1918–19] All ER Rep 661 at 673–674, where he added   b
to the statements of the same principle in the Exchequer Chamber in *Behn v Burness*
(1863) 3 B & S 751, 122 ER 281 and in *Oppenheim v Fraser* (1876) 34 LT 524 his own great
authority.

My Lords, the judgment of Diplock LJ in the *Hong Kong Fir* case is, if I may respectfully
say so, a landmark in the development of one part of our law of contract in the latter part
of this century. Diplock LJ showed by reference to detailed historical analysis, contrary   c
to what had often been thought previously, that there was no complete dichotomy
between conditions and warranties and that there was a third class of term, the
innominate term. But I do not believe he ever intended his judgment to afford an easy
escape route from the normal consequences of rescission to a contract breaker who had
broken what was, on its true construction, clearly a condition of the contract by claiming
that he had only broken an innominate term. Of course when considering whether a   d
particular term is or is not a condition it is relevant to consider to what other class or
category that term, if not a condition, might belong. But to say that is not to accept that
the question whether or not a term is a condition has to be determined solely by
reference to what has to be proved before rescission can be claimed for breach of a term
which has already been shown not to be a condition but an innominate term. Once it is
appreciated that the whole of this part of Diplock LJ's judgment is directed to the   e
consequences of a term which is not a condition but an innominate term and not to the
question of whether or not a particular term is a condition, the difficulties mentioned by
Megaw LJ in his judgment if the passages in question are read too literally, and as the
appellants invite your Lordships to read them, disappear. The only criticism I would
respectfully venture of these passages is the use of the adverb 'expressly' in the passage I
have already quoted (see [1962] 1 All ER 474 at 487, [1962] 2 QB 26 at 70). Surely the   f
same result must follow whether the legal consequences of the breach are also 'impliedly'
provided for in the contract on that contract's true construction. In venturing this
amendment to what Diplock LJ said, I derive comfort from the fact that Lord Diplock
himself in *Photo Production Ltd v Securicor Transport Ltd* [1980] 1 All ER 556 at 566–567,
[1980] AC 827 at 849 speaks of the case where the contracting parties have agreed—

> 'whether by express words or by implication of law [my emphasis], [that *any* (Lord   g
> Diplock's emphasis] failure by one party to perform a particular primary obligation
> ("condition" in the nomenclature of the Sale of Goods Act 1893), irrespective of the
> gravity of the event that has in fact resulted from the breach, shall entitle the other
> party to elect to put an end to all primary obligations of both parties remaining
> unperformed . . .'   h

Thus I think it legitimate to suggest an amendment to the passage in the *Hong Kong Fir*
case [1962] 1 All ER 474 at 487, [1962] 2 QB 26 at 70 either by deleting the word
'expressly' or by adding the words 'or by necessary implication'.

My Lords, your Lordships' House had to consider a similar problem in relation to a
different clause (cl 21) in a different GAFTA contract in *Bremer Handelsgesellschaft mbH v
Vanden Avenne-Izegem* [1978] 2 Lloyd's Rep 109. In passing I would observe the text of   j
that clause is inaccurately quoted in the headnote of the report but will be found
correctly quoted in the speech of Viscount Dilhorne (at 121). Lord Wilberforce said (at
113):

> 'Automatic and invariable treatment of a clause such as this runs counter to the
> approach, which modern authorities recognise, of treating such a provision as

having the force of a condition (giving rise to rescission or invalidity), or of a
contractual term (giving rise to damages only) according to the nature and gravity
of the breach. The clause is then categorised as an innominate term. This doctrine
emerged very clearly in *Hongkong Fir Shipping Co. Ltd. v. Kawasaki Kisen Kaisha Ltd.*
([1962] 1 All ER 474, [1962] 2 QB 26) in relation to the obligation of seaworthiness,
and was as applied to a contract for sale of goods made on GAFTA form 100 in *The
Hansa Nord* ([1975] 3 All ER 739, [1976] QB 44), a decision itself approved by this
House in *Reardon Smith Line v. Hansen-Tangen* (1976] 3 All ER 570, [1976] 1 WLR
989). In my opinion, the clause may vary appropriately and should be regarded as
such an intermediate term: to do so would recognise that while in many, possibly
most, instances, breach of it can adequately be sanctioned by damages, cases may
exist in which, in fairness to the buyer, it would be proper to treat the cancellation
as not having effect. On the other hand, always so to treat it may be often be unfair
to the seller, and unnecessarily rigid.'

The passage I have just quoted was directed to cl 21 of the contract there in question.
All members of your Lordships' House were of the opinion that that clause was not a
condition because it was insufficiently definitive or precise (see the speeches of Lord
Salmon and Lord Russell at 128, 130). But it is important to observe that your Lorships'
House had also to consider cl 22 of that contract. All members of your Lordships' House
held that cl 22 was a condition (see the speeches of Lord Wilberforce and Lord Salmon at
116, 128). I venture to emphasise the statement in the former passage that accurate
compliance with the stipulation in question was essential to avoid commercial confusion
in view of the possibility of long string contracts being involved, a point of especial
importance in the present case.

In short, while recognising the modern approach and not being overready to construe
terms as conditions unless the contract clearly requires the court so to do, none the less
the basic principles of construction for determining whether or not a particular term is
a condition remain as before, always bearing in mind on the one hand the need for
certainty and on the other the desirability of not, when legitimate, allowing rescission
where the breach complained of is highly technical and where damages would clearly be
an adequate remedy. It is therefore in my opinion wrong to use the language employed
by Diplock LJ in the *Hong Kong Fir* case as directed to the determination of the question
which terms of a particular contract are conditions and which are only innominate
terms. I respectfully agree with what Megaw LJ said in the passage in his judgment in
the instant case (see pp 536–537, ante). The explanation of the passage which he quotes
is that which I have just given.

My Lords, counsel for the appellants founded much of this part of his argument on the
decision of your Lordships' House in *United Scientific Holdings v Burnley Borough Council*
[1977] 2 All ER 61, [1978] AC 904 when your Lordships' House, unanimously reversing
two separate decisions of the Court of Appeal, held that the timetable specified in rent
review clauses for the completion of the various steps for determining the rent payable
of the period following a review was not of the essence. Naturally, counsel relied on a
passage in the speech of Lord Diplock which I quote in full ([1977] 2 All ER 62 at 70,
[1978] AC 904 at 928):

'My Lords, I will not take up time repeating here what I myself said in the *Hong
Kong Fir* case, except to point out that by 1873: (1) stipulations as to the time at
which a party was to perform a promise on his part were among the contractual
stipulations which were not regarded as "conditions precedent" if his failure to
perform that promise punctually did not deprive the other party of substantially the
whole benefit which it was intended that he should obtain from the contract; (2)
when the delay by one party in performing a particular promise punctually had
become so prolonged as to deprive the other party of substantially the whole benefit
which it was intended that he should obtain from the contract it did discharge that
other party from the obligation to continue to perform any of his own promises
which as yet were unperformed; (3) similar principles were applicable to determine

whether the parties' duties to one another to continue to perform their mutual obligations were discharged by frustration of the adventure that was the object of the contract. A party's ability to perform his promise might depend on the prior occurrence of an event which neither he nor the other party had promised would occur. The question whether a stipulation as to the time at which the event should occur was of the essence of the contract depended on whether even a brief postponement of it would deprive one or other of the parties of substantially the whole benefit that it was intended that he should obtain from the contract.'

Read literally, the passage might be thought to be of universal application and to suggest that by 1873 terms in contract as to time, whatever their character, were not to be construed as conditions any breach of which would give rise to a right to rescind unless the several prerequisites specified in this passage were fulfilled. My Lords, I do not think that Lord Diplock can possibly have intended this passage to be so read. In the immediately preceding pages he had been dealing with the manner in which the courts of Chancery had been developing the equitable principles which he describes and explaining how contemporaneously the courts of common law were reaching the same result though by a different route. But to read the passage I have just quoted as of universal application and in particular as of application to stipulations as to time in mercantile contracts would be to misread it, for it would be quite inconsistent with many earlier authorities such as *Behn v Burness* (1863) 3 B & S 751, 122 ER 281 as well as later authorities such as *Bowes v Shand* (1877) 2 App Cas 455, *Reuter v Sala* (1879) 4 CPD 239 and *Bentsen v Taylor, Sons & Co (No 2)* [1893] 2 QB 274, to which I have already referred. That this is so is strongly reinforced by the fact that H E Francis QC, whose argument for the appellants was unanimously accepted by your Lordships' House, expressly conceded that the doctrine that Lord Diplock ultimately so clearly expounded (see [1977] 2 All ER 62 at 68–70, [1978] AC 904 at 925–928) did not apply in three classes of cases of which the second was 'where the courts may infer from the nature of the contract or the surrounding circumstances that the parties regard time stipulations as of the essence of their bargains: mercantile contracts . . .' (see [1978] AC 904 at 908), a concession which I think was clearly rightly made.

In reply to this part of counsel's argument for the appellants, counsel for the respondents drew your Lordships' attention to 9 Halsbury's Laws (4th Edn) paras 481 and 482. He was able to show that the penultimate full paragraph in para 481 had been expressly approved by no less than three of your Lordships in the *United Scientific Holdings* case, by Viscount Dilhorne, Lord Simon and Lord Fraser, while Lord Salmon stated the law in virtually identical terms though without an express reference to this particular passage in Halsbury's Laws (see [1977] 2 All ER 62 at 78, 81, 83, 94, 88, [1978] AC 904 at 937, 941, 944, 958, 950). The passage in para 481 reads thus:

'The modern law, in the case of contracts of all types, may be summarised as follows. Time will not be considered to be of the essence unless: (1) the parties expressly stipulate that conditions as to time must be strictly complied with; or (2) the nature of the subject matter of the contract or the surrounding circumstances show that time should be considered to be of the essence; or (3) a party who has been subjected to unreasonable delay gives notice to the party in default making time of the essence.'

The relevant passage in para 482 reads thus:

'Apart from express agreement or notice making time of the essence, the court will require precise compliance with stipulations as to time wherever the circumstances of the case indicate that this would fulfil the intention of the parties. Broadly speaking, time will be considered of the essence in "mercantile" contracts and in other cases where the nature of the contract or of the subject matter or the circumstances of the case require precise compliance.'

Footnote 3 to para 482 refers among other cases to *Reuter v Sala* and *Bowes v Shand*. My

Lords, I agree with counsel for the respondents that the express approval of the passage
a in para 481 cannot be taken as involving implied disapproval of the passage I have just
quoted from para 482.

My Lords, I venture to doubt whether much help is necessarily to be derived in
determining whether a particular term is to be construed as a condition or as an
innominate term by attaching a particular label to the contract. Plainly there are terms
in a mercantile contract, as your Lordships' House pointed out in *Bremer Handelsgesellschaft*
b *mbH v Vanden Avenne-Izegem* [1978] 2 Lloyd's Rep 109, which are not to be considered as
conditions. But the need for certainty in mercantile contracts is often of great importance
and sometimes may well be a determining factor in deciding the true construction of a
particular term in such a contract.

To my mind the most important single factor of counsel's submission for the
respondents is that until the requirement of the 15 consecutive days' notice was fulfilled
c the respondents could not nominate the 'one Gulf port' as the loading port, which under
the instant contract it was their sole right to do. I agree with counsel that in a mercantile
contract when a term has to be performed by one party as a condition precedent to the
ability of the other party to perform another term, especially an essential term such as the
nomination of a single loading port, the term as to time for the performance of the
former obligation will in general fall to be treated as a condition. Until the 15 consecutive
d days' notice had been given, the respondents could not know for certain which loading
port they should nominate so as to ensure that the contract goods would be available for
loading on the ship's arrival at that port before the end of the shipment period.

It follows that in my opinion the umpire, the board of appeal and the Court of Appeal
all reached the correct conclusion, and for the reasons I have given I would dismiss the
appellants' appeal. It will have been observed that I have reached this conclusion as a
e matter of the construction of the relevant clause. I have thus far paid no regard to the
finding in para 5 of the special case that: 'This term in an FOB Contract is regarded in the
trade as of such great and fundamental importance that any breach thereof goes to the
root of the contract.' Naturally, though the crucial question of construction is a matter
of law for the court, the court will give much weight to the view of the trade tribunal
concerned. Though I question whether on the argument of a special case it is permissible
f to look outside the findings of fact in that special case to findings of fact in other special
cases, counsel for the appellants was able to point to a contrary finding of fact by a
different board of appeal of the same association in *Bremer Handelsgesellschaft mbH v J H*
Rayner & Co Ltd [1978] 2 Lloyd's Rep 73 at 81:

> 'Failure of an f.o.b. Buyer to indicate to his Seller the demurrage/despatch rate
g > with the nomination of a vessel or at any time is *not* [my emphasis] customarily
> treated by the trade as being a term of great of fundamental importance to the
> Contract such as to give a Seller the right to reject the nomination or to refuse to ship
> the goods.'

The relevant clause, cl 7, in that case will be found in the judgment of Mocatta J (at
85):
h
> '7. NOMINATION OF VESSEL. Buyer to give nomination of vessel to Seller, in
> writing, in time for Seller to receive with minimum 15 days' notice of earliest
> readiness of tonnage at first or sole port of loading.'

The judge held (at 89) that the finding which I have just quoted did not preclude his
j reaching the conclusion that that clause was as a matter of construction a condition, a
breach of which entitled the innocent party to rescind. The judge's decision was reversed
on appeal on a different point (see [1979] 2 Lloyd's Rep 216). But Bridge LJ (at 234) was
at pains to say that as then advised he was not persuaded that on this question the judge
had reached the wrong conclusion. See also the judgment of Megaw LJ (at 229). With
respect, I think that Mocatta J was plainly correct in his conclusion on this question.

Counsel for the respondents also relied on a number of cases where the argument presently urged by counsel for the appellants might have been but was not advanced. They included *Peter Turnbull & Co Pty Ltd v Mundas Trading Co (Australasia) Pty Ltd* *a* [1954] 2 Lloyd's Rep 198, a decision of the High Court of Australia which included Dixon CJ, and *Carapanayoti & Co Ltd v Comptoir Commercial Andre & Cie SA* [1972] 1 Lloyd's Rep 139, a decision of the Court of Appeal. With respect I doubt whether past omissions, whether for good or bad reasons, greatly advance the solution of the present problem.   *b*

My Lords, I would only add in conclusion that it seems clear from the argument and indeed from the judgment of Parker J in the present case that certain passages in the judgment of Diplock LJ in the *Hong Kong Fir* case and in the speech of Lord Diplock in *United Scientific Holdings v Burnley Borough Council* have been read out of context and thus misunderstood. An excellent illustration of this misunderstanding is shown by the argument advanced and unanimously rejected in *Toepfer v Lenersan-Poortman NV* [1978] *c* 2 Lloyd's Rep 555 (Donaldson J); [1980] 1 Lloyd's Rep 143 (Court of Appeal). There the sellers attempted on the strength of the decision in the *Hong Kong Fir* case to argue that the sellers' obligations regarding time for presentation of the documents against which the buyers had to pay not later than 20 days after the bill of lading date was not a condition a breach of which entitled the buyers to rescind but was only an innominate term. I find myself in complete agreement with the observations of Donaldson J *d* pointing out how the *Hong Kong Fir* case had been misunderstood. I would, therefore, dismiss this appeal with costs.

My Lords, I turn to deal briefly with the respondents' cross-appeal. Both the umpire and the board of appeal awarded the respondents damages on the basis of the mean contract quantity of 5,000 long tons. They clearly reached this conclusion on the strength of the last sentence of cl 22 of GAFTA form 119. The Court of Appeal reduced *e* the damages payable to the respondents by assessing them by reference not to 5,000 long tons but to 4,750 long tons being 5% less than the mean contract quantity, this being the minimum quantity the appellants would have been obliged to take. As a result of the Court of Appeal decision, the board of appeal subsequently made a supplementary award in the respondents' favour for a lesser amount based on the figure of 4,750 long tons.

It was common ground that the reference in the contract 'at vessel's option' meant 'at *f* buyers' option'. My Lords it was also common ground that the Court of Appeal was bound to reach this conclusion by reason of an earlier decision of that court in *Toprak Mahsulleri Ofisi v Finagrain Compagnie Commerciale Agricole et Financière SA* [1979] 2 Lloyd's Rep 98, to which I was a party. In that case the court held that the relevant sentence in the contract applied only to default of shipment by the seller or default of delivery by the seller and not to default by the buyer. In the latter case damages fell to *g* be assessed on ordinary principles.

My Lords, the respondents urged that in this context 'default' bore its primary dictionary meaning of 'failure' or 'want' or 'absence' and that since there had been a 'failure' or 'want' or 'absence' of shipment by the sellers that was sufficient to enable the last sentence of cl 22 to be invoked so as to require the respondents' damages to be assessed on the mean contract quantity.

My Lords, no doubt in some contexts the word 'default' may bear this particular *h* dicionary meaning. But in determining the meaning of the word in any case, the context in which the word is used is of crucial importance. One has only to see the number of times that the word 'default' or 'defaulter' is used in cl 22 to see that the context is one of a breach of contract sounding in damages and not of non-performance without breach. My Lords, I am clearly of the view that 'default' in the last sentence of cl 22 means default *j* by the sellers in breach of their contractual obligations. That sentence has no application to the present case. Accordingly with all respects to the umpire and the board of appeal in the present case I think that *Toprak v Finagrain* was correctly decided. If the trade wishes to have the same result where the relevant default is by the buyer and not by the

seller the terms of GAFTA form 119 and other similar terms will require to be altered.
a   For these reasons I would dismiss the cross-appeal with costs.

Appeal and cross-appeal dismissed.

Solicitors: *William A Crump & Son* (for the appellant buyers); *Sinclair, Roche & Temperley* (for the respondent sellers).

b
Mary Rose Plummer   Barrister.

Westminster City Council v Haymarket Publishing Ltd

c

COURT OF APPEAL, CIVIL DIVISION
LORD DENNING MR, SHAW AND OLIVER LJJ
26th, 27th FEBRUARY, 2nd MARCH 1981

Rates – Surcharge on unused commercial building – Unpaid surcharge constituting charge on
d   *land comprised in hereditament – Scope of charge – Land subject to legal mortgage – Owner's*
interest consisting merely of equity of redemption – Mortgagee exercising power of sale and
selling land to defendant – Whether defendant liable for rates surcharge – Whether charge for
unpaid surcharge having priority over defendant's interest in land – Whether 'charge on land'
imposing charge on all existing interests at time charge created including mortgagee's interest –
Whether charge imposed only on owner's interest at that date consisting of equity of redemption
e   *– General Rate Act 1967, ss 17A(1), 17B(3).*

On 3rd January 1974 a company acquired the freehold of commercial premises. The
next day the company mortgaged the premises by a legal mortgage to a bank to secure
indebtedness to the bank of £6m. By s 17A^d of the General Rate Act 1967 the owner of
unused commercial premises was liable to a rating surcharge while the premises
remained unused, the 'owner' being defined, in s 17B(7)^b of that Act, as 'the person
f   entitled to possession'. By s 17B(3) a surcharge levied under s 17A was a 'charge on the
land comprised in the hereditament'. The company left the premises unused and in
April 1976 the rating authority levied a surcharge on the company for £16,940 and
registered it as a land charge in the local land charges register. The company failed to pay
the surcharge. In July 1977 the bank exercised its power of sale under the mortgage and
g   sold the premises to the defendants for £220,000. The contract of sale provided that the
bank would indemnify the defendants against the charge for the unpaid surcharge if it
was binding on the defendants. The rating authority took out a summons against the
defendants claiming, inter alia, a declaration that its charge had priority over the
defendants' interest in the land, on the grounds (i) that the charge imposed by s 17B(3)
was a charge on all the interests in the premises at the date the charge arose and
h   accordingly was imposed on, and had priority over, the bank's interest in the premises as
mortgagee and therefore had priority over the defendants' interest, and (ii) that if the
charge imposed by s 17B(3) was confined to a charge on the interest of the owner of the
premises at the date the charge arose, there could be more than one such owner and the
bank was included as an owner. The judge ([1980] 1 All ER 289) held that the charge
imposed by s 17B(3) was imposed on all the interests in the land existing when the charge
j   arose and therefore was imposed on the bank's interest in the premises and thus on the
defendants' interest. The defendants appealed, contending (i) that under s 17A a

a   Section 17A, so far as material, is set out at p 557 j, post
b   Section 17B, so far as material, is set out at p 557 j, post

surcharge could be levied only on one owner, namely the person in possession of the
premises at the date of the surcharge, and (ii) that the charge imposed by s 17B(3) was   *a*
imposed on the interest of that owner only, particularly as a surcharge was a penalty, and,
since the company was the owner for the purposes of s 17A when the charge arose and at
that date its interest in the premises consisted merely of the equity of redemption subject
to the mortgage, the charge was imposed only on that interest.

Held – (1) On the true construction of s 17A of the 1967 Act a surcharge could be levied   *b*
only on one owner, namely on the person entitled to exercise possession of the premises,
and where the premises were mortgaged the mortgagor was the owner for the purpose
of s 17A unless and until the mortgagee entered into possession under the mortgage (see
p 558 *a b* and *j* to p 559 *b* and *g*, post).
    (2) On the true construction of s 17B(3) of the 1967 Act the 'charge on the land'
imposed for an unpaid surcharge was not confined to a charge on the owner's interest in   *c*
the premises when the charge arose but extended to a charge on all the estates and
interests in the premises existing when the charge arose. Accordingly, the rating
authority's charge for the unpaid surcharge was imposed not only on the company's
equity of redemption but also on the bank's interest as mortgagee of the premises over
which it had priority. It followed that the rating authority's charge had priority over the
defendants' interest in the premises. The appeal would therefore be dismissed (see p 558   *d*
c and *g* to p 559 *b* and *g*, post); *Birmingham Corpn v Baker* (1881) 17 Ch D 782 and
Paddington Borough Council v Finucane [1928] All ER Rep 428 applied.
    Decision of Dillon J [1980] 1 All ER 289 affirmed.

Notes
For the rating surcharge on unused commercial buildings, see Supplement to 32   *e*
Halsbury's Laws (3rd Edn) para 51A.3.
    For the General Rating Act 1967, ss 17A, 17B (inserted by the Local Government Act
1974, s 16), see 44 Halsbury's Statutes (3rd Edn) 1309, 1310.

Cases referred to in judgments
Birmingham Corpn v Baker (1881) 17 Ch D 782, 46 JP 52, 26 Digest (Repl) 606, 2616.   *f*
Paddington Borough Council v Finucane [1928] Ch 567, [1928] All ER Rep 428, 97 LJ Ch
    219, 139 LT 368, 92 JP 68, 26 LGR 283, 26 Digest (Repl) 685, 29.
Tendring Union Guardians v Dowton [1891] 3 Ch 265, 61 LJ Ch 82, 65 LT 434, CA, 26
    Digest (Repl) 607, 2623.

Cases also cited   *g*
Birmingham Corpn v Baker (1881) 17 Ch D 782, 46 JP 52, 26 Digest (Repl) 606, 2616.
Bristol Corpn v Virgin [1928] 2 KB 622, DC.
London Corpn v Cusack Smith [1955] 1 All ER 302, [1955] AC 337, HL.

Appeal
This was an appeal by the defendants, Haymarket Publishing Ltd, against the judgment   *h*
of Dillon J ([1980] 1 All ER 289) declaring that a charge under s 17B(3) of the General
Rate Act 1967 for £16,940·93 in favour of the plaintiff, Westminster City Council ('the
rating authority'), for an unpaid rating surcharge levied on Shop Investments Ltd as the
owner of commercial property at 22 Lancaster Gate, London W2, had priority over the
defendants' interest in the property, and seeking a declaration that the rating authority's
charge (a) took priority according to the date on which it arose and was registered, and   *j*
therefore ranked after a legal mortgage of the land dated 4th January 1974 between Shop
Investments Ltd and the National Westminster Bank Ltd ('the bank') as mortgagees; and
(b) was overridden by the sale to the defendants under the power of sale in the
mortgage. The grounds of the appeal were that Dillon J was wrong in law (1) in holding
that the rating authority's charge for the unpaid surcharge was a charge on all the interest

in the land, and therefore had priority over the mortgage, and (2) in failing to hold that
a the charge affected only the freehold interest of Shop Investments Ltd subject to the
mortgage. By a respondent's notice the rating authority sought to uphold the judgment
of Dillon J on the additional ground that the bank as legal mortgagee was at all material
times an owner or the owner of the property whether or not Shop Investments Ltd was
also an owner. The facts are set out in the judgment of Lord Denning MR.

b Peter Millett QC and Gregory Hill for the defendants.
W J Mowbray QC and Colin Braham for the rating authority.

LORD DENNING MR. On the north side of Hyde Park there is an elegant period
property, 22 Lancaster Gate. It was very suitable for use as offices by high class
organisations. But it remained empty for many months, like the notorious Centre
c Point. The owners did not try to let it to anyone. It suited them better, in days of
inflation, to let it remain empty, not paying rates.
Parliament did not approve of such goings on. So in 1974 they enacted provisions
under which the local authority could impose a surcharge on commercial buildings left
empty in this way. If a commercial building was left empty for 12 months the surcharge
would be double the normal rates. Treble in the second 12 months. Quadrupled in the
d third 12 months. And so forth.
The question in this case is whether the surcharge applies to commercial buildings
which are mortgaged up to the hilt. Is the surcharge payable by the mortgagor, or by the
mortgagee? If it is not paid, how can it be enforced?
This building at 22 Lancaster Gate was bought on 3rd February 1974 by a company
called Shop Investments Ltd. That company was a subsidiary of a holding company,
e Amalgamated Investment and Property Co Ltd. Shop Investments guaranteed the
indebtedness of the holding company to the National Westminster Bank. It came to over
£6m. As security Shop Investments mortgaged 22 Lancaster Gate to the bank. It was by
way of a charge of legal mortgage on 4th February 1974. A few days later on 8th
February 1974 the Local Government Act 1974 was passed bringing the surcharge into
effect for empty properties left unused.
f Despite the new Act, Shop Investments Ltd left 22 Lancaster Gate empty. They left
it empty for nearly two years. They made no effort to let it. This came to the notice of
the Westminster City Council. They decided to levy a surcharge for the period from 8th
February 1974, when the Act came into force, to 24th October 1975, that being the
period when the mortgagors had made no effort to let it at all. The surcharge came to
£16,940·93. The Westminster City Council registered it in the local land charges
g registry.
In 1977 the holding company went into liquidation, owing the bank £6m. The bank,
as mortgagees, sold the property to Haymarket Publishing Ltd for £220,000. The
Westminster City Council claim that this surcharge of £16,940·93 takes priority over the
mortgage debt. But the bank say that the mortgage debt of £6m takes priority over the
surcharge of £16,940·93. So the practical question is: who gets the £16,940·93?
h Westminster City Council or the bank?
It all comes down to the correct interpretation of two sections which were inserted in
the General Rate Act 1967 by s 16 of the Local Government Act 1974. It is written in by
two supplemental sections, ss 17A and 17B. Section 17A says who is to pay the surcharge:

> 'If for a continuous period exceeding six months a commercial building is not
> used for the purpose for which it was constructed or has been adapted, its owner
i > shall pay in respect of that period . . . a surcharge additional to the rates (if any)
> payable apart from this section.'

So there is the liability to pay put on the owner. The meaning of 'owner' is defined in
s 17B(7): '. . . "owner" means the person entitled to possession . . .' If the owner does not
pay, then s 17B provides for how it can be enforced. Section 17B(3) says: 'A surcharge

imposed under section 17A of this Act in respect of a hereditament shall until recovered
be a charge on the land comprised in the hereditament . . .'
    The first question is: who is liable to pay the rates? Who is the 'owner'? Who is
'entitled to possession' when it is a question between mortgagor and mortgagee? It is
quite plain to my mind that unless and until the mortgagee enters into possession, in
accordance with the mortgage law, and takes the rents and profits, the mortgagor is the
person entitled to possession. He is the person who is entitled to put up advertisements,
to let and do all that is necessary to let, unless and until the mortgagee interferes. It
seems to me that the 'owner' under s 17A is not two, three or more people. It is the one
who really has control of the letting. In this case the 'owner' means the mortgagor, Shop
Investments Ltd. They were liable to pay the surcharge. No doubt Westminster City
Council could sue them for it if they were worth suing, which unfortunately they are
not.
    Then under s 17B we get the provision that the surcharge is 'a charge on the land'.
What does that mean? I agree that it is ambiguous. The meaning is difficult to discover
from the words of the statute. But fortunately there have been a series of cases in the
courts which lead inevitably to the interpretation that it means a charge on 'all the estates
and interests in the land'. I will go through the series of cases which lead to this result.
The first is *Birmingham Corpn v Baker* (1881) 17 Ch D 782. In that case there was a charge
on the 'premises'. Jessel MR said (at 786):

> 'Now, the houses *per se* being inanimate, they cannot bear the burden. If there
> be a charge on the houses it is a charge on the total ownership—if I may call it so,
> on the proprietorship; not on any particular section or portion of the proprietorship,
> but on the whole.'

    The next case is *Tendring Union Guardians v Dowton* [1891] 3 Ch 265. That again was
a question of a charge on the 'premises'. I would pick out the words of Fry LJ (at 269):

> 'All the [Public Health Act 1875] does is to create a charge on the premises—that
> is, on the land—that is, on all the interests of the owners of the land.'

    To finish the citations, I would refer to *Paddington Borough Council v Finucane* [1928] Ch
567, [1928] All ER Rep 428. That was a decision of Russell J who said ([1928] Ch 567 at
575, [1928] All ER Rep 428 at 432) of the Public Health Act 1875:

> '. . . when it confers a charge on the premises, [it] means not a charge only on the
> interests of the rack-rent owner in the premises, but a charge upon the entirety of
> the interests of the premises, the whole of the proprietary interests of the premises.'

    Having regard to that line of authorities, it seems to me that we should interpret the
words in this statute, 'a charge on the land comprised in the hereditament', in the same
sense.
    It was suggested that it should be confined to cases where the charge was in respect of
improvements or expenses incurred on the land, as happened in some of those cases, and
that it should not apply to a charge in respect of a penal provision such as this. That
distinction is not well founded. The issue depends simply on the interpretation of the
words in the statute. It seems to me that 'a charge on the land' means a charge on 'all the
estates and interests in the land'.
    This conforms with the intention of Parliament. Any other view would mean that it
would be open to companies, by manipulation of their affairs between holding and
subsidiary companies, to avoid the charge altogether. The land could be bought in the
name of a subsidiary company with money obtained on mortgage from a holding
company: and, lo and behold, the charge would be gone. That cannot be right. The
judge was quite right in holding that there was a charge on the land in favour of
Westminster City Council; and that it took priority over the mortgage debt which was
owing to the bank.
    I would dismiss the appeal accordingly.

SHAW LJ. I agree. I would only add that support is to be found in the subsection itself
a   for limiting the application of the phrase 'person entitled to possession' where it appears
in s 17B(7) of the General Rate Act 1967 to the person who is at material times actually
exercising that right. It provides for apportionment between persons who become
successively entitled to possession during a period of non-use. This could hardly be apt
in relation to persons who are in law collaterally and contemporaneously entitled to
possession.
b   I would dismiss the appeal.

OLIVER LJ. I also agree. It is quite clear, in my judgment, that s 17A contemplates,
contrary to the submission of counsel for the rating authority, only one owner, a single
individual or persons holding jointly, on whom the surcharge would be levied. But that,
of course, is not conclusive of the matter because the question at issue is the ambit of the
c   charge which is imposed by sub-s (3) of s 17B. In sub-s (2) it is said:

> 'References in section 17A of this Act and this section to a commercial building
> are references to a hereditament . . . whose net annual value falls to be ascertained
> under section 19(2) of this Act . . .'

So quite clearly the hereditament there is the commercial building.
d   Then one comes to sub-s (3), where it is provided that:

> 'A surcharge imposed under section 17A of this Act in respect of a hereditament
> shall until recovered be a charge on the land comprised in the hereditament . . .'

This is a formula which is familiar in other statutes, for instance the Public Health Act
1936 and Housing Acts, and Lord Denning MR has already referred to cases in which
e   similar words have been construed.
What is there in this statute to restrict the words in s 17B(3) in such a way as to lead to
the conclusion that they do not mean exactly what they say? There is the fact, first of all,
that this is a charge imposed by way of a penalty. It may be argued that the statute
should be construed restrictively, but that by itself does not, I think, justify the court in
concluding that the section does not mean exactly what it says. Then it is said that it is
f   very unfair that the effect of the charge is to make the recovery of the rates from persons
such as mortgagees, tenants and owners who are not in possession and were not under an
original liability. But the words of the statute are, as I think, plain and one must start
from the position that Parliament must have been aware of how similar words in
previous statutes had been construed. If it had been intended to confine the charge to the
interest of the owner in the premises, nothing would have been simpler than to have said
g   so. The legislature did not do that.
I agree that the judge came to the right conclusion, and I too would dismiss the appeal.

Appeal dismissed. Leave to appeal to the House of Lords refused.

Solicitors: *Wilde, Sapte & Co* (for the defendants); *Edward Woolf.*

Frances Rustin   Barrister.

Cam Gears Ltd v Cunningham a

COURT OF APPEAL, CIVIL DIVISION
CUMMING-BRUCE, TEMPLEMAN AND OLIVER LJJ
17th FEBRUARY 1981

Landlord and tenant – Opposition to grant of new tenancy of business premises – Intention of b
landlord to occupy holding for purpose of business to be carried on by him – Holding – Demised
premises consisting of vacant site used as car park – Landlord intending to use site in connection
with his existing garage business by building workshop on part of site for car testing – Whether
landlord intending to occupy 'the holding' comprised in the tenancy – Whether proposed
development of site creating new holding – Landlord and Tenant Act 1954, s 30(1)(g).

c
By a lease dated 5th May 1972 the landlord demised to the tenant business premises,
consisting of a vacant site, for a term of seven years. The tenant covenanted to use the site
solely as a car park and not to erect any buildings on it. When the landlord gave notice
in 1978 under the Landlord and Tenant Act 1954 to terminate the lease, the tenant
applied for a new tenancy under that Act. The landlord opposed the grant of a new
tenancy on the ground specified in s 30(1)(g)[a] of the 1954 Act, namely that on the d
termination of the tenancy he intended to occupy the holding for the purposes of a
business to be carried on by him. The landlord wished to expand his existing garage
business and proposed to occupy the demised property as a car testing centre and to erect
a building for that purpose on part of the site. The tenant submitted that since, by virtue
of s 23(3)[b] of the Act, 'the holding' meant the property comprised in the tenancy, and
since that consisted of a vacant site, the erection of a building on the site would amount e
to the creation of a new holding, and that the landlord accordingly intended to occupy
a new holding and not 'the [existing] holding' within s 30(1)(g) and could not therefore
rely on s 30(1)(g) to oppose the grant of a new tenancy. The judge refused the tenant's
application for a new tenancy and the tenant appealed.

Held – A landlord who opposed the grant of a new tenancy on the ground specified in f
s 30(1)(g) of the 1954 Act was not required to show that he did not intend to alter the
demised property but only that he intended to carry on his own business on the holding
comprised in the tenancy. The holding which the landlord intended to occupy was the
same as the holding comprised in the tenancy, since it did not form part of any larger
undertaking and consisted solely of the vacant site, and the fact that the landlord
proposed to erect a building on the site, so that he would be occupying the holding g
comprised in the tenancy plus the building, did not mean that he intended to occupy a
different holding. Accordingly, the landlord had established his ground of opposition to
the grant of a new tenancy and the appeal would be dismissed (see p 563 e to p 564 b and
e to j, post).
Nursey v P Currie (Dartford) Ltd [1959] 1 All ER 497 distinguished.

Notes
For the landlord's right to oppose the grant of a new tenancy of business premises on the
ground that he intends to occupy the holding for his own business, see 23 Halsbury's
Laws (3rd Edn) 894, para 1718, and for cases on the subject, see 31(2) Digest (Reissue)
966–969, 7796–7805.
For the Landlord and Tenant Act 1954, s 30, see 18 Halsbury's Statutes (3rd Edn) 565.

---

a Section 30(1), so far as material, is set out at p 561 g, post
b Section 23(3), so far as material, is set out at p 562 f g, post

Cases referred to in judgments

a *Method Developments Ltd v Jones* [1971] 1 All ER 1027, [1971] 1 WLR 168, 22 P & CR 141, CA, 31(2) Digest (Reissue) 968, 7804.
Nursey v P Currie (Dartford) Ltd [1959] 1 All ER 497, [1959] 1 WLR 273, CA, 31(2) Digest (Reissue) 966, 7799.

Cases also cited

b *Fisher v Taylors Furnishing Stores Ltd* [1956] 2 All ER 78, [1956] 2 QB 78, CA.
McKenna v Porter Motors Ltd [1956] 3 All ER 262, [1956] AC 688, PC.

Appeal

The tenant, Cam Gears Ltd, appealed against the judgment of his Honour Judge Kingham given on 11th January 1980 in the Luton County Court refusing the tenant's application c for the grant of a new tenancy of business premises consisting of land used as a car park at Selbourne Road, Covent Garden Close, Luton, on the ground that the landlord, David Lawrence Cunningham, was entitled to oppose the grant of a new tenancy on the ground, specified in s 30(1)(g) of the Landlord and Tenant Act 1954, namely that he intended to occupy the holding for the purpose of his own business. The facts are set out in the judgment of Oliver LJ.

d
Nicholas Patten for the tenant.
Allan Levy for the landlord.

OLIVER LJ delivered the first judgment at the invitation of Cumming-Bruce LJ. This is an appeal by a tenant of business premises from a decision of his Honour Judge e Kingham which was given on 11th January 1980, refusing the grant of a new tenancy under the provisions of the Landlord and Tenant Act 1954.

The premises with which the application is concerned consist of a vacant site, that is to say a site unencumbered by buildings but with a concrete surface, constituting a car park and situate on the corner of Selbourne Road and Covent Garden Close in Luton. The tenant carries on business nearby, and the premises have been at all material times f used as a car park in connection with that business. The premises were originally let by the landlord to the tenant on a lease dated 5th May 1972 for a term of seven years from 1st January 1972; that term expired in 1979.

The proper notice under the 1954 Act was given by the landlord in July 1978, and there is no dispute that the correct sequence of events envisaged by the Act has taken place; I need not go through its various stages.

g The present dispute arises out of the landlord's opposition to the grant of a new tenancy which, in the notice which was served on the tenant, he put on the ground set out in s 30(1)(g) of the 1954 Act, that is:

'... that on the termination of the current tenancy the landlord intends to occupy the holding for the purposes, or partly for the purposes, of a business to be carried on by him, or as his residence.'

h
The landlord has been in business for some time, originally, I think, in partnership, but more recently through the medium of a limited company, Technical Brakes Ltd, of which he is a director and in which he holds 74 out of the 99 issued shares. That company runs a garage business and, as I understand it, the principal facet of that business is the provision of Ministry of Transport testing facilities for vehicles which are j more than three years of age. In the course of its business, at present carried on in Wingate Road, Luton, it tests about ten thousand vehicles a year.

What the landlord wishes to do is to expand his business. The lease of the present business premises expired in, I think, June 1980 and he needs two new test lanes.

As I have mentioned, the premises the subject matter of this appeal are used at present as a car park. They consist simply of a vacant site with no buildings on it, and the

landlord's project, if he can get possession, is to have erected on the site what is known as
a Banbury prefabricated commercial building, which will cover about one-third of the *a*
total area of the site and will furnish a workshop, an office, a waiting room, toilet
facilities and inspection pits for vehicles. The total cost of that building is likely to be in
the order of £16,000, the total cost of the operation, including erection, being estimated
by the landlord before the judge at £20,000. His evidence, which was accepted by the
judge, was that facilities would be made available to him by his bankers. The judge
accepted the landlord's evidence in toto and he found as a fact that he was bona fide in *b*
forming his intention and that the intention was a practicable one, albeit that he would
have to get detailed planning permission, satisfy the building regulations and obtain a
Ministry of Transport licence. The judge was satisfied that these were not problems
which would stand in the way of a successful outcome of the project.

The tenant's contention before the judge and in this court was that since the only
ground of opposition to the grant of a new tenancy under the Act specified in the *c*
landlord's notice was that which appears in s 30(1)(g) of the 1954 Act, the landlord had
to show that his intention was not just to occupy the site, but that he was to occupy 'the
holding'; that the holding consisted of the present vacant site used as a car park and that
the proposed erection on that site of a new building to be used for the purpose of a testing
workshop constituted the erection of a new and different holding and that therefore the
landlord was not proposing to occupy 'the holding' for the purposes of the business. *d*

The erection of the proposed building was, no doubt, a major work of construction,
which could only be carried out if the landlord obtained possession, and it might indeed
have justified opposition to the grant of a new tenancy under s 30(1)(f); but that was not
the ground that was specified, and since the only ground relied on was the ground in para
(g), that is the ground on which the landlord must rely.

The judge rejected the tenant's contention, which was based on the decision of this *e*
court in *Nursey v P Currie (Dartford) Ltd* [1959] 1 All ER 497, [1959] 1 WLR 273. That
was a case which bears a superficial resemblance to the present case, in that the landlord's
notice in that case was confined to the ground specified in s 30(1)(g) of the 1954 Act, and
what the landlord company proposed to do was to demolish the existing buildings,
which were standing in a yard which was occupied by the landlord, and redevelop the
site as part of a petrol station which it proposed to carry on there. The Court of Appeal *f*
held that the ground of opposition was not made out; and it did so because of the
limiting definition of the word 'holding' in s 23(3) of the 1954 Act.

That subsection defines the word 'holding' as meaning 'the property comprised in the
tenancy': I close the quotation there; there is some more but it is not material for present
purposes. The court held in that case that that definition included the existing
buildings. The landlord, since it intended to remove the existing buildings and replace *g*
them with others, did not therefore intend to occupy 'the holding' but intended to
occupy the new buildings to be erected on the land forming part only of 'the holding'
viewed as a totality, at any rate that is what I apprehend is the ratio of the decision in the
Nursey case, and that is the view of it which was adopted by this court in *Method
Developments Ltd v Jones* [1971] 1 All ER 1027, [1971] 1 WLR 168; I refer particularly to
the judgment of Salmon LJ in that case. *h*

I confess that the *Nursey* decision is one which I find far from easy to understand. The
only argument, so far as can be deduced from the report (see [1959] 1 WLR 273 at 275)
had been that since the landlord intended to demolish the buildings, it could not be
intending to occupy 'the holding' which included the buildings. But Wynn-Parry J, who
delivered the first judgment, seems to have taken the view, at any rate on one reading of
his judgment, that it was fatal to the landlord's claim that the holding was to be occupied *j*
as part of a larger complex and not as a separate holding on its own. He said ([1959] 1 All
ER 497 at 500, [1959] 1 WLR 273 at 277):

'It seems to me that that language circumscribes the use of the phrase "the
holding" in that paragraph [ie para (g)] and makes it necessary to concentrate the

whole of one's attention on the particular piece of land, whether it has buildings on
a it or not, which is the subject-matter of the tenancy in question. So viewed, it
appears to me that the contention for the landlords in the present case is too wide,
and that when one is looking at the material time at "the holding" under para (g),
it is not permissible to take into account the wider scheme which the landlords had
in mind and merely to treat the land comprised in the holding as land which in one
way or another will be used for the purpose of the wider undertaking.'

b
I cannot think that the judge can have intended to do more than to answer the
question: is the holding which the landlord intends to occupy the same holding as that
comprised in the tenancy? Construed in the wider sense that I have indicated, it would
follow that a landlord who carried on a business next door to the demised premises and
who wanted to occupy those premises as one with his existing shop for an expanding
c business, would be unable to rely on s 30(1)(g), and would be able to resist a new lease
only if he intended to reconstruct. For my part, I cannot ascribe so eccentric an intention
to the legislature. Certainly, Willmer LJ confined his judgment to the narrow ground
that the definition of 'the holding' simply involved reading into the subsection, in place
of the words 'the holding', the parcels of the lease, a ratio which hardly helps the present
tenant since the lease in the present case merely refers to 'all that piece or parcel of land
d delineated for the purposes of identification only on the plan annexed hereto and thereon
edged red', and that is precisely what the landlord intends to occupy.
But even if I am wrong in the limits within which, as I think, the judgment of Wynn-
Parry J must be read, and even assuming that the concurrence in that decision of Hodson
LJ renders the wider construction binding on us, it still does not seem to me to help the
tenant in the instant case. There is no wider scheme here in which the holding is
e proposed to be incorporated. The landlord simply intends to place a building on the site
and to use the whole site, together with the new building, for the purposes of his
business.
Counsel for the tenant, who has argued this appeal, if I may say so, with conspicuous
frankness and acumen, seeks to steer a course midway between the construction of
Wynn-Parry J's judgment to which I have referred, and the very limited ratio adopted by
f Willmer LJ. He suggests that the ratio of the Nursey case is that you have to look at the
holding as it is at the termination of the tenancy and to ask yourself the question: does
the landlord intend to occupy the holding for the purposes of his business in substantially
the identical condition as it was at the date of termination? If he intends to occupy the
whole of it, but to make any material alteration to its condition, then he is intending to
occupy a different holding.
g For my part, I find myself unable to follow counsel for the tenant through the gap
which he thus seeks to make between the prongs of Morton's fork. Whatever may be the
true ratio of the Nursey case, I am unable to extract that from it and indeed to do so
would, I think, be to attribute a wholly irrational and capricious intention to the
legislature. Accepting as I must that Nursey is binding on this court, I certainly do not
feel disposed to strain it beyond the narrowest limits within which it is capable of being
h confined.
I think that the determining feature of the Nursey decision was not the purpose for
which the holdings were occupied by the tenant, or the particular condition at the time
of the determination of the tenancy, but the fact that the holding consisted of the
buildings which, under the landlord's proposals, were to be demolished. That may or
may not have been a logical or reasonable construction of the section, and I bear in mind
j Salmon LJ's reservation in the Method Developments case whether it was correctly decided,
although the combined industry of counsel has not succeeded in unearthing the
inconsistent unreported case in the Court of Appeal to which Salmon LJ referred. But it
cannot in any event, in my judgment, have any possible application to a case such as the
present where 'the holding' consists solely of a vacant site on which the landlord proposes
to erect a building, so that what he will occupy is 'the holding' plus something else. He

proposes to occupy everything that is there at the moment, with the sole exception of two lengths of topsoil and subsoil which will be removed to sink the inspection pits. *a* *Nursey v Currie* is, in my judgment, of no assistance to the tenant in such circumstances.
The judge rejected the tenant's submission. So do I, and I would dismiss the appeal.

TEMPLEMAN LJ. I agree.
By a lease dated 5th May 1972 the landlord demised to the tenant 'ALL THAT piece or parcel of land . . . on the plan annexed hereto and thereon edged in red'. The 'tenant *b* covenanted to use the demised premises only for the purposes of a car park and not to erect on the demised land or any part thereof any buildings or structures other than those necessary for the parking of vehicles and, should the tenant so require, for providing shelter for vehicles.
The landlord proposed to occupy the demised premises for the business of a Ministry of Transport car testing centre, and for that purpose needed and planned to erect a *c* building on part of the land.
By s 30(1)(g) of the Landlord and Tenant Act the landlord, having duly determined the lease by notice, is entitled to resist the tenant's present application for a new lease if the landlord, on the determining of the current tenancy, intends to occupy the holding for the purpose of a business to be carried on by the landlord thereon.
By s 23(3) 'the holding' means the property comprised in the tenancy. The lease will *d* determine at the expiration of three months after the final refusal of the tenant's application for a new lease. If there is no appeal from this court the lease will determine three months from today.
Unassisted by authority, it seems to me that, the county court judge having found that the landlord in fact intends to occupy the whole of the demised land for the purposes I have mentioned and has the financial resources and the ability and the will to do so, it *e* follows that the landlord made good his opposition under the 1954 Act.
We were pressed by the decision of this court in *Nursey v P Currie (Dartford) Ltd* [1959] 1 All ER 497, [1959] 1 WLR 273, of which I make the melancholy observation that two bad reasons do not make one good reason although both may be binding on this court. It is plain, however, that the facts of the present case are distinguishable. Taking the test adumbrated by Wynn-Parry J: is this a case where the holding which is to be developed *f* is the same as the holding demised? The answer is Yes; it does not form part of any larger undertaking. Taking the test adumbrated by Willmer LJ, what was comprised in the demise in the present case is a piece of land, and the landlord's business will be carried on on that piece of land. The fact that for the purposes of enhancing that business, or enabling it to be carried on, the landlord intends to put a workshop on part of the land is neither here nor there. The object of para (g) of s 30(1) is not to hand the land back to *g* the landlord in a sterilised form, so that he has to put his hand on his heart, saying in effect: 'I do not intend to make any alteration'. The purpose of the subsection is to hand the land back to the landlord if he wants to carry on his own business there, and that indeed is what this landlord intends to do and that is what he is entitled to do.
Accordingly, I would dismiss the appeal.

h

CUMMING-BRUCE LJ. I agree with both judgments, hoping that such agreement does not give rise to the difficulties which have arisen as a result of Hodson LJ's similar agreement in *Nursey v P Currie (Dartford) Ltd* [1959] 1 All ER 497, [1959] 1 WLR 273.

Appeal dismissed. Leave to appeal to House of Lords refused.

j

Solicitors: *Slaughter & May* (for the tenant); *John Photiades*, Luton (for the landlord).

Henrietta Steinberg   Barrister.

A J Bekhor & Co Ltd v Bilton

COURT OF APPEAL, CIVIL DIVISION
STEPHENSON, ACKNER AND GRIFFITHS LJJ
14th, 15th, 16th JANUARY, 6th FEBRUARY 1981

Injunction – Interlocutory – Danger that defendant may transfer assets out of jurisdiction – Discovery or interrogatories in aid of injunction – Power to make order for discovery or interrogatories in aid of Mareva injunction – Defendant thought to be in breach of terms of Mareva injunction – Whether jurisdiction to order discovery or interrogatories in aid of Mareva injunction – Whether jurisdiction to order discovery of past assets and their disposal to establish breaches – Supreme Court of Judicature (Consolidation) Act 1925, s 45(1) – RSC Ord 24, rr 1(1), 7(1), Ord 26, r 1(1).

The plaintiffs issued a writ against the defendant claiming the sum of £217,077, to which the defendant filed an arguable defence and counterclaim. The plaintiffs subsequently learnt that the defendant had sold a farm which had been his home in the United Kingdom and, fearing that he might remove himself and his assets out of the jurisdiction, they obtained a Mareva injunction restraining him from removing assets out of the jurisdiction except in so far as his assets within the jurisdiction exceeded £250,000. On an application by the defendant and subject to his undertaking not to change the investment of his assets within the jurisdiction so as to cause them to depreciate in value, the Mareva injunction was varied to allow him to take his car, certain personal possessions and £1,250 per month out of the jurisdiction. In an affidavit in support of his application the defendant deposed that his marriage had broken up and that he had taken a one-year lease of a flat in Monte Carlo at a rent of nearly £15,000 where he intended to live with another woman. The defendant later made a further application for a variation of the injunction to permit him to meet financial obligations within the jurisdiction out of assets within the jurisdiction. In affidavits in support of the application the defendant stated that the net proceeds from the sale of the farm were £63,000, which had been transferred to Jersey a week before the Mareva injunction was granted, and that his assets within the jurisdiction totalled £154,000. The affidavits further disclosed that, contrary to his undertakings, he had reduced his assets within the jurisdiction by some £66,000 since the grant of the injunction and that he had no assets capable of producing the £15,000 a year which the court had permitted him to remove out of the jurisdiction for living expenses. The plaintiffs accordingly applied under RSC Ord 24, r 7(1)[a] and Ord 26, r 1(1)[b] for an order for discovery, inter alia, of (i) his assets as at the dates when the injunction was granted, when it was varied, and when discovery was ordered, and (ii) the details of the disposal of any assets between the variation of the injunction and the date of the order for discovery. At the hearing of both applications the judge allowed the defendant's application for a variation of the injunction in part by allowing him to pay solicitors' and accountants' fees out of assets which were subject to the injunction. The defendant was also allowed to continue to remove £1,250 per month for living expenses provided it came out of income and not capital. The judge also granted the plaintiffs' application for an order for discovery and stated that if

---

a   Rule 7(1) provides: 'Subject to rule 8, the Court may at any time, on the application of any party to a cause or matter, make an order requiring any other party to make an affidavit stating whether any document specified or described in the application or any class of document so specified or described is, or has at any time been, in his possession, custody or power, and if not then in his possession, custody or power when he parted with it and what has become of it.'
b   Rule 1(1), so far as material, provides: 'A party to any cause or matter may apply to the Court for an order—(a) giving him leave to serve on any other party interrogatories relating to any matter in question between the applicant and that other party in the cause or matter . . .'

discovery disclosed that the defendant had acted in breach of his undertakings given
when the injunction was first varied the court would of its own motion treat that as a *a*
contempt of court. The defendant appealed against the order for discovery, contending
(i) that the order was not within the ambit of Ord 24, r 7(1) or Ord 26, r 1(1) since it did
not relate to 'matters in question in the action' within Ord 24, r 1(1)ᶜ or to 'matters in
question . . . in the cause or matter' within Ord 26, r 1(1) but merely to the defendant's
ability to satisfy a judgment if the matters in question in the action were decided against
him, and (ii) that the order should not have been made because his answers might tend *b*
to incriminate him. The plaintiffs contended that the power to grant discovery or
interrogatories in aid of a Mareva injunction was conferred by Ord 24, r 7(1) and Ord 26,
r 1(1) or alternatively by s 45(1)ᵈ of the Supreme Court of Judicature (Consolidation) Act
1925, and that in any event the court had an inherent residual jurisdiction to order
discovery wherever the cause of justice required it.

c

Held – (1) Although orders for discovery and interrogatories in aid of a Mareva
injunction could not be made under RSC Ord 24, r 7(1) or Ord 26, r 1(1) because they
would not then relate to 'matters in question in the action' or 'matters in question . . . in
the cause or matter', they could be made under s 45(1) of the 1925 Act, since inherent
and implicit in the power to grant an injunction contained in s 45, from which the
Mareva jurisdiction derived, was the power to make all ancillary orders necessary to *d*
ensure the effectiveness of the Mareva jurisdiction (see p 575 *b* to *j*, p 576 *b c*, p 577 *g* to
j, p 582 *a* to *f*, p 584 *d e*, p 585 *a* to *d*, p 586 *a* to *d* and p 587 *e f*, post); *A v C* [1980] 2 All
ER 347 approved in part; *The Siskina* [1977] 3 All ER 803 distinguished.
    (2) The defendant was not entitled to complain about the grant of the order of
discovery on the grounds that his answers to it might be self-incriminatory, because the
appropriate time for making such an objection was when answering the order and not *e*
when the order was being made (see p 579 *h j*, p 580 *g*, p 582 *h j* and p 587 *e f*, post); *Fisher
v Owen* (1878) 8 Ch D 645 applied; *Rank Film Distributors Ltd v Video Information Centre*
[1980] 2 All ER 273 distinguished.
    (3) However (Griffiths LJ dissenting), the order for discovery made by the judge, by
referring to the defendant's assets in the past and their disposal, was made not for the
purpose of locating and freezing the defendant's remaining assets but to establish if and *f*
to what extent the defendant had not complied with the order varying the injunction or
had breached the undertakings he had given, and was not therefore a proper order for
discovery in aid of a Mareva injunction. The judge, although having jurisdiction to
order discovery, had exceeded his powers in making the order he did. The defendant's
appeal would be allowed and the order quashed (see p 579 *f* to *g*, p 580 *h* and p 586 *j* to
p 587 *b* and *e f*, post).
    Per Stephenson and Ackner LJJ. If the plaintiff or the judge wishes to police a Mareva *g*
injunction to see whether the defendant is in breach of it or of any undertaking he has
given the appropriate method is to order the defendant to be cross-examined on his
affidavits under RSC Ord 38, r 2(3) or to deprive him of the right to take any money or
possessions out of the jurisdiction unless and until he has made full disclosure of his assets
(see p 579 *c d* and p 587 *c d*, post).
    Per Ackner LJ. The Mareva jurisdiction provides a limited exception to the general *h*
rule that the court will not normally grant an injunction to restrain a defendant from
parting with his assets in order that they may be preserved in case the plaintiff's claim
succeeds. The plaintiff, like other creditors of the defendant, must obtain his judgment
and then enforce it. The Mareva jurisdiction is not a form of pre-trial attachment and

—— *j*

c Rule 1(1) provides: 'After the close of pleadings in an action begun by writ there shall, subject to
     and in accordance with the provisions of this Order, be discovery by the parties to the action of the
     documents which are or have been in their possession, custody or power relating to matters in
     question in the action.'
d Section 45(1) is set out at p 584 *e*, post

the courts must be vigilant to ensure that a Mareva defendant is not treated as a
a judgment debtor (see p 577 *a* to *e*, post).

Notes
For injunctions restraining a defendant removing assets out of the jurisdiction, see 24
Halsbury's Laws (4th Edn) para 1018.
   For the Supreme Court of Judicature (Consolidation) Act 1925, s 45, see 25 Halsbury's
b Statutes (3rd Edn) 717.

Cases referred to in judgments
A v C [1980] 2 All ER 347, [1981] 2 WLR 629n, [1980] 2 Lloyd's Rep 200.
Anton Piller KG v Manufacturing Processes Ltd [1976] 1 All ER 779, [1976] Ch 55, [1976]
   2 WLR 162, [1976] RPC 719, CA, Digest (Cont Vol E) 338, *1238b*.
Bankers Trust Co v Shapira [1980] 3 All ER 353, [1980] 1 WLR 1274, CA.
c *Barclay-Johnson v Yuill* [1980] 3 All ER 190, [1980] 1 WLR 1259.
Beddow v Beddow (1878) 9 Ch D 89, 47 LJ Ch 588, 3 Digest (Reissue) 97, *495*.
Blair v Haycock Cadle Co (1917) 34 TLR 39, HL, 18 Digest (Reissue) 224, *1782*.
Bremer Vulkan Schiffbau Und Maschinenfabrik v South India Shipping Corpn [1981] 1 All ER
   289, [1981] 2 WLR 141, HL.
China Transpacific Steamship Co v Commercial Union Assurance Co (1881) 8 QBD 142, 51
d   LJQB 132, 45 LT 647, CA, 18 Digest (Reissue) 69, *481*.
Comet Products UK Ltd v Hawkex Plastics Ltd [1971] 1 All ER 1141, [1971] 2 QB 67, [1971]
   2 WLR 361, [1972] RPC 691, CA, 22 Digest (Reissue) 510, *5185*.
Cretanor Maritime Co Ltd v Irish Marine Management Ltd, The Cretan Harmony [1978] 3 All
   ER 164, [1978] 1 WLR 966, [1978] 1 Lloyd's Rep 425, CA, Digest (Cont Vol E) 333,
   79d.
e *EMI Ltd v Pandit* [1975] 1 All ER 418, [1975] 1 WLR 302, Digest (Cont Vol D) 543,
   1238a.
Fisher v Owen (1878) 8 Ch D 645, 47 LJ Ch 681, 38 LT 577, 42 JP 758, CA, 18 Digest
   (Reissue) 244, *1929*.
Hunnings v Williamson (1883) 10 QBD 459, 52 LJQB 400, 48 LT 581, 47 JP 390, sub nom
   Hummings v Williamson 52 LJQB 273, sub nom *Hemmings v Williamson* 48 LT 392, 18
f   Digest (Reissue) 19, *97*.
*Iraqi Ministry of Defence v Arcepey Shipping Co SA (Gillespie Brothers & Co Ltd intervening),
   The Angel Bell* [1980] 1 All ER 480, [1981] QB 65, [1980] 2 WLR 488, [1980] 1 Lloyd's
   Rep 632.
Lister & Co v Stubbs (1890) 45 Ch D 1, [1886–90] All ER Rep 797, 59 LJ Ch 570, 63 LT 75,
   CA, 1(2) Digest (Reissue) 659, *4513*.
g *London and Counties Securities Ltd v Caplan* (26th May 1978, unreported).
Mareva Compania Naviera SA v International Bulkcarriers SA, The Mareva (1975) [1980] 1
   All ER 213, [1975] 2 Lloyd's Rep 509, CA, Digest (Cont Vol E) 331, *79b*.
Marriot v Chamberlain (1886) 17 QBD 154, 55 LJQB 448, 54 LT 714, CA, 18 Digest
   (Reissue) 204, *1616*.
Mediterranea Reffineria Siciliana Petroli SpA v Mabanaft GmbH [1978] Court of Appeal
h   Transcript 816.
Nippon Yusen Kaisha v Karageorgis [1975] 3 All ER 282, [1975] 1 WLR 1093, [1975] 2
   Lloyd's Rep 137, CA, Digest (Cont Vol D) 534, *79a*.
North London Railway Co v Great Northern Railway Co (1883) 11 QBD 30, 52 LJQB 380, 48
   LT 695, CA, 3 Digest (Reissue) 95, *485*.
Prince Abdul Rahman Bin Turki Al Sudairy v Abu-Taha [1980] 3 All ER 409, [1980] 1 WLR
j   1268, CA.
Rank Film Distributors Ltd v Video Information Centre [1980] 2 All ER 273, [1980] 3 WLR
   487, CA.
*Rasu Maritima SA v Perusahaan Pertambangan Minyak Dan Gas Bumi Negara (Pertamina)
   and Government of Indonesia (as interveners)* [1977] 3 All ER 324, [1978] QB 644, [1977]
   3 WLR 518, [1977] 2 Lloyd's Rep 397, CA, Digest (Cont Vol E) 331, *79c*.

Siskina (Cargo owners) v Distos Compania Naviera SA, The Siskina [1977] 3 All ER 803,
[1979] AC 210, [1977] 3 WLR 818, [1978] 1 Lloyd's Rep 1, HL, Digest (Cont Vol E)   **a**
660, 782a.
Smith v Hegard [1980] Court of Appeal Transcript 603.
Third Chandris Shipping Corpn v Unimarine SA, The Pythia, The Angelic Wings, The Genie
[1979] 2 All ER 972, [1979] QB 645, [1979] 3 WLR 122, [1979] 2 Lloyd's Rep 184, CA, **,**
Digest (Cont Vol E) 333, 79e.
Wickham, Re, Marony v Taylor (1887) 35 Ch D 272, 56 LJ Ch 748, 57 LT 468, CA, 51   **b**
Digest (Repl) 672, 2757.

Cases also cited
Bakarin v Victoria P Shipping Co Ltd [1980] 2 Lloyd's Rep 193.
Bramblevale Ltd, Re [1969] 3 All ER 1062, [1970] Ch 128, CA.   **c**
British Leyland Motor Corpn v TI Silencers Ltd [1980] 1 CMLR 598.
Cook Industries Inc v Galliher [1978] 3 All ER 945, [1979] Ch 439.
Gouriet v Union of Post Office Workers [1977] 3 All ER 70, [1978] AC 435, HL.
Jennison v Baker [1972] 1 All ER 997, [1972] 2 QB 52, CA.
Kangol Industries Ltd v Alfred Bray & Sons Ltd [1953] 1 All ER 444n.
Loose v Williamson [1978] 3 All ER 89, [1978] 1 WLR 639n.   **d**
National Association of Operative Plasterers v Smithies [1906] AC 434, [1904–7] All ER Rep
961, HL.
Norwich Pharmacal Co v Customs and Excise Comrs [1973] 2 All ER 943, [1974] AC 133,
HL.
Ocli Optical Coatings Ltd v Spectron Optical Coatings Ltd [1980] FSR 227, CA.
Protector Alarms Ltd v Maxim Alarms Ltd [1978] FSR 442.   **e**

Interlocutory appeal
By a writ issued on 12th July 1979 the plaintiffs, A J Bekhor & Co Ltd, claimed
£217,077·42 from the defendant, Godfrey Derek Ernest Bilton. On 11th March 1980 a
Mareva injunction was granted by Jupp J on an ex parte application by the plaintiffs **f**
restraining the defendant from removing from the jurisdiction or otherwise disposing
of any of his assets, save in so far as his assets exceeded £250,000. On 18th March 1980
an injunction was granted inter partes on the same terms by Kilner Brown J. On 28th
April 1980 on the defendant's application Parker J varied the terms of the injunction by
allowing the defendant to remove from the jurisdiction personal possessions to the value
of £5,000, his car and the sum of £1,250 per month for living expenses out of income **g**
from his United Kingdom investments, subject to the defendant undertaking not to
change the investment of his assets within the jurisdiction so as to be likely to depreciate
their value. On 17th November 1980 on the hearing of the defendant's application to
vary the order of 28th April and the plaintiffs' application for discovery under RSC Ord
24, r 7(1) and Ord 26, r 1(1), Parker J ordered (i) that the injunction granted by Kilner
Brown J on 18th March 1980 be varied so as to allow the defendant to remove from the **h**
jurisdiction £1,250 per month for his living expenses and to pay accountancy and legal
costs relating to the action out of assets within the jurisdiction and (ii) that the plaintiffs'
application for discovery be granted. The defendant appealed against the order for
discovery to the Court of Appeal out of time pursuant to leave granted by Parker J on 15
December 1980. By a respondent's notice under RSC Ord 58, r 6 the plaintiffs sought an
order requiring the defendant to swear an additional affidavit relating to his assets. The **j**
facts are set out in the judgment of Ackner LJ.

Robert Gatehouse QC and *George Newman* for the defendant.
S A Stamler QC and *Michael Jones* for the plaintiffs.

Cur adv vult

a
6th February. The following judgments were read.

ACKNER LJ (delivering the first judgment at the invitation of Stephenson LJ). The essential point raised by this appeal is whether and to what extent an order for discovery can be made in relation to matters which relate not to the issues in the action but to the
b operation of a Mareva injunction granted against the appellant restraining him from removing from the jurisdiction of the High Court or otherwise dealing with certain of his assets. The question arises out of the following circumstances.

Facts
The respondent company, the plaintiffs in the action, carry on business as
c stockbrokers. On 12th July 1979 they issued a specially indorsed writ for £217,077·42, being the balance of money which they alleged they lent from time to time to the defendant as his stockbrokers. RSC Ord 14 proceedings were threatened, but after a series of adjournments and special appointments this course was abandoned. The defendant delivered a defence and counterclaim, disputing the alleged debt on a number of bases, including the statutory defence provided by s 1 of the Moneylenders Act 1927
d that the transactions relied on by the plaintiffs were nominee transactions and accusing the plaintiffs of negligence. It is accepted that the defence and counterclaim raise arguable points.
Early last year the plaintiffs heard that the defendant had sold two farms and they made an ex parte application for an injunction restraining the defendant from removing from the jurisdiction or otherwise disposing of any of his assets, including in particular
e any moneys in his bank account, including the proceeds of the sale of Rocky Lane Farm, Henley, save in so far as the sum of his assets exceeded £250,000. The order was granted. When the matter was argued, inter partes, a week later, the point was taken on the defendant's behalf that so far from there being evidence that he was resident outside the United Kingdom the evidence filed by the plaintiffs established that he was resident in the United Kingdom. The defendant himself provided no evidence, but his wife
f swore an affidavit referring to the fact that she had been married to the defendant for 18 years, that they had three children and that he had for some five years, until he recently sold it, lived at Rocky Lane Farm. She stated that he was English, as are his father and mother, and that she and he had lived in England during the whole of their married life. The affidavit concealed that for some time they had not been happily married, that he had been close friends with a divorced lady and that he had decided to separate from
g his wife and go and live with this lady and her daughter in Monte Carlo and there start a new life.
Notwithstanding the doubts whether the court then had jurisdiction to make a Mareva injunction where the defendant is resident in the United Kingdom, Kilner Brown J made an order on 18th March, but it restrained the defendant from removing from the jurisdiction 'or otherwise disposing out of the jurisdiction any of his assets etc'.
h   The defendant entered a notice of appeal against the injunction, one of the grounds being 'the Defendant was based or resident in England or within the jurisdiction . . .'
This was probably only a tactical move because within a fortnight the defendant swore an affidavit in support of an application to vary the injunction and in that affidavit disclosed his domestic circumstances, which I have described above. He conceded that he had arranged for the sale of Rocky Lane Farm, but gave no information whether it has
j been sold and if so for how much. He denied that he had sold the other farm, Barnes Farm; this farm belonged to his mother and had been sold by her, he receiving no part of the proceeds. He explained that he had taken a lease for one year, with options to extend, of a flat in Monte Carlo where he and the lady and her daughter were to live, and the rent and service charge for which amounted to nearly £15,000 per year. He asserted that if he had remained he would have been free to spend as he had throughout his life,

'my income from the investment of my assets wherever situated'. He explained that he would be willing to withdraw his appeal and accept that his assets be frozen within the *a* jurisdiction if he was granted leave to take out of the jurisdiction his Citroen motor car, certain personal possessions and the income arising from the investment of his assets. He further stated that the income arising from the investments of such assets as he had out of the jurisdiction, which he did not particularise, would be insufficient even to pay the rent and service charges on the flat.

At the hearing of this application by Parker J on 28th April, the defendant's counsel, *b* who has not appeared in this appeal, informed the judge that the decision taken to advance the contention before Kilner Brown J that the defendant was still genuinely resident within the jurisdiction was on his advice and that therefore no adverse inference should be drawn against his client. Counsel also informed the judge that the defendant's assets within the jurisdiction amounted to between £217,000 and £250,000 and that he was prepared to limit his claim to be allowed to remove income to the sum of £25,000 *c* per annum.

The application to vary was largely successful. It was in the following terms:

'UPON . . . the Defendant by his Counsel undertaking (i) to withdraw his appeal to the Court of Appeal under Notice of Motion dated 1st April 1980 and (ii) not to change the investment of his assets within the jurisdiction so as to be likely to depreciate their value IT IS ORDERED: (1) That the Order dated 18th March 1980 and *d* the Injunction thereby granted be varied by allowing the Defendant to remove from the jurisdiction:—(a) personal possessions to the value of not exceeding £5,000; (b) his Citroen Motor Car; and (c) the sum of £1,250 per month [viz £15,000 per year] out of the income from his United Kingdom investments for living purposes . . .'

e

Within a few months of the injunction being varied, a problem arose with regard to the second of the two undertakings referred to above. The injunction as ordered by Kilner Brown J in no way fettered the defendant's right to deal with his assets within the jurisdiction, in such manner as he thought fit. To meet the possible objection which might have been made by the plaintiffs to the variation sought, the defendant had been advised to give an undertaking that his assets would not be invested in any manner *f* which was likely to depreciate their value, such an undertaking being designed to prevent him investing his capital in a wasting asset for the purpose of producing a very high income. However, the undertaking as incorporated in the order *not to change* the investment of his assets within the jurisdiction etc was capable of being construed so as to prevent the defendant meeting his financial obligations within the jurisdiction from his assets within the jurisdiction. The defendant's solicitors therefore sought the *g* plaintiffs' solicitors agreement to his utilising the assets within the jurisdiction to discharge his commitments there. Understandably the plaintiffs' solicitors stated that before they could agree to any variation of the terms of the undertaking they must know the exact nature of the defendant's assets and the way in which they were invested, as well as the extent of his expenses and obligations in this country which he had to meet. The defendant's solicitors failed to provide this information. They however confirmed *h* that their client was spending capital to meet his commitments in the jurisdiction 'to the extent that *his remaining income* in this country was insufficient'. They asserted, quite wrongly, that a Mareva injunction in standard form in no way prevents a defendant spending within the jurisdiction. They had apparently overlooked the terms of the ex parte order which was indeed in standard form.

On 28th October the defendant's solicitors filed an affidavit making the points referred *j* to above and stated that their client's commitments involved the expense of his making occasional visits to England, paying his professional advisers and maintaining his wife and three children. They sought, on the defendant's behalf, a variation of the undertaking so as to enable the defendant to continue to honour his commitments within the jurisdiction out of his assets within the jurisdiction. The plaintiffs countered

by giving notice that at the restored hearing of the summons they would apply, under
a RSC Ord 24, r 7(1) and Ord 26, r 1(1), for an order that the defendant should swear an
affidavit which, as amended by the judge, obliged him to: (1) disclose the full value of his
assets within the jurisdiction as at (a) 11th March 1980, (b) 28th April 1980, (c) the date
of the order; (2) identify with full particularity the nature of his assets, including the
identity of all bank or other accounts in his name and the sums presently standing in
each account; (3) disclose in so far as the value of his assets do not now total between
b £217,000 and £250,000 all facts within his knowledge as to the present whereabouts of
any assets said on 28th April 1980 to be included in that total, but not now so included,
and further disclose how and when those assets came to be changed and/or disposed of;
(4) identify in a written schedule all relevant documents material to the value,
distribution and disposal or change of his assets between 11th March and the date of the
order.
c   In an affidavit of 11th November the appellant set out his assets in England with their
approximate values as follows:

(a) freehold agricultural land	£75,000
(b) a bank account	£3,500
(c) a helicopter	£48,000

d (He said the helicopter was in fact worth £65,000 but he was purchasing it under a
financial agreement which he did not detail but in respect of which he said there was
approximately £17,000 outstanding.)

(d) a farm tractor	£6,500
(e) a debt owed to him	£7,000
(f) share and loan capital in Lowe Music Ltd	£10,000
(g) money held by solicitors on account of costs	£4,160

e

This totalled £154,000. He then went on to state that on 28th April his total assets
within the jurisdiction were worth approximately £220,000, that they had fallen since
that date to the extent of approximately £66,000, such money having been spent by him
entirely within the jurisdiction on: legal costs, £7,452; accountancy fees, £8,950;
f payments to his wife, approximately £15,000; payments for the helicopter, £25,000;
and the cost of his visits to England, £6,000. He further stated that his commitments
within the jurisdiction in the foreseeable future must inevitably be substantial both in
relation to the legal costs of defending the proceedings, the advice from his accountants
and his obligations to his wife, quite apart from the cost of visits to see his three children.
      On 14th November he swore yet another affidavit, following criticism made at the
g initial hearing of his application on 13th November that his affidavit did not contain
information with regard to his assets and liabilities out of the jurisdiction. In that
affidavit he dealt, for the first time, with the proceeds of the sale of Rocky Lane Farm.
He said the sale had been made in various lots, and completion took place on three
separate dates, namely 3rd March, 10th April and 25th April 1980, the total proceeds
amounting to £532,500. Immediately after the sale on 3rd March, that is a week before
h the ex parte Mareva injunction, he remitted £63,000 to a bank in Jersey. This he said
was all he obtained from the sale of the farm because it was heavily mortgaged, part of
the proceeds of the sale was paid to his wife in satisfaction of her claim and there were
substantial farming and personal debts. No figures or other details were provided of the
mortgage, the payment to the wife or the alleged debts.
      Understandably when the matter came before Parker J on 17th November the
j defendant was subject to considerable criticism. He had commenced the proceedings by
suppressing the fact that he had deliberately decided to leave the country and had
removed one asset, namely the sum of £63,000 as soon as he possibly could. The only
obvious income-producing asset which he had disclosed was £10,000 in the share and
loan capital of Lowe Music Ltd, which clearly was incapable of producing £25,000 a
year, or even the £15,000 a year which the court, by its order of 28th April, had

permitted him to remove. The defendant was living in Monaco in premises which cost him nearly £15,000 a year to run, he was supporting the woman referred to above, her **a** daughter and himself, as well as his wife at the rate of about £16,000 a year. Further, he was apparently running a helicopter and all this was being achieved without any substantial income. Further, he had reduced the value of his assets within the jurisdiction by some £66,000 despite the terms of his undertaking to the court. His affidavit was clearly evasive and deficient in essential particulars.

The judge, following the decision in *Iraqi Ministry of Defence v Arcepey Shipping Co SA* **b** *(Gillespie Brothers & Co Ltd intervening), The Angel Bell* [1980] 1 All ER 480, [1981] QB 65, was prepared to allow the defendant to make payment from his assets in England to his solicitors and accountants in connection with the present proceedings, providing any such payments were notified to the plaintiffs seven days before the payment was made. He, however, varied the injunction by restraining the defendant from otherwise dealing with any of his assets within the jurisdiction, save as to the monthly sum of £1,250 **c** provided for in the order of 28th April 1980, which sum, in accordance with that order, must come out of his income from his United Kingdom investments. Although the notice of appeal seeks the variation of this order, counsel for the defendant had conceded that the only point of attack is the judge's refusal to allow any payment out of assets within the jurisdiction to the defendant's wife. He accepts, however, that the judge was fully entitled to make the criticisms which he did of the defendant's conduct and of the **d** deficiencies in his affidavit and to decide that unless and until he made proper disclosure to the court he should be obliged to make payments to his wife from his assets outside the jurisdiction. Accordingly, the essential subject matter of the appeal is the grant by the judge, subject to certain minor amendments, of the plaintiffs' application for discovery. Parker J accepted that some of the material sought in the application was already to be found in the affidavits before the court, but because of the deficiencies in **e** those affidavits he decided that the matter must proceed de novo. He rejected the suggestion that because a Mareva injunction is not concerned with assets outside the jurisdiction it would be wrong to order discovery in respect of such assets. He accepted that in the ordinary way the foreign assets of a defendant may be irrelevant, but that, when a defendant comes before the court seeking to have certain payments excepted from the full ambit of a Mareva injunction already granted and to obtain certain freedom **f** of movement, then it could be that the foreign assets are of vital importance. The judge also clearly had in mind that the defendant's activities since the order of 28th April might well disclose that he had acted in breach of the order and, in particular, of his undertaking recorded in that order and thus be in contempt of court. He therefore stated, at the conclusion of his judgment, that whether or not the plaintiffs saw fit to make any further application after the defendant had filed his affidavit pursuant to the order the court **g** would, in the light of the affidavit, restore the matter if it appeared that the defendant was in contempt of court.

The Mareva jurisdiction

In *Nippon Yusen Kaisha v Karageorgis* [1975] 3 All ER 282, [1975] 1 WLR 1903 the plaintiff chartered a ship to the defendants from whom a large sum was claimed as **h** hire. There was a strong prima facie case that hire was due. Although the charterers could not be traced there was evidence that they had funds at a bank in London. An ex parte application to grant an injunction restraining the charterers from disposing of or removing from the jurisdiction any of the assets which were within the jurisdiction was refused at first instance but granted in the Court of Appeal. A month later a very similar case came before the Court of Appeal, *Mareva Compania Naviera SA v International* **j** *Bulkcarriers SA* (1975) [1980] 1 All ER 213. This was another ex parte application and a similar injunction was made. It is from this case that the Mareva jurisdiction takes its name. The power to grant this relief was founded on s 45(1) of the Supreme Court of Judicature (Consolidation) Act 1925. This provides that a mandamus or an injunction may be granted or a receiver appointed by an interlocutory order of the court in all cases in which it shall appear to the court to be just or convenient.

The customary form of the order is in very wide terms. It restrains the defendant
a from 'removing from the jurisdiction or otherwise disposing of or dealing with any of
his assets within the jurisdiction including and in particular [a certain specified asset] save
in so far as such assets do not exceed in value the sum of [the plaintiff's claim]'. The order
is made in this wide form in the first instance, but later it may be varied, because for
example the plaintiff desires bona fide to make payments in the ordinary course of his
business or to provide for his own living expenses: see *Iraqi Ministry of Defence v Arcepey*
b *Shipping Co SA.*

The use of the remedy has greatly increased and far from being exceptional it has now
become commonplace. In 1979 applications were being made at the rate of about
twenty per month (per Mustill J in *Third Chandris Shipping Corpn v Unimarine SA* [1979]
2 All ER 972 at 976, [1979] 1 QB 645 at 650). Although it was initially thought that the
jurisdiction only applied in relation to a defendant who was out of the jurisdiction but
c had money or goods in this country (see *Rasu Maritima SA v Perusahaan Petambangan
Minyak Dan Gas Bumi Negara (Pertamina)* [1977] 3 All ER 324, [1978] QB 644), it was
decided at first instance in *Barclay-Johnson v Yuill* [1980] 3 All ER 190, [1980] 1 WLR 1259
and shortly thereafter by the Court of Appeal in *Prince Abdul Rahman Bin Turki Al Sudairy
v Abu-Taha* [1980] 3 All ER 409, [1980] 1 WLR 1268 that the jurisdiction applied even
if the defendant was not a foreigner or foreign based, since the essence of the jurisdiction
d is the risk of the defendant removing his assets from the jurisdiction and so stultifying
any judgment given by the courts in the action.

Clause 37 of the Supreme Court Bill provides for the re-enaction of s 45(1) and further
provides in terms that the power of the court to grant an interlocutory injunction
restraining a party to any proceedings from removing from the jurisdiction of the High
Court or otherwise dealing with assets located within that jurisdiction shall be exercisable
e in cases where that party is, as well as in cases where he is not, domiciled, resident or
present within that jurisdiction.

Discovery

A further step in the process of the evolution of the Mareva jurisdiction took place in
A v C [1980] 2 All ER 347, [1981] 2 WLR 629. In considering what this case decided it
f is important to have in mind the basic facts and the remedies which were being
sought. The plaintiffs claimed to be victims of a fraud, allegedly masterminded by the
first defendant, but which implicated the second, third, fourth and fifth defendants. In
their writ, they claimed against these five defendants damages for conspiracy to defraud
and damages for deceit and against the fifth defendant damages for breach of warranty
in the sum of £5·7 m. In addition, they also claimed to trace the sum of £383,872 which
g they said was paid under a mistake of fact induced by fraud into the account of the sixth
defendant, a bank. There was no allegation of malpractice against the bank, but simply
a claim to trace money into its hands, which the plaintiffs said was their property in
equity. Before the issue of the writ the plaintiffs obtained, ex parte, a Mareva injunction
against the first five defendants limited to £1·5m. They also obtained an injunction
restraining all the defendants from disposing of the sum of £383,872 or any lesser sum
h standing to the credit of accounts in the name of any of the first five defendants or of
another party (WL) at the sixth defendant (the bank). Two issues fell to be decided.
These were (a) whether an order should be made that if the sum of £383,872 was no
longer in WL's account at the bank each defendant should disclose all facts within their
knowledge as to the present whereabouts of that sum, and (b) whether an order should
be made requiring all the defendants to disclose to the plaintiffs forthwith the sums at
j present standing in accounts in the names of any of the first five defendants or WL at the
bank. As regards (a) Robert Goff J described this as relating to the 'proprietary claim'. He
held that in such cases there was good authority that the court may make orders with the
purpose of ascertaining the whereabouts of missing trust funds. In *London and County
Securities Ltd v Caplan* (26th May 1978, unreported) Templeman J made an order for the
purpose of enabling the plaintiffs to trace property acquired by the defendant and so take
steps to seize that property if it derived from their assets. In *Mediterranea Reffineria*

Siciliana Petroli SpA v Mabanaft GmbH [1978] Court of Appeal Transcript 816, which was
concerned with tracing the product of the plaintiff's assets, viz a cargo of oil, delivery of   *a*
which was alleged to have been obtained without the production of bills of lading,
Mocatta J made a sweeping order requiring directors and an employee of the defendant
company to make full disclosure of certain specified facts on affidavits and directed that
one of them should file an affidavit of documents. His order was upheld by the Court of
Appeal, and Templeman LJ said:

> 'The court of equity has never hesitated to use the strongest power to protect and   *b*
> preserve a trust fund in interlocutory proceedings on the basis that, if the trust fund
> disappears by the time the action comes to trial, equity will have been invoked in
> vain.'

Robert Goff J thus held that there was ample authority that in an action in which the
plaintiff seeks *to trace* property, which in equity belongs to him, the court not only has   *c*
jurisdiction to grant an injunction restraining the disposal of that property but may in
addition, at the interlocutory stages of the action, make orders designed to ascertain the
whereabouts of that property. Robert Goff J's decision in *A v C* that the orders sought
were necessary for the purposes of the tracing claim was approved and followed by the
Court of Appeal in *Bankers Trust Co v Shapira* [1980] 3 All ER 353, [1980] 1 WLR 1274.

As regards the second order sought the judge recognised that there was no authority   *d*
to guide him as to the power to make an order for discovery of documents or for
interrogatories in aid of a Mareva injunction. He accordingly dealt with the matter quite
shortly and I will quote from the material parts of his judgment ([1980] 2 All ER 347 at
351, [1981] 2 WLR 629 at 622–623):

> 'Now the exercise of this jurisdiction may lead to many problems. The defendant   *e*
> may have more than one asset within the jurisdiction, for example he may have a
> number of bank accounts. The plaintiff does not know how much, if anything, is
> in any of them nor does each of the defendant bankers know what is in the other
> accounts. Without information about the state of each account it is difficult, if not
> impossible, to operate the Mareva jurisdiction properly; for example, if each banker
> prevents any drawing from his account to the limit of the sum claimed, the   *f*
> defendant will be treated oppressively, and the plaintiff may be held liable on his
> undertaking in damages. Again, there may be a single claim against a number of
> defendants; in that event the same difficulty may arise. Furthermore, the very
> generality of the order creates difficulty for the defendant's bankers, who may for
> example be unaware of the existence of other assets of the defendant's within the
> jurisdiction; indeed, if a more specific order is possible, it may give much needed   *g*
> protection for the defendant's bankers, who are after all simply the innocent holders
> of one form of the defendant's assets ... Furthermore, for the purposes of the
> Mareva jurisdiction, since this is a case involving a number of defendants, it is
> necessary for the proper exercise of that jurisdiction to know how much money is
> standing in the identified bank account; if, for example, that account should be
> unencumbered and in excess of the plaintiff's claim, the Mareva injunction can be   *h*
> restricted to that amount.'

The judge concluded that the court should, where necessary, exercise its powers to
order discovery or interrogatories in order to ensure that the Mareva jurisdiction 'is
properly exercised and thereby to secure its objectives which is ... the prevention of
abuse'.

He then went on to consider the source of that power. He said ([1980] 2 All ER 347   *j*
at 351, [1981] 2 WLR 629 at 633):

> 'That the court has power to order discovery of particular documents and
> interrogatories at an early stage of proceedings is, I think, not in doubt. I refer in
> particular to RSC Ord 24, r 7(1) in relation to discovery of documents, and to the
> general terms of RSC Ord 26, r 1(1) in relation to interrogatories. If necessary,

a　　however, the court's power to make an appropriate order in aid of a Mareva injunction can be derived from the power to make mandatory orders conferred on the court by s 45 of the Supreme Court of Judicature (Consolidation) Act 1925 . . .'

Rules of the Supreme Court

If and in so far as the judge relied for his power to make the order under the Rules of the Supreme Court, then I respectfully think he was in error. The documents which can
b be made the subject of discovery must relate 'to matters in question in the action': see Ord 24, r 1. Order 24, r 7(1), to which the judge drew specific attention and which the plaintiffs in the first three lines of their notice of intention to apply for discovery specifically invoked, although giving the court power at any time to make an order for discovery, in no way departs from Ord 24, r 1. In fact it provides (in r 7(3)) that an application for an order under this rule must be supported by an affidavit stating the
c belief of the applicant that the party from whom discovery is sought has, or at some time had, in his possession, custody or power the document, or class of document, specified or described in the application *and* that it relates to one or more of the matters in question in the cause or matter.

Significantly, although invoking this rule, the plaintiffs did not seek to put in the requisite affidavit in support. The reason for such failure was no doubt attributable to
d the fact that the documents or class of documents in respect of which they sought discovery did not relate to one or more of the matters in question in the cause or matter. The value of the defendant's assets in March, April and November 1980, the nature of those assets, including the identity of all bank or other accounts in his name, and how he had dealt with those assets between March and November 1980 were not matters in question in the action or in the cause or matter (see the definitions of 'action',
e 'cause', and 'matter' in s 225 of the Supreme Court of Judicature (Consolidation) Act 1925). Order 24, r 8, provides that on the hearing of an application for an order under r 3, r 7 or r 7A the court shall refuse to make such an order if and so far as it is of opinion that discovery is not necessary either for disposing fairly of the cause or matter or for saving costs. It is pursuant to the terms of this rule that discovery (as well as interrogatories) solely for the purpose of impeaching the credit of the opposite party will
f not be ordered.

As to interrogatories, the power to grant them is similarly circumscribed. Order 26, r 1(1), to which Robert Goff J made specific reference (see *A v C* [1980] 2 All ER 347 at 351, [1981] 2 WLR 629 at 633) and which was also invoked in the plaintiff's notice of application, provides that a party to any cause or matter may apply to the court for an order giving him leave to serve on any other party interrogatories relating 'to any matter
g in question between the applicant and that other party in the cause or matter'. Order 26, r 1(3) provides that on the hearing of such an application the court shall give leave as to such only of the interrogatories as it considers necessary, either for disposing fairly of the cause or matter or for saving costs. Quite apart from the somewhat unusual form adopted in this case by the plaintiffs to interrogate the defendant, the same general objection, mutatis mutandis, applies. The right to interrogate, although not confined to
h facts directly in issue, extends to any facts the existence or non-existence of which is relevant to the existence or non-existence of the facts directly in issue (per Lord Esher MR in *Marriott v Chamberlain* (1886) 17 QBD 154 at 163). Although it is not necessary that answers to interrogatories should be conclusive on the question at issue, it is enough that they should have some bearing on the question and that they might form a step in establishing liability (see *Blair v Haycock Cadle Co* (1917) 34 TLR 39 at 40 per Lord Finlay
j LC). None of the questions raised by the plaintiffs' application, or indeed those raised in *A v C*, had any relevance to establishing liability in the action.

In my judgment the power to order discovery to ensure that the Mareva jurisdiction is properly exercised and thereby to secure its objective of preventing the defendant removing his assets from the jurisdiction and so stultifying any judgment given by the court in the action cannot be found in the Rules of the Supreme Court. This, to my mind, is by no means surprising, the jurisdiction having, for all practical purposes, only

recently come to light. Counsel for the plaintiffs, while arguing valiantly for the
proposition which I have just rejected, preferred to base the court's power first upon its *a*
inherent jurisdiction, and secondly on s 45 of the Supreme Court of Judicature
(Consolidation) Act 1925, to which I have made reference above. I propose to deal with
the latter point first.

Section 45

Having regard to the authorities referred to above it is now clearly established that the *b*
power of the High Court under s 45(1) includes the power to grant an interlocutory
injunction to restrain a party to any proceedings from removing from the jurisdiction or
otherwise dealing with assets located within the jurisdiction where that party is, as well
as where he is not, domiciled, resident or present within that jurisdiction. Clause 37 of
the Supreme Court Bill is obviously designed to give statutory effect to those
authorities. To my mind there must be *inherent in that power* the power to make all such *c*
ancillary orders as appear to the court to be just and convenient to ensure that the exercise
of the Mareva jurisdiction is effective to achieve its purpose.

The power now contained in s 45 of the 1925 Act was formerly contained in s 25 of
the Supreme Court of Judicature Act 1873. It was referred to by Jessel MR in *Beddow v
Beddow* (1878) 9 Ch D 89 at 93 as embracing the grant of an injunction 'in any case where
it would be right or just to do so'. Applying that decision, Lord Denning MR in *Rasu* *d*
Maritima SA v Pertamina [1977] 3 All ER 324 at 333, [1978] QB 644 at 659–60 stressed
that the section gives the court a very wide discretion to grant an injunction. Counsel for
the defendant contends however that *Siskina (Cargo owners) v Distos Compania Naviera SA,
The Siskina* [1977] 3 All ER 324, [1979] AC 210 and in particular certain observations
made by Lord Diplock in his speech ([1977] 3 All ER 803 at 824, [1979] AC 210 at 256)
prevent any ancillary order being made under s 45 in aid or support of the injunction *e*
granted under that section. He quotes in particular the sentence, 'The right to obtain an
interlocutory injunction is merely ancillary and incidental to the pre-existing cause of
action.' However, in my judgment, this overlooks the context in which this observation
was made. In that case the cargo owners applied ex parte to a judge of the commercial
court (a) for leave to issue a writ against the shipowner and to serve a notice of it out of
the jurisdiction and (b) for an immediate interim injunction to restrain the shipowners *f*
from disposing of their assets within the jurisdiction of the High Court, including, in
particular, the insurance proceeds in respect of the loss of the Siskina.

The shipowners were a Panamanian company. At no time had it any office or agent
in England. The cargo owners were the owners of cargo laden on the Siskina, the only
asset of the shipowners, which had become a total loss. The bills of lading issued in Italy
by the shipowners on the shipment of the cargo contained a clause confirming exclusive *g*
jurisdiction on the court in Genoa. The application was granted ex parte. However,
subsequently, an application was made before Kerr J to set aside the service of the writ
and all subsequent proceedings. He granted the application because the cargo owner's
claim for damages, whether based in contract or in tort, disclosed no cause of action in
respect of which the court had any power to permit service of its process out of the
jurisdiction under RSC Ord 11. There was therefore no substantive claim to pecuniary *h*
relief within the jurisdiction of the court to grant to which the Mareva injunction sought
could be ancillary. In this context, what Lord Diplock was saying in the observation
quoted above, and so strongly relied on by counsel for the defendant, was that you cannot
obtain an interlocutory injunction unless there is some claim for substantive relief on
which jurisdiction can be founded. It is, of course, common ground in this action that
there is a substantive claim which founds jurisdiction. The plaintiffs are claiming to *j*
recover a large sum of money lent within the jurisdiction to the defendant. In my
judgment therefore the decision in *The Siskina* and the basis for that decision is of no
relevance to the issue whether there is inherent in the power to grant the Mareva
injunction a power to make an ancillary order or orders to ensure the effective exercise
of that power.

However, it must be borne in mind that the foundation of the jurisdiction is the need
a to prevent judgments of the court from being rendered ineffective by the removal of the
defendant's assets from the jurisdiction. It provides a limited exception to the general
rule that the court will not normally grant an injunction to restrain a defendant from
parting with his assets so that they may be preserved in case the plaintiff's claim
succeeds. The plaintiff, like other creditors of the defendant, must obtain his judgment
and then enforce it. He cannot prevent the defendant from disposing of his assets
b pendente lite merely because he fears that by the time he obtains judgment in his favour
the defendant will have no assets against which the judgment can be enforced. Were the
law otherwise, the way would lie open to any claimant to paralyse the activities of any
person or firm against whom he makes his claims, by obtaining an injunction freezing
their assets (per Sir Robert Megarry V-C in *Barclay-Johnson v Yuill* [1980] 3 All ER 190 at
193, [1980] 1 WLR 1259 at 1262, referring to the *Lister & Co v Stubbs* (1890) 45 Ch D 1,
c [1886–90] All ER Rep 797 line of authority). The Mareva jurisdiction was not intended
to rewrite the English law of insolvency in this way. The purpose of the Mareva
jurisdiction was not to improve the position of claimants in an insolvency but simply to
prevent the injustice of a defendant removing his assets from the jurisdiction which
might otherwise have been available to satisfy a judgment. It is not a form of pre-trial
attachment but a relief in personam which prohibits certain acts in relation to the assets
d in question (per Robert Goff J in *Iraqi Ministry of Defence v Arcepey Shipping Co SA* [1980]
1 All ER 480, [1980] 2 WLR 488 and *Cretanor Maritime Co Ltd v Irish Marine Management
Ltd* [1978] 3 All ER 164, [1978] 1 WLR 966). It is therefore clear that, although the
Mareva plaintiff, who has satisfied the guidelines set out by Lord Denning MR in *Third
Chandris Shipping Corpn v Unimarine SA* [1979] 2 All ER 972 at 984, [1979] QB 645 at 668,
and in particular has provided adequate grounds for believing that there is a risk of the
e defendant's assets being removed before the judgment or award is satisfied, is in a
privileged position, this privilege must not be carried too far. The courts must be
vigilant to ensure that the Mareva defendant is not treated like a judgment debtor. It
was no doubt with this general principle in mind that Robert Goff J in *A v C* was at pains
to point out that it would not be right to make general use of the power to enable the
plaintiff to discover whether the defendant has any assets here. However, having
f established the existence of the assets, it may, in a particular case, be necessary for the
proper exercise of the jurisdiction that the defendant should provide information about
a particular asset in order for the jurisdiction to be properly exercised. Where, as in *A v
C*, there are several defendants, the ancillary order might well be designed to obtain
information which would enable the court to restrict the injunction to a particular
account, and thus enable the judge to decide on what the Mareva injunction should bite.
g

Inherent jurisdiction
    If I am wrong in concluding that s 45 provides the basis for the jurisdiction to make
the type of ancillary order referred to above, then the question arises whether the court
has an inherent or residual jurisdiction to make such an ancillary order. In so far as
counsel for the plaintiffs contends that there is inherent jurisdiction in the court to make
h effective the remedies that it grants, this seems to me merely another way of submitting
that, where the power exists to grant the remedy, there must also be inherent in that
power the power to make ancillary orders to make that remedy effective. This I have
accepted. However, if and in so far as he contends that the courts have a general residual
discretion to make any order necessary to ensure that justice be done between the parties,
then in my judgment that is too wide and sweeping a contention to be acceptable. Such
j a proposition would seem to come well within the criticism made by Lord Hailsham in
The Siskina [1977] 3 All ER 803 at 829, [1979] AC 210 at 262. Support for this general
proposition was sought from what are now known to be Anton Piller orders and, in
particular, from the observations of Lord Denning MR in *Anton Piller KG v Manufacturing
Processes Ltd* [1976] 1 All ER 779 at 783, [1976] Ch 55 at 61. The source, however, of the
Anton Piller orders was the decision of Templeman J in *EMI Ltd v Pandit* [1975] 1 All ER

418, [1975] 1 WLR 302. It concerned the power of the court to make ex parte orders requiring a defendant to permit the inspection of articles or documents. The difficulty *a* which was sought to be overcome, which in no way arises in this case, was the requirement in Ord 29, r 2(5) that an application for an order for inspection, detention, preservation etc of the subject matter of the cause or matter was to be made 'by summons or by notice'. The reason for the order being sought ex parte was because of the very serious risk that once the defendant was given notice of the application he would destroy the articles or documents and thereby defeat the very purpose of the action. The *b* problem therefore was an entirely different one. Templeman J concluded that, if it appears that the object of the plaintiff's litigation would be unfairly and improperly frustrated by the very giving of the notice which is normally required to protect the defendant, there must be exceptional and emergency cases in which the court can dispense with the notice and, either under power in the rules to dispense with notice or by the exercise of its inherent jurisdiction, make such a limited order, albeit ex parte, as *c* will give the plaintiffs the relief which they would otherwise be unable to obtain (see [1975] 1 All ER 418 at 421, [1975] 1 WLR 302 at 305). The authorities to which Templeman J referred do not appear to me to support the existence of the wide residuary discretion claimed by counsel for the plaintiffs to exist. I do not therefore consider that the Anton Piller line of authorities assist him. However, in view of the opinion which I have expressed in relation to s 45, he does not require to establish the existence of such *d* residual power.

The order made in this case

Given that there is power to make an order for discovery in 'aid' of a Mareva injunction in the limited sense which I have sought to describe above, the question next arises whether the order made by Parker J was such an order. I can find no suggestion that he *e* was seeking to rely on s 45 of the 1925 Act, save in so far as he was relying on the decision in *A v C*. On the face of it, he was purporting to grant an application for discovery and interrogatories made pursuant to the Rules of the Supreme Court. However, this would be no valid basis for attacking his order, if he had jurisdiction to make the same order under s 45.

In order to appreciate the nature and purpose of the judge's order it seems to me *f* necessary to consider again what the defendant had disclosed with regard to his assets in England in the two affidavits of 11th and 14th November, which the judge justifiably found to be evasive and unsatisfactory. The defendant deposed that assets to the value of £154,000 were within the jurisdiction. As stated above they consisted of freehold agricultural land, a helicopter, a farm tractor, a debt, shares, money held by his solicitors on account of costs and a bank account in the sum of £3,500. Further, the defendant's *g* assets had been worth £220,000 approximately some six months earlier when the defendant had last appeared before the judge. Since then he stated that he had expended approximately £66,000 on legal costs, accountancy fees, payments to his wife, payments for the helicopter and visits to England as described previously in this judgment. To my mind, there was no necessity for making any order ancillary to the Mareva injunction in order to ensure the proper exercise of that jurisdiction. It was not suggested by the plaintiffs that they were particularly interested in the identity of the bank where approximately 1½% of the defendant's assets were to be found. There was no question as to on what property the Mareva injunction was to bite. It was to operate in relation to all the assets referred to above.

Apart from the lack of information given in regard to these assets, the judge was clearly concerned, and rightly concerned, at the lack of any income-producing asset, apart from the £10,000 in the share and loan capital of Lowe Music Ltd. This was most unlikely to produce the £25,000 per year income which the defendant had wished to take out of the country, or even the £15,000 per year which the judge had permitted to be removed from the jurisdiction when he varied the order inter partes on 28th April 1980. He was also concerned with the apparent breaches by the defendant of his

undertaking. Anticipating that the affidavit which he had directed the defendant to
a provide might disclose that the defendant had been guilty of contempt of court, he stated
in his judgment that when the affidavit had been filed the plaintiffs were, of course, at
liberty to make a further application to the court with regard to the defendant's
operations since the undertaking was given. Whether or not they saw fit to make any
further application, if it appeared to the court that the affidavit did not contain proper
disclosure in accordance with the order, or proper explanation of the defendant's conduct
b with regard to the hearings on 18th March, and with regard to the undertaking, then the
court would appoint a day when the matter of possible contempt of court and the
appropriate steps to be taken, if such contempt was shown, should be considered.

Counsel for the plaintiffs submits that Parker J was seeking, by his order, to police the
Mareva injunction which he had granted and that this was therefore an order made 'in
aid of' the Mareva injunction.

c   I cannot accept this view. If the plaintiffs, or the court of its own volition, desired to
'police its order', then the plaintiffs could have applied for an order for the cross-
examination of the defendant on his affidavit, or the court itself could have made such
an order (see Ord 38, r 2). No such application was made by the plaintiffs and no such
initiative was taken by the court. From the plaintiffs' point of view, this of course is
understandable enough, since their concern was not the committal of the defendant to
d prison, but the preservation of his assets, so as to avoid the prospect of a barren
judgment. But there was another remedy open to them, or to the judge. The order of
28th April varying the Mareva injunction and allowing the defendant to remove £1,250
per month from the jurisdiction appears to have been obtained without proper disclosure
to the court of the true position of the defendant's assets. The plaintiffs could have
applied for the withdrawal and the judge of his own initiative could have withdrawn
e from the defendant the permission to remove any further money from the jurisdiction
unless and until he made a full and proper disclosure of those matters which the court
thought were necessary to establish the true nature of his assets, and he had given a
proper explanation of his conduct between the material dates. The plaintiffs made no
such application, and the judge, somewhat surprisingly, so far from removing permission
from the defendant to take £1,250 per month out of the jurisdiction permitted him, on
f terms, to pay from his assets within the jurisdiction legal and accountancy costs relating
to the action.

In short, while fully indorsing and approving the judge's desire to put an end to the
defendant's evasiveness and to establish to what extent if at all there had been non-
compliance with his order, or breaches by the defendant of his undertaking, I do not
consider that he had the jurisdiction to achieve it by the order which he made. Having
g regard to the existence of the remedies available to the plaintiffs to 'police' the order that
they had obtained, it would, in my judgment, be quite wrong to seek to create new
machinery which could have far-reaching and undesirable consequences and which are
quite unnecessary for the proper operation of the Mareva jurisdiction.

In the light of the views expressed above it is unnecessary for me to deal with the
defendant's submission that, as the answers to the interrogatories ordered could
h incriminate him, the order should never have been made. However, in deference to the
arguments which have been addressed to us I will shortly express my views on this
submission.

It has long been established that the fact that the answer to interrogatories sought to
be administered would or might tend to incriminate the party interrogated is no ground
to objecting to leave being given to administer them (see *Fisher v Owen* (1878) 8 Ch D 645
j and the other cases cited in the Supreme Court Practice 1979, vol 1, p 450, para
26/1/16). The objection to answer on this ground must be taken in the answer. The only
exception to this general rule arises in an action to recover a penalty (see *Hunnings v
Williamson* (1883) 10 QBD 459). I do not consider that *Rank Film Distributors Ltd v Video
Information Centre* [1980] 2 All ER 273, [1980] 3 WLR 487 in any way detracts from the
general rule referred to above. In that case the plaintiffs, who were film companies

owning the copyright to films produced and made by them, believed the defendants were pirating copies of those films and recording and selling unauthorised video cassettes *a* of them. They obtained Anton Piller orders which went beyond requiring the defendants to permit forthwith representatives of the plaintiffs to enter premises occupied by the defendants for the purpose of inspecting and removing any unauthorised films. The orders further required three of the defendants to disclose (a) the names and addresses of persons who supplied the cassettes and customers who bought them, (b) all invoices and other documents relating to the cassettes and (c) the whereabouts of all pirate cassettes *b* and master copies known to the defendants. These were peremptory orders for discovery and interrogation requiring instant obedience and the defendants were informed by the penal notice on the order that disobedience would expose them to penal consequences. This was therefore no ordinary order for discovery or interrogatories where the party interrogated has the opportunity to consider and take legal advice before deciding whether to comply with the order (see [1980] 2 All ER 273 at 288–289, [1980] 3 WLR *c* 487 at 515 per Templeman LJ). It was accordingly held by the majority of the Court of Appeal that that part of the orders requiring disclosure was contrary to the well-established principle of privilege against self-incrimination and would accordingly be expunged.

Counsel for the defendant further sought to rely on *Comet Products UK Ltd v Hawkex Plastics Ltd* [1971] 1 All ER 1141, [1971] 2 QB 67. That was a passing-off action in which *d* the plaintiffs had obtained an interim injunction restraining the defendants from passing off their product as the plaintiffs'. Before the trial of the action, the plaintiffs alleged that the defendants were guilty of contempt of court in disobeying the injunction and applied for the committal of the second defendant to prison for his contempt. On the hearing of the application affidavits were filed on each side and were read. The plaintiffs sought an order to cross-examine the defendant on his affidavit, such application being *e* made under Ord 38, r 2, which gives the court discretion to make such an order. It is clear from all the judgments of the Court of Appeal that, if the cross-examination was to have been limited to the particular circumstances of the alleged contempt, then it would have been right to have ordered the cross-examination. It is only in very exceptional cases that a judge ought to refuse an application to cross-examine a defendant on his affidavit (see [1971] 1 All ER 1141 at 1147, [1971] 2 QB 67 at 77 per Cross LJ). In the *f* Court of Appeal however, notwithstanding that counsel for the plaintiff had told the judge he did not wish to cross-examine on the subject of the main action, it became apparent that a much wider cross-examination was intended in which the whole circumstances of the alleged passing off was to be investigated. The court accordingly held that as a matter of discretion the cross-examination ought not to be allowed. Again, this case does not detract from the general principle to which I have referred above that, *g* if the answers to interrogatories may tend to incriminate, that is no valid objection to the order for the interrogatories. The objection must be taken when the time comes to answer them.

For the reasons given I would accordingly allow this appeal. The defendant's victory may well be a hollow one, since the plaintiffs will, I anticipate, pursue the remedies to which I have made reference, and restore the matter to Parker J with a view to his either *h* ordering the cross-examination of the defendant and/or varying the Mareva injunction should he think fit.

GRIFFITHS LJ. Until recently the courts have refused to grant an injunction to freeze the assets of a defendant in anticipation of the plaintiff obtaining judgment against him. This general rule is long standing and well established by such authorities as *Lister* *j* *& Co v Stubbs* (1890) 45 Ch D 1, [1886–90] All ER Rep 797.

However, in 1975 an exception to this general rule appeared which came to be known as the Mareva injunction, taking its name from the decision of this court in *Mareva Compania Naviera SA v International Bulkcarriers SA* (1975) [1980] 1 All ER 213. If the court is satisfied that there is a real risk that a defendant will remove his assets from the jurisdiction so that a successful plaintiff will be unable to issue execution against them

and thus be left with a barren judgment it will issue an injunction to restrain the
a defendant from removing sufficient of his assets from the jurisdiction to protect the
plaintiff from this risk. At first the Mareva injunction was only granted against a
defendant resident outside the jurisdiction, but it has recently been extended to include
a resident within the jurisdiction, provided there is a real risk that he intends to defeat
the plaintiff's claim by removing his assets from the jurisdiction (see *Prince Abdul Rahman
Bin Turki Al Sudairy v Abu-Taha* [1980] 3 All ER 409, [1980] 1 WLR 1268). Although the
b primary purpose of the Mareva injunction is to prevent the defendant removing his
assets from the jurisdiction and thus out of reach of execution, the form of order
generally prevents the defendant not only from removing his assets from the jurisdiction
but also from otherwise dealing with them within the jurisdiction. The latter part of the
order is made in order to prevent the defendant passing on his assets to a third party who
then takes them out of the jurisdiction. To mitigate the obvious hardship that may be
c caused to a defendant if a large part of his assets are completely frozen the court will be
prepared to vary the order to enable the defendant to use his assets for legitimate trading
and other purposes within the jurisdiction (see *Iraqi Ministry of Defence v Arcepey Shipping
Co SA, The Angel Bell* [1980] 1 All ER 480, [1981] QB 65).

The power to make the Mareva injunction is derived from s 45(1) of the Supreme
Court of Judicature (Consolidation) Act 1925 on the grounds that such an order is 'just
d and convenient'. Counsel for the defendant has referred to passages in the speeches of
Lord Diplock and Lord Hailsham in *Siskina (Cargo owners) v Distos Compania Naviera SA,
The Siskina* [1977] 3 All ER 803, [1979] AC 210 which he submits cast doubt on the power
of the court to grant a Mareva injunction. But the power to make a Mareva injunction
was not directly in question in that case and whatever may be the outcome if the matter
is finally tested in the House of Lords it must for the moment be taken as settled by
e decisions of this court that such a power exists.

The first question that arises in this appeal is whether the court has jurisdiction to
make an order for discovery in aid of a Mareva injunction. Counsel for the defendant
concedes that it is desirable that the court should have such jurisdiction but submits that
it does not. Until Robert Goff J made an order for discovery in *A v C* [1980] 2 All ER 347,
[1981] 2 WLR 629, it seemed that the jurisdiction had been exercised successfully
f without the defendant being ordered to give discovery. The plaintiff must be able to
satisfy the court that the defendant has assets within the jurisdiction in order to obtain
the injunction and in most cases will probably be able to identify those assets with
sufficient particularity to enable the court to make an effective order. In such cases there
is no need for discovery, and it would be most oppressive to make an unnecessary order
for discovery merely to harass the defendant. However, from time to time cases will
g arise when, although it seems highly probable that the defendant has assets within the
jurisdiction, their precise form and whereabouts are in doubt, or in the case of a number
of defendants they may collectively have sufficient assets but there may be doubt about
their distribution among themselves. In such cases in order that the Mareva injunction
should be effective both the court and the plaintiff require to know the particular assets
on which the order should bite. It must be remembered that the underlying reason for
h making the order is the fear that the defendant may remove his assets and this is most
effectively prevented by the plaintiff serving a copy of the injunction on whoever is
holding the defendant's assets for the time being. Very often this will be the defendant's
bankers, but assets can take many forms and be in the hands of many different persons
to whom it is desirable to give notice of the court's order. To my mind the desirability
of the power to order discovery is obvious and it is particularly needed in the case of a
j defendant who has demonstrated himself to be untrustworthy and evasive. But the
question remains: does the power exist?

In this case the plaintiffs applied for and it appears to me the judge made his order in
purported exercise of his powers to make an order for discovery of particular documents
under RSC Ord 24, r 7(1) and to administer interrogatories under Ord 26, r 1. In doing
so he followed the decision of Robert Goff J in *A v C*. The form of the order he made is
fully set out in the judgment of Ackner LJ. It is an order for discovery of both

documents and facts in wide terms and certainly does not follow the type of order normally made in applications either for discovery of particular documents or for *a* interrogatories.

I agree that the Rules of the Supreme Court give no power to a judge to make such an order.

In both the case of discovery of documents and discovery of facts by way of interrogatories the discovery has to relate 'to matters in question in the action' or 'cause or matter' (see Ord 24, r 1(1) and Ord 26, r 1(1)) and these words must also be read into *b* Ord 24, r 7(1), by necessary implication arising from the fact that an application for particular discovery under r 7(1) must be supported by affidavit stating that documents relate to matters in question in the cause or matter (see r 7(3)).

The phrases 'matters in question in the action' and 'matters in question . . . in the cause or matter' have for generations been understood to refer to the issues to be decided in the litigation. The present existence and whereabouts of the defendant's wealth are not such *c* an issue; they are relevant only to the defendant's ability to satisfy judgment if the 'matters in question in the action' are resolved in the plaintiff's favour. I therefore conclude that the judge had no power to order discovery pursuant to the rules of court and in so far as *A v C* was founded on such a power it was wrongly decided.

However, in *A v C* Robert Goff J derived the power to order discovery not only from the rules but also from the power to make the injunction under s 45 of the Supreme *d* Court of Judicature (Consolidation) Act 1925. Counsel for the plaintiffs relies on this power to support the judge's order. If the court has power to make a Mareva injunction it must have power to make an effective Mareva injunction. If the injunction will not be effective it ought not be made.

For the reasons I have already given it may be necessary to order discovery to make the injunction effective and I would hold that the court has the power to make such ancillary *e* orders as are necessary to secure that the injunctive relief given to the plaintiff is effective. I therefore agree that a judge does have power to order discovery in aid of a Mareva injunction if it is necessary for the effective operation of the injunction.

I feel it unnecessary to express any view on counsel's wider argument based on the inherent jurisdiction of the court to order discovery wherever the cause of justice requires it.   *f*

Assuming that the judge had power to order discovery ought he to have done so on the facts of this case? Counsel for the defendant submits that the judge should not have ordered discovery because it was not necessary to do so and because its primary purpose was not to aid the exercise of the Mareva jurisdiction but to force the defendant to provide material on which he could be punished for contempt of court.

I will deal first with the objection on the ground of self-incrimination. It is true that *g* the judge expressed disapproval of the defendant's behaviour in the proceedings and referred to the possibility of his being in contempt of the court's order. But this possibility must have been present to the minds of all those engaged in the litigation. The defendant's solicitor had himself referred to the possibility in the course of the correspondence. If I thought that this order for discovery was made merely to provide the material for contempt proceedings I would not hesitate to set it aside; it would clearly *h* be an improper exercise of the power and offend against the principle that a man cannot be required to incriminate himself. I cannot accept that the judge made his order with this objective. The fact that an answer to an interrogatory may tend to incriminate the maker is no ground for disallowing the interrogatory; objection on this ground is to be taken in the answer (see the Supreme Court Practice 1979, vol 1, p 450, para 26/1/16 and cases therein cited). It will be open to the defendant to take objection on this ground *j* when he comes to swear his affidavit in this case, if he considers it in his best interests to do so. This is a very different case to *Rank Film Distributors Ltd v Video Information Centre* [1980] 2 All ER 273, [1980] 3 WLR 487 in which the defendants were ordered to give discovery and answer interrogatories backed by a penal order, and I see nothing to take it out of the general rule that it is for the defendant to take his objection on the grounds of self-incrimination when he swears his affidavit. But the question remains, was this

order properly made in aid of the Mareva injunction? Here I have the misfortune to
a differ from Stephenson and Ackner LJJ.
    The power to order a Mareva injunction is discretionary and it follows that the power
to order discovery as an ancillary order to the injunction must also be discretionary. This
court should only interfere with the exercise of the judge's discretion if satisfied that it
has been wrongly exercised; it is not sufficient that members of the court might not have
been disposed to exercise the discretion in a similar manner.
b   The judge was clearly dealing with a very evasive litigant. The affidavits he had put
before the court did not begin to make economic sense. Here was a man seeking leave
to take £25,000 a year out of the jurisdiction from the income produced by his assets, yet
swearing affidavits which revealed no assets capable of producing anything approaching
that sum, and at the same time telling the court that he had already reduced his assets by
£66,000 since the Mareva injunction was first granted. Furthermore the court had been
c misled as to his residence outside the jurisdiction at the hearing in March and he was now
seeking to justify the dissipation of his assets since April 1980 on a strained and, in my
view, clearly wrong construction of the undertaking he had given to the court at that
hearing.
    The judge was, in my opinion, fully justified in taking the view that the defendant's
affidavits as to his assets were so unsatisfactory that he was entitled to refuse to accept
d their contents at their face value and to order the defendant to make a full disclosure of
his financial position. It was a measure that I think was justified to enable the court and
the plaintiffs to identify the assets and to give the plaintiffs the opportunity to serve a
copy of the court's order on the bank or other holders of the assets or take such other steps
as they consider appropriate to ensure that the Mareva order did effectively bite on the
defendant's assets.
e   It is true that the judge might have used other measures to put pressure on the
defendant to induce him to reveal the true state of his finances. He could have ordered
him to come from Monte Carlo to be cross-examined on his affidavits, involving him in
considerable expense and inconvenience. He could have refused to allow him to continue
to take any income out of the jurisdiction for his living expenses in Monte Carlo. He
could have refused to allow him to draw money to pay his solicitors or accountants. The
f fact that these alternative courses were open to the judge does not appear to me to be any
reason why he should not order discovery if he considered that to be the more appropriate
course. It is not without significance that the plaintiffs did not ask the judge to consider
any of these alternatives. The plaintiffs are not concerned to punish the defendant or put
him to any unnecessary inconvenience; all they want is to be able to identify and protect
sufficient of the defendant's assets to satisfy the judgment they hope to obtain against
g him.
    I agree that the power to order discovery in support of a Mareva injunction should be
sparingly exercised and if too readily resorted to could easily become a most oppressive
procedure.
    I am sure that the judges in the Commercial Court have this well in mind. There
should be no question of an order for discovery becoming a usual part of the Mareva
h relief. However, for the reasons I have indicated I am of the opinion that the judge was
fully justified on the facts of this case in ordering this evasive defendant to give full
discovery. I would have dismissed the appeal.

STEPHENSON LJ. If the defendant is regarded with suspicion by the court, he has
only himself to blame. It is hard to conceive a more naked attempt to mislead the court
j than his filing of his wife's affidavit, and his own affidavits have understandably not
reduced but increased the suspicions which led Parker J to make the robust order under
appeal. I would be reluctant to quash a robust order thought necessary by a commercial
judge to make effective such a valuable weapon in the court's armoury as a Mareva
injunction.
    But a court of law can only do what it has power or jurisdiction to do. It is as
important that it should not exceed its powers to interfere in the lives of private citizens

and to compel them to make public what they may wish to keep private as that it should
use them to the full to protect and enforce private and public rights and restrain their *a*
destruction or infringement. Injustice comes from abuse of power, judicial power
included, as well as from failure to exercise it. Counsel for the defendant has submitted
powerful arguments that the judge had no power to order the discovery which he has
required the defendant to make. The courts have, many would say, stretched their
powers beyond what were long considered their limits in granting Mareva injunctions;
it would be an unlawful extension to add to a Mareva injunction an order for discovery, *b*
even if necessary to make it effective; the limits of the court's powers to grant
interlocutory remedies and relief, in particular discovery, are defined by statute and rules
made under statute; such discovery is outside the relevant statute and rules and can only
be derived from the court's inherent jurisdiction and that jurisdiction, he submits, is to
be found only in the authority of established practice and decided cases; there is no
established practice and no decided case, except a recent decision at first instance which *c*
the judge followed and we are asked to overrule.

The plaintiffs applied for this order under RSC Ord 24, r 7(1) and Ord 26, r 1(1). The
judge did not say what the power was under which he made the order; but he said that
their application was based on the decision in *A v C* [1980] 2 All ER 347, [1981] 2 WLR
629, which is the decision counsel for the defendant wishes us to overrule. In that case
Robert Goff J based his decision on s 45 of the Supreme Court of Judicature (Consolidation) *d*
Act 1925, as well as on those rules, and it may therefore be right to treat this order as
based on that section as well as on those rules. While contending for the plaintiffs that
it could rightly be based on either the Act or the rules, their counsel asked us to affirm
the judge's order primarily on the ground that it was within the court's inherent
jurisdiction.

I am not satisfied that either the Act or the rules give the court this power.   *e*

Section 45(1), replacing s 25(8) of the Supreme Court of Judicature Act 1873, provides:

'The High Court may grant a mandamus or an injunction or appoint a receiver
by an interlocutory order in all cases in which it appears to the court to be just or
convenient so to do.'
                                                                                        f
This order is not a mandamus. Certainly a mandamus in its context extends beyond
the prerogative remedy now obtainable on judicial review to an order to a public
authority to produce public documents for inspection, but it does not extend to every
mandatory order enforceable by committal, as are orders for discovery of documents and
for interrogatories by virtue of Ord 24, r 16(2) and (4), and Ord 26, r 6(2) and (4). Nor
is this order an injunction. It is an order in aid of an injunction, or ancillary or auxiliary *g*
to an injunction, whereby the court and the other party can ascertain whether there have
been breaches of the injunction and what and where the assets which are the subject of
the injunction are, so that they can be used to satisfy any judgment against the
defendant. It is not therefore, in my judgment, an order which the court is empowered
to make by s 45 unless indirectly and by implication.

Is it authorised by the Rules of the Supreme Court? Order 24, rr 1(11) and 2(1) are *h*
concerned with discovery of documents in an action and with matters in question in the
action. Order 24, rr 7(3), 11(2) and (3) and 12 and Ord 26, rr 1 and 2, are concerned with
parties to any cause or matter and with matters in question in the cause or matter. The
definitions of 'action', 'cause' and 'matter' in s 225(1) of the 1925 Act do not explain the
substitution but make it unimportant:

'"Action" means a civil proceeding commenced by writ or in such other manner *i*
as may be prescribed by rules of court, but it does not include a criminal proceeding
by the Crown ... "Cause" includes any action, suit or other original proceeding
between a plaintiff and defendant, and any criminal proceeding by the Crown ...
"Matter" includes every proceeding in court not in a cause ...'

As I read these definitions 'matters' are wide enough to include 'causes' and 'causes' to
a include 'actions'. But the judge's order was applied for and made in an action, the action
between the plaintiffs and the defendant and the matters (in a different sense) in question
between these parties to which discovery must relate are matters in issue in the action
between them. The matters in question in the Mareva injunction are not in issue in the
action. The plaintiffs do not have to prove the existence of assets of the defendant within
the jurisdiction and the risk of their being removed out of the jurisdiction in order to
b prove their case or obtain judgment; the plaintiffs want the injunction and discovery in
aid of it in order to preserve something out of which any judgment they may obtain on
proving their case can be executed and satisfied. That is the matter in question to which
this discovery relates.

I therefore reject counsel for the plaintiffs' submission that discovery relating to a
matter in question in an application for a Mareva injunction is discovery within Ord 24
c or Ord 26. The plaintiffs' application, though made under Ords 24 and 26, was not
supported by an affidavit as an application for further discovery is required to be by Ord
24, r 7(3). The requirements in Ord 24, rr 2(5), 8 and 13(1) and Ord 26, r 1(3) that
discovery or interrogatories must be necessary for disposing fairly of the action or of the
cause or matter are intended to restrict discovery and cannot be interpreted to extend it.

I am therefore of opinion that we can only affirm the judge's order on a ground on
d which he did not base it any more than Robert Goff J based his order on it in A v C,
namely the inherent jurisdiction of the court.

Counsel for the defendant has submitted that the court's inherent jurisdiction is very
limited. It has inherent jurisdiction in the four cases which can be derived from the
index to the Supreme Court Practice 1979 (vol 1, p 1768) and in no others. The first two
are its power to strike out or stay proceedings which are frivolous or vexatious or an
e abuse of its process, two aspects of a jurisdiction now recognised by Ord 18, r 19 and s 41
of the 1925 Act respectively. The third is the power to join other persons to proceedings
between parties before it, a jurisdiction recognised by Ord 15, r 6(2). And the fourth is
the recently assumed power to make preservation and inspection orders under Ord 29,
r 2, ex parte in cases of emergency: see *EMI Ltd v Pandit* [1975] 1 All ER 418, [1975] 1
WLR 302 and *Anton Piller KG v Manufacturing Processes Ltd* [1976] 1 All ER 779, [1976]
f Ch 55. But these are, except the last, powers recognised as appertaining to the courts of
Chancery or common law before the Supreme Court of Judicature Acts 1873 and 1875,
and the Anton Piller injunction is merely an exercise ex parte of an old power,
comparable perhaps with the extension made by the Mareva injunction but certainly not
with the addition made by the judge's order for discovery.

It is, however, significant that those curious enough to consult the index to the
g Supreme Court Practice 1976 (vol 1, p 1728) would find there only a reference to the first
two instances of inherent jurisdiction, and the additional references in the 1979 edition
would indicate that the court's inherent jurisdiction may be an uncertain expression
loosely used and signifying a discretionary power which may be developed to meet
circumstances not known to nineteenth century judges.

Such authorities as *China Transpacific Steamship Co v Commercial Union Assurance Co*
h (1881) 8 QBD 142, *Hunnings v Williamson* (1883) 10 QBD 459, *North London Railway Co
v Great Northern Railway Co* (1883) 11 QBD 30 and *Re Wickham, Marony v Taylor* (1887)
35 Ch D 272 clearly show what, a hundred years ago, judges of the newly constituted
Court of Appeal understood to be the effect of the Judicature Acts and the rules made
thereunder; the Rules of the Supreme Court did not cover every matter or define the
jurisdiction of the Supreme Court completely, but that jurisdiction remained what it was
j in the hands of the courts of Chancery and common law before the Acts and rules; what
they could do was neither cut down nor extended thereby. How far those authorities
imprison the courts a century later or fossilize their practice is a question which cannot
be answered without considering the *Anton Piller* and *Mareva* lines of cases. But the
House of Lords has reiterated the old requirement that injunctions must protect a legal
or equitable right, a substantive cause of action in law or equity, in *The Siskina* [1977] 3

All ER 803, [1979] AC 210 and even more recently in *Bremer Vulkan Schiffbau Und Maschinenfabrik v South India Shipping Corpn* [1981] 1 All ER 289, [1981] 2 WLR 141. *a* Somehow the Mareva injunction must be considered to come within this pre-Judicature Acts restriction, and so the *A v C* ancillary order for discovery could also come within it. In my judgment a judge has the duty to prevent his court being misused as far as the law allows, but the means by which he can perform that duty are limited by the authority of Parliament, of the rules of his court and of decided cases. Those means do, however, include what is reasonably necessary to effectively performing a judge's duties and *b* exercising his powers. In doing what appears to him just or convenient he cannot overstep their lawfully authorised limits, but he can do what makes their performance and exercise effective. He has a judicial discretion to implement a lawful order by ancillary orders obviously required for their efficacy, even though not previously made or expressly authorised. This implied jurisdiction, inherent because implicit in powers already recognised and exercised, and so different from any general or residual inherent *c* jurisdiction, is hard to define and is to be assumed with caution. But to deny this kind of inherent jurisdiction altogether would be to refuse to judges incidental powers recognised as inherent or implicit in statutory powers granted to public authorities, to shorten the arm of justice and to diminish the value of the courts.

Whether the court has inherent or implied power to grant a Mareva injunction in its ordinary form of restraining a defendant from removing his assets outside the jurisdiction *d* or disposing of them within the jurisdiction is no longer an open question in this court, and it has received recognition in cl 37 of the Supreme Court Bill now before Parliament. There is no statute directly conferring it, like s 37 of the Matrimonial Causes Act 1973. So it must be presumed to have been within s 45 of the 1925 Act, its express words or by necessary implication. Whether the court has such power to make such an order for discovery in aid of such an injunction as was made by Robert Goff J in *A v C* is *e* still, however, an open question in this court, because although it has twice been accepted in this court, in neither case was its validity challenged in argument and I was wrong to imply in the latter case that it had been approved in the former: see *Bankers Trust Co v Shapira* [1980] 3 All ER 353, [1980] 1 WLR 1274 and *Smith v Hegard* [1980] Court of Appeal Transcript 603 decided by a court consisting of Ackner LJ and myself on 7th August 1980. I was also wrong to describe Robert Goff J's order in *A v C* in aid of a *f* Mareva injunction as an Anton Piller order: it was an order for discovery and inspection inter partes which purported to be made under s 45 of the 1925 Act (rightly) and under RSC Ords 24 and 26 (wrongly), but not under Ord 29, r 2 as was Stocker J's order under appeal in *Smith v Hegard*. That order we set aside as an unjustified 'fishing' attempt to restore and 'police' a Mareva injunction, which had been discharged, by discovery of dealings within the jurisdiction, to reveal breaches of such a non-existent injunction, or *g* of an undertaking which had been offered but refused, and to secure a form of attachment against a potential judgment debtor which should have been obtained, if at all, by conditional leave to defend in Ord 14 proceedings. It was a wrong exercise of jurisdiction, whether or not the judge had it, to pile Piller on Mareva in the circumstances of that case.

In that case both members of this court approved but distinguished Robert Goff J's *h* decision in *A v C* as necessary to the proper and effective exercise of the Mareva jurisdiction for the reason (it may have been the second reason) that he gave, which Ackner LJ has read (see [1980] 2 All ER 347 at 352, [1981] 2 WLR 629 at 634), namely that the case involved a number of defendants and it was necessary to know the amount standing in their accounts with the identified bank so as to exclude from the restriction of the overall injunction any account or accounts providing moneys exceeding the *j* amount of the plaintiff's claim.

Parker J described the plaintiffs' application and his order for discovery as in aid or support of the Mareva injunction and so in a sense they were. But in so far as they relate to the defendant's assets at past dates as distinct from their present whereabouts their purpose seems to be not so much to help the court or the defendant to locate and 'freeze'

particular assets now as to open the way to incriminating and ultimately punishing the
a defendant for contempt of court in formerly disobeying the Mareva injunction and/or
breaking his undertaking. This purpose emerges not only from the wide terms of the
order but from the judge's comments at the end of his judgment. To that extent the
order goes beyond the legitimate purpose of an order for discovery in aid of a Mareva
injunction and Robert Goff J's order in *A v C* and is not necessary for the proper and
effective exercise of the Mareva injunction.

b   It was, however, the defendant himself who first made and invited discovery by giving
the court information (which was obviously incomplete and evasive) about his assets in
his affidavit of 16th April 1980 in support of his application to vary the Mareva
injunction. It was that imperfect discovery which led the plaintiffs to apply for the
further discovery ordered by Parker J and to the defendant giving further discovery (still
imperfect) by his affidavits of 1st and 14th November 1980. Why, matters having gone
c thus far without apparent objection by the defendant, should they not be pursued to the
point of completion required by the judge's order?

In my judgment they have gone far enough in aid of the Mareva injunction and
should be pursued or completed, if desired, by cross-examination on the defendant's
existing affidavits, not as the judge indicated on a further affidavit. The defendant has
already been warned by the judge that he may possibly be in contempt of court, but on
d the authorities cited by Ackner LJ that is no reason for not ordering him to attend for
cross-examination under Ord 38, r 2(3), though it may enable him to refuse to answer
questions put to him in cross-examination. And he is, in my opinion, liable to be
deprived of the right given him by the order of 18th April 1980 to take income or
possessions out of the jurisdiction unless and until he makes full and proper disclosure of
his assets. The judge had jurisdiction to order discovery but exceeded his powers by
e making the order for discovery under appeal.

For these reasons I feel bound to differ with some hesitation from Parker J's order,
particularly as it has been so cogently supported by Griffiths LJ, and to concur with the
order proposed by Ackner LJ that the appeal be allowed and with, in substance, all the
reasons he gives for that conclusion.

f *Appeal allowed.*

*25th February. Parker J in chambers made an order for the cross-examination of the defendant
on his affidavits on a date to be fixed. Leave to appeal against that order was refused.*

*6th March. The Court of Appeal (Stephenson and Ackner LJJ) dismissed an application by the
defendant for leave to appeal against Parker J's order of 25th February 1981.*

Solicitors: *Harbottle & Lewis* (for the defendant); *Coward Chance* (for the plaintiffs).

Patricia Hargrove   Barrister.

London Borough of Hammersmith and Fulham v Harrison and other appeals

a

COURT OF APPEAL, CIVIL DIVISION
WALLER, BRANDON LJJ AND SIR DAVID CAIRNS
9th, 10th, 11th, 15th DECEMBER 1980, 21st JANUARY 1981

b

Housing – Local authority houses – Possession – Notice to quit dwelling house expiring before provisions giving security of tenure to council tenants coming into force – Action for possession commenced before provisions coming into force – Whether provisions giving security of tenure retrospective – Whether tenant entitled to protection of security of tenure provisions – Whether tenant having a licence from local authority to occupy premises if remaining in occupation after expiry of notice to quit – Housing Act 1980, ss 28(1), 33(1), 34(1), 48(1).

c

In three separate cases local authorities served valid notices to quit on tenants of council flats which were let on periodic tenancies. The notices expired and the authorities commenced actions for possession prior to 3rd October 1980, which was the date the provisions of the Housing Act 1980 giving security of tenure to public sector tenants came into force. Judgment in each action was given after that date. In the first action the judge in the county court gave judgment for possession on the ground that the relevant provisions of the 1980 Act were not retrospective and the tenancy had been validly determined and the action for possession commenced before the security of tenure provisions came into force. The tenant appealed against that decision. In the second action the judge dismissed the claim for possession on the ground that the tenant's occupation of the flat was protected by the 1980 Act. The local authority appealed against that decision. In the third action the judge decided on a preliminary issue that the local authority's particulars of claim disclosed a cause of action. The tenant appealed against that decision. On each appeal the local authority submitted that since the relevant tenancy had been determined by a notice to quit before the date on which the action for possession was begun, and a fortiori before determination of the action, there was not at those dates a tenancy under which a dwelling house 'is let' within s 28(1)[a] of the 1980 Act, and therefore the flats were not 'let under a secure tenancy' for the purposes of s 33(1)[b] or s 34(1)[c] of that Act. The tenants submitted that the security of tenure provisions in the 1980 Act were analogous to the security of tenure provisions in the Rent Acts of 1920 and 1949 (ie the Rent and Mortgage Interest Restrictions Acts 1920 to 1939 and the Landlord and Tenant (Rent Control) Act 1949) and were similarly to be construed retrospectively to cover former tenants who had remained in possession after the expiry of valid notices to quit before 3rd October 1980.

d

e

f

g

Held – The Rent Acts of 1920 and 1949 and the 1980 Act were not in pari materia, and on the ordinary and natural meaning of s 28(1) of the 1980 Act a tenancy was a secure tenancy within s 28(1) only if the dwelling house was let on or after the coming into force of the security of tenure provisions in the 1980 Act on 3rd October 1980, and similarly, on the ordinary and natural meaning of the expression 'let under a secure tenancy' in ss 33(1) and 34(1) of the 1980 Act, a tenancy was let under a secure tenancy only if the dwelling house was so let for the purposes of s 33(1) at the date of commencement of the action for possession or for the purposes of s 34(1) at the date of the decision whether to make an order for possession. Since such a construction did not give retrospective effect

h

j

---

a   Section 28(1), so far as material, is set out at p 591 *f*, post
b   Section 33(1) is set out at p 592 *c*, post
c   Section 34(1), so far as material is set out at p 592 *e*, post

to the security of tenure provisions in the 1980 Act, the tenants were not entitled to the
a protection of the 1980 Act. Accordingly, the appeals of the tenants in the first and third
actions would be dismissed and the appeal of the local authority in second action would
be allowed (see p 596 *j*, p 597 *b* to *g* and *j* to p 598 *j*, p 599 *d e*, p 600 *j* to p 601 *a* and *f* to
p 602 *a*, post).

Remon v City of London Real Property Co Ltd [1921] 1 KB 49 and Hutchinson v Jauncey
[1950] 1 All ER 165 distinguished.

b   Per Curiam. Where a council tenant stays on in council premises after the expiry of
a notice to quit before 3rd October 1980 because the authority cannot evict him without
a court order, it cannot be inferred that the local authority, by allowing him to stay on
until the action for possession is determined, is thereby impliedly granting him a licence
to occupy the premises within s 48(1)^d of the 1980 Act. In such circumstances the tenant
might have a statutory licence but that does not make the local authority a licensor
c within s 48(1) (see p 599 *a* to *d* and p 601 *g h*, post).

Notes
For the retrospective effect of statutes, see 36 Halsbury's Laws (3rd Edn) 423–426, paras
643–646.

d **Cases referred to in judgments**
Athlumney, Re, ex parte Wilson [1898] 2 QB 547, [1895–9] All ER Rep 329, 67 LJQB 935,
5 Mans 322, 79 LT 303, 44 Digest (Repl) 294, *1243*.
Hutchinson v Jauncey [1950] 1 All ER 165, [1950] 1 KB 574, CA, 44 Digest (Repl) 299,
1295.
Jonas v Rosenberg [1950] 1 All ER 296, [1950] 2 KB 52, CA, 44 Digest (Repl) 299, *1296*.
e Neale v Del Soto [1945] 1 All ER 191, [1945] 1 KB 144, 114 LJKB 138, 172 LT 65, CA,
31(2) Digest (Reissue) 1009, *8025*.
Remon v City of London Real Property Co Ltd [1921] 1 KB 49, 89 LJKB 1105, 123 LT 617,
18 LGR 691, 84 JP Jo 349, CA, 31(2) Digest (Reissue) 1025, *8123*.

Cases also cited
f American Economic Laundry Ltd v Little [1950] 2 All ER 1186, [1951] 1 KB 400, CA.
Dobson v Richards (1919) 63 Sol Jo 663, NP.
McPhail v persons, names unknown [1973] 3 All ER 393, [1973] Ch 447, CA.
National Real Estate & Finance Co Ltd v Hassan [1939] 2 All ER 154, [1939] 2 KB 61, CA.
Thomas v Sorrell (1673) Vaugh 330, [1558–1774] All ER Rep 107, Ex Ch.
Welby v Parker [1916] 2 Ch 1, CA.
g
Appeals

London Borough of Hammersmith and Fulham v Harrison

The defendant, George Harrison, appealed against the order of his Honour Judge Stucley
dated 13th October 1980 made in the West London County Court adjudging that the
plaintiff, the London Borough of Hammersmith and Fulham, recover possession of
h premises known as 81 Brackenbury Road, London W6 from Mr Harrison. The ground
of the possession order was that as the notice to quit served on Mr Harrison by the
Council had expired before the action for possession was begun, Mr Harrison's tenancy
had been validly determined and Part I, Chapter II of the Housing Act 1980, which came
into operation after the action was begun, could not be invoked by Mr Harrison
retrospectively. The facts are set out in the judgment of Brandon LJ.
j
London Borough of Haringey v Mosner

The plaintiff, the London Borough of Haringey, appealed against the order of his Honour
Judge Tibber made on 28th October 1980 in the Edmonton County Court dismissing the

d Section 48(1) is set out at p 592 *f g*, post

plaintiff's claim for possession of premises known as 206 The Sandlings, Pelham Road, London N22, against the defendant, Mrs Ellen Mosner, on the ground that **a** notwithstanding the expiry of a notice to quit the premises, and the commencement of the proceedings for possession, prior to Part I, Chapter II of the Housing Act 1980 coming into operation, Mrs Mosner's tenancy was protected by that part of the 1980 Act. The facts are set out in the judgment of Brandon LJ.

London Borough of Hackney v Watson   **b**

The defendant, Mrs Jennie Watson, appealed against the order of his Honour Judge Willis made on 10th October 1980 in the Shoreditch County Court declaring, on a preliminary point of law in the trial of the action by the plaintiff, the London Borough of Hackney, for possession of premises known as 50 Corbiere House, Balmes Road, London N1, that the particulars of claim disclosed a cause of action on the ground that the provisions of Part I, Chapter II of the Housing Act 1980 which came into operation **c** after the commencement of the action did not apply to the action. The facts are set out in the judgment of Brandon LJ.

Andrew Bano for Mr Harrison.
Andrew Arden for Mrs Mosner and Mrs Watson.
Colin Braham for the London Borough of Hammersmith and Fulham.   **d**
Simon Goldblatt QC and *Anna Worrall* for the London Boroughs of Haringey and Hackney.

Cur adv vult

21st January. The following judgments were read.   **e**

BRANDON LJ (delivering the first judgment at the invitation of Waller LJ). The court has before it three appeals from the decisions of three different county court judges in possession actions brought by local authority landlords against persons who were in any case formerly, and claim still to be, council tenants. The three appeals raise the same question on the construction of those provisions of the Housing Act 1980 ('the 1980 Act') **f** which relate to security of tenure for public sector tenants and have accordingly been heard together.

Taking the actions in the order in which they were begun, the first action is one brought by the London Borough of Hammersmith and Fulham as plaintiff against George Harrison as defendant in respect of a flat known as Hall Floor, 81 Brackenbury Road, Hammersmith, London W6. The flat had been let by the plaintiff to the defendant **g** on 28th June 1976 on a weekly tenancy and the current rent for it was £11·66. On 23rd June 1980 the plaintiff served on the defendant notice to quit the flat on 21st July 1980. The defendant did not comply with the notice and on 5th August 1980 the plaintiff began an action in the West London County Court to recover possession of the flat. On 13th October 1980 his Honour Judge Stucley gave judgment for the plaintiff, ordering the defendant to give up possession on 10th November 1980. By notice of **h** appeal dated 30th October 1980 the defendant appealed against that decision.

The second action is one brought by the Mayor and Burgesses of the London Borough of Haringey as plaintiffs against Ellen Mosner as defendant in respect of a flat known as 206 The Sandlings, Pelham Road, London N22. The flat had been let by the plaintiffs to the defendant on 9th April 1979 and the current rent for it was £13·88. On 7th June 1980 the plaintiffs served on the defendant notice to quit the flat on 7th July 1980. The **j** defendant did not comply with that notice and on 29th August 1980 the plaintiff began an action in the Edmonton County Court to recover possession of the flat. On 28th October 1980 his Honour Judge Tibber dismissed the action. By notice of appeal dated 21st November 1980 the plaintiffs appealed against that decision.

The third action is one brought by the Mayor and Burgesses of the London Borough

of Hackney as plaintiffs against Jennie Watson as defendant in respect of a flat known as
a 50 Corbiere House, Balmes Road, London N1. The flat had been let by the plaintiffs to
the defendant on a weekly tenancy and the current rent payable for it was £19·08. On
5th June 1980 the plaintiffs served on the defendant notice to quit the flat on 7th July
1980. The defendant did not comply with the notice and on 12th September 1980 the
plaintiffs began an action in the Shoreditch County Court to recover possession of the
flat. On 15th October 1980 his Honour Judge Willis tried a preliminary issue in the
b action, whether, having regard to the provisions of the 1980 Act, the particulars of claim
disclosed any cause of action, and decided that issue in favour of the plaintiffs, giving
leave to appeal. By notice of appeal dated 21st October 1980 the defendant appealed
against that decision.

The 1980 Act was passed on 8th August 1980. The provisions relating to security of
tenure for public sector tenants are contained in Chapter II of Part I of the Act. Section
c 153(2) provided that Chapter II of Part I should come into operation on such day as the
Secretary of State might by order appoint or, if no such order should have been made, on
the expiry of the period of eight weeks beginning with the day on which the Act was
passed. No order was made by the Secretary of State for the coming into operation of
Chapter II of Part I, and that chapter accordingly came into operation eight weeks after
the passing of the Act, that is to say on 3rd October 1980.

d The question of law raised by the three appeals can therefore be formulated as follows:
where a local authority landlord has (a) brought a tenant's periodic tenancy to an end by
service and expiry of a valid notice to quit, and (b) subsequently begun, but not yet
obtained judgment in, a possession action against the tenant, all before 3rd October 1980,
when the provisions of the 1980 Act relating to security of tenure for public sector
tenants came into operation, can the tenant rely on those provisions as a defence to the
e action?

In the three cases now on appeal before us, two of the county court judges concerned
have answered that question of law in the negative, while the third has answered it in the
affirmative.

The sections of Chapter II of Part I of the 1980 Act relating to security of tenure for
public sector tenants provide, so far as material, as follows:
f

'**28.**—(1) A tenancy under which a dwelling-house is let as a separate dwelling is
a secure tenancy at any time when the conditions described below as the landlord
condition and the tenant condition are satisfied . . .

'(2) The landlord condition is that—(a) the interest of the landlord belongs to one
of the bodies mentioned in subsection (4) below . . .
g '(3) The tenant condition is that the tenant is an individual and occupies the
dwelling-house as his only or principal home . . .

'(4) The bodies referred to in subsection 2(a) above are—(a) a local authority . . .

'**29.**—(1) Where a secure tenancy (in this section referred to as "the first tenancy")
is a tenancy for a term certain and comes to an end by effluxion of time or by an
order under section 32(2) below, a periodic tenancy of the same dwelling-house
h arises by virtue of this section unless the tenant is granted another secure tenancy of
the same dwelling-house (whether a tenancy for a term certain or a periodic tenancy)
to begin on the coming to an end of the first tenancy.

'(2) Where a periodic tenancy arises by virtue of this section—(a) the periods of
that tenancy are the same as those for which rent was last payable under the first
tenancy; and (b) the parties and the terms of the tenancy are the same as those of the
j first tenancy at the end of it; except that the terms are confined to those which are
compatible with a periodic tenancy and do not include any provision for re-entry or
forfeiture.

'**32.**—(1) A secure tenancy which is either—(a) a weekly or other periodic
tenancy; or (b) a tenancy for a term certain but subject to termination by the
landlord; cannot be brought to an end by the landlord except by obtaining an order

of the court for the possession of the dwelling-house or an order under subsection (2) below; and where the landlord obtains an order for the possession of the dwelling-house the tenancy ends on the date on which the tenant is to give up possession in pursuance of the order.

'(2) Where a secure tenancy is a tenancy for a term certain but with a provision for re-entry or forfeiture, the court shall not order possession of the dwelling-house in pursuance of that provision; but in any case where, but for this section, the court would have made such an order, it shall instead make an order terminating the secure tenancy on a date specified in the order.

'(3) Section 146 of the Law of Property Act 1925 (restriction on and relief against forfeiture) . . . and any other enactment or rule of law relating to forfeiture shall apply in relation to proceedings for an order under subsection (2) above as if they were proceedings to enforce a right of re-entry or forfeiture.

'**33.**—(1) The court shall not entertain proceedings for the possession of a dwelling-house let under a secure tenancy, unless the landlord has served on the tenant a notice complying with the provisions of this section and, if the tenancy is a periodic tenancy—(a) the proceedings are begun after the date specified in the notice; and (b) the notice is still in force at the time the proceedings are begun.

'(2) A notice under this section must be in a form prescribed by regulations made by the Secretary of State and must specify the ground on which the court will be asked to make an order for the possession of the dwelling-house or for the termination of the tenancy and give particulars of that ground.

'(3) If the secure tenancy is a periodic tenancy the notice—(a) must also specify a date after which proceedings for the possession of the dwelling-house may be begun; and (b) ceases to be in force twelve months after the date specified in it; and the date specified in it must not be earlier than the date on which the tenancy could, apart from this Act, be brought to an end by notice to quit given by the landlord if the notice to quit were given on the same date as the notice under this section . . .

'**34.**—(1) The court shall not make an order for possession of a dwelling-house let under a secure tenancy except on one or more of the grounds set out in Part I of Schedule 4 to this Act . . .

'**47.**—This Chapter applies to tenancies granted before as well as tenancies granted after the commencement of this Chapter.

'**48.**—(1) Where a person who is not the tenant of a dwelling-house has a licence (whether or not granted for a consideration) to occupy the dwelling-house and the circumstances are such that, if the licence were a tenancy, it would be a secure tenancy, then, subject to subsection (2) below, this Part of this Act applies to the licence as it applies to a secure tenancy, and, as so applying has effect as if expressions appropriate to a licence were substituted for "landlord", "tenant", "tenancy" and "secure tenancy".

'(2) Subsection (1) above does not apply to a licence which was granted as a temporary expedient to a person who entered the dwelling-house or any other land as a trespasser (whether or not before the grant another licence to occupy that or another dwelling-house has been granted to him).

'**50.**—(1) In this Chapter . . . "local authority" means . . . the council of a London borough . . .

'(2) For the purposes of this Chapter—(a) a dwelling-house may be a house or part of a house . . .'

In connection with s 33(2) above, para 62 of Part II of Sch 25 to the 1980 Act (entitled 'Transitional Provisions and Savings') provides:

'For the purposes of section 33 of this Act a notice served at any time after regulations are first made for the purposes of subsection (2) of that section, but before the commencement of that section shall be treated as duly served under that

a

section if it would have been so treated had Chapter II of Part I of this Act then been in force.'

The Secretary of State availed himself of the power conferred on him by para 62 of Part II of Sch 25 above by making, in advance of the coming into operation of Chapter II of Part I, anticipatory regulations of the kind authorised by that paragraph. These regulations are contained in the Secure Tenancies (Notices) Regulations 1980, SI 1980 No

b 1339. They were made on 4th September and came into operation on 5th September 1980. The latter date was 28 days before 3rd October 1980, when Chapter II of Part I came into operation, and the inevitable inference is that the Secretary of State was of the opinion that, if a notice in the form prescribed by those regulations was served on the first day on which they came into operation, it would be an effective notice for the purpose of any action brought 28 days later when the restrictions relating to the

c entertainment by the court of actions for possession of dwelling houses let on secure tenancies first came into operation.

The following matters were not in dispute. First, that by virtue of the definition of the expression 'dwelling-house' contained in s 50(2)(a), all the flats concerned in these three appeals were dwelling houses for the purposes of ss 28, 29, 33 and 34 of the 1980 Act. Second, that prior to the termination, by the service and expiry of notices to quit, of the

d tenancies of the three flats concerned, the conditions prescribed in s 28 (2) (3) as the landlord condition and the tenant condition respectively were satisfied. Third, that none of the three local authority landlords concerned had served on their tenants notices of the kind required by s 33 in the form prescribed by the Secure Tenancies (Notices) Regulations 1980. Fourth, that none of the three local authority landlords concerned had based their claims to possession on any of the grounds specified in Part I of Sch 4 to

e the 1980 Act, whether they would have been able to do so or not. On the contrary, they based such claims, and based them solely, on the service on their respective tenants of notices to quit in the ordinary form, which had expired before their respective actions were begun.

It follows from those matters that, if at the dates when the actions for possession were begun, or the dates on which such actions were heard and adjudicated on, or both, the

f flats concerned were 'let under a secure tenancy' within the meaning of that expression as used in ss 33(1) and 34(1), the landlords' claims for possession must fail and be dismissed. This is because s 33(1) prohibits the court from entertaining proceedings for the possession of a dwelling house let under a secure tenancy unless the landlord has previously served on the tenant a notice of the kind required by s 33(2), that is to say a notice in the form prescribed by the Secure Tenancies (Notices) Regulations 1980; and

g s 34(1) further prohibits the court from making an order for the possession of a dwelling house let under a secure tenancy except on one or more of the grounds set out in Part I of Sch 4.

For the local authority landlords it was contended that since valid notices to quit had been served in each case, and had expired before the date on which the relevant action for possession had been begun, and a fortiori before the date on which such action had been

h heard and adjudicated on, it was impossible to say that, at either of these two dates, which were the material dates for the purposes of ss 33 and 34, the flats concerned were let by the landlords to the tenants at all, let alone that they were let to them on secure tenancies.

In support of this contention much reliance was very properly placed on the use of the present tense in the expression 'is let' in the first line of s 28(1), the section in which the nature and characteristics of a secure tenancy are defined and explained.

j In view of the use of the expression 'is let' in s 28(1), it was the duty of the court, it was said, so far as s 33(1) is concerned, to ask itself this simple question as at the date on which each of the three actions for possession was begun: is this flat presently let by the landlords to the tenant at all? And the answer to that simple question which the court would be bound to give itself, having regard to the prior service and expiry of a valid notice to quit, would be: 'No, the flat was formerly let by the landlords to the tenant, but it is no longer presently so let.' Similarly, so far as s 34(1) is concerned, it was the duty of the court to ask itself the same simple question as at the date on which the action was heard and adjudicated on, and the answer which the court would be bound to give itself would be the same.

These contentions are based on the ordinary and natural meaning of the words used in ss 28, 33 and 34, and, as such, must necessarily carry great force. The result of the contentions, if correct, is that, since in each of the three cases concerned the relationship of landlord and tenant had been brought to an end before the relevant action for possession was begun, the defendant who had ceased to be a tenant had no defence to the claim, and the court was bound to make the order for possession sought.

For the tenants it was not disputed that the expression 'let under a secure tenancy' as used in ss 33(1) and 34(1), included the meaning contended for by the local authority landlords. It was, however, contended that the expression as so used was an elastic one which included also the extended meaning 'was previously, prior to the service and expiry of any otherwise valid notice to quit, let under a secure tenancy as defined and explained in section 28'. In support of this contention, reliance was placed on a series of authorities on certain of the earlier Rent Acts, with which it was said that Chapter II of Part I of the 1980 Act was in pari materia, and in conformity with which it was said that questions of construction on analogous provisions in the 1980 Act should be decided.

The first, and by far the most important of the authorities relied on, was *Remon v City of London Real Property Co Ltd* [1921] 1 KB 49. In that case the defendants had in December 1915 let to the plaintiff two rooms for business purposes. In February 1920 the defendants gave the plaintiff a valid notice to quit expiring on 24th June 1920. The plaintiff did not comply with the notice, nor with a solicitor's letter requiring him to give up possession immediately. On 2nd July 1920 the Increase of Rent and Mortgage Interest (Restrictions) Act 1920 came into operation. On the same day, after the plaintiff had finished work, and had locked up the premises and gone home, the defendants took advantage of his absence to have the locks broken and take possession. The plaintiff then brought an action against the defendants in the High Court in which, relying on the protection given to him by the 1920 Act, he claimed an injunction restraining the defendants from interfering with his possession.

The relevant provisions of the 1920 Act were these. By s 12(2), the Act applied to any house or part of a house 'let as a separate dwelling', subject to certain specified limits with regard to the annual amount of the standard rent or the rateable value. By s 5(1), no order or judgment for the recovery of possession of any dwelling house to which the Act applied, or for the ejectment of a tenant therefrom, was to be made or given, except in a number of specified circumstances. By s 15(1) a tenant who, by virtue of the provisions of the Act, retained possession of any dwelling house to which the Act applied, was, so long as he retained possession, to observe and be entitled to the benefit of all the terms and conditions of the original contract of tenancy, so far as the same were consistent with the provisions of the Act. By s 13(1) the Act applied also, subject to certain modifications which are not material, to premises used for business purposes.

It was not in dispute that the Act applied to the premises which had been occupied by the plaintiff, nor did the defendants suggest that there existed any of the various circumstances specified in s 5(1) which would have entitled the court to make an order for possession against the plaintiff.

McCardie J, treating by agreement a summons in chambers by the plaintiff for an interlocutory injunction as the hearing of the action without prejudice to an appeal, held that the plaintiff was entitled to the protection of the 1920 Act and granted him the injunction which he sought. On an appeal by the defendants to the Court of Appeal, consisting of Bankes, Scrutton and Atkin LJJ, the plaintiff's right to the injunction was upheld. The decision of the Court of Appeal is summarised in the headnote as follows (at 49):

'*Held*, that although the agreement of tenancy had come to an end by the notice to quit, the rooms were "let" within the meaning of s. 12, sub-s. 2, and the plaintiff

was a tenant who by virtue of the provisions of the Act retained possession within
a the meaning of s. 15, sub-s. 1, of the Act and the landlords could not lawfully disturb
him in his possession.'

The reasoning of the court appears from the judgments of Bankes and Scrutton LJJ,
with which Atkin LJ agreed. Bankes LJ said (at 54):

'In no ordinary sense of the word was the respondent a tenant of the premises on
b July 2. His term had expired. His landlords had endeavoured to get him out. He
was not even a tenant at sufferance. It is however clear that in all the Rent
Restriction Acts the expression "tenant" has been used in a special, a peculiar sense,
and as including a person who might be described as an ex-tenant, some one whose
occupation had commenced as tenant and who had continued in occupation without
any legal right to do so except possibly such as the Acts themselves conferred upon
c him. The respondent therefore on the coming into operation of the new Act was
a tenant within the meaning of that expression in the Act, and as the Act for the first
time included business premises within its protection, the premises were not
excluded on the ground that they were business premises only.'

Later, dealing with the expression 'let' in s 12(2), Bankes LJ said (at 56):

d 'I have already explained the meaning which must necessarily be given to the
expression "tenant" as used in the Act. I consider that a similar construction must
be placed upon the expression "let" in s. 12, sub-s. 2. The sub-section cannot be
confined to premises in respect of which a letting is in existence at the time when
the protection of the Act is claimed. The expression must be read as sufficiently
elastic to include the letting under which the tenant who claims the protection of
e the Act became tenant.'

Scrutton LJ said (at 58):

'Whom did they mean to include in the term "tenant"? If a tenant by agreement
whose tenancy had expired was not within those terms, the whole purpose of the
Act would have been defeated, for it was obviously intended to allow former tenants
f who were willing to carry out the terms of their old tenancy, as modified by any
permissible statutory increases of rent, to stay on. If this was not so every weekly or
monthly tenant, the small tenant for whose benefit the Acts were obviously framed,
was outside the Act. Unless "tenant" includes a former tenant by agreement holding
over against the will of the landlord, and "letting" includes the landlord's relation to
such a tenant, the whole object of the Acts is defeated.'

g Then, after saying that the persons under consideration could not properly be described
as tenants at sufferance, he continued on the same page:

'Yet I think it is clear Parliament has intended to confirm these people in a
statutory tenancy and to speak of their position as a "letting".'

Finally, dealing with the argument that the words of the Act should be given their
h ordinary and natural meaning, Scrutton LJ said (at 59):

'. . . I feel that I am straining language in speaking of a person whose tenancy has
expired, and who stays in against the active protest of the landlord, as a "tenant," and
of the landlord's relation to him as a "letting"; but such a person appears to be within
the clear intention of the Legislature . . .'

j The second authority relied on for the tenants was *Hutchinson v Jauncey* [1950] 1 All ER
165, [1950] 1 KB 574. In that case the tenant of a house within the protection of the Rent
Acts had sublet two rooms in it, sharing the use of the scullery for cooking with a
subtenant. Later the subtenant purchased the house subject to the tenancy, and in his
capacity as landlord served on the tenant notice to quit expiring on 25th April 1949. The
tenant failed to comply with the notice and on 25th May 1949 the landlord began an

action in the Edmonton County Court claiming possession. As the law stood before the coming into operation of the Landlord and Tenant (Rent Control) Act 1949, a tenancy *a* which involved the sharing of part of the accommodation let to a tenant with a subtenant was not within the protection of the Rent Acts.

On 2nd June 1949, however, the 1949 Act came into operation, and by s 9 extended the protection of the Rent Acts to tenancies involving sharing of this kind. The action came on for hearing in the county court on 22nd June 1949, and the question arose whether the change in the law effected by the 1949 Act was of such retrospective effect *b* as to give the tenant a good defence to the action. It was held by the Court of Appeal, consisting of Evershed MR and Cohen and Asquith LJJ, that the law applicable was that in force at the date of the hearing, rather than that which had been in force at the date of the expiry of the notice to quit or the commencement of the action, and that the county court judge accordingly had no jurisdiction to make an order for possession against the tenant. *c*

The court accepted the general rule that a statute should not, in the absence of express provision, be construed as depriving persons of accrued rights. They considered, however, on the authority of *Remon's* case, that the Rent Acts, in so far as they provided tenants with protection, or additional protection, against eviction, constituted an exception to that general rule. In this connection Evershed MR said ([1950] 1 All ER 165 at 168, [1950] 1 KB 574 at 579): *d*

'The question, therefore, is: Since a summons had been issued before the Act came into force, did the landlord acquire rights pursuant to the law as it stood under the decision in *Neale v. Del Soto* ([1945] 1 All ER 191, [1945] KB 144), and are those rights unaffected by either the express language or by the necessary implication to be drawn by ss. 9 and 10 of the Landlord and Tenant (Rent Control) Act, 1949? Apart from *Remon v. City of London Real Property Co.* I think the point might have *e* been one of serious difficulty, and I do not think that it is an easy one now, but that case seems to me to have laid down the application of a principle to this class of legislation generally, and I think, therefore, that citations from authorities relating to wholly different subject-matters may not be so pertinent to cases of this character.'

The third authority relied on for the tenants was *Jonas v Rosenberg* [1950] 1 All ER 296, *f* [1950] 2 KB 52. That case raised, in substance, the same question as *Hutchinson v Jauncey* had raised with regard to the retrospective effect of s 9 of the 1949 Act in relation to a tenancy involving the sharing of accommodation between a tenant and a subtenant. The only potentially significant difference between the two cases was that in *Jonas v Rosenberg* the hearing of the landlord's action for possession was concluded on 31st May 1949 (just before the 1949 Act came into operation), but judgment in it was reserved and not given *g* until 4th August 1949 (some two months after the 1949 Act came into operation). Much of the argument in the case appears to have turned on the meaning of the words 'or anything done' towards the end of s 10 of the 1949 Act. In the result, however, the Court of Appeal held that the case was indistinguishable from *Hutchinson v Jauncey*, the law applicable being that in force when the county court judge delivered his reserved judgment on 4th August 1949. *h*

The argument for the tenants was founded on the basic proposition that the provisions for security of tenure for public sector tenants contained in Chapter II of Part I of the 1980 Act were in pari materia with the provisions for security of tenure for private sector tenants contained in the earlier Rent Acts, in particular the 1920 Act, with which *Remon's* case was concerned. Relying on this basic proposition, counsel for the tenants argued that since the Court of Appeal in *Remon's* case had found it necessary to give a strained and *j* unnatural meaning to such expressions as 'let' in s 12(1) and 'tenant' in s 15(1) of the 1920 Act, this court should interpret the expression 'let under a secure tenancy' in ss 33(1) and 34(1) of the 1980 Act as including a comparably strained and unnatural meaning.

In my opinion this basic proposition, from which counsel for the tenants sought to derive the result which I have stated, is not, when the characteristics of the two pieces of legislation are looked at and analysed as a whole, a correct proposition.

It is true that there are certain important similarities between the relevant provisions
a of the earlier Rent Acts and those of Chapter II of Part I of the 1980 Act. The first such
similarity is that both pieces of legislation have as their purpose the provision of security
of tenure for tenants of rented homes. The second similarity is that the legislature has
in both cases achieved this purpose by (a) preventing a landlord from obtaining possession
of the premises which he has let except in pursuance of an order of a court, and (b)
prohibiting a court from making such an order for possession unless and until it is
b satisfied by the landlord that certain circumstances exist or certain conditions are fulfilled.

Against these two important similarities, however, there must be set what appear to
me to be two even more important differences. The first difference is between the
housing situation in which, and the social background against which, the two pieces of
legislation were passed. The 1920 Act, in relation to which *Remon's* case was decided, was
passed to deal with the critical housing shortage which followed the demobilisation of
c immense numbers of the armed forces after the end of the 1914–18 war. It was
necessary that legislation to meet that situation should be passed, and that its remedial
qualities should take effect, as quickly as possible.

By contrast, Chapter II of Part I of the 1980 Act was not enacted in order to meet any
immediate or urgent crisis in housing accommodation. Its purpose was rather the social
one of giving to tenants in the public housing sector, so far as reasonably practicable, the
d same kind of protection from being evicted from their homes without good and
sufficient cause as had been enjoyed by tenants in the private housing sector for many
decades under the Rent Acts. This assimilation of rights as between public and private
sector tenants, though no doubt regarded as desirable in the general interests of social
equality and non-discrimination, was not an urgent matter, and no special reason for
setting the earliest possible deadline for such assimilation existed. In this connection it
e is to be observed that, for numerous years past, it had been thought safe and proper to
give to local authority landlords a complete discretion with regard to the eviction of
public sector tenants, and to rely on them to exercise such discretion fairly and wisely.

The second difference is between the method used by the legislature in order to effect
its purpose in the Rent Acts, particularly the earlier Acts prior to 1965, on the one hand,
and that used by it to effect its purposes in Chapter II of Part I of the 1980 Act on the other
f hand.

In the earlier Rent Acts the legislature did not seek to interfere with the common law
principles on which contractural tenancies, whether periodical or for a term certain,
could be brought to an end. In the case of periodical tenancies, the legislature left
landlords free to bring them to an end by the service and expiry of valid notices to quit.
In the case of tenancies for a term certain, the legislature left such tenancies to come to
g an end automatically by effluxion of time. What the legislature did, however, in order
to protect the person who had been a contractual tenant before his contractual tenancy
came to an end, was to create a new relationship between that person and his former
contractual landlord, which Scrutton LJ described, in the second passage from his
judgment in *Remon's* case [1921] 1 KB 49 at 58 which I quoted earlier, as a 'statutory
tenancy', the parties to which were the former contractual tenant, from then on described
h as a 'statutory tenant', and the former contractual landlord or his successor in title. The
concept of a statutory, as distinct from a contractual, tenancy, having been formulated
initially by the court, as a matter of necessary implication, from such provisions as s 15(1)
of the 1920 Act, and accepted for many years thereafter as a convenient description of the
relationship concerned, was in the end formally recognised by the legislature in s 1(4)(b)
of the Rent Act 1965, and still remains, despite subsequent developments with regard to
j 'controlled' and 'regulated' tenancies, ingrained in the Rent Acts legislation as a whole.

By contrast, in the 1980 Act the legislature went about the matter in quite a different
way. It abolished altogether the common law principles on which contractual tenancies,
both periodical and for a term certain, could be brought or come to an end. It did this
by providing, first, that on the expiry of a contractual tenancy for a term certain, there
should come into existence a periodic tenancy in its place, unless a further contractual
tenancy for a term certain should be granted (s 29(1) (2)); and, second, that a periodic

tenancy, whether having that character originally, or coming into being on the expiry of
a term certain, should not be capable of being brought to an end by a landlord except by a
the latter obtaining an order of the court for possession (s 32(1)), or, in cases where
provisions for re-entry or forfeiture are relied on, an order terminating the secure
tenancy (s 32 (2)).

The significance of the first difference between the two pieces of legislation to which
I have referred above is that, in a situation where the legislature, having passed the 1980
Act as a whole on 8th August 1980, has then seen fit not to bring Chapter II of Part I into b
operation until eight weeks later, namely on 3rd October 1980, there is no policy reason
of any kind why the court should seek, by giving a strained and unnatural meaning to
certain expressions in the Act, to give retrospective effect to the provisions of that
chapter.

The significance of the second difference between the two pieces of legislation to
which I have referred is this. Whereas a court interpreting the earlier Rent Acts, such as c
the 1920 Act in *Remon's* case, felt obliged to fill gaps in the express provisions of the Acts
on the basis of necessary implication from their manifest purpose, the 1980 Act deals
much more fully and explicitly with the methods by which the purpose of providing
security of tenure for public sector tenants is to be achieved. The result is that gaps in the
express provisions of the kind which existed in the earlier Rent Acts do not exist in the
1980 Act, and do not therefore require to be filled up by the kind of process of strained d
and unnatural construction to which the Court of Appeal was admittedly driven in
Remon's case.

In my view, when one looks at the differences, as well as the similarities, between the
Rent Acts legislation on the one hand and Chapter II of Part I of the 1980 Act on the
other, it is impossible to say that the two pieces of legislation are in pari materia, so that
a decision on the retrospective effect of certain provisions in the first of these two pieces e
of legislation should be regarded as binding this court to reach a similar decision with
regard to the retrospective effect of what are, to some extent at least, comparable
provisions in the second of the two pieces of legislation.

In *Remon's* case the Court of Appeal felt bound to give strained and unnatural meanings
to perfectly ordinary words, such as 'tenant', 'tenancy', 'letting' and 'let'. It did so for one
reason, and one reason only, namely that unless those words were given strained and f
unnatural meanings, the manifest purpose of the 1920 Act (to protect from eviction
persons whose contractual tenancies had been brought or come to an end) would be
defeated.

In the three cases with which these appeals are concerned, I do not see any compelling
reason why the court should follow its predecessor in *Remon's* case by giving a strained
and unnatural meaning to the expression 'let under a secure tenancy' as used in ss 33(1) g
and 34(1) of the 1980 Act.

The ordinary and natural meaning of the expression is 'let under a secure tenancy at
the date to which each subsection concerned relates', that is to say the date of
commencement of an action for possession in the case of s 33(1) and the date of deciding
whether an order for possession should be made in such an action in the case of s 34(1).

To adopt that ordinary and natural meaning of the expression concerned will not, so h
far as I can see, in any way defeat the purposes of Chapter II of Part I of the 1980 Act. It
will only mean that, since under s 153(2) of the Act Chapter II of Part I did not come into
operation, by the decision of the legislature and the Secretary of State, until eight weeks
after the passing of the Act, namely on 3rd October 1980, only those public sector tenants
whose tenancies were not lawfully brought to an end before that date will benefit from
the provisions of that chapter. j

What I have said disposes of the primary way in which the case for the tenants was
put. It remains, however, for me to deal with a secondary, and very much subsidiary,
argument advanced on their behalf. This alternative argument was based on s 48(1) of
the 1980 Act, which deals with the position of persons occupying dwelling houses as
licensees, and equates their rights with those occupying them as tenants.

The argument was that if, contrary to the tenants' primary case, they did not have, as
a a result of the expiry of their respective notices to quit, secure tenancies of the dwelling
houses which they occupied, they were nevertheless, as a result of staying on after such
notices to quit had expired, licensees of the dwelling houses concerned within the
meaning of s 48(1) referred to above.

I find it impossible to accept this alternative submission. The whole tenor of s 48
makes it clear that it is referring to licences granted by the owner, or other person
b entitled to the possession, of the dwelling house concerned. It was not open to the local
authority landlords to evict their tenants except in pursuance of a court order. In these
circumstances it is impossible to infer that the local authority landlords, by awaiting the
results of their actions for possession, were expressly or impliedly giving their former
tenants licences to remain in their flats. It can, I think, be said that the former tenants
had a statutory licence or dispensation to remain in occupation of their flats unless and
c until orders for possession were made by a court against them. Assuming that to be
right, however, I do not think that the result is to create the relationship of licensors and
licensees between the local authority landlords and their former tenants. I would,
therefore, reject this alternative argument for the tenants based on s 48.

For the reasons which I have given I have come to the conclusion that, since the local
authority landlords (a) terminated their tenants' periodic tenancies by valid notices to
d quit, and (b) subsequently began actions against them for possession, before 3rd October
1980 when the provisions of the 1980 Act relating to security of tenure for public sector
tenants came into operation, the tenants are not entitled to rely on those provisions as a
defence to their actions.

It follows, in my judgment, that the appeals brought by George Harrison against the
judgment of his Honour Judge Stucley and by Jennie Watson against the decision of his
e Honour Judge Willis should be dismissed; but that the appeal brought by the Mayor and
Burgesses of the London Borough of Haringey against the judgment of his Honour Judge
Tibber should be allowed.

f **WALLER LJ.** The question which arises for decision in these three cases is whether the
tenant of a local authority on whom a notice to quit has been served is entitled after the
time of expiry of the notice to quit to the protection of the Housing Act 1980, even
though the notice to quit had expired in each case before the Act had come into effect.

Counsel for Mrs Mosner in his submissions has relied on the phrase in s 28(1) of the
1980 Act, 'let as a separate dwelling' as a connecting link between this Act and the
g Increase of Rent and Mortgage Interest (Restrictions) Act 1920 and subsequent Rent
Acts. Founding his submission on *Remon v City of London Real Property Co Ltd* [1921] 1
KB 49 which was concerned with the 1920 Act, and *Hutchinson v Jauncey* [1950] 1 All ER
165, [1950] 1 KB 574 which was concerned with the Landlord and Tenant (Rent Control)
Act 1949, counsel submitted that expressions in those Acts which were held to cover the
case of ex-tenants remaining in possession should apply to the Housing Act 1980.

h The 1920 Act was an Act passed to protect tenants after the 1914–18 war from increase
of rent and protect them from ejection. There were strong reasons for interpreting the
phrase 'a house let as a separate dwelling' as including a house where the notice to quit
had expired and the word 'tenant' to cover the case of a tenant who had been given notice
to quit on a certain day and was still in possession after that day. Similarly the 1949 Act
was passed in order to cover conditions arising after the 1939–45 war. In that case also
j it was held that tenant included ex-tenant holding over.

If the language used in the Housing Act 1980 were similar to that used in those two
Acts I would, for myself, follow those two decisions even though the circumstances of
the passing of the 1980 Act are very different from those in 1920 and 1949. Counsel for
the London Borough of Haringey submitted, however, that the Rent Act 1968 was a
consolidating statute which repealed all the preceding Rent Acts and replaced the

legislation with somewhat different phraseology. He has also emphasised that the purpose of the 1980 Act was rather different from the earlier Rent Acts.

In *Remon's* case the court was concerned with two sections of the Increase of Rent and Mortgage Interest (Restrictions) Act 1920, namely s 12(2) which read: 'This Act shall apply to a house or part of a house let as a separate dwelling . . .' and s 15(1) which read: 'A tenant who by virtue of the provisions of this Act retains possession of any dwelling-house to which this Act applies . . .' Those two provisions were those which concerned the court. Bankes LJ said (at 54):

'It is however clear that in all the Rent Restrictions Acts the expression "tenant" has been used in a special, a peculiar sense and as including a person who might be described as an ex-tenant, someone whose occupation had commenced as tenant and who had continued in occupation without any legal right to do so except, possibly, such as the Acts themselves conferred upon him.'

Scrutton LJ, after saying that unless the word 'tenant' included a tenant whose tenancy had expired the whole purpose of the Act would have been defeated, went on (at 58):

'Yet I think it is clear Parliament has intended to confirm these people in a statutory tenancy and to speak of their position as a "letting".'

In *Hutchinson v Jauncey* [1950] 1 All ER 165, [1950] 1 KB 574 the Act being considered was the Landlord and Tenant (Rent Control) Act 1949. That Act gave Rent Act protection to subtenants who were sharing part of the accommodation with the landlord. Evershed MR said ([1950] 1 All ER 165 at 166, [1950] 1 KB 574 at 577):

'. . . having regard to *Remon v. City of London Real Property Co.*, if it had not been for the issue of the summons before the Act came into operation the tenant must have been entitled to claim the benefit of s. 9 of the Act of 1949 notwithstanding the service of an effective notice to quit.'

The court went on to hold that the important time at which the matter had to be considered was the time of the hearing of the case and not the time of the issuing of the summons. If therefore those Rent Acts were still in force and the Housing Act 1980 was simply adding additional provisions to them, the arguments of counsel for Mrs Mosner would have great force.

The Rent Act 1965, s 20, gave statutory effect to the decision in the *Remon* case. Specific provision was made for the transitional stage and s 20(1) said:

'Where the tenancy of a dwelling-house has come to an end before the commencement of this Act and the tenancy would have been a regulated tenancy had this Act been then in force, then—(a) no order for the possession of the dwelling-house shall be made which would not be made if this Act had come into force before the termination of the tenancy. . .

This Act was followed by the Rent Act 1968 which repealed most of the earlier Rent Act legislation and in particular the whole of the 1920 Act, the whole of the 1939 Act and the whole of the 1949 Act. It also repealed the Rent Act part of the Rent Act 1965, leaving only Part III which dealt with harassment.

The 1968 Act adopted different phraseology. Section 1(1) read: 'A tenancy under which a dwelling-house . . . is let as a separate dwelling is a protected tenancy for the purposes of this Act . . .' and this phraseology is followed in the 1980 Act. Section 28(1) reads: 'A tenancy under which a dwelling-house is let as a separate dwelling is a secure tenancy at any time when the conditions described below . . .' are in existence. While it is possible to describe 'house . . . let as a separate dwelling' as including a house which has been let as a separate dwelling and 'a tenant who by virtue of the provisions of this Act retains possession of a dwelling house . . .' as still being a tenant when he retains possession after a notice to quit, more particularly when, as Scrutton LJ pointed out in

Remon v City of London Real Property Co Ltd [1921] 1 KB 49 at 58, the whole intention of
a the Act would be defeated if another interpretation was given, it is in my opinion very
difficult to say that the words 'a tenancy under which a dwelling-house . . . is let' shall
include 'a tenancy under which a dwelling house was or has been let' as a separate
dwelling.

Although in the earlier Rent Acts the effect of the decisions that I have already quoted
was to make the Acts retrospective. As Wright LJ said in *Re Athlumney, ex parte Wilson*
b [1898] 2 QB 547 at 551–552, [1895–9] All ER Rep 329 at 331–332:

'Perhaps no rule of construction is more firmly established than this—that a
retrospective operation is not to be given to a statute so as to impair an existing right
or obligation otherwise than as regards matter of procedure, unless that effect
cannot be avoided without doing violence to the language of an enactment. If the
enactment is expressed in language which is barely capable of either interpretation,
c it ought to be construed as prospective only.'

In 1920 in the years immediately after the 1914–18 war there were strong reasons for
preserving as far as possible the restriction on rents and security of tenure. And as
Scrutton LJ pointed out in *Remon's case* (at 58):

'If a tenant by agreement whose tenancy had expired was not within [the terms
d of the Act], the whole purpose of the Act would have been defeated, for it was
obviously intended to allow former tenants who were willing to carry out the terms
of their old tenancy, as modified by any permissible statutory increases of rent, to
stay on.'

Similar circumstances existed after the 1939–45 war, circumstances with which the 1949
e Act was dealing.

The circumstances surrounding the Housing Act 1980 are different and reflect one of
two different approaches to public sector housing. One view is that housing associations
and local authorities should have a greater power over their tenants and be able to make
their own decisions about possession in order to use the housing to best advantage.
Another view is that the courts and only the courts should decide on these matters. The
f 1980 Act which enabled tenants to purchase their houses also gave effect to the latter of
these two views regarding possession. However, in my opinion the purpose of the 1980
Act would in no way be frustrated if the plain meaning of the words in s 28 were
adopted. This would mean that the important date would be the date of coming into
effect of the Act.

There was some argument before us as to the status of an ex-tenant, a tenant to whom
g a notice to quit has been given but who because of statutes such as the Protection from
Eviction Act 1977 could not be said to be a trespasser. The question of whether he is a
tenant at sufferance or whether he is a licensee or whether he has some other status was
discussed before us. If it were necessary to decide it I would be of the opinion that an ex-
tenant would not be a tenant at sufferance nor would he be a licensee of the landlord. It
is possible that there might be a statutory licence but this would not put the landlord in
h the position of licensor. Probably the best description is to call him the ex-tenant.

I have come to the conclusion that s 28 of the Housing Act 1980 has no retrospective
effect. The words 'a tenancy under which a dwelling-house is let as a separate dwelling'
mean one which is let as a separate dwelling at or after the time of coming into force of
the Act. It does not mean in the context of this Act 'a tenancy under which a dwelling-
house was formerly let as a separate dwelling but where the ex-tenant remains in
j possession'. Accordingly I would allow the appeal of the London Borough of Haringey
and dismiss the appeal of Mr Harrison and Mrs Watson.

SIR DAVID CAIRNS. I had the advantage of reading beforehand the two judgments
which have already been delivered.

I entirely agree with the reasoning of both of those judgments, and accordingly I agree that the appeal of the London Borough of Haringey should be allowed, and the other two *a* appeals should be dismissed.

Appeal of Mr Harrison dismissed. Leave to appeal to the House of Lords refused. Stay of execution for 28 days.
Appeal of the London Borough of Haringey allowed. Leave to appeal to the House of Lords refused. Stay of execution for 28 days. *b*
Appeal of Mrs Watson dismissed. Leave to appeal to the House of Lords refused. Stay of execution for 28 days.

Solicitors: *John Ingham* (for Mr Harrison); *P Norton* (for Mrs Mosner); *Louise London* (for Mrs Watson); *C T Mahoney* (for the London Borough of Hammersmith and Fulham); *T F Neville* (for the London Borough of Haringey); *R A Benge* (for the London Borough of *c* Hackney).

William Hoskins Esq   Barrister.

R v Inland Revenue Commissioners, ex parte *d* Chisholm

QUEEN'S BENCH DIVISION (DIVISIONAL COURT LIST)
MCNEILL J
4th MARCH 1981

e

Income tax – Pay as you earn system – Deduction of tax by employer – Failure to deduct tax – Employee receiving emoluments knowing that employer has wilfully failed to deduct tax – Knowing – Wilfully – Director receiving emoluments over a number of years without deduction of tax – Whether material on which commissioners could reasonably form opinion that employee had received emoluments knowing that employer had wilfully failed to deduct tax – Income Tax (Employments) Regulations 1973 (SI 1973 No 334), reg 26(4). *f*

From 1972 to 1977 the applicant, a director and employee of a company, received emoluments from the company without deduction of tax. During those years the applicant had signed the company's accounts as a director and in 1977 his advisers had admitted in correspondence with the Revenue that tax had not been deducted from his remuneration. The Commissioners of Inland Revenue, pursuant to reg 26(4)[a] of the *g* Income Tax (Employments) Regulations 1973, directed that there should be recovered from the applicant the amounts by which the tax deductible from the remuneration paid to him by the company exceeded the amount of tax actually deducted, on the ground that, in view of the admission made on his behalf and his position in the company, the applicant had received his emoluments knowing that the company had wilfully failed to deduct the tax due. The applicant applied for judicial review, seeking an order of *h* certiorari to quash the direction on the ground that there had been no material before the commissioners on which they could reasonably have formed the opinion that the applicant had received his remuneration knowing that the company had wilfully failed to deduct therefrom the amount of tax due. The applicant contended that the material on which the commissioners had decided to make the direction indicated only that the applicant ought to have known and not that he had known that the company had *j* wilfully failed to deduct the tax.

Held – For an employee to receive emoluments 'knowing' that his employer had wilfully (ie intentionally or deliberately) failed to deduct tax therefrom, within reg 26(4)

---

a   Regulation 26(4) is set out at p 604 *b*, post

of the 1973 regulations, the employee had to have actual knowledge of the failure and it
a was not sufficient that the employee ought to have known or that he should have been
suspicious. Thus once it had been acknowledged by the applicant through his advisers
that no tax had been deducted from his emoluments and that the failure to deduct
covered a considerable period it could not in the circumstances be said that the applicant
had been unaware that he had been receiving his emoluments without deduction of tax
or that the failure to deduct had not been wilful. It followed that there was material on
b which the commissioners could form the opinion that the applicant had received his
remuneration knowing that the company had wilfully failed to deduct the tax
therefrom. The application would therefore be refused (see p 605 *e f*, p 607 *f* to *j* and
p 608 *g* to *j*, post).

Notes
c For payment of tax by employer under PAYE system and recovery of unpaid tax from
employee, see 23 Halsbury's Laws (4th Edn) para 737.
    For the Income Tax (Employments) Regulations 1973, reg 26, see 11 Halsbury's
Statutory Instruments (Third Reissue) 61.

Cases referred to in judgment
d *Associated Provincial Picture Houses Ltd v Wednesbury Corpn* [1947] 2 All ER 680, [1948] 1
    KB 223, 177 LT 641, 112 JP 55, 45 Digest (Repl) 215, 189.
R v Secretary of State for the Home Department, ex parte Mughal [1973] 3 All ER 796, [1974]
    QB 313, [1973] 3 WLR 647, 137 JP 846, CA, Digest (Cont Vol D) 25, *101j*.

Cases also cited
e *Atwal v Massey* [1971] 3 All ER 881, DC.
Burton v Bevan [1908] 2 Ch 240.
French v Elliott [1959] 3 All ER 866, [1960] 1 WLR 40.

Application for judicial review
Ian Nigel Gordon Chisholm applied, with the leave of the Divisional Court granted on
f 29th August 1980, for an order of certiorari to quash a direction of the Commissioners
of Inland Revenue made on 3rd June 1980 that, under reg 26(4) of the Income Tax
(Employments) Regulations 1973, SI 1973 No 334, there should be recovered from the
applicant the amounts by which the tax deductible from the emoluments paid to him
during the years 1972–73 to 1976–77 by McQueen of London Sportswear Ltd exceeded
the amount of tax actually deducted. The facts are set out in the judgment.

g
Robin Mathew for the applicant.
Robert Carnwath for the Crown.

McNEILL J. This is an application by the applicant for an order of certiorari to remove
into this court for the purpose of its being quashed a decision of the Commissioners of
h Inland Revenue promulgated on 3rd June 1980, pursuant to reg 26(4) of the Income Tax
(Employment) Regulations 1973, SI 1973 No 334, made pursuant to s 204 of the Income
and Corporation Taxes Act 1970.
    The short factual position which lies behind the application and the direction is this.
From about 1970 onwards the applicant was a director, shareholder and employee of a
company in business manufacturing and wholesaling ladies garments. The company
j had two names and, so far as is material, was known as McQueen of London Sportswear
Ltd. In 1972 the applicant was joined by a Mr Mark Bloom, who became a director of
the company. The applicant and Mr Bloom each held 50% of the shares in the
company. The association lasted until the end of 1976, when the applicant sold out his
interest to Mr Bloom. There is no documentary record of the terms of that sale until a
document dated 6th March 1979, the delay being due apparently to a dispute between
the company and a Canadian supplier. The applicant makes the point that from the time

that Mr Bloom joined him the financial control of the company was in Mr Bloom's
hands.

a

The direction in question relates to the tax due and payable in the years 1972 to 1977
inclusive. The direction is made in pursuance of reg 26(4) which reads as follows:

'If the amount which the employer is liable to pay to the Collector under
paragraph (1) of this Regulation exceeds the amount actually deducted by him from
emoluments paid during the relevant income tax month, and the Commissioners
of Inland Revenue are of the opinion that an employee has received his emoluments   *b*
knowing that the employer has wilfully failed to deduct therefrom the amount of
tax which he was liable to deduct under these Regulations, the said Commissioners
may direct that the amount of the excess shall be recovered from the employee, and
where they so direct the employer shall not be liable to pay the amount of the said
excess to the Collector.'

c

This paragraph is the heart of the machinery for dealing with the PAYE scheme.
Regulation 26(1) puts an obligation on the employer within 14 days of the end of every
income tax month to pay to the collector all amounts of tax which he was liable to deduct
from emoluments paid by him during that month. Paragraph (4) provides for the
situation where the amount of the liability exceeds the amount actually deducted in
circumstances to which I shall return in more detail later.

d

The assessments for the years 1972 to 1977 dealt with in the direction required the
applicant to pay the excess of the amounts which his employers were liable to pay over
the amount actually deducted. I suspect, though it does not expressly appear from the
documents, that the amount actually deducted was nil. It is necessary, therefore, to look
first of all, for the purposes of this application, at the decision which is challenged.
Paragraph (4) provides for the procedure followed here, where 'the Commissioners are of   *e*
the opinion that an employee has received his emoluments knowing that the employer
has wilfully failed to deduct therefrom the amount of tax which he was liable to deduct'.

There is, first of all, this to be borne in mind, that the court is considering only the
opinion which was formed by the commissioners assuming, as is common ground here,
that an opinion was formed. The opinion is, as has not been disputed, an administrative
decision which falls to be considered in accordance with the rules which were adumbrated *f*
in the well-known case of *Associated Provincial Picture Houses Ltd v Wednesbury Corpn*
[1947] 2 All ER 680, [1948] 1 KB 223. I should mention in particular the often repeated
passages from the judgment of Lord Greene MR ([1947] 2 All ER 680 at 682–683, [1948]
1 KB 223 at 228–229). I do not think it is necessary to burden this judgment by a
recitation of those directions.

The matter has further been considered more recently by the Court of Appeal in *R v*   *g*
Secretary of State for the Home Department, ex parte Mughal [1973] 3 All ER 796, [1974] QB
313. I should mention again that the particular well-known passage is from the
judgment of Lord Denning MR and there is a short passage in the judgment of Scarman
LJ (see [1973] 3 All ER 796 at 803, 807–808, [1974] QB 313 at 325, 330–331). Again, I
do not propose to read out those passages, but I follow the directions there contained.

For the purposes of this case the applicant sets out to show that the opinion formed by *h*
the commissioners was one which was not fair or reasonable in the sense in which those
words are used in these cases, to which I have referred, and others dealing with
administrative decisions and/or that there was no or no sufficient material on which a
tribunal, properly instructing itself as to its approach to the facts, could have come to the
conclusion that the commissioners reached here.

There are certain introductory observations that I should make. It was contended by *j*
counsel for the applicant that para (4) was essentially a penal or punitive provision, and
he drew attention to the effect of a direction in so far as the concluding words of the
paragraph, in the event of a direction, relieved the employer of liability for the payment
of tax. I do not think that this is properly called 'penal' or 'punitive'. It is part of a system
for endeavouring to ensure, as best it can be done, that the person in whose hands the
unpaid tax remains pays the tax. Both paras (3) and (4) are parts of a system for ensuring

that object. Of course they are not penal in this sense, that they do not provide for
a penalties on the taxpayer of themselves.

The next point to which I refer, only to view it in the context of this judgment, is
this. Regulation 26(5) does provide machinery for determination of a dispute between
employer and employee as to which of the two holds the unpaid tax. That paragraph
provides:

> *b* 'If a difference arises between the employer and the employee as to whether the
> employer has deducted tax, or having regard to Regulation 23 is deemed to have
> deducted tax, from emoluments paid to the employee . . . the matter shall, for the
> purpose of ascertaining the amount of any tax to be recovered from the employee
> under paragraph (3) or (4) of this Regulation, be determined by such General
> Commissioners as the Commissioners of Inland Revenue having regard to all the
> circumstances shall direct . . .'

c
That paragraph has not been invoked here, though the material before me suggests
that it might have been invoked by the present applicant; but, without investigating
reasons which are no part of my task, at any rate the fact remains that neither by his
solicitors nor by his accountants did he seek to take advantage of that procedure.

The matters on which the commissioners have to form an opinion are these: that the
d employee received his emoluments knowing that the employer has wilfully failed to
deduct therefrom the amount of tax which he was liable to deduct. It is common
ground between the parties that the employer has not paid the tax for which he was
liable in respect of the applicant's emoluments. The material words in the passage I read,
if I may stress them again, are '[the] employee has received his emoluments knowing
that the employer has *wilfully failed to deduct* [those last four words also I stress] therefrom
the amount of tax which he was liable to deduct'.

e
I accept that, for the purpose of construing that regulation, the word 'knowing' means
what it says and does not mean 'ought to have known' or 'should have been suspicious'
or any other weakening of knowledge. Although I shall refer to authority on the
interpretation of that word in the criminal law, I do not think it is necessary to refer to
authority for the proposition that the word 'knowing' means 'knowing' and nothing
f else. I also accept, and it is not really in dispute between the parties, that the word
'wilfully' means 'intentionally' or 'deliberately', and may, in the context of the PAYE
scheme and the collection of tax, import a measure of blameworthiness, at least in the
sense that it is blameworthy not to pay the tax that is due.

Applying those definitions to the material words, I then go to consider whether there
was material on which the commissioners could reasonably and fairly, properly
g instructing themselves about their responsibilities, reach the conclusion which would
lead to the direction which they made. The employee himself, the present applicant,
swore an affidavit in support of his application for leave. In the course of that affidavit
he swore that from the time that Mr Bloom joined the company he, the applicant,
received his salary net of tax. Then he went on to say: 'My emoluments were paid to me
by my drawing my net salary leaving the PAYE liability thereon to be paid direct.'
h When he deals with the severing of his association with Mr Bloom he says:

> 'At the time I left the Company it had very substantial assets and was well able to
> pay the outstanding PAYE tax. Bloom undertook with me that he would ensure
> that payment would be made.'

He annexed to his affidavit the letter to which I have already referred, dated 6th March
j 1979, in the course of which there appears this paragraph over Mr Bloom's signature:

> 'I further confirm that at the date of your ceasing to be a director of the three
> companies above mentioned [which included McQueen of London Sportswear Ltd]
> you were not indebted to any of them and that none of the Companies had any
> claims of any nature whatsoever against you, and that the Companies would
> discharge all or any of their liabilities which might arise out of any payments made
> by the Companies or any of them to you.'

Counsel for the applicant says that can only be read as a clear recognition by Mr Bloom that the employer, McQueen of London Sportswear Ltd, of which he was then in sole and *a* effective control, would discharge the liability for tax arising out of payment of emoluments to the applicant. If the matter stood there, of course, I do not suppose that counsel for the Crown would attempt to support the decision. What appears to have happened is this. The applicant and the employer, at the time at which he was associated with it, had the assistance of professional accountants, Goodman, Jones & Co. The applicant's personal tax matters were dealt with, as it were, in arrears, and it was not until *b* 1978 and 1979 that assessments were made on him in respect of the tax to which his employers were liable but which had not been paid. It was following that that his solicitors began to correspond with the commissioners, but there had been earlier correspondence which, to my mind, is of substantial importance.

In 1977, by letter dated 21st April, Goodman, Jones & Co had pleasure in enclosing the applicant's completed tax returns for the years 1973–74 and 1976–77 with accompanying *c* schedules. 1973–74 certainly was and 1976–77 may in part have been, but probably was not, during the period of the association between the applicant and Mr Bloom. The third paragraph of that letter reads as follows: 'We can advise you that no PAYE tax has been deducted in respect of the remuneration from McQueen of London Sportswear Ltd . . .' That seems to me, I am bound to say, despite all the efforts that counsel has made on the applicant's behalf, to be the plainest possible admission of what it says, namely that no *d* PAYE tax has been deducted in respect of the relevant emoluments.

Counsel for the applicant seeks to say that in accountants' language, or if not in accountants' language then in these accountants' language, that means that no PAYE tax was paid by the employers to the Revenue. To accept that would be straining at least my understanding of the English language, and I see no reason for thinking that Goodman, Jones & Co meant anything other than that no PAYE tax had been deducted in respect *e* of the relevant emoluments.

The amount of those emoluments, the applicant's remuneration, for the period from 1st September 1972 to 30th June 1974 was the sum of £21,000. That sum is referred to in the accounts of the company, which were also available to the commissioners when they were coming to their conclusions. It is to be observed that, although that sum appears as the remuneration of the applicant in the computation of the liability of the *f* employer for corporation tax and the total of directors' emoluments (those of the applicant and Mr Bloom) appear in the profit and loss account, the balance sheet does not contain any reference to the liability for tax. The current liabilities, which included directors' loan accounts and creditors and accrued charges (which is not suggested was included in this item) did make reference to taxation as a current liability in the sum of £18,706, but that sum is United Kingdom corporation tax at the relevant percentages. *g* It is at any rate interesting to observe that the profit and loss account is signed by the applicant as a director and he was, of course, also at that time the secretary of the company.

That is of itself some material, when associated with the accountants' letters, to which I have referred, which the commissioners were entitled to take into consideration when they were approaching an opinion material for reg 26(4), but it does not end there, *h* because in the course of the correspondence between the applicant's solicitors and the commissioners, the commissioners drew the attention of the solicitors to the first of those letters to which I have referred, namely that of 21st April 1977 when, in a letter of 20th March 1980, the gentleman conducting this matter at the Operations Division (Collection Procedures) of the Inland Revenue said this:

j

'Regulation 26(4) provides for the Commissioners of Inland Revenue to form an opinion from the evidence before them that the employee received his emoluments knowing that the company had wilfully failed to deduct tax therefrom. Had the tax been deducted but not paid to the Revenue then a direction would not be sought. That the company wilfully failed to deduct the tax is shown by the non submission of returns accounting for [the applicant's] remuneration and the tax due as required a by the PAYE Regulations or by payment of any of the tax due. In addition [the applicant's] accountants, Messrs Goodman Jones & Co, in their letter of 21 April 1977 to the Inspector confirmed that no PAYE tax had been deducted from [the applicant's] remuneration. In view of this admission and [the applicant's] position in the company I do not see how you can seriously contend that he was not aware of the company's failure to deduct PAYE and in view of this a direction is appropriate.'

b While one might have expected, in those circumstances, the solicitor to have said, 'Stop, you have got it wrong' or words to that effect but more elegantly phrased, what in fact they said in a letter on 14th April 1980 was this. Having asserted that, notwithstanding the applicant was a director, he was very much a junior director and Mr Bloom was the dominating force in the company responsible for the financial affairs, they said:

c
'Whilst it is correct that P.A.Y.E. was not operated as such in relation to the directors' remuneration, nevertheless at all times [the applicant] understood that this would be dealt with and the tax attributable to his salary would be paid by the company.'

d Then they draw attention to the fact that when he severed his connection the company was solvent and, by inference, referred to the letter from Mr Bloom which I have already read.

Again, on 28th April 1980, arguing the position on his behalf, his solicitors wrote:

'When [the applicant] left the company he was assured that these matters would be dealt with and the tax on his remuneration would be paid by the company.
e Consequently [the applicant] until he received the first communications from you on this subject was not aware that Mr. Bloom had not paid the tax which was due and therefore whilst it ultimately transpired that the tax was not deducted and we suppose that you could argue that once it had not been paid there had been a wilful default, it does not follow that [the applicant] was aware of this wilful default.'

f Again, counsel for the applicant has done what he can with that phrase in the solicitors' letter. It does seem to me that, just as the accountants' letter, to which I have referred, was a plain admission that tax had not been deducted, so too in the solicitors' correspondence there is a plain admission that tax had not been deducted. The point then being taken, in April 1980, was that it did not necessarily follow that the applicant was aware of the wilful default. Indeed, so far as the words 'wilful failure to deduct' are g concerned, once it is acknowledged on the applicant's behalf that there was not a deduction, from which in turn it follows that he by his solicitors and accountants acknowledged that he received his emoluments without the deduction of tax, it is at least prima facie the case that the payment was a deliberate and intentional payment, and unless there be some material to suggest that it was a careless mistake or a negligent rather than a deliberate and intentional way of dealing with the matter, I would have h thought that it was really unarguable that the failure to deduct was other than wilful.

I bear in mind that this was not an isolated payment of a single week or for a short period. The sum in question of £21,000 is a sum which was payable over a period from a date in 1972 to the end of June 1974. Did the applicant know? I must start on the basis that he was receiving his full emoluments without deduction. It is difficult to conceive of a man receiving his emoluments in that way without knowing that that was precisely j what was happening. Counsel for the applicant contends with force that when the commissioners approached the opinion which led to the direction they were in error in looking not for knowledge but only for reason to believe, not 'Did the applicant know?' but 'Must the applicant have known?' They are not, of course, the same thing. 'Knowing' has to be, he said, and I agree, construed strictly and 'ought to have known' is not good enough. Counsel for the applicant says the approach which is spoken to by Mr Lister, the Assistant Director of the relevant Division of the Board of Inland Revenue, in his affidavit is wrong. He comments on and criticises the way in which Mr Lister says in his affidavit he fulfilled his responsibilities.

Counsel for the applicant criticises in Mr Lister's affidavit the use by Mr Lister of terms such as 'It seemed to me that the correspondence with the Solicitors confirmed and certainly did not contradict the Accountants' statement that the company had failed to make P.A.Y.E. deductions . . .' and at a later stage, when considering whether the failure was wilful, 'It seemed to me that, unless there were evidence to the contrary, the reasonable inference was that such a failure had been wilful'. Counsel for the applicant is saying that that is really reversing the onus of proof, as it were, and putting on the applicant the obligation of producing evidence to rebut an inference rather than going directly to a conclusion.

Counsel for the applicant also criticises Mr Lister's affidavit where he says:

'I would expect a Director . . . to be well aware whether or not he had received his voted remuneration in full, i.e. without deductions under the P.A.Y.E. system. I therefore scrutinised with care all the correspondence on this point to see if there was any unusual feature of the case which would displace that first impression. I did not find any such unusual feature in the correspondence. . .'

At a later stage in the affidavit Mr Lister said: 'It seemed to me that, even if I had been in doubt—which I was not—that remark served to confirm that the Applicant had at all times been aware of the company's wilful failure to make P.A.Y.E. deductions from his emoluments . . .' and so on.

Finally, this reference in Mr Lister's affidavit dealing with the company's accounts 'ostensibly signed by the Applicant and his co-director' is criticised: 'In my view the accounts showed that, whether or not the co-director was the dominating force, the Applicant participated to a substantial degree in the financial affairs of the company.' Counsel for the applicant says that when you put all that together some of it is irrelevant, though I do not subscribe to that view of the matter. But, taking all that together and with the criticisms of its relevance, counsel says the opinion to which Mr Lister came was an unreasonable conclusion, not that the commissioners were acting in bad faith, but that they were misdirecting themselves on their approach to the matter by, as it were, paraphrasing counsel's words, making assumptions and then attempting to justify them rather than by looking at the evidence in the round and seeing what conclusion and what opinion could be formed. Counsel says that Mr Lister ought to be held to have needed more than he had to reach the opinion that there was actual knowledge of wilful default. Counsel says there is no more than suspicion and there is the possibility of muddle, and it is not sufficient for a concluded opinion of knowledge and wilful failure.

I hope I have canvassed what seemed to me to be the most material parts of the affidavits and the correspondence, all of which have been read or highlighted at least in the course of the argument. At the end of the day, applying the tests which are laid down for me in the cases to which I have referred, I am of the conclusion that there was an abundance of material on which the commissioners were entitled to come to the opinion which they did. At the end of the day it is in no way for me to substitute an opinion for the commissioners' opinion. It would be quite wrong for me to conclude, as a matter of fact, as counsel for the Crown invited me to do in the course of his submissions, that the evidence was conclusive. It is only necessary for me to say that the material was certainly there and an objective view could very well be held that it was conclusive in favour of the opinion that was reached. That being so, there is no ground for interfering with the direction which followed on the opinion so arrived at, and this application fails.

Application dismissed.

Solicitors: *David Lee & Co* (for the applicant); *Solicitor of Inland Revenue.*

Diana Brahams   Barrister.

Dodds v Walker

a

HOUSE OF LORDS
LORD DIPLOCK, LORD EDMUND-DAVIES, LORD FRASER OF TULLYBELTON, LORD RUSSELL OF
KILLOWEN AND LORD ROSKILL
21st MAY, 18th JUNE 1981

b *Landlord and tenant – Business premises – Application for new tenancy – Time – Computation of time – Four months from giving of landlord's notice terminating tenancy – Landlord's notice given on last day of short month, namely on 30th September – Whether four months' period expiring on 30th or 31st of following January – Landlord and Tenant Act 1954, s 29(3).*

On 30th September 1978 the landlord of business premises served a notice on the tenant under s 25 of the Landlord and Tenant Act 1954 terminating his tenancy from 31st *c* March 1979. By s 29(3)[a] of that Act a tenant wishing to apply under s 24(1) of the Act for a new tenancy had to do so not more than 'four months after the giving of the landlord's notice', which, under Sch 1[b] of the Interpretation Act 1978, was four calendar months. The tenant applied to the county court under s 24(1) for a tenancy on 31st January. The registrar, and on appeal, the judge and the Court of Appeal ([1980] 2 All *d* ER 507) dismissed his application on the ground that it was made out of time because the period of four months prescribed by s 29(3) expired on 30th January and not 31st January.

Held – In calculating the period of a month or a specified number of months that had elapsed after the occurrence of a specified event, such as the giving of a notice, the general rule was that the period ended on the corresponding date in the appropriate subsequent *e* month, irrespective of whether some months were longer than others. Thus where a landlord gave notice of termination under the 1954 Act on the last day of a 30-day month, the four calendar months prescribed by s 29(3) of the 1954 Act for service of an application for a new tenancy expired on the 30th day of the fourth succeeding month even if it was a 31-day month. Accordingly, the four-month period within which the tenant had to apply for a new tenancy expired at midnight on 30th January and his *f* application made on 31st January was out of time. The appeal would therefore be dismissed (see p 610 g to j, p 611 c to h and p 612 a to d, post).

Per Curiam. If the month in which the period expires has no corresponding date because it is too short the period given by the notice ends on the last day of that month (see p 611 a e f h j and p 612 c, post).

Decision of the Court of Appeal [1980] 2 All ER 507 affirmed.

g **Notes**

For the computation of a calendar month running from an arbitrary date, see 37 Halsbury's Laws (3rd Edn) 83, para 143.

For application for a new tenancy of business premises, see 23 ibid 891, para 1714.

For the Landlord and Tenant Act 1954, s 29, see 18 Halsbury's Statutes (3rd Edn) 564.

For the Interpretation Act 1978, Sch 1, definition of 'month', see 48 ibid 1319.

h

Cases referred to in opinions

Freeman v Read (1863) 4 B & S 174, 2 New Rep 320, 32 LJMC 226, 8 LT 458, 10 Jur NS 149, 122 ER 425, 45 Digest (Repl) 236, 67.

Lester v Garland (1808) 15 Ves 248, [1803–13] All ER Rep 436, 33 ER 748, 45 Digest (Repl) 254, 211.

Appeal

Robert William Dodds, trading as Cee Bee Autos ('the tenant'), appealed against the

---

a Section 29(3), so far as material, is set out out at p 610 d, post
b Schedule 1, so far as material, provides: '"Month" means calendar month.'

decision of the Court of Appeal (Stephenson and Templeman LJJ, Bridge LJ dissenting)
([1980] 2 All ER 507, [1980] 1 WLR 1061) on 29th February 1980 dismissing the tenant's *a*
appeal against an order made by his Honour Judge Whitehead in the Grantham County
Court on 27th April 1979 dismissing the tenant's appeal from an order of Mr Registrar
Wain made on 23rd March 1979 whereby the registrar dismissed the tenant's application,
under s 24 of the Landlord and Tenant Act 1954, for the grant of a new tenancy under
Part II of that Act of premises at 34 George Street, Grantham, Lincolnshire, of which the
respondent, Kenneth Edward Walker, was the landlord, on the ground that the *b*
application was made out of time under s 29(3) of the 1954 Act. The facts are set out in
the opinion of Lord Diplock.

Mathew Thorpe QC and *Michael Barnes* for the tenant.
The landlord appeared in person.

c
Their Lordships took time for consideration.

18th June. The following opinions were delivered.

LORD DIPLOCK. My Lords, Part II of the Landlord and Tenant Act 1954 entitles a
tenant of business premises, whose tenancy has been terminated by notice given to him *d*
by his landlord in accordance with the provisions of that Act, to apply to the court for a
new tenancy. By s 29(3) the application must be made 'not less than two nor more than
four months after the giving of the landlord's notice'.

In the instant case the (respondent) landlord's notice was given on 30th September
1978; the (appellant) tenant's application to the court for a new lease was made on 31st
January 1979. The only question in this appeal is: was that one day too late? *e*

The registrar and the judge of Grantham County Court both thought that it was too
late. They dismissed the tenant's application on the ground that the court had no
jurisdiction to entertain it. In the Court of Appeal ([1980] 2 All ER 507, [1980] 1 WLR
1061) opinion was divided. Stephenson and Templeman LJJ, agreed that it was one day
too late; Bridge LJ thought that it was just in time; and leave was given by that court to
appeal to your Lordships' House. *f*

My Lords, reference to a 'month' in a statute is to be understood as a calendar
month. The Interpretation Act 1978 says so. It is also clear under a rule that has been
consistently applied by the courts since *Lester v Garland* (1808) 15 Ves 248, [1803–13] All
ER Rep 436 that, in calculating the period that has elapsed after the occurrence of the
specified event such as the giving of a notice, the day on which the event occurs is
excluded from the reckoning. It is equally well established, and is not disputed by *g*
counsel for the tenant, that when the relevant period is a month or a specified number
of months after the giving of a notice the general rule is that the period ends on the
corresponding date in the appropriate subsequent month, ie the day of that month that
bears the same number as the day of the earlier month on which the notice was given.

The corresponding date rule is simple. It is easy of application. Except in a small
minority of cases, of which the instant case is not an example, all that the calculator has *h*
to do is to mark in his diary the corresponding date in the appropriate subsequent
month. Because the number of days in five months of the year is less than in the seven
others the inevitable consequence of the corresponding date rule is that one month's
notice given in a 30-day month is one day shorter than one month's notice given in a 31-
day month and is three days shorter if it is given in February. Corresponding variations
in the length of notice reckoned in days occurs where the required notice is a plurality *j*
of months.

This simple general rule, which Cockburn CJ in *Freeman v Read* (1863) 4 B & S 174 at
184, 122 ER 425 at 429 described as being 'in accordance with common usage . . . and
with the sense of mankind', works perfectly well without need for any modification so
long as there is in the month in which the notice expires a day which bears the same

number as the day of the month on which the notice was given. Such was the instant
a case and such will be every other case except for notices given on the 31st of a 31-day
month and expiring in a 30-day month or in February, and notices expiring in February
and given on 30th or 29th (except in leap years) of any other month of the year. In these
exceptional cases, the modification of the corresponding date rule that is called for is also
well established: the period given by the notice ends on the last day of the month in
which the notice expires.

b   My Lords, I do not personally derive assistance from pursuing metaphysical arguments
about attributing to the one day or the other the punctum temporis between 2400 hrs
on 30th September and 0000 hrs on 1st October at which time began to run against the
tenant. These seem to me quite inappropriate to the determination of the meaning of
a statute which regulates the mutual rights of landlords and tenants of all business
premises and is intended to be understood and acted on by them. It refers to periods to
c be reckoned in months and was passed at a time when the corresponding date rule had
been recognised for more than a century as applicable in reckoning periods of a month
after the occurrence of a specified event. In agreement with the majority of the Court of
Appeal, I would not construe the Act as calling for any departure from the familiar
corresponding date rule where this rule can be applied nor as calling for any greater
modification in the general rule than was already recognised as applicable where there is
d no corresponding date in the month in which the notice expires because it is shorter than
the month in which the notice was given.
      In the instant case the corresponding date rule presents no difficulty. I would apply it
and dismiss the appeal.

LORD EDMUND-DAVIES. My Lords, I am in respectful agreement with the views
e expressed in the speeches of my noble and learned friends Lord Diplock and Lord
Russell, which I have read in draft, and I would accordingly dismiss the appeal.

LORD FRASER OF TULLYBELTON. My Lords, I have had the advantage of
reading in draft the speeches prepared by my noble and learned friends Lord Diplock and
Lord Russell. I agree with them, and for the reasons stated therein I too would dismiss
f this appeal.

LORD RUSSELL OF KILLOWEN. My Lords, it is common ground that in this
case the period of four months did not begin to run until the end of the date of the
relevant service on 30th September, ie at midnight 30th September–1st October. It is
also common ground that ordinarily the calculation of a period of a calendar month or
g calendar months ends on what has been conveniently referred to as the corresponding
date. For example, in a four-month period, when service of the relevant notice was on
28th September, time would begin to run at midnight 28th–29th September and would
end at midnight 28th–29th January, a period embracing four calendar months. It is to
be observed that the number of *days* in the four month period in that example is in one
sense inevitably limited by the fact that September and November each contains but 30
h days. But the application of the corresponding date principle inevitably produces
variation in the number of days involved, depending on the date on which a four-month
notice is served and the irregular allotment of days to different months. Sometimes it is
not possible to apply directly the principle, for instance if a four-month notice is served
on 30th October (the time beginning to run at midnight 30th–31st October), there being
in February but 28 (or 29) days it is not possible to find a corresponding date in February
and plainly a corresponding date cannot be sought in March; the application of the
corresponding date principle in such case can only lead to termination of the four-month
period at midnight 28th February–1st March (or midnight 29th February–1st March in
a leap year). That is an inevitable outcome.
      Bridge LJ in his dissenting judgment in this case adopted a simple stance. Time he
said (correctly) began to run at midnight 30th September–1st October. Stretching ahead

were the four calendar months of October, November, December and January; the
tenant was allowed the whole of those four calendar months including the whole of 31st *a*
January; therefore the application made on 31st January was made in time. I am with
respect unable to accept this departure from the corresponding date principle simply
because the period starts to run at the outset of the first of a month: a departure from the
sound and well-established rule is not required in that one instance, as it is required in the
example given of there being no corresponding date in February. For the tenant it was
submitted that Templeman LJ had fallen into the error of including the whole of 30th *b*
September in the period. I am clearly of opinion that the language used by him was not
to that effect.

Accordingly I am of opinion that the corresponding date principle is applicable in this
case, that the four-month period expired at midnight 30th–31st January, and that the
application made on 31st January was out of time and could not be entertained.
Consequently I also would dismiss this appeal. *c*

LORD ROSKILL. My Lords, I have had the advantage of reading in draft the speeches
of my noble and learned friends Lord Diplock and Lord Russell. For the reasons they
give, I agree that this appeal fails and should be dismissed.

Appeal dismissed.

Solicitors: *Radcliffes & Co*, agents for *Norton & Hamilton*, Grantham (for the tenant). *d*

Mary Rose Plummer   Barrister.

R v Holmes, ex parte Sherman and another

QUEEN'S BENCH DIVISION *e*
DONALDSON LJ AND HODGSON J
26th NOVEMBER, 8th DECEMBER 1980

*Arrest – Arrest without warrant – Preferment of charge – Requirement that arrested person be
charged with offence as soon as there is sufficient evidence – Whether charge can be postponed
when to prefer a charge would prejudice further inquiries into other offences – Judges' Rules* *f*
(revised 1964), Introduction, principle (d).

*Arrest – Requirement that person arrested be taken before a magistrates' court as soon as
practicable – 'As soon as practicable' meaning within 48 hours of arrest in absence of any special
statutory provision – Magistrates' Courts Act 1952, s 38(4).*

The common law rule, embodied in principle (d)[a] in the introduction to the Judges' *g*
Rules, that a person arrested for a suspected offence has to be charged with the offence or
informed that he may be prosecuted for it as soon as there is sufficient evidence to prefer
a charge is a mandatory requirement and cannot be made subject to any qualification by,
for example, the police setting an unduly high standard of 'sufficient evidence' or on the
ground that to prefer a charge would prejudice or make more difficult police inquiries
into other suspected offences (see p 614 g, p 615 c d and p 616 j, post). *h*

The requirement in s 38(4)[b] of the Magistrates' Courts Act 1952 that a person taken
into custody for an offence without a warrant shall be brought before a magistrates' court
'as soon as practicable' means, in the absence of any special statutory provision, that he is
to be brought before a magistrates' court within 48 hours of the arrest (see p 615 g and
p 616 c j, post). *j*

Notes
For charging a suspect, see 11 Halsbury's Laws (4th Edn) para 422.

For bringing an arrested person before a magistrates' court as soon as practicable after
his arrest, see ibid para 118.

a   Principle (d) is set out at p 614 e, post
b   Section 38(4) is set out at p 615 e, post

a For the Magistrates' Courts Act 1952, s 38, see 21 Halsbury's Statutes (3rd Edn) 221.
As from 6th July 1981, s 38 of the 1952 Act has been replaced by s 43 of the
Magistrates' Courts Act 1980.

Cases referred to in judgments
R v Houghton (1978) 68 Cr App R 197, CA.
R v Hudson (1980) Times, 29th October, CA.

b **Applications for habeas corpus**
Clinton John Sherman and Edward Charles Apps applied for writs of habeas corpus ad
subjiciendum in respect of their detention at Kentish Town police station following their
arrest in connection with handling stolen goods. The facts are set out in the judgment
of Donaldson LJ.

Christopher Hookway for the applicants.
c *Alan Rawley QC* and *Tony Docking* for the respondent.

Cur adv vult

8th December. The following judgments were read.

DONALDSON LJ. At 11.30 am on Tuesday, 18th November 1980 the applicants
d were arrested by officers of the Metropolitan Police. They were taken to Kentish Town
police station where they were questioned. Their solicitor made inquiries as to where
they were and was told. However, when by the morning of Thursday, 20th November
they had neither been charged nor brought before a magistrate, he rightly applied to this
court for a writ of habeas corpus.

This application was heard that afternoon and was adjourned until 10.30 am on the
e Friday, the applicants' solicitor being told to notify the respondent, Det Sgt Holmes of the
Metropolitan Police. To our surprise the police were neither present nor represented at
the adjourned hearing. Accordingly, we made an immediate order for the issue of a writ
of habeas corpus requiring Sgt Holmes to produce the applicants in court at 2 pm. Half
an hour later Sgt Holmes arrived in court and explained that the applicants' solicitor had
left notice of the hearing on the counter of the police station without explaining to
f anyone what it was. We accept that explanation, but there is a lesson to be learnt. It is
the duty of applicants and their solicitors to effect proper service on respondents when
ordered so to do.

We then asked Sgt Holmes for an explanation. He said that the applicants had been
arrested and had made certain admissions. On the basis of those admissions and other
evidence, he had been in a position on the Tuesday to charge them with handling the
g proceeds of a single, very recent burglary. However, both the Metropolitan and the
Hertfordshire forces wished to question the applicants in connection with a further 100
burglaries committed over a period of three years in the areas of the two forces. The
investigation was necessarily complex and was not made any simpler by the facts that
two police forces were involved, that due to current industrial action cell space was at a
premium and that the applicants and two other people who might be involved were
h lodged in different police stations.

Sgt Holmes explained that in those circumstances he thought that he was faced with
a problem. If he charged the applicants, he or his senior officer would have to consider
granting bail and, as he assessed the situation, bail would in fact have to be granted. Once
the applicants left police custody, the investigations would become much more
difficult. He told us that in these circumstances, he considered that it was both in the
i interest of the applicants and of the public that the applicants be retained in custody
whilst, as he put it, 'they assisted the police in their inquiries'. He further explained that
he anticipated that all necessary inquiries would be completed by that evening (Friday,
21st November). The applicants would then be charged and brought before a magistrate
on the Saturday morning. By then four days would have elapsed from the time of arrest.

We told Sgt Holmes that if he would undertake to charge the applicants within 1½
hours, that being the minimum practicable time, bearing in mind that he was at the Law
Courts and the applicants were in Kentish Town, the writ of habeas corpus would be

stayed. Otherwise it would issue forthwith and the applicants would have to be produced in court at 2 pm.

It seemed to both Hodgson J and to me that Sgt Holmes was being completely frank *a* with us, that he quite genuinely could not understand what the fuss was about and that he was a good police officer doing his duty as he saw it. If this was right, it seemed to us that any criticism should be directed not at Sgt Holmes but at those in command of the Metropolitan Police whose systems and standing orders had allowed such a situation to arise. We therefore suggested to Sgt Holmes that he should get in touch with his *b* superior officers and with the legal department of the Metropolitan Police and we further adjourned the matter until Monday, 26th November.

On that day counsel appeared for the police and we were informed that the applicants had indeed been charged on the Friday and released on bail. This disposed of the matter only in the sense that the applicants had achieved the relief to which they were entitled. But it left much wider and more serious issues for investigation. Due to the *c* shortness of time available counsel for the police had been inadequately instructed and we further adjourned the matter.

At the resumed hearing counsel for the Metropolitan Police made it clear that, whilst the commissioner would not have shared Sgt Holmes's surprise at our anxiety and would have expressed himself somewhat differently, he would on the facts of this case have been fully prepared to justify the actions of the police. *d*

Let me explain how this comes about. The commissioner's view of the law is set out in his written evidence to the Royal Commission on Criminal Procedure (at pp 42–70, 157–159) and I do not doubt that other chief officers of police share his views. His general orders to the force give effect to this view.

In the instant case there were two matters which caused us particular concern. The first was that Sgt Holmes appeared to display a complete disregard of the fundamental *e* principle of the common law—

'that when a police officer who is making inquiries of any person about an offence has enough evidence to prefer a charge against that person for the offence, he should without delay cause that person to be charged or informed that he may be prosecuted for the offence.'

The quotation is from para (d) of the introduction to the 1964 Judges' Rules (see Practice *f* Note [1964] 1 All ER 237, [1964] 1 WLR 152).

The commissioner accepts this principle which he refers to as 'principle (d)', and I will use the same terminology. However, he says that he does not agree that Sgt Holmes had in fact enough evidence to charge the applicants, at any rate during the initial stages of the detention. This is interesting, but the fact remains that Sgt Holmes was the officer who had to reach a decision; he thought that he had sufficient evidence and accordingly *g* he should have preferred a charge. Furthermore, the fact that he had further inquiries to make, and that these might become more difficult if the applicants were charged, is no justification for disregarding the mandatory requirements of principle (d).

We have not investigated the instant case in detail because to do so in open court might prejudice the subsequent trial of the applicants and, in any event, now that the applicants *h* have been charged and bailed our principal concern is with the system rather than with the instant case.

The commissioner has criticised principle (d) in the following terms:

'17.32. The unsatisfactory nature of principle (d) is that an officer may have sufficient evidence to charge but may wish to defer charging an arrested person to seek advice from his superior officers or to seek legal advice whether or not it is *j* appropriate in all the circumstances of the case to charge. An officer so delaying a charge is in breach of principle (d). Equally he is open to criticism if he does *not* delay and goes ahead and charges although he wanted guidance from his superior officers or legal advice on the exercise of his discretion to prosecute. Additionally an officer may have sufficient evidence to charge a person but wishes to attempt to put that evidence to the test by seeking to obtain corroborative evidence in support. A typical example is that shown in the case [previously] referred to . . . where police

a   received an admission to a murder sufficient to support a charge but the charge was
    delayed in order to test the veracity of the admission and in particular to recover the
    murder weapon from the river where it had been thrown. Had police charged
    immediately after the confession and the confession had proved as false as the earlier
    untrue explanations the suspect had put forward as to his movements police would
    doubtless have been criticised for charging prematurely although certainly they had
    sufficient evidence to charge; by delaying the charging until they had obtained
b   corroborative evidence it could be argued that police were in breach of principle (d).
       '17.33. For these reasons I suggest that the principle in rule (d) be amended to
    recognise the fact that despite the possession by an officer of "enough evidence" to
    prefer a charge there may well be perfectly proper reasons why it is not appropriate
    to charge "without delay".'

c   Suffice it to say that, whilst there may well be strong grounds for amending the law,
    the amendment must be achieved in a constitutional manner and not by a process of
    modification in practice. The law at present is that, as soon as there is enough evidence
    to prefer a charge, the arrested person must *without delay* be charged or informed that he
    may be prosecuted for the offence. The principle is subject to no qualification and no
    qualification should be introduced by, for example, setting an unduly high standard of
d   'sufficient evidence'. The criticism that an officer refrained from charging and retained
    a man in custody is incomparably more serious than that he charged a man on insufficient
    evidence.
       The second aspect of the instant case which caused us concern was the delay in
    bringing the applicants before a magistrates' court. Section 38(4) of the Magistrates'
    Courts Act 1952 is unequivocal and imperative in its terms. It reads as follows:

e   'Where a person is taken into custody for an offence without a warrant and is
       retained in custody, he shall be brought before a magistrates' court as soon as
       practicable.'

       In both *R v Houghton* (1978) 68 Cr App R 197 at 205 and in *R v Hudson* (1980) Times,
    29th October it was I think accepted that save in a wholly exceptional case the period
f   between arrest and appearance before a magistrates' court should not exceed 48 hours.
    The same approach seems to have been adopted in the Prevention of Terrorism
    (Temporary Provisions) Act 1976. The Act abrogates s 38 of the Magistrates' Courts Act
    1952 where it applies but only permits detention in right of an arrest exceeding 48 hours
    if the Secretary of State extends this period. This seems to me to point unmistakably to
    a period of 48 hours as being the maximum permissible period of detention in right of
g   an arrest in the absence of special statutory provision. Counsel for the police drew our
    attention to s 29 (5) of the Children and Young Persons Act 1969, as amended by the Bail
    Act 1976, which requires a young person to be brought before a magistrates' court
    within 72 hours. He submitted that this pointed to a longer period than 48 hours being
    acceptable under s 38 of the 1952 Act. I do not think that this inference can be drawn.
    Section 29 is a self-contained code applying to children and young persons which is
h   designed primarily to achieve their immediate release from arrest or alternatively their
    transfer to the care of a local authority. It is primarily concerned with their welfare. It
    is only in a well-defined and wholly exceptional case that a delay of 72 hours in bringing
    a detained child or young person before a magistrates' court is specially authorised.
       It was against this background that we were told that in a specimen period of three
    months, for which statistics were specially prepared for the Royal Commission, 212
j   persons or 0·43% of those arrested in the Metropolitan Police District were detained for
    more than 72 hours before being brought before a magistrates' court. The percentage
    may be tiny, but we are concerned with people not percentages. No figures are available
    for the number of persons who were so detained for more than 48 hours, but clearly it
    must have been higher.
       What is the reason? I think that it is largely the time lag between arresting on
    suspicion and the stage at which the police consider that they have sufficient evidence to
    charge. Curiously enough, s 38 of the 1952 Act makes no mention of the preferment of

a charge as a precondition of bringing the arrested person before a magistrates' court. However, the commissioner takes the view that this is the position and I know that many *a* lawyers would agree with him. He has recommended that this precondition be removed by giving magistrates power to consider bail before a charge is made and requiring the police to bring an arrested person before a magistrate within 72 hours of arrest.

There is much to be said for this recommendation, but both we and the police have to live not only with but by the law as it is. The arrested person has to be bailed or brought before a magistrates' court 'as soon as practicable'. Practicability is obviously a slightly *b* elastic concept which must take account of the availability of police manpower, transport and magistrates' courts. It will also have to take account of any unavoidable delay in obtaining sufficient evidence to charge, but this latter factor has to be assessed in the light of the power of the police to release on bail conditioned by a requirement to return to the police station when further inquiries have been completed and a power to release and re-arrest when the evidence is more nearly sufficient. Any such release may involve a risk *c* that the arrested person will abscond, commit further crimes or interfere with witnesses, but this risk has to be balanced against the vital consideration that no man is to be deprived of his liberty save in accordance with the law. 'As soon as practicable' still means 'within about 48 hours at most'.

The commissioner in his evidence to the Royal Commission says that:

'A suspect in custody aggrieved about the length of time taken before a charge is *d* preferred is not without remedy because he can apply to the Divisional Court for a writ of habeas corpus. This is by no means a legal remedy that has fallen into disuse but a real and available remedy. In 1977 there were 55 applications to the Divisional Court for writs of habeas corpus.'

This is true, but habeas corpus is a remedy for an abuse of power and it should rarely *e* be necessary to invoke it. Furthermore, if, as the commissioner seems to suggest, an application for such a writ is to be regarded as a routine method whereby any arrested person aggrieved by his detention can find out whether his grievance is justified, this court is going to be extremely busy and a great deal of police time is going to be spent in justifying detentions. This is not an attractive prospect. However, it is right that all should know that the writ of habeas corpus has not fallen into disuse, but is, as the *f* commissioner says, a real and available remedy. They should also know that, if the arrested person is unable to apply for the issue of the writ, others may do so on his behalf. Furthermore, such applications are given absolute priority in the fixing of the business of the court. I would only add the caution that the costs to the applicant of a frivolous application may be considerable, as will be the cost to the police if the application is found to be justified.

The police are undoubtedly carrying out their duties under very considerable *g* difficulties which are both logistic and legal. We are told that the report of the Royal Commission will be published in the fairly near future[1]. Once that report has been published and the recommendations of the commission considered, I hope that Parliament will feel able to treat the clarification and improvement of the law in this field as a matter of the utmost urgency.

In this case the applicants were fully justified in making this application which has *h* resulted in their being charged earlier than would otherwise have been the case and also expedited their release on bail. Their costs will be paid by the police.

HODGSON J. I agree.

Order accordingly.   *j*

Solicitors: *Howard Gross & Co* (for the applicants); *R E T Birch* (for the respondent).

Sepala Munasinghe Esq Barrister.

---

1 Report of the Royal Commission on Criminal Procedure (Cmnd 8092 (January 1981)); The Investigation and Prosecution of Criminal Offences in England and Wales—the Law and Procedure (Cmnd 8092–I (January 1981))

a

Attorney General's Reference (No 4 of 1980)

COURT OF APPEAL, CRIMINAL DIVISION
ACKNER LJ, TUDOR EVANS AND DRAKE JJ
26th MARCH, 2nd APRIL 1981

b

Criminal law – Homicide – Causation – Cause of death – Manslaughter – Death caused by one or other of two or more acts of accused each of which sufficient to establish manslaughter but Crown not able to prove which act caused death – Proper direction to jury – Whether Crown required to prove which act caused death to found conviction for manslaughter.

c

In the course of an argument on the landing of a maisonette the accused pushed the deceased causing her to fall backwards over a handrail and head first onto the floor below. Almost immediately afterwards the accused tied a rope round the deceased's neck and dragged her upstairs by it. He then placed her in the bath and cut her neck with a knife to let out her blood, with the purpose of cutting up her body and disposing of it, which he then did. The body was never found. The accused was charged with manslaughter. There was evidence that the deceased died either as a result of being pushed down the stairs or by being strangled by the rope or by having her throat cut, but the Crown conceded that it was impossible to prove which of those acts had caused the death. In response to a submission by the defence at the close of the Crown's case that there was no case to go to the jury, the judge decided to withdraw the case from the jury and directed an acquittal on the ground that the Crown had failed to prove the cause of the death. The Attorney General referred to the court for its opinion the question whether, if an accused person killed another by one or other of two or more different acts, each of which was sufficient to establish manslaughter, it was necessary to prove which act caused the death in order to found a conviction.

d

e

Held – It had not been necessary for the Crown to prove which act had caused the death in order to found a conviction for manslaughter, since it had been common ground that the deceased had been killed by an act done to her by the accused and there had been material available to the jury which would have entitled them to convict the accused of manslaughter for whichever of his acts had caused the death even though they could not be satisfied which act had caused the death. The proper course for the judge would have been to direct the jury to ask themselves whether they were satisfied that each of the accused's acts had been a sufficient act to establish manslaughter, and if they were so satisfied, they would have been entitled to convict the accused of manslaughter. It followed that the case should not have been withdrawn from the jury (see p 619, *h* to p 620 *b*, post).

f

g

Notes
For absence of the body in homicide cases, see 11 Halsbury's Laws (4th Edn) para 361, for manslaughter in general, see ibid para 1161, and for cases on the corpus delicti, see 14(2) Digest (Reissue) 480–481, 3949–3963.

h

Cases referred to in judgment
R v Church [1965] 2 All ER 72, [1966] 1 QB 59, [1965] 2 WLR 1220, 129 JP 366, 49 Cr App R 206, CCA, 15 Digest (Reissue) 1140, 9656.
Thabo Meli v R [1954] 1 All ER 373, [1954] 1 WLR 228, PC, 14(1) Digest (Reissue) 19, 50.

j

Reference
This was a reference by the Attorney General under s 36 of the Criminal Justice Act 1972 seeking the court's opinion on the following point of law: whether a person who has committed a series of acts against another culminating in the death of that other person, each act in the series being either unlawful and dangerous or an act of gross criminal negligence, is entitled to be acquitted of manslaughter on the ground that it cannot be

shown which of such acts caused the death of the deceased. The facts are set out in the
judgment of the court.

a

Brian Walsh QC and *Keith Lawrence* for the Attorney General.
James Chadwin QC and *Ashraf Khan* (neither of whom appeared below) for the respondent.

Cur adv vult

b

2nd April.   **ACKNER LJ** read the following judgment of the court: This is a reference
to the court by the Attorney General of a point of law seeking the opinion of the court
pursuant to s 36 of the Criminal Justice Act 1972. It raises yet again the problem of the
supposed corpse, and the facts, which I take from the terms of the reference itself, are
inevitably macabre.

The deceased was the fiancée of the accused and for some months before her death   *c*
they had lived together in a maisonette consisting of two floors of a house connected by
two short flights of carpeted wooden stairs. The deceased was employed locally and was
last seen at work on 17th January 1979 at about 5 pm. Thereafter no one, other than the
accused, ever saw her alive again.

The deceased met her death on 18th January 1979, although this fact was not known
until over three weeks later when the defendant so informed a friend. His account, the   *d*
first of a number, was that in the course of an argument on the evening of 17th January
he had slapped her on the face causing her to fall downstairs and bang her head. He said
that he had then put her to bed but discovered next morning that she was dead. He then
took her body to his home town and buried her.

On the following day, 14th February, he gave his second account, telling the same
friend that after the deceased had 'fallen downstairs' he had dragged her upstairs by a   *e*
piece of rope tied round her neck. He subsequently cut up her body with a saw before
burying it. The next day, on the advice of his friend, the accused went to see a superior
and gave an account similar to the one he had given his friend.

We now come to the statements which he made to the police. On 27th February,
having consulted solicitors, the accused was interviewed by the police at his solicitors'
office. He began by giving the police substantially the same account that he had given   *f*
to his friend and his superior but added that instead of burying the deceased he had
'dumped' the various parts of her body on a tip. At the police station later that day he
amplified his statement by saying that the incident when the deceased 'fell downstairs'
occurred at about 7 pm on 17th January and that it was the following day, when he
found her motionless, that he pulled her upstairs by a rope around her neck and then cut
up her body in the bathroom. On the following day after much questioning by the   *g*
police he changed his account stating that everything had happened on Thursday, 18th
January at about 7 am. This is what he then said happened. (i) He and the deceased had
an argument on the landing in the course of which each slapped the other; he seized the
deceased and shook her hard; she dug her nails into him and he pushed her away
instinctively, causing her to fall backwards over the handrail, down the stairs head first
onto the floor. (ii) He went downstairs immediately to find her motionless and on a very   *h*
cursory examination discovered no pulse, and no sign of breath but frothy blood coming
from her mouth. (iii) Almost immediately thereafter he dragged her upstairs by a rope
tied around her neck, placed her in the bath and cut her neck with a penknife to let out
her blood, having already decided to cut up her body and dispose of the pieces.

He agreed that his previous account was untrue and he made a detailed voluntary
statement along the lines set out in (i), (ii) and (iii) above describing how subsequently he   *j*
had cut up and disposed of her body.

In the course of these interviews at the police station, after the defendant had given his
revised account, the following conversation took place:

> '*Officer.* How long was it from the time that she went backwards over the
> handrail to when you started pulling her up the stairs with a piece of rope around
> her neck? *Accused.* I went downstairs when she went backwards. I looked at her,

a   tried her pulse. I tried to lift her and she wee'd, so I put her down again. Then two girls went past [the glass fronted door] so I covered the door with the blanket. Then I got the piece of rope and pulled her up the stairs.'
    '*Officer.* When did you decide you were going to cut the body up and dispose of it? *Accused.* Just before I pulled her up the stairs.'

Later he was questioned by the officer:

b   'Q. Is it correct that you hauled [her] to the bathroom, and put her into the bath and then cut her neck with a knife to let the blood out and these were all a continuous series of events? A. Yes, they all happened together.'

Subsequently the police discovered evidence which corroborated the accused's account of how, where and when he had cut up the body. They also found the saw he had used
c   and the shopkeeper who sold it to him. However, the body of the deceased was never found, only some minute fragments of bone, which were discovered in the maisonette. There was thus no expert evidence as to the cause of death. The deceased died either as a result of being pushed and thus caused to fall backwards over the handrail and backwards down the stairs head first onto the floor, or by being strangled with the rope, or having her throat cut. The Crown conceded that it was not possible for them to prove
d   whether the deceased died as the result of the 'fall' downstairs or from what the accused did to the deceased thereafter.
    The indictment charged the accused with (i) manslaughter, (ii) obstructing the coroner in the execution of his duty, and (iii) preventing the burial of a corpse.
    The accused pleaded guilty to the third count, the Crown offered no evidence on the second and the trial proceeded on the count of manslaughter.
e   At the close of the Crown's case counsel for the accused stated that he proposed to submit that on the facts proved there was no case of manslaughter capable of going to the jury. It is not easy to follow from the transcript the exact basis of his submissions, but what he appears to have been contending was that (a) it was not possible for the jury to be sure what caused the deceased's death and (b) whether the death was caused as a result of her 'fall' down the stairs or from what the accused subsequently did, believing her to
f   be dead, in neither event was there a prima facie case of manslaughter.
    The judge, although expressing his reluctance to accept that the accused could be in a better position as a result of his dismembering the body of the deceased, appeared to have been very concerned at what he described as 'an insuperable problem of sentencing', were the accused to be convicted of manslaughter. He expressed the view that the real criminality of the accused's behaviour was in disposing of the body, a view which this
g   court is unable to accept. These views appear to have influenced his decision, which was to withdraw the case from the jury and to direct an acquittal on the ground that the Crown had failed to prove the cause of the death of the deceased.
    On the above facts this reference raises a single and simple question, viz, if an accused kills another by one or other of two or more different acts each of which, if it caused the death, is a sufficient act to establish manslaughter, is it necessary in order to found a
h   conviction to prove which act caused the death? The answer to that question is No, it is is not necessary to found a conviction to prove which act caused the death. No authority is required to justify this answer, which is clear beyond argument, as was indeed immediately conceded by counsel on behalf of the accused.
    What went wrong in this case was that counsel made jury points to the judge and not submissions of law. He was in effect contending that the jury should not convict of
j   manslaughter if the death had resulted from the 'fall', because the push which had projected the deceased over the handrail was a reflex and not a voluntary action, as a result of her digging her nails into him. If, however, the deceased was still alive when he cut her throat, since he then genuinely believed her to be dead, having discovered neither pulse nor sign of breath, but frothy blood coming from her mouth, he could not be guilty of manslaughter because he had not behaved with gross criminal negligence. What counsel and the judge unfortunately overlooked was that there was material available to the jury which would have entitled them to have convicted the accused of

manslaughter, whichever of the two sets of acts caused her death. It being common ground that the deceased was killed by an act done to her by the accused and it being a conceded that the jury could not be satisfied which was the act which caused the death, they should have been directed in due course in the summing up, to ask themselves the following questions: (i) 'Are we satisfied beyond reasonable doubt that the deceased's "fall" downstairs was the result of an intentional act by the accused which was unlawful and dangerous?' If the answer was No, then they would acquit. If the answer was Yes, then they would need to ask themselves a second question, namely: (ii) 'Are we satisfied b beyond reasonable doubt that the act of cutting the girl's throat was an act of gross criminal negligence?' If the answer to that question was No, then they would acquit, but if the answer was Yes, then the verdict would be guilty of manslaughter. The jury would thus have been satisfied that, whichever act had killed the deceased, each was a sufficient act to establish the offence of manslaughter.

The facts of this case did not call for 'a series of acts direction' following the principle c in *Thabo Meli v R* [1954] 1 All ER 373, [1954] 1 WLR 228. We have accordingly been deprived of the stimulating questions whether the decision in *R v Church* [1965] 2 All ER 72, [1966] 1 QB 59 correctly extended that principle to manslaughter, in particular to 'constructive manslaughter' and if so whether that view was part of the ratio decidendi.

Determination accordingly. d

Solicitors: *Director of Public Prosecutions*; *Kaye & Martin*, Hull (for the defendant).

N P Metcalfe Esq   Barrister.

e

Baxendale v Instow Parish Council and others

CHANCERY DIVISION
SIR ROBERT MEGARRY V-C
5th, 6th, 7th, 14th NOVEMBER 1980 f

Foreshore – Rights over foreshore – Conveyance of portion of foreshore – Whether grant of foreshore conveying fixed piece of land consisting of foreshore as it was at the time of the conveyance – Whether grant conveying movable piece of land consisting of foreshore as it is from time to time – Whether presumption that conveyance granting only movable piece of land.

g

Commons – Registration – Common land and rights of common – Waste land of manor – Land forming part of foreshore – Land conveyed in 1855 to owner of manor – Land contiguous to waste land of manor – Sea and foreshore receding leaving conveyed land above high-water mark – Whether conveyance granting movable freehold consisting of foreshore wherever it might be – Whether land ceasing to be held under 1855 grant because no longer foreshore and becoming part h of waste land of manor – Whether land still held under conveyance and therefore not registrable as waste land of manor – Commons Registration Act 1965, s 22(1)(b).

Commons – Registration – Common land and rights of common – Waste land of manor – Whether waste land 'of' manor including waste land 'reputedly of' manor at time of registration – Commons Registration Act 1965, s 22(1)(b).

j

In 1855 the Crown conveyed to the owner of a manor on the coast 'three several pieces or parcels of land lying between high water mark and low water mark and covered with water at ordinary tides containing by admeasurement 262 acres or thereabouts and situate adjacent to [land of the manor] which pieces or parcels of land are more particularly delineated and described in the Plan drawn in the margin [of the conveyance]

and are thereon colored red and are distinguished by the letters A, B, and C'. The land
a conveyed was then part of the foreshore and was precisely delineated on the plan. At the
time land of the manor was contiguous to the foreshore. Over the years the sea, and with
it the foreshore, receded, leaving the land in the conveyance above the high-water
mark. The county council registered the land in the conveyance as common land under
the Commons Registration Act 1965 on the basis that it was 'waste land of a manor'
within s 22(1)(b)[a] of that Act. The commons commissioner confirmed the registration,
b on the ground that the land conveyed in 1855 was a movable freehold, namely the
foreshore, wherever from time to time it might be, and not the fixed freehold of the
foreshore as it was in 1855, and that as the foreshore had moved with the sea, the land in
the conveyance was no longer held under the 1855 conveyance, but by accretion had
become part of the land to which it was contiguous, and, since the contiguous land was
waste land of the manor, the conveyed land had also become waste land of the manor and
c as such was registrable as common land under s 22(1)(b). The owners of the land
appealed, contending that the 1855 grant had conveyed a fixed freehold consisting of the
foreshore as it was in 1855, so that although the land conveyed was no longer foreshore
it was still held under the 1855 conveyance. The council contended, inter alia, that waste
land 'of' a manor for the purposes of s 22(1)(b) included land which was 'reputedly waste
land of' a manor at the time of registration.

d
Held – The appeal would be allowed for the following reasons—
    (1) There was no rule of law that a grant of foreshore conveyed only a movable piece
of land, namely the foreshore as it was from time to time, since a conveyance of foreshore
was capable of conveying either the foreshore as it was from time to time or a fixed piece
of land consisting of the foreshore as it was at the time of the conveyance. Although
e there might be a presumption that a conveyance of foreshore was intended to convey
only the foreshore as it was from time to time, what was in fact conveyed by a particular
grant depended on the true construction of that grant. Since the 1855 grant conveyed
'land' and not 'foreshore', and having regard to the particularity with which the
conveyance and the plan indorsed on it defined the land conveyed, the presumption (if
it existed) had been rebutted, and on its true construction the 1855 grant conveyed the
f fixed area of land shown on the plan indorsed on the conveyance, and not a piece of land
which moved with the position of the sea. It followed that the commissioner had erred
in law in holding that the 1855 grant conveyed the foreshore as it was from time to time,
and that the land in question remained land held under 1855 grant and had not become
waste land of the manor by accretion. Accordingly, the land should be removed from
the register (see p 627 *a* to *c*, p 628 *g* to *j* and p 631 *f h*, post); *Scratton v Brown* [1824–34]
g All ER Rep 59 distinguished.
    (2) On the true construction of s 22(1)(b) of the 1965 Act, waste land 'of' a manor did
not extend to waste land 'reputedly of' a manor but was confined to land which was in
fact, at the time of registration, waste land of a manor (see p 630 *b d* to *g* and p 631 *e*,
post); *Box Parish Council v Lacey* [1979] 1 All ER 113 considered.
    Per Curiam. In cases stated under the 1965 Act it is the duty of each party to give the
h other party notice at the earliest possible moment of any new point which was not taken
before the commons commissioner, and if this is not done the court may order an
adjournment with costs (see p 629 *e f*, post).

Notes
For common and commonable lands, see 6 Halsbury's Laws (4th Edn) para 506, for waste
j land of a manor, see ibid paras 510, 756, and for cases on the subject, see 11 Digest
(Reissue) 5–23, 2–262, 282–285.
    For the grant of foreshore, see 39 Halsbury's Laws (3rd Edn) 558, para 772, and for
cases on the subject, see 47 Digest (Repl) 709–711, 547–575.
    For the Commons Registration Act 1965, s 22, see 3 Halsbury's Statutes (3rd Edn) 933.

---

a Section 22(1), so far as material, is set out at p 623 *c*, post

Cases referred to in judgment

Attorney General v Hanmer (1858) 27 LJ Ch 837, 31 LTOS 379, 22 JP 543, 4 Jur NS 751, *a*
    11 Digest (Reissue) 23, 283.

Attorney General of Southern Nigeria v John Holt & Co (Liverpool) Ltd [1915] AC 599, [1914–
    15] All ER Rep 444, 84 LJPC 98, 112 LT 955, PC, 47 Digest (Repl) 705, 509.

Box Parish Council v Lacey [1979] 1 All ER 113, sub nom *Re Box Hill Common* [1980] Ch
    109, [1979] 2 WLR 117, 77 LGR 289, 37 P & CR 181, CA, Digest (Cont Vol E) 81,
    366a.   *b*

Bradshaw v Lawson (1791) 4 Term Rep 443, 100 ER 1109, 13 Digest (Reissue) 30, 289.

Britford Common, Re [1977] 1 All ER 532, [1977] 1 WLR 39, 141 JP 179, 75 LGR 317, 33
    P & CR 377, Digest (Cont Vol E) 81, 282a.

Chewton Common, Christchurch, Re [1977] 3 All ER 509, [1977] 1 WLR 1242, 141 JP 674,
    75 LGR 727, 35 P & CR 220, Digest (Cont Vol E) 81, 282c.

Delacherois v Delacherois (1864) 11 HL Cas 62, 4 New Rep 501, 10 Jur NS 886, 11 ER 1254, *c*
    HL, 13 Digest (Reissue) 4, 1.

Doe d Jones v Richards (1798) Peake Add Cas 180, NP, 13 Digest (Reissue) 6, 20.

Doe d Molesworth v Sleeman (1846) 9 QB 298, 1 New Pract Cas 434, 15 LJQB 338, 7 LTOS
    252, 10 Jur 568, 11 ER 1287, 13 Digest (Reissue) 4, 5.

Doe d Clayton v Williams (1843) 11 M & W 803, 12 LJ Ex 429, 1 LTOS 316, 152 ER 1029,
    13 Digest (Reissue) 9, 50.   *d*

Eastwood v Ashton [1915] AC 900, 84 LJ Ch 671, 113 LT 562, HL, 17 Digest (Reissue) 427,
    1889.

Government of the State of Penang v Beng Hong Oon [1971] 3 All ER 1163, [1972] AC 425,
    [1972] 2 WLR 1, PC, Digest (Cont Vol D) 1021, 482a.

Hull and Selby Railway Co, Re (1839) 5 M & W 327, 8 LJ Ex 260, 151 ER 139, 47 Digest
    (Repl) 705, 510.   *e*

Lawrence's Will Trusts, Re [1971] 3 All ER 433, [1972] Ch 418, [1971] 3 WLR 188, Digest
    (Cont Vol D) 726, 455a.

Mellor v Walmesley [1905] 2 Ch 164, 74 LJ Ch 475, 93 LT 574, CA; *rvsg* [1904] 2 Ch 525,
    47 Digest (Repl) 703, 488.

Mercer v Denne [1905] 2 Ch 538, [1904–7] All ER Rep 71, 74 LJ Ch 723, 93 LT 412, 70
    JP 65, 3 LGR 1293, CA, 47 Digest (Repl) 704, 499.   *f*

R v Duchess of Buccleugh (1704) 6 Mod Rep 150, 87 ER 909.

Scratton v Brown (1825) 4 B & C 485, 6 Dow & Ry KB 536, [1824–34] All ER Rep 59, 107
    ER 1140, 13 Digest (Reissue) 9, 63.

Wallington v Townsend [1939] 2 All ER 225, [1939] Ch 588, 108 LJ Ch 305, 160 LT 537,
    55 TLR 531, 40 Digest (Repl) 279, 2329.

Welden v Bridgewater (1595) Cro Eliz 421, 78 ER 663, 2 Digest (Reissue) 50, 211.   *g*

Case stated

William Lloyd Baxendale, Ronald George Price and Peter Baring, the trustees in whom
the Christie Devon Estate was vested ('the applicants'), appealed by way of case stated
under the Commons Registration Act 1965, from the decision of Mr A A Baden Fuller,
a commons commissioner, dated 24th September 1979, confirming the registration *h*
under the 1965 Act of land forming part of the estate, comprising sands, sandhills and
grass above high-water mark at Instow, North Devon, as waste land of a manor. The
respondents to the appeal were the Instow Parish Council, the North Devon District
Council and the Devon County Council. The facts are set out in the judgment.

Derek Wood QC and *K M J Lewison* for the applicants.   *j*
Sheila Cameron for the respondents.

                                                                      Cur adv vult

14th November. **SIR ROBERT MEGARRY V-C** read the following judgment: This
is an appeal by way of case stated under the Commons Registration Act 1965 from a

decision of a commons commissioner, Mr A A Baden Fuller, dated 24th September 1979,
a concerning land at Instow, North Devon. The case raises questions on movable freeholds,
on the law of accretion of land occurring on the imperceptible retreat of the sea, on the
boundaries and nature of manorial waste, and on the construction of a Crown grant
made in 1855, as well as the construction of the 1965 Act. The case was stated on 7th July
1980, but a number of points raised are now not being pursued or have in effect been
resolved by agreement. The dispute is between the applicants, the three trustees in
b whom the Christie Devon Estate is vested as statutory owner under the Settled Land Act
1925, and the respondents, the Instow Parish Council, the North Devon District Council
and the Devon County Council. The land in question is a long strip running mainly
north and south, but following the indentations of the former coastline. The sea has
gradually receded westwards, and this has thrown up the strip of land which, though
formerly below high-water mark of ordinary tides, is now above it. That is the strip in
c dispute. The whole of it falls within the area registered by the county council under the
Act, though that area includes other land as well.

     Under the Act, 'common land' can be registered. By s 22(1), 'common land' means
'(a) land subject to rights of common . . .' and also '(b) waste land of a manor not subject
to rights of common'. No question of any rights of common under para (a) has arisen;
the central question on the Act has been the meaning of the words 'waste land of a
d manor' in para (b). In that phrase there has been no real disagreement on the meaning
of 'waste'. Land is waste if it is open, uncultivated and unoccupied; and it is waste land
of a manor if it is open, uncultivated and unoccupied land which forms part of the manor
and does not constitute part of the lord's demesne: see Re Britford Common [1977] 1 All ER
532, [1977] 1 WLR 39, where Slade J applied to the Act a statement made by Watson B
in Attorney General v Hanmer (1858) 27 LJ Ch 837 at 840 that has been generally accepted
e in the books. Land that once was waste may cease to be waste if it is enclosed or
cultivated or occupied. Yet as was held in Re Britford Common, land does not cease to be
waste merely because the lord takes its produce and cuts the grass for hay or silage; for
by merely taking the natural produce of the waste the lord does not turn that waste into
demesne land.

     With that in mind I may dispose of the car parks with little ado. There are three of
f them in the area registered. One, known as the 'small car park', is now no longer the
subject of any appeal, for counsel for the applicants abandoned it. The other two he
pressed, and counsel for the respondents conceded that they ought to be excluded from
the registration. The commissioner took the view that the land did not cease to be waste
land merely by being used for a profitable purpose 'if that purpose is one of the uses to
which waste land is commonly put'; and he held that the car parking arranged by the
g estate company for the trustees was such a use. On the facts relating to these two car
parks counsel for the respondents was unable to support this conclusion. The
commissioner found that hardcore had been put down and fencing had been erected;
and that, coupled with the actual use as car parks and the consequent occupation of them
by the trustees, seems to me to exclude the car parks from the category of waste. As he
pointed out in the case stated, the commissioner was in the difficulty that at the hearing
h the contention was that none of the registered area was waste land; there was no attempt
by the trustees to divide the registered area into separate parts, and claim (no doubt in the
alternative) that even if much of the registered area was properly registered, there were
some parts that were not. The commissioner did in fact in his decision attach labels to
different parts of the registered area, without defining any boundaries; but this was
merely for the purposes of exposition, and it was not related to any separate issues at the
j hearing. It is plain that the course of argument at the hearing, where the parties were
not represented by counsel, was very different from the course of argument before me.
At all events, I think that it is wrong in law to include the two car parks, since, on the
admitted facts, neither at the time of registration nor at any other material time do they
appear to have had the quality in law of being 'waste'. They must therefore be excluded
from the registration.

     That brings me to the main issue, that of the land which was formerly foreshore but

which, by the gradual receding of the sea, now stands above high-water mark. For the
purpose of elucidating the rival contentions I put before counsel a diagrammatic *a*
representation, consisting in the main of four more or less vertical numbered lines,
roughly parallel to each other but bending from side to side to represent the indentations
of a coastline. Line 1, on the right (or east), represents the western boundary of the
trustees' land and the manor which they hold, as it stood in 1855; that is the line of the
high-water mark, and so the beginning of the foreshore, as it was in those days. Line 2,
further to the left (or west), is the present high-water mark, and so the beginning of the *b*
present foreshore. Line 3, further left (and so further west), is the old low-water mark,
and line 4, further left, and further west again, is the present low-water mark. The area
between lines 1 and 2 is marked A, that between 2 and 3 is B, and that between 3 and 4
is C. The old foreshore is thus A plus B, while the new foreshore is B plus C. B, of course,
has been part of the foreshore throughout, and still is. The dispute is about area A, all of
which is included in the registered area. The trustees say that it should be excluded, *c*
while the councils say that the commissioner rightly held that it should be included. On
behalf of the councils, counsel for the respondents sought to support the commissioner's
decision on two distinct grounds, either of which would suffice for her purpose. The
first ground was that which the commissioner put forward, while the second does not
appear to have been mentioned before him. For brevity, these grounds may respectively
be called the accretion argument and the 'of' argument, from the importance attached *d*
to the word 'of' in the statutory phrase 'waste land of a manor'.
    First, then, the accretion argument. The starting point is the Crown grant of 1855.
This conveyed to Mrs Clevland, the then owner of the manor, all the land lying between
high- and low-water mark, ie areas A and B. (Near the middle of these areas two strips
running east and west were excluded, for reasons which do not appear, but otherwise the
conveyance was of the whole of A and B. Apart from a point on the construction of the *e*
conveyance, nothing, I may say, seems to turn on the exclusion of these strips: I was told
that they appear to have been treated over the years, without demur, as if they had been
included.) The conveyance, it is said, was a conveyance not of a fixed and immovable
area of land, but of whatever for the time being was the land between high- and low-
water mark. Thus when the sea slowly retreated to the west, and the foreshore retreated
with it, the land which was the subject of the 1855 grant moved from its original site and *f*
followed the sea. What was conveyed by the 1855 grant remained throughout what
from time to time constituted the foreshore, wherever it was, and whether it was larger
or smaller than the original foreshore. In other words, whereas what was held under the
grant was areas A and B in 1855, at the time of registration it was areas B and C; and to
area A the grant no longer gave any title. Area A was an emergent area of land which
stood between the manor on the east and the foreshore (held under the grant of 1855) on *g*
the west; and it had been thrown up by the imperceptible receding of the sea.
Accordingly, under the doctrine of accretion, it became part of the land to which it was
contiguous on the east (namely, the manor) and it acquired the characteristics of that to
which it acceded. As that was waste of the manor, so area A became waste of the manor,
and so, by falling within s 22(1)(b) of the 1965 Act, it became registrable.
    Now this view was put somewhat more concisely in the commissioner's decision; but *h*
in its essentials, that appears to be the reasoning, and both counsel for the applicants and
counsel for the respondents made their submissions on that basis. Part of the chain of
reasoning relies considerably on a case cited by the commissioner in his decision, *Mercer
v Denne* [1905] 2 Ch 538, [1904–7] All ER Rep 71. There, the Court of Appeal held that
a custom for fishermen to dry their nets on the land of a private owner near the sea
extended also to contiguous land on the seaward side which had been thrown up by the *j*
gradual recession of the sea, and so had been added to the owner's existing land.
    Counsel for the applicants did not contest this point; his argument was more
fundamental. What was conveyed by the grant of 1855 was the foreshore as it then was;
and when the sea receded, there was no alteration in the boundaries of what had been
conveyed. What had been granted remained where it was, and did not follow the sea.

Area A, which had been registered, was still held under the Crown grant, and was in no
a sense an accretion. Being held under the Crown grant it could not be waste of the
manor, and so it was wrongly registered. Area C, which had previously been part of the
sea bed but had become part of the foreshore, was an accretion to the land held under the
Crown grant (ie areas A and B), but that had not been registered, and no question on it
arose for decision. That was the argument. Let me say at once that I shall decide nothing
on area C, since nothing on it arises for decision, and the Crown, which is not a party to
b these proceedings, may be concerned.

It will be seen that the essential difference between the two arguments lies in the effect
of the grant in 1855. Was it a grant of the foreshore as it then stood, or was it a grant of
the foreshore wherever it might be from time to time? In other words, was the freehold
that it conveyed a freehold in a fixed area of land, or a freehold in a movable area of
land? More shortly, but perhaps rather less accurately, was the fee a fixed fee or a
c movable fee?

Movable fees are little known in the modern law of property; and I must say something
about them. It is well settled that such fees may exist. The fee itself is a continuing
estate, but it is an estate in land which from time to time changes its position. An ancient
example is that of lot meadows. In these, two or more persons each have a fee simple in
a distinct part of a meadow, but the particular part over which rights of ownership are
d from time to time exercisable by each of them is determined by the drawing of lots
annually or at other intervals. Thus in *Welden v Bridgewater* (1595) Cro Eliz 421, 78 ER
663 the plaintiff was entitled to 13 acres out of a meadow of 80 acres, the particular 13
acres being determined from time to time by lot; and the Court of Queen's Bench held
that the plaintiff could maintain an action of trespass in respect of the 13 acres that for the
time he held by allotment, for 'by the allotment, it is the proper soil and freehold of him
e to whom it is allotted' (Cro Eliz 421 at 422, 78 ER 662 at 633). Coke himself recorded
the decision before it had been reported, and he also discussed the method of effecting
livery of seisin (which had to be done on the land being conveyed) in such cases: see Co
Litt at 4a, 48b. In 1657, in advising on a joint case to counsel, Sir Orlando Bridgman
made it plain that in such a case the soil of the lot meadows was vested in the lot
freeholders: see the case and opinion as set out in (1866) 12 Jur NS (Pt II) 103 at 104.

f Another instance of movable freeholds, and one that is very much in point in this case,
may arise on a grant of foreshore; for such a grant may convey an estate in the foreshore
in whatever position it is from time to time. If the sea imperceptibly recedes, the
foreshore recedes with it, and so the grantee's land moves too; if the sea encroaches, the
foreshore that has been granted moves inland. This has to be considered in relation to
the law of accretion and diluvion. Apart from any grant of the foreshore, if there is
g diluvion the movement of the foreshore appears to divest the frontager of some of his
land; for what was his dry land becomes part of the new foreshore, and so belongs to the
owner of the foreshore, usually the Crown: see *Re Hull and Selby Railway* (1839) 5 M & W
327, 151 ER 139. This is justified as being a form of rough justice for the frontager: he
should not complain of losing land since he would have gained land if instead the sea had
retreated. However, if an incursion of the sea extends further inland on to the land of a
h neighbouring owner it is difficult to see why he should suffer, since he would have
gained nothing if there had been accretion instead of diluvion. Fortunately, nothing on
this arises for decision in the present case; and I resist the temptation to discuss the
Delphic last sentence in the judgment of Alderson B in *Re Hull and Selby Railway* 5 M &
W 327 at 333, 151 ER 139 at 141, much quoted though it is.

The leading authority on a freehold in a movable foreshore, and one on which counsel
j for the respondents strongly relied, is *Scratton v Brown* (1825) 4 B & C 485, [1824–34] All
ER Rep 59. In that case, in 1773 the lord of certain manors had conveyed land by lease
and release, and the land had been elaborately described in the parcels clause. The clause
occupies nearly two pages of the report, and I shall summarise the relevant parts. What
was conveyed was all those 'sea-grounds, oyster-layings, shores and fisheries', commonly
called by certain names, in a certain parish or parishes, 'which said sea-grounds, oyster-

layings, shores and fisheries did extend from the south, at low-water mark, to the north at high-water mark', and abutted on certain lands on the east and the west; 'all which said sea-grounds, oyster-layings, shores and fisheries' thereby conveyed contained 'by estimation, 800 acres of land covered with water, or thereabouts, as the same were beaconed, marked, and stubbed out', and were then in the occupation of certain persons. Over the years the sea had encroached on the land, and the action was brought by the lord of the manors for trespass on land which, though no part of the foreshore in 1773, had become part of it since then. The case was thus one in which there had been diluvion rather than accretion; but I think that the references in the judgments to accretion must be treated as using that word as including both categories. The real point of the case was not the operation of either doctrine but the effect of the conveyance.

One issue was whether under the conveyance the defendant had obtained a mere easement or privilege of fishery, or whether there was a grant of the soil; and the latter was held to be the correct view. On that footing, the argument was whether the land conveyed was the foreshore as it stood in 1773 or whether it was the foreshore wherever it stood for the time being; and the Court of King's Bench held that it was the latter. It was argued that there could not be such a thing as a shifting freehold, but this contention did not survive the citation of Co Litt 48b. The question was thus what the deed had in fact conveyed; and it was held that the plaintiff's contention was wrong, and that the deed had conveyed the foreshore as it was from time to time. In reaching this conclusion the court examined and construed the language of the deed; and before I turn to this, I think that I should set out the relevant part of the language of the Crown grant of 1855 in the present case in order to facilitate comparison.

The grant of 1855 is in one continuous sentence, without subdivision; but for ease of reference during the argument I divided the parcels clause into four limbs, and I shall set it out with these subdivisions, though of course this cannot affect the construction. The grant is of—

'ALL THOSE (a) three several pieces or parcels of land lying between high water mark and low water mark and covered with water at ordinary tides (b) containing by admeasurement 262 acres or thereabouts and (c) situate adjacent to certain land belonging to the said Margaret Caroline Clevland in the Parishes of Instow and Westleigh in the said County of Devon (d) which pieces or parcels of land are more particularly delineated and described in the Plan drawn in the margin of these presents and are thereon colored red and are distinguished by the letters A, B, and C.'

The plan lacks any scale, but it gives a considerable amount of topographical detail in the shape of roads, railway, and lime kilns and other buildings on the east of the land, with an appearance of some precision. It shows the red land as running about 14 inches from north to south (including the two uncoloured strips which were not conveyed, which together are about an inch from north to south) and varying in width from east to west from about ½ inch to 3 inches. Despite the absence of a scale, the whole appearance of the plan is one of careful and precise draftmanship.

Counsel for the respondents placed considerable emphasis on features which those parcels had in common with the parcels in *Scratton v Brown*. In that case, neither the statement that the area was 800 acres nor the fact that the land had been 'beaconed, marked, and stubbed out' prevented the deed from conveying the foreshore as it was from time to time. Why, then, should limbs (b) and (d) of the 1855 grant, stating the area and referring to the plan, be any more effective to prevent that grant from conveying a foreshore which was movable and not fixed? Further, 39 Halsbury's Laws (3rd Edn) 558, para 772 states that 'a grant of foreshore conveys not that which at the time of the grant is between high- and low-water marks, but that which from time to time is between these termini'; and, I may add, Coulson and Forbes on the Law of Waters and Land Drainage (6th Edn, 1952, p 24) makes a similar statement. In each case *Scratton v Brown* is cited as the supporting authority.

Such statements appear to be laying down a rule of law. If there is such a rule, it would
a mean that however explicit a conveyance might be that it was conveying only a stationary
portion of what was then the foreshore, and not a part of the foreshore as it might be
from time to time, what would pass would be a movable portion of a movable foreshore.
I cannot see why there should be any such rule, and no authority has been cited to me
which supports a rule of that sort. Certainly *Scratton v Brown* does not support it. I can
see nothing in the nature of the foreshore that requires a rule like that. Instead, I think
b that the law is that a conveyance of foreshore is capable of conveying either the foreshore
as it is from time to time, or else the foreshore as it is at the time of the conveyance, and
that which of these the conveyance does depends on the true construction of the
conveyance. In short, whether the freehold conveyed is movable or fixed depends on
what the conveyance provides.

This, I think, sufficiently appears from *Scratton v Brown* itself, or at any rate from two
c of the three judgments. Bayley J inquired what was the object of the parties to the deed
of 1773, and referred to the construction of the words in the deed (see 4 B & C 485 at 499,
[1824–34] All ER Rep 59 at 63). The most helpful part of his judgment from the point
of view of counsel for the respondents is his statement that the language of the deed must
be construed with reference to the common law as to accretion. This, however, may
merely mean that if what is being conveyed is foreshore, there is something of a
d presumption, in case of doubt, that it is movable rather than fixed foreshore that is to
pass. Against that it might be said that as the vast majority of freeholds are fixed and not
movable, the court should be slow to hold that the intention is to convey something in
the exceptional form of a freehold that is movable.

The judgment of Holroyd J is puzzling. He put his decision on the ground that the
grantee must stand in the position that the grantor would have had, and said (4 B & C 485
e at 502, [1824–34] All ER Rep 59 at 64):

'. . . the accretion follows as an accessary to the principal. The change being
gradual it becomes part of the shore, and belongs to the person who has the shore at
the time when the accretion takes place.'

f As the sea had encroached on the land and the foreshore had moved inland, it is difficult
to see what 'accretion' there was that could have become 'part of the shore'. However
that may be, although the judge had extensively examined the language of the deed in
determining that it was a conveyance of land and not merely the grant of an easement or
privilege, he says nothing about this in determining what land was conveyed. It could
therefore be said that (contrary to my view of the law) he was treating the matter as a rule
g of law rather than a question of construction. If, of course, there had been a simple
accretion by reason of the retreat of the sea, then plainly, as a matter of law, the accretion
would have followed as an accessory to the principal, and would have belonged to the
person who at the time owned the shore.

On the other hand, Littledale J made it abundantly clear that the matter was one of
construction; and he drew a distinction between the words of grant and the subsequent
h words of description (see 4 B & C 485 at 504–505, [1824–34] All ER Rep 59 at 64). What
was granted was the sea-grounds and so on which went by the specified names, and the
only inquiry was what were those sea-grounds. The subsequent words of description
might be true or might be false, but they would not affect the operative words, even if
instead of 800 acres there had in fact been 5,000 acres. Whatever may be said about that,
it is plain that the question was what, on the true construction of the deed, had been
j conveyed. Had the rule been one of law, all this discussion would have been irrelevant.
The judge then added some puzzling words about 'the accretion which has taken place'.

As I have said, I think the question is one of construction, and that both Bayley and
Littledale JJ treated it as such. Further, it may or may not be that in construing the deed
of 1855 there is something of a presumption that a conveyance of foreshore passes the
foreshore as it is from time to time, and not merely the foreshore as it stands at the date

of the conveyance. With that in mind, I return to the parcels in the grant of 1855 in the case before me.

If limbs (a), (b) and (c) stood alone, it might indeed be that the deed would have conveyed a movable and not a fixed freehold. But there is also limb (d); and that seems to me to be another matter. The words, of course, must be construed as a whole. I do not think that the words of limb (d) can be said to be subsequent words of description in the sense in which Littledale J spoke; the words are words of greater particularity in defining what is being conveyed. The grant is to pass three pieces or parcels of land which are described in general terms in limbs (a), (b) and (c), and then there are the words 'more particularly delineated and described' in the plan. If the intention is to convey the foreshore as it is from time to time, why go to the trouble of preparing a detailed plan, and why state that what is to be found on the plan more particularly describes the pieces or parcels of land that have been mentioned, and delineates them? Counsel for the respondents ingeniously suggested that the plan was effective to show the northern and southern boundaries both of what was conveyed and of the strips that were not conveyed, but not to show any of the eastern and western boundaries of any of the land. I suppose that if appropriate language is used, it would be possible to give a plan a selective particularity of this sort; but I can see no grounds for concluding that in this case the plan was intended to operate in this way, or for making ineffective by far the greater part of the delineation on the plan.

In saying that, I bear in mind the authorities on words in a parcels clause such as 'more particularly described' or 'more particularly delineated' in relation to a plan. In *Eastwood v Ashton* [1915] AC 900 at 902–903 the words of the parcels clause fell into four parts, much as in the present case, with the fourth of them being 'all of which said premises are more particularly described in the plan endorsed on these presents and are delineated and coloured red in such plan'; and it was this that the House of Lords held should prevail. I do not think that the distinction made by Littledale J between the words of grant and subsequent words of description was much fortified by the later decision. As Lord Wrenbury pointed out (at 920), the words 'more particularly' excluded the view that what was being conveyed had already been exhaustively described; instead, they meant that the previous description might be insufficient for exact delineation, and that the plan was to cover all deficiencies, if any. In *Wallington v Townsend* [1939] 2 All ER 225, 160 LT 537, 55 TLR 531, this was followed and applied to a description, contained in a contract, of land 'more particularly delineated' on a plan. The reports of the case at [1939] Ch 588 and 108 LJ Ch 305 omit this point.

Even if I give full weight to the possible presumption that a conveyance of foreshore is intended to convey the foreshore as it is from time to time, and not the foreshore as it then is, it seems to me that limb (d) of the parcels, coupled with the detailed plan indorsed on the grant of 1855, suffice to repel the presumption. Furthermore, the grant is not of 'foreshore', eo nomine, or of 'sea-grounds, oyster-layings, shores and fisheries' (as in *Scratton v Brown*), but simply of 'pieces or parcels of land' lying between high- and low-water mark. However much one would expect sea-grounds, oyster-layings, shores and fisheries to follow the sea as it advances or retreats, the same cannot be said of 'land'; land remains land, however the sea moves, and whether or not it is covered with water. In the result, I hold that on its true construction the grant of 1855 conveyed a fixed area of land as shown on the plan, and not land which would vary in its position with the sea. The movement of the sea consequently did not produce any land which lay between the land granted in 1855 and the manor, and so there was nothing that became 'waste land of a manor' within s 22(1)(b) of the 1965 Act so as to become registrable. The land thrown up by the sea was on the west of the land granted in 1855, and may or may not have been acquired by the owners of that land by a simple process of accretion. Area A, being the part of the old foreshore which is not included in the new foreshore, and being the land which has been registered under the 1965 Act, ought not to have been registered, and so should now be removed from the register.

I do not think that this conclusion is affected by *Attorney General of Southern Nigeria v John Holt & Co (Liverpool) Ltd* [1915] AC 599, [1914–15] All ER Rep 444, *Government of*

Penang v Beng Hong Oon [1971] 3 All ER 1163, [1972] AC 425, or *Mellor v Walmsley* [1905]
a 2 Ch 164, which was discussed in that case. The *Holt* case shows that where riparian land
is conveyed, with the sea stated as the boundary, and then the sea recedes, there is an
accretion to the land conveyed. What was said at [1915] AC 612–613 has to be read in
the light of what was said at [1915] AC 610. The *Penang* case was one of land bounded
by the 'sea beach' having land added to it by the receding of the sea. *Mellor v Walmsley*
is made more readily intelligible by examining the plan which is included in the report
b at first instance: see [1904] 2 Ch 525 at 526. In that case the land conveyed was just above
high-water mark of spring tides. So far as it goes it provides a little support for the
importance to be attached to detailed plans (see [1905] 2 Ch 164 at 174, 175, 179),
although it seems a little surprising that the words 'more particularly delineated' did not
receive more attention. Still, at that time *Eastwood v Ashton* [1915] AC 900 lay some ten
years in the future. None of the three cases was concerned with a conveyance of
c foreshore, or whether what was conveyed was fixed or movable; and I say no more about
them.

That brings me to counsel's alternative argument for the respondents, the 'of'
argument. This begins with the words 'waste land of a manor' in s 22(1)(b) of the 1965
Act. The time for determining whether these words are satisfied is the time of
registration. If at that time there is waste land which is not in fact waste land of the
d manor but is reputed to be waste land of the manor, it falls within s 22(1)(b); and area A
was so reputed when it was registered. Therefore the registration should stand. That, in
brief, was the argument.

This argument is altogether new. Nothing to this effect was put before the
commissioner, and counsel for the applicants knew nothing of it until he heard counsel
for the respondents advancing it on Day 2. Not surprisingly, he objected to a new point
e being raised without warning. I was told that there was nothing in any rules which
provided for the giving of the equivalent of a respondent's notice in such circumstances;
it may be that some such provision ought to be made. But quite apart from any statutory
requirement, it seems to me that in cases stated under the 1965 Act it is part of the
forensic duty of an advocate to give his adversary notice at the earliest possible moment
if he wishes to advance a new point which has not been taken before the commissioner.
f If this is not done, then the court may well refuse to hear the point unless the party taken
by surprise is given an adjournment, at the expense of the party taking the point, in
which to consider the matter. In the present case, it was plain that if the point succeeded
as a matter of law, the case would have to go back to the commissioner in order that he
might find the facts, particularly as to repute, which would be needed to support the
point. However, while reserving all rights to counsel for the applicants in this respect,
g it seemed best to permit counsel for the respondents to argue the point, not least because
in view of the way in which the case was proceeding counsel for the applicants would
have the latitude of an overnight adjournment in which to reflect on the argument, and
it was obviously desirable to avoid increasing the costs.

The starting point is, of course, the statutory words 'waste land of a manor'. These are
not defined, and on the face of it there seems to be no particular reason why they should
h not mean what they say, namely that the land must in fact be waste land, and that it must
be waste land of what in fact is a manor. However, counsel for the respondents relied on
what was said by the Court of Appeal in *Box Parish Council v Lacey* [1979] 1 All ER 113,
[1980] Ch 109. There, the Chief Commons Commissioner had expressed the view that
all manors were now reputed manors, so that there could be no waste land of what was
in fact a manor. However, this difficulty, he thought, could be got over by holding, on
j the authority of *Doe d Clayton v Williams* (1843) 11 M & W 803, 152 ER 1029, that there
could be waste land of even a reputed manor. The Court of Appeal said that that case was
not authority for that conclusion, but took the view that in s 22(1)(b) the words 'waste
land of a manor' had been used so as to comprehend waste land of the lord of a reputed
manor. This view was reached after considering the language of the Conveyancing Act
1881, ss 2(iv) and 6(3), and the corresponding provisions of the Law of Property Act
1925, namely ss 205(1)(ix) and 62(3) respectively. Under these provisions in the Acts,

'manor' included a 'lordship, and reputed manor or lordship', and a conveyance of a
manor conveyed with the manor all wastes (and many other things) appertaining or   *a*
reputed to appertain to the manor, and so on. If in s 22(1)(b) of the 1965 Act the words
'waste land of a manor' includes waste land of a reputed manor, why should it not also
include waste land which is only reputedly 'of' a manor? If 'manor' embraces both true
manors and reputed manors, why should not 'waste land of a manor' include both waste
land which was truly 'of' the manor and also waste land which was 'of' the manor only
by repute? If 'repute' could be used to extend 'manor', why should it not also extend   *b*
'of'? Thus ran the argument.

I do not think that this is right. There is a very real difference between the two
categories. For centuries there has been a category of manors known as 'reputed
manors'. If there ceased to be at least two free tenants of a manor, the manor became a
'reputed manor'; for the freeholders were the judges of the court baron, and at least two
were needed so that an only freeholder would not be his own judge: see Scriven on   *c*
Copyholds (7th Edn, 1896, p 3) and *Bradshaw v Lawson* (1791) 4 Term Rep 443, 100 ER
1109. As Lord Denman CJ said, speaking for the Court of Queen's Bench in *Doe d
Molesworth v Sleeman* (1846) 9 QB 297 at 301, 11 ER 1287 at 1288: '. . . a reputed manor
is that which has been a manor, though from some supervening defects it has ceased to
be so.' With the decay of the manorial system, more and more manors became reputed
manors, and so if 'manor' in the 1965 Act had not included reputed manors, much land   *d*
would have remained outside the Act by reason only of the reduction in the number of
freeholders of the manor below two; and the number of freeholders was a matter which
had no discernible relevance to the purposes of the Act.

None of this reasoning has any application to waste land which only by repute can be
said to be 'of' a manor. I have heard nothing to suggest that there is or was any
substantial known category of such land, such that Parliament could be assumed to   *e*
intend to include it. At best there is some authority, to be mentioned shortly, which not
unexpectedly shows that it was possible for some land to be reputed to be 'of' a manor
although it was not in fact such. Further, the statutory material in the property
legislation is more slender and indirect under this head. There is nothing to match the
definition which makes 'manor' include 'reputed manor' and so would make 'of' include
'reputedly of'. There are only the words relating to what a conveyance is to include, and   *f*
these go far wider than mere repute. They include all wastes and many other things
which at the time of conveyance are 'demised, occupied or enjoyed with the [manor], or
reputed or known as part, parcel, or member thereof'. Mere occupation or enjoyment
with the manor suffices, even if there is no repute; and I do not see how the words of the
property statutes can be relied on by way of analogy without carrying the 1965 Act to an
unacceptable width. What the Court of Appeal said on this point in *Box Parish Council v*   *g*
Lacey was, I think, obiter: but accept it to the full, and I still do not see how it carries
counsel's point for the respondents.

There was also a more general argument on this point that I should mention. Initially,
I think, there was a contention that if the lord of a manor acquired waste land, that waste
became waste 'of' the manor. One obvious difficulty in this was the fact that of necessity
a manor had its origin prior to the statute 18 Edw 1, c 1 (Quia Emptores (1289–90)) and   *h*
could not be created subsequently, so that it was at least improbable that subsequent
acquisitions could enlarge the manor. Another difficulty was that on this footing if the
lord of a manor in Cornwall bought waste in Yorkshire, the Yorkshire waste would
become waste of the Cornish manor. Ultimately the argument emerged in a much
narrower form, with a threefold test and a retreat from fact to reputation. If (a) waste
land became vested in the lord of a manor, and (b) the waste was physically situated   *j*
within the manor or adjoining its boundaries, and (c) the waste was reputed to be part of
the manor, then it was waste which was reputedly 'of' the manor, and so fell within
s 22(1)(b) of the 1965 Act. That was the argument in its final form.

It was settled that the boundaries of a manor might be determined on evidence of
reputation (*Doe d Jones v Richards* (1798) Peake Add Cas 180), though this application of
the ordinary rules of evidence does not appear to bear on the substantive law that I have
to consider. It is also clear that if land that was part of a manor was severed from it, that

land could never again truly form part of the manor merely because the lord purchased
a it; it was otherwise if it came back by escheat. The case of a lord purchasing land that had
never formed part of a manor must be a fortiori. However, if land which had once been
part of a manor was purchased by the lord of the manor, and for a considerable time
there was unity of possession, that land might become part of the manor by repute, and
might then pass with the manor on a conveyance of the manor: see *R v Duchess of
Buccleugh* (1704) 6 Mod 150 at 151; *Delacherois v Delacherois* (1864) 11 HL Cas 62 esp at
b 105–106, 11 ER 1254 esp at 1270–1271 per Lord St Leonards. Furthermore, in *Re
Chewton Common* [1977] 3 All ER 509, [1977] 1 WLR 1242 it was contended that such
land fell within the words 'waste land of a manor' in s 22(1)(b) of the 1965 Act, though
Slade J found it unnecessary to decide the point, and did not do so.

None of this goes far enough for counsel for the respondents. As she accepted, she has
to show not merely that waste formerly of the manor may later become waste reputedly
c of the manor, but that waste which was never waste of the manor could also become
waste reputedly of the manor; for plainly area A was Crown land until 1855, and there
is no suggestion that it was ever part of the manor before then. For such a proposition
counsel for the respondents was unable to proffer any authority. In one sense that may
not matter much: it might be that the principles applicable to former land of the manor
would be extended to land never of the manor, with, perhaps, a higher burden of
d proof. But in another sense it seems to me to be of considerable importance: for
Parliament is unlikely to have been legislating in 1965 for something which, unlike
reputed manors, was far from being a matter of notoriety, and has apparently not
emerged until now.

In the result I doubt very much whether there is any real category of waste which,
though never part of a manor, has become waste reputedly of that manor; and in any case
e I do not think that on its true construction s 22(1)(b) of the 1965 Act extends to such
land. Accordingly, this alternative contention by counsel for the respondents fails. In
s 22(1)(b) of the 1965 Act, 'of' means 'of' and not 'reputedly of', for there is no real reason
for construing the word in any other way. There is thus no reason for remitting the case
to the commissioner to find any facts on reputation.

Finally, I may revert to the first point. For the reasons that I have given, I think that
f the commissioner erred in law in holding that the 1855 grant conveyed the foreshore as
it was from time to time instead of holding that it conveyed the foreshore as it then
stood, as on its true construction I have held that it did. That question of construction
does not seem to have been raised before the commissioner; instead, the decision seems
to have been reached by applying the legal principles governing the foreshore as if they
operated irrespectively of any question of construction. In saying that, I must emphasise
g that the commissioner had many other matters to decide, and he heard much less ample
argument on the main issues than I have. He also had considerable difficulty in framing
the case stated, since the correspondence seeking the case left it far from clear what points
really were in issue; and as he stated in para 3 of the case, he had to deal with this as best
he could. Indeed, only when counsel opened the case before me was I able to understand
what the real issues were; and much that appears in the case stated does not now arise for
h decision. At all events, the upshot is that in my judgment the two car parks and also the
land indicated by area A on the diagram, being land which was foreshore in 1855 but was
not foreshore at the date of registration, should be removed from the register. I so hold.
I should add that although I have referred to certain authorities which were not discussed
before me, I have acted on the principle stated in *Re Lawrence's Will Trusts* [1971] 3 All
ER 433 at 447–448, [1972] Ch 418 at 436–437. The additional authorities have not
j altered the result that I would have reached without their aid, and so I have not invited
further argument in which they could be discussed.

Appeal allowed.

Solicitors: *Bower, Cotton & Bower*, agents for *Ashford, Sparkes & Harward*, Tiverton (for
the applicants); *Sharpe, Pritchard & Co* (for the respondents).

Azza M Abdallah   Barrister.

Dennis v McDonald

FAMILY DIVISION

PURCHAS J

16th, 19th JANUARY, 19th FEBRUARY 1981

Tenants in common – Real property – Occupation of whole property by one of tenants in common – Rent – Family home purchased in joint names on trust for sale by man and woman living together – Relationship breaking down and woman leaving home because of man's violence – Some of children of family living with man in home – Whether man liable to pay occupation rent to woman – Whether woman excluded from home – Whether rent to be assessed on basis of man having protected tenancy of house and liable to pay half the fair rent for property to the woman – Whether, if order for sale of house could not be made because prime object of trust for sale was to provide family home, occupation rent could be ordered – Law of Property Act 1925, s 30.

The father and mother had cohabited since 1962 but were not married. In 1970 they bought the freehold of a house for £3,220, £2,000 being obtained on a mortgage and the balance being provided by the parties more or less in equal shares. The house was conveyed into their joint names on trust for sale for themselves as tenants in common. The husband paid all the mortgage instalments and by 1980 the mortgage was paid off. In 1974 the mother left the father because of his violence or threatened violence, taking the five children of the family with her. Later, three of the children, all aged under 16, returned to live with the father in the house while the other two children remained with the mother. Those arrangements were confirmed by a court order. The mother applied under s 30[a] of the Law of Property Act 1925 for an order for the sale of the house under the trust for sale, or alternatively for an order that the father should pay her a rent in respect of his occupation of the house. The father opposed an order for sale and submitted that he was not liable to pay rent to the mother.

Held – (1) The mother, even though she was a mistress, was entitled to all the rights of a joint owner of property held under a trust for sale, but the court would make neither an immediate order for the sale of the house under s 30 of the 1925 Act, because the prime object of the trust for sale was to provide a home for the family, nor an order for sale suspended for a specified period (such as the minority of the youngest child living in the house), because it was not convenient or appropriate to do so (see p 635 h to p 636 c, post); *Re Evers's Trust* [1980] 3 All ER 399 applied.

(2) However, where an association similar to a matrimonial relationship broke down and one party was excluded from the family home by the other party, the principle that a tenant in common was not liable to pay an occupation rent merely by virtue of being the sole occupant did not apply, and the court had power on general principles to order the occupying party who was a tenant in common with the excluded party to pay an occupation rent to the excluded party if it was equitable that such a rent should be paid. Since the father had forced the mother to leave the house by his violence or threatened violence and thereafter had prevented her from returning to the house in circumstances similar to constructive desertion and since it would be unreasonable to expect the mother to exercise her right of occupation as a tenant in common in the circumstances, it was equitable that he should pay her an occupation rent (see p 638 e to h and p 640 h, post); *M'Mahon v Burchell* (1846) 2 Ph 127 and dictum of Stirling J in *Hill v Hickin* [1897] 2 Ch at 581 applied; dictum of Lord Denning MR in *Jones v Jones* [1977] 2 All ER at 235 considered.

---

a   Section 30, so far as material, provides: 'If the trustees for sale refuse to sell . . . or any requisite consent cannot be obtained, any person interested may apply to the court for . . . an order directing the trustees for sale to give effect thereto, and the court may make such order as it thinks fit.'

(3) The occupation rent payable by the father to the mother was to be assessed on the
a basis that he had a tenancy of the house analogous to a protected tenancy, and therefore
that half the fair rent payable for an unfurnished letting of the house under a protected
tenancy was payable to the mother. Accordingly, for the period 1974 to 1976 (being the
early years of the mortgage) the amount payable would be half the mortgage repayments
paid by the father, that being broadly equivalent to the appropriate occupation rent. The
mother would not be required for that period to give credit for the amount representing
b her share of the mortgage repayments because the major element in the repayments
during that period was interest on the capital advanced. For the period from 1977 to the
expiry of the mortgage in 1980 there would be an inquiry as to the appropriate
occupation rent, since it would be higher than half the mortgage repayments paid by the
father, but the mother's share of the mortgage repayments and any capital sums paid by
him to enhance the property would have to be set off against the rent. From 1980
c onwards the occupation rent would be half the fair rent for the property (see p 641 *c* to
j, post); *Leake (formerly Bruzzi) v Bruzzi* [1974] 2 All ER 1196 and *Sutthill v Graham* [1977]
3 All ER 1117 applied.
    Per Curiam. Although s 30 of the 1925 Act does not give power to order payment of
an occupation rent unless an order for sale is being made and the order for payment of
an occupation rent is ancillary to the order for sale, s 30 can be used to enforce payment
d of an occupation rent by indicating that unless the tenant in common in occupation
undertakes to pay an occupation rent an order for sale will be made (see p 640 *g*, post).

Notes
For the incidents of tenancy in common, see 32 Halsbury's Laws (3rd Edn) 341, para 535,
and for cases on the subject, see 38 Digest (Repl) 827–829, 396–409.
e   For the Law of Property Act 1925, s 30, see 27 Halsbury's Statutes (3rd Edn) 385.

Cases referred to in judgment
Buchanan-Wollaston's Conveyance, Re, Curtis v Buchanan-Wollaston [1939] 2 All ER 302,
    [1939] Ch 738, 108 LJ Ch 281, 160 LT 399, CA; *affg* [1939] Ch 217, 108 LJ Ch 132, 159
    LT 601, 38 Digest (Repl) 822, 348.
f *Evers's Trust, Re, Papps v Evers* [1980] 3 All ER 399, [1980] 1 WLR 1327, CA.
Gissing v Gissing [1970] 2 All ER 780, [1971] AC 886, [1970] 3 WLR 255, 21 P & CR 702,
    HL, 27(1) Digest (Reissue) 311, 2303.
Henderson v Eason (1851) 17 QB 701, 21 LJQB 82, 18 LTOS 143, 16 Jur 518, 117 ER 1451,
    Ex Ch; *previous proceedings* (1846) 10 Jur 821, V-C; (1847), 2 Ph 308, LC, 38 Digest
    (Repl) 828, 405.
g *Hill v Hickin* [1897] 2 Ch 579, 66 LJ Ch 717, 77 LT 127, 40 Digest (Repl) 437, 277.
Jones v Jones [1977] 2 All ER 231, [1977] 1 WLR 438, 33 P & CR 147, CA, Digest (Cont
    Vol E) 214, 1590a.
Leake (formerly Bruzzi) v Bruzzi [1974] 2 All ER 1196, [1974] 1 WLR 1528, CA, Digest
    (Cont Vol D) 392, 706a.
M'Mahon v Burchell (1846) 2 Ph 127, 1 Coop *temp* Cott 457, 8 LTOS 289, 41 ER 889, LC,
h   38 Digest (Repl) 828, 407.
Pettitt v Pettitt [1969] 2 All ER 385, [1970] AC 777, [1969] 2 WLR 966, 20 P & CR 991,
    HL, 27(1) Digest (Reissue) 102, 707.
Suttill v Graham [1977] 3 All ER 1117, [1977] 1 WLR 819, CA, Digest (Cont Vol E) 256,
    715c.
Turner v Morgan (1803) 8 Ves 143, 32 ER 307.
j *Williams v Williams* [1977] 1 All ER 28, [1976] Ch 278, [1976] 3 WLR 494, CA, Digest
    (Cont Vol E) 255, 662b.

Action
By an originating summons dated 14th November 1978 issued in the Chancery Division
under ss 30 and 203(5) of the Law of Property Act 1925 the plaintiff, a trustee under a

trust for sale of property, sought the following relief: (1) an order that the property be sold, (2) a declaration that she was entitled to receive one-half of the net proceeds of sale *a* of the property, (3) an order that the trusts affecting the property be carried out with all necessary accounts and inquiries, including an account of the rents of part of the property received by the defendant (with whom the plaintiff had cohabited, and the other trustee under the trust for sale) and (4) further or other relief. On 6th March 1980 the plaintiff issued a summons in the Family Division under the Guardianship of Minors Act 1971 seeking an order that custody of the five children of the family be granted to her. On *b* 10th April Master Cholmondeley Clarke ordered that the action commenced in the Chancery Division be transferred to the Family Division to enable the judge who considered the application under the 1971 Act to decide the action. Both proceedings were heard by Purchas J in chambers but judgment on the originating summons was given in open court. The facts are set out in the judgment.

c

Andrew Walker for the plaintiff.
T A C Coningsby for the defendant.

PURCHAS J. This is an originating summons commenced in the Chancery Division which by order of Master Cholmondeley Clarke of 10th April 1980 has been transferred to the Family Division to be dealt with as if it were originally assigned to the Family *d* Division. The purpose of the transfer was to enable the matter to be considered by the judge who considered an application under the Guardianship of Minors Act 1971 which had been made in relation to the five children who were the issue of the plaintiff. Immediately prior to the hearing of this summons I heard evidence in the guardianship of minors application and delivered judgment. With the consent of the parties I order that the evidence in the guardianship of minors application shall be evidence where *e* relevant in this application. A transcript of my judgment in the guardianship of minors application is filed with the papers in this case.

The plaintiff seeks an order for the sale of property known as 125–127 Strathleven Road, London SW2, in accordance with the trust for sale under which it is held in the joint names of the plaintiff and the defendant as tenants in common. She applies under the provisions of s 30 of the Law of Property Act 1925 for such an order or, alternatively, *f* for such other order as the court may think fit. In the further alternative the plaintiff seeks 'such further or other relief' in support of which application, according to her counsel, she relies on the general principles applied by the courts in doing justice between tenants in common.

Both the plaintiff and the defendant are of Jamaican origin. They have lived in this country since at least 1962. In that year they started to cohabit. Apart from three or four *g* occasions on which the plaintiff left the defendant for periods of varying length the parties lived together until early in 1974, ie for about twelve years. On the occasions when she did leave, the plaintiff took with her such children as had, at the time, been born.

In 1974 the plaintiff left the defendant for the last time and permanently. Again she took with her the five children who formed the family at that time. Apart from the final *h* separation the last substantial departure of the plaintiff from the home occurred in the summer of 1969 when she left with the four children who were then living. In January 1970 the plaintiff and the defendant together bought the premises at Strathleven Road making more or less equal financial contributions towards its purchase. Thereafter the plaintiff, who was then pregnant with the fifth child of the family, whose paternity the defendant does not admit, returned to live with the defendant at Strathleven Road. Here *j* they established a home for themselves and the five children which lasted until the final breakdown of the association about four years later. The defendant accepted the fifth child, Martin, as a member of the family.

It is common ground that the house was purchased and registered in the joint names of the plaintiff and the defendant as tenants in common in equal shares. At one stage during these proceedings, prior to the discovery of a solicitor's attendance note recording

the instructions given by the defendant in relation to the purchase of the property and
a its conveyance into the joint names, there was an issue on this matter. Since that
document was discovered the defendant has admitted the plaintiff's contention that the
property is held by the parties as tenants in common in equal shares.

As I have already mentioned, at the time of the final separation early in 1974 the
plaintiff took all five children with her. Shortly thereafter (ie within a matter of months
and certainly not more than a year later) the two older children returned to live with the
b defendant. Later the third child returned to live with the defendant. These three
children have remained living with the defendant at the family home at Strathleven
Road. Apart from a comparatively short period during which the fourth child lived
with the defendant, the fourth and fifth children have remained with the plaintiff and
still remain with her. The result of the orders which I have made in the guardianship of
minors application stabilises this position. The three older children will remain with the
c defendant in the erstwhile family home whilst the remaining two children will remain
with the plaintiff in a home which she has established in a council house. The ages of the
children now living with the defendant range from 16 to 14 years. The two children
living with the plaintiff are aged 13 and 11 years.

The purchase price of the house including the costs of the purchase was £3,220. Of
this sum £2,000 was obtained on a mortgage. In very rough terms the balance of £1,220
d was provided by the parties paying a sum of approximately £610 each. The defendant
has throughout paid the instalment payments on the mortgage. These were regular
payments of £36·67 per month over a period of ten years. The last such payment was
made in March 1980. The property now stands unencumbered.

The defendant is employed by the Thames Water Board. He earns something in the
region of £7,400 gross per annum although this varies with the amount of overtime
e available. He says that he has no savings and gave evidence as to his means and financial
commitments. I treat his evidence with some reservation, however. I think that he may
well have more assets than he cares to disclose. In any event the means of the parties are
not, in my judgment, relevant. The plaintiff is also in employment earning a little over
£2,000 gross per annum. There is no regular overtime available for her. Again, she has
dealt with her means and declared that she has some very modest savings in the region
f of £300. As with the defendant I do not think that these matters are relevant; but I
accept the plaintiff as an honest and reasonably accurate witness.

Evidence has been produced in the form of letters from two firms of chartered
surveyors. This establishes, in my judgment, that a fair market value at the date of the
hearing of 125–127 Strathleven Road, freehold with the benefit of full vacant possession,
would be £19,000. The defendant has given evidence, which I accept, that he has been
g offered by the appropriate housing authority an improvement grant of £3,500 on
condition that he contributes a further £1,000 towards repairs and improvements to the
premises which will cost £4,500. He would only have to repay this grant if he sold the
property during the ensuing five years. He has, however, been warned that the
improvement in the property would be reflected in an increase in the rates of some
undetermined amount. Depending on the outcome of these proceedings the defendant
h would like to take up this offer. He sees no difficulty in meeting his side of the bargain.

This case raises some interesting questions relating to the rights as between parents
who have established a home but who are not married. Apart from the recent provisions
of the Domestic Violence and Matrimonial Proceedings Act 1976 the law gives no rights
to a mistress arising out of her relationship with her lover per se except as the father of
her children (see the Guardianship of Minors Acts 1971 and 1973). She receives no
j recognition by way of analogy either under the Married Women's Property Act 1882 or
under the Acts which culminated in the Matrimonial Causes Act 1973.

On the other hand, she does not lose any rights at law or in equity which she would
otherwise enjoy merely because she is a mistress. She is, therefore, to be treated in
exactly the same way as any other tenant in common in relation to the joint property.
Counsel for the defendant submitted that no order should be made under s 30 of the Law
of Property Act 1925 but alternatively submitted that if any order were to be made under

that section then I should take into account all the financial liabilities and capabilities of the parties much as the court is required to do under the provisions of s 25 of the *a* Matrimonial Causes Act 1973. To do this, however, would be inconsistent with the position enjoyed in relation to the property by the plaintiff as a tenant in common and I am, therefore, unable to accede to counsel's alternative submission.

In support of his first contention counsel for the defendant relied, inter alia, on *Re Evers's Trust* [1980] 3 All ER 399, [1980] 1 WLR 1327. This case is a clear authority for the proposition that where the circumstances in which the trust for sale originated *b* envisaged as one of the primary objects the provision of a home for the family rather than an immediate sale then the proper approach to the exercise of the discretion granted by s 30 of the 1925 Act is not to make an order for sale. See also the dictum of Lord Denning MR in *Williams v Williams* [1977] 1 All ER 28 at 30–31, [1976] Ch 278 at 285. There is no doubt that this is such a case. Subject to what follows hereafter in this judgment it would not be proper to make an immediate order for the sale of 125–127 *c* Strathleven Road; nor would it be either convenient or appropriate to make such an order suspended during any specific period, eg the minority of the youngest of the children enjoying the property as his home. Counsel for the plaintiff, whilst keeping his options open, has not seriously argued against this proposition.

The main argument has revolved around the right or otherwise of the plaintiff to receive an occupation rent as a co-tenant who is excluded from the property. Counsel for *d* the defendant has referred me to a judgment of Lord Denning MR in *Jones v Jones* [1977] 2 All ER 231 at 235, [1977] 1 WLR 438 at 441–442:

> 'First the claim for rent. It is quite plain that these two people were in equity tenants in common having a three-quarter and one-quarter share respectively. One was in occupation of the house. The other not. Now the common law said clearly *e* that one tenant in common is not entitled to rent from another tenant in common, even though that other occupies the whole ... As between tenants in common, they are both equally entitled to occupation and one cannot claim rent from the other. Of course, if there was an ouster, that would be another matter, or if there was a letting to a stranger for rent that would be different, but there can be no claim for rent by one tenant in common against the other whether at law or in equity.' *f*

In *Jones v Jones* the plaintiff failed not only on the ground that no occupation rent could be claimed by one tenant in common from another but also on the ground of equitable estoppel. Lord Denning MR had been referred to *M'Mahon v Burchell* (1846) 2 Ph 127. In that case the issue as pleaded involved the simple question whether or not a tenant in common by the mere fact of his occupation of the property became liable to pay an occupation rent to any other tenant in common of that property. It had been submitted *g* to Lord Cottenham LC that there was a ruling by Shadwell V-C in *Henderson v Eason* (1846) 10 Jur 821 to the effect that such a liability existed. In his judgment Lord Cottenham LC said (2 Ph 127 at 134–135):

> '... I cannot think that the Vice-Chancellor can have laid down any such doctrine; for the effect would be that one tenant in common, by keeping out of the actual *h* occupation of the premises, might convert the other into his bailiff; in other words, prevent the other from occupying them, except upon the terms of paying him rent. There is nothing in the Acts of Parliament (4 Ann. c. 16, s. 27, and 3 & 4 W. 4, c. 27, s. 12) to lead to that conclusion, which is contrary to the law as clearly established from the time of Lord Coke downwards. I cannot think, therefore, that the Vice-Chancellor intended to lay down such a proposition. Indeed, it has hardly *j* been contended for at the Bar: for the argument has been, that there is enough in the answer to raise a claim to rent which may have arisen in some other manner. There may, no doubt, be various modes of occupation, which would make the party occupying liable for rent to other tenants in common; but there is nothing in these pleadings to entitle the Defendant to an enquiry, whether the Plaintiff's occupation

a was in one of those modes, beyond the statement in the answer to which I have
referred.'

The same case is reported in rather more detail in C P Cooper's Cases (see (1 Coop *temp*
Cott 457). Both in argument and in the judgment the expresion 'exclusion' is used.
Submissions made by counsel involved the proposition (at 464):

b 'There must be either exclusion, or some contract, to make the occupying tenant
in common liable. In the present case the house had been open to all the tenants in
common; it was clear that there was no exclusion. As to contract, none was alleged
by the answer.'

Passing to the judgment, I cite the following extract (at 467–468):

c 'With regard to exclusion it was plain there was none. The answer alleged that
the Plaintiff, William M'Mahon, and one of his brothers and two of his sisters, had
occupied the house during certain periods: but it nowhere alleged that the other
brothers and sisters might not have occupied the house if they had thought fit . . .
The Plaintiffs say, it is very true that the Plaintiff, William M'Mahon, occupied the
house, but he never occupied it to the exclusion of the other tenants in common.
This the Defendants do not think fit to contest. The case set up by the Defendants,
d therefore, was neither contract, nor exclusion, nor anything else except simple
occupation.'

Lord Cottenham LC went on to deal later with this suggestion (at 469):

'There were, no doubt, various modes of occupation which would make the
tenant in common occupying liable to rent to the other tenants in common, but
e those other modes ought not to be the subject of discussion in the Master's office.'

And then later (at 471):

'The question then was, the house being open to all the tenants in common, and
the Plaintiff, William M'Mahon, having been in occupation, but there being no
exclusion of the other tenants in common, and there being an absence of all
f contract, was the Plaintiff, William M'Mahon, liable to rent?'

The report then continues as in Phillips's Reports that in these circumstances no
occupation rent could be claimed by the tenants in common not in occupation, unless by
agreement the occupying tenant in common became bailiff for another tenant in
common and thereby liable to pay.

g Counsel for the plaintiff submitted that when one refers to M'Mahon v Burchell, which
was the basis of Lord Denning MR's comment in *Jones v Jones*, it is clear that in citing the
instances of 'ouster' and 'letting to a stranger for rent' Lord Denning MR was instancing
but two of the occasions on which the courts would hold that a tenant in common might
be liable for an occupation rent. In any event the old meaning of the word 'ouster' was
probably wider than the sense of expulsion which the word carries today. The right of
h a tenant in common to claim his fair share of rent received from a stranger, to which
Lord Denning MR referred, was granted by the statute 3 & 4 Anne c 16, s 27, which was
considered in *Henderson v Eason*. Lord Denning MR did not mention, for instance, the
situation mentioned in *M'Mahon v Burchell* where, by agreement, one tenant in common
became the bailiff for another or other tenants in common and in that way was liable for
occupation rent or alternatively an agreed rent. The reference by Lord Cottenham LC
j to 'other modes of occupation' which might give rise to an occupation rent is clearly
much wider than this. The Court of Chancery was ever ready to inquire into such
matters: see the judgment of Stirling J in *Hill v Hickin* [1897] 2 Ch 579 at 580, where the
description of the issue is as follows:

'The writ was issued in 1890, and judgment given in 1892, and one of the
inquiries thereby directed was what sum was due from the defendant James Hickin

in respect of his occupation of the hereditaments since September 29, 1890 (he having been in occupation during that period without payment of rent), having *a* regard to any previous tenancy thereof.'

In his judgment Stirling J said (at 580–581):

'The defendant James Hickin not having been tenant or bailiff of his co-owners, nothing could have been recovered from him at law; nor does the Statute of Anne (4 Anne, c. 16, s. 27) apply: see *Henderson* v. *Eason* ((1851) 17 QB 701). It has, *b* however, long been the practice of the Court of Chancery and of the Chancery Division to direct such inquiries as have been directed in the present case: see as to occupation rent, *Turner* v. *Morgan* ((1803) 8 Ves 143 at 145).'

Counsel for the plaintiff submitted, I think correctly, that when one looks at the judgment in *M'Mahon v Burchell* together with the extract from the judgment of Stirling J in *Hill v Hickin* the true position under the old authorities was that the Court of *c* Chancery and Chancery Division would always be ready to inquire into the position as between co-owners being tenants in common either at law or in equity to see whether a tenant in common in occupation of the premises was doing so to the exclusion of one or more of the other tenants in common for whatever purpose or by whatever means. If this was found to be the case, then if in order to do equity between the parties an occupation rent should be paid, this would be declared and the appropriate inquiry *d* ordered. Only in cases where the tenants in common not in occupation were in a position to enjoy their right to occupy but chose not to do so voluntarily, and were not excluded by any relevant factor, would the tenant in common in occupation be entitled to do so free of liability to pay an occupation rent.

In the instant case the plaintiff is clearly not a free agent. She was caused to leave the family home as a result of the violence or threatened violence of the defendant. In any *e* event, whatever might have been the cause of the breakdown of the association, it would be quite unreasonable to expect the plaintiff to exercise her rights as a tenant in common to occupy the property as she had done before the breakdown of her association with the defendant. In my judgment she falls into exactly the kind of category of person excluded from the property in the way envisaged by Lord Cottenham LC in *M'Mahon v Burchell*. Therefore, the basic principle that a new tenant in common is not liable to pay an *f* occupation rent by virtue merely of his being in sole occupation of the property does not apply in the case where an association similar to a matrimonial association has broken down and one party is, for practical purposes, excluded from the family home.

I should add that I have thought it proper to consider the wider implications of what I believe to be the wide ambit of the meaning of the word 'exclusion' in the context of joint tenants because I am reluctant to see any extension of the concept of 'constructive *g* desertion' after it has to a large extent been successfully eliminated by the provisions of s 1(2)(b) of the Matrimonial Causes Act 1973. On the particular facts of this case, however, I am satisfied that by his acts of violence and threats of continuing violence the defendant forced the plaintiff to leave the home and thereafter prevented her returning to it in circumstances amounting to constructive desertion. Whatever may be the true test of 'expulsion' or 'ouster' I have no doubt that the plaintiff in this case was expelled by *h* the conduct of the defendant from the property and prevented by him from enjoying her rights as a tenant in common.

Counsel for the plaintiff pointed out that the court in effect ordered the tenant in common in occupation to pay the equivalent of an occupation rent in some of the other cases which were cited in argument. In *Re Evers's Trust* [1980] 3 All ER 399, [1980] 1 WLR 1327, whilst dismissing the appeal the court altered the order made by the judge: *j*

'For these reasons the judge was right not to order an immediate sale, but the form of his actual order is not satisfactory. Under s 30 the primary question is whether the court should come to the aid of the applicant at the "particular moment, and in the particular circumstances when the application is made to it" (*Re Buchanan-Wollaston's Conveyance* [1939] 2 All ER 302 at 308, [1939] Ch 738 at 747). In the present case, at the present moment and in the existing circumstances, it would be wrong to order a sale. But circumstances may change unpredictably. It may not be appropriate to order a sale when the child reaches 16 years, a purely arbitrary date, or it may become appropriate to do so much sooner, for example on the mother's remarriage or on it becoming financially possible for her to buy the father out. In such circumstances it will probably be wiser simply to dismiss the application while indicating the sort of circumstances which would, prima facie, justify a further application. The ensuing uncertainty is unfortunate, but, under this section, the court has no power to adjust property rights or to redraft the terms of the trust. Ideally, the parties should now negotiate a settlement on the basis that neither of them is in a position to dictate terms. We would, therefore, dismiss the father's appeal, but would vary the order to dismiss the application on the mother's undertaking to discharge the liability under the mortgage, to pay the outgoings and maintain the property, and to indemnify the father so long as she is occupying the property.'

(See [1980] 3 All ER 399 at 404, [1980] 1 WLR 1327 at 1334, per Ormrod LJ.)

Counsel for the plaintiff points out that the terms on which the court declined to make an order included an undertaking by the mother who was occupying the premises to discharge the liability under the mortgage. This included not only capital but also interest elements and, therefore, in effect required her to pay an occupation rent for the privilege of continuing to occupy as a tenant in common the whole property adversely to the father.

In *Leake (formerly Bruzzi) v Bruzzi* [1974] 2 All ER 1196, [1974] 1 WLR 1528, which was an application under s 17 of the Married Women's Property Act 1882, the question arose as to what relief the husband who had paid all the mortage instalments should get for having in effect paid the wife's share for which she would otherwise be liable. The court ordered that the husband should have relief only in respect of the capital element of those payments. In effect, by depriving him of relief in respect of the wife's liability for the interest element of the mortgage repayments, the court was charging him indirectly with an occupation rent. Counsel for the plaintiff submitted, in answer to a question put by me, that had the wife not availed herself of the relief afforded by s 17 of the 1882 Act she could just as well have proceeded under s 30 of the Law of Property Act 1925. I cannot see any fallacy in this submission. It would not be satisfactory if differing results could be obtained depending on which cause of action was adopted. *Leake v Bruzzi*, therefore, is support for counsel for the plaintiff's contentions notwithstanding that it was a case brought under the 1882 Act, and not the Law of Property Act 1925. In another case under the Married Women's Property Act 1882, *Suttill v Graham* [1977] 3 All ER 1117, [1977] 1 WLR 819, the husband and wife bought a house on mortgage as a matrimonial home and it was conveyed to them jointly in equal shares. The parties separated and each remarried but the husband continued to occupy the home and pay the mortgage instalments. In an action under s 17 of the 1882 Act and the Matrimonial Proceedings and Property Act 1970 for a declaration that she was entitled to half the beneficial interest of the home and for an order for sale, the husband contended that he should be credited with one-half of the mortgage instalments which he had paid, including both capital and interest, and that the sum claimed by the wife should be reduced accordingly. The judge held that the husband should be credited with one-half of the capital repayments only since they had reduced the principal sum owing and increased pro tanto the value of the property. On appeal Stamp LJ said ([1977] 3 All ER 1117 at 1119–1120, [1977] 1 WLR 819 at 821):

'It must be emphasised at this point that this is not a case where the husband, nor for that matter the wife, is claiming in the divorce suit ancillary relief in the form

of a property adjustment order or lump sum payment. The matter has throughout
been dealt with under the machinery laid down in the 1882 Act as amended. *a*
Accordingly it would be open to the wife, who was not represented and did not
appear on this appeal, to submit first, that applying *Pettit v Pettit* [1969] 2 All ER
385, [1970] AC 777 and *Gissing v Gissing* [1970] 2 All ER 780, [1971] AC 886 the
rights of the parties must be judged on general principles in considering questions
of title to property; and second, that applying those principles a beneficiary entitled
to an equal share in equity of property of which he is a trustee, and which he himself *b*
occupies, is to be charged with at least an occupation rent; so that if as here he seeks
to charge his co-beneficiary trustee with half the outgoings he should be charged
with half the occupation rent. That is not precisely the way in which such a
situation has been approached in the cases to which attention has been called by
counsel on behalf of the husband. But in *Leake v Bruzzi* [1974] 2 All ER 1196,
[1974] 1 WLR 1528 this court arrived at a similar conclusion by regarding the *c*
mortgage interest paid by the husband while in possession as something equivalent
to rent or payment for use and occupation. That will normally produce a fair result
and save costs; and where, as here, the husband in possession does not submit to be
charged with an occupation rent, it must be wrong that he should seek to charge the
wife with half the mortgage interest which he has paid while living in the property
rent free and resisting a sale of the property.' *d*

Since early 1974 the defendant has occupied the property in circumstances in which
he should pay an occupation rent to the plaintiff. I now turn to consider s 30 of the Law
of Property Act 1925. Counsel for the plaintiff submitted that I can make appropriate
orders by virtue of the provision in s 30. After considering the wording of this section
I have come to the conclusion that it does not confer any power on the court to this *e*
effect. As was said in argument, the section was really passed for conveyancing purposes
to help deal with the flood of equitable tenants in common holding under trusts for sale
which resulted from the passing into law of the Law of Property Act 1925. I do not think
that this section enables the court to make orders where an order for sale is not made.
Only orders ancillary to an order for sale which are necessary to implement the sale are
envisaged by the words of the section. The words are 'and the court may make such *f*
order as it thinks fit' and not 'or the court may make such other orders' etc. As is
explained in Megarry and Wade's Law of Real Property (4th Edn, 1975, p 427) s 30 of the
Law of Property Act 1925 is the successor to the old Partition Acts and in particular the
power of sale granted under the Partition Act 1868. In *Turner v Morgan* (1803) 8 Ves 143
at 145, 32 ER 307 at 308 Lord Eldon LC held the threat of making a partition order over
the parties in order to bring them to terms. Although s 30 does not grant a power to the *g*
court to order the payment of an occupation rent it certainly could be used in a manner
similar to that adopted by Lord Eldon LC, by means of indicating that unless an
undertaking to pay an occupation rent was forthcoming from the defendant then the
order for sale would be made.

However, such an indirect method may not be necessary. I think on the general
principles of the law set out in this judgment it is open to the court to make an order that *h*
an occupation rent should be paid. If I am wrong about this then the course outlined
immediately above should be adopted.

Counsel for the plaintiff put the matter in an alternative way which out of respect for
his able argument I refer to here. He submitted that the defendant was seeking equity
and, therefore, under the old maxim must himself do equity. This argument has its
attractions. It is based on the proposition that in resisting an order for sale under s 30 the *j*
defendant is seeking equitable relief. This would be so if the trust for sale had as its sole
object the sale of the property and if its postponement was a matter of seeking the
indulgence of the court. In this case, as I have already said, it is clear that the prime object
of the trust was to provide a home. Whilst it is still being used for this purpose, as

without doubt it still is, then I do not think that it is right to describe the defendant as
a someone who is seeking equity to protect him from the due execution of the trusts for
sale. Whilst the family occupy the house the sale is secondary to the trust to provide a
home for the family.

Counsel for the defendant submitted that if I came to the conclusion that the defendant
was liable to pay an occupation rent then I should not make an order that was
retroactive. The main plank of his argument was that if I made such an order it would
b impose a heavy financial burden on the defendant and might well prejudice him in
taking advantage of the offer made by the housing authority to pay an improvement
grant. It is obviously important for both parties that the value of their joint investment
should be enhanced and that this offer be taken up. I do not think that I can accede to
counsel's submission. I am by no means satisfied that the defendant was wholly frank
about either his means or his capital assets. There is in any event a valuable property here
c which at the moment is unencumbered.

Counsel for the plaintiff submitted that I should deal with the question of occupation
rent to date in two stages. He submitted that between the years 1974 and 1976 inclusive
there should not be any inquiry but that I should order that for this period no credit
should be given either for the capital or interest elements of the plaintiff's share of the
mortgage payments which have in fact been paid by the defendant. This would be in
d line with the approach of Stamp LJ in *Suttill v Graham* and Ormrod LJ in *Leake (formerly
Bruzzi) v Bruzzi.* The basis of his submission is that during the early years the major
element in the mortgage repayment is interest on the capital advanced and that half of
the sums would be broadly equivalent to an occupation rent. This would in my
judgment do rough justice between the parties.

As to the years 1977 to 1980 inclusive, counsel for the plaintiff submitted that an
e occupation rent would be noticeably higher than half the mortgage payments which
would otherwise be due to be paid by the plaintiff. During this period, counsel suggested,
there should be an inquiry as to what the occupation rent ought to be with an order for
the payment of such sums subject to the defendant's entitlement to set off any amount
paid in redemption of the mortgage on behalf of the plaintiff. Since 1980, of course, no
question of mortgage repayment arises and the liability of the defendant to pay an
f occupation rent must be a payment of half the appropriate rent for the property. The
question arises whether such a rent ought to be assessed as a normal rack rent, as the
interest to be paid on a sum equivalent to the value of the property; or should the rent
be assessed as 'a fair rent' such as would be assessed by a rent officer?

I indicated in argument that I did not think that the occupation rent ought to be
assessed in relation to the value of the capital asset involved, or, rather, half of it, as this
g was not the concept behind an occupation rent. Although counsel for the plaintiff again
kept his options open on this score he did not pursue the argument.

The question then reverts to whether it should be a rack rent assessed on the basis that
there is not a protected tenancy involved or whether it should be a fair rent to be assessed
in the ordinary way as with a protected tenancy. There is room for argument here. The
approach which I adopt is that as each party has a right to occupy the property but the
h occupation rent arises as a result of the exclusion of the plaintiff in the manner already
described in this judgment, then the plaintiff's rights as against the defendant must
envisage that the defendant himself has a right to occupy the property akin to the sort of
protection given to a protected tenant. For these reasons I think that the proper way to
assess the amount of the occupation rent for which the defendant is liable is that this
should be half the fair rent which would be assessed by the rent officer for a letting
i unfurnished of the whole of the property to a protected tenant. An inquiry should be
ordered, therefore, to assess this figure for the years 1977 to 1980 inclusive. In such an
inquiry the defendant should be entitled to credit for any sums paid in respect of the
property which enhances its capital value but not for any sums paid in the ordinary
maintenance and repair of the property.

If the defendant gives an undertaking to pay the amount found due by such an inquiry for the years 1977 to 1980 inclusive and for the year 1981 and thereafter undertakes to *a* pay such amount by way of occupation rent as shall be agreed between the parties or otherwise to be determined by the rent officer, then I shall not make an order under s 30 of the Law of Property Act 1925.

Order accordingly.

b

Solicitors: *Eric Hauser & Co* (for the plaintiff); *Robert Thompson & Partners* (for the defendant).

Bebe Chua Barrister.

c

d
Practice Direction

FAMILY DIVISION

Practice – Matrimonial causes – Trial – Directions for trial – Applications for property adjustment – Discovery – Valuation of property – Issue of conduct raised.
e

The experiment in operation from 1st April 1980 to secure the settlement of financial applications at a pre-trial review has resulted in a success rate so low as not to justify its continuance. Consequently pre-trial reviews on such applications will not take place as from 1st July 1981.

Nevertheless the following procedures laid down by the registrar's direction of 12th *f* February 1980 ([1980] 1 All ER 592, [1980] 1 WLR 245) are still useful and should be continued.

(a) After affidavits have been filed mutual discovery should take place without order 14 days from the last affidavit, unless some other period is agreed, with inspection 7 days thereafter.

(b) Where a dispute arises as to the value of any property, a valuation should be made *g* without order by an agreed valuer or, in default of agreement, by an independent valuer chosen by the President of the Royal Institution of Chartered Surveyors. The valuation should be produced to the registrar at the hearing.

(c) If a dispute arises as to the extent of discovery or as to answers in a questionnaire, an appointment for directions should be taken out. Where the registrar considers that to answer any question would entail considerable expense and that there is doubt *h* whether the answer would provide any information of value, he may make the order for the question to be answered at the questioner's risk as to costs. The registrar may refuse to order an answer to a question if he considers that its value would be small in relation to the property or income of the party to whom the question is addressed.

(d) Where an issue of conduct is raised on the affidavits, an appointment for directions should be taken out at which the registrar will inquire whether the issue is being pursued *j* and, if so, will order particulars to be given of the precise allegations relied on.

The registrar's direction of 12th February 1980 is hereby cancelled.

R L BAYNE-POWELL
4th June 1981	Senior Registrar.

Re Marquess of Abergavenny's Estate Act Trusts
Marquess of Abergavenny v Ram and another

CHANCERY DIVISION
GOULDING J
2nd DECEMBER 1980

Settlement – Advancement – Power to advance proportion of trust fund – Trustees advancing prescribed proportion to beneficiary – Retained assets appreciating in value – Whether advances up to prescribed limit at date of advancement exhausting power of advancement – Whether trustees having power to make further advances to bring aggregate of advances up to prescribed limit where balance retained by trustees increasing in value.

The trustees held a settled fund on trust for, inter alios, the plaintiff during his life and had a discretionary power to raise and pay to the plaintiff, for his own use and benefit, any part of the fund up to a value of one-half of the fund.' In 1965 the trustees decided to exercise the discretionary power in full and paid to the plaintiff a sum representing one-half of the value of the fund at the date of the advance. The trustees invested the balance retained, which appreciated considerably in value. In 1980 the plaintiff took out a summons seeking determination of the question whether the trustees could properly make a further payment to bring the advances made to him, including that part already advanced, up to one-half of the existing value of the fund. The trustees were willing to make a further payment if they had power to do so.

Held – Where there was power to make advances to a beneficiary up to a specified proportion of a trust fund, a payment up to that limit exhausted the exercise of the power and it ceased to be exercisable in the future even though the retained assets subsequently increased in value. Accordingly, the summons would be answered by declaring that the trustees' discretionary power had already been fully exercised (see p 646 *a b* and *e* to *h*, post).

Notes

For a trustee's power of advancement, see 38 Halsbury's Laws (3rd Edn) 1019, para 1758, and for cases on the subject, see 47 Digest (Repl) 270–274, 2355–2384.

Cases referred to in judgment

Gollin's Declaration of Trust, Re, Turner v Williams [1969] 3 All ER 1591, [1969] 1 WLR 1858, Digest (Cont Vol C) 1048, 3192a.
Richardson, Re, Morgan v Richardson [1896] 1 Ch 512, 65 LJ Ch 512, 74 LT 12, 24 Digest (Reissue) 743, 7967.

Originating summons

By a summons dated 2nd June 1980 the plaintiff, the Most Hon John Henry Guy Nevill, Marquess of Abergavenny, sought determination whether on the true construction of the trusts, powers and provisions contained in Sch 7 to the Marquess of Abergavenny's Estate Act 1946 (9 & 10 Geo 6 c 1) and in the events which had happened (a) Edward David Abel Ram and Anthony West Ponder, the trustees of the trusts, could properly, on an upward revaluation of the assets comprised in the trust fund, exercise further in favour of the plaintiff their discretionary power to raise and pay to him any part or parts of the trust fund or (b) whether their discretionary power had already been exercised to the full. The facts are set out in the judgment.   *a*

Martin Buckley for the plaintiff.
Hedley Marten for the trustees.

GOULDING J. The Marquess of Abergavenny's Estate Act 1946, chapter 1 of the private Acts of Parliament of that year, was enacted on a Bill which was prepared, as I *b* believe, by the most eminent draftsman of his day. I also have reason to believe that he regarded the Bill as one of his choicest pieces of work. Nevertheless, such is the difficulty of the conveyancer's art, the variety of supervening events, and the ingenuity of the learned, that I have before me today a short question of construction on one of the provisions contained in the statute.

The originating summons on which I am now giving judgment was taken out by the *c* present Lord Abergavenny, who was Earl of Lewes at the time the statute was passed. The defendants to the summons are the present trustees of a certain settlement provided for thereby. Lord Abergavenny himself is tenant for life of the settled property.

I go at once to the relevant legislative provisions. The Act removed from the family estates an unbarrable statutory entail dating from Tudor times and it made a number of provisions for members of the Nevill family. By s 5 of the Act the then trustees for the *d* purposes of the Settled Land Act 1925 of the settlement of the entailed estate were directed by sale, mortgage or other means to raise certain sums of money. One of those sums was a sum of £230,000 referred to in Part IV of Sch 4 to the Act. The trustees were by the same section directed to hold that sum on the trusts and with and subject to the powers and provisions set forth in Sch 7 to the Act. Reference to Sch 7 shows that the sum of £230,000 is governed by trusts, powers and provisions set out in Part I of such Sch *e* 7. The first trust is for the plaintiff during his life with remainders over in strict settlement and an ultimate remainder to the plaintiff himself. Then there are a number of provisos, of which the one that has given rise to the present question is set out in para 2(2) of Part I of Sch 7. It is this:

'In the case of each tenant for life for the time being in possession under the *f* foregoing trusts the Trustees of the settlement shall have power in their discretion from time to time during his life and upon his request in writing to raise and pay to him for his own use and benefit any part or parts not exceeding in all one-half in value of the settled fund of which he becomes tenant for life in possession. And they may for that purpose compute and decide the value of the settled fund or any part thereof in such manner and upon such evidence as they shall think proper...'
                                                                                      g

I should have said that the expression 'the settled fund' is defined near the beginning of Sch 7 as meaning the sum of £230,000 or the investments and property for the time being representing it.

In 1965 the trustees of the settled fund determined to exercise their power under para 2(2) to its full extent in favour of Lord Abergavenny. They took into account certain payments or transfers of assets that had already been made to him in exercise of the *h* power. No question arises as to the values they put on such previously released assets. Nor does any question arise as to the figure which in 1965 they determined would represent the balance of one half share of the settled fund. Nor is it in doubt that in that year, or at any rate very shortly afterwards, Lord Abergavenny received such balance to the full. However, the money value of the retained fund, after giving Lord Abergavenny a half at the time I have mentioned, has very considerably appreciated. The trustees *j* subsequently bought the family landed estate from Lord Abergavenny and, like most land in the south of England, it has gone up a great deal in value. Accordingly, the suggestion is made on behalf of the plaintiff that the trustees, if in their discretion they think fit, should now make over to him a sufficient part of the assets in their hands to bring him up to one-half of the sum of the present value of the property retained by the trustees in 1965, or what now represents it, plus the value in 1965 put on the half share then made over to the plaintiff himself. The trustees say that they would be minded to a make at any rate some further payment to the plaintiff if the court thinks they have power to do so.

It is well known to those who advise on family trusts that a variety of accounting problems arise where you have a power of appointment of advancement exercisable over a fund of fluctuating value and limited by a fractional maximum. It is difficult to lay down any general principles that will solve all such problems. No doubt the learned draftsman of the Bill for the 1946 Act felt that he had done the best he could by giving b the trustees a wide discretionary power to compute and decide the value of the settled fund or any part thereof in such manner and on such evidence as they should think proper when exercising their power to benefit the tenant for life. However, it is not suggested on either side that that discretionary power of valuation enables the trustees to decide the question of construction that is now placed before me.

The point is a short one. It is not, so far as the researches of counsel have revealed, the c subject of any express judicial authority. Counsel for the plaintiff, Lord Abergavenny, has referred me to cases that he submits are applicable by analogy, namely cases where appropriation is necessary to constitute a fractional share of a fund and a partial appropriation has been made in the first place. There the approved practice is, when the balance of the share comes to be appropriated, to require the beneficiary to bring in what he has previously received at a money valuation as at the date when it was previously d allocated to him. That is brought into account and the fund still retained by the trustees or other holders of the fund is valued as at the date of the further appropriation. The cases cited to illustrate that principle are *Re Richardson* [1896] 1 Ch 512, a decision of North J, and *Re Gollin's Declaration of Trust* [1969] 3 All ER 1591, [1969] 1 WLR 1858, decided by Buckley J. The principle regarding successive appropriations being as I have stated, counsel for the plaintiff says that it really should make no difference whether a e limit has been completely reached or nearly reached. If the remainder of the fund appreciates, why should the person previously paid out be entitled to get his benefit from it if he has had almost the whole of his share and yet be debarred from reopening the matter just because the limit has been reached? It is offensive to logic, counsel submits. In the present case, as long as the remaining assets in the trustees' hands remain in settlement, it is submitted that Lord Abergavenny should be entitled to come back, f being himself of course life tenant, see what they are worth, and say, 'Well, taking into account what I have already received I have not had a half yet, consider giving me some more if you think fit.' I put to counsel an illustration suggested to me by *Re Richardson*, but on much simpler facts. Supposing that a testator gives his residue, half to his son absolutely and half in settlement for his daughter and her children, and the son's share is fully paid out in one operation shortly after the testator's death, would anyone suppose g that he could at any time thereafter during his sister's life require a valuation of the half retained for her and her children and, if it had appreciated since the original appropriation, require some more? I think that counsel did not feel able to resist my suggestion that in such a case the son could not reopen the appropriation, but he did draw a distinction between a simple appropriation case and one like the present where there is a continuing discretionary power, intended to be available for repeated exercise h during the whole of a life. The power here is that the trustees in their discretion may raise and pay assets to Lord Abergavenny, or any other life tenant, from time to time during his life and on his request in writing. Another distinction drawn by counsel was that in the case I put of the appropriation between the two children's shares the son would by some express receipt, or at any rate by conduct in taking what was given to him, accept it and agree it as satisfying his whole entitlement under the residuary j bequest, and there is no such requirement at any point, says counsel, in the provisions now under scrutiny. I am not persuaded by that distinction. Looking at the account which has been put in evidence by the plaintiff himself to show what was done in 1965, it does seem to me that he must have accepted it in full satisfaction of what could be given to him under the settlement. Had the question been asked at that time I think he would have unhesitatingly agreed. However, that may be thought speculative and I do not put my judgment on it.

Counsel for the trustees, although they are sympathetic, as I have said, to Lord

Abergavenny's request, has none the less performed his duty of putting the other side of the argument on construction. He suggests, and I agree, that the only true conclusion *a* from the evidence is that Lord Abergavenny received a full one-half of the trust fund as valued in 1965. Then, counsel for the trustees says, as a matter of law, that amounted to an exhaustive exercise of the power which ceased to be exercisable for the future, whatever might happen to the retained assets, that is whether they went up or down in value. In my judgment that is right. I do not think that the authorities on a partial appropriation followed by a supplemental appropriation really assist in the present *b* matter one way or the other. The judges who have had to consider that question have never, so far as I know, had the present point drawn to their attention. Buckley J said in the *Gollin* case [1969] 3 All ER 1591 at 1592, [1969] 1 WLR 1858 at 1861:

> 'I treat the first defendant as having received in specie one-third of the fund in 1947. Having regard to the decision I have reached on the first question in the summons, her entitlement at that time was not one-third of the fund but five- *c* ninths of the fund and that appropriation was insufficient to satisfy her whole absolute entitlement.'

It was against that background that he considered how as a matter of account the first defendant in that case was obliged to bring in what she had previously received. I do not think that on a fair consideration of the questions decided in that and in the earlier *d* *Richardson* case that they really help the present controversy one way or the other.

I think myself that the reason why there is no direct authority on the question is because the answer has always seemed plain. Any layman, and any lawyer I think, without such special and persuasive advocacy as I have heard this morning, would feel that where there is a power to make successive payments to a person up to a limit of a certain fraction of a fund and at a certain date he, the beneficiary, has received assets then *e* fully reaching the prescribed limit thereafter no further exercise of the power is possible. All that the settlor authorised has been done. It would be to my mind strange and unexpected if the object of the power as such retained an interest or possibility of interest in the fund still in settlement, so that he could require accounts from the trustees and demand reconsideration of his position whenever there should be an appreciation of assets. It is perfectly true that even in the partial appropriation cases the beneficiary who *f* has received something early may do very well because he may keep what has been given to him in some asset that appreciates while he only has to bring a cash sum, fixed once and for all, into account; it may of course go the other way. But some such possibility of good or ill fortune is inherent in the very nature of payments made under a duty or a power on successive occasions up to an aggregate limit. There is no reason that I can see why such inequality, or exposure to fortune, should be continued to the possible *g* disadvantage of other beneficiaries after the limit has been reached.

I have endeavoured to give reasons for my view on what is really a very short point and, as I say, it does not seem to me a very difficult one when one looks at the terms of the power. Accordingly, I must answer the question asked by the originating summons by declaring that on the true construction of the 1946 Act and in the events which have happened the power has already been exercised to the full. Unless anyone is going to *h* submit the contrary, I should have thought that it was a case in which the usual order as to costs could be made directing the plaintiff's costs on the common fund basis and the defendants' costs as trustees to be taxed and to be raised and paid out of the capital of the trust fund. It was a question that was brought with propriety, once having been raised.

[Counsel for the trustees agreed and did not resist the proposed order.]

j

Determination accordingly.

Solicitors: *Withers* (for the plaintiff and the trustees).

Evelyn M C Budd   Barrister.

R v Bloxham

COURT OF APPEAL, CRIMINAL DIVISION
DUNN LJ, KILNER BROWN AND TAYLOR JJ
10th, 20th FEBRUARY 1981

Criminal law – Handling stolen goods – Undertaking or assisting in retention etc – Realisation of goods – Realisation of goods to innocent purchaser believing them to be stolen – Accused purchasing car which he subsequently suspected was stolen – Accused disposing of car to innocent purchaser without appropriate documents for less than true value – Whether accused undertaking or assisting in realisation of car 'for the benefit of another person' – Whether person for whose benefit goods realised limited to principal for whom accused acting as agent – Whether person for whose benefit goods realised including anyone deriving benefit from purchase of goods – Theft Act 1968, s 22(1).

In January 1977 the appellant agreed to buy a car for £1,300. Unknown to him, the car was stolen. He paid £500 on account and agreed to pay the balance on production of the registration documents. The documents were never produced and by May 1977 the appellant suspected that the car was stolen. He drove it until August 1977 when the tax on it expired and then decided to dispose of it to avoid further possession of a stolen vehicle. He sold it in December 1977 to someone unknown to him who was prepared to buy it for £200 without the appropriate documents. The appellant was charged with handling stolen goods, contrary to s 22(1)[a] of the Theft Act 1968 which made it an offence if a person 'knowing or believing them to be stolen goods ... dishonestly undertakes or assists in their ... realisation ... for the benefit of another person'. At his trial it was submitted on behalf of the appellant that the facts did not disclose an offence within s 22(1), because realisation 'for the benefit of another person' did not extend to the realisation of stolen goods by a sale to an innocent purchaser but was restricted to a realisation linked to the theft of the goods or the prior dishonest handling of them, since 'another person' for whose benefit the goods were realised would usually be the thief or a prior dishonest handler of the goods. The Crown submitted that the words 'for the benefit of another person' in s 22(1) were clear and unambiguous and that the innocence or otherwise of that other person was irrelevant.

Held – Although the words 'undertakes' and 'assists in' in s 22(1) of the 1965 Act contemplated that the accused was playing a subsidiary role as agent for a principal, the section was not limited to the situation where the goods were realised by an agent for a principal, since the mischief which s 22(1) was aimed at was dishonest handling, and all that was required to constitute the offence was a dishonest realisation of the goods which conferred some benefit on the buyer, and it was not necessary that the buyer had got the better of the transaction between himself and the seller or that the seller had derived no benefit from the realisation. Since in realising the car believing it to be stolen the appellant had acted dishonestly and the buyer had received a benefit, namely the use of a car for which he had paid less than the true value, all the elements of the offence were present and accordingly the appeal against conviction would be dismissed (see p 649 h j, post).

Notes

For handling stolen goods, see 11 Halsbury's Laws (4th Edn) para 1289, and for cases on the subject, see 15 Digest (Reissue) 1362–1363, 11,900–11,904.

For the Theft Act 1968, s 22, see 8 Halsbury's Statutes (3rd Edn) 796.

---

[a]   Section 22(1), so far as material, is set out at p 648 *f g*, post

Cases referred to in judgment

R v Deakin [1972] 3 All ER 803, [1972] 1 WLR 1618, 137 JP 19, 56 Cr App R 841, CA, *a* 14(1) Digest (Reissue) 275, 2083

R v Sloggett [1971] 3 All ER 264, [1972] 1 QB 430, [1971] 3 WLR 628, 135 JP 534, 55 Cr App R 532, CA, 14(1) Digest (Reissue) 275, 2081

Appeal

On 16th January 1980, the appellant, Albert John Bloxham, was convicted on his plea of *b* guilty in the Crown Court at Southampton before his Honour Judge McCreery QC, of the offence of handling stolen goods contrary to s 22(1) of the Theft Act 1968, the judge having ruled against a submission that no offence was disclosed on the facts and that a person who dishonestly assisted in the disposal of stolen property by selling it to an unknown purchaser who benefited thereby, dishonestly assisted in the realisation of the goods 'for the benefit of another', ie the purchaser, within s 22(1). The appellant was *c* given a conditional discharge for 12 months and ordered to pay £250 towards the costs of the defence. He appealed against the conviction on the ground that the judge was wrong to rule on the admitted facts that the appellant was guilty because the admitted disposal of the property in question, a stolen car, was not for the benefit of another, the purchaser, but was solely for the benefit of the appellant. The facts are set out in the judgment of the court. *d*

David Griffiths and *S W Watkins* for the appellant.
Neil Butterfield and *Claudia Ackner* for the Crown.

Cur adv vult

20th February. **KILNER BROWN J** read the following judgment of the court: This *e* application for leave to appeal against conviction raises a point of law and has been treated by the court as an appeal. The appellant was convicted on his plea of guilty on 16th January 1980 in the Crown Court at Southampton before his Honour Judge McCreery QC after the judge had ruled against a submission that the facts did not disclose an offence within the statutory provisions relied on in the indictment. The alleged offence was charged as being contrary to s 22(1) of the Theft Act 1968 the relevant *f* parts of which read as follows:

'A person handles stolen goods if (otherwise than in the course of stealing) knowing or believing them to be stolen goods he . . . dishonestly undertakes or assists in their . . . realisation by or for the benefit of another person . . .'

The meaning and application of these words in the context of the facts of this case has *g* not, so far as we are aware, come up for consideration by the Court of Appeal although this section of the Act was considered in differing circumstances in R v Sloggett [1971] 3 All ER 264, [1972] 1 QB 430 and R v Deakin [1972] 3 All ER 803, [1972] 1 WLR 1618. Neither case dealt with the interpretation to be put on the words 'for the benefit of another'. The situation disclosed by the facts of this case has, however, been considered hypothetically in the academic field and has given rise to obvious difference of opinion. *h*

The facts can be summarised in a sentence or two. In January 1977 the appellant agreed to buy a Ford Cortina motor car for the sum of £1,300 which in fact, though unknown to him, had been stolen and fitted with false number plates. He paid £500 on account and the balance of £800 was to be paid on production of the registration documents. No such documents were forthcoming and the appellant admitted to the police that by May 1977 he suspected that the car might be stolen. He drove it until *j* August 1977 when the tax expired. Desiring to be rid of it and to avoid further possession of a car which might be stolen he sold it in December 1977 for £200 to a man he did not know who was prepared to buy it without the appropriate documents. It was this act in the month of December 1977 which gave rise to the offence alleged against him. By this ruling the judge decided that this was a dishonest realisation of the car for the benefit of another person, namely the unknown buyer. The benefit was the use of

the car at a cheap price even though he had no title to it. The judge ordered a conditional
a discharge but added to the net loss of £300 a further sum of £250 by way of payment of
prosecution costs.

On behalf of the appellant it was argued before us, as it was before the trial judge, that
the section as a whole is intended to link the dishonest receipt of goods or assistance given
by realisation thereof with a theft by another person or a prior dishonest handling by
another person. Thus the 'another' who gets a benefit would often be the thief. The
b section, so it is said, was drafted in this fashion to prevent conviction for dishonest
handling as well as theft being registered against the thief. In this counsel has the
support of Professor Smith in The Law of Theft (4th Edn, 1979, para 420, p 209) and
Smith and Hogan's Criminal Law (4th Edn, 1978, p 611). That being so, it was further
submitted that if the realisation of the goods was to a genuine innocent purchaser, such
realisation was not intended by the legislature to be applied so as to cover the transaction
c in this case because the innocent purchaser derives no benefit from the sale, since he has
no title to the goods. The only person to benefit was the appellant who received the cash
consideration for the sale, and because of the inclusion of the words 'for the benefit of
another' he has committed no offence under the section.

On behalf of the Crown it is argued that whatever the intention of Parliament may
have been, the words 'for the benefit of another' are plain and unambiguous and the
d innocence or otherwise of the 'another' is irrelevant. Nevertheless it has to be recognised
that the convoluted terminology of the section as a whole can give rise to a variety of
interpretations. Thus Professor Griew in his book The Theft Acts 1968 and 1978 (3rd
Edn, 1978, p 147) says: 'Realisation for the benefit of another typically occurs when an
agent sells on behalf of a principal.' We recognise that the use in the section of the words
'assists in' contemplates that the accused is playing a subsidiary role to a principal and that
e the alternative word 'undertakes' also implies that it is to do something for a principal.
So the question is whether the section has to be limited in its application to the situation
where there is a relationship of principal and agent. Professor Smith concentrates, in the
paragraph of his book to which reference has been made, on the thief who sells to an
innocent purchaser, and asserts that the thief cannot be guilty of handling unless merely
performing the contract with the purchaser amounts to acting for the benefit of
f another. Perhaps wisely, he does not advert to the situation, as in the instant case, where
it is not the thief but a purchaser with knowledge or belief in the stolen nature of the
goods who then sells on to another. On the other hand the precise situation was
considered by Mr L W Blake in his article The Innocent Purchaser and Section 22 of the
Theft Act 1968 ([1972] Crim LR 494). He recognised that despite the confusion of
thought in the association of 'by . . . another person' with 'for the benefit of another
g person', the words of the section do not allow for contention that 'If a purchaser for value
discovers that he has bought stolen goods, he may be guilty of obtaining property by
deception if he resells them, but he does not become a handler'. He plainly recognises
that the resale situation is covered by the terminology of the section which makes it a
dishonest handling.

We have come to the same conclusion as Mr Blake, not so much on academic and
h metaphysical grounds as on pragmatic grounds. The mischief at which the section is
aimed is a dishonest handling. If the words permit of a simple approach capable of being
readily understood by a jury this is to be preferred. In this case, although the appellant
received the car innocently, there came a time when he believed it to be stolen. He then
realised the car by selling it. Although he undoubtedly received a benefit, so did the
buyer. He had the use of the car for which he had paid less than its true value. No one
j can tell what he might have done with it. The section does not require that in realising
the car the buyer should have got the better transaction, or that the seller should have no
benefit. It simply requires that the buyer should have derived some benefit. In the view
of this court he did derive a benefit and, it being accepted that the appellant, in realising
the car believing it to be stolen, acted dishonestly all the elements of the offence are
complete. The appeal is dismissed.

Appeal dismissed.

The court refused leave to appeal to the House of Lords but certified, under s 33(2) of the Criminal Appeal Act 1968, that the following point of law of general public importance was involved in the decision: whether a bona fide purchaser for value commits an offence of dishonestly undertaking the disposal or realisation of stolen property for the benefit of another if when he sells the goods on he knows or believes them to be stolen.

9th April. The Appeal Committee of the House of Lords allowed a petition by the appellant for leave to appeal.

Solicitors: *Bernard Chill & Axtell,* Southampton (for the appellant); *R N Bourne,* Winchester (for the Crown).

N P Metcalfe Esq   Barrister.

Habib Bank Ltd v Habib Bank AG Zurich

COURT OF APPEAL, CIVIL DIVISION
STEPHENSON, OLIVER AND WATKINS LJJ
3rd, 4th, 8th, 9th, 10th, 11th, 15th, 16th, 17th, 18th DECEMBER 1980

Passing off – Trade name – Business carried on abroad and in England – Business enjoying international reputation and goodwill – International business setting up branch in England – International business losing control of management of English branch and setting up another branch – Whether goodwill and reputation continuing to attach to international business or becoming exclusive property of English branch.

In 1941 a well-known Indian banking family, the Habibs, founded a bank, Habib Bank Ltd ('the original Habib bank'), which was established in Karachi in 1947 on the partition of India. In 1952 the Habib family (as to 60%) and the original Habib bank (as to 40%) established an associate bank, Habib Bank (Overseas) Ltd ('the overseas bank'), to handle the overseas business of the original Habib bank. The overseas bank set up branches in foreign countries including branches in London and elsewhere in England. In 1967 the family established a separate Habib bank in Switzerland, Habib Bank AG Zurich ('the Zurich bank'), in which, in accordance with Swiss policy, the majority of shares were owned by a Swiss corporation and a minority by the overseas bank. The three banks were in fact run as parts of the same entity. In 1973 the Zurich bank opened a branch in London in a room adjoining the offices of the overseas bank. The arrangements for opening the London branch of the Zurich bank were made by the overseas bank. In 1974 both the original Habib bank and the overseas bank were nationalised by the Pakistan government and merged into a state corporation, the plaintiffs in the action. The Habib family ceased to have any connection with the new corporation which, however, continued to use the name Habib bank. The Zurich bank remained independent of the plaintiffs and continued to be managed by members of the Habib family. In 1974, with the help and co-operation of the plaintiffs, the Zurich bank moved its London office to another address and began to expand its business in England, to the extent that it directly competed with the plaintiffs in some spheres. In July 1977 the Zurich bank moved its London branch to an office just round the corner from the plaintiffs' office. A month later the plaintiffs issued a writ seeking an injunction to restrain the Zurich bank from passing off its bank in England as the Habib bank. The judge dismissed the plaintiffs' action and they appealed to the Court of Appeal, contending (i) that the overseas bank had exclusive right in England to the reputation in the Habib name, and (ii) that the Zurich bank held itself out as being under the same effective management as the overseas bank.

Held – The appeal would be dismissed for the following reasons—
   (1) Where an international business with an international reputation and goodwill

a established a branch in England the goodwill and reputation of the business in England did not become the exclusive property of the branch, but continued to be the goodwill and reputation of the international business and attached to any other branch which the business set up in England. The plaintiffs could not therefore claim, on behalf of the overseas bank, the exclusive right to use the name Habib in respect of a banking business in England. Nor could the plaintiffs claim that the Zurich bank was misrepresenting itself in England as being a subsidiary of, or under the same management as, the overseas

b bank, because the only representation made by the Zurich bank was the entirely correct representation that it was a company associated with the Habib family. Furthermore, the plaintiffs had, on the evidence, failed to establish any substantial damage or probability of damage to the business of the overseas bank arising out of the Zurich bank's activities. In the absence of any misrepresentation or proof of damage, which was of the essence of a claim for passing off, there could be no passing off by the Zurich bank

c (see p 656 *j* to p 657 *a h j*, p 661 *f g*, p 662 *a* to *d*, p 663 *b c e f* and *j* to p 664 *a c* to *h* and p 668 *f g*, post); *A G Spalding Brothers v A W Gamage Ltd* [1914–15] All ER Rep 147 and dicta of Lord Diplock and of Lord Fraser in *Erven Warnink BV v J Townend & Sons (Hull) Ltd* [1979] 2 All ER at 932, 943–944 applied.

(2) The plaintiffs' claim was barred on the grounds of acquiescence, laches and estoppel, having regard to the facts that the plaintiffs did not allege mala fides, that the

d Zurich bank assumed its trading name, style and objects with the consent of the plaintiffs' predecessors (the overseas bank), that the arrangements for the Zurich bank establishing a London branch were made by the overseas bank, that no objection was taken to the Zurich bank's use of the Habib name from 1973 until 1977, and that it would in the circumstances be inequitable for the plaintiffs to succeed in their claim (see p 657 *a*, p 664 *h*, p 667 *g h* and p 668 *d* to *f*, post).

e Per Curiam. The distinction between protecting a legal right or an equitable right is archaic and arcane and has no relevance to the application of the doctrine of laches or acquiescence (see p 666 *f g* and p 668 *f g*, post).

Cases referred to in judgments

f *Alexander Pirie & Sons Ltd's Application* (1933) 149 LT 199, [1933] All ER Rep 956, 50 RPC 147, HL, 46 Digest (Repl) 67, 369.

Amalgamated Investment & Property Co Ltd (in liquidation) v Texas Commerce International Bank Ltd [1981] 1 All ER 923, [1981] 2 WLR 554.

Bulmer (H P) Ltd and Showerings Ltd v J Bollinger SA and Champagne Lanson Père et Fils [1976] RPC 97, [1975] 2 CMLR 479, Digest (Cont Vol E) 631, *1558a*.

g *Burgers v Burgers* (1853) 3 De GM & G 896, [1843–60] All ER Rep 90, 22 LJ Ch 675, 21 LTOS 53, 17 Jur 292, 43 ER 351, LJJ, 46 Digest (Repl) 236, *1535*.

Crabb v Arun District Council [1975] 3 All ER 865, [1976] Ch 179, [1975] 3 WLR 847, 32 P & CR 70, CA, Digest (Cont Vol D) 312, *1250a*.

Erlanger v New Sombrero Phosphate Co (1878) 3 App Cas 1218, 48 LJ Ch 73, 39 LT 269, HL, 35 Digest (Repl) 82, *762*.

h *Erven Warnink BV v J Townend & Sons (Hull) Ltd* [1979] 2 All ER 927, [1979] AC 731, [1979] 3 WLR 68, [1980] RPC 31, HL, Digest (Cont Vol E) 630, *1494a*.

Greasley v Cooke [1980] 3 All ER 710, [1980] 1 WLR 1306, CA.

Inland Revenue Comrs v Muller & Co's Margarine Ltd [1901] AC 217, [1900–3] All ER Rep 413, 70 LJKB 677, 84 LT 729, HL, 45 Digest (Repl) 515, *1002*.

Inwards v Baker [1965] 1 All ER 446, [1965] 2 QB 29, [1965] 2 WLR 212, CA, Digest (Cont Vol B) 242, *1552a*.

Jelley, Son and Jones's Application, Re (1878) 51 LJ Ch 639n, 46 LT 381, 46 Digest (Repl) 73, *398*.

Lindsay Petroleum Co v Hurd (1874) LR 5 PC 221, PC, 21 Digest (Repl) 431, *1424*.

Marengo v Daily Sketch and Sunday Graphic Ltd [1948] 1 All ER 406, [1948] LJR 787, 65 RPC 242, HL, 46 Digest (Repl) 305, *2059*.

Payton & Co v Snelling, Lampard & Co [1901] AC 308, 70 LJ Ch 644, 85 LT 287, 17 RPC 628, HL, 46 Digest (Repl) 268, *1743*.

Ramsden v Dyson (1866) LR 1 HL 129, 12 Jur NS 506, HL, 31(1) Digest (Reissue) 68, 506.
Reddaway (Frank) & Co Ltd v George Banham & Co Ltd [1896] AC 199, [1895–9] All ER **a**
    Rep 133, 65 LJQB 381, 74 LT 289, 13 RPC 218, HL, 46 Digest (Repl) 221, 1454.
Saunders v Sun Life Assurance Co of Canada [1894] 1 Ch 537, 63 LJ Ch 247, 69 LT 755, 8
    R 125, 10 Digest (Reissue) 1385, 8917.
Spalding (A G) Brothers v A W Gamage Ltd (1915) 84 LJ Ch 449, [1914–15] All ER Rep 147,
    113 LT 198, 32 RPC 273, HL, 46 Digest (Repl) 204, 1362.
Taylor Fashions Ltd v Liverpool Victoria Trustees Co Ltd [1981] 1 All ER 897, [1981] 2 WLR **b**
    576n.
Willmott v Barber (1880) 15 Ch D 96, 49 LJ Ch 792, 43 LT 95, 35 Digest (Repl) 129, 245.

Cases also cited
Adrema v Adrema-Werke GmbH [1958] RPC 323.
Banks v Gibson (1865) 34 Beau 566, 55 ER 753.   **c**
Brestian v Try [1958] RPC 161, CA.
Brinsmead (John) & Sons Ltd v Brinsmead & Waddington & Sons Ltd (1913) 30 RPC 493, CA.
British Legion v British Legion Club (Street) Ltd (1931) 48 RPC 555.
Burgess v Burgess (1853) 3 De GM & G 896, [1843–60] All ER Rep 90.
Cluett Peabody & Co Ltd v McIntyre Hogg Marsh & Co Ltd [1958] RPC 335.
Coles (J H) Pty Ltd v Need [1934] AC 82, PC.   **d**
Dent v Turpin (1861) 2 John & H 139, 70 ER 1003.
Draper v Trust [1939] 3 All ER 513, CA.
Electrolux Ltd v Electrix Ltd (No 2) (1953) 71 RPC 23, CA.
Ewing v Buttercup Margarine Co Ltd [1917] 2 Ch 1, [1916–17] All ER Rep 1012, CA.
General Electric Co v The General Electric Co Ltd [1972] 2 All ER 507, [1972] 1 WLR 729,
    HL.   **e**
Guimaraens (M P) & Son v Fonseca & Vasconcellos Ltd (1921) 38 RPC 288.
Jamieson & Co v Jamieson (1898) 15 RPC 169, CA.
Kammins Ballrooms Co Ltd v Zenith Investments (Torquay) Ltd [1970] 2 All ER 871, [1971]
    AC 850, HL.
Lecouturier v Rey [1910] AC 262, HL.
Music Corpn of America v Music Corpn (Great Britain) Ltd (1947) 64 RPC 41.   **f**
Parker Knoll Ltd v Knoll International Ltd [1962] RPC 265, HL.
Roberts Numbering Machine Co v Davis (1935) 53 RPC 79.
Sayers v Collyer (1884) 28 Ch D 103, CA.
Southorn v Reynolds (1865) 12 LT 75.
Turton v Turton (1889) 42 Ch D 128, CA.
Tussaud v Tussaud (1890) 44 Ch D 678.   **g**

Appeal
The plaintiffs, Habib Bank Ltd, a company incorporated in Pakistan, appealed against the
judgment of Whitford J on 12th October 1979 dismissing the plaintiffs' claim against the
defendants, Habib Bank AG Zurich, a company incorporated in Switzerland, for an
injunction restraining the defendants from trading under any name containing the **h**
name Habib or otherwise passing off their business as and for the plaintiffs' business, and
damages. The facts are set out in the judgment of Oliver LJ.

William Aldous QC and *Anthony Watson* for the plaintiffs.
Julian Jeffs QC and *Robin Jacob* for the defendants.

OLIVER LJ delivered the first judgment at the invitation of Stephenson LJ. This is an   **j**
appeal from a judgment of Whitford J delivered on 12th October 1979 in which he
dismissed the plaintiffs' action for passing off. The title to these proceedings indicates the
close similarity of the names of the parties and it is the plaintiffs' contention that in
carrying on their business under their corporate name in the United Kingdom the

defendants are either directly passing off their business as that of the plaintiffs or at least
a holding out to the public that they are a company controlled by or associated with the
plaintiffs. And indeed, so far as association goes, they *are* to some extent associated, as the
history of the matter shows, although counsel for the plaintiffs submits that that factual
association does not justify what his clients claim to be, effectively, a representation by
the defendants that their business forms part of the plaintiffs' banking business.

The history of the matter goes back to the period before the partition of the Indian sub-
b continent into India and Pakistan. The Habibs were and are a well-known banking
family and in 1941 they incorporated a banking company in Bombay. That company
bore the same name as that of the plaintiffs in the action (Habib Bank Ltd) and I will refer
to them as 'the original HBL'. On the partition of India in 1947 the seat of this company
was moved to Karachi. The business of the original HBL was both substantial and
international and in 1952 it was decided to incorporate a further company in Pakistan to
c handle the overseas business. That company was Habib Bank (Overseas) Ltd, which I
refer to as 'HBO' for short, and it was owned as to 40% by the original HBL and as to 60%
by individual members of the Habib family. The affairs of the two companies were,
throughout their joint corporate lives, very closely intertwined. The original HBL dealt
with all business in Pakistan whilst foreign business was undertaken and branches in
foreign countries were operated by HBO. But the separation was more theoretical than
d real, because there seems to have been no practical separation of banking staffs who were
treated as freely interchangeable between the two companies and there can be no doubt
that the two companies were known to the general public as 'the Habib Bank' without
differentiating between the two corporate entities.

From 1970 onwards the two companies operated under the shadow of threatened
nationalisation. In 1970 the elections in West Pakistan were won by Mr Bhutto's People's
e Party whose manifesto included a policy of nationalisation of, inter alia, the banks, but
war with India and the formation of the separate state of Bangladesh intervened and no
immediate nationalisation took place. The writing was, however, very clearly on the
wall and there was an obvious danger of government interference or supervision, a
danger which became more acute when certain major industries were nationalised in
1972. It had, in fact, been on the wall, albeit perhaps in rather fainter characters, since
f early 1967 when Mr Bhutto had formed his party and the directors of the bank saw the
merit (no doubt in the bank's own interest as well as in that of its customers) in forming
a branch or affiliate abroad in a country whose laws prohibited the disclosure of banking
information, so that any attempted interference or inquiry could effectively be blocked.
In July 1967 application was made to the Pakistan State Bank for permission to establish
a branch in Switzerland. That was approved in principle and on 9th August 1967 the
g defendants, the Habib Bank AG Zurich (to which I will refer as HBZ), were established
in Zurich. The attitude of the Swiss authorities was such that the establishment was
much facilitated if the new bank was established with local capital and accordingly HBO
had only a minority of the shares (45% initially) the remainder being issued to a Swiss
company called Thesaurus. HBZ formally opened for business on 12th October 1967.
Thereafter until 1974 HBZ's business was in fact run by the original HBL and HBO as
h part of the Habib Bank business, even though HBO was only a minority shareholder. A
member of the Habib family, Mr Rashid Habib, was chairman of the board and another,
Mr Hyder Habib, was a vice-chairman and the staff of the bank were freely
interchangeable with the staff of HBO and the staff of the original HBL. HBZ were,
effectively, the Zurich branch of the Habib Bank. Contemporary internal correspondence
at the time of its formation indicates that the primary purpose of establishing the Swiss
bank was to provide a haven for customers who desired to place their funds in a hard-
currency area without fear of disclosure.

In May 1973 the board of HBZ decided to open a branch in London. HBO was already
operating there with a small head office at Finsbury Pavement and a substantial number
of branches outside London in cities where there was a substantial immigrant population
from Pakistan. The arrangements for the opening of the London branch of HBZ were

handled in London by HBO. Powers of attorney were given to two senior executives of
HBO in London, Mr Pirbhai and Mr Padiyar, and the latter negotiated the necessary *a*
permission from the Bank of England. It did not really make commercial sense to
establish, in effect, a competitor in the United Kingdom within the same group, but Mr
Padiyar's letter to the Bank of England dated 5th June 1973 indicated, perhaps rather
surprisingly, that the Swiss bank 'find considerable scope for expansion of their business
here and they desire to participate in the banking activities of the City of London and the
United Kingdom'. The primary business of HBO was the remittance to Pakistan of *b*
funds received from immigrants of Pakistan origin and one cannot help doubting
whether in fact the opening of a branch of the Zurich business was intended to do more
than provide on-the-spot facilities for remittance to hard-currency areas without the risk
of disclosure which would have existed if they were channelled through a branch
directly controlled from Pakistan. This is consistent with the object which the then
board of the original HBL had in mind when HBZ was formed as it appears from a letter *c*
from Mr Pirbhai (an executive of HBO in London) to Mr Rashid Habib dated 24th
February 1967. Nevertheless, a contemporary note of a meeting held on 15th February
1974 (that is *after* nationalisation) of representatives of both HBO and HBZ with HBO's
auditors, Messrs Thompson McLintock, indicates that both HBO and HBZ then had it in
contemplation that HBZ would expand into a general banking business in London.

In so far as any conclusion can be drawn from this it seems to me to be merely this, that *d*
it bears out the plaintiffs' case that the Swiss branch in London was treated simply as a
branch of the international business of the Habib Bank and that it was really a matter of
indifference at that time by which corporate entity the actual business was conducted.
The whole group was under the management of members of the Habib family.

The London office of HBZ opened for business in November 1973 in a very modest
way. It consisted of a room adjoining the offices of HBO in 12 Finsbury Pavement. It *e*
had an independent entrance to the outside corridor but was also accessible through the
telex room in HBO's office and in practice it consisted of a room, a desk and a telephone
which was manned by one of the members of the staff of HBO as occasion required. Up
to March 1974 it had done very little business in the United Kingdom. By that time it
had only three accounts, so that apart from such reputation as it may have enjoyed as part
of the Habib banking group it had had very little time or opportunity to build up any *f*
independent goodwill of its own in London. On 1st January 1974 the Damoclean sword
fell. The Pakistan government announced the nationalisation of all the banks in Pakistan,
which included both HBL and HBO. Subsequently in the summer of 1974 both HBL
and HBO were merged in a new state corporation, the present plaintiffs, and it is not
disputed that the effect of this, as a matter of law, was to vest in the plaintiffs all the
goodwill and rights of the original HBL and of HBO. *g*

The effect of nationalisation, however, was to produce a radical change in the
management of the business. All the existing chief executives and directors of HBL and
HBO were removed, so that from the beginning of January 1974 the Habib family ceased
to have any say in the banks' operations. But, of course, that did not apply to HBZ, which
was not susceptible to control from Pakistan, since HBO had only a minority
shareholding. That in fact had been cut down to 22½% as a result of a further issue of *h*
shares in November 1973. Matters came to a head in March 1974. Mr Rashid Habib and
Mr Hyder Habib were persuaded to transfer their own nominee shareholdings to the
direction of the government of Pakistan in July 1974 and this resulted in their vacating
office as directors of HBZ for want of the essential share qualification. They actually
resigned in October 1974. The plaintiffs had, in March 1974, written to HBZ seeking to
appoint their own nominees and had been firmly told that the composition of the board *j*
was a matter for the majority shareholders and on 12th July HBZ refused to appoint the
directors nominated by the plaintiffs. Thereafter in 1976 the proportionate holding of
HBO in the equity of HBZ was further reduced by a rights issue in which the plaintiffs
were not allowed to participate and in May 1976 litigation ensued in Switzerland which
is still proceeding and in which the plaintiffs are seeking (so far unsuccessfully) to
establish control of or increase their shareholding in HBZ.

The important thing for present purposes is the effect of these upheavals on HBZ in
a London. In January 1974 Mr Hyder Habib came to London to discuss the setting up of
an office of HBZ separate from that of the now nationalised HBO. There is a clear history
of assistance and co-operation on the part of HBO in this venture but the evidence
indicates that at this time there was considerable confusion among the London staff
because nobody knew what was going on or exactly what the effect of nationalisation was
going to be. Certainly normal banking transactions between the nationalised HBO and
b HBZ carried on and in May 1974 HBZ moved to 8 City Road with the active co-operation
and help of the management and staff of HBO. They stayed there for a little over a year
and in August 1975 moved to 10 Throgmorton Avenue. There was no hint or murmur
of any protest or dissatisfaction on the part of the plaintiffs until August 1977, just after
HBZ had moved their office once more. The new office was at 92 Moorgate just round
the corner from HBO's office. It took place in July 1977 and on 22nd August the
c plaintiffs' solicitors wrote demanding that HBZ discontinue the use of their corporate
name in the United Kingdom. The writ followed on 23rd September.

The basic ingredients of a passing-off action are not in dispute between the parties.
Nor could they be for they have been well settled for years. They are set out in the speech
of Lord Parker in *A G Spalding Brothers v A W Gamage Ltd* (1915) 84 LJ Ch 449, [1914–15]
All ER Rep 147 at 149:

d
> 'This principle is stated by Lord Justice Turner in BURGESS v. BURGESS ((1853) 3 De
> GM & G 896, [1843–60] All ER Rep 90) and by Lord Halsbury in REDDAWAY v.
> BANHAM & Co. ([1896] AC 199, [1895–9] All ER Rep 133) in the proposition that
> nobody has any right to represent his goods as the goods of somebody else. I prefer
> the former statement, for, whatever doubts may be suggested in the earlier
> authorities, it has long been settled that actual passing-off of a defendant's goods for
e
> the plaintiff's need not be proved as a condition precedent to relief in equity either
> by way of an injunction or an enquiry as to profits or damages ... Nor need the
> representation be made fraudulently. It is enough that it has in fact been made,
> whether fraudulently or otherwise, and that damages may probably ensue, though
> the complete innocence of the party making it may be a reason for limiting the
f
> account of profits to the period subsequent to the date at which he became aware of
> the true facts.'

There is a useful passage with regard to evidence. In particular with regard to
advertisements in that case, Lord Parker said (84 LJ Ch 449 at 452, [1914–15] All ER Rep
147 at 152):

g
> 'It was also contended that the question whether the advertisements were
> calculated to deceive was not one which your Lordships could yourselves determine
> by considering the puport of the advertisements themselves, having regard to the
> surrounding circumstances, but was one which your Lordships were bound to
> determine upon evidence directed to the question itself. I do not take this view of
> the law. There may, of course, be cases of so doubtful a nature that a Judge cannot
h
> properly come to a conclusion without evidence directed to the point, but there can
> be no doubt that in a passing-off action the question whether the matter complained
> of is calculated to deceive—in other words, whether it amounts to a misrepresen-
> tation—is a matter for the Judge, who, looking at the documents and evidence
> before him, comes to his own conclusion, and, to use the words of Lord Macnaghten
> in PAYTON & Co. v. SNELLING, LAMPARD & Co. ([1901] AC 308 at 311) "must not
> surrender his own independent judgment to any witness whatever".'

More recently the principles have been reiterated in the following passages from the
speech of Lord Diplock in *Erven Warnink BV v J Townend & Sons (Hull) Ltd* [1979] 2 All
ER 927 at 932, [1979] AC 731 at 742:

> 'My Lords, *A G Spalding & Bros v A W Gamage Ltd* and the later cases make it
> possible to identify five characteristics which must be present in order to create a

valid cause of action for passing off: (1) a misrepresentation (2) made by a trader in the course of trade, (3) to prospective customers of his or ultimate consumers of goods or services supplied by him, (4) which is calculated to injure the business or goodwill of another trader (in the sense that this is a reasonably foreseeable consequence) and (5) which causes actual damage to a business or goodwill of the trader by whom the action is brought or (in a quia timet action) will probably do so.'

The difficulties, as always, arise in applying these well-known principles to the facts of the individual case. Counsel for the plaintiffs' case is a very simple one. Up to November 1973 the only Habib Bank presence in the United Kingdom was HBO and their branches. HBO (either alone or in conjunction with their associated company HBL) had a substantial goodwill in connection with the banking business carried on from London. HBZ were introduced to London by HBL and HBO as a bank operating under the same management and they were allowed to participate in the goodwill generated by HBO but had no goodwill here of their own. They were simply held out or allowed to hold themselves out as part of the Habib Bank, that is, as a banking organisation substantially under the same management as that of the existing and established business. In March 1974, however, they ceased in fact to be under the same management as the organisation known as the Habib Bank, not because their management had changed, but because the management of the Habib Bank had changed and HBZ had refused to accept the nominee of the now nationalised Habib Bank. They had, therefore, as counsel graphically put it, 'left the club'. From that moment on, they ceased to be entitled to hold themselves out as members of the club by using the Habib name and by continuing to do so they misrepresented to the public that their business was under the same management as the plaintiffs' business and thus passed themselves off as or for a part of the plaintiffs' business when they were not. That, in its essentials, is counsel for the plaintiffs' case, though there are refinements. The case is pleaded as a simple case of an interloper's adoption of the name of an existing business, but counsel has to meet the difficulty that his own clients were responsible both for the establishment of HBZ in Switzerland and for their introduction to London. He meets this difficulty ingeniously, although without the assistance of any clearly pleaded case of a licence, by suggesting that the only way in which HBZ could become entitled to make use of the existing United Kingdom goodwill of HBO is by a licence from HBO or HBL, a licence which impliedly endured only so long as the companies remained substantially under the same management. Counsel skilfully turns the lack of pleading into a weapon by suggesting that the only justification for HBZ's operation in this country under their own corporate name can be either their possession of a goodwill of their own (and they had none when they commenced business) or an irrevocable licence of some sort from the only company which did have any goodwill, namely HBO. And such a licence, he observes, is neither pleaded nor supported by the facts. What was pleaded was that HBZ were established with the active concurrence and support of at least one of the entities now incorporated in the person of the plaintiffs and an open, public and uninterrupted course of business on the part of HBZ, in some respects encouraged, in some respects perhaps merely tolerated, but in no respect ever challanged from November 1973 to August 1977, facts which are prayed in aid in support of a plea of acquiescence, laches and estoppel.

The judge, in a careful and detailed judgment, reviewed the relevant facts and the evidence and his conclusions may be summarised as follows.

(1) The reputation enjoyed by the Habib Bank in this country was a shared reputation, part of which was assumed by HBZ immediately on entry into the United Kingdom. HBZ thus acquired the right to trade in this country under their corporate name and that right remained unaffected by the nationalisation of HBO and the original HBL or by any refusal on their behalf to accept the plaintiffs' dictates as to their future management.

(2) There was, in any event, no misrepresentation. HBZ, HBO and the original HBL had a common right to the use of the name Habib and the defendants were doing no more than to trade under the name by which they were incorporated and known and which they were entitled to use.

(3) No substantial damage to the plaintiffs had in any event been shown.

a (4) Although this did not arise on the view which the judge took, any claim by the plaintiffs would in his view have been barred by acquiescence.

Counsel for the plaintiffs attacks the first of these conclusions on the ground that, as he submits, there was no evidence which could conceivably support a shared reputation. Up to March 1974, after which time HBZ and the plaintiffs were going their separate ways, there was only one reputation here, that of the Habib Bank, as personified by HBO, to whom the reputation adhered. HBZ had substantially no business, they were

b unknown, their only office was a room in HBO's office and in so far as they could claim any reputation or goodwill at all it could only be that which they enjoyed by the permissive use of their corporate name here. That permission determined as soon as they threw off the shackles of the new nationalised management. Counsel for the defendants, whilst naturally seeking to support the judgment, ventures to put the matter

c in a rather different way from that adopted by the judge. It is, he submits, not so much a matter of a shared reputation or goodwill as of an honest and unchallenged concurrent user. There is, he points out, no evidence whatever which can properly support the suggestion that when HBZ came to London there was any limitation of their activities or any condition as to their management or policy implied, understood or agreed to. Two companies, both connected with the well-known Habib banking family, were

d perfectly honestly and properly making a concurrent user of that family name just as, for instance, manufacturers of a substance with a well-known and recognised trade description, such as champagne, may enjoy the right in common to use that description for their products: see *H P Bulmer Ltd and Showerings Ltd v Bollinger SA and Champagne Lanson Père et Fils* [1976] RPC 97.

In the case of a trade mark, s 12(2) of the Trade Marks Act 1938 enables the registrar

e to permit registration of a mark in the name of more than one proprietor where an 'honest concurrent use' can be shown: see, for instance, *Jelley, Son and Jones's Application* (1878) 51 LJ Ch 639 and *Alexander Pirie & Son Ltd's Application* (1933) 149 LT 199, [1933] All ER Rep 956. Now if the statute permits registration of two or more proprietors in the case of trade marks, where there has been honest concurrent use, the case of honest concurrent use of an unregistered name or mark is, counsel for the defendants argues, a

f fortiori.

I think, if I may say so, that counsel's submissions are too ambitious, in this sense, that they seek to elevate into a doctrine dignified by a term of art, 'the doctrine of honest concurrent user', what is, in the sphere of passing off, merely a facet of Lord Diplock's first essential ingredient of misrepresentation. As counsel for the plaintiffs has pointed out, s 2 of the Trade Marks Act 1938 expressly provides that nothing in the Act is deemed

g to affect any rights of action for passing off. The fact, therefore, that two or more people may be entitled to rely on honest concurrent user of a mark to achieve registration leaves quite unaffected the question whether they may be entitled to sue one another in a passing-off action. What I think counsel for the defendants is really saying in propounding his doctrine is really this, that where you find that two traders have been concurrently using in the United Kingdom the same or similar names for their goods or

h businesses you may well find a factual situation in which neither of them can be said to be guilty of any misrepresentation. Each represents nothing but the truth, that a particular name or mark is associated with his goods or business.

It is *mis*representation which lies at the root of the action and counsel for the plaintiffs concedes that if he fails, on the evidence, to demonstrate this then he fails on this appeal. The judge, as I have said, found none, and counsel has to submit that that finding

j was either wrong in law or contrary to the weight of the evidence. It is, therefore, necessary to analyse and examine carefully the major premise on which counsel beguilingly erects the logical structure of his case. We have been treated to a detailed and fascinating guided excursion into the labyrinth of cases relating to the use by traders of their own and others' names, but in the ultimate analysis the question remains: what was the misrepresentation? The Habib Bank AG Zurich was set up in London as the Habib Bank AG Zurich with the express consent and co-operation of the plaintiffs' predecessors. They are still the Habib Bank AG Zurich carrying on the business which they were incorporated to carry on. Their constitution, their management, their business *a* style and their motto remain unchanged. And it is accepted, as it must be accepted on the facts, that when they established their business here there was no misrepresentation.

I have already outlined in summary the way in which counsel for the plaintiffs puts his case and it bases itself, on analysis, on a number of axioms (I say axioms advisedly because they are advanced rather as matters which are self-evident than as matters which can be said to be supported by the evidence or by the learned judge's findings). First, it is said *b* that the reputation and goodwill in this country associated with the name Habib was in November 1973 exclusively the property of HBO because that was the only company which traded here. Then it is said that HBZ were set up here and held out as a bank associated with and '*under the same effective management as* [and these words are crucial to counsel for the plaintiffs' case] the existing United Kingdom business of HBO'. That, the argument proceeds, was done for the limited purpose of enabling HBO's customers in *c* England to make remittances to hard-currency areas. So here, says counsel, is the representation imported by the use by the defendants of the name Habib: 'We are under the same effective management as the bank known as Habib Bank Overseas Ltd and we are here for the purpose of receiving deposits from customers of that bank for hard-currency areas.'

In the spring of 1974, when the now nationalised Habib Bank Ltd sought *d* unsuccessfully to appoint their nominees to the board of HBZ, counsel for the plaintiffs says that all that changed. The representation remained the same but it was no longer true. True it is that in the resulting confusion HBO and their personnel in London assisted HBZ in finding new offices and setting up their business. True it is that HBO and HBZ continued, as they do to this day, to do business together, substantial business, indeed many thousands of transactions. But they are not associated together. They are *e* not under the same effective management. Indeed on 8th April 1974 a meeting of the executives of the nationalised bank resolved as follows: 'Zurich. We should continue business relations with them as before. However, rates of interest etc. should be on competitive basis.'

HBZ over the next few years expanded their activities. They received Bank of England permissions to operate non-resident sterling accounts in June 1974, to issue and confirm *f* credits (June 1974 and March 1975), to remit to resident customers' non-resident dependants in the Middle East (September 1975), to open a US dollar account in New York (June 1975), to open a Deutschmark account in Germany (September 1975) and finally to effect remittances in rupees to resident customers' non-resident dependent relatives in the Indian subcontinent (September 1978). It was really only this latter which trespassed in any way on the plaintiffs' principal business in the United Kingdom *g* which is and has always been that of obtaining remittances for Pakistan.

So, says counsel for the plaintiffs, the defendants 'left the club'. They eschewed the same management. They traded on their own in a way quite other than that contemplated when they were established here. Yet they continued to make use of the plaintiffs' exclusive reputation in the name Habib for the purposes of their now competing business. From March 1974 onwards therefore counsel submits there was a *h* continuing misrepresentation which entitles him now to an injunction. Now it is perhaps not surprising that counsel seeks to concentrate attention on March 1974 when his clients' attempt to obtain effective management of HBZ failed, for it is only thus that he can make out a case for misrepresentation at all. To some extent it does however obscure the issue because it ignores the three and a half years of independent trading which ensued thereafter before the first murmur of discontent was heard which gave rise *j* to this action, and the question ultimately is whether there was a cause of action in passing off at the date of the writ and not whether, three years earlier, one party or the other might have succeeded if proceedings had then been commenced.

But granted for a moment counsel's hypothesis that this is the relevant moment for testing the matter, and leaving aside all questions of laches and acquiescence, one still has to examine with some care whether he can make good his basic factual submissions.

First let me take his tenet that in March 1974 HBO had the exclusive reputation and goodwill in the United Kingdom in the name Habib. For this counsel relies on two passages in the judge's judgment which, he claims, constitute findings in his favour. The judge said this:

> 'Although HBZ were and are a separate legal entity, it is clear on the evidence that they in fact operated as if they were another branch of the Habib organisation, just as had been the case with HBO. Effectively the control over the operations of HBO, HBL and HBZ was the same.'

Later the judge said:

> 'When HBZ entered the United Kingdom, as they did at the instance of and with the approbation and assistance of HBL and HBO, they immediately assumed a part in this shared reputation in this country. At this stage HBZ would be taken, as the plaintiffs' witnesses put it, to be the same bank.'

I am unable to put on these passages the interpretation which counsel for the plaintiffs urges. It seems to me to perfectly plain that when the judge used the expression 'the same bank' he was referring to the whole international banking organisation run by the members of the Habib family whose name was well known to Pakistan's immigrants in this country. That emerges, I think, clearly from these further passages in the judgment. Talking of the action, the judge said:

> 'It has only arisen because of the nationalisation on 1st January 1974 of two banking organisations which, together with the defendant bank prior to that date, constituted an international banking network owned and controlled by members of the family bearing the name Habib. I was told by Mr Tayebi, the plaintiffs' first witness, who is an executive vice-president, chief law officer and secretary of the plaintiffs, that Habib is not a very common name, but it is a name found in Muslim countries. He also told me that, in relation to the business community and in a commercial and banking context the name Habib in Pakistan for many years was associated exclusively with the business of the family who, in 1941, established the Habib Bank Ltd in Bombay. In the years which followed, up to 1974, this bank remained under the control of the family, but in the years intervening there have been a number of changes.'

The judge continued:

> 'Dealing with HBL in Pakistan, or at three overseas branches which HBL ran in Kuala Lumpur, Singapore and New York, and dealing with the branches of HBO, the customers would I think proceed on the basis that they were using the facilities of the Habib Bank without stopping to consider whether or not there were separate organisations running the different branches in different parts of the world and without stopping to consider for one moment who may have held the shares or the majority of the shares in one or other of these organisations. There were these two separate organisations but customers dealing with them could none the less be rightly confident that their interests were safeguarded by reason of the control exercised by the Habib family, whose reputation in commercial and banking circles stood and stands very high, as was said in the evidence of the plaintiffs' witnesses, in particular Mr Bukhari.'

Later the judge said:

> 'I think, on the evidence, the goodwill and repute prior to 1973 which attached to the name Habib was a goodwill attaching to the Habib organisation at large and it was no doubt additionally built up having regard to the confidence felt in the family which started the bank and the esteem in which they continued to be held.'

Earlier the judge had said:

'Staff were moved from one company to the other, but always considered themselves as being servants of the same organisation. The customers, I am sure, *a* whether dealing with HBL, HBO or HBZ, thought they were dealing with one and the same organisation (as indeed, so far as any question of effective control is concerned, they were) and the evidence that was called is in support of this view.'

That was related to the period before nationalisation.

The view of the matter expressed by the judge is I think amply borne out by the *b* evidence. The plaintiffs' own witness, Mr Tayebi, said that the Habib family ranked high in the 22 families who controlled the economy of Pakistan before 1971. Mr Bukhari, another of the plaintiffs' witnesses, was even more explicit. He said:

'*Counsel for the defendants.* You referred to Mr Habib as being really a person of high eminence in the bank? A. Naturally, yes.

'Q. What reputation does the Habib family have as bankers amongst business *c* people of your country? A. A very good reputation. They are conservative, sound bankers with good traditions of banking.

'Q. That was a personal family reputation, was it? A. That is correct; a personal family reputation and also as the owners of the bank.

'Q. Did that reputation in any way assist the bank in obtaining custom or was it immaterial? A. I believe so. *d*

'Q. You believe that it did assist? A. Yes, I agree with you.

'Q. Is the Habib family still well known and respected in business circles in Pakistan or has nationalisation altered that? A. Yes, they are a respected family.

'Q. Would that make any difference whether or not, in your experience of bank customers, a customer would be likely to go to a bank that he knew was being run by a member of that family? A. The reputation that was built up by the Habib *e* Bank Ltd with the Habibs at the helm of affairs was naturally theirs and these two things could not be separated. The Habib Bank Ltd, by its own actions and functions and being led by the Habib family, had reached a certain position of eminence.'

Earlier the same witness stressed the family control of management:

'Q. Tell me about the constitution of the boards of the banks for which you *f* worked at this time, HBO and HBL. Did they have the same directors between the two banks or were the boards differently composed? A. Some of the directors were common and some were different in both these situations.

'Q. How many directors were there approximately? A. I suppose that in [HBO] there were eight or nine directors; I believe that three or four of those would also be in [HBL] and the remainder would be other members of the Habib family who *g* were not directors of [HBL] or their very close friends or associates.

'Q. So that they were all members of the family or close friends? A. Yes.

'Q. Were Mr Rashid Habib and Mr Hyder Habib both directors of HBL and HBO? A. Mr Rashid Habib was definitely the managing director of [HBL] throughout that time. At certain times he might have been a director of [HBO] also, but I am not sure about that. They used to change every two or three years. *h*

'Q. Mr Hyder Habib was the man at the top of it all, was he not? A. Yes.'

The same thing emerged from the evidence of Mr Tayebi. He said this:

'The way in which the Habib Bank was run was that it was a family concern and the top management were of course all members of the Habib family. The second *j* tier of management, which was all the executives of the bank and not the directors, were also members of the Habib family. It was only from the third tier downwards that any non-Habibian was able to come up to that level and continue. The result was that, on nationalisation, the first two tiers had gone and the third tier had come up; and it was a very uphill task to run the bank and put the administration in order

and there was a considerable amount of confusion. It took quite some time to put
a things in order.'

All this is underlined by Mr Bukhari's evidence about the formation of the
defendants. He was referred to a letter to the president of the bank in Karachi in October
1967:

'Q. Had you received this letter, would you have regarded it as a letter from a
b branch of your own bank or from something quite separate? A. If you read the
letter in detail, then the facts are that the two Habibs were there and the rest were
Swiss people; but, internationally in the banking world, everybody thought that the
Habib family had acquired another bank or a branch or a representation in
Switzerland.'

So strong was this family connection that Mr Bukhari, after being asked why after
c nationalisation he had continued to accept instructions from Mr Hyder Habib, was
further asked:

'Q. Was it your habit to act on instructions that you thought were given without
authority? A. For the last 25 to 30 years we were working under the Habib family,
although it was a limited company, but for all practical purposes the Habibs were
d our bosses and we could not break the habit and go against them for any purpose
whatsoever or disregard their advice or instructions immediately after one week of
nationalisation.'

Of course, it is perfectly true, as counsel for the plaintiffs submits, that the exploitation
of the family name in the United Kingdom had taken place through only one of the
three limited companies founded by the family so that in one sense the goodwill
e associated with the name adhered to that company, but it seems perfectly clear from the
evidence (and it must be remembered that the customers were either entirely or
substantially entirely Pakistanis in this country, many of whom were illiterate) that the
reputation attached to the family name, so that an organisation established by that family
under the family name immediately acquired the reputation of the family. The judge
has been criticised for his finding that there was a shared goodwill, which it is said was
f not a reflection of the way in which the case had been argued by either side and it may
be that the expression is perhaps less than precise shorthand. But for my part I cannot see
that in the essentials the judge was wrong. Where an internationally known business
establishes a branch in this country through a limited company, either incorporated here
or abroad, it may be that technically the goodwill and reputation of that business
'belongs' to the limited company in the sense that the company may be the proper and
g only plaintiff in an action taken here to protect it. But it does not cease to be the goodwill
and reputation of the international business because it is also the goodwill and reputation
of the local branch. And that reputation inheres, as it seems to me, equally in any other
local branch which the international business may set up in the same place. The
expression 'goodwill' has been conveniently defined in the following phrase which is
quoted in the *Erven Warnink* case [1979] 2 All ER 927 at 931–932, [1979] AC 731 at 741
h from the speech of Lord MacNaghten in *Inland Revenue Comrs v Muller & Co's Margarine
Ltd* [1901] AC 217 at 223, [1900–3] All ER Rep 413 at 416. After referring to Lord
Parker's speech in *A G Spalding & Sons v A W Gamage Ltd* (1915) 84 LJ Ch 449 at 450,
[1914–15] All ER Rep 147 at 150, Lord Diplock said:

'In a speech which received the approval of the other members of this House,
j [Lord Parker] identified the right the invasion of which is the subject of passing-off
actions as being the "property in the business or goodwill likely to be injured by the
misrepresentation". The concept of goodwill is in law a broad one which is perhaps
expressed in words used by Lord MacNaghten in *Inland Revenue Comrs v Muller &
Co's Margarine Ltd*. It is the benefit and advantage of the good name, reputation and
connection of a business. It is the attractive force which brings in custom."'

At the base of counsel for the plaintiffs' submissions there lies the notion that, even in the case of an international group in the sense used above, once there has been established *a* here a corporate entity making use of their goodwill, the goodwill becomes a localised asset forming part of the exclusive property of the corporate entity, and can be attached to another corporate entity established by the international body only by some transfer from the original user in this country, for instance by assignment or licence, expressed or implied. For my part I think that that displays an unduly and unjustifiably formalistic approach to the matter and to be an approach which ignores both substance and reality. *b* Essentially the evidence and the judge's findings seem to me to justify the proposition that the reputation and the establishment of a branch in this country, whether as a separate corporate entity or not, imports simply that it is part of that international organisation which is run by the Habib family.

I start therefore from the position that for my part I am unable to see that, however he expressed it, the judge went wrong in his rejection of counsel for the plaintiffs' first basic *c* assumption of an exclusive goodwill subsisting in HBO.

I come then to counsel's second axiom, that the establishment here of the defendants' office under the title of HBZ imported a representation that they were a company under the effective management of HBO or HBL or under the same effective management as those two companies. I do not think it imported anything of the sort save to this extent, that all the companies were under the management of members of the Habib family. *d* I can see absolutely no reason why anyone should assume from the name Habib Bank AG Zurich that HBZ were a subsidiary of one or the other of HBO or HBL or that they were their parent company or indeed anything more than that they were loosely associated with them by their ties with the same family. It is indeed instructive to see how this was pleaded. In para 5 of the amended statement of claim it is pleaded as follows:

'The defendants have passed off and intend to continue to pass off their banking *e* business in this country as and for the business of the plaintiffs or as a business connected or associated with the plaintiffs or a branch thereof or as a business under the effective control of the plaintiffs.'

The plaintiffs were asked for particulars of that. They were asked:

'(a) State what is meant by the plaintiffs' "effective control" of the defendants. *f* (b) Identify precisely the date when it is alleged that the defendants ceased to be under the effective control of the plaintiffs. (c) State precisely the period during which it is alleged that the defendants were under the effective control of the plaintiffs and all facts and matters relied upon to establish such effective control. (d) State all facts and matters relied upon to establish that the plaintiffs lost effective control of the defendants. (e) State precisely when the nationalisation and merger *g* are alleged to have taken place.'

That request was answered in these words:

'(a) By "a business under the effective control of the plaintiffs", the plaintiffs mean a business wherein the majority shareholding is the same as that of the plaintiffs and/or in which the executive decisions are made by the same persons who *h* make such decisions in the plaintiff company. (b) The defendants ceased to be under the effective control of the plaintiffs on the date of nationalisation being 1st January 1974 or shortly thereafter. (c) The defendants were under the effective control of the plaintiffs at all times prior to the date of nationalisation. In support hereof the plaintiffs will rely on the fact that prior to 1st January 1974 the majority shareholdings in HBZ and HBO were held by the same persons and that ultimately *j* the executive decisions of the two companies were made by the same persons and in particular by Mr Hyder Habib. [It will be remembered that he remained and still remains to this day one of the controlling persons behind the defendants.] (d) In support of the allegation that the plaintiffs lost effective control of the defendants,

the plaintiffs will rely on the fact that after nationalisation the ownership of HBO
a   and HBL passed to the State of Pakistan and that shortly thereafter the executive
decisions of HBO were taken by persons other than those taking such decisions for
HBZ.'

It then gives the date of nationalisation.

There was never at any time a majority shareholding in HBZ by HBO or by the Habib
family and I confess myself wholly unable to see why the mere establishment by a Swiss
b   company of an office in London where there is already a family company doing business
should import any representation at all about who is responsible for the management
decisions of either. It seems to me that, where you are dealing with Pakistani citizens
who are familiar with affairs in Pakistan and well acquainted with the reputation of a
well-known banking family, all that the name imports is, 'We are a company associated
with the Habib family'. That is as true today as it was in 1973.

c   Then turning to counsel for the plaintiffs' third proposition that there was some
agreed or understood limitation on the activities of HBZ in London, which has somehow
been transcended by the development of a general banking business, there is, apart from
a reference to the original purpose of providing a hard-currency haven safe from the
prying eyes of an inquisitive government, no evidence to support any such agreement or
understanding. HBO's officers in their answers to the State Bank of Pakistan denied any
d   agreement and simply said that the operations were to be governed by the articles of
association (which I should perhaps say cover the carrying on of a general banking
business). The Bank of England was informed that HBZ desired to take part in the
banking activities of the City of London and Mr Hussein's evidence was that he was told
in Zurich to take over the London branch which would be a general banking business.
I find this suggestion of the plaintiffs really wholly unsupported by the evidence, but in
e   any event it seems to me to have relevance only to the question of acquiescence and not
to the logically anterior question of whether there was any misrepresentation.

I think that it will have become evident from what I have said so far that I find myself
wholly unpersuaded that the judge, however he may have expressed himself, erred in
principle in the conclusion at which he arrived that the evidence disclosed no passing off
because there simply is not and was not any misrepresentation. That really was sufficient
f   to dispose of the case and it is sufficient, in my judgment, to dispose of this appeal.

The proposition that a nationalisation decree which deprives individuals in a foreign
jurisdiction of their control of a foreign company can have the effect of forcing those
individuals to give up the use of a name which they have lawfully adopted and are
lawfully using in another jurisdiction is one which, in any event, I find a little startling,
and counsel for the defendants has addressed to us, under his cross-notice, an argument
g   that the English court will not prevent a company lawfully incorporated abroad from
honestly using its corporate name in connection with a business carried on here. In the
view that I take it is unnecessary to decide this interesting point, although it derives some
support from the decision of Stirling J in *Saunders v Sun Life Assurance Co of Canada* [1894]
1 Ch 537, and the judgment of Morton LJ in particular in the Court of Appeal in
Marengo v Daily Sketch and Sunday Graphic Ltd although that decision was subsequently
h   reversed on the facts in the House of Lords ([1948] 1 All ER 406).

But even if I were in doubt about the principal ground for the judge's decision, I think
that the judgment can equally be supported on the other grounds which he gave. First,
the question of damage. Having reviewed the evidence on damage, the judge expressed
himself in these terms:

j   'Had it been necessary for me to come to a conclusion on the question of damage,
I am by no means certain that I could come to the conclusion that the plaintiffs have
satisfactorily established their case under this head.'

I think that if I have a criticism of the judge's judgment, it is only that in this he did not
go far enough. It has to be remembered that damage is of the essence of the claim,

although of course it may be inferred. This appears most clearly from the speech of Lord Fraser in *Erven Warnink BV v J Townend & Sons (Hull) Ltd* [1979] 2 All ER 927 at 943–944, *a* [1979] AC 731 at 755–756:

> 'It is essential for the plaintiff in a passing-off action to show at least the following facts: (1) that his business consists of, or includes, selling in England a class of goods to which the particular trade name applies; (2) that the class of goods is clearly defined, and that in the minds of the public, or a section of the public, in England, the trade name distinguishes that class from other similar goods; (3) that because of *b* the reputation of the goods, there is goodwill attached to the name; (4) that he, the plaintiff, as a member of the class of those who sell the goods, is the owner of goodwill in England which is of substantial value; (5) that he has suffered, or is really likely to suffer, substantial damage to his property in the goodwill by reason of the defendants selling goods which are falsely described by the trade name to *c* which the goodwill is attached.'

But here there really was no evidence of any damage of any significance over the whole period since nationalisation. The witnesses called by the plaintiffs to establish the probability of confusion seem, judging from the transcripts, from the plaintiffs' point of view to have been disappointingly vague. It has to be remembered that these two banks had been trading together in London for three and a half years before the issue of the writ *d* and nearly six years at the date of the hearing. Yet there was not one atom of evidence of any customer who had opened an account at one in mistake for the other, apart from one case in which a gentleman who had opened an account with the defendants had subsequently closed it and transferred his business to the plaintiffs. Since he had previously transferred part of the moneys in his account with the defendants to an account opened with the plaintiffs before finally closing his account with the defendants, *e* this may import dissatisfaction but it hardly looks like a case of confusion. All the other evidence of confusion related to a decreasing amount of postal confusion (much of which was accounted for by carelessness on the part of the Post Office), telex confusion by junior banking staff, and a decreasing quantity of credits or debits to the wrong banks, which were swiftly rectified without loss, although this may have caused some slight administrative inconvenience on both sides. But the evidence did indicate that errors of *f* this sort did occur, though much less frequently, even with other banks.

HBZ have 21 branches in various countries, in many of which the plaintiffs also have branches, sometimes even in the same town. There was no evidence of confusion between the two except in one case of a press report where a guarantee given by the plaintiffs was described as given by the 'Zurich based' Habib Bank.

Counsel for the plaintiffs says that there is a danger of some malpractice of HBZ *g* rubbing off on his clients. That is a two-way traffic. The judge dismissed this as pure speculation, and so it is. Moreover, it is speculation against the background of some twelve years of concurrent international trading during which there is minimal evidence of any substantial confusion, except of a purely mechanical kind. For my part I would be bolder than the judge. I think that the plaintiffs failed to establish any substantial damage or probability of damage. *h*

Finally I turn to the point of acquiescence, laches and estoppel. The judge would have held the claim barred on this ground if he had thought that any claim existed; and so would I. Just consider the facts. It is common ground that the defendants were formed and founded with the active concurrence of the plaintiffs' predecessors and that their staff were used to set them up in London. *After* nationalisation HBZ were established in their new office with the help of HBO's staff in London. It was the evidence of the plaintiffs' *j* own witnesses that thereafter there were literally thousands of transactions between the two banks every year and that the plaintiffs and the defendants entered into a whole series of agency arrangements which were profitable to both sides.

The relationship after nationalisation is summed up in the following very significant evidence from the plaintiffs' own witness, Mr Bukhari. He was asked:

'Q. Can you tell me, if HBO (subsequently the plaintiffs) had decided to do no
business after nationalisation with HBZ, what would be the position in relation to
HBZ? Would they have been able to transact the same business? A Not after
nationalisation; we could not or did not stop our dealings with [HBZ], neither did
they stop dealing with us, because there were so many transactions, so many
accounts mutual and they were so interwoven and so many clients are involved that
it was not possible for us or for them to discontinue relationship between the two
banks.

'Q. I do not think you are answering the question I asked but do finish your
answer. A. I was saying that we in London were looking after all the London
business of [HBZ]. All their investments were made to us, all their money was
placed or transactions relevant were effected with us. So at that time I believe that
[HBZ] could not have done without us. Of course, they could make alternative
arrangements with other banks, but it would take a lot of time.

'Q. What about the agency agreements? Supposing you had said, "We will take
no agency work", could they have transacted that with some other bank? A. Yes,
it is always possible to make agency arrangements with other banks; but, relations
being what they were prior to nationalisation, it was easier and more convenient,
and particularly they needed Habib Bank with a network of branches in Pakistan,
and that is why they approached us and we did make agency arrangements.'

There was also evidence which established that whereas HBZ had from the inception
used a logo consisting of a lion, not dissimilar to that used by the original HBL in
Pakistan, HBO had right from the outset used in the United Kingdom the insignia of a
flying horse. After nationalisation that was abandoned and the plaintiffs elected to use
here the original HBL motif thus bringing themselves nearer to the defendants, a source
of possible confusion compounded by their failure to comply with s 411 of the
Companies Act 1948 by specifying in their letterheads that they were incorporated in
Pakistan. One's initial reaction, looking at the history of the matter, is that there could
hardly be a plainer case of acquiescence than this, but counsel for the plaintiffs says first
that there is no properly pleaded case of acquiescence and second that the essential
ingredients of a defence of acquiescence were never proved.

We were again referred to many authorities on this subject and to the debate which
has taken place whether, in order to succeed in a plea of acquiescence, a defendant must
demonstrate all the five probanda contained in the judgment of Fry J in *Willmott v Barber*
(1880) 15 Ch D 96 (see the recent judgment of Robert Goff J in *Amalgamated Investment
and Property Co Ltd (in liquidation) v Texas Commerce International Bank Ltd* [1981] 1 All ER
923, [1981] 2 WLR 554). Whether all five of those probanda are necessary or not,
counsel for the plaintiffs submits that to succeed the defendants must at least establish
three things. They must show, first, that the defendants have been acting under a
mistake as to their legal rights. That, in the instant case, must mean that they were
unaware that what they were doing (that is to say, carrying on their business under the
name in which they had been incorporated with the active assistance of the plaintiffs'
predecessors) constituted any invasion of the plaintiffs' rights. Second, they must show
that the plaintiffs encouraged that course of action, either by statements or conduct.
Third, they must show that they have acted on the plaintiffs' representation or
encouragement to their detriment.

None of these three essentials, submits counsel, has been pleaded or proved in the
instant case. I will consider that submission in a moment, but I must first notice the
submission of junior counsel for the defendants that in any event these three allegedly
essential ingredients do not constitute the test for a successful plea of acquiescence or
estoppel, at any rate as the law has now developed. The true principle, counsel suggests,
is that to be found in the judgment of the Board in *Lindsay Petroleum Co v Hurd* (1874) LR
5 PC 221 at 239–240 delivered by Sir Barnes Peacock and cited with approval by Lord
Blackburn in *Erlanger v New Sombrero Phosphate Co* (1878) 3 App Cas 1218 at 1279:

'The doctrine of laches in Courts of Equity is not an arbitrary or a technical doctrine. Where it would be practically unjust to give a remedy, either because the *a* party has, by his conduct, done that which might fairly be regarded as equivalent to a waiver of it, or where by his conduct and neglect he has, though perhaps not waiving that remedy, yet put the other party in a situation in which it would not be reasonable to place him if the remedy were afterwards to be asserted, in either of these cases, lapse of time and delay are most material. But in every case, if an argument against relief, which otherwise would be just, is founded upon mere *b* delay, that delay of course not amounting to a bar by any statute of limitations, the validity of that defence must be tried upon principles substantially equitable. Two circumstances, always important in such cases, are, the length of the delay and the nature of the acts done during the interval, which might affect either party and cause a balance of justice or injustice in taking the one course or the other, so far as relates to the remedy.'   *c*

After quoting that passage Lord Blackburn continued (at 1279–1280):

'I have looked in vain for any authority which gives a more distinct and definite rule than this; and I think, from the nature of the inquiry, it must always be a question of more or less, depending on the degree of diligence which might reasonably be required, and the degree of change which has occurred, whether the balance of justice or injustice is in favour of granting the remedy or withholding *d* it. The determination of such a question must largely depend on the turn of mind of those who have to decide, and must therefore be subject to uncertainty; but that, I think, is inherent in the nature of the inquiry.'

To this counsel for the plaintiffs retorts that that applies only where you are considering the doctrine of laches or acquiescence in relation to the assertion of equitable rights and *e* not where you are considering the enforcement by equitable means of legal rights; and we were regaled with authorities on both sides for the purpose of establishing whether a plaintiff in a passing-off action is protecting a legal right or an equitable right.

I have to confess that I detect in myself, despite the erudition displayed by both counsel, a strong predilection for the view that such distinctions are both archaic and arcane and that in the year 1980 they have but little significance for anyone but a legal *f* historian. For myself, I believe that the law as it has developed over the past twenty years has now evolved a far broader approach to the problem than that suggested by counsel for the plaintiff and one which is in no way dependent on the historical accident of whether any particular right was first recognised by the common law or was invented by the Court of Chancery. It is an approach exemplified in such cases as *Inwards v Baker* [1965] 1 All ER 446, [1965] 2 QB 29 and *Crabb v Arun District Council* [1975] 3 All ER *g* 865, [1976] Ch 179. We have been referred at length to a recent judgment of my own in *Taylor Fashions Ltd v Liverpool Victoria Trustees Co Ltd* [1981] 1 All ER 897, [1981] 2 WLR 576 in which I ventured to collect and review the authorities. I said this ([1981] 1 All ER 897 at 915–916, [1981] 2 WLR 576 at 593):

'Furthermore, the more recent cases indicate, in my judgment, that the application of the *Ramsden v Dyson* ((1866) LR 1 HL 129) principle (whether you call *h* it proprietary estoppel, estoppel by acquiescence or estoppel by encouragement is really immaterial) requires a very much broader approach which is directed rather at ascertaining whether, in particular individual circumstances, it would be unconscionable for a party to be permitted to deny that which, knowingly or unknowingly, he has allowed or encouraged another to assume to his detriment rather than to inquiring whether the circumstances can be fitted within the confines *j* of some preconceived formula serving as a universal yardstick for every form of unconscionable behaviour.'

Whilst having heard the judgment read by counsel I could wish that it had been more succinct, that statement at least is one to which I adhere.

But let me, for present purposes, assume in favour of counsel for the plaintiffs the
a three essentials which he propounds. He says that there was no plea, no assertion, no
evidence of the defendants' innocence in what they did; but, I ask, why should there
be? In his statement of claim he asserted that the defendants 'intended' to pass off their
business as one associated with the plaintiffs and he was asked, in a request for particulars,
whether that meant deliberate passing off. That request produced a positive response,
but it is common ground that the allegation was withdrawn well before the trial. So that
b the case from there on proceeded from first to last on the footing that there was no
suggestion of mala fides. Then, again, before the trial the plaintiffs were asked to make
certain admissions and the following facts were all expressly admitted.

It was admitted that HBZ were incorporated under their present name with the
consent of HBO. It was admitted that cl 2 of HBZ's statutes, translated into English,
provided as follows:

c   'The corporation may take up holdings in similar companies, establish branches
          in Switzerland or abroad and in general transact any business directly or indirectly
          connected with realising its objects.'

It was admitted that 'by letter dated 5th June 1973 HBO on behalf of HBZ sought Bank
of England consent to open an office in London'. It was admitted 'that HBZ acquired
d premises at 8 City Road under a lease dated 22nd May 1974'.

It was *not* admitted that the premises were found for HBZ by De Groot Collis (estate
agents) pursuant to instructions given by HBO officials; but in fact that was proved. And
it was admitted that 'The London office of HBZ has maintained an account with HBO
and subsequently the plaintiffs since 3rd July 1973'.

In the reply there was this admission:

e   'It is admitted that until shortly prior to these proceedings neither HBL nor HBO
          objected to the defendants' activities. However the same does not provide any
          defence to this action.'

There is then a very significant deletion, which was the original pleading:

f   'Up till that time the defendants' activities in this country had been very limited
          and had been purely in respect of their Swiss banking business. The first knowledge
          the plaintiffs had that the defendants intended to carry out banking activities in this
          country other than as a necessary part of their activities in Switzerland was when the
          defendants started preparation to open their new premises in Moorgate.'

The whole of that was subsequently deleted on amendment before trial.
g   So here was a company against whom no mala fides was alleged, as to whom it was
admitted that their trading name, style and objects were assumed with the consent of the
plaintiffs' predecessors, that their offices were found for them by the plaintiffs'
predecessors, that their very consent from the Bank of England was obtained by the
plaintiffs' predecessors, and that up to and after the action they had maintained an
account with the plaintiffs; and in relation to whose user of the name it was never alleged
h from first to last that the slightest objection was taken until about a month before the
writ. I am bound to say that it struck me while counsel for the plaintiffs was addressing
us, as it strikes me now, that in these circumstances the calling of a witness to prove what
the facts themselves seem to me to demonstrate beyond a peradventure was a work of
supererogation, for there could not, in the proven circumstances, have been any reason
why, in the absence of any adverse claims by the plaintiffs, anyone should for a moment
j imagine that there could be the slightest objection likely to be raised by them to the
continuation in business of what, essentially, had started life as their own creature.
   As regards the second of counsel's propositions, I challenged him in the course of the
argument to tell us what more the plaintiffs could have done than what they did to
encourage the defendants in the belief that there was no objection to their trading style,
and his answer was that there was more: they could have written a letter expressly stating

that there was no such objection. That answer, I think, really spoke for itself, although
perhaps extracted from counsel in a moment of exasperation, for really when the facts *a*
are examined (and they show a history of continuous mutual trading over the whole
period, even including the sale of equipment by the plaintiffs to the defendants) the case
is really unanswerable.

Finally, there was, says counsel neither express allegation nor express proof that the
defendants had acted on the encouragement. There is certainly an allegation in relation
to estoppel in the defence that the defendants have relied on the right to use their own *b*
name and motif and have been permitted by the plaintiffs to build up a goodwill
therein. That goodwill, in fact, was amply proved by the banking documents and by the
defendants' witnesses. I really cannot think that it was necessary formally to call a
witness to say, 'We did this in reliance on the supposition that we were allowed to use our
corporate name'. That reliance can be inferred from the circumstances, as it was in
Greasley v Cooke [1980] 3 All ER 710 at 711, [1980] 1 WLR 1306 at 1307 per Lord *c*
Denning MR, and I think that the judge was perfectly justified in inferring it from the
evidence before him in this case.

I have to acknowledge my indebtedness to counsel on both sides for some illuminating
arguments, but at the end of them I find myself entirely unpersuaded that the judge
erred in any material respect. He concluded his judgment in this way on the question
of estoppel: *d*

'Of course, estoppel by conduct has been a field of the law in which there has been
considerable expansion over the years and it appears to me that it is essentially the
application of a rule by which justice is done where the circumstances of the
conduct and behaviour of the party to an action are such that it would be wholly
inequitable that he should be entitled to succeed in the proceeding.'
                                                                                  e
That, to my mind, sufficiently appears on the facts of this case.

I, too, think that it would be wholly inequitable that the plaintiffs should succeed even
if, contrary to the view which I have formed, they had established their primary case. I
would, therefore, dismiss the appeal.

WATKINS LJ. I agree, and there is nothing I could possibly add to that judgment. *f*

STEPHENSON LJ. I agree and would like to express my concurrence with what
Oliver LJ has said, both about archaic and arcane distinctions and his statement in *Taylor
Fashions Ltd v Liverpool Victoria Trustees Co Ltd* [1981] 1 All ER 897 at 915–916, [1981] 2
WLR 576 at 593 which he read from his judgment.
                                                                                  g
Appeal dismissed. Leave to appeal to the House of Lords refused.

Solicitors: *Stones, Porter & Co* (for the plaintiffs); *Freshfields* (for the defendants).

Patricia Hargrove   Barrister.

Tehno-Impex v Gebr van Weelde Scheepvartkantoor BV

COURT OF APPEAL, CIVIL DIVISION
LORD DENNING MR, OLIVER AND WATKINS LJJ
2nd, 3rd, 4th FEBRUARY, 12th MARCH 1981

Arbitration – Award – Interest – Damages – Power of arbitrator to award interest – Claim for interest only – Claim for interest on payments made late but before commencement of arbitration – Whether interest can be awarded by way of damages at common law – Whether interest can be awarded by way of damages under Admiralty jurisdiction – Whether interest on interest can be awarded.

By a charterparty containing a London arbitration clause the shipowners agreed with the charterers to ship cement from Yugoslavia to Nigeria. After 12 voyages a dispute arose which was referred to arbitration. The charterers claimed $30,000 demurrage overpaid on the twelfth voyage while the shipowners cross-claimed that demurrage had been paid late on most if not all of the 12 voyages and that they were entitled to interest on all late payments. The arbitrator awarded the charterers the $30,000 claimed, together with interest at $7\frac{1}{2}\%$ from the date of overpayment to the date of the award. In regard to the shipowners' claim the arbitrator considered that where the principal sum had been paid before the commencement of the arbitration, as had happened in the case of all demurrage payments owed by the charterers, and the claim was for interest alone, arising out of the late payment, he was bound to refuse the claim because of the common law rule that, in the absence of any express stipulation in the contract, interest could not be claimed by way of damages in respect of a late or withheld payment due under the contract. The shipowners appealed unsuccessfully to the Commercial Court, and then to the Court of Appeal, contending (i) that the common law rule was merely a rule of practice applicable to common law actions and was not a substantive rule binding on arbitrators, or (ii) that the claim fell within the jurisdiction of the Admiralty Court and under that jurisdiction interest could be claimed and awarded in respect of late payments.

Held – (1) (Lord Denning MR dissenting) An arbitrator deciding a claim in accordance with the rights of the parties under English law was obliged to apply the common law rule that interest could not be claimed or awarded by way of damages in respect of a late or withheld payment due under a contract if the payment was made prior to the commencement of the arbitration, since that rule, whatever its origins, was so entrenched as to be a substantive rule of law (see p 681 *a j* to p 682 *a c* to *f h j*, p 688 *b c* and p 689 *b c*, post); *London, Chatham and Dover Railway Co v South Eastern Railway Co* [1893] AC 429 applied; *Re Badger* (1819) 2 B & Ald 691 doubted.

(2) However (Oliver LJ dissenting), the Admiralty Court, under its inherent equitable jurisdiction, retained power to award as damages interest for non-payment of money due at a particular date, and since by s 1(1)(h)[a] of the Administration of Justice Act 1956 the shipowners' claim could have been brought in the Admiralty Court rather than the Commercial Court the arbitrator was entitled, in view of the charterers' inequitable behaviour, to invoke that jurisdiction and award damages corresponding to the interest

---

a   Section 1(1), so far as material, provides: 'The Admiralty jurisdiction of the High Court shall be as follows, that is to say, jurisdiction to hear and determine any of the following questions or claims . . . (h) any claim arising out of any agreement relating to the carriage of goods in a ship or to the use or hire of a ship . . .'

claimed. Moreover, in making such an award the arbitrator was not prevented by s 3(1)[b] of the Law Reform (Miscellaneous Provisions) Act 1934 from awarding interest on the **a** award even though to do so would in effect be awarding interest on interest. Accordingly, the appeal would be allowed and the shipowners' claim remitted to the arbitrator to consider whether and to what extent the claim for interest should be allowed (see p 674 j to p 675 b, p 677 c d, p 689 d to h and p 690 b to d, post); The Northumbria (1869) LR 3 A & E 6 and The Aldora [1975] 2 All ER 69 applied; The Medina Princess [1962] 2 Lloyd's Rep 17 doubted. **b**

Per Curiam. Modern monetary conditions require an urgent reappraisal of the common law relating to claims for interest for late or withheld payments, and (per Lord Denning MR) on principle arbitrators should be allowed to award damages for nonpayment of money under the ordinary rules as to damages in contract (see p 675 d, p 677 e to g, p 686 f and p 688 b, post).

c

Notes

For claims for interest, see 32 Halsbury's Laws (4th Edn) paras 106–109, and for cases on the subject, see 35 Digest (Repl) 208–214, 153–196.

For the power of an arbitrator to award interest, see 2 Halsbury's Laws (4th Edn) para 580, and for cases on the subject, see 3 Digest (Reissue) 201–203, 1235–1243.

For the Law Reform (Miscellaneous Provisions) Act 1934, s 3, see 25 Halsbury's **d** Statutes (3rd Edn) 752.

For the Adminstration of Justice Act 1956, s 1, see 1 ibid 21.

Cases referred to in judgments

Aldora, The, Tyne Tugs Ltd v The owners of the motor vessel Aldora [1975] 2 All ER 69, [1975] QB 748, [1975] 2 WLR 791, [1975] 1 Lloyd's Rep 617, Digest (Cont Vol D) 834, 7829a. **e**

Alina, The (1880) 5 Ex D 227, 49 LJP 40, 42 LT 517, 4 Asp MLC 257, CA, 1(1) Digest (Reissue) 391, 2760.

Amalia, The (1864) 5 New Rep 164n, 34 LJPM & A 21.

Arnott v Redfern (1826) 3 Bing 353, 4 LJOSCP 89, 11 Moore CP 209, 130 ER 549, 11 Digest (Reissue) 491, 923.

Badger, Re (1819) 2 B & Ald 691, 106 ER 517, 3 Digest (Reissue) 155, 898. **f**

Beldis, The [1936] P 51, [1935] All ER Rep 760, 106 LJP 22, 154 LT 680, 18 Asp MLC 598, CA, 1(1) Digest (Reissue) 219, 1243.

Boddam v Riley (1785) 2 Bro CC 2, 29 ER 1, LC; on appeal (1787) 4 Bro Parl Cas 561, 2 ER 382, HL; previous proceedings (1783) 1 Bro CC 239, LC, 36(2) Digest (Reissue) 735, 1143.

Bremer Vulkan Schiffbau Und Maschinenfabrik v South India Shipping Corpn [1981] 1 All ER **g** 289, [1981] 2 WLR 141, HL.

Cameron v Smith (1819) 2 B & Ald 305, 106 ER 378, 35 Digest (Repl) 203, 106.

Chandris v Isbrandtsen Moller Co Inc [1950] 2 All ER 618, [1951] KB 240, CA, 3 Digest (Reissue) 202, 1241.

De Havilland v Bowerbank (1807) 1 Camp 50, 170 ER 872, NP, 35 Digest (Repl) 206, 131.

Dundee, The (1827) 2 Hag Adm 137, 1(1) Digest (Reissue) 366, 2507. **h**

Eddowes v Hopkins (1780) 1 Doug KB 376, 99 ER 242, 30 Digest (Reissue) 346, 647.

Edwards v Great Western Railway Co (1851) 11 CB 588, 21 LJCP 72, 138 ER 603, 35 Digest (Repl) 209, 167.

Gertrude, The (1887) 57 LT 883, 6 Asp MLC 224, 1(1) Digest (Reissue) 365, 2501.

j

b   Section 3(1), so far as material, provides: 'In any proceedings tried in any court of record for the recovery of any debt or damages, the court may, if it thinks fit, order that there shall be included in the sum for which judgment is given interest at such rate as it thinks fit on the whole or any part of the debt or damages for the whole or any part of the period between the date when the cause of action arose and the date of the judgment: Provided that nothing in this section—(a) shall authorise the giving of interest upon interest . . .'

a *Hadley v Baxendale* (1854) 9 Exch 341, [1843–60] All ER Rep 461, 23 LJ Ex 179, 23 LTOS 69, 18 Jur 358, 2 CLR 517, 156 ER 145, 17 Digest (Reissue) 101, *109.*

Jade, The, The Eschersheim, motor vessel Erkowit (Owners) v Ship Jade (Owners), Owners of cargo lately laden on board motor vessel Erkowit v Ship Eschersheim (Owners) [1976] 1 All ER 920, [1976] 1 WLR 430, [1976] 2 Lloyd's Rep 1, HL, 1(1) Digest (Reissue) 267, *1590.*

b *Jugoslavenska Oceanska Plovidba v Castle Investment Co Inc, The Kozara* [1973] 3 All ER 498, [1974] QB 292, [1972] 3 WLR 847, [1973] 2 Lloyd's Rep 1, CA, Digest (Cont Vol D) 46, *2136a.*

Knox v Simmonds (1791) 3 Bro CC 358, 1 Ves 369, 1 Hov Suppl 146, 29 ER 582, 3 Digest (Reissue) 155, *897.*

Kong Magnus, The [1891] P 223, 65 LT 231, 7 Asp MLC 64, 1(1) Digest (Reissue) 365, *2503.*

c *Liesbosch (Dredger) (Owners) v Owners of Steamship Edison, The Liesbosch* [1933] AC 449, [1933] All ER Rep 144, 102 LJP 73, 149 LT 49, 38 Com Cas 267, 18 Asp MLC 380, 45 Ll L Rep 123, HL, 41 Digest (Repl) 945, *7368.*

London, Chatham and Dover Railway Co v South Eastern Railway Co [1893] AC 429, 63 LJ Ch 93, 69 LT 637, 58 JP 36, 1 R 275, HL, 35 Digest (Repl) 209, *159.*

Manners v Pearson & Son [1898] 1 Ch 581, 67 LJ Ch 304, 78 LT 432, CA, 35 Digest (Repl) d 201, *90.*

Medina Princess, The [1962] 2 Lloyd's Rep 17.

Miliangos v George Frank (Textiles) Ltd [1975] 3 All ER 801, [1976] AC 443, [1975] 3 WLR 758, [1976] 1 Lloyd's Rep 201, HL, Digest (Cont Vol D) 691, *64c.*

Minter (F G) Ltd v Welsh Health Technical Services Organisation (1980) 13 BLR 1, [1980] Court of Appeal Transcript 159.

e *Multiservice Bookbinding Ltd v Marden* [1978] 2 All ER 489, [1979] Ch 84, [1978] 2 WLR 535, 35 P & CR 201, Digest (Cont Vol E) 428, *22a.*

Napier Star, The [1933] P 136, 102 LJP 57, 149 LT 359, 18 Asp MLC 400, 45 Ll L Rep 139, 1(1) Digest (Reissue) 366, *2509.*

Nea Tyhi Maritime Co Ltd of Piraeus v Compagnie Grainiere SA of Zurich, The Finix [1975] 2 Lloyd's Rep 415; *rvsd* [1978] 1 Lloyd's Rep 16, CA, Digest (Cont Vol E) 555, *2483c.*

f *Northumbria, The* (1869) LR 3 A & E 6, 39 LJ Adm 3, 21 LT 681, 3 Mar LC 314; *subsequent proceedings* LR 3 A & E 24, 42 Digest (Repl) 1063, *8811.*

Ozalid Group (Export) Ltd v African Continental Bank Ltd [1979] 2 Lloyd's Rep 231.

Page v Newman (1829) 9 B & C 378, 4 Man & Ry KB 305, 7 LJOSKB 267, 109 ER 140, 6 Digest (Reissue) 304, *2221.*

Parana, The (1877) 2 PD 118, 36 LT 388, 3 Asp MLC 399, CA; *rvsg* (1876) 1 PD 452, 41 g Digest (Repl) 388, *1752.*

Podar Trading Co Ltd, Bombay v Francois Tagher, Barcelona [1949] 2 All ER 62, [1949] 2 KB 277, [1949] LJR 1470, DC, 3 Digest (Reissue) 201, *1240.*

Smith v Kirby (1875) 1 QBD 131, 24 WR 207, 42 Digest (Reissue) 1064, *8815.*

Straker v Hartland (1864) 2 Hem & M 570, 5 New Rep 163, 34 LJ Ch 122, 11 LT 622, 10 Jur NS 1143, 2 Mar LC 159, 71 ER 584, 1(1) Digest (Reissue) 365, *2500.*

h *Theems, The* [1938] P 197, 107 LJP 139, 159 LT 392, 19 Asp MLC 206, 61 Ll LR 178, 42 Digest (Repl) 1064, *8818.*

Trendtex Trading Corpn v Central Bank of Nigeria [1976] 3 All ER 437, [1976] 1 WLR 868; *rvsd* [1977] 1 All ER 881, [1977] QB 529, [1977] 2 WLR 356, [1977] 1 Lloyd's Rep 581, CA, 1(1) Digest (Reissue) 59, *382.*

United Railways of Havana and Regla Warehouses Ltd, Re [1960] 2 All ER 332, [1961] AC j 1007, [1960] 2 WLR 969, HL, 11 Digest (Reissue) 489, *919.*

Wallersteiner v Moir (No 2) [1975] 1 All ER 849, [1975] QB 373, 508n, [1975] 2 WLR 389, CA, Digest (Cont Vol D) 570, *518a.*

Cases also cited

Aldebarau Compania Maritima SA Panama v Aussenhandel AG Zurich, The Darrah [1976] 2 All ER 963, [1977] AC 157, HL.

Bushwall Properties Ltd v Vortex Properties Ltd [1975] 2 All ER 214, [1975] 1 WLR 1649;
    rvsd [1976] 2 All ER 283, [1976] 1 WLR 591, CA.

Carlton v Bragg 15 East 223, 104 ER 828.

Gordon v Swan (1810) 12 East 419, 104 ER 164.

Higgins v Sargent (1823) 2 B & C 348, 107 ER 414.

Jefford v Gee [1970] 1 All ER 1202, [1970] 2 QB 130, CA.

Mecca, The [1968] 2 All ER 731, [1968] P 665.

Norseman, The [1957] 2 All ER 660, [1957] P 224.

Riches v Westminster Bank Ltd [1947] 1 All ER 469, [1947] AC 390, HL.

Swift & Co v Board of Trade [1925] AC 520.

Trans Trust SPRL v Danubian Trading Co Ltd [1952] 1 All ER 970, [1952] 2 QB 297, CA.

Appeal

The respondents to an arbitration, Gebr van Weelde Scheepvartkantoor BV of Holland
('the shipowners'), appealed against the decision of Parker J given on 5th November 1979
refusing to set aside or remit an award made by the arbitrator, Mr Clifford Clark, on 13th
August 1979 in which the arbitrator held that he had no jurisdiction to consider the
shipowners' counterclaim against the claimants, Tehno-Impex of Yugoslavia ('the
charterers'), for the award of damages by way of interest in respect of late payments of
demurrage made by the charterers and for the award of interest on the damages
awarded. The facts are set out in the judgment of Lord Denning MR.

Stewart Boyd and *Jeffrey Gruder* for the shipowners.
Richard Aikens for the charterers.

Cur adv vult

12th March. The following judgments were read.

LORD DENNING MR. This case raises a point of the first importance: to what extent
are arbitrators in the City of London at liberty to award interest on sums due and unpaid?
Especially those who deal with shipping matters. I emphasise shipping matters because
this is a shipping case. If it had come before the courts of law, it would have come within
the scope of the Admiralty jurisdiction.

The facts

This case arises out of the pile-up of ships off Lagos in 1975 which we considered in
Trendtex Trading Corpn Ltd v Central Bank of Nigeria [1977] 1 All ER 881, [1977] QB
529. It led to large sums of money being payable for demurrage. In our present case
Dutch shipowners agreed with Yugoslav charterers to carry 350,000 metric tons of
cement in bags from Split to Lagos or Port Harcourt. It would take many shipments to
take that quantity. They were to be carried between March 1975 and June 1976.
Twelve voyages were performed. The rest were suspended. There were many matters
in difference. There was a clause saying: 'Any dispute arising out of or relating to this
Charter Party shall be referred to the Arbitration in London.' The differences were
referred to the arbitrator, Mr Clifford Clark, who is one of the most experienced of
London maritime arbitrators. He made an interim award raising the point about
interest.

There were cross-claims: the Yugoslav charterers said that they had paid too much
demurrage on a vessel which had performed the twelfth voyage. They had paid $30,000
under a mistake of fact. The Dutch shipowners said that a lot of demurrage had become
payable on the vessels on the 12 voyages. The clause under which it was payable was in
these words:

'Demurrage to be paid . . . at the rate of US$40 (forty dollars . . .) per m/ton loaded
at discharging port . . . Demurrage at discharging port will be paid within 15 days

after receiving Statement of Facts from discharging port, if vessel has maximum 15 days of demurrage. If vessel has over 15 days of demurrage at discharging port, demurrage will be paid every 15 days of demurrage incurred and final settlement of demurrage will be settled within 15 days after receiving Statement of Facts from discharging port for each vessel.'

The Yugoslav charterers were very late in making payments of demurrage. The Dutch shipowners kept a schedule for every vessel showing the amount due every 15 days as required by the charter: the date when payment was received; and the days overdue. Sometimes payment was only a few weeks late, but sometimes as much as six months.

Now comes the point. The arbitrator awarded interest to the charterers on the sum of $30,000 which they had overpaid, at 7½% from the date of payment, 1st January 1977, to the date of his award on 13th August 1979. But he awarded no interest to the shipowners on the sums which were paid late by the charterers during the period from 1975 to 1976, before the arbitration was started.

The arbitrator gave his reasons in his award. He felt that he was bound by a rule of law to refuse interest to the shipowners on the late payments, but he added:

'I wish to make it clear that the rule, if it be the rule, that in the absence of a term in the contract to the contrary effect, a debtor can delay payment as long as he likes and can avoid liability for interest by paying the principal sum at any time, is one which does not accord with justice nor commercial commonsense, especially in times of acute shortage of cash.'

I have no doubt that the arbitrator made his interim award in that form because he wanted the courts to decide whether or not maritime arbitrators in the City of London can award interest on late payments. That is what has happened. The shipowners moved to set aside the award on the ground that it was bad in law on the face of it. Parker J refused to set it aside. The shipowners appeal to this court.

The cases can be divided into three categories. Category I are those cases where the principal sum has not been paid before the award, and the claimant claims both the payment of the principal sum and also interest on it. Category II are those cases where the principal sum has been paid after the commencement of the arbitration, but before the making of the award: late, in breach of contract, and the claimant claims interest or damages for the period during which it was outstanding. Category III are those cases where the principal sum has been paid *before* the commencement of the arbitration, and the claimant claims interest for the period of delay.

CATEGORY I: PRINCIPAL SUM NOT PAID BEFORE THE AWARD

The common law courts

At the time when the common law courts were developing their rules about interest, sterling was a stable currency. Inflation was unknown. Interest was regarded by many with opprobrium. It was stigmatised as usury. But the commercial community viewed it with favour. Blackstone said in 1765 in his Commentaries (2 Bl Com 455):

'that the allowance of moderate interest tends greatly to the benefit of the public, especially in a trading country, will appear from the generally acknowledged principle, that commerce cannot subsist without mutual and extensive credit.'

At the same time, it must be remembered that all actions in the common law courts were tried by *juries*. If a creditor suffered damage by being kept out of his money, it was for the jury to assess his loss. Two of our great Chief Justices would have allowed *juries* to award interest as damages: Lord Mansfield CJ in *Eddowes v Hopkins* (1780) 1 Doug KB 376, 99 ER 242 and Best CJ in *Arnott v Redfern* (1826) 3 Bing 353 at 360, 130 ER 549 at 551–552. But in 1829 Lord Tenterden CJ in *Page v Newman* (1829) 9 B & C 378 at 381, 109 ER 140 at 141 ruled otherwise. He thought it very undesirable that interest should be given by *juries* because it 'would be productive of great inconvenience'. So he held that—

'interest is not due on money secured by a written instrument, unless it appears on the face of the instrument that interest was intended to be paid, or unless it be *a* implied from the usage of trade, as in the case of mercantile instruments.'

Having laid down that rule, however, he took steps in Parliament to modify it. But only in the case of trial by *jury*. Lord Tenterden's Act 1833 (the Civil Procedure Act 1833) allowed a *jury* to award interest 'upon all debts or sums certain, payable at a certain time': or 'otherwise' if a notice in writing were given to the debtor demanding interest. That Act did not give as much help to creditors as might be hoped. This was because of *b* the very restrictive interpretation put by the courts on the words 'a sum certain' and 'a certain time' and the notice of demand. Note that Lord Tenterden, both in *Page v Newman* and in his statute, confined his rules about interest to trial by *jury*: because of the 'great inconvenience' it entailed. He deliberately did not apply his rules to arbitrators. Because he himself with the full King's Bench had already held in 1819 in *Re Badger* 2 B *c* & Ald 691, 106 ER 517 that arbitrators could award interest whenever in their discretion they thought proper. To this I will return.

In 1893 the House of Lords in *London, Chatham and Dover Railway Co v South Eastern Railway Co* [1893] AC 429 affirmed with reluctance the rule of the common law courts as stated in *Page v Newman*. Lord Herschell LC thought that Lord Tenterden's reasoning about 'great inconvenience' was not at all satisfactory; but he felt obliged to follow it. *d* The House did not consider the position in arbitrations. If they had done so, I feel that they would have said that Lord Tenterden's reasoning about 'great inconvenience' did not apply to arbitrations. Just as Lord Tenterden himself (as Abbott CJ) had said in *Re Badger*.

In 1934 the Law Reform (Miscellaneous Provisions) Act 1934 allowed interest to be given on debt or damages but it did not apply to arbitrations. It was expressly confined to 'any proceedings tried in any court of record'. And the Act only applied where *e* judgment was given for the principal sum. Interest was to be 'included in the sum for which judgment is given'. Many astute debtors have taken advantage of this. They delay for months before writ is issued. They delay for many more months till the action is about to come to trial. Then they pay the principal at the last moment before judgment. And thus get out of paying any interest. *f* Such unscrupulous conduct should not be allowed in commercial arbitrations. It can be done by holding that the rules in the common law courts do not apply to arbitrations.

The Chancery courts

There were never any *juries* in the Chancery courts. So the rules in *Page v Newman* never applied to them. We recently had occasion to consider the practice of the Chancery *g* courts in *Wallersteiner v Moir (No 2)* [1975] 1 All ER 849 at 855–856, 870–871, [1975] QB 373 at 388, 406. We there held that the court in its equitable jurisdiction could award interest when it was considered equitable to do so. This is a most flexible jurisdiction. It should not be, and is not, limited by the strict rules of the common law courts or the 1934 Act.

h

The Admiralty Court

Again there were no *juries* in the Admiralty Court. Once liability was established, the amount of debt or damages was assessed by the registrar and merchants. It was the practice of the Admiralty Court from the very earliest times to allow interest on debt or damages awarded in that court. This practice was stated by Lord Stowell in *The Dundee* (1827) 2 Hag Adm 137 at 141: 'If payment is delayed, the claimant is entitled to interest *j* or he will suffer loss ...' It was emphatically affirmed by Sir Robert Phillimore in *The Northumbria* (1869) LR 3 A & E 6 (interest on the amount allowed by the limitation of liability provisions in the Merchant Shipping Acts); by Sir James Hannen in *The Gertrude* (1887) 57 LT 883 (interest on sum awarded for damage to cargo); and by Brandon J in *The Aldora* [1975] 2 All ER 69, [1975] QB 748 (interest on salvage).

The cross-claims in our present case were well within the Admiralty jurisdiction of the

High Court under s 1(1)(h) of the Administration of Justice Act 1956. We have here a
a Dutch owner and a Yugoslav charterer in dispute about the carriage of goods by sea from
Yugoslavia to Nigeria. Nothing to do with England. The dispute only comes here by
virtue of an arbitration clause. If it were not for that clause, it could only have got here
if the ship was arrested in rem in a port in England. If there were such an action in rem,
there is no doubt that, under the Admiralty jurisdiction of the High Court, interest
would have been awarded on both sides of the account.

b

Other legal systems
In all other legal systems of the world the general rule is that the withholding of a debt
entitles the creditor to interest. The position is well set out by the Law Commission in
their Working Paper No 66 ((1976), pp 36–39), and in their Report on Interest ((Law
Com 88 (1978); Cmnd 7229), paras 40–41). Seeing that in most of the arbitrations in
c London the parties (as here) are from countries overseas, it would seem only natural to
them that the arbitrators should be able to award interest.

Arbitration
Looking at the matter on principle, it seems clear that arbitrators should be allowed to
award damages for non-payment of money in those cases where such damage was within
d the reasonable contemplation of the parties under the rule in *Hadley v Baxendale* (1854)
9 Exch 341, [1843–60] All ER Rep 461; and such damage could be assessed by taking a
reasonable rate of interest. The rules about trial by *juries* should not apply to arbitrators
any more than the rules about dismissal for want of prosecution (see *Bremer Vulkan
Schiffbau Und Maschinenfabrik v South India Shipping Corpn* [1981] 1 All ER 289 at 294,
[1981] 2 WLR 141 at 146–147). Much more appropriate for arbitrators are the rules
e about trials in Chancery or in Admiralty where there were no juries. Arbitrations take
place not only on common law matters, but in Chancery matters and in Admiralty
matters. The arbitrators should not be required to place any particular dispute under any
particular category, or to look up recondite law for the purpose. Much better for them
to have a general discretion to award damages in the shape of interest on any debt or
f damages from the date when the sum falls due until the date of the award. This is the
only satisfactory explanation of the arbitration cases in the courts.
The first case is *Re Badger* (1819) 2 B & Ald 691, 106 ER 517, by a strong Court of
King's Bench in its golden age presided over by Lord Tenterden (as Abbott CJ), supported
by some of the best judges ever. It has never been overruled. The case is so important
for present purposes that I must set out a good deal of it. It would appear that the owner
of some houses had entrusted the management of them to an agent who had collected
g the rents from the tenants but had also done work and labour and supplied materials for
which he was entitled to be paid. An action was started in Chancery, but then all matters
in difference were referred to arbitrators. They found that the agent owed rents to the
owner: but that he was entitled to payment for the work done and material supplied.
They allowed interest on both sides of the account. This was to the advantage of the party who
succeeded on balance. The other party moved to set aside the award. Sir James Scarlett
h put it clearly: 'Here the arbitrators have infringed a rule of law by allowing interest and
their award must be set aside.' The Court of King's Bench refused to set it aside. Lord
Tenterden (2 B & Ald 691 at 692, 106 ER 517 at 518) himself distinguished the practice
of the courts of law, saying that it was—

'to avoid that uncertainty which would be productive of very great inconvenience
j   . . . But an arbitrator, to whom a particular cause is referred, is not placed in this
situation; he is not, as it seems to me, bound by those rules of practice which were
adopted by the Court . . .'

And Best J said (2 B & Ald 691 at 693, 106 ER 517 at 693):

'It does not appear that the arbitrators here have violated any general rule of law,
but they have only not complied with the practice of the Court. It is this very

circumstance which, in many cases, makes a decision by an arbitrator preferable to
that of a Court; viz. that the former is not bound by the strict rules of practice, but *a*
may do full justice according to the particular circumstances of the individual case.'

The second case is *Edwards v Great Western Railway Co* (1851) 11 CB 588, 138 ER
603. The claimants there had failed to give a notice of action demanding interest. It
would have been fatal to a claim in an action in the court. But it was held that it was not
fatal to a claim before the arbitrator: see the last five lines of the judgment of the court
on the sixth head of claim (11 CB 588 at 650, 138 ER 603 at 630).   *b*

The third case is *Smith v Kirby* (1875) 1 QBD 131, 24 WR 207. This was an action
against shipowners for damage to cargo. It was tried at Guildhall by a common law
court. The jury found a verdict for the plaintiff on liability. The amount of damages
was referred to an arbitrator. He awarded the full amount allowed on limitation of
liability; and also interest on that sum. The Divisional Court of the Queen's Bench held
that the arbitrator was entitled to apply the Admiralty rule. Quain J said (24 WR 207 at *c*
208): 'It would be absurd to sanction a different rule here from that which prevails in the
Courts of Chancery and Admiralty.' I regard that as an important case. If the arbitrator
had been compelled to apply the rule of the common law courts, he could not have
awarded interest. But, as he was an arbitrator, he applied the Admiralty rule.

The fourth case is *Podar Training Co Ltd, Bombay v Francois Tagher, Barcelona* [1949] 2
All ER 62, [1949] 2 KB 277, where the Divisional Court held that whenever an arbitrator *d*
awarded damages for breach of a contract of sale he could not award interest on the
amount; because he had to follow the common law courts. That case was wrongly
decided, and was overruled in our next case.

The fifth case is *Chandris v Isbrandtsen Moller Co Inc* [1950] 2 All ER 618, [1951] KB
240, when an arbitrator awarded interest on damages for demurrage. The Court of
Appeal held that he was entitled to do so. They put it on the ground that the Law *e*
Reform (Miscellaneous Provisions) Act 1934 could be applied to arbitrations. That is a
very dubious ground, as the Law Commission points out in their Report on Interest
((Law Com 88 (1978); Cmnd 7229), para 175), because the 1934 Act is expressly confined
to 'courts of record', and it cannot by any stretching of words be extended to
arbitrations. The better ground for the decision would have been that the arbitrators
were not bound by the old rules about *juries*; and could give interest in their discretion. *f*

The sixth case is *F G Minter Ltd v Welsh Health Technical Services Organisation* (1980) 13
BLR 1. In a building contract the builder was entitled to be reimbursed for any 'direct
loss or expense' due to a variation. The arbitrator stated a consultative case asking
whether the builder was entitled, in addition to the actual sum expended, to interest on
it. The builder had had to incur finance charges. Parker J, applying the rule of the
common law, rejected the claim for interest. But the Court of Appeal allowed interest *g*
as included in the word 'expenses'. Stephenson LJ said that he regarded the common law
rule as 'an anomaly and an anachronism' which he declined to apply to the case.

Textbooks and practice
The textbooks and arbitrators have treated *Re Badger* as giving arbitrators guidance to *h*
award interest. It was so stated in Russell on Arbitration (7th Edn, 1891, p 120; 10th
Edn, 1919, p 450) and in Hogg on Arbitration (1936, p 129). In *The Finix* [1978] 1
Lloyd's Rep 16 at 19 I stated of my own knowledge that it has been the practice in
commercial arbitrations, certainly in the City of London, for the arbitrator to award
interest on the amounts found to be due without restriction.

Seeing that the practice of arbitrators is of such long standing, going back to 1819, I am *j*
clearly of opinion that the courts should not disturb it now. Numerous awards have
been made on that basis. So on the first category I would hold that, whenever arbitrators
make an award for the whole or part of the principal sum, or on cross-claims, they have
a discretion to award damages in the shape of interest, for the period during which the
debt or damages has been withheld.

CATEGORY II: PRINCIPAL SUM PAID AFTER ARBITRATION STARTED BUT BEFORE AWARD

a   These should come under the same principle as Category I. When a debtor delays paying his creditor, and this causes damage to the creditor, such as falls within the reasonable contemplation of the parties, the creditor should be allowed to recover damages for it. These damages should be recoverable not only when the debtor delays payment of the principal sum until after judgment is given against him but also when he delays for a long time and then pays the principal just before judgment. But in *The*
b *Medina Princess* [1962] 2 Lloyd's Rep 17 Hewson J held otherwise. Wages of seamen fell due on 13th June 1958. A writ was issued for them on 20th July 1959. After pleadings the defendant paid the sums late in 1961. In July 1962 the plaintiffs moved for judgment for interest for the three years' delay. Hewson J refused, saying (at 21):

> 'The words of the section are "shall be included in the sum for which judgment is given". This Court has given no judgment in respect of any sum . . . It seems to
c > me I am bound by the Law Reform (Miscellaneous Provisions) Act, 1934 . . .'

I think that was a mistake. The judge was exercising his Admiralty jurisdiction, under which he was entitled to award interest whenever it was equitable so to do.

So also in an arbitration, when the debtor pays after the commencement of an arbitration and before the making of the award, the arbitrator should be able to award
d interest for the period of delay. In support of this principle, I would venture on a reappraisal.

A reappraisal

During the last twenty years the monetary systems of the world have changed radically. Sterling is no longer a stable currency. It floats in the wind. It changes like a
e weathercock with every gust that blows. Likewise all foreign currencies. The value of money in every country depreciates every year. Inflation is the order of the day. In England recently over 20% a year. Now down to 12%. Interest on bank overdrafts is up to 15% or more. If a debtor deliberately delays payment for a year, he is nothing more nor less than a cheat. At any rate in commercial transactions where traders conduct their business on overdrafts. By withholding the sum due, the debtor saves himself from
f paying interest on the sum, and compels the creditor to pay it instead. To add insult to injury, the value of the money is depreciated in real terms, owing to inflation, by 12% or more.

In this new state of affairs, it is quite unjust that a debtor should be able to withhold payment of the debt till the creditor issues a writ or makes a demand for arbitration. It is quite outrageous that he should be able to delay even afterwards until the day before judgment or award: and by paying then escape all liability for interest. The radical
g changes in the concept of money and its value calls aloud for a reappraisal of the position. It has already been done in the case of awards by allowing them to be given in foreign currency (see *Jugoslavenska Oceanska Plovidba v Castle Investment Co Inc, The Kozara* [1973] 3 All ER 498, [1974] 1 QB 292); so also judgments can now be given in foreign currency (see *Miliangos v George Frank (Textiles) Ltd* [1975] 3 All ER 801, [1976] AC
h 443). It has also been done in the case of index-linked obligations by allowing them to operate according to their terms (see *Multiservice Bookbinding Ltd v Marden* [1978] 2 All ER 489, [1979] Ch 84). Can we not now reappraise the rule too about interest? The London maritime arbitrators have clearly shown the way. Mr Donald Davies, a well-known arbitrator of much experience, has written a letter to this court, saying:

> '. . . I feel that it may be of interest to the Court of Appeal, that until the judgment
j > of Mr. Justice Parker it was my practice, and indeed that of a number of my arbitrator colleagues, to award interest where money was paid late, provided that I was making an Award on another issue in the reference at the same time. I have spoken to the following maritime arbitrators, Cedric Barclay, Bruce Harris, Ralph Kingsley, Michael Mabbs, John Potter, Robert Reed and John Selwyn, who confirm that their practice was, until the Judgment of Mr. Justice Parker, the same as mine.'

Following this lead, I think it is open to arbitrators in the City of London to award interest by way of damages when claimants have suffered loss by being kept out of their *a* money and the respondents pay up at the last moment just before the award is made. If the creditor has suffered real damage by being kept out of his money, and the debtor has made gain by keeping it, then the arbitrator should be able to award damages in the shape of interest for the period that the debt or damages have been withheld.

Compound interest   *b*
    In any case where interest can be awarded, then it is in the discretion of the arbitrator to award it with yearly or half-yearly rests. That is what banks do on overdrafts. It is what we did in *Wallersteiner v Moir (No 2)* [1975] 1 All ER 849 at 855–856, [1975] QB 373 at 388. I know that it is forbidden by the 1934 Act, but arbitrators are not subject to that Act.

c
CATEGORY III: PRINCIPAL SUM PAID BEFORE ARBITRATION IS STARTED
    On like principles, if a debtor delays deliberately for months or years, he should not be able to avoid paying interest by paying just before the notice of appointment of an arbitrator. Take our present case where there are cross-claims. If the charterers are awarded interest on sums overpaid, the arbitrator might think it fair to award the owners interest on the sums paid late. Take *Ozalid Group (Export) Ltd v African Continental Bank* *d* *Ltd* [1979] 2 Lloyd's Rep 231 before Donaldson J. The defendants delayed the payment of US dollars for two months. The rate of exchange fell, with the result that the plaintiffs suffered a currency loss of £2,987 in sterling. The plaintiffs recovered the currency loss, but Donaldson J held that in addition they could recover interest on the principal sum for the period of the delay. He had, we are told, full argument on it. If he could do so, a fortiori an arbitrator should be able to do so.   *e*
    Those are plain cases where interest should be awarded on late payments. But I would suggest that it is in the discretion of the arbitrator. In the ordinary way, when payment is made late, before any arbitration is started, I should think the arbitrators would rarely allow a claim for interest *simpliciter*. It is probable that they would only allow it, as the London maritime arbitrators do, when 'making an award on another issue in the reference at the same time'.   *f*

Conclusion
    In my opinion the arbitrators in the City of London are not bound by the strict rules of the common law courts or of the statutes applicable to them, for this simple reason: that those are rules of practice only which do not govern the practice of arbitrators. Arbitrators have a wide discretion to award interest whenever it is just and equitable to *g* do so. This discretion covers the rate of interest and the period for which it should be allowed, no matter whether the principal sum is paid before or after the arbitration has started, or before or after the award is made. But I should think they will rarely allow it when the principal sum has been paid before the arbitration has started, and the claim is for interest *simpliciter* without any other claim or cross-claim.
    On this view of the law, it follows that the award here is bad for error of law on the face *h* of it. The case should be remitted to the arbitrator for him to consider whether and to what extent interest should be allowed on the late payments of demurrage.
    I would allow the appeal accordingly.

OLIVER LJ. I will not take up time with reciting the facts which have already been summarised in the judgment delivered by Lord Denning MR.   *j*
    I agree that the result of the arbitrator's award is a curious and regrettable one and one which offends one's sense of justice. The respondents, the charterers, because they had not been repaid the $30,000 overpaid prior to the award, are compensated for the time over which they have been out of their money by an award of interest, whilst the appellants, the shipowners, who were without very much larger sums due to them for

a much longer period, receive no similar compensation. The arbitrator regretted being
a compelled to arrive at a conclusion which, he said, did not accord either with justice or
with commercial common sense and his regret was shared by Parker J who likewise felt
compelled for the same reasons to dismiss the appellants' motion. *London, Chatham and
Dover Railway Co v South Eastern Railway Co* [1893] AC 429, he held, was a fatal and
insurmountable obstacle to the shipowners' claim. That that decision represents the
common law of England and is binding on this court is beyond question and if, as a
b matter of law, the arbitrator was bound to apply the common law rule with regard to
interest, it must indeed be fatal to the shipowners.

What counsel for the shipowners submits, however, is that the arbitrator was not
bound to apply the common law rule for two reasons. First he submits that although an
English arbitrator is bound, in making his award, to apply the substantive rules of
English law, he is not bound by what are, on analysis, rules of practice; and the common
c law rule with regard to interest on sums due under contract is, he submits, no more than
a rule of practice, although of course a rule binding on all inferior courts in which it falls
to be applied. Second, and in any event, he relies on a long-standing rule in the former
High Court of Admiralty that interest will be awarded. The instant claim is one which
could, under s 1 of the Administration of Justice Act 1956, have been litigated in what
is now the Admiralty Court and, accordingly, it is submitted, it is open to an arbitrator
d called on to apply the rules of English law to apply the Admiralty rule in preference to
the common law rule.

It is only if one or other of these two submissions stands that this appeal can succeed,
for it is conceded that the construction of the Law Reform (Miscellaneous Provisions) Act
1934, on which the arbitrator relied in reaching his conclusion that no award of interest
under the Act in the shipowners' favour could be made, is correct. It produces the highly
e unsatisfactory result that an astute debtor could avoid the burden of interest by
discharging the principal claim before judgment and can still do so if he can persuade the
plaintiff to accept payment or if he pays before proceedings are commenced; but it
follows inevitably from the words used by the legislature.

This appeal therefore raises two distinct, although interrelated, questions.

First, it is clear, since the decision of this court in *Chandris v Isbrandtsen Moller Co Inc*
f [1950] 2 All ER 618, [1951] 1 KB 240, that an arbitrator has an implied power to award
interest on the analogy of the 1934 Act, but has he any power to award interest in
circumstances where the Act does not apply? Second, and if he has, can he make such an
award by way of damages for late payment, independently of any claim for the sum on
which the interest is computed?

As regards the first question, the view has been expressed by Lord Denning MR in *The
g Finix* [1978] 1 Lloyd's Rep 16 that an arbitrator has an inherent power to award interest,
which is not necessarily related to the 1934 Act or to its predecessor, the Civil Procedure
Act 1833. That view was not adopted by the other two members of the court in that case
(Geoffrey Lane and Cumming-Bruce LJJ) but it was not a view formed without some
apparent support from previous authority. In *Re Badger* (1819) 2 B & Ald 691, 106 ER
517 all matters in dispute in a suit in the Court of Chancery had been submitted to
h arbitration. What the suit was about is not clear from the report but the arbitration
involved the taking of accounts on both sides, accounts of rents received, of moneys
expended, of materials used and so on. The rule in equity seems to have been firmly
established by this time (see *Boddam v Riley* (1785) 2 Bro CC 2, 29 ER 1) that interest
would not be awarded on taking an account except on an account stated, the ground
being that only when an account was stated could it be said that there was a contract to
j pay. The arbitrator seems to have ignored this, and allowed interest on both sides. The
Court of King's Bench (Abbott CJ presiding) was moved to set aside the award on this
ground, but declined to do so on the ground that, whilst the arbitrator was bound by
rules of law, he was not bound by mere rules of practice. The case is one example of the
wider proposition laid down in *Knox v Simmonds* (1791) 3 Bro CC 358, 29 ER 582 that an
arbitrator has a greater latitude than the court in order to do complete justice between

the parties, but the source of the decision in *Re Badger* is interesting because it was Abbott CJ himself who, as Lord Tenterden, subsequently laid down the common law rule with *a* regard to interest on contractual claims, and was responsible for the Civil Procedure Act 1833, which gave only limited powers to juries to award interest in certain circumstances.

Little seems to have been heard of *Re Badger* in the next hundred years. It does not appear to have been treated as an arbitrator's charter to award interest at large, and indeed in *Edwards v Great Western Railway Co* (1851) 11 CB 588, 138 ER 603 it seems to have been conceded that the arbitrator in that case had no power to award interest save by *b* analogy with the 1833 Act. But law is not made by concession, and *Re Badger* has never been overruled. It was cited in the seventh edition of Russell on Arbitration in 1891 as authority for the proposition that an arbitrator is not fettered by mere rules of practice which the courts of law or equity have adopted for general convenience and that interest may be allowed by an arbitrator in cases where the court will not give it. The tenth edition in 1919 (at p 359) more cautiously stated that 'much reliance cannot be placed *c* [on the decision] now that arbitrations are regarded as a recognised form of litigation, to be conducted judicially'. In both the thirteenth edition (1935) and the fourteenth edition (1949) it is simply cited for the proposition that it is the arbitrator's duty to decide according to the legal rights of the parties. On the other hand, it is cited as still good law in both Hogg on Arbitration (1936) and Redman's Law of Arbitrations and Awards (5th Edn, 1932), and the current edition of Russell (19th Edn, 1979, p 231) says in terms *d* that—

'A distinction must be drawn between ... general rules of law and rules of practice of the courts, such as the rules laying down when interest will be given upon a sum of money due to a claimant. These last, it is within the discretion of an arbitrator to disregard.'

e

However, in *Podar Trading Co Ltd, Bombay v Francois Tagher, Barcelona* [1949] 2 All ER 62, [1949] 2 KB 277, a Divisional Court of the King's Bench Division decided that an arbitrator had no power to award interest. The question at issue in that case was, whether interest could be awarded in reliance on s 3 of the Law Reform (Miscellaneous Provisions) Act 1934. Since the section applied, in terms, only to courts of record, the court held that there was no power conferred on the arbitrator by the Act; but it had to *f* consider also the wider question whether, since the Act itself did not apply, there was an inherent power to award interest on the analogy of the Act. The contention that such a power was exercisable was rejected, as I read the decision, on the ground that an arbitrator must act in accordance with the law and that *London, Chatham and Dover Railway Co v South Eastern Railway Co* [1893] AC 429 precluded any award of interest apart from statute. The *Podar* case was overruled subsequently in *Chandris v Isbrandtsen* *g* *Moller Co Inc* [1950] 2 All ER 618, [1951] KB 240 on the ground that the power of an arbitrator to award interest did not derive from the statute but from the submission to arbitration which impliedly gave the arbitrator power to decide the rights of the parties in accordance with the law which would have been applicable if they had litigated the matter in court. Just as, therefore, in *Edwards v Great Western Railway Co* (1851) 11 CB 588, 138 ER 603 the court had upheld an award of interest on the analogy of the Civil *h* Procedure Act 1833 (which gave the power to award interest only to a jury) so an arbitrator equally had power to make an award by analogy with the 1934 Act. The *Chandris* case, however, left untouched the views expressed in the Divisional Court in the *Podar* case with regard to an arbitrator's power to award interest otherwise than by analogy with the statute. In the course of his judgment in *Podar*, Lord Goddard CJ, without casting any doubt on the correctness of the decision in *Re Badger*, expressed the *j* view that it formed no exception to the general rule that an arbitrator must act in accordance with the law. He explained the case on the ground that there was a practice of the Court of Chancery in the method of taking accounts which the arbitrator had not observed, inasmuch as, in taking accounts in equity, interest was not allowed on either side. If I may say so respectfully, that merely states the result of the case without explaining the decision. The equity practice was, in fact, one which, as I understand it,

related back to a positive rule, having the same genesis as the common law rule that
a interest was not allowed save on an account stated, since, until the account was stated,
there could be no implied promise to pay interst. I think that *Re Badger* was to this
extent an exception to the rule, and there is nothing in the subsequent cases which
convinces me that, so far as it states a principle, it is no longer good law.

Indeed, another example of a case in which the practice of arbitrators differed from the
rule applied by the courts is to be found in *Jugoslavenska Oceanska Plovidba v Castle*
b *Investment Co Inc, The Kozara* [1973] 3 All ER 498, [1974] 1 QB 292, where the Court of
Appeal upheld the right of an arbitrator to make an award in a foreign currency although
it had long been the rule that a judgment in an English court had to be in sterling (see
Manners v Pearson & Son [1898] 1 Ch 581; *United Railways of Havana and Regla Warehouses*
Ltd [1960] 2 All ER 332, [1961] AC 1007). The reason for that rule was, as Lord Reid said
in the *Havana* case [1960] 2 All ER 332 at 345, [1961] AC 1007 at 1052), primarily
c procedural and it could, I think, properly be described as a rule of practice. Having said
this, however, the question remains: how far does *Re Badger* assist the appellant
shipowners in the instant case? What, to begin with, is a 'rule of practice', and do the
common law limitations on awarding interest constitute such a rule? Counsel for the
shipowners frankly acknowledges that a classification of rules of law into those of
substance and those of practice presents obvious problems, not least because the method
d of classification may itself depend on the purpose for which it is to be made. The
common law rule, quite clearly expressed in the *London, Chatham and Dover Railway* case,
was that interest could not be given by way of damages for detention of a debt, and the
reason why the House of Lords felt it necessary to affirm it was that it had been too long
established for it to be reopened (see the speech of Lord Herschell LC [1893] AC 429 at
441). That, however, tells one nothing about the nature of the rule. For that, one is
e driven back to the authorities at the beginning of the nineteenth century on which the
rule rested, authorities referred to by Lord Herschell LC in his speech. Whether or not
interest was payable on sums due under contract but remaining unpaid was a question
on which there had been considerable conflict and confusion in the authorities prior to
1829. In *De Havilland v Bowerbank* (1807) 1 Camp 50, 170 ER 872 Lord Ellenborough in
the interests of certainty had attempted to lay down a defined range of cases in which
f interest could be awarded. Nevertheless, the matter clearly remained uncertain for some
years after that. In *Cameron v Smith* (1819) 2 B & Ald 305, 106 ER 378 Abbott CJ
(contrary to the view he subsequently adopted) clearly contemplated the possibility of
the jury awarding interest by way of damages, and Best CJ in the Court of Common Pleas
in *Arnott v Redfern* (1826) 3 Bing 353, 130 ER 549 expressed the view that the jury could
give interest in the shape of damages for money due under contract but wrongfully
g withheld after demand. The modern rule, to alleviate which the Civil Procedure Act
1833 was passed, was established by the Court of King's Bench in *Page v Newman* (1829)
9 B & C 378, 109 ER 140. There the court refused the plaintiff's claim for interest on a
debt which the defendant had failed to pay after demand. In his judgment Lord
Tenterden CJ rejected the views expressed by Best CJ in *Arnott v Redfern* on the ground
that it would create great inconvenience at nisi prius if the jury had, in each case, to
h determine whether proper steps had been taken to obtain payment so as to start interest
running. Thereafter the Civil Procedure Act 1833, s 28 enabled a jury 'on the trial of any
issue, or on any inquisition of damages' to allow interest on certain debts and in certain
limited circumstances.

It seems to me that the following propositions can be deduced from the cases. First,
there was, originally, no positive rule of English common law that any different principle
j applied to damages for breach of a contract to pay money from that which applied to
other breaches of contract. Second, the rule that the court would not award interest on
money withheld was originally a restriction not on the right but on the remedy, and was
introduced for procedural convenience, to promote uniformity and to absolve juries
from what was considered to be a difficult task. Third, the practice of the courts since the
rule was introduced in the early nineteenth century was so consistent and long established
that the House of Lords did not feel able, some sixty years later, to depart from it and

accepted it as a universal rule. These considerations, it may be argued, make it not inappropriate to describe the rule as a rule of practice rather than one of substantive law; *a* and there is a further and important consideration which fortifies this conclusion. It arises from counsel's second argument for the shipowners. Although in the nineteenth century interest would be awarded in the courts of common law only within the relatively narrow framework of the Civil Procedure Act 1833, a quite different practice was applied in relation to Admiralty cases both by the Admiralty Court, which applied the civil law to cases within its jurisdiction, and by the Court of Chancery, which *b* followed the Admiralty Court in Admiralty cases. The extent of that practice will require to be considered in more detail in connection with counsel's second submission for the shipowners. In the present context, however, it is significant because it does underline the view expressed above that the common law rule was in origin one which related rather to the practice of the common law courts than to the substantive law.

The difficulty that I feel, however, is that whatever may have been the origins of a rule *c* there does, as it seems to me, come a time when it has been so long observed, so entrenched and so authoritatively pronounced that it must be accepted as part of the substantive law applied by the courts.

It does not seem to me to be sufficient, to establish a rule as a rule of practice merely to say that the rule had its origins in practical or procedural considerations. Judged by that test, I think that many rules which are recognised as rules of substantive law could *d* be classified merely as rules of practice. It may be that, in some jurisprudence theory, it is possible to classify as a legal right some claims which will not be enforced by the court, but on a practical level the existence of a right depends on the existence of a remedy for its infringement. Speaking for myself, I would respectfully question whether the equitable rule considered in *Re Badger* (1819) 2 B & Ald 691, 106 ER 517 was merely a rule of practice, but, be that as it may, the position at law is clear and is established by a *e* decision which certainly binds this court. Speaking for myself, I do not see how one can apply a different rule to English arbitrations without discarding what is regarded as a basic implied term that the arbitrator shall decide in accordance with the rights of the parties under English law. Here the authorities show that for over a hundred years both the courts and the profession have accepted the proposition that in commercial arbitrations the arbitrator's power to award interest is no greater than the power of the *f* court or, to put it another way, that the power is a matter of substantive law and not merely a rule of practice which the arbitrator can disregard at his discretion. It was conceded in *Edwards v Great Western Railway Co* (1858) 11 CB 588, 138 ER 603; it was a matter of decision in *Podar Trading Co Ltd, Bombay v Francois Tagher, Barcelona* [1949] 2 All ER 62, [1949] 2 KB 277; and it was treated as common ground in *Chandris v Isbrandtsen Moller Co Inc* [1950] 2 All ER 618, [1951] KB 240, if, indeed, that case did not *g* implicitly decide the point. There has been some argument before this court with regard to the current practice of arbitrators and some material has been adduced which was not before the learned judge and which indicates that some arbitrators at least have adopted a practice of awarding interest outside the framework of the 1934 Act, although even here only, it appears, when associated with some other claim. Speaking for myself, I do not feel safe in relying on this. The learned judge, with a very much greater *h* experience in commercial matters of this sort than I have, stated in his judgment that he was unaware of any such practice. Although, therefore, my own interpretation of *Re Badger* is that it did, as a matter of decision, authorise a departure from the rule as to interest then applied in the Court of Chancery, I feel considerable doubt whether, having regard to what I conceive to be the consistent practice over the past 150 years, it can be relied on today to justify ignoring what is clearly established by the House of Lords as the *j* common law rule, however unsatisfactory that rule may be.

Counsel for the shipowners, however, submits that he can, in the instant case at least, arrive at the result for which he contends by a different route. He accepts, as he must accept, that the common law rule is that laid down in the *London, Chatham and Dover Railway* case, and that, if the dispute between the parties falls to be regulated by the common law, he cannot quarrel with the arbitrator's decision. The arbitrator applied

what he conceived to be the rule applicable in the Commercial Court and his award,
a subject to the *Re Badger* point dealt with above, cannot be attacked as being an error in
the application of that rule. But he applied the commercial rule reluctantly, as appears
from the award, and he did so, it seems, because he felt obliged to and had no discretion
in the matter. Here, counsel for the shipowners submits, he was in error. The claim
was, it is true, a claim which could have been litigated in the Commercial Court; but it
could equally well have been litigated in Admiralty, since s 1(1)(h) of the Administration
b of Justice Act 1956 includes in the Admiralty jurisdiction of the High Court 'any claim
arising out of any agreement relating to the carriage of goods in a ship or to the use or
hire of a ship'. This is accepted by counsel for the charterers. In exercising its Admiralty
jurisdiction, the High Court is, it is claimed, the successor to the former High Court of
Admiralty, and the contention is that in that court the common law rule regarding
interest as damages on money remaining unpaid never applied, and equally does not
c apply today in Admiralty cases. It was, therefore, it is argued, open to the arbitrator to
apply the old Admiralty rule to the case before him, and he was not, as he thought,
precluded from awarding damages by way of interest for late payment of demurrage.
    Now the jurisdiction of the old High Court of Admiralty was statutory, and it did not
include claims under charterparties. But that it was the practice of the Admiralty Court
to award interest in cases within its statutory jurisdiction where interest could not have
d been awarded at common law is beyond doubt, the leading case being *The Northumbria*
(1869) LR 3 A & E 6, in which Sir Robert Phillimore explained the rule and, incidentally,
made it quite clear that it was a conscious and deliberate departure from the rule applied
in the common law courts, and that the interest was awarded as damages for non-
payment of the money which was due at the date when the damage occurred. Sir Robert
Phillimore said this (at 10):
e
    'But it appears to me quite a sufficient answer to these authorities to say, that the
    Admiralty, in the exercise of an equitable jurisdiction, has proceeded upon another
    and a different principle from that on which the common law authorities appear to
    be founded. The principle adopted by the Admiralty Court has been that of the
    civil law, that interest was always due to the obligee when payment was not made,
    ex morâ of the obligor; and that, whether the obligation arose *ex contractu* or *ex*
f *delicto*.'

A little later he quotes in his judgment (at 13) from the judgment of Dr Lushington in
The Amalia (1864) 5 New Rep 164n, where the learned jurist said:

    'Upon what grounds, then, was interest given? Interest was not given by reason
    of indemnification for the loss, for the loss was the damage which had accrued; but
g interest was given for this reason, namely, that the loss was not paid at the proper
    time. If a man is kept out of his money, it is a loss in the common sense of the word,
    but a loss of a totally different description, and clearly to be distinguished from a loss
    which has occurred by damage done at the moment of collision.'

That rule was applied equally by the Court of Chancery in relation to Admiralty matters
h (see *Straker v Hartland* (1864) 2 Hem & M 570, 71 ER 584) and has consistently been
applied in the High Court of Admiralty and, after 1873 and up to 1956, in Admiralty
cases formerly justiciable by that court in the Probate, Divorce and Admiralty Division
of the High Court (see, for example, *The Kong Magnus* [1891] P 223, *The Napier Star*
[1933] P 136, *The Theems* [1938] P 197). It was applied also by the House of Lords in *The
Liesbosch* [1933] AC 449 at 469, [1933] All ER Rep 144 at 162–163; and it is interesting
j to see also that it was applied in an arbitration case by a Queen's Bench Divisional Court
in *Smith v Kirby* (1875) 1 QBD 131, 24 WR 207, Quain J remarking that it would be
absurd to sanction in the Queen's Bench Division a rule different from that prevailing in
the Courts of Chancery and Admiralty (see 24 WR 207 at 208). It should, however, be
noted that all these cases concern claims which fell within the jurisdiction of the old
High Court of Admiralty under the Admiralty Court Act 1861.
    Counsel for the charterers does not quarrel with the proposition that the Admiralty

rule was different from and existed alongside the common law rule, but he contends that
it applies only to loss or damage claims and has never yet, in any decided case, been *a*
applied to a late payment of money. The latter contention is, I think, certainly correct
but, although it is perfectly true that the reported cases are almost all cases of loss of
vessels or cargo by collision, I do not read the principle as being in any way restricted to
such cases. The civil law principle is, I think, simply restitutio in integrum and it is
noteworthy that Sir Robert Phillimore states it expressly as applying both to claims ex
delicto and to claims ex contracta. A case once much referred to in remoteness of *b*
damage cases in contract is The Parana (1877) 2 PD 118, a case of a claim by assignees
under s 6 of the Admiralty Court Act 1861. The Court of Appeal there reversed Sir
Robert Phillimore's decision that the assignees of a cargo delivered late as a result of
defects in the carrying ship were entitled to damages for loss of the market. What is
interesting in the present context, however, is that the court restored the report of the
registrar and merchants which had awarded damages by way of interest calculated on the *c*
capital value of the goods. It does not seem therefore as if the principle was confined to
cases of damage or total loss but covered also delay in delivery, and I can see no reason in
principle why it should not have applied to a late payment of demurrage *if* such a claim
had then been justiciable in the Admiralty Court under the 1861 Act.

The principle behind the old Admiralty rule is, as I understand it, a perfectly general
one that a man who has been put out of pocket by the wrongdoing of another should be *d*
restored to the position in which he would have been if the wrong had not occurred.
Thus in The Aldora [1975] 2 All ER 69, [1975] QB 748, a case to which the provisions of
s 3 of the 1934 Act applied, Brandon J, as an alternative ground for his decision, awarded
interest on a salvage award under the inherent Admiralty jurisdiction. Again that was
a case which would have been within the jurisdiction of the Admiralty Court under the
1861 Act. Counsel for the shipowners has, however, to meet the difficulty created by the *e*
decision of Hewson J in The Medina Princess [1962] 2 Lloyd's Rep 17, which both the
arbitrator and Parker J considered to be fatal to this alternative way of putting the
shipowners' claim. In that case the claim was for unpaid seamen's wages (similarly a
claim within the jurisdiction of the former High Court of Admiralty) and for interest
under the 1934 Act. The wages were paid after action brought and the claim for interest
was, on the pleadings, the only claim left. Hewson J regretfully felt bound to reject it *f*
because of the wording of s 3 which ruled out a claim for interest simpliciter when there
was no other sum for which judgment was sought or given. But he went on to consider
an alternative submission that such interest could be awarded under his inherent
jurisdiction. He said this (at 21):

> 'So far as claims for damage arising out of tort are concerned, I have little doubt
> that the Court may, and does, include as part of the damages interest upon the sum *g*
> finally found to be due in respect of that damage; but I have been referred to no case
> of any wages claim for breach of contract where the Court has ever been asked to do
> so, or has done so, as part of the damages for breach of contract. Certainly I can see
> no inherent jurisdiction in that matter.'

Parker J regarded this as an authority against the shipowners' contention and one *h*
which, although not binding on him, he ought to follow. For my part, I find some
difficulty in accepting The Medina Princess as an authoritative ruling on the limits of the
jurisdiction of the High Court to award damages by way of interest in a case which
formerly fell within the jurisdiction of the High Court of Admiralty. Unhappily the
report does not contain any résumé of counsel's argument, but it is at least questionable
how fully the matter can have been gone into. The action was an action in rem and the *j*
application was on motion for judgment in default of defence so that the argument
necessarily had to be limited to what was claimed on the face of the statement of claim.
While it is true that counsel was unable to make good his claim for interest under the
inherent jurisdiction because the learned judge was unpersuaded that he had the
jurisdiction to award it, my doubt whether he intended to give any authoritative ruling

a on the extent of the Admiralty jurisdiction is fortified by his closing remarks in the subsequent discussion as to costs where he is recorded as saying (at 23):

> 'I have not said that they are not entitled to interest. I said that this method of asking for it does not appeal to me.'

Certainly, so far as the short passage which I have quoted from the judgment seeks to suggest that the inherent jurisdiction is limited to claims in tort, it seems to be inaccurate.
b   In my judgment the case is but slender authority against the proposition that such a claim can be entertained under the Admiralty jurisdiction.

What I question, however, is the assumption which lies at the root of counsel's submission for the shipowners, namely that, because the claim is one which now, since s 1 of the Administration of Justice Act 1956, falls within the enlarged Admiralty jurisdiction of the High Court, it therefore follows that the High Court must or can
c apply to it the same civil law rules as those previously applied by the old Admiralty Court to cases previously within the jurisdiction of that court. It does not in my judgment follow that, because the former High Court of Admiralty applied to matters falling within its statutory jurisdiction a rule different from that applicable in the courts of common law and because the jurisdiction of that court was statutorily transferred in 1873 to the Admiralty Division of the High Court, that rule falls subsequently and
d inexorably to be applied also to a quite different subject matter, formerly within the jurisdiction only of another division, simply by reason of the statutory inclusion of that subject matter within the jurisdiction of the Admiralty Division. That result could, in my judgment, follow only if there were some context in the statute which enlarges the jurisdiction so to indicate, and I can see none. The history of the Admiralty Court up to the nineteenth century is one of struggle with the common law courts to capture
e jurisdiction in contractual matters falling within the latter's jurisdiction, with the common law courts carrying the day except in matters where, owing to the nature of the claim, the suitor could not obtain an adequate remedy in those courts. The jurisdiction of the Admiralty Court was statutorily defined in ss 4 to 13 of the Admiralty Court Act 1861 and it did not include purely contractual claims under a charterparty such as the present. The jurisdiction of that court was transferred to the High Court by s 16 of the
f Supreme Court of Judicature Act 1873 and it was provided by s 23 that, in the absence of special provision in the Act and the rules, it should be exercised in the same manner as nearly as may be as it might have been exercised by the court from which jurisdiction was transferred. That simply meant that in those cases previously falling within the Admiralty Court jurisdiction, the High Court continued to apply the same rules, but the Act did not extend those rules to any other case. Section 21 of the 1875 amending Act
g preserved the procedural rules, where not inconsistent with the Act or the rules—

> 'in such and the like cases, and for such and the like purposes, as those to which they would have been applicable in the respective courts of which the jurisdiction is so transferred . . .'

It is in fact quite clear from the authorities that the High Court of Admiralty, and
h subsequently the Probate, Divorce and Admiralty Division of the High Court, did not have any general jurisdiction to entertain claims for demurrage under charterparties. One of the curiosities of the Admiralty jurisdiction was that, although the County Courts' Admiralty Jurisdiction Amendment Act 1869 conferred on county courts exercising Admiralty jurisdiction a power to entertain purely contractual claims in words very similar to those employed in s 1(1)(h) of the Administration of Justice Act
j 1956, this power was not one enjoyed by the High Court of Admiralty (or subsequently by the High Court) until 1926 except on an appeal or transfer from the county court (see *The Alina* (1880) 5 Ex D 227, *The Beldis* [1936] P 51 at 62). I find difficulty in accepting that the 1869 Act, simply by including such cases in the Admiralty jurisdiction of the county court, had the effect of conferring on county courts a power to award interest in cases where no such power existed in any division of the High Court.

The Probate, Divorce and Admiralty jurisdiction was enlarged and defined by s 5 of the Administration of Justice Act 1920 and s 22 of the Supreme Court of Judicature *a* (Consolidation) Act 1925, but there was nothing in those Acts which extended practices peculiar to the former Admiralty Court beyond those cases in which it had exercised jurisdiction before 1873 and the Act contained, in s 103, a similar procedural saving as regards rules, forms and methods of procedure previously in force, restricting them to the 'like cases and for the like purposes' in and for which they would previously have been applicable. *b*

Equally I can find nothing in the Administration of Justice Act 1956 which would have the effect of applying the rules and practice of the former Admiralty Court to the wider subject matter included in the High Court Admiralty jurisdiction by s 1 of the Act, and there is nothing in s 2 of the Administration of Justice Act 1970, to which the present Admiralty Court owes its title, which would produce that result. Part I of that Act was passed to enable the United Kingdom to ratify and comply with its obligations *c* under the International Convention Relating to the Arrest of Seagoing Ships (Cmd 8954) signed four years earlier (see *The Jade* [1976] 1 All ER 920 at 923, [1976] 1 WLR 430 at 434); and it would, to my mind, be an extraordinary consequence if the legislature, simply by including particular existing types of commercial claim heretofore litigated in the Queen's Bench Division in what is described as 'the Admiralty jurisdiction' (the evident intention being simply to enable them to be raised in the manner prescribed by *d* s 3 of the Act by an action in rem), should have opened up a whole new vista of claims which could not previously have been successfully raised in any court. If counsel for the shipowners is right, the legislature has, by a sidewind, freed one branch of the same division of the same High Court from the shackles of the *London, Chatham and Dover Railway* case, leaving the rule standing in all other branches and divisions, so that a plaintiff can produce a quite different legal result by an astute choice of the court in *e* which he commences his proceedings. For my part, I find it impossible to imagine that the legislature can have intended so curious a result or to accept that it did in fact flow simply from an enlarged definition of the Admiralty jurisdiction.

Accordingly, although with the same regret as that felt by the learned judge, I feel compelled to the conclusion that his decision was right.

I should perhaps add that I do not dissent at all from the view expressed by Lord *f* Denning MR that modern conditions require an urgent reappraisal of the common law rule with regard to interest. My doubt is only whether *this* court has the power to put it into effect even in the limited sphere of arbitration without altering fundamentally the implied basis on which English arbitrations are conducted.

Equally, if I am wrong, I can see no reason at all why an award of interest should be linked necessarily to an award of a principal sum in the proceedings. The distinction *g* between interest and damages is, as Brandon J has said, entirely artificial and unreal, and no one who, in the times in which we now live, enjoys banking facilities by way of overdraft could be in any doubt at all that he suffers damage by late payment.

But, for the reasons that I have endeavoured to state, I would regretfully dismiss this appeal.

h

WATKINS LJ (read by Lord Denning MR). Dutch shipowners, the appellants, are in dispute with Yugoslav charterers, the respondents, who by a contract between them of 24th February 1975 hired the owners' ships to carry cement from Yugoslavia to Nigeria. After the completion of 12 voyages the contract was suspended. The parties to it were displeased with one another. On the one hand, the charterers, in respect of the twelfth voyage, had overpaid $30,000 for demurrage and claimed its return from the *j* owners. On the other hand, the charterers, in respect of most, if not all, of the other voyages, in breach of contract paid demurrage in some instances late and in others very late. So the owners claimed interest from the respective due dates of payment to the actual dates of payment and, further, as damages, interest on that interest from the date of payments of demurrage to the date of an award of interest by an arbitrator.

Arbitration of disputes arising out of it was by the contract to take place in London.

It took place in London before Mr Clark, a very experienced arbitrator, on 5th July 1979.
By that time all demurrage owing by the charterers to the owners had been paid.

   At or before the arbitration proceedings the owners conceded the overpayment
reclaimed. Accordingly the arbitrator made an award to the charterers for this sum with
interest at 7½%. The claims for interest by the owners he rejected, effectively for the
reason that he decided in the absence of any contractual term enabling him to do so he
had in all the circumstances no jurisdiction to award interest, stating:

> 'Accordingly, I hold that since on any view the principal sum in this case had been
> paid, and I have not been asked to make any award in respect of demurrage, I have
> no jurisdiction to make any award of interest. I should add that I share the
> reluctance expressed by Hewson J. in The "MEDINA PRINCESS" ([1962] 2 Lloyd's Rep
> 17) in reaching this conclusion. I wish to make it clear that the rule, if it be the rule,
> that in the absence of a term in the contract to the contrary effect, a debtor can delay
> payment as long as he likes and can avoid liability for interest by paying the
> principal sum at any time, is one which does not accord with justice nor commercial
> commonsense, especially in times of acute shortage of cash. It was submitted on
> behalf of the Owners that, as the Admiralty Court has jurisdiction over demurrage
> claims, and as this Court regularly awards interest (see The "ALDORA" ([1975] 2 All
> ER 69, [1975] QB 748)), I should follow their practice. I decided that the appropriate
> Court of record for me to follow is the Commercial Court, and I feel bound by the
> "MEDINA PRINCESS" authority and cannot use my discretion. As far as the
> counterclaim for interest upon interest is concerned, in view of my decision upon
> the main counterclaim, it is inapplicable, but if I had been called upon to decide it
> I would have decided that it could not be awarded under the 1934 Act.'

   Obviously the arbitrator found no comfort in this conclusion. He felt obliged to act
other than in accord with justice and common sense. Arbitrators, Mr Clark included, in
the City of London are renowned for their conspicuous ability in resolving justly and
fairly disputes which arise out of commercial transactions. This is an international
renown, as is evidenced by the number of disputes referred to them by foreign companies
including shipowners and charterers of ships who neither are registered in nor have any
connection with this country. These companies are aware that the decision of the
arbitrators can be, and often are, reviewed where, for instance, there is error on the face
of the record by our courts.

   In this case the owners appealed to Parker J complaining of such an error. His
judgment, one of admirable clarity, was concluded in what was, for the owners, a
disappointing agreement with the arbitrator's decision. So they look to this court for,
one supposes, judgments which accord with justice and common sense.

   Need Mr Clark have decided that he had no jurisdiction to award interest and, as
damages, interest on interest? Apparently not, if the practice of his fellow arbitrators is
is anything to go by. In a letter dated 30th January 1981 Mr Donald Davies, himself a
very experienced arbitrator, wrote as follows:

> 'I refer to the Judgment of the Honourable Mr. Justice Parker of the 5th
> November 1979 in the above case. Towards the end of his Judgment at page 12, Mr.
> Justice Parker refers to whether commercial arbitrators have in practice awarded
> interest on sums not due because already paid. The learned Judge indicated that in
> his view no such practice existed. However, you may like to know, because I feel
> that it may be of interest to the Court of Appeal, that until the judgment of Mr.
> Justice Parker it was my practice, and indeed that of a number of my arbitrator
> colleagues, to award interest where money was paid late provided that I was making
> an Award on another issue in the reference at the same time. I have spoken to the
> following maritime arbitrators, Cedric Barclay, Bruce Harris, Ralph Kingsley,
> Michael Mabbs, John Potter, Robert Reed and John Selwyn, who confirm that their
> practice was, until the Judgment of Mr. Justice Parker, the same as mine.'

In the present case there were cross-claims in the reference to arbitrators: there was an issue other than the claim for interest. Presumably then, Mr Donald Davies and those whom he names in his letter would have entertained the claim for interest, if not that for *a* interest on interest.

This practice is, so we were informed, unknown at least to some experienced practitioners at the commercial Bar and to Parker J. However that may be, and no matter how little known the practice is, it seems to me to be in these days of erratic fluctuations in the value of money in the counting houses of the world and high interest rates to have the twin merits of justice and common sense.   *b*

But arbitrators must have a warrant, a jurisdiction, that is to say, for what they do. This is, of course, only another way of saying that they must not act outside the law of this country. They may ignore the practices which these courts decide should govern them in one way or another from time to time, but they may not act in a way either prohibited by or not permitted by the common law, equity or other judge-made law or by the laws of Parliament.   *c*

This, so it is said, is what Mr Clark would have done had he awarded interest to the owners. He could not have acted within the provisions of s 3(1) of the Law Reform (Miscellaneous Provisions) Act 1934, the common law gave him no power to award interest, there is no equitable power to do that, and the power of the Admiralty Court to deal with claims for demurrage does not extend to awarding interest when the principal debt has been paid before the court is able to give judgment for it.   *d*

There is no doubt that the arbitrator could not have derived the power to award interest from s 3(1), or from any non-statutory jurisdiction other than that which may be exercised by the Admiralty Court or by virtue of the common law.

Accordingly, his power, if any, to award interest must be derived either from the common law or from the jurisdiction of Admiralty or from both.

It was submitted to this court that for almost two centuries, at least, the common law *e* has allowed the grant of interest on outstanding debt. So far as arbitrators are concerned, much reliance was placed by the owners on *Re Badger* (1819) 2 B & Ald 691, 166 ER 517, the ghost of which I imagined during argument still stalks around the Royal Courts of Justice. Alas! I do not believe this to be true. *Re Badger* was, I think, a transitory figure which no doubt in its context fulfilled a certain need in the early part of the last century, after when it subsided into disuse and ineffectiveness. That it is no longer good law *f* emerges, I think, as the opinion of Lord Goddard CJ, from *Podar Trading Co Ltd, Bombay v Francois Tagher, Barcelona* [1949] 2 All ER 62 at 67, [1949] 2 KB 277 at 289. Giving the judgment of the Divisional Court in that case, he held also that arbitrators have no greater powers than the courts possess to award interest. This part of the judgment was not, I think, overruled by anything said in *Chandris v Isbrandtsen Moller Co Inc* [1950] 2 All ER 618, [1951] KB 240.   *g*

No reference to *Re Badger* was made in *London, Chatham and Dover Railway Co v South Eastern Railway Co* [1893] AC 429 at 437, from which one finds the authoritative voice of Lord Herschell LC speaking thus:

'But, my Lords, the appellants contended that even although they might not under the terms of Lord Tenterden's Act be entitled to interest, yet interest might *h* be given by way of damages in respect of the wrongful detention of their debt. I confess that I have considered this part of the case with every inclination to come to a conclusion in favour of the appellants, to the extent at all events, if it were possible, of giving them interest from the date of the action; and for this reason, that I think that when money is owing from one party to another and that other is driven to have recourse to legal proceedings in order to recover the amount due to him, the *j* party who is wrongfully withholding the money from the other ought not in justice to benefit by having that money in his possession and enjoying the use of it, when the money ought to be in the possession of the other party who is entitled to its use. Therefore, if I could see my way to do so, I should certainly be disposed to give the appellants, or anybody in a similar position, interest upon the amount withheld from the time of action brought at all events. But I have come to the conclusion, a   upon a consideration of the authorities, agreeing with the Court below, that it is not possible to do so, although no doubt in early times the view was expressed that interest might be given under such circumstances by way of damages.'

I have not been persuaded by any of the other authorities and quotations from textbooks relied on by the owners that the law on the grant of interest by the courts and by arbitrators has changed since Lord Herschell LC pronounced on it in that way.

b   With the exception of his introduction of the decision in The Medina Princess [1962] 2 Lloyd's Rep 17 into his reasoning, I agree with (generally speaking, for the reasons he provides) the conclusion of Parker J that there is no power at common law to grant interest and that the arbitrator was right to regard himself as disabled from awarding interest on that ground.

I think otherwise, however, about the power which arises out of the jurisdiction to grant interest in the Admiralty Court. Of this I take at the outset leave to adopt the comments made by Oliver LJ on The Medina Princess, save that I regard it as having no persuasive authority so as to support the charterers' contention that the claim for interest made in the present case cannot be entertained under the Admiralty jurisdiction. No relevant authorities seem to have been quoted by Hewson J, and there is no indication in the report of the case that the inherent jurisdiction of the Admiralty Court was argued before him in any other than at most a superficial way.

d   There is no doubt that in awarding interest the Admiralty Court is exercising an equitable jurisdiction; this is a power to be applied in a suitable case at the discretion of the judge. The Admiralty Court has jurisdiction to hear and determine claims for demurrage, but there is no record of it having, so far as I know, awarded interest in claims involving demurrage unpaid at the time of judgment or on demurrage paid late but before judgment.

e   I see nothing incongruous about the Admiralty Court in its modern setting retaining undiluted its inherent equitable jurisdiction, as I think it has done; nor am I affronted with the prospect of a claimant using what I believe is a choice available to him, to decide which court of record he will commence proceedings in, even though his choice is solely motivated by the presence of an advantageous jurisdiction in one which is lacking in all other courts.

f   By the same token I should think it neither surprising nor wrong if an arbitrator were to decide to derive his power to award interest from what he understood was the only remaining court with inherent jurisdiction to award interest, notwithstanding that all other courts, the Commercial Court included, are without it. Indeed, if in that state of mind, that, in my opinion, he should in order to do justice proceed to do if in his judgment an award of interest is called for.

g   Arguments which have led to these observations are, although I have thought it necessary to touch on them, in my opinion, almost if not wholly irrelevant. The sole point is not whether the Admiralty Court has retained its inherent jurisdiction but whether this jurisdiction extends to the granting of interest on principal already paid and, as damages, in the circumstances of this case of interest on interest.

I cannot understand why that question should be answered otherwise than in the affirmative, seeing that it surely is inequitable nowadays anyway to behave as these charterers did.

There are no limitations to the extent of the Admiralty jurisdiction that I can see, although in its Report on Interest the Law Commission (Law Com 88 (1978); Cmnd 7229) refers in its passages on awards of interest in Admiralty to the limited number of cases in which interest may be awarded as part of the Admiralty jurisdiction.

j   In The Aldora [1975] 2 All ER 69 at 74, [1975] 1 QB 748 at 753 Brandon J stated:

'Having considered the matter carefully I do not see any reason why the principle on which the Admiralty Court proceeded in awarding interest in damage actions should not be applied also to salvage actions. The principle is stated to be an equitable one, and, so far as equity is concerned, I should have thought that a person claiming salvage was not less entitled to interest on this claim than a person claiming for damage. Indeed it might be thought that he was even more entitled. The main argument against applying the principle to salvage actions is that it does *a* not appear to have been done before. When what is involved is no more than applying an equitable principle, long established in one class of case, to another class of case in which it is equally or even more appropriate, I do not think that this argument should prevail.'

I think the present case involves claims which fall within the proper application of the equitable principle referred to by Brandon J and would be so regarded now, at any rate *b* by the Admiralty Court.

It may well be that claims of many other kinds entertainable by the Admiralty Court in respect of which interest is claimed and which is not provided for by the Law Reform (Miscellaneous Provisions) Act 1934 would come to be likewise regarded. Just as the categories of negligence are never closed, the power of the Admiralty Court to use its equitable jurisdiction to award interest is not governed by the extent of its usage up to *c* the present time.

I would hold that the arbitrator had the power to do justice and apply common sense to the owners' claims for interest through the Admiralty jurisdiction. In using this power he is not debarred by the provisions of the Law Reform (Miscellaneous Provisions) Act 1934 from awarding damages by way of interest on interest.

Accordingly, I would allow this appeal.   *d*

Appeal allowed and claim remitted to arbitrator. Leave to appeal to the House of Lords granted.

Solicitors: *Thomas Cooper & Stibbard* (for the shipowners); *William A Crump & Son* (for the charterers).

Sumra Green   Barrister.   *e*

Townsend and another v Stone Toms & Partners (a firm) and others

f

COURT OF APPEAL, CIVIL DIVISION
EVELEIGH, WATKINS LJJ AND SIR DAVID CAIRNS
6th, 7th, 11th MAY 1981

Practice – Payment into court – Joint or alternative claims – Defendants sued jointly or in the alternative – Payment in by one of several defendants – Plaintiff bringing action against architect *g* *and builder for defective work – Mutual or overlapping items in claims against architect and builder – Payment in by builder accepted by plaintiff in satisfaction of claim against builder – Whether architect and builder sued 'jointly' or 'in the alternative' in respect of mutual or overlapping items – Whether acceptance of payment in by builder barring claim against architect – RSC Ord 22, r 3(4).*

h

The plaintiffs brought an action against three defendants, a firm of architects, a plumber and a building company, claiming damages in respect of work done on the plaintiffs' house. The plaintiffs alleged against the first defendants, the architects, defective design and defective supervision of the work, and against the third defendants, the builders, defective workmanship. The claim against the second defendant, the plumber, was not pursued. The third defendants paid £30,000 into court in 'satisfaction of all the causes *j* of action in respect of which the Plaintiffs claim' and the plaintiffs accepted that sum 'in satisfaction of the causes of action in respect of which it was paid in and in respect of which the Plaintiffs claim against that Defendant'. A consent order was made in those terms and judgment was entered against the third defendants. At the trial of the claim against them, the first defendants contended that there were mutual and overlapping items in the claims against the first and third defendants and that the plaintiffs were *a* barred from pursuing their claim against them in respect of such items because under RSC Ord 22, r 3(4)[a] the effect of the acceptance of the third defendants' payment into court was to stay all proceedings against the third defendants and 'any other defendant sued jointly with or in the alternative to [them]'. The judge upheld that submission and the plaintiffs appealed.

Held – On the natural meaning of RSC Ord 22, r 3(4) a person was 'sued jointly' only if *b* he was sued in respect of a joint liability, and not when he was merely joined together with another or others as one of a number of defendants in the same proceedings, since otherwise the reference to a defendant being sued 'in the alternative' would be otiose. Since there were separate causes of action against the first defendants and the third defendants and they were not sued in respect of a joint liability, the plaintiffs were not barred by r 3(4) from pursuing the whole of their claim against the first defendants. The *c* appeal would accordingly be allowed (see p 694 *g* to *j*, p 695 *f* to *h*, p 696 *f g* and p 697 *a*, post).

Notes

For payment into court by one or more of several defendants, see 30 Halsbury's Laws (3rd Edn) 382, para 711, and for cases on payment into court where there are joint and *d* alternative claims, see 51 Digest (Repl) 582, 2136–2138.

Cases referred to in judgments

Brooke v Bool [1928] 2 KB 578, [1928] All ER Rep 155, 97 LJKB 511, 139 LT 376, DC, 45 Digest (Repl) 284, 72.

Holbrow v Swan & Moore (Assessors) Ltd [1975] Court of Appeal Transcript 257.

Parkes v Knowles [1957] 3 All ER 600, [1957] 1 WLR 1040, 13 Digest (Reissue) 501, 4140.
e

Cases also cited

Hutchinson v Harris (1978) 10 BLR 19, CA.

Isaacs & Sons v Salbstein [1916] 2 KB 139, [1916–17] All ER Rep 386, CA.

Interlocutory appeal

f By a writ issued on 20th February 1979 the plaintiffs, Colin Michael Victor Townsend and Mary Hay McKay Townsend, his wife, brought an action against the first defendants, Stone Toms & Partners, a firm of architects, the second defendant, A L M Gough, a plumbing consultant, and the third defendants, John Laing Construction Ltd, a building company, claiming damages for breaches of duty under various contracts relating to certain works carried out at Frith Farm, Frome, Somerset in 1973. On 31st January and *g* 13th November 1980 the third defendants paid sums totalling £30,000 into court in satisfaction of all the causes of action in respect of which the plaintiffs claimed against them and that sum was accepted by the plaintiffs in satisfaction of their claim against the third defendants. On 17th December 1980 his Honour Judge John Newey QC as official referee ordered by consent that there should be payment out and judgment entered against the third defendants. On 30th April 1981 his Honour James Leonard, sitting as *h* a deputy circuit judge for official referees' business, ordered that all proceedings in the action against the first defendants in so far as there were mutual and overlapping items in the claim against the first and third defendants be stayed by reason of the acceptance by the plaintiffs of the payment into court made by the third defendants. The plaintiffs appealed against that order. The second defendant took no part in the proceedings at any stage and the claim against him was not pursued. The facts are set out in the judgment *j* of Eveleigh LJ.

A J Butcher QC and *D G Valentine* for the plaintiffs.
D H Gardam QC and *Michael Harvey* for the first defendants.
The third defendants were not represented.

_____

a   Rule 3(4) is set out at p 693 *c*, post

EVELEIGH LJ. The plaintiffs in this case were building owners who sued architects and plumbing contractors and also the main building contractor in respect of their work *a* in relation to reconstruction of the plaintiffs' house. The pleadings in the case are, as Deputy Judge Leonard stated, complex and voluminous. Fortunately, the point that arises on this appeal is a short one, and I therefore do not propose to go into the details of the statement of claim, but to summarise it in the way that was done before the learned deputy judge by counsel, and for that purpose will quote from the judgment. The learned judge said: *b*

'... I think it is sufficient to accept the summary made by counsel for the plaintiffs, and his summary of claims made against the first defendants [that is to say, the architects] is as follows. Category one, defective design; that is a case against the first defendants as architects only. The second category is defective supervision by the first defendants, resulting in bad work, which the third defendants had done and were sued for, getting passed and which will have to be made good. The *c* damage claimed is the same as was claimed against the third defendants, but the breaches of duty arise from different contracts. The third category is over-certification by the architects in various respects, including certification in respect of bad work. This claim is primarily against the first defendants, but it may also be recovered from the third defendants. In the latter event there is still a claim for interest because the plaintiffs have been kept out of their money. There is also a *d* fourth category which counsel for the plaintiffs added and which he specified thus: claim for loss of amenity which will break down, he says, under one head or another, though there is likely to be some overlapping.'

One may shortly state the position, then, as follows. The second defendant does not enter into the picture for the purpose of this appeal. The first defendants are architects, *e* and against them it is alleged, in so far as it is relevant for this appeal, that they failed properly to supervise the work. Against the third defendants, the builders, in so far as is relevant for this appeal, it is alleged they did work badly and are liable therefore to the plaintiffs. In so far as lack of supervision is claimed, it is also claimed in the statement of claim that the first defendants should be liable in respect of loss of amenities suffered by the plaintiffs. I do not find it necessary for this appeal to go more deeply into the precise *f* pleading or the causes of action, or whether or not the second plaintiff is suing in contract or tort or both, because the position has come down to a quite narrow one, namely: where there is overlapping of the items of damage alleged as a result of bad workmanship and also alleged to be the subject of a failure to supervise, should the action be stayed when money paid into court by the builder has been taken out?

The builder in this case, the third defendants, put in a defence denying liability, and *g* also counterclaimed in respect of their charges to the extent which they alleged that they had not been paid. They made two payments in, the second of which was accompanied by a notice dated 13th November 1980 and reads as follows:

'TAKE NOTICE that JOHN LAING CONSTRUCTION LIMITED, the Third Defendants have increased the payment into Court of £7,500 made on the 31st day of January 1980 and have paid the further sum of £22,500 into Court, the said £22,500 together *h* with the said sum of £7,500 is in satisfaction of all the causes of action in respect of which the Plaintiffs claim and after taking into account and satisfying the above-named Defendants' cause of action for £32,363·92. in respect of which it counterclaims.'

By a notice dated 4th December the plaintiffs took out the £30,000 (and I quote from *j* their notice) 'in satisfaction of the causes of action in respect of which it was paid in and in respect of which the Plaintiffs claim against that Defendant'. Subsequently, an application was made to his Honour Judge John Newey QC on 17th December 1980, when he ordered by consent that there should be payment out in the terms of the notice and the acceptance. He further ordered that the first and second plaintiffs recover against the third defendants their costs of the action attributable to the first and second plaintiffs'

claim, and that judgment be given in favour of the first and second plaintiffs against the
a third defendants, and the third defendants' counterclaim be dismissed, in accordance
with the terms of the payment in.

The matter then came on for hearing before the learned deputy judge on 30th April
1981, when a preliminary point was taken to the effect that, in so far as there were
mutual or overlapping items in the claim against the architect and the builder in relation
to lack of supervision and bad workmanship, the action against the architect should be
b stayed, on the ground that the payment in by the third defendants had been accepted.

In support of that application, indeed, the only basis for it, was the wording of RSC
Ord 22, r 3(4), which reads as follows:

'On the plaintiff accepting any money paid into court all further proceedings in
the action or in respect of the specified cause or causes of action, as the case may be,
to which the acceptance relates, both against the defendant making the payment
c and against any other defendant sued jointly with or in the alternative to him shall
be stayed.'

It is not wholly clear to me in this case whether it was alleged that the architect was sued
jointly or in the alternative, that is to say, in the argument before Judge Leonard, but, as
I understand it, the contention in this court is that the expression 'sued jointly' is apt to
d cover the case against the architect because it is said in respect of certain items, whilst in
strict law the cause of action is a separate one, the same damage was covered by the
claim. Judge Leonard took the view that Ord 22, r 3(4) did apply and in consequence
counsel worked out in detail the particular items in the statement of claim that would be
covered by such a decision. In other words, where there was an overlapping of the claim,
counsel drafted the appropriate order, which subsequently became the order of the court,
e to stay the action against the architect in respect of those items. It is against the
judgment on that preliminary matter that the plaintiffs now appeal to this court. The
point is a short one. What is the meaning of Ord 22, r 3(4), in particular the words 'sued
jointly with or in the alternative to him'?

On behalf of the first defendants it has been submitted, as I have said, that 'sued jointly'
does not mean 'sued in respect of joint liability'; it means simply joined together in the
f same proceedings as defendants, or, if any limitation is to be put on it, sued together in
the same proceedings as defendants in respect of the same damage.

Some support was invoked from a note in the Supreme Court Practice 1979 (vol 1,
para 22/4/1, p 379) under Ord 22, r 4. Order 22, r 4(1)(a) reads:

'Where a plaintiff accepts any sum paid into Court and that sum was paid into
Court—(a) by some but not all of the defendants sued jointly or in the alternative
g by him ... the money in Court shall not be paid out except under paragraph (2) or
in pursuance of an order of the Court, and the order shall deal with the whole costs
of the action or of the cause of action to which the payment relates, as the case may
be.'

The note to that rule under the heading 'Several Defendants' reads: 'The term "sued
h jointly" in this rule does not mean the same thing as "joint liability", but only that other
defendants have been joined together in the action.'

The authority for that note does not appear, but it is not unreasonable to assume that
it was prompted by *Parkes v Knowles* as reported in [1957] 3 All ER 600, which has been
relied on in this court by the first defendants as authority for their contention that 'sued
jointly' does not mean 'sued in respect of joint liability', but 'joined together in the same
j proceedings as defendants'. That was a motor accident case in which an innocent
passenger, as he is sometimes called, sued two defendants, the drivers of the two vehicles
involved in the collision. One made a payment in, which was acceptable to the plaintiff,
and counsel appeared before the judge, Lynskey J, at Birmingham Assizes, to inform him
that it was the plaintiff's desire to take the money out and further to ask him to decide
the position as to costs in relation to the other defendant. As the money accepted was
within the jurisdiction of the county court, the question whether the costs should be paid

on a county court scale or a High Court scale arose. Counsel has submitted that that
application, being made as it was, recognised that Ord 22, r 4 meant that 'sued jointly' *a*
was not limited to the case of people sued in respect of joint liability, because in that case
there was no suggestion of joint liability. Further, reliance was placed on some words of
the learned judge, who, after he had delivered his judgment saying what the appropriate
scale of costs for the other defendant was, then said ([1957] 3 All ER 600 at 603):

> 'Under R.S.C., Ord. 22, r. 4, it is not open now, where there are two defendants, *b*
> for the plaintiff to take the money out. He must make an application. Therefore,
> until he comes before the court to make the application he cannot take the money
> out. My order as to costs will include not merely costs up to date of payment in, but
> also the costs of this application.'

However, be that as it may, the decision of the learned judge was in relation to costs.
That was the issue that he had to determine, namely the scale of costs. He said ([1957] *c*
3 All ER 600 at 601, [1957] 1 WLR 1040 at 1041): 'The application now comes before me
under R.S.C., Ord. 22, r. 4(3), on the question what order as to costs shall be made.' Then
he elaborated on the issue. Nowhere was it argued that the leave of the court was
necessary, or unnecessary, for the payment out, and nowhere did a question arise as to
whether the action could be stayed as against the other defendant. It was, as I say,
concerned solely with the question of costs. I also take the view that when it was *d*
intimated to the court that the plaintiff was accepting the liability of one defendant to the
exclusion of that of the other, as was the case, it could rightly be regarded at that stage as
a case where defendants were being sued in the alternative. In a running-down case
where two defendants are blamed on facts similar to those in *Parkes v Knowles*, each
defendant is blamed, but in strict pleading the claim was made severally against them as
separate tortfeasors in respect of the same damage, and also against each in the alternative, *e*
because it very often turns out, as the plaintiff can anticipate, that one defendant alone
will be found liable to him. Therefore, I take the view that *Parkes v Knowles* can be
treated as a case of persons sued in the alternative, and the obiter dicta at the end of
Lynskey J's judgment could be regarded as applying to such a case, or the facts of the case
then before him. But, however that might be, I do not regard that case as deciding the
question that this court has to decide. The principle which is contended for in this case *f*
was never in issue and in no way could be said to be the ratio decidendi of Lynskey J's
decision.

So, I look at this problem for the moment, as indeed I think all such problems of
construction should be treated, by looking at the wording of the rule with which we are
concerned. It says there 'any defendant sued jointly with or in the alternative to him'.
For myself, I would regard the natural meaning of the words 'sued jointly' as relating to *g*
the case of a claim made where there is one cause of action, but more than one defendant
liable thereon jointly with the other or others. The presence of the words 'or in the
alternative to him', to my mind, strengthens that conclusion, because if 'sued jointly'
meant, as counsel for the first defendants contends, any defendant in the same action,
there would be no need to refer specifically to one sued in the alternative. A defendant
who is sued in the alternative is sued for his own several liability, and if any defendant *h*
is covered by this rule because of the words 'sued jointly' so would a person sued in the
alternative be covered, without need for any special reference to him. Counsel for the
first defendants says we can read into the rule a limitation, which limitation may make
it necessary to have specific reference to an alternative defendant, namely the limitation
that the defendants must be sued in respect of the same damage. For myself, I ask: if one
is going to read into it the limitation 'in respect of the same damage', why should not one *j*
read into it the limitation 'in respect of the same cause of action', in other words joint
liability? If it is to be one or the other, I would prefer the construction that means in
respect of joint liability because, strictly speaking, one is not reading it into the paragraph
at all. It arises from what I regard as the natural meaning of the expression 'sued jointly'.

I find some assistance for this in RSC Ord 15, r 4. Paragraph (1) thereof reads:

a
'Subject to rule 5(1), two or more persons may be joined together in one action as plaintiffs or as defendants with the leave of the Court or where—(a) if separate actions were brought by or against each of them, as the case may be, some common question of law or fact would arise in all the actions, and (b) all rights to relief claimed in the action (whether they are joint, several or alternative) are in respect of or arise out of the same transaction or series of transactions.'

b
Then, by para (3):

'Where relief is claimed in an action against a defendant who is jointly liable with some other person and also severally liable, that other person need not be made a defendant to the action; but where persons are jointly, but not severally, liable under a contract and relief is claimed against some but not all of those persons in an action in respect of that contract, the Court may, on the application of any defendant
c
to the action, by order stay proceedings in the action until the other persons so liable are added as defendants.'

That rule clearly to my mind contemplates three different categories of parties to an action, namely where liability is joint, where liability is several and where liability is in the alternative. Examples are given of that in the notes. They are well known. An example of joint liability is the case of joint contractors or of vicarious liability, master
d
and servant, or indeed of joint tortfeasors, such as the well-known case of *Brooke v Bool* [1928] 2 KB 578, [1928] All ER Rep 155. Cases of alternative liability are seen in those of principal and agent, or in the running-down case where the plaintiff is uncertain which of two people drove the offending vehicle, and several liability, of course, cases where one cause of action is alleged against one person only. The Rules of the Supreme Court were much affected, when they were originally drafted, by the common law
e
principles applicable to cases of joint and several liability. They are well known. They have been affected and modified by the Law Reform (Married Women and Tortfeasors) Act 1935 and the Civil Liability (Contribution) Act 1978, but the basic common law principle had an influence on the drafting of the rules of court.

Picking up those three categories from Ord 15, r 4, and turning back again to Ord 22, r 3, one finds only two categories mentioned there, sued jointly or in the alternative.
f
Quite apart, then, from arriving at my conclusion from a strict reading of the words, assistance from r 15, if assistance is necessary, leads me to the conclusion that three categories are envisaged in the rules, and if there are three 'sued jointly' can only mean 'sued in respect of joint liability', leaving the two other cases of alternative and several liability; and Ord 22, r 3 specifically proclaims that it is concerned with only two of them. In the case with which we are concerned it is conceded, as indeed it must be, that
g
there are separate causes of action sued on against the first and third defendants. That being so, I for my part am of the opinion that the case is not covered by Ord 22, r 3(4), and that the action should not have been stayed. If there had been separate actions and a payment in had been accepted in the action against the builder, it is accepted by counsel for the first defendants that there would be no way in which he could obtain a stay in the action against the architects. What the result at the end of the day will be is not a matter
h
for this court to determine at this stage. To what extent money paid will have to be taken into account is a question that may well have to be argued, but I am not concerned to answer it in this case.

I should just mention *Holbrow v Swan & Moore (Assessors) Ltd* [1975] Court of Appeal Transcript 257 which has been cited to the court. It is an unreported judgment of the Court of Appeal of 13th June 1975. There, a plaintiff was injured in a motor accident.
j
He was an infant plaintiff, and the father on his behalf engaged an assessor to make a claim for him on the terms that the father was not to be liable for costs. A solicitor was eventually brought in by the assessor, and the father instructed the solicitor. The son's claim failed and the father found himself liable for costs to the defendants. He brought an action against the assessor and the solicitor, alleging against the assessor that they were in breach of contract in that they had undertaken he would not be liable for costs and

against the solicitors that it was a result of the breach of their professional duty that his
liability had been incurred. The solicitors paid in. An application was made to the court *a*
under CCR Ord 11, r 10(1)(*a*), which reads: 'Where payment into court is made—(*a*) by
one or more of several defendants sued jointly or in the alternative . . . the money in
court shall not be paid out except in pursuance of an order of the court.' An application
was made to the court for the money to be paid out. In the course of his judgment,
Megaw LJ, having recited the facts and the state of the pleadings and the action, said:
'Thereafter the plaintiff filed an application to enable him to take out the £525 which *b*
had been paid into court. That application was necessary by virtue of the County Court
Rules.' He then quoted the rule which I have just read. So, says counsel for the first
defendants here, the words are the same; it was said that application was necessary; it
could only have been necessary on the basis of two defendants sued in the same action,
and they were in that case not sued jointly: they were separate causes of action. I myself
have some doubt whether the transcript has a word omitted in that sentence. I do not *c*
know, and it is not really necessary to come to any conclusion on the matter. It could be
that what had been said was 'That application was thought to be necessary [*or* thought
necessary] by virtue of the County Court Rules'. I know not. The matter was not in
issue. What Megaw LJ did decide in that case was this, that the action against the assessor
should proceed. He said that it was a separate cause of action and, although money had
been accepted and although that would affect the damages recoverable in the action *d*
against the first defendant, the assessor, that action could proceed because there was still
an issue as to the liability for costs between the parties. I refer to that case, and refer to
it rather cursorily, because it has been quoted to this court. I do not find it of direct
assistance to the matter that we have to decide. First, as I say, our problem was not in
issue in that case; and, second, Megaw LJ did say: '. . . the relief claimed against the two
parties was not identical and, properly, was not claimed as being identical.' So, it might *e*
be argued that he would not have come to the same conclusion if there had been precise
overlapping of the damages claimed in the case. I know not. I do, however, regard the
case as pointing in the direction to which our decision should go, namely that, where
there are two separate causes of action, satisfaction of the one should not be a bar to
proceedings in the other.

For those reasons, I am of the opinion that to stay the action against the architects, *f*
albeit in respect of the limited number of heads of claim, was wrong, and that this appeal
should be allowed.

WATKINS LJ. I agree.

SIR DAVID CAIRNS. I also agree. I only want to make an observation about one *g*
further sentence in the judgment of Megaw LJ in *Holbrow v Swan & Moore (Assessors) Ltd*
[1975] Court of Appeal Transcript 257. After saying that the claims against the two
parties were not identical, Megaw LJ went on:

'It is true, of course, that the plaintiff, having received satisfaction for the full
amount of his claim against the second defendants, would not have been entitled to *h*
recover anything in the way of a judgment for damages against the first defendants,
because in the circumstances that would have involved a duplication of damages.'

I do not find that sentence, with great respect to Megaw LJ, entirely free from
ambiguity. If the learned Lord Justice meant that the plaintiff would not be entitled to
have a judgment against the first defendant if he could establish that defendant's liability, *j*
I would respectfully dissent from that. If he meant simply that under such a judgment
he could not obtain any further damages than those already recovered, I would
respectfully agree with what he said. That would be where duplication of damages
would come in, there being in *Holbrow's* case no suggestion that any more than £525
would be the appropriate damages against either defendant.

a I entirely agree with all that Eveleigh LJ has said as to the reasons for allowing the appeal, and I have nothing further to add to them.

Appeal allowed.

Solicitors: *Walters, Fladgate* (for the plaintiffs); *Kennedys* (for the first defendants).

b   Mary Rose Plummer   Barrister.

Customs and Excise Commissioners v Hedon Alpha Ltd and others

c

COURT OF APPEAL, CIVIL DIVISION
STEPHENSON, ACKNER AND GRIFFITHS LJJ
12th, 23rd JANUARY 1981

Company – Officer – Default – Power of court to grant relief from liability – Director of a
d company carrying on business as bookmaker – Liability of director for general betting duty not
paid by company – Director acting honestly and reasonably and not guilty of misconduct –
Whether director entitled to relief from claim for civil liability by a stranger to the company –
Whether claim to recover betting duty a 'proceeding for . . . default' against director – Companies
Act 1948, s 448(1) – Betting and Gaming Duties Act 1972, s 2(2).

e The third defendant was a director of a company which carried on the business of an off-
course bookmaker. When the company failed to pay general betting duty due under
s 2(1)[a] of the Betting and Gaming Duties Act 1972 the Commissioners of Customs and
Excise brought proceedings under s 2(2) of the 1972 Act to recover the duty from the
company, from another director who was the holder of the bookmaker's permit and
betting office licence and from the third defendant as a director of the company, suing
f them jointly and severally. Judgment in default of defence was entered against the
company and the other director but the third defendant served a defence pleading that
he had acted throughout honestly and reasonably and if he was guilty of negligence,
default or breach of duty he ought, in the circumstances of his appointment and his
activities as a director, to be excused therefor and relieved from liability, pursuant to
s 448(1)[b] of the Companies Act 1948. On the trial of a preliminary issue whether s 448
g applied to proceedings under s 2(2) of the 1972 Act against a director of a bookmaker
company, the judge held that it did not and directed that judgment be entered against
the third defendant for the amount of duty claimed. The third defendant appealed,
contending that the action against him was a 'proceeding for . . . default' against an
officer of the company, within s 448(1), and therefore the court had jurisdiction to
relieve him from liability for the claim.

h

Held – The appeal would be dismissed for the following reasons—
    (1) Although s 448(1) of the 1948 Act was expressed in wide language, in its context
of company law and on its true construction the only proceedings for which relief under
s 448 could be claimed were proceedings against a director by, on behalf of or for the
benefit of his company for breach of his duty to the company as a director, or penal
j proceedings against a director for a breach of the 1948 Act. Section 448(1) accordingly
did not apply to claims by a stranger to the company against a director to enforce a civil
liability, e g a debt (see p 701 *d e*, p 702 *b c*, p 703 *d j* and p 704 *e f h*, post).

---

a   Section 2, so far as material, is set out at p 699 *d* to *f*, post
b   Section 448(1), so far as material, is set out at p 700 *a b*, post

(2) Moreover, even if s 448 could apply to a claim by a stranger against a director to enforce a civil liability, it could not apply to the commissioners' claim against the third defendant since that claim was not a 'proceeding for ... default' within s 448(1) of the 1948 Act, because it was the company alone which was in default in failing to comply with its obligation under s 2(1) of the 1972 Act to pay betting duty since s 2(2) did not impose any duty on the third defendant to pay the duty but merely enabled the commissioners to recover it from him, as a director, if it was not paid by the company (see p 701 *b c*, p 702 *d e*, p 703 *a b j* and p 704 *f g*, post).

Per Ackner and Griffiths LJJ. 'Default' in the context of s 448(1) signifies some misconduct by a director in the discharge of his obligations under the 1948 Act but no element of misconduct is contained in a claim against a director under s 2(2)(*d*) of the 1972 Act for unpaid betting duty (see p 703 *c* and p 704 *g*, post).

Notes

For the power of the court to grant an officer of a company relief against liability, see 7 Halsbury's Laws (4th Edn) para 524.

For the Betting and Gaming Duties Act 1972, s 2, see 42 Halsbury's Statutes (3rd Edn) 395.

For the Companies Act 1948, s 448, see 5 ibid 426.

Cases referred to in judgments

Barry and Staines Linoleum Ltd, Re [1934] Ch 227, 103 LJ Ch 113, 150 LT 254, 9 Digest (Reissue) 545, 3252.

Claridge's Patent Asphalte Co Ltd, Re [1921] 1 Ch 543, 90 LJ Ch 273, 125 LT 255, 9 Digest (Reissue) 545, 3251.

Gilt Edge Safety Glass Ltd, Re [1940] 2 All ER 237, [1940] Ch 495, 109 LJ Ch 239, 162 LT 293, 9 Digest (Reissue) 545, 3254.

Cases also cited

Duomatic Ltd, Re [1969] 1 All ER 161, [1969] 2 Ch 365.

Franklin (J) & Son Ltd, Re [1937] 4 All ER 43.

Selangor United Rubber Estates Ltd v Cradock (No 3) [1968] 2 All ER 1073, [1968] 1 WLR 1555.

Appeal

By a writ dated 28th August 1979 the Commissioners of Customs and Excise claimed against the defendants Hedon Alpha Ltd, John Mitchell Lotinga and the appellant, Albert Robert George Gough, the sum of £18,080·15 as the balance of the amount of general betting duty in respect of the period 1st April 1978 to 2nd May 1979 due from the first defendant by virtue of s 2(1) of the Betting and Gaming Duties Act 1972 and alleged to be recoverable from all three defendants by virtue of s 2(2) of the 1972 Act. Judgment in default of defence was entered against the first and second defendants but the appellant put in a defence pleading that he was entitled to be relieved from liability under s 448(1) of the Companies Act 1948. By an order dated 5th June 1980 Master Elton ordered the trial of a preliminary point of law, whether s 448 of the 1948 Act applied to proceedings under s 2(2) of the 1972 Act. On 24th October 1980 Sir Douglas Frank QC sitting as a deputy judge of the High Court gave judgment on the preliminary point and determined that s 448 did not apply to proceedings under s 2(2) of the 1972 Act. By notice of appeal dated 17th November 1980 the appellant appealed against that judgment. The grounds of the appeal were that the judge (i) misdirected himself that the question of 'default' within s 448 did not arise in proceedings under s 2(2) of the 1972 Act and (ii) erred in law in construing s 448 of the 1948 Act as being inapplicable to claims brought by a stranger to a company against a director. The facts are set out in the judgment of Stephenson LJ.

Charles Pugh for the appellant.
John Laws for the commissioners.

Cur adv vult

a
23rd January. The following judgments were read.

STEPHENSON LJ. This appeal raises a short preliminary point on the construction of two statutes: does s 448 of the Companies Act 1948 apply to proceedings under s 2(2) of the Betting and Gaming Duties Act 1972? The judge has answered that question in
b the negative.

It arises out of the failure of a limited company named Hedon Alpha Ltd ('the defendant company'), which carried on the business of an off-course bookmaker, to pay general betting duty on bets made with the company between 1st April 1978 and 2nd May 1979. For the purposes of this appeal it is proved or admitted that in respect of that period the balance of duty due and unpaid is £18,080·15, that the third defendant
c Gough (the appellant) and his co-defendant, Lotinga (the second defendant), were directors of the defendant company, and that the defendant Lotinga was the holder of a bookmaker's permit and betting office licence.

The respondent commissioners by writ dated 29th August 1979 claimed this balance from the defendant company, from Lotinga and from the appellant as recoverable jointly and severally from them all by virtue of s 2(2) of the 1972 Act. Section 2 of that
d Act deals with two things, payment and recovery of general betting duty, and provides:

'(1) The general betting duty in respect of any bet shall, without prejudice to any regulations made under paragraph 2 of Schedule 1 to this Act, be due on the making of the bet, and shall be paid—(a) in the case of a bet with a bookmaker, and without prejudice to subsection (2) below, by the bookmaker . . .

e '(2) The general betting duty chargeable on any bet made with a bookmaker shall be recoverable jointly and severally from all or any of the following persons—(a) that bookmaker; (b) the holder of the bookmaker's permit or betting office licence relating to the business in the course of which, or the premises at which, the bet was made; (c) any person responsible for the management of that business or those premises; (d) where the bookmaker is a company, any director of that company.'

f   Judgment was entered against the first and second defendants in default, but the appellant served a defence on 10th March 1980 on which the master gave him unconditional leave to defend and directed the question I have already stated to be tried as a preliminary point of law. It was raised by para 5 of the appellant's defence in this form:

g   'Further or alternatively in regard to all the acts and matters referred to in the statement of claim the third named defendant says that he acted throughout honestly and reasonably and if (which he denies) he has been guilty of any negligence default or breach of duty he will submit that having regard to all the circumstances of the case he ought fairly to be excused therefor and be relieved from his liability by Order of the Court pursuant to s 448 of the Companies Act 1948.'

h That paragraph was amended on 28th May 1980 to add (with certain other matters) these sentences:

'The relevant circumstances of the case including those connected with the appointment of the third named defendant as a director are as follows: (a) he was told by the second named defendant that his appointment was merely "as a formality"; (b) he did not receive extra salary or any fee as a result of the
i appointment; (c) he was never invited to attend at any Board meeting; (d) he never saw any accounts; (e) he never held any relevant permit or licence; (f) he was never consulted concerning financial matters; (g) he was not permitted to execute a cheque unless it was countersigned by the second-named defendant . . . or the company secretary.'

Section 448 of the 1948 Act provides:

'(1) If in any proceeding for negligence, default, breach of duty or breach of trust
against an officer of a company or a person employed by a company as auditor *a*
(whether he is or is not an officer of the company) it appears to the court hearing the
case that that officer or person is or may be liable in respect of the negligence,
default, breach of duty or breach of trust, but that he has acted honestly and
reasonably, and that, having regard to all the circumstances of the case, including
those connected with his appointment, he ought fairly to be excused for the
negligence, default, breach of duty or breach of trust, that court may relieve him, *b*
either wholly or partly, from his liability on such terms as the court may think fit.

'(2) Where any such officer or person aforesaid has reason to apprehend that any
claim will or might be made against him in respect of any negligence, default,
breach of duty or breach of trust, he may apply to the court for relief, and the court
on any such application shall have the same power to relieve him as under this
section it would have had if it had been a court before which proceedings against *c*
that person for negligence, default, breach of duty or breach of trust had been
brought . . .'

The defendant company being insolvent and the second defendant having disappeared,
the appellant is hopeful of obtaining relief in the exercise of the court's discretion under
s 448, but we are concerned only with the court's jurisdiction to grant him relief. It may *d*
be hard on him if the judge was right in holding that he had no jurisdiction, and the
appellant has therefore to pay all or part of this large sum without the help from his co-
defendants, but if this statutory relief is not available to the defendant as a director of a
limited company which is a bookmaker, who is sued for unpaid betting duty under
s 2(2)(d) of the 1972 Act, he must pay what the commissioners can prove to be due and
unpaid.   *e*

The appellant's case presented by counsel on his behalf has an attractive simplicity.
The court can relieve an officer of a company against whom any proceeding for default
is brought; the appellant is an officer of the defendant company (see s 455(1) of the 1948
Act); a default is a 'failure to perform some legal requirement or obligation' or 'to pay a
sum due' (see the Shorter Oxford English Dictionary and Osborn's Concise Law
Dictionary); the defendant company is guilty of a default in failing to pay the betting *f*
duty due, and so is the appellant; the commissioners' claim to recover what the
defendants are legally obliged to pay is a proceeding for default; and the court may
relieve the appellant from the liability which is or may be his in respect of the
undischarged legal obligation.

He submits that there is no reason in principle or authority for restricting the material
meaning of the words 'in [the] proceeding for . . . default'. The words are, as Astbury J *g*
said of the language of the section's predecessor, s 279 of the Companies (Consolidation)
Act 1908, 'perfectly wide and general': see *Re Claridge's Patent Asphalte Co Ltd* [1921] 1 Ch
543 at 548. Proceedings to which the section applies are not restricted to proceedings in
respect of a director's negligence, default etc or to proceedings in respect of his negligence,
default etc in relation to the company of which he is a director; they cover proceedings
initiated by strangers, eg, an informer or the Board of Trade: *Re Barry and Staines* *h*
Linoleum Ltd [1934] Ch 227 and *Re Gilt Edge Safety Glass Ltd* [1940] 2 All ER 237, [1940]
Ch 495, decisions on s 372 of the Companies Act 1929, which was the immediate
predecessor of s 448 of the 1948 Act and introduced the word 'default' between
'negligence' and 'breach of duty'.

Counsel for the appellant supported this construction of s 448 by the general rule that
directors acting as such within their powers and within the powers of the company and *j*
without negligence or breach of fiduciary duty, incur no personal liability (7 Halsbury's
Laws (4th Edn) para 516) and by the severity of the exception to the rule which s 2(2)(d)
of the 1972 Act would create if it were not mitigated by the relief which s 448 of the
1948 Act could provide. He pointed out that the Social Security Act 1975, s 152(4)
provides that contributions or premiums which a body corporate fails to pay—

'shall be a debt due to the Secretary of State jointly and severally from any director
of the body corporate who knew, or could reasonably be expected to have known,
of the failure to pay the contributions or premiums in question.'

This provision, repeating a restriction on a director's liability which was enacted by
s 95(8) of the National Insurance Act 1965, does not exclude the application of s 448 from
proceedings to recover such contributions or premiums, but makes the imposition of
unrestricted liability on a director for betting duty due from a company so unlikely as to
require the court to restrict it by the application of s 448.

The judge rejected these submissions and accepted the submissions of counsel for the
commissioners. These were and are that the commissioners' action was not a proceeding
for default, which in its context of negligence, breach of duty and breach of trust
involved some fault or guilt or misconduct, but for debt; if there was any default it was
by the defendant company on whom alone rested a duty to pay imposed by s 2(1)(a) and
not by the director against whom s 2(2)(d) provided the commissioners with a right to
recover the company's unpaid debt; and the proceedings in which relief could be granted
must be proceedings for the negligence, default etc of the director (or auditor) himself in
his capacity as director (or auditor, or perhaps as one partner in a firm of accountants
acting as auditors for the negligence, default etc of another partner).

Furthermore, the language of s 448 was apt to describe the area in which a company
director might be in breach of his duties to the company, and the ambit and concern, the
context or matrix, of the section was company law and the relation of the officer (or
auditor) of a company to the company and not to third persons. The proceedings which
qualified for the statutory relief were claims made by companies, or on their behalf or for
their benefit by, e g liquidators, the Board of Trade, private prosecutors, including penal
proceedings for the enforcement of the Companies Act, but not proceedings for the
recovery of debts or the enforcement of civil liability to strangers.

In support of his construction of s 2 of the 1972 Act and s 448 of the 1948 Act counsel
for the commissioners relied on s 152(4) of the Social Security Act 1975 as a pointer to
Parliament's intending that s 448 should not apply either to betting duty or to what are
now social security contributions and premiums. He relied also on the derivation of
s 448 from the Judicial Trustee Act 1896, now s 61 of the Trustee Act 1925, as indicating
that s 448 was concerned with breaches of a director's fiduciary duty to the company
regarded as a beneficiary. He also called attention to the anomaly that if the argument
of counsel for the appellant was right, not only the company, liable under s 2(2)(a) of the
1972 Act, but also the holder of the bookmaker's permit and licence and the bookmaker's
manager, liable under s 2(2)(b) and (c), would have no chance of obtaining the relief
which the company's director could claim against his liability under s 2(2)(d). The
anomaly is, I think, limited by the fact that where the bookmaker is a company the
manager could claim relief as an officer of the company: see s 455(1) of the 1948 Act.

There is a surprising absence of authority (1) on the meaning of 'default' in s 448, and
(2) on the extent of the section's application. As to (1) the word 'default' appears to have
been introduced at the same time as the 1929 Act enacted some 20 new penalties for
'defaults' of company officers: see Palmer's Company Law (13th Edn, 1929, p 217).
Section 440 of the 1948 Act is consistent with the meaning given by counsel for the
respondents to 'default' in s 448 and to the section generally. As to (2), the current
edition of Palmer's Company Law (22nd Edn, 1976, p 683) expresses the opinion—

'that the court's power to grant relief in appropriate circumstances under section
448 is sufficiently wide to extend to actions by third parties as well as actions by the
company, but the point is not free from doubt.'

But an opinion inclining the other way is expressed in Pennington's Company Law
(4th Edn, 1979, p 548):

'... relief can be given against any of the criminal penalties imposed by the
Companies Acts 1948 and 1976, but not, it would seem, against civil liability to

anyone other than the company, and so apparently no relief may be given in the
rare cases where a member or auditor of a company has a personal right to sue its   *a*
directors.'

I agree with the judge in preferring counsel for the commissioners' submissions and
construction of these two statutes, and I agree with both of the judge's grounds for
determining the preliminary question as he did. But I would put his second ground first
and hold that s 448 is inapplicable to the commissioners' claim because it is inapplicable
to any claim by third parties to enforce any liability except a director's liability to his   *b*
company or his director's duties under the Companies Acts. Wide and general though
the opening words of s 448 are, read in their context they do not allow an officer or
auditor of a company to claim relief in 'any' legal proceedings which may be brought
against him in his capacity as an officer or auditor of a company by the rest of the world.
If Parliament had wished to provide a director, whom it exceptionally makes liable to
discharge a company liability, with the protection of s 448 or some other protection, it   *c*
would, in my judgment, have done so by express words, either by subjecting the
statutory liability to the right to claim relief under s 448 or, as in the Social Security Act
1975, by subjecting it to some other restriction. That Parliament has not done in s 2 of
the 1972 Act and it is that Act, not the Companies Act 1948, which governs the
appellant's liability to the respondents for betting duty and imposes an absolute liability
on him irrespective of knowledge or any personal fault. By becoming a director of the   *d*
defendant company he became liable for this debt of the company without qualification.

But I also agree that if s 448 could apply to claims by third parties the commissioners'
claim is not a proceeding for default, since s 2(2) gives a right to recover a debt against a
director who is not in breach of any duty except a duty to pay on demand which he
would not owe had it not been placed on him by the 1972 Act. If there was any default
it was the company's and the appellant did not even, in the words of s 4 of the Statute of   *e*
Frauds (1677), 'promise to answere for the debt default or miscarriages' of the company;
he was required by the statute of 1972 to answer for it and the commissioners' action
against him was not a proceeding in respect of default even if their action against the
company was. I would accordingly dismiss the appeal.

ACKNER LJ. The respondents, the Customs and Excise Commissioners, brought   *f*
proceedings against three defendants, Hedon Alpha Ltd, a company carrying on business
as off-course bookmakers, John Mitchell Lotinga, who was the managing director of the
company and the holder of a bookmakers' permit and betting office licence, and also
against the appellant, Mr Gough, as a director of the company, for the sum of £18,080·15,
being the balance of general betting duty which the commissioners alleged was due
jointly and severally from all three defendants. Judgment in default was signed against   *g*
the company and the second defendant, but the appellant obtained leave to defend and
an order was made for the trial of a preliminary issue. The claim against the appellant
was made by virtue of s 2(2) of the Betting and Gaming Duties Act 1972, which section
Stephenson LJ has set out in full. The preliminary issue was whether s 448 of the
Companies Act 1948 is applicable to proceedings brought against the appellant.

The appellant, being a director, was an officer of the company (see s 455 of the   *h*
Companies Act 1948). Thus in order for s 448 of the 1948 Act to apply the proceedings
brought by the commissioners must be proceedings for 'default' within the meaning of
that section.

Counsel for the appellant argued before us, as he did before Sir Douglas Frank QC
sitting as a deputy judge of the High Court, that the word 'default' should be given its   *i*
ordinary meaning as defined in the Shorter Oxford English Dictionary, viz 'a failure to
perform some legal requirement or obligation'. However, the duty to pay the general
betting duty is, by virtue of s 2(1) of the Betting and Gaming Duties Act 1972, imposed
on the bookmaker, that is the company, Hedon Alpha Ltd. If the bookmaker fails to
comply with its statutory obligation as occurred in this case, then the commissioners
have an additional remedy by virtue of s 2(2) in that the betting duty is recoverable

jointly and severally from all or any of the three categories of persons referred to in s
a 2(2)(b), (c) and (d). Thus s 2(2), in contradistinction to s 2(1), imposes no duty: it merely
provides a statutory right to recover from persons other than those on whom the duty to
pay is imposed.

Assuming that the word 'default' should be given its ordinary meaning not in any way
limited by the context in which it appears in s 448, I would nevertheless take the view,
as did the judge, that it was the company, as bookmaker, which was in default, by failing
b to comply with the obligation imposed on it by s 2(1). Since s 2(2) imposed no duty on
the appellant, but merely gave the commissioners the right to sue in debt, there was no
default by him.

I do not, however, take the view that an unrestricted construction should be given to
the word 'default'. In the context in which it appears in s 448, it signifies a species of
misconduct by an officer of a company or a person employed by a company as auditor,
c against a liability for which a court may relieve him either wholly or in part. It is
common ground that no element of misconduct is to be found in the foundation of a
claim brought by virtue of s 2(2) of the Act. Accordingly the question of default does not
arise.

That is sufficient to dispose of this appeal, but I accept that the true ambit of s 448,
with one limited exception, is restricted to claims by or on behalf of the company or its
d liquidator against the officer or auditor for their personal breaches of duty. The only
exception relates to the criminal process for the enforcement of certain specific duties
imposed by the 1948 Act on the company's officers, eg the requirement to hold a
specified share qualification. Section 448 thus gives similar protection to directors to that
which is accorded to trustees under s 61 of the Trustee Act 1925. Significant support for
the proposition that s 448 operates, with the exception referred to above, only in relation
e to claims by a company against its officer or auditor is provided by the Social Security Act
1975, s 152(4). Where a body corporate fails to pay any sum which it is liable to pay
under ss 150 and 151 of that Act, that sum shall be a debt due to the Secretary of State
jointly and severally from any directors of the body corporate. However, the subsection
goes on to provide that such directors must know or could reasonably be expected to have
known of the failure to pay the contributions or premiums in question. If s 448 could
f be invoked by a director by way of a defence to a claim under s 152(4) then there would
have been no need for the legislature to have provided specifically in the subsection for
the need to establish actual or constructive knowledge.

There is of course much force in the point made by counsel for the appellant in his able
argument, that there may be cases, of which this may well be an example, of considerable
hardship which may arise if the court has no power to grant relief in whole or in part.
g However, a director of the bookmaker company is only one of three other categories
of persons who is jointly and severally liable for betting duty. Harsh though on occasions
indeed it may be for there to be no escape from liability, it would seem to me that it
could work manifest injustice if only the director of the bookmaker company was
entitled to relief, whereas the holder of the bookmaker's permit or betting office licence
or any person responsible for the management of the business if not carried on as a
h company remained in all circumstances absolutely liable. If Parliament had intended to
limit the liability of those whom it decided should be jointly and severally liable for the
general betting duty, I would have expected to have found such limitation in the Act
itself (vide s 152(4) of the Social Security Act 1975). It would be odd indeed if such
limitation, confined essentially only to one category of person, was to be found in a
wholly unrelated Act to which no reference was made.
j I also would therefore dismiss this appeal.

GRIFFITHS LJ. Bookmaking can be a very profitable business; but as this case shows
those who take part in the management of a bookmaking business or who accept office
as directors of a company carrying on a bookmaking business may thereby expose
themselves to grave personal financial risk. The Betting and Gaming Duties Act 1972

imposes a general betting duty on every bet laid with a bookmaker. Section 2(1) provides that this duty shall be paid by the bookmaker but sub-s (2) goes much further and provides that the betting duty is recoverable not only from the bookmaker but jointly and severally from all or any of the following persons, that is, the holder of the bookmaker's permit or betting office licence where the bet was made, any person responsible for the management of the business where the bet was made and in the case of a company carrying on a bookmaking business any director of that company. The effect of this subsection is to make those persons statutory guarantors of the bookmaker's liability to pay betting duty. Their liability to pay is wholly independent of any fault on their part, their liability arises solely out of the position that they have chosen to accept in the bookmaking business. So far as they are concerned it is indeed a draconian section but no doubt thought necessary by Parliament taking into consideration the vast amounts of money spent on gambling and the obvious difficulties that may arise in collecting duty on such a huge flow of swift-moving money.

The appellant is a director of a bookmaking company which it is alleged has failed to pay betting duty in the sum of approximately £18,000. There is apparently no prospect of the commissioners recovering that money from the company and so they have brought proceedings to recover it from the appellant. The appellant contends that he was in no way to blame for the failure of the company to pay the betting duty and that in these circumstances a court has a discretion to allow him relief as an officer of a company pursuant to s 448 of the Companies Act 1948. Before turning to consider that section of the 1948 Act it is to be observed that if this is right it places the director of a company in a more advantageous position than the holder of the bookmaker's permit or betting office licence, or the person responsible for the management of the business who works for a bookmaker that is not carrying on his business as a limited company, neither of whom would be in a position to claim relief as company directors. This would hardly seem a fair state of affairs.

In my judgment s 448 has no application to the present claim. Although the section is expressed in wide language it is in my view clearly intended to enable the court to give relief to a director who, although he has behaved reasonably and honestly, has nevertheless failed in some way in the discharge of his obligations to his company or their shareholders or who has infringed one of the numerous provisions in the Companies Acts that regulate the conduct of directors.

In these proceedings no allegation of any misconduct or breach of any obligation owed to the company or any other person is relied on by the commissioners. It is true that the appellant has not paid the betting duty when called on to do so, but I cannot regard that failure as a default within the meaning of that word where it appears in s 448. The word 'default', where it appears in the section, is to be construed as a failure to conduct himself properly as a director of the company in discharge of his obligations pursuant to the provisions of the 1948 Act.

When banks lend money to private companies they usually require the directors to enter into personal guarantees of the loan. Unhappily directors are not infrequently called on to honour their guarantees. I know of no case in which it has been suggested that s 448 would provide any defence to such a claim by the bank. I agree with Stephenson and Ackner LJJ that s 448 does not apply to claims against directors brought by strangers with the exception of prosecutions brought for breach of the provisions of the Companies Acts.

I would accordingly dismiss the appeal.

Appeal dismissed. Leave to appeal to the House of Lords refused.

Solicitors: *Clark & Son*, Reading (for the appellant); *Solicitor for the Customs and Excise*.

William Hoskins Esq   Barrister.

R v Brophy

HOUSE OF LORDS

LORD DIPLOCK, LORD FRASER OF TULLYBELTON, LORD RUSSELL OF KILLOWEN, LORD KEITH OF KINKEL AND LORD ROSKILL

2nd, 25th JUNE 1981

Criminal evidence – Admissions and confessions – Incriminating admission made at voire dire – Admission relevant to issue in question at voire dire – Admission relating to offence not under consideration at voire dire – Admission relating to admissibility of statements made to police in connection with other offences – Judge ruling that statements inadmissible – Whether admission made by defendant at voire dire admissible against him at substantive trial.

The respondent was charged on an indictment containing 49 counts, including 12 counts of murder arising from an explosion and fire in which 12 people died, 36 counts of causing explosions or possessing explosives or firearms on various occasions between September 1976 and February 1978 and one count (count 49) of belonging to a proscribed organisation, ie the IRA, between specified dates in 1976 and 1978 contrary to s 19(1)(*a*) of the Northern Ireland (Emergency Provisions) Act 1973. The respondent pleaded not guilty to all the charges. There was no evidence to connect him with the crimes except a number of verbal and written statements which he had made or was alleged by the Crown to have made to the police after his arrest. The respondent challenged the admissibility of the statements under s 8(2)[a] of the Northern Ireland (Emergency Provisions) Act 1978 (which consolidated the 1973 Act) on the ground that he had been induced to make them by being subjected to torture or to inhuman or degrading treatment while in custody. The trial judge, sitting without a jury, dealt with the issue of admissibility on a voire dire at which the respondent gave evidence challenging the admissibility of the statements. In his evidence-in-chief in answer to questions from his counsel the respondent stated that he had been a member of the IRA during the greater part of the period charged in count 49. After the voire dire the judge ruled that he was not satisfied that the statements had not been induced by torture or inhuman or degrading treatment and excluded evidence of them from the substantive trial. When the substantive trial resumed the Crown proposed to call the shorthand writer who had recorded the evidence at the voire dire to prove the respondent's statement on the voire dire that he had been a member of the IRA. The objection of counsel for the respondent to the admission of this evidence was overruled by the judge who admitted it on the ground that it was not strictly relevant to the central question in dispute on the voire dire, ie the admissibility of the respondent's statements to the police, and because it had been freely given during the respondent's examination-in-chief. Since the first 48 counts were unsupported by any evidence the respondent was acquitted on those counts but on count 49 he was convicted. The respondent appealed to the Court of Appeal in Northern Ireland which allowed his appeal on the ground that the respondent's evidence at the voire dire as to his membership of the IRA could be regarded as relevant to the issue on the voire dire and accordingly was inadmissible at the substantive trial. The Crown appealed.

---

a Section 8(2) provides: 'If, in any such proceedings where the prosecution proposes to give in evidence a statement made by the accused, prima facie evidence is adduced that the accused was subjected to torture or to inhuman or degrading treatment in order to induce him to make the statement, the court shall, unless the prosecution satisfies it that the statement was not so obtained—(a) exclude the statement, or (b) if the statement has been received in evidence, either—(i) continue the trial disregarding the statement; or (ii) direct that the trial shall be restarted before a differently constituted court (before which the statement in question shall be inadmissible).'

Held – Where evidence was given on a voire dire by an accused person in answer to questions by his counsel, and without objection by counsel for the Crown, his evidence *a* was to be treated as relevant to the issue at the voire dire unless it was clearly and obviously irrelevant, and the accused was to be given the benefit of any reasonable doubt as to relevancy. The respondent's statement that he had been a member of the IRA was relevant to the issue at the voire dire whether he had been subjected to inhuman or degrading treatment, for by showing that he had been a member of the IRA for several years up to a few months before the date of the murders charged and that the police *b* knew or suspected this, he could then ask the court to infer that not only would they be more hostile to him but also that they would have expected him to have received instruction how to avoid succumbing to the normal techniques of interrogation which did not involve ill-treatment. Although it had not been proved that the police did know of his membership of the IRA it was reasonable to assume that if he had been a member of the IRA for six years the police would probably have been aware of that fact. It *c* followed therefore that, since the respondent's evidence as to his IRA membership was relevant to the issue at the voire dire, it was not admissible in the substantive trial and the appeal would be dismissed (see p 707 *d*, p 708 *h* to p 709 *f* and p 710 *g h*, post).

Per Curiam. (1) At a trial before a judge sitting without a jury, it is not normally necessary at the substantive trial to go through the formal step of proving the evidence given by the accused at the voire dire because the judge has himself heard the evidence *d* given at the voire dire and is himself the sole judge of fact at the substantive trial (see p 707 *d*, p 708 *a b* and p 710 *g h*, post).

(2) If, at the voire dire, the accused, whether in answer to questions from his own counsel or not, goes out of his way to boast of having committed the crimes with which he is charged, or if he uses the witness box as a platform for a political speech, his evidence so far as it relates to those matters will almost certainly be irrelevant to the issue *e* at the voire dire, and different considerations will apply to its admissibility at the substantive trial (see p 707 *d*, p 709 *b c*, and p 710 *g h*, post).

(3) The right of the accused to give evidence at the voire dire without affecting his right to remain silent at the substantive trial is absolute and is not to be made conditional on an exercise of judicial discretion (see p 707 *d* and p 710 *c* to *h*, post); dictum of Lord Hailsham in *Wong Kam-ming v The Queen* [1979] 1 All ER at 946–947 applied. *f*

Notes

For the duty of the trial judge in relation to admissibility of confessions, and for use of facts discovered as a result of inadmissible statements, see 11 Halsbury's Laws (4th Edn) paras 413, 418.

For the Northern Ireland (Emergency Provisions) Act 1973, s 19(1)(a), see 43 Halsbury's *g* Statutes (3rd Edn) 1250.

For the Northern Ireland (Emergency Provisions) Act 1978, s 8(2), see 48 ibid 979.

As from 1st June 1978, s 19(1)(a) of the 1973 Act was replaced by s 21(1)(a) of the 1978 Act, 48 ibid 989.

Cases referred to in opinions *h*

R v Sang [1979] 2 All ER 1222, [1980] AC 402, [1979] 3 WLR 263, 143 JP 606, HL, Digest (Cont Vol E) 137, 3913a.

R v Wright [1969] SASR 256.

Wong Kam-ming v The Queen [1979] 1 All ER 939, [1980] AC 247, [1979] 2 WLR 81, 143 JP 525, PC, Digest (Cont Vol E) 140, 4506a.

j

Appeal

The Crown appealed against the decision of the Court of Appeal in Northern Ireland (Lord Lowry LCJ, Gibson LJ and MacDermott J) on 27th March 1981 allowing an appeal by the respondent, Edward Manning Brophy, against his conviction by the Crown Court at Belfast (Kelly J without a jury) on 1st April 1980 and quashing the conviction on count

49 of the indictment (as amended by the judge at the trial) for belonging to a proscribed
a organisation, namely the Irish Republican Army, between 15th August 1976 and 1st
January 1978, contrary to s 19(1)(*a*) of the Northern Ireland (Emergency Provisions) Act
1973. The Court of Appeal certified under s 31 of the Criminal Appeal (Northern
Ireland) Act 1980 that three points of law of general public importance were involved in
the decision and granted the Crown leave to appeal to the House of Lords against the
decision. The facts and the points of law certified are set out in the opinion of Lord
b Fraser.

Ronald Appleton QC, R D Carswell QC and *M J Higgins* (all of the Northern Ireland Bar) for
the Crown.
Richard Ferguson QC and *Terence Mooney* (both of the Northern Ireland Bar) for the
respondent.

c
At the conclusion of argument their Lordships dismissed the appeal stating that their
reasons for doing so would be given at a later date.

25th June. The following opinions were delivered.

d **LORD DIPLOCK.** My Lords, I have had the advantage of reading in draft the speech
of my noble and learned friend Lord Fraser. I agree with it and with the order which he
proposes.

LORD FRASER OF TULLYBELTON. My Lords, this appeal raises a question of
importance to the administration of criminal justice, whether admissions made by an
e accused person in the course of giving evidence at a trial within a trial, or voire dire, can
be used by the Crown at the substantive trial as evidence tending to prove that he is
guilty of the offence charged in the indictment.
 The respondent was tried by Kelly J, sitting without a jury under the Northern Ireland
(Emergency Provisions) Act 1978, on an indictment containing 49 counts. There were
12 counts of murder, arising out of an explosion and fire in which 12 persons were
f burned to death or suffocated. There were 36 counts of causing explosions or possessing
explosives or firearms on various occasions between September 1976 and February
1978. Finally there was one count, the 49th, of belonging to a proscribed organisation,
namely the Irish Republican Army ('IRA'), between specified dates in 1976 and 1978.
The respondent pleaded not guilty to all the charges. There was no evidence of any kind
against him except a number of statements, some written and some oral, which he had
made, or was alleged by the Crown to have made, to the police after his arrest. The
g respondent challenged the admissibility of the statements, under s 8(2) of the 1978 Act,
on the ground that he had been induced to make them by being subjected to torture or
to inhuman or degrading treatment while in custody. The learned trial judge, after a
voire dire, delivered a careful and exhaustive judgment holding that he was not satisfied
that the statements had not been so obtained, and he excluded evidence of them from the
h substantive trial. The first 48 counts were therefore unsupported by any evidence, and
on those counts the accused was acquitted.
 The instant appeal relates only to the 49th count, of belonging to a proscribed
organisation. At an early stage of his evidence-in-chief in the voire dire the respondent
admitted in terms that he had been a member of the IRA during the greater part of the
period charged in count 49. His evidence on this matter could not have been more
i explicit. In answer to a question from his own counsel whether he had joined any
organisation, he replied: 'Yes, I was a member of the IRA'. In answer to the immediately
following questions from his counsel he said that he had joined the IRA in September
1971 and remained a member until December 1977. When the substantive trial was
resumed, the Crown called the shorthand writer who had recorded the evidence given at
the voire dire to prove the evidence given by the respondent. I pause to notice that this

was done, as I understand, to keep the procedure formally the same as it would have been if the judge had been sitting with a jury, but I doubt whether it can have served any *a* practical purpose; the judge had heard the evidence given at the voire dire, and he was himself the sole judge of fact at the substantive trial. In such circumstances, unless the judge wishes to have his recollection of the evidence at the voire dire refreshed, or there is some other practical reason for proving what passed at the voire dire, I do not consider that it is necessary to go through the formal step of proving it to the judge who has already heard it.

Returning to the narrative, when the shorthand writer was called, counsel for the *b* respondent objected to her evidence being admitted, but the judge overruled the objection, the transcript of the evidence at the voire dire was read and the shorthand writer was not cross-examined. The judge considered that the respondent's evidence as to his membership of the IRA was not strictly relevant to the voire dire, and that it was certainly not essential to the central question that had been in dispute at that stage. On *c* that ground he did not regard it as evidence on the question of admissibility of the respondent's statements to the police, and, as it had been freely given during the respondent's examination-in-chief, he held that it was admissible in the substantive trial. On that evidence, which was the evidence against the respondent, he was only convicted on count 49.

The Court of Appeal in Northern Ireland allowed the respondent's appeal against his *d* conviction. They also certified three points of law of general public importance and granted leave to appeal to your Lordships' House. The questions certified by the Court of Appeal are as follows:

'(1) Whether in a criminal trial, after statements made by the accused have been excluded on the *voir dire* as inadmissible, the prosecution may adduce in evidence at the substantive trial admissions made by the accused in the course of the *voir dire* *e* which prove or tend to prove that he is guilty of an offence charged in the indictment;
'(2) Whether any distinction in this respect should be drawn between admissions elicited by cross-examination and other admissions;
'(3) Whether there is any difference in this respect between a trial with a jury and a trial by a judge alone.' *f*

The decision of the Court of Appeal to allow the appeal was made after they had held that the respondent's evidence at the voire dire that he had been a member of the IRA was fully capable of being regarded as relevant to the issue for decision on the voire dire. On that vital matter they differed from the trial judge. That it was vital appears from the statement by Lord Lowry LCJ, delivering the judgment of the Court of Appeal, *g* that 'it is only relevant evidence which is protected' against admission at the substantive trial. I am of opinion that the Court of Appeal were clearly right in holding that the evidence was relevant to the issue at the voire dire. The practical question at that stage was whether the respondent had been subjected by the police to inhuman or degrading treatment. The respondent contended that he had, and the police of course denied it. In relation to that question, it was in my opinion relevant for him to show, if he could, that *h* he had been a member of the IRA for several years, up till a date less than two months before the date of the murders charged in counts 1 to 12 (17th February 1978). If, as would be likely, the police knew or suspected this, not only would they be more hostile to him than if he had not, but also they would expect him to have received instruction how to avoid succumbing to the normal techniques of interrogation which do not involve any physical ill-treatment. Counsel for the Crown argued that the mere fact that *j* the respondent had been a member of the IRA was not relevant unless the police knew of his membership and he said (rightly) that it had not been proved that the police did know of it. Counsel argued that an essential link in the chain was therefore missing, and that the trial judge had been right in treating the respondent's evidence of membership of the IRA as irrelevant. I cannot agree. The argument depends in my opinion on taking

altogether too narrow a view of the matter. If the respondent had been a member of the
a IRA for more than six years, as he had admitted, I think it is reasonable to assume that the
police would probably have been aware of the fact.

I would rest my opinion of relevance also on a wider ground. Where, as in this case,
evidence is given at the voire dire by an accused person in answer to questions by his
counsel, and without objection by counsel for the Crown, his evidence ought in my
opinion to be treated as relevant to the issue at the voire dire, unless it is clearly and
b obviously irrelevant. The accused should be given the benefit of any reasonable doubt.
Of course, if the accused, whether in answer to questions from his own counsel or not,
goes out of his way to boast of having committed the crimes with which he is charged,
or if uses the witness box as a platform for a political speech, his evidence so far as it
relates to these matters will almost certainly be irrelevant to the issue at the voire dire,
and different considerations will apply to its admissibility at the substantive trial. But on
c any reasonable view of the respondent's evidence in this case it cannot be said to be clearly
and obviously irrelevant.

Once it has been held that the material part of the respondent's evidence was relevant
to the issue at the voire dire, a necessary consequence is, in my opinion, that it is not
admissible in the substantive trial. Indeed counsel for the Crown did not argue to the
contrary. If such evidence, being relevant, were admissible at the substantive trial, an
d accused person would not enjoy the complete freedom that he ought to have at the voire
dire to contest the admissibility of his previous statements. It is of the first importance
for the administration of justice that an accused person should feel completely free to
give evidence at the voire dire of any improper methods by which a confession or
admission has been extracted from him, for he can almost never make an effective
challenge of its admissibility without giving evidence himself. He is thus virtually
e compelled to give evidence at the voire dire, and if his evidence were admissible at the
substantive trial, the result might be a significant impairment of his so-called 'right of
silence' at the trial. The right means 'No man is to be compelled to incriminate himself;
nemo tenetur se ipsum prodere': see *R v Sang* [1979] 2 All ER 1222 at 1246, [1980] AC
402 at 455 per Lord Scarman. The word 'compelled' in that context must, in my
opinion, include being put under pressure. So long as that right exists it ought not to be
f cut down, as it would be if an accused person, who finds himself obliged to give evidence
at the voire dire, in order to contest a confession extracted by improper means, and
whose evidence tends to show the truth of his confession, were liable to have his evidence
used at the substantive trial. He would not receive a fair trial, as that term is understood
in all parts of the United Kingdom.

I do not overlook or minimise the risk that accused persons may make false allegations
g of ill-treatment by the police; some of them undoubtedly do. But the detection of
dishonest witnesses on this, as on other matters, is part of the ordinary duty of the courts
and it should be left to them. The possibility, indeed the practical certainty, that some
accused will give dishonest evidence of ill-treatment does not justify inhibiting their
freedom to testify at the voire dire. The importance of the principle was explained by
Lord Hailsham in the recent Privy Council case of *Wong Kam-ming v The Queen* [1979] 1
h All ER 939 at 946–947, [1980] AC 247 at 261, where he said:

> '. . . any civilised system of criminal jurisprudence must accord to the judiciary
> some means of excluding confessions or admissions obtained by improper
> methods. This is not only because of the potential unreliability of such statements,
> but also, and perhaps mainly, because in a civilised society it is vital that persons in
i > custody or charged with offences should not be subjected to ill treatment or
> improper pressure in order to extract confessions. It is therefore of very great
> importance that the courts should continue to insist that before extra-judicial
> statements can be admitted in evidence the prosecution must be made to prove
> beyond reasonable doubt that the statement was not obtained in a manner which
> would be reprobated and was therefore in the truest sense voluntary. For this

reason it is necessary that the accused should be able and feel free either by his own testimony or by other means to challenge the voluntary character of the tendered statement. If, as happened in the instant appeal, the prosecution were to be permitted to introduce into the trial the evidence of the accused given in the course of the voire dire when the statement to which it relates has been excluded, whether in order to supplement the evidence otherwise available as part of the prosecution case, or by way of cross-examination of the accused, the important principles of public policy to which I have referred would certainly become eroded, possibly even to vanishing point.'

Wong Kam-ming v The Queen differs from the present case in two respects. First, the trial there was by a judge and jury. Second, the accused's admission had been elicited in cross-examination at the voire dire. The decision is therefore not directly in point, but neither of these features was essential to the observations by Lord Hailsham in the passage which I have quoted, which were quite wide enough to apply to the facts of this appeal. In my opinion they are applicable here also.

A submission was made by counsel for the Crown that the position of the accused could be adequately safeguarded if his evidence at the voire dire were admissible at the substantive trial, provided that the judge had a discretion to exclude at the trial any such evidence which would prejudice him unfairly. This was the approach favoured by Bray CJ in *R v Wright* [1969] SASR 256, a South Australian case, the actual decision in which cannot stand with *Wong*, and was not supported by counsel for the Crown in this appeal. With all respect, I cannot regard that as a satisfactory solution. The right of the accused to give evidence at the voire dire without affecting his right to remain silent at the substantive trial is in my opinion absolute and is not to be made conditional on an exercise of judicial discretion.

Where an accused has admitted at the voire dire that he is guilty of a charge of such gravity as that contained in the 49th count in the instant appeal, no court can acquit him without most anxious consideration of the issues involved. The Court of Appeal evidently gave such consideration to the issues here, and I have endeavoured to do the same. Having done so, I feel no doubt that the Court of Appeal reached the right decision and that the respondent must be acquitted.

I would answer all the certified questions in the negative and I would dismiss the appeal.

LORD RUSSELL OF KILLOWEN. My Lords, I have had the advantage of reading in draft the speech of my noble and learned friend Lord Fraser. I agree with it and with the order that he proposes.

LORD KEITH OF KINKEL. My Lords, I have had the advantage of reading in draft the speech of my noble and learned friend Lord Fraser. I agree with it, and for the reasons stated by him I too would dismiss the appeal.

LORD ROSKILL. My Lords, I have had the advantage of reading in draft the speech of my noble and learned friend Lord Fraser. For the reasons he gives, I too would answer all the certified questions in the negative and would dismiss this appeal.

Certified questions answered in the negative; order appealed from affirmed and appeal dismissed.

Solicitors: *Director of Public Prosecutions*, agent for *Director of Public Prosecutions for Northern Ireland; Simons, Muirhead & Allan*, agents for *P J McGrory*, Belfast (for the respondent).

Mary Rose Plummer   Barrister.

Forrest v Brighton Justices
Hamilton v Marylebone Magistrates' Court

HOUSE OF LORDS

LORD FRASER OF TULLYBELTON, LORD ELWYN-JONES, LORD SALMON, LORD SCARMAN AND LORD ROSKILL

13th MAY, 18th JUNE 1981

Magistrates – Fine – Committal to prison in default of payment – Issue of committal warrant without a hearing – Issue of committal warrant without notice – Defendant serving sentence of imprisonment at the time – Whether breach of natural justice – Whether power to dispense with presence of defendant at hearing including power to dispense with notice – Criminal Justice Act 1967, s 44(6).

Sentence – Imprisonment – Magistrates' court – Consecutive terms – Aggregate terms imposed by court not to exceed 12 months – Court imposing a term of imprisonment of 12 months for several offences – Court subsequently imposing sentence of imprisonment of 144 days for default in payment of fines – Terms to run consecutively – Whether prescribed maximum period of 12 months exceeded – Validity of order – Magistrates' Courts Act 1952, s 108(1)(2).

On 15th March 1979 the appellant in the first appeal was sentenced by a magistrates' court to consecutive terms of imprisonment totalling 12 months. On 4th April 1979, when he was still in prison, the same court issued a warrant for his imprisonment for a further 144 days, consecutive to the sentences passed on 15th March, in respect of his default in paying a large number of fines which had been imposed by various magistrates' courts since 1975. The appellant was given no notice of the proceedings and had no opportunity of making representations to the court before it issued the warrant for his further imprisonment. The appellant applied for judicial review by way of an order of certiorari to quash the order of 15th March and the warrant of commitment of 4th April, contending (i) that the magistrates had erred in law in committing him to prison without any notice of the hearing and that s 44(6)[a] of the Criminal Justice Act 1967 did not empower them to dispense with notice, and (ii) that the magistrates had acted ultra vires in imposing sentences on 15th March and 4th April which together exceeded the maximum period of 12 months prescribed by s 108(2)[b] of the Magistrates' Courts Act 1952 in respect of indictable offences triable summarily. The appellant contended that the fact that the two periods of imprisonment were imposed on different days was immaterial. The Divisional Court refused the application and the appellant appealed to the House of Lords.

On 12th July 1979 the appellant in the second appeal was sentenced by a magistrates' court to 30 days imprisonment in default of payment of a personal recognisance of £100. The appellant was in custody at the time serving a sentence of five years' imprisonment in respect of another offence. On 22nd October 1979 the same court issued a warrant committing the appellant to prison for a period of 30 days to be consecutive to the period of five years' imprisonment which the appellant was then serving. The appellant was given no notice of the proceedings of 12th July or 22nd October. The appellant applied for judicial review by way of an order of certiorari to quash the two orders. The Divisional Court refused his application and he appealed to the House of Lords.

---

a   Section 44(6), so far as material, is set out at p 715 c, post

b   Section 108(2) provides: 'If two or more of the terms imposed by the court are imposed in respect of an indictable offence tried summarily under section nineteen of this Act, the aggregate of the terms so imposed and any other terms imposed by the court may exceed six months but shall not, subject to the following provisions of this section, exceed twelve months.'

Held – (1) Although the effect of s 44(6) of the 1967 Act was that where an offender was serving a sentence of imprisonment, his actual presence at the hearing before a warrant of committal was issued might be dispensed with, that did not, either expressly or impliedly, mean that the hearing itself was to be dispensed with or that there was no need to give notice of it to the offender. It followed that the magistrates in both cases had been in breach of the principle of natural justice that a person was entitled to adequate notice and opportunity to be heard before any judicial order was pronounced against him, and the appeals would accordingly be allowed (see p 715 g h, p 716 a to f and p 717 f to j, post); R v Dudley Magistrates' Court, ex parte Payne [1979] 2 All ER 1089 overruled; R v Southampton Justices, ex parte Davies [1981] 1 All ER 722 considered.

(2) Section 108(1)ᶜ of the 1952 Act was clear and unambiguous in its terms and imposed a limitation only on the total imprisonment imposed on the same occasion. Accordingly, the magistrates in the first appeal had not been in breach of the limitation imposed by s 108(1) when on 4th April 1979 they imposed the additional period of 144 days to run consecutively to the period of 12 months imposed on 15th March (see p 717 a to j, post); R v Metropolitan Stipendiary Magistrate for South Westminster, ex parte Green [1977] 1 All ER 353 applied.

Notes

For imprisonment for default in the payment of a fine, see 29 Halsbury's Laws (4th Edn) paras 454–455, 457, and for cases on the subject, see 33 Digest (Repl) 380–381, 1950–1958.

For the imposition by magistrates of consecutive terms of imprisonment, see 29 Halsbury's Laws (4th Edn) para 417, and for cases on the subject, see 33 Digest (Repl) 254, 831–832.

For the Magistrates Court Act 1952, s 108, see 21 Halsbury's Statutes (3rd Edn) 278. For the Criminal Justice Act 1967, s 44, see ibid 381.

As from 6th July 1981, s 108 of the 1952 Act has been replaced by s 133 of the Magistrates' Courts Act 1980.

Cases referred to in opinions

Bonaker v Evans (1850) 16 QB 162, 20 LJQB 137, 16 LTOS 536, 15 Jur 460, 117 ER 840, Ex Ch, 19 Digest (Repl) 448, 2657.

R v Dudley Magistrates' Court, ex parte Payne [1979] 2 All ER 1089, [1979] 1 WLR 891, 143 JP 393, DC, Digest (Cont Vol E) 398, 808a.

R v Metropolitan Stipendiary Magistrate for South Westminster, ex parte Green [1977] 1 All ER 353, 141 JP 151, DC, Digest (Cont Vol E) 399, 835c.

R v Southampton Justices, ex parte Davies [1981] 1 All ER 722, [1981] 1 WLR 374, DC.

R v Uxbridge Justices, ex parte Fisc (4th March 1980), unreported, DC.

Appeals

Forrest v Brighton Justices

Peter Charles Forrest applied, with the leave of Sheen J given on 14th September 1979, for judicial review by way of an order of certiorari to quash an order made by the justices of the petty sessional division of Brighton, East Sussex, on 4th April 1979 whereby it was ordered that a warrant be issued committing the appellant to prison for 144 days consecutive to other terms of imprisonment imposed by the justices on 15th March 1979. On 20th October 1980 the Divisional Court of the Queen's Bench Division (Ormrod LJ and Lloyd J) dismissed his application and refused leave to appeal to the House of Lords but certified under s 1(2) of the Administration of Justice Act 1960 that the following points of law of general public importance were involved in the decision: (1) whether a magistrates' court may lawfully issue a warrant of commitment to prison under s 44(6) of the Criminal Justice Act 1967 for a default in payment of a sum of money adjudged to be paid by a conviction without giving notice to the defendant

---

c   Section 108(1) is set out at p 716 j, post

before issuing the warrant and an opportunity to make representations to the court
a either personally or by an advocate on his behalf; (2) whether a magistrates' court may
lawfully impose a term of imprisonment on a defendant under s 108 of the Magistrates'
Courts Act 1952 which is consecutive to other terms of imprisonment imposed on a
previous occasion by a magistrates' court and which will have the effect of imposing an
aggregate term of imprisonment exceeding 12 months. On 18th December 1980 the
Appeal Committee of the House of Lords gave the appellant leave to appeal against the
b decision. The facts are set out in the opinion of Lord Fraser.

Hamilton v Marylebone Magistrates' Court
Michael Francis Hamilton applied with leave of the Divisional Court of the Queen's
Bench Division (Lord Lane CJ and Boreham J) given on 19th June 1980 for judicial
review by way of an order of certiorari to quash an order of 12th July 1979 and a warrant
c of commitment dated 22nd October 1979 made by the stipendiary magistrate sitting at
Marylebone Magistrates' Court whereby the appellant was sentenced to a term of
imprisonment of 30 days to run consecutive to a sentence of five years imprisonment
imposed at the Central Criminal Court on 15th June 1979. On 14th July 1980 the
Divisional Court of the Queen's Bench Division (Lord Lane CJ and Comyn J) refused his
application and refused leave to appeal to the House of Lords but certified under s 1(2) of
d the Administration of Justice Act 1960 that the following point of law of general public
importance was involved in the decision: whether s 44(6) of the Criminal Justice Act
1967 authorises a magistrates' court to issue a warrant of commitment against an
offender in circumstances falling within para (*a*) or para (*b*) of that subsection without
giving prior notice to the offender of its intention so to do. On 18th December 1980 the
Appeal Committee of the House of Lords gave the appellant leave to appeal against the
e decision. The facts are set out in the opinion of Lord Fraser.

Nicholas Nardecchia for the appellant Forrest.
Gordon Bennett for the appellant Hamilton.
D Cocks for the Attorney General as amicus curiae.
The respondents did not appear.

f
Their Lordships took time for consideration.

18th June. The following opinions were delivered.

LORD FRASER OF TULLYBELTON. My Lords, these appeals were heard
g together. They raise two questions, one of which is common to both appeals, and the
other of which arises only in the case of Forrest. I shall consider the common point first.
     On 15th March 1979 the appellant Peter Forrest pleaded guilty to several offences and
was sentenced by the magistrates' court in Brighton to consecutive terms of imprisonment
totalling 12 months. On 4th April 1979, when he was, of course, in prison, the same
court issued a warrant for his imprisonment for a further period of 144 days, consecutive
h to the sentences passed on 15th March, in respect of his default in paying a large number
of fines which had been imposed by various magistrates' courts on various dates since
1975. He was given no notice of the proceedings on 4th April, and he had no opportunity
of making representations to the court before it issued the warrant for his further
imprisonment. The first that he knew of the matter was after the court proceedings on
4th April, when he was informed by the governor of the prison where he was then
j serving his sentence of 12 months that the warrant had been issued and that he would
have to serve an additional 144 days. He applied to the Divisional Court for an order to
quash the order of 4th April on two grounds, the first of which was that the magistrates
had erred in law in committing him to prison without giving him any notice or warning
of the hearing on that day. When his application came before the Divisional Court
(Ormrod LJ and Lloyd J) that court felt itself bound by an earlier decision of the
Divisional Court in *R v Dudley Magistrates' Court, ex parte Payne* [1979] 2 All ER 1089,

[1979] 1 WLR 891 to dismiss the application. But Ormrod LJ, with whose opinion Lloyd J agreed, said that he arrived at his conclusion 'with both surprise and some considerable measure of regret'.

The facts in the appeal by Michael Hamilton do not differ in any relevant respect from those in Forrest's case, although they are perhaps more striking because of the long period which they span. In August 1971 the appellant Hamilton entered into a personal recognisance of £100 to appear at Marylebone Magistrates' Court about a month later in answer to a charge under the Forgery Act 1913. He did not appear, having gone abroad, but on 23rd March 1978 he was eventually brought before the court. On 23rd May 1978 the court ordered that his recognizance be forfeited, giving him seven days to pay. The appellant failed to pay, and on 12th July 1979 the magistrates' court fixed a period of 30 days as the period to be served in default of payment in accordance with the Magistrates' Courts Act 1952, s 65(2). By 12th July 1979 the appellant was serving a sentence of five years' imprisonment in respect of another offence and he failed to pay the £100 recognisance. On 22nd October 1979 the same court issued a warrant committing the appellant to prison for a period of 30 days, to be consecutive to the period of five years imprisonment which he was then serving, and because he was in prison no inquiry into his means had to be held or was held: see s 44(4) and (6) of the Criminal Justice Act 1967. The appellant was given no notice of the proceedings in the Marylebone court on either 12th July or 22nd October 1979. He applied to the Divisional Court for an order of certiorari to quash the orders made by the magistrates on those dates. His application, like that of the appellant Forrest, was refused by the Divisional Court, consisting on this occasion of Lord Lane CJ and Comyn J. The opinion of the court was given by Comyn J who said that the court was bound by the decision in R v Dudley Magistrates' Court 'however difficult we may find it to accept the majority ruling'. Lord Lane CJ agreed with that opinion and said that he felt the same 'hesitation' as Comyn J.

In the light of these expressions of opinion by the (differently constituted) Divisional Courts in the instant appeals, and having regard to the fact that the decision in R v Dudley Magistrates' Court was by a majority (Michael Davies J and Lord Widgery CJ) and that a strong dissenting opinion was expressed by Robert Goff J, the soundness of that decision clearly merits consideration.

The appellants may not be deserving of much sympathy, but the question whether they were entitled to notice of the proceedings in the magistrates' courts concerning them respectively raises an issue of some constitutional importance. One of the principles of natural justice is that a person is entitled to adequate notice and opportunity to be heard before any judicial order is pronounced against him, so that he, or someone acting on his behalf, may make such representations, if any, as he sees fit. That is the rule of audi alteram partem which applies to all judicial proceedings, unless its application to a particular class of proceedings has been excluded by Parliament expressly or by necessary implication. That principle has often been stated, nowhere more clearly than in the passage cited in R v Dudley Magistrates' Court from Bonaker v Evans (1850) 16 QB 162 at 171, 117 ER 840 at 844, by Parke B as follows:

'. . . no proposition can be more clearly established than that a man cannot incur the loss of liberty or property for an offence by a judicial proceeding until he has had a fair opportunity of answering the charge against him, unless the Legislature has expressly or impliedly given an authority to act without that necessary preliminary.'

It was because the learned judges who considered the instant appeals in the Divisional Court were conscious of that rule that they expressed the surprise and hesitation they did at the decisions to which they felt themselves driven by authority. But counsel who appeared as amicus curiae, while accepting (rightly in my opinion) that the proceedings in which magistrates fixed the term of imprisonment in default of payment and issued warrants for committal were judicial proceedings, argued that the application of the rule had been excluded by necessary implication in the legislation which applies to these appeals.

The power of magistrates to commit to prison for default in payment of fines is

derived from the Magistrates' Courts Act 1952, s 64(1) which, so far as relevant, provides
a that—

> 'where default is made in paying a sum adjudged to be paid by a conviction or
> order of a magistrates' court, the court may issue a warrant . . . committing the
> defaulter to prison.'

That power is subject to certain limitations which are now set out in s 44 of the Criminal
b Justice Act 1967 in several subsections which apply to various circumstances in which the
power may fall to be exercised. The subsection relevant here is sub-s (6) which provides
as follows:

> 'After the occasion of an offender's conviction by a magistrates' court, the court
> shall not, unless—(a) the court has previously fixed a term of imprisonment under
> section 65(2) of the Magistrates' Courts Act 1952 which is to be served by the
c > offender in the event of a default in paying a sum adjudged to be paid by the
> conviction; or (b) the offender is serving a term of imprisonment or detention in a
> detention centre; issue a warrant of commitment for a default in paying the sum or
> fix such a term except at a hearing at which the offender is present . . .'

The argument which was accepted by the majority in *R v Dudley Magistrates' Court*,
d and which was advanced by counsel who appeared as amicus curiae in the present case,
was that the effect of that subsection was to dispense with the need for any hearing before
fixing a term of imprisonment or issuing a warrant for imprisonment in the case of an
offender who was already serving a term of imprisonment. Michael Davies J, giving the
opinion of the court in *R v Dudley Magistrates' Court*, after quoting the passage which I
have quoted above from *Bonaker v Evans*, stated his conclusion thus ([1979] 2 All ER
e 1089, [1979] 1 WLR 891 at 895):

> 'As I have already said, in my view it is quite plain that the legislature by s 44(6)
> gave the justices express authority to issue a warrant of commitment in
> circumstances such as these [ie where the offender is serving a term of imprisonment]
> without a hearing and in my judgment it follows that the legislature also bestowed
> on the justices an implied authority to do so without notice to the individual
f > concerned. So there was no breach of the rules of natural justice. That, in my
> judgment, is sufficient to dispose of the short point in this application.'

With the greatest respect to the learned judge, I am unable to accept that view. The
effect of s 44(6) is (relevantly) that, where an offender is serving a term of imprisonment,
a warrant for his commitment for a default in paying a fine may be issued without the
g necessity of 'a hearing *at which the offender is present*'. That is to say, a hearing can proceed
in the absence of the offender. But the subsection does not provide, nor, in my opinion,
does it imply, that a warrant for commitment may be issued without any hearing at
all. Still less does it provide or imply that no notice need be given to an offender that
procedure is about to take place in the magistrates' court which may result in his being
committed to prison for a period consecutive to the sentence which he is already
h serving. I agree with the dissenting opinion of Robert Goff J in *R v Dudley Magistrates'
Court* and particularly with the passage where he says ([1979] 2 All ER 1089 at 1093,
[1979] 1 WLR 891 at 897):

> 'In my judgment, a requirement of "presence" is a very different thing from a
> requirement of "notice" . . . [sub-s (6)] means, in my judgment, what it says, that
> except in the two excluded cases, the actual presence of the offender is required at
j > the hearing before a warrant of commitment is issued. That is because, except in
> the two excluded cases, a means enquiry must take place and for that purpose the
> offender has to attend the hearing.'

The reason why a means inquiry is not required in the case of an offender who is
serving a sentence of imprisonment probably is that the majority of such offenders who
have defaulted in paying fines have no substantial means, so that the inquiry would be

futile. An additional reason may be that any period of imprisonment for default in paying fines will generally be ordered to run concurrently with the sentence which the *a* offender is already serving, so that its length will have little practical effect on him. However that may be, s 44(6) of the 1967 Act is not, in my opinion, capable of being read as dispensing with a hearing altogether or with the need to give notice of it to the offender. It dispenses only with the need for his actual presence, and on a matter of constitutional importance such as this, its meaning ought not to be stretched in such a way as to prejudice the offender. In many cases he may have no excuse to offer for *b* defaulting in payment, and, if he neither appears in person or by a representative, nor sends a written explanation, the 'hearing' will in practice consist simply of the magistrates making an appropriate order. But, if he makes any representations either personally, or through another person or in writing, he is entitled to have them taken into consideration by the magistrates before they make an order. An obvious example of the type of representation that might be made is that any period of imprisonment should run *c* concurrently with his current sentence, on the ground that his default in paying the fine had been due to some cause which was not his fault, such as ill health or loss of his job. Another possible type of representation was suggested by a case that was mentioned in argument to us, *R v Southampton Justices, ex parte Davies* [1981] 1 All ER 722, [1981] 1 WLR 374, where the Divisonal Court (Donaldson LJ and Forbes J) considered the proper method of computing the maximum period of imprisonment that might be imposed by *d* magistrates for default in paying fines. If that case was rightly decided, the calculation in Forrest's case was made on a wrong basis, and the period of 144 days imposed on him exceeded the proper maximum which was only 90 days. Counsel who appeared as amicus curiae conceded that *R v Southampton Justices* had been rightly decided, and counsel for Forrest naturally accepted the concession, but as I am not at present satisfied that the reasoning underlying the decision is correct and as we have not heard full *e* argument on the question, I would reserve my opinion on it. The relevance of the case is only to show that an offender who is in prison may have a real practical interest in making representations to the court before a term of imprisonment is imposed on him for default in paying fines.

I would accordingly anwer the first of the certified questions in the appeal by Forrest and the only certified question in the appeal by Hamilton in the negative.   *f*

The second question which is raised on behalf of the appellant Forrest is whether the magistrates, having sentenced the appellant on 15th March 1979 to consecutive terms of imprisonment amounting in total to 12 months, were entitled to impose an additional period of 144 days imprisonment on 4th April 1979 for default in payment of fines. Counsel for the appellant argued that the magistrates had acted ultra vires on 4th April in respect that the total of all the sentences imposed on that date and on 15th March *g* exceeded 12 months which was the maximum they were entitled to impose under the Magistrates' Courts Act 1952, s 108(2). He submitted that the fact that the 144 days had been imposed on a different day from the 12 months was immaterial and that the total of all sentences, current or pending, imposed by the magistrates was the relevant figure. On the facts of this case, it was enough for counsel for appellant to submit, as he did, that the maximum of six months under sub-s (1) of s 108 or 12 months under *h* sub-s (2) applied to the aggregate of the terms of imprisonment imposed by any one magistrates' court; but, as counsel who appeared as amicus curiae pointed out, it might be argued that the maximum applied to the aggregate of all terms imposed by any magistrates' court. Whichever form the argument takes it depends on the provisions of s 108 and particularly on the latter part of sub-s (1). That subsection provides as follows:

> 'A magistrates' court imposing imprisonment on any person may order that the *j* term of imprisonment shall commence on the expiration of any other term of imprisonment imposed by that or any other court; but where a magistrates' court imposes two or more terms of imprisonment to run consecutively the aggregate of such terms shall not, subject to the provisions of this section, exceed six months.'

The first part of that subsection down to the semicolon contains nothing to suggest

that the date on which the 'other term of imprisonment' was imposed is material. If it
a was imposed by 'the court' (ie by the magistrates' court itself) that might have been
either on the same occasion as the sentence which is to be consecutive to it is imposed, or
on an earlier occasion. But if it was imposed by 'any other court' it must have been
imposed on an earlier occasion. When one comes to the second part of sub-s (1), after the
semicolon, the provision is applicable where a magistrates' court 'imposes two or more
terms of imprisonment to run consecutively' and in my opinion the natural and plain
b meaning of those words is to read them as referring to imposing two or more terms of
imprisonment on the same occasion. I agree with Ormrod LJ and Lloyd J that the
subsection, on its natural reading, does not limit the power of the magistrates' court to
imposing sentences of a total amount of 6 months or 12 months in all circumstances. If
it had done so, it would have been inconsistent with the policy given effect to by sub-s
(4) and while that is not impossible it is unlikely.

c   I recognise that the result of construing the subsection in the way that I consider to be
correct is to leave room for what may seem to be an anomaly; provided that sentences are
imposed on different days there is, in theory, no limit to the aggregate of the terms of
imprisonment that a magistrates' court may impose. But that is only theoretical, because
in practice if the aggregate were going to be greatly in excess of 6 months or 12 months,
as the case may be, the magistrates' court would remit the case to a higher court for
d sentence. In any event, I regard the construction of sub-s (1), which is the only subsection
relevant for this purpose, as too plain to be shaken by consequences which may seem to
some extent anomalous. I am fortified in that opinion by the decision of the Divisional
Court in the instant appeal by Forrest, and also by the decisions in *R v Metropolitan
Stipendiary Magistrate for South Westminster, ex parte Green* [1977] 1 All ER 353, where the
judgment was given by May J with whom Lord Widgery CJ and Croom-Johnson J
e concurred, and in the unreported case of *R v Uxbridge Justices, ex parte Fisc* (4th March
1980) where the judgment of the court, consisting of Lord Widgery CJ and May J was
again given by May J.
    I would answer the second question in Forrest's appeal in the affirmative.
    For these reasons I would allow both appeals.

f **LORD ELWYN-JONES.** My Lords, I have had the advantage of reading in draft the
speech of my noble and learned friend Lord Fraser. For the reasons he gives I would
answer the two certified questions as he proposes. Accordingly, I would allow the two
appeals.

    LORD SALMON. My Lords, I have had the advantage of reading in draft the speech
g of my noble and learned friend Lord Fraser. For the reasons he has given I would answer
the two certified questions as he proposes. Accordingly, I too would allow the two
appeals.

    LORD SCARMAN. My Lords, I have had the advantage of reading in draft the speech
delivered by my noble and learned friend Lord Fraser. For the reasons he gives I would
h answer the two certified questions as he proposes. Accordingly, I would allow the two
appeals.

    LORD ROSKILL. My Lords, I have had the advantage of reading in draft the speech
of my noble and learned friend Lord Fraser. For the reasons he gives I agree that both
appeals should be allowed. I desire to record my respectful agreement with the comment
j which my noble and learned friend makes on the reasoning underlying the decision in
R v Southampton Justices, ex parte Davies [1981] 1 All ER 722, [1981] 1 WLR 374.

Forrest v Brighton Justices
*Order appealed from set aside; the first certified question answered in the negative, the second
certified question answered in the affirmative; case remitted to the Divisional Court with a
direction to quash the order and warrant of committal of the magistrates made on 4th April 1979.*

Hamilton v Marylebone Magistrates' Court
Order appealed from set aside; certified question answered in the negative; case remitted to the a
Divisonal Court with a direction to quash the order of the magistrate of 12th July 1979 and his
warrant of committal of 22nd October 1979.

Solicitors: *Selwood, Leathes & Hooper*, Brighton (for the appellant Forrest); *Gentle, Mathias*
& Co (for the appellant Hamilton); *Treasury Solicitor*.

b

Mary Rose Plummer   Barrister.

Windsors (Sporting Investments) Ltd v Oldfield
Boulton v Coral Racing Ltd and another

c

QUEEN'S BENCH DIVISION
DONALDSON LJ AND FORBES J
23rd, 30th JANUARY 1981

d

Gaming – Betting – Licensed betting office – Advertisement – Elsewhere than in betting office or
on premises giving access to office – Advertisement drawing attention to availability of or facilities
afforded in betting office – Poster affixed to inside of shop window of betting office – Poster facing
outwards so that it could be read only by persons outside office – Whether advertisement published e
outside betting office – Whether poster constituting advertisement drawing attention to betting
office facilities – Betting, Gaming and Lotteries Act 1963, s 10(5)(c).

The licensees of two betting shops fixed outward-facing posters on the inside of their
shop windows so that the posters could be read by persons outside the shop but not by
persons inside the shop. The posters were found, or assumed, to constitute advertisements f
drawing attention to the betting shops and their facilities. The respective licensees were
charged with publishing an advertisement drawing attention to the availability of a
betting shop otherwise than 'in a licensed betting office', contrary to s 10(5)(c)[a] of the
Betting, Gaming and Lotteries Act 1963. In the first case the magistrates convicted the
licensee and on appeal that conviction was upheld by the Crown Court, on the ground
that if the poster was visible to anyone outside the betting shop it was published outside g
the shop. In the second case the stipendiary magistrate held that a poster fixed to the
inside of a shop window of a betting shop so that it could only be read from the outside
did not contravene s 10(5), and accordingly dismissed the information. The licensee in
the first case and the prosecutor in the second case appealed.

Held – (1) An advertisement placed inside a betting shop but visible to, and clearly h
aimed at, persons outside the shop was published outside the shop and displayed outside
the premises. The posters were accordingly published otherwise than 'in a licensed
betting office' in contravention of s 10(5)(c) of the 1963 Act. It followed that the appeal
in the first case would be dismissed (see p 722 e f and p 723 c to e, post); *Dunsford v Pearson*
[1970] 1 All ER 282 and *R v Newcastle upon Tyne Gaming Licensing Committee, ex parte*
White Hart Enterprises Ltd [1977] 3 All ER 961 applied; dictum of Lord Parker CJ in *Roy* j
William Robinson Ltd v Cox (1968) 67 LGR at 195 not followed.
    (2) Whether or not material was an advertisement for the purposes of s 10(5)(c) of the
1963 Act was a question of fact for the magistrates' court. However (per Donaldson LJ),
although the prosecution had to satisfy the court that the material extolled the virtue of

---

a   Section 10(5) is set out at p 720 *h* to p 721 *a*, post

a betting office it was not necessary for the advertisement to state that the premises to
which it was affixed was a licensed betting office for it to constitute an advertisement
'drawing attention to the availability of, or to the facilities afforded [in]' a licensed betting
office for the purposes of s 10(5)(c). Accordingly, the second case would be remitted to
the stipendiary magistrate for him to consider whether the posters in that case constituted
an advertisement (see p 722 *h* to p 723 *a* and *f*, post).

Notes

For the conduct of licensed betting offices, see 4 Halsbury's Laws (4th Edn) para 71, and
for cases on the subject, see 25 Digest (Reissue) 501–502, 4381–4386.

    For the Betting, Gaming and Lotteries Act 1963, s 10, see 14 Halsbury's Statutes (3rd
Edn) 553.

Cases referred to in judgments

Dunsford v Pearson [1970] 1 All ER 282, [1970] 1 WLR 222, 134 JP 180, 68 LGR 61, DC,
    25 Digest (Reissue) 500, 4379.

R v Newcastle upon Tyne Gaming Licensing Committee, ex parte White Hart Enterprises Ltd
    [1977] 3 All ER 961, [1977] 1 WLR 1135, 142 JP 81, CA, Digest (Cont Vol E) 236,
    352Abe.

Robinson (Roy William) Ltd v Cox (1968) 67 LGR 188, 25 Digest (Reissue) 502, 4383.

Cases stated

Windsors (Sporting Investments) Ltd v Oldfield

Windsors (Sporting Investments) Ltd ('Windsors') appealed by case stated from a decision
of the Crown Court at Bradford (Mr Recorder F C Radcliffe) on 27th September 1979
dismissing Windsors' appeal from a decision of the justices for the County of West
Yorkshire acting in and for the petty sessional division of Bradford whereby they
convicted Windsors on 15th June 1979 on an information preferred by the prosecutor,
Chief Inspector Oldfield, that on 6th November 1978 at Bradford, being the licensee of
a licensed betting office at 12 The Green, Idle, Bradford, Windsors published an
advertisement which stated 'Meet the Greyhound Trapper—Every dog has his day—
This could be yours—William Hill where the action is', thereby drawing attention to the
facilities afforded to persons resorting to the betting office, such publication being
otherwise than in the betting office or in the prescribed manner on premises giving
access to the office, contrary to s 10(5) of the Betting, Gaming and Lotteries Act 1963.
The question of law for the opinion of the High Court was whether an advertisement
which was fixed within a licensed betting office was nevertheless published outside that
office if it could be read by persons outside the office. The facts, so far as material, are set
out in the judgment of Donaldson LJ.

Boulton v Coral Racing Ltd and Howells

The prosecutor, Chief Superintendent Sidney Boulton, appealed by case stated from the
decision of Mr D Alan Phillips, the stipendiary magistrate for the County of Mid
Glamorgan acting in and for the petty sessional division of Newcastle and Ogmore, in
respect of his adjudication as a magistrates' court sitting at Bridgend on 12th December
1979, whereby the magistrate dismissed informations laid by the prosecutor against the
defendants, Coral Racing Ltd ('Corals') and Barbara Ann Howells, that they had on 21st
June and 7th September 1979 published advertisements in the shop window of a licensed
betting office in Market Street, Bridgend, in such a manner as to draw attention to the
facilities afforded to persons resorting to the office, contrary to s 10(5)(c) of the Betting,
Gaming and Lotteries Act 1963. Corals were the owner and the second defendant the
manageress of the betting office. The questions of law for the opinion of the High Court
were (i) whether an advertisement affixed to the inside of a clear glass window of a
licensed betting office and facing outwards, legible from outside but not legible from
inside the office, was published outside the premises, and (ii) whether to constitute an
advertisement for the purposes of s 10(5)(c) of the Betting, Gaming and Lotteries Act
1963, an advertisement which drew attention to the facilities provided by licensed
premises must state as a fact that the premises to which it was affixed was a licensed
betting office. The facts, so far as material, are set out in the judgment of Donaldson LJ.

John Marriage QC and *Rodney Smith* for Windsors.
S W Williamson for the prosecutor Oldfield.   *a*
Alun Jones for the prosecutor Boulton.
Gareth Williams QC and *Anthony Evans* for Corals and Barbara Ann Howells.

Cur adv vult

30th January. The following judgments were read.
b

DONALDSON LJ. Windsors (Sporting Investments) Ltd ('Windsors') are part of the
William Hill group of bookmakers with a licensed betting office at 12 The Green, Idle,
Bradford. On 9th April 1979 Chief Inspector Oldfield preferred informations charging
them with (1) publishing an advertisement drawing attention to the facilities afforded to
persons resorting to that office, contrary to s 10(5) of the Betting, Gaming and Lotteries
Act 1963, and (2) exhibiting signs on licensed premises which did not comply with reg *c*
3(2) of the Betting (Licensed Offices) Regulations 1960, SI 1960 No 2332, contrary to s
10(1) of the 1963 Act.
   Windsors were acquitted by the Bradford justices of the charge under the regulations,
but convicted of the charge under s 10(5). They appealed unsuccessfully against that
conviction to the Crown Court at Bradford. They now appeal again, this time by means
of a case stated by the Crown Court.   *d*
   Coral Racing Ltd ('Corals'), as its name implies, is a part of the Coral group of
companies and has a licensed betting office in Market Street, Bridgend, Mid
Glamorgan. The office was managed by Barbara Ann Howells. On 20th September
1979 Chief Superintendent Sidney Boulton laid informations against Corals and their
manageress charging them with two separate offences of publishing advertisements
contrary to s 10(5)(c) of the 1963 Act. The stipendiary magistrate dismissed the charges *e*
and the prosecutor now appeals by case stated.
   Both appeals are in the nature of test cases and both raise the question whether it is
permissible for advertisements to be 'put up', to use a neutral term, *inside* the window of
a licensed betting office in such a way that they cannot, or cannot normally, be read by
anyone inside the betting office, but are fully visible to passers by and others outside the
office. We have accordingly heard the two appeals together and this judgment relates to *f*
both.
   So far as is material, the scheme of the 1963 Act appears to be to provide two different
zones of control, namely (i) in the betting office itself and premises giving access to such
an office, and (ii) elsewhere. Control in the case of the betting office and premises giving
access to it is by s 10(1), rules contained in Sch 4 of the 1963 Act, and the Betting
(Licensed Offices) Regulations 1960 which were continued in force by s 57(3) of the 1963 *g*
Act. Control elsewhere is by s 10(5) of the Act.
   On any view the window of a betting office is on the interface of these two zones and
it is this which has given rise to the problem.
   Section 10(5) of the 1963 Act is in the following terms:

   'If, save in a licensed betting office or in such manner as may be prescribed on *h*
   premises giving access to such an office, any advertisement is published—(*a*)
   indicating that any particular premises are a licensed betting office; or (*b*) indicating
   where any such office may be found; or (*c*) drawing attention to the availability of,
   or to the facilities afforded to persons resorting to, such offices, then, in the case of
   an advertisement in connection with the office or offices of any particular licensee,
   that licensee, and in every case any person who published the advertisement or *j*
   caused or permitted it to be published, shall be guilty of an offence: Provided that
   it shall be a defence for any person charged with an offence under this subsection to
   prove—(i) that he did not know and had no reasonable cause to suspect that the
   advertisement was, and that he had taken all reasonable steps to ascertain that it was
   not, such an advertisement as aforesaid; or (ii) if he is charged by reason only of

a being a licensee, that the advertisement was published without his consent or connivance and that he exercised all due diligence to prevent the publishing of any such advertisement in connection with his office or offices.'

Regulation 3 of the 1960 regulations provides as follows:

'(1) The holder of a betting office licence shall exhibit in a conspicuous manner and in some conspicuous place inside the licensed premises a notice stating that

b persons under the age of eighteen years are not admitted thereto.

'(2) The holder of a betting office licence shall inside the licensed premises exhibit no written matter or sign of any description other than the betting office licence and the notice required to be exhibited by paragraph (1) of this Regulation, except: (a) in such manner that the matter exhibited cannot be read from outside those premises, the rules subject to which betting transactions are effected on those

c premises and information relating to events in connection with which betting transactions may be or have been effected thereon, and a page containing such information taken from a newspaper may be exhibited under this subparagraph notwithstanding that it does not consist solely of such information . . .'

I do not think I need bother with (b) and (c).

d In Windsors case, it is not now disputed that the posters which were displayed constituted an advertisement drawing attention to the availability of, or to the facilities afforded to persons resorting to, a licensed betting office. That issue has not been decided in the Coral case and does not arise for our decision. However, in the interests of simplicity I shall assume that the Coral posters also constitute such advertisements.

This is not the first time on which s 10(5) and the regulations have been considered by this court.

e In *Roy William Robinson Ltd v Cox* (1968) 67 LGR 188 the bookmaker exhibited a facia-like sign on the outside wall of the betting office and over its full length bearing his name and the words, 'Licensed Betting Office: Open 11 a.m. daily'. He was charged and convicted under s 10(5). On appeal to the Divisional Court it was held, not surprisingly, that this notice was not in the betting office or on premises giving access to the betting

f office and so within the exception to s 10(5). However, Lord Parker CJ said (at 195):

'I confess that I have fought against coming to that conclusion because it seems to me that there can be no harm whatever in having a sign on the outside of the building, as there was in this case, when one realises there is nothing in the Act or regulations to prevent a similar sign, indeed not confined in area and size, appearing on the inside of the plate glass window facing outside, and therefore giving exactly

g the same advertisement from the inside of the office as in the present case appears from the outside of the office.'

Ashworth and Willis JJ agreed.

In *Dunsford v Pearson* [1970] 1 All ER 282, [1970] 1 WLR 222 the bookmaker who may have been familiar with the decision in *Robinson v Cox* placed two notices reading

h 'TURF ACCOUNTANT' in the window of the betting office in such a way that they were visible from the highway, but not from inside the office. He was prosecuted for breach of reg 3 of the 1960 regulations. On appeal his acquittal was affirmed because this court held that there was no breach of reg 3 unless the notice could be seen by those inside the premises. As Ashworth J put it ([1970] 1 All ER 282 at 286, [1970] 1 WLR 222 at 227):

j 'Really the issue before this court can be confined in the nutshell of: does exhibition inside involve the proposition that what is exhibited must be visible inside? Counsel for the appellant put it in exactly that form, that, in order to render the present licensee liable for contravention of the regulation, the notice which he exhibited must have been exhibited in such a form that it was visible inside. That is the view which was indicated in *Robinson v Cox*, and it is the view which I take here.'

Lord Parker CJ and Cantley J agreed. Both Lord Parker CJ and Ashworth J affirmed
the dictum of Lord Parker in *Robinson v Cox*, but this affirmation was no more necessary *a*
to the decision than the original dictum since the bookmaker was charged under the
regulations and not under s 10(5).

In *R v Newcastle upon Tyne Gaming Licensing Committee* [1977] 3 All ER 961, [1977] 1
WLR 1135 the Court of Appeal, Civil Division, was concerned with the Gaming Act
1968 under which a notice of intended application for a licence must be 'displayed
outside the entrance to the relevant premises'. The prospective licensee placed the notice *b*
on the inside of the window of the premises facing outwards and this was held to
constitute displaying the notice outside the premises.

The stipendiary magistrate at Bridgend felt that he should follow the twice affirmed
dictum of Lord Parker CJ and, in his position, I should unhesitatingly have done the
same. The Crown Court felt free to depart from this dictum. This may have been a bold
decision, but if the deputy circuit judge was convinced that the dictum was wrong, he *c*
was right to do so. He said:

> 'We were of the opinion that the said advertisement was published outside the
> licensed betting office because, although it was fixed inside it was not visible inside
> and was clearly visible to anyone outside the said premises. We interpreted the
> subsection as banning the publication of advertisements visible on the outside to
> passers-by. The point of publication is not where the advertisement is fixed but *d*
> where it is read.'

In this court we have to give great weight to such a dictum, but it is not binding on us
and it is necessary that we should decide the point.

These advertisements were clearly published, exhibited and displayed. On the binding
authority of *Dunsford v Pearson* they were not exhibited in the betting offices, because *e*
they were not visible to anyone in the premises. Were it otherwise, an offence would
have been committed under reg 3. On the binding authority of *R v Newcastle upon Tyne
Gaming Licensing Committee* these posters were displayed outside the premises. It would
in my view be anomalous to hold that, although they were not exhibited in the betting
office, and were displayed outside it, they were not published outside the betting office,
and I am quite satisfied that, as a matter of law, they were so published. *f*

This conclusion is in my judgment fatal to the appeal of Windsors (Sporting
Investments) Ltd and I would dismiss it.

In the Coral case we are also asked:

> 'Whether to constitute an advertisement for the purposes of s 10(5)(*c*) of the
> Betting, Gaming and Lotteries Act 1963, an advertisement which draws attention
> to the facilities provided by licensed premises must state as a fact that the premises *g*
> to which it is affixed is a licensed betting office.'

I would answer that there is no reason whatsoever why the advertisement should state
that the premises to which it is affixed is a licensed betting office. The offence is
committed if it is affixed to a hoarding deep in the country, provided only that it draws
attention to the availability of, or to the facilities afforded to persons resorting to, such *h*
offices. However, I imagine that the question is really directed to the fact that the section
is only concerned with advertising the availability etc of licensed betting offices, that is
offices involved with cash as opposed to credit betting. This is of course correct and the
prosecution will have to satisfy the court that the advertisement concerned did extol the
virtues of a licensed betting office or offices. The fact that an advertisement is displayed
on or near a licensed betting office may well be a potent factor in deciding on the *j*
meaning to be attributed to any particular advertisement. But that would be a matter
for the court charged with deciding issues of fact and not for this court.

I think therefore that the Coral case will have to be remitted to the stipendiary
magistrate for him to consider such further issues as whether the posters constituted an
advertisement. He may also have to consider the proviso to s 10(5). As to that I would

a only say that if the defendants did not know that their poster was such as to contravene s 10(5) (and I do not see how they could have known this in the light of the state of the art) and if they had considered and accepted the advice contained in the dicta in *Robinson v Cox* or *Dunsford v Pearson* I should have thought that they had an absolutely impregnable defence on this occasion, but not in future.

b **FORBES J.** Shorn of all irrelevancies s 10(5) of the 1963 Act makes it an offence to publish an advertisement otherwise than inside a betting office. To publish an advertisement both inside and outside is thus an offence. The sole question is therefore whether in the circumstances of these cases the advertisements were published solely inside the offices.

It is clear that the advertisements could not be read from inside but only from outside the offices. Both these organisations are commercial enterprises. The only possible *c* commercial purpose of placing, to use a neutral term, material of this character in the windows could have been to advertise to those outside the offices the name or the activities of these organisations. The primary meaning of to 'publish' is to 'make public'. The proposition that advertisements placed inside the offices in such a way as to be invisible to anyone inside while on the other hand visible to and clearly aimed at persons outside the offices are published inside but not outside does such violence to the *d* common usage of language that for myself I could not accept that this is what Parliament intended.

There is nothing in any report of *Robinson's* case to suggest that any argument about the effect of s 10(5) was ever addressed to this court on that occasion. Had they had the advantage of hearing the arguments addressed to us, I feel no doubt that neither Lord Parker CJ nor Ashworth J would have committed themselves to a dictum which can now *e* be seen to be not only obiter but also per incuriam. As such I think this court must be justified in holding itself free not to follow it. For myself I would be content to rule that an advertisement is not published solely inside premises if, as here, it is clearly visible to and intended to be read by persons outside.

I have used the term 'advertisements' as if the material placed in these windows properly fell within the meaning of that word. The question of whether or not any *f* material is an advertisement will depend, in individual cases, on what that material is, and will thus be a question of fact for the justices to decide. I agree that Coral's case must go back to the stipendiary magistrate to consider whether the poster in the window was an advertisement.

If it is objected that this ruling will mean that it is an offence even to indicate that premises, other than premises in multiple occupation, are in fact a betting office I would *g* only say that this would appear to conform to the clear intention of Parliament that these establishments should be difficult to find and, when found, should be internally as dreary as possible.

Appeal of Windsors (Sporting Investments) Ltd dismissed. Coral Racing Ltd's case remitted to the stipendiary magistrate for further consideration.

h The court refused leave to appeal to the House of Lords but certified, under s 1(2) of the Administration of Justice Act 1960 that the following point of law of general public importance was involved in the decision: whether, for the purposes of s 10(5) of the Betting, Gaming and Lotteries Act 1963, an advertisement affixed to the inside of a clear glass window of a licensed betting office and facing outwards, legible from outside but not legible from inside the office, is published outside the premises.

j
Solicitors: *Gosschalk, Wheldon & Co*, Hull (for Windsors); M D *Shaffner* (for the prosecutor Oldfield); J M *Timmons* (for the prosecutor Boulton); *John Morse & Co* (for Coral and Barbara Ann Howells).

Jacqueline Charles   Barrister.

Hadmor Productions Ltd v Hamilton and others

COURT OF APPEAL, CIVIL DIVISION

LORD DENNING MR, WATKINS AND O'CONNOR LJJ

16th, 17th, 18th, 19th MARCH, 9th APRIL 1981

Trade dispute – Acts done in contemplation or furtherance of trade dispute – In contemplation or furtherance of – Secondary action in furtherance of dispute – Claim by party that he had acted in furtherance of trade dispute – Policy of television technicians' union that television stations should not buy in ready-made programmes from outside – Plaintiffs making programmes and agreeing to sell them to television station – Union blacking programmes – Whether union acting in contemplation or furtherance of 'trade dispute' – Whether union's action amounting to interference with plaintiffs' trade or business by unlawful means – Trade Union and Labour Relations Act 1974, ss 13, 29 – Employment Act 1980, s 17.

The plaintiffs were a facility company which made television films for sale to network stations for transmission. In 1979 they made a series of 15 filmed programmes using freelance performers and technicians who were members of the technicians' union. The plaintiffs received an assurance from the national organiser of the union that they would not be prevented by the union from having the programmes shown on television. The first two programmes were transmitted by a network station which then agreed to purchase and transmit the remaining 13 programmes. However, the local branch of the union at the television station resolved that the plaintiffs' programmes should be 'blacked' (ie that union members should refuse to handle them) in accordance with the branch's policy that facility companies should not be used by network stations to make programmes when they could be made in the stations' own studios using permanent staff who were members of the union and who might be threatened with redundancy if ready-made programmes were bought in from outside. Faced with the likelihood of disruption if they continued to transmit the programmes, the television station decided to withdraw them from transmission. The plaintiffs issued a writ against the defendants, three officials of the union, seeking an injunction to restrain them from preventing the plaintiffs' programmes being transmitted. The judge refused the relief sought and the plaintiffs appealed to the Court of Appeal where they were given leave to add the union itself as a defendant. The plaintiffs contended that, consequent on the withdrawal, by s 17(8)[a] of the Employment Act 1980, of the immunity from actions in tort which, by virtue of s 13(3)[b] of the Trade Union and Labour Relations Act 1974, formerly applied to breaches of contract committed in contemplation or furtherance of a trade dispute, the defendants' actions amounted to an interference with the plaintiffs' trade or business by unlawful means.

Held – The appeal would be allowed and an injunction issued against the defendants, for the following reasons—

(1) The defendants' actions were a clear interference with the plaintiffs' business by unlawful means in respect of which the defendants were not entitled to immunity under the 1974 Act since their actions were an attempt by the union to impose its policy on the network station and as such were not connected with a 'trade dispute', within s 29[c] of the 1974 Act, and so could not have been done 'in contemplation or furtherance of a trade dispute', within s 13(1)[d] of that Act (see p 730 *h* to p 731 *a*, p 735 *b c f g*, p 736 *a b* and p 737 *a b d g h*, post).

---

a   Section 17(8) is set out at p 733 g, post

b   Section 13(3) is set out at p 733 c, post

c   Section 29, so far as material, is set out at p 735 h and p 736 g h, post

d   Section 13(1) provides: 'An act done by a person in contemplation or furtherance of a trade dispute shall not be actionable in tort on the ground only—(a) that it induces another person to break a

(Continued on p 725)

(2) (Per Lord Denning MR and Watkins LJ) Furthermore, the effect of the repeal of
a s 13(3) of the 1974 Act by s 17(8) of the 1980 Act was that an act done by a person in
contemplation or furtherance of a trade dispute which induced another person to break
a contract or threatened to induce such a breach was to be regarded as unlawful. It
followed that, although the defendants' actions were not actionable by the network
station (because the immunity from action by an employer conferred by s 13(1) of the
1974 Act remained), they were actionable by a third party, such as the plaintiffs, on the
b ground that inducing employees to break their contracts of employment by blacking the
plaintiffs' programmes was an interference with the plaintiffs' business by unlawful
means (see p 733 *h* to p 734 *b* and p 736 *b c*, post).

(3) (Per Lord Denning MR) The general legislative purpose of s 17 of the 1980 Act was
to retain statutory immunity for 'primary' action, i e picketing or blacking the employer's
premises or goods, but not (subject to certain specific exceptions) for 'secondary' action
c directed against other firms, such as suppliers or customers, with whom the employer
had dealings but who were not parties to the dispute. Since the defendants' actions were
secondary action directed against a third party, the plaintiffs', rather than their employers,
the defendants were, for that reason also, not entitled to statutory immunity (see p 734
e h to p 735 *a*, post).

d **Notes**
For the legal liability of trades unions, see Supplement to 38 Halsbury's Laws (3rd Edn)
para 677B.3.
For the Trade Union and Labour Relations Act 1974, ss 13, 29, see 44 Halsbury's
Statutes (3rd Edn) 1769, 1779.

Cases referred to in judgments
e *Acrow (Automation) Ltd v Rex Chainbelt Inc* [1971] 3 All ER 1175, [1971] 1 WLR 1676, CA,
Digest (Cont Vol D) 909, *221a*.
Allen v Flood [1898] AC 1, [1895–9] All ER Rep 52, 67 LJQB 119, 77 LT 717, 62 JP 595,
HL, 45 Digest (Repl) 280, *38*.
Associated Newspapers Group Ltd v Wade [1979] 1 WLR 697, [1979] ICR 664, [1979] IRLR
210, CA, Digest (Cont Vol E) 612, *1457a*.
f *British Broadcasting Corpn v Hearn* [1978] 1 All ER 111, [1977] 1 WLR 1004, [1977] ICR
685, CA, Digest (Cont Vol E) 610, *1444b*.
Camellia Tanker Ltd SA v International Transport Workers' Federation [1976] ICR 274,
[1976] 2 Lloyd's Rep 546, CA, Digest (Cont Vol E) 613, *1489c*.
Eastham v Newcastle United Football Club Ltd [1963] 3 All ER 139, [1964] Ch 413, [1963]
3 WLR 574, 30 Digest (Reissue) 211, *318*.
g *Express Newspapers Ltd v MacShane* [1980] 1 All ER 65, [1980] AC 672, [1980] 2 WLR 89,
[1980] ICR 42, HL; *rvsg* [1979] 2 All ER 360, [1979] 1 WLR 390, [1979] ICR 210, CA.
General Aviation Services (UK) Ltd v Transport and General Workers Union [1975] ICR 276,
CA, Digest (Cont Vol D) 775, *1524q*.
Greig v Insole, World Series Cricket Pty Ltd v Insole [1978] 3 All ER 449, [1978] 1 WLR 302,
Digest (Cont Vol E) 604, *288d*.
h *Island Records Ltd, Ex parte* [1978] 3 All ER 824, [1978] Ch 122, [1978] 3 WLR 23, CA,
Digest (Cont Vol E) 339, *1238e*.
Nagle v Feilden [1966] 1 All ER 689, [1966] 2 QB 633, [1966] 2 WLR 1027, CA, 25 Digest
(Reissue) 503, *4388*.
Rookes v Barnard [1964] 1 All ER 367, [1964] AC 1129, [1964] 2 WLR 269, [1964] 1
Lloyd's Rep 28, HL, 17 Digest (Reissue) 81, *14*.
j *Stratford (J T) & Son Ltd v Lindley* [1964] 3 All ER 102, [1965] AC 269, [1964] 3 WLR 541,
[1964] 2 Lloyd's Rep 133, HL, 45 Digest (Repl) 309, *228*.

(*Continued from p 724*)
contract or interferes or induces any other person to interfere with its performance; or (*b*) that it
consists in his threatening that a contract (whether one to which he is a party or not) will be broken
or its performance interfered with, or that he will induce another person to break a contract or to
interfere with its performance.'

Torquay Hotel Co Ltd v Cousins [1969] 1 All ER 522, [1969] 2 Ch 106, [1969] 2 WLR 289, CA, 28(2) Digest (Reissue) 1009, 369.

Cases also cited

American Cyanamid Co v Ethicon Ltd [1975] 1 All ER 504, [1975] AC 396, HL.
Boulting v Association of Cinematograph, Television and Allied Technicians [1963] 1 All ER 716, [1963] 2 QB 606.
Conway v Wade [1909] AC 506, [1908–10] All ER Rep 344, HL.
Cory Lighterage Ltd v Transport and General Workers Union [1973] 2 All ER 558, [1973] 1 WLR 792, CA.
Crofter Hand Woven Harris Tweed Co v Veitch [1942] 1 All ER 142, [1942] AC 435.
Daily Mirror Newspapers Ltd v Gardner [1968] 2 All ER 163, [1968] 2 QB 762, CA.
Duport Steels Ltd v Sirs [1980] 1 All ER 529, [1980] 1 WLR 142, QBD, CA and HL.
Edwards v Society of Graphical and Allied Trades [1970] 3 All ER 689, [1971] Ch 354, CA.
Fellowes v Fisher [1975] 2 All ER 829, [1976] QB 122, CA.
Health Computing Ltd v Meek [1980] IRLR 497.
Langston v Amalgamated Union of Engineering Workers (No 2) [1974] ICR 510, NIRC.
Lumley v Gye (1853) 2 E & B 216, 118 ER 749.
Morgan v Fry [1968] 3 All ER 452, [1968] 2 QB 710, CA.
NWL Ltd v Woods, NWL Ltd v Nelson [1979] 3 All ER 614, [1979] 1 WLR 1294, HL.
Radford v National Society of Operative Printers, Graphical and Media Personnel [1972] ICR 484.
Secretary of State for Employment v Associated Society of Locomotive Engineers and Firemen (No 2) [1972] 2 All ER 949, [1972] 2 QB 455, NIRC and CA.
Sorrell v Smith [1925] AC 700, [1925] All ER Rep 1.
Star Sea Transport Corpn v Slater, The Camilla M [1979] 1 Lloyd's Rep 26, CA.
Thomson (D C) & Co Ltd v Deakin [1952] 2 All ER 361, [1952] Ch 646, CA.

Interlocutory appeal

The plaintiffs, Hadmor Productions Ltd, David Heath-Hadfield and Michael Collier, appealed against the refusal of Dillon J on 23rd February 1981 to grant an injunction against Robert Hamilton, Jack S O'Connor and Peter Bould, who were officials of the Association of Cinematograph, Television and Allied Technicians ('the ACTT'). At the Court of Appeal hearing the plaintiffs were granted leave to join the ACTT as fourth defendants. The facts are set out in the judgment of Lord Denning MR.

Alexander Irvine QC and *Christopher Carr* for the plaintiffs.
Jeffrey Burke and *Roy Lemon* for the defendants.

Cur adv vult

9th April. The following judgments were read.

LORD DENNING MR. This is the first case we have had on the new Employment Act 1980. It raises the question: how far is 'blacking' lawful since the passing of the Act? First, the facts.

The Hadmor project

Two men in the entertainment world had an idea. They had played in bands and had recorded music. One was David Heath-Hadfield. The other was Michael Collier. His stage name was 'Mike Morton'. They decided to form a company with the name Hadmor Productions Ltd, derived from their two names. They afterwards formed it. I will call them and their company 'Hadmor', for short. Their project was to produce programmes with music, make video films of the show, and then sell the films to the television companies. They needed finance. They raised it to the tune of £410,000. They got a studio. They bought cameras and equipment. They engaged an orchestra and a group of singers. They prepared a series of thirteen programmes, each lasting half

an hour featuring popular musicians of the 1950s and 1960s. They called the series
a 'Unforgettable'. They negotiated with the television networks so as to sell the films to
them.

(1) *The agreement with the trade unions*
From the beginning Hadmor realised that it would be vital for them to get the co-
operation of the trade unions. Especially of the technicians' union called the Association
b of Cinematograph, Television and Allied Technicians ('ACTT'). This union controlled
the services of all the technicians in the television industry. Some of the ACTT members
worked as permanent employees of the independent television companies. They would
produce the programmes, make the video films and transmit them on television. Other
members of ACTT worked as 'freelances' who got employment on short engagement
with 'facility companies'. Those were companies which had their own cameras and
c broadcasting equipment. Such a company would produce a programme, and make and
finish a video film in its own studio. It would then sell it to a television company for the
purpose of transmission. It would then be transmitted by the permanent employees of
the television company.

Before 1979 ACTT had an approved list of facility companies. Quite a short list. The
technicians union ACTT would co-operate in transmitting a film made by a company on
d the list. If a company was not on the approved list, the union would not co-operate. This
system came under considerable criticism. Cases reached the courts about it. In
consequence, in the middle of 1979 ACTT said they would abandon the system. They
would no longer black a film simply because it had been made by a facility company.

Nevertheless Hadmor realised that their project would never succeed unless they
cleared their position with ACTT. So at the very outset in August 1979 David Heath-
e Hadfield of Hadmor had discussions with Bob Hamilton, the union organiser, at the
ACTT office in Soho Square. They came to an agreement, partly oral and partly in
writing, which David Heath-Hadfield explained in these words:

'... I believed I had been given an assurance that, if I formed a facility company
to make and sell television films to the independent television companies, that
company would not be prevented by ACTT from having its films shown on
f television. It goes without saying that this assurance depended upon our employing
ACTT members and consulting the ACTT. But the plaintiff company had every
intention of doing this and in fact always did so.'

In particular, by letter of 13th August 1979 it was confirmed in writing that (i) there
was no longer an ACTT approved facility company list, (ii) the equipment used by
g Hadmor should come up to the required standard, (iii) that all equipment should be
manned by ACTT members who would be paid the correct union rate, (iv) Hadmor were
free to use multi-track recording studios which had an established ACTT shop, and it was
agreed that 'this will in no way be blocked by [the members of ACTT] in the various T.V.
stations'.

I must say that I would regard that agreement as binding in honour on the union. On
h the faith of it, Hadmor went ahead with their project. They got the cameras and
equipment. They got the studio. They got the orchestra and the singers. They got the
technicians as 'freelance' members of ACTT. They produced the programme. They
made video films, all ready for sale to the television companies.

If this agreement had been made between two commercial concerns, I should have
held that it was a binding contract, by which ACTT would not 'black' a film made by
j Hadmor in accordance with the agreement.

But I fear that it was not a binding contract. It was a 'collective agreement' within
s 30(1) of the Trade Union and Labour Relations Act 1974, relating as it did to the rate of
pay of the workmen, and in which Hadmor were 'employers' within para (*b*) of the
definition inserted by the Employment Protection Act 1975, s 125(1), Sch 16, Part III,
para 7(2).

Being a 'collective agreement' it was not binding, because it did not contain any provision that it was intended to be a legally enforceable contract: see s 18(1)(b) of the 1974 Act.

a

(2) *The agreement with Thames Television*
Having cleared the position with ACTT (as they thought) Hadmor were active also in negotiating with the television companies. Five companies of the independent network showed much interest. Hadmor agreed to make and produce a series of films featuring the music and performers of the 1950s and 1960s.

Thames Television agreed to show the first two at Christmas time 1980 and the others later. Letters passed confirming it. On 20th October Thames Television wrote to Hadmor:

b

'UNFORGETTABLE

'I am writing to confirm that, subject to contract, we will acquire the 2 × 30 minute shows from this series entitled UNFORGETTABLE CHRISTMAS and UNFORGETTABLE NEW YEAR for transmission at 11.30 am on 22 and 29 December. The terms we agreed were £500 per show for a single transmission in the London area . . . the price agreed represents a U.K. figure of around £2,000 which is the going rate within the ITV Network for acquired material of this type . . .'

c

d

Those two films were duly made and transmitted at Christmas time. But, in addition, some time before Christmas, arrangements had been made by which Thames Television were to take another 13 films from January onwards. These arrangements were made in November 1980. Thames Television wrote to Hadmor on 27th November 1980:

'UNFORGETTABLE

e

'This is to confirm that, subject to board approval, we will acquire the London area rights of 13 × 30 minute episodes from this musical series. Terms agreed are £500 per episode . . . it is our intention to schedule this show on a weekly basis from Tuesday 8 January at 15.45 hours . . . As soon as I have formal approval for this purchase, I will let you know and you can then let me have a contract reflecting these terms.'

f

As a result of this letter it is clear that, subject to contract, Thames Television agreed to take the 13 films over the ensuing 13 weeks.

There does not appear ever to have been a formal contract binding Thames Television to take all 13 films. But there was every expectation, as a matter of business, that Thames Television would take all 13 films.

g

Hadmor were based at Croydon. They made the films and began to supply them to Thames Television. They supplied the two Christmas films. They began to supply the series of 13 films. Thames Television transmitted the first on 6th January 1981. They scheduled the remaining programmes at weekly intervals from that date onwards. The programmes were in fact shown on 6th, 13th and 20th January 1981. Then came the first stoppage.

h

The first stoppage
The film due to be shown on 27th January 1981 was stopped. It was stopped by reason of the action of some shop stewards of ACTT. It appears that one of them spotted a small item criticising the series in the Observer newspaper which appeared on Sunday, 25th January 1981. It ran:

j

'TUESDAY 3.45–4.15 UNFORGETTABLE (Thames): Eminently forgettable really. The series features well-preserved pop stars of the 1950s. The project is worth notice because it's produced by a facility company based in Croydon and bought in by

Thames TV. The beginning of a trend? Jeremy Isaacs, chief executive of Channel Four, which will look to independent producers, foresees a rosy future for this kind of company. But I don't think he'd show it on his Channel.'

That item was seen by Michael Cashman, the shop steward at the Teddington premises of Thames Television. He telephoned Peter Bould, the shop steward at the Euston premises of Thames Television. He told Peter Glock, the shop steward at the Hansworth premises of Thames Television. We do not know what they said to one another. But on Monday, 26th January 1981, Peter Bould went to see the director of Thames Television. He was John O'Keefe, the industrial relations director. Peter Bould showed him the newspaper article. We do not know what Peter Bould said. All we know is that John O'Keefe said he would investigate the matter. Pending the investigation, John O'Keefe withdrew the programme scheduled for 27th January. This upset Hadmor greatly. David Heath-Hadfield at once on 28th January sent a telegram to Mr Hamilton (the union organiser who had given the clearance for the series). Bob Hamilton telephoned back to David Heath-Hadfield. He said he was sorry that the programme had not been transmitted. He said that the action did not originate from the head office of the union. He said that it was possibly the result of the action of the shop stewards. David Heath-Hadfield asked for a letter of apology. Bob Hamilton said that he would investigate the matter. Later that day he telephoned David Heath-Hadfield to say that the management of Thames Television had withdrawn the programme of their own volition and that he should pursue the matter with them.

There followed an investigation by the head people of Thames Television and ACTT. As a result, Thames Television decided to restore the programme and told the ACTT representatives. The programme was restored. It was shown again on 3rd February 1981. The only inference I can draw is that, when the shop stewards read the extract in the Observer, they were concerned about it, and this concern led to the withdrawal of 27th January 1981, but that the head office of the union did not share their concern and allowed the programme to go ahead. Perhaps they realised that they had given it clearance, and ought not to go back on it.

The second stoppage

The shop stewards, however, still felt concerned. They did not agree to the series being restored. On 3rd February 1981 the shop steward at Teddington went to Hanworth and addressed an emergency meeting there. Those present resolved unanimously to 'black' the programme.

Further discussions took place, but the upshot of it all was that on 9th February 1981 the union organiser, Bob Hamilton, called a meeting of the union and came to a decision to black the series. Despite all the affidavits, I think the reason for the blacking is to be found in the circular of 10th February 1981 which was sent to all members:

'TO: ALL MEMBERS, TELEVISION BRANCH COMMITTEE
'Dear Member,
'RE: UNFORGETTABLE—HADMOR PRODUCTIONS LTD.
'I am writing to advise you of the text of a Resolution carried unanimously at the Television Branch Committee meeting held on Monday, 9th February 1981. "This Television Branch Committee reaffirms its policy regarding the use of facility companies for ITV productions and endorses the blacking of the programme series 'UNFORGETTABLE' imposed by the joint Thames/ACTT Shops". Please ensure that this Resolution is complied with.'

That resolution turned the scale. It was made known to the head people of Thames Television. They decided to withdraw the programme altogether. So it was not shown on 10th February 1981 or at any time thereafter. The managing director of Thames Television gave this non-committal explanation in a letter of 27th February, 1981:

'Messrs. Hadmor Productions Limited,
183 London Road, Croydon, CRO 2RJ.

a

'Dear Sirs,
'. . . Whilst appreciating the difficulties you have encountered, it remains the case
that Thames Television may show or withdraw programmes at its absolute
discretion whether or not any programme is acquired from an outside source. In
the case of "Unforgettable" we exercised that discretion in the light of the conflicting
information then available to us, but I can say that in so doing we have not sought   *b*
nor would we seek to make any judgment between allegations which might or
might not be true. We will, of course, fulfil all contractual payments due to your
company . . .'

The freelance members
The decision was much to the disadvantage of the freelance members of ACTT, who   *c*
had taken part in the programme. Their attitude is shown by an illuminating letter sent
by Miss Pamela Hicks, a loyal member of 14 years' standing. It was written to Bob
Hamilton, the union organiser. It confirms the clearance which had been given to the
series, and regards the breach of it as discreditable. It was written soon after the
programme had been withdrawn:

d
'I have, as you are obviously aware, worked on several of the "Unforgettable"
series being made by Hadmor Productions, and have done so on the basis of specific
assurances via shop officers from you that the operation was approved by the Union:
since the series had been sold throughout the Network in anticipation of its being
made I find it impossible to believe that any significant relevant matter could, or
should, have escaped Union notice. I cannot believe, from the evidence available to   *e*
me, that in the ensuing dispute the Union has behaved entirely with integrity . . .'

The proceedings
Hadmor were so aggrieved by the second stoppage that within a week they issued a
writ and sought an injunction. It was heard within six days by Dillon J. On the
information before him, he refused an injunction. Hadmor appeal to this court. Both   *f*
sides have adduced further evidence. So virtually we have to consider it all afresh.

Was there a trade dispute?
From the evidence, I would draw the inference that the shop stewards at Hanworth,
Teddington and Euston said to the officers of Thames Television: 'We don't think you
should have agreed to buy these video films from Hadmor without consulting us. It is   *g*
a facility company, and it is our policy that you should not buy films from a facility
company without consulting us. Many of the technicians in our shop are idle without
any work available to them. You ought to have engaged an orchestra and singers and
made music programmes of your own instead of buying films from facility
companies.' There was implied a threat: 'If you do attempt to show the series, we will
black it.' Thames Television replied: 'We take your point. We will withdraw the series   *h*
rather than have any trouble.'
So stated it seems to me that the dispute was not a trade dispute at all. It was an
attempt by ACTT to go back to the system before 1979, by which the use of a facility
company was made subject to their approval. It was an attempt to dictate to Thames
Television the way in which they should conduct their business. The attempt succeeded
here; but that does not make it a trade dispute; any more than the attempt (which failed)   *j*
in *British Broadcasting Corpn v Hearn* [1978] 1 All ER 111 at 117–118, [1977] 1 WLR 1004
at 1011.
Counsel for the shop stewards made a valiant effort to bring the dispute within one or
other of the heads of a 'trade dispute' under s 29(1) of the 1974 Act. He suggested that
the men had fears about being made redundant and so it related to the 'termination or

suspension of employment', as in *General Aviation Services (UK) Ltd v Transport and General Workers Union* [1975] ICR 276 at 290. But that fear was not of any weight in the decision. It found no place in the resolution of 9th February 1981. It would not have come well from the permanent employees of Thames Television, seeing that it would put the freelance employees out of work; so they confined the resolution to their 'policy' against facility companies.

I would say, in passing, that if there had been a trade dispute the demand made by ACTT would be done 'in contemplation of a trade dispute' notwithstanding that Thames Television submitted to it: see s 29(5) of the 1974 Act.

Interference by unlawful means

It seems to me that Hadmor have a legitimate grievance against Bob Hamilton and the shop stewards. Hadmor had cleared the position with the union. On the faith of it, they negotiated with Thames Television. They had a firm business expectation that their video films would be taken, bought and transmitted by Thames Television for the 13 weeks from 8th January 1981. That expectation was shattered by the action of Bob Hamilton and the shop stewards in 'blacking' or threatening to 'black' the series, by inducing the technicians to break their contract of employment. It was the cause of much damage to Hadmor, which is still continuing.

That interference was clearly a wrong done to Hadmor. It is actionable unless there is some statutory immunity available to them. Before the recent Employment Act 1980 there was a clear statutory immunity by reason of the Trade Union and Labour Relations Act 1974, s 13(1) (as substituted by s 3(2) of the 1976 amending Act) and of s 13(3) of the 1974 Act. But those provisions have been much affected by s 17 of the 1980 Act. Does s 17 mean that there is no longer statutory immunity for this kind of 'blacking'? This is a point of the utmost importance. But it involves a most complicated discussion arising out of the legislative history.

Looking at legislative history

In most of the cases in the courts, it is undesirable for the Bar to cite Hansard or for the judges to read it. But in cases of extreme difficulty, I have often dared to do my own research. I have read Hansard just as if I had been present in the House during a debate on the Bill. And I am not the only one to do so. When the House of Lords were discussing Lord Scarman's Bill on the Interpretation of Legislation on 26th March 1981, Lord Hailsham LC made this confession (418 HL Official Report (5th series) col 1346):

> 'It really is very difficult to understand what they [the Parliamentary draftsmen] mean sometimes. I always look at *Hansard*, I always look at the Blue Books, I always look at everything I can in order to see what is meant and as I was a Member of the House of Commons for a long time of course I never let on for an instant that I had read the stuff. I produced it as an argument of my own, as if I had thought of it myself. I only took the trouble because I could not do the work in any other way. As a matter of fact, I should like to let your Lordships into a secret. If you were to go upstairs and you were a fly on the wall in one of those judicial committees that we have up there, where distinguished members of the Bar ... come to address us, you would be quite surprised how much we read ... The idea that we do not read these things is quite rubbish ... if you think that they did not discuss what was really meant, you are living in a fool's paradise.'

Having sat there for five years, I would only say: 'I entirely agree and have nothing to add.' Thus emboldened, I set about the task of finding out what Parliament meant when it passed s 17(8) of the Employment Act 1980.

(i) *The 1906 Act*

The history starts, of course, with s 3 of the Trades Disputes Act 1906, which has two limbs:

'[i] An act done by a person in contemplation or furtherance of a trade dispute shall not be actionable on the ground *only* that it induces some other person to break a contract of employment *or* [ii] that it is an interference with the trade, business, or employment of some other person, or with the right of some other person to dispose of his capital or his business as he wills.'

Notice the word 'only'. Immunity is only given to the specified torts. Not to others. Nor to any new torts. Notice also the words 'a contract of employment'. Not to other contracts. Not to commercial contracts.

(iii) *Rookes v Barnard*

The immunity previously thought to be given by s 3 was greatly cut down by the decision of the House of Lords in *Rookes v Barnard* [1964] 1 All ER 367, [1964] AC 1129, when it was held that it did not protect the new tort of intimidation, or the new tort of interference with the business of another by unlawful means. Lord Reid said (in words which I have slightly amplified for the sake of clarity) ([1964] 1 All ER 367 at 380, [1964] AC 1129 at 1178):

'... s. 3 does not protect inducement of breach of contract where that is brought about by [the tort of] intimidation or other illegal means and the section must be given a similar construction with regard to [the tort of] interference with trade business or employment [by unlawful means].'

(iv) *The 1965 Act*

The ruling in *Rookes v Barnard* was reversed in the next year by the Trade Disputes Act 1965. Immunity was given in respect of the new tort of intimidation. But not in respect of the new tort of interference by unlawful means. Nor in respect of the tort of conspiracy to use unlawful means: see Lord Donovan's Report (Royal Commission on Trade Unions and Employers' Associations 1965–1968 (Cmnd 3623 (1968)) para 854). Those torts had no immunity. Trade union officials could still be made liable for them.

(v) *Unlawful means*

In considering the next development, it is important to recognise that we have now a separate and distinct tort of interference with the business of another by unlawful means. It was stated in *Allen v Flood* [1898] AC 1 at 138, 180, [1895–9] All ER Rep 52 at 88, 104 by Lord Herschell and Lord James; in *J T Stratford & Son Ltd v Lindley* [1964] 3 All ER 102 at 106, 109, [1965] AC 269 at 324, 328 by Lord Reid and Viscount Radcliffe; by this court in *Torquay Hotel Co Ltd v Cousins* [1969] 1 All ER 522 at 530–531, [1969] 2 Ch 106 at 139; in *Acrow (Automation) Ltd v Rex Chainbelt Inc* [1971] 3 All ER 1175 at 1181, [1971] 1 WLR 1676 at 1683; in *Ex parte Island Records Ltd* [1978] 3 All ER 824 at 830, [1978] Ch 122 at 136; and in *Associated Newspapers Group Ltd v Wade* [1979] 1 WLR 697 at 708. It was accepted by Lord Wedderburn in Clerk and Lindsell on Torts (14th Edn, 1975, para 808), and was admitted by counsel for the trade union officers in argument before us.

(vi) *'Not actionable'*

It is also important to remember that the words 'not actionable' were given by Lord Pearce a very limited meaning. He did it in *J T Stratford & Son Ltd v Lindley* [1964] 3 All ER 102 at 114, [1965] AC 269 at 336. Those words only meant that the act was 'not actionable by the employer'. Although not actionable by the employer, the act will still remain unlawful and actionable at the suit of a third person (in the tort of intimidation) or in the use of unlawful means (in the tort of interference with business by unlawful means). Some others of us did not take that view. But all the authorities were carefully reviewed by Templeman J in *Camellia Tanker Ltd SA v International Transport Workers' Federation* [1976] ICR 274 at 285–288, where he came down in favour of the view of Lord Pearce. So much so that, in the subsequent legislation, Parliament assumed that Lord Pearce's view was right, or at any rate might well be right.

(vii) *The 1974 Act*

a   The view of Lord Pearce restricted greatly the immunity of trade union officials. By so doing, it made them liable in many situations. It meant that, if they interfered with a commercial contract (made by the employer with a third person), they might be liable in damages (not to the employer) but to the innocent third person. It was thought by the government in 1974 that the statutory immunity should be extended to these acts also. So they enacted s 13(3) of the 1974 Act for that very purpose. It was enacted, says Lord

b   Wedderburn, so as to resolve all these difficulties (see Clerk and Lindsell on Torts (14th Edn, 1975, para 817), and Kahn-Freund on Labour and the Law (2nd Edn, 1977, pp 258–259). Section 13(3) says:

c   'For the avoidance of doubt it is hereby declared that—(a) an act which by reason of subsection (1) or (2) above is itself not actionable; (b) a breach of contract in contemplation or furtherance of a trade dispute; shall not be regarded as the doing of an unlawful act or as the use of unlawful means for the purpose of establishing liability in tort.'

(viii) *The 1976 Act*

d   In 1976 Parliament extended immunity to interference with any commercial contract. It did so by an amendment to s 13(1) of the 1974 Act by the Trade Union and Labour Relations (Amendment) Act 1976, s 3(2). This meant that trade union officials could interfere with any commercial contract with impunity.

(ix) *Preparation for the 1980 Bill*

    When the government was preparing the 1980 Bill, the Department of Employment issued a Working Paper. It made s 13(3) the subject of comment. They said:

e   'The 1974 Act (section 13(3)) was designed to establish, on a statutory basis, wider immunity in certain cases. For instance, it enabled a person to induce employees to break their contracts of employment as a means, indirectly and without legal liability, of preventing their employer from performing a commercial contract.'

    Together with the 1976 Act, it made the scope of the immunity 'unnecessarily and

f   dangerously wide'.

(x) *The 1980 Act*

    Seeing that s 13(1) and (3) of the 1974 Act had so wide an effect, Parliament decided to alter them. In the Employment Act 1980 at the beginning of s 17 (on secondary action) they made some kinds of secondary action unlawful and actionable: and at the end of

g   s 17 they inserted this sub-s (8):

    'Subsection (3) of section 13 of the 1974 Act shall cease to have effect.'

    I cannot think that the legislature intended by this sentence to throw us back into the era of doubt which had existed before 1974: so that we should have to decide whether Lord Pearce was right or wrong in what he said in *J T Stratford & Son Ltd v Lindley* [1964]

h   3 All ER 102 at 114, [1965] AC 269 at 336. I feel that the effect of s 17(8) is to take away the effect of s 13(3), so that the acts which it said were *'not to be regarded* as unlawful' are now, since the 1980 Act, *'to be regarded* as unlawful'. They are 'not actionable' by the employer, but they are unlawful so as to be available as 'unlawful means' for the purpose of establishing liability in tort.

    This view is supported by the fact that Lord Wedderburn took strong objection to

j   s 17(8) as the Bill proceeded through Parliament: he wanted s 13(3) of the 1974 Act retained in its full import. He made a speech to a committee which Lord Hailsham LC, with more than a touch of irony, described as a 'crowded and excited committee'. It is a most valuable essay on the whole of this subject. He moved an amendment designed to retain s 13(3) of the 1974 Act, but his amendment was defeated. Section 17(8) was passed into law. (See 410 HL Official Report (5th series) cols 673–690.)

    The result is that an act of a trade union official which *induces* a workman to break a contract of employment, or *threatens* to induce it, is to be regarded as 'unlawful means'; and, although it is not actionable by the employer, it can be used by a third person for the *a* purpose of establishing liability in tort. It can be used to establish liability for interference with the business of a third person by unlawful means or conspiracy to do so.

Applied to our present case, it means that the 'blacking' or threatening to black the series (in breach of the men's contract of employment) was unlawful means. It makes the shop stewards liable for the tort of interference with the business of Hadmor by unlawful means.   *b*

Restraint of trade

Counsel for Hadmor flew another kite. He asked us to introduce a new tort into English law. There were some interests, he said, that were entitled to be protected from unjustifiable interference in restraint of trade: such as the lady trainer of racehorses in *Nagle v Fielden* [1966] 1 All ER 689, [1966] 2 QB 633; the footballer in *Eastham v* *c* *Newcastle United Football Club Ltd* [1963] 3 All ER 139, [1964] Ch 413; or the cricketers in *Grieg v Insole* [1978] 3 All ER 449, [1978] 1 WLR 302. Such a tort would not attract any statutory immunity.

I would leave this point till another day. Suffice it for present purposes to have the tort of interference with a business by unlawful means.
                                                                d

'Secondary action'

On reading through the Employment Act 1980, and especially s 17 on secondary action, I confess to a sense of bewilderment. It is the most tortuous section I have ever come across. After a careful rereading, I think I can discern the general legislative purpose of s 17. It is to retain the statutory immunity for primary action, but to remove the immunity for secondary action. It means that trade union officials (who call out men *e* in dispute with their employer) are not liable for acts directed against the employer (primary action), but they are liable for acts directed against his customers or suppliers or other traders (secondary action). Some species of secondary action are given immunity by sub-ss (3), (4) and (5), but these are so confusing that I cannot attempt to summarise them. Suffice it to say that the general legislative purpose is to make secondary action unlawful and actionable when it directly interferes with the business of any customer or *f* supplier or other trader, not party to the dispute, who suffers by it. So the statute in effect overrules the House of Lords in *Express Newspapers Ltd v MacShane* [1980] 1 All ER 65, [1980] AC 672, and restores the Court of Appeal ([1979] 2 All ER 360, [1979] 1 WLR 390); and it affirms the Court of Appeal in *Associated Newspapers Group Ltd v Wade* [1979] 1 WLR 697. It affirms what I there said (at 713):

> 'Thus when strikers choose to picket, not their employers' premises but the *g* premises of innocent third persons not party to the dispute—it is unlawful. "Secondary picketing" it is called.'

It is in complete conformity with this legislative purpose that Parliament should declare that s 13(3) of the 1974 Act should cease to have effect. It so declared in s 17(8) of the 1980 Act. It seems to me that by inserting s 16 on picketing and s 17(8) the legislature *h* intended to protect commercial contracts (made with commercial firms not parties to the dispute) from unwarranted interference by 'picketing' or by 'blacking'. If employees are in dispute with their own employer, they are to be at liberty to picket *his* place of work or 'black' (that is, refuse to handle) goods in *his* premises, or coming into or from *his* premises. That is called 'primary action'. But they are not to be at liberty to picket the premises of other commercial firms or to 'black' goods or services of other commercial *j* firms with whom their employer has commercial contracts, or other traders, and with whom neither they nor their employer are in dispute. That is called 'secondary action'. Such secondary action is direct interference by the employees with the trade or business of the other commercial firms. The 'blacking' of these firms is an unlawful act or the use of unlawful means. Previously the 'blacking' might have been given immunity by

s 13(3) of the 1974 Act; but, when the 1980 Act was passed and declared that s 13(3) was
a no longer to have effect, the 'blacking' has no immunity.

Conclusion

Applying these tests, it seems to me that, when the shop stewards 'blacked' the series
produced by Hadmor, they were acting unlawfully. They were not attacking their own
employers. They were attacking Hadmor because they were a facility company. That
b was a wrong for which they have no immunity.

I think an injunction should go to prevent the present defendants, Bob Hamilton and
Peter Bould, from 'blacking' or inducing the members of the union to 'black' the
'Unforgettable' series produced by Hadmor. They must leave Thames Television to
make their own decision, whether to go on with the series or not, free from any
interference by unlawful means.

c

WATKINS LJ. Television or film technicians employed by the British Broadcasting
Corpn, independent television companies and what are known in the parlance of the
entertainment world as facility companies all belong to the same trade union, the
Association of Cinematograph, Television and Allied Technicians ('ACTT'). Those of
them who are employed in one at least of the independent television companies, namely
d Thames Television Ltd ('Thames'), do not care very much for the facility companies.
They object to films made by these companies, who employ freelance technicians, being
transmitted by Thames without consultation, a word which I take in the circumstances
of this case to bear almost the same meaning as consent. Thames and ACTT developed
what has been called a policy of consult action: facility company films are not admitted
without consultation. Consultation with whom? With, so it would seem, not only the
e organiser of ACTT, but also with shop stewards of this union employed by Thames.

The organiser, Mr Hamilton, was consulted by the plaintiffs before they sought to sell
their films or to grant a licence for their use to Thames. He did not inform the shop
stewards and other union members at Thames of the agreement he had reached with Mr
Heath-Hadfield. Later on Thames did not consult with the shop stewards before
transmitting the plaintiffs' films.

f When the shop stewards discovered this state of affairs, they protested to Thames
saying that the policy had not on this occasion been observed. A storm blew up in the
studios and other premises of Thames. Mr O'Keefe and it may be that other officials of
Thames had a careful look at it, so did Mr Hamilton. Thames decided not to ride it
out. They bowed before it. There was no resistance whatsoever to it. There had been,
in fact, nothing which could be said remotely to resemble a dispute between employers
g and workmen. If it were not for the provisons of s 29(5) of the Trade Union and Labour
Relations Act 1974 I fail to see how the defendants could have begun to contend that a
trade dispute as defined in the Act had taken place. Section 29(5) provides:

> 'An act, threat or demand done or made by one person or organisation against
> another which, if resisted, would have led to a trade dispute with that other, shall,
> notwithstanding that because that other submits to the act or threats or accedes to
h the demand no dispute arises, be treated for the purposes of this Act as being done
> or made in contemplation of a trade dispute with that other.'

However the contention has in the long run proved to have been made in vain for, in
my view, the defendants have failed on the facts as we know them to establish that there
was a trade dispute in connection with any of the matters set out in s 29(1)(*a*) to (*f*)
j inclusive of the 1974 Act.

What is involved here has all the appearance of a kind of restrictive practice dignified
by the word 'policy'. The rights and wrongs of its existence and preservation are of no
consequence to the grant or refusal of interlocutory relief to the plaintiffs. Recognition
of it for what it is is nevertheless important, since by its very nature it clearly signifies
that it has nothing to do with a trade dispute.

It is very much more than likely that the sole object of bringing it forcefully to the
attention of Thames was to destroy that company's new-found relationship with the   **a**
plaintiffs. So it was aimed at keeping out yet another facility company which wanted to
do business with Thames. It was obviously a gross interference with the plaintiffs'
business achieved by the unlawful means of, through the blacking procedure, causing
employees of Thames to break their contracts by refusing to do the work necessary to
transmit the plaintiffs' films.

For the reasons provided by Lord Denning MR, with which I respectfully agree, I am   **b**
of the opinion that the defendants have consequently committed the tort of interference
with the trade or business of a third party, ie the plaintiffs, by unlawful means. The
provisions of s 17(8) of the Employment Act 1980 effectively destroyed the immunity
which s 13(3) of the 1974 Act created. It is once again an actionable wrong to behave as
the defendants did. Accordingly, I too, on this sole ground, would grant the plaintiffs the
relief they seek.   **c**

I wish to say finally that I choose deliberately to refrain from commenting on those
provisions of s 17 of the 1980 Act which do not affect any issue in this appeal. We deal
here with but one species of secondary action for which there is no longer any immunity,
namely action which although taken by workers at the premises of their employers is in
fact directed at a third party. One step at a time in the minefield of industrial relations
is, I think, sufficient unless another calls obviously to be taken. And I am not prepared   **d**
to say that a legally enforceable contract between Mr Hamilton or ACTT and the
plaintiffs was effected. This other interesting field of exploration into which we were led
by counsel for the plaintiffs will have to be tilled by someone else on another day and in
another case the crucial decision in which turns on it.

O'CONNOR LJ. The facts of this case have been set out by Lord Denning MR and   **e**
Watkins LJ and I need not repeat them.

The first question is whether in 'blacking' the transmission of the Hadmor programmes
the defendants were acting in contemplation or furtherance of a trade dispute. The
defendants submit that they were so acting and that the trade dispute was between ACTT
members employed by Thames Television and their employers, that is Thames
Television.   **f**

'Trade dispute' is defined in s 29(1) of the Trade Union and Labour Relations Act
1974. The defendants submit that the evidence discloses that a dispute within para (b)
and/or para (g) was either in existence or at least contemplated. Those paragraphs
provide:

> 'In this Act "trade dispute" means a dispute between employers and workers . . .
> which is connected with one or more of the following, that is to say—(a) terms and   **g**
> conditions of employment, or the physical conditions in which any workers are
> required to work; (b) engagement or non-engagement, or termination or suspension
> of employment or the duties of employment, of one or more workers . . . (g)
> machinery for negotiation or consultation, and other procedures, relating to any of
> the foregoing matters, including the recognition by employers or employers'
> associations of the right of a trade union to represent workers in any such negotiation   **h**
> or consultation or in the carrying out of such procedures.'

Remember that Thames Television had production units at Hanworth and
Teddington. Euston was for transmission. The defendants say that at the end of January
and early February 1981 Hanworth and Teddington were underemployed. They had a
fear of redundancies; so if the employers bought in programmes rather than producing   **j**
them in their own studios 'the termination . . . of employment . . . of one or more
workers' might become an issue (see para b).

Secondly, they say that there was an agreement that the services of facility companies
should not be used without consultation with the union and that it could be argued (and

this means properly argued) that as there had been no consultation before these
a programmes were scheduled for transmission there was or might be an issue within para
(g).

There is no substance in either of these submissions. There had been no threat of
redundancies, no mention of the topic, no discussion. The only evidence is that some
natural wastage had not been replaced. To my mind it is quite impossible to spell out
any dispute under this head.

b As far as consultation is concerned, here again there was no dispute. The truth is that
the shop stewards and Mr O'Keefe acted in complete harmony under what seems to have
been a mutual mistake. The agreement between Thames Television and the union was
that Thames Television would not employ the services of facility companies to produce
programmes without consultation. This was a straightforward arrangement to cover
occasions when the in-house capacity was insufficient for whatever reason. It had
c nothing to do with buying a ready-made programme. The shop stewards and Mr
O'Keefe seem to have thought that Thames Television employed Hadmor to make
series. It turns out that all the reasons given by Mr O'Keefe in his memorandum of 6th
February are ill-founded. There had been no discussion on the question of what
programmes could be acquired ready-made, just like the films with which we are all
familiar. Later the union seeks to bolster its position by saying that Hadmor sold at an
d uneconomical price. Whether this be so or not, and it probably is not so, it has nothing
whatever to do with the decision to black the series.

I am satisfied that the decision to black this series was not an act done in contemplation
or furtherance of a trade dispute.

How does that leave the case? The defendants say that, under the contract made with
Hadmor, Thames Television were not bound to transmit the series and that they have
e not broken that agreement. As there is no issue before the court between Hadmor and
Thames Television, I am not prepared to go beyond saying that there was no express term
in the contract. I cannot think that there can be any doubt about the commercial reality
of the transaction. Hadmor did not make and sell the series for storage in a vault, nor did
Thames Television buy it for that purpose. The series was being transmitted weekly and
Hadmor says that but for the blacking Thames Television would have gone on showing
f the series and other programme companies who were interested might well have bought
it. The defendants say that they made no threats of any kind and that, having had the
piece in the Observer drawn to their attention, Thames Television made their own
inquiries and decided not to transmit any further episodes of the series. I cannot accept
this submission. Even if it is right to think, as I have said, that Mr O'Keefe advised the
suspension of transmission for mistaken reasons, I am sure that the only reason for
g Thames Television not restoring the series is the union's resolution to black the
programmes.

I consider this to be a clear example of the tort of interfering with the business of
Hadmor by unlawful means. In respect of that tort the defendants enjoy no immunity
under the Trade Union and Labour Relations Act 1974 because no trade dispute actual
or contemplated has been established. In addition s 13(3) of that Act has been repealed,
h but for my part I do not consider it necessary to analyse the effect of the repeal.

It remains to consider whether Hadmor should be granted relief. I agree that relief
should be granted and I would order the injunction to go.

Appeal allowed and injunction granted. Leave to appeal to the House of Lords refused.

Solicitors: *Nutt & Oliver* (for the plaintiffs); *Brian Thompson & Partners*, Stanmore (for the
defendants).

Sumra Green   Barrister.

R v National Insurance Comr, ex parte Secretary of State for Social Services

COURT OF APPEAL, CIVIL DIVISION
LORD DENNING MR, DUNN AND O'CONNOR LJJ
3rd, 10th APRIL 1981

National insurance – Attendance allowance – Entitlement – Attention ... in connection with bodily functions – Whether cooking of meals for disabled person constituting 'attention ... in connection with his bodily functions' – Social Security Act Act 1975, s 35(1)(a)(i).

The cooking of meals and the performance of other domestic or household duties for a disabled person are not sufficiently connected with that person's 'bodily functions' to constitute 'attention ... in connection with his bodily functions' within s 35(1)(a)(i)[a] of the Social Security Act 1975 so as to qualify him for an attendance allowance under that section (see p 741 *j*, p 742 *b g* to *j*, p 744 *b* to *d* and p 745 *d* to *g*.

Notes

For attendance allowance and adjudication on attendance allowance, see Supplement to 27 Halsbury's Laws (3rd Edn) paras 1351C, 1363A.4.

For the Social Security Act 1975, s 35, see 45 Halsbury's Statutes (3rd Edn) 1120.

Case referred to in judgments

R v National Insurance Comr, ex parte Stratton [1979] 2 All ER 278, [1979] QB 361, [1979] 2 WLR 389, CA, Digest (Cont Vol E) 445, 12(1).

Appeal

The Secretary of State for Social Services appealed against the judgment of Forbes J, hearing the Divisional Court List, on 24th February 1981 dismissing the Secretary of State's application for an order of certiorari to quash a decision of a National Insurance Commissioner, Mr I O Griffiths, dated 15th January 1980, in which the commissioner set aside a determination dated 7th June 1979 of the Attendance Allowance Board, acting by a delegated medical practitioner, rejecting the claim of Mrs Martha Packer for a higher rate of attendance allowance under s 35(1) of the Social Security Act 1975. The facts are set out in the judgment of Lord Denning MR.

Simon D Brown for the Secretary of State.
David Latham appeared as amicus curiae.

LORD DENNING MR. It seems a small matter to bring to this court. It is whether an old lady of 83 should get an 'attendance allowance' of £14 a week or £21 a week. But there are many old ladies in a similar position. So it is desirable to have the matter cleared up. Especially as there have been conflicting decisions about it by the National Insurance Commissioners. The case comes well within what we said in *R v National Insurance Comr, ex parte Stratton* [1979] 2 All ER 278 at 281–282, [1979] 1 QB 361 at 368–369.

Under our social security system, an 'attendance allowance' is paid to a person who is so disabled that he needs help to cope with his disability. The relevant provision is in s 35(1) of the Social Security Act 1975 which I will set out in full:

'A person shall be entitled to an attendance allowance if he satisfies prescribed conditions as to residence or presence in Great Britain and either—(a) he is so

---

a   Section 35(1) is set out beginning at line *j* 2 above

a   severely disabled physically or mentally that, by day, he requires from another
     person either—(i) frequent attention throughout the day in connection with his
     bodily functions, or (ii) continual supervision throughout the day in order to avoid
     substantial danger to himself or others; or (b) he is so severely disabled physically or
     mentally that, at night, he requires from another person either—(i) prolonged or
     repeated attention during the night in connection with his bodily functions, or (ii)
     continual supervision throughout the night in order to avoid substantial danger to
b   himself or others.'

     You will see that para (a) covers 'by day' and para (b) 'by night'. If the person requires
     a good deal of attention *both* by day and by night he or she gets £21 a week. If *only* by day
     or *only* by night, he or she gets £14 a week.
         Our old lady, Mrs Martha Packer, used to get only £14 a week because it was said that
     she only required attention *by night*. Her daughter now says that she ought to get £21
c   because she requires attention *by day* as well as by night. Strange to relate, after all is said
     and done, the point depends on the cooking of her meals. She cannot cook her own
     meals. Her daughter has to cook them for her. Does 'cooking' come within the words
     'attention . . . in connection with [her] bodily functions'?

d   *The facts of the case*
         I take the facts from the report of the Attendance Allowance Board. The board acted
     through a delegated medical practitioner. He said that Mrs Martha Packer was entitled
     to an attendance allowance for the *night*:

         'With regard to the night conditions, I note from the medical report . . . that
e   attention was required twice a night, for 5–10 minutes at a time, seven nights a
         week when she was helped out of bed to go to the toilet and given a drink to help
         her back to sleep . . . I accept that she requires repeated attention during the night
         in connection with her bodily functions.'

     But the delegated medical practitioner rejected her claim for an allowance for the
     daytime. He said:

f   'Before, however, I can . . . issue a certificate for the higher rate of attendance
         allowance I must be satisfied that in addition to fulfilling the night requirement,
         Mrs Packer also satisfies one of the day conditions . . . In this connection I note that
         Mrs Packer was watched when getting into bed. She could, however, without
         assistance from another person get out of bed, walk, use stairs although she came
         down backwards, dress and undress, wash, bathe, eat, drink and go to the toilet. She
g   was able to be up for 15 hours during the day and was not dependent upon any
         apparatus. She was not incontinent of bowels or bladder, needed no help with
         adjusting her clothes or wiping herself at the toilet . . . Miss Packer says in her
         signed statement . . . "I have to do all the washing and prepare all the meals for my
         mother. I do all the shopping and see to all the accounts".'

h   The delegated medical practitioner then directed himself on the law:

         'However, Mrs Packer's inability to carry out domestic duties is not a factor which
         I can take into account in assessing her need for attention in connection with her
         bodily functions. It is clear that she is able to manage the majority of functions
         connected with daily living and I do not accept that she requires frequent attention
         throughout the day in connection with her bodily functions.'

j   *The commissioner's view*
         The daughter appealed to the National Insurance Commissioner. The discussion
     turned on the question of cooking. He held that it was 'attention' etc. He said:

         'It seems to me that the personal service of an active kind involved in cooking is
         immediately and not remotely connected with the bodily function of eating.

Indeed preparing food for an invalid cannot reasonably be regarded as having any purpose other than satisfying the bodily function of eating. The fact that the statute *a* uses the phrase "in connection with" (which connotes a wider concept than "with") means in my judgment that there must be a sufficient nexus between the personal service and the bodily function it is intended to satisfy. I reject the contention of the Secretary of State that cooking is too remote from the bodily function of eating. In my judgment cooking is an attention in connection with the bodily function of eating.'　　　　　　　　　　　　　　　　　　　　　　　　　　　　　　　　　　　*b*

So the commissioner held that eating is a bodily function, and that cooking is attention in connection with it.

The judge's view

The judge seems to have gone much further than the commissioner. He seems to have interpreted the phrase 'bodily functions' as including cooking. He said that the *c* phrase 'include[s] every mode of action of which the fit body is capable at the dictate of the normal brain . . .' He explained this by saying:

'A man must eat and drink and keep clean. In the normal way he could buy his food and drink, cook it and consume it; he could wash his dishes and his clothes as well as himself. If he is disabled and cannot do some of these things, they may have *d* to be done for him. They involve bodily functions in connection with which attendance may be required.'

So the judge held that 'cooking' itself is a bodily function. He said:

'. . . cooking is an activity which consists of the application of a number of bodily functions to a particular task and . . . if a disabled person cannot perform the *e* requisite bodily functions himself then someone who performs them on his behalf is rendering attention in connection with those bodily functions.'

The divergent views

So we have these divergent views. The judge held that *cooking* is a 'bodily function'. So that if a disabled person cannot cook for himself, and someone has to do it for him, it *f* is attention which qualifies for an attendance allowance.

The commissioner held that *eating* is a 'bodily function'; and that cooking is sufficiently closely connected with it that, if anyone has to do it for a disabled person, it is attention which qualifies.

The department submit that eating is a 'bodily function', but say that cooking is too remote from it for it to be considered as 'attention . . . in connection with [it]'.　　　*g*

Previous decisions

We were given a selection of previous decisions which illustrate the difference of opinion.

1. Mr Robert Lazarus QC on 25th September 1972:

'In my judgment, the word "attention" denotes a concept of some personal service *h* of an active nature; for example, helping the disabled person to bath, or to eat his food, cooking for him, or dressing a wound.'

2. Mr J G Monroe on 23rd October 1974:

'Although it might perhaps be argued that, as eating is a bodily function and as there is an obvious connection between cooking and eating, the person who needs *j* to be cooked for requires attention in connection with one of his bodily functions. I do not consider that there is any substance in such an argument. It is wholly unnatural to say of a man whose wife regularly cooks his meals, that his wife gives him attention in connection with his bodily functions. I consider that the words of a the section refer to a person who needs the relevant degree of attention in connection with the performance of his bodily functions, and that they are directed primarily to those functions which the fit man normally performs for himself.'

3. Mr Robert Lazarus QC on 8th July 1975:

b 'I find myself unwilling to go so far as to say that the preparation of food or drink for a disabled person can never be regarded as an attention in connection with his bodily functions ... In my view, it is open to the determining authority to hold that the heating of liquids in order to have a hot drink is an activity in connection with bodily functions.'

4. Sir Rawden Temple QC on 27th August 1979:

c 'It was a question of fact and degree whether in the particular case the service performed could be said to be attention in connection with bodily functions. He [the Chief Commissioner] rejected the narrow interpretation of physical assistance. His view was that attention in connection with bodily functions should be broadly interpreted. His decision was that cooking was an attention in connection with the bodily function of eating.'

d *The meaning of the words*

The statute contains no definition of the words in controversy. I will first take them separately.

In order to qualify at all, the person must be 'so severely disabled physically or mentally' that he requires attention. This conveys the thought that the attention must be required so as to enable him to cope with his disability, whatever it is.

e In order to get the allowance, the 'attention' must be required 'frequent[ly] throughout the day' or 'prolonged[ly] or repeated[ly] during the night'. 'Frequent' connotes several times, not once or twice. 'Prolonged' means some little time. 'Repeated' means more than once at any rate.

'Attention' is different from 'activity' or 'attendance'. It connotes something personal to the disabled person.

f 'Bodily functions' include breathing, hearing, seeing, eating, drinking, walking, sitting, sleeping, getting in or out of bed, dressing, undressing, eliminating waste products, and the like, all of which an ordinary person, who is not suffering from any disability, does for himself. But they do not include cooking, shopping or any of the other things which a wife or daughter does as part of her domestic duties, or generally which one of the household normally does for the rest of the family.

g It is the words 'in connection with' which give rise to the difficulty. They are very uncertain. Some kinds of attention are closely connected with 'his bodily functions'; other kinds are too remote. It is a question of degree on which different minds may reach different conclusions. As Terence said long ago: 'Quot homines tot sententiae: suo quoique mos' (Phormio, 454), which may be translated: 'So many men, so many opinions: his own a law to each.' In the very question before us, I might say: 'So many commissioners, so many opinions: his own a law to each.'

h Such a situation should not be allowed to continue. These provisions have to be applied, day in and day out, by delegated medical practitioners all over the country. They should be applied uniformly. Else there will be many complaints: 'Why should she get it and not me?' To dispel these complaints, as far as possible, I think the courts should lay down rules for guidance. I would hold that ordinary domestic duties, such as

j shopping, cooking meals, making tea or coffee, laying the table or the tray, carrying it into the room, making the bed or filling the hot-water bottle, do not qualify as 'attention ... in connection with [the] bodily functions' of the disabled person. But that duties that are out of the ordinary, doing for the disabled person what a normal person would do for himself, such as cutting up food, lifting the cup to the mouth, helping to dress and undress or at the toilet, all do qualify as 'attention . . . in connection with [the] bodily functions' of the disabled person.

It will then be for the delegated medical practitioner to add up those items of attention which qualify and decide whether the answer is 'frequent attention throughout the day'.

Conclusion

So far as the present case is concerned, I would take a different view from the commissioner. I should have thought that the services rendered by the daughter in buying the food at the shops and cooking it was not 'attention . . . in connection with [the] bodily functions' of the mother. I see no misdirection by the Attendance Allowance Board. I would, therefore, allow the appeal and restore its decision. But I would add this. It would appear that the daughter gave up her work in order to be at home to look after her mother. She would therefore be entitled to receive an invalid care allowance under s 37 of the Act: payable to her and not to her mother. In that way she will, I hope, be well treated; and everything will be fair all round.

DUNN LJ. This appeal raises a short point of construction of s 35(1) of the Social Security Act 1975 which is set out in full in the judgment of Lord Denning MR.

The judge held in a closely reasoned judgment that cooking and the preparation of food involved bodily functions within the meaning of the section, so that a seriously disabled person who required frequent attention in connection with cooking was entitled to an attendance allowance. Counsel as amicus curiae did not feel able to support the judge's formulation, but he did seek to uphold the reasoning of the National Insurance Commissioner who held that eating was a bodily function and that cooking was an attention in connection with that bodily function.

Counsel as amicus submitted that on its true construction the attention to be provided under the section must be required because of the disability, and must be in connection with a bodily function. He accepted the definition of the word 'attention' in the decision on the commissioner's file CA 6/72 as denoting a concept of some personal service of an active nature. He said cooking fell within that definition and that it was a question of fact and degree in each case whether the cooking was done in connection with the disabled person's bodily functions. While conceding that shopping or growing vegetables were too remote, he submitted that once the food had been brought into the disabled person's house there was or might be a sufficient nexus between the cooking and the bodily function of eating. He pointed out that the words 'in connection with' in the section were wide in scope and should be construed broadly.

I look first at the section without regard to authority. To my mind the word 'functions' in its physiological or bodily sense connotes the normal actions of any organs or set of organs of the body, and so the attention must be in connection with such normal actions. The word 'attention' itself indicates something more than personal service, something involving care, consideration and vigilance for the person being attended. The very word suggests a service of a close and intimate nature. And the phrase 'attention . . . in connection with . . . bodily functions' involves to my mind some service involving personal contact carried out in the presence of the disabled person.

Attractive as were the submissions of counsel as amicus, it seems to me that they would in practice cause more difficulties than they solved. In each case it would be necessary for the delegated medical practitioner to ascertain whether the claimant usually cooked for himself, because if he did not the attention would not be required because of his disability.

In my view, on the construction of the section as a whole, cooking, including the preparation of a special diet, is not as a matter of law capable of being an attention in connection with bodily functions, because it is too remote from them. I reach this conclusion on the construction of the section itself. But there have been conflicting decisions of the commissioners on the question whether cooking is or is not an attention

in connection with bodily functions and, before finally deciding the question, it is right
a to look at those decisions. As Lord Denning MR said in *R v National Insurance Comr, ex
parte Stratton* [1979] 2 All ER 278 at 282, [1979] QB 361 at 369, where there is a
difference of opinion between commissioners, then the High Court should give a ruling.
We are told that until 1979 it was the universal practice of delegated medical
practitioners to exclude cooking as too remote. Then in 1979 came a decision of Sir
Rawden Temple QC, Chief National Insurance Commissioner, decision CA 2/79. In his
b judgment the commissioner said this:

> 'The logical result of confining attention to actual physical assistance given to a
> disabled person is, for example, that he would be receiving attention of the required
> character whilst being bathed, but not whilst the bath was being prepared for him,
> and be receiving attention when his food was being cut up to enable him to eat it,
> but not whilst it was being prepared to enable it to become edible. Such fine
c > distinctions wholly unintelligible I would suppose to those for whose benefit the
> legislation exists, and which fragment the course of personal services given to the
> severely disabled in regard to their bodily functions, do not attract me. In my
> opinion "attention . . . in connection with bodily functions" should be broadly
> interpreted, so to include not only any physical assistance ultimately given to enable
> the disabled person to eat (or drink), but also to include the necessary steps taken by
d > the attendant to prepare the food (or drink) which is to be consumed, with or
> without later physical assistance to do so. For myself, I do not doubt that a disabled
> person waiting for food or drink to be prepared, if asked whether he was being
> attended to, or receiving attention, would answer that he was, and such answer to
> my mind would accord both with common sense and with the fact. I do not believe
> that Parliament intended that a disabled person, waiting whilst an attendant
e > prepared a meal or special diet which he was unable to do for himself because of his
> disability, should be held not to be receiving attention in connection with his bodily
> function. I am fortified in my approach to the scope of "attention" by the
> observation of the Commissioner in the Decision CA 6/72 (unreported) . . . There
> the Commissioner wrote "In my judgment, the word 'attention' denotes a concept
> of some personal service of an active nature; for example, helping the disabled
f > person to bath, or to eat his food, *cooking for him* . . . or dressing a wound". The then
> Chief Commissioner in Decision R(A) 3/74 . . . said "This description of attention is
> correct", and [later] he repeated his endorsement of the description as correct, and
> found no reason to dissent from the example of cooking as constituting "attention".
> I have well in mind that in a decision on Commissioner's file CA 60/74 (unreported)
> another Commissioner expressed the view that the words in the section, referring
g > to a person who needs "attention in connection with his bodily functions", are
> directed primarily to those functions which the fit man normally performs for
> himself, and that "it is wholly unnatural to say of a man whose wife regularly cooks
> his meals that his wife gives him attention in connection with his bodily
> functions". However, in the context of a service to a disabled person who cannot
> prepare food to eat (whether by cooking or not) because of his disabilities, the
h > observation (with respect to the author) has no real application or validity. It was
> considered in the Decision on Commissioner's file CA 77/1974 by the author of the
> Decision CA 6/72 and he then expressed himself as unwilling to go so far as to say
> that the preparation of food or drink for a disabled person can never be regarded as
> an attention in connection with his bodily functions. [In decision CA 77/1974] he
> held in terms that it is open to the determining authority to hold that the heating
j > of liquids in order to have a hot drink is an activity (ie attention) in connection with
> bodily functions.'

The decision CA 60/74 was a decision of Mr J G Monroe.
With great respect to the care with which Sir Rawden Temple set out his decision and

considered all the previous decisions, and indeed to Mr I O Griffiths who followed him in this case, for the reasons that I have given on the construction of the section itself I prefer the decision of Mr Monroe. In particular I think that his concluding words are useful. They are:

> 'I consider that the words of the section refer to a person who needs the relevant degree of attention in connection with the performance of his bodily functions, and that they are directed primarily to those functions which the fit man normally performs for himself.'

That seems to me to provide a useful practical approach for the delegated medical practitioners. The line must be drawn somewhere. I think it should be drawn to exclude cooking, which is essentially a domestic duty. Domestic duties such as cooking, housework and the like do not constitute 'attention' within s 35(1). Indeed, as O'Connor LJ pointed out in the course of the argument, the claimant's daughter in this case could probably claim under s 37 of the Act for invalid care allowance which would cover the kind of domestic duties such as cooking and cleaning which she at present carries out for her mother.

In my judgment the delegated medical practitioner was right to exclude cooking as a factor to be taken into account in considering whether the claimant was entitled to attendance allowance. I would allow the appeal and restore the decision of the delegated medical practitioner.

O'CONNOR LJ. There are many people in the community who are so disabled physically or mentally that they cannot look after themselves. Parliament on behalf of the community has made various provisions to make money available so that they can be cared for in the home. This case is concerned with attendance allowance as provided for by s 35(1) of the Social Security Act 1975. It is payable to the disabled person. The section has been set out and I need not repeat it. It is said by the claimant, Mrs Packer, that she 'requires from another person . . . frequent attention throughout the day in connection with [her] bodily functions'.

When a claim is made it is assessed by the Attendance Allowance Board, in practice, that is, by a medical practitioner to whom the duty is lawfully delegated. In the present case the delegated medical practitioner, in rejecting a claim for daytime allowance under s 35(1)(a)(i), said:

> 'Before, however, I can revise the decision of 3 October 1978 and issue a certificate for the higher rate of attendance allowance I must be satisfied that in addition to fulfilling the night requirement, Mrs Packer also satisfies one of the day conditions overleaf. In this connection I note that Mrs Packer was watched when getting into bed. She could, however, without assistance from another person get out of bed, walk, use stairs although she came down backwards, dress and undress, wash, bathe, eat, drink and go to the toilet. She was able to be up for 15 hours during the day and was not dependent upon any apparatus. She was not incontinent of bowels or bladder, needed no help with adjusting her clothes or wiping herself at the toilet. The medical report dated 19 March 1979 substantially agrees with the earlier report. Miss Packer says in her signed statement in this report "I have to do all the washing and prepare all the meals for my mother. I do all the shopping and see to all the accounts." However, Mrs Packer's inability to carry out domestic duties is not a factor which I can take into account in assessing her need for attention in connection with her bodily functions. It is clear that she is able to manage the majority of functions connected with daily living and I do not accept that she requires frequent attention throughout the day in connection with her bodily functions, or that she has required such attention throughout the period relevant to the claim. So far as supervision is concerned, there is nothing in the medical evidence before me to indicate that Mrs Packer has any disturbances of behaviour

or dangerous tendencies. Miss Packer says that her mother is nervous but I note

a   from her signed statement in the medical report dated 14 September 1978 that she is able to leave her for up to 2 hours. Moreover, I do not accept that the wish to have someone nearby, although perfectly understandable in an old person, constitutes the need for continual supervision for the avoidance of danger. The latest medical report states that Mrs Packer is not mentally deranged and is aware of common danger. She is able to do a bit of cooking and I have no evidence that she gets into

b   dangerous situations. It is stated that she might fall but I consider that the risk of falls occur at predictable times, i e when she is moving about and in my opinion she could be safely left for periods seated in a chair with her immediate needs to hand. The medical report dated 14 September 1978 states that she can be safely left unsupervised for 1–2 hours at a time and, having regard to the evidence as a whole, I do not accept that she requires continual supervision throughout the day in order

c   to avoid substantial danger to herself or others or that she has required supervision throughout the period relevant to the claim.'

An appeal was made to the commissioner, the claimant contending that the delegated medical practitioner had erred in law in excluding from his consideration her inability to cook as being capable of making the cooking done for her 'attention . . . in connection with [her] bodily function' of eating. The commissioner upheld that contention. He

d   reviewed a number of decisions by commissioners. The Secretary of State asked for judicial review of the decision. The judge upheld the decision, but for an entirely different reason. He held that the bodily function involved was not eating but the physical movements needed for cooking. Like Lord Denning MR and Dunn LJ, I cannot agree with that approach and the question is that asked by the commissioner. With great respect to the commissioners who have decided that cooking is capable of being attention

e   in connection with the bodily function of eating, I do not think that it is. It was suggested in argument that a distinction should be drawn between ordinary cooking and the preparation of a special diet. I do not think it right to make any such distinction. I think that cooking is too remote from the proximity that 'attention . . . in connection with [a] bodily function' necessarily requires. Cutting up food for a person and/or feeding it to a person are clearly within the words. Shopping for food is equally clearly

f   not within the words. The line must be drawn somewhere and I think work in the kitchen is outside the ambit of the section.

Separate provision is made in the Act for paying for the care of a severely disabled person which includes domestic work like cooking: see s 37 of the Act. The payment under s 37 is in addition to any payment made under s 35. I appreciate that the money is payable to the person providing the service and not the disabled person, but it is part

g   of the scheme to promote the care of the disabled in the home.

I would allow the appeal and restore the decision of the delegated medical practitioner.

Appeal allowed. Commissioner's decision quashed. Board's decision restored.

Solicitors: *Solicitor to the Department of Health and Social Security; Treasury Solicitor.*

Sumra Green   Barrister.

McCormick v Horsepower Ltd   *a*

COURT OF APPEAL, CIVIL DIVISION
LAWTON, TEMPLEMAN AND O'CONNOR LJJ
5th, 6th MARCH, 13th APRIL 1981

Unfair dismissal – Dismissal in connection with strike or other industrial action – Dismissal not *b*
unfair unless one or more employees of same employer taking part in strike are not dismissed –
Relevance of dates when other employees took part in strike – Relevant employee not dismissed at
same time as strikers but later dismissed for redundancy – Whether relevant employee required
to be dismissed while on strike for complainant's claim to be barred – Whether complainant's claim
barred if relevant employee dismissed by the time claim heard – Employment Protection
(Consolidation) Act 1978, s 62(2)(a).   *c*

Unfair dismissal – Dismissal in connection with strike or other industrial action – Dismissal not
unfair unless relevant employee not dismissed – Relevant employee – Complainant's union going
on strike – Another employee belonging to different union voluntarily refusing to cross picket line
– Other employee not dismissed – Whether other employee a 'relevant employee' for purposes of
determining whether complainant's claim for unfair dismissal barred – Employment Protection   *d*
(Consolidation) Act 1978, s 62(4)(b).

By virtue of s 62(2)(a)[a] of the Employment Protection (Consolidation) Act 1978 an
industrial tribunal was barred from determining whether the dismissal of an employee
on strike was unfair unless, inter alia, it was shown that one or more employees also
taking part in the strike ('the relevant employees') were not dismissed. A 'relevant   *e*
employee' was defined by s 62(4)(b) of that Act as an employee who took part in the
strike. The appellant was employed by a company as a boilermaker. On 2nd October
1978 the boilermakers, including the appellant, went on strike. An engineer who was
a member of another union refused to cross the boilermakers' picket line until 13th
November when he decided to cross the picket lines and return to work. Between 21st
November and 8th December the striking boilermakers, including the appellant, were   *f*
dismissed. On 27th November the engineer was dismissed on the grounds of
redundancy. The appellant complained to an industrial tribunal, claiming that he had
been unfairly dismissed. He contended that the tribunal was not barred by s 62 from
determining his claim, because the engineer had taken part in the strike and had not
been dismissed while he was on strike. The employers contended that the claim was
barred by s 62 because the engineer was not a 'relevant employee' since he had not taken   *g*
part in the boilermakers' strike, but, even if he was, he had been dismissed by the time
the appellant's application was heard. The tribunal held that the engineer was not a
relevant employee and that the appellant's claim was barred by s 62. On appeal, the
Employment Appeal Tribunal held that the engineer was a relevant employee but that
the claim was nevertheless barred by s 62 because the engineer had been dismissed by the
time the appellant's application was heard by the tribunal. The appellant appealed to the   *h*
Court of Appeal, contending that s 62 only barred his claim if a relevant employee was
dismissed while he was on strike, and that a relevant employee, the engineer, had not
been dismissed while he was on strike.

Held – The appeal would be dismissed for the following reasons—
    (1) On the ordinary meaning of s 62 of the 1978 Act, which required the fact that a   *j*
relevant employee had not been dismissed to be 'shown' to the industrial tribunal, the
time for determining whether a relevant employee had not been dismissed was the date
of the hearing before the tribunal. Accordingly, if the engineer was a relevant employee,

---

a   Section 62, so far as material, is set out at p 748 *h j*, post

he had been dismissed by the time the industrial tribunal heard the appellant's claim and
a the fact that he had not been dismissed while on strike did not prevent s 62 barring the
appellant's claim (see p 749 *b f g j* to p 750 *a e f j* and p 751 *d* to *g*, post); *Stock v Frank Jones
(Tipton) Ltd* [1978] 1 All ER 948 applied.

(2) In any event, the engineer was not a 'relevant employee' for the purpose of s 62
because he had acted voluntarily as an individual when refusing to cross the picket line
and not in concert with, or because of any obligation to, the boilermakers to come out on
b strike with them. Accordingly, even if he had not been dismissed, the appellant's claim
would still have been barred under s 62 (see p 750 *b* to *c j* and p 751 *b* to *d g*, post).

Notes

For fair and unfair dismissal in connection with industrial action, see 16 Halsbury's Laws
(4th Edn) paras 633–633:1.
c   For the Employment Protection (Consolidation) Act 1978, s 62, see 48 Halsbury's
Statutes (3rd Edn) 514.

Case referred to in judgments

Stock v Frank Jones (Tipton) Ltd [1978] 1 All ER 948, [1978] 1 WLR 231, [1978] ICR 317,
HL, Digest (Cont Vol E) 620, 1560*a*.

d
Cases also cited

Heath v J F Longman (Meat Salesmen) Ltd [1973] 2 All ER 1228, NIRC.
Wimpey (George) & Co Ltd v British Overseas Airways Corpn [1954] 3 All ER 661, [1955] AC
169, HL.

e ### Appeal

James McCormick appealed against the judgment of the Employment Appeal Tribunal
(Talbot J, Mr T H Goff and Mr T G P Rogers) given on 27th November 1979 dismissing
his appeal and allowing a cross-appeal by Horsepower Ltd ('the employers'), against a
decision of an industrial tribunal (chairman Mr L A Brown) sitting at Liverpool on 20th
February 1979 whereby the tribunal decided by a majority that it did not have
f jurisdiction to hear his complaint under s 67 of the Employment Protection
(Consolidation) Act 1978. The cross-appeal raised the question whether or not Thomas
Brazier, a fellow employee of the appellant's, was a 'relevant employee' within the
meaning of s 62 of the 1978 Act. The industrial tribunal held that he was not and the
Employment Appeal Tribunal held that he was. By their cross-notice of appeal the
employers asked the Court of Appeal to uphold the tribunal's finding. The facts are set
g out in the judgment of Templeman LJ.

David Turner Samuels QC and *Stephen Sedley* for the appellant.
Alan Pardoe for the employers.

Cur adv vult
h
13th April. The following judgments were read.

TEMPLEMAN LJ (delivering the first judgment at the invitation of Lawton LJ). This
appeal raises two problems in connection with s 62 of the Employment Protection
(Consolidation) Act 1978, which debars an industrial tribunal from determining whether
j a dismissed striker has been unfairly dismissed if all the strikers have been dismissed.
The first problem is whether the jurisdiction of the tribunal is ousted if a striker resumes
his employment in the course of the strike but is dismissed before an application is made
by another dismissed striker to the tribunal. The second problem is whether in the
events which happened in the present case an employee who was not one of the original
strikers took part in the strike when he refused to cross the strikers' picket lines.

Section 62 provides that, where an employee claims that he has been unfairly dismissed by his employers and that he was at the time of his dismissal taking part in a strike, an *a* industrial tribunal shall not determine whether the dismissal was fair or unfair unless it is shown that one or more of the employees of the same employer who took part in the strike have not been dismissed.

In the present case the employers, the respondents, Horsepower Ltd, employed boilermakers and engineers represented by different unions. On 2nd October 1978 the boilermakers, who included the appellant, went on strike. The engineers took no *b* industrial action. One of the engineers, a Mr Brazier, was on holiday when the boilermakers began their strike. When Mr Brazier returned from holiday on 9th October 1978 he declined to cross the boilermakers' picket lines and was absent from work until 13th November 1978, when he crossed the picket lines and resumed his work for the employers. Between 21st November and 5th December 1978 the employers dismissed all the striking boilermakers, including the appellant, Mr McCormick. On *c* 27th November 1978 the employers dismissed Mr Brazier because he was redundant. The appellant applied to the industrial tribunal on 7th December 1978 claiming that he had been unfairly dismissed. The employers replied that the tribunal could not determine whether the appellant had been unfairly dismissed because s 62 applied.

The appellant's application came before the industrial tribunal on 20th February 1979. The employers argued that Mr Brazier had not taken part in the boilermakers' *d* strike and, even if he had, he had been dismissed and all the strikers had been dismissed, so that the appellant's claim was barred by s 62. The appellant contended that Mr Brazier had taken part in the boilermakers' strike, that he had not been dismissed while he was on strike and that all the other strikers, including the appellant, who had been dismissed while they were on strike, were not barred by s 62 and were entitled to require the industrial tribunal to determine whether in all the circumstances they had been unfairly *e* dismissed within the meaning of the Act.

The industrial tribunal, by a majority, decided that Mr Brazier had not taken part in the boilermakers' strike and that s 62 therefore barred the appellant's claim.

The Employment Appeal Tribunal decided that Mr Brazier had been on strike but, since Mr Brazier and all the other strikers had been dismissed by the time the appellant's application came before the tribunal, s 62 barred the tribunal from determining whether *f* the appellant had been unfairly dismissed.

The appellant appeals to this court, repeating that Mr Brazier had taken part in the strike and had not been dismissed while he was on strike and arguing that s 62 does not debar the industrial tribunal unless each and every striker is dismissed at a time when he is on strike.

The employers contend that Mr Brazier did not take part in the strike and alternatively *g* that the appellant's claim was barred because all the strikers and Mr Brazier had been dismissed before the contrary could be shown to the tribunal.

Section 62 provides, inter alia:

'(1) The provisions of this section shall have effect in relation to an employee [in this case the appellant] who claims that he has been unfairly dismissed by his employer where at the date of dismissal . . . (b) the employee was taking part in a *h* strike . . .

'(2) In such a case an industrial tribunal shall not determine whether the dismissal was fair or unfair unless it is shown—(a) that one or more relevant employees of the same employer have not been dismissed . . .

'(4) In this section . . . (b) "relevant employees" means . . . (ii) in relation to a strike . . . employees who took part in it . . .' *j*

The appellant was at the time of his dismissal taking part in a strike. If Mr Brazier was one of the 'relevant employees' nevertheless it was shown to the tribunal that all the relevant employees had been dismissed.

Counsel for the appellant argued that since s 62 deals with a claim for unfair dismissal by a striker who was on strike 'at the time of his dismissal' it must be implied as a matter

a of construction that a claim by such a striker for unfair dismissal should be determined by the tribunal unless 'it is shown' to the tribunal that 'one or more relevant employees of the same employer have not been dismissed' *while they were on strike at the times of their respective dismissals.* Mr Brazier had been dismissed, but not whilst he was on strike.

In my judgment, this construction is inadmissible because it limits the apparent ambit and alters the ordinary meaning of the words used in s 62 by the addition of a non-

b existent requirement that all the relevant employees shall have been dismissed while they were on strike.

Counsel for the appellant pointed out that the object of s 62, in the words of Viscount Dilhorne in *Stock v Frank Jones (Tipton) Ltd* [1978] 1 All ER 948 at 951, [1978] 1 WLR 231 at 234—

c 'was to prevent victimisation by an employer of persons who took part in a strike or other industrial action. The dismissal of all who took part in such action must not be regarded as unfair, but discrimination between those who took part either by not dismissing some of those who took part, or by re-engaging some, but not the claimant for compensation, of those who had been dismissed rendered the dismissal unfair if it was for an inadmissible reason'.

d The speech of Viscount Dilhorne was directed towards the provisions of legislation which has been repealed and replaced by the 1978 Act, with some amendments, but that part of Viscount Dilhorne's speech on which counsel for the appellant relies applies equally to the 1978 Act.

If there is a strike and there comes a time when some strikers are willing to resume work on terms which they find acceptable but other strikers reject those terms and

e remain out on strike, the employer is not guilty of discrimination if he allows those who wish to resume work to do so. The employer will be guilty of discrimination if he subsequently dismisses those strikers who remain out, without dismissing the strikers who have resumed employment, and it will then be for the tribunal to determine whether the dismissed strikers have been unfairly dimissed. The dismissals of strikers and employees may well take place on different dates and s 62 fixes the date of the

f hearing before the industrial tribunal as the date on which discrimination must be shown by demonstrating that some strikers have been dismissed while others have not been dismissed.

It is said that if the date for demonstrating discrimination is the date of the hearing before the industrial tribunal there will be anomalies and uncertainties. I do not agree. In the first place an employer will not escape from s 62 if he has been guilty of

g discrimination, which can be demonstrated to the tribunal by reference to the facts existing on that date. In the second place, if all that the employer has done is to allow some strikers to resume work on terms offered to all strikers, it is unlikely that the employer will be willing to dismiss the employees who have rejoined before the date of the hearing before the tribunal in order to rely on s 62. The employer is much more likely to retain those employees who have rejoined and to argue that those strikers who

h stayed out and were ultimately dismissed were not unfairly dismissed. In the third place, the procedure for making claims for unfair dismissal will prevent uncertainty in practice. An applicant to the tribunal will serve his complaint of unfair dismissal. The employer must then determine whether to resist the claim and if so whether the employer wishes to rely on s 62 or wishes to contend that the dismissal was a fair dismissal. If the employer wishes to rely on s 62 he will make this clear in his reply to

j the complaint and he will make sure that all strikers have been dismissed before the date of the hearing before the tribunal.

In *Stock v Frank Jones (Tipton) Ltd* the House of Lords reaffirmed the principle that, if the words used by Parliament are plain, the circumstances in which they can be departed from by the courts are severely limited. In the present case it was not shown to the tribunal, as expressly required by the plain words of s 62, that 'one or more employees of the same employer who took part' in the boilermakers' strike 'have not been dismissed'. In my judgment, that concludes the matter so far as this court is concerned. In the *a* present case no possible injustice can be shown because when Mr Brazier changed his mind and decided to cross the picket line the employers were not guilty of discrimination or strike-breaking or any other unfair industrial action.

This appeal must accordingly fail and it is strictly unnecessary to determine whether Mr Brazier was a relevant employee. For my part, I do not consider that Mr Brazier was a relevant employee because, although he may be said to have gone on strike, he did not *b* take part in the same strike as the appellant. Section 62 requires that the appellant and all relevant employees shall have taken part in the same strike. The boilermakers went on strike and agreed or were instructed to come out together and they were under a mutual obligation to stay out together and go back together. Mr Brazier did not become under any obligation to come out or stay out with the boilermakers. Mr Brazier did not take part in any sympathetic strike by the engineers or any other body of persons because *c* there was no sympathetic strike. Mr Brazier did not agree with any other person or become under any obligation to come out or stay out with the boilermakers, the engineers or any other person. Mr Brazier was an individual who voluntarily decided not to work on 9th October 1978 because the boilermakers were on strike and voluntarily decided to resume work on 13th November 1978 although the boilermakers were still on strike. Mr Brazier did not take part in the boilermakers' strike and for the purposes *d* of s 62 he was an irrelevancy. The employers would not have been guilty of discrimination or victimisation between fellow strikers taking part in the same strike if, having allowed Mr Brazier to resume work on 13th November 1978, they had continued to employ him until after the date of the hearing before the industrial tribunal, having dismissed all the strikers who took part in the boilermakers' strike.

For these reasons I would dismiss the appeal.   *e*

O'CONNOR LJ. I agree with Templeman LJ that this appeal should be dismissed. Like him, I can find no grounds for reading into the clear words of s 62(2)(*a*) of the Employment Protection (Consolidation) Act 1978 the additional words 'while on strike' as contended for by the appellant. I have had more difficulty in concluding that the time for deciding whether a relevant employee has not been dismissed is the time of the *f* hearing before the industrial tribunal.

It will be seen that s 62(1) provides: 'The provisions of this section shall have effect in relation to an employee who claims that he has been unfairly dismissed by his employer . . .' Subsection (2) provides: 'In such a case an industrial tribunal shall not determine . . .' That is in the case of 'an employee who claims that he has been unfairly dismissed'. An employee becomes 'an employee who claims' when he notifies the claim *g* to the employer. This would appear to point to the time of making the claim as the time when it must be shown that 'one or more relevant employees . . . have not been dismissed'. Such a construction would avoid the anomaly created by taking the time of the hearing, namely that it enables an employer to deprive the industrial tribunal of jurisdiction after a claim is made, indeed at any time up to the hearing of the complaint, by dismissing any strikers who have not been dismissed.   *h*

However, the time when 'it is shown' to the industrial tribunal must be the same for both para (*a*) and para (*b*) of s 62(2). Paragraph (*b*) reads 'unless it is shown . . . (*b*) that one or more such employees have been offered re-engagement . . .'

The anomalies that would be created by taking the time when a claim is made are quite unacceptable. If all strikers were not dismissed at the same time but at different times during the strike, as happened in this case, then if the first dismissed made a claim *j* at once there would be jurisdiction but not for the last. The re-engagement provision would be wholly uncertain in its incidence.

For these reasons I agree that the time must be the time of the hearing. Lastly, I agree with Templeman LJ that Mr Brazier was not a relevant employee.

LAWTON LJ. Mr McCormick, as a boilermaker who had been on strike, was not
a entitled to have an industrial tribunal determine whether his dismissal by his employers
was unfair unless it was shown that Mr Brazier, who was employed by the same
employers as an engineer, was a relevant employee within the meaning of s 62(2)(*a*) and
(4)(*b*) of the Employment Protection (Consolidation) Act 1978. He was not a relevant
employee unless he took part in the same strike as Mr McCormick. The statutory words
'who took part in it' (that is, the strike) mean giving help by acting in concert with each
b other and in withdrawing their labour for a common purpose or pursuant to a dispute
which they or a majority of them or their union have with their employer and staying
away from work as long as the strike lasts. Some help by standing on picket lines or by
doing organising work in committee rooms. Evidence of Mr Brazier's refusal to cross
the boilermakers' picket lines even though, as the industrial tribunal found, his refusal
was not brought about by fear, was not in my judgment enough to prove that he was
c taking part in the boilermakers' strike. He was not shown to have had a common
purpose with them or any interest in their dispute with their employers. He was not
acting in concert with them as was shown by the fact that he returned to his work on
13th November 1978 whilst they were still on strike. In my judgment there was
evidence on which the industrial tribunal could find, as it did, that he was not taking part
in the strike and in consequence was not a relevant employee.

d   Even if Mr Brazier had been such an employee, he had been dismissed by the relevant
time which I adjudge to be when the industrial tribunal started to hear Mr McCormick's
application. There was no jurisdiction to determine whether his dismissal had been fair
or unfair unless it was shown that a relevant employee had not been dismissed. The
showing had to be to the industrial tribunal and without a showing there was no
jurisdiction. The words 'have not been dismissed' must relate to a period before the time
e when the showing is done. There are no statutory words to indicate how long before or
whether the dismissal should have been for any reason connected with or relevant to the
strike. The meaning of the words is plain and must be applied by the courts even though
results might follow which some, perhaps many, may consider undesirable. In my
opinion, undesirable results may follow from the application of the plain meaning. For
example, an employer who had enticed back to work one or more strikers could defeat
f claims for unfair dismissal by the other strikers by dismissing those he had taken back a
day or so before the hearings. In such a case he might have to face damages for wrongful
dismissal but in industry such damages would probably be small compared to what
might be awarded by way of compensation for unfair dismissal. This, however, is my
opinion and it remains an opinion even if others may share it. Parliament, for all I know,
may have weighed these consequences against others which they thought beneficial for
g good labour relations and fairness to workers. The only safe and correct way of
construing statutes is to apply the plain meaning of the words.
    I too would dismiss the appeal.

Appeal dismissed. Leave to appeal to the House of Lords refused.

Solicitors: *Seifert, Sedley & Co*, agents for *Casson & Co*, Salford (for the appellant); *Barlow,
Lyde & Gilbert* (for the employers).

                                        Mary Rose Plummer   Barrister.

Jobling v Associated Dairies Ltd   *a*

HOUSE OF LORDS

LORD WILBERFORCE, LORD EDMUND-DAVIES, LORD RUSSELL OF KILLOWEN, LORD KEITH OF KINKEL
AND LORD BRIDGE OF HARWICH

28th, 29th APRIL, 25th JUNE 1981

b

Damages – Personal injury – Amount of damages – Subsequent further injury to plaintiff – Supervening disease – Plaintiff's back injured in accident resulting from defendant's breach of statutory duty – Back injury impairing plaintiff's capacity to work – Plaintiff subsequently rendered totally unfit for work because of spinal disease unconnected with accident – Claim for loss of earnings – Whether damages for injury originally caused by defendant should be reduced by reason of supervening disease.   *c*

In 1973 the appellant slipped and fell in the course of his employment, the accident being caused by the employers' breach of statutory duty. The plaintiff suffered a back injury and was thereafter able to do only light work. His earning capacity was reduced by 50%. He brought an action against his employers, but before the action came on for trial he was found in 1976 to be suffering from a spinal disease which was unrelated to *d* the accident but which rendered him wholly unfit to work. At the trial of the action against the employers in 1979 in respect of the 1973 accident the employers were found to be liable. The trial judge refused to take into account the supervening disease and awarded damages which included loss of earnings based on 50% earning capacity from the date of total incapacity (1976) to the date of trial and for seven years thereafter. On appeal, the Court of Appeal ([1980] 3 All ER 769) held that where an injury caused to a *e* plaintiff by a tort was obliterated by and submerged in a greater injury caused by a supervening illness or other non tortious event the liability of the tortfeasor ceased, and accordingly the employers were not liable for the appellant's loss of earnings from the time when the disease rendered him wholly unable to work. The appellant appealed to the House of Lords, contending that where a disease or illness was not latent or dormant at the time of the injury but was contracted after and independently of the injury it was *f* irrelevant to the assessment of damages for the injury, since the employers were required to take the appellant as they found him, namely as someone who was at the time of the injury a healthy person who might or might not after the injury suffer a supervening and unconnected illness.

Held – In the circumstances the damages awarded to the appellant for loss of earnings *g* were to be assessed according to the principles that the vicissitudes of life were to be allowed for and taken into account when assessing damages so that the plaintiff was not over-compensated, and that a supervening illness apparent and known of before the trial was, whether it was latent or not at the time of the prior injury, at the time of the trial a known vicissitude about which the court ought not to speculate when it in fact knew. Accordingly, the employers were not liable for any loss of earnings suffered by *h* the appellant after the onset of the disease in 1976 and his appeal would be dismissed (see p 755 *b h g*, p 757 *d g h*, p 759 *d h j*, p 760 *a* to *c* and *e f j*, p 764 *a b g*, p 766 *j* to p 767 *a* and *h* to p 768 *a h*, post).

Baker v Willoughby [1969] 3 All ER 1528 not followed.

Per Curiam. When a plaintiff has suffered disabling injuries from two or more successive and independent tortious acts the question whether the supervening disability *j* caused by the second tort should be disregarded when assessing the first tortfeasor's liability for loss of earnings remains open (see p 754 *f g*, p 759 *g*, p 760 *g* to *j*, p 763 *e* to *g* and *j* to p 764 *d f g* and p 768 *b e* to *h*, post); *Baker v Willoughby* [1969] 3 All ER 1528 doubted.

Per Lord Wilberforce. To attempt a solution of the problems arising where there are successive causes of incapacity according to classical juristic principles and common law *a* rules is in many cases no longer possible because other sources of compensation (eg criminal injuries compensation, sickness benefit etc) may, if not taken into account in assessing damages, lead to the plaintiff being ultimately over-compensated (see p 755 *c* to *e* and *j*, post).

Decision of the Court of Appeal [1980] 3 All ER 769 affirmed.

Notes

b For the measure of damages in personal injuries cases, see 12 Halsbury's Laws (4th Edn)' paras 1138–1158, and for cases on the subject, see 17 Digest (Reissue) 112–118, 168–200.

Cases referred to in opinions

Andrews v Grand & Toy Alberta Ltd (1978) 83 DLR (3d) 452, [1978] 1 WWR 577, Digest
c (Cont Vol E) 460, 2612*a*.
Baker v Willoughby [1969] 3 All ER 1528, [1970] AC 467, [1970] 2 WLR 50, HL; *rvsg* [1969] 2 All ER 549, [1970] AC 467, [1969] 2 WLR 489, CA, 17 Digest (Reissue) 115, 186.
Curwen v James [1963] 2 All ER 619, [1963] 1 WLR 748, CA, 36(1) Digest (Reissue) 378, 1522.
d *Harwood v Wyken Colliery Co* [1913] 2 KB 158, 82 LJKB 414, 108 LT 283, 6 BWCC 225, CA, 34 Digest (Repl) 562, 3848.
Hodgson v General Electricity Co Ltd [1978] 2 Lloyd's Rep 210.
Jones v National Coal Board (13th December 1976, unreported).
Mulholland v Mitchell [1971] 1 All ER 307, [1971] AC 666, [1971] 2 WLR 93, HL, Digest (Cont Vol D) 1062, 3829*a*.
e *Paul v Rendell* (29th April 1981, unreported), PC.
Penner v Mitchell [1978] 5 WWR 328, Alta SC.
Phillips v London and South Western Railway Co (1879) 5 CPD 280, [1874–80] All ER Rep 1176, 49 LJQB 223, 42 LT 6, 44 JP 217, CA, 17 Digest (Reissue) 221, 932.

Appeal

f Alexander Jobling appealed against the decision of the Court of Appeal (Stephenson, Ackner LJJ and Dame Elizabeth Lane) ([1980] 3 All ER 769, [1980] 3 WLR 704) on 11th July 1980 allowing the appeal of the respondents, Associated Dairies Ltd, against the judgment of Reeve J at Newcastle upon Tyne on 26th March 1979 awarding the appellant damages of £17,950 and interest in his action against the respondents for negligence and/or breach of statutory duty. The facts are set out in the opinion of Lord Wilberforce.

g
Robin Stewart QC and *Keith Walmsley* for the appellant.
L D Lawton QC and *Simon Hawkesworth* for the respondents.

Their Lordships took time for consideration.

h 25th June. The following opinions were delivered.

LORD WILBERFORCE. My Lords, the question raised by this appeal is whether, in assessing damages for personal injury in respect of loss of earnings, account should be taken of a condition of illness supervening after the relevant accident but before the trial of the action, which illness gives rise to a greater degree of incapacity than that caused by
j the accident.

The chronology is as follows. In January 1973 the appellant slipped at his place of work and sustained injury to his back. The respondents were held liable in damages in respect of this injury. In 1975 the appellant had a fall which aggravated his condition which the judge held was referrable to the injury of 1973. He has not worked since this event. By 1976 his condition was such that by reason of his back injury he was only fit for sedentary work. In 1976, however, there supervened spondylotic myelopathy, which affected the appellant's neck. By the end of 1976 this had rendered him totally unfit for work.

The judge at the trial on 26th March 1979 awarded sums in respect of special damages *a* and general damages for pain, suffering and loss of amenities; the figure for the latter was reduced by the Court of Appeal. No question now arises as regards these items. The figure now in dispute relates to loss of earnings, from the date of total incapacity to the date of the trial and for the future from the date of trial. This loss the judge fixed at £6,825 representing a sum of £13,650 arrived at by using a multiplier, and dividing this *b* by two on the basis of a 50% loss of earning capacity. The Court of Appeal set this figure aside on the basis that the appellant was made totally unfit for work by the supervening myelopathy. They supported this decision by an impressive judgment delivered by Ackner LJ.

The evidence as to myelopathy was provided by agreed medical reports. No doctor was called at the trial. An agreed joint report by a consultant neurologist and a surgeon, *c* dated 5th March 1979, stated:

'(4) At the date of the relevant accident (1973) there was [sic] no discernible signs or symptoms of myelopathy.
'(5) The effect of the myelopathy has of itself been such as to render the Plaintiff totally unfit to work.'

d
Finding (4) has been accepted as establishing that the myelopathy was not a condition existing, but dormant, at the date of the original injury; it was a disease supervening after that event. If it had been dormant but existing it is not disputed that it would have had to be taken into account in the actual condition found to exist at the trial. But the appellant submits that a different result follows if the origination of the disease takes place after the accident, i e after the tortious act which gives rise to the claim. At the very *e* first sight this distinction is unattractive, if only for the (to me compelling) reason that to accept it places in an impossible position both potential medical witnesses and the judge who has to value their evidence.

In an attempt to solve the present case, and similar cases of successive causes of incapacity according to some legal principle, a number of arguments have been invoked.

1. Causation arguments. The unsatisfactory character of these is demonstrated by the *f* case of *Baker v Willoughby* [1969] 3 All ER 1528, [1970] AC 467. I think that it can now be seen that Lord Reid's theory of concurrent causes even if workable on the particular facts of *Baker v Willoughby* (where successive injuries were sustained by the same limb) is as a general solution not supported by the authority he invokes (*Harwood v Wyken Colliery Co* [1913] 2 KB 158) or workable in other cases. I shall not enlarge on this point in view of its more than sufficient treatment in other opinions.

2. The 'vicissitudes' argument. This is that since, according to accepted doctrine, *g* allowance, and if necessary some discount, has to be made in assessing loss of future earnings for the normal contingencies of life, amongst which 'illness' is normally enumerated, so, if one of these contingencies becomes actual before the date of trial, this actuality must be taken into account. Reliance is here placed on the apophthegm 'the court should not speculate when it knows'. This argument has a good deal of *h* attraction. But it has its difficulties: it raises at once the question whether a discount is to be made on account of all possible 'vicissitudes' or only on account of 'non-culpable' vicissitudes (i e such that if they occur there will be no cause of action against anyone, the theory being that the prospect of being injured by a tort is not a normally foreseeable vicissitude) or only on account of 'culpable' vicissitudes (such as per contra). And if this distinction is to be made how is the court to act when a discounted vicissitude happens *j* before trial? Must it attempt to decide whether there was culpability or not? And how is it to do this if, as is likely, the alleged culprit is not before it?

This actual distinction between 'culpable' and 'non-culpable' events was made, with supporting argument, in the Alberta case of *Penner v Mitchell* [1978] 5 WWR 328. One may add to it the rider that, as pointed out by Dickson J in the Supreme Court of Canada in *Andrews v Grand & Toy Alberta Ltd* (1978) 83 (3d) 452 at 470, there are in modern

society many public and private schemes which cushion the individual against adverse
circumstances. One then has to ask whether a discount should be made in respect of (a)
such cases or (b) cases where there is no such cushion. There is indeed in the 'vicissitude'
argument some degree of circularity, since a discount in respect of possible events would
only be fair if the actual event, discounted as possible, were to be taken into account
when happening. But the whole question is whether it should be. One might just as
well argue from what happens in 'actual' cases to what should happen in discountable
cases.

In spite of these difficulties, the 'vicissitude' argument is capable in some, perhaps
many, cases of providing a workable and reasonably just rule, and I would certainly not
discountenance its use, either in the present case or in others.

The fact, however, is that to attempt a solution of these and similar problems, where
there are successive causes of incapacity in some degree, on classical lines ('the object of
damages for tort is to place the plaintiff in as good a position as if etc'; 'the defendant
must compensate for the loss caused by his wrongful act, no more'; 'the defendant must
take the plaintiff as he finds him etc') is, in many cases, no longer possible. We do not live
in a world governed by the pure common law and its logical rules. We live in a mixed
world where a man is protected against injury and misfortune by a whole web of rules
and dispositions, with a number of timid legislative interventions. To attempt to
compensate him on the basis of selected rules without regard to the whole must lead
either to logical inconsistencies or to over- or under-compensation. As my noble and
learned friend Lord Edmund-Davies has pointed out, no account was taken in *Baker v
Willoughby* of the very real possibility that the plaintiff might obtain compensation from
the Criminal Injuries Compensation Board. If he did in fact obtain this compensation he
would, on the ultimate decision, be over-compensated.

In the present case, and in other industrial injury cases, there seems to me no
justification for disregarding the fact that the injured man's employer is insured (indeed
since 1972 compulsorily insured) against liability to his employees. The state has decided,
in other words, on a spreading of risk. There seems to me no more justification for
disregarding the fact that the plaintiff (presumably; we have not been told otherwise), is
entitled to sickness and invalidity benefit in respect of his myelopathy, the amount of
which may depend on his contribution record, which in turn may have been affected by
his accident. So we have no means of knowing whether the plaintiff would be over-
compensated if he were, in addition, to receive the assessed damages from his employer,
or whether he would be under-compensated if left to his benefit. It is not easy to accept
a solution by which a partially incapacitated man becomes worse off in terms of damages
and benefit through a greater degree of incapacity. Many other ingredients, of weight
in either direction, may enter into individual cases. Without any satisfaction I draw
from this the conclusion that no general, logical or universally fair rules can be stated
which will cover, in a manner consistent with justice, cases of supervening events,
whether due to tortious, partially tortious, non-culpable or wholly accidental events.
The courts can only deal with each case as best they can in a manner so as to provide just
and sufficient but not excessive compensation, taking all factors into account. I think
that this is what *Baker v Willoughby* did, and indeed that Lord Pearson reached his decision
in this way; the rationalisation of the decision, as to which I at least have doubts, need and
should not be applied to other cases. In the present case the Court of Appeal reached the
unanswerable conclusion that to apply *Baker v Willoughby* to the facts of the present case
would produce an unjust result, and I am willing to accept the corollary that justice, so
far as it can be perceived, lies the other way and that the supervening myelopathy should
not be disregarded. If rationalisation is needed, I am willing to accept the 'vicissitudes'
argument as the best available. I should be more firmly convinced of the merits of the
conclusion if the whole pattern of benefits had been considered, in however general a
way. The result of the present case may be lacking in precision and rational justification,
but so long as we are content to live in a mansion of so many different architectures this
is inevitable.

I would dismiss the appeal.

LORD EDMUND-DAVIES. My Lords, this appeal relates to the assessment of damages where a party has been injured by another's tort, but, before his action comes on for trial, the plaintiff sustains further injury as a result of a wholly independent and non-tortious event.

The appellant was the 48-year-old manager of the respondents' butcher shop at Newcastle upon Tyne. In January 1973 he slipped on the floor of a meat refrigerator owing to his employers' breach of the Office, Shops and Railways Premises Act 1963 by failing to keep it free from substances likely to cause persons to slip. He sustained a prolapsed intravertebral disc, but, although in considerable pain, which reduced his earning capacity by 50%, he resumed work in a supervisory capacity until September 1976, when he became totally disabled by the manifestation of a hitherto unsuspected condition known as spondylotic myelopathy which was unrelated to the 1973 incident.

The action based on the 1973 incident came before Reeve J in March 1979. He found that, even had the plaintiff sustained no injury therefrom—

'he would since 1976 by reason of his myelopathy have been rendered unfit for work thereafter. Should I have regard to that fact in assessing damages for loss of earnings arising from the 1973 accident? At first blush it might seem that he is only entitled to be compensated for loss of earnings during his working life as limited by the myelopathy.'

But, in the light of certain observations of Lord Reid in *Baker v Willoughby* [1969] 3 All ER 1528, [1970] AC 467, Reeve J concluded: 'I am bound to leave out of account the disability caused to the plaintiff by the myelopathy in assessing the damages resulting from the 1973 incident.' In the result, his award of general damages included the sum of £6,825 for future loss of earnings, on the basis that the plaintiff's back injury must be regarded as continuing in to the future to reduce his earning capacity by 50%. The Court of Appeal unanimously reversed that finding ([1980] 3 All ER 769, [1980] 3 WLR 704), and this appeal has been brought to secure its restoration.

In *Baker v Willoughby* this House found for the plaintiff on the basis of the Court of Appeal decision in *Harwood v Wyken Colliery Co* [1913] 2 KB 158. *Baker v Willoughby* was different in one important respect from the present appeal, for this House was there concerned with successive torts. The plaintiff's left leg was injured in 1964 when he was knocked down by a car negligently driven by the defendant. In 1967, before his action came on for trial, he was shot in the same leg during an armed robbery and the limb had to be amputated well above the knee. The trial judge rejected the defendant's submission that no injury or loss suffered thereafter by the plaintiff could be attributed to his tort since its effect had been obliterated by the amputation, and he awarded damages on the basis of continued weakness and pain in the left ankle and the possibility of later development of arthritis in the leg. Following on its unanimous reversal in the Court of Appeal ([1969] 2 All ER 549, [1970] AC 467), this House restored the decision of the trial judge, Lord Reid (with whom Lord Guest, Viscount Dilhorne and Lord Donovan concurred) basing his conclusion largely on the Court of Appeal decision in *Harwood v Wyken Colliery Co*. That was a case brought under the Workmen's Compensation Act 1906, where a miner, who had for some months been paid compensation for a personal injury by accident arising out of and in the course of his employment, was later disabled for work by heart disease in no way attributable to the accident. Holding that '. . . there is no work which . . . the accident has prevented him from doing which the heart disease would not also have prevented him from doing', the judge found that compensation had ceased to be payable. The Court of Appeal reversed that decision. Hamilton LJ stressed (at 159–170) that the 1906 Act compensated workmen 'in a new and statutory manner in respect of a wholly statutory right', markedly different from that operating in the common law assessment of damages, the latter necessitating regard being had to contingencies such as '. . . the possibility of future diminution or loss of earnings arising independently of the cause of action, from increasing age, from accident or illness in futuro, and so forth'. Hamilton LJ explained (at 170):

'The compensation for workmen under the Act is very different . . . It is based on
what the workman has earned, not on what he will be prevented from earning . . .
Redemption of weekly payments by a lump sum is on the basis of an annuity,
calculated by expectation of life and not by expectation of immunity from further
accident or from growing age and infirmity . . .'

Hamilton LJ further pointed out that, whereas damages are calculated so as to put the
victim of tort in as good a position as he was before the wrong, the Act 'is not founded
on indemnity, and the ideas of retribution for wrong doing and of restitutio in integrum
are foreign to it'.

Notwithstanding this clear differentiation, this House (with the exception of Lord
Pearson), holding that 'causation cannot be different in tort', applied the *Harwood* decision
to the different facts giving rise to the common law claim for damages brought in *Baker
v Willoughby*. Lord Reid could see '. . . no reason why the appellant's present disability
cannot be regarded as having two causes' (see [1969] 3 All ER 1528 at 1532, [1970] AC
467 at 492), and cited in support the following words of Hamilton LJ ([1913] 2 KB 158
at 169):

'. . . [the workman] is not disentitled to be paid compensation by reason of the
supervention of a disease of the heart. It cannot be said of him that partial incapacity
for work has not resulted and is not still resulting from the injury. All that can be
said is that such partial incapacity is not still resulting "solely" from the injury.'

My Lords, I must respectfully decline to follow the route adopted by the majority of
their Lordships in *Baker v Willoughby*. For the decision in *Harwood v Wyken Colliery Co*,
with its different facts requiring to be considered solely in the light of an elaborate
statutory scheme having no counterpart in the common law, was there applied without
qualification or differentiation to the common law claim then under consideration. In
marked contrast was the speech of Lord Pearson, who made no reference to *Harwood* and
who described as 'formidable' the argument of the defendant's counsel that the
consequence of the original accident had been submerged and obliterated by the
supervening event. He nevertheless added ([1969] 3 All ER 1528 at 1535, [1970] AC 467
at 495):

'*But it must not be allowed to succeed, because it produces manifest injustice.* The
supervening event has not made [the plaintiff] less lame nor less disabled nor less
deprived of amenities. It has not shortened the period over which he will be
suffering. It has made him more lame, more disabled, more deprived of
amenities. He should not have less damages through being worse off than might
have been expected.' (Emphasis added.)

I have to say respectfully that I find this approach unrealistic. It involves awarding
damages on the basis of pain and suffering which the plaintiff would have suffered *if* the
amputation had not taken place, and it compensates him for that which no longer
exists. Nor is it correct to compensate him for loss of earnings when the very state which
has produced that loss of earnings has ceased. The loss of earnings sustained after the
amputation of the leg was caused by the amputation, not by the first accident. And the
effect of the amputation was to obliterate completely all the constituents (pain and
suffering, reduced earning capacity, and loss of amenities) of the damages to be awarded
for the injury sustained as a result of that accident.

The key, as I think, to the contrary conclusion arrived at by Lord Pearson is to be found
in the words which followed immediately on the passage quoted above:

'The nature of the *injustice* becomes apparent if the supervening event is treated
as a tort (as indeed it was) and if one envisages [the plaintiff] suing the robbers who
shot him.'

The undoubted attraction of the *Baker v Willoughby* decision is that it avoided what was
there understandably regarded as an unacceptable result, as—

'it provides a greater measure of protection for the victim. For if the whole burden is placed upon the second tortfeasor and he is a man of straw—as would *a* appear to have been the position in *Baker v. Willoughby* itself—or cannot be traced, then the victim is left without any redress.'

(See McGregor on Damages (14th Edn, 1980, p 783, para 1146). But such a view ignores the ex gratia payment of compensation provided under the Criminal Injuries Compensation Scheme in respect of personal injury directly attributable to, inter alia, crimes of violence. Atiyah considered that '. . . the existence of the Criminal Injuries *b* Compensation Board . . . plainly cast a long shadow over the entire proceedings' (see (1969) 85 LQR 475), but were this indeed so it seems inconceivable that the reports contain no mention of the scheme, despite its introduction in August 1964. The simple fact is that it was never adverted to at any stage by anyone.

It cannot be doubted that the injured plaintiff in *Baker v Willoughby* had a valid claim to compensation under the scheme. But it needs to be added that such compensation is *c* assessed on the basis of common law damages, and Baker would naturally be treated as a workman who at the time of the armed robbery had a maimed leg and reduced earning capacity. And the board imposes a compensation limit based on gross average industrial earnings and it applies a strict approach to collateral benefits (see the learned note in (1981) 97 LQR 210 at 212). So the injured plaintiff in *Baker v Willoughby* might still have been better off under the decision of this House than under the scheme, though that *d* must remain a matter of pure speculation. And, even so, what one can say is that the 'injustice', the avoidance of which appears to have led to Lord Pearson's conclusion, did not, at least in its full dimensions, exist.

My Lords, the appellant's counsel submits that no materiality resides in the fact that the present case is not one of successive torts (as in *Baker*), but that of a tort followed by greater and enveloping injury arising from independent natural causes. He accepts (and, *e* indeed, actually relies on) the proposition that a defendant 'must take the plaintiff as he finds him'. He also recognises that, in the assessment of damages, the court must not speculate when it knows the facts, and must therefore have regard to relevant events which have occurred before trial or before the hearing of an appeal (see *Curwen v James* [1963] 2 All ER 549, [1963] 1 WLR 748; *Mulholland v Mitchell* [1971] 1 All ER 307 at 313, [1971] AC 666 at 680 per Lord Wilberforce). But counsel for the appellant draws a novel *f* distinction between (a) cases where at the time of the tort the victim was (whether or not he knew it) already suffering from a disease which later manifested itself and (b) cases where the *inception* of the disease was an event supervening after the tort, and he submits that in the second type of case the later event has no materiality.

In my judgment, the distinction drawn between (a) and (b) is in principle irrelevant and in practice capable of creating great confusion. Indeed, in the present case Reeve J *g* in the course of his careful judgment expressed no conclusion regarding the time of inception of the myelopathy, and simply proceeded on the basis of the 'agreed medical formula' that—

'(4) At the date of the relevant accident (1973) there was [sic] no discernible signs or symptoms of myelopathy.
'(5) The effect of the myelopathy has of itself been such as to render the Plaintiff *h* totally unfit to work.'

Uncertainty as to inception may well arise with frequency and ought not to be determinative of the outcome of proceedings unless legal principle demands. Not only was counsel for the appellant unable to cite authority supporting the drawing of the *j* distinction he advanced, but it is contrary to the principle enunciated in innumerable cases that among the contingencies and vicissitudes of life relevant to the assessment of damages for tort is that that the victim's expectation of both natural and working life may be reduced or terminated by the future development of illness or infirmity: see, for example, the classic words of Brett LJ in *Phillips v London and South Western Railway Co* (1879) 5 CPD 280 at 291; those of Hamilton LJ, already quoted, in *Harwood v Wyken*

Colliery Co; and those of Dickson J in the Supreme Court of Canada in *Andrews v Grand & Toy Alberta Ltd* [1978] 83 DLR (3d) 452.

But the submission of learned counsel for the appellant went even further. He would not restrict the exclusion of post-tort incidents to the inception of illness, for, as Ackner LJ put it ([1980] 3 All ER 769 at 774, [1980] 3 WLR 704 at 710):

> 'It would equally follow on counsel's submission that, if [after the tort] the plaintiff ... as a result solely of his own negligence, was knocked down by a motorcoach and thereby rendered totally incapable of further work, this incapacity would have to be wholly ignored and the plaintiff awarded his future loss of earnings, as if that event had never occurred.'

Despite the attractive manner of their presentation, these bold submissions run so counter to fundamental principles as to be wholly unacceptable. In *Penner v Mitchell* [1978] 5 WWR 328 at 336 the Alberta Supreme Court declined to extend the decision in *Baker v Willoughby* to such cases as the present, Prowse JA saying that 'any event that would otherwise be assessed as a future contingency is a relevant factor for assessing damages if it occurs before trial', and a similar conclusion was arrived at by Latey J in *Hodgson v General Electric Co Ltd* [1978] 2 Lloyd's Rep 210.

My Lords, it is a truism that cases of cumulative causation of damage can present problems of great complexity. I can formulate no convincing juristic or logical principles supportive of the decision of this House in *Baker v Willoughby*, and none were there propounded. Lord Pearson in particular manifestly acceded to the submission of learned counsel for the plaintiff ([1970] AC 467 at 475–476):

> 'The defendant's approach, although based on a neat logical solution, results in culpable injustice and, *therefore*, must be rejected ... If it is necessary to weigh the balance between fairness to the plaintiff and fairness to the defendant, the burden should not fall on the innocent plaintiff rather than the tortious defendant. The present is a case where justice and logic do not go together and in the interests of justice the argument founded on logic by the defendants should be rejected.' (My emphasis.)

Perhaps Glanville Williams was right in saying: 'When the lawyer uses the conception of causation, he is not bound to use it in the same way as a philosopher, or a scientist, or an ordinary man. The concept can be moulded by considerations of policy' (see [1961] CLJ 62 at 75).

Abandoning the search for logical principles and adverting solely to questions of policy, it may therefore be that *Baker v Willoughby* is acceptable on its own facts. Even so, I am shaken by (a) the reliance there mistakenly placed (as I respectfully think) on *Harwood v Wyken Colliery Co* and (b) the misapprehension that, were this House to uphold the Court of Appeal, the innocent yet badly injured workman might be wholly without redress for his injuries. As, however, learned counsel for the respondents was not minded to challenge the correctness of *Baker* on its different facts, the matter does not call for present determination.

But what is clear is that where, as in the present appeal, the question in issue relates to the assessment of damages when, a tort having been committed, the victim is overtaken before trial by a wholly unconnected and disabling illness the decision in *Baker v Willoughby* has no application. Your Lordships are therefore untrammelled by precedent. The effect of the Court of Appeal's decision is that no considerations of policy warrant the imposition on the respondents of liability for the loss of earnings after the emergence of myelopathy. That is in accordance with the long-established and eminently reasonable principle that the onset or emergence of illness is one of the vicissitudes of life relevant to the assessment of damages. And it is of some interest to note that this view was evidently shared at all stages by learned counsel for the plaintiff in *Baker v Willoughby* itself, and had been anticipated as long ago as 1961 by Glanville Williams (see [1961] CLJ 62 at 76). I believe the Court of Appeal decision was entirely correct, and I would dismiss the appeal.

LORD RUSSELL OF KILLOWEN. My Lords, it is well established that, in assessing compensation for damage caused to a plaintiff by a tortfeasor, among other considerations *a* is the consequent loss or reduction in earning capacity in the working life of the plaintiff. It is also well established that it is appropriate, in arriving at an estimated figure under that head, that some allowance or discount should be made for the ordinary vicissitudes of life. It is also well established that, if by the time of trial facts emerge which make known a vicissitude of life as applicable to the plaintiff, that knowledge should replace that which would have been only an estimate: where there is knowledge *b* estimation has no part.

One of these vicissitudes is that a plaintiff might thereafter succumb to a disease (unconnected with the tort) which would abbreviate the plaintiff's working life. Commonly, the discount for such a possibility might well be small; but it is not to be ignored. If before trial the plaintiff does so succumb, in my opinion the evidence of its abbreviating effect must take the place of estimate, and reduce the amount of *c* compensation for the tortious damage under that head. In the instant case the plaintiff (the appellant) succumbed to spondylotic myelopathy which by 1976, before the trial, terminated his working life, which, had its length remained as at the date of the tort, would have continued (albeit at a lower wage earning capacity) for several more years. For the appellant it was contended that, since the evidence did not show that this condition was latent and dormant at the date of the tortious injury, its emergence could *d* not serve to reduce the amount of compensation based on an estimate of working life. But it was conceded that if the condition was in some degree present at the date of the tort the contrary view should prevail.

In the first place I find that this attempted distinction is calculated to produce medical problems virtually impossible of solution. In the joint medical report dated 5th March 1979 all that could be said was that at the date of the tort 'there was [sic] no discernible *e* signs or symptoms of myelopathy'.

In the second place this approach appears to me to intrude on the well-known principle of discount or allowance for the vicissitudes of life, by the wholly irrelevant principle that a tortfeasor takes his victim as he finds him. Among the vicissitudes of life there falls to be included the possibility of *developing* a disease which will shorten or terminate a plaintiff's working life; if that development takes place before trial the vicissitude *f* must, it seems to me, move from the field of estimate to the field of knowledge.

I agree therefore with the approach of the Court of Appeal.

There remains the question of the decision of this House in *Baker v Willoughby* [1969] 3 All ER 1528, [1970] AC 467, the facts in which have been related by others of your Lordships. That was a case of successive torts by two tortfeasors. The first tort severely damaged the plaintiff's leg; the second tort required the removal of that leg by surgery. *g* This House decided that the first tortfeasor could not escape liability for the damage done to the now non-existent leg. The main consideration leading to the decision was that otherwise the second tortfeasor could (on the principle that a tortfeasor is entitled to take his victim as he finds him) reduce the damages against him on the ground that he was only responsible for the removal of an already damaged leg, and not for removal of a sound leg; thus, if the first tortfeasor escaped liability, the plaintiff could not get full *h* compensation for the injuries done to him. I am not prepared to state disagreement with the decision. I am prepared to suggest that physical damage due to a subsequent tort is not to be regarded as a relevant vicissitude. Some of the reasons given in that case are suceptible of being taken as pointing in favour of the appellant in the instant appeal, but they do not persuade me that we are led by *Baker v Willoughby* to take a further step by allowing this appeal. I add that I cannot, with respect, find the reliance of Lord Reid on *j* the workmen's compensation case of *Harwood v Wyken Colliery Co* [1913] 2 KB 158 sound.

In short I am persuaded that the Court of Appeal in the instant case was right, and I would dismiss this appeal.

LORD KEITH OF KINKEL. My Lords, this appeal raises a short but very difficult
a point in connection with the assessment of damages for personal injuries. In January
1973 the appellant, in the course of his employment with the respondents and as a result
of their negligence, suffered an injury to his back in the shape of a slipped disc. This had
the effect of incapacitating him for any but light work. In September 1976 the appellant
was found to be suffering from a condition known as cervical myelopathy, unrelated to
the accident, which by the time his claim came to trial, in March 1979, had resulted in
b a total incapacity for work. According to an agreed medical report, there were no
discernible signs or symptoms of myelopathy at the date of the accident in 1973.

In that state of affairs the question arose whether the respondents were liable to pay
damages for loss of earnings on the basis of a partial incapacity continuing throughout
the period which, in the absence of the myelopathy, would have represented the balance
of the appellant's normal working life, or whether their liability was limited to loss of
c earnings up to the time when the myelopathy resulted in total incapacity.

The trial judge (Reeve J) decided in favour of the greater liability. He took the view
that he was bound, on the authority of *Baker v Willoughby* [1969] 3 All ER 1528, [1970]
AC 467, to leave out of account the disability caused to the appellant by the myelopathy
in assessing the damages resulting from the 1973 accident. The Court of Appeal
(Stephenson, Ackner LJJ and Dame Elizabeth Lane) reversed the decision of Reeve J
d holding that *Baker v Willoughby* did not compel the conclusion that where the victim of
a tortious act suffers a further disability through a supervening event of non-tortious
character, such as natural disease, the consequences of the latter event must be ignored
in the assessment of damages.

The facts in *Baker v Willoughby* were that the plaintiff suffered an injury to his left leg
through the defendant's negligence, resulting in a continuing disability which reduced
e his earning capacity. Before his case came to trial he was shot by a robber in the same leg,
which in consequence had to be amputated. As a result the plaintiff's disability was
rather greater than it had been before. This House, reversing the Court of Appeal, held
that the award of damages for loss of earnings did not fall to be diminished by reason of
the later injuries on the view that they represented no more than a concurrent cause,
along with the original injury, of the plaintiff's disability.

f It was argued for the respondent, defendant in the action, that the second injury
removed the very limb from which the earlier disability had stemmed, and that therefore
no loss suffered thereafter could be attributed to the respondent's negligence. In rejecting
this argument Lord Reid, whose speech was concurred in by Lord Guest, Viscount
Dilhorne and Lord Donovan, said ([1969] 3 All ER 1528 at 1532, [1970] AC 467 at 493):

g
'If it were the case that in the eye of the law an effect could only have one cause
then the respondent might be right. It is always necessary to prove that any loss for
which damages can be given was caused by the defendant's negligent act. But it is
commonplace that the law regards many events as having two causes; that happens
whenever there is a contributory negligence, for then the law says that the injury
was caused both by the negligence of the defendant and by the negligence of the
plaintiff. And generally it does not matter which negligence occurred first in point
h of time.'

Lord Reid took the view that the appellant's disability could be regarded as having two
causes, and he found support for this view in *Harwood v Wyken Colliery Co* [1913] 2 KB
158. That was a workmen's compensation case in which the Court of Appeal held the
plaintiff entitled to compensation, notwithstanding that there had supervened on the
j incapacity resulting from an accident at work an incapacity of similar extent resulting
from heart disease. Lord Reid later went on to distinguish the case where damages
might properly fall to be diminished by reason of the death of the plaintiff before trial,
on the basis that in such a case the supervening event had reduced the plaintiff's loss. He
said ([1969] 3 All ER 1528 at 1534, [1970] AC 467 at 495):

'If the later injury suffered before the date of the trial either reduces the disabilities from the injury for which the defendant is liable, or shortens the period during *a* which they will be suffered by the plaintiff then the defendant will have to pay less damages. But if the later injuries merely become a concurrent cause of the disabilities caused by the injury inflicted by the defendant, then in my view they cannot diminish the damages. Suppose that the plaintiff has to spend a month in bed before the trial because of some illness unconnected with the original injury, the defendant cannot say that he does not have to pay anything in respect of that *b* month; during that month the original injuries and the new illness are concurrent causes of his inability to work and that does not reduce the damages.'

It seems clear from this passage that the principle of concurrent causes which Lord Reid selected as the ratio decidendi of the case would, if sound, apply with the same force where the supervening event is natural disease, as in the present case, as it does where the supervening event is a tortious act.   *c*

Lord Pearson's main reason for rejecting the respondent's argument was that it would produce manifest injustice. He said ([1969] 3 All ER 1528 at 1535, [1970] AC 467 at 495):

'The supervening event has not made the plaintiff less lame nor less disabled nor less deprived of amenities. It has not shortened the period over which he will be *d* suffering. It has made him more lame, more disabled, more deprived of amenities. He should not have less damages through being worse off than might have been expected.'

Lord Pearson went on to illustrate the nature of the injustice by pointing out that, where the supervening event was a tortious act, the later tortfeasor, on the principle that he takes his victim as he finds him, would be liable for damages in respect of loss of *e* earnings only to the extent that the act had caused an additional diminution of earning capacity. If the earlier incapacity were treated, in a question with the first tortfeasor, as submerged by the later, the plaintiff would be left in the position of being unable to recover from anyone a substantial part of the loss suffered after the date of the second tort. So he would not be fully compensated in respect of the combined effects of both torts. It is to be observed that this was the consideration which had been principally *f* urged in the argument for the appellant.

A notable feature of the speeches in *Baker v Willoughby* is the absence of any consideration of the possible implications of what may be termed the 'vicissitudes' principle. The leading exposition of this principle is to be found in the judgment of Brett LJ in *Phillips v London and South Western Railway Co* (1879) 5 CPD 280 at 291:   *g*

'. . . if no accident had happened, nevertheless many circumstances might have happened to prevent the plaintiff from earning his previous income; he may be disabled by illness, he is subject to the ordinary accidents and vicissitudes of life; and if all these circumstances of which no evidence can be given are looked at, it will be impossible to exactly estimate them; yet if the jury wholly pass them over they will go wrong, because these accidents and vicissitudes ought to be taken into account. *h* It is true that the chances of life cannot be accurately calculated, but the judge must tell the jury to consider them in order that they may give a fair and reasonable compensation.'

This principle is to be applied in conjunction with the rule that the court will not speculate when it knows, so that when an event within its scope has actually happened *j* prior to the trial date, that event will fall to be taken into account in the assessment of damages.

In *Harwood v Wyken Colliery Co*, which was founded on by Lord Reid in *Baker v Willoughby* as supporting the view which he took on causation, Hamilton LJ was at pains to stress that compensation under the Workmen's Compensation Acts had nothing in

common with an award of damages for personal injuries, being based on what the
workman has earned in the past, not on what he will be prevented from earning in the
future. He fully recognised the application of the 'vicissitudes' principle in the damages
context, saying (at 169–170):

> 'In assessing damages for injury caused to a plaintiff workman by the tortious
> negligence of the employer or his servants a jury would be directed that, their
> damages being a compensation once for all, they must consider not merely past
> injury, pain and suffering endured, expenses incurred and earnings lost, but also
> future loss. They would have to measure in money the future effects of permanent
> or continuing disablement, but they must consider also the possibility of future
> diminution or loss of earnings arising independently of the cause of action, from
> increasing age, from accident or illness in futuro, and so forth. They would be
> directed that they had to give solatium for suffering and compensation for
> disablement, but so that the tort-sufferer should not make a profit out of the wrong
> done him, the object being by the verdict to place him in as good a position as he
> was in before the wrong, but not in any wise in a better one.'

By way of contrast, under the Workmen's Compensation Acts the workman was given
a guarantee of compensation on the statutory scale where he was subject to an incapacity
resulting from personal injury by accident arising out of and in the course of his
employment. The statute did not say that the incapacity must result *solely* from the
injury. It was therefore irrelevant that the incapacity resulted also to some extent from
heart disease. In the circumstances *Harwood v Wyken Colliery Co* must be regarded as an
infirm foundation for the decision in *Baker v Willoughby*.

It is implicit in that decision that the scope of the 'vicissitudes' principle is limited to
supervening events of such a nature as either to reduce the disabilities resulting from the
accident or else to shorten the period during which they will be suffered. I am of opinion
that failure to consider or even advert to this implication weakens the authority of the
ratio decidendi of the case, and must lead to the conclusion that in its full breadth it is not
acceptable. The assessment of damages for personal injuries involves a process of
restitutio in integrum. The object is to place the injured plaintiff in as good a position
as he would have been in but for the accident. He is not to be placed in a better
position. The process involves a comparison between the plaintiff's circumstances as
regards capacity to enjoy the amenities of life and to earn a living as they would have
been if the accident had not occurred and his actual circumstances in those respects
following the accident. In considering how matters might have been expected to turn
out if there had been no accident, the 'vicissitudes' principle says that it is right to take
into account events, such as illness, which not uncommonly occur in the ordinary course
of human life. If such events are not taken into account, the damages may be greater
than are required to compensate the plaintiff for the effects of the accident, and that
result would be unfair to the defendant. Counsel for the appellant sought to draw a
distinction between the case where the plaintiff, at the time of the tortious injury, is
already suffering from a latent undetected condition which later develops into a disabling
illness and the case where the inception of the illness occurs wholly at a later date. In the
former case, so it was maintained, the illness would properly fall to be taken into account
in diminution of damages, on the principle that the tortfeasor takes his victim as he finds
him, but in the latter case it would not. There is no trace of the suggested distinction in
any of the authorities, and in my opinion it is unsound and apt to lead to great practical
difficulties, providing ample scope for disputation among medical men. What would be
the position, it might be asked, of an individual having a constitutional weakness
making him specially prone to illness generally, or an hereditary tendency to some
specific disease?

I am therefore of opinion that the majority in *Baker v Willoughby* were mistaken in
approaching the problems common to the case of a supervening tortious act and to that
of supervening illness wholly from the point of view of causation. While it is logically

correct to say that in both cases the original tort and the supervening event may be concurrent causes of incapacity, that does not necessarily, in my view, provide the correct *a* solution. In the case of supervening illness, it is appropriate to keep in view that this is one of the ordinary vicissitudes of life, and when one is comparing the situation resulting from the accident with the situation, had there been no accident, to recognise that the illness would have overtaken the plaintiff in any event, so that it cannot be disregarded in arriving at proper compensation, and no more than proper compensation.

Additional considerations come into play when dealing with the problems arising *b* where the plaintiff has suffered injuries from two or more successive and independent tortious acts. In that situation it is necessary to secure that the plaintiff is fully compensated for the aggregate effects of all his injuries. As Lord Pearson noted in *Baker v Willoughby* [1969] 3 All ER 1528 at 1535, [1970] AC 467 at 495 it would clearly be unjust to reduce the damages awarded for the first tort because of the occurrence of the second tort, damages for which are to be assessed on the basis that the plaintiff is already *c* partially incapacitated. I do not consider it necessary to formulate any precise juristic basis for dealing with this situation differently from the case of supervening illness. It might be said that a supervening tort is not one of the ordinary vicissitudes of life, or that it is too remote a possibility to be taken into account, or that it can properly be disregarded because it carries its own remedy. None of these formulations, however, is entirely satisfactory. The fact remains that the principle of full compensation requires *d* that a just and practical solution should be found. In the event that damages against two successive tortfeasors fall to be assessed at the same time, it would be highly unreasonable if the aggregate of both awards were less than the total loss suffered by the plaintiff. The computation should start from an assessment of that total loss. The award against the second tortfeasor cannot in fairness to him fail to recognise that the plaintiff whom he injured was already to some extent incapacitated. In order that the plaintiff may be fully *e* compensated, it becomes necessary to deduct the award so calculated from the assessment of the plaintiff's total loss and award the balance against the first tortfeasor. If that be a correct approach, it follows that, in proceedings against the first tortfeasor alone, the occurrence of the second tort cannot be successfully relied on by the defendant as reducing the damages which he must pay. That, in substance, was the result of the decision in *Baker v Willoughby*, where the supervening event was a tortious act, and to that *f* extent the decision was, in my view, correct.

Before leaving the case, it is right to face up to the fact that, if a non-tortious supervening event is to have the effect of reducing damages but a subsequent tortious act is not, there may in some cases be difficulty in ascertaining whether the event in question is or is not of a tortious character, particularly in the absence of the alleged tortfeasor. Possible questions of contributory negligence may cause additional complications. Such *g* difficulties are real, but are not sufficient, in my view, to warrant the conclusion that the distinction between tortious and non-tortious supervening events should not be accepted. The court must simply do its best to arrive at a just assessment of damages in a pragmatical way in the light of the whole circumstances of the case.

My Lords, for these reasons I would dismiss the appeal.

h

LORD BRIDGE OF HARWICH. My Lords, on 15th January 1973 the appellant injured his back in a fall at the premises where he was employed by the respondents. He sustained a prolapsed intervertebral disc which produced low back pain. In 1976 he developed cervical myelopathy. This condition was wholly unrelated to the 1973 injury. It has also been treated as common ground in the courts below and in your Lordships' House, that the condition of cervical myelopathy was not present in any latent *j* or dormant form at the date of the appellant's accident, but developed subsequently. The effect of the myelopathy was of itself such as to render the appellant totally unfit to work from the end of September 1976 onwards.

The appellant's claim for damages against the respondents was tried by Reeve J who, on 26th March 1979, gave judgment for the appellant, awarded him £6,000 for general

damages (reduced in the Court of Appeal to £4,000) and awarded him special damages
a representing his loss of earnings from the date of the accident to the end of September
1976. No issue is raised as to any of these matters in your Lordships' House. The judge
went on to consider the extent to which the appellant's earning capacity would have been
impaired by the accident injury if the myelopathy had not supervened. He assessed this
impairment at 50%, held that he was bound by authority to disregard the supervening
myelopathy in assessing the damages resulting from the accident, and accordingly
b awarded further special damages to represent half the appellant's lost earnings from
October 1976 to the date of the trial, and a sum in respect of future loss of earnings
calculated by applying a multiplier of seven to a figure representing half the appellant's
annual earning capacity. The respondents appealed against the inclusion of these
elements of damage in the award on the ground that the supervening incapacity of the
appellant attributable to myelopathy put an end to their legal liability for any loss of
c earnings which, but for myelopathy, would have resulted from the appellant's accident
injury in 1973. The Court of Appeal (Stephenson, Ackner LJJ and Dame Elizabeth
Lane), in a unanimous judgment delivered by Ackner LJ, so held and reduced the
damages accordingly. The appellant invites your Lordships to restore the award of the
judge.
    The authority by which the judge held himself bound, and that which is the linchpin
d of the argument for the appellant before your Lordships is the decision of this house in
Baker v Willoughby [1969] 3 All ER 1528, [1970] AC 467. The plaintiff in that case
sustained, by the negligence of the defendant, an injury to his left leg which caused a stiff
and painful left ankle, liability to future arthritis, diminished mobility and loss of
earning capacity. Subsequently, but before the trial, he was shot in the left leg in the
course of a robbery and as a result the leg had to be amputated above the knee. The trial
e judge held that he should not take into account in his assessment of the damages the
amputation of the left leg, since the appellant's actual and prospective loss flowing from
the respondent's negligent act had not been reduced by the subsequent loss of the leg.
The Court of Appeal reduced the damages to such as were appropriate to compensate the
plaintiff for the effects of the injury up to the date of the subsequent amputation but no
longer, holding that the subsequent consequences of the plaintiff's disability were in law
f attributable not to the original injury but to the subsequent amputation. This House
reversed that decision and restored the award of the trial Judge.
    It is significant that the argument for the plaintiff in Baker's case was put by counsel on
the ground that special considerations governed the assessment of damages in the case of
a plaintiff suffering successive injuries, such as those suffered by Mr Baker, where both
were caused tortiously. Counsel appears to have conceded, by implication if not
g expressly, that, if the amputation of the plaintiff's leg had been caused by disease or non-
tortious accident, the Court of Appeal's view of its effect on the assessment of damages for
the previous injury would have been correct. He argued that the trial judge's basis of
assessment was necessary in the case of successive tortious injuries to ensure that the
plaintiff should recover in the sum of the awards against both tortfeasors the aggregate
loss he had sustained from both injuries. This he would not do if the first tortfeasor's
h liability was reduced by the effect of the second injury, and the second tortfeasor was
entitled to take the plaintiff as he found him, ie as an already injured man. The Court
of Appeal rejected this argument as fallacious on the ground that the second tortfeasor
would be liable to compensate the plaintiff not only for the loss of his injured leg, but also
for the diminution of his entitlement to damages against the first tortfeasor attributable
to the loss of the leg.
j   Notwithstanding the course taken by the argument, in the speech of Lord Reid in this
House (with which Lord Guest, Viscount Dilhorne and Lord Donovan agreed) there is no
reference at all to the circumstance that the amputation of the plaintiff's leg was the
result of a tort as a factor relevant to the decision. On the contrary, the reasoning in the
speech applies equally to the effect of a supervening disability arising from illness or non-
tortious accident, as the following passage amply demonstrates ([1969] 3 All ER 1528 at
1532–1534, [1970] AC 467 at 492–494):

'A man is not compensated for the physical injury; he is compensated for the loss which he suffers as a result of that injury. His loss is not in having a stiff leg; it is in his inability to lead a full life, his inability to enjoy those amenities which depend on freedom of movement and his inability to earn as much as he used to earn or could have earned if there had been no accident. In this case the second injury did not diminish any of these. So why should it be regarded as having obliterated or superseded them? If it were the case that in the eye of the law an effect could only have one cause then the respondent might be right. It is always necessary to prove that any loss for which damages can be given was caused by the defendant's negligent act. But it is commonplace that the law regards many events as having two causes; that happens whenever there is contributory negligence, for then the law says that the injury was caused both by the negligence of the defendant and by the negligence of the plaintiff. And generally it does not matter which negligence occurred first in point of time. I see no reason why the appellant's present disability cannot be regarded as having two causes, and if authority be needed for this I find it in *Harwood* v. *Wyken Colliery Co* ([1913] 2 KB 158). That was a Workmen's Compensation Act 1906 case. But causation cannot be different in tort. There an accident made the man only fit for light work. And then a heart disease supervened and it also caused him only to be fit for light work. The argument for the employer was the same as in the present case. Before the disease supervened the workman's incapacity was caused by the accident. Thereafter it was caused by the disease and the previous accident became irrelevant; he would have been equally incapacitated if the accident had never happened. But HAMILTON, L.J., said (at 169): "... he is not disentitled to be paid compensation by reason of the supervention of a disease of the heart. It cannot be said of him that partial incapacity for work has not resulted and is not still resulting from the injury. All that can be said is that such partial incapacity is not still resulting 'solely' from the injury." ... If the later injury suffered before the date of the trial either reduces the disabilities from the injury for which the defendant is liable, or shortens the period during which they will be suffered by the plaintiff then the defendant will have to pay less damages. But if the later injuries merely become a concurrent cause of the disabilities caused by the injury inflicted by the defendant, then in my view they cannot diminish the damages. Suppose that the plaintiff has to spend a month in bed before the trial because of some illness unconnected with the original injury, the defendant cannot say that he does not have to pay anything in respect of that month; during that month the original injuries and the new illness are concurrent causes of his inability to work and that does not reduce the damages.'

In the speech of Lord Pearson there are references to the tortious causation of the supervening injury, but it is certainly not clear that Lord Pearson was treating this as the critical factor and thus adopting the narrow ground for decision advanced by counsel in argument. In any event, the ratio decidendi must be collected from the reasons adopted by the majority and, according to the strict doctrine of precedent, I think Reeve J was right to treat the wide principle expressed in the passages from the speech of Lord Reid which I have cited as binding him to decide the present case as he did.

Counsel for the appellant has naturally relied on *Baker's* case as binding authority supporting the judge's assessment of the damages, but, recognising that it is open to your Lordships to examine critically and, if thought right, to differ from Lord Reid's reasoning, he has sought to reconcile it with those principles of law which the Court of Appeal in the instant case treated as justifying them in reaching a different conclusion from the judge.

The first principle is that, in assessing damages for future loss of earnings, the court makes a discount for the possibility that, apart from the injury in respect of which he claims, the plaintiff's earning capacity may be diminished by some independent cause ('the vicissitudes principle').

The second principle is that, since the court does not speculate when it knows,

damages for loss of earnings, if the plaintiff's earning capacity has before trial been
a actually diminished by some independent cause of the kind to which the court would
have had regard in applying the vicissitudes principle, must be reduced accordingly.

Counsel does not dispute the existence of either of these principles, but he contends
that the scope of the vicissitudes principle must be confined to consideration of those
future possibilities which arise from factors which can be shown at the date of trial to
have been already inherent in some way in the plaintiff's physical make-up, or in his
b situation at the date of the tort, such as a latent but symptomless arthritis or a particular
liability to injury by accident arising from the hazardous nature of his occupation.

Naturally, when such factors *are* shown to have been present, they will materially
affect the extent of the discount to be made in assessing damages, but the judgment of
the Court of Appeal has drawn attention to the absurdities which would flow from the
adoption of any such absolute limitation of the vicissitudes principle as that suggested.
c The limitation would, moreover, be contrary both to authority and to the underlying
theory of legal causation on which the vicissitudes principle itself depends.

In the classic words cited by the Court of Appeal from the judgment of Brett LJ in
Phillips v London and South Western Railway Co (1879) 5 CPD 280 at 291; cf [1874–80] All
ER Rep 1176 at 1180–1181:

d '. . . if no accident had happened, nevertheless many circumstances might have
happened to prevent the plaintiff from earning his previous income; he may be
disabled by illness, he is subject to the *ordinary* accidents and vicissitudes of life; and
if all these circumstances of which no evidence can be given are looked at, it will be
impossible to exactly estimate them; yet if the jury wholly pass them over they will
go wrong, because these accidents and vicissitudes ought to be taken into account.'
(Emphasis added.)

e
In delivering the judgment of the Privy Council in *Paul v Rendell* (29th April 1981,
unreported) on the very day your Lordships concluded the hearing of the appeal in this
case, Lord Diplock said:

'Where, as in the present case, the plaintiff's disability is permanent, it is, their
Lordships are informed, the common practice in Australia to use actuarial tables for
f calculating the present capital value of future annual economic loss resulting from
the reduction in the plaintiff's annual earnings which the judge considers that he
will suffer for the remainder of his working life. From this figure as a starting point
the judge makes such adjustments as he thinks appropriate. Some adjustment
downwards would be needed to take account of all those contingencies such as
unemployment, ill-health or any other disability short of premature death, for
g which allowance is not made in the actuarial tables but which might have deprived
the plaintiff of his earning power or reduced it below the figure adopted for the
purpose of the actuarial calculation.'

The vicissitudes principle itself, it seems to me, stems from the fundamental
proposition of law that the object of every award of damages for monetary loss is to put
h the party wronged so far as possible in the same position, no better and no worse, as he
would be in if he had not suffered the wrong in respect of which he claims. To assume
that an injured plaintiff, if not injured, would have continued to earn his full wages for
a full working life, is very probably to over-compensate him. To apply a discount in
respect of possible future loss of earnings arising from independent cases may be to
under-compensate him. When confronted by future uncertainty, the court assesses the
j prospects and strikes a balance between these opposite dangers as best it can. But, when
the supervening illness or injury which is the independent cause of loss of earning
capacity has manifested itself before trial, the event has demonstrated that, even if the
plaintiff had never sustained the tortious injury, his earnings would now be reduced or
extinguished. To hold the tortfeasor, in this situation, liable to pay damages for a
notional continuing loss of earnings attributable to the tortious injury is to put the
plaintiff in a better position than he would be in if he had never suffered the tortious

injury. Put more shortly, applying well-established principles for the assessment of damages at common law, when a plaintiff injured by the defendant's tort is wholly *a* incapacitated from earning by supervening illness or accidental injury, the law will no longer treat the tort as a continuing cause of any loss of earning capacity.

It follows from the foregoing that I am, with the utmost respect, unable to agree with the opinion of Lord Reid in *Baker's* case, as expressed in the two passages from his speech which I have cited. In particular, I cannot accept that the decision in *Harwood v Wyken Colliery Co* [1913] 2 KB 158 affords any authority in support of Lord Reid's conclusion, *b* or that he was right to say that causation could not be different in tort and under the Workmen's Compensation Acts. In *Harwood's* case, Hamilton LJ, with whose judgment Cozens-Hardy MR agreed, was at pains to stress the very different principles governing a tortfeasor's liability to pay damages at common law on the one hand and the statutory liability of an employer to compensate an injured workman on the other. With reference to the former, he clearly recognised the vicissitudes principle (at 170): *c*

> 'They [sc the jury] would have to measure in money the future effects of permanent or continuing disablement, but they must consider also the possibility of future diminution or loss of earnings arising independently of the cause of action, from increasing age, from accident or illness in future, and so forth.'

With reference to the latter, he founded his view that an injury at work could be a *d* continuing cause of incapacity, which would continue to attract compensation notwithstanding supervening illness, entirely on the construction of the particular language of the statute to be applied.

Having reached the conclusion that the ratio decidendi of *Baker's* case cannot be sustained, it remains to consider whether the case should still be regarded as authority, as a decision on its own facts, for the proposition that, when two successive injuries are *e* both caused tortiously, the supervening disability caused by the second tort should, by way of exception to the general rule arising from the application of the vicissitudes principle, be disregarded when assessing the liability of the first tortfeasor for damages for loss of earnings caused by the first tort. I find it difficult to attribute such authority to the decision, when both the Court of Appeal and this House were expressly invited to adopt that proposition, and both, in different ways, declined the invitation. There is a *f* powerful, perhaps irresistible, attraction in the argument that, in the circumstances envisaged, the aggregate of the damages recoverable by the plaintiff should, provided both tortfeasors can be found and can meet their liability, be sufficient to cover the aggregate loss of earnings, past and future, which results from the combined effect of both injuries. But whether this end is properly achieved, as between the two tortfeasors, by apportioning liability on the principle which commended itself to the Court of *g* Appeal, or on the principle for which counsel for the appellant contended in argument, seems to me a very difficult question. For the reasons I have indicated, I think the speeches in your Lordships' House, by going off on a different tack, ultimately left that question unanswered. In the instant appeal counsel for the respondents was content to accept the decision in *Baker's* case as correct on its facts, so your Lordships have not heard argument on the question. In these circumstances, the proper conclusion seems to me *h* to be that the question should remain open for decision on another occasion, if and when it arises.

However that may be, for the reasons indicated earlier in this speech, I would dismiss the appeal.

Appeal dismissed. *j*

Solicitors: *Elborne, Mitchell & Co* (for the appellant); *Berrymans*, agents for *Crutes*, Newcastle upon Tyne (for the respondents).

Mary Rose Plummer   Barrister.

a

Pascoe v Nicholson

HOUSE OF LORDS

LORD DIPLOCK, LORD FRASER OF TULLYBELTON, LORD RUSSELL OF KILLOWEN, LORD KEITH OF KINKEL AND LORD ROSKILL

10th JUNE, 2nd JULY 1981

b

Road traffic – Specimen for laboratory test to determine driver's blood-alcohol proportion – Conditions precedent to request for specimen – Request for specimen – Whether specimen must be provided at same police station as that at which request for specimen made – Road Traffic Act 1972, s 9(1).

c Where a person suspected of driving or attempting to drive a motor vehicle while under the influence of alcohol has been arrested under s 8[a] of the Road Traffic Act 1972 following a positive breath test, and then, while he is at a police station and after he has been given an opportunity to provide a second specimen of breath, is required by a constable to provide a specimen of blood or urine for a laboratory test pursuant to s 9(1)[b] of that Act, it is not essential that the specimen of blood or urine be provided at the same *d* police station as that at which the requirement is made, and the validity of the procedure for requiring a specimen of blood or urine for a laboratory test is not affected if the arrested person is taken to another police station to provide that specimen (see p 770 c to f, p 774 b c f g and p 775 a, post).

Milne v M'Donald 1971 JC 40 followed.

Butler v Easton [1970] RTR 109 overruled.

e

Notes

For the power to require a specimen of blood or urine for a laboratory test, see Supplement to 33 Halsbury's Laws (3rd Edn) para 1061A.7.

For the Road Traffic Act 1972, s 9, see 42 Halsbury's Statutes (3rd Edn) 1655.

f **Cases referred to in opinions**

Butler v Easton [1970] RTR 109, DC, Digest (Cont Vol C) 929, 322e.

Galloway v Cruickshank (10th October 1969) unreported, HC of Justiciary.

Milne v M'Donald 1971 JC 40, 1971 SLT 291, HC of Justiciary.

Appeal

g On 19th November 1979 the justices for the county of Cornwall acting for the petty sessional division of Penwith sitting as a magistrates' court at Penzance dismissed an information preferred by the appellant, Chief Inspector Peter Pascoe, against the respondent, David Ralph Nicholson, that he on 13th June 1979 at Marazion in Cornwall did drive a motor cycle on the A 394 road having consumed alcohol in such quantity that the proportion thereof in his blood, as ascertained from a laboratory test for which he *h* subsequently provided a specimen under s 9 of the Road Traffic Act 1972, exceeded the prescribed limit contrary to s 6(1) of the Act. The ground of dismissal was that all the procedural requirements of the 1972 Act had not been complied with and therefore the evidence of analysis of the blood sample given by the respondent was inadmissible. The appellant appealed by way of case stated to the Divisional Court of the Queen's Bench Division (Donaldson LJ and Forbes J) which on 30th October 1980 dismissed the appeal *j* holding itself bound to do so by a previous decision of the court. The Divisional Court refused leave to appeal to the House of Lords but certified pursuant to s 1(2) of the

---

a   Section 8, so far as material, is set out at p 771 j to p 772 d, post

b   Section 9(1) is set out at p 772 e, post

Administration of Justice Act 1960 that a point of law of general public importance was
involved in the decision. On 18th December 1980 the House of Lords gave the appellant *a*
leave to appeal against the decision. The facts are set out in the opinion of Lord Roskill.

Michael Hutchison QC and *Claudia Ackner* for the appellant.
J Hampden Inskip QC and *Christopher Jervis* for the respondent.

 b

Their Lordships took time for consideration.

2nd July. The following opinions were delivered.

 c

LORD DIPLOCK. My Lords, I have had the advantage of reading in draft the speech
prepared by my noble and learned friend Lord Roskill, with which I am in full
agreement.

LORD FRASER OF TULLYBELTON. My Lords, I have had the advantage of
reading in draft the speech prepared by my noble and learned friend Lord Roskill. I *d*
agree with it and for the reasons stated in it I would allow this appeal and dispose of the
case as he proposes.

LORD RUSSELL OF KILLOWEN. My Lords, I have had the advantage of reading
in draft the speech about to be delivered by my noble and learned friend Lord Roskill.
I agree with it and with the adoption of the course that he proposes. *e*

LORD KEITH OF KINKEL. My Lords, I have had the benefit of reading in draft the
speech of my noble and learned friend Lord Roskill. I agree with it, and would
accordingly allow the appeal and answer the certified question as he proposes.

LORD ROSKILL. My Lords, all the events giving rise to this appeal, except the last, *f*
took place within less than two hours early on the morning of 30th June 1979. At
12.55 am that morning two police officers suspected that the respondent was driving his
motor cycle with alcohol in his body. Their suspicions were aroused by the manner of
his driving near Marazion in Cornwall. They stopped the vehicle. They smelt alcohol
on his breath. At 1 am one of the officers required the respondent to provide a specimen
of breath. At 1.10 am this specimen was provided. It was positive. The respondent was *g*
arrested and taken to Penzance Police Station. There, at 1.33 am, he provided a second
specimen of breath. It, too, was positive. At 1.37 am, at Penzance Police Station, the
respondent was required to provide a specimen for a laboratory test and, pursuant to
s 9(7) of the Road Traffic Act 1972, was warned of the consequences of any failure to
provide a specimen of blood or of urine. At 1.39 am a police officer requested the
respondent to supply a sample of blood. The respondent then agreed to do so. The *h*
respondent was thereupon taken from Penzance Police Station to Camborne. A specimen
of blood was there taken from him by a doctor. On laboratory testing (the admissibility
of the result of which was in issue) that specimen was found to contain not less than
164 mg of alcohol in 100 ml of blood, more than twice the permitted quantity.
    My Lords, on 9th August 1979 an information was preferred by the appellant against
the respondent for an offence contrary to s 6(1) of the 1972 Act. That information was *j*
heard by the Penzance justices on 5th and 19th November 1979. At the close of the case
for the prosecution it was submitted on behalf of the respondent that there was no case
to answer because the evidence of the result of the analysis of the specimen of blood, to
which I have already referred, was inadmissible. The appellant conceded that, if that
evidence were inadmissible, there was no case to answer. The justices upheld the

submission and dismissed the information. They stated a case for the opinion of the
a   High Court, asking the following question:

> 'Whether the provisions of the Road Traffic Act 1972 and in particular sections 6
> to 12 thereof require that the provisions of a specimen of breath for a breath test at
> a police station, the request for a sample of blood or of urine and the giving of such
> sample of blood or urine, must all take place at the same police station.'

b   My Lords, this submission for the respondent was founded on a decision of the
Divisional Court (Lord Parker CJ, Ashworth and Cantley JJ) in *Butler v Easton* [1970] RTR
109, decided on 22nd October 1969. The attention of the justices was, however, properly
drawn to a later decision of the High Court of Justiciary, *Milne v M'Donald* 1971 JC 40,
decided on 27th May 1971, in which that court (the Lord Justice-General (Clyde), Lords
Migdale and Johnston) in a reserved judgment followed an earlier unreported decision
c   of their own (*Galloway v Cruickshank*, 10th October 1969) and reached the opposite
conclusion from that which had been reached by the Divisional Court, and expressly
declined to follow that earlier decision.

My Lords, the difference of opinion arose on a single issue, namely, whether on the
true construction of s 3(1) of the Road Safety Act 1967, which was the statutory
predecessor of s 9(1) of the 1972 Act, it was essential for the provision of the specimen of
d   blood or of urine to take place at the same police station as that at which the requirement
to provide that specimen had been made. The Divisional Court had held that it was
essential for that requirement to provide the specimen and its actual provision to take
place at the same police station. The High Court of Justiciary held that it was not.

My Lords, the justices sitting at Penzance rightly held that they were bound to follow
the decision of the Divisional Court, though they were referred to and recognised the
e   persuasive authority of the decision of the High Court of Justiciary. It was for this reason
that they held that the evidence of the result of the analysis of the specimen of blood
taken from the respondent at Cambourne Police Station was inadmissible. They
accordingly, and rightly on this view of the law, dismissed the summons.

When the present appeal by the appellant came before the Divisional Court by way of
case stated on 30th October 1980, that court was also bound by its earlier decision.
f   Indeed, the proceedings of the Divisional Court are recorded to have lasted only five
minutes. But the Divisional Court certified the following question as raising a point of
law of general public importance, namely:

> 'Whether the provisions of the Road Traffic Act 1972 and in particular sections 6
> to 12 thereof require that the provisions of a specimen of breath for a breath test at
> a police station, the request for a sample of blood or of urine and the giving of such
g   > sample of blood or urine, must all take place at the same police station'

thus inviting your Lordships to answer the same question as that which the justices had
asked in their case stated.

The Divisional Court refused leave to appeal but that leave was granted by your
Lordships' House on 18th December 1980.
h   My Lords, thus, after an interval of some ten years, your Lordships' House is invited,
for the first time, to decide which of the two decisions to which I have already referred
is right. Those two decision are in principle indistinguishable and, indeed, the present
case is, on its facts, also in principle indistinguishable from those earlier cases.

My Lords, as I have already said, the determination of this appeal depends on the true
construction of s 9(1) of the 1972 Act. But since both learned counsel invited attention
j   to, and indeed sought support for their respective submissions from, other sections of the
statute, I set out for ease of reference those parts of the several sections on which reliance
was thus placed:

> '8.—(1) A constable in uniform may require any person driving or attempting
> to drive a motor vehicle on a road or other public place to provide a specimen of

breath for a breath test there or nearby, if the constable has reasonable cause—(a) to suspect him of having alcohol in his body, or (b) to suspect him of having committed a traffic offence while the vehicle was in motion; but no requirement may be made by virtue of paragraph (b) above unless it is made as soon as reasonably practicable after the commission of the traffic offence.

'(2) If an accident occurs owing to the presence of a motor vehicle on a road or other public place, a constable in uniform may require any person who he has reasonable cause to believe was driving or attempting to drive the vehicle at the time of the accident to provide a specimen of breath for a breath test—(a) except while that person is at a hospital as a patient, either at or near the place where the requirement is made or, if the constable thinks fit, at a police station specified by the constable; (b) in the said excepted case, at the hospital; but a person shall not be required to provide such a specimen while at a hospital as a patient if the medical practitioner in immediate charge of his case is not first notified of the proposal to make the requirement or objects to the provision of a specimen on the ground that its provision or the requirement to provide it would be prejudicial to the proper care or treatment of the patient.

'(3) A person who, without reasonable excuse, fails to provide a specimen of breath for a breath test under subsection (1) or (2) above shall be guilty of an offence . . .

'(7) A person arrested under this section, or under the said section 5(5), shall, while at a police station, be given an opportunity to provide a specimen of breath for a breath test there . . .

'**9.**—(1) A person who has been arrested under section 5(5) or 8 of this Act may, while at a police station, be required by a constable to provide a specimen for a laboratory test (which may be a specimen of blood or of urine), if he has previously been given an opportunity to provide a specimen of breath for a breath test at that station under subsection (7) of the said section 8, and either—(a) it appears to a constable in consequence of the breath test that the device by means of which the test is carried out indicates that the proportion of alcohol in his blood exceeds the prescribed limit, or (b) when given the opportunity to provide that specimen, he fails to do so.

'(2) A person while at a hospital as a patient may be required by a constable to provide at the hospital a specimen for a laboratory test—(a) if it appears to a constable in consequence of a breath test carried out on that person under section 8(2) of this Act that the device by means of which the test is carried out indicates that the proportion of alcohol in his blood exceeds the prescribed limit, or (b) if that person has been required, whether at the hospital or elsewhere, to provide a specimen of breath for a breath test, but fails to do so and a constable has reasonable cause to suspect him of having alcohol in his body; but a person shall not be required to provide a specimen for a laboratory test under this subsection if the medical practitioner in immediate charge of his case is not first notified of the proposal to make the requirement or objects to the provision of a specimen on the ground that its provision, the requirement to provide it or a warning under subsection (7) below would be prejudicial to the proper care or treatment of the patient.

'(3) A person who, without reasonable excuse, fails to provide a specimen for a laboratory test in pursuance of a requirement imposed under this section shall be guilty of an offence . . .

'(5) A person shall not be treated for the purposes of subsection (3) above as failing to provide a specimen unless—(a) he is first requested to provide a specimen of blood, but refuses to do so; (b) he is then requested to provide two specimens of urine within one hour of the request, but fails to provide them within the hour or refuses at any time within the hour to provide them; and (c) he is again requested to provide a specimen of blood, but refuses to do so . . .

'(7) A constable shall on requiring any person under this section to provide a
specimen for a laboratory test warn him that failure to provide a specimen of blood
or urine may make him liable to imprisonment, a fine and disqualification, and, if
the constable fails to do so, the court before which that person is charged with an
offence under section 6 of this Act or this section may direct an acquittal or dismiss
the charge, as the case may require. In this subsection "disqualification" means
disqualification for holding or obtaining a licence to drive a motor vehicle granted
under Part III of this Act . . .

'11. Any person required to provide a specimen for a laboratory test under
section 9(1) of this Act may thereafter be detained at the police station until he
provides a specimen of breath for a breath test and it appears to a constable that the
device by means of which the test is carried out indicates that the proportion of
alcohol in that person's blood does not exceed the prescribed limit.'

My Lords, it was urged for the appellant that nowhere in s 9(1) was there any express
limitation on the place where the specimen for a laboratory test was to be provided. The
subsection properly interpreted contrasted the requirement to provide such a specimen
with its actual provision. The requirement to provide had to be made at the same police
station as that where the opportunity to supply the specimen of breath for the second
breath test had been given pursuant to s 8(7). Only those two events had to take place at
the same police station, but not the third event referred to in s 9(1), namely the actual
provision of the specimen for the laboratory test.

My Lords, your Lordships' attention was drawn to the provisions of s 8(1) and (2) and
of s 9(2) as showing that where the statute intended to limit or define the place at which
a particular event, or events, were to take place, it so provided in specific terms. Thus the
breath test provided for in s 8(1) had to take place 'there or nearby', that is to say, there
or nearby on the road or other public place referred to earlier in that subsection. A
similar provision, subject to the stated exception, is included in s 8(2) in the case of an
accident. Moreover, s 9(2) opens with the words 'A person while at a hospital . . .' may
be requested in certain circumstances to provide 'at the hospital' a specimen for a
laboratory test, words of limitation or restriction as to the place where the requirement
can be made and the specimen provided which are not to be found in s 9(1). Attention
was also drawn to the provisions in s 9(7) regarding warning and to the absence of any
words of limitation or restriction in that subsection as to where the warning should be
given.

My Lords, these were in substance the submissions which found favour with the High
Court of Justiciary. But that court did not in its judgment refer to s 11 (formerly s 4 of
the 1967 Act) which provides for detention 'at *the* police station' (I italicise the definite
article) after the specimen for the laboratory test has been provided, in effect, until the
motorist is fit to drive. It was this section which had impressed the Divisional Court, and
led that court to its conclusion. Lord Parker CJ said [1970] RTR 109 at 111: 'That . . .
clearly shows that it is contemplated that he shall be kept throughout at one and only one
police station.' My Lords, I find it difficult to believe that the High Court of Justiciary
overlooked this section, for they clearly considered, but disagreed with, the decision of
the Divisional Court which was based on its provisions. I think the High Court of
Justiciary must have thought that the statutory predecessor of s 11 was not, of itself,
enough to lead to a different conclusion from that to which the other relevant sections of
the 1967 Act pointed.

Learned counsel for the respondent in his argument founded much on s 11. He
argued that the provisions of this part of the statute, while restricting the liberty of the
individual, were designed to see that those liberties were not unduly restricted. He
urged that the argument for the appellant had precisely the result of imposing undue
restrictions on those liberties. If a motorist were taken to a police station after the first
breath test were positive and then, after any second breath test, were required to provide
a specimen for a laboratory test, and to that end might be taken many miles to another

police station for the provision of that specimen, and there detained until fit to drive, the motorist would be likely when fit to have to go back to the first police station to regain *a* possession of his car in order to go home. It was urged that the appellant's argument ignored the use of the definite article in s 11. If those submissions were sound, it was said that the indefinite article could equally well have been used, as it was used in s 9(1).

My Lords, as my noble and learned friend Lord Keith, pointed out during the argument, if on arrival at a police station the motorist sought a second breath test and there was then no suitable breathalyser available at that police station, there is nothing in *b* the statute which would prevent the police at that juncture taking the motorist to another police station where proper equipment was available. If that be permissible, as like my noble learned friend I think it clearly would be, I see no logical reason why in the absence of express statutory provision, the motorist should not, after being required to supply the specimen for a laboratory test immediately following any second breath test, be taken to another police station where a doctor is more easily available in order to take *c* from him the specimen of blood. It is not difficult to visualise many parts of the United Kingdom where it might be extremely difficult to obtain the services of a doctor at some isolated police station.

My Lords, learned counsel for the respondent also founded an elaborate argument on s 9(5). Suppose, he contended, that the motorist first volunteered to provide a specimen of blood and to that end was taken to a second police station and then was unable, or *d* unwilling, perhaps for some understandable reason to provide that specimen, and sought to fall back on his alternative option to provide a specimen of urine. The motorist might then have to be taken back to the first police station. My Lords, this argument, if I understood it correctly, is based on a misunderstanding of s 9(5), which is concerned with and only with the offence created by s 9(3). A motorist must, before being liable to conviction for an offence against that subsection, namely of failing to provide a specimen *e* for a laboratory test, be shown to have been given but to have failed to have availed himself of the successive opportunities required by s 9(5) to have been accorded to him. That subsection is, to my mind, irrelevant in the present case and sheds no light on the true construction of s 9(1).

My Lords, apart from the provisions of s 11, I would have no doubt that the language of s 9(1) read in isolation and without regard even to s 9(2) imposes no restriction which *f* makes it essential that the specimen for the laboratory test must be provided at the same police station as that at which the requirement that it be provided is made. But I think this conclusion is strongly reinforced by the provisions of s 9(2) and also of s 9(7) regarding the insistence on warning. With profound respect to Lord Parker CJ, I do not regard the language of s 11 as strong enough to require a contrary conclusion, for in the context I think 'the police station' in that section can be legitimately construed as *g* meaning 'the police station where he is'. It follows that, in my view, *Butler v Easton* was wrongly decided and the decision of the High Court of Justiciary in *Milne v M'Donald* is to be preferred. I would, therefore, allow the appeal and answer the certified question in the negative.

My Lords, the question also arose whether your Lordships' House should remit this case to the justices with a direction to continue the hearing, for, as I have already said, the *h* respondent succeeded on a submission, now held to be wrong but correct when made, of no case to answer. Learned counsel for the respondent told your Lordships that it had been proposed to raise by way of substantive defence an issue whether or not the respondent had been properly told of the reason for his arrest. My Lords, learned counsel for the appellant did not ask your Lordships to remit the case, being content to succeed in the appeal solely on the question of law raised. In view of this generous attitude by the *j* prosecution, I think it might leave a sense of injustice in the respondent were he now, some two years after the events in question, to be put in peril afresh of losing his licence as well as of some financial penalty. Your Lordships were told that he is a man with no previous convictions. My Lords, if your Lordships agree, I would propose that exceptionally, and possibly fortunately for the respondent, your Lordships' House should *a*   only allow the appeal and answer the certified question in the negative, for this appeal was brought to clarify the law rather than to punish the respondent.

Certified question answered in the negative: order appealed from set aside.

Solicitors: *Robbins, Olivey & Lake*, agents for *Cornish & Birtill*, Penzance (for the appellant); *Burton, Yeates & Hart*, agents for *Vivian Thomas & Jervis*, Penzance (for the respondent).

b
Mary Rose Plummer   Barrister.

c
Practice Direction

QUEEN'S BENCH DIVISION
LORD LANE CJ AND MICHAEL DAVIES J
26th JUNE 1981

d
Practice – Trial – Estimate of length of trial – Jury trials – Civil actions – Estimates required to be realistic.

LORD LANE CJ gave the following direction at the sitting of the court: The recent trial in the case of *Orme v Associated Newspapers Group Ltd* (31st March 1981, unreported) *e* demonstrates the importance of ensuring that all possible steps are taken to prevent unnecessary hardship to the jury in civil actions. Judges in such cases inquire of prospective jurors whether they will suffer inconvenience or hardship by having to serve for the estimated length of the trial and excuse those who will be so affected.

If the estimate of length is inaccurate, the jurors are misled and may suffer great hardship. It is, therefore, essential that such estimates should be realistic. The court *f* must be informed immediately if, at any time after the action has been set down for trial, there is any change of circumstances likely to alter the probable length of the trial.

N P Metcalfe Esq   Barrister.

R v Lambie   a

HOUSE OF LORDS
LORD DIPLOCK, LORD FRASER OF TULLYBELTON, LORD RUSSELL OF KILLOWEN, LORD KEITH OF
KINKEL AND LORD ROSKILL
3rd, 25th JUNE 1981

b

*Criminal law – Obtaining pecuniary advantage by deception – Deception – Implied representation
– Credit card transaction – Payment guaranteed by bank which issued credit card – Retailer not
concerned with card holder's credit standing at bank – Whether card holder who used card when
over credit limit imposed by bank obtaining pecuniary advantage by deception – Theft Act 1968,
s 16(1).*

c

*Criminal law – Obtaining property by deception – Deception – Credit card – Dishonest use of
credit card to obtain goods from retailer – Card holder using card when over credit limit imposed
by bank or company issuing card – Whether card holder may be charged with obtaining property
by deception – Theft Act 1968, s 15(1).*

Criminal evidence – Inducement – Inference of inducement –Irresistible inference – Transaction d
*of which it would be unreasonable to expect parties to remember details – Result of transaction
such that inference of inducement may well arise – Whether jury may decide whether inference
is in fact irresistible.*

The respondent was issued with a credit card by a bank giving her credit facilities up to
£200, an express condition of use being that it should be used only within the credit e
limit. The bank entered into contracts with retailers prepared to accept the card for the
purchase of goods, by which the bank guaranteed payment of any purchase up to £50
made with the credit card, provided the retailer complied with certain conditions relating
to the validity of the card. The appellant, when well over her credit limit of £200,
purchased goods for £10·35 from a shop using her credit card. The shop complied with
the conditions for a credit card purchase and allowed the respondent to take the goods she f
had selected. The respondent was charged with obtaining a pecuniary advantage by
deception contrary to s 16(1)ᵈ of the Theft Act 1968. At her trial the shop assistant who
made the sale stated that she gave no thought to, and made no assumptions about, the
respondent's credit standing with the bank or whether the respondent could pay the
bank since her only concern was to see that the conditions for a credit card purchase were
complied with in order that the shop would be paid by the bank. In his summing up the g
judge asked the jury whether the shop assistant had relied on the presentation of the card
as being due authority to use the card within the respondent's credit limit at that time.
The jury returned a verdict of guilty and the respondent was convicted. The respondent
appealed to the Court of Appeal ([1981] 1 All ER 332) which allowed her appeal and
quashed her conviction on the ground that in order to obtain a conviction under s 16(1)
it was necessary to show that the shop assistant to whom the representation had been h
made had acted or relied on the representation and there was no evidence that the shop
assistant had been induced by a false representation that the respondent's credit standing
at the bank gave her authority to use the card.

Held – The presentation of a credit card as the means of payment for a purchase implied
a representation on the part of the purchaser that he or she had actual authority to make,
on behalf of the bank or credit card company which issued the card, a contract with the j
retailer to the effect that the bank or company would honour the voucher signed by the

---

a   Section 16(1) provides: 'A person who by any deception dishonestly obtains for himself or another
    any pecuniary advantage shall on conviction on indictment be liable to imprisonment for a term
    not exceeding five years.'

purchaser, and not a representation that the purchaser's credit standing entitled him or
a her to use the card. The only inference to be drawn from the shop assistant's evidence
was that she had been induced to complete the transaction and to allow the respondent
to take the goods by the representation implied in the respondent's presentation of the
credit card as the means of payment, since had she known that the respondent was acting
dishonestly and had no authority to use the card she would not have completed the
transaction. It followed that the respondent was guilty of the offence charged. The
b appeal would be allowed and the conviction restored (see p 778 *a* to *d*, p 779 *j*, p 780 *e j*,
p 781 *f* to *j* and p 782 *h*, post).

Metropolitan Police Comr v Charles [1976] 3 All ER 112 applied.

Per Curiam. Where no one could reasonably be expected to remember a particular
transaction in detail, and the inference of inducement may well be in the circumstances
irresistible, there is no reason in principle why it should not be left to the jury to decide,
c on the evidence, whether that inference is in fact irresistible (see p 778 *a* to *d* and p 782
c to *h*, post); dictum of Humphreys J in R v Sullivan (1945) 30 Cr App R at 136 approved.

Semble. A person who obtains goods from a retailer by the dishonest use of a credit
card may properly be charged with obtaining property by deception contrary to s 15(1)[b]
of the 1968 Act (see p 778 *a* to *d* and p 779 *b c*, post).

Decision of the Court of Appeal [1981] 1 All ER 332 reversed.

d
Notes

For obtaining a pecuniary advantage by deception, see 11 Halsbury's Laws (4th Edn) para
1279, and for cases on the subject, see 15 Digest (Reissue) 1387–1391, *12,138–12,152*.

For the Theft Act 1968, s 16, see 8 Halsbury's Statutes (3rd Edn) 793.

e ### Cases referred to in opinions

Metropolitan Police Comr v Charles [1976] 3 All ER 112, [1977] AC 177, [1976] 3 WLR
431, 140 JP 531, 63 Cr App R 252, HL; *affg* [1976] 1 All ER 659, [1976] 1 WLR 248,
CA, 15 Digest (Reissue) 1390, *12,150*.

R v Laverty [1970] 3 All ER 432, 134 JP 699, 54 Cr App R 495, [1971] RTR 124, CA, 15
Digest (Reissue) 1412, *12,368*.

f R v Sullivan (1945) 30 Cr App R 132, CCA, 15 Digest (Reissue) 1411, *12,354*.

Appeal

On 2nd April 1979 the respondent, Shiralee Ann Lambie, was convicted in the Crown
Court at Bedford before his Honour Judge Counsell and a jury of obtaining a pecuniary
advantage by deception contrary to s 16(1) of the Theft Act 1968. The respondent
g appealed by leave of Park J to the Court of Appeal, Criminal Division (Cumming-Bruce
LJ, Stocker and Smith JJ) ([1981] 1 All ER 332, [1981] 1 WLR 78), which allowed her
appeal on 30th July 1980 and quashed her conviction. The court refused an application
by the Crown for leave to appeal to the House of Lords, but certified under s 33(2) of the
Criminal Appeal Act 1968, that a point of law of general public importance was involved
in its decision. On 6th November 1968 the Appeal Committee of the House of Lords
h allowed a petition by the Crown for leave to appeal to the House. The facts are set out
in the opinion of Lord Roskill.

Richard Curtis QC and Michael Pert for the Crown.
Patrick Back QC and John Plumstead for the respondent.

j Their Lordships took time for consideration.

---

b   Section 15(1) provides: 'A person who by any deception dishonestly obtains property belonging to
another, with the intention of permanently depriving the other of it, shall on conviction be liable
to imprisonment for a term not exceeding ten years.'

25th June. The following opinions were delivered.

LORD DIPLOCK. My Lords, I have had the advantage of reading in draft the speech *a*
prepared by my noble and learned friend Lord Roskill. I agree with it and would allow
the appeal.

LORD FRASER OF TULLYBELTON. My Lords, I have had the advantage of
reading in draft the speech prepared by my noble and learned friend Lord Roskill. I *b*
agree with it and for the reasons stated therein I would answer the certified question in
the negative and allow this appeal.

LORD RUSSELL OF KILLOWEN. My Lords, I have had the advantage of reading
in draft the speech prepared by my noble and learned friend Lord Roskill. I agree with
it and that this appeal should be allowed.   *c*

LORD KEITH OF KINKEL. My Lords, for the reasons given in the speech of my
noble and learned friend Lord Roskill, which I have had the opportunity of reading in
draft and with which I entirely agree, I too would allow the appeal.

LORD ROSKILL. My Lords, on 20th April 1977 the respondent was issued by *d*
Barclays Bank Ltd ('the bank') with a Barclaycard ('the card'). That card was what today
is commonly known as a credit card. It was issued subject to the Barclaycard current
conditions of use, and it was an express condition of its issue that it should be used only
within the respondent's credit limit. That credit limit was £200 as the respondent well
knew, since that figure had been notified to her in writing when the card was issued.
The then current conditions of use included an undertaking by the respondent, as its *e*
holder, to return the card to the bank on request. No complaint was, or indeed could be,
made of the respondent's use of the card until 18th November 1977. Between that date
and 5th December 1977 she used the card for at least 24 separate transactions, thereby
incurring a debt of some £533. The bank became aware of this debt and thereupon
sought to recover the card. On 6th December 1977 the respondent agreed to return the
card on 7th December 1977. She did not, however, do so. By 15th December 1977 she *f*
had used the card for at least 43 further transactions, incurring a total debt to the bank
of £1,005·26.

My Lords, on 15th December 1977 the respondent entered into the transaction out of
which this appeal arises. She visited a Mothercare shop in Luton. She produced the card
to a departmental manager at Mothercare named Miss Rounding. She selected goods
worth £10·35. Miss Rounding completed the voucher, checked that the card was *g*
current in date, that it was not on the current stop list and that the respondent's signature
on the voucher corresponded with her signature on the card. Thereupon, the respondent
took away the goods which she had selected. In due course, Mothermore sent the
voucher to the bank and were paid £10·35 less the appropriate commission charged by
the bank. On 19th December 1977 the respondent returned the card to the bank.

My Lords, at her trial at the Crown Court at Bedford on 1st and 2nd August 1979 *h*
before his Honour Judge Counsell and a jury, the respondent faced two charges of
obtaining a pecuniary advantage by deception contrary to s 16(1) of the Theft Act
1968. These were specimen charges. The first related to an alleged offence on 5th
December 1977 and the second to the events which took place at the Mothercare shop at
Luton which I have just related. The particulars of each charge were that she dishonestly
obtained for herself a pecuniary advantage 'namely, the evasion of a debt for which she *j*
then made herself liable by deception, namely, by false representations that she was
authorised to use a Barclaycard . . . to obtain goods to the value of £10·35'.

The jury acquitted the respondent on the first charge. She was, however, convicted on
the second. The evidence of dishonesty in relation to the Mothercare transaction which
was the subject of the second charge was overwhelming, and before your Lordships'

House counsel for the respondent did not seek to suggest otherwise. Presumably the
a acquittal on the first count was because the jury were not certain that at the earlier date,
5th December 1977, the respondent was acting dishonestly.

My Lords, during the hearing in this House your Lordships inquired of counsel for the
appellant prosecutor why no count of obtaining property by deception on 15th December
1977 contrary to s 15 of the Theft Act 1968 had been included in the indictment. Your
Lordships were told that such a charge had indeed been preferred at the magistrates'
b court during the committal proceedings but had been rejected by the magistrates on a
submission made on behalf of the respondent during those proceedings. My Lords, if
this be so, I find it difficult to see on what basis such a submission could properly have
succeeded, or what defence there could have been had such a charge been the subject of
a further count in the indictment once the jury were convinced, as they were, of the
respondent's dishonesty on 15th December 1977. Had that course been taken, the
c complications which in due course led to the Court of Appeal, Criminal Division,
quashing the conviction on the second count, and consequently, to the prosecutor's
appeal to this House, with your Lordships' leave, following the grant of a certificate by
the Court of Appeal, Criminal Division, would all have been avoided. But the course of
adding a count charging an offence against s 15 of the Theft Act 1968 was not followed,
and accordingly your Lordships have now to determine whether the Court of Appeal,
d Criminal Division, was correct in quashing the conviction on the second count. If it was,
then, as that court recognised in the concluding paragraph of its judgment, a gateway to
successful fraud has been opened for the benefit of the dishonest who in circumstances
such as the present cannot be proceeded against and punished at least for offences against
s 16 of the Theft Act 1968.

My Lords, the committal proceedings were what is sometimes called 'old fashioned',
e that is to say, that advantage was not taken of s 1 of the Criminal Justice Act 1967.
Witnesses were called in the magistrates' court and cross-examined. These witnesses
included Miss Rounding, the departmental manager. Your Lordships were shown a
copy of her deposition. Miss Rounding was not called at the trial at the Crown Court.
Her deposition was read to the jury. It emerged from her evidence, and other evidence
given or read, that, as one would expect, there was an agreement between Mothercare
f and the bank. That agreement does not appear to have been properly proved at the trial,
but, by consent, your Lordships were given a pro forma copy of what is known as a
'merchant member agreement' between the bank and its customer, setting out the
conditions on which the customer will accept and the bank will honour credit cards such
as Barclaycards.

My Lords, at the close of the case for the prosecution, counsel for the respondent
g invited the judge to withdraw both counts from the jury on, it seems from reading the
judge's clear ruling on this submission, two grounds: first, that as a matter of law there
was no evidence from which a jury might properly draw the inference that the
presentation of the card in the circumstances I have described was a representation by the
respondent that she was authorised by the bank to use the card to create a contract to
which the bank would be a party, and, second, that as a matter of law there was no
h evidence from which a jury might properly infer that Miss Rounding was induced by
any representation which the respondent might have made to allow the transaction to be
completed and the respondent to obtain the goods. The foundation for this latter
submission was that it was the existence of the agreement between Mothercare and the
bank that was the reason for Miss Rounding allowing the transaction to be completed
and the goods to be taken by the respondent, since Miss Rounding knew of the
j arrangement with the bank, so that Mothercare was in any event certain of payment. It
was not, it was suggested, any representation by the respondent which induced Miss
Rounding to complete the transaction and to allow the respondent to take the goods.

My Lords, the judge rejected these submissions. He was clearly right to do so, as
indeed was conceded in argument before your Lordships' House, if the decision of this
House in *Metropolitan Police Comr v Charles* [1976] 3 All ER 112, [1977] AC 177 is of

direct application. In that appeal this House was concerned with the dishonest use, not
as in the present appeal of a credit card, but of a cheque card. The appellant defendant *a*
was charged and convicted on two counts of obtaining a pecuniary advantage by
deception, contrary to s 16 of the Theft Act 1968. The Court of Appeal, Criminal
Division, and your Lordships' House both upheld those convictions. Your Lordships
unanimously held that where a drawer of a cheque which is accepted in return for goods,
services or cash, uses a cheque card he represents to the payee that he has the actual
authority of the bank to enter on its behalf into the contract expressed on the card that *b*
it would honour the cheque on presentation for payment.

My Lords, I venture to quote in their entirety three paragraphs from the speech of my
noble and learned friend Lord Diplock ([1976] 3 All ER 112 at 114, [1977] AC 177 at
182–183) which, as I venture to think, encapsulate the reasoning of all those members of
your Lordships' House who delivered speeches:

> 'When a cheque card is brought into the transaction, it still remains the fact that *c*
> all the payee is concerned with is that the cheque should be honoured by the bank.
> I do not think that the fact that a cheque card is used necessarily displaces the
> representation to be implied from the act of drawing the cheque which has just
> been mentioned. It is, however, likely to displace that representation at any rate as
> the main inducement to the payee to take the cheque, since the use of the cheque
> card in connection with the transaction gives to the payee a direct contractual right *d*
> against the bank itself to payment on presentment, provided that the use of the card
> by the drawer to bind the bank to pay the cheque was within the actual or ostensible
> authority conferred on him by the bank.
>
> 'By exhibiting to the payee a cheque card containing the undertaking by the bank
> to honour cheques drawn in compliance with the conditions endorsed on the back
> and drawing the cheque accordingly, the drawer represents to the payee that he has *e*
> actual authority from the bank to make a contract with the payee on the bank's
> behalf that it will honour the cheque on presentment for payment.
>
> 'It was submitted on behalf of the accused that there is no need to imply a
> representation that the drawer's authority to bind the bank was actual and not
> merely ostensible, since ostensible authority alone would suffice to create a contract
> with the payee that was binding on the bank; and the drawer's possession of the *f*
> cheque card and the cheque book with the bank's consent would be enough to
> constitute his ostensible authority. So, the submission goes, the only representation
> needed to give business efficacy to the transaction would be true. This argument
> stands the doctrine of ostensible authority on its head. What creates ostensible
> authority in a person who purports to enter into a contract as agent for a principal
> is a representation made to the other party that he has the actual authority of the *g*
> principal for whom he claims to be acting to enter into the contract on that person's
> behalf. If (1) the other party has believed the representation and on the faith of that
> belief has acted on it and (2) the person represented to be his principal has so
> conducted himself towards that other party as to be estopped from denying the
> truth of the representation, then, and only then, is he bound by the contract
> purportedly made on his behalf. The whole foundation of liability under the *h*
> doctrine of ostensible authority is a representation, believed by the person to whom
> it is made, that the person claiming to contract as agent for a principal has the actual
> authority of the principal to enter into the contract on his behalf.'

If one substitutes in the passage the words 'to honour the voucher' for the words 'to pay
the cheque', it is not easy to see why mutatis mutandis the entire passages are not equally *j*
applicable to the dishonest misuse of credit cards as to the dishonest misuse of cheque
cards.

But the Court of Appeal in a long and careful judgment delivered by Cumming-Bruce
LJ felt reluctantly impelled to reach a different conclusion. The crucial passage in the
judgment which the learned Lord Justice delivered reads thus ([1981] 1 All ER 332 at
339–340, [1981] 1 WLR 78 at 86–87):

'We would pay tribute to the lucidity with which the learned judge presented to
the jury the law which the House of Lords had declared in relation to deception in
a cheque card transaction. If that analysis can be applied to this credit card
deception, the summing up is faultless. But, in our view, there is a relevant
distinction between the situation described in *Metropolitan Police Comr v Charles* and
the situation devised by Barclays Bank for transactions involving use of their credit
cards. By their contract with the bank, Mothercare had bought from the bank the
right to sell goods to Barclaycard holders without regard to the question whether the
customer was complying with the terms of the contract between the customer and
the bank. By her evidence Miss Rounding made it perfectly plain that she made no
assumption about the appellant's credit standing at the bank. As she said: "The
company rules exist because of the company's agreement with Barclaycard." The
flaw in the logic is, in our view, demonstrated by the way in which the judge put
the question of the inducement of Miss Rounding to the jury: "Is that a reliance by
her, Miss Rounding of Mothercare, on the presentation of the card as being due
authority *within the limits as at that time* as with count 1?" In our view, the evidence
of Miss Rounding could not found a verdict that necessarily involved a finding of
fact that Miss Rounding was induced by a false representation that the appellant's
credit standing at the bank gave her authority to use the card.'

I should perhaps mention, for the sake of clarity, that the person referred to as the
appellant in that passage is the present respondent.

It was for that reason that the Court of Appeal, Criminal Division, allowed the appeal,
albeit with hesitation and reluctance. That court accordingly certified the following
point of law as of general public importance, namely:

'In view of the proved differences between a cheque card transaction and a credit
card transaction, were we right in distinguishing this case from that of *Metropolitan
Police Comr v Charles* [1976] 3 All ER 112, [1977] AC 177 on the issue of
inducement?'

My Lords, as the appellant says in his printed case, the Court of Appeal, Criminal
Division, laid too much emphasis on the undoubted, but to my mind irrelevant, fact that
Miss Rounding said she made no assumption about the respondent's credit standing with
the bank. They reasoned from the absence of assumption that there was no evidence
from which the jury could conclude that she was 'induced by a false representation that
the [respondent's] credit standing at the bank gave her authority to use the card'. But,
my Lords, with profound respect to Cumming-Bruce LJ, that is not the relevant
question. Following the decision of this house in *Charles*, it is in my view clear that the
representation arising from the presentation of a credit card has nothing to do with the
respondent's credit standing at the bank but is a representation of actual authority to
make the contract with, in this case, Mothercare on the bank's behalf that the bank will
honour the voucher on presentation. On that view, the existence and terms of the
agreement between the bank and Mothercare are irrelevant, as is the fact that Mothercare,
because of that agreement, would look to the bank for payment.

That being the representation to be implied from the respondent's actions and use of
the credit card, the only remaining question is whether Miss Rounding was induced by
that representation to complete the transaction and allow the respondent to take away
the goods. My Lords, if she had been asked whether, had she known the respondent was
acting dishonestly and, in truth, had no authority whatever from the bank to use the
credit card in this way, she (Miss Rounding) would have completed the transaction, only
one answer is possible: 'No'. Had an affirmative answer been given to this question, Miss
Rounding would, of course, have become a participant in furtherance of the respondent's
fraud and a conspirator with her to defraud both Mothercare and the bank. Leading
counsel for the respondent was ultimately constrained, rightly as I think, to admit that
had that question been asked of Miss Rounding and answered, as it must have been, in
the negative, this appeal must succeed. But both he and his learned junior strenuously

argued that, as Lord Edmund-Davies pointed out in his speech in *Charles* [1976] 3 All ER
112 at 122, [1977] AC 177 at 192–193, the question whether a person is or is not induced   *a*
to act in a particular way by a dishonest representation is a question of fact, and, since
what they claimed to be the crucial question had not been asked of Miss Rounding, there
was no adequate proof of the requisite inducement. In her deposition, Miss Rounding
stated, no doubt with complete truth, that she only remembered this particular
transaction with the respondent because someone subsequently came and asked her
about it after it had taken place. My Lords, credit card frauds are all too frequently   *b*
perpetrated, and if conviction of offenders for offences against s 15 or s 16 of the Theft
Act 1968 can only be obtained if the prosecution are able in each case to call the person
on whom the fraud was immediately perpetrated to say that he or she positively
remembered the particular transaction and, had the truth been known, would never
have entered into that supposedly well-remembered transaction, the guilty would often
escape conviction. In some cases, of course, it may be possible to adduce such evidence   *c*
if the particular transaction is well remembered. But where as in the present case no one
could reasonably be expected to remember a particular transaction in detail, and the
inference of inducement may well be in all the circumstances quite irresistible, I see no
reason in principle why it should not be left to the jury to decide, on the evidence in the
case as a whole, whether that inference is in truth irresistible as to my mind it is in the
present case. In this connection it is to be noted that the respondent did not go into the   *d*
witness box to give evidence from which that inference might conceivably have been
rebutted.

My Lords, in this respect I find myself in agreement with what was said by Humphreys
J giving the judgment of the Court of Criminal Appeal in *R v Sullivan* (1945) 30 Cr App
R 132 at 136:

> 'It is, we think, undoubtedly good law that the question of the inducement acting   *e*
> upon the mind of the person who may be described as the prosecutor is not a matter
> which can only be proved by the direct evidence of the witness. It can be, and very
> often is, proved by the witness being asked some question which brings the answer:
> "I believed that statement and that is why I parted with my money"; but it is not
> necessary that there should be that question and answer if the facts are such that it
> is patent that there was only one reason which anybody could suggest for the person   *f*
> alleged to have been defrauded parting with his money, and that is the false
> pretence, if it was a false pretence.'

It is true that in *R v Laverty* [1970] 3 All ER 432 at 434 Lord Parker CJ said that the
Court of Appeal, Criminal Division, was anxious not to extend the principle in *Sullivan*
further than was necessary. Of course, the Crown must always prove its case and one   *g*
element which will always be required to be proved in these cases is the effect of the
dishonest representation on the mind of the person to whom it is made. But I see no
reason why in cases such as the present, where what Humphreys J called the direct
evidence of the witness is not and cannot reasonably be expected to be available, reliance
on a dishonest representation cannot be sufficiently established by proof of facts from
which an irresistible inference of such reliance can be drawn.   *h*

My Lords, I would answer the certified question in the negative and would allow the
appeal and restore the conviction of the respondent on the second count in the indictment
which she faced at the Crown Court.

*Certified question answered in the negative; order appealed from reversed; conviction on count
2 of the indictment restored.*

Solicitors: *David Alterman & Sewell*, agents for *David Picton & Co*, Luton (for the Crown);
R H Lloyd & Co, St Albans (for the respondent).

Mary Rose Plummer   Barrister.

Brikom Investments Ltd v Seaford

COURT OF APPEAL, CIVIL DIVISION
ORMROD AND GRIFFITHS LJJ
18th, 19th FEBRUARY, 5th MARCH 1981

Landlord and tenant – Implied covenant to repair – Short lease of dwelling house – Short lease – Lease for term of less than seven years – Determination of length of term – Agreement for lease for term of seven years beginning on date of agreement – Lease executed shortly afterwards but not delivered to tenant until two weeks later – Fair rent assessed and correspondence passing between landlord and tenant on basis that landlord liable for repair under implied covenant – Whether lease for term of 'less than seven years' because grant took effect from date of delivery – Whether agreement for lease for term of seven years beginning on or after date of agreement constituting lease for term of seven years and therefore having no implied covenant to repair – Whether acceptance of rent as assessed estopping landlord from denying implied covenant to repair – Housing Act 1961, ss 32(1), 33(1)(3)(5).

On or prior to 1st November 1969 the landlords and the tenant made an agreement for the lease of premises to the tenant for a term of seven years from 1st November 1969. The lease itself was not executed until some days later, possibly on 12th November, and was not delivered to the tenant until 15th November. The habendum of the lease provided that the tenant was to hold the premises from 1st November 1969 for a term of seven years at a stated rent. By ss 32(1)(b)[a] and 33(1)[b] of the Housing Act 1961 a landlord was impliedly liable for certain internal repairs where a dwelling house was leased for 'a term of less than seven years'. In 1979, as in previous years, the fair rent for the premises was assessed on the basis that the landlords were liable for the repairs specified in s 32(1)(b) and in consequence a higher rent was registered than would have been the case if the liability for those repairs had fallen on the tenant. Furthermore, in correspondence between the landlords and the tenant in 1979 the landlords had accepted liability for s 32 repairs. The landlords failed to carry out repairs which fell within s 32(1)(b) and the tenant had them carried out and paid for them. He withheld a proportion of the rent to cover the cost of the repairs. The landlords brought an action against him to recover possession of the premises for non-payment of rent and claimed arrears of rent on the basis that the full registered rent was due from the tenant. In the claim the landlords for the first time disputed liability for s 32 repairs. The tenant filed

---

a defence claiming to set off the cost of the repairs against the rent on the ground that
(i) the lease was for a term of less than seven years within s 33(1) because, although the *a*
habendum referred to a term of seven years from 1st November 1969, the actual term
created by the lease was two weeks short of seven years under the established principle
that the grant of a lease took effect only from the date of delivery of the lease, which in
the event was from 15th November 1969, or (ii) alternatively, the landlords were
estopped from disputing liability for the repairs.

Held – (1) Since by s 32(5) of the 1961 Act the expression 'lease' in that Act included 'an *b*
agreement for a lease' and the 'term' of a lease included the term of an agreement to lease,
an agreement for a lease for a term of seven years which provided for the term to begin
on or after the date of the agreement was, if the term was not backdated to an anterior
date, to be treated as being a lease for not less than seven years for the purposes of s 33(1),
and accordingly was not within s 32(1). Furthermore, the words 'grant' and 'granted' in *c*
s 33(5) were to be read as equivalent to 'made' when the term of an agreement to lease
was in issue and if the agreement provided for the term to begin on or after the date the
agreement was 'made' there was then no part of the term falling before the grant which
was required by s 33(5) to be discounted in computing the term. Since the tenant was,
by the agreement made on or before 1st November 1969, able to say on that date that he
was entitled to remain as tenant for seven years, the agreement was to be treated as a lease *d*
for seven years for the purposes of s 33(1) and the liability for repairs was governed by the
lease and not by s 32(1) (see p 786 *j* and p 787 *b* to *f*, post).
     (2) Alternatively, by virtue of s 33(3), s 32(1) did not apply, because the tenant was a
person who immediately before the lease was granted, ie delivered, was the lessee under
another lease of the flat within s 33(3)(*a*), ie under the agreement to lease, and the
agreement to lease was not a lease to which s 32 applied for the purposes of s 33(3)(ii) (see *e*
p 787 *d e*, post).
     (3) However, the landlords, by taking no steps to have the registered rent changed to
reflect the fact that they were not liable for s 32 repairs and by demanding the full
registered rent from the tenant, had made a representation of fact that they accepted
liability for the s 32 repairs, and so long as the full registered rent was claimed from the
tenant they were estopped from claiming that the tenant was liable for the s 32 repairs *f*
while at the same time claiming from him rent arrears based on the full registered rent.
It followed that the appeal would be allowed (see p 788 *b* to *h*, post).

Notes

For the implied obligation to repair in short leases of dwelling houses, see Supplement to
23 Halsbury's Laws (3rd Edn) para 1253A.   *g*
     For the Housing Act 1961, ss 32, 33, see 16 Halsbury's Statutes (3rd Edn) 351, 352.

Cases referred to in judgment

Bradshaw v Pawley [1979] 3 All ER 273, [1980] 1 WLR 10, Digest (Cont Vol E) 377,
     7773a.
Cadogan (Earl) v Guinness [1936] 2 All ER 29, [1936] Ch 515, 105 LJ Ch 255, 155 LT 404, *h*
     40 Digest (Repl) 366, 2932.
Kai Nam (a firm) v Ma Kam Chan [1956] 1 All ER 783, [1956] AC 358, [1956] 2 WLR 767,
     PC, 21 Digest (Repl) 376, 1130.
London County Territorial and Auxiliary Forces Association v Nichols [1948] 2 All ER 432,
     [1949] 1 KB 35, [1948] LJR 1600, CA, 31(2) Digest (Reissue) 980, 7872.
Roberts v Church Comrs for England [1971] 3 All ER 703, [1972] 1 QB 278, [1971] 3 WLR *j*
     566, CA, 31(1) Digest (Reissue) 176, 1492.

Appeal

By amended particulars of claim dated 17th August 1980 the plaintiffs, Brikom
Investments Ltd ('the landlords'), claimed against the defendant, David Seaford ('the

a tenant'), possession of premises known as Flat 72, Herga Court, Sudbury Hill, Harrow for non-payment of rent and arrears of rent of £336·28 and mesne profits at the rate of £627·58 per annum from the date of the claim until delivery up of possession, contending, inter alia, that s 32 of the Housing Act 1961 did not apply to the tenancy of the premises. By his defence the defendant averred, inter alia, that the landlords were liable under s 32 for certain plumbing and electrical work that had been carried out and paid for by the tenant, in the sum of £405·89, and claimed to set off that sum against the

b landlords' claim. On 27th June 1980 his Honour Judge Honig in the Willesden County Court ordered that the landlords recover possession of the premises and gave them judgment for £777·02. The tenant appealed on the grounds that the judge erred in law (1) in holding that s 32 did not apply to the tenancy and (2) in failing to hold that the landlords were estopped from denying that s 32 applied. The parties gave their written consent to the appeal being heard by two judges. The facts are set out in the judgment

c of the court.

Isaac Jacob for the tenant.
Norman Primost for the landlords.

Cur adv vult

d
5th March. **ORMROD LJ** read the following judgment of the court: This appeal concerns the liability, as between the appellant tenant and the respondent landlords, for certain internal repairs, as defined in s 32(1)(b) of the Housing Act 1961, in respect of Flat 72, Herga Court, Sudbury Hill, a block of flats owned by the landlords, Brikom Investments Ltd.

e The tenant puts his case in two alternative ways. First, he relies on s 32 of the 1961 Act under which there is to be implied into any lease to which the section applies a covenant by the landlord, inter alia, to keep certain installations in the dwelling house for the supply of water, gas, electricity etc in repair and working order, notwithstanding a covenant by the tenant in the lease to the contrary. Alternatively he says that the landlords, in the events which have happened, are estopped from disputing their liability

f for the repairs referred to in the defence and counterclaim.

The first point, which raises a difficult question of construction of ss 32 and 33 of the 1961 Act, was decided against him by his Honour Judge Honig, sitting at Willesden County Court, on 27th June 1980. The second point was not specifically dealt with by the judge.

By s 33(1) of the 1961 Act s 32 applies, subject to the provisions of the section, to 'any

g lease of a dwelling-house granted after the passing of this Act, being a lease for a term of less than seven years'. So the question is whether the tenant had a lease for less than seven years. He contends that his lease was for less than seven years; the landlords contend that the lease was for seven years.

The dates in the case are, therefore, important. It is common ground that this flat was vacant in October 1969 and that the landlords' letting agents, Stackpole & Co, introduced

h the tenant to the flat in that month. He was shown a specimen lease for a term of seven years, which was the standard form used by the landlords. He decided to take the flat on the proposed terms. His references had to be approved by the managing agents, Waite & Sons, on behalf of the landlords, who approved them in due course and, on 1st November 1969, he was allowed into possession and paid in advance a proportion of the quarterly rent in respect of the period 1st November to 25th December 1969. He also

j signed the counterpart of the lease on that day. The landlords did not immediately execute the lease and it is not known precisely when they did so, but the lease itself bears the date 12th November 1969. It was sent by post to the tenant, who received it on 15th November 1969. The evidence was that the date on the lease was filled in by the landlords' solicitors but that it was 'somewhat fortuitous', depending on the conveyancing clerk's arrangements for stamping.

The habendum of the lease provides that the tenant is to hold the premises from 1st November 1969 for a term of seven years at an annual rent of £385 payable by equal quarterly instalments, but it is clear that the lease was not executed by the landlords until some days after 1st November 1969, and not delivered until 15th November 1969. So, once again, the problem arises of determining, for the purposes of a statutory definition, the length of the term of a lease.

It has been held in many cases, of which *Earl Cadogan v Guinness* [1936] 2 All ER 29, [1936] Ch 515, *Roberts v Church Comrs for England* [1971] 3 All ER 703, [1972] 1 QB 278 and *Bradshaw v Pawley* [1979] 3 All ER 273, [1980] 1 WLR 10 are examples (arising, however, in connection with different statutes), that a term defined in a deed as beginning from a date prior to the delivery of the deed, say for ten years from such date, is not a term of ten years. It is a shorter term beginning from the date of delivery of the deed and ending ten years from the earlier date specified in the lease (see per Clauson J in *Earl Cadogan v Guinness* [1936] 2 All ER 29 at 31–32, [1936] Ch 515 at 518), or, as Stamp LJ put it in *Roberts v Church Comrs for England* [1971] 3 All ER 703 at 707, [1972] 1 QB 278 at 285:

'It is well settled that the habendum in a lease only marks the duration of the tenant's interest, and the operation of the lease as a grant takes effect only from the time of its delivery . . .'

Counsel for the tenant in this case accordingly submits that although the habendum refers to a term of seven years from 1st November 1969 the actual term created by the lease is two weeks short of seven years and is, accordingly, a lease for a term of less than seven years and, therefore, falls within s 32 of the 1961 Act.

The question to be decided, however, is what does this phrase 'being a lease for a term of less than seven years' mean in the context of s 33. Counsel for the landlords drew attention to s 33(5), which reads:

'In the application of this section to a lease granted for a term part of which falls before the grant, that part shall be left out of account and the lease shall be treated as a lease for a term commencing with the grant.'

He submitted that if s 33(1) is construed in accordance with the principle laid down in the cases cited, sub-s (5) is wholly unnecessary because in any event the term cannot start before the grant. So he says s 33(1) must refer to the term as described in the habendum, namely seven years from 1st November 1969; the term in the present case is therefore not a term of less than seven years. This submission, however, does not help him because if he is right such a lease is caught later by the same sub-s (5); the part falling before the grant must be left out of account, and the term computed from the date of the grant. So, he is back to square one!

This is obviously an unsatisfactory conclusion. It is difficult to believe that Parliament intended that the application of s 32, which seriously affects the rights of landlords and tenants, should depend on something so essentially fortuitous as the date of the delivery of the lease. Fortunately, there is another way of approaching the problem which the judge in the court below in substance adopted.

The 1961 Act (unlike the Acts with which this court was concerned in other cases) contains a definition section which defines the word 'lease' in relatively broad terms. Section 32(5) provides that 'lease' includes, inter alia, 'an agreement for a lease . . . and any other tenancy', and the word 'term' is to be construed accordingly.

In the present case there was, undoubtedly, an agreement for a lease of seven years beginning on 1st November 1969, made by the parties on or before that date, because by that time the terms of the lease as set out in the specimen lease or in the counterpart had been agreed and there had been part performance by entry into possession and payment and acceptance of rent.

In *Roberts v Church Comrs for England* there was, as Russell LJ emphasised, no agreement for a lease of the length required to satisfy the terms of s 3(1) of the Leasehold Reform Act 1967, namely tenancy for a term of years certain exceeding 21 years. 'Tenancy' in

that Act means a 'tenancy at law or in equity': s 37(1)(*f*). Russell LJ suggested a test
a which the tenant must pass to fulfil that definition, namely that he—

> 'must at some point of time be, or have been, in a position to say that, subject to
> options to determine, rights of re-entry and so forth, he is entitled to remain tenant
> for the next 21 years, whether at law or in equity.'

(See [1971] 3 All ER 703 at 706, [1972] 1 QB 278 at 284.)
b   The tenant in the present case is in a position to fulfill that test, substituting seven
years, which is the relevant period under the 1961 Act. So if this is the right approach
to the 1961 Act, as we think it is, we are entitled to hold that for the purposes of s 33(1)
there was an agreement for a lease, and therefore a lease as defined, for a term which was
not less than seven years.
     But the landlords have still to get over s 33(5), the language of which is not very apt to
c agreements for a lease unless the words 'granted' and 'grant' are to be read as equivalent
to 'made'. If this is permissible the subsection will still be effective to prevent the
mischief at which it was presumably directed, that is to prevent a landlord granting or
agreeing to grant a lease for less than seven years and back dating the term so as to make
it seven years from some anterior date. We do not think that such a construction does
undue violence to the language of these sections read as a whole.
d   If this goes beyond the limits of construction we think the same result follows from
the application of s 33(3), which deals with consecutive leases. The tenant in this case
was a person who immediately before the lease was granted, that is delivered, was the
lessee under another lease, i e under the agreement for the lease which for the purpose of
these provisions is to be regarded as a lease. So he is within s 33(3)(*a*). The other lease,
that is the agreement for the lease, was not a lease to which s 32 applies because it was for
e not less than seven years; so s 33(3)(ii) is satisfied and, accordingly, s 32 does not apply.
     In our judgment, therefore, an agreement for a lease for a term of seven years is not
caught by s 32, provided that the term begins on or after the date of the agreement,
whether or not it is followed by a formal lease. Accordingly we would hold, in agreement
with the judge in the court below, that s 32 does not apply to the lease in the present case,
and that the liability for internal repairs is governed by the terms of the original lease.
f That, however, does not dispose of this appeal because if the tenant is right on the
estoppel point he will still be entitled to succeed in this action.
     The alleged estoppel arises in a curious way. In 1975 the landlords applied, under the
terms of the Rent Act 1968, to the rent officer to register the rent of this flat. The
application itself has not survived but, on 23rd September 1975, the rent officer
determined the rent at the sum of £555, exclusive of rates, with effect from 16th May
g 1975, and duly registered it. In the notification of registration of rent the rent officer set
out very clearly the basis of his determination. Under the heading 'Allocation of liability
for repairs' he referred to the lease and added the words 'and subject to the provisions of
sections 32 and 33 of the Housing Act 1961', plainly indicating that his assessment of the
rent was made on the basis that the landlords were liable for the repairs specified in
s 32(1)(*b*) and that the tenant's covenant in the lease did not apply to such repairs. This,
h of course, resulted in the registration of a higher rent than would have been the case if
the liability had been on the tenant.
     The landlords did not object and thereafter demanded and received rent at the
enhanced rate. In June 1977 the landlords applied again for the registration of a fair
rent. After a full hearing, at which the landlords' representative and several tenants gave
evidence, the rent assessment committee, on 30th January 1978, determined the fair rent
j of this and other flats in Herga Court. In the case of Flat 72 it was accepted by both sides
that ss 32 and 33 applied, that is that the landlords were liable for the s 32 repairs. On
that basis the fair rent for Flat 72 was assessed at £671·92 exclusive. Again the enhanced
rent was demanded and paid.
     Another application was made in 1979 resulting in the registration of a fair rent in the
sum of £930, still on the same basis.
     About the same time correspondence took place between the parties on the subject of

repairs, and it is clear that throughout the landlords accepted that they were liable for the s 32 repairs; but in the event the tenant did the repairs, paid for them, and withheld a proportion of the rent. Eventually the landlords brought the present action for possession and arrears of rent at the enhanced rate, and the tenant filed a defence claiming to set off the cost of the repairs against the rent. Then, for the first time, the landlords disputed their liability and claimed that s 32 did not apply to this lease. Thus, in the same proceedings, they are seeking to recover arrears of the rent fixed on the basis that they were liable for those repairs and claiming that they were not liable for them.

In our judgment it would clearly be inequitable to hold that the tenant was liable for the full amount of the arrears of a rent which reflects, in part, that the landlords were liable for the repairs, and at the same time that the tenant was liable for the cost of such repairs.

This is the classic situation which the doctrine of estoppel was designed to meet. Counsel for the tenant put his case in alternative ways. Either the landlords, by demanding a rent fixed on the basis of the rent officer's allocation of liability for repairs, represented that they accepted liability accordingly, or the landlords, by not taking steps to have the registered rent changed so as to reflect the true position and suing for the enhanced rent, had made their election and could not be heard, in these proceedings, to assert a claim inconsistent with the position they had adopted.

Counsel for the landlords, however, contended that the representation was a representation of law and not of fact, and therefore could not give rise to an estoppel, and that the tenant was seeking to use the estoppel as a sword, that is to recover the cost of the repairs, and not, in the classic phrase, as a shield. He relied on two cases, *London County Territorial and Auxiliary Forces Association v Nichols* [1948] 2 All ER 432, [1949] 1 KB 35 and *Kai Nam (a firm) v Ma Kam Chan* [1956] 1 All ER 783, [1956] AC 358, in neither of which had the party alleging estoppel acted to his detriment, nor had the other party gained any advantage from the representation.

These dichotomies are dangerously neat and apt to mislead. Representations of fact shade into representations of law, and swords, with a little ingenuity, can be beaten into shields, or shields into swords. In this case the shield may have quite a sharp edge but it is nonetheless a shield and the representation was essentially one of fact, ie that the landlords accepted liability for the s 32 repairs to the tenant's flat in return for the enhanced rent. We would hold that so long as the enhanced rent is claimed the landlords cannot put the burden of the s 32 repairs on the tenant. But they can take immediate action to have the fair rent corrected so as to reflect the true position in regard to repairs, and will then be entitled to the benefit of the tenant's covenant. The tenant, therefore, succeeds on this point.

The judge in the court below attempted to deal with the matter on broad commonsense lines by assessing the amount of excess rent paid by the tenant under the rent officer's assessments and allowing credit accordingly. But he had insufficient material on which to estimate the amount of the overpayment and, in our opinion, no jurisdiction to make such an adjustment, although he may have been under the impression that the parties were consenting to his taking this course. In fact, it seems clear from a letter from the tenant's solicitors written shortly after judgment was given that he had not agreed to it.

This appeal must, therefore, be allowed.

Appeal allowed. Case remitted to judge for decision in the light of the court's judgment. Leave to appeal to the House of Lords refused.

Solicitors: *J E Kennedy & Co*, Harrow (for the tenant); *A E Hamlin & Co* (for the landlords).

Avtar S Virdi Esq   Barrister.

Thwaite v Thwaite

COURT OF APPEAL, CIVIL DIVISION
ORMROD, DUNN LJJ AND WOOD J
17th, 18th DECEMBER 1980, 29th JANUARY 1981

Divorce – Financial provision – Variation of order – Jurisdiction – Consent order – Jurisdiction to vary order incorporating terms agreed between spouses – Appeal from consent order – Consent order that husband transfer share in house to wife – Wife undertaking to return children to England and live with them in house – Order providing that on execution of transfer wife's other applications for ancillary relief were to be dismissed – Wife removing children from England before transfer executed – Whether court having jurisdiction to entertain husband's appeal from consent order – Whether jurisdiction to reconsider financial arrangements between the parties – Matrimonial Causes Act 1973, ss 23(1), 24(1), 31(1).

The husband and the wife had three daughters of school age and jointly owned a house which was subject to a mortgage. The marriage broke down and the wife went to live in Australia where she was later joined by the children. In 1977 the husband commenced divorce proceedings in England, in which the wife applied for ancillary relief. Her application was settled by the wife undertaking to return the three children to England and the husband undertaking to pay their school fees and to convey his interest in the house to the wife within 28 days of the children being returned to England in order that the wife could make a home for herself and the children there. On 30th April 1979 the registrar made a consent order which embodied those terms and further ordered that the wife's other applications for ancillary relief (including her application for periodical payments) should stand dismissed from the date of the conveyance of the husband's interest in the house to her. The husband was further ordered, by consent, to make periodical payments of £51 a month for each child. The consent order reserved to each party liberty to apply. The wife returned the children to England in May 1979 but before the husband had completed the conveyance of his interest in the house to her she removed the children from the jurisdiction and returned with them to Australia without informing the husband. The husband declined to complete the transfer of his interest in the house and on 5th October 1979 applied to the registrar to vary the consent order by ordering the wife to transfer her interest in the house to him and dismissing forthwith her applications for ancillary relief. The wife cross-applied to the registrar asking him to enforce the transfer of the husband's interest in the house in accordance with the consent order. On 12th March 1980 the registrar dismissed the husband's application and ordered him to complete the transfer of his interest in the house to the wife. The husband appealed to the judge against that order and also appealed to the judge, with leave, against the consent order of 30th April 1979. The judge also had before him various applications by the wife including applications relating to the children. The judge expressed doubt whether there could be an appeal from a consent order and decided to determine the matters before him under the liberty to apply reserved by the consent order. He allowed the husband's appeal from that part of the order of 12th March 1980 directing him to complete the conveyance of his interest in the house to the wife, on the ground that the wife had broken her side of the bargain underlying the consent order by removing the children from the jurisdiction and, in effect, had failed to fulfil her undertaking to return them to England, and it would be unjust to compel the husband to transfer his interest in the house to her. However, the judge dismissed the husband's appeal against the registrar's refusal to vary the consent order and then considered the question of financial provision de novo, although the wife did not consent to that course. The judge ordered that the house be sold and the proceeds of sale divided equally between the parties, that there be a nominal order for periodical payments to the wife and a lump sum order for payment to her of £1,000, and that the periodical payments for the children be varied by increasing them to £75 a month for each child. The wife appealed, submitting, inter alia, that (i) the judge had no jurisdiction to entertain the husband's appeal because there was no right of appeal from an order of a divorce registrar made with the parties' consent, (ii) the judge had no jurisdiction to consider the matter de novo under the liberty to apply clause because there was no application under that clause and in any event it covered only implementation of the consent order, and (iii) if the judge did have jurisdiction in the matter, the orders he made were wrong.

Held – (1) Unlike consent orders in other types of litigation which derived their force and effect from the parties' agreement, consent orders embodying the financial arrangements agreed between the parties to a divorce derived their legal effect from the court order and not from the parties' agreement, since that was a necessary consequence of the policy underlying ss 23(1) and 24(1) of the Matrimonial Causes Act 1973 to permit the parties to a divorce to make a clean break in financial matters. It followed that consent orders embodying the spouses' financial arrangements were to be treated as orders of the court and dealt with, so far as possible, in the same way as non-consensual orders. Accordingly, if the order fell within s 31(2) of the 1973 Act it could be varied under s 31(1) by the court which made the order, and, further, an appeal lay from a consent order to an appellate court on grounds which were not limited to fraud or mistake but included, for example, the fact that there was fresh admissible evidence. However, where the court of first instance had not adjudicated on the evidence its decision could not be challenged on appeal on the ground that it had reached a wrong conclusion on the evidence (see p 794 *a* to *g*, post); *Minton v Minton* [1979] 1 All ER 79 and dictum of Lord Diplock in *de Lasala v de Lasala* [1979] 2 All ER at 1155 applied.

(2) It followed (a) that since the registrar's order of 12th March 1980 dismissing the husband's application to vary the consent order was not an order within s 31(2) of the 1973 Act but was a final order, the judge had no jurisdiction to vary it and was correct in dismissing the husband's appeal from that part of the order of 12th March, (b) that the judge had jurisdiction to refuse to enforce the consent order in the circumstances prevailing at the time of the appeal to him and therefore his order allowing the husband's appeal from that part of the registrar's order of 12th March directing him to complete the conveyance of his interest in the house was correct, (c) that the judge had jurisdiction to hear an appeal from the consent order of 30th April 1979 and, on the basis of the fresh evidence before him that the wife did not intend to make a home for herself and the children in England, he had jurisdiction to set aside the consent order, but he had, however, been in error in holding that he had jurisdiction to do so under the liberty to apply clause, and (d) that the judge had jurisdiction to make a new order for ancillary relief although the wife did not consent to his doing so, because the conveyance by the husband had never been executed and therefore that part of the consent order dismissing the wife's claims for ancillary relief on the execution of the conveyance had never come into effect and her original application for ancillary relief was still before the court. Furthermore, in all the circumstances, the orders for financial provision made by the judge had been correct. It followed that the wife's appeal would be dismissed (see p 795 *a* to *h*, post).

Per Curiam. If the legal effect of a consent order embodying spouses' financial arrangements depended on the parties' agreement it would be difficult to avoid the conclusion that it was a 'subsisting maintenance agreement' within s 35 of the 1973 Act and consequently subject to variation by the court under that section, which would defeat the policy of a clean break (see p 794 *d e*, post).

Notes

For consent orders embodying spouses' agreement on financial provision, see 13 Halsbury's Laws (4th Edn) para 1158.

For the Matrimonial Causes Act 1973, ss 23, 24, 31, see 43 Halsbury's Statutes (3rd Edn) 564, 566, 576.

Cases referred to in judgment

B (GC) v B (BA) [1970] 1 All ER 913, sub nom *Brister v Brister* [1970] 1 WLR 664, 27(2) Digest (Reissue) 865, 6884.

a
de Lasala v de Lasala [1979] 2 All ER 1146, [1980] AC 546, [1979] 3 WLR 390, PC, Digest
   (Cont Vol E) 354, 708a.
Huddersfield Banking Co Ltd v Henry Lister & Son Ltd [1895] 2 Ch 273, [1895–9] All ER Rep
   868, 64 LJ Ch 523, 72 LT 703, 12 R 331, CA, 21 Digest (Repl) 210, 109.
Minton v Minton [1979] 1 All ER 79, [1979] AC 593, [1979] 2 WLR 31, HL, Digest (Cont
   Vol E) 268, 6702a.
Mullins v Howell (1879) 11 Ch D 763, 48 LJ Ch 679, 28(2) Digest (Reissue) 1154, *1558.*

b *Purcell v F C Trigell Ltd (trading as Southern Window & General Cleaning Co)* [1970] 3 All ER
   671, [1971] 1 QB 358, [1970] 3 WLR 884, CA, Digest (Cont Vol C) 1095, *3232a.*

Interlocutory appeal

The wife, Susan Maria Thwaite, applied for ancillary relief in divorce proceedings
brought by the husband, Anthony Albert Thwaite. On 30th April 1979, Mr Registrar
c Lowis in the Exeter County Court made an order by consent that on the wife undertaking
to return the children of the marriage to England before 30th June 1979 and on the
husband undertaking to pay their school fees, the husband was to convey to the wife his
interest in 19 Howells Road, Exeter (a house which stood in the parties' joint names),
subject to the existing mortgage on it, within 28 days of the children being returned to
England and the wife's other applications for ancillary relief (including an application for
d periodical payments) were to stand dismissed from the date of the conveyance. The
husband was by consent also ordered to make periodical payments for each child at the
rate of £51 per month. Liberty to apply was given to both parties. The children were
returned to England in May 1979 but before the husband executed a conveyance to the
wife of his interest in the house she removed the children from the jurisdiction on 27th
August 1979 without informing the husband. By a summons dated 5th October 1979
e the husband applied to the registrar to vary the consent order of 30th April 1979 by, inter
alia, ordering the wife to convey her interest in the house to him forthwith and by
dismissing forthwith her applications for ancillary relief. On 23rd October the wife
served a counter-summons applying to the registrar to enforce the transfer of the
husband's interest in the house to her in accordance with the consent order of 30th April
1979. On 12th March 1980 Mr Registrar Lowis dismissed the husband's application to
f vary the consent order and ordered him to execute a transfer of his interest in the house
to the wife. He gave each party liberty to apply. The husband appealed against that
order and also, with leave, appealed against the consent order of 30th April 1979. On 1st
August 1980 his Honour Judge Goodall in the Exeter County Court gave judgment. He
expressed doubt whether there could be an appeal from a consent order but did not
decide the point. However, under the liberty to apply in the consent order he allowed
g the husband's appeal from the order of 12th March 1980 directing him to complete the
transfer of his interest in the house to the wife, but dismissed his appeal from the refusal
to vary the consent order, and, determining the question of financial provision de novo,
ordered that the house be sold and the net proceeds divided equally between the parties,
that there be a nominal order for periodical payments for the wife and an order for
payment to her of a lump sum of £1,000, and that the periodical payments for the
h children be varied to £75 a month for each child. The wife appealed. The grounds of
the appeal were, inter alia, (1) that the judge had no jurisdiction to entertain the appeal
because there was no right of appeal from the order of a divorce registrar made with the
consent of the parties, and if there was such a right of appeal, leave of the registrar who
made the order had to be obtained by the appellant and in the instant case the husband
had failed to obtain such leave, (2) in any event the judge had no jurisdiction to consider
j the matter de novo under the liberty to apply clause in the consent order because no
application was made under that clause and such a clause related only to the
implementation of an order and not to matters of substance, and (3) if the judge did have
jurisdiction, the order which he made was wrong on the facts and against the weight of
the evidence. The facts are set out in the judgment of the court.

Barbara Calvert QC and *John Dixon* for the wife.
Joseph Jackson QC and *David Tyzack* for the husband.

Cur adv vult

29th January. **ORMROD LJ** read the following judgment of the court: This is a wife's
appeal from two orders made by his Honour Judge Goodall on 1st August 1980 at Exeter
County Court. By his first order the judge set aside that part of a consent order which
had been made by the registrar on 30th April 1979 which provided that the husband do
convey his interest in the former matrimonial home, 19 Howells Road, Exeter, to the
wife, and that all other applications for ancillary relief be dismissed from the date of the
conveyance. By his second order the judge substituted a new order for financial provision
for the wife, consisting of a nominal order for periodical payments, and a lump sum of
£1,000 payable within three months, and varied the order for periodical payments for
the three children from £51 per month to £75 per month for each child. He also
ordered the house to be sold and the net proceeds of sale divided equally between the
husband and the wife. The house is in their joint names.

Counsel on behalf of the wife contended that the judge had no jurisdiction to make
either of these orders. Counsel for the husband submitted that in the circumstances of
the case there was jurisdiction to make both orders, and that they were properly made.

The facts of the case are as simple as the procedural tangle is formidable, reflecting, as
counsel for the husband says, the confusion prevailing in the profession about consent
orders in the matrimonial jurisdiction. The parties were married in 1967 and there are
three daughters born in 1968, 1970, and 1972, respectively. The husband is employed
by a multi-national company and his work has required him to live abroad in various
places for considerable periods of time. No 19 Howells Road, Exeter, was purchased in
joint names by means of a mortgage as a home in this country, although for most of the
marriage the parties were living abroad. In 1976, they separated while living in
Bombay. The wife, unexpectedly, went to Australia where she set up house with the co-
respondent, Mr Davis. The husband remained in Bombay. The children eventually
joined their mother in Australia, where she commenced proceedings in the Family Court
of Western Australia for maintenance for the children. She made no application on her
own behalf since, on her own admission, she was being supported by Mr Davis.

On 17th January 1977 the husband filed a petition for divorce in England, relying on
adultery by the wife. A decree nisi was pronounced on 25th October 1977, and the wife
applied for ancillary relief in these proceedings. The matter came on eventually for
hearing on 30th April 1979 before Mr Registrar Lowis. The husband was then living in
Trinidad and the wife in Australia, but both were present and gave evidence. These
proceedings were settled and a consent order was made, the material parts of which were
as follows. On the wife's undertaking to return the children to England and Wales
before 30th June 1979 and on the husband's undertaking to pay school fees for each
child, the husband was ordered to convey his interest in 19 Howells Road to the wife
subject to the existing mortgage within 28 days of the family being returned to this
country, and all the wife's other applications for ancillary relief (including her application
for periodical payments) were to stand dismissed from the date of the conveyance. In
addition there was an order for periodical payments for each child at the rate of £51 per
month. Liberty to apply was given to both parties.

In May 1979 the children returned from Australia to England. There was a delay by
the husband's solicitors in completing the conveyance of 19 Howells Road and on 27th
August 1979, before the husband had executed the conveyance, the wife removed the
children from the jurisdiction and returned to Australia without informing the husband
or his solicitors, and rejoined Mr Davis. She had bought air tickets for the children on
6th August, and had a return ticket for herself. The children went back to the same
school in Australia where they had been before. They are still in Australia, although the
children now attend a state school or schools.

In these circumstances the husband declined to complete the transfer of his interest in
19 Howells Road to the wife on the ground that he had agreed to the transfer on the
understanding that the wife would make a home here for the children, and arrange for
them to attend a local fee-paying school. The basis of the agreement had, therefore, been
completely destroyed by the wife's return to Australia with the children.

a   A spate of applications to the court ensued, beginning with an application dated 5th October 1979 by the husband to vary the consent order of 30th April 1979. On 23rd October the wife countered with an application to enforce the order for transfer of the husband's interest in the house. On 12th March 1980 the registrar dismissed the husband's application to vary his consent order and ordered him to complete the transfer of his interest in the house within 28 days.

b   The husband gave notice of appeal to the judge from the order dismissing his application to vary the consent order of 30th April 1979 and the order to execute the conveyance. On 15th May 1980 the husband also obtained leave to appeal out of time against the consent order from his Honour Judge Anthony Cox. These appeals all came on for hearing before the judge on 30th July 1980. He also had before him applications by the wife to commit the husband for contempt in failing to carry out certain undertakings to hand over some books, and to pay school fees. There were also other applications by the wife relating to the children, including an application for leave to keep the children out of the jurisdiction in Australia.

c   The judge rejected the wife's applications to commit the husband. He allowed the husband's appeal from the registrar's order directing him to complete the conveyance of his interest in the house, but dismissed his appeal against the refusal to vary the consent order. He thought that he had no power to allow the husband's appeal from the consent order because, as he put it, an appeal from a consent order seemed 'anomalous'. But he decided that in the circumstances he could set aside the financial provisions of the consent order under the 'liberty to apply'.

d   On the facts, the judge found that the basis of the consent order was, as the husband alleged, that the wife would use the house as a permanent home for the children and send them to St Margaret's School, Exeter, but he acquitted her of what he called a 'deliberate calculated deceit'. On the other hand, he found that she had no settled intention of remaining in England, among other reasons because she had made no definite arrangements with the school and had retained her return ticket to Australia. He rejected her explanation that she was driven to return to Australia because of financial difficulties consequent on the husband's delay in completing the conveyance. He expressed his reasons for allowing the husband's appeal from the registrar's order directing him to execute the conveyance in these words:

f
> 'I therefore allow the appeal on two grounds. First, on the broad ground, that, as the wife has broken her side of the bargain in a very material particular, it would not be right to hold the husband to his, because this was the whole basis of the order. Second, I allow this appeal and dismiss the wife's application for enforcement on the narrow ground that the children have never been effectively returned to this country, and therefore there is no obligation on the husband to convey the house into the wife's name.'

g

h   The judge might have left the matter there because under the consent order of 30th April 1979 the dismissal of the wife's application for ancillary relief took effect only from the date of the conveyance. It was open to her to restore her application immediately or later. But he, not unreasonably, thought that this state of affairs was unsatisfactory, particularly because he concluded that the die was cast, and that the children's future now lay in Australia and that the circumstances under which the order had been made had wholly changed.

j   A curious situation then arose. The judge proposed to make a new order in favour of the wife. The husband consented but the wife refused to agree to his doing so. Notwithstanding the wife's refusal, he decided to proceed and made a nominal order for periodical payments and an order for a lump sum of £1,000, and increased the periodical payments for the children to £75 per month each. He also ordered the house to be sold.

We now turn to the law. The leading case on the effect of consent orders in the matrimonial jurisdiction is the recent case of *de Lasala v de Lasala* [1979] 2 All ER 1146, [1980] AC 546, an appeal to the Privy Council from the Court of Appeal in Hong Kong. In giving the advice of the Judicial Committee, Lord Diplock said ([1979] 2 All ER 1146 at 1155, [1980] AC 546 at 560):

'Financial arrangements that are agreed on between the parties for the purpose of
receiving the approval and being made the subject of a consent order by the court, *a*
once they have been made the subject of a court order no longer depend on the
agreement of the parties as the source from which their legal effect is derived. Their
legal effect is derived from the court order . . .'

This statement of principle is effectively binding on this court because the relevant
provisions of the Hong Kong Ordinance are identical to the corresponding provisions of
the Matrimonial Causes Act 1973. We respectfully adopt it and believe that it removes *b*
much of the confusion about consent orders which has prevailed in this jurisdiction. It
does, however, represent a significant departure from the general principle frequently
stated in cases arising in other divisions of the High Court, that the force and effect of
consent orders derives from the contract between the parties leading to, or evidenced by,
or incorporated in, the consent order (see, for example, *Huddersfield Banking Co Ltd v
Henry Lister & Son Ltd* [1895] 2 Ch 273, [1895–7] All ER Rep 868, and *Purcell v F C Trigell* *c*
Ltd [1970] 3 All ER 671 at 676–677, [1971] 1 QB 358 at 366–367 per Buckley LJ). A
distinction, therefore, has to be made between consent orders made in this and other
types of litigation.

This distinction is a necessary consequence of the decision in the House of Lords in
Minton v Minton [1979] 1 All ER 79, [1979] AC 593 that the policy underlying ss 23(1)
and 24(1) of the Matrimonial Causes Act 1973 is to permit the parties to a divorce to *d*
make a 'clean break' in financial matters, if they wish, from which there is no going
back. If the legal effect of a consent order of this kind depended on the agreement
between the parties it would be difficult to avoid the conclusion that it was a 'subsisting
maintenance agreement' within the terms of s 35, and, consequently, subject to variation
by the court under its powers under this section. This would, of course, defeat the policy
of a 'clean break'.   *e*

The effect of eliminating the contractual basis of these consent orders should simplify
the problems. If their legal effect is derived from the court order it must follow, we
think, that they must be treated as orders of the court and dealt with, so far as possible,
in the same way as non-consensual orders. So, if the order is one of those listed in s 31(2)
of the 1973 Act, it can be varied in accordance with the terms of that section (see *B (G C)*
v B (B A) [1970] 1 All ER 913, [1970] 1 WLR 664). But if it is not within the list, it cannot *f*
be varied by the court of first instance.

Similarly, as orders of the court, they must be subject to the provisions which apply to
appeals from orders made at first instance, though with one important exception. Where
the court of first instance has not adjudicated on the evidence, its decision cannot be
challenged on the ground that the court has reached a wrong conclusion on the evidence
before it. Final orders of all kinds, however, can be challenged on appeal and may be set *g*
aside on other grounds. Lord Diplock referred to two such grounds, fraud or mistake,
but there are others, for example, on fresh evidence properly admitted by the appellate
court. In the matrimonial jurisdiction final orders, which are non-consensual, may also
be set aside on the ground of material non-disclosure. Rule 73(2) of the Matrimonial
Causes Rules 1977, SI 1977 No 344, requires a party, in the circumstances stated in the
rule, to file an affidavit containing full particulars of his property and income. Non- *h*
compliance with this rule would be an irregularity which would give the court discretion
to set aside the order if the interests of justice so required.

Where the order is still executory, as in the present case, and one of the parties applies
to the court to enforce the order, the court may refuse if, in the circumstances prevailing
at the time of the application, it would be inequitable to do so: *Mullins v Howell* (1879) 11
Ch D 763 and *Purcell v F C Trigell Ltd* [1970] 3 All ER 671 at 676–677, [1971] 1 QB 358 *j*
at 367–368. Where the consent order derives its legal effect from the contract, this is
equivalent to refusing a decree of specific performance; where the legal effect derives
from the order itself the court has jurisdiction over its own orders: per Jessell MR in
Mullins v Howell (1879) 11 Ch D 763 at 766.

We do not think that the references to 'fraud or mistake' in Lord Diplock's judgment
in *de Lasala v de Lasala* [1979] 2 All ER 1146 at 1155, [1980] AC 546 at 560 were intended
to confine the powers of the court in these respects in regard to orders based on consent
within narrower limits than those which apply to non-consensual orders.

We can now return to the various orders made by the judge in this case.

(i) The dismissal of the husband's appeal from the registrar's order dismissing his
application to vary the consent order of 30th April 1979 was right. The order in question
was a final order in the sense that it was not an order within s 31(2) of the 1973 Act, so
that there was no jurisdiction to vary it.

(ii) The order allowing the husband's appeal against the registrar's order directing him
to complete the conveyance of his interest, was right. There was jurisdiction to refuse to
make such an order and, in the circumstances, as found by the judge, it would have been
manifestly inequitable to enforce the order.

(iii) The judge was wrong in thinking that he had no jurisdiction to hear an appeal
from the consent order in the circumstances of this case. In our judgment he had
jurisdiction to set it aside on the basis of the fresh evidence, not available on 30th April
1979, as to the wife's intention to make a home for herself and the children at 19 Howells
Road. The order was based on the belief that she had a settled intention to do so; the
fresh evidence proved, as the judge found, that she had no such settled intention. But he
was in error in holding that he had jurisdiction to do this under the liberty to apply
reserved by the order of 30th April 1979.

(iv) The judge was entitled, in his discretion, to make a new order for ancillary relief
in favour of the wife, notwithstanding the refusal of the wife to consent to his doing
so. His jurisdiction arose not from the liberty to apply, as he held, but from the fact that
the wife's original application for ancillary relief was still before the court and awaiting
adjudication. It had not been dismissed since the conveyance had never been executed,
so that that part of the order of 30th April 1979, by which her application was dismissed,
had never come into effect.

We think that the judge correctly exercised his discretion in this respect. It was not
suggested, and is not now suggested, that the judge did not have all the material before
him to enable him to deal properly with the wife's application. No application to call
further evidence was made although the wife was present in court, and no application for
an adjournment was made The nominal order reflects the wife's attitude throughout the
proceedings here and in Australia. She was living with and being supported by the co-
respondent. The nominal order adequately protects her income position in the future.
No question could now arise of a property adjustment order, and there was no alternative
but to sell the house and divide the proceeds according to the existing beneficial
interests. The husband has no capital of any significance apart from the house so that the
lump sum of £1,000 was, if anything, generous to the wife.

It is not necessary, in this case, to consider the alternative procedure referred to by Lord
Diplock, i e by a separate action to set aside the order of 30th April 1979, because there
is no material difference between trying such an action and hearing an appeal from a
registrar, which in itself is a rehearing.

For these reasons the wife's appeal from the order setting aside the order of 30th April
1979, and from the order of 1st August 1980 as drawn is dismissed.

Appeal dismissed. Leave to appeal to the House of Lords refused.

Solicitors: *Fishman, Wallace & Co* (for the wife); *Dunn & Baker*, Exeter (for the husband).

Avtar S Virdi Esq   Barrister.

Re Fullard (deceased)

a

COURT OF APPEAL, CIVIL DIVISION
ORMROD LJ AND PURCHAS J
30th JANUARY 1981

Family provision – Former spouse – Reasonable provision for maintenance – Court's approach b
to application by former spouse – Former wife and deceased settling financial matters on their
divorce – Settlement resulting in division between them of sole family asset – Wife purchasing
deceased's half share in matrimonial home and both parties acknowledging that neither party
entitled to periodical payments from other – Deceased leaving small estate consisting mainly of
sum paid to him by wife – Deceased making no provision in will for wife – Deceased dying less
than two years after dissolution of marriage – Whether former wife entitled to reasonable c
provision out of his estate – Whether financial settlement made on divorce relevant – Whether
deceased having any further obligation to wife – Whether costs of unsuccessful application by a
former spouse should be paid out of deceased's estate – Inheritance (Provision for Family and
Dependants) Act 1975, ss 1(1)(b), 2(1), 3(1)(g).

The former wife married the deceased in 1939 and obtained a divorce from him in d
1977. Both had worked throughout the marriage and although their earnings were low
each had managed to save about £3,000. Both were drawing old age pensions. The only
family asset was the matrimonial home which was worth £9,000, subject to a
mortgage. After negotiations following the divorce, the parties settled their financial
arrangements by agreeing to split the sole family asset between them by the former wife
paying to the deceased £4,500 for the transfer to her of his share in the home. Both e
parties in effect acknowledged that neither party was entitled to an order for periodical
payments against the other. The deceased moved out of the home in 1977 and, having
nowhere else to go, went to live in a house belonging to a lady friend with whom he
shared the house. Soon after moving in with his friend he made a will leaving his estate,
amounting to £7,100, to her. The greater part of the estate consisted of the £4,500 paid
to him by the former wife. The deceased died in January 1978. His former wife applied f
for financial provision out of his estate under s 1[a] of the Inheritance (Provision for Family
and Dependants) Act 1975. The judge dismissed the application on the ground that in
all the circumstances it was reasonable that the deceased did not make any financial
provision in his will for the former wife. The judge ordered the wife's costs of the
application to be paid out of the deceased's estate. The wife appealed against the dismissal
of her application.

g

Held – (1) In view of the court's powers under the Matrimonial Causes Act 1973 to make
capital adjustments between spouses on a divorce (by property adjustment orders and
orders for lump sum payments) there would be few cases in which it would be possible
for a former spouse to satisfy the condition precedent contained in s 2(1)[b] of the 1975 Act
for the award of financial provision out of a deceased's estate, namely that the court had h
to be satisfied that the deceased's will, or the intestacy, did not make reasonable financial
provision for the former spouse, and where the deceased's estate was small the former

---

a   Section 1, so far as material, provides:
        '(1) Where after the commencement of this Act a person dies domiciled in England and Wales
    and is survived by . . . (b) a former wife . . . of the deceased who has not remarried . . . that person j
    may apply to the court for an order under section 2 of this Act on the ground that the disposition
    of the deceased's estate effected by his will . . . is not such as to make reasonable financial provision
    for the applicant.
        '(2) In this Act "reasonable financial provision" . . . (b) in the case of [an] application made by
    virtue of [inter alia, sub-s (1)(b)] above, means such financial provision as it would be reasonable in
    all the circumstances of the case for the applicant to receive for his maintenance . . .'
b   Section 2(1), so far as material, is set out at p 799 d, post

spouse had a heavy onus of satisfying that condition because the application for financial
a provision would diminish the estate and cause great hardship to the deceased's
beneficiaries if they were ultimately successful. It was impossible to determine whether
the condition precedent in s 2(1) had been satisfied without considering what the
deceased ought to have done and that in turn raised the question of his moral obligation
to the former spouse. Thus, the fact that the applicant had been divorced from the
deceased and the terms of the financial arrangements made by them on the divorce were
b relevant matters for the court to have regard to, under s 3(1)(g)^c of the 1975 Act, and (per
Purchas J) where the parties had settled their financial affairs on divorce with legal advice,
there had to be exceptional developments or conditions present at the date of death to
show that reasonable maintenance within s 1(2)(b) had not been made for the former
spouse by the agreed settlement (see p 799 *a* to *c* *e* h, p 800 *c* *d*, p 802 *h* and p 803 *h* to
p 804 *a* and *g*, post); *Re Coventry (deceased)* [1979] 3 All ER 815 applied.
c   (2) Accordingly, the question for the court was whether it was reasonable in the
circumstances for the deceased to have made no financial provision in his will for the
former wife. Having regard to the deceased's assets and the arrangements he made with
his former wife to settle their financial affairs, and since he had no other legal or moral
obligations to his former wife it was reasonable for him to have made no financial
provision for her. Accordingly, the former wife had not satisfied the condition precedent
d to the exercise of the court's jurisdiction under the 1975 Act and her appeal would be
dismissed (see p 800 *h*, p 801 *f* to *h*, p 802 *d* to *j*, p 803 *c* *d* and p 804 *f* *g*, post).
     Per Curiam. (1) Examples of circumstances where an application by a former spouse
for financial provision under the 1975 Act may be successful are where a long period of
time has elapsed since the dissolution of the marriage in which there has been a
continuing obligation by the deceased to make periodical payments to the former spouse
e and where the deceased is found to have a reasonable amount of capital in his estate, or,
where the death unlocks a substantial capital sum from which the deceased, had he made
a will immediately before his death, ought, within the criteria of the 1975 Act, to have
made some provision for the surviving former spouse, but (per Purchas J) it is doubtful
whether the mere accretion of wealth after the dissolution of the marriage would of itself
justify an application by a former spouse for financial provision out of the estate (see
f p 801 *j* to p 802 *a* h and p 804 *b* to *e*, post).
     (2) In unsuccessful applications by a former spouse for financial provision out of the
deceased's estate, judges should look closely at the merits of the application before
ordering that the estate pay the applicant's costs (see p 799 *c* *d* and p 802 *h*, post).
     (3) The court and legal advisers when considering the terms of financial provision on
a divorce may be well advised to remember s 15^d of the 1975 Act and to persuade a
g former spouse to agree to a provision in accordance with s 15 being written into an order
for financial provision (see p 802 *c* and *h*, post).

Notes
For matters to which the court is to have regard on an application for financial provision
from a deceased's estate, see 17 Halsbury's Laws (4th Edn) para 1337.
h   For the Inheritance (Provision for Family and Dependants) Act 1975, ss 1, 2, 3, 15, see
45 Halsbury's Statutes (3rd Edn) 496, 498, 501, 517.

Case referred to in judgments
Coventry (deceased), Re [1979] 3 All ER 815, [1980] Ch 461, [1979] 3 WLR 802, CA; *affg*
     [1979] 2 All ER 408, [1980] Ch 461, [1979] 2 WLR 853, Digest (Cont Vol E) 224,
j 7680a.

Case also cited
Shanahan (deceased), Re [1971] 3 All ER 873, [1973] Fam 1.

---

c Section 3(1), so far as material, is set out at p 799 *f* *g*, post
d Section 15, so far as material, is set out at p 802 *b*, post

Appeal

By an originating summons dated 4th August 1978 the applicant, the former wife of the *a* deceased, applied under s 1(1)(b) of the Inheritance (Provision for Family and Dependants) Act 1975 for an order for reasonable financial provision out of the deceased's estate. The respondents to the application were the personal representatives of the deceased's estate and the sole beneficiary under his will. On 17th November 1980 Bush J gave judgment dismissing the application and ordered that the costs of the applicant and the respondents be paid out of the deceased's estate. The applicant appealed. The parties gave their *b* written consent to the appeal being heard by two judges. The facts are set out in the judgment of Ormrod LJ.

Robert Reid QC for the applicant.
Donald McConville for the respondents.

c

ORMROD LJ. This is an appeal by a former wife, who is the plaintiff in proceedings under the Inheritance (Provision for Family and Dependants) Act 1975, asking for provision to be made by the court for her out of the estate of her former husband, now deceased. The case is of some importance because it seems to be the first case to reach this court where the applicant is a former spouse, that is somebody who comes under s 1(1)(b) of the 1975 Act. It is therefore of some significance. *d*

The matter was heard at length by Bush J and on 17th November 1980 he dismissed the application because (in his own words) he held that 'No financial provision for the former wife/applicant was reasonable financial provision.' Perhaps it would have been neater to put it round the other way and say that he held that it was not reasonable for financial provision for the former wife to be made having regard to all the circumstances of the case. *e*

In approaching these applications by a party who has been divorced, I think it is important to bear in mind two things: first, the history of the legislation and, second, the fact that proceedings of this kind are an open invitation to dissatisfied (and perhaps spiteful) spouses to start proceedings which they cannot lose, because the practice seems to be to order the costs in any event to be paid by the estate, so, win or lose, the applicant diminishes the estate and therefore diminishes the amount the beneficiary receives. This *f* is a serious consideration in these cases.

To go to the history briefly, the 1975 Act is a composite of the former Family (Inheritance Provision) Act 1938 and what was originally s 3 of the Matrimonial Causes (Property and Maintenance) Act 1958. Section 3 of the 1958 Act provided:

> '(1) Where after the commencement of this Act a person dies . . . and is survived by a former wife of his who has not re-married, the former wife may apply to the *g* High Court for an order under this section on the ground that the deceased has not made reasonable provision for her maintenance after his death . . .
> '(2) If on an application by a former wife under this section the court is satisfied—
> (a) that it would have been reasonable for the deceased to make provision for her maintenance, and (b) that the deceased has made no provision or has not made reasonable provision for her maintenance, the court may order such reasonable *h* provision for her maintenance as the court thinks fit shall be made out of the net estate of the deceased . . .'

It is very important to remember that at the time that section first came into existence the court had no power to deal with capital adjustments between spouses. At that period the court's powers were greatly restricted in relation to ancillary relief because they could *j* not deal adequately with the situation when (usually) a husband came into a substantial capital sum, either because he earned it or inherited it or for some other reason, after the ancillary relief order had been made. So there were many cases in and around that time where ex-wives were in receipt of periodical payments which ceased on the death of their former husbands and were placed in a position of extreme difficulty. There is no doubt that that section was passed originally to give the court power to deal with that sort of

situation when it arose. With the coming into effect of the Matrimonial Proceedings and
a Property Act 1970 with the new powers to make property adjustment orders and very
much freer power to order lump sums, the court now has power to make appropriate
capital adjustments as between spouses after divorce and those powers, although they are
not necessarily comprehensive (and that is plain from s 15 of the 1975 Act which clearly
contemplates that proceedings may be taken under the 1975 Act after divorce)
nonetheless the number of cases in which it would be possible for an applicant to bring
b himself (or herself) within the terms of s 2 of the 1975 Act, in my judgment, would be
comparatively small. Where the estate, like this one, is small, in my view the onus on an
applicant of satisfying the conditions in s 2 is very heavy indeed and these applications
ought not to be launched unless there is (or there appears to be) a real chance of success,
because the result of these proceedings simply diminishes the estate and is a great
hardship on the beneficiaries if they are ultimately successful in litigation. For that
c reason I would be disposed to think that judges should reconsider the practice of ordering
the costs of both sides in these cases to be paid out of the estate. That is probate litigation;
this is something quite different. I think judges should look very closely indeed at the
merits of each application before ordering that the estate pays the applicant's costs if the
applicant is unsuccessful.

In my judgment s 2, which is applicable of course to all classes of applicant under the
d 1975 Act, provides quite clearly and simply for the conditions under which the court
may exercise its powers under the later section of the Act. Section 2(1) reads:

'Subject to the provisions of this Act, where an application is made for an order
under this section, the court may, if it is satisfied that the disposition of the
deceased's estate effected by his will or the law relating to intestacy, or the
combination of his will and that law, is not such as to make reasonable financial
e provision for the applicant, make any one or more of the following orders . . .'

It is therefore a condition precedent to the exercise of the court's powers under this Act
that the court should be satisfied that the will (or the intestacy) did not make reasonable
financial provision for the applicant.

Section 3(1) provides that—
f

'. . . the court shall, in determining whether the disposition of the deceased's
estate effected by his will or the law relating to intestacy, or the combination of his
will and that law, is such as to make reasonable financial provision for the applicant
and, if the court considers that reasonable financial provision has not been made, in
determining whether and in what manner it shall exercise its powers under that
g section, have regard to the following matters . . .'

The 'following matters' are set out as guidelines. It is not necessary to read them at
length. They are in a sense the obvious ones. But para (g) is important; that reads:

'any other matter, including the conduct of the applicant or any other person,
which in the circumstances of the case the court may consider relevant.'
h
So that gives the court the widest possible powers to take into account any matter
which is relevant. Plainly where the application is made by an ex-wife (or ex-husband)
of the deceased, the fact that the parties have been divorced and the result of that divorce
in financial terms is plainly another matter which is relevant, and which is highly
relevant.
j These sections were considered at great length and in meticulous detail by Oliver J in
Re Coventry (deceased) [1979] 2 All ER 408, [1980] Ch 461. His judgment was
subsequently examined with meticulous care in this court, mainly by Goff LJ ([1979] 3
All ER 815, [1980] Ch 461). There was no difference of opinion whatever between the
three members of this court. Goff LJ, in giving the final judgment of the court, analysed
the matter in great detail, approving in every respect the judgment of Oliver J in the
court below. One matter, which I need not refer to in any depth, which exercised both

Oliver J and the Court of Appeal was the meaning to be attributed to the word
'maintenance' where it occurs in the definition of reasonable provision in such cases in s 2   *a*
of the 1975 Act. Goff LJ came to consider the question of whether or not the disposition
made reasonable provision for the applicant. Oliver J had been criticised because it was
said that he introduced the question of moral obligation into his consideration at this
point, but that criticism did not commend itself to Goff LJ who said ([1979] 3 All ER 815
at 821–822, [1980] Ch 461 at 487):

> 'It is true that he said a moral obligation was required, but in my view that was   *b*
> on the facts of this particular case, because he found nothing else sufficient to
> produce unreasonableness.'

The judge in the court below explained this proposition time and time again. That is
clearly right. It is impossible to answer the question, 'Is the provision reasonable, or
alternatively is it reasonable to make no provision, without considering what ought to   *c*
have been done for the applicant?' Once one introduces the word 'ought', one inevitably
introduces in some way or other some moral question. In *Re Coventry (deceased)* Oliver
J was saying the only way in which it could be argued that the fact that no provision was
made for the son was unreasonable was by finding a moral obligation of some kind to
make such provision. This case is very close to that same proposition. For the sake of
convenience, I would refer briefly to what Geoffrey Lane LJ said, because he sums up the   *d*
issues very simply and in a very useful manner. He said ([1979] 3 All ER 815 at 825,
[1980] Ch 461 at 492):

> 'The questions to be answered by the judge were these. First of all, did the
> statutory provisions relating to intestacy operate in this particular case so as not to
> make reasonable financial provision for the applicant's son; secondly, if they did so
> operate (that is to say, if there was no reasonable provision), should the court in its   *e*
> discretion exercise its power to order some provision to be made; and, thirdly, if so,
> in what manner should that provision be ordered?'

Geoffrey Lane LJ agreed with Oliver J's conclusion that it was not reasonable to make
any financial provision. Buckley LJ put it even more succinctly where he formulated the
question thus ([1979] 3 All ER 815 at 827, [1980] Ch 461 at 494):   *f*

> 'Was it, or was it not, reasonable in the circumstances of the present case that the
> deceased made no financial provision for the applicant?'

I hope that it will now be possible to apply these statutory provisions in a way in which
I am sure they were intended to be applied, which is sensibly and simply. It is very easy
to over-complicate the analysis of words like 'reasonable' which are used in legislation.   *g*
The court should decide what is reasonable in the circumstances. It is complicated, of
course, by discussion of 'objective tests' and 'subjective tests' but, when all is said and
done, it comes back to the same question: in the circumstances is it or is it not
reasonable? So I start, looking at the facts of this case, by asking the same question as
Buckley LJ formulated: was it or was it not reasonable, in the circumstances of the
present case, that the deceased made no financial provision for the applicant?   *h*

Now I can go back to the facts. The applicant was married to the deceased on 13th
August 1938. They had two children, of course long since grown up. They lived
together (apparently not at all happily) for 40 years. Things went wrong in 1976, or
wrong to the extent of forcing the wife to take some action. She filed a divorce petition
and got a decree nisi against her husband on the ground of his behaviour (which he did
not defend) on 12th November 1976. The decree was made absolute on 31st December   *j*
1976. The history was that the deceased and his wife had worked and been employed
throughout the marriage. The husband was a gardener and the wife had all sorts of
jobs. No doubt she worked extremely hard. When the time came for them to split up
it was quite plain that she was at least as well off (if that is the right word) as her
husband. She had something like £3,000 in savings, no doubt accumulated with

a   enormous difficulty and great struggles throughout her life. The husband had about that or possibly, as the judge thought, slightly less. So they were people on a very low standard of living. They were both drawing old age pensions. She was over 60 and he was over 65. The only asset they had between them was the matrimonial home which had been bought years ago in joint names. It was valued at £9,000 and that was the sum total of their assets.

b   There was, of course, discussion between the solicitors as to how to dispose of the house. At one stage it was suggested that the house be sold and the proceeds be divided equally, but that of course would have meant that they would both have had to give up the house and the wife (I am sure reasonably) decided that it would be better for her, as she had some savings and a small mortgage-raising capacity, to buy the husband out. In the event it was agreed that she should pay him £4,500 in cash and let him take what furniture he wanted. That was done and he conveyed his share of the house to her. She

c   paid him £4,500 in cash. She had to use a substantial part of her savings to raise that sum.

After some delay the husband moved out. He had nowhere to go, of course. He went, first, to stay with, and then began to share a house with, the beneficiary in this case (whom I need not name). They had been friendly for some time, a platonic friendship, and they were both lonely people. He needed a house and she had some spare

d   accommodation. So he just went to live there as a matter of convenience. Unfortunately he had not been there very long, about six months, when he died on 30th January 1978.

He made a will on 28th September 1977 (that is after fixing up the house and after moving out of the former matrimonial home) a simple will leaving virtually everything to the lady whose house he was sharing. No doubt he was grateful to her for taking him in.

e   If one does a comparison between the two ladies concerned, it works out that they are very much on similar terms. Each has a house of her own. The wife has a mortgage on hers. Their pensions of course are the same. The wife is working; the beneficiary is not. The beneficiary has rather more savings than the wife.

The question is, and it is a simple question to my mind: is it unreasonable, or was it unreasonable, that this man made no financial provision by his will for his former

f   wife? He thought he and his wife had sorted out their financial claims as between each other when they reached the agreement about the house. It is right to say that if the wife had been dissatisfied with that arrangement, she had her remedy. She could have applied to the court for an order and she might have succeeded in getting the whole of the house transferred to her without having to pay anything, or perhaps on payment of very much less.

g   The final irony of this case is to be seen in looking at the estate of the deceased which amounted to £7,100, the greater part of which consisted of the £4,500 which his former wife had paid for his share of the house. So, if she is right on this application, what she is in fact doing is asking for her money back. It is as simple as that. It does not get any less simple and any less stark by going through all the steps that s 3(1) of the 1975 Act directs the court to do. We come back to the same position which is: is it reasonable to

h   expect a husband with assets of this kind who has made arrangements with his former wife which settled their financial affairs or is it reasonable for the court in his place to make provision for the wife out of his estate? To my mind the answer is plain and obvious. It is obviously No.

As I mentioned at the beginning of this judgment, it seems to me that the number of cases which, since the court acquired its wide powers under the 1970 Act to make property adjustments, can now get in within the umbrella of the 1975 Act post-divorce

j   must be comparatively few. In the course of argument I suggested one case where a periodical payments order has been going on for a long time and the husband is found to have a reasonable amount of capital in his estate. That is one. Counsel for the applicant suggested that there was another possible situation, where a substantial capital fund was unlocked by the death of the deceased, such as insurance or pension policies.

Those are cases which could come within the 1975 Act. Apart from those, it seems to me there cannot be many cases which qualify.

Counsel for the applicant rightly draws attention to the provisions of s 15(1) of the 1975 Act which provide:

> 'On granting a decree of divorce, a decree of nullity of marriage or a decree of judicial separation or at any time thereafter, the court may, if the court considers it just to do so and the parties to the marriage agree, order that either party to the marriage shall not be entitled on the death of the other party to apply for an order under section 2 of this Act.'

Certainly that provides a form of security against such applications as this.

On one view it might be said that the court, and legal advisers acting in these cases, might be well advised to remember s 15 and, if they can persuade the other side to agree, to write into an order the appropriate provision. I regard s 15 as the form of insuring against applications under the 1975 Act which some people may very reasonably wish to do having made financial provision of a capital nature for the former spouse. People obviously have other commitments: second wives (or husbands) and children and so on. I do not regard s 15 as materially affecting the question the court has to answer as the condition precedent to these applications.

For those reasons I have no doubt whatever that the judge arrived at the correct result. In the course of his judgment he did not approach the case quite in the same way as I have done. I think he asked himself the correct question when he said:

> 'The question this court has to answer is, In this case is no financial provision reasonable financial provision for the former wife?'

That is the same question, put in different words, as I have suggested, and he answered it in the negative.

I only make one passing comment. When he was performing the exercise required by s 3(1), taking into account the factors set out there, when he was dealing with responsiblity or obligations of the deceased, he said quite rightly that the deceased had no legal obligations or responsibilities for the beneficiary. To my mind he had no legal or moral obligations or responsibility either, in the circumstances of this case, to his former wife (the applicant). The judge referred to his having towards his former wife (as he said): 'The responsibility and obligations of a former husband for the maintenance of his former wife.' I am not quite clear what he had in mind because the responsibility and obligations of a former husband for the maintenance of a former wife are to comply with such orders as the court has made or that the parties may have agreed between themselves. There are certainly no other legal obligations. In these days it might be quite difficult to say that he had a moral obligation, though there may be cases where it could be argued that he had.

The result is, I think, that the judge arrived at the right answer which is the same as this court reached in *Re Coventry (deceased)*, namely that the applicant does not get over the first hurdle and cannot satisfy the condition precedent to the court exercising its jurisdiction under the 1975 Act.

For those reasons I would therefore dismiss this appeal.

PURCHAS J. I agree. I would only add a few words of my own in view of the fact that counsel for the applicant draws our attention to the fact that there has not been a case specifically concerning a former spouse who brings herself within s 1(1)(b) of the Inheritance (Provision for Family and Dependants) Act 1975.

The application of the Act has already been exhaustively considered in *Re Coventry (deceased)* [1979] 3 All ER 815, [1980] Ch 461. The only contribution that this case can make is to point out any distinction, if there be distinctions, in the particular circumstances involved with a former spouse.

a
The applicant in *Re Coventry* (*deceased*) came under s 1(1)(c), that is a child of the deceased. Therefore, like the applicant in this case, the definition of 'reasonable financial provision' for the purposes of the Act was that contained in s 1(2)(b). Rightly counsel for the applicant has not sought to go outside the analysis of what in all the circumstances the applicant in that case should receive for his maintenance within that definition. He adopts the extract from the judgment of Goff LJ ([1979] 3 All ER 815 at 819–820, [1980] Ch 461 at 485):

b
'What is proper maintenance must in all cases depend on all the facts and circumstances of the particular case being considered at the time, but I think it is clear on the one hand that one must not put too limited a meaning on it; it does not mean just enough to enable a person to get by, on the other hand, it does not mean anything which may be regarded as reasonably desirable for his general benefit or welfare.'

c
In this case the applicant has to satisfy the court, within the terms of s 2(1), that the provisions of the will, which were made shortly after the resolution of the matrimonial matters following on the divorce, were not such as to make reasonable financial provision for her. In this case, as in *Re Coventry* (*deceased*), there were no financial provisions made for the applicant so the question resolves itself to a consideration whether in all the d circumstances it is reasonable that no financial provision should be made. The approach to be adopted by the court is set out in s 3(1) and (2). So far as the provisions of s 3 are concerned, it is to be remembered that they apply, not merely to an ex-spouse, but also to a spouse whose marriage is still existing at the date of the death. If and in so far as some of the criteria set out in those subsections apply, especially to a spouse whose marriage survives, those features must be qualified when one is dealing with an ex-
e spouse. That is effected by s 3(1)(g), a matter to which the judge referred specifically in his judgment. He referred not only to the phrase 'all the circumstances of the case' in s 1(2)(b), but also to the conduct of the applicant and any other person (and so on) in s 3(1)(g).

In this case the parties had, after some protracted negotiations, agreed to a settlement between them. Counsel for the applicant in his able argument attempted to draw f distinctions between a formal agreement, which was nearly reached, to sell the house and split the proceeds equally and what happened thereafter, but one must look, not at the form but at the substance of the events. It is clear that, in the face of the suggestion by the applicant's solicitors that she might even have earned herself more than a 50/50 share in the assets of the family that were to be distributed on the dissolution of the marriage, the arrangement finally agreed was in effect a split of the assets and an acknowledgement g that neither party had any practical chance of obtaining an order for periodical payments against the other.

Counsel for the applicant has criticised the judge for saying that there was an inference that the applicant had abandoned any right to periodical payments if in the event of further circumstances she might become entitled to them. I do not accept that submission. The judge investigated the position. He had in mind (and referred to) s 15 h of the 1975 Act and commented that nothing was done under that section to prevent the applicant from coming back to the court, but the approach he made (which I respectfully adopt) is that, where the parties have, with the assistance of legal advisers, clearly gone into the whole situation, it must weigh heavily with the court in considering the various criteria, and in particular the matters referred to under s 3(1) and (2). It would be, in my judgment, unreal to take a position that the applicant, advised as she was, was content to j come to an arrangement which did not provide on the face of it reasonable maintenance for herself within at least the definition of that expression to which I have referred in *Re Coventry* (*deceased*). In cases such as this, therefore, there must be some exceptional developments or conditions present which would make the analysis of what is reasonable as at the date of the death, which is the time when considerations under the Act must be made, different from the circumstances which existed at the dissolution of the marriage when these matters were carefully canvassed and resolved. In this case, unhappily, there *a* was very short period of time between the dissolution of the marriage and the death. There were no further developments which could possibly have affected the situation other than the matter of the death itself. That would not justify a change of attitude such as that contended for on behalf of the applicant which, as Ormrod LJ has said, in effect was that of asking for her money back. That would not be a proper criterion under the sections of the Act. *b*

There may well of course be developments which would enable an ex-spouse to seek relief with some chances of success under this Act, such as Ormrod LJ has already mentioned (and at the risk of repetition I mention them again here). Where there has been a long period of time since the dissolution of the marriage in circumstances in which a continuing obligation to support the ex-spouse has been established by an order of the court, by consent or otherwise, under which periodical payments have been, and *c* continue to be, made up to the date of the death. There may be circumstances such as envisaged by counsel for the applicant, where the death itself unlocks a substantial capital sum of which the testator should have been aware, and from which, had he made a will at the time immediately before his death, he ought, within the criteria of the 1975 Act, have made some provision. There may be other incidents, of further accretion of wealth, but I doubt that the mere fact of accretion of wealth after the dissolution of the marriage *d* would of itself justify an application. An application would only be justified if all the circumstances of the case and all the considerations set out in the Act made it reasonable that the testator should have made some provision as at the time of his death for the applicant.

In my judgment the points which counsel for the applicant has challenged in the judgment in the court below are not substantiated. I do not think the judge in fact was *e* influenced by the inference that there was an abandonment of any claim for periodical payments. Nor do I think that he was led in any way from the correct consideration of the matter by what counsel for the applicant has described as 'a subjective test', whatever may be the significance or meaning of that expression. In this case the test relates to the actual facts established and the circumstances surrounding the making of the will and the circumstances existing at the date of the death. *f*

In my judgment the judge applied all the correct criteria. He examined exhaustively all aspects of the case within the terms of s 3(1) and (2) and came to the correct decision that it was reasonable that no provision should be made by the testator in the will concerned.

For the reasons I have given, as well as those given by Ormrod LJ, I would dismiss this appeal. *g*

Appeal dismissed.

Solicitors: *Stanleys & Simpson, North*, agents for *Rutherfords*, Birmingham (for the applicant); *Philip Baker-King & Co* (for the respondents).

Avtar S Virdi Esq   Barrister.

R v Statutory Committee of Pharmaceutical Society of Great Britain, ex parte Pharmaceutical Society of Great Britain

QUEEN'S BENCH DIVISION

LORD LANE CJ AND WEBSTER J

10th, 11th NOVEMBER 1980

Tribunal – Domestic tribunal – Disciplinary committee of professional society – Misconduct rendering convicted person unfit to be on register of society – Members of society conditionally discharged on conviction of criminal offence – Whether disciplinary committee prohibited from hearing evidence of facts leading to conviction in support of complaint of misconduct – Whether maxim that person not to be punished twice for same offence applicable to disciplinary committee – Powers of Criminal Courts Act 1973, s 13(3).

The respondents, three students at the London School of Pharmacy who were student members of the Pharmaceutical Society, were involved in a fracas in which another student was seriously injured. The respondents were convicted at the Central Criminal Court of unlawful wounding, contrary to s 20 of the Offences against the Person Act 1861, but each was conditionally discharged. The society made a complaint to its disciplinary committee that the respondents were guilty of misconduct rendering them unfit to be on the register of pharmaceutical chemists. The secretary of the disciplinary committee wrote to each respondent indicating that in support of the complaint the facts leading to their convictions would be relied on but not the convictions themselves. By the date of the hearing of the complaint two of the respondents had qualified as chemists and in their case it was suggested that their names ought to be removed from the register for misconduct. On a submission to the committee on behalf of the respondents that s 13(3)[a] of the Powers of Criminal Courts Acts 1973 prohibited the committee from receiving evidence of facts on which the respondents were convicted at the Central Criminal Court and that it therefore deprived the committee of jurisdiction, the legally qualified chairman ruled that the committee did not have jurisdiction to hear the complaints because (i) under s 13(3) there was no jurisdiction to allow evidence of the facts which led to the convictions to be adduced before the committee, and (ii) to allow such evidence to be adduced would violate the legal maxim that a person ought not to be punished twice for the same offence. The society applied for judicial review of the committee's decision seeking an order of certiorari to quash the decision and an order of mandamus directing the committee to proceed with the hearing of the complaint.

Held – The application would be allowed for the following reasons—

(1) Assuming that the removal of a name from the register was a disqualification or disability within s 13(3) of the 1973 Act, a tribunal such as the disciplinary committee was not prevented by s 13(3) from acting on facts leading to a conviction in a criminal court since the tribunal was merely prohibited by s 13(3) from relying on a conviction itself as evidence of misconduct. Accordingly, on its true construction s 13(3) did not prevent the allegations of misconduct against the respondents being supported by proof of facts which had been adduced at the respondents' trial at the criminal court (see p 809 *b c* and p 811 *b c* and *f g*, post); *R v Harris* [1950] 2 All ER 816 applied.

(2) The maxim that a person ought not to be punished twice for the same offence did not apply to proceedings before the disciplinary committee because the offences before it and the findings it would make were totally different from the offences before, and findings made in, the criminal court. Moreover, a tribunal such as the disciplinary

---

a Section 13(3) is set out at p 807 *h*, post

committee was not a court of competent jurisdiction to which the maxim applied (see p 811 e to g, post).

a

Notes
For the effect of a conditional discharge on an enactment imposing disqualification on a convicted person, see 11 Halsbury's Laws (4th Edn) para 538.

For the Powers of Criminal Courts Act 1973, s 13, see 43 Halsbury's Statutes (3rd Edn) 306.

b

Cases referred to in judgment
Connelly v Director of Public Prosecutions [1964] 2 All ER 401, [1964] AC 1254, [1964] 2 WLR 1145, 128 JP 418, 48 Cr App R 183, HL, Digest (Cont Vol B) 250, 472a.
Lewis v Morgan [1943] 2 All ER 272, [1943] KB 376, 112 LJKB 313, 169 LT 156, 107 JP 156, 41 LGR 139, DC, 14(1) Digest (Reissue) 458, 3899.

c

Medical Practitioner, Re a [1959] NZLR 784, 21 Digest (Reissue) 106, 754.
R v Harris [1950] 2 All ER 816, [1951] 1 KB 107, 114 JP 535, 34 Cr App R 184, 49 LGR 37, CCA, 14(2) Digest (Reissue) 502, 4119.
R v Hogan [1960] 3 All ER 149, [1960] 2 QB 513, [1960] 3 WLR 426, 124 JP 457, 44 Cr App R 255, CCA, 37 Digest (Repl) 445, 47.
Simpson v General Medical Council (1955) Times, 9th November, PC.

d

Application for judicial review
The Pharmaceutical Society of Great Britain applied, with the leave of the Divisional Court granted on 14th June 1979, for (i) an order of certiorari to quash a decision of the second respondents, the society's statutory committee, made on 14th March 1979 dismissing a complaint made by the society against the first respondents, Michael Richard *e* Shutt, Jerome Frederick Brookman and Keith Frank Martin, and (ii) an order of mandamus requiring the statutory committee to proceed with an inquiry into the facts of the complaint. The grounds of the application were that the statutory committee erred in law in holding that s 13 of the Powers of Criminal Courts Act 1973 and/or the legal maxim nemo debet bis puniri pro uno delicto deprived the statutory committee of jurisdiction to inquire into the complaint. The facts are set out in the judgment of the *f* court.

Richard Du Cann QC and *Robert Webb* for the society.
J K Toulmin QC for the statutory committee.
The first respondents appeared in person.

g

LORD LANE CJ delivered the following judgment of the court: This is an application for judicial review by way of certiorari and mandamus. It arises in the following way. The first respondents are three young men, who at the time of the events I am about to describe were students at the London School of Pharmacy. They are not represented before us here in this court, but they have put in a document which we have considered.

The case arose out of an incident on 12th March 1977 in which those three respondents *h* were concerned. It was a fracas at a student discotheque at the London School of Pharmacy. As a result of that fracas another student (apart from the three I have mentioned) was seriously injured. Amongst other injuries he suffered a fractured skull. As a result of that incident criminal proceedings were instituted against these three at the Central Criminal Court under s 18 of the Offences against the Person Act 1861. In the upshot they were acquitted of the s 18 offence and convicted of the lesser *j* offence under s 20 of that same Act. His Honour Judge Buzzard, having heard the records of their antecedent history, imposed on them a conditional discharge. He also ordered them to pay £50 compensation and £50 towards the prosecution costs.

Those matters were considered by the ethics committee of the Pharmaceutical Society, of which the three were student members; the ethics committee resolved to refer the *a* matter to the disciplinary committee, which is called the statutory committee, in order for them to consider the matter, the suggestion being that the conduct exhibited by the three on that occasion rendered them unfit to be on the Register of Pharmaceutical Chemists.

There was a gap in the proceedings, time elapsed, and in the upshot by the time the proceedings came to be heard Shutt and Brookman had become qualified, so the suggestion was that the names of those two should be removed from the register.

b In November 1978 there was a letter directed to the statutory committee, and in due course, on 9th February 1979 the secretary wrote to the three young men making it clear what the allegation against them was. I read the letter which was directed to one of the respondents because they were all in the same form. It reads as follows:

c 'On behalf of the Statutory Committee of the Pharmaceutical Society of Great Britain, I give you notice that the Committee have received a complaint from the Council of the Pharmaceutical Society of Great Britain, 1 Lambeth High Street, London, S.E.1, from which it appears that on 3rd August, 1978 you were before the Central Criminal Court in London on a charge of causing grievous bodily harm to a Mr. David Thompson. You pleaded not guilty. You were made subject to a Conditional Discharge Order for two years, and ordered to pay £50 compensation *d* and £50 costs towards the cost of the prosecution. The Council allege that you may have been guilty of such misconduct as to render you unfit to be on the Register of Pharmaceutical Chemists.'

It is to be noted that in that letter there was no mention at all of the word 'conviction', a point which will become of importance in a moment.

e The statutory committee sat on 12th March 1979. It was, as the statute requires, presided over by a legally qualified chairman in the person of Sir Gordon Willmer. Counsel there on behalf of the respondents raised the question of whether the committee was entitled to receive as evidence of misconduct the same evidence as that on which these three young men had been found guilty of an offence under s 20 of the 1861 Act at the Central Criminal Court. The argument was that s 13 of the Powers of Criminal Courts Act 1973 prohibited that. Section 13 reads as follows:
f

'(1) Subject to subsection (2) below, a conviction of an offence for which an order is made under this Part of this Act placing the offender on probation or discharging him absolutely or conditionally shall be deemed not to be a conviction for any purpose other than the purposes of the proceedings in which the order is made and of any subsequent proceedings which may be taken against the offender under the *g* preceding provisions of this Act.

'(2) Where the offender was of or over seventeen years of age at the time of his conviction of the offence in question and is subsequently sentenced under this Part of this Act for that offence, subsection (1) above shall cease to apply to the conviction.

'(3) Without prejudice to the preceding provisions of this section, the conviction of an offender who is placed on probation or discharged absolutely or conditionally *h* under this Part of this Act shall in any event be disregarded for the purposes of any enactment or instrument which imposes any disqualification or disability upon convicted persons, or authorises or requires the imposition of any such disqualification or disability . . .'

The point raised by counsel in that way was certainly a novel point, and it is certainly *j* a point which, if correct, would have some remarkable effect on disciplinary proceedings before statutory professional bodies, be they bodies of dentists, or bodies of veterinary surgeons, bodies of doctors, medical men, or bodies of pharmacists.

The chairman, Sir Gordon Willmer, reserved his judgment in the matter. There had been cited before him no authority on the matter, which in retrospect was perhaps unfortunate. On 14th March he gave his judgment. The material part reads as follows:

'I accordingly rule that in the light of s 13(3) of the 1973 Act this committee is without jurisdiction to hear and pronounce on the complaint now put forward by *a* the council. In my judgment, to allow evidence to be adduced before this committee as to the same facts as led to the decision of the criminal court would be a violation of the well-known maxim nemo bis vexari debet. It follows that, without proceeding any further, the present complaint by the council against these three parties must be dismissed.'

The learned chairman seems to base himself on two foundations: first of all, the *b* provisions of s 13 of the 1973 Act; and second on the maxim, a truncated version of which he gave in that passage in his judgment.

The contents of that judgment, and particularly the passage which I have read, caused some considerable concern to the Pharmaceutical Society, and consequently they wished the matter to be determined by this court as to whether that ruling is correct or not. They were concerned, says counsel for the society, for a number of reasons. If that *c* judgment is right it might very well be better for the society not to prosecute breaches, for example, of the Pharmacy Act 1954 at all, on the basis that it would be preferable to ensure that the member or student no longer practised or belonged to the society than that he should have a conviction recorded against him, a finding of guilt, which might be simply followed by an absolute or conditional discharge or a probation order.

As a matter of practice the society deal with cases either as 'conviction cases' or *d* misconduct cases, the latter including cases where a probation order, or an order of absolute discharge, or an order of conditional discharge is made. This instant case, as the letter which I read indicates, was expressly alleged as a misconduct case.

There are, as counsel for the society rightly pointed out to us, three questions to be asked. First of all, does s 13 of the 1973 Act apply at all in the present circumstances? Second, if it does, how does it affect such proceedings, as opposed to criminal *e* proceedings? Third, is the Latin maxim relevant?

First of all, it is right to point out, on the third point, that the full version of the maxim is not as the learned chairman cited it, but is as follows: nemo debet bis vexari, si constat curiae quod sit pro una et eadem causa, or in its alternative form: nemo debet bis puniri pro uno delicto (no one ought to be twice punished for the same offence).

It is necessary, first of all, to read the relevant sections of the Pharmacy Act 1954. *f* Section 7, which reads as follows, sets up the statutory committee:

'For the purposes of this Act there shall be appointed a committee of the Society (to be known as "The Statutory Committee"), and the provisions of the First Schedule to this Act shall have effect in relation to the Statutory Committee.'

Section 8, which is the important section reads, so far as is material, as follows: *g*

'(1) Where—(a) a person applying to have his name registered, or (b) a registered pharmaceutical chemist or any person employed by him in the carrying on of his business, or (c) a person whose name has been removed from the register under section twelve of this Act or any person employed by him as aforesaid, has been convicted of any such criminal offence or been guilty of such misconduct (being in *h* a case falling within paragraph (c) of this subsection a conviction or misconduct which took place either before or after the removal of the name) as in the opinion of the Statutory Committee renders the convicted or guilty person unfit to have his name on the register, the Committee may, after enquiring into the matter . . .'

and then it sets out the powers of the committee in those circumstances.

It is clear from those sections and subsections that whatever the criminal offence or *j* whatever the punishment has been the committee is required and bound to inquire and to consider whether it is such as to render the offender unfit to have his name on the register. In other words, they must inquire into the matter, and they cannot simply take the conviction on its own, simpliciter, as being the basis of whatever determination they choose to make.

The Powers of Criminal Courts Act 1973 was a consolidating Act. It replaced s 12 of
a the Criminal Justice Act 1948 without making any significant alteration to the
wording. Section 12 of the 1948 Act was new, for two reasons. First of all, prior to 1948
there was no such thing as an absolute discharge or a conditional discharge at all. They
did not exist, and at that stage probation orders could be made without any conviction
being recorded against the subject of the order. Therefore, when the 1948 Act came into
force the position with regard to probation orders had to be preserved, and also new
b provisions had to be made in respect of orders of absolute and conditional discharge,
those being new forms of order, hence s 13 of the Powers of Criminal Courts Act 1973.

One can assume for the purposes of argument that the removing of a name from the
register is a disqualification or disability within the provisions of s 13(3) of the 1973 Act,
although it is perhaps a somewhat tortuous way of describing it, but it seems to us clear
that whatever s 13 may do, it does not purport to prevent a tribunal such as this one from
c acting on the facts which underlie the finding of guilt.

This indeed was the view taken by the Privy Council in *Simpson v General Medical
Council* (1955) Times, 9th November, a case which was before them under the Medical
Act 1950. It was decided on 8th November 1955 before Viscount Simonds, Lord Keith
and Lord Somervell. The reasoning of the Board was given by Viscount Simonds. The
relevant passage from the speech reads as follows. Viscount Simonds starts by quoting
d s 29 of the Medical Act (1858):

> 'If any registered medical practitioner shall be convicted [by any court in the
> United Kingdom or the Republic of Ireland, of any felony, misdemeanour, crime or
> offence], or shall, after due inquiry, be judged by the General Council to have been
> guilty of infamous conduct in any professional respect, the General Council may, if
> they see fit, direct the registrar to erase the name of such medical practitioner from
e > the register.'

His Lordship continued:

> 'The relevant facts are not in dispute and can be briefly stated. The appellant was
> at Chelmsford Assizes in November, 1954, charged with, and pleaded guilty to, a
f > number of very grave offences against his female patients which clearly constituted
> infamous conduct in a professional respect unless effect is given to the plea now
> advanced on his behalf. Having pleaded guilty he was duly convicted, but the
> learned Judge, having heard medical evidence, did not pass any sentence upon him
> but placed him on probation, the condition of the probation order being that he
> should submit to treatment as a resident patient at the Runwell Mental Hospital,
> Wickford, Essex, for 12 months or such less period as the Superintendent might
g > direct and should thereafter submit to treatment by and under the direction of the
> Superintendent of the said hospital. The result of these proceedings was that by
> virtue of Section 12 of the Criminal Justice Act, 1948, the appellant's conviction
> could not be deemed to be a conviction for any purpose other than for the purposes
> of these proceedings and must be disregarded for the purposes of any enactment
> which imposes any disqualification or disability on convicted persons or authorises
h > or requires the imposition of any such disqualification or disability. It was therefore
> not open to the Committee whose duty it was to review the conduct of the appellant
> to proceed upon the footing that he had been convicted of a crime. It was for them
> to determine after due enquiry whether he had been guilty of infamous conduct in
> any professional respect and, if they so determined, then, if they saw fit, to direct the
> Registrar to erase his name from the Register. It was agreed by the appellant before
j > the hearing by the Committee that the depositions of certain witnesses taken at the
> Magistrates' Court should be put in as evidence and at the hearing the facts alleged
> in the charge were agreed and admitted on his behalf . . . The Medical Acts are
> designed at the same time to protect the public and to maintain the high professional
> and ethical standard of an honourable calling. If a practitioner, having committed
> the grave offences of which the appellant has been guilty, can upon such a plea

successfully resist the charge of infamous conduct and the erasure of his name from
the Register, the public will lack their proper protection and the honour of the *a*
profession may be endangered by the continued practices of one who can still claim
to be of their number.'

On that basis their Lordships humbly advised Her Majesty that the appeal of the
practitioner should be dismissed. The point was not specifically argued in that case, but
nevertheless that speech demonstrates clear approval of the arguments addressed to this *b*
court by counsel for the society.

The situation under the Medical Acts is not precisely the same as it is under the
Pharmaceutical Act. We have not overlooked that point. Nevertheless, that seems to us
to be powerful persuasive authority that what the committee did here was incorrect.

We were referred to a decision of the Court of Criminal Appeal in *R v Harris* [1950]
2 All ER 816, [1951] 1 KB 107. The Court of Criminal Appeal was composed of *c*
Humphreys, Morris and Sellers JJ. I read the headnote in the All England Law Reports
which is as follows:

> 'HELD: under s. 12(1) of the Act of 1948 the conviction of Dec. 13, 1949, was not
> to be regarded for the purpose of another case as a conviction, and, therefore, the
> certificate of conviction should not have been accepted in evidence, but evidence
> would have been admissible by a witness who had heard the appellant confess in *d*
> court to the charge of having been found in possession of housebreaking implements
> or had heard him convicted of that offence and conditionally discharged.'

Humphreys J, delivering the judgment of the court, said this ([1950] 2 All ER 816 at 818;
cf [1951] 1 KB 107 at 113):

> 'In the present case the offence was under the Vagrancy Act, 1824, s. 4, which was
> amended by the Prevention of Crimes Act, 1871, s. 15 (headed "Amendment of
> criminal law in certain cases"). Section 15 of the Act of 1971 provides that: ". . . in
> proving the intent to commit a felony it shall not be necessary to show that the
> person suspected was guilty of any particular act or acts tending to show his purpose
> or intent, and he may be convicted if on the circumstances of the case, and from his *f*
> known character as proved to the justice of the peace or court before whom or
> which he is brought, it appears to such justice or court that his intent was to commit
> a felony . . ." That section obviously renders admissible in such a case that which
> would otherwise, according to the common law of England, be inadmissible, that
> is to say, evidence of the previous bad character of the accused person although he
> has not himself put his character in issue. No possible objection, in our view, could *g*
> have been taken to the procedure adopted in this case if the detective constable,
> whose deposition I have read, had been present at the trial and had given evidence
> to the following effect: "I was present at the court on the day named when the
> accused was there. I heard him confess to a charge of having been found in
> possession of certain implements of housebreaking, and he was then discharged
> subject to the condition that he commit no offence during the period of 12 months *h*
> thereafter." That would have been, not merely the proof of a previous conviction,
> but proof of the appellant's "known character" in that he was a person who had
> admitted in a court of justice that he had committed a certain offence. What was
> done was merely to produce a document which purported to be a record of a
> conviction in regard to the appellant, and no other evidence was given in regard to
> the matter. In any future case we think that courts—whether courts of summary *j*
> jurisdiction or courts trying a case on indictment with a jury—should be careful to
> see that evidence is given, not that the accused has been previously convicted,
> because the conviction itself is not to be regarded for the purpose of any other case
> as a conviction, but that he was seen doing this, that, or the other, which showed
> that he was a person of bad character.'

That citation from *R v Harris* seems to us to put precisely the contention of counsel for
a the society and to demonstrate its correctness.

Counsel on behalf of the statutory committee submits that although the word
'conviction' was not used in the letter of complaint which I have read yet nevertheless it
was clear that the conviction was to be relied on. We respectfully disagree with that
contention. What was to be relied on, and the letter makes it perfectly plain, were the
facts which lay behind the conviction, namely the use by these young men of disastrous
b force on the body of the injured student.

My conclusion is that on the wording of s 13 of the 1973 Act there was nothing to
prevent the allegation of misconduct being supported by the proof of facts which were
adduced in the first instance at the Central Criminal Court before Judge Buzzard. There
is nothing in s 13 to suggest that the underlying facts in that way should be
disregarded. Apart from any other reasons, it seems to me, if it had been intended that
c not only the conviction but the facts underlying the conviction should be disregarded in
any future proceedings, then the Act should have said so and it did not.

We have had our attention drawn to an Act which does make specific provision to that
effect. That is the Rehabilitation of Offenders Act 1974, and particularly s 4 and its
various subsections. There is no need for us to read those particular provisions. So much
for the first point arising under the terms of s 13.

d   Our attention has been drawn to a number of authorities in respect of the second issue,
that is to say the maxim. I will give the reference to those authorities: *Lewis v Morgan*
[1943] 2 All ER 272, [1943] KB 376; *R v Hogan* [1960] 3 All ER 149, [1960] 2 QB 513;
Connelly v Director of Public Prosecutions [1964] 2 All ER 401, [1964] AC 1254; and *Re a
Medical Practitioner* [1959] NZLR 784.

I can, however, deal with this matter very briefly because counsel for the statutory
e committee has not sought to argue against the contention advanced by the society that
the maxim, in whatever form one chooses to relate it, has no reference to tribunals such
as this one at all. First of all, although the facts might be the same before the Central
Criminal Court and before the tribunal the offence and the findings are totally distinct;
and second, it is plain on the authorities that a tribunal such as this is not a court of
competent jurisdiction to which the maxim applies.

f   In those circumstances it is enough for me to say that the second leg of the argument
based on the so-called maxim fails. The result is that the request that certiorari and
mandamus should issue in this case is good, and they must issue. What the penalty may
be when the case goes back, in all the circumstances, is none of our affair, though
doubtless the committee will take fully into account the matters which have been urged
on us in the document I have mentioned, which was put before us by the three young
g men. The appeal must, in the circumstances, be allowed.

Application allowed; orders of certiorari and mandamus issued.

Solicitors: *Walker, Martineau & Co* (for the society); *Le Brasseur & Bury* (for the statutory
committee).

N P Metcalfe Esq   Barrister.

CBS Inc & others v Ames Records & Tapes Ltd

CHANCERY DIVISION
WHITFORD J
4th, 5th, 6th, 13th FEBRUARY 1981

Copyright – Infringement – Authorising infringement without licence of owner – Authorises – Sound recordings tape recorded at home in breach of copyright – Defendants operating record lending library – Defendants indifferent whether borrowers taping borrowed records at home – Whether defendants 'authorising' home taping in breach of copyright – Copyright Act 1956, s 1(2).

The defendants, the owners of a chain of record shops, opened a record lending library in two of their shops because retail sales of records were falling. Subscribers under the lending scheme paid an initial subscription of £5 to borrow one long-playing record at a time or £8 to borrow two records or a double album. Subscribers also paid a borrowing fee of between 50p and £1 in respect of each record or two records borrowed. The scheme was similar to those run by public libraries except that the defendants included a larger selection of popular records than most public libraries, and borrowers were entitled to purchase borrowed records at a discount price. The defendants were aware that records might be borrowed for home tape recordings on blank tapes, which cost as little as 50p, but claimed that they did not encourage home taping of records. The plaintiffs, who were the copyright owners and manufacturers of pop music records included in the defendants' scheme, formed the view that people would become subscribers to the defendants' scheme solely in order to home tape borrowed records, thereby obtaining for as little as £1 a sound recording which normally retailed for £5, and that the defendants' scheme would be detrimental to retail sales of records. After a warning from the plaintiffs the defendants displayed notices in their shops and on their records to the effect that home taping was an infringement of copyright. The plaintiffs sought an injunction restraining the defendants from hiring out records purchased by them from the plaintiffs, alleging that the defendants had infringed the plaintiffs' copyright in their sound recordings. The plaintiffs claimed that the defendants, without the licence of the copyright owner, had 'authorised' another person, ie any borrower under their scheme, to infringe the copyright, contrary to s 1(2)ᵃ of the Copyright Act 1956. The plaintiffs relied on previous authority to the effect that 'authorises' in s 1(2) meant 'sanction, approve and countenance' and claimed that the defendants by their lending scheme had countenanced home taping in breach of copyright or that the defendants had been so indifferent to the possibility of home taping that authorisation could be inferred. The plaintiffs further claimed that the sale of records to the defendants for the purposes of resale did not licence the defendants to publish the copyright literary and artistic work on record sleeves by way of hiring those works.

Held – The plaintiffs' claim would be dismissed for the following reasons—
(1) Although the defendants' record lending scheme enabled subscribers to the scheme to tape records at home in breach of the plaintiffs' copyright in the records, the defendants could not be said to have 'authorised' such taping within s 1(2) of the 1956 Act merely because illegal home taping resulted from the scheme or because the defendants remained indifferent to the possibility of that result, since the defendants had not provided recording equipment or facilities to their borrowers and their indifference did not in the circumstances amount to authority to borrowers to tape records at home (see p 821 c d f g, p 823 c d, p 824 a, p 825 e and p 829 g to j, post); *Falcon v Famous Players Film*

---

a Section 1(2) is set out at p 820 *g h*, post

Co [1926] 2 KB 474 applied; *Performing Right Society Ltd v Ciryl Theatrical Syndicate Ltd*
a [1924] 1 KB 1 and *Vigneaux v Canadian Performing Right Society Ltd* [1945] 1 All ER 432
considered; *Winstone v Wurlitzer Automatic Phonograph Co of Australia Pty Ltd* [1946] VLR
338 and *Moorhouse and Angus & Robertson (Publishers) Pty Ltd v University of New South
Wales* [1976] RPC 151 distinguished.

(2) The plaintiffs could not claim that hiring the records infringed the copyright in
the literary and artistic work on the record sleeves because once the plaintiffs sold the
b records to the defendants, the latter were entitled to sell them, give them away, hire
them, destroy them or otherwise deal with them as they pleased provided they did not
reproduce the literary and artistic work or the recordings themselves (see p 830 *b* to *d*,
post).

Notes
c For authorising infringement, see 9 Halsbury's Laws (4th Edn) paras 909, 923, and for
cases on the subject, see 13 Digest (Reissue) 117, 967.

For infringement by hiring, see 9 Halsbury's Laws (4th Edn) para 920, and for cases on
the subject, see 13 Digest (Reissue) 140, 1151–1157.

For the Copyright Act 1956, s 1, see 7 Halsbury's Statutes (3rd Edn) 129.

d **Cases referred to in judgment**
Adelaide (City) v Australian Performing Right Association Ltd (1928) 40 CLR 481, [1928]
Argus LR 127.
Evans v E Hulton & Co Ltd (1924) 131 LT 534, [1924] All ER Rep 224, 13 Digest (Reissue)
117, 967.
Falcon v Famous Players Film Co Ltd [1926] 2 KB 474, 96 LJKB 88, 135 LT 650, CA, 13
e Digest (Reissue) 84, 737.
Infabrics Ltd v Jaytex Ltd [1980] 2 All ER 669, [1980] Ch 282, [1980] 2 WLR 882, CA; *rvsd*
[1981] 1 All ER 1057, [1981] 2 WLR 646, HL.
Karno v Pathé Frères (1909) 100 LT 260, CA, 13 Digest (Reissue) 136, 1116.
Liverpool City Council v Irwin [1975] 3 All ER 658, [1976] QB 319, [1975] 3 WLR 663, 31
P & CR 34, CA; *affd in part* [1976] 2 All ER 39, [1977] AC 239, [1976] 2 WLR 562, 74
f LGR 392, HL, Digest (Cont Vol E) 366, 4870a.
Lyon v Knowles (1864) 5 B & S 751, 10 LT 876, 122 ER 1010, Ex Ch, 13 Digest (Reissue)
141, 1167.
Monaghan v Taylor (1886) 2 TLR 685, 13 Digest (Reissue) 142, 1169.
Monckton v Pathé Frères Pathephone Ltd [1914] 1 KB 395, 83 LJKB 1234, 109 LT 881, CA,
13 Digest (Reissue) 109, 899.
g *Moorhouse and Angus & Robertson (Publishers) Pty Ltd v University of New South Wales* [1976]
RPC 151, 6 ALR 193, 13 Digest (Reissue) 119, *130.
Performing Right Society Ltd v Ciryl Theatrical Syndicate Ltd [1924] 1 KB 1, 92 LJKB 811,
129 LT 653, CA, 13 Digest (Reissue) 131, 1089.
Stauffer Chemical Co's Application, Re [1977] RPC 33, CA, Digest (Cont Vol E) 484, 4319a.
Vigneux v Canadian Performing Right Society Ltd [1945] 1 All ER 432, [1945] AC 108,
h [1945] 2 DLR 1, 4 CPR 65, 4 Fox Pat C 183, PC, 13 Digest (Reissue) 133, *152.
Winstone v Wurlitzer Automatic Phonograph Co of Australia Pty Ltd [1946] VLR 338.

Cases also cited
A & M Records Inc v Audio Magnetics Inc (UK) Ltd [1979] FSR 1.
Ash v Hutchinson & Co (Publishers) Ltd [1936] 2 All ER 1496, [1936] Ch 489, CA.
j *Betts v Willmott* (1871) LT 6 Ch App 239.
Fox's Glacier Mints Ltd v Joblings (1932) 49 RPC 352.
Microbeads AG v Vinhurst Road Markings Ltd [1975] 1 All ER 529, [1975] 1 WLR 218, CA.
Performing Right Society Ltd v Bray Urban District Council [1930] AC 377, PC.
Stillitz (C) (a firm) v Jones & Higgins (1942) 60 RPC 15.
Townsend v Haworth (1875) 12 Ch D 831n.

Action

By a statement of claim dated 27th August 1980, the plaintiffs, CBS Inc and CBS United *a*
Kingdom Ltd, suing on behalf of themselves and all other members of the British
Phonographic Industry Ltd, sought (1) an injunction restraining the defendants, Ames
Records & Tapes Ltd, from infringing the copyright in any sound recording or in any
artwork or literary work used on or in relation to any sound recording belonging to the
plaintiffs and any other member of the British Phonographic Industry Ltd, (2) an
injunction restraining the defendants from hiring out records purchased from the *b*
plaintiffs or any other member of the British Phonographic Industry Ltd in breach of
contract and (3) damages or an account of profits for infringement of copyright or breach
of contract. The facts are set out in the judgment.

Hugh Laddie for the plaintiffs.
A Kynric Lewis QC and *N J G Howarth* for the defendants.	*c*

Cur adv vult

13th February. **WHITFORD J** read the following judgment: The plaintiffs are in
business manufacturing and selling sound recordings in the form of discs and tapes. *d*
They claim to sue in a representative capacity, suing not only on their own behalf but also
on behalf of a large number of other manufacturers who, like the plaintiffs, belong to a
trade association, British Phonographic Industry Ltd (BPI). There can be no doubt that
the plaintiffs and the other members of BPI are the owners of copyright in a large
number of sound recordings. I was asked to assume for the purposes of this action that
the copyright in the particular recordings the subject of the action is vested in the *e*
plaintiffs.

Records in the form of discs are sold in so-called sleeves, on which are printed literary
and artistic works. The tapes are sold in cassettes which also carry literary and artistic
material on their covers. I was asked to assume that the plaintiffs or other members of
BPI own the copyright in the relevant literary and artistic works.

The plaintiffs and other members of BPI supply records to companies such as the *f*
defendants on standard conditions. Among these forms there is a standard form used by
the plaintiffs, but for reasons which will become apparent the plaintiffs place no particular
reliance on the terms of supply, and I need not refer to them in detail.

The defendants have been customers of the plaintiffs for some time. They run a chain
of retail shops, I think 13 in number, in the north of England. The moving spirit in the
defendant company is Mr Philip Ames, who has had 21 years in the record business. *g*

Times are bad for trade, particularly perhaps in the North and North West, where
unemployment is high. Mr Ames, whom I found to be a straightforward and reliable
witness, told me that over the last year trading has been so bad in the North that retailers
generally have been turning to special offers, discounts and other schemes to get
customers into the shops. Blackburn and Burnley, the latter especially, for it has the
second highest unemployment rate in the area, are two towns where Ames have shops. *h*
Mr Ames decided to introduce at these shops a scheme to promote business. He decided
that as an alternative to direct sales he would offer his customers a record lending
library. Basically he was doing no more than public lending libraries hiring out records
have been doing for many years. He envisaged putting a rather larger selection of pop
records into his library than most public libraries do, though on the evidence it would
appear that in Burnley at least the public library offers a good selection of pop records. *j*
Mr Ames's scheme was described in a memorandum which was sent to the Burnley and
Blackburn shops in April 1980. It starts by saying:

'Subscription fees. £5—1 L.P. system. £8—2 L.P. or 1 Double Album system.
The amount is payable straightaway upon joining. The borrowing fee is 50p for the
first week and 10p for each week thereafter up to a maximum of £1 in all. (This

a   includes the first 50p). The borrowing fee is payable on return. On joining a member is issued a numbered card, prefixed by the first two letters of the issuing shop. In your case the prefix will be BB.'

Then there is a description of the way in which the cards are to be filled in and marked so as to ensure that there is a record of lendings and the necessary information is recorded to enable the appropriate fee to be collected. There is a provision that if records are returned in a damaged condition a charge can be made of 25p to £1 for what is described *b* as a single album (this I understand to be no more than one record in its cover) and 35p to £1·75 for a double album. The cards, it is said, are not transferrable, but if a member loses his card there may be a reissue. That I think is all that is material so far as the lending terms are concerned.

There was an addition to the memorandum in these terms:

c   'As a special promotion which we expect to last a few weeks, we will be issuing, free of charge. to all who join the record library, a special discount card. This will allow the library member discount of 10 per cent off all stock except blank tapes (which will be at 5 per cent), and our top charge L.P.s which are already on special offer (no discount on these). See the Ames Record Library Sheet (attached) for all details.'

d Then there is further material which I do not think at the moment is of any particular relevance. I can leave the scheme with that brief description.

Contemporaneously with the introduction of this scheme, shoppers were in fact also being offered, without becoming library members, a special discount scheme on payment of some appropriate sum entitling them to a 10% discount on all goods other than tapes, on which again only a 5% discount was being offered.

e   There are a number of journals dealing with items of interest in the record world. On 2nd June 1980 an item appeared in the magazine Record Business which came to the attention of the plaintiffs. It forms part of an exhibit to an affidavit of Mr John Deacon, the director general of BPI. It is in these terms:

f   'Ames launches rent-a-disc library plan. A controversial scheme to rent out L.P.s for 50p a week has been launched by Philip Ames, owner of the Preston-based record retail chain. So far the disc libraries are only being run in his Burnley and Blackburn branches as an experiment. But if the initial success is maintained Ames plans to extend the scheme into another 10 of his 25 outlets. For an introductory subscription of £5 a customer can borrow any album for 50p a week and for up to six weeks for £1. Singles are not included in the scheme. Ames commented: "We *g* obviously know the reason why many people are renting the albums and we wish we didn't have to do it. But we've been forced into it because of the reduced margins. We have to pay our rents, rates and wages somehow." Ames added: "Since we started up the pilot scheme, the response has grown steadily and it's now quite heavy with about 150 subscriptions taken out altogether. To begin with people thought it was too good to be true."'

h   Retail traders are not the only people who are suffering from the present recession. The evidence goes to this: that the record industry is having a lean time. Labour and material costs have forced up prices to such an extent that the recommended full retail price for a pop LP now stands at about £5. Pop records form the profitable side of the record business. Sales of pop records have been eaten into by sales of pirated copies, by which I mean infringing reproductions made by third parties and sold on the market. *j* To some extent such infringements can be dealt with by the bringing of court proceedings.

A more difficult problem has arisen out of home taping. In recent years tape recorders which make a fair quality reproduction have been available at decreasing prices. The most expensive tapes that are on offer of a length sufficient to record both sides of a £5 pop record can be bought for about half that price. The evidence indeed was that you can

buy blank tape capable of recording 40 minutes, the length of a double sided LP, for a
sum rather less than 50p. Music can be taped from records or tapes borrowed, for *a*
example, from public libraries, or from friends. Music can be taped from radio or
television broadcasts, from the soundtrack of film or from the soundtrack of video
cassettes. Home taping is a cheap way of building up a collection. The temptation to
tape must be enormous and the chances of any individual home taper getting caught by
a copyright owner and having proceedings brought against him is no doubt extremely
slender.   *b*

As soon as they came across this article the plaintiffs decided that the scheme being
operated by Mr Ames was likely to lead to a significant increase in home taping. On the
strength of this article they also, I think, concluded that the scheme had been introduced
by Mr Ames so that he could cash in on the home taping industry at the expense of the
record companies. They formed the view that everyone borrowing pop records from
one of the Ames libraries would be borrowing to home tape, for it was not in their view *c*
to be believed that anybody would be prepared to pay an entrance fee of £5 plus 50p for
one week's hire just to listen to a record or even to listen to a succession of records. It is
the case of the plaintiffs that this scheme was embarked on by Mr Ames in full knowledge
of the fact that the record companies would object, in full knowledge of the fact that it
would be detrimental to the interests of the record companies, and in full knowledge
that substantially all the people hiring would be home taping. This, they say, is apparent *d*
from the press reports, one of which I have read, and certain correspondence to which I
shall be coming.

It was the evidence of Mr Ames that the picture painted by the plaintiffs is wrong.
While he accepts that he at all times realised that records borrowed from his library
might be home taped, as indeed records purchased may be by friends of the purchaser,
he did not start the library scheme in order to make money out of home taping.   *e*

I will turn first to the other press reports which are to be found in Mr Deacon's
exhibit. There is a report taken from Music Week of 7th June 1980 which reads:

> 'Ames' own shops in Blackburn and Burnley have started a record library system
> that is likely to be viewed by manufacturers as tantamount to encouraging home
> taping. Customers can join his scheme for an annual subscription, an annual
> membership fee and a small charge each time they borrow an album. And the *f*
> library members are also allowed a 5 per cent discount on blank tapes.'

There is an article in Billboard for 21st June 1980, which is quite a long article, under
the heading 'Album rental scheme sparks controversy'. It refers to Mr Philip Ames being
currently the most talked about figure in the United Kingdom record industry, and goes
on to say:
                                                                                                                  g
> 'His most controversial move? To rent out albums for roughly $1·20 a week on
> a library basis. [This is apparently an American journal. It continues:] He accepts
> that record companies will see his move as being tantamount to open encouragement
> of home taping, particularly as it runs alongside a 5 per cent discount for library
> members on blank tape purchases.'

I do not think I need read anything more from that article.   *h*

There is an article in Music Week for, I think, 28th June 1980 which is entitled 'Ames
is worrying record chiefs'. Perhaps the most relevant paragraph is one which purports
to quote from Ames who, it is said, has told Music Week that he intends to continue with
his scheme at least in the Blackburn and Burnley shops, adding:

> 'The scheme is pinpointing the difference in record customer attitude in areas *j*
> where economic circumstances are different. Blackburn is quite prosperous, but
> Burnley as a town seems to be disintegrating as factories and businesses close down
> and put people out of work. It is in Burnley that the lending scheme has really
> taken off.'

It refers to the fact that there has been no statement from the BPI of any official reaction.

Then there is another reference to Billboard of 5th July 1980 which deals with reaction
a to what is described as the album lending library scheme, started by controversial United
Kingdom retailer Philip Ames in some of his north of England stores.   There is a
purported quotation from the deputy managing director of WEA Records to the effect
that it is highly damaging to the industry.   He apparently added:

> *b* 'The advisability of record companies supplying such operations, or indeed record
> libraries in general, has to be questioned closely. In the longer run, if home taping
> can't be prevented, the industry can only survive if there is a substantial royalty on
> the sale of blank tapes.'

Those were the press reports put forward by the plaintiffs to support their contention
that it was apparent that this scheme had been started with a particular purpose in mind.
The plaintiffs, so far as the correspondence is concerned, rely particularly on two letters
c passing between a firm of solicitors and Mr Ames.   There is a letter of 23rd June 1980
sent to Mr Ames by a firm of solicitors, Joynson-Hicks & Co.   Having referred to the fact
that the operations in Burnley and Blackburn have come to their attention, Joynson-
Hicks say:

> *d* 'The act of hiring out records lawfully manufactured with the consent of the
> relevant copyright owner in the United Kingdom is not in itself an infringement of
> copyright, but our clients are extremely concerned to find that you are sanctioning
> the reproduction of the records incorporating the relevant musical works on to tapes
> . . . We have advised our clients that their members may have possible grounds for
> proceedings against you for authorising infringements of copyright by sanctioning
> and approving the taping of records hired from you. However, our clients have
> *e* first asked us to write to you and explain the position, and in particular to stress the
> importance of this matter to the music industry as a whole. As you will know, one
> of the great problems which the industry is facing at the moment is that of home
> taping, and we cannot believe that it is in your long term interests to encourage the
> practice, which is so much contributing to the decline of the industry in this
> country. We must stress that our clients take a very serious view of the matter
> *f* indeed, and they are prepared to take proceedings against you unless you cease to
> encourage infringement of copyright by home taping. We enclose notices setting
> out the copyright position together with stickers which can be placed on individual
> records. Many record libraries have adopted this form of warning people of the
> possibilities of infringement. May we please therefore hear from you within the
> next seven days with your confirmation that: (1) You will not sanction, approve or
> *g* encourage in any way the taping of records hired from any record library run by
> you at any of your branches. (2) That you will display in a prominent position in
> each of such branches a poster in the form enclosed with this letter, and will affix to
> each record hired out by you a sticker of the type also enclosed. Further copies of
> such posters and stickers can be obtained direct from our clients. (3) That you will
> inform all the subscribers to any record library run by you that home taping is an
> *h* infringement of copyright except in the circumstances set out above.'

The letter was in fact sent by the solicitors at the instance of the Mechanical-Copyright
Protection Society Ltd (MCPS), who, however, work in close co-operation with BPI. I
was told that the form of warning notice referred to in the letter was one which had been
discussed by BPI and MCPS, but it is not accepted by the plaintiffs that the display of
j warning notices or the application of stickers carrying the warning notices would be
adequate to get over their assertion that the carrying on of a library of this kind is an
infringement of copyright. It is perhaps only of interest to note on this letter that it had
been observed, before even Mr Ames came on the scene, that other record libraries were
in existence, who apparently have been prepared, and MCPS have accepted that it was
adequate, to adopt the form of warning which they suggested Mr Ames should adopt.

Mr Ames replied to this letter. I do not need to read the whole of his letter. He does indicate that he has fought against home taping, which he says in some part has been *a* developed by the very industry that is complaining against him. In the second paragraph he says:

'We shall not encourage anyone to tape any records hired. Our employees will be briefed as to what conditions apply when a recording is made by the hirer. Because of the economic situation and the state that the record industry has forced itself into, *b* I have had to find a source of revenue to make up for the problems, and I have simply applied the local authority lending library system. The more we are forced into a corner, mostly by some of our suppliers' terms, the more we have got to do to stay alive!'

Then he goes on to deal with some of the steps which he says the industry has taken *c* which have landed them in their present difficulty. On the second page of the letter he says:

'An interesting point to relate to your client is that we also are offering the hirer an option to buy the album at 10 per cent discount on the album's retail price, and we are able to confirm that a surprising amount of people have bought the records *d* that they have borrowed, so there is a positive side to it—it has encouraged the sale of some albums. However, I still cannot understand an industry that has invented its own rope and noose, and now complains that it is hanging itself. I am simply taking advantage of something that is already there.'

Particular reliance was placed by counsel for the plaintiffs in his address to me on these *e* concluding words which he put it to Mr Ames in cross-examination indicate that Mr Ames was thereby acknowledging that he was taking advantage of home taping. That Mr Ames denies. He said in his evidence that he was in fact by these words doing no more than suggest that he was taking advantage of a situation under which he was perfectly entitled to carry on such a lending library business as was, for example, carried on by local authority lending libraries.   *f*

I may at this stage add that I am satisfied on the evidence that at no time has Mr Ames expressly sanctioned, approved or encouraged home taping. I am satisfied that warning notices are now displayed as requested by Joynson-Hicks on behalf of MCPS and stickers attached to the records hired as also requested. I am satisfied on the evidence that all library members have now signed a new form of library sheet in which they sign under a form of warning in the terms required by MCPS, and I did not understand it to be *g* disputed by the plaintiffs that this is the case.

I may also say at this stage that I reject the assertion that the whole of this scheme was set up by Mr Ames to enable him to make money from members of the public who he must have known would only be borrowing records to make tapes from them. He was, as I have already indicated, a frank and fair witness. He accepted that he undoubtedly knew and indeed he undoubtedly must have known that there would be likely to be *h* some home taping of the library records.

I should also I think make it plain that he was not prepared to accept that the quotations attributed to him in the magazine articles to which I referred are literally correct. He told me that he was asked questions and gave answers out of which these reports evolved. Reports tend to try to stress anything that is likely to be controversial. To give one example I take the comment quoted in Record Business. Mr Ames has no *j* doubt that he was asked if he knew that rented albums were being or were likely to be taped. He cannot recall, as I can well understand, exactly what his answer was. He said that he would have replied that he would have expected in some cases records could be so taped.

Mr Ames's main idea, he said, was to introduce a scheme to get people into his shops. It was his evidence that to this extent the scheme has worked and that people are not only

borrowing records but are also buying records which have been borrowed and other
a items which are on sale.

The evidence also goes to this: that there has been no real increase in tape sales since the
introduction of the scheme. I accept Mr Ames's evidence that his intention in
introducing the scheme was to enhance business generally and not just to make money
out of a scheme designed to encourage home taping. The question still remains,
however, whether in so doing it can be said that he has infringed the plaintiffs' rights.

b Before I come to the questions of law there are some other matters to which I should
make brief reference. The plaintiffs, prior to issuing the writ, took the precaution of
causing investigations to be made at Burnley and Blackburn with a view to finding out
just how this scheme was being operated. Two private investigators retained by BPI
were instructed to visit the defendants' shops in Burnley and Blackburn. They were a Mr
Foster and a Mr Thompson. On 21st June 1980 Mr Foster went to Burnley to make some
c preliminary inquiries. He was told how the scheme was operated. It was his evidence
that he was told by an assistant, on this occasion gratuitously, that he could copy the
records on his own tapes and could be supplied with blank tapes but not with recording
equipment. The 21st June was a Saturday, a day on which casual assistants are employed
at the premises in question. I have had the advantage of hearing the evidence of two
assistants who were in permanent employ at Burnley at the relevant time. They do not
d recollect Mr Foster visiting on that date. Mr Foster also visited Blackburn on the same
date, where he made similar inquiries and where also, on his evidence, he was told,
following an inquiry, that the shop had no objection to home taping, but again none of
the assistants who were called from Blackburn can recall this event.

Counsel for the defendants described the various visits of these investigators as trap
orders and reminded me of the many references to be found in judgments in passing-off
e or trade mark cases to the desirability of the person springing the trap disclosing the
reason for the inquiry immediately after it has been made and answered. The reason for
this is plain. The person making the inquiry, knowing that exact words used may be of
some importance, will usually make some written or mental note. So far as the person
from whom the inquiry is made is concerned, in the case of a busy retail shop, it is in the
highest degree improbable, unless they are alerted to the importance of remembering
f exactly what has happened, that they will remember with any exactitude exactly what
took place months, weeks or even days after the event. This undoubtedly accounts for
some lack of evidence on the defendants' side as to exactly what was said by the
investigators. The inquiries made on the preliminary visits may have been made of
assistants who were only in the shop on a temporary basis. In any event, much of the
divergence as to what took place during the course of these investigations when the
g assistants did recall the inquiries was no doubt due to the fact that the assistant in
question at the time would have had no particular reason to pay particular attention to
what was being said.

On June 26th, Mr Foster returned to Burnley and joined the library, borrowing two
records. He says that he asked for a tape long enough to record them. He says that he
was sold such a tape. On this occasion he was served by Mrs Booth, who told me in
h evidence that she remembers Mr Foster's visit on this occasion. She remembers it
because she was surprised that someone living in Bury should want to join a library in
Burnley. Mr Foster had to give his address when he was enrolled. It was her evidence
that he did not say anything about wanting to record. Mrs Booth was a good witness and
I am sure that she does not remember anything being said about tapes. I am sure too that
Mr Foster's account is incomplete. He says he bought and was sold a tape and no more
j than that. The price of blank tapes varies quite widely. There must have been something
more said about the type of tape that he wanted or the price that he was prepared to
pay. In the end however I am in no doubt that Mr Foster said something about wanting
to tape. He went to the shop intending to see what their reaction to such a suggestion
would be. Whatever he said, it appears to have made no impression on Mrs Booth. Miss
Wild, the other assistant there at this time, had no recollection of ever having seen Mr
Foster.

Mr Foster then went on to carry out a similar transaction at Blackburn. Miss Billington who served him denied that there was any talk about home taping and denied that she *a* sold him a cassette. Her recollection was confirmed by Miss Davidson, who also remembers seeing Mr Foster in the shop at the time when he was served by Miss Billington. Miss Davidson told me that Mr Foster chatted them up and it may well be that his conversation about boy friends and what to do on evenings out was of more interest to them than anything he may have said about tapes or taping. Here again I have no doubt that he said something, but exactly what was said and how it was said must *b* remain a matter of doubt.

On a further visit by Mr Foster to Blackburn, when he borrowed two further records, he was shown the MCPS notice, but on his evidence he was still sold a tape which he said he explained he wanted in order to record from the albums he was borrowing. It was the evidence of Miss Billington that there was no talk about recording on this further occasion and she cannot recall selling a cassette.   *c*

I do not think it is necessary for me to go in detail through Mr Thompson's evidence touching his visits to the defendants' shops in Blackburn and Burnley. He appears to have made some impression due to the fact that he stayed for a very long period in one of the shops, apparently, according to him, looking for warning notices, but in general his evidence followed the same pattern as the evidence of Mr Foster, as did the evidence of the assistants.   *d*

I have already said that I am satisfied that the library scheme was not initiated merely to take advantage of home taping. Up to the time of the MCPS intervention my view is that the defendants were indifferent to the possibility or indeed the probability that a proportion of borrowers would home tape. Since the MCPS intervention I am satisfied, as I have already said, that warning notices have been displayed and that the stickers have been applied to the protective sleeves used for the library records. Indeed there was no *e* cross-examination to the defendants' evidence in this particular regard.

What then is the position in law? I was told that the parties are anxious to treat this as a test case, seeking a speedy resolution to two questions, which is why I have been asked to assume that the plaintiffs' title to copyright in the recordings and any relevant literary and artistic matter is a good one.

Section 1 of the Copyright Act 1956 is in these terms: *f*

> '(1) In this Act "copyright" in relation to a work (except where the context otherwise requires) means the exclusive right, by virtue and subject to the provisions of this Act, to do, and to authorise other persons to do, certain acts in relation to that work in the United Kingdom or in any other country to which the relevant provision of this Act extends. The said acts, in relation to a work of any description, are those acts which, in the relevant provision of this Act, are designated as the acts *g* restricted by the copyright in a work of that description.
>
> '(2) In accordance with the preceding subsection, but subject to the following provisions of this Act, the copyright in a work is infringed by any person who, not being the owner of the copyright, and without the licence of the owner thereof, does, or authorises another person to do, any of the said acts in relation to the work in the United Kingdom or in any other country to which the relevant provision of *h* this Act extends . . .'

Section 12 of the Act gives the owner of the copyright in a sound recording, inter alia, the sole right to make a record embodying the recording. So far as literary and artistic works are concerned, there is a series of acts reserved to the copyright owner, including reproducing the work in any material form, publishing the work, performing the work *j* in public and so on.

Ames are not of course making records embodying the plaintiffs' original work. The plaintiffs' first and principal point as put to me in argument, however, was that by the operation of the library scheme Ames are authorising home taping by borrowers. Asked whether in the circumstances which I have outlined it could be said that Ames have

authorised such home taping, I cannot believe that anybody other than a lawyer would
a have any difficulty in saying No. Any ordinary person would, I think, assume that an
authorisation can only come from somebody having or purporting to have authority and
that an act is not authorised by somebody who merely enables or possibly assists or even
encourages another to do that act, but does not purport to have any authority which he
can grant to justify the doing of the act.

The fact that in this country no defined law of unfair competition has developed has
b resulted in this, that the law of copyright, like the law relating to passing off, has been
stretched to give protection to creative talents and activities the protection of which was
probably never in the contemplation and indeed in some cases cannot have been in the
contemplation of those who from time to time have been responsible for the framing of
successive statutes. Language can be and has been stretched beyond the limits that most
people would attribute to the words used in successive Copyright Acts, but there must be
c a breaking point. The question is whether it has been reached.

I would say at once that in the absence of authority I should have no hesitation in
regarding the plaintiffs' contention on this aspect of the case as being untenable. It seems
to me, just considering the language of the statute and the meaning which ought to be
attributed to such a word as 'authorising', to be contrary to common sense to say that the
defendants are authorising home taping by operating the library system. I am in no
d sense out of sympathy with the plaintiffs. I accept the evidence that home taping is
having a very detrimental effect on sales. Of course you can home tape from bought
records, borrowed records, borrowed from friends or public libraries, from the playing
of records over the radio, and indeed, at no expense, from records which can be obtained
for trial periods on introductory offers from many record clubs who advertise in the
papers, who are prepared to let you have up to three or four records for a limited period
e of trial free of any charge whatsoever. Specimen advertisements relating to such offers
are to be found in the agreed supplementary bundle. Are these clubs, the broadcast
authorities, the public libraries, vendors of records and individuals lending records to
friends authorising their taping? The answer may differ depending on the circumstances
of each particular case. In the circumstances of this case counsel for the plaintiffs, as I
understand it, submits that the operation of a library amounts to 'authorising' if the
f persons running the library know that what they are doing is going to result in home
taping. Of course what all the category of persons I have referred to above are doing
would enable home taping to take place and will assist home taping, but if persons do no
more than some act which may result in home taping then I do not think it can be said
that they are 'authorising' home taping.

Counsel urges that the vice of Mr Ames's library system is that it positively encourages
g home taping and was designed to take advantage of the desire to home tape, and that one
must proceed on this basis: that whatever Mr Ames's intention may have been, we are
faced with the fact that he is positively encouraging home taping in a way which makes
it sensible to describe the activities of his library as being activities which amount to an
authorising of home taping. Of course if one considers the situation where the warning
notices and stickers are applied, I am bound to say that it appears to me to be almost
h impossible to suggest that a library operating with warnings of this kind could be said to
be encouraging home taping. I think there is some significance in the evidence that the
bringing into operation of the system, apart from the sales made to the investigators,
does not really appear to have led to any very great increase in the sales of blank tapes.
The discount which is offered to library users is available to anybody who goes into the
shop, whether they join the library or not.

j Whatever the present position may be, there undoubtedly was a period during which
no warning notices were displayed and no stickers were applied to the sleeves of the
albums in the library. I turn now to consider this position.

In *Re Stauffer Chemical Co's Application* [1977] RPC 33 Roskill LJ dealt with the
meaning properly to be attached to the words 'fairly based' in connection with patent
applications. In dealing with these words Roskill LJ questioned the use of paraphrases of

single words and simple phrases as used in Parliament in statutes. Referring to earlier authority he observed (at 61):

    a

    'These two cases afford an interesting and at the same time curious illustration of the haphazard and sometimes unsatisfactory way in which the English law develops through successive judicial decisions. A judge uses a phrase in a judgment; a phrase, which may or may not have been carefully chosen, is used as apposite to a particular background of fact. Some years later that phrase is borrowed, maybe by another court or by counsel arguing another case, and applied to facts widely different from *b* those with which the first case was concerned. Perhaps half a century later those two decisions (and perhaps others which have been given during the intervening period) are sought to be applied to yet another case where the facts are entirely different and the phrase originally used in relation to particular facts of restricted application becomes elevated into a rule of law, the purpose of the original use of the phrase and the background to that original use having been meanwhile overlooked *c* or forgotten or sometimes completely misunderstood.'

    With these observations in mind I turn to the authorities to which my attention was drawn by counsel on the plaintiffs' behalf, taking first of all *Falcon v Famous Players Film Co* [1926] 2 KB 474. Mr Falcon owned the motion picture rights so far as performance in this country was concerned in a particular film. The defendants purported to let the *d* right to exhibit the film to a cinema proprietor. It was held that in so doing they had authorised what would amount to an infringement of Mr Falcon's performing right in the film. Bankes LJ said (at 490–491):

    'The definition of "copyright" in s. 1, sub-s. 2, includes "the sole right ... to perform ... the work" and also "the sole right to authorise any such act". It has been said, and I think the comment is not an unfair one, that the use of that word *e* "authorise" adds nothing to the definition, because, strictly speaking, the sole right of performance must necessarily include the right to authorize performance. But when the definition of "copyright" is read in connection with that of "infringement", I think it becomes fairly apparent that the object of introducing the word "authorise" was to get rid of the effect of certain decisions, of which *Karno* v. *Pathé Frères* ((1900) 100 LT 260) was the most recent, in which it was held upon the language of earlier *f* statutes that a defendant who for reward gave permission to a third person to represent a play in breach of the owner's copyright did not "cause it to be represented," unless the person so representing it was the servant or agent of the defendant. In the present statute that language has been deliberately dropped, and for the word "cause" has been substituted the word "authorise"; and the decision of Tomlin J. in *Evans* v. *Hulton* ((1924) 131 LT 534) and the dictum of Buckley L.J. in *g* *Monckton* v. *Pathé Frères* ([1914] 1 KB 395) both clearly indicate that in the opinion of those learned judges the present expression is to be understood in its ordinary dictionary sense of "sanction, approve and countenance". If that is the true view I think McCardie J. was, upon the materials before him, amply justified in coming to the conclusion that the first three defendants had infringed the plaintiff's sole right to authorize the performance of the play. For these reasons I am of opinion that the *h* appeal should be dismissed.'

    Scrutton LJ concurred in the finding that there was on the facts an authorisation. I can go to the judgment of Atkin LJ where he said (at 498–499):

    'There remains the question of infringement. Upon that I agree with the view *j* expressed by my Lord. The plaintiff possessed the sole right to perform the play or to authorize its performances, and by the terms of s. 2 the defendants infringed that right if they either performed the play themselves or authorized its performance by others. To my mind the hiring out of the film for three days on the terms of the contract of hiring, which is before us, amounts to an authorization by the defendants

a to Chetham to perform the play, and is an infringement of the right of the plaintiff, who alone has the right to give such an authorization. For the purposes of this case it appears to me that to "authorize" means to grant or purport to grant to a third person the right to do the act complained of, whether the intention is that the grantee shall do the act on his own account, or only on account of the grantor; and that construction of the word "authorize" seems to have been the one adopted by Buckley L.J. in *Monckton* v. *Pathé Frères*, where he held that the seller of a
b gramophone record authorizes the use of the record, and by Tomlin J., who in *Evans* v. *Hulton* held that a person who sold to a publisher serial rights in stories written by the plaintiff authorized the printing and publication of them. I think the view taken by those two learned judges was right. I agree that the appeal should be dismissed.'

c On the facts of the present case it appears to me that the defendants have neither granted nor purported to grant any right to home tape. Adopting the approach of Bankes LJ one does of course see that he refers to the sense undoubtedly given in the dictionaries to the word 'authorise', namely 'sanction, approve and countenance'. Observing that these words are used disjunctively, counsel for the plaintiffs fastened on the word 'countenance', being the word capable of the widest meaning, as covering the
d activities of the defendants. 'Countenance' in itself is a word of wide meaning. It may mean sanction, encourage, support or condone. If Parliament had intended to give copyright owners the sole right to give countenance to infringing acts, then no doubt they would have said so in plain terms.

In my judgment, in the context of *Falcon v Famous Players Film Co*, it is quite plain that a person who hires out a film to a cinema proprietor can sensibly be said to be purporting to grant authority for the showing of the film, and there is no doubt that anybody
e purchasing a record would immediately assume that he was being authorised to play it, but no more than that. The decision in *Falcon v Famous Players Film Co* I think went against the defendants because they plainly purported to grant the right to show the film. Indeed Scrutton LJ went so far as to say that the distributor-defendants would be liable as performers of an infringing act.

f Before I continue with the cases relied on by counsel for the plaintiffs, I should make reference to another decision of the Court of Appeal, in which the same three Lords Justices were sitting, given two years earlier, that being the case of *Performing Rights Society Ltd v Ciryl Theatrical Syndicate Ltd* [1924] 1 KB 1. It was a case in which the defendant-appellant had authorised or was alleged to have authorised the performance of a musical work. He was the managing director of the company which employed a band who gave an infringing performance. The company was held liable for authorising it.
g The question was whether the managing director was liable, he not being privy, as the Court of Appeal found, to the tortious act. He did not know what pieces were being performed, he gave no instructions to the band, and he was not indeed in the country at the time of the performance.

Bankes LJ said (at 9):

h 'In order to succeed the respondents had to adduce evidence either of authority given by the appellant for the performance, or of permission to use the theatre for the performance, of these pieces. I agree with Mr. Henn Collins that the Court may infer an authorization or permission from acts which fall short of being direct and positive; I go so far as to say that indifference, exhibited by acts of commission or omission, may reach a degree from which authorization or permission may be
j inferred. It is a question of fact in each case what is the true inference to be drawn from the conduct of the person who is said to have authorized the performance or permitted the use of a place of entertainment for the performance complained of.'

I pause at this point to say that attention was particularly drawn by counsel to the reference to the fact that 'indifference exhibited by acts of commission or omission' may reach a degree from which authorisation or permission may be inferred, adding only this, that Bankes LJ does make it plain that the inference proper to be drawn is a question of fact depending on the circumstances of each particular case.

Bankes LJ continued (at 9–10):

'In the present case I cannot draw the inference which the learned judge drew from the conduct of the appellant. The band was employed and paid by the Syndicate; in July, 1921, the appellant was abroad; there is no evidence that he either knew or had reason to anticipate or suspect that the band in his absence were likely to give performances which would be infringements of copyright. A letter was written to him on July 15 calling his attention to an alleged infringement by the band, but there is no evidence that it ever reached him. A second letter was written on July 28 again complaining of an infringement by the band. The appellant was still abroad. He does not seem to have returned until some time in September, as I gather from a letter of August 10 from the respondents' representative. Then there is a letter from the appellant dated August 10 to which the learned judge attached an importance which I do not think it deserves. It does not appear from where it was written. [Then some letters were read.] I agree that those letters do show indifference of a kind, but I say emphatically not of a kind to warrant the inference of authorization or permission. It was the indifference of one who did not consider it his business to interfere, who had no desire to see another person's copyright infringed, but whose view was that copyright and infringement were matters for the conductor or bandmaster to consider. The indifference from which permission or authorization is to be inferred is of a very different character, of which *Monaghan* v. *Taylor* ((1886) 2 TLR 685) is an example. The performance there was by an agent introduced to sing whatever songs he chose, the principal's conduct indicating that he did not care whether the performance was an infringement of copyright or not. In addition it appears that the performance was heard in whole or in part by the principal himself. In those circumstances the question was left to the jury whether they inferred that the principal authorized the infringement. The jury found for the plaintiff and a Divisional Court confirmed the decision, holding that no objection could be taken to the summing up of the learned judge, and that the verdict should stand.'

Scrutton LJ concurred in the view of Bankes LJ, saying (at 12):

'It was argued that under s. 2 copyright is infringed by anyone who, without consent of the owner of the copyright, authorizes the performance of a work in public, and no doubt he does infringe; but the answer to that argument seems to me to be that the band were not the servants or agents of the appellant, who as agent for the company appointed the band to the position of servants or agents of the company. As in *Lyon* v. *Knowles* ((1864) 5 B & S 751) a person in the appellant's position was held not to have caused a work to be performed, so the appellant cannot be held to have authorized this work to be performed.'

Atkin LJ said (at 15):

'If the directors themselves directed or procured the commission of the act they would be liable in whatever sense they did so, whether expressly or impliedly. In this case there is no suggestion that the appellant was privy to the commission of this wrongful act. He was away at the time. He had no idea what pieces were being performed. He gave no instructions or directions to the band to play the works in question. No one would think of holding a managing director responsible for all the wrongful acts committed by servants of the company in such circumstances. How does this particular wrongful act differ from others? It is said that the appellant authorized the performance within the meaning of the Act. I think the plain answer is that he did not. The employers of the band may be said to have authorized the performance in pursuance of a general authority, on the footing that

an employer may be deemed to authorize acts done by his servants in the general
scope of his employment; but that doctrine does not apply to a servant whose
business is to engage other employees, and even to dismiss them, and in the general
scope of whose business the act complained of does not fall. To make such a servant
liable he must be privy to the tortious act.'

Of course every case differs on its facts. Quite plainly here we have a case differing
from the present case in this sense, that on the findings of the Court of Appeal there is no
evidence that the managing director even knew or which could lead him to suspect that
infringement might be taking place, whereas in the present case, as I have already
indicated, Mr Ames is prepared to accept that he knew that, in connection with record
borrowers as in connection with any other dealing in records, home taping might take
place.

Counsel for the plaintiffs, as I have already indicated, drew particular attention to the
fact that authorisation may be inferred from indifference. He says that at the very least
Mr Ames was indifferent to the possibility of home taping, and that we can derive from
various matters: from his omission in the early stages at least to display warning notices;
from the selling of blank tapes at a discount, albeit a lower discount than that given for
any other goods, and so forth. But of course the question so far as the point of indifference
is concerned goes back really to what Bankes LJ said about the matter. Is this again a case
of the indifference of somebody who did not consider it his business to interfere, who
had no desire to see another person's copyright infringed, but whose view was that
copyright and infringement were matters in this case not for him, but for the owners of
the copyright?

It must be recalled that the most important matter to bear in mind is the circumstances
established in evidence in each case.

Counsel went from the 1920s to more recent authority, drawing my attention quite
rightly to a case in the Privy Council of *Vigneux v Canadian Performing Right Society Ltd*
[1945] 1 All ER 432, [1945] AC 108. Counsel reminded me that this is not an authority
binding on me, and indeed it is not. I confess that I find the judgment of the Privy
Council in relation to the relevant point of little assistance for reasons which will
emerge. It was a case concerned with what have become known as juke boxes, namely,
record reproducers which operate by inserting a coin. Vigneux was a company whose
business it was to install and service equipment of this kind. They supplied the
equipment; they also supplied and changed, at the request of the persons to whom they
were supplying, the records which could be played by the machine. The instrument in
connection with which the proceedings were brought was hired out to a company called
Rae Restaurants Ltd, who ran a chain of restaurants. Each week a representative of
Vigneux called to collect the hiring charge and to change the records if so required.

The principal question in the case was the extent to which Rae were protected by a
provision of the Canadian Act which is not material to be considered in the context of the
present case, but the Board considered the question of authorisation by Vigneux. The
point was not I think germane to any live issue, because if, as was found, Rae were saved,
then Vigneux were going to be saved also.

The matter is dealt with very briefly in the judgment of the Board given by Lord
Russell ([1945] 1 All ER 432 at 439, [1945] AC 108 at 122–123):

'In regard to Vigneux, no doubt in law they are the owners of the gramophone.
As such they might, if necessary, claim to be protected by the section. But in their
case no such claim is necessary, because, as their Lordships think, they neither gave
the public performance of *Star Dust*, nor did they authorise it. They had no control
over the use of the machine; they had no voice as to whether at any particular time
it was to be available to the restaurant customers or not. The only part which they
played in the matter was, in the ordinary course of their business, to hire out to Raes
one of their machines and supply it with records, at a weekly rental of $10. Their
Lordships are unable to accept the view of MACLEAN, P., (accepted by SIR LYMAN

DUFF, C.J., and DAVIES, J.) that Raes and Vigneux were carrying on: ". . . a distinct
class of business, a venture of publicly performing musical works purely for *a*
profit." They can see no foundation on which such a view can be based. As stated
above, Raes hired a machine which they thought would attract custom to their
restaurant. Vigneux supplied the machine in the ordinary course of their business,
at a fixed rental; they had no interest beyond that. To hold, on those materials, that
"they are virtually partners in a distinct class of business" and to decide the case on
that ground, cannot, in their Lordships' opinion, be justified.' *b*

I find it somewhat curious that no reference was made in this judgment to the fact that
Vigneux, in addition to supplying the equipment for playing the records, also supplied
the records, and could quite plainly only anticipate that any records they were supplying
would be taken as records which it was open to customers to have played on the insertion
of an appropriate coin. On any basis the case against Vigneux was very much stronger
than the present case. It was a case of supplying both records and the equipment which *c*
could perform and would perform what would be a limited repertoire of records.

The *Vigneux* case was distinguished by the Supreme Court of Victoria in *Winstone v
Wurlitzer Automatic Phonograph Co of Australia Pty Ltd* [1946] VLR 338, a case in which
it was held that the owner of a coin operated gramophone authorised public performances
given in a shop in which the machine was installed. It was again a case where the owner
supplied the machine and the records. Herring CJ referred to the *Vigneux* case and said *d*
(at 351):

'According to the report before the Judicial Committee the argument was
concerned entirely with the proper interpretation of the relevant legislation. There
was no suggestion made apparently therein that apart from the subsection Vigneux
were not liable for infringement. Their Lordships state their conclusions as *e*
follows. [Then he cited the passage I have just read from the *Vigneux* case, and
continued:] Owing to the similarity that exists between the facts of this case and the
present one great reliance was placed on the dictum of their Lordships that in the
circumstances of the case Vigneux neither gave the public performance of "Star
Dust" nor did they authorise it. As Vigneux were on their Lordships' view entitled
to the protection of the subsection, as was contended on their behalf, the dictum *f*
would appear to be obiter and on a matter which, as far as can be seen from the
reports, was outside the scope of the defences raised and never debated. The only
control moreover referred to by their Lordships was control over the use of the
machine, which was the means of giving the performance complained of. No
consideration was apparently given to the question of control over the content of the
performances, that could be given by means of the machine. And it would seem *g*
relevant to the question whether Vigneux, to apply the test of Atkin L.J. in *Falcon
v. Famous Players Film Co* ([1926] 2 KB 474), granted or purported to grant to Raes
and his customers the right to do the act complained of, to know whether or not
they controlled the selection of the records that were to be placed in the "juke box"
from time to time, and so determined what musical compositions could, if and
when it was put in operation by Raes' customers, be performed thereon. Actually *h*
as appears from the extract from the judgment of Rinfret J. set out above, it was not
clear just what the position was in this regard.'

Having drawn attention to the somewhat curious nature of the decision in the Privy
Council in relation to the issue of authorisation, Herring CJ then went on nevertheless to
draw distinctions which he said in any event led to a different conclusion. In fact the *i*
finding in that case was that quite plainly there was a joint venture out of which both *j*
defendants were going to profit. Of course there are no comparable facts so far as this
case is concerned.

That brings me to the case on which I think the greatest reliance was placed on the
plaintiffs' side, namely, *Moorhouse and Angus & Robertson (Publishers) Pty Ltd v University*

of New South Wales [1975] RPC 454. Tape recording is by no means the only recent
a development which has given rise to problems in the copyright field. Photocopying is
but one of a number of other developments which present difficulties. The university,
no doubt with a view to assisting students, installed a number of photocopying machines
in the university library. Under the Australian Act, as under our Act, there are provisions
safeguarding copying for the purposes of research and private study. Such a machine can
however be used for copying for any purpose. Moorhouse procured the services of a
b graduate to copy a book of short stories. Among other questions, one of the questions,
and one of interest for present purposes, that arose was whether the university were
'authorising' the copying which was carried out at the behest of Moorhouse. There was
a good deal of evidence as to the degree of control exercised by the library over the
machine and what notices, if any, were displayed from time to time, giving warnings
about copyright infringement. That some consideration was given to the need for the
c introduction of some form of notice was accepted by Hutley JA, the trial judge. He said
(at 463–464):

> 'The notices were never attached to the machines in this library. It is not
> necessary to decide whether they would be sufficient to eliminate any liability of a
> University for misuse of copying machines . . . The only basis of liability seriously
> pressed against the University was that it authorized such breaches of copyright [and
d > then there is the citation from the relevant provisions of the Australian Copyright
> Act]. Authorization, for the purposes of the Copyright Act 1911 (UK) and the
> Copyright Act 1912 (Aust), has received authoritative exposition and, in my
> opinion, the section does not alter the law laid down in relation to that Act. In
> *Falcon v. Famous Players Film Co Ltd* ([1926] 1 KB 393 at 491) it is said: "the present
> expression [ie. authorise] is to be understood in its ordinary dictionary sense of
e > sanction, approve and countenance". His Lordship was adopting the words of
> Tomlin, J. in *Evans v. E. Hulton & Co* ([1924] WN 130 at 131) where his Lordship
> defined authorize as "to give formal approval to; to sanction, approve, countenance".
> It was suggested in argument because of the presence of the word "and", the three
> terms sanction, approve, countenance, were cumulative not alternative descrip-
> tions. This is, in my view, unsound. Each of the terms stands on its own. This is
f > made clear by the judgment of the High Court in *Adelaide Corporation v. Australasian
> Performing Right Association* ((1928) 40 CLR 481 at 497). There Higgins, J. treated
> "authorize" as meaning: "sanction, approve *or* countenance". Countenance is the
> widest of the terms and most appropriate in the term under which any liability of
> the University is most likely to be subsumed. As the judgment of Gavan Duffy and
> Stark J.J. shows, countenance can occur by reason of inactivity. Their Honours said
g > (at 504): "It is said, however, that this permission should be inferred because when
> the Corporation learned that the performance was about to take place it did
> nothing. Mere inactivity or failure to take some steps to prevent the performance
> of the work does not necessarily establish permission. Inactivity or 'indifference,
> exhibited by acts of commission or omission, may reach a degree from which an
> authorisation or permission may be inferred'." Higgins, J. took a narrower line and
h > certain passages in his judgment might be read as making it very difficult for any
> act of mere indifference to be treated as authorization.'

Hutley JA continued (at 464):

> 'It was submitted by counsel for the University that there could not be
> authorization unless it was express. In my opinion this is unsound. It would
j > certainly render it easy to undermine the privileges given to authors by the
> Copyright Act 1968 if this were so. It was further argued that unless the acts relied
> upon to constitute authorization were the acts of the council or the Vice-Chancellor,
> they were not the acts of the University for these purposes. I do not agree. In my
> opinion, in order to determine whether the University authorized a breach of

copyright in these circumstances it is necessary to look, not only at what its
controlling bodies did behind closed doors, but at how it, through its organs, acted *a*
towards the users of the library.'

Then he went on to deal with questions of inspection and so forth. He continued (at
467):

> 'The University can only be liable in this case if it authorized the breach of
> copyright committed by Mr. Brennan. It can only have authorized the breach if its *b*
> acts or omissions were factors contributing to the commission of the breach. There
> is no proof that Mr. Brennan was induced to do what he did by a study of the library
> guides, the careful consideration of the notices attached to the machines, or was
> influenced by the atmosphere of disregard for authors' rights which the University
> has encouraged. In other words, his particular breach of copyright has not been
> shown to have been authorized by the University. The tort of authorization implies *c*
> that there is some causative relationship, however tenuous, between the conduct of
> the University and the breach by the actual operative. In this regard I find such
> evidence as there is points the other way. A trespasser who trespasses to prove that
> the fence surrounding a property is scaleable or that the guards were ineffective does
> not thereby prove that the owner of the property authorized his exploit. I find that
> this part of the claim fails.' *d*

The judge then went on to consider the question of the making of a declaration. I do
not think I need read further, because the findings when the case went to the High Court
were somewhat different. On the facts the High Court came to the conclusion that the
university were granting or purporting to grant a general authority. The report ([1976]
RPC 151) shows that they in fact came to a different conclusion on the declaration, the
point on which the case went in favour of Moorhouse below, but that is of no particular *e*
significance. The real significance of the judgment of the High Court lies in relation to
the question of authorisation on which, in the High Court, Moorhouse succeeded.

McTiernan ACJ concurred in the judgment of Gibbs J. Gibbs J said (at 158–159):

> 'The word "Authorise" in legislation of similar intendment to section 36 of the
> [Copyright Act 1968 (Aust)] has been held judicially to have its dictionary meaning *f*
> of "sanction, approve, countenance". [Then there is a reference to two cases,
> including *Falcon v Famous Players Film Co Ltd* [1926] 2 KB 474 at 491.] It can also
> mean "permit", and in *Adelaide Corporation* v. *Australasian Performing Right
> Association Ltd* 40 CLR 481 at 489, 497, "authorise" and "permit" appear to have been
> treated as synonymous. A person cannot be said to authorise an infringement of
> copyright unless he has some power to prevent it (at 497–498, 503). Express or *g*
> formal permission or sanction, or active conduct indicating approval, is not essential
> to constitute an authorisation: "Inactivity or indifference, exhibited by acts of
> commission or omission, may reach the degree from which an authorisation or
> permission may be inferred" (at 504). However, the word "authorise" connotes a
> mental element and it could not be inferred that a person had, by mere inactivity,
> authorised something to be done if he neither knew nor had reason to suspect that *h*
> the act might be done. Knox, C.J. and Isaacs, J. referred to this mental element in
> their dissenting judgments in *Adelaide Corporation* v. *Australasian Performing Right
> Association Ltd*. Knox, C.J. (at 487) held that indifference or omission is "permission"
> where the party charged (amongst other things) "knows or has reason to anticipate
> or suspect that the particular act is to be or is likely to be done". Isaacs, J. (at 490–
> 491) apparently considered that it is enough if the person sought to be made liable *j*
> "knows or has reason to know or believe" that the particular act of infringement
> "will or may" be done. This latter statement may be too widely expressed [and an
> authority is referred to]. It seems to me to follow from these statements of principle
> that a person who has under his control the means by which an infringement of
> copyright may be committed—such as a photocopying machine—and who makes

a it available to other persons, knowing, or having reason to suspect, that it is likely to be used for the purpose of committing an infringement, and omitting to take reasonable steps to limit its use to legitimate purposes, would authorise any infringement that resulted from its use. [Authority is again referred to.] Although in some of the authorities it is said that the person who authorises an infringement must have knowledge or reason to suspect that the particular act of infringement is likely to be done, it is clearly sufficient if there is knowledge or reason to suspect that

b any one of a number of particular acts is likely to be done, as for example, where the proprietor of a shop installs a gramophone and supplies a number of records any one of which may be played on it.'

Then there is a reference to *Winstone v Wurlitzer Automatic Phonograph Co of Australia Pty Ltd* [1946] VLR 338. Gibbs J continued (at 159):

c
'In the present case the University made available to a section of the public the books in its library—at least those in the open shelves—and provided in the library the machines by which copies of those books could be made. It seems to me that the University must have known that it was likely that a person entitled to use the library might make a copy of a substantial part of any of those books. It is true that

d the machines were not used exclusively for the purpose of copying books; they were extensively used to copy lecture notes and other private documents. Moreover, not all of the books which might be copied were subject to copyright. However, in the nature of things it was granted that some of the books which were subject to copyright and which were in the open shelves might be copied by use of the machines in a manner that would constitute an infringement of copyright unless

e some means were adopted to prevent that from being done.'

I do not think I need read any further. The other judgment in the case was given by Jacobs J. I do not propose to read all of his observations (see 164–165). They follow in the same line as that which had been taken already in the judgment of Gibbs J, but he concluded by saying (at 165):

f
'The acts and omissions of the alleged authorising party must be looked at in the circumstances in which the act comprised in the copyright is done.'

There then is the *Moorhouse* case, an interesting one, but one which on the facts is very different from the present case. It was a case in which the university were supplying not only, as in this case the works which might be copied, but also the equipment by which

g such copying was going to take place, together with the material on which copying was going to take place. It is true that a person joining the library scheme can buy tapes at Mr Ames's shops, or possibly and indeed, on the evidence, probably more cheaply at some other shops. If Mr Ames had installed equipment to enable the person joining the library to make copies on tapes at a fee, however modest, the *Moorhouse* case would be of direct application, but in the light of the authorities which I have cited and considering

h all the circumstances of the case it appears to me to be quite impossible to suggest that, indifferent or not, by operating their library scheme Ames are authorising an infringement of copyright, a conclusion which seems to me to accord with a common-sense approach to the meaning of the language of the Act, and the plaintiffs' action under this head accordingly fails.

The second point was argued briefly and I can deal with it briefly. On the sleeves of

j records there are pictorial representations and written matter which for present purposes I am asked to assume is matter in which the plaintiffs have a copyright interest. It was first said by counsel for the plaintiffs that in the light of the decision of the Court of Appeal in *Infabrics Ltd v Jaytex Shirt Co Ltd* [1980] 2 All ER 669, [1980] Ch 282 every hiring of a record plus its sleeve is a publication of the artistic and literary material on the sleeve and hence unless authorised an infringement of copyright. Counsel for the defendants did not argue that hiring is not a publication. I shall take this accordingly as being the law as at present.

a

At one time there was a plea by the plaintiffs that there could be implied into the terms of their agreements for sale a provision that Ames could only resell but were not entitled to hire out the records supplied. Accepting that in the light of the opinions in *Liverpool City Council v Irwin* [1976] 2 All ER 39, [1977] AC 239 the point is not open to him, counsel for the plaintiffs sought to turn this case to his advantage by saying that there can be no implied licence in respect of publication by hiring, though he was forced to *b* concede that there must at the very least be an implied licence to publish by sale.

In truth, in my judgment, once the plaintiffs parted with their records on sale, the purchasers, including the defendants, were perfectly entitled to sell them, give them away, hire them or destroy them. They were of course no more entitled to reproduce any of the literary or artistic work than they were entitled to reproduce any of the recordings, but the articles as articles were licensed in the defendants' hands short of *c* reproduction or some other act in which, under the provisions of the statutes, the interest is reserved to the plaintiffs, and Ames were otherwise entitled to deal with the records and their sleeves as they pleased. I would only finally observe that if a claim under this heading were correct a number of lending libraries dealing in books would be likely to find themselves in considerable difficulty.

In the result the finding is in favour of the defendants on both points argued, and I will *d* hear counsel on the form of the order.

Action dismissed with costs.

Solicitors: *A E Hamlin & Co* (for the plaintiffs); *Donald Race & Newton*, Colne (for the defendants).

Evelyn M C Budd   Barrister.

Practice Direction

a

Magistrates – Clerk – Functions – Advice on questions of law, mixed law and fact, practice and procedure – Evidence and issues – Penalties – Manner of performance of functions.

1. A justices' clerk is responsible to the justices for the performance of any of the
b functions set out below by any member of his staff acting as court clerk and may be called in to advise the justices even when he is not personally sitting with the justices as clerk to the court.

2. It shall be the responsibility of the justices' clerk to advise the justices as follows: (a) on questions of law or of mixed law and fact; (b) as to matters of practice and procedure.

3. If it appears to him necessary to do so, or he is so requested by the justices, the
c justices' clerk has the responsibility to (a) refresh the justices' memory as to any matter of evidence and to draw attention to any issues involved in the matters before the court, (b) advise the justices generally on the range of penalties which the law allows them to impose and on any guidance relevant to the choice of penalty provided by the law, the decisions of the superior courts or other authorities. If no request for advice has been made by the justices, the justices' clerk shall discharge his responsibility in court in the
d presence of the parties.

4. The way in which the justices' clerk should perform his functions should be stated as follows. (a) The justices are entitled to the advice of their clerk when they retire in order that the clerk may fulfil his responsibility outlined above. (b) Some justices may prefer to take their own notes of evidence. There is, however, no obligation on them to do so. Whether they do so or not, there is nothing to prevent them from enlisting the
e aid of their clerk and his notes if they are in any doubt as to the evidence which has been given. (c) If the justices wish to consult their clerk solely about the evidence or his notes of it, this should ordinarily, and certainly in simple cases, be done in open court. The object is to avoid any suspicion that the clerk has been involved in deciding issues of fact.

5. For the reasons stated in the Practice Direction of 15th January 1954 ([1954] 1 All ER 230, [1954] 1 WLR 213), which remains in full force and effect, in domestic
f proceedings it is more likely than not that the justices will wish to consult their clerk. In particular, where rules of court require the reasons for their decision to be drawn up in consultation with the clerk, they will need to receive his advice for this purpose.

6. This Practice Direction is issued with the concurrence of the President of the Family Division.

2nd July 1981   LANE CJ

Practice Direction

FAMILY DIVISION

Probate – Practice – Non-contentious probate – Grant of representation – Fee – Cases not requiring Inland Revenue account – Value of estate – Oath required with application for grant – Non-Contentious Probate Fees Order 1981 (SI 1981 No 861) – Capital Transfer Tax (Delivery of Accounts) Regulations 1981 (SI 1981 No 880).

The Inland Revenue have laid before Parliament the Capital Transfer Tax (Delivery of Accounts) Regulations 1981 which provide that, in certain types of case therein specified, it will no longer be necessary to deliver an Inland Revenue account for the purposes of applying for a grant of representation. It is anticipated that, subject to acceptance, the regulations will come into force at the beginning of August next. [See now SI 1981 No 880, made on 22nd June 1981 and coming into operation on 1st August 1981.]

As from 3rd August 1981, the Non-Contentious Probate Fees Order 1981, SI 1981 No 861, will provide, inter alia, for the payment of a flat fee of £40 on application for a grant of representation in cases in which the net value of the estate passing under the grant exceeds £10,000 but does not exceed £25,000. No fee will be payable if the value does not exceed £10,000.

Consequently as from that date, in those cases in which an Inland Revenue account is not required to be delivered, it will be sufficient to state in the oath to lead the grant the brackets into which the estate falls. Every oath must contain a statement by the applicant as follows:

> 'To the best of my knowledge, information and belief the gross estate passing under the grant does not exceed/amounts to* £   and the net estate does not exceed/amounts to* £   [and this is not a case in which an Inland Revenue account is required to be delivered]*.'

The alternatives marked with an asterisk should be deleted as appropriate.

In addition, as from that date, every oath must state the age of the deceased. In those cases in which the exact age is not known, the applicant should give the best estimate he can.

It is to be emphasised, however, that inquiries whether or not an Inland Revenue account must be delivered in any particular case should *not* be made to the Probate Registries but to the Capital Taxes Office, Minford House, Rockley Road, London W14 0DF.

R L BAYNE-POWELL
Senior Registrar.

23rd June 1981

a

R v Marcus

COURT OF APPEAL, CRIMINAL DIVISION
SHAW LJ, TUDOR EVANS AND SHELDON JJ
23rd MARCH, 9th APRIL 1981

b *Criminal law – Administering poison or other destructive or noxious thing – Noxious thing –*
Substance not likely to cause danger in common use – Sleeping tablets in milk – Whether
intrinsically harmless drug can be noxious when administered in excessive quantity – Whether
'noxious' confined to substance causing injury to bodily health – Offences against the Person Act
1861, s 24.

c The appellant put eight sedative and sleeping tablets into her neighbour's bottle of
milk. She was charged with attempting to cause to be taken a noxious thing with intent
to injure, aggrieve or annoy, contrary to s 24ᵃ of the Offences against the Person Act
1861. The expert evidence was that little harm would have resulted from the toxicity of
the drugs in the milk but that they would have caused sedation and possibly sleep and
were therefore a potential danger to someone who drank the milk and then carried out
d a normal but potentially hazardous operation such as driving a car. The trial judge
directed the jury that it was for them to decide, as a matter of fact and degree, whether
the drugs in the milk were a noxious thing. The appellant was convicted. She appealed,
submitting that the drugs in the milk were not a 'noxious thing' within s 24 because (i)
the drugs were intrinsically harmless and could not be regarded as 'noxious' merely
because the appellant had attempted to administer them in an excessive quantity, and
e (ii) the word 'noxious' in s 24 meant harmful in the sense of causing injury to bodily
health, and did not cover impairment of faculties, and on the evidence there was no risk
of injury to bodily health.

Held – The appeal would be dismissed for the following reasons—
(1) Since the offence created by s 24 of the 1861 Act involved an intention to injure,
f aggrieve or annoy, the concept of 'noxious thing' in s 24 involved not only the quality or
nature of the substance but also the quantity administered or sought to be administered.
A substance which might be harmless in small quantities could therefore be 'noxious' if
the quantity administered was sufficient to injure, aggrieve or annoy. It followed that,
as the judge had rightly directed, the jury had to consider the substance in regard to both
its quality and its quantity (see p 837 *a* to *c j* and p 838 *a*, post); *R v Hennah* (1877) 13 Cox
g CC 547 and *R v Cramp* (1880) 5 QBD 307 applied; dictum of Lord Widgery CJ in *R v Cato*
[1976] 1 All ER at 268 explained.
(2) The meaning of 'noxious' in s 24 was not limited to substances which caused
injury to bodily health. In any event there was evidence before the jury that in the
quantity present in the milk the drugs were potentially capable of causing injury to
bodily health because of the danger to someone who carried out a normal but potentially
h hazardous operation whilst his faculties were impaired by the drugs (see p 835 *c*, p 837
e f h and p 838 *a*, post).

Notes
For causing a noxious thing to be administered, see 11 Halsbury's Laws (4th Edn) para
1204, and for cases on the subject, see 15 Digest (Reissue) 1197–1198, 10,277–10,288.
j   For the Offences against the Person Act 1861, s 24, see 8 Halsbury's Statutes (3rd Edn)
155.

---

a   Section 24, so far as material, provides: 'Whosoever shall unlawfully and maliciously . . . cause to
      be . . . taken by any other person any poison or other destructive or noxious thing, with intent to
      injure, aggrieve, or annoy such person, shall be guilty of [an offence].'

Cases referred to in judgment

Donoghue v Stevenson [1932] AC 562, [1932] All ER Rep 1, LJPC 119, 147 LT 281, 37 Com   *a*
Cas 350, 1932 SC 31, 1932 SLT 317, HL, 36(1) Digest (Reissue) 144, 562.

R v Cato [1976] 1 All ER 260, [1976] 1 WLR 110, 140 JP 169, 62 Cr App R 41, CA, 15
Digest (Reissue) 1198, *10,293*.

R v Cramp (1880) 5 QBD 307, 39 LJMC 44, 42 LT 442, 44 JP 411, 14 Cox CC 401, CCR,
1200, *10,300*.

R v Hennah (1877) 13 Cox CC 547, 15 Digest (Reissue) 1198, *10,287*.   *b*

Appeal

On 13th December 1979 at the Central Criminal Court before his Honour Judge Buzzard
the appellant, Lily Marcus, was convicted of attempting to cause to be taken a noxious
thing with intent to injure, aggrieve or annoy, contrary to s 24 of the Offences against the
Person Act 1861. She appealed against the conviction, inter alia, on the ground that the   *c*
judge wrongly decided that a quantity of nitrazepan and dichloralphenazone, the
chemical constituents of Mogadon and Welldorm, proprietory brands of sleeping tablets
in common use, was or was capable of being a noxious thing within s 24. The facts are
set out in the judgment of the court.

Hugh Torrance (assigned by the Registrar of Criminal Appeals) for the appellant.   *d*
Arthur French for the Crown.

Cur adv vult

9th April. **TUDOR EVANS J** read the following judgment of the court: This is an   *e*
appeal against conviction on a point of law. On 13th December 1979, the appellant was
convicted at the Central Criminal Court of an attempt to cause to be taken a noxious
thing with intent to injure, aggrieve or annoy contrary to s 24 of the Offences against the
Person Act 1861. On 7th February 1980 the appellant was made subject to an order to
enter into her own recognisance in the sum of £300 to come up for judgment if called
on within the three years. She was also ordered to pay £150 towards the legal aid costs   *f*
of her defence.

The appellant lived very close to a family named Laskey. There had been trouble
between them for a number of years. For some days before 15th May 1978 the Laskey
family had noticed that there was something wrong with the milk that was being
delivered to their house. At first they blamed the dairy, but eventually they became
suspicious and informed the police. On 12th May one of the milk bottles was handed in   *g*
for analysis. On the morning of 15th May a police officer started to keep watch. He first
saw the appellant with some children in the yard area between her house and the
Laskeys' house. At 8.40 am a milkman delivered two bottles of red top milk at the
Laskeys' back door leaving them in a basket. By that time the Laskeys had left home for
the day. The police officer who was concealed in a ground floor room then saw the
appellant hurry over to the Laskeys' back door and remove the two bottles of milk. She   *h*
took them into her own house. Very shortly afterwards she was seen to emerge from her
own house carrying two bottles of red top milk. She replaced them in the basket at the
Laskeys' back door. The red top on one of the bottles was found to be intact. The top of
the other bottle was slightly loose.

A toxicologist, Mr Wilson, was called to give evidence on behalf of the Crown. He
analysed the contents of the bottle which the Laskeys had handed in on 12th May, as well   *j*
as the bottle which had been found to have a slightly loose top. The bottle handed in on
12th May gave a positive test for some type of household detergent. Mr Wilson was of
the opinion that the detergent present could not be harmful. The incident of 12th May
did not form part of the indictment. However, Mr Wilson found that the contents of the
other bottle were contaminated by two powdered substances which he identified as
nitrazepan and dichloralphenazone. These chemical substances were used in the

preparation of well-known types of sedative and sleeping tablets. The former was sold
a only under the trade name Mogadon. The latter was used in sleeping tablets sold under
a number of trade names but most commonly under the name Welldorm. Mr Wilson
found that the powdered drugs were impacted up to a level of half an inch from the
bottom of the bottle. He also found, in the contents of the bottle, a trace of a well-known
pain killer called paracetamol. The presence of paracetamol in the milk could have been
explained if the person who had put the sleeping tablets into the milk had just been
b handling a drug containing paracetamol.

Mr Wilson and Mr Tozeland, a toxicologist called for the defence, were agreed that
there were three to four doses of each of the sleeping tablets in the bottle. Mr Tozeland
thought that at least eight tablets had been put into it. They were also agreed that the
dose of the drugs would be likely to cause sedation and even sleep. The speed at which
the drugs would operate would depend on the amount taken and on the contents of the
c stomach at the time. The greater the amount of food in the stomach, the longer it would
take for the drugs to have effect; if taken on an empty stomach, the effect would be more
immediate and deeper.

Mr Wilson said in evidence that in his opinion little harm would arise from the
toxicity of the drugs themselves but that there was a danger to someone carrying out
potentially hazardous operations, for example, driving a car. He said that he would
d never describe a drug as harmless since the object of a drug is to affect the physiology of
the person who takes it. Although this may operate in an appropriate case beneficially,
there may be concurrent adverse side effects. Mr Tozeland substantially agreed with
him.

According to the appellant, on the morning of 15th May she had seen two bottles of
red top milk on her draining board. She was unable to remember if she had brought the
e bottles into her house. At some stage, because she had had a bad night, she had in her
hands a couple of tablets known as Solpadeine. These were pain-killing tablets containing
paracetamol, a trace of which was subsequently found in the bottle containing the
sleeping tablets. The appellant said that she had pushed the top of one of the bottles
down but then, because of the colour of the top, she realised that the milk was not hers
and she then put them outside the Laskeys' back door.

f There was evidence before the jury that the appellant had previously taken sleeping
tablets, (including Mogadon but not Welldorm) but that she did not have sleeping tablets
at the time of the alleged offence. When interviewed by the police, the appellant denied
putting anything into the milk but later she said that she had been upset and annoyed by
the Laskeys and had put two Solpadeine tablets into their milk.

There was ample evidence before the jury on which they could find that the appellant
g had put at least eight tablets into the milk bottle and that, when she did so, she intended
to injure, aggrieve or annoy the Laskeys. But counsel for the appellant contends that an
offence was not committed because the tablets were not a 'noxious thing' within s 24 of
the Act.

Two submissions are made. First, it is said that for a thing to be noxious within the
meaning of s 24, it must be noxious in itself. A thing which is intrinsically harmless
h cannot become noxious or harmful because it is given in excess quantity. In support of
this submission, counsel relied on obiter dicta of Lord Widgery CJ in *R v Cato* [1976] 1
All ER 260, [1976] 1 WLR 110. Second, it is submitted that the word 'noxious' means
harmful and that the meaning is necessarily confined to injury to bodily health. The
word cannot mean harm involving an impairment of faculties. Counsel submits that on
the undisputed evidence there was in fact no risk of injury to bodily health. If any one
j member of the Laskey family had drunk the milk, or any part of it, he or she would have
been sedated or at most would have been caused to fall asleep.

In *R v Cato* the appellant had been convicted of manslaughter and of an offence under
s 23 of the Offences against the Person Act 1861 by the administration of heroin. Section
23 is in language similar to s 24, but concerns the endangering of life or the causing of
grievous bodily harm. Lord Widgery CJ observed, speaking of s 23 ([1976] 1 All ER 260
at 268, [1976] WLR 110 at 119):

'The thing must be a "noxious thing" and it must be administered "maliciously". What is a noxious thing, and in particular is heroin a noxious *a* thing? The authorities show that an article is not to be described as noxious for present purposes merely because it has a potentiality for harm if taken in overdose. There are many articles of value in common use which may be harmful in overdose, and it is clear on the authorities when looking at them that one cannot described an article as noxious merely because it has that aptitude. On the other hand, if an article is liable to injure in common use, not when an overdose in the *b* sense of an accidental excess is used but is liable to cause injury in common use, should it then not be regarded as a noxious thing for present purposes?'

It was then held that heroin was a noxious thing for the purposes of s 23.

Counsel for the appellant, relying on those observations, submits that the sleeping tablets, being harmless in themselves, could not be regarded as noxious within s 24 simply because the appellant had attempted to administer or cause to be administered an *c* excess quantity of them. The question whether a thing could be noxious within the 1861 Act if administered in excessive quantity was considered in a number of authorities in the last century. It was held in cases to which we shall refer that although a substance may be harmless if administered in small quantities, it may nevertheless be noxious if administered in excessive quantities.

In *R v Hennah* (1877) 13 Cox CC 547, the defendant was charged with administering *d* cantharides contrary to s 24 of the 1861 Act. In his judgment, Cockburn CJ clearly envisaged that although a substance may be harmless in small quantities, it may be noxious within the section if a sufficient quantity is administered. He is reported as saying (at 549):

'Upon the medical evidence before us, cantharides, or, as it is commonly called, *e* Spanish Fly, is administered medicinally and in small quantities, and up to a certain extent, is incapable of producing any effect. What is important to the present case is that the quantity administered was incapable of producing any effect. The statute makes it an offence to administer, although not with the intention of taking life or doing any serious bodily harm, any noxious thing with intent to cause injury or annoyance. But unless the thing is a noxious thing in the quantity administered, it *f* seems exceedingly difficult to say logically there has been a noxious thing administered. The thing is not noxious in the form in which it has been taken; it is not noxious in the degree or quantity in which it has been given and taken. We think, therefore, the indictment will not hold. It would be very different if the thing administered, as regards either its character or degree, were capable of doing mischief.' *g*

In *R v Cramp* (1880) 5 QBD 307 the appellant was convicted of an offence under s 58 of the 1861 Act which, inter alia, makes it an offence to procure or attempt to procure an abortion by administering or causing to be administered any poison or other noxious thing. The poison or noxious thing administered was a half ounce of juniper. It was submitted on behalf of the defendant, as it is in this case, that the offence consists of administering a thing in itself noxious and that the statute does not make it an offence *h* to administer harmless substances even in excessive doses. The submission was unanimously rejected by a court of five judges. We need refer only to two passages. Lord Coleridge CJ said (at 309):

'The intent with which the oil of juniper was given was proved, and it was further proved that it was noxious in the quantity administered. What is a poison? That *j* which when administered is injurious to health or life, such is the definition of the word poison. Some things administered in small quantities are useful, which, when administered in large quantities are noxious.'

Denman J said (at 309):

'Where a person administered with the improper and forbidden intent large

a

quantities of a thing which so administered is noxious, though when administered in small quantities it is innocuous, the case falls within the statute.'

We are of the opinion that for the purposes of s 24 the concept of 'noxious thing' involves not only the quality or nature of the substance but also the quantity administered or sought to be administered. If the contention of the appellant is correct, then, on the assumption that the drugs were intrinsically harmless, it would follow that if the appellant had attempted to administer a dose of 50 tablets by way of the milk, an amount

b

which, if taken, would have been potentially lethal, she would have committed no offence. We do not consider that such a result can follow from the language of s 24. The offence created by the section involves an intention to injure, aggrieve or annoy.

We consider that the words 'a noxious thing' mean that the jury has to consider the very thing which on the facts is administered or sought to be administered both as to quality and as to quantity. The jury has to consider the evidence of what was

c

administered or attempted to be administered both in quality and in quantity and to decide as a question of fact and degree in all the circumstances whether that thing was noxious. A substance which may have been harmless in small quantities may yet be noxious in the quantity administered. Many illustrations were put in the course of the argument; for example, to lace a glass of milk with a quantity of alcohol might not amount to administering a noxious thing to an adult but it might do so if given to a

d

child.

We do not consider that Lord Widgery CJ in R v Cato was intending to lay down the general proposition that a substance harmless in itself and in small quantities could never be noxious within s 24 of the 1861 Act if administered in large quantities. R v Cato was a very different case from the present. The court was concerned with heroin, plainly a dangerous substance. R v Cramp was not cited to the court.

e

We shall now consider the second submission for the appellant that the word 'noxious' means harmful in the sense of injury to bodily health. Counsel took us through the relevant sections of the 1861 Act. In a number of sections (including s 24) the words 'poison or other destructive or noxious thing' appear. It was submitted that the meaning of the word 'noxious' must take colour from the preceding words. We do not accept that construction. It seems to us, looking at the relevant sections, that the statute is dealing

f

with offences in a declining order of gravity and that by 'noxious' is meant something different in quality from and of less importance than poison or other destructive things.

On this part of his argument counsel relies on evidence from the toxicologists on both sides that the dose would do no more harm than cause sedation or possibly sleep and was therefore harmless. In fact, the evidence was not so confined. In the course of his summing up the judge, having referred to the evidence relating to sedation and sleep,

g

continued:

'Mr Wilson said that little harm is likely to arise, in his opinion, from the toxicity of the drugs themselves, but there is a danger to someone carrying out normal but potentially hazardous operations, for example, driving whilst their faculties are impaired. You may think that it would not have to be driving, it might be crossing a London street, for example; one could think of a lot of things.'

h

There was therefore evidence before the jury that the drugs in the quantity in which they were present in the milk were potentially harmful in the sense of being capable of causing injury to bodily health. The result of the evidence was that the milk might have had a direct physical effect on the victim. But we do not consider that the word 'noxious' bears the restricted meaning for which counsel contends.

j

In the course of his summing up the judge quoted the definition of 'noxious' from the Shorter Oxford English Dictionary, where it is described as meaning 'injurious, hurtful, harmful, unwholesome'. The meaning is clearly very wide. It seems to us that even taking its weakest meaning, if for example a person were to put an obnoxious (that is objectionable) or unwholesome thing into an article of food or drink with the intent to annoy any person who might consume it, an offence would be committed. A number of illustrations were put in argument, including the snail said to have been in the ginger

beer bottle (to adapt the facts in *Donoghue v Stevenson* [1932] AC 562, [1932] All ER Rep 1).
If that had been done with any of the intents in the section, it seems to us that an offence
would have been committed.   *a*

The judge when summing up to the jury reminded them fully of the evidence and
directed them that it was matter of fact and degree for them to decide whether the drugs
in the milk were noxious. His direction in law was unexceptionable. The appeal must
be dismissed.

Appeal dismissed.   *b*

Solicitors: *R E T Birch.*

April Weiss   Barrister.

c

EMI Records Ltd v Riley and others

CHANCERY DIVISION
DILLON J   *d*
13th MARCH 1981

*Practice – Parties – Representative proceedings – Infringement of copyright – Claim for
injunction and damages – Member of class which produced, made or distributed most of sound
recordings in country suing on behalf of itself and the other members of the class – Sale of pirate
recordings – Defendant admitting infringements of copyright and assertions as to members of* *e*
*class – Whether member of class entitled in representative capacity to injunction and to inquiry
as to damages.*

The plaintiff was a member of the British Phonographic Industry Ltd ('BPI') whose
members produced, made and distributed nearly all the sound recordings made in
England. The member responsible for each recording owned the copyright in it or was *f*
the exclusive licensee under the copyright. The plaintiff, suing on its own behalf and on
behalf of and as representing all other members of BPI, brought an action against the
defendant, a market trader, alleging that she was concerned in manufacturing, selling
and distributing 'pirate records', i e sound recordings made from recordings in which BPI
members owned the copyright or were exclusive licensees under the copyright. The
plaintiff sought as against the defendant an injunction restraining her from infringing *g*
the copyright of BPI members and an inquiry as to the damages sustained by BPI
members by reason of the defendant's infringements of copyright and conversion by sale
of infringing recordings. The plaintiff asserted in the statement of claim that the
members of BPI had consented to any damages recoverable being paid to BPI to defray
the expenses of detecting and suppressing the pirate record trade. The defendant denied
making, but admitted selling, some 2,900 pirate records. She also admitted that most *h*
sound recordings were produced, made or distributed by BPI members. On a motion by
the plaintiff for judgment,

Held – (1) The plaintiff on its own behalf and in its representative capacity was entitled
to an injunction against the defendant restraining her from ordering, selling, exposing
for sale, inviting offers to acquire or parting with any pirate record (see p 840 *f* to *h* and
p 841 *f*, post).   *j*

(2) Furthermore, having regard to the fact that BPI members produced, made or
distributed most sound recordings in the country (which the defendant admitted), thus
giving BPI a special position in the record industry, and having regard also to the fact that
any damages would be paid by the plaintiffs to BPI, it was appropriate that damages
should be recoverable by the plaintiff in its representative capacity since that would avoid

the procedural complication that for the purpose of the inquiry into damages either all
a the members of BPI would have to be joined as co-plaintiffs or they would have to issue
separate writs and apply for consolidation with the plaintiff's claim (see p 841 c to h,
post); *Prudential Assurance Co Ltd v Newman Industries Ltd* [1979] 3 All ER 507
distinguished.

Notes

b For representative actions, see 7 Halsbury's Laws (4th Edn) paras 771–772, and for cases
on representative proceedings in general, see 50 Digest (Repl) 465–470, *1603–1637*.

Case referred to in judgment

Prudential Assurance Co Ltd v Newman Industries Ltd [1979] 3 All ER 507, [1980] 2 WLR
339, Digest (Cont Vol E) 661, *1620a*.

c **Motion for judgment**

By a writ issued on 19th October 1978 the plaintiffs, EMI Records Ltd, suing on behalf
of themselves and on behalf of and as representing all other members of the British
Phonograph Industry Ltd ('BPI'), sought as against, inter alios, the defendant, Mrs Grace
Riley, an injunction restraining infringement of BPI members' copyright in sound
recordings and an inquiry as to the damages sustained by BPI members by reasons of the
d alleged infringement and the conversion by sale of infringing recordings. The defendant
admitting infringing members' copyright by selling pirate records. On 13th March
1981 the plaintiffs issued a motion for judgment in the action seeking, inter alia, an
injunction restraining the defendant from making or assisting in making or selling any
recording made directly or indirectly from a sound recording in which the copyright was
owned by members of BPI and an inquiry as to the damages sustained by members of
e BPI by reason of the defendant's infringements of copyright and conversion of infringing
copies of sound recordings. The facts are set out in the judgment.

Peter Prescott for the plaintiffs.
The defendant appeared in person.

f **DILLON J.** This is a motion for judgment on admissions. The action is brought by
EMI Records Ltd, suing on behalf of themselves and on behalf of and as representing all
other members of the British Phonographic Industry Ltd ('BPI'), against a Mrs Riley, as
first defendant. There were a number of other defendants originally named in the
proceedings, and the proceedings remain on foot against one of them, Mr Patrick
Buckley, but no claim against him is before me today.

g   The action was started in 1978, and the statement of claim was served on 8th June
1979. The admissions by the defendant, Mrs Riley, which are relied on are contained in
two documents. One is called 'Reply to Plaintiff's Statement of Claim' and it is signed by
Mrs Riley and dated 19th November 1979. This was, I think, intended to represent Mrs
Riley's defence to the action, but it was not accepted as satisfactory in form, and
accordingly a little later she served a document which is substantially to the same effect,
h headed 'Defence of Grace Riley, First Defendant', which is signed and dated 22nd
November 1979.

The action concerns the sale of pirate cassettes. The statement of claim sets out in para
1 certain definitions. The definition of 'pirate record' is a 'record made directly or
indirectly from a sound recording without the licence of the United Kingdom copyright
owner or exclusive licensee, being a member of the class', and the 'class' is 'all members
j of the B.P.I.', which is a company limited by guarantee. The statement of claim then sets
out in paras 2 and 3 that the 'Plaintiff is a legitimate record company and a member of
the BPI and sues on behalf of and representing and for the benefit of the Class', and that
'Nearly all records in this country are produced, made or distributed by members of the
Class', and in her defence Mrs Riley agrees both those paragraphs. Paragraph 4 of the
statement of claim sets out that the 'members of the Class are continually and frequently
producing, making or distributing records embodying new sound records. The member

of the Class responsible for each sound recording owns the copyright therein or is the
exclusive licensee thereunder'; Mrs Riley in her defence expressly does not deny the   *a*
existence of copyright.

Paragraph 8 of the statement of claim (I shall have to come back to para 7 in a moment)
asserts:

> 'The Defendants and each of them had been concerned in a business in this
> country of making pirate records and/or authorising them to be made, and/or
> selling and/or distributing for trade purposes records which to their knowledge   *b*
> were pirate. Said business occurred on a massive scale and over a considerable
> period . . .'

and that particulars are served separately with the statement of claim.

As to that Mrs Riley denies ever making a pirate record in her life, but she says that she
did order them to be made and she did authorise her daughter to sell them for her. She   *c*
denies that the business occurred on a massive scale over a considerable period, but she
does say that the business was conducted for some 25 weeks on 25 Saturdays in Portobello
Market, 12 days in Carnaby Street, and 32 days in Oxford Street, and she says that the
total number of the tapes sold was approximately 2,980, and that the probable quantity
affecting members of the class was 2,900 tapes, on the assumption that her sales affected
members of the class. She claims that her sales were too small to affect the large record   *d*
companies, but I take this to mean that she is accepting that 2,900 out of the 2,980 tapes
she admits selling were pirated versions of recordings made by members of the class.

Paragraph 7 of the statement of claim asserts that the members of the class have
consented to all pecuniary remedies granted in respect of actions for, inter alia,
infringement of copyright in sound recordings and selling counterfeit records and all
sums paid in settlement of such actions, being actions conducted by the solicitors to the   *e*
BPI, being paid to the BPI in order to defray the expenses of detecting and suppressing
the pirate and counterfeit record and like trades, and it asserts further that the action is
being conducted by the solicitors to the BPI. Mrs Riley in her defence says that she has
no comment on that, by which I take her to mean that she does not dispute it. She has
also said that she does not want this action complicated and extended by massive
inquiries.   *f*

It seems to me that on the admissions in Mrs Riley's defence and in the reply to the
statement of claim, which is to the same effect and on the further admissions in a sworn
statement by Mrs Riley which is dated 17th November 1978, which she has put before
me, the plaintiffs are entitled to an injunction against Mrs Riley. They are entitled to
relief in respect of goods seized under an Anton Piller order, and they are entitled to the
costs of the action, but the entitlement is not entirely in the form of the draft minutes of   *g*
order, because the draft minutes of order set forth a form of injunction which would
restrain Mrs Riley, for instance, from making or assisting in the making of pirate records,
and she has expressly denied that she has ever made such a record or assisted in the
making of such a record. I think the plaintiffs are entitled to an injunction restraining
her from ordering or selling or exposing for sale or inviting offers to acquire or parting
with any pirate record, that is to say, any record made directly or indirectly from a sound   *h*
recording without the licence of the United Kingdom copyright owner or exclusive
licensee being a member of the class.

I think the plaintiffs are also entitled to an order that their solicitors may deliver to the
plaintiffs or to their order all pirate records, including the packaging thereof, which are
currently in the custody of the solicitors as a result of the Anton Piller order which was
executed at the inception of the proceedings, but there should be an order that the   *j*
solicitors release to the defendant all genuine cassettes which are in their possession as a
result of the Anton Piller order.

The minutes of order then ask for an inquiry as to what damages the members of the
class have sustained by reason of the defendant's infringements of copyright and
conversion of infringing copies, the costs of the inquiry to be reserved, and that the

a   plaintiffs do recover judgment for such sums as are found due together with interest thereon without prejudice to the plaintiffs' obligations to hold or apply the sums in such manner if any as may be required of them at law or in equity.

Counsel for the plaintiffs has taken me to the judgment of Vinelott J in *Prudential Assurance Co Ltd v Newman Industries Ltd* [1979] 3 All ER 507, [1980] 2 WLR 339, where the judge expressed the view that it was not appropriate to award damages to a plaintiff in a representative capacity. A plaintiff in a representative capacity might be entitled to
b   relief by way of declaration or injunction, but not to relief by way of damages. Counsel for the plaintiffs has submitted that that case is distinguishable on its facts from the present case, and he has referred me to orders made by Foster and Whitford JJ who on motions for judgment in default of defence directed inquiries as to damages suffered by the plaintiffs or any other member of the BPI.

I think the fundamental factor is the special position in this particular trade of the
c   BPI. This is not a case of a small number of manufacturers getting together as a self-constituted association where there would be a serious likelihood that other pirate cassettes which Mrs Riley may have sold would have nothing to do with the members of the association, because she herself has admitted that nearly all records in this country, and 'record' includes discs or tapes or similar contrivances for reproducing sound, are produced, made or distributed by the members of the BPI. The matter of substance that
d   underlies this is that if the plaintiffs can only recover damages in respect of tapes in which they individually own the copyright they will have considerable difficulty in establishing which pirate EMI tapes were sold by Mrs Riley among the 2,980 tapes which she admits having sold or among whatever higher number it is found she had sold, but given the admission that nearly all records including tapes are produced, made or distributed by the members of the BPI, on an inquiry as to damages suffered by all members of the BPI
e   the task will be much simpler since it will be clear and seems to be admitted that nearly all the tapes which Mrs Riley has sold were tapes the copyright in which belongs to members of the BPI.

In the circumstances of the BPI and the pleaded allegations, including para 7 of the statement of claim, and I have already referred to the defence to these, it seems to me that it is appropriate that damages should be recoverable by the plaintiffs in the representative
f   capacity in which they are entitled to sue for an injunction, and it would be a wholly unnecessary complication of our procedure if the court were to insist that for the purposes of the inquiry as to damages all members of the BPI must be joined as co-plaintiffs, or alternatively, all members except for EMI Records Ltd must issue separate writs and apply for them to be consolidated with the claim for damages of EMI Records Ltd.

g   Therefore, in my judgment, it is appropriate that the inquiry as to damages should be in the form set out in the draft minutes of order, but it must be clear that there is to be no duplication of damage in so far as there are claims outstanding against other defendants. That is a matter which counsel for the plaintiffs mentioned at an early stage in his submissions, but did not in fact elaborate as the argument proceeded.

Finally, the plaintiffs must be entitled as against Mrs Riley to their costs of the action
h   to date, including the costs of obtaining and executing the Anton Piller order, such costs to be taxed if not agreed, but the costs of the inquiry and all future further costs after today's date are reserved.

Order that if the plaintiffs elected to proceed on the inquiry ordered they would not be entitled to seek any further inquiry as to damages as against any other defendant in the action.

Solicitors: *A E Hamlin & Co* (for the plaintiffs).

Evelyn M C Budd   Barrister.

Payne v Lord Harris of Greenwich and another

COURT OF APPEAL, CIVIL DIVISION
LORD DENNING MR, SHAW AND BRIGHTMAN LJJ
23rd, 24th, 25th FEBRUARY, 12th, 19th MARCH 1981

Prison – Release on licence – Refusal to release on licence – Reasons for refusal – Whether Parole Board or local review committee required to inform prisoner of reasons for refusal to recommend release – Whether contrary to natural justice not to inform prisoner of reasons – Criminal Justice Act 1967, ss 59 to 62 – Local Review Committee Rules 1967 (SI 1967 No 1462).

The plaintiff was convicted of murder and sentenced to life imprisonment in 1968. As a life-sentence prisoner he did not qualify for any remission of sentence although he might be released on licence by the Secretary of State acting under s 61 of the Criminal Justice Act 1967 after consultation with the Parole Board which in turn made recommendations to the Secretary of State after studying a report made by the local review committee. The plaintiff was a model prisoner who had been placed in the lowest security category in prison. He made a number of requests for release on licence but these were refused. He issued a writ against the chairman of the Parole Board, the Secretary of State and the local review committee claiming, inter alia, a declaration that he was entitled to know the reasons for the refusal to release him on licence. He contended that he was entitled to know the reasons for the refusal in order to be in a position to make representations for his release and that it was contrary to natural justice for him not to be informed of the reasons. The judge refused the declarations sought and the plaintiff appealed to the Court of Appeal.

Held – The appeal would be dismissed for the following reasons—
(1) Sections 59 to 62 of the 1967 Act and the Local Review Committee Rules 1967 made thereunder provided a comprehensive code for the procedure for determining whether to release prisoners on licence, and there was no provision in that code for a prisoner to be informed of the reasons for a refusal to release him on licence (see p 845 *a b*, p 846 *g*, p 847 *e f*, p 849 *b c e* to *g*, p 850 *g*, p 851 *j*, p 852 *j*, and p 853 *e f* and *j*, post).
(2) Since neither the Parole Board nor the local review committee were under a duty to inform the plaintiff of their reasons not to recommend him for release, they had not acted unfairly towards him in refusing to inform him of their reasons for so deciding, and accordingly they had not acted contrary to the rules of natural justice (see p 846 *e* to *g*, p 850 *g*, p 851 *j*, p 852 *c e* to *j* and p 853 *d e* and *j*, , post).

Notes

For the natural justice that a person should be given the opportunity to be heard, see 2 Halsbury's Laws (4th Edn) para 76, and for cases on the subject, see 1(1) Digest (Reissue) 200–201, 1172–1176.

For the Criminal Justice Act 1967, ss 59 to 62, Sch 2, see 25 Halsbury's Statutes (3rd Edn) 887–893, 900.

For the Local Review Committee Rules 1967, see 18 Halsbury's Statutory Instruments (Third Reissue) 33.

Cases referred to in judgments

Cinnamond v British Airports Authority [1980] 2 All ER 368, [1980] 1 WLR 582, CA.
Golder v United Kingdom (21st February 1975) Publications of the European Court of Human Rights, Series A, no 18.
Heywood v Hull Prison Board of Visitors [1980] 3 All ER 594, [1980] 1 WLR 1386.

Kanda v Government of the Federation of Malaya [1962] AC 322, [1962] 2 WLR 1153, PC.

a *McInnes v Onslow Fane* [1978] 3 All ER 211, [1978] 1 WLR 1520, 142 JP 590, Digest (Cont Vol E) 45, 62a.

Pergamon Press Ltd, Re [1970] 3 All ER 535, [1971] Ch 388, [1970] 3 WLR 792, CA, 9 Digest (Reissue) 651, 3904.

R v Gaming Board for Great Britain, ex parte Benaim [1970] 2 All ER 528, [1970] 2 QB 417, [1970] 2 WLR 1009, 134 JP 513, CA, Digest (Cont Vol C) 397, 352Aa.

b *R v Secretary of State for the Home Department, ex parte Santillo* p 897, post, [1981] 2 WLR 362, CJEC, QBD & CA.

Thompson v Goold & Co [1910] AC 409, 79 LJKB 905, 103 LT 81, 3 BWCC 392, HL, 34 Digest (Repl) 652, 4494.

Wiseman v Borneman [1969] 3 All ER 275, [1971] AC 297, [1969] 3 WLR 706, 45 Tax Cas 540, [1969] TR 279, 48 ATC 278, HL; *affg in part* [1967] 3 All ER 1045, [1968] Ch 429,

c [1968] 2 WLR 320, CA, 28(1) Digest (Reissue) 493, 1760.

Cases also cited

De Verteuil v Knaggs [1918] AC 557, PC.

Fairmount Investments Ltd v Secretary of State for the Environment [1976] 2 All ER 865, [1976] 1 WLR 1255, HL.

d *HK (an infant), Re* [1967] 1 All ER 226, [1967] 2 QB 617, DC.

Howarth v National Parole Board [1976] 1 RCS 453.

K (infants), Re [1963] 3 All ER 191, [1965] AC 201, HL.

R v Board of Visitors of Hull Prison, ex parte St Germain [1979] 1 All ER 701, [1979] QB 425, CA.

Ridge v Baldwin [1963] 2 All ER 66, [1964] AC 40, HL.

e
Appeal

Roger John Payne appealed against the refusal of McNeill J on 24th July 1979 to grant him declarations against the first defendant, Lord Harris of Greenwich, the chairman of the Parole Board, sued on behalf of himself and other members of the board, the second defendant, Peter Timms, the chairman of the Maidstone Local Review Committee, sued

f on behalf of himself and other members of the committee, and the third defendant, the Secretary of State for the Home Department, that (i) the defendants were bound to apply the rules of natural justice in deciding whether to recommend the plaintiff for early release on licence, (ii) the first and second defendants' decisions, on various dates between January and June 1977, declining to recommend the plaintiff for early release on licence were null and void, (iii) the plaintiff was entitled to make representation to the first and

g second defendants as to his case for early release, and they were bound to acquaint him with the nature of the case for declining to recommend it when his sentence was last reviewed, and (iv) the third defendant was bound to acquaint the plaintiff with any reason for not complying with any recommendation made by the Parole Board or the local review committee for the plaintiff's early release on licence and to consider the plaintiff's representations thereon. The grounds of appeal were (i) that the judge erred

h in deciding that fairness did not require a prisoner to be informed shortly of the reasons why his application for parole had failed, (ii) that the judge failed to give sufficient weight to the argument that a right to make representations was only properly and adequately effective if the person having such right knew enough about the case which he had to meet to be able to make cogent representations directed thereto, (iii) that the judge misconstrued the effect of ss 59 to 62 of the Criminal Justice Act 1967, (iv) that the

j judge wrongly held that if natural justice applied that would necessarily require such a full statement of reasons as would involve the full panoply of particularisation, discovery, interrogatories etc and a breach of judicial confidentiality, and (v) that the judge failed sufficiently to consider whether the Local Review Committee Rules 1967 had been applied fairly in the circumstances. The facts are set out in the judgment of Lord Denning MR.

David Turner-Samuels QC and *Brian Langstaff* for the plaintiff.
Simon D Brown and *John Laws* for the defendants.

a

Cur adv vult

19th March. The following judgments were read.

LORD DENNING MR. Nearly thirteen years ago, on 24th May 1968, Roger John *b*
Payne, being then aged about 26, was convicted of the murder of a woman and was
sentenced to life imprisonment. (He had two previous convictions when he was about
18 and 23 years old. Each of them involved an assault on a woman.)
  On 4th December 1968 he was placed in prison in category A as being a man whose
escape would be highly dangerous to the public. He was in that category for seven years
until 7th July 1975, when he was placed in category B as being a man for whom escape *c*
must be made very difficult. Three years later, on 23rd March 1978, he was placed in
category C as one for whom simple basic precautions would be sufficient. He is now in
category D. He is still in prison in that category.
  Throughout his time in prison he has been exceptionally well behaved. He is described
as a model prisoner. He is in the 'blue band' allocated to the educational department at *d*
Maidstone Prison.
  Being a life-sentence prisoner, Roger Payne does not qualify for remission, whereas, a
prisoner who is given a determinate sentence may, if he is well behaved, get one-third of
his sentence remitted, in which case he is released unconditionally without being liable
to recall.
  Yet even a life-sentence prisoner may be released on licence, subject always to
conditions, and in particular to being liable to recall. It is so provided in s 61 of the *e*
Criminal Justice Act 1967.
  Roger Payne has sought to be released on licence ever since he had completed six years
in prison. But he has never been granted a licence. His case has been reviewed from
time to time, but he has never been let out on parole. He has asked to be told the reasons
for refusal. He wants them, he says, so as to be able to prepare his representations for the *f*
next review.
  Now he has brought an action in the High Court seeking a declaration that he is
entitled to know the reasons. McNeill J rejected his claim. He appeals to this court.
  I would like to say that, instead of seeking a declaration, it would have been more
appropriate to proceed by judicial review: see *Heywood v Hull Prison Board of Visitors*
[1980] 3 All ER 59, [1980] 1 WL 1386. But, as the case is before us, we will deal with it. *g*

The procedure
  The procedure is governed by ss 59 to 62 of the Criminal Justice Act 1967 and the
Local Review Committee Rules 1967, SI 1967 No 1462. The stages are as follows.
  The prisoner, if he is willing, is interviewed by a member of the local review
committee. At that interview 'he shall be given a reasonable opportunity to make any *h*
representations which he wishes to be considered by the committee'. The member
writes a report of the interview. He includes in it any representations made by the
prisoner. The local review committee consider the report of their member. They then
make a report to the Secretary of State of the suitability of the prisoner for release on
licence. The Secretary of State then refers the case to the Parole Board. The Parole Board
advises the Secretary of State. If they recommend that the man should be released on *j*
licence, the Secretary of State may then release a life-sentence prisoner, but only after
consultation with the Lord Chief Justice and the trial judge. If the Parole Board do not
recommend that he be released on licence, that is the end of the matter, until his case
comes up for a further review.

The interpretation of the provisions

a   It seems to me that the statute and the rules together form a comprehensive code. They set out the procedure in such detail that there is nothing more needed to supplement it. They set out the occasions when a man is entitled to make representations, and when he is to be informed of reasons. In particular, it is specifically provided in s 62(3) of the 1967 Act that, if he is recalled, he 'shall on his return to prison be informed of the reason for his recall'. There is no corresponding provision when he is refused a
b   licence. That goes to show that the legislature did not think that reasons were necessary.

But I hesitate to decide this case on that simple ground. In a parallel case when we thought it sufficient to go by the procedure laid down by the state (see *Wiseman v Borneman* [1967] 3 All ER 1045, [1968] Ch 429), the House of Lords said that natural justice was still to be considered (see especially [1969] 3 All ER 275 at 285, [1971] AC 297 at 317 per Lord Wilberforce).

c
Natural justice

No doubt it is the duty of all those concerned, from the member of the local review committee, to the Parole Board, to the Secretary of State, to act fairly. That is the simple precept which now governs the administrative procedure of all public bodies. But the duty to act fairly cannot be set down in a series of set propositions. Each case depends on
d   its own circumstances. As Sachs LJ said in *Re Pergamon Press Ltd* [1971] 3 All ER 535 at 542, [1971] Ch 388 at 403:

'In the application of the concept of fair play, there must be real flexibility, so that very different situations may be met without producing procedures unsuitable to the object in hand.'

e   Sometimes fairness may require that the man be told the outline of the case against him. As in *R v Gaming Board for Great Britain, ex parte Benaim* [1970] 3 All ER 528 at 534, [1970] 2 QB 417 at 431 I said:

'... without disclosing every detail, I should have thought that the board ought in every case to be able to give to the applicant sufficient indication of the objections raised against him so as to enable him to answer them.'
f
That is what counsel for Payne urged here.

At other times it may not be necessary to have a hearing or even to tell the man the case against him, because it must be obvious to him. As, for instance, in *Cinnamond v British Airport Authority* [1980] 2 All ER 368 at 374–375, [1980] 1 WLR 582 at 590–591 and *R v Secretary of State for the Home Department, ex parte Santillo* p 897 at pp 920, 922,
g   post.

Submissions on behalf of Roger Payne

Counsel for Payne submitted that, in the case of life-sentence prisoners at any rate, it was only fair that they should be given the reason, at any rate in outline, why they were refused to be let out on licence. One reason was because he would be better able to make
h   adequate representations on the next occasion when his case was reviewed. Another reason was that it would be beneficial to the man, as a human being, to be told the reasons for refusal. In support of this view, Payne's counsel called Mr Blom-Cooper QC, who said:

'It can only be beneficial in helping the prisoner grapple with the problems of perhaps long confinement or even to grapple with the probability of a release which
j   may be some years away.'

Mr Blom-Cooper QC also said that James LJ was very much in favour of giving reasons in the parole system, and he quoted Lord Hunt, the first chairman of the Parole Board as saying:

'It is a moral right that cannot be indefinitely denied and it is a failure of natural justice which has lasted for far too long.'   *a*

Only a few days ago Payne's counsel drew to our notice *Golder v United Kingdom* in the European Court of Human Rights (21st February 1975, Publications of the European Court of Human Rights, Series A, no 18). Golder complained that it was a wrong statement in his prison record that prevented him being recommended for parole.

Submissions to the contrary   *b*

There are equally strong submissions to the contrary. The first is the practical difficulty of giving the reasons of a body of five members. One or two may have a different reason from the other three or four. Some may be spoken. Others unspoken. The next is the danger that the reasons, if given, would tend to become short and stereotyped, rather than full and informative. So they would be of little avail. If they were full and informative, they would give the prisoner an opening with which he could   *c* challenge the refusal. He could lodge an application for judicial review complaining that the board took things into account which they should not have done, or that their decision was unreasonable. If he were refused judicial review, he would harbour a grievance which would become obsessive, just as much as if he is refused parole without reasons being given.

Apart from these practical considerations, I would suppose that in most cases the man *d* will know the reasons well enough himself. He will have known the gravity of his crime. He will know whether he is thought to be a danger or not. He will know whether he has behaved well in prison or not. He will be able to deal with all these points in the representation which he is allowed to make. If there should be any new factor adverse to him, of which he is unaware, the Parole Board might well arrange for one of their members to interview him so as to ascertain his reaction to it. This is *e* contemplated by s 59(4)(*b*) of the 1967 Act. Thus fairness will be ensured here just as we envisaged in *R v Secretary of State for the Home Department, ex parte Santillo* at pp 919–920, post.

On balance

In the end I think the problem comes down to this: what does public policy demand *f* as best to be done? To give reasons or to withhold them? This is more a matter for the Secretary of State than for the courts. But, so far as I can judge of the matter, I should think that in the interests of the man himself, as a human being facing indefinite detention, it would be better for him to be told the reasons. But, in the interests of society at large, including the due administration of the parole system, it would be best not to give them. Except in the rare case when the board themselves think it desirable, *g* as a matter of fairness, to ask one of the members to interview him. That member may then think it appropriate to tell him.

This is not a case for any declaration. I would dismiss the appeal.

SHAW LJ. The Criminal Justice Act 1967 introduced what was, in the United Kingdom, a new and dramatic concept in our penal system. Part III of the Act under the *h* heading 'Treatment of Offenders' made provision for the possible release of prisoners on licence. The concept was not a novel one. It had, in differing forms, been applied in other countries for some years. Their experience was known and had been studied. The impulse which led to the adoption of a system of parole in this country was of a complex nature. It derived from considerations which were humanitarian, sociological, moral and practical and which in combination made early release a justifiable expedient. If the *j* reformation of a prisoner appeared to have been securely achieved before the expiry of his sentence, that circumstance might (though not necessarily if it stood alone) justify his earlier release. So too might his need (and his capacity) to make his own way and meet his own responsibilities, domestic and general, in an open society to which he had the ability to make a useful contribution. It may be added without any cynical inflection that by the end of the 1960s prisons had become very overcrowded with a resultant deterioration in conditions and standards. If it was possible, without involving an undue threat of some detriment to society as a whole, to relieve the pressure on the walls of prisons by a system providing for the premature release of prisoners that system was worth pursuing though with due caution and always bearing in mind the general well-being of society.

I have embarked on this preamble as it seems to me important to set the scene for a consideration of the rights and responsibilities which are created by the provisions of Part III of the 1967 Act. Those provisions relate to persons who, ex hypothesi, are in the process of serving custodial sentences lawfully imposed. Those sentences are primarily to be served in designated institutions, namely prisons, and for their full term subject only to remission for good conduct. When a prisoner is so discharged his sentence is exhausted and he cannot be recalled even though he commits a further offence during the period represented by remission. At common law there was no power to release a prisoner before the due expiry of his sentence otherwise than by the exercise of the Crown's prerogative of mercy to which recourse was appropriate only in exceptional situations.

The object and effect of Part III of the 1967 Act is to empower the Secretary of State for Home Affairs to release a prisoner on licence before the expiry of his sentence. This power is exercisable only on the recommendation of the Parole Board set up under s 59(1). In the absence of such a recommendation the Secretary of State cannot order a release on licence. On the other hand, he is not bound to follow such a recommendation if it should be made, though in practice he generally does. If, following a recommendation in that regard, release on licence is directed, the duration of the sentence is unaffected. The effect of the licence is that, subject to the power of recall vested in the Secretary of State if recommended by the Parole Board, the residue of the sentence is served (that is to say, worked out) free from confinement.

The mechanics of the operation whereby the Secretary of State may release a prisoner on licence are prescribed in ss 59 to 62 of the Act and in the Local Review Committee Rules 1967, SI 1967 No 1462, made under it. Nowhere in the Act or in the rules is there any reference to 'granting parole' though this is the phrase generally heard in colloquial usage. The statutory expression is simply 'release on licence'. The Secretary of State does not, in directing release on licence, accede to a claim by a prisoner to the benefit of the statute. As I see it, he is doing an executive act which is considered to be justified in the immediate interests of the prisoner and, no less importantly, in the general interests of society when those interests appear to coincide. Whether they do so or not, it is the responsibility of the Parole Board to determine and to make their recommendation to the Secretary of State in accordance with their determination.

To ensure so far as practicable that all aspects of a prisoner's situation may be duly considered by the Parole Board called on to decide whether to recommend release on licence, the constitution of the board is prescribed by Sch 2 to the Act. It is there provided that among its members (of whom there must be not less than five) there shall be included (a) a person who holds or has held judicial office, (b) a registered medical practitioner who is a psychiatrist, (c) a person appearing to the Secretary of State to have knowledge and experience of the supervision or after care of discharged prisoners, and (d) a person appearing to the Secretary of State to have made a study of the causes of delinquency or the treatment of offenders.

I reproduce these requirements not merely to emphasise the breadth of the disciplines involved as safeguards for the interests of a candidate for parole but as indicating also the wide area in which members trained in different disciplines may travel in arriving at their respective conclusions. In the result, whether they agree or differ, they may assign different reasons for the view they reach.

The Local Review Committee Rules 1967, to which I have referred, provide for the creation of a local review committee for every prison. The constitution of these committees is also prescribed. They must include a probation officer who is not a prison

welfare officer and a member of the board of visitors, but no prison officer other than the
governor. It is their function to meet at least once a year to review prisoners' cases in *a*
accordance with the rules.

In regard to any individual prisoner, no review of his case may proceed until he has
been interviewed by a member of the committee (not being the prison governor) if he
is willing to be interviewed. Rule 3(2) provides:

> 'When a prisoner is interviewed he shall be given a reasonable opportunity to *b*
> make any representations which he wishes to be considered by the committee.'

The interviewing member is required to make a report of the interview for the
consideration of the local review committee and a copy of the report must be sent to the
Secretary of State together with the committee's report on the prisoner's suitability for
release.

The interviewing member of the local review committee is thus the only direct link *c*
between a prisoner whose case is to be reviewed and the ensuing parole process. Counsel
for the plaintiff has contended that this is too precarious a means of communication and
that it might in practice be inadequate and unrevealing. The prisoner might be
inarticulate or illiterate or both so that some matter of consequence in relation to his
prospect of parole might not become known or fully understood.

This contention may have some substance but it ignores practicalities. A full-scale *d*
system of interviewing by the local review committee as a body or by the Parole Board
would perhaps be the ideal method of inquiry, but such a procedure would be
unworkable and the parole scheme would succumb. In any case a prisoner can seek
assistance not only from the interviewing member but in advance of the interview from
the prison welfare officer or the chaplain or from the prison doctor or a prison visitor.
Not even the most obtuse prisoner is bereft of all resource when he sees a hope of *e*
freedom. For those who can read, the Home Office provides easily understood pamphlets
dealing comprehensively with all material questions which may arise in relation to
parole.

This argument was put forward as reinforcing what was the main contention of the
plaintiff, namely that where a prisoner is not recommended for parole he should be told
why. Without surrendering the generality of his proposition, counsel for the plaintiff *f*
argued that in the case of a prisoner serving a sentence of imprisonment for life it was
imperative that he should be informed of the matters which militated against his release
on parole. Unlike a prisoner serving a finite sentence, he could not assess his prospect of
release on any scale of time. If the obstacle to parole was remediable, how could a life
prisoner set about meeting the requirements of the Parole Board if he was left to
conjecture and to speculate as to what the factors were which influenced the board *g*
against recommending parole?

The argument is not without substance. It has been the subject of much debate by
experienced and informed protagonists of divergent views. Ethical and moral
considerations play their part, but so also does expediency and the well-being of the law-
abiding section of society. The courts are concerned with the legalities, that is to say with
rights and obligations which have their source in the law or in its proper administration. *h*
It is requisite, therefore, to begin with the statutory provision as to the release on licence
of a person serving a sentence of life imprisonment. Section 61 of the 1967 Act enacts
that the Secretary of State may, if recommended to do so by the Parole Board, release such
a prisoner on licence but shall not do so except after consultation with the Lord Chief
Justice together with the trial judge if available.

Although the issue whether parole should be recommended assumes a different *j*
dimension in the case of a prisoner sentenced to life imprisonment, the essential problem
remains the same. It will generally speaking involve a more onerous responsibility.
Whether the sentence was imposed on a conviction for murder or for some other grave
crime, the prospect of releasing such a prisoner into society must be fraught with very
great anxiety. The validity of parole may be called in question if a person so released

commits murder again, as has indeed happened. Unlike the case of a person serving a
a fixed term whose case is reviewed after he has been detained for a third of his sentence
or for one year, whichever is the longer, the case of a prisoner sentenced to life
imprisonment is reviewed only when the Secretary of State directs it. This is not to say
that such a direction will be captiously withheld, but at what stage it will be given must
depend in part on the circumstances of the crime itself. It will not be until after the lapse
of some years from conviction.

b   It is now necessary to look back to discover what legal rights, if any, are conferred on
persons serving sentences of imprisonment by the 1967 Act or by the rules made under
it.

     In relation to the release of a prisoner on licence, I cannot deduce from the statute itself
any right with which a person serving a sentence of imprisonment can claim to be
invested. The Act, as I read it, sets up an administrative procedure in accordance with
c which the Secretary of State is empowered to release such a person before the natural
expiry of his sentence. In this regard what the Act does is to invest the Parole Board with
responsibilities which it owes to the Secretary of State and to no one else.

     The Local Review Committee Rules 1967, in giving shape to the parole procedure,
does confer certain rights on a prisoner. If he is serving a determinate sentence and does
not indicate that he does not wish to be considered for parole, the local review committee
d is under a duty to review his case. Rule 3(1) then requires that before such review the
prisoner, if willing, shall be interviewed by a member of the committee. By r 3(2), a
prisoner being interviewed must be given a reasonable opportunity to make any
representations he wishes to be considered by the committee. Rule 4 provides that,
before the review, a prisoner must be told that he has a right to make written
representations to the committee. The duties so imposed in regard to incidental matters
e of substance confer corresponding rights on the prisoner concerned; he is entitled to
complain if those duties are not observed and to insist that they should be duly carried
out. What he cannot do is to require something to be done where there is no specific
obligation placed on the Parole Board or the local review committee to do something to
or with the prisoner. There is nowhere any reference to informing any prisoner of the
reasons for not recommending release on licence. This situation is in sharp contrast to
f the position created under s 62 of the 1967 Act, which deals with the revocation of a
licence by the Secretary of State on the recommendation of the Parole Board. Where
such a revocation does occur, it is provided by s 62(3):

> 'A person recalled to prison . . . may make representations in writing with respect
> to his recall and shall on his return to prison be informed of the reasons for his recall
> and of his right to make such representations.'

g

     There is no equivalent statutory requirement that the Parole Board should give to a
prisoner information as to the reasons for not recommending his release on licence; nor
is there any such requirement that the Secretary of State should do so. The actual
decision is, of course, his, though it is related to the recommendation of the board. By
a late reamendment of the statement of claim there was added to the relief sought a
h prayer for—

> 'a declaration that on the occasion of any interview by a member of the Local
> Review Committee under rule 3 of the Local Review Committee Rules 1967, or by
> a member of the Parole Board under Section 59(4)(*b*) of the Criminal Justice Act,
> 1967, matters which may weigh against the recommendation of a release on licence
j > should be put to the plaintiff except to the extent that the same are against public
> interest.'

     The difficulties to which I have already referred do not disappear by using the
interviewing member of the local review committee as the means of communicating the
reasons. He will not know them save in so far as they are expressed in some cryptic

formula such as 'not recommended on account of nature and circumstances of offence'
or 'risk of re-offending unacceptable'.

It is not easy, even if it were desirable, to give expression to or to define the subjective
reasons in the minds of the members of the board; it is often virtually impossible to
communicate them in exact terms via a third party.

Not only is there no statutory requirement to disclose to a prisoner the reasons for an
adverse recommendation as to release on licence, but I doubt whether there is any
statutory authority to make such a disclosure.

Notwithstanding what I think is a statutory inhibition against disclosing reasons for
not recommending parole, counsel for the plaintiff advanced a powerful argument
founded on the principle of natural justice or fairness in the exercise of administrative
functions. If no disclosure is made to a prisoner, it may be that some adverse factor
which should not in truth relate to him at all may have affected the board's decision; and
the error may survive in records and affect the next consideration of the case and any
succeeding one. He cited *Golder v United Kingdom* (21st February 1975, Publications of
the European Court of Human Rights, Series A, no 18) as an illustration of how matters
may go wrong so that injustice results. However, in the best of regulated procedures
something may sometimes go awry; the question is whether the safeguards against
possible error may not bring greater risks of injustice than what is prevented. A prisoner
might find in being told the reason for refusal a specious and insincere means of creating
a totally misleading impression by his conduct thereafter.

A person sentenced to imprisonment could not *expect* to be released before the due
expiry of his sentence. Since the introduction of parole he may *hope* that part of his
sentence may be served outside prison. If his offence was of a heinous kind, even that
hope will be a frail one. When he seeks release on licence, he cannot undo the past. No
doubt he will strive to convey to the Parole Board all the redeeming and more favourable
aspects of his history. He needs no special information to enable him to do this; nor is
the case he puts forward one to be argued. It will make its impact one way or the
other. Of course the board must act fairly, as must any body discharging a public duty
which affects the interests of individuals. In the well-known case of *R v Gaming Board of
Great Britain, ex parte Benaim* [1970] 2 All ER 528 at 533, [1970] QB 417 at 430, Lord
Denning MR said:

'It is not possible to lay down rigid rules as to when the principles of natural
justice are to apply; nor as to their scope and extent. Everything depends on the
subject-matter.'

In a context in which the public interest may be put at risk by the inopportune release
of a prisoner on licence, no constraints or pressures should weigh on the Parole Board in
coming to what must in the end be a decision in which expediency must be an important
influence.

I agree with the conclusion of McNeil J. I would dismiss the appeal.

BRIGHTMAN LJ. This appeal involves the proper construction and application of
ss 59 to 62 of the Criminal Justice Act 1967 and the Local Review Committee Rules
1967, SI 1967 No 1462. The parole procedure can be summarised as follows.

(1) A prisoner can only be released on licence by a decision of the Secretary of State.
In the case of a person imprisoned for life, the decision of the Secretary of State must be
preceded by consultation with the Lord Chief Justice and the trial judge if available: see
ss 60(1) and 61(1).

(2) Every such decision of the Secretary of State must be preceded by a
'recommendation' of the Parole Board to that effect, unless the case is in the special
category to which s 35 of the Criminal Justice Act 1972 applies; if in that category, the
Home Secretary may reach his decision on the 'recommendation' of the local review
committee instead of the Parole Board.

(3) Every such 'recommendation' of the Parole Board must be preceded by a 'report'

of the local review committee to the Secretary of State: see r 3(3). This 'report' is not a
a 'recommendation'. The statutory function exercised by the committee in relation to
prisoners is 'to report to the Secretary of State on their suitability for release on licence':
see r 1(1). The distinction drawn between a 'recommendation' and a 'suitability report'
clearly emerges from the language of s 59(6)(a) and rr 1(1) and 3(3), which refer to
suitability reports of the local review committee, and ss 60(1) and 61(1) of the 1967 Act
and s 35 of the 1972 Act which refer to recommendations of the Parole Board. The local
b review committee does not make a 'recommendation' except in a s 35 case. The plaintiff
does not fall into the s 35 category. We are not therefore concerned with any
'recommendations' by the local review committee but only with 'suitability reports' by
that body. I shall omit hereafter any reference to the s 35 procedure, although my
conclusions would equally apply to a s 35 case.

(4) The 'recommendation' of the Parole Board is also preceded by an interview
c between a member of the board and the prisoner if the board consider such an interview
necessary: see s 59(4)(b).

(5) Every 'suitability report' of the review committee must be preceded by an
interview between a committee member and the prisoner if the prisoner is willing: see
r 3(1). On this occasion the interview depends not on the decision of the authority but
on the decision of the prisoner.

d (6) On the occasion of his interview by a member of the review committee (if the
interview takes place) the prisoner is to be given 'a reasonable opportunity to make any
representations which he wishes to be considered by the committee': see r 3(2).

(7) Rule 4 gives the prisoner a further right, independent of any interview taking
place, to make written representations to the committee.

The plaintiff was informed in 1975 and 1977 that the Parole Board had decided not to
e recommend his release on licence. As will be seen from my analysis of the Act and the
rules, each such adverse recommendation will have been preceded by a suitability report
by the local review committee. I have laboured the distinction between a 'recommendation' and a 'suitability report' because the Act and the rules clearly draw that distinction,
but it is overlooked in the pleaded case. A suitability report will not necessarily contain
any recommendation at all. It could properly consist, and for all I know may in this case
f consist, only of an assessment of the pros and cons.

The rights which the plaintiff possesses under the Act and the rules therefore include
the following: (i) a right to be considered for release on licence if his case is referred by
the Secretary of State to the local review committee: see r 5; (ii) a right, prior to such
consideration, to be interviewed by a member of the review committee: seer 3(1); (iii) a
right on the occasion of such interview to be given a reasonable opportunity to make any
g representations which he wishes to be considered by the committee: see r 3(2); (iv) a
right independently of such interview to make written representations to the committee
before they review his case: see r 4.

The plaintiff's purpose in these proceedings is to establish his right to know the
reasons, or the gist of the reasons, why he has not in the past been recommended for
release on licence, in order to assist him in the exercise of his statutory right to make
h representations for his future release on licence. The case has proceeded in the pleadings
and to some extent in the argument on the basis that the review committee as well as the
Parole Board have declined to recommend the plaintiff for release on licence. So far as
the Parole Board are concerned, that is correct. The plaintiff does not know, nor do we
know, what recommendations (if any) the review committee have made. That is not
their statutory function in the plaintiff's case.

j A 'right to know' is not expressly given to a prisoner in Payne's situation by any statute
or statutory instrument. Nor is there any general principle of law which imposes on a
decision maker a duty to make known the reasons for his decisions. I agree with what
was said by Sir Robert Megarry V-C in this respect in McInnes v Onslow Fane [1978] 3 All
ER 211 at 219ff, 1 WLR 1520 at 1531ff.

To succeed in this action, therefore, the plaintiff must rely either on the application of

some principle of natural justice or on an implication which ought to be made into the
Act or the rules as a matter of construction. No other foundation for the plaintiff's claim   *a*
has been suggested.

So far as natural justice is concerned, both the board and the committee accept that
they are under a duty to act fairly in the exercise of their statutory functions. So the
question that has to be asked is whether fairness requires that a prisoner in the situation
of the plaintiff ought to be apprised of the reasons why he has not heretofore been
recommended by the board for release on licence, or at least the gist of the reasons, or of   *b*
matters which may tend to weigh against him.

In *Kanda v Government of the Federation of Malaya* [1962] AC 322 the plaintiff, an
inspector of police, had under the constitution of the federation to be heard before being
dismissed from the police service. The Judicial Committee observed (at 337): 'If the
right to be heard is to be a real right which is worth anything, it must carry with it a right
in the accused man to know the case which is made against him.'   *c*

That is the basis of the plaintiff's claim in this present action. In my judgment there
is no close comparison between the two cases. The function of the Parole Board is to
make a recommendation and of the review committee to make a suitability report. In
neither case is it to investigate charges. The board and the committee will each, no
doubt, make an assessment of the prisoner's character and his likely reaction to a free
environment, and also, perhaps more importantly, an assessment of the public interest.   *d*
According to the undisputed evidence, the committee's suitability report, and the board's
recommendation, will be based on a consideration of the prisoner's file, including all
reports which have been made from time to time by prison staff and reports specially
prepared for the review, and also the representations (if any) made by the prisoner. The
suitability report of the review committee and the representations of the prisoner form
part of the material placed before the Parole Board to enable them to exercise an advisory   *e*
function. I can see no principle of fairness which requires that the prisoner should be
informed, even in outline, of the reasons which accompanied previous suitability reports
of the review committee or recommendations of the Parole Board, or of the adverse
matters which may weigh against him. Indeed, the prisoner will be only too well aware
of the adverse factors likely to feature in reports made about him. He will not be better
able to formulate effective representations because he has been told of the character   *f*
assessments and the assessments of the public interest which may also feature in the file.

The scope and extent of the principles of natural justice depend on the subject matter
to which they are sought to be applied; see *R v Gaming Board for Great Britain, ex parte
Benaim* [1970] 2 All ER 528 at 533, [1970] 2 QB 417 at 430. They apply to the present
case, as conceded, to the extent that they impose on the board and the committee, and
each member of it, a duty to act fairly. That duty does not, in my judgment, require that   *g*
any disclosure is made to the prisoner of adverse material which the board and the
committee have in their possession to assist them in their advisory and reporting
functions.

There are other problems in applying the principles of natural justice so as to produce
the results which the plaintiff seeks. One problem would be to define in legally
intelligible language the limits of the disclosure which must be made if the plaintiff is   *h*
right. The local review committee's report will be a report on the plaintiff's suitability
for release on licence. It is not claimed that he is to be given a copy of that report. Is he
to be given a précis of it? If so, why not the whole report? If not a précis, how is one to
define in legal language what has to be given? Much the same questions must be asked
in relation to disclosure of the Parole Board's conclusions on which their recommendation
is founded.   *j*

Once the conclusion is reached that natural justice, ie fairness, does not require
disclosure to be made, it is difficult to see how the same goal can be reached as a matter
of construction of the Act and the rules. As I have said, there is nothing in the Act or the
rules which expressly requires disclosure to be made. So the duty, if it exists, must be an
implied duty. The law is, I think, correctly expressed in Maxwell on Interpretation of
Statutes (12th Edn, 1969, p 33):

a   'It is a corollary to the general rule of literal construction that nothing is to be
           added to or taken from a statute unless there are adequate grounds to justify the
           inference that the legislature intended something which it omitted to express.'

The authority cited for that proposition is an observation in the speech of Lord Mersey
in *Thompson v Goold & Co* [1910] AC 409 at 420: 'It is a strong thing to read into an Act
of Parliament words which are not there, and in the absence of clear necessity it is a
b   wrong thing to do.'
    It was submitted that r 3(2) by necessary implication imposed on the interviewing
member of the committee the obligation to make known to the prisoner the matters
which might weigh against him. The prisoner is to be given 'a reasonable opportunity'
to make representations; that reasonable opportunity is to be given at the interview;
therefore it is to be implied, so the argument runs, that the interviewer is under a duty
to direct the prisoner's attention to those aspects of his case which need to be answered:
c   it is not easy to plead to an undisclosed case. The statement of claim was amended during
the argument in order to raise this point. Clearly the interviewing member of the
committee should brief himself in advance of the interview. So he is likely to know the
probable impediments to release on licence if impediments exist. I found this approach
attractive at one time, and not inconsistent with the common sense of the situation.
    However on reflection I feel no doubt at all that such an implication, even if it could be
d   formulated with sufficient precision, is unjustified in the absence of necessity. There is
no 'necessity' that such an inference should be made, particularly if I am right in
concluding that natural justice does not so require. The system has apparently worked
for the last ten years or more without disclosure being made. I can understand the
argument that disclosure might be helpful to a prisoner who wishes to exercise his
statutory right to make effective representations, but it is not 'necessary'. As Lord
e   Mersey said, it is a strong thing to imply what Parliament has omitted. Furthermore, we
have in s 62(3) of the 1967 Act an express provision that a person who is recalled to prison
shall be informed of the reasons for his recall. He, too, has a statutory right to make
representations. As the duty to give reasons is expressly imposed where recall to prison
is in issue, but not where release on licence is in issue, it seems fairly obvious that the
f   duty was not intended to be imposed in the latter case.
    When this case was restored for further argument, we were referred to the decision in
Golder v United Kingdom (21st February 1975, Publications of the European Court of
Human Rights, Series A, no 18). Golder was serving a term of imprisonment for
robbery. In 1969 a prison riot took place. It was thought that Golder had taken part.
Charges were prepared against him for offences against prison discipline. The charges
were dropped but his prison record referred to their existence and to the fact that they
g   were not proceeded with. In due course Golder was considered for parole but was not
recommended. He complained to the European Commission of Human Rights in
relation to stoppage of mail and refusal of access to a solicitor. Later the abandoned
charges were expunged from his prison record. As I understand it, we were referred to
this case merely to illustrate the truism that misleading material is capable of finding its
h   way into a prisoner's record. This might be an argument for disclosing to a prisoner the
factual matters which appear on his record, so that he can check their accuracy, but it is
not an argument for disclosing to him the assessments, reasons, opinions and
recommendations on his file, which are the material the plaintiff is seeking. The case is
not therefore in my opinion illustrative of anything relevant to this appeal.
    I, too, would dismiss the appeal.

j   *Appeal dismissed.*

Solicitors: *Gulland & Gulland*, Maidstone (for the plaintiff); *Treasury Solicitor*.

Frances Rustin   Barrister.

R v Holt and another   *a*

COURT OF APPEAL, CRIMINAL DIVISION
GRIFFITHS LJ, LAWSON AND BALCOMBE JJ
3rd, 13th MARCH 1981

Criminal law – Theft – Evasion of liability by deception – Attempt – Defendants attempting to   *b*
evade payment of bill for meals in restaurant by deception that meals already paid for –
Defendants charged with intent to make permanent default on liability to pay by attempting to
induce creditor to 'forgo' payment – Defendants convicted of offence charged – Whether
defendants should have been charged with dishonestly securing 'remission' of liability to pay –
Whether evading liability by deception comprising a single offence or consisting of three separate
offences – Theft Act 1978, s 2(1)(a)(b).
                                                                 c

The defendants, who were eating in a restaurant, planned to evade payment for their
meals by the device of pretending to the person asking for payment that they had already
made payment to another member of the restaurant's staff. An off-duty police officer
who was in the restaurant overheard their plan and when the defendants were presented
with the bill and advanced the deception he prevented them from carrying it out. The   *d*
defendants were charged with attempted deception in that with intent to make a
permanent default on an existing liability they had attempted to induce a servant of the
restaurant 'to forgo payment' of the price of the meals by falsely representing that
payment had been made to another servant of the restaurant, contrary to s 2(1)(b)[a] of the
Theft Act 1978. At the close of the Crown's case the defendants submitted that they
should have been charged with attempting to secure 'the remission of the whole or part
of [an] existing liability to make a payment', contrary to s 2(1)(a) of the 1978 Act and   *e*
should not have been charged under s 2(1)(b) because if their attempt had succeeded their
liability to pay for the meals would have been 'remitted' within s 2(1)(a) and not merely
'forgone' under s 2(1)(b), and further submitted that the former term imported different
legal consequences from the latter term. The trial judge rejected the submission and the
defendants were convicted. They appealed against the convictions.   *f*

Held – Although the offences defined in paras (a), (b) and (c) of s 2(1) of the 1978 Act had
common features, namely the use of deception on a creditor in relation to a liability,
dishonesty in the use of deception, and the use of deception to gain an advantage in time
or money, they were separate offences and there were substantial differences in the
elements of each offence. An intent to make permanent default on the whole or part of
an existing liability was unique to the offence under para (b), and since the jury, on a   *g*
proper direction, had concluded that the defendants' conduct was motivated by the
intent to make permanent default in payment of the bill for their meals, and since the
other elements necessary to constitute an offence under para (b) were present, namely the
use of deception dishonestly to induce a creditor to forgo payment, the defendants had
been properly charged and convicted and their appeals would be dismissed (see p 856 d   *h*
to h and p 857 a, post).
    Per Curiam. The differences between the offences in s 2(1)(a), (b) and (c) relate
principally to the different situations in which the debtor-creditor relationship arises (see
p 856 h j, post).

_____

a   Section 2(1), so far as material, provides: '. . . where a person by any deception—(a) dishonestly   *j*
     secures the remission of the whole or part of any existing liability to make a payment, whether his
     own liability or another's; or (b) with intent to make permanent default in whole or in part on any
     existing liability to make a payment . . . dishonestly induces the creditor or any person claiming
     payment on behalf of the creditor . . . to forgo payment; or (c) dishonestly obtains any exemption
     from or abatement of liability to make a payment; he shall be guilty of an offence.'

Notes

a   For evasion of liability by deception, see Supplement to 11 Halsbury's Laws (4th Edn) para 1279A.

For the Theft Act 1978, s 2, see 48 Halsbury's Statutes (3rd Edn) 313.

Applications for leave to appeal against convictions

b   The appellants, Victor Reginald Holt and Julian Dana Lee, were charged with attempting to evade liability by deception contrary to the common law. The particulars of the offences made it clear that the charges were of attempts to commit an offence under s 2(1)(b) of the Theft Act 1978. On 16th July 1980 in the Crown Court at Liverpool before his Honour Judge Edward Jones the appellants were convicted of the offences charged. They applied for leave to appeal against the convictions on the grounds, inter alia, that on the facts of the case they ought to have been charged under s 2(1)(a) of the

c   1978 Act because (i) s 2(1) created in paras (a), (b) and (c) three separate offences and not one offence, (ii) there was a difference between securing the 'remission' of an existing liability under para (a) and inducing a creditor to 'forgo' payment with intent to make permanent default under para (b) since 'remission' connoted an act of a creditor which had the effect in law of cancelling or extinguishing the legal liability to make the payment in question, whereas 'forgoing' payment did not require or connote any

d   modification of the legal relationship between a creditor and debtor but only a forbearance by the creditor to enforce unaltered rights, and (iii) the Crown had alleged an attempt by the appellants to obtain cancellation of their liability to pay which was conduct contrary to s 2(1)(a) since it was an attempt to secure remission of their liability and not an attempt to induce a forbearance to enforce the debt. The facts are set out in the judgment of the court.

e

Paul C Reid (assigned by the Registrar of Criminal Appeals) for the appellants.
John Leach for the Crown.

f   At the conclusion of argument Griffiths LJ announced that the application would be refused for reasons to be given later.

13th March. **LAWSON J** read the following judgment of the court: Victor Reginald Holt and Julian Dana Lee apply to the full court for leave to appeal against their convictions at the Crown Court at Liverpool on 16th July 1980 of attempting, contrary

g   to the common law, to evade liability by deception, that is to say, an attempt to commit an offence contrary to s 2(1) of the Theft Act 1978. This court granted leave to appeal and treated the hearing of the application as the hearing of the appeal.

The charge on which they were convicted was as follows. The statement of the offence was attempted evasion of liability by deception, contrary to common law. The particulars of the offence were that the appellants, on 9th December 1979, by deception with intent

h   to make permanent default on an existing liability, did attempt to induce Philip Parkinson, servant of Pizzaland Restaurants Ltd, to forgo payment of £3·65 by falsely representing that payment had been made by them to another servant of the said Pizzaland Restaurants Ltd.

From the use of the expressions 'with intent to make permanent default' and 'to induce (the creditor's agent) to forgo payment', it is clear that the attempt charged was

j   one to commit the offence defined by s 2(1)(b) of the 1978 Act.

The facts of the case were that in the evening of 9th December 1979, the appellants consumed meals costing £3·65 in the Pizzaland Restaurant in Southport. There was a police officer off duty also having a meal in the restaurant and he overheard the appellants planning to evade payment for their meals by the device of pretending that a waitress had removed a £5 note which they had placed on the table. When presented with their

bill, the appellants advanced this deception and declined payment. The police officer
concerned prevented them from leaving the restuarant and they were shortly afterwards   *a*
arrested and charged.

At the close of the prosecution case in the Crown Court counsel who has also conducted
this appeal, made a submission which was overruled, the main point of which was that
assuming the facts as we have recounted them to be correct, the attempt to evade thus
emerging was an attempt to commit an offence not under s 2(1)(*b*) as charged but under
s 2(1)(*a*) of the 1978 Act since, he submitted, had the attempt succeeded, the appellants'   *b*
liability to pay for their meals would have been 'remitted' and not just 'forgone', to use
the contrasting terms contained in the respective subsections.

Counsel further developed his submission before us. As we understand it, he submits
that the vital differences between the two offences defined in the first two paragraphs of
s 2(1) of the Act are that 'remission' involves that, first, the creditor who 'remits' the
debtor's existing liability must communicate his decision to the debtor and, second, the   *c*
legal consequence of the 'remission' is to extinguish the debt, whereas the 'forgoing of an
existing liability', to use the words of sub-s 2(1)(*b*), need not be communicated to the
debtor and has not the consequence in law of extinguishing such liability. We find great
difficulty in introducing these concepts into the construction of the subsection. We will
later return to the matter.

Counsel further submitted that the effect of s 2(1) of the Act was to create three   *d*
different offences but conceded that there could be situations in which the conduct of the
debtor or his agent could fall under more than one of the three paragraphs of s 2(1).

The elements of the offence defined by s 2(1)(*b*) of the Act relevant to the present case
are clearly these: first, the defendant must be proved to have the intent to make
permanent default on the whole or part of an existing liability. This element is unique
to s 2(1)(*b*); it has no application to the offences defined in s 2(1)(*a*) or (*c*). Second, given   *e*
such intent, he must use deception. Third, his deception must be practised dishonestly
to induce the creditor to forgo payment.

It must always be remembered that in the present case, whatever offence was being
attempted, the attempt failed. The creditor was not induced by the dishonest deception
and did not forgo payment. It is clear on the evidence that the appellants' conduct
constituted an attempt to evade liability by deception, and the jury, who were properly   *f*
directed, clearly concluded that the appellants' conduct was motivated by the intent to
make permanent default on their supper bill. Thus, all the elements needed to enable an
attempt to commit the offence defined in s 2(1)(*b*) were found to be present, so that the
appellants were rightly convicted as charged.

Reverting to the construction of s 2(1) of the Act, as to which the commentators are
not at one, we are not sure whether the choice of expressions describing the consequences   *g*
of deception employed in each of its paragraphs, namely in para (*a*) 'secures the remission
of any existing liability', in para (*b*) 'induces a creditor to forgo payment' and in para (*c*)
'obtains any exemption from liability', are simply different ways of describing the same
end result or represent conceptual differences.

Whilst it is plain that there are substantial differences in the elements of the three
offences defined in s 2(1), they show these common features: first, the use of deception   *h*
to a creditor in relation to a liability, second, dishonesty in the use of deception, and
third, the use of deception to gain some advantage in time or money. Thus the
differences between the offences relate principally to the different situations in which the
debtor-creditor relationship has arisen.

The practical difficulty which counsel's submissions for the appellants failed to
confront is strikingly illustrated by cases of attempting to commit an offence under   *j*
s 2(1)(*a*) or s 2(1)(*b*). If, as he submits, s 2(1)(*a*) requires communication of remission to
the debtor, whereas s 2(1)(*b*) does not require communication of the 'forgoing of payment'
but, as the case is a mere attempt, the matter does not *end* in remission of liability or
forgoing of payment, then the prosecution would be in a dilemma since it would either
be impossible to charge such an attempt or the prosecution would be obliged to charge

a   attempts in the alternative in which case, since any attempt failed, it would be quite uncertain which of the alternatives it was.

These appeals are accordingly dismissed.

Applications for leave to appeal granted. Appeals dismissed.

Solicitors: *R H Nicholson*, Liverpool.

b

Sepala Munasinghe Esq   Barrister.

c

Foley v Foley

COURT OF APPEAL, CIVIL DIVISION
EVELEIGH, WATKINS LJJ AND SIR DAVID CAIRNS
15th, 18th MAY 1981

d   *Divorce – Financial provision – Conduct of parties – Duty of court to have regard to conduct – Conduct prior to ceremony of marriage – Relevance – Weight to be given to premarital cohabitation – Parties cohabiting as a family for seven years before marrying – Marriage lasting five years – Whether two periods should be treated differently – Matrimonial Causes Act 1973, s 25(1).*

e   The husband and the wife began living together in 1962 when each was married to someone else. They lived together for some seven years, until their marriage in 1969, and during that period had three children. The husband owned an investment property (worth £62,000 at the date of trial) which the wife helped to renovate and manage during the period of cohabitation. The property provided a substantial income from lettings and was the most substantial family asset. The parties had a good standard of
f   living during the period of cohabitation and marriage. In 1974 the marriage broke down and was dissolved in 1977, following which the husband remarried. At the date of trial the wife was aged 40 and earning £90 per week as a hairdresser. She lived in a rented flat, had realisable assets of £10,000 and for some years to come would be able to maintain the style of life she had previously enjoyed. The husband was aged 52, was not working because of ill health, and was being supported by his new wife, a nurse. His
g   only asset was the investment property and he and his new wife planned to buy and run a smallholding. The wife applied for ancillary relief, contending that the appropriate starting point for calculating the amount to be awarded to her, having regard to the combined period of cohabitation and marriage, was one-third of the assets of the parties (ie £14,000). The judge rejected that approach and awarded the wife a lump sum payment of £10,000. In doing so the judge differentiated between the periods of
h   marriage and cohabitation. The wife appealed, contending that the judge had failed to take into account or give sufficient weight to the period of cohabitation.

Held – The two periods of cohabitation and marriage were not the same and, whereas the court was expressly required by s 25(1)[a] of the Matrimonial Causes Act 1973 to have regard to 'the duration of the marriage', the period of cohabitation was merely one of the
j   other 'circumstances' to which the court was required to have regard, and the weight to be attached to the period of cohabitation as one of the other circumstances of the case was a matter for the court's discretion. The court was entitled to take the view that what happened during the period of cohabitation did not carry the same weight as the events

---

a   Section 25(1), so far as material, is set out at p 861 *d e*, post

during the period of marriage, although where the parties were unable to legitimise the relationship the court could take into account what happened during the period of *a* cohabitation as a very weighty factor. Since the judge had not dismissed the period of cohabitation as irrelevant but had merely decided to attach less weight to it than to the period of marriage, he had not been wrong in the exercise of his discretion. Nor had the judge been wrong in refusing to apply the one-third principle since it was not a rule of law, and he had taken into account all the proper considerations in arriving at a lump sum figure of £10,000. The appeal would accordingly be dismissed (see p 861 *e* to p 862 *b* *d*, post).

Campbell v Campbell [1977] 1 All ER 1 and Kokosinski v Kokosinski [1980] 1 All ER 1106 considered.

Notes

For financial provision after a decree of divorce and matters which the court must have *c* regard, see 13 Halsbury's Laws (4th Edn) para 1060.

For the calculation of the amount to be awarded by way of financial provision, see ibid, para 1066.

For the Matrimonial Causes Act 1973, s 25, see 43 Halsbury's Statutes (3rd Edn) 567.

Cases referred to in judgments

Campbell v Campbell [1977] 1 All ER 1, [1976] Fam 347, [1976] 3 WLR 572, Digest (Cont *d* Vol E) 264, 6614*b*.

Kokosinski v Kokosinski [1980] 1 All ER 1106, [1980] Fam 72, [1980] 3 WLR 55.

Cases also cited

Dipper v Dipper [1980] 2 All ER 722, [1981] Fam 31, CA.

O'Donnell v O'Donnell [1975] 2 All ER 993, sub nom O'D v O'D [1976] Fam 83, CA.   *e*

Interlocutory appeal

The wife, Annick Rouillon Foley, appealed against an order of Balcombe J made in chambers on 12th December 1980 whereby on an application by the wife for ancillary relief he ordered that the husband, Anthony Michael Foley, should pay the wife a lump sum of £10,000 by 30th June 1981 and that he should pay the wife's costs up to 8th *f* October 1980 and thereafter that both parties should pay their own costs. The facts are set out in the judgment of Eveleigh LJ.

Joseph Jackson QC and *Peter Warburton-Jones* for the wife.
Roger Gray QC and *Isaac Jacob* for the husband.

g
EVELEIGH LJ. In this case the wife claimed a lump sum and agreed that her claim for periodical payments should be dismissed. The learned judge awarded her the sum of £10,000, ordered that her application for periodical payments should be dismissed and also ordered that there be a payment of £7·50 per week to the son D'Arcy until he attained 17 years of age. He also ordered that the husband should pay the wife's costs up to but not beyond 8th October 1980.   *h*

The husband was 52 years of age at the date of the hearing in December 1980 and the wife 40. The wife was French. She came to England in 1960. She was a trained hairdresser. On 2nd May 1961 she married a Mr Nunn in Edinburgh. It was a marriage of convenience. She never lived with Mr Nunn, but in 1962 she started to live with Mr Foley, who was himself a married man. In March 1963 a daughter Natasha was born. At first Mr Foley denied parentage but he later accepted her as his child. In 1963 Mr *j* Foley's marriage was dissolved. On 26th February 1966 the son D'Arcy Lord Foley was born. On 11th June 1969 a son Carl was born. On 8th August 1969 the parties married. In 1974 they separated. In December 1976 there was a decree nisi and in 1977 the decree was made absolute. Mr Foley married again in October 1977.

The husband had an unusual career with various occupations. He was described as a bullion dealer, a firearms dealer, a dealer in antiques. He and the wife lived well during

the period of their cohabitation and the period of their marriage. At first they lived in
a mews flat at 12 Pindock Mews, London W9. In 1972 they moved to a spacious flat in
Ashworth Mansions, London W9. That was a rented flat and the wife now lives there.
In 1959, before meeting his wife, Mr Foley bought a freehold property, 55 Upper
Montague Street, London W1, for £5,250. He and his first wife converted the ground
floor to a sandwich bar and they let it and it remains let. The top two floors were in a bad
condition. They were let, however, on controlled tenancies. In the mid-1960s the
second Mrs Foley, who was, of course, not at that date married to Mr Foley, helped in the
renovation of the upper floor of that property and Mr Foley spent some £45,000 on
improvements. The wife (and I shall call her 'the wife' for the purposes of this judgment)
helped in furnishing those flats and in the decoration and she collected the rents when
they fell due.

Today, as the learned judge has found, the wife is an attractive woman, who dresses
well. She is employed as a hairdresser in the Edgware Road at £75 a week and the
learned judge estimated that she received tips of about £15 a week. She lives in the flat
and she has the furniture. The learned judge made this finding, that the wife will be able
to maintain the style of life that she has enjoyed over the last few years for some years to
come. He assessed her capital at £10,000 and this was jewellery, paintings, a fur coat and
some cash, her current realisable assets, as the learned judge called them. The two boys,
because the daughter, it will be appreciated, was of responsible years, at first lived with
the husband but in 1980 D'Arcy went to live with the wife.

As to the husband, he was in arrears for maintenance to his first wife and the learned
judge found that his free assets did not exceed his debts. He had the property 55 Upper
Montague Street, which was valued or, as the learned judge found, was worth £62,500
after allowing for capital gains tax. At the time of the hearing the husband was not
earning. It is said that he had hypertension and back trouble. The learned judge
accepted that he was indeed not earning and was unable to work certainly at that time.
However, it seems that he regarded the husband's condition with some scepticism, but
he made no positive finding as to what the husband's future prospects were. Having said
that, it is quite clear from his judgment that he did not regard them as good from a
financial point of view. He said that the present wife was the breadwinner. She is a
nurse and a lady with some veterinary knowledge. The husband and the present Mrs
Foley have in mind buying a smallholding in the country and running that. As I have
said, the learned judge came to the conclusion that the proper sum to award the wife was
£10,000.

The wife now appeals and the first ground of her appeal is to the effect that the learned
judge failed to take into account the period of cohabitation, that is to say, the period
when the parties were living together before the marriage. It is said 'the learned judge
was wrong in law in that he held that he should only take into account the five years of
actual marriage, whereas the parties had cohabited between 1962 and 1969 and (a) the
three children of the family were born during the said seven year period of cohabitation
and (b) the learned judge had found that the petitioner was at all times a "good mother
and housewife" and had helped the respondent with the renovation and management of
the house at 55 Upper Montague Street, which house had not only provided significant
income from lettings but also, by the time of the hearing, constituted the most substantial
family asset; (c) the petitioner had helped the respondent in his business activities'.

It was further pleaded that the learned judge was wrong in holding that one-third was
not an appropriate starting point for computing the appropriate lump sum. The notice
of appeal goes on to say: 'On the figures of disposable capital found by the learned judge
an application of the "one-third" principle would have given the petitioner £14,000
instead of £10,000.' Then the notice of appeal specifies certain matters of fact which it
is said should have influenced the learned judge's judgment to be more favourable to the
wife. It is not necessary to go into those in detail.

The gravamen of the criticism of the learned judge was that he failed to take into
account or give sufficient weight to the period of cohabitation. It is, therefore, necessary
to see what he in fact said in that regard. He said:

'The first question I have to decide is: what length of marriage do I take? I have
already given the facts; that they started living together in 1962 when each was   *a*
married to somebody else. They lived as a family unit and did not get married until
1969, and the marriage broke up in 1974.'

Balcombe J then referred to what Baker P said in *Campbell v Campbell* [1977] 1 All ER 1
at 6, [1976] Fam 347 at 352:

'Counsel for Mrs Campbell attempts to persuade me that the 3½ years of   *b*
premarital cohabitation should be taken into account in assessing the length of the
marriage. The way he puts it is: "She was for 3½ years performing wifely duties
before marriage." Now I entirely reject that argument. This was a married woman
with a large number of children, most of them in care, living with a youngster.
There is an increasing tendency, I have found in cases in chambers, to regard and,
indeed, to speak of the celebration of marriage as "the paper work". The phrase   *c*
used is: "We were living together but we never got round to the paper work." Well
that is, to my mind, an entirely misconceived outlook. It is the ceremony of
marriage and the sanctity of marriage which count; rights, duties and obligations
begin on the marriage and not before. It is a complete cheapening of the marriage
relationship, which I believe, and I am sure many share this belief, is essential to the
well-being of our society as we understand it, to suggest that premarital periods,   *d*
particularly in the circumstances of this case, should, as it were, by a doctrine of
relation back of matrimony, be taken as a part of marriage to count in favour of the
wife performing, as it is put, "wifely duties before marriage". So it comes to this
that I take this as a marriage of two years and a month or two, and it ended.'

Balcombe J after quoting that passage, said: *e*

'I would say with respect that I wholly agree with everything that is said there.
Campbell v Campbell was distinguished in a recent case before Wood J of *Kokosinski v
Kokosinski* [1980] 1 All ER 1106, [1980] Fam 72, where the facts were exceptional.'

Balcombe J then read the headnote to *Kokosinski v Kokosinski* [1980] Fam 72–73):   *f*

'The respondent husband left Poland in 1939, leaving behind a wife and child,
and settled in this country. In 1947 he began to live with the petitioner, and their
son was born in 1950. During the period of cohabitation the petitioner was faithful,
loving and hard-working. She played a significant role in building up the husband's
business and from her earnings she contributed substantially to the maintenance of
the household. In 1969 the husband's Polish wife divorced him and in 1971 the   *g*
husband and petitioner were married. Early in 1972 cohabitation ceased and, in
1977, the petitioner obtained a decree nisi on the grounds of the husband's desertion
... *Held*, that section 25(1) of the Matrimonial Causes Act 1973 required the court
not only to consider the duration of the marriage but "all the circumstances of the
case" and the conduct of the parties; that the facts that the petitioner had been
loving, faithful and hardworking over many years and had helped to build up the   *h*
family business were matters to be taken into account under the subsection ...'

Balcombe J then commented:

'Again with respect, I would not wish in any way to dissent from that conclusion   .
on the facts of that case, and of course it is clear that one has to take into account all   *j*
the circumstances of the case, s 25 says I should do so, and indeed I have endeavoured
to do so.'

So for my part I would far from consider the learned judge to be saying that the years
of cohabitation were irrelevant. He says that all the circumstances must be taken into
account and he had endeavoured to do so, but he then went on to say:

'But in so far as s 25(1)(d) refers to the duration of the marriage for my part I am
not prepared to treat this as a marriage which subsisted more than the five years
which it actually subsisted, by which I mean from the date of the marriage to the
date of the break-up.'

What he is saying, as I understand it, is not that the other matters are irrelevant, that the
period of cohabitation and contributions of the wife during that period are irrelevant.
He is saying, however, that the duration of the marriage begins with the date of the
ceremony.

It is clear to my mind that the learned judge was regarding the period of cohabitation
as relevant. He finished by saying:

'Contributions made by each to the welfare of the family I have really covered.
During the period they were living together it is not suggested that the wife was
other than a good mother to the children and a good housekeeper. At the end of the
day I have to take some figure.'

He arrived at the figure of £10,000 and went on to say: 'It gives some adequate
recognition to her contributions to the family, so long as there was a family.' Again I do
not regard those words as limited to the period of the duration of the marriage.

He did, however, differentiate between marriage and cohabitation and he was doing
so in the light of the wording of s 25(1) of the Matrimonial Causes Act 1973, which reads:

'It shall be the duty of the court in deciding whether to exercise its powers under
section 23(1)(a), (b) or (c) or 24 above in relation to a party to the marriage and, if so,
in what manner, to have regard to all the circumstances of the case including the
following matters, that is to say . . . (d) the age of each party to the marriage and the
duration of the marriage.'

Does the fact that the learned judge clearly differentiated between cohabitation and
marriage invalidate his judgment? In my view, the two periods, namely cohabitation
and marriage, are not the same. What weight will be given to matters that occurred
during those periods will be for the learned judge to decide in the exercise of his
discretion, but one cannot say that those two periods are the same. Ten years of
cohabitation will not necessarily have the same effect as ten years of marriage. During
the period of cohabitation the parties were free to come and go as they pleased. This is
not so where there is a marriage. In the great majority of cases public opinion would
readily recognise a stronger claim founded on years of marriage than on years of
cohabitation. On the other hand, in deciding these difficult financial problems there
may be cases where the inability of the parties to sanctify and legitimise their relationship
calls for a measure of sympathy which will enable the court to take what has happened
during the period of cohabitation into account as a very weighty factor. *Kokosinski v
Kokosinski* is one such case. *Campbell v Campbell* is certainly not.

I do not regard Balcombe J as saying that the years of cohabitation are irrelevant. He
simply says that they are not years of marriage within s 25(1)(d). That section requires
the court to have regard to all the circumstances. Circumstances may be relevant for
consideration in one case which would not be relevant in another, and the two cases,
Campbell v Campbell and *Kokosinski v Kokosinski*, provide examples of this. But the matters
specifically listed in s 25 will always be relevant, because Parliament has said so.

I therefore see no error in the approach of the learned judge to the problem and I
cannot say that he wrongly exercised his discretion in this case, in so far, for the moment,
as he considered what weight should be given to the years of cohabitation.

But the second ground of appeal is that the learned judge should have started on the
basis that one-third was the proper proportion for the wife. Counsel for the wife argued
that, starting from one-third, the wife, on the facts of this case, should actually have
received more than the £14,000 which a 'one-third' calculation would have produced,
and he referred the court to the authorities relating to the 'one-third' proportion. As I see
it, one-third in many cases is a very useful starting point for the court in deciding what

should be the final figure. It is a useful proportion to take and then adjust one way or another as the case demands. But it is in no way a rule of law, as I see it. It is an aid to *a* the mental process when arriving at the appropriate figure and there are many cases where the 'one third' figure would not enter the mind of the court, because it would be obvious from the start that the proportion would be nothing like that. For example, the young marriage that lasts but a day or two. It is an extreme case but it is not unknown in this court. So I do not find it possible to criticise the learned judge because he in fact said that he did not regard one-third as the starting point in this case.   *b*

In so far as an overall criticism is made of the figure at which he arrived, I find myself unable to support that criticism. The learned judge made an important finding, that the wife could maintain herself for some years in the manner to which she had been accustomed while living with the husband. The capital which the husband will retain in this case is in fact for him a source of income and that I regard as a very important consideration. But I find no need in this case, indeed I do not think that I am called on, *c* to go through the exercise of arriving at a figure that I would have awarded. Suffice it to say that the learned judge did have all the proper considerations in mind. He arrived at a figure which, to my mind, is wholly tenable and I can see no reason for interfering with his discretion. Therefore, in relation to the appeal as to the lump sum, I would dismiss it.

There is another subject matter of appeal and that relates to the costs of the action. *d* Counsel for the wife says it was wrong of the learned judge to deprive the wife of her costs against the husband after October 1980, because, he says, the wife was not given sufficient information by the husband, indeed he says the husband concealed the true position, on which the wife, or her advisers, could assess the value of her claim. It is said, and rightly said, that the husband stated the house, 55 Upper Montague Street, to be worth only £15,000. It is said that the husband had not made tax returns for some years, *e* although he led the wife and her advisers to think that tax returns could reveal useful information. But the centre of this matter is the value of the house. On 9th August 1979 the husband made an offer of £10,000. At the end of that year the wife's solicitors were informed that there had been an offer of £105,000 for the house. There was not a sale. There was some disagreement, it is not necessary to go into the details, between the husband and the wife as to who should have control, and to what extent, of the proceeds *f* of that sale. On 25th July 1980 the wife's solicitors were told that there had been another offer, this time of £75,000. There had been an order under which the wife's surveyor could inspect the property and consequentially value it. On 14th November 1980 the wife's solicitors were saying that the property was worth £80,000. After the trial had started, I think I am right in saying two days after, a figure of £80,000 was agreed between the parties as the value of that house.   *g*

In those circumstances, it seems to me that the wife did have available to her all the necessary information, or the means of obtaining the necessary information, in order to decide what was the proper figure for her to accept. For myself, I think the learned judge was right in refusing to limit the husband's liability for costs to the date of the first offer on 9th August 1979, and I see no reason to criticise him in the exercise of his discretion in saying that there had to be a line drawn somewhere and the proper place to draw it was *h* in October 1980, as indeed he did.

I therefore would dismiss this appeal on that matter also.

WATKINS LJ. I agree.

SIR DAVID CAIRNS. I also agree.   *j*

Appeal dismissed. Husband to pay to wife the lump sum of £10,000 by 31st August 1981.

Solicitors: *Heald & Nickinson* (for the wife); *Elfords* (for the husband).

Mary Rose Plummer   Barrister.

R v Cunningham

HOUSE OF LORDS

LORD HAILSHAM OF ST MARYLEBONE LC, LORD WILBERFORCE, LORD SIMON OF GLAISDALE, LORD EDMUND-DAVIES AND LORD BRIDGE OF HARWICH

2nd, 3rd, 4th JUNE, 8th JULY 1981

Criminal law – Murder – Intent – Grievous bodily harm – Intent to cause grievous bodily harm – Accused not intending to kill – Whether sufficient mens rea for murder.

The appellant attacked the deceased in a public house and hit him repeatedly with a chair. The deceased died from his injuries and the appellant was charged with murder. The attack was motivated by jealousy but the appellant claimed that he did not intend to kill the deceased. At his trial the judge directed the jury that if the appellant was found to have intended really serious harm to the deceased he ought to be convicted of murder. He was convicted and appealed to the Court of Appeal, contending that the judge had misdirected the jury. The Court of Appeal dismissed his appeal and he appealed to the House of Lords, contending that murder ought to be restricted to cases where an accused desired or foresaw the likely consequences of his act as being the death of another, and thus that the Crown ought to be required to prove an intention to kill or to endanger life before the accused could properly be convicted of murder. The appellant submitted that previous House of Lords authorities contrary to his contention ought to be overruled.

Held – In order to prove intent in the crime of murder it was sufficient for the Crown to establish an intention to cause grievous bodily harm, even though such intention might fall short of an intention to kill or to endanger life (see p 868 *g* to *j*, p 870 *e* and *h* to p 871 *d g h* and p 872 *b* to *d*, post).

R v Vickers [1957] 2 All ER 741, *Director of Public Prosecutions v Smith* [1960] 3 All ER 161 and *Hyam v Director of Public Prosecutions* [1974] 2 All ER 41 approved.

Observations on overruling previous House of Lords decisions and the practice of maintaining stare decisis, especially in the criminal law (see p 870 *e* to *h* and p 871 *d* to *g*, post); *Note (judgment: judicial decision as authority: House of Lords)* [1966] 3 All ER 77 referred to.

Notes

For the mental element of murder, see 11 Halsbury's Laws (4th Edn) para 1157, and for cases on the subject, see 15 Digest (Reissue) 1109–1111, 9313–9338.

Cases referred to in opinions

Director of Public Prosecutions v Smith [1960] 3 All ER 161, [1961] AC 290, [1960] 3 WLR 546, 124 JP 473, 44 Cr App R 261, HL, 15 Digest (Reissue) 1133, 9569.

Hyam v Director of Public Prosecutions [1974] 2 All ER 41, [1975] AC 55, [1974] 2 WLR 607, 138 JP 374, 59 Cr App R 91, 15 Digest (Reissue) 1111, 9338.

Knuller (Publishing, Printing and Promotions) Ltd v Director of Public Prosecutions [1972] 2 All ER 898, [1973] AC 435, [1972] 3 WLR 143, 136 JP 728, 56 Cr App R 633, HL, 14(1) Digest (Reissue) 140, 966.

La Fontaine v R (1976) 136 CLR 62, HC of Aust.

Miliangos v George Frank (Textiles) Ltd [1975] 3 All ER 801, [1976] AC 443, [1975] 3 WLR 758, [1976] 1 Lloyd's Rep 201, HL, Digest (Cont Vol D) 571, 678b.

R v Ashman (1858) 1 F & F 88, 175 ER 638, 15 Digest (Reissue) 1180, 10,070.

R v Malcherek, R v Steel p 422, ante, [1981] 1 WLR 690, CA.

R v Metharam [1961] 3 All ER 200, 45 Cr App R 304, CCA, 15 Digest (Reissue) 1183, 10,110.

R v Vickers [1957] 2 All ER 741, [1957] 2 QB 664, [1957] 3 WLR 326, 121 JP 510, 41 Cr App R 189, CCA, 15 Digest (Reissue) 1110, 9324.

Shaw v Director of Public Prosecutions [1961] 2 All ER 446, [1962] AC 220, [1961] 2 WLR
    897, 125 JP 437, 45 Cr App R 113, HL, 14(1) Digest (Reissue) 139, 965.   *a*
Woolmington v Director of Public Prosecutions [1935] AC 462, [1935] All ER Rep 1, 104
    LJKB 433, 153 LT 232, 25 Cr App R 72, 30 Cox CC 234, HL, 14(2) Digest (Reissue)
    474, 3919.

Appeal

Anthony Barry Terence Cunningham appealed against the decision of the Court of   *b*
Appeal, Criminal Division (Lord Lane CJ, Boreham and Ewbank JJ) on 4th December
1980 dismissing his appeal against conviction by the Crown Court at Maidstone before
Lawson J and a jury on 18th February 1980 of the offence of murder. The Court of
Appeal refused leave to appeal to the House of Lords but certified, under s 33(2) of the
Criminal Appeal Act 1968, that a point of law of general public importance was involved
in the decision. On 19th March 1981 the Appeal Committee of the House of Lords gave   *c*
the appellant leave to appeal against the decision. The facts are set out in the opinion of
Lord Hailsham LC.

Giles Rooke QC and *Anthony Speaight* for the appellant.
Louis Blom-Cooper QC and *Laurence Giovene* for the Crown.

                                                                     d

Their Lordships took time for consideration.

8th July. The following opinions were delivered.

LORD HAILSHAM OF ST MARYLEBONE LC. My Lords, on 14th February
1980 the appellant was arraigned on an indictment accusing him of the murder of a   *e*
Persian national named Korosh Amine Natghie (known as 'Kim') on 8th October 1979.
There was a second count of unlawful wounding with which we are not concerned. To
the charge of murder the appellant pleaded that he was indeed guilty of the manslaughter
of Kim, but that he was not guilty of his murder. He was tried before Lawson J and a
Kent jury and on 18th February 1980 he was duly convicted of murder. His appeal
against conviction was dismissed by the Court of Appeal, Criminal Division, consisting   *f*
of Lord Lane CJ, Boreham and Ewbank JJ on 4th December 1980. They refused leave to
appeal to the House of Lords, but certified that the following point of law of general
public importance was involved in the appeal, viz: 'Whether a person is guilty of murder
by reason of his unlawfully killing another intending to do grievous bodily harm.'
    On 19th March 1981 the appellant was given leave to appeal by an Appeal Committee
of your Lordships' House. In these circumstances the appeal comes before your   *g*
Lordships for decision.
    Broadly speaking the facts are not in dispute. The victim died on 8th October 1979
when, in view of the fact that he was virtually already dead, the breathing machine on
which he had been placed on 5th October was finally switched off. Kim's death was due
to a fracture of the base of the skull and a subdural haemorrhage as the result of an
incident on 30th September 1979 at the Royal Albion public house, Margate. These   *h*
injuries were caused by blows received from the appellant, which included repeated
blows from a chair or part of a chair, some of which were inflicted while Kim lay
defenceless on the ground. The attack by the appellant on Kim was unprovoked, but
motivated by jealousy. The appellant suspected Kim, wrongly it seems, of associating
sexually with the appellant's former mistress whom the appellant planned to marry.
    At no time did the appellant deny the attack or that the attack was the cause of   *j*
death. The point decided by the Court of Appeal in *R v Malcherek* p 422, ante, was
neither taken nor argued. From the start, however, he asserted that he had not intended
to kill the deceased. There was, however, ample evidence from which the jury could
infer, as they evidently did, that he did intend to inflict grievous bodily harm, whether
or not this is defined as 'really serious injury'.

Constrained by previous authorities, Lawson J directed the jury that the sole question
a for them was:

'As a matter of law, the question of fact on which your verdict depends is solely
this . . . at the time when the defendant inflicted the injuries on Kim . . . did he
intend to do him really serious harm? If the answer to that question is Yes, you find
him guilty of murder. If the answer to the question is No, then you find him not
b guilty of murder, but guilty of manslaughter.'

There were further directions to the same effect later in the summing up, and on a
subsequent request by the jury for further instruction on the difference between murder
and manslaughter, but they do not alter the point at issue. This direction was rightly
characterised by Lord Lane CJ in the course of delivering the judgment of the Court of
Appeal as 'by reason of a number of decisions . . . binding on this court . . . correct and
c impeccable'. The sole question, therefore, for your Lordships' House is whether these
decisions, binding on both courts below, were correctly or wrongly decided. The
assumption which must be made for the purpose of determining the appeal is that the
appellant in inflicting the fatal injuries on the deceased did intend to inflict really serious
injury, but did not intend to kill him. In the circumstances of the judge's direction,
there can be no question of applying the proviso.

d   Murder has been traditionally defined as unlawful killing with malice aforethought.
It was this element of malice aforethought which rendered the offence unclergiable after
the reign of Henry VIII (see my speech in *Hyam v Director of Public Prosecutions* [1974] 2
All ER 41 at 45, [1975] AC 55 at 66). It is, of course, common ground that malice
aforethought at least includes an intention to kill. The question is how nearly to this
intention malice must be confined to constitute the offence of murder. The Homicide
e Act 1957 abolished the species of malice known as 'constructive' but it has hitherto been
accepted doctrine that the 1957 Act did not abolish the doctrine, in my view rather
unfortunately, known as 'implied malice': see s 1(1) of the Act, *R v Vickers* [1957] 2 All
ER 741 at 743–744, [1957] 2 QB 664 at 671–672 and *Hyam*. I call the label unfortunate
because the 'malice' in an intention to cause grievous bodily harm is surely express
enough. The question is whether the fact that it falls short of an intention to kill and
f may fall short of an intent to endanger life is enough to exclude an unlawful killing
resulting from an act inspired by this intention from the ambit of the crime of
murder. The intermediate doctrine which adds on an intention to endanger life to the
positive intention to kill as sufficient mens rea to complete the offence need not be
considered until I consider Lord Diplock's dissenting speech in *Hyam*. At the other end
of the spectrum, it is established that, since s 8 of the Criminal Justice Act 1967, the test
g whether malice is express or implied is subjective (see *Hyam*). The definition of grievous
bodily harm means 'really serious bodily harm' in current English usage (see *Director of
Public Prosecutions v Smith* [1960] 3 All ER 161, [1961] AC 290, *R v Metharam* [1961] 3 All
ER 200, *Hyam v Director of Public Prosecutions* [1974] 2 All ER 41 at 46–47, [1975] AC 55
at 68, all disapproving *R v Ashman* (1858) 1 F & F 88, 175 ER 638).

Counsel for the appellant understandably founded his case on the powerful dissenting
h opinion of Lord Diplock in *Hyam*, concurred in by Lord Kilbrandon, and asked, if
necessary, your Lordships to avail themselves of the practice direction on judicial
precedent (*Note* [1966] 3 All ER 77, [1966] 1 WLR 1234) to give effect to it. I say 'if
necessary', because counsel properly drew our attention to the somewhat Delphic
italicised phrase employed by Lord Cross ([1974] 2 All ER 41 at 72, [1975] AC 55 at 98)
in adding his weight to the opinions of what became the majority in an otherwise
j equally divided House. In order to dispose first of this minor point I do not believe that
your Lordships could give effect to the submission of counsel that *R v Vickers* was
wrongly decided without invoking the practice direction. However apparently
ambiguous the italicised phrase, there is no doubt on which side Lord Cross's vote was
cast, and, even if there were any doubt about this, *Vickers* was effectively indorsed by
your Lordships' House in *Director of Public Prosecutions v Smith*, which for this purpose has

not been overtaken by the Criminal Justice Act 1967. In order to determine the appeal in favour of the appellant and to give effect to Lord Diplock's opinion it would be *a* necessary, in my view, not merely to override *Vickers* but to disregard the indorsement of it in *Smith* and *Hyam* notwithstanding that the exact point in *Hyam* was concerned with the proposition formulated in art 264(*b*) in Stephen's Digest of the Criminal Law (9th Edn, 1950, p 212), whilst the present case is concerned with the part of the proposition in art 264(*a*). (As to these, see the quotation which follows.)

Before I embark on an analysis of Lord Diplock's argument, on your Lordships' *b* attitude to which, substantially, I regard the appellant's case to stand or fall, there are one or two preliminary observations as to the history of the crime of homicide and the language employed in defining them on which I would desire to comment. As I pointed out in *Hyam* [1974] 2 All ER 41 at 45, [1975] AC 55 at 66, the expression 'malice aforethought', in whatever tongue expressed, is unfortunate since neither the word 'malice' nor the word 'aforethought' is construed in its ordinary sense. In construing the *c* word 'aforethought' an intention to kill or, if Lord Diplock's dissenting opinion be followed, to endanger life, however lacking in premeditation, is admittedly enough to constitute the mens rea in murder in the absence of the availability of such mitigating factors as self-defence, provocation, insanity or diminished responsibility, notwithstanding that, five minutes before his act, the killer may have been innocent of any such intention. As regards 'malice', the necessary intention for the purposes of the present *d* appeal is either an intention to kill or endanger life (as Lord Diplock's speech in *Hyam* would have had it) or the intention to kill or cause really serious harm (or the addition to it decided in *Hyam*) as the five-judge Court of Appeal and your Lordships' House have decided it to be in *Vickers, Smith* and *Hyam* respectively. Each state of mind is something which may exist without the assailant being consciously activated by 'malice' in the popular sense of the word. *e*

Stephen's Digest of the Criminal Law (9th Edn by L F Sturge, 1950, pp 211–213, art 264) defined 'malice aforethought' as follows:

'Murder is homicide not excused or justified by the exceptions laid down in Chapter XXX, and with malice aforethought as hereinafter defined.

'Malice aforethought means any one or more of the following states of mind *f* preceding or co-existing with the act or omission by which death is caused, and it may exist where that act is unpremeditated. (*a*) An intention to cause the death of, or grievous bodily harm to, any person, whether such person is the person actually killed or not [this is the state of mind affirmed in *Vickers*]; (*b*) knowledge that the act which causes death will probably cause the death of, or grievous bodily harm to, some person, whether such person is the person actually killed or not, although such knowledge is accompanied by indifference whether death or grievous bodily harm *g* is caused or not, or by a wish that it may not be caused [this is approximately the state of mind affirmed in *Hyam*]; (*c*) an intent to commit any felony whatever; (*or* SUBMITTED an intent to commit any felony of such a kind that the actual commission thereof would involve the use or at least the threat of force against the person killed) [this state of mind was excluded by the Homicide Act 1957]; (*d*) an intent to oppose *h* by force any officer of justice on his way to, in, or returning from the execution of the duty of arresting, keeping in custody, or imprisoning any person whom he is lawfully entitled to arrest, keep in custody, or imprison, or the duty of keeping the peace or dispersing an unlawful assembly, provided that the offender has notice that the person killed is such an officer so employed [this state of mind too was excluded by the Homicide Act 1957].'

j

This definition was the result of a long and careful research into the earlier cases and authors, beinning with Coke and ending with East, as set out at length in Stephen's original Note XIV (now Note VIII in Mr Sturge's edition). It represents the author's view of what the law of murder was independently of the doctrine of 'constructive malice' contained in paras (*c*) and (*d*) of the definition now effectively abolished by the Homicide Act 1957.

By the time *Vickers* was decided, the terminology of the law thus recognised three
a classes of malice aforethought as sufficient to constitute the crime of murder, viz 'express',
'implied' and 'constructive' malice, the last mentioned, as I have said, having been
abolished by the Homicide Act 1957, but corresponding to paras (*c*) and (*d*) of Stephen's
classification. These last are sometimes labelled 'felony murder' and 'arrest murder'. For
myself, as I have observed before (see *Hyam* [1974] 2 All ER 41 at 46, [1975] AC 55 at 67),
I find the terminology inconvenient. I can understand well enough how a contract can
b be express (when expressed in words oral or written) or implied (eg when to be inferred
from conduct, from a course of dealing or by necessary implication). I find much greater
difficulty in applying this distinction to a state of mind. Since a mental state must
necessarily be subjective, there is an argument for saying that all states of mind must be
express. Since a mental state can only be inferred, whether from the deeds or words of
the subject, or, as Lord Diplock points out in *Hyam* [1974] 2 All ER 41 at 66, [1975] AC
c 55 at 90, from his own subsequent account of the matter on oath in the witness box,
there is an equally strong case for saying that all states of mind must be implied.
Nevertheless, though I personally find the terminology misleading and inappropriate, it
was expressly recognised by the draftsman of the Homicide Act 1957 (s 1(1)) as being
current law at the time, and by the reinforced Court of Appeal in *Vickers*. Despite the
summing up of Hinchcliffe J in *Vickers* [1957] 2 All ER 741 at 744, [1957] 2 QB 664 at
d 672, and the fact (of which I am fairly certain) that the phrase 'implied malice' has not
been used consistently at all (Stephen in his History of the Criminal Law uses it at least
once in the sense of 'constructive malice'), I was at one time tempted to the view that
'express malice' was originally used to refer to Stephen's para (*a*) (the *Vickers* point) and
'implied malice' to Stephen's para (*b*) (the *Hyam* point). However in deference to the
authority of *Vickers* where the phrase is not used in this sense either by the Court of
e Appeal or by Hinchcliffe J, I do not now think it safe to express this opinion, attractive
as I still find it. Whatever the truth of the matter, the language of decided cases and of
s 1(1) of the Homicide Act 1957 compels one to accept the nomenclature as established
legal usage, and to assume a tripartite division between express and implied malice, on
the one hand, and constructive malice on the other.
    This brings me to Lord Diplock's dissenting opinion which is really central to the
f appellant's case. Like myself, he is offended by the express/implied terminology, which
is, however, inescapable in discussing the previous learning. For this terminology Lord
Diplock substitutes the far more convenient 'actual malice' and 'constructive malice'. I
do not myself consider that this innovation, by itself an improvement, necessarily affects
the validity, or otherwise, of his argument, though it does enable him to skate over the
difficulty created by the express retention by the draftsman of the 'implied' category in
g s 1(1) of the 1957 Act.
    The real nerve of Lord Diplock's argument, however, does, as it seems to me, depend
on the importance to be attached to the passing in 1803 of Lord Ellenborough's Act (43
Geo 3 c 58) by which, for the first time, wounding with the intent to inflict grievous
bodily harm became a felony. This, Lord Diplock believes, rendered it possible to apply
the doctrine of 'felony murder' as defined in Stephen's category (*c*), abolished in 1957, to
h all cases of felonious wounding, where death actually ensued from the wound. The
abolition of 'felony murder' in 1957 was thus seen to enable the judiciary to pursue the
mental element in murder behind the curtain imposed on it by the combined effect of
the statutory crime of felonious wounding and the doctrine of constructive malice, and
so to arrive at a position in which the mental element could be redefined in terms either
of an intention to kill, or an intention actually to endanger human life, to correspond
j with the recommendations of the Fourth Report of Her Majesty's Commissioners on
Criminal Law (8th March 1839).
    It seems to me, however, that this highly ingenious argument meets with two
insuperable difficulties. I accept that it appears to be established that the actual phrase
'grievous bodily harm', if not an actual coinage by Lord Ellenborough's Act, can never be
found to have appeared in print before it, though it has subsequently become current
coin, and has passed into the general legal jargon of statute law, and the cases decided

thereon. But counsel, having diligently carried us through the institutional writers on homicide, starting with Coke, and ending with East, with several citations from the a meagre reports available, only succeeded in persuading me at least that, even prior to Lord Ellenborough's Act of 1803, and without the precise label 'grievous bodily harm', the authors and the courts had consistently treated as murder, and therefore unclergiable, any killing with intent to do serious harm, however described, to which the label 'grievous bodily harm', as defined by Viscount Kilmuir LC in *Director of Public Prosecutions v Smith* [1960] 3 All ER 161 at 171, [1961] AC 290 at 334, reversing the 'murder by b pinprick' doctrine arising from *R v Ashman* (1858) 1 F & F 88, 175 ER 638, could properly have been applied. It would be tedious to pursue the citations all in detail. We were referred successively to 3 Co Inst 47–52, 1 Hale PC 424–477, 1 Hawk PC 85–88, 4 Bl Com 191–201, Foster's Discourse on Homicide (Crown Law) 255–267 and 1 East PC 103, 214–233. But the further we went into these passages the more hopeless appeared to be the view that, irrespective of constructive malice, malice aforethought had ever c been limited to the intention to kill or endanger life. On the contrary, these authorities reinforced the conclusion arrived at by Stephen's original Note XIV (in the Sturge edition Note VIII). This is the more striking in that the last few lines of the note demonstrate clearly that the possible combined effect of the felony-murder rule and the existence of a statutory crime of felonious wounding was consciously present to the author's mind.

There is a second difficulty in the way of treating Lord Ellenborough's Act as providing d the kind of historical watershed demanded by Lord Diplock's speech and contended for in the instant appeal by the appellant's counsel. This consists in the fact that, though the nineteenth century judges might in theory have employed the felony-murder rule to apply to cases where death ensued in the course of a felonious wounding, they do not appear to have done so in fact. No case was cited where they did so. On the contrary, there appears to be no historical discontinuity between criminal jurisprudence before e and after 1803. Stephen never so treated the matter (either in his text, or, except in the last few lines, in his Note XIV). It was not so treated in the Australian case of *La Fontaine v R* (1976) 136 CLR 62 (after *Hyam*, but in a jurisdiction in which the constructive malice rule still applied). It was pointed out by counsel for the Crown that the relevant felony created by Lord Ellenborough's Act was limited to cutting or stabbing and did not extend, for example, to beating, which would effectively have excluded the felony- f murder doctrine from many cases where death ensued from an act intended to inflict grievous bodily harm. For myself, I think that there is a logical difficulty not based on this narrow point of construction, which prevented the judges from adoping the principle. Felonious wounding intrinsically involves proof by the prosecution of the requisite intention and therefore gives no added force to the earlier law, if I have correctly interpreted the learning before 1803. The way is thus clear on any view to g accept as decisive what I myself had always understood to be the law prior to 1957. This is contained in the statement of Lord Goddard CJ representing the court of five judges in *Vickers* [1957] 2 QB 664 at 670; cf [1957] 2 All ER 741 at 743:

> 'Murder is, of course, killing with malice aforethought, but "malice aforethought" is a term of art. It has always been defined in English law as either an express h intention to kill, as could be inferred when a person, having uttered threats against another, produced a lethal weapon and used it on a victim, or implied where, by a voluntary act, the accused intended to cause grievous bodily harm to the victim, and the victim died as the result.'

I should, however, make at least a passing reference to the valid observation made by Lord Diplock in *Hyam* [1974] 2 All ER 41 at 67, [1975] AC 55 at 91 where he points out j that, at one point in his History, Stephen appears to treat his draft code (which clearly would have supported Lord Diplock's formulation) as 'exactly corresponding' with his formulation in the Digest (which it clearly does not). As to this, I can only say, on this point, Stephen was surely in error. The two documents do not 'exactly correspond'.

Counsel for the appellant used one further ground, not found in Lord Diplock's opinion, for supporting the minority view in *Hyam*. This was the difficulty which, as he

a
suggested, a jury would find in deciding what amounted to an intention to inflict 'grievous bodily harm' or 'really serious bodily harm' as formulated in *Smith*. I do not find this argument convincing. For much more than a hundred years juries have constantly been required to arrive at the answer to precisely this question in cases falling short of murder (eg the s 18 cases). I cannot see that the fact that death ensues should render the identical question particularly anomalous, or its answer, though admittedly more important, any more difficult. Nor am I persuaded that a reformulation of murder

b
so as to confine the mens rea to an intention to endanger life instead of an intention to do really serious bodily harm would either improve the clarity of the law or facilitate the task of juries in finding the facts. On the contrary, in cases where death has ensued as the result of the infliction of really serious injuries I can see endless opportunity for fruitless and interminable discussion of the question whether the accused intended to endanger life and thus expose the victim to a probable danger of death, or whether he simply

c
intended to inflict really serious injury.

I must add one or two words about the arguments presented in the view of the minority in *Hyam* [1974] 2 All ER 41 at 66, [1975] AC 55 at 90. I readily accede to the view that the task of the modern judge in applying the criminal law is rendered more difficult by the paucity of reliable reports of criminal cases prior to the establishment of a proper pyramid of criminal appeals. I also accept the relevance of the fact that prior to

d
Woolmington v Director of Public Prosecutions [1935] AC 462, [1935] All ER Rep 1 the burden of proof was erroneously supposed to be on the defence in a number of cases where a voluntary act resulting in death had been proved by the prosecution, and that prior to 1898 criminal courts had never the advantage of the testimony of the accused. I also genuflect before the miracles of modern surgery and medicine, though I express some doubt whether these may not have been offset to some extent by the increased

e
lethal characteristics of modern weaponry (particularly in the fields of automatic weaponry, explosives and poisons), and the assistance to criminality afforded by the automobile, the motorway and international air transport. I also take leave to doubt whether in the case of injuries to the skull in particular or indeed really serious bodily harm in general these advances have made the difference between inflicting serious bodily harm and endangering life sufficiently striking as to justify judicial legislation on

f
the scale proposed. But, more important than all this, I confess that I view with a certain degree of scepticism the opinion expressed in *Hyam* [1974] 2 All ER 41 at 65–68, [1975] AC 55 at 90–93 that the age of our ancestors was so much more violent than our own that we can afford to take a different view of 'concepts of what is right and what is wrong that command general acceptance in contemporary society'. In the weeks preceding that in which this appeal came before your Lordships both the Pope and the President of the

g
United States have been shot in cold blood, a circuit judge has been slain, a police officer has given evidence of a deliberate shooting of himself which has confined him to a wheeled chair for life, five soldiers have been blown up on a country road by a mine containing over a thousand pounds of high explosive, the pillion passenger has been torn from the back of a motor bicycle and stabbed to death by total strangers apparently because he was white, and another youth stabbed, perhaps because he was black, petrol

h
bombs and anti-personnel weapons have been thrown in the streets of London and Belfast at the bodies of the security forces, cars have been overturned and set on fire in Brixton and Bristol, and the press has carried reports that our own Sovereign moves about the streets of her own country protected by bodyguards armed with automatic weapons. If I moved a few months back I could cite the siege of the Iranian embassy and other terrorist sieges where hostages have been taken by armed men, the shooting in the

j
streets of London of foreign refugees at the hand of their political opponents, and many other acts of lawlessness, violence and cruelty. I doubt whether what seemed clear in 1974, when the *Hyam* appeal was heard, would have seemed so obvious seven years later in 1981. Like 'public policy', 'concepts of what is right and what is wrong that command general acceptance in contemporary society' are difficult horses for the judiciary to ride, and, where possible, are arguably best left to the legislature to decide. It must be added that the legislature has been relatively slow to act. Commission after commission,

committee after committee have reported both before and after Sir James Stephen's draft Bill was stillborn after examination by a Victorian select committee of the House of Commons in 1874. Few of the recommendations of these successive inquiries have exactly coincided with one another, and fewer still have reached the statute book. One cannot but feel sympathy with Lord Kilbrandon's plea (*Hyam* [1974] 2 All ER 41 at 72, [1975] AC 55 at 98) for a single, and simplified, law of homicide especially since the death penalty for murder has been abolished. But I venture to think that the problem involves difficulties more serious than is supposed. Few civilised countries have identical laws on the subject of homicide or apply them in the same way. To name only two broad issues of policy, are we to follow s 5 of the Homicide Act 1957 and categorise certain classes of murder in which the prohibited act is arbitrarily adjudged to be worse than in others? The fate of s 5 after the abolition of the death penalty, and its history before that, do not encourage emulation. Or, are we to follow Lord Kilbrandon's inclination and create a single offence of homicide and recognise that homicides are infinitely variable in heinousness, and that their heinousness depends very largely on their motivation, with the result that the judge should have absolute discretion to impose whatever sentence he considers just from a conditional discharge to life imprisonment? I can see both difficulty and danger in this for the judiciary. After conviction of the new offence of homicide, judges would have to be the judges of fact for themselves, unaided by any precise jury verdict as to the exact facts found or any guidance from the legislature as to the appropriate penalty. I doubt whether in practice they would relish the responsibility with greater enthusiasm than that with which Parliament would be eager to entrust them with it.

In the meantime we must administer the law as we consider it to be without either the zeal of the reformer or the unwillingness to admit error which characterises the reactionary. In my opinion, *Vickers* was a correct statement of the law as it was after amendment by the Homicide Act 1957, and in *Smith* and *Hyam* your Lordships were right to indorse *Vickers*.

Having reached this conclusion, I doubt whether I possess moral or intellectual agility to discern exactly what I would have done with regard to the practice direction had I reached an opposite view. But I am impressed by the stance Lord Reid took in *Knuller (Publishing, Printing and Promotions) Ltd v Director of Public Prosecutions* [1972] 2 All ER 898 at 903, [1973] AC 435 at 455, where he refused to invoke the practice direction in support of his own previous dissent in *Shaw v Director of Public Prosecutions* [1961] 2 All ER 446, [1962] AC 220 and I am impressed by the arguments of Lord Morris and Lord Simon in the same case in favour of caution. Nor can I disregard the fact that had I reached a different conclusion I should have been saying that between 1957 and the abolition of capital punishment for murder, a number of persons (including Vickers himself) would have been executed when they ought only to have been convicted at common law of manslaughter had the trial judge anticipated my putative decision. Under the express terms of the practice direction stare decisis is still the indispensable foundation of the use by your Lordships of the appellate jurisdiction of the House and its normal practice. Especially must this be so in criminal law, where certainty is indeed a condition of its commanding and retaining respect.

In the event, I am spared these conscientious difficulties, and, without refusing to invoke the practice direction, I am able to say with sincerity that, on the law as it is, and on its merits, the appeal should be dismissed.

LORD WILBERFORCE. My Lords, I have had the privilege of reading in advance the speeech delivered by Lord Hailsham LC. I agree entirely with it.

I wish to add to what the noble and learned Lord has said my firm recognition of the value of his opinion with reference to the issue now relevant, in *Hyam v Director of Public Prosecutions* [1974] 2 All ER 41, [1975] AC 55. Taken together with *R v Vickers* [1957] 2 All ER 741, [1957] 2 QB 664 and the indorsement of that case by this House in *Director of Public Prosecutions v Smith* [1960] 3 All ER 161, [1961] AC 290, with the history of the development of the law relating to murder over nearly four hundred years, and with the *a* authority of Stephen, this makes the case for the minority opinions in *Hyam*, as statements de lege lata, with respect, unarguable at the present time. And, furthermore, if it were possible for this House, judicially, to change the existing law (so as to require an intention to endanger life rather than an intention to do 'grievous bodily harm'), whatever defects the present law may possess, that particular change would in my opinion be for the worse, not for the better, in providing a test both uncertain and practically unworkable. I am happy to see that Lord Hailsham LC agrees in this.

b I would dismiss the appeal and answer the certified question in the affirmative.

LORD SIMON OF GLAISDALE. My Lords, I have had the privilege of reading in draft the speech delivered by my noble and learned friend on the Woolsack. I agree with it; and I would therefore dismiss the appeal.

c
LORD EDMUND-DAVIES. My Lords, I gratefully accept everything that Lord Hailsham LC has propounded in his speech which I have had the advantage of reading in draft, and I venture to add no more than a footnote.

The cases are probably rare where your Lordships' House would think it right to invoke the practice direction on judicial precedent (*Note* [1966] 3 All ER 77, [1966] 1
d WLR 1234) notwithstanding the conclusion that a relevant earlier decision had been *correctly* arrived at. But that such a power exists is recognised in the practice direction itself, and *Miliangos v George Frank (Textiles) Ltd* [1975] 3 All ER 801, [1976] AC 443 is an instance of this House, while not condemning as wrong a decision it had delivered 15 years earlier, declining to follow it on the ground that the instability which had meanwhile overtaken major currencies was such that, in the words of Lord Wilberforce,
e 'To change the rule would . . . avoid injustice in the present case' (see [1975] 3 All ER 801 at 812, [1976] AC 443 at 467).

Even where an earlier decision is *not* approved of, the practice direction stresses '. . . the especial need for certainty as to the criminal law', and in *Knuller (Publishing, Printing and Promotions) Ltd v Director of Public Prosecutions* [1972] 2 All ER 898 at 903, [1973] AC 435 at 455 Lord Reid emphasised that—

f   '. . . our change of practice in no longer regarding previous decisions of this House as absolutely binding does not mean that whenever we think that a previous decision was wrong we should reverse it.'

The minority dissents of Lord Diplock and Lord Kilbrandon, in *Hyam v Director of Public Prosecutions* [1974] 2 All ER 41, [1975] AC 55 were based on their conclusions that the
g law as to intent in murder had been incorrectly stated by this House in *Director of Public Prosecutions v Smith* [1960] 3 All ER 161 at 172, [1961] AC 290 at 335, and that exposure of the error should lead to a quashing of Hyam's conviction for murder. In the present case, on the other hand, your Lordships have unanimously concluded and now reiterate that the law as to murderous intent was correctly stated in *R v Vickers* [1957] 2 All ER 741, [1957] 2 QB 664. Even so, is now the time and is this House the place to reveal and
h declare (so as to 'avoid injustice') what *ought* to be the law and, in the light of that revelation, here and now to recant from its former adoption of *Vickers*?

My Lords, I would give a negative answer to the question. I say this despite the fact that, after much veering of thought over a period of years, the view I presently favour is that there should be no conviction for murder unless an intent to kill is established, the wide range of punishment for manslaughter being fully adequate to deal with all less
j heinous forms of homicide. I find it passing strange that a person can be convicted of murder if death results from, say, his intentional breaking of another's arm, an action which, while undoubtedly involving the infliction of 'really serious harm' and, as such, calling for severe punishment, would in most cases be unlikely to kill. And yet, for the lesser offence of attempted murder, nothing less than an intent to kill will suffice. But I recognise the force of the contrary view that the outcome of intentionally inflicting serious harm can be so unpredictable that anyone prepared to act so wickedly has little

ground for complaint if, where death results, he is convicted and punished as severely as
one who intended to kill.

a

So there are forceful arguments both ways. And they are arguments of the greatest
public consequence, particularly in these turbulent days when, as Lord Hailsham LC has
vividly reminded us, violent crimes have become commonplace. Resolution of that
conflict cannot, in my judgment, be a matter for your Lordships' House alone. It is a task
for none other than Parliament, as the constitutional organ best fitted to weigh the
relevant and opposing factors. Its solution has already been attempted extra-judicially on *b*
many occasions, but with no real success. My Lords, we can do none other than wait to
see what will emerge when the task is undertaken by the legislature, as I believe it should
be when the time is opportune.

Be that as it may, in respectful and complete concurrence with the Lord Chancellor,
I hold that the direction of Lawson J in the present case was impeccable and I would
therefore dismiss the appeal.

c

LORD BRIDGE OF HARWICH. My Lords, I have had the advantage of reading
in draft the speech of my noble and learned friend on the Woolsack. I respectfully and
unreservedly agree with it. Accordingly I would answer the certified question in the
affirmative and dismiss the appeal.

d

Certified question answered in affirmative; order appealed from affirmed and appeal dismissed.

Solicitors: *Boxall & Boxall*, agents for *Godfrey Davis & Waitt*, Ramsgate (for the appellant);
Director of Public Prosecutions.

Mary Rose Plummer   Barrister. *e*

R v Crown Court at Huntingdon and others,
ex parte Jordan

f

QUEEN'S BENCH DIVISION
DONALDSON LJ AND BINGHAM J
4th FEBRUARY 1981

Crown Court – Appeal to Crown Court – Power of court on appeal – Appeal against conviction *g*
by magistrates – Jurisdiction to allow change of plea – Plea of guilty entered in magistrates' court
– Plea appearing to magistrates to be unequivocal plea of guilty – Plea entered under duress –
Whether Crown Court having jurisdiction to inquire into plea which appeared to be unequivocal
plea of guilty.

A wife was charged with her husband before a magistrates' court with theft by *h*
shoplifting. Both pleaded guilty. The wife's plea appeared to be an unequivocal plea of
guilty and was therefore accepted. Following her sentence the wife appealed to the
Crown Court against her conviction, submitting that her guilty plea was procured by the
husband's duress because he had forced her to assist him in the shoplifting by threatening
her with violence and had then forced her to plead guilty by nudging her in court when
their pleas were being taken to remind her that he would ill-treat her if she pleaded not *j*
guilty. On the assumption that those facts were correct the Crown Court nevertheless
held that it had no jurisdiction to entertain the appeal, on the ground that the Crown
Court could only intervene if a guilty plea was equivocal and should have been treated
as a not guilty plea. The wife applied for judicial review of the Crown Court's decision
by way of certiorari to quash the decision and mandamus to direct the Crown Court to

inquire into the issue whether her plea of guilty was a nullity because of the husband's
a coercion.

Held – Where it was alleged that a plea of guilty in a magistrates' court had been entered
under duress or coercion the Crown Court had jurisdiction to inquire into the matter in
order to determine whether the plea should have been treated as being an equivocal plea
requiring a plea of not guilty to be entered, notwithstanding that the duress or coercion
b was not apparent to the magistrates' court or that there was nothing to indicate to that
court that the plea might have been equivocal. Accordingly, the application would be
granted (see p 874 *j* to p 875 *d* and *j* to p 876 *a* and *e* to *j*, post).
    R v Marylebone Justices, ex parte Westminster City Council [1971] 1 All ER 1025 explained.

Notes
c For the right of appeal to the Crown Court from a magistrates' court in criminal cases and
the Crown Court's jurisdiction to hear an appeal against conviction by a person who has
unequivocally pleaded guilty, see 11 Halsbury's Laws (4th Edn) para 677.

Cases referred to in judgment
R v Inns (1974) 60 Cr App R 231, CA, 14(1) Digest (Reissue) 328, 2603.
d R v Marylebone Justices, ex parte Westminster City Council, R v Inner London Quarter Sessions,
    ex parte Westminster City Council [1971] 1 All ER 1025, [1971] 1 WLR 567, 135 JP 239,
    DC, Digest (Cont Vol D) 636, 1289c.
R v Crown Court at Snaresbrook, ex parte Gavi Burjore (20th December 1979, unreported),
    DC.

e **Cases also cited**
Foster (P) (Haulage) Ltd v Roberts [1978] 2 All ER 751, DC.
R v Brentford Justices, ex parte Catlin [1975] 2 All ER 201, [1975] QB 455, DC.
R v Coventry Crown Court, ex parte Manson (1978) 67 Cr App R 315, DC.
R v Durham Quarter Sessions, ex parte Virgo [1952] 1 All ER 466, [1952] 2 QB 1, DC.
R v Hull Prison Board of Visitors, ex parte St Germain [1978] 2 All ER 198, [1978] QB 678,
f   DC; rvsd [1979] 1 All ER 701, [1979] QB 425, CA.
R v Inner London Crown Court, ex parte Sloper (1978) 69 Cr App R 1, DC.
R v Tottenham Justices, ex parte Rubens [1970] 1 All ER 879, [1970] 1 WLR 800, DC.
S (an infant) v Manchester City Recorder [1969] 3 All ER 1230, [1971] AC 481, HL.

Application for judicial review
g Mrs Eileen June Jordan applied, with the leave of the Divisional Court granted on 13th
March 1980, for (i) an order of certiorari to bring up and quash the decision of the Crown
Court at Huntingdon (his Honour Judge Hammerton sitting with justices) dated 19th
December 1979 whereby the court dismissed Mrs Jordan's appeal against conviction for
theft before the Peterborough Magistrates' Court on 6th September 1979 on her plea of
guilty, (ii) an order of mandamus requiring the Crown Court to hear and determine the
h issue whether the plea of guilty was a nullity by reason of coercion by Mrs Jordan's
husband (who was jointly charged with her and appeared with her in the magistrates'
court), (iii) an order of certiorari to bring up and quash Mrs Jordan's election before the
magistrates' court for summary trial, and (iv) an order of mandamus requiring the
magistrates' court to put her to her election as to the mode of her trial. The facts are set
out in the judgment of Donaldson LJ.
j
Owen Davies for Mrs Jordan.
Timothy Barnes for the prosecution.

DONALDSON LJ. This is an application for judicial review brought on behalf of Mrs
Jordan, against the Crown Court at Huntingdon, seeking an order to quash a decision of

the Crown Court which held that it had no jurisdiction to deal with Mrs Jordan's application, to which I will come in a moment. First let me set the historical scene.

Mrs Jordan appeared before the Peterborough magistrates on 6th September 1979 charged with theft. Charged with her was her husband. Both of them pleaded guilty to theft and indeed Mrs Jordan asked for 11 other offences to be taken into consideration. She was fined and so was her husband. Thus far there appears to be no ground for any appeal to the Crown Court so far as conviction is concerned. They were both convicted on their own pleas of guilty, and there was no apparent ground for coming to this court for any form of judicial review.

But when Mrs Jordan appeared before the Crown Court on her own appeal, she wanted to put forward a somewhat unusual story, and the story was this. She wanted to say that in March 1977 she was married to David John Jordan her co-accused. He was suffering from some form of mental illness and throughout the marriage he ill-treated her in a most violent manner. She gives particulars of that. In January 1979 she had left her husband and indeed had taken the step of instructing solicitors to institute divorce proceedings. However in early August 1979 her husband discovered her whereabouts and persuaded her to return to him. He then took up his former habit of maltreating her, and in addition took to shoplifting. Whilst out shopping together her husband threatened that he would physically ill-treat her if she gave information to anybody about his shoplifting, and further, under threat of physical violence, he required her to assist him with his shoplifting. She was so doing on 25th August when their activities were detected and it was that incident which led to this charge.

Under s 47 of the Criminal Justice Act 1925 a wife has a defence to a charge of this nature if she can prove that the offence was committed in the presence and under the coercion of her husband. It follows that if Mrs Jordan had raised these issues before the magistrates, they would, I have no doubt, have investigated them, and if she had been able to bring herself within s 47, she would have been entitled to be acquitted. But of course she did not raise the matter before the magistrates; she simply pleaded guilty. When she got to the Crown Court she then added the information (at least I assume that this was before the Crown Court) that the husband had threatened her in much the same way in the magistrates' court itself. He said that he would physically ill-treat her if she did other than plead guilty. It is now said that while they were standing together and being asked how they pleaded he nudged her with his foot, or otherwise reminded her of the physical consequences which would follow if she entered a plea of not guilty. So she raises a submission that her plea of guilty, like the offence itself, was procured by duress.

The Crown Court judge held that, assuming that those facts were established (he did not investigate them), there was no jurisdiction in the Crown Court to give her any relief. The basis of that decision, as I understand it, was that the jurisdiction of the Crown Court, once there has been a plea of guilty accepted by the magistrates, is very limited. It can of course entertain an appeal against sentence. That is clear from s 83 of the Magistrates' Courts Act 1952. It can (this is established by a long line of cases) inquire to see whether there was a real plea of guilty, in the sense of inquiring whether the plea was equivocal.

An equivocal plea has been described by Lord Goddard CJ, and by Lord Parker CJ when he succeeded him, as a 'guilty but' plea (see *R v Marylebone Justices, ex parte Westminster City Council, R v Inner London Quarter Sessions, ex parte Westminster City Council* [1971] 1 All ER 1025 at 1026, [1971] 1 WLR 567 at 570). It is a common experience of all who sit in magistrates' courts that those who are charged with theft sometimes come forward and say 'Yes, I plead guilty, because I took it, but I thought that it was mine', or 'I thought nobody would object', and all sorts of other excuses, some of which at least nullify the plea of guilty which has just been given. In those circumstances, where the magistrates recognise that an equivocal 'guilty but' plea is being made, they quite rightly enter a plea of 'not guilty'.

There is no doubt that the Crown Court has jurisdiction to investigate the matter where it is alleged that there has been an equivocal plea in that sense and, if satisfied that *a* there was an equivocal plea, it can send the matter back to the magistrates to enable them to, in effect, rehear the case, because the plea should have been treated as not guilty.

It is equally clear (it was made clear to us in argument here) that that situation is to be distinguished from the situation which arises where there is an unequivocal plea of guilty and at a later stage the accused person comes to the conclusion that he should never have pleaded guilty and he asks to change his plea. In such cases magistrates have a discretion to allow a change of plea up to the time when sentence has been passed. There *b* are also special situations where trial and sentence are split between the magistrates' court and the Crown Court, but I need not bother with that.

What is submitted in this case is that there is no other way in which a Crown Court can intervene. It is said that if Mrs Jordan is seeking to change her plea, then she is too late. For my part I would accept that that is so. It is said that this is not a case of an equivocal plea. As to that I am not so sure. It may be a case of an equivocal plea or it may *c* be a case which is sui generis. But whichever it be, I am satisfied that the Crown Court had jurisdiction to inquire into this matter, and should have inquired into it. If it came to the conclusion that Mrs Jordan, when uttering the words 'guilty' was doing an act which, if she had been applying pen to paper, would have qualified for the description 'non est factum', in other words her mind was overborne by the will of another, then they could have so found and sent the case back to the magistrates.

d But I must explain why. I am satisfied first of all that the Crown Court ought to have jurisdiction. It is a wholly absurd situation if it is a defence for a wife to prove that she committed the crime under coercion from her husband but she loses the right to put that defence forward or to rely on that defence if the coercion is of so grave a character that she is unable to put forward a plea of not guilty. That is not to say that the law is that. I am saying that the law ought to be that.

e A similar case was considered by this court in *R v Crown Court at Snaresbrook, ex parte Gavi Burjore* (20th December 1979, unreported). The court was composed of Shaw LJ and Kilner Brown J. That was a case in which duress was alleged and Kilner Brown J, in giving the judgment, with which Shaw LJ agreed, stated:

f '. . . in the case of an appeal to the Crown Court against conviction before the magistrate which had proceeded to the passing of sentence, there is no power in the Crown Court to reopen the question of the validity of the plea of guilty. There are, however, certain exceptions to that general statement of principle: one is where it can be shown that the plea of guilty was entered under a mistake as to the law and the other, which is relevant in the present case, is the possibility of the reconsideration of a plea of guilty if it can be shown that it was entered under duress. Authority for the latter proposition is to be found in *R v Inns* (1974) 60 Cr App R 231.'

g

That passage has been criticised by counsel for the prosecution on a number of grounds. First it is said that there is no authority anywhere for the proposition that a plea of guilty entered under a mistake of law can be investigated by the Crown Court. For my part I would not wish to express any view about that at all. That seems to be a quite different case from one of duress. I would observe in passing that, as is clear from the *h* passage that I have cited, this was obiter and not necessary for the decision of the court in that case. Somebody at some time may have to decide this matter. We do not in this case.

Then it is said that anyway this passage is itself obiter. There I part company with counsel for the prosecution, because, whilst it is true that what the Divisional Court was deciding in that case was whether the Crown Court should have extended the time for *j* an application, if this court had come to the conclusion that an extension of time would have been completely idle because the court would have had no jurisdiction to deal with the substance of the application, it could not conceivably have acted as it did and ordered the Crown Court to extend the time. It was I think part of the ratio of that decision and we are bound by it. But I would go further than that and say that, speaking for myself, I think that decision was right, because where you have a plea of guilty given under duress (it may not be this case), it seems to me that you are either in a position that there is no plea at all, which is a possible view, or, alternatively, you are in the position of a 'guilty but' plea: a 'The reason why I am pleading guilty is that I am being forced to do *a* so' situation.

It is said by counsel for the prosecution that this cannot be regarded as a 'guilty but' plea because there are a number of cases, notably *R v Marylebone Justices, ex parte Westminster City Council* [1971] 1 All ER 1025 at 1026, [1971] 1 WLR 567 at 570, where it was said by Lord Parker CJ:

'The enquiry in each case is as to what took place before the magistrates' court to *b* see whether the court acted properly in accepting an apparent plea of guilty as an unequivocal plea.'

Quite plainly the magistrates acted properly in this case on what they knew. There was nothing they could have done but accept this plea. But I do not believe that those words would have been used by Lord Parker CJ in the *Marylebone Justices* case if he had *c* been considering a case such as this. He did not in fact say that the inquiry must be confined to what was 'apparently' happening in the magistrates' court. He said 'what took place'. It is the essence of duress that what is happening is not only what is apparent to anybody in the court but what is actually happening there, albeit in an unapparent or latent form.

Two situations were put in argument by Bingham J, with husband and wife as co- *d* accused. In the first the husband lifts a revolver, puts it to his wife's head in the sight of all and says, 'My dear, you plead guilty or else'. If she did plead guilty, that would undoubtedly be an equivocal plea. In the second the co-defendant keeps the revolver in his pocket and manipulates it so that she can feel it pressing against her, and she then, enters an apparently unequivocal plea of guilty. It would be a travesty of justice if the law treated these two cases differently. In my judgment it does not. *e*

For these reasons I would remit the matter to the Crown Court with a direction that it has jurisdiction to investigate the case and that it should investigate the case. Nothing that I say must lead the Crown Court to think that I have formed any view whether Mrs Jordan's allegations are correct. Also, and this may be more important in the light of the submissions of counsel for the prosecution, I think that if this case is proved by Mrs Jordan on investigation, it is a case of the greatest rarity indeed, and it would be most *f* unfortunate if every married woman thought that she could apply to the Crown Court with a view to having her plea of guilty treated as equivocal merely on an allegation that her husband was not as good a husband as he might have been. It is a matter which should be investigated by the Crown Court.

Let me add this. If, but only if, the Crown Court decides that this plea of guilty was produced by duress and that the matter should go back to the magistrates for rehearing, *g* then the magistrates would be able to reconsider the mode of trial. Certainly they might well take the view that if this lady was acting under duress in pleading guilty, the same considerations may have applied to her consent to summary trial. At all events it seems unlikely that anyone who is sufficiently under the influence of her husband to plead guilty could be making a free choice on whether she should be tried summarily or not. They may in those circumstances think it right to reconsider that aspect too. *h*

We quash the decision of the Crown Court and order that a rehearing of the application take place. We make no order against the magistrates.

BINGHAM J. I agree. Counsel for the prosecution has referred to a number of clear statements of principle to the effect that pleas of guilty may only be reopened before sentence or if equivocal. It must be remembered, when considering these statements, *j* that the court in none of the cases was dealing with a situation of coercion or duress such as is alleged in the case before us. The only clear case in which such a situation has been said to have existed is *R v Crown Court at Snaresbrook, ex parte Gavi Burjore* (20th December 1979, unreported), and an order was there made by the court that the matter should be inquired into by the Crown Court.

Accordingly in my judgment the statements of principle must be read subject to the

important reservation that the judges in those cases did not have the present situation in
a mind, because it was not raised before them.

Application granted. Case remitted to Crown Court.

*The court refused leave to appeal to the House of Lords but certified, under s 1(2) of the
Administration of Justice Act 1960, that the following point of law of general public importance
was involved in the decision: whether, on appeal from a magistrates' court in a case where an*
b *accused person has pleaded guilty to an offence, has been sentenced for it and there have been no
circumstances which indicated to the court that the plea was or might be equivocal, the Crown
Court has power to investigate the voluntariness of the plea.*

*12th May. The Appeal Committee of the House of Lords (Lord Fraser of Tullybelton, Lord
Scarman and Lord Roskill) dismissed a petition by the prosecution for leave to appeal.*

c Solicitors: *Bowling & Co* (for Mrs Jordan); *D C Beal*, Huntingdon.

Sepala Munasinghe   Barrister.

Faith Panton Property Plan Ltd v Hodgetts
d   **and another**

COURT OF APPEAL, CIVIL DIVISION
WALLER, BRANDON LJJ AND SIR DAVID CAIRNS
15th, 16th, 17th, 18th DECEMBER 1980, 21st JANUARY 1981

e *Injunction – Interlocutory – Principle governing grant – Judgment for costs to be taxed – Danger
of defendant disposing of assets before taxation – Defendant indicating by conduct that he
intended to dispose of assets and become bankrupt in order to defeat order for costs – Whether
plaintiff entitled to injunction before taxation restraining defendant from disposing of assets –
Supreme Court of Judicature (Consolidation) Act 1925, s 45(1).*

f Following the termination in March 1979 of an agreement between the plaintiffs, who
were interior decorators, and the defendants, who were manufacturers of bathroom
equipment, the plaintiffs, in April 1979, brought an action against the defendants
seeking, inter alia, an injunction to restrain them from passing off their goods or business
as the plaintiffs' goods or business. The defendants by a counterclaim claimed the
copyright in certain moulds of bathroom equipment and ownership of a patent, and
g alleged infringement of the copyright and patent. The plaintiffs sought interlocutory
relief in the action as the result of which the defendants, in April and August 1979, gave
certain undertakings to the court until the trial of the action. Subsequently the plaintiffs
alleged that the defendants were in breach of their undertakings and issued motions for
their committal for breach of the undertakings. On 3rd November 1980 the judge gave
judgment in favour of the plaintiffs and ordered the plaintiffs' costs of the motions to be
h taxed on a full indemnity basis and paid by the defendants forthwith after taxation. The
costs, which were estimated to be about £12,000, not having been taxed, the plaintiffs
were not therefore able to enforce judgment for them. The defendants by their
ambivalent conduct indicated that they might divest themselves of their assets, including
the alleged copyright, the moulds and the patent, and make themselves bankrupt. To
safeguard their judgment for costs the plaintiffs, on 9th December 1980, applied to the
j court for an injunction, under either the Mareva jurisdiction or s 45[a] of the Supreme
Court of Judicature (Consolidation) Act 1925, restraining the defendants from assigning
or otherwise disposing of the copyright, the moulds and the patent, but the judge, in the
exercise of his discretion, refused to grant the injunction under either jurisdiction. The
plaintiffs appealed.

---

a   Section 45(1) is set out at p 880 *h*, post

Held – On analogy with the pre-Mareva practice whereby the court had power to enforce an order for costs which had not been taxed by appointing a receiver of the *a* property of the person liable for the costs, the court had power under s 45(1) of the 1925 Act to protect a party in whose favour an order for costs had been made by granting, prior to the taxation of the costs, an injunction restraining the other party from disposing of his assets. In the circumstances the court would exercise its discretion under s 45(1) to grant the injunction sought by the plaintiffs and, accordingly, the appeal would be allowed (see p 882 *d* to *g*, p 884 *f g* and p 886 *f* to *h*, post).   *b*

Cummins v Perkins [1899] 1 Ch 16 applied.

Lister & Co v Stubbs [1886–90] All ER Rep 797 distinguished.

Notes

For the statutory jurisdiction to grant, and the principles on which the court acts in granting, interlocutory injunctions, see 24 Halsbury's Laws (4th Edn) paras 917–919, and for cases on the subject, see 28(2) Digest (Reissue) 966–973, 60–103.   *c*

For the Supreme Court of Judicature (Consolidation) Act 1925, s 45, see 25 Halsbury's Statutes (3rd Edn) 717.

Cases referred to in judgments   *d*

Allen v Jambo Holdings Ltd [1980] 2 All ER 502, [1980] 1 WLR 1252, CA.

Barclay-Johnson v Yuill [1980] 3 All ER 190, [1980] 1 WLR 1259.

Beddow v Beddow (1878) 9 Ch D 89, 47 LJ Ch 588, 28(2) Digest (Reissue) 959, 22.

Blunt v Blunt [1943] 2 All ER 76, [1943] AC 517, 112 LJP 58, 169 LT 33, HL, 27(1) Digest (Reissue) 565, 4119.

Brewis v Brewis [1893] WN 6, 27(2) Digest (Reissue) 938, 7578.   *e*

Bullus v Bullus (1910) 102 LT 399, 27(2) Digest (Reissue) 935, 7544.

Burmester v Burmester [1913] P 76, 82 LJP 54, 108 LT 272, 27(2) Digest (Reissue) 849, 6773.

Chartered Bank v Daklouche [1980] 1 All ER 205, [1980] 1 WLR 107, CA.

Cummins v Perkins [1899] 1 Ch 16, 68 LJ Ch 57, 79 LT 456, 27(1) Digest (Reissue) 294, 2193.   *f*

Gebr Van Weelde Scheepvaart Kantoor BV v Homeric Marine Services Ltd, The Agrabele [1979] 2 Lloyd's Rep 117, Digest (Cont Vol E) 334, 79g.

Gillet v Gillet (1889) 14 PD 158, 58 LJP 84, 61 LT 401, 27(2) Digest (Reissue) 682, 5183.

Jagger v Jagger [1926] P 93, [1926] All ER Rep 613, 95 LJP 83, 135 LT 1, CA, 27(2) Digest (Reissue) 849, 6774.

Lister & Co v Stubbs (1890) 45 Ch D 1, [1886–90] All ER Rep 797, 59 LJ Ch 570, 63 LT 75, *g* CA, 1(2) Digest (Reissue) 659, 4513.

Mareva Compania Naviera SA v International Bulkcarriers SA, The Mareva (1975) [1980] 1 All ER 213, [1975] 2 Lloyd's Rep 509, CA, Digest (Cont Vol E) 331, 79b.

Newton v Newton (1885) 11 PD 11, 55 LJP 13, 27(2) Digest (Reissue) 938, 7570.

Newton v Newton [1896] P 36, 65 LJP 15, 27(2) Digest (Reissue) 849, 6772.

Nippon Yusen Kaisha v Karageorgis [1975] 3 All ER 282, [1975] 1 WLR 1093, [1975] 2 *h* Lloyd's Rep 137, CA, Digest (Cont Vol D) 534, 79a.

Prince Abdul Rahman Bin Turki Al Sudairy v Abu-Taha [1980] 3 All ER 409, [1980] 1 WLR 1268, CA.

Rasu Maritima SA v Perusahaan Pertambangan Minyak Dan Gas Bumi Negara (Pertamina) and Government of Indonesia (as interveners) [1977] 3 All ER 324, [1978] QB 644, [1977] 3 WLR 518, [1977] 2 Lloyd's Rep 397, CA, Digest (Cont Vol E) 331, 79c.   *j*

Scott v Scott [1950] 2 All ER 1154, [1951] P 193, CA, 27(1) Digest (Reissue) 105, 717.

Sidney v Sidney (1867) 17 LT 9, 27(2) Digest (Reissue) 849, 6770.

Siskina (Cargo owners) v Distos Compania Naviera SA, The Siskina [1977] 3 All ER 803, [1979] AC 210, [1977] 3 WLR 818, [1978] 1 Lloyd's Rep 1, HL, Digest (Cont Vol E) 660, 782a.

Ward v James [1965] 1 All ER 563, [1966] 1 QB 273, [1965] 2 WLR 455, CA, 51 Digest
a (Repl) 808, 3640.
Waterhouse v Waterhouse [1893] P 284, 62 LJP 115, 69 LT 618, 6 R 630, CA, 27(2) Digest
   (Reissue) 849, 6771.
Wright v Wright [1954] 1 All ER 707, [1954] 1 WLR 534, 27(2) Digest (Reissue) 938,
   7576.

b **Cases also cited**
A v C [1980] 2 All ER 347, [1981] 2 WLR 629n.
Anton Piller KG v Manufacturing Processes Ltd [1976] 1 All ER 779, [1976] Ch 55, CA.
Bankers Trust Co v Shapira [1980] 3 All ER 353, [1980] 1 WLR 1274, CA.
Carter v Carter [1896] P 35.
Cretanor Maritime Co Ltd v Irish Marine Management Ltd [1978] 3 All ER 164, [1978] 1
c WLR 966, CA.
Fanshawe v Fanshawe [1927] P 238.
Lloyds Bank Ltd v Marcan [1973] 3 All ER 754, [1973] 1 WLR 1387, CA.
Mills v Northern Railway of Buenos Ayres Co (1870) 5 Ch App 621
Norwich Pharmacal Co v Comrs of Customs and Excise [1973] 2 All ER 943, [1974] AC 133,
   HL.
d *Robinson v Pickering* (1881) 16 Ch D 660.
Stewart Chartering Ltd v C & O Managements SA [1980] 1 All ER 718, [1980] 1 WLR 460.
Third Chandris Shipping Corpn v Unimarine SA, The Pythia, The Angelic Wings, The Genie
   [1979] 2 All ER 972, [1979] QB 645, CA.
Twentyman v Twentyman [1903] P 82.

e **Interlocutory appeal**
By a writ dated 6th April 1979 the plaintiffs, Faith Panton Property Plan Ltd, sought an
injunction restraining the defendants, Alexander Charles Hodgetts and Sheila Hodgetts
(trading as Dekor Bathroom Laminates), from passing off the defendants' goods as those
of the plaintiffs, causing or procuring breaches of contracts made with the plaintiffs,
unlawfully interfering with the plaintiffs' business, making or publishing malicious
f falsehoods about the plaintiffs and wrongfully interfering with the plaintiffs' goods. The
plaintiffs also sought delivery up of any material the use of which would be a breach of
the terms of the injunction claimed, delivery up of various goods and chattels alleged to
be their property and an inquiry as to damages suffered as a result of the acts complained
of. The plaintiffs moved for interlocutory relief and by orders dated 10th April, and 8th
and 29th August 1979 the defendants gave certain undertakings to the court until trial
g of the action. By motions issued on 28th, 29th, 30th and 31st October 1980 the plaintiffs
applied for committal of the defendants for breaches of the undertakings. On 3rd
November 1980, Foster J held that the defendant Alexander Charles Hodgetts was in
breach of the undertakings given on 10th April, 8th August and 29th August 1979 and
ordered him to pay to the plaintiffs their costs of the motions for committal, such costs
to be taxed on the basis of a full indemnity. To safeguard their order for costs which had
h not yet been taxed, the plaintiffs applied on 9th December 1980 to Vinelott J for (i) an
order restraining the defendants until judgment or further order from assigning selling
or otherwise dealing in, without the plaintiffs' licence, an alleged copyright relating to,
and moulds for, bathroom and sanitary ware formerly manufactured by the defendants
for the plaintiffs, and letters patent no 1541444 and any rights in or under the letters
patent or any interest therein, and (ii) an order that the defendants disclose within seven
j days of the date of order the names and addresses of any person, firm or company to
whom they had assigned any of the aforementioned assets. Vinelott J refused the
injunction. The plaintiffs appealed. The facts are set out in the judgment of Waller LJ.

C A Brodie QC and *Malcolm Warner* for the plaintiffs.
The first defendant appeared in person.

Cur adv vult

21st January. The following judgments were read.   *a*

WALLER LJ. This is an appeal from a judgment of Vinelott J in which he refused an
injunction against both defendants. The plaintiffs have a business of interior decorators,
designers and suppliers of bathroom equipment. The defendants also manufacture
fibreglass baths and other bathroom equipment. In 1978 and early 1979 there was an
agreement between the plaintiffs and either the first defendant or both defendants *b*
concerning the manufacture of bathroom equipment. In March 1979 that agreement
was determined and there followed a number of proceedings in the High Court. The
plaintiffs brought proceedings alleging passing off, procuring breaches of contract,
slander of goods and malicious falsehood and moved for interlocutory relief as a result of
which a number of undertakings were given to the court until trial. There was also a
counterclaim in the same proceedings raising claims to copyright and the ownership of *c*
a patent and alleging infringement of the copyright and patent. There was also a reply
and defence to that counterclaim. Those were proceedings in the Chancery Division and
there was also an action in the Queen's Bench Division.

On 8th November 1979 the plaintiffs obtained judgment in the Queen's Bench
Division for £9,679·23 but a stay of execution was granted pending the determination
of the Chancery proceedings. On 23rd January 1980 both defendants were ordered to *d*
pay costs which were subsequently taxed at £526·24 on a motion to set aside a subpoena
on Mrs Steedman, the majority shareholder in the plaintiff company. On 3rd November
1980 the first defendant was ordered to pay the costs of four motions before Foster J. The
judge directed that the costs were to be taxed on an indemnity basis and paid
forthwith. They have not yet been taxed and it is estimated they will not be taxed for
some four or five months but they they will be assessed at approximately £12,000.   *e*

The first defendant has said that he intends to go bankrupt, and has said falsely that he
had an offer from a substantial company for his assets. He then said after that that he had
received another offer and accepted it and that he has spent the purchase money. He has
told the plaintiffs' solicitors that he intends to sell his copyright and patents to a
substantial company; he also has said that moulds which are estimated to be worth
£1,000 each are in his possession but that he had sold them in March 1979 on terms that *f*
he was allowed to remain in possession of them.

The plaintiffs are anxious about the enforcement of the order for costs of approximately
£12,000 and in this application they apply to restrain the defendants from dealing in any
rights that they may have in the alleged copyrights, patents or in the moulds, and they
also seek an order that each of the defendants disclose on oath the names of the persons
to whom they have assigned or transferred the copyrights, letters patent or moulds.   *g*

The plaintiffs claim that the company is entitled to the injunction under s 45 of the
Supreme Court of Judicature (Consolidation) Act 1925, on the authority of the Mareva
decisions. Section 45(1) of the 1925 Act reads:

> 'The High Court may grant a mandamus or an injunction or appoint a receiver,
> by an interlocutory order in all cases in which it appears to the court to be just or *h*
> convenient so to do.'

Counsel for the plaintiffs submits that the discretion given to the court is one which is
unfettered and relies on the cases of *Beddow v Beddow* (1878) 9 Ch D 89, *Blunt v Blunt*
[1943] 2 All ER 76, [1943] AC 517 and *Ward v James* [1965] 1 All ER 563, [1966] 1 QB
273. In the latter case Lord Denning MR said ([1965] 1 All ER 563 at 571, [1966] 1 QB *j*
273 at 295):

> 'The cases all show that, when a statute gives discretion, the courts must not fetter
> it by rigid rules from which a judge is never at liberty to depart. Nevertheless the
> courts can lay down the considerations which should be borne in mind in exercising
> the discretion and point out those considerations which should be ignored.'

Where however a plaintiff is asking for an injunction in proceedings which are pending,
a Cotton LJ in *Lister & Co v Stubbs* (1890) 45 Ch D 1 at 13, [1886–90] All ER Rep 797 at 799
said:

> 'I know of no case where, because it was highly probable that if the action were
> brought to a hearing the plaintiff could establish that a debt was due to him from
> the defendant, the defendant has been ordered to give security until that has been
> established by the judgment or decree.'

b   We have been referred to a number of matrimonial cases both in the 19th century and
the first half of this century in which injunctions were granted or refused and it would
seem that in practice an injunction was only granted where the sum due was a liquidated
sum which had been ordered by the court. See, for example, *Newton v Newton* (1885) 11
PD 11, *Jagger v Jagger* [1926] P 23, *Scott v Scott* [1950] 2 All ER 1154, [1951] P 193 and
a number of other cases. These cases are no longer good law because as Brandon LJ
c pointed out in the course of argument Parliament has reversed them in matrimonial
cases.

       Cummins v Perkins [1899] 1 Ch 16 (which was not a matrimonial case) showed that an
order for costs could be the subject of an order for a receiver of married woman's separate
estate even though those costs had not been taxed. Lindley MR (at 19–20) made the
order for a receiver on the ground that the court was 'dealing with equitable estates and
d a judgment that a debt [was] to be paid out of a particular equitable estate.' He went on
(at 20):

> 'That is the principle on which the learned judge has acted here—a perfectly
> sound principle, even without invoking the aid of s. 25 of [the Supreme Court of
> Judicature Act 1873]. But the introduction of that section does not curtail the
> power of the Court to grant injunctions or to appoint receivers: it enlarges it. It has
e not revolutionised the law, but it has enabled the Court to grant injunctions and
> receivers in cases in which it used not to do so previously. I will not say where it had
> no jurisdiction to do so, that would be going too far, but where in practice it never
> did so . . .'

       Counsel for the plaintiffs has also relied on the Mareva line of cases, *Nippon Yusen
f Kaisha v Karageorgis* [1975] 3 All ER 282, [1975] 1 WLR 1093, *Mareva Compania Naviera
SA v International Bulkcarriers SA, The Mareva* [1980] 1 All ER 213, *Rasu Maritima SA v
Perusahaan Pertambangan Minyak Dan Gas Negara (Pertamina) and Government of Indonesia
(as interveners)* [1977] 3 All ER 324, [1978] QB 644, *The Siskina* [1977] 3 All ER 803,
[1979] AC 210 and *Prince Abdul Rahman Bin Turki Al Sudairy v Abu-Taha* [1980] 3 All ER
409, 1 WLR 1268 and others, as altering the practice which had hitherto governed such
g cases. He has submitted that, although the Mareva line of cases all concerned either
foreign defendants who had assets in this country which were liable to be removed or, as
in the *Rahman* case, a foreign defendant apparently living in this country in similar such
circumstances, the only logical explanation of the exercise of the jurisdiction was on the
basis of jeopardy; that unless some such order was made the plaintiffs would be
jeopardised by being deprived of the fruits of any judgment that he might get. It was
h submitted that jeopardy does not depend solely on the risk of assets being removed out
of the jurisdiction and reliance was placed on the judgment of Lord Denning MR in the
Rahman case [1980] 3 All ER 409 at 412, [1980] 1 WLR 1268 at 1273 as showing that the
Mareva injunction is not to be confined to cases where assets are likely to be removed out
of the jurisdiction. Lord Denning MR said:

> 'So I would hold that a Mareva injunction can be granted against a man even
j though he is based in this country if the circumstances are such that there is a danger
> of his absconding, or a danger of the assets being removed out of the jurisdiction or
> disposed of within the jurisdiction or otherwise dealt with so that there is a danger
> that the plaintiff, if he gets judgment, will not be able to get it satisfied.'

Emphasis was placed on the words 'disposed of within the jurisdiction'. It was submitted
that removal out of the jurisdiction was logically only one way in which jeopardy could

occur. In the *Pertamina* case [1977] 3 All ER 324 at 337, [1978] QB 644 at 664 Orr LJ
expressed the view: 'Whether it is right or just to exercise this particular jurisdiction	*a*
must depend on all the circumstances of a given case and not, in my judgment, on any
single factor.' And then Orr LJ went on to enumerate the factors such as the apparent
strength or weakness of the plaintiff's case, whether it is restricted to money, the effect
on the defendant and so on. For myself I see the force of this argument but to accept it
would, in my opinion, be a considerable extension of the Mareva doctrine and I would
wish to reserve my opinion until the facts of the case make it necessary so to consider.	*b*
I find it unnecessary to make the decision whether or not a Mareva injunction would
apply in the circumstances suggested by counsel for the plaintiffs. All of the authorities
before the Mareva cases go to show that injunctions will not be granted before
judgment. This is an intermediate case. It is not a case where it is highly probable that
if the action is brought to a hearing the plaintiff would be able to establish a debt such as
Cotton LJ was considering in *Lister v Stubbs* 45 Ch D 1, [1886–90] All ER Rep 797. It is	*c*
a case where the defendant has been ordered to pay the costs of a hearing on an
indemnity basis, a hearing that took four days. It is only because of the delay which must
inevitably take place before taxation that the plaintiffs have not been enabled to execute
the judgment. The principle in *Lister v Stubbs* depends on there being no order or
judgment. In this case there is a judgment which cannot be enforced for some months
because of the difficulties of taxation. In *Cummins v Perkins* [1899] 1 Ch 16 an order for	*d*
costs which had not been taxed was treated as an order which could be enforced by
appointing a receiver. In my opinion there is nothing in any of the authorities which
would make it wrong to grant an injunction in this case.
Are the circumstances of this case such that an injunction should be granted? The
defendant has shown by his behaviour that he intends to divest himself of his assets if he
can. He has shown a lack of frankness to the court in not disclosing to whom he has sold	*e*
some of his assets when asked by this court. The hearing before Foster J was for
contempt of court and more serious consequences might have followed. In my
judgment this is a case where the court should ensure so far as possible that its orders are
not thwarted, and I would grant an injunction as prayed until after the costs have been
taxed and paid.
I have arrived at this conclusion differing from Vinelott J with reluctance. He accepted	*f*
that where there was a substantial judgment, not finally quantified, an injunction might
be granted but came to the conclusion that this was not such a case. There has, however,
been fuller argument before this court and in particular we have been referred to a
number of cases which were not before Vinelott J. Furthermore as I have mentioned
above there has been before this court a lack of frankness.
With regard to the prayer for the disclosure of the names of the persons to whom the	*g*
defendants have assigned or transferred to copyright, letters patent or moulds, this
appears to me to be an inquiry of a fishing nature. The case put forward by the plaintiffs
is based largely on the suspicion that the first defendant had transferred the assets to the
second defendant. On this basis the plaintiffs are adequately protected without any
further order. The possibility of the assets having been transferred elsewhere is remote
and is based on suspicion rather than evidence. If any have been transferred the	*h*
difficulties of tracing them would be almost insuperable. I would therefore refuse this
part of the application.

BRANDON LJ. The facts which constitute the background of this case have been
stated in the judgment of Waller LJ and it is not necessary that I should repeat them.
By their notice of motion dated 2nd December 1980 and amended on 9th December	*j*
1980 the plaintiffs applied for two orders in respect of (a) the defendants' alleged
copyright relating to moulds for 'Palace Bathroom' furniture, (b) the moulds themselves
and (c) patent no 1541444 relating to an allegedly original design of a water closet.
In para (i) of the notice of motion the plaintiffs asked, on the basis that the defendants
had not already assigned or otherwise disposed of the alleged copyright, moulds, and
patent owned by them, for an injunction restraining them from doing so. In para (ii) of

the notice of motion the plaintiffs asked, on the basis that the defendants had already

a assigned or otherwise disposed of the alleged copyright, moulds and patent owned by them, for an order that they do disclose on oath within seven days the person, persons, firm or company to whom they made any such dispositions.

The reason why the plaintiffs asked for these two alternative kinds of relief in this way was that the first defendant had claimed to have sold the moulds in March 1979, although on terms which allowed him to keep them in his possession, and to have

b assigned the copyright and patent on 5th November 1980; but that, due to discrepancies, omissions and ambivalence in the first defendant's various accounts of these transactions, there was a serious doubt whether his claim to have made such sale and assignments was true.

So far as the first kind of relief asked for is concerned, namely an injunction against dealing with the copyright, moulds or patent, the appeal appears to me to raise two

c questions, each primarily of law. The first question is whether to grant the injunction asked for would be in accordance with the practice in such matters established over many years prior to the development, from 1975 onwards, of the doctrine of the Mareva injunction. The second question is whether, if the answer to the first question is in the negative, to grant the injunction would be in accordance with the recently developed doctrine to which I have referred.

d I shall consider first what may conveniently be called the pre-Mareva practice. The basic tenet of that practice was expressed by Cotton LJ in *Lister & Co v Stubbs* (1890) 45 Ch D 1 at 13, [1886–90] All ER Rep 797 at 799:

'I know of no case where, because it was highly probable that if the action was brought to a hearing the plaintiff could establish that a debt was due to him from the defendant, the defendant has been ordered to give security until that has been

e established by the judgment or decree.'

The practice as so stated was applied mainly in matrimonial cases, in which a basic distinction was drawn between cases in which a wife had obtained against her husband an order for the payment of a specific sum of money by way of alimony, maintenance, costs or security for costs on the one hand, and cases in which she had applied for such an

f order but not yet obtained it on the other hand. Examples of the first category of cases are *Sidney v Sidney* (1867) 17 LT 9, *Gillet v Gillet* (1889) 14 PD 158, *Waterhouse v Waterhouse* [1893] P 284, *Brewis v Brewis* [1893] WN 6, *Newton v Newton* [1896] P 36, and *Bullus v Bullus* (1910) 102 LT 399. Examples of the second category of cases are *Newton v Newton* (1885) 11 PD 11, *Burmester v Burmester* [1913] P 76, *Jagger v Jagger* [1926] P 93, [1926] All ER Rep 613, *Scott v Scott* [1950] 2 All ER 1154, [1951] P 193 and *Wright v*

g *Wright* [1954] 1 All ER 707, [1954] 1 WLR 534.

In *Jagger v Jagger* Scrutton LJ said ([1926] P 93 at 102, [1926] All ER Rep 613 at 618):

'I am not aware of any statutory or other power in the Court to restrain a person from dealing with his property at a time when no order against him has been made.'

The distinction between the two categories of cases referred to above operated unjustly

h to wives, who often had little control over the speed with which their applications for financial relief were carried through to judgment, especially having regard to the manifold opportunities available to husbands to delay that process. This injustice was recognised by Parliament, which dealt comprehensively with the prevention of wives being deprived of their just dues by their husbands' disposal or other dissipation of their assets before proceedings for financial relief were concluded, in the Matrimonial Causes

j (Property and Maintenance) Act 1958, s 2. These provisions have since been re-enacted in later Matrimonial Causes Acts, and are presently to be found in s 37 of the 1973 Act.

The present case does not fall clearly into either of the two categories of cases discussed above. On the one hand it is a case when an order was made on 3rd November 1980 that the first defendant should pay to the plaintiffs their costs of the applications for committal for contempt to be taxed by the taxing master on the basis of a full indemnity. On the other hand taxation of the costs has not yet taken place, and we have been told that, due to the delays presently occurring in such matters, it is unlikely to take place for another five months or so. The amount ultimately payable is, however, by no means at large, for there is evidence before the court, which I see no reason not to accept as reasonably reliable, that the amount is likely to be in the region of £12,000.

How should the court, acting in accordance with the pre-Mareva practice, deal with an intermediate case of this kind? Assistance on this is, in my view to be found, first, in common sense, and, second, in a further authority on the practice of the court to which I have not yet referred.

First, as to common sense. It seems to me to verge on the absurd that, if the costs had already been taxed at £12,000, the court would have power to grant an injunction against the defendants restraining them from dealing with their assets (if they still hold them), but that, because the costs have not yet been taxed, although there is sufficient evidence that they will in fact amount to about £12,000, the court has no power to grant such an injunction.

Second, as to further authority. This is to be found in *Cummins v Perkins* [1899] 1 Ch 16. In that case an action brought by a married woman had been dismissed with costs, to be paid out of her separate estate. The defendants' solicitor had brought in a bill of costs amounting to £270. The plaintiff had no, or virtually no, separate estate, except a share in the estate of her deceased sister which was due to her but had not yet been paid. It was held that, in such circumstances, the court had power to appoint a receiver of the share of the plaintiff's deceased sister's estate which was coming to her, and an order for the appointment of such a receiver was made. It is to be observed that the order against the plaintiff was that the defendants' costs should be paid out of her separate estate, not out of any particular fund which might constitute such estate.

It is true that this case is complicated by the fact that the court was dealing with a married woman and ordering the costs to be paid out of her separate estate. For myself, however, I cannot see any significant distinction between that situation and the situation in an ordinary modern case like the present one, in which costs are ordered to be paid by a defendant, whether male or female. The order will not, of course, direct payment out of any separate estate, because there is no need for it to do so. But the effect is in practice the same. Further, assuming that the court could properly appoint a receiver in such a case, I see no reason why it should not afford protection to the party in whose favour the order for costs has been obtained by the alternative method of granting an injunction.

I am further of the opinion that, having regard to the peculiar, inconsistent and ambivalent conduct of the first defendant with regard to what dispositions, if any, he has made of the alleged copyright, moulds and patent, the court should exercise its discretion by granting the first injunction asked for by the plaintiffs in the present action.

On the footing that the court has power, under the pre-Mareva practice, to grant the first kind of injunction asked for by the plaintiffs, and that it would be right, in the circumstances of this case, to exercise such power, it is not necessary to examine the plaintiffs' alternative case based on the recent development of the doctrine of Mareva injunctions. Since, however, considerable argument was addressed to us on the subject, I think it would be right for me to make some observations on it.

Originally Mareva injunctions were granted only in cases where the defendants were foreigners with assets in the jurisdiction, which they could easily remove in time to avoid execution of any money judgment which might subsequently be obtained by the plaintiffs: see *Nippon Yusen Kaisha v Karageorgis* [1975] 3 All ER 282, [1975] 1 WLR 1093, *Mareva Compania Naviera SA v International Bulkcarriers SA, The Mareva* [1980] 1 All ER 213, *Rasu Maritima SA v Perusahaan Pertambangan Minyak Dan Gas Bumi Negara (Pertamina) and Government of Indonesia (as interveners)* [1977] 3 All ER 324, [1978] QB 644. These were all commercial cases, but the same principle was later applied in an action for personal injuries: see *Allen v Jambo Holdings Ltd* [1980] 2 All ER 502, [1980] 1 WLR 1252.

In *Gebr Van Weelde Scheepvaart Kantoor BV v Homeric Marine Services Ltd, The Agrabele* [1979] 2 Lloyd's Rep 117, Lloyd J held that there was a settled practice against granting

Mareva injunctions against defendants resident within the jurisdiction. In *Chartered*
a *Bank v Daklouche* [1980] 3 All ER 502, [1980] 1 WLR 107, however, this court held that
mere residence here did not prevent the grant of a Mareva injunction against a defendant
of foreign nationality, when her residence here might well be temporary only, and a
serious risk of removal of assets from the jurisdiction existed.

Similarly in *Barclay-Johnson v Yuill* [1980] 3 All ER 190, [1980] 1 WLR 1259 Sir Robert
Megarry V-C granted a Mareva injunction against an English defendant who, although
b he had previously been ordinarily resident within the jurisdiction, had since taken
himself off abroad for an indefinite period. The Vice-Chancellor stressed in that case that
the crucial factor justifying the grant of an injunction was the risk of the defendant
removing assets from the jurisdiction in order to defeat the plaintiff's claim. This
decision was approved by this court in *Prince Abdul Rahman bin Turki al Sudairy v Abu-Taha*
[1980] 3 All ER 409, [1980] 1 WLR 1268, where an injunction was granted against
c foreign defendants who claimed to be resident within the jurisdiction, but, in the
affidavits which they filed, failed to disclose their 'place of residence' as required by RSC
Ord 41, r 1(4).

It is right to observe, I think, that, although the modern doctrine of the Mareva
injunction has developed rapidly since it was first applied by this court in 1975, it has
never yet been applied to a case like the present one in which no foreign element of any
d kind exists. It was argued by counsel for the plaintiffs that there was no logicality in
insisting on the presence of a foreign element, and that the only issue on which the grant
of a Mareva injunction should depend was that of jeopardy, by which he meant a real risk
that a defendant, whatever his nationality, domicile or residence might be, against
whom a plaintiff had a good claim, might dispose of or dissipate his assets, either abroad
or here, in such a way as to prevent the plaintiff from executing any judgment which he
e might later obtain.

I see the force of this argument, and indeed it was fully recognised by Lord Hailsham
in *The Siskina* [1977] 3 All ER 803 at 829, [1979] AC 210 at 261, when he said in what I
may perhaps be permitted to describe as a particularly prescient passage in his speech:

f
> 'I believe the truth to be that sooner or later the courts or the legislature will have
> to choose between two alternatives. Either the position of a plaintiff making a
> claim against an English based defendant will have to be altered, or the principle of
> the Mareva cases will have to be modified.'

It now seems highly likely that it will be the first of the two alternatives referred to by
Lord Hailsham in that passage which will be chosen, namely the alteration of the
position of a plaintiff making a claim against an English based defendant, and further
g that it will be the legislature which will before long be making the choice. In this
connection I refer to the Supreme Court Bill, recently introduced in the House of Lords
in its legislative capacity. Clause 37 of this Bill, which is designed to replace s 45 of the
Supreme Court of Judicature (Consolidation) Act 1925, is in these terms:

h
> '(1) The High Court may by order (whether interlocutory or final) grant an
> injunction or appoint a receiver in all cases in which it appears to the court to be just
> and convenient to do so . . .
> '(3) The power of the High Court under subsection (1) to grant an interlocutory
> injunction restraining a party to any proceedings from removing from the
> jurisdiction of the High Court, or otherwise dealing with, assets located within that
> jurisdiction shall be exercisable in cases where that party is, as well as in cases where
> he is not, domiciled, resident or present within that jurisdiction.'

j
With fresh legislation of this kind in the offing, I think that it would be undesirable
for this court to express a judicial opinion on what the law would have been without it,
unless it was necessary to do so. Since I am of opinion, for the reasons which I gave
earlier, that the plaintiffs in the present action are entitled to the grant of the first
injunction sought by them in accordance with the pre-Mareva practice, I do not propose

to express any opinion on the question whether they could, on the law as it exists at present, obtain such an injunction on the basis of the Mareva doctrine as well.

I turn now to the second order asked for by the plaintiffs. That order was, as I indicated earlier, that the defendants, on the assumption that they had assigned or otherwise dealt with the copyright, moulds or patent, should disclose on oath within seven days to whom such assignment or other disposition had been made.

I cannot see any good reason for making such an order. As I understand the plaintiffs' case, they are not, at present at least, asserting any proprietary interest, legal or equitable, in the three assets concerned, that is to say the copyright, the moulds and the patent. That being so, even if there has been an assignment of one or more of these assets to a third party or parties, I do not see how knowledge of the identity of such third party or parties will assist the plaintiffs at this stage. The assets would not be traceable by the plaintiffs in the hands of their present holders, and knowledge of the identity of such holders would not therefore assist the plaintiffs in obtaining security for the enforcement of their judgment on costs in the motions for contempt when these have finally been taxed.

There is the further point in this connection that the defendants were earlier ordered to pay to Mrs Faith Marian Steedman, the managing director of the plaintiffs, costs later taxed at £526·24 in respect of a successful application by her to set aside a subpoena served on her by them. In relation to this judgment debt an order has been made under RSC Ord 48, r 1(1), for the attendance of the defendants for oral examination on 20th January 1981 and it should be possible to elicit from them in the course of that examination the kind of information which the plaintiffs seek.

For these reasons I agree with Vinelott J that the court should not make the second order asked for by the plaintiffs.

I recognise that, in coming to a different conclusion from that of the judge with regard to the first order asked for by the plaintiffs, I am disagreeing with him in a matter which involved an exercise of discretion by him. I think, however, that this court has had the advantage of a much fuller exposition of the relevant authorities than the judge had and that, in the light of that fuller exposition, we are entitled, even though an exercise of discretion is involved, to take a different view of the matter from that which he took.

For the reasons which I have given I would allow this appeal so far as it relates to the order asked for in para (i) of the notice of motion, and dismiss it so far as it relates to para (ii).

SIR DAVID CAIRNS. I agree that the appeal against the refusal of an injunction restraining the defendant from disposal of assets should be allowed, and that the injunction be granted in the terms indicated by Waller LJ.

I also agree that the appeal against the refusal of an order for the discovery of certain names should be dismissed.

In both cases my agreement is for the reasons given in the judgments already delivered, to which I have no further reasons of my own to add.

Appeal against refusal of injunction allowed. Appeal against refusal of an order for discovery dismissed.

Solicitors: *Dawson & Co* (for the plaintiffs).

William Hoskins Esq   Barrister.

a
Schiffahrtsagentur Hamburg Middle East Line GmbH v Virtue Shipping Corpn
The Oinoussian Virtue

b
QUEEN'S BENCH DIVISION (COMMERCIAL COURT)
ROBERT GOFF J
19th JANUARY, 5th FEBRUARY 1981

Arbitration – Appeal – Leave to appeal – Exercise of discretion – Decision by commercial arbitrator on construction of charterparty – Arbitrator voluntarily giving reasons for decision – Whether leave to appeal should be granted – Whether appeal on question of law – Whether
c *failure to ask for reasoned award precluding grant of leave to appeal – Arbitration Act 1979, s 1(3)(4)(6).*

Arbitration – Award – Remission – Grounds for remission – Remission for further findings of fact – Procedure – Cases arising under new arbitration procedure – Whether jurisdiction to remit for statement of arbitrator's 'reasons' including jurisdiction to remit for findings on relevant facts –
d *Whether remission for further findings of fact should be made under new procedure rather than under former procedure – Arbitration Act 1950, s 22(1) – Arbitration Act 1979, s 1(5).*

The owners time chartered a vessel to the charterers for a voyage to the Persian Gulf under a charterparty on the New York Produce Exchange Form which provided, by
cl 36(b), that 'Any additional war risk insurance premiums over and above normal war
e risk insurance premiums ... [shall] be for the Charterers' account'. Having regard to the itinerary of the vessel the owners decided to take out additional full war risks insurance and claimed reimbursement from the charterers under cl 36(b). The charterers denied liability and the dispute was referred to arbitration. At the hearing of the arbitration the charterers submitted, inter alia, that under cl 36(b) they were only liable for any addition to the normal premium payable for war risk cover found to be due after the date of the
f charterparty, and not for any abnormal war risk cover taken out by the owners after the date of the charterparty. The arbitrator found in favour of the owners, on the ground that 'additional war risk insurance premiums' in cl 36(b) referred to special cover for abnormal war risks and not merely to any increase in, or additional premium for, normal cover. The arbitrator, although not asked by either party for a reasoned award, voluntarily gave his reasons for the award in order to inform the parties of the basis of his
g decision. The charterers applied under s 1(3)[a] of the Arbitration Act 1979 for leave to

---

a   Section 1, so far as material, provides:
    '... (2) Subject to subsection (3) below, an appeal shall lie to the High Court on any question of law arising out of an award made on an arbitration agreement ...
    '(3) An appeal under this section may be brought by any of the parties to the reference—(a)
h with the consent of all the other parties to the reference; or (b) subject to section 3 below, with the leave of the court.
    '(4) The High Court shall not grant leave under subsection (3)(b) above unless it considers that, having regard to all the circumstances, the determination of the question of law concerned could substantially affect the rights of one or more of the parties to the arbitration agreement; and the court may make any leave which it gives conditional upon the applicant complying with such conditions as it considers appropriate.
j   '(5) Subject to subsection (6) below, if an award is made and, on an application made by any of the parties to the reference,—(a) with the consent of all the other parties to the reference, or (b) subject to section 3 below, with the leave of the court, it appears to the High Court that the award does not or does not sufficiently set out the reasons for the award, the court may order the arbitrator or umpire concerned to state the reasons for his award in sufficient detail to enable the
(Continued on p 888)

appeal against the arbitrator's decision on the same grounds put forward at the arbitration. In support of the application for leave the charterers submitted that the *a* appeal was on questions of law arising out of the award, within s 1(2) of the 1979 Act, namely the construction of cl 36(b), and that since determination of those questions would substantially affect the parties' rights within s 1(4) of the 1979 Act the court ought to exercise its discretion to grant leave to appeal. The charterers further submitted that the court ought not to impose conditions on the grant of leave despite the fact that the charterers were in financial difficulty, since that arose because they were trading with a *b* country suffering internal upheaval (Iran) and otherwise they were efficient businessmen who were not pursuing the appeal merely to postpone an inevitable liability. The charterers also applied under s 22(1)^*b* of the Arbitration Act 1950 for remission of the award to the arbitrator for further stated findings of fact. The owners opposed the grant of leave to appeal on the grounds (i) that the charterers' arguments turned on what were normal war risk insurance premiums and that was a question of fact decided by the *c* arbitrator and not a question of law, (ii) that the court ought not to give leave to appeal under s 1(3) where the parties had not asked for a reasoned award, because the court was then precluded by s 1(6) from ordering the arbitrator, under s 1(5), to state his reasons, in which case an appeal would be impossible, (iii) that reasons stated voluntarily by an arbitrator for the parties' information were not necessarily sufficient reasons to enable the court to decide an appeal and, moreover, if leave were granted when an arbitrator *d* voluntarily gave reasons that might discourage arbitrators from voluntarily giving reasons in the future, and (iv) that the court should exercise its discretion to refuse leave where the decision of a commercial arbitrator turned on the meaning of the words in a commercial contract, even though the decision raised a point of law, because in such a case the arbitrator was more likely than a judge to be right.

e

Held – (1) The charterers would be given leave to appeal, conditional on providing security for costs, for the following reasons—

(a) the questions at issue on the appeal were questions of construction of the charterparty and therefore questions of law (see p 891 *g* to *j* and p 894 *g* to *j*, post);

(b) as a matter of construction the 1979 Act did not preclude the grant of leave to appeal where the parties had not requested the arbitrator to give a reasoned award but he *f* had nevertheless given his reasons voluntarily, since the court was only precluded by s 1(6) from requiring the arbitrator to state his reasons if no reasons had been asked for and none given. As a matter of practice, where reasons were given by an arbitrator voluntarily they would normally be sufficient not only to inform the parties of the basis of the arbitrator's decision but also to enable the court to review the decision, and the granting of leave to appeal where reasons were given voluntarily ought not to deter *g* arbitrators from giving reasons voluntarily (see p 892 *b* to *d* and p 894 *g* to *j*, post);

(c) where an appeal was on a question of law, including the interpretation of a commercial contract, the only limit on the court's discretion to grant leave was whether determination of the question would substantially affect the rights of the parties, and, if it did so, the court was not entitled to fetter its discretion by giving leave in some cases but not in others according to predetermined guidelines (see p 893 *j* and p 894 *a b d* to *j*, *h*

(*Continued from p 887*)

court, should an appeal be brought under this section, to consider any question of law arising out of the award.

'(6) In any case where an award is made without any reason being given, the High Court shall not make an order under subsection (5) above unless it is satisfied—(*a*) that before the award was *j* made one of the parties to the reference gave notice to the arbitrator or umpire concerned that a reasoned award would be required; or (*b*) that there is some special reason why such a notice was not given . . .'

b   Section 22(1) provides: 'In all cases of reference to arbitration the High Court or a judge thereof may from time to time remit the matters referred, or any of them, to the reconsideration of the arbitrator or umpire.'

a post); dictum of Lord Denning MR in *Pioneer Shipping Ltd v BTP Tioxide Ltd, The Nema*
[1980] 3 All ER at 124–125 not followed.

(2) An application to remit an award for further findings of fact in a case arising under
the 1979 Act should ordinarily be made under s 1(5) of the 1979 Act, and not under s 22
of the 1950 Act, because (a) the expression 'reasons for the award' in s 1(5) included the
relevant facts on which the arbitrator's conclusion was based and was not limited to the
arbitrator's 'reasoning' and therefore there was jurisdiction under s 1(5) to remit an
b award for further findings of fact, and (b) the general power to remit in s 22 of the 1950
Act was concerned with the special case procedure which had been abolished by the 1979
Act. Accordingly, treating the charterers' application to remit as if it had been made
under s 1(5) of the 1979 Act, the court would, in all the circumstances, remit the award
for the further findings of fact asked for (see p 895 d to j and p 896 c, post).

c Per Curiam. It is to be hoped that it will become the general practice of arbitrators to
give reasoned awards as a matter of course (see p 892 d e, post).

Notes
For appeal to the High Court from an arbitrator's decision, see 2 Halsbury's Laws (4th
Edn) para 627.
d   For jurisdiction and procedure to remit an award, see paras 615–617, and for cases on
remitting an award, see 3 Digest (Reissue) 298–300, 2002–2014.
For the Arbitration Act 1950, s 22, see 2 Halsbury's Statutes (3rd Edn) 451.
For the Arbitration Act 1979, s 1, see 49 ibid 59.

Cases referred to in judgment
e *Angelia, The, Trade and Transport Inc v Iino Kaiun Kaisha Ltd* [1973] 2 All ER 144, [1973]
1 WLR 210, [1972] 2 Lloyd's Rep 154, Digest (Cont Vol D) 823, 1355a.
*British Launderers' Research Association v Central Middlesex Assessment Committee and Hendon
Rating Authority* [1949] 1 All ER 21, [1949] 1 KB 462, [1949] LJR 646, 113 JP 72, 47
LGR 113, 41 R & IT 564, CA, 38 Digest (Repl) 583, 627.
f *Mondial Trading Co GmbH Ltd v Gill and Duffus Zuckerhandelsgesellschaft mbH* [1980] 2
Lloyd's Rep 376
Pilgrim Shipping Co Ltd v State Trading Corpn of India, The Hadjisakos [1975] 1 Lloyd's Rep
356, CA.
Pioneer Shipping Ltd v BTP Tioxide Ltd, The Nema [1980] 3 All ER 117, [1980] QB 547,
[1980] 3 WLR 326, [1980] 2 Lloyd's Rep 339, CA.
g *Universal Cargo Carriers Corpn v Citati* [1957] 2 All ER 70, [1957] 2 QB 401, [1957] 2
WLR 713, [1957] 1 Lloyd's Rep 174; *affd* [1957] 3 All ER 234, [1957] 1 WLR 979,
[1957] 2 Lloyd's Rep 191, CA, 12 Digest (Reissue) 419, 3057.

Motion
By a notice of motion the applicants, Schiffahrtsagentur Hamburg Middle East Line
h GmbH, Hamburg ('the charterers'), applied to the Commercial Court (i) for an order
pursuant to s 22 of the Arbitration Act 1950 or under the inherent jurisdiction of the
court that the interim award of an arbitrator, Mr Cedric Barclay, dated 6th October 1980,
be remitted to him in order that he might make further findings of fact relevant to the
question of law decided by him in the arbitration and (ii) for leave to appeal to the High
Court against the arbitrator's determination that they were liable to the respondents,
j Virtue Shipping Corpn, Monrovia ('the owners'), in the sum of $US203,282·53 pursuant
to cl 36(b) of the charterparty dated 7th February 1980 made between the parties. The
facts are set out in the judgment.

Kenneth Rokison QC and *Patricia Phelan* for the charterers.
Stewart Boyd for the owners.

Cur adv vult

a

5th February. **ROBERT GOFF J** read the following judgment: There is before the
court an application under s 1 of the Arbitration Act 1979 by Schiffahrtsagentur
Hamburg Middle East Line GmbH, Hamburg ('the charterers') for leave to appeal against
an arbitration award made by a single arbitrator, Mr Cedric Barclay, dated 6th October
1980.

The dispute arose under a charterparty dated 7th February 1980 on the New York   b
Produce Exchange Form, under which Virtue Shipping Corpn, Monrovia ('the owners')
time chartered their ship Oinoussian Virtue to the charterers for a trip from the time of
arrival at the pilot station at Flushing, via safe port(s) always within institute warranty
limits, to the Persian Gulf. The charterparty contained the following clause, under
which the dispute has arisen:

c

> '36. (a) Owners guarantee that the vessel is entered for full cover and shall remain
> entered for the duration of the Charter in a P. & I. Association, namely, U.K. Mutual
> Steamship (Bermuda) Limited and is thus covered in respect of Owners' liability for
> personal accidents or injuries incurred to third parties, including the servants of the
> Charterers, on board or about the vessel.
> '(b) Any additional war risk insurance premiums over and above normal war risk   d
> insurance premiums and any war risk bonuses, if any, to be for Charterers'
> account. Such premium to be paid promptly on receipt by Charterers of debit notes
> submitted by Owners' underwriters.
> '(c) Charterers have the benefit of any return insurance premium receivable by
> Owners from Underwriters (as and when received from Underwriters) by reason of
> the vessel being in port for minimum 30 days, provided the vessel remained on   e
> hire.'

The owners claimed $US305,720 as due to them from the charterers under cl 36(b),
that sum being the total of additional premiums with which they had been debited by
the Hellenic Mutual War Risk Association for crossing the Suez Canal, for penetrating
into the Persian Gulf, and remaining there between 13th March 1980 and early May
1980. The charterers denied liability for this sum. The arbitrator held the charterers   f
liable to pay $203,282.53, consisting of $196,425.13 additional war risks premiums for
the Persian Gulf, and $6,857.40 for the Suez Canal. The arbitrator reached his conclusion
by allowing the owners' claims, subject to two points: (a) he held that the parties should
share equally the additional premium for the Suez Canal, because this additional
premium covered a whole year and it seemed likely that the ship would, during that
year, pass through the canal again after the termination of the charter; and (b) he   g
deducted certain commission and discounts, which were in substance a rebate refundable
to the owners.

At the arbitration two principal submissions were advanced by the charterers. Their
first submission was that under cl 36(b) they were only liable for any increase in war risk
premiums after the date of the charterparty; they said that since, after the charterparty
date, war risk premiums were going down, they were under no liability at all to the   h
owners under the clause. The arbitrator rejected this submission. In his reasoned award,
he said:

> 'I FIND AND HOLD that the Charterers' reading of Clause 36 to have been in error.
> Normal War Risk premiums must be distinguished from "Additional War Risk
> premiums", although admittedly these four words do give rise to equivocation.   j
> The "additional" does not relate to an increase in premium, but to a distinct and
> somewhat different type of insurance. The premium is in part the cost of reinstating
> a policy which has been cancelled. "Additional War Risk" should be understood as
> a generic term, a term of art, and a special type of cover which is not an increase or
> addition to the normal rates, but a fresh type of insurance above the normal War
> Risk Cover . . .'

The charterers' second submission related to the quality of cover afforded by the
a Hellenic Mutual War Risks Association, the mutual assurance association in which the
owners had entered their ship for war risks. The additional premium quoted by the
association gave an option to members to choose between two rates, full policy conditions
(0·475%) and cover which excluded 'blocking and trapping risks' (0·1%). The charterers
contended that if they were liable at all, their liability should be restricted to the latter
cover. This construction, if right, would have made a substantial difference to the award,
b because it would have reduced the award from about $200,000 to about $60,000.
However, the arbitrator rejected this submission also, stating that he could see no good
reason why the owners should restrict the scale and extent of their cover just because of
its cost to the charterers.

The charterers now seek leave to appeal in order to pursue both these points before the
courts. They submitted that the principles to be applied by the court in deciding
c whether to grant leave were as follows: (1) The court has an over-riding discretion
whether to grant leave. (2) An appeal can however only lie on a question of law arising
out of the award (s 1(2) of the 1979 Act), and it is a prerequisite of granting leave that the
determination of the question of law could substantially affect the rights of one or more
of the parties (s 1(4)). (3) The court has the power to make any leave which it gives
conditional on the applicant complying with such conditions as it considers appropriate
d (s 1(4)).

Here, submitted the charterers, the appeal which they sought to pursue was on
questions of law, viz the construction of the charterparty, and in particular cl 36; and
plainly those questions did substantially affect the rights of the parties. Furthermore,
said the charterers, there was no good reason why the court should exercise its discretion
against granting leave, or should even impose conditions. True, they were in financial
e difficulties (and indeed could not at the moment satisfy any requirement that the money
be brought into court). But they were described by the arbitrator as 'excellent charterers
... known as good businessmen', and their present financial difficulties arose from the
fact that their trade was with Iran (a situation which might be expected to improve now
that the American hostages had been released). Furthermore this was not a case in which
the appeal was being pursued simply to postpone an inevitable liability, as was evidenced
f by the fact that their appeal was being supported by their own P & I club.

Counsel for the owners opposed the charterers' application. His first submission was
that no question of law was involved. He said that both of the charterers' arguments
really hinged on the question of what were *normal* war risk insurance premiums, and
that question was essentially a question of fact which had been determined by the
arbitrator. I am unable to accept this submission. The arbitrator plainly regarded the
g charterers' first argument as raising a question of construction of the charterparty, a
question to be decided, no doubt, against the admissible commercial background of the
contract, but a question of construction none the less; and in this he was plainly right.
The charterers' second argument was explained to me by counsel on behalf of the
charterers, as follows. He said that the question at issue was this: did the charterers have
to pay a *premium* which was over and above the normal *premium*; or did the word
h 'additional' qualify the words 'war risk *insurance*', so that the charterers were obliged to
pay for any additional war risk *insurance* over and above normal war risk *insurance*. The
charterers' submission was that it could not possibly have been the intention that they
should be compelled to pay for abnormal cover; but that, they said, was the effect of the
arbitrator's award. Now that question too, in my judgment, is also a question of
construction of the contract and therefore a question of law.

j Counsel's second submission for the owners was founded on the fact that neither party
had in fact given notice to the arbitrator that a reasoned award was required. In those
circumstances, of course, if the arbitrator had not made a reasoned award, the court
would (in the absence of any special reason why a notice requiring him to do so had not
been given) be precluded by s 1(6) of the 1979 Act from making an order under s 1(5)
that the arbitrator should state his reasons, in which event an appeal would not be
possible. Here however (in accordance with what I understand to be now the normal

practice, at least in maritime arbitrations) the arbitrator has voluntarily given his reasons, as a matter of course. Counsel for the owners submitted that, if neither party has asked *a* the arbitrator for a reasoned award, the court should not ordinarily give leave to appeal. He suggested that if neither party asked for a reasoned award the arbitrator, if he voluntarily made a reasoned award, would only set out such reasons as were necessary to inform the parties of the basis of his decision, which would not necessarily be sufficient to enable a court to consider the question on appeal. Furthermore, to allow appeals on awards where reasons had been given voluntarily might discourage arbitrators from *b* giving reasons except in cases where they were asked to give them. I am unable to accept this submission. First of all, I can see no basis for it as a matter of construction of the 1979 Act. All the Act does is to preclude an order for reasons where none have been given and none have been asked for. I have little doubt in point of fact that this was to prevent the court ordering reasons in circumstances where the arbitrator might well be no longer in a position, after a lapse of time, to respond to the order. Nor can I see any *c* basis for the submission as a matter of practice. First, I do not accept the distinction drawn by counsel for the owners between reasons given to inform the parties and reasons given to enable the court to review the matter. I would expect arbitrators simply to give reasons for their award; and reasons given to explain why they have reached their decision should ordinarily be sufficient both to inform the parties of the basis of the decision, and to enable the court, if appropriate, to review the matter on appeal. Second, *d* I do not expect the rejection of the argument of counsel for the owners to deter arbitrators from giving reasons, even where neither party has asked for them, unless the case is one (such as a 'look-sniff' arbitration) where reasons are not appropriate. It is widely believed that one of the chief benefits of the 1979 Act is that reasoned awards will be readily given; it is, I believe, the general practice of maritime arbitrators to give reasoned awards as a matter of course, and I trust that it either has, or will, become the *e* general practice of all English arbitrators to do so.

Counsel's third submission for the owners was that the court should not ordinarily give leave to appeal from a commercial arbitration on a question which turns on the commercial meaning of words, or the construction of words in their commercial context. This submission is founded on certain dicta of Lord Denning MR in *Pioneer Shipping Ltd v BTP Tioxide Ltd* [1980] 3 All ER 117, [1980] QB 547 in the course of which *f* he expressed regret that leave to appeal had been given in that case. In fact, the decision of the judge to give leave to appeal had previously been affirmed by the Court of Appeal (Lord Denning MR, Goff LJ and Sir George Baker); it follows that the subsequent observations of Lord Denning MR, regretting that leave had been given, are strictly obiter dicta, though obviously they are entitled to, and will certainly receive, the greatest respect.

g

The observations of Lord Denning MR were as follows ([1980] 3 All ER 117 at 124–125, [1980] QB 547 at 564–565):

'The first guideline is given by s 1(4) of the [Arbitration Act 1979]. Leave is not to be given unless the point of law could "substantially affect the rights" of one or both of the parties. In short, it must be a point of practical importance, not an *h* academic point, nor a minor point. The second guideline is given by s 1(2), (3) and (7). The decision of the arbitrator is final unless the judge gives leave. Once he gives leave, the judge is to hear the appeal. His decision is final unless he certifies that the question is one of general importance, or is one which for some other special reason should be considered by the Court of Appeal. This finality gives rise to these reflections. Take a case where the sole question is the proper interpretation *j* of a commercial contract. Not a standard form. But a "one-off" clause in a "one-off" contract. The interpretation of it is unlikely ever to arise again. The parties agree, as here, to the "final arbitrament" of an arbitrator carrying on business in the City of London. To my mind, in the ordinary way, once the arbitrator has given his award, containing his interpretation of the clause, the judge should not give leave to appeal. Not even when a large sum of money is involved. For this reason. On such a clause, the arbitrator is just as likely to be right as the judge, probably more likely. Because he, with his expertise, will interpret the clause in its commercial sense, whereas the judge, with no knowledge of the trade, may interpret the clause in its literal sense. And, once the judge has decided it, there is no appeal; because it is not a case for a certificate. Then as between the arbitrator and the judge, whose decision is to be preferred? I should say that in general, in the absence of some special reason, it should be the decision of the arbitrator; because it was he to whom the parties agreed to submit it on the basis that his decision was to be final, and not the judge's. But if the arbitrator intimated that he would welcome an appeal, that would be a special reason for giving leave. It is different with a clause in a standard form, and a question arises which is likely to come up again and again. The decision on such a question may well be one of general public importance within s 1(8) of the 1979 Act. If a judge is prepared so to certify, he may often consider it desirable to give leave. But, even then, he should hesitate a little before giving it. He must remember that, even in a standard form, a commercial arbitrator is better placed to interpret it in a commercial sense, or in a sense acceptable to the parties, than the judge himself is. He should not give leave unless it is a really debatable point. If the arbitrator has put on the clause the meaning generally accepted in the trade, leave should be refused, because that is what the parties would have expected when they agreed to the arbitration. I would repeat what I said in *Pilgrim Shipping Co Ltd v State Trading Corpn of India Ltd, The Hadjitsakos* [1975] 1 Lloyd's Rep 356 at 360–361 in the hope that the commercial judges will accept it as the correct approach since the 1979 Act. Take then a case like the present, in which the point is whether a contract was ended by frustration or not. In *Universal Cargo Carriers Corpn v Citati* [1957] 2 All ER 70 at 83, [1957] 2 QB 401 at 435, Devlin J said: ". . . while the application of the doctrine of frustration is a matter of law, the assessment of a period of delay sufficient to constitute frustration is a question of fact": whereas, in *The Angelia, Trade and Transport Inc v Iino Kaiun Kaisha Ltd* [1973] 2 All ER 144 at 154, [1973] 1 WLR 210 at 221 Kerr J said that it was "an inference of law to be drawn by the court from the facts found in the special case". I must say that I prefer the approach of Devlin J. It is mixed law and fact. But, whichever way it is put, the decision of the arbitrator on frustration should normally be accepted. He is just as likely to be right as a judge. He is as well able to make the "assessment" or to draw the "inference" as a judge. His decision should be accepted unless it is an "assessment" or an "inference" which could not reasonably be drawn from the facts: see *British Launderers' Research Association v Central Middlesex Assessment Committee and Hendon Rating Authority* [1949] 1 All ER 21 at 25–26, [1949] 1 KB 462 at 471–472. Leave to appeal should normally be refused. Especially in a case like the present (where the parties sought and obtained a speedy ruling from the arbitrator) so as to know what the vessel was to do on her next voyage. Was she to go across to Sorel under the charterparty? Were the owners at liberty to fix her for a fresh voyage elsewhere? Once the arbitrator gives his decision, the parties should abide by it. Even though both parties asked for a reasoned award, still they should abide by it, unless it is manifest that the arbitrator has gone wrong.'

I have to say, with the utmost respect, that I do not feel free to apply these principles in deciding whether or not to give leave to appeal under the 1979 Act, because I am unable to discover any basis for them in the Act itself. First, I can find nothing in the Act which indicates that, in considering whether or not to give leave to appeal from an arbitrator's award, any limit should be placed on 'the question of law', except that it must be such that its determination could substantially affect the rights of one or more of the parties. Of course, if the argument which the applicant seeks to advance is flimsy, then the court may conclude that leave should only be given subject to conditions (see, eg, *Mondial Trading Co GmbH Ltd v Gill and Duffus Zuckerhandelsgesellschaft mbH* [1980] 2

Lloyd's Rep 376). It is plain that one of the mischiefs which the Act was intended to remove was the abuse of the old special case procedure by taking trivial or flimsy points *a* for the purpose of delaying payment of an arbitrator's award. But I can find nothing in the Act which, as a matter of construction, suggests that the court should give leave in the case of some questions of law, but decline to give leave in others, as Lord Denning MR proposes; I cannot see that the Act was designed to achieve any such purpose. In particular, it appears to me to be irrelevant that the parties have agreed to submit their dispute to the 'final arbitrament' of the arbitrator, if they have not taken advantage of the *b* procedure open to them (under ss 3 and 4 of the Act) to exclude the right of appeal after the commencement of the arbitration; nor can I, with all respect, see the relevance of the more stringent limits imposed by s 1(7) on appeals to the Court of Appeal, when considering whether to give leave to appeal from an arbitrator. Furthermore, I must with all respect demur to Lord Denning MR's conclusion founded on his belief that the arbitrator may, in a particular type of case, be as likely or more likely to be right than the *c* court. In my judgment, the difference between arbitrator and judge is not one of competence or experience, but of function. I am only too well aware that, in for example maritime arbitrations, the arbitrator may be a retired Lord Justice, a barrister (silk or junior) or solicitor in commercial practice, a broker, a marine surveyor, a marine engineer, a former ships master, a gentleman from the world of insurance, or possibly from some other profession. He may be an experienced arbitrator; he may not. The case *d* may or may not be within his particular experience or expertise. It is impossible therefore to predicate that in any particular type of case the arbitrator will or will not be as likely or more likely to be right than the judge. But in any event, in my judgment, whoever the arbitrator may be, it is the *function* of the court to decide on questions of law which substantially affect the rights of the parties, the main purpose of the exercise of this function being to ensure that the principles of law are applied in arbitrations, *e* thereby preventing the injustice which will arise if the law is not consistently applied.

Of course, it goes without saying that the conclusion of a commercial arbitrator carries great weight with the Commercial Court. The commercial judges and the commercial arbitrators in this country hold each other, I believe, in mutual respect, and understand well each other's respective functions. Moreover, whenever the commercial context is important to the construction of a contract, the arbitrator's findings concerning that *f* context may be of great, even decisive, weight in the decision of the question of construction, and his conclusion on the question of construction itself will carry great weight. But I am unable to accept the fetter on the court's discretion to grant leave to appeal under the Act proposed by counsel for the owners in his argument in the present case. I therefore reject this submission.

It follows that I am unable to accept any submissions of counsel for the owners, and I *g* approach the matter as follows. Plainly, both points which the charterers wish to pursue raise questions of law, which are questions of law which substantially affect the rights of both parties. On the other hand, it seems to me that the argument of the charterers on their first point (viz that, on a true construction of cl 36(b) they were only liable for any increase in war risk premiums after the date of the charterparty) is by no means strong; I have therefore considered whether I should impose any terms in respect of that *h* particular point. I have come to the conclusion that I should not do so. I am satisfied that unconditional leave should be given in respect of the second point; and it seems to me that the two points are so closely linked that it would be unrealistic to impose terms in respect of one, but not the other. I accordingly decide to give the charterers leave to appeal against the arbitrator's award which is unconditional except for one matter. That is that, having regard to the admitted impecuniosity of the charterers and the fact that *j* they are outside the jurisdiction of the court, and bearing in mind the further fact that their application is supported by their P & I club, this is in my judgment an appropriate case to order that the leave to appeal against the arbitrator's award is conditional on the charterers furnishing to the owners security in a form reasonably satisfactory to the owners' solicitors for the costs of the appeal, including the costs of this application.

I come now to the second matter before me, which is an application by the charterers, pursuant to s 22 of the Arbitration Act 1950, that the award be remitted to the arbitrator to make further findings of fact. In the affidavit evidence before the court, a number of findings of fact were referred to, but in the course of argument these were reduced to the following: (1) when was the Persian Gulf designated an additional premium area; (2) whether any increase in premium was imposed after the contract was made; (3) the full terms of the rules of the Hellenic War Risks Association; (4) the text of the Institute War Clauses; (5) the text of the RJM exclusion 'J' wording (which I understand to be a form of amended war risks cover now used to some extent in the City of London), and a statement of the circumstances in which, and the extent to which, such cover was at the material time in use.

Now in point of fact, with the possible exception of (5), there should be very little difficulty in obtaining these findings. It became plain that the first two items (which are directed towards the first of the two issues in the case) could without difficulty be agreed. So far as items (3), (4) and (5) are concerned (which are presumably directed towards the commercial background of the clause), (3) was referred to by the arbitrator, and could no doubt also be agreed, (4) is a standard document, which could certainly be agreed, and the text of (5) is no doubt available and should be capable of agreement. There remains only the explanation concerning the use of (5), which may have to be considered by the arbitrator.

The application to remit was made under s 22 of the 1950 Act which, unlike s 21, was not repealed by the 1979 Act. Since s 22 of the 1950 Act sets out the court's general power to remit, it is scarcely surprising that it was not repealed. However, there is now a parallel, though more limited, jurisdiction under s 1(5) of the 1979 Act under which the court may order an arbitrator to state the reasons for his award in sufficient detail to enable the court, should an appeal be brought under s 1 of the 1979 Act, to consider any question of law arising out of the award. Furthermore, in my judgment the expression 'reasons' in this subsection cannot be limited to 'reasoning', but must include the relevant facts on which the arbitrator's conclusion is based. Of course, a reasoned award need not take any particular form; though a typical form of reasoned award which now comes before the court is one in which the arbitrator, having set the general scene and identified the dispute between the parties, then sets out the parties' respective contentions, makes any further findings of fact which may be desirable for the purpose of considering those contentions, and then sets out his conclusion and reasons for reaching that conclusion. In such an award, facts found by the arbitrator appear to me to form an inseparable part of the total reasons for his award.

A question therefore arises as to the relationship between applications to the court for an order under s 22 of the 1950 Act to remit the award for further findings of fact, and applications under s 1(5) of the 1979 Act, where the applicant is asking for an order that the arbitrator should state further facts as part of his reasons. In my judgment, such an application should, in a case arising under the 1979 Act, ordinarily be made under s 1(5) of the 1979 Act and not under s 22 of the 1950 Act. It is to be remembered that applications of this kind under s 22 of the 1950 Act were generally concerned with special cases, which are formal documents in which the arbitrator found certain facts and then stated a question of law for the opinion of the court, and which have now been abolished. Furthermore, it appears to me that when a new procedure for the review of arbitration awards is contained in a statute and that procedure embodies a process for obtaining further findings of fact, one should look rather to that process for that purpose than to the general power to remit contained in a previous statute.

It is to be observed that the court's power to order further reasons to be stated under s 1(5) of the 1979 Act is unfettered, except by s 1(6); and should in my judgment be construed in its context as part of the flexible, new procedure. Under the old procedure, it became established over the years that it was for the parties to ensure that so far as possible the relevant facts were found in the award; in the absence of evidence of this, courts were reluctant to remit awards for further facts to be found. This approach has led to a most time-wasting and expensive practice under which, in many arbitrations, counsel draft long and complicated documents which are submitted to an arbitrator after *a* the conclusion of the arbitration specifying every fact which his client wishes to be found. I cannot think that this undesirable consequence of the old procedure should be perpetuated under the new procedure. As I have said, the court's discretion under s 1(5) of the 1979 Act is unfettered by s 1(6). But generally speaking, if the further reasons sought form part of an argument fairly raised below, the court may be ready to make an order under s 1(5); but it may desist from making an order if, for example, the applicant *b* requires new reasons in order to advance a point not taken below which, on established principles, the court may not in the interests of justice allow him to take, and if the court feels that the applicant has in any sense contributed to the absence of the relevant matter in the arbitrator's award the court may, if it thinks it appropriate to do so, make an order of costs against him.

I therefore propose to consider the present application as though it had been made *c* under s 1(5) of the 1979 Act. In all the circumstances of this case, I can see no reason why I should not make an order that the arbitrator should make the further findings of fact asked for by the charterers; but I will hear any submissions which counsel may wish to address to me on the question whether, as a condition of any such order, I should impose any terms as to costs.

[After a discussion on costs his Lordship said:] I would have thought that the principle *d* ought to be that the normal order, when leave to appeal is given, is that the costs of the application should be costs in the appeal unless there was no reasonably arguable ground on which the court might be persuaded to dismiss the application, or to impose terms; but if leave to appeal is refused, the normal order will be that the applicants will pay the costs of the application.

[After further discussion following counsel's application for the owners for leave to *e* appeal to the Court of Appeal his Lordship said:] Normally, therefore, I would have been most reluctant to accede to counsel's application. But bearing in mind the fact that there is on the face of this judgment a difference of opinion between Lord Denning MR and this court, I feel that it would be proper for this court to give leave to appeal to enable the Court of Appeal to consider that conflict of opinion and for that reason, and for that reason alone, I propose to accede, I must confess with reluctance, to counsel's application. *f*

Application for leave to appeal granted. Application for remission of award granted. Leave to appeal to the Court of Appeal.

Solicitors: *Richards, Butler & Co* (for the charterers); *Holman, Fenwick & William* (for the owners).

K Mydeen Esq   Barrister.

R v Secretary of State for the Home Department, ex parte Santillo

(Case 131/79)

COURT OF JUSTICE OF THE EUROPEAN COMMUNITIES
JUDGES O'KEEFFE (ACTING PRESIDENT), TOUFFAIT (PRESIDENTS OF CHAMBERS), MERTENS DE WILMARS, PESCATORE, LORD MACKENZIE STUART, BOSCO AND KOOPMANS
ADVOCATE-GENERAL J-P WARNER
6th, 27th FEBRUARY, 22nd MAY 1980

QUEEN'S BENCH DIVISION
DONALDSON LJ AND COMYN J
8th, 18th JULY 1980

COURT OF APPEAL, CIVIL DIVISION
LORD DENNING MR, SHAW AND TEMPLEMAN LJJ
4th, 5th, 19th DECEMBER 1980

European Economic Community – Directives – Direct application in member states – Circumstances in which rights conferred by directives enforceable by individuals in courts of member states – Provisions of directive sufficiently well defined and specific to enable them to be relied on and to be applied.

European Economic Community – Freedom of movement – Restriction on freedom – Restrictions justified on grounds of public policy, public security or public health – Expulsion of EEC national following conviction of criminal offence – Court imposing sentence recommending deportation of defendant – Deportation order made at conclusion of $4\frac{1}{2}$-year prison term – Whether court's recommendation for deportation an 'opinion' – Whether court of trial a 'competent authority' – Whether lapse of time between recommendation and order depriving 'opinion' of its validity – EEC Council Directive 64/221, art 9(1).

Alien – Deportation – Order – Validity – Lapse of time between recommendation for deportation and deportation order – Deportation following conviction of criminal offences – Defendant refused parole while serving prison sentence – Medical evidence that defendant likely to commit further similar offences on release from prison – Whether lapse of time between recommendation and order depriving recommendation of its validity.

Alien – Deportation – Order – Validity – Natural justice – Deportation recommended by trial judge on defendant's conviction of criminal offences – Deportation ordered at conclusion of defendant's $4\frac{1}{2}$-year prison sentence – Defendant not showing that recommendation or order unfair – Whether Secretary of State under absolute duty to disclose all information on which deportation order based – Whether defendant denied natural justice.

The defendant, an Italian national, came to the United Kingdom in 1967. In 1973 he was convicted in the Central Criminal Court of buggery, rape, indecent assault and assault causing actual bodily harm on two prostitutes. He was sentenced to 8 years' imprisonment with a recommendation for deportation. The Court of Appeal refused his application for leave to appeal. In 1976 and 1977 the parole review committee refused to recommend the applicant for parole, and in 1978 the Secretary of State for the Home Department decided not to release the applicant on licence. There was recent evidence from the prison medical officer that the experience of the prison sentence was unlikely to prevent the applicant committing similar offences in the future. In September 1978,

ie some $4\frac{1}{2}$ years after the applicant was convicted, the Secretary of State, acting on the
recommendation of the trial judge, ordered the defendant to be deported to Italy. No *a*
reasons other than the recommendation were given for the order. The defendant
applied to the Divisional Court for an order of certiorari to quash the deportation order
on the ground that it infringed art 9(1)[a] of EEC Council Directive 64/221. The directive
made provision for certain limitations on the power of a member state to deport EEC
nationals, and in particular art 9(1) provided that before the administrative authority of
a member state ordered deportation it had first to obtain the 'opinion' of an independent *b*
'competent authority'. The defendant contended that the recommendation of the trial
judge did not qualify as such an 'opinion' and that, even if it were to be regarded as an
'opinion', as it had been given $4\frac{1}{2}$ years before the deportation order a further opinion
ought to have been obtained. The defendant further contended that the Secretary of
State had breached the rules of natural justice in not disclosing to the defendant all the
information available to the Secretary of State on which the decision to order the *c*
defendant's deportation was based. On a reference to the Court of Justice of the European
Communities by the Divisional Court of certain questions concerning the interpretation
of the directive,

Held (by the Court of Justice of the European Communities) – (1) The provisions of art
9(1) of Directive 64/221 were sufficiently well defined and specific to enable them to be *d*
relied on by any person concerned and were capable of being applied by any national
court (see p 911 *a b* and p 912 *e*, post).

(2) Since the criminal courts in the United Kingdom were independent of the
administration, which was responsible for making any deportation order, and since the
person concerned had the right to be represented and exercise his rights of defence before
such courts, it followed that a recommendation for deportation made by a criminal court *e*
on passing sentence could constitute 'an opinion' obtained from a competent authority,
within art 9(1), provided it was made sufficiently proximate in time to the decision
ordering expulsion to ensure that there were no new factors to be taken into consideration
and provided both the administrative authority and the person concerned were in a
position to take cognisance of the reasons which had led the court to make the
recommendation. A lapse of time amounting to several years between the recommen- *f*
dation for deportation and the decision by the administration was liable to deprive the
recommendation of its function as an 'opinion' within art 9(1), because it was essential
that the social danger resulting from a foreigner's presence was assessed at the very time
when the decision ordering expulsion was made, since the factors to be taken into
account, particularly those concerning his conduct, were likely to change in the course
of time (see p 911 *c* to p 912 *h*, post); *R v Bouchereau* p 924, post, applied. *g*

Accordingly, **Held** (by the Court of Appeal) – (1) Applying the answers given by the
European Court to the facts of the case, it was clear that the Central Criminal Court was
a 'competent authority' which had expressed an 'opinion' that the applicant be expelled
and that the Secretary of State, the administrative authority, was entitled to act on that
opinion in ordering the applicant's expulsion. In the circumstances, the lapse of $4\frac{1}{2}$ years *h*
between the date when the court recommended the applicant's deportation and the date
when the deportation order was made by the Secretary of State was not sufficient to
deprive the recommendation of its function as an opinion, since there had not arisen in
that time any new factors which invalidated the opinion, such changes as there had been,
such as the refusal of the parole review committee to recommend the applicant's release
on licence and the prison medical officer's evidence that there was a real risk that the *j*
applicant might commit similar offences in the future, only serving to reinforce the
recommendation for deportation (see p 918 *c d*, p 919 *c* to *g*, p 920 *d e g* to *j*, p 921 *d*,
p 922 *e* and p 923 *c* to *f*, post).

(2) Furthermore, it could not be said that the applicant had been denied natural

_____

a   Article 9(1) is set out at p 910 *b c*, post

justice, because there was no absolute duty on the Secretary of State when exercising the
a power of acting on a deportation recommendation to disclose to the person concerned all
the information available to the Secretary of State, and because (per Templeman LJ) the
applicant had not put forward any positive reason why the trial judge should not have
made the deportation recommendation, why the Secretary of State should not have made
the deportation order or why the deportation order should not be implemented. It
followed that the applicant's appeal against the Divisional Court's refusal to grant an
b order of certiorari to quash the deportation order would be dismissed (see p 920 *b* to *f* and
j, p 921 *j* to p 922 *a* and *h j* and p 923 *a* and *g h*, post).

Per the Advocate-General. (1) A member state's failure to implement a provision of a
directive does not of itself mean that that provision may be directly invoked by private
persons. That result follows only where the provision in question is of such a kind as to
require the member state to confer, by its own law, rights on private persons. Since art
c 9(1) imposes on each member state an obligation to afford to nationals of other member
states procedural safeguards of the kind that it prescribes, it is capable of being relied on
by private persons (see p 904 *e f* and p 905 *e f*, post); *Van Duyn v The Home Office (No 2)*
[1975] 3 All ER 190 applied.

(2) All the material on which the executive may base its decision to deport must be
placed before the court and the person concerned must have the opportunity to make
d representations (see p 905 *j*, p 906 *a b* and p 907 *b*, post).

(3) In the case of an English criminal court an oral statement by the judge or the
presiding magistrate of its reasons for recommending deportation is enough to satisfy the
requirement that the opinion be reasoned. The statement need not be long, provided it
is not incomplete (see p 907 *j* to p 908 *a*, post).

e **Notes**

For enforcement of Community law, see Supplement to 39A Halsbury's Laws (3rd Edn)
paras 29–32, 54.

For the restriction on the movement of EEC nationals within the Community, see ibid
para 124.

f For the deportation of non-patrials, see 4 Halsbury's Laws (4th Edn) para 1011, and for
cases on deportation, see 2 Digest (Reissue) 208–214, 1177–1224.

For the rules of natural justice, see 1 Halsbury's Laws (4th Edn) para 64, 66, and for
cases on the subject, see 1(1) Digest (Reissue) 200–201, 1172–1175.

For EEC Council Directive 64/221, art 9, see 42A Halsbury's Statutes (3rd Edn) 132.

g **Cases cited**

Delkvist (Knud Oluf) v Anklagemyndigheden Case 21/78 [1978] ECR 2327, [1979] 1 CMLR
    372, [1979] RTR 161, CJEC, 21 Digest (Reissue) 272, 1762.
Enka BV v Inspecteur der Invoerrechten en Accijnzen, Arnhem Case 38/77 [1977] ECR 2203,
    [1978] 2 CMLR 212, CJEC, 21 Digest (Reissue) 245, 1647.
K (H) (an infant), Re [1967] 1 All ER 226, [1967] 2 QB 617, [1967] 2 WLR 962, DC, 2
h   Digest (Reissue) 204, 1163.
Pecastaing (Josette) v Belgian State Case 98/79 [1980] ECR 691, [1980] 3 CMLR 685, CJEC.
Pubblico Ministero v Tullio Ratti Case 148/78 [1979] ECR 1629, [1980] 1 CMLR 96, CJEC,
    21 Digest (Reissue) 247, 1656.
R v Bouchereau Case 30/77 p 924, post, [1978] QB 732, [1978] 2 WLR 250, [1977] ECR
    1999, [1977] 2 CMLR 800, 66 Cr App R 202, CJEC.
j *R v Nazari* [1980] 3 All ER 880, [1980] 1 WLR 1366, 71 Cr App R 87, CA.
Rutili (Roland) v Minister for the Interior Case 36/75 [1975] ECR 1219, [1976] 1 CMLR 140,
    CJEC, 21 Digest (Reissue) 254, 1684.
Simmenthal SpA v Amministrazione delle Finanze dello Stato Case 70/77 [1978] ECR 1453,
    [1978] 3 CMLR 670, CJEC.
Van Duyn v The Home Office (No 2) Case 41/74 [1975] 3 All ER 190, [1975] Ch 358, [1975]
    2 WLR 760, [1974] ECR 1337, [1975] 1 CMLR 1, CJEC, 21 Digest (Reissue) 245, 1645.

Verbond van Nederlandse Ondernemingen v Inspecteur der Invoerrechten en Accijnzen Case
51/76 [1977] ECR 113, [1977] 1 CMLR 413, CJEC, 21 Digest (Reissue) 245, 1646.   *a*

Reference

Mario Santillo, an Italian national, applied, with the leave of the Divisional Court of the
Queen's Bench Division given on 5th December 1978, for an order of certiorari to quash
an order dated 5th October 1978 made by the Secretary of State for the Home
Department pursuant to s 5(1) of the Immigration Act 1971 requiring the applicant to   *b*
leave and prohibiting him from entering the United Kingdom so long as the order
remained in force. On 10th April 1979 the Divisional Court (Lord Widgery CJ, Michael
Davies and Robert Goff JJ) heard the application and, on hearing counsel for the applicant
and for the Secretary of State, referred, by order dated 30th July 1979, certain questions
(set out at p 910 *d* to *f*, post) as to the interpretation of art 9(1) of EEC Council Directive
64/221 to the Court of Justice of the European Communities for a preliminary ruling   *c*
under art 177 of the EEC Treaty. The United Kingdom, the applicant and the
Commission of the European Communities submitted written observations to the
European Court. The language of the case was English. The facts are set out in the
opinion of the Advocate-General.

Louis Blom-Cooper QC and *Alan Newman* for the applicant.   *d*
Simon D Brown for the United Kingdom.
Anthony McClellan, agent for the EC Commission, *Stephen O'Malley* with him, for the
   Commission.

27th February. **The Advocate-General (J-P Warner)** delivered the following
opinion: My Lords, in this case the court is once again concerned with EEC Council   *e*
Directive 64/221 'on the co-ordination of special measures concerning the movement
and residence of foreign nationals which are justified on grounds of public policy, public
security or public health'. More particularly the court is concerned with the effect of that
directive in relation to deportation orders made in England by the Secretary of State for
Home Affairs on the recommendation of criminal courts under the procedure that I
described in my opinion in *R v Bouchereau* pp 927–929, post.   *f*

The case comes before the court by way of a reference for a preliminary ruling by a
Divisional Court of the Queen's Bench Division of the High Court of Justice of England
and Wales. The applicant in the proceedings before that court is Mr Mario Santillo. The
respondent is the Secretary of State for the Home Department.

The facts are these. The applicant, who was born in 1941 and is an Italian national,
went to the United Kingdom as a migrant worker in 1967 and was in full employment   *g*
there until December 1973. He is married to an Italian national and has two children,
both born in the United Kingdom.

On 13th December 1973 the applicant was convicted at the Central Criminal Court in
London of offences of buggery, rape, indecent assault and assault causing actual bodily
harm. The victims of the offences were prostitutes. In sentencing the applicant, which
he did on 21st January 1974, the learned trial judge described the offences as 'very grave   *h*
... callous, cruel and ruthless'. He sentenced the applicant to a total of eight years'
imprisonment and recommended him for deportation.

Before passing that sentence and making that recommendation the judge heard
counsel on behalf of the applicant. From the transcript of the hearing, which is among
the papers before us, it seems that counsel made three points. The first was to the
possibility of the applicant responding to treatment, the second (on which counsel placed   *j*
the most emphasis) was as to the situation of his wife and children, and the third was that
he had no previous convictions. At an earlier hearing, on 11th January 1974, counsel had
said that the United Kingdom's accession to the EEC did not mean that a deportation
order could not be made in respect of the applicant. (He was not the same counsel as
appeared for the applicant in the Divisional Court and in this court).

On 18th February 1974 the applicant applied to the Court of Appeal, Criminal
a Division, for leave to appeal against his sentence and against the recommendation for
deportation. The grounds put forward on his behalf were mostly concerned with the
length of the sentence, though mention was made of the situation of his wife and
children, and of the fact that he had previously been a hard-working man 'of good
character'. On 10th October 1974 a full court of the Court of Appeal refused the
application.

b On 28th September 1978 (that is some 4½ years after the recommendation for
deportation had been made and nearly four years after the case had been considered by
the Court of Appeal) the Secretary of State, pursuant to ss 3(6) and 5(1) of the Immigration
Act 1971, made a deportation order in respect of the applicant based on the
recommendation of the trial judge. By the last paragraph of that order the Secretary of
State, pursuant to para 2 of Sch 3 to the Act, authorised the applicant to be detained until
c he should be removed from the United Kingdom. No reason for the Secretary of State's
decision was given in the deportation order itself, save the existence of the
recommendation.

The applicant was at the time still serving his sentence at Maidstone prison. It was
expected that, having earned remission for good conduct, he would complete his sentence
on 3rd April 1979.

d On 5th October 1978 there was addressed to him on behalf of the Secretary of State a
document headed 'Directions for removal on deportation', informing him that the
Secretary of State had given directions for his removal from the United Kingdom 'on 2nd
April 1979 or as soon as possible thereafter by air to Italy'. The document also stated that
there was no appeal against deportation, but that he was entitled to appeal against the
removal directions to the independent appellate authorities established under the
e Immigration Act 1971 on the ground that he ought not to be removed to Italy but ought
to be removed to some other country or territory specified by him. The document went
on to indicate the procedure on such an appeal.

The order for reference records that the applicant had been afforded 'no further
hearing' between the date when the Court of Appeal refused his application and the date
when the Secretary of State made the deportation order. We were told however at the
f hearing in this court that written representations, to the effect that he ought not to be
deported, had been made on his behalf to the Secretary of State in 1975 and again in
1978.

An affidavit sworn in the proceedings before the Divisional Court by an official of the
Immigration and Nationality Department of the Home Office mentions the factors
taken into account by the Secretary of State in considering whether the applicant should
g be deported. The deponent says that the Secretary of State took into account the
applicant's status as a national of an EEC member state and the considerations set out in
para 47 of the Statement of Immigration Rules for Control after Entry: EEC and other
Non-Commonwealth Nationals (HC Paper (1972–73) no 82). Those are rules laid down
by the Secretary of State under s 3(2) of the Immigration Act 1971. Paragraph 47
provides (so far as material):

h
'In considering whether to give effect to a recommendation for deportation made
by a court on conviction the Secretary of State will take into account every relevant
factor, including—age; length of residence in the United Kingdom; strength of
connections with the United Kingdom; personal history, including character,
conduct and employment record; domestic circumstances; the nature of the offence
of which the person was convicted; previous criminal record; compassionate
j circumstances; any representations received on the person's behalf.'

The affidavit goes on to say that the Secretary of State took into account in particular: (i)
the applicant's domestic circumstances; (ii) the nature and circumstances of his conviction
including the fact that it arose from two separate incidents involving different women;
and (iii) the fact that the parole review committee of Maidstone prison had refused to

recommend him for parole in 1976 and 1977 and that the Secretary of State himself had
decided not to release him on licence in 1978 (this was an allusion to the application, or   *a*
rather non-application, in the applicant's case of the provisions of s 60 of the Criminal
Justice Act 1967, under which the Secretary of State may, if recommended to do so by the
Parole Board created by that Act, release on licence a person serving a sentence of
imprisonment after he has served one-third of his sentence or 12 months of it, whichever
expires later). The affidavit concludes:

> 'As a matter of public policy and in the interests of public safety the Secretary of   *b*
> State reached the conclusion that in all the circumstances there would be an excessive
> risk to the public from offences of the same or similar sort as those of which the
> Applicant had been convicted, which out-weighed the arguments in favour of
> allowing the Applicant to remain . . . in the United Kingdom on completion of his
> sentences of imprisonment.'

c

There has also been filed in the proceedings before the Divisional Court an affidavit by
the senior medical officer of Maidstone prison. That affidavit is before us too. It is about
the relations between the applicant and his wife and children, and about the likelihood
of his committing similar offences again. We were told however that no report by that
officer was before the Secretary of State when he made the deportation order, though
other medical reports may have been. We were also told that the Secretary of State had   *d*
before him information to the effect that the police suspected the applicant of having
committed other offences similar to the ones for which he had been convicted.

The proceedings before the Divisional Court are proceedings for judicial review (under
RSC Ord 53) in which the applicant seeks an order of certiorari to quash the deportation
order. They are thus proceedings in which the Divisional Court has jurisdiction in
respect of the legal validity of the deportation order but not in respect of its merits.   *e*

It was submitted on the applicant's behalf before the Divisional Court that that order
was a nullity as being in breach of art 9(1) of EEC Council Directive 64/221, which is (so
far as material) in these terms:

> 'Where there is no right of appeal to a court of law, or where such appeal may be
> only in respect of the legal validity of the decision . . . a decision . . . ordering the
> expulsion of the holder of a residence permit from the territory shall not be taken   *f*
> by the administrative authority, save in cases of urgency, until an opinion has been
> obtained from a competent authority of the host country before which the person
> concerned enjoys such rights of defence and of assistance or representation as the
> domestic law of that country provides for. This authority shall not be the same as
> that empowered to take the decision . . . ordering expulsion.'

g

It was further submitted on the applicant's behalf, in reliance on the judgment of this
court in the *Bouchereau* case, that before any deportation order was made in the case of an
EEC national the authorities had to be satisfied that he presented 'a present threat to the
requirements of public policy' and that a court recommendation made over 4½ years
before the deportation order could not comply with that rule.

Finally, as regards the facts, I must mention that the applicant did complete his   *h*
sentence, as expected, on 3rd April 1979. He was thereafter detained for some months
under the deportation order. In the summer of 1979, however, the Home Office
arranged for him to go to Italy pending the outcome of the Divisional Court
proceedings. His wife and children are, we were told, still in England.

I must also mention, before I turn to the questions referred to this court by the
Divisional Court, that there were cited to us on behalf of the applicant a number of cases   *j*
in the Court of Appeal, Criminal Division, in which that court has considered the
principles on which an English criminal court should exercise its discretion whether or
not to recommend an alien for deportation. It was submitted that those authorities were
unsatisfactory and to some extent inconsistent with each other. None of them seems to
me directly in point. Some of them were decided before the United Kingdom became
a member state of the Community. Those decided after that date are either cases where

the Court of Appeal has set aside the recommendation for deportation made by the court
a of trial or cases where the Court of Appeal has ascertained the nationality of the convicted person and found that it was (in one case) Nigerian or (in the other) Israeli. The general tenor of at all events the later cases seems to me, however, to be to the effect that an English criminal court should, before making a recommendation for deportion, consider all relevant factors, to the exclusion only of the risk to the convicted person of persecution or ostracism in his or her country of origin. Those risks, the Court of Appeal has held,
b the English courts do not have the machinery for investigating, and their evaluation must be left to the Secretary of State. Since such risks do not exist (or at least should not exist) in any member state of the Community, the exception is in my opinion irrelevant for present purposes.

The questions referred to this court by the Divisional Court are, in slightly abbreviated form, these. (1) Whether art 9(1) of EEC Council Directive 64/221 confers on individuals
c rights which are enforceable by them in the national courts of a member state and which the national courts must protect. (2) (a) What is the meaning of the phrase 'an opinion has been obtained from a competent authority of the host country' in art 9(1) of the directive? and (b) in particular, can a recommendation for deportation made by a criminal court on passing sentence constitute 'an opinion'? (3) If the answer to question 2(b) is Yes, (a) must 'a recommendation' be fully reasoned? (b) in what (if any)
d circumstances does the lapse of time between the making of 'a recommendation' and the taking of the decision ordering the expulsion preclude 'a recommendation' from constituting 'an opinion'? (c) in particular, does the lapse of time involved in serving a sentence of imprisonment have the effect that 'a recommendation' ceases to be 'an opinion'?

It was submitted on behalf of the applicant and of the Commission that the first
e question should be answered in the affirmative; on behalf of the United Kingdom government that it should be answered in the negative.

The starting point of the United Kingdom government's argument was that the problem to be solved was whether art 9(1) of the directive was 'self-executing. In my opinion that expression, which is taken from American law, is in the present context best avoided, because it blurs the distinction between direct applicability and direct effect.
f Those two concepts are different and it is confusion between them that leads to the fallacious argument that one sometimes hears that, because art 189 of the EEC Treaty says that a regulation shall be 'directly applicable in all Member States' and says nothing of the kind in the case of directives, no provision of a directive can have direct effect. Unquestionably every provision of every regulation is directly applicable, but not every provision of every regulation has direct effect, in the sense of conferring on private
g persons rights enforceable by them in national courts. One can point to numerous examples of provisions of regulations that confer no direct rights on private persons. Conversely it is, as the Advocate-General (G Reischl) said in *Pubblico Ministerio v Ratti* [1979] ECR 1629 at 1650, 'certainly inappropriate to speak of the direct applicability of a directive'. But it does not follow that a directive can never have a direct effect. As the court has said more than once, 'whilst under art 189 regulations are directly applicable
h and, consequently, by their nature capable of producing direct effects, that does not mean that other categories of acts covered by that article can never produce similar effects': see *Van Duyn v The Home Office (No 2)* [1975] 3 All ER 190 at 205, [1975] Ch 358 at 376–377 (para 12), *Verbond van Nederlandse Ondernemingen v Inspecteur der Invoerrechten en Accijnzen* [1977] ECR 113 at 126 (para 21), *Delkvist v Anklagemyndigheden* [1978] ECR 2327 at 2339 (para 19) and the *Ratti* case [1979] ECR 1629 at 1641 (para 19). The United
j Kingdom government indeed acknowledged that that was so.

What then is it that makes a provision of a directive have direct effect? In *Enka BV v Inspecteur der Invoerrechten en Accijnzen, Arnhem* [1977] ECR 2203 at 2226 I said:

'The crucial consideration seems to me to be this. Article 189 of the Treaty, although it leaves to each Member State the choice of the "form and methods" whereby it is to give effect to a directive, does not allow it the choice of not giving effect to the directive at all, or of giving effect to it only in part. On the contrary Article 189 says in terms that a directive "shall be binding, as to the result to be *a* achieved, upon each Member State to which it is addressed". A Member State that fails fully to give effect to a directive is in breach of the Treaty, so that to allow it (through its executive or administrative authorities) to rely upon that fact as against a private person in proceedings in its own Courts would be to allow it to plead its own wrong.'

Similarly, in the *Ratti* case [1979] ECR 1629 at 1650, the Advocate-General (G Reischl) *b* said:

'The essence of such effects is that in certain cases, which however constitute the exception to the rule, Member States which do not comply with their obligations under the directive are unable to rely on provisions of the internal legal order which are illegal from the point of view of Community law, so that individuals become *c* entitled to rely on the directive as against the defaulting State and acquire rights thereunder which the national courts must protect.'

That view was clearly adopted by the court in the *Ratti* case [1979] ECR 1629 at 1642 (para 22), where it said:

'Consequently a Member State which has not adopted the implementing *d* measures required by the directive in the prescribed periods may not rely, as against individuals, on its own failure to perform the obligations which the directive entails.'

Of course a member state's failure to implement a provision of a directive does not of itself mean that that provision may be directly invoked by private persons. That result *e* follows only where the provision in question was of such a kind as to require the member state to confer, by its own law, rights on private persons. The test in each case is whether 'the nature, general scheme and wording of the provision' are such as to entail such a requirement; consider *Van Duyn v The Home Office (No 2)* [1975] 3 All ER 190 at 205, [1975] Ch 358 at 376–377 (para 12).

It was submitted on behalf of the United Kingdom government that a provision of a *f* directive could never have direct effect unless it satisfied three conditions: (i) it must be 'clear', (ii) it must be 'unconditional or at least subject only to clearly defined conditions' and (iii) it must leave 'no element of discretion to member states in regard to its application'. The United Kingdom government went so far as to submit that those conditions had been laid down by this court in its judgments on the direct effect of directives. In my opinion that is not so. Those conditions are, more or less, those that *g* the court has held must be satisfied before a provision of the Treaty can have direct effect. But the court has never, so far as I am aware, held that they apply in the case of a directive. Nor, as it seems to me, could the court have so held without qualification.

Take the third condition, that no element of discretion should be left to member states in the application of the directive. It is of the very essence of a directive that it should, in the words of art 189, 'leave to the national authorities the choice of form and *h* methods'. Of course the width of that choice will depend on the subject matter and content of the directive, but some element of discretion there will nearly always be.

The United Kingdom government submitted that a distinction should be drawn between those articles of EEC Council Directive 64/221 that were concerned with substantive rights (arts 2, 3 and 4) and those concerned with procedural safeguards (arts 5 to 9). The substantive provisions, it was said, created rights for individuals as to the *j* scope of which member states had no discretion, whereas the procedural provisions admitted of a variety of methods of compliance adapted to 'the varied administrative and judicial processes of the individual member states'. I do not doubt that that is right. But it does not mean that, if a member state should fail to provide a procedural safeguard of a kind required by any of the provisions of arts 5 to 9, or should provide it only imperfectly, an individual thereby adversely affected can have no remedy. The member

state has 'the choice of form and methods', but it must in some form and by some
a method afford to the individual the safeguards required by the directive. As was pointed
out to us on behalf of the Commission, those procedural safeguards may in practice be
as important to him as his substantive rights.

That the provision in question must be unconditional is obviously right. Indeed, if
the application of a provision in a directive is subject to a condition and that condition is
not fulfilled, that provision can have no effect at all. We had a very good example of such
b a situation in *Simmenthal v Amministrazione delle Finanze dello Stato* [1978] ECR 1453. But
the United Kingdom government has here interpreted the word 'conditional' in quite a
different sense. It has fastened on the introductory words of art 9(1), 'Where there is no
right of appeal to a court of law, or where such appeal may be only in respect of the legal
validity of the decision . . .', and suggested that those words import a relevant condition.
In my opinion they do nothing of the kind. They merely describe the circumstances in
c which art 9(1) is to apply.

Lastly there is the first condition enunciated on behalf of the United Kingdom
government; that the provision should be 'clear'. Clear of course it must be, in the sense
of precise enough to give rise to a legal right or to legal rights (see para 23 of the
judgment in the *Ratti* case [1979] ECR 1629 at 1642). But the United Kingdom
government interpreted 'clear' in this context as meaning not 'precise' but 'unambigu-
d ous'. It submitted that the 'want of clarity [of art 9(1)] is perhaps best demonstrated by
the competing contentions as to its proper meaning' advanced by the parties in this
case. Ambiguity in legislative provisions is one of the things that courts exist to resolve.
It is not the same as lack of precision. We are only too familiar in this court with
ambiguities in regulations. No one ever suggested however, and quite rightly, that an
ambiguity in a regulation meant that it could not have direct effect. The same is true of
e directives, as the court held in the *Van Duyn* case [1975] 3 All ER 190 at 206, [1975] Ch
358 at 377 (para 14).

Thus, in my opinion, the answer to the Divisional Court's first question really depends
on whether one should infer from 'the nature, general scheme and wording' of art 9(1)
that it imposed on each member state an obligation to afford to nationals of other
member states procedural safeguards of the kind that it prescribed. To my mind the
f answer can only be Yes.

So I turn to the Divisional Court's second question.

On that it was submitted on behalf of the applicant and of the Commission that a
recommendation of the kind here in question could not constitute an 'opinion' for the
purposes of art 9(1). On behalf of the United Kingdom government it was submitted
that it could.

g It was common ground that no legislation had been introduced in the United Kingdom
specifically to give effect to EEC Council Directive 64/221. Those responsible considered
at the time of accession that the United Kingdom's existing laws complied with the
directive. This case in effect raises the question whether they were right. Manifestly a
member state the law of which already complies with the provisions of a directive at the
time when the directive becomes binding on it need not enact new legislation to
h implement the directive (consider in that respect the *Delkvist* case [1978] ECR 2327).

The main point taken on behalf of the applicant was that the Secretary of State would
often have available to him information about the offender that was not before the court
of trial. That was illustrated by this case, where the Secretary of State was informed of
the suspicions of the police, of the views of parole review committee, and so forth.

That is undoubtedly a valid criticism of the way in which the procedure was operated
j in this case and may have been operated in other cases. The scheme of arts 8 and 9 of the
directive is plainly that the person concerned should be afforded the opportunity of
having the merits of his case considered by a body independent of the administrative
authority in which is vested the power of decision. That independent consideration may
come about by virtue of art 8. If not it must (save in 'cases of urgency') come about by
virtue of art 9. I respectfully agree with the view expressed by the Advocate-General
(F Capotorti) in the opinion that he delivered recently in *Pecastaing v Belgian State* [1980]

ECR 691 that, in a case where art 9 applies, and subject to the exception for national security made by the last few words of art 9(2), the person concerned must be supplied with all the material on which the administrative authority may found its decision, so that he may at least make representations thereon to the independent body. The reference in art 9(1) to 'rights of defence' clearly imports that the person concerned should have the protection of what English-speaking lawyers generally call 'the rules of natural justice' and French-speaking lawyers call 'les droits de la défense'. It is contrary to those rules to withhold from a person, so that he cannot comment on it, material that is to be taken into account in reaching a decision affecting him. (I should add that the words 'such rights . . . as the domestic law of that country provides for' in the English text of art 9(1) cannot be interpreted as meaning that the host country is free to deny such rights to the person concerned. Reference to the other five texts shows that the discretion of that country is only as to the procedure according to which he is to exercise his rights. Thus the French text has '. . . l'intéressé doit pouvoir faire valoir ses moyens de défense . . . dans les conditions de procédure prévues par la législation nationale'.)

To say that in the present case (and possibly in other cases) the procedure was operated in a manner incompatible with art 9(1) is not to say that a recommendation made by a criminal court on passing sentence cannot be an opinion for the purposes of that article. The procedure will not be incompatible with the requirements of art 9(1) if all the material on which the Secretary of State may base his decision is placed before the court and the court considers it, together with any representations made by or on behalf of the convicted person, before deciding whether or not to make a recommendation.

The Commission for its part put forward two arguments of a more technical kind.

The first was that, since (as was to be deduced from the judgment of the court in the Bouchereau case p 924, post) a recommendation of a criminal court made under the Immigration Act 1971 was a 'measure' within the meaning of that expression in art 3 of the directive, it could not be an 'opinion' for the purposes of art 9. I disagree. Such a recommendation clearly has the effect of conveying to the Secretary of State the opinion of the court that the person concerned ought to be deported. It was held in the Bouchereau case to be a 'measure' for the purposes of art 3 because it affected the right of free movement of that person in two ways: it was a necessary step in the process of arriving at any decision to make a deportation order under s 3(6) of the 1971 Act and it enabled the person concerned to be deprived of his liberty under para 2 of Sch 3 thereto (see paras 21 to 24 of the judgment, p 939, post). A 'necessary step in the process of arriving at any decision to make a deportation order' is a precise description of an opinion obtained under art 9(1). Thus 'measure' in art 3 and 'opinion' in art 9 are not mutually exclusive. Nor indeed is there any reason why they should be.

The Commission's other argument was based on the words 'not until an opinion has been obtained' in art 9(1). Those words, said the Commission, showed that what the authors of the directive envisaged was that the administrative authority, as soon as it was minded to take a decision ordering the expulsion of the holder of a residence permit, should inform an independent body of that fact and ask that body to give its opinion whether or not the decision would be justified. I agree that the phrase 'not until an opinion has been obtained' in the English text of art 9(1) suggests that the initiative should come from the administrative authority rather than from the independent advisory body. If, however, the phrase were 'only after an opinion has been given', it would then be quite neutral, in the sense that it would equally cover a case where the initiative came from the independent body. It is the equivalent of the latter formula that one finds in the Dutch, French, German and Italian texts. The French text, for instance, has 'qu'après avis donné'. The sense of the Danish text is midway between that of the English and that of the others. That illustrates, in my opinion, how mistaken it can be to seek to interpret a Community instrument on the basis of a semantic analysis of its text in only one language. Bearing in mind the manifest purpose of art 9(1) (which I have already stated) I see no reason why the opinion of the independent body should not precede consideration of the case by the administrative authority having the power of decision.

a   One last point on this question: in his opinion in the *Pecastaing* case the Advocate-General (F Capotorti) seems to have assumed that the independent body, the 'competent authority', referred to in art 9(1) must be an administrative one. In the circumstances of that case it was unnecessary for the Advocate-General to consider whether that body might not be a court. There is, in my opinion, plainly no reason why it should not be.

I would therefore answer the Divisional Court's second question by saying that a recommendation for deportation made by a criminal court of the host country on
b   passing sentence can constitute an opinion for the purposes of art 9(1) of the directive provided that all the material on which the administrative authority of that country may base its decision has been placed before that court and that the court has considered it, together with any representations made by or on behalf of the convicted person, before deciding whether or not to make the recommendation.

The Divisional Court's question 3(a) is, your Lordships remember, 'must "a
c   recommendation" be fully reasoned?' As was pointed out in argument before us, the real question is: must an 'opinion', in order to satisfy the requirements of art 9(1), be fully reasoned?

For the applicant and for the Commission it was submitted that that question should be answered in the affirmative. For the United Kingdom government it was submitted that it should be answered in the negative.

d   On behalf of the applicant it was asserted that a recommendation for deportation made by an English criminal court was virtually never reasoned. It is not of course for this court to say whether that assertion is correct, but I did find it surprising, if only because in this very case the learned trial judge gave his reasons for making the recommendation, albeit briefly and albeit in terms which, in the light of later judgments of this court (in particular the judgment in the *Bouchereau* case p 924, post), can be seen not to have been
e   entirely appropriate. I will not take up your Lordships' time by reading from the transcript of what the learned judge said.

The United Kingdom government rested its submission on two grounds. First, it pointed out that there was no express requirement in art 9(1) that an opinion should be fully reasoned or, indeed, reasoned at all. This contrasted with the provisions of art 6 of the directive which clearly required reasons to be given for a 'decision'. An 'opinion'
f   under art 9(1) was not a 'decision'. Second, said the United Kingdom government, no requirement that an opinion should be reasoned was necessarily to be implied into art 9(1).

I agree of course that art 6 applies only to decisions and does not apply to opinions. Nor do I think that the court held otherwise in paras 36 to 39 of its judgment in *Rutili* case [1975] ECR 1219 at 1233, to which we were referred on behalf of the applicant and
g   of the Commission. It does not, however, in my opinion follow that an opinion need not, in order to comply with art 9(1), be reasoned. Whether an opinion needs to be reasoned must depend on its purpose. It seems to me that an opinion that was a bare statement of the independent body's conclusion would be of scant assistance to the administrative authority in making up its mind and a scant safeguard to the person whose expulsion was under consideration. It must in that connection be borne in mind
h   that, although under the English system a recommendation is always positive (in the sense that, if the court does not think that an offender should be deported, it simply refrains from making any recommendation in his case), art 9(1) is wide enough to encompass a system where a negative opinion given by the independent body may be followed by a positive decision (ie a decision to expel) taken by the administrative authority.

j   I would hesitate however to answer the Divisional Court's question simply in the affirmative, because to say that an opinion must be 'fully reasoned' might convey the impression that a lengthy document was called for. The authors of the directive clearly intended that the procedural traditions of the different member states should be respected. In the case of an English criminal court, I think that an oral statement by the judge or by the presiding magistrate of its reasons for recommending deportation (of which a transcript can be made available) must suffice. The statement need not be long, provided it is not incomplete. I would accordingly answer the question by saying that, in order to satisfy the requirements of art 9(1), the 'competent authority' therein referred to must state the reasons for its opinion.

I come lastly to paras (b) and (c) of the Divisional Court's third question, relating to lapse of time between 'opinion' and 'decision', and in particular lapse of time due to the person concerned serving a sentence of imprisonment. As to that counsel for the United Kingdom government very helpfully placed some figures before us which enabled us to get the magnitude of the problem into focus. In the past three years (1977, 1978 and 1979) the number of EEC nationals recommended for deportation by English criminal courts was 73, 60 and 72 respectively. Of those, about half received non-custodial sentences, so that the problem of lapse of time did not arise in their case, and something of the order of another third received sentences of under six months, so that the problem in their case was negligible. Recipients of sentences of six months or more have numbered about a dozen a year.

The crux of the problem is of course that, if there is a substantial lapse of time, new factors may arise, rendering the opinion stale. Much emphasis was laid on behalf of the applicant and of the Commission on the formula used by this court in the *Bouchereau* case, 'a present threat to the requirements of public policy' (see p 940, post). In my opinion, however, if a court has made a finding that a person's conduct is a present threat to those requirements, that threat may reasonably be assumed to continue unless and until some new factor comes to light. Mere lapse of time therefore would not, I think, invalidate an opinion. But the reality is that the more time passes the less probable the absence of new factors becomes. If a new factor does arise (such as for instance a report of a parole review committee) there is a dilemma. Either the administrative authority must ignore it, which could be detrimental to the person concerned or, alternatively, to the public in the host country, or that authority must take it into account although it has not been considered by the independent 'competent authority'. Neither course would in my opinion accord with the scheme of art 9(1).

During the course of the hearing one of your Lordships suggested that in England the dilemma might be solved by the Secretary of State sending the case back to the court of trial for reconsideration in the light of the new factor or factors. Counsel for the United Kingdom government accepted that that might be practicable in some circumstances. I imagine that, generally speaking, it would be practicable only in cases where the lapse of time had not been too great.

In the result, I would answer the Divisional Court's questions 3(b) and (c) by saying that, whilst lapse of time between the date of the opinion envisaged by art 9(1) and the making of a decision ordering the expulsion of the person concerned does not itself invalidate the opinion, it will do so if it is such that a new factor arises which ought to be taken into account in making the decision and which the 'competent authority' has had no opportunity of considering.

22nd May. **THE COURT OF JUSTICE** delivered its judgment which, having summarised the facts, procedure and submissions of the parties, dealt with the law as follows:

1. By an order of 30th July 1979 received at the court on 10th August 1979 the High Court of Justice, Queen's Bench Division, Divisional Court, referred several questions to the court under art 177 of the EEC Treaty concerning the interpretation of, in particular, art 9(1) of EEC Council Directive 64/221 of 25th February 1964 on the co-ordination of special measures concerning the movement and residence of foreign nationals which are justified on grounds of public policy, public security or public health with a view to the exercise of its powers of judicial review following an application made by an Italian national resident in the United Kingdom as an employed person to set aside a deportation order made against him pursuant to a criminal conviction.

2. It emerges from the file and from the observations made in the course of the oral
a procedure that the United Kingdom has not introduced any specific legislation to
implement Directive 64/221. The law applied in this case, namely the law regulating
immigration (the Immigration Act), dates back to 1971. It provides that any person
described as 'non-patrial' is subject in the United Kingdom to controls which include
liability to be deported in the circumstances set out below. Under s 3(5):

b
    '(a) if, having only a limited leave to enter or remain, he does not observe a
    condition attached to the leave or remains beyond the time limited by the leave; or
    (b) if the Secretary of State deems his deportation to be conducive to the public good;
    or (c) if another person to whose family he belongs is or has been ordered to be
    deported'

and under s 3(6):

c
    '... if ... he is convicted of an offence for which he is punishable with
    imprisonment and on his conviction is recommended for deportation by a court ...'

The system of appeals differs according to whether the case is within s 3(5) or s 3(6). If
s 3(5) applies, the decision by the Secretary of State to make a deportation order is subject
to an appeal to an adjudicator from whose decision there is a further appeal to the
d Immigration Appeal Tribunal. If s 3(6) applies, the recommendation for deportation
made by a court may be appealed against but no appeal may be brought after the making
of a subsequent deportation order and there is no machinery for making representations
before the decision to make the order is taken.

3. It may be seen from the order making the reference and the documents in the file
that on 13th December 1973 the applicant was convicted before the Central Criminal
e Court of buggery and rape committed on 18th December 1972 on a prostitute and of
indecent assault and assault occasioning bodily harm on 14th April 1973 on another
prostitute. On 21st January 1974 he was sentenced to a total of eight years' imprisonment
for these four offences. When giving judgment the Central Criminal Court made a
recommendation for deportation under the Immigration Act 1971.

4. On 10th October 1974 the Court of Appeal, Criminal Division, refused the
f applicant leave to appeal against the prison sentence and the recommendation for
deportation. On 28th September 1978 the Secretary of State made a deportation order
against him to take effect when his prison sentence was completed. Having completed
his prison sentence on 3rd April 1979 after remission of one-third for good behaviour,
the applicant was due to be released but remained in detention under the Immigration
Act 1971. On 10th April 1979 the applicant applied to the High Court to set aside the
g deportation order on the ground that, having been made more than four years after the
recommendation for deportation by the Central Criminal Court, it infringed his
individual rights for failure to comply with the provisions of art 9(1) of EEC Council
Directive 64/221.

5. Article 48 of the EEC Treaty ensures freedom of movement for workers within the
Community. This comprises the right of nationals of member states, subject to
h restrictions justified on grounds of public policy, public security or public health, to
move freely in the territory of member states and to stay in a member state to take up a
post there in accordance with the laws, regulations and administrative provisions
governing the employment of national workers.

6. According to the third recital in the preamble to Directive 64/221, one of the aims
which it pursues is that 'in each Member State, nationals of other Member States should
j have adequate legal remedies available to them in respect of the decisions of the
administration' in the sphere of public policy, public security and public health.

7. Under art 8 of the same directive the person concerned must, in respect of any
decision affecting him, have 'the same legal remedies ... as are available to nationals of
the State concerned in respect of acts of the administration'. In default of this, the person

concerned must, under art 9, at least be able to exercise his rights of defence before a competent authority which must not be the same as that empowered to take the decision *a* ordering expulsion.

8. Article 9(1) of the directive provides as follows:

'Where there is no right of appeal to a court of law, or where such appeal may be only in respect of the legal validity of the decision, or where the appeal cannot have suspensory effect, a decision refusing renewal of a residence permit or ordering the expulsion of the holder of a residence permit from the territory shall not be taken *b* by the administrative authority, save in cases of urgency, until an opinion has been obtained from a competent authority of the host country before which the person concerned enjoys such rights of defence and of assistance or representation as the domestic law of that country provides for. This authority shall not be the same as that empowered to take the decision refusing renewal of the residence permit or ordering expulsion.' *c*

9. It is settled in English law that the legal remedies available against a deportation order relate only to the legal validity of that order. It follows that the deportation order itself may be made only in accordance with the provisions of art 9 of the directive, which makes express provision for such a case.

10. These were the circumstances in which the High Court of England and Wales, *d* Queen's Bench Division, came to refer the following questions to the Court of Justice for a preliminary ruling:

'1. Whether art 9(1) of EEC Council Directive 64/221 confers on individuals rights which are enforceable by them in the national courts of a member state and which the national courts must protect.

'2. (a) What is the meaning of the phrase "an opinion has been obtained from a *e* competent authority of the host country" within art 9(1) of EEC Council Directive 64/221 ("an opinion")? and (b) in particular, can a recommendation for deportation made by a criminal court on passing sentence ("a recommendation") constitute "an opinion"?

'3. If the answer to question 2(b) is Yes, (a) must "a recommendation" be fully reasoned? (b) in what (if any) circumstances does the lapse of time between the *f* making of "a recommendation" and the taking of the decision ordering the expulsion preclude "a recommendation" from constituting "an opinion"? (c) in particular, does the lapse of time involved in serving a sentence of imprisonment have the effect that "a recommendation" ceases to be "an opinion"?'

11. Article 9(1) of the directive is one of a number of provisions designed to ensure *g* that the rights of nationals of a member state regarding the freedom of movement and residence in the territory of other member states are observed. Articles 3 and 4 of the directive restrict the grounds for deportation or for refusing a worker leave to enter a member state. Article 6 provides that the person concerned shall be informed of the grounds of public policy, public security or public health on which the decision taken in his case is based, unless this is contrary to the interests of the security of the state *h* involved. Article 7 provides, inter alia, that the person concerned shall be notified of any decision to refuse the issue or renewal of a residence permit or to expel him from the territory. Article 8 gives the person concerned access to the same legal remedies as are available to nationals in respect of acts of the administration.

12. The provisions of art 9 are complementary to those of art 8. Their object is to ensure a minimum procedural safeguard for persons affected by one of the measures *j* referred to in the three cases set out in para (1) of that article. Where the right of appeal relates only to the legal validity of a decision, the purpose of the intervention of the 'competent authority' referred to in art 9(1) is to enable an exhaustive examination of all the facts and circumstances including the expediency of the proposed measure to be

carried out before the decision is finally taken. Furthermore the person concerned must
be able to exercise before that authority such rights of defence and of assistance or
representation as the domestic law of that country provides for.

13. These provisions, taken together, are sufficiently well defined and specific to
enable them to be relied on by any person concerned and capable, as such, of being
applied by any court. This conclusion justifies a positive reply to the first question
submitted by the national court.

14. The requirement contained in art 9(1) that any decision ordering expulsion must
be preceded by the opinion of a 'competent authority' and that the person concerned
must be able to enjoy such rights of defence and of assistance or representation as the
domestic law of that country provides for can only constitute a real safeguard if all the
factors to be taken into consideration by the administration are put before the competent
authority, if the opinion of the competent authority is sufficiently proximate in time to
the decision ordering expulsion to ensure that there are no new factors to be taken into
consideration and if both the administration and the person concerned are in a position
to take cognisance of the reasons which led the 'competent authority' to give its opinion,
save where grounds touching the security of the state referred to in art 6 of the directive
make this undesirable.

15. As regards the question what is the significance of the phrase 'opinion . . . obtained
from a competent authority of the host country' and whether a recommendation for
deportation made by a criminal court at the time of conviction constitutes such an
opinion, it should be noted that the directive does not define the expression 'a competent
authority'. It refers to an authority which must be independent of the administration,
but it gives member states a margin of discretion in regard to the nature of the authority.

16. It is common ground that the criminal courts in the United Kingdom are
independent of the administration, which is responsible for making the deportation
order, and that the person concerned enjoys the right to be represented and to exercise
his rights of defence before such courts.

17. A recommendation for deportation made by a criminal court at the time of
conviction under British legislation may, therefore, constitute an opinion within the
meaning of art 9 of the directive provided that the other conditions of art 9 are satisfied.
As the court has already stressed in its judgment in *R v Bouchereau* p 940, post, a criminal
court must take account in particular of the provisions of art 3 of the directive inasmuch
as the mere existence of criminal convictions may not automatically constitute grounds
for deportation measures.

18. As regards the time at which the opinion of the competent authority must be
given, it must be observed that a lapse of time amounting to several years between the
recommendation for deportation and the decision by the administration is liable to
deprive the recommendation of its functions as an opinion within the meaning of art 9.
It is indeed essential that the social danger resulting from a foreigner's presence should
be assessed at the very time when the decision ordering expulsion is made against him
as the factors to be taken into account, particularly those concerning his conduct, are
likely to change in the course of time.

19. These considerations lead to a reply in the following terms to the second and third
questions submitted by the High Court of Justice:

The directive leaves a margin of discretion to member states for defining the
'competent authority'. Any public authority independent of the administrative authority
called on to adopt one of the measures referred to by the directive which is so constituted
that the person concerned enjoys the right of representation and of defence before it may
be considered as such an authority.

A recommendation for deportation made under British legislation by a criminal court
at the time of conviction may constitute an opinion under art 9 of the directive provided
that the other conditions of art 9 are satisfied. The criminal court must take account in
particular of the provisions of art 3 of the directive inasmuch as the mere existence of

criminal convictions may not automatically constitute grounds for deportation measures.

The opinion of the competent authority must be sufficiently proximate in time to the *a* decision ordering expulsion to ensure that there are no new factors to be taken into consideration, and that both the administration and the person concerned are in a position to take cognisance of the reasons which led the 'competent authority' to give its opinion, save where grounds touching the security of the state referred to in art 6 of the directive make this undesirable.

A lapse of time amounting to several years between the recommendation for *b* deportation and the decision by the administration is liable to deprive the recommendation of its function as an opinion within the meaning of art 9. It is indeed essential that the social danger resulting from a foreigner's presence should be assessed at the very time when the decision ordering expulsion is made against him as the factors to be taken into account, particularly those concerning his conduct, are likely to change in the course of time.   *c*

Costs

20. The costs incurred by the government of the United Kingdom and by the Commission of the European Communities, which have submitted observations to the court, are not recoverable. As these proceedings are, in so far as the parties to the main action are concerned, in the nature of a step in the action pending before the national *d* court, the decision on costs is a matter for that court.

On those grounds, the court, in answer to the questions referred to it by the High Court of Justice, Queen's Bench Division, Divisional Court, by an order of 30th July 1979, hereby rules: (1) art 9 of EEC Council Directive 64/221 of 25th February 1964 imposes obligations on member states which may be relied on by the persons concerned before *e* national courts; (2)(a) the directive leaves a margin of discretion to member states in regard to the definitions of the 'competent authority'. Any public authority independent of the administrative authority called on to adopt one of the measures referred to by the directive which is so constituted that the person concerned enjoys the right of representation and of defence before it may be considered as such an authority; (b) a recommendation for deportation made under British legislation by a criminal court at *f* the time of conviction may constitute an opinion under art 9 of the directive provided that the other conditions of art 9 are satisfied. The criminal court must take account in particular of the provisions of art 3 of the directive inasmuch as the mere existence of criminal convictions may not automatically constitute grounds for deportation measures; (3)(a) the opinion of the competent authority must be sufficiently proximate in time to the decision ordering expulsion to ensure that there are no new factors to be taken into *g* consideration, and that both the administration and the person concerned are in a position to take cognisance of the reasons which led the 'competent authority' to give its opinion, save where grounds touching the security of the state referred to in art 6 of the directive make this undesirable; (b) a lapse of time amounting to several years between the recommendation for deportation and the decision by the administration is liable to deprive the recommendation of its function as an opinion within the meaning of art 9. *h* It is indeed essential that the social danger resulting from a foreigner's presence should be assessed at the very time when the decision ordering expulsion is made against him as the facts to be taken into account, particularly those concerning his conduct, are likely to change in the course of time.

Agents: *Alexander & Partners*, Willesden (for the applicant); *G Dagtoglou*, Treasury *j* Solicitor's Department (for the United Kingdom); *Anthony McClellan*, Legal Service of the EC Commission (for the Commission).

Andrew Durand Esq   Barrister.

Application for judicial review

a Following the receipt by the Divisional Court of the Queen's Bench Division of the answers to the questions referred by it to the Court of Justice of the European Communities, the application was heard by the Divisional Court.

Louis Blom-Cooper QC and *Alan Newman* for the applicant.
Simon D Brown for the Secretary of State.

b
　　　　　　　　　　　　　　　　　　　　　　　　　　　　　　Cur adv vult

18th July. The following judgments were read.

DONALDSON LJ. On 21st January 1974 the applicant, an Italian citizen, was
c convicted of rape and buggery before his Honour Judge Rees at the Central Criminal Court. He was sentenced to eight years' imprisonment and a recommendation was made for his deportation. His application for leave to appeal was dismissed by the Court of Appeal, Criminal Division.

On 28th September 1978 the Secretary of State made a deportation order under s 3(6) of the Immigration Act 1971, effective when the applicant should be released from
d imprisonment. This event occurred on 3rd April 1979 and the applicant was thereafter detained under the 1971 Act. In these proceedings he challenges the validity of the deportation order.

On 30th July 1979 this court referred to the Court of Justice of the European Communities several questions arising in connection with his application (see p 910 d to f, ante). We have now to reach a decision on the application in the light of the judgment
e of that court.

Counsel for the applicant submits that, irrespective of the provisions of Community law as incorporated into English law, the deportation order should be quashed on the ground that there was a breach of the right of audi alteram partem. The basis of this submission is that, as appears from an affidavit sworn by Mr Youngs of the Home Office, the Secretary of State, in reaching the conclusion that, as a matter of public policy and in
f the interests of public safety, there would be an excessive risk to the public from offences of the same or a similar sort as those of which the applicant was convicted if he were allowed to remain in the United Kingdom, took account of four matters without informing the applicant that he was doing so and without giving him any opportunity of being heard in relation thereto. These four matters were that (a) in February 1972 the applicant was acquitted of robbery from a prostitute when she failed to attend court to
g give evidence for the prosecution, (b) that the police considered that the applicant was responsible for other similar offences of which insufficient evidence existed to prove his guilt, (c) that in 1976 and 1977 the parole review committee refused to recommend the applicant for parole and (d) that in 1978 the Secretary of State had decided not to release the applicant on licence.

Counsel for the Secretary of State does not challenge the importance of the right of
h audi alteram partem, but submits that it is not universally applicable. In the present instance a convicted person has a right to have notice that a recommendation for deportation may be made, to be heard in opposition to the making of such a recommendation and to appeal against it if made (see s 6 of the 1971 Act). But once those rights have been exhausted, the person concerned is 'liable to deportation' under s 3(6) of the Act and, whilst any representations which he cares to make within a
j reasonable time before the order takes effect should and would be considered in the context of whether, as an act of grace, the order should be revoked, nothing can affect his status as a person who is and remains *liable* to deportation. In a word, he is irremediably at mercy. Since the subject of the deportation order has no legal right to complain of the order being made and executed, he can have no right to be heard in opposition to this

course and no right to complain to the Secretary of State, as part of the decision-making process, taking account of matters of which the convicted person may be unaware and which may indeed be irrelevant or untrue.

In my judgment, counsel's submission is correct in law, but I would hope and expect that the Secretary of State, in deciding what weight to attach to matters which appear to tell against deciding, as an act of grace, not to make a deportation order, would take full account of the fact (if such it be in the circumstances) that the convicted person has not had an opportunity of being heard and of the possibility that, if he had been heard, these matters might have had no weight or less weight. This is an exercise in fair judgment which is in this instance exclusively within the province of the Secretary of State and is not open to review in this court.

I now turn to the submissions based on EEC Council Directive 64/221, which is designed to further the unification of Europe by removing or inhibiting obstacles to the freedom of citizens to live, work and travel freely within the territory of the Community.

The applicant's principal complaint is based on art 9(1) of the direction which is in the following terms:

'Where there is no right of appeal to a court of law, or where such appeal may be only in respect of the legal validity of the decision, or where the appeal cannot have suspensory effect, a decision refusing renewal of a residence permit or ordering the expulsion of the holder of a residence permit from the territory shall not be taken by the administrative authority, save in cases of urgency, until an opinion has been obtained from a competent authority of the host country before which the person concerned enjoys such rights of defence and of assistance or representation as the domestic law of that country provides for. This authority shall not be the same as that empowered to take the decision refusing renewal of the residence permit or ordering expulsion.'

The European Court has given guidance on the meaning of this article in the following terms (see pp 911–912, ante):

'The directive leaves a margin of discretion to member states for defining the "competent authority". Any public authority independent of the administrative authority called on to adopt one of the measures referred to by the directive which is so constituted that the person concerned enjoys the right of representation and of defence before it may be considered as such an authority. A recommendation for deportation made under British legislation by a criminal court at the time of conviction may constitute an opinion under art 9 of the directive provided that the other conditions of art 9 are satisfied. The criminal court must take account in particular of the provisions of art 3 of the directive inasmuch as the mere existence of criminal convictions may not automatically constitute grounds for deportation measures. The opinion of the competent authority must be sufficiently proximate in time to the decision ordering expulsion to ensure that there are no new factors to be taken into consideration, and that both the administration and the person concerned are in a position to take cognisance of the reasons which led the "competent authority" to give its opinion, save where grounds touching the security of the state referred to in art 6 of the directive make this undesirable. A lapse of time amounting to several years between the recommendation for deportation and the decision by the administration is liable to deprive the recommendation of its function as an opinion within the meaning of art 9. It is indeed essential that the social danger resulting from a foreigner's presence should be assessed at the very time when the decision ordering expulsion is made against him as the factors to be taken into account, particularly those concerning his conduct, are likely to change in the course of time.'

That guidance is expressed in general terms and it is our duty to apply it to the facts of this case.

The only opinion from a competent authority which can be relied upon in this case is
a   the recommendation of the trial judge. That was expressed on 21st January 1974, a little
under five years before the decision was taken to make a deportation order. It was thus
very stale and *liable* to have ceased to perform its function as an opinion of the competent
authority within the meaning of art 9. I take the word 'liable' from the European Court's
answer to question 3(b). But in fact there is not a scintilla of evidence that the position
had in any way changed or that any of the considerations which caused the trial judge to
b   make his recommendation had been altered at least in a sense favourable to the
applicant. Accordingly, in my judgment, the recommendation not only brought s 3(6)
of the 1971 Act into operation, it also continued, down to and including the date when
the decision to deport was taken, to constitute a valid opinion of the competent authority
within the meaning of art 9.

The only other matter to which I need make specific reference is the complaint that
c   neither the Secretary of State nor the trial judge had regard to art 3 of the directive as
explained in *R v Bouchereau* p 924, post.

Article 3, so far as is material, is in these terms:

'1. Measures taken on grounds of public policy or of public security shall be based
exclusively on the personal conduct of the individual concerned.

'2. Previous criminal convictions shall not in themselves constitute grounds for
d   the taking of such measures . . .'

In their judgment, the Court of Justice of the European Communities said (see
pp 939–940, post):

'27. The terms of art 3(2) of the directive, which states that "previous criminal
convictions shall not in themselves constitute grounds for the taking of such
e   measures", must be understood as requiring the national authorities to carry out a
specific appraisal from the point of view of the interests inherent in protecting the
requirements of public policy, which does not necessarily coincide with the
appraisals which formed the basis of the criminal conviction.

'28. The existence of a previous criminal conviction can, therefore, only be taken
into account in so far as the circumstances which gave rise to that conviction are
f   evidence of personal conduct constituting a present threat to the requirements of
public policy.

'29. Although, in general, a finding that such a threat exists implies the existence
in the individual concerned of a propensity to act in the same way in the future, it
is possible that past conduct alone may constitute such a threat to the requirements
of public policy.'
g
In my judgment, it is clear that both the trial judge and the Secretary of State did in
fact approach the matter in a way which was consistent with art 3 as explained by the
European Court. The learned judge expressly said that he made the recommendation
'in the interests of the community and the protection of the community'. According to
Mr Youngs's affidavit, the Secretary of State made the deportation order because he
h   considered that a failure to deport the applicant would expose the public to an excessive
risk of further offences of the same sort being committed by the applicant. This is
precisely the consideration which art 3 allows to be taken into account. It stipulates only
that the fact of previous criminal convictions is irrelevant save in so far as past personal
conduct throws light on the likely pattern of future personal conduct and that likelihood
justifies the deportation as a matter of public policy or public security.

j   So the position reached is this. Whilst the Secretary of State could have sought an
updated opinion from some competent authority, on the facts of this case Community
law did not require him to do so because the original recommendation was still effective
for the purposes of art 9. And, even if he had done so, there is not the slightest ground
for believing that such an updated opinion would have differed from that of the trial
court.

Furthermore, it should be remembered that a recommendation by the trial court unleashes the Secretary of State's power under s 3(6) of the 1971 Act irretrievably. If, on *a* the facts of a particular case, that recommendation becomes out of date for the purposes of art 9 and the Secretary of State is required by that article to obtain a further opinion, that further opinion is advisory only and does not bind the Secretary of State whether it recommends for or against an order of deportation.

For the reasons which I have given I do not consider that there are any grounds for granting the relief sought. However, it is clear that courts which are minded to make *b* recommendations for deportation should have their attention drawn to two matters.

The first is that to which I have already referred, namely that the existence of previous criminal convictions is not of itself a basis for making a recommendation. This is not only the law in accordance with art 3 of the directive. It is also only common sense and fairness. No one can reasonably recommend the deportation of a foreigner solely because he has a criminal record. If he is, or will on release from prison be, completely *c* rehabilitated, he is a threat to no one. But the position is quite different if the court considers that the previous record of the accused, including the offence with which the court is directly concerned, renders it likely that he will offend again. This possibility of reoffending, a matter which has to be taken into account under the Bail Act 1976 when considering whether to grant bail pending trial, is a very important factor in deciding whether to recommend deportation and taking account of it is permitted by the directive. *d*

The second is the decision of the Court of Appeal in *R v Nazari* [1980] 3 All ER 880, [1980] 1 WLR 1366, which pointed out that no court should make an order recommending deportation without full inquiry into all the circumstances, gave some guidance on the principles involved and held that the court should give reasons for its decision if a recommendation is to be made. It would avoid subsequent argument if those reasons included some indication of the extent to which the current and previous *e* criminal convictions of the accused have been taken into account and, in so far as this has been done, the light which, in the view of the court, such conviction or convictions throw on the likely nature of the accused's personal conduct in the future. The giving of reasons is not only in accordance with this decision, it is also consistent with the philosophy disclosed by art 6 of the directive which requires that the person concerned shall be informed of the grounds of public policy, public security or public health on *f* which the decision taken by the Secretary of State in his case is based, unless it is contrary to the interests of the security of the state.

This only leaves the question of how a procedure can be devised which will give the Secretary of State the benefit of an 'opinion . . . from a competent authority' in cases in which the convicted person has been imprisoned for such a term as, in the circumstances of his case, has deprived the trial court's recommendation for deportation of its status as *g* such an opinion for the purposes of art 9. This is a matter for the Secretary of State, and we were told that it is receiving active consideration. He may, however, consider that, whatever procedure is adopted, it is most undesirable that the competent authority should in fact or in form conduct an appeal in respect of the original recommendation. In so far as there was a right of appeal in respect of the sentence of imprisonment, there will also have been a right of appeal in respect of the recommendation. That should end *h* the matter. What the competent authority should consider is whether, given that the recommendation was justified when made, circumstances have so changed that it can no longer be treated as effective. This is a quite different concept. It involves no challenge to the original recommendation, but only a consideration of whether the convicted person should be relieved of its effect. It would be no novelty if Parliament decided that in such cases the competent authority should be the court which made the original *j* recommendation. The courts are already empowered to review their own previous orders for disqualification for holding or obtaining driving licences (see the Road Traffic Act 1972, s 95). But if it was decided to remit the matter to a different competent authority, for example, an Immigration Act adjudicator, it may be thought to be of some importance that that authority should adopt a similar approach.

I would dismiss the application.

COMYN J. I agree with the judgment that has just been given and that the application
a should be dismissed.

I wish only to add a few words on one matter which I regard as being of some
importance. In deciding finally whether to deport or not, the Home Secretary is acting
administratively and must therefore have a very wide discretion as to what he does or
does not take into account.

In that connection two things have been specifically mentioned in this case which I
b think need to be clarified, namely taking account of an acquittal and taking account of
suspicions of criminality which cannot be turned into proof. In my view, neither
acquittals nor suspicions should be taken into account against somebody unless there are
good reasons for making it just and fair to do so. Good reasons would exist, for example,
if an acquittal were on purely technical grounds or if the suspicions had a strong basis of
provable fact.

c I am satisfied that none of the matters taken into account by the Secretary of State here
had been in any way improperly taken into account. I agree that the application should
be dismissed.

Application dismissed.

d   Dilys Tausz   Barrister.

Appeal

The applicant appealed to the Court of Appeal.

Alan Newman for the applicant.
e *Simon D Brown* for the Secretary of State.

Cur adv vult

19th December. The following judgments were read.

f **LORD DENNING MR.** Mario Santillo came from Italy in October 1967. He
obtained work here. When we joined the European community in 1973 he became
entitled to all the rights accorded to workers here by art 48 of the EEC Treaty. In
particular to remain here and not be expelled except on grounds of public policy as
spelled out in EEC Council Directive 64/221 of 25th February 1964. That directive is
directly applicable here and must be applied by our courts as part of our law.
g Now Santillo turned out be a criminal. He was a menace to our society. He committed
horrible offences against women. Such as rape, buggery, robbery and bodily harm. He
was convicted on 11th January 1974 at the Central Criminal Court. At the hearing the
question arose whether he should be recommended for deportation. The judge
adjourned the case for ten days for it to be looked into. On 21st January 1974 the judge
was told that his wife and children were in a council flat and wanted to stay in this
h country. It was suggested that it would be rather hard for her if, after serving his
sentence, he should be deported. The judge gave sentence in these words:

> 'Mario Santillo, you have been found guilty by the jury of offences which were
> very grave. They were callous, cruel and ruthless, and I propose to deal with you on
> that basis. The medical reports on you show that you are not in any need of medical
j > or psychiatric treatment and you are of sound mind . . . you go to prison for . . .
> eight years in all. As regards the matter of the notice of deportation served on you,
> I take into account all that [counsel] has said regarding the position of your wife and
> small daughters, for whom I sympathise, but I think my duty requires me to
> recommend that an order of deportation be made in your case in the interests of the
> community and the protection of the community. I recommend that an order of
> deportation be made in your case.'

Mario Santillo applied for leave to appeal, but it was refused, not only on the sentence but on the recommendation for deportation. He went to prison and was sufficiently well conducted as to earn remission of one-third of his sentence. So he was due to be released after serving just over five years, that is, in April 1979. Six months before that date the Home Secretary considered whether he should be deported or not. The Home Secretary had before him full details of the offences which Mario Santillo had committed; but also these additional matters: (i) in February 1972 he was charged with robbery from a prostitute, but acquitted after she had failed to attend court to give evidence; (ii) in addition to the offences of which he was convicted in January 1974, the police considered that he was responsible for other similar offences, but that not sufficient evidence existed to prove this was the case; (iii) in 1976 and 1977 the parole review committee of Maidstone prison refused to recommend him for parole; (iv) in 1978 the Home Secretary decided not to release him on licence.

In addition the senior medical officer of the prison was of opinion that 'Clearly Mario Santillo was driven by a strong urge to commit these offences . . . I doubt that the experience of custodial sentence would have the effect of enabling him to suppress those urges again'.

In other words, there was still a risk that, after his release, he might commit similar offences again.

On these materials the Home Secretary decided to make a deportation order. His reasons were as follows:

'As a matter of public policy and in the interests of public safety the Secretary of State reached the conclusion that in all the circumstances there would be an excessive risk to the public from offences of the same or similar sort as those which the Applicant had been convicted, which out-weighed the arguments in favour of allowing the Applicant to remain, if he were allowed to remain in the United Kingdom on completion of his sentences of imprisonment. Accordingly the Secretary of State felt that the proper course was to act on the Court's recommendation . . . he decided to make a Deportation Order . . .'

The deportation order itself was dated 28th September 1977 and was signed by Mr Merlyn Rees, the Home Secretary, himself. It said: '. . . I by this order require the said . . . Mario SANTILLO to leave and prohibit him from entering the United Kingdom so long as this order is in force.'

On 3rd April 1979 Mario Santillo completed his prison sentence. In the ordinary way he would have been deported within few days. But everything has been held up for 2½ years because he has contended that our machinery for deportation contravenes Community law. On 10th April 1979 counsel made an application to the Divisional Court on his behalf. He asked that the deportation order be quashed on the ground that the United Kingdom had failed to comply with the articles of the EEC Treaty and with the directives. The Divisional Court decided to refer some questions to the Court of Justice of the European Communities at Luxembourg. The questions were answered in a judgment of the European Court of 22nd May 1980 (see pp 908–912, ante). Their answers were considered by the Divisional Court on 18th July 1980 (see pp 913–917, ante). The Divisional Court held that the proceedings for deportation had not broken any of the provisions of Community law, and that the deportation order was valid. Mario Santillo now appeals to this court. Pending his appeal he has gone back to Italy, but if his appeal is allowed, he will be brought back.

Article 48 of the EEC Treaty

By art 48 Mario Santillo was entitled to the benefit of freedom of movement within the European Community and to stay here 'subject to limitations justified on grounds of public policy . . .' There has been no breach of that article. The deportation order was a limitation which was justified on grounds of public policy. The presence here of Mario *a* Santillo constituted a genuine and serious threat to the peace and good order of our society: see *R v Bouchereau* p 940, post.

EEC Council Directive 64/221

The directive is worded in European fashion. It starts with recitals and goes on to detailed articles. I do not propose to set out the directive in full here; nor the rulings of the European Court on it. That would take up too much space and also too much time. *b* I would only say that arts 3 and 6 were clearly complied with. The deportation order was a measure taken on grounds of public policy. It was based exclusively on the personal conduct of Mario Santillo. He was informed of the grounds on which the decision was based, at the time he was sentenced.

The only difficulty is art 9(1). I find it difficult to reconcile the provisions of art 9(1) with the procedure of the United Kingdom in relation to deportation. It seems to me *c* that those who drafted art 9(1) had no knowledge of the procedure for deportation adopted by the United Kingdom in cases under s 3(6) of the Immigration Act 1971, that is, in cases where a court has made a recommendation for deportation. In order to reconcile the directive with our procedure, I would say:

(1) The Central Criminal Court on 21st January 1974 was a 'competent authority of the host country'. Mario Santillo enjoyed before that court full rights of defence and of *d* assistance and representation such as our domestic law provided for.

(2) That court, the competent authority, did express its 'opinion' recommending that Mario Santillo should be expelled.

(3) The Home Secretary was the 'administrative authority' which ordered expulsion. The Home Secretary had before him the opinion of the competent authority. That was sufficient for him to act on.

e (4) Now this is the important point: in my opinion the word 'until' in the directive should be construed as if it said 'except after'. That is necessary to effect the reconciliation.

(5) The opinion of the competent authority (the Central Criminal Court) was sufficiently proximate in point of time to be a valid opinion, on which the administrative authority (the Home Secretary) could act, because there were no new factors which were such as to invalidate the opinion. The only new factors were factors which were adverse *f* to Mario Santillo, and these served to reinforce the recommendation for deportation.

(6) The lapse of time here, 4½ years, was not such as to invalidate the recommendation for deportation. Santillo had spent all those years in prison. That was because he was such a bad man, and there was a risk of his offending again. It does not deprive the recommendation of its force in the slightest.

For these reasons I am of opinion that the procedure adopted by this country in *g* relation to deportation (after a court has recommended deportation) is in conformity with Community law as set out in the directive. There is no reason for it to be changed in any way.

Natural justice

It was submitted that the Home Secretary, in making the deportation order, took into *h* account some considerations which he ought not have done, adverse to Mario Santillo, without giving him an opportunity of dealing with them. Such as the prosecution for which he was acquitted, or the suspicion of other offences, or the refusal of parole, or of licence. It was said that, although the Home Secretary was an administrative authority, nevertheless on the modern authorities it was incumbent on him to act fairly (see *Re K (H) (an infant)* [1967] 1 All ER 226, [1967] 2 QB 617), and that it was not fair of him to *j* take those matters into account as he did.

The answer to this submission is that the rules of natural justice, or of fairness, are not cut and dried. They vary infinitely. In the present case, where a court of law has already recommended deportation, the Home Secretary can and should be trusted to act fairly. In the latest immigration rules (Statement of Changes in Immigration Rules (HC Paper (1979–80) no 394)) it is provided by r 141:

'In considering whether to give effect to a recommendation for deportation made by a court on conviction the Secretary of State will take into account every relevant *a* factor known to him, including: age; length of residence in the United Kingdom; strength of connections with the United Kingdom; personal history, including character, conduct and employment record; domestic circumstances; the nature of the offence of which the person was convicted; previous criminal record; compassionate circumstances; any representations received on the person's behalf . . .'
b

It seems to me that so long as the Secretary of State follows that rule he does all that fairness requires, and that there is no need for him to have a hearing or to put this or that matter to the person. If there should come to his notice that there is a new factor which is adverse to the person, there ordinarily is no need for the Home Secretary to invite him to deal with it. If the case for deportation is already so strong that the new factor simply reinforces it, the Home Secretary need not put it to him. But there may be special cases *c* where the case for deportation is so doubtful that the new adverse factor may turn the scale against the man. In those circumstances the Home Secretary should invite him to deal with it. No doubt in this case the grounds for deportation were so strong that there was no need to put these four new factors to Santillo.

It seems to me that the Home Secretary acted perfectly fairly. There was no breach of the rules of natural justice.
d

Conclusion

It was very proper that these proceedings should have been brought so as to see that our procedure for deportation was in conformity with Community law. I trust that we have now made it clear that it is. I would dismiss the appeal, accordingly.
e

SHAW LJ (read by Templeman LJ). I agree. At the root of the matter is the fact that the deportation order was made in pursuance of s 3(6) of the Immigration Act 1971. The recommendation made by the court of trial is itself based on a consideration of all available relevant information and the defending advocate at the trial has an opportunity to make submissions and to put forward arguments against the making of a recommendation. If it is none the less made, there is an appeal by leave to the Court of *f* Appeal. Thus two competent authorities consider the propriety of making a recommendation following on a conviction. The directive does not contemplate a procedure involving such a high degree of investigation and review. The English system so far as it relates to recommendation for deportation following on a conviction contains in-built safeguards for the interests of the prospective deportee.

The heart of the matter so far as the applicant is concerned lies in the proposition that, *g* where a recommendation relates to a person who is sentenced to a long term of imprisonment, his personality and character may have changed in a radical way by the date of his release. His deportation may no longer be necessary for the good health of society and there should accordingly be a further review on or before that date. In such circumstances it would, as I see it, be for the prospective deportee to raise the matter by making representations in that regard when the time for his release approached. If he *h* should do so the Secretary of State would be bound to consider them and to act fairly in making his decision. He may indeed take the initiative and decide that further consideration is appropriate even though no representations in that regard are made to him. The lapse of time, even of a long time, may bring no material change. The telling factors remain as the conviction and the circumstances which gave rise to it. There are ample safeguards in the English system which meet the total requirements of the *j* directive. In my view it is unnecessary to change that system in any respect. On the facts of the present appeal and notwithstanding the recital of irrelevant and immaterial matter in the list of facts which were considered by the Secretary of State, I am quite satisfied that he acted fairly and reasonably and that his decision was a proper one. I would dismiss the appeal.

TEMPLEMAN LJ. By ss 3(6) and 6(1) of the Immigration Act 1971 the applicant,
a being a non-patrial allowed into this country in 1967, was liable to deportation if he was
convicted of a criminal offence, sentenced to a term of imprisonment and recommended
for deportation by the trial judge. By s 5(1) the Secretary of State was authorised to make
a deportation order in response to a deportation recommendation.

On 21st January 1974 the applicant was convicted of buggery and rape committed
against one victim on 18th December 1972 and of indecent assault and assault occasioning
b actual bodily harm against another victim on 14th April 1973 and he was sentenced to
eight years' imprisonment.

The trial judge described the offences of which the applicant was convicted as 'very
grave ... callous, cruel and ruthless'. The learned judge observed that the medical
reports on the applicant showed that he was not in need of medical or psychiatric
treatment and was of sound mind. Finally the learned judge said:

c
> '... I take into account all that [your counsel] has said regarding the position of
> your wife and small daughters, for whom I sympathise, but I think my duty
> requires me to recommend that an order of deportation be made in your case in the
> interests of the community and the protection of the community.'

The applicant applied for leave to appeal against his sentence and against the
d deportation recommendation but the full court refused leave.

There is no evidence that anything happened after 21st July 1974 when the deportation
recommendation was made to cast doubt on the justice or propriety of the deportation
recommendation or to support representations against the making or implementation of
a deportation order. The parole review committee refused to recommend the applicant
for parole in 1976 and 1977 and the Secretary of State decided not to release the applicant
e on licence in 1978. On 28th September 1978 the Secretary of State made a deportation
order against the applicant under s 5(1) of the Immigration Act 1971.

On 27th November 1978 the applicant applied to the Divisional Court to quash the
deportation order.

On 30th March 1979 the senior medical officer of Maidstone prison where the
applicant was serving his sentence deposed in an affidavit as follows:
f
> '7. ... I cannot point to any new factor which would demonstrate that [the
> applicant] would not commit these offences again.
> '8. Clearly [the applicant] was driven by a strong urge to commit these offences.
> Having particular regard to the fact that [the applicant] still denies the sexual
> offences were committed by him, I doubt that the experience of a custodial sentence
> would have the effect of enabling him to suppress those urges again.
g
> '9. In my experience this type of condition can only be modified by long term
> Psychiatric treatment and the utmost co-operation from the patient.'

On 30th July 1979 the Divisional Court was obliged to turn its back on reality and to
propound certain questions to the European Court. Immersed in the cloudy generality
of its functions under art 177 of the EEC Treaty, the European Court was also obliged to
h ignore reality but furnished replies which enable this court now to approach the moment
of truth.

The truth is that the Secretary of State, applying principles of public policy preserved
by Community law and weighing under English law his responsibilities to the applicant,
his responsibility to other criminals liable to deportation and his responsibility to the
community whose citizens, whose laws and whose moral principles have been so brutally
j violated, would have failed in his duty if he had not ordered the deportation of the
applicant.

In connection with his application to the Divisional Court on 27th November 1978
and throughout this litigation since that date, the applicant has received the benefit of
expert legal advice. At no time has the applicant put forward any positive reason why
the trial judge should not have made the deportation recommendation, why the Secretary

of State should not have made the deportation order or why the deportation order should not be implemented.

On behalf of the applicant two negative submissions have been made; first, that the Secretary of State received information which under English law he was under a duty to refer to the applicant for comment; and, second, that the Secretary of State made no deportation order valid under Community law because he did not obtain the opinion of a competent authority at the time he purported to make the deportation order.

It is said that consistently with English law the Secretary of State should have disclosed to the applicant that the information available to the Secretary of State included unproved and hearsay allegations of other crimes by the applicant and other information including the fact that parole had been refused.

It is clear that the applicant was aware of some of the allegations of other crimes made against him and that he was aware of the decisions of the parole review committee and it is naive to think that he did not know in general that this information would be available to the Secretary of State in some form.

More importantly, it is equally clear in my judgment that the information of which the applicant now complains could have had no influence on the Secretary of State. The crimes which justified the deportation recommendation were the crimes of which the applicant stood convicted and they needed no embellishment. The applicant was free to make representations to the Secretary of State before and after the deportation order was made and he took advantage of his opportunities. The applicant has been free to put forward evidence to this court. Representations and evidence by the applicant would be directed to asserting and supporting the assertion that he is fit to be trusted at large in England. The decisions of the parole review committee only reflect the fact that the applicant has been unable to convince anyone that he is fit to be trusted. The evidence of the chief medical officer of Maidstone prison illustrates and confirms the fact that the applicant is and remains unable to convince anyone that he is fit to be trusted. If all the information of which the applicant now complains had been eliminated and never been made available to the Secretary of State, the result must have been the same. I decline to turn my back on reality.

With all respect to the earnest and fluent submissions of counsel on behalf of the applicant, this appeal is regardless and reckless of facts which have been buried under a mass of authorities dealing with natural justice. Those authorities disclose the principle which this court will always uphold that an individual should be treated fairly by a minister exercising a discretionary power. I do not subscribe to the views expressed by Donaldson LJ in the Divisional Court that the applicant was at mercy or that the Secretary of State was asked to perform an act of grace. The applicant has rights and the Secretary of State has responsibilities. The rights of the applicant are to make representations and to be treated fairly. The responsibilities of the Secretary of State are to treat the applicant fairly and to determine whether the public interest requires his deportation.

The authorities do not disclose an absolute duty on the Secretary of State exercising the power of acting on a deportation recommendation to disclose all the information available to him. In fairness the Secretary of State should disclose information of which the criminal is unaware and which the Secretary of State considers to be persuasive. But it is impossible and undesirable to lay down any hard and fast rules; for example, some information will be of a nature which should not be disclosed in the public interest or in the interests of the criminal himself or in the interests of his family. This means that the Secretary of State must be trusted to decide what information is persuasive and liable to disclosure. In the context of the duties imposed on the Secretary of State by the Immigration Act 1971 and in particular by s 5(1) of that Act, it seems to me that this consequence is inevitable and acceptable.

There are practical safeguards. Every Secretary of State will endeavour to be fair. Unfairness, like murder, will out. The court will investigate and adjudicate on allegations

of unfairness. European Community law has now, as revealed by the ruling of the
a European Court in this case, imposed further safeguards in the event of a deportation
recommendation losing its validity as a result of lapse of time. It suffices for present
purposes that in the light of all the evidence and all the argument I am satisfied that the
applicant received full and fair treatment at the hands of the Secretary of State and that
the rules of natural justice and other rules of English law have not been breached.

But then it was said by counsel that by the law of the European Community the
b Secretary of State was debarred from making a deportation order in the absence of an
opinion from a competent authority obtained at or about the time of the making of the
deportation order. The European Court in its replies delivered on 22nd May 1980 to the
questions referred for a preliminary ruling in this case declared that a reasoned
recommendation for deportation by the trial judge before whom the person concerned
has rights of defence and representation may constitute the opinion of a competent
c authority required by art 9 of EEC Council Directive 64/221. In my judgment the
reasoned deportation recommendation in the present case was the opinion of a competent
authority for the purposes of art 9.

At the same time, in their replies, the European Court declared that 'The opinion of
the competent authority must be sufficiently proximate in time to the decision ordering
expulsion to ensure that there are no new factors to be taken into consideration' (see
d p 912, ante), and it is now argued on behalf of the applicant that the deportation
recommendation made on 21st July 1974 was not sufficiently proximate in time to the
deportation order made on 28th September 1978.

But in the present case no new factor has been suggested by the applicant. The
evidence in this case makes it clear that no new factor has emerged, let alone a new factor
which might militate against the making of a deportation order, and it is plain from the
e uncontradicted and uncontradictable evidence of the senior medical officer of Maidstone
prison that the lapse of time between the deportation recommendation and the
deportation order had and could have no effect whatsoever and did not operate to deprive
the deportation recommendation of its force and effect or raise any doubts concerning
the continuing validity of the deportation recommendation at the date of the deportation
order.

f   Counsel for the Secretary of State agreed that there is no machinery under English law
to enable the Secretary of State when contemplating a deportation order to obtain a
second opinion where a deportation recommendation ceases to be an adequate expression
of opinion within art 9 of directive 64/221 as a result of lapse of time. I cannot usefully
add anything to the debate on this problem.

So far as this appeal is concerned, I have reached the conclusions that by the law of
g England the Secretary of State was empowered to make a deportation order provided he
acted fairly and that he did act fairly towards the applicant. Community law did not in
the present circumstances require any further reference to a competent authority for a
second opinion before the Secretary of State exercised the powers conferred on him by
English law. Applying both English law and Community law, it is difficult to see how
the Secretary of State as a responsible minister could have refrained from exercising his
h powers. The appeal must be dismissed.

Appeal dismissed. Leave to appeal to the House of Lords refused.

*9th April 1981. The Appeal Committee of the House of Lords (Lord Russell of Killowen, Lord
Scarman and Lord Bridge of Harwich) dismissed a petition by the applicant for leave to appeal.*

j
Solicitors: *Alexander & Partners*, Willesden (for the applicant); *Treasury Solicitor*.

Sumra Green   Barrister.

Note
R v Bouchereau

(Case 30/77)

COURT OF JUSTICE OF THE EUROPEAN COMMUNITIES

JUDGES KUTSCHER (PRESIDENT), SØRENSEN, BOSCO (PRESIDENTS OF CHAMBERS), DONNER, MERTENS
DE WILMARS, PESCATORE, LORD MACKENZIE STUART, O'KEEFFE AND TOUFFAIT
ADVOCATE-GENERAL J-P WARNER

5th JULY, 28th SEPTEMBER, 27th OCTOBER 1977

*European Economic Community – Freedom of movement – Restriction on freedom – Restrictions
justified on grounds of public policy, public security or public health – Measures taken on grounds
of public policy – Measures – Public policy – Whether recommendation for deportation made by
national court of member state to executive authority of that state constituting a 'measure' –
Whether previous criminal convictions can be taken into account only in so far as they manifest
present or future propensity to act in manner contrary to public policy – Whether 'public policy'
incorporating concept of threatened breach of peace – EEC Treaty, art 48(3) – EEC Council
Directive 64/221, art 3(1)(2).*

*European Economic Community – Treaty provisions – Obligations under Treaty – Failure to
fulfil obligation – Whether member state failing to fulfil obligation when one of its courts reaches
wrong decision on Community law – EEC Treaty, art 169.*

In December 1975 the defendant, a French national who was employed in the United
Kingdom, pleaded guilty in a magistrates' court to unlawful possession of drugs. He was
conditionally discharged for 12 months. In March 1976 he again pleaded guilty in a
magistrates' court to unlawful possession of drugs. He thereupon became liable to be
sentenced for both offences. The magistrate deferred sentence while he considered
whether to recommend the defendant for deportation. The defendant submitted that he
was a worker to whom art 48[a] of the EEC Treaty applied and that his deportation was
precluded by art 3[b] of EEC Council Directive 64/221. Article 48(3) of the Treaty allowed
limitations on the freedom of movement of workers within the Community on grounds
of, inter alia, public policy. Article 3 of the directive provided that measures restricting
the movement of EEC nationals taken on the grounds of public policy were to be based
exclusively on the personal conduct of the individual concerned and that previous
criminal convictions should not 'in themselves' constitute grounds for the taking of such
measures. The magistrate referred to the Court of Justice of the European Communities
for a preliminary ruling the questions whether a recommendation for deportation made
by a national court was a 'measure' within art 3(1) and (2) of the directive, whether the

---

a Article 48, so far as material, provides:
    '1. Freedom of movement for workers shall be secured within the Community by the end of
the transitional period at the latest.
    '2. Such freedom of movement shall entail the abolition of any discrimination based on
nationality between workers of the Member States as regards employment, remuneration and
other conditions of work and employment.
    '3. It shall entail the right, subject to limitations justified on grounds of public policy, public
security or public health: (a) to accept offers of employment actually made; (b) to move freely
within the territory of Member States for this purpose; (c) to stay in a Member State for the purpose
of employment in accordance with the provisions governing the employment of nationals of that
State laid down by law, regulation or administrative action; (d) to remain in the territory of a
Member State after having been employed in that State, subject to conditions which shall be
embodied in implementing regulations to be drawn up by the Commission ...'

b Article 3, so far as material, is set out at p 829 f, post

a inclusion of the words 'in themselves' in art 3(2) of the directive meant that previous criminal convictions were only relevant in so far as they manifested a present or future propensity to act in a manner contrary to public policy, and whether 'public policy' within art 48 of the Treaty was to be interpreted as incorporating the concept of a threatened breach of the peace or in some wider sense.

Held – (1) Since it was essential to protect nationals of other member states from any
b exercise of the right to limit their right of free movement going beyond that justified on grounds of, inter alia, public policy, it followed that where national courts were involved in the adoption of a decision to make a deportation order they were required to ensure that Directive 64/221, which was designed to co-ordinate national rules on the control of aliens, was correctly applied and that the limitations it imposed were taken into account. It followed therefore that the concept of 'measures' in art 3 of that directive included the
c action of a court which was required by national law to recommend in certain cases that a national of another member state be deported (see p 938 j to p 939 c and p 940 j to p 941 a, post).

(2) The terms of art 3(2) were to be understood as requiring national authorities to carry out a specific appraisal from the point of view of the interests inherent in protecting the requirements of public policy, which did not necessarily coincide with the appraisals
d which formed the basis of the criminal conviction. The existence of a previous criminal conviction could, therefore, only be taken into account in so far as the circumstances which gave rise to that conviction were evidence of personal conduct constituting a present threat to the requirements of public policy. Although, in general, a finding that such a threat existed implied the existence in the individual concerned of a propensity to act in the same way in the future, it was possible that past conduct alone could constitute
e such a threat to the requirements of public policy. It was for the authorities and, where appropriate, the national courts to consider that question in each individual case in the light both of the particular legal position of persons subject to Community law and of the fundamental nature of the principle of the free movement of persons (see p 939 j to p 940 c and p 941 a b, post).

(3) The concept of public policy in the context of the Community, particularly where
f it was used as a justification for derogating from the fundamental principle of freedom of movement for workers, was to be interpreted strictly, so that its scope could not be determined unilaterally by each member state without being subject to control by the institutions of the Community. However, the particular circumstances justifying recourse to the concept of public policy could vary from one country to another and from one period to another, and it was therefore necessary to allow the competent national
g authorities an area of discretion within the limits imposed by Community law. In so far as it justified certain restrictions on the free movement of persons subject to Community law, recourse by a national authority to the concept of public policy presupposed the existence, in addition to the perturbation of the social order which any infringement of the law involved, of a genuine and sufficiently serious threat to the requirements of public policy affecting one of the fundamental interests of society (see p 940 e to h and
h p 941 b c, post); *Van Duyn v The Home Office (No 2)* [1975] 3 All ER 190 applied.

Per the Advocate-General. For the purposes of art 169[c] of the EEC Treaty, a member state does not fail to fulfil an obligation under the Treaty simply because one of its courts has reached a wrong decision on Community law. In such a case there would be such a failure only when a court had deliberately ignored or disregarded Community law (see p 931 d e, post).

j ————————————————————————————————————

c   Article 169 provides: 'If the Commission considers that a Member State has failed to fulfil an obligation under this Treaty, it shall deliver a reasoned opinion on the matter after giving the State concerned the opportunity to submit its observations. If the State concerned does not comply with the opinion within the period laid down by the Commission, the latter may bring the matter before the Court of Justice.'

Notes

For the freedom of movement for workers who are nationals of EEC countries, see **a**
Supplement to 39A Halsbury's Laws (3rd Edn) paras 108–113, and for cases on the
subject, see 21 Digest (Reissue) 252–267, *1675–1742*.

For the EEC Treaty, arts 48, 169, see 42A Halsbury's Statutes (3rd Edn) 751, 432.

For EEC Council Directive 64/221, art 3, see ibid 131.

Cases cited **b**

Bonsignore (Carmelo Angelo) v Oberstadtdirektor der Stadt Köln Case 67/74 [1975] ECR 297,
[1975] 1 CMLR 472, CJEC.

EC Commission v Italian Republic Case 39/72 [1973] ECR 101, [1973] CMLR 439, CJEC.

EC Commission v Kingdom of Belgium Case 77/69 [1970] ECR 237, [1974] 1 CMLR 203,
CJEC, 21 Digest (Reissue) 289, *1841.*

Foster v Driscoll, Lindsay v Attfield, Lindsay v Driscoll [1929] 1 KB 470, [1928] All ER Rep **c**
130, 98 LJKB 282, 140 LT 479, CA, 11 Digest (Reissue) 483, *885.*

Meyer-Burckhardt (Martin) v EC Commission Case 9/75 [1975] ECR 1171, CJEC.

R v Akan [1972] 3 All ER 285 [1973] QB 491, [1972] 3 WLR 866, 136 JP 766, 56 Cr App
R 716, CA, 2 Digest (Reissue) 212, *1205.*

R v Edgehill [1963] 1 All ER 181, [1963] 1 QB 593, [1963] 2 WLR 170, 47 Cr App R 41,
CCA, 2 Digest (Reissue) 219, *1226.* **d**

R v Immigration Appeal Tribunal, ex parte Mehmet [1977] 2 All ER 602, [1977] 1 WLR 795,
141 JP 430, DC, 2 Digest (Reissue) 221, *1235.*

R v Marlborough Street Stipendiary Magistrate, ex parte Bouchereau [1977] 3 All ER 365,
[1977] 1 WLR 414, 142 JP 27, [1977] 1 CMLR 269, 66 Cr App R 195, DC, 21 Digest
(Reissue) 235, *1612.*

R v Secretary of State for the Home Department, ex parte Hosenball [1977] 3 All ER 452, **e**
[1977] 1 WLR 766, 141 JP 626, CA, 2 Digest (Reissue) 214, *1224.*

Richardson v Mellish (1824) 2 Bing 229, [1824–34] All ER Rep 258, 1 C & P 241, 9 Moore
CP 435, Ry & M 66, 3 LJOSCP 265, 130 ER 294, 22 Digest (Reissue) 381, *3781.*

Royer (Jean Noël) Case 48/75 [1976] ECR 497, [1976] 2 CMLR 619, [1977] ICR 314, CJEC,
21 Digest (Reissue) 254, *1685.*

Rutili (Roland) v Minister for the Interior Case 36/75 [1975] ECR 1219, [1976] 1 CMLR 140, **f**
CJEC, 21 Digest (Reissue) 254, *1684.*

Sagulo (Concetta), Gennaro Brenca and Addelmadjid Bakhouche Case 8/77 [1977] ECR 1495,
[1977] 2 CMLR 585, CJEC, 21 Digest (Reissue) 255, *1687.*

Van Duyn v The Home Office (No 2) Case 41/74 [1975] 3 All ER 190, [1975] Ch 358, [1975]
2 WLR 760, [1974] ECR 1337, [1975] 1 CMLR 1, CJEC, 21 Digest (Reissue) 245, *1645.*

Watson (Lynne) and Allessandro Belmann Case 118/75 [1976] ECR 1185, [1976] 2 CMLR **g**
552, CJEC, 21 Digest (Reissue) 251, *1670.*

Reference

The Marlborough Street Magistrates' Court referred certain questions (set out at p 929 g,
p 932 b and p 933 h, post) as to the interpretation of art 48(3) of the EEC Treaty and art **h**
3(1) and (2) of EEC Council Directive 64/221 to the Court of Justice of the European
Communities for a preliminary ruling under art 177 of the Treaty. The questions arose
out of the prosecution of the defendant, Pierre Roger André Bouchereau, for unlawful
possession of drugs. The Commission of the European Communities, the United
Kingdom, the Metropolitan Police and the defendant submitted written observations to
the European Court. The language of the case was English. The facts are set out in the **j**
opinion of the Advocate-General.

Alan Newman for the defendant.
Peter Gibson for the United Kingdom.
Anthony McClellan, agent for the EC Commission, for the Commission.

28th September. **The Advocate-General (J-P Warner)** delivered the following
a opinion: My Lords, in this case the court is once more called on to interpret, in specific
respects, the provisions of Community law under which member states are enabled to
make exceptions 'on grounds of public policy, public security or public health' to the
general principles of non-discrimination between nationals of member states and, more
particularly, of freedom of movement for workers within the Community, that are
enshrined in the EEC Treaty. The permissible scope of such exceptions has already been
b defined to some extent by the decisions of the court in *Van Duyn v The Home Office (No 2)*
[1975] 3 All ER 190, [1975] Ch 358, *Bonsignore v Oberstadtdirektor der Stadt Köln* [1975]
ECR 297, *Rutili v Minister for the Interior* [1975] ECR 1219, *Royer* [1976] ECR 497, *Watson
and Belmann* [1976] ECR 1185 and most recently *Sagulo, Brenca and Bakhouche* [1977] ECR
1495.

The present case comes to the court by way of a reference for a preliminary ruling by
c a metropolitan stipendiary magistrate, sitting at Marlborough Street Magistrates' Court
in London. Pending before that court are criminal proceedings against the defendant, a
French national who is now 21 years of age. Since May 1975, apart from a brief period
of unemployment at the time of his arrest in March 1976, the defendant has been
employed in the United Kingdom as a motor mechanic.

There is in force in the United Kingdom a statute, the Misuse of Drugs Act 1971,
d which is described by its long title as making provision 'with respect to dangerous or
otherwise harmful drugs and related matters, and for purposes connected therewith'. It
replaces earlier United Kingdom legislation about the misuse of drugs. Section 5 of that
statute makes it unlawful, subject to exceptions none of which is material here, for a
person to have certain types of drugs in his possession. The defendant has twice pleaded
guilty before magistrates' courts in London to offences under that section. The first
e occasion was on 7th January 1976, when he pleaded guilty before the Marylebone
Magistrates' Court to unlawful possession, on 10th December 1975, of small quantities
of methyl amphetamine and of cannabis. For that offence he was conditionally
discharged for 12 months and ordered to pay £5 costs. The effect of an order for
conditional discharge under English criminal law is, shortly stated, that the person
concerned is not punished for the offence unless he commits another offence during the
f period specified in the order. If he does so, he is liable to be sentenced both for the
original offence and for the new one (see the Powers of Criminal Courts Act 1973, s 7,
which replaces earlier legislation dating from 1948). On 10th March 1976 the defendant
was again found in unlawful possession of drugs: 28 tablets of LSD and three packets of
salt of amphetamine. To those offences he pleaded guilty before the Marlborough Street
Magistrates' Court on 9th June 1976. He has not yet been sentenced for them, or indeed
g for his first offence. It seems that the magistrate has deferred sentence until he has
decided whether to recommend the defendant for deportation.

The power for a court in the United Kingdom to recommend an alien for deportation
is conferred by the Immigration Act 1971. This too is a statute that replaces earlier
legislation, dating back to 1914. Before that the control of the movements of aliens was
a matter that pertained, in the United Kingdom, to the royal prerogative. In other words
h it was governed by the common law.

The 1971 Act contains two distinct provisions laying down circumstances in which a
person is to be 'liable to deportation from the United Kingdom'. The first is s 3(5), under
which a person who is not 'patrial' (ie is not a British subject having the right of abode
in the United Kingdom) is to be so liable—

j   '(a) if, having only a limited leave to enter or remain, he does not observe a
          condition attached to the leave or remains beyond the time limited by the leave; or
          (b) if the Secretary of State deems his deportation to be conducive to the public good;
          or (c) if another person to whose family he belongs is or has been ordered to be
          deported.'

Manifestly that subsection has to be read subject to considerable modification in the case of a national of another member state of the Community. But I need not pursue that topic in detail here, for the present case is not one where s 3(5) applies.

The second provision, which is material in this case, is s 3(6), which is in these terms:

'Without prejudice to the operation of subsection (5) above, a person who is not patrial shall also be liable to deportation from the United Kingdom if, after he has attained the age of seventeen, he is convicted of an offence for which he is punishable with imprisonment and on his conviction is recommended for deportation by a court empowered by this Act to do so.'

The courts empowered by the Act to recommend deportation are defined by s 6(1). In short, they are the courts empowered to sentence the person concerned for the offence in question.

The power to make an actual deportation order is contained in s 5(1) of the Act. It is conferred on the Secretary of State and is expressed to arise 'where a person is under section 3(5) or (6) above liable to deportation'.

The system of appeal differs according to whether the case is within s 3(5) or s 3(6). In a case under s 3(5) the Act envisages that, before any deportation order may be made, there should first be a 'decision' by the Secretary of State to make it. Against that decision the Act provides for an appeal to an adjudicator and for a further appeal from him to the Immigration Appeal Tribunal. In certain circumstances the appeal is direct to the tribunal. Not until the possibilities of appeal have been exhausted may a deportation order be made. On an appeal, the adjudicator and the tribunal may review all aspects of the case, including the merits of making a deportation order (see ss 12 and 15 of the Act and the recent judgment of the Queen's Bench Divisional Court in *R v Immigration Appeal Tribunal, ex parte Mehmet* [1977] 2 All ER 602, [1977] 1 WLR 795). Section 15(3) of the Act makes an exception if the ground of the decision to make a deportation order is that the deportation of the alien concerned—

'is conducive to the public good as being in the interests of national security or of the relations between the United Kingdom and any other country or for other reasons of a political nature.'

In such a case there can be no appeal to an adjudicator or to the Immigration Appeal Tribunal. Instead there is an extra-statutory procedure for reference of the case to a panel whose duty it is to advise the Secretary of State (see *R v Secretary of State for the Home Department, ex parte Hosenball* [1977] 3 All ER 452, [1977] 1 WLR 766). Of course the adjudicators, the Immigration Appeal Tribunal and the Secretary of State himself are (as the cases to which I have referred of *ex parte Mehmet* and *ex parte Hosenball* illustrate) at all stages subject to the supervisory jurisdiction of the High Court, in particular in proceedings for an order of certiorari. Certiorari will lie to quash a decision of an inferior court or tribunal, or of any public authority, where there is an error of law on the face of it, or where it is in excess or abuse of jurisdiction, or where it has been reached in a manner contrary to the rules of natural justice.

Where s 3(6) applies the appeal system that I have just described is excluded. An appeal against a recommendation for deportation made by a court lies through the normal hierarchy of criminal courts, the recommendation being treated for this purpose as if it were a sentence (see s 6(5) of the Act) and the appellate courts being free to review the recommendation on its merits (see *R v Akan* [1972] 3 All ER 285, [1973] 1 QB 491). There again, however, no actual deportation order may be made so long as any appeal is pending (see s 6(6)). But the recommendation enables the alien concerned to be detained 'pending the making of a deportation order in pursuance of the recommendation' unless the court or the Secretary of State otherwise directs (see s 5(5) of the 1971 Act and para 2 of Sch 3 thereto). I should perhaps emphasise that those are the only respects in which a recommendation for deportation is to be assimilated to a sentence. It has been laid down that a recommendation for deportation is not to be regarded as part of the punishment for an offence: the court should impose on the defendant the sentence that

he deserves and then deal with the question of deportation quite separately (see *R v*
a *Edgehill* [1963] 1 All ER 181 at 183, [1963] 1 QB 593 at 597). The point at which the
procedure where s 3(6) applies rejoins as it were, that where s 3(5) applies is when the
Secretary of State comes to make a deportation order. He is then in either case amenable
to the supervisory jurisdiction of the High Court that I have mentioned.

I should perhaps also emphasise that I have, in the foregoing, sought only to summarise
the law as it applies in England. The procedure in Scotland is not in all respects the
b same. But we are not concerned in this case with the position in Scotland.

I revert to the facts of this case. It appears that, the magistrate having indicated that
he was minded to recommend the defendant for deportation, and the case against him
having been adjourned so as to enable the appropriate notice to be served on him (as
required by s 6(2) of the Act), it was submitted on the defendant's behalf that he was a
worker to whom art 48 of the EEC Treaty applied and that, in the circumstances,
c Community law precluded his deportation. In the result the magistrate, on 20th
November 1976, made an order referring three questions to this court under art 177 of
the Treaty. There followed a delay while the question was considered how the defendant
could be afforded legal aid in the proceedings before this court. That question was a
novel one, since this is the first case ever to have been referred to the court by an English
criminal court. It was resolved by a decision of a Queen's Bench Divisional Court on
d 17th January 1977 holding that the legal aid order made in the defendant's favour in the
magistrates' court extended to the proceedings in this court (see *R v Marlborough Street*
Stipendiary Magistrate, ex parte Bouchereau [1977] 3 All ER 365, [1977] 1 WLR 414).
Following that decision the order for reference was received at the registry of this court
on 2nd March 1977.

Of the three questions referred to the court by the magistrate, the first two are
e questions of interpretation of EEC Council Directive 64/221 of 25th February 1964 'on
the coordination of special measures concerning the movement and residence of foreign
nationals which are justified on grounds of public policy, public security or public
health', an instrument that the court has already had to consider in a number of the cases
that I mentioned at the outset.

Your Lordships will remember that the first two paragraphs of art 3 of the directive
f provide:

'1. Measures taken on grounds of public policy or of public security shall be based
exclusively on the personal conduct of the individual concerned.
'2. Previous criminal convictions shall not in themselves constitute grounds for
the taking of such measures.'

g The first question referred to the court by the magistrate is:

'Whether a recommendation for deportation made by a national court of a
member state to the executive authority of that state (such recommendation being
persuasive but not binding on the executive authority) constitutes a "measure"
within the meaning of art 3(1) and (2) of EEC Council Directive 64/221.'

h The Metropolitan Police, who are responsible for the defendant's prosecution, submit
that a recommendation for deportation made by a United Kingdom court to the Secretary
of State does not constitute a 'measure' within the meaning of those provisions. In
support of that submission the Metropolitan Police argue that 'in reality a recommendation for deportation is no more than a notification to the Secretary of State that a
particular foreign national who is capable of being deported has been convicted of an
j offence punishable with imprisonment' and they draw attention to the fact that all
previous reported cases in this court regarding the interpretation of art 48 of the EEC
Treaty and of the directive concerned actual decisions leading directly to restrictions on
the free movement of workers within the Community.

The United Kingdom government, which assisted the court with observations
independent of those of the Metropolitan Police, concedes however that the argument

put forward on behalf of the Metropolitan Police goes too far. A recommendation for deportation made by a United Kingdom court is not a mere notification to the Secretary of State of particular facts. It has legal consequences. Not only does it render the alien concerned liable to be detained, it empowers the Secretary of State to make a deportation order in respect of him without the need, in any circumstances, for the decision to that effect to be subjected to review by an adjudicator or by the Immigration Appeal Tribunal.

The United Kingdom government makes two submissions. The first is that a judicial decision by a national court, as distinct from action by the legislature or executive of a member state, cannot constitute a 'measure' for the purposes of art 3(1) and (2) of the directive. Secondly the United Kingdom Government submits that, if a judicial decision can constitute a 'measure', a recommendation by a court, which does not bind the executive authority to which it is made, and which does not of itself terminate the right of the alien concerned to reside in that member state, does not constitute a 'measure'. With those submissions the United Kingdom Government couples a concession that, nonetheless, it would not be open to a court in a member state to ignore the provisions of the directive, and that such a court must have regard to those provisions in dealing with any matter to which they are relevant.

At first sight the attitude of the United Kingdom government is puzzling. What can be the purpose of saying in one breath that a judicial decision is not a measure to which the directive applies and, in the next breath, that the courts of the member states are bound by the provisions of the directive?

It transpired that underlying that attitude was concern lest, if a decision of a court of a member state were held to be a measure within the meaning of the directive, the member state itself might be held, under art 169 of the EEC Treaty, to have failed to fulfil an obligation under the Treaty if that decision were inconsistent with Community law. The United Kingdom government referred in this connection to the views expressed by one of your Lordships in an article published in 1970 ('Proceedings against Member States for failure to fulfil their obligations', by J Mertens de Wilmars and I M Verougstraete [1970] CML Review 385 at 389–390) and it emphasised that, whilst an executive authority in a member state (such as the Secretary of State in the present context) was bound, before reaching a decision, to appraise itself of all relevant factors, so as to ensure among other things that its decision was compatible with Community law, a court, or at all events an English court, had no such investigative powers: it could act only on the basis of the facts as presented to it by the parties.

In my opinion, it would be incorrect to say that particular action or inaction on the part of a court of a member state could never constitute a failure on the part of that state to fulfil an obligation under the Treaty, nor do I read the article referred to as expressing that view. The locus classicus on this subject is, I think, the opinion of Advocate-General J Gand in *EC Commission v Belgium* [1970] ECR 237. I quote from the original (Rec 1970 (1) at 247):

'Un tel raisonnement méconnaîtrait que les sujets de droits—ou d'obligations—sont les *États membres* de la Communauté. Ce sont eux qui, en vertu de l'article 5, doivent prendre "toutes mesures générales ou particulières" propres à assurer l'exécution des obligations découlant du traité. L'engagement qu'ils ont ainsi contracté s'étend aux domaines les plus divers et peut, par suite, nécessiter de leur part des mesures de nature juridique très différentes: il s'agira d'instituer, de modifier ou d'abroger une législation ou une réglementation de portée générale, comme aussi bien de prendre des décisions de portée individuelle destinées à assurer l'exécution du traité et de ses textes d'application. Savoir si, dans un cas donné, cette exécution requiert le concours de l'un seulement ou de plusieurs des pouvoirs qui constituent la structure de l'État est une question dont la solution dépend du système constitutionnel de cet État, mais elle ne peut modifier, l'étendue des obligations qui doivent s'imposer également à tous et les organes communautaires n'ont pas à en connaître. Sans doute ceux-ci, conformément à la pratique

a traditionelle des relations internationales, n'ont-ils comme interlocuteurs que les gouvernements, mais il ne s'ensuit pas que seuls les actes ou les abstentions du pouvoir exécutif et des services placés sous son autorité constituent des manquements au sens de l'article 169 du traité. Ceux-ci peuvent exister dès lors que l'État membre ne s'acquitte pas des obligations qui lui incombent, sans qu'il y ait lieu de rechercher lequel de ses organes se trouve à l'origine de l'inexécution reprochée.'

b That was followed by the court, which held succinctly (see para 15 of its judgment, [1970] ECR 237 at 243):

'The obligations arising from Article 95 of the Treaty devolve upon States as such and the liability of a Member State under Article 169 arises whatever the agency of the State whose action or inaction is the cause of the failure to fulfil its obligations, even in the case of a constitutionally independent institution.'

c To the same effect in substance are the opinion of the Advocate-General (H Mayras) and the judgment of the court in *EC Commission v Italy* [1973] ECR 101. No doubt the constitutionally independent institution whose action, or rather inaction, in each of those cases lay at the root of the default of the member state concerned was its Parliament, but the relevant principle, as there stated, is wide enough to apply also to the judiciary of a member state. Indeed it must logically do so. I am reminded that, in *Meyer-Burckhardt* **d** *v EC Commission* [1975] ECR 1171 at 1187, I felt no hesitation about that.

It is obvious on the other hand that a member state cannot be held to have failed to fulfil an obligation under the Treaty simply because one of its courts has reached a wrong decision. Judicial error, whether due to the misapprehension of facts or to misapprehension of the law, is not a breach of the Treaty. In the judicial sphere, art 169 could only come into play in the event of a court of a member state deliberately ignoring **e** or disregarding Community law. So I think that the United Kingdom government's concern in this respect is ill-founded.

Were it correct, however, that judicial error could constitute a breach of the Treaty, I do not see how it could make any difference for present purposes whether one held that a decision of a court was a 'measure' within the meaning of the directive or held that, whilst that was not so, a court was bound to have regard to the directive. In either case **f** the same possibility of judicial error would exist.

I can, I think, deal more shortly with the United Kingdom government's alternative submission. The word 'measure' is not one of precise import. Its interpretation requires a consideration of the context in which it is found. Plainly a recommendation by an official to his minister would not constitute a 'measure' in the present context, for it would have no legal effect. But one cannot assimilate to such a recommendation a **g** recommendation of the kind here in question, which does have legal effects. To hold that such a recommendation was not a relevant 'measure' would have bizarre consequences. It would mean, for instance, that, so far at all events as the express terms of the directive were concerned, such a recommendation could be made on the ground of previous criminal convictions alone, even though the deportation order that it envisaged could not. On this, the semantic aspect of the case, if I may so describe it, it is **h** no answer to say (as counsel for the United Kingdom said at the hearing in answer to questions of mine and of one of your Lordships) that a national court must in any event 'have regard' to the terms of the directive. Indeed, assuming that 'must' here imports a legal obligation, that answer virtually contradicts the submission itself.

I should, I think for the sake of completeness, lastly refer to some submissions that were made on behalf of the United Kingdom at the hearing, based on arts 8, 9 and 10 of **j** the directive. It does not seem to me that any of those articles throws much light on the interpretation of art 3. Articles 8 and 9 do not use the word 'measures'. In art 10 the word 'measures' is used but clearly in a sense different from that in which it is used in art 3: it relates to general legislative or administrative provisions, not to action taken in an individual case. (As regards the terms used, the foregoing is equally true as respects the

Dutch, English, French and German texts of the directive. In the Danish text the terms equivalent to 'measure' are different in arts 3, 8, 9 and 10. In the Italian text the same term 'provvedimenti' is used in arts 3, 8 and 9, whilst the term 'misure' is used in art 10.)

In the result I am of the opinion that, in answer to the first question referred to the court by the magistrate, your Lordships should rule that a recommendation for deportation made by a court of a member state to the executive authority of that state constitutes a 'measure' within the meaning of art 3(1) and (2) of the directive if, although not binding on that authority, it has legal consequences.

The magistrate's second question is:

'Whether the wording of art 3(2) of EEC Council Directive 64/221, namely that previous criminal convictions shall not "in themselves" constitute grounds for the taking of measures based on public policy or public security means that previous criminal convictions are solely relevant in so far as they manifest a present or future propensity to act in a manner contrary to public policy or public security; alternatively, the meaning to be attached to the expression "in themselves" in art 3(2) of Directive 64/221.'

It appears from the order for reference that the reason why that question is asked is that, before the magistrate, it was submitted on behalf of the defendant that art 3(2) meant that previous criminal convictions were solely relevant in so far as they manifested a present or future intention to act in a manner contrary to public policy or public security, and that there was no evidence to support such a conclusion in his case; whereas it was submitted on behalf of the prosecution that art 3(2) meant that the court could not make a recommendation for deportation on grounds of public policy based on the fact alone of a previous conviction, but was entitled to take into account the past conduct of the defendant which resulted in the previous conviction.

I will say at once that, in my opinion, the prosecution was, in that respect, clearly right. Article 3(2) cannot be interpreted in such a way that it would result in the existence of a conviction being a bar to deportation in circumstances in which the conduct of the person concerned would otherwise justify the step. Nor can it be interpreted as requiring evidence as to that person's intentions.

The question as framed by the magistrate does not however refer to evidence of intentions. It refers to 'a present or future propensity'. The real question thereby posed is, I think, whether art 3(1) and (2) read together mean that the conduct of the person concerned, in order to justify his deportation, must manifest a propensity on his part to act in a manner contrary to public policy or public security.

On behalf of the Commission, as well as, of course, on behalf of the defendant, it is submitted in effect that that question should be answered in the affirmative. But on behalf of the United Kingdom government, as well as on behalf of the Metropolitan Police, it is submitted that to give an affirmative answer to the question would be to lay down too narrow a test. The United Kingdom government in particular points out that cases do arise, exceptionally, where the personal conduct of an alien has been such that, whilst not necessarily evincing any clear propensity on his part, it has caused such deep public revulsion that public policy requires his departure. I agree. I think that in such a case a member state may exclude a national of another member state from its territory, just as a man may exclude from his house a guest, even a relative, who has behaved in an excessively offensive fashion. Although therefore, in the nature of things, the conduct of a person relevant for the purposes of art 3 will generally be conduct that shows him to have a particular propensity, it cannot be said that that must necessarily be so.

I accordingly agree with the United Kingdom government's submission that this court should adhere to the test that it laid down in *Rutili v Minister for the Interior* [1975] ECR 1219, where it held (at 1231 (para 28)) that 'restrictions cannot be imposed on the right of a national of any Member State to enter the territory of another Member State, to stay there and to move within it unless his presence or conduct constitutes a genuine and sufficiently serious threat to public policy'. I observe that, in so declaring, the court a followed the view expressed by the Advocate-General (H Mayras) not only in that case but in the earlier *Bonsignore* case [1975] ECR 297 where, specifically in relation to art 3 of the directive, he said (I cite from the original, Rec 1975 at 311):

b 'Les auteurs de la directive ont donc voulu qu'indépendamment de toute condamnation les autorités nationales ne puissent décider l'expulsion que dans la mesure où le comportement personnel du ressortissant communautaire, auteur d'une infraction, ait comporté ou risque de comporter dans l'avenir une menace telle, pour l'ordre public national, que la présence de l'individu concerné sur le territoire pays d'accueil devienne intolérable.'

and again (at 315):

c 'La directive exige en vérité que l'atteinte à l'ordre public national, en tant qu'elle résulte du comportement personnel, soit telle que l'expulsion s'impose soit parce que l'ordre public a été gravement perturbé par les faits commis, soit parce que le renouvellement d'actes anti-sociaux est à redouter de la part de l'intéressé.'

I am not of course saying that the defendant's conduct has been such as to render his continued presence on United Kingdom territory intolerable. It is for the English courts not for this court to judge his conduct. But this court must give to the learned
d magistrate's question as comprehensive and accurate an answer as the circumstances allow.

I have one minor, verbal, reservation. The language of the *Rutili* case was French and the phrase used in the authentic text of the judgment in that case 'une menace réelle et suffisamment grave pour l'ordre public' is of course unimpeachable French. But its literal translation into English involving as it does the use of the phrase a 'threat to public
e policy' reads somewhat oddly. In the present case, where the authentic text of the judgment will be in English, it might be better to refer to 'a threat to the requirements of public policy'.

I am therefore of the opinion that your Lordships should answer the magistrate's second question by saying that art 3(2) of the directive means that a deportation order on grounds of public policy or public security may not be based on the fact alone of the existence of previous convictions but that such an order can only be justified if the
f presence or conduct of the individual concerned constitutes a genuine and sufficiently serious threat to the requirements of public policy or of public security.

Inherent of course in the use there of the adverb 'sufficiently' is an allusion to the principle spelt out by the court in the *Watson and Belmann* case [1976] ECR 1185, and reaffirmed in the *Sagulo* case [1977] ECR 1495, that measures taken by member states in respect of nationals of other member states must be reasonable and not disproportionate
g to the gravity of their conduct.

The third question referred to the court by the magistrate is in these terms:

'Whether the words "public policy" in article 48(3) of the EEC Treaty, on the grounds of which limitations to the rights granted by art 48 must be justified, are to be interpreted (a) as including reasons of state even where no breach of the public
h peace or order is threatened, or (b) in a narrower sense in which is incorporated the concept of some threatened breach of public peace, order or security, or (c) in some other wider sense.'

Three of the expressions there used seem to me to call for comment. The first is 'reasons of state', the second 'breach of the public peace' and the third 'order' or 'public order'.
j 'Reasons of state' (as distinct from 'act of state') is not an expression that belongs to English legal terminology, nor do I know of any authority for its use in the context of Community law. The court invited submissions at the hearing as to its meaning in the magistrate's question, but counsel were not able to give us much assistance. I think that probably counsel for the United Kingdom came nearest to the answer when he said that he took it as intended to cover justification on grounds of public interest wider than

breaches of the peace and public order. In my opinion, it is an expression of such
indefinite import that it is best eschewed.

The use of the expression 'breach of the public peace' in the present context seems to
have its origin in a mistranslation in the English text of the judgment of the court in the
Bonsignore case [1975] ECR 297 at 307, which reads:

> 'As departures from the rules concerning the free movement of persons constitute
> exceptions which must be strictly construed, the concept of "personal conduct"
> expresses the requirement that a deportation order may only be made for breaches
> of the peace and public security which might be committed by the individual
> affected.'

In the authentic text of the judgment, however, which is the German text, the words
corresponding to 'breaches of the peace and public security which might be committed
by the individual affected' are 'Gefährdungen der öffentlichen Ordnung und Sicherheit
... die von der betroffenen Einzelperson ausgehen könnten', which, I understand,
literally means 'threats to public policy and security that could be occasioned by the
person affected', the expression 'öffentliche Ordnung' being that which corresponds to
'public policy' in art 48 of the Treaty. The mistranslation is particularly unfortunate
because, as was pointed out on behalf of the United Kingdom government, 'breach of the
peace' has a distinct meaning in English law, where it constitutes a criminal offence. In
fairness to the translation service of the court, I suspect that they resorted to the expression
in order to avoid the oddity of using in English the phrase 'threats to public policy',
although they accepted that oddity when they came to translate the *Rutili* judgment.

The use of the expression 'public order' seems to reflect a submission put forward on
behalf of the defendant to the effect that the expression 'public policy' in art 48 should be
given a narrow meaning akin to that of 'public order'. We were referred by counsel for
the defendant to various international instruments, such as the European Convention for
the Protection of Human Rights and Fundamental Freedoms (TS 71 (1953); Cmd 8969),
in the English text of which 'public order' is used, instead of 'public policy', where the
French text has 'ordre public' (see in particular arts 6 and 9 of that convention). All this
might be helpful if 'public order' had a clear meaning in English legal terminology. But
it does not. It is, so far as I am aware, an expression unknown to the common law. Its
only use that I know of in statute law is in the title to the Public Order Act 1936, a statute
of limited scope, which was passed to deal with the activities, in the 1930s, of the British
fascist movement. As appears from the text of that statute, its main purposes were to
prohibit the wearing of uniforms in connection with political objects and the
maintenance by private persons of associations of a military or similar character. It also
made provision for the preservation of order on the occasion of public meetings and
processions, particularly by the prohibition of the possession of offensive weapons, and
of the use of threatening, abusive or insulting words or behaviour, on such occasions.

Unlike 'public order', 'public policy' is a concept known to the common law. We were
referred on behalf of the defendant to an illuminating article by Professor Lyon-Caen
('La réserve d'ordre public en matière de liberté d'établissement et de libre circulation'
(1966) Revue Trimestrielle de Droit Européen 693) in which he discusses the meaning
of the phrase 'ordre public', which corresponds in the French text of the Treaty to 'public
policy' in the English text, in the light of the laws of the six original member states.
Professor Lyon-Caen observes at the outset that the role of the concept of 'ordre public'
is so wide that it has lost all precision. He discerns, as I understand him, three spheres in
which it may be invoked. The first is in relations between private persons. There it may
be invoked to negative freedom of contract or the application of a foreign law that would
normally be applicable. In this sphere it corresponds to the common law concept of
'public policy', the most usual manifestations of which are in the law of contract (to
invalidate a contract that would otherwise be binding), in private international law (to
exclude a foreign law that would otherwise be applicable) and in the law of property (to
invalidate a disposition that would otherwise be effective). Of course the 'public policy'

here in question is the public policy not of government but of the law, developed by the courts. Nonetheless it has been described by eminent common law judges as an 'unruly horse' for them to ride (see per Burrough J in *Richardson v Mellish* (1824) 2 Bing 229 at 252, [1824–34] All ER Rep 258 at 266 and per Scrutton LJ in *Foster v Driscoll* [1929] 1 KB 470 at 498, [1928] All ER Rep 130 at 139). The second sphere in which Professor Lyon-Caen discerns the application of the concept of 'ordre public' is that of 'public law'. There, he says, 'on y a recours pour restreindre ou supprimer une liberté au nom d'exigences supérieures'. This too sounds familiar to an English lawyer, even though the expression 'public law' has no technical meaning for him, and though he would generally tend, in the context of administrative law, to refer to the 'public interest' rather than to 'public policy'. A feature that Professor Lyon-Caen identifies as being common to the first two spheres in which 'ordre public' may be invoked, is that it operates so as to make an exception to whatever legal rule would normally apply. In the third sphere in which it operates, however, that of the control of aliens ('police des étrangers'), that feature is absent. Reliance on 'l'ordre public' is there no longer the exception, but the very foundation of the law. It is seen as justifying the exercise by the executive of a virtually unlimited discretion. Professor Lyon-Caen calls this 'un ordre public "spécial"'. It appears to me to correspond, in English terminology, to the 'public good' of which the Immigration Act 1971 speaks.

Among the conclusions drawn by Professor Lyon-Caen is the valuable one that, in relation to those nationals of the member states to whom the Treaty applies, the Treaty must be taken to have abolished that 'ordre public "spécial"'. 'L'ordre public', he says (at p 696), 'est ramené à son rôle de mécanisme exceptionnel'. That must be right, since the role of 'public policy' (or 'ordre public') under the Treaty is to afford a ground for making an exception to the general principle of non-discrimination between such nationals. Professor Lyon-Caen's analysis also shows, I think, that, otherwise, little guidance as to the meaning of the phrases 'public policy', 'ordre public', 'öffentliche Ordnung' etc, in the Treaty, is to be derived from a consideration of their meanings in the national laws of the member states.

There is another way in which the wording of the Treaty seems to me to give an indication of the scope of 'public policy' as there used. This lies in the collocation of phrases 'public policy, public security or public health', which shows, in my opinion, that the authors of the Treaty envisaged them as connoting three distinct concepts, albeit perhaps overlapping ones.

Beyond that, the authors of the Treaty appear to have left the concept of 'public policy' to be defined and developed by Community secondary legislation and by decisions of this court.

The judgments of the court, particuarly in the *Van Duyn* and *Rutili* cases make it clear, that, in the result, to quote from the judgment in the latter case ([1975] ECR 1219 at 1231) 'Member States continue to be, in principle, free to determine the requirements of public policy in the light of their national needs'. That freedom is however limited and its exercise is subject to control by the institutions of the Community.

The problem confronting the magistrate in the present case cannot therefore be solved without inquiring whether any specific provision of Community law limits, either expressly or by necessary implication, the discretion exercisable by a member state in circumstances such as those of that case.

In that connection the Commission referred in its written observations to paras (1) and (2) of art 4 of Directive 64/221. The other parties did not, but the court invited submissions from them thereon at the hearing. Those paragraphs are in the following terms:

'1. The only diseases or disabilities justifying refusal of entry into a territory or refusal to issue a first residence permit shall be those listed in the Annex to this Directive. 2. Diseases or disabilities occurring after a first residence permit has been issued shall not justify refusal to renew the residence permit or expulsion from the territory.'

The annex referred to in para 1 is in two parts. Part A, which is headed 'Diseases which might endanger public health' is not here in point. But Part B, headed 'Diseases and disabilities which might threaten public policy or public security', lists:

> '1. Drug addiction; 2. Profound mental disturbance; manifest conditions of psychotic disturbance with agitation, delirium, hallucinations or confusion.'

Although I do not think it really relevant, I should, I think, record that we were told at the hearing on behalf of the United Kingdom government that a first residence permit had been issued to the defendant on 28th January 1977, ie long after the date of his second conviction and while the reference to this court was pending. That fact was accepted on behalf of the defendant.

Of more importance, in my opinion, is the fact that it was agreed by everyone at the hearing that there was no evidence that the defendant was a drug addict. There was evidence only that he had been in unlawful possession of drugs. This induced counsel for the Commission to resile somewhat from the submission it had made in its written observations and to concede that art 4 was not here directly relevant.

That ready consensus reflected the distinction that exists in English law between unlawful possession of harmful drugs, which is a criminal offence, and drug addiction, which, in itself, is not, though it may be a consequence of earlier criminal conduct. We were referred in that connection to the Misuse of Drugs (Notification of and Supply to Addicts) Regulations 1973, SI 1973 No 799, made by the Secretary of State under powers conferred by the Misuse of Drugs Act 1971 and replacing earlier regulations of the same kind made under previous legislation. Those regulations, putting it shortly, enable a doctor to obtain from the Secretary of State a licence to supply drugs to a person whom he considers to be a drug addict on furnishing to the chief medical officer at the Home Office the name and certain other particulars of that person. Possession by an addict of drugs supplied to him under such a licence is not unlawful. An addict is defined for the purposes of the regulations as one who 'has as a result of repeated administration become so dependent on the drug that he has an overpowering desire for the administration of it to be continued'. The regulations apply only to certain kinds of drugs, which are listed in a schedule. It may be observed that they do not include any of the drugs that were found in the defendant's possession, presumably because none of these is regarded as addictive (which, of course, is a different thing from saying that it is not regarded as harmful).

So far as I have been able to ascertain there is nothing quite like those regulations in the law of any other member state. As one would expect, the law about drugs differs from member state to member state and, in some member states at least, is very complex. It seems however that, in all member states except Italy, the unauthorised possession of harmful drugs is a criminal offence. In Italy the only sanction against the unlawful possession of drugs, as such, is that they are liable to confiscation in so far as their quantity exceeds that compatible with use for therapeutic purposes (see art 80 of Statute 685 of 22nd December 1975, Gazz Uff 342 of 30th December 1975). On the other hand, unlawful trafficking in drugs is a punishable offence in Italy, as in other member states. There are two member states, namely Denmark and the Netherlands, where, apparently, the possession by a person for his own use of cannabis or of its derivatives, as distinct from the possession of other drugs, is, whilst an offence, treated as a trivial one. There is, in most member states, to be found an assimilation, to a greater or lesser degree, of drug addiction to illness and in two cases (namely the Federal Republic of Germany and Ireland) specifically, in certain respects, to mental illness. In many member states provisions have been enacted to secure the medical treatment of addicts rather than their punishment: see in particular art 9 of the Belgian statute of 24th February 1921 as amended by the statute of 9th July 1975 (Moniteur Belge, 26th September 1975), the French statute No 70-1320 of 31st December 1970 (JO de la République Française of 3rd January 1971, pp 74–76) introducing new articles L 355-14 to L 355-21 and L 626 to L 630-2 into the Code de la Santé Publique, s 28 of the Irish Misuse of Drugs Act 1977, art a 100 of the Italian statute to which I have already referred, and arts 23 to 30 of the Luxembourg statute of 19th February 1973 (Memorial A 12 of 3rd March 1973, p 319).

Of more importance, I think, than the position in individual member states is the approach of the directive itself. Article 4, as its terms evince, applies only to 'diseases and disabilities'. The effect of para 2 thereof is that no disease or disability whatever, occurring after a first residence permit has been issued, can justify expulsion. The significance of the annex is that it lists a number of exceptional diseases and disabilities b which, under para 1, can justify refusal of entry or refusal to issue a first residence permit. No disease or disability not so listed can justify even that.

The argument put forward at the hearing on behalf of the defendant, as I understood it, was, in a nutshell, that, if he were a drug addict, he could not be deported on that ground; a fortiori could he not be deported on the 'mere' ground that he had been found in unlawful possession of drugs. In my opinion that is a non sequitur. Certainly the c defendant, at all events if he became a drug addict after the issue to him of his first residence permit, could not be deported on that ground. But art 4 does not forbid the deportation of a drug addict on grounds other than his drug addiction, unless of course such grounds consist in some other disease or disability. Suppose that a person were at once a scientologist and a drug addict. He could clearly be deported from the United Kingdom on the ground of his association with scientology, though not on the ground d of his drug addiction. The unlawful possession of drugs is not a disease or disability, even though it shares with drug addiction a connection with drugs. So art 4 does not apply to it and does not exclude it as a ground for deportation. In a member state where it is regarded as a criminal offence or otherwise as socially harmful, the provisions of the directive that are relevant in relation to it are those of art 3.

It remains to consider how your Lordships should answer the magistrate's third e question. The United Kingdom government suggests that it would be enough for your Lordships to say that the concept of 'public policy' in art 48 of the Treaty is not limited to the threatened breach of public peace, order or security. Perhaps it would, but I think that it might be more helpful if your Lordships were somewhat more specific and added that that concept is not to be interpreted as excluding, as a potential ground for limiting the rights conferred on a worker by that article, the fact of his having been found f repeatedly in unlawful possession of harmful drugs.

g 27th October. **THE COURT OF JUSTICE** delivered its judgment which, having summarised the facts, procedure and submissions of the parties, dealt with the law as follows:

1. By order of 20th November 1976, received at the court on 2nd March 1977, the Marlborough Street Magistrates' Court, London, referred to the Court of Justice three questions concerning the interpretation of art 48 of the EEC Treaty and of certain provisions of EEC Council Directive 64/221 of 25th February 1964 on the co-ordination of special measures concerning the movement and residence of foreign nationals which are justified on grounds of public policy, public security or public health.

h 2. The questions arose within the context of proceedings against a French national who had been employed in the United Kingdom since May 1975 and who was found guilty in June 1976 of unlawful possession of drugs, which is an offence punishable under the Misuse of Drugs Act 1971.

3. On 7th January 1976 the defendant had pleaded guilty to an identical offence before another court and had been conditionally discharged for 12 months.

j 4. The Marlborough Street Magistrates' Court was minded to make a recommendation for deportation to the Secretary of State pursuant to its powers under s 6(1) of the Immigration Act 1971 and the appropriate notice was served on the defendant, who maintained, however, that art 48 of the EEC Treaty and the provisions of EEC Council Directive 64/221 prevented such a recommendation from being made in that instance.

5. As the national court considered that the action raised questions concerning the

interpretation of Community law it referred the matter to the Court of Justice under art 177 of the EEC Treaty.

The first question

6. The first question asks—

'whether a recommendation for deportation made by a national court of a member state to the executive authority of that state (such recommendation being persuasive but not binding on the executive authority) constitutes a "measure" within the meaning of art 3(1) and (2) of EEC Council Directive 64/221.'

7. That question seeks to discover whether a court which, under national legislation, has jursidiction to recommend to the executive authority the deportation of a national of another member state, such recommendation not being binding on that authority, must, when it does so, take into account the limitations resulting from the EEC Treaty and from EEC Council Directive 64/221 on the exercise of the powers which, in that area, are reserved to the member states.

8. According to the observations submitted by the government of the United Kingdom in accordance with art 20 of the Protocol on the Statute of the Court of Justice of the European Economic Community, the question referred to the court raises two separate problems: whether a judicial decision can constitute a 'measure' for the purposes of the directive and, if the answer is in the affirmative, whether a mere 'recommendation' by a national court can constitute a measure for the purposes of that same directive.

9. Article 2 of EEC Council Directive 64/221 states that the directive relates to all 'measures' (dispositions, Vorschriften, provvedimenti, bestemmelser, voorschriften) concerning entry into the territory, issue or renewal of residence permits or expulsion from their territory taken by member states on grounds of public policy, public security or public health.

10. Under paras (1) and (2) of art 3 of that directive, 'measures' (mesures, Maßnahmen, provvedimenti, forholdsregler, maatregelen) taken on grounds of public policy or public security shall be based exclusively on the personal conduct of the individual concerned and previous criminal convictions shall not in themselves constitute grounds for the taking of such measures.

11. Although the government of the United Kingdom declares that it accepts unreservedly that paras (1) and (2) of art 3 are directly applicable and confer rights on nationals of member states to which the national courts must have regard, with the result that it is not open to a court of a member state to ignore those provisions on any matter coming before the court to which they are relevant, it submits that a judicial decision of a national court cannot constitute a 'measure' within the meaning of art 3.

12. On that point the government observes that the fact that the term 'measures' is used in the English text in both arts 2 and 3 shows that it is intended to have the same meaning in each case and that it emerges from the first recital in the preamble to the directive that when used in art 2 the expression only refers to provisions laid down by law, regulation or administrative action, to the exclusion of actions of the judiciary.

13. A comparison of the different language versions of the provisions in question shows that with the exception of the Italian text all the other versions use different terms in each of the two articles, with the result that no legal consequences can be based on the terminology used.

14. The different language versions of a Community text must be given a uniform interpretation and hence in the case of divergence between the versions the provision in question must be interpreted by reference to the purpose and general scheme of the rules of which it forms a part.

15. By co-ordinating national rules on the control of aliens, to the extent to which they concern the nationals of other member states, EEC Council Directive 64/221 seeks to protect such nationals from any exercise of the powers resulting from the exception relating to limitations justified on grounds of public policy, public security or public

health, which might go beyond the requirements justifying an exception to the basic
a principle of free movement of persons.

16. It is essential that at the different stages of the process which may result in the
adoption of a decision to make a deportation order that protection may be provided by
the courts where they are involved in the adoption of such a decision.

17. It follows that the concept of 'measure' includes the action of a court which is
required by the law to recommend in certain cases the deportation of a national of
b another member state.

18. When making such a recommendation, therefore, such a court must ensure that
the directive is correctly applied and must take account of the limits which it imposes on
the action of the authorities in the member states.

19. That finding is, moreover, in line with the point of view of the government of the
United Kingdom which 'is not suggesting that it would be open to a court of a member
c state to ignore the provisions of art 3(1) and (2) of the directive on any matter coming
before the court to which the articles are relevant' but on the contrary accepts 'that the
provisions of those articles are directly applicable and confer rights on nationals of
Member States to which the national courts must have regard'.

20. As regards the second aspect of the first question, the government of the United
Kingdom submits that a mere recommendation cannot constitute a 'measure' within the
d meaning of art 3(1) and (2) of EEC Council Directive 64/221, and that only the
subsequent decision of the Secretary of State can amount to such a measure.

21. For the purposes of the directive, a 'measure' is any action which affects the right
of persons coming within the field of application of art 48 of the EEC Treaty to enter and
reside freely in the member states under the same conditions as the nationals of the host
state.

e 22. Within the context of the procedure laid down by s 3(6) of the United Kingdom
Immigration Act 1971, the recommendation referred to in the question raised by the
national court constitutes a necessary step in the process of arriving at any decision to
make a deportation order and is a necessary prerequisite for such a decision.

23. Moreover, within the context of that procedure, its effect is to make it possible to
deprive the person concerned of his liberty and it is, in any event, one factor justifying
f a subsequent decision by the executive authority to make a deportation order.

24. Such a recommendation therefore affects the right of free movement and
constitutes a measure within the meaning of art 3 of the directive.

The second question

25. The second question asks—

g   'whether the wording of art 3(2) of EEC Council Directive 64/221, namely that
     previous criminal convictions shall not "in themselves" constitute grounds for the
     taking of measures based on public policy or public security means that previous
     criminal convictions are solely relevant in so far as they manifest a present or future
     propensity to act in a manner contrary to public policy or public security;
     alternatively, the meaning to be attached to the expression "in themselves" in art
h   3(2) of Directive 64/221.'

26. According to the terms of the order referring the case to the court, that question
seeks to discover whether, as the defendant maintained before the national court,
'previous criminal convictions are solely relevant in so far as they manifest a present or
future intention to act in a manner contrary to public policy or public security' or, on the
j other hand, whether, as counsel for the prosecution sought to argue, although 'the court
cannot make a recommendation for deportation on grounds of public policy based on
the fact alone of a previous conviction [it] is entitled to take into account the past conduct
of the defendant which resulted in the previous conviction'.

27. The terms of art 3(2) of the directive, which states that 'previous criminal
convictions shall not in themselves constitute grounds for the taking of such measures'

must be understood as requiring the national authorities to carry out a specific appraisal from the point of view of the interests inherent in protecting the requirements of public *a* policy, which does not necessarily coincide with the appraisals which formed the basis of the criminal conviction.

28. The existence of a previous criminal conviction can, therefore, only be taken into account in so far as the circumstances which gave rise to that conviction are evidence of personal conduct constituting a present threat to the requirements of public policy.

29. Although, in general, a finding that such a threat exists implies the existence in *b* the individual concerned of a propensity to act in the same way in the future, it is possible that past conduct alone may constitute such a threat to the requirements of public policy.

30. It is for the authorities and, where appropriate, for the national courts, to consider that question in each individual case in the light of the particular legal position of persons subject to Community law and of the fundamental nature of the principle of the free *c* movement of persons.

The third question

31. The third question asks whether the words 'public policy' in art 48(3) of the EEC Treaty are to be interpreted as including reasons of state even where no breach of the public peace or order is threatened or in a narrower sense in which is incorporated the *d* concept of some threatened breach of the public peace, order or security, or in some other wider sense.

32. Apart from the various questions of terminology, this question seeks to obtain a definition of the interpretation to be given to the concept of 'public policy' referred to in art 48.

33. In its judgment in *Van Duyn v The Home Office (No 2)* [1975] 3 All ER 190 at 206, *e* [1975] Ch 358 at 378 the court emphasised that the concept of public policy in the context of the Community and where, in particular, it is used as a justification for derogating from the fundamental principle of freedom of movement for workers must be interpreted strictly, so that its scope cannot be determined unilaterally by each member state without being subject to control by the institutions of the Community.

34. Nevertheless, it is stated in the same judgment that the particular circumstances *f* justifying recourse to the concept of public policy may vary from one country to another and from one period to another and it is therefore necessary in this matter to allow the competent national authorities an area of discretion within the limits imposed by the EEC Treaty and the provisions adopted for its implementation.

35. In so far as it may justify certain restrictions on the free movement of persons subject to Community law, recourse by a national authority to the concept of public *g* policy presupposes, in any event, the existence, in addition to the perturbation of the social order which any infringement of the law involves, of a genuine and sufficiently serious threat to the requirements of public policy affecting one of the fundamental interests of society.

Costs

36. The costs incurred by the government of the United Kingdom and the *h* Commission of the European Communities, which have submitted observations to the court, are not recoverable.

37. As these proceedings are, in so far as the parties to the main action are concerned, in the nature of a step in the action pending before the national court, the decision on costs is a matter for that court.

On those grounds, the court, in answer to the questions referred to it by the *j* Marlborough Street Magistrates' Court hereby rules: (1) any action affecting the right of persons coming within the field of application of art 48 of the EEC Treaty to enter and reside freely in the member states under the same conditions as the nationals of the host state constitutes a 'measure' for the purposes of art 3(1) and (2) of EEC Council Directive 64/221. That concept includes the action of a court which is required by the law to recommend in certain cases the deportation of a national of another member state, where *a* such recommendation constitutes a necessary prerequisite for a decision to make a deportation order; (2) art 3(2) of Directive 64/221, according to which previous criminal convictions do not in themselves constitute grounds for the imposition of the restrictions on free movement authorised by art 48 of the EEC Treaty on grounds of public policy and public security, must be interpreted to mean that previous criminal convictions are relevant only in so far as the circumstances which gave rise to them are evidence of personal conduct constituting a present threat to the requirements of public policy; (3) *b* in so far as it may justify certain restrictions on the free movement of persons subject to Community law, recourse by a national authority to the concept of public policy presupposes, in any event, the existence, in addition to the perturbation to the social order which any infringement of the law involves, of a genuine and sufficiently serious threat affecting one of the fundamental interests of society.

c Agents: *Alexander & Partners* (for the defendant); *Treasury Solicitor*; *Anthony McClellan*, Legal Service of EC Commission (for the Commission).

Andrew Durand Esq   Barrister.

d
Re Edwards's Will Trusts
Edwards v Edwards

COURT OF APPEAL, CIVIL DIVISION
BUCKLEY, EVELEIGH AND BRIGHTMAN LJJ
e 17th, 18th DECEMBER 1980, 6th FEBRUARY 1981

Court of Appeal – New trial – Jurisdiction to order new trial – Civil action –Judgment obtained in party's absence – Whether jurisdiction of Court of Appeal coexisting with trial court's jurisdiction to order new trial – Whether Court of Appeal's jurisdiction limited to motions for new trial where trial by jury – Supreme Court of Judicature (Consolidation) Act 1925, s 30(1)
f *– RSC Ord 35, r 2(1), Ord 59, rr 10, 11.*

Administration of estates – Assent – Legal estate in land – Administrator beneficially entitled failing to execute written assent vesting legal estate in himself – Administrator in beneficial occupation of land for many years – Administrator devising land to his executors on trust for sale – Whether land passing to executors in absence of written assent vesting legal estate in administrator – Whether assent to vesting of equitable estate in administrator to be inferred from
g *his conduct – Whether inferred assent passing land to executors under administrator's will.*

The testator's wife died intestate in 1930. The testator was the administrator of her estate and her sole beneficiary. The wife's estate included two plots of land ('the two plots') on one of which was a house which she and the testator had occupied and which the testator *h* occupied after the wife's death until his own death in 1950. The testator enjoyed the beneficial occupation of the two plots after the wife's death but failed in his capacity as administrator to execute a written assent of the legal estate in the two plots in his own favour as beneficial owner, so that the legal estate remained vested in him merely as administrator. The testator also owned a strip of land ('the access strip') which formed part of a third plot lying between the two plots and a road, and had for many years extensively used the third plot for the purpose of access to the house and the two plots. *j* By his will the testator appointed his two sons, who were the plaintiff and defendant, to be executors and trustees of his estate and devised the house and the two plots to them on trust for sale for themselves and the defendant's wife. In 1950, following the testator's death, the sons purported to execute an assent vesting the legal estate in the two plots in themselves on the will trusts. After the testator's death the defendant, with the consent of his wife and the plaintiff, occupied the house and the two plots, and, like the testator, used the third plot for the purposes of the house and the two plots. In 1965 there was a dispute between the defendant and a third party about the ownership of the third plot which was compromised by the third party conveying the access strip to the defendant *a* and the defendant abandoning any claim to the remainder of the third plot. The object of the compromise was to retain a means of access to the road for the benefit of the occupier of the house and the two plots. In 1977 there was a dispute between the plaintiff and the defendant regarding the beneficial ownership of the access strip. The plaintiff maintained that the access strip was subject to the will trusts whilst the defendant maintained it was solely his property. The plaintiff brought an. action against the *b* defendant seeking a declaration that at all material times the access strip was subject to the will trusts and an order removing the defendant from the trusteeship of the will trusts and appointing the defendant's wife in his place. Although the defendant was served with the summons and notified of the date of the hearing, he failed to attend the hearing of the summons and in his absence the judge (without giving reasons) gave judgment for the plaintiff and granted him the relief he sought. The defendant appealed *c* to the Court of Appeal and applied for an order for a new trial on the ground that the summons ought not to have been heard and determined in his absence. He submitted that the Court of Appeal had jurisdiction to order a new trial under RSC Ord 59, r 10[a], which gave the Court of Appeal all the powers of the High Court, since those powers included, by Ord 35, r 2(1)[b], power to order a new trial where judgment in a civil action was obtained in a party's absence. The defendant also contended (i) that the two plots *d* were never subject to the will trusts, because the testator had failed to execute an assent of the legal estate in his own favour with the consequence that the plots had never passed to his executors and remained unadministered assets of the wife's estate, and (ii) that there was insufficient evidence that the access strip was subject to the will trusts. The plaintiff submitted that the Court of Appeal had no jurisdiction to order a new trial since, by virtue of Ord 59, r 2, the applications for a new trial which the Court of Appeal could *e* entertain on an appeal were limited to motions for a new trial which came within s 30(1)[c] of the Supreme Court of Judicature (Consolidation) Act 1925 and those were restricted to motions for a new trial where there had been trial with a jury.

Held – (1) Notwithstanding the existence of the trial court's jurisdiction to order a new trial under RSC Ord 35, r 2(1), on the true construction of Ord 59, rr 10 and 11 the Court *f* of Appeal had jurisdiction on an appeal from a judgment given in a civil action tried without a jury to set aside the judgment and order a new trial if the judgment had been obtained in the absence of a party. However, as a general rule, the absent party who sought a new trial should first apply to the trial court for a new trial and only then if the application was refused appeal from the refusal to the Court of Appeal (see p 949 *a* to *e* and p 951 *d*, post); dictum of Brett LJ in *Oastler v Henderson* (1877) 2 QBD at 579, *Jones* *g* *v Hough* (1879) 5 Ex D 115, *Vint v Hudspith* (1885) 29 Ch D 322 and *Armour v Bate* [1891] 2 QB 233 applied.

---

a Order 59, so far as material, provides:
  '1. This Order applies, subject to the provisions of these rules with respect to particular appeals, to every appeal to the Court of Appeal . . . not being an appeal for which other provision is made by these rules. *h*
  '2. This Order (except so much of rule 3(1) as provides that an appeal shall by way of rehearing and except rule 11(1)) applies to an application to the Court of Appeal for a new trial or to set aside a verdict, finding or judgment after trial with or without a jury, as it applies to an appeal to that Court, and references in this Order to an appeal and to an appellant shall be construed accordingly
  . . .
  '10.—(1) In relation to an appeal the Court of Appeal shall have all the powers and duties as to *j* amendment and otherwise of the High Court . . .
  '11.—(1) On the hearing of any appeal the Court of Appeal may, if it thinks fit, make any such order as could be made in pursuance of an application for a new trial or to set aside a verdict, finding or judgment of the court below . . .'
b Rule 2(1) is set out at p 946 j, post
c Section 30(1) provides: 'Every motion for a new trial, or to set aside a verdict, finding or judgment, in any cause or matter in the High Court in which there has been a trial thereof or of any issue therein with a jury, shall be heard and determined by the Court of Appeal.'

(2) However, in the circumstances because of the lapse of time no purpose would be
a served in requiring the defendant to apply to the judge for a new trial and the Court of
Appeal would decide the matter. On that issue, a new trial would be refused because (a)
the two plots were subject to the will trusts even though the testator had never assented
to the vesting of the legal estate in himself, since an assent to the vesting of an equitable
estate was not required to be in writing and by his conduct in enjoying beneficial
occupation of the plots over a period of 20 years it was to be inferred that the testator had
b assented to the vesting of the equitable estate in himself, and accordingly the equitable
estate in the two plots had passed to his executors and become subject to the will trusts,
(b) the defendant had acquired the access strip under the compromise in consequence of
his occupation in the capacity of a trustee under the will trusts of the house and the two
plots and therefore held the access strip as a constructive trustee under those trusts, and
(c) the jurisdiction to remove a trustee being discretionary, the court would not be
c justified, having regard to all the circumstances, in interfering with the judge's order
removing the defendant from his position as trustee (see p 949 e f and h to p 950 b d and
g to p 951 d, post); Keech v Sandford [1558–1774] All ER Rep 230 applied.
   Per Curiam. On its true construction, s 30(1) of the 1925 Act has no application to a
case tried without a jury (see p 949 b c and p 951 d, post).

d **Notes**
For the appellate jurisdiction of the Court of Appeal, see 10 Halsbury's Laws (4th Edn)
para 900, and for cases on the subject, see 16 Digest (Reissue) 243–245, 2377–2393.
   For an assent by an administrator to the vesting of a legal estate, see 17 Halsbury's Laws
(4th Edn) paras 1349–1350, and for cases on assents by administrators and executors, see
24 Digest (Reissue) 730–738, 7859–7934.
e For the Supreme Court of Judicature (Consolidation) Act 1925, s 30, see 7 Halsbury's
Statutes (3rd Edn) 589.

Cases referred to in judgments
Armour v Bate [1891] 2 QB 233, 60 LJQB 433, 65 LT 137, CA, 51 Digest (Repl) 667, 2717.
Hodge, Re, Hodge v Griffiths [1940] Ch 260, 109 LJ Ch 185, 162 LT 155, 48 Digest (Repl)
f   248, 2237.
Jones v Hough (1879) 5 Ex D 115, 49 LJQB 211, 42 LT 108, 4 Asp MLC 248, CA, 46 Digest
   (Repl) 483, 306.
Keech v Sandford (1726) Cas temp King 61, [1558–1774] All ER Rep 230, 2 Eq Cas Abr
   741, 25 ER 223, LC, 47 Digest (Repl) 104, 749.
King's Will Trusts, Re, Assheton v Boyne [1964] 1 All ER 833, [1964] Ch 542, [1964] 2 WLR
g   913, 24 Digest (Reissue) 733, 7878.
Oastler v Henderson (1877) 2 QBD 575, 46 LJQB 607, 37 LT 22, CA, 31(2) Digest (Reissue)
   874, 7257.
Vint v Hudspith (1885) 29 Ch D 322, 54 LJ Ch 844, 52 LT 741, CA, 51 Digest (Repl) 668,
   2732.

h **Appeal**
By an originating summons dated 8th December 1977, as amended, the plaintiff, Francis
Lindsay Edwards, sought the following relief: (1) a declaration that a piece or parcel of
land ('the access strip') conveyed to the defendant, Alfred Kenneth Edwards, pursuant to
an order of the court made on 8th March 1972 in an action entitled Morton v Edwards
was at all material times until 21st March 1977 part of the property subject to the trusts
j of the will dated 18th June 1949 of Arthur Sydney Edwards deceased; (2) an account of
all money received by the defendant in respect of the access strip; (3) if and so far as
necessary execution of the will trusts; (3a) an order appointing the defendant's wife,
Ellen Elizabeth Edwards, to be a trustee of the will trusts in place of the defendant and
(4) further or other relief. By an order made on 28th July 1978 Sir Robert Megarry V-C
granted the plaintiff the relief sought in the absence of the defendant who failed to
appear at the hearing. The defendant appealed, seeking (1) to set aside the order and (2)
an order that the access strip was his sole property and that he be reinstated as a trustee

of the will trusts and his wife be removed from the trusteeship. The grounds of the
appeal were (1) that there was no sufficient evidence on which the judge could find that   *a*
the access strip formed part of the property subject to the will trusts and (2) that the judge
was wrong to hear the matter in the defendant's absence and the absence of counsel or a
solicitor on his behalf, the defendant having received no sufficient notice of the hearing
and having been unable to appoint a solicitor and counsel. On the hearing of the appeal
the defendant applied for an order for a new trial. The facts are set out in the judgment
of Buckley LJ.

b

Terence Etherton for the defendant.
John P Brookes for the plaintiff.

Cur adv vult

c

6th February. The following judgments were read.

BUCKLEY LJ. This is an appeal from an order made by Sir Robert Megarry V-C on
3rd August 1978 on the hearing of the originating summons in this matter. That order
was made in the absence of the defendant in circumstances which will appear hereafter.

The plaintiff and the defendant are brothers. At the date of her death on 4th July 1930   *d*
their mother ('Mrs Edwards') was the owner in fee simple of two adjoining plots of land
at Peacehaven in East Sussex which are shown numbered 1 and 2 respectively in the plan
attached to the Vice-Chancellor's order. At that time each of the two plots extended
southwards to a frontage on Firle Road. At the end of plot 2 remote from Firle Road
there stood, and still stands, a house now known as 128 Phyllis Avenue. [A plan appears
at p 951, post.]

e

Mrs Edwards was survived by her husband ('Mr Edwards'). She died intestate and Mr
Edwards was the sole beneficiary of her estate. From the death of Mrs Edwards until his
own death on 3rd January 1950 Mr Edwards occupied the two plots in question, residing
in 128 Phyllis Avenue. Letters of administration of Mrs Edwards's estate were granted
to Mr Edwards on 27th August 1930, but he never executed any assent in writing in his
own favour in respect of the two plots or any part of them. This may very probably be   *f*
explained by the fact that until the decision in *Re King's Will Trusts* [1964] 1 All ER 833,
[1964] Ch 542 it was fairly generally thought by conveyancers that, where the legal estate
in land had become vested in a person beneficially entitled to that land but had become
so vested in some capacity (eg as the executor of the previous owner) other than the
capacity of beneficial owner, no assent in writing was necessary to clothe that person with
the legal estate in his capacity as beneficial owner.

g

Mr Edwards appointed the plaintiff and the defendant executors of his last will which
they proved on 29th March 1950. On 25th April 1950 they executed what purported to
be a written assent in respect of the two plots. This purported to assent to the fee simple
in the two plots vesting in themselves on a trust for sale declared by Mr Edwards's will.
If, however, *Re King's Will Trusts* was rightly decided, and the contrary has not been
suggested, the purported assent cannot have had that effect, for the legal estate was never   *h*
vested in Mr Edwards in any capacity other than that of administrator of Mrs Edwards's
estate. The plaintiff and the defendant have subsequently together obtained a grant of
administration de bonis non to their mother's estate but they have made no written
assent in respect of the legal estate in the two plots.

From the death of Mr Edwards until the compulsory purchase which I shall shortly
refer to, the two plots were occupied by the defendant with the consent of his brother,   *j*
the plaintiff, and he resided in 128 Phyllis Avenue. The only beneficiaries under Mr
Edwards's will were the two brothers and the defendant's wife, who also presumably
consented to the defendant's occupation of the property.

The southern extremity of each of the two plots fronting onto Firle Road was sold
off. When this took place does not appear from the evidence except that an indorsement
on the assent referred to earlier indicates that part of the southern extremity of plot 2 was
conveyed by the plaintiff and the defendant to a named company on 16th March 1965.

a The only significance of these transactions is that they left the remainder of the two plots (which I shall henceforth refer to as 'the property') land-locked except so far as access could be obtained thereto from Phyllis Avenue (a road which runs north and south to the east of the two plots) across a piece of land, numbered 3 on the plan annexed to the Vice-Chancellor's order, which occupies an area lying between Phyllis Avenue and plot 2. It is apparently common ground that, in addition to the property, Mr Edwards owned at his death a narrow strip of land measuring approximately 12 feet by 80 feet forming the

b northern extremity of plot 3 and extending from the eastern boundary of the property to the western verge of Phyllis Avenue. The evidence in support of the originating summons relating to plot 3 is this:

> 'For very many years both before and after the death of the Testator [ie Mr Edwards] extensive use was for the purpose of the property made of the unoccupied plot to the east known as [plot] 3 which gave access to Phyllis Avenue.'

c In or about 1965 a dispute arose between one John Albert Morton and the defendant about the ownership of plot 3. In an action entitled *Morton v Edwards*, Mr Morton claimed to be the true owner of plot 3, and the defendant counterclaimed a possessory title to it. This action was compromised on terms under which Mr Morton conveyed to the defendant free of charge a piece of land measuring 80 feet by 40 feet extending from

d the eastern boundary of plot 2 to the western verge of Phyllis Avenue and the defendant abandoned his claim to any other part of plot 3. This piece of land is shown hatched blue on the plan annexed to the Vice-Chancellor's order. It is there referred to as 'the access strip' and I shall so call it. It is with the access strip that we are concerned in this appeal. By his originating summons the plaintiff claimed, and in the event he obtained from the Vice-Chancellor, a declaration that at all material times the access strip was

e subject to the trusts of Mr Edwards's will. From the time of its conveyance to the defendant until it became vested in the East Sussex County Council in pursuance of the compulsory purchase on 21st March 1977, the access strip was used for the purpose of obtaining access to and from the property from and to Phyllis Avenue.

The evidence contains no indication of what has happened since 25th April 1950 to the strip of land at the northern extremity of plot 3 mentioned earlier, or of who now owns

f it.

When the county council obtained its compulsory purchase order, which comprised not only the property but also the access strip, the consequent negotiations of the compensation to be made brought to a head a difference between the plaintiff and the defendant about the beneficial ownership of the access strip. The plaintiff consequently issued the originating summons in these proceedings on 8th December 1977. In its

g original form it asked merely for the declaration which I mentioned earlier and certain consequential relief. The summons in this form was served on the defendant on 4th April 1978 together with a notice of an appointment for a hearing before Master Gowers on 27th April 1978. There must, however, have been some form of earlier service of the summons, for appearance was entered by the defendant personally on 19th December 1977. In February 1978 the defendant, through a firm of London solicitors, applied for

h legal aid. When the defendant received the notice of the appointment for hearing to take place on 27th April 1978, he forwarded this to the solicitors in question, who replied saying that they could not act for him until he had been granted legal aid, and advising him to attend the hearing in person. He did not do so, but instead, on 26th April 1978, he wrote to the registrar of the Chancery Division explaining that he was the defendant in these proceedings, of which there was to be a hearing on 27th April, and explaining

j the position regarding his legal aid application. We do not know whether this letter was brought to the master's attention on 27th April. It seems that at the hearing on that day Master Gowers directed that the matter should be set down within 14 days for an early hearing. It was, I think, unfortunate that no intimation of this direction was given either by the court or by the plaintiff to the defendant. The time for setting down was later extended by the court, but the defendant does not seem to have known anything about this. He subsequently received by post from the court a notice dated 17th July 1978 saying that the originating summons had been entered for trial in the non-witness list.

This communication contained no reference to an early hearing. The words 'You should watch the weekly warned list for further information' were deleted from it. In the *a* meantime the originating summons was by leave amended on 1st June 1978. The amendment consisted of the addition of a paragraph asking for the appointment of the defendant's wife as a trustee of Mr Edwards's will in the place of the defendant and jointly with the plaintiff; that is to say, the defendant's removal as a trustee was sought. The defendant was served personally with the amended originating summons on 6th June 1978. *b*

The defendant was notified that he had been granted legal aid by a letter dated 23rd June 1978. He accepted that offer by a letter post on 27th June 1978. He had then had notice of an application to be heard by Master Gowers on 30th June 1978, but he does not seem to have transmitted this information to his solicitors, notwithstanding that he had been granted legal aid. The solicitors presumably had no knowledge of the appointment. The defendant was not present or represented on that occasion, when the *c* master gave directions as to filing further evidence and extended the time for setting down.

The defendant heard nothing more until about 4 pm on 27th July 1978, when a letter from the plaintiff's solicitors, practising in Peacehaven, was delivered by hand at his residence, 128 Phyllis Avenue, which was in the following terms: 'Please note the Hearing is due on the 28th July 1978 at 10.30 am in Court 16 before the Vice *d* Chancellor.' The letter contained no identification of the matter to which it referred. The defendant says in his affidavit, which we admitted in this court, that he did not know exactly what to make of this letter, but I can entertain no doubt that he was in fact perfectly well aware that it referred to the hearing of the originating summons in this matter. If he had been genuinely in doubt, he had only to telephone the solicitors in Peacehaven, which he did not do. But it is fair to say that the letter was very short notice *e* indeed having regard to the fact that, according to the defendant, he would have had to leave Peacehaven at 6.30 am the following day to reach the Strand in time for the hearing. The defendant apparently received no letter or other intimation from the court that the hearing would take place on 28th July.

In these circumstances the defendant unwisely took the view that to travel to London on 28th July would be 'a wild-goose chase'. He did not travel to London, or attempt to *f* communicate with the plaintiff's solicitors or the court or his own solicitors. Consequently the defendant was neither present nor represented when the originating summons was before the Vice-Chancellor, and the Vice-Chancellor was ignorant of the defendant's position. In my view, the defendant has only himself to thank for the fact that the court was not even aware of such difficulties as he found himself in. The defendant had filed no evidence. *g*

The Vice-Chancellor did not deliver a reasoned judgment. He granted the plaintiff the relief he sought as to both the declaration and the appointment of a new trustee in place of the defendant.

The defendant appeals from the Vice-Chancellor's order on these grounds: (1) that there was insufficient evidence on which to find that the access strip forms part of the property subject to the trusts of Mr Edwards's will; (2) that plots 1 and 2 have never been *h* subject to those trusts; (3) that there was no sufficient evidence to justify the removal of the defendant as a trustee of the will, and (4) that the judge should not have heard the matter in the absence of the defendant.

It will, I think, be convenient to say something about the fourth head first. Counsel for the defendant has asked us to direct a new trial under RSC Ord 35, r 2 which provides as follows: *j*

'(1) Any judgment, order or verdict obtained where one party does not appear at the trial may be set aside by the Court, on the application of that party, on such terms as it thinks just.

'(2) An application under this rule must be made within 7 days after the trial.'

Order 1, r 4(2) provides that in the Rules of the Supreme Court unless the context otherwise requires 'the Court' means the High Court, which does not, of course, include

the Court of Appeal; but counsel says that under Ord 59, r 3(1) an appeal to this court is
a by way of rehearing and that under r 10 of the same order this court has, in relation to
an appeal, all the powers of the High Court. So, it is submitted, this court is as well able
to order a new trial in the present case as the High Court would be.

Counsel for the plaintiff, on the other hand, contends that this court has no jurisdiction
to entertain this application for a new trial. He submits that an application for a new trial
is not an appeal and that Ord 59 has no application to the former except so far as the
b contrary is expressly provided. He says that Ord 59, r 2, which makes Ord 59 applicable
to applications to the Court of Appeal for a new trial or to set aside a verdict, finding or
judgment after trial with or without a jury, relates only to those cases in which the
Supreme Court of Judicature (Consolidation) Act 1925, s 30 lays down that motions for
a new trial shall be heard by the Court of Appeal. The present case, he contends, is not
such a case, because there was no trial with a jury, so that s 30 is inapplicable. Section 30
c cannot, in my opinion, apply to this case unless the words 'in any cause or matter in the
High Court in which there has been a trial thereof ... with a jury' govern only the
preceding words 'or to set aside a verdict, finding or judgment' and not the words 'for a
new trial'.

Consideration of this question of jurisdiction requires a short historical excursus.

The Court of Appeal was brought into existence by the Supreme Court of Judicature
d Act 1873, and its jurisdiction is statutory. Among the jurisdictions vested in it at its
creation was the jurisdiction theretofore vested in the Court of Exchequer Chamber: see
the Supreme Court of Judicature Act 1873, s 18(4). Immediately before the
commencement of that Act the Court of Exchequer Chamber was the court of error, ie
the appellate court, for all civil actions tried in the common law courts of this country.
The Court of Exchequer Chamber, however, had no power to disturb a verdict of a
e jury. If a party wished to displace a verdict of a jury, he had to move that court in which
the case had been tried sitting in banc for a new trial.

Until the Common Law Procedure Act 1854 came into operation, all actions in the
three common law courts were tried by judge and jury. Under s 1 of that Act it became
possible for the first time for the parties to an action to agree to its being tried by a judge
alone. In a trial by judge and jury all issues of fact were submitted to the arbitrament of
f the jury, with whose verdict neither the trial judge nor the court of error could
interfere. Where an action was tried by a judge alone, he necessarily determined all
issues of fact arising in the case. If he went wrong in determining an issue of fact, the
court of error was as competent and as appropriate a tribunal to determine that issue
correctly as the trial judge was except that the trial judge had had the advantage of
observing the witnesses. By correcting such an error the court of error was not invading
g the distinct function of a jury.

This state of affairs was not affected by the Judicature Acts of 1873 and 1875 except
that a motion for a new trial in a case tried whether with or without a jury in any of the
three common law divisions of the new High Court had to be made to a Divisional
Court: see s 48 of the 1873 Act and Ord 39 in Sch 1 to the 1875 Act. Section 19 of the
1873 Act provided that the Court of Appeal should have jurisdiction and power to hear
h and determine appeals from any judgment or order of the High Court subject to the
provisions of that Act and to any rules and orders made pursuant to it, and that for all the
purposes of and incidental to the hearing of any appeal the Court of Appeal should have
all the power, authority and jurisdiction vested in the High Court. That Act, however,
contained no provisions corresponding to s 30 of the 1925 Act, and the Court of Appeal
could not order a new trial in any case to which Ord 39, r 1 applied.

j In December 1876 Ord 39 was amended to provide that a motion for a new trial in a
cause or matter tried with a jury in any of the three common law divisions should be to
a Queen's Bench Divisional Court and that, where there had been a trial without a jury,
the application should be by appeal to the Court of Appeal. This was changed in 1890,
when the Supreme Court of Judicature Act of that year contained, in s 1, a provision in
similar terms to s 30 of the 1925 Act.

In 1879 this court decided in *Jones v Hough* 5 Ex D 115 that, where an action had been
tried before a judge alone, the Court of Appeal had jurisdiction on an appeal to review

the judge's findings as to fact without a rule for a new trial having been obtained. Bramwell LJ said (at 122):

a

'Where the jury find the facts, the Court cannot be substituted for them, because the parties have agreed that the facts shall be decided by a jury; but where the judge finds the facts, there the Court of Appeal has the same jurisdiction that he has, and can find the facts whichever way they like.'

Cotton LJ agreed and Thesiger LJ (at 127) said:

b

'It appears to me that, with one exception, there was no necessity in a case of this kind for any motion for a new trial. That one exception relates to motions upon the ground of surprise. There I think it would be proper that a motion for a new trial should be made, although upon that motion it would be open to this Court not to send back the case to the judge who tried it, but, it might itself, instead of doing that, take the additional evidence, and so try the whole case.'

c

It will be observed that in that case the Court of Appeal disposed of the matter as an appeal. That they had jurisdiction to do so may be justified either on the ground that such jurisdiction vested in them as the heirs to the jurisdiction of the Court of Exchequer Chamber or on the ground that such jurisdiction was vested in them by s 19 of the 1873 Act. The latter is, I think, the better view.

d

In *Oastler v Henderson* (1877) 2 QBD 575 an action in the Queen's Bench Division to recover arrears of rent was tried before a judge alone, who entered a verdict and judgment for the plaintiffs. The defendant thereafter obtained some further evidence on which he sought to rely in support of an implied acceptance by the plaintiffs of a surrender of the lease. The defendant moved the Divisional Court for a new trial. The court granted an order nisi but this was later discharged on the ground that the Divisional Court had no jurisdiction, the trial having taken place before a judge alone. Order 39, r 1 of the Rules of the Supreme Court then in force required the application for a new trial in a case which had been tried by a judge alone to be made to the Court of Appeal. The defendant then appealed to the Court of Appeal. Cockburn CJ and Bramwell LJ dealt with the matter purely on its merits, dismissing the appeal and refusing a new trial. Brett LJ, however, not only dealt with the merits but also referred to the *f* jurisdiction point, saying (at 579):

e

'I am, however, on that point of opinion that the Court below were right, and that in cases of trials by a judge without a jury, all applications for a new trial must be made to the Court of Appeal whatever the ground of the application may be.'

In *Vint v Hudspith* (1885) 29 Ch D 322 an action was dismissed with costs against a *g* plaintiff who did not appear at the trial. The plaintiff had known nothing about the trial. He appealed to the Court of Appeal. The court clearly took the view that they had jurisdiction to hear the appeal, but declined to do so. Cotton LJ said (at 323):

'We are of opinion that the Plaintiff's proper course was to apply to the Judge to restore the cause on the ground that the Plaintiff was absent per incuriam. I am far from saying that this Court cannot entertain an appeal from a judgment made by *h* default, but in a case like the present it is important to prevent the Court of Appeal from being flooded by having to hear cases in the first instance.'

Bowen LJ expressed similar views.

In *Armour v Bate* [1891] 2 QB 233 a plaintiff employee sued his employer for repayment of £300 admittedly deposited by the plaintiff with the defendant. The defendant *j* pleaded that dishonest or negligent conduct by the plaintiff entitled him to indemnify himself out of the deposit. The defendant also counterclaimed. The plaintiff did not appear at the trial. The defendant abandoned his counterclaim and asked for judgment. Wills J, who sat without a jury, entered judgment for the defendant. The plaintiff thereafter did not apply to the judge under the then Ord 36, r 33 to have the judgment set aside but, after the time for such an application had expired, he gave notice of appeal. The Court of Appeal entertained the appeal and held that the judge should have dismissed the action instead of giving judgment for the defendant. They dismissed

a the appeal with costs but amended the judgment so as to dismiss the action in conformity with the then Ord 36, r 32.

This review of the statutes, rules and cases, in my opinion, establishes the following propositions, in which I make reference to the current Rules of the Supreme Court. (1) Where a civil action has been tried without a jury, the Court of Appeal has jurisdiction, on hearing an appeal, to set aside the judgment of the trial judge and to

b order a new trial, or to correct any error by the trial judge of fact or law and to vary the judgment appropriately: see Ord 59, rr 10 and 11. (2) Where the action has been tried with a jury any verdict, finding or judgment can be set aside on motion to the Court of Appeal and the Court of Appeal can on motion direct a new trial: see s 30 of the 1925 Act. In my judgment the words 'in any cause or matter in the High Court in which there has been a trial thereof or of any issue therein with a jury' in that section govern all

c that goes before them, so that the section has no application to any case tried without a jury. The reason for the enactment of this section appears to me to have been the historic view that without statutory authority no court could interfere with a verdict of a jury, so long as it was not perverse, or with any judgment properly founded on it. (3) Where any judgment, order or verdict has been obtained in the absence of any party, the Court of Appeal can entertain an appeal. They can deal with any such appeal on its merits or

d alternatively set the judgment, order or verdict aside and order a new trial. (4) But if the party who has been absent from the trial wants to apply for a new trial he should apply under Ord 35, r 2 not to the Court of Appeal but the court which tried the action and, if possible, to the trial judge himself. From a refusal of such an application an appeal will lie to the Court of Appeal. But the existence of the jurisdiction of the trial court under Ord 35, r 2 does not negative the coexistence of the Court of Appeal's jurisdiction under

e (1) above.

The present case falls under heads (1), (3) and (4) above. The proper course for the defendant to have adopted would have been to apply to the Vice-Chancellor under Ord 35, r 2 for a new trial and for any necessary extension of the time limit under that rule; but this court is not without jurisdiction to order a new trial on hearing this appeal. It does not seem to me that any useful purpose would be served in the present case by

f requiring the defendant to make an application to the Vice-Chancellor, the proper time for which has long since expired. I think that we should decide the matter here.

I propose to deal next with the question whether the property, as I have defined that term, has ever been subjected to the trusts of Mr Edwards's will. The argument presented by counsel for the defendant has been that, since Mr Edwards as administrator of his wife's estate never made any written assent in respect of the property or any part of it in

g his own favour as the sole beneficiary entitled to it, the legal estate was at his death vested in him as such administrator and so did not pass to his executors but remained an unadministered asset of Mrs Edwards's estate. He relied on *Re King's Will Trusts* [1964] 1 All ER 833, [1964] Ch 542. I proceed on the basis that this is correct. It does not follow that the equitable beneficial interest in the property did not vest in Mr Edwards in his lifetime so as to form part of his estate at his death: see *Re Hodge* [1940] Ch 260 at 264.

h Mr Edwards enjoyed the beneficial occupation of the property for nearly twenty years after Mrs Edwards's death. Nothing in the evidence suggests that during the greater part of that period any liabilities of Mrs Edwards's estate remained outstanding.

It is evident that when the plaintiff and the defendant executed the assent of 25th April 1950 they regarded the property as having vested beneficially in Mr Edwards. They were clearly not aware that the legal estate might have then been outstanding. The

j assent may have been ineffective to vest the legal estate, but this does not deprive it of significance as evidence of the executors' views where the beneficial interest was when Mr Edwards died. An assent to the vesting of an equitable interest need not be in writing. It may be inferred from conduct. In my judgment there are ample grounds for inferring that Mr Edwards assented in his lifetime to the vesting in himself of the full beneficial interest in the property. If so, that beneficial interest passed to his executors on his death and became subject to the trusts of his will. For these reasons I am of the opinion that the property is subject to the trusts of Mr Edwards's will.

The next question is whether the access strip is subject to the same trusts. This depends, in my opinion, on whether on the evidence before this court the access strip is *a* subject to a constructive trust. It is well-established law that a trustee cannot use his position or his powers as a trustee to acquire property for his own benefit. If he purports to do so, however innocently, he is held to be a constructive trustee of that property for the persons beneficially interested under the trust of which he is a trustee. The leading case on this topic is *Keech v Sandford* (1726) Cas *temp* King 61, [1558–1774] All ER Rep 230. *b*

The defendant was, and is, an executor and trustee of Mr Edwards's will. He was from the death of Mr Edwards until after his acquisition of the access strip in occupation of the property by the consent or licence of his co-executor and co-trustee, the plaintiff. He could not, in my judgment, make use of that situation to acquire any other property for his own benefit without being affected by a constructive trust in accordance with the doctrine just referred to. Does the evidence before the court justify the view that the *c* defendant's acquisition of the access strip was a consequence of his occupation of the property?

I have already read what is to be found in the plaintiff's evidence about the use of plot 3 'for very many years both before and after the death' of Mr Edwards. This evidence is devoid of particulars about the kind of use made of plot 3, but it is described as use 'for the purpose of the property' and there is an express reference to the fact that plot 3 gave *d* access to Phyllis Avenue. This evidence to my mind indicates clearly that the use or uses in question was or were ancillary to the enjoyment of the property.

In para 4 of his affidavit introduced in this court, the defendant asserts that in the *Morton v Edwards* action he had claimed the entirety of plot 3 by virtue of his own acts of adverse possession. He says that the acts of adverse possession on which he relied were not committed on behalf of the trustees of his father's will and that he did not rely on the *e* acts of anyone other than himself and his agents. He asserts that he entered into possession of plot 3, worked it and occupied it on his own account. The defendant, however, does not specifically deny any part of the statement contained in the plaintiff's affidavit.

It cannot, I think, be disputed that the object of stipulating for the conveyance of the access strip under the compromise of the action was to retain or secure a means of access *f* from the property to Phyllis Avenue.

Notwithstanding that the acts relied on by the defendant may have been done by the defendant on his own account and not on behalf of the plaintiff and himself as executors or trustees of this will, this would not avoid the inference of a constructive trust if the acts were acts which he was in a position to do by reason of his occupation of the property.

In my judgment the evidence to which I have referred, taken as a whole, indicates that *g* plot 3 was used, both by Mr Edwards during his lifetime and thereafter by the defendant, from Mr Edwards's death until the compromise of the action, or at any rate until the dispute with Mr Morton arose, by the occupier for the time being of the property for purposes ancillary to the enjoyment of the property, and that the object of the compromise was to retain a means of access to Phyllis Avenue for the benefit of the occupier of the property. *h*

If this is right, the effect of the evidence before this court is, in my opinion, to establish that the circumstances of the defendant's acquisition of the access strip were such as to fix him with a constructive trust of the access strip on the trusts of Mr Edwards's will. The relevant evidence adduced on each side is of a very sketchy nature, but the defendant has had ample time to furnish more cogent evidence, had he so wished or been so advised. In my judgment, insufficient grounds are shown to justify ordering a new trial; and this *j* court would not, in my judgment, be justified on the evidence in interfering with the declaration contained in the order of the Vice-Chancellor.

There remains the question whether the order which had the effect of removing the defendant from his position as a trustee of Mr Edwards's will was justified. Such an order should only be made on cogent grounds, but the jurisdiction is undoubtedly discretionary. The defendant must show that the Vice-Chancellor erred on some point

of principle. As he delivered no reasoned judgment, it is hard to know precisely on what
a grounds he acted. The defendant in his supplementary notice of appeal dated 5th
December 1980 says that there was no, or no sufficient, evidence on which the Vice-
Chancellor could conclude that it was expedient to remove the defendant from his
trusteeship. The complaint against the defendant is that when the East Sussex County
Council was prepared to make an advance payment of £27,000 on account of the
compensation in respect of the compulsory purchase of the property (not including the
b access strip) the defendant refused to accept it. The offer of the advance payment was
expressly made without prejudice to the amount of compensation finally to be agreed.
The defendant was adopting the attitude that the property was worth much more than
the £30,000 suggested by the district valuer. The Vice-Chancellor probably, I think,
took the view that the defendant's attitude about the advance payment was unreasonable
and damaging to the interests of the beneficiaries under Mr Edwards's will. In these
c circumstances, I would not feel justified in interfering with the Vice-Chancellor's decision
in the exercise of an essentially discretionary jurisdiction.

I would accordingly dismiss this appeal.

EVELEIGH LJ. I agree.

d **BRIGHTMAN LJ.** I also agree.

Appeal dismissed.

Solicitors: *Outred & Co*, agents for *Donne, Mileham & Haddock*, Newhaven (for the
defendant); *Bedford & Co*, Peacehaven (for the plaintiff).

Diana Brahams   Barrister.

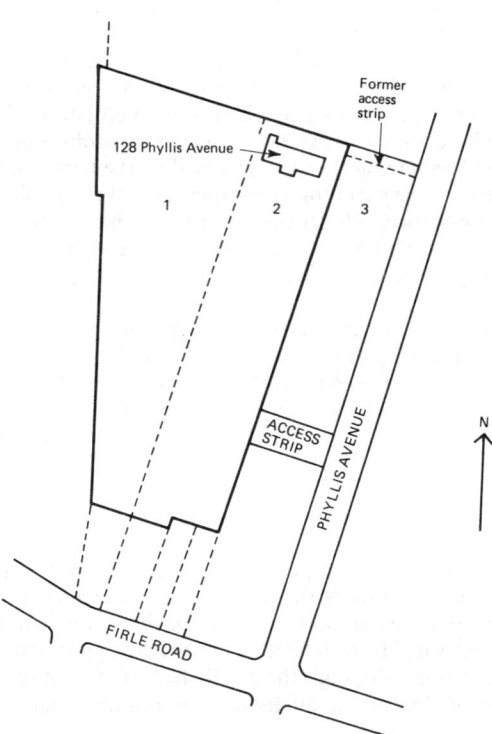

Re S (a barrister)

VISITORS OF THE INNER TEMPLE
VINELOTT, MCNEILL AND ANTHONY LINCOLN JJ
20th MARCH, 15th APRIL 1981

Counsel – Disciplinary jurisdiction – Senate of the Inns of Court and the Bar – Disciplinary tribunal – Whether Senate through its disciplinary tribunal acting as judge in its own cause – Whether tribunal consisting mostly of barristers capable of considering fairly a charge of misconduct brought against fellow barrister.

Tribunal – Domestic tribunal – Disciplinary committee of professional society – Impartiality – Whether disciplinary committee of professional society capable of considering fairly a charge of misconduct brought against fellow member of society.

The appellant, a barrister, was found guilty by a disciplinary tribunal of the Senate of the Inns of Court and the Bar of a number of charges of professional misconduct, namely touting for instructions, demanding and accepting a fee from a lay client whom he subsequently represented in court without the intervention of a solicitor, and requiring a client to execute building and decorating work at his home in lieu of part payment of his fee. The tribunal, which, pursuant to byelaws made by the Senate, was governed by the rules of natural justice and which, pursuant to the regulations of the Senate, consisted of a judge of the High Court who was a member of the Senate, a lay representative from a panel appointed by the Lord Chancellor and three practising barristers who were members of the Senate at least one of whom was a member of the appellant's Inn, sentenced the appellant to be disbarred and expelled from his Inn of Court. The appellant appealed against the decision to the visitors of his Inn. He did not dispute the findings of the tribunal, but he contended, inter alia, that the constitution of the tribunal infringed the principle that no man should be a judge in his own cause and that its findings in consequence were a nullity. Although he accepted that there was no suggestion of actual bias against him on the part of any member of the tribunal, he submitted that a tribunal the majority of which were members of the Senate, which in turn included as a subordinate part the Bar Council, a committee of which was charged with investigating and preferring the charges heard by the tribunal, was not one which would be regarded by ordinary and informed members of the public as free from every suspicion of bias or prejudice. He further submitted that a tribunal the majority of which were practising barristers was incapable of considering fairly a charge of misconduct brought against a fellow barrister.

Held – A tribunal which had the duty of hearing a disciplinary complaint against a member of a profession relating to the question whether he was guilty of a breach of the code of conduct governing the exercise of that profession could not be said to be partial merely because the majority of the members of the tribunal were members of that profession. It had always been accepted that, because of their knowledge of the reasons which had led to the acceptance by the profession of a code of conduct and from their experience of the difficulties which might confront both the practitioner in observing and the profession in enforcing proper standards of conduct, professional men were peculiarly well fitted to determine whether there had been a breach of the code of conduct governing the profession and to judge the gravity of it if it had been proven. Nor, in the circumstances, was there the appearance of partiality in the composition of the disciplinary tribunal, since the conduct of the appellant of which complaint had been made had not been motivated by or related in any way to opposition to the Senate or the Inns of Court. Furthermore, although the public had an interest in ensuring that those charged with the regulation of the affairs of a profession should investigate, and in

a appropriate cases determine, charges of professional misconduct in a fair and impartial way, it was not necessary that the regulations concerning the conduct of the profession, if they were to accord with the standards of natural justice and ensure the confidence of the public in the proper regulation of the affairs of the profession, should go further and provide that complaints of professional misconduct be heard by a tribunal having a majority of members who were not members of the profession. It followed that the appeal would be dismissed (see p 957 d to f, p 958 f g j and p 959 g h, post).

b le Compte v Belgium [1980] 3 ECC 294 distinguished.

Per the visitors. Those charged with the proper regulation of a profession should be careful in framing the constitution of the governing body and of its disciplinary tribunals to ensure that the task of investigating and presenting a complaint and the task of adjudication on it and, if it is proved, determining the appropriate sentence are in different hands (see p 957 f g, post).

c ### Notes

For the Senate of the Inns of Court and the Bar, see 3 Halsbury's Laws (4th Edn) para 1108, for disciplinary authority see ibid para 1134, and for cases on the subject of discipline and disbarring, see 3 Digest (Reissue) 746–748, 4452–4461.

d ### Cases referred to in decision

Delcourt v Belgium [1980] 1 EHRR 355.

le Compte v Belgium [1980] 3 ECC 294.

Leeson v General Council of Medical Education and Registration (1889) 43 Ch D 366, [1886–90] All ER Rep 78, 59 LJ Ch 233, 61 LT 849, CA, 33 Digest (Repl) 521, 33.

S (a barrister), Re [1969] 1 All ER 949, [1970] 1 QB 160, [1969] 2 WLR 708, 3 Digest

e (Reissue) 747, 4461.

Appeal

S, a barrister, appealed to Her Majesty's Judges sitting as visitors of the Honourable Society of the Inner Temple against an order of the disciplinary tribunal of the Senate of the Inns of Court and the Bar that he be disbarred and expelled from membership of his

f Inn. The respondent to the appeal was the Professional Conduct Committe of the Bar Council. The visitors heard the appeal in private but, with the consent of the parties, pronounced their findings in public. The facts are set out in the decision of the visitors.

Louis Blom-Cooper QC and Alan Newman for the appellant.
Stephen Powles for the respondent.

g
Cur adv vult

15th April. **VINELOTT J** read the following decision of the visitors: In this appeal we sit not as a court of law but as visitors of the Inns of Court. The Lord Chancellor and all the judges of the High Court of Justice are visitors of the Inns of Court and as visitors it

h is their duty to hear appeals by barristers who have been found guilty of professional misconduct and who have been disbarred or disciplined by suspension from practice for a period or by the imposition of a fine or who have been reprimanded. Under rules made on behalf of all the judges of the High Court by the Lord Chancellor, the Lord Chief Justice, the President of the Family Division and the Vice-Chancellor, appeals to the judges as visitors are heard by not fewer than three judges nominated by the Lord

j Chief Justice after consultation with the Lord Chancellor. We have been so nominated to hear an appeal by a barrister who has been found guilty by the Disciplinary Tribunal of the Senate of the Inns of Court and the Bar of very serious charges of misconduct. He was sentenced to be disbarred and expelled from the Inn of Court of which he was a member. Normally, the visitors sit and give their decision in private. In this case we heard the appeal in private, but, as a question of principle has been raised by counsel for the appellant, we have decided, with the consent of counsel for the appellant and the Professional Conduct Committee, to pronounce our findings in public.

For nearly seven hundred years the judges have had the constitutional duty and right, derived from the Crown, of providing and ordaining lawyers to serve and transact the business of the court. Over many centuries, two important objects of the Inns of Court were the training of persons to be advocates in disputes before the judges and ensuring that those who are such persons remain fit persons to be advocates. Accordingly, by the middle of the seventeenth century it was accepted by the judges that, provided the call had been published in the Inn and the oaths of allegiance and supremacy taken, no further qualification was required to entitle the person called to the Bar of his Inn to appear as an advocate in what were then the King's courts. So the Inns of Court, with the concurrence of the judges, performed the duty of selecting those persons who were fit and proper persons to be called to the Bar and entitled to a right of audience in the courts, and the duty of suspending or prohibiting such persons from practice or of fining or reprimanding them for improper conduct subject, of course, to the visitatorial jurisdiction of the judges.

In 1966 the Inns of Court resolved to create a new body, the Senate of the Inns of Court. They also resolved that their disciplinary powers over barristers (other than the power to pronounce and carry into effect any sentence in respect of misconduct) should vest in the Senate and that the Masters of the Bench of each of the Inns would pronounce and carry into effect any sentence decided on or recommended by the Senate. That resolution was confirmed by a resolution by all the judges. In *Re S (a barrister)* [1969] 1 All ER 949, [1970] 1 QB 160 Paull, Lloyd-Jones, Stamp, James and Blain JJ, sitting as visitors on behalf of the Lord Chancellor and all the judges, held that the resolutions of the Inns and of the judges effectively transferred the duty of disciplining members of the Bar to the Senate.

At the time of that decision there also existed an elected body representing the Bar. Although that body, the General Council of the Bar, did not itself have disciplinary powers, a committee of the council, the Complaints Committee, investigated complaints against barristers and, if necessary, referred them to the Disciplinary Committee of the Senate and instructed counsel to appear before the Disciplinary Committee to present the charges.

In 1974 these constitutional arrangements were changed. A new Senate was formed, the Senate of the Inns of Court and the Bar. The General Council of the Bar became a part of it. Again, the judges with the concurrence of the Inns of Court resolved that, after 27th July 1974, disciplinary powers over barristers should be exercised in accordance with the regulations governing the new Senate. Although the General Council of the Bar ceased to exist as a separate entity, the constitution of the Senate contains provisions designed to ensure that it will operate as an independent body. The members of the Senate include 39 Bar representatives who are elected by the Bar. The Bar Council consists of the chairman and the vice-chairman of the Senate (both of whom are required to be practising barristers), the treasurer of the Senate (if and so long as he is a practising barrister), the Attorney General, the Solicitor General, the leader of each circuit (or his deputy) and the 39 elected Bar representatives. Regulation 11 of the Regulations of the Senate of the Inns of Court and the Bar provides: 'The Bar Council shall be an autonomous body for the purposes of its separate powers and functions in the performance of which it shall not be subject to any directions from the Senate . . .'

One of the committees of the Bar Council is the Professional Conduct Committee. The membership of the Professional Conduct Committee consists of the vice-chairman of the Senate and 14 members of the Senate elected by the Bar Council. The Professional Conduct Committee has power to co-opt one or more lay representatives selected from a panel appointed by the Lord Chancellor. At all times since the formation of the Senate the Professional Conduct Committee has included at least one lay member.

The Professional Conduct Committee has (amongst others) the following powers and functions: '(i) To investigate and sift complaints. (ii) To prefer charges of professional

misconduct before Disciplinary Tribunals as provided by Regulation 20 and be
responsible for prosecuting any such charges before such Tribunals' (see reg 31(2)(B)).

a

Regulation 20 sets out the composition and functions of the disciplinary tribunal,
which is a committee of the Senate. Paragraph (a) provides that any charge of professional
misconduct preferred by the Professional Conduct Committee shall be heard and
determined by the disciplinary tribunal. The disciplinary tribunal acts in the name and
on behalf of the Senate and has the powers contained in the standing orders of the
Disciplinary Committee of the old Senate and such other powers as are conferred on it by

b

the new Senate.

Paragraph (b) provides that the disciplinary tribunal is to consist of the following five
persons, namely, as chairman of the tribunal a judge of the High Court who is a member
of the Senate, a lay representative from a panel appointed by the Lord Chancellor and
three practising barristers who are members of the Senate including at least one who is
a member of the Inn of the barrister charged.

c

Under para (c) the President of the Senate is required to nominate two practising
barristers who are members of the Senate to act as spare members for the purpose of
filling vacancies in the membership of the tribunal which may arise before the start of
a hearing.

Paragraph (d) provides that notwithstanding paras (b) and (c) the president may
appoint as members or spare members one or more barristers who are not members of

d

the Senate if, in the exercise of his discretion, he deems such appointment to be expedient.

Paragraph (e) is important. It reads as follows:

> 'A barrister who was a member of the Professional Conduct Committee at any
> time when the matters to which the charge relates were being considered by that
> Committee shall not be eligible to serve on the Disciplinary Tribunal which hears

e

> and determines the charge.'

Regulation 48 confers powers on the Senate by extraordinary resolution to make and
rescind and amend byelaws and it is provided that such byelaws shall be effective only so
far as they are consistent with the regulations. Byelaws have been made pursuant to this
power which amplify reg 20. Paragraph 11(b) of the byelaws provides:

f

> 'The proceedings of the Tribunal shall be governed by the rules of natural justice,
> subject to which the Chairman may give all such directions with regard to the
> conduct of and procedure at the hearing and with regard to the admission of
> evidence thereat as he considers appropriate for securing that the barrister charged
> has a proper opportunity of answering the charge.'

g

As we have said, in this case serious charges were preferred against the appellant. He
was found guilty on some, but not all, of them. He was sentenced to be disbarred and
expelled from his Inn. By his notice of appeal to the visitors, the appellant appealed
against these findings on the ground that having regard to the evidence before the
tribunal the findings were unsafe and unsatisfactory. He also appealed against the
sentence as being unduly severe having regard to his record and to the sentences imposed

h

in other cases. Before us, counsel made it clear when opening his appeal that the appeal
so far as founded on the claim that on the evidence before the tribunal its findings were
unsafe and unsatisfactory would not be pursued. But he mounted a fundamental attack
on the constitution of the tribunal. He submitted that the constitution of the tribunal
infringed the principle nemo judex in causa sua and that its findings were in consequence
a nullity.

j

In its narrower formulation counsel's submission was that the Senate is legislator,
investigator, prosecutor, judge and jury. He repudiated any suggestion that there was
any element of actual bias against the appellant on the part of any member of the
tribunal. But he submitted that a tribunal the majority of the members of which are
members of the Senate, which in turn includes as a subordinate part a body, the Bar
Council, a committee of which is charged with the duty of investigating and preferring

the charges heard by the tribunal, is not one which would be regarded by ordinary and informed members of the public as free from every suspicion of bias or prejudice and that accordingly its findings should not be allowed to stand.

There may be room for doubt whether it would be open to us as visitors sitting on behalf of the Lord Chancellor and the judges of the High Court to hold the findings of a disciplinary tribunal constituted in accordance with the regulations of the Senate, a body to which the exercise of disciplinary powers in accordance with those regulations has been entrusted by resolution of the judges of the High Court, to be invalid on this ground. This question has not been argued before us and we express no opinion on it. In our opinion there is no substance in counsel's objection. The principle that he who is an accuser cannot be a judge is stated by Bowen LJ, in a passage in the case of *Leeson v General Council of Medical Education and Registration* (1889) 43 Ch D 366 at 384–385, [1886–90] All ER Rep 78 at 86 which has often been cited, in these terms:

'. . . nothing can be clearer than the principle of law that a person who has a judicial duty to perform disqualifies himself for performing it if he has a pecuniary interest in the decision which he is about to give, or a bias which renders him otherwise than an impartial judge. If he is an accuser he must not be a judge. If he has a pecuniary interest in the success of the accusation he must not be a judge. Where such a pecuniary interest exists, the law does not allow any further inquiry as to whether or not the mind was actually biased by the pecuniary interest. The fact is established from which the inference is drawn that he is interested in the decision, and he cannot act as a judge. But it must be in all cases a question of substance and of fact whether one of the judges has in truth also been an accuser. The question which has to be answered by the tribunal which has to decide—the legal tribunal before which the controversy is waged—must be: Has the judge whose impartiality is impugned taken any part whatever in the prosecution, either by himself or by his agents?'

In that case the defendant council held an inquiry in which they adjudged a medical practitioner to be guilty of infamous conduct in a professional respect. The proceedings were instituted by the managing body of the Medical Defence Union, one of whose objects was to suppress and prosecute unauthorised practitioners. Two of the twenty-nine persons who held the inquiry were members of the Medical Defence Union. But they were not members of the managing body and had nothing to do with the making of the complaint. The majority of the Court of Appeal, Cotton and Bowen LJJ, held that the two members did not have such an interest as to disqualify them from taking part in the inquiry. Fry LJ took a stricter view. He said (43 Ch D 366 at 390, [1886–90] All ER Rep 78 at 89):

'I think that it is a matter of public policy that, so far as is possible, judicial proceedings shall not only be free from actual bias or prejudice of the judges, but that they shall be free from the suspicion of bias or prejudice: and I do not think that subscribers to associations for the purpose of carrying on prosecutions can be said to be free from suspicion of bias or prejudice in the case of prosecutions instituted by the associations to which they subscribe. It is needless for me to disclaim any intention, in arriving at that conclusion, of holding that the two gentlemen in question were in fact influenced by any bias. That appears to me a point which is not really open to us, because I put my decision on the ground of public policy, and I disclaim any right to inquire whether in fact they were or they were not biased. I need hardly say that I do not believe they were.'

The regulations of the Senate were clearly framed with these observations of Fry LJ in mind. As we have pointed out, the Bar Council, while part of the Senate, acts as an autonomous body for the purposes of its separate powers and duties and in relation to those powers and duties is not subject to any direction from the Senate. Further, para (e) of reg 20 precludes any barrister who was a member of the Professional Conduct

a
Committee when the matters to which a charge relates was considered by that committee from serving on the disciplinary tribunal which determines the charge.

But counsel for the appellant founded his submission on another and wider ground. He submitted that a tribunal the majority of the members of which are practising barristers is incapable of considering fairly a charge of misconduct brought against a fellow barrister. He professed to find support for this heterodox proposition in a passage from Professor de Smith's Judicial Review of Administrative Action (4th Edn, 1980,

b
p 256), which reads as follows:

'Finally, the administration of internal discipline in educational institutions, trade unions, clubs and even professional associations is apt to present special problems. Those who have to make decisions can hardly insulate themselves from the general ethos of their organisation; they are likely to have firm views about the proper regulation of its affairs, and they will often be familiar with the issues and the

c
conduct of the parties before they assume their role as adjudicators. Application of the rules against interest and bias must be tempered with realism; for instance, it may be right to require evidence of actual bias rather than mere likelihood of bias before a decision is set aside by a court.'

d
Again, there may be room for doubt whether it would be open to us to hold the regulations to be invalid on this ground. But, again, we do not think it necessary or desirable to express any opinion on this point. For, in our opinion, the submission is wholly misconceived. There is nothing in the passage from the late Professor de Smith's work which has been cited or elsewhere in that work, nor is there anything in any decided case, which supports the proposition that professional men who are members of the governing body of their profession are incapable of hearing impartially a complaint of professional misconduct against a member of their own profession. Indeed, it has

e
always been accepted that professional men are peculiarly well fitted from their knowledge of the reasons which led to the acceptance by the profession of a code of conduct and from their experience of the difficulties which may confront both the practitioner in observing and the profession in enforcing proper standards of conduct to determine whether there has been a breach of the code of conduct governing the profession and to judge the gravity of it if it is proven. Of course, as Professor de Smith

f
observed, the administration of the internal discipline of a profession does present special problems and it is no doubt wise that those charged with the proper regulation of a profession should be careful in framing the constitution of the governing body and of its disciplinary tribunals to ensure that the task of investigating and presenting a complaint and the task of adjudication on it and, if it is proved, determining the appropriate sentence are in different hands. We have already drawn attention to the provisions of the

g
Senate regulations designed to achieve this separation of function.

It has also been increasingly recognised in recent years that the public has an interest in ensuring that those charged with the regulation of the affairs of a profession should investigate, and in appropriate cases determine, charges of professional misconduct in a fair and impartial way. It is for this reason that reg 20 provides that every disciplinary

h
tribunal must include a lay representative. That was done in this case. But the suggestion that the regulations, if they are to accord with the standards of natural justice and ensure the confidence of the public in the proper regulation of the affairs of a profession, must go further and provide for complaints of professional misconduct to be heard by a tribunal the majority of the members of which are not members of the profession is, in our opinion, inconsistent with principle and authority.

j
Counsel for the appellant referred us, in this connection, to a recent opinion of the European Commission of Human Rights in the case of le Compte v Belgium [1980] 3 ECC 294. In that case three Belgian doctors were in dispute with their professional association. The complaints made against them had been heard by a tribunal the membership of which included a majority of doctors who were also members of the association. The complaints related to behaviour on the part of the three doctors which

was motivated by their opposition to the association and which were not related in any way to clinical practice. One of the questions before the commission was whether the tribunal was an independent and impartial tribunal complying with art 6(1) of the European Convention for the Protection of Human Rights and Fundamental Freedoms (TS 71 (1953); Cmd 8969). The majority of the commission were of opinion that the tribunal did not conform to this standard. The complaint by the Belgian doctors was accordingly referred to the European Court of Human Rights where in due course it will be finally determined. It is the duty of the commission to decide whether a complaint is admissible, not whether it is well founded. However, the majority of the members of the commission made it clear that in their opinion—

> 'the participation of doctors, either on a majority or equal number basis, in the Association's organs, namely the provincial council and the appeal council, does not necessarily imply that these organs are partial when deciding a disciplinary complaint against a doctor.'

They based their opinion that the three doctors had a valid complaint as to the constitution of the disciplinary tribunals that had heard the charges against them on the special circumstances that they—

> 'were the subject of disciplinary proceedings on account of behaviour motivated by their opposition to the Medical Association, as such, and in particular to their obligation to become members of this association.'

Having regard to this particular circumstance they concluded:

> '. . . one cannot automatically assume that the medical members of the disciplinary organs were impartial. On the contrary, it appears that these members had interests very close to those of one of the parties to the proceedings. In this connection the Commission refers to the European Court of Human Rights judgment in *Delcourt v Belgium* ([1980] 1 EHRR 355) where it was conceded that the English legal maxim "justice must not only be done, it must also be seen to be done" also expresses one of the ideas contained in Article 6 of the Convention.'

(See para (78) of the opinion at 320–321.)

In the present case the conduct of the appellant of which complaint was made was not motivated by or related in any way to opposition to the Senate or the Inns of Court. The opinion of the majority supports the view we take that a tribunal which has the duty of hearing a disciplinary complaint against a member of a profession which relates to the question whether he has been guilty of a breach of the code of conduct governing the exercise of that profession cannot be said to be partial merely because the majority of the members of the tribunal are members of that profession.

One member of the commission took a different view. Mr Melchior in a separate opinion said (at 331, para (12)):

> 'In my opinion the requirements of Article 6(1) of the Convention could be completely satisfied in Belgian law if the judicial functions of the Association relating to the determination of civil rights and obligations were taken away and conferred on an objectively impartial court, while the Association retained its powers of initiating "disciplinary" proceedings, investigating the cases and making rules, subject to judicial control of the conformity of these rules with the law in the broad sense.'

But that was the opinion of only one of the eleven members of the commission which heard the complaint.

In our opinion, therefore, the objections raised by counsel for the appellant to the constitution of the disciplinary tribunal are wholly without substance.

The charges which the tribunal found proved fall into three categories. First, the tribunal found that on two separate occasions the appellant gave to a man who had done

a some electrical work at his house a number of visiting cards showing both his chambers and home addresses with telephone numbers without having been asked for them or for the information printed on them, with a view to their distribution and in doing so was guilty of touting for instructions. Second, the tribunal found that the appellant had on two separate occasions without the intervention of a solicitor demanded and accepted a fee from a lay client whom he subsequently represented in court. Third, the tribunal found that the appellant had required a client whom he had represented in the Crown
b Court to execute building and decorating work at his home in lieu of payment for part of his fee for representing him.

Counsel stressed that the appellant came here in 1965, when he was 26 years old, from Bangladesh where he was born and brought up. He took his degree in law at the University of Dacca. He was admitted a student of the Inner Temple in April 1965 and was called in 1970. He did not undertake a pupillage until 1975 and did not commence
c his practice until January 1976. All the offences with which he was charged occurred during his first year of practice or shortly thereafter. Counsel for the appellant pointed out that in Bangladesh there is a single fused profession and that as a necessary consequence there is no rule prohibiting a member of the legal profession from dealing directly with and accepting payment from a member of the public even in relation to a matter in which he is instructed as an advocate. He submitted that given his background
d the appellant might not have appreciated fully the very serious nature of the offences with which he was charged even though, as counsel accepts, he must be taken to have known that the offences, or at least those within the second and third categories, were breaches of the code of conduct governing members of the Bar.

It is possible that if the appellant had admitted his guilt and had put these matters fairly before the tribunal, the tribunal might have been persuaded not to go to the length
e of deciding that the appellant should be disbarred and expelled from his Inn. The tribunal heard the appellant and could have evaluated the sincerity of his explanation. We are in no position to do so, although it is relevant to point out that when the appellant started to practise here he had been here for eleven years and that he had spent five years as a student at his Inn and had completed a year's pupillage. However, this explanation was not put before the tribunal. The case put before the tribunal, in particular in relation
f to the charges in the second and third categories, was that the evidence of the witnesses called to substantiate those charges was fabricated and that they had fabricated this evidence because of the grievance they felt at the fact that his advocacy had not resulted in an acquittal. Any force which this plea by counsel might have had is destroyed by the nature of the defence relied on by the appellant. Although the appellant was not found guilty of all the charges made against him, the misconduct of which he was found guilty,
g in particular bargaining for and accepting a fee from a lay client without the intervention of a solicitor, was of the gravest nature and strikes at the root of the independence of the Bar and of the barrister on which the courts and the public are entitled to rely.

In these circumstances the disciplinary tribunal in our opinion had no alternative but to order that this appellant be disbarred and expelled from his Inn.

We were informed by counsel that the appellant is a polio victim and in addition in
h October 1980 suffered a serious coronary heart attack and will shortly have to return to hospital for major heart surgery. It is, of course, a serious and distressing thing that a member of the Bar should be disbarred and expelled from his Inn and deprived of the prospect of success in his profession. We are not indifferent to the consequences to the appellant. At the same time we have to consider the wider interests of the profession and the public.

j

Appeal dismissed.

Solicitors: *Bernard Sheridan & Co* (for the appellant).

Jacqueline Metcalfe   Barrister.

Tandon v Trustees of Spurgeon's Homes   *a*

COURT OF APPEAL, CIVIL DIVISION
ORMROD, WATKINS AND GRIFFITHS LJJ
20th FEBRUARY 1981

Landlord and tenant – Leasehold enfranchisement – House – House reasonably so called – **b**
Purpose-built shop with flat above in parade of similar premises – Shop occupying greater area
of premises than flat – Whether building 'reasonably . . . called' a house – Leasehold Reform Act
1967, s 2(1).

The premises occupied by the tenant formed part of a small parade of similar premises
which had been designed as purpose-built shops with living accommodation above and *c*
originally let as such in 1881. The premises were subsequently divided into separate
units, 75% of the floor area consisting of a shop on the ground floor and 25% consisting
of a flat on the floor above containing a living room and two bedrooms. The tenant
applied under the Leasehold Reform Act 1967 for a declaration that he was entitled to
acquire the landlord's freehold interest. By s 1(1) of the 1967 Act the right to leasehold
enfranchisement was restricted to the tenant of 'a house' which, by s 2(1)*[a]* of that Act, *d*
included any building which was 'reasonably . . . called' a house. The county court judge
concluded that the premises were reasonably to be called a house within s 2(1) and
accordingly made the declaration sought by the tenant. The landlord appealed.

Held (Ormrod LJ dissenting) – Taking into account the fact that the premises were at all
times a purpose-built shop with living accommodation above and part of a parade of such *e*
shops, the premises could not reasonably be called a house for the purposes of s 2(1) of the
1967 Act, and were properly to be described as a shop with living accommodation
above. Accordingly, the appeal would be allowed (see p 962 *b* to *h*, post).
   Lake v Bennett [1970] 1 All ER 457 distinguished.

Notes   *f*
For the meaning of house for the purpose of the right to leasehold enfranchisement, see
Supplement to 23 Halsbury's Laws (3rd Edn) para 1748, and for cases on the subject, see
31(1) Digest (Reissue) 176, 1489–1491.
   For the Leasehold Reform Act 1967, ss 1, 2, see 18 Halsbury's Statutes (3rd Edn) 634,
636.

g

Cases referred to in judgments
Lake v Bennett [1970] 1 All ER 457, [1970] 1 QB 663, [1970] 2 WLR 355, 21 P & CR 93,
   [1970] RVR 56, CA, 31(1) Digest (Reissue) 176, *1489.*
Peck v Anicar Properties Ltd [1971] 1 All ER 517, 21 P & CR 919, [1970] RVR 738, CA,
   31(1) Digest (Reissue) 176, *1490.*

h

Appeal
The trustees of Spurgeon's Homes, the landlords of premises known as 116 Mitcham
Lane, Streatham, London, appealed against the judgment of his Honour Judge
Coplestone-Boughey given on 11th June 1980 at Wandsworth County Court declaring
that Mr Ajeet Kumar Tandon, the tenant, was entitled under the Leasehold Reform Act
1967 to acquire the freehold of the premises. The grounds of the appeal were that the *j*
judge was wrong in fact and law to hold that he was bound by *Lake v Bennett* [1970] 1 All
ER 457, [1970] 1 QB 663 to find that the premises were a house reasonably so called
within s 2(1) of the 1967 Act and ought to have held on the evidence before him that the

---

a   Section 2(1), so far as material, is set out at p 961 *h*, post

premises could not reasonably be called a house and therefore to have dismissed the
a tenant's application for a declaration that he was entitled to acquire the freehold. The
facts are set out in the judgment of Griffiths LJ.

Patrick Ground for the landlords.
David Parry for the tenant.

b **GRIFFITHS LJ** delivered the first judgment at the invitation of Ormrod LJ. This is an
appeal from a decision of his Honour Judge Coplestone-Boughey, in which he held that
a tenant was entitled to the enfranchisement of his lease pursuant to the provisions of the
Leasehold Reform Act 1967. There is no dispute in this case that the tenant was entitled
to enfranchisement providing that the building in question of which he was tenant could
be said to be a house 'reasonably so called' within the meaning of s 2 of the 1967 Act.
c   I cannot improve on the description of the property contained in the county court
judge's judgment and I now read the description from that judgment:

> 'The property is clearly shown by the agreed plan, description and photographs
> which are before me. [I interpolate to say that the members of this court have had
> the advantage of seeing that plan and photographs.] The site is a long narrow plot
> with a frontage of about 21 feet on Mitcham Lane. The ground floor is a shop
d > fronting the main road and is one of four identical shops with varying shop fronts.
> There is a first floor above containing three effective rooms in the main part of the
> building and a back addition. Behind this building there was originally a narrow
> open path running beside the back addition and behind that an open space leading
> to a two-storey stable which in turn gave access to a rear service road. At some
> uncertain time but certainly before 1962, when Mr Kirkaldie inspected the
e > premises, a roof, treated for London building consent as temporary, was erected
> over the whole of the yard except an outside water closet. This roof runs from and
> is attached to the rear of the main building and extends right back to the stable. The
> doors are arranged so that there is internal communication from the shop in front
> through the original open space to the stable and service road at the back. The
f > interior layout is that at the rear of the main building there is an opening to the
> right which forms the access to the upper part of the building and also to the
> combined bathroom and water closet at ground level. The stairs rise by a right
> angle to the right and open on the first floor. At present the whole of the ground
> floor, including the covered yard and stable, are used as a shop, and the first floor is
> residential. In 1962 the layout was the same but the first floor was used as offices.'

g   We have seen the photographs of the premises and it consists of one of a small parade
of shops. Each shop has living accommodation above it; each consists essentially of a flat
above a shop. The premises now consist, as to their area, of about 75% of the area being
used as a shop, because the whole of the yard which is covered in is now used as storage
for the shop, and about 25% for the modest living accommodation, comprising living
room and two bedrooms on the first floor.
h   I turn now to s 2(1) of the 1967 Act which provides:

> 'For purposes of this Part of this Act, "house" includes any building designed or
> adapted for living in and reasonably so called, notwithstanding that the building is
> not structurally detached, or was or is not solely designed or adapted for living in,
> or is divided horizontally into flats or maisonettes . . .'

j   These premises were originally let by a lease in 1881 and were originally let not solely
as a house but (I quote from the lease) as a 'messuage or dwellinghouse and shop'. So
these are premises which started as a shop with living accommodation.
     The judge was referred to the decision of this court in *Lake v Bennett* [1970] 1 All ER
457, [1970] 1 QB 663. He held that that decision applied to the facts in this case and
concluded it in favour of the tenant. The premises in *Lake v Bennett* were, in my view, of
a markedly different character to the present premises and we have had the advantage of

seeing photographs of them. In *Lake v Bennett* the premises in question consisted of a house in a parade of houses, which, from looking at the photographs, were quite clearly *a* built as a terrace of dwelling houses. It was a house that consisted of a basement, a ground floor and first and second floors. In the course of time the ground floor was converted into a betting shop. The Court of Appeal held that, notwithstanding that the ground floor was now a betting shop, the building as a whole was 'reasonably . . . called' a house, and that conclusion differed from that of the county court judge who tried the case at first instance. The Court of Appeal held that they were free to differ from the *b* judge because, he having found the primary facts, this court was free to say whether or not, on those primary facts, the house fulfilled the condition in s 2(1), namely that it was 'reasonably . . . called' a house.

The judge having found the primary facts in this case, in my view this court is free to apply its own views of whether these premises are reasonably called a house. In approaching this decision, I bear in mind that the right to enfranchisement is only given *c* to householders. A person who lives in a flat has no right to enfranchise the flat. Furthermore, I bear in mind that Parliament does provide protection for those who carry on businesses and when their leases end they can apply, under the relevant statutory provision, for a new lease, and if they cannot agree with their landlords then there are provisions for the court to fix a fair rent for the parties.

In *Lake v Bennett*, although the court in that case, on those facts, was satisfied that that *d* building was reasonably to be called a house, Lord Denning MR realised that in future other difficult questions might arise in regard to other buildings. I, for my part, think that this is such a case. I am bound to say that, looking at the photographs and taking into account that this was at all times a purpose-built shop with living accommodation above it and part of a parade of such shops, I do not think that it can reasonably be called a house. I share the view of the very experienced surveyor who gave evidence before the *e* judge and who said that it was not properly to be described as a house but as a shop with living accommodation above it.

I appreciate that, in the course of their judgments in *Lake v Bennett*, both Salmon and Cross LJJ pointed out that there might be a case in which one person would describe the building as a shop with living accommodation above it but equally another person could reasonably describe it as a house with the ground floor made into a shop. Of course, *f* there will be such borderline cases, but in my view this case is not a borderline case and for my part I do not think that these premises could reasonably be described as a house. Although the judge, I accept, applied the right test, and I take into account that he said that he would have come to the conclusion, quite apart from *Lake v Bennett*, that it could reasonably be called a house, I take the view that, on the facts that he has found, he came to the wrong conclusion. Accordingly, for my part, I would, for those reasons, allow this *g* appeal.

I should perhaps just add that we were also referred to *Peck v Anicar Properties Ltd* [1971] 1 All ER 517, where, in respect of premises which appear to me to be almost identical to those in *Lake v Bennett*, it was assumed without argument that the premises were a house. I do not think that case carries the matter any further than the authority of *Lake v Bennett*.   *h*

For those reasons, I would allow this appeal.

WATKINS LJ. I agree and have nothing to add.

ORMROD LJ. I arrive at the opposite conclusion in this matter. The definition in s 2(1) of the Leasehold Reform Act 1967 is not at all easy to construe. It begins by saying *j* that '"house" includes any building designed or adapted for living in', it goes on to say 'and reasonably so called', and then proceeds with the words 'notwithstanding that the building is not structurally detached, or was or is not solely designed or adapted for living in'. So Parliament plainly contemplated that a house within the meaning of this Act might well be a house with a double user, partly for living in, partly for some other

purpose. So the fact that this house was originally built in 1881 as a dwelling house and
a shop does not, in my judgment, take it outside the definition in s 2(1).

It seems to me that one has to look at the building as a whole and answer the question,
allowing for the fact it is used for two quite different purposes, whether it still can
reasonably be called a house. That seems to me to introduce a degree of flexibility into
the application of the definition, which is highly unusual in a statute but, of course, is
designed to enable the court responsible for making the decision to arrive at what one
b might call a broadly sensible conclusion without being tied down by a technical
definition.

Consequently, I have some considerable difficulty in overruling the judge who, having
seen the property and having considered the matter and applied, as I think, the right
tests, came to the independent conclusion, as he plainly did because he says in terms:
'Even if the matter were free from authority, I should conclude that the present building
c was reasonably called a house.' I find great difficulty in differing from him on facts as
narrow as these in the present case.

To my mind the approach which this court adopted in *Lake v Bennett* [1970] 1 All ER
457, [1970] 1 QB 663 makes it still more difficult to hold that these particular premises
are not reasonably described as a 'house'. The approach which the court adopted in *Lake
v Bennett* seems to have been in accordance with the definition, because the court began
d by saying that, looking at the premises in *Lake v Bennett*, for many statutory purposes the
building would be called a 'house'. One knows that there is, in other statutes, a definition
of a 'house' which is very wide indeed. The court construed the words 'and reasonably
so called' as, in a sense, words of limitation, starting from the assumption that, without
those words, there could be no doubt but that the property in *Lake v Bennett* was a
house. That being the approach that this court adopted in *Lake v Bennett*, I feel
e considerable difficulty in adopting a different approach in this particular case.

If that is the right way of approaching it, then I find myself unable to disagree with the
judge's view. I accept that it is open to anybody to adopt the surveyor's description of this
property and I bear in mind that in the report of *Lake v Bennett*, which includes an extract
from the county court judge's judgment in that case, the judge said ([1970] 1 QB 663 at
665):

f

> 'I have formed the definite opinion that it would not be called a "house" in
> ordinary speech in the present century. A person looking for a house to buy would
> be surprised to be directed to 61, Gayton Road. On seeing it he would say: "I asked
> for a house and they have sent me to a shop. I have been misled".'

No doubt exactly the same point can be made on the facts of the present case.

g   So I feel the greatest diffidence in distinguishing this case from *Lake v Bennett*. There
are, of course, certain distinctions. First, there is the historical distinction that in *Lake v
Bennett* the property had started life unquestionably as a house and had been subsequently
converted to use as a shop on the ground floor. It is fair comment that both Salmon and
Cross LJJ used language which indicated that the fact of the conversion was not irrelevant
to their minds. But the county court judge in this case dealt with that point and dealt
h with it, I think, correctly. The only other distinction from *Lake v Bennett*, it seems to me,
is to say that in this case the area of the property which was used as a shop was very much
greater. But that seems to introduce a quantitative consideration which could be
extremely difficult. The fact which influences my mind very much is that, looking at
the photographs we have been supplied with, looking at these present premises from the
point of view of somebody standing in the street and comparing the appearance of these
j premises with the appearance of the premises which were the subject matter of *Lake v
Bennett*, it seems a little bizarre to hold that the premises at 61 Gayton Road in *Lake v
Bennett* and the premises at 41 Lee High Road in another case were houses and yet that
the present premises are not reasonably called a house.

I think that Parliament has left the decision on the fine distinctions in this type of case
to the trial judge and I am not prepared to differ from his conclusion in this court,

although I agree with Watkins and Griffiths LJJ that, starting afresh and without *Lake v Bennett* as a guide, I think I should have come to the same conclusion as they do. But I do *a* not think that this case can properly be distinguished from *Lake v Bennett*. Therefore, I would dismiss the appeal.

Appeal allowed. Leave to appeal to the House of Lords granted.

Solicitors: *Pothecary & Barratt* (for the landlords); *Radia & Co, Kilburn* (for the tenant).　*b*

Avtar S Virdi Esq　Barrister.

R & T Thew Ltd v Reeves
Reeves v R & T Thew Ltd and another

c

COURT OF APPEAL, CIVIL DIVISION
LORD DENNING MR, DUNN AND O'CONNOR LJJ
2nd, 6th, 7th, APRIL, 6th MAY 1981

d

Legal aid – Unassisted person's costs out of legal aid fund – Costs incurred by unassisted party – Costs incurred in proceedings between him and party receiving legal aid – Costs of counterclaim where defendant legally aided – Defendant admitting claim but pleading set off of counterclaim against claim – Application for legal aid for defendant limited to defence of claim – No application for legal aid to prosecute counterclaim – Legal aid certificate giving authority only to defend claim – Certificate amended shortly before hearing to cover counterclaim – Action settled *e* *in plaintiff's favour – Plaintiff applying for order for costs of counterclaim out of legal aid fund – Whether judge entitled to hold original certificate issued containing a mistake and that it covered counterclaim – Whether certificate conclusive of proceedings covered by it – Legal Aid Act 1974, s 13(1) – Legal Aid (General) Regulations 1971 (SI 1971 No 62), regs 2(2), 9(1).*

Legal aid – Unassisted person's costs out of legal aid fund – Severe financial hardship – Company *f* *– Whether company able to suffer severe financial hardship – Legal Aid Act 1974, s 13(3)(b).*

By a writ dated 31st January 1977 the plaintiff company, a small private company of which a husband and wife were the sole shareholders, brought an action against the defendant to recover a debt. In March 1977 the defendant delivered a defence, in which he admitted the debt, and counterclaimed for rescission of a contract between the parties and damages for fraud and negligence. The husband was joined personally as a defendant *g* to the counterclaim. The plaintiff company responded by amending its statement of claim to include a claim for sums payable under the contract. The defendant then amended his defence to plead that his counterclaim be set off against the plaintiff company's claims. On 16th August 1977 the defendant applied for legal aid. His application, which was made by an inexperienced articled clerk, stated that the *h* proceedings for which legal aid was sought were 'to defend in court proceedings commenced already by the . . . writ of [31st January 1977]', and did not refer to the counterclaim. The papers appended to the application included copies of the defence and counterclaim and also a synopsis of the case prepared by the local Law Society which indicated that the real issue between the parties arose from the counterclaim and that the defendant admitted the plaintiff company's claim for the debt. On 23rd August 1977 *j* the legal aid committee decided to grant the application and on 21st November 1977 a legal aid certificate was issued to the defendant to defend the action to recover the debt. The hearing of the action was fixed for 10th March 1980. Shortly before that date the defendant's solicitors realised that the certificate did not cover the counterclaim and on 6th March they applied by letter to the local Law Society for an extension of the

certificate to cover the counterclaim. On 7th March the secretary of the local Law
a Society, acting under his delegated powers, granted the application and certified that the
legal aid certificate had been amended to cover prosecution of the counterclaim against
the plaintiff company. The amended certificate did not cover prosecution of the
counterclaim against the husband personally. Soon after the commencement of the
hearing of the action the proceedings were settled on terms, the effect of which was that
the plaintiff company and the husband succeeded on the claim and counterclaim. The
b company, which had no liquid assets and a substantial bank overdraft, and the husband
applied under s 13(1)^d of the Legal Aid Act 1974 for payment out of the legal aid fund of
the costs they had incurred in the counterclaim since 21st November 1977. The judge
held that, although the certificate issued on 21st November 1977 on its face covered only
the defence to the claim for the debt, the documents enclosed with the application
showed that that was a mistake and that the application and the certificate were intended
c to cover the counterclaim and joinder of the husband as a party to the counterclaim. The
judge in effect rectified the mistake by holding that the certificate issued in November
1977 covered the counterclaim and joinder of the husband as a party to it. He further
held that the counterclaim was a proceeding instituted by the party receiving legal aid
(the defendant) which had been decided in favour of the unassisted parties (the plaintiff
company and the husband), that it was just and equitable that their costs of the
d counterclaim should be provided out of public funds, and that both the company and the
husband would suffer severe financial hardship within s 13(3)(b) if an order was not made
under s 13(1). Accordingly, he made an order for payment out of the legal aid fund of
the company's and the husband's costs incurred since November 1977. The Law Society
appealed, submitting that the judge had no jurisdiction to make the order, because (i) in
regard to the husband personally, the defendant had never received legal aid to prosecute
e the counterclaim against him, (ii) the certificate as issued in November 1977 did not
cover legal aid to prosecute the counterclaim and therefore legal aid to prosecute it
against the plaintiff company was not received until 7th March 1980, and (iii) in any
event, the company was not entitled to recover the costs of the counterclaim incurred
since 7th March 1980 because, under the taxation rule that costs of a counterclaim were
to be treated as costs in the claim, the costs incurred since 7th March 1980 were costs in
f the claim and not costs of the counterclaim and therefore did not qualify for an order
under s 13(1). The Law Society conceded that both the company and the husband would
suffer severe financial hardship if an order was not made in their favour under s 13(1).
The plaintiffs and the husband contended that they should not be penalised by a mistake
made by the defendant in his application for legal aid.

g **Held** – The appeal would be allowed for the following reasons—
    (1) (Lord Denning MR dissenting) The legal aid scheme contained in the 1974 Act
and the regulations made thereunder showed that the legal aid certificate was the corner-

---

a   Section 13, so far as material, provides:
        '(1) Where a party receives legal aid in connection with any proceedings between him and a
h   party not receiving legal aid (in this and section 14 below referred to as "the unassisted party") and
    those proceedings are finally decided in favour of the unassisted party, the court by which the
    proceedings are so decided may, subject to the provisions of this section, make an order for the
    payment to the unassisted party out of the legal aid fund of the whole or any part of the costs
    incurred by him in those proceedings.
        '(2) An order may be made under this section in respect of any costs if (and only if) the court is
    satisfied that it is just and equitable in all the circumstances that provision for those costs should
j   be made out of public funds. . . .
        '(3) Without prejudice to subsection (2) above, no order shall be made under this section in
    respect of costs incurred in a court of first instance, whether by that court or by any appellate court,
    unless—(a) the proceedings in the court of first instance were instituted by the party receiving
    legal aid; and (b) the court is satisfied that the unassisted party will suffer severe financial hardship
    unless the order is made . . .'

stone of the scheme and that the extent of the legal assistance granted to a litigant was to be derived from the certificate, which in turn controlled and defined the rights of the *a* unassisted party under the scheme. An applicant was under a duty to apply for the appropriate certificate, since, in general, a legal aid committee was required to grant legal aid in accordance with the application for legal aid and was under no duty to go behind the application to decide what proceedings were to be covered by the certificate. Furthermore, on the true construction of the Act and the regulations the judge was not entitled to look behind the certificate to see whether the authority conferred by the *b* certificate was wider than that shown on its face. A mistake in a certificate could only be amended by the area committee, in accordance with reg 9(1)[b] of the Legal Aid (General) Regulations 1971, and could not be enlarged or varied under reg 2(2)[c] of those regulations which applied only to questions of the validity of a certificate. It followed that the certificate issued in November 1977 was conclusive as to the proceedings which it covered and that it did not, therefore, cover prosecution of the counterclaim prior to 7th *c* March 1980. In any event the certificate only covered prosecution from that date of the counterclaim against the plaintiff company and not against the husband personally (see p 980 *h* to p 981 *a e f* and *h*, p 982 *b* to *h*, p 983 *b h*, p 984 *e* to *j* and p 986 *g h*, post); *Lacey v W Silk & Son Ltd* [1951] 2 All ER 128, *Wallace v Freeman Heating Co Ltd* [1955] 1 All ER 418 and *Francis v Francis and Dickerson* [1955] 3 All ER 836 applied.

(2) A limited company could suffer 'severe financial hardship' for the purposes of *d* s 13(3)(*b*) of the 1974 Act, and since the company might have to go into liquidation if it had to bear the costs of the litigation, the judge had been entitled to find, and the Law Society had been right to concede, that the plaintiff company would suffer severe financial hardship if its costs were not paid out of the legal aid fund. Accordingly, the court had jurisdiction to order payment of the company's costs out of the legal aid fund but (per Dunn and O'Connor LJJ), having regard to the terms of the certificate, only in *e* respect of the company's costs incurred after 7th March 1980 and not in respect of the husband personally at all (see p 973 *j* to p 974 *a*, p 983 *d e h* and p 984 *b c*, post).

(3) Since the costs of the company incurred since 7th March 1980 could be divided between the claim and the counterclaim the costs of the counterclaim were not required to be treated solely as costs in the claim, and accordingly costs incurred by the company on the counterclaim could properly be taxed as such and an order made in respect of *f* them under s 13(1) of the 1974 Act. Accordingly (per Dunn and O'Connor LJJ), the company was entitled to recover from the legal aid fund the costs of the counterclaim incurred after 7th March 1980 (see p 975 *f*, p 976 *e*, p 981 *c*, p 983 *g h*, p 984 *j* and p 986 *f* to *h*, post); *Millican v Tucker* [1980] 1 All ER 1083 distinguished.

Per O'Connor LJ. An area committee has no power to make an amendment to a legal aid certificate on the ground of mistake which would have the effect of backdating legal *g* aid so as to affect the right to costs which has accrued in the meantime (see p 984 *h j*, post).

Notes

For the award of costs to an unassisted party out of the legal aid fund, see Supplement to 30 Halsbury's Laws (3rd Edn) para 933A.

For the Legal Aid Act 1974, s 13, see 44 Halsbury's Statutes (3rd Edn) 1053.

For the Legal Aid (General) Regulations 1971, regs 2, 9, see 5 Halsbury's Statutory *h* Instruments (Fourth Reissue) 322, 333.

As from 1st January 1981 regs 2 and 9 of the 1971 regulations have been replaced by reg 50 and by regs 10 to 14, 16 and 17, respectively, of the Legal Aid (General) Regulations 1980, SI 1980 No 1894.

Cases referred to in judgments

Atlas Metal Co v Miller [1898] 2 QB 500, 67 LJQB 815, 79 LT 5, CA, 40 Digest (Repl) 473, 577.

---

b   Regulation 9(1), so far as material, is set out at p 981 *d* and *g*, post
c   Regulation 2(2) is set out at p 980 *a*, post

Boys v Chaplin [1968] 1 All ER 283, [1968] 2 QB 1, [1968] 2 WLR 328, CA; *affd on other*
a   *grounds* [1969] 2 All ER 1085, [1969] 3 WLR 322, [1969] 2 Lloyd's Rep 487, HL,
Digest (Cont Vol C) 594, *709a*.

Christie v Platt [1921] 2 KB 17, 90 LJKB 555, 124 LT 649, CA, 40 Digest (Repl) 472, *571*.

Cinema Press Ltd v Pictures & Pleasures Ltd [1945] 1 All ER 440, [1945] KB 356, 114 LJKB
368, 172 LT 295, CA, 51 Digest (Repl) 926, *4691*.

Federal Commerce and Navigation Ltd v Molena Alpha Inc, The Nanfri, The Benfri, The Lorfri
b   [1978] 3 All ER 1066, [1978] QB 927, [1978] 3 WLR 309, [1978] 2 Lloyd's Rep 132,
CA; *affd* [1979] 1 All ER 307, [1979] AC 757, [1978] 3 WLR 991, [1979] 1 Lloyd's Rep
201, HL, Digest (Cont Vol E) 109, *3036a*.

Francis v Francis and Dickerson [1955] 3 All ER 836, [1956] P 87, [1955] 3 WLR 973,
Digest (Cont Vol A) 778, *5364c*.

Gilbert-Ash (Northern) Ltd v Modern Engineering (Bristol) Ltd [1973] 3 All ER 195, [1974] AC
c   689, [1973] 3 WLR 421, 72 LGR 1, HL, Digest (Cont Vol D) 86, *419d*.

Hamilton v Farrer (1831) 8 Bing 10, 1 Moo & S 143, 1 LJCP 5, 131 ER 303, 17 Digest
(Reissue) 406, *1706*.

Hanlon v Law Society [1980] 1 All ER 763, [1980] 2 WLR 756, CA; *on appeal* [1980] 2 All
ER 199, [1980] 2 WLR 756, HL.

Hatton v Harris [1892] AC 547, 62 LJPC 24, 67 LT 722, 1 R 1, HL, 50 Digest (Repl) 531,
d   *1977*.

Henriksens Rederi A/S v PHZ Rolimpex, The Brede [1973] 3 All ER 589, [1974] QB 233,
[1973] 3 WLR 556, [1973] 2 Lloyd's Rep 333, CA, Digest (Cont Vol D) 829, *3514a*.

Lacey v W Silk & Son Ltd [1951] 2 All ER 128, 50 Digest (Repl) 489, *1716*.

Lawrie v Lees (1881) 7 App Cas 19, 51 LJ Ch 209, 46 LT 210, HL, 33 Digest (Repl) 667,
1134.

e   *Lim Poh Choo v Camden and Islington Area Health Authority* [1979] 1 All ER 332, [1979] QB
196, [1978] 3 WLR 895, QBD and CA; *varied* [1979] 2 All ER 910, [1980] AC 174,
[1979] 3 WLR 44, HL, Digest (Cont Vol E) 457, *1285a*.

Manley v Law Society [1981] 1 All ER 401, [1981] 1 WLR 335, CA.

Medway Oil and Storage Co Ltd v Continental Contractors Ltd [1929] AC 88, [1928] All ER
Rep 330, 98 LJKB 148, 140 LT 98, HL, 40 Digest (Repl) 471, *565*.

f   *Megarity v D J Ryan & Sons Ltd (No 2)* [1981] 1 All ER 641, [1981] 2 WLR 335, HL.

Millican v Tucker [1980] 1 All ER 1083, [1980] 1 WLR 640, CA.

Nowotnik v Nowotnik (Hyatt intervening) [1965] 3 All ER 167, [1967] P 83, [1965] 3 WLR
920, CA, Digest (Cont Vol B) 370, *5365e*.

Padwick v Scott, Re Scott's Estate (1876) 2 Ch D 736, 3 Char Pr Cas 107, 45 LJ Ch 350, 50
Digest (Repl) 80, *665*.

g   *Pearlman (Veneers) SA (Pty) Ltd v Bartels* [1954] 3 All ER 659, [1954] 1 WLR 1457, CA, 50
Digest (Repl) 99, *815*.

Price v Mann [1942] 1 All ER 453, 58 TLR 197, CA, 31(2) Digest (Reissue) 896, *7424*.

Salmon v Duncombe (1886) 11 App Cas 627, 55 LJPC 69, 55 LT 446, PC, 44 Digest (Repl)
266, *914*.

Saner v Bilton (1879) 11 Ch D 416, 48 LJ Ch 545, 40 LT 314, 40 Digest (Repl) 473, *572*.

h   *Storer v Wright* [1981] 1 All ER 1015, [1981] 2 WLR 208, CA.

Uvedale v Halfpenny (1723) 2 P Wms 151, 24 ER 677, 17 Digest (Reissue) 406, *1704*.

Wallace v Freeman Heating Co Ltd [1955] 1 All ER 418, [1953] 1 WLR 172, 50 Digest
(Repl) 498, *1769*.

Whittam v W J Daniel & Co Ltd [1961] 3 All ER 796, [1962] 1 QB 271, [1961] 3 WLR 1123,
CA, 32 Digest (Reissue) 727, *5269*.

j   *Whitehouse v Jordan* [1980] 1 All ER 650, CA; *affd* [1981] 1 All ER 267, [1981] 1 WLR
246, HL.

Cases also cited

Box (W R) v Midland Bank Ltd [1980] Court of Appeal Transcript 926.

Hanak v Green [1958] 2 All ER 141, [1958] 2 QB 9, CA.

Hanning v Maitland [1969] 3 All ER 1558, [1969] 1 WLR 1885, CA.
Hanning v Maitland (No 2) [1970] 1 All ER 812, [1970] 1 QB 580, CA.   *a*
Miller v Littner [1979] Court of Appeal Transcript 717.
Mills v Mills [1963] 2 All ER 237, [1963] P 329, CA.
Practice Direction [1965] 3 All ER 732, [1966] 1 WLR 23.
Wilkinson v Wilkinson [1962] 1 All ER 922, [1963] P 1, CA.

Interlocutory appeal   *b*
The Law Society appealed against an order of his Honour Judge Curtis, sitting as an
official referee of the High Court at Oldham, dated 25th July and 7th August 1980,
ordering that so much of the costs of the plaintiffs, R & T Thew Ltd and Robert Thew,
as were incurred by them in proceedings between them and the defendant, Alan Reeves,
should be paid to them out of the legal aid fund pursuant to s 13 of the Legal Aid Act
1974, together with the costs of their application for such order, as from 21st November *c*
1977, the date when a legal aid certificate was first issued to the defendant. The facts are
set out in the judgment of Lord Denning MR.

Duncan Matheson for the Law Society.
Charles Bloom for the plaintiff.

                                                                                        d

                                                                    Cur adv vult

6th May. The following judgments were read.

LORD DENNING MR. Much of the litigation today is dominated by legal aid. The   *e*
state subsidises one side by giving him unlimited financial assistance. It pays his lawyers'
fees almost in full. It leaves the other side, who is often of very moderate means, entirely
unassisted. He has to bear his own costs with no recourse against the other side even
when he wins. This is a grave injustice to the unassisted party. Parliament has done
something to remedy it but the remedy is far from adequate. This case will show up the
defects in the statute and in the regulations. It looks very much as if a hard-working *f*
husband and wife will be ruined by the fact that the other side was granted legal aid.
     The case will, I hope, also bring home to the profession the responsibilities which they
owe not only to their own client for whom they get legal aid but also to the other side
who is unassisted. Unless carefully watched, legal aid may be used unfairly to harass the
other side who is not assisted.

                                                                                        g
R & T THEW LTD
     Like many other young men coming back from the war, Robert Thew in 1947 set up
in business. That was 34 years ago. It was in the photographic business. At Middleton
in the Manchester area. Robert Thew and his wife made it into quite a good business.
They formed a small private company. They called it R & T Thew Ltd. Robert Thew
and his wife were the sole shareholders. Their sons grew up and joined them in it. In *h*
turn they made it into two separate businesses in adjoining premises. Both were owned
by the company R & T Thew Ltd.

(i) *The photographic business*
     One business undertook the usual activities of photographers in a commercial town.
They took photographs of weddings, works presentations and local functions of all *j*
kinds. I will call it 'the photographic business'.

(ii) *The processing business*
     The other business developed films and processed them, made prints, both in colour
and in black and white, and so forth. They did this work not only for their own
photographic business but also for other professional photographers to whom they
charged commercial rates. I will call it 'the processing business'.

(iii) Sale of the photographic business

a
In 1975 R & T Thew Ltd decided to sell the photographic business but to keep the processing business. A local photographer called Alan Reeves was keen to buy. He was aged 35 and knew all about the businesses because he lived in the place. On 9th November 1975 the parties entered into an agreement for sale. R & T Thew Ltd sold the photographic business to Mr Reeves for £14,000, of which £5,500 was payable almost at once and the balance of £8,500 by 60 equal monthly instalments of £141·66
b commencing in November 1976. Mr Reeves paid the £5,500 but, as I will relate, he never paid any of the monthly instalments.

After the sale Mr Reeves took possession of the photographic business. R & T Thew Ltd continued the processing business. Mr Reeves sent his films to the processing business to be developed and processed. But unfortunately Mr Reeves turned out not to be a good payer. He fell into arrear with his payments to the processing business. By
c November 1976 he owed R & T Thew Ltd £849·04 for this processing work.

(iv) A cock-and-bull story

On 31st January 1977 R & T Thew Ltd issued a writ for £849·04 for the work done. There was no possible defence to this claim. But Mr Reeves went to his solicitors and told them a cock-and-bull story. At least we now know that it was a cock-and-bull story. He
d put it up in order to avoid paying his just debts. He alleged that he had been induced to buy the photographic business by fraud. Robert Thew, he said, had made false representations about the takings and profits of the photographic business. Mr Reeves's solicitors accepted this cock-and-bull story at its face value. Mr Reeves was their client and they had to accept his word. They put it before counsel and asked whether they should start a separate cross-action or put in a counterclaim in the existing action. Counsel advised that a counterclaim be made, and that Robert Thew personally should
e be made a defendant to the counterclaim. So on 28th March 1977 the solicitors for Mr Reeves delivered a defence and counterclaim, joining Robert Thew as a defendant to the counterclaim. In it they admitted the £849·04 was owing for the processing and developing; but they said Mr Reeves had a counterclaim for fraud on the photographic purchase. Notice that this was pure counterclaim. It was not available as equitable set-
f off because it arose out of an entirely separate transaction on the photographic business. It had nothing to do with the £849·04 owing to the processing business. It ought not to have been made by counterclaim but only by cross-action (see s 39(1)(b) of the Supreme Court of Judicature (Consolidation) Act 1925 and *Padwick v Scott, Re Scott's Estate* (1876) 2 Ch D 736). But, as no objection was taken to it being made by counterclaim, we must let it pass as a point of procedure only.

g
(v) The disturbing counterclaim

This counterclaim was most disturbing to R & T Thew Ltd and Mr Robert Thew. Here they were, simple creditors seeking to recover the sum due to them, and they were faced with a counterclaim for fraud. They were good honest folk who had never been treated like that before. They went to their solicitors and took their advice. They were
h not eligible for legal aid. A limited company is not allowed legal aid. So they had to bear all their own solicitors' costs themselves.

(vi) The amendment of the writ

On the advice of their solicitors, on 8th August 1977, R & T Thew Ltd amended their writ. It was done in order to meet the counterclaim for fraud. Mr Reeves had defaulted
j on all the instalments on the sale of the photographic business. He had paid none of them. Ten instalments were due of £141·66 a month. This default was so grave that the whole of the balance had become due. So R & T Thew Ltd claimed the balance of £8,500 payable under the sale of the photographic business. Although framed as an amendment to the writ, it was in truth a response to the counterclaim. It was in law just the same as if Mr Reeves had brought, as he should have done, a cross-action for fraud on the sale of the photographic business against R & T Thew Ltd and Robert Thew; and as if, in reply, R & T Thew Ltd had claimed the balance due on the sale.

(vii) *The application for legal aid*

It was at this stage that Mr Reeves sought legal aid. He could not pay any legal costs. So if his counterclaim for fraud was to be pursued, it had to be done on legal aid. His solicitors decided to apply for legal aid on his behalf. They entrusted it to a young articled clerk. He had passed the examination but had not yet been admitted as a solicitor. He had no experience of applying for legal aid. He had never applied for it before. So he went to the Law Society in Manchester where they deal with legal aid. He saw a young lady. She produced the forms. She explained them to him and told him how to fill them in. He asked her questions, such as 'What do I put in here?', and she told him. She told him that solicitors usually put in 'To defend' and so forth.

I am afraid that, between the two of them, these two young people bungled the whole thing. They made a complete botch of the application form. For instance, the application referred to two writs (one copy writ of 31st January 1977 and one amended writ of 8th August 1977), whereas there was only one writ of 31st January 1977 which was amended on 8th August 1977. And the articled clerk put in that legal aid was sought 'to defend' whereas it was obviously sought for the counterclaim for fraud, for that was the only matter in dispute.

In the most important space, the young articled clerk filled in this as the application:

'to defend in court proceedings commenced already by the below mentioned writs of 31.1.1977 & 8.8.1977.'

But fortunately he did append all the papers. These would show the legal aid authorities what the case was all about.

These were:

'1. Court Writ of 31.1.1977.
'2. Copy Defence and Counterclaim. [This included Robert Thew as defendant to the counterclaim as well as R & T Thew Ltd.]
'3. Copy Amended Writ of 8.8.77.
'4. Copy Instructions to Counsel referred to Writ of 31.1.77.
'N.B. The papers referred to in the above-mentioned Instructions to Counsel are available if required from my below mentioned solicitor.'

The application form had to be signed, of course, by the client Mr Reeves. So the articled clerk got Mr Reeves to sign it. Mr Reeves, no doubt, thought that it covered all the proceedings thenceforward in the action. It was dated 16th August 1977.

(viii) *The synopsis*

One of the clerks in the Law Society then prepared a synopsis for submission to the legal aid committee. It shows that he understood full well that the sole dispute was on the counterclaim for fraud and that legal aid was sought for that dispute. This synopsis is so important that I set out the material parts here:

'On the Advice of Counsel, which is not submitted with the Application as Advice was given orally at a conference, the Applicant has issued a Defence and Counter-claim. The basis of his counter-claim is that prior to the acceptance of the Contract, fraudulent misrepresentation was made as to the projected net profit of the business, or alternatively this information was made negligently. The Counter-claim goes on to say "Robert Thew had access to all information necessary to ascertain the true annual tradings of the said business and failed to observe the inaccuracy of the figures set out in the [said] document and/or take any effective steps to trace the same and/or ensure that the same were compiled on the basis of accurate information. Further and in the alternative, the said representations were incorporated in and became the terms of the said Agreement, or alternatively constituted a Warranty collateral to and in consideration thereof, and by the falsity of the said representations the Plaintiffs and/or the said Thew are in breach of the

Agreement and/or the said Warranty ... (as a result of this) the Defendant has
suffered loss and damage and is entitled to rescind the said Agreement."
'The Applicant admits being indebted to the Plaintiffs for the sum claimed, but
seeks to use his Counter-claim to set off and extinguish the Plaintiffs' claim.

DOCUMENTS SUBMITTED: Copy Pleadings.
                        Copy Instructions to Counsel.'

(ix) *Offer of legal aid*
I would repeat the last sentence of the synopsis: 'The Applicant admits being indebted
to the Plaintiffs for the sum claimed, but seeks to use his Counter-claim to set off and
extinguish the Plaintiffs' claim.' That shows plainly that the application was for legal aid
for the counterclaim.
On 23rd August 1977 the legal aid committee decided to grant the application subject
to the determination of the financial resources of Mr Reeves. These were ascertained.
His contribution was fixed at £54·50. Then an offer of legal aid was made. I was sorry
to say that the clerk who drew up the form of offer bungled it also. He made a complete
botch of it. Instead of giving legal aid for the counterclaim (as the synopsis showed), the
clerk seems to have copied out the botched application of the articled clerk. Under the
heading 'Description of legal aid offered', the clerk wrote:

'TO DEFEND PROCEEDINGS IN THE HIGH COURT OF JUSTICE, QUEENS BENCH DIVISION,
OLDHAM DISTRICT REGISTRY, NO. 77 R 32 BETWEEN R. & T. THEW LIMITED (PLAINTIFF) AND
ALAN REEVES (DEFENDANT).'

The offer was subject to the payment by Mr Reeves of £54·50 as a maximum
contribution. He accepted the offer and paid £54·50. The certificate was issued on 21st
November 1977.

(x) *The effect of the certificate*
No one treated the certificate as confined to the 'defence' by Mr Reeves. He had no
defence to the action. Legal aid would not have been granted for a defence which did not
exist. Everyone treated the certificate as extending to the 'counterclaim' by Mr Reeves
for fraud on the sale of a business, a fraud which was charged against Mr Robert Thew
and R & T Thew Ltd as defendants to the counterclaim. I am quite sure that Mr Reeves's
solicitors treated the legal aid as extending to the counterclaim. They went to great
expense on the counterclaim. They prepared very voluminous particulars. They
prepared a Scott schedule. They made it so detailed that the action was referred to an
official referee. The solicitors for Mr Reeves would get not a penny for all this work
unless they got it from the legal aid fund, by virtue of the legal aid certificate.
The judge accepted this view of the documents. He said that the wording of the
application by the articled clerk was 'slipshod', but he added:

'... there was also some responsibility on the Law Society's side to ensure that the
certificate should cover what it was intended to cover. Somebody must have read
the documents which accompanied the application. That person must have
appreciated that what was being applied for was legal aid to cover the whole
proceedings, not only the proceedings brought by the plaintiffs against Reeves, but
also the proceedings brought by Reeves against the plaintiffs and Thew. That was
what was intended by the grant of the application.'

So we reach the cause of all the trouble. The young articled clerk botched up the
application, so that it did not correctly state the description of the legal aid desired. This
led to the certificate itself being botched up by the clerk of the legal aid committee; so
that in turn it did not correctly state the description of the legal aid that was granted.
Can this botching up be rectified?

(xi) *The mistake is discovered*

From 21st November 1977 (when the legal aid certificate was granted) onwards *a* everyone acted as if the legal aid granted to Mr Reeves covered the whole proceedings. Mr Reeves's solicitors made all the expensive interlocutory proceedings on that basis. So did Mr Thew's solicitors. The trial was fixed to start on Monday, 10th March 1980. Then suddenly on the previous Thursday, 6th March, the young articled clerk (who by this time had been admitted as a solicitor) happened to look at the legal aid certificate. At once he took alarm. It only said 'to defend'. It did not say 'and counterclaim'. He *b* telephoned the Law Society and was told, 'You had better put in an amended application'.

On that Thursday briefs had not been delivered to counsel. The young solicitor (as he now was) was so perturbed that he told all concerned: 'Hold everything. Do not deliver briefs until the position is cleared.'

The clerks at the Law Society were very accommodating. They must have realised that a mistake had been made. They did their best to rectify it. They did it at once *c* without reference to the committee.

(xii) *An amendment is made*

On that Thursday, 6th March, the young solicitor wrote to the Law Society:

'Further to our telephone conversation this morning we write to confirm our application on behalf of our above-named client for an extension of the above *d* numbered legal aid certificate so that the certificate will cover our client's counterclaim in the matter.'

The Law Society lost no time. On the next day, Friday, 7th March, they replied:

'This is to certify that the legal aid certificate issued to the above named has been amended as follows:—By adding the words "and counterclaim in" after the word *e* "defend" in the description of the legal aid.'

(xiii) *The effect of the amendment*

No doubt an amendment of substance cannot be backdated. But this was not an amendment of substance. It was only an amendment of a verbal slip. Everyone knew *f* that it was a slip. The amendment was made with the consent of all concerned. As such it dated back to the original certificate. The judge said: 'The amendment of 7th March 1980 should in my view be regarded as having been made nunc pro tunc so that it relates back to November 1977.'

I entirely agree. It is the sensible solution to the whole problem.

As soon as that amendment was received, the solicitors for both sides delivered their *g* briefs. On the Friday for the case to start on the Monday. Everyone thought that everything was now all right.

(xiv) *The hearing of the action*

The case started on Monday, 10th March 1980. It soon became obvious, says the judge, that Mr Thew was 'a thoroughly honest man who had given truthful information *h* about the business and had produced genuine records'. The solicitors for Mr Reeves realised this. They could see that Mr Reeves could not possibly establish his case of fraud or misrepresentation against Mr Thew. They negotiated for a settlement. In the negotiations they were in a strong position. It did not hurt Mr Reeves to continue the case because all his costs were being paid by the legal aid fund. But it did hurt R & T Thew Ltd because they had to pay their own costs out of their own pocket. The longer *j* the case went on, the worse for R & T Thew Ltd. In addition, Mr Reeves had no money, so they could not expect to get much out of him. So they took judgment for far less than they were entitled to. Instead of the £849·04 and £8,500 to which they were entitled, they took £5,500 (without interest) payable by monthly instalments over the next three years. A big loss for them of moneys owing to them, all due to Mr Reeves being granted legal aid.

(xv) The costs of R & T Thew Ltd and Robert Thew

a   Apart from this, however, there are all the costs to which R & T Thew Ltd had been put. They came to £7,000. These costs made the whole case a financial disaster for R & T Thew Ltd and Mr Thew. They had been put to all these costs, simply because the legal aid fund had backed Mr Reeves. The fund had supported his groundless charge of fraud. They had given him all the financial assistance needed for it. If they had not given him legal aid, it would have died a natural death, for want of sustenance. As a

b   matter of simple justice, the legal aid fund ought to pay the whole of the costs to which R & T Thew Ltd and Mr Thew have been put by reason of the groundless charge of fraud made against them.

So R & T Thew Ltd and Mr Robert Thew applied to the judge for an order against the legal aid fund. He made the order. He had tried the case and knew all about it. His judgment is quite first class. It covers every point admirably. The legal aid fund appeal

c   to this court.

(xvi) The 'unacceptable face' of British justice

The judge realised that the legal aid fund might appeal. So he added this pertinent comment which I would adopt as my own:

d   'If it were to be held by higher authority that the Law Society, having given every appearance of providing Reeves with legal aid and thereby being responsible for this litigation being taken up to the third day of the hearing of the action, can now turn round and say to the unassisted parties, "Owing to the defective form of the legal aid certificate which we granted to your opponent, we are not liable to you for your costs for which we would otherwise be responsible", then Mr and Mrs Thew will no doubt ascribe the disastrous consequences of their successful litigation to what in

e   modern jargon might well be described as the "unacceptable face" of British justice.'

(xvii) The Legal Aid Act 1974

The 1974 Act has prescribed the conditions under which an unassisted party can get his costs paid out of the legal aid fund. I will deal with them in order.

f   *Section 13(3)(a)* An unassisted party can never get an order against the legal aid fund unless 'the proceedings in the court of first instance were instituted by the party receiving legal aid'. To apply this provision in this case, it is important to distinguish between the claim of R & T Thew Ltd for £849·04 and the counterclaim by Mr Reeves for fraud. The claim for £849·04 (for processing films and developing them) was made under an entirely different contract from Mr Reeves's counterclaim for fraud (on the sale of the

g   photographic business). Seeing that the counterclaim arose out of an entirely separate transaction which had no connection whatever with the claim, it was not available as a set-off, legal or equitable (see *Henriksens Rederi A/S v PHZ Rolimpex, The Brede* [1973] 3 All ER 589 at 596–597, [1974] QB 233 at 248–249 and *Federal Commerce and Navigation Co Ltd v Molina Alpha Inc* [1978] 3 All ER 1066 at 1079, [1978] QB 927 at 976). Seeing that it was made against Mr Robert Thew as well as the company, it ought to have been

h   brought as a cross-action. On counsel's advice it was not made by a cross-action but by a counterclaim. But that cannot alter the case. This counterclaim was itself a proceeding instituted not by the Thews but by Mr Reeves. It was a 'separate proceeding' for which a separate writ and certificate could have been granted to Mr Reeves: see reg 2 of the Legal Aid (Costs of Successful Unassisted Parties) Regulations 1964, SI 1964 No 1276. In consequence of this counterclaim, R & T Thew Ltd amended their writ, but this was

j   itself the result of a counterclaim, just as if there had been a cross-action. So all the costs incurred after the counterclaim were the result of it.

Section 13(3)(b) The court must be 'satisfied that the unassisted party will suffer severe financial hardship unless the order is made'. The judge was so satisfied. Although R & T Thew Ltd is a limited company, and thus disqualified from getting legal aid itself, nevertheless there is nothing to disqualify it from getting an order for costs against the legal aid fund. R & T Thew Ltd are virtually Mr and Mrs Robert Thew. The company will be ruined if it has to bear the £7,000 costs. It will, beyond doubt, suffer severe financial hardship.

Section 13(2) The court must be 'satisfied that it is just and equitable in all the circumstances that provision for those costs should be made out of public funds'. The judge was so satisfied here. So would everyone be. Justice does demand that the legal aid fund should bear all the costs of the counterclaim.

Section 13(1) 'Where a party receives legal aid in connection with any proceedings ...' Here is where the difficulty arises. The Law Society say that in order to find out what are the 'proceedings' it is necessary to look at the legal aid certificate. It is issued under reg 6 of the Legal Aid (General) Regulations 1971, SI 1971 No 62. The legal aid fund say that the certificate is sacrosanct. It is conclusive. In this case the certificate shows that on 21st November 1977 Mr Reeves was granted legal aid only for the *defence*: to *defend* the claim of R & T Thew Ltd for the sum owing to them. Mr Reeves was not granted leave to *counterclaim* until 7th March 1980 and then only against R & T Thew Ltd and not Mr Robert Thew. The legal aid fund say that a legal aid certificate cannot be back-dated. So R & T Thew Ltd cannot get any costs against the legal aid fund for the counterclaim except for the costs incurred after 7th March 1980. It follows, too, that the solicitors for Mr Reeves cannot get any of their costs on the counterclaim out of the legal aid fund until after 7th March 1980. That will be extremely hard on them too.

I must say that this attitude of the legal aid fund is extremely unmeritorious. They acknowledge it. But they say they must stand by it in order to administer the fund properly.

To show how unmeritorious is their attitude, I would point out that the legal aid fund called no one from their office to explain their part in it at all. No doubt the young articled clerk made a mistake. He bungled the application form. But the young lady in the Law Society helped him to make it. No mistake was made by the legal assistant who prepared the synopsis. He said quite clearly that the debt was admitted and that the legal aid was required for the counterclaim. But a mistake was made by the clerk who drew up the offer of legal aid. He bungled it by copying out the words of the botched application form, whereas he should have got in touch with the young articled clerk and got the application form amended at that stage so as to represent the true position. It is significant that when, on 7th March 1980, attention was drawn to the mistake, the clerks immediately rectified it. They did it without reference to the legal aid committee. They did it because they realised that a mistake had been made and that it should be put right at once.

(xviii) *The slip rule*

So I come to the real point in the case: can the mistake in the certificate of 21st November 1977 be rectified so as to cover the counterclaim as from that date? I think it can. There is a rule recognised by the law when there is an obvious slip in the wording of a document, when the slip is so obvious that no one has been deceived or misled by the slip in any way, when everyone who was concerned in the making of the document knew what it was intended to convey and when everyone who has acted on it has acted on the meaning so intended by the makers. In such a case the parties themselves can correct it at any time; or, if they do not agree, the court itself can correct the slip, without recourse to the doctrine of rectification or anything of that sort. Thus the court has omitted words which were erroneously inserted, as in *Price v Mann* [1942] 1 All ER 453. It has transposed words such as 'demandant' and 'tenant' or 'plaintiff' and 'defendant' (see *Hamilton v Farrer* (1831) 8 Bing 10, 131 ER 303). It has transposed whole provisions (see *Uvedale v Halfpenny* (1723) 2 P Wms 151, 24 ER 677). It has corrected a misnomer or misdescription by giving the right name or the right description (see *Whittam v W J Daniel & Co Ltd* [1961] 3 All ER 796, [1962] 1 QB 271). The general principle is that when the object and intent of a document is obvious, and known to all concerned, the court will not allow it to be defeated by the draftsman's unskilfulness or ignorance of the facts or the law or by his slipshod use of words (see the decision of the Privy Council in

Salmon v Duncombe (1886) 11 App Cas 627 at 634). The parties can correct the slip
a themselves. If they do not do it, the court itself can correct the slip so as to give the
document the effect which it was intended by all to have.

The most familiar instance of this principle is when a slip is made in drawing up an
order of the court. The court itself has an inherent power to correct the record of the
court so as to bring it into harmony with the order which the judge obviously intended
to pronounce (see *Lawrie v Lees* (1881) 7 App Cas 19 at 35). The rule is now embodied in
b RSC Ord 20, r 11.

All the cases show that, when a slip is corrected in this way, the correction dates back
to the date when the document originally took effect, unless anything has happened in
the meantime to make it inexpedient or unjust to do so (see *Hatton v Harris* [1892] AC
547 at 560 by Lord Watson and *Pearlman (Veneers) SA (Pty) Ltd v Bartels* [1954] 3 All ER
659 at 660, [1954] 1 WLR 1457 at 1459).

c   This seems to me a plain case for the application of the slip rule. The certificate of legal
aid of 21st November 1977 contained an obvious slip. It omitted the words 'and
counterclaim'. But everyone treated it as containing those words; and it was corrected as
soon as it was discovered. The amendment dates back to the time of the original grant,
ie 21st November 1977.

d *(xix) What were the costs incurred on the counterclaim?*

There is a side issue of much importance. Assuming that the Thews can get their costs
on the counterclaim, what do they get? Counsel for the Law Society submitted that they
come to nothing. He cited the cases on taxation of costs. He said that the main costs
were on the claim and very little on the counterclaim. He relied on the cases leading up
to *Medway Oil and Storage Co Ltd v Continental Contractors Ltd* [1929] AC 88, [1928] All ER
e Rep 330. But those cases only apply when the same issues are contested on both claim
and counterclaim. They do not apply when the claim (as here) is admitted and the whole
fight is on the counterclaim. In such a case *Christie v Platt* [1921] 2 KB 17 applies. It was
approved and explained by Lord Blanesburgh in the *Medway Oil* case [1929] AC 88 at
106–108, [1928] All ER Rep 330 at 339–340.

I desire to say, however, that those cases on taxation of costs do not apply here. We are
f only concerned with the costs of the proceedings instituted by Mr Reeves for fraud, in so
far as they were incurred after 21st November 1977 when he got legal aid. Those costs
were the whole costs from that time: because the whole fight was on the counterclaim
for fraud.

(xx) Millican v Tucker

g   There remains to consider *Millican v Tucker* [1980] 1 All ER 1083, [1980] 1 WLR
640. The plaintiffs there were two men of the highest integrity. The defendants took
unfair advantage of them. They induced the plaintiffs to enter into transactions which
the judge described as 'iniquitous'. The plaintiffs sued the defendants, asking for the
iniquitous transactions to be set aside. The defendants denied their iniquity. They got
legal aid to defend the case and also to counterclaim for a declaration that the iniquitous
h transactions were binding. After the hearing had gone on for several days and was still
part heard, the defendants gave up their defence and counterclaim. They surrendered
and acknowledged that the transactions were not binding.

There is no doubt that it was the legal aid fund which enabled the defendants to fight
the case. If it were not for legal aid, the defendants would probably not have contested
the case at all or at any rate they would probably have given in much earlier.

j   The plaintiffs then sought an order for the costs of the counterclaim to be paid out of
the legal aid fund. Browne-Wilkinson J held that the counterclaim was a 'separate
proceeding instituted by the defendants'. He ordered the costs of the counterclaim to be
paid out of the legal aid fund. But then the point arose: how much were the costs of the
counterclaim? Browne-Wilkinson J did the fair thing, or at any rate the fairest thing
permitted by the statute. He gave the plaintiffs one-half of the costs common to claim

and counterclaim. But the Court of Appeal (consisting of only two Lords Justices) gave
the plaintiffs nothing (see [1980] 1 All ER 1083, [1980] 1 WLR 640 at 651). They felt *a*
that they were bound by the decisions on taxation of costs. Another disaster for
unassisted plaintiffs who had won their case. They had to pay all their own costs without
any recourse against anyone. They applied to the House of Lords for leave to appeal but
it was refused.

Now we have often held that a decision of two Lords Justices is not binding on a court
of three (see *Boys v Chaplin* [1968] 1 All ER 283, [1968] 2 QB 1). And it is clear that a *b*
refusal by the House of Lords of leave to appeal does not imply any approval by the
House of the decision (see *Gilbert Ash (Northern) Ltd v Modern Engineering (Bristol) Ltd*
[1973] 3 All ER 195 at 214, [1974] AC 689 at 715 by Lord Diplock).

I must say that I think that *Millican v Tucker* was rightly decided by Browne-Wilkinson
J and I regret that his decision was reversed by the Court of Appeal. To my mind the
decisions about taxation of costs should not be applied to these cases about legal aid costs. *c*

(xxi) *The majority view*

I have been privileged to read in advance the judgments prepared by my brethren. I
am distressed to find that they feel that the mistake made in the legal aid certificate
cannot be remedied in any way. It must remain uncorrected forever. The result is that
the solicitors for Mr Reeves cannot get any of their costs out of the legal aid fund, nor can *d*
R & T Thew Ltd either, for any of the work done in the 2½ years from 21st November
1977 to 7th March 1980, during which there were very expensive interlocutory
proceedings. All they can get is the costs of the counterclaim for the five days from 7th
to 12th March 1980: and then only because of the lucky chance that the young solicitor
happened at that late stage to spot the mistake: and got it amended just in time to cover
those five days. The Law Society said that even then the costs for those five days were not *e*
recoverable, because of the decision of this court in *Millican v Tucker*. But I am glad to say
that my brethren do hold they are recoverable. They do manage to 'distinguish' *Millican
v Tucker*, and thus enable R & T Thew Ltd to save a little from the wreck. I hope that
every court in future will be able likewise to 'distinguish' it.

This small crumb will do little to satisfy the hunger of the Thews, for justice. Just
think of the costs to which they have been put in making this very application to the *f*
courts, in an attempt to get justice. They have been put to all the costs in the court below
and in this court. They have failed on the main argument, and only succeeded in getting
a crumb from a side issue. They may well find themselves having to pay all their own
costs of the application, and maybe having to pay some of the costs of the Law Society as
well.

If the Thews should seek leave to appeal to the House of Lords, I hope that it may be *g*
given. But I do not suppose for a moment that the Thews will be able to take the case up
there. They cannot afford it. They cannot get legal aid. And who in their place would
take the risk of an appeal to the House of Lords, with all that that entails: costs against
them if they fail?

(xxii) *Most ugly* *h*

So here we have presented to us at its most ugly the 'unacceptable face' of British
justice. The Thews came to the courts of law to obtain sums from a debtor which were
undoubtedly due to them. They were baulked by the grant of legal aid to the
defendant. Their own costs came to £7,000. When they sought to recover those costs
from the legal aid fund, they were met by the plea: 'You cannot recover them because a
mistake was made in the legal aid certificate and it cannot be corrected.' That plea has *j*
succeeded. I hang my head in shame that it should be so.

(xxiii) *Law reform*

In *Millican v Tucker* the judges expressed the hope that Parliament would intervene so
as to remedy the injustice done to unassisted parties when the other side is granted legal

aid (see [1980] 1 WLR 640 at 650 per Brown-Wilkinson J, and [1980] 1 All ER 1083 at
a   1088, [1980] 1 WLR 640 at 656 per Buckley LJ). But Parliament seems to pay no heed
to the hopes or prayers of the judges. In *Lim Poh Choo v Camden and Islington Area Health
Authority* [1979] 2 All ER 910, [1980] AC 174 the House of Lords agreed with me that a
radical reappraisal of the law was needed. But when, I ask, will it take place? That is why
I think the judges should be more courageous themselves. They should do their utmost
to remedy the injustice in the instant case, rather than leave it to the delay and uncertainty
b   of intervention by Parliament years ahead. In any case, Parliament will never be able to
remedy the injustice in the instant case. In our present case it means that the unassisted
party is left to suffer 'severe financial hardship' without recourse from anyone. It is a blot
indeed on our system of justice.

This case, and other cases of late in this court, have shown up the need for reform of
the Legal Aid Act 1974, and of the system itself.
c   The first thing is the immense power which the system puts into the hands of the
legally aided person as against the other side who is not legally aided. The legally aided
person is backed by the unlimited financial resources of the state. He has the power to
carry on the litigation indefinitely till the other side is exhausted. The certificate is often
expressed in such wide terms that it covers the whole conduct of the suit, through all the
interlocutory proceedings, right through to the end, as in *Hanlon v Law Society* [1980] 1
d   All ER 763 at 770, [1980] 2 WLR 756 at 776. It sometimes gives the solicitor a 'blanket'
authority to consult experts and to call them at the trial, as in *Storer v Wright* [1981] 1 All
ER 1015, [1981] 2 WLR 208. In some cases the expense is colossal, as in the medical
negligence cases like *Whitehouse v Jordan* [1980] 1 All ER 650, CA; [1981] 1 All ER 267,
[1981] 1 WLR 246, HL. If there are negotiations for a settlement, the legally aided
person can, and sometimes does, say to the other, 'Unless you settle on my terms, I will
e   go on with the trial, at no expense to me, but at your expense entirely', as in *Manley v Law
Society* [1981] 1 All ER 401, [1981] 1 WLR 335; with the result that unassisted defendants
will often pay the demand of the legally aided plaintiff rather than spend money on
fighting the case; or an unassisted plaintiff will take much less than is due to him from
a legally aided defendant because it is not worthwhile spending any more money on the
case, as in *Millican v Tucker* and this present case. The most significant reform would be
f   that, when the legally aided person fails in his action or defence, the legal aid fund should
pay the costs of the unassisted party, just as any other litigant who fails.

I know that the legal aid system has done great good for a great many people. But the
profession must remember that, when seeking legal aid, they are under a special
responsibility to see that it is wisely and carefully administered. It is to be used only in
cases where it is justified: and not to support thin cases of little merit: nor the
g   uncorroborated word of dubious parties. It must not be used so as to incur extravagant
or unnecessary expense: or so as to take unfair advantage of the unassisted party.

CONCLUSION

For myself I would affirm the judge and dismiss the appeal. But my brethren would
set aside the judge's order and only allow the costs of the counterclaim after 7th March
h   1980.

DUNN LJ. The plaintiff company is a small private company of which Mr and Mrs
Thew are the sole shareholders. Down to 1975 the company carried on a photographic
business at two shops, one at Oldham and one at Middleton where there was also a
processing laboratory. In 1975 the company decided to sell the Middleton shop but not
j   the laboratory, and on 9th November 1975 an agreement was made for the sale of the
shop by the company to the defendant. The purchase price was payable partly by way
of a down payment, partly by way of a deferred payment, and the balance by 60 equal
monthly instalments. The down payment and the deferred payment were duly made
according to the agreement, and also the initial monthly payments. The defendant was
also a customer of the processing laboratory in respect of which he was sent monthly

accounts. By November 1976 his account for laboratory work was in debit to the sum
of £849. On 31st January 1977 a writ was issued on behalf of the plaintiff company a
claiming that sum. On 23rd February 1977 a summons was issued under RSC Ord 14
returnable in April. In March the defendant delivered a defence whereby he admitted
the claim, subject to a counterclaim alleging fraud and negligent misrepresentation in
relation to the sale of the business. It claimed rescission of the sale agreement and
damages, and joined Mr Thew as a personal defendant to the counterclaim. At that stage
the defendant was an unassisted person. On receipt of the counterclaim the plaintiffs b
amended their statement of claim to claim damages for breach of the agreement to sell
the business. The defence was subsequently amended to admit the sale agreement
subject to the counterclaim, which was set off against the claim in extinction or
diminution thereof. So, although there was originally only a counterclaim, as a result of
the plaintiffs' amendment and the consequential amendment by the defendant a true
equitable set off by way of defence to the claim was set up. c

On 16th August 1977 the defendant applied for legal aid. The application was made
by a young and inexperienced man employed by his solicitors. It was his first application
for legal aid and he was quite unsupervised. He went to the local Law Society at
Manchester to obtain the forms for two applications, the application in this case and
another case. He asked the advice of a young lady in the office as to how he should fill
up the forms. She said: 'They usually put in "to defend court proceedings".' It was a d
general inquiry: there was no special inquiry in relation to this case. The young man
took the forms back to the office and completed them. The completed application
appears in our bundle and, as Lord Denning MR has read the material parts, it is not
necessary for me to do so. The application was sent to the local Law Society where, in
accordance with the usual practice, it was considered by the secretary who prepared a
synopsis for the benefit of the local committee who were to consider the application. e
The material parts of the synopsis have also been read by Lord Denning MR. The local
committee granted the application and accordingly an offer of legal aid was made to the
defendant in the following terms:

> 'TO DEFEND PROCEEDINGS IN THE HIGH COURT OF JUSTICE, QUEENS BENCH DIVISION,
> [and then the number] BETWEEN R. & T. THEW LIMITED (PLAINTIFF) AND ALAN REEVES
> (DEFENDANT).' f

The offer was accepted by the defendant and a legal aid certificate was duly issued to him
on 21st November in the terms of the offer, that is to say it was confined to defending the
proceedings between the company and the defendant. It did not grant authority to
counterclaim or to join Mr Thew as a personal defendant.

The action was fixed for hearing before his Honour Judge Curtis, sitting as an official g
referee, for 10th March 1980. Shortly before the hearing the young man thought that
the legal aid certificate was not sufficiently wide, and on 6th March 1980 he applied for
authority so that the certificate would cover the counterclaim. The application was
made by letter of that date asking for an extension of the legal aid certificate 'so that the
certificate will cover our client's counterclaim in the matter'. The application was
considered by the secretary under his delegated powers by virtue of reg 1(5) of the Legal h
Aid (General) Regulations 1971 and was granted the following day. The terms of the
authorisation were:

> 'This is to certify that the legal aid certificate issued to the above named has been
> amended as follows:—By adding the words "and counterclaim in" after the word
> "defend" in the description of the legal aid.'
j

The amended certificate still did not extend to cover Mr Thew as a party to the
counterclaim.

The hearing started on 10th March, and it soon became apparent that the defendant
would not succeed on his counterclaim. Negotiations took place on 12th March, and the
judge dealt with the situation in his judgment. He said:

a

'It soon became obvious that the defendant would be faced with an impossible task in establishing his case against the plaintiffs and Thew. The negotiations on the part of the plaintiffs were conducted by Thew who impressed me as a thoroughly honest man who had given truthful information about the business and had produced genuine records and when he had to make an assessment rather than give a precise figure did his best to give an accurate assessment.'

b The action was eventually settled on terms that the defendant would pay the plaintiffs £5,500 by instalments, the whole amount to be secured on the defendant's house which was in fact in his wife's name. Although the settlement was considerably less than the claim, it was accepted that the plaintiffs had substantially succeeded in the action, particularly as the money was secured on the property in the wife's name.

c After the terms of settlement had been incorporated in a Tomlin order, application was made for the plaintiffs' costs to be paid from the legal aid fund. The judge held, as he was bound to do before considering such an application, that in the ordinary way he would have made an order for costs against the defendant. In fact he made no order because of the provisions of the Legal Aid Act 1974. He adjourned the application for the Law Society to be represented.

d The adjourned hearing took place on 11th July 1980, and the Law Society submitted that the judge had no jurisdiction to make an order in favour of the company before 7th March 1980 in any event because the certificate did not cover the counterclaim until that date, and further submitted that the judge had no jurisdiction to make an order in favour of Mr Thew at all because there was no certificate authorising the joining of Mr Thew as a defendant to the counterclaim. On 11th July the judge gave a judgment and once again adjourned the application for evidence to be called as to the circumstances in which

e the certificate was granted. The adjourned hearing took place on 7th August. The plaintiffs called the young man who had applied for legal aid on behalf of the defendant but no evidence was called by the Law Society, although the judge had indicated that he would be assisted by evidence. Having heard the young man, the judge gave another judgment described as 'addendum to judgment'. He held that the original certificate of 7th November 1977 had been issued by mistake, that the Law Society must have

f intended to grant legal aid to cover the counterclaim and also the joining of Mr Thew, and he held accordingly that he had jurisdiction to make an order for the costs of both plaintiffs to be paid out of the legal aid fund, which he duly did.

It was accepted here and before the judge that Mr Thew will suffer severe financial hardship unless an order is made for payment of his costs by the legal aid fund. It was also accepted before the judge, and the judge held, that the company will suffer severe

g financial hardship, but although the point was not taken here it was properly pointed out by counsel for the Law Society that there is a question whether a limited company can ever suffer severe financial hardship, and that as this goes to jurisdiction under s 13(3)(b) of the Legal Aid Act 1974 it is not a point which the court can ignore. The point not being raised before the judge, he based himself on s 13(1) and held that proceedings had been finally decided in favour of the unassisted party, the plaintiffs. This was accepted

h here and below. The judge also held that it was just and equitable in all the circumstances that provision for the plaintiffs' costs should be made out of public funds, so that s 13(2) of the Act was satisfied. This also was not challenged if there was jurisdiction to make the order. The judge finally held that the provisions of s 13(3)(a) of the Act were satisfied because the only issue in the proceedings arose on the counterclaim, which were proceedings instituted by the party receiving legal aid, that is to say the defendant.

j Although the certificate on its face only covered the defence, the documents enclosed with the application showed that there was a mistake which the judge held that he had power in effect to rectify. It is that decision which has been the principal target of the submissions in this court of counsel for the Law Society.

Counsel for the plaintiffs has put the matter as attractively as it could be put. He referred first, as did the judge, to s 14(1)(a) of the Act, which provides that regulations

may make provision for determining proceedings which are or are not to be treated as
separate proceedings for the purpose of s 13. He referred to the Legal Aid (General) *a*
Regulations 1971, reg 2(2) of which provides:

> 'Any document purporting to be a certificate issued in accordance with these
> regulations shall, until the contrary is proved, be deemed to be a valid certificate
> issued to the person named therein and for the purposes there set out.'

He submitted that that regulation showed that the certificate was not conclusive, and he *b*
relied on certain findings of fact by the judge made after hearing the evidence of the
defendant's young solicitor. Those findings of fact appear in the judgment. The judge
said:

> 'I accept the explanation of [the young man] of the circumstances under which
> the application was made in the slipshod form which merits criticism. But there
> was also some responsibility on the Law Society's side to ensure that the certificate *c*
> should cover what it was intended to cover. Somebody must have read the
> documents which accompanied the application. That person must have appreciated
> that what was being applied for was legal aid to cover the whole proceedings, not
> only the proceedings brought by the plaintiffs against Reeves, but also the
> proceedings brought by Reeves against the plaintiffs and Thew. That was what was
> intended by the grant of the application. Unfortunately the slipshod wording *d*
> remained uncorrected. I find as a fact that there is a mistake in the certificate of
> November 1977 in that it was not expressed to cover the counterclaim and made no
> mention of R Thew although it was intended to cover the proceedings against him
> and that it was and is open to the appropriate area committee to amend the
> certificate so that their member Messrs Goulty & Goodfellow may be paid for the
> work which they have done in the bona fide belief that they were covered by the *e*
> certificate of November 1977. The amendment of 7th March 1980 should in my
> view be regarded as having been made nunc pro tunc so that it relates back to
> November 1977.'

So, said counsel for the plaintiffs, the defendant was a party in receipt of legal aid in
connection with the proceedings, a certificate had been issued to him and that certificate *f*
was intended to cover not only the defence but also the only live issue at the trial, that is
to say the counterclaim and the joining of Mr Thew as a defendant to the counterclaim.
All the other requirements of s 13 being fulfilled, the judge had jurisdiction to make the
order.

I wish I could accept the submissions of counsel for the plaintiffs as it is plain that all
the merits are on his side. The judge said in his judgment:
g

> '. . . I consider it would be unjust and inequitable that the unassisted party who
> was driven to compromise the action, not through any lack of confidence on his part
> or the part of his advisers as to the strength of their case but by considerations of the
> opponent's ability to satisfy a judgment, should also be placed in the position of
> defraying the whole of his own costs.'

h
But there are unfortunately formidable obstacles in the way of accepting the submissions
on behalf of the plaintiffs. The whole scheme for legal aid depends on the terms of the
1974 Act and the regulations made thereunder. The corner-stone of the scheme is the
certificate on which everything depends. Regulation 1 of the Legal Aid (General)
Regulations 1971 is the interpretation regulation. The phrase 'assisted person' means a
person in respect of whom a certificate is in force. And 'certificate' means a civil aid *j*
certificate issued in accordance with these regulations entitling a person to legal aid, and
includes an amendment to a certificate issued under reg 9(4)(a) and an emergency
certificate. Regulation 2, which I have just cited, only goes to the validity of the
certificate and not to its amendment. The certificate may be set aside but cannot be

enlarged or varied under that regulation. Certificates are issued on application on the
prescribed form under reg 3. The application is made to a local committee. Regulation
6 deals with the issue of certificates. Paragraph (2) provides:

'Unless a certificate otherwise provides it shall not without the authority of the
appropriate committee given under regulation 15(1) extend to—(a) the addition of
any further parties except in matrimonial proceedings, or (b) any steps having the
same effect as a cross action or a reply thereto or to a cross appeal.'

Regulation 2 of the Legal Aid (Costs of Successful Unassisted Parties) Regulations 1964,
SI 1964 No 1276, provides:

'Any proceedings in respect of which a separate civil aid certificate could properly
be issued under the General Regulations to a person receiving legal aid shall be
treated as separate proceedings for the purposes of the Act.'

It follows that a counterclaim can be treated as separate proceedings: see *Millican v Tucker*
[1980] 1 All ER 1083, [1980] 1 WLR 640. But even so, although a separate civil aid
certificate could properly be issued to cover a counterclaim, the counterclaiming party
would not be an 'assisted person' unless and until a certificate has been issued.

In this case the original certificate did not cover the counterclaim or the joining of Mr
Thew as a defendant. The question is: can it be amended or rectified?

Regulation 9 of the 1971 regulations deals with the amendment of certificates.
Paragraph (1) provides:

'The appropriate area committee may amend a certificate where in their
opinion—(a) there has been some mistake in the certificate . . .'

Regulation 9(5) provides: 'The decision of an area committee on any question relating to
the amendment of a certificate shall be final.' It follows that the decision may only be
challenged by way of judicial review. The mistake referred to in reg 9(1)(a) is the
mistake of the area committee in issuing the certificate, and not the mistake of the
applicant. It is the duty of the applicant to apply for the appropriate certificate;
applications are invariably made by solicitors, and it is their duty to apply for the
appropriate certificate; it is not the duty of the legal aid committee to go behind the
application and decide what proceedings the certificate should cover. Indeed paras (6),
(7) and (8) of reg 5 show that the powers of the committee to grant legal aid other than
in accordance with the application are limited. In this case, however, no application was
made on the ground of mistake. The application was made under reg 9(1)(f) which
provides that the area committee may amend a certificate where in their opinion 'under
regulation 15(1) a solicitor should be authorised to take any steps referred to in regulation
6(2)(a) or (b)'. Regulation 15(1) provides:

'Where it appears to the assisted person's solicitor necessary for the proper conduct
of the proceedings to take any of the steps referred to in regulation 6(2) he shall,
unless authority has been given in the certificate, apply to the appropriate area
committee for such authority.'

And that regulation takes one back to reg 6(2) which opens with the words: 'Unless a
certificate otherwise provides . . .' That was what was done in this case. There was no
application and no authority for the certificate to extend to the counterclaim until 7th
March, and it is plain from the words of the regulation that such authority cannot be
retrospective. Regulation 14(1) provides:

'Where, after proceedings have been instituted in any court, any party becomes
an assisted person in regard to those proceedings, the provisions of section 2(2)(e)
[now s 8(1)(e)] of the Act shall apply only to so much of the costs of the proceedings
as are incurred while a certificate is in force.'

Section 8(1) provides:

> 'Where a person receives legal aid in connection with any proceedings . . . (e) his
> liability by virtue of an order for costs made against him with respect to the
> proceedings shall not exceed the amount (if any) which is a reasonable one for him
> to pay having regard to all the circumstances, including the means of all the parties
> and their conduct in connection with the dispute.'

If any authority can be given retrospectively it would follow that an unassisted party
would be unable to recover against an assisted party costs incurred before the date when
the authority was given save as provided by s 8(1)(e). This would be contrary to the
whole scheme.

Regulation 17 deals with the service of notices and provides in para (2) that all other
parties are to be served with notice of the issue of a certificate. This regulation again
emphasises the importance of the certificate: the other parties must know what certificate
has been issued to whom and what proceedings it covers. By reg 15(2) the certificate is
to go to the assisted person's counsel. And of the Notes for Guidance as to the scope of the
certificate, note 28 makes it plain that it is the duty of counsel to check the certificate so
that he can be satisfied that what he advises falls within the scope of the certificate, or he
should advise that an authority be obtained for an amendment of the certificate.
Regulation 17(7) provides that copies of certificates shall be provided for the use of the
judge at the trial. All this emphasises the importance of the certificate. Whatever the
financial hardship suffered by the plaintiffs in this case (and I recognise that it is
considerable) one cannot just brush all these regulations aside, and say that there was in
fact authority to counterclaim and to join Mr Thew as a defendant to the counterclaim,
and that that authority had been given before the certificate was issued, and that the
judge had found as a fact that the area committee intended that the defendant should be
granted legal aid to cover those matters. Nor do I think that the judge was entitled on
the construction of the statute and the regulations to look behind the certificate and find
on the evidence as a fact that the authority went wider than shown on the face of the
certificate itself.

To hold otherwise seems to me quite inconsistent with the elaborate code for the
granting of legal aid which is set out in the regulations to which I have referred. The
question of mistake in the certificate is expressly covered by reg 9 and the only body
which has power to amend the certificate on the ground of mistake is the area committee
itself. The extent and scope of the legal aid authorised is covered wholly by the certificate
itself. To hold otherwise would seem to me to involve immense practical difficulties.
Unassisted parties would not know from the certificates the extent to which their assisted
opponents were covered by legal aid and they have no other means of knowing. Costs
might be taxed as between solicitor and client under the provisions of the Act on the basis
of a certificate, and it might then subsequently be held that the certificate did not in fact
cover the whole authority for legal aid which had been given by the legal aid
committee. All this would give rise to uncertainty and confusion, and would be
detrimental to unassisted parties.

The view which I have formed based on a consideration of the Act and of the
regulations is supported by authority. In *Lacey v W Silk & Son Ltd* [1951] 2 All ER 128
Slade J held that he had no power to antedate a certificate. In *Wallace v Freeman Heating
Co Ltd* [1955] 1 All ER 418, [1955] 1 WLR 172 Pearson J held that approval must be
obtained in a certificate before any expense incurred by a solicitor acting for an assisted
person was incurred. He went on to say that if in fact the expense had been authorised
but did not appear on the certificate then the certificate might be amended (but the
amendment would be under the predecessor to reg 9 of the 1971 regulations, by the area
committee). He did not suggest that the court had the power to go behind the legal aid
certificate and impute an intention to the legal aid committee which did not appear in
the certificate itself. In *Francis v Francis and Dickerson* [1955] 3 All ER 836, [1956] P 87
Sachs J emphasised the importance of ensuring that legal aid certificates were clear and

a unambiguous on their face, thus again emphasising the importance of the certificate itself.

There would have been no need for the elaborate arguments in *Hanlon v Law Society* [1980] 1 All ER 763, [1980] 2 WLR 756, CA; [1980] 2 All ER 199, [1980] 2 WLR 756, HL as to what proceedings were covered by the certificate, if all the court had to do was to exercise its inherent jurisdiction and rectify the certificate so as to define its scope more precisely.

b In my judgment the extent of the legal assistance granted to a litigant is to be derived from the certificate itself, and the certificate can only be amended on the ground of mistake by the area committee concerned.

I now turn to consider whether it is possible as a matter of law for a limited company to suffer severe financial hardship. In *Nowotnik v Nowotnik (Hyatt intervening)* [1965] 3 All ER 167 at 172, [1967] P 83 at 103 Lord Denning MR said:

c   'If the [unassisted person] is a company in a considerable way of business, it may suffer financial loss by having to pay its own costs but it does not suffer severe financial hardship.'

That shows that a company may suffer severe financial hardship. Whether it does or not is a question of fact in each case. The plaintiff company is not a public company to which *d* different considerations might well apply. It is a private 'close' company. Indeed it might, having regard to the shareholdings, be said to be no more than the alter ego of Mr and Mrs Thew. It has no liquid assets and a substantial overdraft at the bank. If it were obliged to pay its own costs of these proceedings, its capital would undoubtedly be seriously depleted and it might be forced into liquidation. In those circumstances there was ample evidence to support the judge's finding that this company would in fact suffer *e* financial hardship if its costs were not paid out of public funds.

Finally it was submitted by counsel for the Law Society that on the basis that the court had jurisdiction to order the payment of the plaintiff company's costs as from 7th March 1980, out of public funds, the only costs which the company was entitled to recover were those additional costs attributable to the counterclaim as being the costs of separate proceedings, and did not extend to the costs of defending the action which were *f* practically the whole of the costs. This submission depended on the well-established rule that where, as here, the defence consists of a counterclaim which is properly set off so as to reduce or extinguish the claim the costs of the counterclaim are properly to be regarded as the costs of defending the claim, except and in so far as those costs are solely attributable to the counterclaim, for example by proving the amount of damage which would arise thereunder. This is the rule in *Saner v Bilton* (1879) 11 Ch D 416.

g So far as this point is concerned, having read a draft of the judgment of O'Connor LJ, I am content to adopt his reasoning and to hold that *Millican v Tucker* [1980] 1 All ER 1083, [1980] 1 WLR 640 is distinguishable from this case on the ground that in this case it is possible for the taxing master to divide the costs between claim and counterclaim.

I would accordingly allow the appeal and replace the judge's order by an order that the plaintiff company should recover from the legal aid fund such sum as is found due on *h* taxation to be costs of the counterclaim after 7th March 1980.

O'CONNOR LJ (read by Lord Denning MR). I adopt with gratitude the statement of the facts set out by Dunn LJ in his judgment.

We are told that Mr Thew and his company have incurred costs of the order of £7,000 in this litigation. At no time did Mr Reeves suggest that he was not indebted to the *j* company in the sum of £849 claimed in the writ for work done by the company for him. He sought to avoid payment of this sum by raising a counterclaim against the company and Mr Thew making broad allegations of fraud which turned out in the end to be entirely without substance. The reality is that this disastrous litigation was only made possible because from November 1977 Mr Reeves was in receipt of legal aid.

Mr Thew and the company applied for an order under s 13 of the Legal Aid Act 1974 for the payment of their costs incurred since November 1977 out of the legal aid fund. In due course the judge made the order. The Law Society as custodians of the legal aid *a* fund appeal against that decision.

The Law Society concede as follows: (i) that the counterclaim qualifies as a separate proceeding for the purposes of s 13 of the Act (see s 14(1)(a) and the regulations made thereunder); (ii) that those proceedings have been finally decided in favour of the unassisted parties; (iii) that both Mr Thew and the company will suffer severe financial hardship unless the order is made. *b*

This last concession raises a point of jurisdiction, namely whether a limited company can suffer severe financial hardship. In the present case we are dealing with a private close company incorporated to run what is a family business. On the facts there is no dispute that the liability for costs imposes a grave financial burden on Mr Thew and his company. The word 'hardship' connotes a degree of personal suffering which a company by definition cannot feel. Here the words are 'financial hardship', and in my judgment *c* those words are apt to cover the present situation. I would hold that the concession made by the Law Society was properly made.

The Law Society contend as follows: (i) that Mr Reeves never received legal aid to bring any proceedings against Mr Thew personally; (ii) that Mr Reeves did not receive legal aid to prosecute the counterclaim against the company until 7th March 1980; (iii) that the costs incurred by the company are costs in the claim and therefore do not *d* qualify under s 13 of the Act.

Legal aid is a creature of statute. There is a complex code found in the Act and the regulations made thereunder. The grant of legal aid to one party to litigation has a serious impact on the unassisted party or parties. I think it is of the greatest importance that the unassisted party should know with certainty the exact extent of legal aid granted to the assisted party. The provisions of the legislation point unerringly to the certificate *e* as the document that controls and defines the respective rights of the assisted and unassisted parties.

In the present case Mr Reeves never asked for nor did he receive legal aid to bring any proceedings against Mr Thew personally. Mr Reeves never asked for nor did he receive legal aid to pursue a counterclaim against the company until March 1980. In my judgment the certificates are conclusive on this issue. The judge thought that he had *f* power in effect to amend the certificate on the ground that the local legal aid committee in November 1977 must have intended to grant legal aid to Mr Reeves to pursue the counterclaim against both the company and Mr Thew. The pleadings which were before them showed that the only live issue was the counterclaim or at least originated from the counterclaim, for it must be remembered that the company had amended its statement of claim to claim damages for breach of contract and/or for money due under the *g* agreement for the sale of the business. Search as I will, I can find no provision in the legislation which enables the court to do this. Regulation 9(1)(a) of the Legal Aid (General) Regulations 1971 enables 'the appropriate area committee to amend a certificate where in their opinion there has been some mistake in the certificate'. The area committee has never been asked to amend this certificate and for my part I do not think that there was any mistake in the certificate. The mistake was in the application; it was *h* the mistake of Mr Reeves's solicitor; on each occasion he got exactly what he asked for. In the present case I am not prepared to speculate as to what kind of mistake the area committee is entitled to correct, but I am satisfied that it would have no power to make an amendment which would have the effect of backdating legal aid so as to affect the right to costs which had accrued in the meantime. In my judgment the order made by the judge cannot be supported. Mr Thew personally is not entitled to any order. *j* Mercifully, that is of no real importance because the amount of his costs is minimal. The company is entitled to an order in respect of costs referable to the counterclaim as from 7th March 1980.

The third contention of the Law Society depends on the following propositions: (i) that the costs of defending a claim are to be taxed as the costs of the claim; (ii) that where

the only defence to a claim is an equitable set-off itself depending on a counterclaim the
a   costs of the issues raised by the counterclaim are to be taxed as costs in the claim; (iii) that
in this case the only order which the court can make under s 13 of the Legal Aid Act 1974
is in respect of costs which could properly be taxed as costs of the counterclaim, and the
submission is that there are none.

It is submitted that this strange result is required by the rule in *Saner v Bilton* (1879) 11
Ch D 416, as applied by this court in *Millican v Tucker* [1980] 1 All ER 1083, [1980] 1
b   WLR 640. The rule in *Saner v Bilton* is that where a court orders that a claim and
counterclaim be dismissed or allowed with costs the rule of taxation is that the claim
should be treated as if it stood alone and the counterclaim should bear only the amount
by which the costs of the proceedings have been increased by it. In *Millican v Tucker* the
litigation arose out of a management contract between the plaintiffs who were
entertainers and the defendants. The plaintiffs claimed declarations to set aside the
c   management agreements on the grounds of fraud and oppression and claimed an account
of moneys received by the defendants. The individual defendants obtained legal aid,
they alleged that the agreements were binding and they counterclaimed for an account
of moneys received by the plaintiffs and remuneration said to be owing to them. In due
course the case was settled, as is the position in the present case, on terms which showed
that the plaintiffs had succeeded on claim and counterclaim. In that case the issues raised
d   by the claim and the issues raised by the counterclaim were for practical purposes the
same. The trial judge apportioned the costs of the action equally between claim and
counterclaim and made an order under s 13 in respect of the half share that he had
apportioned to the counterclaim. The Court of Appeal allowed the appeal. Donaldson
LJ said ([1980] 1 All ER 1083 at 1087–1088, [1980] 1 WLR 640 at 655):

e   'The order under appeal seeks by the special direction to include in the costs of the
counterclaim costs which are not occasioned by it but were saved because the issues
had already been raised by the claim and defence . . . It is quite clear from the *Atlas*
case [1898] 2 QB 500 and the *Medway Oil* case [1929] AC 88 that costs incurred in
connection with the claim can never be appropriated to the counterclaim either
wholly or by apportionment so as to become part of the costs of the counterclaim.
However dealt with by the judge's order they remain part of the costs of the claim.'
f

It is necessary to go back to the *Medway Oil* case. In that case claim and counterclaim
had both been dismissed with costs, the same as the order in *Saner v Bilton*. Viscount
Haldane pointed out ([1929] AC 88 at 95):

        'The question [in *Saner v Bilton*] was whether the defendant ought to pay only so
much of the costs pertaining to the claim as were occasioned by the counterclaim or
g   whether the costs of all the proceedings which related to both claim and
counterclaim should be apportioned.'

In *Saner v Bilton*, Fry J decided that there should be no apportionment and the House
of Lords approved that decision in the *Medway Oil* case. Viscount Haldane reviewed the
authorities. In considering *Christie v Platt* [1921] 2 KB 17 Viscount Haldane said ([1929]
h   AC 88 at 99–100):

        'I share the sense of Atkin L.J. that there was something in the result of the
taxation which on the face of it must have been wrong. For although the defendant
had recovered the larger amount on what was a cardinal question between the
parties, the plaintiff was given on her case, which was practically uncontroverted,
j   214*l*., while the defendant only got 3*l*. 0*s*. 5*d*. to cover the whole of her costs. I agree
with Atkin L.J. that this must have been wrong. There were obviously costs
incurred in common; the single fee on the brief given by the plaintiff is an
example. It may be that this fee would not have been too much if there had been
no counterclaim to meet. But that does not affect the fact that it was paid to the
plaintiffs' counsel to cover his services in both proceedings. It ought therefore to

have been divided for the purposes of taxation. The same thing appeared to have been true of a good deal of the evidence put forward on the two sides . . . My Lords, the distinction between division and apportionment may in certain circumstances be a thin one. But under the rule as laid down by Lindley M.R., and by the judges in the earlier case also, the distinction is fundamental.'

This distinction between apportionment and division was considered by this court in *Cinema Press Ltd v Pictures and Pleasures Ltd* [1945] 1 All ER 440, [1945] KB 356. The headnote reads ([1945] KB 356):

'When in an action an order is made that the plaintiff shall have the costs of the action, except that the costs on the issue of damages as from the date of payment into court with a denial of liability shall be the defendants, the costs of the issue of damages are confined to increased costs, but the taxing master must, in taxing the costs, divide the costs in respect of any item incurred after the date of payment in and attributable both to the issue of damages and to any other issues in the action, and give to the defendants so much of these costs as is attributable to the issue of damages.'

Lord Goddard, giving the judgment of the court, expressly applied the passage from the speech of Viscount Haldane which I have quoted and later he had this to say ([1945] 1 All ER 440 at 443–444, [1945] KB 356 at 363):

'While the answer of the master in the present case, "that there is no apportionment of costs in issue cases," is correct as far as it goes, this does not deal with the question as to whether there are not some items which must be divided, nor would it appear that he has applied his mind to that question. Though it may well be that the result of this case will be trifling, for as I have already said, it is possible that there will be no division of brief fee and instruction for brief, this case is of some general importance as calling attention to the fact that it is the *Medway* case that is now the governing authority and taxing officers must in these cases consider the question of the division of certain items common to both issues in the light of that decision, as distinct from apportionment in accordance with the former, but now rejected, practice of the Chancery Taxing Office.'

The *Cinema Press* case was cited to the court in *Millican v Tucker* but is not referred to in the judgments. I think that it is possible to distinguish *Millican v Tucker* from the present case. In *Millican v Tucker* it seems to me the court must have come to the conclusion that no division was possible. If that be not so, it is in conflict with the earlier case. On the facts of the present case I am satisfied that division is certainly possible and for my part I would have thought may well result in a substantial award of costs to the company.

I would set aside the order of the judge and substitute for it an order that the company should recover from the legal aid fund such sum as is found due on taxation to be the costs of the counterclaim after 7th March 1980.

Appeal allowed. Order that plaintiff recover from legal aid fund costs of counterclaim after 7th March 1980.

Solicitors: *David Edwards*, Secretary, Legal Aid (for the Law Society); *Kirk, Jackson & Co*, Eccles (for the plaintiffs).

Sumra Green   Barrister.

a Re a debtor (No 6864 of 1980, High Court), the debtor v Slater Walker Ltd

COURT OF APPEAL, CIVIL DIVISION
EVELEIGH, WATKINS LJJ AND SIR DAVID CAIRNS
18th, 19th, 20th MAY 1981

b

Bankruptcy – Act of bankruptcy – Non-compliance with bankruptcy notice – Debtor wanting to set up counterclaim equalling or exceeding judgment debt after expiry of ten days from date of notice – Debtor applying for extension of time to file affidavit setting up counterclaim – Whether jurisdiction to extend time after expiry of ten days and act of bankruptcy committed – Bankruptcy Act 1914, ss 1(1)(g), 109(4) – Bankruptcy Rules 1952 (SI 1952 No 2113), rr 138, 139.

c

On 30th September 1980 the petitioning creditor obtained judgment by consent against the debtor for a sum of money. There was no stay of execution. On 22nd January 1981 the creditor served a bankruptcy notice on the debtor pursuant to the Bankruptcy Rules 1952 requiring him to satisfy the judgment debt or to satisfy the court that he had, inter alia, a counterclaim equalling or exceeding the debt, within ten days of service of the *d* notice. The notice stated, pursuant to r 137, that if he had such a counterclaim he should, within seven days, file an affidavit applying to set aside the notice on the ground of the counterclaim. The debtor failed either to satisfy the debt or to file an affidavit setting up a counterclaim within ten days of the notice and therefore, by virtue of s 1(1)(g)*ᵃ* of the Bankruptcy Act 1914, he was deemed on the expiry of the ten days to have committed an act of bankruptcy. On 4th February the creditor presented a *e* bankruptcy petition. On 13th February the debtor filed an affidavit pursuant to r 137 in which he applied (i) to set aside the bankruptcy notice on the ground that he had a counterclaim and (ii) for an extension of the time for filing the affidavit, under s 109(4)*ᵇ* of the 1914 Act. The registrar refused an extension of time, on the ground, inter alia, that he had no jurisdiction to extend the time for filing the affidavit once the ten days prescribed by s 1(1)(g) had expired. The debtor appealed, submitting that s 109(4) *f* conferred a general power on the court to extend time to file an affidavit applying to set aside a bankruptcy notice, and that the power could be exercised after the ten days had expired.

Held – The court had no jurisdiction under s 109(4) of the 1914 Act to extend beyond the ten days prescribed by s 1(1)(g) of that Act the time prescribed by r 138 of the 1952 *g* rules for filing an affidavit applying to set aside a bankruptcy notice, because once the ten days had expired without the debtor having satisfied the debt or having satisfied the court that he had a counterclaim equalling or exceeding it, the act which was a condition precedent to, and gave rise to, the deemed act of bankruptcy under s 1(1)(g), namely the debtor's failure to do anything under the bankruptcy notice, had been completed and an act of bankruptcy occurred by operation of law which could not be set aside by *h* proceedings under r 139 of the 1952 rules. Furthermore, although there was power under s 109(4) to extend the seven days prescribed by r 138, that power could not be used to extend the time for filing an affidavit applying to set aside a bankruptcy notice beyond the ten-day period. Accordingly, the appeal would be dismissed (see p 991 *a* to *e g* and p 992 *a* to *d* and *h j*, post).

Notes
j For the effect of a counterclaim, set-off or cross-demand on a bankruptcy notice, see 3 Halsbury's Laws (4th Edn) para 271, for setting aside a bankruptcy notice, see ibid para 273, and for cases on the subject, see 4 Digest (Reissue) 113–115, 990–998.

---

a Section 1(1), so far as material, is set out at p 989 *f* to *h*, post
b Section 109(4) is set out at p 990 *e*, post

For the Bankruptcy Act 1914, ss 1, 109, see 3 Halsbury's Statutes (3rd Edn) 38, 136.
    For the Bankruptcy Rules 1952, rr 137 to 139, see 3 Halsbury's Statutory Instruments   *a*
(Fourth Reissue) 246.

Cases referred to in judgments
Debtor (No 10 of 1953), Re a, ex parte the debtor v Ampthill Rural District Council [1953] 2 All
    ER 561, [1953] 1 WLR 1050, DC, 4 Digest (Reissue) 147, 1292.
Debtor (No 138 of 1980), Re a (1981) Times, 28th January, 125 Sol Jo 133, CA.
                                                                                            b
Cases also cited
Foster, Re, ex parte Basan (1885) 2 Morr 29, CA.
Hastings, Re, ex parte Dearle (1884) 14 QBD 184, CA.
Lennox, Re, ex parte Lennox (1885) 16 QBD 315, [1881–5] All ER Rep 1025, CA.
Moore (a bankrupt), Re (1969) 113 Sol Jo 791, [1969] Court of Appeal Transcript 287, CA.
                                                                                            c
Appeal
By a writ issued on 13th May 1980 the petitioning creditor, Slater Walker Ltd, brought
an action against the debtor claiming repayment of £432,702·62 as money lent. On
30th September 1980 Parker J, in chambers, ordered that judgment by consent be
entered against the debtor for the sum plus interest. On 8th December 1980 the
petitioning creditor issued a bankruptcy notice in respect of the judgment debt which *d*
was served on the debtor on 22nd January 1981. The debtor failed to comply with the
notice and accordingly, was deemed by s 1(1)(g) of the Bankruptcy Act 1914 to have
committed an act of bankruptcy. On 4th February the petitioning creditor presented a
bankruptcy petition. On 13th February the debtor filed an affidavit pursuant to r 137 of
the Bankruptcy Rules 1952 in which he applied under s 109(4) of the 1914 Act for an
extension of time for filing an affidavit to set aside the bankruptcy notice on the ground *e*
that he had a counterclaim equalling or exceeding the judgment debt and to set aside the
notice. On 17th February 1981 Mr Registrar Dewhurst refused the application. The
debtor appealed. The grounds of the appeal were (1) that the registrar erred in law in
failing to hold that he had power under s 109(4) to extend the time for service of the
debtor's affidavit under rr 137 to 139 of the 1952 rules beyond the expiration of ten days
from the service of the notice, (2) he erred in exercising his discretion by not extending *f*
the time for service of the affidavit by holding that the debtor's reasons were insufficient
grounds for exercising the discretion by extending the time, and (3) erred in holding that
the debtor's counterclaim could have been raised in the action in which the judgment for
the debt was obtained. The facts are set out in the judgment of Eveleigh LJ.

Gabriel Moss for the debtor.
Michael Crystal for the petitioning creditor.   *g*

EVELEIGH LJ. On 13th May 1980 Slater Walker Ltd issued a specially indorsed writ
against the debtor claiming the repayment of money lent. On 16th July 1980 the debtor
wrote a letter, addressed to 'The Directors, Slater, Walker Limited', in the following
terms: *h*

> 'Dear Sirs, 'High Court Action 1980 S. No. 2866.
> 'I hereby acknowledge and accept that I have no defence to the above action ("the
> action"). I further confirm that, in consideration of your agreement not to sign
> judgment in default of defence for a period of three months from 5 June 1980, I will
> not enter a defence to the action and will take no other steps to defend the action and
> I will consent to Slater, Walker Limited entering judgment against me on 5 *j*
> September 1980 for the full amount of your claim, namely, £432,702·60 together
> with interest and costs.'

On 30th September judgment was signed against him. On 22nd January 1981 a
bankruptcy notice was served. That was in the prescribed form and stated that execution
had not been stayed and that he was required within ten days to satisfy the debt or to

satisfy the court that he had a counterclaim, set-off or cross-demand which 'equals or
exceeds the sum claimed'. The notice concluded by saying:

> 'If, however, you have a Counterclaim, Set-off or Cross-demand which equals or
> exceeds the amount claimed by SLATER, WALKER LIMITED in respect of the Judgment
> and which you could not set up in the Action or other proceedings in which the said
> Judgment was obtained, you must within *seven* days apply to this Court to set aside
> this Notice, by filing with the Registrar an Affidavit to the above effect.'

The ten days in fact expired, allowing for dies non, on 3rd February 1981. The last
sentence of the notice which I have just quoted reflects the Bankruptcy Rules 1952, SI
1952 No 2113, in particular r 137, which requires every notice to be indorsed with an
intimation to the effect stated.

The filing of such an affidavit is made to operate as an application to set aside the
bankruptcy notice. That is the effect of r 139(1), which reads as follows:

> 'The filing of the affidavit referred to in Rule 137 shall operate as an application
> to set aside the bankruptcy notice, and thereupon the Registrar shall, if he is satisfied
> that sufficient cause is shown, fix a time and place for hearing the application, and
> shall give not less than three clear days' notice thereof to the debtor, the creditor, and
> their respective solicitors, if known.'

Rule 139(2) reads:

> 'If the application cannot be heard before the time specified in the notice for
> compliance with its requirements, the Registrar shall extend the time, and no act of
> bankruptcy shall be deemed to have been committed under the notice until the
> application has been heard and determined.'

Rule 138 as amended in 1977 prescribes the time for filing the affidavit, which in the
case of a notice served in England is seven days.

If an affidavit had been filed in time the registrar would have to ask himself if he was
satisfied that sufficient cause was shown and, on being so satisfied, he would then fix a
date for hearing the application. In fact in this case nothing at all was done. No affidavit
was filed. The debt was not satisfied. Therefore, on 3rd February 1981, the debtor had
committed an act of bankruptcy. That is the effect of s 1(1)(g) of the Bankruptcy Act
1914. Section 1(1) begins: 'A debtor commits an act of bankruptcy in each of the
following cases . . .' There are then listed a number of cases; para (g) reads as follows:

> 'If a creditor has obtained a final judgment or final order against him for any
> amount, and, execution thereon not having been stayed, has served on him in
> England, or, by leave of the court, elsewhere, a bankruptcy notice under this Act,
> and he does not, within ten days after service of the notice, in case the service is
> effected in England, and in the case the service is effected elsewhere, then within the
> time limited in that behalf by the order giving leave to effect the service, either
> comply with the requirements of the notice or satisfy the court that he has a
> counter-claim set off or cross demand which equals or exceeds the amount of the
> judgment debt or sum ordered to be paid, and which he could not set up in the
> action in which the judgment was obtained, or the proceedings in which the order
> was obtained . . .'

On 4th February 1981 a bankruptcy petiton was presented. On 13th February the
debtor filed an affidavit and applied to the registrar to fix a date for the hearing of his
application to set aside the bankruptcy notice. In his affidavit he alleged that he had a
counterclaim or counterclaims. There is no need for me to list them in detail. Suffice it
to say that one related to the selling of his shares by Slater Walker, which he alleges were
sold at too low a price. Another claim related to an alleged agreement to refund interest
to him, which interest was payable under a separate agreement granting a loan. It was
alleged that interest then had not been paid. It was further alleged in the affidavit that
the debtor was unable to set up the claim in the action. The reason for that was the letter

of 16th July 1980. The affidavit did not specifically aver that the amount of the counterclaim was equal to or exceeded the amount of the judgment debt. Indeed, for *a* my part, I find it quite impossible to arrive at any sort of figure for the alleged counterclaim.

The registrar refused to extend the time for filing the affidavit. He said that the reasons given by the debtor were insufficient and he added: '... in any case [it is] doubtful whether I have power to extend time beyond service of bankruptcy notice'. By that he clearly meant beyond the expiration of the ten days. He said: *b*

'If I am wrong the counterclaim or cross-claim referred to in ... the debtor's affidavit sworn on 13th February 1981 and in ... his supplemental affidavit dated 16th February 1981 could have been raised in the action in which judgment was obtained. The document dated 16th July 1980 signed by the debtor precluded him from raising them.'

c

He concluded by saying: 'He cannot rely on his own act now to say that he has a counterclaim or cross-claim which could not be raised in the action.'

The debtor appeals to this court on the grounds that the registrar was influenced or inhibited in arriving at his decision by his doubt whether or not he had jurisdiction and it is submitted that the registrar did in fact have jurisdiction to extend the time. It is said that he should have extended the time for the affidavit and also extended the ten days *d* (that must of course follow) for compliance under s 1(1)(g). It is further said that he should have fixed a time for hearing, namely a day within the extended term. It was also submitted that the registrar was wrong in concluding that the debtor was precluded from raising the counterclaim as stated by the registrar.

In so far as the question of jurisdiction is concerned, counsel has relied on s 109(4) of the Act. That reads as follows: *e*

'Where by this Act, or by general rules, the time for doing any act or thing is limited, the court may extend the time either before or after the expiration thereof, upon such terms, if any, as the court may think fit to impose.'

He argues that that is a general power which can be exercised retrospectively and gives power to extend the time not only of seven days for the filing of the affidavit but also the *f* ten days referred to in s 1(1)(g) of that Act. He relied also on a decision of the Court of Appeal in *Re a debtor (No 138 of 1980)* (1981) Times, 29th January 1981. It is but a short report, and as there is no other report of that case I shall read The Times report in full:

'Lord Justice Ormrod, sitting with Lord Justice Brightman and Mr Justice Reeve in the Court of Appeal, said in a judgment of the court that a registrar in bankruptcy had a discretionary power under section 109(4) of the Bankruptcy Act, 1914, to *g* extend the time for allowing a debtor to file an affidavit relating to a counterclaim, set-off or cross-demand against his creditor: rule 137(b) of the Bankruptcy Rules, 1952. The statement to the contrary in *Williams on Bankruptcy* (19th Edn, 1979, p 467) was based on a misunderstanding of *In re a Debtor* ([1953] 2 All ER 561, [1953] 1 WLR 1050) and was not correct. In the present case the Affidavit was filed after the expiry of the seven-day period appropriate under rule 138 (as amended) *h* but before the expiry of the 10-day period before an act of bankruptcy was committed under section 1(1)(g) of the Act. The debtor had asked that the affidavit be admitted as a valid claim although it was filed two days out of time.'

That case was dealing with an application made within the ten-day period. The judgment indeed, in the words I have quoted, emphasises that. However, counsel for the *j* debtor says that the same power must exist in the present case, because the power derives from s 109(4) and that is of general application.

So in the present case, on 3rd February 1981 an act of bankruptcy had been committed. That was a fact. The question is whether this court has power under s 109 to extend time in such a way as to cancel that act or to revoke it or to deem it never to

have occurred. That means that the debtor in this case has to satisfy the court that there
a is a retrospective power to alter the effect of s 1 of the Bankruptcy Act 1914.

Turning to s 1(1)(g), one sees that the time prescribed there of ten days relates to a
failure of the debtor to satisfy the court. The words used are: 'If . . . he does not, within
ten days after service of the notice . . . satisfy the court . . .' Now 'if he does not', in my
view, is equivalent to saying 'if he fails'. Once the ten days are up the act which gives rise
to the consequential act of bankruptcy has been completed. That act is his failure. Seen
b in this way, the court, in my opinion, is concerned to determine whether a condition has
been fulfilled so that an act of bankruptcy has been committed and not to decide whether
there is an act which remains to be done. The act has been done: his failure is complete.
If the court extends the ten days after the failure is complete it will be refusing to
recognise the consequences which Parliament has said have ensued. In my opinion, we
cannot do this. Once the ten days have expired the failure within that period of the
c debtor to satisfy the court is properly to be seen as a condition which has been fulfilled
and which gives rise to the consequences, namely, that an act of bankruptcy has been
committed.

I accept that the court can extend the seven days in r 139 and can do so
retrospectively. But in the present case the registrar was asked to do this for the purpose
of revoking a condition that had already been fulfilled, that is to say, for the purpose of
d extending the ten days. To grant an extension of time for the seven days would be of no
effect if the ten-day period were not to be extended and, as I have said, in my opinion, we
cannot extend the ten days retrospectively. The power to extend the seven days must be
exercised for a proper purpose. It cannot be used for the purpose of extending the ten
days. In my opinion, the court has no jurisdiction to exercise the power under s 109(4)
for this purpose.

e It is interesting to see the provision contained in s 1(1)(e), that is to say, an act of
bankruptcy is committed—

> 'If execution against him has been levied by seizure of his goods under process in
> any action in any court, or in any civil proceedings in the High Court, and the goods
> have been either sold or held by the sheriff for twenty-one days.'

f The holding of goods for 21 days by the sheriff is a condition on the fulfilment of which
an act of bankruptcy is committed. Once the 21 days has expired (I say nothing as to the
power of the court before that time) I would find it difficult, and indeed impossible, to
say that the court could alter that period. In the same way I find it impossible to say that
the court can extend the ten-day period once it has expired.

Consequently, I would hold that the court has no jurisdiction. But if I am wrong on
g that, in my opinion, this affidavit so lacks precision and clarity that I would hesitate to say
that the registrar or the court should be satisfied, as r 139 requires. Indeed, the note in
Williams on Bankruptcy (19th Edn, 1979, p 583) emphasises the importance of the
words 'if he is satisfied that sufficient cause is shown'. They were inserted in 1952—

> 'reinforcing earlier decisions that if the affidavit does not show on the face of it
> that the counterclaim, set-off or cross-demand equals or exceeds the judgment debt,
h > the rule does not come into operation; the debtor must therefore quantify his
> counterclaim and give full particulars.'

The strict interpretation of those words may be relaxed where 'the shortness of time for
filing the affidavit may not permit the debtor to state more than the outline of the case',
but in the present case that cannot apply. The proceedings were commenced in 1980.
j The debtor must have known then whether or not he had any counterclaim. There was
ample time for him to investigate the matter. The history of this case indicates to my
mind that he was not anxious to proceed with dispatch in any way; for, having served
notice of this appeal, he then opposed an application by the judgment creditor for the
appeal to be expedited. As there will, or may, be further proceedings in this matter in
relation to the validity of the counterclaims and their value and their effect in bankruptcy

proceedings, I feel that I ought not to comment on whether or not the registrar was right in saying that the debtor could not set up the counterclaims now, because he had *a* precluded himself by his own act from doing so in the action. I prefer to say nothing on that aspect of this case, but for the reasons which I have stated I would dismiss this appeal.

WATKINS LJ. I agree and have nothing to add.

SIR DAVID CAIRNS. I also agree. I am satisfied that there is no jurisdiction under *b* s 109(4) of the Bankruptcy Act 1914 to extend the period of seven days within which an affidavit setting up a counterclaim may be filed under r 138 of the Bankruptcy Rules 1952, as amended in 1977, beyond the ten days at the expiration of which an act of bankruptcy is deemed to have occurred under s 1(1)(g) of the 1914 Act as amended by s 4 of the Insolvency Act 1976. There is no provision in the Acts for extending the ten days. Section 109(4) does not apply to it, because there is no 'act or thing' to be done *c* within the ten days. When a bankruptcy notice has been given and nothing occurs before the expiratation of the ten days to hold up its operation, then the act of bankruptcy takes place by operation of law. There is nothing in the Acts or the rules to suggest that, once there has been an act of bankruptcy, it can be set aside by proceedings under rr 137 to 139. Therefore, extension of the time for filing the affidavit after the tenth day has passed would be nugatory. Parliament cannot have intended by s 109 to authorise a *d* futile extension.

That is the formal reason for saying that there is no such jurisdiction. There are good practical reasons too. If the time could be extended after the tenth day there is no limit to the possible extensions. Counsel for the debtor conceded that, if his argument is right, there could be an application for extension at any time in the course of the bankruptcy proceedings, even after adjudication. This would lead only to inconvenience, expense *e* and delay. Moreover, it has to be remembered that an act of bankruptcy enures to the benefit not only of the creditor who has served the bankruptcy notice but of any other creditor who may wish to present a petition. It would be unsatisfactory if such a right could be defeated as a result of an application on which no creditor has the right to be heard.

If there were jurisdiction to extend the time in this case I would still say that there was *f* no ground for extending it. In my view, the letter signed by the debtor on 16th July 1980 constitutes an agreement by him not to enter a defence and an acknowledgment that he has no defence to the action. The only counterclaims set up in the debtor's affidavits are claims arising out of the same transaction or series of transactions on which the plaintiffs' claim was based. Therefore, if valid, they would constitute not only counterclaims but set-offs, and a set-off is a defence. *g*

Next, I was inclined to agree with the registrar that the words 'counterclaim . . . which he could not set up in the action' are not apt to include a counterclaim which the debtor has debarred himself from setting up in the action. Having regard to the caveat entered by Eveleigh LJ, I express no final opinion on that matter. But, lastly in the affidavits filed by the debtor he did not depose to a counterclaim which equalled or exceeded the amount of the judgment debt. *h*

I mention all these various matters because each of them formed the subject matter of argument before this court and each separate ground which I have given is, in my judgment, a sufficient reason for dismissing the appeal. The fact that I have mentioned them is not to be taken as any indication that I have any doubt about the primary ground for dismissing the appeal, namely the absence of jurisdiction.

j

Appeal dismissed.

Solicitors: *Janzen & Co* (for the debtor); *Freshfields* (for the petitioning creditors).

Mary Rose Plummer   Barrister.

a   # André & Cie SA v Marine Transocean Ltd
    # The Splendid Sun

COURT OF APPEAL, CIVIL DIVISION
LORD DENNING MR, EVELEIGH AND FOX LJJ
b   19th, 20th FEBRUARY, 8th APRIL 1981

Arbitration – Practice – Want of prosecution – Injunction restraining claimant from proceeding with arbitration – Delay – Rescission – Frustration – Neither party taking any action in arbitration for eight years – Whether parties impliedly agreeing to terminate arbitration agreement – Whether agreement rescinded – Whether agreement frustrated because delay c *making fair arbitration impossible.*

In May 1969 a vessel under charter to the charterers grounded as she was berthing at the port of discharge in Venezuela and sustained damage costing $US221,733 to repair. The owners claimed that the charterers had ordered the vessel to discharge at an unsafe berth and were therefore liable. The charterers claimed that the captain was at fault and that d the owners were liable. Under the terms of the charterparty the dispute was referred to arbitration in London, and in September and October 1969 each side appointed an arbitrator. Nothing further happened and in 1973 the charterers closed their file on the claim. In February 1975 the arbitrator appointed by the charterers died and no appointment was made to replace him. Again nothing further happened, until December 1977 when the owners delivered their points of claim. The charterers sought e and were granted an injunction restraining the owners from proceeding with the arbitration, on the ground that the delay of eight years made it impossible for the charterers to prepare their defence (which depended on the evidence of ships' officers in Venezuela at the time), and that the arbitration agreement had been frustrated. The owners appealed, contending that it was not open to the judge to hold that the agreement had been frustrated by the owners' delay, because the charterers were under the same f duty as the owners to keep the arbitration moving.

Held – The appeal would be dismissed for the following reasons—
    (1) It was to be inferred from the lapse of eight years between the appointment of arbitrators and the delivery of the owners' points of claim during which nothing happened that the parties had impliedly agreed to terminate the arbitration agreement, g so that by 1978, when they received the owners' points of claim, the charterers had, as they were entitled to, already accepted the contract as being rescinded (see p 996 *a b d*, p 999 *a b*, p 1000 *d e*, p 1002 *e f j*, p 1005 *h j* and p 1006 *a* to *g*, post); *Forslind v Bechely-Crundall* 1922 SC (HL) 173 and dictum of Rowlatt J in *Pearl Mill Co Ltd v Ivy Tannery Co Ltd* [1918–19] All ER Rep at 704 applied; *Bremer Vulkan Schiffbau Und Maschinenfabrik v South India Shipping Corpn* [1981] 1 All ER 289 distinguished.
h   (2) (Per Lord Denning MR, Fox LJ dissenting) An arbitration agreement could be frustrated either by mutual default of both parties or repudiatory breach by one party of the agreement to refer the dispute to arbitration if the delay caused by the mutual default or the conduct of one party was such that a fair arbitration was impossible. Having regard to the owners' delay, the arbitration agreement had been frustrated by the owners' delay or their repudiatory breach (see p 997 *j*, p 998 *c* to *j* and p 999 *a b*, post); dicta of j Lord Diplock, Lord Fraser and Lord Scarman in *Bremer Vulkan Schiffbau Und Maschinenfabrik v South India Shipping Corpn* [1981] 1 All ER at 297, 306, 310–311 applied and of Lord Diplock at 299, 301 not followed.

Notes
For the court's power to restrain arbitration proceedings by injunction, see 2 Halsbury's

Laws (4th Edn) para 518, for an arbitrator's powers generally, see ibid para 577, and for
cases on restraint of arbitration by injunction, see 3 Digest (Reissue) 95–98, 484–500.   *a*

 For dismissal of actions for want of prosecution, see 30 Halsbury's Laws (3rd Edn) 410,
para 771.

 For frustration of contract, and the application of the doctrine to charterparties, see 9
Halsbury's Laws (4th Edn) paras 450, 452–453, and for cases on the subject, see 12 Digest
(Reissue) 484–491, 3435–3465.

 For repudiation of contract, see 9 Halsbury's Laws (4th Edn) paras 546–549, and for   *b*
cases on the subject, see 12 Digest (Reissue) 411–416, 3032–3049.

Cases referred to in judgments

Bremer Vulkan Schiffbau Und Maschinenfabrik v South India Shipping Corpn [1980] 1 All ER
 420, [1980] 2 WLR 905, CA; *on appeal* [1981] 1 All ER 289, [1981] 2 WLR 141, HL.   *c*
Carswell v Collard (1893) 20 R (HL) 47.
Davis Contractors Ltd v Fareham Urban District Council [1956] 2 All ER 145, [1956] AC 696,
 [1956] 3 WLR 37, 54 LGR 289, HL, 12 Digest (Reissue) 507, 3518.
Forslind v Bechely-Crundall 1922 SC (HL) 173.
Freeth v Burr (1874) LR 9 CP 208, [1874–80] All ER Rep 751, 43 LJCP 91, 29 LT 773, 12
 Digest (Reissue) 413, 3042.   *d*
Mersey Steel and Iron Co Ltd v Naylor, Benzon & Co (1884) 9 App Cas 434, [1881–5] All ER
 Rep 365, 53 LJQB 497, 51 LT 637, 32 WR 989, HL, 12 Digest (Reissue) 413, 3038.
National Carriers Ltd v Panalpina (Northern) Ltd [1981] 1 All ER 161, [1981] 2 WLR 45,
 HL.
Pearl Mill Co Ltd v Ivy Tannery Co Ltd [1919] 1 KB 78, [1918–19] All ER Rep 702, 88 LJKB
 134, 120 LT 28, 24 Com Cas 169, DC, 21 Digest (Repl) 482, 1700.   *e*
R v Inhabitants of Gresham (1786) 1 Term Rep 101, 99 ER 996, 12 Digest (Reissue) 445,
 3215.

Cases also cited   *f*

Constantine (Joseph) Steamship Line Ltd v Imperial Smelting Corpn Ltd, The Kingswood [1941]
 2 All ER 165, [1942] AC 154, HL.
Crawford v A E A Prowting Ltd [1972] 1 All ER 1199, [1973] 1 QB 1.
Denmark Productions Ltd v Boscobel Productions Ltd [1968] 3 All ER 513, [1969] 1 QB 699,
 CA.
Maritime National Fish Ltd v Ocean Trawlers Ltd [1935] AC 524, [1935] All ER Rep 86, DC.   *g*
North London Railway Co v Great Northern Railway Co (1883) 11 QBD 30.
Pioneer Shipping Ltd v BTP Tioxide Ltd, The Nema [1980] 3 All ER 117, [1980] QB 547, CA.
Turriff Ltd v Richards & Wallington (Contracts) Ltd [1981] Com LR 39.

Appeal   *h*

By an originating summons dated 24th July 1978, the plaintiffs, André & Cie SA ('the
charterers'), a body corporate of Lausanne, Switzerland, sought against the defendants,
Marine Transocean Ltd ('the owners'), a body corporate of Monrovia, (i) a declaration that
Mr Cedric Barclay, being the arbitrator appointed by the owners in a dispute between the
owners and the charterers relating to a charterparty of the vessel Splendid Sun dated 27th
February 1969, had no jurisdiction to make any order or award in the arbitration, (ii) an   *j*
injunction restraining the owners from appointing Mr Barclay as sole arbitrator in the
arbitration or otherwise attempting further to pursue the arbitration, and (iii)
alternatively, a declaration that such arbitrator or arbitrators as might be appointed in the
arbitration had jurisdiction, if so advised, to dismiss the owners' claim, whether by
making an award in favour of the charterers or otherwise, for want of prosecution. On

a 25th June 1979 Lloyd J granted the charterers the first declaration and the injunction sought. The owners appealed. The facts are set out in the judgment of Lord Denning MR.

Michael Collins for the owners.
Nicholas Phillips QC and *Richard Aikens* for the charterers.

b   *Cur adv vult*

8th April. The following judgments were read.

LORD DENNING MR. Everything in this case took place eleven years ago. In February 1969 the m v Splendid Sun was let by her owners on a voyage charter. She was to load a cargo at a safe port on the West Coast of Mexico and carry it to Puerto Cabello *c* in Venezuela, and discharge it at 'one/two safe berths PUERTO CABELLO'.

In April 1969 the vessel went to Manzanillo, Mexico. She loaded 10,400 metric tons of maize. A bill of lading was issued, incorporating the terms of the charterparty, including the Centrocon arbitration clause. This provides for arbitration in London by two commercial arbitrators (one arbitrator appointed by each party) with power to appeal to an umpire.

d On 10th May 1969 the vessel arrived in the roads off Puerto Cabello. On 31st May 1969 the receivers of the cargo ordered her to proceed to berth 10 in order to discharge. As she was getting near, she grounded. Her rudder was damaged. Temporary repairs were done there. Permanent repairs were done in Italy. The expense was $US221,733·18.

The owners put the blame on the charterers. They wrote a letter on 7th June 1969 to the charterers: 'It is obvious, being the demonstration in "re ipsa", that the assigned berth *e* was not safe as under the terms of the C/P.'

The charterers put the responsibility on the owners. They wrote a letter on 24th June 1969 to the owners: 'We hereby repudiate any liability as it was the captain's duty to bring his vessel to the assigned berth, which is customarily used for other vessels of similar size.'

f Each side appointed nautical surveyors to examine the vessel. Each side appointed an arbitrator. On 18th September 1969 the owners appointed Mr Cedric Barclay. On 1st October 1969 the charterers appointed Mr R J Lynn.

Now, this is the amazing thing. Nothing more happened on this dispute for over eight years. The period of limitation of six years came and went. Mr Lynn died on 5th February 1975. No one was appointed in his place. Then out of the blue on 29th December 1977 the solicitors for the owners wrote to the charterers a letter received on *g* 3rd January 1978:

'"SPLENDID SUN"—C/P 27.9.69—GROUNDING AT PUERTO CABELLO—
'We act for Marine Transocean Limited in connection with this matter and now enclose Points of Claim on their behalf. You will recall that on 1.10.69 you appointed Mr. R. J. Lynn to act as your Abritrator, and that Mr. Cedric Barclay was *h* appointed on behalf of our clients. We have today written to Mr. Barclay requesting him to make the order for directions.
'Yours faithfully,
'Holman, Fenwick, & Willan.'

j The solicitors enclosed in that letter points of claim drafted and signed by counsel. The charterers were aghast at this sudden revival of the claim. Their solicitors made inquiries and went out to Puerto Cabello to see if there was any evidence available to meet the claim. None was available. As a result the judge said:

'... it is now virtually impossible to prepare a defence to the claim in the arbitration. If the correct test is, as I believe it to be, whether the delay of the owners

in pursuing their claim in [the] arbitration has been such as to frustrate the
arbitration agreement, I would unhesitatingly hold that it has.'   *a*

Abandonment

For myself, I would be prepared to decide this case on the same lines as *Pearl Mill Co
Ltd v Ivy Tannery Co Ltd* [1919] 1 KB 78 at 82, [1918–19] All ER Rep 702 at 704. The
lapse of time, over eight years, was so long that 'the proper inference to be drawn [is] that
each party was justified in assuming that the matter was off altogether'. I look at it in this   *b*
way. It was the owners who were making the claim for damage to the ship. It was their
master who was navigating it into the berth. It was for him and the crew to say how she
came to be grounded, to give some evidence that the berth was unsafe, and that the
grounding was not due to the bad navigation of the master.

As soon as the two arbitrators were appointed in 1969, it was for the owners to take the
next step. Either by applying to the arbitrators for directions, or (as they eventually did)   *c*
omitting that step and delivering points of claim. By failing to take that step, it would
look as if they, or their insurers, had little confidence in the claim. They may have
suspected it was the master's own fault. Then, after five years, one of the arbitrators, Mr
Lynn, died. Still the owners did nothing. I do not see why the charterers at that stage
should have been expected to appoint anyone in Mr Lynn's place. It was for the owners,
if they were pursuing their claim, to serve the charterers with notice to appoint a   *d*
substitute for Mr Lynn (see s 7(b) of the Arbitration Act 1950). By doing nothing, the
inference was that the owners were not pursuing their claim. So much so that three
years later the charterers were justified in assuming that the arbitration was at an end.

The Bremer Vulkan case

The recent ruling of the House of Lords in *Bremer Vulkan Schiffbau Und Maschinenfabrik*   *e*
v South India Shipping Corpn [1981] 1 All ER 289, [1981] 2 WLR 141 has given much
anxiety to many. It would appear to put on each party to an arbitration a duty to get on
with the case. If the claimant does nothing, it is the duty of the respondent to apply to
the arbitrator. If the respondent does not fulfil that duty, the claimant can delay
indefinitely, even for years, and then restore the case for hearing before the arbitrators;
and the arbitrators must go on and hear and determine the case. That is the interpretation   *f*
which we were asked to put on the words of Lord Diplock. He said ([1981] 1 All ER 289
at 299, 301, [1981] 2 WLR 141 at 153, 155):

'. . . the obligation is, in my view, mutual: it obliges each party to co-operate with
the other in taking appropriate steps to keep the procedure in the arbitration
moving, whether he happens to be the claimant or the respondent in the particular
dispute . . . if what is done voluntarily by way of preparation is done so tardily that   *g*
it threatens to delay the hearing to a date when there will be a substantial risk that
justice cannot be done, it is in my view a necessary implication from their having
agreed that the arbitrators should resolve their dispute that both parties, respondent
as well as claimant, are under a mutual obligation to one another to join in applying
to the arbitrators for appropriate directions to put an end to delay.'

h

This mutual obligation comes as something of a surprise to everyone; especially to the
denizens of Essex Court and St Mary Axe. Nothing of the kind was propounded before
the judge, or before us in the Court of Appeal. It appears for the first time in the speech
of Lord Diplock in the House of Lords. It is, I suppose, too late for any words of mine to
make any difference. It is for us to come to terms with it. It is said to be based on an
implication. As such it goes beyond anything that I have hitherto understood. To my   *j*
way of thinking the implication is neither obvious, nor reasonable, nor necessary. Nor
does it accord with reality. If the claimant does not pursue his claim, if he makes no
application to the arbitrator, it is said that the respondent is bound himself to do so. Who
ever hears of a respondent doing any such thing? Take this very case. It was not the
charterers who were claiming any money. It was the owners. If they wanted to pursue

their claim, they should have taken steps to put in their points of claim, or to apply for
directions. It was not for the charterers to do so. Just as the owners started the arbitration
by taking the first step. So they should have continued it by taking the second or
succeeding steps as they came around to be done. As we all know, the cases are legion in
which arbitrators are appointed and nothing more is heard of the case. Sometimes it is
settled. At other times the claimant simply lets it drop, and the respondent does
nothing. Does that mean that the claimant can revive it five, eight, fifteen or twenty
years later on? I cannot believe that the House of Lords intended any such thing. I think
that we must have misunderstood the ruling in some way or other. Take this very case.
If there really is a mutual obligation, the charterers, at the end of 1969, ought themselves
to have roused the sleeping shipowners or have applied to the arbitrators for directions;
and, as they did not do so, they are now in 1981 being faced with an arbitration, when
all their evidence is lost. It would be most unjust to put such an obligation on the
charterers, which no one had ever thought of before.

Lord Diplock made striking reference to the maxim vigilantibus non dormientibus
jura subveniunt: the laws help the vigilant, not the sleepers. But that maxim can work
both ways. If the shipowners had been vigilant and watchful, the laws ought indeed to
help them, as against the sleeping charterers. But these shipowners were not vigilant:
they went to sleep themselves. So they should have no claim on the laws to help them.
The maxim simply does not apply. Two of their Lordships (Lord Edmund-Davies and
Lord Russell) agreed with the speech of Lord Diplock without giving separate reasons of
their own. So we have no help there to correct the misunderstanding, if such it be, of
Lord Diplock's speech.

The alternative

Lord Fraser and Lord Scarman differed. They took a view which it is easy to
understand. It seems to me, at any rate, to be much more in accord with sound
jurisprudence. They start off with a precept of natural justice which cannot be denied.
Each party to a dispute has a right to a fair trial. Not only in a court of law or in a
domestic tribunal. But also in an arbitration. But, seeing that arbitration is consensual,
there is a corollary which is equally indisputable. Each is to do his part as it comes round
to him to do it. Neither party will do anything that he ought not to do, or omit to do
anything that he ought to do, in order to ensure a fair trial. The claimant will put in his
points of claim as it comes round for him to do it; the respondent will put in his answer
when it comes to his turn. A failure on either side entitles the other to such redress as the
justice of the case requires. Ubi jus ibi remedium. The manner and scope of the redress
depends on the circumstances. Lord Fraser found this redress by resort to equitable
principles ([1981] 1 All ER 289 at 306, [1981] 2 WLR 141 at 162):

> '... I would rest my opinion in favour of the respondents in this appeal on the
> principle that they have an equitable right not to be harassed by arbitration
> proceedings which cannot result in a fair trial.'

Lord Scarman found it by resort to the common law. He rested it on a term necessarily
to be implied ([1981] 1 All ER 289 at 310–311, [1981] 2 WLR 141 at 166–167):

> 'Where parties agree to refer present or future differences to arbitration, they
> enter into a contract, an implied term of which is that each has a right to a fair
> arbitration ... there are mutual obligations to be implied into the parties'
> agreement not to obstruct or frustrate the purpose of the agreement, ie a fair
> arbitration to be conducted in accordance with the terms of their agreement.'

If this view were to prevail, it would enable us to give a short answer in this case. The
shipowners would fail. After their long delay of eight years, they are now harassing the
charterers by resurrecting this arbitration. Their delay has been such as to obstruct and
frustrate the purpose of the agreement. They should not be allowed to proceed.

The solution

Although the views of the majority and minority seem so divergent, there is one *a* sentence in Lord Diplock's speech which points the way to a solution. It is this ([1981] 1 All ER 289 at 297, [1981] 2 WLR 141 at 150):

'I would accept that the unperformed primary obligations of the parties under an arbitration agreement, like other contracts, may be brought to an end by frustration, or at the election of one party where there has been a repudiatory breach of that agreement by the other party.' *b*

That looks to me very like Lord Scarman's view. In so far as any principle of law is to be gathered from the *Bremer Vulkan* case, I would find it in that one sentence of Lord Diplock, coupled with the allied principles stated by Lord Fraser and by Lord Scarman. It leaves it open to the courts to apply the doctrines of frustration or repudiatory breach, as they always have done. To these, therefore, I now turn. *c*

Frustration

In our present case Lloyd J had no doubts. He held without hesitation that the delay in this case was so great as to frustrate the arbitration agreement completely. I entirely agree with him. The delay was so great that a fair trial was impossible. Any arbitration at this length of time would be one-sided in favour of the shipowners. They had the *d* evidence of the master of the ship to help them. But the charterers had nothing. All their evidence had been made unavailable because of the delay. The harbour records had been lost or destroyed. Witnesses had lost their minds or could not remember anything.

But here is the problem: the doctrine of frustration is always stated in the formula that performance has become impossible '*without* the default of either party', as for instance the classic formula by Lord Radcliffe in *Davis Contractors Ltd v Fareham Urban District* *e* *Council* [1956] 2 All ER 145 at 160, [1956] AC 696 at 729 and the recent formula by Lord Simon in *National Carriers Ltd v Panalpina (Northern) Ltd* [1981] 1 All ER 161 at 175, [1981] 2 WLR 45 at 63. In our present case it is said that if there is a 'mutual obligation' as stated by Lord Diplock the impossibility of performance was '*with* the default of both parties'. So this case cannot be fitted into the formula.

But that formula is not exhaustive. There can be frustration by the mutual default of *f* both parties. In my opinion there can be frustration of an arbitration agreement where it is delayed by the mutual default of both sides, if it continues for so long a time that a fair trial is impossible.

Repudiatory breach

Another way of reaching the same result is the other exception stated by Lord Diplock *g* ([1981] 1 All ER 289 at 297, [1981] 2 WLR 141 at 150): '. . . at the election of one party where there has been a repudiatory breach of [the] agreement by the other party': or, as stated by Lord Scarman ([1981] 1 All ER 289 at 310, [1981] 2 WLR 141 at 166): '. . . frustration of the right, ie conduct of a party making the fair arbitration of a dispute impossible, will be a repudiatory breach at least of the agreement to refer that *dispute* to arbitration' (my emphasis). *h*

When one party is guilty of prolonged delay (in applying to the arbitrator) it is a breach which goes to the root of the contract. It is then open to the other to elect to accept it; and he does accept it by not himself applying to the arbitrator, thus treating himself as discharged from further performance.

In our present case the failure of the shipowners for over eight years to apply to the arbitrators was a breach going to the root of the arbitration. It was open to the charterers *j* to accept it as discharging them from any further performance of the contract. They did accept it by their own conduct, in not applying to the arbitrator themselves.

Conclusion

I would try my hand at expressing the result of the *Bremer Vulkan* case. It is binding so far as the actual decision goes: that the court has no jurisdiction to intervene in an *a* arbitration by way of dismissing the plaintiff's claim for want of prosecution. But the reasoning of the majority is so capable of being misunderstood that we should await its further consideration before acting on it. Meanwhile it is open to the court to find that an arbitration has come to an end by abandonment, or by frustration, or by repudiatory breach. Applied to this case, I would hold that the arbitration was abandoned by both sides long ago, or, alternatively, that it was frustrated by the long delay, or by repudiatory breach by the shipowners. I would dismiss the appeal.

b

EVELEIGH LJ. On 18th September 1969 the owners appointed their arbitrator. On 1st October 1969 the charterers appointed their arbitrator, Mr R J Lynn. Dr Wirth, a director of the charterers, stated in his affidavit that the last record on the charterers' files of any meeting with the owners was of one on 30th January 1970 and the last correspondence between the parties was in February 1970. He had by then learned that *c* hull underwriters were expected to make a payment of $110,000 shortly. As nothing more had been heard from the owners, their club or the vessel's underwriters, the charterers' file was closed some time in 1973 and put in the archives. Mr Lynn died on 5th February 1975. It seems highly probable that the parties and their advisers would have known this almost immediately or at the latest by September when Dr Monducci, the appellants' lawyer, says he was told by Dr Wirth. No new arbitrator was appointed *d* by the charterers and the owners made no request that they should do so. Dr Monducci claims that he was told of Mr Lynn's death in a chance encounter with Dr Wirth in the street. He says that he mentioned to Dr Wirth that 'We were going ahead with arbitration' and that Dr Wirth had said that 'Mr. Lynn had died and that they would have to substitute him'. Further Dr Monducci says that he told Dr Wirth that he had been ill and that this was making things lengthy. Dr Wirth, while conceding that he might have *e* mentioned the death of Mr Lynn, denies the rest of the alleged conversation. Neither person has a record of the conversation. On 29th December 1977 the owners wrote to the charterers enclosing their points of claim. This letter was received on 3rd January 1978. From that date right back to February 1970 there had been no step taken in the arbitration and no communication between the parties save what occurred at the chance encounter in the street between Dr Monducci and Dr Wirth.

f The charterers clearly treated the owners' claim and any intention to proceed with the arbitration as abandoned. They probably did so in 1973. Whether they were entitled to take this view at that time is another matter. They certainly had done so by 1975 and quite clearly by January 1978 when the points of claim arrived they had long since treated the whole matter as at an end. In legal language they had treated the owners as having rescinded the arbitration agreement in so far as this claim was concerned and had *g* themselves agreed that it should be rescinded. The question is whether or not they were entitled to do so and to ask for an injunction to restrain the owners from proceeding with the arbitration.

Bremer Vulkan Schiffbau Und Maschinenfabrik v South India Shipping Corpn [1981] 1 All ER 289, [1981] 2 WLR 141 clearly establishes that the relationship between the parties to an arbitration clause is governed by the law of contract and not by considerations *h* applicable to an action at law. The arbitration clause is, in the words of Lord Diplock, 'an agreement between the parties as to what each of them will do if and whenever there occurs an event of a particular kind' (see [1981] 1 All ER 289 at 298, [1981] 2 WLR 141 at 151). Lord Diplock went on to say:

j 'The event is one that either party can initiate by asserting against the other a claim under or concerning the shipbuilding agreement which they have not been able to settle by agreement. In that event, each is obliged to join with the other in referring the claim to arbitration and to abide by the arbitrator's award. The arbitration clause itself creates no obligation on either party to do or refrain from doing anything unless and until the event occurs, and even then the mutual obligations that arise are *in relation to the particular claim that constitutes the event*. The primary obligations of both parties that arise then are contractual, whether express, or implied by statute or included by necessary implication in the arbitration clause.' (My emphasis.)

It must follow that if the party who initiated the event then withdraws or abandons his claim he must, at least prima facie, be taken to annul the event and to seek the cancellation of the arbitration *'in relation to the particular claim that constitutes the event'*. It may be that the other party will wish for a decision of the arbitrator, for there may be other claims which could be affected. On the other hand, he might gladly accept the position and consent to the arbitration being at an end. The fact that he has himself failed to proceed diligently with the appropriate steps in the arbitration will not prevent him from doing so. There is no implied term that he will not be dilatory. Lord Diplock made this clear for, as the Arbitration Act 1950 itself provided machinery to put an end to delay, there was no necessity to imply such a term. The highest it might be put, and Lord Diplock did not decide the point, is that there is a mutual obligation which 'obliges each party to co-operate with the other in taking appropriate steps to keep the procedure in the arbitration moving, whether he happens to be the claimant or the respondent in the particular dispute' (see [1981] 1 All ER 289 at 299, [1981] 2 WLR 141 at 153). When the other party is not operating there is nothing with which to co-operate. Even if there is a breach of some obligation on both sides, that clearly cannot prevent the parties from agreeing to put an end to their obligations under it.

In the present case, however, it is said that the owners did not seek to put an end to the arbitration and did not intend to withdraw or abandon their claim. In my opinion, however, they must be taken to intend that which any reasonable man would conclude that they intended, particularly when the other party has acted to his detriment in consequence. That the charterers did so act is quite apparent. They made no further preparations for their defence, they treated the matter as at an end, and as time went on evidence ceased to be available to them. The fact that it is not necessary to prove an actual intention to rescind or withdraw the claim clearly emerges from the authorities, among which perhaps *Forslind v Bechely-Crundall* 1922 SC (HL) 173 is the most emphatic. The defender had contracted to fell timber and sell it to the pursuer who had paid £5,000, part of the price, in advance. There was considerable delay. The pursuer made various excuses but from time to time offered to deliver some of the trees. Viscount Haldane said (at 179):

> 'But the case made by the appellant is, not that a reasonable time had elapsed so that in this respect there was a breach of contract, but that the conduct of the respondent was such as to evince the intention to make default in the performance of the contract as a whole, in such a fashion that the appellant was entitled to treat it as repudiated *in toto*, without waiting for the arrival of the time at which specific implement could in the ordinary course be demanded. Whether what amounted to such repudiation actually took place is largely a question of fact, to be determined by consideration of the circumstances and of the action of the respondent in these circumstances ... If the defender has behaved in such a way that a reasonable person would properly conclude that he does not intend to perform the obligations he has undertaken, that is sufficient. *The defender's words and the state of his mind are less important than the intention to be gathered from what he does, as evidenced by his attitude.*' (My emphasis.)

He observed that the law in Scotland was the same as in England. Viscount Finlay, who dissented on the facts, said (at 184):

> 'The law bearing upon this point has been clearly settled by a series of decisions, of which *Freeth v. Burr* ((1874) LR 9 CP 208, [1874–80] All ER Rep 751) and the *Mersey Steel and Iron Co.'s* case ((1884) 9 App Cas 43 at 438–439, 446, [1881–5] All ER Rep 365 at 367–368, 371) are the most important. If one of the parties to a contract, either in express terms or by conduct, leads the other party to the reasonable conclusion that he does not mean to carry out the contract, this amounts

a to a repudiation which will justify the other in treating the contract as at an end and claiming damages on that footing, without waiting for the time when, by the contract, performance was to have taken place.'

Lord Dunedin said (at 190):

b 'There is a case decided by this House which has not received the attention it deserves from the fact of its being only reported in the Scottish reports (*Carswell* v. *Collard* ((1893) 20 R (HL) 47)). I cite it because I think Lord Chancellor Herschell put the true criterion which is to be applied to the facts in a case when a party to a contract says he is entitled to be free of it owing to repudiation on the other contractor's part. Lord Herschell says (at 48): "Of course the question was not what actually influenced the defender, but what effect the conduct of the pursuer would be reasonably calculated to have upon a reasonable person." Applying this criterion

c to the facts of the present case I take the same view as that expressed by Lord Haldane, which is also the view of the Lord Ordinary.'

Lord Shaw said (at 191–192):

d 'I desire to add this reference to the decided cases. *Freeth* v. *Burr* was referred to in this House with approval in *Mersey Steel and Iron Co.* v. *Naylor, Benzon, & Co.* The language of Lord Coleridge is well-known and I do not dissent from it. It may be too late to do that; but I must keep myself right by saying that I incline to go further than the noble Lord. His language is (LR 9 CP 208 at 213, [1874–80] All ER Rep 751 at 753): "Where the question is whether the one party is set free by the action of the other, the real matter for consideration is whether the acts or conduct of the one do or do not amount to an intimation of intention *to abandon* and altogether to

e refuse performance of the contract." In other passages his Lordship says (LR 9 CP 208 at 213): "The true question is whether the acts and conduct of the party evince an intention no longer to be bound by the contract." But, in one view of the matter, it may be an extremely difficult task for a person willing to be bound by his contract to enter the region of the mind of the other and to say: "I gather from what you have

f done what is your intention, and your intention is to back out of the contract." This may in many cases be plain to see, but there are other cases in which the psychological operations within the mind of a party to a contract may be very difficult to analyse into an intention one way or another . . . I think that upon the whole it is fair, without abandoning the idea underlying Lord Coleridge's language, to take the proper and more workable propositions of Lord Selborne in the *Mersey*

g *Steel and Iron Co.* case (9 App Cas 434 at 438–439, [1881–5] All ER Rep 365 at 367–368)—"you must look at the actual circumstances of the case in order to see whether the one party to the contract is relieved from its future performance by the conduct of the other"—and of Lord Herschell in *Carswell v Collard* (20 R (HL) 47 at 48). [Lord Shaw went on to say]: . . . the question whether the stage has been reached when procrastination or non-performance may be so construed is an inference of

h fact upon which I should be slow to disturb the verdict of a jury or a Judge of first instance.' (My emphasis.)

Lest the references to repudiation and refusal to perform in the above quotations lead to the suggestion that they are applicable only to a claim for breach of contract, I should emphasise that their Lordships were in fact dealing with the question of rescission. There had been initially a claim for breach of contract and a cross-action for damages for

j breach of contract, but the position is clearly stated by Viscount Finlay (at 183):

'The pleadings have, by consent of all parties, been treated as claiming by amendment that the appellant was entitled to treat the contract as rescinded, owing to the respondent's failure to implement the contract . . . The only question raised on this appeal is whether the appellant was entitled to rescind the contract, and did rescind it. The appellant asks for the restoration of the decision of the Lord Ordinary, but there was no appeal against the dismissal of the cross-action.'   *a*

Referring to the proceedings in the Inner House, Viscount Haldane said (at 182):

> 'The ground taken by the Lord Justice-Clerk was that the appellant could not be taken to have established that the respondent had ever intimated an intention to rescind or had in fact rescinded. He thought that the respondent professed himself *b* anxious to keep the contract alive, notwithstanding a possible claim for damages. But the real question was not what the respondent said, but what *he did, and the inference which the appellant was entitled to draw.*' (My emphasis.)

In so far as it is said in the present case that the delay was occasioned by the illness of Dr Monducci, it is interesting to note that in the above case the delay was said to have *c* been caused by the refusal of the landowner, on whose land the trees were growing, to allow them to be cut. Viscount Haldane said (at 182):

> 'Lord Salvesen took a similar view to Lord Dundas. He thought that the delay, having been occasioned by circumstances over which the respondent had no control, could not be evidence of an intention to repudiate. But the delay was the fault of *d* the respondent, and the source of that fault he had from the beginning failed to disclose to the appellant.'

In so far as Dr Monducci's affidavit says that in September 1975 he told Dr Wirth that he had been ill, that information came too late to affect the position. The charterers had already accepted the contract as rescinded. In my opinion justifiably. In Chitty on *e* Contracts (24th Edn, 1977, para 1370) we read: 'A contract which is rescinded is completely discharged and cannot be revived.' In my opinion that is an accurate statement of the law: see *R v Inhabitants of Gresham* (1786) 1 Term Rep 101, 99 ER 996. Whilst the parties might agree to revive their old rights and obligations, such an agreement is a new one and to be enforceable as a contract must comply with the necessary conditions for enforceability. On neither version of the meeting in September *f* 1975 can I find a new and enforceable contract.

The owners have sought to rely strongly on the *Bremer Vulkan* case. That case was not dealing with the question of rescission. It decided: (1) the principles applicable to delay in bringing proceedings in the High Court are not applicable to an arbitration; (2) an arbitration is governed by the law of contract; (3) an injunction may be obtained to restrain a party from proceeding with an arbitration to protect or enforce some legal or *g* equitable right; (4) the Arbitration Act 1950 provides procedure by application to the arbitrator for putting an end to delay; (5) no such application had been made and there was no room for the implication of a term obliging a party to act with dispatch because an application to the arbitrator was the contemplated procedure; (6) whatever obligation might be implied, for example to co-operate with the other party, there was no obligation fundamental to the arbitration agreement which had been broken.   *h*

The facts of *Bremer Vulkan* were very different from the present case. Over the years the parties had been in frequent negotiation. Settlements were discussed. In 1974 another claim arose and in 1975 the parties agreed that it should be included in the points of claim along with the other claim. In my opinion it would have been impossible in that case to argue that the claimants had evinced an intention to abandon their claims. They were in fact adding to them as time went on. Far from regarding Lord Diplock's *j* speech as assisting the owners, I see it as clearly indicating the proper approach to the present case which is one that leads to a conclusion unfavourable to the owners. Lord Diplock makes it quite clear that the court may grant an injunction in accordance with the ordinary principles of the law of contract.

I would dismiss this appeal.

FOX LJ. I approach this case on the basis that, because of the loss of evidence by reason
a of the very great lapse of time since the arbitration proceedings were instituted, a fair
trial of the dispute is now probably impossible. I refer, in particular, to the matters
mentioned by Lloyd J in his judgment, in relation to the evidence of Captain de
Lesparda, Captain Velasquez, Captain Figallo and the loss of documentary evidence.

The crucial question is the effect of the decision of the House of Lords in *Bremer Vulkan
Schiffbau Und Maschinenfabrik v South India Shipping Corpn* [1981] 1 All ER 289, [1981] 2
b WLR 141; it is said that it is a complete answer to this claim. In *Bremer Vulkan* the
dispute related to claims arising out of a shipbuilding agreement for the construction of
five ships. The ships were delivered over a period of some 13 months between November
1965 and December 1966. A number of complaints were made in relation to alleged
defects in each of the vessels; some of those complaints were accepted, some were not.
Discussions took place between the parties but no agreement was reached. In January
c 1972 a sole arbitrator was appointed.

There was no application to the arbitrator for a preliminary appointment. In April
1972 it was agreed between the parties that South India should deliver a statement of
claim so that Bremer Vulkan could plead a time bar on which it relied under the
contract.

Later in 1972 the parties agreed that claims relating to further alleged defects be added
d to the points of claim. There was a similar agreement in April 1975 in relation to a
further alleged defect. Points of claim were not delivered until 23rd April 1976. No
application to the arbitrator for directions was ever made by either party. Apart from his
notice of appointment in 1972 the arbitrator knew nothing of the matter.

On 25th April 1976 Bremer Vulkan issued a writ in the High Court claiming, inter
alia, an injunction restraining South India from proceeding with the arbitration.

e It is clear that the whole case proceeded in a dilatory way but it was with the delay
between January 1972 and the delivery of the points of claim in April 1976 that the court
was concerned. As to the consequences of that delay, the judge found that the delay had
caused Bremer Vulkan serious prejudice in two ways: first, the loss of witnesses by reason
of death, retirement and persons having left Bremer Vulkan's service and, second, in the
effect of the delay on their ability to collect evidence to ensure that justice could be
f done. Lord Edmund-Davies dealt with the case on the basis that, if it had been a civil
action, the court would have been justified in dismissing the action on the ground 'that
the plaintiffs' inordinate and inexcusable delay had resulted in a fair trial being
impossible' (see [1981] 1 All ER 289 at 302–303, [1981] 2 WLR 141 at 157).

Lord Fraser said that the appeal was concerned with the question whether the court
had jurisdiction to restrain a claimant by injunction from pursuing a claim in an
g arbitration 'after he has been guilty of such inordinate and inexcusable delay that a fair
hearing is no longer possible' (see [1981] 1 All ER 289 at 303, [1981] 2 WLR 141 at
157). Lord Scarman said that he accepted that the appellants had been guilty of delay
which made it impossible for the respondents to collect the evidence necessary to ensure
that justice could be done at the hearing of the arbitration (see [1981] 1 All ER 289 at 309,
[1981] 2 WLR 141 at 165).

h Lord Diplock referred merely to 'the risk' that a fair trial of the dispute would not be
possible (see [1981] 1 All ER 289 at 302, [1981] 2 WLR 141 at 157). But I do not read his
speech as disagreeing in any way with the view of the judge which he describes as being
that the delay 'had given rise to so substantial a risk that a fair trial of the issues could not
be had that *if the arbitration had been an action* it ought to have been dismissed for want of
prosecution' (see [1981] 1 All ER 289 at 293, [1981] 2 WLR 141 at 145–146; Lord
j Diplock's emphasis).

I think it is plain that in *Bremer Vulkan* there was, at the very least, a serious risk that
a fair trial was impossible. I see no difference in principle between *Bremer Vulkan* and
this case in that respect.

So much for the facts. I come to the law. *Bremer Vulkan*, it seems to me, is authority
for the following.

First, the court has no inherent jurisdiction to control the conduct of arbitrations.

Second, if the court is to interfere with the course of an arbitration, that is done for the *a* enforcement or protection of a legal or equitable right.

Third, that the unperformed primary obligations of parties to an arbitration agreement like any other contract may be brought to an end by frustration or at the instance of one party when there has been a repudiatory breach of the agreement by the other party. And the court then has jurisdiction, by way of protecting the right of the party not in default from being harassed by the making of a purported award against him, to grant *b* an injunction restraining the other party from proceeding with the arbitration.

Fourth, the parties are under mutual obligations to each other to take steps by way of application to the arbitrator for directions to prevent such delay in the course of the arbitration as would give rise to the risk that a fair trial could not be achieved.

Last, if the parties fail to take these steps, both are in breach of their contractual obligations to one another and neither can rely on the other's breach as giving him a right *c* to treat the primary obligations of each as at an end.

Accordingly, in *Bremer Vulkan* the application for an injunction failed.

The present case was decided at first instance before *Bremer Vulkan* reached the House of Lords. The judge said that he saw no reason why the agreement contained in the arbitration clause, namely to submit disputes to arbitration, should not be repudiated; and if it could be repudiated he could see no reason why it should not be repudiated by *d* delay in performance, though there was no special logic in regarding the degree of delay necessary as being that which would justify dismissing an action for want of prosecution. He thought that perhaps the test should be the same as in other cases of delay, namely such delay as would frustrate the arbitration agreement.

So far as repudiation is concerned, it appears from *Bremer Vulkan* that the charterers cannot rely on the owners' breach of contract in failing to proceed with the arbitration *e* with due diligence (and consequently to prejudice a fair trial) since the charterers are themselves in breach.

Now as regards frustration, the first question is: what is the cause of the frustration which is alleged? It can I think only be the existence of the risk that a fair trial is impossible. But that circumstance was equally present in *Bremer Vulkan*. In both cases the risk was, at least, substantial. If frustration is an answer in this case, it was an answer *f* in *Bremer Vulkan* also. I cannot think that it was in any way overlooked in *Bremer Vulkan*. Lord Diplock said ([1981] 1 All ER 289 at 297, [1981] 2 WLR 141 at 150):

'I would accept that the unperformed obligations of the parties under an arbitration agreement, like other contracts, may be brought to an end by frustration, or at the election of one party where there has been a repudiatory breach of that *g* agreement by the other party.'

Lord Scarman said ([1981] 1 All ER 289 at 310–311, [1981] 2 WLR 141 at 167):

'In a contract of arbitration I accept that there are mutual obligations to be implied into the parties' agreement not to obstruct or frustrate the purpose of the *h* agreement, ie a fair arbitration is to be conducted in accordance with the terms of their agreement.'

Further, the issue of frustration was evidently before the Court of Appeal in *Bremer Vulkan*. Thus Lloyd J's treatment of the present case as a case of frustration was approved by the Court of Appeal (see [1980] 1 All ER 420 at 431, 433, [1980] 2 WLR 905 at 916, *j* 919).

In my view it is inconsistent with the majority speeches and the decision in *Bremer Vulkan* to treat the circumstance that there has been such delay as to render a fair trial impossible as constituting a frustration of the arbitration agreement. Lord Diplock at the end of his speech said ([1981] 1 All ER 289 at 302, [1981] 2 WLR 141 at 157):

a
'For failure to apply for such directions before so much time had elapsed that there was a risk that a fair trial of the dispute would not be possible, both claimant and respondent were in my view in breach of their contractual obligations to one another; and neither can rely on the other's breach as giving him a right to treat the primary obligations of each to continue with the reference as brought to an end.'

b
That seems to me, having regard to Lord Diplock's formulation of the position in relation to frustration and repudiatory breach, which I have quoted, to be ruling out any contention that the primary obligations of the parties are brought to an end either by frustration or in consequence of repudiatory breach because the parties, in breach of their mutual obligations, have been so dilatory that a fair trial is prejudiced.

Further, the House of Lords in *Bremer Vulkan* concluded that the reference was still on foot. That, I think, is inconsistent with the proposition that the agreement to refer was
c frustrated.

In the circumstances, I do not feel able to support the judge's conclusion on the basis of frustration.

That, however, is not the end of the matter. The present case is quite different from *Bremer Vulkan* in this respect: there was not in *Bremer Vulkan* that complete absence of any activity between the parties in relation to the arbitration over a very long period
d which is such a striking feature of the present case. Thus, in *Bremer Vulkan* the parties agreed in 1972 that claims relating to further alleged defects should be added to the points of claim. The same thing happened in April 1975 in relation to a further alleged defect. Within about a year before the issue of the writ, therefore, both sides were clearly treating the arbitration as still on foot.

In the present case the sequence of the material events was as follows:
e   *18th September 1969*: the owners appointed their arbitrator.
1st October 1969: the charterers appointed their arbitrator, Mr Lynn.
30th January 1970: this, according to Dr Wirth's affidavit is the last record on the correspondence file of any meeting with the owners.
February 1970: the last correspondence between the parties.
Also by February 1970 the charterers were aware that hull underwriters were expected
f to make a payment before long.
1973: some time in 1973 the charterers, having heard no more, closed their file on the matter.
5th February 1975: Mr Lynn died.
The charterers did not appoint a new arbitrator and were never asked to do so. The owners were aware of the death of Mr Lynn by, at the very latest, September 1975 when
g Dr Monducci, the owners' lawyer, met Dr Wirth by chance. He says that Dr Wirth told him that Mr Lynn had died and that there would have to be a substitute. Dr Monducci says that he told Dr Wirth that he had been ill which had delayed matters. The meeting is admitted by Dr Wirth but the conversation is denied by him.
29th December 1977: the owners wrote to the charterers enclosing their points of claim.
3rd January 1978: the charterers received the points of claim.
h There was, therefore, a period of nearly eight years in which nothing whatever happened in relation to the arbitration.

The House of Lords did not have to deal with any such situation in *Bremer Vulkan* where there was continuing activity in relation to the arbitration up to a late stage. It is said that the long period of inactivity had no effect on the continued validity of the arbitration and it is said that *Bremer Vulkan* is authority for that. I do not feel able to
j agree. The reference to arbitration was contractual. The parties could put an end to that contract by agreement whenever they liked. The question in the present case is whether it can be inferred that, having regard to the very long period of total inactivity, the parties have impliedly agreed to put an end to the agreement. Thus in *Pearl Mill Co Ltd v Ivy Tannery Co Ltd* [1919] 1 KB 78 at 82, [1918–19] All ER Rep 702 at 704 Rowlatt J refers to 'a lapse of time allowed to pass by both sides so long as to induce the Court to

draw the inference that both parties thought that each of them had treated the contract as at an end'. And later Rowlatt J refers to the fact that the lapse of time had been 'so long *a* on both sides that . . . the proper inference to be drawn was that each party had put an end to the agreement'.

It seems to me that, by the end of 1973, the charterers regarded the whole matter as at an end. They closed their file and put it away. It may be that they were not justified in doing that in 1973. But I think that they were justified by, at the very latest, 1978 when the points of claim were delivered. I do not think that the meeting between Dr *b* Morducci and Dr Wirth alters that. Let me suppose that, at the meeting, and contrary to the charterers' evidence, some indication was given that the arbitration was continuing. Nevertheless by the end of 1977 (over 2¼ years later) the charterers had heard no more, though 8½ years had elapsed since the Splendid Sun had grounded. In these circumstances, I think that any person in the position of the charterers would reasonably have supposed that the matter was quite dead. *c*

The owners say that they never intended to put an end to the arbitration. I do not think that the owners can be heard to say that. It seems to me that they must be taken to intend what a reasonable person would conclude from their acts. That, I think, is the principle stated in the passage from the speech of Viscount Haldane in *Forslind v Bechley-Crundall* 1922 SC (HL) 173 at 179, to which Eveleigh LJ has referred. In my opinion the lapse of time in this case, unaccompanied by any activity from the parties, is so great that *d* the reasonable inference in January 1978 is that the owners had decided not to proceed with the arbitration and that the charterers had accepted that and were agreeable to it. If that is not so, I find it difficult to suppose that complete inactivity for any period, be it ten or twenty years, would ever justify the conclusion that the claimants were not proceeding. The illness of Dr Morducci seems to me to be irrelevant. The question is the impact of the events, or rather the absence of events, on the charterers. I conclude that *e* the proper inference from the facts is that, by January 1978, the parties had indicated an intention not to proceed with the reference and had put an end to the contract to refer. That is not in my opinion contrary to anything decided in *Bremer Vulkan*. That case was not concerned with the implication through lapse of time of any agreement between the parties to put an end to the arbitration. The facts could not have supported it. The essence of the decision was that the parties are under mutual obligations to prevent such *f* delay as would prevent a fair trial. If they fail to prevent that delay, both are in breach and neither can rely on the other's breach as giving him a right to treat the primary obligation as at an end.

The reason why, as it seems to me, this contract came to an end was not because of breach or its consequences but because the inference is that both sides accepted that it should be terminated; that is not necessarily connected at all with any question of *g* whether a fair trial is possible. If it was terminated, then the charterers are entitled to the protection of an injunction to prevent the owners from seeking to proceed.

I would dismiss the appeal.

Appeal dismissed. Leave to appeal to the House of Lords granted.

Solicitors: *Holman, Fenwick & Willan* (for the owners); *Richards, Butler & Co* (for the charterers).

Sumra Green Barrister.

a

Note
Re a company

CHANCERY DIVISION
VINELOTT J

b

2nd, 3rd MARCH 1981

Company – Oppression – Alternative remedy in cases of oppression – Compromise – Application for order requiring company or directors to purchase petitioner's shares – Petitioner not seeking compulsory winding up of company – Whether order staying petition pending implementation of compromise agreed by parties an appropriate alternative remedy – Companies Act 1948, s 210.

c **Notes**

For alternative remedies for a member of a company in cases of oppression, see 7 Halsbury's Laws (4th Edn) paras 1010–1012, and for cases on the subject, see 10 Digest (Reissue) 943–945, 5526–5530.

d

For effect of a compromise, see 30 Halsbury's Laws (3rd Edn) 405, para 763, and for a case on the form of minutes where the terms of a compromise are contained in a schedule, see 51 Digest (Repl) 736, 3246.

Petition

A contributory of a company petitioned under s 210 of the Companies Act 1948 for an order requiring the company or its directors to purchase the petitioner's shares in the company at the fair value prescribed by the company's articles of association. Following

e resolution of differences between the shareholders the parties sought the court's approval of an order staying the petition pending the implementation of a compromise agreed by the parties and scheduled to the order (a 'Tomlin order'). The facts are set out in the judgment.

f

Ralph Instone for the petitioner.
Eben Hamilton for the company.

VINELOTT J. This is a petition under s 210 of the Companies Act 1948. It does not seek the winding up of the company, and accordingly it has not been advertised. The only relief sought is an order requiring the company or its directors, who are also

g majority shareholders, to purchase the shares of the petitioner at the fair value prescribed by the articles but on the footing that the profits of the company are treated as increased by the addition of certain sums which it is said were either wrongly charged against profits or wrongly diverted to another company. The petitioner is supported by the trustees of the will of a former shareholder. The petitioner and the supporting trustees together own approximately 28% of the shares of the company. The differences between

h the shareholders have now been resolved. A scheme has been agreed which provides amongst other things for the distribution of exceptional dividends by the company during the current fiscal year and in the early weeks of the next fiscal year and for the purchase of the minority shareholding. In order to mitigate capital gains tax that purchase will take place over a three-year period. These terms have been embodied in a Tomlin order, and I have to decide whether this is a form of order appropriate to be made

j where an application under s 210 is compromised.

I can see no reason why this form of order should not be employed in such a case provided that the petitioner does not seek an order for the compulsory winding up of the company. If the petitioner does seek such an order, then it is clearly wrong that the proceedings should be stayed while the terms of compromise are carried into effect since if an order for the compulsory winding up of the company were to be subsequently

made it would relate back to the service of the petition. I understand that no order in
Tomlin form has been made on the compromise of an application under s 210. The *a*
explanation may well be that such petitions commonly do seek an order for the
compulsory winding up of the company as an alternative to an order under s 210. In the
present case there are clear advantages to the parties in embodying the agreed terms of
compromise in an order in Tomlin form so that if any dispute arises in carrying out the
terms of the compromise, the matter can be expeditiously and inexpensively referred to
the court. I can see no possible prejudice to any other persons concerned with the *b*
company, in particular creditors, if the petition remains on the file during the period
required to complete the sale and transfer of the minority shareholding. On the other
hand I think it would be undesirable that the petition should remain on the file
indefinitely, and I shall ask the petitioners for an undertaking to apply to dismiss the
petition when the terms of compromise have been fully implemented.

c

Form of order approved.

Solicitors: *William F Prior & Co*, agents for *Dibb, Lupton & Co*, Leeds (for the petitioner);
Harrisons, Leeds (for the company).

Jacqueline Metcalfe   Barrister. *d*

R v Lucas

COURT OF APPEAL, CRIMINAL DIVISION
LORD LANE CJ, COMYN AND STUART-SMITH JJ   *e*
29th APRIL, 19th MAY 1981

*Criminal evidence – Corroboration – Accomplice – Jury preferring accomplice's evidence to that
of defendant – Whether amounting to corroboration.*

Criminal evidence – Corroboration – Rejection of defendant's evidence – Defendant's lies told out *f*
*of court as corroboration – Circumstances in which defendant's lies told out of court may provide
corroboration against him.*

The fact that a jury may prefer an accomplice's evidence to that of the defendant does not
of itself provide corroboration of the accomplice's otherwise uncorroborated evidence.
It is only if the accomplice's evidence is believed that there is any necessity to look for *g*
corroboration of it (see p 1010 *j* to p 1011 *a*, post).
    For a lie told by a defendant out of court to provide corroboration against him that lie
must be deliberate, it must relate to a material issue, the motive for it must be a
realisation of guilt and a fear of the truth, and it must be clearly shown to be a lie by
evidence other than that of an accomplice to be corroborated, ie by admission or by
evidence from an independent witness (see p 1011 *e f*, post); dicta of Lord Dunedin in *h*
Dawson v M'Kenzie 1908 SC at 649 and of Orr LJ in *R v Boardman* [1974] 2 All ER at 963
approved; *R v Chapman* [1973] 2 All ER 624 explained.

Notes
For the nature of corroboration in criminal proceedings, see 11 Halsbury's Laws (4th
Edn) para 454, and for cases on the subject, see 15 Digest (Reissue) 962–964, 8320–8342. *j*
    For corroboration and the evidence of accomplices, see 11 Halsbury's Laws (4th Edn)
para 457, and for cases on the subject, see 14(2) Digest (Reissue) 608–621, 4942–5078.

Cases referred to in judgment
Credland v Knowler (1951) 35 Cr App R 48, DC, 15 Digest (Reissue) 1234, 10,540.

Dawson v M'Kenzie 1908 SC 648, 45 Sc LR 473, 15 SLT 951, 32 Digest (Reissue) 75, *352.

a *R v Boardman* [1974] 2 All ER 958, [1975] AC 421, [1974] 3 WLR 673, CA; *affd* sub nom
   Boardman v Director of Public Prosecutions [1974] 3 All ER 887, [1975] AC 421, [1974]
   3 WLR 673, 60 Cr App R 165, HL, 14(2) Digest (Reissue) 527, 4296.

   R v Chapman [1973] 2 All ER 624, [1973] QB 774, [1973] 2 WLR 876, 57 Cr App R 511,
   137 JP 525, CA, 14(2) Digest (Reissue) 608, 4947.

   R v Knight [1966] 1 All ER 647, [1966] 1 WLR 230, 130 JP 187, 50 Cr App R 122, CCA,
b 15 Digest (Reissue) 1234, 10,541.

   Tumahole Bereng v R [1949] AC 253, [1949] LJR 1603, PC, 14(2) Digest (Reissue) 617,
   *3967.

Appeal

On 23rd November 1979 at the Crown Court at Reading before his Honour Judge
c Murchie and a jury the appellant, Iyabode Ruth Lucas, was convicted on two counts of
being knowingly concerned in the fraudulent evasion of the prohibition on importation
of a controlled drug, cannabis, contrary to s 304 of the Customs and Excise Act 1952, as
amended by s 26 of the Misuse of Drugs Act 1971, by a majority of ten to two on count
1 and unanimously on count 2. She was sentenced to two years' imprisonment on count
1 and three years' imprisonment concurrent on count 2. The case is reported on whether
d the trial judge gave a correct direction to the jury on the question of corroboration of an
accomplice and on when statements made out of court can amount to corroboration.
The facts are set out in the judgment of the court.

William E M Taylor (assigned by the Registrar of Criminal Appeals) for the appellant.
Douglas Blair for the Crown.

e At the conclusion of argument Lord Lane CJ announced that the appeal on count 1
would be allowed and that on count 2 would be dismissed as to both conviction and
sentence for reasons to be given later.

19th May. **LORD LANE CJ** read the following judgment of the court: This is an
appeal pursuant to leave of the full court by Iyabode Ruth Lucas against conviction at the
f Crown Court at Reading on 23rd November 1979 on two counts of being knowingly
concerned in the fraudulent evasion on the prohibition of the importation into this
country of a controlled drug, namely cannabis, contrary to the Misuse of Drugs Act
1971. The first count was in respect of an importation on 12th December 1978 through
Gatwick airport and related to 25·17 kg of the drug; the second was in respect of an
importation some two months later through Heathrow airport of 18·12 kg. In both
g cases the appellant had arrived here from Nigeria.

The jury first brought in a verdict of guilty on the Heathrow count. That verdict was
unanimous. Then, after a majority direction, they returned 22 minutes later giving a
ten to two majority verdict of guilty on the Gatwick count.

The judge sentenced the appellant to three years' imprisonment on the Heathrow
count and two years' imprisonment on the Gatwick count to run concurrently.

h In both counts the appellant was charged together with a man called Fritz Emanuel
Bastian. Bastian originally pleaded not guilty to the Gatwick count but guilty to the
Heathrow count. During the trial he changed his plea to one of guilty on the Gatwick
count also.

The appellant and Bastian were admittedly together on both occasions. On the first
occasion they were accompanied by a man called Crike Areh. Areh was charged
j independently with an offence in the terms of the Gatwick count, pleaded guilty to it at
the Crown Court at Lewes, and was sentenced to 18 months' imprisonment. He took no
part at all in the Heathrow matter. At the trial of this appellant and Bastian, Areh gave
evidence in detail implicating both of them in the Gatwick count. The only material
point in this appeal is whether the judge gave a correct direction on the question of
corroboration of Areh's evidence.

Counsel for the appellant therefore directs his main attack against the Gatwick conviction, that is count 1, but seeks to keep alive his contention that the conviction on *a* count 2 (Heathrow) is tainted by any defect in the conviction on count 1.

We can dispose of that matter at once. The fault which we are constrained to say occurred in respect of the Gatwick count does not, in our judgment, in any way affect the validity of the conviction on the second, the Heathrow, count. The judge most carefully pointed out to the jury that the two counts were separate and had to be considered by them separately. That they fully heeded that direction was plain from the different form *b* of their verdicts: unanimous in regard to the Heathrow count, a ten to two majority in respect of the Gatwick count. It only remains to say of the Heathrow count that there was very strong evidence implicating the appellant and that the keys of the suitcase containing cannabis which Bastian tried to smuggle through customs were found shortly afterwards in the appellant's fur coat. His and her attempted explanation that he put them there unknown to her was plainly and understandably rejected by the jury. The *c* appeal in respect of the second count fails.

What counsel for the appellant says about the Gatwick count is this. Areh was undoubtedly an accomplice; therefore it was incumbent on the judge to give the usual warning to the jury about the dangers of convicting on his uncorroborated evidence, and then to point out any potentially corroborative facts. There is no dispute that the warning was given in impeccable terms. The complaint is confined to the way in which *d* the judge directed the jury as to what might be considered by them as corroboration.

Having explained to the jury that they were entitled to convict on the evidence of the accomplice even though uncorroborated, provided they heeded the warning of the dangers of so doing, he went on to explain that such corroboration could sometimes be found in the evidence of the defendant herself. He correctly directed the jury that, when a defendant tells lies, there may be reasons for those lies which are not connected with *e* guilt of the offences charged and that one of their tasks would be to decide, if the defendant had told lies, what their purpose was.

He went on to say:

> 'In the same way it is said that the defendant lied to you on various matters, and you will consider those aspects ... If you weigh the defendant's evidence, if you reject it on many aspects, you are entitled to say: "Why has this evidence, which we *f* the jury reject, been given to us by the defendant?" If there is only one possible answer (for example, that Mr Areh, though wholly unsupported, was telling the truth) you are entitled to give your answer to that question in your two verdicts, providing you bear in mind my warning to look for independent support of the evidence of a tainted man.'

g

Apart from that passage, there is nothing in the direction which suggests to the jury what, if anything, is capable of amounting to corroboration of the accomplice's evidence. Although read literally the judge does not say so, the jury may have received the impression that they were entitled to ask themselves whether they rejected the defendant's evidence given before them and, if the answer was Yes, to use their consequent conclusion that she had lied to them as corroboration of Areh's evidence. *h* This was certainly what counsel for the Crown thought the judge was saying, because at the close of the summing up, in the absence of the jury, he invited the judge to clarify the matter. That invitation was not accepted.

We accept that the words, used in the context in which they were, were probably taken by the jury as a direction that lies told by the defendant in the witness box could be considered as corroborative of an accomplice's evidence, and we approach the case on *j* that footing.

The fact that the jury may feel sure that the accomplice's evidence is to be preferred to that of the defendant and that the defendant accordingly must have been lying in the witness box is not of itself something which can be treated by the jury as corroboration of the accomplice's evidence. It is only if the accomplice's evidence is believed that there is any necessity to look for corroboration of it. If the belief that the accomplice is truthful

means that the defendant was untruthful and if that untruthfulness can be used as
a corroboration, the practical effect would be to dispense with the need of corrobation
altogether.

The matter was put in this way by Lord MacDermott in *Tumahole Bereng v R* [1949] AC
253 at 270:

b
> 'Nor does an accused corroborate an accomplice merely by giving evidence which
> is not accepted and must therefore be regarded as false. Corroboration may well be
> found in the evidence of an accused person; but that is a different matter, for there
> confirmation comes, if at all, from what is said, and not from the falsity of what is
> said.'

There is, without doubt, some confusion in the authorities as to the extent to which
lies may in some circumstances provide corroboration and it was this confusion which
c probably and understandably led the judge astray in the present case. In our judgment
the position is as follows. Statements made out of court, for example statements to the
police, which are proved or admitted to be false may in certain circumstances amount to
corroboration. There is no shortage of authority for this proposition (see, for example,
R v Knight [1966] 1 All ER 647, [1966] 1 WLR 230 and *Credland v Knowler* (1951) 35 Cr
App R 48). It accords with good sense that a lie told by a defendant about a material issue
d may show that the liar knew that if he told the truth he would be sealing his fate. In the
words of Lord Dunedin in *Dawson v M'Kenzie* 1908 SC 648 at 649, cited with approval
by Lord Goddard CJ in *Credland v Knowler* (at 55):

e
> '. . . the opportunity may have a complexion put upon it by statements made by
> the defender which are proved to be false. It is not that a false statement made by
> the defender proves that the pursuer's statements are true, but it may give to a
> proved opportunity a different complexion from what it would have borne had no
> such false statement been made.'

To be capable of amounting to corroboration the lie told out of court must first of all
be deliberate. Secondly it must relate to a material issue. Thirdly the motive for the lie
must be a realisation of guilt and a fear of the truth. The jury should in appropriate cases
f be reminded that people sometimes lie, for example, in an attempt to bolster up a just
cause, or out of shame or out of a wish to conceal disgraceful behaviour from their
family. Fourthly the statement must be clearly shown to be a lie by evidence other than
that of the accomplice who is to be corroborated, that is to say by admission or by
evidence from an independent witness.

As a matter of good sense it is difficult to see why, subject to the same safeguard, lies
g proved to have been told in court by a defendant should not equally be capable of
providing corroboration. In other common law jurisdictions they are so treated: see the
cases collated by Professor J D Heydon ((1973) 89 LQR at 561) and cited with apparent
approval in Cross on Evidence (5th Edn, 1979, p 210).

It has been suggested that there are dicta in *R v Chapman* [1973] 2 All ER 624, [1973]
QB 774 to the effect that lies so told in court can never be capable of providing
h corroboration of other evidence given against a defendant. We agree with the comment
on this case in Cross on Evidence (5th Edn, 1979, pp 210–211) that the court there may
only have been intending to go no further than to apply the passage from the speech of
Lord MacDermott in *Tumahole Bereng v R* which we have already cited.

In our view the decision in *R v Chapman* on the point there in issue was correct. The
decision should not, however, be regarded as going any further than we have already
j stated. Properly understood, it is not authority for the proposition that in no
circumstances can lies told by a defendant in court provide material corroboration of an
accomplice. We can find ourselves in agreement with the comment on this decision
made by this court in *R v Boardman* [1974] 2 All ER 958 at 963, [1975] AC 421 at 428.
That point was not subsequently discussed when that case was before the House of Lords.

The main evidence against Chapman and his co-defendant Baldwin was a man called
Thatcher, who was undoubtedly an accomplice in the alleged theft and dishonest

handling of large quantities of clothing. The defence was that Thatcher was lying when he implicated the defendants and that he must himself have stolen the goods. The judge gave the jury the necessary warning about accomplice evidence and the requirement of corroboration, and then went on to say this ([1973] 2 All ER 624 at 626, [1973] QB 774 at 779):

> 'If you think that Chapman's story about the disappearance of the van and its contents is so obviously untrue that you do not attach any weight to it at all—in other words, you think Chapman is lying to you—then I direct you that that is capable of corroborating Thatcher because ... if Chapman is lying about the van, can there be any explanation except that Thatcher is telling the truth about how it came to disappear? ... My direction is that it is capable in law of corroborating Thatcher. Similarly in the case of Baldwin, if you think that Baldwin's story about going up to London and buying these goods ... is untrue—in other words he has told you lies about that—then ... that, I direct you, so far as he is concerned, is capable of amounting to corroboration of Thatcher.'

That being the direction which this court was then considering, the decision is plainly correct, because the jury were being invited to prefer the evidence of the accomplice to that of the defendant and then without more to use their disbelief of the defendant as corroboration of the accomplice.

Providing that the lies told in court fulfil the four criteria which we have set out above, we are unable to see why they should not be available for the jury to consider in just the same way as lies told out of court. So far as the instant case is concerned, the judge, we feel, fell into the same error as the judge did in *R v Chapman*. The lie told by the defendant was clearly not shown to be a lie by evidence other than that of the accomplice who was to be corroborated and consequently the apparent direction that a lie was capable of providing corroboration was erroneous. It is for that reason that we have reached the conclusion that the conviction on the Gatwick count, that is count 1, must be quashed and the appeal to that extent is allowed.

Appeal allowed in part. Conviction on count 1 quashed

Solicitors: *Solicitor for the Customs and Excise.*

N P Metcalfe Esq   Barrister.

Boorman and another v Godfrey

COURT OF APPEAL, CIVIL DIVISION
DONALDSON AND ACKNER LJJ
6th, 11th MARCH 1981

Legal aid – Assisted person's liability to pay costs – Certificate limited to steps or procedures to be taken by legal advisers – Certificate limited to representation of plaintiff on an interlocutory application and obtaining counsel's opinion on plaintiff's claim – Defendant succeeding on another interlocutory application for further and better particulars of claim before counsel's opinion on plaintiff's claim obtained – Whether plaintiff liable to pay costs of that interlocutory application – Legal Aid Act 1974, s 8(1)(e).

In November 1979 the plaintiff began proceedings in the county court claiming from the defendant the balance of the price of goods sold and delivered. The defendant put in a counterclaim. On 30th June 1980 the plaintiff was granted an emergency legal aid certificate which, on 22nd July, was superseded by an ordinary certificate. The legal aid was described as allowing the plaintiff 'To continue to take' the proceedings in the county court between him and the defendant but under the 'Conditions and limitations' heading it was stated that legal aid was limited to representation on an interlocutory application in the proceedings made by the defendant to be heard on 1st July 1980 and thereafter to

a preparation of papers for counsel and obtaining counsel's opinion on evidence, merits and quantum in regard to the plaintiff's claim. The certificate required that the papers and counsel's opinion were then to be referred to the area committee to decide whether the certificate should be amended or discharged. On 15th September 1980, before the plaintiff had obtained counsel's opinion, the defendant applied for and was granted an order for further and better particulars of the plaintiff's claim. At the hearing of that

b application the judge had before him a letter from the plaintiff's solicitors explaining that they would not be attending the hearing because their attendance was not covered by the legal aid certificate. The judge ordered the plaintiff to pay the defendant's costs of the application for further and better particulars in any event. On 23rd October the plaintiff applied to the judge to amend the order for costs by adding a proviso that the plaintiff was an assisted person and the order should not be enforced unless there was a

c determination under s 8(1)(e)ᵃ of the Legal Aid Act 1974 of the amount of costs it was reasonable for him to pay, having regard to all the circumstances. The judge refused the plaintiff's application on the ground that he was not an assisted person in regard to the application on 15th September, in view of the limitations on the legal aid granted to him. Accordingly, the plaintiff was liable for the full costs of the application. The plaintiff appealed, contending that where a legal aid certificate was limited to particular

d steps or procedures to be taken by the assisted person's legal advisers, he was entitled to legal aid until those steps or procedures were taken. The defendant contended that the relevant 'proceedings' for the purpose of s 8(1) was the application on 15th September and, since the plaintiff was not in receipt of legal aid in connection with that proceeding within s 8(1), an inquiry under s 8(1)(e) was not required.

e **Held** – Where a certificate limited legal aid by reference to the steps or procedures which could be undertaken with legal aid by an assisted person's legal advisers, then, until they had done that which the certificate authorised them to do and the certificate had been discharged, the assisted person was entitled, by s 8(1)(e) of the 1974 Act, to have his costs limited to what was a reasonable amount for him to pay, in relation to all the costs incurred by the other party during that period. Since the limitation on the legal aid

f granted to the plaintiff referred to the steps or procedures which could be undertaken by his legal advisers (ie it was a limitation by reference to time) and was not a limitation by reference to part of the proceedings (ie it was not a limitation by reference to issues), the plaintiff was an assisted person in relation to the whole of the county court proceedings until the authorised steps had been undertaken. Accordingly, he was entitled to the benefit of s 8(1)(e) in regard to the order for costs. The appeal would therefore be allowed

g (see p 1017 *a* to *c e f* and *h j*, post).

Dugon v Williamson [1963] 3 All ER 25 applied.

Mills v Mills [1963] 2 All ER 237 and Herbert (otherwise Bridgeman) v Herbert [1964] 1 All ER 915 distinguished.

Notes

h For costs awarded against an assisted person, see 30 Halsbury's Laws (3rd Edn) 502, para 933.

For the Legal Aid Act 1974, s 8, see 44 Halsbury's Statutes (3rd Edn) 1045.

Cases referred to in judgments

Dugon v Williamson [1963] 3 All ER 25, [1964] Ch 59, [1963] 3 WLR 477, CA, 50 Digest

j (Repl) 494, *1751*.

Herbert (otherwise Bridgeman) v Herbert [1964] 1 All ER 915, [1964] 1 WLR 471, 27(2) Digest (Reissue) 769, *6143*.

Megarity v Law Society, Gayway Linings Ltd v Law Society [1981] 1 All ER 641, [1981] 2 WLR 335, HL.

---

a   Section 8(1) is set out at p 1015 *d e*, post

Mills v Mills [1963] 2 All ER 237, [1963] P 329, [1963] 2 WLR 831, CA, 50 Digest (Repl) 494, *1752*.

a

Interlocutory appeal

The plaintiff, Edward George Boorman, appealed against an order of his Honour Judge McDonnell made on 23rd October 1980 dismissing the plaintiff's application to set aside the judge's order made on 15th September 1980 that the plaintiff pay the defendant's costs of an application for further and better particulars granted on 15th September 1980 *b* without an inquiry under s 8(1)(e) of the Legal Aid Act 1974 as to the costs it was reasonable for the plaintiff to pay. The grounds of the appeal were that the judge misdirected himself in holding that the plaintiff was not in receipt of legal aid in connection with the application for further and better particulars and therefore failed to limit the order for costs to such amount (if any) which it was reasonable in all the circumstances for the plaintiff to pay. The facts are set out in the judgment of Donaldson *c* LJ.

Robert Beecroft for the plaintiff.
Gordon Murdoch for the defendant.

Cur adv vult *d*

11th March. The following judgments were read.

DONALDSON LJ. This appeal concerns the position of an assisted litigant against whom an order for costs is made when his legal aid certificate is subject to limitations.

In November 1979 the plaintiff began proceedings in the Lambeth County Court *e* claiming the balance of the price of goods sold and delivered. He was met with a counterclaim which included a claim for an injunction restraining him from entering the defendant's premises. There were a number of interlocutory 'activities', to use a neutral term, but we are only concerned with two. The first was an application by the defendant for an injunction and committal which was to be heard, and may well have been heard, on 1st July 1980. How the making of the order could have been combined *f* with committal, presumably for its breach, is not explained and does not matter. The second was an application by the defendant for an order requiring the plaintiff to deliver further and better particulars of the particulars of claim. This application was made on 15th September 1980. It was successful and the plaintiff was ordered to pay the defendant's costs in any event.

I now turn to the legal aid situation. On 30th June 1980 the plaintiff was granted legal *g* aid under an emergency certificate in the following terms:

'Description of legal aid—To continue to take proceedings in the Lambeth County Court Plaint Number 79 15929 between Edward George Boorman Plaintiff and Maurice Godfrey Defendant.
'Conditions and limitations (if any)—Limited to representation on the Defendant's *h* application for an Injunction and committal to be heard on the 1st July 1980.'

This was superseded on 22nd July 1980 by an ordinary certificate as follows:

'Description of legal aid—To continue to take proceedings in the Lambeth County Court Plaint No. 79 15929 between Edward George Boorman Plaintiff and Maurice Godfrey Defendant.
'Conditions and limitations (if any)—Limited to representation on the Defendant's *j* application for an Injunction and committal to be heard on the 1st July 1980. Thereafter limited to preparation of papers for Counsel and obtaining Counsel's Opinion on evidence, merits and quantum after a conference at which the Assisted Person should attend. Papers and Counsel's Opinion to be referred to the Area Committee for decision whether Certificate be amended or discharged.'

When on 15th September 1980 his Honour Judge McDonnell ordered the plaintiff to
a pay the defendant's costs of the application in relation to particulars in any event, he had
before him a letter from the plaintiff's solicitors stating, as was the fact, that they
represented the plaintiff under a limited civil aid certificate which would not cover them
for that hearing and that for this reason they would not be attending.

On 23rd October, the plaintiff applied to the judge to amend the order of 15th
September by adding a proviso that the order should not be enforced unless there was a
b determination made under s 8 of the Legal Aid Act 1974. Both parties were represented
by counsel. The judge rejected the application, holding on the authority of *Mills v Mills*
[1963] 2 All ER 237, [1963] P 329 and *Herbert (otherwise Bridgeman) v Herbert* [1964] 1 All
ER 915, [1964] 1 WLR 471 that the plaintiff had not been an assisted person quoad the
application of 15th September. Unfortunately, he was not referred to *Dugon v Williamson*
[1963] 3 All ER 25, [1964] Ch 59 which like *Mills v Mills* is a decision of this court. He
c thus escaped the problem of having to reconcile these two decisions. This task now falls
to us on the plaintiff's appeal from the judge's refusal to amend his order.

The key statutory provision is s 8(1) of the 1974 Act, which is in the following terms:

'Where a person receives legal aid in connection with any proceedings—(a) the
expenses incurred in connection with the proceedings, so far as they would
ordinarily be paid in the first instance by or on behalf of the solicitor acting for him,
d shall be so paid, except in the case of those paid direct from the legal aid fund as
provided by section 10 below; (b) his solicitor and counsel shall not take any
payment in respect of the legal aid except such payment as is directed by section 10
below to be made out of the legal aid fund; (c) he may be required to make a
contribution to the legal aid fund in respect of the sums payable out of that fund on
his account; (d) any sums recovered by virtue of an order or agreement for costs
e made in his favour with respect to the proceedings shall be paid into the legal aid
fund; (e) his liability by virtue of an order for costs made against him with respect
to the proceedings shall not exceed the amount (if any) which is a reasonable one for
him to pay having regard to all the circumstances, including the means of all the
parties and their conduct in connection with the dispute.'

f In *Mills v Mills* [1963] P 329 at 330 the legal aid certificate entitled the husband—

'to be heard as respondent in the High Court of Justice, Probate, Divorce and
Admiralty Division (Divorce) in proceedings entitled: Rhoda Jean Mills, petitioner,
and Thomas Leonard Lanty Mills, respondent, in respect of the claim in the prayer
of the petition for alimony and maintenance, to include application to determine
liability for costs.'

g The appeal turned on the construction of the Legal Aid and Advice Act 1949, but there
is no material difference between that Act and the 1974 Act. This court held, to quote
the headnote (at 330):

'On its true construction "proceedings" in section 2(2) of the Legal Aid and Advice
Act, 1949, had a narrower meaning than the whole of a cause, action or matter, and
h an assisted person was not protected by section 2(2)(e) from paying the full costs of
that part of the cause, action or matter to which his certificate did not extend.
Accordingly, the husband was liable to pay the full costs of the petition.'

In *Herbert v Herbert* [1964] 1 All ER 915, [1964] 1 WLR 471 at 472 the legal aid
certificate entitled the husband—

j 'to legal aid to be represented in a suit . . . as to the claims made by the prayer of
the petition for alimony pending suit, maintenance, a secured provision, and costs.'

Cairns J applied *Mills v Mills* and ordered the husband to pay the full costs incurred by his
wife in obtaining the decree on the basis that that was a separate part of the proceedings.

In *Dugon v Williamson* the certificate was 'Limited to obtaining transcript of judgment,
preparation of papers for counsel, and counsel's opinion thereafter on merits and
prospects of success of the appeal' (see [1964] Ch 59 at 60). The papers were in fact

referred to the committee together with counsel's opinion and the committee discharged
the certificate. This court held, to quote the headnote—   *a*

> 'that it was within the jurisdiction of the area committee to grant a civil aid
> certificate for the limited purpose of preparing the papers for counsel and getting
> counsel's opinion since, even if counsel's opinion was adverse, it was reasonable to
> get it, and that, therefore, the defendant was an assisted person from the date when
> the certificate was granted until the date when it was discharged; the costs incurred
> during that period, accordingly, were incurred while the defendant was an assisted *b*
> person within section 2 of the [1949] Act so that by virtue of regulation 13(6)(*b*) of
> the regulations of 1962, section 2(2)(*e*) applied and his liability for costs did not
> exceed the amount which was reasonable for him to pay in all the circumstances
> and, in those circumstances, it was reasonable to make no order in regard to those
> costs.'

At this point it may be convenient to refer to the Legal Aid (General) Regulations   *c*
1971, SI 1971 No 62. These regulations were made under the 1949 Act, but are kept in
force and are deemed to refer to the corresponding provisions of the 1974 Act by s 42 of
that Act. Regulation 13(6) differs slightly from the corresponding regulation under the
1962 regulations referred to in *Dugon v Williamson*, but the differences are not material.
Regulation 13(6) provides: *d*

> 'Where a certificate has been discharged, the person to whom the certificate was
> issued shall remain liable for the payment of his maximum contribution, if any, as
> determined by the appropriate committee or as determined or redetermined by the
> Commission up to the amount paid or payable by The Law Society under paragraph
> (3)(*b*) and where he continues to assert or dispute the claim or to take, defend or be
> a party to the proceedings to which the certificate related, section 2(2)(*e*) of the Act *e*
> shall apply in so far as the costs were incurred while he was an assisted person.'

Regulation 14(1) provides:

> 'Where, after proceedings have been instituted in any court, any party becomes
> an assisted person in regard to those proceedings, the provisions of section 2(2)(*e*) of
> the Act shall apply only to so much of the costs of the proceedings as are incurred *f*
> while a certificate is in force.'

Regulation 15(9) provides:

> 'Where a certificate has been issued in connection with any proceedings, the
> assisted person's solicitor or counsel shall not take any payment for work done in
> those proceedings during the currency of that certificate (whether within the scope *g*
> of the certificate or otherwise) except such payments as may be made out of the
> fund.'

Regulation 20(1) provides:

> 'Where proceedings have been concluded in which an assisted person (including,
> for the purpose of this Regulation, a person who was an assisted person in respect of *h*
> those proceedings) is liable or would have been liable for costs if he had not been an
> assisted person, no costs attributable to the period during which his certificate was
> in force shall be recoverable from him until the court has determined the amount
> of his liability in accordance with section 2(2)(*e*) of the Act: Provided that where the
> assisted person's certificate does not relate to or has been amended so that it no
> longer relates to the whole of the proceedings, the court shall nevertheless make a *j*
> determination in respect of that part of the proceedings to which the certificate
> relates.'

Counsel for the plaintiff submits that a legal aid certificate can be limited in two
different ways with quite different consequences. First, it can be limited to part of the
proceedings. This was the case in *Mills v Mills* and in *Herbert v Herbert*. The consequence
was that the husbands were assisted persons only quoad those parts of the proceedings to

which the certificate extended. Second, it can be limited by reference to the steps or
a procedures which can be undertaken by the assisted person's legal advisers. This was the
position in *Dugon v Williamson*. If this latter course is adopted, the consequences may be
surprising. However little the assisted person's legal advisers may be authorised to do,
until they have done it and the certificate has been discharged, the assisted person has the
benefit of s 8(1)(e) of the 1974 Act in relation to all costs incurred by the other party
during that period.

b   Counsel for plaintiff submits that in this case the legal aid authorities chose to adopt
the *Dugon* method of limitation. Legal aid extended to the whole of the county court
proceedings and the limitation bit only on what the plaintiff's legal advisers were
allowed to do, namely represent the plaintiff on 1st July 1980 and to advise. It follows,
as he submits, that the plaintiff is entitled to the benefit of s 8(1)(e) from 30th June 1980,
when the emergency certificate was granted and in particular in relation to the costs of
c the defendant's application on 15th September 1980.

It is conceded by counsel for the plaintiff that, in the light of reg 20(1) of the 1971
regulations, it may well be that there was no need to amend the judge's order and that
the correct course would have been to resist any attempt to recover the costs at a later
stage. But this would only be to defer the problem which now confronts us, and both
parties ask us to determine the question on this appeal.

d   Counsel for the defendant submits that *Mills v Mills* is authority on the meaning of
'proceedings' and *Dugon v Williamson* on 'in connection with'. The relevant 'proceedings'
in the instant case was the application on 15th September 1980, and the plaintiff obtained
no assistance in relation to that application. He also points out that if the plaintiff's
submissions are correct and he had wanted to be represented on the hearing of that
application neither his solicitors nor counsel could have been instructed and paid
e 'privately': see reg 15(9) of the 1971 regulations.

For my part I accept that this is the consequence of the plaintiff's submissions, but in
the light of *Dugon v Williamson* I am driven to the conclusion that the plaintiff was an
assisted person in relation to the whole of the county court proceedings notwithstanding
that as a result of the limitation on the certificate the assistance was conspicuous by its
absence in relation to the application on 15th September. If this is not right, it is
f necessary to identify a more limited part of the proceedings in respect of which the
plaintiff was an assisted person. In the present case it might be arguable that this was the
application on 1st July 1980, but in other cases, of which *Dugon v Williamson* is an
example, in which the only authorised work was of an advisory nature, the submission
of counsel for the defendant would lead to the conclusion that the litigant was not
assisted in relation to any part of the proceedings. This is clearly fallacious.

g   While preparing this judgment my attention was drawn to the decisions of the House
of Lords in *Megarity v Law Society, Gayway Linings Ltd v Law Society* [1981] 1 All ER 641,
[1981] 2 WLR 335. These relate to the liability of the legal aid fund for the costs of
unassisted persons and are not directly material. However, I note that Lord Diplock,
who had given the leading judgment in *Mills v Mills*, expressed the view that where legal
aid is given in relation to part of the proceedings as contrasted with the whole
h proceedings, that part might be defined either by time or by reference to issues (see
[1981] 1 All ER 641 at 648, [1981] 2 WLR 335 at 343). The legal aid regulations to
which I have referred are drawn on the same assumption. In my judgment, in the
instant case the limitation was by reference to time and not to issues.

I would allow the appeal. I am not clear quite what order is asked for, but that can be
discussed.

j **ACKNER LJ.** I agree.

Appeal allowed.

Solicitors: *Daniel Davies & Co* (for the plaintiff); *Simanowitz & Brown* (for the defendant).

William Hoskins Esq   Barrister.

Re Cleaver (deceased)
Cleaver v Insley and others

a

CHANCERY DIVISION
NOURSE J
15th, 16th, 17th, 18th, 19th DECEMBER 1980

b

Will – Mutual wills – Requirements for enforceable mutual wills – Evidence required to establish enforceable agreement to dispose of property pursuant to mutual wills – Husband and wife making wills on same date in similar terms – Wife taking benefit under husband's will in accordance with his will – Wife making new will differing from terms of mutual wills – Whether wife under legal obligation to dispose of her estate in accordance with terms of mutual wills – Whether mere fact of simultaneity of wills in similar terms sufficient to establish enforceable   c
agreement – Whether constructive trust arising out of enforceable agreement for mutual wills.

The testator and the testatrix married in October 1967 when he was aged 78 and she was aged 74. He had three children, she had none. They each had assets of their own and kept their finances separate. On 19th December 1967 and 12th June 1970 they made d
successive wills in similar terms whereby each, after directing the payment of certain legacies, left the remainder of his or her estate to the survivor absolutely and in default of survival left their respective residuary estates to the testator's children in equal shares. By 1974 the testator had determined that one of his children ('the daughter') should receive only a life interest in his residuary estate because he did not wish her husband to benefit from the estate. The testatrix either shared that wish or was prepared to fall in with it. Accordingly, on 7th February 1974, the testator and the testatrix made e
further wills similar to those they had made in 1967 and 1970 except that the daughter's interest was cut down to a life interest in one-third of the residuary estates with a gift over on the daughter's death to the testator's other two children in equal shares. The testator died in the early hours of 27th February 1975. That evening the testatrix had a conversation with the testator's son in which she recognised that she had an obligation to the testator to dispose of her estate in accordance with her 1974 will. The testator's will f
was duly proved and, after payment of the legacies the testator had bequeathed, the testatrix became absolutely entitled to his estate. In May 1975, within three months of the testator's death, the testatrix made a new will which in every material respect was identical to her 1974 will. In November 1975 she made a further will by which she left her residuary estate to the testator's three children absolutely in equal shares, thus breaching the arrangement regarding the daughter's share which she and the testator g
had made in 1974 and given effect to in their 1974 wills. In June 1977 the testatrix made her last will, by which she left her residuary estate to the daughter and her husband absolutely in equal shares and left nothing to the testator's two other children, the plaintiffs. The testatrix died in 1978. In 1979 the plaintiffs brought proceedings seeking a declaration that the executors of the testatrix held her estate on trust to give effect to her 1974 will, and an order that the executors administer and distribute her estate h
accordingly, on the ground that there was an enforceable agreement between the testator and the testatrix that they would execute mutual wills disposing of their property in identical terms in pursuance of the agreement.

Held – For mutual wills to be enforceable it had to be established by clear and satisfactory j
evidence that on the balance of probabilities there had been an agreement between the makers of the two wills to dispose of their respective property in a similar way under mutual wills. The mere simultaneity of wills and the similarity of their terms was not enough by itself to establish the necessary agreement, but the fact that there were such wills was a relevant circumstance to be taken into account. If there was an enforceable agreement to execute mutual wills equity would interfere to impose a constructive trust

a on the survivor's property on the principle that equity would not permit a person to whom property had been transferred on the faith of an agreement that it would be dealt with in a particular way for the benefit of a third party to deal with it inconsistently with that agreement. In all the circumstances there was clear and satisfactory evidence that the 1974 wills were executed in pursuance of an enforceable agreement between the testator and the testatrix which imposed mutual obligations on them to dispose of their property in a similar way and accordingly, since the testatrix had had the benefit of the

b testator's estate, a constructive trust was imposed on her estate for the benefit of the plaintiffs. Her executors were therefore bound to administer and distribute the estate in accordance with her 1974 will. It followed that the declaration and order sought would be made (see p 1022 d e and j to p 1023 a, p 1024 d to j, p 1026 a b, p 1028 a to c and j to p 1029 a and h to p 1030 a, post).

Dufour v Pereira (1769) 1 Dick 419, Gray v Perpetual Trustee Co Ltd [1928] All ER Rep
c 758 and Birmingham v Renfrew (1937) 57 CLR 666 applied.

Notes

For mutual wills, see 39 Halsbury's Laws (3rd Edn) 847, para 1280, for restrictions by taking a benefit under a mutual will, see ibid 853, para 1289, and for cases on the subject, see 48 Digest (Repl) 22–25, 95–118.

d **Cases referred to in judgment**

Birmingham v Renfrew (1937) 57 CLR 666, HC of Aust.
Dufour v Pereira (1769) 1 Dick 419, 21 ER 332, LC, 48 Digest (Repl) 24, *110*.
Gray v Perpetual Trustee Co Ltd [1928] AC 391, [1928] All ER Rep 758, 97 LJPC 85, 139
    LT 469, PC, 48 Digest (Repl) 24, 112.
Oldham, Re [1925] Ch 75, [1924] All ER Rep 288, 95 LJ Ch 148, 132 LT 658, 48 Digest
e   (Repl) 24, *114*.
Ottaway v Norman [1971] 3 All ER 1325, [1972] Ch 698, [1972] 2 WLR 50, Digest (Cont
    Vol D) 1007, 475a.
Pearson Fund Trusts, Re (21st October 1977, unreported).
Walpole (Lord) v Lord Orford (1797) 3 Ves 402, 30 ER 1076, LC, 48 Digest (Repl) 14, 8.

f **Cases also cited**

Adams and Kensington Vestry, Re (1884) 27 Ch D 394, CA.
Gillespie, Re [1969] 1 OR 585.
Green (deceased), Re [1950] 2 All ER 913, [1951] Ch 148.
Hagger, Re [1930] 2 Ch 190.
Heys (deceased), In the estate of [1914] P 192.
g Stone v Hoskins [1905] P 194.
Szabo v Boros (1966) 58 WWR 247; affd (1967) 60 WWR 754.

Action

By a writ issued on 20th August 1979 the plaintiffs, Arthur Cleaver and Florence Zetterberg, suing as residuary legatees under the will dated 7th February 1974 of Flora
h Cleaver deceased ('the testatrix') sought, by para (1) of the prayer for relief, a declaration that the first defendants, George Ernest Insley and David Richard Aldersey, executors of the testatrix's will, held her estate on trust to give effect to the provisions of her will dated 7th February 1974 and, by para (2) an order that the first defendants administer and distribute her estate accordingly. The second to seventh defendants, Martha Noble ('Mrs Noble'), Desmond Noble ('Mr Noble'), Nigel Noble, Elizabeth Noble, Joanne Noble and
j Katie Noble, were beneficiaries under a will of the testatrix dated 23rd June 1977. The facts are set out in the judgment.

John Hicks QC for the plaintiffs.
D J M Campion for the first defendants.
Martin Keenan for Mr and Mrs Noble.
The fourth to seventh defendants did not appear.

NOURSE J. This is a case in which it is alleged that mutual wills are enforceable. By
that I mean that it is one where it is alleged that two persons (in this case husband and
wife) made an enforceable agreement as to the disposal of their property and executed
wills in substantially identical terms in pursuance thereof. The husband died first
without having revoked his will. The wife accepted benefits under the husband's will
and later made her last will in substantially different terms. She is now dead. The
question is whether the persons who would have been the beneficiaries under the wife's
original will can claim that her estate should be held on the trusts of that will and not of
her last will.

The persons concerned and the state of their families are as follows. The testator was
Arthur Cleaver and the testatrix was Flora Cleaver. They were married in about October
1967. It was the testator's third marriage, his second wife having died in 1966. The
testator had had three children by his first marriage which was dissolved in about
1918. In order of seniority they are the second defendant Martha Noble, the second
plaintiff Florence Zetterberg and the first plaintiff Arthur Cleaver junior. There are two
years between each of them and Mr Arthur Cleaver is now 64. The testatrix never had
a child but two nieces of hers play a minor role in the story. Mrs Noble's husband is the
third defendant Desmond Noble. The fourth defendant is their son and the fifth is his
wife. The sixth and seventh defendants are two young children of theirs. I should also
mention that the testator had a sister, Emma Cleaver, who died in 1959 leaving a net
estate sworn for probate of about £8,500. She left legacies of £100 to the testator, £500
to Mr Arthur Cleaver and three legacies amounting to £700 to others. Then she left
legacies of £100 each to two of Mrs Noble's sons and her residuary estate to Mrs Noble
absolutely. That would appear to have been worth £7,000 or thereabouts.

At the time of their marriage the testator was aged 78 and the testatrix about 74. A
few days beforehand the testator purchased flat 4, Basing House, Wilderton Road, Poole,
which is just over the boundary from Bournemouth. They lived there until about
November 1971 when they took a lease on flat 3, Albany House, Balcombe Road, Poole,
which was only about 50 yards away from Basing House, a corner property, on the other
side of the road. In May 1972 the flat at Basing House was sold for £6,300 and the net
proceeds were paid to the testator.

On 19th December 1967 the testator and testatrix each made a will primarily in
favour of the other in substantially identical terms. The testator gave everything to the
testatrix subject to her surviving him for a period of one month, in default of which he
gave pecuniary legacies to the two nieces of the testatrix and directed his net residue to
be equally divided between Mrs Noble, Mrs Zetterberg and Mr Arthur Cleaver or the
survivor or survivors absolutely. The testatrix's will was in the same form mutatis
mutandis except that she gave one of her nieces some specific items of property instead
of a pecuniary legacy. Instructions for these wills were taken by Mr George Ernest
Insley, then a partner in the firm of Greenwood & Insley of Bournemouth. The testator
and the testatrix visited him together for that purpose and he was handed instructions for
both wills written out in what he believes to have been the testator's handwriting.

On 12th June 1970 the testator and the testatrix each made a further will. On this
occasion however there was a difference between the two gifts over of residue. If the
testator was the survivor then his residue was to go as before to his three children or the
survivors or survivor of them, in equal shares, but if the testatrix was the survivor then
her two nieces, if surviving, were to come in and share equally with the testator's three
children or the survivor or survivors of them. There is no evidence worth talking of as
to the circumstances in which these two wills were made.

On 7th February 1974 the testator and the testatrix made the allegedly enforceable
mutual wills with which this case is concerned. I shall return to the circumstances in
which these wills were made in some detail later. The testator's will gave a legacy of
£500 to each of his three children. It then gave his residuary estate to the testatrix
absolutely, subject to her surviving him for a period of one month. If she did not so
survive him then the residue was directed to be divided into three equal parts with one

going to Mrs Zetterberg absolutely and the second to Mr Arthur Cleaver absolutely. The
third part was settled on trust for Mrs Noble for life with remainder to Mrs Zetterberg
and Mr Arthur Cleaver absolutely in equal shares with two provisos, one immaterial and
the other to the effect that if Mrs Zetterberg and Mr Arthur Cleaver should predecease
Mrs Noble then her share should go to Maureen Cleaver, the adopted daughter of Mr
Arthur Cleaver, absolutely. The testatrix's will was in identical terms mutatis mutandis
except that she gave legacies of £500 to each of her two nieces instead of legacies of the
same amount to each of the testator's three children.

The testator died on 27th February 1975 and his 1974 will was duly proved by the
testatrix as sole executrix on 25th April 1975. Apart from the legacies of £500 to each
of the testator's three children, she thus became absolutely entitled to the whole of the
testator's net estate which in due course was paid or transferred to her. The net value of
the testator's residuary estate was about £6,500. The principal assets were a sum of about
£3,500 (including accrued interest) standing to his credit with a building society and a
Bournemouth bond of £4,000. He also owned a freehold house, 48 Pytchley Road,
Rugby. That was subject to a rent controlled tenancy and its value was sworn for probate
at a figure of £500.

It appears that on 15th May 1975, less than three months after the testator's death, the
testatrix gave someone in the firm of Greenwood & Insley instructions to make her a new
will and on 2nd June she did indeed execute a new will. Except for the natural
disappearance of all reference to the testator and the reduction of one of her niece's
legacies from £500 to £100, that will was in identical terms to those of her 1974 will.
On 13th November 1975 the testatrix made a further will by which she gave each of her
two nieces a legacy of £500 and directed her residuary estate to be divided in equal shares
absolutely between Mrs Noble, Mrs Zetterberg and Mr Arthur Cleaver or the survivors
or survivor of them. That was a return to her first will of 19th December 1967 but it
clearly involved a breach of the alleged agreement between the testator and the testatrix,
if such there was, in so far as it restored Mrs Noble's interest to an absolute one. On 27th
January 1976 the testatrix made a codicil to her will which is not material for present
purposes. On 23rd June 1977 the testatrix made what was to be her last will. By that she
gave pecuniary legacies to the fourth to seventh defendants and her net residuary estate
to Mrs Noble and her husband Mr Desmond Noble or the survivor of them if more than
one in equal shares absolutely. That will made no provision for Mrs Zetterberg, Mr
Arthur Cleaver or either of the testatrix's two nieces.

There is no evidence worth talking of as to the circumstances in which any of the
testatrix's testamentary dispositions between her will of 7th February 1974 and the
codicil of 27th January 1976 came to be made. There is some evidence as to the
circumstances in which her last will came to be made and I will deal with that in due
course.

After the testator's death the testatrix continued to live on at the flat in Albany House
but in about February 1976 she moved to a nursing home about three-quarters of a mile
away. I believe that she returned home for a period but her second visit was a permanent
one. She was certainly there when she made her last will on 23rd June 1977.

The testatrix died on 30th May 1978. Her last will was duly proved on 9th October
1978 by Mr Insley and his partner Mr David Richard Aldersey, who are also defendants
in this action. The net value of her estate was sworn for probate at just over £18,000.
The principal assets were sums standing to her credit with two building societies of an
aggregate amount of about £13,500, about £550 in the National Savings Bank and the
house in Rugby which had formerly belonged to the testator and was now sworn at a
figure of £4,000. On 7th June 1978, about a week after the testatrix's death, Mr Arthur
Cleaver informed Mr Insley's firm by telephone that he would be contesting the last will
of the testatrix. By the beginning of January 1979 that claim had been effectively
formulated by solicitors acting on behalf of Mrs Zetterberg and Mr Arthur Cleaver. That
caused Mr Insley and Mr Aldersey to commence proceedings in the Chancery Division
for leave to distribute the testatrix's estate in accordance with the terms of the 1977

will. When those proceedings came before the master he very rightly took the view that Mr Arthur Cleaver and Mrs Zetterberg should commence an action against the Noble family; Mr Insley and Mr Aldersey would also be necessary parties. He stayed the administration proceedings accordingly.

The writ in this action was issued on 8th November 1979. Mr Arthur Cleaver and Mrs Zetterberg, the plaintiffs, claim a declaration that Mr Insley and Mr Aldersey, the first defendants, hold the estate of the testatrix on trust to give effect to the provisions of her 1974 will and an order that they administer and distribute the estate accordingly. Mr Insley and Mr Aldersey have very properly submitted to act as the court shall direct, but Mr and Mrs Noble, the third and second defendants, have appeared by counsel and have throughout contested the plaintiffs' claim. The fourth to seventh defendants have entered appearances and served a defence but they have not appeared and have not been represented at the hearing before me.

Before I deal with further facts of a more controversial nature it will be convenient for me to deal with the principles of law which are applicable to a decision of this case. There cannot now be much doubt about the nature of those principles, but there is no modern authority in England in which they have been fully explored.

The foundation of the plaintiffs' claim is the well-known case of *Dufour v Pereira* (1769) 1 Dick 419, 21 ER 332. That case is fully discussed in Hargrave's Juridical Arguments (1799, vol 2, pp 304ff). That was a case where Lord Camden, relying as it appears only on the terms of a joint will executed by a husband and wife, concluded that there had been a prior agreement. There have not been so very many cases on the subject since, but in one of them, *Gray v Perpetual Trustee Co Ltd* [1928] AC 391, [1928] All ER Rep 758, the Privy Council decided in clear terms that the mere simultaneity of the wills and the similarity of their terms are not enough taken by themselves to establish the necessary agreement. I will read what appear to me to be the material passages in the judgment of the Board, which was delivered by Viscount Haldane. The first reads as follows ([1928] AC 391 at 399–400, [1928] All ER Rep 758 at 761):

> 'In *Dufour* v. *Pereira* the conclusion reached was that if there was in point of fact an agreement come to that the wills should not be revoked after the death of one of the parties without mutual consent, they were binding. That they were mutual wills to the same effect was at least treated as a relevant circumstance, to be taken into account in determining whether there was such an agreement. But the mere simultaneity of the wills and the similarity of their terms do not appear, taken by themselves, to have been looked on as more than some evidence of an agreement not to revoke. The agreement, which does not restrain the legal right to revoke, was the foundation of the right in equity which might emerge, although it was a fact which had in itself to be established by evidence, and in such cases the whole of the evidence must be looked at.'

Their Lordships then proceeded to mention two authorities, the second of which was the decision of Astbury J in *Re Oldham* [1925] Ch 75. The judgment continues ([1928] AC 391 at 400, [1928] All ER Rep 758 at 762):

> 'Their Lordships agree with the view taken by Astbury J. The case before them is one in which the evidence of an agreement, apart from that of making the wills in question, is so lacking that they are unable to come to the conclusion that an agreement to constitute equitable interests has been shown to have been made. As they have already said, the mere fact of making wills mutually is not, at least by the law of England, evidence of such an agreement having been come to. And without such a definite agreement there can no more be a trust in equity than a right to damages at law.'

As to the penultimate sentence of that passage it must, in the light of the earlier passage, be read as meaning that the mere fact of making mutual wills is not by itself sufficient evidence of such an agreement having been come to.

It is therefore clear that there must be a definite agreement between the makers of the two wills, that that must be established by evidence, that the fact that there are mutual wills to the same effect is a relevant circumstance to be taken into account, although not enough of itself, and that the whole of the evidence must be looked at.

I do not find it necessary to refer to any other English case, but I have derived great assistance from the decision of the High Court of Australia in *Birmingham v Renfrew* (1936) 57 CLR 666. That was a case where the available extrinsic evidence was held to be sufficient to establish the necessary agreement between two spouses. It is chiefly of interest because both Latham CJ and more especially Dixon J examined with some care the whole nature of the legal theory on which these and other similar cases proceed. I would like to read three passages from the judgment of Dixon J, which state, with all the clarity and learning for which the judgments of that most eminent judge are renowned, what I believe to be a correct analysis of the principles on which a case of enforceable mutual wills depends. First (at 682–683):

> 'I think the legal result was a contract between husband and wife. The contract bound him, I think, during her lifetime not to revoke his will without notice to her. If she died without altering her will, then he was bound after her death not to revoke his will at all. She on her part afforded the consideration for his promise by making her will. His obligation not to revoke his will during her life without notice to her is to be implied. For I think the express promise should be understood as meaning that if she died leaving her will unrevoked then he would not revoke his. But the agreement really assumes that neither party will alter his or her will without the knowledge of the other. It has long been established that a contract between persons to make corresponding wills gives rise to equitable obligations when one acts on the faith of such an agreement and dies leaving his will unrevoked so that the other takes property under its dispositions. It operates to impose upon the survivor an obligation regarded as specifically enforceable. It is true that he cannot be compelled to make and leave unrevoked a testamentary document and if he dies leaving a last will containing provisions inconsistent with his agreement it is nevertheless valid as a testamentary act. But the doctrines of equity attach the obligation to the property. The effect is, I think, that the survivor becomes a constructive trustee and the terms of the trust are those of the will which he undertook would be his last will.'

Next (at 689):

> 'There is a third element which appears to me to be inherent in the nature of such a contract or agreement, although I do not think it has been expressly considered. The purpose of an arrangement for corresponding wills must often be, as in this case, to enable the survivor during his life to deal as absolute owner with the property passing under the will of the party first dying. That is to say, the object of the transaction is to put the survivor in a position to enjoy for his own benefit the full ownership so that, for instance, he may convert it and expend the proceeds if he choose. But when he dies he is to bequeath what is left in the manner agreed upon. It is only by the special doctrines of equity that such a floating obligation, suspended, so to speak, during the life-time of the survivor can descend upon the assets at his death and crystallize into a trust. No doubt gifts and settlements, *inter vivos*, if calculated to defeat the intention of the compact, could not be made by the survivor and his right of disposition, *inter vivos*, is, therefore, not unqualified. But, substantially, the purpose of the arrangement will often be to allow full enjoyment for the survivor's own benefit and advantage upon condition that at his death the residue shall pass as arranged.'

Finally (at 690):

> 'In *In re Oldham Astbury*, J., pointed out, in dealing with the question whether an agreement should be inferred, that in *Dufour v. Pereira* the compact was that the

survivor should take a life estate only in the combined property. It was, therefore, easy to fix the corpus with a trust as from the death of the survivor. But I do not see any difficulty in modern equity in attaching to the assets a constructive trust which allowed the survivor to enjoy the property subject to a fiduciary duty which, so to speak, crystallized on his death and disabled him only from voluntary dispositions *inter vivos.*'

I interject to say that Dixon J was there clearly referring only to voluntary dispositions inter vivos which are calculated to defeat the intention of the compact. No objection could normally be taken to ordinary gifts of small value. He went on:

'On the contrary, as I have said, it seems rather to provide a reason for the intervention of equity. The objection that the intended beneficiaries could not enforce a contract is met by the fact that a constructive trust arises from the contract and the fact that testamentary dispositions made upon the faith of it have taken effect. It is the constructive trust and not the contract that they are entitled to enforce.'

It is also clear from *Birmingham v Renfrew* that these cases of mutual wills are only one example of a wider category of cases, for example secret trusts, in which a court of equity will intervene to impose a constructive trust. A helpful and interesting summary of that wider category of cases will be found in the argument of counsel for the plaintiffs in *Ottaway v Norman* [1972] Ch 698 at 701–702. The principle of all these cases is that a court of equity will not permit a person to whom property is transferred by way of gift, but on the faith of an agreement or clear understanding that it is to be dealt with in a particular way for the benefit of a third person, to deal with that property inconsistently with that agreement or understanding. If he attempts to do so after having received the benefit of the gift equity will intervene by imposing a constructive trust on the property which is the subject matter of the agreement or understanding. I take that statement of principle, and much else which is of assistance in this case, from the judgment of Slade J in *Re Pearson Fund Trusts* (21st October 1977, unreported; the statement of principle is at p 52 of the official transcript). The judgment of Brightman J in *Ottaway v Norman* is to much the same effect.

I would emphasise that the agreement or understanding must be such as to impose on the donee a legally binding obligation to deal with the property in the particular way and that the other two certainties, namely those as to the subject matter of the trust and the persons intended to benefit under it, are as essential to this species of trust as they are to any other. In spite of an argument by counsel for Mr and Mrs Noble to the contrary, I find it hard to see how there could be any difficulty about the second or third certainties in a case of mutual wills unless it was in the terms of the wills themselves. There, as in this case, the principal difficulty is always whether there was a legally binding obligation or merely what Lord Loughborough LC in *Lord Walpole v Lord Orford* (1797) 3 Ves 402 at 419, 30 ER 1076 at 1084 described as an honourable engagement.

Before turning in detail to the evidence which relates to the question whether there was a legally binding obligation on the testatrix in the present case or not I must return once more to *Birmingham v Renfrew*. It is clear from that case, if from nowhere else, that an enforceable agreement to dispose of property in pursuance of mutual wills can be established only by clear and satisfactory evidence. That seems to me to be no more than a particular application of the general rule that all claims relating to the property of deceased persons must be scrutinised with very great care. However, that does not mean that there has to be a departure from the ordinary standard of proof required in civil proceedings. I have to be satisfied on the balance of probabilities that the alleged agreement was made, but before I can be satisfied of that I must find clear and satisfactory evidence to that effect.

Before I come to the oral evidence in detail I must remark on a number of background facts and surrounding circumstances as to the existence of which there can I think be

little dispute. In the course of a very clear argument on behalf of the plaintiffs counsel
relied on the following facts and circumstances in support of his contention that there
was here an enforceable agreement for mutual wills. First, he relied on the simultaneity
and similarity of the terms of the wills. Second, he relied on the pattern of successive
wills made together. Third, he relied on the significance of the cutting down of Mrs
Noble's absolute interest to a mere life interest. He said that until that point there was
nothing particularly remarkable, but that that fact did point to a definite decision and a
likelihood of agreement between the parties. Fourth, he pointed to the fact that only the
testator had children and that the testatrix was in fact agreeing to benefit her
stepchildren. Fifth, he pointed to the ages of the parties. They were 78 and 74
approximately in 1967 and 84 and 80 approximately in 1974. Sixth, he said that the
testatrix had received at least one substantial benefit from the testator before his death.
I shall come to that later, but it is clear that the testator did at some time between the sale
of the flat in Basing House in May 1972 and the beginning of January 1974 give to the
testatrix the sum of £2,000. Seventh, and finally, he relied on the faithful terms of the
first will which the testatrix made after the testator's death.

For the plaintiffs evidence was given by both Mr Arthur Cleaver and Mrs Zetterberg
themselves and also by a Mr Gray, a gentleman who moved with his wife into the flat
above the Cleavers in Basing House in 1970. He and his wife became friendly with the
Cleavers and remained so until the testator's death, and afterwards with the testatrix
until she went into the nursing home. It appears that after the first six months or so of
their acquaintance the testator began to talk quite freely about family matters in the
presence of Mr and Mrs Gray and also of the testatrix. Mr Insley also gave evidence.
Neither Mr Noble nor Mrs Noble gave evidence. No other evidence was adduced on
their behalf. All the witnesses gave truthful evidence to the best of their recollection. In
particular I should say that both Mr Arthur Cleaver and Mrs Zetterberg appeared to me
to be scrupulously honest. As so often happens in a case where the principal parties are
dead, both Mr Arthur Cleaver and Mrs Zetterberg had opportunities of improving on
their recollection, had they chosen to do so, but in neither case did I detect anything but
a desire to give the court the benefit of that recollection and no more. Their evidence
could only have been given by people who were telling the truth. I therefore accept their
evidence, and indeed that of all the other witnesses, in its entirety and I need say no more
about that.

There was a great deal of evidence which clearly established that by the time of the
1974 wills the testator was determined that Mr Noble should not benefit in any way and
that Mrs Noble should be penalised or at least put in a position where she could not get
the free use of capital. Mr Gray said that the appropriate way of describing the testator's
attitude to the Nobles was that he disliked them. He also described the testator as a very
determined man. There appear to have been two principal causes of complaint around
which the testator's mind revolved so far as the Nobles were concerned. First, he appears
to have thought, with what justification I do not know, that Mrs Noble had brought
pressure on his sister Emma to leave her the bulk of her estate. In relation to that matter
Mr Arthur Cleaver gave evidence of a conversation which he had with the testator
shortly after the death of the testator's second wife Dorothy in 1966. On that occasion
the testator said to Mr Arthur Cleaver, 'You know that Martha got most of Emma's
money by threatening to report her for pushing Auntie Rose downstairs'. The testator
went on to say that he was a little bit horrified that Emma had left her money to
Martha. 'Auntie Rose' was Miss Emma Cleaver's aunt. Later on the testator also told Mr
Gray about the 'Aunt Emma' incident. It seems likely that he came back to it on more
than one occasion, but Mr Gray remembers him referring to it in this way, or in words
to this effect: 'I am determined Martha does not see any of my money'. Second, the
testator thought, again with what justification I do not know, that Mr Desmond Noble
had been fiddling him over the house at Rugby which Mr Noble, who lived with his
family nearby, managed on the testator's behalf. It was always coming up in conversation
when the Grays and the Cleavers were together. The testatrix, who appears mostly to

have been a lady of few words, never took much part in these conversations but Mr Gray's evidence was that he always understood her to be in agreement with the testator *a* over these matters. An on one occasion she herself spoke to Mr Arthur Cleaver in forceful terms about Mr Noble's management of the house in Rugby.

I am satisfied on the evidence as a whole that by the date of the 1974 wills the testator was determined to deal with the Nobles in the way I have described and that this determination was either shared by the testatrix at that time or at least that she was prepared to fall in with the testator's wishes. Counsel for Mr and Mrs Noble did not *b* really dispute this.

Against that background I must now come to some important evidence concerning the making of the 1974 wills. Mrs Zetterberg, who has lived in Sweden since 1952, visited the Cleavers in January 1974. She could not remember whether it was at the end of that month or at the beginning of February, but I am satisfied that she was there either on 7th February or perhaps on 22nd January. Mrs Zetterberg said that on one day when *c* she was there her father asked her to go out because the solicitors were coming to take notes for the making of their wills. When she came back she was told that the solicitor had been. They all sat round the fire and the testator said that he was going to tell Mrs Zetterberg 'what we have put in our wills'. This was all in the presence of the testatrix. Mrs Zetterberg said that she remembers the occasion very clearly. Her father told her that in the event of his death before his wife she, that is the testatrix, should have the 'use' *d* of his money. He then went on to say that the estate was to be divided equally between his three children with restrictions on Mrs Noble's share. Having dealt with what those restrictions were, the testator then explained his reasons for imposing them. They were because he thought that Mrs Noble had very unfairly got Aunt Emma's money and the other reason was so that if she died Mr Desmond Noble and the children could not receive anything afterwards. Mrs Zetterberg said that the testatrix did not say anything, *e* or anything very much, during this conversation except at the stage when the testator said that they had made the same wills. At that stage the testatrix interrupted and said, 'Except for small legacies to my nieces'. Later on on the same day when Mrs Zetterberg and the testatrix were alone together, the testatrix said to Mrs Zetterberg words to this effect: 'You know I did not marry your father for his money.' Then she said this, and Mrs Zetterberg said that these were her actual words, 'I really do love him, but you need not *f* be afraid that I shall take any money away from you children; you will get your share.'

There were a number of other conversations to which Mrs Zetterberg was a party during this visit. In one of them there was talk going on about shopping and the cost of living in England on the one hand and in Sweden on the other. The testatrix apparently complained about the cost of living in England and she said to the testator, 'You know, I have to pay half of everything and my capital is getting low', to which the testator said, *g* 'You do not have to grumble now because I have just given you £2,000 to even it up.' After that the conversation continued generally.

Mr Arthur Cleaver gave similar evidence of a conversation which took place on Boxing Day 1974. That apparently was not a very happy day for the testator and the testatrix, but I need not go into that. At one stage during that day the testator said to Mr Arthur Cleaver: 'I gave Flora £2,000 and she is supposed to have paid the rent sometimes but she *h* has never done so.' The testator said he had also given it to her to even up her savings a little.

At some time after the execution of the 1974 will Mr and Mrs Gray were going to take the Cleavers to Southampton in their car. Before they left, the testator asked Mr Gray to make a diversion so that the testator could drop his and the testatrix's wills in at the solicitors. Mr Gray originally thought that this incident occurred in the summer but it *j* then appeared that it could have been in February or indeed later. What he really remembered was that it was a sunny day. In any event his recollection was very clear that after the testator got back into the car he was smiling all over his face and that he said, 'That has settled [or 'That has cooked'] his hash.' Nothing more was said on the subject but it was obvious to everybody what the testator meant. He was referring to Mr *a* Noble. The testatrix of course was in the car, but she said nothing. Mr Gray's understanding was that she agreed with what the testator had said.

As I have already said the testator died on 27th February 1975, just over a year after the making of the 1974 wills. He died in the early hours and Mr Arthur Cleaver got down to Bournemouth from Weybridge, where he lives, later that morning to help the testatrix with the funeral arrangements and so forth. That evening there was an important conversation between the two of them. The testatrix said to Mr Arthur

b Cleaver: 'I expect you would like to see your father's will. It is in the attaché case over there. You can read it.' She then said that he could also read her will as well. He demurred at that suggestion but the testatrix said: 'I want you to. I want you to see that our wills are exactly the same. You will also notice that Martha does not come off very well in that because your dad was very cross with her because of the way she got hold of most of Emma's money.' Then she said: 'Your dad [or 'Your father'] wanted to put it

c right with you and Flo.' That of course was a reference to Mrs Zetterberg. Then Mr Arthur Cleaver very candidly said that he did not recall the testatrix having said anything on that occasion as to how the wills, or will, had come to be made. As counsel for the plaintiffs correctly observed, it was clear at that stage that the only way in which things could be put right with Mr Arthur Cleaver and Mrs Zetterberg was by the testatrix disposing of her estate in accordance with the terms of her 1974 will, and it seems to me

d that that conversation is powerful evidence to the effect that she then recognised not merely that she herself wanted to do that but that she was under an obligation to her newly deceased husband to do so. In other words it points strongly towards obligation and not mere honourable engagement. And, although this could not in itself be in any way conclusive, it seems that that is how Mr Arthur Cleaver himself saw the matter. I say that because in May 1975 he tried to arrange a meeting with Mr Insley for the

e purpose of warning him that Mrs Noble might find a way of persuading the testatrix to change her will in the same way as she was said to have done in the case of Emma Cleaver. He thought that Mr Insley should remind the testatrix of the agreement which she had with the testator. Nothing in fact came of this because he saw someone else in the firm with whom he was not able to discuss the matter in the way he would have liked.

f The next important event occurred at the end of June 1977 when Mr Arthur Cleaver, on another of his regular visits to Bournemouth, went to see the testatrix at the nursing home. On 9th June Mr Oram, of Mr Insley's firm, had been to see the testatrix to take instructions for what became her last will of 23rd June. The material part of his attendance note on that occasion reads as follows:

g 'Attending Mrs. Cleaver at Alumhurst Road [that was the nursing home] taking instructions for new will. She said certain beneficiaries named in her existing will, 1975, were not in need and her principal beneficiaries in new will were to be Mrs. Martha Noble, stepdaughter, and her husband Desmond who were very good to her.'

h The original attendance note contains a wavy line under the words 'were very good'. That could either be read as being an emphasis of those three words or it could be read as dividing the first part of the note from what followed, which was clearly the second part of the note. I do not think that anything very much turns on that particular fact, but it does mean that the testatrix did tell Mr Oram that the Nobles were very good to her.

j Mr Arthur Cleaver's evidence about his visit at the end of this month of June was as follows. The testatrix had just returned from two weeks in Rugby with the Nobles. I infer from that that she had been to stay with them before she gave instructions for her new will to Mr Oram on 9th June. Mr Arthur Cleaver remembers the testatrix saying that her solicitor had been to see her and a couple of days later he asked her why she needed him. She said this: 'Your father only left me £1,500 and I have had to live on my own savings. Martha told me I can leave my money to whom I like, I do not have to worry about promises made to dad, he is dead now and can do nothing about it.' On one view of all this I could entertain a strong suspicion that that which Mr Arthur Cleaver *a* had all along feared had come to pass and that when the testatrix, who was at that time about 84 years of age, had been to stay with the Nobles in Rugby Mrs Noble had indeed persuaded her to cut Mr Arthur Cleaver and Mrs Zetterberg out of her will. However, that matter is not relevant to this case and I altogether disregard it. What is important is that the testatrix acknowledged that she had made a promise to the testator, but that since he was dead she did not have to worry because he could do nothing about it. It *b* seems to me that this again was a recognition by the testatrix that she had made a promise to the testator, not in the sense of an honourable engagement, but of a solemn contract with him which obliged her to honour the terms of her 1974 will. If he had been alive he would, as she thought, have been able to do something about it; it was because he was dead that she did not have to worry. That again seems to me to point strongly towards obligation rather than an honourable engagement. *c*

I do not think that I need deal specifically with any of the other events described in the evidence of Mr Arthur Cleaver, Mrs Zetterberg or Mr Gray, but I must now deal with that of Mr Insley. I have left him to the last because he can truly be said to have been an independent witness who very properly came to give what evidence he could. He said that on 22nd January 1974 he went to see the Cleavers at their flat to take instructions for new wills. There seemed to be some urgency about it. Mr Insley made a note of his *d* attendance on that occasion. It is headed: 'Mr Cleaver at his house, re will'. Then there is a date. Then the note reads as follows: 'Life interest to Martha only and after her death capital to Florence but if she predeceases then to Maureen Cleaver, his adopted daughter. The same for Mrs Cleaver and delete Olive and Lilian from residue.' Olive and Lilian were the testatrix's two nieces. Mr Insley said that he remembered only two things about that visit. The first is immaterial. The second was that he remembered the *e* testator looking at the testatrix and saying to her, 'I suppose we had not better leave Arthur out or there will be trouble', to which the testatrix shrugged her shoulders. Mr Insley said that this registered in his mind because he thought it was a rather odd remark. There was some debate in argument as to what all this was about, but with the help of Mr Insley's own surmise on the question I think that the testator's remark was directed only to the possibility of leaving Mr Arthur Cleaver out of the gift over of Mrs *f* Noble's settled share. However, counsel for Mr and Mrs Noble correctly said that Mr Insley's evidence was the only direct evidence of the making of any part of the alleged agreement. He said it was significant that the testatrix merely shrugged her shoulders. I do not myself attach much significance to that particular fact. It may well have been that the testatrix did not think it very important whether Mr Arthur Cleaver came in at that stage or not, and I would be inclined to agree with her. I do not think that if I was *g* otherwise satisfied that there was an enforceable agreement that fact could displace my finding. More significant at first blush was Mr Insley's evidence that he was completely unaware, if such was the case, that the Cleavers intended an enforceable agreement. He was sure in his own mind that if there had been any question of that he would have taken steps to put it on a proper footing. He never remembered having made mutual wills of that character in the whole of his long professional experience. In cross-examination he *h* agreed that this meant that he could not remember a case where he had had clients who had asked him to deal with it on that footing, but he agreed that that did not mean that he might not have had cases where there was an agreement of which he was not aware. Again therefore it seems to me that there is nothing in Mr Insley's evidence on this point which could displace a finding of an enforceable agreement if I was duly satisfied that the Cleavers had in fact arrived at one beforehand. *j*

I have now reviewed what appear to me to have been the main features of the evidence in the present case, but there was of course a lot of other evidence which I have not mentioned. I must look at the whole of the evidence. Having done that as fully and carefully as I can, I find that I am satisfied on what I believe to be clear and satisfactory evidence that the testator and the testatrix did make an agreement which they intended should impose mutual legal obligations as to the disposal of their property, that the 1974

wills were executed in pursuance of that agreement, and that the 1974 wills correctly
reproduced its terms. I have already indicated a number of matters which have led me
to this conclusion but I can summarise my view of the evidence as a whole as follows.
Within three months of their marriage at the ages of 78 and 74 respectively the testator
and the testatrix, who each had assets of their own, had made mutual wills under which
the ultimate residuary beneficiaries were to be the testator's three children. The pattern
of identity continued down to and included the 1974 wills with a variation only in the
case of the testatrix's June 1970 will, which is not in my view of any great significance.
In every case the survivor was to take absolutely the bulk of the estate of the first to die.
They kept their finances separate, there being no suggestion that they had a joint
banking account or anything like that. I am satisfied on the evidence that it was at the
beginning of 1974 that the testator gave £2,000 to the testatrix, as he said, to even things
up but with the intention that the testatrix should pay some of the rent. All this suggests
to me that they dealt with their joint financial affairs on a more commercial basis than
is sometimes the case with other, particularly younger, married couples, but it also
suggests that the testator recognised that the testatrix might need capital to live on after
his death. That I think is strongly confirmed by what he said to Mrs Zetterberg at the
beginning of 1974. He said that in the event of his dying first he wanted the testatrix to
have the 'use' of his money. I should have said that Mrs Zetterberg confirmed on two
occasions that that was the word which he used. To my mind when one is considering
persons in the circumstances of the testator and testatrix that means that the testator
wanted the testatrix to have the security after his death which a free power of disposal
over his estate would give her. At the same time he was a very determined man and
everything suggests that he would, so far as he could, have wanted to ensure that
anything which was left at her death should go back to his side of the family. I therefore
start by approaching the crucial period of January and February 1974 in the belief that
it is at the least possible that the testator did do a deal with the testatrix at the beginning
of that year. I think he may well have said that he would leave his estate to her if she as
survivor would leave hers back to his children. I think that the £2,000 may very well
have been part of an overall arrangement to this effect. As counsel for the plaintiffs
pointed out, the testator did by that stage, if not before, have a particular motive for
wishing to tie things up in that he wanted Mrs Noble to have no more than a life interest
and Mr Noble to have no interest at all and, as I think counsel for Mr and Mrs Noble
accepts, the testatrix at that time clearly looked on the Nobles in the same way as the
testator did. However, although I do not have to decide this point, I think that had the
matter rested on these considerations alone it would have been difficult for the plaintiffs
to make out their case. And I am not certain that what was said to Mrs Zetterberg at the
end of January or the beginning of February 1974, both in the three-sided conversation
round the fire and by the testatrix to her alone afterwards, would necessarily have carried
the plaintiffs home. But to the later events I do attach considerable importance. First
there was the 'That has settled [or 'That has cooked'] his hash' incident. That suggests to
me that the testator did think that he had tied everything up and that that did have the
testatrix's tacit agreement. Then there are the events after the testator's death, in
particular the two conversations which the testatrix had with Mr Arthur Cleaver, the
first on the evening of the testator's death and the second at the end of June 1977. I have
already dealt with those conversations at some length. Having added them to all the
other evidence in the case I find that I am in the end fully satisfied as to the existence of
an enforceable agreement. I should however add that I do also attach some importance
to the fact that within three months after the testator's death the testatrix did make a
fresh will which faithfully followed her 1974 will in every material respect. There was
no need for her to make a fresh will. It could perhaps be partly explained as a tidying-up
operation and I can understand that she might not have wished to have a will which
made any mention of her deceased husband. However, in the absence of any evidence
as to the circumstances in which that will was made, it must I think be of some
significance that the testatrix apparently regarded herself as being under more than a
moral duty to dispose of her estate in accordance with her 1974 will.

In the result, and perhaps contrary to my expectation when the case was opened, I am
driven to the conclusion that the plaintiffs are entitled to succeed in this action. Subject
to any point which counsel may have on the wording of the relief sought I propose to
make a declaration in the terms of para (1) of the prayer for relief and an order in the
terms of para (2).

Declaration and order accordingly.

Solicitors: *R Nichols Marcy*, Walton-on-Thames (for the plaintiffs); *Sharpe, Pritchard & Co*,
agents for *Insley & Partners*, Bournemouth (for the first defendants); *Le Brasseur & Bury*
(for Mr and Mrs Noble).

                                         Hazel Hartman   Barrister.

Pioneer Shipping Ltd and others v BTP Tioxide Ltd
The Nema

HOUSE OF LORDS
LORD DIPLOCK, LORD FRASER OF TULLYBELTON, LORD RUSSELL OF KILLOWEN, LORD KEITH OF
KINKEL AND LORD ROSKILL
15th, 16th, 17th, 18th JUNE, 16th JULY 1981

*Shipping – Charterparty – Frustration – Delay – Consecutive voyage charterparty – Shipowners
chartering vessel to charterers for six or seven consecutive voyages in 1979 season – Strike
starting after completion of first voyage – Only two more voyages likely to be possible before end
of 1979 season – Shipowners agreeing in addendum to charterparty to charter vessel to charterers
for seven voyages in 1980 season – Whether 1979 and 1980 voyages separate adventures –
Whether charterparty frustrated in whole or only in part.*

*Arbitration – Award – Leave to appeal against award – Factors to be considered by court when
deciding whether to grant leave – Arbitration Act 1979, s 1(3)(b).*

By a charterparty dated 2nd November 1978 the owners of a vessel chartered her to the
charterers for six or seven consecutive voyages for the carriage of cargo from Sorel in
Canada to ports in Europe between April and December 1979, that being the period
when Sorel was not ice-bound. The charterparty was a standard single voyage form
modified by the parties to cover multiple voyages. Under the terms of the charterparty
the charterers were entitled to cancel the vessel for any voyage for which she was not
ready for loading by 5th December 1979 and were not liable to pay freight in respect of
time lost in loading on account of strikes. A strike broke out at Sorel while the vessel was
away on the first voyage and was still in progress when she arrived back at Sorel on 20th
June 1979, thus preventing her from being loaded for the second voyage. Discussions
took place between the owners and the charterers about the effect of the strike as a result
of which the charterparty was further modified by the addition of addendum 2 and
addendum 3 by which the charterers agreed to release the vessel to the owners for one
intermediate voyage to Glasgow at the end of which if the strike was still continuing the
situation was to be 'discussed without obligation', and the owners agreed to carry a
further seven cargoes in the 1980 season. At the end of the intermediate voyage to
Glasgow the strike was still in progress, so the owners asked permission from the
charterers to extend the intermediate voyage. The charterers refused but the owners
nevertheless arranged for the vessel to go on to Brazil and then to Portugal. The owners
claimed that the charterparty was partly or wholly at an end by reason of frustration.

a The parties agreed to submit to arbitration the question whether the owners were obliged to return the vessel to Sorel at the end of the voyage to Glasgow or were free to send it on to Brazil. At the date of the arbitration hearing the strike at Sorel was still continuing. The arbitrator decided that the whole of the charterparty had been frustrated and that the owners were not obliged to return the vessel to Sorel at the end of the voyage to Glasgow. In his award he stated that his decision related only to the seven consecutive voyages for 1979, that he had disregarded addenda 2 and 3 in arriving at his

b conclusion, that he could not foretell when the strike would end, and that he had decided that the charterparty had been frustrated because by 26th September the vessel had completed only one of the seven consecutive voyages and, after taking into account the prospective delay due to the strike, no more than two further contractual voyages were likely during the remainder of the 1979 season, and the performance of only three out of seven contractual voyages constituted something radically different from what had

c originally been agreed by the owners. The strike ended on 5th October. The charterers applied to a judge for leave to appeal under the Arbitration Act 1979 against the award. The judge gave leave and allowed the appeal on the grounds that the arbitrator had wrongly considered the 1979 season separately, because the original charterparty and the two subsequent addenda constituted one indivisible contract extending over two seasons with a necessary break because of the climatic conditions during the winter, and that

d when the two seasons were taken together under one contract the delay did not amount to frustration of the contract. On appeal, the Court of Appeal ([1980] 3 All ER 117) held that the arbitrator had been correct in deciding both that the voyages for the 1979 and 1980 seasons were separate and divisible adventures and that the charterparty had been frustrated in respect of the 1979 season. The court accordingly reversed the judge and restored the arbitrator's award. Lord Denning MR further held that the judge had been

e wrong to grant leave under s 1(3)*ᵃ* of the 1979 Act because the arbitrator was just as likely as the judge to be right when interpreting a one-off contract or clause and it was contrary to the purpose of that Act to give leave unless the arbitrator was clearly wrong on a question of law. The charterers appealed to the House of Lords.

Held – The appeal would be dismissed for the following reasons—

f (1) Having regard to the purpose of the 1979 Act, which was to promote greater finality in arbitration awards than had previously been the case under the special case procedure, judicial interference with an arbitrator's award was only justified if it was shown that the arbitrator had misdirected himself in law or had reached a decision which

---

g *a* Section 1, so far as material, provides:
'(1) In the Arbitration Act 1950 ... section 21 (statement of case for a decision of the High Court) shall cease to have effect and, without prejudice to the right of appeal conferred by subsection (2) below, the High Court shall not have jurisdiction to set aside or remit an award on an arbitration agreement on the ground of errors of fact or law on the face of the award.
'(2) Subject to subsection (3) below, an appeal shall lie to the High Court on any question of law arising out of an award made on an arbitration agreement; and on the determination of such an

h appeal the High Court may by order—(a) confirm, vary or set aside the award; or (b) remit the award to the reconsideration of the arbitrator or umpire together with the court's opinion on the question of law which was the subject of the appeal; and where the award is remitted under paragraph (b) above the arbitrator or umpire shall, unless the order otherwise directs, make his award within three months after the date of the remission.
'(3) An appeal under this section may be brought by any of the parties to the reference—(a) with the consent of all the other parties to the reference; or (b) subject to section 3 below, with the

j leave of the court.
'(4) The High Court shall not grant leave under subsection (3)(b) above unless it considers that, having regard to all the circumstances, the determination of the question of law concerned could substantially affect the rights of one or more of the parties to the arbitration agreement; and the court may make any leave which it gives conditional upon the applicant complying with such conditions as it considers appropriate ...'

no reasonable arbitrator could have reached. In particular, in the case of a one-off clause
or contract the judge ought usually to exercise his discretion under s 1(3)(b) of the Act by   a
refusing leave unless it was apparent from the award itself, without argument at a
hearing, that the arbitrator had obviously ascribed the wrong meaning to the clause or
contract. Since the addition of addenda 2 and 3 to the already modified standard form
made the charterparty a one-off contract peculiar to the particular voyages contemplated
by the parties and since the arbitrator's award was not obviously wrong, the judge had
been wrong to grant the charterers leave to appeal from the award in favour of the   b
owners (see p 1034 a b, p 1039 h to p 1040 d, p 1041 d to g, p 1042 a to d and p 1048 h,
post); dictum of Lord Radcliffe in *Edwards (Inspector of Taxes) v Bairstow* [1955] 3 All ER
at 57 applied; *Czarnikow v Roth, Schmidt & Co* [1922] All ER Rep 45 and *Halfdan Grieg
& Co A/S v Sterling Coal & Navigation Corpn, The Lysland* [1973] 2 All ER 1073
distinguished; *Schiffahrtsagentur Hamburg Middle East Line GmbH v Virtue Shipping Corpn,
The Oinoussian Virtue* p 887, ante, overruled.   c

(2) On the substantive issues, on the true construction of the charterparty as varied by
the addenda the voyages for the 1979 and 1980 seasons were separate and distinct
adventures, since the performance of the one was not dependent on the performance of
the other. Treating the voyages for the 1979 season as a separate adventure, the arbitrator
was justified on the facts and correct in law in holding that the 1979 adventure was
frustrated (see p 1034 a b, p 1041 d to g, p 1046 a to e and p 1048 b e f and h, post); dictum   d
of Lord Atkinson in *Larrinaga & Co Ltd v Société Franco-Américaine des Phosphates de
Médulla, Paris* [1923] All ER Rep at 7–8 applied.

Per Curiam. (1) Although the question of frustration is never a pure question of fact
and ultimately always involves a question of law whether the frustrating event has made
performance of the contract something which is radically different from that which was
undertaken by the contract, that is not in itself sufficient to justify the court in granting   e
leave to appeal from the arbitrator or in imposing its own view in place of that of the
arbitrator (see p 1034 a b, p 1041 d to g and p 1047 e to j, post); *The Angelia, Trade and
Transport Inc v Iino Kaiun Kaisha Ltd* [1973] 2 All ER 144 doubted.

(2) There is no reason in principle why a strike should not be capable of causing
frustration of an adventure by delay. It cannot be right to divide causes of delay into
classes and then say that one class can and another class cannot bring about frustration of   f
an adventure. It is not the nature of the cause of delay which matters so much as the
effect of that cause on the performance of the obligation which the parties have assumed
towards each other (see p 1034 a b, p 1041 d to g and p 1048 g, post).

(3) Massive citation of authority in cases where the relevant legal principles have been
clearly and authoritatively determined is of little or no assistance to the court and should
be firmly discouraged (see p 1034 a b, p 1041 d to g and p 1046 f, post).   g

Observations on when the court should grant leave to appeal against an arbitrator's
award under the 1979 Act (see p 1037 a and f to p 1038 c, p 1039 g to p 1040 b d to f and
j to p 1041 d, post).

Decision of the Court of Appeal [1980] 3 All ER 117 affirmed.

Notes

For frustration of contract generally, and the application of the doctrine to charterparties,   h
see 9 Halsbury's Laws (4th Edn) paras 450, 452, and for cases on the subject, see 12 Digest
(Reissue) 484–498, 3435–3488.

For frustration caused by delay, see 9 Halsbury's Laws (4th Edn) para 453, and for cases
on the subject relating to charterparties, see 12 Digest (Reissue) 484–491, 3435–3465.

For the Arbitration Act 1979, s 1, see 49 Halsbury's Statutes (3rd Edn) 59.

Cases referred to in opinions   j
Angelia, The, Trade and Transport Inc v Iino Kaiun Kaisha Ltd [1973] 2 All ER 144, [1973]
    1 WLR 210, [1972] 2 Lloyd's Rep 154, Digest (Cont Vol D) 823, 1355a.
Czarnikow v Roth, Schmidt & Co [1922] 2 KB 478, [1922] All ER Rep 45, 92 LJKB 81, 127
    LT 824, 28 Com Cas 29, CA, 3 Digest (Reissue) 178, 1082.
Davis Contractors Ltd v Fareham Urban District Council [1956] 2 All ER 145, [1956] AC 696,
    [1956] 3 WLR 37, 54 LGR 289, HL, 7 Digest (Reissue) 368, 2356.

a   *Edwards (Inspector of Taxes) v Bairstow* [1955] 3 All ER 48, [1956] AC 14, [1955] 3 WLR
    410, 36 Tax Cas 207, [1955] TR 209, 34 ATC 198, 48 R & IT 534, HL, 28(1) Digest
    (Reissue) 566, 2089.
    Halfdan Grieg & Co A/S v Sterling Coal & Navigation Corpn, The Lysland [1973] 2 All ER
    1073, [1973] QB 843, [1973] 2 WLR 904, [1973] 1 Lloyd's Rep 296, CA, Digest (Cont
    Vol D) 42, 1144a.
    International Sea Tankers Inc of Liberia v Hemisphere Shipping Co Ltd of Hong Kong, The
b   *Wenjaing* (21st May 1981, unreported).
    Larrinaga & Co Ltd v Société Franco-Américaine des Phosphates de Médulla, Paris (1923) 92
    LJKB 455, [1923] All ER Rep 1, 129 LT 65, 16 Asp MLC 133, 29 Com Cas 1, HL, 41
    Digest (Repl) 157, 32.
    National Carriers Ltd v Panalpina (Northern) Ltd [1981] 1 All ER 161, [1981] 2 WLR 45,
    HL.
c   *Penelope, The* [1928] P 180, 97 LJP 127, 139 LT 355, 17 Asp MLC 486, 41 Digest (Repl)
    341, 1354.
    *Schiffahrtsagentur Hamburg Middle East Line GmbH v Virtue Shipping Corpn, The Oinoussian
    Virtue* p 887, ante, [1981] 1 Lloyd's Rep 533.
    Tsakiroglou & Co Ltd v Noblee Thorl GmbH [1961] 2 All ER 179, [1962] AC 93, [1961] 2
    WLR 633, [1961] 1 Lloyd's Rep 329, HL, 12 Digest (Reissue) 497, 3488.

d

Appeal

BTP Tioxide Ltd appealed by leave of the House of Lords granted on 23rd July 1980
against the decision of the Court of Appeal (Lord Denning MR, Templeman and Watkins
LJJ) ([1980] 3 All ER 117, [1980] 3 WLR 326) on 22nd May 1980 allowing an appeal by
the respondents, Pioneer Shipping Ltd and Armada Marine SA, the owners of the vessel
e Nema and the claimants in the arbitration, against the judgment of Robert Goff J dated
21st December 1978 and restoring the decision of the sole arbitrator, Mr Donald Ashford
Davis, given in an award published on 3rd October 1979 declaring that the charterparty
dated 2nd November 1978 whereby the respondents chartered the Nema to the
appellants for the carriage of titanium slag in bulk from Sorel in Canada to Calais or
Hartlepool became frustrated by 26th September 1979 and that the Nema was not
f obliged to return to Sorel during the 1979 open season. The facts are set out in the
opinion of Lord Roskill.

A B R Hallgarten QC and *Bernard Rix QC* for the appellants.
Anthony Diamond QC and *Bernard Eder* for the respondents.

g Their Lordships took time for consideration.

16th July. The following opinions were delivered.

LORD DIPLOCK. My Lords, this is the first case to come before this House under the
new procedure for judicial review of arbitrators' awards that was instituted by the
h Arbitration Act 1979. Leave to appeal was given by an Appeal Committee of the House
itself. This was not because of any intrinsic general importance of the points of law
involved in the arbitrator's award. If ever there were a case which under the new
procedure ought never to have been allowed to get any further than the arbitrator's
award, this was one. The reason why leave was given to bring the matter before this
House was because the proceedings in the instant case and in cases that have come before
j the Commercial Court since the judgment of the Court of Appeal was given show that
there exist significant differences of opinion between the individual judges themselves
who sit in the Commercial Court, and between one of them at least and the guidelines
laid down in the instant case by Lord Denning MR (with whom Watkins LJ agreed) as
to the considerations which should influence the judge in deciding how to exercise his
discretion under s 1 of the Arbitration Act 1979 to grant or to refuse leave to appeal to the
High Court on a question of law arising out of an arbitrator's award.

The dispute submitted to the arbitration of a London maritime arbitrator of great   *a*
experience arose between charterers and owners under a consecutive voyage charterparty.
The relevant terms of the charterparty, the dispute between the parties to it and the
circumstances in which that dispute was submitted to arbitration will be dealt with in
the speech of my noble and learned friend Lord Roskill with whose reasons for dismissing
the appeal and upholding the award of the arbitrator I find myself in such unqualified
agreement that I am able to confine my own speech to the question of the discretion to
grant leave to appeal under s 1 of the new Act which has given rise to divergences of   *b*
opinion between those judges called on to exercise it. These, if permitted to continue,
may well endanger the maintenance of the reputation of London arbitration as a forum
for the resolution of commercial disputes.

It is sufficient for my purpose to mention that the reason why the parties submitted
the dispute to speedy arbitration was that they wanted to know, not later than the end of
September 1979, how they then stood as respects the employment of the chartered   *c*
vessel, the Nema, during the remainder of the 1979 St Lawrence River open water season
at the loading port under the charter, Sorel, in the Province of Quebec. Was she, as the
charterers claimed, bound to proceed forthwith from Spain, where she then lay, to Sorel
and wait there at the owners' expense until either the strike at Sorel ended and she could
be loaded or the end of the open water season had made loading impossible, whichever
should first occur? Or, as the owners claimed, had their contractual obligation to   *d*
perform any further voyages in the 1979 open water season been dissolved by frustration?

My Lords, as mentioned by my noble and learned friend, there had been three
contested interlocutory applications in this matter before the application for leave to
appeal from the arbitrator's award was made. At the first two, before Mars-Jones J and
before Donaldson J, undertakings were given by the owners not to fix the Nema for any
further voyage otherwise than in accordance with the charterparty, pending arbitra-   *e*
tion. The third interlocutory application came before Mocatta J after the arbitrator had
telexed to the parties that his award was in favour of the owners, but before he had had
time to set out in writing the reasons for his decision. Mocatta J discharged the owners
unconditionally from their undertaking; but what for my purposes is significant in the
reasons that he gave for doing so (of which a note was taken) was the expression of his
opinion that in the circumstances in which the arbitration had arisen the way in which   *f*
any judge would exercise his discretion would be to refuse leave to appeal from the
arbitrator's award when his reasons had been given, even though the judge might have
doubts as to the correctness of the arbitrator's reasons for his conclusions on any question
of law involved. According to Mocatta J a similar view that the arbitration award would
be treated by the court as final and not one in which leave to appeal to the court would
be granted under s 1 of the Act had also been expressed by Mars-Jones J and by   *g*
Donaldson J on the two earlier interlocutory applications.

My Lords, the particular circumstance in which the parties wanted a quick decision as
to where they stood as respects the future employment of the Nema are, no doubt,
exceptional. In my view, they are in themselves sufficient to make a grant of leave to
appeal from the arbitrator's award under s 1 of the Arbitration Act 1979 an unjudicial
exercise of the discretion conferred on the judge by that section. Such was the view of   *h*
those who were then the two most senior judges of the Commercial Court and such (on
second thoughts) was the view of Lord Denning MR; but the dispute had other
characteristics that are likely to recur in other cases and have caused those divergencies
of views as to the weight that should be given to them in deciding how to exercise that
discretion.

As will appear from my noble and learned friend Lord Roskill's speech, the terms of   *j*
the charterparty and its addenda that are relevant to the disputed issue of frustration are
unique; it is almost inconceivable that they will be found again in any other charter. The
same may be said of the events that preceded and led up to the dispute between the
parties. If one were seeking to exemplify what is meant by the convenient neologism
'a one-off case' it would be hard to find a better exemplar than the case that is now before
your Lordships.

Of course the dispute involves some question of law. It is difficult to conceive of a
dispute under a charterparty that does not do so. The dispute is likely to be about what
the parties have agreed shall be their respective legal rights and obligations in events that
have actually happened or, it may occasionally be, in events that it is anticipated may
happen. The answer must depend on the true construction of the agreement between
the parties; and in English jurisprudence, as a legacy of the system of trial by juries who
might not all be literate, the construction of a written agreement, even between private
parties, became classified as a question of law. The object sought to be achieved in
construing any commercial contract is to ascertain what the mutual intentions of the
parties were as to the legal obligations each assumed by the contractual words in which
they (or brokers acting on their behalf) chose to express them; or, perhaps more
accurately, what each would have led the other reasonably to assume were the acts that
he was promising to do or to refrain from doing by the words in which the promises on
his part were expressed. In the case of a one-off contract where the exact combination of
words and phrases that fall to be construed has not only never been used before and so did
not possess an already established meaning of which each party was entitled to assume
the other knew when he entered into the contract but is also unlikely to be used in future
by any other parties, it is not self-evident that an arbitrator or arbitral tribunal chosen by
the parties for his or their experience and knowledge of the commercial background and
usages of the trade in which the dispute arises is less competent to ascertain the mutual
intentions of the parties than a judge of the Commercial Court, a Court of Appeal of
three Lords Justices or even an Appellate Committee of five Lords of Appeal in
Ordinary. A lawyer nurtured in a jurisdiction that did not owe its origin to the common
law of England would not regard it as a question of law at all. This, I believe, was all that
Lord Denning MR meant to convey by his vivid, if somewhat less than tactful, phrase
([1980] 3 All ER 117 at 124, [1980] 3 WLR 326 at 335): 'On such a clause, the arbitrator
is just as likely to be right as the judge, probably more likely.' Nevertheless, despite the
disappearance of juries, literate or illiterate, in civil cases in England, it is far too late to
change the technical classification of the ascertainment of the meaning of a written
contract between private parties as being 'a question of law' for the purposes of judicial
review of awards of arbitrators or decisions of administrative tribunals from which an
appeal to a court of justice is restricted by statute to an appeal on a question of law.

My Lords, the great majority of international maritime and commercial contracts
which contain a London arbitration clause, and typically those falling within the
categories of disputes in respect of which it is, at least for the time being, forbidden by
s 4 of the Arbitration Act 1979 to enter into an 'exclusion agreement' covering disputes
that have not already arisen are made on standard printed forms on which the particulars
appropriate to the contract between the actual parties are inserted, and any amendments
needed for reasons special to the particular contract are either made to the printed clauses
or dealt with in added clauses, which sometimes may themselves be classified as
standard. Business on the Baltic, the insurance market and the commodity markets
would be impracticable without the use of standard terms to deal with what are to be the
legal rights and obligations of the parties on the happening of a whole variety of events
which experience has shown are liable to occur, even though it be only rarely, in the
course of the performance of contracts of those kinds.

It was in the context of a standard term agreement that in the classic judgment of the
Court of Appeal in *Czarnikow v Roth, Schmidt & Co* [1922] 2 KB 478, [1922] All ER Rep
45 Bankes, Scrutton and Atkins LJJ stated the reasons why the inclusion in an agreement
to refer future disputes to arbitration of an undertaking by the parties not to require any
case to be stated by the arbitral tribunal on a question of law for the opinion of the High
Court was unenforceable as being contrary to public policy at that time. As Atkin LJ put
it ([1922] 2 KB 478 at 491, [1922] All ER Rep 45 at 52):

'The jurisdiction that is ousted is . . . the special statutory jurisdiction of the Court
to intervene to compel arbitrators to submit a point of law for determination by the
Courts. This appears to me to be a provision of paramount importance in the

interests of the public. If it did not exist arbitration clauses making an award a condition precedent would leave lay arbitrators at liberty to adopt any principles of law they pleased. In the case of powerful associations such as the present [sc the Refined Sugar Association], able to impose their own arbitration clauses upon their members, and by their uniform contract, conditions upon all non-members contracting with members, the result might be that in time codes of law would come to be administered in various trades differing substantially from the English mercantile law.'

Bankes and Scrutton LJJ, too, explained the policy that underlay the statutory jurisdiction of the court, as it existed from 1889 to 1979, as being directed to secure that 'the settled principles of law' should be applied by arbitrators as well as by the courts of law.

My Lords, when contracts are entered into which incorporate standard terms it is in the interests alike of justice and of the conduct of commercial transactions that those standard terms should be construed and treated by arbitrators as giving rise to similar legal rights and obligations in all arbitrations in which the events which have given rise to the dispute do not differ from one another in some relevant respect. It is only if parties to commercial contracts can rely on a uniform construction being given to standard terms that they can prudently incorporate them in their contracts without the need for detailed negotiation or discussion. Such uniform construction of standard terms had been progressively established up to 1979, largely through decisions of the courts on special cases stated by arbitrators. In the result English commercial law has achieved a degree of comprehensiveness and certainty that has made it acceptable for adoption as the appropriate proper law to be applied to commercial contracts wherever made by parties of whatever nationality. So, in relation to disputes involving standard terms in commercial contracts an authoritative ruling of the court as to their true construction which is binding also on all arbitrators under the sanction of an appeal from an award of an arbitrator that has resulted from his departing from that ruling performs a useful function that is lacking in that performed by the court in substituting for the opinion of an experienced commercial arbitrator its own opinion as to the application of a one-off clause to the particular facts of a particular case. It was this useful function that it was the plain intention of the 1979 Act to preserve by s 4, for at least an experimental period during which it would be subject to scrutiny by the Commercial Court Users' Committee to see whether the new provisions of ss 1 and 2 relating to leave to appeal from arbitrators' awards and the determinations of preliminary points of law would operate in practice to prevent the continuance of abuses that had become notorious of recent years under the previous system of cases stated.

My Lords, in the instant case there arose out of the arbitrator's award the two interdependent questions of law that are discussed in the speech of my noble and learned friend Lord Roskill. One, which I shall call the question of divisibility, was a question of construction of the charterparty and in particular the one-off clauses in addendum 2; the other was the question of frustration which, as was held unanimously by this House in *Tsakiroglou & Co Ltd v Noblee Thorl GmbH* [1961] 2 All ER 179, [1962] AC 93, is never a pure question of fact but does in the ultimate analysis involve a conclusion of law whether the frustrating event or series of events has made performance of the contract a thing radically different from that which was undertaken by the contract, however closely that conclusion of law may seem to follow from a commercial arbitrator's findings as to mercantile usage and the understanding of mercantile men about the significance of the commercial differences between what was promised and what in the changed circumstances would now fall to be performed.

Lord Denning MR, in laying down guidelines as to the proper exercise of the judicial discretion conferred on a High Court judge by s 1 of the new Act, which led him to the conclusion that in the instant case leave to appeal ought not to have been granted, did not find it necessary to embark on a detailed analysis of the various provisions of the Act. Where the question of law involved is simply the construction of the clause he drew the

distinction that I have already indicated between a one-off clause in a one-off contract and
a clause that is a standard term in a particular class of commercial contract. If what he
said about the former was to be understood as meaning that leave should *never* be given
on a question of interpretation of a one-off clause (and I do not think that this was what
he intended) I consider that would go rather too far; and I shall be suggesting later what,
in my view, in the absence of exceptional circumstances, the appropriate criteria should
be. What he said on the issue of frustration was that the judge should have accepted the
decision of the arbitrator as final unless it was shown 'either (i) that the arbitrator
misdirected himself in point of law or (ii) that the decision was such that no reasonable
arbitrator could reach' (see [1980] 3 All ER 117 at 126, [1980] 3 WLR 326 at 337). With
this I entirely agree and shall explain briefly my reasons for doing so later.

In his vigorous and critical rejection of these guidelines in the subsequent case,
*Schiffahrtsagentur Hamburg Middle East Line GmbH v Virtue Shipping Corpn, The Oinoussian
Virtue* p 887, ante, Robert Goff J founded himself on what in his view was the true
construction of the 1979 Act. He professed himself unable to find in s 1 anything 'which
indicates that, in considering whether or not to give leave to appeal from an arbitrator's
award, any limit should be placed on "the question of law", except that it must be such
that its determination could substantially affect the rights of one or more of the parties'
(see p 893, ante). He accepted that the purpose of the latter part of s 1(4) was to enable
the court to impose conditions on the grant of leave to appeal if it considered that the
argument which the applicant sought to advance was flimsy; but he could 'find nothing
in the Act which, as a matter of construction, suggests that the court should give leave in
the case of some questions of law, but decline to give leave in others . . .' (see p 894,
ante). In his subsequent decision in *International Sea Tankers Inc of Liberia v Hemisphere
Shipping Co Ltd of Hong Kong, The Wenjaing* (21st May 1981, unreported) he made it clear
that in his view whenever any question of construction of a written contract could be
discerned as arising out of an arbitrator's award then, except where its determination
could not substantially affect the rights of any of the parties, the only proper exercise of
his discretion by the judge was to grant leave to appeal, though if the argument that the
arbitrator had erred in point of law appeared to the judge to be flimsy it was open to him
to impose conditions, such as payment of the whole or part of the amount of the award
into court or the provision of security.

My Lords, with great respect, I do not think that the learned judge's reasoning, in
concentrating as it appears to have done on sub-s (4) of s 1, pays sufficient regard to the
general discretion of the High Court to *refuse* leave absolutely. This is conferred not by
sub-s (4) but by sub-s (3)(*b*). Nor, as it seems to me, has he given proper effect to the terms
in which the right of appeal is conferred in sub-s (2).

The judicial discretion conferred by sub-s (3)(*b*) to refuse leave to appeal from an
arbitrator's award in the face of an objection by any of the parties to the reference is in
terms unfettered; but it must be exercised judicially; and this, in the case of a dispute
that parties have agreed to submit to arbitration, involves deciding between the rival
merits of assured finality on the one hand and on the other the resolution of doubts as to
the accuracy of the legal reasoning followed by the arbitrator in the course of arriving at
his award, having regard in that assessment to the nature and circumstances of the
particular dispute.

My Lords, in weighing the rival merits of finality and meticulous legal accuracy there
are, in my view, several indications in the Act itself of a parliamentary intention to give
effect to the turn of the tide in favour of finality in arbitral awards (particularly in non-
domestic arbitrations of which the instant case is one), at any rate where this does not
involve exposing arbitrators to a temptation to depart from 'settled principles of law'.
Thus s 1(1) removes a former threat to finality by abolishing judicial review (formerly
certiorari) for error of law on the face of the award. Section 1(3) withdraws the previous
power of an arbitrator to accede to a request to state his award in the form of a special case
if such request was made by any party to the reference.

It is notorious, particularly after the decision of the Court of Appeal in *Halfdan Grieg*

& Co A/S v Sterling Coal & Navigation Corpn, The Lysland [1973] 2 All ER 1073, [1973] 1
QB 843, that, if such request were made, it was virtually impracticable for an arbitrator   *a*
to refuse it.

Except when all parties to the reference consent, the first part of s 1(4) places an
absolute bar on the grant of leave to appeal unless the determination of the disputed
point of law would substantially affect the rights of one or more parties to the reference,
and this, be it noted, even though the point might have arisen under a standard form
contract and be of outstanding importance to the trade generally. I find it impossible to   *b*
infer from the inclusion of a power to impose conditions in the latter part of the same
subsection a parliamentary intention that whenever that absolute bar did not operate
leave to appeal *should* be granted, albeit that it might be made subject to conditions.

Section 1(7) is another provision in favour of reaching finality as soon as possible; the
stringent conditions imposed on a further appeal from the judge to the Court of Appeal
are clearly adapted from the provisions of the Criminal Appeal Act 1968 relating to   *c*
appeals to the House of Lords in criminal matters, another field of law in which speedy
finality is much to be desired. The subsection also draws a significant distinction between
a question of law which arises in connection with a one-off case and a question of law of
general importance to a substantial section of the commercial community, such as may
arise under standard term contracts. I add parenthetically that it is one of the ironies of
the instant case that if the judge's initial error in granting leave to appeal to the High   *d*
Court had not been compounded by his also giving a certificate and leave to appeal to the
Court of Appeal under this subsection (which a fortiori in such a one-off case he never
should have done) the owners would have been left with a decision against them which,
although it is not one of general public importance, both the Court of Appeal and this
House have unanimously held to be wrong.

Section 3 gives effect to a reversal of public policy in relation to arbitration as it had   *e*
been expounded more than half a century before in *Czarnikow v Roth, Schmidt & Co.*
Exclusion agreements, which oust the statutory jurisdiction of the High Court to
supervise the way in which arbitrators apply the law in reaching their decisions in
individual cases, are recognised as being no longer contrary to public policy. In principle
they are enforceable, subject only to the special limitations imposed, for the time being,
by s 4 in the case of awards made in respect of certain limited classes of contracts which,   *f*
important as they are to the role of London as a forum for international arbitrations,
represent what is numerically only a small fraction of the total arbitrations, large and
small, that take place in England.

The classes of contracts listed in s 4 in respect of which the right to make exclusion
agreements is not unfettered but is subjected to some qualifications are those in which
(i) the use of standard forms of contract, in the vast majority of transactions, is a   *g*
commercial necessity, (ii) English law is very widely chosen as the 'proper law' of the
contract, even though the parties are foreign nationals and no part of the transaction is
to take place in England, and (iii) provision is very frequently made for London
arbitration. I have already drawn attention to the fact that decisions of the English courts
on cases stated by arbitrators under the previous system had made an important
contribution in giving to English commercial law the comprehensiveness and certainty   *h*
that makes it a favoured choice as the 'proper law' of contracts in the classes listed, and
London arbitration as the favoured curial law for the resolution of disputes arising under
them. Even in respect of contracts falling within these classes, however, an exclusion
agreement may be made and will be enforceable if entered into after the dispute arose.
What is not enforceable is an exclusion agreement covering possible future disputes
under the contract before they have arisen. Nevertheless, when a dispute under the   *j*
contract has arisen and the award of an arbitrator made, an appeal to the High Court on
a point of law arising out of it is not as of right: it is still subject to the discretion of the
judge under s 1(3)(*b*).

My Lords, it seems to me quite evident that the parliamentary intention evinced by
s 4 in maintaining for the time being a prohibition on pre-dispute exclusion agreements

only was to facilitate the continued performance by the courts of their useful function of

a   preserving, in the light of changes in technology and commercial practices adopted in various trades, the comprehensiveness and certainty of English law as to the legal obligations assumed by the parties to commercial contracts of the classes listed, and particularly those expressed in standard terms; it was not Parliament's intention to encourage appeals from arbitrators' awards even under those classes of contracts where such appeals would not fulfil this purpose. That Parliament was alert to the possibility

b   of such abuse in the case of any or all of the listed classes of contracts appears to me to follow from the provision in s 4(3) that the Secretary of State may at any time *remove* the ban on pre-dispute exclusion agreements in respect of all or any of the classes of contracts included in the list but he has no power to *add* any other class of contract to them.

My Lords, I can deal much more briefly with the terms in which the right of appeal to the High Court is conferred by s 1(2). The power to require an arbitrator to state an

c   award in the form of a special case for the opinion of the High Court under the previous Arbitration Acts from 1889 to 1950 was not conferred in terms that restricted it expressly to cases in which questions stated for the opinion of the High Court were confined exclusively to points of law. Parliament had been content to allow any such restriction to be implied from its use of the phrase 'special case for the opinion of the . . . Court' which, by 1889, had become a term of legal art; and many and varied (and, if I may be

d   forgiven for saying so, at times confusing) were the authorities as to findings of arbitrators in particular cases that could or could not be upset by the High Court in the exercise of this power. The right of appeal to the High Court, on the other hand, under the substituted procedure for challenging an arbitrator's award which is provided by s 1(2), viz 'an appeal . . . to the High Court on any question of law arising out of' an award, is given in terms which expressly confine the appeal to questions of law and which, ever

e   since the decision of this House 25 years ago in *Edwards (Inspector of Taxes) v Bairstow* [1955] 3 All ER 48, [1956] AC 14, have been understood (at least where the tribunal from which such appeal lies is not itself a court of law) as bearing the precise meaning as to the function of the court to which an appeal on a question of law is brought that is stated in the classic passage to be found in the speech of Lord Radcliffe ([1955] 3 All ER 48 at 57, [1956] AC 14 at 36):

f   'If the case contains anything ex facie which is bad law and which bears on the determination, it is, obviously, erroneous in point of law. But, without any such misconception appearing ex facie, it may be that the facts found are such that no person acting judicially and properly instructed as to the relevant law could have come to the determination under appeal. In those circumstances, too, the court must intervene. It has no option but to assume there has been some misconception

g   of the law and that this has been responsible for the determination. So there, too, there has been error in point of law.'

Or, as Lord Denning MR summarised it in dealing with the question of frustration in the instant case: to justify interference with the arbitrator's award it must be shown (i) that the arbitrator misdirected himself in law or (ii) that the decision was such that no

h   reasonable arbitrator could reach.

My Lords, in view of the cumulative effect of all these indications of Parliament's intention to promote greater finality in arbitral awards than was being achieved under the previous procedure as it was applied in practice, it would, in my view, defeat the main purpose of the first four sections of the 1979 Act if judges, when determining whether a case was one in which the new discretion to grant leave to appeal should be

j   exercised in favour of an applicant against objection by any other party to the reference, did not apply much stricter criteria than those stated in *The Lysland* which used to be applied in exercising the former discretion to require an arbitrator to state a special case for the opinion of the court.

Where, as in the instant case, the question of law involved is the construction of a one-off clause the application of which to the particular facts of the case is an issue in the

arbitration, leave should not normally be given unless it is apparent to the judge, on a
mere perusal of the reasoned award itself without the benefit of adversarial argument, *a*
that the meaning ascribed to the clause by the arbitrator is obviously wrong; but if on
such perusal it appears to the judge that it is possible that argument might persuade him,
despite impression to the contrary, that the arbitrator might be right, he should not
grant leave; the parties should be left to accept, for better or for worse, the decision of the
tribunal that they had chosen to decide the matter in the first instance. The instant case
was clearly one in which there was more than one possible view as to the meaning of the *b*
one-off clause as it affected the issue of divisibility. It took two days' argument by counsel
before the learned judge to satisfy him that the arbitrator was wrong on this and on the
interdependent question of frustration, four days' argument before the Court of Appeal
to convince them that the judge was wrong and the arbitrator right and over three days'
argument in trying to persuade this House to the contrary, even though it was not found
necessary to call on the respondents to address us on the merits. Even apart from the *c*
reasons special to this case mentioned at the outset, which led Mocatta J and Donaldson
J to conclude that it was a case in which no court would grant leave to appeal from the
arbitrator's award, it is in my view typical of the sort of case in which leave to appeal on
a question of construction ought not to be granted.

For reasons already sufficiently discussed, rather less strict criteria are in my view
appropriate where questions of construction of contracts in standard terms are *d*
concerned. That there should be as high a degree of legal certainty as it is practicable to
obtain as to how such terms apply on the occurrence of events of a kind that it is not
unlikely may reproduce themselves in similar transactions between other parties engaged
in the same trade is a public interest that is recognised by the 1979 Act, particularly in
s 4. So, if the decision of the question of construction in the circumstances of the
particular case would add significantly to the clarity and certainty of English commercial *e*
law it would be proper to give leave in a case sufficiently substantial to escape the ban
imposed by the first part of s 1(4), bearing in mind always that a superabundance of
citable judicial decisions arising out of slightly different facts is calculated to hinder
rather than to promote clarity in settled principles of commercial law. But leave should
not be given, even in such a case, unless the judge considered that a strong prima facie
case had been made out that the arbitrator had been wrong in his construction; and when *f*
the events to which the standard clause fell to be applied in the particular arbitration
were themselves one-off events stricter criteria should be applied on the same lines as
those that I have suggested as appropriate to one-off clauses.

The other question of law arising out of the award in the instant case if the construction
of the charterparty as respects the 'divisibility' of the adventures for the 1979 season and
the 1980 season respectively were to be decided in favour of the owners, as the arbitrator *g*
held it should, was whether in the events that had happened by 26th September 1979
(which were very much one-off events) the adventure for the 1979 season had by then
become frustrated. Disputes on questions whether contractual obligations have been put
an end to by frustration and the somewhat analogous questions whether one party to a
commercial contract is entitled to refuse to continue to perform his own obligations
under the contract in consequence of a fundamental breach or breach of condition by the *h*
other party are frequent subjects of commercial arbitration.

The legal concept of frustration, as my noble and learned friend Lord Roskill points
out, can be expressed in the short and simple language used by Lord Radcliffe in *Davis
Contractors Ltd v Fareham Urban District Council* [1956] 2 All ER 145, [1956] AC 696.
Whether a particular event or series of events have made further performance something
radically different from that which was undertaken by the contract involves, as is *j*
indicated by Lord Radcliffe's adverb and its oft-used variant 'fundamentally', a question
of degree on which, though faced with the same facts, different opinions may not
unreasonably be held by different men.

In deciding how to exercise his discretion whether to give leave to appeal under s 1(2)
what the judge should normally ask himself in this type of arbitration, particularly

a
where the events relied on are one-off events, is not whether he agrees with the decision reached by the arbitrator, but: does it appear on perusal of the award either that the arbitrator misdirected himself in law or that his decision was such that no reasonable arbitrator could reach. While this should, in my view, be the normal practice, there may be cases where the events relied on as amounting to frustration are not one-off events affecting only the transaction between the particular parties to the arbitration but events of a general character that affect similar transactions between many other persons

b
engaged in the same kind of commercial activity; the closing of the Suez Canal, the United States soya bean embargo, the war between Iraq and Iran, are instances within the last two decades that spring to mind. Where such is the case it is in the interests of legal certainty that there should be some uniformity in the decisions of arbitrators as to the effect, frustrating or otherwise, of such an event on similar transactions, in order that other traders may be sufficiently certain where they stand as to be able to close their own

c
transactions without recourse to arbitration. In such a case, unless there were prospects of an appeal being brought by consent of all the parties as a test case under s 1(3)(a), it might be proper exercise of the judge's discretion to give leave to appeal in order to express a conclusion as to the frustrating effect of the event that would afford guidance binding on the arbitrators in other arbitrations arising out of the same event, if the judge thought that in the particular case in which leave to appeal was sought the conclusion

d
reached by the arbitrator, although not deserving to be stigmatised as one which no reasonable person could have reached, was, in the judge's view, not right. But such was far from being the instant case.

For all these reasons this was the sort of case in which in my opinion leave to appeal from the arbitrator's award ought never to have been given.

e
LORD FRASER OF TULLYBELTON. My Lords, I have had the advantage of reading in draft the speeches of my noble and learned friends Lord Diplock and Lord Roskill. I agree with them and, for the reasons stated in those speeches, I would dismiss this appeal.

LORD RUSSELL OF KILLOWEN. My Lords, I have had the advantage of reading

f
in draft the speeches of my noble and learned friends Lord Diplock and Lord Roskill. I agree with them and, for the reasons stated in those speeches, I would dismiss this appeal.

LORD KEITH OF KINKEL. My Lords, I agree with the speeches of my noble and learned friends Lord Diplock and Lord Roskill, which I have had the benefit of reading in draft, and, for the reasons which they give, I would dismiss the appeal.

g
LORD ROSKILL. My Lords, this appeal by the appellant charterers to your Lordships' House against a decision of the Court of Appeal (Lord Denning MR, Templeman and Watkins LJJ) ([1980] 3 All ER 117, [1980] 3 WLR 326) dated 22nd May 1980 in favour of the respondent owners of the Greek motor vessel Nema raises two entirely separate questions. The first is whether what I shall call 'the 1979 venture' agreed on between the

h
appellants and the respondents on the terms of a consecutive voyage charterparty dated 2nd November 1979 'for 6 voyages, Charterers option 7 voyages' during 1979 from Sorel, Province of Quebec to either Calais or Hartlepool was, in the events which occurred, frustrated. This is the central issue between the parties to which the appellants' printed case was entirely directed. That issue is of great importance to them and your Lordships were told that a substantial sum of money is involved.

j
But the second question is of wide general importance. Yet it is mentioned only in passing in the respondents' printed case and then principally only in a postscript of that document. My Lords, this is the first occasion on which your Lordships' House has had to consider the Arbitration Act 1979, and it was to enable that consideration to be given, especially to the principles on which leave should be granted by the High Court to appeal from a decision of an arbitral tribunal under s 1(2) and (3)(b) of the 1979 Act and also the

principles on which any certificate which by reason of s 1(7) of that Act is an essential prerequisite to a further appeal from the High Court to the Court of Appeal should be *a* granted, that leave to appeal to your Lordships' House was given on 23rd July 1980.

My Lords, I have had the advantage of reading in draft the speech prepared by my noble and learned friend Lord Diplock on the second question. I entirely agree with it and respectfully adopt the criticisms which he has made of the several judgments of Robert Goff J on this question in the instant case ([1980] 2 Lloyd's Rep 83) and in the two subsequent cases, *The Oinoussian Virtue* p 887, ante, and *The Wenjaing* (21st May 1981, *b* unreported), in which that learned judge felt free not to follow the decision of the Court of Appeal in the instant case. I would only add with profound respect to Robert Goff J that if the learned judge's view were allowed to prevail I find it difficult to see what useful purpose had been served by the passing of the 1979 Act which had as one of its primary targets the abolition of the special case, since it seems to me that if leave to appeal from an arbitral tribunal to the High Court is to be given in accordance with the principles *c* which the learned judge there enunciated the notoriously unsatisfactory results to which special cases have given rise in recent years will be perpetuated, albeit in a different form.

If the views expressed by my noble and learned friend Lord Diplock are shared by all your Lordships it follows that not only ought leave to appeal to the High Court not to have been granted by Robert Goff J in the present case but also that the certificate under s 1(7) and indeed leave to appeal to the Court of Appeal itself ought also not to have been *d* granted by the learned judge. It is therefore somewhat ironical that it is because two successive appeals from the arbitrator were wrongly permitted that your Lordships' House has now to determine what I have called the first question, that of the alleged frustration of the 1979 adventure. The arbitrator held that it was frustrated. Robert Goff J reversed that decision. The Court of Appeal restored it. Your Lordships' House must now decide between these conflicting opinions, and it is to this, the first question, *e* that I now turn.

My Lords, I begin by setting out the relevant clauses of the charterparty dated 2nd November 1978 as they stood when that charterparty was first concluded. The parties used a standard form, C (Ore) 7, as the basis of their agreement, but since that form is designed for use for a single voyage it naturally required, and indeed received, substantial amendment and addition; so much that the finished product well justifies the application *f* of my noble and learned friend Lord Diplock's word 'one-off'. Even so, understandably in the circumstances, there are some loose ends and some somewhat untidy drafting which could sometimes leave doubt whether a particular clause was directed to the charterparty as a whole or only to individual voyages made under that charterparty or conceivably only to the first voyage made thereunder. None the less, the essential provisions are clear enough and read thus: *g*

> '2. ... proceed with all convenient speed to SOREL, P.Q. and there load ... a full and complete Cargo of Titanium Slag ... 15000 long tons 5% more or less in Owners' option ... and being so loaded ... proceed to CALAIS or HARTLEPOOL in Charterers option ...
>
> '3. Freight to be paid at ... the rate of ... per ton ...
>
> '5. The Cargo to be shipped at the rate of ... and to be discharged at the rate of *h* ... Time lost by reason of ... any of the following causes shall not be computed in the loading or discharging time ... Strikes, Lock-outs, stoppage of ... essential to the Working, Carriage, Delivery, Shipment or Discharge ... whether partial or general ... or any other cause beyond control of Charterers, unless steamer is already on demurrage ...
>
> '10. ... should the Steamer not be in Loading Port and ready to load on or before *j* 30th April, 1979 for first voyage (see Clause No. 38), it shall be at the option of the Charterer whether or not he will load the vessel. Laydays are not to count before 1st April, 1979 except by Charterers consent ...
>
> '19. Ship to apply to QUEBEC IRON & TITANIUM CORP., P.O. BOX 40, SOREL, P.Q. ... for Cargo ...

'27. In the event of any general strike, riot, insurrection, revolution or war, which may prevent Shipment of Titanium Slag under this Charter, the Owners in the event of no cargo having been loaded, have the option of cancelling this Charter or if any cargo has been loaded they have the right to proceed on the voyage with the cargo so loaded . . .

'37. This Charter Party to remain in force for 6 voyages, Charterers option 7 voyages, such option declarable at termination of 5th voyage or 30th September, 1979, whichever is the sooner. Intervals between voyages minimum 30 days/maximum 50 days. Owners have the option of return cargoes, but same limited to a maximum of three.

'38. Charterers have the option of cancelling the vessel for any voyages for which she has not presented at loading port by 5th December, 1979.'

It is clear from these provisions that both parties recognised that, since Sorel was on the St Lawrence River and might, therefore, become ice bound before the end of 1979, the vessel might not be able to perform all seven voyages which the 1979 adventure contemplated when the charterparty was signed.

My Lords, the relevant facts found by the arbitrator are set out with such admirable clarity by him in 15 numbered paragraphs in section F of his reasoned award that I hesitate even to attempt to summarise them in an inevitably shorter and no doubt less clear form. But I fear some reference to them is essential. The more important findings include the following. (a) The first voyage was performed between 17th May and 20th June 1979. On or about 21st June 1979 the appellants exercised their option for the seventh voyage. Industrial action, whether a strike or a lockout is irrelevant, had begun at the plant of the shippers named in cl 19 on 6th June 1979 and thenceforth there was a total shutdown at that plant. This began before the vessel returned to Sorel to load for the second voyage. (b) On 22nd June 1979 the owners claimed to cancel the whole charterparty under cl 27. This claim was later that day limited to a claim to cancel the second voyage. Discussion thereupon took place as a result of which addendum 2 was signed. I shall later set out the relevant clauses of addendum 2 in full since much of the argument for the appellants was founded on it. Suffice it for the present to say that provision was there made, inter alia, for a further seven voyages in 1980 ('the 1980 adventure') and that the respondents were also given the right to fix the vessel for a transatlantic voyage in place of the second voyage. In the event the respondents were unable to take advantage of this latter concession by the appellants. Accordingly, on 11th July 1979 addendum 3 was signed under which the appellants agreed to pay the respondents $2,000 per day from 1st July until the end of the strike or until the appellants agreed to release the vessel for an intermediate voyage. (c) On 20th July the appellants did so release the vessel for an ore cargo to Glasgow. Another request by the respondents was refused but the respondents were allowed to carry a return cargo to Canada. (d) In August 1979 the prospects for the end of the strike were gloomy; but the appellants refused to release the vessel for a further round voyage. Whereupon on 14th August 1979 the respondents rejected the appellants' instructions to return to Sorel for another voyage and on 16th August 1979 they fixed her for an intermediate voyage for their own account which would not be completed until towards the end of September. The rejection of the appellants' instructions led to an application by them for an injunction. Such an injunction was granted ex parte on 17th August 1979 but it was lifted on the following day by the vacation judge (Mars-Jones J) on his learning that the vessel was already fixed for the unauthorised August voyage, the respondents giving an undertaking not to fix the vessel for another voyage pending an arbitration on the question whether they would be entitled to do so. An arbitration was thereupon fixed for hearing for 26th September, the parties varying the Centrocon arbitration clause which had been incorporated into the charterparty and appointing a very experienced maritime arbitrator, Mr Donald Davies, as sole arbitrator. A further application came before Donaldson J at which the undertaking was renewed and the matter was adjourned until 2nd October 1979, the beginning of the legal term. As it happened, on 26th

September 1979, the day when the arbitration took place, the vessel had just completed discharge under the non-approved voyage and subject to the result of the arbitration was *a* ready to sail back to Canada for a further voyage under the charterparty. By 2nd October 1979 the arbitrator had already announced that the award was in favour of the respondents though he had not yet published his reasons. At the adjourned hearing in the High Court by Mocatta J the respondents were discharged from their undertaking. (e) In para 15 of section F the arbitrator found as follows: 'As at September 26 there were no immediate prospects for the ending of the strike. The earliest probable date, for the *b* resumption of loading of titanium slag, is the end of October.' The result of his award was notified to the parties on 28th September, but in that paragraph I think the arbitrator is stating the position as he saw it on 26th September when the arbitration took place and not when his reasoned award was later published on 3rd October. (f) Your Lordships were told that in the event the strike ended on 5th October 1979 and work had begun again on 18th October 1979.

c

My Lords, it seems from section G of the arbitrator's award that the now crucial question whether the 1979 adventure was frustrated was never fully argued for the respondents at the arbitration. Mr Rix QC, who appeared for the appellants in the arbitration, told your Lordships that this possible conclusion was only mentioned in the course of his address to the arbitrator. The respondents seem only to have argued (see section G of the award) first, that each individual voyage was severable and susceptible of *d* frustration, second, that the whole of the consecutive voyage charterparty, by which was meant the entirety of the adventure (which by 26th September 1979 covered 1980 as well as 1979), had been frustrated, and, third, that by cl 27 the respondents were entitled to cancel the charterparty. None of those arguments was advanced in your Lordships' House. The arbitrator in section H, para 1 of his reasoned award rejected the first and third of the three contentions I have mentioned. As for the second, in section H, para *e* 1(a) he said: 'The whole of the consecutive voyage charterparty, dated November 3 [sic], 1978, was frustrated by September 26 1979.' Read in isolation this conclusion would seem to mean that the entirety of the adventure both for 1979 and 1980 was, in his view, frustrated, thus accepting the respondents' second contention as already set out. But in section H, para 6 the arbitrator added:

'For the sake of completeness I should mention that I have disregarded addendums *f* Nos. 2 and 3 while arriving at my conclusions. My decision only adverts to the seven consecutive voyages for 1979. No consideration has been given by me to the part of addendum No. 2 relating to the seven voyages contemplated for the 1980 season.'

Thus it seems clear from this statement that the arbitrator in the conclusion above *g* referred to in section H, para 1(a) was intending to hold that only what I have called 'the 1979 adventure' was frustrated leaving the mutual obligations of the parties in 1980 to be performed in the fullness of time. Not unnaturally in these circumstances the solicitors for the parties were puzzled and in connection with the projected appeal to Robert Goff J sought enlightenment from the arbitrator in a joint letter dated 15th November 1979. The arbitrator replied in a telex dated 16th November 1979 which was *h* followed by a letter of 21st November 1979.

My Lords, I must confess that I do not find this interchange enlightening. I think, whatever criticism may be made of the actual language which the arbitrator used in his award, and it must be remembered that this award was prepared with admirable clarity in a great hurry, the arbitrator's intention is plain enough. He was intending to hold and clearly did hold, notwithstanding that the point had never been firmly taken before on *j* behalf of the respondents, that the 1979 adventure was, but the 1980 adventure was not, frustrated. It is implicit in his contention that the two adventures were on the true construction of the charterparty as varied by addendum 2 separate and distinct adventures. It is this view which the Court of Appeal has accepted but which Robert Goff J rejected.

My Lords, in order to determine which of these two views is correct two separate
a questions must be asked and answered. First, on the true construction of the charterparty
as varied by addendum 2, were the 1979 and 1980 adventures separate and distinct
adventures? If they were not it was common ground that this appeal must succeed.
Second, if the 1979 and 1980 adventures were separate and distinct adventures, was the
arbitrator, on the facts found by him, entitled to hold that the 1979 adventure was
frustrated or has he erred in point of law in so doing?

b My Lords, on the first issue your Lordships were referred to a number of decisions on
consecutive voyage charterparties. I do not propose to refer to them for each was a
decision on the particular contract then in issue and decisions on one particular contract
are of no assistance whatever in interpreting another and quite different contract and
ought not to be cited for this purpose. In *Larrinaga & Co Ltd v Société Franco-Américaine
des Phosphates de Médulla, Paris* (1923) 92 LJKB 455 at 460–461, [1923] All ER Rep 1
c at 7–8 Lord Atkinson, in the context of a very different type of contract from the present,
where the question was whether the obligation to perform three later separate adventures
under a tonnage agreement had survived the abandonment during the 1914–18 war of
three earlier adventures, described the particular contract as one which 'dealt with six
wholly distinct, separate, and severable adventures between which there was no
interdependence in the sense that the carrying out of any one of them was made to
d depend in any way upon the carrying out or abandonment of any of the others'.

If I may borrow Lord Atkinson's language and apply it to the present charterparty as
varied by addendum 2, the question is whether the 1979 and 1980 adventures are in any
way interdependent so that the carrying out of the 1980 adventure depended in any way
on whether or not the 1979 was performed. I have already set out the relevant clauses in
the charterparty as it was originally executed. I will now set out the relevant clauses in
e addendum 2 which bore the date 28th June 1979.

'ADDENDUM NO. 2 to "NEMA" C/P dated 2nd November, 1978 Sorel/Calais or
Hartlepool . . .

'2. In consideration of the strike situation presently existing at Sorel, Charterers
agree that "NEMA" be permitted to now undertake one transatlantic voyage with Iron
f Ore, St. Lawrence to Glasgow or Birkenhead (or as otherwise mutually agreed)
thereafter returning in ballast to load her next cargo at Sorel. Except as provided in
Clause No. 8 (of this Addendum), this voyage shall in all respects replace voyage 2
under this Charter Party 2.11.78.

'3. (a.) It is further hereby mutually agreed that this Charter Party is extended
for a subsequent 7 (seven) further cargoes to be lifted in the period commencing
g laydays 1st April, 1980/cancelling 30th April, 1980, Charterers having the right of
cancelling any voyages for which the vessel has not presented by 31st December,
1980. (b.) Rates of freight for these further 7 cargoes to be U.S. $16·50 . . . per ton
for Calais or U.S. $17·50 . . . per ton for Hartlepool . . .

'4. For the postponed voyage No. 2 of 1979 (in spite of having declared
Hartlepool), Charterers have the option restored of declaring discharging port
h Hartlepool or Calais.

'5. In consideration of the foregoing Charterers agree to increase freight rates for
voyages still to be performed in 1979 (eventually FOW 1980 per Clause No. 8 of this
Addendum) i.e. voyages Nos. 2–7 under Charter Party 2.11.78 by U.S. $1·00 per ton
to U.S. $13·00 Calais and U.S. $14·00 Hartlepool . . .

'7. If the current strike at Sorel is still in existence on completion of discharge of
j the Iron Ore cargo or other replacement voyage cargo (if mutually agreed), the
situation to be discussed without obligation.

'8. If Charterers have to charter another vessel to lift a Sorel cargo of Slag with
loading prior to presentation of "NEMA" for her second lifting Owners to remain
obligated to perform a replacement voyage in 1979 if possible, otherwise FOW
1980, at the rate of freight applicable for 1979 per item 5 above.'

Reliance was placed on behalf of the appellants on the fact that the addendum 2 was described as an extension of the charterparty dated 2nd November 1978, and also on the obligation imposed on the respondents by cl 8 of that addendum to replace the second voyage dealt with in cl 2 by an extra voyage either in 1979 or if not possible FOW (ie first open water) 1980, at the revised 1979 freight rate. But, my Lords, what one might call the cross-references in the addendum 2 to both the 1979 and the 1980 adventures does not mean that the performance of one is wholly dependent on the performance of the other. The 1979 adventure could end prematurely because of some wholly extraneous cause, for example serious damage to the vessel herself or to the loading facilities at Sorel, and yet the 1980 adventure be capable of timeous and complete performance in the event of the vessel or those loading facilities, as the case might be, being sufficiently repaired in time for 1980.

My Lords, two considerations seem to me to point strongly to the independence and against the interdependence of the two adventures. The first is that cl 3(a) of addendum 2 provides completely new and different cancelling dates for the 1980 adventure from those in cll 10 and 38 of the charterparty of 2nd November 1978 for the 1979 adventure. Secondly, the possible interposition of the substitute voyage for which para 8 of addendum 2 provides is to take place (in events which did not in fact happen) first open water 1980, a date which is not linked with either 1st or 30th April 1980, which are, respectively, commencing and cancelling lay days under cl 3(a) of addendum 2. This seems to me to be a further indication of the independent nature of the obligations for which addendum 2 provides. My Lords, on this question I find the reasoning of Templeman LJ ([1980] 3 All ER 117 at 127–128, [1980] 3 WLR 326 at 339–340) entirely persuasive and convincing and I respectfully adopt it. Like the learned Lord Justice, I wholly decline to join the two adventures together in the manner which appealed to Robert Goff J.

I therefore turn to the second question, namely whether the arbitrator was, on the facts found by him, entitled in point of law to hold that the 1979 adventure was frustrated. Before considering the grounds on which his conclusion was attacked on behalf of the appellants, I venture to offer certain preliminary observations. First, I hope I shall not be thought discourteous or unappreciative of the industry involved in the preparation of counsel's arguments if I say that today massive citation of authority in cases where the relevant legal principles have been clearly and authoritatively determined is of little or no assistance and should be firmly discouraged. Some citation merely lengthens hearings and adds to costs without in any way leading to the avoidance of judicial error. In *National Carriers Ltd v Panalpina (Northern) Ltd* [1981] 1 All ER 181, [1981] 2 WLR 45 your Lordships' House recently reviewed the doctrine of frustration and, by a majority, held that it was susceptible of application to leases. It is clear, reading the speeches of your Lordships, that the House approved the now classic statement of the doctrine by Lord Radcliffe in *Davis Contractors Ltd v Fareham Urban District Council* [1956] 2 All ER 145 at 160, [1956] AC 696 at 729, whatever may have been said in other cases at earlier stages of the evolution of the doctrine of frustration:

'. . . frustration occurs whenever the law recognises that, without default of either party, a contractual obligation has become incapable of being performed because the circumstances in which performance is called for would render it a thing radically different from that which was undertaken by the contract. Non haec in foedera venti. It was not this that I promised to do.'

It should therefore be unnecessary in future cases, where issues of frustration of contracts arise, to search back among the many earlier decisions in this branch of the law when the doctrine was in its comparative infancy. The question in these cases is not whether one case resembles another, but whether, applying Lord Radcliffe's enunciation of the doctrine, the facts of the particular case under consideration do or do not justify the invocation of the doctrine, always remembering that the doctrine is not lightly to be invoked to relieve contracting parties of the normal consequences of imprudent commercial bargains.

Second, in some cases where it is claimed that frustration has occurred by reason of the happening of a particular event, it is possible to determine at once whether or not the doctrine can be legitimately invoked. But in others, where the effect of that event is to cause delay in the performance of contractual obligations, it is often necessary to wait on events in order to see whether the delay already suffered and the prospects of further delay from that cause will make any ultimate performance of the relevant contractual obligations 'radically different', to borrow Lord Radcliffe's phrase, from that which was undertaken by the contract. But, as has often been said, businessmen must not be required to await events too long. They are entitled to know where they stand. Whether or not the delay is such as to bring about frustration must be a question to be determined by an informed judgment based on all the evidence of what has occurred and what is likely thereafter to occur. Often it will be a question of degree whether the effect of delay suffered, and likely to be suffered, will be such as to bring about frustration of the particular adventure in question. Where questions of degree are involved, opinions may and often legitimately do differ. Quot homines, tot sententiae. The required informed judgment must be that of the tribunal of fact to whom the issue has been referred. That tribunal, properly informed as to the relevant law, must form its own view of the effect of that delay and answer the critical question accordingly. Your Lordships' House in *Tsakiroglou & Co Ltd v Noblee Thorl GmbH* [1961] 2 All ER 179, [1962] AC 93 decided that, while in the ultimate analysis whether a contract was frustrated was a question of law, yet as Lord Radcliffe said in relation to that case 'that conclusion is almost completely determined by what is ascertained as to mercantile usage and the understanding of mercantile men' (see [1961] 2 All ER 179 at 189, [1962] AC 93 at 124).

My Lords, in *Edwards (Inspector of Taxes) v Bairstow* [1955] 3 All ER 48 at 57, [1956] AC 14 at 36 Lord Radcliffe made it plain that the court should only interfere with the conclusion of special commissioners if it were shown either that they had erred in law or that they had reached a conclusion on the facts which they had found which no reasonable person, applying the relevant law, could have reached. My Lords, when it is shown on the face of a reasoned award that the appointed tribunal has applied the right legal test, the court should in my view only interfere if on the facts found as applied to that right legal test no reasonable person could have reached that conclusion. It ought not to interfere merely because the court thinks that on those facts and applying that test it would not or might not itself have reached the same conclusion, for to do that would be for the court to usurp what is the sole function of the tribunal of fact.

My Lords, there have been suggestions in some of the decided cases that, because questions of frustration are ultimately questions of law, it is always open to the court to impose its own view rather than adopt that of the arbitral tribunal. My Lords, I think, with respect, that this is what Kerr J did in *The Angelia, Trade and Transport Inc v Iino Kaiun Kaisha Ltd* [1973] 2 All ER 144, [1973] 1 WLR 210 and what Robert Goff J has done in the present case, and I think they were each wrong to do so. I respectfully question whether *The Angelia* was rightly decided in the light of the findings of fact by the very experienced arbitrators there concerned. For the future I think that in those cases which are otherwise suitable for appeal the court should only interfere with the conclusion on issues such as those which arise in cases of frustration expressed by arbitrators in reasoned awards either if they are shown to have gone wrong in law and not to have applied the right legal test or if, whilst purporting to apply the right legal test, they have reached a conclusion which no reasonable person could, on the facts which they have found, have reached. On this matter too I find myself in entire agreement with what was said by Templeman LJ (see [1980] 3 All ER 117 at 130, [1980] 3 WLR 326 at 342). Templeman LJ pointed out that the arbitrator had correctly directed himself in accordance with *Davis Contractors Ltd v Fareham Urban District Council*, had made a large number of findings of fact and had reached the conclusion that the 1979 adventure had been frustrated. Templeman LJ went on to say that in those circumstances he was not prepared to substitute the decision of the court for that of the arbitrator. I respectfully and entirely agree with him.

It was contended for the appellants that this conclusion would lead arbitrators to assert that they had applied the right legal test by quoting what Lord Radcliffe had said in *Davis Contractors Ltd v Fareham Urban District Council*, and then seek to apply the doctrine of frustration to facts to which it could not properly be applied. My Lords, I question whether this is in fact likely to happen, but if I am wrong and it should happen such an error is likely quickly to emerge from any reasoned award, and the court would then be well justified in interfering in accordance with the principles which I have just endeavoured to state.

Like Templeman LJ, I am entirely satisfied that the arbitrator directed himself correctly in point of law. Do these findings of fact then justify his conclusion that the 1979 adventure was frustrated? They have been assailed by learned counsel for the appellants in a number of respects. Complaint was made that the arbitrator had given too little weight to what had happened in June and July 1979, and to the ability of the respondents to perform a substitute voyage in lieu of the second voyage, and to the payment made under addendum 3. The arbitrator had, it was said, treated the provision for a seventh voyage as if it were an absolute obligation. He had ignored the limitation on the number of voyages which might be performed by the cancelling date in December 1979. It was also alleged that the arbitrator had ignored the possibility of a sudden collapse of the strike, which in the event happened, and the number of voyages which might then still have been fitted in between its collapse and Sorel becoming ice-bound. It was argued that both parties had treated the contract as a going concern throughout the summer and early autumn of 1979 and that, by allowing the respondents to use the ship for their own purposes in August and September 1979, the charterers had shown how anxious they were to maintain the 1979 adventure in being. It was argued that there was no change in that position by the time the arbitration was held on 26th September 1979.

My Lords, these are powerful arguments. I see nothing to suggest that the arbitrator did not consider them carefully. In my judgment he made his findings of fact with reference to considerations of that kind, and he duly reached his conclusion. Another arbitrator might have reached a different conclusion, for clearly there were many points which had to be taken into consideration both ways. But I am quite unable to say that the conclusion which Mr Davies reached was one which he was not, on the facts which he found, fully entitled to reach.

It was not suggested that a strike could never bring about frustration of an adventure. But it was pointed out that most attempts to invoke strikes as a cause of frustration have in the past failed. *The Penelope* [1928] P 180 is almost the only example of success, and in that case the underlying reasoning of the judgment is far from easy to follow, even though the decision may well be correct.

My Lords, I see no reason in principle why a strike should not be capable of causing frustration of an adventure by delay. It cannot be right to divide causes of delay into classes and then say that one class can and another class cannot bring about frustration of an adventure. It is not the nature of the cause of delay which matters so much as the effect of that cause on the performance of the obligations which the parties have assumed one towards the other.

In the result I have reached the conclusion that Robert Goff J was wrong in reversing the arbitrator's award, and that the conclusion reached by the Court of Appeal was right. I would, therefore, dismiss this appeal.

Appeal dismissed.

Solicitors: *Sinclair, Roche & Temperley* (for the appellants); *Holman, Fenwick & Willan* (for the respondents).

Mary Rose Plummer   Barrister.

R v Mellor

COURT OF APPEAL, CRIMINAL DIVISION
EVELEIGH LJ, CANTLEY AND KILNER BROWN JJ
28th OCTOBER, 5th DECEMBER 1980

Sentence – Young offender – Restriction on prison sentence – Restriction not applying to person serving sentence of imprisonment when sentence passed – Offence committed and sentence passed while defendant released on parole following sentence of imprisonment for earlier offence – Whether defendant 'serving a sentence of imprisonment' while on parole – Whether restriction on sentence applicable to defendant – Criminal Justice Act 1961, s 3(1)(2) – Criminal Justice Act 1967, s 60.

While serving a sentence of imprisonment the defendant was released on licence on the recommendation of the Parole Board acting under s 60(1)[a] of the Criminal Justice Act 1967. The defendant then committed further offences and was sentenced to 18 months' imprisonment. The defendant, who was at all material times under 21, appealed against the sentence of 18 months' imprisonment on the ground that because he was under 21 the court was precluded by s 3(1)[b] of the Criminal Justice Act 1961 from passing a sentence of between six months and three years on him. By virtue of s 3(2) of the 1961 Act that restriction on sentencing did not apply to a person who was 'serving a sentence of imprisonment at the time when the court passe[d] sentence'. The defendant contended that notwithstanding that he was on parole he was not 'serving a sentence of imprisonment' at the time he was sentenced for the further offences and therefore the exception in s 3(2) to the restriction on sentence did not apply in his case.

Held – Section 3(2) of the 1961 Act was to be considered in the light of the system of release of prisoners on licence which had been introduced by s 25[c] of the Prison Act 1952 and replaced by s 20[d] of and Sch 3[e] to the 1961 Act, and the reference in s 3(2) of the 1961 Act to 'release subject to supervision or on licence' applied only to persons who had been released under that system and not to persons who had been released on parole under the 1967 Act. It followed therefore that, having regard to the fact that release from a prison sentence on parole under the 1967 Act did not entail total liberty and was subject to constraints by virtue of that sentence, a person released on parole was 'serving a sentence of imprisonment' for the purposes of s 3(2) of the 1961 Act, and the restrictions on sentencing imposed by s 3(1) of that Act did not apply to such a person. Accordingly, the court, when sentencing the defendant for the further offences, had been entitled to impose a sentence of 18 months' imprisonment. The appeal would therefore be dismissed (see p 1051 a to c and p 1052 g to j, post).

Notes

For restrictions on prison sentences imposed on young offenders, see 11 Halsbury's Laws (4th Edn) para 552, and for cases on the subject, see 14(2) Digest (Reissue) 728–734, 6090–6159.

For the Criminal Justice Act 1961, s 3, see 8 Halsbury's Statutes (3rd Edn) 502.

For the Criminal Justice Act 1967, s 60, see 25 ibid 888.

Section 25 of the Prison Act 1952, so far as material, and s 20 of and Sch 3 to the 1961 Act were repealed by the 1967 Act.

---

a   Section 60(1) provides: 'The Secretary of State may, if recommended to do so by the Parole Board, release on licence a person serving a sentence of imprisonment, other than imprisonment for life, after he has served not less than one-third of his sentence or twelve months thereof, whichever expires the later.'

b   Section 3, so far as material, is set out at p 1050 h j, post

c   Section 25, so far as material, is set out at p 1052 b to e, post

d   Section 20, so far as material, is set out at p 1051 e f, post

e   Schedule 3, so far as material, is set out at p 1051 h j, post

Application for leave to appeal against sentences

On 29th February 1980, in the Crown Court at Warwick before his Honour Judge
Blennerhassett QC, the defendant, Gary Mellor, pleaded guilty to the offence of taking a
conveyance without the consent of the owner or other lawful authority and the offence
of theft of a car radio. On 9th April 1980, in the Crown Court at Warwick before his
Honour Judge Harrison-Hall, the defendant pleaded guilty to a count of dishonestly
receiving stolen goods knowing or believing them to be stolen. Those offences were
committed whilst he was released on licence by recommendation of the Parole Board
from serving a sentence of imprisonment for an earlier offence. The defendant was
sentenced to 12 months' imprisonment for the first offence, to 6 months for the second
offence to run concurrently and 6 months for the third offence to run consecutively,
making a total sentence of 18 months' imprisonment. He applied for leave to appeal
against the sentences on the grounds that, as he was aged 20 when the sentences were
passed, s 3(1) of the Criminal Justice Act 1961 applied and prohibited a sentence of 18
months for, although he was on parole licence when the sentences were passed, he was
not a person who was then serving a sentence of imprisonment within s 3(2) of the 1961
Act so as to prevent the application of s 3(1). The single judge referred the application to
the full court who granted leave to appeal and treated the hearing as the hearing of an
appeal. The facts are set out in the judgment of the court.

Anthony Engel (assigned by the Registrar of Criminal Appeals) for the defendant.
Stephen Waine for the Crown.

Cur adv vult

5th December. **EVELEIGH LJ** read the following judgment of the court: This case
was referred by the single judge to the full court, which treated that reference as an
appeal against sentence and gave the necessary leave.

On 9th April 1980 in the Crown Court at Warwick the appellant was sentenced to a
total period of 18 months' imprisonment. That sentence was made up of 12 months'
imprisonment for taking a vehicle without consent, 6 months' imprisonment concurrent
for theft and 6 months' imprisonment consecutive for handling. Two offences were
taken into consideration. He was 20 years of age at that time.

On 16th June 1978 the appellant had been sentenced to three years' imprisonment.
He had been released on parole on 14th November 1979 and his licence was due to expire
on 23rd April 1981. The first two offences were committed on 27th November 1979,
two weeks after his release from prison, when he was staying at a probation hostel. He
was arrested that very same day but was granted bail. The third offence was committed
on 5th December 1979, while he was on bail.

It is, however, submitted that the court had no power to pass a sentence of 18 months'
imprisonment because of the restrictions placed on the sentencing of young offenders by
s 3(1) of the Criminal Justice Act 1961. That subsection reads:

'Without prejudice to any other enactment prohibiting or restricting the
imposition of imprisonment on persons of any age, a sentence of imprisonment
shall not be passed by any court on a person within the limits of age which qualify
for a sentence of borstal training except—(a) for a term not exceeding six months;
or (b) (where the court has power to pass such a sentence) for a term of not less than
three years.'

The case is clearly covered by those words, but the question now arises whether or not
it falls within the provisions of s 3(2), which reads as follows:

'Subsection (1) of this section shall not apply in the case of a person who is serving
a sentence of imprisonment at the time when the court passes sentence; and for the
purpose of this subsection a person sentenced to imprisonment who has been
recalled or returned to prison after being released subject to supervision or on
licence, and has not been released again or discharged, shall be treated as serving the
sentence.'

Were it not for the second half of that subsection, we would be of the opinion that a
a   person released on parole was serving a sentence of imprisonment. On revocation of the
parole licence by the Secretary of State or by the court, s 62 of the Criminal Justice Act
1967 provides that the offender shall be liable to be detained in pursuance of his
sentence. However his sentence has not been suspended while on parole (as it is for
example in the case of a person discharged temporarily on account of ill-health): see s 28
of the Prison Act 1952; and he will be required to serve the time remaining from the date
b   of revocation to the end of the sentence (with remission) or 30 days, whichever is the
greater: see para 4 of the Practice Note of 19th December 1975 ([1976] 1 All ER 271,
[1976] 1 WLR 122). A person released on parole is not free to do exactly as he wishes, but
is under some constraints by virtue of his prison sentence. In such circumstances, ie the
progressive reduction of the period to be served and the lack of total liberty, he is in fact
serving his sentence but doing so 'in the community'. He is not behind the prison walls
c   but he is still subject to his prison sentence.
It is submitted however that the second half of s 3(2), by making special provision in
relation to supervision or licence, indicates that a person released on supervision or on
licence is not serving a sentence of imprisonment. By analogy it is said that a person
released on parole is also not serving a sentence of imprisonment. It therefore becomes
necessary to see why the references to supervision and licence were made in the Criminal
d   Justice Act 1961.
Section 20 of that Act (repealed by the Criminal Justice Act 1967, ss 60(7), 103(2) and
Sch 7, Part I; see now s 63 of the 1967 Act) made provision for supervision of certain
prisoners after release. That section reads:

'(1) The provisions of Part I of the Third Schedule to this Act shall have effect
with respect to the supervision after release from prison of persons to whom this
e   section applies, and the return to prison of such persons in the event of failure to
comply with the requirements of their supervision.
'(2) This section applies to persons serving the following sentences of imprisonment (being sentences commencing after such date as may be prescribed by order
of the Secretary of State), that is to say—(a) a sentence for a term of four years or
more; (b) a sentence for a term of six months or more passed on a person who has
f   served at least one previous sentence, being a sentence of imprisonment for a term
of three months or more or a sentence of corrective training, preventive detention
or borstal training; and (c) a sentence for a term of six months or more passed on a
person appearing to the Prison Commissioners to have been under the age of
twenty-six at the commencement of the sentence, but does not apply to a person
serving a sentence of imprisonment for life . . .'
g
By para 1 of Sch 3 the period of supervision is 12 months from the date of release.
Paragraph 5 provides for the return to prison for a term—

'not exceeding whichever is the shorter of the following, that is to say—(a) a
period equal to one third of the term of imprisonment to which he was originally
h   sentenced, or, if that period exceeds six months, a period of six months; (b) a period
equal to so much of the period of supervision as was unexpired at the date of the
laying of the information by which the proceedings were commenced.'

There are various situations which could result in a person being detained in a prison
after the date of the expiration of his original sentence. Not every person detained in
prison is 'serving a sentence of imprisonment', for example a person on remand. The
j   status of a person returned to prison in case of breach of supervision might be thought
to be equivocal. This difficulty is recognised in para 16 of Sch 3, for it provides:

'For the purposes of Part III of this Act, a person who has been sent back to prison
under paragraph 5 or paragraph 10 of this Schedule, and has not been released again,
shall be deemed to be serving part of his original sentence, whether or not the term
of that sentence has in fact expired.'

However, while that paragraph was treating such a person as serving part of his original sentence, it was doing so only for the purposes of Part III of the Act. Section 3(1) *a* is contained in Part II of the Act. In order to remove any ambiguity with regard to s 3(2), a special reference was necessary to the position of a person under supervision.

Section 25 of the Prison Act 1952 provided for remission for good conduct. The relevant subsections read:

'(2) If it appears to the Prison Commissioners that a person serving a sentence of imprisonment was under the age of twenty-one years at the commencement of his *b* sentence, they may direct that instead of being granted remission of his sentence under the rules he shall, at any time on or after the day on which he could have been discharged if the remission had been granted, be released on licence under the following provisions of this section.

'(3) A person released on licence under this section shall until the expiration of his sentence be under the supervision of such society or person as may be specified *c* in the licence and shall comply with such requirements as may be specified . . .

'(6) Where the unexpired part of the sentence of a person released under subsection (2) of this section is less than six months, subsections (3) to (5) of this section shall apply to him subject to the following modifications—(*a*) the period for which he is under supervision under subsection (3) and is liable to recall under subsection (4) shall be a period of six months from the date of his release under the *d* said subsection (2); (*b*) if he is recalled under subsection (4) the period for which he may be detained thereunder shall be whichever is the shorter of the following, that is to say—(i) the remainder of the said period of six months; or (ii) the part of his sentence which was unexpired on the date of his release under the said subsection (2), reduced by any time during which he has been so detained since that date; and he may be released on licence under subsection (5) at any time before the expiration *e* of that period.'

(Subsections (2) to (6) have been repealed by the Criminal Justice Act 1967, s 103(2) and Sch 7, Part 1.)

Thus again it is possible for a person to be detained at a time when his original sentence will have expired. While sub-s (3) of s 25 speaks of such a person as being under supervision, strictly speaking he is released on licence under sub-s (2). The marginal note *f* to s 25 reads: 'Remission for good conduct and release on licence of persons sentenced to terms of imprisonment.' Thus we find a reference to licence in s 3(2) of the Criminal Justice Act 1961.

In our opinion, therefore, the references in s 3(2) of the 1961 Act were necessitated by the provisions of s 20 of the 1961 Act and s 25 of the 1952 Act. They were dealing with those special cases and the reasons for doing so can have no application to the position of *g* a person on parole by virtue of the provisions of a subsequent Act of Parliament, namely the Criminal Justice Act 1967. The appellant in the present case therefore was a person serving a sentence of imprisonment and the restrictions imposed in s 3(1) of the 1961 Act do not apply.

We now turn to the sentence of 18 months itself. That matter can be shortly dealt with. The defendant had been sentenced on 16th June 1978 to three years' imprisonment *h* for robbery. That sentence had not expired by the time the sentence of 18 months' imprisonment now appealed against was imposed. One has only to say in this case that he was on parole at the time of the commission of the first of the offences for which he was sentenced on 9th April 1980, and one of those, the third offence, was committed, as has been said, while he was on bail.

It is quite obvious that this appellant had no intention whatsoever of observing the *j* law, and this court is of the view that the sentence of 18 months was correct in every way.

This appeal therefore is dismissed.

Appeal dismissed.

Solicitors: *Field & Sons*, Leamington Spa.

April Weiss   Barrister.

R v Orpwood and another

COURT OF APPEAL, CRIMINAL DIVISION
LORD LANE CJ, THOMPSON AND GLIDEWELL JJ
12th FEBRUARY 1981

Sentence – Young offender – Restriction on prison sentence – Restriction not applying to person serving sentence of imprisonment when sentence passed – Offence committed and sentence passed while defendant released from prison on licence subject to supervision – Whether defendant 'serving a sentence of imprisonment' while released on licence – Whether restriction on sentence applicable to defendant – Criminal Justice Act 1961, s 3(1)(2).

The appellant, who was at all material times under 21, had been sentenced in 1977 to three years' imprisonment for an offence and then released on licence subject to supervision. While he was on licence he committed another offence for which he was sentenced to 15 months' imprisonment. He appealed against that sentence, contending that he had not been 'serving a sentence of imprisonment' within s 3(2)[a] of the Criminal Justice Act 1961 when he committed the second offence while on licence and that therefore, because he was a young offender, a sentence of 15 months was prohibited in his case by s 3(1) of that Act.

Held – On the true construction of s 3(2) of the 1961 Act a young person who had been released from prison on licence and had not been recalled to prison was not to be treated as 'serving a sentence of imprisonment'. It followed that s 3(1) of that Act prohibited a sentence of 15 months being passed on the appellant. Accordingly, the court would allow the appeal and reduce the appellant's sentence to six months' imprisonment (see p 1055 b d and g, post).

R v Mellor p 1049, ante, distinguished.

Notes

For restrictions on prison sentences imposed on young offenders, see 11 Halsbury's Laws (4th Edn) para 552, and for cases on the subject, see 14(2) Digest (Reissue) 728–734, 6090–6159.

For the Criminal Justice Act 1961, s 3, see 8 Halsbury's Statutes (3rd Edn) 502.

Case referred to in judgment

R v Mellor p 1049, ante, CA.

Applications for leave to appeal against sentences

On 22nd September 1980 at Dartford Magistrates' Court the appellants, Arthur Keith Orpwood and Gary Patrick Brooker, pleaded guilty to a joint charge of attempted burglary. They were committed to the Crown Court for sentence under s 29 of the Magistrates' Courts Act 1952. On 21st October 1980 in the Crown Court at Canterbury before his Honour Judge Edie each was sentenced to 15 months' imprisonment. They applied for leave to appeal against sentence. Brooker's ground of appeal was that, as he was under 21 when the sentence was passed, s 3(1) of the Criminal Justice Act 1961 applied and its application was not precluded by s 3(2) thereof because, although when the sentence was passed he was on release from prison on licence subject to supervision, he was not to be treated as a person serving a sentence of imprisonment within s 3(2). The applications were treated as appeals. The Crown did not oppose the applications. The facts are set out in the judgment of the court.

Greville Davis for the appellants.

---

a   Section 3, so far as material, are set out at p 1054 e to h, post

LORD LANE CJ delivered the following judgment of the court: On 22nd September 1980 at Dartford Magistrates' Court, these appellants, as they now are, leave having been given, pleaded guilty to a joint charge of attempted burglary. They were committed for sentence. They appeared in the Crown Court at Canterbury on 21st October and each was sentenced to 15 months' imprisonment.

They both now appeal against that sentence, Brooker also applying for an extension of time of 87 days, which we grant.

The facts of the case are these. On 18th July 1980, shortly after midnight, a 72-year-old man was in bed at his home in Swanley, when he was awakened by these two youths knocking at his front door. They had equipped themselves with stockings, which they had pulled over their heads in order to conceal their features. They went round to the back of the house. They removed a piece of plastic which in fact covered a ventilator. They apparently thought it covered a whole pane of glass. By removing it, they thought, they would have been enabled to enter the house. That was wrong. They went round to the front of the house once again, knocked on the door. The elderly gentleman opened the door and saw the appellants. They ran off. He slammed the door and shouted to his neighbours. The police were called and they arrested these two appellants very shortly afterwards.

They prevaricated for a time but eventually admitted the offence. They said that they were trying to get into the house in order to steal money from the meter. They said that they knocked on the door to see whether the house was empty (it seems unnecessary to have equipped themselves with masks if that had been the case) and that they had been drinking.

The burden of this case is a technical one, and it arises in this way. At the time of the sentence Brooker was 20 years of age. Thus the power to pass a sentence of imprisonment on him was governed by s 3(1) of the Criminal Justice Act 1961, the section which has given this court so much trouble in the past. It reads as follows:

> 'Without prejudice to any other enactment prohibiting or restricting the imposition of imprisonment on persons of any age, a sentence of imprisonment shall not be passed by any court on a person within the limits of age which qualify for a sentence of borstal training except—(a) for a term not exceeding six months; or (b) (where the court has power to pass such a sentence) for a term of not less than three years.'

That upper limit of three years is in certain circumstances reduced to 18 months (see s 3(3) of the 1961 Act), but in this case there is no doubt that Brooker's record would lead the court, had it been so minded, to pass a sentence of 18 months or more.

But the problem arises thus. Section 3(2) of the 1961 Act reads as follows:

> 'Subsection (1) of this section shall not apply in the case of a person who is serving a sentence of imprisonment at the time when the court passes sentence; and for the purpose of this subsection a person sentenced to imprisonment who has been recalled or returned to prison after being released subject to supervision or on licence, and has not been released again or discharged, shall be treated as serving the sentence.'

Brooker's position was this. He had been sentenced in 1977 to three years' imprisonment for robbery and wounding with intent at the Crown Court at Maidstone. That sentence was imposed on him on 7th November 1977. He was then a young person and, owing to the various provisions which it is not necessary for this court to read, young persons are not given remission, but are released on licence subject to supervision, and indeed that had happened to Brooker. At the time when the instant offence was committed, he was on licence.

The question is: can it be said that he was serving a sentence of imprisonment at the time when the court, that is to say the court we are considering, passed sentence? It appears to this court prima facie that the second half of that subsection, which I will read

a again in a moment, makes it clear that he was not serving a sentence. The words are:

> '... and for the purpose of this subsection a person sentenced to imprisonment who has been recalled or returned to prison after being released subject to supervision or on licence, and has not been released again or discharged, shall be treated as serving the sentence.'

b   We have had our attention drawn to a decision of this court on 5th December 1980 *R v Mellor* p 1049, ante, where a person had been released on parole licence.

It seems to us that, whatever may have been the situation in *R v Mellor*, the words of s 3(2) of the Criminal Justice Act 1961 must mean that a person who has, as a young person, been released on licence and not recalled is not serving a sentence of imprisonment. Had it been intended that such a person should be regarded as serving

c a sentence, the section would have read as follows: '... and for the purpose of this subsection a person sentenced to imprisonment who has been released subject to supervision or on licence, whether or not he has been recalled or returned to prison thereafter, shall be treated as serving the sentence.' But it does not so read.

Consequently we have reluctantly come to the conclusion that the sentence imposed on Brooker of 15 months was not a sentence which was open to the court to pass. It

d should have been a sentence either of 6 months or less or 18 months or more. Consequently so far as Brooker is concerned, although we are reluctant to do so, we are forced to reduce his sentence from 15 months to 6 months.

That leaves the problem of Orpwood. May we say immediately that in the view of this court, for the sort of offence they have committed, 15 months was a lenient sentence, and this court, if left to its devices at the trial, would have sentenced each of these young

e men to 18 months' imprisonment at a minimum. But once again the tentacles of s 3(2) have grasped the court. We have been forced to reduce Brooker's sentence against our better judgment. The question is whether justice demands that Orpwood should have his sentence likewise reduced.

His counsel disclaims that there would be any feeling of unfairness in Orpwood's mind were we to leave his sentence, which was perfectly legal, at 15 months. We feel

f however, in the light of their respective records, Brooker being much the more serious criminal according to his previous record, that it would be unfair were we to leave Orpwood at 15 months, having been forced to reduce Brooker's sentence. Consequently Orpwood, who should consider himself exceedingly lucky in at least three respects, as a matter of fairness should likewise have his sentence reduced.

Consequently each of these appeals is allowed to the extent that the sentence of 15

g months' imprisonment in each case is reduced to 6.

Appeals allowed. Sentences varied.

Solicitors: *Chancellor & Ridley*, Dartford (for the appellants).

N P Metcalfe Esq   Barrister.

Practice Direction

a

FAMILY DIVISION

Divorce – Practice – Children – Report of court welfare officer – Court to specify matters on which report to be made – Reporting officer to bring any other relevant matters to court's attention – Attendance of reporting officer at hearing – Parties to agree convenient date for attendance of reporting officer.

b

In order to make the best use of welfare officers' reports and of their time the President draws attention to the following points:

1. The time of the busy Divorce Court Welfare Service will be better spent and the time of busy judges saved if the court specifies those matters on which the report is to be made.

c

2. Such specification should never prevent the reporting officer from bringing to the notice of the court any other matters which he considers the court should have in mind.

3. If any party considers it desirable that the reporting officer should attend the hearing, the proper course is to ask the registrar so to direct or, if time does not permit, to inform the reporting officer that it is proposed at the hearing to ask the judge to direct that he attends.

d

4. Bearing in mind that contested custody cases often take several days to hear, the parties should agree a convenient date and time for the attendance of the reporting officer in cases where his attendance is required, so that his valuable time is not wasted.

Issued with the concurrence of the Lord Chancellor.

e

16th July 1981

R L BAYNE-POWELL
Senior Registrar.

a

Attorney General's Reference (No 6 of 1980)

COURT OF APPEAL, CRIMINAL DIVISION
LORD LANE CJ, PHILLIPS AND DRAKE JJ
13th APRIL, 7th MAY 1981

b

Criminal law – Assault – Defence – Fight – Fight otherwise than in course of sport or game – Whether consent a defence to charge of assault – Whether any distinction between fight in public place and fight in private.

Where two persons fight (otherwise than in the course of properly conducted games and
c sports) intending to cause or causing actual bodily harm, it is not a defence for one of
those persons to a charge of assault arising out of the fight that the other consented to the
fight, whether the fight occurs in private or in public, because it is not in the public
interest that people should try to cause or should cause each other actual bodily harm for
no good reason and because, if the participants intend to and/or do cause actual bodily
harm, they are (subject to any question of self-defence) guilty of assault, ie the actual
d intended use of unlawful force to another person without his consent or any other lawful
excuse (see p 1058 *g h* and p 1059 *e g*, post); dictum of James J in *Fagan v Metropolitan
Police Comr* [1968] 3 All ER at 445 adopted; *R v Coney* (1882) 8 QBD 534 and *R v Donovan*
[1934] All ER Rep 207 explained; *Smart v HM Advocate* 1975 SLT 65 not followed.

Properly conducted games and sports, lawful chastisement or correction, reasonable
surgical interference, dangerous exhibitions etc can be justified as apparent exceptions to
e otherwise illegal conduct as involving the exercise of a legal right, in the case of
chastisement or correction, or as needed in the public interest, in the other cases (see
p 1059 *f*, post).

Notes
f
For consent to assault, see 11 Halsbury's Laws (4th Edn) para 1213, and for cases on the
subject, see 15 Digest (Reissue) 1175–1177, 9992–10,029.

Cases referred to in judgment
g
Fagan v Metropolitan Police Comr [1968] 3 All ER 442, [1969] 1 QB 439, [1968] 3 WLR
1120, 133 JP 16, 52 Cr App R 700, DC, 15 Digest (Reissue) 1175, 9992.
R v Coney (1882) 8 QBD 534, 51 LJMC 66, 46 LT 307, 46 JP 404, 15 Cox CC 46, CCR, 15
Digest (Reissue) 916, 7850.
R v Donovan [1934] 2 KB 498, [1934] All ER Rep 207, 103 LJKB 683, 152 LT 46, 98 JP
409, 25 Cr App R 1, 32 LGR 439, 30 Cox CC 187, CCA, 14(1) Digest (Reissue) 36, *142*.
h
Smart v HM Advocate 1975 SLT 65.

Reference
This was a reference by the Attorney General under s 36 of the Criminal Justice Act 1972
for the opinion of the Court of Appeal on the following point of law: where two persons
j fight (otherwise than in the course of sport) in a public place can it be a defence for one
of those persons to a charge of assault arising out of the fight that the other consented to
fight? The facts are set out in the judgment of the court.

Richard Rougier QC and *Richard Inglis* for the Attorney General.
Allan Green as amicus curiae.

Cur adv vult

7th May. **LORD LANE CJ** read the following opinion of the court: This is a reference   *a*
to the court by the Attorney General under s 36 of the Criminal Justice Act 1972. The
point of law on which the court is asked to give its opinion is as follows:

> 'Where two persons fight (otherwise than in the course of sport) in a public place
> can it be a defence for one of those persons to a charge of assault arising out of the
> fight that the other consented to fight?'   *b*

The facts out of which the reference arises are these. The respondent, aged 18, and a
youth aged 17 met in a public street and argued together. The respondent and the youth
decided to settle the argument there and then by a fight. Before the fight the respondent
removed his watch and handed it to a bystander for safe keeping and the youth removed
his jacket. The respondent and the youth exchanged blows with their fists and the youth   *c*
sustained a bleeding nose and bruises to his face caused by blows from the respondent.
    Two issues arose at the trial: (1) self-defence and (2) consent. The judge directed the
jury in part as follows:

> 'Secondly, if both parties consent to a fight then that fight may be lawful. In that
> respect I disagree with [counsel for the prosecution's] description of the law. It may
> well be that a fight on the pavement is a breach of the peace or fighting in public or   *d*
> some other offence but it does not necessarily mean that both parties are guilty of an
> assault. So that if two people decide to fight it out with their fists then that is not
> necessarily an assault. If they use weapons or something of that nature, other
> considerations apply. So you have to consider those two matters in this case. Was
> [the youth] acting in self-defence? Was this a case of both parties agreeing to fight
> and using only reasonable force?'   *e*

Thus the jury were directed that the respondent would, or might, not be guilty of
assault if the victim agreed to fight, and the respondent only used reasonable force. The
respondent was acquitted.
    Leading counsel who appeared for the Attorney General at the hearing of the reference
submitted that this direction was incorrect, that the answer to the point of law was No,   *f*
and that if an act (ordinarily constituting an assault) is unlawful per se no amount of
consent can render it lawful. Thus an act committed in public might, he submitted, be
an assault, even though it would not be if committed in private, since if committed in
public it would be a breach of the peace and for that reason unlawful.
    Counsel as amicus curiae drew the attention of the court to the relevant authorities and
textbooks. He pointed out that though the conclusions in the cases are reasonably   *g*
consistent the reasons for them are not.
    For convenience we use the word 'assault' as including 'battery', and adopt the
definition of James J in *Fagan v Metropolitan Police Comr* [1968] 3 All ER 442 at 445,
[1969] 1 QB 439 at 444, namely 'the actual intended use of unlawful force to another
person without his consent', to which we would respectfully add 'or any other lawful
excuse'.   *h*
    We think that it can be taken as a starting point that it is an essential element of an
assault that the act is done contrary to the will and without the consent of the victim; and
it is doubtless for this reason that the burden lies on the prosecution to negative
consent. Ordinarily, then, if the victim consents, the assailant is not guilty.
    But the cases show that the courts will make an exception to this principle where the
public interest requires: see *R v Coney* (1882) 8 QBD 534 (the prize-fight case). The   *j*
eleven judges were of the opinion that a prize-fight is illegal, that all persons aiding and
abetting were guilty of assault, and that the consent of the actual fighters was
irrelevant. Their reasons varied as follows: Cave J, that the blow was struck in anger and
likely to do corporal hurt, as opposed to one struck in sport, not intended to cause bodily
harm; Mathew J, the dangerous nature of the proceedings; Stephen J, what was done was

a   injurious to the public, depending on the degree of force and the place used; Hawkins J, the likelihood of a breach of the peace, and the degree of force and injury; Lord Coleridge CJ, breach of the peace and protection of the public.

b   The judgment in *R v Donovan* [1934] 2 KB 498, [1934] All ER Rep 207 (beating for the purposes of sexual gratification), the reasoning in which seems to be tautologous, proceeds on a different basis, starting with the proposition that consent is irrelevant if the act complained of is 'unlawful . . . in itself', which it will be if it involves the infliction of bodily harm.

Bearing in mind the various cases and the views of the textbook writers cited to us, and starting with the proposition that ordinarily an act consented to will not constitute an assault, the question is: at what point does the public interest require the court to hold otherwise?

c   In answering this question the diversity of view expressed in the previous decisions, such as the two cases cited, make some selection and a partly new approach necessary. Accordingly we have not followed the dicta which would make an act (even if consensual) an assault if it occurred in public, on the ground that it constituted a breach of the peace, and was therefore itself unlawful. These dicta reflect the conditions of the times when they were uttered, when there was little by way of an established police force and prize-fights were a source of civil disturbance. Today, with regular policing, conditions are *d*   different. Statutory offences, and indeed byelaws, provide a sufficient sanction against true cases of public disorder, as do the common law offences of affray etc. Nor have we followed the Scottish case of *Smart v HM Advocate* 1975 SLT 65, holding the consent of the victim to be irrelevant on a charge of assault, guilt depending on the 'evil intent' of the accused, irrespective of the harm done.

The answer to this question, in our judgment, is that it is not in the public interest that *e*   people should try to cause or should cause each other actual bodily harm for no good reason. Minor struggles are another matter. So, in our judgment, it is immaterial whether the act occurs in private or in public; it is an assault if actual bodily harm is intended and/or caused. This means that most fights will be unlawful regardless of consent.

Nothing which we have said is intended to cast doubt on the accepted legality of *f*   properly conducted games and sports, lawful chastisement or correction, reasonable surgical interference, dangerous exhibitions etc. These apparent exceptions can be justified as involving the exercise of a legal right, in the case of chastisement or correction, or as needed in the public interest, in the other cases.

Our answer to the point of law is No, but not (as the reference implies) because the fight occurred in a public place, but because, wherever it occurred, the participants *g*   would have been guilty of assault (subject to self-defence) if (as we understand was the case) they intended to and/or did cause actual bodily harm.

The point of law referred to us by the Attorney General has revealed itself as having been the subject of much interesting legal and philosophical debate, but it does not seem that the particular uncertainty enshrined in the reference has caused practical inconvenience in the administration of justice during the last few hundred years. We *h*   would not wish our judgment on the point to be the signal for unnecessary prosecutions.

Determination accordingly.

Solicitors: *Director of Public Prosecutions* (for the Attorney General); *Treasury Solicitor.*

N P Metcalfe Esq   Barrister.

R v Galbraith

COURT OF APPEAL, CRIMINAL DIVISION
LORD LANE CJ, PAIN AND STUART-SMITH JJ
12th, 19th MAY 1981

Criminal law – Trial – No case to answer – Guidelines to be followed by trial judge on submission of no case to answer.

On a submission of no case to answer at the end of the prosecution case, the trial judge should stop the case and direct an acquittal if there is no evidence that the crime alleged against the accused was committed by him. However, if there is some evidence but it is of a tenuous character (eg because of inherent weakness or vagueness or because it is inconsistent with other evidence), it is the judge's duty, on a submission of no case, to stop the case if he comes to the conclusion that the prosecution evidence, taken at its highest, is such that a jury properly directed could not properly convict on it; but, where the prosecution evidence is such that its strength or weakness depends on the view to be taken of a witness's reliability or on other matters which are generally speaking within the province of the jury and where on one possible view of the facts there is evidence on which a jury could properly come to the conclusion that the accused is guilty, then the judge should allow the matter to be tried by the jury (see p 1062 *e* to *g*, post).

R v Barker (1977) 65 Cr App R 287 applied.
R v Mansfield [1978] 1 All ER 134 not followed.

Notes
For the submission of no case to answer, see 11 Halsbury's Laws (4th Edn) para 290, and for cases on the subject, see 14(1) Digest (Reissue) 368–369, 3064–3079.

Cases referred to in judgment
R v Barker (1977) 65 Cr App R 287, CA.
R v Mansfield [1978] 1 All ER 134, [1977] 1 WLR 1102, 142 JP 66, 65 Cr App R 276, CA, Digest (Cont Vol E) 139, 4405*a*.
R v Tobin [1980] Crim LR 731.

Cases also cited
R v Falconer-Atlee (1974) 58 Cr App R 348, CA.
R v Hipson [1969] Crim LR 85, CA.

Application for leave to appeal against conviction and sentence
On 13th November 1979 at the Central Criminal Court before Mars-Jones J and a jury the applicant, George Charles Galbraith, was convicted by a majority verdict of 10 to 2 of affray and was sentenced to four years' imprisonment. He applied for leave to appeal against conviction and sentence. The applications were referred to the full court by McNeill J and the main ground of appeal against conviction, in respect of which the case is reported, is the procedure to be followed following a submission of no case to answer at the end of the prosecution case. The facts are set out in the judgment of the court.

Robin Simpson QC and *Howard Godfrey* for the applicant.
Allan Green and *Susan Edwards* for the Crown.

At the conclusion of argument Lord Lane CJ announced that leave to appeal against conviction would be refused for reasons to be given later. His Lordship also announced that the application for leave to appeal against sentence would be granted and that the sentence would be varied from four to two years' imprisonment.

19th May. **LORD LANE CJ** read the following judgment of the court: On 13th
a November 1979 at the Central Criminal Court the applicant was convicted by a majority
verdict of affray and was sentenced to four years' imprisonment. He now applies for
leave to appeal against that conviction, the application having been referred to this court
by the single judge.

The facts of the case were these. On 20th November 1978 at the Ranelagh Yacht Club,
Putney Bridge, in the early hours of the evening a fight broke out in the bar. There were
b a number of people present, amongst them being Darke, Begbe, Bohm, Dennis and
Bindon. Knives were used. At least three men were stabbed, Darke fatally, Bindon
seriously, and Dennis less so. There was in these circumstances no doubt that there had
been an affray. The only question for the jury to decide was whether it had been
established with a sufficient degree of certainty that the applicant had been unlawfully
taking part in that affray.

c At the close of the Crown's evidence, a submission was made by counsel for the
applicant that there was no case for the applicant to answer. The judge rejected that
submission. The principal ground of appeal to this court is that he was wrong in so
doing. There are other subsidiary grounds of appeal which we shall have to examine in
due course.

We are told that some doubt exists as to the proper approach to be adopted by the
d judge at the close of the Crown's case on a submission of 'no case' (see Archbold on
Pleading, Evidence and Practice in Criminal Cases (40th Edn, Fifth Supplement to §575)
and *R v Tobin* [1980] Crim LR 731).

There are two schools of thought: (1) that the judge should stop the case if, in his view,
it would be unsafe (alternatively unsafe or unsatisfactory) for the jury to convict; (2) that
he should do so only if there is no evidence on which a jury properly directly could
e properly convict. Although in many cases the question is one of semantics, and though
in many cases each test would produce the same result, this is not necessarily so. A
balance has to be struck between on the one hand a usurpation by the judge of the jury's
functions and on the other the danger of an unjust conviction.

Before the Criminal Appeal Act 1966 the second test was that which was applied. By
s 4(1)(*a*) of that Act however the Court of Appeal was required to allow an appeal if it was
f of the opinion that the verdict should be set aside on the grounds that 'under all the
circumstances of the case it is unsafe or unsatisfactory'. It seems that thereafter a practice
grew up of inviting the judge at the close of the Crown's case to say that it would be
unsafe (or sometimes unsafe or unsatisfactory) to convict on the Crown's evidence and on
that ground to withdraw the case from the jury. Whether the change in the powers of
the Court of Appeal can logically be said to justify a change in the basis of a 'no case'
g submission, we beg leave to doubt. The fact that the Court of Appeal has power to quash
a conviction on these grounds is a slender basis for giving the trial judge similar powers
at the close of the Crown's case.

There is however a more solid reason for doubting the wisdom of this test. If a judge
is obliged to consider whether a conviction would be 'unsafe' or 'unsatisfactory', he can
scarcely be blamed if he applies his views as to the weight to be given to the Crown's
h evidence and as to the truthfulness of their witnesses and so on. That is what Lord
Widgery CJ said in *R v Barker* (1977) 65 Cr App R 287 at 288 was clearly not permissible:

> '... even if the *judge* had taken the view that the evidence could not support a
> conviction because of the inconsistencies, he should nevertheless have left the
j > matter to the jury. It cannot be too clearly stated that the judge's obligation to stop
> the case is an obligation which is concerned primarily with those cases where the
> necessary minimum evidence to establish the facts of the crime has not been
> called. It is not the judge's job to weigh the evidence, decide who is telling the
> truth, and to stop the case merely because he thinks the witness is lying. To do that
> is to usurp the function of the jury ...' (Our emphasis.)

Although this was a case where no submission was in fact made, the principle is affected.

Some of the difficulties have arisen from the subsequent case of *R v Mansfield* [1978] 1 All ER 134 at 140, [1977] 1 WLR 1102 at 1106–1107. Lawton LJ said:

'Unfortunately since this practice started [sc withdrawing a case from the jury on the ground that a conviction on the evidence would be unsafe] . . . there has, it seems, been a tendency for some judges to take the view that if they think that the main witnesses for the prosecution are not telling the truth then that by itself justifies them in withdrawing the case from the jury. Lord Widgery CJ in his judgment in *R v Barker* pointed out that this was wrong . . . [Lawton LJ then cited part of the passage we have already quoted, and continued:] Counsel for the appellant intended to submit to the judge that some of the evidence was so conflicting as to be unreliable and therefore if the jury did rely on it the verdict would be unsafe. In our judgment he was entitled to make that submission to the judge and the judge was not entitled to rule that he could not.'

On one reading of that passage it might be said to be inconsistent both with *R v Barker* and with the earlier part of the judgment itself. It is an illustration of the danger inherent in the use of the word 'unsafe'; by its very nature it invites the judge to evaluate the weight and reliability of the evidence in the way which *R v Barker* forbids and leads to the sort of confusion which now apparently exists. 'Unsafe', unless further defined, is capable of embracing either of the two schools of thought and this we believe is the cause of much of the difficulty which the judgment in *R v Mansfield* has apparently given. It may mean unsafe because there is insufficient evidence on which a jury could properly reach a verdict of guilty; it may on the other hand mean unsafe because in the judge's view, for example, the main witness for the Crown is not to be believed. If it is used in the latter sense as the test, it is wrong. We have come to the conclusion that, if and in so far as the decision in *R v Mansfield* is at variance with that in *R v Barker*, we must follow the latter.

How then should the judge approach a submission of 'no case'? (1) If there is no evidence that the crime alleged has been committed by the defendant, there is no difficulty. The judge will of course stop the case. (2) The difficulty arises where there is some evidence but it is of a tenuous character, for example because of inherent weakness or vagueness or because it is inconsistent with other evidence. (a) Where the judge comes to the conclusion that the Crown's evidence, taken at its highest, is such that a jury properly directed could not properly convict on it, it is his duty, on a submission being made, to stop the case. (b) Where however the Crown's evidence is such that its strength or weakness depends on the view to be taken of a witness's reliability, or other matters which are generally speaking within the province of the jury and where on one possible view of the facts there *is* evidence on which a jury could properly come to the conclusion that the defendant is guilty, then the judge should allow the matter to be tried by the jury. It follows that we think the second of the two schools of thought is to be preferred.

There will of course, as always in this branch of the law, be borderline cases. They can safely be left to the discretion of the judge.

We turn now to the evidence in this case. It was admitted that the applicant had gone to the club with Darke and Begbe and, using a false name, had signed them in. They had later been joined by Bohm. It was further not disputed that at the conclusion of the fighting the applicant was in the bar and, much to his credit, was helping a dying Darke. He did not go into the witness box, but the account of events which he gave in a self-exculpatory statement to the police, reiterated in a statement from the dock, was that he had at the material time when the affray was in progress not been in the bar at all but had been downstairs in the lavatory.

There were two principal pieces of evidence called by the Crown which tended to disprove that assertion and to show that he was in the bar taking an active part in the affray. The first was a witness called John Gilette. He said that Darke had attacked Bindon and that at that time there were three men with Darke. They all had knives. He *a* then described the three men. One description plainly referred to Begbe, another to Bohm and the third was an accurate description of the applicant. These men were described by Gilette as standing by the fight watching with knives out in a threatening way. He had attended an identification parade on 19th February 1979. On that parade the applicant was standing. Gilette, however, said he was not able to point out anyone on that parade whom he recognised as having been in the club that night.

The second piece of evidence was from a witness called Cook. He was the doorman of *b* the club and was a very reluctant witness. Leave was eventually given to treat him as hostile. Cook described how the applicant, or a man who, from the description given by Cook, was plainly and admittedly the applicant, had signed Darke and Begbe into the club at about 4.15 pm. At 6.15 pm he heard glass breaking and people shouting in the bar, so he went upstairs. When he got there Dennis had told him that he had been stabbed and pointed to a group of people standing by the juke box. This group was *c* described by Cook as being 'John Darke's party, the man with the beard, the fair-haired chap and the bloke with the twisted nose'. The reference to the fair-haired chap was plainly intended to be a reference to the same person as had signed the other two in at the door two hours previously, namely the applicant.

In cross-examination he said that he could have been mistaken in thinking that the fair-haired man with Darke by the juke box was the same blonde man who signed them *d* in.

In addition to these two pieces of evidence there was a further witness called Stanton who gave evidence that, when Darke was attacking Bindon as Bindon lay on the floor, a little guy went up to Darke and said, 'Stop it John, you'll kill him.' This man was described by Stanton in a way which would fit the applicant. However, in cross-examination, Stanton said the little guy was not the applicant. There was a body of *e* evidence which seemed to indicate that there had been some form of agreement between the witnesses that they would, so far as possible, back-pedal from the statements which they had made to the police immediately after the incident had taken place.

In these circumstances it seems to us that this was eminently a case where the jury should be left to decide the weight of the evidence on which the Crown based their case. It was not a case where the judge would have been justified in saying that the Crown's *f* evidence taken at its highest was such that the jury properly directed could not properly convict on it.

Of the remaining subsidiary grounds which the applicant advances in his perfected grounds of appeal, the only one that has any substance is the complaint that the learned judge misdirected the jury in directing them that they could regard Bindon's evidence of having shaken hands with the co-defendants Bohm and the applicant and having said *g* to them 'let bygones be bygones' in a cell at the magistrates' court as evidence against the applicant. We are inclined to agree that strictly speaking that was a misdirection. The evidence was certainly part of the background of the case and an important part of the background, but it could not properly be said to be evidence against the applicant. However, this minor error on the part of the judge can have had no possible effect on the outcome of the case and can safely be disregarded.

h   There is nothing in the other grounds of appeal which makes it necessary to comment on them.

Accordingly, as indicated at the close of the argument before us, the application for leave to appeal against conviction is refused. We have already dealt with the question of sentence.

j *Application refused. Appeal against sentence allowed in part and varied.*

Solicitors: *Henry Milner & Co* (for the applicant); *Director of Public Prosecutions.*

N P Metcalfe Esq   Barrister.

I Congreso del Partido   a

HOUSE OF LORDS

LORD WILBERFORCE, LORD DIPLOCK, LORD EDMUND-DAVIES, LORD KEITH OF KINKEL AND LORD BRIDGE OF HARWICH

11th, 12th, 13th, 14th, 18th, 19th MAY, 16th JULY 1981

Constitutional law – Foreign sovereign state – Immunity from suit – Exceptions – Commercial transaction – Admiralty – Action in rem – Ship owned by foreign sovereign state – Ordinary trading ship – Foreign sovereign state defaulting in commercial transaction for foreign policy reasons – Ship owned by Republic of Cuba – Ship used for commercial purposes – Ship delivering cargo from Cuba to Chile pursuant to contract – Diplomatic relations between Cuba and Chile severed – Ship diverted from Chile and cargo disposed of elsewhere on orders of Cuban government – Action in rem against ship brought by cargo owners in respect of non-delivery of cargo – Whether Republic of Cuba entitled to claim immunity from suit.

Early in 1973 a Cuban state enterprise, Cubazucar, agreed to sell to a Chilean company a quantity of sugar to be delivered in monthly instalments between January and October 1973. The August instalment was dispatched on two ships, the Playa Larga and the Marble Islands. Both ships were under voyage charter to Cubazucar from Mambisa, another Cuban state enterprise. Although Cubazucar and Mambisa were not departments of the government of Cuba, they were both under the direct control of the Cuban government. Mambisa was described in the charterparty as the owner of the Playa Larga and was the demise charterer of the Marble Islands. On 11th September, while the Playa Larga was in the course of discharging her cargo at Valparaiso in Chile, and the Marble Islands was still on the high seas bound for Chile, the government in Chile, which had been on friendly terms with the Cuban government, was overthrown and replaced by a new government which the Cuban government found to be politically repugnant. Diplomatic relations between the two countries were severed and Cuba decided to have no further commercial dealings with Chile. The Cuban government ordered the Playa Larga to leave Valparaiso immediately and the Marble Islands not to go to Chile. The Playa Larga returned to Cuba with the remainder of her cargo and the Marble Islands went to North Vietnam. During the course of the voyage to North Vietnam the Marble Islands was purchased by the Republic of Cuba. The cargoes on both ships were then disposed of by Mambisa. In September 1975 Mambisa, acting on behalf of the Republic of Cuba, took delivery in England of a new ship, the Congreso, which was an ordinary trading ship registered in the name of the Republic of Cuba and was intended to be operated and managed by Mambisa. After Mambisa had taken delivery of the Congreso, the plaintiffs, the Chilean owners of the cargoes of sugar on board the Playa Larga and the Marble Islands, brought actions in rem, pursuant to s 3(4)(b)[a] of the Administration of Justice Act 1956, against the Congreso as a ship beneficially owned by the Republic of Cuba, which, the plaintiffs claimed, would have been liable on claims in actions in personam for damages for conversion and/or breach of contract for non-delivery of the cargoes under s 1(1)(g) and (h)[b] of that Act. The Congreso was subsequently arrested in

---

a   Section 3(4), so far as material, provides: 'In the case of any . . . claim arising in connection with a ship, where the person who would be liable on the claim in an action in personam was, when the cause of action arose, the owner or charterer of, or in possession or in control of, the ship, the Admiralty jurisdiction of the High Court may (whether the claim gives rise to a maritime lien on the ship or not) be invoked by an action in rem against—(a) that ship, if at the time when the action is brought it is beneficially owned as respects all the shares therein by that person; or (b) any other ship which, at the time when the action is brought, is beneficially owned as aforesaid.'

b   Section 1(1), so far as material, provides: 'The Admiralty jurisdiction of the High Court shall be as follows, that is to say, jurisdiction to hear and determine any of the following questions or claims . . . (g) any claim for loss of or damage to goods carried in a ship; (h) any claim arising out of any agreement relating to the carriage of goods in a ship or to the use or hire of a ship . . .'

England. The Republic of Cuba moved to have the plaintiffs' writs set aside on the
a ground that it was entitled to invoke sovereign immunity in respect of the proceedings.
At the hearing of the motion the plaintiffs contended that when a sovereign state
engaged in commerce or descended into the market place it could not later claim
sovereign immunity in regard to any default by it in its transactions. The Republic of
Cuba, while conceding that it was not entitled to absolute immunity from suit,
contended that it was entitled to claim immunity in the circumstances because its action
b in preventing delivery of the sugar to the Chilean consignees was done in the exercise of
its sovereign authority (jus imperii) as part of its foreign policy. The judge ([1978] 1 All
ER 1169) upheld the republic's claim to sovereign immunity and the plaintiffs
appealed. The Court of Appeal ([1981] 1 All ER 1092) dismissed the appeals. The
plaintiffs appealed to the House of Lords.

c **Held** – (1) Actions, whether commenced in personam or in rem, were to be decided
according to the restrictive theory of sovereign immunity so that a sovereign state had no
absolute immunity as regards commercial or trading transactions. Whether an act of a
sovereign state attracted sovereign immunity depended on whether the act in question
was a private act (jure gestionis) or a sovereign or public act (jure imperii), and the fact
that the act was done for governmental or political reasons would not convert what
d would otherwise be an act jure gestionis or an act of private law into one done jure
imperii. In considering whether state immunity should be granted, the court had to
consider the whole context in which the claim against the state was made, with a view
to deciding whether the relevant act on which the claim was based should, in the context,
be considered as fairly within an area of activity, trading or commercial or otherwise, of
a private law character in which the state had chosen to engage or whether the relevant
e act should be considered as having been done outside that area and within the sphere of
governmental sovereignty (see p 1070 *a* to *j*, p 1071 *d e*, p 1072 *g*, p 1074 *a* to *d g h*,
p 1078 *d e*, p 1080 *j*, p 1081 *c* to *e* and p 1082 *d* and *j* to p 1083 *c*, post); *The Philippine
Admiral* [1976] 1 All ER 78 applied.
(2) In the case of the Playa Larga, the acts done by the Republic of Cuba in deciding
not to complete unloading at Valparaiso, or to discharge in Chile, were acts done as
f owners of the vessel and it invoked no governmental authority and exercised no
sovereign powers. In the case of the Marble Islands (Lord Wilberforce and Lord Edmund-
Davies dissenting) the acts complained of, the discharge and sale of the cargo, were
effected under private law and not in the exercise of any sovereign powers. It followed
therefore that the Republic of Cuba was not entitled to sovereign immunity in respect
of the plaintiffs' claims and the appeals would be allowed (see p 1075 *c* to *h*, p 1079 *g*,
g p 1080 *a* to *d* and *g* to *j*, p 1082 *d* to *g* and p 1083 *c* to *h*, post).
Decision of the Court of Appeal [1981] 1 All ER 1092 reversed.

Notes
For sovereign immunity from suit, see 8 Halsbury's Laws (4th Edn) para 410, and for
cases on the subject, see 1(1) Digest (Repl) 54–56, 358–366.
h For sovereign immunity and actions in rem and in personam in Admiralty
proceedings, see 1 Halsbury's Laws (4th Edn) paras 304, 310, and for cases on those
subjects, see 1(1) Digest (Reissue) 219–223, 238–232, 1240–1251, 1292–1305.
For the Administration of Justice Act 1956, ss 1, 3, see 1 Halsbury's Statutes (3rd Edn)
21, 26.
The immunity from the jurisdiction of the courts which foreign sovereign states can
j claim is now regulated by the State Immunity Act 1978.

Cases referred to in opinions
Alfred Dunhill of London Inc v Republic of Cuba (1976) 425 US 682, 48 US L ed 2d 301, 96
S Ct 1854 (US Supreme Court).
Bank of United States v Planters' Bank of Georgia (1824) 9 Wheat 904, 22 US 904 (US
Supreme Court).

Charkieh, The (1873) LR 4 A & E 59, 42 LJ Adm 17, 28 LT 513, 1 ASP MLC 581, 1(1)
Digest (Reissue) 57, *373*.   *a*
Charkow, The (LG Bremen, 21st December 1959).
Claim against the Empire of Iran Case (1963) 45 ILR 57.
Collision with Foreign Government-owned Motor Car (Austria) Case (1961) 40 ILR 73.
Compania Naviera Vascongada v Steamship Cristina [1938] 1 All ER 719, [1938] AC 485,
107 LJP 1, 159 LT 394, 19 Asp. MLC 159, HL, 1(1) Digest (Reissue) 228, *1297*.
Czarnikow (C) Ltd v Centrala Handlu Zagranicznego 'Rolimpex' [1978] 2 All ER 1043, *b*
[1979] AC 351, [1978] 3 WLR 274, [1978] 2 Lloyd's Rep 305, HL, Digest (Cont Vol E)
525, *2748b*.
Danish State Railways in Germany, Re (1953) 20 ILR 178.
Ohio v Helvering (1934) 292 US 360.
Parlement Belge, The (1880) 5 PD 197, [1874–80] All ER Rep 104, 42 LT 273, 4 Asp MLC
234, CA, 1(1) Digest (Reissue) 220, *1244*.   *c*
Philippine Admiral (Owners) v Wallem Shipping (Hong Kong) Ltd [1976] 1 All ER 78, [1977]
AC 373, [1976] 2 WLR 214, [1976] 1 Lloyd's Rep 234, PC, 1(1) Digest (Reissue) 229,
1301.
Porto Alexandre, The [1920] P 30, [1918–19] All ER Rep 615, 89 LJP 97, 122 LT 661, 15
Asp MLC 1, 1 Ll L Rep 191, CA, 1(1) Digest (Reissue) 228, *1298*.
Trendtex Trading Corpn v Central Bank of Nigeria [1977] 1 All ER 881, [1977] QB 529, *d*
[1977] 2 WLR 356, [1977] 1 Lloyd's Rep 581, CA, 1(1) Digest (Reissue) 59, *382*.
United States of America v Dollfus Mieg et Compagnie SA [1952] 1 All ER 572, [1952] AC
582, HL, 1(1) Digest (Reissue) 60, *388*.
Victory Transport Inc v Comisaria General de Abastecimientos y Transportes (1964) 336 F 2d
354.
Ysmael (Juan) & Co Inc v Government of the Republic of Indonesia [1954] 3 All ER 236, [1955] *e*
AC 72, [1954] 3 WLR 531, [1954] 2 Lloyd's Rep 175, PC, 1(1) Digest (Reissue) 231,
1304.

Interlocutory appeals

The plaintiffs, the owners of cargoes lately laden on board the vessels Marble Islands and
Playa Larga, appealed with leave of the Court of Appeal against the orders of the Court *f*
of Appeal (Lord Denning MR and Waller LJ) ([1981] 1 All ER 1092) given on 1st October
1979 dismissing their appeal against the decision of Robert Goff J ([1978] 1 All ER 1169,
[1978] QB 500) dated 28th January 1977 setting aside their writs of summons and all
subsequent proceedings in their actions against the owners of the vessel I Congreso del
Partido, on the grounds that the owners of that vessel were the government of the
Republic of Cuba which was entitled to claim, and had claimed, sovereign immunity *g*
from the court's jurisdiction. The two members of the Court of Appeal disagreed; Lord
Denning MR gave judgment for the plaintiffs and would have allowed the appeals while
Waller LJ gave judgment for the defendants and would have dismissed the appeals. The
Court of Appeal being evenly divided the orders of Robert Goff J were affirmed. The
facts are set out in the opinions of Lord Wilberforce and Lord Diplock.

h

Robert Alexander QC, Bernard Rix QC and *Rosalyn Higgins* for the appellants.
Brian Davenport QC, Timothy Saloman and *Robert Jennings* for the respondents.

Their Lordships took time for consideration.

16th July. The following opinions were delivered.   *j*

LORD WILBERFORCE. My Lords, these two appeals raise questions of importance
as to the scope of the restrictive theory of state immunity as it existed in the law of this
country in 1973–75 when the relevant events happened. The law in question is the
common law before this was superseded by statute (the State Immunity Act 1978); it will
continue to form part of the corpus of international law.

The proceedings

a   There are two separate actions, the common feature of which is that both were
brought against the owners of the vessel I Congreso del Partido ('I Congreso'), which was
constructed, found and arrested in this country. There is no doubt that this vessel was
constructed to be used for normal trading purposes. The claims relate not to anything
done on or by this ship, but to two sister ships, the Marble Islands and the Playa Larga;
they are brought by the owners of cargo formerly laden on them.

b
As regards Marble Islands

It is interesting to see the basis on which proceedings were first launched. This was
that the cargo owners had a claim against a Cuban state enterprise known as Empresa
Navegación Mambisa ('Mambisa') and that Mambisa was the owner of I Congreso. An
action was started on this basis on 9th September 1975. However, this was met by the

c   contention, supported by affidavit, that I Congreso was owned not by Mambisa but by
the Republic of Cuba. The appellants thereupon started another action on the basis that
I Congreso was owned by the Republic of Cuba and that the Republic of Cuba was liable
to the appellants in an action in personam as owner or in possession or control of Marble
Islands. This immediately gave rise to a claim of state immunity on the part of the
Republic of Cuba, which in turn was met by the contention that, under the restrictive

d   theory, immunity should be denied. This action is the subject of one of the instant
appeals.

As regards Playa Larga

The proceedings concerning Playa Larga were commenced on 12th December 1975,
when I Congreso was again arrested on the application of the owners of cargo formerly

e   laden on Playa Larga, now the appellants. Their claim was based on an alleged breach of
contract by non-delivery of part of the cargo, the contract in question being a bill of
lading signed by the master of Playa Larga. There was also a claim in tort (detinue,
conversion or breach of duty). Ultimately, the same issue emerged: whether the
Republic of Cuba as owner of I Congreso and of Playa Larga could raise a claim of state
immunity or whether the restrictive theory applied. This action is the subject of the

f   other of the instant appeals.

Outline of facts

The facts, in outline, are as follows. I shall expand them when the point of decision is
reached. In February 1973 a contract for the sale of sugar was made between a Cuban
state trading enterprise, Empresa Exportadora de Azucar, known as 'Cubazucar', as

g   sellers and a Chilean company, Industria Azucarera Nacional SA, known as 'Iansa', as
buyers (the status of Iansa is not material). The contract was for 128,395 tons of sugar to
be shipped in eight shipments of 10,000 to 20,000 tons. Cubazucar was to obtain
payment by negotiation of documents against a letter of credit to be opened by Iansa.
These proceedings are concerned with two of the agreed shipments.

One shipment was of 10,476 tons, carried on Playa Larga; this was a Cuban flag vessel,

h   owned by the Republic of Cuba, and operated by Mambisa.

Mambisa is a state trading enterprise which manages and operates all Cuban state-
owned ships. It is not an 'emanation' or department of the Cuban state; it has
independent legal existence, and it is not claimed that it would be entitled to state
immunity. It is subject however to direction and control by the Cuban government
which provides all the funds necessary for its operation. It may be added here that

j   Cubazucar and another concern to be shortly referred to (Alimport) are also Cuban state
trading enterprises of similar status to Mambisa. It has never been claimed that either of
these are agencies of, or that they contracted on behalf of, the Cuban State. State-
controlled enterprises, with legal personality, ability to trade and to enter into contracts
of private law, though wholly subject to the control of their state, are a well-known
feature of the modern commercial scene. The distinction between them, and their
governing state, may appear artificial, but it is an accepted distinction in the law of

England and other states (see *C Czarnikow Ltd v Centrala Handlu Zagranicznego 'Rolimpex'* [1978] 2 All ER 1043, [1979] AC 351). Quite different considerations apply to a state-controlled enterprise acting on government direction on the one hand and a state, exercising sovereign functions, on the other. This distinction is crucial in relation to these appeals.

Returning to the facts, Playa Larga was chartered for the voyage to Chile by Cubazucar under a normal form of commercial voyage charter; in the charterparty Mambisa was described as owners of the vessel. Bills of lading were issued for the shipment in Mambisa's standard form, signed by the master. They were negotiated to Iansa against payment of the price under commercial letter of credit; Iansa sold the sugar to another Chilean company.

The other shipment was of 10,890 tons carried on Marble Islands. She was owned by Blue Seas Shipping Co Ltd, a Liechtenstein corporation, and flew the Somali flag. She was chartered to Mambisa on a demise charter and sub-chartered by Mambisa to Cubazucar for the voyage to Chile. Bills of lading were issued for the shipment and negotiated as for Playa Larga.

The events which occurred in September 1973 are described in lucid detail by Robert Goff J in his judgment ([1978] 1 All ER 1169, [1978] QB 500). Briefly, on 11th September 1973 Playa Larga was at Valparaiso, Chile, having commenced discharge of the cargo. Marble Islands was at sea nearing her destination. On that day a coup d'état took place in Chile; the government of President Allende (friendly to Cuba) was replaced by a government under President Pinochet of which the government of Cuba strongly disapproved. There was some military action in Santiago; diplomatic relations between Chile and Cuba were terminated. There seems to have been no violence at Valparaiso, and nothing occurred to prevent Playa Larga from continuing to discharge; however she was ordered by Mambisa, which had itself been so instructed by the Cuban government, to leave Valparaiso and join Marble Islands. Consequently, she left Valparaiso without port clearance, taking with her 7,907 tons of her sugar cargo; there was some attempt to stop her leaving but she was able to proceed.

Playa Larga met Marble Islands at sea, and, on instructions, both vessels proceeded to Callao in Peru. It appears that the Chilean authorities, through their embassy, requested discharge at that port, which would have been practicable, but both masters refused to discharge. On 20th September 1973 Playa Larga left Callao and returned to Cuba, where she discharged the balance cargo on 5th October, and where it was later sold by Mambisa. These events seem to establish a prima facie case of tortious action and (see below for further discussion) possibly of breach of contract by the owner of Playa Larga, to which there may or may not be available defences. We are, of course, not concerned with these; the only question is whether, since the owner of Playa Larga is the Republic of Cuba, a plea of state immunity can be raised so as to deny jurisdiction. Whether an action could be maintained against Mambisa is irrelevant, since Mambsia is not the owner of the sister ship I Congreso.

Marble Islands left Callao on 27th September 1973 intending also to return to Cuba, but she was arrested at the Panama Canal on the application of Iansa. She broke arrest and sailed west for North Vietnam. In the course of her voyage her ownership and flag were transferred to the Republic of Cuba. After arrival at Haiphong, her cargo, having been discharged, was sold by the master to another Cuban state enterprise ('Alimport') and by it donated to the people of North Vietnam in part fulfilment of Cuba's programme of donations to that people. In this case too, it would appear that, subject to defences, a prima facie cause of action by the cargo owners could be raised against Mambisa. The involvement (if any) of the Republic of Cuba is another matter which will have to be examined. It can be observed at this stage, however, that, by contrast with the case of Playa Larga, no claim in contract is made or appears to lie against the Republic of Cuba.

The law

I must now attempt to ascertain the state of English law as to state immunity as existing in 1973–75. Certain points can be cleared away.

a 1. If these matters had arisen as at the present date, they would be governed by the State Immunity Act 1978. This Act, which came into force on 22nd November 1978, introduced, by statute, a restrictive theory of state immunity into English law by means of a number of detailed exceptions to a general rule of state immunity. It was not retrospective. However, the appellants made use of it in the following way. There is a presumption, they said, that English legislation is intended to be in conformity with international law; therefore the Act may be used as evidence of what international law

b at its date was. I cannot accept this contention; to argue from the terms of a statute to establish what international law provides is to stand the accepted argument on its head. In the particular case, it is clear that international law, in a general way, in 1978, gave support to a restrictive theory of state immunity; we do not need the statute to make this good. On the other hand, the precise limits of the doctrine were, as the voluminous material placed at our disposal well shows, still in course of development and in many

c respects uncertain. If one state chooses to lay down by enactment certain limits, that is by itself no evidence that those limits are generally accepted by states. And particularly enacted limits may be (or presumed to be) not inconsistent with general international law, the latter being in a state of uncertainty, without affording evidence what that law is. I shall make no further reference to this English statute, nor for similar reasons to the analogous United States statute passed in 1976.

d 2. The appellants invoked at considerable length the International Convention for the Unification of Certain Rules concerning the Immunity of State-owned Ships 1926 (Brussels; Misc 2 (1938); Cmd 5672) both generally and in respect of particular articles in it, especially arts 1, 2 and 3. This convention was only ratified by the United Kingdom in 1979 and has never been accepted by the Republic of Cuba. The number of states bound by it has always been limited and has not included states important in maritime

e commerce. Yet it is invoked, as I understood the argument, as a statement of generally accepted international law. Now there may be cases in which a multilateral convention may become part of general international law so as to bind states not parties (a proposition not uncontroversial) but at the least the convention must bear a legislative aspect and there must be a wide general acceptance of it as law-making, over a period, before this condition is satisfied. The Brussels convention does not nearly meet these requirements:

f it was a limited agreement between a limited number of states. At the very most it may, together with its progressive, though not numerous, ratifications and accessions, be evidence of the gradual seepage into international law of a doctrine of restrictive immunity. For that purpose we do not need it. What the appellants need, and what they seek to extract from it, is precise definition of the scope and conditions of the doctrine, through the use of particular words and phrases. This is clearly impermissible

g and, I may add, not supported by international publicists of authority. I shall make no further reference to this convention, nor (a fortiori) to the European Convention on State Immunity of 1972 (Misc 31 (1972); Cmnd 5081).

I can now try to state the English law. This can be done without complication up to a certain point. Until 1975 it would have been true to say that England, almost alone of influential trading nations (the United States of America having changed its position

h under the Tate letter in 1952, ie the letter addressed on 19th May 1952 by J B Tate, the acting legal adviser of the State Department, to the then acting Attorney General of the United States notifying him of a change in the policy of the Department of State with regard to the granting of sovereign immunity to foreign governments), continued to adhere to a pure, absolute, doctrine of state immunity in all cases. The classic formulation of this was that of Lord Atkin in *Compania Naviera Vascongada v Steamship Cristina* [1938]

j 1 All ER 719, [1938] AC 485, which is too well known to require citation, and, as regards trading vessels, *The Porto Alexandre* [1920] P 30, [1918–19] All ER Rep 615, purportedly applying *The Parlement Belge* (1880) 5 PD 197, [1874–80] All ER Rep 104. In 1977 there were reported two landmark cases: *The Philippine Admiral (Owners) v Wallem Shipping (Hong Kong) Ltd* [1976] 1 All ER 78, [1977] AC 373 and *Trendtex Trading Corpn Ltd v Central Bank of Nigeria* [1977] 1 All ER 881, [1977] QB 529. In *The Philippine Admiral* the Judicial Committee of the Privy Council, in an appeal from Hong Kong, declined to follow *The Porto Alexandre* and decided to apply the restrictive doctrine to an action in rem against a state-owned trading vessel. In the comprehensive judgment which was *a* delivered on behalf of the Board, it was said that to do so was more consonant with justice. It was further commented that it was open to the House of Lords to move away from the absolute rule of immunity in actions in personam. Sitting in this House I would unhesitantly affirm as part of English law the advance made by *The Philippine Admiral* with the reservation that the decision was perhaps unnecessarily restrictive in, apparently, confirming the departure made to actions in rem. In truth an action in rem *b* as regards a ship, if it proceeds beyond the initial stages, is itself in addition an action in personam, viz the owner of the ship (see *The Cristina* [1938] 1 All ER 719 at 722, 730, [1938] AC 485 at 492, 504 per Lord Atkin and Lord Wright), the description in rem denoting the procedural advantages available as regards service, arrest and enforcement. It should be borne in mind that no distinction between actions in rem and actions in personam is generally recognised elsewhere so that it would in any event be desirable to *c* liberate English law from an anomaly if that existed. In fact there is no anomaly and no distinction. The effect of *The Philippine Admiral* if accepted, as I would accept it, is that, as regards state-owned trading vessels, actions, whether commenced in rem or not, are to be decided according to the 'restrictive' theory.

The other landmark authority (*Trendtex*), a decision of the Court of Appeal, establishes that, as a matter of contemporary international law, the restrictive theory should be *d* generally applied. In that case what was involved was not a claim relating to a trading ship but one based on a commercial letter of credit arising out of a purchase of cement. The case was not appealed to this House, and since there may be appeals in analogous cases it is perhaps right to avoid commitment to more of the admired judgment of Lord Denning MR than is necessary. Its value in the present case lies in the reasoning that, if the act in question is of a commercial nature, the fact that it was done for governmental *e* or political reasons does not attract sovereign immunity.

On the basis of these cases I have no doubt that the restrictive doctrine should be applied to the present case, though the relevant events chronologically preceded both *The Philippine Admiral* and *Trendtex*. Indeed this was not disputed by either side in these appeals. The issue is as to the limits of the doctrine; merely to state that the restrictive doctrine applies is to say little more than that a state has no absolute immunity as regards *f* commercial or trading transaction, but where immunity begins and ends has yet to be determined.

It is necessary to start from first principle. The basis on which one state is considered to be immune from the territorial jurisdiction of the courts of another state is that of 'par in parem . . .', which effectively means that the sovereign or governmental acts of one state are not matters on which the courts of other states will adjudicate. *g*

The relevant exception, or limitation, which has been engrafted on the principle of immunity of states, under the so-called restrictive theory, arises from the willingness of states to enter into commercial, or other private law, transactions with individuals. It appears to have two main foundations. (a) It is necessary in the interest of justice to individuals having such transactions with states to allow them to bring such transactions before the courts. (b) To require a state to answer a claim based on such transactions does *h* not involve a challenge to or inquiry into any act of sovereignty or governmental act of that state. It is, in accepted phrases, neither a threat to the dignity of that state nor any interference with its sovereign functions.

When therefore a claim is brought against a state (I include in this expression, and shall not repeat, direct and indirect claims; cf *United States of America v Dollfus Mieg et Cie SA* [1952] 1 All ER 572, [1952] AC 582) and state immunity is claimed, it is necessary to *j* consider what the relevant act is which forms the basis of the claim: is this, under the old terminology, an act 'jure gestionis' or is it an act 'jure imperii'; is it (to adopt the translation of these catchwords used in the Tate letter) a 'private act' or is it a 'sovereign or public act', a private act meaning in this context an act of a private law character such as a private citizen might have entered into? It is on this point that the arguments in these appeals are focused.

a   The appellants contend that we have here (I take the case of Playa Larga for the present so as to avoid complication of statement) a commercial transaction, viz a trading vessel, owned by the Republic of Cuba, carrying goods under normal commercial arrangements. Any claim arising out of this situation is, they assert, a claim of private law, and it is irrelevant that the purpose for which the act giving rise to the claim was committed may have been of a political character (sc, briefly, to break off trading relations with a state, Chile, with which Cuba was not friendly). The appellants were able to cite a good

b   deal of authority to support the proposition that it is the character of the relevant act that is decisive, not its purpose. I may mention a decision of the Swiss Federal Court of 10th February 1960 (86 BGE 1, p 23), of the Austrian Supreme Court of 10th February 1961 (*Collision with Foreign Government-owned Motor Car (Austria) Case* 40 ILR 73) and of the German Federal Constitutional Court (*Claim against the Empire of Iran Case* (1963) 45 ILR 57 at 80 (passage quoted below)).

c   In my opinion this argument, though in itself generally acceptable, burkes, or begs, the essential question, which is: what is the relevant act?; it assumes that this is the initial entry into a commercial transaction and that this entry irrevocably confers on later acts a commercial, or private law, character. Essentially it amounts to an assertion 'once a trader always a trader'. But this may be an over-simplification.

If a trader is always a trader, a state remains a state and is capable at any time of acts of

d   sovereignty. The question arises, therefore, what the position is where the act on which the claim is founded is quite outside the commercial, or private law, activity in which the state has engaged, and has the character of an act done jure imperii. The restrictive theory does not and could not deny capability of a state to resort to sovereign, or governmental, action: it merely asserts that acts done within the trading or commercial activity are not immune. The inquiry still has to be made whether they were within or

e   outside that activity.

In many cases the process of deciding on the character of the relevant act presents no difficulty. In *The Philippine Admiral*, once it was accepted that the contract for goods, the obligation to repay disbursements and the charterparty were of a trading or commercial character, the breach of these obligations was clearly within the same area, none the less because committed by a state. Other reported shipping cases are of the same character:

f   *The Charkieh* (1873) LR 4 A & E 59 (collision), *The Porto Alexandre* [1920] P 30, [1918–19] All ER Rep 615 (salvage; the case should have been decided the other way). In *Trendtex*, similarly, and the same is true of the acts in issue in other countries relating to the Nigerian cement purchases, the relevant act was simply a breach of a commercial contract and was treated as such, none the less though committed by a state or department of state for reasons of government. The purpose for which the breach was committed

g   could not alter its clear character. Of cases in other jurisdictions one of great clarity is the leading case of *Claim against the Empire of Iran*, decided by the Federal Constitutional Court of the German Federal Republic in 1963. This was a claim for the cost of repairs to the heating system of the Iranian Embassy. The judgment contains the following passage (45 ILR 57 at 80):

h   'As a means for determining the distinction between acts *jure imperii* and *jure gestionis* one should rather refer to the nature of the State transaction or the resulting legal relationships, and not to the motive or purpose of the State activity. It thus depends on whether the foreign State has acted in exercise of its sovereign authority, that is in public law, or like a private person, that is in private law.'

j   And later (at 81):

'This Court has therefore examined the argument that the conclusion of the contract for repair is to be regarded as a non-sovereign function of the foreign State, and has accepted this proposition as correct. It is obvious that the conclusion of a contract of this kind does not fall within the essential sphere of State authority. It does not depend . . . on whether the conclusion of the contract was necessary for the regular transaction of the Embassy's affairs and therefore stood in a recognizable relationship with the sovereign functions of the sending State. Whether a State is entitled to immunity does not depend on the purpose of the function which the foreign State is thereby pursuing.'

Clearly a breach of a contract of that character was within the area of private law. Similar cases in tort are *Re Danish State Railways in Germany* (1953) 20 ILR 178 and *The Charkow* (LG Bremen, 21st December 1959). These are cases which present no difficulty. The problems with which they were concerned were simply (i) whether it could be said that the relevant contract was concluded for governmental purposes and (ii) whether it was relevant that governmental motives were advanced for breaching the contract.

In other situations it may not be easy to decide whether the act complained of is within the area of non-immune activity or is an act of sovereignty wholly outside it. The activities of states cannot always be compartmentalised into trading or governmental activities; and what is one to make of a case where a state has, and in the relevant circumstances clearly displayed, both a commercial interest and a sovereign or governmental interest? To which is the critical action to be attributed? Such questions are the more difficult since they arise at an initial stage in the proceedings and, in all probability, on affidavit evidence. This difficulty is inherent in the nature of the restrictive doctrine, introducing as it does an exception, based on a certain state of facts, to a plain rule. But as was said in *Claim against the Empire of Iran Case* 45 ILR 57 at 79–80:

> 'The fact that it is difficult to draw the line between sovereign and non-sovereign State activities is no reason for abandoning the distinction. International law knows of other similar difficulties ... The distinction between sovereign and non-sovereign State activities cannot be drawn according to the purpose of the State transaction and whether it stands in a recognizable relation to the sovereign duties of the State. For, ultimately, activities of State, if not wholly then to the widest degree, serve sovereign purposes and duties, and stand in a still recognizable relationship to them. Neither should the distinction depend on whether the State has acted commercially. Commercial activities of States are not different in their nature from other non-sovereign State activities.'

Even cases based on the plain absolute rule might involve similar problems (cf *Juan Ysmael & Co Inc v Government of the Republic of Indonesia* [1954] 3 All ER 236, [1955] AC 72, *United States of America v Dollfus Mieg et Compagnie SA* [1952] 1 All ER 572, [1952] AC 582). Under the restrictive theory the court has first to characterise the activity into which the defendant state has entered. Having done this, and (assumedly) found it to be of a commercial, or private law, character, it may take the view that contractual breaches, or torts, prima facie fall within the same sphere of activity. It should then be for the defendant state to make a case (cf *Juan Ysmael*) that the act complained of is outside that sphere, and within that of sovereign action.

I have so far discussed this matter on such English decisions as are relevant, and on principle. But since, in this area, English courts are applying, or at least acting so far as possible in accordance with, international law, it is necessary to see what assistance can be gained. If the determination of the character of the relevant act has to be made by municipal courts, they should do so, so far as possible, in conformity with accepted international standards. For this purpose we are entitled to consider judgments of foreign courts of authority, and writings of reputed publicists. We have been invited also to consider affidavits of a number of eminent professors, filed on either side. As to these I must strike a note of caution. In so far as they express opinions as to how the present case should or would be decided in the courts of their country, the reservation must be made that these opinions are based on a statement of facts which is controversial and in some respects incomplete. They had not the benefit of the much more detailed and complete examination made by the trial judge, on which our decision must be based. Leaving this aside, I have, myself, derived much assistance from the reasoning

and learning contained in these affidavits and for the explanations which their deponents
a give of decisions of their courts, direct resort to which may be hazardous.

As regards the United States, I have already mentioned the Tate letter which in 1952,
after reviewing the contemporary state of international law, announced the movement
of the State Department towards, and encouraged the courts to adoption of, the restrictive
theory of state immunity. Two subsequent cases are of importance. In *Victory Transport
Inc v Comisaria General de Abastecimientos y Transportes* (1964) 336 F 2d 354 the Second
b Circuit Court of Appeals was concerned with an in personam action against a department
of the Spanish government under a charterparty. The court held that the chartering of
the ship for the supply of wheat to the people of Spain was not a strictly public or political
act: it partook far more of the character of a private commercial act. The judgment drew
attention to the difficulty of differentiating between a sovereign's private and public acts,
whether according to the nature, or to the purpose of the transaction (at 360):

c
> 'The conceptual difficulties involved in formulating a satisfactory method of
> differentiating between acts *jure imperii* and acts *jure gestionis* have led many
> commentators to declare that the distinction is unworkable . . . The purpose of the
> restrictive theory of sovereign immunity is to try to accommodate the interest of
> individuals doing business with foreign governments in having their legal rights
> determined by the courts, with the interest of foreign governments in being free to
d
> perform certain political acts without undergoing the embarrassment or hindrance
> of defending the propriety of such acts before foreign courts.'

The judgment then listed certain criteria which I do not reproduce because they are
stated (in conformity with United States constitutional doctrine) to be subject to
directions given by the State Department. This formula is not suitable for use by our
e courts.

The second case is that of *Alfred Dunhill of London Inc v Republic of Cuba* (1976) 425 US
682, a case on the United States doctrine of act of state.

The majority of the Supreme Court (five justices) held that no act of state had
occurred. Within this majority four justices in a separate part of the opinion expressed
the opinion that the concept of act of state should not be extended to include the
f repudiation of a purely commercial obligation owed by a foreign sovereign (at 695):

> 'Repudiation of a commercial debt cannot, consistent with this restrictive
> approach to sovereign immunity, be treated as an act of state; for if it were, foreign
> governments, by merely repudiating the debt before or after its adjudication, would
> enjoy an immunity which our government would not extend them under
> prevailing sovereign immunity principles in this country. This would undermine
g
> the policy supporting the restrictive view of immunity, which is to assure those
> engaging in commercial transactions with foreign sovereignties that their rights
> will be determined in the courts whenever possible.'

The scope of this pronouncement may be seen from references made to previous Supreme
Court decisions. In *Bank of United States v Planters' Bank of Georgia* (1824) 9 Wheat 904 at
h 907 Marshall CJ said:

> 'It is, we think a sound principle, that when a government becomes a partner in
> any trading company, it devests itself, *so far as concerns the transactions of that
> company*, of its sovereign character, and takes that of a private citizen.'

And in *Ohio v Helvering* (1934) 292 US 360 at 369 the court said:

j
> 'When a state enters the market place seeking customers it divests itself of its *quasi*
> sovereignty *pro tanto*, and takes on the character of a trader . . .'

(My emphasis in each case.)

We are entitled to be impressed by this reasoning, which, while denying immunity to
breaches of commercial agreements, even though for governmental reasons, seems to

recognise the legitimacy of inquiring whether the act in question is within the area of commercial activity into which the state has descended.

As regards other countries, in particular the Federal Republic of Germany and Italy, both of which accept the restrictive theory, I need not comment on individual cases. I have already referred to *Claim against the Empire of Iran Case*, the judgment of which contains an instructive review of the law of state immunity over a wide area. I accept that there is support in them for the proposition that the existence of a governmental purpose or motive will not convert what would otherwise be an act jure gestionis, or an act of private law, into one done jure imperii, but beyond this proposition (which is not decisive here) they do not give direct guidance on the questions we have to consider.

The conclusion which emerges is that in considering, under the restrictive theory, whether state immunity should be granted or not, the court must consider the whole context in which the claim against the state is made, with a view to deciding whether the relevant act(s) on which the claim is based should, in that context, be considered as fairly within an area of activity, trading or commercial or otherwise of a private law character, in which the state has chosen to engage or whether the relevant act(s) should be considered as having been done outside that area and within the sphere of governmental or sovereign activity.

Application to the facts

(a) *Playa Larga*   She was at all material times owned by the Republic of Cuba, operated by Mambisa, and chartered by Mambisa to Cubazucar under a charter probably governed by Cuban law. The appellants claim that the Republic of Cuba was contractually liable to the cargo owners under the bills of lading, signed by the master on behalf of 'the owner of the above-mentioned ship'. I venture the opinion that this is far from clear. The bills of lading appear to be governed by the law of Cuba, and in view of the presence of a similar provision in the bills of lading issued from Marble Islands, in which the word 'owner' seems certainly to refer to Mambisa, I cannot regard this as more than an assertion yet to be proved. The appellants also claim that the Republic of Cuba, as owner of Playa Larga, is liable to Iansa (or its sub-purchasers) for detinue or conversion of the sugar, first by refusing to deliver it at Valparaiso, second, by refusing to deliver it at Callao and, third, by selling it in Cuba. There are no doubt possible defences to each of these claims, but these will have to be adjudicated on if the action proceeds. At the present stage it is sufficient that there is a basis for a claim in personam against the Republic of Cuba.

Whether the Republic of Cuba can claim immunity depends, if I am right as to the law, on an examination of those acts in respect of which the claim is asserted. The appellants are certainly able to show, as a starting point, that this vessel was engaged in trade with the consent, if not with the active participation, of the Republic of Cuba. They were 'doing business with a foreign government', to use the *Victory Transport* formulation. The question is whether the acts which gave rise to an alleged cause of action were done in the context of the trading relationship or were done by the government of the Republic of Cuba acting wholly outside the trading relationship and in exercise of the power of the state. That this is not an easy question to answer is shown by the difference of judicial view, Robert Goff J and Waller LJ holding that Cuba's acts were governmental, Lord Denning MR that they were not. In my opinion it must be answered on a broad view of the facts as a whole and not on narrow issues as to Cuba's possible contractual liability. I do not think that there is any doubt that the decision not to complete unloading at Valparaiso, or to discharge at Callao, was a political decision taken by the government of the Republic of Cuba for political and non-commercial reasons. I need not restate the history of events between 11th and 20th September 1973 which is very fully and clearly given by the learned judge. The change of government in Chile, and the events at Santiago in which the Cuban Embassy was involved, provoked a determination on the part of the government of Cuba to break off and discontinue trading relations with Chile. There may also have been concern for the safety of Playa

Larga at Valparaiso. I do not think that, for present purposes, the judge's finding can be
a improved on ([1978] 1 All ER 1169 at 1177, [1978] QB 500 at 509):

> 'The Ministry of Merchant Marine and Ports became concerned about the safety
> of the Playa Larga, which was then discharging her cargo at Valparaiso; a decision
> was taken that for her safety she should leave Chilean waters, and this decision was
> communicated to Mambisa. There was no evidence of any prior communication
> with the vessel, about the state of affairs at Valparaiso or at all, before this decision
b > was taken. The ship's log, which was verified by the master on affidavit, recorded
> that at 16.30 hours that day [11th September 1973] the ship received a cable from
> Mambisa ordering the ship to proceed with her exit from Valparaiso.'

Does this call for characterisation of the act of the Republic of Cuba in withdrawing
Playa Larga and denying the cargo to its purchasers as done jure imperii? In my opinion
c it does not. Everything done by the Republic of Cuba in relation to Playa Larga could
have been done, and, so far as evidence goes, was done, as owners of the ship: it did not
exercise, and had no need to exercise, sovereign powers. It acted, as any owner of the ship
would act, through Mambisa, the managing operators. It invoked no governmental
authority. I have not overlooked Law No 1256 which recited in vivid terms the (no
doubt governmental) reaction of Cuba to the events in Chile, a law enacted on 27th
d September 1973 (and so subsequent to the decisive acts concerning the Playa Larga)
though retrospective to 11th September 1973. But it seems to me clear that it was not
this law, mainly a 'freezing' or 'blocking' enactment, which brought about, or had any
effect on, action taken by Playa Larga prior to the ultimate sale of the cargo: that action
was caused by instructions issued by the Cuban government as owner to Mambisa as
operator of the vessel.
e   It may well be that those instructions would not have been issued, as they were, if the
owner of Playa Larga had been anyone but a state; it is almost certainly the case that there
was no commercial reason for the decision. But these consequences follow inevitably
from the entry of states into the trading field. If immunity were to be granted the
moment that any decision taken by the trading state were shown to be not commercially,
but politically, inspired, the restrictive theory would almost cease to have any content
f and trading relations as to state-owned ships would become impossible. It is precisely to
protect private traders against politically inspired breaches, or wrongs, that the restrictive
theory allows states to be brought before a municipal court. It may be too stark to say of
a state 'once a trader always a trader'; but, in order to withdraw its action from the sphere
of acts done jure gestionis, a state must be able to point to some act clearly done jure
imperii. Though, with much hesitation, I feel obliged to differ on this issue from the
g conclusion of the learned judge, I respectfully think that he well put this ultimate test
([1978] 1 All ER 1169 at 1192, [1978] QB 500 at 528):

> 'it is not just that the purpose or motive of the act is to serve the purposes of the
> state, but that the act is of its own character a governmental act, as opposed to an act
> which any private citizen can perform.'

h   As to the Playa Larga, therefore, I find myself in agreement with Lord Denning MR
and would allow the appeal.
    (b) *Marble Islands* The facts regarding this ship are more complicated. Initially, and
until after her departure from Callao, where her master refused to discharge the cargo,
she was owned by Blue Seas Shipping Co Ltd, a Liechtenstein corporation, and flew the
Somali flag. She was chartered on a demise charter to Mambisa, and Mambisa had sub-
j chartered her to another Cuban state enterprise on behalf of Cubazucar. Bills of lading
were issued in respect of the shipment of sugar signed by the master. These contained
the provision:

> 'This contract of carriage is entered into between the shipper designated above
> and the owner of the above-named ship. The carrying vessel and her owner are
> referred to in this bill of lading as the carrier.'

Since Mambisa was in possession of the ship as demise charterer it is, as the judge found, highly unlikely that the master had the authority of the Liechtenstein owners to **a** sign the bills of lading on their behalf so that the contract probably took effect as a contract with Mambisa as disponent owners. At all events, the Republic of Cuba had no concern with, interest in, or responsibility for the cargo or for the operation of the ship or for the actions of the master or the crew. It was, of course, in a position to control the acts of Mambisa, but the commercial venture was exclusively that of Mambisa. The cargo owners did not do any business with a sovereign state. **b**

After Marble Islands had left Balbao, Panama, for North Vietnam she was purchased on 13th October 1973 by the Republic of Cuba. There is no evidence as to the reason for this; it may have had to do with the desirability of entering North Vietnam with a Cuban flag. There is equally no evidence as to the subsistence, after the sale, or otherwise, of the demise charter. Counsel for the Republic of Cuba did not seek to rely on its continuance in existence. However, I can find no basis on which it can be said that the cargo owners **c** entered into any business relationship with the Republic of Cuba. There can be no doubt, as subsequent events showed, that Marble Islands continued to be operated by Mambisa, and, though the ownership of Marble Islands by the Republic of Cuba is a factor to be considered, what is decisive on the question of immunity is what the Republic of Cuba did as regards the cargo when the ship arrived at Haiphong. There is a good deal of evidence as to this. **d**

1. (a) Dr Carlos Amat Fores, a high official in the Ministry of External Relations of the Republic of Cuba, states, on oath, that the donation and delivery for the people of North Vietnam of 10,800 tons of sugar discharged in Haiphong by Marble Islands was carried out in accordance with the express instructions issued in this matter by the government of Cuba in compliance with Law No 1256. (As I have stated above, this law was enacted on 27th September 1973 and provided for the freezing and blocking of Chilean assets.) **e**

(b) Dr Balmaseda Remedios, in September 1973 senior legal adviser of the Cuban Ministry of Merchant Marine, refers to the enactment of Law No 1256, which made it illegal for Marble Islands to deliver the cargo to Chile. Orders were therefore given to Mambisa to proceed first to Balbao (Panama) and later to Haiphong.

'The decision was taken at a very high level in the Government of Cuba that her **f** cargo should be given to the people of Vietnam . . . and I was directed to proceed to Haiphong to supervise this operation.'

He went to Haiphong early in November 1973. The cargo was then discharged and deposited in a warehouse of Agroexport (a Vietnamese undertaking), the discharge and deposit being presumably acts of Mambisa. By a sale contract dated 22nd November 1973 the master of Marble Islands, on behalf of Mambisa, sold the cargo to Alimport, a **g** Cuban state undertaking concerned with food importing. Alimport lodged the proceeds of sale with the National Bank of Cuba under Law No 1256. 'Upon completion of these formalities the sugar itself was given to the people of Vietnam by Alimport.'

2. As regards Mambisa. (a) On 6th November 1973 the captain of Marble Islands requested the port commander to unload the cargo of sugar and deposit it with Agroexport (see above). He confirmed that this deposit was made by him as **h** representative of the transporting company and under cll 2 and 8 of the bills of lading. (b) Also on 6th November 1973 the captain signed an 'Act of Protest' at Haiphong. This narrated the course of the voyage of Marble Islands from Cuba, via Callao, and Balbao, to Haiphong. It stated his intention, for the good of the cargo, to deposit it and subsequently to sell it at Haiphong and his entitlement to do so under the bills of lading and the Commercial Code. It then reserved his claim for expenses due to his shipowner. (c) On **j** 2nd November 1973 the captain, 'acting in the name and in representation of his shipowner, Empresa Navegación Mambisa, operator in the name of the Cuban state of [Marble Islands]' and on behalf of whoever might prove to be the legitimate owners of the sugar, by a sales contract, sold the deposited sugar to Alimport. In cl 5 he confirmed that he was making the sale in the name of whoever should prove to be the legitimate

a owner of the said goods in his capacity of legal representative of the transporting
company, Mambisa, in accordance with the provisions of the Cuban Commercial Code,
and cll 2 and 8 of the bill of lading.

These are all the material documents. The result of them, and of the evidence of the
Cuban officials, is clear. All the operations of carriage, deposit and sale of the cargo were
made by Mambisa. These, as the references to the bills of lading and to the Commercial
Code make clear, were carried out (legally or illegally) as trading operations governed by
b contract and by private law.

The Republic of Cuba never entered into these operations. The captain did not
purport to act on its behalf (references to his shipowner are clearly references to
Mambisa). It was never in trading relations with the cargo owners. Its actions were
confined to directing transfer of the sugar to North Vietnam, and to the enactment of
Law No 1256. All of this was done in a governmental capacity; any attack on its actions
c must call in question its acts as a sovereign state.

Lord Denning MR dealt with the case of Marble Islands briefly in these words ([1981]
1 All ER 1092 at 1104):

d
> 'In the case of the Marble Islands the origin of all that happened was a simple
> commercial transaction by which one of the state organisations of Cuba agreed to
> carry sugar to Chile and deliver it to the Chilean importers. The Cuban government
> induced its state organisation to repudiate that contract and ordered it to carry the
> sugar to North Vietnam.'

However, the commercial transaction was not that of the Cuban state, but of an
independent state organisation. The status of these organisations is familiar in our
courts, and it has never been held that the relevant state is in law answerable for their
e actions.

He continues:

f
> 'The Cuban government then bought the vessel and, by its conduct, adopted the
> repudiation as their own. They continued the repudiative act and went on to carry
> the sugar to North Vietnam and handed it to the people there. The nature of the
> transaction was again the repudiation of a purely commercial obligation. Its
> purpose was twofold: to show their hostility to Chile and to help the people of
> Vietnam. But the purpose does not matter. The act by its very nature was an act of
> repudiating a binding commercial obligation. Such an act does not give rise to
> sovereign immunity.'

I regret that I cannot accompany this reasoning. Assuming that the actions of Mambisa
g amounted to a repudiation of contract, the action of the state, ex hypothesi, and in fact,
not involved in any trading relationship, in ordering that repudiation cannot, with
respect, amount to a repudiation by the state, or the distinction between jure imperii and
jure gestionis would simply disappear. I cannot agree that there was ever any purely
commercial obligation on the Republic of Cuba or any binding commercial obligation:
the republic never assumed any such obligation; it never entered the trading area; the
h cargo owners never entered into a commercial relation with it. I agree that the purpose,
above, is not decisive but it may throw some light on the nature of what was done. The
acts of the Republic of Cuba were and remained in their nature purely governmental.
The fact is that if any wrong (contractually or delictually) was done as regards the cargo
it was done by Mambisa. Indeed (see above) the initial proceedings were started on this
basis. Unfortunately, Mambisa turned out not to be the owners of I Congreso, so a fresh
j action had to be brought against the Republic of Cuba, who were the owners of that
ship. But in my opinion, in agreement with the learned judge, the acts complained of
as regards the Republic of Cuba were acts jure imperii and so covered by immunity. I
would dismiss the Marble Islands appeal.

There are two other points which require some brief attention. 1. It may be a question
in some cases where it is claimed that a restrictive doctrine of immunity should be

applied, ie that jurisdiction should be asserted against a sovereign state, whether it is
necessary to show some territorial connection of the claim with the state of the forum. *a*
In my opinion this does not arise in this case (i) since I Congreso is within the jurisdiction
(or was until released), (ii) since the claim is in respect of Playa Larga and Marble Islands,
an Admiralty claim as to which territoriality is not a requirement for jurisdiction, (iii) in
view of s 3(8) of the Administration of Justice Act 1956. However, if any case of a
different character should arise, and which is not covered by the State Immunity Act
1978, I should wish to regard this point as open. 2. It was argued by the respondents that *b*
even if the Republic of Cuba might appear to be entitled to plead state immunity, it
should be denied that right on various grounds: that its acts were contrary to international
law, or to good faith, or were discriminatory, or penal. On the view which your
Lordships take these arguments do not arise, but I would wish to express my agreement
with the judge and with Waller LJ as to their invalidity. The whole purpose of the
doctrine of state immunity is to prevent such issues being canvassed in the courts of one *c*
state as to the acts of another.

LORD DIPLOCK. My Lords, the practical importance of these appeals as respects
commercial transactions entered into by governments or departments of governments
of foreign states is much diminished by the coming into force of the State Immunity Act
1978 after the occurrence of the events on which the appellants ('Iansa') base their claims *d*
against the government of Cuba. Since I agree with my noble and learned friend Lord
Wilberforce that at the relevant time when I Congreso was arrested in 1975 the United
Kingdom should be regarded as having ceased to be odd man out among nations by
continuing to adhere to the theory of absolute state immunity, and since I agree broadly
with his analysis of the restrictive theory that replaced it until the 1978 Act came into
force, I can be, perhaps uncharacteristically, brief even though I have the misfortune to *e*
differ from him on the consequences of the application of the restrictive theory to the
case of the Marble Islands.
  The facts of the two cases are set out in considerable detail in the judgment of Robert
Goff J ([1978] 1 All ER 1169, [1978] QB 500). To Lord Wilberforce's summary of them,
which I gratefully adopt, I would make five additions.
  1. The charterparties between Mambisa and Cubazucar as charterers under which the *f*
cargoes were shipped on Playa Larga and Marble Islands each contained a cesser clause:
the charterers' liability, except as regards charter rate freight, deadfreight and demurrage,
was to cease on the master's signing bills of lading. So a direct contractual relationship
was created between the 'owner' of the vessel on whose behalf the master signed and
Iansa as consignee.
  2. In the charterparty relating to the voyage of Playa Larga, although Mambisa was *g*
described as 'owner', the evidence discloses that Mambisa was not in Cuban law the
owner of the Playa Larga but fulfilled the role of managing operator of the ship on behalf
of the true owner, the Cuban government itself, a type of arrangement that is by no
means unknown in ordinary non-governmental maritime trade. So once the bills of
lading had been signed by the master and negotiated to Iansa, there came into existence
as respects the cargo laden on Playa Larga an ordinary commercial contract for the *h*
carriage of goods by sea between the government of Cuba as carrier and Iansa as
consignee.
  3. At the time the charterparty for Marble Islands was entered into between Mambisa
and Cubazucar, the owner of the vessel was a Liechtenstein company but Mambisa as
demise charterers had possession and control of it. We know nothing about the terms of
the demise charter but in the voyage charter of the vessel to Cubazucar Mambisa was *j*
described as 'disponent owner'. Accordingly in signing bills of lading the master of
Marble Islands would do so on behalf of Mambisa and not on behalf of either the
Liechtenstein company or the government of Cuba, which at that time had no interest
in the vessel. So there was no contractual relationship between Iansa and the government
of Cuba covering the carriage of the consignment of sugar in Marble Islands.

4. The evidence about the purchase of Marble Islands from the Liechtenstein company by the Cuban government on 13th October 1973 and her transfer from the Somali to the Cuban register is scanty. It seems however to be incompatible with the general evidence filed by the respondents about the relationship both in fact and in Cuban law between Mambisa and the Cuban government that the demise charter should have survived the change in ownership. So the position which I think must be accepted by your Lordships at this stage of the proceedings is that on 13th October 1973 while Marble Islands was on the high seas the Cuban government acquired the ownership and (through their agent Mambisa) possession and control of a trading vessel that was carrying a cargo of sugar which was still the subject of an existing contract between Mambisa and Iansa for Mambisa to carry it to Valparaiso. But any civil liability to Iansa of the Cuban government itself must be based on events occurring after that date. So Iansa cannot rely, as it can in the case of Playa Larga, on the refusal by Mambisa to discharge the cargo on Marble Islands at Callao on 15th September 1973, a refusal which it claims to have been wrongful under the terms of the contract evidenced by the bills of lading in respect of the consignments on each vessel.

5. Lastly, I attach considerable significance to the elaborate legal machinery that was adopted to discharge and dispose of the cargo of Marble Islands at Haiphong. Permission to discharge the sugar at Haiphong was apparently required from the port commander. It was applied for on 6th November 1973 by the master as representative not of the owners of the cargo but of the carriers, Mambisa, and was expressed to be in exercise of the carriers' contractual rights under cll 2 and 8 of the bills of lading. On the same date the master executed an act of protest in which he asserted that Marble Islands had been prevented from performing the contract voyage to Valparaiso because of danger at Chilean ports. He went on to state that the cargo had been damaged by sea water and was in danger of deteriorating if it remained on board and that in these circumstances he intended to deposit it in Haiphong and sell it there. The sixth paragraph read as follows:

> '... that these deposit and sales procedures will be undertaken within the framework of the facilities which he holds, shown in the bills of lading covering the said merchandise, particularly in its second and eighth clauses as well as in accordance with the provisions of the Commercial Code in force in Cuba, with none of which the legal provisions in force in the Democratic Republic of Vietnam are in conflict.'

The right asserted by the master to discharge and sell the perishable cargo in Haiphong is thus fairly and squarely based on private law (jus gestionis), the contractual terms contained in the bills of lading and the Commercial Code in force in Cuba. There is no suggestion that the cargo had been requisitioned by the Cuban government jure imperii nor is there any mention of Law No 1256 of 27th September 1973 ('the freezing law') which froze all property and assets 'located in Cuban territory' belonging to juridical persons such as Iansa in which the Chilean State owned an interest. Since the cargo on Marble Islands was then located not in Cuban territory but in the territory of Vietnam the words of the freezing law that I have quoted may account for the fact that no reliance was placed at that time on any jus imperii.

The discharge of the cargo at Haiphong was followed on 22nd November 1973 by its sale by the master (describing himself as acting on behalf of Mambisa) to another Cuban enterprise Alimport at a price stated to be the spot price in Cuban currency according to world market quotation. The agreement provided that the price was to be paid in Havana, Cuba to an account at the National Bank of Cuba in favour of 'IANSA or whoever should prove to be the legitimate owner of the said sugar'. Once credited to that account the sale price would, no doubt, be blocked under the freezing law; but the actual contract of sale contained no reference to the freezing law. It was stated to be made by the master in his capacity as legal representative of the transporting company, Mambisa, 'in accordance with the provisions of the Commercial Code in force in Cuba and the second and eighth clauses of the bill of lading covering this consignment'. So all that was done in Haiphong in November to Iansa's sugar laden on Marble Islands was *a* done on the instructions of the Cuban government in purported reliance on Mambisa's rights in private law (jus gestionis) and not on any jus imperii of the Cuban State itself. It was only after the property in the sugar had been purportedly transferred to Alimport under the terms of the sale contract by delivery of the warehouse warrants that the sugar was then handed over by Alimport as a gift by the State of Cuba to the government of Vietnam. *b*

My Lords, counsel for the Cuban government has invited your Lordships to treat the form that these transactions took as devoid of legal significance and to regard them as mere 'formalities' recorded for internal accounting purposes of the government. For my part I see no basis in the evidence for doing this or for treating them as a mere charade, a word which counsel hesitated to use. I think that your Lordships are justified in holding that this evidence is sufficient to sustain an arguable case that Mambisa, at any *c* rate, was treating the contract of carriage evidenced by the bill of lading as still subsisting between 13th October and 22nd November 1973, and was relying on that contract as authorising the deviation to Haiphong and the discharge and sale of the cargo there. Your Lordships at this stage of the proceedings are in no way concerned whether or not such reliance was justified under whatever may turn out to be the proper law of the contract of carriage. *d*

So the legal position of the Cuban government after 13th October 1973 was that it then acquired the ownership of a trading vessel, Marble Islands, then in mid-Pacific engaged in carrying cargo belonging to Iansa on a voyage which the master claimed was authorised by a power to deviate contained in the bill of lading under which the cargo had been shipped. Mambisa from being demise charterer of Marble Islands had become managing operator of the vessel on behalf of the Cuban government, and legal possession *e* of the cargo laden on her passed from Mambisa as former disponent owner to the Cuban government itself which in terms of English law became the 'bailee' of Iansa's sugar. Thereafter, as the evidence discloses, everything that was done by the master was done on the express directions of the Cuban government, the director and senior legal adviser of the Ministry of Merchant Marine and Ports being sent to Haiphong in November to supervise what the master did there and the legal form and nature of the steps he took. *f*

My Lords, the events principally complained of in relation to the cargo laden on Marble Islands after she passed into the ownership of the Cuban government took place in Haiphong. There is no evidence before this House as to the law of delict or civil wrongs in Vietnam, so your Lordships for present purposes must proceed on the assumption that it is the same as the English law of tort, an assumption that may be less improbable in relation to the international carriage of goods by sea than in some other *g* fields of private law.

Unless the master's assertions in the documents that the discharge and sale of the cargo was authorised by the bills of lading was right in law, the facts to which I have particularly referred would disclose in English law a prima facie case of conversion of the cargo by the Cuban government as bailee when the master sold and delivered it to Alimport on the instructions of the government in purported exercise of rights under *h* private law. The relevant transaction, viz the discharge and sale of the cargo to Alimport at Haiphong was, as it seems to me, deliberately treated by the Cuban government as being effected under private law and not in the exercise of any sovereign powers.

For these reasons I for my part would allow the appeal in the case of the Marble Islands as well as in the case of the Playa Larga.

j

LORD EDMUND-DAVIES. My Lords, your Lordships are at one that the appeal brought by the owners of the Playa Larga sugar cargo should be allowed and I propose to say nothing more about that appeal than that I respectfully concur. But your Lordships are unhappily divided as to the proper outcome of the appeal brought by the owners of

the cargo carried by the vessel Marble Islands. Having studied with great advantage
a drafts of the speeches prepared by my noble and learned friends Lord Wilberforce and
Lord Diplock, I propose to indicate briefly why I have respectfully concluded that the
former is correct in the reasoning which has led him to hold that the appeal in the case
of Marble Islands should be dismissed.

I approach the application of the restricted doctrine of state immunity on the following
basic principles: (1) that enunciated in *Victory Transport Inc v Comisaria General de*
b *Abastecimientos y Transportes* (1964) 336 F 2d 354 at 360 that 'Sovereign immunity is a
derogation from the normal exercise of jurisdiction by the courts and should be accorded
only in clear cases'; (2) that propounded in *Claim against the Empire of Iran Case* (1963) 45
ILR 57 at 80 that—

> 'As a means for determining the distinction between acts *jure imperii* and *jure*
c   *gestionis* one should rather refer to the nature of the State transaction or the resulting
> legal relationships, and not to the motive or purpose of the State activity. It thus
> depends on whether the foreign State has acted in exercise of its sovereign authority,
> that is in public law, or like a private person, that is in private law;

(3) that, as was said in *Ohio v Helvering* (1934) 292 US 360 at 369, 'When a state enters the
d market place seeking customers it divests itself of its *quasi*-sovereignty *pro tanto* and takes
on the character of a trader . . .'; (4) that, while it is common ground that, even before the
State Immunity Act 1978, the doctrine of state immunity had become restricted, it
emphatically has not been rendered obsolete. Any such idea as 'once a trader, always a
trader' can lead into error, for, to quote my noble and learned friend Lord Wilberforce,
'If a trader is always a trader, a state remains a state and is capable at any time of acts of
e sovereignty . . . The restrictive theory does not . . . deny [this] capability'.

My Lords, I can see no scope for the 'trader' theory in relation to the Marble Islands
claim, the factual basis of which others of your Lordships have set out. It was brought
by the owners of the sugar cargo aboard Marble Islands, and was originally instituted
against Mambisa on the basis that they owned I Congreso del Partido, and secondly
(when the error was exposed) against the Republic of Cuba when it was discovered that
f *they* owned the vessel. The plaintiffs' claim was—

> 'in respect of a consignment of sugar carried on board the "Marble Islands" . . .
> and is for the return of the said consignment or its value and damages for its
> detention, alternatively damages for the wrongful conversion thereof, and/or for
> damages for breach of duty with respect thereto.'
g

When the Marble Islands cargo left Cuba for Valparaiso, Chile, that vessel was owned by
a Liechtenstein corporation, held by Mambisa under a demise charter and sub-chartered
to Cubazucar. Following the Chilean coup d'état of 11th September 1973, the Republic
of Cuba took it on itself to order its master not to proceed to Valparaiso, Chile, its
h designated destination, but to change course northwards and link up with the Playa
Larga. This was done, and both vessels reached Callao, Peru, on 15th September. There
the Cuban ambassador ordered both vessels not to discharge their cargoes, and this
against the request for discharge made by the Chilean ambassador, whose government
had already bought and paid for both cargoes. On 20th September Playa Larga left
Callao and returned to Cuba, and on 27th September (the day when Cuban Law No 1256
j with its retrospective provision to 11th September was enacted) Marble Islands set out for
Haiphong, North Vietnam. It was only during that voyage that on 13th October the
Republic of Cuba acquired ownership of Marble Islands. It reached Haiphong on or
about 6th November, where its cargo was unloaded at the master's request and was
subsequently sold to Alimport (a Cuban State enterprise) which in its turn seemingly
donated the sugar to the North Vietnamese people.

In the words of Lord Denning MR ([1981] All ER 1092 at 1099): 'The Cuban
government ... clearly converted the sugar when she reached Haiphong on 6th *a*
November 1973. They unloaded it and presented it to the people of Haiphong as a
gift.' Hence the claim instituted by the cargo owners, a claim which (unlike that
advanced by the owners of the Playa Larga cargo) did not sound in contract at all. This
was clearly right, for there never was any contractual relationship between the parties to
the action. The question that arises is: was there between those parties at any time *any*
commercial relationship falling within the ambit of the restricted doctrine of sovereign *b*
immunity and now preventing the Republic of Cuba from relying on it?

My Lords, if in these circumstances it be held that the Republic of Cuba cannot rely
on state immunity, I find it impossible to imagine circumstances where the doctrine *can*
operate. Whether or not I find the conclusion palatable is neither here nor there, but in
my judgment the plea is clearly one which should be upheld. I therefore concur with
my noble and learned friend Lord Wilberforce in holding that the Marble Islands appeal *c*
should be dismissed.

LORD KEITH OF KINKEL. My Lords, I have had the benefit of reading in draft the
speeches of my noble and learned friends Lord Wilberforce and Lord Diplock. I find
myself in full agreement with the opinion expressed by my noble and learned friend *d*
Lord Wilberforce regarding the principles which at the material time represented the
law of England in the field of sovereign immunity. I am also in agreement with him as
to the result which must follow from the proper application of these principles to the
actions of the Cuban government in relation to the cargo laden aboard Playa Larga.

As regards the cargo laden aboard Marble Islands, on the other hand, I agree with the
analysis made by my noble and learned friend Lord Diplock of the relationship which *e*
existed between Iansa and the Cuban government following the latter's acquisition of the
vessel on 13th October 1973. I also agree that, for the reasons which he gives, the actions
of the master of Marble Islands in connection with the discharge and sale of the cargo at
Haiphong, carried out on the instructions of the Cuban government and under the
supervision of its representatives, are properly to be regarded as having been done under
private law and not as an exercise of sovereign powers. The Cuban government did not *f*
profess to be exercising any such powers. The transactions which it instructed were
presented as being authorised by the terms of the bills of lading and the Cuban
Commercial Code. It follows that I would repel the plea of sovereign immunity in
respect of the Marble Islands cargo.

My Lords, I would accordingly allow the appeal in both cases.

g

LORD BRIDGE OF HARWICH. My Lords, this is the first time the courts of this
country have had to decide, applying the restrictive doctrine of sovereign immunity,
how the boundary is to be drawn in international law between the acts of a sovereign
state that are still entitled to immunity and those that are not. Happily it is probably also *h*
the last, since the matter is now governed by the State Immunity Act 1978. The
restrictive doctrine itself is a novelty in English law, having been so recently accepted as
supplanting absolute immunity. But it is not only on account of its novelty that the
problem of attempting to delimit the scope of the doctrine presents such difficulty for
English judges. This difficulty has been very generally felt by the judges of many
countries and nowhere satisfactorily resolved. *j*

I could not possibly hope to emulate, let alone improve on, the penetrating analysis of
the relevant principles, derived from the welter of material put before us, which is set out
in the speech of my noble and learned friend Lord Wilberforce, and with which I broadly
agree. But I venture, with diffidence, to add a footnote to it. It does seem to me that two
propositions can be derived from the relevant authorities which may often, and do in this

case, provide a useful guide in deciding whether or not a claim to sovereign immunity
can be sustained. First, if a sovereign state voluntarily assumes a purely private law
obligation, it cannot, when that obligation is sought to be enforced against it, claim
sovereign immunity on the ground that the reason for assuming the obligation was of a
sovereign or governmental character. Example: State A orders uniforms for its army
from a supplier in State B; when sued for the price in the courts of State B, State A cannot
claim immunity on the ground that the maintenance of its army is a sovereign
function. This is really elementary. But it leads on logically to the second proposition
that, having assumed a purely private law obligation, a sovereign state cannot justify a
breach of the obligation on the ground that the reason for the breach was of a sovereign
or governmental character. Example: State A, having ordered uniforms for its army
from a supplier in State B, repudiates the contract; when sued in the courts of State B for
damages, State A cannot claim immunity on the ground that, since the placing of the
contract, a government of a new political complexion has made a sovereign decision,
pursuant to a policy of total disarmament, to disband its army.

Since your Lordships are all agreed that the appeal in the case of Playa Larga should be
allowed, I need do no more than record my assent to that view.

With regard to the appeal in the case of Marble Islands, I have had the advantage of
reading all your Lordships' speeches in advance. Your Lordships appear to be radically
divided rather on the interpretation of the evidence and the significance of the particular
facts than on any question of legal principle. This is the more unfortunate since a
decision has to be reached at this stage when the evidence, all by affidavit, is manifestly
incomplete. My own view of the facts and their significance accords with that expressed
in the speech of my noble and learned friend Lord Diplock. In my opinion, two
considerations are decisive. First, when the Republic of Cuba acquired ownership of
Marble Islands in mid-Pacific, it not being suggested that the demise charter continued,
the evidence in the affidavits filed on behalf of the respondents justifies the inference that
the relationship between the republic and its creature Mambisa, in respect of all state-
owned ships, was such that the republic took legal possession of Marble Islands through
Mambisa as its agent. There is no suggestion that the acquisition of Marble Islands was
itself a sovereign act. Taking possession of the vessel, the republic also took possession of
the cargo which the vessel was carrying, thereby, in English law, assuming towards the
cargo owners the obligations of bailee to bailor. Bailment may be a concept peculiar to
English law. But I cannot suppose that any civilised system of law would not recognise
that an international carrier of goods acquiring a laden vessel in mid-voyage from
another incurs private law obligations to the cargo owners. Second, as Lord Diplock has
demonstrated in detail, all the contemporary documents relating to the disposal of the
cargo at Haiphong show that it was effected in purported exercise of private law rights.
It follows from these two considerations, in my view, that, assuming a conversion of the
cargo by the Republic of Cuba (an assumption necessarily to be made at this stage), this
was a breach of a private law obligation previously assumed when Marble Islands was
acquired. Hence, immunity cannot be claimed in respect of it on the ground that the
reasons for the disposal of the cargo were of a sovereign and governmental character.

Accordingly, I would allow the appeals in both cases.

Appeals allowed.

Solicitors: *Bischoff & Co* (for the appellants); *Coward Chance* (for the respondents).

Mary Rose Plummer   Barrister.

Raymond v Honey

QUEEN'S BENCH DIVISION
ORMROD LJ AND WEBSTER J
25th MARCH, 7th APRIL 1981

Contempt of court – Obstruction of legal proceedings – Obstruction of person's right of access to courts – Prisoner – Legal communications – Governor stopping communications – Letter by prisoner to solicitor when party to proceedings alleging theft by assistant governor – Letter stopped by governor but prisoner told he could rewrite letter without allegation – Prisoner shortly due to see his solicitor in prison – Subsequent application by prisoner to commit governor for contempt – Application accompanied by letter – Governor stopping application – Whether application a 'letter or communication' – Whether governor guilty of contempt – Whether stopping of letter not calculated to obstruct or interfere with due course of justice – Whether stopping of application to commit and accompanying letter contempt by hindering prisoner's access to courts – Prison Rules 1964 (SI 1964 No 388), r 33(3).

The applicant, who was serving a sentence of imprisonment, was, in June 1980, a party to certain legal proceedings. On about 24th June he wrote a letter to his solicitor which was read by a prison officer and stopped by the governor of the prison because it contained an allegation that an assistant governor of the prison had committed theft. The applicant was, however, told that he could rewrite the letter omitting the allegation of theft, and, in any event, he was due in the next few days to be visited by his solicitor when he could have raised the allegation. Later in June and arising out of the stopping of the letter of 24th June, the applicant prepared an application to the High Court for leave to commit the governor for contempt of court, which consisted of the necessary documents and an accompanying letter, and gave them to the prison authorities to be forwarded to the Crown Office at the Royal Courts of Justice. The governor stopped them. The applicant applied to a Divisional Court to commit the governor for contempt and submitted that any obstruction of a party to legal proceedings, by breaching the confidentiality between him and his solicitors, constituted contempt. The governor relied on r 33(3)[a] of the Prison Rules 1964 as authorising him to stop both the letter of 24th June and the later documents and letter.

Held – Although the obstruction of a party to legal proceedings by breaching the confidentiality of communications between him and his solicitor was contempt if it was calculated to prejudice his right to unhindered access to the courts or to obstruct or interfere with the due course of justice or with lawful process, provided he was a person whose common law rights had not already in some material respect been restricted, and, although a person confined to prison retained all his civil rights except those which had been expressly or impliedly taken from him in law, (i) the stopping of the letter of 24th June was not, in the circumstances that the applicant was told he could rewrite the letter and was due to be visited by his solicitor, conduct calculated to obstruct or interfere with the due course of justice or with lawful process and did not therefore constitute contempt of court, whether or not the governor had been entitled under r 33(3) of the 1964 rules to stop the letter, but (ii) the stopping of the documents and accompanying letter constituting the application to commit the governor for contempt did amount to conduct calculated to prejudice the requirement that a citizen should have unhindered access to the courts, and in stopping them the governor had been guilty of contempt, since they constituted the issuing of process, and, although they included a letter, r 33(3) did not apply to confer power to stop them since they could not be regarded as a 'letter or communication' within that rule. In the circumstances, however, since the application had been only temporarily delayed, the court would make no order (see p 1086 g h, p 1087 a b and j to p 1088 d, post).

---

a   Rule 33, so far as material, is set out at p 1087 c d, post

a   Dicta of Lord Russell CJ in *R v Gray* [1900–3] All ER Rep at 62, of Lord Morris and of Lord Diplock in *Attorney General v Times Newspapers Ltd* [1973] 3 All ER at 66, 72 and *Solosky v R* (1980) 105 DLR (3d) 745 applied.

Notes

For letters to and from a prisoner, see 30 Halsbury's Laws (3rd Edn) 611, para 1175.

For conduct amounting to contempt of court, see 9 Halsbury's Laws (4th Edn) para 7,
b   and for cases on criminal contempt committed outside the court, see 16 Digest (Reissue) 19–38, *193–385*.

For the Prison Rules 1964, r 33, see 18 Halsbury's Statutory Instruments (Third Reissue) 20.

Cases referred to in judgment

c   *Attorney General v Times Newspapers Ltd* [1973] 3 All ER 54, [1974] AC 273, [1973] 3 WLR 298, HL, 16 Digest (Reissue) 23, *221*.

R v Gray [1900] 2 QB 36, [1900–3] All ER Rep 59, 69 LJQB 502, 82 LT 534, 64 JP 484, DC, 16 Digest (Reissue) 47, *452*.

R v Hull Prison Board of Visitors, ex parte St Germain [1979] 1 All ER 701, [1979] QB 425, [1979] 2 WLR 42, 68 Cr App R 212, CA, Digest (Cont Vol E) 488, *6a*.

d   *Solosky v R* (1980) 105 DLR (3d) 745.

Cases also cited

Becker v Home Office [1972] 2 All ER 676, [1972] 2 QB 407, CA.

Cherter v Bateson [1920] 1 KB 829, DC.

Waugh v British Railways Board [1979] 2 All ER 1169, [1980] AC 521, HL.
e

Application to commit for contempt

The applicant, Steven Patrick Raymond, a prisoner serving a sentence of imprisonment for theft at HM Prison, Albany, Isle of Wight, and awaiting further criminal charges, applied to commit for contempt of court the respondent, Colin Peter Honey, the
f   governor of Albany prison. The grounds on which the committal was sought were (1) that the respondent had acted in a manner calculated to prejudice the fair trial of a pending cause in that (i) by his unlawful and improper interference with the confidential correspondence passing between the applicant and his legal advisers, he had prevented, and by his servants, agents and colleagues, he continued to prevent, the applicant from informing his legal advisers as to the nature of his defence to the further criminal charges he faced, (ii) he had unlawfully and improperly endeavoured to influence the applicant
g   to alter and/or withdraw certain parts of that defence and (iii) he had unlawfully and improperly instructed his servants, agents and colleagues to inquire into various aspects of the defence with a view to instituting prison disciplinary charges against the applicant, and (2) that the respondent had acted in a manner calculated to interfere with the due and proper administration of justice in that he prevented the applicant from applying to
h   the High Court for leave to make an application in a matter already pending before the court. The facts are set out in the judgment of the court.

Louis Blom-Cooper QC and *Andrew Trollope* for the applicant.
Andrew Collins for the respondent.

j   *Cur adv vult*

7th April. **WEBSTER J** read the following judgment of the court: In this case counsel on behalf of the applicant moves to commit the respondent for contempt of court. At all material times the applicant was a prisoner in HM Prison, Albany, Isle of Wight, and the respondent was the governor of that prison. Two matters are relied on in support of the application.

In June 1980 the applicant was engaged in legal proceedings, the precise nature of
which is immaterial. On about 24th or 26th June (the date is uncertain) he wrote a letter *a*
to his solicitors. The letter was read by a prison officer and stopped by the respondent.
That is the first matter on which the applicant relies.

Later, and arising out of that incident, the applicant prepared an application to the
High Court for leave to commit the respondent, and Mr Bagshaw, an assistant governor
of the prison, for contempt of court. He gave the documents, consisting of a statement,
his unsworn affidavit, a bundle of exhibits and a covering letter dated 30th June 1980, to *b*
the prison authorities to be forwarded to the Crown Office at the Royal Courts of
Justice. These documents were also stopped by the respondent, and that is the second
matter on which the applicant relies in support of the application.

In both instances the respondent relied on the Prison Rules 1964, SI 1964 No 388, as
his authority to stop the letters and other documents; but before considering the
provisions of those rules we will state what in our view the relevant law is.   *c*

The classic general statement of the law of contempt is that of Lord Russell CJ in *R v
Gray* [1900] 2 QB 36 at 40, [1900–3] All ER Rep 59 at 62, where he said: '... any act
done ... calculated to obstruct or interfere with the due course of justice or the lawful
process of the Courts is a contempt of Court.'

More recently, in *Attorney General v Times Newspapers Ltd* [1973] 3 All ER 54 at 66,
[1974] AC 273 at 302, Lord Morris said: *d*

> 'In the general interests of the community it is imperative that the authority of
> the courts should not be imperilled and that recourse to them should not be subject
> to unjustifiable interference ... There can be no such thing as a justifiable contempt
> of court.'

Lord Diplock said ([1973] 3 All ER 54 at 72, [1974] AC 273 at 309):   *e*

> 'The due administration of justice requires *first* that all citizens should have
> unhindered access to the constitutionally established courts of criminal or civil
> jurisdiction for the determination of disputes as to their legal rights and
> liabilities ... [Having dealt with the second and third requirements Lord Diplock
> concluded:] Conduct which is calculated to prejudice any of these three requirements
> or to undermine the public confidence that they will be observed is contempt of *f*
> court.'

Counsel for the applicant submits that any obstruction of a party to legal proceedings,
by breaching the confidentiality of communication between that party and his solicitors,
constitutes a contempt. In our judgment that submission is too wide. Applying the
dicta of Lord Russell and of Lord Diplock to which we have just referred, such conduct *g*
can only be categorised as contempt if it is calculated to prejudice that party's unhindered
access to the courts or to obstruct or interfere with the due course of justice or the lawful
process of the court; and then only if the common law rights of the party in question are
not restricted in some material way.

The applicant, as we have said, has been at all material times a prisoner, and no
authority is needed to support the proposition, which is self-evident, that by having been *h*
committed to custody a prisoner thereby loses many of his ordinary rights. None the
less, as Shaw LJ said in *R v Hull Prison Board of Governors, ex parte St Germain* [1979] 1 All
ER 701 at 716, [1979] QB 425 at 455:

> '... despite the deprivation of his general liberty, a prisoner remains invested
> with residuary rights appertaining to the nature and conduct of his incarceration. *j*
> Now the rights of a citizen, however circumscribed by a penal sentence or otherwise,
> must always be the concern of the courts unless their jurisdiction is clearly excluded
> by some statutory provision. The courts are in general the ultimate custodians of
> the rights and liberties of the subject whatever his status and however attenuated
> those rights and liberties may be as the result of some punitive or other process.'

In *Solosky v R* (1980) 105 DLR (3d) 745 at 760, a case arising out of facts very similar
a to those of the first of the two matters on which the applicant relies in this case,
Dickson J, in a judgment with which all the other members of the Supreme Court of
Canada agreed, said: '. . . a person confined to prison retains all of his civil rights, other
than those expressly or impliedly taken from him in law.'

That principle, which was accepted by counsel on behalf of the respondent, is in our
view the principle to be applied in the present case. It is therefore necessary to examine
b the extent to which the relevant rights of the applicant and other prisoners are removed
or restricted, in particular by the Prison Rules 1964 (as amended by SI 1972 No 1860 and
SI 1974 No 713), rules which it is common ground have been properly made pursuant
to s 47 of the Prison Act 1952 as amended by the Criminal Justice Act 1961.

Of these rules, it is only necessary to recite the following:

'*Letters and visits generally*
c '**33.**—(1) The Secretary of State may, with a view to securing discipline and good
order or the prevention of crime or in the interests of any persons, impose
restrictions, either generally or in a particular case, upon the communications to be
permitted between a prisoner and other persons.

'(2) Except as provided by statute or these Rules, a prisoner shall not be permitted
to communicate with any outside person, or that person with him, without the
d leave of the Secretary of State.

'(3) Except as provided by these Rules, every letter or communication to or from
a prisoner may be read or examined by the governor or an officer deputed by him,
and the governor may, at his discretion, stop any letter or communication on the
ground that its contents are objectionable or that it is of inordinate length . . .

'*Further facilities in connection with legal proceedings*
e '**37A.**—(1) A prisoner who is a party to any legal proceedings may correspond
with his legal adviser in connection with the proceedings and unless the Governor
has reason to suppose that any such correspondence contains matter not relating to
the proceedings it shall not be read or stopped under Rule 33(3) of these Rules . . .'

Against that background, we return to the first of the two incidents of which the
f applicant complains. We have already stated that, at the time of that incident, the
applicant was a party to legal proceedings. He had, therefore, by virtue of r 37A, a right
to correspond with his legal adviser in connection with those proceedings; conversely, in
those circumstances and depending on the precise construction of the two rules in
question, the power to read and stop that correspondence, conferred by r 33(3), was taken
away 'unless the Governor [had] reason to suppose that any such correspondence
g [contained] matter not relating to the proceedings'.

Without reciting the circumstances giving rise to the suspicion, we accept the evidence
contained in the respondent's affidavit, not challenged by counsel for the applicant, that
he had reason for such a supposition in relation to the applicant's letter of 24th or 26th
June 1980.

The probable effect of that fact is, in our judgment, simple (although it is not necessary
h finally to decide it): it enabled the respondent to invoke the powers conferred by r 33(3)
and, therefore, to read or examine the letter (or to have it read or examined by an officer
deputed by him) and to stop it if he reasonably believed that its contents were
objectionable.

The respondent stopped the letter because it contained an allegation that Mr Bagshaw
had stolen a book referred to in the letter. In stopping the letter for that reason the
j respondent was relying on Ord 26(4)(*b*)(ix) of the Prison Standing Orders which provides
that allegations against officers should not be included in an outgoing letter. Without
considering the question whether those standing orders have any legislative authority (a
question about which we were left in some doubt) we would be inclined to take the view
that the respondent, for that reason, was entitled to regard the contents of the letter as
objectionable, that he therefore had a discretion to stop it and that in stopping it he did

so in the proper exercise of that discretion. But it is not necessary to decide that question, because according to the respondent's evidence (which was not challenged) he told the applicant that he could rewrite the letter omitting the allegation of theft against Mr Bagshaw; moreover, according to his evidence, the applicant was to the respondent's knowledge due to be visited by his solicitor within the next few days when he could, in the course of an interview with him, have told him anything he wished.

In these circumstances, whether or not the respondent was entitled to stop the letter, we are satisfied that his conduct was not conduct calculated to obstruct or interfere with the due course of justice or the lawful process of the courts and that it was not therefore a contempt of court.

Different considerations, however, apply to the second matter relied on by the applicant, namely the stopping by the respondent of the applicant's application to the High Court to commit him, the respondent, and Mr Bagshaw for contempt of court. We were not referred to any rule (other than r 33) which could give the respondent power to stop that application. In our judgment such an application to the court, which constitutes the issuing of proceedings, cannot be regarded as a 'letter or communication' to which r 33(3) applies, even if that application is accompanied by a covering letter. In stopping that application the respondent was, in our judgment, guilty of conduct calculated to prejudice what Lord Diplock in *Attorney General v Times Newspapers* described as the requirement that all citizens should have unhindered access to the courts, and therefore guilty of contempt.

The application which was stopped and therefore temporarily delayed has, however, now been made; and in all the circumstances we do not propose to make any order on the present motion other than as to costs on which we would like to hear counsel.

Judgment accordingly. Leave to the respondent to appeal. Leave to the applicant to cross-appeal.

Solicitors: *Hallinan, Blackburn Gittings & Co* (for the applicant); *Treasury Solicitor.*

N P Metcalfe Esq   Barrister.

a R v London Borough of Hillingdon, ex parte Islam

COURT OF APPEAL, CIVIL DIVISION

LORD DENNING MR, ACKNER LJ AND SIR DENYS BUCKLEY

b 11th, 12th, 13th, 22nd MAY 1981

Housing – Homeless person – Person becoming homeless intentionally – Act or omission causing applicant to cease occupying accommodation available for him – Applicant coming from Bangladesh and settling in England – Applicant's wife and children residing at his parents' home in Bangladesh – Wife and children subsequently coming to England – Applicant's accommodation inadequate to house him and them – Applicant and family having no accommodation because of
c *inadequacy of his accommodation – Whether applicant entitled to be permanently housed by local authority – Whether applicant homeless intentionally – Housing (Homeless Persons) Act 1977, ss 16, 17(1).*

The applicant came to England from Bangladesh (then East Pakistan) in 1965 and ever
d since had lived and worked in the London borough of Hillingdon, where he had thus become settled. On his Bangladesh passport his parents' address in Bangladesh was given as his permanent address. From time to time he revisited Bangladesh and during those visits married there and had four children. His wife and children lived with his parents in Bangladesh. In September 1974 the applicant's passport was indorsed with a United Kingdom entry certificate and in the same year his wife applied for entry clearance for herself and the children to enter the United Kingdom. In August 1979 the applicant
e moved from his existing accommodation in Hillingdon to new accommodation in Hillingdon which consisted of one shared room which was inadequate to house both him and his family. At the end of 1979 permits for the wife and children to enter the United Kingdom were issued and they arrived in England in April 1980. The applicant's landlord accommodated them temporarily but in July 1980 gave the applicant and his family notice to quit and in September 1980 ejected them. The applicant applied to
f Hillingdon council for accommodation as a homeless person under the Housing (Homeless Persons) Act 1977. The council determined (i) that he was homeless but was not in priority need of accommodation within s 2(1)[a] of that Act, because his children were not persons who might reasonably be expected to reside with him as they had lived apart from him (ie in Bangladesh) for the previous seven years, and (ii) that, even if he were in priority need, he was to be treated as having become homeless intentionally
g within s 17(1)[b] of the 1977 Act, because he had deliberately arranged for his wife and children to leave accommodation in Bangladesh which it would have been reasonable for them to continue to occupy. Accordingly, the council decided that the applicant and his family were not entitled under the 1977 Act to be permanently housed by the council. The applicant applied for judicial review of the council's decision by way of an, inter alia, order of certiorari to quash the decision. The judge held that the applicant was in
h priority need of accommodation within s 2(1) but that, in bringing his wife and family to England from Bangladesh without ensuring there was permanent accommodation available for them in England, he had rendered himself and them homeless intentionally within s 17(1). The applicant appealed.

Held (Ackner LJ dissenting) – The applicant had become homeless intentionally within
j s 17(1) of the 1977 Act and the appeal would be dismissed, for the following reasons—
     (1) (Per Lord Denning MR) Although the 1977 Act spoke in the singular of 'a person' being homeless, the Act was concerned with the family unit, and under s 17(1) the court

---

a Section 2(1), so far as material, is set out at p 1094 f, post
b Section 17(1), so far as material, is set out at p 1094 j, post

had to consider whether the family unit had became homeless intentionally.
Accordingly, 'a person' with a family became homeless intentionally if he deliberately   *a*
did or failed to do anything in consequence of which he or his family ceased to occupy
accommodation which was available for his or their occupation and which it would have
been reasonable for him or them to continue to occupy. Since the family's abode was the
applicant's parents' home in Bangladesh and the applicant was only in lodgings in
England and whilst there was occupying, by his wife and children, his parents' home, it
followed that, by arranging for his family to come to England, he had deliberately done   *b*
something in consequence of which both he and his family had 'ceased to occupy
accommodation which was available for occupation' by him and them and which it
would have been reasonable for him and them to continue to occupy, within s 17(1).
Accordingly, the applicant was homeless intentionally and was not entitled under the
1977 Act to permanent accommodation (see p 1092 *e* to p 1093 *e*, post); *De Falco v
Crawley Borough Council* [1980] 1 All ER 913 and *Lewis v North Devon District Council*   *c*
[1981] 1 All ER 27 considered.

(2) (Per Sir Denys Buckley) Although at all relevant times the applicant's home for the
purpose of the 1977 Act was in Hillingdon, he had, by bringing his family to England,
deliberately done something in consequence of which he had ceased to occupy
'accommodation which was available for his occupation', ie his shared room, within
s 17(1) of that Act, for, by s 16^c of that Act 'available accommodation' meant   *d*
accommodation which was available for occupation by a person and 'any other person
who might reasonably be expected to reside with him' and, on the arrival of the
applicant's family in England as permitted immigrants, they had become 'persons who
might reasonably be expected to reside with him' within s 16 and accordingly, on their
arrival, the applicant's shared room, which was totally inadequate to house both him and
them, had ceased to be, by his deliberate act in bringing the family to England,   *e*
accommodation which was 'available' for occupation by him and them, for the purpose
of s 17(1). It followed that, as his homelessness was due to his deliberate act, he had to be
treated as intentionally homeless (see p 1096 *f* to p 1097 *c* and *g*, post).

Observations on what constitutes the home of a person who has accommodation
available for him in two places which are a considerable distance from one another (see
p 1097 *e* to *g*, post).   *f*

Notes

For a housing authority's duty to house homeless persons and the inquiries into possible
homelessness a housing authority must make, see 22 Halsbury's Laws (4th Edn) paras
511–513.

For the Housing (Homeless Persons) Act 1977, ss 2, 16, 17, see 47 Halsbury's Statutes   *g*
(3rd Edn) 317, 330.

Cases referred to in judgments

De Falco v Crawley Borough Council [1980] 1 All ER 913, [1980] QB 460, [1980] 2 WLR
     664, 78 LGR 180, CA.
Lewis v North Devon District Council [1981] 1 All ER 27, [1981] 1 WLR 328.   *h*

Cases also cited

Dyson v Kerrier District Council [1980] 3 All ER 313, [1980] 1 WLR 1205, CA.
Lally v Kensington and Chelsea Royal Borough (1980) Times, 27th March.
R v Bristol City Council, ex parte Browne [1979] 3 All ER 344, [1979] 1 WLR 1437, DC.
R v Bristol Corpn, ex parte Hendy [1974] 1 All ER 1047, [1974] 1 WLR 498, CA.   *j*
R v Hillingdon Borough Council, ex parte Streeting [1980] 3 All ER 413, [1980] 1 WLR 1425,
     DC and CA.
Tickner v Mole Valley District Council [1980] Court of Appeal Transcript 215.

---

c   Section 16, so far as material, is set out at p 1092 *g*, post

Appeal

a Tafazzul Islam applied, with the leave of the Divisional Court granted on 20th October 1980, for (1) an order of certiorari to quash those parts of a decision made by the homeless families panel of the London Borough of Hillingdon on 2nd October 1980 whereby it decided (a) that the applicant was not in priority need of accommodation pursuant to s 2(1) of the Housing (Homeless Persons) Act 1977 and (b) that, if he was, he was intentionally homeless pursuant to s 17 of that 1977 Act, (2) an order of mandamus

b requiring Hillingdon council to make appropriate inquiries pursuant to s 3 of the 1977 Act, (3) various related declarations and (4) an injunction ordering Hillingdon council to provide accommodation for the applicant and his family. On 30th January 1981 Glidewell J, hearing the Divisional Court List, dismissed the application. The applicant appealed. The ground of the appeal was that the court erred in law in upholding the decision of the homeless families panel because there was no material before either the

c panel or the court on the basis of which the applicant could be deemed to be intentionally homeless within s 17. The facts are set out in the judgment of Lord Denning MR.

Andrew Arden for the applicant.
Lionel Read QC and *R A Barratt* for the council.

d

Cur adv vult

22nd May. The following judgments were read.

LORD DENNING MR. The applicant, at the age of 23, came in 1965 from
e Bangladesh (then East Parkistan) to England. He got work in Uxbridge and was in lodgings at 5 Cowley Mill Road, Uxbridge. He went back to Bangladesh from time to time. On a visit in 1968 he married his wife there. On other visits she conceived and had children. She lived there in Bangladesh in his parents' home with the children. He returned to England to work and sent money back to Bangladesh for his wife and the children. He had a Bangladesh passport in which his permanent address was given as at
f Syhlet in Bangladesh. He was, however, ordinarily resident here, and 'settled' here with indefinite leave to stay here under the Immigration Act 1971, s 1(2).

In 1974 the applicant applied for a visa to permit his wife and children to come to this country. This took a long time to come through but eventually on 15th February 1980 they were granted entry clearance as being the 'dependants' of a person who is already in the United Kingdom and 'settled' here. They were his wife and four children (sons aged
g 11, 6 and 2 and a baby daughter aged 1). As the applicant was settled here before 1973, they were entitled under the immigration rules to indefinite leave to enter without any special requirements as to support or accommodation: see the Statement of Changes in Immigration Rules (HC Paper (1979–80) no 394), r 42.

As soon as they had been granted entry clearance, the applicant arranged for them to come here. He took new lodgings at 120 Cowley Mill Road from a Mr Rahman at £13
h a week. They consisted of one room and a shared use of another room. But when the wife and children arrived Mr Rahman refused to allow them to stay in his house. They went from pillar to post. A few days later Mr Rahman relented a little. He did allow them to stay for four weeks but then said they could stay no longer. The applicant applied to the Hillingdon council for accommodation as they were homeless. Several meetings were held which I need not relate, but eventually on Thursday, 2nd October
j 1980 the homeless families panel of the council came to this conclusion:

'RESOLVED—(1) That the applicant be considered homeless, but not in priority need, as his dependent children might not reasonably be expected to reside with him having lived apart for the past seven years. (2) That, even if he were in priority need, the applicant be considered to have become homeless intentionally, having

deliberately arranged for his wife and children to leave accommodation which it
would have been reasonable for them to continue to occupy. (3) That *a*
accommodation continue to be secured for the applicant and his family up to and
including 16 October 1980.'

Thereupon the applicant got legal aid and applied for judicial review of the council's
decision. On 30th January 1981 Glidewell J held that the council were wrong in holding
that he was not in priority need. It was clear that he had dependent children who were *b*
residing with him, within s 2(1)(a) of the 1977 Act. He had therefore a priority need.
But Glidewell J held that the council were entitled to decide that he was 'intentionally
homeless' within s 17. He said that '. . . in bringing his wife and family to England from
Bangladesh without ensuring that there was permanent accommodation available to
them, the applicant had rendered himself, and them also, homeless intentionally'.

Now an application is made to this court. It is said that this case is distinguishable *c*
from *De Falco v Crawley Borough Council* [1980] 1 All ER 913, [1980] 1 QB 460. In that
case the whole family, husband, wife and children, came together from Italy to
England. The *husband* had become homeless intentionally because *he* had ceased to
occupy accommodation which was available (in Italy) for himself and his family. So the
case came directly within s 17(1) of the 1977 Act. But in the present case the husband
was already *here.* *He* had not ceased to occupy accommodation which was available for *d*
his occupation in Bangladesh. So *he* did not come within s 17(1).

This raises a point of much importance. In past years many men have come to
England from the Indian subcontinent and elsewhere. They have come to find work and
have found it. They have settled here. They have left their wives and children back in
their homeland. Under our immigration laws they are entitled to bring them over here
to join them. When they arrive, and are homeless here, can they then call on the local *e*
council to house them permanently?

The 1977 Act, throughout its length, speaks in the singular. It speaks of 'a person'
being homeless. It speaks of 'a person' applying for accommodation. It speaks of 'he', or
'him', or 'his', and so forth. But the use of the singular is deceptive. If you look a little
deeper into the Act, you will see that it is concerned not so much with 'a person' as with
a family unit of which he is the head. Thus, in considering whether 'he' is homeless, you *f*
have to take into account 'any other person who normally resides with him as a member
of *his* family': see s 1(1)(a). In considering whether he has a priority need, you have to
take into account any 'dependent children who are residing with him or who might
reasonably be expected to reside with him': see s 2(1)(a). In considering whether
accommodation is available for a person's occupation, you have to take into account 'any
other person who might reasonably be expected to reside with him': see s 16. *g*

In the light of all these provisions, it seems to me that we should look in every case at
the family unit, and treat the words 'person', 'he', 'him' and 'his' as referring to him as the
head of the family unit. We should regard the home as the home of the family unit. So
that 'he' is homeless when the family unit is homeless.

Applying this concept to s 17 it means that 'a person' with a family becomes homeless
intentionally if he deliberately does or fails to do anything in consequence of which he *h*
or his family cease to occupy accommodation which is available for his or their
occupation and which it would have been reasonable for him or them to continue to
occupy.

Applied to this case, it seems to me that the 'home' of the applicant and his family was
not in England. It was in Syhlet in Bangladesh. That is where his wife and family were
living. That is where he returned on holidays or on leave. It was the abode of the family *j*
unit. He was only in lodgings in England. It is like many of our English families. The
menfolk go off to work in countries overseas and leave their wives and children at home
in England. The home of the family is in England and not in the country overseas. The
man 'occupies' the home by his wife and family even whilst he is overseas. So the
applicant 'occupied' the home in Bangladesh by his wife and family even whilst he was

in lodgings in England. When they ceased to occupy it and came to England, he ceased
a to occupy it also.

Looking at s 17 in this way, it seems to me that when the applicant arranged for his
wife and children to come to England, *he* deliberately did something in consequence of
which *he* and his family ceased to 'occupy' accommodation in Bangladesh which was
available for *his* and their occupation and which it would have been reasonable for *him*
and them to continue to occupy. That accommodation was available for occupation both
b by *him* and by any other person who might reasonably be expected to reside with him.

We were referred to *Lewis v North Devon District Council* [1981] 1 All ER 27, [1981] 1
WLR 328. I agree with the decision in that case, but I would prefer to put it on the
ground that the man was the head of the family unit; and when he became homeless
intentionally, it affected the whole of the family. So that the woman (so long as they
lived together as a family) would stand or fall with him. But if there was a separation of
c the family so that she became the head of her own separate family unit, then she could
make her own application which should be considered on its own merits. The 1977 Act
intended, I am sure, that the application should always be made by the head of the family
unit. The object was to keep the family together, so far as possible, and not separate.

Accordingly I agree with the judge that the applicant was homeless intentionally. He
is therefore not entitled to permanent accommodation. The only duty of the council is
d to furnish him with advice and appropriate assistance and, so as to enable him to secure
accommodation for himself and his family, give him accommodation for a short time:
see s 4(2) and (3) of the 1977 Act.

The moral of this case is that men from overseas should not bring their wives and
children here unless they have arranged permanent and suitable accommodation for
them to come to. The applicant is homeless intentionally. He is not entitled to
e permanent accommodation. He will not take priority over young couples here who are
on the waiting list for housing accommodation. I would dismiss the appeal.

ACKNER LJ. The applicant's country of origin was East Pakistan, now Bangladesh.
He first came to the United Kingdom in 1965 and thereafter has lived and worked in
f Hillingdon and has thus become 'settled' in England. In 1968 he returned to Bangladesh
in order to marry. He thereafter visited his wife on five occasions of unspecified
duration. As a result of those visits they have four children. His wife and his children
lived in Bangladesh at an address which is the home of the applicant's parents. This
address is shown as the applicant's permanent address in his Bangladesh passport, issued
to him in August 1974. In September 1974 the applicant had an entry certificate
g indorsed on his passport and in the same year his wife applied for entry clearance to enter
the United Kingdom for herself and her children, then two in number. Some six years
later, in February 1980, an entry visa was indorsed on the wife's passport to entitle her
and their children to join him in this country, such a visa being valid for presentation
within six months.

Since the applicant had become settled in the United Kingdom prior to 1973, the
h immigration rules restricting the admission for settlement of his dependents are not
applicable. He does not, inter alia, have to be able to accommodate them in
accommodation of his own or which he occupies himself (see the Statement of Changes
in Immigration Rules (HC Paper (1979–80) no 394), r 42).

On 27th April 1980 the applicant's wife and children arrived in the United
Kingdom. They stayed overnight at 5 Cowley Hill Road, Hillingdon, where for some 14
j years the applicant had lived in a single room. The applicant had, since August 1979,
been himself sharing a room in the home of a Mr Rahman at 120 Cowley Hill Road,
Uxbridge. Mr Rahman refused to permit him to bring his wife and children to stay
there, although the applicant asserts that he thought his landlord would accommodate
him and his family. The applicant then attended the homeless families unit of the
London borough of Hillingdon for their assistance. Mr Rahman appears to have agreed

to accommodate on a purely temporary basis the applicant and his family until about
July 1980 when a notice to quit was served. In September he was ejected by his *a*
landlord. The council granted the applicant and his family bed and breakfast
accommodation at 21 Sheepcote Road, Harrow, pending an application to the Uxbridge
County Court, but on 2nd October an application for an interim injunction against the
landlord was dismissed. In the evening of that same day the council's homeless family
panel made the following decision relative to the applicant's application made initially on
29th April and again on 8th September claiming to be homeless and to be entitled to *b*
have accommodation secured for him by the council under s 4(5) of the Housing
(Homeless Persons) Act 1977:

> '(1) That the applicant be considered homeless, but not in priority need, as his
> dependent children might not reasonably be expected to reside with him having
> lived apart for the past seven years. (2) That, even if he were in priority need, the *c*
> applicant be considered to have become homeless intentionally, having deliberately
> arranged for his wife and children to leave accommodation which it would have
> been reasonable for them to continue to occupy. (3) That accommodation continue
> to be secured for the applicant and his family up to and including 16 October 1980.'

Section 1(1) of the 1977 Act gives a definition of homelessness. It provides:
d
> 'A person is homeless for the purpose of the Act if he has no accommodation
> ... (a) which he, together with any other person who normally resides with him as
> a member of his family or in circumstances in which the housing authority consider
> it reasonable for that person to reside with him—(i) is entitled to occupy by virtue
> of an interest in it or an order of a court, or (ii) has, in England and Wales, an express
> or implied licence to occupy ...'
e
The council conceded, and rightly conceded, that on 2nd October 1980, and indeed
from 8th September onwards, the applicant was homeless within the meaning of the
1977 Act. The council then had to decide the following questions: (a) was the applicant
in 'priority need' within the meaning of the Act? and (b) if so, was his homelessness
intentional or not?
Section 2(1) defines 'priority need' in the following terms: *f*

> 'For the purposes of this Act a homeless person ... has a priority need for
> accommodation when the housing authority are satisfied that he is within one of
> the following categories:—(a) he has dependent children who are residing with him
> or who might reasonably be expected to reside with him ...'

Glidewell J in the Divisional Court had no difficulty in deciding that under s 2(1)(a) *g*
the question 'might reasonably be expected to reside' with the homeless person only
arises if at the material time the dependent children are not residing with him. The
word 'or' does not mean 'and'. He therefore held that the council were wrong in
concluding that the applicant was not in priority need. Against this decision there is no
cross-appeal.
Accordingly the only issue which we have to consider is: was there material available *h*
to the council which could properly justify their decision that the applicant had become
homeless intentionally?
The material sections of the 1977 Act are ss 16 and 17. Section 16 defines the meaning
of 'accommodation available for occupation'. I will therefore set out the material terms
of s 17 with that incorporation: *j*

> '(1) ... a person becomes homeless intentionally if he deliberately does or fails to
> do anything in consequences of which he ceases to occupy accommodation which
> is [available for occupation both by him and by any other person who might
> reasonably be expected to reside with him] and which it would have been reasonable
> for him to continue to occupy ...'

a It will be recalled that the decision of the council that the applicant intentionally rendered himself homeless was based on the contention that he had 'deliberately arranged for his wife and children to leave accommodation which it would have been reasonable for them to continue to occupy'. This is a reference to the Bangladesh accommodation and not the accommodation at 120 Cowley Hill Road, which the applicant had been occupying since August 1979. Counsel for the council submits, and in my judgment rightly submits, that the English accommodation cannot qualify as accommodation
b which is available for his occupation, because it was so obviously quite inadequate to accommodate the applicant and his family, his wife and children being by the date of the decision persons who might reasonably be expected to reside with him.

Counsel seeks to justify the council's decision by what he accepts, quite frankly, is an artificial view of the facts. He contends that the accommodation in the parents' home in Bangladesh was available for occupation both by the applicant and his family. As I have
c already indicated, the evidence on this is sparse indeed, five visits of an undefined period and no description of the accommodation. Counsel submits that when the Act provides that 'he ceases to occupy' such accommodation that must be read as including both the applicant and those who are residing with him. I would not seek to criticise such an interpretation, but can *he* be said in reality to have been 'occupying' that accommodation? In the context of the Act, where there are frequent references to the word 'reside',
d the word 'occupy' must have some element of permanence. It cannot, in my judgment, be extended to rare visits.

But, if I am wrong about that, where is the material to justify the conclusion that it would have been reasonable for *him* to continue to occupy the Bangladesh room or rooms? Significantly the decision of the council was that it would have been reasonable for the *wife* and *children* to continue to occupy those premises. They do not suggest that
e it would have been reasonable for the applicant as well to continue to occupy the Bangladesh premises. This is in no way surprising. There was no material to suggest that there was any opportunity for the applicant to make a gainful living in Bangladesh. The evidence was all one way. He had chosen over all these years to separate himself from his family, sending them such financial support as he could afford. It was clearly not a separation that he desired, since for the last six or more years he had been
f trying to get his wife and family to join him and had only recently obtained the requisite permission. The fallacy, in my respectful judgment, in the approach of counsel for the council is to be found in the circular argument which it appears to create. Unless the applicant finds accommodation to house himself and his family before they come to this country, then it is said he is intentionally making himself and his family homeless. But it is not suggested that he failed to take any steps reasonably open to him to find such
g accommodation. So how is he ever to implement the permission and get his family to join him, unless he can qualify for assistance from the council?

I fully appreciate that by virtue of s 113(2) of the Housing Act 1957, as amended by s (2) of the Housing (Homeless Persons) Act 1977, the applicant by bringing to this country his wife and four children, as he has been specifically authorised to do, has obtained priority on the housing list, which if he had continued to live alone would not
h have been available. He may well have thus achieved, under the points system that operates, priority over a husband and wife and a smaller family who have for long lived in unsatisfactory accommodation in the borough. However open to criticism that situation is or may be, it seems to me to be the result of the absence of that immigration control to which I have referred not applying to the applicant because he is a person who has settled in the United Kingdom before 1973. The 1977 Act is part of our social
j welfare legislation. It is concerned with homelessness in this country. One of its main purposes and functions is to keep the family unit together (see *Lewis v North Devon District Council* [1981] 1 All ER 27, [1981] 1 WLR 328). Much as I may regret the unanticipated advantages which the Act gives to persons in the position of the applicant, I cannot accept that the unrealistic approach to its interpretation, which the council seeks to put forward, can be justified.

I would accordingly decide that there was no material on which the council could properly have concluded that the applicant became homeless intentionally, within the meaning of the 1977 Act, and I would therefore have reluctantly allowed the appeal.   *a*

SIR DENYS BUCKLEY. The applicant came to this country from Bangladesh (then East Pakistan) in 1965 and has ever since lived and worked here in the London borough of Hillingdon. He has from time to time revisited his country of origin, Bangladesh, where his parents live. On one of these occasions in 1968 he married, and on that and *b* subsequent visits by the applicant to Bangladesh he and his wife have begotten four children. His wife and children have lived with the applicant's parents in Bangladesh. In August 1979 the applicant moved from other accommodation which he had occupied for many years at 5 Cowley Mill Road, Hillingdon, to new accommodation at 120 Cowley Mill Road consisting of a shared room. It seems that entry permits for the applicant's wife and the four children were issued in December 1979 authorising them *c* to come to this country. They arrived here on 27th April 1980 and have since been here with the applicant.

Until the arrival of his family in this country the applicant was not homeless for the purposes of the Housing (Homeless Persons) Act 1977. At all times before their arrival he had accommodation, and there was no one who normally resided with him as a member of his family or in circumstances in which it might have been considered *d* reasonable for that person to reside with him who fell to be taken into account under s 1(1) of the Act.

The 1977 Act emphasises in numerous places the importance placed by Parliament on any person who is homeless or threatened by homelessness being able to provide a home for himself and any dependent children who are living with him or who might reasonably be expected to live with him (see ss 1(1)(*a*) and 2(1)(*a*); see also ss 5, 16 and 18 *e* which contain several references to 'any person who might reasonably be expected to reside with him'). Until they reached this country the applicant's wife and children were certainly not residing with him in this country, nor were they then persons who might reasonably be expected to reside with him, for until they obtained entry permits and could travel to this country they could not enter the country. But as soon as they arrived in this country as permitted immigrants they became, in my opinion, persons who *f* might reasonably be expected to reside with him.

Section 16 of the 1977 Act provides that for the purposes of the Act accommodation is only available for a person's occupation if it is available for occupation both by him and by any other person who might reasonably be expected to reside with him. Such accommodation must obviously be reasonably adequate to house the applicant and any such other persons as aforesaid. In my judgment the share of a room at 120 Cowley Mill *g* Road could not possibly be regarded as available for occupation both by the applicant and his wife and four children, for it was accommodation of a kind which was inherently unsuitable and entirely inadequate to house the applicant and his family. Accordingly, in my judgment, the share of a room at 120 Cowley Mill Road thereupon ceased to be 'available' for the applicant's occupation for the purposes of the Act, with the consequences that the applicant ceased to have any accommodation and became homeless within the *h* meaning of s 1(1) of the Act.

If I am right that the applicant's children might in these circumstances be reasonably expected to reside with him, the applicant became a homeless person having a priority need (see s 2(1)(*a*)).

It would then be incumbent on the housing authority to inquire whether the applicant had become homeless intentionally (see s 3(2)(*b*)(ii)). Section 17(1) of the Act provides *j* that for the purposes of the Act a person becomes homeless intentionally if he deliberately does or fails to do anything in consequence of which he ceases to occupy accommodation which is available for his occupation and which it would have been reasonable for him to continue to occupy. By bringing his family here or by procuring that they came to join him here, the applicant, in my opinion, deliberately did something which had the effect of rendering the shared room at 120 Cowley Mill Road accommodation which was

a no longer available for his occupation within the terms of s 17(1). This would, it seems to me, have been so even if the applicant in fact continued to occupy his share of that room himself, for this share of the room would nevertheless have ceased to be 'available' for his occupation within s 17(1) by reason of s 16 of the Act.

With deference to Lord Denning MR, I do not feel able to regard the applicant's home as having been in Bangladesh throughout the period down to April 1980. In my view,

b he was resident in England at all relevant times and had his home here, notwithstanding that by force of circumstances he had to leave his wife and children in Bangladesh. What accommodation he then had was presumably adequate to his need, living on his own; but when his family arrived the position was completely changed. What had been adequate accommodation for himself alone was wholly unsuited for himself and his family as a family unit. He therefore ceased to occupy accommodation available for

c occupation by that family unit. It is on that ground that, in my judgment, the applicant must be regarded as homeless; and, since that homelessness was due to a deliberate act on the applicant's part in bringing his family to this country, he must be treated as having become homeless intentionally.

A possible alternative view might be that before April 1980 the applicant had accommodation available for himself and his family taking into account both the

d accommodation which he himself occupied in England and the accommodation occupied by his wife and children in Bangladesh and that by giving up the accommodation in Bangladesh the applicant ceased to occupy accommodation which was previously available for occupation by himself and his family and which it would have been reasonable for him to continue to occupy (see s 17(1)). Considerations of this kind would have been equally germane if the applicant's family had lived in the North of England

e instead of Bangladesh, too far from Hillingdon to enable the applicant to live there with them and remain in his employment at Hillingdon. It may be legitimate to regard the accommodation at Hillingdon and that in the North of England or in Bangladesh, as the case might be, as together constituting the home of the applicant and his family for the purposes of the Act. In such circumstances, in my view, the applicant would on vacating the accommodation in the North of England or in Bangladesh have ceased to occupy

f accommodation which had theretofore been available for occupation by himself and by other persons who might reasonably be expected to reside with him, leaving himself only with accommodation unsuitable and inadequate to accommodate his family unit and consequently not to be treated as 'available' for his occupation (see s 16). If the removal of his family from the North of England or from Bangladesh were the applicant's deliberate act and it would have been reasonable for him to continue to occupy the

g vacated accommodation, he would have become homeless intentionally under s 17(1) of the Act.

For these reasons I would dismiss this appeal.

Appeal dismissed. Leave to appeal to the House of Lords granted. Council to undertake to house applicant until hearing of appeal.

Solicitors: *Edward Mackie & Co*, Greenford (for the applicant); *J A Kosky*, Uxbridge (for the council).

Francis Rustin   Barrister.

R v Kelly and others

a

HOUSE OF LORDS
LORD WILBERFORCE, LORD EDMUND-DAVIES, LORD FRASER OF TULLYBELTON, LORD KEITH OF
KINKEL AND LORD ROSKILL
13th, 14th, 28th JULY 1981

b

*Criminal law – Jurisdiction – Ship – Foreign ship on high seas – Offence of criminal damage
committed by British subject on board foreign ship on high seas – Whether English courts having
jurisdiction to try offender – Whether offender 'belonging' to foreign ship on which he was a
passenger – Merchant Shipping Act 1894, s 686(1).*

The appellants, who were British subjects, damaged or destroyed various fittings on a *c*
Danish ship on which they were travelling as passengers between Denmark and
England. The ship was on the high seas at the time. The appellants were later charged
with criminal damage, contrary to s 1(1) of the Criminal Damage Act 1971, and,
notwithstanding that the offences occurred on a foreign ship on the high seas, were tried
and convicted in the Crown Court on the basis that the court had jurisdiction under
s 686(1)[a] of the Merchant Shipping Act 1894 to try them because they were each a British *d*
subject charged with having committed an offence 'on board [a] foreign ship to which he
[did] not belong'. They appealed, contending (i) that the acts committed by them were
not offences triable by an English court because at common law extra-territorial
jurisdiction on the high seas was confined to British ships and there was no express
provision in the 1971 Act extending that Act so as to apply to British subjects on board
foreign ships, and s 686(1) did not extend the ambit of English criminal law but was *e*
concerned only with establishing a venue for the trial of those offences committed
outside the United Kingdom which were otherwise justiciable under the criminal law in
England or Scotland, or, alternatively, (ii) that the appellants 'belonged' to the ship and
therefore s 686(1) did not apply. The Court of Appeal ([1981] 1 All ER 370) dismissed
their appeals. The appellants appealed to the House of Lords.

f

Held – The appeal would be dismissed for the following reasons—
(1) Section 686(1) of the 1894 Act was general in character and extended the ambit of
the jurisdiction of the English criminal courts to the various classes of persons mentioned
in the section. Accordingly, the jurisdiction conferred on English courts by s 686(1)
extended to any offence against English law committed by a British subject on board a
foreign ship on the high seas provided he did not 'belong' to the ship (see p 1099 *f* to *j*, *g*
p 1102 *h j*, p 1103 *b h j* and p 1104 *d e*, post).
(2) The appellants could not be described as 'belonging to the ship' in the ordinary
meaning of those words when used in the context of s 686(1) and accordingly, since they
had been on board a foreign ship to which they did not belong at the time the offences
were committed, the English court had power to try them for the offences (see p 1099 *f*
to *j* and p 1104 *b* to *e*, post); *The Fusilier* (1865) 3 Moo PCCNS 51 distinguished. *h*
Per Curiam. In considering whether a person 'belongs' to a ship no distinction should
be drawn between persons not members of the crew who are on board only for the
duration of a short voyage and those who are on board for a longer period of time, the
duration of the stay on board not being relevant (see p 1099 *f* to *j* and p 1104 *c d*, post).
Decision of the Court of Appeal [1981] 1 All ER 370 affirmed.

Notes

j

For offences on the high seas, see 11 Halsbury's Laws (4th Edn) para 78, and for cases on
the subject, see 14(1) Digest (Reissue) 158–161, 1103–1132.
For jurisdiction in respect of crimes committed out of England, see 11 Halsbury's

---

a   Section 686(1) is set out at p 1101 *c d*, post

Laws (4th Edn) para 87, and for cases on the subject, see 14(1) Digest (Reissue) 161–162,

a   *1133–1139*.

For the Merchant Shipping Act 1894, s 686, see 31 Halsbury's Statutes (3rd Edn) 383.
For the Criminal Damage Act 1971, s 1, see 41 ibid 409.

Case referred to in opinions

Fusilier, The (1865) 3 Moo PCCNS 51, Brown & Lush 341, 5 New Rep 453, 12 LT 186, 11

b   Jur NS 289, 2 Mar LC 177, 16 ER 19, PC, 1(1) Digest (Reissue) 388, 2716.

Appeals

The appellants, William Robert Kelly, David James Murphy and Stephen Paul Avison,
were convicted in the Crown Court at Newcastle upon Tyne on 18th October 1979
before his Honour Judge Stroyan QC on charges of causing criminal damage on the high
seas contrary to s 1(1) of the Criminal Damage Act 1971, having pleaded guilty to those
c   charges following a ruling by the judge that s 686 of the Merchant Shipping Act 1894
extended the English criminal law generally to acts of British subjects when passengers
on foreign ships on the high seas, and that the acts alleged against the appellants were
therefore subject to the English criminal law and within the jurisdiction of the Crown
Court. The appellants appealed. On 24th October 1980 the Court of Appeal, Criminal
Division (Lord Lane CJ, Stocker and Glidewell JJ) ([1981] 1 All ER 370, [1981] 2 WLR
d   112) dismissed the appeals and refused leave to appeal to the House of Lords but certified,
under s 33(2) of the Criminal Appeal Act 1968, that a point of law of general public
importance was involved in the decision. On 18th December 1980 the Appeal
Committee of the House of Lords gave the appellants leave to appeal against the
decision. The facts are set out in the opinion of Lord Roskill.

e   *Robin Stewart QC* and *Stephen Rich* for the appellants.
David Robson QC and *Brian Forster* for the Crown.

Their Lordships took time for consideration.

f   28th July. The following opinions were delivered.

LORD WILBERFORCE. My Lords, I have had the advantage of reading in draft the
speech of my noble and learned friend Lord Roskill, with which I concur and with the
answers that he proposes to the certified question. For the reasons given by him I would
dismiss these appeals.

g   **LORD EDMUND-DAVIES.** My Lords, for the reasons developed in the speech of
my noble and learned friend Lord Roskill, which I have had the advantage of reading in
draft, I would answer as he does the question of law certified by the Court of Appeal,
Criminal Division, and I would accordingly dismiss these appeals.

LORD FRASER OF TULLYBELTON. My Lords, I have had the advantage of
h   reading in draft the speech of my noble and learned friend Lord Roskill, and I agree with
it and with the answers that he proposes to the certified question. For the reasons given
by him I would dismiss these appeals.

LORD KEITH OF KINKEL. My Lords, I agree with the speech to be delivered by
my noble and learned friend Lord Roskill, which I have had the opportunity of reading
in draft, and would accordingly answer the certified questions as proposed by him, and
j   dismiss the appeals.

LORD ROSKILL. My Lords, on 16th October 1979 at the Crown Court at Newcastle
upon Tyne, all three appellants faced charges of criminal damage committed on board
the Danish motor vessel Winston Churchill, when on the high seas in November 1978,
contrary to s 1(1) of the Criminal Damage Act 1971. The appellants Kelly and Murphy
faced one such charge (count 1) and the appellant Avison two (counts 2 and 3). Avison

also faced two counts of theft but these were not proceeded with and are no longer
relevant. Unusually, written demurrers were signed on behalf of all the appellants at the
outset of the trial. These averred that the Crown Court ought not to take cognisance of
the indictment since the offences there charged were not committed within the
jurisdiction of the court. Elaborate legal argument followed over some two days, and on
18th October 1979 the trial judge, his Honour Judge Stroyan QC, delivered a long and
careful judgment overruling the demurrers. He held that the court possessed the
requisite jurisdiction and that in those circumstances the trial must proceed.

My Lords, in those circumstances the appellants pleaded guilty to the three counts I
have mentioned. Each was then sentenced to undergo a period of community service
and to pay £300 compensation. The appellants thereupon appealed against their several
convictions, the issue of law being that previously raised on the demurrers in the Crown
Court at Newcastle. The appeal was heard by the Court of Appeal, Criminal Division
(Lord Lane CJ, Stocker and Glidewell JJ). On 24th October 1980 that court in a judgment
prepared by Glidewell J dismissed the appeal ([1981] 1 All ER 370, [1981] 2 WLR 112)
but at the request of counsel for the appellants certified the point of law as one of general
public importance:

'Whether the English criminal law, and more particularly the Criminal Damage
Act 1971, extends to the acts of British subjects when passengers on foreign ships
when on the high seas and whether the English courts have power to try such
persons for such acts by virtue of section 686 subsection 1 of the Merchant Shipping
Act 1894 or any other rule of law.'

The Court of Appeal, Criminal Division, refused leave to appeal to your Lordships'
Houses but that leave was subsequently granted by this House.

My Lords, as will later emerge, I venture to question whether the formulation of the
point of law certified, which appears to have emanated from counsel for the appellants,
is susceptible of a monosyllabic answer, whether in the affirmative or the negative. But
it is plain enough that the central question intended to be raised by the appeal is whether,
by reason of s 686(1) of the Merchant Shipping Act 1894, the Crown Court had
jurisdiction to try the appellants, all British subjects, for the offences charged, since the
acts relied on as constituting those offences took place on a foreign ship on the high
seas. Leading counsel for the appellants, in his clear and able argument, did not shrink
from condemning the behaviour of the appellants on board the Winston Churchill as
disgraceful. So it was. But, however unmeritorious their conduct, they must not be
allowed to be convicted of the offences charged unless the law of this country clearly
provides that in the events in question the Crown Court had jurisdiction to try them.

My Lords, it is a remarkable fact that it is nearly ninety years since s 686(1) of the 1894
Act first appeared on the statute book. But the arguments presented in the present
appeals have never before been advanced. One imagines that in that period there must
have been many cases where British subjects have misbehaved on board foreign ships on
the high seas and been prosecuted to conviction by virtue of this subsection. Indeed,
leading counsel for the Crown told your Lordships that his information was that there
had been such cases over the years, heard in magistrates' courts on the north-east, east and
south-east coasts of England. Yet the present submissions have never previously been
advanced for the purpose of denying jurisdiction in the court before whom the offenders
have been brought. Tribute should therefore be paid to the ingenuity of those to whom
the possibility of advancing these submissions first occurred, for as the arguments before
your Lordships' House developed it became clear that the submissions had considerable
force, especially when s 686(1) is looked at historically.

My Lords, for ease of reference I will set out all those sections of the 1894 Act to which
reference was made, as well as s 686(1):

'**511.**—(1) Where a British or foreign vessel is wrecked, stranded, or in distress at
any place on or near the coasts of the United Kingdom or any tidal water within the
limits of the United Kingdom, the receiver of wreck for the district in which that

a
place is situate shall, upon being made acquainted with the circumstance, forthwith proceed there, and upon his arrival shall take the command of all persons present, and shall assign such duties and give such directions to each person as he thinks fit for the preservation of the vessel and of the lives of the persons belonging to the vessel (in this Part of this Act referred to as shipwrecked persons) and of the cargo and apparel of the vessel . . .

b
'544.—(1) Where services are rendered wholly or in part within British waters in saving life from any British or foreign vessel, or elsewhere in saving life from any British vessel, there shall be payable to the salvor by the owner of the vessel, cargo, or apparel saved, a reasonable amount of salvage, to be determined in case of dispute in manner herein-after mentioned . . .

'686.—(1) Where any person, being a British subject, is charged with having committed any offence on board any British ship on the high seas or in any foreign
c
port or harbour or on board any foreign ship to which he does not belong, or, not being a British subject, is charged with having committed any offence on board any British ship on the high seas, and that person is found within the jurisdiction of any court in Her Majesty's dominions, which would have had cognizance of the offence if it had been committed on board a British ship within the limits of its ordinary jurisdiction, that court shall have jurisdiction to try the offence as if it had been so
d
committed . . .

'687. All offences against property or person committed in or at any place either ashore or afloat out of Her Majesty's dominions by any master, seaman, or apprentice who at the time when the offence is committed is, or within three months previously has been, employed in any British ship shall be deemed to be offences of the same nature respectively, and be liable to the same punishments respectively,
e
and be inquired of, heard, tried, determined, and adjudged in the same manner and by the same courts and in the same places as if those offences had been committed within the jurisdiction of the Admiralty of England . . .'

My Lords, the argument founded on s 686(1) was twofold. First, it was said that the subsection did not in any way extend the ambit of English or, indeed, Scottish criminal
f
law: it was not, to borrow the language of counsel for the appellants, an offence-making section. It was concerned only with establishing a venue for the trial of those offenders whose offences committed outside the United Kingdom were otherwise justiciable under the criminal law of England or Scotland. Second, it was said that, even if the subsection did have the overall effect contended for by the Crown, the appellants, being passengers on the Winston Churchill, 'belonged' to her and were therefore in any event not within the subsection. The validity of these submissions must depend on the true construction
g
of the subsection.

My Lords, the argument from the appellants started from the undoubted, and indeed admitted, fact that Criminal Damage Act 1971 does not have extra-territorial effect. In other words, a British subject who does an act outside England and Wales, which if done in England and Wales would constitute an offence against that Act, is not liable to prosecution and conviction in England or Wales for that act so done outside. As Professor
h
Glanville Williams QC expresses the point in the first of three valuable articles entitled Venue and the Ambit of Criminal Law ((1965) 81 LQR 276, 395, 518) criminal jurisdiction is linked with territory. There are, of course, a number of well-known statutory exceptions to this rule, for example, s 9 of the Offences against the Person Act 1861 (murder or manslaughter by a British subject committed on land outside the
j
United Kingdom) and s 31(1) of the Criminal Justice Act 1948 (offences by servants of the Crown committed outside the United Kingdom). See also Archbold's Pleading, Evidence and Practice in Criminal Cases (40th Edn, 1979, §§192–204). But, so the appellants' submissions ran, the basic rule is clear and s 686(1) of the 1894 Act does not on its true construction render a British subject who does an act of criminal damage on a foreign vessel on the high seas liable to prosecution and conviction in England for an offence against the Criminal Damage Act 1971, since it is conceded that that Act has no extra-

territorial effect. Section 686(1) must, therefore, be construed as concerned only with venue for the trial of those offences committed abroad which are otherwise justiciable *a* here.

My Lords, I propose first to examine these submissions by reference only to the language of the subsection and without regard to its genealogy, for it is common ground that the subsection, though also in part reproducing s 21 of the Merchant Shipping Act Amendment Act 1855 and s 11 of the Merchant Shipping Act 1867 introduced additional provisions beyond those previously on the statute book. In passing I note that it appears *b* to be the curious fact that these two last-mentioned sections, though seemingly overlapping, remained concurrently in force until repealed by Sch 22 to the 1894 Act.

My Lords, s 686(1) of the 1894 Act is directed to two classes of person. First, British subjects and, second, non-British subjects. It is directed to those British subjects who commit offences, which I take to mean who do acts which if done in England and Wales or Scotland would be offences against the respective criminal law of those countries, *c* either on board a British ship on the high seas or in any foreign port or harbour or on board any foreign ship to which they do not belong. It is further directed to non-British subjects who commit offences on a British ship on the high seas. The subsection then provides that, if any such person (be he British subject or non-British subject) is found within the jurisdiction of any court in any of Her Majesty's dominions which would have had jurisdiction to try that person for that offence if committed on board a British *d* ship 'within the limits of its ordinary jurisdiction', that court shall have the jurisdiction to try the offences in question 'as if it had been so committed', that is to say committed on board a British ship within the limits of the ordinary jurisdiction of that court.

My Lords, your Lordships' House is presently only concerned with that part of the subsection which affects British subjects on foreign ships. In the second of the articles to which I have already referred (81 LQR 395 at 411) Professor Glanville Williams asks: *e*

> 'Was this section intended to extend the English law of indictable offences *generally* to British subjects travelling on foreign ships, or was it intended merely as a venue provision applicable only where such British travellers were otherwise subject to the law . . . ?'

The learned author gives as an illustration of the latter situation what might be regarded *f* as the somewhat improbable example of bigamy committed by a British subject on a foreign ship.

If the construction contended for by the appellants be correct, and the subsection be construed as concerned only with venue, its practical effect would be negligible. I therefore ask why in order to achieve so little so drastic an alteration was made to the law in 1894. Pressed to say what disciplinary control there could be over miscreant British *g* subjects on board foreign ships were his submission to be correct, counsel for the appellants was constrained to say that their offences would fall to be dealt with by the courts of the country to which the vessel belonged in accordance with the law of the vessel's flag. But this is hardly a satisfactory form of control of miscreants returning to the United Kingdom on a foreign ship, and were the flag to be one of what is today called 'convenience' the power of control and punishment would be likely, in most cases, to be *h* for all practical purposes non-existent.

My Lords, I find it difficult to believe that Parliament in 1894 can have intended this result. It seems infinitely more likely that the underlying intention was to enable miscreant British subjects on foreign ships to be dealt with in the courts of the place where they were 'found', the offending acts which they had done outside the jurisdiction being treated as offences committed within the jurisdiction of the court where these *j* persons were found. It is, as I think, the reiterated emphasis in the subsection on the word 'offence' which points the way to the correct construction of this subsection. First, regard must be had to the offence with which the offenders are charged, that is to say the acts done on the foreign ship alleged to constitute the offence. The offenders are then to be tried in the relevant part of the United Kingdom or of other parts of Her Majesty's dominions as if those acts had been committed on a British ship within the limits of the

ordinary jurisdiction of the courts within the jurisdiction of which the offenders are
a found.

In my opinion, all the indications are that the intention of the relevant part of the
subsection is directed to ensuring that these offenders are swiftly brought to justice
wherever they may be found. The subsection, of course, applies equally to Scotland as to
England and Wales, though this seemingly was overlooked in argument in the courts
below. The Crown would have to show in each case that the acts done constituted an
b offence against the relevant criminal law, whether of England and Wales or of Scotland
as the case might be. I accordingly have reached the same conclusion as the trial judge
and the Court of Appeal, Criminal Division, simply as a matter of the construction of the
subsection.

But it was argued for the appellants that, if the genealogy of the subsection be
examined, its legislative history supports the view for which the appellants contended.
c Counsel for the appellants helpfully drew your Lordships' attention to a series of statutes
beginning with the Offences at Sea Act 1536 and followed by the Offences at Sea Act
1799, the Admiralty Offences Act 1844 and the Admiralty Offences (Colonial) Act
1849. My Lords, I agree that if regard be paid only to these statutes there is much to be
said in favour of the view that the relevant parts, to which it is not necessary to refer in
detail, were concerned only with venue and not with creating offences. But when one
d comes first to the 1855 and then to the 1867 Acts, it seems to me that a different pattern
emerges. Section 21 of the 1855 Act reads thus:

> 'If any person, being a British subject, charged with having committed any crime
> or offence on board any British ship on the high seas or in any foreign port or
> harbour, or if any person, not being a British subject, charged with having
> committed any crime or offence on board any British ship on the high seas, is found
e > within the jurisdiction of any court of justice in Her Majesty's dominions which
> would have had cognizance of such crime or offence if committed within the limits
> of its ordinary jurisdiction, such Court shall have jurisdiction to hear and try the
> case as if such crime or offence had been committed within such limits . . .'

Section 11 of the 1867 Act provides:
f
> 'If any *British* subject commits any Crime or Offence on board any *British* Ship, or
> on board any Foreign Ship to which he does not belong, any Court of Justice in Her
> Majesty's Dominions, which would have had Cognizance of such Crime or Offence
> if committed on board a *British* Ship within the Limits of the ordinary Jurisdiction
> of such Court, shall have Jurisdiction to hear and determine the Case as if the said
> Crime or Offence had been committed as last aforesaid.'
g
My Lords, one thus finds in these two sections indications of a change of policy
designed, as I think, to enable persons to be tried in any court in any part of Her Majesty's
dominions for offences committed in the several circumstances respectively dealt with in
these sections as if those offences had been committed within the jurisdiction of such a
court. In 1894 this policy is taken one step further by the provisions enacted in
h s 686(1). Clearly, this subsection is not confined to offences created by the 1894 Act
itself. It is entirely general in character and to my mind was designed, like the two
earlier sections to which I have referred, to extend the territorial aspect of the criminal
law to the various classes of persons mentioned in this section, including British subjects
on foreign ships to which they did not belong.

Counsel for the appellants also sought support for his submissions from s 687 of the
j 1894 Act. I do not however think that this section sheds any light on the present
problem since although it immediately follows s 686 it has a completely different origin:
see s 267 of the Merchant Shipping Act 1854.

I can deal more briefly with the second submission, namely, that the appellants as
passengers 'belonged to the ship' and are therefore in any event without the subsection.
This argument was founded on the decision in *The Fusilier* (1865) 3 Moo PCCNS 51, 16
ER 19, a decision on s 458 of the 1854 Act (see now ss 511 and 544 of the 1894 Act). In

their context of entitlement to life salvage, the words were construed as including
passengers as well as crew, a decision obviously sensible in that context. Counsel for the **a**
appellants argued that similar words in the same statute should be given the same
meaning, and that, when Parliament in s 686(1) used the phrase 'or on board any foreign
ship to which he does not belong' after the decision in *The Fusilier*, it must be taken to
have intended that the same meaning be given to that phrase as had previously been
given to similar words in s 458 of the 1854 Act. In my view this argument is weakened
by a number of considerations. First, the context in which the phrase appears in s 686(1) **b**
is wholly different from that of the subsection which was construed in *The Fusilier*.
Second, successive editions of Temperley's Merchant Shipping Acts in a note to s 686(1)
have questioned, rightly in my view, whether the reasoning in *The Fusilier* has any
application to the phrase when used in that subsection. My Lords, I do not believe that
anyone using ordinary language would for one moment describe the appellants 'as
belonging' to the Winston Churchill. In my view this submission is unsound and fails. **c**
I would only add that with respect I find myself unable to agree with the distinction
suggested at the end of the judgment of the Court of Appeal, Criminal Division, between
persons not members of the crew who are on board only for the duration of a short
voyage and those who are on board for a longer period of time. I do not think that the
duration of the stay on board is relevant to this question.

My Lords, I have already said that the certified question does not permit of a simple **d**
monosyllabic answer. I would answer it by saying that 'by virtue of s 686(1) of the
Merchant Shipping Act 1894 the Crown Court had jurisdiction to try the appellants for
the several offences against the Criminal Damages Act 1971 with which they stood
charged'.

My Lords, I would therefore affirm the convictions of the appellants and dismiss these
appeals. **e**

Appeals dismissed.

Solicitors: *Park Nelson & Doyle Devonshire*, agents for *Molyneux, McKeag & Cooper*,
Gosforth (for the appellants); *Collyer-Bristow*, agents for *D E Brown*, Newcastle upon Tyne
(for the Crown). **f**

Mary Rose Plummer   Barrister.

Practice Direction **g**

FAMILY DIVISION

Probate – Grant – Trust corporation – Corporation appointed executor on terms and conditions
in existence at date of will – Terms and conditions not limiting corporation's power to take full
grant – Production of terms and conditions not necessary where oath contains statement to that **h**
effect.

The following practice is to be followed on all applications for grants made on or after 3rd
August 1981 by trust corporations where the corporation has been appointed as executor
on terms and conditions specifically referred to as being in existence at the date of the
will or of its republication as the case may be. **j**

Provided that the oath contains a statement to the effect that nothing in these terms
and conditions limits the corporation's power to take a full grant, it will not normally be
necessary to produce them on the application.

R L BAYNE-POWELL
30th July 1981   Senior Registrar.

a

Re T (a barrister)

VISITORS OF LINCOLN'S INN
WHITFORD, EWBANK AND BINGHAM JJ
1st, 19th MAY 1981

b *Counsel – Disciplinary jurisdiction – Judges as visitors of Inns of Court – Jurisdiction – Validity of rules of professional conduct – Whether disciplinary proceedings appropriate place to consider validity of rules of professional conduct.*

Counsel – Professional misconduct – Advising without intervention of a solicitor – Non-contentious business – Validity of rule requiring intervention of a solicitor.

c
Counsel – Professional misconduct – Inquiries on behalf of client – Inquiries concerning prosecuting authorities' policy as to prosecuting dishonest conduct – Whether professional misconduct to make such inquiries.

The appellant, a barrister, represented F who, with other defendants, was tried on
d indictment for conspiracy to defraud, the nature of the fraud alleged being what was known as a 'carbon paper fraud'. F was acquitted. Following the trial, the appellant agreed at two meetings with F to give legal advice to F and companies under F's control or management on the conduct and disposition of his and their affairs in consideration of a retainer of £100 a week. No solicitor was concerned in the making of the agreement or in the retainer. Shortly afterwards the appellant telephoned the police sergeant who
e had been in charge of the prosecution of F to make inquiries on F's behalf to find out whether the police were still investigating carbon paper frauds and whether the Director of Public Prosecutions had directed that no more carbon paper frauds were to be prosecuted. A disciplinary tribunal of the Senate of the Inns of Court and the Bar found the appellant guilty of attempting, while acting on behalf of F, to elicit information from the police sergeant as to the policy which in future would be adopted by the Director of
f Public Prosecutions which might have been of assistance to F and of accepting a total of £400 from one of F's companies for providing legal advice without the intervention of a solicitor. The tribunal ordered the appellant to be suspended from practice as a barrister for four months. The appellant appealed to the judges of the High Court as visitors of his Inn of Court, contending that the adoption by the Bar of a general rule prohibiting the acceptance of direct instructions from a paying client in non-contentious
g matters was without legal effect unless or until it received the approval of the judges, and that, even if the rule had been adopted by the Bar and was prima facie binding on members, the visitors had the right to quash any conviction based on the rule if they considered the rule to be contrary to the public interest and in the circumstances they should do so. The appellant further contended that barristers frequently made inquiries of official sources concerning current policy and that in the circumstances the appellant
h had not been guilty of any professional misconduct in making inquiries of the police sergeant.

Held – The appeal against the findings of the tribunal and its order would be dismissed for the following reasons—
    (1) The rules of professional conduct of the Bar (as of most other professions) were rules
j which were, and were properly, determined by the profession itself in the light of tradition and experience, changing and developing over the years as circumstances changed. Although a rule which was acceptable to the Bar but which was held by the judges, in whatever capacity, to be contrary to public policy or to be liable to undermine the proper administration of justice would be ineffective, the responsibility for formulating rules of professional conduct rested with the Bar through its appropriate procedure, and rules so formulated did not require the sanction of the judges as a

condition of their validity (see p 1109 j to p 1110 a d e and j, post); dictum of Lord Campbell CJ in *Doe d Bennett v Hale* (1850) 15 QB at 186 explained.

(2) There had never been a right to obtain the advice of counsel in non-contentious matters without the intervention of a solicitor, since for such a right to exist there would have had to have been a duty on counsel to give such advice in a proper case when asked and no such duty had ever existed (see p 1109 h j and p 1110 d e j, post).

(3) Even if the visitors possessed power to decline to sanction the rule that it was wrong for a barrister to do non-contentious legal work for clients in the course of his profession for fees without instructions, it was not in the circumstances appropriate for the visitors to determine issues of policy with potentially far-reaching implications within the confines of a hearing in which most interested parties were necessarily unrepresented and most of the relevant material was not before the visitors (see p 1110 b to e and j, post).

(4) In relation to conduct which was plainly dishonest it was improper conduct for a barrister to make inquiries of the prosecuting authorities to discover where they drew the line between conduct which would lead to criminal proceedings and conduct which would not. Furthermore, the impropriety of such an inquiry was compounded by making the approach to a very junior police officer on the strength of a casual acquaintance in an earlier case (see p 1110 e to j, post).

Notes

For the necessity for the intervention of a solicitor, see 3 Halsbury's Laws (4th Edn) paras 1120–1121, and for cases on the subject, see 3 Digest (Reissue) 758, 4564–4566.

For disciplinary authority over barristers, see 3 Halsbury's Laws (4th Edn) para 1134, and for cases on the subject, see 3 Digest (Reissue) 746–748, 4452–4461.

Case referred to in decision

Doe d Bennett v Hale (1850) 15 QB 171, 19 LJQB 353, 15 LTOS 136, 14 Jur 830, 117 ER 423, 3 Digest (Reissue) 758, 4564.

Cases also cited

Rondel v Worsley [1967] 3 All ER 993, [1969] 1 AC 191, HL.
S (a barrister), Re [1969] 1 All ER 949, [1970] 1 QB 160, Visitors of Gray's Inn.
Saif Ali v Sydney Mitchell & Co (a firm) [1978] 3 All ER 1033, [1980] AC 198, HL; *rvsg* [1977] 3 All ER 744, [1978] QB 95, CA.

Appeal

T, a barrister, appealed to Her Majesty's Judges sitting as visitors of the Honourable Society of Lincoln's Inn against the findings and order of the disciplinary tribunal of the Senate of the Inns of Court and the Bar made on 13th December 1980 that he be suspended from practice as a barrister and from enjoyment of all rights and privileges as a member of Lincoln's Inn for a period of four months. The respondent to the appeal was the Professional Conduct Committee of the Bar Council. The visitors heard the appeal in private but pronounced their findings in public. The facts are set out in the decision of the visitors.

Quentin Edwards QC for the appellant.
F B Smedley QC for the respondent.

Cur adv vult

19th May. **WHITFORD J** read the following decision of the visitors: This is an appeal by a barrister of Lincoln's Inn against the findings and order of a disciplinary tribunal of the Senate made on 13th December 1980. We hear this appeal as judges nominated to act as visitors of Lincoln's Inn.

The charges preferred against the appellant were (1) that on 9th February 1979, when acting on behalf of a client, Michael Finch, who was the subject of an investigation by a Det Sgt Robin James, of the Metropolitan and City Police company fraud branch, he

improperly attempted to elicit information from Det Sgt James as to the policy which in
a future would be adopted by the Director of Public Prosecutions which information
might have been of assistance to his client and (2) that he between 9th February and 23rd
March 1979 accepted a total of £700 from a company, Foilcroft Ltd, for providing legal
advice without the intervention of a solicitor.

The factual basis of the Senate's case was succinctly summarised in the appellant's
petition of appeal, in these terms:

b
'(a) Finch was tried, together with other defendants, upon an indictment alleging
conspiracy to defraud. The nature of the fraud alleged was what is known as a
'carbon paper fraud'. The trial of the indictment was at the Central Criminal Court
from 6th November to 21st December, 1978. Finch was represented by the
Appellant, did not give evidence and was acquitted.

'(b) By an agreement made at two meetings between the Appellant and Finch, the
c first in the Appellant's chambers at the end of January, 1979 and the second in a
restaurant on 5th February, 1979, the Appellant agreed to give legal advice to Finch
and to companies under his control or management upon the conduct and
disposition of his and their affairs in consideration of a retainer of £100 a week. No
solicitor was concerned in the making of this agreement or in the retainer.

'(c) On 9th February, 1979 the Appellant telephoned Sergeant James, who had
d been the officer in charge of the prosecution in the trial mentioned in (a) above. The
gist of the conversation was that the Appellant asked Sergeant James to discuss with
him areas considered by the police to amount to criminal acts in stationery sales
methods. The Appellant said that he was making the inquiry on behalf of Finch.
Sergeant James said that, as counsel, the Appellant should know what the situation
was. Former cases of "carbon paper" frauds were briefly mentioned and the
e Appellant said that he wanted to study in depth the areas amounting to deception.
The Appellant went on to ask whether the police were still continuing inquiries on
"carbon paper" frauds, to which Sergeant James gave a general answer that
complaints would continue to be investigated. The Appellant then asked whether
the Director of Public Prosecutions had directed that no more "carbon paper" frauds
should be prosecuted because of the expense and Sergeant James said that he
f doubted whether any such directive had been given as any criminal offence would
be investigated. In the course of the conversation the Appellant invited Sergeant
James to have a meal or a drink with him.

'(d) The Appellant received the following payments, by cheques drawn by
Foilcroft Ltd., pursuant to the agreement mentioned in 1(ii) above:—

g
9.2.79.	£100	
16.2.79.	£100	
23.2.79.	£100	
9.3.79.	£200	
23.3.79.	£200	£700.'

h   The Senate did not accept this summary in its entirety, but their reservations are not
in our judgment material for present purposes.

The tribunal found both charges to be proved. In so finding , however, the tribunal
made it plain that they did not find that the appellant was at any material period aware
that there were currently pending inquiries with regard either to Mr Finch or the
companies with which he was concerned. Further, with regard to the second charge, the
j tribunal found the charge proved to the extent of £400 only, and not £700.

The tribunal ordered that the appellant should be suspended from practice as a
barrister and from enjoyment of all rights and privileges as a member of Lincoln's Inn
for a period of four months. The appeal before us is against both the findings and the
order of the tribunal.

In the course of his skilful and attractive submissions counsel for the appellant
contended that the first charge preferred against the appellant disclosed no conduct

amounting to professional misconduct and that the second was bad in law. This second submission largely occupied the hearing before us, and it is convenient to deal with it *a* first. It raises questions of some general importance, and for this reason we have thought it right to pronounce our findings in public.

The tribunal's finding on the second charge is plainly founded on the basic proposition of the Senate that it was professionally improper for the appellant to advise Mr Finch or his company for reward in non-contentious matters without being instructed to do so by a solicitor. That the matters to be advised on were non-contentious follows from the *b* conclusion that the appellant at the relevant time knew of no current inquiries (still less proceedings) affecting Mr Finch or his companies. Counsel strongly attacked the Senate's basic proposition. If, he submitted, the Bar had ever purported to adopt a general rule prohibiting the acceptance of direct instructions from a paying client in non-contentious matters (and he criticised the mode of adoption as quite inadequate in all the circumstances), such adoption was without legal effect unless or until it received the *c* approval of the judges, with whom lies the ultimate responsibility for overseeing and regulating the conduct of members of the Bar. Furthermore, he submitted, even if this rule had been adopted by the Bar and was prima facie binding on members, we have as visitors the right to quash any conviction based on a rule which we consider to be contrary to the public interest and we should do so in this instance.

In support of his submissions counsel referred us to the background history of the *d* present rule (if it be such) which we would summarise briefly as follows.

1. In 1850 it was the approved practice that counsel appearing in court, whether in a criminal or a civil matter, should be instructed by a solicitor, but there was no rule of law that he had to be. So much emerges from *Doe d Bennett v Hale* (1850) 15 QB 171, 117 ER 423, where a new trial was ordered because counsel not instructed by an attorney had been prevented from cross-examining or addressing the jury. It was a matter on which, *e* said Lord Campbell CJ, a rule could have been laid down but had not been. But the Lord Chief Justice made plain his preference for the prevailing practice (15 QB 171 at 186, 117 ER 423 at 429):

'Exceptional cases may again occur, though very rarely, when it may be fit for barristers to plead in civil suits, instructed only by the parties; but I hope that they will continue generally to adhere to what has been considered the etiquette of the *f* Bar. Although conscientiously bound and ever ready to render their best assistance for the discovery of truth and the vindication of right, they are at liberty, under the controul of the Courts, to lay down conditions upon which, for the public good, their services are to be obtained.'

2. In 1888 the professional rule hardened. A member of the Bar wrote to Sir Richard Webster QC, the Attorney General of the day, and raised the questions: 'May a barrister *g* advise and otherwise act for the outside client, and receive a fee direct, without the intervention of a solicitor? To what extent, if at all, is this right limited after a writ has been issued?' The Attorney General replied in a letter which was published in the Law Times on 7th July 1888 (85 LT Jo 176). The material passage reads as follows:

'It is essential to keep in view throughout the distinction between contentious *h* and non-contentious business. With reference to contentious business, in my opinion neither before nor after litigation is commenced should a barrister act or advise without the intervention of a solicitor. One very grave reason for this rule is obvious. In contentious business, which frequently affects the rights of other persons, it is most important that the facts should be, as far as possible, accurately ascertained before advice is given. For this purpose, as a barrister cannot himself *j* make proper inquiry as to the actual facts, it is essential that he should be able to rely on the responsibility of a solicitor as to the statement of facts put before him. As regards non-contentious business, the case is, in my opinion, somewhat different. It is scarcely possible to state the rule in a way which will be absolutely accurate under all circumstances, but speaking generally, there is, in my opinion, no objection to a barrister seeing and advising a lay client, without the intervention of a solicitor a   upon points relating to the lay client's own personal conduct or guidance or the management or disposition of his own affairs or transactions. I only desire to add that great care should be exercised by members of the Bar who do advise lay clients to abstain from advising upon matters which are in effect of a contentious character.'

The Attorney General was then the mouthpiece of the Bar and it is not doubted that his opinion was regarded as an authoritative statement during the years which followed.

b   3. At the annual general meeting of the Bar on 11th July 1955 the Attorney General (Sir Reginald Manningham-Buller QC) said:

'While it is not a breach of etiquette for a barrister to give advice free on legal matters to a friend or relative, or to poor persons, it is wrong for a barrister to do non-contentious legal work for clients in the course of his profession for fees without instructions, save in particular cases, such as, for example, advising a foreign lawyer on non-contentious matters in which no litigation in this country is contemplated or in progress.'

c

This statement was published in the Annual Statement of the General Council of the Bar 1955 (p 20). Sir Richard Webster's opinion was also referred to, followed by the observation that 'The Council has taken the view that the above opinion is no longer in accord with existing practice'.

d   4. This publication provoked opposition among some members of the Bar. Notice was given of a motion, to be moved at the 1956 annual general meeting, seeking the reinstatement of Sir Richard Webster's ruling. This motion was, however, withdrawn. At the annual general meeting on 9th July 1956 the Attorney General referred to his statement the previous year and to Sir Richard Webster's ruling and reiterated that in his view it was now generally improper for a barrister to do legal work for clients in the

e   course of his profession without instructions and for fees. He acknowledged, however, that the new ruling recognised exceptions, and the council intended to publish a list of them for the guidance of the Bar. (A list was duly published later in the year.) When the adoption of the council's annual statement for 1955 was moved, the resolution was carried nem con. The new rule was never submitted to the judges for their approval, but it has not (so far as we know) been the subject of any formal challenge in the years since

f   1956. The recently promulgated Code of Conduct (which appeared well after the matters giving rise to this appeal) reflects the 1956 ruling.

While suggesting that a rule of this importance should have been specifically submitted to members of the Bar for their approval, counsel was constrained to acknowledge that approval of the 1955 annual statement necessarily involved approval of the ruling on professional conduct which it contained. He therefore urged that, even

g   if the Bar had adopted this ruling, it had no power to do so. The public had a right, recognised by usage since time immemorial, to consult counsel in non-contentious matters without the intervention of a solicitor. This was a right (it was said) which could be taken away only by Parliament or the judges, not by the Bar alone. The 1955 statement and the 1956 resolution were accordingly devoid of legal effect.

We cannot accept this submission. In the first place, there has never been a *right* to

h   obtain the advice of counsel in non-contentious matters without the intervention of a solicitor. For such a right to exist there would have to be a duty on counsel to give such advice in a proper case when asked (as, on the familiar 'cab rank' principle, there is ordinarily a duty to accept instructions to appear in court). But Sir Richard Webster's ruling certainly suggests no such duty and there is no ground known to us for believing that such a duty has ever existed, before or after 1888. In the second place, we consider

j   that the rules of professional conduct of the Bar (as of most other professions) are rules which are, and are properly, determined by the profession itself in the light of tradition and experience, changing and developing over the years as circumstances change. If any rule acceptable to the Bar were held by the judges (in whatever capacity) to be contrary to public policy or to be liable to undermine the proper administration of justice, that rule would of course be ineffective, but subject to that the responsibility for formulating rules of professional conduct rests with the Bar through its appropriate procedure. Rules so formulated do not require the imprimatur of the judges as a condition of their validity. This, we think, is what Lord Campbell CJ meant when he said in *Doe d Bennett v Hale* that barristers 'are at liberty, under the controul of the Courts, to lay down conditions upon which, for the public good, their services are to be obtained'.

Even if the Bar had properly adopted the rule, with authority to do so, counsel submitted that we none the less had power as visitors to decline to sanction the rule, and we should decline here because this rule was restrictive of the public's access to the Bar, was anomalous (because riddled with exceptions) and was contrary to the interests of the Bar. There were issues of policy here on which, he contended, we were entitled and bound to give effect to our opinion.

Even on the assumption that we possess the powers which counsel attributes to us, we should be reluctant in the extreme, in a case such as this, to determine issues of policy with potentially far-reaching implications within the confines of a hearing in which most interested parties are necessarily unrepresented and most of the relevant material is not before us. Nor can we overlook the fact that the Royal Commission on Legal Services which recently gave prolonged and detailed consideration to the practices of the legal profession did not see fit to criticise the rules with which we are concerned. In a plain case or one where the rule under attack impinged directly or indirectly on the administration of justice a different course might be taken, but this is not such a case. We should, however, record that the criticisms made of the rule have not to any extent persuaded us that the rule is other than beneficial. The material placed before us in this case (to much of which we have not referred) vividly illustrates the value of the rule and the protection which it affords to members of the public.

It follows that the attack made on the second charge, and the finding based on it, fails. On the facts found a breach of the rule was plainly established.

The first charge, based on the telephone conversation with the detective sergeant, was quite independent of the second, since it in no way depended on the absence of a solicitor. Counsel's submission for the appellant quite simply was that barristers frequently make inquiries of official sources concerning current policy and that the facts here involved no professional misconduct of any kind. We consider that everything turns on the facts of the particular case, and in the present case we unhesitatingly share the view of the tribunal. The crucial ingredient of a carbon paper fraud, as of any other, is dishonesty, and the appellant's plain duty was to advise Mr Finch to avoid any conduct which was or could reasonably be thought to be dishonest. On the evidence it appears that the appellant did advise to this effect but the client was dissatisfied. This being so the only purpose in approaching the detective sergeant was to attempt to discover where the prosecuting authorities drew the line between conduct which would lead to criminal proceedings and conduct which would not. Such an inquiry is in itself improper, but the impropriety was here compounded by the making of the approach to a relatively very junior police officer on the strength of a casual acquaintance formed during the earlier case. The fact that the inquiry was most unlikely to yield anything of value makes it more ill-advised but does not make it less improper. This charge also was in our judgment clearly proved.

It was urged that the sentence of four months' suspension was harsh and unreasonable having regard to the appellant's long years of practice, the evidence given of his good character by a number of prominent practitioners and others, the financial consequences of a suspension, his health and the long period of anxiety which these proceedings have involved. These matters were all before the tribunal and were fully considered. We should interfere with the tribunal's sentence only if we were satisfied it was wrong. We are not so satisfied, and indeed consider the sentence to be just.

In the result, therefore, we dismiss the appeal against both findings and order.

Appeal dismissed.

Sepala Munasinghe Esq   Barrister.

a Re Eloc Electro-Optieck and Communicatie BV

CHANCERY DIVISION

NOURSE J

b 24th FEBRUARY, 13th MARCH 1981

Company – Compulsory winding up – Unregistered company – Foreign company – Jurisdiction – Essentials to establish jurisdiction – Assets within jurisdiction – Nature of assets – Benefit likely to accrue to petitioner from winding-up order – Petitioners former employees in England of foreign company – Petitioners obtaining judgment against company for arrears of pay – Company becoming insolvent and ceasing to carry on business – Company having no assets within *c* *jurisdiction and unable to satisfy judgment debt – Petitioners likely to be able to claim on Redundancy Fund in respect of debt if winding-up order made – Whether court having jurisdiction to make winding-up order – Whether likelihood that petitioners would obtain payments from source outside company, namely from fund, if winding-up order made sufficient to found jurisdiction – Companies Act 1948, s 399(5) – Employment Protection (Consolidation) Act 1978, s 122(1).*

d

A foreign, unregistered company which carried on business in England but had no place of business there employed the petitioners in England to carry out its business there. Later the company unfairly dismissed the petitioners from its employment. The petitioners obtained judgment in England against the company for sums in respect of unpaid salary and remuneration owed to them The company became insolvent and *e* ceased to carry on business. It had no assets in England to meet the judgment debts. The petitioners therefore applied to the Secretary of State for payments out of the Redundancy Fund pursuant to s 122(1)*[a]* of the Employment Protection (Consolidation) Act 1978 but were informed that no payments could be made to them out of the fund unless the company was insolvent within s 127(1)*[b]* of the 1978 Act, ie unless a winding-up order was made with respect to it. The petitioners petitioned the Companies Court under *f* s 399*[c]* of the Companies Act 1948 for an order winding up the company and submitted that the court had jurisdiction to make a winding-up order under s 399 although the company owned no assets within the jurisdiction.

Held – Although there had to be assets of a foreign company within the jurisdiction and also a reasonable possibility of benefit accruing to the petitioning creditor from the *g* making of a winding-up order before the court had jurisdiction to make a winding-up order in respect of such a company, (i) the assets could be of any nature and did not have to be in the company's ownership, and could, therefore, come from a source outside the company, and (ii) the benefit likely to accrue to the petitioning creditor did not have to be obtained through the liquidator. Since there was a reasonable possibility that if a winding-up order were made the petitioners would obtain payments from a source of

h

---

a Section 122(1) is set out at p 1114 *a*, post

b Section 127(1), so far as material, is set out at p 1114 *b*, post

c Section 399, so far as material, provides:

   '(1) Subject to the provisions of this Part of this Act, any unregistered company may be wound up under this Act, and all the provisions of this Act with respect to winding up shall apply to an *j* unregistered company, with the exceptions and additions mentioned in the following provisions of this section . . .

   '(5) The circumstances in which an unregistered company may be wound up are as follows:— (*a*) if the company is dissolved, or has ceased to carry on business, or is carrying on business only for the purpose of winding up its affairs; (*b*) if the company is unable to pay its debts; (*c*) if the court is of opinion that it is just and equitable that the company should be wound up . . .'

assets directly related to their employment by the company, namely from the
Redundancy Fund, there were sufficient assets within the jurisdiction and a sufficient
possibility of benefit accruing to the petitioners out of those assets from the making of
a winding-up order to found the court's jurisdiction. Accordingly, on the petitioners'
undertaking to indemnify the Official Receiver in regard to all liability, costs, charges
and expenses he might incur as liquidator of the company, the court would make an
order for the winding up of the company (see p 1114 *f* to p 1115 *c*, post).

Re Compania Merabello San Nicholas SA [1972] 3 All ER 448 applied.

Notes

For the winding up of a foreign company, see 7 Halsbury's Laws (4th Edn) para 1865, and
for cases on winding up unregistered companies, see 10 Digest (Reissue) 1275–1278,
8048–8066.

For the Companies Act 1948, s 399, see 5 Halsbury's Statutes (3rd Edn) 399.

For the Employment Protection (Consolidation) Act 1978, s 122, see 48 ibid 577.

Cases referred to in judgment

Banque des Marchands de Moscou (Koupetschesky) v Kindersley [1950] 2 All ER 549, [1951]
Ch 112, CA, 10 Digest (Reissue) 1396, 8956.

Compania Merabello San Nicholas SA, Re [1972] 3 All ER 448, [1973] Ch 75, [1972] 3 WLR
471, [1972] 2 Lloyd's Rep 268, 10 Digest (Reissue) 1277, 8066.

Winding-up petition

Paul James Knulty and Albert Henry Madeksho by a petition dated 13th January 1981
prayed for an order that Eloc Electro-Optieck and Communicatie BV, a company
established under the laws of the Netherlands, be wound up pursuant to s 399 of the
Companies Act 1948, in the circumstances that it was an unregistered company which
had ceased to carry on business and was unable to pay its debts and that it was just and
equitable that it should be wound up. The facts are set out in the judgment.

Nicholas Leviseur for the petitioners.
The company was not represented.

Cur adv vult

13th March. **NOURSE J** read the following judgment: This is a petition seeking the
winding up by the court of a company called Eloc Electro-Optieck and Communicatie
BV, which was established under the laws of the Netherlands in 1975 as a company with
limited liability. The objects for which the company was established were to carry on
business in relation to the exploitation of industrial property and wholesale trading in
electronic products. The company's principal place of business was Amsterdam, but it
was authorised to operate throughout the world. In or about 1975 it commenced
business in England, but it never had a place of business here.

The petitioners are two foreign nationals, Mr Paul James Knulty and Mr Albert Henry
Madeksho, who were employed by the company in the carrying on of its business in
England and Wales. The company later unfairly dismissed them from its employment. On 22nd August 1978 the petitioners obtained a final judgment against the
company in the Queen's Bench Division. Mr Knulty obtained judgment for £11,394·30
in respect of unpaid salary and remuneration due and owing to him by the company.
Mr Madeksho obtained judgment for £3,303 in respect of unpaid salary and
remuneration likewise due and owing to him. In November 1979 the petitioners'
solicitors were informed by the company's legal advisers in Amsterdam that the company
had ceased operations, that it was not expected that it would ever be in a position to
continue its activities and that it was not in a position to pay its outstanding debts. It
therefore seems clear that the circumstances mentioned in both paras (*a*) and (*b*) of

s 399(5) of the Companies Act 1940 exist in relation to the company. The company has
a been duly served with the proceedings, but it has not been represented at the hearing of
the petition.

Paragraph 8 of the petition contains this sentence:

> 'The company has no assets within the jurisdiction sufficient to meet the said
> judgment debt and your petitioners by reason of their poverty have not sought thus
> far to have enforced a judgment which they know could not be satisfied by the
b > company in the United Kingdom.'

Counsel for the petitioners, to whom I am indebted for an argument which fully drew
my attention to the difficulties in their way, told me that that must in truth be read as
an acknowledgment that the company has no assets within the jurisdiction at all. That
would appear to suggest that one of the essential requirements for the making of a
c winding-up order in respect of a foreign company is not satisfied in the present case.
Those essentials were summarised, so far as *normal* cases are concerned, in the judgment
of Megarry J in *Re Compania Merabello San Nicholas SA* [1972] 3 All ER 448 at 460, [1973]
Ch 75 at 91–92. The third essential was expressed by the judge in this way:

> 'A proper connection with the jurisdiction must be established by sufficient
> evidence to show (a) that the company has some asset or assets within the
d > jurisdiction, and (b) that there are one or more persons concerned in the proper
> distribution of the assets over whom the jurisdiction is exercisable.'

There is no difficulty about (b), because the petitioners are persons over whom the
jurisdiction is exercisable. But there is clearly a difficulty about (a).

The way in which counsel for the petitioners seeks to overcome that difficulty is this.
e He says that there is in reality no overriding requirement that the company should have
some asset or assets within the jurisdiction. He says that if you look at the authorities you
will find that reliance on the existence of assets here as a means of founding the
jurisdiction was developed in an effort to mitigate the hardships caused by the earlier
well-recognised objection that there was no jurisdiction where the company had not had
a place of business in this country. The existence of assets here was taken to constitute
f the indicia of a business formerly conducted here. Therefore, says counsel, what is
important is not the place of business but the carrying on of business in this country. For
that proposition he relies on two passages in the judgment of Evershed MR in *Banque des
Marchands de Moscou (Koupetschesky) v Kindersley* [1950] 2 All ER 549 at 556, [1951] Ch
112 at 125–126, on two earlier passages in the judgment of Megarry J in *Re Compania
Merabello San Nicholas SA* [1972] 3 All ER 448 at 455, 457, [1973] Ch 75 at 86, 88 and on
g the first two essentials in the summary itself. For reasons which will appear it is
unnecessary for me to decide whether counsel for the petitioners can make out that
proposition or not. It would in any event be most undesirable for me to express a view
on a general question of that kind in a case where I have not been able to hear an
argument to the contrary and where the earlier authorities have either not been cited or
not been fully considered.

h In a normal case there would be no point in the court making a winding-up order in
respect of a foreign company which had no assets within the jurisdiction, because there
would be nothing which could be realised for the benefit of the creditors. That accords
with the fundamental principle that the court will not wind up a company if there is no
likelihood that any advantage will be achieved by the petitioner. In Megarry J's summary
of the essentials that is the sixth, and it is expressed in this way ([1972] 3 All ER 448 at
j 460, [1973] Ch 75 at 92):

> 'If it is shown that there is no reasonable possibility of benefit accruing to
> creditors from making the winding-up order, the jurisdiction is excluded.'

As to that, the position in the present case is this. It is provided by s 122(1) of the
Employment Protection (Consolidation) Act 1978:

'If on an application made to him in writing by an employee the Secretary of State is satisfied—(a) that the employer of that employee has become insolvent; and (b) *a* that on the relevant date the employee was entitled to be paid the whole or part of any debt to which the section applies, the Secretary of State shall, subject to the provisions of this section, pay the employee out of the Redundancy Fund the amount to which in the opinion of the Secretary of State the employee is entitled in respect of that debt.'

b

Section 127(1), so far as material, provides:

'For the purposes of sections 122 to 126, an employer shall be taken to be insolvent if, but only if, in England and Wales ... (c) where the employer is a company, a winding up order is made ... with respect to it ...'

The petitioners claim that they have rights, inter alia, under s 122, but it is evident *c* from s 127 that they cannot pursue them unless and until a winding-up order is made with respect to the company.

The petitioners have already been awarded small redundancy payments under the 1978 Act and they have since applied to the Secretary of State in writing for arrears of salary in amounts somewhat less than the judgment debts on which the petition is based. I have seen correspondence which has passed between the petitioners' solicitors *d* and the Department of Employment, and the attitude of the department to the claim in respect of arrears of salary is concisely expressed in the following extract from a letter to the petitioners' solicitors dated 25th January 1980:

'The matter has been considered by our Headquarters and I am instructed to inform you that we cannot provide funds to make any payments unless the company *e* is insolvent in this country, that is insolvent in the terms of section 127. We cannot give a guarantee at this stage that payments would be made if the definition of insolvency was satisfied. Any claims would if accepted be subject to the limits imposed by section s 122. I regret that I cannot be more helpful.'

The department was given notice of the hearing of this petition, but indicated that it did not wish to attend. *f*

Although the department, no doubt very properly, has not been able to commit itself, it does nevertheless seem to me from the 1978 Act and from the correspondence which has passed between the two sides that there is a reasonable possibility of benefit accruing to the petitioners from the making of a winding-up order with respect to the company. The benefit would consist of assets coming into the hands of the petitioners not from the company but from an outside source which can only be tapped if an order is made. In *g* the light of that consideration and of the facts, first, that the company did carry on business in England and Wales, second, that it employed the petitioners in that business, and, third, that the potential source of assets is directly related to that employment, there is, in my judgment, sufficient to found the jurisdiction of the court. To put it in another way, it would, in my judgment, be a lamentable state of affairs if the court's jurisdiction was excluded by the mere technicality that the assets in respect of which the reasonable *h* possibility of benefit accruing to the petitioners derived belonged not to the company but to an outside source. I think that support for this view is to be found in the fourth and fifth essentials in Megarry J's summary ([1972] 3 All ER 448 at 460, [1973] Ch 75 at 92):

'(4) It suffices if the assets of the company within the jurisdiction are of any *j* nature; they need not be "commercial" assets, or assets which indicate that the company formerly carried on business here. (5) The assets need not be assets which will be distributable to creditors by the liquidator in the winding-up: it suffices if by the making of the winding-up order they will be of benefit to a creditor or creditors in some other way.'

That shows, first, that the assets can be of any nature and, second, that the consequential
a benefit accruing to a creditor or creditors need not be channelled through the hands of
the liquidator. To my mind that confirms that the ownership of the assets by the
company is not a matter of crucial importance. I must again observe that Megarry J's
summary of the essentials was directed to normal cases. I would, if necessary, say that
this was not a normal case.

In all the circumstances I am satisfied that this is a case in which the court has
b jurisdiction to wind up the company. I am also satisfied that I ought, in the exercise of
my discretion, to make an order. The modern practice in these cases is to require an
undertaking from the petitioner to indemnify the Official Receiver as to all liability,
costs, charges and expenses which he may incur in the course of acting as liquidator of
the company. If the petitioners are prepared to give that undertaking in the present case
I will make the usual order for the compulsory winding up of the company by the court.

c
Order accordingly.

Solicitors: *Friedman, Friedman & Co* (for the petitioners).

Hazel Hartman   Barrister.
d

Practice Direction

e
FAMILY DIVISION

*Adoption – Jurisdiction – Practice – Preliminary examination of jurisdiction – Application to be
referred to judge only if it appears court may be required to dismiss or not proceed with adoption
proceedings – Hearing date and notice – Adoption (High Court) Rules 1976 (SI 1976 No 1645),*
f *r 11.*

The Practice Direction of 17th November 1976 ([1976] 3 All ER 864, [1976] 1 WLR
1267) which, inter alia, set out the procedure to be followed for a preliminary
examination of the court's jurisdiction under r 11 of the Adoption (High Court) Rules
1976, SI 1976 No 1645, is hereby amended.

g The revised procedure under that rule will be as follows:
All applications for adoption in the High Court which appear to be governed by r 11
will be referred to a judge for a preliminary examination only if a registrar considers at
any stage, either of his own motion or on the ex parte application of the applicant or the
guardian ad litem, that the court may be required to dismiss or not proceed with the
adoption proceedings.

h In those cases in which the preliminary examination is referred to a judge, the
registrar will fix a hearing date and give notice thereof to the applicant, the guardian and,
unless otherwise directed, any parent of the child who is not an applicant.

R L BAYNE-POWELL
Senior Registrar.

3rd August 1981

Robinson (Inspector of Taxes) v Scott Bader Co Ltd

COURT OF APPEAL, CIVIL DIVISION
WALLER, OLIVER AND FOX LJJ
7th, 8th, 19th MAY 1981

Income tax – Deduction in computing profits – Expenditure wholly and exclusively laid out for purposes of trade – Purposes of expenditure – Subsidiary company – Parent company incurring expenditure in respect of its employee seconded to manage its subsidiary – Expenditure incurred for sole benefit of parent company – Whether expenditure incurred wholly and exclusively for purposes of parent company's trade – Whether payment in nature of capital expenditure – Income and Corporation Taxes Act 1970, s 130(a)(f).

In March 1975 the taxpayer company acquired a 100% interest in a French company. It then seconded F, one of its employees, to the French company to act as manager to provide that company with the necessary technical and marketing skills on the basis that it would pay his salary, expenses and social costs while he was in post in France. In computing its taxable profits for the accounting period ending on 2nd July 1976, the taxpayer company claimed to deduct under s 130(a)[a] of the Income and Corporation Taxes Act 1970 the payments which it had made to F in respect of his salary, expenses and social costs. The inspector of taxes disallowed the claim on the grounds (i) that the payment was not expenditure wholly and exclusively laid out or expended for the purposes of the taxpayer company's trade but was in part for the benefit of the French company and (ii) that the payment was in the nature of a capital expenditure within s 130(f) of the 1970 Act. The General Commissioners found as a fact that the taxpayer company had undertaken the rescue operation of the French company to further its own business in France and Europe and determined that the payment to F was an allowable deduction. The judge ([1980] 2 All ER 780) upheld that determination, holding that the test to be applied in determining the purpose of the taxpayer company in making the payment was a subjective one and, applying that test, on the facts found by the commissioners the payment to F was an allowable deduction in arriving at the profits of the taxpayer company for tax purposes. The Crown appealed.

Held –The phrase 'for the purposes of' in s 130(a) of the 1970 Act contained an ingredient of intention and it was difficult to determine intention without some element of subjectivity. On the evidence, it was perfectly reasonable for the commissioners to conclude that the rescue operation had been taken to further the taxpayer company's business in Europe, and that was a finding strongly in favour of the payments having been made to F for the purposes of the taxpayer company's trade. Furthermore, the payments, being expenditure for the purpose of the trading of the company, were not capital within s 130(f) of the 1970 Act. It followed that the payments in question were allowable deductions in computing the taxable profits of the taxpayer company. The Crown's appeal would, therefore, be dismissed (see p 1119 g to j and p 1120 a to h, post).

Decision of Walton J [1980] 2 All ER 780 affirmed.

---

a   Section 130, so far as material, provides: '. . . in computing the amount of the profits or gains to be charged under Case I or Case II of Schedule D, no sum shall be deducted in respect of—(a) any disbursements or expenses, not being money wholly and exclusively laid out or expended for the purposes of the trade, profession or vocation . . . (f) any capital withdrawn from, or any sum employed or intended to be employed as capital in, the trade, profession or vocation . . .'

Notes

a For deduction of expenditure laid out wholly and exclusively for trade purposes, see 23 Halsbury's Laws (4th Edn) paras 305–312, and for cases on the subject, see 28(1) Digest (Reissue) 141–158, 421–505.

For the Income and Corporation Taxes Act 1970, s 130, see 33 Halsbury's Statutes (3rd Edn) 182.

b **Cases referred to in judgments**

Bentleys, Stokes and Lowless v Beeson (Inspector of Taxes) [1952] 2 All ER 82, 33 Tax Cas 491, 31 ATC 229, [1952] TR 239, 45 R & IT 461, CA, 28(1) Digest (Reissue) 150, 465.

Edwards (Inspector of Taxes) v Bairstow [1955] 3 All ER 48, [1956] AC 14, [1955] 3 WLR 410, 36 Tax Cas 207, 34 ATC 198, [1955] TR 209, 48 R & IT 534, HL, 28(1) Digest (Reissue) 566, 2089.

c Smith's Potato Estates Ltd v Bolland (Inspector of Taxes), Smith's Potato Crisps (1929) Ltd v Inland Revenue Comrs [1948] 2 All ER 367, [1948] AC 508, 30 Tax Cas 267, [1948] LJR 1557, 41 R & IT 373, HL, 28(1) Digest (Reissue) 151, 470.

Cases also cited

Inland Revenue Comrs v Mills [1974] 1 All ER 722, [1975] AC 38, [1974] STC 130, HL.

d Marshall Richards Machine Co Ltd v Jewitt (Inspector of Taxes) (1956) 36 Tax Cas 511.

Milnes (Inspector of Taxes) v J Beam Group Ltd [1975] STC 487.

Morgan (Inspector of Taxes) v Tate and Lyle Ltd [1954] 2 All ER 413, [1955] AC 21, 35 Tax Cas 367, HL.

Odhams Press Ltd v Cook [1940] 3 All ER 15, 23 Tax Cas 233, HL.

e **Appeal**

The Crown appealed against the order of Walton J ([1980] 2 All ER 780, [1980] STC 241) made on 21st February 1980 dismissing the Crown's appeal by way of case stated (set out at [1980] 2 All ER 781–784, [1980] STC 242–245) from the determination of the Commissioners for the General Purposes of the Income Tax for the Division of Wellingborough that Scott Bader Co Ltd ('the taxpayer company') was entitled to deduct f from its taxable profits payments made to one of its employees seconded to a subsidiary company. The facts are set out in the judgment of Waller LJ.

D C Potter QC and Michael Hart for the Crown.
John Tallon for the taxpayer company.

g   *Cur adv vult*
19th May. The following judgments were read.

WALLER LJ. This is an appeal from a decision of Walton J ([1980] 2 All ER 780, [1980] STC 241) dismissing an appeal from the Commissioners for the General Purposes of Income Tax for the Division of Wellingborough. The taxpayer company had claimed h to deduct the sum of £16,354 from an assessment to corporation tax but the inspector had not allowed the deduction. The appeal to the commissioners was allowed and Walton J dismissed an appeal from their decision.

The accounting period with which the case is concerned was a period of 53 weeks ending on 2nd July 1976. The principal activity of the taxpayer company during that period was the manufacture and marketing of chemical intermediates and synthetic j resins. In addition to its subsidiary and associated companies the taxpayer company derives royalty income from licensees in Germany, Italy, Switzerland, South Africa, the United States of America and Australia.

The taxpayer company trades in a specialised field dealing with the manufacture and supply of synthetics for fibreglass making. It provides its synthetics as raw materials for its subsidiary and associated companies, licensees and other customers for their

manufacturing trades. The taxpayer company also furnishes technical and marketing
expertise by means of its own personnel to its subsidiary and associated companies.

At the beginning of that accounting period the company had acquired the whole of
the share capital of the French subsidiary having previously owned 50% of it. After
acquiring the 100%, an employee of the taxpayer company, Mr S Fearon, was seconded
to the French company on the basis that the taxpayer company would pay his salary and
expenses whilst he was in post in France. The sum of £16,354 represents the payments
made to him over a period of six months. At the end of that period of six months Mr
Fearon became the managing director of the French company, paid directly by it.

The decision of the General Commissioners was that the deduction should be allowed
as coming within s 130(a) of the Income and Corporation Taxes Act 1970. That
paragraph prohibits the deduction of any disbursements 'not being money wholly and
exclusively laid out or expended for the purposes of the trade, profession or vocation'.

It is not necessary to set out the whole of the facts in the case stated, but I shall start
with a board meeting held on 25th November 1974 at which a number of representatives
of the taxpayer company were present. The case finds (in para 5(g)) that 'the [taxpayer
company's] determination to continue activities in France was minuted . . .' as follows:

> 'Papers were before the meeting from Mr. Trueman setting out the position and
> from Mr. Broome itemising the points for and against the continuing operations in
> France. [And there followed an account of how the French subsidiary was being
> operated in France] in a very lean manner as far as staff were concerned and output
> was high the margin on sales was low and, if these margins could not be increased,
> added throughput would be needed to get above break-even level. [And the
> minutes went on:] After further discussion, particularly on the desirability for our
> continuing operation in Europe, it was unanimously agreed to go ahead with Scott
> Bader Sturge SA with strong support and backing from Wollaston.'

The minute went on to say there were two further decisions to be made. The case stated
continued (para 5(h)):

> 'On 31st March 1975 the [taxpayer company] acquired a 100% interest in the
> French Company and following the departure of the Managing Director of the
> French Company, Mr. S. Fearon, an employee of the [taxpayer company], acted as
> Manager, which provided the French Company with necessary technical and
> marketing expertise.'

Mr Fearon was seconded to the French company on the basis that the taxpayer
company would pay his salary, expenses and social costs whilst he was in post in
France. This was done and, as I have already said, he was paid £16,354 in respect
thereof. There followed in the case certain findings of fact:

> '(j) There is another firm in France named Wauquier SA, which is not a
> subsidiary or associated company of the [taxpayer company], and with which the
> [taxpayer company] deals at arm's length as an ordinary customer. Primarily the
> [taxpayer company's] business and trading in France is served directly through the
> French Company. (k) Direct sales by the [taxpayer company] to Wauquier SA were
> of specialist products for use only with prerequisite basic products. These basic
> products were supplied by the French Company because substantial transportation
> costs ruled out supply from the U.K. Without the French Company to supply the
> basic products, sales by the [taxpayer company] of specialist products to Wauquier
> SA would have been lost. (l) The position of the French Company vis-a-vis the
> [taxpayer company] was unique, the rescue operation being undertaken to further
> the [taxpayer company's] business in France and in Europe.'

The only other part of the case stated that I need quote is para 9, which said:

> 'We decided on the evidence (see para 5(l) above) that: (a) The [taxpayer company]
> and the French Company contribute to and are dependent upon an international

unitary business. (b) The nature of that business includes marketing and extension
of markets. (c) The deduction of £16,354 from the [taxpayer company's] profits
should be allowed.'

The Crown submitted that the only reasonable conclusion from the findings of fact
made by the General Commissioners was that there were two purposes for the payment
of Mr Fearon, namely that the money was laid out or expended for the purposes of the
subsidiary company as well as the purposes of the taxpayer company. Counsel for the
Crown submitted that the judge was wrong in regarding the test as a subjective one and
submitted to this court that it was an objective test. Quoting paras (h), (k) and (l), he
submitted that there were four facts of importance: (1) that the taxpayer company
owned the entire share capital of the French company and that their trades were separate;
(2) that, by providing Mr Fearon as manager, the taxpayer company gave the French
company technical and marketing expertise; (3) that the French company had to provide
basic products to enable the taxpayer company to sell their products to Wauquier SA; and
(4) that the use of the word 'business' in the phrase of the rescue operation included the
whole of the business of the subsidiary as well as the taxpayer company. He summarised
his argument by saying that, the test being objective, the purpose of the expenditure was
partly to increase the value of the assets in the French company and partly to prevent loss
of the English company's products in Wauquier SA.

The circumstances in which this court can interfere with the findings of the
commissioners set out in a special case were considered in *Edwards (Inspector of Taxes) v
Bairstow* [1955] 3 All ER 48 at 57, [1956] AC 14 at 36, 36 Tax Cas 207 at 229. Lord
Radcliffe set out the principles on which the court can interefere:

'When the Case comes before the court, it is its duty to examine the determination
having regard to its knowledge of the relevant law. If the Case contains anything
ex facie which is bad law and which bears on the determination, it is, obviously,
erroneous in point of law. But, without any such misconception appearing ex facie,
it may be that the facts found are such that no person acting judicially and properly
instructed as to the relevant law could have come to the determination under
appeal. In those circumstances, too, the court must intervene. It has no option but
to assume that there has been some misconception of the law, and that this has been
responsible for the determination. So there, too, there has been error in point of
law.'

Against the background of this test I will consider first the argument that the test is
objective and not, as the judge found, subjective. The phrase with which the case is
concerned is 'for the purposes of'. In my judgment 'purpose' contains an ingredient of
'intention'. It is very difficult, but perhaps not impossible, to determine this without
some element of subjectivity. Indeed, in many cases the test will be wholly subjective.
When deciding whether or not a solicitor is entertaining a client to lunch, the test must
be wholly subjective. The solicitor is entertaining; it may be because it is an old client;
it may be because it is the only opportunity to discuss the business. The court has to
decide the real purpose, if it is for the trade, vocation or profession, and whether it is
independent, i e independent of the business purposes to be served (see *Bentleys, Stokes and
Lowless v Beeson (Inspector of Taxes)* [1952] 2 All ER 82 at 85–86, 33 Tax Cas 491 at 504–
505). It would be impossible in such a case to do other than make the decision
subjectively. In considering the purposes of a company there may be room for some
objectivity, but it will normally be to assist in making the subjective decision.

There may be a case where the evidence shows that something was done in a different
capacity altogether, e g *Smith's Potato Estates Ltd v Bolland (Inspector of Taxes), Smith's Potato
Crisps (1929) Ltd v Inland Revenue Comrs* [1948] 2 All ER 367, [1948] AC 508, 30 Tax Cas
267, where it was held that something done as a taxpayer could not be for the purposes
of the trade, profession or vocation. In my opinion, in spite of the submission of counsel
for the Crown to the contrary, that does not arise in this case.

In the present case the payments made to Mr Fearon could not possibly be solely for

the benefit of the subsidiary company. There were therefore two possibilities which had
to be considered by the commissioners: either the payments were made partly for the
purposes of the subsidiary and partly for the purposes of the taxpayer company or the
real purposes for which they were made were the purposes of the taxpayer company.

In considering the findings of fact which I have quoted above, it seems to me that para
5(l) describing the rescue operation being taken to further the taxpayer company's
business in Europe is a finding strongly in favour of the real purpose being for the trade,
profession or vocation of the taxpayer company. And, while I am not prepared to say
that 'business' could not include the business of the subsidiary, in my opinion it could
certainly be construed as meaning the taxpayer company's trading operation and,
although it is irrelevant, this, in my view, would be the right construction in this case.
Furthermore, the findings at sub-paras (k) and (j) both point in the same direction. 'The
[taxpayer company's] business and trading in France' is important and the French
company's supply of basic products is necessary to support the taxpayer company's
trading. In my judgment this finding also tends to support the finding that the real
purpose was for the taxpayer company.

The inevitable result of sending Mr Fearon at the taxpayer company's expense to
France would be to improve the running of the French company and no doubt this
would improve that company's financial position. But it does not follow that that was
the real purpose of making the payments. It was one of the results, albeit it may well be
an inevitable result. It was vis-à-vis the company in much the same position as the
provision of lunch by the solicitor in the case referred to above.

I have considered whether in this case there was any positive evidence which would
tend to show that the commissioners were wrong. The only possible finding is that at
para 9(a), a finding not very happily worded. In my judgment, however, the phrase
'international unitary business' in the context of all the findings in this case cannot be
construed to indicate that it was the group as a whole which was being considered. This
was the commissioners' phrase to describe what had been described earlier in the
paragraphs I have already quoted. In my judgment it is quite impossible to say that the
facts found are such that no person acting judicially and properly instructed as to the
relevant law could have come to the determination under appeal. On the contrary, it
appears to me to be a perfectly reasonable conclusion at which to arrive.

I should add that an alternative submission was that this was capital, and that
accordingly it would come within s 130(f) of the Income and Corporation Taxes Act
1970; but in my opinion it is quite impossible to say that this was capital. It was being
expended for the purposes of the trading of the company and could not be described as
capital.

I would dismiss this appeal.

OLIVER LJ. For the reasons given in the judgment which has just been delivered by
Waller LJ I agree that the appeal should be dismissed.

FOX LJ. I also agree.

Appeal dismissed. Leave to appeal to the House of Lords refused.

Solicitors: *Solicitor of Inland Revenue; Jacques & Co* (for the taxpayer company).

Edwina Epstein   Barrister.